# The Negro Almanac
## A Reference Work on the
# African American

# The Negro Almanac
## A Reference Work on the
# African American

**Fifth Edition**

Compiled and Edited by
HARRY A. PLOSKI
New York University
and
JAMES WILLIAMS
Director of Public Relations
NAACP



Gale Research Inc. • DETROIT • NEW YORK • FORT LAUDERDALE • LONDON

Harry A. Ploski and James Williams, *Editors*

**Gale Research Inc. Staff**

Mary Beth Trimper, *Production Manager*
Marilyn Jackman, *External Production Assistant*
Arthur Chartow, *Art Director*
C. J. Jonik, *Keyliner*

Laura Bryant, *Production Supervisor*
Louise Gagné, *Internal Production Associate*
Sharana M. Wier, *Internal Production Assistant*


835 Penobscot Bldg.
Detroit, MI 48226-4094

Library of Congress Catalog Card Number 86-72654
ISBN 0-8103-7706-3

Printed in the United States of America

## Editorial Staff for the Fifth Edition



## Research and Support Personnel

# PREFACE

With this fifth edition of *The Negro Almanac,* Gale Research Inc. proudly assumes publication of one of the premier reference works on the African American experience. Although the publisher and the cover are new, this thorough update and revision of the book has been prepared by the same editorial team that produced the preceding editions so successfully under the Bellwether Publishing Company imprint.

## SCOPE

The detailed table of contents reveals the depth and breadth of coverage offered in the thirty-three chapters of this edition of *The Negro Almanac.* A combination of historical narrative, biographical sketches, and statistical tables and graphs present in great detail nearly five hundred years of history, from the fifteenth-century voyages of discovery to today's headlines. The greatest attention goes to the current situation of blacks in American society, whether in politics and the law; business, labor, and the economy; education; the family; religion; or any variety of the arts, sports, or science; but it always comes with a thorough grounding in what paved the way for the present. Moreover, the history of the African continent and a synopsis of conditions in present-day nations there and a summary of the black experience throughout the western hemisphere are covered in separate chapters, thus providing a worldwide perspective. Other chapters present a listing of "Black Firsts" and descriptions of "Historic Landmarks of Black America" certain to enrich study of African American heritage. An extensive bibliography will direct those seeking further information to valuable resources. Throughout the volume, abundant illustrations and dozens of clear and concise tables and charts enhance the text.

## ABOUT THIS EDITION

All the powerful and useful features of previous editions of *The Negro Almanac* remain. Some sections have been totally rewritten, and to all appropriate sections, new facts have been added. The sections on jazz and on the family, in particular, have been enhanced in this way. Biographies as well as socioeconomic, cultural, and historical material reflect the most current data and research. The editors have used the latest statistical information available at the time of publication. Expanded coverage distinguishes the chapters on national organizations and landmarks, while the number of documents, both historic and contemporary, in the chapter on this subject has also grown.

Information on the extensive range of topics covered here could be obtained only from multiple sources in a few specialized library collections and therefore has been relatively inaccessible to all but highly trained and well-placed researchers before the publication of *The Negro Almanac.* By laying the groundwork for a far broader dissemination of such information in a single compendium, this book provides the widest audience with an accurate, comprehensive, and well-documented study of black culture in the United States and around the world.

## COMMENTS AND SUGGESTIONS WELCOME

The editors of *The Negro Almanac* will appreciate suggestions for additions or changes that will make the book as useful as possible. Please send any comments to:

*The Negro Almanac*
Gale Research Inc.
387 Park Avenue South
New York, NY 10016

# CONTENTS

*Hiram Revels is sworn in as Senator from Mississippi, the first black man to occupy the office.*

# CHRONOLOGY: A HISTORICAL REVIEW

**Major Events in Black History (1492-1953) ■ The Civil Rights Revolution (1954-1964) ■ The March of News (1965-1970) ■ Consolidation and Reverses (1971-1989)**

Black history in the Western Hemisphere can probably be traced back to the *Santa Maria,* with Columbus's crewman Pedro Alonzo Niño identified as a black sailor. Without any doubt, black seamen and explorers figured importantly in many of the subsequent Spanish expeditions as well as in the successful English colonization that birthed the United States of America. Nevertheless, standard references have largely ignored the historical role of the black American. For the most part blacks have been viewed as outside the mainstream of American history rather than as active participants in its creation and greatness. The following chronology attempts to redress this error by specifically reviewing the important events of Afro-American history. In addition to providing a developmental outline of the black American presence, the chronology stands as a record of the contributions of blacks to the nation's growth, achievements, and vitality that should not be overlooked. Subsequent sections of this volume will flesh out the record with respect to specific eras and fields, but the chronology by itself documents the great range and depth of the black contribution to the social, cultural, and economic strength of this nation.

## MAJOR EVENTS IN BLACK HISTORY (1492-1953)

**1492, The New World** Blacks are among the first explorers to the New World. Pedro Alonzo Niño, identified by some scholars as a black, arrives with Columbus; other blacks accompany Balboa, Ponce de Leon, Cortes, Pizarro, and Menendez on their travels and explorations.

**1501, Spain** The Spanish throne officially approves the use of black slaves in the New World.

**1502, Latin America** Portugal lands its first slave cargo in the Western Hemisphere.

**1513, Latin America** Spain authorizes the use of black slaves in Cuba. Thirty blacks accompany Balboa when he discovers the Pacific Ocean.

**1526, South Carolina** The first group of blacks to set foot on what is now the United States are brought by a Spanish explorer to South Carolina to erect a settlement. However, they soon flee to the interior and settle with the native Americans.

**1538, Arizona** New Mexico Estevanico, a black explorer, leads an expedition from Mexico into the territory of the American Southwest and is credited with the discovery of what is now Arizona and New Mexico.

**1562, Hispaniola** Britain enters the slave trade when John Hawkins sells a large cargo of blacks to Spanish planters. Though Queen Elizabeth allows Hawkins to include the figure of a bound black in his coat of arms, she denies that he transports slaves.

**1600, Latin America** Historical records indicate that by 1600, 900,000 slaves have been brought to Latin America. In the next century, 2,750,000 are added to that total. Slave revolts in the sixteenth century were reported in Hispaniola, Puerto Rico, Panama, Cuba, and Mexico.

**1618, England** The government grants monopolies to a group of companies, established for the purpose of slave trading.

**1619, Jamestown, Virginia** The forerunner of slavery in the English colonies begins with the arrival of 20 black indentured servants aboard a Dutch vessel. Most indentured servants are released after serving a term, usually seven years, and are allowed to own property and participate in political affairs.

**1624, New Amsterdam** The Dutch, who had entered the slave trade in 1621 with the formation of the Dutch West Indies Co., import blacks to serve on Hudson Valley farms. According to Dutch law, the children of manumitted (freed) slaves are bound to slavery.

**1629-1637, The English Colonies** Black slaves are imported into Connecticut (1629), Maryland and Massachusetts (1634), and New York City (1637).

**1630, Massachusetts** A law protecting slaves who flee owners because of ill treatment is enacted.

**1639, Salem, Massachusetts** New England seamen enter slave trade as Captain William Pierce sails to West Indies and exchanges Indian slaves for blacks.

**1640-1650, The "Western Hemisphere"** Spurred by the increasing use of sugar as a money crop, the slave population of the West Indies multiplies rapidly, but growth in mainland English colonies is slow. The black slave population in Barbados, for example, grows from a few hundred in 1640 to 6,000 in 1645. But by 1649, there are only 300 black slaves in Virginia, and by 1671 only 2,000.

**1640-1699, The English Colonies** Punitive fugitive laws applying to both indentured servants and slaves are enacted in Connecticut, Maryland, New Jersey, South Carolina, and Virginia. The Virginia law, passed in 1642, penalizes people sheltering runaways, 20 pounds worth of tobacco for each night of refuge granted. Slaves are branded after a second escape attempt.

***These half-starved and physically weak slaves have just disembarked in America.***

**1641, Massachusetts** Massachusetts becomes the first colony to legalize slavery, adding a modification that forbids capture by "unjust violence." This provision was subsequently adopted by all of the New England colonies.

**1643, New England** The groundwork is laid for eighteenth and nineteenth century fugitive slave laws in the United States when an intercolonial agreement of the New England Confederation declares that mere certification by a magistrate is sufficient evidence to convict a runaway slave.

**1651, North Hampton, Virginia** Anthony Johnson, himself a black, imports five servants and thus qualifies to receive a 200 acre land grant along the Puwgoteague River in Virginia. Other blacks soon join Johnson and attempt to launch an independent black community. At its height, the settlement has 12 black homesteads with sizable holdings.

**1662, Virginia** The colony passes a law which provides

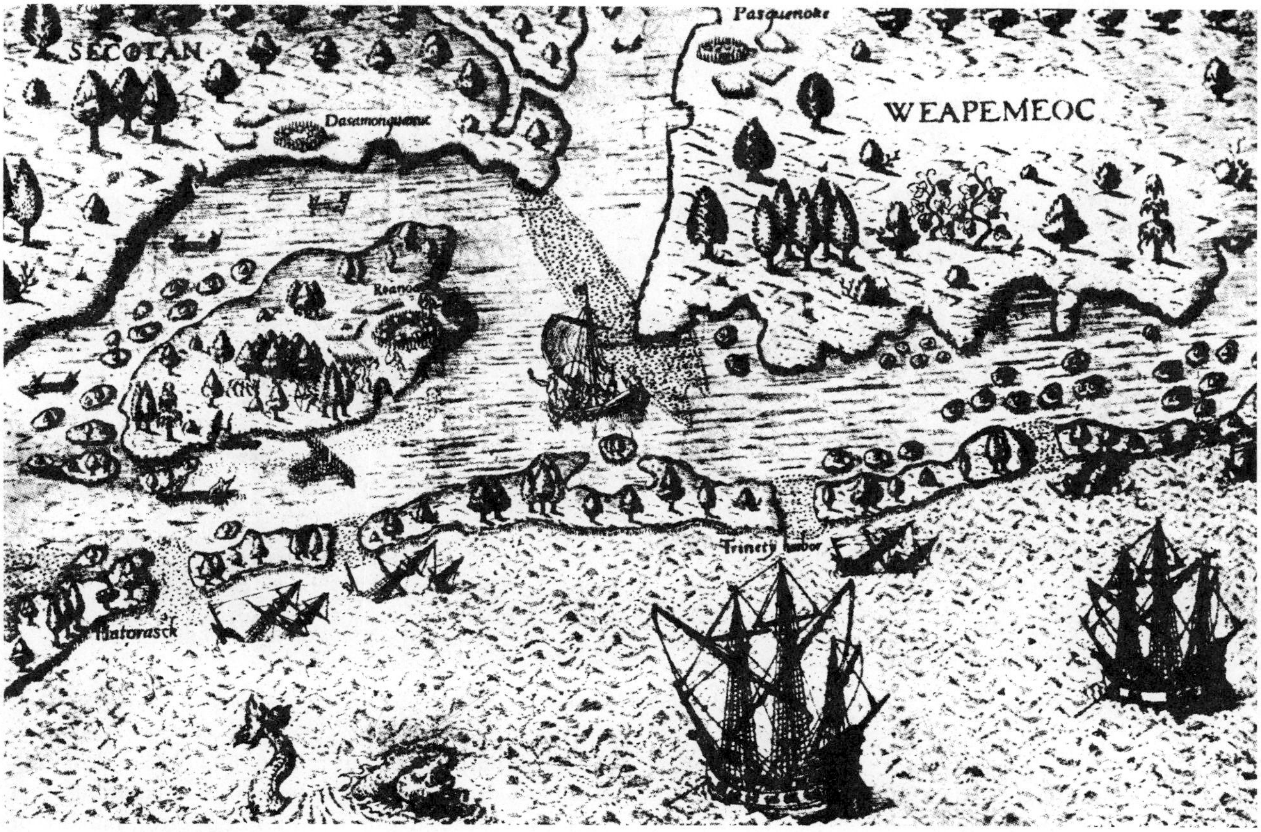


*The earliest English settlement in America was on Roanoke Island in Pamlico Sound, shown here on a sixteenth-century navigator's map. The sinking ships warned captains of the banks.*

that the status of children—bound or free—will be determined by the condition of the mother.

**1663, Gloucester, Virginia** A planned uprising, involving many black slaves and white indentured servants, is betrayed by a house servant.

**1663, Maryland** Settlers pass a law stipulating that all imported blacks are to be given the status of slaves. Free white women who marry black slaves are to be slaves during the lives of their spouses; children of the union are also classified as slaves. Ironically, children born of white servant women and blacks are regarded as free by a later law (1681).

**1670, Virginia** Voting rights are removed from recently freed slaves and indentured servants. All non-Christians imported to the territory, "by shipping," are to be slaves for life, whereas those who enter by land are to serve until the age of 30 if they are adult men and women when their period of servitude commences.

**1672, Virginia** A law is enacted providing for a bounty on the heads of "Maroons"—black fugitives who form communities in the mountains, swamps, and forests of southern colonies. Many Maroon communities attack towns and plantations.

**1685, French West Indies** The French Code Noir is enacted. It requires religious instruction for slaves, permits intermarriage, outlaws working of slaves on Sundays and holidays, but forbids liberation of mulatto children reaching 21 if their mothers are still enslaved. However, the Code is largely ignored by the French settlers.

**1688, Germantown, Pennsylvania** Mennonite Quakers sign an anti-slavery resolution, the first formal protest against slavery in the Western Hemisphere. In 1696, Quakers importing slaves are threatened with expulsion from the Society.

**1700, English North American Colonies** Slave population is placed at 28,000, with 23,000 in the South.

**1704, New York City** Elias Neau, a French immigrant, opens the "Catechism School" for black slaves.

**1705, Virginia** The Assembly declares that "no Negro, mulatto, or Indian shall presume to take upon him, act in or exercise any office, ecclesiastic, civil or military." Blacks are forbidden to serve as witnesses in court cases and are condemned to lifelong servitude, unless they have either been Christians in their native land or free men in a Christian country.

**1711, Pennsylvania** Spurred by the Mennonites and Quakers, the colonial legislature outlaws slavery but is overruled by the British Crown.

*New slaves being unloaded in America, they were welcomed with harsh, inhuman treatment.*

**1712, New York City** An early slave revolt claims the lives of nine whites and results in the execution of 21 blacks. Six others commit suicide.

**1723, Virginia** The colony enacts laws to limit the increase of free blacks to those who are born into this class or manumitted by special acts of the legislature. Free blacks are denied the right to vote and forbidden to carry weapons of any sort.

**1727, Philadelphia** The Junto, a benevolent association founded by Benjamin Franklin, opposes slavery.

**1735, New York** Dutch Burgher John Van Zandt whips his slave to death for being picked up outside of his quarters. Van Zandt is tried by a coroner's jury which asserts that the slave was killed "by the visitation of God."

**1739, South Carolina** Three black revolts occur, resulting in known deaths to 51 whites and many more slaves. One of the insurrections led by the slave, Cato, results in the death of 30 whites.

**1740, South Carolina** The colony passes a slave code which forbids slaves from raising livestock, provides that any animals owned by slaves be forfeited and fixes severe penalties for slaves who make "false appeals" to the governor on the grounds that they have been placed in bondage illegally.

**1741, New York** A series of arsonist acts throughout the city prompts a massive white backlash which results in the burning of 11 blacks and the hanging of 18 others. Public suspicion of slaves stems solely from their presence, rather than from any circumstantial or direct proof of their connection with the crimes.

**1744, Virginia** The colony amends its 1705 law declaring that blacks cannot serve as witnesses in court cases; it decides, instead, to admit "any free Negro, mulatto, or Indian being a Christian," as a witness in a criminal or civil suit *involving another Negro*, mulatto, or Indian.

**1746, Deerfield, Massachusetts** Slave poet Lucy Terry pens *Bars Fight,* a commemorative poem recreating the Deerfield Massacre. Terry, generally considered the first black poet in America, later tried unsuccessfully to convince the Board of Trustees at Williams College to admit her son to the school.

**1747, South Carolina** The Assembly commends black slaves for demonstrating "great faithfulness and courage in repelling attacks of His Majesty's enemies." It then makes cautious provisions for utilizing black recruits in the event of danger or emergency. No more than half of all able-bodied slaves aged 16-20 is authorized to enlist. Once mustered in, slaves are to be integrated among the companies so that they never constitute more than one-third of the white men in the company.

**1749, Georgia** Prohibitions on the importation of slaves are repealed in a law which also attempts to protect slaves from cruel treatment and from being hired out.

**1750, Framingham, Massachusetts** Crispus Attucks, later to become one of the first heroes of the American Revolution, escapes from his master.

**1750, The English Colonies** Slave population reaches 236,400, with over 206,000 of the total living south of Pennsylvania. Slaves comprise about 20% of the colonies' population, and over 40% of Virginia's.

**1752, Mount Vernon, Virginia** There are 18 slaves in Mount Vernon at the time George Washington acquires the estate there. Under Washington, the number grows to 200. Washington's record shows a concern for their physical welfare, but vacillation about their right to freedom and his willingness to dispense with their services.

**1754, Philadelphia** Quaker John Woolman publishes *Some Considerations On the Keeping Of Negroes*, an exhortation to fellow members of the Society of Friends to consider manumitting their slaves on grounds of morality. Three years later, some Quakers take formal action against members who ignore this plea and continue to own slaves.

**1754, Baltimore** Benjamin Banneker, a 22-year-old free black, becomes the first person in the North American colonies to build a clock, though he has never before seen one. The clock chimes the hour accurately for more than 20 years.

**1760, New York City** Jupiter Hammon, a black poet, publishes *Salvation By Christ With Penitential Cries.*

**1760, Rhode Island** Despite the exhortation of some Friends and official statements from other Quaker communities, Quaker policy is not uniform on the slavery issue. One group in Rhode Island continues to be active in the slave trade. A few Quakers in the Carolinas and Virginia refuse to relinquish slaves.

**1764, Massachusetts** Slave ship captains and merchants oppose efforts to raise the price of sugar and molasses, declaring them essential to the slave trade, which they deem the "vital commerce" of New England. But, representing another viewpoint, Samuel Adams refuses the offer of a slave for his sick wife. Though penniless, Adams insists the woman be freed before she enters his house.

*Slaves are accused , without hard evidence, of arsonist acts in New York City. Eleven blacks are burned, eighteen are hung.*

**1766, Virginia** George Washington orders that one of his slaves, "Negro Tom," who had run away, be sold in the West Indies for molasses, rum, limes, tamarinds, sweet meats, and good old spirits.

**1767, Boston** Phyllis Wheatley, a 14-year-old slave to the wife of a prosperous Boston tailor, authors *A Poem by Phyillis, A Negro Girl, On the Death of Reverend Whitefield*. It is printed in 1770 by *The University of Cambridge in New England* . She is soon hailed as a prodigy and feted in New England and London.

**1769, Virginia** In the Virginia House of Burgesses, Thomas Jefferson unsuccessfully presses for a bill to emancipate slaves.

**1770, Boston, Massachusetts** Crispus Attucks is shot and killed during the Boston Massacre.

**1770, Philadelphia, Pennsylvania** Led by Anthony Benezet, the Quakers open a school for blacks.

**1773, Savannah, Georgia** George Lisle and Andrew Bryan organize the first Negro Baptist church in the state.

**1774, The Continental Colonies** The Continental Congress demands elimination of the slave trade and economic embargoes on all countries participating in it. Rhode Island enacts a law freeing slaves henceforth brought into the colony, but not those presently there.

**1775, Germany** Johann Friedrich Blumenbach publishes the first telling attack on theories declaring blacks to be racially inferior. In *On the Natural Variety of Mankind,* Blumenbach proves that the skulls and brains of blacks are the same as those of Europeans. Blumenbach's paper serves as a counter to the views of Voltaire, Hume, and Linne that blacks are akin to apes.

**1775, Philadelphia** Organization of the first abolitionist society in the United States.

**1775, Fort Ticonderoga** Black patriots join Ethan Allen and the Green Mountain Boys in the capture of Fort Ticonderoga.

**1775, Bunker Hill** Peter Salem, Salem Poor, and others are among blacks to fight heroically at Bunker Hill.

**1775, Philadelphia** The Continental Congress bars blacks from the American Revolutionary army.

**1775, Virginia** Lord Dunmore, British governor of Virginia, offers freedom to all male slaves who join the loyalist forces. General George Washington, originally opposed to the enlistment of blacks, is alarmed by the response to the Dunmore proclamation and orders recruiting officers to accept free blacks for service.

**1776, Philadelphia** Adoption of the amended form of the Declaration of independence, which eliminates the Jefferson proposal denouncing slavery.

**1776, The Continental Colonies** Lafayette praises black soldiers for successfully covering Washington's retreat to Long Island. Blacks also help cover Washington's retreat at Trenton and Princeton, but many rebel leaders oppose

*Above: Newspaper woodcuts for runaway slave notices.*

*Right: This handbill circulated in Charleston, South Carolina, during a smallpox epidemic.*

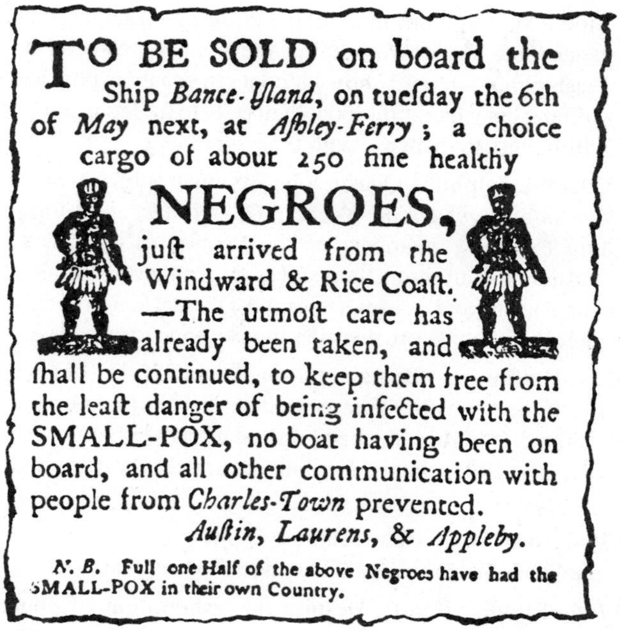

TO BE SOLD on board the Ship *Bance-Yland*, on tuesday the 6th of *May* next, at *Ashley-Ferry*; a choice cargo of about 250 fine healthy

NEGROES,

just arrived from the Windward & Rice Coast. —The utmost care has already been taken, and shall be continued, to keep them free from the least danger of being infected with the SMALL-POX, no boat having been on board, and all other communication with people from *Charles-Town* prevented.

*Austin, Laurens, & Appleby.*

N. B. Full one Half of the above Negroes have had the SMALL-POX in their own Country.

integrated forces and two all-black companies are formed.

**1776, Delaware River** Two blacks, Prince Whipple and Oliver Cromwell, cross the Delaware with Washington enroute to an attack on the British and their Hessian mercenaries in Trenton, New Jersey.

**1778, Rhode Island** A black battalion consisting of 300 former slaves is formed. They are compensated on a par with their white comrades-in-arms and promised freedom after the war. In August, the battalion kills 1,000 Hessians and later sees action under Colonel Green at Ponts Bridge in New York.

**1779, New York** Alexander Hamilton endorses the plan of South Carolina's Henry Laurens to use slaves as soldiers in the south. "I have not the least doubt that the Negroes will make very excellent soldiers," says Hamilton, "....for their natural faculties are as good as ours. "Hamilton reminds the Continental Congress that the British will make use of Negroes if the Americans do not. In Hamilton's words: "The best way to counteract the temptations they will hold out, will be to offer them ourselves."

**1781, Virginia** Black soldiers participate in defeat of Cornwallis at Yorktown. Maroon attacks on plantations and an uprising in Williamsburg are reported.

**1782, Virginia** Thomas Jefferson's *Notes on Virginia* exhibits a curious mixture of perception and naivete with regard to blacks. On the one hand, Jefferson believes that "the whole commerce between master and slave is a perpetual exercise of the most boisterous passions," on the other, he invents the fantasy that black's "griefs are transient."

**1782, Massachusetts** Deborah Gannet, a female black disguised as a man, serves in the 4th Massachusetts Regiment and is later cited for bravery.

**1783, The United States** The war ends. Some 10,000 blacks had served in the continental armies, 5,000 as regular soldiers. The famed "Black Regiment" is deactivated.

**1783, Massachusetts** Slavery in The Commonwealth is abolished by the Massachusetts Supreme Court. Blacks in taxable categories are granted suffrage.

**1785, Wilmington, North Carolina** Birth of black abolitionist David Walker, who in 1827 establishes a second-hand clothing business in Boston, and two years later, writes *Walker's Appeal*, a call to revolt in the South. The document creates such a furor among slave owners that at least one southern legislature makes circulation of it a capital offense.

**1787, Philadelphia** Black preachers Richard Allen and Absalom Jones organize the Free African Society. Prince Hall organizes the first black Masonic Lodge in America—African Lodge No. 459.

**1787, Northwest Territory** Congressional passage of the "Northwest Ordinance" forbids the extension of slavery into this area.

**1787, New York City** Opening of the African Free School by the New York Manumission Society.

**1787, The United States** The Constitution is adopted. In it, importation of slaves cannot be prohibited before 1808, and five slaves are considered the equivalent of three freemen in Congressional apportionment.

**1788, Newport, Rhode Island** The Negro Union advocates emigration of free blacks to Africa. Its stand is opposed by the Philadelphia Free African Society.

**1790, The United States** According to the first census, there are 757,000 blacks in the United States, comprising 19% of the total population. Nine percent of blacks are free.

**1790, West Indies** Blacks comprise seven-eighths of the islands' 529,000 inhabitants. Less than 3% are free.

*Two black soldiers were with General George Washington when he crossed the Delaware River. They were Oliver Cromwell and Prince Whipple.*

Mulattoes in French Santo Domingo own 10% of the slaves and land.

**1790, The Western Territories** Jean Baptiste Pointe du Sable, the son of a French mariner and African slave mother, establishes the first permanent settlement at what is to become Chicago.

**1791, Haiti** Toussaint L'Ouverture, a self-educated slave, leads an unsuccessful uprising, but the French grant suffrage to mulattoes born of free parents.

**1791, Louisiana** Twenty-three slaves are hanged and three white sympathizers deported, following suppression of a black revolt.

**1791, District of Columbia** On the recommendation of Thomas Jefferson, Benjamin Banneker—astronomer, inventor, mathematician and gazetteer—is appointed to serve as a member of the commission charged with laying out plans for the city of Washington.

**1791, Philadelphia** Congress excludes blacks and Indians from peacetime militia. Kentucky is admitted as a slave state.

**1793, Philadelphia** Passage of the Fugitive Slave Act, which makes it criminal to harbor a slave or prevent his arrest.

**1793, Mulberry Grove, Georgia** Eli Whitney patents the cotton gin, which strengthens slavery by vastly increasing profits in cotton growing.

**1793, Virginia** Passage of a state law which forbids free blacks from entering the state.

**1794, Philadelphia** Dedication of the First African Church of St. Thomas, the first black Episcopal Congregation in

*The British prison ship Jersey, aboard which many white and black Revolutionary soldiers died.*

*Arab slavers enter a West African village. As the slave trade intensified, European guns made tribal resistance futile.*

the United States. In the same year, Richard Allen organizes the Bethel Church, a Negro Methodist Episcopal Church. Allen and Absalom Jones are well known to the citizens of Philadelphia, having been commended by the Mayor for organizing blacks to minister to the sick and bury the dead during an outbreak of yellow fever.

**1795, Louisiana** More slave uprisings are suppressed with some 50 blacks killed and executed.

**1795, Virginia** George Washington advertises for the return of one of his slaves, stipulating that the notice for his retrieval not be run north of Virginia. This same year, John Adams writes: "I have never owned a Negro or any other slave ( even ) when it has cost me thousands of dollars for the labor and sustenance of free men, which I might have saved by the purchase of Negroes at times when they were very cheap."

**1796, Tennessee** Admission of Tennessee to the Union as a slave state. The state's constitution, however, does not deny suffrage to free blacks.

**1796, New York City** Organization of the Zion Methodist Church.

**1797, North Carolina** Congress refuses to accept the first recorded anti-slavery petition seeking redress against a North Carolina law which requires that slaves, although freed by their Quaker masters, be returned to the state and to their former condition.

**1797, Hurley, New York and Chapel Hill, North Carolina** Births of Sojourner Truth and George Moses Horton. Miss Truth, freed in 1827, feels herself singled out for a divinely inspired crusade involving emancipation and women's liberation. During the Civil War, she is a nurse; later, she is a touring lecturer. A janitor, George Moses Horton writes love poems for students and later publishes a book of verse. Horton is freed after the Civil War and finishes a second volume, *Naked Genius*.

**1798, Washington, D.C.** Secretary of the Navy Stoddert forbids the deployment of black sailors on men-of-war, thus disrupting a nonracial enlistment policy which had been operative in the Navy for many years. Nevertheless, a few blacks slip past the ban, including William Brown, a "powder monkey" on the *Constellation* and George Diggs, quartermaster of the schooner *Experiment*. Enlistments in the Marine Corps are also forbidden.

**1799, Mount Vernon, Virginia** George Washington's will declares: "It is my will and desire that all the slaves which I hold in my right, shall receive their freedom."

**1799, Boston** First minstrel performance is given by Gottlieb Graupner, a young German who had studied songs sung by blacks in Charleston. Graupner later forms the Boston Philharmonic Society.

**1800, Richmond** Betrayal of Gabriel Prosser's plan to lead thousands of slaves in an attack on Richmond. Prosser and 15 of his followers are later hanged.

**1800, Washington, D.C.** By a vote of 85 to 1, Congress rejects petition by free blacks of Philadelphia to gradually end slavery in the United States.

**1803, South Carolina** The Legislature, which had been trying to limit importation of slaves, reopens slave trade with Latin America and the West Indies.

**1803, New York City** Blacks of New York burn parts of the city and destroy several homes.

**1804, Ohio** The legislature enacts the first of the "Black

Laws" restricting the rights and movements of blacks. Other Western states soon follow suit. Illinois, Indiana, and Oregon later have anti-immigration clauses in their state constitutions.

**1804, New Jersey** New Jersey passes an emancipation law. All states north of the Mason-Dixon Line now have laws forbidding slavery or providing for its gradual elimination. However, there are to be some slaves in New Jersey right up to the Civil War.

**1807, New Jersey** The state alters its 1776 Constitution by limiting the vote to free white males.

**1807, Washington, D.C.** Congress bars the importation of any new slaves into the territory of the United States (effective January 1, 1808). The law is widely ignored.

**1808, United States** Ban on the importation of slaves is scheduled to take effect. There are one million slaves in the country.

**1810, Louisiana** Courts declare, in *Adelle v. Beauregard,* that a black is free unless it is other wise proven.

**1811, Westport, Connecticut** Paul Cuffee (1759-1818), son of black and Indian parents and later a wealthy shipbuilder, sails with a small group of blacks to Sierra Leone to underscore his advocacy of a black return to Africa.

**1811, Delaware** The state forbids the immigration of free blacks and declares that any native-born free black who has been out of Delaware for more than six months will be deemed a nonresident.

**1811, Louisiana** U.S. troops suppress a slave uprising in two parishes some 35 miles from New Orleans. The revolt is led by Charles Deslands. Some 100 slaves are killed or executed.

**1812, Louisiana** Admission of Louisiana to the Union as a slave state. State law enables freedmen to serve in the state militia.

**1813, Lake Erie** Out of Admiral Perry's victorious force in a naval battle with the British, 10 to 25% are blacks. Many are cited for bravery.

**1814, The United States** Blacks participate in victories at Plattsburg and on Lake Champlain. Andrew Jackson praises blacks for bravery in battle.

**1815, New Orleans** Six hundred blacks, many led by black officers, fight with Andrew Jackson in successful defense of New Orleans.

**1815, Fort Blount, Florida** Blacks and Creek Indians capture the fort from Seminoles and use it as a haven for escaped slaves, and base for attacks on slave owners. But an American army detachment eventually recaptures the fort.

**1816, Louisiana** State law prohibits slaves from testifying against whites and free blacks, except in cases involving slave uprisings.

**1816, Philadelphia** Organization of the African Methodist Episcopal Church.

**1816, Washington, D.C.** Organization of the American Colonization Society, which seeks to transport free blacks to Africa. (Protest meetings are subsequently held by many such blacks in opposition to the Society's efforts "to exile us from the land of our nativity.")

**1816, Virginia** Failure of slave rebellion led by George Boxley, a white man.

**1816, Baltimore** Founding of Bethel Charity School for Negroes by Daniel Coker, a black.

**1816, New Orleans** James P. Beckwourth, who was to become one of the great explorers of the nineteenth century, signs on as a scout for General Henry Ashley's Rocky

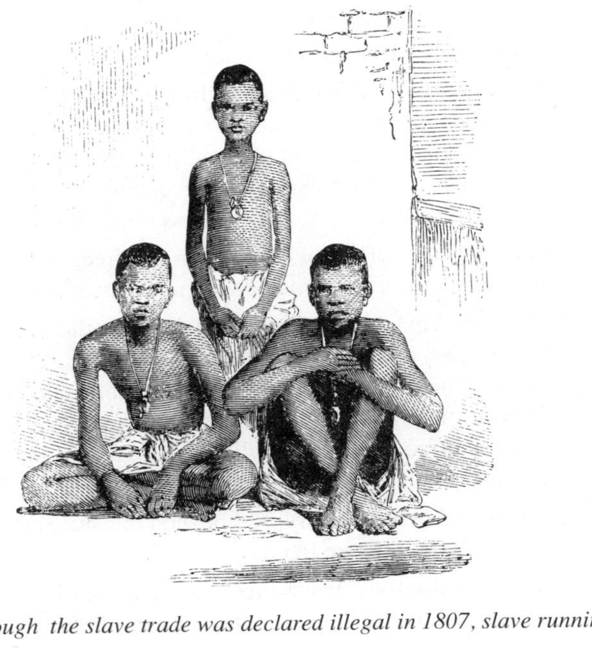

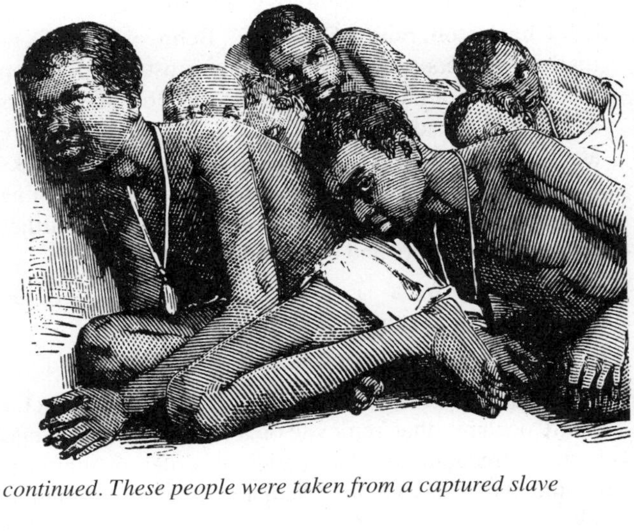

*Although the slave trade was declared illegal in 1807, slave running continued. These people were taken from a captured slave schooner.*

Mountain expedition.

**1817, The United States** Mississippi enters the union as a slave state. New York passes a gradual abolition act.

**1818, Connecticut** Blacks are disenfranchised.

**1818, Philadelphia** Free blacks form the Pennsylvania Augustine Society "for the education of people of colour." Schools for blacks receive public aid.

**1819, Washington, D.C.** James Madison, who wishes slavery to cease but believes in separatism, argues that slavery should end gradually and that slaves be allotted land in the West because the barriers to "incorporation of the people are insuperable."

**1819, Alabama** Alabama enters the Union as a slave state, although its constitution provides the Legislature with the power to abolish slavery and compensate slave owners. Other measures include jury trials for slaves figuring in crimes above petty larceny, and penalties for malicious killing of slaves.

**1820, Washington, D.C.** The Missouri Compromise provides for Missouri's entry into the Union as a slave state and Maine's entry as a free state. There are thus 12 slave and 12 free states in the United States. All territory north of 36 30 is declared free; all territory south of that line open to slavery. The Army is forbidden from accepting blacks and mulattoes.

**1820, New York City** The *Mayflower of Liberia* sails for the west coast of Africa (Sierra Leone) with 86 blacks aboard.

**1821, New York** The State Constitutional Convention alters the voting requirements of the 1777 N.Y. Convention by establishing higher property and longer residence requirements for blacks.

**1821, New York City** Founding of the African Methodist Episcopal Zion Church, with James Varick as its first bishop.

**1821, New York** The African Company performs Shakespeare in a theater on Mercer Street.

**1822, Charleston, South Carolina** Betrayal of the Denmark Vesey conspiracy, one of the most elaborate on record. Vesey, a sailor and carpenter, and 36 collaborators are hanged, an additional 130 blacks and four whites are arrested, and stricter controls are imposed on free blacks and slaves. Following this insurrection, South Carolina and other slave states adopt laws and policies that further restrict the mobility and education of blacks.

**1822, Western Africa** Liberia is founded by blacks of the American Colonization Society.

**1822, Rhode Island** Free blacks are disenfranchised.

**1823, Washington, D.C. and Philadelphia** U.S. Circuit Court declares that removal of a slave to a free state bestows freedom and that malicious, cruel, or inhuman treatment of a slave is an indictable offense of a common law.

*The cotton gin made slave labor more "essential" in the South.*

**1823, Mississippi** Law prohibiting teaching of reading and writing to blacks and meetings of more than five slaves or free blacks is enacted.

**1824, The United States** As the country moves toward universal male suffrage, more states in the North and West as well as the South move to deny the vote to blacks. Illinois, Indiana, Iowa, and Michigan require blacks to post bond in guarantee of good behavior.

**1825, Maryland** Josiah Henson, prototype for the original "Uncle Tom," leads a group of slaves to freedom in Kentucky. Henson later crosses the border into Ontario and becomes leader of a community of ex-slaves.

**1826, London** Frederick Ira Aldridge, a black actor born in New York City and educated in The African Free School, makes his London debut playing Othello at the Royal Theater. Aldridge is later acclaimed in Europe as one of the great actors of the nineteenth century.

**1826, Virginia** Thomas Jefferson's will frees only five of his many slaves, the remainder being bequeathed to heirs.

**1827, New York City** *Freedom's Journal*, the first black newspaper, begins publication on March 16. States the publication: "In the spirit of candor and humility we intend to lay our case before the public with a view to arrest the progress of prejudice, and to shield ourselves against its consequent evils."

**1827, New York** Slavery is abolished in New York State on July 4; 10,000 are freed.

**1828, Bennington, Vermont** William Lloyd Garrison begins attacks on slavery in the *National Philanthropist*.

**1829, Cincinnati** After a riot in which whites attack black

*An international anti-slavery society was planned by William Garrison, George Thompson, and Wiliam Phillips.*

residents and loot and burn their homes, 1,200 blacks flee to Canada.

**1829, Boston** Publication by David Walker, a free black, of a militant anti slavery pamphlet *An Appeal to the Colored People of the World* which is distributed throughout the country and arouses a furor among slaveholders.

**1830, North Carolina** Masters fearing violation of state law manumit more than 400 slaves to Quaker residents of North Carolina, who retain theoretical ownership, but allow slaves virtual freedom until they can afford to transport them to free states.

**1830, Washington, D.C.** The U.S. Census Bureau reports that 3,777 Negro heads of families own slaves, mostly in Louisiana, Maryland, Virginia, North Carolina, and South Carolina.

**1830, Philadelphia** Chaired by Richard Allen, the first National Negro Convention meets from September 20 to 24 at Philadelphia's Bethel Church. It launches a church-affiliated program to improve the social status of the American Negro.

**1830, The United States** As a counter to the increasing strength of the abolitionist movement a number of states pass laws restricting the education, legal safeguards, and citizenship rights of slaves and free blacks. Many states require the deportation of free blacks; slave codes are enforced more strictly and the number of manumissions decline.

**1831, Boston** The *Liberator,* an abolitionist organ, is founded by William Garrison. Proclaims Garrison: "I am in earnest—I will not equivocate—I will not excuse—I will not retreat a single inch—AND I WILL BE HEARD!"

**1831, Southampton County, Virginia** Nat Turner, a brilliant and moody slave, leads the greatest slave rebellion in history. Some 60 whites are killed and the entire South is thrown into panic. Turner is captured on October 30 and hanged in Jerusalem (Virginia) 12 days later.

**1831, Philadelphia** Convocation of the first Annual Convention of the People of Color at Wesleyan Church, where delegates from five states resolve to study black conditions, explore settlement possibilities in Canada, and raise money for an industrial college in New Haven. Delegates oppose the American Colonization Society and recommend annual meetings.

**1831, Virginia** Thomas Dew, a legislator, proudly refers to Virginia as a "Negro-raising state" for other states. Between 1830 and 1860, Virginia exports some 300,000 slaves, and South Carolina exports 179,000.The price of slaves increases sharply due to expanding territory in which slaves are permitted and a booming economy in products harvested and processed by slave labor.

**1832, Boston** The New England Anti-Slavery Society is established by 12 whites at the African Babtist Church on Boston's Beacon Hill.

**1833, Philadelphia** Black, and white abolitionists organize the American Anti-Slavery Society.

**1833, Canterbury, Connecticut** Miss Prudence Crandall, a white liberal, is arrested for conducting an academy for black girls.

**1833, Ohio** Founding of Oberlin College, integrated from the outset and a leader in the abolitionist cause. At the start of the Civil War, blacks constitute one-third of Oberlin's students.

**1834, British Empire** Parliament abolishes slavery in the British Empire; 700,000 are liberated at a cost of 20 million British pounds sterling.

**1834, South Carolina** State enacts a law prohibiting the teaching of black children, free or slave.

**1835, Washington, D.C.** President Jackson seeks to restrict the mailing of abolitionist literature to the South.

**1835, North Carolina** The last southern state to deny suffrage to blacks, North Carolina repeals a voting rights provision of the state constitution. The state also makes it illegal for whites to teach free blacks.

**1836, The United States** The Methodist Church softens its opposition to slavery and declares its intention to avoid interference in civil and political relationships between masters and slaves.

**1836, Washington, D.C.** The House of Representatives adopts the "gag rule" which prevents Congressional action on antislavery resolutions or legislation.

**1837, Alton, Illinois** Elijah P. Lovejoy is murdered by a mob in Alton after refusing to stop publishing antislavery material.

**1837, Florida** John Horse, a black, is a commander of Seminole Indians in their victory over American troops at the Battle of Okeechobee.

**1837, New York City** James McCune Smith establishes medical practice after studying medicine in Scotland.

**1837, Boston** Series of abolitionist works are published, including Reverend Hosea Eaton's *A Treatise on the Intellectual Character and Political Condition of the Colored People of the United States.*

**1837, Virginia** The price for a slave "prime field hand," that is, a black male between 18 and 25 years of age, in good physical condition reaches $1,300, then declines in wake of a recession.

**1837, Canada** Blacks are given the right to vote.

**1838, Southern States** Black preachers are increasingly forbidden to conduct services, as slaves are required to worship under the supervision of their masters.

**1838, Montauk, Long Island** The slaveship *Amistad* is brought into Montauk by a group of Africans who have revolted against their captors. The young African leader Cinque and his followers are defended before the Supreme Court by former President John Quincy Adams, and awarded their freedom.

**1839, Washington, D.C.** The State Department rejects a black's application for a passport on the grounds that blacks are not citizens.

**1839, Warsaw, New York** Founding of the first antislavery political organization, the Liberty Party, with black abolitionists Samuel Ringgold Ward and Henry Highland Garnet among its leading supporters. Party urges boycotts and exclusion of southern crops and products.

**1840, The Vatican** Pope Gregory XVI declares opposition to slavery and the slave trade.

**1840, New York and Vermont** Jury trial for fugitive slaves is instituted. Vermont law is overturned in 1843, reinstated in 1850.

**1840, Massachusetts** Running counter to a nationwide trend, Massachusetts repeals law forbidding intermarriage between whites and blacks, mulattoes, or Indians.

**1841, Virginia** Slaves revolt on the vessel *Creole* enroute from Hampton, Virginia to New Orleans. Overpowering the crew and sailing the ship to the Bahamas, the slaves are granted asylum and freedom.

**1841, Massachusetts** Frederick Douglass begins his career as a lecturer with the Massachusetts Anti-Slavery Society.

**1841, The United States** Increasingly restrictive segregation statutes are enacted. The New York State Legislature grants school districts the right to segregate their educational facilities. South Carolina forbids white and black mill hands from looking out the same window. Whites and blacks in Atlanta are required to swear on different bibles in court.

**1842, Boston** The capture of George Latimer, an escaped slave, precipitates the first of several famous fugitive slave cases straining North-South relations. Latimer is later purchased from his master by Boston abolitionists. Agitation for Latimer is marked by Frederick Douglass's first appearance in print.

**1842, Rhode Island** Suffrage is granted to blacks.

**1842, Pennsylvania** An early challenge to the Fugitive Slave Act (of 1793) occurs when a state court convicts Edward Prigg of kidnapping for his recapture of an escaped slave, Margaret Morgan. The Pennsylvania Court denies that the Fugitive Slave Law applies in Prigg's behalf, on grounds that it must be enforced by federal officials. An early dispute between immigrant and black laborers erupts in coal mining areas, where black and Irish

*The Amistad at anchor in Long Island Sound after America's most famous slave mutiny.*

miners clash.

**1843, Buffalo, New York** Henry Highland Garnet calls for a slave revolt and general strike while addressing the National Convention of Colored Men. Garnet, Samuel R. Ward, and Charles B. Ray participate in the Liberty Party convention, becoming the first blacks to take part in a national political gathering.

**1843, Massachusetts and Vermont** Legislatures defy the Fugitive Slave Act and forbid state officials from imprisoning or assisting federal authorities in the recapture of escaped slaves.

**1843, Washington, D.C.** Approval of Webster-Ashburton Treaty in which Britain and the United States agree to keep ships off African Coast to suppress the slave trade there. No agreement is reached, however, to restrict slave trade within the Western Hemisphere.

**1844, Philadelphia** Birth of Richard Greener, the first black to receive a degree from Harvard (1870). Active as a teacher and editor, Greener is admitted to the South Carolina bar in 1876 and becomes dean of Howard's Law School in 1879.

**1844, California** Jim Beckwourth discovers a pass through the Sierra Nevada Mountains to California and the Pacific Ocean.

**1845, Worcester, Massachusetts** Macon B. Allen becomes the first black formally admitted to the bar in the United States.

**1845, Washington, D.C.** Congress overturns the gag rule of 1836. Texas is admitted to the Union as a slave state.

**1846, Louisiana** Norbert Rillieux, son of a white engineer and free mulatto mother, patents the multiple-effect vacuum evaporation process which becomes the basic method for processing sugar.

**1847, New York** Abolitionist Gerritt Smith's plans to parcel up thousands of acres of his land in New York fails to attract prospective black farmers. Lack of capital among blacks and the infertility of the land doom the project. New York voters reject a constitutional amendment to grant equal suffrage to blacks.

**1847, St. Louis** Dred Scott files suit for his freedom in the Circuit Court of St. Louis.

**1847, Rochester, New York** Frederick Douglass publishes the first issue of his abolitionist newspaper, *The North Star*.

**1848, Buffalo** The convention of the Free Soil Party is attended by a number of black abolitionists.

**1848, Virginia** Postmasters are forced to inform police of the arrival of pro-abolition literature and turn it over to authorities for burning.

**1849, Maryland** Harriet Tubman, soon to be a conductor on the "Underground Railroad," escapes from slavery. Tubman later returns to the South no less than 19 times to help transport more than 300 slaves to freedom. In the same year, the Maryland legislature enacts laws to override restrictions on the importation of slaves.

*A political cartoon from the 1850's depicting the Fugitive Slave Act.*

**1849, Maryland** The state's Supreme Court establishes the "separate but equal" doctrine in response to a suit brought by Benjamin Roberts to have his daughter admitted to a white school.

**1850, Washington, D.C.** The Clay Compromise is enacted, strengthening the 1793 Fugitive Slave Act. Federal officers are now offered a fee for the slaves they apprehend. California is admitted to the union as a free state.

**1850, New York** Samuel R. Ward becomes president of the American League of Colored Laborers, a union of skilled black workers who develop black craftsmen and encourage black-owned business.

**1851, Virginia** New laws require freed slaves to leave the state within a year or be enslaved again.

**1852, Akron, Ohio** Sojourner Truth addresses the National Women's Suffrage Convention.

**1852, Rochester** Frederick Douglass delivers his scathing "What to the Slave is the Fourth of July ?" oration—"....your celebration a sham; your boasted liberty an unholy license, your national greatness, swelling vanity...."

**1852, Boston** Publication of the first edition of Harriet Beecher Stowe's controversial *Uncle Tom's Cabin*.

**1852, Cincinnati** Some 200 of the 3,500 Cincinnati blacks are prosperous property owners whose aggregate worth is $500,000 and who pay real estate taxes on their accumulated wealth. However, violent incidents between white and black communities are frequent.

**1853, London** William Wells Brown publishes *Clotel*, the first novel written by an American black.

**1853, The United States** Moves to deport free blacks to

*Two perceptions of John Brown, abolitionist: On the left, a kindly, gentile person is led to the gallows. Above, a militant, fiery giant, John Brown, with Bible and rifle is depicted battling to make Kansas a free state.*

Africa gain support. Virginia imposes poll tax on free blacks to obtain funds for deportation and the *New York Herald Tribune* declares that black "racial inferiority" renders their emigration desirable.

**1853, Oxford, Pennsylvania** Lincoln University, the first black college, is founded as Ashmum Institute.

**1854, Boston** Anthony Burns, a fugitive slave, is arrested and escorted through streets lined with abolitionist sympathizers, by U.S. troops prior to being returned to his master, who refuses an offer of $1,200 from Boston citizens attempting to purchase his freedom.

**1854, Washington, D.C.** The Kansas-Nebraska Act, authored by Stephen Douglas, admits the territories of Kansas and Nebraska to the Union without slavery restrictions, in direct contradiction to the provisions of the Missouri Compromise of 1820.

**1854, Paris, France** James Augustine Healy, later the first American black Roman Catholic bishop, is ordained a priest in Notre Dame Cathedral.

**1854, Ohio** John Mercer Langston, who was born a slave in Virginia, is admitted to the Ohio bar. Langston is to become dean of Howard University and the first black to win elective office in the history of the United States.

**1854, New England** The New England Emigration Society organizes to settle ex-slaves in Kansas.

**1854, Peoria, Illinois** In his first statement on slavery, Abraham Lincoln opposes its extension to Western Territories.

**1855, New York** The Liberty Party nominates Frederick Douglass for Secretary of State, the first black nominated for statewide office.

**1855, Maine, Massachusetts, and Michigan** The slavery issue is further polarized by enactment, in these states, of laws forbidding state officials from aiding the federal government in enforcement of the Fugitive Slave Laws. The Massachusetts Legislature abolishes school segregation and integration proceeds without incident

**1856, Ohio** Wilberforce University is founded by the Methodist Episcopal Church. Blacks in Ohio are given control of their own schools.

**1856, Missouri and Kansas** Pro-slavery forces sack the town of Lawrence, noted for its abolitionist, free-soil sentiment.

**1856, The United States** George Vashon publishes an anthology of his poetry, including *Victor Oge*, an antislavery work about a Haitian mulatto.

**1856, Washington, D.C.** Senator Sumner of Massachusetts is severely beaten on the Senate floor by Representative Brooks of South Carolina; Sumner is in the midst of attacking slave owners and those who favor pro-slavery legislation.

**1857, Washington, D.C.** In the Dred Scott decision, the U.S. Supreme Court, by a 6 to 3 vote, opens federal territory to slavery, denies citizenship rights to blacks, and decrees that slaves do not become free when taken into free territory. (Scott himself is freed by his owner.) The Dred Scott decision is followed by a ruling that blacks are not entitled to land grants.

**1857, Maine and New Hampshire** Continuing to defy Fugitive Slave Laws, these states grant freedom and citizenship to people of African descent.

**1858, Illinois** In debates with Douglas, Lincoln states opposition to slavery, but declares that equality between the races is impossible.

**1858, Washington, D.C.** U.S. Attorney rules slaves cannot patent inventions because they are not citizens. Jefferson Davis is unable to patent a boat propeller invented by a slave of his, Benjamin Montgomery, because slaves cannot assign inventions to owners.

**1858, Vicksburg, Mississippi** The Southern Commercial Convention calls for reestablishment of the slave trade, despite opposition from Tennessee and Florida delegations.

**1859, Harpers Ferry** John Brown and his band (13 whites, 5 blacks) attack Harpers Ferry. Two blacks are killed, two are captured, one escapes. (Brown is later hanged at Charles Town, West Virginia.)

**1859, Baltimore** Businessmen complain at slaveholders convention that free black laborers and entrepreneurs monopolize some service industries. However, a resolution to expel free blacks from the state fails.

**1860, The United States** Policies of pro- and anti-slave forces continue to polarize, as the country edges toward Civil War. In Virginia, a law provides that free blacks can be sold into slavery for committing imprisonable offenses. Maryland forbids manumission. President Buchanan advocates a constitutional amendment confirming the Fugitive Slave Acts. The Democratic Party platform supports the Dred Scott decision. The Republican platform opposes the expansion of slavery into the western territories, and Lincoln, still a moderate on the subject of abolition, is elected President. On December 17, South Carolina secedes from the Union.

**1861, The Confederacy** The Confederates attack Fort Sumter, South Carolina, marking the beginning of Civil War. Jefferson Davis is elected President of Confederate States of America and defends slavery as necessary to "self-preservation." The Confederates conscript slaves for military supporting jobs. Some Confederate states use free blacks in armed forces.

**1861, Washington, D.C.** The Secretary of the Navy solicits enlistment of blacks, but most black offers to help militarily are rejected. Federal policy toward liberated slaves is erratic, depending mostly on the viewpoint of individual commanders. Lincoln moves warily, countermanding General Freemont's order that slaves of masters who fight against the Union are to be "declared free men."

**1861, Boston** William C. Nell is appointed a post office clerk, becoming the first black person to hold a federal civilian job.

**1862, Washington, D.C.** President Lincoln proposes plan for gradual, compensated emancipation of slaves. Included is a provision to subsidize emigration to Haiti or Liberia. Lincoln's cautious policies are clarified in a letter to Horace Greeley in which he states his paramount objective as saving the Union "not either to save or destroy slavery." However, Lincoln does sign bills abolishing slavery in the territories and freeing slaves of masters disloyal to the United States. Military commanders are forbidden from returning fugitive slaves to owners and, in September, Lincoln issues an ultimatum giving hostile areas until January 1 to cease fighting or lose their slaves.

**1862, New York** Formation of the National Freedmen's Relief Association, one of many groups dedicated to assist the black slave in making the transition to freedom. Groups in Philadelphia, Cincinnati, and Chicago are eventually consolidated as the American Freedmen's Aid

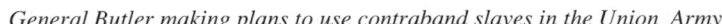

*General Butler making plans to use contraband slaves in the Union Army.*

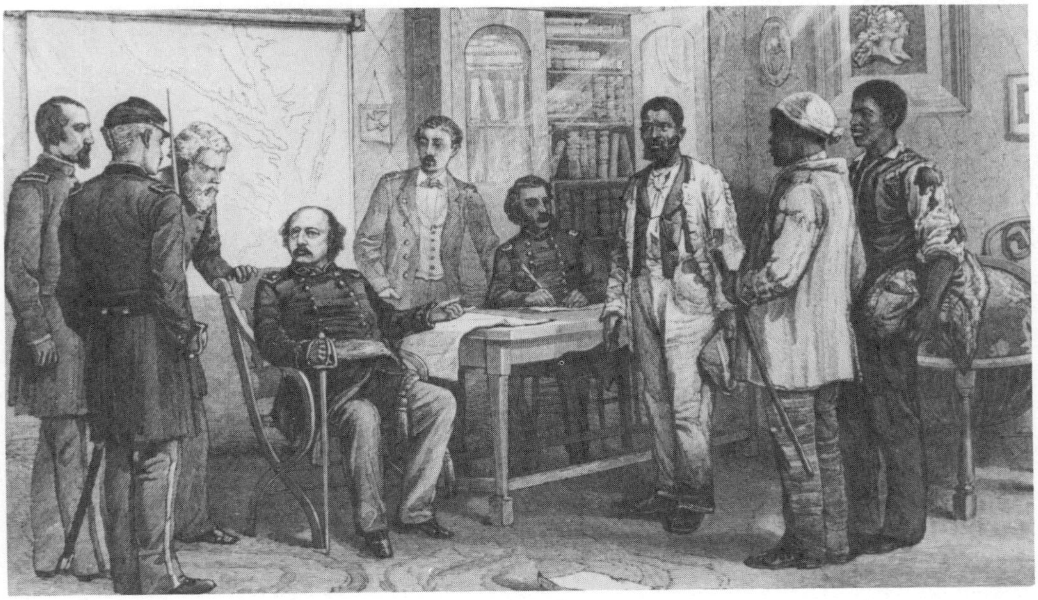

Commission.

**1862, Charleston, South Carolina** Black pilot Robert Smalls, later a congressman, sails the *Planter,* a Confederate steamer, out of Charleston harbor and turns the ship over to Union forces as war booty.

**1862, Washington, D.C.** Congress authorizes the enlistment of blacks for military service.

**1862, The Confederacy** Captured black union troops are hanged or pressed into forced labor. Union generals using black troops are declared subject to execution.

**1863, Washington, D.C.** Lincoln issues Emancipation Proclamation, declaring all slaves in rebellious areas to be free. The War Department forms the USCT (United States Colored Troops) group to federalize black regiments. Between 75 and 100 blacks become officers, most of them serving in Louisiana, many with distinction.

**1863, New York** In anti-draft riots, 1,200 people, mostly blacks, are killed. Riot is spurred in part by provision that exemption from military service can be bought for $300, a provision bitterly resented by poor white immigrants, who vent their frustrations on blacks.

**1863, Cow Island, Haiti** Lincoln sends ship to bring back 500 black settlers as colonization attempt fails.

**1864, The Louisiana Territory** Legislature, elected under auspices of occupying Union forces, votes to abolish slavery, but denies suffrage to blacks.

**1864, The Union** Reports of ill-treatment and withheld wages of black troops and officers continue despite efforts of the Department of War to improve matters.

**1864, Virginia** Fourteen of 37 Congressional Medal of Honor winners at Battle of Chaffin's Farm are black.

**1865, Washington, D.C.** John Rock becomes the first black admitted to practice before the Supreme Court. Congress approves the Thirteenth Amendment and establishes the Freedmen's Bureau.

**1865, Montgomery, Alabama** Jefferson Davis authorizes the Confederacy to fill its military quota by enlisting blacks in number not to exceed 25% of the able-bodied slave population. The measure comes one month before Appomatox and is too late to have an impact on the war.

**1865, Appomatox, Virginia** The Confederacy surrenders: of the 179,000 blacks who served in the Union army, 3,000 were killed in battle, 26,000 died from disease, 14,700 deserted. Blacks represented 9 to 10% of the armed forces and 7% of the desertions.

**1865, Washington, D.C.** Death of Abraham Lincoln. The new President, Andrew Johnson, calls for ratification of the Thirteenth Amendment, which forbids slavery, but opposes black suffrage.

**1865, Southern States** All-white legislatures in many states enact black codes, which seek to maintain many features of prewar restrictions on blacks. Laws impose heavy penalties for "vagrancy," "insulting gestures," "curfew violations," and "seditious speeches." South Carolina requires blacks entering the state to pose a $1,000 bond in guarantee of good behavior and entitles employers to whip black employees.

**1865, Davis Bend, Mississippi** Blacks are settled on confiscated land, but President Johnson pardons owners and returns land to them. Johnson is also to return confiscated land in Georgia and South Carolina.

**1865, The Union** Wisconsin, Connecticut, and Minnesota deny suffrage to blacks.

**1865, Tennessee** The Ku Klux Klan is formed with the purpose of reasserting white supremacy and minimizing the influence of the Union in the South.

**1866, Massachusetts** Edward G. Walker and Charles L. Mitchell are elected to the Massachusetts House of Representatives, becoming the first blacks to serve in a legislative assembly in the United States.

**1866, Nashville, Tennessee** Opening of Fisk University.

**1866, Washington, D.C.** Passage of the Civil Rights Bill of 1866 despite President Johnson's veto. Its intention is to nullify the black codes. A bill is introduced in the District of Columbia to provide for black suffrage. White voters are asked to indicate their sentiments in a referendum. Over 6,500 vote against extension of the franchise to blacks; only 35 favor it. The Fourteenth Amendment passes the House and Senate despite opposition from Johnson. After considerable wrangling, a compromise bill, modestly extending the authority of the Freedman's Bureau, is passed over a Johnson veto. The bill provides for military protection of blacks, distribution of food to

*Ex-slaves formed a pool of cheap labor.*

members of both races, expansion of educational facilities, and return of expropriated land to original owners.

**1866, Tennessee and Louisiana** In a race riot in Memphis, 48 blacks and two white sympathizers are killed. Also, 35 blacks are killed in a riot in New Orleans.

**1866, Washington** Two black cavalry units are formed to serve in the west.

**1866, London** The *London Art Journal* selects Robert Duncanson, a black painter born in Cincinnati, as one of the day's outstanding landscape artists.

**1867, Atlanta and Washington, D.C.** Openings of Morehouse College and Howard University.

**1867, Washington, D.C.** Congress passes, over another veto by President Johnson, the first Reconstruction Act, which provides for military rule pending organization of state governments loyal to the Union. The Act requires occupied states to ratify the Fourteenth Amendment and guarantee the vote to blacks. Secretary of War Sumner fails in efforts to have Act order Freedman's Bureau to provide homes and schools for blacks.

**1867, Southern and Border States** Enforcement of the Reconstruction Act provides blacks with majority of vote in most southern states and alliances of blacks and white Republicans control in border states.

**1867, The West** Iowa and Dakota grant suffrage to blacks, Ohio rejects it.

**1868, Hampton, Virginia** Opening of Hampton Institute by an ex-Union officer, Samuel Chapman Armstrong.

**1868, Southern States** Oscar Dunn, an ex-slave and captain in the Union army, is elected Lieutenant Governor of Louisiana. Blacks outnumber whites 87 to 40 in South Carolina Legislature, but whites have majority in state Senate.

**1868, Washington, D.C.** The Fourteenth Amendment is ratified, establishing the concept of "equal protection" for all citizens under the U.S. Constitution. President Johnson's veto of the bill granting vote to blacks in the District of Columbia is overridden by Congress. Congress passes the Fifteenth Amendment guaranteeing the vote to blacks, and a bill denying the Supreme Court the right to rule on cases involving constitutionality of the Reconstruction Act. The Senate declines by one vote short of needed two thirds (35 to 19) to find Johnson guilty of offenses for which he was indicted by the House of Representatives.

**1868, Louisiana** Louisiana's senators and representatives are readmitted to the U.S. Congress. The move follows the systematic terror initiated by the Ku Klux Klan against members of the Republican Party and emancipated blacks. Killings, lynchings, and beatings are recorded in several Louisiana parishes.

**1868, The South** Many states are readmitted to the Union. The Alabama legislature votes to segregate races in schools

**1868, North and West** Nine states grant suffrage to blacks, but two deny it. The Republican platform omits demand for black suffrage in northern states.

**1868, Great Barrington, Massachusetts** Birth of William DuBois, the great activist and writer, an early advocate of racial pride.

**1869, Washington, D.C.** Organization of The Colored National Labor Union advocates purchase and distribution of land. Ebenezer Don Carlos Bassett, believed to be the first black to receive an appointment in the diplomatic service, becomes U.S. Minister to Haiti.

**1870, Washington, D.C.** The Fifteenth Amendment, guaranteeing all citizens the right to vote, is ratified. In "Ku Klux Klan Acts," the Army is empowered to maintain order in federal elections. The Supreme Court refuses to

*Schoolhouse and chapel at the Trent River settlement.*

review the Reconstruction Act. Hiram Revels of Mississippi, America's first black senator, delivers his maiden speech on March 16 and says: "I maintain that the past record of my race is a true index of the feelings which today animate them...They aim not to elevate themselves by sacrificing one single interest of their white fellow citizens." Between 1870 and 1900, 22 blacks, 13 of them ex-slaves, are to serve in Congress. The Census of 1870 finds only 19% of blacks literate. The figure reaches 43% in 1890.

**1870, Washington, D.C.** Recruitment of blacks for cavalry intensifies. By 1890, 14 were to receive Congressional Medals of Honor for bravery in Indian Wars.

**1870, The South** Democrats regain control of many states from Republicans. Some attribute this to intimidation by the Ku Klux Klan. A Congressional investigation reports that in nine South Carolina counties, the Klan murdered 35 men and whipped 262 men and women. The Florida Secretary of State reports 153 Klan murders in Jackson County.

**1871, Nashville** The renowned Fisk Jubilee Singers go on an international tour to raise money for the college and to present black spirituals to wider and ever-growing audiences.

**1872, Washington, D.C.** Charlotte E. Ray becomes the first black woman to graduate from a university law school (Howard) in the United States.

**1872, Louisiana** P. B. S. Pinchback becomes acting governor of the state upon impeachment of the incumbent.

**1872, Washington, D.C.** Congress passes Amnesty Act, enabling officials of the Confederacy to hold office. Ku Klux Klan Act expires and is not renewed.

**1874, Washington, D.C.** Reverend Patrick F. Healy, S. J., is named President of Georgetown, the oldest Catholic University in the United States.

**1874, Virginia** State rearranges election districts and local government system thereby reducing political power of blacks.

**1875, Washington, D.C.** Congress passes the Civil Rights Bill of 1875, prohibiting discrimination in such public accommodations as hotels, theaters, and amusement parks. A key piece of legislation in the post-Civil War era, it seeks to "....mete out equal and exact justice to all, of whatever nativity, race, color, or persuasions, religious or political..."

**1875, Mayesville, South Carolina** Birth of Mary McLeod Bethune, who was to become the advisor on youth affairs to President Franklin Roosevelt.

**1875, Washington, D.C.** Blanche K. Bruce of Mississippi becomes the only black man to serve a full term in the Senate until the middle of the twentieth century. Bruce soon becomes a respected and articulate advocate for blacks, whose rights and influence he feels are insufficiently protected by Congress or President Grant.

**1875, Kentucky** Oliver Lewis, a black jockey, rides Aristides to victory in the first Kentucky Derby.

**1876, Washington, D.C.** The Senate, after three years of controversy, refuses to seat H. R. Pinchback, a black who had been elected in Louisiana in 1873. In two decisions, the Supreme Court decides that the Fourteenth and Fifteenth Amendments do not guarantee suffrage. In *U.S. v. Cruikshank* the Court declares that the Fourteenth Amendment provides blacks with equal protection under the law but does not add anything "to the rights which one citizen has under the Constitution against another." The Court rules that "the right of suffrage is not a necessary attribute of national citizenship."

**1876, South Carolina** Federal troops are sent by President Grant to restore order after five blacks are killed in Hamburg.

**1876, Philadelphia** Black landscape painter Robert Bannister and sculptress Edmonia Lewis, born of black and Indian parents, win critical praise at a Centennial Exhibition.

**1877, The United States** Many historians regard 1877 as the start of a prolonged, adverse period, in which the legal and economic status of blacks declines. Major factors involved are the re-establishment of white political control in the South and the widespread use of blacks as cheap labor and strike breakers in the nation's rapid economic expansion.

**1877, Washington, D.C.** In the aftermath of the inconclusive presidential election of 1876, Rutherford Hayes, a Republican, promises southern delegates he will withdraw federal troops from the South. This contributes to his selection for the presidency over Samuel J. Tilden by the House of Representatives. Democrats control Congress, deny funds to the Army, and in 1878 remove presidential authority to use troops to guarantee fair elections.

**1878, Washington, D.C.** The U.S. Attorney General reveals widespread intimidation of blacks attempting to vote and stuffing of ballot boxes in several southern states.

**1879, The South** Frustrated by poverty and discrimination, large numbers of blacks start to emigrate north and west. A leader of the emigration movement is Benjamin Singleton, a mulatto ex-slave who had earlier escaped to Canada and favors separate black communities. Emigration is vigorously opposed by many whites, some of whom prevent ships from transporting blacks on the Mississippi River. Between 1870 and 1880, 21% of black males between 15 and 34 in Alabama leave.

**1880, The United States** Garfield is elected President, promising protection to southern blacks. Only two blacks are elected to Congress. Bruce is defeated for reelection to the Senate as whites regain control of the state's legislature.

**1881, Washington, D.C.** Chester Arthur succeeds Garfield,

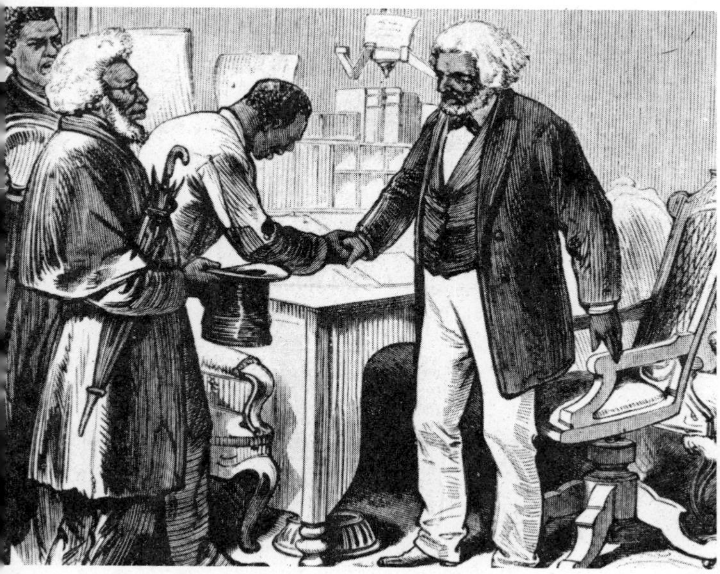

*Frederick Douglass accepts congratulations on his appointment as minister to Haiti.*

who is assassinated, and implies the belief that blacks are not sufficiently educated to vote. Ex-Senator Bruce is appointed Registrar of the Treasury after refusing two other minor federal appointments, one a ministerial post in Brazil.

**1881, Tennessee** Tennessee passes a "Jim Crow" railroad law which sets a trend soon taken up by Florida (1887), Mississippi (1888), Texas (1889), Louisiana (1890), and a host of other southern and border states.

**1881, Tuskegee, Alabama** Booker T. Washington opens Tuskegee Institute with a $2,000 appropriation from the Alabama Legislature.

**1881, Washington, D.C.** Patent for the first incandescent electric lamp with carbon filament is granted Lewis Latimer, a black inventor. Latimer also makes drawings for Alexander Graham Bell's telephone and eventually becomes chief draftsman for General Electric and Westinghouse.

**1883, Washington, D.C.** The Supreme Court declares the Civil Rights Act of 1875 unconstitutional.

**1883, Lynn, Massachusetts** The shoe-lasting machine of Jan Matzeliger, a black from Dutch Guiana, so revolutionizes the industry that Lynn becomes the "shoe-capital of the world."

**1884, New York** The first issue is published of the *New York Age*, a successful black newspaper by T. Thomas Fortune, a mulatto born in Florida.

**1884, Washington, D.C.** Former black Reconstruction Congressman John Roy Lynch is elected temporary chairman of the Republican convention—the first black to preside over a national political gathering.

**1887, Chicago** Formation of the first black baseball team, the Union Giants.

**1888, Richmond and Washington, D.C.** Founding of two black banks—The Savings Bank of the Grand Fountain United Order of True Reformers in Virginia and the Capital Savings Bank in Washington.

**1889, Washington, D.C.** Frederick Douglass is appointed U.S. Minister to Haiti. Three blacks, one each from North Carolina, South Carolina, and Virginia, take seats in Congress.

**1890, Mississippi** The Mississippi Constitutional Convention begins the systematic exclusion of blacks from the political arena by adopting literacy and other complex "understanding" texts as prerequisites to voting. Seven other southern states follow suit by 1910.

**1890, Washington, D.C.** In the *In Re Green* decision, the Supreme Court sanctions control of elections by state officials, thus weakening federal protection for southern black voters. The Court also permits states to segregate public transportation facilities.

**1891, Baffin Bay, Greenland** Matthew Henson, a Maryland-born black, accompanies Admiral Perry in exploration of the Arctic. Henson, a skilled navigator with fluent command of the Eskimo language, is indispensable to the expedition's success.

**1891, Chicago, Illinois** Dr. Daniel Hale Williams founds Provident Hospital, with the first training school for black nurses in the United States.

**1891, Washington, D.C.** The number of lynchings in the United States is reported to be 112. The great majority of victims are blacks residing in the South.

**1892, St. Louis** Georgia Populists, at the Populist Convention, strive to unite poor black and white farmers in the South, who, according to gubernatorial candidate Tom Watson, are kept at loggerheads by landed interests. Watson argues that wealthy Southerners perpetuate racial antagonisms so that poor whites and their black counterparts will resent each other, rather than cooperate for mutually advantageous ends.

**1893, Washington, D.C.** George Murray of South Carolina is the only black to take a seat in the 53rd Congress. The national lynch count is 117.

**1893, Cambridge, Massachusetts** William Henry Lewis, a black football player at Harvard, makes Walter Camp's all-American team.

**1894, Cambridge, Massachusetts** William DuBois becomes the first black to be awarded a Ph.D. by Harvard.

**1894, Washington, D.C.** A section of the Emancipation Act dealing with the right of blacks to vote is repealed.

**1894, Detroit, Michigan** Publication of *Appointed*, a militant, politically conscious novel by William Anderson and Walter Stowers.

**1895, Washington, D.C.** George Murray is, again, the only black to take a seat in Congress.

**1895, Atlanta, Georgia** Booker T. Washington delivers his famous "Atlanta Compromise" address at the Cotton Exposition—"To those of my race who depend on bettering their condition in a foreign land, or who underestimate the importance of cultivating friendly relations with the Southern white man I would say: "Cast down your bucket where you are..."

**1896, Washington, D.C.** The Supreme Court in the *Plessy v. Ferguson* decision upholds the doctrine of "separate but equal," paving the way for segregation of blacks in all walks of life. Justice Harlan, dissenting, calls the ruling as "pernicious as the Dred Scott case."

**1896, Cambridge, Massachusetts** DuBois, who is emerging as a militant counterforce to Booker T. Washington, publishes *Suppression of the African Slave Trade*, the first of some 20 annual sociological studies of blacks in the United States.

**1896, The Southern States** Riots erupt in bitter elections, as diverse factions seek to control or eliminate the black vote. Racism increases within Populist ranks. G. H. White of North Carolina is the only black elected to Congress.

**1896, Washington, D.C.** Formation of The National Association of Colored Women, a politically active self-help group.

**1897, United States** Andrew J. Beard is awarded $50,000 for the invention of the railroad coupler.

**1898, Santiago, Cuba** Four black regiments in the regular army compile an outstanding combat record in and around Santiago during the Spanish-American War. Five blacks receive Congressional Medals of Honor. At the close of the war, over 100 blacks are officers.

**1898, Louisiana** An addition of a "grandfather clause" to the Constitution enables poor whites to qualify for the franchise while curtailing black registration. In 1896, there were over 130,000 black voters on the Louisiana rolls. Four years later, the number is about 5,000.

**1900, London, England** W. E. B. DuBois attends the conference of the African and New World Intellectuals, where he delivers an address incorporating his famous dictum: "The problem of the twentieth century is the problem of the color line." DuBois also attends the first Pan-African Congress, an international body of concerned African nations protesting Western imperialism and promoting the concept of self-government among colonized peoples.

**1900, Boston** Formation by Booker T. Washington of the National Negro Business League.

**1900, The United States** Two contrasting works by blacks receive wide attention. Booker T. Washington's *Up from Slavery* describes success through acceptance of white domination. Charles W. Chestnutt's *The House Behind the Cedars* portrays the desperate plight of the mulatto, whom he perceives as an outcast from both black and white worlds.

*Booker T. Washington*

**1901, Washington, D.C.** Congressman George White delivers his farewell address in the House of Representatives "in behalf of an outraged, heart-broken, bruised and bleeding, but God-fearing people, faithful, industrious, loyal people—rising people, full of force." No black was to serve in Congress again until 1928.

**1901, The United State** Joe Walcott becomes the welterweight champion, and Joe Gans becomes the lightweight champion.

**1902, Richmond, Virginia** Virginia joins other southern states in adopting the "grandfather clause."

**1902, Paris, France** *Off Bloomingdale Asylum*, a satirical comedy, is the first film to use blacks.

**1903, The United States** John D. Rockefeller starts large donations to the General Education Board, which stresses training of black teachers for southern schools. Within six years, Rockefeller donates over $50 million to the Board.

**1903, New York City** A black real estate man starts promoting Harlem as a community for blacks. The poet Countee Cullen is born.

**1903, Georgia and Ohio** Whites attack blacks in riots, which are spurred by charges that blacks have murdered whites.

**1904, Atlanta** Financier Andrew Carnegie brings together a parcel of prominent black leaders, including Booker T. Washington and W. E. B. DuBois, who discuss "the interests of the Negro Race." The personal and ideological clash between the two men is evident at the meeting, though there is agreement that the group should press for "absolute civil, political, and public equality." The group shows little fire in advancing familiar proposals for black self-help.

**1905, Fort Erie, New York** Twenty-nine militant black intellectuals from 14 states organize the Niagara Movement (a forerunner of the NAACP) in opposition to the conciliatory policies of Booker T. Washington. Delegates to the convention demand the abolition of all distinctions based on race.

**1906, Atlanta** An extended riot, in which respected black citizens are killed, brings the city to a standstill for several days. After the riot interracial groups are formed to better conditions for blacks, but many blacks emigrate and moderates lose influence.

**1906, Brownsville, Texas** Several black soldiers of the 25th Infantry Division are involved in a riot with Brownsville police and merchants. Following the incident, President Roosevelt dishonorably discharges three companies without a trial. These dishonorable discharges are finally reversed by the Army in 1972. The lone survivor is awarded $25,000 by the Army in 1973.

**1907, Washington, D.C.** The Supreme Court upholds the right of railroads to segregate passengers traveling between states, even when this runs counter to the laws of states in which the train is traveling.

**1908, Washington, D.C.** The first black sorority, Alpha Kappa Alpha, is founded at Howard University.

**1909, New York City** Partly in reaction to continuing riots, the National Association for the Advancement of Colored People (NAACP) is founded in New York, on the 100th anniversary of Lincoln's birth. The signers of the original charter of incorporation include Jane Addams, John Dewey, Dr. W. E. B. DuBois, William Dean Howells, and Lincoln Steffens. Booker T. Washington is opposed to the group. The NAACP concentrates on legal abuses of blacks. In 1910, it succeeds in having a Baltimore residential segregation statute declared unconstitutional, although the city succeeds later with more carefully drafted laws. In New Jersey, the NAACP secures the release of two blacks being held without evidence on murder charges.

**1909, North Pole** Matthew Henson places the flag of the United States at the North Pole. Henson, a black, was part of the Admiral Robert E. Peary expedition.

**1909, Memphis, Tennessee** William Handy composes campaign music for Edward Crump, the "Mayor Crump Blues."

**1909, The United States** *Sambo* and *Rastus* comedy shorts, in which blacks are depicted as childlike and incompetent, become popular.

**1910, New York** The first edition of *Crisis Magazine*, edited by W. E. B. DuBois, appears. Only 1,000 copies are in print, but before the end of the decade circulation of the magazine has increased one-hundred fold. Among the articles in the first edition, is one by DuBois in which he

*Lieutenant Colonel Charles Young on the trail of Pancho Villa.*

*This "Silent Protest Parade" was held in New York City, in 1917, by blacks protesting lynchings in the South.*

maintains that individuals should be free to marry whomever they choose. He concedes, however, that such an enlightened policy would cause a social calamity in the United States.

**1910, Reno, Nevada** Jack Johnson wins heavyweight championship from James Jeffries in fifteenth round knockout.

**1910, England** On separate lecture tours of Great Britain, DuBois and Washington paint contrasting versions of the black condition in the United States. Washington tells the British that blacks are making strides; DuBois underscores injustices and claims Washington kowtows to powerful white interests. In 1911, DuBois joins the Socialist Party and publishes a novel, The *Quest of the Silver Fleece* , which relates racism to economic causes.

**1911, New York City** The National Urban League is founded with support from wealthy whites and Booker T. Washington. The League stresses employment and industrial opportunities for blacks. Eugene Kinckle Jones is the first executive secretary.

**1911, Jamaica** Marcus Garvey forms the Universal Negro Improvement Association.

**1912, The United States** Despite his southern background and apparent indifference to black rights, Woodrow Wilson is supported for President by DuBois and the NAACP, who feel Wilson is a decent and principled man.

**1912, New York** James Weldon Johnson's *The Autobiography of an Ex-Colored Man* is published, spurring white recognition of black culture and the advent of the "Harlem Renaissance." Theaters in New York City are desegregated.

**1913, Washington, D.C.** President Wilson refuses to appoint a National Race Commission to study the social and economic status of blacks, rejecting a proposal sponsored by Oswald Garrison Villard. The President also appoints white foreign service officers to Haiti and Santo Domingo, among the few consular posts open to blacks by custom and practice.

**1914, The United States** Blacks make the first noteworthy appearance in films. Bert Williams stars in *The Darktown Jubilee* and Sam Lucas plays Uncle Tom. Heretofore, blacks had been portrayed by whites in blackface.

**1915, Southern States** Spurred by boll weevil devastation of cotton crops, the great migration of blacks to the north begins. In a year and a half, the total is 350,000. Dr. Carter G. Woodson establishes the Association for the Study of Negro Life and History and launches the *Journal of Negro History*, with himself as its editor.

**1915, Washington, D.C.** U.S. Supreme Court in *Guinn v. United States* declares the "grandfather clause" in the Oklahoma constitution unconstitutional.

**1916, New York City** Oswald Villard resigns from the NAACP Board in protest against DuBois's militancy. Black leaders meet at the home of Joel Spingarn and agree that suffrage, equal education, and cessation of violence against blacks are priorities. The NAACP expands to the South, naming James Weldon Johnson to organize local chapters there.

**1916, Mexico** Colonel Charles Young, the highest ranking black in the U.S. Army, commands a squadron in an expedition against Pancho Villa.

**1917, Washington, D.C.** The U.S. Supreme Court declares that the Louisville "block" segregation ordinance is unconstitutional.

**1917, New York City** Some 10,000 blacks parade down Fifth Avenue in protest against lynchings and the East St. Louis riot. Marchers include DuBois and James Weldon Johnson.

**1917, Washington, D.C.** The United States enters World War I. Joel Spingarn presses the War Department to establish an officers' training camp for blacks, thus alienating many of his NAACP colleagues who feel that such a camp only perpetuates segregation and in effect gives substance to the notion of black inferiority. Others concede that the move is prudent, since it is the only way for black officers to be trained. The organization ultimately puts itself on record in favor of separate camps. In October, over 600 blacks are commissioned officers, and 700,000 blacks register in the draft.

**1918, The United States** Most blacks and black papers support the War, as 365,000 blacks are drafted for military service. Blacks comprise 11% of troops sent overseas.

**1918, France** Two black infantry battalions are awarded the Croix de Guerre and two black officers win the French Legion of Honor as blacks are in the forefront of fighting from 1917 until the defeat of Germany.

**1919, Atlantic City** Samuel Gompers of the American Federation of Labor delivers an address to the Federation's annual conference in which he vows to remove "every class and race distinction" from the movement and pledges himself to the total abolition of all discrimination in union membership. Gompers professes to see a new era in the struggle for black rights "as well as an advance in the history of political and economic liberty in America." However, Gompers does not support antidiscrimination resolutions at the AFL conventions of 1921 and 1924.

**1919, The United States** Membership of the NAACP approaches 100,000 despite attempts in some areas, such as Texas, to make it illegal. During the second half of the year, there are 75 lynchings and 27 race riots, the severest in Chicago and Washington, D.C. Charles Evans Hughes, leading jurist and defeated Presidential candidate, supports the NAACP efforts to have lynching outlawed.

**1919, West Virginia** The State Supreme Court rules blacks should be admitted to juries.

**1919, Paris** W. E. B. DuBois organizes the first Pan-African Congress at the Grand Hotel; says DuBois: "The Natives of Africa must have the right to participate in the government as fast as their development permits." Jazz and ragtime sweep the French capital. A representative of the Casino de Paris comes to New York to assemble an orchestra of 50 blacks.

**1920, New York** James Weldon Johnson becomes the first black secretary of the NAACP and campaigns for the withdrawal of U.S. troops occupying Haiti.

**1921, St. Louis** At the age of 15, Josephine Baker runs away from home, becomes Bessie Smith's maid, and soon proves her own singing ability.

**1921, Tulsa, Oklahoma** Twenty one blacks and ten whites are killed in a riot.

**1922, Washington, D.C.** After it is approved by the House, Republican Senators vote to abandon the Dyer Anti-Lynching Bill, which provides severe penalties and fines for "any state or municipal officer" convicted of negligence in affording protection to individuals in custody who are attacked by a mob bent on lynching, torture, or physical intimidation. The Bill had also provided for compensation to the families of victims.

**1922, New York** Publication of *Harlem Shadows* by Claude McKay.

**1923, New York** Marcus Garvey, sentenced to a five-year term for mail fraud, charges that most of his troubles stem "from my opponents of the colored race... light colored Negroes who think that the Negro can always develop in this country...resent... that I, a black Negro, am their leader."

**1924, Washington, D.C.** New York Representative Emanuel Cellar introduces legislation to provide for the formation of a blue-ribbon panel to study the racial question. The idea is met with disdain from the black press, particularly the *Chicago Defender,* which editorializes: "We have been commissioned to death...We have too many studies and reports already." *The Defender* asserts that blacks need only to look after their own interests through the creation of a strong party vehicle and potent political leadership in the halls of Congress.

**1924, Washington, D.C.** Immigration Act excludes blacks of African descent from entering the country.

**1925, New York** Publication of *Color*, poetry by Countee Cullen and *The New Negro*, an anthology of poetry edited by Alain Locke.

**1925, New York** Black physicians are admitted to practice in Harlem Hospital.

**1926, The United States** Founding of the Brotherhood of Sleeping Car Porters by A. Philip Randolph.

**1926, Washington, D.C.** President Coolidge tells Congress that the country must provide "for the amelioration of race prejudice and the extension to all elements of equal opportunity and equal protection under the laws, which are guaranteed by the Constitution." Twenty-three blacks are reported lynched during the year.

**1926, New York** Controversy rages among the black intelligentsia after publication of *Nigger Heaven* by white writer Carl van Vechten. The book glamorizes the free wheeling style of Harlem life amid the general contention that blacks are less ashamed of sex and more morally honest than whites. DuBois finds the assumptions deplorable; James Weldone Johnson, on the other hand, believes the treatment is neither scandalous nor insulting.

**1926, Washington, D.C.** Negro History Week is introduced by Dr. Carter G. Woodson and the Association for the Study of Negro Life and History.

**1926, New York City** Langston Hughes, writing in *The Nation* magazine, urges black artists to write from their experience and to stop imitating white writers.

**1927, The United States** In assorted legislation and judicial verdicts, Colorado, Illinois, and New Jersey lessen segregation in schools, but segregation statutes are firmed in southern states.

**1927, Chicago** Urban League organizes boycott of stores that don't hire blacks. In 1929, boycotts are started in several other Midwest cities.

**1927, Atlanta** Marcus Garvey is released from prison and deported to the British West Indies.

**1927, New York City** Formation of the Harlem Globetrotters basketball team. Bill "Bojangles" Robinson and Ethel Waters star on Broadway in *Blackbirds*.

**1927, Pennsylvania and West Virginia** Nonunion black labor is brought from the South to the coal fields, weakening the position of the United Mine Workers. Racial strife ensues as hysterical rumors of rape and miscegenation spread through white mining communities.

**1927, Washington, D.C.** The U.S. Supreme Court strikes down the Texas law which bars blacks from voting in party primaries. Texas then enacts a law allowing local committees to determine voter qualifications.

**1928, Illinois** The election of Oscar De Priest, a Republican, as the first black Congressman from a northern state.

**1929, New York** Oscar De Priest tells an audience of 2500 gathered at a rally at Harlem's Abyssinian Baptist Church that blacks will never make substantial progress until they elect political leaders whose fortunes are dependent on their ability to fight for black interests in Congress. De Priest concludes:"No one can really lead you but one who has been Jim Crowed as you have."

**1930, Washington, D.C.** An NAACP campaign helps prevent confirmation of U.S. Supreme Court nominee John H. Parker, one-time self-admitted opponent of the franchise for blacks. The NAACP also helps unseat three of the senators who voted for him in later Congressional elections.

**1930, Detroit, Michigan** Founding, by Fard Mohammed, of the Temple of Islam, later to become the "Black Muslims."

**1931, Alabama** First trial of the Scottsboro Nine results in a battle between the NAACP and the International Labor Defense, a Communist-controlled group, for the right to represent the young defendants who are charged with rape. The case, which becomes a worldwide *cause celebre* and important propaganda weapon for Communists, drags on for 20 years despite the recanting of a charge by one of the two plaintiffs and medical testimony that rape was not committed.

*Langston Hughes at Tuskegee Institute in 1926 with Jessie Fauset and Zora Neale Hurston. Hughes urged black writers to draw on their own experiences and stop imitating white writers.*

**1932, The United States** Franklin Roosevelt is elected President, but with little support from blacks who observe omission of their objectives from the Democratic Platform. However, in coming years Roosevelt's popularity rises as he appoints blacks to responsible posts and his wife, Eleanor, shows sensitivity to black problems.

**1933, The United States** More than one-fourth of urban blacks are on relief. New Deal programs aid housing and education of blacks, but traditional segregation policies are generally followed. One exception is the Civilian Conservation Corps camps in New England and the Pacific states, which are integrated.

**1934, The United States** In northern and border states 52% of blacks, compared with about 12% of whites, are on relief. The American Federation of Labor's organization committee rejects a resolution introduced by A. Philip Randolph to end discrimination, stating that no discrimination exists in the labor organization.

**1934, Chicago** Arthur Mitchell becomes the first black Democrat of the twentieth century to be elected to Congress, succeeding De Priest.

**1934, Washington, D.C.** Antilynch bill fails, as Roosevelt does not support it. American troops are withdrawn from Haiti.

**1934, Chicago** Black Muslim Headquarters are established. Elijah Muhammed is leader.

**1935, New York City** Founding by Mary McLeod Bethune of the National Council for Negro Women.

**1935, Washington, D.C.** U.S. Supreme Court Justice Roberts upholds the Texas law that prevents blacks from voting in the Texas Democratic primary. The decision is a setback to the NAACP, which has waged several effective legal battles to equalize the ballot potential of the black voter.

**1935, St. Louis** The NAACP bitterly criticizes Roosevelt for failure to present or support civil rights legislation.

**1935, The United States** Percy Julian, a black chemist, develops physostigmine, a drug for treatment of glaucoma.

**1936, The United States** Roosevelt wins an overwhelming reelection victory, gains increasing support from blacks who feel he would like to achieve more for them than Congress allows.

**1936, Berlin, Germany** Jesse Owens wins four gold medals in the 1936 Olympics, but is snubbed by the Chancellor of Germany, Adolf Hitler.

**1936, Washington, D.C.** The U.S. Supreme Court requires Maryland University to admit a black student, Donald Murray, to its graduate law school.

**1937, Virgin Islands** William H. Hastie is confirmed Judge of the Federal District Court in the Virgin Islands, thereby becoming the first black to serve as a federal judge in the history of the United States.

**1937, The United States** Blacks continue to benefit from New Deal programs but not to the same degree as whites. In South, black tenants leave farms as government policies encourage use of wage labor. U.S. Supreme Court rules that picketing is a legal means for blacks to seek redress of grievances.

**1937, Pennsylvania** New law denies many state services to unions discriminating against blacks.

**1937, New York** Richard Wright becomes editor of *Challenge Magazine*, changes the title to *New Challenge*, and urges blacks to write with greater "social realism."

**1937, Spain** Between 60 to 80 of the 3200 Americans who fight for the Republican side in the Civil War are black. Oliver Law, a black from Chicago, commands the Lincoln Battalion.

**1938, New York** Adam Clayton Powell, Jr. and other black leaders convince white merchants in Harlem to hire at least one third blacks and to promise equal promotion opportunities.

**1938, New York** Billie Holiday appears with Artie Shaw's band. Boogie Woogie is popularized at a Carnegie Hall concern given by three blacks. Boxer Henry Armstrong defeats Barney Ross for the welterweight championship and Lou Ambers for the lightweight championship. Armstrong is also featherweight champion and thus holds three championships concurrently.

**1938, Pennsylvania** Crystal Bird Fauset of Philadelphia, the first black woman state legislator, is elected to the Pennsylvania House of Representatives.

**1939, Washington, D.C.** Marian Anderson, denied the use of Constitution Hall by the Daughters of the American Revolution, sings on Easter Sunday before 75,000 people assembled at the Lincoln Memorial.

**1939, New York City** Jane Bolin is appointed Judge of the Court of Domestic Relations in New York City, becoming the first female black judge in the United States.

**1939, Miami, Florida** Intimidation and cross-burning by the Ku Klux Klan in the black ghetto of Miami fail to discourage over 1,000 of the city's registered blacks from appearing at the polls. The Klan parades with effigies of blacks who will allegedly be slain for daring to vote.

**1940, Washington, D.C.** The census places black life expectancy at 51 years, and white at 62. Nearly one-fourth of blacks live in the North and West. The U.S. Supreme Court rules that black teachers cannot be denied wage parity with white teachers.

**1940, Virginia** The Virginia Legislature chooses *Carry Me Back to Ole Virginny*, written by black composer James A. Bland, as the official state song.

**1940, Washington, D.C.** Appointment of Benjamin O. Davis Sr. as the first black general in the history of the U.S. Armed Forces. Responding to NAACP pressure, Franklin Delano Roosevelt announces that black strength in the Armed Forces will be proportionate to black population totals. Several branches of the military service and several occupational specialties are to be opened to blacks. But Roosevelt rules out troop integration because it will be "destructive to morale and detrimental to....preparation for national defense." At the start of Selective Service, less than 5000 of 230,000 men in the Army are black and there are only two black combat officers. Approximately 888,000 black men and 4,000 black women are to serve in the Armed Forces during World War II. Blacks are mostly confined to service units.

**1940, New York** In a mass meeting of West Indians here, they oppose the transfer of West Indian islands to the United States.

**1940, Southern States** Eighty thousand blacks vote in eight southern states. Five percent of voting age blacks are registered.

**1941, Washington, D.C.** Dr. Robert Weaver is appointed director of the government office charged with integrating blacks into the National Defense program.

**1941, Washington, D.C.** The U.S. Supreme Court, in a case brought by Congressman Arthur Mitchell, rules that separate facilities in railroad travel must be *substantially* equal.

**1941, Washington, D.C.** The blacks' threat to stage a massive protest march on the nation's capital results in the issuance of Executive Order 8802, prohibiting discrimination in the defense establishment. The order states: "There shall be no discrimination in the employment of workers in defense industries or Government because of race, creed, color or national origin."

**1941, Pearl Harbor** Dorie Miller, messman aboard the *USS Arizona,* mans a machine gun during the Pearl Harbor attack, downs four enemy planes, and wins the Navy Cross.

**1941, Washington, D.C.** Dr. Charles R. Drew, a black physician, sets up the blood bank.

**1942, Washington, D.C.** The Justice Department threatens to file suit against a number of black newspapers which it believes are guilty of sedition in their strong criticism of the government's racial policies in the armed services. The NAACP steps in to suggest guidelines which will satisfy the Justice Department. The clear alternative is suppression of the black press, should it remain unruly.

**1942, Chicago** Founding of the Congress of Racial Equality (CORE), a civil rights group dedicated to a direct-action, nonviolent program. In 1943, CORE stages its first sit-in in a Chicago restaurant.

**1944, The European Theater of War** The black 99th Pursuit Squadron flies its 500th mission in the Mediterranean Theater. The 92nd Division enters combat in Italy. On D-Day, 500 blacks land on Omaha Beach, France, among them the 761st tank battalion which spends 183 days in action and is cited for conspicuous courage. Also cited in January 1945, is the 969th Field Artillery Battalion, for support in the defense of Bastogne.

**1944, Washington, D.C.** Restrictions of black seamen to shore duty are ended, as is exclusion of blacks from the Coast Guard and Marine Corps. The War Department officially ends segregation in all Army posts, but the order is widely ignored. The U.S. Supreme Court rules that "white primaries" violate the Fifteenth Amendment.

**1944, New York City** Adam Clayton Powell Jr., is elected to the House of Representatives, becoming the first black congressman from the Northeast.

**1944, Guam, San Francisco, and New York** NAACP secures release of servicemen detained for protests of discrimination in Armed Forces.

**1944, New York City** Frank Yerby wins O. Henry short story award.

**1945, Kentucky** Benjamin O. Davis Jr., is named Commander of Godman Field.

**1945, New York** The first state Fair Employment Practices Commission (FEPC) is established in New York as a result of the Ives-Quinn Bill.

*Messman Dorie Miller (left) wears Navy Cross he won at Pearl Harbor. When Japanese bombers attacked U.S. ships, Miller voluntarily manned a deck machine gun and downed four enemy planes.*

*President Truman (below) presents scroll to Brigadier General Davis upon his retirement after 50 years of Army service.*

*U.N. Undersecretary Ralph Bunche is shown conferring with Roy Wilkins of the NAACP.*

**1945, Washington, D.C.** Congress denies funds to federal FEPC established during the war to enforce fair employment policies. Ralph Bunche becomes a division head in the State Department.

**1945, European Theater** Black troops are in the forefront of victorious assaults in Germany and Northern Italy. However, the use of black troops in World War II was more confined and beset by prejudice than in World War I or the Spanish-American War. Despite efforts by some enlightened Naval officers, over 90% of blacks in the Navy are still messmen when the war ends.

**1946, Washington, D.C.** The U.S. Supreme Court rules that segregation on interstate buses is unconstitutional.

**1947, Atlanta** The Southern Regional Council releases figures which demonstrate that only 12% (c. 600,000) of the blacks in the Deep South meet voting qualifications. In the states of Louisiana, Alabama, and Mississippi, the figure is approximately 3%. In Tennessee more than one in four adult blacks meets state voting requirements.

**1947, Washington, D.C.** The Truman Committee on civil rights formally condemns racial injustice in America in the widely quoted report, "*To Secure These Rights.*"

**1947, Tuskegee, Alabama** Tuskegee statistics indicate the 3,426 blacks have been lynched in the United States in the period 1882-1947. Of these, 1,217 were lynched in the decade 1890-1900. From 1947 to 1962, 12 blacks are lynched.

**1947, Winston Salem, North Carolina** A black is elected to the City Council.

**1947, Southern States** CORE's first "freedom ride" travels through southern states to integrate transportation facilities.

**1947, New York City** Jackie Robinson breaks the color bar in major league baseball, playing second base for the Brooklyn Dodgers.

**1948, Washington, D.C.** The U.S. Supreme Court in *Shelley v. Kraemer* rules that federal and state courts may not enforce restrictive covenants. But the Court does not declare the covenants illegal.

**1948, Washington, D.C.** President Truman issues Executive Order 9981 directing "equality of treatment and opportunity" in the Armed Forces and creates the Fair Practices Board of the Civil Service Commission to deal with complaints of discrimination in government employment.

**1948, New York** Ralph Bunche is confirmed by the U.N. Security Council as Acting U.N. mediator in Palestine.

**1948, California** The California Supreme Court declares the state statute banning racial intermarriage unconstitutional.

**1948, The United States** Truman is elected President in a surprise victory. The States Rights (Dixiecrat) Party takes four states.

**1949, Connecticut** The state becomes the first in the Union to extend the jurisdiction of the Civil Rights Commission into the domain of public housing.

**1949, Washington, D.C.** Congressman William L. Dawson becomes the first black to head a Congressional committee, when he is named Chairman of the House Committee on Government Operations.

**1949, New York City** Jackie Robinson is voted most valuable player in the National League. Joe Louis retires from boxing after holding the heavyweight championship for 11 years.

**1950, Chicago** Gwendolyn Brooks is awarded a Pulitzer Prize for poetry—the first black so honored.

**1950, New York City** Edith Sampson is appointed an alternate delegate to the United Nations.

**1950, Oslo, Norway** Ralph Bunche wins the Nobel Peace Prize.

**1950, Washington, D.C.** Census puts net 10-year black emigration from South at 1.6 million. Various U.S. Supreme Court decisions open university facilities to blacks. A special committee reports to President Truman that black servicemen are still barred from many military specialties and training programs, but that the Armed Forces has largely been desegregated.

**1950, Korea** The black 24th Infantry Regiment recaptures city of Yech'on, the first American victory in the Korean War.

**1951, Korea** Private-First-Class William Thompson is awarded the Congressional Medal of Honor during the Korean War, becoming the first black since the Spanish-American War to win the nation's highest military citation.

**1952, The United States** In a series of legal maneuvers, the NAACP and other black groups succeed in desegregating a number of colleges and high schools in southern and border areas. In addition, public housing projects are opened to blacks in some northern and western cities and desegregation is achieved in several businesses and unions. A public swimming pool is integrated in Kansas City, a golf course in Louisville, and Ford's Theater in Baltimore.

**1952, The United States** Eisenhower is elected President, though he gets only 21% of the black vote. In the South over one fourth of voting-age blacks register to vote.

**1952, Tuskegee** A Tuskegee report indicates that, for the first time in its 71 years of tabulation, no lynchings have occurred in the United States.

**1953, Washington, D.C.** The U.S. Supreme Court asks to re-hear five school segregation cases first argued in 1942. Sensing a major opportunity, the NAACP puts 100 lawyers, scholars and researchers to work in preparation. The NAACP also files complaint with the Interstate Commerce Commission to execute earlier Supreme Court desegregation orders in transportation facilities.

**1953, New York City** Hulan Jack is sworn in as Borough President of Manhattan.

**1953, District of Columbia** D.C. Commissioners order the abolition of segregation in several district agencies. The Fire Department is among those which escape the mandate. The Defense Department orders an end to segregation in schools on military bases and in Veterans Hospitals.

## THE CIVIL RIGHTS REVOLUTION(1954-1964)

**1954, Washington, D.C.** On May 17, by a unanimous 9 to 0 vote, the Supreme Court declares that "separate but equal" educational facilities are "inherently unequal" and that segregation is therefore unconstitutional. The decision is reached in the case of *Brown v. Board of Education,* (of Topeka) and overturns the "separate but equal" doctrine that since 1896 has legitimized segregation. In another case, the court rules that the University of Florida must admit blacks regardless of any "public mischief" it might cause.

**1954, The United States** In the autumn following the *Brown* decision, 150 formerly segregated school districts in eight states and the District of Columbia integrate. But a number of groups opposing segregation emerge in the South. Most prominent among these are White Citizens Councils, which soon claim 80,000 members and propose constitutional amendments reinstating segregation.

**1954, Washington, D.C.** President Eisenhower appoints a black, J. Ernest Wilkins, to be Undersecretary of Labor, but pointedly does not endorse Civil Rights Legislation. The Department of Defense reports that "all-Negro" units in the Army no longer exist. However, some bases still evade integration. The Veteran's Administration announces

*(Left to Right) George Hayes, Thurgood Marshall, and James Nabrit congratulate each other for their victory which found segregation in schools unconstitutional.*

their hospitals have been desegregated, but the Department of Health, Education and Welfare declares it will continue to give funds to segregated hospitals. Charles H. Mahoney becomes the first black American appointed as a permanent delegate to the United Nations.

**1955, Montgomery, Alabama** Mrs. Rosa Parks takes a seat in the front of a Cleveland Avenue bus, refuses to surrender it to a white man, and is arrested. Four days later, on December 5, the Reverend Martin Luther King Jr. urges the city's black community to boycott the buses. Thus begins the Montgomery Bus Boycott which was to end with desegregation the following year and start the era of passive resistance that culminated in the Civil Rights Acts of the 1960s.

**1955, Washington, D.C.** U.S. Supreme Court orders school boards to draw up desegregation procedures "with all deliberate speed." In accordance with Supreme Court edicts, the Interstate Commerce Commission outlaws segregated buses and waiting rooms for interstate passengers, but many communities ignore the order.

**1955, The Southern States** While such states as Kansas, Oklahoma, Missouri, and parts of Texas desegregate schools with minimal fuss, states in the Deep South dig in to fight. Georgia's Board of Education adopts a resolution revoking the license of any teacher who teaches integrated classes. Mississippi repeals its compulsory school attendance law and establishes a branch of government for the sole purpose of maintaining segregation. White Citizens Councils in Mississippi initiate economic pressures against blacks who try to register to vote, while more extreme groups resort to direct terror.

**1955, Washington, D.C.** The Eisenhower administration continues to discourage civil rights legislation. The House of Representatives defeats attempts by Adam Clayton Powell, Jr. to deny funds to segregated schools.

**1955, New York State** The Metcalf-Baker Law is passed, forbidding discrimination in housing assisted by FHA or Veterans Administration funds. Robert Weaver is appointed State Rent Commissioner.

**1955, New York City** Walter White, head of the NAACP since 1931, dies and is succeeded by Roy Wilkins. Marian Anderson becomes the first black to sing on the stage of the Metropolitan Opera House, appearing in Verdi's *The Masked Ball*.

**1956, Southern States** By the fall term, some 800 school districts containing 320,000 black children had desegregated since the 1954 Supreme Court decision. However, nearly 2.5 million black children remain in segregated schools and there are still no desegregated districts in Virginia, North and South Carolina, Georgia, Florida, Mississippi, Alabama, and Louisiana. Autherine Lucy is admitted to the University of Alabama by court order, but riots ensue and she is expelled on a technicality.

**1956, Washington, D.C.** Southern senators, led by Harry

*The civil rights revolution ended segregation and "Jim Crow" in most segments of American society.*

*The arrest of Rosa Parks, one of the leading figures in the civil rights movement; she refused to go to the back of the bus.*

*Among the first to ride the buses were activist ministers Ralph David Abernathy (front) and Martin Luther King, Jr. (rear).*

Byrd of Virginia, fight integration. Byrd obtains signatures of 100 congressmen on a "Southern Manifesto," which attacks the Supreme Court. Southern nonsigners include Senators Kefauver and Gore of Tennessee and Lyndon B. Johnson of Texas.

**1956, Washington, D.C.** U.S. Supreme Court rules bus segregation unconstitutional. Montgomery boycott ends in victory for boycotters on December 21.

**1957, Southern States** President Eisenhower orders paratroopers to Little Rock to enforce an integration order for 18 black pupils in Central High School. Token school desegregation starts in some North Carolina cities. Tennessee announces desegregation of state universities to start in 1958. The Southern Christian Leadership Conference is formed by Martin Luther King Jr., Bayard Rustin, and Stanley Levinson to coordinate activities of nonviolent groups devoted to integration and citizenship for blacks.

**1957, Washington, D.C.** A civil rights bill, affirming the right to vote, is enacted after provisions strengthening school integration are withdrawn.

**1957, Milwaukee** Henry Aaron is voted the most valuable player in the National League and wins his first home run title, with 44.

**1958, Southern States** Black voter registration rises slowly, as states institute complicated delaying tactics. Black registration reaches 72% in Tennessee, 39% in Florida, and 36% in North Carolina and Texas, but is only 3% in Mississippi.

**1959, Southern States** Blacks are elected to local offices in North Carolina. In other areas, however, blacks are disenfranchised and in Tennessee, black landowners registering to vote are denied their usual preharvest loans. In Virginia, Prince Edward County abolishes its public school system rather than comply with an integration order.

**1959, Western States** California abolishes antimiscegenation act and passes a law forbidding discrimination in public housing.

**1960, Washington, D.C.** President Eisenhower signs a bill authorizing judges to appoint referees to aid blacks to register and vote in federal elections. The bill also outlaws bombing and mob action to restrict voting.

**1960, The United States** John F. Kennedy, the Democratic candidate for President, telephones Coretta King to express concern about her husband's arrest during an Atlanta sit-in. Kennedy then sends his brother, Robert, to speak to the judge handling the case. The Republican candidate, Richard Nixon, remains aloof. Kennedy's actions are credited with tipping the states of Michigan and Illinois into his column and enabling him to win in a very close election. In all, Kennedy receives over two thirds of the black vote.

**1960, Southern States** The "sit-in" era starts at a Woolworth lunch counter in Greensboro, North Carolina, when four blacks from a local college sit down and refuse to move. Soon blacks and white supporters are being

*New York college youths sit-in at a Woolworth's lunch counter.*

*More than 200,000 Americans of all races advanced toward the Lincoln Memorial in the "March on Washington," the largest protest in the nation's history.*

trained in passive resistance techniques by the Congress of Racial Equality. Sit-ins spread to Nashville, Montgomery, and other cities. Before the year is over, lunch counters in Greensboro, San Antonio, and other places are desegregated. In Atlanta, the *Student Non-Violent Coordinating Committee* is formed to organize activities. Church kneel-ins and beach wade-ins soon join lunch counter and bus station sit-ins. Houston desegregates schools, but delay tactics stall progress in other parts of the South.

**1960, New York** The Negro American Labor Council is founded by A. Philip Randolph, who believes the AFL-CIO is paying little more than lip service to desegregation in unions.

**1960, New Rochelle, New York** The first integration suit in the North occurs as black parents sue to end *de facto* segregation of New Rochelle schools. The case is won in 1961.

**1961, Washington, D.C.** Several bus loads of Freedom Riders organized by CORE set out on a ride through the South to test compliance of bus stations with the Interstate Commerce Commission desegregation order. They are arrested and attacked in many places. Attorney General Robert Kennedy orders 600 federal marshalls to Montgomery, Alabama to maintain order. Adam Clayton Powell Jr. becomes Chairman of the House Education and Labor Committee. Robert Weaver is appointed Administrator of the Federal Housing and Home Finance Administration. James P. Parsons is appointed to the Federal District Court, becoming the first black District Judge. Fred Moore becomes the first black sentry to guard the tomb of the unknown soldier.

*Bayard Rustin, the organizing genius of the March on Washington.*

**1961, The United States** Six more states pass laws forbidding desegregation in housing, raising the total to 10.

**1962, Washington, D.C.** The Kennedy Administration issues orders banning segregation in southern paper mills and federally financed housing. Military commanders are ordered to actively oppose discriminatory practices in the Armed Forces.

**1962, Jackson, Mississippi** Twelve thousand federal troops are ordered to the University of Mississippi campus to maintain order as riots erupt in protest over the admission of James Meredith, a 29-year-old black veteran, to the university.

**1962, Washington, D.C.** Army reports 3% of its officers and 12% of its enlisted men are black. Figures for the Navy are much lower, only 3% officers and 5% enlisted men. The Navy appoints its first black to a ship command, Lt. Commander Samuel L. Gravely to destroyer escort, *U.S.S. Falgout*. Gravely later becomes the first black Admiral.

**1963, Jackson, Mississippi** Medgar Evers, a prominent civil rights leader, is assassinated in the doorway of his home.

**1963, Washington, D.C.** President Kennedy becomes the

first President to declare that segregation is "morally wrong." More than 200,000 Americans of all races and colors gather at the Lincoln Memorial in the "March on Washington," the largest protest in the nation's history. Marchers demand legislation to end discrimination in education, housing, and employment, and courts. On the day of Evers' funeral, President Kennedy asks Congress to vote equal rights in public accommodations and to outlaw discrimination in employment, housing, and labor unions.

**1963, Birmingham, Alabama** Four black children are killed in the bombing of the 16th Street Baptist Church.

**1963, Southern States** Less than 10% of black public school students attend integrated classes in the fall term. Governor George Wallace of Alabama declares: "I draw the line in the dust and toss the gauntlet before the feet of tyranny and I say "segregation now, segregation tomorrow, segregation forever.'" Martin Luther King Jr. targets Birmingham for a drive against discrimination. This soon results in famous, televised confrontations between demonstrators and the policemen and police dogs of Birmingham Police Chief Eugene "Bull" Connor.

**1963, Dallas, Texas and Washington, D.C.** President Kennedy is assassinated. His successor, Lyndon B. Johnson, promises to support strong civil rights legislation.

**1964, Washington, D.C.** A major Civil Rights Bill, forbidding discrimination in public accommodations and employment, is enacted with strong support from President Johnson, as the Senate finally votes cloture to shut off filibuster by southern opponents.

**1964, Oslo, Norway** Martin Luther King Jr. wins the Nobel Peace Prize.

**1964, Philadelphia, Mississippi** Three young civil rights volunteers, James Chaney, Michael Schwerner, and Andrew Goodman, the latter two whites, are murdered. A number of arrests on federal charges, less severe than murder, follow. Among the 19 suspects are the sheriff and a deputy sheriff of Neshoba County. But no convictions are obtained and charges are dismissed in December.

**1964, Tuskegee, Alabama** Two blacks are elected to the City Council.

**1964, Northern Cities** Blacks in New York and Cleveland stage brief school boycotts to protest inadequate facilities.

**1964, New York City** One person is killed, 140 injured, and 500 arrested in a riot in Harlem. This is generally considered to be the first of the wave of large riots that were to strike urban black neighborhoods during the sixties. Shortly after the Harlem disturbances, riots erupt in Brooklyn and Rochester, New York, and Jersey City and Paterson, New Jersey. The riots produce a split in the civil rights movement, with Roy Wilkins condemning the "criminal elements" which instigate them, while other blacks are more reserved in their criticism.

**1964, New York City** Malcolm X resigns from the Black Muslim Movement and forms the Organization for Afro-American Unity.

*Malcolm X (top) Civil Rights leader, was a black nationalist spokesman and dissident. Martin Luther King Jr. (below) is congratulated by King Olav V of Norway after receiving the 1964 Nobel Peace Prize.*

**1964, The United States** George Wallace receives a large number of votes in the Democratic Party primaries, including 30% in Indiana and 43% in Maryland. However, Lyndon B. Johnson is renominated easily and reelected in a landslide over Senator Barry Goldwater. Johnson receives about 95% of the black vote.

**1964, Forest Hills, New York** Arthur Ashe becomes the first black man to win the American singles tennis championship and to play on the U.S. Davis Cup Team.

**1964, Miami Beach, Florida** Cassius Clay, to become known as Muhammad Ali, knocks out Sonny Liston in the seventh round of a scheduled 15-round fight and wins the heavyweight championship of the world.

## THE MARCH OF NEWS (1965-1970)

An epochal point in the march of Afro-American history was reached when the Supreme Court in *Brown v. Board of Education* (May 17, 1954) ruled that racial segregation in the nation's public schools was unconstitutional. This major legal victory was viewed by blacks as a breakthrough in the painstaking process of achieving total integration into the cultural fabric of the United States. From hopes raised by the *Brown* decision came the militancy and activism now known as the Civil Rights Revolution (see Civil Rights section). The Voting Rights Act of 1965 was enacted, and under Martin Luther King's urging, the question "What is America for?" was brought up for national reappraisal. Questions regarding civil rights, human rights, activism, militancy, and "black power" dominated media attention. What followed was a turbulent period of progress, backlash, action, and reaction. Major events from 1965 to 1970 are arranged chronologically here to help recapture the prevailing mood of those years.

**1965, January 2-23** On January 2, Reverend Martin Luther King Jr. announces his intention to call for demonstrations if Alabama blacks are not permitted to register and vote in appropriate numbers. Twelve blacks, including Dr. King himself, book rooms on January 18 at Selma's Hotel Albert, becoming the first blacks accepted for this formerly all-white hotel. While signing the register, Dr. King is accosted by a white segregationist who is later fined $100 and given a 60-day jail sentence. On January 19, Sheriff James G. Clark arrests 62 blacks in Selma after they refuse to enter the Dallas County court-house through an alley door. Clark and his deputies arrest 150 other black voter-registration applicants the very next day. A federal district court order issued on January 23 bars law enforcement officials from interfering with voter registration and warns against violence.

*Sheriff blocks a black man from registering to vote in Montgomery, Alabama.*

**1965, January 4** The U.S. House of Representatives votes to seat five white Congressmen elected from Mississippi. Some 600 blacks assemble in protest outside the House chamber.

**1965, January 15** A Jackson, Mississippi federal grand jury hands down indictments for the June 1964 slaying of three civil rights workers—James E. Chaney, Andrew Goodman, and Michael Schwerner. The following day, 18 men (including two law enforcement officers from the state of Mississippi) are arrested.

**1965, February 1-4** Reverend Martin Luther King Jr. and some 770 blacks are arrested in Selma, Alabama during protest demonstrations against discrimination in black voter registration (February 1). Dr. King remains in jail for four days before posting bond. During this time, more than 3,000 persons are arrested. On February 4, a federal district court orders the county board of registrars to refrain from using an unduly difficult literacy test on voter applicants or from rejecting their application on petty technicalities.

### The Selma Story

Martin Luther King and thousands of civil rights supporters made a five-day, 54-mile march from Selma to the Alabama state capital of Montgomery from March 21 to 25, 1965, in an effort to dramatize the denial of voting rights to blacks who had attempted to register in Selma.

When the march ended in front of the state capitol building, the number of participants had swelled to 25,000.Dr. King addressed the throng, and later sought to present an equal rights petition to Governor George C. Wallace, who twice turned away a delegation before finally meeting with it on March 30.

The march, which captured national headlines, was first attempted on March 7, 1965, at which time some 200 Alabama state troopers and posse men of the Dallas County Sheriff's office halted the 525 black marchers by charging into their ranks, using tear gas, nightsticks, and whips in a reputed effort to enforce Governor Wallace's order banning the demonstration. Seventeen blacks were hospitalized and 67 others treated for injuries of varying severity, including exposure to tear gas.

On March 8, Governor Wallace denied that the police had made an intemperate display of force, and maintained further that police action in dispersing marchers had undoubtedly saved many black lives. Dr. King then returned to Selma to lead another March on Montgomery.

On March 9, President Lyndon B. Johnson stated that he was certain that all Americans "joined in deploring the brutality with which a number of black citizens of Alabama were treated when they sought to dramatize their deep and sincere interest in attaining the precious right to vote."

On the same day, 1500 blacks and whites, among them hundreds of northern clergymen and civil rights workers, began a second march to Montgomery, with Martin Luther King in the front rank. By that time, however, Federal Judge Frank M. Johnson, Jr. had already issued a restraining order against the march. The demonstrators again turned back, although they were allowed to pass a few minutes in prayer before doing so.

On March 17, Judge Johnson upheld the right of black demonstrators to stage the march as originally planned and enjoined Governor Wallace and other Alabama officials from intimidating the participants in any way. Furthermore, the judge ordered the governor to provide police protection for the march.

After the march had begun, some 2,900 of the original 3,200 participants returned to Selma on the evening of March 21. Thereafter, in accordance with a court order, the number of marchers was limited to 300 each day.

**1965, February 16** Three blacks and a white woman from Canada (described by police as pro-Castro left-wingers) are arrested in New York City on charges of plotting to blow up the Statue of Liberty, the Liberty Bell, and the Washington Monument.

**1965, February 18** Some 300 school-boycotting black students sweep through the streets of downtown Brooklyn, New York, hurling bricks at policemen and breaking store windows. The following day, an estimated 5,500 students are absent from 27 schools.

**1965, February 21** Malcolm X, 39-year-old black nationalist leader and former member of the Black Muslim sect, is shot to death in the Audubon Ballroom, New York City,

*Mississippi: Freedom marchers approach Jackson, a center of Klan power.*

*Troopers charge into freedom marchers in Selma.*

as he is about to deliver an address before a rally of several hundred followers.

After the murder, Black Muslim headquarters in New York City and San Francisco are burned, and most Muslim leaders are placed under heavy police guard. Three blacks—Talmadge Hayer, Norman 3X Butler, and Thomas 15X Johnson—are later taken into custody, and charged with first-degree murder. The trio is convicted and sentenced to life imprisonment on March 10,1966.

Suspended from the Black Muslims by Elijah Muhammad after he had referred to President John F. Kennedy's assassination as a case of "chickens coming home to roost," Malcolm X had retired for a time to the Middle East, where he had engaged in a serious study of the Moslem faith before returning to the United States and founding his own nationalist group, the Organization of Afro-American Unity.

**1965, February 25** U.S. District Court Judge W. Harold Cox dismisses a federal indictment against 17 of the men accused of conspiracy in the June 1964 murder of three civil rights workers in Philadelphia, Mississippi. (See January 15 entry.)

**1965, February 26** Jimmie Lee Jackson, a 26-year-old black, dies in Selma, eight days after having been clubbed and shot during a night march in Marion, Alabama.

**1965, March 9-15** Three white Unitarian ministers are beaten on March 9, in Selma, Alabama while assisting in the civil rights drive being directed by Martin Luther King Jr. Reverend James J. Reeb, a 38-year-old white Boston minister, is critically injured and dies in a Birmingham hospital on March 11. A federal judge arranges with law-enforcement officials in Selma to allow more than 2,000 white and black sympathizers to hold memorial services there on March 15.

**1965, March 13** Colonel Al Lingo, head of the Alabama Highway Patrol, admits that Jimmie Lee Jackson (see February 26 entry) was shot in Marion by a state trooper.

**1965, March 26-30** President Johnson announces the arrest of four Ku Klux Klan members in connection with the murder of Mrs. Viola Gregg Liuzzo, a 39-year-old white civil rights worker from Detroit, slain on a Lowndes County highway during the Selma-to-Montgomery Freedom March. The President goes on to declare war on the Klan, calling it a "hooded society of bigots." Robert M. Shelton Jr. Imperial Wizard of the United Klans of America, Inc., answers the President's charges by branding him "a damn liar." On March 30, the House Un-American Activities Committee votes to open a full investigation of the activities of the Klan. The Committee chairman, a Louisiana Democrat, asserts that the Klan is perpetrating "shocking crimes."

**1965, April 1-2** Martin Luther King Jr. announces plans for an economic boycott of Alabama during a meeting of the executive board of the Southern Christian Leadership Conference (SCLC) in Baltimore. The three-stage program outlined by King calls for: (1) suspension by the business community of all plant location and expansion in Alabama, (2) withdrawal of federal tax funds from Alabama banks coupled with an appeal to private institutions,

*Martin Luther King, Jr., fellow Nobelist Ralph Bunche, and Coretta King lead the last lap of the Selma march.*

churches, and labor unions to make certain their investments are not used to support racism in the state, and (3) a boycott of Alabama-produced goods. President Johnson warns against full execution of such a program, maintaining that it would endanger the security of innocent people.

**1965, April 13** A grand jury in Selma, Alabama indicts three white men for the murder of Reverend James J. Reeb. (See March 9-15 entry.) They are William S. Hoggle, Namon O. Hoggle (his brother), and Elmer L. Cook.

**1965, April 23** Martin Luther King Jr. leads a three-mile civil rights demonstration in Boston, parading from the predominantly black section of Roxbury to the Boston Common. There he tells a crowd of 20,000 that America cannot afford to become a nation of "on lookers" in the struggle against segregation.

**1965, April 29** The autumn of 1967 is set by the federal government as a deadline for integration at all grade levels of public schools seeking to qualify for federal funds. In addition, Commissioner of Education Francis Keppel states that school districts must also show a "good faith substantial start" toward desegregation by September of 1965. (This is defined as desegregation of at least four of the first 12 grades.)

*K.K.K. membership reached its high point during the mid 1960's.*

**1965, May 3-7** A mistrial is declared in the trial of Collie Leroy Wilkins, a Ku Klux Klansman charged with the murder of Mrs. Viola Gregg Liuzzo. (See entry dated March 26.) The all-male, all-white jury is hopelessly deadlocked after two days of deliberation, the vote being split 10-2 in favor of conviction. At the opening of the trial (May 3), FBI informer and undercover agent Gary Thomas Rowe Jr., who was allegedly in the car at the time of the murder, testifies that Wilkins and a fellow passenger fired shots at Mrs. Liuzzo after driving their own car along side hers. The FBI presents the weapons as evidence, indicating that tests prove the bullets which killed Mrs. Liuzzo were fired from them. The defense attorney, however, attempts to discredit Rowe as a witness by maintaining that he has broken the oath of secrecy associated with membership in the Ku Klux Klan (Rowe had joined the organization as part of his assignment) and, therefore, cannot be believed. Moreover, witnesses are produced who testify that they have seen Wilkins elsewhere at the approximate time of the shooting. In closing, the defense attorney maintains that what happened to Mrs. Liuzzo was her own fault since she was riding in a vehicle with a black passenger. The jury is instructed that it can convict Wilkins on a lesser charge than first-degree murder and quickly settles on a charge of first-degree manslaughter.

**1965, May 26** The Senate passes the Voting Rights Bill, 77-19.

**1965, May 30** Vivian Malone becomes the first black to graduate from the University of Alabama.

**1965, June 6** Louisiana law-enforcement officials express growing concern over the activities of the Deacons for Defense and Justice, an armed black group with the professed aim of protecting blacks from terrorism by whites. Members of this group are reported to have twice fired on whites who were caught harassing blacks.

**1965, June 10-16** Mass demonstrations, marches to City Hall, and other gestures of protest begin in Chicago on June 10, drawing attention to the slow pace of desegregation in the city's public school system. On June 11, 225 persons are arrested, including comedian Dick Gregory and CORE director James Farmer. Within four days, the arrest total reaches 530. On June 16, a final march culminates in a meeting between Chicago Mayor Richard Daley and a delegation led by the Reverend John Porter, leader of the Chicago branch of the NAACP.

**1965, June 17** Pope Paul VI names John Patrick Cody of New Orleans, a staunch advocate of civil rights, to the post of Archbishop of Chicago, the nation's largest Roman Catholic see.

**1965, June 18** More than 850 persons are arrested in Jackson, Mississippi after five days of protest demonstrations there.

**1965, July 1-19** Between July 1 and July 5, the Congress of Racial Equality (CORE) lays the groundwork for a

*Six days of burning and looting reduced Watts, California, to a disaster area.*

"major assault" in Bogalusa, Louisiana, scene of alleged police brutality against blacks. On July 7, a march is made on the Bogalusa City Hall to present desegregation demands. The following day, during a second march, a white man attacks two blacks, one of whom shoots and seriously wounds the man. On July 10, a federal district court judge enjoins Bogalusa authorities from blocking civil rights demonstrations, and orders protection for blacks who are being harassed by whites. Marches resume on July 11 with James Farmer of CORE in the vanguard. On July 12, Louisiana Governor John J. McKeithen flies to Bogalusa and appeals for a 30-day cooling-off period. On July 19, as the marches still continue, the Justice Department files criminal and civil contempt actions against Bogalusa officials. On July 22, the governor announces the formation of a 40-member biracial committee.

**1965, July 2** Title VII of the 1964 Civil Rights Act prohibiting job discrimination in private business goes into effect.

**1965, July 13** Thurgood Marshall is nominated as Solicitor General of the United States, the first black to hold this office.

**1965, July 24-26** Martin Luther King Jr. and the Southern Christian Leadership Conference (SCLC) conduct a civil rights campaign in Chicago, leading 18 rallies and church services in black neighborhoods, as well as in the primarily white suburb of Winnetka. On July 26, King and some 10,000 to 20,000 marchers assemble at the city hall, where King assails the city's *de facto* segregation patterns.

**1965, August 6** President Johnson signs the 1965 Voting Rights Act, providing for the registration by federal examiners of those black voters turned away by state officials.

**1965, August 8** Some 700 members of the Ku Klux Klan stage a silent march and memorial service in Americus, Georgia for a white youth slain in a racial conflict.

**1965, August 11-21** A six-day orgy of looting, burning, and rioting plunges the predominantly black section of Watts, Los Angeles into a state of virtual anarchy. Thousands of National Guardsmen and state police are rushed in to quell the rioting which is traced to the arrest and alleged mistreatment of a black youth by white policemen on charges of drunken driving. The death toll is 35; 883 are injured, 3598 arrested. Fire damage: 175 million dollars. Property damage: 46 million dollars.

**1965, August 20** President Johnson denounces the Los Angeles rioters, comparing them in one sense to Ku Klux Klan extremists. He declares that the existence of legitimate grievances in such communities as Watts is no justification for lawlessness. "We cannot... in one breath demand laws to protect the rights of all our citizens, and then turn our back... and... allow laws to be broken that protect the safety of our citizens."

**1965, September 27-30** An all-white Alabama jury acquits part-time deputy sheriff Thomas L. Coleman of manslaughter charges in connection with the slaying of Jonathan M. Daniels, 26, a white Episcopal seminarian and civil rights worker from Keene, New Hampshire (September 30). State Attorney General Richmond Flowers calls the verdict "appalling" and a "license to kill."

**1965, October 2** Pope Paul appoints the first black bishop in the United States in the twentieth century, the Very Reverend Harold R. Perry (Auxiliary Bishop of New Orleans).

**1965, October 19** The House Un-American Activities Committee opens public hearings in the nation's capitol on the activities of the Ku Klux Klan. Robert M. Shelton, Jr., Imperial Wizard of the largest Klan group, invokes his constitutional rights and refuses to answer any of the committee's questions. Federal investigators charge Klan leaders with misappropriation of funds and the frequent use of violence against individuals and groups they consider to be enemies.

**1965, October 22** An all-white Alabama jury acquits Ku Klux Klansman Collie Leroy Wilkins in the slaying of Mrs. Viola Gregg Liuzzo. (See entries dated March 26-30; May 3-7.) The verdict is greeted with a storm of applause in the courthouse. The first Wilkins trial (see entry dated May 3-7) ended in a hung jury. At the second trial, the prosecution was handled by State Attorney General Richmond Flowers, who said of Wilkins: "The blood of this man's sins, if you do not find him guilty, will stain the very soul of our country for an eternity." Flowers attempted to disqualify the jury after several members admitted they felt civil rights workers were inferior beings.

The Alabama Supreme Court, however, ruled against him, with the result that six self-styled white supremacists and eight present or former members of the White Citizens Council were selected to pass judgment on the case.

**1965, November 23** A federal court in Montgomery, Alabama nullifies state court injunctions against the enrollment of federally registered voters in six Alabama counties.

**1965, December 2** Segregationist Hubert D. Strange, 23, is convicted by a state court in Anniston, Alabama of second-degree murder in the slaying of Willie Brester, a 38-year-old black. Strange is sentenced to 10 years in prison by an all-white jury.

**1965, December 3** An all-white jury convicts Collie Leroy Wilkins, 22, Eugene Thomas, 42, and William Orville Eaton, 42, on charges of conspiracy in the murder of Mrs. Viola Gregg Liuzzo. (See entries dated March 26; May 3; October 22.) Convictions are based on an 1870 federal civil rights law.

**1965, December 10** A Selma, Alabama jury acquits three white businessmen charged with the murder of Reverend James J. Reeb, a Boston clergyman slain in Selma civil rights demonstrations.

**1966, January 13** Robert Weaver is named head of the Department of Housing and Urban Development (HUD), the first black appointed to serve in a Presidential cabinet in U.S. history.

**1966, January 15** President Johnson names Lisle Carter, a black, as an assistant secretary in the Department of Health, Education and Welfare (HEW).

**1966, January 25** Constance Baker Motley, former NAACP lawyer and Borough President of Manhattan, becomes the first black woman to be named to a federal judgeship in the history of the United States.

**1966, February 7** A federal court finds Lowndes County, Alabama guilty of "gross, systematic exclusion of members of the black race from jury duty." County officials are ordered to prepare a new jury list, one taking into account the added fact that an Alabama law barring women from juries has been declared unconstitutional. Lowndes County is also ordered to desegregate its school system within two years, to close 24 black-schools staffed with only one teacher each, and to introduce remedial programs designed to close the educational gap between white and black pupils.

**1966, March 7** The Office of Education, Department of Health, Education and Welfare (HEW), issues tighter guidelines to end discrimination in schools and hospitals, threatening to cut off federal funds in both areas.

**1966, March 15** A renewed outbreak of violence in Watts results in two deaths, injury to 26 people, 34 arrests, and damage to 15 buildings. Government studies indicate little change in the economic prospects of the average Watts citizen, with unemployment still running around 35%.

**1966, March 25** The U.S. Supreme Court outlaws the poll tax for all elections, a ruling which complements the Twenty-Fourth Amendment to the U.S. Constitution, barring such a tax in federal elections.

**1966, April 12** Emmett Ashford becomes the first black major league umpire when he opens the season umpiring an American League game between Washington and Cleveland.

**1966, April 1-24** The first World Festival of Black Arts is held in Dakar, Senegal. Black art the world over is brought for exhibit, with several American black artists being awarded prizes for their work.

**1966, April 29** President Johnson sends his third civil rights bill to Congress. This one makes the racial murder of a civil rights worker, a student seeking education, or a citizen attempting to vote a federal crime punishable by life imprisonment. The Johnson bill is also designed to force the desegregation of schools and other public facilities, and to outlaw discrimination on racial and religious grounds in the sale, rental, or occupancy of all housing.

**1966, May 4** Over 80% of Alabama's more than 235,000 registered blacks turn out for the Democratic primary election in which Lurleen Wallace is nominated by the party to succeed her husband as governor of the state. Sheriffs James Clark (Selma) and Al Lingo (Birmingham) fail in their bid for renomination.

**1966, May 16** Stokely Carmichael is named as the new head of the Student Nonviolent Coordinating Committee(SNCC), replacing John Lewis, while Ruby Smith Robinson is appointed to fill the post of James Forman as SNCC executive secretary. The shakeup is interpreted to mean that the organization is charting a more militant course.

**1966, June 6** James Meredith is shot from ambush shortly after beginning a 220-mile voting rights pilgrimage from Memphis, Tennessee to Jackson, Mississippi. Aubrey James Norvell, 40, is arrested at the scene and taken to jail where, according to authorities, he admits to the shooting. Meredith suffers multiple injuries, but recovers.

**1966, June 22** A federal grand jury in Biloxi, Mississippi returns indictments against 15 alleged members of the Ku Klux Klan in connection with the January 10 slaying of Vernon F. Dahmer, a black active in promoting voter registration.

**1966, June 26** The Mississippi march begun by James Meredith ends with a rally in front of the state capitol in Jackson. Addresses are delivered by Meredith himself, Martin Luther King Jr., and Stokely Carmichael, who urges the 15,000 blacks in attendance to "build a power base... so strong that we will bring them (whites) to their knees every time they mess with us." (The "Meredith March Against Fear," taken up on June 7 by an assortment of civil rights groups, covers 260 miles, and results in the registration of about 4,000 blacks.)

**1966, July 1-4** The national convention of the Congress of Racial Equality (CORE) votes to adopt a resolution endorsing the concept of "black power" as enunciated by Stokely Carmichael during the "Meredith March." CORE National Director Floyd McKissick says: "As long as the white man has all the power and money, nothing will happen, because we have nothing. The only way to achieve meaningful change is to take power."

**1966, July 4-9** The National Association for the Advancement of Colored People (NAACP) disassociates itself from the "black power" doctrine.

**1966, July 10** Martin Luther King Jr. launches a drive to make Chicago an "open city," addressing a predominantly black crowd of 30,000 to 45,000 at Soldier Field. The rally is sponsored by the Coordinating Council of Committee Organizations (CCCO), a coalition consisting of some 45 local civil rights groups.

**1966, July 12-15** Three nights of rioting sweep Chicago's West Side black district in the wake of a police decision to shut off a fire hydrant which had been open illegally to give black children relief from the stifling heat. Two blacks are killed, scores of police and civilians wounded, and 372 persons are arrested.

**1966, July 18-23** Shooting, fire-bombing, and looting sweeps through the black area of Hough on Cleveland's East Side. Four are killed and 50 are injured amid widespread property damage. Most of the 164 persons arrested are charged with looting.

**1966, July 22** John Lewis resigns from the Student Nonviolent Coordinating Committee, vowing to remain active in the civil rights movement.

**1966, July 29-31** Martin Luther King launches demonstrations in a Southwest Side Chicago neighborhood as part of the "open city" campaign begun by his Southern Christian Leadership Conference (SCLC). Jeering whites pelt marchers with rocks and bottles before being driven off by police. In the Gage Park section, some 300 white hecklers overturn five cars belonging to black demonstrators.

**1966, August 5** Martin Luther King is stoned in Chicago as he leads a march of 600 demonstrators through crowds of angry white residents in the Gage Park section of Chicago's Southwest Side. Near rioting ensues between 4,000 whites and 960 policemen, including 160 members of a riot-control force. King leaves Chicago on August 6, but pledges to "keep coming back until we are safe from harassment."

**1966, August 9** By a vote of 259-157, the House of Representatives passes and sends to the Senate an amended version of the Administration's proposed Civil Rights Bill of 1966. Most of the long debate centers around the bill's controversial "open housing" section embodied in Title IV. The Mathias Amendment, added to the bill, exempts some 60% of the nation's housing from its anti-discrimination provisions. Other sections of the bill concern jury selection, interference with the civil rights of individuals, and initiation of court action to desegregate schools and public accommodations.

*Roy Wilkins of the NAACP.*

**1966, October** Huey Newton and Bobby Seale found the Black Panther Party in Oakland, California. They propose a 10-point program, which includes reparations for past abuses of blacks, release of all black prisoners, and trial of blacks by all-black juries.

**1966, October** Bill Russell becomes the first black to coach a major professional athletic team, as a player-coach with the Boston Celtics of the National Basketball Association.

**1966, November 8** Edward Brooke, a Massachusetts Republican, becomes the first black elected to the U.S. Senate since Reconstruction. Floyd McCree, a black, is elected Mayor of Flint, Michigan.

**1967, January-March** Representative Adam Clayton Powell Jr. of New York is stripped of his chairmanship of the House Committee on Education and Labor, and then barred from assuming his seat in the 90th Congress. A Congressional committee investigating the case later proposes public censure, loss of seniority, and a $40,000 fine, stipulating, however, that he be returned to his seat. Congress, on the other hand, votes for exclusion, whereupon Powell and his lawyers indicate their intention to challenge the constitutionality of this decision in federal court.

**1967, February 15** President Johnson requests that Congress consider and pass new civil rights legislation in the area pertaining to the sale and rental of housing. In his special message, Johnson outlines the scope of the proposed bill, specifying that it be designed to end discrimination in jury selection, to permit the Equal Opportunity Commission (EEOC) to issue cease-and-desist orders, to extend the life of the U.S. Commission on Civil Rights, and to authorize 2.7 million dollars in appropriations for the Community Relations Service. Violators are to be subject to court orders and fines issued by the Secretary of Housing and Urban Development. The law is also to address itself to the matter of the civil rights to individuals, particularly insofar as it will enable them to file damage suits in cases where they are being victimized by discrimination. Civil rights workers, too, would be in a position to seek injunctions to combat discriminatory practices.

**1967, February 27** A federal grand jury returns federal conspiracy indictments against 19 men in connection with the 1964 slayings of civil rights workers Michael Schwerner, Andrew Goodman, and James Earl Chaney. Another 12 men are indicted in connection with the 1966 firebombing of black leader Vernon Dahmer.

**1967, March 1-8** Representative Powell is barred from the 90th Congress by a vote of 307-116, and immediately files suit in U.S. District Court to combat his ouster. Powell argues that he has met all Constitutional requirements for House membership: citizenship, age, and residency. The Congressman also charges that his constituency is left without representation, and hence subject to discrimination.

**1967, March 7-13** James Meredith announces he will run against Adam Powell, calling the impending special election "one of the most important in the history of this country." Though he declares himself an independent Democrat, Meredith plans to run on the Democratic ticket. Meredith withdraws on March 13 after meeting with CORE leader Floyd McKissick and Charles Evers, NAACP field secretary from Mississippi.

**1967, March 22** A three-judge federal court in Montgomery, Alabama orders the state board of education and the governor to begin desegregation of public schools in the fall term. This is the first instance in which an entire state is under a single injunction to end discrimination.

**1967, March 29** The 5th Circuit Court of Appeals upholds the legality of revised federal school desegregation guidelines, in an 8-4 ruling, which calls for the desegregation of all students, teachers, school transportation facilities, and school-related activities in six Deep South states. The guidelines establish rough percentage goals to be used in determining compliance with the Civil Rights Act of 1964.

**1967, April 7-11** Adam Clayton Powell appeals a U.S. District Court dismissal of his suit seeking reinstatement in the House. The Court declares it has no jurisdiction in the matter and is unable to tell Congress how to govern itself. Powell next seeks and receives a popular mandate, being returned to office by more than 74% of the Harlem electorate in a special election. The Congressman conducts his campaign from his Bimini retreat partly because he would risk possible arrest on contempt charges if he were to return to New York, but also as a means of demonstrating his enormous popularity. He is a landslide winner in the special runoff election for the 18th Congressional District, which has been left unrepresented since Powell's exclusion from the House. Powell wins 27,900 votes to 4,091 for Republican candidate Lucille Pickett Williams and only 427 for Reverend Erwin Yearling, Conservative Party standard bearer.

**1967, April 11-24** Demonstrations escalate in Louisville, Kentucky following rejection of a proposed open-housing ordinance by the city's Board of Aldermen. In the vanguard of the march are Reverend A. D. Williams King and comedian/activist Dick Gregory. White youth harassing the marchers chant "We Want Wallace," and carry banners saying "We Don't Want Any Niggers." On April 13, a band of some 75 whites burn a cross on the lawn of the Southern Junior High School. A circuit court judge issues a restraining order seeking to curb the marches, but attorneys for the demonstrators petition to dissolve the injunction. Police use tear gas and smoke bombs to disperse whites who interfere with the march, and arrest black demonstrators for violating the injunction. Demonstrations are extended into affluent white suburbs and exclusive east side sections of Louisville; arrests, trials, and convictions follow in their wake. On April 24, county and city leaders agree to hold "hard bargaining sessions" to resolve the problems.

**1967, April 15-24** Ignoring the criticisms of some of his black colleagues, Martin Luther King Jr. signals his full-fledged entry into the peace movement by leading thousands of demonstrators through New York's Central Park to the U.N. building, where he and other prominent leaders deliver a series of forceful addresses attacking U.S. policy in Vietnam. More than 100,000 attend the rally, only one of several staged at campuses and in cities across the country. King later announces the formation of Negotiation Now, a pressure group dedicated to the accumulation of one million signatures on a peace petition to be submitted to the President.

**1967, May 3** A federal district court in Montgomery overturns the Alabama statute countering guidelines for school desegregation. The court rules that no state may nullify the action of "a federal department or agency without initiating Court action" which the U.S. Supreme Court can review.

**1967, May 10-13** A black delivery man, Benjamin Brown, on his way to a restaurant, is shot and killed during riots on the campus of Jackson State College. Within full view of police, Brown is left at the scene unattended until he is taken to the University Hospital by black bystanders. Rioters are apparently "not rioting over any specific grievance," according to Kenneth Dean, director of the Mississippi Council of Human Relations. Police, unable to contain the demonstrators whose ranks are swelled by participants from nearby Tougaloo College, are reinforced by more than 1,000 National Guardsmen.

**1967, May 12-16** H. Rap Brown replaces Stokely

Carmichael as chairman of the Student Non-Violent Coordinating Committee. Brown calls a news conference to announce that SNCC's Black Power policy will remain intact, and pledges to build a strong anti-draft program and movement among black youth. Carmichael vows to stay on at SNCC as field secretary in Washington, D.C.

**1967, June 2-5** Scores of persons are injured; 75-100 are arrested in an outbreak of rioting in Boston's predominantly black section of Roxbury. The disturbance occurs in the wake of an attempt by welfare mothers to barricade themselves inside a building as a protest against departmental policies and police rudeness. Police who try to enter the building are struck by stones and bottles; others inside the building form a flying wedge and charge out the center, only to be bombarded by various missiles.

**1967, June 6** Legal Defense Fund director/counsel Jack Greenberg announces the creation of a new educational project to inform blacks of their rights in housing, health, and employment. The program, known as the Division of Legal Information and Community Service and funded by a matching $300,000 Rockefeller grant, is headed by Jean Fairfax.

**1967, June 12-15** More than 300 persons are arrested in Cincinnati racial disturbances which include incidents of looting and arson. H. Rap Brown arrives in the city on June 15, advising city fathers to remove National Guard patrols and "honkie cops" and urging that 12 imprisoned blacks be released. The cause of the rioting, originally identified as a protest aired against a death sentence imposed on a black convict, turns out to be the familiar litany of grievances associated with urban unrest, primarily police brutality, and lack of job opportunity.

**1967, June 13** Thurgood Marshall is appointed an Associate Justice of the Supreme Court, the first black so designated. President Johnson calls Marshall "the right man," the Court "the right place," and the appointment "the right thing to do."

**1967, June 14** Nine prominent civil rights leaders, meeting secretly in Suffern, New York, announce plans to ease racial tensions in Cleveland, a city they regard as one in which "underlying causes of unrest and despair" have reached crisis proportions. One of the leaders, Martin Luther King Jr., confirms SCLS's previously announced plans for initiating organized civil rights action during the summer, and singles out the bread industry for a selective buying campaign. The NAACP's Roy Wilkins expresses reservations about King's plans to "stir up trouble," although he hastens to add that slums, poor schools, and lack of jobs are the real causes of trouble. The FBI's J. Edgar Hoover faults King for issuing an "open invitation" to summer violence by naming cities where it is likely to occur.

**1967, June 12-17** The "long hot summer" begins in earnest in Newark, New Jersey, scene of the most devastating riot to sweep an urban center since the 1965 Watts uprising.

**1967, June 18-22** Stokely Carmichael is arrested as he joins a crowd of 200-500 persons gathered in the Dixie Hill section of Atlanta to protest the arrest of a citizen accused of "malicious mischief." Carmichael tells the crowd that the police have "everybody marked, ready to shoot" and exhorts them to take to the streets. State Senator Leroy Johnson tries to organize a youth patrol to cool tempers, but the move does not prevent a confrontation between police and crowds gathered in a shopping center. One black is killed; three others are injured. Carmichael is convicted on June 22 of fomenting a riot and sentenced to 50 days in jail.

**1967, June 19** U.S. District Judge J. Skelly Wright rules that *de facto* segregation of blacks in the District of Columbia is unconstitutional, and orders the public school system to abolish the "track system," the assignment of some children to special courses for gifted students. Wright orders the complete desegregation of D.C. schools by the fall.

**1967, June 24** James Meredith and four others resume the "March Against Fear" in Mississippi mainly, as Meredith says, to complete unfinished business, to demonstrate that local police can protect blacks if they choose to, and because "the black has a whole history of failure and in completions," based on the fear which he seeks to expose and extinguish.

**1967, June 27-30** Three days of rioting in Buffalo, New York, result in more than 85 injuries, 205 arrests, and property damage estimated at $100,000.

**1967, July 10-15** The fifty-eighth NAACP convention is a tense and at times bitter affair in which Executive Director Roy Wilkins defends black militants for shaking up the establishment, but warns against the endorsement of the kind of radicalization that will force whites out of the movement altogether.

**1967, July 19** The House of Representatives passes legislation which declares it a federal crime to cross state lines or to use interstate facilities for the purpose of inciting a riot. The bill is aimed at alleged professional agitators who travel from city to city to inflame the people. New York's Emanuel Celler finds the bill "neither preventive nor curative," and fears it will only arouse black hostility even further.

**1967, July 20-23** Despite objections by New Jersey Governor Hughes, a four-day conclave of black leaders, many of them Black Power advocates, convenes in Newark. Militancy and a call for separate nationhood dominates the meeting, as most delegates concur with the estimate offered by one participant. Alfred Black of the Newark Human Relations Commission: "The black today is either a radical or an Uncle Tom. There is no middle ground." On July 22, riots erupt in Detroit.

**1967, July 25-28** "You'd better get yourselves some guns. The only thing honkies respect is guns." These words, attributed to SNCC leader H. Rap Brown, are cited as the cause of the rioting and arson that inflict wholesale damage on the black business section of Cambridge, Maryland. Governor Spiro Agnew later tours the district and tells the press that Brown is responsible for the trouble. The Governor orders 700 National Guardsmen to take up positions in Cambridge. On July 28, the Governor calls the city "sick" and obviously segregated.

**1967, July 27** President Johnson appoints a blue-ribbon panel to "investigate the origins of the recent disorders in our cities." The President instructs the commission to leave aside political considerations and concern itself solely with the health and safety of American society and its citizens. The President imposes only three guidelines on the panel, three basic questions which he deems it indispensable to answer: (1) what happened (2) why did it happen, and (3) how can it be prevented from happening again.

**1967, August 10** The National Advisory Commission on Civil Disorders urges President Johnson to increase the number of blacks in the Army and Air National Guard. The panel also recommends increased riot-control training for the Guard, as well as a review of promotion procedures. The recommendations, delivered in a letter to LBJ, are forwarded to Defense Secretary Robert McNamara.

**1967, August 14-22** H. Rap Brown is indicted *in absentia* by a Dorchester County grand jury on charges of inciting to riot, arson, and other related actions inimical to the

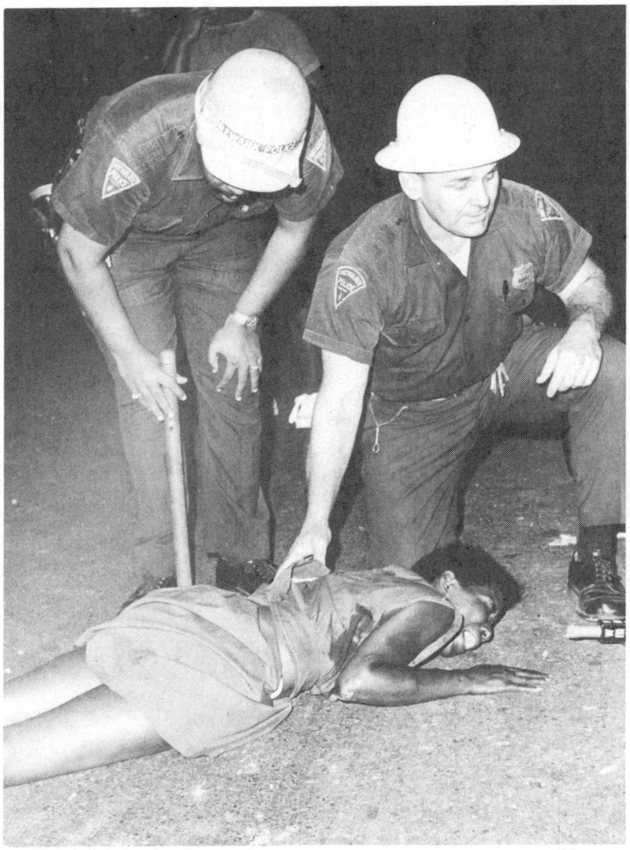

*Police with an injured woman during the Newark riot of 1964.*

*An aerial view of the widespread destruction caused during the Detroit riot.*

public peace. Brown is arrested in New York on August 19 and charged with carrying a gun across state lines while under indictment. After strenuous objections are voiced by his white lawyer, William Kunstler, Brown's bail is reduced to $15,000 on August 22, and he is released in time to address a crowd of 100 blacks on the steps of the Foley Square courthouse. Pointing to whites nearby, Brown says: "That's your enemy out there. And you better not forget, because I ain't going to."

**1967, August 14-21** The Student Nonviolent Coordinating Committee (SNCC) publishes an article in its newsletter denouncing Zionism and charging Israelis with inflicting atrocities against the Arabs. The article accuses Israel of practicing segregation against Arabs still in their country, and of assigning second-class status to dark-skinned Jews. Author Harry Golden and folksinger Theodore Bikel resign from SNCC following the charges posted in the article. The article is later defended by SNCC as being anti-Zionist, not anti-Jewish.

**1967, August 16** The House passes an amended Administration bill to defend persons exercising federally protected civil rights. The vote is 326-93.

**1967, August 19-23** Nearly 450 persons are arrested during five days of looting, arson, and vandalism in New Haven, Connecticut. No serious injuries are reported, and no shots are fired by police despite frequent curfew violations. New Haven Mayor Richard C. Lee declares: "We've done a lot, but for everything we've done, there are five that we haven't."

**1967, September 6** President Johnson discloses he will nominate Walter E. Washington to head the newly reorganized municipal government of Washington, D.C. Washington is the first black to govern a major American city.

**1967, September 19** An open-housing ordinance is introduced in the Milwaukee Common Council following weeks of open-housing demonstrations led by the militant Catholic priest, Reverend James E. Groppi. Committeemen fail to agree on specific provisions of the ordinance.

**1967, October 3-5** Black power at the polls is evidenced by the Democratic primary victory of Representative Carl Stokes, who unseats incumbent Ralph Locher in the race for Cleveland mayor. Wealthy black lawyer and businessman A. W. Willis Jr. is less successful, however, running a poor fourth in a nonpartisan election for mayor of Memphis on October 5.

**1967, October 6** The Equal Employment Opportunity Commission (EEOC) declares that there is widespread discrimination against blacks in the nation's drug industry. EEOC Chairman Clifford Alexander meets with Food and Drugs Commissioner James L. Goddard and some 24 representatives of the industry whose companies account for 70% of the drug business. Alexander threatens to institute the "complaint process" unless hiring and up-

*Thurgood Marshall was the first black justice appointed to the U.S. Supreme Court.*

grading of blacks commences immediately.

**1967, October 20** An all-white Mississippi federal jury of five men and seven women returns a verdict of guilty in the 1964 murder trial of three civil rights workers near Philadelphia. Seven men are convicted of conspiracy; eight, however, are acquitted, and three are declared to be victims of mistrial. Among the guilty are Chief Deputy Sheriff Cecil Price and Sam Bowers, Imperial Wizard of the Ku Klux Klan.

**1967, November 7** Richard Hatcher is elected Mayor of Gary, Indiana, Carl Stokes of Cleveland, Ohio.

**1967, November 28** Martin Luther King Jr. announces significant victories for SCLC's Operation Breadbasket, a program of skillful buying and selective pressure designed to convince white chain stores operating in ghetto neighborhoods to hire and upgrade more blacks.

**1967, December 4** Martin Luther King, Jr. announces plans for a massive civil disobedience campaign scheduled for Washington, D.C. in the spring of 1968 and designed to apply pressure on Congress and the Johnson Administration to end poverty by providing jobs and income for all of America's citizens.

**1967, December 27** Roy Innis is named to succeed Lincoln Lynch as Associate National Director of CORE. Innis, a militant black nationalist, was formerly chairman of CORE's New York (Harlem) chapter.

**1968, January 4** Black poet-playwright Imamu Amiri Baraka (Leroi Jones) is sentenced to $2\,{}^{1}/_{2}$- 3 years in prison and fined $1,000 for illegal possession of firearms during the July 1967 riots in Newark. Two others are sentenced with Baraka, but their terms are far less severe.

**1968, January 8** NAACP Executive Director Roy Wilkins concedes that his organization's membership decreased by 3% in 1967, with a consequent loss in operating revenue as well. Wilkins attributes the decline to the problems of central cities, and the violence which invariably produces a loss of sympathy for all black organizations. He ignores reference to the appeal of other militant black groups at odds with NAACP strategy.

**1968, January 8-13** Adam Clayton Powell, rejected by the House in 1967 after having been excluded from that body due to irregularities in the use of Congressional funds, goes on a speaking tour of California campuses, exhorting his white listeners "to join the Black Revolution" and classifying Black Power as "the saving grace of the United States."

**1968, January 16** Lucius Amerson is elected Sheriff of Macon County, Alabama, the first black sheriff in the South since Reconstruction.

**1968, January 24** President Johnson appeals to Congress to enact his pending 1967 civil rights proposals in the areas of housing, jobs, jury selection, and federal protection of persons exercising their civil rights. The President recognizes that minorities in America are subject to social, educational, and economic disparities, not merely the equities or inequities of law. He places heavy stress on the denial of equal justice and opportunity as the primary factors behind the tragedy of urban riots, but he insists that such lawlessness must be curbed, if only because its prime victims are ghetto residents themselves.

**1968, February 5-26** Three black youths are shot to death and more than 30 people are wounded in a racial outburst involving police and students at Orangeburg's South Carolina State College. The violence is the culmination of student protest against the segregation of a local bowling alley. Students begin the protests on February 5 and continue them the next evening when 15 are arrested on trespassing charges. One policeman and seven students are injured and hospitalized. On February 7, the campus is sealed off and classes are suspended in the wake of rock and bottle-throwing incidents. The three students shot on February 8 are fired on by police who mistakenly believe one of their troopers has been shot when, in reality, he has been knocked down by a piece of lumber heaved by a demonstrator. On February 9, Governor McNair orders a curfew, and attributes the violence to "Black Power" advocates, including Cleveland Sellers, state coordinator for SNCC. Sellers, under arrest, is held on $50,000 bond. On February 11, local blacks call for the removal of the National Guard, and announce plans for a boycott of white business. The city fathers counter by establishing a Human Relations Commission which resolves to prevent further outbreaks by determining the causes of the present one. On February 13, the NAACP criticizes the commission for failing to consult with it before appointing the black members. On February 24, the Southern Regional Council issues a report analyzing the Orangeburg upheaval and tracing it to such things as the emotional appeal of black power to young blacks, white overreaction against this euphoria, the tendency of blacks to see violence as being more and more necessary in the face of continued failure to enforce federal laws (in this case, the 1964 Civil Rights Act), and the expectation by whites that police power and military force must be utilized to cope with all forms of public demonstrations. The analysis does not prevent later violence after the resumption of classes at the College on February 26.

**1968, February 15-17** McGeorge Bundy of the Ford Foundation says his organization will work to eliminate racial prejudice even if it is forced to lend its support to black separatists. The Foundation announces grants to three experimental projects in school decentralization in New York City—the IS 201 complex, Ocean Hill-Brownsville in Brooklyn, and Two Bridges in lower New York.

**1968, February 29** The President's National Advisory Commission on Civil Disorders issues an exhaustive report on the causes of the civil disorder that disrupted the nation in 1967. The commission identifies the major cause of the rioting as the existence of two separate bodies in America—"one black, one white, separate and unequal." It charges that white racism, more than anything else, was the chief catalyst in the already explosive mixture of discrimination, poverty, and frustration that ignited so many urban ghettos in the tragic summer of 1967. It reminds white America how deeply it is implicated in the existence of the ghetto. "White institutions created it, white institutions maintain it, and white society condones it." To overcome this terrible and crushing legacy, the Commission implores the nation to initiate a massive and sustained commitment to action and reform, and appeals for unprecedented levels of "funding and performance" in housing, education, employment, welfare, law enforcement, and the mass media.

**1968, March 11** The Senate passes the Civil Rights Bill of 1968, prompting President Johnson to hail the "nation's commitment to human rights under law." Among its major provisions are sweeping housing and anti-riot measures which go far beyond the federal protections offered to civil rights workers in the 1967 House version of the bill.

**1968, March 12** Though he was victorious in the primary, Charles Evers is defeated by a 2-1 margin in the special run off election for the Congressional seat in Mississippi's Third District. His rival, Charles Griffin, out polls him 87,761 to 43,083. Evers carries two of the district's 12 counties, Jefferson and Claiborne.

**1968, March 18** The Department of Health, Education and Welfare (HEW) extends its school desegregation guidelines to northern schools. It calls for the elimination of such concrete examples of unequal treatment as overcrowded classes, lower per-pupil expenditures, less-qualified teachers, and inadequate text books.

**1968, March 22-24** Adam Clayton Powell returns to New

*President Johnson signs the Voting Rights bill into law; Roy Wilkins is among those looking on.*

York City and surrenders on criminal contempt-of-court charges. On March 24, Powell tells his congregation at Abyssinian Baptist Church that nonviolence is no longer the most effective strategy in the civil rights struggle. Powell says black leadership is in the hands of a "new breed," dedicated to retaliatory violence. His words: "Think big, think black, and think like a child of God."

**1968, March 29** A teen-aged black youth is slain in Memphis after a protest march led by Martin Luther King Jr. deteriorates into violence and looting. The march culminates six weeks of labor strike activity involving the sanitation workers of the city, 90% of whom are black. The workers seek a pay raise, a dues checkoff system, seniority rights, health and hospitalization insurance, and recognition of the American Federation of State, County and Municipal Employees as bargaining agents. City officials, including the mayor, contend the strike is illegal under the terms of a State Supreme Court decision banning strikes by public employees. Civil rights leaders and black ministers call for a boycott of downtown business and urge massive civil disobedience to express support for the strikers. Such action broadens the thrust of the strike and transforms it into a general civil rights action. On the day of the march, disturbances begin almost immediately. Some black students who have been refused the right to leave school and participate in the march begin pelting police with bricks; others smash department store windows along Beale Street and steal merchandise. Still, most of the marchers (estimates vary from 6,000 to 20,000) are peaceful until city and county police join the National Guard in quelling the disturbances. After Dr. King is spirited away to safety at a near by hotel, tear gas is fired at the crowds, and more than 150 persons are arrested, 40

*Union municipal workers of the AFL-CIO, in the city of Baltimore, go on strike against the city. Here they march to attract attention to their grievances .*

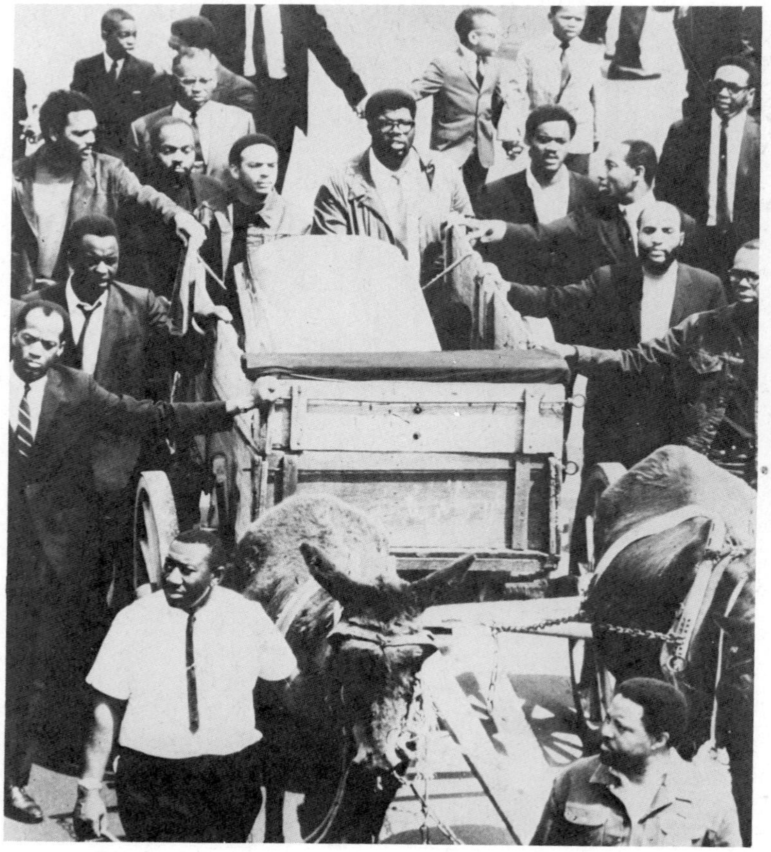

Assassin's view of Martin Luther King, Jr.'s balcony is recaptured down a rifle barrel.

The slain leader is carried to his grave in a farm wagon pulled by two Georgia mules.

of them on looting charges.

**1968, April 4-11** The world is shocked by the assassination of Martin Luther King, by a sniper's bullet in Memphis. The killing triggers a wave of violence in over 100 cities, including such urban centers as Baltimore, Chicago, Kansas City, Missouri, and Washington, D.C., where looting, burning, and shooting are most pronounced. Some 70,000 federal troops and guardsmen are dispatched to restore order. Official figures report 46 dead: 41 blacks, five whites. Thousands are injured and arrested.

Felled by a single bullet fired from a distance of only 50-100 yards from the point of impact, Dr. King was pronounced dead at St. Joseph's Hospital at 7:05 P.M. CST, barely an hour after he had been hit. Attorney General Ramsey Clark, on hand to conduct the preliminary investigation in person, declares that the early evidence points to the crime as being the work of a single assassin. Witnesses report seeing a white man running from the doorway of a rooming house at 420 South Main Street minutes after the shooting. On April 5,Reverend Ralph Abernathy is named to succeed King and discloses that SCLC's first public gesture will be to lead the march King himself was planning. Three days later, Coretta Scott King takes her place in the front ranks of the marchers, locking arms with two of the 42,000 people on hand for the demonstration. King's body is put on public view at Ebenezer Baptist Church on April 6. He is buried at South View Cemetery on April 9 after funeral services are held at the church and a general memorial service is conducted at Morehouse College, his alma mater. There is an eerie magnificence and a sublime dignity to the last gesture in the proceedings before interment, when the coffin is carried through the streets on a faded green farm wagon pulled by two Georgia mules. In accordance with a request of Mrs. King, the tape-recorded voice of King echoes through the crowd at the funeral service as a last reminder of the man and a vivid testimony to his courage: "Say... that I tried to love and serve humanity... say that I was a drum major for peace... for righteousness..." Following King's death, riots break out in several cities.

**1968, April 10-11** The assassination moves the House to submit to the President a Senate-passed civil rights bill prohibiting racial discrimination in the sale or rental of 80% of the nation's housing. The President signs the measure on April 11, and counsels the nation to stay on the road to progress by recognizing "the process of law."

**1968, April 16** An accord is reached in the Memphis sanitation men's strike, the issue which brought Martin Luther King Jr. to the beleaguered southern city. Most of the workers' demands are met, including dues checkoff, recognition of a bargaining agent, and an immediate pay raise.

**1968, April 23** Roman Catholic bishops call on the faithful to "declare war" on racism in housing, education, and employment. The National Conference of Catholic Bishops appropriates $25,000 to "Operation Connection," an interfaith group raising money to finance black-sponsored programs in five cities.

**1968, May 11-June 10** Nine caravans of poor people begin arriving in Washington, D.C., the vanguard of the Poor People's Campaign. The Defense Department alerts "selected troop units" to help D.C. police in the event of violence. On Mother's Day, May 12, Coretta Scott King leads a march of welfare mothers from 20 cities and declares at a subsequent rally that she will try to enlist the support of all the nation's women "in a campaign of conscience." The next day, Ralph Abernathy, clad in blue denims and using carpenter's tools, presides at the christening of Resurrection City, the plywood shanty town erected within walking distance of the White House and the Capitol. Demonstrations follow almost immediately as the SCLC staff leadership begins to put pressure on Congress and the Administration to declare its dedication to the goal of eliminating poverty in the United States. Meanwhile, bad weather contributes to the mounting internal crises being faced by residents of the city. Inadequate cooking, bathing, and sanitation facilities create health hazards for some, and induce others to leave the campsite. Bayard Rustin, called in to lead a special Solidarity Day March on June 19, resigns on June 7 following a dispute among staff hierarchy as to the exact nature of Rustin's role. The controversy stems from Rustin's association with reformist sentiments and pressure on Abernathy from other quarters to adopt a more revolutionary stance. Abernathy explains that Rustin does not intend to press for jobs, a minimum guaranteed income, major housing and welfare reform, and an end to the war in Vietnam. Rustin's replacement, Sterling Tucker of the Washington Urban League, drafts a revised list of demands which include the establishment of strong federal gun control laws and a commitment to de-escalate the Vietnam war. On the positive side, Abernathy is able to report, as the campaign draws to a close, that certain gains have been recorded. The Department of Agriculture, for instance, agrees to "provide food to the neediest counties in this country"; the Senate approves an amendment removing restrictions on the Agriculture Department's use of contingency funds for this purpose; the Senate approves a bill to increase low-income housing construction; and the OEO allocates 25 million dollars for expanded programs, including one encouraging participation of the poor.

**1968, June 5-8** Senator Robert Kennedy is shot and killed in Los Angeles moments after leaving a rally in celebration of his victory over Eugene McCarthy in the California Democratic primary. Seized almost immediately after the shooting is Sirhan Sirhan, a young Jordanian resident of

*Poor People's Crusade: escorted by supporters, Reverend Ralph D. Abernathy and other leaders march toward Labor Department.*

*"Resurrection City", the architect designed shantytown where 2,500 camped out to bring poverty home to the nation's legislators.*

*Robert Kennedy—moments before he was assassinated. Behind his left shoulder stands bodyguard Roosevelt Grier, who disarmed the assailant.*

the Los Angeles area who is disarmed by Roosevelt Grier, one of the black bodyguards and aides who had been accompanying Kennedy throughout his California campaign to protect him from excitable crowds. (The other two are Rafer Johnson, former Olympic decathlon champion, and Deacon Jones, Los Angeles football player.) Kennedy is flown by presidential jet to New York on June 6. Among the passengers consoling his grieving widow Ethel are Mrs. Martin Luther King Jr. and Mrs. Medgar Evers, both of whom have seen their own husbands fall victim to the assassin's bullet.

**1968, June 8** James Earl Ray, alleged assassin of Dr. Martin Luther King Jr. is arrested at a London airport on June 8, the same day on which Senator Kennedy is buried at Arlington. Four days later, the United States applies for extradition, ending what is said to have been the most extensive manhunt in U.S. history. Ray had been under indictment as Eric Starvo Galt since April 23, and was first indicted under his real name on May 7. After Ray's capture, rumors of conspiracy again multiply, but Attorney General Ramsey Clark continues to make numerous public statements discounting them.

**1968, June 25-27** Ralph Abernathy is sentenced to 20 days in jail for leading an unlawful assembly at the foot of Capitol Hill. From his cell, he issues a letter encouraging the clergy to join in a demonstration the next day. The letter, reminiscent of Dr. King's Letter from a Birmingham Jail, is distributed nationally, but less than 25 clergymen respond. Abernathy announces his intention to fast for spiritual strength.

**1968, July 8** CORE National Director Floyd McKissick takes a leave of absence from the organization, whereupon Roy Innis assumes the directorship. Innis pledges to tighten up the organization and give it direction.

**1968, July 16** Black comedian Dick Gregory is released from an Olympia, Washington jail after being held for six weeks following his conviction on charges of illegal net fishing during a 1966 Indian fishing-rights demonstration. While in custody, Gregory fasted for six weeks in order to call attention to the civil rights struggle of the Indian minority.

**1968, July 23-27** A racial outburst in Cleveland's Glenville district results in the death of 11 persons, eight of them black (including three labeled as nationalists) and three white policemen. Black Mayor Carl Stokes helps restore order with relative rapidity after a night of burnings and lootings which result in over a million dollars worth of property damage. Over 3,000 National Guardsmen are on the scene, but they are not widely utilized. Blame for the attack is laid to Ahmed (Fred) Evans, 37-year-old anti-poverty worker and head of the Black Nationalists of New Libya. At the height of the shoot-out, followers of Evans occupy several Glenville buildings, exchanging gunfire with black community leaders who agree to help organize citizen's patrols and assist regular police to maintain order. The distressed areas are cordoned off, but the renewed outbreak of looting and violence forces Stokes to send in guard units once more, albeit sparingly. Within a day, calm is restored, and the Stokes 9 P.M. to 6 A.M. curfew is lifted. On June 26, Ahmed Evans is arraigned on three charges of first degree murder; a day later, Stokes offers an analysis of the incident in which he claims it is "uniquely different" from those experienced elsewhere in the country. In this case, Stokes feels that the episode was part of a deliberate, premeditated attempt to attack police in a revolutionary manner. SNCC program director Phil Hutchings confirms this estimate in a New York press conference.

**1968, July 27** The Kerner Commission releases preliminary findings that indicate a sharp rise in the number of blacks who accept urban riots as a justifiable or inevitable response to conditions prevailing in the nation's ghettos. One study totally rejects the so-called riffraff theory, the assumption that the riots were caused by a small dissatisfied portion of the black community subjected to outside agitation.

**1968, August 1** President Johnson signs into law the Housing and Urban Development Act of 1968, authorizing more than 5 billion dollars worth of funds for a three-year program aimed at providing 1.7 million units of new or rehabilitated housing for families with low-income status. The bill sets up a home ownership assistance program that will provide eligible low-income purchasers with an interest-rate subsidy. Other subsidies cover construction or rehabilitation of rental and cooperative housing.

**1968, August 6** Representatives of the Poor People's Campaign put in various appearances at the convention headquarters of various Republican Presidential hopefuls, receiving an enthusiastic welcome from New York's Governor Rockefeller, a lukewarm reception from the Nixon entourage, and a flat rejection from California's Governor Reagan, who bars them from his news conference. Claiming to represent the "51st state—that of poverty," Abernathy calls for a platform "to end poverty and injustice in America," and declares that Rockefeller is the last hope of the party to capture "the black vote."

**1968, August 7-8** Two days of looting, fire bombing, and shooting in the black section of Miami culminate in Florida Governor Claude Kirk's decision to summon the National Guard to quell disorders. Despite Ralph Abernathy's plea for "an end to this violence," crowds of blacks battle police in the eight-block area which the latter have cordoned off. On August 8, three blacks are killed in gun battles with law enforcement officials. Although Dade County Mayor Chuck Hall accuses outsiders of instigating the trouble, particularly to gain exposure before a nationwide audience, the 10% rate of unemployment, particularly among blacks in the 16-22 age bracket, is certainly a factor producing the explosive situation.

**1968, August 29** Ralph Abernathy, appearing with his Poor People's entourage, addresses an August 29 rally in Chicago and accuses Democratic officials of rebuffing his requests to address the convention and offering little encouragement or support for Poor People campaigners. Abernathy demands a personal apology from Democratic nominee Hubert Humphrey. Elsewhere on the streets, comedian Dick Gregory and 300 other demonstrators marching toward the convention site are halted by police, who arrest 150 persons and disperse the others by using tear gas.

**1968, August 29** Dr. Nathan Wright announces that white newsmen will be barred from the Third National Conference on Black Power due to the allegedly false stories they filed at the previous conference. During the four-day meeting, some 4,000 delegates approve more than 100 formal proposals in such areas as politics, education, and economics. One of them calls for a national black party.

**1968, September 4** More than 150 whites, many said to be off-duty policemen, allegedly attack a handful of Black Panthers and white sympathizers standing in a hallway of Brooklyn's Criminal Court building. The policemen, said to be members of a right-wing group within the department, are reported to have proclaimed themselves "the white tigers" and to have swung blackjacks while stomping the outnumbered group. Mayor Lindsay orders an investigation, but no arrests are made, nor is disciplinary action taken.

**1968, September 8-27** Black Panther Huey P. Newton is tried and convicted of manslaughter in the October 28, 1967 fatal shooting of a white patrolman. Nearly three weeks later, Newton is sentenced to 2-15 years imprisonment. The trial and the conviction introduce the nation at large to a new and formidable organization of black militants: the Black Panthers. Who they are and what they represent is the subject of occasionally hysterical inquiry.

**1968, September 9** Opening day of the New York teacher's strike immobilizes the public school system in the city and keeps a million pupils out of the schools for several weeks. The dispute carries strong racial overtones, centering as it does on the Ocean Hill-Brownsville School Demonstration District, a predominantly black and Puerto Rican district in Brooklyn, most of whose 500 teachers are white. Teachers, fearing student and community harassment, and administrators, seeking to implement the notion of community control or involvement in the operation of the schools, clash head-on over jurisdiction, procedures, tenure, seniority, the right to teach, etc. The union vows to remain out on strike until its members are assured they cannot be arbitrarily dismissed. The community, on the other hand, feels the teachers show callous disregard for the needs of the children, plus a disturbing unwillingness to submit to some form of periodic evaluation or quality control. Battle lines in the dispute crystallize around three basic positions: complete retention of the status quo, creation of a decentralized system recognizing neighborhood or local residential patterns, the establishment of full-fledged community control based on local self-determination in matters pertaining to funding, hiring and firing, and direction of curriculum.

**1968, September 10** The Gallup poll reports that 50% of union members interviewed in the South favor Governor Wallace over both major party nominees, Humphrey (29%) and Nixon (16%). The poll shows that labor's traditional support of the Democratic nominee is being overridden by increasing blue-collar disenchantment with the pace of black progress in the labor market and with the social strength of the black movement.

**1968, September 17-24** News that Eldridge Cleaver has been asked to deliver a series of 10 lectures at the Berkeley campus of the University of California touches off a furious battle between radical student supporters of the idea and conservatives who denounce the Black Panther leader as an "advocate of racism and violence." Governor Reagan is among those who oppose Cleaver; the Board of Regents takes the stand that he should be allowed to appear as a one-time guest lecturer; students demand that all conditions restricting his appearance be rescinded. Cleaver eventually delivers a single lecture entitled "The Roots of Racism." The lecture is well received and regarded as scholarly and moderate.

**1968, October 1-20** More than half the professional basketball players opening the season are black. Nearly one third of major league football and baseball players are also black.

**1968, October 8** Some 250 Washington, D.C. blacks protest the fatal shooting of a black pedestrian by a motorcycle policeman who reportedly tried to stop the victim on a jaywalking charge. Demonstrators set fires and block traffic until police reinforcements disperse them with tear gas. The patrolman is eventually charged by a federal grand jury and exonerated of guilt.

**1968, October 4** Gary Mayor Richard Hatcher and Detroit Congressman John Conyers, members of an all-black National Committee of Inquiry, propose that black voters withhold their support of Democratic nominee Hubert Humphrey unless he takes an unequivocal stand on the war in Vietnam and agrees in advance to support programs designed to cope meaningfully with problems indigenous to all-black communities across the nation.

**1968, November 5** Richard Nixon defeats Hubert Humphrey for President in a very close election. Some 90% of the black vote goes to Humphrey despite his weaker advocacy of the black cause than in his previous campaigns. However, blacks are unresponsive to Nixon's "law and order" campaign and promises of aid to blacks wishing to go into business for themselves. In local and state elections, seven blacks become mayors, 97 are elected to state legislatures, Shirley Chisholm becomes the first black woman elected to the House of Representatives. Four hundred blacks are elected to various local offices in the eleven states of the old Confederacy, compared to 70 in 1965.

**1968, November 13-19** Two gun battles involving Panthers in California keep the feud between the party and the police in the national spotlight. On November 13, in Berkeley, one Panther and one patrolman are injured in a shooting fracas after police stop a car whose driver is accused of a traffic violation. Six days later, three police are wounded in a gunfight with eight blacks wanted for questioning in a service station holdup. The eight blacks are in possession of a panel truck identified as a vehicle of "The Black Panther Black Community News Service."

**1968, November 27-29** Eldridge Cleaver, Black Panther Minister of Information and Presidential candidate of the Peace and Freedom Party, is sought by police as a parole violator on a fugitive warrant issued in San Francisco. Cleaver is believed to have left the United States for Montreal to attend an international conference of antiwar militants. Local officials ask the FBI to join in the manhunt.

**1968, December 1-5** Three members of the Panthers are arrested on charges of carrying out a machine gun attack on a Jersey City police station on November 29. A Panther spokesman claims that a December 1 bombing of party headquarters in Newark is in response to the Jersey City attack. A police sergeant cites the arrest of seven Newark Panthers on November 28 as the cause of the precinct attack. Amid such frequent speculation and wholesale accusations on both sides, little explanation can be offered save the conscientious reporting of the kaleidoscopic incidents and the conflicting versions of what happened.

**1969, January 3** After long and entangled debate concerning his qualifications and conduct, the House of Representatives votes to seat Adam Clayton Powell. However, it fines him $25,000 for alleged misuse of payroll funds and travel allowances, and demotes him to freshman status by stripping him of his seniority rank.

**1969, January 29** Barely a week after his inauguration, President Nixon stirs the apprehensions of the liberal alliance by postponing, for 60 days, a deadline that would have cut off federal funds for five southern school districts which have failed to abolish segregated schooling. HEW secretary Robert Finch asks for more time to study the cases, but others interpret the moves as a calculated and familiar stall.

**1969, February 6** President Nixon admits he is not regarded as "a friend by many of our black citizens," professing instead a desire to be a "friend to all the people." At his press conference, he reaffirms his reluctance to cut off federal funds to school districts refusing to foster integration. Nixon appoints only three blacks to important cabinet positions, James Farmer as an Assistant Secretary of Health, Education and Welfare, Arthur Fletcher as an Assistant Secretary of Labor, and William Brown III, as Chairman of the Equal Employment Opportunities Commission.

**1969, March 10** Confessed murderer James Earl Ray is

sentenced to 99 years for the slaying of Dr. Martin Luther King Jr. The Department of Justice brings no evidence to bear that Ray was part of a larger conspiracy, although it leaves open that possibility by continuing its investigation.

**1969, April 8** The Justice Department moves against Cannon Mills, a Southern textile company, accusing it of bias in employment and housing. The move marks the first time the government has exerted legal pressure in the question of company-owned housing facilities which are segregated by design.

**1969, April 9** Harvard-trained Alexander Jr., resigns as Chairman of the Equal Employment Opportunity Commission (EEOC), citing "a crippling lack of administration support" as the main grounds of his departure. Mr. Alexander alludes specifically to a threat made by Republican Senator Dirksen to have him ousted for harassing businessmen on the issue of job discrimination.

**1969, April 19-20** Student members of the campus Afro-American Society seize a student center at Cornell University, protesting, among other things, the alleged harassment of black coeds and the burning of a cross on campus. Whites try unsuccessfully to remove them, and four are injured in the brief skirmish. After the administration yields to their demands, students relinquish control of the building and leave peacefully, though with weapons poised for action. Campus radicals cheer; most students and faculty are appalled.

**1969, April 22-26** More than 700 striking Charleston hospital workers are led by Reverend Ralph Abernathy of the Southern Christian Leadership Conference (SCLC) in a march designed to dramatize their deplorable working conditions and draw national support for their unionizing efforts. Coretta Scott King lends her presence to support the strikers. On April 26, 100 black students are thrown in jail when they try to march down the city's main street in support of the workers. National Guardsmen and state troopers on duty in the city arrest over 200 people.

**1969, May 2** The Department of Health, Education and Welfare (HEW) authorizes Antioch College to operate an all-black studies program on the condition that non-blacks are excluded only on the ground that their background is not "relevant" to the courses, not because of arbitrary distinctions based on race, color, or national origin.

**1969, May 6** Howard Lee is elected Mayor of Chapel Hill, North Carolina, the first black man to hold such an office in a predominantly white North Carolinian city.

**1969, May 13** Charles Evers joins a host of successful black candidates who win assorted political posts in the state of Mississippi. Evers defeats a white incumbent in an election free from violence and harassment and becomes Mayor of Fayette.

**1969, May 28** Los Angeles City Councilman Thomas Bradley, a heavy favorite, is upset by incumbent Mayor Sam Yorty in a mayoralty election that is riddled with unsavory campaign tactics and blatant appeals to prejudice. Yorty resorts to unsubstantiated smears and guilt-by-association moves that polarize the voting community and heighten racial tension.

**1969, June 6-20** Testimony released in a federal court in Houston, Texas indicates that the telephones of Martin Luther King Jr. and Elijah Muhammad were tapped by the FBI, despite the fact that President Johnson had ordered a halt to all wiretaps in 1965. The loophole in the order stems from the Attorney General's discretion in reported cases of "national security." Former Attorney General Ramsey Clark labels as misleading the statement FBI Director J. Edgar Hoover made that Robert Kennedy ordered wire-

*Armed black students occupied Cornell University building in protest.*

taps on Dr. King.

**1969, June 16** The Supreme Court slaps down the House of Representatives' suspension of Harlem Congressman Adam Clayton Powell and terms that action a violation of the U.S. Constitution.

**1969, July 3** The Nixon Administration affirms its intention to hold Southern school districts to the September deadline for school desegregation, but its exemption of some districts from the mandate on grounds that they have "bona fide... problems causes the NAACP's Roy Wilkins to accuse the government of breaking the law."

**1969, July 6** James Forman of the National Black Economic Development Conference receives a check for $15,000 from the Washington Square United Methodist Church in New York City. The church is the first predominantly white organization to come up with some money in the aftermath of Forman's earlier demand made on American churches that they owe 500 million dollars in reparations for helping to perpetuate slavery.

**1969, July 9** The Justice Department accuses the Chicago Board of Education and the State Board in Georgia of practicing segregation. The latter group is said to be maintaining a dual system that is unconstitutional, while the former is singled out for segregating faculty.

**1969, July 18** The 113-day-old Charleston hospital strike comes to a close. Its most notable achievement is the cooperation achieved between labor and civil rights groups seeking union representation and racial justice.

**1969, July 29** Black candidates win four of five seats on the County Commission of Alabama's Green County and also capture two of the five school board seats in a special election victory which Ralph Abernathy calls "the most significant achievement by black men since the Emancipation."

**1969, August 1** The Justice Department files suit against the state of Georgia to end segregation in its schools in the first desegregation suit against an entire state. Governor Lester G. Maddox condemns the action as criminal and declares the state will "win the war against these tyrants."

**1969, August 18-23** President Nixon nominates Southern judicial conservative Clement Haynsworth Jr. to occupy the seat vacated by departing Justice Abe Fortas. Investigation of Haynsworth's holdings reveals that the judge tried a 1963 case involving a textile concern depending for supplies on a vending-machine company in which he owned stock.

*Black Panthers demonstrate outside Manhattan Criminal Court during the murder trial of the "Harlem Six." Beginning as an organization basically dedicated to the defense of the black poor against the police, the Panthers, especially in California, have since expanded their power and range of operations by working within the political system.*

**1969, August 20** Bobby Seale's defense attorney accuses the Justice Department of initiating a national campaign to intimidate and harass the Black Panther Party. Seale, being held on $25,000 bail, is under indictment for the May 1969 slaying of an alleged Panther informer in Connecticut.

**1969, August 21-25** The 600 delegates at the National Welfare Rights Organization convention in Detroit assail President Nixon's $1600 annual minimum family assistance figure as inadequate, and call for a figure of $3,200.

**1969, August 25-29** Five construction sites in Pittsburgh are closed by several hundred black construction workers and members of the Black Construction Coalition to protest "discriminatory hiring practices." Four hundred angry white workers stage counter demonstrations on August 28 and 29 to protest the work stoppage agreed to by the construction project owner while negotiations for a black job training project were in progress.

**1969, August 26-27** Civil rights lawyers in the Nixon Administration make known their dissatisfaction with the government's request in the application of desegregation guidelines. The lawyers say that the Nixon brain trust is instituting a slowdown in virtually all areas of civil rights enforcement. When news reaches them that the government has called for a delay in Mississippi school integration, more than half of the Justice Department's Civil Rights Division joins in protest against the decision.

**1969, September 2** After a comparatively quiet summer, the nation is stunned at the news that Hartford, Connecticut is the scene of widespread ghetto disorders including fire bombings and snipings. Scores of people are placed under arrest, and a dusk-to-dawn curfew is imposed.

**1969, September 2** Governor Nelson Rockefeller of New York urges a federal takeover of all welfare costs at the meeting of the National Governors Conference in Colorado Springs.

**1969, September 3** The Episcopal Church's House of Deputies votes James Forman's Black Economic Development Conference $200,000, part of the 500 million dollars the organization has demanded for injustices to the black man.

**1969, September 3** General Leonard F. Chapman Jr., Marine Corps Commander, orders an end to discrimination against blacks in promotions, assignments, and social activities on marine posts.

**1969, September 12** A 105-page report by the U.S. Commission on Civil Rights, chaired by Father Theodore Hesburgh, President of Notre Dame University, charges the Nixon administration with choosing the wrong school desegregation policy and covering its actions with overly optimistic statistics.

**1969, September 12** Black militant Robert F. Williams lands in Detroit and is arrested in connection with a kidnapping charge. The kidnapping was supposed to have occurred in North Carolina eight years previously. Since that time Williams had been in self-imposed exile in Cuba, China, and Africa.

**1969, September 23** Labor Secretary George P. Schultz orders federally assisted construction projects in Philadelphia to follow the guidelines for minority hiring suggested in the so-called "Philadelphia Plan."

**1969, October 17** Dr. Clifton Reginald Wharton Jr., a black economist from New York City, is elected President of Michigan State University. Dr. Wharton becomes the first black to head a major public and predominantly white university.

**1969, October 29** The Supreme Court orders an end to all school desegregation "at once." The decision replaces the Warren court's doctrine of "all deliberate speed," and is regarded as a setback for the Nixon administration.

**1969, October 29** Judge Julius J. Hoffman orders Bobby Seale, on trial for conspiracy to incite to riot in Chicago, gagged and chained after Seale disrupts court proceeding by jumping up and shouting insults at the judge.

**1969, November 4** Carl B. Stokes is reelected Mayor of Cleveland. He is the first black mayor of a major American city.

**1969, November 5** Black Panther leader Bobby Seale is sentenced to four years in prison for contempt of court by Chicago 7 Judge Julius Hoffman.

**1969, November 21** The Senate rejects the nomination of Clement F. Haynsworth Jr. of South Carolina to the Supreme Court by a vote of 55 to 45.

**1969, December 4** Two Black Panther leaders, Fred Hampton and Mark Clark, are killed by police in Chicago, four others are wounded. Panthers charge police with premeditated murder and a Grand Jury later calls police action "excessive."

**1970, January 2** J. Edgar Hoover, Director of the Federal Bureau of Investigation, states that in 1969, there were over 100 attacks on police by "hate-type" black groups, among which he includes the Black Panthers.

**1970, January 3** Mississippi Governor John Bell Williams announces his intention to submit to the state legislature a proposal to authorize income tax credits of up to $500 a year for contributors to "private" educational institutions. The plan is designed to create a "workable alternative" to school desegregation. That same day, HEW reports that a comprehensive survey indicates that 61% of the nation's black students and 65.6% of its white students were attending segregated schools as of 1968.

**1970, January 5-6** Black children are enrolled in three formerly all-white Mississippi districts under the watchful eyes of federal marshals and Justice Department officials. Scores of white parents picket the schools, while others keep their children home, relying on the new private schools which have been chartered to circumvent desegregation. HEW Secretary Robert Finch supports a counter move to cut off tax exemptions for the 300-400 "private schools" which have opened in the South since the 1964 Civil Rights Act was enacted.

**1970, January 10-23** Four southern governors—Maddox of Georgia, Brewer of Alabama, McKeithen of Louisiana, and Kirk of Florida—promise to reject all busing plans designed for their states by the federal government or the courts. Each moves independently to block the busing order. Maddox asks the legislature to abolish compulsory attendance; McKeithen reveals no plan, but describes himself as one "drawing the line in the dust"; Brewer denies the courts have the constitutional authority to order busing as a device to achieve racial balance and promises to use his full executive powers to prevent it; Kirk vows to issue an executive order to block further desegregation of Florida schools.

**1970, January 12** The Supreme Court refuses to review the ruling of an Ohio State Court which upholds an equal employment plan comparable to the Nixon Administration's "Philadelphia Plan." The plan requires state contractors to give assurances that they will employ a specified number of black workers in projects constructed with federal funds or sponsored *in toto* by the federal government. The Ohio contractor who brought suit in the case had refused to provide such assurances.

**1970, January 13** A three-judge federal court orders the Internal Revenue Service to refuse tax-exemption status for more segregated private academies in Mississippi. Those already in existence are immune from the ruling.

**1970, January 14** The Supreme Court overturns a December 1, 1969 Circuit Court of Appeals ruling which sets September 1, 1970 as a pupil desegregation deadline date for six Southern states. The Court sets February 1, 1970 as the new deadline, rejecting a Justice Department bid for postponement. Four Justices concur without reservation in reaffirming the conclusion of the Court's October 29, 1969 ruling in *Alexander v. Holmes Board of Education* (see that entry). The words "at once" are requoted from the Alexander decision.

**1970, January 15** Though the day is not yet a national holiday, the anniversary of the birth of Martin Luther King Jr. is celebrated with impressive ceremonies, eulogies, and church services in many parts of the country. Public schools are closed in many cities; in others, they are kept open for formal study of Dr. King's work and utterances. In Atlanta, Coretta King dedicates the Martin Luther King Jr. Memorial Center, which includes his home, the Ebenezer Baptist Church, and the crypt where his remains are housed.

**1970, January 16** Black Panther Warren Kimbro, head of the party's New Haven chapter, pleads guilty to second-degree murder in the killing of alleged Panther informer Alex Rackley. Kimbro faces a possible life term.

**1970, January 19** Florida Governor Claude Kirk petitions the U.S. Supreme Court for a rehearing of its January 14 ruling ordering immediate school desegregation. Kirk claims the state is "financially and physically unable" to meet the Court's deadline, and says he will instruct school districts not to change their calendar in mid-year. Two attorneys representing school districts in Louisiana inform the Court that they are encountering insurmountable difficulties in complying with the Court order.

**1970, January 19-20** The nomination to the U.S. Supreme Court of G. Harrold Carswell draws the immediate fire of civil rights advocates.

**1970, January 20** A Los Angeles District Court judge orders the Pasadena school district to submit a desegregation plan for its public schools no later than February 16, 1970. Pasadena is the first northern school district pressed by the federal government to produce an educational plan in which no single school has a majority of nonwhite students. The plan is slated to take effect in September 1970.

**1970, January 21-27** Civil rights organizations and labor groups begin a salvo of criticism against the Carswell Supreme Court nomination. On January 21, the NAACP leads off by condemning his "pro-segregation record." Two days later, the SCLC's Ralph Abernathy sends a telegram to Senate leaders pleading for "reassurance to the black community that there is... understanding and support... for our needs." AFL-CIO President George Meany calls the appointment "a slap in the face to the nation's black citizens." Testifying before the Senate Judiciary Committee on January 27, Carswell states: "I am not a racist. I have no notions, secretive or otherwise, of racial superiority." This statement contrasts sharply with a 1948 remark that Carswell would yield to no man "in the firm, vigorous belief in the principles of white supremacy." Carswell is also accused of helping form a private golf club in 1956 in an effort to prevent desegregation.

**1970, February 1** Three districts in Louisiana, two in Mississippi, and one in Florida comply with the Supreme Court order setting February 1 as the date for establishing integration. About 15 others are granted delays by district court judges, whereas 20 districts choose to disobey the order either by closing schools or supporting parent-organized boycotts. Vice President Agnew announces a Presidential plan to appoint a cabinet-level committee to advise the districts on how best to implement the court's order without causing wholesale disruption. Elsewhere, South Carolina (January 27) announces that it will comply with the desegregation mandate.

**1970, February 5-9** Senators John Stennis and Strom Thurmond demand that northern school districts be obliged to observe federal desegregation guidelines in the same way as their southern counter parts. On February 9, Connecticut Senator Abraham Ribicoff endorses the Stennis Amendment, a rider to the House-passed education bill then before the Senate. The Stennis bill is a virtual duplication of the text of the 1969 New York State bill prohibiting the assignment of students to schools according to race. Ribicoff condemns northern liberals who blame the South for resistance to integration while, at the same time, failing to recognize and assail similar policies in the North. He chides northern communities for their "systematic and consistent" denial of educational opportunity to black children.

**1970, February 6** Some one-third of Denver buses slated to put into effect the city's plan to achieve racial balance by busing the city's school children are destroyed by dynamite bombs believed to have been set by fanatic opponents of busing.

**1970, February 7** The NAACP asks the U.S. government to examine and ban a fourth-grade Alabama history textbook that "glorifies the Ku Klux Klan" by claiming that the vigilante organization appeared only sporadically, and then only to prevent carpetbaggers from taking refuge behind unjust laws.

**1970, February 11-16** Black neurosurgeon Dr. Thomas W. Matthew, head of the National Economic Growth and Reconstruction Organization (NEGRO), criticizes the NAACP for its continued harassment of Supreme Court nominee G. Harrold Carswell. Matthew endorses Carswell, citing his "public renunciation of racist views." The Senate Judiciary Committee clears the Carswell nomination on February 16.

**1970, February 16** President Nixon establishes a cabinet-level task force to assist and counsel local school districts which have been ordered to desegregate their school immediately. The objective is to spare the public school system undue disruption while, at the same time, insuring compliance with the law.

**1970, February 16** Joe Frazier knocks out Jimmy Ellis to assume undisputed possession of the heavyweight championship of the world. After the match, Frazier indicates he will retire unless a match can be arranged with Muhammad Ali, the former title holder.

**1970, February 17** Leon E. Panetta, Director of the Office for Civil Rights in the Department of Health, Education and Welfare (HEW), resigns in protest against the Nixon Administration's lax enforcement of the nation's civil rights laws. Panetta states that, though Nixon himself may be sincere in wishing for greater unity among Americans, he is surrounded by others who are perfectly willing to subvert that goal if it is necessary to win the next election.

**1970, February 18** The Senate passes, by a 56-36 margin, an amendment to deny federal funds to *all school districts* whose racial imbalance stems from residential segregation. Mississippi Senator Stennis hails the move as an endorsement of his proposal to force northern districts to grapple with the same guidelines and policies which are being imposed on the South.

The text of the Stennis amendment reads as follows: It is the policy of the U.S. that guidelines and criteria pursuant to Title VI of the Civil Rights Act of 1964 and Section 182 of the Elementary and Secondary Amendments of 1966 shall be applied uniformly in all regions of the U.S. in dealing with conditions of segregation by race, whether *de jure or de facto*, in the schools of the local education agencies of any state without regard to the origin or cause of such segregation.

**1970, February 18** Hearings on the extension of the 1965 Voting Rights Act open in Congress with the NAACP's Clarence Mitchell seeking to reinstate the government's power to veto allegedly discriminatory voting laws in the South. The House amendments to the law seek to curb the government's veto power, a policy which would reduce the pressure on these states to conform to federally approved voting guidelines. The use of federal registrars and the reliance on the enforcement power of the Attorney General's office have added almost 900,000 blacks to the voting rolls in the South.

**1970, February 19** Southerners in the House and Senate incorporate, into two appropriation bill's, riders designed to restore "freedom-of-choice" school plans and to prevent the federal government from resorting to busing as a vehicle to promote racial balance.

**1970, February 21-23** Texas Governor Preston Smith recommends a statewide referendum to give voters the opportunity to declare approval or rejection of public school busing. Governors Maddox and McKeithen sign bills prohibiting busing and student/teacher transfers to

*Busing in Woodville, Mississippi—part of the court ordered plan to end segregation in the nation's schools.*

achieve racial balance. Governor Brewer calls a special session of the legislature to sponsor a similar bill for Alabama.

**1970, February 21-25** Three gasoline bombs explode in front of the New York home of State Supreme Court Justice John Murtaugh, presiding judge at the Panther hearings. Though no one is injured, there is some property damage and a warning scrawled on the pavement: "Free the Panther 21." On February 25, Murtaugh halts the hearings, demanding from the defendants a written pledge to observe American courtroom procedures.

**1970, February 28** The Senate approves the Education Appropriations Bill after first voting down three southern riders aimed at diluting the government's power to enforce school desegregation laws. The Senate succeeds entirely in blocking southern efforts to reinstate "freedom of choice" plans. The Mathias Amendment weakens the restrictive language of the House's anti-busing amendment by making it conform to the requirements of the Constitution, which already required integration.

**1970, February 28** The "benign neglect" memorandum from Daniel Patrick Moynihan to President Nixon is revealed. In this memo, Moynihan, domestic advisor to the President, counseled him that "the time may have come when the issue of race could benefit from a period of "benign neglect.' " Moynihan explains that the memo was intended to suggest ways that the "extraordinary black progress" in the last decade could be "consolidated." However, black leaders such as Bayard Rustin and Representative John Conyers, charge that the memo is "symptomatic of a calculated, aggressive, systematic effort of the Nixon Administration to wipe out civil rights progress of the past 20 years."

**1970, March 3** State troopers intervene with riot guns and tear gas to dispense an angry mob, armed with ax handles and baseball bats, that smashes windows and menaces a bus transporting 39 black students to an all-white school in Lamar, South Carolina. Two empty buses are overturned; both troopers and mob members are injured, none severely.

**1970, March 4-7** White House Aide John D. Ehrlichman says he is opposed to school integration if its real purpose is to foster social integration without an accompanying improvement in the caliber of education. Sociologist James S. Coleman, however, suggests that integration is the most effective instrument yet discovered to upgrade the education of poor black children.

**1970, March 6** The Mississippi State Senate clears a tax relief bill designed to grant financial support to white parents who intend to enroll their children in private academies.

**1970, March 9** The U.S. Supreme Court orders the Memphis school system, consisting of 74,000 black students and 60,000 whites, to end racial segregation, and remands the case to a lower court where it issues instructions to develop an effective desegregation plan.

**1970, March 21** Federal Reserve Board member Andrew Brimmer, a leading black economist, declares that there is "a deepening schism" in the black community, despite the economic gains that are being recorded. Upon studying the figures further, Brimmer concludes that the gap is widening between the able and the less able, between the more prepared and those with few skills. In Brimmer's view, this accounts, in part for the growing militancy at the bottom end of the scale, where the disparity is most keenly felt.

**1970, March 24** President Nixon's long-awaited statement on school desegregation expected with hope by some blacks, affirms his "personal belief" that the 1954 Supreme Court decision (*Brown v. Board of Education* ) is right "in both constitutional and human terms." The President vows to bring the full force of his office and authority to bear toward eliminating *de jure* segregation, but balks at applying the same standard to the question of *de facto* segregation, stating that the courts have not yet provided clear-cut mandates in this domain. Nixon, however, rejects the concept of school busing and offers instead financial aid to upgrade ghetto schools. Most civil rights groups regard the statement as bland, evasive, and retrogressive.

**1970, March 2 5** After a long, self-imposed exile, Stokely Carmichael testifies before a closed session of the Senate Internal Security Subcommittee in Washington, D.C. Carmichael discusses his travels and associations in Cuba, Africa, China, and Puerto Rico, and explains that his return is linked to his desire to curb drug abuse in the black community. Some observers brand the sessions "an inquisition," others are vexed that they were uninformed about schedules for the proceedings.

**1970, April 7** HEW Secretary Finch predicts the number of black children in schools with whites will double by the fall of 1970. Finch maintains that busing will be one of the practices used to enforce desegregation, claiming that 90% of the South's schools already utilize buses for comparable functions. The Secretary admits, however, that the decision as to whether discrimination is *de facto* or *de jure* will have to be rendered on an individual basis.

**1970, April 7** The recessed pretrial hearings of 13 Black Panthers are resumed in a courtroom atmosphere of calm and restraint on both sides. Justice Murtaugh, unable to obtain a signed pledge from the defendants to uphold the decorum of the court, proceeds nonetheless with the legal issue at hand.

**1970, April 7** The Detroit school board approves a busing plan for some 3,000 high school students and announces the initiation of a decentralization plan aimed at dispersing white minority students among the city's secondary schools. In Detroit, 63% of the system's 294,000 students are nonwhite, as are 42% of the teachers.

**1970, April 8** In what is regarded as a major Administration defeat, Supreme Court nominee G. Harrold Carswell is rejected by the Senate in a 51-45 vote. Among the key swing senators who influence the outcome are Winston Prouty of Vermont and Margaret Chase Smith of Maine. Instrumental in the defeat of Carswell are the quiet and diplomatic moves of Senator Edward A. Brooke. Brooke's gentle prodding of Republican colleagues and his constant reminders that Carswell's record not only stamps him as racially biased but as judicially intemperate are held as vital factors influencing some of the last-minute shifts which upended Carswell.

**1970, April 11** The Commission on Civil Rights criticizes President Nixon's March 24 policy statement as inadequate, over cautious, and indicative of a possible retreat in the area of school integration. The panel maintains that *de jure* segregation is not confined to the South, and indicates that the President could apply great pressure to eliminate it in this area of the country as well.

**1970, April 20** Sociologist Kenneth Clark, Director of the Metropolitan Applied Research Center, testifies that segregation is even more damaging to white school children than to those from minority groups. Clark maintains that the President's March 24 statement constitutes an important withdrawal from the situation, a failure to assess its moral, ethical, and educational implications, and a slackening of the momentum generated by the courts and by some segments of society.

**1970, April 22-23** A student strike is called at Yale in support of the eight Black Panthers awaiting trial in New Haven. Yale President Kingman Brewster asserts he is "skeptical" that such black revolutionaries can have a fair trial in the United States.

**1970, May 4** A warrant is issued for the arrest of H. Rap Brown who again fails to appear in court to resume his trial. Brown's bond is forfeited, and the FBI is asked to join Maryland authorities in the search. Days later, Brown's name is added to the list of the nation's 10 most-wanted fugitives.

**1970, May 8** All charges against seven Panthers indicted on January 30 on charges of instigating a shootout with Chicago police are dropped. The State Attorney admits that the evidence gathered may not satisfy "judicial standards of proof."

**1970, May 12** Six blacks are shot and 20 other people are wounded in Augusta, Georgia, during a night of violence punctuated by looting, burning, and sniper activity. The immediate cause of the violence is said to be the killing of a black youth in a county jail a few days earlier. Autopsies of the slain blacks establish that they were shot in the back. The *New York Times* later reports that at least three of the dead were unarmed bystanders.

**1970, May 14-17** Two black students are shot and killed after a night of violence outside a women's dormitory at Jackson State College in Mississippi. Witnesses charge that police simply moved in and indiscriminately blasted

*Clement F. Haynsworth Jr. (left) and G. Harrold Carswell, two unsuccessful Nixon Supreme Court nominees.*

the residence hall with shotguns. President Nixon dispatches Justice Department officials to ferret out the facts, but contradictory explanations make it impossible to assemble a wholly coherent story. On May 17, the Mississippi United Front vows to provide students and other groups with independent protection.

**1970, May 23** A five-day, 100-mile march against repression ends in downtown Atlanta with a rally by the SCLC and the NAACP. Speakers include Ralph Abernathy, Coretta King, and Senator George McGovern. Jointly, they condemn racism, the Vietnam war, student killings at Kent State and Jackson State, and alleged police brutality in Augusta.

**1970, May 29** A California Court of Appeals overturns the manslaughter conviction of Huey Newton, finding that procedural errors had deprived the Black Panther leader of a fair trial.

**1970, June 13** The NAACP announces a $50,000 grant to a panel of independent citizens created in December 1969 to study clashes between the Black Panthers and the police in various cities across the United States. The commission, hoping for funds from the Ford Foundation, is disappointed at the lack of interest shown by this group, and confesses it will be unable to function until it can raise its budget to $150,000.

**1970, June 29** Spottswood Robinson and a host of other black leaders who address the sixty-first annual NAACP convention brand the Nixon Administration anti-black and catalog a list of grievances to support their contention. These include the signing of defense contracts with firms practicing discrimination, the retreat on enforcement of school desegregation, the nominations of Supreme Court Justices whose record and outlook brand them as insensitive to black aspirations, and the systematic attempt to emasculate the Voting Rights Act.

**1970, July 1** Kenneth Gibson becomes Mayor of Newark, New Jersey, defeating Hugh Addonizio, whose administration had been racked by charges of kickbacks from contractors doing business with the city.

**1970, July 10** The Internal Revenue Service announces its intention to tax private academies practicing racial discrimination in their admissions policies. The greatest impact of the policy is expected to be felt in the South, although schools there will presumably receive ample time to adjust their policies should they be branded racist. Thus, the new policy promises these schools sufficient flexibility to avoid immediate revocation of their tax-exempt status.

**1970, July 19** Whitney Young refuses to follow the hard line taken by the NAACP in denouncing Administration policy toward the black. Instead, Young characterizes that policy as "pro-political," designed exclusively to win political votes from a beguiled majority. To offset this "white magic" policy, Young encourages the total spectrum of black groups—from the Panthers to the Baptists—to enter the arena of decision-making by forging a coalition of agreement on vital issues affecting the total black community.

*Raised black fists respond to the shattered windows of Jackson State.*

*Whitney Young urged the total spectrum of black groups—from the Panthers to the Baptists—to forge a coalition on vital issues affecting the total black community.*

**1970, August 1** Figures released by the Pentagon reveal a decline in the proportion of black fatalities in the Indo-China War. In 1969, blacks accounted for 13.5% of battle deaths and represented only 9.5% of troops there. In the first three months of 1970, however, blacks represented about 10% of the total force and 8.5% of battle fatalities

**1970, August 7** A dramatic shootout outside the San Rafael courthouse results in the death of Superior Court Judge Harold Haley and three other men—all black prisoners on trial. The shootout follows a daring escape plan in which weapons are smuggled into the courtroom, while the court is in session, by a 17-year-old youth. The prisoners take control of the court, seize the judge and members of the jury at gunpoint, and try to effect their escape. Police reinforcements open fire on the escape van, killing its driver and the other fugitives. The judge, too, is slain by a shotgun blast from the weapon of one of the fugitives. Later investigation traces the sale of the weapons used in the shootout to Angela Davis, controversial UCLA professor and longtime defender of the so-called Soledad Brothers. Davis, a self-admitted Communist, has been the center of considerable dispute over her right to teach at UCLA. Though dismissed by the Board of Regents, she has strong faculty and student backing, and benefits from a court decision invalidating dismissal for political beliefs. After the shootout, Davis disappears. In accordance with California law, she is charged with murder and kidnapping. The FBI places her on its list of the 10 most-wanted fugitives in the nation.

**1970, August 29** Some whites in Fort Pierce, Florida threaten to remove bodies of relatives from a local all-white cemetery, after a federal judge orders it to accept the remains of Poindexter E. Williams, a black soldier killed in action in Vietnam. The burial plot had been given to William's family by a white women.

**1970, September 1-10** Some 300,000 black children are integrated in over 200 southern school districts, but parental boycotts and delaying tactics by states and cities slow desegregation pace. Whites opposed to desegregation are encouraged by the Nixon Administration's "southern policy" which delays enforcement of integration orders and seeks exemptions for private "academies." However, the Internal Revenue Service revokes a large number of these exemptions.

**1970, September 12** California's Governor Reagan signs a bill forbidding busing of school children without the written consent of their parents or guardians.

**1970, September 13** Eldridge Cleaver, in exile in Algiers, presides at an "international section" meeting of the Black Panther Party. The Algerian government had granted the party status of a "liberation movement."

**1970, October 1** A three-judge federal court convening in Buffalo declares void New York States anti-busing law which made it illegal for appointed school boards to reshuffle pupil assignment plans for the purpose of achieving racial balance. The law had been copied by several southern school districts to forestall desegregation. Earlier, Governor Reagan had signed into California law a bill prohibiting the busing of students "for any... reason without the written permission of the parent or guardian."

**1970, October 1** On October 19, the NAACP files suit against HEW, charging it with general and calculated default in enforcement of desegregation guidelines.

**1970, October 1-30** Two northern cities, Pontiac, Michigan and Trenton, New Jersey, are the scenes of violent clashes connected with integration efforts. Four whites and one black are shot in Pontiac. Trenton schools are shut for two days following fights between 100 white and black students.

**1970, October 12** Father Theodore M. Hesburgh, Chairman of the U.S. Commission on Civil Rights, announces in a 1,115-page report that there has been a "major breakdown" in the enforcement of national mandates outlawing racial discrimination. The Commission maintains that the absence of pressures from the White House contributes to the general breakdown in the enforcement of pertinent laws.

**1970, October 13** Angela Davis is arrested in New York and arraigned in federal court on charges of unlawful flight to avoid prosecution for her alleged role in a California kidnap-escape plot. Seized with Davis is David R. Poindexter, a 36-year-old Chicago black accused of knowingly aiding a fugitive.

**1970, October 19** The government dismisses conspiracy charges against Bobby Seale in connection with the Chicago riot of 1968, but Seale must still contend with a four-year prison term for contempt of court plus kidnapping and murder charges in connection with the slaying, in New Haven, of Alex Rackley.

**1970, October 24-November 24** Violent confrontations erupt in a number of northern cities between police and extremist black groups. In Cicero, Illinois, a group of blacks fire at the police station. There are no injuries. In Detroit, 15 blacks, reputedly connected with the National Committee to Combat Fascism, are arrested after the slaying of a black policeman. In Arkansas, a riot erupts on the Cumming Prison Farm following agitation for racially segregated living quarters.

**1970, November 5** Shooting and fires break out in Henderson, North Carolina, where blacks had been protesting a decision to reopen an all-black school. The National Guard was called out to restore order and the Board of Education agreed to close the school. Over 100 arrests are made.

**1970, November 30** Senator Abraham Ribicoff of Connecticut introduces legislation to bring about total integration of the nation's schools, both urban and suburban. The target date: 1982.

**1970, December 7** James Farmer resigns as Assistant Secretary for Administration of the Department of Health, Education and Welfare. Farmer declines to criticize Nixon Administration policies.

**1970, December 17** A Pentagon task force reports "frustration and anger" among black troops stationed in Germany. At stake is the morale of black troops subjected to racial indignities by the civilian population.

**1970, December 30** A U.S. Court of Appeals in Philadelphia rules that the Department of Housing and Urban Development must promote fair housing when it considers applications for mortgage insurance and rent supplements.

*Rifle-bearing policeman guards downtown Asbury Park, New Jersey , after the town was rocked by several days of disturbances.*

## CONSOLIDATION AND REVERSES (1971-1975)

The period between 1971 and 1975 was full of contrasts. Political leaders increasingly cooled to the political and economic demands of the black electorate, yet there were more black officeholders than at any time in American history, many elected in areas where whites comprise a majority. Opposition to school integration spread from the South to the North, and within the black community, but more blacks than ever were attending integrated schools and colleges. Discontent among blacks in the Armed Forces was manifest, particularly in the Navy, but there were more black servicemen and officers than ever. Many blacks, popularly classified as radicals, were apparently singled out for surveillance, harassment, and prosecution by federal and local officials, but black defendants were successful in a number of landmark courtroom battles. The federal government and much of the business sector clearly failed to follow up on the promise of the civil rights legislation and job training programs of the 1960s, yet more blacks than ever held skilled and responsible positions.

Much of the period was ugly. An increasing number of politicians appealed to, even stimulated, the fears and prejudices of white "ethnics." Instances of extra legal action by the police seemed to increase. But blacks increasingly united, at a series of caucuses and conventions, to present their demands and proclaim pride in their race and culture. This closing of the ranks was symbolized at the Gary Convention in 1972 where Coretta King, widow of the Reverend Martin Luther King Jr., and Bobby Seale, a leader of the Black Panthers, sat side by side on the same podium.

**1971, January 1** James A. Floyd, a black, is appointed Mayor of Princeton, New Jersey, an affluent university town. His Chief of Police is also black.

**1971, January 4** Reverend Leon Howard Sullivan is elected to the Board of Directors of General Motors, the first black man to participate in the direction of a U.S. auto company.

**1971, January 5** Bethlehem Steel is charged with job bias through the use of a seniority system which effectively discriminates against blacks. Bethlehem denies the charge, but agrees to establish new hiring, training, and promotion quotas for black employees.

**1971, January 6** J. Edgar Hoover reports that attacks on police by black extremists are increasing, but that racial incidents in schools are declining. He concludes that America is "far from the realization of racial harmony."

**1971, January 16** Preliminary reports on the 1970 census indicate that since 1960 black population in cities increased 3 million, and white urban population decreased about 2.5 million. Reports also indicate that 1.4 million blacks emigrated from the South in the 1960s and nearly half of these settled in New York or California. Since 1940, the percentage of blacks living in the South has declined from 77 to 53%.

**1971, February 4** Eight black federal employees file suit in federal court claiming that the principal test qualifying college graduates for civil service posts is "culturally and racially discriminatory." Defendants in the suit include HUD Secretary Romney.

**1971, March 8** FBI files stolen from a Pennsylvania office and released to the press reveal that in November 1970, J. Edgar Hoover ordered an investigation of all groups "organized to project the demands of black (college) students, because they posed a threat to the nation's stability and security."

**1971, March 29** President Nixon grants audience to the Congressional black caucus which had been trying to see him for months. The black Congressmen request stronger welfare services, desegregation, housing, and social justice programs. President Nixon reportedly promises stronger enforcement of civil rights laws. In May, he promises "jobs, income and tangible benefits." Caucus leaders express disappointment.

**1971, April 8** Heavyweight champion Joe Frazier becomes the first black man to address the South Carolina Legislature since Reconstruction. He chides the Legislature for not having invited a black sooner.

**1971, April 23** The African Heritage Studies Association meeting in Baton Rouge, Louisiana, urges black scholars to study their African heritage and use it to unify their "fragmented race."

**1971, April 30** The Joint Center for Political Studies in Washington, D.C. reports that 1,860 blacks now hold elective office in the United States; almost four times the 475 who held office in 1967. However, only three of every 1,000 officeholders in the United States are black, while blacks now represent 12% of the population.

**1971, May 4** Georgia's Governor Carter says that it is fortunate the North forced the South to deal with its racial problems and that the South now has a healthier racial climate than the North. Governor Carter's remarks come a week after Tom Wicker, Southern-born columnist for the *New York Times*, noted that Carter and Governor West of South Carolina believe that white Southerners are tired of old racial patterns and think the battle to maintain them has been lost.

**1971, May 5** A riot erupts in the Brownsville section of Brooklyn, New York, after thousands of residents take to the streets to protest cuts in state welfare, Medicaid, food stamps, and educational programs. One policeman is shot; 12 are injured. Residents blame police for firing first shots. Police say it was in self-defense. The government is forced by a District Judge to release David Hilliard, Chief of Staff of the Black Panther Party, when it refuses to reveal wiretaps of Hilliard conversations. Hilliard had been arrested on charges of threatening the life of President Nixon during a speech in San Francisco.

**1971, May 13** Thirteen Black Panthers are acquitted on all of 156 counts of conspiracy to bomb police stations and department stores in New York. The trial lasts nine months, the longest in the history of New York City.

**1971, May 17** Senator McGovern of South Dakota urges the government to divert $31 billion of current federal spending in an effort to end racial discrimination by the end of the century. Dr. Milton Eisenhower, former Chairman of President Johnson's Commission on Causes and Preventions of Violence, warns that the United States faces a racial war if it does not remedy the social injustice, inequitable law enforcement, and easy availability of firearms that pervade the nation.

**1971, June 1** By a vote of 5 to 4, the Supreme Court declares unconstitutional a Cincinnati city ordinance making it unlawful for small groups of people to loiter in an annoying manner in public places. Blacks claimed the ordinance had been used by police to harass them. Other cities passed similar laws in recent years.

**1971, June 2** President Nixon invites a group of 36 black Republicans from various parts of the country to the White House for a briefing on his replies to the Congressional black caucus. The meeting occurs just before representatives of the Congressional caucus are to appear on a television program to criticize the President's response to their demands. The White House denies that it is considering a counter caucus.

**1971, June 4** The Department of Labor announces it is removing support from the voluntary "Chicago Plan," which was to hire 4,000 blacks and Spanish-speaking Americans for construction jobs on federal projects. After 18 months, less than 900 had been accepted in training programs and only a few had been admitted to Chicago construction unions. Plans are to replace the Chicago Plan with a compulsory program similar to the Philadelphia Plan which requires a quota on federal construction projects costing more than $500,000.

**1971, June 7** The Supreme Court rules unanimously that people can sue in Civil Court against individuals who conspire to deprive them of their civil rights. The decision orders a hearing in the Federal District Court of Mississippi on a suit by four blacks who were beaten by two whites who mistook them for civil rights workers. The decision reverses a 1951 decision that such suits could only be filed against public officials.

**1971, June 15** By a vote of 5 to 4, the Supreme Court rules that a community can close publicly owned recreational facilities rather than desegregate them. The ruling upholds the closing of the Jackson, Mississippi swimming pools in 1963 after federal courts ordered them integrated. Justice Hugo Black, known as a stalwart of integration, wrote the majority decision, a factor widely interpreted as indicating growing resistance of the court to expanding integration. Jackson contended it closed pools to both races from economic need and desire to avert violence.

**1971, June 15** Governor King of New Mexico summons the National Guard to quell a disturbance attributed to marauding bands of blacks, Chicanos, and white "hippies." Thirty-three people including four policemen are injured and some 200 are arrested. Violence started after a public rock concert was canceled and five youths were arrested for drinking. The Black Berets, a coalition of Chicanos and blacks, is allowed to hold a meeting in a public park at which the state Attorney General promises to investigate charges of police brutality.

**1971, June 24** Secretary of Defense Laird states that civilian authorities in the Johnson Administration, not the military, ordered the Army to spy on black leaders after the riots following the assassination of Martin Luther King Jr. in 1968. The Administration's directive was implemented after Clark Clifford, then Secretary of Defense, ordered the establishment of a riot command center at the Pentagon. In a related statement, J. Edgar Hoover, Director of the Federal Bureau of Investigation declares that terrorism by black extremists is rising and necessitates more federal investigation. A spokesman for the New York City Police Department states that the slaying of a white and a black policeman in Harlem may signal the beginning of guerrilla warfare by radical blacks against the police, but feels the shootings were directed more against the "establishment" than against whites.

**1971, June 27** James Meredith announces that he is returning to Mississippi from New York because the South now has a better racial climate than the North. Meredith says he will try to get blacks to concentrate more on attaining economic power.

**1971, June 28** By an 8 to 0 vote, with Justice Marshall abstaining, the Supreme Court overturns draft evasion charges against Muhammad Ali. In its decision, the Court agreed that Ali, a Black Muslim, was objecting to military service sincerely and on religious grounds, rather than on a political basis, as the Department of Justice had charged.

**1971, July 5** Addressing the annual convention of the NAACP, Roy Wilkins, Executive Director, states that young black activists differ most markedly from their predecessors in their distrust of white men. Black youth, he adds, may have repudiated, NAACP's "slow and careful methods," but not its basic philosophy. Indeed, he states, most contemporary black groups have adopted policies that are essentially variations of NAACP themes.

**1971, July 17** Vice President Agnew, while traveling from Africa to Spain, criticizes American blacks who have "arrogated unto themselves the positions of black leaders and spend their time in querulous complaint and constant recrimination against the rest of society instead of undertaking constructive action." Agnew adds that American black leaders, who he would not identify, could learn much from African leaders, who more truly represent the wishes of their constituents. American blacks, says Agnew, refuse to recognize efforts made on their behalf. Black leaders criticizing Agnew's remarks include R. L. Grant, Special Assistant to HUD, Assistant Secretary Hyde, and Representative William Clay of Missouri, who reportedly charges that the Vice President is "seriously ill" and then refuses a demand of Republican House Leader Gerald Ford that he apologize to the Vice President. Grant is dismissed from his post on July 30 by HUD Secretary Romney.

**1971, July 24-27** Fifteen blacks are arrested and several hospitalized during racial disturbances in Columbus, Georgia, following the dismissal of eight black policemen. Fire bombings and snipings are reported. Seventy-five state troopers are summoned to maintain order as both black and white communities become apprehensive of bloodshed.

**1971, August 4** The U.S. Civil Rights Commission writes detailed recommendations to Representative Wilbur Mills, Chairman of the House Ways and Means Committee, warning that without strong antidiscrimination provisions the Administration's $5 billion revenue-sharing plan will be used to continue racial discrimination. Representative Mills notes that these recommendations confirm his opposition to revenue sharing because they threaten state and local governments with extensive federal controls.

**1971, August 7-14** Julian Bond, a member of the Georgia House of Representatives, tours his state to spark the political interests of blacks who remain unregistered six years after the passage of the Voting Rights Act. Bond notes that due to a blend of apathy and activism many blacks do not perceive the ballot as an effective political weapon that can be used to bring a change in their lives. Bond cites as an example the failure of blacks in 1970 to elect black officials in an area where they were a majority of registered voters. However, leaders of the Southern Leadership Conference announce that their goal of electing a Southern black to Congress is feasible in view of the redistricting in a number of southern states.

**1971, August 21** Roy Innis, Executive Director of CORE, upon his return from a four-week African trip, urges massive American support for black African interests, including a Washington lobby, economic assistance, and a response to military threats from foreign attacks. Innis includes Caribbean and South American countries in his definition of Africa.

**1971, August 18-23** Eleven members of the Republic of New Africa, including I. Obadele, leader of the organization, are charged with murder and assault of federal officers after the death of Lieutenant I. Skinner, a Mississippi policeman. Skinner was shot when police and FBI agents raided the Jackson headquarters of the Republic of New Africa, a black separatist organization, in order to

*Insurrectionary Attica inmates dispute terms conveyed by State Correction Commissioner Russell G. Oswald (lower left). Refusing to visit the scene personally, Governor Rockefeller ordered heavily armed police to retake the prison; 35 persons were killed and some 80 others wounded in the ensuing attack.*

serve fugitive warrants on three members. The FBI claims that the separatists were tipped off about the coming raid by informers hired and paid by the FBI. Mississippi Attorney General Summer says the incident would not have occurred if U.S. Attorney General John Mitchell had complied with a request made by the state for action to be taken against the group. Following the death of Lieutenant Skinner, the District Attorney of Hinds County asks a special grand jury to charge the 11 separatists with treason and requests the Justice Department to allow these charges to take precedence over any federal prosecution.

**1971, August 28** Blacks differ on events leading to the death of George Jackson, author of *Soledad Brothers*, and a folk hero to many black and white radicals. Jackson was shot and killed while trying to escape from San Quentin Prison in California. Some supporters of Jackson claim he was "set-up" for assassination. Others feel the official version is essentially correct and that Jackson was shot during a serious, premeditated escape attempt.

**1971, August 30** Roy Wilkins, at ceremonies honoring his seventieth birthday, reports that the term "colored" must remain part of his organization's title because the initials NAACP are too well known to drop.

**1971, August 31** The indictment is revealed of 14 Chicago lawmen for conspiring to obstruct justice in the investigation of the December 1969 deaths of Mark Clark and Fred Hampton, leaders of the Illinois Black Panther Party. Among those indicted is the Chief Prosecutor of Cook County, Edward V. Hanrahan, widely regarded as the heir apparent to Richard Daley as Mayor of Chicago. The Grand Jury cited 20 examples of police and official misconduct.

**1971, September 4** Trade reports a box office boom in black movies. The gross of *Sweet Sweetback's Baadaass Song* reportedly reaches $10 million. The more recently released *Shaft*, directed by Gordon Parks, grosses $6 million.

**1971, September 4** A massive return of blacks to the South is urged by Dr. J. Cashin, Chairman of the National Democratic Party of Alabama, an interracial group that is challenging control of the state's regular party. Dr. Cashin believes blacks are becoming disillusioned with the North and that an additional 200,000 to 400,000 blacks in each southern state would effect dramatic and positive changes in them.

**1971, September 5** A survey conducted by Michigan University's Social Research Institute indicates Americans think police should shoot, but not shoot to kill, blacks in order to control riots.

**1971, September 9-13** During a riot by 1,200 inmates at the Attica Correctional Facility, Attica, New York, 32 inmates and 11 correctional employees die. Of the 43, 39 are killed and some 80 others wounded during a 15-minute attack by New York State police to retake the prison. Of 11 slain prison employees, 10 were hostages killed by police gunfire during the assault. The Attica riot was spawned and compounded by a number of elements: black and Puerto Rican militancy, a growing "law and order" political climate, poor prison conditions, and rehabilitation programs, and after the riot started, false and exaggerated reports of castration and other brutality to the 39 white hostages by black inmates. The demands of the prisoners ranged from popularly accepted but perpetually rejected areas of penal reform, such as better food, library facilities, and legal assistance, to proposals for complete amnesty for rioters and an option for them to relocate to "nonimperialist" nations. A number of prominent citizens, including Bobby Seale of the Black Panthers and Jose Paris of the Young Lords, a Puerto Rican group, attempted to mediate the dispute and persuade Governor Rockefeller to show his concern for better conditions by visiting Attica personally. But the Governor refuses, negotiations collapse, and the assault is ordered.

**1971, September 20** The National Urban Coalition's Committee on Cities reports that if present trends continue, the majority of American cities will be predominantly black, brown, and bankrupt by 1980. The Committee, headed by Senator Harris of Oklahoma and Mayor Lindsay of New York, is encouraged by the growth of black self-help organizations, but contends that conditions in slums have become more polarized and that the commitment of the federal government to correct urban problems has eased.

**1971, October** "Black Expo," a cultural and business exposition attracts some 800,000 people during its four day run in Chicago. The exposition is run by Jesse Jackson, of "Operation Breadbasket," and a number of black businessmen.

**1971, October** Dick Gregory, black comedian and presidential candidate in 1968, urges blacks to have large families as a counter to "genocide" attempts by whites to reduce the black population. Gregory adds that whites want to dictate the bedroom habits of blacks.

**1971, November** The Newark, New Jersey Board of Education votes to hang the Black Liberation flag in all schools where blacks comprise a majority, but implementation of the decision is prevented by a New Jersey state court.

**1971, November** Decline of confidence by blacks in the government is indicated by an attitude survey conducted by the University of Michigan which reports that only 34% of blacks believe that the government is run for the benefit of all people. In 1958, some 78% of blacks held this view.

**1971, November** For the third time in 1971, the U.S. Commission on Civil Rights accuses the government of inadequate enforcement of civil rights laws. The Commission grants that in many cases enforcement machinery has been set up, but objects that little progress has stemmed from this.

**1971, December** The National Opinion Research Center reports that whites seem more ready to accept racial integration than in 1942. It concedes that many whites who claim to favor integration may be hiding their true feelings, but adds that whites will respond affirmatively if the government's presentation of the case for integration is positive.

**1972, January** A federal judge in Richmond, Virginia orders consolidation of Richmond's predominantly black school system with the nearly all-white system of two suburbs. Judge Robert Mehirge bases his decision on the failure of state officials to take *positive action* to reverse *de facto* segregation. The decision goes beyond recent verdicts of courts in Detroit and Pontiac, Michigan, which required busing because officials *condoned* segregation. Richmond announces it will appeal the decision.

**1972, January** Hunter Nicolas, an 18-year-old researcher from Boston, becomes the first pre-college student in the United States to present a paper to the American Federation for Clinical Research.

**1972, January** In the worst violence in the South for two years, two white policemen and two young blacks, identifying themselves as Black Muslims, are killed in a shootout in Baton Rouge, Louisiana. After 31 bystanders are wounded, 700 National Guardsmen are sent by the Governor to establish order. Black Muslim headquarters in Chicago disavows the blacks.

**1972, March** President Nixon proposes a moratorium until July 1973 on all court-ordered busing, and diversion of $1.5 billion for "impoverished" schools. Blacks in Congress claim the President is suggesting a return to separate but equal schools and that the moratorium would be unconstitutional. Roy Wilkins warns that the plan will precipitate a constitutional crisis.

**1972, March** Some 8,000 blacks, representing a wide spectrum of political views, attend the first National Black Political Convention in Gary, Indiana. The convention is chaired by Imamu Amiri Baraka of Newark. Mayor Richard Hatcher of Gary is the keynote speaker. The group approves a political platform, the "Black Agenda," which demands reparations, proportional Congressional representation for blacks, an increase in federal spending to combat crime and drug traffic, reduction of the military budget, and a guaranteed annual income of $6,500 for a family of four. The Caucus also approves, after heated debate, a solution opposing integration of schools, demanding as an alternative control of schools by local school boards. The Congressional Black Caucus, however, repeats its support of busing and school integration. The Convention does not take a position in support of the many candidates for the Democratic Party's presidential nomination. A resolution to support Congresswoman Shirley Chisholm does not come to a vote.

**1972, May** Mrs. Esther Hunt Moore, the first black woman to register in Hickory, North Carolina, becomes the second black "mother of the year" in the award's 37-year history.

**1972, May** Stanford University rejects a proposal by Dr. William Shockley, Nobel Prize winning physicist, to teach a graduate course in which he would present his views that blacks are genetically inferior to whites. The University's rejection is based on grounds that Shockley's suggested reading material for the course is biased and that he is insufficiently familiar with the field of genetics. Shockley continues with the University as a teacher of electrical engineering.

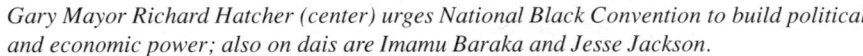

*Gary Mayor Richard Hatcher (center) urges National Black Convention to build political and economic power; also on dais are Imamu Baraka and Jesse Jackson.*

*Frank Wills, who captured the Watergate burglars in the act, is honored by Ralph Abernathy at a 1974 ceremony. If not for Wills, Nixon's "secret police" operations and other subversions of democracy might never have been revealed to the American public.*

**1972, June** Hank Aaron hits home run number 648 to tie Willie Mays, now with the New York Mets, for second place on the all-time home run list. Following the game, Aaron expresses belief he has a chance to surpass Babe Ruth's record of 714.

**1972, June** A U.S. Appeals Court, by a 5 to 1 vote, overturns the "Richmond" decision that would have required busing of school children between the city and two nearly "all-white" suburbs.

**1972, June** In San Jose, California, after 13 hours of deliberation, a jury of 11 whites and one Mexican-American acquits Angela Davis of murder and other charges in connection with the 1970 "court house shootout" in San Rafael, California.

**1972, June** Frank Wills, a black security guard in Washington, D.C.'s Watergate office complex, detects and detains a group of men installing surveillance equipment in the Democratic Party National Headquarters. The men are arrested by the city police whom Wills summons and within a year the highest reaches of the Nixon Administration are racked by the Watergate scandal. Congressman Andrew Young of Georgia later asserts that Wills refused to accept bribes from the intruders in return for letting them escape.

**1972, June** Jerome H. Holland, former Ambassador to Sweden, becomes the first black to be nominated a director of the New York Stock Exchange.

**1972, July** At the sixty-third annual NAACP convention, Herbert Hill charges that minority membership in building trades unions is actually declining despite federally-prodded programs in Chicago, Philadelphia, Pittsburgh, and New York City.

**1972, July** Senator George McGovern of South Dakota obtains the Democratic nomination for the presidency at a convention in which 400 blacks (15% of the total) are delegates. The vote of black delegates is largely divided between McGovern and Shirley Chisholm. Chisholm's showing is lessened by the fact that the black vote in the primaries was divided. Her total never exceeded 6%. After his nomination, McGovern names State Senator Basil Patterson of New York, Deputy Chairman of the Democratic Party.

**1972, August** Attorney General Richard Kleindienst files suit against Los Angeles and Montgomery, Alabama for discrimination in hiring for public service jobs. Montgomery is accused of assigning whites to better jobs than blacks and with paying less to blacks in the same jobs as whites. Los Angeles is accused of discriminating against blacks in hiring and promotion of minorities in the Fire Department, which has only 48 blacks, 94 Mexican-Americans, and no Americans of Asian descent.

**1972, August** James Baker, a 37-year-old diplomat, is appointed by the U.S. State Department to a post in the intensely segregated Union of South Africa, and coolly announces he will be able to live in the same area as whites because he is a "distinguished foreigner." Baker's appointment follows a controversy in March in which Roy Wilkins denied defending the role of American businesses operating in South Africa. Wilkins had noted he was unsure South African blacks were better off working for South African than American employers.

**1972, August** The "Coalition Against Blax-ploitation," a combination of major civil rights groups in Los Angeles, announces its intention to rate black films, notes that "the transformation from the stereotype Stepin Fetchit to Super Nigger on the screen is just another form of cultural genocide."

**1972, August** American black athletes become embroiled in a number of issues at the Munich Olympic Games. Some support African blacks in an attempt to deny acceptance of the team from Rhodesia. Two American runners are severely criticized for appearing lackadaisical on the victory stand during the playing of the Star Spangled Banner.

**1972, August** Richard Nixon, renominated for President at Miami Beach, restates his opposition to busing and "statistical targets" for use by blacks and other minorities in jobs and education. Says Nixon: "The way to end discrimination against some is not to begin discrimination against others." Many observers interpret Nixon's comments as a step in the rejection of special programs and quotas for blacks in construction and other skilled trades.

**1972, September** A special New York State Commission, reporting on the 1971 uprising at Attica prison, criticizes inmates for taking hostages and New York State authorities for "clearly indiscriminate firing by men who did not value inmates' lives." The report confirms that hostages were killed by gunfire from state forces retaking the prison.

**1972, October** Algernon Cooper, the great-great grandson of a black slave and a Confederate general, is inaugurated Mayor of Prichard, Alabama, a town of 41,000. A moderate who seeks to attract business to his community, Cooper pays a call on Governor George Wallace, who is recovering from an assassination attempt.

**1972, October** Demonstrations by white parents in Canarsie and other sections of Brooklyn and Queens, New York, successfully halt busing of black children to three schools. Parents' groups say they do not favor segregation but feel the schools are "tilting" too strongly to a black student body.

**1972, November** Richard Nixon is reelected President in a landslide victory over Senator George McGovern, despite the fact that some 86% of the black vote went to McGovern. However, blacks achieve a number of electoral successes. Among them are: an increase of black Congressmen from 12 to 15; election of the first black Congress members from the South since the days of Reconstruction, Andrew Young from Atlanta and Yvonne Jordan from Houston; a landslide victory for Republican Senator Edward Brooke in Massachusetts, even though Massachusetts was the only state to be carried by George McGovern; an increase in black representation in state legislatures, from 206 in 31 states before the election to 229 in 39 states after the election; election of blacks to the Arkansas state legislature for the first time in the history of that state; and election of blacks to the Minnesota and Oregon legislatures, where they were not represented in the previous session. Blacks also suffered some setbacks. Black candidates for statewide offices lost in Indiana, Washington, and Pennsylvania. Blacks were unseated from state legislatures in the same states. The percentage of blacks of voting age who cast a ballot was 44 compared with 54 in 1968, but whites also voted in lesser numbers, 55 compared with 69 in 1968.

**1972, November** The Association for the Study of Black Life History, meeting in Cincinnati for its fifty-seventh annual convention, changes its name to the Association for the Study of African American History. The change is based on a mail ballot of the Association's membership, some two-thirds of whom opted to substitute "African-American" for "black" in the title. Prominent speakers at the convention include Andrew F. Brimmer, a governor of the Federal Reserve Board; Congressman Louis Stokes of Cleveland; Dr. John Hope Franklin, Professor of History at the University of Chicago; and Dr. Rayford W. Logan, Distinguished Professor of History at Howard University.

**1972, November** Admiral Elmo R. Zumwalt Jr., Chief of Naval Operations, and Secretary of the Navy John W. Warner summon some 90 admirals and Marine Corps generals to a "stern lecture" on the "failure" of the commanders to achieve racial harmony on their ships and stations. Admiral Zumwalt orders the commanders to punish any act of bias or violation of its equal opportunity program. The issue was brought to a head by disturbances, strikes, and sabotage aboard a number of warships in Asia and domestic waters and the ensuing arrest pattern in which black sailors were questioned and confined in much greater numbers than whites. Zumwalt notes the incidents "were clearly due to the failure of commands to implement new racial programs with a whole heart." Blacks only were arrested in October after disturbances aboard the aircraft carrier *Kitty Hawk* and the Navy oiler *Hassayampa*. A multimillion dollar fire on the carrier *Forrestal* on July 10 and sabotage on the carrier *Ranger* were linked to racial tensions and anti-war feeling despite the fact that sailors arrested for these actions were white. A number of Admirals and Congressmen reply that the Navy has been too "permissive" with blacks.

**1972, November** Secretary of Defense Laird releases and praises a report by a bi-racial panel of military officers and civilians which declares that systematic and intentional discrimination exists against blacks in the military services.

**1972, November** Father Theodore M. Hesburgh, President of Notre Dame University, resigns as Chairman of the U.S. Commission on Civil Rights. The White House concedes it had sought the resignation of Father Hesburgh, an outspoken critic of President Nixon's anti-busing policy, and the Commission's five other members. Father Hesburgh had served on the Commission since its formation in 1957.

**1972, November** Two young black men, Denver A. Smith and Leonard Douglas Brown, are killed on the Baton Rouge, Louisiana campus of Southern University during a confrontation between students, state police and sheriff deputies of East Baton Rouge Parish. The students had been pressing for the resignation of University President Dr. G. Leon Netterville, whom they charged had arbitrarily dismissed teachers he regarded as militant and was unreceptive to student demands for better living and academic facilities.

Following the shootings, Louisiana Governor Edwin W. Edwards closes the school and sends the National Guard to the Baton Rouge campus. After declaring that law enforcement officers had not used firearms in the Baton Rouge confrontation, the Governor concedes that a deputy might have mistaken a shot gun shell for a tear gas shell which resembled it. Students declare that they had not attacked police except to hurl back a tear gas shell that had been fired into their ranks.

Earlier in November, students had occupied the administration building of the New Orleans campus until the campus administrator, Dr. Emmet W. Bashful, resigned. However, the state Board of Education did not accept the resignation and the issue was cloudy at the time of the violence in Baton Rouge.

**1972, November** A Newark, New Jersey Superior Court judge lifts a temporary restraining order that had halted construction of the Kawaida Towers apartment building in a white middle-class neighborhood. The 16-story, 210-apartment project is sponsored by Temple Kawaida, whose spiritual leader is Imamu Baraka. Court action to halt construction was brought by a group of four whites, led by Assemblyman Anthony Imperiale. Numerous battles in court and the City Council ensue before construction proceeds.

**1972, November** The NAACP announces opposition to the nomination of Peter J. Brennan as Secretary of Labor. Roy Wilkins charges that the appointment of Brennan, President of the New York Building Trades Council, is "appalling in the nature of a disaster" and that Brennan did nothing to aid the acceptance of blacks and other minority members into craft union membership programs." President Nixon replies that Brennan has been "instrumental" in helping minorities gain access to such programs.

*Imamu Baraka and Anthony Imperiale head the opposing factions in Newark's Kawaida Towers housing controversy.*

*Father Theodore Hesburgh, President of Notre Dame College and an outspoken critic of ex-President Nixon's civil rights policies.*

**1972, December** In a guarded statement in the Black Panther newspaper, Huey P. Newton, Chief of the Panthers, offers assistance to Eldridge Cleaver, former head of the Panthers, in the event that Cleaver should return from exile in Algeria to face trial in the United States. Cleaver, who once headed the Panthers, and Newton had split over policy, with Cleaver generally believed to hold the more revolutionary philosophy. Cleaver, who authored the best-selling autobiography *Soul On Ice,* fled the country in 1968 when he was scheduled to go to prison for parole violation. Cleaver had recently announced an intention to return to the United States and demand a trial. Newton states that the Panthers cannot forget Cleaver's attacks, but adds that Cleaver is "not an oppressor, but is himself oppressed."

**1972, December** The Supreme Court rules unanimously that residents of racially segregated housing projects can sue to integrate them. The decision states that white residents suffer social and economic injury as do people denied entry to them, and can thus be stigmatized as residents of a "white ghetto."

**1972, December** The Reverend W. Sterling Cary, 45-year-old Administrator of the United Church of Christ's Greater

New York District, becomes the first black President of the National Council of Churches when he is elected unanimously in Dallas by the Council's General Assembly at its triennial meeting. After his election, Reverend Cary advocates that the financing of nonprofit housing programs by the 33 Protestant and Orthodox denominations belonging to the Council can "help to pull the country together again." Cary adds that white liberals are suffering from "battle fatigue." The meeting is calmer than the session in 1969 at which James Forman pressed for reparations to blacks, and a black candidate challenged Dr. Cynthia C. Wedel, the woman president whom Reverend Cary is succeeding. In an address to the Council, Imamu Baraka notes that organized religion must espouse representative government and "equitable distribution of wealth or be destroyed."

**1972, December** Leaders of the East Harlem Parents Council in New York announce the end of a school boycott which had kept over 10,000 of the area's 13,000 pupils out of 13 elementary schools for nearly two weeks. The boycott fails in its attempt to force the New York City Board of Education to restore funds and personnel cuts from local schools, but does focus widespread attention on the neighborhood's educational problems. It also indicates a high level of cooperation between blacks and Puerto Ricans.

**1972, December** Johnnie Rodgers, controversial black halfback for the University of Nebraska, is awarded the Heisman Trophy as the "country's outstanding college football player." Rodgers, once convicted for a holdup, was opposed by some people who felt this selection would set a bad example for American youth, who presumably wish to emulate athletic heroes. But Nebraska coach Bob Devaney supports Rodgers, as does O. J. Simpson, the 1968 winner, who observes: "I just missed getting into some scrapes when I was growing up and so did everybody else from the ghettoes."

**1973, January** The American Telephone and Telegraph Company settles a suit by the Federal Equal Employment Opportunities Commission when it promises to pay $15 million in back wages to 15,000 women and minority group men. A T & T also agrees to give $23 million in raises to 36,000 employees who had been advanced to more responsible positions, but allegedly had not been granted sufficient wage increases. EEOC officials promise more suits would follow if business did not act on its own.

**1973, January** At the start of its second term in office, spokesmen for the Nixon Administration note the following policies and claims with respect to blacks: Hiring preference for blacks to make up for past injustices and oversights is to be replaced by a merit system, ostensibly without regard to race; Civil rights laws are to be enforced less stringently; Discrimination clearly in violation of the law must be established for the government to act; The government will no longer attempt to force integration in schools or suburban housing; Busing is to be opposed, if necessary by a constitutional amendment; And welfare legislation will be pursued, but with less emphasis on cost cutting, work requirements and establishment of eligibility than in the 1969 Bill which was not enacted. The Administration claims that between 1969 and 1973 it increased appropriations to enforce civil rights legislation, helped minority business enterprises, and raised the number of children in legally depressed schools in the South from 32 to 91%.

**1973, April** Paul Robeson is honored on his seventy-fifth birthday by Rutgers University, which he attended, and many other institutions and groups. The homage to Robeson, who is ill at the time, marks attempts at reconciliation between American institutions and the great singer, actor, and long-time Communist sympathizer.

**1973, April** Bobby Seale, running as a Democrat, finishes second in the mayoral race in Oakland, California, and earns the right to a runoff against the incumbent, John Reading, who just fails to attain the needed 50% necessary for election without a runoff.

**1973, May** The Supreme Court, in a 4 to 4 tie, fails to overturn a circuit court rejection of the Mehirge decision which would have required Richmond, Virginia to integrate its school system with that of two suburbs. Thus, for the time being at least, the Court rejects the concept that racial imbalance in a few schools justifies revision of school boundaries.

**1973, June** Thomas Bradley, a former policeman, who is the son of a sharecropper, is elected Mayor of Los Angeles, defeating the incumbent Sam Yorty by 100,000 votes. Yorty had defeated Bradley in 1969 in a vote in which Bradley's race had been a major issue.

**1973, June** Howard University's Joint Center for Political Studies reports that as of April 1973, 2,621 blacks hold 2,627 elective offices in the United States at every level from school boards to the Congress. When the first list was compiled, in 1969, the total was 1,185. In 1972 the figure was 2,264. Michigan leads the states with 179, followed in order by New York, Mississippi, Alabama, and Arkansas.

**1973, July** Alonzo Crim, Atlanta's new, black Superintendent of Schools, launches a "school compromise plan" which would leave some 80 of the city's 140 schools all-black, limit busing to 3% of the school population, and increase the number of desegregated schools by only eight. A number of blacks, among them Roy Wilkins, condemn the plan, as setting a dangerous precedent. Defenders feel the plan is the best route to effective education and racial harmony.

**1973, September** Willie Mays, now of the New York Mets, announces his retirement as an active player, though he is to appear in the World Series. Mays's lifetime batting average is .302, his homer total 660. Hank Aaron ends the season with 713 home runs, one short of Babe Ruth's record.

**1973, November** The number of black elected officials in the United States rises from 370 to 2,991, in an election held mostly for municipal and county offices. The number of black mayors rose from 81 to 108 with notable victories in Detroit and Atlanta.

**1973, November** Governor George Wallace of Alabama is warmly applauded as he addresses a meeting of the National Conference of Black Mayors in Tuskegee. The black mayor of Tuskegee, Johnny Ford, stresses the need for black mayors to forget old racial hostilities and get along with Wallace, but many blacks attack the spread of "creeping respectability" for the Alabama Governor. In May 1974, Wallace and the Reverend Ralph Abernathy, head of The Southern Christian Leadership Conference, meet and shake hands.

**1974, January** A group of prominent black leaders, including Roy Wilkins, Reverend Jesse Jackson, Floyd McKissick, and Mayors Bradley, Young, and Jackson, visit Vice President Ford and report that the meeting was courteous and say they hope blacks now have a friendly ear in the Nixon Administration.

**1974, January** Rabbi Balfour Brickner of the New York Federation of Reform Synagogues urges both blacks and Jews, in the spirit of the late Martin Luther King Jr., to reestablish the cooperation that prevailed in the 1960s, and says that the negative atmosphere in New York City is partly attributable to separatism within both communities.

**1974, March** The Department of Justice releases memos revealing that in the 1960s, and early 1970s, the Federal Bureau of Investigation had waged a campaign designed to disrupt, discredit, and neutralize black nationalist groups, including the Black Panther Party. A major objective of the effort, according to the memo, was to prevent the emergence of a black leader capable of uniting disparate factions and inspiring violence. Reverend Jesse Jackson asserts the documents give credence to charges that the FBI figured in the deaths of Malcolm X, Reverend King, and Fred Hampton.

**1974, March** The Second Black National Political Convention meets in Little Rock. Mayors Hatcher of Gary and Jackson of Atlanta and Imamu Baraka are among the speakers. However, many prominent black leaders are absent, among them Representative Charles Diggs who resigned as co-chairman.

**1974, April** Henry Aaron of the Atlanta Braves ties Babe Ruth's home run record of 714 in his team's opening game in Cincinnati, breaking it with number 715 a few days later in Atlanta against Al Downing of the Los Angeles Dodgers.

**1974, May** Alvin F. Poussaint, a black Harvard professor, charges that the women's liberation movement is regarded as a threat by many blacks who feel it is being used as an excuse to perpetuate discriminatory practices in employment. While praising the contributions of the women's movement to human rights, Poussaint asks women to be aware of efforts by racists to use them as pawns.

**1974, June** A draft report of the Senate "Watergate" investigating staff indicates that reelection efforts on behalf of President Nixon in 1972 sought to gain the support or neutrality of prominent blacks by means of an expeditious proffering and withholding of federal aid. Two black targets were the Reverend Jesse Jackson, head of Operation PUSH, and James Farmer, an official during Nixon's first term.

**1974, July** By a vote of 5 to 4, the Supreme Court nullifies an attempt to effect "metropolitan integration" of predominantly black schools in Detroit with those of nearby white suburbs. Chief Justice Burger in his majority decision declares that segregation in a city's schools does not justify its combination with schools in its suburbs. Justice Thurgood Marshall, dissenting, calls the decision an emasculation of the constitutional guarantee of equal opportunity.

**1974, August** Richard Nixon resigns as President as likelihood of his conviction and removal from office on three counts of impeachment becomes apparent. Three blacks, Conyers, Jordan, and Rangel, serve on the Committee. Nixon is succeeded by Vice President Gerald Ford who, a few days after the inauguration, holds a meeting with the Congressional Black Caucus. Though Ford promises little in the way of civil rights activity, the meeting is cordial, a marked change from encounters between the Caucus and the Nixon Administration.

**1974, November** The number of black elected officials rises at federal, state, and local levels. All blacks in Congress are reelected and one new member, Harold Ford of Memphis, Tennessee is added. Blacks are elected lieutenant governor in California and Colorado.

**1974, December** Riots against integration of public schools in Boston peak as police struggle to restrain violence which wrenches much of the city. President Ford deplores the violence, but is criticized by black leaders as actually encouraging it by his comment that he opposes busing to integrate schools.

**1975, February** A wide range of black leaders attack President Ford's budget which proposes to reduce and eliminate humanitarian programs and to raise the cost of food stamps. Democrats declare opposition to much of the plan.

**1975, March** William T. Coleman is appointed Secretary of Transportation by President Ford, becoming the second black in the nation's history to hold a cabinet post.

**1975, May** Department of Labor figures report the national unemployment rate at 9%, the black rate at 15%. Vernon L. Jordan Jr. of the National Urban League reports that the black rate is actually 26% when undercounts and

*General Daniel "Chappie" James becomes the first black four star general in U.S. History. Gen. James commands North American air defenses.*

"discouraged" workers are considered.

**1975, June** *Focus* the publication of the Joint Center for Political Studies, charges that the proportion of blacks being recruited for the Armed Forces is being deliberately reduced.

**1975, June** President Ford addresses the NAACP's annual convention in Washington, D.C. He asks blacks, in the interest of economic stability, to accept his reduced spending policies, which mean lower aid to minorities and poor people. Black leaders differ strongly with the President's programs.

**1975, July 1** Wallace Muhammed, supreme minister of the Nation of Islam, delivers a historic speech, opening the Muslim Nation to members of all races.

**1975, July** The NAACP's sixty-sixth annual convention in Washington, D.C. focuses on the country's bitter economic situation with over 12% of adult black workers and as much as 40% of black youth unemployed. Discussion centers on programs for creating new jobs and on organized labor's seniority system, which unintentionally, but automatically, discriminates against blacks. President Ford addresses the convention but refuses to create special programs for unemployed or under employed blacks.

**1975, August 18** District of Columbia Appellate Court Judge Julia Cooper is confirmed by the Senate, becoming the highest ranking black woman in the federal courts.

**1975, August 20** Senator Edward Brooke calls for a $10 billion federal employment program to end the economic "depression" in black America by creating 1 million public service jobs.

**1975, August 22** In a celebrated North Carolina trial, 21-year-old Joan Little is freed of the charge of murdering a white jailer while she was a prisoner in a county jail; the defense contended she slew the jailer while being raped.

**1975, August 29** General Daniel "Chappie" James Jr., becomes commander-in-chief of the North American Air Defense Command (NORAD). On the same day he is promoted to become the first black four-star general in U.S. history.

**1975, September** The U.S. Civil Rights Commission rebukes President Ford for voicing public opposition to a federal court's busing plan for Boston, saying that the President's stand has contributed to the entrenched and sometimes violent resistance to busing.

**1975, September 27-28** The Congressional Black Caucus, now 17 members strong, holds its fifth annual dinner, an event that has grown into a two-day, 2,800-person civil rights convention. The major theme of the affair is "From Changing Structures to Using Structure—1879-1976." Panelists recommend federal takeover of the welfare system and poverty assistance, that the states assume more fiscal responsibility for education, and that Caucus-directed programs develop a national black position on matters of policy.

**1975, September 3** The case of Rubin "Hurricane" Carter and John Artis, who have been serving life sentences for murder since 1967, despite the fact that the two chief prosecution witnesses recanted in September 1974 (asserting they were coerced into perjury by the Passaic County Prosecutor's office) was sent by New Jersey Governor Byrne to the Assembly Judiciary Committee for review and to determine whether pardons should be granted. Carter has long claimed that he was framed because of his outspoken views about racism and police brutality in Paterson.

**1975, September 29** WGPR-TV, the first black-owned, black-operated television station in the United States, goes on the air in Detroit.

**1975, December** U.S. Attorney General Edward Levy opens an official review of the Martin Luther King assassination. Although self-confessed James Ray was convicted of the crime, many facts point to a conspiracy and suggest that those really responsible for the murder are still at large. These facts move the Justice Department to open a secret investigation as early as 1970, but the FBI refuses to turn over necessary records. The major questions are: Could Ray, a stranger to Memphis, find the perfect assassination spot in just 2 $^1/_2$ hours if he were acting alone? What are the New Orleans connections the assassin was afraid to discuss even while on trial for his life? Where did his escape money come from?

**1975, December 4** Pointing to recently discovered graves and statues, archaeologists announce that Africans, rather than Columbus or the Vikings, were the first overseas explorers to set foot in the New World. Probably the first to come, perhaps as early as 4000 B.C., were fishermen from the Liberian area. Mali King Zabu Bakiri II is believed to have headed one of the last expeditions from Africa to the New World in the early 1300s, using compasses and navigational instruments developed for crossing the Sahara desert. The great Olmec civilization of ancient Mexico is now thought to have been a largely black culture.

**1976, March 24** The Supreme Court decides that blacks who have been denied jobs in violation of the 1964 Civil Rights Act must receive retroactive seniority once they have been hired in those jobs.

**1976, April 20** The Supreme Court rules that federal courts may order minority low-cost public housing in white suburbs of a city even when those suburbs have not been guilty of racially discriminatory housing practices. The Department of Housing and Urban Development can be ordered to provide such housing.

**1976, April 26** The Metropolitan Applied Research Center, a major black research organization founded to serve as advocate for the urban poor, announces that it must close due to declining funds

**1976, June 1** A study by The Joint Center for Political Studies shows that blacks hold almost 4,000 elected posts in government, more than any other time in history. Still blacks comprise only 0.05% of the total elected officials in the country.

**1976, June 14** The Supreme Court refuses without comment to review court-ordered busing for desegregation of Boston public schools. In January, the U.S. Court of Appeals for the First Circuit upheld a May 1975 ruling by U.S. District Court Judge Arthur Garrity ordering busing to achieve racial integration in the Boston school system. In April of that same year, a period of prolonged violence erupts in Boston after the topic of busing becomes the object of a bitter and simmering dispute.

**1976, July** Mayor Kenneth A. Gibson of Newark, New Jersey is elected the first black president of the 43-year old U.S. Conference of Mayors.

**1976, August 31** A Chancellery Court in Mississippi awards $1,250,058 to 12 white, Port Gibson merchants in damages from the NAACP due to the organization's successful boycott in 1966.

**1976, October 2** U.S. Agriculture Secretary Earl Butz is reprimanded by President Gerald Ford for making "highly offensive" remarks about blacks. Butz issues an apology for his remarks.

**1976, November 2** Blacks play a vital role as Jimmy Carter narrowly defeats President Gerald Ford in the presidential election. Carter received about 94% of some 6.6 million black votes.

**1976, November 14** The congregation of President-Elect Jimmy Carter's Baptist church in Plains, Georgia votes to drop its 11-year ban on attendance by blacks.

**1976, December 16-21** President-Elect Jimmy Carter appoints Andrew Young as Chief Delegate to the United Nations and Patricia Roberts Harris as Secretary of the Department of Housing and Urban Development.

**1977, January 20** Clifford Alexander Jr. is sworn in as the first black Secretary of the Army. Appointees by President Carter include 19 blacks in the White House and 37 in other executive positions.

**1977, February 6** Griffin Bell is confirmed as Attorney General despite opposition from leading blacks. Bell soon appoints two blacks—Wade H. McCree as Solicitor General and Drew Days as Assistant Attorney General for Civil Rights. However, Coretta King declares that Bell has an image that is almost segregationist and Congressman Parren Mitchell reveals Bell's membership in three social clubs that exclude blacks. During the Senate confirmation hearings, Bell saw himself as a voice of moderation, and despite the efforts of the NAACP to keep the hearings open, the hearings went behind closed doors and after a bitter Senate battle Bell was confirmed.

**1977, March 2** Representative Charles C. Diggs of Michigan is indicted on charges of taking kickbacks from three Congressional employees and keeping on his payroll three other employees who did not work in Congress.

**1977, March 9** Joseph Lawson Hawze is installed as Bishop of the Roman Catholic Diocese of Biloxi, Mississippi. He becomes the first black bishop of an American diocese since James Healy of Portland, Maine in 1875. The diocese has over 42 parishes with 48,000 Catholics, including about 9,000 blacks.

**1977, April 19** Author Alex Haley receives a special Pulitzer Prize for his book *Roots*. The book becomes a best seller among blacks and its popularity is further boosted through the television movie *Roots*.

**1977, July 2** Colston A. Lewis, a member of the EEOC, charges President Carter with racism and failure to keep his promise to bring more blacks into the Administration. He then defies a White House order to vacate his office immediately.

**1977, July 18** The once radical Black Panther Party becomes integrated into the political system of Oakland, California, as it works to elect Lionel Wilson as the city's first black mayor and John George as the first black Alameda County supervisor.

**1977, July 24-25** National Urban League Executive Director Vernon Jordan, thought to be one of the black leaders closest to President Carter, criticizes the Administration's policies in a speech to his organization. Carter replies that he has no apologies for his record on blacks and the poor.

**1977, July 29** Roy Wilkins, a 42-year veteran of the NAACP serving the last 22 as Executive Director, announces his intention to retire during the organization's sixty-eighth annual convention in St. Louis, his hometown. Wilkins was 75 when he announced his retirement.

**1977, May 14** Reverend Jesse Jackson accuses President Carter of assuming a conservative stance on blacks and the poor, and moves to organize a coalition of all groups of blacks and whites to secure economic and social justice. In June, NAACP Chairwoman Margaret Bush Wilson attacks Carter, stating that his means of attempting a balanced budget will be harmful to the interests of blacks.

**1977, September 4** A meeting of 15 black leaders at the National Urban League produces two general agreements: A loose coalition of members will work against perceived anti-black sentiment in the nation and top priority would be given to increasing job opportunities for minorities.

**1977, October 27** Dr. Clifton R. Wharton, President of Michigan State University, is appointed President of the State University of New York, the nation's largest state university.

**1977, November 19** Robert E. Chambliss, a 73-year-old former member of the Ku Klux Klan, is convicted of first-degree murder in the 1963 bombing of the 16th Street Baptist Church where four black girls were killed. He is sentenced to life in prison. Chambliss protests his innocence.

*In 1978, after the retirement of Roy Wilkins, Benjamin Hooks became executive director of the NAACP.*

**1977, December 28** Karen Farmer becomes the first black member of the Daughters of American Revolution, when she proves her worthiness by tracing her ancestry to William Hood, a soldier in the patriot army during the American Revolution.

**1978, January 8** Benjamin Hooks, the new Executive Director of the NAACP, announces plans to revitalize the civil rights organization with new chapters and a greater stress on fund raising.

**1978, January 17** Major Guion S. Bluford Jr., Major Frederick D. Gregory, and Dr. Ronald E. McNair join the space program and begin training as astronauts for future space missions.

**1978, May 2** Ernest Morial, a former judge, is inaugurated as the first black mayor of New Orleans.

**1978, May 23** Wallace D. Muhammad, leader of the World Community of Islam in the West, says that his organization will abandon its separatist philosophy and be a patriotic group in the belief that minorities may have asked too much and not done enough for themselves.

**1978, May 29** Files made public by the FBI reveal that an unidentified black leader worked with the agency during the 1960s in an effort to remove Dr. Martin Luther King from national prominence in the civil rights movement. The information released is from files of J. Edgar Hoover.

**1978, June 9** The Church of the Latter Day Saints (Mormons) revokes its 148-year-old policy of excluding black men from the priesthood.

**1978, June 28** The Supreme Court, in a 5-4 decision, orders that white student Allan P. Bakke be admitted to The University of California, Davis's Medical College, indicating that the refusal to admit Bakke was tantamount to reverse discrimination and that use of racial or ethnic quotas was an improper means of achieving racial balance. The Court held that the college affirmative action program was invalid since it had the effect of discriminating against qualified white applicants although the Court perceived the goal of attaining a diverse student body constitutional and permissible. The decision, however, creates a need to reevaluate affirmative action programs in general and how best to achieve greater minority equality in education and the economy. Justice Thurgood Marshall writes a separate opinion (see Legal section).

**1978, June 30** Assistant Attorney General Drew Days states that federal agencies will be able to continue vigorous enforcement of antidiscrimination laws in wake of the Bakke decision, but must be more careful in doing so.

**1978, July** Debate rages within the civil rights movement over charges that many groups and leaders serve two masters by accepting large donations and board of directors positions with large corporations. The greatest argument centers on the NAACP's generally favorable position on deregulation of energy prices. Some black opponents of deregulation contend that the NAACP had difficulty achieving objectivity on the issue because members of its energy committee were employed by energy interests.

**1979, July 20** Patricia Roberts Harris moves within the Carter Administration from Secretary of Housing and Urban Development to Secretary of Health, Education and Welfare.

**1978, July 22** NAACP leader Benjamin Hooks asserts that if the Republican Party's efforts to gain more black political support were to be effective, the party would have to demonstrate more concern for the needs of disadvantaged Americans, and that programs such as lower taxes for those in lower income brackets and full employment legislation would be basic considerations. The Republican Party had announced a $640,000 public relations campaign to garner more black votes.

**1978, August 14-18** The House of Representatives holds public hearings on the assassinations of Dr. Martin Luther King and President John F. Kennedy. James Earl Ray, convicted of killing Dr. King, denies his guilt and charges that he was framed.

**1978, September 9** President Carter acts to heal a rift with the Congressional Black Caucus following an angry meeting during which Representative John Conyers walks out after a heated verbal exchange with Carter and Vice President Mondale. Conyers was demanding a "Camp David summit" to discuss employment.

**1978, October 10** Representative Charles Diggs (D., Mich.), considered the "dean" of blacks in the House of Representatives, is convicted on 11 counts of mail fraud and 18 counts of falsified Congressional payroll vouchers. He announces his intention to appeal and is later reelected despite the conviction.

**1978, October 27** President Carter signs the Humphrey-Hawkins Full Employment Bill, which states the government's desire to reduce unemployment to 4% and continue the CETA program for four more years. However, it does not provide for funds to pursue its goals.

**1978, November 8** U.S. Senator Edward Brooke of Massachusetts, the only black in the upper house of Congress, loses to Paul T. Songas following a period of bad publicity about his divorce and personal finances.

**1978, December 3** The Census Bureau reports that during the period of 1960 to 1977, the number of blacks living in suburbs increased from 2.4 million to 4.6 million, and that 55% of the 24.5 million blacks in the United States live in central cities, indicating a decline from the 1970 figure of 59%.

**1979, January 24** President Carter sends his budget to Congress and the response of most blacks in government and in leadership positions across the nation is negative. Ronald H. Brown of the Washington-based operations committee of the National Urban League states, "we're concerned and disturbed about any budget that doesn't meet the needs of the poor and this one doesn't."

**1979, January 30** Franklin A. Thomas, former president of Bedford-Stuyvesant Restoration Corporation and a director of New York Life Insurance Company, becomes the first black president of the Ford Foundation.

**1979, February 18** It is reported that the most rapidly growing minority group in America, the Hispanics, at the present growth rate, will displace blacks as the nation's largest minority by 1985.

**1979, February 24** President Carter honors Jesse Owens, Reverend Martin Luther King Sr., and 15 other elderly blacks selected for their contributions by the National Caucus on Black Aged.

**1979, February 27** The Department of Housing and Urban Development announces it will foreclose the financially troubled Soul City, a new town in rural North Carolina that was to have been controlled by blacks but open to all. Since 1969, when Floyd B. McKissick announced the idea for the city, $27 million had been spent by federal, state, and local sources. McKissick vows to continue efforts to keep the project alive.

**1979, March 28** In a bid to become the first black mayor of Kansas City, Missouri, Bruce R. Watkins fails as the city divides along racial rather than political lines, and elects Republican Richard L. Berkley by a 20,000 plurality.

**1979, April 15** Imperial Wizard Bill Wilkinson leads 100 members of the KKK through Selma, Alabama shouting "white power." They are confronted by stone-throwing blacks who attempt to disrupt the procession.

**1979, April 20** The National Association of Black Social Workers calls for a national black political convention in 1980 to develop strategies to counteract racism in health, housing, employment, and social programs.

**1979, May 1** New York State Senator Vander Beatty announces he has collected 63,000 signatures calling for the City Council in New York City to schedule a referendum in the fall on whether a recall procedure should be included in the City Charter. Beatty started his campaign accusing Mayor Edward Koch of racism. However, Beatty's efforts failed.

**1979, May 2** The Congressional Black Caucus and delegates from 11 southern states set up an "action alert communications network" to help them exert pressure on at least 100 white Congressional representatives from heavily black districts to vote with the caucus on important issues.

**1979, May 16** News of a series of private meetings between middle-level black officials in the Carter Administration becomes known. The group meets over a period of several months to discuss its concerns over the Administration's record on minority issues.

**1979, May 27** A march led by Reverend Joseph Lowery of SCLC erupts into a fight with some 100 KKK members as the Klan attempts to block the march. Two Klansmen are shot during the disturbance.

**1979, June 11** Statistics gathered by the tribunal of the U.S. Supreme Court demonstrates that the majority of individuals employed by the courts are white and male and that black employees are concentrated at the lowest levels. There have been only two black law clerks in the Court's history.

**1979, June 19** The Bureau of the Census announces a study indicating that despite the fact that black Americans have made enormous advances in employment, income, health, housing, political power, and other measures of social well-being in recent decades, they remain far behind white Americans.

**1979, June 25** Amalya L.Kearse receives an appointment to the U.S. Court of Appeals for the Second Circuit and becomes the first woman to sit on that bench and the second black ever in such a position. The first black was Thurgood Marshall, who is now a justice of the Supreme Court.

**1979, June 29** The U.S. Supreme Court rules 5-2, in *U.S. Steel v. Brian Weber*, that private employers can legally give special preference to black workers to eliminate "manifest racial imbalance" in traditionally white jobs.

**1979, July 26** The U.S. Justice Department announces that it will sponsor a seminar for police officials on the use of deadly force as a result of policemen killing nonwhites in controversial circumstances in several cities during previous months.

**1979, August 1** The House of Representatives votes 408-1 to place a bust of Martin Luther King Jr. in the Capitol. The work will be the first to honor any black American in Congress.

**1979, August 16** Andrew Young resigns as Chief U.S. Delegate to the United Nations after being publicly criticized for unauthorized talks with the Palestine Liberation Organization in New York. The resignation sets off a storm of controversy and animosity between segments of the Jewish and black communities.

**1979, September 10** The NAACP announces plans to establish ties with representatives of African and Caribbean nations in a move to increase the influence of blacks on world affairs.

**1979, September 15** The FBI admits it planted a rumor in 1970 that actress Jean Seberg, who later committed suicide, was pregnant by a member of the Black Panther Party. The rumor was circulated in an effort to discredit her support for the black nationalist movement.

**1979, September 20** A delegation of 10 black Americans representing the Southern Christian Leadership Conference meets in Lebanon with guerrillas of the Palestine Liberation Organization. The visit stems from the resignation of Andrew Young from his post as U.S. Ambassador to the United Nations.

**1979, September 20** A survey conducted by the Southern Regional Council of 11 southern states, and four cities in other areas of the country, discloses that three of five southern judges belong to all-white social organizations and the probability exists that such is the case throughout the country.

**1979, September 24** Donald McHenry replaces Andrew Young as U.S. Ambassador to the United Nations.

**1979, September 25** One of every five firms receiving federal aid for minority businessmen and the disadvantaged has been demonstrated to be a front for white contractors, an audit by the Small Business Administration concludes. In effect, of the 1,505 firms granted assistance, 256 should not have been funded.

**1979, October 3** Councilman Richard Arrington of Birmingham, Alabama is elected as that city's first black mayor. Arrington garnered 52% of the vote.

**1979, October 17** Sir Arthur Lewis, a professor at Princeton, is named winner of the Nobel Prize in Economic Science for his work in the subject of problems of developing nations. He shares the award with Theodore W. Schultz of the University of Chicago.

**1979, October 18** Benjamin Hooks, M. Carl Holman, James Farmer, Dr. Kenneth Clark, and Vernon Jordan express concern that meetings between black leaders and the Palestine Liberation Organization could damage the black movement.

**1979, November 19** Ayatollah Khomeini releases eight blacks and five white women while continuing to hold other hostages at the U.S. Embassy in Teheran.

**1979, December 22** The Joint Center for Political Studies reveals that between 1978 and 1979 the number of blacks elected to public office increased by 104. This 2% increase is considered meager, especially because such officials were elected in states with substantial black populations.

**1980, January 18** A survey conducted by Data Black, a major black commercial polling organization, indicates widespread dissatisfaction with President Carter's efforts among blacks.

**1980, February 6** The Congressional Black Caucus attacks President Carter's fiscal 1981 budget proposals, criticizing increases in military spending that lead to cuts for social programs. Caucus members promise to initiate legislation to reduce military spending increases and pronounce the budget "an unmitigated disaster for the poor, the unemployed and minorities."

**1980, February 6** Georgia State Senator Julian Bond suffers a political setback in a bid for a largely ceremonial post of majority whip. He is defeated in a Democratic caucus by Senator Loyce Turner of Valdosta by a vote of 27 to 21.

**1980, February 6** The American Bar Association votes to defer action on a measure requiring law schools to adopt affirmative action plans for the admission of minority students. The measure would amend the Standards for the Approval of Law Schools and would require schools seeking to obtain or maintain accreditation to demonstrate "concrete action" in expanding opportunities for racial minorities and women in the study and entry into the law profession.

**1980, March 3** The "National Conference for a Black Agenda" meets with limited success. A special "presidential forum" in which the presidential candidates were to discuss issues of importance to black Americans, is canceled when Senator Edward Kennedy, Representative John Anderson, and Governor Jerry Brown decide not to attend. However, 1,000 national black leaders conduct in-depth discussions on strategies and goals pertaining to maximizing black political clout, employment, housing, and affirmative action. The conference is sponsored by organizations such as the NAACP, the National Urban League, PUSH—groups that had already endorsed President Carter—so that candidates saw no purpose in speaking.

**1980, March 17** A study released by the Radio and Television News Directors Association indicates that women are making greater employment advances than minorities in the broadcasting industry. Only 71% of all television stations employed minorities, while 94% of those stations

*In 1980 Representative Charles C. Diggs, (shown here in better days), abruptly resigned his house seat after conviction on mail fraud and payroll kickbacks.*

employed women, according to the survey conducted in 1979. In radio, only 20% of the country's stations employ minorities, a figure unchanged in 9 years.

**1980, April 22** The U.S. Supreme Court, in a 6-3 decision, overturns a lower court ruling that an at-large city electoral system in Mobile, Alabama is unconstitutional because it dilutes the voting strength of blacks.

**1980, April 23** In an unprecedented decision, the Supreme Court votes 6 to 3 that intentional discrimination must be proven to declare a local election system unconstitutional. Mobile, Alabama's, at-large voting system was found constitutional, overturning the rulings of two lower courts. Not one black had been elected city commissioner or to the county school board in the city's history, although blacks comprise 35.4% of its population. Justices William Brennan, Byron White, and Thurgood Marshall wrote dissenting opinions.

**1980, April 30** Amoco Oil Co., a division of Standard Oil of Indiana, agrees to pay a record civil penalty of $200,000 to settle charges of discrimination against blacks, Hispanics, and women, in the issuance of credit cards. The company's use of zip codes to determine which applicants obtained credit fostered the discrimination charges, and Amoco agreed to reconsider, upon request, applicants rejected over the past three years. The action could result in 30,000 to 50,000 new card holders. The civil penalty is the largest ever levied under the Equal Credit Opportunity Act.

**1980, May 11** Early primary results reveal that the black community is supporting President Carter's second-term bid despite criticism of his record by national black leaders, according to reports. The "resounding" victories won by Carter in the southern primaries are interpreted as blacks lacking faith in their ability to enact a "Great Society-style social renewal" agenda as proposed by Senator Edward M. Kennedy.

**1980, May 14** J. B. Stoner, a white supremacist, is convicted for the 1958 bombing of a black church in Birmingham, Alabama.

**1980, May 18** The black Liberty City area and predominantly black Coconut Grove section of Miami erupt into riotous violence, ending with 9 dead and 163 injured, following the acquittal of four white Dade County police officers in the beating death of a black man. In the night-long unrest, stores are looted, property burned, and whites fatally beaten. During the violence, blacks are heard screaming the name "McDuffie" (Arthur), the black insurance executive beaten to death following a high-speed chase with Dade County police officers for a traffic violation. Dade County officials impose an 8 P.M. to 6 P.M. curfew; 350 National Guard troops set up headquarters in an armory, with 450 more enroute from Orlando.

**1980, May 29** Vernon E. Jordan Jr., President of the National Urban League, is shot and seriously wounded by an unknown assailant in Fort Wayne, Indiana. Stating that the shooting evidenced "an element of premeditation," William H. Webster, Director of the Federal Bureau of Investigation, says, "the shooting was not accidental, and was in furtherance of an apparent conspiracy to deprive Vernon Jordan of his civil rights." The shooting occurred just outside Jordan's motel room.

**1980, June 4** Representative Charles C. Diggs Jr. (D. Mich.) abruptly resigns his House seat after the Supreme Court refuses to review his case presented to the U.S. Court of Appeals, which was denied. Diggs, a senior black Congressman, ends a 26-year career marred by formal House censure, resignation of committee and subcommittee chairmanships, and conviction on charges of mail fraud and the diversion of $60,000 in payroll kickbacks. He agrees to pay $40,000 and will leave Congress with a "clear conscience."

**1980, June 14** Based on a recent ruling by the U.S. Supreme Court, the Justice Department drops a voting rights discrimination suit against Hattiesburg, Mississippi because of their inability to prove intentional dicrimination. The high court ruled in Mobile, Alabama that it must be proven that "at large" voting systems were intentionally established and excluded black voters. The Justice Department contendedd that "at large" elections for three members of the Hattiesburg City Commission diluted black voting strength in violation of the Voting Rights Act of 1965 and the Fourteenth and Fifteenth Amendments.

**1980, June 25** The nomination of Alabama State Senator U. W. Clemon is unanimously approved by the Senate Judiciary Committee. Ranking Republican committee member Senator Strom Thurmond endorses Clemon and says although he does not condone his (Clemon's) late filing of tax returns, there was "no indication whatsoever of fraud." If confirmed by the Senate, Clemon would be the thirty-second black appointed to a federal judgeship by President Carter. At the start of his administration, only 19 blacks sat on the bench.

**1980, July 1** Presidential candidate Ronald Reagan declines an invitation to address the NAACP national convention. Executive Director Benjamin Hooks then criticizes the candidate for "writing off" black votes. Reagan soon responds by accepting an invitation to speak at the National Urban League convention.

**1980, July 2** The U.S. Supreme Court decides that Congress' award of federal funds on the basis of race was to redress racial discrimination.

**1980, July 3** A ruling authorizing Congress to impose racial quotas to remedy past discrimination against minority contractors in federal jobs programs is upheld by the Supreme Court in a 6-3 vote. It validates the 10% minority set-aside of federal public works contracts, challenged by white contractors in *Fullilove v. Klutznick.*

**1980, July 3** In a consent decree with the Justice Department, the City of Cincinnati agrees to hire and promote more blacks and women within the police department. The decree permanently enjoins the city from engaging in any employment discrimination. Over a 5-year period, 34% of new police officer vacancies will be filled by blacks and 23% by women. The Fire Department of the City of Chicago, in a similar action (April 2, 1980), was permanently prohibited from discriminating against any candidate for promotion on the basis of race or national origin. The settlement of this discrimination action was filed in federal district court and resulted from a suit charging violations of the Civil Rights Act of 1964 and the Federal Sharing Act of 1972. In New York City, the U.S. Court of Appeals (August 1,1980) overturned a lower court ruling that 50% of all new police officer hirings be black and Hispanic. The Appeals Court, however, ruled that the written test used for hiring had "significant disparate racial impact" in violation of the Civil Rights Act of 1964. It concluded that until a new test was implemented one-third of all newly hired police must be black or Hispanic.

**1980, July 18** A federal district court in Montgomery rules that the State of Alabama cannot prosecute Gary Thomas Rowe Jr., a chief informant of the FBI during the 1960s, even though the Justice Department issued a report indicating that the FBI knew about and apparently covered up illegal acts by Rowe, including attacks on blacks, civil rights activists, and newsmen.

**1980, September 3** St. Louis schools are desegregated peacefully after eight years of struggle. Over 16,000 students are bused on the first day of classes under court-

*Representatives Charles Rangel (center), Cardiss Collins (right center), Walter Fauntroy , Bennett Stewart (right), and William Gray meet with reporters in front of the Capitol to comment upon a speech made by President Ronald Reagan.*

ordered power. No violence is reported.

**1980, September 26** Federal District Judge Horace W. Gilmore invalidates the 1980 census on the ground that it undercounts blacks and Hispanics, thus violating the one-person, one-vote principle. The action was precipitated by a suit initiated by the city of Detroit with support from dozens of other cities. The census was later upheld in higher courts.

**1980, September 26** The Congressional Black Caucus marks its tenth anniversary with its annual legislative weekend. The group of bipartisan representatives cite as their major achievements the Humphrey-Hawkins Full Employment Bill and the 10% "minority-set-aside," law established to ensure minority firms a nearly representative share of federal contracts. The caucus identifies its current concern as the potential reapportionment of congressional districts affected by the outcome of the 1980 census.

**1980, September 29** Blacks are warned to mobilize against growing evangelical Christian political organizations to protect their social progress by the Congressional Black Caucus. During its legislative weekend, the caucus announces plans to spearhead the mobilization effort, which will include other national leaders.

**1980, September 29** The Schomburg Center for Research in Black Culture opens a new $3.8 million building in New York City's Harlem.

**1980, September 30** The first annual Black College Day in Washington, D.C. is attended by 18,000 black students. Speeches on the preservation of black colleges and universities are given by black officials and student leaders. The march is organized by black journalist Tony Brown in an effort to draw public attention to the impact of integration and merging of black private and public colleges and universities. Brown contends seven out of 10 blacks attending predominantly white colleges do not graduate.

**1980, October 17** The candidacy of Republican nominee Ronald Reagan for President is endorsed by two long-time civil rights leaders, the Reverend Ralph David Abernathy and Hosea Williams. Reverend Abernathy cited President Carter's broken 1976 campaign promises as spurring the endorsement, which came after a private meeting with Reagan.

**1980, October 24** Discrimination against blacks and women by the South's largest bank, Republic National, is found in a 272-page ruling by U.S. District Judge Patrick Higginbotham. Discrimination in salaries, promotions, and hiring occurred over a 10-year period, according to Higginbotham. Out of the bank's 570 officers, only 15 were black and none had reached the rank of vice president.

**1980, November** By an electoral landslide of 483 to 49, Ronald Reagan sweeps Jimmy Carter out of the presidency. The wake of his victory sweeps some of the best senatorial liberal friends of blacks away as well. Heroic liberals such as George McGovern, Frank Church, Birch Bayh, Warren Magnusson, and John Culver lose their senate seats to Republicans and for the first time in almost 30 years, conservatives control the U.S. Senate. Very few voters are enthralled by either Carter or Reagan and had it not been for Carter's maneuvering of the Iranian hostage crisis for his advantage, he might well have lost the nomination to Senator Edward Kennedy. Kennedy's campaign got off to a slow start, but as the months wore on and the disillusion with Carter grew, Kennedy's primary victories increased. It was generally believed that the contest between Carter, a virtually discredited president, and Reagan, the most conservative Republican nominee since Herbert Hoover, would be much closer than the final result. The vast majority of blacks, are disillusioned with Carter, and many chose to stay home along with whites as only 52% of registered voters vote. Ronald Reagan is elected by only 26% of the eligible voters. With the election of Ronald Reagan and the loss of a Democratic Senate, blacks have little to cheer about and voice concern about the future of the hard-won gains of the past 50 years. There is a small minority of blacks, an emerging group with conservative thoughts, such as Gloria Toote, a black senior advisor in Reagan's successful campaign, who says, "Governor Reagan's approach, our approach, is the economic approach. We talk in terms of entrepreneurship and reducing welfare roles simultaneously with increasing work opportunities and full employment." Says Urban League President Vernon Jordan, "We survived Nixon and we can survive Reagan... If you take Mr. Reagan at his word that he is going to put America back to work again, he can't put just white people back to work."

*Because of President Carter's "broken promises" to blacks, the Reverand Ralph Abernathy endorsed 1980 presidential candidate Ronald Reagan.*

**1980, November 23** About 1,000 people from 25 states attend a convention in Philadelphia and form the National Black Independent Party. The idea grows out of a National Black Political Assembly in Gary, Indiana in 1972.

**1980, November 30** A special report says that violence and rioting erupted in Miami on May 17 because of the black community's perception of racist conditions and of a local political system stacked against them. Issued by an eight-member private citizens's committee appointed by Governor Bob Graham, it also criticizes the State Attorney's office handling of the Arthur McDuffie case (the black insurance executive beaten to death while in police custody). The report also pointed to the underlying problems of poverty, slum housing, functional illiteracy, and others as causing the rioting.

**1980, December 4** Congress sends a $9.1 billion appropriations bill, with controversial legislation preventing the Justice Department from ordering busing to achieve school desegregation, to President Carter. The constitutionality of the anti-busing rider, which prohibits the use of funds "to bring any sort of action to require" busing, is publicly questioned by Attorney General Benjamin Civiletti. In addition, black leaders meet with President Carter to urge him to veto the measure, and on December 14, 1980 President Carter vetoes the funding bill which includes an anti-busing rider that prohibits the Justice Department from initiating court cases to require busing to achieve school desegregation. A spokesman for House Speaker Thomas (Tip) O'Neill Jr. says no attempt will be made to override the veto. Anti-busing proponents vow to resume their efforts in the next session of Congress.

**1980, December 12** Testifying for the government in the civil rights trial of a former Dade County police officer, Dr. Roland Wright says that Arthur McDuffie "died of blunt impact injuries on the head (caused) by a beating." Dr. Wright's testimony challenges police claims that the black insurance executive died from injuries resulting from a motorcycle accident. The officer, Charles Veverka, 30, is charged with assisting in the falsification of reports to make the beating appear an accident. The trial is conducted in San Antonio after being switched from three other cities because of racial tension.

**1980, December 12** Black leaders of the nation's major civil rights organizations meet with President-Elect Ronald Reagan, who says he will defend the civil rights of minorities. The leaders urge him to appoint a black to a Cabinet

*Samuel Pierce, Reagan's Secretary of Housing and Urban Development*

position in his Administration, and include Vernon E. Jordan Jr., President of the National Urban League, Benjamin Hooks, Executive Director, NAACP, and Dorothy I. Height, President of the National Council of Negro Women.

**1980, December 18** A federal grand jury acquits Charles Veverka, 30, of four counts of violating the civil rights of Arthur McDuffie, a black who was beaten to death while in police custody. The jury deliberated for 16 hours, finally breaking an 11-1 deadlock that threatened a mistrial. Veverka was indicted following violent riots in Miami resulting from the acquittal of four white police officers accused of executing the fatal beating.

**1980, December 23** Samuel R. Pierce Jr., 58, is named by President-Elect Reagan to the Cabinet post of Secretary of the Department of Housing and Urban Development. As such, Pierce is the highest ranking black appointee of the new Administration. According to reports, Pierce is a lifelong Republican, widely respected in legal, financial, and civil rights circles.

**1981, January 14** Ruth B. Love, 48, is voted the first black general superintendent of Chicago's schools, following the rejection of a black deputy superintendent who has been with the school system for 26 years. The school board, comprised of five blacks, three Hispanics, and three whites, voted 8 to 2 to hire Love. The initial vote rejecting Manford Byrd Jr., by the white and Hispanic board members was reportedly a reaffirmation of their efforts to bring in an outsider for the job. Love, who had been superintendent of Oakland Public Schools, is also a member of the board of trustees of the National Urban League.

**1981, January 17** President Carter disavows the urban policy findings of the President's Commission for a National Agenda for the Eighties, stating that he disagrees with the Commission's recommendation that the federal government should play a role in facilitating the population trend from the Frost Belt to the Sun Belt, and that "we cannot abandon our older urban areas." After receiving a copy of the 44-member Commission's final report, Carter says he agrees with many of its recommendations, but that he opposes many others. He says the older urban areas of the Northeast and Midwest have "unique values and resources" and that their present and future contributions to the national economy must be recognized. The Commission was appointed by Carter in 1979.

**1981, January 23** Samuel Pierce Jr. receives Senate confirmation as Secretary of Housing and Urban Development. He is the only black member of the Reagan Cabinet.

**1981, February 7** Three Miami youths are convicted of murder, in connection with the beating deaths of three whites during the Liberty City riots in May 1980. A fourth youth, who was tried with the others, is acquitted. Attorneys for the defendants announce plans to appeal the verdicts.

**1981, April 7** The Southern Regional Council issues a report entitled "A Decade of Frustration," finding that public schools in the "black belt" of the Deep South remain inferior to other southern schools despite desegregation efforts. An 18-month examination of these schools in 34 rural counties in Georgia and Alabama, where blacks constitute a majority of the population, found that inferior public schools are often a result of local government decision making. According to the report, exceptions result from two factors—mandatory state and federal standards and school boards with a black majority.

**1981, April 16** Incumbent Mayor Tom Bradley of Los Angeles wins his third term with 63.6% of the vote, beating 18 opponents. According to the report, part of Bradley's success is attributed to a successful campaign strategy in which he stayed away from the city's volatile busing issues and was projected as thoughtful and articulate on the issues of fiscal restraint and crime.

**1981, May 7** Representative Robert S. Walker (R. Penn.) introduces a bill which prohibits the use of numerical quotas devised to increase the hiring or school enrollment of minorities and women. Entitled the "Equal Employment Opportunity Act," it seeks to amend the Civil Rights Act of 1964 and prevents the federal government from imposing rules on employers or schools to hire workers or to admit students on the basis of race, sex, or national origin. In effect, the proposal no longer requires companies and educational institutions to make up for past discrimination by taking on a set number of minorities and women within a specified time frame.

**1981, May 13** The Labor Department proposes revisions of Executive Order 11246 (prohibiting employment discrimination by federal contractors based on race, sex, color, national origin, or religion) in its continuing effort to ease job-discrimination rules for federal contractors. The contents of an internal memorandum reveal the effort seems targeted toward reducing the record-keeping and affirmative action requirements for small contractors and eliminating "unnecessary confrontations" with all contractors. Timothy Ryan, Labor Department Solicitor, says that the revisions make the program more manageable and cuts the number of companies covered by two-thirds for certain requirements. Secretary Raymond Donovan maintains that a final decision on revisions within the Office of Federal Contracts Compliance Programs has not been made. Administration officials plan to alter the proposal before its effective date of June 29.

**1981, May 17** A special study conducted for the Ford Foundation concludes that the Miami riots of 1980 were dramatically different from those of the 1960s, noting that such spontaneous uprisings by blacks to beat or kill whites have not occurred since the slave uprisings before the Civil War. According to the report, unlike the rioters of the 1960s, the Liberty City rioters were from a more law-abiding and representative group.

**1981, May 23** Calling them "ineffective" and unfair remedies to discrimination, Attorney General William French Smith announces that the Justice Department will no longer continue its vigorous pursuit of mandatory busing and the use of racial quotas in employment discrimination cases. In effect, the Department will no longer intervene in school desegregation cases dealing with mandatory busing and will abandon its advocacy of affirmative action plans, including quotas in the Supreme Court and elsewhere. It also considers amendments which would make "reverse discrimination" illegal under the Civil Rights Act of 1964.

**1981, June 10** The House once again approves an anti-busing provision by a vote of 265 to 122, forbidding the Justice Department from taking any direct or indirect action to require the busing of students to schools other than those closest to where they live, with the exception of cases involving special education needs. The provision is known as an "anti-busing rider" because of its attachment to the Department's $2.3 billion authorized bill.

**1981, June 16** The Reagan Administration, in a letter to Attorney General William French Smith, requests the Justice Department to determine whether the political rights of minority Americans are best served by the Voting Rights Act of 1965. Stating that the act marks the nation's commitment to full equality for all Americans, the Administration says that what must be answered is whether the act continues to be the most appropriate means of guaranteeing their rights. The completed report is due October 1.

**1981, June 21** Wayne B. Williams, a 23-year-old talent scout and freelance photographer, is charged with the slaying of two of 28 young blacks murdered in Atlanta. He is indicted within a month and the reports of missing persons drop in the city. Williams pleads not guilty.

**1981, June 30** Speaking to the NAACP national convention in Denver, President Reagan states that government programs have created a "new kind of bondage for blacks" and calls on the delegates to join him in an effort to allow business and industry to bring about "economic emancipation" for the poor. Generally, the President receives a cold reception from the audience.

**1981, July 1** A bipartisan group of 12 Senators takes exception to efforts by "conservative" legislators to limit the role of federal courts in school busing desegregation cases in a "Dear Colleague" letter. The Senators contend that such efforts will "radically alter our basic constitutional framework," and they specifically criticize the business measure sponsored by Senators Jesse Helms (R. N.C.) and J. Bennett Johnston (D. La.). The letter reflects growing concern among "liberals," constitutional scholars, and rights groups, on 25 bills before Congress which seek to restrict the authority of federal courts in school desegregation cases and other controversial issues. Among the senators signing the letter were Edward M. Kennedy (D. Mass.) and Lowell P. Weicker Jr. (R. Conn.).

**1981, July 16** The Reagan Administration sends mixed signals to blacks on its affirmative action and civil rights policy by cutting back the enforcement powers of the Justice Department and by weakening regulations against racial discrimination in employment. A July deadline date for the publication of affirmative action guide lines, by the

Office of Federal Contract Compliance Practices, is delayed until August 26. In addition, the Justice Department's civil rights division only initiates five civil lawsuits on discrimination issues as compared to 17 filed by the Carter Administration in its first six months in office. According to William Bradford Reynolds, Assistant Attorney General-Designate for Civil Rights in the Department, the Administration's actions are not indicative of its unwillingness to litigate civil rights violations but instead constitute its intention to "look at more remedies than those tried in the past that failed."

**1981, July 30** According to this report, the House reaches a tentative agreement on a compromise for the extension of the Voting Rights Act of 1965. In what would be a major change in the existing law, some counties would no longer be required to undergo federal review of their local election practices, once they have met stringent requirements dealing with their voting records. Counties in the states covered by the provision would have to prove their compliance with "the letter and spirit of the act," for 10 years. If the proposal is approved, nine states including seven in the South, and portions of 13 other states, may win exemption from seeking Justice Department approval when making changes in local election laws or voting procedures.

**1981, August 13** The Reagan Administration undertakes its review of 30 federal regulations, including rules on civil rights guidelines, to determine whether they are "burdensome, unnecessary or counter productive." The review is the third in a series conducted by the Presidential Task Force on Regulatory Relief, which will examine, among other such rules, Title IX regulations requiring companies to maintain hiring guidelines and records to prevent job discrimination against blacks and other minorities. According to Vice President Bush, who announced the start of the study, the regulations are to receive a fair review, which is intended to help stimulate the economy by reducing the rules and record-keeping load on business.

**1981, September 9** Roy Wilkins, former head of the NAACP and one of the key players in the Civil Rights movement of the 1960s, dies at New York University Medical Center of uremia at the age of 80.

**1981, September 10** Vernon Jordan announces his plans to resign as Executive Director of the National Urban League and join the Dallas-based law firm of Akin, Grump, Hauer and Field. Jordan's office will be in Washington, D.C.

**1981, September 11** In a brief to the Supreme Court, the Justice Department indicates that a Washington state law barring a voluntary busing plan in Seattle is no longer considered unconstitutional. Filed by the solicitor general, Rex E. Lee, and William Bradford Reynolds, head of the civil rights division, it may affect some 10,000 students being bused under the voluntary plan. The Department's reversal is characterized as "unethical and a breech of legal canons" by a school board attorney. A previous ruling by the Ninth U.S. Circuit Court of Appeals found that the law violated the equal protection clause of the constitution's Fourteenth Amendment.

*Popular Mayor of Los Angeles Tom Bradley, loses bid to become the nation's first black governor.*

**1981, September 13** William Bradford Reynolds, in a reversal of his earlier action, disapproves a staff recommendation that the Justice Department file a legal brief supporting allegations that the voting rights of blacks in Edgefield County, South Carolina have been violated. Black residents contend the county violated the Voting Rights Act by changing its local government from an appointed to an elected form, without submitting the plan to either the Justice Department or the federal district court, as law requires.

**1981, October 7** A House vote, 389-24, in favor of extending the Voting Rights Act of 1965, seems to ensure the likelihood of an equally strong measure in the Senate, according to Capitol Hill analysts. The House version makes the pre-clearance provisions of the act permanent (requiring six southern states and Alaska to submit proposed changes in election laws to the Justice Department before implementation), but also features the so-called bailout provision that exempts jurisdiction from the requirement if they can prove a clean 10-year, voting rights record and efforts to encourage minority voting.

**1981, October 29** Andrew Young defeats Sidney Marcus to succeed Maynard Jackson as Mayor of Atlanta, Georgia.

**1981, November 28** The nomination of Clarence M. Pendleton, President of the Urban League of San Diego, to head the U.S. Commission on Civil Rights, results in divided opinion over his suitability for the post. Pendleton's selection is controversial because of his promotion of private industry as a cure-all for black economic problems and because of his opposition to other positions taken traditionally by the civil rights movement on issues such as busing and affirmative action.

**1981, December 8** William Bradford Reynolds, Assistant Attorney General of the Justice Department's civil rights division, announces plans to seek a ruling by the Supreme Court which would find it unconstitutional to give minorities and women preference in hiring and promotion. Reynolds wants a reversal of the high court's decision in *Weber v. Kaiser Aluminum and Chemical Corp.*, which upheld the legality of affirmative action hiring and promotion practices negotiated by the company and the United Steel Workers of America. Reynolds contends the *Weber* decision was "wrongly decided" and that different sets of rules for the public sector and the private sector should not exist. Under his direction, the Justice Department has ceased such hiring preferences; the action sought by Reynolds would prohibit individuals, the Labor Department, or the Equal Employment Opportunity Commission from seeking such preferences.

**1981, December 8** The selection of John E. Jacob, 46, to succeed Vernon E. Jordan Jr., as President of the National Urban League is announced at a news conference at the agency's headquarters in New York City. Jacob, the NUL's Executive Vice President, is unanimously selected by a special search committee as the best choice among the final contenders. The League's Board of Trustees approves the recommendation. In accepting the appointment, effective January 1, 1982, Jacob says his task is to "make a difference—to help guide the Urban League movement to new heights of effectiveness, to help educate the nation to its unfinished responsibilities, and to help bring fresh opportunities to the black and poor people who are the constituency of the Urban League."

**1981, December 11** A filibuster against an anti-busing amendment in the Senate is halted by a vote of 64 to 35. The amendment by Senator J. Bennett Johnston (D. La.) would ban judges deciding school desegregation cases from requiring busing of students for more than five miles or 15 minutes away from their homes. Senator Lowell Weicker Jr.(R. Conn.), who conducted the filibuster, succeeds in delaying a vote on the measure by proposing a series of procedural motions. Weicker views the entire bill as an unconstitutional attempt by Congress to usurp the authority of the judicial and executive branches.

**1982, January** Stating that rent in its current New York office headquarters would quadruple, the NAACP asks for help from the offices of Mayor Edward Koch as it sought a new location for its national headquarters. A search committee announced that the civil rights organization was surveying other cities and the group did receive some criticism for allegedly failing to seek out a location in a black neighborhood such as New York City's Harlem.

**1982, January 2** Mayor Tom Bradley of Los Angeles opens his campaign to become the first black governor of California. The 64-year-old former policeman has been elected to the mayoralty three times.

**1982, January 4** Former U.S. Ambassador to the United Nations Andrew Young is inaugurated as Mayor of Atlanta. Young becomes mayor following a runoff election with white State Representative Sidney Marcus.

**1982, January 20** Two black civil rights workers, Julia Wilder and Maggie Bozeman, are imprisoned in Alabama after multiple appeals and pleas for leniency, charged with vote fraud.

**1982, January 25** Sandra Antoinette Wilson is ordained as the first black female priest in New York City's Episcopal Diocese. She is the fourth in the nation to be ordained.

**1982, January 27** Before a Senate Judiciary subcommittee, the Reagan Administration throws its support behind extension of key provisions of the Voting Rights Act. The Administration, in doing so, states that there is a continuing need to protect the rights of voters who are minorities.

**1982, February 1** Representative Shirley Chisholm, a Democrat of New York and the first black woman to win a seat in Congress, announces that she will not seek another term. She has served the Brooklyn communities of Bedford-Stuyvesant and Bushwick since 1968.

**1982, February 1** The Justice Department proposes that the City of Chicago be allowed to try to desegregate its schools following a plan that would rely mainly on voluntary student transfers rather than mandatory busing.

**1982, February 5** Mayor Ernest N. "Dutch" Morial, the first black to be elected mayor in New Orleans, wins a second term of office.

**1982, February 6** A small band of southern civil rights workers, followed by 300 sympathizers, start a 140-mile march in support of the Federal voting Rights Act and in protest against the vote fraud conviction of two black political activists. The marchers travel from Carrollton, Alabama through Selma to the state capitol, Montgomery, a route made famous in early civil rights marches.

**1982, February 7** A key person in the Mississippi voter registration drive in the 1960s, Amzie Moore, dies at the age of 69. Mr. Moore was responsible for bringing students into the state to register voters and also recruited local students to work.

**1982, February 8** Wesleyan University ends an admission policy that does not consider the student's ability to pay, which in effect will bar some poor students because of proposed cuts in federal student aid.

**1982, February 9** John E. Jacob, new President of the Urban League, announces that the organization will concentrate on four priority issues: pregnancy among black teenagers, the plight of poor households headed by women, crime in black neighborhoods, and voting registration and education.

**1982, February 10** The Black and Puerto Rican Caucus of the State Legislature of New York sues to force the body's leaders to adopt new Senate, Assembly, and congressional district lines by March 1.

**1982, February 12** Bowing to opposition from civil rights groups and several Democratic senators, President Reagan withdraws the nomination of William M. Bell as chairman of the Equal Employment Opportunity Commission and announces that he will instead nominate Clarence Thomas, an Assistant Secretary for Civil Rights in the Department of Education.

**1982, February 13** The American Civil Liberties Union accuses southern states of continuous discrimination against black voters in light of the federal enforcement under the Voting Rights Act of 1965.

**1982, February 14** Hundreds of voting rights marchers going from Carrollton to Montgomery march peacefully across the four-lane Edmund Pettus Bridge, where as police wielding clubs attacked participants in the Selma-to-Montgomery march.

**1982, February 14** The New York State Black and Puerto Rican Legislative Caucus meet for its eleventh Legislative Weekend with 700 participants present, and listen to chairman Assemblyman Albert Vann call for more effort to increase the political power of minority groups in the state.

**1982, February 17** Sixty rank-and-file lawyers of the Justice Department's Civil Rights Division question their boss William Bradford Reynolds about his policies, especially tax exemptions for private segregationist schools. Earlier, both the White House and the Justice Department stated that those who had objected to the Administration's policies were free to resign.

**1982, February 25** President Reagan announces his decision to request the Supreme Court for a decision about whether racially discriminatory schools should receive tax-exempt status. The move is the latest in a series of moves to resolve a politically explosive issue precipitated by the Administration's support for tax-exempt status for such schools.

**1982, February 27** A jury in Atlanta finds Wayne Williams guilty in the sensational murder case involving two slain young men. He is sentenced to consecutive life terms but indicates he will seek a new trial. Within days after the conviction, Atlanta authorities dismantle the task force which had worked for months to solve the murders of 28 young black people in Atlanta.

*Highly regarded Representative, Shirley Chisholm, in a surprise announcement in 1982, stated that she will not seek reelection.*

**1982, March** Reverend Sam B. Hart, nominated by President Reagan for a position on the U.S. Civil Rights Commission, resigns after pressure against his nomination due to outrage by a number of groups over positions he had taken regarding individual rights, and some concern about his past financial status.

**1982, March 2** Representative Parren J. Mitchell makes public a 63-page report, "Urban Policy Issues," and states that the national policy is in disarray and that the cities will not be aided by President Reagan's proposed Urban Enterprise Zone program designed to encourage business development of inner cities through tax incentives.

**1982, March 3** After the Senate passes a sweeping anti-busing bill by a vote of 57-37 (following a filibuster of eight months), House Speaker Thomas P. O'Neill Jr. says he will take no action on the legislation unless asked to do so by two key committee chairmen.

**1982, March 4** The Federal Bureau of Investigation is asked by the White House to reopen an investigation into the background of Clarence M. Pendleton, who had been nominated for the chairmanship of the U.S. Commission on Civil Rights.

**1982, March 13** The Reagan Administration is defended by Assistant Attorney General William Bradford on its rejection of preferential hiring and promotion of minority groups. Reynolds states that "this administration is firmly committed to the view that the Constitution and laws of the United States protect the rights of every person, whether black or white, male or female, to pursue his or her goals in an environment of racial and sexual neutrality."

**1982, April 4** The Bureau of Census reports that the 1980 census missed counting 1.3 million blacks and that the undercount represented 4.8% of the nation's 28 million blacks. The Bureau says that in 1970 the census missed 1.9 million out of 24.4 million blacks.

**1982, April 14** Eight surviving black members of "the Golden 13" hold a reunion at sea aboard the *U.S.S. Kidd* off Virginia. The Golden 13 were the first blacks to wear the gold stripes of commissioned officers.

**1982, April 18** A study of national test results shows that black children closed the gap on whites in educational achievement tests during the 1970s. Dr. Lyle V. Jones, author of the study, says that blacks probably had an increased motivation to succeed.

**1982, April 27** Private Joseph C. Christopher, a 26-year-old white Army private is found guilty of murdering four blacks in Buffalo and a Hispanic man in New York City.

**1982, June 8** Mayor Tom Bradley of Los Angeles wins the Democratic nomination for Governor of California. Bradley will face Attorney General George Deukmejian in the general election. If elected, Bradley would become the first black governor in the United States.

**1982, June 15** Kenneth A. Gibson is elected to a record fourth term as Mayor of Newark, New Jersey, defeating City Council President Earl Harris in a runoff election. Gibson is the Mayor of New Jersey's largest city.

**1982, June 18 and 23** The Senate approves the landmark Voting Rights Act of 1965 by a vote of 85-8, as a quarter-century renewal of the enforcement provisions designed to guarantee free access to the polls for blacks and other minorities. Senator Jesse Helms of North Carolina delayed the voting for 10 days after he vowed to block the extension of the bill. The House approved the extension on June 23.

**1983, January 12** A majority of the Civil Rights Commission charges that the Reagan administration's Justice Department has been moving in the direction of getting judicial approval to end affirmative action. The two and a half page text issued by the majority asserts that cases in several cities, given the current position of the Justice Department, could result in continued discrimination. The committees assertion is opposed by the chairman of the committee Clarence Pendelton, a black Reagan appointee.

**1983, January 17** "I draw the line in the dust and toss the gauntlet before the feet of tyranny and I say segregation now, segregation tomorrow, segregation forever." So spoke the Governor of Alabama George Wallace as Dr. Martin Luther King Jr. targeted Birmingham and their policies of discrimination in 1963. Twenty years later George Wallace takes the oath of office, achieving his unprecedented fourth term. with the help of blacks, and calls for mercy and justice for all. Two blacks are appointed to important and influential cabinet posts, as well as four black legislators appointed as committee chairmen.

**1983, January 28** The NAACP takes the NAACP Legal Defense Fund to court, asserting that continued use of the initials NAACP' by the Legal Defense and Education Fund causes public confusion between the identities of the fund and the National Association for the Advancement

**1983, February 23** The Supreme Court of the United States rules 6 to 3, validating a new electoral system in Lockhart, Texas, which may have a discriminating effect upon Mexican Americans. Justice Thurgood Marshall in a dissenting opinion states in effect, that a system that allows discrimination and dilutes existing minority voting strength undermines the intent of the Voting Rights Act.

**1983, March** A test case of the Justice Department to eliminate court-ordered busing to desegregate public schools is turned down by the U.S. Supreme Court. It was the contention of the Justice Department that a desegregation plan in Nashville, Tennessee was contributing to "white flight" from the city.

**1983, March 29** In 1939, for tax purposes, the NAACP Legal Defense Fund had become a separate arm of the NAACP and in 1959 it officially became divorced from its parent organization. Since the separation the organizations had been in some conflict over contributions and celebrity. Because of these conflicts The National Asso-

*Representative Parren J. Mitchell attacked Reagan's Urban Enterprise Zone program.*

ciation for the Advancement of Colored People sued the NAACP legal Defense Fund for "name infringement." On March 28, 1983 Judge Thomas P. Jackson ruled that the Legal Defense Fund was infringing upon the association's trademark by continuing to use the initials after it had become a separate and independent agency, thereby, ordering them to stop using the initials NAACP. The Legal Defense Fund plans to appeal the ruling according to its chairman, William T. Coleman Jr.

**1983, April 13** Rep. Harold Washington ( D Ill), a member of the house of representatives since 1980, challenges the previously impervious Chicago political machine to become the Democratic nominee and wins the election to become the first black to hold that office in the city's history. Washington received 656,727 votes (51%), while his opponent, Bernard Epton received 617,159 votes (48%). The voting followed racial lines with 90% of the votes in black areas going to Washington, as well as some 44% of the vote in the cities white liberal areas.

**1983, April 19** The 175 member Leadership Conference on Civil Rights charges that the Reagan Administration's proposal for changes in Executive Order 11246, which requires federal contractors to have affirmative action programs and anti-discrimination requirements , will have the effect of voiding the equal employment opportunity aspects of the original Order, thereby recreating the problems it was created to cure.

**1983, April 19** William Bradford Reynolds, head of the Civil Rights Division of the Department of Justice , states that any racial quota system is morally wrong and that the Reagan Administration would never use quotas or condone them to remediate any perceived pattern of discrimination.

**1983, April 22** After 29 months of investigation, a federal grand jury indicts six Ku Klux Klansmen and three members of the American Nazi Party in the deaths of five members of the Communist Workers Party who participated in a "Death-to-the-Klan" rally in Greensboro, N.C. in 1979.

**1983, May 18** With a record turnout Wilson Goode wins the Philadelphia Democratic primary over former Mayor Frank Rizzo. Goode received 312,219 votes (53.2%), while his opponent Frank Rizzo received 270,115 votes (46.8%). Goode did exceptionally well with the blacks getting 97% of their votes. He also received 20% of the white vote to give him the majority needed to defeat Rizzo. Blacks comprise 44% of the cities 887,816 registered Democrats.

**1983, May 18** Benjamin L. Hooks' executive director of the National Association for the Advancement of Colored People is suspended indefinitely by the association's chairman, Margaret Bush Wilson. The controversy was said to have begun with Mrs. Wilson's criticism of some internal aspects as to how well the organization was doing. Management and image were reported to be among the issues. There was some report as to a severe decline in NAACP membership from some 400,000 to about 125,000. Hooks and Bush are unavailable for comment on the action.

**1983, May 24** Jesse L. Jackson, by invitation, becomes the first black since Reconstruction to address a joint session of the Alabama State Legislature

**1983, May 25** In an 8 to 1 decision the Supreme Court rules that private schools which discriminate on the basis of race are not eligible for tax exemptions. The high court rejects the Reagan Administration's contention that because there is nothing in the internal revenue service code banning such exemptions, they are permissible. The opinion, rendered by Chief Justice Warren E. Burger, stated that racial discrimination in education violates deeply and widely accepted views of elementary justice, and ''that to grant tax exempt status to racially discriminatory educational entities would be incompatible with the concepts of tax exemption."

**1983, May 26** President Reagan presents three nominees to replace three current members of the U.S. Commission on Civil Rights. If confirmed, the administration would have a majority of its appointees on the six-member commission. A storm of protest and controversy arises from civil rights groups and members of congress accusing the President of efforts to pack the Commission. The three nominees are John H. Bunzel, San Jose State University, CA, Morris B. Abram, a lawyer and former president of Brandeise University, MA., and Robert A. Destro, an assistant law professor at Catholic University in Washington, D.C. The commissioners to be replaced are Mary Frances Berry, Rabbi Murray Saltzman and Blandina Cardenas Ramirez. However, lawyers from various private and governmental agencies indicated that the President probably does not have the legal authority to dismiss personnel who in effect are members of an independent bipartisan deliberative body with no powers. Jack Greenberg of the NAACP Legal Defense and Education Fund stated that it was illegal for the President to do what he proposes and that the Fund would represent the Commissioners if they decided to mount a challenge.

**1983, May 28** The National Association for the Advancement of Colored People's executive director Benjamin L. Hooks is reinstated to his post after an eight-day suspension by board chairman Margaret Bush Wilson. Wilson states that the objective of the action has been achieved and its continuance no longer serves a useful purpose.

**1983, June 15** The U.S. Commission on Civil Rights cites White House data showing that only 4.1% of President Reagan's appointees to high level positions are blacks as compared to 12% for the Carter Administration. A decline in the appointment of women from 12.1% in the previous administration to 8% in Reagan's is also cited. Commission Chairman Clarence Pendleton, Jr., while voting in favor of sending the report to the President, states that it ignores "political realities" and that he does not agree with many of the contentions of his colleagues

**1983, June** Black political leaders endorse the notion of a black presidential candidate and the development of a black coalition to support such a candidacy, and also create a "people's platform" to increase minority registration and develop greater bargaining strength within the Democratic Party. The Rev. Jesse L. Jackson, a participant at the meeting, indicates the possibility of his candidacy. However, Benjamin Hooks, NAACP Executive Director, asserts that the support of a black and unelectable candidate could siphon off votes in the primaries from the more minority oriented candidates on the issues, and hand the nomination to a more conservative Democrat less enthusiastic about the concerns of blacks. Mayor Richard G. Hatcher, (Gary, Ind.), is seen as accepting the idea of a black presidential candidate. As chairman of a committee exploring the notion, he is reportedly seen as encouraging the Rev. Jesse L. Jackson to make a run for the presidency. With the growing determination of blacks to put forth a National Presidential Candidate, The Southern Christian Leadership Conference urges it's president, the Rev. Joseph Lowery to seek the nomination of the Democratic Party for the 1984 election, which he later does.

**1983, July 13** The Reagan administration is charged by the U.S. Commission of seriously injuring American education if the proposed 13% cut in funds is passed. The commission cites many successful programs that will have to be cut if the education budget is slashed by two billion dollars.

**1983, July 14** In an article in the New York Times Kenneth B. Clark, professor emeritus City University of New York, famed for his research cited by the Supreme Court in it's 1954 ruling eliminating segregation in the Nation's public schools, states that the NAACP is verging on irrelevance. Outlining the previous intellectual and programmatic historic profundity of the organizations vitality and leadership skills of the likes of W.E.B. DuBois, Walter White, Roy Wilkins, and Thurgood Marshall, he portrays a rather dismal picture for the future of the organization. Philosophy, programs, policies and structure "must be reexamined " and the trend toward succumbing to black separatism and becoming a racially segregated institution must be reversed if it is to continue to be a potent force for constructive change.

**1983, July 15** Vice President George Bush is loudly booed several times at the NAACP's 74th Annual Convention in a speech defending the civil rights policies of the Reagan Administration. He states that the President is not inaccessible to them and that their perceptions of "laxity" on the part of the administration are "dead wrong."

**1983, July 18** The average income gap between blacks and whites is as large today as it was in 1960. This in part was one of the conclusions issued in a non-partisan report by The Center for the Study of Social Policies, an agency headed by a former official of the Nixon Administration Mr. Tom Joe. "The economic gap between whites and blacks remains wide and is not diminishing. On measures of income, poverty and unemployment, wide disparities between blacks and whites have not lessened or have worsened since 1960."

**1983, July 28** In the resulting furor over administration policies to remake the U.S. Commission on Civil Rights, and with national criticism by those who had been in the forefront of the so called "civil rights revolution" as to the lack of enforcement of civil rights legislation on the books, many in the administration come to the President's defense. Attorney General William French Smith in this effort calls Reagan "more committed than any other administration to finding remedies for discrimination that promise to work." He calls many of the previous means utilized "ineffective" (i.e. busing, quotas etc.) and charges that criticisms that the Justice Department does not enforce civil rights laws are done so "to create hostility among minority Americans."

**1983, August** Surveys in the state of Mississippi indicate a probability that enforcement of the Voting Rights Act will be extremely difficult in many counties. As a result Assistant Attorney General William Bradford Reynolds announces that he will send 300 federal observers into the

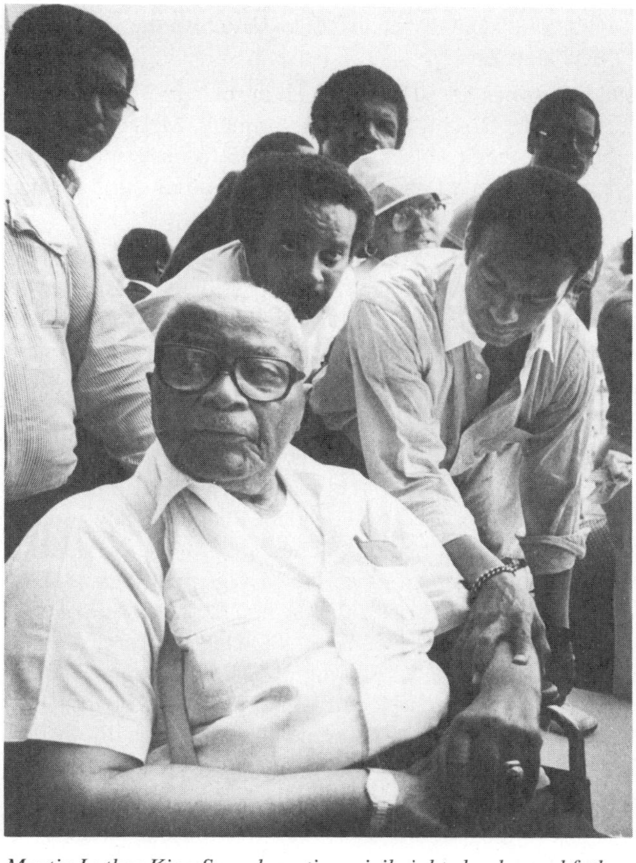

*Martin Luther King Sr., a long time civil rights leader and father of slain martyr Martin Jr., died after a long illness.*

state to see that the Act is enforced. Many civil rights leaders believe the response to be totally inadequate and the Rev. Jesse Jackson believes that the planned observers are untrained and will be unable to see or understand many violations.

**1983, September 12** In remarks made before the U.S. Commission on Civil Rights and the nation's 50 state advisory committees, William Bradford Reynolds Assistant Attorney General, considered by many to be the administrations point man in negating many gains won by minorities, likened the civil rights stance of the President to that of Dr. Martin Luther King and former Vice President Hubert Humphry. The theme was that justice should be colorblind and therefore programs that were instituted for particular groups because of minority status were unjustified. Herbert Hill's (chairman, civil rights advisory committee) answer to the Reynolds' comparison of Reagan with King and Humphry was "rhetorical claptrap" and "a demonstration as to how the devil can quote scripture for his own purposes." Chairman Thomas Pugh of the Illinois committee called Mr. Reynolds' statements "a preposterous insult to his audience."

**1983, September 18** Representing New York State, Vanessa Williams becomes the first black Miss America in the 62-year history of the Atlantic City pageant. The first runner-up is Suzette Charles representing New Jersey, who coincidentally is also black and also the first black Miss New Jersey

**1983, October 12** Though receiving only 34% of the votes cast in the Boston Democratic primary, Melvin H. King becomes the first black in Boston's 350-year history to win a mayoral runoff and the Democratic nomination for the November general election.

**1983, October 13** Richard Arrington is reelected mayor of Birmingham, Alabama by a fairly strong bi-racial coalition. Needing white support , Arrington wins 20% of the white vote.

**1983, October 20** By a vote of 78 to 22 action is completed in the Senate and the President signs into law a bill making the third Monday of each January a day honoring the memory of slain civil rights leader Dr. Martin Luther King Jr. Initially opposed by President Reagan, many prominent Republican Senators urged and got the president's support of the bill thus insuring passage in the Senate. The bill had previously passed in the house by a margin of 338 to 90. Senator Jesse Helms (R-N.C.) led an effort to defeat the bill. Helms accused King of "Marxist" ways. Helms also attempted to have controversial FBI tapes on Dr. King opened and made public in the hope that such disclosure would create public scandal. Sen. Edward Kennedy (D-Mass.) is outraged by Helms and asks for a renunciation of the Senator in the nation and in his home state

**1983, October 25** In a surprise move President Reagan fires three members from the Civil Rights Commission ostensibly because their views are critical of many aspects of the administration's policies in this area. The move was unexpected in light of the efforts of Republicans and Democrats in the Congress to work out a bi-partisan solution to changes demanded by the President. Those fired were Mary Francis Berry, a professor of history and law at Howard University, Cardenas Ramirez of San Antonio, and Rabbi Murray Saltzman of Baltimore; all highly regarded as effective spokespersons for minorities. Miss Berry charged that it was the administration's way to "shut up" criticism and that it essentially was a demonstration that the Commission had been effective.

**1983, November 4** What had been anticipated for some time becomes a reality as the Rev. Jesse L. Jackson declares his candidacy for the 1984 Democratic Presidential nomination. In announcing his candidacy Jackson states that it is aimed toward serving "the nation at a level where I can help restore a moral tone, a redemptive spirit and a sensitivity to the poor and the dispossessed of this nation." Jackson, outlining the reasons for his candidacy, speaks for three hours.

**1983, November 10** In general elections throughout the nation, blacks make some significant gains. W. Wilson Goode is elected mayor of Philadelphia, becoming that cities first black to serve in such capacity and making his city the fourth of the nation's six largest cities to have a black as chief executive. Other black winners are Democrat Harvey Gantt, who becomes the first black elected mayor of Charlotte, N.C.; James A. Sharp Jr., the first elected black mayor of Flint, Mich.; Thirman Milner wins a second term in Hartford, Conn.; and Mayor Richard Hatcher wins a fifth term in Gary, Indiana. On the other side of the ledger Melvin King losses his bid to become Boston's first black mayor. Although both candidates in the election stressed racial harmony and neighborhood revitalization, it was thought that careless statements by King during the campaign cost enough votes to lose the election.

**1983, November 15** In a preliminary injunction by U.S. District Court Judge Norma Johnson, President Reagan is prevented from carrying out an order of his to fire three members of the U.S. Commission on Civil Rights.

**1983, December 1** In a supposed compromise bill President Reagan signs into law a newly reorganized U.S. Commission on Civil Rights comprised of four presidential and four congressional appointees. As the first of his appointments Reagan reappoints Clarence M. Pendleton Jr. as chairman of the new commission.

**1983, December 9** Charging that they were "double-crossed" by the Reagan Administration and Republican congressional leaders, civil rights leaders indicated that there was a failure of the President and Republicans to live up to terms of a compromise on the new U.S. Commission on Civil Rights inasmuch as they failed to reappoint Mary Louise Smith and Jill Ruckelshaus.

**1984, January 1** The Supreme Court of the United States upholds a court of Appeals decision allowing the city of Detroit to go forward with a plan for the promotion of black police officers until there are as many black Lieutenants as white, thus rejecting the Reagan Justice Department's assertion that such a plan was unconstitutional.

**1984, January 3** W. Wilson Goode takes the oath of office as the first black mayor of Philadelphia.

**1984, January 4** The Rev. Jesse L. Jackson obtains the release of Navy Lt. Robert O. Goodman from Syria. Lt. Goodman was shot down in a retaliation raid by the U.S. Navy, ordered by the President, against terrorist positions in Lebanon

**1984, January 9** A Joint Center for Political Studies report shows that in 1983 there was an 8.6% increase in the number of blacks holding political office, thus reversing an eight year decline. The number of black public officials is reported to be 5,606.

**1984, January 18** "The United States Commission on Civil Rights, with a new majority firmly in control, today denounced the use of numerical quotas for the promotion of blacks and prodded the Supreme Court to adopt a similar position. ". The Commission deplored the use of the quota system as adopted by the Detroit Police Department. The commission stated that it has separated itself from past policies and recommendations regarding actions for specific civil rights cases currently pending. The Commission also decided to cancel a study on the effects of budget cuts in financial aid to predominantly minority colleges and alleges a lowering of academic standards with increased affirmative action in colleges.

**1984, February 27** After a long and bitter struggle to win state recognition for a day memorializing the slain civil rights leader Dr. Martin Luther King Jr., the Virginia State Legislature enacts a bill making his birthday a state holiday.

**1984, March 29** At the age of 89 Dr. Benjamin Mays a major national civil rights advocate, educator, and an inspiring selfless leader dies in Atlanta, Georgia.

**1984, March & April** The Rev. Jesse Jackson demonstrates strong black support for the presidential nomination in Illinois where he garners 79% of the black vote. With a large black turnout in the first round of the Virginia Caucuses he comes in second to Walter Mondale; while in New York State Jackson turns out the largest black vote in the states history and comes in second to Walter Mondale in the city and third in the state behind Mondale and Gary Hart.

**1984, April 20** A Florida Judge's ruling taking away the custody of a white women's three year old white child because she marries a black man is unanimously overturned by the U.S. Supreme Court. They state that racial prejudice should not be a part of any custody decision.

**1984, May 2 & 7** By winning the primary in the District of Columbia Jesse Jackson has his first major victory taking some 63% of the votes cast. Mondale places second with 28% and Gary Hart third with 8%. This is followed by his first State win in the primaries as Louisiana's blacks turn out in record numbers to give "Jesse" their enthusiastic support.

**1984, May 10** Rep. Katie Hall Indiana's first black congresswomen loses her bid for a second term to Peter Visclosky in the democratic primary. Hall was charged by Visclosky of neglecting her white constituents

**1984, May 15** State and local set-aside programs for minority contractors will continue to be challenged by the Reagan Administration's Justice Department, so states Assistant Attorney General William Bradford Reynolds after one such action was turned aside by a Federal Appeals Court in Dade County, Florida in a case by a contractors group ( the Department joined).

**1984, May 28** Because of under representation in the broadcast industry a member of a minority group may be awarded preferential treatment over a white applicant for a broadcast licence. Such ruling was made by the FCC and upheld in the U.S. Court of Appeals for the District of Columbia.

**1984, June 6** Margret Bush Wilson former chairman of the NAACP losses the battle to get herself reinstated as a member of the association's governing board. After her suspension of the Executive Director Benjamin Hooks in 1983, she apparently lost an internal political power struggle related to her position. Mrs. Wilson was the first female to be Chairman of the NAACP and had been a member of the national board of directors since 1963.

**1984, June 12** After several months of attempting to make an out-of-court settlement with the city of Yonkers, N.Y., the Justice Department moves forward with it's suit against the city contending that the city has not corrected discrimination in education and housing.

**1984, June 13** In a 6-3 decision the U. S. Supreme Court invalidated a U.S. District Court decision that allowed the layoff of three white firefighters who had seniority over three black firefighters. The Supreme Court decided that affirmative action employment gains are not preferential when jobs must be decreased and that "legitimate" seniority systems are protected from court intervention. However, a dissenting opinion by justices Blackman, Brennan and Marshall argued that under Title 7 of the Civil Rights Act of 1964 race related preferential practice was an acceptable application. As a result of the high court decision the Justice Department announces that it will reexamine all federal anti-discrimination settlements and as well will advise government agencies to not continue the practice of using racial employment quotas when negotiating affirmative action plans.

**1984, June 28** In a unanimous ruling the Supreme Court

invalidates the dismissal of a discrimination suit filed against officials of Coppin State College because of the expiration of a six-month statute of limitations set by the Maryland Human Rights Commission. The Supreme Court states that it is "inappropriate" for federal judges to use deadlines established by a state's administrative grievance procedure, a procedure which has as it's goal the resolution of employment discrimination complaints without going into court; and in effect such an administrative grievance committee cannot be the determinant as to whether or not a civil rights lawsuit is to reach federal court.

**1984, July 6** Secret tapes of President John F. Kennedy are made public and demonstrate a sincere effort by Kennedy to get mayors, governors and congressmen to accept integration and support his civil rights programs. The recordings made during the Kennedy presidency also reveal a dramatic conversation with Dr. Martin Luther King Jr. in which Dr. King, after a bombing in Birmingham, Alabama in which 4 children at a black church are killed, calls upon the President to send Federal troops into the city to help protect the black community and to prevent riots. In a conversation with Mayor Allen Thompson of Jackson, Mississippi, the President urges him to hire black police officers. After the Mayor assures the President that he will hire blacks, he say's to Kennedy "don't get your feelings hurt" about public statements he may have to make about the President, to which Kennedy replies "Well, listen I give you full permission to denounce me in public as long as you don't do it in private."

**1984, Sept. 28** The Senate, in a narrow vote, approves the attachment of civil rights legislation to an omnibus government spending bill to further ensure its consideration for passage. Those in support of the action say it is essential for civil rights. The legislation, the Civil Rights Act of 1984, would overturn the Supreme Court decision in the Grove City College v. Bell case. The decision of the Supreme Court dictates that federal funds may not be denied to an entire institution if a program within the institution is guilty of discrimination, that funds can only be denied to the specific program.

**1984, November 8** As expected President Ronald Reagan gets a second term as he defeats Walter Mondale in a landslide victory. Reagan wins 59% of the popular vote and 525 electoral votes. Mondale receives 90% of the black vote.

**1984, November 14** The Supreme Court rules that redistricting plans and election laws that have discriminatory results are affirmed to be illegal under a provision of the

*After Pan-American trip, Jesse Jackson meets with members of the Congressional Black Caucus.*

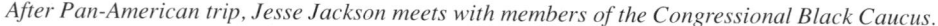

1982 Voting Rights Act. The ruling came as a result of a Mississippi redistricting plan in the Second Congressional District.

**1984, November 21** In a 600-page decision Federal District Court Judge Leonard Sand rules that the city of Yonkers, (NY) ''illegally and intentionally'' segregated its public schools and housing on the basis of race. The judge states that the pattern of segregation has existed since 1949 and resulted from deliberate actions taken by city and school officials.

**1984, November 12** The Rev. Martin Luther King Sr. dies of a heart ailment at the age of 82 in Atlanta, Georgia. The father of murdered civil rights leader Martin Luther King Jr., he was often referred to as "Daddy King" by friends and others as a term of endearment. For 44 years he had been pastor of the Ebenezer Baptist Church and was one of the South's most influential black clergymen for decades and as well was a prominent member of the NAACP's' Social Action Committee and involved in the civil rights struggles for many years helping to create a base for future gains.

**1984, December 13** The U.S. Court of Appeals for the 6th Circuit rules that Detroit's affirmative action hiring and promotion plan is legal. The court's unanimous decision upholds a lower court ruling that the plan to redress previous discriminatory practices does not violate the civil rights of 38 firemen for whom the suit was filed.

**1985, January 5** Rep. William H. Gray (D-Pa.) becomes Chairman of the House Budget Committee, a distinguished position which has a powerful voice in governmental budgetary affairs. Gray, a black congressman, had enormous competition for the prized position which he had sought for several years.

**1985, January 5-13** Sen. Edward Kennedy visits South Africa at the invitation of Noble Peace Prize recipient Bishop Desmond Tutu and forcefully speaks out against the country's apartheid system. Many South African blacks cheer him, however, the Azanian People's Organization (Azapo), a radical black group that is opposed to any cooperation with whites in their antiapartheid struggle, followed the Senator's tour and jeered him at every speaking event. Kennedy visited Winnie Mandela, the wife of jailed black nationalist Nelson Mandela, but his request to meet with the imprisoned leader was refused by the government.

**1985, January 16** President Reagan holds a meeting with 20 little known blacks from a variety of fields for the purpose of discussing an "agenda for black progress." No nationally recognized black leaders are included, thereby creating the impression of a symbolic gesture purely to enhance an image, and also, within the black community, representing "callousness" toward the underprivileged and programs for their health and well-being, even those underscored by the administration such as self-help programs. Writing about the meeting in the New York Times, Diane Compton asks the question "Where's the support even for programs involving self-help?", and indicates that federal loans for minority and small business were down as were "set asides" for minority contractors. Robert L. Woodson, leader of the group meeting with the President, stated that the purpose of the meeting was to "establish a strategic alliance between the black community and the Reagan Administration."

*Reagan's civil rights commissioner, Clarence Pendelton Jr., thought equal pay for women was "looney."*

**1985, January 19** President Reagan states many black leaders distort his civil rights record for partisan political reasons since they are committed to the Democratic Party, and to "keep their constituencies aggrieved."

**1985, January 29** A dispute between the NAACP and the NAACP Legal Defense and Education Fund may not be at an end even though a three-judge panel from the appellate court decided that the NAACP Legal Defense and Education Fund could continue to use the initials NAACP in it's name. Ruling that the length of time that the parent organization had allowed the fund to use it's name, negated the claim that the parent group had exclusive rights. Wrote Judge David Bazelon, "these two great organizations, like brilliant but quarreling family members must continue to share the NAACP initials with which they were born." The NAACP intends to take the decision to the Supreme Court. The fund was at one time the legal arm of its parent and had fought and won many landmark civil rights cases.

**1985, February 1** Clarence Pendleton, Chairman of the United States Commission on Civil Rights, and Vice Chairman Morris Abram, state that they support the Supreme Court decision invalidating affirmative action plans in conflict with 'legitimate' on the job seniority programs.

**1985, February 21** As a cost-savings measure the NAACP will move from its headquarters in New York City to Baltimore by 1986. The association is negotiating the purchase of a suitable building for $2 million in Baltimore after being unable to find, in New York City, a suitable and economically sound location not in conflict with their budget.

**1985, February 25** Libyan leader, Col. Muammar Qaddafi, in a 40-minute speech via satellite to the Nation of Islam annual Conference, urges black servicemen to leave the military and form their own army to create an independent and separate black state

**1985, Feb. 26** The U.S. Commission on Civil Rights gives enthusiastic support to a Supreme Court decision giving the seniority systems in place in cities that have affirmative action programs preference over recently hired blacks when layoffs are necessary; even though the blacks were hired to remedy previously contended discriminatory hiring practices. U. S. Civil Rights Commissioners Mary Frances Berry and Blandina Cardenas Ramirez, in heated disagreement with the Supreme Court and the Civil Rights Commission's report, state that civil rights laws are designed to protect blacks, minorities, and women, not white men. The statement creates new controversy as to the meaning of the existence of the Civil Rights Commission.

**1985, March 7** Charging that the U.S. Commission on Civil Rights had already decided to oppose such measures as timetables and quotas, national civil rights groups boycott hearings on the use of such goals to achieve racial balance or to remedy discriminatory hiring practices.

**1985, March 9** The late Clarence M. Mitchell Jr., often referred to as the Senate's 101st Senator because of his ability to get his message across effectively as a lobbyist for the NAACP, with whom he had a relationship for some 40 years, is honored in Baltimore with the renaming of Court House West to the Clarence M. Mitchell Court House. This is in commemoration of his years of service to the cause of equality and justice. The ceremony is attended by hundreds of friends, supporters, and family, including Supreme Court Justices Thurgood Marshall and William Brennan.

**1985, March 13** Clarence Pendleton, Chairman of the U.S. Commission on Civil Rights, estimates that after the issue of preferential treatment is settled the Civil Rights Commission should be abolished. Responsibility for civil rights, says Pendelton, should be in the hands of the Justice Department and the Equal Employment Opportunity Commission

**1985, March 22** At the Joint Center for Political Studies Annual Dinner, black economist Andrew Brimmer contends that economic progress for blacks is being hindered not by discrimination alone, but by a lack of education and/or marketable skills. Brimmer argues that although discrimination is part of the problem, ''Certain problems are not a matter of circumstance but a matter of choice for black people, '' and cites, as contributory, high teenage pregnancy rates and black youth joblessness caused by frustrated job search efforts .

**1985, March 22** According to the Joint Center for Political Studies, there were more black mayors elected (31) in 1984 than in any other single year. This was attributed to the presidential candidacy of Jesse Jackson, the enthusiasm for him and his ability to turn out the black vote. There are currently 286 black mayors in the nation, a figure doubled since 1975.

**1985, March 24** Patricia Roberts Harris, former Cabinet secretary, diplomat and lawyer, dies of cancer at the age of 60, in Washington, D.C. (see biography in section on Voter and Elected Office Holder)

**1985, May 1** A statue of Martin Luther King Jr., is dedicated at the Washington Cathedral (Washington, D.C.), as a memorial to his comprehensive contributions and celebrated leadership in the struggle for civil rights.

**1985, May 6** The Federal Government and the state of Maryland reach tentative agreement on a plan to desegregate the state's public colleges and universities White enrollment at traditionally black colleges will be increased to 19% and black enrollment at predominantly white schools will reach 15% from 11% The implementation of such plan is to take 5 years

**1985, May 10** Warith Deen Muhammad, son of the late Elijah Muhammad, founder of The Nation of Islam, disbands the organization inherited from his father and renamed the "American Muslim Mission." He urges his followers to join the international Muslim community.

**1985, The Philadelphia Siege Story (May-October-November)** On May 13, in a residential section of West Philadelphia, a state police helicopter drops a bomb upon the roof of an Osage street house, igniting a can of gasoline and causing a six alarm conflagration which kills 11 members, 4 of whom were children, of a black radical group known as MOVE, and destroys two city blocks of homes leaving some 300 people homeless.

Since the arrival of MOVE in 1982, a group described as believing in anarchism and the rejection of technology, neighbors had filed numerous complaints and accusations with the police. However, no effective action was taken until an appeal for direct involvement was made to Mayor Wilson Goode who, after initial hesitation, gave in to community pressure and sent in the police, citing housing violations and unpaid utility bills. —The mayor had felt that prosecuting the previously violent MOVE members

*Eleven were dead and another 300 were left homeless after the dropping of a bomb by police in an effort to evict a group known as MOVE from their headquarters in Philadelphia. Reviewing the devastation is Mayor Wilson Goode and Sen. John Heinz.*

may instigate another confrontation.— After numerous fruitless attempts to dislodge the group, using tear gas, water cannon, and even tunneling into the basement, the mayor consented to the use of a small bomb to create a hole for tear gas and water.

Hearings between October 8th and November 6th, reveal disagreement, disarray, misinformation, and misleading information in the handling of the crisis. The original "two-pound Tovex bomb" was actually three and a quarter pounds and contained a powerful explosive known as C-4, and police apparently could clearly see a gasoline can on the roof, most probably the cause of the rapid spread of the fire. Also, according to the fire commissioner, fire fighters wait one-and-a-half hours because of gunfire before acting to fight the fire .

In the meantime, residents of the community filed a $10,000,000 lawsuit against the city for lost property as they asserted that three years of procrastination lead to the disaster.

**1985, June 17** The Supreme Court refuses to hear an appeal by the NAACP against an appellate court ruling which allowed the NAACP Legal Defense and Education Fund to use the initials NAACP. (See January 29, 1985)

**1985, June 28** Attorney General Edwin Meese's nominee, Assistant Attorney General William Bradford Reynolds, for promotion to the post of Associate Attorney General of the Justice Department is rejected by the Senate Judiciary Committee by a vote of 10-8. Reynolds has long been accused by civil rights leaders and many Democrats and some Republicans of being inattentive to the enforcement of civil rights laws, and of making misleading statements about his handling of cases in sworn testimony. Republican Senators Arlen Specter of Pennsylvania and Charles Mathias Jr. of Maryland, side with Democrats to reject confirmation. It is suggested by some Senators that Reynolds should resign his post.

**1985, August 1** Dr. Laval S. Wilson becomes the first black to be selected as the Superintendent of schools for the city of Boston. The student population is 48% black, 28% white and 24% other minorities. Racial discord has been a part of the Boston school system for a decade.

**1985, August 2** Because of its policy of apartheid, the House gives final approval to a bill imposing economic sanctions against the South African Government by a vote of 380 to 48. The Reagan Administration remains opposed to the legislation.

**1985, August 9** Attorney General Edwin Meese III brands civil rights organizations that successfully lobbied against the appointment of William Bradford Reynolds as Associate Attorney General, as a "very pernicious lobby." Meese tried to lead an attempt to bring the nomination to a vote in the full Senate but failed in the attempt. Meese called the defeat of Reynolds a "tragedy."

**1985, September 20** Rep. Don Edwards (D-Calif.), Chairman of the House Judiciary subcommittee and who is white, expresses his concern over a "noticeable decrease" in the numbers of minorities and women serving on new state advisory panels. In response, U.S. Commission on Civil Rights Chairman Clarence Pendleton accuses the House subcommittee chairman of racism for repeatedly raising questions about why more blacks, minorities and women have not been appointed. Rep. Edwards says Pendleton's statements show he is unqualified to head the commission.

**1985, October 8** Lt. Cmdr. Donnie Cochran becomes the first black pilot in the U.S. Navy to fly with the Navy's elite special flying squadron the Blue Angels. The precision flight team was formed some 40 years ago and has performed its highly sophisticated aerobatics in air shows here and in Europe.

**1985, December 6** Stating that "discriminatory housing practices" on the part of Yonkers, New York, were responsible for the segregation of blacks from whites in the city's schools, U.S. District Court Judge Leonard B. Sand indicated for the first time in school desegregation cases that a city's housing policies are inextricably linked to school segregation. Judge Sand held that since 1949 Yonkers public housing had been deliberately sited in low income neighborhoods which had the effect of confining students to "inferior and racially unmixed schools." The Justice Department in 1980 charged the city of Yonkers with bias in housing and schools, and received from the city a tentative plan in 1984 to build public housing in predominantly white East Yonkers. The case could have landmark implications since busing had been the primary means for cities to comply with desegregation rulings.

**1985, December 23** Federal District Judge Sam Pointer Jr. dismisses a reverse discrimination suit instituted on behalf of 14 white firefighters in Birmingham, Alabama. It was claimed that the 14 whites were denied advancement because of a city hiring and promotion plan favoring less qualified blacks. Judge Pointer ruled that the city accepted the consent decree along with the Justice Department in 1981 and therefore the decree is valid, and that the firefighters failed to prove the plan violated that agreement.

**1986, January 11** Douglas Wilder becomes the first black lieutenant governor of the State of Virginia. Douglas, the grandson of a slave, was a Bronze Star winner in the Korean War and a former member of the State Senate.

**1986, January 12** In a by-lined story by Susan Rasky in the New York Times, Rasky indicates that there is an ever growing demand to collect preserve and disseminate the history of blacks in the United States. She cites an effort in Philadelphia to obtain forty acres of Fairmont Park to establish an African-American Hall of Fame, and also in California the descendents of Allen Allensworth (an escaped slave and the first black American to reach the rank of Colonel in the United State Army) are attempting to restore Allensworth , a black community in the San Joakin Valley in California founded by the colonel in 1908.

**1986, January 18** A poll conducted by the *Washington Post* and *ABC* reports that 56% of America's blacks consider President Ronald Reagan a racist. The report was

*Peter Rodino (D-NJ ), a long-time congressional friend of civil rights, is awarded the NAACP's Walter White award by Benjamin Hooks. Rodino's retirement enabled Donald Payne to become New Jersey's first black congressman.*

released at the same time that the President quoted Dr. Martin Luther King's "we want a colorblind society" to make the point that there should be no quotas in a truly colorblind society so that all can have the opportunity to succeed on merit.

**1986, January 20** Dr. Martin Luther King's birthday, as a federal holiday, is observed for the first time.

**1986, February 11** A trial balloon regarding the possibility that President Reagan may alter Executive order 11246, an affirmative action plan signed by President Lyndon Johnson twenty years earlier, is criticized by two black Republican groups, the National Black Republican Council and the Council of 100, both urge President Reagan not to change Johnson's Order. In a letter to President Reagan, the Council of 100 says of the 20-year old order, "we fear that the proposed change will be the trigger that aborts the development of black businesses and employment and could unleash another era of discrimination. ''

**1986, February 16** Benjamin Hooks, Executive director of the NAACP, defends the organization against critics who believe that its political clout has been lost and that a previous strong financial base has been eroded. States Hooks, ".(the organization )...is financially solvent and programmatically fine-tuned."

**1986, April 16** Black Republican Robert Brown, former official of the Nixon Administration, speaking for a group of prominent black Republicans calls for the resignation of the Reagan appointed chairman of the U.S. Commission on Civil Rights, Clarence Pendelton. Says Brown, "we are tired and will no longer stand for Pendelton ....to be looked on as a leader of black Republicans."

*Coretta Scott King, in South Africa, meets with Mrs. Winnie Mandela, wife of the imprisoned anti-apartheid spokesman.*

**1986, March 19** The Supreme Court, in the first of three major affirmative action decisions, rules 5-4 that broad affirmative action plans including hiring goals are permissible if they are carefully tailored to remedy past discrimination. Ruling on a case involving teachers laid off in Jackson, Michigan, the court sends a mixed signal by deciding that public employers cannot give affirmative action plans as a substitute for seniority when reducing their work forces .

**1986, June 16** The U.S. Supreme Court denies an injunction sought by black parents that would prevent the Norfolk, Va. , school board from ending school busing to stem "white flight" from the city's public schools. According to the petition, the change would result in "a general resegregation of the public schools of the South. ''

**1986, July 2** The United States Supreme Court ruling on an action regarding Cleveland printers and New York sheet-metal workers, upholds the use of affirmative action plans designed to remedy past discrimination. It rejects the Reagan Administration's argument that only specific victims of discrimination are entitled to such relief.

**1986, July 26** Between the years 1984 and 1985 there was a 6.1% increase in the number of black elected officials in the United States, though blacks hold only a total of 1.3% of the total number of 490,000, states a report issued by the Joint Center for Political Studies.

**1986, August 5** At his confirmation hearing Supreme Court nominee Antonin Scalia states that he supports affirmative action programs for people who are poor and disadvantaged even if every one so benefited were to turn out to be of one race.

**1986, September 5** In the 1970's and reiterated in the early 80's the Federal Communications Commission had a policy which sought to help blacks and women get a toehold in the broadcast industry by giving them some preferences in obtaining radio and television licences. Such practice was developed to give some balance to an industry that had been particularly white and male, however, in an abrupt shift of policy the FCC tells a federal court in the District of Columbia that such practice is unconstitutional and should be abandoned.

**1986, September 11** Coretta Scott King visits South Africa, meets with Archbishop Desmond Tutu, cancels a meeting with the prime minister and later visits Winnie Mandela, wife of the imprisoned South African antiapartheid leader.

**1986, October 3-4** In an effort to win Senate support for his veto of a sanctions bill against South Africa for their apartheid policies, Ronald Reagan appoints a black career diplomat, Edward J. Perkins, to be the new American ambassador to that country. The bill had been overridden by a wide majority (313 to 83) in the House, however, the Senate, despite the appointment, votes with the house by a vote of 78 to 21 to override the veto.

**1986, October 7** The 32-year-old case of *Brown v. Board of Education of Topeka, Kansas* is reopened by the original plaintiff and others who maintain that the school district has failed to integrate fully its schools or to eradicate the remaining elements that permitted racial separation in the past. Richard Jones, the lawyer for the plaintiffs, says he will show that the school board approved boundaries that perpetuate racially separate schools and have allowed white parents to avoid compliance with desegregation efforts by offering school attendance alternatives.

**1986, October 20** Four days of dedication ceremonies commence as The National Association for the Advancement of Colored People opens its new headquarters in Baltimore, Md. The NAACP was founded in New York in 1909 and maintained its headquarters there until this move. There is official indication that the organization will include new and diverse programs, which among other things will include business development, in addition to its more fundamental activities such as voter registration and protest demonstrations in its general goal of social and economic justice.

**1986, November 4** The Supreme Court declines to review two school desegregation cases, one which allows the city of Norfolk to end its busing plan, and another that attempts to sanction the authority of the Oklahoma City School Board to end busing for students in grades one through four. It is speculated that some high court justices want to leave the lower courts with the means of interpreting law on a local and regional basis. In the Norfolk case, black parents had claimed that the lower court ruling ending busing would have the effect of reinstating school segregation.

**1986, November 7** With a heavy turnout and massive support from blacks throughout areas of the South, four Democrats win senatorial seats. The four are Terry Sanford (N.C.), Richard Shelby (Ala), Wyche Fowler Jr.(Ga.), and John B. Breaux (La.).

**1986, December 2** A federal district judge rejects a reverse discrimination suit of 14 white firefighters and another municipal employee of the city of Birmingham, Alabama, who allege they have been denied promotions in favor of blacks whom they consider less qualified. The judge rules that the plaintiffs have failed to show the city to be in violation of a 1981 consent decree signed with the Justice Department designed to encourage the hiring and promotion of blacks and minorities.

**1986, December 21** Michael Griffith a 23-year-old black man is struck by an auto and killed while seeking safety from a white mob beating him with bats and fists. The incident occurred in the white community of Howard Beach, Queens, New York. The whites were reported as shouting, "niggers, you don't belong here!" The youths were in the neighborhood looking for a tow for their disabled car.

**1986, December 30** Three whites allegedly involved in the racial attack that resulted in the death of Michael Griffith, a black man, are charged with murder, manslaughter and assault, however Judge Ernest Bianchi dismisses charges citing insufficient evidence when the key witness for the prosecution, another black who was a victim of the attack, refuses to testify. He was advised not to testify by his attorney because of "a bad-faith investigation and prosecution". The attorney charged that the man who struck Griffith with his car was also involved in the attack, although an investigation by the police did not demonstrate any connection.

**1987, January 7** New regulations are issued to strengthen the federal Government's authority to reject changes in local election law that have a discriminatory result. No longer does the legal process have to prove that the intent of the local law was to discriminate, it need only demonstrate that it could have a discriminatory result.

**1987, January 13** Blacks of Springfield, Illinois win a class action voting rights lawsuit against 5 members of the city council. U.S. District Judge Harold Parker in deciding the case rules that blacks of that city have suffered the effects of 75 years of segregation and have been denied, since 1911, an opportunity to gain any seats on the city council.

**1987, January 21** Charging that the Reagan administration has failed to enforce affirmative action hiring laws for federal contractors, Joseph Cooper, director of the Labor Department's Office of Federal Contract Compliance resigns in protest and he identifies Attorney General Edwin Meese III and William Bradford Reynolds as officials in the administration seeking to circumvent rules requiring numerical hiring goals of some 20,000 companies that employ 23 million workers.

**1987, February 11** In Howard Beach, Queens N.Y., three white teenagers who participated in a racial attack against three black youths were charged with murder as a result of the death of one of the black youths who was killed by an auto along an adjacent parkway as he attempted to escape from his white attackers.

**1987, February 24** Mayor Harold Washington of Chicago beats back a challenge by former Mayor Jane Byrne in a very close election. Most of the voting was along racial lines with Washington picking up 96% of the black vote and Byrne getting 76% of the white vote. A watchdog committee states that both sides were guilty of massive vote fraud and other election irregularities.

**1987, February 26** In an effort to remedy long-standing, blatant, and pervasive discrimination the Supreme Court in a 5 to 4 ruling upholds the authority of judges to order strict racial promotion quotas. The case came about as the result of a challenge to an 1983 decision requiring Ala-

*In Howard Beach, Queens, New York, demonstrators call for justice after a racial attack that resulted in the death of Michael Griffith.*

bama to hire one black state trooper for each new white trooper hired. The Reagan administration had argued that such quotas are "excessive" and "profoundly illegal" and should be tailored instead to reflect the percentage of blacks applying for state police jobs.

**1987, April 5** Rep. Charles Rangel (D-N.Y.) introduces two measures in Congress to have the late revolutionary civil rights leader Marcus Garvey exonerated of mail fraud charges of which he was convicted of in 1924. The move by Rangel came after Robert Hill, editor of the Marcus Garvey papers project at the University of California at Los Angeles, discovered new evidence which could indicate that Garvey's conviction may have been politically motivated. In 1927 Garvey's sentence was commuted by President Calvin Coolidge after which he was deported to Jamaica, his place of birth.

**1987, April 7** Mayor Harold Washington wins reelection to a second four-year term and his supporters win control of the city council for the first time. Voting was along strong racial lines with Washington receiving 97% of the black vote cast, and his white opponent Edward R. Vrdolyak receiving 74% of the white vote. Hispanics cast 57% of their vote for Washington.

**1987, April 16** After a nine-week trial the a federal jury finds the *New York Daily News* guilty of discriminating against four of its black editorial reporters in promotions, salaries, and assignments. As a result of testimony by more than 40 witnesses the jury found that the *News* had discriminated against the employees in 12 out of 23 separate cases. The *News* says it will appeal the decision.

**1987, April 18** Vice president Al Campanis of the Los Angeles Dodgers who was in charge of player personnel, is pressured to resign from his job after stating that blacks might not be qualified to be managers or hold executive positions in baseball. The remarks were made by Campanis on the ABC News program "*Nightline*."

**1987, April 24** Rep. Harold Ford (D-Tenn), the only black congressman from Tennessee, is indicted in Memphis on Federal fraud and conspiracy charges which allege that he sold political favors to convicted bank swindler C. H. Butcher Jr. Ford claims that the charges are racially motivated.

**1987, April 25** A federal grand jury in Fort Smith, Ark., indites ten white supremacists on charges of conspiring to assassinate federal officials including a judge, and to kill members of ethnic groups through bombings. Richard Girnt Butler the leader of the Aryan Nations Church, was named in the indictment, along with nine others affiliated with the church and other white supremacist groups such as The Order and the Ku Klux Klan.

**1987, April 27** Johnetta Cole is named president of Spelman College in Atlanta, Ga. Previous to her appointment she was a professor of anthropology and Afro-American studies at Hunter College in New York. She succeeds Donald Stewart, who is named as the new president of The College Board in New York

*Honorable Harry Blackmun (left) and William Brennan (center), two liberal Supreme Court Justices, and Justice John Paul Stevens, who is often a swing vote.*

**1987, May 3** Japanese Prime Minister Yasuhiro Nakasone meets with the Congressional Black Caucus and other black leaders after being accused of making racial slurs in a speech angering blacks and other ethnic groups. Following the meeting Nakasone agreed to pursue Japanese investments in minority-owned American banks, to exchange programs between Japanese colleges and black American colleges, and to locate Japanese companies in predominantly black areas.

**1987, July 1** As a result of his decision to rescind state observance of Dr. Martin Luther King's birthday Gov. Evan Mecham (R) of Arizona faces a citizens' effort to recall him as the governor of the state. The plan has strong state support from both parties and many Republicans wear "Recall Mecham" buttons.

**1987, July 28** After 15 years a tentative settlement is reached between the Alabama State Police Department and the Justice Department. Accordingly there will be an increase in the number of blacks at various ranks on the force to as high as 25 percent over a three-year period. The department will promote 15 blacks to the rank of corporal in a month, and will eventually have blacks comprise 20 percent of its sergeants, 15 percent of its lieutenants, and 10 percent of its captains. Federal District Judge Myron Thompson, who originally ordered the police department to hire one black officer for every white officer hired, has to approve the suggested settlement.

**1987, July 29** The City Council of Selma, Alabama gets its first black majority as seventy-one-year-old Ed Moss is sworn in to replace a white councilman who resigned. In the 1965 voting rights march across the Edmund Pettus Bridge, in which Moss was a participant, the demonstrators were attacked by mounted, club- swinging troops.

**1987, August 24** Long-time civil rights activist, and Executive Director of the A. Philip Randolph Institute, Bayard Rustin dies after suffering a heart attack. He was 77 years old. In 1941, Rustin helped organize a march on Washington to demand better jobs for blacks in the defense industry, however, the march never came off because of President Franklin D. Roosevelt's issuance of an executive order banning racial discrimination in all industries with government contracts. In 1947, he participated in a "freedom ride" to show the effect of segregation on public accommodation. Rustin, always active in an enormous array of social issues ranging from restriction of nuclear armaments to independence for African nations as well as American civil rights, joined the staff of Dr. Martin Luther King in 1955. It was with Dr. King's SCLC that he became chief architect of the 1963 March on Washington.

**1987, September 8** The Rev. Jesse Jackson announces in Pittsburgh, Pa. that he will be a candidate for the Democratic presidential nomination in 1988, and that he has an initial funding for his campaign of $1,000,000. October 10 is picked as the date to make a formal announcement of his candidacy, a date that coincides with the National Rainbow Coalition convention in Raleigh, North Carolina.

**1987, September 22** In 1986 the number of black elected officials increased by four percent, rising from 6,424 to 6,681, according to a report released by the Joint Center for Political Studies in Washington, D.C.

**1987, October 23** In what was probably the single worst Reagan administration defeat since the President took office, the U.S. Senate soundly rejects Judge Robert Bork for appointment to the United States Supreme Court by a vote of 58 to 42. On July 2, 1987 President Reagan announced he would nominate Judge Robert Bork to the Supreme Court, and in doing so immediately galvanized opposition to the appointment from many diverse sections of the electorate. The horrendous outpouring of opposition resulted from the Judge's reputation as an ideological conservative who would unhesitatingly tip the balance of the Court in an extreme right-wing direction. Director of the NAACP Benjamin Hooks says that his organization will focus on the defeat of Judge Bork, and Sen. Edward Kennedy (D-Mass) moves quickly to unite liberals to gird up for the coming battle. The President counts on his personal popularity and the general conservative mode in the nation to bring forth a Bork victory. He assures the country that Bork is a scholar and a judge who would interpret the law rather than create it, unlike liberal judges who "legislate law." The first Republican to oppose Judge Bork is Sen. Robert Packwood saying that Bork would do "everything possible to overturn the Court's decisions on abortion and the right of privacy." As senate hearings progress, lawyers, lawyer groups such as the New York Bar Association, professors, journalists, women's groups, as well as moderate Republicans and some conservative Democrats move toward defeating the nomination. On October 23, Judge Robert Bork becomes the 27th Supreme Court nomination in the nation's history to be defeated.

**1987, October 27** John Oliver Killens, novelist, film writer, educator and a founder of the Harlem Writers Guild, dies of cancer at the Metropolitan Jewish Geriatric Center in Brooklyn, New York, at the age of 71. Killens had worked with many notable black writers among them Nikki Giovanni, Richard Perry, Arthur Flowers, Wesley Brown, and Barbara Sommers.

**1987, November 25** Chicago Mayor Harold Washington suffers a heart attack at his desk, and dies two hours later at Northwestern Memorial Hospital without regaining consciousness. Washington had won reelection to a second term in April, and gained control of the city council at that time. Among Washington's accomplishments were to increase services to minority neighborhoods and give access to city contracts for minority-owned businesses .

**1987, December 3** Eugene Sawyer, a black alderman, by a vote of 29 to 19, is chosen as acting mayor of Chicago after a boisterous debate and 12 hours of street demonstrations. Twenty of Sawyer's votes came from white aldermen who had been opponents of Harold Washington. Blacks in Chicago are angered by the selection of Sawyer, having had a strong preference for another black alderman Timothy Evans, a close colleague of the late mayor.

**1987, December 12** Supreme Court Justice Thurgood Marshall in an unusual interview with columnist Carl Rowan calls the Attorney General Edwin Meese to task for attempting "to undermine the Supreme Court itself," charging that department is unable to separate its ideology from sound legal argument. Justice Marshall adds that the Reagan administration's labeling of the criticism of Supreme Court nominee Robert Bork as a "lynch mob" was unfair.

**1987, December 18** New Acting Mayor of Chicago, Eugene Sawyer, in an effort to soothe the bitterness among blacks, begins scheduling a series of private "unity prayer meetings" with black ministers and politicians.

**1987, December 21** The recall movement against Arizona Gov. Evan Mecham obtains enough valid signatures to force a recall election.

**1988, January 14** The third anniversary of Dr. Martin Luther King's birthday as a national holiday indicates far wider acceptance and commemoration than many expected. Currently 43 states observe the holiday, an increase of 3 over 1987. The seven states that do not observe the holiday are Arizona, Hawaii, Idaho, Montana, New Hampshire, South Dakota, and Wyoming. In the state of Arizona, Gov. Bruce Babbitt (D) in 1986 issued an order making King's birthday a state holiday.

**1988, January 14** National Urban League President John E. Jacob decries the lack of economic advancement for blacks during the 7-year period of economic growth the country has had during the 1980's. Said Jacob, "While America was riding an economic boom, black poverty rose and we've slipped further back from our goal of parity with white citizens." He noted that the white poverty rate was 11% while for blacks it was 31%, and that inequities in education and job opportunity have not demonstrated any improvement.

**1988, January 16** Noted sports odds maker and CBS TV Football personality Jimmy "the Greek" Snyder is fired by CBS for making remarks viewed as racist. During an interview with a local TV reporter in Washington, D.C. Snyder is reported to have said, "the black athlete is the better athlete and he practices to be the better athlete and he's bred to be the better athlete because this goes all the way back to the Civil War when the slave owner would breed his big women so that they would have a big black kid." Snyder later apologized for his remarks

**1988, January 17** On the 20th anniversary year of Dr. Martin Luther King's death, Richard Bernstein in an article in the *New York Times* reflects on the inner city black poor and their continued and increasing difficulties. Progress for the black middle class is noted, but the poor seem to languish in a limbo that needs deeper reflection than the notion that discrimination is still the core problem. Bernstein, quoting Dr. William Julius Wilson's book *The Declining Significance of Race* , adds "I do not think that the accomplishments of King have benefited significantly the poor, and he was one of the first black leaders to recognize this. Despite the spectacular victories of the civil rights movement, he recognized a more fundamental set of problems attacking the black poor which had yet to be resolved. The question of civil rights alone being the answer is challenged, and weather self-defeating patterns of behavior established in the inner city ghettos, albeit due to past discrimination, can be overcome without far greater understanding of factors perpetuating these patterns in the black "underclass".

**1988, March 8** Presidential candidate Jesse Jackson scores extremely well in "Super Tuesday" primaries demonstrating that he is a serious candidate for the Democratic nomination for president. Jackson wins in Alabama, Georgia, Louisiana, Mississippi, and Virginia. He comes in second in North Carolina, Massachusetts, Missouri and Texas, and holds the second largest number of delegates to the convention behind Gov. Michael Dukakis.

**1988, March 10** Four white students at Dartmouth College are disciplined by the school after being charged with harassing a black professor. All four were members of an off-campus politically conservative newspaper, the *Dartmouth Review.* The incident, which precipitated the disciplinary action, took place when the four students confronted Professor William S. Cole of the music department to get his reaction to an article printed in the Dartmouth Review that termed the professor's class "American Music in Oral Tradition," "one of the most academically deficient courses" taught at the school. The confrontation became a shouting match and witnesses asserted that the 'Review' students were the aggressors and provoked the incident. Three of the students, John H. Sutter, a senior, Christopher L. Baldwin, a junior, and John W. Quilhot, a sophomore were found guilty of disorderly conduct, harassment and invasion of privacy. The fourth student, Sean P. Nolan, a freshman, was found guilty of disorderly conduct. Two of the four, Sutter and Baldwin, were suspended from the college in Hanover, N.H. until the fall semester of 1989. Quilhot, was suspended until the fall of 1988, and Nolan, was placed on probation for one year. The four asserted that they were being prosecuted because they were conservative journalists.

**1988, March 12** The great American artist, Romere Beardon, dies at the age of 75. Beardon had been suffering from bone cancer for almost two years, but his death came as the result of a stroke. Beardon was part of the 'new generation' of African-American artists who migrated from the South to the urban areas of the North. His work reflects the myriad images and facets of life in the big city. In 1960 he moved in the direction of expression in collages and became one of the worlds greatest collagists

**1988, March 15** Eugene Antonio Marino becomes the first black Roman Catholic archbishop in the United States as he is named archbishop of the Atlanta archdiocese. Marino was one of three auxiliary bishops in Washington, D.C.

**1988, March 19** Rep. Peter Rodino (D-N.J.) announces that he will retire at the end of his present term, leaving the way open for a black to represent the district which over the years has lost much of its white population. The stronghold of the district is Newark, which has had major black representation in the city for a number of years. Rodino is remembered as a fairly liberal democrat who represented all of the people of his district, and is best remembered as the chairman of the House Judiciary committee hearings on the impeachment of President Richard Nixon.

**1988, March 23** As a result of legal action brought by the EEOC charging Honda of America with job bias, Honda of America agreed to pay $6,000,000 in settlement to 370 persons, blacks (male and female) and women (all races) who applied for jobs and were turned down during a period between 1983 and 1986. All were later hired and will receive an average award of about $16,200 each.

**1988, April** President Reagan, in a statement about the Democratic primaries, suggested that Jesse Jackson was being protected from greater scrutiny because of his race. Reagan told a group of newsmen that more attention was being paid to Jackson because of his color than to what he had to say. Said Reagan, "I have to believe that a great many of us would find ourselves in great disagreement with the policies that he is proposing and would perhaps be more vocal about them if it wasn't for concern that it would be misinterpreted into some kind of racial attack."

**1988, April** In a stunning Supreme Court 5-4 decision the Court decides to revisit and review a 1976 decision that is often cited as the precedent for many anti-discrimination court decisions that have followed, in housing, education and as well in many other areas of social interaction. Liberals on the Court deplored the decision as an unwarranted "activism," and said it does not bode well for innumerable cases that have long been thought to be resolved regarding anti-discrimination law. Justice Paul Stevens, in dissent, wrote, "If the court decides to cast itself adrift from the constraints imposed by the advisory process and to fashion its own agenda.(then).. the consequences for the nation and for the future of this court as an institution_will be even more serious than any temporary encouragement of previously rejected forms of racial discrimination. The court has inflicted a serious and unwise wound upon itself today." The dissenting opinion was joined by Justices Brennan, Blackmun and Marshall. The Justices favoring a review were Chief Justice Rehnquist, and Associate Justices White, O'Connor, Kennedy, and Scalia. The later three named Justices were appointed by President Reagan. In the 1976 decision, the Court ruled 7-2 that a private school in Virginia could not bar enrollment of two black children on the basis of race. The precedent for that decision was an 1866 civil rights law that said, regardless of color, citizens "shall have the same right to make and enforce contracts as enjoyed by white citizens." Stated Justice Blackmun, "I am at a loss to understand the motivation of five members of this court to reconsider an interpretation of a civil rights statute that so clearly reflects our society's earnest commitment to ending racial discrimination."

**1988, May 3** Philadelphia Mayor Wilson Goode (D) and his top aides, after a 2-year inquiry, are cleared of criminal responsibility for the fire bombing of a house in Philadelphia in order to remove a cult group known as MOVE from their quarters for disturbing the peace of the community. The bombing resulted in the loss of 11 lives and the destruction of 61 homes in this predominantly black area of the city. A separate investigation by a federal grand jury is attempting to ascertain whether the victim's civil rights had been violated.

**1988, May 5** Racial tensions heated up once again in Chicago as a result of speechs attacking whites and Jews made by an aide of Mayor Eugene Sawyer The aide, Steve Cokley, stated among other things, that Jews were involved in an international conspiracy to rule the world, that the crucifix was a symbol of white supremacy and that Jewish doctors were injecting black babies with the AIDS virus. The mayor was accused of failing to act forthrightly to the racial slurs of Cokley, having taken a week to fire his aide which angered whites, religious groups and moderate blacks.

**1988, May 19** Landell Williams and his wife Tammy Williams are arrested for possession of an illegal rifle modified to be an automatic weapon. The charge grew out of a supposed threat to kill presidential candidate Jesse Jackson. In a conversation taped by the Secret Service, Mr. Williams stated that The Covenent, the Sword and the Arm of the Lord, a white supremacist organization, had plans to murder Rev. Jackson. The Jackson campaign has reported numerous death threats against the candidate.

**1988, May 20** Diverted by his duties as chairman of the Jesse Jackson presidential campaign, California's flamboyant and hard-working assembly speaker Willie Brown (D-Calif.), on the verge of losing his powerful state assembly position gets the assistance of five Democratic conservatives to hold on, winning along party lines by a 41-36 vote.

**1988, June.5** Clarence M. Pendelton, a controversial black conservative and president Reagan's appointee to head the U.S. Commission on Civil Rights, dies unexpectedly of a heart attack during a workout at a health center. Pendelton was constantly at odds with most civil rights leaders and black community leaders for his opposition to affirmative action programs for jobs, and busing to achieve school desegregation.

**1988, June 7** With a primary win in California, Gov. Michael Dukakis clinches the Democratic Party nomination for president. Jesse Jackson, the last remaining competition for Dukakis, received a very respectable 35% of the California vote and demonstrated a highly creditable run during the primaries, finishing second in the overall national delegate count.

**1988, June 8** Dukakis and Jackson meet to discuss issues of the Democratic Party after the nomination is secured for Dukakis. After the meeting Jackson states that he deserved not only to be considered as a possible nominee for vice-president but that Dukakis should offer the nomination to him. Jackson appeared to be the first choice for the position by a majority of Democratic voters.

**1988, June 29** In a unanimous decision the Supreme Court states that women and minorities need not prove intentional discrimination in hiring and promotion in cases where decisions by employers are based upon subjective criteria; thereby overruling an Appellate Court decision (*Watson* v. *Fort Worth Bank and Trust*) in which the Appellate Court turned down (a black women) Clara Watson's attempt to use statistical information to demonstrate that discrimination existed inasmuch as less black applicants were hired than white applicants for a similar position. In 1971 in a landmark decision, Griggs v. Duke Power Co., the Supreme Court declared that if there was

*Enthusiastic supporters await the arrival of presidential candidate Jesse Jackson in Houston, Texas.*

"a racial impact" as a result of personnel tests upon which minorities on average did not do as well as whites, and that the test did not demonstrate a relationship between the test scores and job performance, that the use of such test as hiring criteria was illegal.

**1988, July 19** In a stirring, fervent 50-minute speech before the Democratic National Convention Jesse Jackson implores the less fortunate to "keep hope alive." Said Jackson, " Suffering breeds character, character breeds faith, in the end faith will not disappoint. You must not surrender...America will get better and better. Keep hope alive. Keep hope alive . Keep hope alive for tomorrow night and beyond." Earlier Jackson's name was placed in nomination for President of the United States by Machinist Union labor leader William Winpisinger. The candidacy of the Rev. Jesse Jackson was considered as a substantial and serious run at the nomination and not simply a symbolic gesture. His stature as a future contender for the presidential nomination became enhanced by his ability to draw strong white support in many sections of the country.

**1988, July 21** Gov. Michael Dukakis accepts the Democratic Party's nomination for president and pledges to depart from the "cramped ideals and limited ambitions of the Reagan era" In his acceptance address Dukakis stated "My friends, if anyone tells you that the American dream belongs to the privileged few and not to all of us tell them that the Reagan era is over." Dukakis saluted Jesse Jackson's efforts and ideals saying that Jackson was "a man who lifted so many hearts with the dignity and hope of his message throughout the campaign, a man who has said to every child, aim high; to every citizen, you count...to every American, you are a full shareholder in our dream." The strain in the relationship between Jackson and Dukakis over the vice-presidential nomination appeared to have abated as the convention concluded.

**1988, August 2** U.S. District Court Judge Leonard Sand holds Yonkers, New York, in contempt of an order for the city to desegregate, and imposed fines of $500 a day on each member of the city council who voted against the housing plan, and a fine of $100 to be doubled every day for the municipality; such fine would bankrupt the city in 22 days. In 1985,Judge Sand had ruled that for 40 years the city had deliberately fostered segregation in both schools and housing and that such condition must be remedied. An acceptable school plan had been put in place, however, the city council failed to put a low-income integrated housing program into effect that was acceptable to the court.

**1988, August 3** By a vote of 413-3 the House of Representatives votes to impeach U.S. District Court Judge Alcee L. Hastings, the first black to be seated on the federal bench in Florida, for high crimes and misdemeanors. Hastings thus became the 15th federal official and the 11th judge, to be impeached by the House since 1787. The major charge against Hastings was that he conspired to get a $150,000 bribe from defendants being tried for racketeering in his court. In a criminal case Hastings was found not guilty, however, the federal appeals court in Atlanta was requested by two federal judges to investigate possible misconduct by Hastings and did so. After a four-year inquiry the appellate court concluded that Hastings had won acquittal through perjury and that he, in fact, had been guilty of the charges that had been made against him. A House judiciary sub-committee, headed by black Rep. John Conyers Jr. (D-Mich.), after a 15-month investigation, voted unanimously to recommend impeachment. In a solemn and somber session, before the entire House, Rep. Conyers listed the charges against Hastings and his reasons for concluding that the charge was true. He told the House that he began the investigation as a skeptic, suspicious that the situation may be one of "political harassment or outright racism" but instead "found a conspiracy to sell justice." Conyers continued "A black public official must be held to the same standard as every other public official is held to…a lower standard would be patronizing; a higher standard would be racism…Race should never insulate an individual from wrongful conduct." The House accorded Conyers a standing ovation.

**1988, August 9** M. Carl Holman, one of the leading strategists and organizers of the Civil Rights Movement for several decades, dies of cancer at the age of 69 in Washington, D.C. Often described as the godfather of the Movement he had the ability to form coalitions between diverse groups finding that one unifying ingredient that enabled them to work together for a common purpose.

**1988, August 12** In June, the House of Representatives approved by a 376-23 vote a long-stalled fair-housing bill that would expand protection against housing discrimination and expedite review of complaints, and would require the Department of Housing and Urban Development to investigate discrimination complaints and act on behalf of victims of discrimination. On August 2, the Senate also passed the legislation and on August 12 the law became effective. There had been a 20-year dispute between civil rights advocates, real estate interests and the legislature preventing the enactment of such legislation. The new legislation is in effect an amendment to the Civil Rights Act of 1968, commonly called the Federal Fair Housing Law of 1968. The Act to amend the 1968 Fair Housing Law (House Rule 1158 — August 1988) was designed to give greater specificity in defining the coverage and the penalties of Title VIII of the 1968 law. Before this newest legislation, the U.S. government was allowed to intervene only if its lawyers detected a pattern of discrimination against a particular group, requiring individuals to bring expensive and lengthy lawsuits. The measure would also ban discrimination against the disabled and forbids limitations on renting to families with children, except in clearly defined retirement communities. (see Document section for copies of these laws).

*Demonstrators in Yonkers, New York, protest low-income housing ordered by the Federal Court .*

**1988, August 15** The predominantly black, Bishop College of Dallas Texas, at one time the largest black college in the west, closes its doors unable to pay creditors $20,000,000. Founded in 1881 in Marshall, Texas, Bishop moved to Dallas in 1961. In 1967 Bishop had an enrollment of 1,500, in 1987 its enrollment had dwindled to 300.

**1988, August 26** In an effort to prevent a housing settlement between the City of Boston and the United States Department of Housing from being implemented, the NAACP filed suit to have the agreement blocked, stating that a housing settlement, among other things, should include monetary compensation for people previously denied public housing because of their race and therefore forced to pay higher rentals. The Housing Authority of the City of Boston was the largest housing authority in the country to enter into a fair housing voluntary compliance agreement with the Federal Government.

**1988, August 27** Since the death of Mayor Harold Washington of Chicago, in 1987, there has been increasing racial tension in the city regarding the next mayoralty election in which a number of black community leaders are trying to insure a "black only" mayor. Lu Palmer a black political organizer held a meeting with 500 church and community leaders to find one black candidate that all blacks could agree on, in an effort to prevent a white from winning the next mayoralty election. Many newspapers and community leaders, both black and white, condemn the meeting as a step backwards for the city's attempts to find racial harmony.

**1988, August 27** Commemoration of the 25th anniversary of the largest protest demonstration in the nation's history, referred to as the "March on Washington" which brought some 200,000 people into the nation's capital and helped catapult Dr. Martin Luther King Jr. and the civil rights movement into national history. Although small in comparison, about 55,000, the event gave excellent exposure to the Rev. Jesse Jackson and Democratic Party Presidential nominee Gov. Michael Dukakis. The Republican Presidential nominee, George Bush, was invited to attend but declined the invitation.

**1988, August 31** In an effort to get diverse factions of the Democratic Party working together for the November presidential election, Gov. Mario Cuomo attempts to get the Rev. Jesse Jackson and New York's Mayor Ed Koch to put differences aside and work together for the election of Michael Dukakis. The difficulty between Jackson and Koch had been long standing and the New York presidential primary brought feelings between the two to a boiling point. In 1979, Jackson alienated Jews by a seeming acceptance of the Palestine Liberation Organization (PLO) and Yasir Arafat. In 1984 statements by Louis Farrakhan describing Judaisim as a "gutter religion" were not repudiated by Jackson causing a further rift with Jews. Koch, in his support of Al Gore for president stated that any Jew who voted for Jackson "had to be out of his mind." The Jackson camp asserted that Koch was creating racial disharmony. While the Jewish population did not vote for Jackson to any extent, they also did not vote for Koch's candidate Al Gore, but gave a majority of their votes to Michael Dukakis. Many Jews in New York were extremely critical of Mayor Koch for his tactless handling of the situation and called upon Mayor Koch not to run for reelection when his current term was over.

**1988, August 31** A report issued by the Census Bureau on 1987 data, indicated that family income for higher income groups was growing extremely well, however, the poor were just about staying where they were. The median income for white families in 1987 rose to a record high of $30,850, while for black families median income fell almost 1% to $18,098. The richest 20% of all families (those with incomes above $52,910) earned 47.7% of all income, while the poorest 20% earned only 4.6% of all income. The report indicated that 34,500,000 Americans live below the poverty level having family incomes of less than $11,611 (the arbitrary definition by government standards of poverty). While 'poverty' declined among whites by less than 1/2 of 1%, it rose for black families by 2% and for Hispanics by about 1%. Approximately 10.5% of all white families live below the poverty line, while 33.1% of all black families live below the poverty line as do 28.2% of the Hispanic families. Of all children in the U.S. 20% live below the poverty line while approximately 48% of all black children live below the poverty. line. White House spokesman Marlin Fitzwater stated, after the release of the report, "The growing economy has indeed lifted the standards of everyone," causing someone to refer to the spokesman as "Merlin" Fitzwater.

**1988, September 6** Lee Roy Young, a 14-year veteran of the Texas Department of Public Safety becomes the first Texas Ranger in the 165-year history of this famed state police force that, in legend, 'tamed' the early western frontier and whose 'daring heroic exploits' are enshrined forever in hundreds of grade B cowboy movies. Young, at a news conference, said that it was his dream to become a Texas Ranger ever since he was a little boy.

**1988, October 4** The General Accounting Office of the Federal Government made public a report charging that the Equal Employment Opportunity Commission failed to properly investigate as many as 82% of the claims made regarding job discrimination filed with the Commission during a three-month period. Said Augustus F. Hawkins (D-Calif.), "I find it outrageous that there are people across the country who may have had a legitimate job discrimination claim denied because the EEOC mishandled the case...(or)... did not enforce the law." Clarence Thomas, Chairman of the EEOC disagreed with the report and criticized the criteria used by the GAO.

**1988, October 25** The Invisible Empire Knights of the Ku Klux Klan, the Southern White Knights and 11 individuals are ordered, after losing a civil suit, to pay close to $1,000,000 to demonstrators who, during a "brotherhood march" in predominantly white Forsythe County, were harassed and pelted with stones and bottles by about 200 whites who attempted to disrupt the event. The Rev. Hosia Williams, one of the organizers of the demonstration, withdrew as a plaintiff stating that the assets of the whites were meager and it would be "unchristian" to seize what little personal belongings they had. There were few, if any, of the other plaintiffs who agreed with the position of Rev. Williams.

**1988, November 8** Vice-president George Bush is elected as the countries 41st President defeating Massachusetts Gov. Michael Dukakis. Bush wins 426 electoral votes to 112 for Dukakis, and carries 40 states. The popular vote is 54% Bush, 46% Dukakis. The campaign was considered extremely negative with usually inconsequential issues dominating the campaign. The 'pledge of allegiance,' an issue which presumably died with a supreme court decision in 1910, was the focus for many days of the campaign with the implication being that since Dukakis did not back state legislation for the recitation of the pledge in the classroom that he was weak on patriotism. Issues important to blacks were rarely directly mentioned during the campaign nor were the major concerns of all citizens, black or white. Bush throughout the campaign maintained his central theme and did so extremely effectively. He varied little from his game plan to paint Dukakis as a liberal extremist who would undermine conventional values of patriotism and toughness on crime. The Dukakis campaign began to flounder immediately after the Democratic convention as Dukakis seemed to stay aloof and detached from the attacks waged by Bush and the Republicans. Not until the last two weeks of the campaign, when defeat seemed inevitable, did Dukakis fire up. He proved to be an extremely effective campaigner when he decided to take off his jacket, mingle with the people and mount his own attack. There is no question that whoever advised Dukakis on strategy was little in touch with street brawling or guerrilla warfare. A big disappointment for those who know the real Michael Dukakis was that he put a cap on his well-known debating skills to appear likeable and in the process his subtle dynamic intellectual, sometimes hostile, wit lay dormant.

**1988, November 8** Democrat Donald M. Payne becomes New Jersey's first black congressmen with his election to the congressional seat of the 10th district. Payne succeeds the retiring Peter Rodino (D) who had represented the 10th district since 1948. Mr. Payne had been a City Councilman in Newark.

**1988, November 26** As tensions increased between Jews and blacks in the city of Chicago, the Rev. Jesse Jackson meets with Jewish leaders in an effort to reduce the anger and heal the wounds. The Congregation Hakafa turned out to overflow capacity to hear Rev. Jackson deliver the evening sermon and say, "The sons and daughters of the holocaust, and the sons and daughters of slavery, must find common ground again. "The tension between Jews and blacks reached a zenith in May when Mayor Sawyer of Chicago was severely criticized for taking a week to condemn the anti-Jewish remarks made by Steve Cokley, an aide to the Mayor. Underlying the problem is the political struggle for power in Chicago. In 1983, Jews gave Harold Washington almost 50% of their votes and helped give Chicago its first black Mayor; in that race Washington defeated the white Republican candidate, Bernard Epton, who was Jewish.

**1988, December 1** Lieut. Gen. Colin Powell, President Reagan's national security advisor and the top black official in the administration is nominated to become one of 10 four-star generals in the United States Army. Along with the rank goes the assignment to command all U.S. troops in the continental borders of the country and to be responsible for mainland defense. The new rank also puts Gen. Powell in a strong position to become Chief of Staff as early as 1991 when the post becomes vacated with the retirement of Gen Carl E. Vuono. General Powell is credited with helping President Reagan's summit meetings in Moscow and Washington to become diplomatic successes.

**1988, December 19** The U.S. Navy in a self-critical portrait indicates that while there have been very few overt racial incidents there is an underlying subtle bias toward black and Hispanic sailors. According to the report blacks and Hispanics usually receive lower evaluation marks and as a consequence are not promoted at the same pace as are whites. The report also describes the Navy's failure to attract better educated blacks and Hispanics who are prepared to enter training centers for specialized technical positions, and indicates that the goal of 11% minorities for its officer recruitment program may not be realized for years.

**1989, January 4** A report finds that the U.S. Navy has the lowest percentage of black officers and enlisted personnel of all the armed services. Figures from 1987 show black representation in the Navy to be 15% in enlisted ranks, and 3.4% in officer ranks. Comparable percentages in other arms of the service were: 29.9% enlisted and 10.2% officers in the Army; 20.7% enlisted and 4.8% officers in the Marine Corps; and 17.2% enlisted and 5.3% officers in the Air Force.

**1989, January 18** African students in Nanjing, China are harassed on campus for trying to date Chinese women.

**1989, January 23** Six members of the Ku Klux Klan receive jail sentences and fines for their part in harassing blacks in a civil rights march conducted ten years earlier in Decatur, Alabama. The May 1979 march had been to protest the jailing of Tommy Lee Hines, a retarded black man convicted of raping three white women. Hines' 30-year jail sentence was overturned in 1980 and he was committed to a Montgomery mental hospital.

**1989, January 23** The Supreme Court strikes down a law in Richmond, Va., which required 30% of public works funds to be channeled to minority-owned construction companies. The landmark decision was decried by minority leaders, hailed by anti-quota officials, and predicted to have national impact on affirmative action and set-aside programs. The "Richmond decision," which was written by Associate Justice Sandra Day O'Connor and carried by a 6 to 3 majority, said set-aside programs were only justified if they redressed "identified discrimination." O'Connor specifically suggested that "rigid numerical quotas" be avoided, in order to avoid racially motivated hirings of any kind. The ruling only pertains to the disposition of federal, state and local government contracts and does not affect affirmative action programs in private industry.

**1989, January 24** In the National Urban League's 14th annual State of Black America report, president John Jacob says he is "cautiously optimistic" about the future of blacks under the Bush Administration. In the same report, Jacob notes that life expectancy of blacks has declined from 69.7 years to 69.4 in the period 1984-1986. White life expectancy rose during the same time, from 75.3 years to 75.4.

**1989, January 26** Virginia Lieutenant Governor L. Douglas Wilder announces his candidacy for governor. If successful, he would become the nation's first black elected to a governorship.

**1989, January** Rodney S. Patterson, an ordained Baptist minister, starts the first "black" church in Vermont, which Ebony magazine has dubbed "the whitest state in America" due to its tiny black population. Patterson, who moved to Burlington, Vt., to join the staff at the University of Vermont, named the church the New Alpha Missionary Baptist Church.

**1989, February 1** The death of suspected drug dealer Edgar Allen Price while in police custody touches off two nights of violence in a black neighborhood in Tampa, Fla. Medical tests indicate that Price, who was either intoxicated or stunned, apparently suffocated when he was laid face-down in the squad car.

**1989, February 3** In Morristown, N.J., the death while in police custody of John (Tony) Jackson, a black youth, prompts complaints of police brutality and racism. Jackson was arrested for failing to appear in court on a motor vehicle violation, and died while in the police car. Explanations for his death ranged from an asthma attack to his being choked by police.

**1989, February 7** The American Council on Education reports that the number of black men attending college is declining. In 1976, 470,000 black males were enrolled in college. Ten years later, that number dropped to 436,000. Meanwhile the number of black female students grew during the same period, from 563,000 in 1976 to 645,000 in 1986. Reasons for the decline of black male collegians were military enrollment, prohibitive college costs, "school phobia" and the seduction of crime or drugs.

**1989, February 10** Washington lawyer Ronald H. Brown, who held high-level positions in the presidential campaigns of Senator Ted Kennedy and Reverend Jesse Jackson, is elected chairman of the Democratic National Committee. The election of Brown marks the first time a black has been chosen to lead a major American political party.

**1989, February 10** FBI Director William Sessions orders sweeping changes in the bureau's affirmative action program after finding that the bureau had discriminated against minority employees. Black and Hispanic agents were immediately placed on lists for promotions. Mr. Sessions then ordered that FBI employees receive training in racial sensitivity, and that the equal employment office budget be increased. Ironically, the FBI is the agency charged with enforcing the nation's civil rights laws.

**1989, February 10** Dr. Louis W. Sullivan, on sabbatical leave as president of Morehouse School of Medicine in Georgia, becomes Secretary of the Department of Health and Human Services. He is the only black selected in the first round of Cabinet posts in the Bush Administration.

**1989, February 11** Episcopal Reverend Barbara Harris, a black, becomes the first female bishop in the worldwide

*Ron Brown, chairman of the Democratic National Committee, and the first black to be selected to lead a Major political party.*

Anglican communion. The ordination, which took place in Boston, was expected to pose "serious obstacles" for the reconciliation of the Catholic and Anglican churches, which have been separated for some 450 years. The Anglican church decided in 1976 that women could be ordained as priests. The Catholic church has staunchly resisted such a decision.

**February 9, 1989** Michael Manley, leader of the left-leaning People's National Party, becomes Jamaica's prime minister after defeating incumbent Edward Seaga at the polls. Manley, who moderated his political views to become more of a "social democrat," was prime minister from 1972 to 1980.

**March 1989** A media report finds South African trade relations improving with a number of black African countries. The thaw followed the late 1988 visit of South African President P. W. Botha to the Ivory Coast, Zaire, Malawi and Mozambique.

**March 6, 1989** Raymond Barthe the noted sculptor dies at age 88 at his home in Pasadena, California.

**March 1989** Rev. Jesse Jackson was scored publicly for throwing his support to a black third-party hopeful in the hotly contested Chicago mayoral election. Many Democrats believed Jackson should have shown solidarity with Richard M. Daley, the Democratic candidate, instead of independent candidate Timothy C. Evans. Daley later won.

**March 1989** Washington, D.C. Mayor Marion Barry, at one time so popular he was dubbed "Mayor for Life," saw support from his once-faithful bi-racial coalition evaporate in the wake of new charges against colleagues and administration officials. Instead, Washington leaders are privately urging Barry not to seek reelection, and are searching for another candidate.

**March 1989** Statistics show that Washington, D.C. has already taken the lead for having the highest homicide rate in the country. Local police figures show the homicide rate as 55.1% higher than the same time in 1988. Figures from the District of Columbia Office of Criminal Justice said 80% of the time, the motive for the murders was related to drug activity.

**March 1989** Atlantic City's first black Mayor James L. Usry Jr. was invited to attend the installation of the first four black members in England's House of Commons andthe formation of a Parliamentary Black Caucus. The event marks the first time in the United Kingdom's 1,000 years of existence that blacks have been elected to the House of Commons. The House of Lords has one black member. Mayor Usry is president of the National Conference of Black Mayors.

**March 1989** U.S. Civil Rights Commission Chairman William Allen Barclay apologizes to an Apache tribe council for apprehending a 14-year-old Indian girl who was the focus of a custody fight between an adoptive white family and her natural mother. Mr. Allen said his intentions were to interview the girl; the mother had had him arrested and charged with kidnapping.

**April 1, 1989** Former St. Louis Cardinal first baseman Bill White assumes office as president of the National League, becoming the first black to head a professional sports league.

**April 12, 1989** "Sugar Ray" Robinson, pound for pound the greatest boxer in history, died at the age of 67 in Culver City California at Brothman Medical Center.

**April 1989** Shirley Jackson, the first black woman to receive a doctorate in physics in the United States, was one of six women selected to receive the New Jersey Women of Achievement Awards from Rutgers University. Ms. Jackson earned her doctorate at MIT, after which she held positions at the Fermi National Accelerator laboratory in Illinois, and at the European Center for Nuclear Research. She is currently a theoretical physicist at AT&T Bell Laboratories.

**April 1989** Los Angeles Mayor Tom Bradley wins reelection to a fifth term by aplurality of 157,000 votes.

**April 21, 1989** The nation's first nonpartisan African-American summit convenes April 21-23 in New Orleans. Its purpose is to discuss "an African-American agenda for the next four years and onto the year 2000," said General Chairman and Democratic party leader Richard Hatcher. More than 4,000 delegates from the United States, the District of Columbia and the Virgin Islands were invited.

# SIGNIFICANT DOCUMENTS IN AFRICAN-AMERICAN HISTORY (1688-1989)

**Resolutions ■ Declarations ■ Constitutional Provisions and Amendments ■ Editorials ■ Laws ■ Proclamations ■ Speeches ■ Executive Orders ■ Manifestos**

The documents included in this section—whether they be resolutions, legislative enactments, amendments to the Constitution, executive proclamations, or presidential speeches—have all been chosen because they bear a special relevance to black history in the United States. Some—like the Declaration of Independence, the Constitution, the Emancipation Proclamation—are household words which are an explicit part of every American's heritage; others, though less known, deserve comparable status. In themselves, they offer eloquent testimony to the impact of the black on American history—as slave, as freedman, and, ultimately, as full-fledged American citizen.

## THE GERMANTOWN MENNONITE RESOLUTION AGAINST SLAVERY (1688)

*The Germantown Mennonite Resolution Against Slavery represents the earliest such protest formally voiced in Colonial America. It was passed 69 years after the introduction of the first black slaves in America—at a time when the number of slaves in the Colonies was comparatively small. It was not until 1775, however, that the Quakers, a religious group similarly opposed to the institution, formed the first antislavery society in the Colonies.*

This is to the monthly meeting held at Richard Worrell's:

These are the reasons why we are against the traffic of men-body, as followeth: Is there any that would be done or handled at this manner? viz., to be sold or made a slave for all the time of his life? How fearful and faint-hearted are many at sea, when they see a strange vessel, being afraid it should be a Turk, and they should be taken, and sold for slaves into Turkey. Now, what is *this* better done, than

*A black man being sold as a slave in New Amsterdam (now New York City).*

Turks do? Yea, rather it is worse for them, which say they are Christians; for we hear that the most part of such negers are brought hither against their will and consent, and that many of them are stolen. Now, though they are black, we cannot conceive there is more liberty to have them slaves, as it is to have other white ones. There is a saying, that we should do to all men like as we will be done ourselves; making no difference of what generation, descent, or colour they are. And those who steal or rob men, and those who buy or purchase them, are they not all alike? Here is liberty of conscience, which is right and reasonable; here ought to be likewise liberty of the body, except of evil-doers, which is another case. But to bring men hither, or to rob and sell them against their will, we stand against. In Europe there are many oppressed for conscience-sake; and here there are those oppressed which are of a black colour. And we who know that men must not commit adultery—some do commit adultery *in* others, separating wives from their husbands, and giving them to others: and some sell the children of these poor creatures to other men. Ah! do consider well this thing, you who do it, if you would be done at this manner—and if it is done according to Christianity! You surpass Holland and Germany in this thing. This makes an ill report in all those countries of Europe, where they hear of (it), that the Quakers do here handel men as they handel there the cattle. And for that reason some have no mind or inclination to come hither. And who shall maintain this your cause, or plead for it? Truly, we cannot do so, except you shall inform us better hereof, viz.: that Christians have liberty to practice these things. Pray, what thing in the world can be done worse towards us, than if men should rob or steal us away, and sell us for slaves to strange countries; separating husbands from their wives and children. Being now this is not done in the manner we would be done at; therefore, we contradict, and are against his traffic of men-body. And we who profess that it is not lawful to steal, must, likewise, avoid to purchase such things as are stolen, but rather help to stop this robbing and stealing, if possible. And such men ought to be delivered out of the hands of the robbers, and set free as in Europe. Then is Pennsylvania to have a good report, instead, it hath now a bad one, for this sake, in other countries; especially whereas the Europeans are desirous to know in what manner *the Quakers* do rule in *their* province; and most of them do look upon us with an envious eye. But if this is done well, what shall we say is done evil?

If once these slaves (which they say are so wicked and stubborn men) should join themselves—fight for their freedom, and handel their masters and mistresses, as they did handel them before; will these masters and mistresses take the sword at hand and war against these poor slaves, like, as we are able to believe, some will not refuse to do? Or, have these poor negers not as much right to fight for their freedom, as you have to keep them slaves?

Now consider well this thing, if it is good or bad. And in case you find it to be good to handel these black in that manner, we desire and require you hereby lovingly, that you may inform us herein, which at this time never was done, viz., that Christians have such a liberty to do so. To the end we shall be satisfied on this point, and satisfy likewise our good friends and acquaintances in our native country, to whom it is a terror, or fearful thing, that men should be handelled so in Pennsylvania.

This is from our meeting at Germantown, held ye 18th of the 2d month, 1688, to be delivered to the monthly meeting at Richard Worrell's.

Garret Henderich,
Derick op de Graeff,
Francis Daniel Pastorius,
Abram op de Graeff.

## THE DECLARATION OF INDEPENDENCE (1776)

*The final version of the Declaration of Independence, as accepted by Congress, did not contain an anti-slavery clause written by Thomas Jefferson as part of an initial draft of the document: (See following document)*

When in the Course of human events, it becomes necessary for one people to dissolve the political bands which have connected them with another, and to assume among the Powers of the earth, the separate and equal station to which the Laws of Nature and of Nature's God entitle them, a decent respect to the opinions of mankind requires that they should declare the causes which impel them to the separation.

We hold these truths to be self-evident, that all men are created equal, that they are endowed by their Creator with certain unalienable Rights, that among these are Life, Liberty and the pursuit of Happiness. That to secure these rights, Governments are instituted among Men, deriving their just powers from the consent of the governed, That whenever any Form of Government becomes destructive of these ends, it is the Right of the People to alter or to abolish it, and to institute new Government, laying its foundation on such principles and organizing its powers in such form, as to them shall seem most likely to effect their Safety and Happiness. Prudence, indeed, will dictate that Governments long established should not be changed for light and transient causes; and accordingly all experience hath shown, that mankind are more disposed to suffer, while evils are sufferable, than to right themselves by abolishing the forms to which they are accustomed. But when a long train of abuses and usurpations, pursuing invariably the same Object evinces a design to reduce them under absolute Despotism, it is their right, it is their duty, to throw off such Government, and to provide new Guards for their future security.—Such has been the patient sufferance of these Colonies; and such is now the necessity which constrains them to alter their former Systems of Government. The history of the present King of Great Britain is a history of repeated injuries and usurpations, all having in direct object the establishment of an absolute Tyranny over these States. To prove this, let Facts be submitted to a candid world.

*When his attacks on the Crown shocked other Virginia legislators, Patrick Henry shouted "Give me liberty or give me death!"*

He has refused his Assent to Laws, the most wholesome and necessary for the public good.

He has forbidden his Governors to pass Laws of immediate and pressing importance, unless suspended in their operation till his Assent should be obtained; and when so suspended, he has utterly neglected to attend to them.

He has refused to pass other Laws for the accommodation of large districts of people, unless those people would relinquish the right of Representation in the Legislature, a right inestimable to them and formidable to tyrants only.

He has called together legislative bodies at places unusual, uncomfortable, and distant from the depository of their Public Records, for the sole purpose of Fatiguing them into compliance with his measures.

He has dissolved Representative Houses repeatedly, for opposing with manly firmness his invasions on the rights of the people.

He has refused for a long time, after such dissolutions, to cause others to be elected; whereby the Legislative Powers, incapable of Annihilation, have returned to the People at large for their exercise; the State remaining in the mean time exposed to all the dangers of invasion from without, and convulsions within.

He has endeavoured to prevent the population of these States; for that purpose obstructing the Laws of Naturalization of Foreigners; refusing to pass others to encourage their migration hither, and raising the conditions of new Appropriations of Lands.

He has obstructed the Administration of Justice, by refusing his Assent to Laws for establishing Judiciary Powers.

He has made Judges dependent on his Will alone, for the tenure of their offices, and the amount and payment of their salaries.

He has erected a multitude of New Offices, and sent hither swarms of Officers to harass our People, and eat out their substance.

He has kept among us, in times of peace, Standing Armies without the Consent of our legislature.

He has affected to render the Military independent of and

*The reading of the Declaration of Independence to the colonial army of revolution under the command of George Washington.*

superior to the Civil Power.

He has combined with others to subject us to a jurisdiction foreign to our constitution, and unacknowledged by our laws; giving his Assent to their acts of pretended legislation:

For quartering large bodies of armed troops among us:

For protecting them, by a mock Trial, from Punishment for any Murders which they should commit on the Inhabitants of these States:

For cutting off our Trade with all parts of the world:

For imposing taxes on us without our Consent:

For depriving us in many cases, of the benefits of Trial by Jury:

For transporting us beyond Seas to be tried for pretended offences:

For abolishing the free System of English Laws in a neighbouring Province, establishing therein an Arbitrary government, and enlarging its Boundaries so as to render it at once an example and fit instrument for introducing the same absolute rule into these Colonies:

For taking away our Charters, abolishing our most valuable Laws, and altering fundamentally the Forms of our Governments:

For suspending our own Legislature, and declaring themselves invested with Power to legislate for us in all cases whatsoever.

He has abdicated Government here, by declaring us out of his Protection and waging War against us.

He has plundered our seas, ravaged our Coasts, burnt our towns, and destroyed the lives of our people.

He is at this time transporting large armies of foreign mercenaries to compleat the works of death, desolation and tyranny, already begun with circumstances of Cruelty & perfidy scarcely paralleled in the most barbarous ages, and totally unworthy the Head of a civilized nation.

He has constrained our fellow Citizens taken Captive on the high Seas to bear Arms against their Country, to become the executioners of their friends and Brethren, or to fall themselves by their Hands.

He has excited domestic insurrections amongst us, and has endeavoured to bring on the inhabitants of our frontiers, the merciless Indian Savages, whose known rule of warfare, is an undistinguished destruction of all ages, sexes and conditions.

In every stage of these Oppressions We have Petitioned for Redress in the most humble terms: Our repeated Petitions have been answered only by repeated injury. A Prince, whose character is thus marked by every act which may define a Tyrant, is unfit to be the ruler of a free People.

Nor have We been wanting in attention to our British brethren. We have warned them from time to time of attempts by their legislature to extend an unwarrantable jurisdiction over us. We have reminded them of the circumstances of our emigration and settlement here. We have appealed to their native justice and magnanimity, and we have conjured them by the ties of our common kindred to disavow these usurpations, which would inevitably interrupt our connections and correspondence. They too have been deaf to the voice of justice and of consanguinity. We must, therefore, acquiesce in the necessity, which denounces our Separation, and hold them, as we hold the rest of mankind, Enemies in War, in Peace Friends.

We, therefore, the Representatives of the United States of America, in General Congress, Assembled, appealing to the Supreme Judge of the world for the rectitude of our intentions, do, in the Name, and by Authority of the good People of these Colonies, solemnly publish and declare, That these United Colonies are, and of Right ought to be Free and Independent States; that they are Absolved from all Allegiance to the British Crown, and that all political connection between them and the State of Great Britain, is and ought to be totally dissolved; and that as Free and Independent States, they have full Power to levy War, conclude Peace, contract Alliances, establish Commerce, and to do all other Acts and Things which Independent States may of right do. And for the support of this Declaration, with a firm reliance on the Protection of Divine Providence, we mutually pledge to each other our Lives, our Fortunes and our sacred Honor.

JOHN HANCOCK.

*Massachusetts-Bay*
Saml. Adams,
John Adams,
Robt. Treat Paine,
Elbridge Gerry.

*New Hampshire*
Josiah Bartlett,
Wm. Whipplf,
Matthew Thornton.

*Rhode Island*
Step. Hopkins,
William Ellery.

*Pennsylvania*
Robt. Morris,
Benjamin Rush,
Benja. Franklin,
John Morton,
Geo. Clymer,
Jas. Smith,
Geo. Taylor,
James Wilson,
Geo. Ross.

*Connecticut*
Roger Sherman,
Sam'el Huntington,
Wm. Williams,
Oliver Wolcott,
Geo. Read,
Tho. M'Kean.

*Georgia*
Button Gwinnett,
Lyman Hall,
Geo.Walton.

*Delaware*
Caesar Rodney.

*North Carolina*
Wm. Hooper,
Joseph Hewes,
John Penn.

*Maryland*
Samuel Chase,
Wm. Paca,
Thos. Stone,
Charles Carroll
of Carrollton.

*New York*
Wm. Floyd,
Phil. Livingston,
Frans. Lewis,
Lewis Morris.

*South Carolina*
Edward Rutledge,
Thos. Heyward, Junr.,
Thomas Lynch, Junr.,
Arthur Middleton.

*New Jersey*
Richd. Stockton,
Jno. Witherspoon,
Fras. Hopkinson,
John Hart,
Abra. Clark.

*Virginia*
George Wythe,
Richard Henry Lee,
Th. Jefferson,
Benja. Harrison,
Ths. Nelson, Jr.,
Francis Lightfoot Lee,
Carter Braxton.

## THE OMITTED ANTI-SLAVERY CLAUSE (1776)

*Thomas Jefferson's attitudes to blacks varied during his lifetime. In his early years, Jefferson thought blacks were biologically inferior, then decided that slavery had a destructive conditioning effect which stamped blacks with "odious peculiarities." With this view, and spurred by his conviction that "natural rights" accrued to all men, Jefferson penned a short, passionate attack on King George III's indulgence of the slave traffic, for inclusion in the Declaration of Independence. But, at the behest of delegates from South Carolina and Georgia, and with the indulgence of northern delegates whose ports sheltered and profited from slave ships, the clause was omitted from the final version.*

He [King George III] has waged cruel war against human nature itself, violating its most sacred rights of life and liberty in the persons of a distant people who never offended him, captivating and carrying them into slavery in another hemisphere, or to incur miserable death in their transportation thither. This piratical warfare, the opprobrium of *infidel* powers, is the warfare of the *Christian* king of Great Britain. Determined to keep open a market where MEN should be bought and sold, he has prostituted his negative for suppressing every legislative attempt to prohibit or restrain this execrable commerce.

(The omission of this passage reflected the awareness on the part of some Congressmen that a number of New England merchants were profitably engaged in the slave trade. Other legislators were simply in favor of slavery as an institution, and felt that the inclusion of such sentiments would prejudice the case for its continuation.

Many historians and critics have understandably concluded that the elimination of this passage offers adequate proof that the American black, unlike his white counterpart, was never meant to share in the fruits of independence and equality in his adopted homeland.)

## THE CONSTITUTION OF THE UNITED STATES (1787)

*Although we have chosen to print the Constitution and the Bill of Rights in their entirety, we are more concerned—within the framework of this volume—with two passages in particular: Sections 2 and 9 of Article I. Section 2, containing the so-called three-fifths compromise (see paragraph 3, section 2, first sentence set in italic), in effect defines the black ("other Persons") as three-fifths of the white man ("free Persons"). Section 9 (the first two paragraphs of which are also in italic) provides both for the extension of the slave trade for a 20-year period, and for the return of runaway slaves. Such passages attest to the strong element of conservatism that existed in the United States in the critical period following the Revolutionary War.*

We the People of the United States, in Order to form a more perfect Union, establish Justice, insure domestic Tranquility, provide for the common defence, promote the general Welfare, and secure the Blessings of Liberty to ourselves and our Posterity, do ordain and establish this Constitution for the United States of America.

ART. I

SEC. 1. All legislative Powers herein granted shall be vested in a Congress of the United States, which shall consist of a Senate and House of Representatives.

*Jefferson's denunciation of the slave trade was voted out of the Declaration of Independence.*

SEC. 2. The House of Representatives shall be composed of Members chosen every second Year by the People of the several States, and the Electors in each State shall have the Qualifications requisite for Electors of the most numerous Branch of the State Legislature.

No person shall be a Representative who shall not have attained to the Age of twenty-five Years, and been seven Years a Citizen of the United States, and who shall not, when elected, be an Inhabitant of that State in which he shall be chosen.

*Representatives and direct Taxes shall be apportioned among the several States which may be included within this Union, according to their respective Numbers, which shall be determined by adding to the whole Number of free Persons, including those bound to Service for a Term of Years, and excluding Indians not taxed, three-fifths of all other Persons.* The actual Enumeration shall be made within three Years after the first Meeting of the Congress of the United States, and within every subsequent Term of ten Years, in such Manner as they shall by Law direct. The Number of Representatives shall not exceed one for every thirty Thousand, but each State shall have at Least one Representative; and until such enumeration shall be made, the State of New Hampshire shall be entitled to chuse three, Massachusetts eight, Rhode-Island and Providence Plantations one, Connecticut five, New York six, New Jersey four, Pennsylvania eight, Delaware one, Maryland six, Virginia ten, North Carolina five, South Carolina five, and Georgia three.

When vacancies happen in the Representation from any State, the Executive Authority thereof shall issue Writs of Election to fill such Vacancies.

The House of Representatives shall chuse their Speaker and other Officers; and shall have the sole Power of Impeachment.

SEC. 3. The Senate of the United States shall be composed of two Senators from each State, chosen by the Legislature thereof, for six Years; and each Senator shall have one Vote.

Immediately after they shall be assembled in Consequence of the first Election, they shall be divided as equally as may be into three Classes. The Seats of the Senators of the first Class shall be vacated at the Expiration of the second Year, of the second Class at the Expiration of the fourth Year, and of the third Class at the Expiration of the sixth Year, so that one third may be chosen every second Year; and if Vacancies happen by Resignation, or otherwise, during the Recess of the Legislature of any State, the Executive

*Colonial slave markets such as this one were given a twenty-year lease by the Constitution.*

thereof may make temporary Appointments until the next Meeting of the Legislature, which shall then fill such Vacancies.

No Person shall be a Senator who shall not have attained to the Age of thirty Years, and been nine Years a Citizen of the United States, and who shall not, when elected, be an Inhabitant of that State for which he shall be chosen.

The Vice President of the United States shall be President of the Senate, but shall have no Vote, unless they be equally divided.

The Senate shall chuse their other Officers, and also a President protempore, in the Absence of the Vice President, or when he shall exercise the Office of President of the United States.

The Senate shall have the sole Power to try all Impeachments. When sitting for that Purpose, they shall be on Oath or Affirmation. When the President of the United States is tried, the Chief Justice shall preside: And no Person shall be convicted without the Concurrence of two thirds of the Members present.

Judgment in Cases of Impeachment shall not extend further than to removal from Office, and disqualification to hold and enjoy any Office of honor, Trust or Profit under the United States: but the Party convicted shall nevertheless be liable and subject to Indictment, Trial, Judgment and Punishment, according to Law.

SEC. 4. The Times, Places and Manner of holding Elections for Senators and Representatives, shall be prescribed in each State by the Legislature thereof; but the Congress may at any time by Law make or alter such Regulations, except as to the Places of chusing Senators.

The Congress shall assemble at least once in every Year, and such Meeting shall be on the first Monday in December, unless they shall by Law appoint a different Day.

SEC. 5. Each House shall be the Judge of the Elections, Returns and Qualifications of its own Members, and a Majority of each shall constitute a Quorum to do Business; but a smaller Number may adjourn from day to day, and may be authorized to compel the Attendance of absent Members, in such Manner, and under such Penalties as each House may provide.

Each House may determine the Rules of its Proceedings, Punish its Members for disorderly Behaviour, and, with the Concurrence of two thirds, expel a Member.

Each House shall keep a Journal of its Proceedings, and from time to time publish the same, excepting such Parts as may in their Judgment require Secrecy; and the Yeas and Nays of the Members of either House on any question shall, at the Desire of one fifth of those Present, be entered on the Journal.

Neither House, during the Session of Congress, shall, without the Consent of the other, adjourn for more than three days, nor to any other Place than that in which the two Houses shall be sitting.

SEC. 6. The Senators and Representatives shall receive a Compensation for their Services, to be ascertained by Law, and paid out of the Treasury of the United States. They shall in all Cases, except Treason, felony and Breach of the Peace, be privileged from Arrest during their Attendance at the Session of their respective Houses, and in going to and returning from the same; and for any speech or Debate in either House, they shall not be questioned in any other Place.

No Senator or Representative shall, during the Time for which he was elected, be appointed to any civil Office under the Authority of the United States which shall have been created, or the Emoluments whereof shall have been encreased during such time; and no Person holding any Office under the United States, shall be a Member of either House during his Continuance in Office.

SEC. 7. All Bills for raising Revenue shall originate in the House of Representatives; but the Senate may propose or concur with Amendments as on other Bills.

Every Bill which shall have passed the House of Representatives and the Senate, shall, before it becomes a Law, be presented to the President of the United States; If he approves he shall sign it, but if not he shall return it, with his Objections to that House in which it shall have originated, who shall enter the Objections at large on their Journal, and proceed to reconsider it. If after such Reconsideration two thirds of that House shall agree to pass the Bill, it shall be sent, together with the Objections, to the other House, by which it shall likewise be reconsidered, and if approved by two thirds of that House, it shall become a Law. But in all such Cases the Votes of both Houses shall be determined by Yeas and Nays, and the Names of the Persons voting for and against the Bill shall be entered on the Journal of each House respectively. If any Bill shall not be returned by the President within ten Days (Sundays excepted) after it shall have been presented to him, the Same shall be a Law, in like Manner as if he had signed it, unless the Congress by their Adjournment prevent its Return, in which Case it shall not be a Law.

Every Order, Resolution, or Vote to which the Concurrence of the Senate and House of Representatives may be necessary (except on a question of Adjournment) shall be presented to the President of the United States; and before the Same shall take Effect, shall be approved by him, or being disapproved by him, shall be repassed by two thirds of the Senate and House of Representatives, according to the Rules and Limitations prescribed in the Case of a Bill.

SEC. 8. The Congress shall have Power To lay and collect Taxes, Duties, Imposts and Excises, to pay the Debts and provide for the common Defence and general Welfare of the United States; but all Duties, Imposts and Excises shall be uniform throughout the United States;

To borrow Money on the credit of the United States;

To regulate Commerce with foreign Nations, and among the several States, and with the Indian Tribes;

To establish a uniform Rule of Naturalization, and uniform Laws on the subject of Bankruptcies throughout the United States;

To coin Money, regulate the Value thereof, and of foreign Coin, and fix the Standard of Weights and Measures;

To provide for the Punishment of counterfeiting and Securities and current Coin of the United States;

To establish Post Offices and post Roads;

To promote the Progress of Science and useful Arts, by securing for limited Times to Authors and Inventors the exclusive Right to their respective Writings and Discoveries;

To constitute Tribunals inferior to the supreme Court;

To define and punish Piracies and Felonies committed on the high Seas, and Offences against the Law of Nations;

To declare War, grant Letters of Marque and Reprisal, and make Rules concerning Captures on Land and Water;

To raise and support Armies, but no Appropriation of Money to that Use shall be for a longer Term than two Years;

To provide and maintain a Navy;

To make Rules for the Government and Regulation of the land and naval Forces;

To provide for calling forth the Militia to execute the Laws of the Union, suppress Insurrections and repel Invasions;

To provide for organizing, arming, and disciplining, the Militia, and for governing such Part of them as may be employed in the Service of the United States, reserving to the States respectively, the Appointment of the Officers, and the Authority of training the Militia according to the discipline prescribed by Congress;

To exercise exclusive Legislation in all Cases whatsoever, over such District (not exceeding ten Miles square) as may, by Cession of particular States, and the Acceptance of Congress, become the Seat of the Government of the United States, and to exercise like Authority over all Places purchased by the Consent of the Legislature of the State in which the Same shall be, for the Erection of Forts, Magazines, Arsenals, dock-Yards, and other needful Buildings;—And

To make all Laws which shall be necessary and proper for carrying into Execution the foregoing Powers, and all other Powers vested by this Constitution in the Government of the United States, or in any Department or Officer thereof.

SEC. 9. *The Migration or Importation of such Persons as any of the States now existing shall think proper to admit, shall not be prohibited by the Congress prior to the Year one thousand eight hundred and eight, but a Tax or duty may be imposed on such Importation, not exceeding ten dollars for each Person.*

The Privilege of the Writ of Habeas Corpus shall not be suspended, unless when in Cases of Rebellion or Invasion the public Safety may require it.

No Bill of Attainder or ex post facto Law shall be passed.

No Capitation, or other direct, Tax shall be laid, unless in Proportion to the Census or Enumeration before directed to be taken.

No Tax or Duty shall be laid on Articles exported from any State.

No Preference shall be given by any Regulation of Commerce or Revenue to the Ports of one State over those of another: nor shall Vessels bound to, or from, one State, be obliged to enter, clear, or pay Duties in another.

No Money shall be drawn from the Treasury, but in Consequence of Appropriations made by Law; and a regular Statement and Account of the Receipts and Expenditures of all public Money shall be published from time to time.

No Title of Nobility shall be granted by the United States: And no Person holding any Office of Profit or Trust under them, shall, without the Consent of the Congress, accept of any present, Emolument, Office, or Title, of any kind whatever, from any King, Prince or foreign State.

SEC. 10. No State shall enter into any Treaty, Alliance, or Confederation; grant Letters of Marque and Reprisal; coin Money; emit Bills of Credit; make any Thing but gold and silver Coin a Tender in Payment of Debts; pass any Bill of Attainder, ex post facto Law, or Law impairing the Obligation of Contracts, or grant any Title of Nobility.

No State shall, without the Consent of the Congress, lay any Imposts or Duties on Imports or Exports, except what may be absolutely necessary for executing its inspection Laws: and the net Produce of all duties and Imposts, laid by any State on Imports or Exports, shall be for the Use of the Treasury of the United States; and all such Laws shall be subject to the Revision and Control of the Congress.

No State shall, without the Consent of Congress, lay any Duty of Tonnage, keep Troops, or Ships of War in time of Peace, enter into any Agreement or Compact with another State, or with a foreign Power, or engage in War, unless actually invaded, or in such imminent Danger as will not admit of delay.

## ART. II

SEC. 1. The executive Power shall be vested in a President of the United States of America. He shall hold his Office during the Term of four Years, and, together with the Vice President, chosen for the same Term, be elected, as follows

Each State shall appoint, in such Manner as the Legislature thereof may direct, a Number of Electors, equal to the whole Number of Senators and Representatives to which the State may be entitled in the Congress: but no Senator or Representative, or Person holding an Office of Trust or Profit under the United States, shall be appointed an Elector.

The electors shall meet in their respective States, and vote by Ballot for two Persons, of whom one at least shall not be an inhabitant of the same State with themselves. And they shall make a List of all the Persons voted for, and of the Number of Votes for each; which List they shall sign and certify, and transmit sealed to the Seat of the Government of the United States, directed to the President of the Senate. The President of the Senate shall, in the Presence of the Senate and House of Representatives, open all the Certificates, and the Votes shall then be counted. The Person having the greatest Number of Votes shall be the President, if such Number be a Majority of the whole Number of Electors appointed; and if there be more than one who have such Majority, and have an equal Number of Votes, then the House of Representatives shall immediately chuse by Ballot one of them for President; and if no person have a Majority, then from the five highest on the List the said House shall in like Manner chuse the President. But in chusing the President, the Votes shall be taken by States, the Representation from each State having one Vote; A quorum for this Purpose shall consist of a Member or Members from two thirds of the States, and a Majority of all the states shall be necessary to a choice. In every case, after the choice of the president, the person having the greatest number of Votes of the Electors shall be the Vice President. If there should remain two or more who have equal Votes, the Senate shall chuse from them by Ballot the Vice President.

The Congress may determine the Time of chusing the Electors, and the Day on which they shall give their Votes; which Day shall be the same throughout the United States.

No Person except a natural born Citizen, or a Citizen of the United States, at the time of the Adoption of this Constitution, shall be eligible to the Office of President; neither shall any Person be eligible to that Office who shall not have attained to the Age of thirty-five Years, and been fourteen Years a Resident within the United States.

In Case of the Removal of the President from Office, or of his Death, resignation, or Inability to discharge the Powers and Duties of the said Office, the Same shall devolve on the Vice President, and the Congress may by Law provide for the Case of Removal, Death, Resignation or Inability, both of the President and Vice President, declaring what Officer shall then act as President, and such Officer shall act accordingly, until the Disability be removed, or a President shall be elected.

The President shall, at stated Times, receive for his Services, a Compensation, which shall neither be encreased nor diminished during the Period for which he shall have been elected, and he shall not receive within that Period any other Emolument from the United States, or any of them.

Before he enter on the execution of his Office, he shall take the following Oath or Affirmation:—"I do solemnly swear (or affirm) that I will faithfully execute the Office of President of the United States, and will to the best of my Ability, preserve, protect and defend the Constitution of the United States."

SEC. 2. The President shall be Commander in Chief of the Army and Navy of the United States, and of the Militia of the several States, when called into the actual Service of the United States; he may require the Opinion, in writing, of the principal Officer in each of the executive Departments, upon any Subject relating to the Duties of their respective Offices, and he shall have Power to grant Reprieves and Pardons for Offences against the United States, except in cases of Impeachment.

He shall have Power, by and with the Advice and Consent of the Senate, to make Treaties, provided two thirds of the Senators present concur; and he shall nominate, and by and with the Advice and Consent of the Senate, shall appoint Ambassadors, other public Ministers and Consuls, Judges of the Supreme Court, and all other Offices of the United States, whose Appointments are not herein otherwise provided for, and which shall be established by Law; but the Congress may by Law vest the Appointment of such inferior Officers, as they think proper, in the President alone, in the Courts of Law, or in the Heads of Departments.

The President shall have Power to fill up all Vacancies that may happen during the Recess of the Senate, by granting Commissions which shall expire at the end of their next Session.

SEC. 3. He shall from time to time give to the Congress Information of the State of the Union, and recommend to their Consideration such Measures as he shall judge necessary and expedient; he may, on extraordinary Occasions, convene both Houses, or either of them, and in Case of Disagreement between them, with Respect to the Time of Adjournment, he may adjourn them to such Time as he shall think proper; he shall receive Ambassadors and other public Ministers; he shall take care that the Laws be faithfully executed, and shall Commission all the Officers of the United States.

SEC. 4. The President, Vice President and all civil Officers of the United States, shall be removed from Office on Impeachment for, and Conviction of, Treason, Bribery, or other high Crimes and Misdemeanors.

## ART. III

SEC. 1. The judicial Power of the United States, shall be vested in one supreme Court. And in such inferior Courts as the Congress may from time to time ordain and establish. The Judges, both of the supreme and inferior Courts, shall hold their Offices during good Behaviour, and shall, at stated Times, receive for their Services, a Compensation which shall not be diminished during their Continuance in Office.

SEC. 2. The judicial Power shall extend to all Cases, in Law and Equity, arising under this Constitution, the Laws of the United States, and Treaties made, or which shall be made, under their Authority;—to all Cases affecting Ambassadors, other public Ministers and Consuls;—to all Cases of admi-

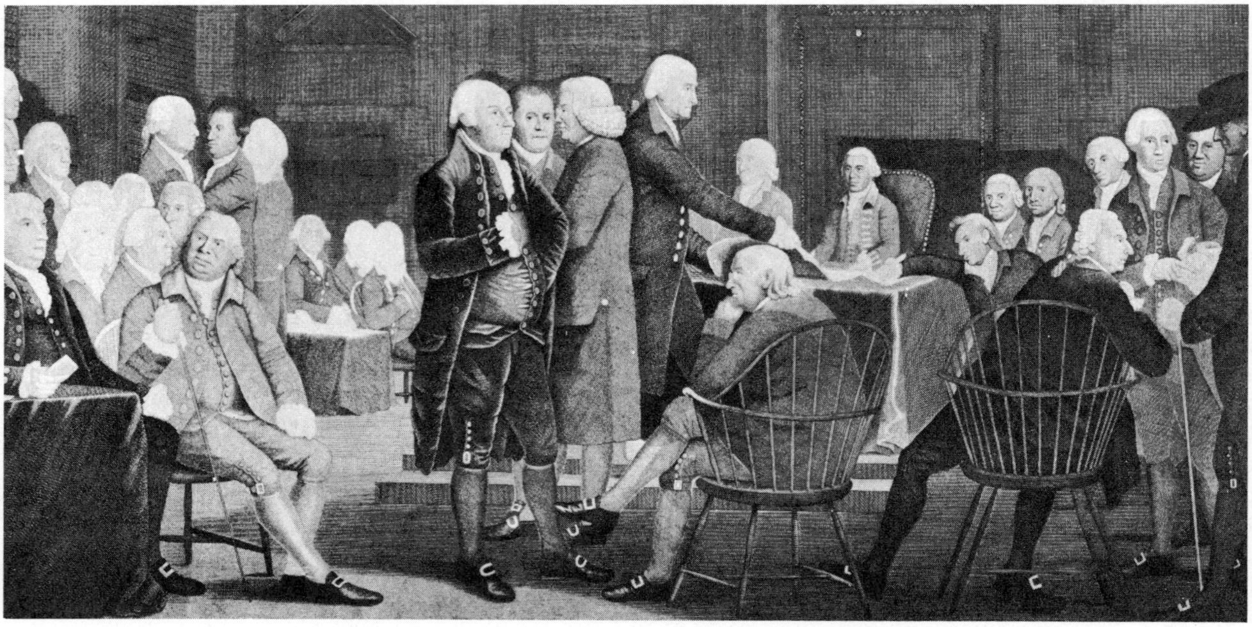

*Many of the revolutionaries who declared independence from Britain reconvened to draw up the Constitution.*

ralty and maritime Jurisdiction;—to Controversies to which the United States shall be a Party;—to Controversies between two or more States;—between a State and Citizens of another State;_between Citizens of different states,—between Citizens of the same State claiming Lands under Grants of different States, and between a State, or the Citizens thereof, and foreign States, Citizens or Subjects.

In all Cases affecting Ambassadors, other public Ministers and Consuls, and those in which a State shall be Party, the supreme Court shall have original Jurisdiction. In all the other Cases before mentioned, the supreme Court shall have appellate Jurisdiction, both as to Law and Fact, with such Exceptions, and under such Regulations as the Congress shall make.

The Trial of all Crimes, except in Cases of Impeachment, shall be by Jury; and such Trial shall be held in the State where the said Crimes shall have been committed; but when not committed within any State, the Trial shall be at such Place or Places as the Congress may by Law have directed.

SEC. 3. Treason against the United States, shall consist only in levying War against them, or in adhering to their Enemies, giving them Aid and Comfort. No Person shall be convicted of Treason unless on the Testimony of two Witnesses to the same overt Act, or on Confession in open Court.

The Congress shall have Power to declare the Punishment of Treason, but no Attainder of Treason shall work Corruption of Blood, or Forfeiture except during the Life of the Person attainted.

ART. IV

SEC. 1. Full Faith and Credit shall be given in each state to the Public Acts, Records, and judicial Proceedings of every other State. And the Congress may by general Laws prescribe the Manner in which such Act, Records and Proceedings shall be proved, and the Effect thereof.

SEC. 2. The Citizens of each State shall be entitled to all Privileges and Immunities of Citizens in the several States.

A Person charged in any State with Treason, Felony, or other Crime, who shall flee from Justice, and be found in another State, shall on Demand of the executive authority of the State from which he fled, be delivered up, to be removed to the State having Jurisdiction of the Crime.

No Person held to Service or Labour in one State, under the Laws thereof, escaping into another, shall, in Consequence of any Law or Regulation therein, be discharged from such Service or Labour, but shall be delivered up on Claim of the Party to whom such Service or Labour may be due.

SEC. 3. New States may be admitted by the Congress into this Union; but no new States shall be formed or erected within the Jurisdiction of any other State; nor any State be formed by the Junction of two or more States, or Parts of States, without the Consent of the Legislatures of the States concerned as well as of the Congress.

The Congress shall have Power to dispose of and make all needful Rules and Regulations respecting the Territory or other Property belonging to the United States; and nothing in this Constitution shall be so construed as to Prejudice any Claims of the United States, or of any particular State.

SEC. 4. The United States shall guarantee to every State in this Union a Republican Form of Government, and shall protect each of them against Invasion; and on Application of the Legislature, or of the Executive (when the Legislature cannot be convened) against domestic Violence.

ART. V

The Congress, whenever two thirds of both Houses shall deem it necessary, shall propose Amendments to this Constitution, or, on the Application of the Legislatures of two thirds of the several States, shall call a Convention for proposing Amendments, which, in either Case, shall be valid to all Intents and Purposes, as Part of this Constitution, when ratified by the Legislatures of three-fourths of the several States, or by Conventions in three-fourths thereof, as the one or the other Mode of Ratification may be proposed by the Congress; Provided that no Amendment which may be made prior to the Year One thousand eight hundred and eight shall in any Manner affect the first and fourth Clauses in the Ninth Section of the first Article; and that no State, without its Consent, shall be deprived of its equal Suffrage in the Senate.

ART. VI

All Debts contracted and Engagements entered into, before the Adoption of this Constitution, shall be as valid against the United States under this Constitution, as under the Confederation.

This Constitution, and the Laws of the United States which shall be made in Pursuance thereof; and all Treaties made, or which shall be made, under the authority of the United States, shall be the supreme Law of the Land; and the Judges in every State shall be bound thereby, any Thing in the Constitution or Laws of any state to the Contrary notwithstanding.

The Senators and Representatives before mentioned, and the Members of the several State Legislatures, and all executive and judicial Officers, both of the United States and of the several States, shall be bound by Oath or Affirmation, to support this Constitution; but no religious Test shall ever be required as a Qualification to any Office or public Trust under the United States.

ART. VII

The Ratification fo the Conventions of Nine States, shall be sufficient for the Establishment of this Constitution between the States so ratifying the Same.

Done in Convention by the Unanimous Consent of the States present the Seventeenth Day of September in the Year of our Lord one thousand seven hundred and Eighty seven and of the Independence of the United States of America the Twelfth. In witness whereof We have hereunto subscribed our Names,

GO WASHINGTON—Presidt
and deputy from Virginia

New Hampshire
JOHN LANGDON
NICHOLAS GILMAN

Massachusetts
NATHANIEL GORHAM
RUFUS KING

Connecticut
WM SAML JOHNSON
ROGER SHERMAN

New York
ALEXANDER HAMILTON

New Jersey
WIL: LIVINGSTON
DAVID BREARLY
WM PATERSON
JONA: DAYTON

Pennsylvania
B FRANKLIN
THOMAS MIFFLIN
ROBT MORRIS
GEO. CLYMER
THOS FITZSIMONS
JARED INGERSOLL
JAMES WILSON
GOUV MORRIS
GEO: READ

Delaware
GUNNING BEDFORD jun
JOHN DICKINSON
RICHARD BASSET
JACO: BROOM

Maryland
JAMES MCHENRY
DAN of ST. THOS. JENIFER
DANL. CARROLL

Virginia
JOHN BLAIR
JAMES MADISON JR

North Carolina
Wm. BLOUNT
RICHD DOBBS SPAIGHT
HU WILLIAMSON

South Carolina
J. RUTLEDGE
CHARLES COTESWORTH PINCKNEY
CHARLES PINCKNEY
PIERCE BUTLER

Georgia
WILLIAM FEW
ABR BALDWIN Trust

## THE BILL OF RIGHTS (1791)

ART. I

Congress shall make no law respecting an establishment of religion, or prohibiting the free exercise thereof; or abridging the freedom of speech, or of the press; or the right of the people peaceably to assemble, and to petition the government for a redress of grievances.

ART. II

A well regulated Militia, being necessary to the security of a free State, the right of the people to keep and bear Arms, shall not be infringed.

ART. III

No Soldier, shall, in time of peace be quartered in any house, without the consent of the Owner, nor in time of war, but in a manner to be prescribed by law.

ART. IV

The right of the people to be secure in their persons, houses, papers, and effects, against unreasonable searches and seizures, shall not be violated, and no Warrants shall issue, but upon probable cause, supported by Oath or affirmation, and particularly describing the place to be searched, and the persons or things to be seized.

ART. V

No person shall be held to answer for a capital, or otherwise infamous crime, unless on a presentment or indictment of a Grand Jury, except in cases arising in the land or naval forces, or in the Militia, when in actual service in time of War or public danger; nor shall any person be subject for the same offence to be twice put in jeopardy of life or limb; nor shall be compelled in any criminal case to be a witness against himself, nor be deprived of life, liberty, or property, without due process of law; nor shall private property be taken for public use, without just compensation.

ART. VI

In all criminal prosecutions, the accused shall enjoy the right to a speedy and public trial, by an impartial jury of the State and district wherein the crime shall have been committed, which district shall have been previously ascertained by law, and to be informed of the nature and cause of the accusation; to be confronted with the witnesses against him; to have compulsory process for obtaining witnesses in his favor, and to have the Assistance of Counsel for his defence.

ART. VII

In Suits at common law, where the value in controversy shall exceed twenty dollars, the right of trial by jury shall be preserved, and no fact tried by a jury, shall be otherwise reexamined in any Court of the United States, than according to the rules of the common law.

ART. VIII

Excessive bail shall not be required, nor excessive fines imposed, nor cruel and unusual punishments inflicted.

ART. IX

The enumeration in the Constitution, of certain rights, shall not be construed to deny or disparage others retained by the people.

ART. X

The powers not delegated to the United States by the Constitution, nor prohibited by it to the States, are reserved to the States respectively, or to the people.

## THE FUGITIVE SLAVE ACT OF 1793

*The Fugitive Slave Act of 1793 was designed to secure enforcement of Article IV, Section 2 of the Constitution and incur penalties against those who aided or abetted attempts of slaves to escape bondage.*

SEC. 1. *Be it enacted by the Senate and House of Representatives of the United States of America in Congress assembled,* That whenever the executive authority of any state in the Union, or of either of the territories northwest or south of the river Ohio, shall demand any person as a fugitive from justice, of the executive authority of any such state or territory to which such person shall have fled, and shall moreover produce the copy of an indictment found, or an affidavit made before a magistrate of any state of territory as aforesaid, charging the person so demanded, with having committed treason, felony or other crime, certified as authentic by the governor or chief magistrate of the state or territory from whence the person so changed fled, it shall be the duty of the executive authority of the state or territory to which such person shall have fled, to cause him or her to be arrested and secured, and notice of the arrest to be given to the executive authority making such demand, or to the agent of such authority appointed to receive the fugitive, and to cause the fugitive to be delivered to such agent when he shall appear: But if no such agent shall appear within six months from the time of the arrest, the prisoner may be discharged. And all costs or expenses incurred to the state or territory making such demand, shall be paid by such state or territory.

SEC. 2. *And be it further enacted,* That any agent, appointed as aforesaid, who shall receive the fugitive into his custody, shall be empowered to transport him or her to the state or territory from which he or she shall have fled. And if any person or persons shall by force set at liberty, or rescue the

*This drawing headlined newspaper advertisements for runaway slaves.*

fugitive from such agent while transporting, as aforesaid, the person or persons so offending shall, on conviction, be fined not exceeding five hundred dollars, and be imprisoned not exceeding one year.

SEC. 3. *And be it also enacted,* That when a person held to labour in any of the United States, or in either of the territories on the northwest or south of the river Ohio, under the laws thereof, shall escape into any other of the said states or territory, the person to whom such labour or service may be due, his agent or attorney, is hereby empowered to seize or arrest such fugitive from labour, and to take him or her before any judge of the circuit or district courts of the United States, residing or being within the state, or before any magistrate of a county, city or town corporate, wherein such seizure or arrest shall be made, and upon proof to the satisfaction of such judge or magistrate, either by oral testimony or affidavit taken before and certified by a magistrate of any such state or territory, that the person so seized or arrested, doth, under the laws of the state or territory from which he or she fled, owe service or labour to the person claiming him or her, it shall be the duty of such judge or magistrate to give a certificate thereof to such claimant, his agent or attorney, which shall be sufficient warrant for removing the said fugitive from labour, to the state or territory from which he or she fled.

SEC. 4. *And be it further enacted,* That any person who shall knowingly and willing obstruct or hinder such claimant, his agent or attorney in so seizing or arresting such fugitive from labour, or shall rescue such fugitive from such claimant, his agent or attorney when so arrested pursuant to the authority herein given or declared; or shall harbor or conceal such person after notice that he or she was a fugitive from labour, as aforesaid shall, for either of the said offences, forfeit and pay the sum of five hundred dollars. Which penalty may be recovered by and for the benefit of such claimant, by action of debt, in any court proper to try the same; saving moreover to the person claiming such labour or service, his right of action for or on account of the said injuries or either of them.

## AN ADDRESS TO THE PUBLIC BY BENJAMIN FRANKLIN (1798)

*The failure of the Constitutional Convention to include Thomas Jefferson's antislavery proposal did not diminish the debate between the pro-slavery states of the South and many antislavery Congressmen of the North. Influential antislavery groups attempted to exert pressure on the Congress to enact an antislavery amendment to the Constitution. Among such groups was the Pennsylvania Society for Promoting the Abolition of Slavery and the Relief of Free Negroes unlawfully held in Bondage. Over the signature of the President of the Society, Benjamin Franklin, the following "Address to the Public," urging abolition, was sent to the Congress of the United States.*

It is with peculiar satisfaction we assure the friends of humanity, that, in prosecuting the design of our association, our endeavors have proved successful, far beyond our most sanguine expectations.

Encouraged by this success, and by the daily progress of that luminous and benign spirit of liberty which is diffusing itself throughout the world, and humbly hoping for the continuance of the divine blessing on our labors, we have ventured to make an important addition to our original plan; and do therefore earnestly solicit the support and assistance of all who can feel the tender emotions of sympathy and compassion, or relish the exalted pleasure of beneficence.

Slavery is such an atrocious debasement of human nature, that its very extirpation, if not performed with solicitous care, may sometimes open a source of serious evils.

The unhappy man, who has long been treated as a brute animal, too frequently sinks beneath the common standard of the human species. The galling chains that bind his body do also fetter his intellectual faculties, and impair the social affections of his heart. Accustomed to move like a mere

*Benjamin Franklin termed slavery "an atrocious debasement of human nature."*

machine, by the will of a master, reflection is suspended; he has not the power of choice; and reason and conscience have but little influence over his conduct, because he is chiefly governed by the passion of fear. He is poor and friendless; perhaps worn out by extreme labor, age, and disease.

Under such circumstances, freedom may often prove a misfortune to himself, and prejudicial to society.

Attention to emancipated black people, it is therefore to be hoped, will become a branch of our national police; but, as far as we contribute to promote this emancipation, so far that attention is evidently a serious duty incumbent on us, and which we mean to discharge to the best of our judgment and abilities.

To instruct, to advise, to qualify those who have been restored to freedom, for the exercise and enjoyment of civil liberty; to promote in them habits of industry; to furnish them with employments suited to their age, sex, talents, and other circumstances; and to procure their children an education calculated for their future situation if life,—these are the great outlines of the annexed plan, which we have adopted, and which we conceive will essentially promote the public good, and the happiness of these our hitherto too much neglected fellow-creatures.

A plan so extensive cannot be carried into execution without considerable pecuniary resources, beyond the present ordinary funds of the Society. We hope much from the generosity of enlightened and benevolent freemen, and will gratefully receive any donations or subscriptions for this purpose which may be made to our Treasurer, James Starr, or to James Pemberton, Chairman of our Committee of Correspondence.

Signed by order of the Society,
B. FRANKLIN, *President*

Philadelphia, 9th of November, 1789

## GEORGE WASHINGTON'S LAST WILL AND TESTAMENT: THE FIRST PRESIDENT FREES HIS SLAVES (1799)

*During the eighteenth century, Negro slavery was a firmly entrenched institution of American life, particularly in the South where it was justified mainly as an economic necessity. This argument notwithstanding, it was Washington's decision, at the writing of his last will and testament in 1799, to free all those slaves which he held in his "own right." Washington's will also reflected his concern for the financial welfare and educational support of his former charges.*

### In the Name of God Amen

I George Washington of Mount Vernon—a citizen of the United States, —and lately President of the same, do make, ordain and declare this Instrument; which is written with my own hand and every page thereof subscribed with my name, to be my last Will & Testament, revoking all others... Upon the decease of my wife, it is my Will & desire that all the Slaves which I hold in my *own right,* shall receive their freedom... And whereas among those who will receive freedom according to this devise, there may be some, who from old age or bodily infirmities, and others who on account of their infancy, that will be unable to support themselves; it is my Will and desire that all who come under the first & second description shall be comfortably cloathed & fed by my heirs while they live;—and that such of the latter description as have no parents living, or if living are unable, or unwilling to provide for them, shall be bound by the Court until they shall arrive at the age of twenty five years;—and in cases where no record can be produced, whereby their ages can be ascertained, the judgment of the Court upon its own view of the subject, shall be adequate and final.—The Negros thus bound, are (by their Masters or Mistresses) to be taught to read & write; and to be brought up to some useful occupation, agreeably to the Laws of the Commonwealth of Virginia, providing for the support of Orphan and other poor Children.—And I do hereby expressly forbid the Sale, or transportation out of the said Commonwealth of any Slave I may die possessed of, under any pretence whatsoever.—And I do moreover most pointedly, and most solemnly enjoin it upon my Executors hereafter named, or the Survivors of them, to see that th*is* clause respecting Slaves, and every part thereof be religiously fulfilled at the Epoch at which it is directed to take place; without evasion, neglect or delay, after the Crops which may then be on the ground are harvested, particularly as it respects the aged and infirm;—Seeing that a regular and permanent fund be established for their Support so long as there are subjects requiring it; not trusting to the uncertain provision to be made by individuals.—And to my Mulatto man William (calling himself William Lee) I give immediate freedom; or if he should prefer it (on account of the accidents which have befallen him, and which have rendered him incapable of walking or of any active employment) to remain in the situation he now is, it shall be optional in him to do so: In either case however, I allow him an annuity of thirty dollars during his natural life, which shall be independent of the victuals and cloaths he has been accustomed to receive, if he chuses the last alternative; but in full, with his freedom, if he prefers the first;—& this I give him as a testimony of my sense of his attachment to me, and for his faithful services during the Revolutionary War.

*General Washington at his Mt. Vernon home.*

## THE ACT TO PROHIBIT THE IMPORTATION OF SLAVES (1807)

*The Act of 1807 (which, although dated March 2, 1807, actually went into effect on January 1, 1808, and thereby did not interfere with the provisions of Article I, Section 9 of the U.S. Constitution) sought to end the slave trade by prohibiting the importation of "men-body" onto the North American mainland. The act, however, was not rigidly enforced, despite the appeals of Presidents Martin Van Buren and John Tyler. Evidence of this can be found in the fact that, between 1808 and 1860, some 250,000 slaves were illegally imported into the United States.*

An Act to prohibit the importation of Slaves into any port or place within the jurisdiction of the United States, from and after the first day of January, in the year of our Lord one thousand eight hundred and eight.

*Be it enacted,* That from and after the first day of January, one thousand eight hundred and eight, it shall not be lawful to import or bring into the United States or the territories thereof from any foreign kingdom, place, or country, any negro, mulatto, or person or colour, as a slave, or to be held to service or labour.

SEC. 2. That no citizen of the United States, or any other person, shall, from and after the first day of January, in the year of our Lord one thousand eight hundred and eight, for himself, or themselves, or any other person whatsoever, either as master, factor, or owner, build, fit, equip, load or to otherwise prepare any ship or vessel, in any port or place within the jurisdiction of the United States, nor shall cause any ship or vessel to sail from any port or place within the same, for the purpose of procuring any negro, mulatto, or person of colour, from any foreign kingdom, place, or country, to be transported to any port or place whatsoever within the jurisdiction of the United States, to be held, sold, or disposed of as slaves, or to be held to service or labour: and if any ship or vessel shall be so fitted out for the purpose aforesaid, or shall be caused to sail so as aforesaid, every such ship or vessel, her tackle, apparel, and furniture, shall be forfeited to the United States, and shall be liable to be seized, prosecuted, and condemned in any of the circuit courts or district courts, for the district where the said ship or vessel may be found or seized...

SEC. 4. If any citizen or citizens of the United States, or any person resident within the jurisdiction of the same, shall, from and after the first day of January, one thousand eight hundred and eight, take on board, receive or transport from any of the coasts or kingdoms of Africa, or from any other foreign kingdom, place, or country, any negro, mulatto, or person of colour in any ship or vessel, for the purpose of selling them in any port or place within the jurisdiction of the United States as slaves, or be to held to service or labour, or shall be in any ways aiding or abetting therein, such citizen or citizens, or person, shall severally forfeit and pay five thousand dollars, one moiety thereof to the use of any person or persons who shall sue for and prosecute the same to effect...

SEC. 6. That if any person or persons whatsoever, shall, from and after the first day of January, one thousand eight hundred and eight, purchase or sell any negro, mulatto, or person, of colour, for a slave, or to be held to service or labour, who shall have been imported, or brought from any foreign kingdom, place, or country, or from the dominions of any foreign state, immediately adjoining to the United States, after the last day of December, one thousand eight hundred and seven, knowing at the time of such purchase or sale, such negro, mulatto, or person of colour, was so brought within the jurisdiction of the United States, as aforesaid, such purchaser and seller shall severally forfeit and pay for every negro, mulatto, or person of colour, so purchased or sold as aforesaid, eight hundred dollars...

SEC. 7. That if any ship or vessel shall be found, from and after the first day of January, one thousand eight hundred and eight, in any river, port, bay, or harbor, or on the high seas, within the jurisdictional limits of the United States, or hovering on the coast thereof, having on board any negro, mulatto, or person of colour, for the purpose of selling them as slaves, or with intent to land the same, in any port or place within the jurisdiction of the United States, contrary to the prohibition of the act, every such ship or vessel, together with her tackle, apparel, and furniture, and the goods or effects which shall be found on board the same, shall be forfeited to the use of the United States, and may be seized, prosecuted, and condemned, in any court of the United States, having jurisdiction thereof. And it shall be lawful for the President of the United States, and he is hereby authorized, should he deem it expedient, to cause any of the armed vessels of the United States to be manned and employed to cruise on any part of the coast of the United States, or territories thereof, where he may judge attempts will be made to violate the provisions of this act, and to instruct and direct the commanders of armed vessels of the United States, to seize, take, and bring into any port of the United States all such ships or vessels, and moreover to seize, take, or bring into any port of the U.S. all ships or vessel of the U.S. wheresoever found on the high seas, contravening the provisions of this act, to be proceeded against according to law...

***Chained for the voyage, Africans were at the mercy of brutal crewmen.***

## THE MISSOURI COMPROMISE (1819-1821)

*Under the terms of the Missouri Compromise (1819-1821), Missouri was admitted to the Union as a slave state.(It was followed in short order by Maine, a free state.) However, slavery was prohibited from that time onward in all Louisiana Territory lying north of latitude 36 30'. For a certain period, the Compromise appeased both pro and antislavery spokesmen. However, the question of slavery once again vaulted into the national spotlight with the outbreak of the Mexican War, which gave promise of greatly increasing the potential territory open to slavery. (See Compromise of 1850 entry.)*

### 1. The Tallmadge Amendment
### February 13, 1819

*And provided also,* That the further introduction of slavery or involuntary servitude be prohibited, except for the punishment of crimes, whereof the party shall be duly convicted; and that all children of slaves, born within the said state, after the admission thereof into the Union, shall be free but may be held to service until the age of twenty-five years.

### 2. The Taylor Amendment
### January 26, 1820

The reading of the bill proceeded as far as the fourth section; when

MR. TAYLOR, of New York, proposed to amend the bill by incorporating in that section the following provision:

Section 4, line 25, insert the following after the word "States"; "And shall ordain and establish, that there shall be neither slavery nor involuntary servitude in the said State, otherwise than in the punishment of crimes, whereof the party shall have been duly convicted: *Provided, always,* That any person escaping into the same, from whom labor or service is lawfully claimed in any other State, such fugitive may be lawfully reclaimed, and conveyed to the person claiming his or her labor or service as aforesaid: *And provided, also,* That the said provision shall not be construed to alter the condition or civil rights of any person now held to service or labor in the said Territory."

*James Monroe, fifth President of the United States. His administration designed the Missouri compromise in an effort to appease both both slavery and antislavery factions.*

### 3. The Thomas Amendment
### February 17,1820

*And be it further enacted,* That, in all that territory ceded by France to the United States, under the name of Louisiana, which lies north of thirty-six degrees and thirty minutes north latitude, excepting only such part thereof as is included within the limits of the State contemplated by this act, slavery and involuntary servitude, otherwise than in the punishment of crimes whereof the party shall have been duly convicted, shall be and is hereby forever prohibited: *Provided always,* That any person escaping into the same, from whom labor or service is lawfully claimed in any State or Territory of the United States, such fugitive may be lawfully reclaimed, and conveyed to the person claiming his or her labor or service, as aforesaid.

### 4. Missouri Enabling Act
### March 6, 1820

*An Act to authorize the people of the Missouri territory to form a constitution and state government, and for the admission of such state into the Union on an equal footing with the original states, and to prohibit slavery in certain territories.*

*Be it enacted* That the inhabitants of that portion of the Missouri territory included within the boundaries hereinafter designated, be, and they are hereby, authorized to form for themselves a constitution and state government, and to assume such name as they shall deem proper; and the said state, when formed, shall be admitted into the Union, upon an equal footing with the original states, in all respects whatsoever.

SEC. 2. That the said state shall consist of all the territory included within the following boundaries, to wit: Beginning in the middle of the Mississippi river, on the parallel of thirty-six degrees of north latitude; thence west, along that parallel of latitude, to the St. Francois river; thence up, and following the course of that river, in the middle of the main channel thereof, to the parallel of latitude of thirty-six degrees and thirty minutes; thence west, along the same, to a point where the said parallel is intersected by meridian line passing through the middle of the mouth of the Kansas river, where the same empties into the Missouri river, thence, from the point aforesaid north, along the said meridian line, to the intersection of the parallel of latitude which passes through the rapids of the river Des Moines, making the said line to correspond with the Indian boundary line; thence east, from the point of intersection last aforesaid, along the said parallel of latitude, to the middle of the channel of the main fork of the said river Des Moines; thence down and along the middle of the main channel of the said river Des Moines, to the mouth of the same, where it empties into the Mississippi river; thence, due east, to the middle of the main channel of the Mississippi river; thence down, and following the course of the Mississippi river, in the middle of the main channel thereof, to the place of beginning...

SEC. 3. That all free white male citizens of the United States, who shall have arrived at the age of twenty-one years, and have resided in said territory three months previous to the day of election, and all other persons qualified to vote for representatives to the general assembly of the said territory, shall be qualified to be elected, and they are hereby qualified and authorized to vote, and choose representatives to form a convention...

SEC. 8. That in all that territory ceded by France to the United States, under the name of Louisiana, which lies north of thirty-six degrees and thirty minutes north latitude, not included within the limits of the state, contemplated by this act, slavery and involuntary servitude, otherwise than in the punishment of crimes, whereof the parties shall have been duly convicted, shall be, and is hereby, forever prohibited: *Provided always,* That any person escaping into the same, from whom labour or service is lawfully claimed, in any state or territory of the United States, such fugitive may be lawfully reclaimed and conveyed to the person claiming his or her labour or service as aforesaid.

## 5. The Constitution of Missouri
## July 19, 1820

SEC. 26. The general assembly shall not have power to pass laws—

1. For the emancipation of slaves without the consent of their owners; or without paying them, before such emancipation, a full equivalent for such slaves so emancipated; and,
2. To prevent *bona-fide* immigrants to this State, or actual settlers therein, from bringing from any of the United States, or from any of their Territories, such persons as may there be deemed to be slaves, so long as any persons of the same description are allowed to be held as slaves by the laws of this State.

They shall! have power to pass laws—

1. To prevent *bona-fide* immigrants to this State of any slaves who may have committed any high crime in any other State or Territory;
2. To prohibit the introduction of any slave for the purpose of speculation, or as an article of trade or merchandise;
3. To prohibit the introduction of any slave, or the offspring of any slave, who heretofore may have been, or who hereafter maybe, imported from any foreign country into the United States, or any Territory thereof, in contravention of any existing statute of the United States; and,
4. To permit the owners of slaves to emancipate them, saving the right of creditors, where the person so emancipating will give security that the slave so emancipated shall not become a public charge.

It shall be their duty, as soon as may be, to pass such laws as may be necessary

1. To prevent free negroes end [and] mulattoes from coming to and settling in this State, under any pretext whatsoever; and,
2. To oblige the owners of slaves to treat them with humanity, and to abstain from all injuries to them extending to life or limb.

## 6. Resolution for the Admission of Missouri
## March 2,1821

Resolution *providing for the admission of the State of Missouri into the Union, on a certain condition.*

*Resolved,* That Missouri shall be admitted into this union on an equal footing with the original states, in all respects whatever, upon the fundamental condition, that the fourth clause of the twenty-sixth section of the third article of the constitution submitted on the part of said state to Congress, shall never be construed to authorize the passage of any law, and that no law shall be passed in conformity thereto, by which any citizen, of either of the states in this Union, shall be excluded from the enjoyment of any of the privileges and immunities to which such citizen is entitled under the constitution of the United States: *Provided ,* That the legislature of the said-state, by a solemn public act, shall declare the assent of the said state to the said fundamental condition, and shall transmit to the President of the United States, on or before the fourth Monday in November next, an authentic copy of the said act; upon the receipt whereof, the President, by proclamation, shall announce the fact; whereupon, and without any further proceeding on the part of Congress, the admission of the said state into this Union shall be considered as complete.

## THE INAUGURAL EDITION OF FREEDOM'S JOURNAL: THE FIRST NEGRO NEWSPAPER IN THE UNITED STATES (1827)

*Freedom's Journal, owned and edited by Samuel Cornish and John B. Russwurm, put its first issue on the streets of New York City in 1827. This editorial, printed here in its entirety, devoted itself to slavery and discrimination.*

### To Our Patrons

In presenting our first number to our Patrons, we feel all the diffidence of persons entering upon a new and untried line of business. But a moment's reflection upon the noble objects, which we have in view by the publication of this Journal; the expediency of its appearance at this time, when so many schemes are in action concerning our people—encourage us to come boldly before an enlightened publick. For we believe, that a paper devoted to the dissemination of useful knowledge among our brethren, and to their moral and religious improvement, must meet with the cordial approbation of every friend to humanity.

The peculiarities of this Journal, renders it important that we should advertise to the world our motives by which we are actuated, and the objects which we contemplate.

We wish to plead our own cause. Too long have others spoken for us. Too long has the publick been deceived by misrepresentations, in things which concern us dearly, though in the estimation of some mere trifles; for though there are many in society who exercise towards us benevolent feelings; still (with sorrow we confess it) there are others who make it their business to enlarge upon the least trifle, which tends to the discredit of any person of colour; and pronounce anathemas and denounce our whole body for the misconduct of this guilty one. We are aware that there are many instances of vice among us, but we avow that it is because no one has taught its subjects to be virtuous; many instances of poverty, because no sufficient efforts accommodated to minds contracted by slavery, and deprived of early education have been made, to teach them how to husband their hard earnings, and to secure to themselves comfort.

Education being an object of the highest importance to the welfare of society, we shall endeavour to present just and adequate views of it, and to urge upon our brethren the necessity and expediency of training their children, while young, to habits of industry, and thus forming them for becoming useful members of society. It is surely time that we should awake from this lethargy of years, and make a concentrated effort for the education of our youth. We form a spoke in the human wheel, and it is necessary that we should understand our pendence on the different parts, and theirs on us, in order to perform our part with propriety.

Though not desiring of dictating, we shall feel it our incumbent duty to dwell occasionally upon the general principles and rules of economy. The world has grown too enlightened, to estimate any man's character by his personal appearance. Though all men acknowledge the excellency of Franklin's maxims, yet comparatively few practise upon them. We may deplore when it is too late, the neglect of these self-evident truths, but it avails little to mourn. Ours will be the task of admonishing our brethren on these points.

The civil rights of a people being of the greatest value, it shall ever be our duty to vindicate our brethren, when oppressed; and to lay the case before the publick. We shall also urge upon our brethren, (who are qualified by the laws of the different states) the expediency of using their elective franchise; and of making an independent use of the same. We wish them not to become the tools of party.

And as much time is frequently lost, and wrong principles instilled, by the perusal of works of trivial importance, we shall consider it a part of our duty to recommend to our young readers, such authors as will not only enlarge their stock of useful knowledge, but such as will also serve to stimulate them to higher attainments in science.

We trust also, that through the columns of the FREEDOM'S JOURNAL, many practical pieces, having for their bases, the improvement of our brethren, will be presented to them, from the pens of many of our respected friends, who have kindly promised their assistance.

It is our earnest wish to make our Journal a medium of intercourse between our brethren in the different states of this great confederacy: that through its columns an expression of our sentiments, on many interesting subjects which concern us, may be offered to the publick: that plans which apparently are beneficial may be candidly discussed and properly weighed; if worth, receive our cordial approbation; if not, our marked disapprobation.

Useful knowledge of every kind, and everything that relates to Africa, shall find a ready admission into our columns; and as that vast continent becomes daily more known, we trust that many things will come to light, proving that the natives of it are neither so ignorant nor stupid as they have generally been supposed to be.

And while these important subjects shall occupy the columns of the FREEDOM'S JOURNAL, we would not be unmindful of our brethren who are still in the iron fetters of bondage. They are our kindred by all the ties of nature; and though but little can be effected by us, still let our sympathies be poured forth and our prayers in their behalf, ascend to Him who is able to succour them.

From the press and the pulpit we have suffered much by being incorrectly represented. Men whom we equally love and admire have not hesitated to represent us disadvantageously, without becoming personally acquainted with the true state of things, nor discerning between virtue and vice among us. The virtuous part of our people feel themselves sorely aggrieved under the existing state of things—they are not appreciated.

Our vices and our degradation are ever arrayed against us, but our virtues are passed by unnoticed. And what is still more lamentable, our friends, to whom we concede all the principles of humanity and religion, from these very causes seem to have fallen into the current of popular feeling and are imperceptibly floating on the stream-actually living in the practice of prejudice, while they abjure it in theory, and feel it not in their hearts. Is it not very desirable that such should know more of our actual condition; and of our efforts and feelings, that in forming or advocating plans for our amelioration, they may do it more understandingly? In the spirit of candor and humility we intend by a simple representation of facts to lay our case before the public, with a view to arrest the progress of prejudice, and to shield ourselves against the consequent evils. We wish to conciliate all and to irritate none, yet we must be firm and unwavering in our principles, and persevering in our efforts.

If ignorance, poverty and degradation have hitherto been our unhappy lot; has the Eternal decree gone forth, that our race alone are to remain in this state, while knowledge and civilization are shedding their enlivening rays over the rest of the human family? The recent travels of Denham and Clapperton in the interior of Africa, and the interesting narrative which they have published; the establishment of the republic of Haiti after years of sanguinary warfare; its subsequent progress in all the arts of civilization; and the advancement of liberal ideas in South America, where despotism has given place to free governments, and where many of our brethren now fill important civil and military stations, prove the contrary.

The interesting fact that there are FIVE HUNDRED THOUSAND free persons of colour, one half of whom might peruse, and the whole be benefitted by the publication of the Journal; that no publication, as yet, has been devoted exclusively to their improvement—that many selections from approved standard authors, which are within the reach of few, may occasionally be made—and more important still, that this large body of our citizens have no public channel—all serve to prove the real necessity, at present, for the appearance of the FREEDOM'S JOURNAL.

It shall ever be our desire so to conduct the editorial department of our paper as to give offence to none of our patrons; as nothing is farther from us than to make it the advocate of any partial views, either in politics or religion. What few days we can number, have been devoted to the improvement of our brethren; and it is our earnest wish that the remainder may be spent in the same delightful service.

In conclusion, whatever concerns us as a people, will ever find a ready admission into the FREEDOM'S JOURNAL, interwoven with all the principal news of the day.

And while every thing in our power shall be performed to support the character of our Journal, we would respectfully invite our numerous friends to assist by their communications, and our coloured brethren to strengthen our hands by their subscriptions, as our labour is one of common cause, and worthy of their consideration and support. And we most earnestly solicit the latter, that if at any time we should seem to be zealous, or too pointed in the inculcation of any important lesson, they will remember, that they are equally interested in the cause in which we are engaged, and attribute our zeal to the peculiarities of our situation; and our earnest engagedness in their well-being.

## THE LIBERATOR: THE MOST FAMOUS ABOLITIONIST NEWSPAPER IN THE UNITED STATES (1831)

*The Liberator was published weekly in Boston, Massachusetts from 1831 to 1865. Most of its subscribers were blacks, though its founder, William L. Garrison ("I have a system to destroy, and I have no time to waste") was himself white.*

*A key organ of abolitionist propaganda, The Liberator succeeded in shifting the sentiment of much of the nation away from the notion of gradual emancipation, and more toward that of total abolition.*

... During my recent tour for the purpose of exciting the minds of the people by a series of discourses on the subject of slavery, every place that I visited gave fresh evidence of the fact, that a greater revolution in public sentiment was to be effected in the free states—and particularly in New England—than at the south. I found contempt more bitter, opposition more active, detraction more relentless, prejudice more stubborn, and apathy more frozen, than among slave owners themselves. Of course, there were individual exceptions to the contrary. This state of things afflicted, but did not dishearten me. I determined, at every hazard, to lift up the standard of emancipation in the eyes of the nation, within sight of Bunker Hill and in the birth place of liberty. That standard is now unfurled; and long may if float, unhurt by the spoliations of time or the missiles of a desperate foe—yea, till every chain be broken, and every bondman set free! Let Southern oppressors tremble—let their secret abettors tremble—let their Northern apologists tremble—let all the enemies of the persecuted blacks tremble—

I am aware, that many object to the severity of my language; but is there not cause for severity? I will be as harsh as truth, and as uncompromising as justice. On this subject, I do not wish to think, or speak, or write, with moderation. No! No! Tell a man whose house is on fire, to give a moderate alarm; tell him to moderately rescue his wife from the hands of the ravisher; tell the mother to gradually extricate her babe from the fire into which it has fallen;—but urge me not to use moderation in a cause like the present. I am in earnest—I will not equivocate—I will not excuse—I will not retreat a single inch—AND I WILL BE HEARD...

WILLIAM LLOYD GARRISON

*Foes cartooned William Lloyd Garrison as helping southern secessionists destroy the Union.*

## INDICTMENT OF SLAVERY (1839)

*In 1839, The American Anti-Slavery Society compiled a massive portfolio of testimony which sought to document the inhumanities and illegalities of slavery. The introduction was written much as a prosecutor would address a court. The following introduction, by Theodore D. Weld of New York, stirred abolitionist sentiments in the North while being attacked as demagogic in the South.*

READER, YOU *are* empanelled as a juror to try a plain case and bring in an honest verdict. The question at issue is not one of law, but of fact—"What is the actual condition of slaves in the United States?"

A plainer case never went to a jury. Look at it. TWENTY SEVEN HUNDRED THOUSAND PERSONS in this country, men, women, and children, are in SLAVERY. Is slavery, as a condition for human beings, good, bad, or indifferent?

We submit the question without argument. You have common sense, and conscience, and a human heart—pronounce upon it. You have a wife, or a husband, a child, a father, a mother, a brother or a sister—make the case your own, make it theirs, and bring in your verdict.

The case of Human Rights against Slavery has been adjudicated in the court of conscience times innumerable. The same verdict has always been rendered—"Guilty;" the same sentence has always been pronounced "Let it be accursed;" and human nature, with her million echoes, has rung it round the world in every language under heaven. "Let it be accursed..."

As slaveholders and their apologists are volunteer wit-

witnesses in their own cause, and are flooding the world with testimony that their slaves are kindly treated; that they are well fed, well clothed, well housed, well lodged, moderately worked, and bountifully provided with all things needful for their comfort, we propose,—first, to disprove their assertions by the testimony of a multitude of impartial witnesses, and then to put slaveholders themselves through a course of cross-questioning which will draw their condemnation out of their own mouths.

We will prove that the slaves in the United States are treated with barbarous inhumanity; that they are overworked, underfed, wretchedly clad and lodged, and have insufficient sleep; that they are often made to wear round their necks iron collars armed with prongs, to drag heavy chains and weights at their feet while working in the field, and to wear yokes and bells, and iron horns; that they are often kept confined in the stocks day and night for weeks together, made to wear gags in their mouths for hours or days, have some of their front teeth torn out or broken off, that they may be easily detected when they run away; that they are frequently flogged with terrible severity, have red pepper rubbed into their lacerated flesh, and hot brine, spirits of turpentine, &c., poured over the gashes to increase the torture; that they are often stripped naked, their backs and limbs cut with knives, bruised and mangled by scores and hundreds of blows with the paddle, and terribly torn by the claws of cats, drawn over them by their tormentors; that they are often hunted with blood-hounds and shot down like beasts, or torn in pieces by dogs; that they are often suspended by the arms and whipped and beaten till they faint, and when revived by restoratives, beaten again till they faint, and sometimes till they die; that their ears are often cut off, their eyes knocked out, their bones broken, their flesh branded with red hot irons; that they are maimed, mutilated and burned to death, over slow fires. All these things, and more, and worse, we shall *prove*...

We shall show, not merely that such deeds are committed, but that they are frequent; not done in corners, but before the sun; not in one of the slave states, but in all of them; not perpetrated by brutal overseers and drivers merely, but by magistrates, by legislators, by professors of religion, by preachers of the gospel, by governors of states, by "gentlemen of property and standing," and by delicate females moving in the "highest circles of society."

We know, full well, the outcry that will be made by multitudes, at these declarations; the multiform cavils, the flat denials, the charges of "exaggeration" and "falsehood" so often bandied, the sneers of affected contempt at the credulity that can believe such things, and the rage and imprecations against those who give them currency. We know, too, the threadbare sophistries by which slaveholders and their apologists seek to evade such testimony. If they admit that such deeds are committed, they tell us that they are exceedingly rare, and therefore furnish no grounds for judging of the general treatment of slaves; that occasionally a brutal wretch in the *free* states barbarously butchers his wife, but that no one thinks of inferring from that, the general treatment of wives at the North and West.

They tell us, also, that the slaveholders of the South are proverbially hospitable, kind, and generous, and it is incredible that they can perpetrate such enormities upon human beings; further, that it is absurd to suppose that they would thus injure their own property, that self-interest would prompt them to treat their slaves with kindness, as none but fools and madmen wantonly destroy their own property; further, that Northern visitors at the South come back testifying to the kind treatment of the slaves, and that the slaves themselves corroborate such representations. All these pleas, and scores of others, are bruited in every corner of the free States; and who that hath eyes to see, has not sickened at the blindness that saw not, at the palsy of heart that felt not, or at the cowardice and sycophancy that dared not expose such shallow fallacies. We are not to be turned from our purpose by such vapid babblings. In their appropriate places, we propose to consider these objections and various others, and to show their emptiness and folly.

*Pro-slavery hoodlums destroy an abolistionist printing press.*

## THE NORTH STAR: THE ABOLITIONIST ORGAN OF FREDERICK DOUGLASS (1847)

*Frederick Douglass, a leading Negro spokesman in the abolitionist movement, founded his newspaper on December 3, 1847 in Rochester, New York. Douglass conceded in his first editorial that he would plead the cause of the Negro before all else, but did not exclude the possibility that several other major topics might also occupy the editorial spotlight from time to time.*

### To Our Oppressed Countrymen

We solemnly dedicate the *North Star* to the cause of our long oppressed and plundered fellow countrymen. May God bless the offering to your good! It shall fearlessly asset your rights, faithfully proclaim your wrongs, and earnestly demand for you instant and even-handed justice. Giving no quarter to slavery at the South, it will hold no truce with oppressors at the North. While it shall boldly advocate emancipation for our enslaved brethren, it will omit no opportunity to gain for the nominally free, complete enfranchisement. Every effort to injure or degrade you or your cause—originating wheresoever, or with whomsoever—shall find in it a constant, unswerving and inflexible foe.

We shall energetically assail the ramparts of Slavery and Prejudice, be they composed of church or state, and seek the destruction of every refuge of lies, under which tyranny may aim to conceal and protect itself...

While our paper shall be mainly Anti-Slavery, its columns shall be freely opened to the candid and decorous discussions of all measures and topics of a moral and humane character, which may serve to enlighten, improve, and elevate mankind. Temperance, Peace, Capital Punishment, Education,—all subjects claiming the attention of the public mind may be freely and fully discussed here.

While advocating your rights, the *North Star* will strive to throw light on your duties: while it will not fail to make known your virtues, it will not shun to discover your faults. To be faithful to our foes it must be faithful to ourselves, in all things.

Remember that we are one, that our cause is one, and that we must help each other, if we would succeed. We have drunk to the dregs the bitter cup of slavery; we have worn the heavy yoke; we have sighed beneath our bonds, and writhed beneath the bloody lash;—cruel mementoes of our oneness are indelibly marked in our living flesh. We are one with you under the ban of prejudice and proscription—one with you under the slander of inferiority—one with you in social and political disfranchisement. What you suffer, we suffer; what you endure, we endure. We are indissolubly united, and must fall or flourish together...

We shall be the advocates of learning, from the very want of it, and shall most readily yield the deference due to men of education among us; but shall always bear in mind to accord most merit to those who have labored hardest, and overcome most, in the praiseworthy pursuit of knowledge, remembering "that the whole need not a physician, but they that are sick," and that "the strong ought to bear the infirmities of the weak."

Brethren, the first number of the paper is before you. It is dedicated to your cause. Through the kindness of our friends in England, we are in possession of an excellent printing press, types, and all other materials necessary for printing a paper. Shall this gift be blest to our good, or shall it result in our injury? It is for you to say. With your aid, cooperation and assistance, our enterprise will be entirely successful. We pledge ourselves that no effort on our part shall be wanting, and that no subscriber shall lose his subscription—"The *North Star* Shall Live."

## THE COMPROMISE OF 1850

*The Compromise of 1850 was occasioned by a revival of the slavery question pursuant to the Mexican War. Henry Clay, chief architect of the compromise, made five key points upon which the document is based:*

1. *That California be admitted to the Union as a free state.*
2. *That territorial governments be established in New Mexico and Utah without any immediate decision as to whether they would be slave or free.*
3. *That a stricter fugitive slave law be passed.*
4. *That the slave trade be abolished in the District of Columbia.*
5. *That the Texas-New Mexico boundary be settled, and that the federal government liquidate any debts incurred by Texas.*

### Clay's Resolutions
### January 29, 1850

1. *Resolved,* That California, with suitable boundaries, ought, upon her application to be admitted as one of the States of this Union, without the imposition by Congress of any restriction in respect to the exclusion or introduction of slavery within those boundaries.

2. *Resolved,* That as slavery does not exist by law, and is not likely to be introduced into any of the territory acquired by the United States from the republic of Mexico, it is inexpedient for Congress to provide by law either for its introduction into, or exclusion from, any part of the said territory; and that appropriate territorial governments ought to be estab-

lished by Congress in all of the said territory, not assigned as the boundaries of the proposed State of California, without the adoption of any restriction or condition on the subject of slavery.

3. *Resolved,* That the western boundary of the State of Texas ought to be fixed on the Rio del Norte, commencing one marine league from its mouth, and running up that river to the southern line of New Mexico; thence with that line eastwardly, and so continuing in the same direction to the line as established between the United States and Spain, excluding any portion of New Mexico, whether lying on the east or west of that river.

4. *Resolved,* That it be proposed to the State of Texas, that the United States will provide for the payment of all that portion of the legitimate and bona fide public debt of that State contracted prior to its annexation to the United States, and for which the duties on foreign imports were pledged by the said State to its creditors, not exceeding the sum of_____dollars, in consideration of the said duties so pledged having been no longer applicable to that object after the said annexation, but having thenceforward become payable to the United States; and upon the condition, also, that the said State of Texas shall, by some solemn and authentic act of her legislature or of a convention, relinquish to the United States any claim which it has to any part of New Mexico.

5. *Resolved,* That it is inexpedient to abolish slavery in the District of Columbia whilst that institution continues to exist in the State of Maryland, without the consent of that State, without the consent of the people of the District, and without just compensation to the owners of slaves within the District.

6. *But, resolved,* That it is expedient to prohibit, within the District, the slave trade in slaves brought into it from States or places beyond the limits of the District, either to be sold therein as merchandise, or to be transported to other markets without the District of Columbia.

7. *Resolved,* That more effectual provision ought to be made by law, according to the requirement of the constitution, for the restitution and delivery of persons bound to service or labor in any State, who may escape into any other State or Territory in the Union. And,

8. *Resolved,* That Congress has no power to promote or obstruct the trade in slaves between the slaveholding States; but that the admission or exclusion of slaves brought from one into another of them, depends exclusively upon their own particular laws.

## THE TEXAS AND NEW MEXICO ACT (1850)

*An Act proposing to the State of Texas the Establishment of her Northern and Western Boundaries, the Relinquishment by the said State of all Territory claimed by her exterior to said Boundaries, and of all her claims upon the United States, and to establish a territorial Government for New Mexico.*

FIRST. The State of Texas will agree that her boundary on the north shall commence at the point at which the meridian of one hundred degrees west from Greenwich is intersected by the parallel of thirty-six degrees thirty minutes north latitude, and shall run from said point due west to the meridian of one hundred and three degrees west from Greenwich; thence her boundary shall run due south to the thirty-second degree of north latitude; thence on the said parallel of thirty-two degrees of north latitude to the Rio Bravo del Norte, and thence with the channel of said river to the Gulf of Mexico.

SECOND. The State of Texas cedes to the United States all her claim to territory exterior to the limits and boundaries which she agrees to establish by the first article of this agreement.

THIRD. The State of Texas relinquishes all claim upon the United States for liability of the debts of Texas, and for compensation or indemnity for the surrender to the United States of her ships, forts, arsenals, custom-houses, custom-house revenue, arms and munitions of war, and public buildings with their sites, which became the property of the United States at the time of the annexation.

FOURTH. The United States, in consideration of said establishment of boundaries, cession of claim to territory, and relinquishment of claims, will pay to the State of Texas the sum of ten millions of dollars in a stock bearing five per cent interest, and redeemable at the end of fourteen years, the interest payable half-yearly at the treasury of the United States...

*A slave attempting to gain his freedom through flight.*

## FUGITIVE SLAVE ACT (1850]

*An Act to amend, and supplementary to, the Act entitled "An Act respecting Fugitives from Justice, and Persons escaping from the Service of their Masters," approved—[February 12,1793].*

SEC. 5. That it shall be the duty of all marshals and deputy marshals to obey and execute all warrants and precepts issued under the provisions of this act, when to them directed; and should any marshal or deputy marshal refuse to receive such warrant, or other process, when tendered, or to use all proper means diligently to execute the same, he shall, on conviction thereof, be fined in the sum of one thousand dollars, to the use of such claimant,... and after arrest of such fugitive, by such marshal or his deputy, or whilst at any time in his custody under the provisions of this act, should such fugitive escape, whether with or without the assent of such marshal or his deputy, such marshal shall be liable, on his official bond, to be prosecuted for the benefit of such claimant, for the full value of the service or labor of said fugitive in the State, Territory, or District whence he escaped: and the better to enable the said commissioners, when thus appointed, to execute their duties faithfully and efficiently, in conformity with the requirements of the Constitution of the United States and of this act, they are hereby authorized and empowered, within their counties respectively, to appoint,... any one or more suitable persons, from time to time, to execute all such warrants and other process as may be issued by them in the lawful performance of their respective duties;

SEC. 6. That when a person held to service or labor in any State or Territory of the United States, has heretofore or shall hereafter escape into another State or Territory of the United States, the person or persons to whom such service or labor may be due,... may pursue and reclaim such fugitive person, either by procuring a warrant from some one of the courts, judges, or commissioners aforesaid, of the proper circuit, district, or county, for the apprehension of such fugitive from service or labor, or by seizing and arresting such fugitive, where the same can be done without process, and by taking, or causing such person to be taken, forthwith before such court, judge, or commissioner, whose duty it shall be to hear and determine the case of such claimant in a summary manner; and upon satisfactory proof being made, by deposition or affidavit, in writing, to be taken and certified by such court, judge, or commissioner, or by other satisfactory testimony, duly taken and certified by some court,... and with proof, also by affidavit, of the identity of the person whose service or labor is claimed to be due as aforesaid, that the person so arrested does in fact owe service or labor to the person or persons claiming him or her, in the State or Territory from which such fugitive may have escaped as aforesaid, and that said person escaped, to make out and deliver to such claimant, his or her agent or attorney, a certificate setting forth the substantial facts as to the service or labor due from such fugitive to the claimant, and of his or her escape from the State or Territory in which he or she was arrested, with authority to such claimant,... to use such reasonable force and restraint as may be necessary, under the circumstances of the case, to take and remove such fugitive person back to the State or Territory whence he or she may have escaped as aforesaid.

SEC. 7. That any persons who shall knowingly and willingly obstruct, hinder, or prevent such claimant, his agent or attorney, or any person or persons lawfully assisting him, her, or them, from arresting such a fugitive from service or labor, either with or without process as aforesaid, or shall rescue, or attempt to rescue, such fugitive from service or labor, from the custody of such claimant,... or other person or persons lawfully assisting as aforesaid, when so arrested,... or shall aid, abet, or assist such person so owing service or labor as aforesaid, directly or indirectly, to escape from such claimant,... or shall harbor or conceal such fugitive, so as to prevent the discovery and arrest of such person, after notice or knowledge of the fact that such person was a fugitive from service or labor... shall, for either of said offences, be subject to a fine not exceeding one thousand dollars, and imprisonment not exceeding six months... ; and shall moreover forfeit and pay, by way of civil damages to the party injured by such illegal conduct, the sum of one thousand dollars, for each fugitive so lost as aforesaid...

SEC. 9. That, upon affidavit made by the claimant of such fugitive,... that he has reason to apprehend that such fugitive will be rescued by force from his or their possession before he can be taken beyond the limits of the State in which the arrest is made, it shall be the duty of the officer making the arrest to retain such fugitive in his custody, and to remove him to the State whence he fled, and there to deliver him to said claimant, his agent, or attorney. And to this end, the officer aforesaid is hereby authorized and required to employ so many persons as he may deem necessary to overcome such force, and to retain them in his service so long as circumstances may require.

## ACT ABOLISHING THE SLAVE TRADE IN THE DISTRICT OF COLUMBIA (1850)

*An Act to suppress the Slave Trade in the District of Columbia.*

*Be it enacted...* That from and after January 1, 1851, it shall not be lawful to bring into the District of Columbia any slave whatever, for the purpose of being sold, or for the purpose of being placed in depot, to be subsequently transferred to any other State or place to be sold as merchandize. And if any slave shall be brought into the said District by its owner, or by the authority or consent of its owner, contrary to the provisions of this act, such slave shall thereupon become liberated and free.

## WHAT TO THE SLAVES IS THE FOURTH OF JULY?: FREDERICK DOUGLASS' INDEPENDENCE DAY ADDRESS (1852)

*Perceiving full well the irony implicit in his delivering an address which commemorated the coming of independence to the United States, Frederick Douglass lost little time in laying bare the contradiction inherent in allowing slavery to exist within a society professedly dedicated to individual freedom.*

**Fellow Citizens**

Pardon me, and allow me to ask, why am I called upon to speak here today? What have I or those I represent to do with your national independence? Are the great principles of political freedom and of natural justice, embodied in that Declaration of Independence, extended to us? And am I, therefore, called upon to bring our humble offering to the national altar, and to confess the benefits, and express devout gratitude for the blessings resulting from your independence to us?

Would to God, both for your sakes and ours, that an affirmative answer could be truthfully returned to these questions. Then would my task be light, and my burden easy and delightful. For who is there so cold that a nation's sympathy could not warm him? Who so obdurate and dead to the claims of gratitude, that would not thankfully acknowledge such priceless benefits? Who so stolid and selfish that would not give his voice to swell the hallelujahs of a nation's jubilee, when the chains of servitude had been torn from his limbs? I am not that man...

I am not included within the pale of this glorious anniversary! Your high independence only reveals the immeasurable distance between us. The blessings in which you this day rejoice are not enjoyed in common. The rich inheritance of justice, liberty, prosperity, and independence bequeathed by your fathers is shared by you, not by me. The sunlight that brought life and healing to you has brought stripes and death to me. This Fourth of July is *yours,* not *mine. You* may rejoice, I must mourn. To drag a man in fetters into the grand illuminated temple of liberty, and call upon him to join you in joyous anthems, were inhuman mockery and sacrilegious irony. Do you mean, citizens, to mock me, by asking me to speak today?...

Fellow citizens, above your national, tumultuous joy, I hear the mournful wail of millions, whose chains, heavy and grievous yesterday, are today rendered more intolerable by the jubilant shouts that reach them. If I do forget, if I do not remember those bleeding children of sorrow this day, "may my right hand forget her cunning, and may my tongue cleave to the roof of my mouth!" To forget them, to pass lightly over their wrongs, and to chime in with the popular theme, would be treason most scandalous and shocking, and would make me a reproach before God and the world. My subject, then, fellow citizens, is "American Slavery." I shall see this day and its popular characteristics from the slave's point of view. Standing here, identified with the American bondman, making his wrongs mine, I do not hesitate to declare, with all my soul, that the character and conduct of this nation never looked blacker to me than on this Fourth of July. Whether we turn to the declarations of the past, or to the professions of the present, the conduct of the nation seems equally hideous and revolting. America is false to the past, false to the present, and solemnly binds herself to be false to the future. Standing with God and the crushed and bleeding slave on this occasion, I will, in the name of humanity, which is outraged, in the name of liberty, which is fettered, in the name of the Constitution and the Bible, which are disregarded and trampled upon, dare to call in question and to denounce, with all the emphasis I can command, everything that serves to perpetuate slavery—the great sin and shame of America! "I will not equivocate; I will not excuse"; I will use the severest language I can command, and yet not one word shall escape me that any man, whose judgment is not blinded by prejudice, or who is not at heart a slave-holder, shall not confess to be right and just.

But I fancy I hear some of my audience say it is just in this circumstance that you and your brother Abolitionists fail to make a favorable impression on the public mind. Would you argue more and denounce less, would you persuade more and rebuke less, your cause would be much more likely to succeed. But, I submit, where all is plain there is nothing to be argued. What point in the anti-slavery creed would you have me argue? On what branch of the subject do the people of this country need light? Must I undertake to prove that the slave is a man? That point is conceded already. Nobody doubts it. The slave-holders themselves acknowledge it in the enactment of laws for their government. They acknowledge it when they punish disobedience on the part of the slave. There are seventy-two crimes in the State of Virginia, which, if committed by a black man (no matter how ignorant he be), subject him to the punishment of death; while only two of these same crimes will subject a white man to like punishment. What is this but the acknowledgment that the slave is a moral, intellectual, and responsible being? The manhood of the slave is conceded. It is admitted in the fact that Southern statute-books are covered with enactments, forbidding, under severe fines and penalties, the teaching of the slave to read and write. When you can point to any such laws in reference to the beasts of the field, then I may consent to argue the manhood of the slave. When the dogs in your streets, when the fowls of the air, when the cattle on your hills, when the fish of the sea, and the reptiles that crawl, shall be unable to distinguish the slave from a brute, then I will argue with you that the slave is a man!

*As a fugitive slave, Frederick Douglass held uncommon views about Independence Day.*

For the present it is enough to affirm the equal manhood of the Negro race. Is it not astonishing that, while we are plowing, planting, and reaping, using all kinds of mechanical tools, erecting houses, constructing bridges, building ships, working in metals of brass, iron, copper, silver, and gold; that while we are reading, writing, and cyphering, acting as clerks, merchants, and secretaries, having among us lawyers, doctors, ministers, poets, authors, editors, orators, and teachers; that while we are engaged in all the enterprises common to other men—digging gold in California, capturing the whale in the Pacific, feeding sheep and cattle on the hillside, living, moving, acting, thinking, planning, living in families as husbands, wives, and children, and above all, confessing and worshipping the Christian God, and looking hopefully for life and immortality beyond the grave—we are called upon to prove that we are men?

Would you have me argue that man is entitled to liberty? That he is the rightful owner of his own body? You have already declared it. Must I argue the wrongfulness of slavery? Is that a question for republicans? Is it to be settled by the rules of logic and argumentation, as a matter beset with great difficulty, involving a doubtful application of the principle of justice, hard to understand? How should I look today in the presence of Americans, dividing and subdividing a discourse, to show that men have a natural right to freedom, speaking of it relatively and positively, negatively and affirmatively? To do so would be to make myself ridiculous, and to offer an insult to your understanding. There is not a man beneath the canopy of heaven who does not know that slavery is wrong *for him.*

What! Am I to argue that it is wrong to make men brutes, to rob them of their liberty, to work them without wages, to keep them ignorant of their relations to their fellow men, to beat them with sticks, to flay their flesh with the last, to load their limbs with irons, to hunt them with dogs, to sell them at auction, to sunder their families, to knock out their teeth, to burn their flesh, to starve them into obedience and submission to their masters? Must I argue that a system thus marked with blood and stained with pollution is wrong? No; I will not. I have better employment for my time and strength than such arguments would imply.

What, then, remains to be argued? Is it that slavery is not divine; that God did not establish it; that our doctors of divinity are mistaken? There is blasphemy in the thought. That which is inhuman cannot be divine. Who can reason on such a proposition? They that can, may; I cannot. The time for such argument is past.

At a time like this, scorching irony, not convincing argument, is needed. Oh! had I the ability, and could I reach the nation's ear, I would today pour out a fiery stream of biting ridicule, blasting reproach, withering sarcasm, and stern rebuke. For it is not light that is needed, but fire; it is not the gentle shower, but thunder. We need the storm, the whirlwind, and the earthquake. The feeling of the nation must be quickened; the conscience of the nation must be roused; the propriety of the nation must be startled; the hypocrisy of the nation must be exposed; and its crimes against God and man must be denounced.

What to the American slave is your Fourth of July? I answer, a day that reveals to him more than all other days of the year, the gross injustice and cruelty to which he is the constant victim. To him your celebration is a sham; your boasted liberty an unholy license; your national greatness, swelling vanity; your sounds of rejoicing are empty and heartless; your denunciation of tyrants, brass-fronted impudence; your shouts of liberty and equality, hollow mockery; your prayers and hymns, your sermons and thanksgivings, with all your religious parade and solemnity, are to him mere bombast, fraud, deception, impiety, and hypocrisy—a thin veil to cover up crimes which would disgrace a nation of savages. There is not a nation of the earth guilty of practices more shocking and bloody than are the people of these United States at this very hour.

Go where you may, search where you will, roam through all the monarchies and despotisms of the Old World, travel through South America, search out every abuse and when you have found the last, lay your facts by the side of the every-day practices of this nation, and you will say with me that, for revolting barbarity and shameless hypocrisy, America reigns without a rival.

## THE KANSAS-NEBRASKA ACT (1854)

*The Kansas-Nebraska Act repealed the Missouri Compromise, placing in the hands of the territories themselves the ultimate decision as to whether they would be slave or free.*

### An Act to Organize the Territories of Nebraska and Kansas

*Be it enacted...* That all that part of the territory of the United States included within the following limits, except such portions thereof as are hereinafter expressly exempted from the operations of this act, to wit: beginning at a point in the Missouri River where the fortieth parallel of north latitude crosses the same; thence west on said parallel to the east boundary of the Territory of Utah, on the summit of the Rocky Mountains; thence on said summit northward to the forty-ninth parallel of north latitude; thence east on said parallel to the western boundary of the territory of Minnesota; thence southward on said boundary to the Missouri River; thence down the main channel of said river to the place of beginning, be, and the same is hereby, created into a temporary government by the name of the Territory of Nebraska; and when admitted as a State or States, the said Territory, or any portion of the same, shall be received into the Union with or without slavery, as their constitution may prescribe at the time of their admission:...

SEC. 14. *And be it further enacted,...* That the Constitution, and all laws of the United States which are not locally inapplicable, shall have the same force and effect within the said Territory of Nebraska as elsewhere within the United States, except the eighth section of the act preparatory to the admission of Missouri into the Union, approved March 6, 1820, which, being inconsistent with the principle of nonintervention by Congress with slavery in the States and Territories, as recognized by the legislation of eighteen hundred and fifty, commonly called the Compromise Measures, is hereby declared inoperative and void; it being the true intent and meaning of this act not to legislate slavery into any Territory or State, nor to exclude it therefrom, but to leave the people thereof perfectly free to form and regulate their domestic institutions in their own way, subject only to the Constitution of the United States: *Provided,* That nothing herein contained shall be construed to revive or put in force any law or regulation which may have existed prior to the act of March 6, 1820, either protecting, establishing, prohibiting, or abolishing slavery...

SEC. 19. *And be it further enacted,* That all that part of the Territory of the United States included within the following limits, except such portions thereof as are hereinafter expressly exempted from the operations of this act, to wit, beginning at a point on the western boundary of the State of Missouri, where the thirty-seventh parallel of north latitude crosses the same; thence west on said parallel to the eastern boundary of New Mexico; thence north on said boundary to latitude thirty-eight; thence following said boundary westward to the east boundary of the Territory of Utah, on the summit of the Rocky Mountains; thence northward on said summit to the fortieth parallel of latitude; thence east on said parallel to the western boundary of the State of Missouri; thence south with the western boundary of said state to the place of beginning, be, and the same is hereby, created into a temporary government by the name of the Territory of Kansas; and when admitted as a State or States, the said Territory, or any portion of the same, shall be received into the Union with or without slavery, as their constitution may prescribe at the time of their admission:...

*(Left) In Kansas, ballot boxes being stuffed with fraudulent votes. ( right) Stephen Douglas as a squatter prepared to defend slavery .*

## THE EMANCIPATION PROCLAMATION (1863)

*The Emancipation Proclamation, drafted in 1862 and put into effect on January 1, 1863, freed the slaves in those states that had seceded from the Union. All other slaves—and there were some 800,000 unaffected by the provisions of this act—were not yet free.*

### By the President of the United States of America: A Proclamation

Whereas on the 22d day of September, A.D. 1862, a proclamation was issued by the President of the United States, containing, among other things, the following, to wit:

"That on the 1st day of January, A.D. 1863, all persons held as slaves within any State or designated part of a State the people whereof shall then be in rebellion against the United States shall be then, thenceforward, and forever free; and the executive government of the United States, including the military and naval authority thereof, will recognize and maintain the freedom of such persons and will do no act or acts to repress such persons, or any of them, in any efforts they may make for their actual freedom.

"That the executive will on the 1st day of January aforesaid, by proclamation, designate the States and parts of States, if any, in which the people thereof, respectively, shall then be in rebellion against the United States; and the fact that any State or the people thereof shall on that day be in good faith represented in the Congress of the United States by members chosen thereto at elections wherein a majority of the qualified voters of such States shall have participated shall, in the absence of strong countervailing testimony, be deemed conclusive evidence that such State and the people thereof are not then in rebellion against the United States."

Now, therefore, I, Abraham Lincoln, President of the United States, by virtue of the power in me vested as Commander-in-Chief of the Army and Navy of the United States in time of actual armed rebellion against the authority and government of the United States, and as a fit and necessary war measure for suppressing said rebellion, do, on this 1st day of January, A.D. 1863, and in accordance with my purpose so to do, publicly proclaimed for the full period of one hundred days from the first day above mentioned, order and designate as the States and parts of States wherein the people thereof, respectively, are this day in rebellion against the United States the following, to wit:

Arkansas, Texas, Louisiana (except the parishes of St. Bernard, Plaquemines, Jefferson, St. John, St. Charles, St. James, Ascension, Assumption, Terrebonne, Lafourche, St. Mary, St. Martin, and Orleans, including the city of New Orleans), Mississippi, Alabama, Florida, Georgia, South Carolina, North Carolina, and Virginia (except the forty-eight counties designated as West Virginia, and also the counties of Berkeley, Accomac, Northhampton, Elizabeth City, York, Princess Anne, and Norfolk, including the cities of Norfolk and Portsmouth), and which excepted parts are for the present left precisely as if this proclamation were not issued.

And by virtue of the power and for the purpose aforesaid, I do order and declare that all persons held as slaves within said designated States and parts of States are, and henceforward shall be, free; and that the Executive Government of the United States, including the military and naval authorities thereof, will recognize and maintain the freedom of said persons.

And I hereby enjoin upon the people so declared to be free to abstain from all violence, unless in necessary self-defense; and I recommend to them that, in all cases when allowed, they labor faithfully for reasonable wages.

And I further declare and make known that such persons of suitable condition will be received into the armed service of the United States to garrison forts, positions, stations, and other places, and to man vessels of all sorts in said service.

And upon this act, sincerely believed to be an act of justice, warranted by the Constitution upon military necessity, I invoke the considerate judgment of mankind and the gracious favor of Almighty God.

*Northern soldiers read the Proclamation's message of freedom to astonished slaves throughout the South.*

## THE FREEDMEN'S BUREAU (1865)

*The Freedmen's Bureau, brought into being in 1865, was designed to provide basic health and educational services for freedmen and to administer all land abandoned in the South. The life of the bureau was extended after the war, despite the veto of President Andrew Johnson.*

### An Act to Establish a Bureau for the Relief of Freedmen and Refugees

*Be it enacted,* That there is hereby established in the War Department, to continue during the present war of rebellion, and for one year thereafter, a bureau of refugees, freedmen, and abandoned lands, to which shall be committed, as hereinafter provided, the supervision and management of all abandoned lands, and the control of all subjects relating to refugees and freedmen from rebel states, or from any district of country within the territory embraced in the operations of the army, under such rules and regulations as may be prescribed by the head of the bureau and approved by the President. The said bureau shall be under the management and control of a commissioner to be appointed by the President, by and with the advice and consent of the Senate.

SEC. 2. That the Secretary of War may direct such issues of provisions, clothing, and fuel, as he may deem needful for the immediate and temporary shelter and supply of destitute and suffering refugees and freedmen and their wives and children, under such rules and regulations as he may direct.

SEC. 3. That the President may, by and with the advice and consent of the Senate, appoint an assistant commissioner for each of the states declared to be in insurrection, not exceeding ten in number, who shall, under the direction of the commissioner, aid in the execution of the provisions of this act;... And any military officer may be detailed and assigned to duty under this act without increase of pay of allowances...

SEC. 4. That the commissioner, under the direction of the President, shall have authority to set apart, for the use of loyal refugees and freedmen, such tracts of land within the insurrectionary states as shall have been abandoned, or to which the United States shall have acquired title by confiscation or sale, or otherwise, and to every male citizen, whether refugee or freedman, as aforesaid, there shall be assigned not more than forty acres of such land, and the person to whom it was so assigned shall be protected in the use and enjoyment of the land for the term of three years at an annual rent not exceeding six per centum upon the value of such land, as it was appraised by the state authorities in the year eighteen hundred and sixty, for the purpose of taxation, and in case no such appraisal can be found, then the rental shall be based upon the estimated value of the land in said year, to be ascertained in such manner as the commissioner may by regulation prescribe. At the end of said term, or at any time during said term, the occupants of any parcels so assigned may purchase the land and receive such title thereto as the United States can convey, upon paying therefor the value of the land, as ascertained and fixed for the purpose of determining the annual rent aforesaid...

The Freedmen's Bureau sought to keep peace between bands of white southeners and former slaves.

## THE THIRTEENTH AMENDMENT (1865)

*Brief and to the point, the Thirteenth Amendment to the U.S. Constitution, ratified December 18, 1865, abolishes slavery "within the United States," thus completing the job begun by the Emancipation Proclamation.*

SEC. 1. Neither slavery nor involuntary servitude, except as a punishment for crime whereof the party shall have been duly convicted, shall exist within the United States, or any place subject to their jurisdiction.

SEC. 2. Congress shall have power to enforce this article by appropriate legislation.

## THE BLACK CODES OF MISSISSIPPI (1865)

*With emancipation many states sought to impose restrictions on blacks to prevent them from having equal social status with whites and to maintain them not only in a subordinate condition but to impose restrictions upon them not unlike those which prevailed before the Civil War. The first state to enact "Black Code Laws" was Mississippi in November 1865, just seven months after the surrender of General Lee at Appomatox Court House in Virginia. "Black Code Laws" imposed heavy penalties for "vagrancy", "insulting gestures" curfew violations and "seditious speeches." The Mississippi "Codes" forced young blacks under the age of eighteen to be apprenticed to their former owners if they were orphaned or if it were determined that their parents did not have the ability to support them, if an apprentice should leave employment without the consent of "the master" he could be pursued, captured and returned to his employer. The Mississippi laws attracted widespread criticism in the North as a strategy to negate Lincoln's Emancipation Proclamation.*

**An Act to Regulate the Relation of Master and Apprentice, as Relates to Freedmen, Free Negroes, and Mulattoes.**

SEC. 1. It shall be the duty of all sheriffs, justices of the peace, and other civil officers of the several counties in this State, to report to the probate courts of their respective counties semiannually, at the January and July terms of said courts, all freedmen, free negroes, and mulattoes, under the age of eighteen, in their respective counties, beats, or districts, who are orphans, or whose parent or parents have not the means or who refuse to provide for and support said minors; and thereupon it shall be the duty of said probate court to order the clerk of said court to apprentice said minors to some competent and suitable person on such terms as the court may direct, having a particular care to the interest of said minor: Provided, that the former owner of said minors shall have the preference when, in the opinion of the court, he or she shall be a suitable person for that purpose.

SEC. 2. The said court shall be fully satisfied that the, person or persons to whom said minor shall be apprenticed shall be a suitable person to have the charge and care of said minor, and fully to protect the interest of said minor. The said court shall require the said master or mistress to execute bond and security, payable to the State of Mississippi, conditioned that he or she shall furnish said minor with sufficient food and clothing; to treat said minor humanely; furnish medical attention in case of sickness; teach, or cause to be taught, him or her to read and write, if under fifteen years old, and will conform to any law that may be hereafter passed for the regulation of the duties and relation of master and apprentice: Provided, that said apprentice shall be bound by indenture, in case of males, until they are twenty-one years old, and in case of females until they are eighteen years old.

SEC. 3. In the management and control of said apprentices, said master or mistress shall have the power to inflict such moderate corporeal chastisement as a father or guardian is allowed to inflict on his or her child or ward at common law: Provided, that in no case shall cruel or inhuman punishment be inflicted.

SEC. 4. If any apprentice shall leave the employment of his or her master or mistress, without his or her consent, said master or mistress may pursue and recapture said apprentice, and bring him or her before any justice of the peace of the county, whose duty it shall be to remand said apprentice to the service of his or her master or mistress; and in the event of a refusal on the part of said apprentice so to return, then said justice shall commit said apprentice to the jail of said county, on failure to give bond, to the next term of the county court; and it shall be the duty of said court at the first term thereafter to investigate said case, and if the court shall be of opinion that said apprentice left the employment of his or her master or mistress without good cause, to order him or her to be punished, as provided for the punishment of hired freedmen, as may be from time to time provided for by law for desertion, until he or she shall agree to return to the service of his or her master or mistress: Provided, that the court may grant continuances as in other cases: And provided further, that if the court shall believe that said apprentice had good cause to quit his said master or mistress, the court shall discharge said apprentice from said in denture, and also enter a judgment against the master or mistress for not more than one hundred dollars, for the use and benefit of said apprentice, to be collected on execution as in other cases.

SEC. 5. If any person entice away any apprentice from his or her master or mistress, or shall knowingly employ an apprentice, or furnish him or her food or clothing without the written consent of his or her master or mistress, or shall sell or give said apprentice ardent spirits without such consent, said person so offending shall be guilty of a misdemeanor, and shall, upon conviction there of before the county court, be punished as provided for the punishment of persons enticing from their employer hired freedmen, free negroes or mulattoes.

SEC. 6. It shall be the duty of all civil officers of their respective counties to report any minors within their respective counties to said probate court who are subject to be apprenticed under the provisions of this act, from time to time as the facts may come to their knowledge, and it shall be the duty of said court from time to time as said minors shall be reported to them, or otherwise come to their knowledge, to apprentice said minors as hereinbefore provided.

SEC. 9. It shall be lawful for any freedman, free negro, or mulatto, having a minor child or children, to apprentice the said minor child or children, as provided for by this act.

SEC. 1O. In all cases where the age of the freedman, free negro, or mulatto cannot be ascertained by record testimony, the judge of the county court shall fix the age...

**An act to amend the vagrant laws of the State.**

SEC. 1. All rogues and vagabonds, idle and dissipated persons, beggars, jugglers, or persons practicing unlawful games or plays, runaways, common drunkards, common night-walkers, pilferers, lewd, wanton, or lascivious persons, in speech or behavior, common railers and brawlers, persons who neglect their calling or employment, misspend what they earn, or do not provide for the support of themselves or their families, or dependents, and all other idle and disorderly persons, including all who neglect all lawful business, habitually misspend their time by frequenting houses of ill-fame, gaming-houses, or tippling shops, shall be deemed and considered vagrants, under the provisions of this act, and upon conviction thereof shall be fined not exceeding one hundred dollars, with all accruing costs, and be imprisoned, at the discretion of the court, not exceeding ten days.

SEC. 2. All freedmen, free negroes and mulattoes in this State, over the age of eighteen years, found on the second Monday in January, 1866, or thereafter. with no lawful employment or business, or found unlawfully assembling themselves together, either in the day or night time, and all white persons assembling themselves with freedmen, free negroes or mulattoes, or usually associating with freedmen, free negroes or mulattoes, on terms of equality, or living in adultery or fornication with a freed woman, freed negro or mulatto, shall be deemed vagrants, and on conviction thereof shall be fined in a sum not exceeding, in the case of a freedman, free negro or mulatto, fifty dollars, and a white man two hundred dollars, and imprisonment at the discretion of the court, the free negro not exceeding ten days, and the white man not exceeding six months.

SEC. 3. All justices of the peace, mayors, and aldermen of incorporated towns, counties, and cities of the several counties in this State shall have jurisdiction to try all questions of vagrancy in their respective towns, counties, and cities, and it is hereby made their duty, whenever they shall ascertain that any person or persons in their respective towns, counties and cities are violating any of the provisions of this act, to have said party or parties arrested, and brought before them, and immediately investigate said charge, and, on conviction, punish said party or parties, as provided for herein. And it is hereby made the duty of all sheriffs, constables, town constables, and all such like officers, and city marshals, to report to some officer having jurisdiction all violations of any of the provisions of this act, and in case any officer shall fail or neglect any duty herein it shall be the duty of the county court to fine said officer, upon conviction, not exceeding one hundred dollars, to be paid into the county treasury for county purposes.

SEC. 4. Keepers of gaminghouses, houses of prostitution, prostitutes, public or private, and all persons who derive their chief support in the employments that militate against good morals, or against law, shall be deemed and held to be vagrants.

SEC. 5. All fines and forfeitures collected under the provisions of this act shall be paid into the county treasury for general county purposes, and in case of any freedman, free negro or mulatto shall fail for five days after the imposition of any fine or forfeiture upon him or her for violation of any of the provisions of this act to pay the same, that it shall be, and is hereby, made the duty of the sheriff of the proper county to hire out said freedman, free negro or mulatto, to any person who will, for the shortest period of service, pay said fine and forfeiture and all costs: Provided, a preference shall be given to the employer, if there be one, in which case the employer shall be entitled to deduct and retain the amount so paid from the wages of such freedman, free negro or mulatto, then due or to become due; and in case said freedman, free negro or mulatto cannot hire out, he or she may be dealt with as a pauper.

SEC. 6. The same duties and liabilities existing among white persons of this State shall attach to freedmen, free negroes or mulattoes, to support their indigent families and all colored paupers; and that in order to secure a support for such indigent freedmen, free negroes, or mulattoes, it shall be lawful, and is hereby made the duty of the county police of each county in this State, to levy a poll or capitation tax on each and every freedman, free negro, or mulatto, between the ages of eighteen and sixty years, not to exceed the sum of one dollar annually to each person so taxed, which tax, when collected, shall be paid into the county treasurer's hands, and constitute a fund to be called the Freedman's Pauper Fund, which shall be applied by the commissioners of the poor for the maintenance of the poor of the freedmen, free negroes and mulattoes of this State, under such regulations as may be established by the boards of county police in the respective counties of this State.

SEC. 7. If any freedman, free negro, or mulatto shall fail or refuse to pay any tax levied according to the provisions of the sixth section of this act, it shall be *prima facie* evidence of vagrancy, and it shall be the duty of the sheriff to arrest such freedman, free negro, or mulatto, or such person refusing or neglecting to pay such tax, and proceed at once to hire for the shortest time such delinquent taxpayer to any one who will

*A political cartoon showing White Leaguers keeping blacks from voting.*

pay the said tax, with accruing costs, giving preference to the employer, if there be one.

SEC. 8. Any person feeling himself or herself aggrieved by judgment of any justice of the peace, mayor, or alderman in cases arising under this act, may within five days appeal to the next term of the county court of the proper county, upon giving bond and security in a sum not less than twenty-five dollars nor more than one hundred and fifty dollars, conditioned to appear and prosecute said appeal, and abide by the judgment of the county court; and said appeal shall be tried *de novo* in the county court, and the decision of the said court shall be final...

**An act to confer civil rights on freedmen, and for other purposes.**

SEC. 1. All freedmen, free negroes and mulattoes may sue and be sued, implead and be impleaded, in all the courts of law and equity of this State, and may acquire personal property, and chooses in action, by descent or purchase, and may dispose of the same in the same manner and to the same extent that white persons may: Provided, That the provisions of this section shall not be so construed as to allow any freedman, free negro or mulatto to rent or lease any lands or tenements except in incorporated cities or towns, in which places the corporate authorities shall control the same.

SEC. 2. All freedmen, free negroes and mulattoes may intermarry with each other, in the same manner and under the same regulations that are provided by law for white persons: Provided, that the clerk of probate shall keep separate records of the same.

SEC. 3. All freedmen, free negroes or mulattoes who do now and have herebefore lived and cohabited together as husband and wife shall be taken and held in law as legally married, and the issue shall be taken and held as legitimate for all purposes; and it shall not be lawful for any freedman, free negro or mulatto to intermarry with any white person; nor for any white person to intermarry with any freedman, free negro or mulatto; and any person who shall so intermarry shall be deemed guilty of felony, and on conviction thereof shall be confined in the State penitentiary for life; and those shall be deemed freedmen, free negroes and mulattoes who are of pure negro blood, and those descended from a negro to the third generation, inclusive, though one ancestor in each generation may have been a white person.

SEC. 4. In addition to cases in which freedmen, free negroes and mulattoes are now by law competent witnesses, freedmen, free negroes or mulattoes shall be competent in civil cases, when a party or parties to the suit, either plaintiff or plaintiffs, defendant or defendants; also in cases where freedmen, free negroes and mulattoes is or are either plaintiff or plaintiffs, defendant or defendants. They shall also be competent witnesses in all criminal prosecutions where the crime charged is alleged to have been committed by a white person upon or against the person or property of a freedman, free negro or mulatto: Provided, that in all cases said witnesses shall be examined in open court, on the stand; except, however, they may be examined before the grand jury, and shall in all cases be subject to the rules and tests of the common law as to competency and credibility.

SEC. 5. Every freedman, free negro and mulatto shall, on the second Monday of January, one thousand eight hundred and sixty-six, and annually thereafter, have a lawful home or employment, and shall have written evidence thereof as follows, to wit: if living in any incorporated city, town, or village, a license from the mayor thereof; and if living outside of an incorporated city, town, or village, from the member of the board of police of his beat, authorizing him or her to do irregular and job work; or a written contract, as provided in Section 6 in this act; which license may be revoked for cause at any time by the authority granting the same

SEC. 6. All contracts for labor made with freedmen, free negroes and mulattoes for a longer period than one month shall be in writing, and a duplicate, attested and read to said freedman, free negro or mulatto by a beat, city or county officer, or two disinterested white persons of the county in which the labor is to be performed, of which each party shall have one: and said contracts shall be taken and held as entire contracts, and if the laborer shall quit the service of the employer before the expiration of his term of service, without good cause, he shall forfeit his wages for that year up to the time of quitting.

SEC. 7. Every civil officer shall, and every person may, arrest and carry back to his or her legal employer any freedman, free negro, or mulatto who shall have quit the service of his or her employer before the expiration of his or her term of service without good cause; and said officer and person shall be entitled to receive for arresting and carrying back every deserting employe aforesaid the sum of five dollars, and ten cents per mile from the place of arrest to the place of delivery; and the same shall be paid by the employer, and held as a set off for so much against the wages of said deserting employe: Provided, that said arrested party, after being so returned, may appeal to the justice of the peace or member of the board of police of the county, who, on notice to the alleged employer, shall try summarily whether said appellant is legally employed by the alleged employer, and has good cause to quit said employer. Either party shall have the right of appeal to the county court, pending which the alleged deserter shall be remanded to the alleged employer or otherwise disposed of, as shall be right and just; and the decision of the county court shall be final.

SEC. 8. Upon affidavit made by the employer of any freedman. free negro or mulatto, or other credible person, before any justice of the peace or member of the board of police, that any freedman, free negro or mulatto legally employed by said employer has illegally deserted said employment, such justice of the peace or member of the board of police shall issue his warrant or warrants, returnable before himself or other such officer, to any sheriff, constable or special deputy, commanding him to arrest said deserter, and return him or her to said employer, and the like proceedings shall be had as provided in the preceding section; and it shall be lawful for any officer to whom such warrant shall be directed to execute said warrant in any county in this State; and that said warrant may be transmitted without endorsement to any like officer of another county, to be executed and returned as aforesaid; and the said employer shall pay the costs of said warrants and arrest and return, which shall be set off for so much against the wages of said deserter.

SEC. 9. If any person shall persuade or attempt to persuade, entice, or cause any freedman, free negro or mulatto to desert from the legal employment of any person before the expiration of his or her term of service, or shall knowingly employ any such deserting freedman, free negro or mulatto, or shall knowingly give or sell to any such deserting freedman, free negro or mulatto, any food, raiment, or other thing, he or she shall be guilty of a misdemeanor, and, upon conviction, shall be fined not less than twenty-five dollars and not more than two hundred dollars and costs; and if the said fine and costs shall not be immediately paid, the court shall sentence said convict to not exceeding two months imprisonment in the county jail, and he or she shall moreover be liable to the party injured in damages: Provided, if any person shall, or shall attempt to, persuade, entice, or cause any freedman, free negro or mulatto to desert from any legal employment of any person, with the view to employ said freedman, free negro or mulatto without the limits of this State, such person, on conviction, shall be fined not less than fifty dollars, and not more than five hundred dollars and costs; and if said fine and costs shall not be immediately paid, the court shall sentence said convict to not exceeding six months imprisonment in the county jail.

SEC. 1O. It shall be lawful for any freedman, free negro, or mulatto, to charge any white person, freedman, free negro or mulatto by affidavit, with any criminal offense against his or her person or property, and upon such affidavit the proper process shall be issued and executed as if said affidavit was made by a white person, and it shall be lawful for any freedman, free negro, or mulatto, in any action, suit or controversy pending, or about to be instituted in any court of law equity in this State, to make all needful and lawful affidavits as shall be necessary for the institution, prosecution or defense of such suit or controversy.

SEC. 1l. The penal laws of this State, in all cases not otherwise specially provided for, shall apply and extend to all freedmen, free negroes and mulattoes...

## THE CIVIL RIGHTS ACT (1866)

*The Civil Rights Act of 1866 was designed to protect the freedman from the Black Codes and other repressive legislation. This measure conferred citizenship on Negroes and set the stage for the more inclusive Fourteenth Amendment.*

### An Act to Protect All Persons in the United States in Their Civil Rights, and Furnish the Means of their Vindication

*Be it enacted,* That all persons born in the United States and not subject to any foreign power, excluding Indians not taxed, are hereby declared to be citizens of the United States; and such citizens, of every race and color, without regard to any previous condition of slavery or involuntary servitude, except as a punishment for crime whereof the party shall have been duly convicted, shall have the same right, in every State and Territory in the United States, to make and enforce contracts, to sue, be parties, and give evidence, to inherit, purchase, lease, sell, hold, and convey real and personal property and to full and equal benefit of all laws and proceedings for the security of person and property, as is enjoyed by white citizens, and shall be subject to like punishment, pains, and penalties, and to none other, any law, statute, ordinance, regulation, or custom, to the contrary notwithstanding.

SEC. 2. *And be it further enacted,* That any person who, under color of any law, statute, ordinance, regulation, or custom, shall subject, or cause to be subjected, any inhabitant of any State or Territory to the deprivation of any right secured or protected by this act, or to different punishment, pains, or penalties on account of such person having at any time been held in a condition of slavery or involuntary servitude, except as a punishment for crime whereof the party shall have been duly convicted, or by reason of his color or race, than is prescribed for the punishment of white persons, shall be deemed guilty of a misdemeanor, and, on conviction, shall be punished by fine not exceeding one thousand dollars, or imprisonment not exceeding one year, or both, in the discretion of the court.

SEC. 3. *And be it further enacted,* That the district courts of the United States,... shall have, exclusively of the courts of the several States, cognizance of all crimes and offences committed against the provisions of this act, and also, concurrently with the circuit court of the United States, of all causes, civil and criminal, affecting persons who are denied or cannot enforce in the courts or judicial tribunals of the State or locality where they may be any of the rights secured to them by the first section of this act...

SEC. 4. *And be it further enacted,* That the district attorneys, marshals, and deputy marshals of the United States, the commissioners appointed by the Circuit and territorial courts of the United States, with powers of arresting, imprisoning, or bailing offenders against the laws of the United States, the officers and agents of the Freedmen's Bureau, and every other officer who may be specially empowered by the President of the United States, shall be, and they are hereby, specially authorized and required, at the expense of the United States, to institute proceedings against all and every person who shall violate the provisions of this act, and cause him or them to be arrested and imprisoned, or bailed, as the case may be, for trial before such court of the United States or territorial court as by this act has cognizance of the offence...

SEC. 8. *And be it further enacted,* That whenever the President of the United States shall have reason to believe that offences have been or are likely to be committed against the provisions of this act within any judicial district, it shall be lawful for him, in his discretion, to direct the judge, marshal, and district attorney of such district to attend at such place within the district, and for such time as he may designate, for the purpose of the more speedy arrest and trial of persons charged with a violation of this act; and it shall be the duty of every judge or other officer, when any such requisition shall be received by him, to attend at the place and for the time therein designated.

SEC. 9. *And be it further enacted,* That it shall be lawful for the President of the United States, or such person as he may empower for that purpose, to employ such part of the land or naval forces of the United States, or of the militia, as shall be necessary to prevent the violation and enforce the due execution of this act.

SEC. 10. *And be it further enacted,* That upon all questions of law arising in any cause under the provisions of this act a final appeal may be taken to the Supreme Court of the United States.

## THE FREEDMEN'S BUREAU EXTENSION ACT (1866)

*The Congress, on March 3, 1865, created the Bureau of Refugees, Freedmen, and abandoned Lands—commonly known as the Freedmen's Bureau. The War Department was given the responsibility of overseeing the program which was designed to provide basic health services and educational services for freedmen and displaced whites in areas occupied by the federal forces. The bureau headed by Major General Oliver 0. Howard was to carry out the responsibilities imbued in the law and cease its function one year after the cessation of the War. In July 1866, Congress passed legislation extending the life of the Freedmen's Bureau and strengthening certain provisions. President Johnson vetoed the legislation indicating that he felt that too much power was being given to the military over civilian rule. Said the New York Tribune in an Editorial " Mr. Johnson has made a grave mistake... Hereafter whatever wrongs may be inflicted upon or indignities suffered by the Southern blacks, will be charged to the President, who has left them naked to their enemies." Congress overrode President Johnson's veto and extended the life and powers of the bureau.*

**Be it Enacted...That the Act to Establish a Bureau for the Relief of Freedmen and Refugees, Approved March Third, Eighteen Hundred and Sixty-Five, Shall Continue in Force for the Term of Two Years From and After the Passage of this Act.**

SEC. 2. The supervision and care of said bureau shall extend to all loyal refugees and freedmen, so far as the same shall be necessary to enable them as speedily as practicable to become self-supporting citizens of the United States, and to aid them in making the freedom conferred by the proclamation of the Commander-in-Chief, by emancipation under the laws of the States, and by constitutional amendment, available to them and beneficial to the Republic.

SEC. 3. The President shall, by and with the advice and consent of the Senate, appoint two assistant commissioners, in addition to those authorized by the act to which this is an amendment, who shall give like bonds and receive the same annual salaries provided in said act; and each of the assistant commissioners of the bureau shall have charge of one district containing such refugees or freedmen, to be assigned him by the Commissioner, with the approval of the President. And the Commissioner shall, under the direction of the President, and so far as the same shall be, in his judgment, necessary for the efficient and economical administration of the affairs of the bureau, appoint such agents, clerks and assistants as may be required for the proper conduct of the bureau. Military officers or enlisted men may be detailed for service and assigned to duty under this act; and the President may, if in his judgment safe and judicious so to do, detail from the Army all the officers and agents of this bureau; but no officer so assigned shall have increase of pay or allowances. Each agent or clerk, not heretofore authorized by law, not being a military officer, shall have an annual salary of not less than

$500, nor more than $1,200, according to the service required of him. And it shall be the duty of the Commissioner, when it can be done consistently with the public interest, to appoint, as assistant commissioners, agents, and clerks, such men as have proved their loyalty by faithful service in the armies of the Union during the rebellion. And all persons appointed to service under this act and the act to which this is an amendment, shall be so far deemed in the military service of the United States as to be under the military jurisdiction and entitled to the military protection of the Government while in the discharge of the duties of their office.

SEC. 4. The officers of the Veteran Reserve Corps or of the volunteer service, now on duty in the Freedmen's Bureau as assistant commissioners, agents, medical officers, or in other capacities, whose regiments or corps have been or may hereafter be mustered out of service, may be retained upon such duty as officers of said bureau, with the same compensation as is now provided by law for their respective grades; and the Secretary of War shall have power to fill vacancies until other officers can be detailed in their places without detriment to the public service.

SEC. 5. The second section of the act to which this is an amendment shall be deemed to authorize the Secretary of War to issue such medical stores or other supplies and transportation and afford such medical or other aid as here may be needful for the purposes named in said section: Provided that no person shall be deemed "destitute," "suffering," or "dependent upon the Government for support," within the meaning of this act, who is able to find employment, and could, by proper industry or exertion, avoid such destitution, suffering, or dependence.

SEC. 6. Whereas, by the provisions of [an act of February, 6, 1863] certain lands in the parishes of St. Helena and St. Luke, South Carolina, were bid in by the United States at public tax sales, and by limitation of said act the time of redemption of said lands has expired; and whereas, in accordance with instructions issued by President Lincoln on [September 16, 1863] to the United States direct tax commissioners of South Carolina, certain land bids in by the United States in the parish of St. Helena, in said State were in part sold by the said tax commissioners to "heads of families of the African race," in parcels of not more than twenty acres to each purchaser; and whereas, under the said instructions, the said tax commissioners did also set apart as "school farms" certain parcels of land in said parish, numbered on their plats from one to thirty three inclusive, making an aggregate of six thousand acres, more or less: *Therefore, be it further enacted*, That the sales made to "heads of families of the African race," under the instructions of President Lincoln to the United States direct tax commissioners for South Carolina... are hereby confirmed and established; and all leases which have been made to such "heads of families" by said direct tax commissioners, shall be changed into certificates of sale in all cases wherein the lease provides for such substitution; and all the lands now remaining unsold, which come within the same designation, being eight thousand acres, more or less, shall be disposed of according to said instructions.

SEC. 7. All other lands bid in by the United States at tax sales, being thirty eight thousand acres, more or less, and now in the hands of the said tax commissioners as the property of the United States, in the parishes of St, Helena and St. Luke, excepting the "school farms," as specified in the preceding section, and so much as may be necessary for military and naval purposes at Hilton Head, Bay Point, and Land's End, and excepting also the city of Port Royal on St. Helena island, and the town of Beaufort, shall be disposed of in parcels of twenty acres, at one dollar and fifty cents per acre, to such persons, and to such only, as have acquired and are now occupying lands under and agreeably to the provisions of General Sherman's special field order, dated at Savannah, Georgia, [January 16, 1865] and the remaining lands, if any, shall be disposed of in like manner to such persons as had acquired lands agreeably to the said order of General Sherman but who have been dispossessed by the restoration of the same to former owners: Provided, That the lands sold in compliance with the provisions of this and the preceding section shall not be alienated by their purchasers within six years from and after the passage of this act.

SEC. 8. The "school farms"... shall be sold... and the proceeds of said sales... shall be invested in United States bonds, the interest of which shall be appropriated, under the direction of the Commissioner, to the support of schools, without distinction of color or race, on the islands in the parishes of St. Helena and St. Luke.

SEC. 9. The assistant commissioners for South Carolina and Georgia are hereby authorized to examine all claims to lands in their respective States which are claimed under the provisions of General Sherman's special field order, and to give each person having a valid claim a warrant upon the direct tax commissioners for South Carolina for twenty acres of land; and the said direct tax commissioners shall issue to every person, or to his or her heirs, but in no case to any assigns, presenting such warrant, a lease of twenty acres of land, as provided for in section seven, for the term of six years; but at any time thereafter, upon the payment of a sum not exceeding one dollar and fifty cents per acre, the person holding such lease shall be entitled to a certificate of sale of said tract of twenty acres from the direct tax commissioner or such officer as may be authorized to issue the same; but no warrant shall be held valid longer than two years after the issue of the same.

SEC. 10. The tax commissioners for South Carolina are hereby authorized and required, at the earliest day practicable, to survey the lands designated in section seven into lots of twenty acres each, with proper metes and bounds distinctly marked, so that the several tracts shall be convenient in form, and as near as practicable have an average of fertility and woodland...

SEC. 11. Restoration of lands occupied by freedmen under General Sherman's field order dated at Savannah, Georgia, [January 16, 1865] shall not be made until after the crops of the present year shall have been gathered by the occupants of said lands, nor until a fair compensation shall have been made to them by the former owners of such lands, or their legal representatives, for all improvements or betterments erected or constructed thereon, and after due notice of the same being done shall have been given by the assistant commissioner.

SEC. 12. The Commissioner shall have power to seize, hold, use, lease, or sell all buildings, and tenements, and any lands appertaining to the same, or otherwise, formerly held under color of title by the late so-called Confederate States, and not heretofore disposed of by the United States, and any building or lands held in trust for the same by any person or persons, and to use the same or appropriate the proceeds derived therefrom to the education of the freed people; and whenever the bureau shall cease to exist, such of said so-called Confederate States as shall have made provision for the education of their citizens without distinction of color shall receive the sum remaining unexpended of such sales or rentals, which shall be distributed among said States for educational purposes in proportion to their population.

SEC. 13. The Commissioner of this bureau shall at all times co-operate with private benevolent associations of citizens in aid of freedmen, and with agents and teachers, duly accredited and appointed by them, and shall hire or provide by lease, buildings for purposes of education whenever such associations shall, without cost to the Government, provide suitable teachers and means of instruction; and he shall furnish such protection as may be required for the safe conduct of such schools.

SEC. 14. In every State or district when the ordinary course of judicial proceedings has been interrupted by the rebellion, and until the same shall be fully restored, and in every State or district whose constitutional relations to the Government have been practically discontinued by the rebellion, and until such State shall have been restored in such relations, and shall be duly represented in the Congress of the United States, the right to make and enforce contracts, to sue, be parties, and give evidence, to inherit, purchase, lease, sell, hold, and convey real and personal property and to have full and equal benefit of all laws and proceedings concerning personal liberty, personal security, and the acquisition, enjoyment, and disposition of estate, real and personal, including the constitutional right to bear arms, shall be secured to and enjoyed by all the citizens of such State or district without respect to race or color, or previous condition of slavery. And whenever in either of said States or districts the ordinary course of judicial proceedings has been interrupted by the rebellion, and until the same shall be fully restored, and until such State shall have been restored in its constitutional relations to the Government, and shall be duly represented in the Congress of the United States, the President shall, through the Commissioner and the officers of the bureau, and under such rules and regulations as the President, through the Secretary of War, shall prescribe, extend military protection and have military jurisdiction over all cases and questions concerning the free enjoyment of such immunities and rights; and no penalty or punishment for any violation of law shall be imposed or permitted because of race or color, or previous condition of slavery, other or greater than the penalty or punishment to which the white persons may be liable by law for the like offense. But the jurisdiction conferred by this section upon the officers of the bureau shall not exist in any State where the ordinary course of judicial proceedings has not been interrupted by the rebellion, and shall cease in every State when the courts of the State and the United States are not disturbed in the peaceable course of justice, and after such State shall be fully restored in its constitutional relations to the Government, and shall be duly represented in the Congress of the United States.

SEC. 15. That all officers, agents, and employees of this bureau, before entering upon the duties of their office, shall take the oath prescribed in the first section of the act to which this is an amendment [i.e., the "ironclad" test oath]...

## THE FIRST RECONSTRUCTION ACT (1867)

*The First Reconstruction Act of 1867 contained the general principles which governed Congressional Reconstruction. President Andrew Johnson vetoed the bill in vain, inasmuch as the Radical Republicans were able to muster the two-thirds majority necessary to override his veto.*

### An Act to Provide for the More Efficient Government of the Rebel States

Whereas no legal State governments or adequate protection for life or property now exists in the rebel States of Virginia, North Carolina, South Carolina, Georgia, Mississippi, Alabama, Louisiana, Florida, Texas, and Arkansas; and whereas it is necessary that peace and good order should been forced in said States until loyal and republican State governments can be legally established: Therefore,

*Be it enacted,* That said rebel States shall be divided into military districts and made subject to the military authority of the United States as hereinafter prescribed, and for that purpose Virginia shall constitute the first district; North Carolina and South Carolina the second district; Georgia, Alabama, and Florida the third district; Mississippi and Arkansas the fourth district; and Louisiana and Texas the fifth district.

SEC. 2. That it shall be the duty of the President to assign to the command of each of said districts an officer of the army, not below the rank of brigadier-general, and to detail a sufficient military force to enable such officer to perform his duties and enforce his authority within the district to which he is assigned.

SEC. 3. That it shall be the duty of each officer assigned as aforesaid, to protect all persons in their rights of persons and property, to suppress insurrection, disorder, and violence, and to punish, or cause to be punished, all disturbers of the public peace and criminals; and to this end he may allow local civil tribunals to take jurisdiction of and to try offenders, or, when in his judgment it may be necessary for the trial of offenders, he shall have power to organize military commissions or tribunals for that purpose, and all interference under color of State authority with the exercise of military authority under this act, shall be null and void.

SEC. 4. That all persons put under military arrest by virtue of this act shall be tried without unnecessary delay, and no cruel or unusual punishment shall be inflicted, and no sentence of any military commission or tribunal hereby authorized, affecting the life or liberty of any person, shall be executed until it is approved by the officer in command of the district, and the laws and regulations for the government of the army shall not be affected by this act, except in so far as they conflict with its provisions: *Provided,* That no sentence of death under the provisions of this act shall be carried into effect without the approval of the President.

SEC. 5. That when the people of any one of said rebel States shall have formed a constitution of government in conformity with the Constitution of the United States in all respects, framed by a convention of delegates elected by the male citizens of said State, twenty-one years old and upward, of whatever race, color, or previous condition, who have been resident in said State for one year previous to the day of such election, except such as may be disfranchised for participation in the rebellion or for felony at common law, and when such constitution shall provide that the elective franchise shall be enjoyed by all such persons as have the qualifications herein stated for electors of delegates, and when such constitution shall be ratified by a majority of the persons voting on the question of ratification who are qualified as electors for delegates, and when such constitution shall have been submitted to Congress for examination and approval, and Congress shall have approved the same, and when said State, by a vote of its legislature elected said constitution, shall have adopted the amendment to the Constitution of the United States, proposed by the Thirty-ninth Congress, and known as article fourteen, and when said article shall have become a part of the Constitution of the United States said State shall be declared entitled to representation in Congress, and senators and representatives shall be admitted therefrom on their taking the oath prescribed by law, and then and thereafter the preceding sections of this act shall be inoperative in said State: *Provided,* That no person excluded from the privilege of holding office by said proposed amendment to the Constitution of the United States, shall be eligible to election as a member of the convention to frame a constitution for any of said rebel States, nor shall any such person vote for members of such convention.

SEC. 6. That, until the people of said rebel States shall be by law admitted to representation in the Congress of the United States, any civil governments which may exist therein shall be deemed provisional only, and in all respects subject to the paramount authority of the United States at any time to abolish, modify, control, or supersede the same; and in all elections to any office under such provisional governments all persons shall be entitled to vote, and none others, who are entitled to vote, under the provisions of the fifth section of this act; and no persons shall be eligible to any office under any such provisional governments who would be disqualified from holding office under the provisions of the third *article* of said constitutional amendment.

## THE FOURTEENTH AMENDMENT (1868)

*The Fourteenth Amendment, ratified July 23, 1868, defined U.S. citizenship and reversed the traditional federal-state relationship by providing for the intervention of the federal government in cases where state governments were accused of violating the Constitutional rights of the individual.*

SEC. 1. All persons born or naturalized in the United States, and subject to the jurisdiction thereof, are citizens of the United States and of the State wherein they reside. No state shall make or enforce any law which shall abridge the privileges or immunities of citizens of the United States; nor shall any State deprive any person of life, liberty, or property, without due process of law; nor deny to any person within its jurisdiction the equal protection of the laws.

SEC. 2. Representatives shall be apportioned among the several States according to their respective numbers, counting the whole number of persons in each State, excluding Indians not taxed. But when the right to vote at any election for the choice of electors for President and Vice President of the United States, Representatives in Congress, the Executive and Judicial officers of a State, or the members of the Legislature thereof, is denied to any of the male inhabitants of such State, being twenty-one years of age, and citizens of the United States, or in any way abridged, except for participation in rebellion, or other crime, the basis of representation therein shall be reduced in the proportion which the number of such male citizens shall bear to the whole number of male citizens twenty-one years of age in such State.

SEC. 3. No person shall be a Senator or Representative in Congress, or elector of President and Vice President, or hold any office, civil or military, under the United States, or under any State, who, having previously taken an oath, as a member of Congress, or as an officer of the United States, or as a member of any State legislature, or as an executive or judicial officer of any State, to support the Constitution of the United States, shall have engaged in insurrection or rebellion against the same, or given aid or comfort to the enemies thereof. But Congress may by a vote of two-thirds of each House, remove such disability.

SEC. 4. The validity of the public debt of the United States, authorized by law, including debts incurred for payment of pensions and bounties for services in suppressing insurrection or rebellion shall not be questioned. But neither the United States nor any State shall assume or pay any debt or obligation incurred in aid of insurrection or rebellion against the United States, or any claim for the loss or emancipation of any slave; but all such debts, obligations and claims shall be held illegal and void.

SEC. 5. The Congress shall have power to enforce, by appropriate legislation, the provisions of this article.

## THE FIFTEENTH AMENDMENT(1870)

*Ratified March 30, 1870, the Fifteenth Amendment, like the Thirteenth a model of brevity, established the right to vote for all citizens.*

SEC. 1. The right of citizens of the United States to vote shall not be denied or abridged by the United States or by any State on account of race, color, or previous conditions of servitude.

SEC. 2. The Congress shall have power to enforce this article by appropriate legislation.

## KU KLUX KLAN ACT (1871)

*Soon after the Civil War white terrorist groups began to spring up in various locations throughout the South. These early groups consisted mainly of Confederate veterans still obsessed with the goals and aspirations of their Southern heritage. They terrorized blacks who sought greater free participation in their communities and whites who participated in teaching blacks about their rights in the new society and the way to achieve them. They were known as the Knights of the White Camelia, the Jayhawkers or the Ku Klux Klan. By 1867 the Klan was becoming somewhat well organized and under the leadership of its Grand Wizard, former Confederate General Nathan Bedford Forrest, brought its fear tactics into many areas of the old confederacy. Coercion could start with a mild message , then a beating, being forced out of a home or locale or execution. A Klan "Knight" was delegated the responsibility as local enforcer of "proper conduct" for blacks which was designed to prevent them from achieving any social standing or political participation. The Grand Wizard Gen. Forrest declared the Klan disbanded in 1869 as a hoax in an effort to detract from Northern efforts to enact strong civil rights laws and anti-Klan strong enforcements. The Ku Klux Klan Act of 1871 was an attempt to force acceptance of black suffrage in the South and end intimidation and violence, acts which were declared "high crimes" by the statute. The law, however, failed to exterminate the Klan or to eliminate the continued use of terror tactics against blacks and those whites who gave support to black concerns.*

*Be it enacted...* That any person who, under color of any law, statute, ordinance, regulation, custom, or usage of any State, shall subject, or cause to be subjected, any person within the jurisdiction of the United States to the deprivation of any rights, privileges, or immunities secured by the Constitution of the United States, shall, any such law, statute, ordinance, regulation, custom, or usage of the State to the contrary notwithstanding, be liable to the party injured in any action at law, suit in equity, or other proper proceeding for redress; such proceeding to be prosecuted in the several district or circuit courts of the United States, with and subject to the same rights of appeal, review upon error, and other remedies provided in like cases in such courts, under the provisions of the [Civil Rights Act of April 9, 1866]... and the other remedial laws of the United States which are in their nature applicable in such cases.

SEC. 2. That if two or more persons within any State or Territory of the United States shall conspire together to overthrow, or to put down, or to destroy by force the government of the United States, or to levy war against the United States or to oppose by force the authority of the government of the United States, or by force, intimidation, or threat to prevent, hinder, or delay the execution of any law of the United States, or by force to seize, take, or possess any property of the United States contrary to the authority thereof, or by force, intimidation, or threat to prevent any person from accepting or holding any office or trust or place of confidence under the United States, or from discharging the duties thereof, or by force, intimidation, or threat to induce any officer of the United States to leave any State, district, or place where his duties as such officer might lawfully be performed, or to injure him in his person or property on account of his lawful discharge of the duties of his office, or to injure his person while engaged in the lawful discharge of the duties of his office, or to injure his property so as to molest, interrupt, hinder, or impede him in the discharge of his official duty, or by force, intimidation, or threat to deter any party or witness in any court of the United

THE CHRISTIAN (?) TURKS.
"Reforming" colored voters South.

*A political cartoon attacking the KKK. The caption reads: "Reforming ... colored voters (in the) south" .*

States from attending such court, or from testifying in any matter pending in such court fully, freely, and truthfully, or to injure any such party or witness in his person or property on account of his having so attended or testified, or by force, intimidation, or threat to influence the verdict, presentment, or indictment, of any juror or grand juror in any court of the United States, or to injure such juror in his person or property on account of any verdict, presentment, or indictment lawfully assented to by him, or on account of his being or having been such juror, or shall conspire together, or go in disguise upon the public highway or upon the premises of another for the purpose, either directly or indirectly, of depriving any person or any class of persons of the equal protection of the laws, or of equal privileges or immunities under the laws, or for the purpose of preventing or hindering the constituted authorities of any State from giving or securing to all persons within such State the equal protection of the laws, or shall conspire together for the purpose of in any manner impeding, hindering, obstructing, or defeating the due course of justice in any State or Territory, with the intent to deny to any citizen of the United States the due and equal protection of the laws, or to injure any person in his person or in his property for lawfully enforcing the right of any person or class of persons to the equal protection of the laws, or by force, intimidation, or threat to prevent any citizen of the United States lawfully entitled to vote from giving his support or advocacy in a lawful manner towards or in favor of the election of any lawfully qualified person as an elector of President or Vice President of the United States, or as a member of the Congress of the United States, or to injure any such citizen in his person or property on account of such support or advocacy, each and every person so offending shall be deemed guilty of a high crime, and, upon conviction thereof in any district or circuit court of the United States or district or supreme court of any Territory of the United States having jurisdiction of similar offenses shall be punished by a fine not less than five hundred nor more than five thousand dollars, or by imprisonment, with or without hard labor, as the court may determine, for a period of not less than six months nor more than six years, as the court may determine, or by both such fine and imprisonment as the court shall determine. And if any one or more persons engaged in any such conspiracy shall do, or cause to be done, any act in furtherance of the object of such conspiracy, whereby any person shall be injured in his person or property, or deprived of having and exercising any right or privilege of a citizen of the United States, the person so injured or deprived of such rights and privileges may have and maintain an action for the recovery of damages occasioned by such injury or deprivation of rights and privileges against any one or more of the persons engaged in such conspiracy, such action to be prosecuted in the proper district or circuit court of the United States, with and subject to the same rights of appeal, review upon error, and other remedies provided in like cases in such courts under the provisions of the [Civil Rights Act]...

SEC. 3. That in all cases where insurrection, domestic violence, unlawful combinations, or conspiracies in any State shall so obstruct or hinder the execution of the laws thereof, and of the United States, as to deprive any portion or class of the people of such State of any of the rights, privileges, or immunities, or protection, named in the Constitution and secured by this act, and the constituted authorities of such State shall either be unable to protect, or shall from any cause fail in or refuse protection of the people in such rights, such facts will be deemed a denial by such State of the equal protection of the laws to which they are entitled under the Constitution of the United States; and in all such cases, or whenever any such insurrection, violence, unlawful combination, or conspiracy shall oppose or obstruct the laws of the United States or the due execution thereof, or impede or obstruct the due course of justice under the same, it shall be lawful for the President, and it shall be his duty to take such measures, by the employment of the militia or the land and naval forces of the United States, or of either, or by other means, as he may deem necessary for the suppression of such insurrection, domestic violence, or combinations; and any person who shall be arrested under the provisions of this and the preceding section shall be delivered to the marshal of the proper district, to be dealt with according to law.

SEC. 4. That whenever in any State or part of a State the unlawful combinations named in the preceding section of this act shall be organized and armed, and so numerous and powerful as to be able, by violence, to either overthrow or set at defiance the constituted authorities of such State, and of the United States within such State, or when the constituted authorities are in complicity with, or shall connive at the unlawful purposes of, such powerful and armed combinations; and whenever, by reason of either or all of the causes aforesaid, the conviction of such offender and the preservation of the public safety shall become in such district impracticable, in every such case such combinations shall be deemed a rebellion, against the government of the United States, and during the continuation of such rebellion, and within the limits of the district which shall be so under the sway thereof, such limits to be prescribed by proclamation, it shall be lawful for the President of the United States, when in his judgment the public safety shall require it, to suspend the privileges of the writ of habeas corpus, to the end that such rebellion may be overthrown: *Provided*, That all the provisions of the second section of an act entitled "An act relating to habeas corpus... [of March 3,1863] which relate to the discharge of prisoners other than prisoners of war, and to the penalty for refusing to obey the order of the court, shall be in full force so far as the same are applicable to the provisions of this section. *Provided further*, That the President shall first have made proclamation, as now provided by law, commanding such insurgents to disperse: *And provided Also*, That the provisions of this section shall not be in force after the end of the next regular session of Congress.

SEC. 5. That no person shall be a grand or petit juror in any court of the United States upon any inquiry, hearing, or trial of any suit, proceeding or prosecution based upon or arising under the provisions of this act who shall, in the judgment of the court, be in complicity with any such combination or conspiracy; and every such juror shall, before entering upon any such inquiry, hearing, or trial, take and subscribe an oath in open court that he has never, directly or indirectly, counselled, advised, or voluntarily aided any such combination or conspiracy; and each and every person who shall take this oath, and shall therein swear falsely, shall be guilty of perjury, and shall be subject to the pains and penalties declared against that crime, and the first section of the act [of June 17, 1862, relating to jurors in United States courts]... be, and the same is hereby, repealed.

SEC. 6. That any person, or persons, having knowledge that any of the wrongs conspired to be done and mentioned in the second section of this act are about to be committed, and having power to prevent or aid in preventing the same, shall neglect or refuse so to do, and such wrongful act shall be committed, such person or persons shall be liable to the person injured, or his legal representatives, for all damages caused by any such wrongful act which such first-named person or persons by reasonable diligence could have prevented; and such damages may be recovered in an action on the case in the proper circuit court of the United States, and any number of persons guilty of such wrongful neglect or refusal may be joined as defendants in such action: *Provided*, That such action shall be commenced within one year after such cause of action shall have accrued; and if the death of any person shall be caused by any such wrongful act and neglect, the legal representatives of such deceased person shall have such action therefor, and may recover not exceeding five thousand dollars damages therein, for the benefit of the widow of such deceased person, if any there be, or if there be no widow, for the benefit of the next of kin of such deceased person.

SEC. 7. That nothing herein contained shall be construed to supersede or repeal any former act or law except so far as the same may be repugnant thereto; and any offenses heretofore committed against the tenor of any former act shall be prosecuted, and any proceeding already commenced for the prosecution thereof shall be continued and completed, the same as if this act had not been passed, except so far as the provisions of this act may go to sustain and validate, such proceedings.

## THE CIVIL RIGHTS ACT (1875)

*The Civil Rights Act of 1875 concerned itself primarily with the prohibition of racial discrimination in places of public accommodation. Eight years later, however, the Supreme Court ruled that the law was unconstitutional, stating that Congress did not have the authority to regulate the prevalent social mores of any state. This decision virtually removed the federal government from the civil rights arena, particularly as regarded enforcement of the Fourteenth Amendment.*

### An Act to Protect All Citizens in Their Civil and Legal Rights

Whereas it is essential to just government we recognize the equality of all men before the law, and hold that it is the duty of government in its dealings with the people to mete out equal and exact justice to all, of whatever nativity, race, color, or persuasion, religious or political; and it being the appropriate object of legislation to enact great fundamental principles into law: Therefore,

*Be it enacted,* That all persons within the jurisdiction of the United States shall be entitled to the full and equal enjoyment of the accommodations, advantages, facilities, and privileges of inns, public conveyances on land or water, theaters, and other places of public amusement; subject only to the conditions and limitations established by law, and applicable alike to citizens of every race and color, regardless of any previous condition of servitude.

SEC. 2. That any person who shall violate the foregoing section by denying to any citizen, except for reasons by law applicable to citizens of every race and color, and regardless of any previous condition of servitude, the full enjoyment of any of the accommodations, advantages, facilities, or privileges in said section enumerated, or by aiding or inciting such denial, shall, for every such offense, forfeit and pay the sum of five hundred dollars to the person aggrieved thereby,... and shall also, for every such offense, be deemed guilty of a misdemeanor, and upon conviction thereof, shall be fined not less than five hundred nor more than one thousand dollars, or shall be imprisoned not less than thirty days nor more than one year...

SEC. 3. That the district and circuit courts of the United States shall have, exclusively of the courts of the several States, cognizance of all crimes and offenses against, and violations of, the provisions of this act...

SEC. 4. That no citizen possessing all other qualifications which are or may be prescribed by law shall be disqualified for service as grand or petit juror in any court of the United States, or of any State, on account of race, color, or previous condition of servitude; and any officer or other person charged with any duty in the selection or summoning of jurors who shall exclude or fail to summon any citizen for the cause aforesaid shall, on conviction thereof, be deemed guilty of a misdemeanor, and be fined not more than five thousand dollars.

SEC. 5. That all cases arising under the provisions of this act... shall be renewable by the Supreme Court of the U.S., without regard to the sum in controversy...

# BOOKER T. WASHINGTON'S "ATLANTA COMPROMISE" SPEECH (1895)

*Booker T. Washington, at one time the sole voice in the movement for Negro advancement, is often criticized today for having encouraged the Negro to cultivate a spirit of peaceful coexistence with the white Southerner. Washington advocated technical and industrial self-help programs for the Negro, even if they tended to discount the importance of his cultivating intellectual and aesthetic values as well.*

Mr. President and Gentlemen of the Board of Directors and Citizens:

One-third of the population of the South is of the Negro race. No enterprise seeking the material, civil, or moral welfare of this section can disregard this element of our population and reach the highest success. I but convey to you, Mr. President and Directors, the sentiment of the masses of my race when I say that in no way have the value and manhood of the American Negro been more fittingly and generously recognized than by the managers of this magnificent Exposition at every stage of its progress. It is a recognition that will do more to cement the friendship of the two races than any occurrence since the dawn of our freedom.

Not only this, but the opportunity here afforded will awaken among us a new era of industrial progress. Ignorant and inexperienced, it is not strange that in the first years of our new life we began at the top instead of at the bottom; that a seat in Congress or the State Legislature was more sought than real estate or industrial skill; that the political convention or stump speaking had more attractions than starting a dairy farm or truck garden.

A ship lost at sea for many days suddenly sighted a friendly vessel. From the mast of the unfortunate vessel was seen a signal: "Water, water; we die of thirst!" The answer from the friendly vessel at once came back: "Cast down your bucket where you are." A second time the signal, "Water, water; send us water!" ran up from the distressed vessel, and was answered: "Cast down your bucket where you are." And a third and fourth signal for water was answered: "Cast down your bucket where you are." The captain of the distressed vessel, at last heeding the injunction, cast down his bucket, and it came up full of fresh, sparkling water from the mouth of the Amazon River. To those of my race who depend on bettering their condition in a foreign land, or who underestimate the importance of cultivating friendly relations with the Southern white man, who is their next door neighbor, I would say: "Cast down your bucket where you are"—cast it down in making friends in every manly way of the people of all races by whom we are surrounded.

Cast it down in agriculture, mechanics, in commerce, in domestic service, and in the professions. And in this connection it is well to bear in mind that whatever other sins the South may be called to bear, when it comes to business, pure and simple, it is in the South that the Negro is given a man's chance in the commercial world, and in nothing is this Exposition more eloquent than in emphasizing this chance. Our greatest danger is, that in the great leap from slavery to freedom we may overlook the fact that the masses of us are to live by the productions of our hands, and fail to keep in mind that we shall prosper in proportion as we learn to dignify and glorify common labor, and put brains and skill into the common occupations of life; shall prosper in proportion as we learn to draw the line between the superficial and the substantial, the ornamental gewgaws of life and the useful. No race can prosper till it learns that there is as much dignity in tilling a field as in writing a poem. It is at the bottom of life we must begin, and not at the top. Nor should we permit our grievances to overshadow our opportunities.

To those of the white race who look to the incoming of those of foreign birth and strange tongue and habits for the prosperity of the South, were I permitted, I would repeat what I say to my own race, "Cast down your bucket where you are." Cast it down among the 8,000,000 Negroes whose habits you know, whose fidelity and love you have tested in days when to have proved treacherous meant the ruin of your firesides. Cast down your bucket among these people who have, without strikes and labor wars, tilled your fields, cleared your forests, builded your railroads and cities, and brought forth treasures from the bowels of the earth, and helped make possible this magnificent representation of the progress of the South. Casting down your bucket among my people, helping and encouraging them as you are doing on these grounds, and, with education of head, hand and heart, you will find that they will buy your surplus land, make blossom the waste place in your fields, and run your factories. While doing this, you can be sure in the future, as in the past, that you and your families will be surrounded by the most patient, faithful, law-abiding, and unresentful people that the world has seen. As we have proved our loyalty to you in the past, in nursing your children, watching by the sick bed of your mothers and fathers, and often following them with tear-dimmed eyes to their graves, so in the future, in our humble way, we shall stand by you with a devotion that no foreigner can approach, ready to lay down our lives, if need be, in defense of yours, interlacing our industrial, commercial, civil, and religious life with yours in a way that shall make the interests of both races one. In all things that are purely social we can be as separate as the fingers, yet one as the hand in all things essential to mutual progress.

There is no defense or security for any of us except in the highest intelligence and development of all. If anywhere there are efforts tending to curtail the fullest growth of the Negro, let these efforts be turned into stimulating, encouraging, and making him the most useful and intelligent citizen. Effort or means so invested will pay a thousand percent interest. These efforts will be twice blessed—"blessing him that gives and him that takes."

There is no escape through law of man or God from the inevitable:

*Accepting Booker T. Washington's (center) invitation, Theodore Roosevelt adresses the National Negro Business League.*

*The laws of changeless justice bind*
*Oppressor with oppressed;*
*And close as sin and suffering joined*
*We march to fate abreast.*

Nearly sixteen millions of hands will aid you in pulling the load upwards, or they will pull against you the load downwards. We shall constitute one-third and more of the ignorance and crime of the South, or one-third its intelligence and progress; we shall contribute one-third to the business and industrial prosperity of the South, or we shall prove a veritable body of death, stagnating, depressing, retarding every effort to advance the body politic.

Gentlemen of the Exposition, as we present to you our humble effort at an exhibition of our progress, you must not expect over much. Starting thirty years ago with ownership here and there in a few quilts and pumpkins and chickens (gathered from miscellaneous sources), remember the path that has led from these to the invention and production of agricultural implements, buggies, steam engines, newspapers, books, statuary, carving, paintings, the management of drug stores and banks, has not been trodden without contact with thorns and thistles. While we take pride in what we exhibit as a result of our independent efforts, we do not for a moment forget that our part in this exhibition would fall far short of your expectations but for the constant help that has come to our educational life, not only from the Southern States, but especially from Northern philanthropists, who have made their gifts a constant stream of blessing and encouragement.

The wisest among my race understand that the agitation of questions of social equality is the extremist folly, and that progress in the enjoyment of all the privileges that will come to us must be the result of severe and constant struggle rather than of artificial forcing. No race that has anything to contribute to the markets of the world is long in any degree ostracized. It is important and right that all privileges of the law be ours, but it is vastly more important that we be prepared for the exercise of those privileges. The opportunity to earn a dollar in a factory just now is worth infinitely more than the opportunity to spend a dollar in an opera house.

In conclusion, may I repeat that nothing in thirty years has given us more hope and encouragement, and drawn us so near to you of the white race, as this opportunity offered by the Exposition; and here bending, as it were, over the altar that represents the results of the struggles of your race and mine, both starting practically empty-handed three decades ago, I pledge that, in your effort to work out the great and intricate problem which God has laid at the doors of the South, you shall have at all time the patient, sympathetic help of my race; only let this be constantly in mind that, while from representations in these buildings of the product of field, of forest, of mine, of factory, letters, and art, much good will come, yet far above and beyond material benefits will be that higher good, that let us pray God will come, in a blotting out of sectional differences and racial animosities and suspicions, in a determination to administer absolute justice, in a willing obedience among all classes to the mandates of law. This, coupled with our material prosperity, will bring into our beloved South a new heaven and a new earth.

## PLESSY V. FERGUSON (1896)

*The* Plessy *case was a test of the constitutionality of an 1890 Louisiana law providing for separate railway carriages for whites and blacks.*
*The information filed in the criminal District Court charged in substance that (Homer) Plessy, being a passenger between two stations within the state of Louisiana, was assigned by officers of the company to the coach used by the race to which he did not belong. Plessy refused to move and was arrested for violation of the law. A suit was filed by Plessy in Louisiana State Court that questioned the constitutionality of the Louisiana law, judge John Ferguson denied the Plessy contention and the case was appealed to the Supreme Court as* Plessy *v* Ferguson.

*The lawyer for the defense summed up the case in one sentence* "Instead of being intended to promote the general comfort and moral well being, this act is plainly and evidently intended to promote the happiness of one class by asserting its supremacy and the inferiority of another class."

*In the majority opinion of the Court,* "separate but equal" *accommodations for blacks constituted a "reasonable" use of state police power. Furthermore, it was said that the Fourteenth Amendment* "could not have been intended to abolish distinctions based on color, or to enforce social... equality, or a co-mingling of the two races upon terms unsatisfactory to either."

Justice John Marshall Harlan delivered a dissenting opinion in this case which proved to be a prophetic one:

"The judgment this day rendered will, in time, prove to be quite as pernicious as the decision made by this tribunal in the Dred Scott case. The thin disguise of equal accommodations for passengers in railroad coaches will not mislead anyone nor atone for the wrong this day done."

*In effect, at the time, the Supreme Court had effectively reduced the significance of the Fourteenth and Fifteenth Amendments of the Constitution which were designed to give blacks specific rights and protections. The ruling was termed the* "separate but equal" *doctrine of the Supreme Court and paved the way for segregation of blacks in all walks of life. The decision stood until the* Brown v. Board of Education *decision of 1954.*

This case turns upon the constitutionality of an act of the General Assembly of the state of Louisiana, passed in 1890, providing for separate railway carriages for the white and colored races...

The constitutionality of this act is attacked upon the ground that it conflicts both with the Thirteenth Amendment of the Constitution, abolishing slavery, and the Fourteenth Amendment, which prohibits certain restrictive legislation on the part of the states.

**1.** That it does not conflict with the Thirteenth Amendment, which abolished slavery and involuntary servitude, except as a punishment for crime, is too clear for argument. Slavery implies involuntary servitude—a state of bondage; the ownership of mankind as a chattel, or at least the control of the labor and services of one man for the benefit of another, and the absence of a legal right to the disposal of his own person, property, and services...

A statute which implies merely a legal distinction between the white and colored races—a distinction which is founded in the color of the two races, and which must always exist so long as white men are distinguished from the other race by color—has no tendency to destroy the legal equality of the two races, or reestablish a state of involuntary servitude. Indeed, we do not understand that the Thirteenth Amendment is strenuously relied upon by the plaintiff in error in this connection.

**2.** By the Fourteenth Amendment, all persons born or naturalized in the United States, and subject to the jurisdiction thereof, are made citizens of the United States and of the state wherein they reside; and the states are forbidden from making or enforcing any law which shall abridge the privileges or immunities of citizens of the United States, or shall deprive any person of life, liberty, or property without due process of law, or deny to any person within their jurisdiction the equal protection of the laws...

The object of the amendment was undoubtedly to enforce the absolute equality of the two races before the law, but in the nature of things it could not have been intended to abolish distinctions based upon color, or to enforce social, as distinguished from political, equality, or a commingling of the two races upon terms unsatisfactory to either. Laws permitting, and even requiring, their separation in places where they are liable to be brought into contact do not necessarily imply the inferiority of either race to the other, and have been generally, if not universally, recognized as within the competency of the state legislatures in the exercise of their police power. The most common instance of this is connected with the establishment of separate schools for white and colored children, which has been held to be a valid exercise of the legislative power even by courts of states where the political rights of the colored race have been longest and most earnestly enforced...

So far, then, as a conflict with the Fourteenth Amendment is concerned, the case reduces itself to the question whether the statute of Louisiana is a reasonable regulation, and with respect to this there must necessarily be a large discretion on the part of the legislature. In determining the question of reasonableness it is at liberty to act with reference to the established usages, customs, and traditions of the people, and with a view to the promotion of their comfort, and the preservation of the public peace and good order. Gauged by this standard, we cannot say that a law which authorizes or even requires the separation of the two races in public conveyances is unreasonable or more obnoxious to the

Fourteenth Amendment than the acts of Congress requiring separate schools for colored children in the District of Columbia, the constitutionality of which does not seem to have been questioned, or the corresponding acts of state legislatures.

We consider the underlying fallacy of the plaintiff's argument to consist in the assumption that the enforced separation of the two races stamps the colored race with a badge of inferiority. If this be so, it is not by reason of anything found in the act, but solely because the colored race chooses to put that construction upon it. The argument necessarily assumes that if, as has been more than once the case, and is not unlikely to be so again, the colored race should become the dominant power in the state legislature, and should enact a law in precisely similar terms, it would thereby relegate the white race to an inferior position. We imagine that the white race, at least, would not acquiesce in this assumption. The argument also assumes that social prejudices may be overcome by legislation and that equal rights cannot be secured to the Negro except by an enforced commingling of the two races. We cannot accept this proposition. If the two races are to meet upon terms of social equality, it must be the result of natural affinities, a mutual appreciation of each other's merits, and a voluntary consent of individuals... Legislation is powerless to eradicate racial instincts or to abolish distinctions based upon physical differences, and the attempt to do so can only result in accentuating the difficulties of the present situation. If the civil and political rights of both races be equal, one cannot be inferior to the other civilly or politically. If one race be inferior to the other socially, the Constitution of the United States cannot put them upon the same plane.

It is true that the question of the proportion of colored blood necessary to constitute a colored person, as distinguished from a white person, is one upon which there is a difference of opinion in the different states, some holding that any visible admixture of black blood stamps the person as belonging to the colored race... others that it depends upon the preponderance of blood... and still others that the predominance of white blood must only be in the proportion of three-fourths... But these are questions to be determined under the laws of each state and are not properly put in issue in this case. Under the allegations of his petition it may undoubtedly become a question of importance whether, under the laws of Louisiana, the petitioner belongs to the white or colored race.

The judgment of the court below is therefore, *Affirmed.*

## MR. JUSTICE HARLAN DISSENTING

In respect of civil rights, common to all citizens, the Constitution of the United States does not, I think, permit any public authority to know the race of those entitled to be protected in the enjoyment of such rights. Every true man has pride of race, and under appropriate circumstances when the rights of others, his equals before the law, are not to be affected, it is his privilege to express such pride and to take such action based upon it as to him seems proper. But I deny that any legislative body or judicial tribunal may have regard to the race of citizens when the civil rights of those citizens are involved. Indeed, such legislation, as that here in question, is inconsistent not only with that equality of rights which pertains to citizenship, national and state, but with the personal liberty enjoyed by everyone within the United States.

The Thirteenth Amendment does not permit the withholding or the deprivation of any right necessarily inhering in freedom. It not only struck down the institution of slavery as previously existing in the United States, but it prevents the imposition of any burdens or disabilities that constitute badges of slavery or servitude. It decreed universal civil freedom in this country. This Court has so adjudged. But that amendment having been found inadequate to the protection of the rights of those who had been in slavery, it was followed by the Fourteenth Amendment, which added greatly to the dignity and glory of the American citizenship, and to the security of personal liberty, by declaring that "all persons born or naturalized in the United States, and subject to the jurisdiction thereof, are citizens of the United States and of the state wherein they reside," and that "no state shall make or enforce any law which shall abridge the privileges or immunities of citizens of the United States; nor shall any state deprive any person of life, liberty, or property without due process of law, nor deny to any person within its jurisdiction the equal protection of the laws." These two amendments, if enforced according to their true intent and meaning, will protect all the civil rights that pertain to freedom and citizenship. Finally, and to the end that no citizen should be denied, on account of his race, the privilege of participating in the political control of his country, it was declared by the Fifteenth Amendment that "the right of citizens of the United States to vote shall not be denied or abridged by the United States or by any state on account of race, color, or previous condition of servitude."

These notable additions to the fundamental law were welcomed by the friends of liberty throughout the world. They removed the race line from our governmental systems.

It was said in argument that the statute of Louisiana does not discriminate against either race but prescribes a rule applicable alike to white and colored citizens. But this argument does not meet the difficulty. Everyone knows that the statute in question had its origin in the purpose, not so much to exclude white persons from railroad cars occupied by blacks, as to exclude colored people from coaches occupied by or assigned to white persons. Railroad corporations of Louisiana did not make discrimination among whites in the matter of accommodation for travelers. The thing to accomplish was, under the guise of giving equal accommodation for whites and blacks, to compel the latter to keep to themselves while traveling in railroad passenger coaches. No one would be so wanting in candor as to assert the contrary. The fundamental objection, therefore, to the statute is that it interferes with the personal freedom of citizens. If a white man and a black man choose to occupy the same public conveyance on a public highway, it is their right to do so, and no government, proceeding alone on grounds of race, can prevent it without infringing the personal liberty of each.

It is one thing for railroad carriers to furnish, or to be required by law to furnish, equal accommodations for all whom they are under a legal duty to carry. It is quite another thing for government to forbid citizens of the white and black races from traveling in the same public conveyance, and to punish officers of railroad companies for permitting persons of the two races to occupy the same passenger coach. If a state can prescribe, as a rule of civil conduct, that whites and blacks shall not travel as passengers in the same railroad coach, why may it not so regulate the use of the streets of its cities and towns as to compel white citizens to keep on one side of a street and black citizens to keep on the other? Why may it not, upon like grounds, punish whites and blacks who ride together in streetcars or in open vehicles on a public road or street? Why may it not require sheriffs to assign whites to one side of a courtroom and blacks to the other? And why may it not also prohibit the commingling of the two races in the galleries of legislative halls or in public assemblages convened for the consideration of the political questions of the day? Further, if this statute of Louisiana is consistent with the personal liberty of citizens, why may not the state require the separation in railroad coaches of native and naturalized citizens of the United States, or of Protestants and Roman Catholics?

The answer given as the argument to these questions was that regulations of the kind they suggest would be unreasonable and could not, therefore, stand before the law. Is it meant that the determination of questions of legislative power depends upon the inquiry whether the statute whose validity is questioned is, in the judgment of the courts, a reasonable one, taking all the circumstances into consideration? A statute may be unreasonable merely because a sound public policy forbade its enactment. But I do not understand that the courts have anything to do with the policy or expediency of legislation. The white race deems itself to be the dominant race in this country. And so it is, in prestige, in achievements, in education, in wealth, and in power. So, I doubt not, it will continue to be for all time, if it remains true to its great heritage and holds fast to the principles of constitutional liberty. But in view of the Constitution, in the eye of the law, there is in this country no superior, dominant, ruling class of citizens. There is no caste here. Our Constitution is colorblind and neither knows nor tolerates classes among citizens. In respect of civil rights all citizens are equal before the law. The humblest is the peer of the most powerful. The law regards man as man and takes no account of his surroundings or of his color when his civil rights, as guaranteed by the supreme law of the land, are involved. It is, therefore, to be regretted that this high tribunal, the final expositor of the fundamental law of the land, has reached the conclusion that it is competent for a state to regulate the enjoyment by citizens of their civil rights solely upon the basis of race...

The sure guarantee of the peace and security of each race is the clear, distinct, unconditional recognition by our governments, national and state, of every right that inheres in civil freedom, and of the equality before the law of all citizens of the United States without regard to race. State enactments, regulating the enjoyment of civil rights, upon the basis of race, and cunningly devised to defeat legitimate results of the war, under the pretense of recognizing equality of rights, can have no other result than to render permanent peace impossible, and to keep alive a conflict of races, the continuance of which must do harm to all concerned...

The arbitrary separation of citizens, on the basis of race, while they are on a public highway, is a badge of servitude wholly inconsistent with the civil freedom and the equality before the law established by the Constitution. It cannot be justified upon any legal grounds.

If evils will result from the commingling of the two faces upon public highways established for the benefit of all, they will be infinitely less than those that will surely come from state legislation regulating the enjoyment of civil rights upon the basis of race. We boast of the freedom enjoyed by our people above all other peoples. But it is difficult to reconcile that boast with a state of the law which, practically, puts the brand of servitude and degradation upon a large class of our fellow-citizens, our equals before the law. The thin disguise of "equal" accommodations for passengers in railroad coaches will not mislead anyone, nor atone for the wrong this day done...

I am of opinion that the statute of Louisiana is inconsistent with the personal liberty of citizens, white and black, in that state, and hostile to both the spirit and letter of the Constitution of the United States. If laws of like character should be enacted in the several states of the Union, the effect would be in the highest degree mischievous. Slavery, as an institution tolerated by law, would, it is true, have disappeared from our country, but there would remain a power in the states, by sinister legislation, to interfere with the full enjoyment of the blessings of freedom; to regulate civil rights, common to all citizens, upon the basis of race, and to place in a condition of legal inferiority a large body of American citizens, now constituting a part of the political community called the People of the United States, for whom, and by whom through representatives, our government is administered. Such a system is inconsistent with the guarantee given by the Constitution to each state of a republican form of government, and may be stricken down by congressional action, or by the courts in the discharge of their solemn duty to maintain the supreme law of the land, anything in the constitution or laws of any state to the contrary notwithstanding.

For the reasons stated, I am constrained to withhold my assent from the opinion and judgment of the majority...

## THE UNIVERSAL NEGRO IMPROVEMENT ASSOCIATION: SPEECH AT LIBERTY HALL, NEW YORK CITY (1922)

*The Universal Negro Improvement Association (UNIA) was founded by Marcus Garvey—a West Indian Negro who, in the decade following World War I, won a large following in the United States. Garveyism was the precursor of present-day black nationalist movements. It represented a sharp repudiation of Washington's ideas, as did the work of Negro scholar W. E. B. DuBois, one of the founding fathers of the NAACP.*

Over five years ago the Universal Negro Improvement Association placed itself before the world as the movement through which the new and rising Negro would give expression of his feelings. This Association adopts an attitude not of hostility to other races and peoples of the world, but an attitude of self-respect

... Wheresoever human rights are denied to any group, wheresoever justice is denied to any group, there the U.N.I.A. finds a cause. And at this time among all the peoples of the world, the group that suffers most from injustice, the group that is denied most of those rights that belong to all humanity, is the black group... even so under the leadership of the U.N.I.A., we are marshaling the 400,000,000 Negroes of the world to fight for the emancipation of the race and of the redemption of the country of our fathers.

We represent a new line of thought among Negroes. Whether you call it advanced thought or reactionary thought, I do not care. If it is reactionary for people to seek independence in government, then we are reactionary. If it is advanced thought for people to seek liberty and freedom, then we represent the advanced school of thought among the Negroes of this country. We of the U.N.I.A. believe that what is good for the other folks is good for us. If Government is something that is worth while; if government is something that is appreciable and helpful and protective to others, then we also want to experiment in government. We do not mean a government that will make us citizens without rights or subjects without consideration. We mean a kind of government that will place our race in control, even as other races are in control of their own government.

... The U.N.I.A. is not advocating the cause of church building, because we have a sufficiently large number of churches among us to minister to the spiritual needs of the people, and we are not going to compete with those who are engaged in so splendid a work; we are not engaged in building any new social institutions,... because there are enough social workers engaged in those praiseworthy efforts. We are not engaged in politics because we have enough local politicians,... and the political situation is well taken care of. We are not engaged in domestic politics, in church building or in social uplift work, but we are engaged in nation building.

In advocating the principles of this Association we find we have been very much misunderstood and very much misrepresented by men from within our own race, as well as others from without. Any reform movement that seeks to bring about changes for the benefit of humanity is bound to be misrepresented by those who have always taken it upon themselves to administer to, and lead the unfortunate...

... The Universal Negro Improvement Association stands for the Bigger Brotherhood; the Universal Negro Improvement Association stands for human rights, not only for Negroes, but for all races. The Universal Negro Improvement Association believes in the rights of not only the black race, but the white race, the yellow race and the brown race. The Universal Negro Improvement Association believes that the white man has as much right to be considered, the yellow man has as much right to be considered, the brown man has as much right to be considered as the black man of Africa. In view of the fact that the black man of Africa has contributed as much to the world as the white man of Europe, and the brown man and yellow man of Asia, we of the Universal Negro Improvement Association demand that the white, yellow and brown races give to the black man his place in the civilization of the world. We ask for nothing more than the rights of 400,000,000 Negroes. We are not

*Marcus Garvey believed in black nationalism*

seeking, as I said before, to destroy or disrupt the society of the government of other races, but we are determined that 400,000,000 of us shall unite ourselves to free our motherland from the grasp of the invader...

The Universal Negro Improvement Association is not seeking to build up another government within the bounds or borders of the United States of America. The Universal Negro Improvement Association is not seeking to disrupt any organized system of government, but the Association is determined to bring Negroes together for the building up of a nation of their own. And why? Because we have been forced to it. We have been forced to it throughout the world; not only in America, not only in Europe, not only in the British Empire, but wheresoever the black man happens to find himself, he has been forced to do for himself.

To talk about Government is a little more than some of our people can appreciate... The average man... seems to say, "Why should there be need for any other government?" We are French, English or American. But we of the U.N.I.A. have studied seriously this question of nationality among Negroes—this American nationality, this British nationality, this French, Italian or Spanish nationality, and have discovered that it counts for nought when that nationality comes in conflict with the racial idealism of the group that rules. When our interests clash with those of the ruling faction, then we find that we have absolutely no rights. In times of peace, when everything is all right, Negroes have a hard time, wherever we go, wheresoever we find ourselves, getting those rights that belong to us in common with others whom we claim as fellow citizens; getting that consideration that should be ours by right of the constitution, by right of the law; but in the time of trouble they make us all partners in the cause, as happened in the last war...

We have saved many nations in this manner, and we have lost our lives doing that before. Hundreds of thousands—nay, millions of black men, lie buried under the ground due to that old-time camouflage of saving the nation. We saved the British Empire; we saved the French Empire; we saved this glorious country more than once; and all that we have received for our sacrifices, all that we have received for what we have done, even in giving up our lives, is just what you are receiving now, just what I am receiving now.

You and I fare no better in America, in the British Empire, or any other part of the white world; we fare no better than any black man wheresoever he shows his head...

The U.N.I.A. is reversing the old-time order of things. We refuse to be followers anymore. We are leading ourselves. That means, if any saving is to be done,... we are going to seek a method of saving Africa first. Why? And why Africa? Because Africa has become the grand prize of the nations. Africa has become the big game of the nation hunters. Today Africa looms as the greatest commercial, industrial and political prize in the world.

The difference between the Universal Negro Improvement Association and the other movements of this country, and probably the world, is that the Universal Negro Improvement Association seeks independence of government, while the other organizations seek to make the Negro a secondary part of existing governments. We differ from the organizations in America because they seek to subordinate the Negro as a secondary consideration in a great civilization, knowing that in America the Negro will never reach his highest ambition, knowing that the Negro in America will never get his constitutional rights. All other organizations which are fostering the improvement of Negroes in the British Empire know that the Negro in the British Empire will never reach the height of his constitutional rights. What do I mean by constitutional rights in America? If the black man is to reach the height of his ambition in this country—if the black man is to get all of his constitutional rights in America—then the black man should have the same chance in the nation as any other man to become president of the nation, or a street cleaner in New York. If the black man in the British Empire is to have all his constitutional rights it means that the Negro in the British Empire should have at least the same right to become premier of Great Britain as he has to become street cleaner in the city of London. Are they prepared to give us such political equality? You and I can live in the United States of America for 100 more years, and our generations may live for 200 years or for 5000 more years, and so long as there is a black and white population, when the majority is on the side of the white race, you and I will never get political justice or get political equality in this country. Then why should a black man with rising ambition, after preparing himself in every possible way to give expression to that highest ambition, allow himself to be kept down by racial prejudice within a country? If I am as educated as the next man, if I am as prepared as the next man, if I have passed through the best schools and colleges and universities as the other fellow, why should I not have a fair chance to compete with the other fellow for the biggest position in the nation?...

We are not preaching a propaganda of hate against anybody. We love the white man; we love all humanity... The white man is as necessary to the existence of the Negro as the Negro is necessary to his existence. There is a common relationship that we cannot escape. Africa has certain things that Europe wants, and Europe has certain things that Africa wants,... it is impossible for us to escape it. Africa has oil, diamonds, copper, gold and rubber and all the minerals that Europe wants, and there must be some kind of relationship between Africa and Europe for a fair exchange, so we cannot afford to hate anybody.

The question often asked is what does it require to redeem a race and free a country? If it takes man power, if it takes scientific intelligence, if it takes education of any kind, or if it takes blood, then the 400,000,000 Negroes of the world have it.

It took the combined power of the Allies to put down the mad determination of the Kaiser to impose German will upon the world and upon humanity. Among those who suppressed his mad ambition were two million Negroes who have not yet forgotten how to drive men across the firing line... when so many white men refused to answer to the call and dodged behind all kinds of excuses, 400,000 black men were ready without a question. It was because we were told it was a war of democracy; it was a war for the liberation of the weaker peoples of the world. We heard the cry of Woodrow Wilson, not because we liked him so, but because the things he said were of such a nature that they appealed to us as men. Wheresoever the cause of humanity stands in need of assistance, there you will find the Negro ever ready to serve.

He has done it from the time of Christ up to now. When the whole world turned its back upon the Christ, the man who was said to be the Son of God, when the world cried out "Crucify Him," when the world spurned Him and spat upon Him, it was a black man, Simon, the Cyrenian, who took up the cross. Why? Because the cause of humanity appealed to him. When the black man saw the suffering Jew, struggling under the heavy cross, he was willing to go to His assistance, and he bore that cross up to the heights of Calvary. In the spirit of Simon, the Cyrenian, 1900 years ago, we answered the call of Woodrow Wilson, the call to a larger humanity, and it was for that that we willingly rushed into the war...

We shall march out, yes, as black American citizens, as black British subjects, as black French citizens, as black Italians or as black Spaniards, but we shall march out with a greater loyalty, the loyalty of race. We shall march out in answer to the cry of our fathers, who cry out to us for the redemption of our own country, our motherland, Africa.

We shall march out, not forgetting the blessings of America. We shall march out, not forgetting the blessings of civilization. We shall march out with a history of peace before and behind us, and surely that history shall be our breast-plate, for how can man fight better than knowing that the cause for which he fights is righteous?... Glorious shall be the battle when the time comes to fight for our people and our race.

We should say to the millions who are in Africa to hold the fort, for we are coming 400,000,000 strong.

## EXECUTIVE ORDER 8802 (1941)

*Executive Order 8802, signed by President Franklin D. Roosevelt, eliminated discriminatory practices in the defense industry during World War II. Since then, such orders have often been supplemented by comprehensive legislation designed to cope with the very grievances outlined by men like Garvey.*

... I do hereby reaffirm the policy of the United States that there shall be no discrimination in the employment of workers in defense industries or Government because of race, creed, color, or national origin, and I do hereby declare that it is the duty of employers and of labor organizations, in furtherance of said policy and of this order, to provide for the full and equitable participation of all workers in defense industries, without discrimination because of race, creed, color, or national origin...

*The armed forces were integrated by President Truman's Executive Order 9981.*

## EXECUTIVE ORDER 9981 (1948)

*Executive Order 9981, signed by President Harry S. Truman, ended segregation in the Armed Forces of the United States.*

Whereas it is essential that there be maintained in the armed services of the United States the highest standards of democracy, with equality of treatment and opportunity for all those who serve in our country's defense:

Now, therefore, by virtue of the authority vested in me as President of the United States, by the Constitution and the statutes of the United States, and as Commander-in-Chief of the armed services, it is hereby ordered as follows:

1. It is hereby declared to be the policy of the President that there shall be equality of treatment and opportunity for all persons in the armed services without regard to race, color, religion or national origin. This policy shall be put into effect as rapidly as possible, having due regard to the time required to effectuate any necessary changes without impairing efficiency or morals.
2. There shall be created in the National Military Establishment an advisory committee to be known as the President's Committee on Equality of Treatment and Opportunity in the Armed Services, which shall be composed of seven members to be designated by the President.
3. The Committee is authorized on behalf of the President to examine into the rules, procedures and practices of the armed services in order to determine in what respect such rules, procedures and practices may be altered or improved with a view to carrying out the policy of this order. The Committee shall confer and advise with the Secretary of Defense, the Secretary of the Army, the Secretary of the Air Force, and shall make such recommendations to the President and to said Secretaries as in the judgment of the Committee will effectuate the policy hereof.
4. All executive departments and agencies of the Federal Government are authorized and directed to cooperate with the Committee in its work, and to furnish the Committee such information or the services of such persons as the Committee may require in the performance of its duties.
5. When requested by the Committee to do so, persons in the armed services or in any of the executive departments and agencies of the Federal Government shall testify before the Committee and shall make available for the use of the Committee such documents and other information as the Committee may require.
6. The Committee shall continue to exist until such time as the President shall terminate its existence by Executive order.

## THE CIVIL RIGHTS ACTS OF 1957 AND 1960

*The Civil Rights Acts of 1957 and 1960, both passed during the Eisenhower Administration, represented the first comprehensive federal legislation in this area in the twentieth century. (Both these documents are presented in summary form.)*

### Provisions of the Act of 1957

#### Title I

Created an executive Commission on Civil Rights composed of six members, not more than three from the same political party, to be appointed by the President with the advice and consent of the Senate.

Established rules of procedure for the Commission.

Authorized the Commission to receive in executive session any testimony that might defame or incriminate anyone.

Provided that penalties for unauthorized persons who released information from executive hearings of the Commission would apply only to persons whose services were paid for by the Government.

Barred the Commission for issuing subpenas for witnesses who were found, resided or transacted business outside the state in which the hearing would be held.

Placed the pay for Commissioners at $50 per day—plus $12 per day for expenses away from home.

Empowered the Commission to investigate allegations that U.S. citizens were being deprived of their right to vote and have that vote counted by reason of color, race, religion, or national origin; to study and collect information concerning legal developments constituting a denial of equal protection of the laws under the Constitution; to appraise the laws and policies of the Federal Government with respect to equal protection of the laws.

Directed the Commission to submit interim reports to the President and Congress and a final report of its activities, findings and recommendations not later than two years following enactment of the bill.

Authorized the President, with the advice and consent of the Senate, to appoint a full-time staff director of the Commission whose pay would not exceed $22,500 a year.

Barred the Commission from accepting or utilizing the services of voluntary or uncompensated personnel.

*Black leaders meet with President Eisenhower at the White House in 1958. Left to right: Martin Luther King, Jr., E. Frederic Morrow, President Eisenhower, A. Philip Randolph, Attorney General William Rogers, Presidential Assistant Rocco Siciliano, and Roy Wilkins.*

Title II

Authorized the President to appoint, with the advice and consent of the Senate, one additional Assistant Attorney General in the Department of Justice.

Title III

Extended the jurisdiction of the district courts to include any civil action begun to recover damages or secure equitable relief under any act of Congress providing for the protection of civil rights, including the right to vote.

Repealed a statute of 1866 giving the President power to employ troops to enforce or to prevent violation of civil rights legislation.

Title IV

Prohibited attempts to intimidate or prevent persons from voting in general or primary elections for federal offices.

Empowered the Attorney General to seek an injunction when an individual was deprived or about to be deprived of his right to vote.

Gave the district courts jurisdiction over such proceedings, without requiring that administrative remedies be exhausted.

Provided that any person cited for contempt should be defended by counsel and allowed to compel witnesses to appear.

Title V

Provided that in all criminal contempt cases arising from the provisions of the Civil Rights Act of 1957, the accused, upon conviction, would be punished by fine or imprisonment or both.

Placed the maximum fine for an individual under those provisions at $1,000 or six months in jail.

Allowed the judge to decide whether a defendant in a criminal contempt case involving voting rights would be tried with or without a jury.

Provided that in the event a criminal contempt case was tried before a judge without a jury and the sentence upon conviction was more than $300 or more than 45 days in jail, the defendant could demand and receive a jury trial.

Stated that the section would not apply to contempts committed in the presence of the court or so near as to interfere directly with the administration of justice, nor to the behavior or misconduct of any officer of the court in respect to the process of the court.

Provided that any U.S. citizen over 21, who had resided for one year within a judicial district would be competent to serve as a grand or petit juror unless: (1) he had been convicted of a crime punishable by imprisonment for more than one year and his civil rights not restored; (2) he was unable to read, write, speak and understand the English language; (3) he was incapable, either physically or mentally, to give efficient jury service.

### Provisions of the Act of 1960

Title I

Provided that persons who obstructed or interfered with any order issued by a federal court, or attempted to do so, by threats or force, could be punished by a fine of up to $1,000, imprisonment of up to one year, or both. Such acts could also be prevented by private suits seeking court injunctions against them.

Title II

Made it a federal crime to cross state lines to avoid prosecution or punishment for, or giving evidence on, the bombing or burning of any building, facility or vehicle, or an attempt to do so. Penalties could be a fine of up to $5,000, or imprisonment of up to five years, or both.

Made it a federal crime to transport or possess explosives with the knowledge or intent that they would be used to blow up any vehicle or building. Allowed the presumption, after any bombing occurred, that the explosives used were transported across state lines (therefore allowing the FBI to investigate any bombing case), but stipulated that this would have to be proved before the person could be convicted. Penalties could be imprisonment of up to one year and/or $10,000 fine; if personal injury resulted, 10 years and/or $10,000 fine; if death resulted, life imprisonment or a death penalty if recommended by a jury.

Made it a federal crime to use interstate facilities, such as telephones, to threaten a bombing or give a false bombscare, punishable by imprisonment of up to one year or a fine of up to $1,000, or both.

Title III

Required that voting records and registration papers for all federal elections, including primaries, must be preserved for 22 months. Penalties for failing to comply or for stealing, destroying or mutilating the records could be a fine of up to $1,000, and/or imprisonment for one year.

Directed that the records, upon written application, be turned over to the Attorney General "or his representative" at the office of the records' custodian.

Unless directed otherwise by a court, the Justice Department representative must not disclose the content of the records except to Congress, a government agency, or in a court proceeding.

Title IV

Empowered the Civil Rights Commission, which was extended for two years in 1959, to administer oaths and take sworn statements.

Title V

Stated that arrangements might be made to provide for the education of children of members of the armed forces when the schools those children regularly attended had been closed to avoid integration and the U.S. Commissioner of Education had decided that no other educational agency would provide for their schooling. Amended the laws on aid to impacted school districts (PL 81-815, PL 81-874) to this effect.

Title VI

Provided that after the Attorney General won a civil suit brought under the 1957 Civil Rights Act to protect Negroes' right to vote, he could then ask the court to hold another adversary proceeding and make a separate finding that there was a "pattern or practice" of depriving Negroes of the right to vote in the area involved in the suit.

If a court found such a "pattern or practice," any Negro living in that area could apply to the court to issue an order declaring him qualified to vote if he proved (1) he was qualified to vote under state law; (2) he had tried to register after the "pattern or practice" finding; and (3) he had not been allowed to register or had been found unqualified by someone acting under color of law. The court would have to hear the Negro's application within 10 days and its order would be effective for as long a period as that for which he would have been qualified to vote if registered under state law.

State officials would be notified of the order, and they would then be bound to permit the person to vote. Disobedience would be subject to contempt proceedings.

To carry out these provisions, the court may appoint one or more voting referees, who must be qualified voters in the judicial district. The referees would receive the applications, take evidence, and report their findings to the court. The referee must take the Negro's application and proof in an *ex parte* proceeding (without cross-examination by opponents) and the court may set the time and place for the referee's hearing.

The court may fix a time limit of up to 10 days, in which state officials may challenge the referee's report. Challenges on points of law must be accompanied by a memorandum and on points of fact by a verified copy of a public record or an affidavit by those with personal knowledge of the controverting evidence. Either the court or the referee may decide the challenges in accordance with court-directed procedures. Hearings on issues of fact could be held only when the affidavits show there is a real issue of fact.

If a Negro has applied for a court certificate 20 or more days before the election, his application is challenged, and the case is not decided by election day, the court must allow him to vote provisionally, provided he is "entitled to vote under state law," and impound his ballot pending a decision on his application. If he applies within 20 days before the election, the court has the option of whether or not to let him vote.

The court would not be limited in its powers to enforce its decree that these Negroes be allowed to vote and their votes be counted and may authorize the referee to take action to enforce it.

The referees would have the powers conferred on court masters by rule 53 (c) of the Federal Rules of Civil Procedure. (Rule 53 (c) gives masters the right to subpena records, administer oaths and cross-examine witnesses.)

In any suit instituted under these provisions, the state would be held responsible for the actions of its officials and, in the event state officials resign and are not replaced, the state itself could be sued.

## EXECUTIVE ORDER 10730 (1957)

*Executive Order 10730, signed by President Dwight D. Eisenhower, ended segregation in Little Rock's Central High School.*

Whereas on September 23, 1957, I issued Proclamation No. 3204 reading in part as follows:

Whereas certain persons in the State of Arkansas, individually and in unlawful assemblages, combinations, and conspiracies, have wilfully obstructed the enforcement of orders of the United States District Court for the Eastern District of Arkansas with respect to matters relating to enrollment and attendance at public schools, particularly at Central High School, located in Little Rock School District, Little Rock, Arkansas; and

Whereas such wilful obstruction of justice hinders the execution of the laws of that State and of the United States, and makes it impracticable to enforce such laws by the ordinary course of judicial proceedings; and

Whereas such obstructions of justice constitutes a denial of the equal protection of the laws secured by the Constitution of the United States and impedes the course of justice under those laws;

Now, therefore, I, Dwight D. Eisenhower, President of the United States, under and by virtue of the authority vested in me by the Constitution and Statutes of the United States, including Chapter 15 of Title 10 of the United States Code, particularly sections 332, 333 and 334 thereof, do command all persons engaged in such obstruction of justice to cease and desist therefrom, and to disperse forthwith, and

Whereas the command contained in that Proclamation has not been obeyed and wilful obstruction of enforcement of said court orders still exists and threatens to continue:

Now, therefore, by virtue of the authority vested in me by the Constitution and Statutes of the United States, including Chapter 15 of Title 10, particularly sections 332, 333 and 334 thereof, and section 301 of Title 3 of the United States Code, it is hereby ordered as follows:

SEC. 1. I hereby authorize and direct the Secretary of Defense to order into the active military service of the United States as he may deem appropriate to carry out the purposes of this Order, any or all of the units of the National Guard of the United States and of the Air National Guard of the United States within the State of Arkansas to serve in the active military service of the United States for an indefinite period and until relieved by appropriate orders.

SEC. 2. The Secretary of Defense is authorized and directed to take all appropriate steps to enforce any orders of the United States District Court for the Eastern District of Arkansas for the removal of obstruction of justice in the State of Arkansas with respect to matters relating to enrollment and attendance at public schools in the Little Rock School District, Little Rock, Arkansas. In carrying out the provisions of this section, the Secretary of Defense is authorized to use the units, and members thereof, ordered into the active military service of the United States pursuant to Section 1 of this Order.

SEC. 3. In furtherance of the enforcement of the aforementioned orders of the United States District Court for the Eastern District of Arkansas, the Secretary of Defense is authorized to use such of the armed forces of the United States as he may deem necessary.

SEC. 4. The Secretary of Defense is authorized to delegate to the Secretary of the Army or the Secretary of the Air Force, or both, any of the authority conferred upon him by this Order.

## EXECUTIVE ORDER 11053 (1962)

*Executive Order 11053, signed by President John F. Kennedy, authorized the use of federal troops in integrating the University of Mississippi.*

Whereas on September 30, 1962, I issued Proclamation No. 3497 reading in part as follows:

Whereas the Governor of the State of Mississippi and certain law enforcement officers and other officials of that State, and other persons, individually and in unlawful opposing and obstructing the enforcement of orders entered by the United States District Court for the Southern District of Mississippi and the United States Court of Appeals for the Fifth Circuit; and

Whereas such unlawful assemblies, combinations, and conspiracies oppose and obstruct the execution of the laws of the United States, impede the course of justice under those laws and make it impracticable to enforce those laws in the

*President Eisenhower initiated the use of Army troops to override southern obstructions to school desegregation.*

State of Mississippi by the ordinary course of judicial proceedings; and

Whereas I have expressly called the attention of the Governor of Mississippi to the perilous situation that exists and to his duties in the premises, and have requested but have not received from him adequate assurances that the orders of the courts of the United States will be obeyed and that law and order will be maintained:

Now, therefore, I, John F. Kennedy, President of the United States, under and by virtue of the authority vested in me by the Constitution and laws of the United States, including Chapter 15 of Title 10 of the United States Code, particularly sections 332, 333 and 334 thereof, do command all persons engaged in such obstructions of justice to cease and desist therefrom and to disperse and retire peaceably forth-with; and

Whereas the commands contained in that proclamation have not been obeyed and obstruction of enforcement of those court orders still exists and threatens to continue:

Now, therefore, by virtue of the authority vested in me by the Constitution and laws of the United States, including Chapter 15 of Title 10, particularly Sections 332, 333 and 334 thereof, and Section 301 of Title 3 of the United States Code, it is hereby ordered as follows:

SEC. 1. The Secretary of Defense is authorized and directed to take all appropriate steps to enforce all orders of the United States District Court for the Southern District of Mississippi and the United States Court of Appeals for the Fifth Circuit and to remove all obstructions of justice in the State of Mississippi.

SEC. 2. In furtherance of the enforcement of the aforementioned orders of the United States District Court for the Southern District of Mississippi and the United States Court of Appeals for the Fifth Circuit, the Secretary of Defense is authorized to use such of the armed forces of the United States as he may deem necessary.

SEC. 3. I hereby authorize the Secretary of Defense to call into the active military service of the United States, as he may deem appropriate to carry out the purposes of this order, any or all of the units of the Army National Guard and of the Air National Guard of the State of Mississippi to serve in the active military service of the United States for an indefinite period and until relieved by appropriate orders. In carrying out the provisions of Section 1, the Secretary of Defense is authorized to use the units, and members thereof, ordered into the active military service of the United States pursuant to this section.

SEC. 4. The Secretary of Defense is authorized to delegate to the Secretary of the Army or the Secretary of the Air Force, or both, any of the authority conferred upon him by this order.

## THE BIRMINGHAM MANIFESTO (1963)

*In 1963, a series of events in Birmingham, Alabama dramatized the Negro's plight to the nation at large. Black citizens were arrested en masse during peaceful demonstrations which were subsequently quelled by local police using dogs and by firemen using hoses. The Manifesto, dated April 3, 1963, embodied the hope of the Negro community in Birmingham that law, order, and peace would somehow prevail.*

The patience of an oppressed people cannot endure forever. The Negro citizens of Birmingham for the last several years have hoped in vain for some evidence... [of the]... resolution of our just grievances.

Birmingham is part of the United States and we are bona fide citizens. Yet the history of Birmingham reveals that very little of the democratic process touches the life of the Negro in Birmingham. We have been segregated racially, exploited economically, and dominated politically. Under the leadership of the Alabama Christian Movement for Human Rights, we sought relief by petition for the repeal of city ordinances requiring segregation and the institution of a merit hiring policy in city employment. We were rebuffed. We then turned to the system of the courts. We weathered set-back after set-back, with all of its costliness, finally winning the terminal, bus, parks and airport cases. The bus decision has been implemented begrudgingly and the parks decision prompted the closing of all municipally-owned recreational facilities with the exception of the zoo and Legion Field...

We have always been a peaceful people, bearing our oppression with superhuman effort. Yet we have been the victims of repeated violence, not only that inflicted by the hoodlum element but also that inflicted by the blatant misuse of police power... For years, while our homes and churches were being bombed, we heard nothing but the rantings and ravings of racist city officials.

The Negro protest for equality and justice has been a voice crying in the wilderness. Most of Birmingham has remained silent, probably out of fear. In the meanwhile, our city has acquired the dubious reputation of being the worst big city in race relations in the United States. Last fall, for a flickering moment, it appeared that sincere community leaders from religion, business and industry discerned the inevitable confrontation in race relations approaching. Their concern for the city's image and commonweal of all its citizens did not run deep enough. Solemn promises were made, pending a postponement of direct action, that we would be joined in a suit seeking the relief of segregation ordinances. Some merchants agreed to desegregate their restrooms as a good faith start, some actually complying, only to retreat shortly thereafter. We hold in our hands now, broken faith and broken promises. We believe in the American Dream of democracy, in the Jeffersonian doctrine that "all men are created equal and are endowed by their Creator with certain inalienable rights, among these being life, liberty and the pursuit of happiness."

Twice since September we have deferred our direct action thrust in order that a change in city government would not be made in the hysteria of a community crisis. We act today in full concert with our Hebraic-Christian traditions, the law of morality and the Constitution of our nation. The absence of justice and progress in Birmingham demands that we make a moral witness to give our community a chance to survive. We demonstrate our faith that we believe that the beloved community can come to Birmingham. We appeal to the citizenry of Birmingham, Negro and white, to join us in this witness for decency, morality, self-respect and human dignity. Your individual and corporate support can hasten the day of "liberty and justice for all." This is Birmingham's moment of truth in which every citizen can play his part in her larger destiny...

## LETTER FROM A BIRMINGHAM JAIL (1963)

*In the spring of 1963, Martin Luther King Jr. was hauled off to jail in the aftermath of the Birmingham confrontation with Public Safety Commissioner "Bull" Connor and municipal authorities. Beatings, hosings, and the unleashing of vicious dogs could not deter thousands of demonstrating Negroes from risking serious injury, even death, in peaceful parades into the heart of downtown Birmingham. When King was criticized by a group of white clergymen who blamed him for precipitating the violence, he penned a subdued, but passionate letter of reply to his colleagues, smuggling it out on toilet tissue, the margins of newspapers, indeed any scrap of paper available to him. Excerpts of the letter indicate more than just extreme despair and anxiety; they offer eloquent testimony to the flaming moral concern for oppressed humanity which was King's legacy to his fellow Americans.*

We have waited for more than 340 years for our constitutional and God-given rights. The nations of Asia and Africa are moving with jetlike speed toward the goal of political independence, and we still creep at horse-and-buggy pace toward the gaining of a cup of coffee at a lunch counter. I guess it is easy for those who have never felt the stinging darts of segregation to say "wait."

But when you have seen vicious mobs lynch your mothers and fathers at will and drown your sisters and brothers at whim; when you have seen hate-filled policemen curse, kick, brutalize and even kill your black brothers and sisters; when you suddenly find your tongue twisted and your speech stammering as you seek to explain to your six-year-old daughter why she can't go to the public amusement park that has just been advertised on television, and see tears welling up in her little eyes when she is told that "Funtown" is closed to colored children, and see the depressing clouds of inferiority begin to form in her little mental sky, and see her begin to distort her little personality by unconsciously developing a bitterness toward white people; when you are humiliated day in and day out by nagging signs reading "white" and "colored," when your first name becomes "nigger" and your middle name becomes "boy" (however old you are) and your last name becomes "John," and when your wife and mother are never given the respected title "Mrs."; when you are harried by day and haunted by night by the fact that you are a Negro, living constantly at tiptoe stance, never quite knowing what to expect next, and plagued with inner fears and outer resentments; when you are forever fighting a degenerating sense of "nobodyness"—then you will understand why we find it difficult to wait.

In your statement you asserted that our actions, even though peaceful, must be condemned because they precipitate violence. Isn't this like condemning the robbed man because his possession of money precipitated the evil act of robbery? Isn't this like condemning Socrates because his unswerving commitment to truth and his philosophical delvings precipitated the misguided popular mind to make him drink the hemlock? Isn't this like condemning Jesus because his unique God-consciousness and never-ceasing devotion

*Martin Luther King, Jr., calmly faces his arraignment in Birmingham Jail, after arrest by "Bull" Connor.*

to God's will precipitated the evil act of the Crucifixion?

The question is not whether we will be extremist but what kind of extremist will we be. Will we be extremists for hate or will we be extremists for love? Will we be extremists for the preservation of injustice—or will we be extremists for the cause of justice? In that dramatic scene on Calvary's hill, three men were crucified for the same crime—the crime of extremism. Two were extremists for immorality, and thus fell below their environment. The other, Jesus Christ, was an extremist for love, truth, and goodness, and thereby rose above his environment. So, after all, maybe the South, the nation and the world are in dire need of creative extremists.

Before the Pilgrims landed at Plymouth, we were here. Before the pen of Jefferson etched across the pages of history the majestic words of the Declaration of Independence, we were here. For more than two centuries, our foreparents labored in this country without wages; they made cotton "king," and they built the homes of their masters in the midst of brutal injustice and shameful humiliation—and yet out of a bottomless vitality, they continued to thrive and develop. If the inexpressible cruelties of slavery could not stop us, the opposition we now face will surely fail. We will win our freedom because the sacred heritage of our nation and the eternal will of God are embodied in our echoing demands.

## A DIGEST OF THE CIVIL RIGHTS ACT OF 1964

*The Civil Rights Act of 1964 is subdivided into 11 titles, as follows:*

| | |
|---|---|
| *Title I* | *Voting* |
| *Title II* | *Public accommodations* |
| *Title III* | *Public facilities* |
| *Title IV* | *Public schools* |
| *Title V* | *Civil Rights Commission* |
| *Title VI* | *Federal aid* |
| *Title VII* | *Employment* |
| *Title VIII* | *Statistics* |
| *Title IX* | *Courts* |
| *Title X* | *Conciliatory services* |
| *Title IX* | *Miscellaneous* |

Title I (voting) prohibits registrars to apply different standards for Negro and white voting applicants, and prevents registrars from disqualifying applicants due to trivial mistakes made on their forms. It also establishes written literacy tests (except for the blind), and provides that an applicant be given a copy of the questions and his answers, should he desire to have it. A sixth-grade education is considered to be a sufficient basis for the presumption of literacy.

Title II (public accommodations) prohibits discrimination in the use of public accommodations—i.e., hotels, motels, restaurants, gasoline stations, and places of amusement whose operations involve inter state commerce. The constitutionality of this title has already been upheld by the Supreme Court of the United States in two test cases, both of which were decided on December 14, 1964. These are: *Heart of Atlanta* v. *United States,* and *Katzenbach* v. *McClung* (379 U.S. 802, 803). Title II also enables the Attorney General to bring suit in a federal court against all persons or groups found to be resisting enforcement of its provisions.

Title III (public facilities) is designed to guarantee that Negroes be accorded equal access to, and treatment in, all public-owned and-operated facilities, including parks, stadiums, and swimming pools. As in the case of Title II, this section makes it possible for the Attorney General to bring suit for its enforcement if private individuals are unable to do so.

Title IV (public schools) authorizes the federal government to provide technical and financial aid to all school districts engaged in the process of desegregation. Once again, the Attorney General is empowered to sue for school desegregation, provided private citizens are not in a position to do so.

Title V (Civil Rights Commission) extends the tenure of the Civil Rights Commission until January 31, 1968.

Title VI (federal aid) guarantees that no person shall be subject to any form of racial discrimination in any program which is receiving federal financial aid. It also empowers federal agencies to take appropriate steps to counteract any such discrimination, particularly by denying federal funds to any state or local agencies which practice discrimination.

Title VII (employment) prohibits discrimination on the part of employers or unions with more than 100 employees or members during the first year from the date the Act takes effect. Four years from that date, the number of employees for both unions and employers is to be reduced to 25. This title also establishes a commission to investigate charges of discrimination in employment or employee organizations and, where necessary, to take appropriate steps in mediating such charges. Where a "pattern or practice" of resistance to the provisions of this title becomes definitely identifiable, the Attorney General is empowered to bring suit before a three-judge federal court.

Title VIII (statistics) directs the Census Bureau to compile voting statistics by race in areas of the country designated by the Civil Rights Commission.

Title IX (courts) allows higher federal courts to prevent lower federal courts from sending a civil rights case back to a state or local court—particularly when such a step by the lower court might compromise the case of an appellant. This reverses a former trend whereby the decision of such a federal court to return a case to a state or local court could not be voided.

Title X (conciliatory services) establishes a Community Relations Service (CRS) in the Department of Commerce for the purpose of mediating racial disputes at the local level. The CRS generally intervenes only after it has received a request to do so from appropriate local officials.

Title XI (miscellaneous) assures the right of jury trial in criminal contempt cases which grow out of any part of the act, save Title I. This title in no way supersedes state laws which already afford protection similar to that which is offered in the provisions of the Civil Rights Act. Furthermore, it provides that the Civil Rights Act as a whole will not be affected by the possible invalidation of any single portion of it...

## PRESIDENT JOHNSON'S VOTING RIGHTS ADDRESS: WE SHALL OVERCOME

*In an address delivered before a joint session of Congress on March 15, 1965, President Lyndon B. Johnson placed the full weight of his office behind the passage of legislation needed to enforce the Fifteenth Amendment, which guarantees all Americans the right to vote. The speech takes its name from the following lines:*
*"... it's not just Negroes, but really it's all of us who must overcome the crippling legacy of bigotry and injustice. And we shall overcome."*

Mr. Speaker, Mr. President, members of the Congress, I speak tonight for the dignity of man and the destiny of democracy.

I urge every member of both parties, Americans of all religions and of all colors, from every section of this country, to join me in that cause.

At times, history and fate meet at a single time in a single place to shape a turning point in man's unending search for freedom.

So it was at Lexington and Concord. So it was a century ago at Appomattox. So it was last week in Selma, Ala.

There, long suffering men and women peacefully protested the denial of their rights as Americans. Many were brutally assaulted. One good man—a man of God—was killed...

There is no Negro problem. There is no Southern problem. There is no Northern problem. There is only an American problem.

Our fathers believed that if this noble view of the rights of man was to flourish it must be rooted in democracy. The most basic right of all was the right to choose your own leaders.

The history of this country in large measure is the history of expansion of that right to all of our people. Many of the issues of civil rights are very complex and most difficult. But about this there can and should be no argument: every American citizen must have an equal right to vote...

Wednesday, I will send to Congress a law designed to eliminate illegal barriers to the right to vote...

This bill will strike down restrictions to voting in all elections, Federal, state and local, which have been used to deny Negroes the right to vote.

This bill will establish a simple, uniform standard which cannot be used, however ingenious the effort, to flout our Constitution. It will provide for citizens to be registered by officials of the United States Government, if the state officials refuse to register them.

It will eliminate tedious, unnecessary lawsuits which delay the right to vote.

Finally, this legislation will insure that properly registered individuals are not prohibited from voting.

I will welcome the suggestions from all the members of Congress—I have no doubt that I will get some—on ways and means to strengthen this law and to make it effective.

But experience has plainly shown that this is the only path to carry out the command of the Constitution. To those who seek to avoid action by their national Government in their home communities, who want to and who seek to maintain purely local control over elections, the answer is simple: Open your polling places to all your people.

Allow men and women to register and vote whatever the color of their skin...

There is no constitutional issue here. The command of the Constitution is plain. There is no moral issue. It is wrong—deadly wrong—to deny any of your fellow Americans the right to vote in this country.

There is no issue of states rights, or national rights. There is only the struggle for human rights...

So I ask you to join me in working long hours and nights and weekends, if necessary, to pass this bill.

And I don't make that request lightly, for from the window where I sit with the problems of our country I recognize that from outside this chamber is the outraged conscience of a nation, the grave concern of many nations and the harsh judgment of history on our acts.

But even if we pass this bill the battle will not be over.

What happened in Selma is part of a far larger movement which reaches into every section and state of America. It is the effort of American Negroes to secure for themselves the full blessings of American life.

Their cause must be our cause too. Because it's not just Negroes, but really it's all of us who must overcome the crippling legacy of bigotry and injustice. And we shall overcome...

A century has passed—more than 100 years—since equality was promised, and yet the Negro is not equal.

A century has passed since the day of promise, and the promise is unkept. The time of justice has now come, and I tell you that I believe sincerely that no force can hold it back. It is right in the eyes of man and God that it should come, and when it does, I think that day will brighten the lives of every American.

For Negroes are not the only victims. How many white children have gone uneducated? How many white families have lived in stark poverty?

How many white lives have been scarred by fear?...

There is really no part of America where the promise of equality has been fully kept. In Buffalo as well as in Birmingham, in Philadelphia as well as Selma, Americans are struggling for the fruits of freedom. This is one nation. What happens in Selma and Cincinnati is a matter of legitimate concern to every American...

And I have not the slightest doubt that good men from everywhere in this country, from the Great Lakes to the Gulf of Mexico, from the Golden Gate to the harbors along the Atlantic, will rally now together in this cause to vindicate the freedom of all Americans.

For all of us owe this duty and I believe that all of us will respond to it. Your President makes that request of every American.

The real hero of this struggle is the American Negro. His actions and protests, his courage to risk safety, and even to risk his life, have awakened the conscience of this nation. His demonstrations have been designed to call attention to injustice, designed to provoke change; designed to stir reform.

He has called upon us to make good the promise of America. And who among us can say that we would have made the same progress were it not for his persistent bravery and his faith in American democracy?

For at the real heart of the battle for equality is a deep-seated belief in the democratic process. Equality depends, not on the force of arms or tear gas, but depends upon the force of moral right—not on recourse to violence, but on respect for law and order.

There have been many pressures upon your President and there will be others as the days come and go. But I pledge you tonight that we intend to fight this battle where it should be fought—in the courts, and in the Congress, and in the hearts of men.

We must preserve the right of free speech and the right of free assembly.

But the right of free speech does not carry with it—as has been said—the right to holler fire in a crowded theatre.

We must preserve the right to free assembly. But free assembly does not carry with it the right to block public thoroughfares to traffic.

We do have a right to protest. And a right to march under conditions that do not infringe the constitutional rights of our neighbors. And I intend to protect all those rights as long as I am permitted to serve in this office.

We will guard against violence, knowing it strikes from our hands the very weapons which we seek—progress, obedience to law, and belief in American values...

*President Johnson is congratulated after delivering an effective civil rights speech at Howard University.*

The bill I am presenting to you will be known as a civil rights bill.

But in a larger sense, most of the program I am recommending is a civil rights program. Its object is to open the city of hope to all people of all races, because all Americans just must have the right to vote, and we are going to give them that right.

All Americans must have the privileges of citizenship, regardless of race, and they are going to have those privileges of citizenship regardless of race.

But I would like to caution you and remind you that to exercise these privileges takes much more than just legal right. It requires a trained mind and a healthy body. It requires a decent home and the chance to find a job and the opportunity to escape from the clutches of poverty.

Of course people cannot contribute to the nation if they are never taught to read or write; if their bodies are stunted from hunger; if their sickness goes untended; if their life is spent in hopeless poverty, just drawing a welfare check.

So we want to open the gates to opportunity. But we're also going to give all our people, black and white, the help that they need to walk through those gates...

I want to be the President who helped to feed the hungry and to prepare them to be taxpayers instead of tax eaters.

Above the pyramid on the great seal of the United States it says in Latin, "God has favored our undertaking." God will not favor everything that we do. It is rather our duty to divine His will. But I cannot help believe that He truly understands and that He really favors the undertaking that we begin here tonight.

# THE VOTING RIGHTS ACT OF 1965

*The 1965 Voting Rights Act was an outgrowth of the protest demonstrations organized by blacks to draw attention to discriminatory voter-registration practices in several Southern states. These were particularly prevalent in Alabama, Arkansas, Mississippi, Texas, and Virginia, which, until passage of the Twenty-Fourth Amendment to the U.S. Constitution, still required payment of a poll tax as a prerequisite for voting in national elections.*

*The 1965 law abolished literacy, knowledge, and character tests as qualifications for voting in those states where less than one-half of the eligible population had voted, or been entitled to vote, in November 1964. It empowered federal registrars to register potential voters in any county where such tests had been suspended, and where, in the judgment of the Attorney General of the United States, registrars were indeed necessary to enforce the Fifteenth Amendment. The Attorney General also was given the right to take whatever legal action he deemed necessary to eliminate any equivalent of the poll tax.* The text of the act follows.

*Be it enacted by the Senate and House of Representatives of the United States of America in Congress assembled, That this Act shall be known as the "Voting Rights Act of 1965."*

SEC. 2. No voting qualification or prerequisite to voting, or standard, practice, or procedure shall be imposed or applied by any State or political subdivision to deny or abridge the right of any citizen of the United States to vote on account of race or color.

SEC. 3. (a) Whenever the Attorney General institutes a proceeding under any statute to enforce the guarantees of the fifteenth amendment in any State or political subdivision the court shall authorize the appointment of Federal examiners by the United States Civil Service Commission in accordance with section 6 to serve for such period of time and for such political subdivisions as the court shall determine is appropriate to enforce the guarantees of the fifteenth amendment (1) as part of any interlocutory order if the court determines that the appointment of such examiners is necessary to enforce such guarantees or (2) as part of any final judgment if the court finds that violations of the fifteenth amendment justifying equitable relief have occurred in such State or subdivision: *Provided,* That the court need not authorize the appointment of examiners if any incidents of denial or abridgement of the right to vote on account of race or color (1) have been few in number and have been promptly and effectively corrected by State or local action, (2) the continuing effect of such incidents has been eliminated, and (3) there is no reasonable probability of their recurrence in the future.

SEC. 4. (a) To assure that the right of citizens of the United States to vote is not denied or abridged on account of race or color, no citizen shall be denied the right to vote in any Federal, State, or local election because of his failure to comply with any test or device in any State with respect to which the determinations have been made under subsection (b) or in any political subdivision with respect to which such determinations have been made as a separate unit, unless the United States District Court for the District of Columbia in an action for a declaratory judgment brought by such State or subdivision against the United States has determined that no such test or device has been used during the five years preceding the filing of the action for the purpose or with the effect of denying or abridging the right to vote on account of race or color: *Provided,* That no such declaratory judgment shall issue with respect to any plaintiff for a period of five years after the entry of a final judgment of any court of the United States, other than the denial of a declaratory judgment under this section, whether entered prior to or after the enactment of this Act, determining that denials or abridgments of the right to vote on account of race or color through the use of such tests or devices have occurred anywhere in the territory of such plaintiff.

(2) No person who demonstrates that he has successfully completed the sixth primary grade in a public school in, or a private school accredited by, any State or territory, the District of Columbia, or the Commonwealth of Puerto Rico in which the predominant classroom language was other than English, shall be denied the right to vote in any Federal, State, or local election because of his inability to read, write, understand, or interpret any matter in the English language, except that in States in which State law provides that a different level of education is presumptive of literacy, he shall demonstrate that he has successfully completed an equivalent level of education in a public school in, or a private school accredited by, any State or territory, the District of Columbia, or the Commonwealth of Puerto Rico in which the predominant classroom language was other than English.

SEC. 5. Whenever a State or political subdivision with respect to which the prohibitions set forth in section 4(a) are in effect shall enact or seek to administer any voting qualification or prerequisite to voting, or standard, practice, or procedure with respect to voting different from that in force or effect on November 1, 1964, such State or subdivision may institute an action in the United States District Court for the District of Columbia for a declaratory judgment that such qualification, prerequisite, standard, practice, or procedure does not have the purpose and will not have the effect of denying or abridging the right to vote on account of race or color, and unless and until the court enters such judgment no person shall be denied the right to vote for failure to comply with such qualification, prerequisite, standard, practice, or procedure.

*The Voting Rights Act of 1965 ensured all people of their constitutional right.*

SEC. 9. (a) Any challenge to a listing on an eligibility list prepared by an examiner shall be heard and determined by a hearing officer appointed by and responsible to the Civil Service Commission and under such rules as the Commission shall by regulation prescribe.

SEC. 10. (a) The Congress finds that the requirement of the payment of a poll tax as a precondition to voting (i) precludes persons of limited means from voting or imposes unreasonable financial hardship upon such persons as a precondition to their exercise of the franchise, (ii) does not bear a reasonable relationship to any legitimate State interest in the conduct of elections, and (iii) in some areas has the purpose or effect of denying persons the right to vote because of race or color. Upon the basis of these findings, Congress declares that the constitutional right of citizens to vote is denied or abridged in some areas by the requirement of the payment of a poll tax as a precondition to voting.

SEC. 11. (a) No person acting under color of law shall fail or refuse to permit any person to vote who is entitled to vote under any provision of this Act or is otherwise qualified to vote, or willfully fail or refuse to tabulate, count, and report such person's vote.

(b) No person, whether acting under color of law or otherwise, shall intimidate, threaten, or coerce, or attempt to intimidate, threaten or coerce any person for voting or attempting to vote, or intimidate, threaten, or coerce, or attempt to intimidate, threaten, or coerce any person for urging or aiding any person to vote or attempt to vote, or intimidate, threaten, or coerce any person for exercising any powers or duties under section 3 (a), 6, 8, 9, 10, or 12(e)...

SEC. 14. (a) All cases of criminal contempt arising under the provisions of this Act shall be governed by section 151 of the Civil Rights Act of 1957 (42 U.S.C. 1995).

(b) No court other than the District Court for the District of Columbia or a court of appeals in any proceeding under section 9 shall have jurisdiction to issue any declaratory judgment pursuant to section 4 or section 5 or any restraining order or temporary or permanent injunction against the execution or enforcement of any provision of this Act or any action of any Federal officer or employee pursuant hereto.

(c) (1) The terms "vote" or "voting" shall include all action necessary to make a vote effective in any primary, special, or general election, including, but not limited to, registration, listing pursuant to this Act, or other action required by law prerequisite to voting, casting a ballot, and having such ballot counted properly and included in the appropriate totals of votes cast with respect to candidates for public or party office and propositions for which votes are received in an election.

SEC. 16. The Attorney General and the Secretary of Defense, jointly, shall make a full and complete study to determine whether, under the laws or practices of any State or States, there are preconditions to voting, which might tend to result in discrimination against citizens serving in the Armed Forces of the United States seeking to vote. Such officials shall, jointly, make a report to the Congress not later than June 30, 1966, containing the results of such study, together with a list of any States in which such preconditions exist, and shall include in such report such recommendations for legislation as they deem advisable to prevent discrimination in voting against citizens serving in the Armed Forces of the United States.

## BLACK PANTHER MANIFESTO (1966)

*The tightly knit, close-fisted Black Panther Party relies on a strict and uncompromising regimen to mold its members into a unified and cohesive revolutionary force. Like the Muslims, the party denounces all intoxicants, drugs, and artificial stimulants "while doing party work." The intellectual fare of every party member is the 10-point program (supplemented by daily reading of political developments), which every member is obliged to know and understand, presumably even to commit to memory. Military training and political education courses are mandatory; strict adherence to central directives is also prescribed. Grants, poverty funds, and other "outside money" may not be accepted by chapters, branches, or members of the party unless National Headquarters first lends its approval. Apart from policy, there is the matter of consistent ideology. This is embodied in the 10-point program drafted in 1966 and enumerated below.*

**1. We want freedom. We want power to determine the destiny of our Black Community.**

We believe that black people will not be free until we are able to determine our destiny.

**2. We want full employment for our people.**

We believe that the federal government is responsible and obligated to give every man employment or a guaranteed income. We believe that if the white American businessman will not give full employment, then the means of production should be taken from the businessmen and placed in the community so that the people of the community can organize and employ all of its people and give a high standard of living.

**3. We want an end to the robbery by the CAPITALIST of our Black Community.**

We believe that this racist government has robbed us and now we are demanding the overdue debt of forty acres and two mules. Forty acres and two mules was promised 100 years ago as restitution for slave labor and mass murder of black people. We will accept the payment in currency which will be distributed to our many communities. The Germans are now aiding the Jews in Israel for the genocide of the Jewish people. The Germans murdered six million Jews. The American racist has taken part in the slaughter of over fifty million black people, therefore, we feel that this is a modest demand that we make.

**4. We want decent housing, fit for shelter of human beings.**

We believe that if the white landlords will not give decent housing to our black community, then the housing and the land should be made into cooperatives so that our community, with government aid, can build and make decent housing for its people.

**5. We want education for our people that exposes the true nature of this decadent American society. We want education that teaches us our true history and our role in the present-day society.**

We believe in an educational system that will give to our people a knowledge of self. If a man does not have knowledge of himself and his position in society and the world, then he has little chance to relate to anything else.

**6. We want all black men to be exempt from military service.**

We believe that Black people should not be forced to fight in the military service to defend a racist government that does not protect us. We will not fight and kill other people of color in the world who, like black people, are being victimized by the white racist government of America. We will protect ourselves from the force and violence of the racist police and the racist military, by whatever means necessary.

**7. We want an immediate end to POLICE BRUTALITY and MURDER of black people.**

We believe we can end police brutality in our black community by organizing black self-defense groups that are dedicated to defending our black community from racist police oppression and brutality. The Second Amendment to the Constitution of the United States gives a right to bear arms. We therefore believe that all black people should arm themselves for self-defense.

**8. We want freedom for all black men held in federal, state, county and city prisons and jails.**

We believe that all black people should be released from the many jails and prisons because they have not received a fair and impartial trial.

**9. We want all black people when brought to trial to be tried in court by a jury of their peer group or people from their black communities, as defined by the constitution of the United States.**

We believe that the courts should follow the United States Constitution so that black people will receive fair trials. The 14th Amendment of the U.S. Constitution gives a man a right to be tried by his peer group. A peer is a person from a similar economic, social, religious, geographical, environmental, historical and racial background. To do this the court will be forced to select a jury from the black community from which the black defendant came. We have been, and are being tried by all-white juries that have no understanding of the "average reasoning man" of the black community.

**10. We want land, bread, housing, education, clothing, justice and peace. And as our major political objective, a United Nations-supervised plebiscite to be held throughout the black colony in which only black colonial subjects will be allowed to participate, for the purpose of determining the will of black people as to their national destiny.**

When, in the course of human events, it becomes necessary for one people to dissolve the political bands which have connected them with another, and to assume, among the powers of the earth, the separate and equal station to which the laws of nature and nature's God entitle them, a decent respect to the opinions of mankind requires that they should declare the causes which impel them to the separation.

We hold these truths to be self-evident, that all men are created equal; that they are endowed by their Creator with certain inalienable rights; that among these are life, liberty, and the pursuit of happiness. **That, to secure these rights, governments are instituted among men, deriving their just powers from the consent of the governed; that, whenever any form of government becomes destructive of these ends, it is the right of the people to alter or to abolish it, and to institute a new government, laying its foundation on such principles, and organizing its powers in such form, as to them shall seem most likely to effect their safety and happiness.** Prudence, indeed, will dictate that governments long established should not be changed for light and transient causes; and, accordingly, all experience hath shown, that mankind are more disposed to suffer, while evils are sufferable, than to right themselves by abolishing the forms to which they are accustomed. **But, when a long train of abuses and usurpations, pursuing invariably the same object, evinces a design to reduce them under absolute despotism, it is their right, it is their duty, to throw off such government, and to provide new guards for their future security.**

## THE CIVIL RIGHTS ACT OF 1968: PROVISION FOR OPEN HOUSING

*Just as the 1964 Civil Rights Bill reflected the nation's belatedly noble attempt to pay tribute to the memory of an assassinated President, John F. Kennedy, so too did the 1968 Civil Rights Act represent a memorial gesture in honor of an assassinated national figure, Martin Luther King Jr. In both cases it was Lyndon B. Johnson who presided over the formal passage of the legislation. As originally drafted in the House, the bill was impotent and uninspiring; in the Senate, however, liberal Democrats and Republicans shaped an open-housing provision with some teeth in it and created an expanded package covering the Constitutional rights of Indians and containing two antiriot clauses. Had it not been for King's death, however, chances are that the conservative mood of the 1968 House would have prevailed, and the bill would have been shelved. With the death of Dr. King, however, the issue became, in the words of House Speaker John McCormack, one of "human dignity" rather than political partisanship. Within a week of King's death, the bill passed the House by a 249-171 margin. NAACP lobbyists for the bill were delighted; black militants, on the other hand, branded the legislation a colossal hoax. To the moderates, the opening of 80% of the nation's housing to Negroes represented the key to unlocking the prison of the ghetto; to the militants, however, 80% of the nation's housing was out of the economic reach of most ghetto residents and so nothing more than an unattainable luxury.*

### Discrimination in the Sale or Rental of Housing

SEC. 804. As made applicable by section 803 and except as exempted by sections 803(b) and 807, it shall be unlawful—

(a) To refuse to sell or rent after the making of a bona fide offer, or to refuse to negotiate for the sale or rental of, or otherwise made unavailable or deny, a dwelling to any person because of race, color, religion, or national origin.

(b) To discriminate against any person in the terms, conditions, or privileges of sale or rental of a dwelling, or in the provision of services or facilities in connection therewith, because of race, color, religion, or national origin.

(c) To make, print, or publish or cause to be made, printed, or published any notice, statement, or advertisement, with respect to the sale or rental of a dwelling that indicates any preference, limitation, or discrimination based on race, color, religion, or national origin, or an intention to make any such preference, limitation, or discrimination.

(d) To represent to any person because of race, color, religion, or national origin that any dwelling is not available for inspection, sale, or rental when such dwelling is in fact so

*Flanked by lawmakers, President Johnson signs the Civil Rights Act of 1968 into law. Among the witnesses are Sen. Edward Brooke and Justice Thurgood Marshall. Johnson's administration produced more civil rights legislation than any of his predecessors.*

available.

(e) For profit, to induce or attempt to induce any person to sell or rent any dwelling by representations regarding the entry or prospective entry into the neighborhood of a person or persons of a particular race, color, religion, or national origin.

### Title IX—Prevention of Intimidation in Fair Housing Cases

SEC. 901. Whoever, whether or not acting under color of law, by force or threat of force willfully injures, intimidates or interferes with, or attempts to injure, intimidate or interfere with—

(a) any person because of his race, color, religion or national origin and because he is or has been selling, purchasing, renting, financing, occupying, or contracting or negotiating for the sale... of any dwelling... shall be fined not more than $1,000, or imprisoned not more than one year, or both; and if bodily injury results shall be fined not more than $10,000, or imprisoned not more than ten years, or both; and if death results shall be subject to imprisonment for any term of years or for life.

### Title I—Interference with Federally Protected Activities

(b) Whoever, whether or not acting under color of law, by force or threat of force willfully injures, intimidates or interferes with, or attempts to injure, intimidate or interfere with—

(1) any person because he is or has been, or in order to intimidate such person or any other person or any class of persons from—

(A) voting or qualifying to vote, qualifying or campaigning as a candidate for elective office, or qualifying or acting as a poll watcher, or any legally authorized election official, in any primary, special, or general election;...

(2) any person because of his race, color, religion or national origin...

(3) during or incident to a riot or civil disorder, any person engaged in a business in commerce or affecting commerce... shall be fined not more than $1,000, or imprisoned not more than one year, or both;and if bodily injury results shall be fined not more than $10,000, or imprisoned not more than ten years, or both; and if death results shall be subject to imprisonment for any term of years or for life.

## THE NIXON DOCTRINE ON SCHOOLS, THE COURTS, SOCIETY, AND RACE: "THE COMPROMISE OF 1970"

*On March 24, 1970, the Nixon Administration issued a carefully drafted comprehensive 8,000-word statement on the status of school desegregation in the United States. The President attempted to establish two philosophical and administrative priorities: one, to provide compensatory educational help to minority group children in* de facto *segregated classrooms; two, to relieve the pressure on local districts to conform to* de jure *federal desegregation guidelines. The President also summarized the findings of various court rulings which have sought to untangle the complexities stemming from support for neighborhood school patterns in the North and freedom of choice plans in the South. His conclusion:* de facto *segregation does not violate the Constitution;* de jure *desegregation as practiced in the South does "in both Constitutional and human terms." The statement was attacked by most members of the black middle-class establishment as a retreat on school desegregation ("desegregation yes, integration no"), and a tacit endorsement of tax-exempt status for separate white "private" schools in the South. At the NAACP convention in July 1970, critics of Nixon ticked off other grievances: Nixon's retreat on the use of federal registrars to enforce the Voting Rights Act of 1965, his emasculation of the cease-and-desist powers of the Equal Employment Opportunity Commission (EEOC), his willingness to sign defense contracts with textile companies not complying with desegregation guidelines, and his Supreme Court nominations. Although this statement does not explicitly contend with all these accusations, it does summarize Nixon's views on the principles for human advancement and the policies he was prepared to back in order to guarantee black progress within the framework of American society. The document is printed in its virtual entirety as a statement of the President's intention to press for "a free and open society" in hiring, housing practices, and higher education.*

My purpose in this statement is to set forth in detail this Administration's policies on the subject of desegregation of America's elementary and secondary schools.

My specific objectives in this statement are:

To reaffirm my personal belief that the 1954 decision of the Supreme Court in *Brown v. Board of Education* was right in both constitutional and human terms.

To assess our progress in the 16 years since Brown and to point the way to continuing progress.

To clarify the present state of the law, as developed by the courts and the Congress, and the Administration policies guided by it.

To discuss some of the difficulties encountered by courts and communities as desegregation has accelerated in recent years, and to suggest approaches that can mitigate such problems as we complete the process of compliance with Brown.

To place the question of school desegregation in its larger context, as part of America's historic commitment to the achievement of a free and open society.

**The Context**

Progress toward school desegregation is part of two larger processes, each equally essential:

The improvement of educational opportunities for all of America's children.

The lowering of artificial racial barriers in all aspects of American life.

Only if we keep each of these considerations clearly in mind—and only if we recognize their separate natures—can we approach the question of school desegregation realistically.

It may be helpful to step back for a moment and to consider the problem of school desegregation in its larger context.

The school stands in a unique relationship to the community, to the family and to the individual students. It is a focal point of community life. It has a powerful impact on the future of all who attend.

It is a place not only of learning, but also of living—where a child's friendships center, where he learns to measure himself against others, to share, to compete, to cooperate—and it is the one institution above all others with which the parent shares the child...

**Overburdening the Schools**

One of the mistakes of past policy has been to demand too much of our schools: They have been expected not only to educate, but also to accomplish a social transformation. Children in many instances have not been served, but used—in what all too often has proved a tragically futile effort to achieve in the schools the kind of a multiracial society which the adult community has failed to achieve for itself.

If we are to be realists, we must recognize that in a free society there are limits to the amount of government coercion that can reasonably be used; that in achieving desegregation we must proceed with the least possible disruption of the education of the nation's children; and that our children are highly sensitive to conflict, and highly vulnerable to lasting psychic injury.

Failing to recognize these factors, past policies have placed on the schools and the children too great a share of the burden of eliminating racial disparities throughout our society. A major part of this task falls to the schools. But they cannot do it all or even most of it by themselves.

Other institutions can share the burden of breaking down racial barriers, but only the schools can perform the task of education itself. If our schools fail to educate, then whatever they may achieve in integrating the races will turn out to be only a Pyrrhic victory...

**Policies and Enforcement: The Nixon Approach**

It will be the purpose of this Administration to carry out the law fully and fairly. And where problems exist that are beyond the mandate of legal requirements, it will be our purpose to seek solutions that are both realistic and appropriate.

I have instructed the Attorney General, the Secretary of Health, Education and Welfare and other appropriate officials of the Government to be guided by these basic principles and policies:

Deliberate racial segregation of pupils by official action is unlawful, wherever it exists. In the words of the Supreme Court, it must be eliminated "root and branch"—and it must be eliminated at once.

Segregation of teachers must be eliminated. To this end, each school system in this nation, North and South, East and West, must move immediately, as the Supreme Court has ruled, toward a goal under which "in each school the ratio of white to Negro faculty members is substantially the same as it is throughout the system."

With respect to school facilities, school administrators throughout the nation, North and South, East and West, must move immediately, also in conformance with the Court's ruling, to assure that schools within individual school districts do not discriminate with respect to the quality of facilities or the quality of education delivered to the children within the district.

In devising local compliance plans primary weight should be given to the considered judgment of local school boards—provided they act in good faith and within constitutional limits.

The neighborhood school will be deemed the most appropriate base for such a system.

Transportation of pupils beyond normal geographic school zones for the purpose of achieving racial balance will not be required.

Federal advice and assistance will be made available on request, but Federal officials should not go beyond the requirements of law in attempting to impose their own judgment on the local school district

**Job Incentives**

We have inaugurated new minority business enterprise programs—not only to help minority members get started in business themselves, but also, by developing more black and brown entrepreneurs, to demonstrate to young blacks, Mexican-Americans and others that they, too, can aspire to this same sort of upward economic mobility.

In our education programs, we have stressed the need for far greater diversity in offerings to match the diversity of individual needs—including more and better vocational and technical training, and a greater development of two-year community colleges.

Such approaches have been based essentially on faith in the individual—knowing that he sometimes needs help, but believing that in the long run he usually knows what is best for himself...

We have overcome many problems in our 190 years as a nation. We can overcome this problem. We have managed to extend opportunity in other areas. We can extend it in this area. Just as other rights have been secured, so too can these rights be secured—and once again the nation will be better for having done so.

I am confident that we can preserve and improve our schools, carry out the mandate of our Constitution, and be true to our national conscience.

## CONGRESSIONAL BLACK CAUCUS: LEGISLATIVE AGENDA, 94TH CONGRESS (1975)

*On February 27, 1975, Representative Charles Rangel of New York announced the legislative program and objectives of the Congressional Black Caucus to the House of Representatives. It was the first formal statement of legislative goals and activities by the Caucus for an upcoming session of Congress.*

*Though it received little attention in the general press, the document was remarkable for its thorough and concise discussion of the problems and solutions of paramount importance to blacks and other minorities, and for the perception with which it drew on the legislative achievements of the 1960s to further the cause of the minorities and low-income groups in the 1970s.*

*Following is an abridged version of the Agenda.*

### Areas of Major Legislative Focus

### Full Employment

The Congressional Black Caucus sees as one of its highest priorities, the passage of comprehensive legislation which establishes both the policy and the mechanism for guaranteeing the right to useful and meaningful employment for all adult Americans able and willing to work. It is most important that the full employment concept be understood as reaching far beyond the public service program to create both the right and the opportunity to meaningful jobs.

As unemployment skyrockets, with some predicting that January's 8.2 percent national unemployment rate will pass 10 percent this year, the need for relief is unquestioned. Black unemployment in January was over 13 percent and black teenage unemployment in the same month was at 41 percent. However, even many of those who recognize the need to not fully understand that Bureau of Labor Statistics figures show that the real national unemployment rate—which included the under-employed, those employed part-time who seek full-time work, and those who need work but are discouraged from looking—is over 15 percent. For blacks, that means a real unemployment rate in the neighborhood of 30 percent nationally, and even higher in depressed areas.

The major thrust of the effort to attain full employment legislation centers around a bill introduced by Caucus member Augustus Hawkins. That measure would create a Job Guarantee Office and a Standby Job Corps, as well as requiring the President to develop a national full employment and production program. Full employment would be achieved through both private and public employers. Central to the proposal is the concept that there is no tolerable level of official unemployment for a narrowly-defined labor force in contrast to present practice.

As the legislative process proceeds, the specifics of a full employment program will, of course, be refined and sharpened. Complementary proposals, such as that of Congressman John Conyers to require the federal government to become the employer of last resort, will also help shape the final legislation. There should also be legislation passed providing for flexible working hours, as in Congresswoman Burke's Career Opportunity Act. Any legislation supported by the Caucus must have an adequate mechanism at the local level for ensuring jobs and eliminating red tape.

Congressman Hawkins has also introduced a bill providing for an additional one million public service jobs, which the Caucus supports. Further, a youth unemployment program aimed at getting young people from school into the labor force, including provisions for summer jobs must be established immediately.

### Tax Reform

If we are to solve our nation's basic problems of unemployment, inadequate housing, health care, public education and other social ills, it will take lots of money. When the question is raised "how shall we fund these programs," the inevitable answer given is that the average American taxpayer is already overburdened with the cost of government and simply is not willing to have taxes raised to fund desperately needed human needs programs.

The Congressional Black Caucus agrees with that assessment. We also agree that if the money to attack these basic domestic problems—which just happen to be reflected most acutely in the black experience—is ever to be raised, it must come through extensive tax reform that will close up gaping loopholes in the tax law by which rich individuals and multinational corporations get away with over $50 billion a year in revenues which would come to the federal Treasury were they taxed today. That amounts to an enormous "welfare payment," "a free ride" for the rich in our nation today.

The noted Brookings Institution economist and Director of the Congressional Budget Office, Alice Rivlin, believes that with the annual yield from tax reform applied to our national budget we could house all of our low and moderate income families, and fund health manpower, health research, and a health care system that would meet the needs of all our citizens. Over several years, we could also create jobs for all our unemployed and train less-skilled people to fill socially useful jobs on a permanent basis and substantially increase our spending on public education at every level from pre-school through college. The Congressional Black Caucus agrees.

For too long, we have seen no fundamental change in our national policies and priorities in response to domestic needs. In the 1930's, the Great Depression led to a system of Social Security. Following the War, the Employment Act of 1946 was passed. In the 1960's major civil rights laws were passed. And in the mid-'60's, a belated and only partial response to the problems of poverty was begun.

Today, we face a period of economic turmoil following closely an era of tragic international and American political turmoil. Yet, as in the '30's, these great events have served to create a common understanding among most Americans as to our common dilemma. It is not the rich against the poor, black against white. Instead, there is a mutual recognition that any of us may be the next victim of unemployment, and that all of us will most certainly be the next victim of inflation.

The Congressional Black Caucus has as its motto that "we have no permanent friends and no permanent enemies, only permanent interests." At this time of economic distress, we feel we have many more friends than enemies, as our interests are even more clearly those of the nation. While our foremost concerns are those of blacks, those concerns and their remedies are inextricably intertwined with those of all Americans.

This legislative agenda begins to address both economic and political problems common to the nation and the black community.

There are several legislative issues to be decided this year which the Caucus considers of primary importance. These are bills of broad scope with major implications for blacks and others, on which major national attention will be focused. They fall into three broad categories: (1) economic issues, (2) access and political participation issues, and (3) issues involving federal domestic assistance programs.

### 1. Economic issues

Our economic program will focus on full employment, tax reform, and a careful review of congressional appropriations in the framework of national priorities... The Caucus does not agree that every time Congress asks for more money it adds to the deficit, for the reordering of priorities will permit the use of old funds for new purposes.

### 2. Political participation issues

The second major goal of the Caucus' program this year, will be to increase voter participation by removing barriers to voting.

### 3. Federal domestic assistance programs

Our third major priority will involve federal domestic assistance programs. Four broad and timely issues here are revenue sharing, health care, social insurance, and education.

At the same time as we press the legislative agenda, the Caucus will expand its oversight of federal activities, continuously evaluating the impact of federal programs on our constituents, to review civil rights enforcement, affirmative action, and substantive program effectiveness and equity. We have a particular concern this year with surveillance activities of the CIA and FBI, much of which appears to have been directed at black organizations and individuals. A more aggressive Congress will, we hope, further this oversight function. Further, we will be carefully scrutinizing nominees for federal appointive posts for their suitability with respect to the black community.

The Congressional Black Caucus will be pressing in the 94th Congress, therefore, to effect such reforms of the tax law as:

Repeal of the oil depletion allowance.

Enactment of a minimum tax to ensure that those who earn incomes are taxed on it.

Restructuring of capital gains provisions to fully tax

*The 1971 House Black Caucus accuses the Nixon administration of trying to justify their status quo position.*

income from whatever source.

Elimination of hobby-farm tax deductions.

Repeal of tax credit provisions which enable multinational corporations to fully deduct foreign taxes from their U.S. tax obligations and thereby avoid U.S. taxes.

Elimination of tax incentives for foreign investments that move industry and jobs from the U.S., thereby eroding the domestic tax base.

Tightening of provisions for business activity to present taxpayer subsidies of a high standard of living not legitimately related to business activity.

### The Budget and Appropriations Process

While we can agree that there must be limits on federal spending, for us the key issue is where cuts and limits should be made. We have already worked to defeat the Administration's proposed cuts in the Food Stamp program and we will continue to work to keep the burden of antirecessionary measures from the backs of the poor.

The time is ripe for a more realistic view of the military and foreign aid budgets and a hard questioning of the premises on which they are built.

There are numerous budget areas which deserve paring. These include:

The B-1 Bomber

The Trident Submarine.

Overseas troop level, by 100,000 troops.

AWACS Air Warning System.

MARV Counterforce.

Additional military aid to Southeast Asia.

$2.3 billion for inflationary costs for shipbuilding.

$1.6 billion for 20 percent increase in research and development.

### Voting Rights Act of 1965

The Voting Rights Act of 1965 has been perhaps the most effective piece of civil rights legislation ever passed. Focusing on areas where the exclusion of black voters was greatest, largely in the South, the Voting Rights Act has resulted in the registration of over 1 million persons since 1965. Black registration rates in covered areas in the South have risen from about 30 percent of those of voting age in 1965 to 57 percent of those eligible in those same areas in 1972. Black elected officials have increased from fewer than 100 in these same areas in considerable evidence such as in the recent U.S. Civil Rights Commission Study, that the problems persist, and that without the Act, there would be serious regression in black voting rights.

The Congressional Black Caucus strongly supports extension of the Voting Rights Act for an additional 10 years. We feel that it is particularly crucial that the extension be for 10 years so as to cover reapportionment which will follow the 1980 census. Experience under the Act has shown it to be especially effective in overcoming racial gerrymandering. The Caucus also supports a permanent ban on literacy tests. Section 5 of the Act, which requires submission of any "change with respect to voting" in covered areas to the Justice Department or C.D. Federal District Court, has proved to be the heart of the legislation. It must be retained in the extension. Congresswoman Barbara Jordan has introduced a bill to extend the protections of the Act.

Further, the Caucus supports efforts to extend the Act's coverage to Spanish-speaking and other minorities who face severe problems of disenfranchisement.

### Universal Voter Registration

The continuing decline in voter participation since 1960 challenges the nation's democratic principles. While voter registration and participation among blacks has increased greatly since the Voting Rights Act of 1965, it still lags significantly behind that for whites. The nationwide voter participation rate has declined from 64% of those eligible in 1960 to 55% of those eligible in 1975. In 1974 only 39% of those eligible voted in the congressional elections. Black voter participation in 1974 is estimated at under 30% of those eligible.

Over the past several years, proposals have been made to institute a system of universal voter registration. Largely, they have been bills which would simplify registration through the use of postcards for registering for federal elections. Provisions to protect against fraud and to give financial incentives for states and localities to utilize the federal postcard registrations have been included in the major bills.

Last year, H.R. 8053, the Voter Registration Act, failed to gain a rule in the House by a vote of 197 to 204. The members of the Congressional Black Caucus supported that bill, and continue to strongly support similar legislation this year.

The states of Maryland, Minnesota, Texas and New Jersey have systems of registration by mail and have found them to be tremendously successful.

### General Revenue Sharing

Revenue sharing was initially proposed during the mid-1960's as a means of distributing a budget surplus to states and localities as a flexible additional sum of money to supplement categorical programs. Under the Nixon Administration, general revenue sharing became a political weapon to shift the focus of decision-making to units of government less responsive to social needs of poor and minorities. Categorical program cutbacks, despite promises to contrary, heightened the withdrawal from commitments to national priorities supported by the Congressional Black Caucus and its constituents. Reports and studies which have appeared to date, such as those by the National Clearinghouse on Revenue Sharing, civil rights organizations, the General Accounting Office, and the Brookings Institution, generally indicate the general revenue sharing funds have gone to purposes other than to meet most basic social needs. Few benefits of revenue sharing expenditures have reached blacks and the poor.

We understand the need for continuing funds for general city services at a time of financial crisis. Yet we see the review and debate concerning general revenue sharing as a focal point for discussion of our national priorities.

Any extension of the general revenue sharing program should contain... Stronger civil rights provisions, which put a greater responsibility for effective enforcement on the federal government.

There must be a specific requirement for citizen participation in the decision-making process for fund use. Citizen participation should include at least public hearings, better notification of minority groups, and public reports on planned and actual uses which indicate the nature and type of projects as well as the real impact in terms of a locality's overall budget.

The formula and permissible use categories must result in greater benefits to lower-income communities and individuals.

Data used in the formula [must] be responsive to the known census undercount.

### Health Care

The United States is the only industrialized nation in the world that does not have a comprehensive health care system. Medicaid and Medicare reach only a minimal number of people and with a relatively low level of benefits. A large number of persons have no medical plan at all, and even those with medical plans frequently do not have regular preventive care.

Unfortunately, the medical industry and the country have forced us to choose between the high costs of comprehensive coverage and a gamble with our own health.

Caucus members Congressman Andrew Young and Congressman Ronald Dellums will introduce major health care legislation. There are a number of principles which must be incorporated in any bill finally passed.

1. It must include preventive services, health maintenance and community education for personal and community health.
2. Health care must be recognized as a right, not merely as a privilege.
3. Health coverage must include the full range of health care, preventive, diagnosis, treatment and rehabilitation regardless of one's ability to pay.
4. There must be progressive trust fund financing so that health care is insured of continuation as a permanent program.
5. Consumers must be permitted and encouraged to participate in health care program operations.
6. Finally, the health care program must be reinforced with adequate financing for research, planning and administration.

### Social Insurance

Welfare or income security must be addressed this year both in terms of the amount of money and resources consumed by the program.

In particular, we will take a close look at the concept of a negative income tax.

However, any measure which receives final Caucus approval cannot be laden down with punitive, counter-productive amendments, such as has happened in the past. As one simple example, it is ludicrous to talk about forced work requirements at a time of spiraling unemployment. Moreover, it is necessary to remove procedures and activities which result in invasions of privacy. It is also crucial to recognize that the majority of welfare recipients are heads of single-parent households, frequently with young children.

Any welfare replacement or income supplement program is doomed to failure unless it is tied to job development, job training, a vastly expanded child care program, and a thorough and far-reaching program to eradicate sex and racial discrimination in education, job training and unemployment.

We also support expansion and increased funding of programs authorized by the Older Americans Act of 1965.

### Education

During the past several years, important education policy questions have taken second place to a misleading, and emotional debate over the question of busing. As misdirected discussion continues to take place, education for black children, as well as for many others, continues to suffer. While elementary and secondary education are of primary importance for our constituents, legislative activity in education this year will mostly concern higher education and vocational education.

Two major pieces of legislation, the Higher Education Act and Vocational Education Act expire this year and are likely to be renewed. We support their renewal, but we are concerned that they be strengthened, and not weakened.

In extending the Higher Education Act, there are three important issues which must be addressed: 1. Eligibility criteria must concentrate on aiding those students with the greatest needs; 2. The Strengthening Developing Institutions program must be continued at least at the same funding level: 3. There must be no provisions which restrict the affirmative action obligations of institutions to hire and promote minorities.

A renewed Vocational Education Act must contain provisions to ensure that handicapped and disadvantaged students receive substantial benefits from the program. Moreover, legislative provisions must be added to see that administrative costs at the state level are substantially diminished.

### Individual Legislative Initiatives

In addition to the preceding areas of major focus, following are some forty pieces of legislation in ten major categories which are being introduced by members of the Congressional Black Caucus.

#### 1. Child-care (Chisholm)

Would establish federally aided child development programs to provide comprehensive services to children under the age of six. Building on the Headstart experience, there would be multi-service programs for young children and their families. While the program would serve a broad population definite priorities are established for poor children and those with special needs including migrants, handicapped and bilingual children. This would also include children of working mothers and single-parent families. The bill would allow public and private organizations and institutions to operate programs.

**2. Civil and political rights and liberties**

Voting Representation for the District of Columbia (Fauntroy, Diggs). A bill to be introduced later this year will provide for full voting members of the Senate and House from Washington, D.C.

To ameliorate the severe and inequitable social and economic consequences of dishonorable discharges, legislation is being introduced to require that there be only a single category of discharge from the armed forces and that reasons for separation be kept confidential.

Amnesty (Dellums). Provides automatic general amnesty for failing to comply with any requirement of, or relating to service in the Armed Forces during our Indochina involvement.

Discrimination in Bar Examination (Hawkins). Would provide for federal bar examiners for temporary periods in those states in which there is substantial and long standing evidence of discrimination in the administration of bar examinations.

Psychosurgery Prohibition (Stokes). Under proposed legislation psychosurgery, including lobotomy, psychiatric surgery, behavioral surgery to modify thoughts, action and behavior would be prohibited in any federally connected health care facility.

Mexican-American Land Rights (Hawkins). Two bills have been introduced to guarantee, protect and, when necessary, to restore the community land grants belonging to descendants of former Mexican Citizens. Further, the civil, religious, political and property rights of these persons are protected, as is their right to self determination.

**3. Criminal justice**

Gun Control (Dellums, Fauntroy, Metcalfe, Nix). The use of handguns and other firearms has become an overwhelming threat to the life and safety to Americans of all races. Black on black crime is an especially prevalent problem. Several bills offered by Caucus members and by others would ban the importation, manufacture, sale, purchase, transfer, transportation, receipt, possession and ownership of handguns, except in certain circumstances. These special circumstances would involve gun clubs, collectors, security guards and similar persons. An effective registration and reporting system would be established. A tax credit system for turning in handguns is proposed in some bills. The Caucus supports the strongest bill using these elements which can be passed.

Grand Jury Reform (Conyers, Rangel). The Grand Jury Reform Act of 1975 provides rules and safeguards assuring the appearance of witnesses, protecting their constitutional rights and apprising grand jury members of their inquiry powers. A witness could be given immunity and a corresponding order to testify only if he or she agrees to this exchange. A favorable vote by a grand jury majority would be necessary to subpoena a witness and to request a contempt citation. Use immunity would be eliminated.

*The Congressional Black Caucus seeks to insure that all children, regardless of color, can get a good education.*

Commodity Price Marketing (Ford). To protect consumer's right and ability to accurately determine prices, particularly in food stores, price marking on individual commodity items must be made mandatory. A bill to this end has been introduced in response to the growing use of computer checkout pricing in the supermarkets. In addition, the Caucus strongly supports the establishment of an independent consumer protection agency with the power to investigate anticonsumer activities and go to court with its own attorneys.

**4. Consumer protection**

F.U.E.L. Subsidy Program for Energy Costs (Stokes). To relieve the burden of rising energy costs on lower-income families, the F.U.E.L. program would make subsidies available for electricity, heating fuel and gas, allowing voluntary participation by needy families.

Antitrust (Jordan). To increase the effectiveness of antitrust laws by such means as permitting state Attorneys General the authority to file class action antitrust suits in federal courts, repealing state fair trade laws, and by preventing leading conglomerates from controlling alternative sources of energy. Also the antitrust exemption for agricultural cooperatives should be re-evaluated.

**5. Foreign affairs**

Rhodesian Chrome (Diggs). The Byrd Amendment passed in 1971, authorizes the President, in disregard of the United Nations sanctions, to import Rhodesian Chrome. The world community recognizes the illegitimacy of the Rhodesian regime.

Fair Employment Practices for U.S. Firms in South Africa (Diggs). Contracts between the U.S. Government and any person or firm doing business in South Africa should be prohibited unless such person or firm is doing business in accordance with fair employment practices.

African Development Funding Act (Young). Would provide for multilateral trade and technical assistance commitments based on the development priorities of African nations.

**6. Governmental structure and responsibility**

Bureaucratic Accountability (Dellums). In response to hearings on governmental lawlessness held by the Congressional Black Caucus in 1972, the Bureaucratic Accountability Act has been introduced to insure that citizens may obtain information and redress concerning federal activities. The bill would extend due process requirements under the Administrative Procedures Act to social programs and other aspects of positive governments.

Census Undercount (Rangel). Would require federal agencies administering domestic assistance programs utilizing population based formulas to adjust data in determining allocations to be responsive to census undercount rates determined by the U.S. Bureau of the Census.

Cabinet Level Minority Enterprises Agency (Mitchell). The minority business components of the Small Business Administration, the office of Minority Business Enterprise and those within the Department of Health, Education, and Welfare would be combined into a single cabinet level agency.

Independent Office of Civil Rights Enforcement (Hawkins). The Civil Rights Enforcement Act of 1975 would create the Civil Rights Enforcement Agency as an independent agency of the federal government with a director as chief executive officer who would be appointed by the Supreme Court of the United States and confirmed by the Senate.

Veterans' Pensions (Ford). Legislation should be enacted to ensure that recipients of Veterans' pension and compensation will not have the amount reduced because of increase in monthly social security benefits.

Hatch Act Reform (Clay). Federal government employees, who are presently prohibited from participating in partisan politics should be permitted to participate in election campaigns and other aspects of the political process.

Social Security Disability Benefits (Stokes). To provide that an individual may qualify for disability insurance benefits and the disability freeze if he has enough quarters of coverage to be fully insured for old-age benefit purposes, regardless of when such quarters were earned.

Criminal Justice Reform (Conyers, Jordan, Rangel). (1) Citizens should be enlisted in the war against crime by such programs as citizens patrols and block security programs. (2) Criminal offenses, especially non-violent victimless crimes should be redefined. (3) Programs of deferred prosecution in federal criminal cases should be created. (4) A federal grand jury investigating executive branch officials should have the opportunity to appoint a special prosecutor if it is felt that the investigation is being compromised.

**7. Health**

Narcotics (Rangel). Legislative and appropriations efforts to (1) increase the Drug Enforcement Agency's budget, (2) provide funding for supportive services such as education and employment counseling.

Mobile Health Units (Burke). Under the Mobile Health Units Act, health care delivery assistance to medically underserved urban and rural areas would be provided through special project grants for the purchase of mobile health units.

Amniocentesis Research (Burke). To further research into the early detection of birth defects, funds should be provided for research to extend the availability of amniocentesis to those who cannot now afford such tests.

**8. Housing**

Low-Income Housing (Mitchell). A 3-year emergency housing program based on legislation now on the books, should be put into effect. Three million units in three years are required: one million public housing; one million 236 or 515 with rent supplements; one million 235 or 502 with interest credits. Sixty percent of the units should be in metropolitan areas, forty percent outside.

Limited Moratorium on Repayment of FHA and Va-Guaranteed Loans (Burke). Persons faced with loss of employment, temporary layoffs, etc. would be permitted to defer loan repayment under FHA and VA guarantee program for six months without penalty.

Condominium Conversion Protection (Collins). Would provide national condominium standards for condominium projects utilizing federal funds, and would create the post of Assistant Secretary of HUD for Condominiums to administer the protections for condominiums.

**9. Martin Luther King Birthday National Holiday (Conyers)**

January 15th of each year, the date of Dr. Martin Luther King's birth, should be designated as a legal public holiday. Making Dr. King's birth date a national holiday would provide at least one day during the year when all Americans would have an opportunity to reflect on the ideals for which Dr. King lived and died.

**10. Women's Rights**

Rape Prevention and Control (Burke). To provide financial assistance for a research and demonstration program into the causes, consequences, prevention, treatment and control of rape.

Pap Smear Test (Collins). To provide for coverage under the Medicare program for routine Papanicolaou (Pap) tests for the diagnosis of uterine cancer.

Social Security Coverage for Homemakers (Jordan). A bill has been introduced which recognizes household employees as self-employed workers and provides them with all the social security benefits available to other workers.

## KEYNOTE ADDRESS OF VERNON E. JORDAN AT THE ANNUAL CONFERENCE OF THE NATIONAL URBAN LEAGUE (1981)

*The keynote speech that Vernon E. Jordan delivered on Sunday, July 18, 1981, at the Sheraton Washington Hotel in Washington, D.C., to open the Annual Conference of the National Urban League was his last as president of the agency. Several months later he announced that after ten years as the head of the League, he was stepping down. While no one in the audience knew that they were witnessing a historic event, Jordan's eloquent and passionate speech, describing the hardships imposed on blacks and the poor by the Reagan Administration and calling for a "return to basics," was regarded as one of his finest moments.*

My first Urban League Conference address was in 1971. Then too, it dealt with a conservative Administration in Washington. But that Administration, while hostile to black people, was pragmatic. It had to be. There was still a strong national consensus that operated to preserve black gains. The Congress was a bulwark against attempts to dismantle important social programs. We had a two-party system then.

Today, there is another conservative Administration in Washington. But this time, much has changed.

This Administration is wedded to an ideology of radical conservatism. This Administration has introduced a new political vocabulary—"budget reconciliation," "truly needy," "supply side economics," and other phrases. But it has dropped from the political vocabulary the one word that makes government relevant to the governed, the one word that grants legitimacy to its laws—"compassion."

This is not mere semantics. The Administration's refusal to temper ideology with compassion makes it a clear and present danger to black people and to poor people...

Yes, outmoded. The President claims to be bringing us new ideas and new policies. But they are actually a recycled version of ideas and policies that were buried in the Great Depression. And with good reason.

What are the new ideas the Administration is ramming down the throats of the nation? Get government off our backs. Give power and programs to the states. Federal programs have failed. Rely on the free enterprise system. Build more missiles.

Black people don't need to be told that government is on our backs because we know it has been by our side, helping to counterbalance the vicious racism that deprived us of our lives, our liberty, and our rights.

Black people don't need to be told that power and programs should go to the states, because we know the few, feeble programs that have helped us were those mandated by Washington. It was the state and local governments that excluded us from everything from voting to paved streets. And it is they who will trample on our interests again if this Administration dumps the programs we need into block grants.

Black people don't need to be told federal programs have failed because we know many have succeeded. The Pentagon may not be able to land helicopters in Iran, but the Food Stamp program has fed the hungry; social security has wiped out poverty for most older citizens; CETA has put the jobless to work, compensatory education programs have improved reading scores of disadvantaged youth, and Legal Services has given poor people access to the justice system.

Black people don't need to be told to rely on the free enterprise system. We believe in the free enterprise system. We want to be part of it. We want our fair share of it.

And we know that will not happen without a federal government that pushes the private sector into affirmative action programs. It will not happen without a federal government that has set asides for minority enterprises and job and training programs for the disadvantaged.

America, we will not get our fair share unless there is more for everyone. But we also know that we will not get our fair share just because there is more. America has managed to push us from the table of prosperity in good times as in bad.

So it is not enough just to have growth. What we want to know is "economic growth for whom?" "A rising tide lifts all boats" is no answer. A rising tide lifts only those boats in the water; our boats are in the drydock of America's economy. And we know we will be stranded on dry land, far from the rising tide, unless government steps in with the programs and protection that help launch us into the mainstream.

That will not happen with an economic program that gives to the wealthy in the vague hopes that some of it will trickle down to the poor. What little trickles down is soaked up long before it reaches us.

Let us cut through the rhetoric of a supply-side economics that supplies misery to the poor: this Administration's economic program amounts to a massive transfer of resources from the poor to the rich.

It takes money, programs, and opportunities from poor people and promises them in return an end to inflation and prosperity for all. It says to poor people: give up the little you have today and we promise you a lot more in the bye and bye. Well, black people aren't buying pie-in-the-sky economics...

A brief look at what happened to some of the major domestic programs will demonstrate that black people are the major victims of a budget that tears huge, gaping holes in our safety net:

Social security. The minimum benefit—a measly $122 a month is eliminated. Who gets hurt? Poor black people who spent their working lives on their knees cleaning floors. Disability benefits are tightened. Who gets hurt? Workers who are injured or fall sick and can't work anymore—a disproportionate number of them black.

Food Stamps—A million people will lose their food stamps, millions more will have their benefits reduced. Who gets hurt? The working poor. Over a third of all food stamp recipients are black.

Public service jobs ended; CETA training cut back—Who

gets hurt? Over a third of all CETA workers are black.

Medicaid is capped; poor people will suffer reductions in access to health care—Who gets hurt? Over a third of Medicaid recipients are black.

Legal Services—The Administration wanted to kill it, but our compassionate Congress just cut its budget by two-thirds. Who gets hurt? People who can't afford a lawyer. Poor people. A third are black.

Welfare is cut and a forced work program authorized in the hope that unpleasant make-work jobs will drive people off the rolls—Who gets hurt? Almost half the recipients are black children and black mothers. Who gets hurt most? Working mothers who get small welfare checks to supplement their low earnings.

Education aid cut heavily—Who gets hurt? Disadvantaged children, over a third of them black.

Defenders of that budget will tell us black people are not being singled out. That's true. It's only poor people who are being victimized. And we are twelve percent of the population but a third of the poor—so we are the main victims.

We are told the nation can no longer afford to help the poor. But it can afford to throw one-and-a-half trillion dollars at the Pentagon over the next five years.

We are told social programs don't help poor people: they help the people in social service professions. Tell that to the families deprived of their food stamps, their welfare checks, their public service jobs.

We are told social programs breed dependency. Tell that to the working mothers who will have to quit their jobs or lose benefits. Tell it to young people in training programs who will lose their chance to learn and to earn their way out of poverty. Tell it to sick people whose public health clinics are shut down.

We are told that it's bad to look to government for special help—everyone should be treated the same. Tell that to the affluent who will get huge tax cuts on top of their loopholes. Tell it to the corporations on welfare. Tell it to the special interests who still get their subsidies while poor people lose their life-lines.

Last month, with no real debate, the programs that help the poor were cut to ribbons. With no real debate, years of slow, patient progress were swept out to sea by the rising tide of radical conservatism.

Never have so few taken so much from so many in so little time!

Where was the outcry against that outrage? Where were the Democrats? Where were the liberals? Where were the Congressmen who once fought for the programs that give poor people opportunities?

With some honorable exceptions, they were in a last-ditch fight to save benefits for the middle class and farm interests. Roosevelt led a party concerned with the "ill-housed, ill-clad, ill-nourished." Today his successors are concerned with the upper-middle class.

Democrats and Republicans alike need some arithmetic lessons. They need to learn that poll results still show significant public support for social programs that work.

They need to learn that when they cut social programs whose beneficiaries are one-third to one-half black, the remainder are white. Whites make up half to two-thirds of the victims of the cuts.

When the poor have no more programs left to cut, the cuts will start reaching into the middle-class constituency the Democrats are now courting.

One last word for the Democrats who take the black vote for granted—an opposition that does not oppose is not worthy of governing.

But the silence extends well beyond a passive Congress. When aid to the arts is cut, there are full-page newspaper ads of protest. There are petitions, and loud protest. When an aggressive foreign policy is implemented, there is the same. But where are the voices raised in behalf of poor people? Where are the churches, the universities, the other sectors of our society that once marched with us and supported us?

And where is the enlightened business community? Will they keep their silence as the price for their tax cuts? Will they choose short-term profits over the long-term social stability that ultimately is the surest guarantee of the free enterprise system? Will they silently pocket billions in tax cuts without speaking out on behalf of poor working people who lose their food stamps?

The silence is frightening because the real issue extends beyond the specific budget cuts. The real issue is the grand design of substituting charity for entitlements, local tyranny for federal protection, and unbridled, law-of-the-jungle capitalism for a balanced cooperation between the public and private sectors...

Thus, the real issue is the nature of our society... The black community today feels itself under siege. It is victimized by the budget cuts. It is harassed by attacks on affirmative action. It is alarmed that state legislatures will redistrict our representatives out of the Congress and out of local offices. It is outraged by the Administration's tilt toward racist South Africa. It is threatened by block grants.

And it is burdened by events beyond the political arena: by growing racial insensitivity and rising anti-black attitudes; by the murders of black children in Atlanta and violence against blacks elsewhere; by the continued deterioration of black neighborhoods; by the flow of drugs and the increase of crime; and by the rise of the fanatics of the far right like the Klan and the Nazis.

... The fight for voting rights symbolizes the erosion of black gains. We are now fighting the fight we fought sixteen years ago. And in some ways, we are dealing with basic issues like better race relations that were issues of the 1950s. We moved far beyond that stage, and now we are thrust back to square one.

... The complexities of today's racial, economic, and political issues are such that there is no one grand strategy or leader to deliver us. We will have to draw on our immense resources of survival skills to get us through these hard times. And we will have to cultivate our bonds of unity to once again overcome.

In many ways, it is back to basics for black people. That means a recommitment to the slow, agonizing work of building community strengths and community institutions. Throughout history, it has been our churches, our press, our colleges, our community organizations that have fought on our behalf.

Back to basics also means a recommitment to group progress. We reject completely the notion that individual progress is meaningful while half of our black brothers and sisters are mired in ghetto poverty.

Back to basics also means a recommitment to excellence. There is no margin granted to black Americans—we've got to be better than others in order to get what other Americans take for granted.

Back to basics also means political action. It's hard to break through the cynicism that grips people who have been subjected to brutalizing poverty and hopelessness.

Back to basics also means building coalitions. We've got to reach across class and ethnic lines to win victories for all people. America's tragedy is the racism that drives a wedge between whites and blacks who have so much to gain by working together.

Back to basics also means devising new strategies, alternatives for a nation that thinks old ideas that led to the Great Depression are new ideas for an uncertain future; alternatives like the Urban League's income maintenance plan.

Back to basics also means challenging America's institutions. It means challenging the Administration and the Congress to discover compassion, to make their conservatism humane. It means challenging the private sector to live up to its job creation and affirmative action obligations. It means challenging the churches to practice the morality they preach. It means challenging weak-kneed liberals and hard-hearted conservatives wherever they may be found. It means reminding America's institutions that black people are Americans too, that our blood, sweat, and tears helped make this country what it is, and all we want is our fair share.

And back to basics means back to protesting our condition. Protest has been the basic response of black Americans, from the protest of the slave revolts to the protest of the March on Washington.

Now, when all about us is dark with despair, now is the time to raise high a fresh banner of protest. Now is the time to speak out loud and clear. Now is the time to tell the Administration that poor people can't live on a diet of jellybeans, to tell local officials they can't close our hospitals, to tell corporations they can't hire us last and fire us first, to tell the school boards they are failing their duty to our children, to tell all of America's institutions that they must root out the racism at the core of our national life.

That is our duty, to our nation, to ourselves, to our children, and to our children's children. Let us then get back to the basic job of building new foundations for a new thrust for equality. Let us get back to the basic job of making America America again—this time for everyone!

*Executive director of the National Urban League Vernon E. Jordan, with President Ford.*

## DEMOCRATIC NATIONAL CONVENTION SPEECH OF JESSE L. JACKSON 1988

*In 1984 Jesse L. Jackson became a candidate for president and sought the nomination of the Democratic Party. Many thought that the reason for the candidacy was to give Jackson leverage at the Democratic party's convention in order to influence the party's platform and to some extent Jackson succeeded, if such was his intent. In 1988 Jackson made a second run at the presidential nomination and the consensus was that he would not do much better than in his previous attempt. Jackson, however gained the support of most black leaders, and with excellent support from African-Americans and many liberal whites, Jackson made the primaries of 1988 memorable. His appearances in the debates during the presidential primaries raised the level of the dialog from political rhetoric to meaningful issues. In a field of seven candidates, Jackson was one of the two who survived up until convention time. Jackson ran an extremely credible race, coming in second behind the winner, Michael Dukakis, and gave notice that he would be an even more formidable candidate in the future.*

*Following are excerpts from the speech to the Democratic National Convention July 19, 1988 by Democratic presidential candidate Rev. Jesse L. Jackson.*

Tonight, we pause and give praise and honor to God for being good enough to allow us to be at this place at this time. When I look out at this convention, I see the face of America, red, yellow, brown, black and white. We are all precious in God's sight—the real rainbow coalition. All of us—all of us who are here think that we are seated. But we're really standing on someone's shoulders. Ladies and gentlemen, Mrs. Rosa Parks. The mother of the civil rights movement...

My right and my privilege to stand here before you has been won—won in my lifetime—by the blood and the sweat of the innocent... Dr. Martin Luther King Jr. lies only a few miles from us tonight. Tonight he must feel good as he looks down upon us. We sit here together, a rainbow coalition—the sons and daughters of slavemasters and the sons and daughters of slaves sitting together around a common table, to decide the direction of our party and our country. His heart would be full tonight.

As a testament to the struggles of those who have gone

*After an eloquent and emotional speech at the 1988 Democratic Convention, the family of Jesse Jackson stands on the podium with him amidst the roar of the crowd. His daughter Jacqueline is at his side. To his left is his son Yusef, to his right his son Jesse Jr.. Standing alongside Jesse Jr. is Jackson's daughter Santita with her arm around Mrs. Jackson.*

before; as a legacy for those who will come after; as a tribute to the endurance, the patience, the courage of our forefathers and mothers; as an assurance that their prayers are being answered, their work has not been in vain, and hope is eternal, tomorrow night my name will go into nomination for the presidency of the United States of America.

**Meeting at the Crossroad**

We meet tonight at the crossroads, a point of decision. Shall we expand, be inclusive, find unity and power; or suffer division and impotence.

We've come to Atlanta, the cradle of the old South, the crucible of the new South.

Tonight there is a sense of celebration because we are moved, fundamentally moved from racial battlegrounds by law, to economic common ground, with the moral challenge to move to higher ground; common ground!... Common ground! That's the challenge of our party tonight.

Left wing. Right wing. Progress will not come through boundless liberalism nor static conservatism, but at the critical mass of mutual survival.

When we divide, we cannot win. We must find common ground as a basis for survival. The day when we debated, differed, deliberated, agreed to agree, agree to disagree, when we had the good judgment to argue a case and then not self-destruct, George Bush was just a little further away from the White House and a little closer to private life.

Tonight I salute Gov. Michael Dukakis. He has run—He has run a well-managed and dignified campaign.

No matter how tired or how tried, he always resisted the temptation to stoop to demagoguery. I have watched a good mind fast at work, with steel nerves guiding his campaign out or the crowded field without appeal to the worst in us.

I have watched his perspective grow as his environment has expanded. I've seen his toughness and tenacity close up, knew his commitment to public service...

His foreparents came to America on immigrant ships. My foreparents came to America on slave ships. But whatever the original ships, we are in the same boat tonight...

Our choice? Full participation in a Democratic government or more abandonment and neglect. And so this night, we choose not a false sense of independence not our capacity to survive and endure. Tonight we choose interdependency, and our capacity to act and unite for the greater good...

**Finding Common Ground**

We find common ground at the plant gate that closes on workers without notice. We find common ground at the farm auction where a good farmer loses his or her land to bad loans or diminishing markets. Common ground at the schoolyard where teachers cannot get adequate pay, and students cannot get a scholarship, and can't make a loan. Common ground at the hospital admitting room, where somebody tonight is dying because they cannot afford to go upstairs to a bed that's empty waiting for someone with insurance to get sick. We are a better nation than that. We must do better than that...

Common ground. America is not a blanket, woven from one thread, one color, one cloth. When I was a child growing up in Greenville, South Carolina, and grandmomma could not afford a blanket, she didn't complain and we did not freeze. Instead she took pieces of old cloth—patches—wool, silk, gabardine, crockersack—only patches, barely good enough to wipe your shoes with. But they didn't stay that way very long With sturdy hands and a strong cord, she sewed them together into a quilt, a thing of beauty and power and culture. Now, Democrats, we must build such a quilt.

Farmers, you seek fair prices, and you are right—but you cannot stand alone, your patch is not big enough. Workers, you fight for fair wages, you are right—but your patch of labor is not big enough. Women, you seek comparable worth and pay equity, you are right—but your patch is not big enough. Women, mothers, who seek Head Start, and day-care and prenatal care on the front side of life, relevant jail care and welfare on the back side of life, you are right—but your patch is not big enough. Students you seek scholarships, you are right—but your patch is not big enough.

Blacks and Hispanics, when we fight for civil rights, we are right—but our patch is not big enough. Gays and lesbians, when you fight against discrimination and a cure for AIDS, you are right—but your patch is not big enough. Conservatives and progressives, when you fight for what you believe, right wing, left wing, hawk, dove, you are right from your point of view—but your point of view is not enough.

But don't despair. Be as wise as my grandma. Pull the patches and the pieces together, bound by a common thread. When we form a great quilt of unity and common ground, we'll have the power to bring about health care and housing and jobs and education and hope... We the people can win...

Based on the belief that the rich had too little money and the poor had too much. That's classic Reaganomics. They believe that the poor had too much money and the rich had too little money so they engaged in reverse Robin Hood—took from the poor and gave to the rich, paid for by the middle class. We cannot stand four more years of Reaganomics in any version, in any disguise.

How'd I document that case: Seven years later, the richest 1% of our society pays 20% less in taxes. The poorest 10% pay 20% more. Reaganomics.

Reagan gave the rich and the powerful a multibillion-dollar party. Now the party's over, he expects the people to pay for the damage.

I take this principal position: let us not raise taxes on the poor and the middle class, but those who had the party, the rich and the powerful, must pay for the party.

**Common Sense in High Places**

I just want to take common sense to high places. We're spending $150 billion a year defending Europe and Japan 43 years after the war is over. We have more troops in Europe tonight than we had seven years ago. Yet the threat of war is ever more remote.

Germany and Japan are now creditor nations, that means they got a surplus; we are a debtor nation, it means we are in debt. Let them share more of the burden of their own defense. Use some of that money to build decent housing. Use some of that money to educate our children. Use some of that money for long-term health care. Use some of that money to wipe out these slums and put America back to work.

I just want to take common sense to high places. We can bail out Europe and Japan. We can bail out Continental Bank and Chrysler and Mr. Iacocca, makes $8,000 an hour, we can bail out the family farmer.

I just want to make common sense. It does not make sense to close down 650,000 family farms in this country while importing food from abroad subsidized by the U.S. government. Let's make sense. It does not make sense to be escorting all our tankers up and down the Persian Gulf paying $2.50 for every $l worth of oil we bring out while oil wells are capped in Texas, Oklahoma and Louisiana. I just want to make sense.

Leadership must meet the moral challenge of its day. What's the moral challenge of our day? We have public accommodations We have the right to vote. We have open housing. What's the fundamental challenge of our day? It is to end economic violence. Plant closings without notice. Economic violence...

Most poor people are not lazy. They're not black. They're not brown. They're mostly white and female and young. But whether white, black or brown, a hungry baby's belly turned inside out is the same color...

Most poor people are not on welfare. Some of them are illiterate and can't read the want-ad section and when they can, they can't find a job that matches the address. They work hard every day. I know, I live amongst them... They catch the early bus. They work every day. They raise other people's children. They work every day. They clean the streets. They work every day... No, they're not lazy. Someone must defend them because it's right and they cannot speak for themselves...

We need a real war on drugs. You can't just say no. It's deeper than that. You can't just get a palm reader or an astrologer. It's more profound than that.

We are spending $15O billion on drugs a year. We've gone from ignoring it to focusing on the children. Children cannot buy $150 billion worth of drugs a year. A few high-profile athletes, athletes are not laundering $150 billion a year. Bankers are.

I met children in Watts who unfortunately in their despair, their grapes of hope have become raisins of despair and they're turning on each other and they're self-destructing. They say we don't have Saturday night specials anymore. They say we buy AK47s and Uzis, the latest make of weapons. We buy them across the counter on Long Beach Boulevard. You cannot fight a war on drugs unless, until you're going to challenge the bankers and the gun sellers and those who grow them. Don't just focus on the children. Let's stop drugs at the level of supply and demand...

**The Moral Challenge**

Leadership must face the moral challenge of our day. In the nuclear age, buildup is irrational. Strong leadership cannot desire to look tough and let that stand in the way of the pursuit of peace.

Leadership must reverse the arms race. At least we should pledge no first use. Why? Because first use begets first retaliation. And that's mutual annihilation. That's not a rational way out...

When Mr. Reagan and Mr. Gorbachev met there was a big meeting. They represented together one-eighth of the human race. Seven-eighths of the human race was locked out of that room...

We're losing ground in Latin America, Middle East, South Africa because we're not focusing on the real world—that real world. We must use basic principles... Support human rights, we believe in that. Support self-determination, we're built on that. Support economic development, you know it's right...

I am often asked, Jesse, why do you take on these toughies? They're not very political. You can't win that way. If an issue is morally right, it will eventually be political. It may be political and never be right...

We can win. We must not lose to the drugs and violence, premature pregnancy, suicide, cynicism, pessimism and despair. We can win. Wherever you are tonight, now I challenge you to hope and to dream. Don't submerge your dreams. Exercise above all else—even on drugs, dream of the day you are drug-free. Even in the gutter, dream of the day that you will be up on your feet again. You must never stop dreaming...

Dream of peace. Peace is rational and reasonable. War is irrational... and unwinnable.

And I was not supposed to make it. You see, I was born of a teenage mother, who was born of a teenage mother. I understand. I know abandonment, and people being mean to you, and saying you're nothing and nobody and can never be anything. I understand...

Wherever you are tonight, you can make it. Hold your head high. Stick your chest out. You can make it. It gets dark sometimes, but the morning comes. Don't you surrender. Suffering breeds character, character breeds faith, in the end faith will not disappoint.

You must not surrender. You may or may not get there but just know that you're qualified and you hold on and hold out. We must never surrender.

America will get better and better. Keep hope alive. Keep hope alive. Keep hope alive for tomorrow night and beyond. Keep hope alive. I love you very much. I love you very much.

## LIFT EVERY VOICE AND SING (1900)

*"Lift Every Voice and Sing" was written by the noted black poet and civil rights leader James Weldon Johnson. It was originally intended for use in a program given by a group of Jacksonville, Florida schoolchildren to celebrate Lincoln's birthday. Inasmuch as its words tend to convey a sense of birthright and heritage, it is often referred to as the "Negro National Anthem" and sung at the opening of various public gatherings.*

Lift every voice and sing
Till earth and heaven ring,
Ring with the harmonies of Liberty;
Let our rejoicing rise
High as the listening skies,
Let it resound loud as the rolling sea.
Sing a song full of the faith that the dark past has taught us,
Sing a song full of the hope that the present has brought us,
Facing the rising sun of our new day begun
Let us march on till victory is won.

Stony the road we trod,
Bitter the chastening rod,
Felt in the days when hope unborn had died;
Yet with a steady beat,
Have not our weary feet
Come to the place for which our fathers sighed?
We have come over a way that with tears have been watered,
We have come, treading our path through the blood of the slaughtered,
Out from the gloomy past,
Till now we stand at last
Where the white gleam of our bright star is cast.

God of our weary years,
God of our silent tears,
Thou who has brought us thus far on the way;
Thou who has by Thy might
Led us into the light,
Keep us forever in the path, we pray.
Lest our feet stray from the places, Our God, where we met Thee,
Lest, our hearts drunk with the wine of the world, we forget Thee;
Shadowed beneath Thy hand,
May we forever stand.
True to our GOD,
True to our native land

## DECLARATION OF THE RIGHTS OF THE CHILD (1959)

*The Declaration of the Rights of the Child was adopted on November 20, 1959 as an extension of the Universal Declaration of Human Rights. Its general objective is to create a climate in which the children of the world can enjoy a safe, happy, and wholesome life.*

*The document, consisting of a preamble and 10 "principles," addresses itself not only to governments, but also to parents, voluntary organizations, and local authorities—encouraging them to recognize the rights of children and to adopt appropriate legal and social measures for the safeguarding of these rights. Great care was taken by various UN agencies to formulate the principles in a way that would not conflict with the political, religious, and ideological beliefs of any member nations.*

### Preamble

*Whereas* the peoples of the United Nations have, in the Charter, reaffirmed their faith in fundamental human rights, and in the dignity and worth of the human person, and have determined to promote social progress and better standards of life in larger freedom,

*Whereas* the United Nations has, in the Universal Declaration of Human Rights, proclaimed that everyone is entitled to all the rights and freedoms set forth therein, without distinction of any kind, such as race, color, sex, language, religion, political or other opinion, national or social origin, property, birth or other status,

*Whereas* the child, by reason of his physical and mental immaturity, needs special safeguards and care, including appropriate legal protection, before as well as after birth,

*Whereas* the need for such special safeguards has been stated in the Geneva Declaration of the Rights of the Child of 1924, and recognized in the Universal Declaration of Human Rights and in the statutes of specialized agencies and international organizations concerned with the welfare of children.

*Whereas* mankind owes to the child the best it has to give,
*Now therefore,*
*The General Assembly*
*Proclaims* this *Declaration of the Rights of the Child* to the end that he may have a happy childhood and enjoy for his own good and for the good of society the rights and freedoms herein set forth, and calls upon parents, upon men and

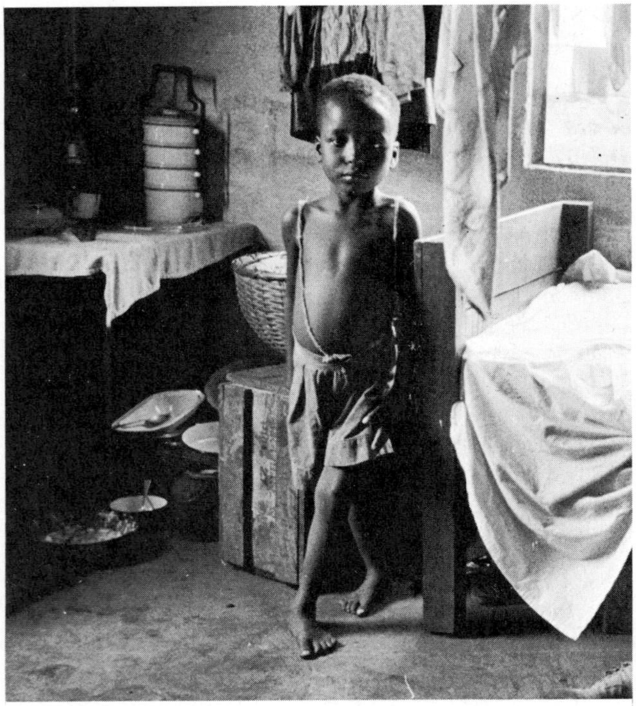

*A boy from the Republic of Cameroon, West Africa.*

women as individuals and upon voluntary organizations, local authorities and national Governments to recognize these rights and strive for their observance by legislative and other measures progressively taken in accordance with the following principles:

**Principle 1**
The child shall enjoy all the rights set forth in this Declaration. All children, without any exception whatsoever, shall be entitled to these rights, without distinction or discrimination on account of race, color, sex, language, religion, political or other opinion, national or social origin, property, birth or other status, whether of himself or of his family.

**Principle 2**
The child shall enjoy special protection, and shall be given opportunities and facilities, by law and by other means, to enable him to develop physically, mentally, morally, spiritually and socially in a healthy and normal manner and in conditions of freedom and dignity. In the enactment of laws for this purpose the best interests of the child shall be the paramount consideration .

**Principle 3**
The child shall be entitled from his birth to a name and a nationality.

**Principle 4**
The child shall enjoy the benefits of social security. He shall be entitled to grow and develop in health; to this end special care and protection shall be provided both to him and to his mother, including adequate pre-natal and post-natal care. The child shall have the right to adequate nutrition, housing, recreation and medical services.

**Principle 5**
The child who is physically, mentally or socially handicapped shall be given the special treatment, education and care required by his particular condition.

**Principle 6**
The child, for the full and harmonious development of his personality, needs love and understanding. He shall, wherever possible, grow up in the care and under the responsibility of his parents, and in any case in an atmosphere of affection and of moral and material security; a child of tender years shall not, save in exceptional circumstances, be separated from his mother. Society and the public authorities shall have the duty to extend particular care to children without a family and to those without adequate means of support. Payment of State and other assistance towards the maintenance of children of large families is desirable.

**Principle 7**
The child is entitled to receive education, which shall be free and compulsory, at least in the elementary stages. He shall be given an education which will promote his general culture, and enable him on a basis of equal opportunity to develop his abilities, his individual judgment, and his sense of moral and social responsibility, and to become a useful member of society.

The best interest of the child shall be the guiding principle of those responsible for his education and guidance; that responsibility lies in the first place with his parents.

The child shall have full opportunity for play and recreation, which should be directed to the same purposes as education; society and the public authorities shall endeavor to promote the enjoyment of this right.

**Principle 8**
The child shall in all circumstances be among the first to receive protection and relief.

**Principle 9**
The child shall be protected against all forms of neglect, cruelty and exploitation. He shall not be the subject of traffic in any form.

The child shall not be admitted to employment before an appropriate minimum age; he shall in no case be caused or permitted to engage in any occupation or employment which would prejudice his health or education, or interfere with his physical, mental or moral development.

**Principle 10**
The child shall be protected from practices which may foster racial, religious and any other form of discrimination. He shall be brought up in a spirit of understanding, tolerance, friendship among peoples, peace and universal brotherhood and in the consciousness that his energy and talents should be devoted to the service of his fellow men.

# HISTORIC LANDMARKS OF BLACK AMERICA

**A Survey of Afro-American Historic Sites, Buildings, Monuments, and Shrines Across the United States**

No more substantial testimony to the black role in the growth and development of this nation can be found than the numerous historical landmarks in various regions of the country which are associated with black Americans. Many of these—like the Alamo and Bunker Hill—are not conventionally known as sites involving black participation in the making of American history.

## ALABAMA

### Florence

*Handy Heights Housing Development and Museum*

The Development and Museum is named for composer W. C. Handy, who was born in Florence in 1873. It includes a restored cabin in which are housed his piano, trumpet, and other mementoes.

### Mobile

*Fort Gaines (on Dauphin Island)*

Fort Gaines is the site of the Battle of Mobile Bay (August 1864) during the Civil War. One of the key battles of the day was the engagement between Admiral David Farragut's flagship, the Hartford, and the Confederate ironclad, Tennessee. During the battle, black naval hero John Lawson manned his duty station despite serious injury. His role in keeping Union guns operative may well have saved the ship from destruction. For his valor, the Pennsylvania black was awarded the Medal of Honor. Black infantry units also participated in the capture of Fort Gaines, and later, the capture of Mobile itself. When nearby Fort Blakely fell, nine black regiments were included in the 1st Division of the federal force commanded by General John Hawkins.

### Montgomery

*Dexter Avenue Baptist Church*
*454 Dexter Avenue*

The Dexter Avenue Baptist Church is the church where Dr. Martin Luther King Jr. organized the black boycott of segregated city buses in Montgomery in 1955. The church, which has been in existence since 1878, was declared a National Historic Landmark by the Department of Interior on March 30, 1974. Dr. King pastored the church from 1954 to 1959. In the church is a mural depicting scenes and related data of the civil rights movement as well as a Dr. Martin Luther King Library containing personal mementoes of Dr. King and his family and resource data on him. It was the boycott of buses in Montgomery, which he led, that brought Dr. King into national prominence as a civil rights leader.

## Talladega
*Talladega College and Swayne Hall*

Home of the first college for blacks in Alabama, Talladega was founded by the American Missionary Association as a primary school in 1867. Its Slavery Library houses three fresco panels by Hale Woodruff (the celebrated Amistad Murals). Professor Woodruff studied abroad in France under the renowned Henry Ossawa Tanner, and also at the Herron Institute in Indianapolis.

Swayne Hall, built in 1857, is the oldest building on the campus of Talladega College. The building was declared a National Historic Landmark by the Department of Interior on December 2, 1974. The building was built by slave labor before the school was established. Talladega pursued a liberal arts program at a time when vocationalism dominated Negro education.

*The Battle of Mobile Bay, where John Lawson, a Pennsylvania black, was awarded the Medal of Honor.*

## Tuskegee
*Tuskegee Institute*

The Institute is a world-famous center for agricultural research and extension work. First opened on July 4, 1881 with a $2,000 appropriation from the Alabama State Legislature, it consisted of a single shanty, a student body of 30, and one teacher—Booker T. Washington. Tuskegee functioned originally as a normal school for the training of black teachers, the first of its kind established in the United States. Eventually it came to specialize in agricultural and manual training, areas which were to make both the school and Booker T. Washington famous.

In 1882, Washington moved the school to a 100-acre plantation and began a self-help program which enabled students to finance their education. Most of the early buildings were built with the aid of student labor.

Next to Washington, the most famous person to be associated with the Institute was George Washington Carver, who became its director of agricultural research in 1896. Carver persuaded many Southern farmers to plant peanuts, sweet potatoes, and other crops instead of cotton, which was rapidly depleting the soil. Ultimately, Carver's research programs helped develop 300 derivative products from peanuts and 118 from sweet potatoes. At one point, he even succeeded in making synthetic marble from wood pulp.

Today, Tuskegee covers nearly 5,000 acres and has more tan 150 buildings. Notable places to visit there include the Founder's Marker (the site of Washington's original shanty), the Oaks (Washington's home), the Booker T. Washington

*The John A. Andrew Memorial Hospital wing at Tuskegee Institute.*

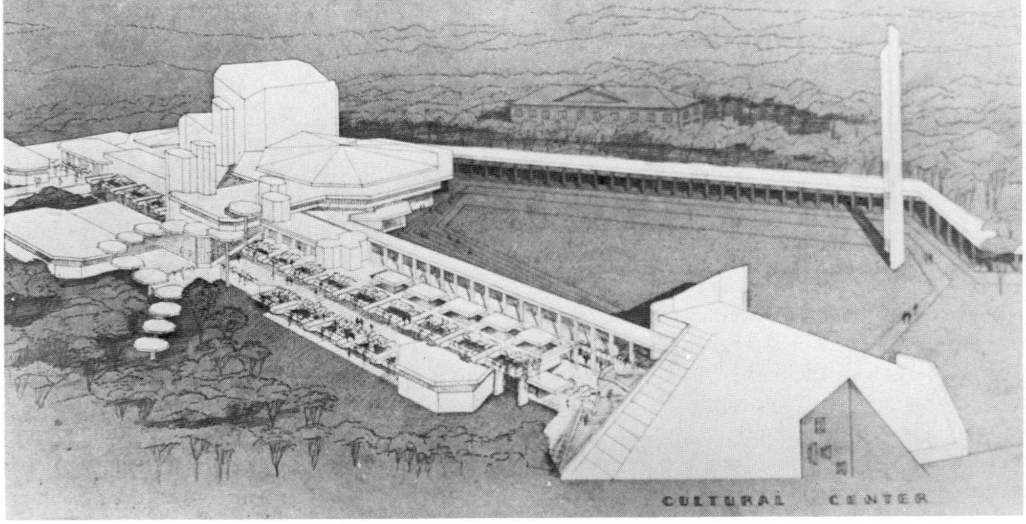

*Fort Apache, Arizona, in 1877. Black troops were quartered here after the Civil War.*

Monument, and the George Washington Carver Museum.

The Carver Museum houses the scientist's plant, mineral, and bird collections, and includes exhibits of various products he developed, as well as a number of his paintings and research papers.

Tuskegee is also the home of the George Washington Carver Foundation, a research center founded by Carver in 1940.

## ALASKA

### Fairbanks
*Pioneers Home*

One of the few surviving black pioneers of Alaska is Mattie Crosby, who first came to the wilderness in 1900 with a Maine family that adopted her. Miss Crosby later opened a bathhouse and became famous as one of Alaska's best cooks. Some blacks came into the territory during the era of the Gold Rush, and others were occasionally seen on board ships which brought in supplies. Still, for nearly 17 years, Mattie Crosby lived in Fairbanks without meeting another black. In her advancing years, she wrote a book about her experiences, but it has unfortunately since been lost.

## ARIZONA

### Bowie
*Fort Bowie*

Established in 1862 in Kochese County, Fort Bowie was the focal point of military operations against Geronimo. Two of the eight cavalry regiments were black "buffalo soldier" regiments.

### Apache
*Geronimo Monument*

Geronimo was one of the last Apache chieftains to resist the oncoming hordes of white settlers and immigrants moving into the Southwest. Black cavalrymen finally escorted Geronimo and his renegades into exile at Fort Dickens, Florida and later returned with him to Fort Sill, where he died.

*On steep mountainside trails, cavalrymen became foot soldiers.*

### Bonita
*Old Fort Grantt*

This is the site of a fort at which black soldiers were housed during the Indian Wars. Two soldiers of the fort, Isaiah Mays and Benjamin Brown, received Congressional Medals of Honor while on duty at this station.

### Fort Apache
*Old Fort Apache*

Another fort at which black units served during the Indian Wars. The punitive expedition led by John Pershing in search of Pancho Villa originated at this point, the 10th Cavalry in the vanguard. This unit was stationed at the fort beginning in 1913, after having seen service in Cuba and the Philippines.

### Fort Thomas
*Camp Thomas*

This camp was a base of operations from which both black cavalry units operated in their mission to keep peace among the Apache tribes. One black, Sergeant William McBryar, won the Congressional Medal of Honor for demonstrating "coolness" and "bravery" under combat stress during the pursuit of a renegade Apache.

*A cavalryman of the Old West.*

### Phoenix
*State House*

Among the eight murals at the State Capitol Building in Phoenix depicting vital episodes from Arizona's history, is one portraying Estevanico, the black guide of Fray Marcos de Niza, the Franciscan missionary whose search for the Seven Cities of Gold brought him into Arizona in 1539. Estevanico was killed at one of the seven Zuni pueblos after trying to escape.

### San Carlos
*San Carlos Indian Reservation*

The 9th and 10th Cavalry, black regiments formed after the Civil War, were often sent out to combat the Cheyenne and Apache Indians in the American Southwest. The Indians called them *Buffalo Soldiers;* their own white officers referred to them as *The Brunettes*. What ever their designation, however, they were considered to be among the best troops in the area. The first black officer assigned to the 10th Cavalry was Lieutenant Henry O. Flipper, who was the first black to graduate from West Point.

Blacks were among the troops under General Crook's command at the time of the surrender of the famed Apache chief Geronimo in 1876.

Today, the tribal council of the San Carlos Apaches meets regularly on the site where the reservation of the Warm Springs Apaches was once found.

### Sierra Vista
*Fort Huachuca*

Fort Huachuca quartered troops of the 9th and 10th Cavalry during the Indian Wars. Elements of the 10th were stationed here in the first decade of the twentieth century. During World War II, the men of the all-black 92nd Division trained here before being sent overseas to Africa and Europe.

### Springerville
*Apache National Forest*

Site, in the White Mountains, where troopers of the 10th Cavalry captured Mangas Coloradas on September 18, 1886. Coloradas was one of those fierce Apache chiefs who fought desperately for choice grazing lands for his people. Today the reservation at Springerville contains millions of acres of fertile land, the legacy of the tenacious resistance of the Apaches.

### Tombstone
*John Swain (Slaughter) Grave in Boot Hill*

Born a slave in 1845, John Swain went to Tombstone in 1879 as a cowhand in the employ of John Slaughter, who was later to become sheriff of this town. Swain was an expert rider, and only one of several blacks to work for Slaughter.

In 1884, Swain fought and lost a one-round boxing match with John L. Sullivan, then heavyweight champion of the world. He died just three months short of his hundredth

*The National Guard escorts children from Little Rock Central High School.*

birthday, and was buried with honors by the citizens of Tombstone. A special tablet stands on the grave site, commemorating the close ties between the two men.

### Tortilla Flat
*Battle of the Caves*

Site, during 1872-1873, of General Crook's campaign to wipe out Apache bands holed up in distant, and virtually inaccessible, mountain retreats. Black units approached the Indian hide-out under cover of darkness, pinned down the enemy in their cave, and scored a notable victory. Few of the marauders escaped, and several were killed by ricocheting bullets.

## ARKANSAS

### Camden
*Poison Spring State Park*

The Poison Spring State Park is the site of an 1864 Civil War battle in which the 1st Kansas Colored Regiment suffered heavy casualties, some of which were apparently inflicted by Confederates on captured or wounded black soldiers. Black troops, as they did at Fort Pillow, vowed to take no more rebel prisoners.

### Helena
*The Battle of Helena*

Among the defenders of this Mississippi River port were members of the 2nd Infantry Regiment of African Descent. Black soldiers fought shoulder to shoulder with whites in repulsing a Confederate siege of the city in July 1863. The experience of one black unit stationed there—the 56th U.S. Colored Troops—is typical of many which confronted blacks during the war. Disease was an even more potent enemy than combat. Only a handful of men lost their lives as a result of armed conflict, whereas literally hundreds fell victim to disease and poor medical treatment.

### Little Rock
*Philander Smith College*

Opened in 1877 under the sponsorship of the Methodist Episcopal Church, Philander Smith (then known as Walder College) was renamed five years later after receiving a large donation which enabled the school to construct a permanent brick edifice.

*Little Rock Central High School*

Here, in the fall of 1957, the first major confrontation over implementation of the Supreme Court's 1954 decision outlawing racial segregation in public school took place. President Eisenhower use of troops to enforce the court's order to desegregate "with all deliberate speed" was an affirmation of the Supreme Court decision by the nation's chief executive.

### Sheridan
*Jenkins Ferry State Park*

Two weeks after the Poison Spring engagement—on April 30, 1864, to be exact—the 1st and 2nd Kansas Colored Regiments saw action along the Sabine River, where they overran a Confederate battery, shouting, "Remember Poison Spring" and inflicting 150 casualties on the enemy.

## CALIFORNIA

### Allensworth
*Allensworth Colony*

The town of Allensworth, an all black community, was founded by Allen Allensworth in 1910 and is still in existence. Now a historic monument, this landmark is being developed by a black historical group as a memorial to the founder. The town is named after Allen Allensworth, who as a slave, just prior to the Civil War, was a well-known racing jockey in Louisville, Kentucky. With the beginning of the Civil War, Allensworth was allowed to enter the Navy where he advanced

*Allensworth, California, was founded by a famous nineteenth-century jockey.*

to rank of Chief Petty Officer. After the War, Allensworth studied for the ministry and returned to the military service as Chaplain of the famed 24th U.S. Infantry. Around 1900 he migrated to California where he dedicated himself to improving the lot of his black brothers. The founding of Allensworth was a result.

### Arcadia
*Santa Anita Race Track*

Santa Anita Race Track is located on the former site of the E. J. "Lucky" Baldwin ranch, a spread at which John Fisher, a black man and former slave, was a prominent breeder and trainer. Fisher, a native of St. Louis, was at first reluctant to follow Baldwin to California out of fear of Indians, but was eventually persuaded to join him. He later became a foreman on the ranch.

### Beckwourth
*Beckwourth Pass*
*(U.S. Alt. 40, east of the junction with U.S. Rte. 395)*

Beckwourth Pass, which runs through the Sierra Nevada mountains, was discovered by James P. Beckwourth, one of a number of black traders and trappers dubbed *The Mountain Men* by many writers of American history.

Fond of telling a good yarn, Beckwourth not surprisingly added spice to his own life with a number of romantic legends, in which it is often difficult to separate fact from fantasy.

One such story has it that, toward the end of his life, he killed a man in an argument in Denver, and was held in custody for a time before being acquitted on a plea of self-defense. Beckwourth, who claimed to be a Crow chief, was subsequently welcomed by the tribe, which believed him to be a symbol of good fortune. When he talked of leaving, the Crow decided to keep their "talisman" with them forever by planning a sumptuous feast in his honor and then poisoning the stew.

A less embellished account of his end has it that he died on the trail two days after leaving Denver for a rendezvous with the Crow.

### Beverly Hills
*Beverly-Wilshire Hotel*

Black architect Paul R. Williams designed this plush hotel, one of the most elegant in the area. Many stunning private residences of famous Hollywood stars have been designed by Williams, the Spingarn medalist for 1953.

*Black and white prospectors washing gold at Spanish Flats, California, in 1852.*

*Jim Beckwourth, the black frontiersman for whom Beckwourth Pass in the Sierras is named.*

### Downieville
*The Pioneer Museum*

Site of an 1849 gold strike involving a Scotch immigrant, William Downie, and 10 blacks. One of the black adventurers was Waller Jackson, an Easterner who journeyed "round the Horn" in 1849 and found his fortune with the rest of the prospecting party.

### Folsom Lake
*"Negro Bar" Marker*

Folsom Lake now covers the site of an old mining camp anonymously associated with black gold miners. Remains of these intrepid pioneers have been reburied at nearby Mormon Island Pioneer Cemetery.

### Fremont Park
*Fremont Peak State Park*

John C. Fremont—soldier of fortune, explorer, writer, politician—was a key figure in the development of California and in the war which was fought against Mexico to make this vast territory a part of the Union.

Fremont led four exploratory and mapping missions into California and took along blacks on two of them. John Dodson, a free black who was a servant of Fremont's father-in-law, Senator Thomas Hart Benton, accompanied the second of these expeditions, while Saunders Jackson, likewise a servant of Benton, volunteered for the fourth in order to raise the $1,700 needed to buy his family's freedom.

After considerable hardship, the ill-fated fourth expedition ended with Fremont and his party finally arriving in California via a southern route. Once there, Fremont discovered that in his absence gold had been discovered on land he owned. Jackson was given permission to prospect for gold and within a few days had dug out nuggets valued at $1,700. He then returned to Missouri, emancipated his family as planned, and disappeared from history.

Having become a millionaire, Fremont, whose political ideology was abolitionist, was to experience several ups and downs, both in military and in political affairs, during his later career. Ultimately, however, he became territorial governor of Arizona before his death in 1890.

### Hollywood
*Grauman's Chinese Theater*

In 1967, Sidney Poitier became the first black actor to record his footprints in the concrete of Grauman's Chinese Theater, a ritual which has become synonymous with stardom and success in Hollywood film circles.

### Hornitos
*Gold Mining Camp*

Home of Moses Rodgers, a successful and affluent black mine owner who was one of the finest engineers and metallurgists in the state. Rodgers was only one of several black miners who struck it rich in gold and quartz. One black, known to history only as Dick, reputedly amassed a fortune of more than $100,000 but lost it all on the Sacramento gaming tables, and in despair, blew his brains out.

### Mokelumme Hill
*Gold Discovery Marker*

Site of a legendary strike involving a black miner allegedly the butt of a white prank. According to the story, a befuddled black prospector asked his white colleagues where to dig and was told, with great fanfare, that a barren hillside in town was the most likely place to strike it rich. What took shape as an elaborate joke turned out, however, to be a startling prophecy, fulfilled inside of two days by a happy black prospector carrying a sack of gold. The butt of the joke had returned to thank his "friends" for their generous and abundant advice.

### Oakland
*Oakland Art Museum*

The museum has several pieces done by prominent black artists, including Sargent Johnson's Forever Free and lithographs by Grafton T. Brown, believed to be the first black artist active in the state.

### Red Bluff
*Oak Hill Cemetery*

The burial place of Aaron Coffey, the only black man in the Society of California Pioneers. Coffey, descendant of an officer who fought under Jackson at New Orleans, came to

California a slave in 1849. By day, he worked at his master's claim, and by night, as a cobbler, accumulating money toward his $1,000 emancipation fee. Betrayed by his owner, he was forced to return to Missouri, where he was again sold. Coffey pleaded with his new master to allow him to return to California and earn the necessary money to free himself and his family, which he left behind as collateral. That mission accomplished, Coffey returned to Red Bluff, took up farming, and settled down to a contented family life.

**Sacramento**

*St. Andrew's African Methodist Church*

The first AME church in California, organized in a private residence in 1850. Within four years, the congregation organized a school for black, Oriental, and Indian children in the church basement.

**San Francisco**

*Leidesdorff Street*

Named after William Alexander Leidesdorff, a wealthy and influential California pioneer of black and Danish ancestry and a native of the Danish West Indies. A merchant, Leidesdorff operated the first steamer to pass through the Golden Gate, was later appointed U.S. vice-consul, and ultimately became a civic and educational leader in San Francisco.

**Sequoia**

*Sequoia National Park*

In 1903, Captain Charles Young, the third black man to graduate from the United States Military Academy at West Point, became the first black superintendent of an American National Park. Captain Young distinguished himself during his tenure as Sequoia National Park Superintendent as he did during his entire military career. He rose to the rank of full colonel and died in 1923 while on an official mission to Africa. Colonel Young was buried in the Arlington National Cemetery with full honors.

## COLORADO

**Breckenridge**

*Barney Ford Hill (just southeast of city limits)*

A fugitive slave who went to Colorado in 1860 in search of gold, Barney Ford had once operated a station in Chicago's Underground Railroad and been involved with the famed revolutionary John Brown.

Ford found gold but was cheated out of his claim by outlaws. He managed to get back to Denver, where rumors began to spread that he had buried a fortune in the hill which now bears his name.

Ford actually became a wealthy hotel owner and restaurateur (repeating the success he had originally had in Nicaragua), but in spite of this, people persisted in believing his wealth was really derived from the hillside treasure-trove. The result was that, over the years, the hill became pockmarked with the diggings of those who refused to believe Ford's protestations and denials. Later in life, Ford was beleaguered by hoodlums and other riffraff who insisted on spying upon his every move in the hope that he would one day betray a vital clue to the whereabouts of the alleged treasure.

*Charity worker Clara Brown became the leading citizen of Central City, Colorado.*

**Central City**

*"Aunt Clara" Brown Chair*
*(Central City Opera House)*

This chair is a tribute to "Aunt Clara" Brown, believed to have been the first black resident of Colorado. Aunt Clara died in 1877, in her eighties.

Born a slave in Virginia, Aunt Clara moved to Missouri where her husband and children were sold before she herself gained freedom through her master's last will and testament. From Missouri she headed for Kansas and then for the gold fields of Colorado, where she opened the territory's first laundry. From her earnings she soon began putting aside money for the purchase of her family.

Even though the Emancipation intervened and her immediate family was set free, she nonetheless returned to Missouri and brought back with her to Central City a group of 38 relatives. She remained in the mining community for the rest of her life, nursing the sick and performing other charitable works.

She was buried with honors by the Colorado Pioneers Association, of which she was a member. Her chair was dedicated in 1932.

**Denver**

*Inter-Ocean Hotel*
*16th and Market Streets*

The Inter-Ocean Hotel, once a showplace for millionaires and presidents, was built by Barney Ford, a black entrepreneur active during the gold rush days. (See first Colorado entry.)Ford and his cohorts joined the fight over the organization of the Colorado territory and the question of statehood. Originally allowed to vote, they had seen this privilege abrogated by the territorial constitution, and as a result, sought to delay statehood for the territory until black voting rights were reinstated. Enlisting the aid of the famed Massachusetts abolitionist Senator Charles Sumner, Ford urged President Andrew Johnson to veto the bill for statehood.

Ultimately, Johnson adopted this course of action, and as an ironic consequence, Colorado was unable to vote on the question of Johnson's impeachment. Had the territory become a state then, it is believed likely that the two provisional senators would have voted for impeachment, inasmuch as they were known to be vehemently anti-Johnson.

In Colorado, Ford was blamed for attempting to block statehood and for keeping Johnson in office. Once the Fifteenth Amendment had been passed, however, Ford began to work vigorously on behalf of statehood. He supported the Republican state legislature and its representatives on the electoral commission which voted in the Hayes-Tilden election. Some claimed Ford was responsible for the deciding commission vote. In any event, the advent of Hayes to the presidency signaled the end of Reconstruction and paved the way for a series of laws which soon deprived the black throughout the South of his precious and newly won voting right.

Ford retired and spent the remainder of his life in Denver where he died in December 1902. He is buried alongside his wife Julia in Denver's Riverside Cemetery.

### Pueblo
*The El Pueblo*

The museum houses a replica of the Gantt-Blackwell Fort which Jim Beckwourth, black explorer, scout, and trader, claimed to have founded in 1842. The validity of the claim has not been established, inasmuch as Beckwourth is known to have had something of a reputation as a teller of tall tales.

## CONNECTICUT

### Canterbury
*Home of Prince Goodin*

A parcel of land in Canterbury, once the home of Prince Goodin, a free black who fought with the British against the French in the French and Indian War. Goodin enlisted in 1757 after hearing a fiery speech of Canterbury's Reverend James Cogswell which stressed the danger of encroachment against "properties, liberties, religion and our lives." He served at Fort William Henry and was captured during a French attack upon the fort and taken to Montreal where he was sold into slavery. After three years of captivity he was freed when the British took the city in 1760. Goodin later petitioned the colony of Connecticut for compensation.

### Farmington
*First Church of Christ*
*(Hartford County)*

As the center of the community life of the Amistad captives after their famous 1840-1841 trial, the First Church of Christ commemorates the importance of this famous trial in the history of the abolition movement. The church was designated a National Historic Landmark on December 8, 1976.

### Groton Heights
*Fort Griswold State Park*

Freeman was the black orderly of the American commander Colonel William Ledyard, who was forced to surrender the fort to superior British forces. The British officer who accepted the surrender behaved ignobly, however. Ledyard was first induced to give up the sword and then run through with his own weapon, presumably in revenge for the death

*Fugitive slave Barney L. Ford discovered gold in California.*

*Barney Ford's hotel in Denver, Colorodo.*

*Jeff Liberty's Grave marker placed by the Sons of the American Revolution.*

of a British officer at the hands of Freeman. Another black, Lambert Latham, avenged Ledyard's death by killing the treacherous British officer.

### Washington
*Jeff Liberty Grave*

In the Judea Cemetery in Washington, Connecticut, lies the grave of Jeff Liberty, a soldier in the Continental Army during the Revolution. His grave marker, erected by the Sons of the American Revolution, states simply "in remembrance of Jeff Liberty and his colored patriots." Liberty, a slave at the time of the rebellion, asked his owner to be allowed to serve in the struggle for independence. His request granted, he fought throughout the revolution with a black Connecticut regiment and was granted freedman status at the end of the war.

### New Haven
*James Weldon Johnson Collection*
*Temple Street Church*

Temple Street Church was one of the foremost stopping-off points for fugitive slaves en route to Canada. It was founded by two Underground Railroad agents, Reverends Simeon S. Jocelyn and Amos G. Beman, the latter of whom was the church's first black pastor. The town of New Haven lived up to its name both prior to and during the Civil War, providing shelter to many slaves bound for freedom. Many New Haven citizens were involved in the work.

## DELAWARE

### *Wilmington*
*Asbury Methodist Episcopal Church*

This church, located at Third and Walnut Streets, was dedicated in 1789 by the distinguished orator Bishop Francis Asbury. Tradition has it that on one occasion a number of the town's leading citizens, many of whom were eager to hear Asbury preach but considered Methodism beneath them socially, refused to enter the church but stayed outside within hearing distance of the sermon. The listeners were impressed by the eloquence of the man they heard—not, as it turned out, the bishop, but his black servant Harry whose compelling testimony reached their ears and inspired their admiration. By 1805, however, blacks had left this church, driven out by the decision of white worshippers to confine black members to the gallery. The blacks who left formed their own church.

## DISTRICT OF COLUMBIA

*Association for the Study of Negro Life and History*
*1538 Ninth Street, N.W.*

The Association was long the sole professional agency concerned with preserving the historical record of the black in American life. The organizing pioneer behind the Association was Carter Woodson, a scholar and lecturer who began publication of the *Journal of Negro History* in 1916. Ten years later, Woodson inaugurated observance of "Negro History Week," during which leaders of the black freedom struggle were appropriately honored, primarily in schools. Negro History Week is always celebrated in February, as close as possible to the birthdays of both Frederick Douglass and Abraham Lincoln. Woodson and his later colleague, Dr. Charles Wesley of Central State, collaborated on many historical studies.

*Mary McLeod Bethune*

### *Mary McLeod Bethune Memorial*

The Mary McLeod Bethune Memorial, unveiled in 1974, is the first monument to a black person, or a woman, erected on public land in the nation's capitol. The $400,000 monument is located in Lincoln Park. It is inscribed with the words:

I leave you love, I leave you hope. I leave you the challenge of developing confidence in one another. I leave you a thirst for education. I leave you respect for the use of power. I leave you faith. I leave you racial dignity.

Mrs. Bethune was a black educator who was concerned about the children of the laborers who worked on the Florida East Coast Railroad.

In 1904, she established the Daytona Normal and Industrial Institute for black girls. In 1926, she merged with Cookman Institute of Jacksonville to form the Bethune and Cookman College.

Mrs. Bethune helped President Roosevelt organize the National Youth Administration, and in 1936 she became Director of the Division of Black Affairs. She received the Spingarn Award in 1935.

### *Bethune Museum and Archives*
### *1318 Vermont Avenue, N.W.*

Named for Mary Mcleod Bethune, the Bethune Museum and Archives national historic sight was opened in November 1979 and granted national historic sight status in April 1982. The Bethune Museum and Archives which is a fully independent non-profit organization preserves the historic and contemporary contributions made by black women and enriches the lives of America's children through educational material programs and other services.

### *Black Revolutionary War Patriots Memorial*

This memorial will honor the 5,000 Afro-Americans who fought during the American Revolution.

### *Blanche K. Bruce House*
### *909 M Street, N.W.*

A Senator from Mississippi, Blanche K. Bruce was the first black American to serve a full term in the U.S. Senate from 1875 to 1881. Bruce was born in Farmville, Virginia and learned the printer's trade in Missouri. In 1861, prior to the Civil War, he escaped to Hannibal, Missouri and set up a school for blacks. He studied at Oberlin College in Oberlin, Ohio and after moving to Mississippi he became a wealthy planter. His positions in Mississippi included that of sheriff, tax collector, a member of the levee board in Mississippi, and superintendent of schools for the county. A Republican, Bruce was elected by the Mississippi state legislature to the U.S. Senate in 1874. The Blanche K. Bruce House was designated a National Historic Landmark on May 15, 1975.

### *Mary Ann Shadd Cary House*
### *1421 W Street, N.W.*

Mary Ann Shadd Cary was the first black newspaper woman in America and lived in the house between 1881 and 1886. She was also a writer, educator, lawyer, and anti-slavery abolitionist. A forceful lecturer, she appeared before audiences throughout the country, usually speaking on topics of slavery and women's suffrage. During the Civil War she held the position of recruiting officer for the Union Army. The house was designated a National Historic Landmark on December 8, 1976.

*Ceder Hill, home of Frederick Douglass.*

*Freed slaves contributed the money for this statue of Lincoln the Emancipator.*

### Frederick Douglass Home
### 1411 W Street, S.E.

Cedar Hill, the 20-room colonial mansion in which Frederick Douglass lived for the last 13 years of his life, has been preserved as a monument to the great nineteenth-century abolitionist. In 1964, Secretary of the Interior Stewart Udall declared it a national shrine.

Credit for the restoration and preservation of the home belongs largely to the National Association of Colored Women's Clubs, which worked hand in hand with the Douglass Association.

### Birthplace of Edward Kennedy "Duke" Ellington
### 1212 T Street, N.W.

On 1212 T Street N.W., Washington, D.C. stands the building in which "Duke" Ellington was born on April 29, 1899. Ellington, one of the world's great exponents of jazz, was enormously versatile. In addition to being a great bandleader, Ellington was a talented pianist, and a composer in his idiom without peer. He died in May 1974.

### Emancipation Statue: Lincoln Park

Former black slaves were responsible for financing and erecting the oldest memorial to Abraham Lincoln in the Washington, D.C. area.

After Lincoln's assassination in 1865, the first five dollars for the statue was donated by a Mrs. Charlotte Scott of Marietta, Ohio. Contributions were soon pouring in, whereupon Congress finally set aside appropriate grounds for Thomas Bell's statue of Lincoln breaking slavery's chains. The memorial was dedicated on April 14, 1876—the eleventh anniversary of the assassination of the Great Emancipator.

### Charlotte Forten Grimkea House
### 1608 R Street, N.W.

Charlotte Forten Grimkea, born of wealthy free black parents in Philadelphia, was among the first wave of northerners engaged in educating slaves in the occupied Union territories of the South. Her activities as a female black activist, writer, poet, and educator forged a path for the participation of other females in education, social welfare, and humanitarian endeavors. The house was designated a National Historic Landmark on May 11, 1976.

### General Oliver Otis Howard House

The house was the residence of the Union Civil War General who became head of the freed men's bureau to help rehabilitate former slaves during the reconstruction period. Howard University is named in honor of General Howard and his residence is the only one of four original university buildings still standing at this distinguished institution.

### Howard University

Howard University, founded in 1867, is the largest institution of higher learning established for the black in the immediate post-Civil War period.

Covering more than 50 acres on one of the highest elevations in the District of Columbia, the campus grounds and the physical plant are valued at more than 40 million dollars. Of particular interest is the famed Founders Library, which contains more than 300,000 volumes and includes the Moorland Collection, one of the finest collections on black life and history in the United States.

### Lincoln Memorial

The Lincoln Memorial has been the site of several important events underscoring the black's quest for dignity and struggle for opportunity. One of these events involved the 1963 March on Washington which was climaxed by the Reverend Martin Luther King's " I have a dream" speech. Another event involved refusal of permission for Marian Anderson to sing at Constitution Hall, an auditorium owned by the Daughters of the American Revolution. The DAR offered no explanation beyond the fact that it was conforming to local custom in excluding her. The District of Columbia public school system followed suit by refusing to allow Miss Anderson to appear, prompting an aroused and indignant public to question local policy toward blacks in every area of public accommodations. Rejection of such arbitrary exclusion of blacks led to the eventual integration of amusement parks and places of entertainment in the city. For Miss Anderson, the episode was a prelude to one of her greatest triumphs—an Easter Sunday concert on the steps of the Lincoln Memorial. Her rendition of "Nobody Knows the Trouble I've Seen" prompted NAACP Executive Secretary Walter White to foresee the advent of "a new affirmation of democracy." In 1968, the mall before the Memorial was the site of Resurrection City, the encampment erected for participants in the "Poor People's March."

### *Mary Church Terrell House*
### *326 T Street N. W.*

The house was the residence of the civil rights activist who achieved national prominence as the first president of the National Association of Colored Women.

### *National Gallery of Art*
### *6th Street and Constitution Avenue, N.W.*

The Gallery houses many of the world's greatest paintings, and has in recent years, at least, sought to find representative samples of early Americana by black painters. Among its paintings is one by the first black American portraitist, Joshua Johnston. Known as *The Westwood Children,* it was probably done during Johnston's most active period, roughly 1796-1824. Many of the families who owned Johnston's work thought he was a slave, but he is listed as a "free householder of color" in the Baltimore directory of 1817.

### *Phillips Gallery*
### *612 21st Street, N.W.*

Thirty pieces out of Jacob Lawrence's famous 60-panel study on black migration in America, are housed in the Phillips Gallery. (Others are in the permanent collection of the New York Museum of Modern Art.) Lawrence, a native of Atlantic City, New Jersey paints in a stark and vivid style that brings to life the human despair implicit in many of the historical situations he uses as subject matter. Lawrence's work has been exhibited in most of the nation's top museums. In 1970, he was the recipient of the NAACP's coveted Spingarn Medal, emblematic of special preeminence in his field.

### *St. Luke's Episcopal Church*
### *15th and Church Streets, N.W.*

From 1879 until 1934, the pulpit of St. Luke's Episcopal Church was filled by Alexander Crummell, a talented and articulate black scholar who became a leading spokesman for black liberation both at home and in Africa. He was the founder of the American Negro Academy, established with the intention of forming a cadre of black intellectuals and scholars. The church was designated a National Historic Landmark on May 11, 1976.

### *Carter G. Woodson House*
### *1538 Ninth Street, N.W.*

This was the home of Carter G. Woodson from 1915 until his death in 1950. Recognizing the need for recording black contributions in the development of the nation and for correcting distortions, Woodson established the Association for the Study of Negro Life and History, the Associated Publishers, and the official organ of the Association, the *Journal of Negro History*. Each of them helped bring to the consciousness of the nation the roles and contributions of Afro-Americans in the development and progress of America. On May 11, 1976, the Carter G. Woodson house was designated a National Historic Landmark.

### *Tidal Basin Bridge*

It is often said that the Tidal Basin Bridge commands the most impressive view of the annual cherry blossom extravaganza in Washington, D.C. each spring. Few are aware that the bridge was engineered and built by a black designer, Archie A. Alexander, once governor of the Virgin Islands. An "outstanding graduate" of the class of 1912 at the State University of Iowa, Alexander was known as a fair minded and witty man who enjoyed his work and expected to be judged for his ability, not his color. He once removed the "White" and "Colored" signs adorning segregated bathrooms, and replaced them with the words "Skilled" and "Unskilled."

*Battle of Olustee, fought by the 8th and 54th Colored Troops.*

## FLORIDA

### Daytona Beach

*Bethune-Cookman College*

One of the leading institutions in the South for the training of Negro teachers, Bethune-Cookman College was founded in 1904 by Mary McLeod Bethune on "faith and a dollar-and-a-half."

In her day, Mrs. Bethune, advisor to Presidents Franklin D. Roosevelt and Harry S. Truman, was one of the most powerful and influential blacks in the United States.

*Mary McLeod Bethune Home*
*Campus of Bethune-Cookman College*

The two-story frame house belonging to the black activist Mary McLeod Bethune was built in 1920 on the campus of the school she established in 1904. Following the tradition of Mary McLeod Bethune, the college has made important and significant contributions to black education in the South. The house was proclaimed a National Historic Landmark on December 2, 1974.

### Dry Tortugas, Key West, Monroe County

Black artisans and laborers worked in the construction of this fort which helped control the Florida Straits. The largest all-masonry fortification in the western world, it served as a prison until 1873. Among the prisoners was Doctor Samual A. Mudd who had set John Wilkes Boothe's broken leg after the assassination of Abraham Lincoln.

### Fort George Island

*Kingsley Plantation*

Kingsley traded extensively in slaves, and the headquarters for his operation was on his plantation on Fort George Island. It is the oldest known plantation house in Florida and was established in 1763. Kingsley was known for training slaves to be exceptionally skilled craftsmen and productive farmers. The plantation, which has been restored as a house museum, displays exhibits and furnishings that reflect the plantations and island life during the period 1763-1783.

### Franklin County

*British Fort Gadsen (six miles southwest of Sumatra)*

This British fort was a place where runaway slaves lived alongside Seminole Indians. Its destruction in 1816 precipitated the First Seminole War. In 1814, the British built the fort as a base for recruiting Indians and blacks during the War of 1812. The British abandoned it to their allies in 1815 along with its artillery and military supplies. It became known as the Negro Fort and served as a beacon for rebellious slaves and a threat to supply vessels on the river. On May 15, 1975, British Fort was named a National Historic Landmark.

### Gulf Islands National Seashore

Fortifications within the Gulf Islands National Seashore were built with the aid of black artisans and laborers. During the Civil War these forts were occupied by soldiers of the 25th and 86th U. S. Colored Infantry.

### Olustee

*Olustee Battlefield Historic Memorial*

Olustee was the site of a bloody Civil War battle during which the unseasoned soldiers of the 8th U.S. Colored Troops lost more than 300 men, many of them untutored in the operation of their weapons and equipment. The veteran 54th Massachusetts, one of the two other black regiments serving among Union forces there, fared better in the battle, checked the enemy, and held its position while it covered the retreat of the corps it had been sent in to rescue. Cited for valor in combat, Stephen A. Swails became the first black to be commissioned in the 54th. Federal troops retired to Jacksonville after the engagement at Olustee, remaining there until the end of the war.

## GEORGIA

### Andersonville

*Andersonville Prison*

Andersonville, the infamous Confederate prison where thousands of Union soldiers perished as a result of the inhuman manner in which they were confined, is now a national monument. Andersonville was the shame of the Confederacy. Here on July 19, 1864, Corporal Henry Gooding of the black 54th Massachusetts regiment was imprisoned and died. It was Corporal Gooding who had started a protest with the military regarding the pay of black soldiers and went over the heads of brass to write President Lincoln. At that time the pay of blacks was a flat $7 per month. For whites, it ranged from $9 to $30. Encouraged by Colonel Robert Shaw, the black soldiers of the 54th refused to accept any remuneration unless it was equal to that of white comrades. This financial inequity was subsequently rectified. But, with tragic irony, Corporal Gooding died at Andersonville without ever having drawn a day's pay.

### Atlanta

*Martin Luther King Jr. Historic District*

The district, within several blocks of Atlanta's Auburn Avenue and Boulevard, includes Dr. Martin Luther King Jr.'s birthplace home, grave site, and the church where King served as assistant pastor. The environs of his childhood are largely intact. Private efforts to create a living monument to Dr. King and his beliefs are carried on primarily through the Martin Luther King Jr. Center for Non-Violent Social Change, Inc., which is building a Freedom Hall complex adjacent to the present memorial. Surrounding the prime historic area are two National Register Historic Districts: The Martin Luther King Jr. National Register Historic District and the Sweet Auburn National Landmark Historic District. The MLK Historic District was designated a National Historic Landmark on May 5, 1977.

*Atlanta University held its first classes in abandoned railway cars.*

### *Atlanta University System*

The campus of the Atlanta University System (consisting of Atlanta University and Morris Brown, Clark, Morehouse, and Spelman Colleges) is one of the most beautiful to be found anywhere in the South.

### *Ebenezer Baptist Church*

Ebenezer Baptist Church had as its associate pastor the Reverend Martin Luther King Jr., the most celebrated spokesman for nonviolent protest America has produced in the twentieth century. It was from this church that Dr. King radiated outward through the rest of the South, organizing chapters of the Southern Christian Leadership Conference (SCLC), the civil rights coalition which he served as president. Funeral services for Dr. King were held in this church, attended by a host of notables from all over the world. As millions watched on television, mourners lined up for miles behind the mule drawn wagon that carried Dr. King from Ebenezer to Morehouse College, his alma mater. There, the eulogies were delivered, and more than 150,000 paid their last respects to a great and fearless American martyr.

### *South View Cemetery*

Dr. King was laid to rest in South View Cemetery, where a marble crypt was inscribed with the words he used to conclude his famous speech delivered on the occasion of the 1963 March on Washington. The words, taken from an old slave song, are: "Free at last, free at last, thank God Almighty I'm free at last." South View was founded in 1886 by blacks who balked at a prevailing policy which required that they be buried in the rear of the municipal cemetery.

### *Stone Hall*

Built in 1882, Stone Hall is most closely associated with the history of Atlanta University. The institution was founded in 1866 by the American Missionary Association to provide education for freed Negroes. Noted writer W. E. B. DuBois taught at the university. The building was named a National Historic Landmark on December 2, 1974.

### *Sweet Auburn Historic District*
### *Auburn Avenue*

Although only a remnant of its original sprawling expanse of one mile, Sweet Auburn Historic District typifies the rapid growth of black enterprise in the post-Civil War period, forced to adjust to segregated residential and commercial patterns. Auburn Avenue was once called the "richest Negro street in the world." The district was designated a National Historic Landmark December 8, 1976.

## **Columbus**
### *"Blind Tom" Marker (U.S. Rte. 27A)*

The "Blind Tom" Marker refers visitors and pedestrians to the grave site of the famous black pianist "Blind Tom" Bethune, son of a slave, but a remarkably gifted prodigy whose astonishing talent brought him into the salons of Europe, where royalty marveled at his virtuoso performances.

*Martin Luther King and his place of birth.*

"Blind Tom" also toured his own country and excited the wonder and admiration of appreciative audiences everywhere.

*Bragg Smith Marker*

The Bragg Smith Marker, located in the Columbus Colored Cemetery, marks the grave site and marble memorial built by the city in memory of Bragg Smith, who was killed while attempting to rescue the city engineer from a cave-in.

**Savannah**

*Reverend George Lisle Monument*
*(First Bryan Baptist Church, 559 West Bryan Street)*

The Reverend George Lisle Monument is dedicated to the first American black Baptist missionary.

## ILLINOIS

**Chicago**

*Robert S. Abbott House*
*4742 Martin Luther King Drive*

The house was occupied by Robert Stengstacke Abbott from 1926 to 1940, the year of his death. Under Abbott, the Chicago Defender, a newspaper appealing to black readers, encouraged southern blacks to migrate northward, particularly to Chicago. Probably more than any other publication, the Defender was responsible for the large northward migration of blacks during the first half of the twentieth century. The house was named a National Historic Landmark on December 8, 1976.

*The Art Institute*

Among the Nation's great art galleries, the Art Institute has works by black artists and sculptors, including Tanner's The Two Disciples at the Tomb, Richard Hunt's Hero Construction, and Marion Perkins' Man of Sorrows.

*Oscar Staton DePriest House*
*45336-4538 Dr. Martin Luther King Jr. Drive*

The house is the residence of the first black American elected to the House of Representatives from a northern state. DePriest was born in Florence, Alabama but moved with his family to Kansas and later to Chicago. He was a real estate broker in Chicago. In 1928, Oscar DePriest was elected to the U.S. House of Representatives as a Republican. He was a congressman for three terms and following his tenure, he returned to the real estate business but was still involved politically in Chicago. DePriest was also vice chairman of the Cook County Republican Committee. The DePriest home was designated a National Historic Landmark on May 15, 1975.

*Du Sable Marker*

According to records in Cahokia, Illinois, Du Sable was married to a Potawatamie Indian in the year 1788. The earliest known reference to him appears in an army report by a British colonel in 1779, but there are several other descriptions of him and his home after that date. For instance, he is known to have owned a farm in Peoria, Illinois, as well as other property in St. Charles, Missouri, where his son eventually settled.

In 1796, Du Sable sold his Chicago home, and went to live with his son in St. Charles, where he died in 1814.

The site of DuSable's home is marked by a plaque on the northeast approach to the Michigan Avenue Bridge. Two other plaques exist—one in the Chicago Historical Society, the other in the lobby of Du Sable High School, at 49th and State Streets.

### The Historical Society

Among the treasures and exhibits of the Chicago Historical Society are many which relate to blacks, including a replica of the cabin built by Jean Du Sable (see entry above) and numerous other artifacts relative to the days of slavery. John Jones (1811-1879), a successful businessman who settled in Chicago in 1845 and was Cook County Commissioner from 1871 to 1875, and his wife Mary are preserved for posterity by two Aaron Darling portraits. Other material explores the role played by black units from Illinois during campaigns of the Civil War.

### Museum of African-American History and Art

The Museum of African-American History and Art was founded recently by Mrs. Margaret Burroughs in an effort to "inspire Afro-American people by acquainting them with contributions other members of their race have made to society in the past." Of the many artifacts, including books and periodicals, relating to the black, perhaps the most distinctive is the powder horn carried during the Revolutionary War by the black fifer Barzillai Lew.

*PFC Milton Olive III saved five comrades from death by leaping on an enemy grenade thrown into their midst and smothering the explosion with his body.*

### Milton L. Olive Park

Milton L. Olive Park was dedicated by Chicago Mayor Richard Daley in honor of the first black soldier to be awarded a Congressional Medal of Honor during the Vietnam conflict. Olive died in action after exhibiting extraordinary heroism which saved the lives of several other soldiers exposed to a live grenade.

### Jean Baptiste Point Du Sable Homesite
### 401 North Michigan Avenue

Jean Baptiste Point Du Sable, a black man born in Haiti to a French mariner father and a black mother, immigrated to French Louisiana and became a fur trapper. He established trading posts on the sites of the present cities of Michigan City, Indiana, Peoria, Illinois, and Port Huron, Michigan but the most important post was on the site of Chicago, Illinois. This site, where he constructed a log home for his wife and family, is recognized as the first settlement of Chicago. The homesite was designated a National Historic Landmark on May 11, 1976.

*Jean Baptiste Point DuSable and the fur trading settlement which became the city of Chicago.*

*Provident Hospital and Training School*
*51st Street and Vincennes Avenue*

Provident Hospital and Training School is the first training school for black nurses in the United States. It was founded by Dr. Daniel Hale Williams, the renowned surgeon who performed the first successful operation on the human heart in 1893.

*Underground Railway Marker*

An Underground Railway Marker, which represents an in-transit point for slaves escaping into Canada, is located at 9955 South Beverly Avenue.

*Victory Monument*
*35th Street and South Park Way*

Victory Monument is a memorial statue by Leonard Crunelle honoring the black soldiers of Illinois who served in World War I. Just opposite this statue is the Lake Meadows Shopping Center and Housing Development. The monument and tomb of Stephen A. Douglas, once the owner of much of the land in the area, is likewise located near 35th Street.

*Ida B. Wells-Barnett House*
*3624 S. Dr. Martin Luther King Jr. Drive*

The home of the 1890s civil rights advocate and crusader for the rights of black women, Ida Wells-Barnett, who carried on her crusades in the pages of her newspaper, the Memphis Free Speech. The Wells house was designated a National Historic Landmark on May 30, 1974.

*Daniel Hale Williams House*
*445 East 42nd Street*

This is the home of one of America's first black surgeons, whose accomplishments include one of the first successful heart operations in 1893 and the establishment of quality medical facilities for blacks. Daniel Hale Williams was born in Hollidaysburg, Pennsylvania. He had operated a barber shop prior to apprenticing under Dr. Henry Palmer, who was surgeon-general of Wisconsin. In 1883, Williams received his M.D. degree from Chicago Medical College and later opened an office in Chicago. He was the first black to win a fellowship from the American College of Surgeons. The Williams home was designated a National Historic Landmark on May 15, 1975.

## INDIANA

### Bloomingdale

*Underground Railroad Marker (U.S. Rte. 41)*

This marker is only one of several once used to assist fugitive slaves brave enough to risk death by fleeing from the South and seeking freedom and safety in Canada. One of these, William Trail, liked Indiana so much he decided instead to stay on and go into farming. His efforts were met with success, and he became one of many prosperous farmers active in Union County, Indiana.

*Slaves like these sought escape from the South via the Underground Railroad.*

*Levi Coffin, referred to as "President of the Underground Railway"*

### Fountain City
*Levi Coffin Home, North Main Street*

Levi Coffin, a Quaker abolitionist referred to as "The President of the Underground Railroad," used his own home as a way station in which, from 1827 to 1847, he hid more than 300 slaves heading for Illinois, Michigan, or Canada.

Born in North Carolina in 1798, Coffin moved to Fountain City (then known as Newport) at the age of 28. From there he went to Ohio where he continued his activities, eventually helping over 3,000 slaves escape from the South. One of the founders of the Freedmen's Bureau (1865), he was still engaged in the resettlement of former slaves long after the Civil War had ended. Coffin died in Avondale, Ohio in 1877.

## IOWA

### Clinton
*Underground Railroad Station*

Before the Lafayette Hotel was built, the small house that once stood at Sixth Street South and South Second Street is known to have been a point of shelter and sustenance for black fugitives escaping from Missouri. Iowa was a free territory by virtue of both the Northwest Ordinance (1787) and the Missouri Compromise of 1820. Many Quakers who had come to the state before the Civil War took great pains to organize an efficient and effective Underground Railroad network.

### Des Moines
*Fort Des Moines Provisional Army Officer Training School*

Fort Des Moines Provisional Army Officer Camp Des Moines was an all black "West Point" established during World War I, on June 15, 1917, for the purpose of training talented black soldiers to hold officer's rank. On October 14, 1917, 639 black soldiers were commissioned as Second Lieutenants and assigned to the American Expeditionary Forces being sent to France. Black units led by men trained at the school were assembled in France as the 92nd Division.

The camp was abandoned at the end of the war. The site was designated a National Historic Landmark on May 30, 1974.

### Sioux City
*Pearl Street*

Once the city's main thoroughfare, Pearl Street is named for a black pioneer who arrived in the town by boat more than a century ago and achieved widespread popularity as a cook. Another black cook, Aunty Wooden by name, impressed many leading citizens with her specialty, an opossum dinner. Civil War veteran Henry Riding was another black pioneer who staked a claim to Iowa land and had a successful career as a homesteader. He once prevented a railroad crew at gunpoint from laying track across his land, and forced the company to settle for $21,000 before granting them the right of access. Sioux City was a refuge for many slaves escaping from Missouri.

## KANSAS

### Beeler
*George Washington Carver Marker*

Along Route K-96 in Ness County lies the plot of land once homesteaded by George Washington Carver, famed black agricultural scientist. He spent two years there before going to college in Iowa.

*Fort Scott*

Fort Scott was the home of the First Kansas Colored Volunteers, a black unit organized by the Union Army in August 1862. The first such unit to go into combat during the Civil War, it beat back a superior Confederate force at the battle of Island Mount, Missouri on October 28, 1862.

### Dodge City
*Fort Dodge*

Established in 1865, Fort Dodge was often used as a base of operations by the all-black 10th U.S. Cavalry, a unit which saw much action on the plains protecting settlers, pioneers, and cattlemen from Indian uprisings, but which was equally active in Dodge City itself, a haven for gamblers, rustlers, and even desperate killers. When a black named Taylor was murdered, the Fort Dodge commandant decided to take action against the town's criminal element. County government and a string of fearless sheriffs eventually quieted the town, reducing the major crime to less serious proportions. Many of the black cowboys active on the trail stopped at Dodge and many of them matched their white counterparts in letting off steam and raising Cain. Ben Hodges was not among these transients, partly because his game called for a smoother operation. Hodges was fond of bilking ranchers by posing as a wealthy man and getting financial backing for supposedly reputable projects. Though he was eventually unmasked as an imposter, he was spared the rope or the bullet and lived to a ripe old age, regaling youngsters with pioneer tales and eventually coming to be regarded as a revered and respectable old-timer.

### Fort Scott, Urban County
*Fort Scott National Historic Sight*

The fort commemorates historic events in Kansas before and during the Civil War. Black "buffalo soldier" regiments were stationed here.

### Larned, Pawnee County
*Fort Larned National Historic Sight*

Black "buffalo soldier" regiments were stationed at this fort during the Indian War of 1868-69. The fort was the key to protection of the Sante Fe Trail.

### Leavenworth
*Fort Leavenworth*

Fort Leavenworth was the first home of the 10th Cavalry, the all-black unit which not only participated in many important battles during the Indian Wars, but also served with valor and distinction during the Spanish-American War. It was at Leavenworth that the Independent Kansas Colored Battery, a unit with several black officers, was recruited in 1864. Among its members was Captain H. Ford Douglass, son of the noted abolitionist Frederick Douglass. The younger Douglass joined the Illinois Volunteers as far back as 1862.

*An outpost sentry of the 10th Cavalry, as seen by Frederic Remington.*

### Nicodemus
*Nicodemus Colony*

Located along U.S. Rte. 24 two miles west of the Rooks-Graham county line, Nicodemus Colony is the last of three now-virtually-deserted colonies which were founded by the Exodusters—a group of black homesteaders active in Kansas during the 1870s. The name "Nicodemus" was derived from a slave who, according to legend, foretold the coming of the Civil War.

Arriving in 1877, the first settlers lived in dugouts and burrows during the cold weather. From the outset, they were plagued by crop failures. Although never more than 500 in number, they managed nonetheless to create a real community—with teachers, ministers, civil servants, etc. The state of Kansas has commemorated this site with a historical marker located in a roadside park in Nicodemus.

### Osawatomie
*John Brown Memorial State Park*

This state park, named in honor of the fiery insurrectionist, contains the cabin in which he lived during his brief sojourn in Kansas.

*Sod houses were built by the first settlers of Nicodemus.*

### Topeka
*Sunler Elementary School*
*330 Western Avenue*

In the case of Brown vs Board of Education of Topeka 1954, their school refused to enroll Linda Brown because she was black. As a result of this suit, the court concluded that "separate education facilities are inherently unequal." This decision struck down the legal basis for segregation in public schools.

### Wallace
*Fort Wallace*

Only a road side marker and a cemetery are left as identifying marks of Fort Wallace, another of the military outposts used by the 10th Cavalry. One white officer who came to Fort Wallace as commandant of the 5th Cavalry after having refused a regiment of black troopers changed his attitude in the field when black soldiers whom he fought alongside proved their mettle in battle against the Cheyenne. The black cavalrymen marched 230 miles in nine days and killed 10 Cheyenne who had surrounded the escort party which was taking the major to his new regiment.

## KENTUCKY

### Berea (Madison County)
*Lincoln Hall, Berea College*

Lincoln Hall was built in 1887 at Berea College. Berea is significant in the history of black education in that it was the first college established in the United States for the specific purpose of educating blacks and whites together. Lincoln Hall, closely associated with Berea's history, was designated by the Department of Interior as a National Historic Landmark on December 2, 1974.

*Lincoln Ridge*

This is the birthplace and boyhood home of Whitney M. Young Jr. executive director of the National Urban League from 1961 to 1971.

## LOUISIANA

### Baton Rouge
*Southern University*

Located in Baton Rouge since 1914, Southern University is the successor to an institute founded in New Orleans after the Civil War. The modern and well-financed plant now serves some 12,000 students on a breathtakingly landscaped site that includes a huge lake. The two university satellites now in existence are located in Shreveport and New Orleans.

### New Orleans
*Chalmette National Historical Park—Louisiana*
*Chalmette*

National Historical Park is the more precise site of what is usually recorded in history as the Battle of New Orleans, fought during the War of 1812. The battle pitted the motley forces of General Andrew Jackson against 5,400 seasoned English veterans of the Napoleonic campaigns fighting under Sir Edward Pakenham. About 200 of Jackson's soldiers

*About 200 of General Andrew Jackson's soldiers at New Orleans were free black riflemen who volunteered for the battle.*

were free blacks commanded by Colonel Joseph Savary. These men, according to Jackson, manifested great bravery, "although they were poorly armed and sometimes forced to fight with empty guns used as clubs." After the first attack on December 23, 1814, Jackson withdrew his men to Chalmette, where he built a defensive breastwork which shielded his 4,000-man force. On Christmas Day, Pakenham arrived with his men, and sought immediately to engage Jackson's Creoles, Indians, Negroes, Kentuckians, and pirates. The Americans repulsed two attacks before girding for the decisive engagement on January 8. Pakenham was felled in this last desperate charge, struck, according to Jackson, "from the bullet of a freeman of color, who was a famous rifle shot and came from the Attakapas region of Louisiana." Among the hundreds of Negroes who had contributed to the victory was Jordan Noble, a 14-year-old drummer boy whose drum has been preserved at the Louisiana State Museum.

*James H. Dillard Home*
*571 Audubon Street*

The home was built during the nineteenth century and James Dillard lived there from 1894 to 1913. Dillard played an important role in black education in the nineteenth century, strengthening vocational and teacher-training programs. Dillard's home was designated a National Historic Landmark on December 2, 1975 by the Department of Interior. Dillard University was named for the educator.

*The Louisiana State Museum*

The Louisiana State Museum contains a tablet inscribed in the memory of Norbert Rillieux, the New Orleans "quadroon libre" whose invention of the sugar evaporating pan revolutionized the sugar refining industry by reducing labor and costs to a bare minimum. Rillieux's father was a wealthy engineer and plantation owner. His mother was a slave.

*Jean Lafitte National Historical Park, Chalmette Unit*

The battle of New Orleans in the War of 1812, at Chalmette Plantation, was a stunning victory over British forces in the War of 1812. General Andrew Jackson commanded about 5000 troups which included two battalions of " free men of color" who fought in the battle on January 8, 1815.

*Sharpesburg, Washington County, Battle of Antietam*

This was a critical battle of the Civil War which stopped General Robert E. Lee's invasion of the north and threat to Washington D. C. Blacks were employed by the quartermaster departments of both armies. President Lincoln used the occasion of the Antietam victory to announce on September 22, 1862, that on the first day of the following year he would issue the Emancipation Proclamation.

**Melrose**
*Yucca Plantation*

The plantation was established by a former slave who became a wealthy business woman. It is located on Louisiana Rte. 119, just east of the intersection with Louisiana Rte. 493, Natchitoches Parish. The plantation was established during the eighteenth and nineteenth centuries. The African House on the plantation, which is a unique structure with an umbrella like roof, may be of direct African derivation. The site was declared a National Historic Landmark by the Department of Interior on May 30, 1974.

*Port Hudson*
*Port Hudson Siege Marker*

The besieged city of Port Hudson was the scene of numerous acts of gallantry involving black troops from the 1st and 3rd Louisiana Native Guards—freed men who were recruited in New Orleans by Union general Ben Butler. The city fell in July, but the bombardment began as far back as March of 1863. The New York *Times* wrote:

*Official testimony settles the question that the Negro race can fight with great prowess. Those black soldiers had never before been in any severe engagement. They were comparatively raw troops, and were yet subjected to... he charging upon fortifications through the crash of belching batteries. The men, white or black, who will not flinch from that, will flinch from nothing. It is no longer possible to doubt the bravery and steadiness of the colored race.*

The great majority of the Negro units in the battle were led by Negro officers, including Captain Andre Cailloux, who was given a state funeral after he fell on the battlefield. The funeral pageant was "the like of which" had never before been seen "in honor of a dead Negro." The site was declared a National Historic Landmark by the Department of Interior on July 1, 1974.

## MARYLAND

### Annapolis
*Matthew Henson Plaque*

The Matthew Henson Plaque honors the memory of the only man to accompany Admiral Robert E. Peary on all of his polar expeditions. Henson was also the first man actually to reach the North Pole (April 6, 1909). Peary himself, barely able to walk, arrived there after Henson had taken a reading of his posistion and proudly planted the flag of the United States.

*The first man to walk on the North Pole was Matthew Henson.*

**Baltimore**

*Morgan State College Frederick Douglass Monument*

Morgan State College has an interesting collection of artifacts on Benjamin Banneker, noted astronomer, compiler of almanacs, and—together with L'Enfant—surveyor of the District of Columbia. It also houses a number of artifacts on Fredrick Douglass and Matthew Henson. On the campus of Morgan State College, in Baltimore, is the Fredrick Douglass Memorial statue created by the noted black sculptor James Lewis. The work, completed in 1956, stands 12 feet tall with pedestal. Its simple inscription reads, "Fredrick Douglass 1817-1895 Humanitarian, Statesman."

**Baltimore County**

*Banneker Marker*

*Westchester Avenue at Westchester School*

This marker is a tribute to Benjamin Banneker, the black mathematician, astronomer, and inventor who, in 1792, produced an almanac regarded as one of the most reliable of his day. His scientific knowledge, as well as the international renown that accrued to him, led to his assignment as a member of the surveying and planning team which helped lay out the nation's capital.

Banneker's correspondence with President Thomas Jefferson can be seen at the Library of Congress.

**Rockville**

*Uncle Tom's Cabin*

Site of the log cabin believed to be the birthplace of Josiah Henson, the escaped slave immortalized as Uncle Tom in Harriet Beecher Stowe's famous abolitionist study. Born in 1789, Henson was sold at auction at an early age and transferred to many masters until he managed to escape in 1830. After setting up a community for fugitive slaves in Dawn, Canada, Henson frequently returned to the South to liberate others. Later a minister and mill owner, Henson journeyed to London in 1851, meeting the Archbishop of Canterbury, who asked him from which university he had graduated. Henson replied cryptically: "The University of Adversity." Two years earlier, he had met Mrs. Stowe and given her the outline of his slave experiences which formed the bases for her celebrated story. In the introduction to Henson's autobiography, published some years later, she acknowledged his story as the source of her own tale.

*A scene from an early dramatization of the novel.*

*"Uncle Tom" as he appeared in theater posters. Between 1852 and 1931, Uncle Tom was playing continually somewhere in the United States.*

# MASSACHUSETTS

## Boston

### *African American National Historic Site*

This area contains the largest concentration of pre-Civil War black history sites anywhere in the United States. Among the sites in this area is the African Meeting House, a national historic landmark.

#### *African Meeting House*
#### *8 Smiths Court*

This is the first black church in Boston and oldest surviving black church building in the United States. Designated May 30, 1974, and now a part of the Boston African American National Historic Site.

#### *Crispus Attucks Monument*

The Crispus Attucks Monument, located in the Boston Common, was dedicated in 1888 to honor the five victims of the Boston Massacre—Crispus Attucks, Samuel Maverick, James Caldwell, Samuel Gray, and Patrick Carr. The site of the Massacre is marked by a plaque on State Street, near the Old State House.

Attucks is believed by many historians to have been the same man who in 1750 was advertised as a runaway black slave from Framingham, Massachusetts. A stranger to Boston, he led a group which converged on a British garrison quartered in King Street to help enforce the Townshend Acts. One of the soldiers of the garrison panicked and fired, and Attucks was the first to fall. (Gray and Caldwell were also killed on the same spot. Maverick and Carr died later of wounds sustained during the clash. The British soldiers were later tried for murder and acquitted.)

The five men are buried in Granary Burying Ground, together with such famous Revolutionary War figures as John Adams and John Hancock, as well as Governor William Bradford of Plymouth Colony.

#### *Bunker Hill Monument*

Standing in the Charlestown district of Boston, the Bunker Hill Monument commemorates the famous Revolutionary War battle, which—contrary to popular belief—was actually fought on Breed's Hill on June 17, 1775.

A number of blacks fought alongside the colonists during the battle, including Peter Salem, Salem Poor, Titus Coburn, Cato Howe, Alexander Ames, Seymour Burr, Pomp Fiske, and Prince Hall, founder of the Negro Masonic order.

The cornerstone for the monument was laid by the Marquis de Lafayette in 1825. A ceremony at which Daniel Webster was a featured speaker marked the completion of the monument in 1843.

#### *Longfellow National Historic Site*

A wealthy black merchant, John Craigie, sold his house to the poet Henry Wadsworth Longfellow in 1837. George Washington's headquarters were located here during the Siege of Boston (1775-7610).

*The Crispus Attucks Monument.*

*William C. Nell Residence*
*3 Smith Court*

From the 1830s to the end of the Civil War, William C. Nell was a leading black abolitionist and spokesman for his race. He was born in Boston and studied law in the office of William I. Bowditch. Nell refused to take an oath to be admitted to the bar because he did not want to support the Constitution of the United States, which he felt compromised the powers of slaves. He then began organizing meetings and lecturing in support of the antislavery movement. Nell's residence was designated a National Historic Landmark by the Department of Interior on May 11, 1976.

*Shaw Monument*

Executed by the famed sculptor Augustus Saint-Gaudens the Shaw monument, on Beacon Street facing the State House, is a group statue of Colonel Robert Gould Shaw and the 54th Massachusetts Volunteers, a black regiment which served in the Union Army. The regiment particularly distinguished itself in the battle for Fort Wagner during which Colonel Shaw was killed. Sergeant William H. Carney's valiant exploits during this battle later won him the Congressional Medal of Honor.

### Cambridge

*Maria Baldwin House*
*196 Prospect H Street*

This house was the permanent address of Maria Baldwin from 1892 until her death in 1922. As principal and later as "master" of the Agassiz School in Cambridge, as a leader in community organizations such as the League for Community Service, as a gifted and popular speaker on the lecture circuit, and as a sponsor of charitable activities like the first kindergarten in Atlanta, Georgia, Maria Baldwin exemplified the achievements that were attainable by a black person in a predominantly white society. The house was designated by the Department of Interior as a National Historic Landmark on May 11, 1976.

*Phillis Wheatley Folio*

During her celebrated trip to England in 1773, Phillis Wheatley, the first American black woman to write a book, was presented with a folio edition of John Milton's *Paradise Lost*. It now resides in the library of Harvard University.

Miss Wheatley, who came to America in 1761 as a child of seven or eight, made rapid strides in mastering the English language, and by the time she was 14, had already completed her first poem. Always in delicate health, she died in Boston on December 5, 1784.

*Central Village*
*Memorial to Paul Cuffe*

Cuffe, son of a freedman, was born in 1759, became a prosperous merchant seaman, and resolved to use his wealth and position to campaign for the extension of civil rights for blacks. On one occasion, Cuffe refused to pay his personal property tax on the grounds that he was being denied full citizenship rights. A court of law eventually upheld his action, whereupon he was granted the same privileges and immunities enjoyed by white citizens of the state. In 1815, Cuffe transported 38 blacks to Sierra Leone in what was intended to become a systematic attempt at repatriating the black inhabitants of the United States. With the growth of abolitionist sentiment in the colonies, repatriation lost favor among both blacks and whites as a means of solving the black question.

*W.E.B. DuBois, prominent writer and civil rights organizer.*

*William E. B. DuBois Boyhood Homesite*
*Route 23*

This is the boyhood homesite of William E. B. DuBois, the prominent black sociologist and writer who was a major figure in the Negro civil rights movement during the first half of the twentieth century. DuBois advocated the elimination of discrimination and inequality against blacks through his writing, as a college professor, and as a lecturer. He received his B.A. degree in 1888 from Fisk University and another B.A. degree from Harvard University in 1890. The DuBois homesite was designated May 11, 1976 as a National Historic Landmark by the Department of Interior.

### Great Barrington

*DuBois Memorial Marker*

William Edward Burghardt DuBois was born here in Great Barrington on February 23, 1868. He is considered one of the most influential black intellectuals of the twentieth century. A founder of the NAACP and author of many books, DuBois died in 1963 at the age of 95. At his homesite, the people of Great Barrington have erected a memorial to one of the city's great citizens.

### Lynn
*Jan Ernst Matzeliger Statue*

The Matzeliger Statue is one of the few extant honors accorded the black inventor whose shoe-last machine revolutionized the industry and made mass-produced shoes a reality in the United States. A native of Dutch Guiana, Matzeliger came to the United States in 1876, learned the cobbler's trade, and set out to design a machine which would simplify shoe manufacture. Sickly, he died at an early age, unable to capitalize on his successful patent, which was purchased by the United Shoe Machinery Company of Boston. After his death, Matzeliger was awarded a gold medal at the 1901 Pan-American Exposition.

### Nantucket
*Nantucket Whaling Museum*

In the whaling museum on beautiful Nantucket Island is stored a treasury of whaling lore among which are recorded the names and histories of blacks who participated in the whaling industry such as Peter Green, a black sailor and second mate of the whaling ship John Adams. In August 1823, after a violent storm in which the captain and first mate were lost at sea, Green brought his ship and crew out of the maelstrom to safety.

### Suffolk County
*William Monroe Trotter House*
*97 Sawyer Avenue*

This is the home of William Monroe Trotter, noted black journalist and militant civil rights activist during the first decades of the twentieth century. Trotter was the first black member of Phi Beta Kappa. He was an insurance and mortgage broker in Boston from 1897 to 1906. In 1901, he became publisher and editor of *The Guardian*, which was a crusading newspaper, and he edited the publication until his death in 1934. The Sawyer Avenue house was designated a National Historical Landmark by the Department of Interior on May 11, 1976.

### Westport
*Paul Cuffe Farm*
*1504 Drift Road*

Paul Cuffe was a self-educated black man who became a prosperous merchant. He also pioneered in the struggle for minority rights in the eighteenth and early nineteenth centuries. Cuffe was also active in the movement for black settlement in Africa. The Paul Cuffe Farm was designated by the Department of Interior as a National Historic Landmark on May 30, 1974.

## MICHIGAN

### Battle Creek
*Sojourner Truth Grave*

The Sojourner Truth Grave in Oak Hill Cemetery marks the resting place of one of the most powerful abolitionist lecturers of the nineteenth century.

Sojourner settled in Battle Creek after the Civil War but continued to travel on lecture tours until a few years before her death in 1883, at the approximate age of 85.

### Cassopolis
*Underground Railroad Marker*

There is an Underground Railroad Marker located 2½ miles east of Cassopolis on Route M-60.

*The most important man in a whaleboat was the harpooner, who was often black.*

### Detroit
*Detroit Public Library*
*5201 Woodward Avenue*

The Azalia Hackley Memorial Collection is one of the major treasures available for public perusal at the Detroit Public Library. Madame Hackley did pioneering work in the field of music, promoting black concert talent and seeking recognition for works by black composers. Talented black musicians like Clarence Cameron White and Nathaniel Dett were among those who benefited from scholarship aid provided by this tireless crusader. Included in her collection of artifacts, clippings, and memorabilia are more than 600 books, sheet music for many popular songs, assorted photographs, and printed programs.

*Douglass-Brown Marker*

The Douglass-Brown Marker, on East Congress Street and St. Antoine, marks the site of the William Webb House, where fellow abolitionists John Brown and Frederick Douglass met in March of 1859 to map out the strategy which ultimately led to the abortive Harpers Ferry revolt. Douglass was strongly opposed to this course of action.

### Marshall
*Crosswhite Boulder*

In Triangle Park, on Michigan Avenue and Mansion Street, stands *Crosswhite Boulder*—the site of the pitched battle fought in 1846 in defense of Adam Crosswhite, a fugitive slave who had fled from Kentucky. The Crosswhite case is said to have been instrumental in the enactment of the Fugitive Slave Law of 1850.

## MINNESOTA

### St. Paul
*Fort Snelling State Park*

Fort Snelling was that outpost in the Wisconsin Territory to which the slave, later to become known as Dred Scott, was transported from Illinois in 1836.

Scott met and married his wife Harriet at the fort, and also saw his first child born there. After having been taken to Missouri by his master, he filed suit for his freedom and became a national figure as his case was tried, from 1847 to 1857, before numerous tribunals enroute to the U.S. Supreme Court. Scott argued that he should be considered free by virtue of his having previously resided in Illinois and at Fort Snelling.

(See St. Louis, Missouri entry for discussion of the Dred Scott decision.)

## MISSISSIPPI

### Alcorn
*Oakland Memorial Chapel, Alcorn University*

The chapel on the Alcorn campus was built in 1838. It is the oldest and the most venerable building on the Alcorn University campus. Oakland Chapel symbolizes the importance of Alcorn as the first black land grant college in the United States. The chapel was designated a National Historic Landmark by the Department of Interior on May 11, 1976.

*Sojourner Truth believed God had assigned her the mission of traveling across the country to spread the truth about slavery. Huge crowds gathered to hear her speak, for she had a very sharp mind and great powers of oratory.*

### Mound Bayou
*I. T. Montgomery House*
*West Main Street*

This is the home of Isiah Thornton Montgomery, who in 1887 founded in the town of Mound Bayou a place where black Americans could obtain social, political, and economic rights in a white supremacist South. The house was declared a National Historic Landmark by the Department of Interior on May 11, 1976.

### Natchez
*Natchez National Cemetery*

This cemetery is the final resting place of many black war dead, including landsman Wilson Brown, a Medal of Honor recipient during the Civil War. Brown and fellow seaman John Lawson received their medals for courage in action while serving aboard the U.S.S. Hartford in its Mobile Bay engagement of August 5, 1864. Another prominent black from Natchez, Hiram R. Revels, was the first black elected to the U.S. Senate. A Methodist minister, Revels recruited blacks for the Union side during the war, and served as Chaplain of a Union regiment from Mississippi. He later became president of Alcorn A & M, and is buried in Holly Springs.

### Tupelo Lee County
*Brices Crossroads and Tupelo National Battlefield Sites*

During a battle at Brices Crossroads in June 1864, General Samual D. Sturgis was in command of Union forces including the 55th and 59th Colored Infantry regiments and battery F of the 2nd Colored Light Infantry. In July 1864, the battle of Tupelo commanded by General A. J. Smith included battery one of the second Colored Light Artillery regiment and the 59th, 61st, and 68th Colored Infantry regiments. Men of the 59th infantry had also participated in the battle of Brices Crossroads. The black soldiers served with distinction and General A. J. Smith was so impressed by their service that he requested inclusion of their forces to capture Mobile, Alabama.

*Vicksburg National Military Park*

Blacks worked as laborers to erect confederate defenses at this Civil War battlefield site. Laborers also served in the crew of the ironclad gunboat, *Cairo*, which was sunk on the Yazoo River on December 12, 1862.

## MISSOURI

### Diamond
*Carver National Monument*

Located in a park, Carver National Monument commemorates the place where the great black scientist George Washington Carver was born and spent his early childhood.

Kidnapped when he was just six weeks old, Carver was eventually ransomed for a horse valued at $300. Raised in Missouri by the family of Moses Carver, his owner, he made his way through Minnesota, Kansas, and Iowa before being "discovered" by Booker T. Washington in 1896. That same year, Carver joined the faculty of Tuskegee Institute where he conducted most of the research for which he is famous.

The monument is the first created in honor of a black. It contains a statue of Carver as a boy, and encloses several trails leading to places of which he was particularly fond. The park also houses a visitors' center and a museum displaying many of his discoveries and personal belongings, as well as other artifacts of his day. It can be reached on U.S. Alt. 71, just west of Diamond.

### Kansas City
*Mutual Musicians Association Building*
*1823 Highland Avenue*

The building was the home of the American Federation of Musicians Local 627 from the 1920s to the 1940s. Its members created the Kansas City style of jazz and have included such jazz greats as Count Basie, Hershel Evens, Lester Young, and Charlie Burg Parker.

### Jefferson City
*Lincoln University*

More than $6,000 raised by the black fighting men of the 62nd and 65th U.S. Colored Infantry constituted the initial endowment for a 22-foot-square room in which classes first began in 1866 at what is now Lincoln University in Jefferson City. Known then as Lincoln Institute, the school began receiving state aid to expand its teacher-training program in 1870. It became a state institution nine years later, and instituted college-level courses in 1887. It has been known as Lincoln University since 1921, and has had graduate school status since 1940. The more than 2,000 students now attending the school are often reminded that Lincoln was launched through the generous philanthropy of former slaves, many of them illiterate, who fought for their freedom and the freedom of succeeding generations.

### St. Joseph
*Pony Express Station*

The famed pony express was a privately owned postal service which carried mail from St. Joseph, Missouri to Sacramento, California in 1860. The riders, a most select group, had to make the run in 10 days, riding in relays, regardless of the weather, terrain, food, or hostile Indians. At its height, the service employed 125 riders, 400 station men

*Dred Scott sued for his freedom in 1847 on the grounds that his master had taken him to live in Minnesota, which did not allow slavery. The southern-dominated Supreme Court denied Scott's suit, ruling that slaves were not American citizens.*

*Plaque commemorating Fort Shaw, home base of the 25th Infantry.*

and assistants, and 420 horses. Two of the most famous, well known for their other exploits, were Buffalo Bill Cody and Wild Bill Hickok. Two black men, for the most part forgotten, who rode the pony express were George Monroe and William Robinson. Little else is known of them except that they made their contribution to this epic saga in western history.

### St. Louis

*Old Courthouse*
*(Jefferson National Expansion Memorial)*

It was in the Old Courthouse in 1847 that Dred Scott, the most famous fugitive slave of his day, first filed suit to gain his freedom. For the next 10 years, the Dred Scott case was a burning political and social issue across the country. In 1857, it reached the Supreme Court. There, Chief Justice Roger Taney handed down the decision that slaves could not become free by escaping—or by being taken—into free territory, nor could they be considered American citizens.

Ironically, a few weeks after the decision was rendered, Scott was set free by his new owner. He died a year later.

*Scott Joplin Residence*
*2685-A Morgan Street*

The Scott Joplin residence was built in the 1890s and was the last surviving residence of Joplin. He was called the "king of ragtime" and was one of the most creative black musicians of the late nineteenth and early twentieth centuries. Joplin was born in Texarkana, Texas but he left home to earn a living when he was 14 years of age. Joplin played piano in the St. Louis and Sedalia, Missouri area in such places as saloons, gambling parlors, and vaudeville houses. His residence was declared a National Historic Landmark by the Department of Interior on December 8, 1976.

## MONTANA

### Big Horn Station

*Fort Manuel Marker*

Captain William Clark and his party, including the lively and valuable slave York, camped at this site on July 26, 1806, a year before Manuel Lisa established Montana's first trading post. This site, too, was chosen by Major Andrew Henry as the Rocky Mountain Fur Company's first trading post. Leader of that expedition was Edward Rose, another of the famed black mountain men and explorers active in the territory.

### Crow Agency

*Custer Battlefield National Monument—Reno-Benteen Battlefield National Monument*

These two monuments commemorate the famed Battle of the Little Big Horn, in which three batteries commanded by General George Armstrong Custer were slaughtered on June 25, 1876 by a group of Indian tribes led by Chief Sitting Bull.

The first skirmish that day involved an advance party under the command of Major Marcus Reno. One of the first to fall was Isaiah Dorman, a black who had lived among the Sioux and was serving as an army interpreter. Dorman was known to the Indians as "Teat," or sometimes referred to as the "black white man."

According to one account, the dying black was found by Sitting Bull himself, who ordered that his body not be mutilated in any way.

### Fort Shaw

*Site of Fort Shaw*

This military outpost was founded in 1867 and named after Colonel Robert Gould Shaw, commandant of the heroic 54th

*Indians did not believe Lewis and Clark's slave York was black. They tried to rub off his color.*

Massachusetts who fell during his unit's spirited, valiant, and unsuccessful charge against the breastworks of Fort Wagner during the Civil War. Fort Shaw was the home base of the 25th Infantry, one of the units sent into the wilderness to protect the territory's few pioneering settlers and indefatigable miners from Indian attacks.

*Pompey's Pillar*

This pillar, named for the Indian Pomp, was discovered by Captain William Clark of the famed Lewis and Clark expedition. One of the members of Clark's group was a slave named York, a giant of a man who proved to be an invaluable asset to Clark—not only because of his prodigious strength and endurance, but also because he got along so well with the Indians, who were impressed with his dancing ability.

## NEVADA

### Reno

*The Jim Beckwourth Trail*

In the early days of pioneer settlement, the barren stretch of trail between Reno and the California line was the last obstacle to be overcome before passing through the gateway to the Golden West. The original trail was laid out by a black man, the loquacious and cantankerous Jim Beckwourth, one of the legendary mountain men whose exploits lend spice and sparkle to the Western saga. Beckwourth Pass helped put the city of Reno on the map, particularly after the railroad decided to put a station there and began selling acreage in the neighborhood. Reno was later the site of the famous Jim Jeffries-Jack Johnson heavyweight fight, won by the famed black champion who had bested Tommy Burns in Australia, in 1908. Johnson held the crown for seven years, losing it to Jess Willard on a 26-round knockout.

## NEW HAMPSHIRE

### Jaffrey

*Amos Fortune Grave*

The Amos Fortune Grave is the resting place of an eighteenth-century black slave who purchased his freedom in 1770 at the age of 60 and went on to become one of the leading citizens of Jaffrey, his adopted hometown.

Nine years later, Fortune was able to buy freedom for his wife, Violet Baldwin, and his adopted daughter, Celyndia. In 1781, he moved to Jaffrey and set himself up as a tanner, employing both black and white apprentices. In 1795, six years before his death, Fortune founded the Jaffrey Social Library, and in his will, directed that money be left to the church and to the local school district.

The school fund begun by Fortune is still in existence, having grown from $233 to the present total of $1,600. Proceeds from the fund are used to provide annual prizes for high-school debating and oratorical contests.

Each year during July and August, the Amos Fortune Forum is held as a memorial to the Old Meeting House where the ex-slave attended church services. Both Fortune and his wife lie in the meeting house burial ground.

Fortune's freedom papers and several receipt slips for the sale of his leather are on file at the Jaffrey Public Library. Similarly, the Fortune house and barn still stand intact.

## NEW JERSEY

### Red Bank

*T. Thomas Fortune House*
*94 West Bergen Place*

From 1901 to 1915 the West Bergen Place address was the home of T. Thomas Fortune, the crusading black journalist who in his newspapers articulated the cause of Negro rights at the turn of the twentieth century. Fortune was born a slave in Marianna, Florida. He was freed by proclamation in 1865. He received training as a printer as a youngster and founded the *New York Age* newspaper. Fortune was a close friend and advisor to Booker T. Washington. The Fortune house was designated a National Historic Landmark on December 8, 1976.

### Newark
*The Newark Museum*

This museum, located at 43-49 Washington Street, owns the paintings of such famous black artists as Henry Ossawa Tanner *(The Good Shepherd)*, Charles W. White *(Sojourner Truth and Booker T. Washington)*, and Hale Woodruff *(Poor Man's Cotton)*. Tanner was a student under Thomas Eakins and spent most of his life abroad. He excelled in religious subjects and sacred themes. White and Woodruff are among the most prominent black painters at work today.

## NEW MEXICO

### Columbus
*Fort Stanton*

It was from Fort Stanton that black troopers of the 9th Cavalry fanned out in pursuit of the Apache chief Victorio and his warriors in 1879. Two black troopers—Sergeants Thomas Boyne and John Denny—were awarded Medals of Honor for heroism displayed during this engagement with the Apaches. At least one other frontier military post in New Mexico was the scene of a fierce battle involving Victorio: Fort Tularosa. There, in May 1880, Sergeant George Jordan and a detachment of 25 cavalrymen held off the Apache chieftain and 100 braves. Jordan, too, was awarded the Medal of Honor for gallantry under fire.

*The Pancho Villa Expedition*

After one of his patented border raids had resulted in the burning of half of Columbus and the loss of many lives, Pancho Villa and his bandit army so aroused the ire of the U.S. government that it dispatched a punitive expedition into Mexico to track down Villa and eliminate him. "Black Jack" Pershing was in command of the 10th U.S. Cavalry during the strenuous journey. With only two days' rations in their knapsacks, the black troopers were forced to live off the land while in pursuit of the canny and fearless Mexican outlaw. The 10th engaged the Villistas at Carrizal, Mexico, and lost 10 men in a bloody skirmish. The expedition then returned to Fort Huachuca, its permanent base.

### Folsom
*Archaeological Folsom Man Discovery*

In the spring of 1925 George Majunkin, a black cowhand, while riding the range and arroyos in the northeast corner of New Mexico near the town of Folsom, chanced to see a glittering object in the back of a tree. In examining the oddity, he took out his knife and began to pry out a number of bone fragments and a spear tip. With acute curiosity, he sent his find to J.D. Figgers, director of the Colorado Museum of Natural History, who determined that they were the bones of a bison that became extinct some 10,000 years ago. Figgers directed excavations at the site of Majunkins find and established proof that the weapon and the animal belonged together and that man had been in that area over 10,000 years ago.

*Troopers of the 10th Cavalry photographed during their expedition to capture Pancho Villa's rebel band. Since speed and flexibility were essential, the cavalrymen were forced to live off the land in Mexico's desolate mountains for several months.*

### Lincoln
*Old Court House*

During the Lincoln County Cattle War of 1877-1878, Billy the Kid, the notorious outlaw, was held in custody at the Old Court House, now a frontier museum. Black cowhands were involved on both sides of this struggle and, on one occasion, a group of black cavalry men surrounded Billy the Kid during a particularly bloody battle. The outlaw, however, managed to escape the ambush. (Incidentally, it was a black trooper who delivered Governor Lew Wallace's proclamation declaring a cessation to hostilities and the granting of amnesty to all those involved.)

### Watrous
*Fort Union National Monument*

American blacks left their mark on Fort Union which was a major military post on the frontier and Sante Fe Trail between 1851 and 1891. Several companies of the U. S. 9th cavalry regiment were stationed at this post with the balance of the regiment serving at other garrisons throughout the New Mexico territory. They spent much of their time subduing civil unrest in the Lincoln and Colfax County wars, guarding telegraph and supply lines, and campaigning against hostile Apache tribesmen. In the post-Civil War Indian Wars, 14 congressional medals of honor were awarded to black regular soldiers, and 11 were won by members of the 9th cavalry. Nine of the medals of honor were awarded for combat actions in New Mexico between 1877 and 1881.

*After escaping from slavery herself, Harriet Tubman led at least 19 missions into the South to conduct hundreds of others to freedom on the Underground Railroad.*

### Zuni
*Zuni Pueblo*

Zuni Pueblo was discovered in 1539 by Estevanico, a Moorish slave who was one of the original party of Spanish explorers to land in Tampa Bay in 1528. After a succession of disasters, the party was ultimately reduced to four (including Estevanico) who, marooned on the Texas shore near what is now Galveston, were soon captured and enslaved by Indians. After seven years in captivity, Estevanico and the others escaped to New Spain.

Having heard of the legend of the Seven Cities of Gold, reputed to be located in the Southwest, Estevanico signed on as an advance scout for an expedition led by a Father Marco. Often traveling ahead of the main party, Estevanico sent most of his messages back via friendly Indians. His last message—a giant cross emblematic of a major discovery—led the expedition to the Zuni Pueblo, which Estevanico apparently thought was part of the legendary Seven Cities. By the time the expedition arrived, however, the suspicious Zuni had already put Estevanico to death.

Today, Estevanico is credited with the discovery of a territory which comprises the states of Arizona and New Mexico.

## NEW YORK

### Albany
*Emancipation Proclamation*

The New York State Library houses President Abraham Lincoln's original draft of the preliminary Emancipation Proclamation issued in September 1862. It was purchased by Gerritt Smith, a wealthy abolitionist and patron of the famed revolutionary John Brown. The January 1, 1863 version of the proclamation resides in the National Archives of Washington, D.C. The draft of this document was destroyed in the Chicago fire of 1871.

### Auburn
*Harriet Tubman Home*

The Harriet Tubman Home stands as a monument to the woman who is believed to have led some 300 slaves to freedom via the Underground Railroad.

Miss Tubman settled in this home at the close of the Civil War—years after it had outlived its original function as a major way station on the north bound freedom route of fugitive slaves. In 1953, the house was restored at a cost of $21,000. Born a slave in Maryland, Miss Tubman fled at the age of 25, only to return South at least 19 times to lead others to freedom. Rewards of up to $40,000 were offered for her capture, but she was never arrested, nor did she ever lose one of her passengers in transit. During the Civil War, she served as a spy for Union forces.

*Harriet Tubman Home for the Aged*
*180-182 South Street*

The Home for the Aged was established in 1908 for aged and indigent Negroes by the most famous "conductor" on the Underground Railroad. Harriet Tubman had led more than 300 slaves to freedom. The home was declared a National Historic Landmark by the Department of Interior on May 30, 1974.

### Greenburgh (Westchester County)
*Villa Lewaro*

Designed by the noted black architect Vertner Woodson Tandy for Madame C. J. Walker, the successful cosmetics manufacturer, Villa Lewaro illustrates the achievements of Negroes in both architecture and business. The Villa Lewaro was declared a National Historic Landmark on May 11, 1976.

### New York City
*African Methodist Episcopal Zion Church*

The African Methodist Episcopal Zion (AMEZ) Church was dedicated in 1801 on a plot of land located at Church and Leonard Streets in New York City. A year later, the trustees of the church signed an agreement with the General Conference of the Methodist Episcopal Church, thereby consenting to place themselves under the jurisdiction of the bishops from this latter church. The conference was also given the right to appoint a preacher for the black church. By 1820, however, the AMEZ Church had found this arrangement so unsatisfactory that it bolted from the General Conference. At this juncture, the leader of the black congregation was a former slave named Peter Williams. The first three ordained black ministers of the new church were Abraham Thompson, James Scott, and Thomas Miller, while the first exhorter (an unordained person authorized to preach) was William Miller. James Varick was the first bishop.

*Amsterdam News*
*2340 Frederick Douglass Boulevard*

The Amsterdam News, now New York City's largest Negro-owned newspaper as well as the largest weekly community paper in the United States, was founded on December 4, 1909 in the home of James H. Anderson (132 West 65th Street). At that time one of only 50 black "news sheets" in the country, the Amsterdam News had a staff of 10, consisted of six printed pages, and sold for 2 cents a copy. Since then, the paper has been printed at several Harlem addresses.

Altogether, the Amsterdam News must be considered one of the most vital organs of information in any campaign to reach blacks in New York City. Its pages have historically

*The Apollo Theater as it appears today on 125th street.*

reflected the interests and concerns of black Americans. It is currently the largest circulating black weekly in the country and publishes on Thursday of each week. The New York Amsterdam News Building, at 2293 Seventh Avenue, was designated a landmark on May 11, 1976 by the Department of Interior.

*Apollo Theater*
*125th Street, between 7th and 8th Avenues*

The Apollo Theater in Harlem, an entertainment mecca for all races, is one of the last great vaudeville houses in the United States. For 50 weeks of every year, the Apollo presents live entertainment—featuring rising young stars as well as established black professionals who play there not so much for the financial reward as for the importance of exposure to a popular audience.

*Louis Armstrong House*
*3456 107th Street, Corona, Queens*

For years this was the home of Louis Armstrong, the famous jazz musician whose talents entertained millions throughout the world. Whenever Louie was at his Corona home on a break from his concert dates, he was a favorite with neighborhood youngsters. He would often entertain them in his home and on the street. His wife, Lucille, still lives at the address. The house was designated a historical landmark on May 11, 1976 by the Department of Interior.

### *Bethel A.M.E. Church*
### *60 West 132nd Street*

In the autumn of 1819 Bishop Richard Allen of Philadelphia dispatched William Lambert to New York City for the purpose of organizing an African Methodist Episcopal church there. Mother Bethel Church, the oldest and largest AME church in Manhattan, came into being both as a religious body and as a kind of protest organization.

### *Booker T. Washington Plaque*

Booker T. Washington, educator and founder of Tuskegee Institute, is the only black honored by a plaque in the Hall of Fame, New York University.

### *Ralph Bunche House*
### *115-125 Grosvenor Road, Kew Gardens, Queens*

The home of Ralph Bunche, the distinguished Afro-American diplomat and scholar who served as Undersecretary of the United Nations and who received the Nobel Peace Prize for his 1949 contribution to peace in the Middle East. The house was designated a National Historic Landmark on May 11, 1976 by the Department of Interior.

### *Calvary Baptist Church*
### *111-10 New York Boulevard, Jamaica, Queens*

Reverend Walter S. Pinn has been pastor of Calvary Baptist Church since 1946, at which time it was still housed in a tiny, one-story building with a seating capacity of only 100. Today it is the largest black congregation on Long Island, meeting in a beautiful, spacious structure which can seat some 2,000 persons. The new building contains several classrooms and meeting halls, a wedding chapel, and a modern kitchen. There are two Sunday services, supplemented by a 150-voice chorale under the direction of Mr. Samuel Daniels.

### *Cornerstone Baptist Church*
### *Lewis and Madison Streets, Brooklyn*

The Cornerstone Baptist Church, a congregation now boasting over 5,000 members, was founded on September 10, 1917 by eight faithful churchgoers assembled for communal worship in a single room of a private residence at 933 DeKalb Avenue, Brooklyn, New York. The church began to expand rapidly under the pastorship of Reverend T. W. Fentress, who linked it in 1932 with the Unity Baptist Church.

### *Will Marion Cook House*
### *221 West 138th Street*

This was the home of the early-twentieth-century black composer Will Marion Cook, whom Duke Ellington called "the master of all masters of our people." Cook was born in Washington, D.C. He began studying violin at 13 years of age, and at 15 he won a scholarship to study with Joseph Joachim at the Berlin Conservatory. Syncopated ragtime music was introduced to theater goers in New York City for the first time with Cook's operetta Clorinda. The house was designated a National Historic Landmark by the Department of Interior on May 11, 1976.

### *Edward Kennedy "Duke" Ellington Residence*
### *935 St. Nicholas Avenue, Apt. 4A*

When Duke Ellington recorded "Take the A Train" to Harlem, he meant just that because the A train express stops on St. Nicholas Avenue and it was the quickest and fastest way for Ellington to get home. The St. Nicholas Avenue address was the long-term residence of Ellington, who has been regarded by critics as the most creative Afro-American composer of the twentieth century. The residence was designated a National Historic Landmark by the Department of Interior on May 11, 1976.

*Restored to its Revolutionary elegance, Fraunces Tavern is a popular New York restaurant.*

### *Franks Restaurant*
### *312 West 125th Street*

The largest black-owned restaurant in Harlem is Franks, run by the eminent East Coast restaurateur Lloyd Von Blaine and the equally well-known caterer Selwyn Joseph. Franks has been the place for quality dining along Harlem's "main stem" for over 50 years.

### *Fraunces Tavern*
### *Broad and Pearl Streets*

One of the most famous landmarks in New York City, Fraunces Tavern was bought in 1762 from a wealthy Huguenot by Samuel Fraunces, a West Indian of black and French extraction. In those days, Fraunces called his establishment the Queen's Head Tavern. Before the Revolutionary War began it served as a kind of meeting place for numerous patriots already chafing under the tyranny of King George III.

On April 24, 1774, the Sons of Liberty and the Vigilance Committee met at the tavern to map out much of the strategy later used during the war. George Washington himself was a frequenter of the tavern, as were many of his senior officers. Washington's association with Fraunces continued for a number of years, with Fraunces eventually coming to be known as "Steward of the Household" in New York City. It was at Fraunces Tavern, in fact, that Washington took leave of his trusted officers in 1783 before retiring to Mount Vernon.

Much of the tavern's original furnishings and decor are still intact. The third floor—now a museum—contains several Revolutionary War artifacts, while on the fourth floor one can find a historical library featuring paintings by John Ward Dunsmore. A restaurant, patronized by leading New York citizens as well as by tourists from all over the country, is maintained on the ground floor.

### *Freedom National Bank*
### *275 West 125th Street*

Freedom National Bank is Harlem's first black-chartered, black-run commercial bank. Founded in 1965, it already has 10,000 customers and assets of over 10 million dollars—a figure which, by comparison with other banks maintaining branches in Harlem (Chase Manhattan, Citibank, Manufacturers, Hanover, Chemical,) is small.

The most significant thing about this bank, however, is the fact that the Harlemite has come to refer to it as his bank, a symbolic phrase for residents of an area in which most fixed property and real estate continue to be controlled by white people. A former chairman of the board of Freedom National was Jackie Robinson, the baseball great. The president is William R. Hudgins, who has lived and worked in Harlem for the past 37 years.

(The first bank in Harlem—the Dunbar Bank—was founded by John D. Rockefeller in 1928 but folded 10 years later. In 1949 the Carver Federal Savings and Loan Association was established, with Hudgins serving as a member of the board. Today, Carver has two branches—one in Manhattan, the other in Brooklyn—and assets totaling some 30 million dollars.)

### *Matthew Henson Residence*
### *Dunbar Apartments, 246 West 150th Street*

This was a late home of Matthew Henson, a black explorer who served as an assistant to Robert E. Peary and whose best known achievement came in 1909 when he became the first man to reach the North Pole. The residence was designated a National Historic Landmark by the Department of Interior on May 15, 1975.

### *Hotel Theresa*
### *2090 7th Avenue (corner of 125th Street)*

Built in 1913, the Hotel Theresa was once a luxury hotel serving white clientele from lower Manhattan and accommodating "white only" dinner patrons in its luxurious Skyline Room. In 1936, a corporation headed by Love B. Woods tried to take over the hotel and transform it into a black business establishment. This move failed when Seidenberg Estates, the Realtors, set a price on it beyond the reach of the group. Woods did eventually manage to purchase the hotel. (Its most publicized guest in recent years has been Cuban premier Fidel Castro.) Nowadays, the hotel has lost some of its original lustre.

### *James Weldon Johnson Residence*
### *187 West 135th Street*

From 1925 to 1938, this was the home of James Weldon Johnson, the versatile black composer of popular songs, as well as being a poet, writer, general secretary of the NAACP and a civil rights activist. Johnson is best known for composing such songs as *"Congo Love Song," "Since You Went Away,"* and *"Lift Every Voice and Sing." "Lift Every Voice and Sing"* has been called the national anthem for black people. Johnson was born in Jacksonville, Florida and did graduate study at Columbia University. The residence was named a National Historic Landmark by the Department of Interior on May 11, 1976.

### *Maiden Lane—First Slave Revolt in New York*

In 1712, on Maiden Lane and William Street the first organized slave revolt in New York City occurred. Approximately 30 slaves organized and attempted to fight their way to freedom. Many people were injured in the melee which ensued as the slaves took to the woods with the militia close behind. Surrounded in the woods, several slaves committed suicide. The rest were captured and subsequently executed.

### *Claude McKay Residence*
### *180 West 135th Street*

From 1941 to 1946, this was the residence of the black poet and writer Claude McKay, who has often been called the father of the Harlem Renaissance. McKay was born in Jamaica, British West Indies and was in Kingston's constabulary prior to coming to the United States. His residence was named a National Historic Landmark by the Department of Interior on December 8, 1976.

*Remington chronicled the life of black infantrymen in the Old West.*

### *Messiah Baptist Church*
### *866 Sutter Avenue, Brooklyn*

Messiah Baptist Church has been in existence since March 1965, having been founded by its current pastor, Reverend Elijah Pope. Starting with a group of 15, the congregation has already grown to over 200. The dedicatory sermon was preached by Reverend Sandy F. Ray, pastor of Brooklyn's famous Cornerstone Baptist Church.

Reverend Pope has already organized several auxiliaries, as well as a Boy Scout troop and a street block association.

### *Florence Mills House*
### *220 West 135th Street*

This was the home of the popular black singer who in the 1920s achieved stardom on Broadway and in Europe. Following that, she became a symbol of success for black Americans. The Mills residence was designated a National Historic Landmark by the Department of Interior on December 8, 1976.

### *Paul Robeson Residence*
### *555 Edgecomb Avenue*

This was the residence of the famous black actor and singer Paul Robeson. In the 1940s and the 1950s, Robeson suffered public condemnation for his political sympathies while he was widely acclaimed for his artistic talents. The residence was named a National Historic Landmark on December 8, 1976 by the Department of Interior.

### *John Roosevelt "Jackie" Robinson Residence*
### *5224 Tilden Street, Brooklyn*

This was the home of Jackie Robinson, the baseball player who in 1947 became the first black to play in the major leagues. His signing to a baseball contract broke the color barrier to full black participation in professional sports. While a Brooklyn Dodger, Robinson lived for many years in the same borough of New York City where he played baseball. The residence was designated a National Historic Landmark on May 11, 1976.

### *St. George's Episcopal Church*
### *Third Avenue and First Street*

This was the home church of Harry Thacker Burleigh, the black composer, arranger, and singer who helped establish the Negro spiritual as an integral part of American culture. The church was designated a National Historical Landmark by the Department of Interior on December 8, 1976.

### *Schomburg Collection of Negro Literature and History*
### *103 West 135th Street*

The Schomburg Collection of Negro Literature and History is a library and archives of materials devoted to black life around the world.

This collection is built around the private library of Arthur A. Schomburg, a Puerto Rican of African descent. It contains books, pamphlets, manuscripts, photographs, art objects, and recordings which cover virtually every aspect of black life—from ancient Africa to present-day black America.

Among the treasured items in the collection are:

1. The work of America's first black poet—Jupiter Hammon's Address to the blacks in the State of New York (1787).
2. Manuscript poems and early editions of the works of Phillis Wheatley.
3. Copies of the 1792 and 1793 Almanacs of Benjamin Banneker.

4. The scrapbook of Ira Aldridge, the black Shakespearean actor who achieved fame in Europe in the nineteenth century.
5. Clotel, the first novel by an American black (William Wells Brown).

Material in the Schomburg is not circulated but can be used or viewed in the library. G. K. Hall and Co., 97 Oliver Street, Boston, Massachusetts has published a nine-volume edition of the Dictionary Catalog of the Schomburg Collection of Black Literature and History, priced at $605.00.

*Sugar Hill, Harlem*

Sugar Hill is a handsome residential section in uptown Harlem. It is bordered on the west by Amsterdam Avenue, on the north by 160th Street, on the east by Colonial Park, and on the South by 145th Street. An area of tall apartment buildings and private homes, it is peopled largely by middle-class blacks, sometimes referred to as the *black bourgeoisie*. Its only counterparts in the area of central Harlem are Riverton and Lenox Terrace.

### North Elba

*John Brown's Grave*

Just six miles south of Lake Placid on Rte. 86A, John Brown's Grave is located on a farm he purchased after he had left Ohio. Brown lived there until he joined the free-soil fight in Kansas.

The farm was part of 100,000 acres set aside for both freedmen and slaves by Gerritt Smith, a wealthy abolitionist. Smith hoped to build an independent community peopled by former slaves who had learned farming and other trades. Brown joined Smith in the venture, but the idea failed to take hold and was eventually abandoned.

### Ogdensburg

*Remington Art Memorial*

Artist/journalist Frederic Remington is easily the greatest visual chronicler of the saga and splendor of the Old West. Remington fashioned several durable portraits and sketches of black cavalrymen in action in the field, on bivouac, and even during ceremonial exercises. Remington was also a correspondent during the Spanish-American War, and did a painting entitled *The Charge of the Rough Riders at San Juan Hill*. The painting shows only one of the many blacks who accompanied Teddy Roosevelt's men on their celebrated charge. The Ogdensburg Museum houses the Remington portrait in its permanent collection.

### Rochester

*Frederick Douglass Monument*

New York Governor Theodore Roosevelt dedicated the Frederick Douglass Monument in 1899. The noted black abolitionist had helped organize all-black volunteer regiments during the Civil War and saw two of his sons volunteer for duty.

### South Granville

*Lemuel Haynes House*
*Route 149*

The house, located in Washington County, was built in 1793. It was the later-day home of Lemuel Haynes, the first black ordained minister in the United States. Haynes was also the first black minister to a white congregation. The South Granville home site was declared a National Historic Landmark by the Department of Interior on May 15, 1975.

### Stillwater

*Saratoga National Historic Park*

Victories in the battles of Saratoga in the Fall of 1777 have been called the turning point of the Revolutionary War. Free blacks served in patriot militia units, and were also utilized as musicians, livers and servants by the Hessian forces supporting the British.

### Ticonderoga

*Fort Ticonderoga*

Leading the Revolutionary War assault on the fort at Ticonderoga were Ethan Allen and his famed Green Mountain Boys, many of whom were blacks, including Lemuel Haynes, Primus Black, and Epheram Blackman. After the American victory, some of the cannons were transported to Boston, where they were instrumental in providing heavy weapons support for General George Washington's thrust into, and capture of, the city.

## NORTH CAROLINA

### Durham

*North Carolina Mutual Life Insurance Company*
*114-116 West Parish Street*

The Parish Street address is the home office of North Carolina Mutual Life Insurance Company, which is a black-managed enterprise founded in 1898. The company achieved financial success in an age of Jim Crow. The site was declared a National Historical Landmark by the Department of Interior on May 15, 1975.

### Milton

*The Yellow Tavern*
*Also known as Union Tavern*

For more than 30 years, the Yellow Tavern was the workshop of Tom Day, one of the great black artisans and furniture makers of the Deep South prior to the Civil War. Day began making hand-wrought mahogany furniture in 1818 and within five years accumulated enough money to convert the old Yellow Tavern into a miniature factory. Both white apprentices and black slaves were taught this skilled trade under his coveted tutelage. Day's artistry was so revered by the citizens of Milton that they went to great pains to secure a special dispensation from a North Carolina law which made it illegal for any free black or mulatto to migrate into

*The British storming Fort Ticonderoga after it was taken by American patriots, many of whom were black.*

the state. The dispensation was needed because Day had married Acquilla Wilson in 1829, two years after the law took effect. The legislature actually went so far as to pass a law which exempted Day and his wife from the "fines and penalties of the Act of 1827."

Day also found an ingenious way to integrate the Presbyterian church in Milton by offering to replace the worn-down mahogany pews on the main floor of the church—in return for the "privilege" of sitting in them, rather than in the gallery, during services. Day built the pews, but he confounded the parishioners by using maple instead of mahogany. The church, the pews, the Yellow Tavern, and Tom Day's home and grave have all survived and are accessible to this day. The Yellow Tavern was declared a National Historic Landmark by the Department of Interior on May 15,1975.

### Raleigh

*John Chavis Memorial Park*
*E. Lenoir at Worth Street*

This park is named after John Chavis, a black educator and preacher who founded an interracial school in Raleigh which later numbered among its graduates several important public figures, including senators, congressmen, and governors. As a result of the abortive Nat Turner slave rebellion in 1831, however, blacks were barred from preaching in North Carolina, obliging Chavis to retire from the pulpit. He died in 1838.

## OHIO

### Akron

*John Brown Monument*

The John Brown Monument was built in honor of the fiery abolitionist whose ill-fated Harpers Ferry revolt led to his conviction for treason and execution by hanging in 1859.

### Cincinnati

*Harriet Beecher Stowe Home*

The Harriet Beecher Stowe Home has been preserved as a memorial to the internationally known author of *Uncle Tom's Cabin.*

*Taft Museum*

An exceptionally fine black American artist, Robert S. Duncanson, took up residence in Cincinnati sometime during the 1840s. A friend and patron of Duncanson was the philanthropist Nicholas Longworth, who commissioned him to do the decorative work on the walls of the main entrance of the mansion. Duncanson completed a series of eight murals and several pieces for over doors. The building was sold to the Tafts of Cincinnati and later became the Taft Museum of Art.

### Dayton

*Paul Laurence Dunbar Home*
*219 Summit Street*

The Paul Laurence Dunbar Home has been preserved much as the poet left it at the time of his death in 1906, just prior to his thirty-fourth birthday. Along with his personal effects, several original manuscripts can be seen.

Dunbar, the first black poet after Phillis Wheatley to gain anything approaching a national reputation in the United States, was also the first to concentrate on dialect poetry and exclusively black themes. His first collection of poetry, *Oakand Ivory,* was published before he was 20. By 1896, his book *Majors and Minors* had won critical favor in a *Harper's Weekly* review. Dunbar contracted tuberculosis in 1899 and was in failing health until his death on February 9, 1906.

*John Mercer Langston House*
*207 East College Street*

This was the home of John Mercer Langston, the first black American to be elected to public office in 1855. Langston later served the Freedman's Bureau and was the first dean of the Howard University Law School. He was also a minister to Haiti. The house was designated a National Historical Landmark by the Department of Interior on May 15, 1975.

**Oberlin**
*Oberlin College*

Before the Civil War, Oberlin was one of the centers of underground abolitionist planning and a haven for activists of every stamp and hue. On one occasion, 20 Oberlin villagers actually snatched away a black fugitive who was being returned to his Kentucky owner by Federal agents. Later, three of John Brown's raiding party at Harper's Ferry were identified as blacks from Oberlin.

After the war, Oberlin was able to devote more time to its stated mission: providing quality education to all regardless of race. Among the distinguished alumni of Oberlin was Blanche Kelso Bruce, who served a full term in the U.S. Senate (1875-1881). Another Oberlin graduate was Moses "Fleet" Walker, who once played baseball with Toledo of the American Association, then recognized as a major league. (Jackie Robinson was the first black player to play major league baseball in the accepted modern sense of that term.)

**Put-in-Bay**
*Battle of Lake Erie Memorial National Monument*

The memorial draws attention to the Battle of Lake Erie, fought during the War of 1812, and to the impatient and impetuous American sea captain who became immortal by virtue of his defeat of the British: Oliver Hazard Perry. Perry had at first criticized his superior, Commodore Isaac Chauncey, for sending him a motley lot of replacements, including blacks. After the actual battle, however, these same men prompted him to revise his original estimate and praise the black seamen for being "absolutely insensible to danger."

**Ripley**
*John Rankin House Museum*

An Underground Railroad station prior to the Civil War, the John Rankin House Museum is believed to have been the haven of the fugitive slave on whose story the novelist Harriet Beecher Stowe based the flight incident in *Uncle Tom's Cabin.*

**Upper Sandusky**
*Wyandotte Indian Mission Church*

John Stewart, self-appointed missionary to the Wyandotte Indians, was of French, black, and Indian stock. His missionary labors among this tribe began in 1816. He was assisted in this work by Jonathan Poynter, a black who had been raised by the Wyandottes and acted as Stewart's interpreter.

Stewart converted the Indians to Christianity with the help of a fine tenor voice which he used to good advantage in singing them the spirituals and hymns he had learned in Virginia. He died in 1823, one year before the construction of his church was completed.

When the Wyandottes signed the treaty which resulted in their move to Kansas, one of its conditions was that the church remain within the Methodist Episcopal Conference. In 1960, the latter listed the Stewart grave and the missionary church among the 10 official shrines of American Methodism.

**Wilberforce**
*Colonel Charles Young House*
*Columbus Pike between Cliffton and Stevenson Roads*

The Columbus Pike address was the residence of the highest ranking black officer in World War I and the first black military attache. Colonel Charles Young was the son of former slaves and was born in Mays Lick, Kentucky. The Army had declared Young unfit physically because of high blood pressure, so to prove that he was physically fit, he rode horseback 500 miles from Wilberforce to Washington, D.C. in 16 days. The Army, however, still stuck by its ruling. The house was declared a National Historical Landmark by the Department of Interior on May 30,1974.

## OKLAHOMA

**Boley**
*Boley Historic District*

This is the largest of the Negro towns established in Oklahoma to provide black Americans with the opportunity for self-government in an era of white supremacy and segregation. The Boley Historic District was designated a National Historic Landmark by the Department of Interior on May 15, 1975.

**Lawton**
*Fort Sill*

Units of the 10th Cavalry and the 24th Infantry were among those which served at Fort Sill in the aftermath of the Civil War. Like most black troopers in the territories, they did escort and patrol duty, but they were often called upon to round up cattle thieves and whiskey runners. It was to Fort Sill that the black cavalrymen of the 10th escorted the famed Apache chieftain Geronimo. Geronimo spent his last days at the fort and is buried in the Apache cemetery.

**Marland (Kay County)**
*101 Ranch Historic District*

This is a large cattle ranch and home base of the 101 Wild West Show, which featured Bill Pickett, the well-known black cowboy who invented steer wrestling and who was elected to the Cowboy Hall of Fame. The ranch was established in 1879. On May 15, 1975, the ranch was declared a National Historic Landmark.

### Ponca City

*101 Ranch (five miles south of Ponca City)*

During the latter part of the nineteenth century, the 101 Ranch was one of the largest and most famous in the West. In its prime, it employed several black cowhands, the most celebrated of whom was Bill Pickett.

The originator of the art of bulldogging or steer wrestling, Pickett also perfected a unique style unlike any used by current rodeo participants. He would leap from his horse, grab the steer around the neck or by the horns, and then sink his teeth into the animal's upper lip. In Mexico City, he once wrestled a fighting bull for a full six minutes to win a bet. In March 1932, though then in his seventies, Pickett was still active—the last of the original 101 hands. He died a month later, on April 21, 1932, after being kicked by a horse, and was buried on a knoll near the White Eagle Monument.

## OREGON

### Astoria Clatsop County

*Fort Clatsop National Memorial*

Named for the local Clatsop Indians, Fort Clatsop was built by the Lewis and Clark Expedition as quarters for the winter of 1805-1806. Clark's black servant York was a member of these historic expeditions.

*Bill Pickett of the 101 Ranch.*

## PENNSYLVANIA

### Erie

*Harry T. Burleigh Birthplace Marker*

A friend of famed Czech composer Dvorak, and a composer/arranger in his own right, Harry T. Burleigh was born in 1866. Burleigh set to music many of the stirring poems of Walt Whitman and arranged such unforgettable spirituals as *Deep River*. He died in 1949.

### Lancaster

*Thaddeus Stevens Grave*

When Thaddeus Stevens was dying, he was attended by Lydia Smith and two nuns from a charity hospital for blacks that Stevens had helped with a grant of $30,000 from Congress.

Upon his death five black and three white pallbearers escorted the body to Washington, D.C., where it lay in state on the same catafalque that had borne the body of Lincoln and was guarded by black soldiers of a Massachusetts Regiment. Two days later the body was returned to Lancaster, where over 10,000 blacks attended the funeral, and was buried in Schreiner's Cemetery, a cemetery for blacks. Stevens, a white abolitionist and civil rights activist, in his will, rejected burial in a white cemetery because of the segregation policy.

### Lower Merion Township (Montgomery County)

*James A. Bland Grave*

In Montgomery County lies the grave of black composer James A. Bland, who wrote *Carry Me Back to Old Virginny,* now the state song of Virginia.

### Philadelphia

*Frances Ellen Watkins Harper House*
*1006 Bainbridge Street*

This was the home of the black writer and social activist Frances Ellen Watkins Harper, who participated in the nineteenth-century abolitionist, Negro rights, woman's suffrage, and temperance movements. The house was named a National Historical Landmark on December 8, 1976.

*Mother Bethel African Methodist Episcopal Church*
*419 S. Sixth Street*

The Mother Bethel African Methodist Episcopal (AME) Church was the fourth church to be erected on the site where Richard Allen and Absalom Jones founded the Free African Society in 1787. This later grew into the AME, one of the largest black religious denominations in the United States.

Allen, the first black bishop, was born a slave and became a minister and circuit rider after winning his freedom. In 1814, he and James Forten organized a force of 2,500 free blacks to defend Philadelphia against the British. Sixteen years later, Allen organized the first black convention in Philadelphia and was instrumental in getting the group to adopt a strong platform denouncing slavery and encouraging

*James Bland wrote the state song of Virginia.*

abolitionist activities. Allen died in 1831 and was buried in a basement vault at Mother Bethel's.

As for Forten, he had been born free in 1766, and despite his youth, served aboard a Philadelphia privateer during the Revolutionary War. In 1800, he was one of the signers of a petition requesting Congress to alter the Fugitive Slave Act of 1793. Opposed to the idea of resettling slaves in Africa, Forten chaired an 1817 meeting held at Bethel to protest existing colonization schemes. In 1833, he put up the funds which William Lloyd Garrison needed to found *The Liberator*.

After his death, Forten's work was continued by his offspring, who remained active in the abolitionist cause throughout the Civil War, and on behalf of the freedmen during Reconstruction. The Forten home was a meeting place for many of the leading figures in the movement.

The church was named a National Historic Landmark by the Department of Interior on May 30, 1974.

*Negro Soldiers Monument*
*Lansdowne Drive, West Fairmount Park*

The Negro Soldiers Monument was erected by the state of Pennsylvania in 1934 to pay tribute to her fallen black soldiers.

*Henry O. Tanner Homesite*
*2903 West Diamond Street*

This was the boyhood home of the late nineteenth- and early twentieth-century black expatriate painter Henry O. Tanner, whose work earned recognition in Europe and the United States. Tanner was born in Pittsburgh, Pennsylvania. He was the first black to be elected to the National Academy of Design. The homesite was designated a historical landmark by the Department of Interior on May 11, 1976.

*Thaddeus Stevens, a dedicated anti-slavery spokesman.*

*Valley Forge*
*Valley Forge State Park*

Blacks were among those who endured the winter hardships of Valley Forge with the bedraggled Continental Army of George Washington in 1777. One of the blacks who died was Phillip Field, a New Yorker. Among those who survived was Salem Poor, the very same black who had fought at Bunker Hill as a member of Colonel Frye's Massachusetts Regiment and been officially cited for having "behaved like an experienced officer, as well as an excellent soldier." The citation concluded as follows: "...in the person of this said black centers a brave and gallant soldier."

## RHODE ISLAND

### Portsmouth

*Site of the Battle of Rhode Island*

This was the site of the only Revolutionary War battle in which an all-black unit, the 1st Rhode Island Regiment, participated. The unit joined John Sullivan's army in attacking British garrison troops in Newport. The site was named a National Historic Landmark on May 30, 1974.

## SOUTH CAROLINA

### Beaufort

*Robert Smalls House*
*511 Prince Street*

Robert Smalls was a former slave who served in the state legislature and in Congress. He had lived in Beaufort both as a slave and as a free man. Smalls fought for black rights while in office. His house was designated a National Historic Landmark on May 30, 1973.

*Robert Smalls and the captured gunboat* Planter.

**Charleston**

*Denmark Vesey House*
*56 Bull Street*

This was the residence of Denmark Vesey, a free black Charleston carpenter whose 1822 plans for a slave insurrection illustrated Negro resistance to slavery. The Denmark Vesey House was declared a National Historic Landmark on May 11, 1976.

*Dubose Hayward House*
*76 Church Street*

Dubose Hayward, the author of *Porgy*, the book upon which George Gershwin's opera *Porgy and Bess* was based, lived here from 1919 to 1924. It was designated a national historic landmark on November 11, 1971.

Fort Sumter National Monument

Site of the first shelling of the Civil War on April 12, 1861, Fort Sumter is an important site in black history due to the daring exploits of a black coastal pilot, Robert Smalls. On May 13, 1862, Smalls took control of the Confederate steamboat Planter, loading into it his family and a few other brave crewmen who endorsed his resourceful and cunning escape plan. Smalls sailed the ship past the Confederate checkpoints, imitating the captain at each vital juncture during which he was being observed from a distance. Once beyond the reach of Confederate shore batteries, Smalls hoisted the white flag of surrender, and delivered the ship into Union hands. Smalls was later elected to several terms as U.S. Congressman from South Carolina.

**Charleston County**

*Stono River Slave Rebellion Site*
*Rantowles Vicinity*

This was the site of a serious slave insurrection in the Colonial period. It was during that time when some 100 escaped slaves burned plantations and murdered whites before being stopped by the militia. The site was named a National Historic Landmark on July 4, 1974.

**Columbia**

*Chapelle Administration Building*
*1530 Harden Street*

This building was one of the finest works of John Anderson Lankfor, a pioneer black architect who helped gain recognition for Afro-American architects among the architectural community. The building was named a historical landmark by the Department of Interior on December 8, 1976.

**Frogmore**

*Penn School Historic District*

The northern missionaries organized one of the first southern schools for Negroes in Frogmore. The Penn School Historic District pioneered in health services and self-help programs. It is the oldest existing structure in Brick Church. On December 2, 1974, the district was named a National Historic Landmark.

**Georgetown**

*909 Prince Street*
*Joseph H. Rainey House*

Joseph Hayne Rainey (1832-1887), former slave, was the first black to serve in the U. S. House of Representatives from 1870 to 1879. His election, along with the election of Hiram R. Rebels the first black citizen to be elected to the U. S. Senate in 1870, marked the beginning of black participation in the federal legislative process. Designated April 20, 1984.

## SOUTH DAKOTA

### Deadwood

*Adams Memorial Museum*

Only one of the legendary claimants to the title of "Deadwood Dick" is a black, but he can back his assertion with a colorful and richly tapestried autobiography which takes the reader through his childhood in slavery, his early bronco-busting efforts, and his fabled life as a range rider and Indian fighter in the old West. Nat Love claimed he won the title during a public competition held in Deadwood on the Fourth of July in 1876. The presence of other black cowboys, gambling house operators, and escort soldiers in the area during these years, as well as the convincing style of Love's narrative, lend a high degree of credibility to his adventurous tales although, like Jim Beckwourth, he was probably given to moments of wanton exaggeration.

*Indian fighter Nat Love claimed the title "Deadwood Dick" after a public competition on July 4, 1876. Born a slave, he grew up to live the fabled life of a cowboy and range rider in the Old West.*

## TENNESSEE

### Fairvue Farm

*4 miles south of Gallatin, Sumner County*

Built between 1832 and 1839, Fairvue was the home of Isaac Franklin and his family. Isaac Franklin, along with his partner John Armfield, of 16 years, developed a very successful slave-trading operation from which he retired in 1835. The original Fairvue contained 2,000 acres with a beautiful Georgian mansion. It also contained 16 brick slave houses, an overseers house, a blacksmith shop, commissary, grist mill, cotton gin, hostelry house, and a two-storey spring house. The spring supplied water for all of the inhabitants which included 129 slaves. Fairvue has since passed into the hands of several different owners and has been sub-divided with approximately 700 acres going with the mansion. Fairvue reflects the lifestyle of antebellum planters in the upper south. It was designated a national historic landmark December 22, 1977.

### Henning

*Fort Pillow Marker*

Taken originally by Union Forces in 1862, Fort Pillow was recaptured by Confederate troops under the command of the wily Nathan B. Forrest on April 12, 1864. The few black survivors of the engagement testified before the Federal Committee on the Conduct of the War, and documented several instances of massacre after their surrender. Southerners claimed the defenders had simply refused to surrender. The fort was declared a National Historic Landmark by the Department of Interior on May 30, 1974.

### Jackson

*Casey Jones Railroad Museum*

On Chester Street in Jackson, Tennessee one will find the Casey Jones Railroad Museum filled with memorabilia of a bygone era. Jones was immortalized through the song about Casey Jones' legendary train ride. The song, which became popularized in vaudeville and music halls, was written by Wallace Saunders, a black fireman aboard Jones' locomotive. The Railroad Museum is a symbolic inclusion that represents the enormous unsung contributions of blacks to the railroad industry in the United States.

### Memphis

*Beale Street Historic District*

*Beale Street from Main to 4th Streets, Memphis*

The "blues", a unique black contribution to American music, was born on a Beale Street lined with saloons, gambling halls, and theaters, and immortalized by William Christopher Handy who composed among others, *Beale Street Blues*, *Memphis Blues*, and *St. Louis Blues*. Beale Street was designated a National Historic Landmark on May 23, 1966.

*W. C. Handy Park*

The city of Memphis pays tribute to famed blues composer W. C. Handy in the form of a park and a heroic bronze statue

*Blacks deserve much credit for the growth of the U.S. railroad industry from its earliest days. Memorabilia of those times are preserved in the Casey Jones Railroad Museum in Tennessee. The famous song about Casey was written by Wallace Saunders, the black fireman aboard his locomotive.*

overlooking the very same Beale Street which he immortalized. The statue shows Handy standing with horn poised, about to play. Executed by Leone Tomassi of Italy, it was dedicated in 1960 at the close of a memorial campaign instituted by the city shortly after Handy's death in 1958. (Though born in Florence, Alabama, Handy lived most of his life in the Tennessee city.)

*Tom Lee Memorial*
*(foot of Beale Street on the river bank)*

The 30-foot-high Tom Lee granite memorial was erected in 1954 to honor a black who, on May 8, 1925, saved the lives of 32 passengers aboard the M. E. Norman, an excursion boat which had capsized some 20 miles below Memphis near Cow Island. Alerted to the disaster, Lee pulled 32 people from the water onto his skiff. He was honored for his feat by the Memphis Engineers Club, which provided him with money for the duration of his life. A fund was also raised to purchase him a home. After his death in 1952, a committee raised the money needed to erect the memorial.

*Lorraine Hotel*

It was on the balcony of the Lorraine Hotel that Martin Luther King Jr. was assassinated while emerging from a second-floor room, in the presence of a pair of his trusted advisers, Ralph Abernathy and Jesse Jackson. King died in the emergency room of St. Joseph's Hospital on April 4,1968.

### Nashville

*Fisk University, Meharry Medical School and Jubilee Hall*

Founded in 1866, Fisk University is today one of the most prestigious institutions of higher learning originally for blacks in the United States. Much the same can be said of Meharry Medical School, one of the leading training centers for black doctors in the U.S.A.

Jubilee Hall is of Victorian Gothic structure and is the oldest building on the Fisk University campus. Fisk was founded by the American Missionary Association to provide a liberal arts education for blacks following the Civil War. When Fisk first began operation, it was called Fisk Free School. The hall was named a National Historic Landmark on December 2, 1974.

## TEXAS

### Amarillo

*First Black School*

Matthew Bones Hooks was born in central Texas in 1867. The story goes that he rode wild horses at 8, had his first paid job as a cowhand at the age of 10, and later herded cattle for Colonel Charles Goodnight, taking them from Texas to Dodge City, Kansas. Hooks homesteaded in New Mexico, rode broncos in Romfa, Texas in 1910, and then moved to Amarillo, where he established the first school for blacks in that city. The school was in the north heights section, an all-black community. He also founded the Dogie Club, an organization for underprivileged boys in cooperation with the Boy Scouts. He was the only black member of the old Settlers Association of Amarillo and the first black of Amarillo to serve on a grand jury.

### San Antonio

*The Alamo*

Mystery shrouds the identity of all who fought at The Alamo in 1836, but evidence exists that there were some blacks serving with the Texas troops defending this post. The most famous of them is known only as "Joe," the slave of Colonel W. B. Travis (a senior officer at the Alamo). After his release

*W. C. Handy, "Father of the Blues."*

by the Mexican general Santa Ana, Joe reported the results of the battle to another contingent of Texas troops in what is believed to be the first known description of the Mexican assault.

It is also believed that Joe was later reenslaved. According to a newspaper ad dated in 1837, a slave named Joe who had survived The Alamo had stolen a horse and run away from his master. No records exist to verify whether Joe or the horse was ever found.

### Fort Davis
*Fort Davis National Historic Site*

Black "buffalo soldier" regiments were stationed at Fort Davis from 1867 to 1885. Black units, like the 9th and 10th cavalry and 24th and 25th infantry, participated in the Indian Wars of the late-nineteenth century. These units compiled a notable record of military accomplishment against their Comanche and Apache antagonists. In respect, the Indians called them "Buffalo Soldiers". The fort was a key post in the west Texas defense system along the San Antonio-El Paso road.

## UTAH

### Fort Douglas
*The Old Fort*

Home of the 24th Infantry Regiment, a black unit which served in the trenches of San Juan Hill and later was utilized to combat the yellow fever epidemic at Siboney. Weakened and reduced in number because of the sickness, the men returned to a huge welcome in New York but were barely able to get through the parade after their strenuous ordeal. More men died of yellow fever in Cuba than of combat wounds sustained in battle.

## VIRGINIA

### Alexandria
*1315 Duke Street*
*Franklin and Armfield Office*

This office, of the Franklin and Armfield slave-trading company, was from 1828 to 1836 the south's largest slave-trading firm. Designated June 2, 1978.

Colonial National Historic Park

Jamestown Island is where the first black slaves arrived in the English colonies (1619); at the battle of Yorktown in 1781, three blacks served in patriot militia units and also worked for the Hessian forces as musicians and servants.

### Arlington
*Arlington National Cemetery*

Being interred at the Arlington National Cemetery is reserved to those men and women who served in the military. It is the resting place of the Unknown Soldier and also President

*Several blacks were among the 179 Texans who died, rather than surrender the Alamo to a Mexican Army.*

*The first blacks arrived on Jamestown Island, Virginia, as indentured servants in 1619, a year before the Pilgrims landed at Plymouth Rock.*

John Kennedy and Senator Robert Kennedy. Many black soldiers are buried here and their grave sites may be visited. Among them is Lieutenant Colonel A. T. Augusta of the Medical Corps during the Civil War, known as a strong civil rights activist. Also buried at Arlington is Colonel Charles Young, the third black cadet to graduate from West Point.

*Benjamin Banneker: SW-9 Intermediate 18th and Van Buren Streets*
*Boundary Stone*

The boundary stone commemorates the accomplishment of Benjamin Banneker, who helped survey the city of Washington, D.C. and who was perhaps the most famous black man in Colonial America. Banneker, a mathematician and scientist, was born in Ellicott Mills, Maryland and received his early schooling with the aid of a Quaker family. Banneker was known as a national hero for black people and many schools have been named for him. The boundary stone was declared a National Historic Landmark on May 11, 1976.

*Charles Richard Drew House*
*2505 First Street South*

This was the home address of Charles Richard Drew from 1920 to 1939. Drew was the noted black physician and teacher best remembered for his pioneer work in discovering means to preserve blood plasma. The house was named a National Historic Landmark by the Department of Interior on May 11, 1976.

### Fort Monroe

This was one of the few military posts not seized by the Confederacy at the outbreak of the Civil War and hence became a haven for fugitive blacks escaping into Union lines. Known as "contraband" (the term was extended by Union General Ben Butler to cover runaways), these able-bodied blacks were put to work building roads, erecting fortifications, and as teamsters and foragers. Many eventually saw combat duty in the Army of the James after restrictions on enlistments were lifted.

### Chatham

*Pittsylvania County*
*Pittsylvania County Courthouse*
*U. S. Business Route 29*

Associated with the case of *Ex parte Virginia* (1878), which concerned the denial to black Americans of participation on juries. It involved the clear attempt by a state official to deny citizens the equal protection of the laws guaranteed by the fourteenth amendment to the constitution. This case showed that the federal government now had a qualified, but potentially effective, power to protect the rights of minority groups. Designated May 4, 1987.

### Capahosic

*Gloucester County*
*Holley Knoll (Robert R. Moton House)*

From 1935 to 1959, the retirement home of Robert R. Moton who succeeded Booker T. Washington as head of Tuskegee Institute in 1915, and guided the school's growth until 1930. He was an influential educator and active in many Afro-American causes.

Petersburg National Battlefield Cite

Black troops played prominent roles in the Union attacks on June 15 and July 30, 1864.

### Glen Allen

*Virginia Randolph Cottage*
*2200 Mountain Road*

Under the Jeanes Fund set up by a wealthy Philadelphia Quaker to aid black education, Virginia Randolph became the first Jeanes supervisor, working to upgrade black vocational training. The cottage was named a National Historic Landmark on December 2, 1974.

### Hampton

*Hampton Institute*

One of the earliest institutions of higher learning for blacks in the United States, Hampton Institute was attended by the

*The campus of Hampton Institute—one of the most beautiful in the entire South.*

great Booker T. Washington before he went to Tuskegee. Washington also taught for a time at Hampton.

**Richmond**
*Jackson Ward Historic District*
*Bounded by 4th, Marshall, and Smith Streets and the Richmond-Petersburg Turnpike*

This is the foremost Afro-American community of the nineteenth and early twentieth centuries and an early center for ethnic social organizations and protective banking institutions. The district was named a National Historic Landmark on June 2, 1978.

*Richmond National Battlefield Park*

The area around Richmond was the scene of several combat engagements involving black troops active in the Civil War. Among these engagements were Chaffin's Farm, New Market Heights, and Deep Bottom. General Butler found that the gallantry of these men merited special consideration, and so authorized the issuance of 200 medals which he presented personally to those outstanding soldiers who were recommended to his attention.

*Maggie Lena Walker House*
*110A East Leigh Street*

In 1903, Maggie Lena Walker, a black woman, founded the successful Saint Luke Penny Savings Bank and became the first woman to establish and head a bank. The life and career of Maggie Walker have inspired many. In addition to being the first woman president of a bank, she was editor of a newspaper which was considered to be one of the best journals of its class in America. She was also a concerned community leader. The house is located in the Jackson Ward Historic District of Richmond and is an impressive two-story red brick structure. It was declared a National Historic Landmark May 15, 1975.

**Rocky Mount**
*Booker T. Washington National Monument*

The Burroughs plantation, on which Booker T. Washington was born a slave in 1856, can be found in a 200-acre park located in Rocky Mount.

## WASHINGTON

**Centralia**
*George Washington Park*

The park is named after a liberated slave who escaped from slavery in Virginia when he was adopted by a white couple and taken to Missouri. He then left Missouri with a wagon train heading for the Pacific Northwest, settling on a homestead along the Chehalis River which was ultimately reached by the Northern Pacific Railroad. Washington subsequently laid out a town, setting aside acreage for parks, a cemetery, and churches. Soon over 2,000 lots were in the hands of a thriving population which formed the nucleus of Centerville.

## WEST VIRGINIA

**Harpers Ferry**
*Harpers Ferry National Monument*

Harpers Ferry derives its historical fame from the much-publicized anti-slavery raid conducted by John Brown and a party of 18 men (including five blacks) from October 16 to 18, 1859. Brown hoped to set up a fortress and refuge for fugitive slaves which he could transform into an important way station for escapees en route to Pennsylvania.

Brown lost two of his sons in the battle and was himself seriously wounded. Later tried and convicted of treason, he was hanged at Charles Town on December 2, 1859.

**Malden**
*Booker T. Washington Monument*

This monument, erected in 1963, marks the site where the great black educator labored for several years in the salt works. At the time, Washington credited his employer, Mrs. Violla Ruffner, with having encouraged him to pursue a higher education at Hampton Institute.

*John Brown's fort at Harpers Ferry.*

## WISCONSIN

### Madison

*State Historical Society of Wisconsin*

The Wisconsin Historical Society has taken the impressive initiative of building up an archival collection of documents and other written materials relating to the modern-day civil rights struggle. Although it goes back only to 1960, archivists have already amassed the papers of more than 300 civil rights workers and agencies. The purpose of the collection is to create a repository of information for later historians and scholars who will seek to interpret the movement and extract its vital essence. Also included in the collection are broadsides of the black in the Civil War, and items pertaining to slavery.

### Milton

*Milton House Museum*

The Milton House Museum (the oldest cement building in the United States) was once used as a hideaway for fugitive slaves escaping by means of the Underground Railroad.

### Portage

*Silver Lake Cemetery*

Ansel Clark, "born a slave, died a respected citizen," settled in Wisconsin after the Civil War, during which he served as an impressed laborer in the Confederate cause for a time, then escaped. He became a nurse in a Union hospital. There he tended a Wisconsin resident who brought him home after the war to settle in Portage, where he became town constable and deputy sheriff. For 30 years he worked in law enforcement, standing up to the town's rough characters and keeping them in line with "firmness and dignity." It was said, however, that he was such a gentle man with animals that his undertaker feared to crack the whip on the horses driving his hearse lest "Old Anse be out of that box and on my neck."

## WYOMING

*Fort Washakie Blockhouse*

The blockhouse served as headquarters for both the 9th and 10th Cavalry regiments during their assorted campaigns on the Indian frontier. On one occasion, the 9th rescued a unit of infantry from Fort Steele, which was being attacked by a Ute war party. The dug-in infantrymen, exhausted and low on provisions, were relieved to be reinforced by the black troopers who drove off the Indians and stayed at the site to start construction on what was to become Fort Duchesne.

# CIVIL RIGHTS ORGANIZATIONS AND BLACK POWER ADVOCATES—PAST AND PRESENT

**A Brief History of Civil Rights in the United States ■ Civil Rights Organizations ■ Past Civil Rights and Black Militant Groups ■ Civil Rights and Black Power Leaders ■ Former Contemporary Civil Rights Leaders ■ Past Civil Rights Leaders ■ National Private Organizations with Civil Rights Programs ■ State and Federal Agencies with Civil Rights Responsibilities**

The history of the struggle of blacks to gain equality and freedom in America can be divided into three broad phases. Two of them are over, the third is still in progress, and it is not inconceivable that there may still be more phases to come. Simply stated, the first phase involved bringing down the house of slavery. The second was concerned with achieving equality under the law. The third is the current effort to secure economic equity with the supposition that this carries social equity with it. The pursuit of these goals has, at the very least, been consistent in Black America. There have been peaks and valleys—a spurt of effort and then a leveling off. Nevertheless, when viewed from a broad historical perspective, the struggle has never really stopped nor, given the realities that still separate black and white, does it seem likely to stop in the near future.

Consistency, however, has not meant uniformity. There have been different approaches to the black struggle from its beginning, just as there are today. Arrayed on one side have been those blacks who have seen the redemption of their dreams of freedom coming within the framework of an integrated pluralistic society. Their values, to a large measure, reflect those of the mainstream of American society—race excepted—and they form the backbone of the traditional Civil Rights Movement. An opposite view has been taken by those who favor an independent black society built outside of white-controlled and dominated institutions. Those who take this view see integration as a sham, a device to keep blacks in some form of bondage. It has been called black nationalism and, more recently, black power.

*Free blacks were frequently kidnapped and sold into slavery.*

What must be pointed out, however, is that the line between the two views is not always sharply drawn and they are not totally at war with each other. One can favor the civil rights approach and still work to build independent black institutions. And those who hold black power views can still, on a pragmatic basis, recognize the need to maintain some degree of contact with white groups and institutions.

Both civil rights and black power advocacy go back to the early days of colonial America. Concepts of liberty and equality, common to the civil rights movement, were stated in the Mennonite Quaker Resolution of 1688, which defended the right of "negers" to the liberty of their bodies. Black power may have an even older history on these shores. As far back as 1671 Maroons (escaped slaves) had established separate communities in Rappahannock and Middlesex counties, Virginia, surviving for years before being hunted down by white settlers and troops.

In the not too distant past, historians assumed that blacks had acquiesced almost completely to their status as slaves. The notion was put forth that blacks are fundamentally childlike and docile and that slavery was therefore necessary for their protection and contentment. This "southern view" was widely disseminated in American education and literature until the 1930s, at which time a more thoughtful approach gained acceptance. This view stated that blacks are not docile or incompetent but had to accept their inferior status because of oppression and social conditioning. Blacks were far from content with their lot. But the sheer strength of white police and military power plus the fragmentation of black families and social organization by slavery rendered protest or resistance physical and emotional impossibilities.

Proponents of this view wanted to be fair and unprejudiced, but they underestimated the efforts of blacks to improve their position. Historical records, recently examined, reveal that during colonial and early days of the Republic, many blacks struggled bravely, and occasionally successfully, for their freedom and rights.

## Early Movements

Foremost among black protest and self-help efforts was the Free African Society organized in 1787 in Philadelphia by the Reverend Richard Allen and Absalom Jones. As with many black movements to follow, the Free African Society was somewhat religious in its principles and program. Indeed, Jones was to become Rector of a Protestant Episcopal Church for blacks and Allen to form the Bethel African Methodist Church.

The Free African Society was an important source of political consciousness and welfare for blacks throughout the country. It combined economic and medical aid for poor blacks with support of abolition and sub rosa communication with blacks in the South.

As was to be the case with civil rights leaders of the nineteenth and twentieth centuries, Allen, who eventually became sole leader of the Society, had a strong appeal to whites. The Free African Society was formed in response to insistence by whites that Allen not preach to integrated congregations.

Blacks were also leaders in plans to resettle them in Africa, plans which led to the founding of Liberia in 1820.Paul Cuffee, a black merchant and ship builder who lived in Connecticut, was a leader of recolonization efforts but withdrew in disillusionment at the growing association between recolonization and the pro-slavery forces of Senator John Calhoun.

The Abolitionist Movement, customarily dated from the first publication of *The Liberator* in 1831, reflected both civil rights and black power strains. Such black abolitionist leaders as Harriet Tubman, Frederick Douglass, and Henry Highland Garnet were concerned not only with erasing slavery but with the growing discrimination and cruelty against free blacks in both the South and North.

The first obvious influence of blacks on a presidential

election occurred in 1844 when the Liberty Party, which counted Douglass and Garnet among its leaders, deprived Henry Clay of enough votes in New York to swing the state and the White House to James Polk.

On the whole, black abolitionists opposed separatist doctrines and favored working with whites to change the system. They foresaw a society in which blacks and whites would cooperate peacefully. However, some very potent black abolitionists, such as Garnet and David Walker, stressed the uniqueness of blacks and from the early days of the abolitionist movement urged that slavery be abolished, if necessary, by violence. The differences between Garnet, who advocated the overthrow of slavery by armed revolt and a general strike, and Douglass, who proposed more moderate methods, were in many respects forerunners of disputes which were to split the civil rights movement more than a century later, in the 1960s.

Both moderates and militants had a profound effect on events leading up to the Civil War and on the thinking of an articulate young politician from the West, Abraham Lincoln.

## Slave Insurrections

While the Abolitionist movement was forming and flowering in the North, many slaves in the South escaped to found their own communities, in defiance of their overlords and military authorities.

Historians sympathetic to the black cause have concentrated their research and writing on the underground slave "escape trains" and more recently on the slave uprisings of Nat Turner and Denmark Vesey. Still unexplored and relatively unknown are the numerous Maroon communities which thrived in the South nearly two centuries before the Civil War.

Maroon societies have, until recently, been regarded as a phenomenon almost exclusive to Latin American and Caribbean countries. Maroon groups in Brazil, Jamaica, Surinam, and other areas survived for centuries, came to number thousands and attained official recognition of their freedom from colonial authorities. In Surinam, the Saranaka Maroon society remains viable today, over 300 years after its founding by escaped slaves, a tribute to the economic and military prowess of its seventeenth-century forebears.

Maroon achievements in the United States were less dramatic but nonetheless real and of great concern to Southern slaveholders and military commanders.

Southern newspapers and military proclamations of the seventeenth, eighteenth, and nineteenth centuries attest to numerous battles and occasional trade between whites and communities of escaped slaves and free blacks. Some 50 such communities are known to have existed during the 200 years preceding the Civil War. Many lasted for years. And today, communities reflecting intermarriage between Maroons and Indians can be found in the hills and swamps from New Jersey to Florida, westward from Florida to Texas and across the border into Mexico.

*The Pennsylvania abolition society, as with other such groups, was an important source of political consciousness and welfare for blacks.*

The following example of a battle between whites and Maroons appears in *Maroon Societies*, edited by Richard Price, associate professor of anthropology at Yale:

*A letter of August 25, 1856 to Governor Thomas Bragg of North Carolina, signed by Richard A. Lewis and twenty-one other citizens, informed him of a "very secure retreat for runaway blacks" in a large swamp between Bladen and Robison Counties (Governor's Letter Book, No. 43, pp. 514-515, Historical Commission, Raleigh). There "for many years past, and at this time, there are several runaways of bad and daring character—destructive to all kinds of stock and dangerous to all persons living by or near said swamp." Slaveholders attacked these blacks on August 1, 1856 but accomplished nothing and saw one of their own number killed. "The blacks ran off cursing and swearing and telling them to come on, they were ready for them again."* The Wilmington Journal *of August 14 mentioned that these runaways "had cleared a place for a garden, had cows in the swamp."*

Such reports abounded throughout the antebellum South. In several South Carolina counties in 1830, slaveholders complained that the example of Maroons induced slaves to become almost uncontrollable. Maroons comprised much of the leadership and strength of Seminole forces in their six-year war (1837 to 1843) against the United States. In 1851, some 1500 ex-slaves were reported fighting as allies of the Comanche Indians against Texas slaveholders. During the Civil War, Maroons together with the white deserters from the Confederate Army evoked requests for martial law in parts of Florida, Alabama, and Virginia.

*Hidden behind their bedsheet masks KKK terrorists tried to keep southern blacks in virtual slavery.*

*Many escaped slaves joined maroon bands deep in the wilderness.*

Acknowledgment of the Maroons and the teachings of such blacks as Garnet and David Walker provide an essential balance to the understanding of black history in the United States. For it then becomes clear that blacks have sought to assert their identity as well as to attain acceptance and justice within white-dominated institutions.

## Civil Rights after the Civil War

Perhaps the era in which blacks were least assertive in their own cause extends from the end of Reconstruction in the 1870s to the formation of the Niagara Movement in 1905. During the period, some blacks sought unsuccessfully to forge alliances with whites in labor unions and political parties. Others, through such leaders as Booker T. Washington, tried to assuage fears of whites that blacks sought "social equality." In the 1890s, however, William Edward Burghardt DuBois—a young black historian who had recently been awarded a Ph.D. at Harvard for his thesis on the slave trade—emerged as an aggressive civil rights advocate. A brilliant debater, DuBois was soon to capture the interest and respect of blacks, who were being oppressed by Klan-style violence in the South and urban riots in the West and North.

## Civil Rights (1905-1963)

W. E. B. DuBois challenged Washington's passive policies in a series of stinging articles and speeches and then, in 1905, played a leading role in the formation of the Niagara Movement, a coalition of black intellectuals which pressed for full citizenship rights for blacks and public understanding of their contributions to America's stability and progress.

The Niagara Movement marked a turning point in black history. No longer would black leadership be dominated by men who felt it necessary to promise whites that blacks would settle for second-class citizenship and jobs. The Niagara Movement, however, suffered from weak finances and a policy which restricted membership to black intellectuals. A movement with appeal to all blacks and sympathetic whites seemed called for. And so, in 1909, most of the blacks in the Niagara Movement together with a number of whites, formed the National Association for the Advancement of Colored People. The NAACP soon emerged as the first black organization with the expertise and finances to fight for justice in America's courts and legislatures.

While the Niagara Movement was fusing into the NAACP, the Urban League was emerging from groups formed to aid blacks who had recently emigrated to northern cities. The NAACP and Urban League were in many respects complementary. The NAACP stressed civil rights, the Urban League stressed jobs and job training.

The civil rights movement suffered many defeats in the first half of the twentieth century. Repeated efforts to obtain passage of federal anti-lynching bills failed, as a series of presidents expressed sympathy but would not exert sufficient pressure on a Senate dominated by Southerners. The all-white primary, which effectively disenfranchised southern blacks, resisted numerous court challenges. The Depression worsened conditions on farms and in ghettos.

On the positive side, the growing political power of blacks in northern cities and an increasing liberal trend in the Supreme Court portended the legal and legislative victories of the 1950s and 1960s.

From the very beginning, the Urban League and the NAACP believed that blacks could benefit from stressing their American heritage and working closely with whites. Less conspicuous was the view that blacks must stress their black heritage and strive for equality on their own. Early in the century, this "black power" approach was maintained by William Monroe Trotter, a cohort of DuBois in the Niagara Movement. Trotter, however, refused to join the NAACP because he said, blacks could not trust whites to work for integration. Trotter also felt that the NAACP was too moderate.

Black consciousness was heightened by the Harlem Renaissance of the 1920s. And Marcus Garvey's preaching of black unity instilled a sense of pride and African Heritage.

*Dr. W. E. B. DuBois works at his desk in the old Crisis office.*

## The Civil Rights Movement (1954)

Unchanged, however, were the rampant discrimination and segregation that were a way of life in America. In the South, they were supported by law, and in other sections of the country, custom was just as effective as law. The United States was, in fact, an overtly racist country.

The bulk of the civil rights struggle throughout this period was carried on by the NAACP, which had begun chipping away at the roots of legalized segregation in a series of successful lawsuits. Its major breakthrough came in 1954 when the Supreme Court ruled in *Brown vs. Topeka Board of Education* that discrimination in education was unconstitutional.

Not since the *Plessy Ferguson* decision of 1896, which legalized separate but equal treatment for blacks, had there been such a momentous decision in a racial case, or one that was to have such far-ranging implications. Today's critics may argue that the *Brown* decision made little real difference, that even several decades later, blacks are still seeking full equality. The fallacy in this is that without the *Brown* decision, the legal basis for segregation and discrimination would still be in place. The *Brown* decision was a start, and should be viewed as that.

*Meeting of leaders of Civil Rights movement of the early 60's including (left to right) Bayard Rustin, Jack Greenburgh,Whitney Young, James Farmer, Roy Wilkins, Martin Luther King, John Lewis, and A. Philip Randolph.*

If any one person can be credited with lighting the match that set off the fire of the Civil Rights Movement that was to burn throughout the rest of the 1950s and 1960s, it was a humble Montgomery, Alabama seamstress, Rosa Parks, who decided on December 1, 1955 that because she was tired she would not give up her seat on a bus to a white man as the law required. Mrs. Parks went to jail and the Montgomery bus boycott, to be led by a 26-year-old Baptist minister, Martin Luther King Jr., was born.

The eventual success of the bus boycott encouraged a wave of massive demonstrations that swept across the South like a flood tide. In Greensboro, North Carolina, in 1960, a group of students denied service at a lunch counter started the sit-in movement. That same year, the Student Non-Violent Coordinating Committee (SNICK) was created and would number among its college student members Julian Bond, H. Rap Brown, Stokely Carmichael, John Lewis, and Marion Berry.

The Civil Rights Movement mobilized blacks and sympathetic whites as nothing had ever done before. It was not easy. Thousands of people were jailed because they defied Jim crow laws. Others were murdered. Homes and churches were bombed. People lost their jobs and their homes because they supported the Movement. The Movement itself made mistakes, but the momentum was too great to be stopped.

The Movement probably reached its zenith August 1963, when more than 300,000 People poured into Washington, D.C. for a massive "March for Jobs and Freedom" that has never been duplicated. A year later, as representatives of the Movement gathered around him, President Lyndon B. Johnson signed the Civil Rights Act of 1964 which, among

*"Stride Toward Freedom" speech.*

other things, outlawed discrimination in public accommodations and employment.

But despite this victory, the end of the Movement was already in sight. Dr. King's philosophy of nonviolence was losing its appeal.

### Urban Violence (1964-1968)

Civil rights laws and court decisions were slow to be implemented. And slowly, the racial battleground was shifting dramatically, out of the South and into Northern and Western ghettos, where residents and leaders were more concerned with the conditions of daily life than with citizenship rights. By 1964, the main focus of activity was no longer in the South but in the stores and streets of Northern and Western ghettos. Militants espousing radical change and "black power" challenged the gradualists and pacifists of the civil rights movement for leadership in the struggle. The peacefulness of the Movement was about to be replaced by urban riots.

### The Harlem Riot (1964)

The first violent eruption to receive national attention occurred in Harlem in the summer of 1964. The Harlem riot erupted two days after the shooting of a 15-year-old black youth by an off-duty patrolman in the Yorkville section of New York. Crowds of blacks roamed through the streets, breaking windows, looting stores, menacing policemen, and threatening the few white people found in the area. They faced helmeted police patrols who fired volley after volley into the night air in a futile attempt to disperse the crowds. In comparison with what was to come, the Harlem casualty figures were paltry. One man died, and 144 were injured. Prophetically, though, things had exploded in Harlem, the prototype black ghetto in the consciousness of white America. Few cared then that virtually every major American city was structured in the same way New York was, with an invisible wall encircling the black ghetto and buttressing white city

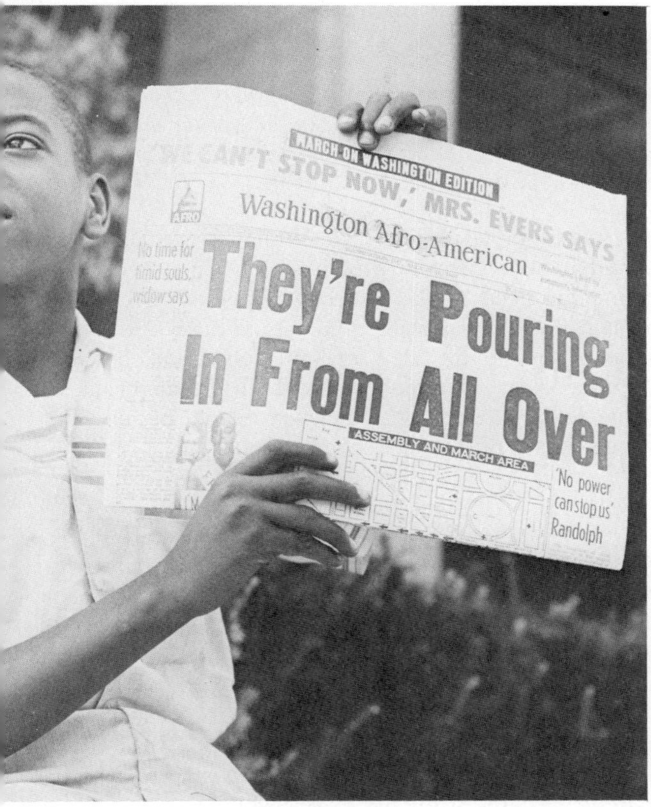

*Washington newsboy vends special edition. (above)*

*The March on Washington (right) was the peak of civil rights mass action.*

dwellers from exposure to, and contact with, their black counterparts.

### The Watts Riot (1965)

The Watts section of southwest Los Angeles, a 20-square-mile black ghetto with an estimated population of 90,000, was the scene of one of the worst riots in the history of the United States, August 11-16, 1965. Thirty-five people were killed, and property damage due to looting and arson reached the staggering total of 200 million dollars. Black deaths numbered 28.

Stores were looted; entire city blocks burned to the ground;buses and ambulances were stoned; and firemen, policemen, and airplanes were shot at in a 150-block area which, after six days, lay under a virtual state of siege.

The incident that sparked the outburst occurred on August 11 when state highway patrolmen chased an automobile around a six-block area and arrested its driver on a charge of drunken driving.

A crowd gathered as word of the arrest spread, and rumors of brutality were passed on by eyewitnesses. Rocks were thrown, and police summoned to disperse the rioters, who soon began stoning cars and smashing windows. A semblance of order was restored by 3 the next morning, but rioting again broke out on the evening of August 12.

Los Angeles Mayor Samuel Yorty and Chief of Police William Parker summoned the National Guard to assist beleaguered police and deputies. Between August 13 and August 16, 12,634 guardsmen, 1,430 city police, 1,017 county sheriff's deputies, and 68 state highway patrolmen served on riot duty.

### Causes of the Riots

A number of causes were advanced to explain the riots. Among them were:

1. Poverty and lack of job opportunities.
2. "Racial humiliation," the failure of whites to accept the dignity of blacks.
3. Lack of black leadership.
4. Agitation of the civil rights movement.
5. Police brutality.
6. Hot weather.
7. The criminal element.

Whatever the relative weight of these factors, the riots demonstrated the axiom that violence is an inevitable result of failure to cope with the root causes underlying discontent.

Statistics told much of the story. At the time, two-thirds of Watts residents had less than a high school education; one-eighth were illiterate. Only one in eight homes in the area was less than 25 years old, the remainder being in various stages of decay and disrepair. Three of every ten school children came from broken homes. The school dropout rate in Watts was 2.2 times above the Los Angeles average. And children grew up among an assortment of social outcasts—prison parolees, prostitutes, narcotics addicts, and the like.

*Large sections of the black Watts community were burned down in the 1965 riots.*

Many black and white observers believed that the riots boosted the pride of blacks. Noted black psychiatrist J. Alfred Cannon:

*They have developed a feeling of potency. They feel the whole world is watching now. And out of the violence, no matter how wrong the acts were, they have developed a sense of pride.*

The rallying cry of the mob ("Get Whitey") revealed another aspect of the problem. Aggressive "Get Whitey" cries were counterbalanced by the protective signs of "Brother" or "Blood" which appeared in the windows of black shopkeepers. In the view of some observers, however, "Whitey"—the white policeman, the white merchant, the white social worker—was attacked mainly because they were symbols of the black's oppression.

### "Black Power" Surfaces

A further indication that nonviolence was becoming less relevant occurred in June 1966, when Stokely Carmichael of the Student Non-Violence Coordinating Committee used the phrase "black power" in Greenville, Mississippi. Carmichael, along with other civil rights leaders, had come to the state after James Meredith, the first black to be admitted to the University of Mississippi, had been shot as he attempted a protest march across the state.

In the days following the Mississippi march, many civil rights leaders analyzed and condemned the concept of "black power." Martin Luther King Jr., for example, whose philosophy of nonviolence appeared to be antithetical to the position taken by the advocates of black power, said:

*I happen to believe that a doctrine of Black Supremacy is as evil as White Supremacy. I don't think that anything can be more tragic than the attitude that the Black Man can solve his problems by himself.*

On July 5, the NAACP heard its executive secretary, Roy Wilkins, denounce black power at its annual convention in Los Angeles:

*No matter how endlessly they try to explain it, the term "black power" means anti-white power. In a racially pluralistic society, the concept, the formation and the exercise of an ethnically tagged power means opposition to other ethnic powers.*

*In the black-white relationship, it means that every other ethnic power is the rival and the antagonist of "black power." It has to mean "going it alone." It has to mean separatism.*

The National Urban League, the last of the civil rights groups to comment on the controversy, issued a press release on July 11, disassociating itself from black power both semantically and philosophically:

*The National Urban League does not intend to invent slogans, however appealing they may be to the press. What we will continue to do through our unique structure is expand and develop positive programs of action which bring jobs to the unemployed, housing to the dispossessed, education to the deprived, and necessary voter education to the disenfranchised. The Urban League is dedicated to an interracial approach to solving the problems faced by the nation. We are equally dedicated to the expansion of the services and programs which have helped hundreds of thousands of people find jobs and get the training, education, and counseling they need. Our interracial staff is at work in 76 cities with programs, not slogans.*

The Congress of Racial Equality (CORE), on the other hand, adopted a resolution at one of its conventions endorsing the concept of black power in these terms:

*Black Power is not hatred. It is a means to bring the Black Americans into the covenant of Brotherhood. Black Power is not Black Supremacy; it is a unified Black Voice reflecting racial pride in the tradition of our heterogeneous nation.*

Stokely Carmichael elaborated further on the subject:

*Black power seems to me a number of things. Number one, that black people in this country are oppressed for one reason—and that's because of their color, and that's what*

*Mississippi freedom marchers enter a small farm town. CORE chairman Floyd McKissick (left front) hails onlookers to join march. CORE's leadership role in confronting racial injustice throughout the United States was built by activist members dedicated to principles of what James Farmer called "nonviolent self-sacrifice."*

*this country has to face their rally cry must be the issue around which they are oppressed, as it was for unions. The workers came together, they were oppressed because they were workers. And we must come together around the issue that oppressed us—which is our blackness. Unions—they needed power to stop their oppression. We need power to stop ours. So it's black power. And black power just means black people coming together and getting people to represent their needs and to stop that oppression.*

Some observers explained black power in terms of the collective frame of mind inevitable in a people emerging from a long period of inferior status. Others found that black power reflected a new ethnic integrity among blacks. Still others interpreted it as a phenomenon embracing many deep-seated antiwhite emotions, and saw in it further a rejection of existing political and social institutions, a voluntary form of separatism nurtured by personal pride, and a desire to meet violence with counter violence.

## The Newark Riot (1967)

Further evidence that nonviolence had perhaps reached the point of diminishing returns was provided later in the summer of 1966 when Martin Luther King attempted to take his philosophy to Chicago in an assault on segregated housing and was greeted with mobs of hostile and violent whites. So entrenched was the opposition that the effort had to be abandoned.

Rioting broke out again in the summer of 1967 first in Newark, New Jersey, and then in other cities, with such ferocity that the "long hot summer" became a catch phrase.

The spark of Newark's ghastly and tragic uprising in the summer of 1967 was a single arrest and the false rumors it generated. On the evening of July 12, black cabdriver John Smith tried to hurry past a prowl car patrolling in a black neighborhood. Carrying a passenger, Smith darted by the slow-moving vehicle, was cut off by police, and was hauled down to the station following a heated argument. (It developed that he was an illegal driver since his license had been revoked for numerous violations and accidents.) Central Ward witnesses who saw police dragging a limp and stiff body into the station concluded hastily that a hackie had been beaten up and killed. (Smith's injuries were serious enough to require a doctor's treatment.) He seems to have been roughed up to such an extent that he could not have cooperated peacefully with arresting officers even if he were so disposed.

Reports of death on the ghetto grapevine, however, escalated the tension and pushed residents and police toward open confrontation. By midnight, rocks and bottles were clattering against the walls of the station house. Inside, the police girded for action; outside, the grapevine telegraphed a message calling for more manpower and other reinforcements.

Meanwhile, civil rights leaders, black militants, community officials, and police authorities met to sort out the facts and quiet the hostility and hysteria of the gathering throng. As black participants at the meeting were attempting to persuade

*Riot police take command of the Newark riot.*

police to initiate an investigation to determine just how Smith had been injured, the unruly people outside became a matter of pressing concern. Soon Molotov cocktails were hurled against the wall of the station house, starting minor fires. These were quickly extinguished, but they were ominous enough to persuade the police to set up a line of defense in front of the station.

Once the moderating black leaders sensed they could not disperse the crowd, they decided shrewdly to try to organize an instantaneous march on City Hall to protest Smith's arrest and demand a thorough investigation. Some of the crowd positioned itself for such a march; others, however, milled around, disgruntled and unappeased. People in the line of march were struck by rocks; windows continued to be shattered; a car was set afire. Seeing the situation deteriorating still further, police rushed the crowd and sent it fleeing in all directions. Late-night reports of the episode carried references to a few isolated lootings, but otherwise indicated that the disturbances had run their course.

Police Chief Dominick Spina, however, sensed the seriousness of the situation, and realized that tensions had been aroused beyond a simple outburst. The next evening, a "Police Brutality Protest Rally" was organized by assorted black power advocates, including the Black Muslims, the United Afro-American Association, and other black nationalists. Together, they planned to picket the Fourth Precinct Station.

Despite the announcement that the Smith incident would be investigated, the blacks remained unsatisfied. In short order, the police station was again under a virtual state of siege, whereupon police once again charged into the crowds, hurrying them off into the night. They did not, however, return to their homes or quiet their anger.

In the early morning hours of Friday, July 14, Mayor Hugh Addonizio finally conceded the situation was beyond his control, and sent in an urgent request to New Jersey Governor Richard J. Hughes for state police and National Guard units.

After daybreak, more than 2,600 National Guard reinforcements were deployed throughout the area. Arrests were made systematically, and roadblocks effectively deterred entrance into, or flight from, the area. Command of the anti-riot operations was assumed by the governor, who declared Newark a city in open rebellion and defined the restoration of order as his first priority. Hughes ordered all guns and ammunition confiscated from stores that were selling them, imposed three separate curfews, and toured the area accompanied by a protective task force which arrested looters on sight.

However, neither the armored personnel carriers, the .50 caliber rifles, nor the other war equipment could diminish the defiance of looters and the persistent barrage of small arms sniper fire.

A three-year-old girl lost the sight of an eye and the hearing of an ear when she was hit by a police bullet fired at fleeing snipers; a 73-year-old man was felled by another police bullet fired as part of a sortie aimed at a group of looters who had attracted a crowd of milling spectators. The imprudent spectators, too, were quickly dispersed by the barrage of bullets, and innocent people were exposed to danger and injury simply by being on the scene. A garage mechanic was shot in the side while jacking up a car; a man standing on a porch was hit in the eye by a bullet; a 10-year-old boy riding in the family car was shot through the head.

Later testimony before the House of Representatives uncovered a hideous skein of events in which it became apparent that the amount of sniper fire was being grossly exaggerated and that, in many cases, it was more likely that frightened Guardsmen and fidgety police were exchanging gunfire.

Other incidents of brutality, anonymous killing, and savage behavior were too numerous to report; official reports after state police and Guardsmen were recalled on July 17 read as follows: 23 dead (21 of them black and two of them—a policeman and a fireman—white). Of these, six were black women, and two black children. Damage was over 10 million dollars, about 20% of it to buildings and fixtures, and the overwhelming majority due to stock loss at supermarkets, liquor stores, clothing shops, and other stores. More than 1,000 people were injured, and another 1,600 under arrest. Among them was black poet/activist Imamu Baraka, who was snatched from a Volkswagen, beaten, and hauled off to jail after being relieved of two .32 caliber pistols.

And Newark was only the first city to burn in 1967.

## The Detroit Riot (1967)

The Detroit riot also stemmed, on the surface at least, from an arrest that attracted widespread attention on the ghetto streets. It began at 3:45 A.M. Sunday morning, July 22 when the police raided a so-called blind pig, an after-hours drinking and gambling spot crowded with patrons attending a party thrown in honor of a group of black servicemen, two of whom had recently returned from Vietnam. All 82 patrons were arrested. As they were being carted off, however, a crowd of 200 gathered, and a mood of ugly resentment soon prevailed.

Shortly after 5 A.M., an empty bottle smashed into a police car, and a litter basket was hurled through a store window. Police reinforcements were summoned as riot tensions mounted, but few police were on duty in the immediate riot area. By 6 A.M., hundreds of irate blacks were already massed on the street. Assorted window-smashing and looting had begun along 12th Street, a high-density area of substandard and deteriorating housing.

A curfew ordered by the mayor had little effect on the situation. Looters continued to raid supermarkets recklessly, and street fights, beatings, knifings, and gun battles were common. A 23-year-old white woman was hit at close range after she and her husband had dropped off two black friends; less than two hours later, she was dead. A 45-year-old white man collaborating with black companions was shot from a car by the owner of the supermarket he was looting. A 68-year-old white shoe repairman was beaten to death by a black youth for interfering with looters cleaning out a nearby store. Fallen power lines killed a white fireman and a black homeowner.

By 2 A.M. Monday, 8,000 National Guardsmen were on their way to bolster the 800 state police officers and 1,200 National Guardsmen already on duty. By this time, Governor Romney and Mayor Cavanaugh had both decided to request federal assistance. The Attorney General's office replied that if state and local police could not control the situation, the governor would have to declare a "state of insurrection." Romney declined to follow this course once he realized that insurance companies would be relieved of financial responsibility for the damages pursuant to such a declaration.

President Johnson then authorized the sending of a paratrooper task force which arrived at Selfridge Air Force Base near the city at about 4 P.M. Monday.

By 11:30 P.M., federal observers (primarily Cyrus Vance and General John L. Throckmorton) advised President Johnson to authorize the use of paratroopers. The President signed the executive order federalizing the Guard, and thus committed the jittery young guardsmen to what amounted to a complex battle situation.

The casualties in the Detroit riot outstripped those of Newark. Altogether, 43 persons were killed, 33 of them black and 10 white. Two of the 17 looters who died were white; the rest, black. Fifteen citizens (four whites), one white National Guardsman, one white fireman, and one black private guard fell victim to gunshot wounds. Property damage soared to 22 million dollars, not counting business stock, private furnishings, churches, and charitable institutions, many of which were covered by insurance.

In all, over 7,000 persons were arrested—3,000 on the second day of the riot and over 4,000 by midnight Monday. Some were kept in such makeshift jails as buses and underground garages.

When the curfew was lifted and the National Guard removed from the city on Saturday, July 29, most of Detroit's black area was a charred mess of tangled rubble and waterlogged ashes. For some, dreams were broken; for others, hopes were seemingly shattered. Some blacks who had lost the work of a lifetime sobbed in dismay and gave up hope; conversely, others who had never accumulated many possessions seemed relieved of rage and inclined to build.

For the white establishment—another day of reckoning had passed, with many still too timid or too angry to press for real change. Walter Reuther found the words to describe the needs dramatized by Detroit:

*Those Americans [who] do not feel a part of society don't behave like responsible people. Only when they get their fair share of America will they respond in terms of responsibility.*

## The Kerner Report (1968)

While the riots in Newark and Detroit were the most serious during the summer of 1967, a number of other disturbances also broke out and President Lyndon B. Johnson appointed a Commission on Civil Disorders to study what happened, why it happened, and what could be done. The Commission, which was given a year to make its report, subsequently came to be known as the Kerner Commission, after its chairman, Governor Otto Kerner of Illinois.

It did not require a full year for the 11-member Kerner Commission to issue its provocative report on the mangled status of black society in the United States in the aftermath of the urban riots of 1967. One reason for the early appearance of the report may have been the fear that procrastination might only serve as fuel for a possible repetition of the holocaust. Another was assuredly the elementary recognition that the causes of the rioting were implicit in the situations and conditions of ghetto life, and these were not, after all, mysteriously unknown factors.

In gathering the facts, the Commission discovered that mass hysteria and exaggeration had reached as far as the nation's media, which had rendered estimates of damage and destruction far out of proportion to true figures. There were, in truth, 164 disorders—eight of them "major,"33 of them "serious," and the rest hardly worthy of attention under normal circumstances. No evidence existed to substantiate the notion that the uprisings were caused by a deliberate conspiracy, Communist or otherwise. Each riot had its own unique and complex character, and was a product of both general grievances and particular circumstances. Most rioters were young men, aged 15-24, high school dropouts, lifelong ghetto residents with a growing measure of racial pride, hostility toward the middle class ( black or white), and a basic distrust of the political system and the role of police enforcers.

Among the facts cited and exhaustively documented were a distressing crime rate (sometimes 35 times higher than in white neighborhoods), the lack of health facilities and municipal services (infant mortality among blacks was reported to be 58% higher than among whites; poor garbage collection and sanitation provisions helped account for 14,000 cases of rat bite in 1965 alone), and the increasing compression of poor black citizens within the urban ghetto itself. These problems were compounded by poor educational opportunity, inadequate recreational facilities, biased administration of justice, discriminatory credit and consumer practices, feeble welfare programs, and incredibly high unemployment. In other words, it was not possible to contemplate wholesale escape, nor was it likely that internal change could be undertaken effectively without wholesale assistance.

The recommendations outlined by the Commission called for a program "equal to the dimension of the problems." Such proposals did not take into account matters of obvious caste or political opposition; instead, they concentrated strictly on the issues and the policies which exacerbated tensions and produced an atmosphere of popular readiness to riot.

The proposals constituted an irrefutable admission that the nation was in fact racially polarized, and that blacks were now so aroused that, whenever it suited their strategy or their mood, they would not shy away from open racial warfare. Nevertheless, a fundamental gulf remained between the Kerner Commission's analysis of the situation (with which black militants generally concurred) and the mood of the nation. To the militants, it was clear that, though the message was couched in urgent, indeed "shocking" terms, it was still being directed to a sluggish and unresponsive source: the

U.S. government, Congress, the Establishment in general.

President Johnson accepted the report but never endorsed it and very little was done to implement its recommendations.

### The Assassination Riots (April 4-11, 1968)

The Kerner Commission issued its report in March 1968. A month later, on April 4, Martin Luther King, the man who had played the leading role in the Civil Rights Movement, was shot and killed by an assassin in Memphis, Tennessee. Gunfire, looting, and burning erupted in some 125 cities following his death.

The government's prompt, strong reaction to these riots marked a turning point in black history and American politics. Unlike the response to earlier riots in Watts, Newark, and Detroit, troops were summoned immediately. In some cities, seasoned troops were dispatched, rather than the relatively green National Guardsmen. Undoubtedly, the existence of rioting in many cities at once, and the fact that one of the cities was the nation's capital, was a factor in these actions. Fear of the growing anti-Vietnam War movement and occasional violence on college campuses may also have played a part, even though black participation in antiwar disturbances was minimal. But whatever provoked such a large scale use of troops (the total reached 70,000) from this point on, the incidence and intensity of urban riots subsided and many militant black leaders became blunt in their counsel to "cool it."

The riots had another effect. The fear they engendered among whites contributed to a "law and order" reaction that was to exert a strong influence on the American political scene for years to come.

H. Rap Brown, president of SNCC, called for violence.

*Black Panthers leaders Bobby Seale (left) and Huey Newton (right).*

### The Fading of Militancy (1964-1974)

Following the riots of 1968, violence and influence of black leaders who seemed to advocate it declined. The summer of 1969, and those that followed, were "cool, " outbreaks increasingly becoming limited in duration and scope.

It could be argued, from a fatalistic point of view at least, that black discontent and frustration had simply reached a pitch of frenzy which had to subside, just as a convulsive attack of epilepsy runs its course for no precisely discernible reason. Far more encouraging and constructive explanations for the cessation of violence could be advanced, however. For one thing, both ghetto residents and black middle-class leaders recognized the excruciating reality that the riots only destroyed their own turf and left many homeless, totally unprotected, and utterly devoid of marketable resources. Militant groups, such as the Black Panthers, while able to attract the interest of the media were unable to sell their messages on a broad scale in the black community. Eventually they faded into impotence.

### The Black Power Conferences (1966-1970)

In the waning days of the nonviolent Civil Rights Movement, the shape of organized "black power" began to emerge. The First National Conference on Black Power was convened in Washington, D.C. on September 3, 1966, by Congressman Adam Clayton Powell. It was attended by 169 delegates from 37 cities, 18 states, and 64 organizations. Out of this grew the Second National Conference on Black Power held in Newark July 20-23, 1967.

The largest and most broadly representative gathering of black Americans ever to attend such a meeting poured into Newark—more than 1,000 strong from 36 states and 42 cities. Its atmosphere and style were distinctly different from any previously scheduled meeting of national consequence involving black leaders. For one thing, white authorities—the Administration and the press—were not given ringside seats at the event, nor were their opinions and analyses solicited. The meeting was a closed-circuit black affair, a four-day private parley that took place at the conference headquarters of Cathedral House in the heart of Newark's Episcopal Diocese.

The serious nature of the issues produced a shroud of secrecy which enveloped the participants in the 14 workshops organized to grapple with the theme and establish key points of programmatic accord. The black representatives clearly wished to keep their divergent opinions private until they could hammer out some form of unified approach to a particular aspect of the problem.

The spectrum of black organizations represented at the meeting ranged from so-called conservative groups like the NAACP, the SCLC, and the Urban League to the so-called orthodox radicals (CORE and SNCC) to the more abrasive and occasionally strident (Ron Karenge's US of Los Angeles and Charles 37X Kenyatta's Mau Mau of New York ). The sporadic reports of violence bubbling up in several American cities lent added vigor to the proclamations of the paramilitary groups who advocated organized military training for black youth and self-defense courses for all black families, castigation of Christianity as a selfish and corrupt religion preaching love and practicing hate and materialism, and rejection of the word "Negro" for the word "black." Other resolutions called for the formal partitioning of the United States into two separate nations, the refusal of blacks to accept induction into the Armed Forces, the censure of all Congressmen who voted to unseat Congressman Adam Clayton Powell, and the support of a black boycott of the 1968 Olympics in the event Muhammad Ali's title remained unrestored.

At the Third National Conference on Black Power, held in Philadelphia in the last week of August 1968, more than 3,000 delegates were in attendance. Not all resolutions of the Conference were made public. Among those released to the press were:

*Neutrality in the Nigeria-Biafra war and a statement that both sides move for a settlement*
*Immediate withdrawal of U.S. forces from Vietnam*
*Boycott of the draft by all eligible black youths*
*Implementation of the goal of creating a black urban army in the city's ghettos for the protection of black citizens*
*Denunciation of the term "ghetto"*

In 1969, delegates to the black power confab took a different approach, scheduling the meeting for Hamilton, Bermuda, and viewing it as an attempt to create an international black power organization. Delegates who attended came from the United States, Africa, Canada, and the Caribbean.

As in the previous year, the resolutions offered by the Black Power Conference dwindled in number. They included:

*An end to media distortion of the black population*
*A return of all documents, art, and artifacts relating to black people from the world's museums*

*The Second National Conference on Black Power pressed beyond traditional civil rights goals toward black control of all black affairs.*

*A protest against the trial of black Canadian students*
*A call for immediate withdrawal from Vietnam and a boycott of draft induction by black youths*

The 1970 conference was held in Atlanta amid the continuing rhetoric that its aim was to develop institutions that would promote the liberation of black people. Significantly, the term black power was removed from the title of the conference, and the scope of the group was broadened to further upgrade the identity of other-than-American black people. Hence the name: The Congress of African People.

The meeting was attended by delegates from North America, Latin America, the Caribbean, and Africa. The internationalist outlook of the participants was apparent in the tendency to identify people by religion rather than by nation.

What was clear from five years of conferences, meetings, encounters, confrontations, violent upheavals, and position papers was that black power was a new driving force in the black community, not just a clever slogan that achieved momentary fashion and then faded into oblivion. Every black leader has had more than just an incidental curiosity about its real meaning; each has somehow been subject to its demands even as he has sought to harness and comprehend its implications.

## Inflation, Recession, and Populism (1974-1975)

In the early 1970s the very successes of the black power concept began to lessen its strengths. The black leaders who met in Gary, Indiana, in 1972 for another black power conference, were conspicuous by the fact that they had succeeded within the system. The host, Richard Hatcher, was mayor of Gary; the chairman, Imamu Amiri Baraka, was accepted, though often resentfully, as a leading writer and political advocate. In 1972, enough blacks were elected to Congress (16) to make the Congressional Black Caucus an important political force. And blacks were being elected mayors of major cities.

These successes contributed to a blurring of the sharp divisions between advocates of black power and the civil rights leaders who, though moving toward greater militancy, had persisted in pursuing traditional paths of reconciliation and integration.

But perhaps of greater long-term importance in the early 1970s was the reemergence, after a lapse of some 70 years, of a populist feeling among blacks, a belief that low—and low—middle income whites and blacks had vital interests in common and should work together toward guarantees of these interests.

The most conspicuous early supporter of this position was Dr. George Wiley, founder of the National Welfare Rights Organization. Wiley's untimely death greatly weakened the NWRO, but with the advent of "double digit" inflation in 1973 and the economic decline of 1974, both moderate and militant black leaders increasingly advocated reconciliation between the races and pursuit of such goals as minimum welfare standards, rent controls, increased taxes on corporations, National Health Insurance subsidies, and improvement of mass transit and other measures that would balance income and provide every citizen with guarantees of a decent living standard.

Included in this shift to interracial cooperation by low— and middle-income whites and blacks were such diverse leaders as black power advocate Imamu Baraka, who tended to a Marxist position, and Vernon Jordan of the Urban League. More moderate policies were also discernible among such groups as the Black Panthers and Black Muslims.

The Civil Rights Movement had produced new leaders, and others emerged from the ranks of black power advocates, to be joined by those who had been provided with leadership opportunities because of the War on Poverty and its funding of community groups.

## The Period of Retrenchment (1976-1981)

By the mid-1970s it was evident that the Civil Rights Movement had entered a new era, completely different from that of the 1950s and 1960s when it had achieved notable substantive victories and a respected status throughout the

*Playwright Imamu Baraka leads the fight for Kawaida Towers housing in Newark, New Jersey.*

land. Basically, what the Movement accomplished during the 1950s and 1960s was to force the removal of the legal base that supported racial discrimination and segregation, forge a broad-based consensus which believed that overt acts of racism were not morally tolerable in American society, enlist the support of the national government in the pursuit of racial equality, and establish a powerful coalition that brought together the church, labor, intellectuals, idealists, other ethnic groups, and the young. It also created the public image of a highly moral and vibrant crusade led by strong and committed black leaders (most notably Martin Luther King) who spoke in a united voice and accurately reflected the hopes and aspirations of their followers.

At its zenith, the Civil Rights Movement was the most important event taking place in America. It aroused the national conscience as it pitted the forces of good (as represented by the Movement) against the forces of evil (as represented by racist police). Through demonstrations, sit-ins, marches, and soaring rhetoric, the Movement aroused widespread public indignation, primarily through television, which was its passport into millions of living rooms, at the injustices being inflicted on a suffering people in the name of the law, thus creating a political atmosphere in which it was possible to make changes.

Once the oppressive laws had been rendered null and void, however, the Movement began to lose momentum. It had won major victories through the Civil Rights Act of 1964, the Voting Rights Act of 1965, court decisions and Presidential directives, but these were behind it and the challenges that it faced in the 1970s and beyond had more to do with the results of discrimination and segregation than with the law.

The accomplishments of the Civil Rights Movement were indeed remarkable and accounted for more progress in less time than blacks had made since they first arrived in America in 1619.The legal structure that kept blacks in the back of the bus in the South, out of hotels and restaurants and other places of public accommodation was outlawed. The segregation of public schools was effectively ended. The Voting Rights Act enfranchised millions of black voters and helped elect hundreds of southern blacks to public office. The Movement brought a fresh sense of pride to many blacks who, while they may not have been a part of it, drew inspiration from its achievements. And, the Movement helped to develop a whole new generation of black leaders.

## Despite Success, Many Untouched

As momentous as these achievements were, however, they failed to materially alter the lives of the mass of black people who remained disproportionately poor, badly educated, and unable to avail themselves of the opportunities that went to better prepared blacks. The Movement hardly touched them at all. Unemployment for blacks remained at double the rate for whites, the ghettos continued to deteriorate, crime still plagued black neighborhoods, and the various government programs that sought to address these problems were never funded at the proper level or maintained long enough to make any real difference.

Bluntly stated, the successes of the Civil Rights Movement did not improve the economic and social conditions of the masses of blacks, nor did they reach to the depth and complexity of the subtle racism that permeates almost every aspect of American life. One astute commentator, Carey Mc Williams, noted:

*The struggle for civil rights was not a social revolution. It has limited objectives, though objectives of critical importance. Legal barriers and discrimination had to be removed before more significant progress could be made.*

Unfortunately, the same type of national consensus that helped bring about the victories of the Civil Rights Movement could not be developed to deal with the endemic economic and social problems of the black community, or with ingrained racism that said in effect that blacks could come so far, and then no further. The mass of people that could be mobilized to demonstrate and march so that the walls of segregation would come tumbling down could not be mobilized over such issues as unemployment, welfare reform, better housing, improved health care. The glamour had gone out of the Movement.

## Progress Slows—Coalitions Break Down

Additionally, as long as the Movement concentrated its energies on attacking the most odious manifestations of racial injustice in the South, it benefited from general public support. But when the emphasis shifted to securing economic equality for blacks and dismantling institutional racism, the support dwindled primarily because many whites saw such actions as jeopardizing their own status. This "me first" attitude became more pronounced as the national economic picture worsened.

The roots for the disintegration of the consensus can be traced back to the urban riots of the 1960s, which did, in fact, whether rightly or wrongly, frighten a number of white people and lessen their ardor for black-oriented causes. At about this same time, the role of national leadership in supporting the Movement began to diminish as President Lyndon B. Johnson turned his attention away from what he had called The Great Society and to the waging of the war in Vietnam. The Nixon-Ford Administration, with its attitude of "benign neglect" ( from a memorandum from Patrick Moynihan to Richard Nixon) toward blacks and coolness toward many of the goals of the Movement, helped further dilute the consensus. For its part, the Carter Administration squandered what political capital it had in such an untidy fashion and was faced with some other critical issues (e.g., Iran and a souring economy) that it could do little in rebuilding consensus.

The Movement was further weakened when old allies began to break ranks because they had either grown weary, felt that they were no longer needed or wanted, turned to other causes such as Vietnam and the antiwar mood, the environment, or equal rights for women, or encountered philosophical differences with civil rights leadership. This latter was most pronounced in the deterioration of relationships between blacks and Jews over two matters—affirmative action and Andrew Young. The former involved primarily black and Jewish leadership while the latter was so emotionally charged that it went far beyond the ranks of the leaders to touch a sizable part of the black community.

At the center of the falling out over affirmative action—a process for assuring that blacks were treated equitably in hiring and in promotions—was the use of numbers or quotas as a method of insuring that affirmative action was actually working. Blacks took the position that quotas were essential. Jews, on the other hand, recalling that quotas had traditionally been used to limit their entry into certain professions and occupations, were opposed to them.

## The Bakke Case

This clash of views simmered for several years and finally came to a critical point in 1978 over the Bakke Case. The plaintiff, Alan Bakke, a white man, sued the medical school at the University of California at Davis because it had reserved 16 places for minorities out of the 100 available spaces for first-year students. Bakke's contention was that the establishment of a quota for minority students denied Bakke admittance even though on the basis of his test scores he was more qualified than some of the minority group members who were admitted.

Bakke's position was supported by a number of the most powerful Jewish groups in the country and unanimously opposed by black civil rights leadership. By a vote of 5-4, the U.S. Supreme Court sustained Bakke and ruled that the special program at Davis, and presumably others molded along the same lines, violated the 14th Amendment because Bakke had been rejected on the basis of his race. Black leaders were especially bitter over the decision since it came at a time when the concept of affirmative action was coming under increased assault by some whites as a form of "reverse discrimination." Blacks felt they had been deserted by their former Jewish allies, and they feared that an adverse decision in Bakke would have a "chilling effect" on other schools with affirmative action programs. Whether Bakke was to blame or not, black enrollments in professional schools did in fact decline after Bakke.

This feeling of an alliance gone wrong was reinforced in 1979 when the two groups once again found them selves on opposite sides of the affirmative action question. The case was *Weber vs. Kaiser Aluminum* and it involved a claim by Brian Weber, a white man, that a voluntary training program set up by Kaiser to train blacks for positions that had previously been closed to them was unconstitutional since he had been denied admittance to the program. In this instance, the Supreme Court ruled 5-2 that such voluntary plans were constitutional, but once again blacks and Jews were at odds.

## Black-Jewish Relations

Black-Jewish relations were further damaged that same year over the Young- PLO incident. Young, once a close and trusted associate of the late Martin Luther King, a civil rights leader in his own right, a former congressman from Atlanta, and one of the most admired blacks in America, was at that time serving as the U.S. Ambassador to the United Nations.

*Black and Jewish relations were severely damaged by Ambassador Andrew Young's violation of U. S. policy by secretly meeting with the Palestine Liberation Organization.*

Under heavy criticism by some whites because of his candor and outspokenness, Young violated official U.S. policy by meeting with a representative of the Palestine Liberation Organization. The policy prohibited any U.S. official from meeting with any PLO representative as long as that organization refused to recognize the right of Israel to exist as a state. The restriction was a matter of great concern not only to Israelis but to American Jews as well because of the violent enmity of the PLO toward Israel.

Young's meeting was secret but news of it leaked out, producing a formal protest from Israel and cries of outrage from American Jews. Initially, Young told the State Department that the meeting had been a chance encounter, but he later conceded that it had been planned and received an official reprimand. Several days later, under mounting pressure, Young submitted his resignation to President Carter, and it was accepted.

The reaction from individual blacks was swift and angry and much of it was directed toward the Jewish community, which was held responsible for forcing Young's resignation. The first organized black response came from the Black Leadership Forum, which had been initiated in 1977 by Vernon Jordan, president of the National Urban League, in an effort to more effectively coordinate the activities of a number of black groups and ease some of the strain existing between them. In addition to the League, other groups comprising the Forum, which is still active, were the National Business League, Legal Defense and Education Fund, National Council of Negro Women, National Urban Coalition, NAACP, Operation PUSH, Martin Luther King Jr. Center for Social Change, Southern Christian Leadership Conference, Congressional Black Caucus, National Black Caucus of Local Elected Officials, A. Philip Randolph Institute, Opportunities Industrialization Centers, and the Joint Center for Political Studies.

The Forum stopped short of directly blaming Jews for Young's troubles but it did issue a sharp statement that took issue with the manner in which Young was treated and condemned President Carter's action in accepting the Ambassador's resignation.

Then, on August 22, over 200 blacks representing the great range of opinion within the black community including many civil rights, fraternal, professional, religious, and grass roots groups, as well as those organizations at the earlier Forum meeting, gathered in an unprecedented meeting at the New York City headquarters of the NAACP to take up the Young matter. Even at the height of the Civil Rights Movement such a diverse group had not been brought together, so that the meeting indicated the seriousness with which the black community viewed the situation.

Several sharply worded statements came out of the meeting, accusing the Carter Administration of applying a double standard in dealing with Young, reaffirming the right of blacks to become involved in all foreign policy issues, and attributing a major share of the responsibility for Young's departure to Jewish influence. A day later, the National Jewish Community Relations Advisory Board, representing all major national Jewish organizations, responded by denying any involvement in Young's resignation—which was commonly conceded to have been forced. This was the sharpest dispute that had ever occurred between blacks and Jews, and while leaders on both sides sought to repair the rift, the scars were slow in healing.

The dispute also produced division within the ranks of black leadership itself when Jordan, one of the most prominent of the black leaders in the 1970s, criticized Jesse Jackson of Operation PUSH, a powerful leader, and others, for meeting with Yasir Arafat, head of the PLO, in the Middle East, a short time after the Young incident and the exchange of statements.

Jordan warned that "black-Jewish relations should not be endangered by ill-considered flirtations with terrorist groups devoted to the extermination of Israel." Jordan in turn was the object of a barrage of criticism for publicly attacking another black leader and for what some saw as taking the Jewish side.

## The Miami Riots of 1980

If white Americans believed, as some of them did, that the absence of major urban riots since the late 1960s indicated that the potential for violence in the inner cities had disappeared, the belief proved to be a fallacy in May 1980 when the city of Miami exploded in an outbreak of rage that left 16 people dead, 371 injured, another 450 under arrest, and property damage in the millions. The spark that touched off the conflagration was the acquittal of white Dade County police officers in the death of a black insurance man, Arthur McDuffie. There was convincing evidence introduced at the trial that the officers had inflicted a brutal beating on a helpless McDuffie after he was in their custody on a traffic charge. But an all-white jury freed the policemen and black anger spilled over into a full-scale riot.

Several national civil rights leaders, including Benjamin Hooks of the NAACP and Jesse Jackson of Operation PUSH, went to Miami in an effort to calm down the situation, but, as in the past, the peacemaking attempts of "establishment" black leaders were not effective and the rioting went on until it finally sputtered out. The failure of black leaders to exert any influence over the rioters was indicative of the sheer intensity of the problems in the black community that the Civil Rights Movement, the black power advocates, and the most militant of the militant black groups had not been able to solve. Writer Francis Ward several months later in *First World* summed up this state of affairs in the following words:

*Miami was a dramatic but timely demonstration that they (younger low-income blacks) have little if any confidence in black leadership, local or national. Black leadership has no message for the black dispossessed, no offer of jobs, education or new opportunities it can offer to lure the new generation of surly, angry blacks away from potential violence.*

And, as in other riots, a report—this one from a special governor's committee—was made and it pointed to all too familiar causes: the black community's perception of racist conditions and a local political system stacked against it, and the always present and underlying problems of poverty, slum housing, functional illiteracy and joblessness. And, once again, it was filed and forgotten.

## Vernon Jordan Ambushed

It was also in May that the National Urban League's president, Vernon E. Jordan, was ambushed and seriously wounded by an unknown gunman as he was about to enter his motel after delivering a speech to the Fort Wayne, Indiana Urban League. The bullet from a 30.06 rifle struck Jordan in the back, leaving a hole that physicians described as "almost large enough to put a fist in." Through a strange twist of fate, Jordan's life was saved by another black man, Dr. Jeffrey H. Towles, a gifted surgeon, who performed the initial operation on the civil rights leader.

The FBI mounted a far-ranging investigation but as late as the end of 1981, no arrest had been made in the case. The FBI did identify the prime suspect as a white man possessed of a virulent hatred for blacks who had been convicted of the murders of two black joggers in Salt Lake City, but they admitted they did not have enough evidence to bring him to trial in the Jordan shooting.

After a 90-day stay in the hospital, Jordan returned to his Urban League offices on November 5 and continued as president of that organization until December 31,1981, when he resigned to become a partner in a major white law firm in Washington, D.C.

## Return of the KKK

The mid-1970s and early 1980s also witnessed a rising tide of violence directed against blacks by such hate groups as the Ku Klux Klan, the Nazis, and the Aryan Nation. In 1980 alone, at least 24 blacks were killed in unprovoked and obviously racially inspired murders in places as far apart as Cincinnati, Indianapolis, Oklahoma City, Johnstown (Pa.), and Salt Lake City. Aided by extensive media coverage, the Klan and its sister groups, though still relatively small, were able to attract additional converts to their ranks, creating the potential for violence.

By the late 1980s, Klan membership had dropped by half to between 6, 000 and 8, 000 . A notable exception to this general decline in the Klan's strength was in North Carolina, where the Klan remained active and even gained members. Part of the Klan's attraction, observers theorized, could be its new image—as paramilitary guerillas— fighting for racial survival. Examples of groups espousing this belief included the White Patriots (formerly the Carolina Knights of the KKK) and The Order, based in the Pacific Northwest.

The KKK has not abandoned its notorious activity of cross-burnings. The Klanswatch Project of the Southern Poverty Law Center reported 45 cases of arson and cross-burning as well as hundreds of acts of vandalism from 1985 to 1987.

There have been other displays of power, as well. In June 1987, 150 Klansmen marched in Greensboro, North Carolina, in their first public demonstration since a shootout between armed Klansmen and leftists in 1979 left five persons dead. The most publicized confrontations with the Klan occurred in Forsyth County, Georgia. Forsyth has been an all-white county since 1912, when three black men were hung for raping a white woman, and the rest of the black population was driven out. In 1986, local Klansmen harassed civil rights activists commemorating Dr. Martin Luther King Jr. Day. As a result, fifty demonstrators sued the Klan for conspiring to deny them their right to free expression. In November 1988, a court ruled that the Klan owed the marchers $950, 400 in damages. In 1987—before the court judgment—a march on the same holiday drew an even larger confrontation. A crowd of KKK members and other whites threw bottles and stones at marchers, causing it to be halted in Cummings, Georgia. The march was resumed a few days later, this time with more than 12, 000 marchers, making it the largest civil rights demonstration since the 1960s. When Klansmen from 20 states staged a counterdemonstration, the National Guard was called out to protect the marchers. No injuries were reported but 55 people, including former KKK leader David Duke, were arrested or detained.

The National Urban League addressed the continued existence of the Klan in its "State of Black America—1981" report:

*It should be remembered that the old Klan went into decline when the so-called "good people," who had never burned crosses or terrorized the frightened and helpless, became embarrassed at their own racism and withdrew their support. But now racism is becoming legitimized again and there is a direct line between the sophisticates who feel free to make derogatory remarks about blacks and all other racial groups and by the primitives who kill and terrorize. They are only separated by the degree of their activity.*

Keeping pace with the times, the Klan in some localities, primarily in the far and mid-west, adopted a more sophisticated approach coaching its racism in code words and availing itself of public access cable television to spread its message. In February 1989, former Ku Klux Klan imperial wizard David Duke, was elected to the Louisiana legislature in a runoff election on the Republican ticket. Both President Bush and former President Reagan campaigned against Duke, but the virtually all-white New Orleans suburb of Metairie elected Duke by little more than a 200-vote margin.

In addition to Ku Klux Klan-related events, there were two other racial clashes which gained national attention.

On December 21, 1986, three black youths were driving by an all-white neighborhood in Howard Beach, N.Y. When their car broke down, the trio sought a tow. A group of white youths spotted them, picked up some bats and began to chase the blacks, shouting racial epithets. One of the black youths, 23-year-old Michael Griffith, ran into a street and was struck and killed by an automobile. The white youths were brought to trial: three whites were given lengthy prison terms for manslaughter, and three others were given weekend prison sentences for misdemeanor charges.

On January 16-19, 1989, rioting broke out in the black neighborhoods of Overtown and Liberty City in Miami to protest the shooting death of a black motorcyclist by a Hispanic police officer. The motorcyclist's male companion, who was riding on the back of the speeding bike, also died. The rioting left 27 stores burned, six people injured by gunshots, and 400 persons arrested. In one sad episode, a black man, Hilliet Williams, came upon two black men beating up a white man. Mr. Williams intervened, allowing the white man an avenue for escape. The two black assailants were so enraged by Mr. Williams' action, though, that they beat him instead. A month later, Mr. Williams died of his injuries. Overtown was also the scene of racial disturbances between blacks and Hispanics in 1980 and 1982, as well.

From a historical perspective, the rise in the level of activities of the various hate groups, the violence in Miami, Howard Beach and Forsyth County were part of something even larger and even more disturbing to civil rights leaders and others—the resurgence of racism.

## The Resurgence Of Racism

In the 1980s, civil rights organizations found themselves faced with a resurgence of racist feelings that exploded not only in such well publicized episodes as Howard Beach and Forsyth County, but spread like a stain to many areas of the country, sometimes blatant, sometimes subtle, but present to a degree that clearly indicated racism was still very much a fact of American life. The NAACP Legal Defense and Educational Fund in its report, "The Unfinished Agenda of Race in America," based on a national survey by the highly respected pollster Louis Harris, found that in the late 1980s the nation is still "the haven of much racism and even racial hatred."

Gone in the 1980s were the feelings of compassion, understanding and support—not universally accepted but shared by enough people to make a difference—that helped insure the success of the civil rights movement. They had been replaced by feelings at best of indifference and at worst hostility that Newsweek Magazine in a special report on "Black and White in America" described as "less caring" than in the 1960s. District of Columbia Rep. Walter Fauntroy, a veteran of the civil rights movement, took much the same view noting there is a "new meanness" in human relations in which "the internal brakes are off."

A longtime baseball executive tells a national television audience that, 40 years after Jackie Robinson broke the color barrier in baseball, blacks probably don't have the qualifications to be managers. The police chief of a suburb outside New Orleans issues an order to stop and question all young black males going through the area. The manager of a country club in affluent Montgomery County, just outside Washington, D.C., contemptuously refers to a black caller—over an open telephone line—as a "nigger" and only the threat of a boycott brings a reluctant apology.

Separate incidents to be sure but they sum up the nature of racism which W.E.B. DuBois described in his "Dusk of Dawn":

*It still remains possible in the United States for a white American to be a gentleman and a scholar, a Christian and a man of integrity, and yet flatly and openly refuse to treat as a fellow human being any person who has Negro ancestry.*

Racism posed a thorny problem for civil rights groups. They could speak out against it and in some instances take limited action, but against the enormity of the deep-seated problem, their traditional methods had little impact in halting its spread.

Of particular concern was the marked increase of racially motivated incidents on college campuses in every area of the country—from Ivy League schools to state universities. The National Institute Against Prejudice and Violence listed 163 incidents over the school years 1986-1987, 1987-1988, and it is generally conceded that many other incidents were either overlooked or not reported since there is no national collection system for such data.

What lends special importance to these campus incidents is that they took place in a setting where diversity and tolerance have traditionally been viewed as welcomed strengths and where the future leaders of the nation are being molded. If "the best and the brightest" are engaged in racist acts, then what does that say for other of their generation?

The incidents themselves ranged from simple harassment to violent assault.

- A fraternity at a Big Ten university placed a caricature of a black man with a bone in his nose on the front lawn of its home.
- A black woman walking across the campus of a school in Pennsylvania was harassed with racial epithets and hit by a bottle of urine thrown from a residence hall window.
- At a Texas university, two masked men attempted to throw a black student activist through his residence window.

The factors underlying such acts are not all that far removed from the factors that help produce racist acts in the larger society. Among the factors identified on campus by the National Association of Student Personnel Administrators are the following:

- A perception among many students that prejudicial attitudes and behaviors are more permissible and even condoned among their peers and the society at large
- Resentment and backlash among white students who feel minority students receive preferential treatment in higher education programs and services.
- Influence of right wing campus and off-campus groups
- More organized and assertive minority student groups on campus.

To their credit, school administrators, by and large, responded to the incidents with a series of positive actions that ran from disciplinary crackdowns to the aggressive recruitment of more black students and faculty members. What remains, however, are the sure signs that college campuses are reflective of the community outside and racism remains alive and well in the country.

Civil rights groups, most notably the NAACP and the National Urban League continued to warn that racism drives a wedge between black America and white America but the chasm seemed wider as the decade came to a close then it did at its beginning.

## The Reagan Years 1980-1988

The election of Ronald Reagan in 1980 brought a deep sense of gloom to black civil rights leaders who feared that under his Administration the enforcement of civil rights laws would be curtailed, social programs for the poor—and blacks were disproportionately poor—would be slashed with a draconian hand, efforts would be made turn back the clock on progress blacks had made to date, and racism would show its ugly head again. The same assessment was made by the mass of blacks of whom only 5% voted for him in 1980 and only one out of nine for his reelection in 1984.

This sense of unease was heightened by the recognition that the nation's growing economic problems would stiffen resistance to further black progress and that the rising tide of

*The Reagan administration, especially through its Supreme Court appointments, has and will continue, to adversely effect the course of the Civil Rights movement.*

conservatism did not auger well for black social and economic concerns.

Throughout Reagan's terms in office, a conscious effort was made to discredit black leadership by snubbing it, by continually charging that it was out of touch with the masses of black people, and by questioning its integrity. The Administration also attempted to establish new black national leadership from the ranks of black neo-conservatives but this proved fruitless since they could never garner any real support in the black community.

For the first time since the pre-Franklin D. Roosevelt days, with the advent of the Reagan years, black leadership found itself without any allies within the White House. Even the Nixon administration, despite its public rhetoric, had desegregated southern schools at a faster rate than the Democrats, stepped up funding for job training programs, expanded government hiring of blacks, and greatly increased Federal aid to minority business, banks and colleges, as well as Federal spending on civil rights enforcement.

Fears were validated when the Reagan Administration began to move immediately to either terminate or drastically reduce various social service programs which disproportionately affected black people: job training, CETA, welfare, and food stamps.

The Reagan Administration also took steps to alter or eliminate some of the gains that had been made in the name of civil rights. For example:

March 1981: The Labor Department announced plans to withdraw a regulation that would bar employers from paying membership fees in private clubs that have discriminatory policies.

August 1981: The Labor Department moved to relax anti-discriminatory rules for contractors doing business with the Federal government.

September 1981: the Justice Department said it would no longer go to court to seek the use of goals and timetables by employers found guilty of racial and sexual discrimination.

November 1981: The Office of Management and Budget told the Federal Communications Commission it could abandon a questionnaire used to determine if broadcasters are treating minorities and women fairly in employment.

The Administration also allowed the Equal Employment Opportunity Commission to drift for over a year without a chairman. In the interim, President Reagan nominated a black man who was so blatantly unqualified that black leaders, traditionally reluctant to criticize another black, mounted such an outcry that the nomination had to be pulled back. Eventually, Clarence Thomas, a black, was appointed.

The Voting Rights Act, universally regarded as the most effective civil rights law ever passed, was a political football during the Reagan years. In 1982, with a lukewarm endorsement from the White House, the Act was updated by Congress to give Federal courts authority to strike down voting regulations that resulted in political exclusion of minorities. Judges, who were instructed to examine the "totality of circumstances" in each case, were soon besieged with political hot potatoes. Legal wrangling occurred over local election laws, voter registration, redistricting, and multimember districts. A key battle occurred in North Carolina, where the voting power of black communities was purposely "diluted" by district dividing lines. The July 1986 Supreme Court ruling in the North Carolina case, Thornburg v. Gingles, was in favor of the black community. North Carolina Attorney General Lacy Thornburg had been supported by the Reagan Justice Department.

Then, early in 1982, the Administration touched off a firestorm when it announced that it was reversing a policy, in existence for more than a decade and supported by several Federal court decisions, and would no longer deny tax-exempt status to private schools that practiced racial discrimination. The case in point was the Bob Jones University, which forbade interracial dating. A Supreme Court decision in May 1983 upheld that private schools which practiced discrimination were not eligible for tax exemption.

During his eight years in office, President Reagan met just once with members of the Black Congressional Caucus.

Despite the president's protestations that he was personally free of any racial bias, the actions of his Administration produced a high level of alarm among civil rights leaders, who felt that not only was there retrogression in civil rights and social programs, but that, given the mood of the country, they had little leverage with which to alter the course of the Administration.

There were exceptions. In 1986, Reagan vetoed a bill to impose sanctions against South Africa in protest of its apartheid policies. In October 1986, both the House and Senate voted to override that veto. The next year, after a heated battle with the White House, the Senate voted to deny the nomination of Judge Robert Bork for the Supreme Court. The civil rights community had united in opposition to the nomination. Bork had said, among other things, that the public accommodations section of the Civil Rights Act embodied "a principle of unsurpassed ugliness."

On October 20, 1983, President Reagan signed into law a bipartisan bill which declared the third Monday of each January a day to honor Dr. Martin Luther King Jr. The bill had not been unanimously supported. Reagan was initially opposed to the holiday, and Senator Jesse Helms of North Carolina led an effort to defeat the bill accusing the late civil rights leader as having had links to Marxists. The bill passed the House 338 to 90, and the Senate, 78 to 22.

Federal observance of Martin Luther King Jr. commenced on January 20, 1986. In 1988, seven states did not recognize the holiday: Arizona, Hawaii, Idaho, Montana, New Hampshire, South Dakota and Wyoming.

Reagan's second term could be characterized as a continuous and vigorous effort to halt civil rights progress and reverse past gains, or at least create a legal climate which discouraged enforcement of civil rights. His Administration's dogged adherence to self-help projects and urging of more black college graduates rang hollow with black leaders who wanted the attention turned to the majority of blacks, with their employment, housing and poverty-life style needs.

A source of much bitterness during the Reagan years centered on the Justice Department's Attorney General Edwin Meese III and his assistant attorney general for civil rights, William Bradford Reynolds, both of whom were outspoken foes of affirmative action, and held that rights inhere in individuals, not in groups. Discrimination, therefore, should be remedied on an individual basis, not in groups. Quotas, or color-sensitive rules, therefore, were unfair. In 1987, however, the Supreme Court, which had been ambiguous in previous rulings, ruled that judges could order strict racial promotion quotas to remedy long-standing, blatant and pervasive discrimination. In April 1986, U.S. Civil Rights Commission Chairman Clarence Pendleton recommended a suspension of Federal programs that are served, or set-aside, money or contracts for businesses owned by blacks or minorities. (Federal agencies had awarded $5 billion in such contracts in 1985, and the volume had increased steadily.) After a public outcry by civil rights leaders, Reagan later opposed the recommendation. (Note—the Richmond Case did not touch federal set-asides.)

In March 1987, Congress overrode Reagan's veto of the civil Rights Restoration Act, a measure designed to reverse a 1984 Supreme Court decision that restricted the reach of laws prohibiting discrimination by institutions which received federal funds.

To many civil rights activists, Reagan's most lasting legacy is now taking substance: his appointments to the Supreme and Federal Courts. The three Reagan appointees, critics noted, create a clear conservative majority in the Supreme Court. On Federal benches, Reagan was able to appoint nearly half the judges now sitting. The actual count is 385 and of this number only seven are black. By contrast, President Jimmy Carter appointed 265 judges including 38 blacks, and President Richard Nixon named 238, including seven blacks.

*In retrospect, President Nixon's administration was effective in enforcing civil rights laws and increasing aid for many sectors of minority concern.*

In April 1988, a bitterly divided Supreme Court voted, 5-4 to review a major 1976 decision that prohibited private entities from discriminating on the basis of race. The 1976 rule was often cited as a precedent and applied to many other cases to prohibit discrimination in housing, education and other areas. The decision to reopen the case—and perhaps reverse the decision—sent shock waves through the civil rights community which had regarded the 1976 ruling as the final word on the matter.

## Reagan Policies and Economics

When President Reagan took office in 1980, polls showed that while an increasing number of whites were committed to the concept and idea of integration, many of them believed that true equality of opportunity had been achieved as the result of the passage of the civil rights laws and that there was no longer a need to help blacks through government programs and spending.

As late as 1988, a Newsweek poll revealed that when asked the question "Is the federal government doing too much, too little, or about the right amount to help American blacks?; 71% of blacks answered "too little," while only 29% of whites did. Blacks from all points on the economic spectrum contend that racial discrimination still exists at all levels of employment, job opportunities, and housing. They also felt that things were getting worse. These differing views vividly illustrate the gap in perceptions between blacks and whites and make it clear why Reagan could leave office with his popularity high among whites, and at rock bottom with blacks.

Statistics in the early Reagan years tended to support this view. At the end of 1981, for example, black unemployment stood at 15.5% when workers who had become discouraged and stopped looking for work and those who held part-time jobs only because they could not find full-time employment were added, the unemployment rate skyrocketed to well over 25%. Youth unemployment in the summer of 1981 reached 45.7%. There was also an alarming rise in the number of black households headed by women and in other indices used to measure economic and social well-being.

By the end of the 1980s, these figures were not so brutal, but continued to reflect a poorer standard of living for many blacks. Black unemployment declined with the rest of the nation's but continued to remain significantly higher than white unemployment. Twice as many black youths were out of work as white youths. In 1986, 1 in 3 blacks, as compared to 1 in 20 whites, lived below the poverty line ($11,208 for a family of four). In 1988 the median income for blacks was 57% of that of whites, down from 61.3% in 1970.

In an assessment of the economic status of blacks as the Reagan years came to an end, Dr. David H. Swinton, Dean of the School of Business, Jackson State University, writing in "The State of Black America 1988" said:

*The empirical evidence does show that some individual blacks have made impressive economic gains. In fact, there has been an increase in the proportion of blacks who can be classified as upper middle class. This limited upward mobility for the few cannot offset the stagnation and decline experienced by the large number of black Americans whose economic status has deteriorated. The central tendency for the group as a whole is revealed by the trends in the averages. And these trends tell a consistent story of stagnation or decline.*

Thus, while some black Americans did well during the Reagan years, some 2.5 million of them remained or sunk into poverty forming what has come to be known by the unflattering term "the underclass", distinguished by unemployment, generation after generation on welfare, non-working males, teenage pregnancy and single-parent families.

In recent history, no American president has been viewed by civil rights leaders as negatively as Reagan. Norman Amaker, a law professor at Loyola University in Chicago, in his book, *Civil Rights and the Reagan Administration* put his finger on the reason when he compared other presidents and concluded that Reagan dramatically slowed a historical march toward equality. He noted that on a range of issues, from support of segregated colleges to attacks on affirmative action, the Reagan Administration consistently antagonized blacks, forcing them to refight battles considered won.

Reagan could not leave office without one final blast and a week before he quit Washington in 1989, he used an appearance on CBS-TV's "60 Minutes" to say of black leaders:

*Sometimes I wonder if they really want what they say they want because some of those leaders are doing very well leading organizations based on keeping alive the feeling that they're victims of prejudice.*

The Los Angeles Times commented:

*But most black people say they do not need black activists to keep alive their perception that racial prejudice exists and they see such comments as attacks on racial equality.*

## The Black Neoconservatives

Black neoconservatives, truly a minority among a minority, multiplied in the 1980s. Led by Dr. Thomas Sowell, an economist and senior fellow at Stanford University's Hoover Institution in California, these political mavericks, occasionally described as "post-civil rights thinkers," took up positions which diametrically opposed long-held opinions of black leaders and many black Americans.

Black conservatives rejected two traditional black viewpoints: that white racism was the fundamental cause of black problems, and that more and bigger Federal programs were needed to alleviate black problems. Black conservatives viewed Federal social programs as counterproductive, dependency-producing and even co-producers of problems with crime, teenage pregnancy and unemployment.

The solution, they said, lay with blacks taking primary responsibility to solve problems in their community and pushing themselves in order to achieve higher standards of living. Sowell was among the first to speak these themes. Since the 1980s, he has argued that social class and family stability, rather than skin color, were the most important factors in determining success. Glenn Loury, a political economist, wrote in New Republic Magazine that the problems of the ghetto "have taken on a life of their own and cannot be effectively reversed by civil rights policies. Both Loury and Sowell have castigated civil rights leaders for "taking the wrongs of the past as an excuse for the failures of the present."

Not all "post-civil rights thinkers" consider themselves "conservatives." William Julius Wilson, a University of Chicago sociologist, describes himself as a "social democrat." Wilson agrees that "historical racial prejudice and discrimination" have created disadvantages in the black community, and does not reject assistance from government programs. Still, Wilson tackled the sacred cow of white-racism-is-the-cause-of-it-all evils in his controversial 1978 book, "The Declining Significance of Race." After studying the stratification of the black population since the civil rights victories of the 1960s, Wilson concluded that "economic class is clearly more important than race in predetermining job place and occupational mobility." His current study of the black underclass in Chicago is expected to be equally controversial.

Traditional leadership has not taken easily to such 'blasphemies'. NAACP leader Benjamin Hooks has called Loury and other critics "treasonous." Others have criticized the "new thinkers" for taking pot shots at past programs without presenting new, concrete resolutions.

After the Reagan victory in 1980, Sowell emerged as the favored black spokesman for the administration, and was approached numerous times for government positions. He turned them all down, reportedly because he didn't want to compromise his independence. Conservative blacks who accepted government posts—Clarence Pendleton, the first black chairman of the U.S. Commission on Civil Rights, for example—found themselves constantly in the political crosshairs of black and white liberals.

Black conservatism remains unpopular with traditional black leadership and much of the black population. However, it has found support in the growing number of prosperous blacks. Pointing out that people who make it economically lose interest in helping those less fortunate, whether black or white.

A number of surveys have revealed that in the main, blacks are economic liberals and differ markedly from conservatives on the role of government in socioeconomic programs. Blacks favor more government aid; conservatives favor less. Noted political scientist, Dr. Charles V. Hamilton had this to say:

*To the extent that the black leadership articulates policies aimed at continued and increased government participation in such areas as education, welfare, housing, and health, that leadership speaks in the same way as the mass of blacks.*

Black conservatives remain a minority voice. They attempted to consolidate their efforts as a group came in December 1980, one month after the Reagan victory, when they held a conference in San Francisco that attracted several hundred persons and major media attention. That meeting failed to produce a conservative black agenda, however, and a planned follow-up meeting was never held. The conservatives also announced that they would form their own national organization to challenge traditional black leadership, but this has not materialized.

Among those gaining reputations as black conservatives in the 1980s are:

•Walter Williams, a former professor at Temple University and an outspoken free-marketer.

•Glenn Loury, a political economist at Harvard's John F. Kennedy School of Government.

•Robert Woodson, a former official of the National Urban Lea~ue and head of the National Center for Neighborhood Enterprise, 1 which coordinates community-based, self-help groups.

•Nathan Wright Jr., author and a chairman of the National Assault on Illiteracy Program.

•Jay. Parker, a former chairman of the conservative Young Americans for Freedom.

•Rev. James Bevel, a civil rights organizer most noted for planning the 1963 Children's Crusade in Birmingham, now executive director of Students for Education and Development in Chicago.

•Ambassador Alan Keyes, a resident scholar at the American Enterprise Institute, who ran unsuccessfully for Maryland Senator in 1988.

Less than 5% of the Reagan Administration appointees were black, although some unprecedented appointments were made. Among those who served in the Reagan Administration were:

•Wendell Wilkie Gunn, former vice president of Chase Manhattan Bank and former executive for Pepsi Co. Inc., special assistant/executive secretary of Cabinet Council on Commerce and Trade.

•Samuel Pierce, secretary of Housing and Urban Development. Held the highest post of any black in the administration.

•Clarence Pendleton, chairman of the U.S. Commission on Civil Rights, the first black to hold that post. Died of a heart attack on June 5, 1988.

•Jake Simmons, under secretary, department of the Interior.—Harold E. Daly, director of the Mineral Management Service, Department of the Interior.

•Melvin Bradley, consultant on Urban Affairs in the White House Office of Policy Development.

•Richard Douglas, deputy assistant secretary, Department of Agriculture—Arthur Teele Jr., administrator of the Urban Mass Transportation.

### The Bush Administration

The inauguration of President George Bush in January 1989 opened the door for rapprochement between the White House and the black community. Unlike his predecessor, he entered office with a reservoir of good will among civil rights leaders, most of whom he knew on a first name basis and with whom he had met during the campaign. In a speech before the 1988 annual convention of the NAACP, then Vice President Bush said:

*I will have a positive civil rights agenda. I guarantee you, I will be personally involved in protecting the civil rights of all Americans... To me, this is not just a matter of social policy, but of fundamental right—the inherent equality of all men and women.*

One of the first things president-elect Bush did was attend a prayer breakfast with black supporters, where he denounced bigotry and praised Dr. Martin Luther King Jr. as a "hero" and "a great gift from God." This praise alone set Bush apart

*President George Bush talks with Benjamin Hooks, executive director of the NAACP.*

from Reagan, who had initially opposed the creation of the Martin Luther King holiday and glibly answered a question about King's alleged connection to communists with, "Well, we'll know in about 35 years (when FBI files are opened) won't we?"

As president, Bush pointedly referred to uplifting America's poor and disadvantaged in several significant speeches early in his administration. He appointed a black, Dr. Louis Sullivan to the Cabinet post of secretary of the Department of Health and Human Services. Black leaders who had resisted olive branches from the Reagan White House were more forthcoming with the Bush White House. Coretta Scott King was a prominent guest on several occasions. Urban League President John Jacob, who had consistently blasted Reagan in his annual State of Black America reports, said he was "cautiously optimistic" about the new; administration. NAACP leader Benjamin Hooks said that while disagreements were bound to occur, he anticipated finding "common ground" with Bush.

Still, within days of Bush's inauguration, conflicts arose. The Supreme Court, now composed of several Reagan appointees, handed down an anti-quota decision, known as "the Richmond decision," which held wide ramifications for minority-owned businesses. The case involved the local government in Richmond, VA, where 30% of all government contracts were mandated by a "set-aside" system to be given to black businesses. A white contractor took this to court. The Supreme Court eventually ruled that such a stipulation was unfair, and that government "set-asides" could only be maintained in cases where they remedied "known discrimination."

Civil rights leaders were further dismayed with the Bush nomination of black lawyer, former FBI agent, and Wayne County (Michigan) executive, William Lucas as head of the Justice Department's Civil Rights Division. Lucas, they claimed, did not have "a major identification" with civil rights issues.

## The Decline Of Civil Rights Organizations

During the 1970s, the influence of the black militants and Black Power advocates, was on the wane. Locally, some of the groups continued to function or served as the parents of other self-help and community organizations, but by the beginning of the 1980s, on the national level, the militants and the Black Power advocates were virtually invisible. It was as if after a brief moment in the sky, they had faded like dying rockets. Certainly their leaders from the 1960s were all gone and no others had emerged to take their places.

Eldridge Cleaver of the Black Panthers was a born-again Christian who frequently lectured on the subject of his conversion. H. Rap Brown, the successor to Stokely Carmichael as the head of the Student Non-Violent Coordinating Committee (SNCC), after serving time for armed robbery, was a storekeeper in Atlanta. Carmichael himself was dividing his time between Africa and America without any real base of power. Huey Newton of the Panthers, after losing in an effort to become mayor of Oakland, California, dropped from sight.

As for the five major organizations that were most active during the Civil Rights Movement of the sixties—the NAACP, the National Urban League, CORE, SNCC, and the Southern Christian Leadership Conference—only the first two continued to thrive.

CORE was still on the scene but it had long since ceased to be a truly national organization and its membership was concentrated in New York City under the long-term and stormy leadership of Roy Innis, who was named its national director in 1968. The organization was also buffeted by charges of fraud in connection with its fund raising activities and expenditures of funds, and allegations of intimidation of dissident members, so that its credibility was badly damaged.

Without the dynamic leadership of Martin Luther King, the Southern Christian Leadership Conference was a shadow of its former self, confining its sporadic activities primarily to the South. SNCC had simply gone out of business.

Even within the oldest and most stable of the groups, the NAACP and the Urban League, there were changes. Roy Wilkins, after 22 years as Executive Director of the NAACP, retired in 1977 to be replaced by Benjamin L. Hooks, a Baptist minister, attorney, and a former commissioner on the Federal Communications Commission. (Mr. Wilkins died in 1981.) Vernon Jordan, after ten years at the helm of the Urban League as the successor to the late Whitney M. Young, stepped down at the end of 1981. His post was taken over by John E. Jacob, who had served for several years as the League's executive vice president.

The NAACP during this period experienced a decline in its membership and resulting financial problems. The former was most critical since the strength of the organization has always resided in its broad base of dues-paying members who not only gave it a degree of independence from white philanthropy, but who could be mobilized quickly in more than 1,000 communities whenever the need arose. Its membership is in fact the strength of the NAACP and, fully aware of this, the organization has moved to increase these ranks aided by the fact that it is usually the NAACP black people turn to in times of trouble.

In recent years the NAACP has shifted its emphasis from lobbying for legislation—at which it was very successful—to seeing that the laws it helped put on the books are properly carried out. Therefore, it has increased the number of court cases it argues on behalf of blacks including legal fights for fair housing, voting parity, school desegregation, and social justice.

Unlike the NAACP, the Urban League does not maintain a national membership, depending for its strength instead on a network of over 100 affiliates staffed by paid personnel. But it also faced financial problems when much of the federal funding it had been receiving to conduct job training and other programs was cut off in the Reagan economy drive. This reduction in resources forced the League to cut back on staff and terminate several of its largest programs, just as the nation was entering a recession and black unemployment was on the rise. Facing this dilemma, Vernon Jordan, in what was to be his last keynote speech as head of the League, told its 1981 conference:

*The complexities of today's racial, economic and political issues are such that there is no one grand strategy or leader to deliver us. We will have to draw on our immense resources of survival skills to get us through these hard times, and to cultivate our bonds of unity to once again overcome.*

He suggested that the future agenda for the League lay in a return to "basics" such as building community strengths and institutions, developing more political muscle, and establishing coalitions. If the League is to do this, the chances are that it will have to continue its traditional focus on funds from the private sector, and this means corporate America.

Under the guidance of the Reverend Jesse Jackson, Operation PUSH (People United to Save Humanity) was the other important national civil rights organization on the scene during this period. In contrast to the NAACP and the League, which had relatively large permanent staffs at their national headquarters and chapters or affiliates across the country, PUSH lacked a national structure of any size, engaged in no legal cases on behalf of constituents, and operated only a single program, on an experimental basis, to improve educational achievement. By the end of the 1980s, however, there were questions raised by the government about the financial integrity of PUSH and the manner in which the organization kept accounting books and the Department of Education suggested that $1.4 million was owed the Federal Government.

Of all the civil rights leaders, the future appeared to be brightest for Jesse Jackson. Invigorated by his back-to-back presidential campaigns and already designated a Democratic front runner for the 1992 elections, Jackson remained one of the most visible black leaders on the American scene. In addition to his political forays, Jackson has remained in the public eye by his frequent trips to campuses to denounce drug use. A major goal, he announced in 1989, was to see the adoption of "African American" as the term of choice to describe blacks. "African American," Jackson argued, contains a "cultural integrity and historical accuracy" which is absent in the word black.

## The Future

In May of 1984, an event took place on the campus of historic Fisk University in Nashville, Tenn., that many observers saw as a watershed in the history of the civil rights movement—the signaling of new directions. Alarmed at what it saw as the rapid deterioration of the strength and stability of the black family as reflected in such indices as the rise in single female headed households, teen pregnancy, school dropouts and crime, the NAACP issued a call for a unique "Black Family Summit" to "bring together the organizational and institutional resources of the black community in order to examine the crisis facing black families, as well as to map strategies for family survival."

The National Urban League later joined as a co-sponsor and when the summit opened some 175 persons, representing some 30 groups, were present. The groups were as diverse as Alpha Phi Alpha Fraternity, the Association for the Study of Afro-American Life and History, National Association of Black Social Workers, Jack and Jill of America, the Black Congressional Caucus, National Medical Association, National Black Police Association, and the National Council of Negro Women.

Dr. Benjamin L. Hooks, Executive Director of the NAACP, set forth the purpose of the Summit.

*Our focus is clear. We will view in context the black family's heroic struggle for survival against overwhelming odds. Our task, and you have chosen to accept it, is to involve our society as a whole in combating the conditions adversely affecting all American families and impacting on us in a very disproportionate manner.*

John E. Jacob, President of the National Urban League, said:

*In seeking to alleviate the problems of black families, we are not alone. Many of the organizations represented here today have similar concerns. But separately, operating in isolation from each other, we can have only limited impact on the problems. Together, sharing our experiences and concerns, we can become more effective.*

With the exception of several general meetings, called to hear reports from the various task forces, the deliberations at the Summit were closed to the media to encourage fuller and more candid discussions on such matters as crime and violence, jobs and economic security, single-parent black families, and male/female relationships in black families.

Paramount in the proceeding was the consensus that while government and other institutions should not be allowed to ignore their responsibilities in revitalizing and enhancing black families, seen as the traditional glue that holds black communities together, black institutions themselves had to do more to address the problems.

This was not the type of "self help" envisioned by conservatives where solutions are left to the individual—and in truth the black community has always engaged in self help efforts, even with limited resources—but a "self help" effort that would have black institutions at every end of the spectrum more deeply involved in preserving and enhancing the black family—whatever its form.

A series of action recommendations were developed and approved by the Summit participants—a not inconsiderable feat given the broad diversity of the groups represented.

Since then, a number of the groups have embarked on programs aimed at the black family. For example, the Urban League has launched a Male Responsibility Program seeking to reduce teenage pregnancy by encouraging young black males to delay fatherhood until they are fully able to assume that responsibility. The NAACP has launched a Back in School/Stay in School Program to target at-risk youngsters for support programs that will help keep them in school and encourage them to return if they have dropped out.

As to the future, civil rights groups, whether national or local, face a new set of challenges growing out of a changing environment which will test their sophistication, their endurance and their ability to devise new strategies to meet these challenges.

Schools that fail to teach, about the scourge of drug and alcohol abuse, black on black crime, and broken homes drain the economic, social and moral strength of all too many black communities, but they will not yield to traditional protest or litigation, thus requiring the civil rights movement to adopt new approaches if it is to remain relevant.

In a succinct comment on one of the major problems of the 1980s, Dr. Benjamin Hooks, Executive Director of the NAACP, repeatedly warned "crack and cocaine are doing more to destroy our young people than the KKK ever did."

Most vulnerable are young blacks growing up in poverty, who are entering a world where job opportunities require more skills and training, and where racism still plays a role in who gets what. Sadly, the enrollment of black men in colleges has declined, although that of black women has steadily increased. Jobs of the future are going to demand education of high school level and beyond, as hi-tech positions replace those of semi-skilled labor.

Although by the 1980s, the workplace was becoming increasingly integrated, racial demarcation lines continued to exist in housing. In 1980, 31% of blacks lived in neighborhoods which were 90% black. Six out of 10 whites lived in neighborhoods which were virtually all white. The number of discrimination complaints received by the Department of Housing and Urban Development continued unabated.

In August 1988, the 25th anniversary of the "March on Washington" was commemorated in the nation's capital, drawing some 55,000 persons. Still, to many young people coming of age in the 1980s. the Civil Rights Movement seemed to mean little. They were not around when it was at its apex and they can see nothing or very little that it has done or is doing to make their lives any better. Civil rights may have won the right to check into a hotel, but the ability to check out of that hotel—meaning economic stability and prosperity—still eluded a significant number of blacks.

Helping to create jobs, improving education, protecting the rights of the disadvantaged, maintaining vigilance to see that the gains of the paste are not wiped out, and enriching the quality of life for black people is unglamorous and sometimes harsh. But this is the task that faces the Civil Rights Movement in the 1990s and beyond.

Future leadership for the black community will come from several directions. Strengths will continue to be shown from traditional leadership groups, such as civil rights alumni, the church and academia. Black conservatism which premiered during the Reagan years is expected to grow under the more moderate Bush Administration.

Other leaders will emerge form the growing number of black elected officials, a group which has grown from a handful in the early 1960s to more than 7,000 in the late 1980s.

Other groups include:

•Blacks who are managing large public and private (predominantly white) institutions such as Franklin Thomas at the Ford Foundation and Dr. Clifton Wharton at the State University of New York. Blacks who are executives in corporate America.

•Black leaders who developed through the War on Poverty programs. Many of these are originally grassroots supporters, who once placed in the position of leadership, developed their potential.

•Black businessmen who have succeeded in nontraditional fields.

America, as a whole, is changing, so must the civil rights movement.

## CIVIL RIGHTS ORGANIZATIONS

### The National Association for the Advancement of Colored People

*I bring you greetings from the oldest, largest, most effective, most consulted, most militant, most feared and to us the most loved of all the civil rights organizations in the world.*

From 1961 until his death in 1974, Bishop Stephen Gill Spottswood (African Methodist Episcopal Zion Church) as chairman of the board of the National Association for the Advancement of Colored People, traditionally used those words to open the organization's annual conference. His description was accurate in almost every respect, for the NAACP has more than earned its niche as America's preeminent civil rights organization.

The NAACP came into being on February 12, 1909—the hundredth anniversary of the birth of Abraham Lincoln. It was largely the brainchild of three people: William English Walling, a white Southerner who feared that racists would soon carry "the race war to the North"; Mary White Ovington, a wealthy young white woman who had attended the 1906 meeting of the Niagara group as a reporter for the *New York Evening Post* and had experience with conditions in the black ghettos of New York City; and Dr. Henry Moskowitz, a New York social worker. This trio proposed that a conference be called "for the discussion of present evils, the voicing of protests, and the renewal of the struggle for civil and political liberty."

The three-day conference (May 30-June 1) was followed by four meetings, the results of which were an increase in membership and the choice of an official name: The National Negro Committee. In 1910 the organization adopted its present name and was incorporated in New York state. A year earlier the Niagara movement and the NAACP had merged. By 1914 the association had already established some 50 branches throughout the country.

With the founding of the NAACP, Crisis magazine, edited by W. E. B. DuBois, became its chief organ for propaganda and a major vehicle for the dissemination of educational and social programs. (*Crisis* is still being published on a monthly basis.)

Over the years, the NAACP attempted to better the black's lot through "litigation, legislation, and education." Perhaps its most significant judicial victory was won in 1954 when the historic *Brown vs. Board of Education* case threw out the "separate but equal" doctrine established in *Plessy v. Ferguson,* thus opening the door for the elimination of segregation in public education.

While other black organizations have tended in recent years to gravitate toward racial separatism, the NAACP has clung tenaciously to its goal of promoting racial integration. It has sought to improve the status of blacks in many fields, including jobs and schools, and has pushed doggedly and perseveringly for civil rights legislation.

Following the failure of legal decisions and legislation championed by the NAACP to evoke fundamental changes in America's racial climate, the NAACP was attacked by many militants and black power advocates as "irrelevant" to the needs of most blacks. These charges reached a climax in 1972 when members of the now defunct National Economic Growth and Reconstruction Organization (NEGRO) occupied part of NAACP's New York office for a few hours in protest against NAACP's alleged "unresponsiveness" to the needs of the black masses.

Such criticism was short-lived, however, as the NAACP launched a new series of programs that included providing assistance to coalitions of minority contractors to qualify for major construction jobs, the establishment of day care centers in several communities, the setting-up of "Project Rebound" to aid the reorientation of former prison inmates, and the investigation of military justice in Alaska and West Germany and on some Navy ships.

The leadership of the NAACP changed in 1977 when Roy Wilkins, who had served as executive director for over 25 years, retired and was succeeded by Benjamin L. Hooks, a lawyer, minister, civil rights activist, and at the time of his selection, a commissioner at the Federal Communications Commission—the first black to hold such a post.

With its efforts to secure civil rights legislation crowned by success, the NAACP has in recent years devoted more of its attention to seeing that the laws are carried out. It argues many court cases on behalf of blacks, including legal fights for fair housing, school desegregation, and political equality. The NAACP Legal Department has been active in 38 states and the District of Columbia, filing motions, arguing cases,

*J. W. Johnson, former secretary of the NAACP.*

meeting with local branch people, interviewing clients, or conferring with cooperating retained counsel.

As an organization, the NAACP endured some internal upheavals in the early 80s. Membership, which was more than half a million in the 1960s, officially dropped to 350,000 by 1983. Critics suggested that number should be halved. In May 1983, NAACP Chairman Margaret Bush Wilson suspended Executive Director Hooks for "mismanaging" the organization. Hooks was reinstated after eight days, but the bitter feelings engendered by the rift continued. Wilson was eventually stripped of her power and asked to resign by the NAACP board.

The NAACP in the 1980s tackled economic issues. "Racism can no longer be the basic reason for our existence," Hooks said in a 1987 interview. "Our new thrust must be in the areas of self-help, of economic development, of quality education, of self-discipline by ridding our communities of crime, drugs, ignorance..."

Under its Fair Share program, the NAACP sought to persuade private industry to buy goods and services from black-owned businesses. Its non-profit subsidiary, National Economic Development Corporation (NEDCO), worked to stimulate minority businesses and jobs. One NEDCO project was to establish an industrial park complex in Hartford, Conn., which would offer modestly priced office space to minority-owned light industry and hi-tech businesses.

In 1987 Hooks and the NAACP did demonstrate that it still could muster a great deal of support as the efforts of the organization contributed to kill the nomination of President Ronald Reagan's attempt to put ultra-conservative, Judge Robert Bork, on the Supreme Court. The nomination was thwarted by a powerful alliance between civil rights groups, liberals, concerned conservative Democrats—a number of whom owed their election to black voters— and moderate Republicans; it was Ronald Reagan's worst political defeat.

Recently the organization has put increased efforts in voter registration, and encouraging more blacks to run for political office. It has also been working with the plight of black farmers and conditions of southern blacks; Also on the agenda for the organization are stepped up efforts to gain economic parity and the development of black enterprises, community activities designed to reclaim and rehabilitate the inner city, more health-care facilities and, as well, fighting apartheid in South Africa.

In 1986, after 77 years in New York City, the national headquarters was relocated to a $3 million, five-story building in Baltimore. The State of Maryland was so pleased with the move that it gave the NAACP $1.1 million with the contingency that it would not have to be repaid if the NAACP stayed in Baltimore for at least 15 years.

## The National Urban League

The National Urban League, in existence since 1919, began as an organization to help black migrants to New York City find suitable employment and make as smooth a transition as possible from rural southern to urban northern life.

Black migrants to the cities stemmed largely from an agricultural environment, and had often lived in virtual peonage in the Black Belt. Unschooled and unguided, they faced the competition of the northern labor markets, including the craft unions, with virtually no preparation, and without the protection of any governmental guidelines for their prospective employers.

*Roy Wilkins outlines a needed federal program to President Johnson.*

*President of the National Urban League, John E. Jacob.*

In 1906, at the urging of William H. Baldwin, president of the Long Island Railroad, a group of blacks and whites met for the purpose of studying the work needs of the black. This group, known as the Committee for Improving the Industrial Conditions among Negroes in New York, studied the racial aspects of the labor market (particularly the attitudes and policies of employers and unions), and sought to find openings for qualified blacks.

At the same time, the League for the Protection of Colored Women was established to provide similar services for black women who were coming into New York and Philadelphia from various parts of the South. These women often had no friends or relatives to meet and welcome them, and so fell prey to unscrupulous employment agencies which led them into jobs at wages far less than they had expected to receive.

A third organization, the Committee on Urban Conditions Among Negroes, appeared on the New York scene in 1910. It was organized by Mrs. Ruth Standish Baldwin, widow of the former Long Island Railroad president, and Dr. George Edmond Haynes, one of only three trained black social workers in the country and the first black person to receive a doctorate from Columbia University. Haynes was named as the first executive secretary of the new agency and a year later it merged with the Committee for the Improvement of Industrial Conditions Among Negroes in New York and the National League for the Protection of Colored Women to form the National League on Urban Conditions Among Negroes. That name was later shortened to the now-familiar National Urban League.

From the outset, the Committee focused more on dealing with the social and economic needs of blacks than it did with the civil rights aspect of their existence. The latter area was one in which the NAACP was active and the League sought instead to involve itself in the training of black social workers, and in housing, health, sanitation, recreation, self-improvement, and job assistance.

The organizational model that the League had established in New York City attracted attention and soon affiliates began to be formed in various cities across the country. Traditionally, the affiliates, like the prototype, were full-time operations, staffed by professionals, and dependent on private philanthropy for funding. A major goal of the League and its affiliates was to broaden economic opportunities for blacks by using the techniques of persuasion and conciliation to open up doors that had been closed before.

The NUL was one of the first black organizations to become involved in research. This occurred in 1920 when Dr. Charles S. Johnson, a classic figure in black scholarship, organized the NUL's Research Department. Dr. Johnson produced numerous landmark studies on the black condition and also edited the magazine *Opportunity: Journal of Negro Life,* which became a mainstay of what was known as "the Harlem Renaissance" of the 1930s, publishing almost every leading black poet and writer of the day.

It was not, however, until the 1960s when Whitney M. Young Jr. became its new leader that the League began to emerge as a force in the civil rights struggle. The League's strategy was to deal with fundamental social problems through influencing decision makers and becoming part of the process by which basic decisions affecting black people are made. Thus a typical technique of the sixties was for the League to work with more obviously militant organizations

*Original Seal of the National Urban League.*

whose marches the League backed up in boardroom and public policy confrontations.

In the late sixties the League embarked on a program called "New Thrust," which was designed to assist inner-city residents to increase their own economic and political power through programs and community organization. This grassroots involvement has continued.

Young had achieved status as a major spokesman for black people when his career was cut short in a drowning accident off the coast of Africa in 1971. He was succeeded by Vernon E. Jordan Jr., a lawyer and the first non-social worker to head the League. Jordan continued the forceful advocacy of Young, enhancing the civil rights posture of the League. In his ten years at the helm (Jordan resigned December 31, 1981) he took the League into new programmatic fields such as energy and the environment, challenged national leadership over its failure to deal with the problems of the poor, and increased the number of League affiliates from 99 to 118 with over 4,200 employees and 30,000 volunteers.

The growth of the League was due primarily to expansion of its direct services, which annually provided over one million people with programs like job training, education, health, housing, criminal justice. The League, over a period of years, had demonstrated an ability to operate such programs effectively and as a result, under both Democrats and Republicans, it received a large number of government grants. However, with the decision of the Reagan Administration when it took office in 1981 to cut back on domestic spending, the League lost a sizable portion of its Federal funding, which in the fiscal year ending June 30, 1981 totaled some $19 million. But still intact was the basic general budget of the League of some $5 million raised in the main from the corporate community and foundations.

The League has been brought under attack by some critics who charge that it is middle class in orientation and therefore cannot be responsive to the needs of the mass of black people. The League responds by pointing out that while it relies for staff on trained professionals, who are middle class, the overwhelming majority of its activities are geared toward improving the economic and social status of the black poor.

Headquartered in New York City, the National Urban League also has four regional offices, in Atlanta, Chicago, Los Angeles, and New York City. In addition, it has a Washington Bureau and Research Department in Washington, D.C.

The Urban League has been interracial since its founding. It has a board of some 60 members drawn from all sectors of the community. The League is headed by a chairman of the board and a president and chief executive officer who is responsible for the day-to-day operation of the agency. The former has traditionally been white and the latter black. The League now describes itself as "an interracial, non-profit community service organization that uses the tools and methods of social work, economics, law and other disciplines, to secure equal opportunity in all sectors of our society for black Americans and other minorities."

The current president of the League is John E. Jacob, a social worker, who succeeded Vernon Jordan on January 1, 1982. Mr. Jacob had served in the number two position at the League as Executive Vice President since February 1, 1979. At the time of his election by the board, he had served in the Urban League Movement for over 15 years.

In 1987, public support to the League which included contributions, special events, grants and contracts from government agencies, direct mail campaign and in-kind contributions totaled $20 million.

The League's programs, administered through 113 affiliates across the United States include a National Education Initiative program which is an effort to mobilize the black community to improve the education of black students, its Male Responsibility program which build bridges to manhood, responsible parenting as well as healthier family units, advocacy for the homeless and its campaign to mobilize communities against crime.

The League is currently concentrating on mobilizing minority communities around a National Educational Initiative, designed to improve black students' academic achievements. It has also put resources into assisting black female heads of households; one such program has 16 computer training centers around the country.

The League continues to issue its State of Black America report every January. Noting that the economic gap between blacks and whites widened during the Reagan years, League President Jacob said in the 1989 report, "I expect the Bush White House to be a very different place from the Reagan White House."

### The Southern Christian Leadership Conference

Born out of the Montgomery bus boycott of the 1950s, the Southern Christian Leadership Conference came into being just as the civil rights movement in the American south was about to explode. Even as young as it was, SCLC was destined to play a leading role in that explosion.

And the time was right for an organization such as SCLC. In some areas of the South, the NAACP was prohibited from operating and the Urban League, with its traditional emphasis on social work as opposed to direct action, was in no position to provide direction for the growing movement. However, led by a gifted young black minister, Martin Luther King Jr., the Montgomery Improvement Association, after a nonviolent struggle that lasted over a year, achieved its goal of desegregating the bus system in a city that was known for its harsh racial attitudes.

Encouraged by this demonstration of the power that could be employed through a mass movement, representatives from ten southern states, consisting mainly of black ministers at the grassroots level, met at Atlanta's Ebenezer Baptist Church in January 1957, shortly after the victory in Montgomery, and organized SCLC. They elected Dr. King as president.

SCLC appealed to blacks "to assert their human dignity by refusing further cooperation with evil." Specifically, SCLC contended that blacks should feel a moral obligation to reinforce traditional legal action in the courts with nonviolent direct action to desegregate public transportation, public places, and public schools. Beyond these accomplishments, the ballot and civil rights laws stood as goals to be achieved.

For the rest of the decade of the 1950s and until the assassination of Dr. King in 1968, SCLC, as one of the most influential and effective of all the civil rights groups, espoused, most often through the eloquence of Dr. King, a doctrine of nonviolent protest and passive resistance in its assault on segregation and discrimination.

The basic strength of SCLC was rooted in the black church, the single most important and influential institution within Black America. By emphasizing the morality of the civil rights crusade, by sharply drawing in religious terms the contrast between racial justice and racial injustice, and by the predominance of ministers in leadership positions, SCLC secured the support of a sizable part of the black church community which gave freely of its resources, even in the face of threatened or actual violence directed against it. The church also encouraged its members to support SCLC. Further, the appeal of SCLC, under King's leadership, to basic principles of humanity, was so great that it drew support from the white community as well.

SCLC was a driving force under King. Its confrontations with the forces of bigotry in such places as Birmingham and Selma, Alabama helped not only arouse the conscience of what had until then been a complacent America, but also spurred the passage of the various civil rights laws of the 1960s. The murder of Dr. King dealt SCLC a severe blow. More than any other person, he had come to symbolize SCLC and there was real concern that without his charismatic leadership the organization would fall apart.

The Reverend Ralph David Abernathy, one of Dr. King's closest associates, was elected by the SCLC board to succeed the slain leader. Prior to his death, Dr. King had planned a massive "Poor People's Campaign" that was to bring thousands of people of all races from all across the country

*Reverend Martin Luther King Jr. leads Chicago march for housing.*

to Washington, D.C. in the spring of 1968 to demand help from the government for the poor. The campaign was continued under Dr. Abernathy, but it was plagued from the very start by a series of almost insurmountable difficulties, including inadequate logistics, internal disputes, general public indifference and seemingly unending rainstorms that turned "Resurrection City," the site where tents had been erected for the demonstrators, into a sea of mud and misery that sapped the spirit and morale of the demonstrators. This was the last major public demonstration that SCLC was to mount outside the South, but in that area of the country, where it had its greatest strength, it continued as a viable organization, albeit with a lower profile. Many of SCLC's recent activities have been centered on its efforts to strengthen the black family, and since 1980 it has held an annual Martin Luther King Jr. Memorial Weekend at which it brings together experts and concerned citizens to examine various aspects of the black family. SCLC has also taken an interest in foreign affairs, particularly those related to the Mideast and Africa. It maintains its on going commitment to protecting and increasing the political power of blacks, and in 1982, as a renewal of the Voting Rights Act of 1965 was being debated in Congress, it duplicated the historic march of Dr. King from Selma to Montgomery, which has been credited with having a major influence in the passage of the original legislation.

SCLC is interracial in character and has supporters among

*Operation PUSH dinner in 1972; Manhattan Borough President Percy Sutton, Reverend Jesse Jackson, presidential candidate George McGovern (left to right).*

people of all faiths, religions, and creeds. Its headquarters is in Atlanta and it maintains affiliates in six Southern and boarder states. Its board of some 50 members is composed of both ministers and lay people. Board chairman is Representative Walter Fauntroy (a Democrat from Washington, D.C.), who was one of the earliest members of SCLC. The president is Reverend Joseph Lowery, who was elected in 1977.

Individuals hold membership in SCLC through such affiliated organizations as churches, fraternal orders, and civic bodies. Bona fide affiliates are restricted to the 17 southern states and the District of Columbia, but supporting affiliates are not under this geographical restriction.

Funds for SCLC are raised through the fees and pledges of affiliated organizations, mass rallies, and direct mail appeals. SCLC does not make available the size of its staff or its annual budget.

One of the major interests of SCLC is its Operation Breadbasket, which it formed in 1962 to deal with the problems blacks faced as workers, consumers, professionals, and businessmen.

The SCLC has created the most news with its staunch stand against apartheid in South Africa . A notable example was its successful boycott of the Win-Dixie grocery chain, which caused it to cease its sales of South African imported fish and fruit

## Operation PUSH (People United to Save Humanity)

Through the leadership of its founder and president, the Reverend Jesse Jackson, Operation PUSH has developed, within a short time, into a nationally known and respected civil rights organization. One of the most sought after speakers in the country, gifted with the ability to communicate with virtually every sector of society, Jackson through his organization has been especially effective in motivating young people through the PUSH-EXCEL Program.

Basically, the program instills a sense of pride in young high school students, builds up their confidence that they can succeed, and encourages disciplined study. PUSH-EXCEL operates in seven cities—Buffalo, N.Y.; Chattanooga, Tenn.; Kansas City, Mo.; Chicago; Denver; Tacoma Park, Md.; and Rochester, N.Y. PUSH also awards a $10,000 annual scholarship through the program.

In the early 1980s PUSH scored major breakthroughs on the economic front when it negotiated national agreements with Coca Cola and Hueblein, Inc. to expand the number of black distributors and wholesalers handling their products, increase employment opportunities, use black media more for advertising, place money in black banks, and generally put more financial resources in the black community. This approach is continuing with other major firms.

This type of activity is not new to PUSH, for in 1972 it signed a similar agreement with the Joseph Schlitz Brewing Co. for blacks to comprise 15% of its work force and black business to receive 15% of its advertising, insurance, and construction expenditures. A similar agreement with the General Food Corp. increased that company's employment of blacks and use of black business.

Operation PUSH's viewpoint is stated in the following preamble and 15-point platform, signed by leading members of its board of directors.

Although PUSH's programs continued, by the late 1980s, the organization was beset with financial problems. According to an audit published in 1987, the combined debt for various PUSH entities approached $2 million. At the same time, the Department of Education determined that PUSH-Excel owed the government $1.4 million in misspent and undocumented federal funds. Additional criticism faulted PUSH-Excel for failing to demonstrate improvement in school attendance or test scores.

## Operation PUSH Platform

We, the People United to Save Humanity, believe that humanity will be saved and served only when justice is done for all people. We believe that we must challenge the economic, political, and social forces that make us subservient to others; and that we must assume the power (of being) given us by the Power of God. We believe that our worth as humane people is expressed in our united efforts to secure justice for all persons. We, therefore, state our declaration of goals.

1. PUSH for a comprehensive economic plan for the development of Black and poor people. This plan will include status as underdeveloped enclaves entitled to consideration by the World Bank and the International Monetary Fund.
2. PUSH for human alternatives to the welfare system.
3. PUSH for the revival of the labor movement to protect organized workers and to organize unorganized workers.
4. PUSH for a survival Bill of Rights for all children up to the age of 18 guaranteeing their food, clothing, shelter, medical care and education.
5. PUSH for a survival Bill of Rights for the aging, guaranteeing adequate food, clothing, shelter, medical care and meaningful programs.
6. PUSH for full political participation including an automatic voter registration as a right of citizenship.
7. PUSH to elect to local, state and federal offices persons committed to humane economic and social programs.
8. PUSH for humane conditions imprisons and sound rehabilitative programs.
9. PUSH for a Bill of Rights for veterans whose needs are ignored.
10. PUSH for adequate health care for all people based
11. PUSH for quality education regardless of race, religion or creed.
12. PUSH for economic and social relationships with the nations of Africa in order to build African/Afro-American unity.
13. PUSH for national unity among all organizations working for the humane economic, political and social development of people.
14. PUSH for a relevant theology geared to regenerating depressed and oppressed peoples.
15. PUSH for black excellence.

We are dedicated to reaching our goals through the research, education, development and execution of direct action programs that provide for economic, political and cultural independence.

## Congress of Racial Equality

The Congress of Racial Equality (CORE) was founded in 1942 by James Farmer as the result of a campaign protesting discrimination at a Chicago restaurant which developed the "sit-in" technique that was to prove so successful during the civil rights movement of the 1960s. CORE began life as an interracial passive-resistance organization committed to confronting racism and discrimination with direct action.

From Chicago, it moved on to other cities and other causes: drug and department stores in St. Louis, a legitimate theater in Baltimore, registration drives in South Carolina, movie theaters in Columbia, Missouri—all the while growing slowly. Then came Greensboro, North Carolina, where in 1960 four young black male students from A&T College staged a sit-in at a Woolworth lunch counter which refused to serve them. Under the auspices of CORE, the sit-ins began to spread rapidly throughout the South, and in many instances they achieved the desegregation of public places. CORE thus began to establish national visibility for itself.

Its status was further enhanced in 1961 when it sponsored a series of Freedom Rides across the South to test compliance with an order of the Interstate Commerce Commission to desegregate bus travel and stations. The riders, both black and white, were brutally assaulted in several cities but the demonstration set the stage for eventual enforcement of the ruling.

In assessing the importance of CORE during those days, the Reverend Jesse Jackson said: "It was the very soul of the civil rights movement. In 1963, it had more people marching

*Flanked by co-workers, Floyd McKissick speaks at a CORE rally in Soul City, North Carolina.*

for desegregation in Greensboro than Dr. King had in Birmingham." Another evaluation called it more activist than the NAACP, more integrated than the Southern Christian Leadership Conference, and more established and respected than the Student Non-Violent Coordinating Committee (SNCC).

CORE began to change directions in 1966 as the Black Power philosophy was coming to the fore. Farmer, the founder, turned the national leadership over to Floyd McKissick, a North Carolina lawyer. The new leader began to move CORE closer to being all-black in membership and staff and in 1967 it moved, at its convention, to eliminate the word "multiracial" from its constitution.

When McKissick left in 1968 he was replaced by the present national director, Roy Innis, former chairman of the Harlem chapter of CORE.

In recent years CORE has been beset by a number of difficulties. Its membership and affiliates have dwindled sharply from some 70,000 members and almost 100 affiliates in 33 states and the District of Columbia that it reported in the late 1960s. Innis became embroiled in a lawsuit which charged him with misappropriation of corporate funds for personal use, and for illegal fund raising. By the end of the 1980s, most CORE chapters were no longer active and Innis was concentrating on his political career

## The Black Leadership Forum

The Black Leadership Forum is an informal group of the heads of 14 national predominantly black organizations who meet on a periodic basis to exchange information, discuss mutual concerns, and plan joint strategies where appropriate. The meetings are private and media coverage is discouraged to ensure the confidentiality of the discussions.

However, the Forum does from time to time issue joint statements on matters of specific interest to blacks. It was created in 1977 following a suggestion by Vernon E. Jordan Jr., then president of the National Urban League, that such a group was needed to better coordinate the various efforts being made on behalf of black people.

One of the first issues to face the Forum was the *Bakke* case involving a white man's claim of reverse discrimination in his failure to be accepted by a medical school. The Forum appealed to the Carter Administration to file a brief in opposition to Bakke's claim.

The Forum can be viewed as a descendant of the Council for United Civil Rights Leadership that was active in the 1950s and 1960s as a coordinating mechanism for the Civil Rights Movement and included the NAACP, the National Urban League, the National Council of Negro Women, the NAACP Legal Defense and Educational Fund, CORE, the Southern Christian Leadership Conference, and the Student Non-Violent Coordinating Committee.

Groups now holding membership in the Forum—and membership is confined to only the leader of each group—are the NAACP, National Urban League, National Business League, NAACP Legal Defense and Education Fund, National Council of Negro Women, National Urban Coalition, Operation PUSH, Martin Luther King Jr. Center for Social Change, Congressional Black Caucus, National Black Caucus of Local Elected Officials, A. Philip Randolph Institute, Opportunities Industrialization Centers, and Joint Center for Political Studies.

The leadership of the Forum alternates on an annual basis. The current chairman is Dorothy Height, National Council of Negro Women.

*Dorothy Height, president of the National Council of Negro Women, is also the current chairman of Black Leadership Forum.*

## The Leadership Conference on Civil Rights

The Leadership Conference on Civil Rights was established in 1950 by A. Philip Randolph, Roy Wilkins, and Arnold Aronson to implement the historic report of President Truman's Committee on Civil Rights, "To Secure These Rights."

Beginning with 30 organizations, the Conference has grown in numbers, scope, and effectiveness. It currently consists of approximately 157 national organizations representing blacks, Hispanics, Asian Americans, labor, the major religious groups, women, the handicapped, the aged, and minority businesses and professions.

These organizations speak for a substantial portion of the population and together comprise the most broadly based coalition in the nation. The member groups differ in size, structure, and broad objectives, but are united in seeking an integrated, democratic, plural society, in which each individual is accorded equal rights, equal opportunities, and equal justice without regard to race, sex, religion, ethnic origin, handicap, or age.

Starting with the Civil Rights Act of 1957, the Leadership Conference coordinated the campaigns that resulted in the passage of all the civil rights legislation of this century, including the Civil Rights Acts of 1960 and 1964, the Voting Rights Act of 1965, and the Fair Housing Act of 1968.

The Leadership Conference is committed to establishing, as a matter of right, a useful job at a decent wage for all who are employable or who can be made so by training or retraining, an income sufficient to provide all others with the essentials for living in dignity and self-respect, decent housing in a decent environment for all, medical care for all in health, sickness, and disability, and education to the limit of each person's capacity to benefit from it.

Among the member groups of the Leadership Conference are the African Methodist Episcopal Church, AFL-CIO, Anti-Defamation League of B'nai B'rith, Kappa Alpha Psi Fraternity, Mexican American Legal Defense and Education Fund, the NAACP, the National Urban League, and the Organization of Chinese Americans.

## The Black United Front

The newest of the national civil rights organizations, the Black United Front, was organized in July 1980, when 1,000 delegates from 34 states gathered at a Brooklyn church in response to a call from Reverend Herbert Daughtry, a Brooklyn Pentecostal minister. Included among the delegates were many long-time activists who saw the need to build a strong grassroots black movement in light of unemployment and other problems affecting blacks.

Daughtry contended that the situation has reached" genocidal dimensions for blacks" and that there was a vacuum in national black leadership, and "our people are searching for new leaders and new vehicles."

The BUF announced that it would seek to enroll black youth, the elderly, churches, the middle class, and professionals. The only groups that it said it would not recruit was "black leaders created by whites who have sold out to whites and who function to keep community leaders from developing."

Among those present for the organizing session were Imamu Amiri Baraka, the poet and playwright; Amiri Obodeli, President of the New Republic of Africa; Skip Robinson, President of the United League of Mississippi; and Prince Ashiel Ben Israel, Ambassador from the Hebrew Israelites of Dimona, Israel.

## The NAACP Legal Defense and Educational Fund, Inc.

Established in 1939 by the NAACP, the NAACP Legal Defense and Educational Fund has had its own board, program, staff, office, and budget for some 20 years. Through the years, it has been in the forefront of legal assaults against discrimination and segregation and has an outstanding record of victories, a tribute to the meticulous care with which it traditionally prepares its cases.

Throughout the years, the LDF has won extremely important legal victories for minorities. In 1972 it succeeded in getting the Supreme Court to nullify the death penalty and to rule that towns with heavy concentrations of white students could not secede from largely black school systems.

Recently, it has been deeply involved in employment, education, the administration of criminal justice, affirmative action, housing, and health care. The greatest concentration has been on employment, where, in the space of just under two years, the LDF secured $10.1 million in back pay

*Lawyers for the NAACP Legal Defense and Educational Fund, Inc. including (left to right) Louis L. Redding, Robert L. Carter, Oliver W. Hill, Thurgood Marshall, Spottswood W. Robinson III, Jack Greenberg, James M. Nabrit Jr., George E. C. Hayes.*

awards for minority workers who had been discriminated against. The LDF was also instrumental in reaching agreement with the Federal government to phase out its Professional and Administrative Career Examination (PACE) because of its severe adverse impact on blacks and other minorities.

As it looked to the 1980s, the LDF predicted that its role as the premiere legal defender of the rights of black Americans would not diminish and that the civil rights of blacks would be affected in the following ways:

- Across-the-board attacks on affirmative action through executive then legislative and budgetary means.
- Appointment of judge unsympathetic to civil rights claims.
- Structural changes in the civil rights enforcement authority of agencies such as the Office of Federal Contract Compliance, the Equal Employment Opportunity Commission, and the Departments of Education and Housing and Urban Development.
- Support of congressional efforts aimed at crippling effective school desegregation remedies.
- Redistricting with the intent to reduce minority representation.

In its 1980 annual report, the LDF said "agencies like LDF will have a more important role in the defense of basic civil rights in the next few years than at any time in the recent past."

In addition to its litigation, the LDF provides scholarships and training for young lawyers, advises lawyers on legal trends and decisions, and monitors federal programs which often fail to deliver their intended services.

The Director-Counsel of LDF is Julius Chambers, who in 1984 succeeded Jack Greenburg; Greenburg had succeeded Thurgood Marshall upon the latter's appointment to the Supreme Court in 1961.

Heading the LDF Los Angeles office are Theodore Shaw, who served with the Justice Department's civil rights division from 1979 to 1982, and Patrick Peterson, a former UCLA law professor.

In 1939, for tax purposes, the NAACP Legal Defense Fund had become a separate arm of the NAACP and in 1959 it officially became divorced from its parent organization. Since the separation the organizations had been in some conflict over identity and it was the contention of the parent organization that there was name confusion and to eliminate the confusion The National Association for the Advancement of Colored People sued the NAACP legal Defense Fund for "name infringement."

After several months of legal wrangling, a federal court ruled that the LDF could keep NAACP in its name, since the NAACP is its parent organization.

## CIVIL RIGHTS AND MILITANT GROUPS OF THE PAST

The cause of blacks in the United States has been represented by a great diversity of organizations. Some, such as the Free African Societies, emerged from organized religious groups; others, such as the Niagara Movement and the Student Non-Violent Coordinating Committee, from intellectuals and students. Following are short descriptions of organizations, no longer active, that have rendered important contributions to the black struggle for equality and respect.

### The Free African Society

The Free African Society was formed in Philadelphia in 1787 by Richard Allen and Absalom Jones, two ministers, to help blacks of "orderly and sober life to support one another in sickness and for the benefit of their widows and children." Though it adhered to its moral tenets intently, and expelled members who violated them, the Free African Society soon began to help blacks who ran a foul of the law because of opposition to slavery. However, it avoided, wherever possible, all appearances of racial militancy, promising to exclude from membership any person who violated "the laws of their country."

Despite such caution, The Free African Society cooperated with the Pennsylvania Abolition Society and counseled other, more militant, "Free African" groups to form in other northern cities. Similar groups in the South were forbidden by law.

### The American Anti-Slavery Society

A number of antislavery societies developed in the eighteenth century, particularly among the Quakers of Pennsylvania, but they lost strength to recolonization movements and the increased demand for slaves to labor on cotton plantations.

Anti-slavery groups that did exist were generally weak and conservative. Total membership in 1825 did not exceed 8,000 and many advocated recolonization of freed blacks. Several of these groups communicated with one another loosely through the American Anti-Slavery Society.

However, in the early 1830s William Lloyd Garrison formed the New England Anti-Slavery Society and through it succeeded in directing the American Anti-Slavery Society to a stronger position, though many chapters remained moderate. Membership boomed, exceeding 300,000 by 1840.

The influence of the Society in the overall abolitionist movement increased. Blacks, pleased with the Society's stand for racial equality, joined, formed their own chapters, and sent delegates to national meetings. Some, however, such as Henry Highland Garnet, were to find the Society's position too reserved and called for revolution to end slavery. And in 1851 Frederick Douglass broke with Garrison when Douglass demanded that the Society attack the Constitution as a document which favors slavery. The split weakened the Society, but its contribution as a catalyst and focal point of anti-slavery sentiment had been fulfilled.

### The Niagara Movement

The Niagara Movement was founded by a group of 29 black intellectuals—headed by W. E. B. DuBois, a professor at Atlanta University—who met July 11-13, 1905 in Buffalo, New York.

The Niagara Movement represented a formal renunciation of the policy of accommodation which had been the keynote of Booker T. Washington's program for the black since his famed "Atlanta Compromise" address of 1895. Washington advocated manual and industrial training for the black as a means of gaining economic security, and preferred conciliation rather than agitation as a means of gaining social equality. "It is important and right," he said, "that all privileges of the law be ours, but it is vastly more important that we be prepared for the exercise of those privileges."

The Niagara Movement, on the other hand, maintained that it was even more important for blacks to press for the immediate implementation of their civil rights. In the words of DuBois:

*We want full manhood suffrage and we want it now...*

*We want the Constitution of the country enforced...*

*We want our children educated... We are men! We will be treated as men. And we shall win!*

The organization held national conferences in 1906 and 1907 at Harper's Ferry and Boston, respectively, and initiated protest rallies in several American cities in 1908. Every aspect of the black's case was laid before the nation: voting rights, educational and economic opportunity, justice in the

*Abolitionist newspaperman William Lloyd Garrison raised public outcry for immediate and total abolition of slavery.*

*Militant Stokely Carmichael headed the Student Nonviolent Coordinating Committee.*

courts (the "separate but equal" doctrine of *Plessy v. Ferguson* was a particular bone of contention), recognition in labor unions and in the military establishment, acceptance in the Christian church. Moreover, the leaders of the Niagara Movement appended certain duties to its list of basic grievances:

The duty to vote.
The duty to respect the rights of others.
The duty to work
The duty to obey the laws.
The duty to be clean and orderly.
The duty to send our children to school.
The duty to respect ourselves, even as we respect others.

In 1909, the Niagara Movement was absorbed into the framework of the National Association for the Advancement of Colored People (NAACP), an organization founded on many of the same principles.

## The Student Non-Violent Coordinating Committee

Often referred to as "Snick" (SNCC), the Student Non-Violent Coordinating Committee was formed in 1960 to coordinate the activities of students engaged in direct action protest such as sit-ins and jail-ins in the South. SNCC achieved enormous results in the desegregation of public facilities and earned respect from the country for its determination to act peacefully, no matter how violent or demeaning the provocation.

After the 1964 Democratic Convention, however, Stokely Carmichael, a leader of SNCC, tended increasingly to feel that the American system could not be turned around without being threatened by wholesale violence and disruption. Failure to seat the delegation of the SNCC-founded Mississippi Freedom Democratic Party (also known as the Lowndes County Freedom Organization or Black Panther Party) at the convention apparently sealed Carmichael's fate as an advocate of black power and supporter of urban-based guerrilla violence.

The Panthers to whom Carmichael moved represented what was believed to be the new thrust of the liberation movement. SNCC, however, depended heavily on the influx of middle-class black and white youths into what was essentially a civil rights movement. Once aggressive northern ghetto youths roared into the picture, SNCC was left without a constituency.

By leaving the South, SNCC surrendered an essential base of support and a concrete program around which to organize. Never a large membership organization, it lost many of its remaining supporters to graduate study, antipoverty work, teaching, law, etc.

SNCC did not recover its sense of direction or central focus once Carmichael departed. H. Rap Brown, formerly minister of justice in the old organization, renamed the new organization the Student National Coordinating Committee in the summer of 1969, at which time he indicated SNCC would retaliate violently if the situation so demanded.

Brown outlined plans for a new SNCC dimension, the creation of a Peoples Medical Center and a Peoples Sewing Center in Brooklyn. However, Brown's legal troubles made it virtually impossible for him to support these programs with any consistent leadership. As a result, SNCC became virtually defunct.

## The Black Panthers

By the 1980s, the Black Panthers, once a powerful force in Black America, especially among inner city youth, had virtually faded from the scene. Under siege by the police, who often brutally trampled on their rights, beset by internal difficulties, with the membership growing older and no new recruits to take their place, the force of the Black Panthers had been spent.

It was not always like this. From its founding by Huey P. Newton and Bobby Seale in October 1966, the Black Panther Party departed from the platform and tactics of all established civil rights organizations.

It condemned institutional structure which, in its view, made American society corrupt; it disavowed established channels of authority and operation which either oppressed or overlooked significant portions of the black community; it rejected middle-class values because they contributed to callous indifference toward, or contempt for, the disinherited youth of the black ghetto. It was, therefore, a revolutionary organization that drew its support almost exclusively from rootless young blacks trapped in large urban slums.

It was to unemployed, undisciplined ghetto youth that the Panthers held out the promise of a bright future, or at least a safer one. The Panthers imposed party discipline on many young males who were responsive to their militaristic regimen, their aggressive rhetoric, and their glorification of machismo. By insisting on the fundamental right of self-defense, the Panthers sought to establish themselves as champions of the black poor against the police.

### The National Welfare Rights Organization

Created in 1966, at a time when the nation's attention was focused on the poor through the War on Poverty, the National Welfare Rights Organization at one time had some 800 local groups of welfare recipients and low-income people located in all 50 states. Its founder and moving force was George Wiley, a chemistry professor from Syracuse. Most of its membership was black, although most welfare recipients are white.

At the time of its greatest influence, NWRO spoke in a militant voice for the rights of people on welfare, advocating a minimum annual income of $7,500 for a family of four and adequate health and legal services for the poor. NWRO's stated purpose was to "provide for bread, justice, dignity, and democracy for welfare recipients." In 1973 NWRO won a suit against the Department of Health, Education and Welfare denying federal funds for sterilization of human beings.

NWRO provided a forum, for the first time, for welfare recipients to speak out on their own behalf and it helped develop a number of powerful spokesmen. As the welfare recipients themselves became more skilled at organizing, a rift developed with Wiley, the professional, and he resigned early in 1973. Wiley died that same year in a drowning accident.

In 1975 NWRO closed its national office in Washington. Since then there has been no national structure, although a number of local chapters are still active.

*Black Panthers await arraignment in Los Angeles following the gun battle that broke out when police raided their headquarters.*

## CURRENT CIVIL RIGHTS LEADERS

Following are biographical sketches of civil rights leaders who are now active on the national scene. In the main, they head national organizations that work in the field of civil rights on a day-to-day basis. Since the last edition of the *Negro Almanac* in 1983, several of the individuals who were included have gone on to other endeavors so that they can no longer be properly included in this category (they appear in other sections). Some of the names that follow will be new to the reader; their inclusion indicates the changing nature of civil rights leadership. The listing of a fairly limited number of individuals in this section should not be construed as indicating that there are not other persons in leadership roles in civil rights. There are in fact many individuals who work on behalf of civil rights in their own communities and on a state and regional basis. It would be impossible to list them all. Finally, the reader will note that none of the leaders connected with the Black Power Movement that flourished during the 1960s and the early 1970s appear. The passing years have seen a marked decline in the Movement on the national level, so that it presently lacks national spokesmen, though it is still a force within some communities.

### IMAMU AMIRI BARAKA
### Community Organizer

Imamu Amiri Baraka, formerly Leroi Jones, is another militant who is successfully using the system to help blacks. Baraka was born in Newark in 1934, the son of a postal superintendent father and social worker mother. He was a scholarship student at Rutgers University and then attended Howard.

After serving in the Air Force, Baraka became a teacher and writer, publishing his first book, *Preface to a Twenty Volume Suicide Note* in 1961. His poetry and fiction won him a John Hay Whitney Fellowship in 1961. Within a few years he had taken powerful steps into the white literary establishment, but he abruptly rejected the values of that world and began to create a radical black literature of highly charged poetry. In 1964 his play Dutchman was acclaimed by New York audiences and critics, receiving the Obie award for the best Off-Broadway play of the season. The shocking honesty of Baraka's treatment of racial conflict in this and later plays became the hallmark of his work. In 1966 Baraka's play The Slave won second prize in the drama category at the First World Festival of Dramatic Arts in Dakar, Senegal.

Later, the prolific Baraka published *Four Black Revolutionary Plays* (1969), *Baptism and The Toilet* (1967), and many other plays in black drama anthologies, in magazines, or as booklets. He edited with Larry Neal *Black Fire: An Anthology of Afro-American Writing* (1968), *Afrikan Congress: A Documentary of the First Modern Pan-African Congress* (1972), and other books. In fiction he published *The System of Dante's Hell* (novel, 1965) and *Tales* (short stories, 1967).

In nonfiction, Baraka has published *Black Music* (1967), *Blues People: Negro Music in White America* (1963), *Home: Social Essays* (1966), *In Our Terribleness: Some Elements and Meanings in Black Style* (with Billy Abernathy, 1969), *Raise Race Rays Raze: Essays Since 1965* (1971), It's *Nation time, Kawaida Studies: The New Nationalism, A Black Value System and Strategy and Tactics of a Pan Afrikan Nationalist Party*. In poetry, in addition to *Preface*,

*Imamu Amiri Baraka, a civil rights organizer as well as an educator and prominent writer.*

he has published *The Dead Lecturer: Poems* (1964) and *Black Magic: Sabotage, Target Study, Black Art: Collected Poetry 1961-1967* (1969). In the 1970s, Baraka, who had earlier gone from avant garde to black nationalism, changed again to his own version of Marxism-Leninism. Since this ideological metamorphosis, he has published *The Motion of History, Six Other Plays* (1978), which also has the play *Slave Ship; Selected Plays and Prose of Amiri Baraka/LeRoi Jones* (1979), which also has a chapter from his autobiographical unpublished novel *Six Persons*; and *Selected Poetry of Amiri Baraka/LeRoi Jones* (1979), containing some new poems and many poems long out of print. In 1984, he published his autobiography, "The Autobiography of LeRoi Jones," and in 1987, introduced his first book on jazz in nearly 20 years: "Reflections on Jazz and Blues." There are five books about Baraka and his writings and three bibliographies of his works.

In the late sixties, though he continued to write, Baraka became a leading black power spokesman in Newark. He was sentenced to prison on a gun-carrying charge and later became head of the Temple of Kawaida, which Baraka describes as an "African religious institution—to increase black consciousness." The Temple and Baraka soon became a focal point of black political activism in the racially polarized city. In 1971 Baraka successfully, and quietly, steered a tax abatement application through the white-dominated Newark City Council and obtained approval of a $6.4 million mortgage through the New Jersey State Finance Agency, for the construction of Kawaida Towers. The site of this 16-story low and middle income housing project is in Newark's north ward, an area of the city that is 70% white and presumed to be the turf of Assemblyman Anthony Imperiale, head of the militant white North Ward Citizens Committee.

The ensuing attempts of Imperiale groups to halt construction of Kawaida Towers marked an important point in black history, for Baraka had so successfully used the system to pave the way for his project, it was Baraka's white opponents, rather than Newark's blacks, who found themselves cast in the role of the disgruntled minority. In a series of political, court, and street protest actions, Imperiale tried to stall construction of the Towers, while Baraka urged his supporters to act with restraint and fought off Imperiale's efforts in the courts.

In 1972 Baraka achieved prominence as a black leader as chairman of the often stormy National Black Political Convention in Gary, where he tried adroitly, though not always successfully, to resolve conflicting positions among the 8,000 nationalist and moderate blacks who attended.

As of 1985, Baraka was an associate professor of African studies at the State University of New York at Stony Brook. He continues to be active in Newark politics, especially on education issues. He belongs to the League of Revolutionary Struggle, a Marxist organization, and edits its publication, Black Nation. He also speaks at forums and rallies nationwide and has lately called for black businesses and professionals to utilize their resources to build institutions for black art, culture, education and commerce.

## MARIAN WRIGHT EDELMAN
### President, Children's Defense Fund

The civil rights of children has been one of the principal concerns of Marian Wright Edelman throughout her career. Founder and president of the Children's Defense Fund, based in Washington, D.C., since its inception in 1973 she has been an outspoken advocate of the rights of children, with special emphasis on minority children.

A native of Bennettsville, South Carolina, Edelman received her undergraduate degree from Spelman College and her law degree from Yale. Her civil rights involvement began in 1963 when she joined the NAACP Legal Defense and Education Fund as staff attorney. A year later she founded the NAACP Legal Defense and Education Fund in Jackson, Mississippi, serving as its director until 1968 when she founded the Washington Research Project of the Southern Center for Public Policy that later developed into the Children's Defense Fund.

As CDF President, Edelman has become the nation's most effective lobbyist on behalf of children, according to the Congressional Quarterly. The CDF annually turns out more than 2,000 pages of reports, which note, for instance, that 12 million American children live below the federally defined poverty level. Edelman uses these reports so effectively to put pressure on Congress that Senator Edward Kennedy once described her as the "101st senator on children's issues."

Edelman managed to score some victories even while the Reagan administration was cutting social spending. In 1986, nine federal programs known as "The Children's Initiative" received a $500 million increase in its $36 billion budget for families and children's health care, nutrition and early education.

*Marian Wright Edelman, president of the Childrens Defense Fund.*

The most visible focus of CDF is its teen pregnancy prevention program. Through Edelman's efforts, Medicaid coverage for expectant mothers and children was boosted in 1984. In 1985, Edelman began holding an annual Pregnancy Prevention Conference, bringing thousands of religious leaders, social and health workers and community organizations to Washington to discuss ways of dealing with the problem.

In her 1987 book, "Families in Peril: An Agenda for Social Change," Edelman wrote, "As adults, we are responsible for meeting the needs of children. It is our moral obligation. We brought about their births and their lives, and they cannot fend for themselves."

Edelman was a member of the Yale University Corporation and the Carnegie Council on Children. She served on the Board of Directors of the NAACP Legal Defense and Education Fund and the Aetna Life and Casualty Foundation. She is the author of many articles and several books on children, including *Children Out of School in America; School Suspensions: Are They Helping Children?*, and *Portrait of Inequality: Black and White Children in America.* Special honors include nine honorary degrees.

## DICK GREGORY
## Comedian, Civil Rights Activist

Dick Gregory was one of America's best known comedians and, more than anyone else, is responsible for creating the precedent which has since enabled other top-flight black humorists to present personal racial humor to the general public.

Born in St. Louis in 1932, Gregory struggled through the depths of the Depression, determined originally to escape from the ghetto on the strength of his athletic ability. As a high school miler, he won the Missouri State mile championship in 1951 and repeated his victory a year later.

He later attended Southern Illinois University on a track scholarship. While there, he was named the school's outstanding athlete in 1953, but he left after two years to join the army. Once in the service, he began working as a comedian in Special Service shows.

After leaving Southern Illinois for the last time in 1956, he worked at various jobs while trying to establish himself in his chosen field. In 1960 part of his Chicago nightclub routine was seen on a television documentary, and he began to receive a few sporadic offers.

On January 13, 1961, he filled in at Chicago's Playboy Club for an ailing comedian and was such an astonishing success that he was held over, given special coverage in *Time* magazine, and booked into the country's top night spots.

Gregory has been an avid campaigner in the civil rights movement, often at great personal expense. While attempting to quiet the Watts rioters in 1965, he was shot in the leg, but was not seriously injured.

Perhaps no entertainer entered the civil rights movement with the commitment and courage of Gregory. Within a year of his Playboy Club success, he was going broke from fines, legal fees, and travel expenses incurred while appearing on

*Brilliant satirist Dick Gregory has been jailed several times for his tireless, nonviolent acts of protest.*

protest picket lines. He was jailed several times. When told by friends he could achieve more as a comedian than activist, Gregory replied tartly, "They didn't laugh Hitler out of existence, did they?"

In 1966 he ran for Mayor of Chicago against Richard Daley, and in 1968 he ran for President, to highlight his "militant but humble" philosophy of confrontation and nonviolence.

Now a wealthy man—from records, writing, and lecture tours, Gregory continues to propound the truth as he sees it to largely white audiences.

Though he amuses audiences with his entertainer's flair, Gregory takes his position very seriously. He has declared that the CIA plans to wipe out black and nonconforming Americans. He frequently fasts for lengthy periods to clean out his system and protest policies such as the Vietnam War, which he opposed. Typical of Gregory's commitment to causes in which he believes was his 46-day fast in 1981 for hunger research.

In the 1980s, Gregory has become known as health guru. His Chicago-based Dick Gregory Health Enterprises, Inc. markets a weight loss powder which claims to help people lose between five and 10 pounds a week. Gregory has gone on talk shows and appeared at a congressional hearing to talk about obesity. His most famous client was 1,200-pound Walter Hudson, who hadn't left his bed in 18 years. Using Gregory's Slim-Safe Bahamian Diet, Hudson lost nearly 400 pounds.

Gregory continues to discuss political topics, including sanctions against South Africa, CIA involvement in drug smuggling and treatment of Cuban refugees.

### BENJAMIN L. HOOKS
### Executive Director, National Association for the Advancement of Colored People

Benjamin L. Hooks was unanimously elected Executive Director of the National Association for the Advancement of Colored People by the NAACP National Board of Directors on January 10, 1977, and formally assumed office on August 1, 1977. He succeeded the legendary Roy Wilkins, who retired.

Hooks' highly successful career spans a number of fields. He first gained nationwide recognition upon his nomination in 1972 to serve on the Federal Communications Commission as its first black member. Once on the FCC he became a driving force to improve the portrayal and employment and ownership opportunities for blacks in the electronic media.

As a lawyer in Memphis, he was an assistant public defender and later was the first black judge to serve in the Shelby County (Memphis) Criminal Court. As an ordained minister, he is on leave from both the Middle Baptist Church in Memphis and the Greater New Mt. Moriah Baptist Church in Detroit. As a prominent local businessman, he was the co-founder and vice president of the Mutual Federal Savings and Loan Association in Memphis for 15 years (1955-1969).

Under his progressive leadership, the NAACP took a more aggressive posture on U.S. policies toward African nations through a successful demonstration in Nashville to protest South Africa's participation in the Davis Cup tennis matches, and through testimony before the House Subcommittee on Africa opposing the lifting of sanctions against Rhodesia.

*Executive director of the NAACP Benjamin Hooks (third from left) with friends.*

Among his many battles on Capitol Hill, Hooks, led the historical Prayer Vigil in Washington, D.C. in 1979 against the Mott anti-busing amendment, which was eventually defeated in Congress; led in the fight for passage of the D.C. Home Rule bill; and was instrumental in gathering important Senate and House votes on the Humphrey-Hawkins Full Employment Bill.

Through such new programs as the Emergency Relief Program to assist victims of natural disasters and the urban assistance program in Miami following the riots of 1980, he also continues the NAACP's tradition of providing technical and financial assistance to the black community. In 1980 Hooks scored another first by becoming the first national figure to address both national political conventions in the same year.

Hooks was born in Memphis and attended LeMoyne College there and Howard University in Washington, D.C. He received his J. D. degree from DePaul University College of Law in 1948. He is a World War II veteran and served in the 92nd Infantry Division's campaign in Italy. He is known for his highly effective and persuasive oratory.

At the NAACP's national convention in 1986, Hooks received the association's highest honor, the Spingarn Medal.

*Roy Innis labels busing "obsolete and dangerous."*

## ROY INNIS
### National Director, Congress of Racial Equality

Born June 6, 1934 in St. Croix, Virgin Islands, Innis has lived in the United States since he was 12. He attended Stuyvesant High School in New York City and went on to serve two years in the service, disguising his age as 18 though he was only 16. Back in civilian life, he majored in chemistry at City College of New York and did not originally plan to pursue a career in the civil rights movement.

By 1963, however, he was active in CORE circles, promoting the theme of economic competition and male assertiveness while down grading the value of integration to blacks. Allies were few at this time, since the organization was multiracial in character and seemed to be irrevocably committed to integration. Patient and persuasive, however, Innis was elected chairman of Harlem CORE in 1965 and went on to become associate national director some three years later. By this time, he was effectively preaching the abandonment of the nonviolent philosophy in favor of a policy of self-defense.

On the economic front, Innis founded the Harlem Commonwealth Council, an agency designed to create black-owned businesses and black-directed economic institutions in Harlem. To promote his ideas, he also took a plunge into journalism, serving with William Haddad as co-editor of the *Manhattan Tribune*, a weekly New York tabloid stressing the affairs of Harlem and the upper West Side. In print and in action, Innis has continued to stress black strength and black advancement over all other themes.

Innis' leadership of CORE, however, has been marked with controversy. Numerous members have dropped out, charging that Innis has run the organization as a one-man show. CORE was also the subject of a three-year investigation by the New York State Attorney General's Office into allegations that it had misused charitable contributions. An agreement was reached in 1981 that did not require CORE to admit to any wrong doing in its handling of funds, but stipulated that Innis would have to contribute $35,000 to the organization over the next three years.

Innis also faced a challenge in the early 1980s when a group of former CORE members, headed by James Farmer, the founder and former chairman of CORE, attempted to oust him. The effort failed and Innis continues to head the organization.

While remaining president of the largely inactive CORE, Innis has sought to build a political base in Brooklyn. He has run for public office twice, most recently as a Republican candidate in the 1986 congressional elections for Brooklyn's 12th District, but has lost both times.

He continues to cause controversy. In a 1987 interview in the Christian Science Monitor, Innis said that crime was a more destructive problem than racism. "We don't need more civil rights laws," he said. "We need to clear our neighborhoods of drugs and crime. In November 1988, while appearing on Geraldo Rivera's talk show, Innis scuffled with John Metzger, a representative of the racist White Aryan Resistance Youth, after Metzger called him an "Uncle Tom." A melee broke out with the audience and Geraldo suffered a broken nose. Innis was also in an on-air shouting match on the Morton Downey Jr. Show that focused on the Tawana Brawley rape case. In that show, Innis pushed Rev. Al Sharpton to the floor.

## JESSE JACKSON
### President, People United to Save Humanity

Jesse Jackson is possibly the most exciting and dynamic young black leader who has decided to work within the system while, at the same time, retaining the appearance, the ardor, and the fervor of a black nationalist or revolutionary. Reared in the black ministry, Jackson has relied on the techniques of pulpit oratory to capture a huge and diverse following, but he has resisted efforts to be cast in the role of a "successor"—particularly to Martin Luther King. "You can be an orator or an organizer," he says. "I am an organizer."

Had Jackson been born white, he could possibly have become another Joe Namath or Tom Seaver. Capable of throwing a football 70 yards and averaging 17 strikeouts per game as a high school pitcher, Jackson won an athletic scholarship to the University of Illinois in 1959 where he was expected to burn up the gridirons and diamonds of the "big Ten."

But Jackson, the son of an Alabama sharecropper, was born black and could not abide the humiliation many white colleges had often inflicted on black athletes. Because he was black, Jackson was not allowed to play at the quarterback position of the football team and was as well subtly excluded from concerts and social events—even those at which black artists, such as Lionel Hampton, performed. Jackson left Illinois for a black college in Greensboro, North Carolina—North Carolina A & T.

*Jesse Jackson, a charismatic civil rights leader and twice a runner for the Democratic nomination for the Presidency.*

While there, Jackson became the "point man" at Greensboro sit-ins. Jackson would enter "whites-only" restaurants alone and when refused service, blacks would start to picket. Such efforts speeded up integration in Greensboro. Upon graduation, Jackson enrolled in the Chicago Theological Seminary. While there he worked briefly, at the precinct level, for a future rival, Mayor Richard Daley, but quit when he concluded that working for the city's Democratic party machine was an affront to his self-respect.

In 1963 Jackson joined the SCLC. He quickly earned a reputation for organizing ability by rallying Chicago's black clergymen behind King. In 1966 Jackson helped unite the SCLC and the Chicago Coordinating Council of Community Organizations into the Chicago Freedom Movement, a group which pressed for integrated schools and open housing. The campaign was one of the first of the postwar years to challenge northern racism, particularly in the Chicago suburb of Cicero, and success in this effort was minor. Shortly thereafter, Operation Breadbasket was launched and Jackson led the campaigns for enlightened hiring and trade policies by the Country Delight Dairy and the A & P. Other businesses in Chicago gradually altered their employment policies, many from fear of the Breadbasket campaign. Recalls Jackson: "You can't calculate the number of jobs made available because they heard those footsteps coming."

While engaged in these battles, Jackson became increasingly concerned about the tendency for money earned and spent by blacks to leave the black community. In part, Breadbasket's effort sought to counter this, but Jackson felt the matter required greater organization and thought. So he formed a group of black leaders and held informal strategy sessions every Saturday morning at the Chicago Theological Seminary. Soon Jackson's Saturday sessions became a platform for Jackson to discuss his views on black pride and a magnet for blacks from all over the country. They are now held in a theater before audiences of several thousand.

Jackson was with King in Memphis when the man he so greatly admired was killed. Two weeks later, in Chicago, after sitting through a eulogy to King by Richard Daley, who had opposed King, Jackson rose and in tears said to Daley, "This blood is on the chest and hands of those who would not have welcomed him here yesterday... (The best tribute) would not be to sit here looking sad and pious... but to behave differently." That Saturday, attendance at Jackson's "strategy session" increased tenfold and to many blacks and whites, Jackson, not Ralph Abernathy, was the inheritor of King's crown.

Through the disappointing years that followed, the failure of the Poor People's March, and the ascendancy of white backlash, Jackson emerged increasingly as the black leader with the organizing ability and charisma necessary to keep the problems and aspirations of blacks before the public eye.

In 1971 Jackson led a march on Springfield, (the capitol of Illinois) which prevented a reduction in state welfare payments. In 1972 he was keynote speaker at the Gary black power convention, where he urged formation of a separate black political party to endorse candidates of both major parties and occasionally run its own.

Jackson has tried to maintain amicable relations with the SCLC and Reverend Abernathy since he left them in 1971. However, the break was not friendly and Jackson's Operation PUSH clearly intrudes on turf SCLC regarded as Breadbasket's. The split occurred in 1971, when Abernathy suspended Jackson for 60 days after learning that Jackson had organized the black fair called "Black Expo" under a separate corporation rather than the aegis of SCLC. Jackson, who had long wanted to go his own way, set up Operation PUSH.

From that point on, Jackson was on his way to becoming the most visible and sought-after civil rights leader in the country. His magnetic personality came across as appealing on television, and while he described himself as "a country preacher," his command of issues and his ability to reach the heart of matters marked him as an individual of intellectual depth.

Of all the civil rights leaders, Jackson was the one who could relate best to the young. He was possessed with a gift of being able to summon out the best in them, in a phrase that became his trademark, "I am somebody."

Out of this came Jackson's program, PUSH-EXCEL, which sought to motivate young school children to do better academically. In 1981 *Newsweek* magazine credited Jackson with building a struggling community improvement organization into a nationwide campaign to revive pride, discipline, and the work ethic in inner-city schools. It also characterized him as the charismatic spokesman for Black America. And when *Black Enterprise* magazine conducted a poll in 1980 to determine who was viewed as the premiere spokesman for blacks, Jackson's name led all the rest.

With funding from the federal government under President Carter, the PUSH-EXCEL program was placed in Chicago and five other cities as a demonstration project. The initial evaluations were mixed as to the success of the programs, and the Reagan Administration revealed that it would reduce funding. Some observers attributed this not only to the evaluation report but to the fact that Jackson had been a supporter of President Carter, whom Reagan defeated.

The Jesse Jackson of the 1980s will be best remembered for his two runs for the Democratic nomination for the Presidency. In 1983, many, but not all, black political leaders endorsed the idea of a black presidential candidate to create a "people's" platform, increase voter registration and have a power base from which there could be greater input into the political process. In a sense the candidacy of Jackson in 1984 was symbolic. His 1984 campaign was launched under the aegis of the "Rainbow Coalition," an umbrella organization of minority groups. Black support was divided, however, between Jackson and former Vice President Walter Mondale, due in part to Mondale's long history of civil rights activism. During this campaign, Jackson attracted considerable media coverage with controversial remarks and actions, demonstrating a lack of familiarity with national politics.

His candidacy in 1988, was another story. The 1988 campaign of Jackson showed enormous personal and political growth, his candidacy was no longer a symbolic gesture but was a real and compelling demonstration. of his effectiveness as a candidate. By the time the Democratic convention rolled around, media pundits were seriously discussing the likelihood of Jackson's nomination as the Democratic presidential candidate, and "what to do about Jesse" became the focus of the entire Democratic leadership. At the end of the primary campaign, Jackson had finished a strong second to Gov. Michael Dukakis, and changed forever the notion that a black President in America was inconceivable. In his 1988 campaign, Jackson avoided controversies, and steadily racked up delegates in Democratic primaries until his delegate count rivaled that of front runner Massachusetts Governor Michael Dukakis. After the convention, which saw the nomination of Dukakis, with Texas Senator Lloyd Bentsen as running mate, the Jackson steamroller stopped. Shelved again by the Democrats, Jackson sat out the rest of the campaign and watched Dukakis get swamped by Republican candidate, President George Bush. Jackson's post-election political cache appeared to be far greater than that of Dukakis', who announced his retirement as Massachusetts governor soon after the election. Jackson, who had won 92 % of the black vote and 20% of the white vote—6.6 million votes_in the 1988 Democratic primaries. In early 1989 Jackson was being suggested as a mayoral candidate for troubled Washington, D.C., and was already being described as a "frontrunner" in the 1992 presidential sweepstakes.

## JOHN E. JACOB
## President, National Urban League

Trained as a social worker and a veteran of the Urban League Movement, John E. Jacob had a large pair of shoes to fill when he replaced Vernon E. Jordan Jr. as president of the NUL on January 1, 1982. In the space of 10 years at the League, Jordan had established a national reputation as an effective and forceful civil rights leader who exerted tremendous influence. He resigned from the League to enter private law practice December 31, 1981, and the board selected Jacob as his successor.

The new president had served since 1979 as executive vice president, the number two staff position at the League, so he was not new to the job. In accepting the new post, Jacob described it as a "signal honor" and added:

*This is my goal as I assume this important post: to make a difference; to help guide the Urban League Movement to new heights of effectiveness; to help educate the nation to its unfinished responsibilities; and to help bring fresh opportunities to the black and poor people who are the constituency of the Urban League.*

Early in his tenure, Jacob clearly indicated that he would put his own mark on the NUL Presidency by speaking out against the budget cuts of the Reagan Administration, by calling on the black community to resist any efforts to turn back the clock on racial gains, and by setting forth several new areas of interest for the League—the plight of single-female-headed households, teenage pregnancy, voter education and registration, and crime in the black community.

His career with the National Urban League began in 1965

when he was named Director of Education and Youth Incentives at the Washington, D.C. Urban League. He held a number of increasingly important positions with the NUL affiliate, serving as director of its Northern Virginia Branch (1966), associate director for administration of the affiliate (1967), and as its acting executive director from 1968 until 1970. He also spent several months as director of community organization training in the Eastern Regional Office of the NUL.

He left the Washington Urban League to serve as executive director for the San Diego Urban League, a post he held $4\frac{1}{2}$ years (1970-1975) until his return to the Washington Urban League as its president. He remained there until 1979 when he joined the national office.

Prior to joining the Urban League Movement he worked for the Department of Public Welfare in Baltimore as a Case Supervisor in the areas of services to families, children's services, protective and medical services.

Jacob is chairman of the Howard University Board of Trustees. He serves as a member of the Board of the Local Initiatives Support Corporation, a national nonprofit enterprise that helps selected local organizations draw new private and public resources into their efforts to revitalize communities and neighborhoods. He is a member of the Board of "A Better Chance, Inc.," a national nonprofit organization whose goal is to increase substantially the number of well-educated minority people who can assume responsibility and leadership in American society. He is also a member of the Community Advisory Board of New York Hospital and the National Advertising Review Board.

He has served as a member of the D.C. Manpower Services Planning Advisory Council and as a member of the Board of Trustees, D.C. Legal Aid Society. Jacob also served as a member of the Judicial Nominating Commission—U.S. District Court and the U.S. Circuit Court for the District of Columbia.

Born in Trout, Louisiana on December 16, 1934, Jacob grew up in Houston. He received his undergraduate and masters degrees from Howard University.

In 1985, he launched the NUL's "Male Responsibility Campaign," which sought to encourage responsible sexual behavior among black teenage boys. Its advertising message was "Don't Make A Baby If You Can't Be A Father."

Jacob was arrested for the first time in 1986, leading a demonstration against apartheid at the South African Embassy. About 1500 supporters were with him at the time of his arrest.

## VERNON E. JORDAN, JR.
### Former President, National Urban League

Vernon E. Jordan Jr. was born in Atlanta in 1935 and grew up there. After graduating from De Pauw University in 1957 and from Howard Law School in 1960, he returned to Georgia, becoming a civil rights lawyer and, in 1962, field secretary for the Georgia branch of the NAACP. Between 1964 and 1968 Jordan was director of the Voter Education Project of the Southern Regional Council and led its successful drives that registered nearly 2 million blacks in the south, leading to an eightfold increase of elected black officials there, from 72 to 564.

*Vernon E. Jordan Jr. has cut channels into the power centers of government.*

In 1970 Jordan moved north to become executive director of the United Negro College Fund, helping to raise record sums for its member colleges until he was tapped by the Urban League as the successor to the late Whitney Young.

Taking over as NUL executive director in January 1972, the energetic Jordan moved the League into new areas, such as voter registration in northern and western cities, while continuing and strengthening the League's traditional social service programs and its role as advocates for the cause of black people and as a bridge to the white community.

While forcefully denouncing the Nixon Administration's racial policies, opposing just about every domestic program offered by it, he was successful in establishing personal links with the White House that softened some federal policies and helped bring federal program contracts to the Urban League and other black institutions.

An outspoken advocate of the cause of the black and the poor, Jordan has taken strong stands in favor of busing, an income maintenance system that ends poverty, scatter-site housing, and a federally financed and administered, consumer-oriented national health system, among others.

As the economy faltered in the early 1970s, Jordan became a leader in the fight for a national full employment policy that "guarantees a decent job at a decent wage for all." Maintaining that the "issues have changed," since the 1960s, Jordan has called for "equal access and employment up to and including top policy-making jobs."

As president of the National Urban League, Jordan's schedule saw him traveling over 100,000 miles a year and often working 70 to 80 hours a week. Much in demand as a speaker, Jordan became one of the most visible and influential leaders of the Civil Rights Movement. In 1977 he was one of the first national spokesmen to criticize the Carter Administration for its emphasis on fiscal conservatism at the expense of human service programs. Still, Jordan maintained his close ties with the President, a fellow Georgian, and with the Administration.

The nation was stunned on May 29, 1980 when Jordan, who had just delivered an address to the Fort Wayne Urban League, was shot in the back by a sniper as he returned to his motel in that city. The bullet was fired from a high-powered rifle and an investigation disclosed that the assailant had lain in wait for some time on a small grassy knoll across from Jordan's room. Jordan narrowly escaped death in the attack and was confined to the hospital, first in Fort Wayne and later in New York City, for some 90 days. He returned to his office in early September 1980. Despite an intensive and widespread investigation by the FBI, as late as May 1982 no suspect had been charged in the shooting.

Jordan made a complete recovery and resumed his demanding schedule within a matter of months. On September 9,1981, he announced that after 10 years as head of the League, he was stepping down effective December 31, 1981, to enter the private practice of law as partner in the Washington office of a major law firm, Akin, Gump, Strauss, Hauer and Feld. At the time of his resignation, Vernon Jordan said:

*My resignation is based on the belief that it is time for a change, personally and institutionally....The goals of the Urban League and the cause of racial equality will always be dearest to my heart and soul.*

During Jordan's tenure, the League increased its affiliates from 99 to 118; employees from 2,100 to 4,200; and its overall budget, involving the affiliates and the national office, from $40 million annually to $150 million.

Jordan now keeps a low profile, declining most speaking engagements and addressing issues publicly infrequently, as in 1983, when he criticized the legal profession for not hiring more minority professionals. Jordan serves on eight of the nation's largest corporate boards, including Revlon, American Express, Bankers Trust and Xerox.

### CORETTA SCOTT KING
### Civil Rights Activist

After her husband's assassination, Coretta Scott King made a swift transition from a dedicated wife and parent living in comparative seclusion to a dynamic civil rights and peace crusader in her own right. During her husband's life, she accommodated herself to the mother/wife role; with him gone, it seemed imperative that she carry on his life's work and perpetuate his ideals actively and publicly.

Born one of three children on April 27,1927, Mrs. King is a native of Heiberger, Alabama. During the Depression she was forced to contribute to the family income by hoeing and picking cotton, but she resolved early to overcome adversity, seek treatment as an equal, and struggle to achieve a sound education.

In 1945 she entered Antioch College in Yellow Springs, Ohio on a scholarship, majoring in education and music. A teaching career appealed to her, but she became badly disillusioned when she was not allowed to do her practice teaching in the public schools of the town. No black had ever taught there, and she was not destined to be the first to break the tradition.

Musical training in voice and on piano absorbed much of her time, with the result that, upon graduation, she decided to continue her studies at the New England Conservatory of Music in Boston, attending on a modest fellowship which

*Coretta Scott King works to make her late husband's dream a reality.*

covered tuition but made part-time work a necessity. Paradoxically, her financial situation improved when she began receiving state aid from Alabama. (Such aid was available to blacks studying outside the state, but not for black applicants seeking to attend schools within the state itself.)

Her meeting with Martin Luther King thrust her into a whirlwind romance, and also presented her with the opportunity to marry an exceptional young minister whose intense convictions and concern for humanity brought her a measure of rare self-realization early in life. Sensing his incredible dynamism, she suffered no regrets at the prospect of relinquishing her own possible career.

Completing her studies in 1954, Mrs. King moved back South with her husband, who became pastor of Drexel Avenue Baptist Church in Montgomery, Alabama. Within a year, King had led the Montgomery bus boycott, and given birth to a new era of civil rights agitation. Two years later, he was the head of the Southern Christian Leadership Conference (SCLC).

By 1964 Mrs. King was the mother of four children: Yolanda (born 1955); Martin Luther, III (born 1957); Dexter Scott (born 1961); and Bernice Albertine (born 1963).

Over the years, Mrs. King did some teaching and fund-raising work for SCLC, becoming more accustomed to the limelight, particularly after her trip to Oslo in 1964. In was more than such exposure, however, that gave her the strength, the courage, and the determination to deal with the assassination, and, later, to deliver the speeches he had drafted in rough form.

*Eddie N. Williams heads the very important Joint Center for Political Studies.*

Her speech on Solidarity Day, June 19, 1968, is often identified as a prime example of her emergence from the shadow of her husband's memory. In it, she called upon American women to "unite and form a solid block of women power" to fight the three great evils of racism, poverty, and war.

Much of her subsequent activity revolved around building plans for the creation of a Martin Luther King Jr. Memorial in Atlanta. Mrs. King later published a book of reminiscences, *My Life With Martin Luther King Jr.*

Today, Mrs. King still remains an eloquent and respected spokesperson on behalf of black causes and nonviolent philosophy. Her children are grown and carving their own careers, and she devotes most of her time to the Martin Luther King Jr. Center for Social Change in Atlanta, which has grown into a well-respected institution visited by persons from across the world.

Mrs. King has been a champion for the anti-apartheid cause. In 1985, she and two of her children were arrested for demonstrating outside the South African embassy in Washington, D.C. In 1986, she visited South Africa for eight days, meeting with businessmen and anti-apartheid leaders. She called her meeting with Winnie Mandela "one of the greatest and most meaningful moments of my life."

## JOSEPH E. LOWERY
## President, Southern Christian Leadership Conference

Reverend Joseph E. Lowery continues a tradition begun with the late Dr. Martin Luther King of having the Southern Christian Leadership Conference headed by a clergyman. In 1977 he succeeded Reverend Ralph David Abernathy, who had been picked by Dr. King as his successor. From his first official statement to SCLC, Reverend Lowery made clear what his course would be:

*It is with both humility and honor that I accepted the presidency of the Southern Christian Leadership Conference. The mantle was handed from Martin Luther King Jr. to Ralph Abernathy, and now to me. Yet, I have accepted the challenge with prayer and determination, for the "dream" remains unfulfilled...*

*Yes, we are still engaged in the struggle to replace violence and poverty with a system that will assure the dignity of every person. Much of our struggle, in communities across the nation, is unheralded by the media—struggles against racism expressed in denial of the ballot, unjust wages, high unemployment, inadequate housing and medical care, lack of economic opportunities and oppression in the criminal justice system.*

Soft-spoken and unassuming, Reverend Lowery received his first broad-scale national and international exposure when he led a delegation of 10 persons from SCLC on a fact-finding mission to the Mideast in 1979, in the wake of the furor that erupted over a meeting held by U.S. Ambassador Andrew Young with a representative of the Palestine Liberation Organization. Such meetings were contrary to U.S. policy and Young was forced to resign, touching off a squabble between black and Jewish leaders.

On his overseas trip, Lowery met with PLO leaders, and as a consequence, Israeli leaders refused to meet with the SCLC president, touching off massive news coverage.

Reverend Lowery was born in Huntsville, Alabama, and holds several degrees. He has been minister of the Centennial Unity Methodist Church since 1968. His ministry began in 1952 at the Warren Street Church in Birmingham, where he served until 1961 when he became administrative assistant to Bishop Golden. From there he moved on to become pastor of St. Paul Church from 1964 to 1968. He was one of the founders of the Southern Christian Leadership Conference and held several positions with the organization before becoming its president.

Under his leadership, SCLC has broadened its activities to include the reinstitution of its Operation Breadbasket to encourage businesses that earn substantial profits in the black community to reinvest equitably and employ blacks in equitable numbers; involvement in the plight of Haitians who were jailed by the American government after they sought asylum here; and a march from Selma to Washington, D.C. in connection with the renewal of the Voting Rights Act of 1982.

In 1984, Lowery made a bid for the Democratic nomination for president. He is otherwise seen most frequently speaking on anti- apartheid issues.

### EDDIE N. WILLIAMS
### President, Joint Center for Political Studies

Regarded as the most knowledgeable person in America about the operation of blacks within the political structure, Eddie N. Williams has headed the Joint Center for Political Studies since 1972.While he maintains a low profile, it is generally conceded that through the Center, Williams has been instrumental in strengthening the black presence in politics. Specifically, the Center keeps its eyes on the changing tides of politics, shares this information on a wide basis, and provides supportive services to black elected officials.

Before joining the Center, Williams was Vice President of Public Affairs and Director of the Center for Policy Study, both at the University of Chicago.

Trained as a journalist, Williams received his undergraduate degree from the University of Illinois and pursued graduate studies in political science at Atlanta University. He was a reporter for the Atlanta *Daily World*. Williams also served in the State Department for seven years as director of the Department's Office of Equal Employment Opportunity, as staff assistant to the assistant secretary for Near Eastern and South Asian Affairs, and as protocol officer. From 1958 to 1960 he was staff aide to Senator Hubert H. Humphrey. He is also the author of numerous magazine and newspaper articles.

Williams received a B.S. in Journalism from the University of Illinois and has received honorary doctorate degrees from Bowie State University and the University of the District of Columbia as well as numerous other professional and achievement awards.

## FORMER CONTEMPORARY CIVIL RIGHTS LEADERS

### RALPH D. ABERNATHY
### Former President, Southern Christian Leadership Conference

Reverend Ralph David Abernathy headed the Southern Christian Leadership Conference from the time of Martin Luther King's death in 1968 until 1977, when he resigned to run for the Congressional seat being vacated by his fellow Atlantan, Andrew Young, who had accepted an appointment from President Jimmy Carter as the Ambassador to the United Nations.

The race went badly for Abernathy, who came in fourth in the 13-man Democratic primary election with less than 5% of the vote. Abernathy laid the blame at the doorstep of the Atlanta voters and said that they obviously thought that he should remain in civil rights and not go to Congress. However, in the succeeding years, Abernathy became less and less involved with the Movement and turned more of his attention to pastorship at Atlanta's West Hunter Street Baptist Church and to the lecture circuit.

When Martin Luther King lost his life to an assassin's bullet, he had already made it clear that if he fell, his successor was to be his trusted confidante, Reverend Abernathy. The mantle of leadership thus passed smoothly and Abernathy rallied the SCLC staff and thousands of supporters to the side of the garbage workers, who won a settlement of their grievances in short order.

Abernathy continued as a leading figure in the Movement until his resignation in 1977, although SCLC never recovered the influence it had had under King.

### H. RAP BROWN
### Former Chairman, Student Nonviolent Coordinating Committee

As chairman of the Student Nonviolent Coordinating Committee, H. Rap Brown emerged with Stokely Carmichael in 1966 as a stormy advocate of black power. In 1968 he was charged with inciting a riot in Cambridge, Maryland and was convicted in New Orleans on a federal charge of carrying a gun between states. Brown disappeared in 1970, after being slated for trial in Maryland, and in 1972 he was shot,

*Joining hands to sing "We Shall Overcome" in Selma, 1965 were (from left) James Foreman, Reverend Fred Shuttlesworth, unidentified man, Reverend Martin Luther King, Reverend Ralph Abernathy, and Reverend James Bevel.*

arrested, and eventually convicted for a saloon holdup in New York City.

In 1974, while still in prison, Brown remained a controversial figure among blacks. Some claimed he had succumbed indulgently to violence, others that he had been framed and harassed by law enforcement officials who feared him.

While in prison, Brown converted to the Islamic faith and took the name of Jamil Abdullah Al-Amin. On his release, he went to Atlanta where he opened a grocery store.

### STOKELY CARMICHAEL
### Former Chairman, Student Nonviolent Coordinating Committee

If there was one individual during the sixties who stood at the forefront of the Black Power Movement it was Stokely Carmichael. Gifted, handsome, and articulate, he soared to fame as popularizer of the dynamic phrase "black power" and as leader, until 1977, of the Student Nonviolent Coordinating Committee. In the short life of SNCC, he was its most powerful and influential leader.

The son of a carpenter, Carmichael was born in Trinidad in 1941 and came to the United States when he was 11. As a teenager, Carmichael was jolted by ghetto life in which "black" and "impotent" seemed to be synonymous terms. He was not reassured later when he was admitted to the Bronx High School of Science, encountered white liberals, and felt he had been adopted by them as a "mascot."

In 1960 Carmichael joined CORE in its efforts to integrate public accommodations in the South. Though offered scholarships to white universities, he entered Howard, graduating in 1964. He then joined SNCC, was elected its leader, and was instrumental in altering its orientation from peaceful integration to "black liberation."

Carmichael not only drove a wedge into the civil rights movement but emerged as the foremost spokesman for the black power concept and became a symbol of violence to whites fearful at the time of uprisings in America's cities.

Carmichael subsequently resigned from SNCC and joined the Black Panthers.

However, he differed with Eldridge Cleaver's view that coalitions could be formed with white radicals, and he soon resigned from the Panthers. In 1969, he and his wife, South African singer Mariam Makeba whom he married in 1968, moved to Guinea where he still resides.

In 1972 he returned briefly to the United States and espoused his Pan-African ideology, which he depicted as an increased awareness and acceptance by American blacks of the culture, heritage, and ideals of Africans. He stresses that this is not a new course but the ultimate extension of black power.

His activities as a civil rights figure have virtually ceased, and rarely is he heard from.

### ELDRIDGE CLEAVER
### Former Minister of Information, Black Panther Party

It was in the late 1970s that the life of Eldridge Cleaver underwent a dramatic change from that of a black militant to that of a "born-again Christian" who shunned all forms of violence. Cleaver first came to prominence as a revolutionary social critic and as the chief theoretician and spokesman for the Black Panther Party. He was also the author of *Soul on Ice*, a collection of impassioned love letters and brilliant essays probing the depth and conundrums of the modern black psyche.

Born in 1935 in Wabbeseka, Arkansas (near Little Rock), Cleaver was convicted of possessing marijuana at age 18 and, in 1954, began a 12-year cycle of assorted prison terms at Soledad, Folsom, and San Quentin. While in prison, he obtained a diploma from Bay View High School, was converted to the Black Muslim faith (he was an ardent follower of Malcolm X), and began writing for the first time

*Expatriate Eldridge Cleaver has returned to the United States.*

in earnest.

After his release from prison, he became a staff writer for *Ramparts* magazine and much-publicized lecturer on college campuses, where he sought to inspire and motivate black students, particularly those with ghetto backgrounds. He was once invited to address a group of Berkeley students as a black studies lecturer, a move roundly opposed by California governor Ronald Reagan. The course Social Analysis 139X was never conducted regularly.

In 1969 Cleaver left the United States secretly, fleeing a prison sentence which had been imposed on him for violating parole and for alleged involvement in a shoot-out with Oakland police. He was found by a Reuters correspondent in Havana, ostensibly working on a sequel to *Soul on Ice*. Later that year, however, he emerged in Moscow, where he granted an interview which confirmed his connection with the "international proletarian movement." Critical of both the Soviet Union and Red China for pursuing "narrow interests," Cleaver contended that "big communist countries" should invest in the future by pooling their arsenals, supplying more generous arms supplies to fledgling liberation movements, and facing up to the imperialism of the United States.

At this juncture, it developed that Cleaver, his wife, and young son were residing in Algeria.

For a time, Cleaver lived amicably in Algeria, praising its "third world" position between the two giant power blocs of East and West. However, in 1972 a rift between Cleaver and his host government was reported on the issue of skyjacking ransom money. The Algerians, contrary to Cleaver's desire, wished it returned to the airlines which had paid it. In 1973 Cleaver was reported to be under house arrest in Algiers. Meanwhile, reports circulated in California that Cleaver's former associates in the Black Panther Party, with whom he had broken, wanted to reconcile their differences with him.

Cleaver returned to the United States in 1979 and in return for his pleading guilty to assaulting an Oakland policeman more than 10 years earlier, the old murder charge against him was dismissed. He was placed on probation and ordered to do 2,000 hours of community service.

A changed man after his stay out of the country, Cleaver announced that he was a "born-again Christian" and began to make a number of appearances at fundamentalist churches in various sections of the country to speak of his conversion and to urge others to follow suit. Once a critic of the United States, Cleaver told a group of students at Yale University in 1982 that America was the "freest and most democratic country in the world."

## JAMES FARMER
## Founder and Former National Director, Congress of Racial Equality

Much of the life of James Farmer has been involved with the Congress of Racial Equality in one way or another. He was one of its founders in 1942 and served as its national director until 1966. CORE was established on the basis of interracial cooperation and during its early years it clung to this philosophy.

During the mid-1960s, CORE moved toward racial separatism and it was at this point that Farmer left, though it was obvious that he did so with regret.

Born in Marshall, Texas on January 12, 1920, Farmer attended public schools throughout the South, and later earned his B.S. in chemistry from Wiley College. At first interested in medicine, he later enrolled in the School of Religion at Howard University with the intention of preparing for the Methodist ministry. Active in the Christian Youth Movement, and once vice-chairman of the National Council of Methodist Youth and the Christian Youth Council of America, Farmer received his Bachelor of Divinity degree in 1941 but refused ordination when confronted with a realization that he would have to practice in a segregated ministry.

In 1941 Farmer accepted a post as race relations secretary of the Fellowship of Reconciliation, a pacifist group. The following year he and a group of University of Chicago students organized CORE, the first American black protest organization which utilized the techniques of nonviolence and passive resistance advocated by the Indian revolutionary Mohandas K. Gandhi. In June 1943 CORE staged the first successful sit-in demonstration at a restaurant in the Chicago Loop. The organization soon supplemented this maneuver with what came to be known as the standing-line, which involved the persistent waiting in line by CORE groups at places of public accommodation where blacks were being denied admission.

Throughout the 1950s Farmer was active on a number of different fronts in the civil rights struggle. In 1958 he was one of a five-man delegation sent to 15 African countries by the International Confederation of Free Trade Unions. He also served as a radio and television commentator on programs sponsored by the United Auto Workers in Detroit, and functioned as program director for the NAACP while contributing several articles to *Crisis* magazine.

In 1961 CORE introduced the Freedom Ride into the vocabulary and methodology of civil rights protest, dispatching a group of bus riders into the South for the purpose of testing whether terminal facilities there had been desegregated. Attacked in Alabama and later arrested in Mississippi, the Freedom Riders eventually succeeded in securing compliance with the Supreme Court decision of 1960 which had outlawed segregated bus terminals.

Farmer left CORE in 1966, phasing out his association with the organization as soon as he discerned what he deemed an irreversible trend toward separatism, and also to restrict the activities of whites who had made a significant commitment to the goals of the organization. Originally, he was slated to head a nation wide literacy program sponsored by the Johnson Administration and funded with a $900,000 grant from the Office of Economic Opportunity (OEO). The project was canceled, however, ostensibly because some urban politicians feared it would produce a black voter registration drive that would disrupt the voting patterns which kept them in power. Farmer later ran for Congress against Shirley Chisholm but was defeated despite the fact that his name appeared on both the Liberal and the Republican line.

*John Lewis heads the Voter Registration Project, which is changing southern politics.*

President Nixon appointed Farmer as Assistant Secretary of Health, Education and Welfare in 1969, creating a furor in some black circles where it was felt that it was inappropriate for a former civil rights leader to serve in such an Administration. However, the appointment was praised by many who thought it necessary for blacks to be represented in all political parties. Farmer, himself, found that there was little of substance that he could do in the post and he resigned in a short period of time.

He began to give lectures and for a while headed a "think tank" at Howard University. In 1976 he broke all ties with CORE, criticizing its leader, Roy Innis, for such things as attempting to recruit black Vietnam veterans as mercenaries in Angola's civil war. In 1977 Farmer became executive director of the Coalition of American Public Employees in Washington, D.C., a post that he still retains.

Disturbed over the course that CORE had taken, Farmer and a score of former CORE members attempted to create a new racially mixed civil rights organization in 1980. Farmer and Floyd McKissick later met with Innis at McKissick's Soul City, in an effort to reach an agreement about the future of the organization, but nothing developed and Innis remained in command. Farmer's civil rights activities ceased at this point.

## JOHN LEWIS
### Former Chairman, Student Nonviolent Coordinating Committee

John Lewis was always the quiet but totally dedicated young man of the Civil Rights Movement. A graduate of Fisk and a Baptist minister, Lewis headed the Student Nonviolent Coordinating Committee from 1963 to 1966, when he was defeated by forces less devoted than he to the nonviolent approach.

Lewis joined the sit-in Movement when he was a seminarian in Nashville, and soon, in addition to Bible training, he had a jail record, much to the grief of his mother, who tried to get him to serve the Movement in some way other than going to jail. However, Lewis told her he felt compelled to act "according to my convictions and according to my Christian conscience."

His most traumatic experience probably occurred at the March on Washington in 1963 when he, as the youngest, was to join such speakers as Martin Luther King, Walter Reuther of the United Auto Workers, Whitney Young of the National Urban League, Roy Wilkins of the NAACP, and Catholic Archbishop Patrick O'Boyle of Washington, D.C., before several hundred thousand people.

Lewis had prepared a strong speech in which he lashed out at the Kennedy Administration and urged basic changes in the social order to correct brutalities and injustices suffered by blacks and civil rights workers in the Deep South. Objections were raised by some of his elders and Archbishop O'Boyle threatened to withdraw if the program was to be too radical.

Under this pressure, Lewis dropped certain parts of the speech. After leaving SNCC, Lewis remained active in the

*Floyd McKissick is an advocate of black economic power.*

Movement, later heading the Voter Education Project, an Atlanta-based organization that coordinates voter registration drives and provides assistance to elected black officials in the South.

After the election of Jimmy Carter as President in 1976, Lewis went to Washington as an official with ACTION, the government agency that was responsible for volunteer activities such as VISTA. When Carter left office, Lewis returned to Atlanta, where he was elected a city councilman in 1981.

From 1982 to 1986, Councilman Lewis was a strong advocate for blacks. He then gave up his seat to run for Georgia's 5th Congressional District, which includes most of Atlanta. He faced opposition from three blacks, including State Senator Julian Bond who had endorsements from Atlanta mayors Andrew Young and Maynard Jackson. Lewis campaigned hard, though, and won the seat by a 4% margin. In 1988, he won reelection.

## FLOYD B. MCKISSICK
## Former National Director, Congress of Racial Equality

When Floyd Bixler McKissick replaced James Farmer as head of CORE on January 3, 1966, the organization completed a 180-degree turn that saw it change from an interracial, integrationist civil rights agency pledged to uphold nonviolence into a militant and uncompromising advocate of the ideology of black power.

McKissick refused to support Martin Luther King's call for massive nonviolent civil disobedience in northern cities, concentrating instead on programs aimed at increasing the political power and improving the economic position of the ghetto dweller.

It was also under McKissick's leadership that CORE moved in 1967 to eliminate the word "multiracial" from its constitution. McKissick and Roy Innis, who at that time was the head of the Harlem chapter of CORE, were close allies, and when McKissick left CORE in 1968, Innis took over.

After leaving CORE, McKissick launched a plan to build a new community, Soul City, on Warren County, North Carolina farmland.

Born in Asheville, North Carolina on March 9, 1922, McKissick did his undergraduate work at Morehouse and North Carolina colleges, and later graduated from the University of North Carolina Law School.

During World War II McKissick served in the European theater as a sergeant. After the war, he began legal practice in Durham, North Carolina, where he once represented his own daughter in her successful bid to gain admission to a previously all-white public school.

Despite the victory, McKissick later decided that "integration" itself only magnified the perils faced by many black children, McKissick bitterly recalled that his children had been taunted and harassed: "Patches cut out of their hair, pages torn out of books, water thrown on them in the dead of winter, ink down the front of their dresses"—a demoralizing array of constant and relentless pressures designed to crack their composure and destroy their will to learn. The adversity no doubt deepened McKissick's nascent radicalism and militant zeal.

As a lawyer, McKissick's most publicized efforts involved a segregated black local in the Tobacco Workers International, an AFL-CIO member. McKissick pressed to have black workers admitted to the skilled scale without loss of their seniority rating. McKissick also successfully defended "sit-in" protestors in the south.

It was at this time that the rupture widened between the older, established civil rights groups, dependent for their programming on a coalition of educated blacks and affluent white liberals, and the younger, more rancorous black militants who turned their backs on most institutional white support. The militants argued that the civil rights groups did not appreciate the urgency of many problems affecting black urban majorities, particularly in the job area where technology often reduced people to useless ciphers.

McKissick saw Soul City as an integrated community with sufficient industry to support a population of 55,000. For his venture, he received a $14 million bond issue guarantee from the Department of Housing and Urban Development and a loan of $500,000 from the First Pennsylvania Bank.

Soul City, however, ran into difficulties and despite the best efforts of McKissick, the project never developed as he had anticipated. Finally, in June 1980, the Soul City Corporation and the federal government reached an agreement that would allow the government to assume control the following January. Under the agreement, the company retained 88 acres of the project, including the site of a mobile home park and a 60,000 square foot building that had served as the project's headquarters.

The Department of Housing and Urban Development paid off $10 million in loans and agreed to pay an additional $175,000 of the project's outstanding debts. In exchange, McKissick agreed to drop a lawsuit brought to block HUD from shutting down the project.

*Huey P. Newton, who with Bobby Seale established the Black Panther Party for Self-defense.*

## HUEY P. NEWTON
### Supreme Commander, Black Panther Party

The youngest of seven children, Newton was born in Monroe, Louisiana on February 17, 1942. He attended Oakland City College, where he founded the Afro-American Society, and later studied at San Francisco Law School.

In 1966 Newton and Bobby Seale joined forces to establish the Black Panther Party for Self-defense. The pair systematically set out to survey police practices in the ghetto, scouting through the area with cameras and loaded shotguns.

Newton and his partner almost immediately became the targets of sharp police resentment and uneasiness. The hostility came to a climax in the 1967 fracas during which Newton allegedly killed an Oakland officer. His eight-week trial was a cause celebre in which more than 2,500 demonstrators surrounded the courthouse chanting Panther slogans and demanding his release. It was also one of the first public appearances of large numbers of the incipient Black Panther Party. Some 250 strong, they wore the berets and leather jackets which have since become a trademark in the public consciousness.

After his September 1968 conviction on a voluntary manslaughter charge, Newton was sent to the California Men's Colony and placed in solitary confinement for his refusal to work in the mess hall. He agreed, however, to take a job in the institution's industrial training program.

His conviction was overturned by the California Court of Appeals on the grounds that the jury had not received proper instruction from the presiding judge. The Appeals court ruled that the judge should have instructed the jury to recognize Newton's defense as a complete one if it accepted his contention that he was unconscious at the time of the killing. Besides the "omitted instructions," the court cited several other prejudicial errors as grounds for overturning the conviction.

Newton, out on $50,000 bail, was slated for retrial on a manslaughter charge stemming from the shooting of the patrolman.

As early as 1972, Newton gave signals that he was beginning to moderate his position. "The gun itself is not revolutionary," he said, adding that the Panthers had "defected from black people" by becoming too militant.

Newton fled to Cuba in 1974 and voluntarily returned to the United States in 1977. He was convicted again in 1978 of the shooting of the policeman, but that conviction was reversed. He went on trial again on a murder charge stemming from the shooting of a woman in 1974, but after two juries could not reach a verdict, the charge was dropped.

In 1980 Newton received his Ph.D. degree from the University of California. His doctoral thesis was "War Against the Panthers—Study of Repression in America." Newton is no longer active in the Black Power Movement.

He has not been able to avoid scrapes with the law. He was arrested in 1985 for embezzling state and federal funds from an educational and nutritional program he headed in California. In 1987, he was convicted of possessing firearms and was sentenced to a prison term of not more than three years.

## BOBBY SEALE
### Co-Founder, Black Panther Party

In 1966 there were but three Black Panthers: Huey P. Newton, Bobby Seale, and Bobby Hutton. Newton and Seale were summer youth workers for the Richmond, California poverty program; Hutton was only 15 and a high school dropout.

At 29, Seale, then foreman in a car wash, was in a position to carve out a satisfactory career in the poverty program, concentrating on "trades and technical skills,... a little black history... and then cleaning lawns, repairing houses, chopping weeds."

When Seale took up residence at the North Oakland Service Center, his patience with such a program was wearing thin; it disintegrated completely one night when he led a group of black youths on a tour of Oakland's police headquarters and heard a white police lieutenant advise members of the party to turn in "people who burn down houses. Why don't you give us their names?"

Sensing then that he was involved in what he regarded as an insidious attempt to propagandize these youths and to distort their loyalties and sense of justice, Seale and Newton withdrew from such work, deciding instead to patrol the ghetto in their own fashion, "unified around the gun." Their objective: to monitor the movement of cops on the beat. The effort was designed to establish a mutual tolerance, Seale said, not to challenge the right of police to do their duty. It was also designed to show young blacks that they had every right to demand respect and due process from police who patrolled their area.

Still, such a policy invariably involved more racial confrontation than programmatic performance. Seale and his cohorts succeeded in luring many youngsters away from the rootlessness and spiritual starvation of ghetto streets but were unable to attract the kind of support from black intellectuals and professionals that might have complemented their emotionally resuscitating ideology.

By 1969 the cream of the Panther hierarchy—men like Huey Newton, Eldridge Cleaver, Fred Hampton, and Bobby Hutton—were either dead or in exile. Seale himself was in jail on charges stemming from the 1968 Chicago convention riots, and was one of the 13 Panthers being held in custody for the alleged execution of suspected Panther informer Alex Rackley.

Some encouragement stemmed from the party's attempts to enlist radical support in 1969 from such lawyers as Charles R. Garry of New York and William M. Kunstler of New York. That same year, the Panthers convoked a three-day conference of 3,500 young radicals from more than 300 organizations.

Significant among the changes evident in the Panther positions was the group's emphasis on "people's" problems, rather than just those of the black ghetto. Seale spoke at the 1969 meeting, stressing "unity of the people" and pledging that Panthers would "not fight racism with more racism."

Seale was shifting the emphasis away from the issue of race and committing the Panthers to the idea that class struggle was the deciding factor in American life:

*We will not fight capitalism with more capitalism—black capitalism. We will fight it with basic socialistic programs. We will not fight fire with fire. The best way to put out fire is with water.*

Seale thus acknowledged the need to resort to propaganda, organization, and political activity as alternate tactics beyond arming people and tutoring them in guerilla warfare. In 1973, Seale ran unsuccessfully for Mayor of Oakland, California, finishing second in a field of eight and thus forcing the incumbent to engage in a runoff election.

In 1974 Seale resigned as chairman of the Black Panther Party and later wrote his autobiography, *A Lonely Rage*. In recent years Seale has lectured widely and is reported to be writing another book. He is no longer active in the Black Power Movement.

Seale has been affiliated with Temple University as a faculty member. In 1987, he authored a book on another of his favorite topics—barbeque. Proceeds from the sale of "Barbeque with Bobby," a 100-recipe cookbook, was to go to "grass roots political groups seeking political and economic change," he told the media.

*Awaiting trial for the murder of a fellow Black Panther member, Bobby Seale (left) describes his experiences in San Francisco City Jail to television producer Francisco Newman.*

## CIVIL RIGHTS AND BLACK POWER LEADERS OF THE PAST

Following are brief biographies of blacks, no longer living, who made profound contributions to the civil rights and political awareness of blacks in the United States. The Negro Almanac has selected this group on the basis of the contributions and fame of each individual. All shades of the political spectrum are represented, from carefully moderate Booker T. Washington to William DuBois, who supported the Communist Party in his late years.

### RICHARD ALLEN
### 1760-1831

Richard Allen was among the first black preachers to become prominent as a political activist. When still in his teens, Allen converted his master to Christianity and was permitted to buy his freedom.

Allen thought of people first as children of God and only then as members of a racial group. He believed that he could preach to both whites and blacks, and in this view Allen was supported by the Bishop of the Methodist Church. However, in 1787 Allen encountered intense bigotry at a church in Philadelphia and as a result, together with Absalam Jones, established the first black church in the United States, the African Methodist Episcopal. In 1816 Allen organized black Methodist congregations from several states into one group and was elected bishop.

Allen was aware that the prejudice which denied him the means to address integrated congregations also denied blacks the means to live in dignity. In 1787 he founded the Free African Society, which sought to further the social welfare and racial and religious awareness of blacks.

Allen remained a patriot throughout his life, strongly supporting the United States in the war of 1812 against Great Britain. In 1830 he formed a movement for settling blacks in Canada but opposed with intensity and vigor all efforts to resettle blacks in Africa.

### FREDERICK DOUGLASS
### 1817-1895

One of a handful of names which immediately leaps to mind at the mention of the American black is that of Frederick Douglass, probably the foremost voice in the abolitionist movement of the nineteenth century.

Born in February 1817 in Talbot County, Maryland, Douglass was sent to Baltimore as a house servant at the age of eight. He learned to read and write under the instruction of his mistress. At the death of her husband, Douglass was sent to the country as a field hand. In his early teens, he began to teach in a Sunday school which was forcibly shut down by hostile Southerners. Douglass himself was severely flogged for his resistance to slavery.

After one unsuccessful attempt to escape, Douglass managed to make his way to New York disguised as a sailor. Once in the North, he found his true calling—leader in the antislavery crusade. Taken on as an agent by the Massachusetts Anti-Slavery Society, he began his great life work.

Douglass soon became an increasingly familiar figure to abolitionists throughout the country. In 1845, after having published his Narrative at great personal risk (that of reenslavement as a fugitive), he went to England, where he raised enough money, through lectures on slavery and women's rights, to buy his freedom. Upon his return to his native shores, he founded the famous newspaper *The North Star*. Later he was forced to flee to Canada when the governor of Virginia swore out a warrant for his arrest on charges that he had conspired with John Brown, leader of the Harpers Ferry revolt.

With the outbreak of the Civil War, Douglass—once again back in the United States—met with President Lincoln and assisted him in recruiting the celebrated 54th and 55th Massachusetts Negro regiments.

In 1871, during the Reconstruction period, he was appointed to the territorial legislature of the District of Columbia; in 1872 he served as one of the presidential electors-at-large for New York and, shortly thereafter, became secretary of the Santo Domingo Commission.

In 1877, after a short term as a police commissioner of the District of Columbia, Douglass was appointed marshal—a post he held until he was named recorder of deeds in 1881.

Eight years later, in return for his support of the presidential campaign of Benjamin Harrison, Douglass was appointed to the most important federal posts he was to hold—minister resident and consul general to the Republic of Haiti and, later, charge d'affaires for Santo Domingo. However, when he saw his efforts being undermined by unscrupulous American businessmen interested solely in exploiting Haiti, he resigned his post in 1891.

Four years later, Frederick Douglass died at his home in Washington, D.C.

### W. E. B. DUBOIS
### 1868-1963

An outstanding critic, editor, scholar, author, and civil rights leader, William Edward Burghardt DuBois is certainly among the most influential blacks of the twentieth century.

Born in Great Barrington, Massachusetts on February 23, 1868, DuBois received a bachelors degree from Fisk University and went on to win a second bachelors, as well as a Ph.D., from Harvard. He was for a time professor of Latin and Greek at Wilberforce and the University of Pennsylvania, and also served as a professor of economics and history at Atlanta University.

One of the founders of the National Association for the Advancement of Colored People (NAACP) in 1909, DuBois served as that organization's director of publications and editor of *Crisis* magazine until 1934. In 1944 he returned from Atlanta University to become head of the NAACP's special research department, a post he held until 1948. Dr.

*Reverend Richard Allen founded the Free African Society.*

*Frederick Douglass.*

DuBois emigrated to Africa in 1961 and became editor-in-chief of the *Encyclopedia Africana,* an enormous publishing venture which had been planned by Kwame Nkrumah, since then deposed as president of Ghana. DuBois died in Ghana in 1963 at the age of 95.

His numerous books include *The Suppression of the Slave Trade* (1896), *The Philadelphia Negro* (1899), *The Souls of Black Folk* (1903), *John Brown* (1909), *Quest of the Silver Fleece* (1911), *The Negro* (1915), *Darkwater* (1920), *The Gift of Black Folk* (1924), *Dark Princess* (1928), *Black Folk: Then and Now* (1939), *Dusk of Dawn* (1940), *Color and Democracy* (1945), *The World and Africa* (1947), *In Battle for Peace* (1952), and a trilogy, *Black Flame* (1957-1961).

It is this enormous literary output on such a wide variety of themes which offers the most convincing testimony to DuBois' lifetime position that it was vital for blacks to cultivate their own aesthetic and cultural values even as they made valuable strides toward social emancipation. In this he was opposed by Booker T. Washington, who felt that the black should concentrate on developing technical and mechanical skills before all else.

In 1961 at age 93, DuBois joined the Communist Party. He died two years later.

It was DuBois' affiliation with the Communist Party that prompted a spirited protest against the plan to erect a memorial in his hometown in 1969. Though DuBois was a lifelong radical, he functioned within the pale of society as an American during his most productive years.

## T. THOMAS FORTUNE
## 1856-1928

T. Thomas Fortune was one of the most prominent black journalists involved in the flourishing black press of the post-Civil War era.

Born in Florida, the son of a Reconstruction politician, Fortune was particularly productive before his thirtieth year, completing such important literature as *Black and White: Land, Labor and Politics in the South* and *The Negro in Politics* while in his twenties.

Fortune attended Howard University for two years, leaving to marry Miss Carrie Smiley of Jacksonville, Florida. The couple went to New York in 1878, with Fortune taking a job as a printer for the New York Sun. In time, Fortune caught the attention of Sun editor Charles A. Dana, who eventually promoted him to the editorial staff of the paper.

Fortune also edited *The Globe,* a black daily, and was later chief editorial writer and polemicist on the staff of *The Negro World*. In 1900 Fortune joined Booker T. Washington in helping to organize the successful National Negro Business League. His later activity with Washington gained him more notoriety than his earlier writing, although the latter is clearly more vital in affording him an important niche in the history of black protest.

In 1883 Fortune founded the *New York Age*, the paper with which he sought to "champion the cause" of his race. In time, the *Age* became the leading black journal of opinion in the United States. One of Fortune's early crusades was against the practice of separate schools for the races in the New York educational system.

Fortune was later responsible for coining the term "Afro-American" as a substitute for Negro in New York newspapers. He also set up the Afro-American Council, an organization which he regarded as the precursor of the Niagara Movement. In 1907 Fortune sold the *Age*, although he remained active in journalism as an editorial writer for several black newspapers.

At the time of his death in 1928, Fortune was writing for the *Negro World.*

## HENRY HIGHLAND GARNET
## 1815-1882

Like Frederick Douglass, Henry Highland Garnet achieved fame as an antislavery crusader and in his later years served his country in appointed office.

Garnet was born a slave in Maryland, escaped with his parents to Pennsylvania when he was nine, and graduated from Oneida Institute in 1840. His eloquent antislavery oratory soon gained him a following. In 1843 he made his famous speech at the Free Colored People Convention in Buffalo, in which he called for a general strike and armed rebellion. The speech was too rousing, even for Douglass, who recessed the meeting to let the assemblage cool down. But Garnet, a pastor as well as a political activist, continued to advocate violence to end slavery, if peaceful methods failed.

After the Civil War, Garnet was a pastor in Washington and New York, president of Avery College in Pittsburgh, and U.S. Minister to Liberia.

## MARCUS GARVEY
## 1887-1940

*Marcus Garvey was one of the pioneer advocates of Black Nationalism.*

Marcus Garvey was a West Indian by birth and a revolutionary by disposition. Garvey dedicated his life to what he called the "uplifting" of the black people of the world through the creation of the Universal Negro Improvement Association (UNIA) and the African Communities League. Like Malcolm X a generation later, he believed that blacks could never achieve equality unless they became independent—founding their own nations, governments, businesses, industrial enterprises, and military establishments—in short, those same institutions by which other peoples of the world had risen to power.

The youngest of 11 children, Garvey moved to Kingston at age 14, found work in a printshop, and became acquainted with the abysmal living conditions of the laboring class. He quickly involved himself in social reform, participating in the first Printers' Union strike on Jamaica and setting up a newspaper called *The Watchman*. Leaving the island to earn money to finance his projects, he visited Central and South America, amassing evidence that black people everywhere were victims of discrimination.

Back in Jamaica in 1911, he laid the groundwork of the Universal Negro Improvement Association, to which he was to devote his life. Undaunted by lack of enthusiasm for his plans, Garvey left for England in 1912 in search of additional financial backing. While there, he worked for an Egyptian scholar and learned much of the history of Africa—particularly with reference to the exploitation of black peoples by colonial powers.

In 1916, acquainted with the work of Booker T. Washington, he came to the United States, where he formulated what he called the "Back to Africa" program for the resettlement of the black in his ancestral homeland. In New York City particularly his ideas attracted popular support, and thousands enrolled in the UNIA. He began publishing the newspaper *The Negro World* and toured the United States preaching black nationalism to popular audiences. In a matter of months, he had founded over 30 UNIA branches and launched some ambitious business ventures, notably the Black Star Line, a black steamship company. On the negative side, he ran into trouble with the New York District Attorney's Office, which he had publicly criticized, and other enemies began to appear.

In 1920 the UNIA convened a 31-day international conclave in Madison Square Garden, where they presented a policy statement on the Back to Africa program and proclaimed a formal Declaration of Rights for blacks all over the world. Following this, Garvey set himself the task of negotiating for the repatriation of blacks to Liberia. Rumors that Garvey's real intention was to seize power in Liberia and build a personal empire there caused Liberia to withdraw all support from the venture, leaving Garvey stunned from the realization that he had actually been rebuffed by a black African nation.

With the Black Star Line in serious financial difficulties, Garvey promoted two new business organizations—the African Communities League and the Negro Factories Corporation. He also tried to salvage his colonization scheme by sending a delegation to appeal to the League of Nations for transfer to the UNIA of the African colonies taken from

Germany during World War I.

Financial betrayal by trusted aides and a host of legal entanglements (based on charges that he had used the U.S. mails to defraud prospective investors) eventually led to Garvey's imprisonment in Atlanta Federal Penitentiary for a five-year term. In 1927 his half-served sentence was commuted, and he was deported to Jamaica by order of President Calvin Coolidge.

Garvey then turned his energies to Jamaican politics, campaigning on a platform of self-government, minimum wage laws, and land and judicial reform. He was soundly defeated at the polls, however, because most of his followers did not have the necessary voting qualifications.

In 1935 Garvey left for England where, in near obscurity, he died five years later in a cottage in West Kensington.

Critics have labeled Garvey a pretentious mountebank, whereas his supporters call him a genius. From a historical viewpoint he must be regarded as a fanatic visionary, a man literally driven by the notion that the blacks' sole means for surviving in the twentieth century was through the foundation of a unified, separatist empire in Africa. Although his ideas were rejected by most people of his day, it is clear that, since then, these very ideas have strongly influenced the policies of black leaders all over the world.

In 1987, New York Congressman Charles Rangel introduced two bills to have Garvey exonerated of the 1924 mail fraud charges. Rangel's efforts came after Robert Hill, editor of a Garvey research project at the University of California at Los Angeles, discovered evidence which pointed to political motivations for Garvey's conviction.

## LESTER B. GRANGER
## 1896-1976

Lester Granger served as executive director of the National Urban League from 1941 to 1961. His vigorous leadership transformed the League into an effective instrument for integrating blacks into the war effort and was responsible for greatly increasing the size and strength of the organization.

Born in Newport News, Virginia, Granger graduated from Dartmouth College in 1917 and served in the 92nd Infantry Division in France during World War I. A social worker by professional training and disposition, he joined the New Jersey Urban League in 1919 and rose to the national directorship in 1941. During the ensuing world war, he worked tirelessly as a special assistant to the Secretary of the Navy, traveling more than 60,000 miles to talk with servicemen, defense contractors, and workers. Presenting him with the Medal of Merit for his work, President Truman said that Granger had contributed "more than any other person to the effective utilization of Negro personnel in the service."

Granger was responsible for a number of major innovations within the League, including the development of a Pilot Placement Project in which blacks were placed in significant jobs previously barred to them, and the establishment of a Commerce and Industry Council and Trade Union Advisory Council. During his tenure in office, the number of League affiliates grew from 41 to 65, and the budget increased from $600,000 to $4.5 million.

When he retired in 1961, Granger was praised by President Eisenhower as a "man of the highest character and integrity." From a historical vantage, it is clear that Granger's contributions both to the League and to the course of American life were profound.

## GEORGE EDMUND HAYNES
## 1875-1960

Dr. George E. Haynes, co-founder and first executive secretary of the Department of Race Relations of the Federal Council of Churches of Christ in America, was born in Pine Bluff, Arkansas. He received an A.B. from Fisk University and later became the first black to receive a doctorate from New York's Columbia University. While studying economics and social science in New York, Haynes developed a keen sensitivity to the urban problems of recently migrated southern blacks and in 1910, along with Ruth Baldwin and Frances Kellor, he launched the National Urban League. He served as executive director until resigning in 1918 to become a special assistant to the Secretary of Labor for three years. Beginning in 1921, he took on the executive secretaryship with the Federal Council of Churches, a post to which he devoted 26 years of service. Following World War II, he organized the Interracial Clinic, an agency dedicated to easing racial tensions.

## M. CARL HOLMAN
## President, National Urban Coalition
## 1919-1988

Often moving behind the scenes, M. Carl Holman was one of the leading strategists in the Civil Rights Movement. From 1971 to his death by cancer in 1988 at age 69, he headed the National Urban Coalition. Since 1971 he has headed the National Urban Coalition, which has come to be recognized as the only broad-based national organization in the country that focuses on the survival and success of the American city, its people, its institutions, its business and industry, and its economic and fiscal well-being.

Holman was born in Minter City, Mississippi, and grew up in St. Louis. He graduated magna cum laude from Lincoln and received masters degrees from Yale University (as a recipient of a Whitney Fellowship) and the University of Chicago. He began his professional career in 1949 as an English professor at Clark College in Atlanta, and also taught at Atlanta University and Hampton Institute.

When the Civil Rights Movement began to develop in the South in the 1950s, Holman emerged as one of its truly important, if unsung heroes, by serving as a wise and compassionate strategist for the student demonstrators who turned to him for guidance, and as a respected and trusted advisor to many civil rights leaders.

In 1962 he joined the U.S. Commission on Civil Rights as its deputy staff director and along with several other highly placed blacks was a member of what was considered the unofficial black cabinet of the Kennedy and Johnson administrations.

## JAMES WELDON JOHNSON
## 1871-1938

Like DuBois, black intellectual James Weldon Johnson played a vital role in the civil rights movement of the twentieth century—as poet, teacher, critic, diplomat, and NAACP official. Johnson is perhaps most often popularly remembered as the lyricist for *Lift Every Voice and Sing*, the poem which is often referred to as the black national anthem.

Born in 1871 in Jacksonville, Florida, Johnson was educated at Atlanta and Columbia universities. His career included service as a school principal, a lawyer, and a diplomat (U.S. Consul at Puerto Cabello, Venezuela and, later, in Nicaragua). From 1916 to 1930 he was a key policy maker of the NAACP, eventually serving as the organization's executive secretary.

In his early days, Johnson's fame rested largely on his lyrics for popular songs, but in 1917 he completed his first book of poetry, *Fifty Years and Other Poems*. Five years later, he followed this with *The Book of American Negro Poetry*, and in 1927 he established his literary reputation with *God's Trombones*, a collection of seven folk sermons in verse. Over the years, this work has been performed countless times, on stage and television.

In 1930 Johnson finished *St. Peter Relates an Incident of the Resurrection* and, three years later, his lengthy autobiography, *Along This Way*.

Johnson died in 1938 following an automobile accident in Maine.

## EUGENE KINCKLE JONES
## 1884-1951

Eugene K. Jones had a long career with the National Urban League, serving as its second executive director from 1918 to 1941, and held many important government posts. Born in Richmond, Virginia, he was educated at Virginia Union and Cornell University. In addition to helping structure the Urban League, he served as Negro Affairs advisor to the U.S. Department of Commerce from 1933 to 1943, chaired the Negro Advisory committees for the Texas Centennial Exposition of 1936 and the New York World's Fair of 1939, and joined the Fair Employment Board of the U.S. Civil Service Commission in 1948.

## MARTIN LUTHER KING JR.
## 1929-1968

Any number of historic moments in the civil rights struggle have been used to identify Martin Luther King Jr.—prime mover of the Montgomery bus boycott (1956), keynote speaker at the March on Washington (1963), youngest Nobel Peace Prize laureate (1964). But in retrospect, single events are less important than the fact that King, and his policy of nonviolent protest, was the dominant force in the civil rights movement during its decade of greatest achievement, from 1957 to 1968.

King was born Michael Luther King in Atlanta on January 15, 1929—one of the three children of Martin Luther King, Sr., pastor of Ebenezer Baptist Church, and Alberta (Williams) King, a former schoolteacher. (He did not receive the name of "Martin" until he was about six years of age.)

After attending grammar and high school locally, King enrolled in Morehouse College (also in Atlanta) in 1944. At this time he was not inclined to enter the ministry, but while there he came under the influence of Dr. Benjamin Mays, a scholar whose manner and bearing convinced him that a religious career could have its intellectual satisfactions as well. After receiving his B.A. in 1948, King attended Crozer Theological Seminary in Chester, Pennsylvania, winning the Plafker Award as the outstanding student of the graduating class, and the J. Lewis Crozer Fellowship as well. King completed the course work for his doctorate in 1953, and was granted the degree two years later upon completion of his dissertation.

Married by then, King returned South, accepting the pastorate of the Dexter Avenue Baptist Church in Montgomery, Alabama. It was here that he made his first mark on the civil rights movement, by mobilizing the black community during a 382-day boycott of the city's bus lines. Working through the Montgomery Improvement Association, King overcame arrest and other violent harassment, including the bombing of his home. Ultimately, the U.S. Supreme Court declared the Alabama laws requiring bus segregation unconstitutional, with the result that blacks were allowed to ride Montgomery buses on equal footing with whites.

A national hero and a civil rights figure of growing importance, King summoned together a number of black leaders in 1957 and laid the groundwork for the organization now known as the Southern Christian Leadership Conference (SCLC). Elected its president, he soon sought to assist other communities in the organization of protest campaigns against discrimination, and in voter-registration activities as well.

After completing his first book and making a trip to India, King returned to the United States in 1960 to become co-pastor, with his father, of Ebenezer Baptist Church.

Three years later, King's nonviolent tactics were put to their most severe test in Birmingham, Alabama during a mass protest for fair hiring practices, the establishment of a biracial committee, and the desegregation of department-store facilities. Police brutality used against the marchers dramatized the plight of blacks to the nation at large with enormous impact. King was arrested, but his voice was not silenced as he issued his classic "Letter from a Birmingham Jail" to refute his critics.

Later that year King was a principal speaker at the historic March on Washington (1963), where he delivered one of the most passionate addresses of his career. At the beginning of the next year *Time* magazine designated him as its Man of the Year for 1963. A few months later he was named recipient of the 1964 Nobel Peace Prize.

Upon his return from Oslo, where he had gone to accept the award, King entered a new battle, in Selma, Alabama, where he led a voter-registration campaign which culminated in the Selma-to-Montgomery Freedom March.

King next brought his crusade to Chicago where he launched a slum-rehabilitation and open-housing program.

In the North, however, King soon discovered that young

and angry blacks (such as the ones in Watts who once replied "Martin Luther Who?" to a question about whether the civil rights leader would approve of their behavior) cared little for his pulpit oratory and even less for his solemn pleas for peaceful protest.

Their disenchantment was clearly one of the factors influencing his decision to rally behind a new cause and stake out a fresh battleground: the war in Vietnam. King himself antagonized many civil rights leaders by declaring the United States to be "the greatest purveyor of violence in the world." His clear aim was to fuse a new coalition of dissent based on equal support for the peace crusade and the civil rights movement.

The rift was immediate. The NAACP saw King's shift of emphasis as "a serious tactical mistake"; the Urban League warned that the "limited resources" of the civil rights movement would be spread too thin; Bayard Rustin claimed black support of the peace movement would be negligible; Ralph Bunche felt King was undertaking an impossible mission in trying to bring the campaign for peace in step with the goals of the civil rights movement.

From the vantage point of history, King's timing could only be regarded as superb. In announcing his opposition to the war, and in characterizing it as a "tragic adventure" which was playing "havoc with the destiny of the entire world," King again forced the white middle class to concede that no movement could dramatically affect the course of government in the United States unless it involved deliberate and restrained aggressiveness, persistent dissent, and even militant confrontation. These were precisely the ingredients of the civil rights struggle in the South in the early 1960s.

Speaking at the U.N., King again found words to prod the conscience of white America:

*Let us save our national honor—stop the bombing.*

*Let us save American lives and Vietnamese lives—stop the bombing.*

*Let us take a single instantaneous step to the peace table—stop the bombing.*

*Let our voices ring out across the land to say the American people are not vain glorious conquerors—stop the bombing.*

As students, professors, intellectuals, clergymen and reformers of every stripe rushed into the movement (in a sense forcing fiery black militants like Stokely Carmichael and Floyd McKissick to surrender their control over antiwar polemics), King turned his attention to the domestic issue which, in his view, was directly related to the Vietnam struggle: the War on Poverty.

At one point, he called for a guaranteed family income, he threatened national boycotts, and spoke of disrupting entire cities by nonviolent "camp-ins." With this in mind, he began to draw up plans for a massive march of the poor on Washington, D.C. itself, envisioning a popular demonstration of unsurpassed intensity and magnitude designed to force Congress and the political parties to recognize and deal with the unseen and ignored masses of desperate and downtrodden

*Martin Luther King addresses thousands who gathered for the "March on Washington".*

Americans.

King's decision to interrupt these plans to lend his support to the Memphis sanitation men's strike was based in part on his desire to discourage violence, as well as to focus national attention on the plight of the poor, unorganized workers of the city. The men were bargaining for little else beyond basic union representation and long-overdue salary considerations.

Though he was unable to eliminate the violence which had resulted in the summoning and subsequent departure of the National Guard, King stayed on in Memphis and was in the process of planning for a march which he vowed to carry out in defiance of a federal court injunction if necessary.

On the night of April 3, 1968, he told a church congregation: "Well I don't know what will happen now... But it really doesn't matter... (At other times, musing over the possibility he might be killed, King had assured his colleagues that he had "the advantage over most people" because he had "conquered the fear of death.")

Death came for King on the balcony of the black-owned Lorraine Motel just off Beale Street on the evening of April

4. While standing outside with Jesse Jackson and Ralph Abernathy, a shot rang out. King fell over, struck in the neck by a rifle bullet which left him moribund. At 7:05 he was pronounced dead at St. Joseph's Hospital.

King's death caused a wave of violence in such major cities as Washington, D.C. (11 dead; 24 million dollars property damage, over 8,000 arrests, over 1,000 injuries); Chicago (nine dead, 11 million dollars property damage, nearly 3,000 arrests, 500 injured), and Baltimore (6 dead, 14 million dollars property damage, 5800 arrests, and 900 injured). Without restraint against looters, death tolls would have been even higher. Both grief and anger suffused the black community. The anger was assuredly all the more fanatic precisely because King had been so irretrievably dedicated to nonviolence.

King's birthday, January 15, is now recognized as a national holiday.

## MALCOLM X
## 1925-1965

Malcolm X was one of the most fiery and controversial blacks of the twentieth century.

Born Malcolm Little in Omaha on May 19, 1925, Malcolm was the son of a Baptist preacher who was an avid supporter of Marcus Garvey's United Negro Improvement Association. At an early age, Malcolm moved to Lansing, Michigan with his parents, both of whom were tragically lost to him in childhood. (His father was run over by a streetcar, and his mother was committed to a mental institution.)

Leaving school after the eighth grade, Malcolm made his way to New York, working for a time as a waiter at Smalls Paradise in Harlem. Soon part of the seamy underworld life of the ghetto, Malcolm began selling and using drugs, turned to burglary, and was sentenced to a 10-year prison term in 1946.

While in prison, he became acquainted with the Black Muslim sect headed by Elijah Muhammad and was quickly converted to it's utopian and racist point of view. Paroled from prison in 1952, he soon became an outspoken defender of Muslim doctrines, accepting the basic argument that evil was an inherent characteristic of the "white man's Christian world."

Unlike Muhammad, Malcolm sought publicity, making several provocative and inflammatory statements to predominantly white civic groups and college campus audiences. Branding white people "devils," he spoke bitterly of a philosophy of vengeance and "an eye for an eye." When, in 1963, he characterized the Kennedy assassination as a case of "chickens coming home to roost," he was suspended from the Black Muslim movement by Elijah Muhammad, and soon formed his own protest group, the Organization of Afro-American Unity.

The group had built only a small following at the time of Malcolm X's murder in 1965. He was buried as Al Hajj Malial-Shabazz, the name he had taken in 1964 after making his holy pilgrimage to Mecca.

Malcolm X had a profound influence on both blacks and whites. Many blacks responded to a feeling that he was a man of the people, experienced in the ways of the street rather than the pulpit or the college campus, which traditionally have provided the preponderance of black leaders. And many young whites responded to Malcolm's blunt, colorful language and unwillingness to retreat in the face of hostility. By the 1970s, it had become apparent that Malcolm X would be lionized, or even beatified, by those who sought as much to revere his memory as to promote their own distorted view of the true meaning of his ideology and striving. In practical terms, he was an advocate of self-help, self-defense, and education; as a philosopher and pedagogue, he succeeded in integrating history, religion, and mythology to establish a framework for his ultimate belief in world brotherhood and inhuman justice. Faith, in his view, was a prelude to action; ideas were feckless without policy. At least three books published since his death effectively present his most enduring thoughts. They are his own classic *Autobiography,* a collection of *Speeches*, given at Harvard, and *Malcolm X: The Man and His Times.*

## KELLY MILLER
## 1863-1939

A voice of reason and scholarship, Kelly Miller was one of the major black spokesmen and teachers of the early twentieth century. His thoughtful essays analyzed racial problems in terms of their global development, the potency and promise of the black race, and viable solutions. For Miller, who devoted his life to teaching, the surest release from the house of bondage was by the road of education.

Born in Winnsboro, South Carolina, during the Civil War, he worked his way through school, graduating from Howard University in 1886, studying postgraduate mathematics and physics at Johns Hopkins (1887-1889), and eventually earning from Howard his A.M. (1901) and LL.D. (1903) degrees. After a short stint teaching in the public schools of Washington, D.C., he joined Howard's faculty, where he was to remain for most of his academic career, serving variously as professor of mathematics, chairman of the department of sociology, dean of the junior college, and dean of the College of Arts and Sciences. In addition to his collegial responsibilities, he published many important essays, became the first black academician to write a regular column for the black press, and helped W. E.B. DuBois edit the journal *Crisis.*

In the face of prevailing pessimism about race relations, Miller emphasized the great capacity for progress the black race had shown in the 50 years since emancipation. Literacy had increased enormously, a managerial and professional class was crystallizing, property ownership had swelled, and the masses' need for self-expression and self-government had given birth to the unique socio-religious institution of the black church. Armed with the belief that no people in world history had made such great advances in so brief a span, and convinced of the inherently democratizing effect of American institutions, Miller proclaimed certainty that the black race would eventually assume its rightful position of equality in the United States. Unlike DuBois, who felt that color would always single blacks out for prejudicial treatment,

*Fiery Malcolm X rose from the underworld to become an outspoken Black Muslim apostle; he was assassinated after starting his own movement.*

Miller held that the evolution of similar behavior patterns would obviate the import of physical differences.

Miller's major publications were *Race Adjustment* (1903), *Out of the House of Bondage* (1917), *History of the World War and the Important Part Taken by the Negroes* (1919), and *The Everlasting Stain*(1924).

## BAYARD RUSTIN
## Executive Director, A. Philip Randolph Institute
## 1910-1987

Bayard Rustin could easily be identified with any number of civil rights organizations, pacifist groups, massive popular demonstrations, etc., but it is through his 30-year association with A. Philip Randolph, and his present directorship of the A. Philip Randolph Institute that he is able to give shape to his most abiding and progressive ideas on civil rights, labor management and economic planning.

As executive director of the Institute since its inception in 1964, Rustin has worked unstintingly to develop and promote sound radical programs designed to cure the economic and social ills of the country. Though he does not totally discount the value of federally sponsored poverty programs and other schemes for ensuring every American family a guaranteed annual income, he feels, nonetheless, that real progress can occur only in the wake of a government decision to mobilize all employable persons and assign to them the basic task of improving their environment: rebuilding ghetto neighborhoods, ghetto schools, and ghetto hospitals at public expense.

Tax money allocated for this objective would not only provide decent income for the unemployed but would generate real growth in a sector of the nation which traditionally cannot produce the taxes needed to finance its progress, and so becomes dependent on regular public assistance. In Rustin's view, it is the nation's incredible distortion of public priorities that has led to the blood baths of the inner city, the wholesale carnage, destruction, and looting, the ascendancy of the riot mentality, and the burning tempers of disillusioned and explosive youth. Poverty money can only relieve such conditions for a time; it cannot, by definition, assuage the anger because it does not reach the heart of the problem.

Rustin defines the problem as the onslaught of a technology that fails to take into account basic human needs, that displaces unskilled and semiskilled laborers without concern for their welfare or economic adaptability, thus indirectly causing social fragmentation, urban decay, family disintegration, and loss of hope. The solution he advocates calls for the orderly seizure of political power by responsible groups able to agree on the defects and to map strategy for their elimination. The groups which, in his view, engineered such impressive movements as the March on Washington, the passage of the 1964 Civil Rights Act, and the Johnson

*Bayard Rustin designed radical socioeconomic programs enlisting government support.*

landslide, must increase their power base, stimulate greater support for their ideology of social reconstruction, and force government to respond tote needs of predominantly urban constituencies. The four identifiable groups present in Rustin's sturdy coalition are: the black community, white liberals, religious parties, and labor unions.

Rustin, in other words, advocates the growth and strengthening of those organizations and agencies identified with the non-Communist political left. He feels black separatism and guerrilla warfare rhetoric are not only suicidal but also criminally destructive and self-defeating. Inevitably, he argues, they play into the hands of reactionary groups able to capitalize on internecine squabbling and disruptive fragmentation.

Rustin's philosophy has not been conceived in Olympian aloofness. More than just a theoretician, he has been arrested 23 times in the cause of peace and civil rights, and has demonstrated time and again his willingness to take to the streets in defense of his beliefs and in promotion of his ideology.

Born in West Chester, Pennsylvania in March 1910, Rustin was raised by his grandparents, though he was particularly influenced by his grandmother, a devout Quaker. At school, he was an honor student and star athlete, experiencing his first real anger at discrimination when he was refused restaurant service in Pennsylvania while on tour with the football team.

After graduation, he studied literature and history at Cheyney State and Wilberforce Colleges, but his most serious interests already lay in politics. In 1936 Rustin joined the Young Communist League, becoming an organizer two years later. Rustin earned an irregular livelihood in New York singing at the old Cafe Society with such notables as Josh White and Leadbelly.

Rustin left the Party in 1941, joining the Fellowship of Reconciliation, a nonviolent antiwar group. That same year, he became a youth organizer for A. Philip Randolph's projected March on Washington to demand better job opportunities for blacks in the defense industry. During World War II, Rustin was imprisoned as a conscientious objector, serving some 2 1/2 years behind bars. Released in 1945, he immediately joined the Indian independence movement and was again jailed for demonstrating before the British Embassy.

In 1947 Rustin participated in a historic "journey of reconciliation," an event now popularly known as a Freedom Ride. The experience brought with it another jail term, but enabled Rustin to expose chain gang abuses in North Carolina which were subsequently abolished. By this time Rustin was not only identified with the Congress of Racial Equality (CORE), the organization which had pioneered in the Freedom Ride movement, but also with A. Philip Randolph's Committee Against Discrimination in the Armed Forces.

Until 1955 Rustin was preoccupied with various peace conventions, efforts to restrict nuclear armaments, and movements toward African independence. That year, he joined Martin Luther King's Southern Christian Leadership Conference (SCLC), again in an organizational capacity as King's Special Assistant. In 1963 he was named chief logistics expert and organizational coordinator of the March on Washington.

In the late 1960s Rustin was increasingly hard pressed to maintain support for the nonviolent philosophy to which he had dedicated his life. His charismatic appeal, relentless logic, and debating effectiveness carried him through crisis after crisis, however. Nonviolence, he argued, was not outdated; it was a necessary and inexorable plan called for by the black's condition in the United States. Guerrilla warfare and armed insurrection, Rustin explained, required friendly border sanctuaries, a steady source of arms and equipment, and the support of the majority of a country's inhabitants.

Still, Rustin was equally appalled by the ignorance and shallowness of government groups who failed to respond to the legitimate appeals of young blacks for better education, increased job opportunity, improved housing, and general medical care. When blacks went on a rampage in Watts in 1965, Rustin, as he had previously in Harlem in 1964, braved jeers and insults in a desperate attempt to explain the hopelessness of violence and to restore order, but he was hooted down by angry militants and the uncontrollable mob.

In response to the difficulty, Rustin set his sights on the enunciation of a broad platform of economic proposals geared primarily to advance the poor and the underprivileged of all races. The general solution involved the acquisition of political power by such groups and a rapid refashioning of the nation's economic priorities.

By taking over the Randolph Institute, Rustin came too occupy a post where his considerable intellectual abilities and rare organizational talents could be combined to create a clearinghouse of information on the viable alternatives to senseless violence and Communist demagoguery.

In 1972 Rustin, writing in *Newsweek* magazine, reasserted his belief in coalition rather than racial solutions to the problems faced by blacks.

*"Black power,"* he wrote *"was born in bitterness and frustration—has left us with a legacy of polarization, division and political nonsense.—Black power was (always)—likely to produce basically conservative answers—The challenge we face is to rebuild abroad-based coalition which embraces intellectuals, organized labor, young people, minorities and liberals.*

Years later, in 1981, when he was 70 and still heading the A. Philip Randolph Institute, Rustin clung to his beliefs.

*I do not think it is practical to separate the problems of black poverty from poverty as such. It makes it look as if we're asking for special privileges unless we do it within the context of asking for the elimination of poverty for all.*

And he added:

*The economic impact of the Reagan Administration is not directed toward blacks. We mustn't fear that. It is directed toward a class of people—the have nots. Today, what you must ask for is education, jobs, hospital care for an entire class of people. So new leadership that will emerge cannot just be a replacement for King, Jordan, Whitney Young and the others.*

Rustin continued to be active in the Civil Rights Movement as its leading and most respected theoretician until his death in August 1987 at the age of 77.

## WILLIAM MONROE TROTTER
## 1872-1934

Many Civil Rights leaders of the past 100 years, men such as DuBois, Johnson, Wilkins, and Fortune, have been writers. William Monroe Trotter was perhaps the most militant of them. An honor student and Phi Beta Kappa at Harvard, Trotter founded the Guardian, a militant newspaper, in 1901, for the purpose of "propaganda against discrimination."

In 1905 Trotter joined DuBois in founding the Niagara Movement but refused to move with him into the NAACP because he felt it would be too moderate. Instead, Trotter formed the National Equal Rights League. In 1919 Trotter appeared at the Paris Peace Conference in an unsuccessful effort to have it outlaw racial discrimination. The State Department had denied him a passport to attend, but he had reached Paris nonetheless, by having himself hired as a cook on a ship.

Because of his strident unwillingness to work with established groups, the Civil Rights Movement has been slow to recognize Trotter. But many of his methods were to be adopted in the 1950s, notably his use of nonviolent protest. In 1903 Trotter deliberately disrupted a meeting in Boston at which Booker T. Washington was preaching support of segregation; Trotter's purpose was to be arrested to gain publicity for his militant position. Trotter also led demonstrations against plays and films which glorified the Ku Klux Klan.

## SOJOURNER TRUTH
## 1797-1883

*Sojourner Truth, born Isabella Baumfree, a gifted orator who traveled across the nation to speak against the evils of her time.*

Isabella Baumfree—popularly known as Sojourner Truth—became famous in her lifetime as a preacher, abolitionist, and lecturer. Born, it is believed, in 1797 in Ulster County, New York, she is known to have been freed from slavery by the New York State Emancipation Act of 1827, and to have lived for a time in New York City.

Soon disillusioned with life there, she adopted the name Sojourner Truth (a name she felt God had given her) and assumed as her "mission" in life the task of traveling across the country and spreading" the truth." It was not long before this self-styled prophetess had become famous as an itinerant preacher. Wherever she appeared, huge crowds would gather to hear her, for she was reputed to have not only "mystical gifts" but great powers of oratory as well.

Since black women were early and active participants in the antislavery movement, it was not surprising that, before long, Sojourner Truth was addressing countless meetings in the abolitionist cause. She soon became friendly with such leading white abolitionists as James and Lucretia Mott and Harriet Beecher Stowe.

With the outbreak of hostilities, she raised money to buy gifts for the soldiers, and went into the army camps to distribute them herself. She also aided blacks who had managed to escape North, helping them to find work and places to live.

After the war, Sojourner Truth continued traveling on behalf of her people, campaigning in particular for better educational opportunities. Her Narrative, published in 1875, recounts her war experiences, as well as a meeting with Abraham Lincoln.

Age and ill health finally forced her to give up traveling and then even the less demanding schedule of lectures at her Battle Creek sanatorium.

She died in Michigan on November 26, 1883.

*Harriet Tubman (left with pan) was the Underground Railroad's best known conductor.*

## HARRIET ROSS TUBMAN
## 1820-1913

The greatest "conductor" on the Underground Railroad—an organized network of way stations which helped black slaves escape from the South to the free states and as far north as Canada—was a former slave and a woman, Harriet Ross Tubman.

Believed to have been born about 1820 in Dorchester County, Maryland, Tubman had a childhood similar to that of most slave children—no schooling, little play, much hard work, and often severe punishment. In 1848 she succeeded in escaping from this life, leaving her husband John Tubman, who threatened to report her to their master.

Once free, she began to devise practical ways to help other slaves escape. Over the next 10 years, she made some 20 trips from the North to the South, rescuing more than 300 slaves. A price of $40,000 was set on her head.

Harriet Tubman's reputation spread rapidly. She won the admiration of leading white abolitionists, some of whom sheltered her "passengers."

One of her major disappointments was the ultimate failure of John Brown's raid on Harpers Ferry. She had met and aided Brown in recruiting soldiers for his cause (in fact, he called her "General Tubman"), and she was always to regard him, rather than Lincoln, as the true emancipator of her people.

In 1860 Harriet Tubman began to canvass the nation, appearing at antislavery meetings and speaking on behalf of women's rights. Shortly before the outbreak of the Civil War, she was forced for a time to leave for Canada, but she soon returned to the United States, serving the Union cause openly and actively as nurse, soldier, spy, and scout. She was particularly valuable in this latter capacity, since her work on the Railroad had made her thoroughly familiar with much of the terrain.

Two years after the end of the war, John Tubman died, and in 1869 Harriet Tubman married Nelson Davis, a war veteran. A year earlier, her biography had been written by Sarah Bradford, and the proceeds from the sales of the book were given to her to help ease her financial burden.

Despite her many honors and tributes (including a medal from Queen Victoria of England), Harriet Tubman spent her last years in poverty. She did not receive a pension until more than 30 years after the close of the Civil War. Awarded $20 a month for the remainder of her life, she used most of this money to help found a place for the aged and needy—later to be called The Harriet Tubman Home.

She died in Auburn in March 1913.

## DAVID WALKER
## 1785-1830

David Walker is something of a mystery, both as a literary figure and as a man. His fame rests exclusively on a small but explosive pamphlet which circulated clandestinely through the antebellum South and "rumored" slave uprisings as the only possible solution to the black problem. The full title of Walker's work is Walker's *Appeal in Four Articles Together With A Preamble to the Colored Citizens of the World, But in Particular and Very Expressly to Those of the United States* (1829).

Born of a free mother and a slave father, Walker left his native North Carolina while in his teens, and settled in Boston, where he earned a living as a dealer in old clothes. After his Appeal was published, his life was threatened, but he refused to flee to Canada and seek anonymity. Instead, he vowed to fight on. He died shortly thereafter, in circumstances which led many abolitionists to believe that he had been murdered. The blacks of Boston believed him a true martyr to their cause.

## BOOKER TALIAFERRO WASHINGTON
## 1856-1915

Educator and statesman Booker T. Washington was Frederick Douglass' successor as the black leader of his day. Unlike Douglass, Washington was never to hold federal office, but he managed, nonetheless, to exert considerable influence on several areas of public affairs.

Washington was born a slave in Hale's Ford, Virginia, reportedly in April 1856. He entered Hampton Institute in 1872 and graduated four years later. After teaching a while, he continued his studies at Wayland Seminary in Washington, D.C. Washington founded Tuskegee Institute in 1881, at the same time becoming its first president. Later, in addition to instituting a variety of programs for rural extension work, he helped establish the National Negro Business League.

In sharp contrast to Douglass, Washington was intent on setting forth a conciliatory policy with respect to civil rights. Already in 1884 he emphasized that the best cause to pursue in regard to civil rights in the South is to let it alone... and it will settle itself.

Some 11 years later, in his famous speech at the opening of the Cotton States Exposition, he expounded moderate views that were to turn black intellectuals against him. It was feared that his stand would encourage the foes of equal rights.

Washington's theme was that blacks would best protect their constitutional rights through their own economic and moral advancement; hence his major task was to win over diverse elements among southern whites, without whose support the program he envisaged would have been impossible.

At the time of his death in 1915, Washington's philosophy had been largely discredited by more militant black groups working toward the achievement of their aims through activist agencies. In the South, however, Washington still managed to play a major role in motivating blacks to improve their lot through self-help programs and the development of skilled labor.

In 1896, shortly after the election of President William McKinley, a movement was set in motion urging that Washington be named to a cabinet post, but Washington withdrew himself from consideration, preferring to work outside the political arena.

## WALTER WHITE
## 1893-1955

Walter White, who could have passed for white, chose instead to identify with his black ancestry, and ultimately came to be the most ardent protagonist in the fight to stamp out lynching in America, particularly after World War I. His most famous work was *Rope and Faggot:A Biography of Judge Lynch* (1929).

Born in Atlanta and educated in that Georgia city as well as in New York, White worked as secretary of the National Association for the Advancement of Colored People (NAACP). He completed his important study after two years as a Guggenheim Fellow. This work stood alongside two earlier novels, *Fire in the Flint* (1924) and *Flight* (1926). White's other work appeared in the leading periodicals of the day, including *Harper's, The Nation,* and *New Republic. White* was awarded a Spingarn Medal in 1937 in recognition of his tireless efforts on behalf of all black Americans.

## ROY WILKINS
## 1910-1981

On September 8, 1981, Roy Wilkins, who had served as Executive Secretary of the NAACP for 22 years, died quietly in New York City at the age of 80. He had retired from the NAACP in 1977 and since then had been in declining health. His death removed from the scene the last of the towering leaders who had played major roles in the Civil Rights Movement of the fifties and sixties—Martin Luther King, Whitney Young, Malcolm X, A. Philip Randolph.

Of his passing, *Newsweek* magazine said:

*He was among the last of a generation of civil rights leaders who pulled and tugged and cajoled the nation through decades of change so profound that many Americans cannot imagine, still less remember, what segregation was like.*

Once asked to describe what he did for a living, Wilkins said, "I work for Negroes." He could never bring himself to use the word "black, "and this, along with his thoughtful, deliberate pace, made him seem out of date to younger blacks. In fact, there were rumblings within the NAACP, even before he retired, that he should step down, but he remained in his position until it became physically impossible for him to continue.

A courtly and gracious man, he was sustained by a determined optimism and a steady faith that "there are more people who want to do good than do evil."

When asked to describe his greatest satisfaction in life, he pointed to the *Brown* decision of 1954 that ended segregation

*One of the great leaders of the Civil Rights Movement, the quiet, gentle, but most effective Roy Wilkins.*

in the public schools and heralded the end of legalized segregation in the country.

Born in St. Louis on August 30, 1901, Wilkins was reared in the home of an aunt and uncle living in St. Paul, Minnesota. Though poor, he was able to attend integrated schools in the city, and he grew up in what might be termed a racially mixed community.

Wilkins majored in sociology and minored in journalism while attending the University of Minnesota, supporting himself by doing a variety of odd jobs. He also served as night editor of the *Minnesota Daily* (the school paper) and edited a black weekly, the St. Paul *Appeal*. After receiving his B.A. in 1923, he joined the staff of the Kansas City *Call,* a leading black weekly. While in Missouri, Wilkins gained his first insight into segregation as an entrenched system, and resolved to broaden his activities in the NAACP, an organization which he had first joined while in college.

In 1931 Wilkins left the *Call* to serve under Walter White as assistant executive secretary of the NAACP. A year later, he substantiated charges of discrimination on a federally financed flood control project in Mississippi and played an instrumental role in getting Congress to take action to curb its practice there.

In 1934 he joined a picket march in Washington, D.C., protesting the failure of the Attorney General to include lynching on the agenda of a national conference on crime. For his pains, he suffered the first arrest of his career. Beginning in this same year, Wilkins put his editorial talent to work for the NAACP, succeeding W. E. B. DuBois as editor of *Crisis* magazine. (He held this post for some 15 years.) In 1945, after having served as an advisor in the War Department, he acted as a consultant to the American delegation at the United Nations conference in San Francisco.

Wilkins was named acting executive secretary of the NAACP in 1949, the year Walter White took a year's leave of absence from the organization. At the same time, he functioned as chairman of the National Emergency Civil Rights Mobilization, a pressure group which sent numerous lobbyists to Washington, D.C. to campaign for civil rights and fair employment legislation.

Wilkins assumed his position as executive secretary of the NAACP in 1955, upon the death of Walter White. He quickly established himself as one of the most articulate spokesmen in the civil rights movement. He testified before innumerable Congressional hearings, conferred with all the Presidents, and wrote extensively for all manner of publications. His training as a journalist stood him in good stead, for he never used a ghost writer.

Although Wilkins and the NAACP became more militant in the 1970s, both he and his organization were, nevertheless, subjected to attack by more radical groups, such as the Black Muslims. However, he never wavered in his determination to use all constitutional means at his disposal to help blacks achieve the rights of full citizenship within the democratic framework of American society.

For a number of years, Wilkins was the chairman of the Leadership Conference on Civil Rights, a group composed of over 100 national civic, labor, fraternal, and religious organizations. He was a trustee of the Eleanor Roosevelt Foundation, the Kennedy Memorial Library Foundation, and the Estes Kefauver Memorial Foundation. He was also a member of the Board of Directors of the Riverdale Children's Association, the John LaFarge Institute, and the Stockbridge School, as well as Peace with Freedom, an international organization working toward the goals described in its name.

Among the numerous awards conferred on Wilkins were the Anti-Defamation League's American Democratic Legacy Award, the Alpha Phi Alpha Fraternity's Medal of Honor, the Omega Phi Psi fraternity's Outstanding Citizen Award, the American Jewish Congress' Civil Rights Award, and the Boy Scout's Scout of the Year Award. He received the Outstanding Alumni Achievement Award of the University of Minnesota, and awards from the Japanese-American Citizens' League, the Unitarian Fellowship for Social Justice, B'nai B'rith Lodges, the Jewish War Veterans, the Postal Alliance, the National Medical Association, and the Eastern Star Lodge. He also holds the Russwurm Award of the National Newspaper Publishers Association. In 1964 the NAACP honored him with its own Spingarn Medal.

In 1972, Jesse Jackson, director of Operation PUSH, joined other militants who are increasingly praising Wilkins. Jackson told the NAACP convention that blacks need both the vitality of the Panthers and the wisdom of Wilkins.

Toward the end of his life there was a reevaluation of Wilkins by younger blacks. Recognition was given to the many positive things the NAACP had accomplished for blacks under his leadership and there was a growing understanding of how important he had been to Black America.

In a final tribute, President Reagan ordered American flags flown at half staff on all government buildings and at all installations.

## WHITNEY M. YOUNG, JR.
## 1922-1971

Whitney M. Young Jr., executive director of the Urban League from 1961 to 1971, was born in Lincoln Ridge, Kentucky, and received his B.S. degree at Kentucky State College in 1941. He later did graduate work at Massachusetts Institute of Technology and earned an M.A. in social work from the University of Minnesota in 1947.

From 1954 to 1961 Young served as dean of the Atlanta University School of Social Work. During the academic year 1960-1961 he was a visiting scholar at Harvard University under a Rockefeller Foundation grant.

A prominent lecturer and author of several articles which appeared in professional journals, Young completed his first full-length book, *To Be Equal,* in 1964. A second, *Beyond Racism,* was published in 1969.

Young was president of the National Association of Social Workers and the National Conference on Social Welfare. He served on the boards and advisory committees of the Rockefeller Foundation, Urban Coalition, and Urban Institute, and on seven Presidential Commissions of the Kennedy and Johnson administrations.

In 1969 Young was one of the 20 Americans selected by President Johnson to receive the Medal of Freedom, the nation's highest civilian award.

Young's many friendships with business and political leaders of the United States stirred much controversy within the black community. Though these relationships were important to the achievement of the Urban League's objectives of jobs for blacks, the epithet "Uncle Tom" was frequently hurled at him. Young, however, was far from an Uncle Tom. He spoke out forcefully, right up to his untimely death, against the slow pace with which businesses and government agencies were fulfilling their promises to blacks. But to Young, the important point was to maintain communication with America's centers of financial and political power, no matter how tense race relations might become in the nation's streets and schools.

Young died while visiting Africa in 1971.

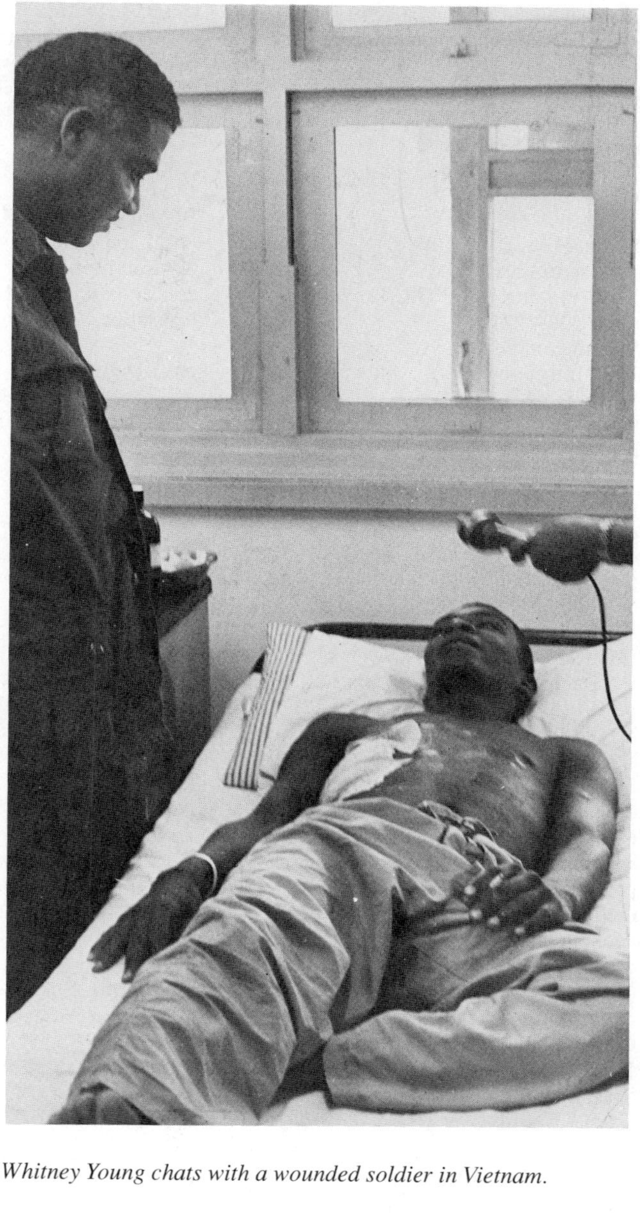

*Whitney Young chats with a wounded soldier in Vietnam.*

## NATIONAL PRIVATE ORGANIZATIONS WITH CIVIL RIGHTS PROGRAMS

**Alpha Kappa Alpha**
5211 South Greenwood Avenue
Chicago, IL 60615
(312) MU 4-1282
National black sorority. Voter education program and voter registration campaigns, providing transportation and baby sitting services.

**Alpha Phi Alpha**
4432 South King Drive
Chicago, IL 60653
(312) DR3-1819
National Negro fraternity. Program includes political action and education and sponsorship of an annual citizenship week to encourage voter registration.

**American Civil Liberties Union**
156 Fifth Avenue
New York, NY 10010
(212) 675-5990) or
Press Relations
(212) 989-7702
Southern Regional Office:
5 Forsyth Street
N. W. Atlanta, GA 30303
(404) 523-2721
Washington Office:
1424 16th Street, N. W. Suite 501
Washington, DC 20036
(202) 483-9832
National legal assistance group. Concerned with abuses of civil liberties, administration of justice, and local and national problems.

**AFL-CIO**
Department of Civil Rights
815 16th Street, N. W.
Washington, DC 20006
(212) 293-5270
Department of Civil Rights is staff arm to AFL-CIO Committee of Civil Rights. It helps to implement AFL-CIO policies on equal opportunity, handles complaints involving any form of union discrimination, prepares materials concerning civil rights issues and programs, aids affiliates in the development of affirmative programs and policies, and serves as official liaison with civil rights organizations and government agencies working in the field of equal opportunity.

**American Federation of Teachers, AFL-CIO**
1012 14th Street, N. W. 6th Floor
Washington, DC 20005
(202) 737-6141
Organization to improve status of teachers and public education in United States. Civil rights programs include Freedom Schools in Mississippi and various conferences on Negro history, especially pertaining to textbooks in elementary and secondary schools.

**American Veterans Committee (AVC) Inc.**
1333 Connecticut Avenue, N. W.
Washington, DC 20036
(202) 293-4890
National veterans organization with strong civil rights program. Has served as watchdog on integration of Regular Armed Forces, Reserves, and National Guard. Veterans claims activities focus on discriminatory situations. Has been member of Leadership Conference on Civil Rights, assisted in planning 1963 March on Washington, and lobbied for civil rights and voting legislation.

**Americans for Democratic Action**
1424 16th Street, N. W.
Washington, DC 20036
(202) 265-5771
National political action organization concerned with local and national civil rights legislation, education, and poverty programs.

**Anti-Defamation League of B'nai B'rith**
315 Lexington Avenue
New York, NY 10016
(212) MU-97400
National human relations organization. Develops extensive resource materials for community education programs (including audiovisual), and research on intergroup relations. Educational and human relations arm of B'nai B'rith.

**Board of Christian Social Concerns of the United Methodist Church**
Division of Human Relations
100 Maryland Avenue, N. E.
Washington, DC 20002
(202) 546-1000
Conducts programs of research, education, and action centering around the following Christian social concerns: race relations, civil liberties, public policy on education, church and state relations, civic responsibility, labor-management relations.

**Board of Social Ministry Lutheran Church in America**
Justice and Social Change—Urban Crisis
231 Madison Avenue
New York, NY 10016
(212) LE 2-3410
Designed to help people understand the nature of prejudice, see their own share in bringing about and perpetuating conditions of deprivation and injustice for minority groups, and take effective action.

**Brotherhood-in-Action, Inc.**
560 Seventh Avenue
New York, NY 10018
(212) LW4-0350
To foster intergroup progress and understanding, offering programs, services, and facilities to qualified intergroup relations agencies for conferences and training programs.

**California Rural Legal Assistance**
1212 Market Street
San Francisco, CA 94102
(415) 863-4911
Established in 1966, California Rural Legal Assistance gives legal aid to the poor without fee in civil cases in rural California. It is nonprofit organization funded by the Office of Economic Opportunity.

**Chamber of Commerce of the U.S. Human Resources Development Group**
1615 H Street, N. W.
Washington, DC 20006
(202) 659-6100
Serves as educational arm to U.S. Chamber of Commerce. Concerned with civil rights policies affecting employment and other aspects of management-employee relations.

**Church Women United**
475 Riverside Drive
New York, NY 10027
(212) 870-2353
Civil Rights program called "Assignment Race." Councils sponsor direct action programs to end discrimination in housing, education, and employment.

**Citizens' Advocate Center**
1211 Connecticut Avenue, N. W. Suite 304
Washington, DC 20036
(202) 293-1515
The Citizens' Advocate Center functions as a privately funded ombudsman to receive complaints and to monitor the administration of Federal programs.

**Congress of Racial Equality(CORE)**
200 West 135th Street
New York, NY 10030
(212) 281-9650
New Orleans Office:
2209 Dryad Street
New Orleans, LA 70113
(504) 523-7625
National human relations, direct action

group. Initiates nonviolent direct action to end discrimination in education, housing, employment, and public accommodations. Program being extended into social, economic, and political fields.

**Leadership Conference on Civil Rights**
2027 Massachusetts Avenue NW
Washington, D.C. 20036
(202) 667-1780
The NAACP Legal Defense And Education Fund, Inc.
10 Columbus Circle
New York, New York 10019
(212) 586-8397

**National Newspaper Publishers Association**
2400 S. Michigan Avenue
Chicago, IL 60616
National professional society. Membership comprised of publishers of Negro newspapers. Initiates action programs, disseminates information, supports other phases of civil rights movement.

**National Office for the Rights of the Indigent(NORI)**
10 Columbus Circle Suite 2030
New York, NY 10019
(212) JU6-8397
Established in 1966 by Ford Foundation grant under sponsorship of NAACP Legal Defense and Educational Fund, Inc., to plan and coordinate significant legal actions affecting rights of the poor. Principal task is making precedents in courts dealing with poverty law.

**National Afro-American Labor Council**
13 Astor Place
New York, NY 10003
(212) 673-5120
National association of Negro trade union members working to eliminate discrimination in employment and in unions. Committed to militant trade union movement. Works in cooperation with official labor bodies.

**Omega Psi Phi Fraternity**
2714 Georgia Avenue, N.W.
Washington, DC 20001
(202) 667-7158
National Negro fraternity. Social action committee develops civil rights programs involving employment, housing, public accommodations, and political action.

**National Sharecroppers Fund, Inc.**
112 East 19th Street
New York, NY 10003
(212) GR3-0284
Created to aid in the solution of the problems of the needy southern United States agricultural population by financing and otherwise fostering constructive efforts to improve their conditions of life.

**National Urban League**
500 East 62nd Street
New York, NY 10021
(212) 644-6500

*Washington Bureau:*
425 13th Street, N.W. Suite 515
Washington, DC 20004
(202) 393-4332

*Region I:*
Eastern Regional Office
420 Madison Avenue
New York, NY 10017
(212) 751-0300

*Region II:*
Mideastern Regional Office
1316 First National Tower
106 South Main Street
Akron, OH 44308(
216) 726-6233

*Region III:*
Midwestern Regional Office
7212 Olive Street Suite 1012
St. Louis, MO 63101
(314) 421-6393

*Region IV:*
Southern Regional Office
136 Marietta Street, N. W.
Atlanta, GA 30303
(404) MU8-8778

*Region V:*
Western Regional Office
955 South Western Avenue
Los Angeles, CA 90006
(213) 731-8261

**Field Services Department**
1424-16th Street, N.W.
Washington, DC 20036
A professional community service organization committed to securing equal opportunities for Negroes and other minorities in all areas of American life. It is nonpartisan and interracial in its leadership and staff. Not largely a membership organization. Community Chest funds support many local affiliates.

**Opportunities Industrialization Center Institute, Inc.**
100 West Coulter Street
Philadelphia, PA 19144
(215) 849-3010
The national and three regional directors operate out of the Philadelphia headquarters. Western Region office is at 100 McAllister Street, San Francisco, CA. The local OIC programs are designed to motivate, train, develop, and utilize the technical skills of members of our communities, regardless of race, creed, color, or sex, in manufacturing and industrialization.

**A. Philip Randolph Institute**
260 Park Avenue South
New York, NY 10010
(212) 533-8000
Group formed to raise economic issues that underlie the civil rights movement. Services all existing civil rights groups by preparing educational materials—pamphlets, testimony, conference programs.

**Scholarship, Education and Defense Fund for Racial Equality, Inc.**
164 Madison Avenue
New York, NY 10016
(212) 532-8216
Formed to develop leadership programs and community organization techniques, handle legal problems, engage in voter registration, and provide scholarship assistance to students who have demonstrated leadership in civil rights activities.

**Southern Christian Leadership Conference (SCLC)**
334 Auburn Avenue, N.E.
Atlanta, GA 30303
(404) 522-1420
National civil rights group organized around affiliate organizations that operate out of Negro churches. Program includes nonviolent direct action, voter registration, citizenship schools, and selective buying campaign. Founded by the late Dr. Martin Luther King Jr.

**Southern Conference Educational Fund, Inc.**
3210 West Broadway
Louisville, KY 40211
(502) 778-3348
Group works with community groups and other civil rights organizations. Gives staff and financial assistance on education, social welfare, voter registration, and community organizing.

**Southern Regional Council**
5 Forsyth Street, N. W.
Atlanta, GA 30303
(404) 522-8764
Regional development program with emphasis on race relations. One hundred persons from throughout the South are the members. No general membership. Cooperates closely with Councils on Human Relations in the 11 Southeastern states.

**United Automobile Workers Fair Practices Department**
8000 East Jefferson Street
Detroit, MI 48214
(313) 926-5000
Acting as the civil rights department of the UAW, it serves its membership in all civil rights matters. It is the contact agent between

UAW, other international unions, and private organizations.

**United Church Board for Homeland Ministries**
Amistad Research Center and Race Relations Department
Fisk University Nashville, TN 37203
To promote better human relations through research and education. Collecting source materials for study of Negro life and history.

**United Farm Workers Organizing Committee, AFL-CIO**
P.O. Box 130
Delano, CA 93215
(805) 725-1314
*Washington:*
*United Farm Workers Organizing Committee Boycott, Washington, DC*
7332 Piney Branch Road
Tacoma Park, MD 20012
(202) 587-0510
Organization to represent farm laborers for collective bargaining purposes. Civil rights, poverty, and clearinghouse programs handled through Delano office.

**United States Catholic Conference Department of Social Development**
1312 Massachusetts Avenue, N. W.
Washington, DC 20005
(202) 659-6600
Action and public affairs agency of Catholic Church in United States. Divisions of Urban Life, Rural Life, Family Life. Task force on urban problems is information and coordinating agency for race-and poverty-related programs conducted in 156 dioceses in United States.

**United States Jaycees Program for Human Resource Development Box 7**
Tulsa, OK 74102
(918) 584-2481
Programs are aimed at helping the disadvantaged of all races and creeds help themselves. The program concentrates on employment, education, recreation, government awareness, personal development, environmental improvement, and housing.

**The Urban Coalition**
2100 M Street, N. W.
Washington, DC 20037
(202) 293-1530
Seeks to alleviate the crisis in the nation's urban centers through all-out attack on the unemployment problem. The Coalition works with businessmen to promote programs for the recruitment, training, and employment of the hard-core unemployed. Assists local communities in organizing coalitions to solve local problems.

**Western Center on Law and Poverty**
1709 West 8th Street
Los Angeles, CA 90017
(213) 483-1491
Legal services resource for the war on poverty in Southern California. It engages in test cases and appellate litigation and seeks toad neighborhood law offices for the poor and to help improve their effectiveness.

**Women's International League for Peace and Freedom**
1738 Pine Street
Philadelphia, PA. 19103
(215) 546-6082
Has human rights division with active committees on civil rights and civil liberties. Members of local branches carry on variety of civil rights community projects.

**Young Men's Christian Association**
National Board
291 Broadway
New York, NY 10007
(212) DI9-0700
Advisory group formed to advance racial integration in YMCA and to work in area of special racial problems. Additional programs also include developing plans for action, studies, and intercultural programs.
Young Women's Christian Association

**Office of Racial Justice National Board**
600 Lexington Avenue
New York, NY 10022
(212) 753-4700
Seeks to be an agent of social change, keeping abreast of developments in civil and human rights, pressing toward full integration in all aspects of its own life and in local community.

**Zeta Phi Beta Sorority, Inc.**
1734 New Hampshire Avenue, N.W.
Washington, DC 20009
(202) 387-3103
National Negro sorority. Program includes leadership development, human and civil rights, youth and adult leadership programs, and social and welfare projects.

## STATE AND FEDERAL AGENCIES WITH CIVIL RIGHTS RESPONSIBILITIES

### ALASKA

**Alaska State Commission for Human Rights**
520 MacKay Building
338 Denali Street
Anchorage, 99501
(907) 272-9504

### ARIZONA

**Arizona Civil Rights Division**
**Arizona State Department of Law**
1502 West Jefferson Street
Phoenix, 85007
(602) 271-5263

### CALIFORNIA

**California Fair Employment Practices Commission**
455 Golden Gate Avenue
San Francisco, 94102
(415) 557-2000

### COLORADO

Colorado Civil Rights Commission
**312 State Services Building**
1525 Sherman Street
Denver, 80203
(303) 892-2621

### CONNECTICUT

**Connecticut Commission on Human Rights and Opportunities**
90 Washington Street
Hartford, 06106
(203) 566-3350

### DELAWARE

**Department of Labor and Industrial Relations Division Against Discrimination**
618 North Union
Wilmington, 19801
(302) 658-9251 Ext. 276, 277

### DISTRICT OF COLUMBIA

**District of Columbia Human Relations Commission Room 5**
District Building
14th and E Street, N. W.
(202) 629-4723

### FLORIDA

**Florida Commission on Human Relations Department of Community Affairs**
2711 Apalachee Parkway
Tallahassee, 32301
(904) 878-1489

### GEORGIA

**Governor's Council on Human Relations Room 104**
State Capital Atlanta, 30334
(404) 656-1735

### HAWAII

**Department of Labor and Industrial Relations**
825 Mililani Street
Honolulu, 96813
(808) 548-3150

### IDAHO

**Idaho Commission on Human Rights**
State House Boise, 83702
(208) 384-3550

### ILLINOIS

**Illinois Commission on Human Relations**
160 North LaSalle Street
Chicago, 60601
(312) 793-2893

### INDIANA

Indiana Civil Rights Commission
**319 State Office Building**
100 North Senate Avenue
Indianapolis, 46204
(317) 633-4855

### IOWA

**Iowa Civil Rights Commission**
State Capitol Building
Des Moines, 50319
(515) 281-5129

### KANSAS

**Kansas Commission on Civil Rights**
Room 1155 W. State Office Building
Topeka, 66612
(913) 296-3206

### KENTUCKY

**Kentucky Commission on Human Rights**
Mammoth Life Building
600 West Walnut Street
Louisville, 40203
(502) 585-3363

### LOUISIANA

**Louisiana Commission on Human Relations, Rights, and Responsibilities**
State Office Building
150 Riverside Mall, Suite 402
Baton Rouge, 70801
(504) 389-6601

### MAINE

**Maine Human Rights Commission**
State House Augusta, 04330
(207) 289-2326

### MARYLAND

**Maryland Commission on Human Rights**
The Mount Vernon Building
701 St. Paul Street
Baltimore, 21202
(301) 383-3680

### MASSACHUSETTS

**Massachusetts Commission Against Discrimination**
120 Tremont Street
Boston, 02108
(617) 727-3990

### MICHIGAN

**Michigan Civil Rights Commission**
1000 Cadillac Square Building
Detroit, 48226
(313) 222-1810

### MINNESOTA

**Department of Human Rights**
60 State Office Building
St. Paul, 55155
(612) 296-2931

### MISSOURI

**Missouri Commission on Human Rights P.O. Box 1129**
314 East High Street
Jefferson City, 65101
(314) 751-3325

### MONTANA

**Montana Department of Labor and Industry**
**1336 Helena Avenue**
Helena, 59601
(406) 449-3472

### NEBRASKA

**Nebraska Equal Opportunity Commission**
233 South 14th
Lincoln, 68508
(402) 471-2024

### NEVADA

**Nevada Commission on Equal Rights of Citizens**
State Office Building Room 100-B
215 East Bonanza
Las Vegas, 89101
(702) 385-0104

### NEW HAMPSHIRE

**New Hampshire Commission on Human Rights**
66 South Street
Concord, 03301
(603) 271-2767

### NEW JERSEY

**New Jersey Division on Civil Rights**
1100 Raymond Boulevard
Newark, 07102
(201) 648-2700

### New Mexico

**Human Rights Commission of New Mexico**
120 Villagra Building
Santa Fe, 87501
(505) 827-2713

### New York

**New York State Division of Human Rights**
270 Broadway
New York, 10007
(212) 488-7610

### NORTH CAROLINA

**North Carolina Human Relations Commission**
P.O. Box 12525
Raleigh, 27605
(919) 829-7996

### OHIO

**Ohio Civil Rights Commission**
240 Parsons Avenue

Columbus, 43215
(614) 469-2785

### OKLAHOMA

**Oklahoma Human Rights Commission**
P.O. Box 52945
Oklahoma City, 73105
(405) 521-2360

### OREGON

**Civil Rights Division**
466 State Office Building
Portland, 97201
(503) 229-5741

### PENNSYLVANIA

**Pennsylvania Human Relations Commission**
100 North Cameron Street, 4th Floor
Harrisburg, 17001
(717) 787-4410

### RHODE ISLAND

**Rhode Island Commission for Human Rights**
244 Broad Street
Providence, 02903
(401) 277-2661

### SOUTH DAKOTA

**South Dakota Human Relations Commission**
State Capitol Building
Pierre, 57501
(605) 224-3692

### TENNESSEE

**Tennessee Commission for Human Development**
Cordell Hull Building
Nashville, 37219
(615) 741-2424

### TEXAS

**Good Neighbor Commission of Texas**
P.O. Box 12007
Austin, 78711
(512) 475-3581

### UTAH

**Anti-Discrimination Division**
Industrial Commission of Utah State Office Building
Salt Lake City, 84114
(801) 328-5552

### VERMONT

Vermont State Human Rights Commission
**c/o Attorney General's Office**
Montpelier, 05602
(802) 828-2717

### WASHINGTON

**Washington State Human Rights Commission**
W.E.A. Building
319 Seventh Avenue
East Olympia, 98501
(206) 753-6770

### WEST VIRGINIA

**West Virginia Human Rights Commission**
1591East Washington Street
Charleston, 25305
(304) 348-2616

### WISCONSIN

**Equal Rights Division**
Department of Industry
310 Price Place
Madison, 53702
(608) 266-3145

### WYOMING

**Department of Labor and Statistics**
304 State Capitol Building
Cheyenne, 82001
(307) 777-7261

## FEDERAL AGENCIES WITH CIVIL RIGHTS OFFICES

**Department of Health, Education, and Welfare**
Office for Civil Rights
North Building
300 Independence Avenue, S.W.
Washington, DC 20201

**Department of Housing and Urban Development**
Equal Opportunity Office
415 Seventh Street, S.W.
Washington, DC 20410

**Department of Justice Civil Rights Division**
Constitution Avenue and Tenth Street, S.W.
Washington, DC 20530

**Department of Transportation**
**Departmental Office of Civil Rights**
400 Seventh Street, S.W.
Washington, DC 20590

**Department of Transportation**
**National Highway Traffic Safety Administration**
Office of Civil Rights
400 Seventh Street, S.W.
Washington, DC 20590

**Department of Transportation**
**Urban Mass Transportation Administration**
Office of Civil Rights and Service Development
400 Seventh Street, S.W.
Washington, DC 20590

**Environmental Protection Agency**
**Office of Civil Rights and Urban Affairs**
Waterside Mall West Tower
401 M Street, S.W.
Washington, DC 20460

**Equal Employment Opportunity Commission Room 1246**
1800 G Street, N. W.
Washington, DC 20506

**Small Business Administration**
**Office of Minority Enterprise**
1441 L Street, N.W.
Washington, DC 20416

**Small Business Administration**
**Office of Equal Employment Opportunity and Compliance**
1441 L Street, N.W.
Washington, DC 20416

# THE LEGAL STATUS OF BLACK AMERICANS

**Recent Status ■ Blacks and the Supreme Court ■ Important Cases ■ Notable Adverse Supreme Court Decisions ■ State Antidiscrimination Laws ■ Lynching ■ Blacks and Police ■ Blacks and the Legal Profession ■ Blacks in the Judiciary ■ Judicial Appointments of Black Federal Judges ■ Biographies of Black Federal Judges ■ Roster of Black Judicial Officers ■ Organizations Related to the Legal Profession**

On January 20, 1989, George Bush became President of the United States, and surprisingly, black leadership expressedoptimism about developing a working relationship with the new Chief of State. Shortly after his election, Bush , unlike Ronald Reagan, met with black civil rights leaders and black elected officials to assure them of his dedication to the elimination of bigotry and unequal justice. The black leadership seemed buoyed by the meeting with Bush and the prospect of a new direction. There was hope that with the election of George Bush the concerted assault by the Reagan administration to strip away many of the precious gains of the modern civil rights movement was over. However, the legacy of the administration could have a far-reaching impact both on blacks in particular and liberal policies in general because of the Reagan administration's achieved goal of an ideologically conservative majority on the Supreme Court. An immediate post-Reagan setback for blacks resulted from the Reagan Court's ruling on January 23, 1989, which found a Richmond Virginia affirmative action set-aside program unconstitutional. The program was originally designed to assist small black businesses develop and grow where they had previously been unable to compete. The full national impact of the Court's decision regarding set-aside programs is as yet undeterminable.

Before the Reagan administration entered office there was a sense that, even though there were some major battles still ahead, progress toward desegregation and equal opportunity was beginning to take root and flourish. There was impetus from the great Court and from political victories in the fifties and sixties, and although there was apprehension in the seventies, the essential thrust was not retrogressive. In a very important sense blacks had won. Racist doctrine was no longer embedded in law. Legal segregation had all but disappeared from public life. But for all this, the march toward equal opportunity in the eighties was being stymied and even turned back by a series of events and policies that were thwarting the translation of legal equality into daily reality.

The roadblocks stemmed from all branches of government. The Supreme Court was proving receptive to claims that affirmative action for minorities produced "reverse discrimination" against whites. Congress was legislating limits and exemptions to measures vital to the actual achievement of equality, such as limits on busing. And, most threatening of all, the Reagan Administration was rapidly detaching itself from enforcement of civil rights laws. As a result, the legal status of equality for which blacks had fought long to achieve was losing strong enforcement. To many blacks such gains were coming to resemble a trophy for past victories rather than a body of rules by which the nation would live.

As the administration of Ronald Reagan unfolded, it became increasingly apparent that a part of the administration's agenda was to thwart, stall, and prevent future gains, and where possible reverse the current legal status. In previous administrations, the Justice Department enforced civil rights legislation and instituted new cases to further Civil Rights, and as well attempted substantial enforcement of court decisions and enacted legislation. The Reagan administration's Justice Department not only softened, or in instances changed the rules of enforcement, but became a hostile opponent reviewing cases to overturn programs designed by cities to meet the standards of previous court rulings. Virtually every area of civil rights gains was under siege: school desegregation, voting rights, policies and practices of the EEOC, employment discrimination, and affirmative action , among others. Also, over a storm of protest the president in late 1983 in a restructure of the Commission dismissed three highly regarded members of the U.S. Commission on Civil Rights and attempted to "stack" the Commission with replacements having the administration's point of view thereby stifling a previously effective voice for civil rights. Those fired were Mary Francis Berry, a professor of history and law at Howard University, Cardenas Ramirez of San Antonio, and Rabbi Murray Saltzman of Baltimore; all highly regarded as effective spokespersons for minorities. However, because of strong congressional and public opposition the president was forced to compromise with Congress on the restructure of the Commission regarding the number of appointments the President could make. In the Congressional plan for restructure of the Commission each, the President and Congress, would have four appointments. The man chosen by the President to head the U.S. Civil Rights Commission, was a black, Clarence Pendelton , an outspoken critic of civil rights policies of the past several decades. From 1983 until the departure of Reagan in 1989, the U.S. Commission on Civil Rights took an oppositional position toward policies and practices, in the area of civil rights, that had been acceptable just prior to the Reagan era.

*NAACP Legal Defense and Educational Fund lawyers who argued* Brown v. Board of Ed. *decided by the U.S. Supreme Court in 1954. (left to right) John Scott, James M. Nabrit Jr., Spottswood W. Robinson lll, Frank D. Reeves, Jack Greenburg, Thurgood Marshall, Louis C. Redding, U. Simpson Tate, George Hayes.*

## BLACKS AND THE SUPREME COURT

For most of the twentieth century, the Supreme Court exercised a profound beneficial effect on the progress of blacks. In case after case the Court invalidated legal and regulatory barriers which had legitimized the withholding of first-class citizenship from minorities. Decisions favorable to minorities occurred most frequently during the 16-year tenure of Chief Justice Earl Warren, from 1953 to 1969. During that period, the Court declared separate school facilities unconstitutional, sought to guarantee the rights of people under arrest, and in scores of other decisions, to erase discrimination in education, due process, housing, employment, recreation, jury service, transportation, and other areas.

Starting in 1969, however, the Court's decisions reflected a more conservative view. Under Warren Burger, who replaced Chief Justice Warren, and with three new justices appointed by President Nixon, decisions tended to allow state and local governments more discretion in law enforcement and integration procedures, with a resultant relaxation of efforts to end discriminatory practices. A factor in the change was the reduction of government representations to the Court on behalf of minorities, and liberal views of due process. During the Eisenhower, Kennedy, and Johnson administrations, the Solicitor General and federal agencies frequently urged the Court to reach "liberal" decisions. But after 1969, the government frequently counseled enforcement delays or reversals of earlier liberal verdicts.

By early 1975, "court-watchers" differed in their forecasts of the Court's path. Some feared the Court might retreat to a course of decisions that would again make discrimination respectable. Most observers, however, felt that progress was still possible and that despite its retreats, the Court had no wish to return to the era of "legal racism."

With the election of Ronald Reagan in 1980, it soon became clear that as vacancies on the Supreme Court became available, fairly young, ideological conservatives would be appointed in order to insure many years of conservative interpretation of the law. Subsequently, Reagan appointed Sandra Day O'Connor, Antonin Scalia and Anthony Kennedy, all in their forties, to the Court, as well as William Renquist, age 62, as Chief Justice upon the retirement of Warren Burger in 1986.

### Retreat and Dismantlement

An important group to suffer extensively from the Reagan Administration's policies was the Legal Services Corporation, which over the years has provided services to millions of poor people through 320 local programs. Though it survived attempts to eliminate it completely in fiscal year 1982, LSC's funding and powers were sharply curtailed in the spring of 1982. President Reagan was still advocating its eradication in fiscal year 1983.

LSC's 1982 funds were reduced by one-third. Its lawyers were prohibited from filing class action suits against federal, state, or local governments and from providing legal help related to segregation. The government's opposition to class action suits extended to other areas, such as affirmative action in employment, where it proposed that discrimination suits could be filed only by individuals. Such a rule would place a heavy financial burden on disadvantaged individuals seeking to use the courts to achieve equality, and additionally, would restrict the impact of the legal victories they might win.

The administration also proposed enactment of a Federal Assistance Reform Act, which would reduce the Congress's ability to examine and amend block grant proposals. The probable result would be evasion of enforcement procedures that have been made part of civil rights programs. Between 1980 and 1982, the number of class action suits filed by EEOC dropped from 62 to 0, and the number of cases brought by the Office of Federal Contract Compliance was cut by 58%. It became announced public policy that the EEOC would no longer enforce affirmative action plans and would no longer seek affirmative action solutions as a remedy for discrimination.

Other proposals affecting civil rights included:

Limiting the jurisdiction of courts to correct discrimination.

Attempts through legislation to weaken the Voting Rights Act, whereby intent to discriminate rather than a de facto result of discrimination had to be proven to obtain redress.

Constitutional amendments to prohibit affirmative action and busing.

Many of the steps taken by the administration involved administrative dismantlement of existing laws through nonenforcement, under funding, and rule changes. Among these were:

Relaxing requirements for enforcement agencies, such as the Department of Justice, to conduct legally required investigations.

Rules requiring victims to bear the burden of proof in discrimination cases and exempting employers from maintaining records to prove they are not discriminating.

Elimination of efforts by the Justice Department to use busing to integrate schools, even where discrimination has been proven.

Granting tax-exempt status to private schools that discriminate against blacks.

Included here are selected examples of positions taken by the Reagan administration:

In June, 1981, the Reagan administration requested the Justice Department to determine whether the Voting Rights Act of 1965 best served the political rights of minorities, and whether the Act continued to be the most appropriate means of guaranteeing voting rights.

In the first six months of the Reagan administration, the Justice Department instituted 5 civil lawsuits as compared with 17 by the Carter administration. Assistant Attorney General William Bradford Reynolds stated that the administration is looking for "more remedies than those tried in the past and failed."

In December, 1981, Assistant Attorney General Reynolds planned to seek a new ruling from the Supreme Court finding it unconstitutional to give minorities and women preference in hiring, which would effectively end affirmative action programs previously upheld by the Court as a legal means to rectify past discriminatory practices.

In June, 1982, the Justice Department indicted and charged with vote fraud several black Civil Rights community organizers who were registering black voters in Alabama and Georgia. Julia Wilder and Maggie Bozemen were found guilty and imprisoned in Alabama.

In February, 1982, the Justice Department proposed that the city of Chicago desegregate its schools through voluntary student transfers rather than mandatory busing.

In February, 1982, sixty rank and file lawyers of the Justice Department's Civil Rights division were sharply critical of the Administration's policies regarding Civil Rights, especially Attorney General Meese's position allowing tax exemptions for private segregationist schools.

In March, 1983, a test case of the Justice Department to eliminate court-ordered busing was turned down by the Supreme Court, the administration contending that a desegregation plan in Nashville, Tennessee, was contributing to a "white flight" from the city.

In May, 1983, the Supreme Court rejects the Justice Department's contention that there is nothing in the Internal Revenue tax code which would ban tax exemption for private schools that discriminate on the basis of race.

In August, 1983, Assistant Attorney General William Bradford Reynolds was forced into sending federal observers into Mississippi for the enforcement of the Voting Rights Act after it had become obvious that blatant discrimination was present. Civil rights leaders called the extent of the response totally inadequate.

In October, 1983, Mary Francis Berry, Cardenas Ramirez, and Murry Saltzman were fired from the U.S. Civil Rights Commission because of critical views toward the administration.

In January, 1984, the Supreme Court rejects the Justice Department's contention that the plan to promote black police officers as part of a discrimination settlement was unconstitutional.

In January, 1984, with a Reagan majority on the U.S. Commission on Civil Rights, the Commission stated that it had separated itself from past policies and recommendations regarding actions for specific Civil Rights cases pending, and announced that the Commission deplores affirmative action quota remedies for past discrimination. The Commission also canceled a study on the effect of budget cuts on predominantly minority colleges.

In May, 1984, state and local set-aside programs for minorities will continue to be challenged, stated Assistant Attorney General Reynolds after one such action was turned aside by a Federal Appeals Court.

In January, 1985, President Reagan holds a meeting with 20 relatively unknown blacks to discuss an "agenda for the future." No nationally recognized black leaders were included and the meeting was perceived as a public relations attempt to alter the "callous" image of the administration towards the underprivileged.

In March, 1985, head of the U.S. Commission on Civil Rights, Clarence Pendelton, stated that affirmative action programs should be eliminated, and once that is accomplished the Commission on Civil Rights should itself be abolished.

In June, 1985, the Senate Judiciary Committee votes against the promotion of Assistant Attorney General William Bradford Reynolds, considered the point man in the Department of Justice in reversing previous civil rights gains. Many Democrats and some Republicans have long contended that Reynolds was inattentive to the enforcement of civil rights laws and made misleading statements about his handling of cases in sworn testimony.

In February, 1986, the Reagan Administration tests the idea of altering a 20-year executive order of President Lyndon Johnson's for an affirmative action plan for minority business. The National Black Republican Council fears that the proposed change would abort the development of black business and employment.

In July, 1986, the Supreme Court once again upholds the use of affirmative action plans against the protestation of the Justice Department.

In January, 1987, Joseph Cooper director of the Labor Department's Office of Federal Contract Compliance resigns in protest and identifies Attorney General Meese and Assistant Attorney General Bradford as seeking to circumvent rules requiring numerical hiring goals of some 20,000 companies that employ 23 million workers.

In February, 1987, the Supreme Court upholds the authority of judges to order strict racial quotas to remedy long-standing, blatant and pervasive discrimination. The Reagan Administration had argued that the remedies were "excessive" and "profoundly illegal."

In January, 1988, the Justice Department made an all out charge against minority set-aside programs designed to assure a designated percentage of jobs and government contracts for blacks specifically in Richmond, Virginia, and Dade County, Florida, and in some 200 state and local programs.

It is estimated that the Justice Department is, or has been involved, in more than 150 school desegregation cases in which "unitary" status is the central issue. The administration has taken the position that once a school implements a court ordered plan for desegregation then the system becomes "unitary" and it can have existing court orders withdrawn and implement their own new plans which would have the effect of resegregating the previously court ordered desegregated school system. In effect, "unitary" means that the school district is released from court supervision after it has adopted an

*Robert Bork , a Reagan Supreme Court nominee, was not confirmed.*

approved plan and implemented a court approved plan.

The Reagan Administration issued a directive which allowed the Department of Education to permit all states covered by *Adams* v. *Richardson,* requiring the state system of higher education to desegregate, to no longer meet desegregation requirements.

There is also the suggestion that Reagan appointees to the Federal bench were unsympathetic to previously accepted civil rights opinion, and sought to overturn established legal principles.

When President Reagan announced that he would nominate Judge Robert Bork to the Supreme Court there was an immediate galvanization from many diverse sections of the electorate to defeat Bork's ascension to the High Court. Civil rights groups, among others, in their analysis of Judge Bork's writings, speeches and opinions declared that his views are contrary to mainstream thinking regarding civil rights, abortion, and the right to privacy, among other opinions. Their efforts were rewarded with the defeat of the Bork nomination.

## Federal Legislation Affecting Blacks

A compilation of significant federal legislation enacted by the Congress since the Civil Rights Act of 1957 indicates that the fight for equality has shifted from civil rights to economic rights. A summary of the salient features of such legislation is included here (a more detailed presentation is made in the Documents section; chapter 2 ).

**Civil Rights Act of 1957**
Created the Commission on Civil Rights and empowered it to investigate allegations of deprivation of a U.S. citizen's right to vote, and to appraise laws and policies of the federal government with respect to equal protection of the law, and to submit a report to the President and to the Congress within two years.

**Civil Rights Act of 1960**
Provided for criminal penalties in the event a person crossed state lines to avoid legal process for the actual or attempted bombing or burning of any vehicle or building, and provided penalties for persons who obstructed or interfered with any order of a federal court.

**Civil Rights Act of 1964**
Prohibited discrimination in the use of public accommodations whose operations involve interstate commerce, and provided enforcement remedies to ensure equal access to public facilities. Also prohibited racial discrimination in any program receiving federal aid, and prohibited discrimination in most areas of employment.

**Voting Rights Act of 1965**
Struck down restrictions such as literacy and knowledge tests and poll tax payments which had been used to restrict black participation in voting, and provided for federal registrars to register voters should state registrars refuse to do so. It further provided that registered voters not be prohibited from voting.

**Civil Rights Act of 1968**
Provided for open housing by prohibiting discrimination based on race, color, religion, or national origin.

**Housing and Urban Development Act of 1968**
Provided for equal employment opportunities for lower income persons by requiring that minimum numbers of minorities be hired to work on housing projects funded by the federal government, and provided for housing for lower income families.

**Equal Employment Opportunity Act of 1972**
Provided the Equal Employment Opportunity Commission (which was established by the Civil Rights Act of 1964) with the authority to issue judicially enforceable cease and desist orders in cases involving discriminatory employment practices.

**Equal Opportunity Act of 1972 [Revision]**
Expanded the coverage of the Act, which prohibits discriminatory employment practices, to include federal, state and local government employers. In addition, the Act provided the Equal Opportunity Commission (which was established by the Civil Rights Act of 1964) with the authority to file lawsuits.

**Comprehensive Employment and Training Act of 1973 (CETA)**
Provided federal funding to employ and train unskilled minority workers in various federally assisted programs.

**Public Works Employment Act of 1977**
Provided that 10% of funds expended as a result of federal grants be earmarked for and paid to minority business

enterprises (so-called set-asides).

**Full Employment and Balanced Growth Act of 1978 (Humphrey-Hawkins Bill)**
Asserted the responsibility of the federal government to promote full employment, production, and real income, and required the President to set forth explicit short- and medium-term economic goals each year.

**Voting Rights Act of 1965 Amendment of 1982**
This was Congress' response to the Supreme Court's ruling in *City of Mobile* v. *Bolden* [see Important Cases-Voting, this section] that required proof of discriminatory intent in voting rights cases. Section 2 of the Act prohibits any voting practice or procedure "imposed or applied by any state or political subdivision in a manner which results in a denial or abridgement of the right of any citizen of the United States to vote on account of race or color..."

**Civil Rights Commission Act of 1983**
Creates an eight member bipartisan commission with four members appointed by the president, and two by the Senate and House, respectively. The Commissioners are appointed to four or six year terms and can be fired "only for neglect of duty or malfeasance in office." The statute was enacted after President Reagan attempted to fire Commissioners who did not express his views on civil rights. The Act extended the life of the Civil Rights Commission Authorization Act of 1978 which was scheduled to terminate in 1983.

**Civil Rights Restoration Act of 1988**
After four years of stalemate Congress enacted legislation, known informally as "Grove City", in response to the Supreme Court's 1984 opinion in *Grove City College* v. *Bell,* holding that discrimination was barred only in programs that received federal funds directly. The Act makes it clear that Title IX of the Education Amendments of 1972, which prohibits discrimination by public and private institutions receiving federal dollars, is to be read broadly and to apply to all programs within schools and universities receiving federal aid.

**Federal Amendments Act of 1988**
These Amendments to the Fair Housing Act of 1968 strengthen the law by fortifying and enhancing enforcement mechanisms. Under the Amendments, HUD has the authority to issue a discrimination charge, and the Attorney General is required to commence and maintain meritorious claims in the federal district court. Another Amendment provides for administrative law judges to review housing discrimination cases. One of the most significant Amendments removes the $1000 limit on punitive damages that a victim of discrimination may receive under the Act.

**Federal Contract Compliance and Work Force Development Act of 1988**
The dual purposes of the Act are to improve the effectiveness of the enforcement of non-discrimination and affirmative action requirements in federal contracts, and to create a fund to be used to establish educational and training programs for minorities and women.

### Mixed Signals on Civil Rights

During the 1970s and early 1980s, signals from the Supreme Court were mixed. Many busing and affirmative employment action plans were upheld, especially those reached voluntarily between institutions and minorities, as in the *Weber* and *AT&T* cases. On the other hand, as noted, the Court acceded to charges of reverse discrimination against whites, as in *Bakke*. Also, in the Mobile, Alabama voting rights case, the Court stated that intent to discriminate, rather than mere result, had to be established to prove that the Voting Rights Act had been violated.

In 1981, in a sharp departure from its predecessors, the Reagan Administration stated an intention to use the Court to reverse steps taken toward integration and affirmative action. Notable among these was its announced intention to seek reversal of the voluntary affirmative action plan approved in *Weber* and a voluntary integration plan reached between minorities and the Seattle School Board. With conservative appointees now a majority of the Court and liberals the eldest justices, there was concern among blacks that the Court would become receptive to such petitions.

Congressional conservatives also indicated interest in reversing civil rights gains through constitutional amendments. An amendment prohibiting busing was receiving the most attention.

## IMPORTANT CASES

The following important cases are presented in digest form and arranged in general categories.

### Due Process

***Moore v. Dempsey***
261 US 86 (1923)
Justice Holmes delivered the opinion.

In 1919, during an Arkansas race riot, one white man was killed and several people of both races were injured. At the trial, 12 blacks were sentenced to death and 67 to lengthy prison terms.

Black witnesses appearing at the trial were whipped until they consented to testify against the accused. The all-white jury heard the case in the presence of a mob threatening violence if there were no convictions. The court-appointed counsel did not ask for a change of venue and called no witnesses, not even the defendants themselves. The trial lasted 45 minutes, and the jury brought in a verdict of guilty after five minutes.

NAACP attorneys then applied for a writ of habeas corpus on the grounds that the trial was a trial in form only and no due process was accorded in view of the mob pressure. The petition was at first dismissed. The U.S. Supreme Court ultimately ruled that the petition should be heard, and reversed the decision of the Arkansas District Court, with Justice Holmes stating in his opinion that "counsel, jury and judge were swept to the fatal end by an irresistible wave of public passion."

***United States v. Adams, Bordenave and Mitchell States***
319 US 312 (1943)

The three defendants in this case were convicted in a local U.S. court of the rape of a civilian while within the confines of Camp Claiborne, Louisiana. They were represented by a court-appointed lawyer, and sentenced to death. The men then appealed for assistance to the NAACP, which applied for a writ of habeas corpus on the ground that the local court was without jurisdiction. The U.S. Court of Appeals for the Fifth Circuit, unable to decide the issue, forwarded the case to the U.S. Supreme Court.

This Court ruled that the lower court was without jurisdiction in the case, with the result that the men were subsequently released from the custody of civilian authorities and returned to the Army for court-martial proceedings.

***Sniacach v. Family Finance Corp.***
395 US 337 (1969)

The Supreme Court ruled that a debtor's wages cannot be garnisheed without court determination in a fair proceeding with notice to the debtor that a debt does exist and an opportunity extended to defend. In this case, the plaintiff 's wages had, under Wisconsin law, been withheld without proving the existence of a debt. In all, 17 states had permitted courts to tie up half an employee's wages without establishing proof of debt.

***Williams v. Illinois***
399 US 235 (1970)

An indigent defendant was convicted of a misdemeanor, sentenced to one year in jail, and fined $500, as permitted by state law. He was required to remain in jail and work off, at a rate of $5 per day, the amount to which he might be in default of the fee at the expiration of his imprisonment.

The defendant's appeal of the work-off provision of the sentence was denied by the trial judge. The Supreme Court, however, ruled for the defendant, declaring the work-off portion to be in violation of the Fourteenth Amendment because the aggregate imprisonment of an indigent would exceed the maximum period fixed by the statute and noted that a person with sufficient funds would not have been subjected to such a penalty.

***Furman v. Georgia***
408 US 238 (1972)

The Supreme Court declared the death penalty to be cruel and unusual punishment in violation of the Eighth Amendment, since it is generally applied arbitrarily by judges and juries. However, the Court left room for state legislators to enact laws in which capital punishment would be applied less capriciously.

***Tennessee v. Garner***
471 US 1 (1985)

Garner, a black unarmed teenager, was shot down by a police officer using "dum dum" bullets, a type of bullet that is so powerful that it causes the body to explode upon impact and which has been prohibited in international warfare. The officer alleged that he believed the fleeing youth had burglarized an unoccupied residence. The evidence demonstrated that the city's policy of shooting unarmed felony suspects applied disproportionately against blacks. The Supreme Court ruled that the state's "Fleeing Felon" statute, which authorized a police officer to shoot to kill a fleeing felon, even if the officer or others were not in immediate danger, was unconstitutional.

## Education

***State of Missouri, ex rel. Lloyd Gaines v. University State of Missouri***
305 US 337 (1938)
Chief Justice Hughes delivered the opinion.

After Lloyd Gaines, a black, had been refused admission to the law school of the State University of Missouri, he applied to state courts for an order to compel admission on the grounds that refusal constituted a denial of his rights under the Fourteenth Amendment of the U.S. Constitution.

The University of Missouri defended its action by maintaining that Lincoln University (a predominantly black institution of higher learning) would eventually establish its own law school, which Gaines could then attend, and that, in the meantime, he could exercise the option of pursuing his studies outside the state on a scholarship. The Supreme Court of Missouri dismissed Gaines' petition for mandamus, and upheld the university's decision to reject his application. The U.S. Supreme Court, however, reversed this decision, maintaining that the state of Missouri was obliged to provide equal facilities for Negroes or, in the absence of such facilities, to admit them to the existing facility.

*Lloyd Gaines disappeared after winning 1938 case for admission to University of Missouri Law School.*

*G. W. McLaurin won a court order to end segregation at the University of Oklahoma.*

**Sipuel v. University of Oklahoma**
332 US 631 (1948)

Ada Lois Sipuel, a black, was denied admission to the law school of the University of Oklahoma, and thereupon promptly requested legal assistance from the NAACP which filed a petition in the Oklahoma courts requesting an order directing her admission. The petition was denied on the grounds that the *Gaines* decision (see above) did not require a state with segregation laws to admit a black to its white schools. Further, the Oklahoma court maintained that the state itself was not obligated to set up a separate school unless first requested to do so by blacks desiring a legal education. The decision was affirmed by the Supreme Court of Oklahoma. The U.S. Supreme Court, however, reversed this decision, and held that the state was required to provide Negroes with equal educational opportunities as soon as it did so for whites.

**Sweatt v. Painter**
339 US 629 (1950)
Chief Justice Vinson delivered the opinion.

The black petitioner in this case was refused admission to the law school of the University of Texas on the grounds that substantially equivalent facilities were already available in another Texas school open to blacks only.

The US Supreme Court ruled that the petitioner be admitted to the University of Texas law school, since "in terms of number of the faculty, variety of courses and opportunity for specialization, size of the student body, scope of the library, availability of law review and similar activities, the University of Texas Law School is superior."

**McLaurin v. Oklahoma State Regents for Higher Education**
339 US 637 (1950)
Chief Justice Vinson delivered the opinion.

After having been admitted to the state university, G. W. McLaurin, a black, was required to occupy a special seat in the classroom and a designated table in both the library and the cafeteria—all because of his race.

The U.S. Supreme Court declared unanimously that the black student must receive the same treatment at the hands of the state as other students, and could not be segregated.

**Gray v. University of Tennessee**
342 US 517 (1952)

This case resulted from the refusal of a three-judge U.S. District Court to accept jurisdiction in the matter of enjoining the exclusion of blacks from a state university. The lone judge to whom the matter was then referred ruled that plaintiffs were entitled to admission but did not order the university to do so.

The Supreme Court was asked to refer the case back to the three-judge District Court for further proceedings. Pending this appeal, however, one of the students seeking admission was in fact admitted. Since the court found no suggestion that persons "similarly situated would not be afforded similar treatment," the case was dismissed as moot.

**Brown v. Board of Education**
347 US 483 (1954)
Chief Justice Warren delivered the opinion.

This case involved the practice of denying black children equal access to state public schools due to state laws requiring or permitting racial segregation. The U.S. Supreme Court unanimously held that segregation deprived the children of equal protection under the Fourteenth Amendment to the U.S. Constitution. The "separate but equal" doctrine of *Plessy v. Ferguson* was overruled. After reargument a year later, the case was remanded (along with its four companion cases) to the District Court, which was instructed to enter such orders as were necessary to ensure the admission of all parties to public schools on a racially nondiscriminatory basis.

**Hawkins v. Board of Control**
347 US 971 (1954)

This case resulted from a ruling of the Florida Supreme Court which denied a black the right to enter the University of Florida on the grounds that he had failed to show that a separate law school for blacks was not substantively equal to the one for whites. The U.S. Supreme Court vacated the judgment and remanded the case to the Florida Supreme Court for a decision in light of the ruling in *Brown* which overruled the separate but equal doctrine.

After two years, the Florida Supreme Court was still denying the petitioner the right to enter the University of Florida. By that time, however, it had appointed a commissioner to determine when in the future he could be admitted "without causing public mischief." This time, the U.S. Supreme Court ruled that the petitioner should be admitted to the school promptly, since there was no palpable reason for any delay.

**_Turead v. Board of Supervisors_**
347 US 971 (1954)

This case stemmed from a provisional injunction requiring the admittance of blacks to Louisiana State University. The State Court of Appeals reversed this action, declaring that it required the decision of a District Court of three judges. The U.S. Supreme Court vacated this judgment and remanded the case for consideration, again in light of *Brown*.

**_Frazier v. University of North Carolina_**
350 US 979 (1956)

The U.S. Supreme Court affirmed a district court judgment that blacks may not be excluded from institutions of higher learning because of their race or color.

**_Cooper v. Aaron_**
358 US 1 (1958)

The Supreme Court voted unanimously to set aside a 2 1/2 year delay in the integration of Central High School, Little Rock.

**_Lucy v. Adams_**
224 F. Supp 79 (1963)

The University of Alabama was ordered by a Federal District Court to admit two black students, Vivian Malone and James Hood. Governor Wallace of Alabama tried to thwart their admission by "standing in the school house door," but he backed down when President Kennedy mobilized the National Guard.

**_Lee v. Macon County Board of Education_**
389 US 25 (1967)

The Supreme Court affirmed a lower court decision ordering the desegregation of Alabama's school districts and declared state school grants to whites attending segregated private schools unconstitutional.

**_Alexander v. Holmes County Board of Education._**
396 US 19 (1969)

The Supreme Court ended the "all deliberate speed" doctrine when, by a vote of 8 to 0, it ordered 33 districts in Mississippi to desegregate. The Department of Health, Education and Welfare had asked that the districts be granted more time to desegregate. This was the first time HEW had sought a delay in integration, but the Court ordered that integration proceed "at once."

*The NAACP generated nationwide pressure for 1954 Brown decision making segregated public schools illegal.*

"All the News That's Fit to Print"

The New York Times.

LATE CITY EDITION
Fair and cool today. Mostly sunny, continued cool tomorrow.

Copyright, 1954, by The New York Times Company.

VOL. CIII ... No. 35,178. NEW YORK, TUESDAY, MAY 18, 1954. FIVE CENTS

# HIGH COURT BANS SCHOOL SEGREGATION; 9-TO-0 DECISION GRANTS TIME TO COMPLY

## McCarthy Hearing Off a Week as Eisenhower Bars Report

SENATOR IS IRATE

Communist Arms Unloaded in Guatemala By Polish Port, U. S. Learns

Embassy Says Nation of Central America May Buy Munitions Anywhere

REACTION OF SOUTH

'Breathing Spell' for Adjustment Tempers Region's Feelings

By JOHN N. POPHAM

1896 RULING UPSET

'Separate but Equal' Doctrine Held Out of Place in Education

Text of Supreme Court decision is printed on Page 15.

By LUTHER A. HUSTON
Special to The New York Times.
WASHINGTON, May 17—The Supreme Court unanimously outlawed today racial segregation in public schools.

Chief Justice Earl Warren read two opinions that put the stamp of unconstitutionality on school systems in twenty-one states and the District of Columbia where segregation is permissive or mandatory.

The court, taking cognizance of the problems involved in the integration of the school systems concerned, put over until the ...

***Swann v. Charlotte Mecklenburg Board of Education***
402 US 1 (1971)

The Supreme Court affirmed the use of busing and faculty transfers to overcome the effects of dual school systems. Writing the decision, Chief Justice Burger noted that "bus transportation has long been a part of all public educational systems and it is unlikely that a truly effective remedy could be devised without continued reliance upon it." However, the decision left local district judges the authority to decide whether a desegregation plan was constitutionally adequate.

***Wright v. City of Emporia***
407 US 451 (1972)

***Cotton v. Scotland Neck Board of Education***
407 US 485 (1972)

The Supreme Court held that two towns with heavy concentrations of white students could not secede from a largely black county school system and form its own school district in an attempt to frustrate integration.

***Richmond, Virginia School Board v. State Board of Education***
412 US 92 (1973)

By a 4 to 4 vote, the Supreme Court declined to order the integration of the predominantly black schools in Richmond with those of two white suburbs. Though the Court wrote no decision, integrationists expressed concern that permitting de facto segregation to stand in this manner will hinder corrective action in other metropolitan areas, perpetuate "neighborhood" one-race schools, and lessen the extent of integration in unitary school systems.

***Keyes v. School District***
1413 US 189 (1973)

The Supreme Court, for the first time, ordered integration in a northern school system. By a 7 to 1 vote, it ruled that a substantial part of the schools of Denver were administratively segregated, that the system must therefore be considered "dual" and thus be desegregated. The suit had been brought by 11 black, Hispanic, and white parents, marking a trend for black and Hispanic minorities to cooperate.

***University of California Regents v. Bakke***
438 US 265 (1978)

See Affirmative Action Cases

***Bob Jones University v. IRS***
461 US 574 (1983)

Contrary to long-standing IRS policy, the Administration sought to extend tax-exempt status to schools that discriminate on the basis of race. The Supreme Court recognized the inability of the Justice Department to argue the case fairly, and requested former Secretary of Transportation William T. Coleman to present the argument. The Supreme Court rebuffed the Justice Department's arguments and unanimously agreed with Coleman's position that the denial of tax-exempt status to racially discriminatory schools is unconstitutional.

***Jenkins v. Missouri***
807 F.2d 657 (8th Circuit, 1986)

Black parents of school children in Kansas City, Missouri achieved a major victory in this case challenging housing discrimination and school segregation. The evidence produced by plaintiffs revealed that local real estate brokers engaged in racial steering and sanctioned racially restricted covenants; state banking institutions denied blacks housing loans; and state agencies selected public housing sites in a discriminatory manner. The plaintiff's claim that discriminatory housing patterns caused segregated school districts, was upheld by the federal court of appeals. To remedy the unlawful discrimination the court ordered the State of Missouri to invest $300 million in the creation of programs designed to enhance educational opportunities for blacks.

## Forced Confessions

***Brown, Ellington and Shields v. State of Mississippi***
297 US 278 (1936)
Chief Justice Hughes delivered the opinion.

On April 4, 1934, a few days after the murder of one Raymond Stewart, three blacks were indicted for the crime. They were arraigned, tried, found guilty and sentenced to death.

The only evidence presented against them during the trial was that they had confessed, admittedly after both force and physical torture had been applied. One had been hanged by a rope to a tree, severely beaten, and then permitted to return home after still refusing to "confess." A day or two later, he was again seized and whipped until he agreed to confess. At the time of the trial, the marks of violence were still visible on this victim's neck.

The conviction in this case was affirmed by the Supreme Court of Mississippi, but it was reversed by the U.S. Supreme Court, which held that the rack and the torture chamber could not be used in place of, or as a prelude to, the witness stand.

***Chambers v. Florida***
309 US 227 (1940)
Justice Black delivered the opinion.

This case involved four blacks convicted of murder in Pompano, Florida. The U.S. Supreme Court reversed the conviction on the grounds that the confessions used to convict the men had been extorted by force and violence, and thus denied the defendants due process as guaranteed by the Fourteenth Amendment.

***Canty v. Alabama***
309 US 629 (March 11, 1940)

The U.S. Supreme Court—in a memorandum opinion—in view of the Chambers case, reversed without argument the decision of the Supreme Court of Alabama which had upheld the conviction and sentence of Dave Canty for murder.

***White v. Texas***
309 US 631 (1940)

On the authority of the *Chambers* and *Canty* cases, the U.S. Supreme Court reversed the conviction and sentencing of Bob White, which had been upheld by the Texas Court of Criminal Appeals.

***Ward v. State of Texas***
316 US 547 (1942)

This case involved William Ward, a black, who, in 1939, was indicted in Texas for the murder of a white man. At his first trial, the jury was unable to agree on a verdict. At the second one, he was found guilty of murder (without malice) and sentenced to three years in the state penitentiary. The Texas Court of Criminal Appeals affirmed the lower court decision, but it was reversed by the U.S. Supreme Court on the grounds that Ward had originally been convicted as the result of a forced confession.

***Lee v. Mississippi***
332 US 742 (1948)
Justice Murphy delivered the opinion.

Albert Lee, a 17-year-old black, was indicted and convicted of assault with the intent to rape; his conviction having been based on a confession which had allegedly been coerced. The Mississippi Supreme Court affirmed the conviction, but the U.S. Supreme Court reversed it on the grounds that the confession had been coerced.

***Watts v. Indiana***
338 US 49 (1949)

The U.S. Supreme Court reversed the conviction and death sentence of a black in a rape and murder case on the grounds that the confession had been coerced.

***Reeves v. Alabama***
348 US 891 (1954)

The defendant, sentenced to death for rape, attacked the conviction on the ground that it was based on a coerced confession and that blacks had been improperly excluded from service on the jury. The U.S. Supreme Court reversed the conviction holding that a conviction based on a coerced confession denied the due process guarantees of the Fourteenth Amendment to the U.S. Constitution.

***Fikes v. Alabama***
352 US 191 (1957)
Chief Justice Warren delivered the opinion

Sentenced to death for the crime of burglary with intent to rape, the defendant attacked the conviction on the grounds that it was based on a coerced confession and because blacks had been systematically excluded from service on the jury. The U.S. Supreme Court reversed the conviction on a number of grounds, including the fact that the prisoner was mentally retarded and had not had the assistance of counsel while being held incommunicado.

## Housing (Right of Sale and Restrictive Covenants)

***Buchanan v. Warley***
245 US 60 (1917)
Justice Day delivered the opinion.

The plaintiff, Buchanan, brought an action in this case for the performance of a sale of certain real estate in Louisville, Kentucky. The purchaser, Warley (a black), maintained that he would be unable to occupy the land since it was located

within what was defined by a Louisville ordinance as a white block. (The ordinance prohibited whites from living in black districts, and vice versa.) Buchanan alleged that the ordinance was in conflict with the Fourteenth Amendment to the U.S. Constitution.

The U.S. Supreme Court maintained that the ordinance was unconstitutional.

***Harmon v. Tyler***
273 US 668 (1927)

On the authority of *Buchanan v. Warley*, a similar New Orleans residential ordinance which was upheld by the lower court was declared unconstitutional by the U.S. Supreme Court.

***City of Richmond v. Deans***
281 US 704 (1930)

The U.S. Supreme Court, again on the basis of *Buchanan v. Warley*, struck down the ruling of a lower court and declared a Richmond residential segregation ordinance unconstitutional.

***Shelley v. Kraemer***
334 US 1 (1948)

***Hurd v. Hodge***
334 US 26 (1948)
Chief Justice Vinson delivered both opinions.

On August 11, 1945, a black family, the Shelleys, received a warranty deed to a parcel of land which, unknown to them, was subject to a restrictive covenant barring its sale to blacks. Suit was subsequently brought in the Circuit Court of St. Louis seeking to divest the Shelleys of the title to the land. The Supreme Court of Missouri directed the trial court to strip the petitioners of said title.

The U.S. Supreme Court reversed this decision, maintaining that restrictive covenants, though valid contracts, could not be enforced by state courts. In the *Hurd v. Hodge* case, involving a similar set of circumstances, federal courts were similarly prohibited from enforcing such restrictive covenants.

***Barrows v. Jackson***
346 US 249 (1953)

The U.S. Supreme Court in this case held it to be a violation of the equal protection and due process clauses of the Fourteenth Amendment for a state court to award damages for the violation of a restrictive covenant.

***Reitman v. Mulkey***
387 US 369 (1967)

In 1964, the California electorate voted in favor of a referendum granting "absolute discretion" to real estate owners in the sale and rental of real property, in effect voiding the state's fair housing laws. Lincoln Mulkey filed suit against property owners in Orange County to challenge the validity of the referendum. Mulkey's position failed in the lower courts but was sustained 5 to 2 by the California Supreme Court on the grounds that the California referendum violated the Fourteenth Amendment of the U.S. Constitution. The U.S. Supreme Court upheld the decision.

***Thorpe v. Housing Authority***
393 US 268 (1969)
Chief Justice Warren delivered the opinion.

The Supreme Court declared that tenants of federally assisted housing projects cannot be evicted without being first informed of the reason and given an opportunity to reply or explain.

***Kennedy Park Homes Assn. v. City of Lackawanna***
401 US 1010 (1971)

The Supreme Court refused to review a lower court decision granting blacks the right to build a low-income housing project in a section of the city largely inhabited by whites.

***Trafficante v. Metropolitan Life Insurance***
409 US 205 (1972)
Justice Douglas delivered the opinion.

The Supreme Court ruled that a complaint of racial discrimination in housing may be brought by parties who have not themselves been refused accommodation but who, as members of the same housing unit, allege injury by discriminatory housing practices. The suit had been filed by

*Political cartoons of the nineteenth century spotlighted abuses and pushed for reforms. Resistance to Jim Crow on Nashville streetcars (above) led blacks to pool finances and buy their own buses. Thomas Nast's "Justice" (left) points out racist inequity of numbers of death penalties.*

a black and a white resident of a housing development in San Francisco, who contended that the owner of the development, in maintaining a "white ghetto," was depriving plaintiffs of the right to live in a racially integrated community.

***James v. Valtierra***
402 US 137 (1971)

The Supreme Court upheld a ruling that local voters could veto projected plans for low-rent housing projects. The ruling affirmed a decision which held that no low-income projects could be developed without the majority vote of a city, town, or county in a referendum where such process was duly provided for in law.

***Jones v. Alfred H. Mayer, Co.***
392 US 409 (1968)

Joseph Lee Jones alleged that the sole reason a Realtor refused to sell him a home was because he was black. The Supreme Court held that 42 U.S.C. 1982, a federal statute created during the Reconstruction era to eliminate the vestiges of slavery, prohibits all racial discrimination, public and private in the sale or rental of property.

***Gladstone Realtors v. Village of Bellwood***
441 US 91 (1979)

The Supreme Court held that even though the plaintiffs were not in fact seeking to purchase homes but were acting as "testers" to determine whether real estate brokerage firms engaged in racial steering, they had suffered racial discrimination, including the loss of social and professional benefits, as well as economic injury.

***Willis v. H & M Enterprises***
Unreported, Docket No. 87-2623-NHJ-PJA
(D.D.C. 1988)

Using the Fair Housing Act as her weapon, Barbara Willis filed a lawsuit against the Washington, D.C. Realtor who refused to rent her an apartment on account of her race. The 1988 settlement in the amount of $325,000 is said to be the largest won by an individual in a housing discrimination case.

## Jury Service

***Batson v. Kentucky***
476 US 79 (1986)

Writing for a majority of seven, Justice Powell held that the prosecution may not use its "preemptory challenge", those challenges to an individual juror for which no cause need be stated, to exclude black jurors in a case involving a black defendant.

***Hollins v. Oklahoma***
295 US 394 (1935)

Charged with rape, the defendant in this case was convicted on December 29, 1931 at a trial held in the basement of the jail in Sapula, Oklahoma. Three days before the scheduled execution, the NAACP secured a stay, and later, a reversal of his conviction by the Supreme Court of Oklahoma.

The U.S. Supreme Court—in a memorandum opinion—affirmed the principle that the conviction of a black by a jury from which all blacks had been excluded was a denial of the equal protection clause of the Fourteenth Amendment to the U.S. Constitution.

***Hale v. Commonwealth of Kentucky***
303 US 613 (1938)

Charged with murder in McCracken County, Kentucky in 1936, Joe Hale moved to set aside the indictment on the grounds that the jury commissioners had systematically excluded blacks from jury lists.

Hale established that one out of every six residents of the county was black, and that there were at least 70 blacks out of a total of 6,700 persons qualified for jury duty. Still, there had not been a black on jury duty between 1906 and 1936. Hale's conviction and death sentence were upheld by the Court of Appeals of Kentucky, but both were struck down by the U.S. Supreme Court on the grounds that he had been denied equal protection of the laws.

***Patton v. Mississippi***
332 US 463 (1947)
Justice Black delivered the opinion.

This case involved Eddie Patton, a black who was indicted,

tried, and convicted of the murder of a white man in Mississippi. At his trial and as part of his appeal, Patton alleged that all qualified blacks had been systematically excluded from jury service in Lauderdale County (the place of the trial) solely because of race. The state maintained that, since jury service was limited by statute to qualified voters, and since few blacks were qualified to vote, such a procedure was valid in the eyes of the law.

The U.S. Supreme Court, however, reversed Patton's conviction on the grounds that such a jury plan, resulting in the almost automatic elimination of blacks from jury service, constituted an infringement of his rights under the Fourteenth Amendment.

***Shepherd v. Florida***
341 US 50 (1951)

The U.S. Supreme Court reversed the conviction of a state court involving black defendants solely on the grounds that the method of selecting the grand jury discriminated against blacks.

***Taylor v. Louisiana***
419 US 522 (1985)

The Supreme Court held that the exclusion of any cognizable group from the jury constitutes a denial of the 6th Amendment rights to have a representative group on the jury rolls. The Court made it clear that groups may not be excluded on the basis of race, sex, or national origin.

***Turner v. Fouche***
396 US 346 (1970)

The Supreme Court affirmed the right to bring an action in Federal Court to end discrimination in jury selection.

***Castanda v. Partida***
430 US 482 (1977)

The Supreme Court upheld the use of statistical evidence demonstrating that Mexican-Americans had been systematically excluded from jury selection, and that such discrimination on the basis of race or color violated the equal protection clause of the Constitution. The principle established in this case, that statistical evidence can be used to prove intentional discrimination, has been used in cases involving employment, housing, voting and education.

***Vasquez v. Hillery***
106 S.Ct. (1986)

The Supreme Court reaffirmed its 1880 ruling that blacks may not be systematically excluded in grand jury selection.

***Turner v. Murray***
106 US 1683 (1986)

The Supreme Court expanded the right of black defendants in capital cases to question potential white jurors to uncover their racial prejudices and biases.

*A mixed jury in 1867. The Fourteenth Amendment protects black people from conviction by juries which exclude black jurors.*

## Public Accommodations

***Katzenbach v. McClung***
379 US 802
***Heart of Atlanta v. United States***
379 US 803
Both cases were decided on the same day in 1964;
both opinions were delivered by Justice Clark.

In the *Katzenbach* case, the Attorney General of the United States sued Ollie's Barbecue Restaurant in Birmingham, Alabama for its refusal to serve blacks in its dining accommodations, a direct violation of the anti-discriminatory public accommodations clause of the 1964 Civil Rights Act. The U.S. District Court, Northern District of Alabama, held that the Civil Rights Act could not be applied under the Fourteenth Amendment to the U.S. Constitution, inasmuch as there was no "demonstrable connection" between food purchased in interstate commerce and sold in a restaurant that would affect commerce. The U.S. Supreme Court, however, held that "the Civil Rights Act of 1964, as here applied, [is] plainly appropriate in the resolution of what . [Congress has] . found to be a national commercial problem of the first magnitude."

*Heart of Atlanta* dealt with a Georgia motel which solicited patronage in national advertising and had several out-of-state residents as guests from time to time. The motel had already instituted the practice of refusing to rent rooms to blacks prior to the passage of the 1964 Civil Rights Act, and stated thereafter that it intended to continue this practice. The motel owner filed suit, maintaining that the 1964 Civil Rights Act violated both the Fifth and the Thirteenth Amendments. The United States countered with the argument that the refusal to accept Negroes interfered with interstate travel, and that the Congress in voting to apply nondiscriminatory standards to interstate commerce was not violating either amendment. The U.S. Supreme Court upheld the right of Congressional regulation, stating that the power of Congress was not confined to the regulation of commerce among the states. "It extends to those activities intrastate which so affect interstate commerce, or the exercise of the power of Congress over it, as to make regulation of them appropriate means to the attainment of a legitimate end."

***Bell v. Maryland***
378 US 226 (1964)

The Supreme Court ordered a Maryland district court to reconsider its affirmation of a state court conviction of 12 blacks for trespass, when they refused to leave a restaurant that refused to serve them entirely on the basis of their color.

***Shuttlesworth v. Birmingham***
394 US 147 (1969)

The Supreme Court invalidated Birmingham's Parade-Permit law which had been used in 1963 to harass Martin Luther King Jr.'s Easter March.

*Demonstrators organized by the NAACP picket the New York's posh Stork Club in 1952 after the club refused to serve international star, Josephine Baker.*

***New York State Club Association v. City of New York***
108 S.Ct. 2225 (1988)

In a unanimous decision, the Supreme Court upheld the constitutionality of a New York City ordinance that forbids so-called private clubs from discriminating against women and minorities.

## Recreation

***Rice v. Arnold***
340 US 848 (October 16, 1950)

This case involved the successful attempt to abolish segregation on a Miami (Florida) golf course owned and operated by the city. The U.S. Supreme Court granted a writ of certiorari and vacated the judgment of the Florida Supreme Court which authorized the segregated use of the course—in light of the *McLaurin* and *Sweatt* decisions. (See education section above.)

### *Muir v. Louisville Park Theatrical Association*
347 US 971 (1954)

Blacks were refused admission to an amphitheater located in a Louisville city park, leased and operated by a privately owned group not affiliated in any way with the city. The Kentucky Court of Appeals found no evidence of unlawful discrimination, but the U.S. Supreme Court vacated this judgment and remanded the case for consideration in the light of the prevailing legal climate as articulated in *Brown v. Board of Education.*

### *Mayor and City Council of Baltimore v. Dawson*
350 US 377 (1955)

The U.S. Supreme Court affirmed a judgment that the enforcement of racial segregation in public beaches and bathhouses maintained by public authorities is unconstitutional.

### *Holmes v. Atlanta*
350 US 859 (1955)

This case involved a suit brought by blacks to integrate a city-owned and city-operated golf course in Atlanta. The segregated arrangements were ordered sustained by the lower court, but that order was vacated by the U.S. Supreme Court and the case remanded to the District Court with directions to enter a decree for plaintiffs in conformity with the Baltimore case above.

### *Evans v. Newton*
382 US 296 (1966)

The Supreme Court ruled that transfer of a city park from municipal ownership to a board of private trustees does not remove its obligations under the Fourteenth Amendment.

## Transportation

### *Morgan v. Commonwealth of Virginia*
328 US 373 (1946)
Justice Reed delivered the opinion.

Irene Morgan, a black, refused to move to the rear seat of a Greyhound bus which was traveling from Virginia to Washington, D.C., and was subsequently convicted in the lower Virginia courts for violating a state statute requiring segregation of the races on all public vehicles.

NAACP attorneys then carried the case through the Virginia courts and on to the U.S. Supreme Court, where it was decided that the Virginia statute could not apply to interstate passengers or motor vehicles engaged in such traffic. (The ruling was of such a nature that it lent itself to application on railroads, in airplanes, etc.)

### *Bob-Lo v. Michigan*
333 US 28 (1948)
Justice Rutledge delivered the opinion.

In this case, the operator of a line of vessels used to transport patrons from Detroit to an amusement park, owned by the city, on an island in Canadian waters, was convicted of violating the Michigan Civil Rights Act for refusing passage to a black.

The U.S. Supreme Court upheld the application of the Michigan statute.

### *Flemming v. South Carolina Electric*
351 US 901 (1956)

This case involved a suit brought by a black passenger against a bus company for damages due to the bus driver's having required her to change seats in accordance with South Carolina's segregation law. The trial judge dismissed the case on the grounds that the statute in question was valid, but the Court of Appeals reversed this decision, holding that the "separate but equal" doctrine was no longer valid. The U.S. Supreme Court upheld the Court of Appeals.

### *Gayle v. Browder*
352 US 114 (1956)

This action challenged the constitutionality of state statutes and ordinances in effect in the city of Montgomery, Alabama, which required the segregation of whites and blacks on public buses.

These statutes were first declared unconstitutional by the decision of a three-judge federal district court. The U.S. Supreme Court then affirmed this judgment.

*Rosa Parks, the "Little Lady Who Started It All" in Montgomery, is honored by civil rights leaders.*

### Voting (Registration and Primaries)

***Guinn v. United States***
238 US 347 (1915)
Chief Justice White delivered the opinion.

By an amendment passed in 1910, the Constitution of Oklahoma restricted the franchise according to a "grandfather clause" which provided that no illiterate person could be registered to vote. The clause, however, granted an exemption for such a person provided he had lived in a foreign country prior to January 1, 1866; had been eligible to register prior to that date, or if his lineal ancestor was eligible to vote at that time. Since no blacks were eligible to vote in Oklahoma prior to 1866, the law disenfranchised all blacks.

The U.S. Supreme Court held the grandfather clause invalid in Oklahoma, as well as in any other state where one was in effect.

***Nixon v. Herndon***
273 US 536 (1927)
Justice Holmes delivered the opinion.

By reason of a state statute providing that no black shall be "eligible to participate in a Democratic Party election held in the State of Texas," Dr. L. A. Nixon, a black, was refused the right to vote in a Texas primary election. Nixon filed suit against the election officials, and his case ultimately reached the U.S. Supreme Court. In his opinion, Justice Holmes said: "It is too clear for extended argument that color cannot be made the basis of a statutory classification affecting the right set up in this case," and, as such, declared the Texas statute unconstitutional.

***Nixon v. Condon***
286 US 73 (1932)
Justice Cardozo delivered the opinion.

Pursuant to the decision in the above case, the Texas legislature passed a new statute, empowering the state Democratic executive committee to set up its own rules regarding the primary. The party promptly adopted a resolution stipulating that only white Democrats be allowed to participate in the primary. Dr. Nixon again filed suit, and his right to vote was again upheld by the U.S. Supreme Court.

***Lane v. Wilson***
307 US 268 (1939)
Justice Frankfurter delivered the opinion.

In an attempt to restrict voter registration, the Oklahoma legislature provided that all those who were already registered would remain qualified voters, but that all others would have to register within 12 days (from April 30 to May 11, 1916) or be forever barred from the polls. In 1934, I. W. Lane, a black, was refused registration on the basis of this statute. The U.S. Supreme Court declared that the statute was in conflict with the Fifteenth Amendment to the U.S. Constitution, and, as such, was unconstitutional.

***Smith v. Allwright***
321 US 649 (1944)

The Texas State Democratic party, in convention, limited the right of membership to white electors, thereby denying nonwhites the right to participate in a Democratic party primary. In *Grovey v. Townsend* (295 US 45), the Supreme Court had upheld this limitation as not being unconstitutional because the determination was made by the party in convention, not by a party executive committee as in *Condon*. Here the Supreme Court overruled *Grovey,* stating, "The United States is a constitutional democracy. Its organic law grants to all citizens a right to participate in the choice of elected officials without restriction by any state because of race." The Court noted that the political party makes its selection of candidates as an agency of the state and, as such, could not exclude participation based on race and remain consistent with the Fifteenth Amendment.

***Baker v. Carr***
369 US 186 (1962)

This case was brought by electors in several counties of the state of Tennessee, who asserted that the 1901 legislative reapportionment statute was unconstitutional because the numbers of voters in the various districts had changed substantially since then. The plaintiffs requested that the court either direct a reapportionment by mathematical application of the Tennessee constitutional formula to the 1960 census, or instruct the state to hold direct at-large elections. The district court dismissed the case on the grounds that it was a political question and, as such, did not fall within the protection of the Fourteenth Amendment. The U.S. Supreme Court ruled that the case involved a basic constitutional right and thereby was within court jurisdiction, and remanded the case to the district court.

***Gomillion v. Lightfoot***
364 US 339 (1960)

In this case black citizens challenged an Alabama statute that redefined the boundaries of the City of Tuskegee. The statute altered the shape of Tuskegee and placed all but four of Tuskegee's 400 black voters outside of the city limits, while not displacing a single white.

***Allen v. State Board of Elections***
393 US 110 (1969)

The Supreme Court emphasized that subtle, as well as obvious state regulations, "which have the effect of denying citizens their right to vote because of their race" are prohibited. The Court confirmed that Section 5 of the Voting Rights Act covered a variety of practices other than voter registration.

***Georgia v. United States***
411 US 526 (1973)

This case confirmed the propriety of the Voting Rights Act

of 1965, which forbids certain states (including Alabama, Georgia, Louisiana, Mississippi, North Carolina, South Carolina and Virginia, which all had a history of depriving blacks of the right to vote) from implementing any change in voting practices and procedures without first submitting the proposed plan to the U.S. Attorney for approval.

***White v. Regester***
412 US 755 (1973)

The Supreme Court struck down a Texas multi-member districting scheme that was being used invidiously to prevent blacks from being elected to public office. The Court upheld a finding that even though there was no evidence that blacks faced official obstacles to registration, voting and running for office, they had been excluded from effective participation in the political process in violation of the Equal Protection Clause of the Constitution.

***Thornburg v. Gingles***
478 US 30 (1986)

This was the Supreme Court's first decision interpreting the provisions of Section 2 of the Voting Rights Act, as amended in 1982, which prohibits voting schemes that result in a denial or abridgement of the right to vote due to race or color. In this landmark decision, the Court ruled that the redistricting plan adopted by the North Carolina legislature, which led to racially polarized voting by whites, and diluted black voting strength, is in violation of the Act which prohibits voting requirements that have a discriminatory effect, as well as those that are intentionally discriminatory.

## Requirements for Legislative Membership

***Bond v. Floyd***
251 F. Supp 333 (1966)

This was the first of two crucial admissions cases involving issues other than the legal qualifications of an elected official to serve in a state legislature. Julian Bond, duly elected to the Georgia House of Representatives, was prevented from taking the oath of office as constitutionally required of such representatives, and thus excluded from membership in two successive sessions of the Georgia House. Grounds for his exclusion involved alleged statements he had either made or supported, in which U.S. policy in Vietnam, as well as the operation of the Selective Service laws, were attacked. Bond then brought an action in U.S. District Court, Northern District of Georgia, on the grounds that the House action depriving him of his seat was unauthorized and a clear violation of his rights under the First Amendment. The District Court, Griffin Bell, Circuit Judge, declared that it had jurisdiction to decide the Constitutionality of the case, that the Georgia House was authorized by state law to take such exclusionary action, and that the plaintiff's right to free speech was not violated. The Supreme Court, however, ruled that Bond's statements did not constitute any incitement to violation of law and reversed the lower court on the question of his right to freedom of expression as guaranteed by the First Amendment.

***Powell v. McCormack***
395 US 486 (1969)

According to the Constitution, only three basic factors govern eligibility to serve as a legislator in the U.S. House of Representatives: the proper age, the possession of U.S. citizenship, and the fulfillment of the state's residency requirement. When Congressman Adam Clayton Powell Jr. was excluded from the 90th Congress on the grounds that he had misused public funds and defied the courts of his home state, the duly elected Congressman from New York's 18th Congressional District filed suit in Federal Court in an attempt to force the House to review only the necessary credentials for membership. The district court dismissed the first petition on the grounds that it lacked jurisdiction. By the time the case was finally heard before the U.S. Supreme Court, the 90th Congress had adjourned. Powell, however, was reelected and finally seated in the 91st Congress, a gesture which in the view of the court did not moot the case. The legal point on which the case hinged involved the distinction between "expulsion" and "exclusion." Despite the more than two-thirds majority required for expulsion, the

*Julian Bond went to Court to be seated in the Georgia legislature.*

*Congress tried but failed to exclude Adam Clayton Powell.*

Court ruled that the intent of the House was to "exclude," not to "expel." Many House members entertained severe doubts about their ability to expel a member for misconduct occurring during a prior session. The Court summation stated flatly that "the House was without power to exclude him from its membership."

## Employment

***Quarles v. Philip Morris***
279 F. Supp 505 (1968)

A Federal Court required equal pay for equal work and maintenance of seniority when an employee is promoted from one department to another. The effect of this decision was to be felt in a number of subsequent administrative decisions including the Labor Department's 1973 order to Bethlehem Steel to make sweeping changes in its seniority system at its Sparrows Point, Md. plant, and an agreement in 1973 signed between the government and The American Telephone and Telegraph Co. in which the latter agreed to promote and grant retroactive pay increases to thousands of minority employees.

***Ali v. State Athletic Commission***
316 F. Supp 1246 (1970)

A federal district court ruled that Muhammad Ali was discriminated against when the New York State Athletic Commission denied him the right to box because of a Selective Service violation and ordered the commission to renew his boxing license. Ali's claim to be a conscientious objector had been denied by Selective Service officials, but was under appeal. The Court noted that boxers convicted of more serious crimes than Ali's had not been deprived of their licenses. (In 1971, the Supreme Court declared Ali to be a sincere conscientious objector and reversed his five-year jail term; 403 US 698.)

***Griggs v. Duke Power***
401 US 424 (1971)

The Supreme Court ruled that under Title VII of the 1964 Civil Rights Act, tests for hiring and promotion must be related to job performance and cannot be used to exclude minorities, even though the tests, such as high school IQ tests, seem to be neutral on their face. In writing the decision, approved by an 8 to 0 vote, Chief Justice Burger stated that "any tests used must measure the person for the job and not the person in the abstract." The case was initiated by 13 black employees of the Duke Power Co., in Draper, N.D., who had been denied promotion.

***Teamsters v. United States***
431 US 324 (1977)

In enforcing the Civil Rights Act of 1964, the Supreme Court held that because of proven union and employer discrimination post-1964 Act discrimination victims were entitled to full relief available to make them whole, including retroactive seniority. However, the court required proof of "intent to discriminate," to establish that a given seniority system is illegal. (Subsequent late 1970s cases in lower Federal Courts have resulted in relief being granted which, in addition to retroactive seniority, included retroactive back pay.)

***Kaiser Aluminum v. Weber***
443 US 193 (1979)

The Supreme Court held that Kaiser Aluminum's voluntary affirmative action plan, created as a result of collective bargaining between Kaiser and the United Steel Workers of America, which granted preference to black employees over more senior white employees in advancement, did not violate the antidiscrimination sections of the 1964 Civil Rights Act. In 1981, the U.S. Department of Justice indicated it would seek to have this decision reversed.

***Fullilove v. Klutznick***
448 US 448 (1980)

See Affirmative Action Cases

***Gulf Oil Company v. Bernard***
68L Ed 2d693 (1981)

In an employee class action suit, an order limiting communications to class members was held to be an abuse of the discretion provided under the Federal Civil Procedure Rules. Here, Gulf proposed to provide back pay to alleged victims of discrimination in exchange for waivers releasing the company from all discrimination claims. However, some employees felt that proposal, fostered by the Equal Employment Opportunity Commission, was inadequate and sought to initiate proceedings to secure what they thought would be adequate relief.

A district court imposed a "gag order" which restricted the dissidents from communicating their point of view to other Gulf employees. The Supreme Court invalidated the gag order as an unconstitutional prior restraint on the First Amendment right of expression because there was no showing of a need to justify such a restraint.

***McDonnell Douglas Corp. v. Green***
411 US 792 (1973)

The plaintiff, a black technician and activist in the civil rights movement, challenged his employer's decision to fire him. Green had participated in a "stall-in" and "lock-in" in protest of the company's decision and the company's treatment of blacks, generally. Green applied for re-employment in response to the advertisements for qualified mechanics. McDonnell refused to rehire Green allegedly because of his participation in the protests. Green filed a lawsuit contending that he was not rehired because of his race and involvement in the civil rights movement.

This case, one of the most significant in the area of employment discrimination, established the framework by which the factual issue of an employee's motivation is resolved. The Supreme Court determined that the initial burden of establishing a prima facia case of discrimination rests with the plaintiff who must show that he/she: (1) is within a protected class (racial, ethnic or female); (2) applied for a job for which the employer was seeking applicants; (3) was rejected despite his/her qualifications and (4) the employer continued to seek applicants. Green proved these factors and won his case.

***Albemarle Paper Co. v. Moody***
422 US 405 (1975)

Black employees of a paper mill in Roanoke Rapids, North Carolina successfully challenged the company's use of written tests which allegedly measured numerical and verbal intelligence. Based upon the standards enunciated in *Griggs* v. *Duke Power Co.*, the Court determined that the tests were discriminatory because they were not job-related and did not predict success on the job. More importantly, the Supreme Court held that the plaintiffs were entitled to "complete justice" and necessary relief that would "make them whole." The Court awarded the black employees back pay and made it clear that back pay should rarely be denied once there has been a showing of discrimination. The Court stated that back pay will not be denied simply because the employer acted in good faith or did not intend to discriminate.

***Hazelwood School District v. United States***
433 US 299 (1977)

Plaintiffs, blacks seeking teaching positions in the suburban part of St. Louis, Missouri offered statistical data to prove that they had been denied employment opportunities. Plaintiffs attempted to prove their case by showing that the percentage of black students was greater than the percentage of black teachers in the school district.
Although the Supreme Court affirmed that "statistics can be an important source of proof in employment discrimination cases," it rejected the plaintiffs' statistical evidence as irrelevant. The Court concluded that the proper comparison was between the percentage of blacks in the relevant geographical area who were qualified to teach and the percentage of blacks in Hazelwood's teaching staff.

*Court decisions in the past guaranteed equal pay for equal work and required that tests for hiring and promotion must be related to job performance and cannot be used to exclude minorities.*

***Meritor Savings Bank, FSB v. Vinson***
106 S.Ct. 2399 (1985)

Mechelle Vinson, a black woman employed as a teller at a bank in Washington, D.C., claimed that she had been sexually harassed for more than two months by her supervisor, Sidney Taylor, a white male. Vinson admitted that Taylor did not condition his denial or granting of employment benefits upon her acceptance of sexual favors, which included sexual intercourse during banking hours.

In this first Supreme Court ruling on sexual harassment, the Court firmly condemned sexual harassment that creates an intimidating, hostile and offensive working environment even when the harassment does not have economic ramifications. The unanimous ruling made it clear that Title VII of the Civil Rights Act embraces both sexual harassment that involves economic reprisals and that involving a hostile and sexually charged atmosphere in the workplace.

Although *Meritor* was not based upon a claim of racial discrimination, it is significant in light of the historic discrimination black women have experienced in the labor markets of America due to their sex and race.

### *Saint Francis College v. Al-Khazraji*
107 S.Ct. 2022 (1987)

In this action, the plaintiff, a U.S. citizen born in Iraq, alleged that he was denied tenure as a professor due to his Arabian racial origin. He alleged that the College's actions violated 42 U.S.C. {1981, a federal statute promulgated during the Reconstruction era to address the problems of freed slaves. The Supreme Court rejected the College's argument that Section 1981 does not cover claims of discrimination by one Caucasian against another and held that all ethnic groups are protected by the statute. The Court pointed out that although Jews and Arabs might be classified as Caucasians in this century, they were considered distinct ethnic or racial groups during the 1800s. Therefore, the Court determined that Congress intended to protect from discrimination "persons who are subjected to intentional discrimination solely because of their ancestry or ethnic characteristics." The Court concluded that if an individual can prove "that he was subjected to intentional discrimination based on the place or nation of his origin or religion," he will have made out a case.

The Supreme Court applied the reasoning in *Saint Francis* to *Shaare Tefila Congregation* v. *Cobb,* an action instituted by a synagogue alleging that the destruction of the Congregation's property was racially discriminatory.

### *Watson v. Fort Worth Bank & Trust*
108 US 2777 (1987)

Clara Watson, a black woman, alleged that she was repeatedly denied promotion to supervisory positions which were awarded to white employees with equivalent or lesser experience. The bank contended that its promotion decisions were based on various subjective criteria including experience, previous supervisory experience and the ability to get along with others.

The Supreme Court held that Watson did not have to prove intentional discrimination. The Court concluded that subjective facially neutral selection devices which disadvantage blacks in much the same way as objective criteria written tests are unlawful.

## Affirmative Action

Affirmative action, the conscious use of race, sex or national origin to rectify the effects of historical discrimination and to prevent discrimination in the future has been endorsed by Congress, past presidents, state and local governments, unions and employers. The use of affirmative action in cases involving housing, education, employment and government contracting has been endorsed by the courts.

In a national poll taken in 1982, Louis Harris reported that 75% of all Americans believe that special efforts to assure equal opportunity are "fair" and necessary to overcome past discrimination.

### *U.S. Steelworkers v. Brian Weber*
433 US 193 (1979)

The United Steelworkers of America and Kaiser Aluminum Company entered into a collective bargaining agreement including a voluntary affirmative action plan designed to eliminate conspicuous racial imbalances in Kaiser's almost exclusively white skilled workforce. The Plant in Gramercy, Louisiana agreed to reserve 50% of the openings in the skilled job training programs for blacks until the percentage of black skilled workers was equal to the percentage of blacks in the local labor force. Brian Weber, a white production worker, who was turned down for the training program although he had more seniority than many accepted blacks, sued, claiming that the affirmative action program discriminated against whites.

The Supreme Court limited the issue to the narrow question of whether Title VII forbids private employers and unions from establishing voluntary affirmative action plans. In a 5-2 opinion the Court upheld the affirmative action plan and established three factors to determine the validity of racial preference. The Court approved the plan because it was: (1) designed to break down Kaiser's historic patterns of racial segregation; (2) did not unnecessarily trammel the interests of white employees since it did not require the firing of white employees and (3) was a temporary measure not intended to maintain racial balance but simply to eliminate an imbalance.

### *Fullilove v. Klutznik*
448 US 448 (1980)

The U.S. Supreme Court upheld a provision of the Public Works Employment Act of 1977 that required a 10% set-aside of Federal funds for minority business enterprises on local public work projects. The provision had been challenged as violative of the equal protection clause of the Fifth Amendment.

### *Firefighters Local Union No. 1784 v. Stotts*
467 US 561 (1984)

In May 1981, for the first time in its history, the City of Memphis announced lay-offs of city employees, due to a projected budget deficit. The lay-offs, which included the Fire Department, were to be made on a "last hired, first fired" city-wide seniority system that had been adopted in 1973. Carl Stotts, a black firefighter, sued to stop the layoffs. Blacks had been hired pursuant to the affirmative action provisions of a 1980 court decree. They would be laid off in far greater numbers than their white co-workers.

In a 6 - 3 decision the Supreme Court held that since the 1980 court decree did not say that blacks had special protection during a lay-off, the lay-offs had to be made according to the 1973 seniority system.

### *Wygant v. Jackson Board of Education*
476 U.S. 267 (1986)

The Supreme Court dealt a tremendous blow to affirmative action in this case involving a public school system's affirmative action plan. The record reflected that the first black school teacher was not hired in Jackson, Michigan until 1953. By 1969, only 3.9% of the teachers were black although 15.2% of the students were black. In response, the school board developed an affirmative action plan which protected black faculty members during lay-offs.

Although the Supreme Court had approved affirmative action plans in prior cases, it rejected the Jackson plan. The Court found that the goal of the plan, to remedy societal discrimination and afford positive role models to black students, was nebulous and not sufficiently compelling.

### *Local No. 93, International Association of Firefighters v. City of Cleveland*
106 S.Ct. 3063 (1986)

The City of Cleveland, which had a long and ugly history of racial discrimination, negotiated a consent decree with black firefighters who had filed a lawsuit alleging that they had been unlawfully denied jobs and promotions. The decree included an affirmative action plan with numerical goals for promotion of blacks to supervisor.

In response to the union's challenge on behalf of white firefighters, the Supreme Court ruled that the lower courts had broad discretion to approve decrees in which employers settle discrimination suits by agreeing to preferential promotions of blacks, in spite of the objections of white employees.

### *Local 28, Sheet Metal Workers International Association v. EEOC*
106 S.Ct. 3019 (1986)

After finding that the all-white union had discriminated against blacks and Hispanics seeking to enter the sheet metal trades for more than a decade, the trial court ordered the union to establish a 29% non-white membership goal. The court also ruled that the union would have to pay substantial fines if the union failed to meet the goals. After the union failed to reach the goal, the court found the union in contempt and established a new goal of 29.3%. The union challenged the court's order.

In a complex opinion, the Supreme Court upheld the affirmative action goal in light of the union's "persistent or egregious discrimination" and to eliminate "lingering effects of pervasive discrimination." This was the first time the Court expressly approved the use of race conscious relief to blacks and Hispanics who were not identified victims of discrimination.

### *United States v. Paradise*
480 US 149 (1987)

This case started in 1972 when the NAACP sued the Alabama Department of Highways because of its long-standing history of racially discriminating employment practices. More than eleven years later, after the Department had failed to hire or promote blacks, the trial court ordered the promotion of one black trooper for every white. The U.S. Attorney General challenged the constitutionality of the plan. The Supreme Court upheld the use of strict racial quotas and found that the plan was "narrowly tailored to serve a compelling government

*Demonstrators sponsored by the National Committee to Overturn the Bakke Decision march in Washington.*

interest" — remedying "egregious" past discrimination against blacks.

***Johnson v. Transportation Agency, Santa Clara County, California***
480 US 616 (1987)

The Supreme Court held that the State Transportation agency's voluntary affirmative action plan, under which a female had been promoted to the position of road dispatcher over a male whose score was slightly higher, was consistent with Title VII of the Civil Rights Act of 1964. The Court held that an employer does not have to admit or prove that it has discriminated in order to justify efforts designed to achieve a more racially balanced workforce. The employer only needs to demonstrate that there is a "conspicuous ... imbalance in traditionally segregated job categories."

### Racial Intermarriage

***Loving v. Virginia***
388 US 1 (1967)

This case virtually nullified the antimiscegenation laws, many of which remain in southern state constitutions and legal codes. It concerned a white man and black woman, residents of Virginia, who married in Washington, D.C. Virginia indicted and convicted them of violating its laws against racial intermarriage when the couple returned to Virginia and attempted to reside there, but released them when the couple agreed not to reside in the state for 25 years. The Lovings, however, decided to challenge the agreement and the law. Their appeal was rejected by the Virginia courts but upheld by the U.S. Supreme Court, which ruled the Virginia law unconstitutional. Soon thereafter, federal district courts in other states which forbade intermarriage were ordering local officials to issue marriage licenses to interracial couples applying for them. (Text of antimiscegenation statutes and state constitutional restrictions can be found in the second edition of the *Negro Almanac*, pages 254-263).

*Mr. and Mrs. Richard P. Loving vanquished Virginia's miscegenation law.*

## NOTABLE ADVERSE U.S. SUPREME COURT DECISIONS

In two cases, *Scott* v. *Sandford* and *Plessy* v. *Ferguson,* the U.S. Supreme Court issued monumental decisions which adversely affected the legal progress of blacks in the United States. The *Dred Scott* case denied blacks all rights of citizenship in accordance with the U.S. Constitution while the *Plessy* dictum not only institutionalized the concept of "separate but equal" facilities in public carriers but also paved the way for the development of the "Jim Crow" system throughout the South. Also, in *Regents of University of California v. Allan Bakke,* the Court's decision effectively negated past gains through affirmative action special admissions programs.

***Regents of University of California v. Allan Bakke***
438 US 265 (1978)

A white male, Allan Bakke, who had been denied admission to the University of California Medical School at Davis for two consecutive years, instituted an action for declaratory and injunctive relief against the Regents of the University in the Superior Court of Yolo County, citing the equal protection clause of the Fourteenth Amendment, a provision of the California constitution, and the proscription in Title VI of the Civil Rights Act of 1964 against racial discrimination in any program receiving Federal financial assistance, in alleging the invalidity of the medical school's special admission program under which only disadvantaged members of certain minority races were considered for 16% of the 100 places in each year's class. Whereas members of any race could qualify under the school's general admission program for the other 84 places in the class, the plaintiff had been denied admission to the school under the general admission program even though applicants with substantially lower entrance examination scores had been admitted under the special admissions program. Finding that the special admissions program operated as a racial quota because minority applicants in the special program were rated only against one another, and 16 places in the class of 100 were reserved for them, the trial court (1) declared that the school could not take race into account in making the admissions decision, and (2) held that the challenged admissions program violated the federal and state constitutions and Title VI, but (3) refused to order the plaintiff's admission because he had failed to prove that he would have been admitted but for the existence of the special program. On direct appeal, the Supreme Court of California affirmed the trial court's judgment insofar as it determined that the special admissions program was invalid under the equal protection clause, but reversed it insofar as it denied an injunction ordering that the plaintiff be admitted to the medical school, having ruled that the university had the burden of demonstration that the plaintiff would not have been admitted even in the absence of the special admissions program, and the university conceded its inability to carry that burden.

### *Scott v. Sandford*

(1856)

Chief Justice Taney delivered the opinion.

In 1835, Dred Scott, born a slave in Virginia, became the property of John Emerson, an Army doctor, in the slave state of Missouri. From there, he was taken into the free state of Illinois and later to the free territory of Minnesota.

In 1847, Scott instituted suit in the Circuit Court of the County of St. Louis, Missouri, arguing that he should be given his freedom by virtue of his having resided on free soil. After nine years, his case was certified to the U.S. Supreme Court, where five of the nine justices, including Chief Justice Taney, were Southerners.

The Court considered three basic questions:

1. Was Scott a citizen of Missouri, and hence within the jurisdiction of the Federal Court there?
2. Did residence in a free area of the United States automatically entitle Scott to his freedom?
3. Was the Missouri Compromise constitutional?

In delivering his opinion, Chief Justice Taney declared that, by virtue of both the Declaration of Independence and the Constitution, blacks could not be regarded as citizens of the United States. Moreover, the Court could not deprive slaveholders of their right to take slaves into any part of the Union, North or South. In effect, therefore, the Missouri Compromise, as well as other antislavery legislation, was declared to be unconstitutional.

*...If the Constitution recognizes the right of property of the master in a slave, and makes no distinction between that description of property and other property owned by a citizen, no tribunal, acting under the authority of the United States, whether it be legislative, executive, or judicial, has a right to draw such a distinction, or deny to it the benefit of the provisions and guarantees which have been provided for the protection of private property against the encroachments of the government...*

*Key figures in the historic Dred Scott case, which denied blacks the rights of citizenship, were Chief Justice Roger B. Taney (below), and Dred Scott (left).*

*Upon the whole, therefore, it is the judgment of this court, that it appears by the record before us that the plaintiff in error is not a citizen of Missouri, in the sense in which that word is used in the Constitution; and that the Circuit Court of the United States, for that reason, had no jurisdiction in the case, and could give no judgment in it.*

**Plessy v. Ferguson**
(1896)
Justice Brown delivered the opinion.

The *Plessy* case was a test of the constitutionality of an 1890 Louisiana law providing for separate railway carriages for whites and blacks.

*The information filed in the criminal District Court charged in substance that (Homer) Plessy, being a passenger between two stations within the state of Louisiana, was assigned by officers of the company to the coach used by the race to which he did not belong.*

In the majority opinion of the Court, "separate but equal" accommodations for blacks constituted a "reasonable" use of state police power. Furthermore, it was said that the Fourteenth Amendment "could not have been intended to abolish distinctions based on color, or to enforce social... equality, or a co-mingling of the two races upon terms unsatisfactory to either."

## Civil Rights Cases (1883)

This group of civil rights cases was heard before the Supreme Court in an effort to determine the constitutionality of the 1875 Civil Rights Act, the first piece of national legislation which attempted to guarantee people of all races "full and equal enjoyment" of all public accommodations, including inns, public conveyances, theaters, and other places of amusement. The Court ruled, however, that the Act was unconstitutional inasmuch as it did not spring directly from the Thirteenth and Fourteenth amendments to the Constitution. In the view of the Court, the Thirteenth Amendment was concerned exclusively with the narrow confines of slavery and involuntary servitude. The Fourteenth Amendment, by a comparable yardstick of interpretation, did not empower Congress to enact direct legislation to counteract the effect of state laws or policies. The effect of this ruling was to deprive blacks of the very protections which the three postwar Freedom Amendments were designed to provide.

***American Tobacco Company v. John Patterson, et al.***
No. 80-1199 (1982)
Justice White delivered the opinion.

The petitioner, American Tobacco Company, operates two plants in Richmond, Virginia, one of which manufactures cigarettes and the other, pipe tobacco. Each plant is divided into a prefabrication department, which blends and prepares tobacco for further processing, and a fabrication department, which manufactures the final product. It is uncontested that prior to 1963 the company and the union, The Bakery, Confectionary and Tobacco Workers Union, and its affiliate Local 182 had engaged in overt racial discrimination. The union maintained two segregated locals, and black employees were assigned to jobs in the lower-paying prefabrication departments. Higher-paying jobs in the fabrication departments were largely reserved for white employees. An employee could transfer from one of the predominantly black prefabrication departments to one of the predominantly white fabrication departments by forfeiting his seniority.

On January 3, 1969, respondent John Patterson and two other black employees filed charges with the Equal Employment Opportunity Commission alleging that the petitioners had discriminated against them on the basis of race. After conciliation failed, the employees filed a class action suit in District Court in 1973 charging the American Tobacco Company with racial discrimination.

In November 1968, the company proposed the establishment of nine lines of progression, six of which were at issue in the case. Four of the six lines of progression at issue consisted mainly of all-white top jobs from the fabrication departments linked with nearly all-white bottom jobs from the fabrication departments. The other two consisted of all-black top jobs from the prefabrication departments linked with all-black bottom jobs from the prefabrication departments. The top jobs in the white lines of progression were among the best paying jobs in the plant. The actions were consolidated for trial and injunctive relief was initially granted, but ultimately the Court of Appeals, without deciding whether the lines of progression were part of a seniority system, held that even if they were, Section 703(h) does not apply to seniority systems adopted after the effective date of the Civil Rights Acts.

***City of Mobile, Alabama v. Wiley L. Bolden et al.***
446 US 55 (1980)

A class action was brought in the U.S. District Court for the Southern District of Alabama on behalf of a class of all-black citizens of Mobile, alleging among other things that the defendant city's practice of electing commissioners at large by a majority vote unfairly diluted the voting strength of blacks in violation of the Fourteenth and Fifteenth amendments. The District Court, although finding that blacks in the city registered and voted without hindrance, nonetheless held that the plaintiff's Constitutional rights had been violated, and entered a judgment in their favor, ordering that Mobile's city commissioners be disestablished and replaced by a municipal government consisting of a mayor and a city council composed of members selected from single member districts (423F Supp 384).

***Louis Swint and Willie Johnson v. Pullman Standard United Steelworkers of America***
72L Ed 2d66 (1982)
Justice White delivered the opinion.

Black employees of Pullman Standard brought a suit in Federal District Court against Pullman Standard and against the union, alleging that Title VII of the Civil Rights Act of 1964 was violated by a seniority system. The District Court found "that the difference in terms, conditions or privileges of employment resulting from the seniority system are not the result of an intention to discriminate because of race or color" and held, therefore, that the system satisfied the requirements of Section 703(h) of the Civil Rights Act. In reversing the decision, the Court of Appeals for the Fifth Circuit said, "because we find the differences in the terms, conditions and standards of employment for black workers and white workers at Pullman Standard resulted from an intent to discriminate because of race, we hold that the system is not legally valid under section 703(h) of Title VII US. C. 2000e-2(h)."

***Allen v. Wright***
488 US 737 (1984)

Parents of black children instituted a nationwide lawsuit claiming that the IRS's failure to deny tax-exempt status to racially discriminating private schools constituted federal financial aid to racially segregated institutions and diminished the ability of their children to receive a racially desegregated education. The court refused to hear the case or the merits on the grounds that the plaintiffs did not have "standing" because they failed to show that the injury suffered was "fairly traceable" or caused by the conduct of the IRS. Further the court maintained that the remedy was "speculative" since there was no showing that the withdrawal of tax-exempt status would cause schools to end their racially discriminatory practices and desegregate. The Court's imposition of such an artificial and stringent standing requirement, which had not been used in other cases not involving school desegregation, effectively denied the black parents their day in court.

***Reddick v. School Board of Norfolk***
784 F. 2d 521 (4th Cir. 1986)

The Supreme Court refused to accept this case to review the Fourth Circuit's determination that a school system which declared unity after carrying out a court ordered plan may then dismantle the plan and resegregate its schools, even though there is evidence that the decision to declare the school unity was intentionally racially discriminatory.

***McKlesky v. Kemp***
481 US 279 (1987)

In April 1987, the Supreme Court decided one of the most significant cases involving the imposition of the death penalty in America. Warren McKlesky, a 38-year-old black man accused of killing a police officer while robbing a furniture store, was sentenced to death by the State of Georgia. In support of his claim that the sentence violated his constitutional rights, McKlesky introduced a sophisticated statistical study that analyzed more than 2,000 murder cases in Georgia. The study demonstrated that there is a disparity in the imposition of the capital sentence based on the race of the victim, as well as the race of the defendant.

Defendants charged with killing white persons received the death penalty in 11% of the cases, but defendants charged with killing blacks received the death penalty in only 1% of the cases. The study further showed that prosecutors asked for the death penalty in 70% of the cases involving black defendants and white victims, and only 19% of the cases involving white defendants and black victims. In sum, the analysis revealed that blacks who kill whites are 4.3 times more likely to receive the death sentence.

In the 5 - 4 opinion, written by Justice Powell, the Supreme Court acknowledged that it had accepted statistics as proof of intent to discriminate in employment, housing and voting cases. However, despite the compelling statistical evidence the Court rejected McKlesky's claim that the death penalty in Georgia is applied in a racially discriminatory manner. The Court's reasoning was that although McKlesky showed the existence of racial discrimination in sentencing, generally, he failed to prove that "racial considerations played a part in his sentence."

Finally, Justice Powell expressed concern that acceptance of McKlesky's argument would open the floodgates of litigation by black defendants seeking to introduce statistical evidence to demonstrate that race affected the outcome of their case.

## STATE ANTIDISCRIMINATION LAWS

In 1974, 33 states encompassing three-fourths of the nation's population had laws on the books which were specifically designed to protect minorities from discrimination in one or more of the following categories: housing, employment, recreation, and education. Most of these laws were enacted prior to the federal civil rights acts of the 1960s and sought to have an educative rather than coercive effect. Enforcement was usually in response to a complaint of discrimination filed by one or a few people and was rarely applied as a whole to industries, large employers, or real estate developers.

With the passage of the Federal Civil Rights Acts in 1964, 1965, and 1968, activity on the state level receded still more in expectation that Washington would assume the role of fighting discrimination. However, such enforcement has not been vigorous and state laws and commissions remain important, especially in two respects. They act:

As a course of redress for victims of discrimination who find the federal machinery cumbersome or indifferent.

As a legal weapon for civil rights advocates who feel agreements between the federal government and specific industries are insufficiently protective of minorities. An example of such use of state laws occurred in April 1974 when the Legal Defense Fund sued in federal court to reverse a consent agreement between the government and steel company employers and unions. The Legal Defense Fund charged that the consent decree violated the Fair Employment laws of some 17 states.

## LYNCHING

For the first half of the twentieth century, lynching, far more than desegregation or voting rights, was regarded as the major issue facing blacks. Lynching has not been an easy term to define. The following is a paraphrase of the definition which has been offered in most proposed federal antilynching legislation:

*Lynching is an act of mob violence which results in the death or maiming of a person or persons in the custody of a peace officer, or suspected of, charged with, or convicted of, a serious crime, often one punishable by death.*

Other criteria for lynching were established in a conference arranged by F. D. Patterson at Tuskegee Institute in 1940. These include:

1. Legal evidence of a person's illegal death.
2. Group participation in a killing under the pretext of service to justice, race, or tradition.

Since 1882, the trend in lynchings in the United States has gone downward, as an examination of the following tables provided through the courtesy of Tuskegee Institute will clearly show. In 1963, Tuskegee Institute ceased issuing data on lynchings. Though blacks are still victims of mob violence performed under the guise of justice, death from lynch mobs has become very rare.

## BLACKS AND POLICE

Tensions between blacks and local judicial and law enforcement officials persisted in many areas throughout the 1970s and into the 1980s. One problem involved excessive time required to bring defendants to trial. As a result, many persons spent long periods of time in jail when they were in fact innocent of the charges against them.

The most explosive issue, however, was the frequent failure of law enforcement agencies to forestall use of excessive force against minorities during arrest and incarceration procedures. An extreme example occurred in Miami, when Arthur McDuffie, a black insurance executive, died shortly after his arrest by white police officers. The Miami Liberty City riots of May and July 1980, in which 16 people were killed, erupted when officers charged with murdering McDuffie were acquitted.

Serious confrontations between blacks and police also occurred in Brooklyn, New York following the death by strangulation of a black businessman in a police car after his arrest.

In 1985 and 1986, in New York City, where tension between the police and the black community had been fairly good for a number of years, events reached an almost explosive point with two incidents which many regarded as avoidable. One case involved a 300-pound 67-year-old black women, Eleanor Bumpers who was killed by a shotgun blast fired by a housing policeman who allegedly was attempting to evict her from her home; she supposedly was threatening the policeman with a knife. The second case was that of Michael Stewart, a young black artist who was beaten so severely by transit police that it apparently caused his death.

In Los Angeles, a black man, who presented no danger to the police, was placed in a chokehold by city police. His suit to enjoin the city police from using chokeholds reached the Supreme Court in *City of Los Angeles v. Lyons*, 461 U. S. 95 (1983). The Court rejected his claim stating that Lyons did not have a case because he was no longer in danger of being a victim of a chokehold, and that it was unlikely that he would ever be chokeholded in the future.

For the most part, lawsuits challenging police misconduct

*One of the causes of tension between African-Americans and police has been the charge that police sometimes use excessive force when it does not appear to be necessary.*

have not been successful. Trial judges and jurors are sometimes reluctant to convict police officers. Furthermore, recent Supreme Court rulings have severely limited lawsuits attacking the unlawful behavior of law enforcement officers and government agencies.

The degree of polarization found in some cities was underscored in 1981 by a poll of attitudes toward police in Milwaukee where a young black, Ernest Lacy, died while in custody for a rape he did not commit. Two-thirds of whites felt the Milwaukee police were doing a good job, while two-thirds of blacks felt they were not.

An issue in Milwaukee was the absence of high-ranking blacks on the police force. A consent decree in 1975 between the city and the EEOC induced the city to hire some 200 black police, but by December 1981 no black held higher rank than sergeant.

The Reagan Administration's decision in 1982 to dismantle the Law Enforcement Assistance Administration (LEAA), which had designed nation-wide programs to investigate and address allegations of police abuse, stymied the advances made to alleviate police misconduct, and placed the responsibility of challenging abusive police actions on civil rights and community based groups.

Beginning in the early 1980s community groups began to effectively use their political strength to influence police department policies and to eliminate abusive police tactics. These efforts included monitoring police activities, legislative initiatives and litigation. In many cities, including New York, Chicago, and Philadelphia, community-based groups developed comprehensive approaches to institutionalized police misconduct. These groups have urged the creation of civilian review boards to investigate and redress claims of police misconduct.

Throughout the 1980s the NAACP Legal Defense Fund and other civil rights groups and lawyers pursued challenges attacking the racially discriminatory hiring and promotion practices of police departments in Detroit, Michigan, New Orleans, Louisiana, Canada, New Jersey and other cities across the nation. In one such action against the City of Louisville, Kentucky, the Fund in 1987 reached a settlement of $3.2 million in back pay for 96 blacks who had been denied positions as police officers. This litigation has produced enormous gains as to the number of black police officers throughout the country. In 1970, 6.3 percent of the police officers were black; by 1980, more than 10 percent of the nation's police officers were black.

The relevance of a fair representation of black police officers is reflected in a lawsuit involving the police department of Detroit, Michigan. In that case, it was demonstrated that black-white community relations improved; fewer officers were killed or injured in the line of duty; there was as well a substantial increase in the number of homicide cases that were solved.

Another positive sign from the white community was that a jury in Wisconsin awarded $1.8 million to the family of Daniel Bell, a black man killed by Milwaukee police in 1958, and a Boston jury awarded $150,000 to the wife of James Bowden, shot to death by police in 1975. In 1981, Milwaukee's District Attorney took a firm public position against police excesses. And during the 1970s, the EEOC achieved gains toward recruitment of minorities for the police forces in several cities (See employment section.)

## BLACKS AND THE LEGAL PROFESSION

### A Brief History and Current Status

During the 19th century, handfuls of black lawyers dotted the nation. In 1890, of the country's 89,630 lawyers 431 were black. By 1900, the number of black lawyers had increased to 728 of the total of 114,703 lawyers. It was not until the 20th century that black lawyers moved from being generally excluded to the periphery of the profession. By 1930, there were roughly 1,100 black lawyers, and by 1940 that number had increased by only 300 or to 1,400. After the launching of the NAACP's campaign for civil rights, and after World War II, blacks began to more aggressively pursue law careers. By 1970, there were roughly 4,000 black lawyers. Today, it is estimated that there are 19,000 black lawyers in the United States.

Nearly 150 years after the first American State bar admitted its first black lawyer, blacks are still under represented in the profession. Current statistics reflect that blacks represent only 6% of the total number of lawyers in the nation.

The enrollment of blacks in law schools increased by nearly 20 percent in the past decade. According to the American Bar Association more than 1500 black students will graduate from law school in the year 1990. Today, blacks constitute 8 percent of all law students. However, these numbers are trailing off and the percentage of blacks in law school has declined in recent years.

The reasons for the declining enrollment appear to be related to the Supreme Court's 1978 ruling in Bakke, after which many schools abandoned their affirmative-action programs. The soaring costs of tuition coupled with cuts in federal grants and loans for students had a particularly adverse impact on black students.

During the 1980s, the legal profession began to extend employment opportunities to blacks, yet, it is generally recognized that subtle barriers still exist and it is still extremely difficult for black lawyers to join major and mid-sized firms. Such circumstance denies black lawyers access to better paid positions and the maximization of professional opportunities.

The most frequently offered unofficial explanation for the minimal participation of black attorneys in many law firms, is that white clients would prefer not to have frequent contact with, or depend upon, black attorneys. Title VII of the Civil Rights Act of 1964 proscribes employment discrimination stemming from perceived racial prejudices of clients or customers as violation of that act. This principle has been so clear that it has seldom merited explicit discussion in the context of a race discrimination case. In the area of sex discrimination, where employers have occasionally attempted to openly justify employment practices on the basis of customer preferences, it has been declared "totally anomalous...to allow the preferences and prejudices of the customers to determine whether...discrimination was valid."

Since the Supreme Court's 1971 ruling in *Diaz v. Pan American Airways*, it has been axiomatic that employers may not discriminate on the basis of client's preferences, and the elimination of employment practices that cater to such prejudices has been a primary target of Title VII.

Another explanation offered for the exclusion of blacks is that the minority lawyer will not "fit in" socially with an otherwise all-white establishment. Title VII which was intended to eliminate decision-making based on "stereotyped characterizations" provides that men and woman shall be employed on the basis of their qualifications, . not as colored citizens, but as citizens of the United States.

Surveys conducted in 1988 demonstrate that the proportion of blacks in the nation's 250 largest law firms, that employ approximately 42,000 lawyers, has changed very little during the 1980s. Blacks account for 1.5 percent of all lawyers in major firms. In fact, while the numbers of lawyers in these firms have increased slightly, the percentages of black lawyers in the firms have steadily declined from 1.60 in 1981 to 1.50 in 1985. The percentages of black partners have increased slightly from .47 in 1981, to .73 in 1985 and 1988.

Blacks continue to have employment and promotional difficulties in many of the nations federal, state, and local legal agencies. The Federal Trade Commission, the National Labor Relations Board and the Maritime Administration have all been charged with discriminatory practices.

The vast majority of black lawyers have their own practices or are members of small black law firms. Such lawyers and law firms find it virtually impossible to break through long established networks and get some degree of access to the more lucrative corporate and governmental contract work.

Many academic sectors of the profession have questionable hiring practices, inasmuch as 33% of the 170 accredited law schools in the country did not employ blacks as full time faculty members as of 1988.

The National Bar Association, the American Bar Association, state bar associations, and local black bar organizations across the country have begun to develop programs designed to ameliorate the problems facing black lawyers in the 80s and beyond. In 1986, the American Bar Association created a sixteen member Commission on Opportunities for Minorities in the Profession and appointed Honorable Dennis Archer to Chair the Commission.

The stated purposes and goals of the Commission are to:

Develop and promote minority legal education opportunities; increase minority hiring, retention and promotion opportunities; coordinate activities within the ABA and with other legal organizations, law schools and law firms; evaluate the performance of the ABA and the profession; serve as a clearing house to publicize, disseminate and draft plans and programs; study and research the problems and solutions.

## BLACKS IN THE JUDICIARY

### An Overview

Inasmuch as blacks have not always been able to regard the law as an impartial, justice-seeking force, it is not surprising that they do not have a long and extensive history in the legal profession. In some states in particular, the law tended to become an instrument of oppression, rather than a vehicle of redress. Before the Civil War, for example, the law constituted one of the forces that prevented the black's escape from slavery. Again, toward the end of Reconstruction, the laws of the South were clearly intended in part to institutionalize the practices of white supremacy.

Despite these obstacles, blacks gradually began to enter the legal profession, albeit predominantly in the North, where they were given some degree of status and the right to represent their clients on equal footing with their white counterparts. The formation of the National Association for the Advancement of Colored People (NAACP) played a vital role in broadening the legal horizons of both the black citizen and the prospective practitioner of law in the twentieth century. By 1939, the year the NAACP Legal Defense and Educational Fund was incorporated, the black had ample reason to believe that the legal institutions of the nation were undergoing a profound metamorphosis—judging particularly from the large number of cases regularly being won by black petitioners before the U.S. Supreme Court. Most legal landmarks in the black's fight for constitutional privileges have been won with the assistance of the NAACP, many by a host of lawyers now active as federal judges in the courts of the United States.

Almost all black judges currently on the bench have received their appointments only since the mid-1960s. Only one black has served as a member of the U.S. Supreme Court, Thurgood Marshall. Marshall's appointment to the Court in 1967 was among the most momentous decisions rendered during the Johnson Administration. Although the qualifications of the former NAACP counsel and Solicitor General were subject to severe criticism by some conservatives who described Marshall's legal outlook as "activist" and as such, a judicial liability, a majority of U.S. Senators rallied to support the nomination and he was confirmed by a vote of 69-11. Marshall pledged for all, "I shall be ever mindful of my obligation to the Constitution and to the goal of equal justice under law." On October 2, 1967, in the presence of President Lyndon Johnson, Marshall took the oath before the court's oldest member, Hugo Black.

## A Brief History

The history of blacks in the judiciary began in 1852 when the Governor of Massachusetts appointed Robert Morris magistrate in Boston. The next appointment of a black to the bench did not occur until 1870 when the South Carolina legislature elected Jonathan Jasper Wright to the South Carolina State Supreme Court. In 1872, George Lee was elected as a trial court judge in North Carolina, and upon his death, in 1873, the legislature elected Macon B. Allen as his successor. These early beginnings of blacks as jurists were followed by a slow trickling stream:

**1873** Mifflin W. Gibbs received an appointment in Little Rock, Arkansas and became the first municipal court judge.

**1883** George Ruffin, a graduate of Harvard Law School and the first black to finish any law school, was appointed to the municipal court in Charleston, Massachusetts, becoming the first black to obtain a judicial position higher than that of magistrate in the North.

**1890** John W. Ballon was appointed to state court in Florida.

**1901** Robert H. Terrell was appointed to municipal court in Washington, D.C. He was the first black to receive a federal judgeship. Terrell, who was reappointed by Presidents Taft, Wilson and Harding, was succeeded successively by three blacks, James A. Cobbs, Armond W. Scott, and Austin Fickling.

**1915** Scipio A. Jones was appointed to the bench in Little Rock, Arkansas.

**1926** James A. Cobb succeeded Robert Terrell to the municipal court in Washington, D.C.

**1937** William H. Hastie was appointed to the federal court in the U.S. Virgin Islands, becoming the nation's first black judge appointed to a federal district court.

**1939** Jane Matilda Bolin became the first black woman judge in the United States when she was appointed to the Domestic Relations Court in New York City.

**1949** William H. Hastie was elevated to the Third Circuit Court of Appeals, becoming the first black judge to serve on the federal appellate level.

**1966** Constance Baker Motley was appointed to the federal district court in New York City, becoming the first black woman moved to a federal bench and the first woman judge in the Southern District of New York.

**1967** Thurgood Marshall was appointed to serve on the United States Supreme Court, becoming the first and only black member of the nation's high court.

**1979** Amalya A. Kearse received an appointment to the Court of Appeals for the Second Circuit in New York, which makes her the only black female to sit on the appellate bench and the highest ranking black female judge.

## Current Status

In 1978, at the time that Congress created the Omnibus Judgeship Act, there was a paucity of black federal judges. Fewer than 20 of the 399 federal district court judges were black, and of the 97 judges at the federal appellate level only 5 were black.

Once the bill was passed, President Carter implemented a selection process designed to enhance the representation of blacks, Hispanics and women on the federal bench. His efforts included the formation of selection commissions composed of persons from diverse racial, political, socioeconomic and professional backgrounds. This was the first time in recent modern history that lay persons participated in the judicial nomination process. He invited civil rights organizations to recommend potential nominees for the newly created vacancies and encouraged senators to identify qualified blacks from their states.

President Carter's earnest commitment to equal justice and "justices" is reflected in his outstanding record in appointing blacks, Hispanics, Asians and women to the federal bench. The Omnibus Judgeship Act, which expanded the federal judiciary by almost 30 percent, created 152 additional federal judgeships, including 117 in the district courts and 35 in the courts of appeal. As a result of President Carter's efforts 38 of his 258 federal judgeships were filled by blacks.

President Reagan had the opportunity to make more judicial appointments than any president in the history of the nation. In fact, 348, almost one-half of the 716 active federal judges were appointed during Reagan's two terms in office,of theseonly seven "qualified" blacks were selected.

## Number and Distribution of Black Judges

Between 1971 and 1974, the number of black judges sitting in Federal Supreme, Appellate, and District level courts increased from 18 to 20. Blacks still comprise only about 5% of the judges sitting on the Appellate and Supreme courts (five of 104) and only about 3% of the judges sitting on Federal District level courts (15 of 437). Also, significantly, black federal judges sit in only eight states and territories, none of them in the South..

During the period of 1974 to 1980, the number of black state judges totaled 291, a decrease from the previous six years. There were still no black state judges in Arkansas and Mississippi, and during that time, West Virginia was also without a black judge either in the federal or state court.

As of 1985, 465 or 3.8% of the country's 12,093 state court judges were black, including 9 black judges on courts of last resort (2.7%) and 33 on intermediate appellate courts. The majority of black judges are concentrated in six major metropolitan cities: Chicago, Detroit, Los Angeles, New York, Philadelphia, and Washington, D.C. Significantly, a higher percentage of blacks chosen were chosen through the appointive process, as compared to the elective system.

The total number of federal judges tripled from 245 in 1948, to 717 in 1988. In 1988, blacks constituted 50 or 6.9 percent of the federal judiciary. Notably, 38 of the blacks currently on the bench were appointed by President Carter.

## JUDICIAL APPOINTMENTS OF BLACK FEDERAL JUDGES

(appointments are made by the President of the United States)

**Franklin D. Roosevelt**
**1933-1945**

**WILLIAM H. HASTIE** (D) — Virgin Islands
1937
**HERMAN E. MOORE** (D) — Virgin Islands
1939
Total Appointed: 224 — Total Black: 2
% Black .89

**Harry S. Truman**
**1945-1953**

**IRWIN C. MOLLISON** — (D)Customs Court
1945
**HERMAN E. MOORE** (S) — Virgin Islands
1949
**WILLIAM HASTIE** (D) — 3rd Circuit (Virgin Islands)
1949
Total appointed: 160 — Total Black: 3
% Black 1.8

**Dwight D. Eisenhower**
**1953-1961**

**SCOVEL RICHARDSON** — (D)Customs Court
1957
**WALTER GORDAN** (D) — Virgin Islands
1958
Total appointed: 180 — Total Black: 2
% Black 1.1

**John J. Kennedy**
**1961-1963**

**JAMES B. PARSONS** — Illinois
**WADE H. MCCREE** — Michigan
1961
**THURGOOD MARSHALL** — 2nd Circuit (NY)
1961
Total appointed: 131 — Total Black: 3
% Black 2.2

**Lyndon B. Johnson**
**1963-1969**

**A. LEON HIGGINBOTHAM** — Pennsylvania
1964
**SPOTTSWOOD ROBINSON** (D) — District of Columbia
1964
**WILLIAM B. BRYANT** — District of Columbia
1965
**AUBREY E. ROBINSON JR.** — District of Columbia
1966
**CONSTANCE B. MOTLEY** — New York
1966
**WADE H. MCCREE** (D) — 6th Circuit (MI)
1966
**JAMES L. WATSON** — Customs Court
1966
**THURGOOD MARSHALL** — U.S. Supreme Court
1967
**JOSEPH C. WADDY** (D) — District of Columbia
1967
**DAMON KEITH** — Michigan
1967
Total appointed: 178 — Total Black: 11
% Black 6.1

**Richard M. Nixon**
**1969-1974**

**ALMERIC CHRISTIAN** — Virgin Islands
1969
**BARRINGTON PARKER** — District of Columbia
1969
**DAVID W. WILLIAMS** — California
1969
**CLIFFORD SCOTT GREEN** — Pennsylvania
1971
**LAWRENCE W. PIERCE** — New York
1971
**ROBERT L. CARTER** — New York
1972
**ROBERT L. DUNCAN** — Military Court of Appeals
1972
**ROBERT L. DUNCAN** — Ohio
1974
Total appointed: 231 — Total Black: 7
% Black 3.0

**Gerald Ford**
**1974-1977**

**HENRY BRAMWELL** — New York
1974
**MATTHEW PERRY** — Military Court of Appeals
1976
**GEORGE N. LEIGHTON** — Illinois
1976
**CECIL F. POOLE** — California
1976
Total appointed: 62 — Total Black: 4
% Black 6.4

**James E. Carter**
**1977-1981**

**A. LEON HIGGINBOTHAM** — 3rd Circuit (PA)
1978
**DAMON KEITH** — 6th Circuit (MI)
1978
**THEODORE MCMILLAN** — 8th Circuit (MO)
1978
**ROBERT F. COLLINS** — Louisiana
1978

| | |
|---|---|
| **JACK E. TANNER**<br>1978 | Washington |
| **MARY JOHNSON LOWE**<br>1978 | New York |
| **JULIAN A. COOK JR.**<br>1978 | Michigan |
| **PAUL A. SIMMONS**<br>1978 | Pennsylvania |
| **DAVID S. NELSON**<br>1978 | Massachusetts |
| **JOSEPH W. HATCHETT**<br>1978 | 11th Circuit (FL) |
| **AMALYA A. KEARSE**<br>1979 | 2nd Circuit (NY) |
| **J. JEROME FARRIS**<br>1979 | 9th Circuit (WA) |
| **CECIL F. POOLE**<br>1979 | 9th Circuit (CA) |
| **NATHANIEL R. JONES**<br>1979 | 6th Circuit (OH) |
| **HARRY T. EDWARDS**<br>1979 | D.C. Circuit |
| **JOSEPH C. HOWARD**<br>1979 | D.C. Circuit |
| **JOHN G. PENN**<br>1979 | District of Columbia |
| **MATTHEW PERRY**<br>1979 | South Carolina |
| **BENJAMIN F. GIBSON**<br>1979 | Michigan |
| **GABRIELLE MCDONALD** (R)<br>1979 | Texas |
| **ANNE E. THOMPSON**<br>1979 | New Jersey |
| **TERRY HATTER**<br>1979 | California |
| **JAMES GILES**<br>1979 | Pennsylvania |
| **HORACE T. WARD**<br>1979 | Georgia |
| **ANNA DIGGS TAYLOR**<br>1979 | Michigan |
| **ALICE L. HASTINGS (R)**<br>1979 | Florida |
| **ODELL HORTON**<br>1979 | Tennessee |
| **U.W. CLEMON**<br>1979 | Alabama |
| **MYRON H. THOMPSON**<br>1979 | Alabama |
| **CONSUELA B. MARSHALL**<br>1980 | California |
| **THELTON E. HENDERSON**<br>1980 | California |
| **NORMAN H. JOHNSON**<br>1980 | District of Columbia |
| **CLYDE S. CAHILL JR.**<br>1980 | Missouri |
| **GEORGE HOWARD JR.**<br>1980 | Arkansas |
| **RICHARD C. ERWIN**<br>1980 | North Carolina |
| **GEORGE WHITE**<br>1980 | Ohio |
| **EARL GILLIAM**<br>1980 | California |
| Total appointed: 259<br>% Black 14.6 | Total Black: 38 |

**Ronald E. Reagan**
**1981-1988**

| | |
|---|---|
| **LAWRENCE PIERCE**<br>1981 | 2nd Circuit (NY) |
| **REGINALD GIBSON**<br>1983 | U.S. Court of Claims |
| **JOHN R. HARGROVE**<br>1984 | Maryland |
| **ANN C. WILLIAMS**<br>1985 | Illinois |
| **HENRY T. WINGATE**<br>1985 | Mississippi |
| **JAMES R. SPENCER**<br>1986 | Virginia |
| **KENNETH HOYT**<br>1988 | Texas |
| Total appointed: 343<br>% Black 2.0 | Total Black: 7 |

**(D) Deceased**
**(R) Retired or resigned**

*Wade McCree, Solicitor General under Jimmy Carter, is now a state court justice in Michigan.*

## BIOGRAPHIES OF BLACK FEDERAL JUDGES

### Supreme Court and District Courts

**WILLIAM BENSON BRYANT**
**U.S. District Judge**
**District of Columbia**

Born in Wetumpka, Alabama on September 18, 1911, Bryant received both his A.B. and LL.B. degrees from Howard University.

Before going on active military duty during World War II (he was honorably discharged with the rank of lieutenant-colonel), Bryant had served briefly with the Works Project Administration (WPA) and then with the Bureau of Intelligence in the Office of War Information.

In 1948, he opened a law office in Washington, D.C., practicing there until 1951 when he entered federal service as an assistant in the office of the U.S. Attorney for the District of Columbia. After three years, Bryant resigned from this post in order to become a member of a private law firm. He had already become a partner in this firm when in 1965 President Lyndon B. Johnson announced his appointment to the federal bench.

**ROBERT LEE CARTER**
**U.S. District Judge**
**Southern District of New York**

Judge Carter was appointed U.S. District Judge for the Southern District of New York in 1972, capping a distinguished career for this veteran of scores of civil rights campaigns.

Carter was born in Florida in 1917, received his A.B. degree from Lincoln University in 1937, and law degrees from Howard and Columbia universities in 1940 and 1942. During World War II Carter served in the Air Force.

After the war, Carter was appointed to a number of challenging posts including: Vice Chairman of the New York City Community Action for Legal Services; a member of the New York State Special Commission on Attica; a member of the Temporary Commission on the State Court System; a member of the Mayor's Committee on the Judiciary; a member of the Mayor's Special Task Force on Minority Employment in the Construction Trades; a member of the Mayor's Advisory Panel to the Board of Higher Education; Special Assistant U.S. Attorney for the Southern District of New York; and a member of the Departmental Committee on Court Administration of the First and Second Judicial Department, Supreme Court of New York.

**ALMERIC CHRISTIAN**
**Judge of the District Court**
**Territory of the Virgin Islands**

Judge Christian was born in Christiansted on the Virgin Island of St. Croix in 1919, only two years after the United States acquired the islands from Denmark. He attended the University of Puerto Rico, then came to the mainland where he graduated with an A.B. degree from Columbia University

*Judge Robert L. Carter served on the Special Commission on Attica.*

in 1942. In 1947, he received his Bachelor of Laws (LL.B.) degree from the Columbia Law School.

Christian was appointed Judge for the Virgin Islands District Court by President Nixon in 1969. In 1970, he became Chief Judge.

**ROBERT F. COLLINS**
**U.S. District Judge**
**Eastern District of Louisiana**

Judge Robert Frederick Collins was born January 27, 1931 in New Orleans. He received his undergraduate degree in 1951 from Dillard University, and his law degree from Louisiana State University in 1954. Judge Collins was a former city attorney with the New Orleans police department, and from 1967 to 1969 he was judge ad hoc of the traffic court of the city of New Orleans. Prior to his appointment to the U.S. District Court, Judge Collins was Judge Magistrate to the Criminal District Court in Orleans Parish, Louisiana.

**JULIAN ABELE COOK JR.**
**U.S. District Judge**
**Eastern District of Michigan**

Julian Abele Cook Jr. was appointed U.S. District Judge for the Eastern District of Michigan, September 23, 1978 by President Jimmy Carter. Judge Cook was born June 22, 1930 in Washington, D.C. He is the co-author of "Some Current Problems of Human Relations Administration" (*Journal of Urban Law, Volume 49, 1971*). He has received a number of honors and awards, among them the Distinguished Citizen of the Year in 1970, from the NAACP of Oakland County, Michigan; a Citation of Merit in 1971 by the Pontiac, Michigan Area Urban League; and the Pathfinders Award from Oakland University in 1977. Judge Cook is a member of a number of community organizations and a participant in numerous activities benefiting his local Michigan area.

### RICHARD C. ERWIN
### U.S. District Judge
### Middle District of North Carolina

Judge Erwin was born August 23, 1923 in McDowell County, North Carolina. He was appointed U.S. District Judge October 31, 1980. From January 1978 to October 1980, he was judge for the North Carolina Court of Appeals and the first black person in the history of that state to win a statewide race for any elective office.

Judge Erwin received his undergraduate degree from Johnson C. Smith University in Charlotte, North Carolina, and his law degree from Howard University. He is a member of the North Carolina Penal Study Commission, a life member of the North Carolina P.T.A. Association, a member of the Board of Visitors of Johnson C. Smith University, and a trustee of the Western North Carolina Conference of the Methodist Church.

### CLIFFORD SCOTT GREEN
### U.S. District Judge
### Eastern District of Pennsylvania

Born in Philadelphia in 1923, Green received his undergraduate and graduate degrees from Temple University, obtaining a Doctor of Laws (J.D.) in 1951.

Judge Green was formerly, in 1964, an Assistant Deputy Attorney General of Pennsylvania; Judge of the Court of Common Pleas of Pennsylvania, from 1964-1972; a member of the Juvenile Court Judges' Commission, from 1965-1972; Co-Chairman of the Philadelphia City White House Conference on Children and Youth, in 1970; a member of the Philadelphia Regional Selection Panel of the President's Commission on White House Fellows; and a member of the President's Advisory Council on Intergovernmental Personnel Policy. During World War II he served in the United States Air Force.

He was appointed to his current position in December 1971.

### JOSEPH W. HATCHETT
### U.S. Circuit Judge
### Fifth Circuit, Tallahassee, Florida

Judge Joseph W. Hatchett was appointed a U.S. Circuit Judge of the United States Court of Appeals on October 1, 1981. He received his undergraduate degree in political science from Florida A&M University in 1954, and his law degree from Howard University in 1959.

Judge Hatchett has written a number of articles for law journals and received numerous awards. He is listed in Who's Who in the South and Southwest, Who's Who in American Law, Who's Who Among Black Americans, The American Bench, Notable Americans, Who's Who in America, and he is also listed as a Notable Black American. Judge Hatchett was the first black to be appointed to the highest court of a state since Reconstruction and the first black to serve on a federal appellate court in the South.

*A. Leon Higginbotham, the first black commissioner in the Federal Trade Commission.*

### A. LEON HIGGINBOTHAM, JR.
### U.S. Circuit Judge
### Third Circuit

Leon Higginbotham Jr. was appointed October 13, 1977 by President Jimmy Carter as U.S. Circuit Judge. Just prior to this appointment, he had served on the Federal Trade Commission—the first black and the youngest person ever to hold the post of commissioner.

Higginbotham was born in Trenton, New Jersey in 1927. Originally an engineering student at Purdue University, he later enrolled at Antioch College as a liberal arts student, and received his LL.B. in 1952 from Yale.

He was soon appointed assistant district attorney in Philadelphia, then joined a private law firm, and later was chosen by Pennsylvania's Governor David Lawrence to serve as a member of the Pennsylvania Human Rights Commission.

In 1959, he was elected president of the Philadelphia chapter of the NAACP, and four years later, was cited as "one of the 10 outstanding young men in America" by the U.S. Junior Chamber of Commerce.

*Judge Odell Horton placing a memorial wreath for Martin Luther King.*

Judge Higginbotham has published more than 40 articles in major scholarly journals and his recent book, *In the Matter of Color: Race and the American Legal Process; The Colonial Period,* has received several national awards.

### ODELL HORTON
### U.S. District Judge
### Western District of Tennessee

Judge Odell Horton received his law degree from Howard University in 1956, and his undergraduate degree from Morehouse College in Atlanta in 1951. He is a native of Bolivar, Tennessee. Judge Horton was one of three Memphis attorneys selected by the Memphis City Council to investigate citizen complaints against the Memphis Police Department. In 1962, Horton was appointed Assistant U.S. Attorney for the Western District of Tennessee by Attorney General Robert F. Kennedy, on the recommendation of Senators Estes Kefauver and Albert Gore and the Shelby County Democratic Club. As an Assistant U.S. Attorney, Horton represented the United States in the prosecution of persons charged with violating criminal laws of the United States as well as civil and criminal legal matters arising in the Western District of Tennessee. Judge Horton also served as president of LeMoyne-Owen College in Memphis from 1970 to 1974.

He has received numerous awards and citations and has held directorships in a number of educational, private, and community organizations.

### NATHANIEL R JONES
### U.S. Court of Appeals, Sixth Circuit
### Ohio, Michigan, Kentucky, Tennessee

Judge Nathaniel R. Jones is a former NAACP general counsel, and during his tenure, he coordinated the attack against northern school segregation and twice argued in the U.S. Supreme Court the Detroit school case *Bradley v. Milliken.* In addition, in 1979, he successfully organized the presentation to the Supreme Court of the issues in the Dayton and Columbus, Ohio school desegregation cases. Judge Jones also directed the NAACP's response to the attacks against affirmative action and led an inquiry into discrimination against black servicemen. President Jimmy Carter appointed Jones to the Sixth Circuit Court of Appeals in Cincinnati, Ohio on October 15, 1979. Judge Jones is a graduate of Youngstown University, where he received his Bachelor of Arts degree in 1951 and his law degree in 1956. He also received honorary doctor of law degrees from Youngstown University in 1970 and from Syracuse University in 1972.

### DAMON JEROME KEITH
### U.S. District Judge
### Eastern District of Michigan

Keith, a judicial appointee of President Lyndon Johnson, was born in Detroit in 1922. He received his A.B. degree from West Virginia State College in 1943, and then served three years in the Army. Upon his return to civilian life, he entered Howard Law School, receiving a Bachelor of Laws degree in 1949.

From 1951 to 1955, Keith was with the Office of the Friend of the Court in Detroit. He then returned to college, obtaining his Master of Law Degree from Wayne State

*Judge Nathaniel R. Jones*

University in 1956. From 1958 to 1967, he was President of the Detroit Housing Commission. From 1964 to 1967, he was also Chairman and Co-Chairman of the Michigan Civil Rights Commission.

### THURGOOD MARSHALL
### Associate Justice
### Supreme Court of the United States

In July 1965, Thurgood Marshall was appointed to one of the most prestigious positions ever held by a black in the federal government; that of Solicitor General of the United States. Marshall assumed the task of acting as the government's chief legal spokesman in cases brought before the Supreme Court.

*Thurgood Marshall speaks with Senator Robert Kennedy after being confirmed as U. S. Solicitor General in 1965. Two years later, Marshall became the nation's first black Supreme Court justice.*

Marshall was born in Baltimore, Maryland on July 2, 1908. After receiving a B.A. degree from Lincoln University as a pre-dental student, he decided instead to become a lawyer and was admitted to Howard University's Law School, graduating in 1933 at the top of his class.

After five years of private practice in Baltimore, Marshall began what was to become a long and distinguished career with the NAACP, interrupted only briefly by an assignment as President John F. Kennedy's personal representative to the independence ceremonies of Sierra Leone.

In 1938, as national special counsel, he handled all cases involving questions of Negro constitutional rights. Then, in 1950, he was named director-counsel of the organization's 11-year-old Legal Defense and Educational Fund. In 1954, as part of an imposing team of lawyers, he played a key role in the now-historic Supreme Court decision on school desegregation. He also figured prominently in such important cases as *Sweatt v. Painter* (requiring the admission of a qualified black student to the law school of Texas University), and *Smith v. Allwright* (establishing the right of Texas Negroes to vote in Democratic primaries).

In 1961, Marshall sat on a federal bench as circuit judge for the Second Circuit. His outstanding achievements in the field of law led in 1946 to his winning the coveted Spingarn Medal, only one of the numerous citations he holds.

The climax of Marshall's legal and judicial career came in 1967 when he was nominated for a seat on the U.S. Supreme Court. At 59, the son of a sleeping-car porter and great-grandson of a slave, became the ninety-sixth man—and the first black—to sit among the nine Supreme Court justices.

### GABRIELLE K. McDONALD
### U.S. District Judge
### Southern District of Texas

Judge Gabrielle K. McDonald was born April 12, 1942 in St. Paul, Minnesota and received her law degree from Howard University in 1966. While at Howard, Judge McDonald was presented with the Kappa Beta Pi Legal Sorority award for academic excellence as well as the Book Award, The Petitioners, for best oral argument and brief in Appellate Practice. She graduated first in her class at Howard.

Judge McDonald was employed as a staff attorney, from 1966 to 1969, with the NAACP Legal Defense and Educational Fund in New York City. She has received awards from the National Bar Association, the Houston Citizens Chamber of Commerce, and Howard University.

### CONSTANCE BAKER MOTLEY
### U.S. District Judge
### Southern District of New York

Born in Connecticut of West Indian parents, Constance Baker Motley was appointed, in 1966, by President Johnson to the U.S. District Court for Southern New York, thus becoming the nation's first black woman federal judge. The appointment marked the high point of her long career in politics and civic affairs.

While still a law student at Columbia University, Mrs. Motley began working with the NAACP Legal Defense and

Educational Fund, Inc., beginning an association that was to make her famous as a defender of civil rights. After receiving her law degree, she began to work full-time with this organization, eventually becoming one of its associate counsels.

Before leaving the organization, in 1964, to run for the New York State Senate, Mrs. Motley had argued nine successful NAACP cases before the U.S. Supreme Court, and participated in almost every important civil rights case that had passed through the courts since 1954—from Autherine Lucy in Alabama to James Meredith in Mississippi. By winning election to the state senate in February of 1964, Mrs. Motley became the first Negro woman in New York state history to sit in the upper chamber.

Then, one year later, the state senator ran for the position of Manhattan Borough President, emerging the victor by the unanimous final vote of the City Council. She thus became the first woman to serve as a city borough president, and therefore, also the first woman on the Board of Estimate.

A resident of Manhattan's Upper West Side, Judge Motley hopes that her career "will be an inspiration to other Negro women," and feels that "it is important for women, and especially black women, to become involved and to hold public office."

In June 1982, Judge Constance Baker Motley was named chief judge of the Federal District Court that covers Manhattan, the Bronx, and six counties north of New York City. Judge Motley succeeded Judge Lloyd F. MacMahon.

*President Johnson announcing he will nominate Constance Baker Motley to be a federal judge for the southern district of New York.*

### BARRINGTON DANIELS PARKER
### U.S. District Judge
### District of Columbia

Judge Parker was born in Rosslyn, Virginia in 1915, and attended Lincoln University where he received an A.B. degree in 1936. He was awarded an M.A. degree from the University of Pennsylvania in 1938 and his law degree from the University of Chicago in 1947.

Following his graduation, Judge Parker was active in private law practice in Washington, D.C. He was a partner in the firm of Parker & Parker when President Nixon appointed him to the District Court in 1969.

### JAMES BENTON PARSONS
### U.S. District Judge
### Northern District of Illinois

James Benton Parsons, chosen by President John F. Kennedy in 1961, and installed on the bench the following year, became the first black appointed a lifetime federal district judge within the continental United States (U.S. District Court for the Northern District of Illinois). Prior to this, he had been elected judge of the Superior Court of Cook County, Illinois, and had also held the office of Assistant U.S. Attorney.

A native of Kansas City, Missouri, Parsons was born on August 13, 1911. At first a student of music at the James Milliken University and Conservatory of Music, and from 1938 to 1940, acting head of the Department of Music at Lincoln University, he attended summer sessions at Wisconsin University with an eye toward changing his major to political science. This plan was temporarily interrupted by four years of military service, but with the end of World War II, he pursued his graduate studies this time at the University of Chicago. He ultimately received an M.A. in political science in 1946 and a Doctor of Laws Degree three years later.

After a brief stint as a teacher at the John Marshall School of Law, Parsons worked for two years as assistant corporation counsel for the City of Chicago, appearing often before the Illinois Appellate Court as well as the State Supreme Court. He was then appointed to the U.S. Attorney's Office, serving there with distinction for nine years. During this period, he was particularly active with cases relating juvenile delinquency and rehabilitation, as well as with those involving both civil rights and the selective service. For his success in prosecuting some 60 selective service violators, Parsons was presented with the first Selective Service System Certificate of Appreciation.

### WARREN LAWRENCE PIERCE
### U.S. District Judge
### Southern District of New York

Judge Pierce was born in 1924 in Philadelphia. He received

his B.S. from St. Joseph's College there in 1948, and his law degree from Fordham in 1951.

From 1954 to 1961, Pierce was an Assistant District Attorney in Brooklyn, New York. In 1961, he was named Deputy Commissioner of the New York City Police Department. In 1963, he became Director of the New York State Division for Youth, and in 1966,Chairman of the New York State Narcotic Addiction Control Commission. Thus Judge Pierce had a solid foundation in law enforcement procedures and problems when he was appointed to the federal bench in 1970.

### SCOVEL RICHARDSON
### U.S. Customs Court Judge

In 1957, Scovel Richardson was named judge to the U.S. Customs Court for New York State, having previously acquired considerable legal experience both as a practicing lawyer and a professor of law.

Born in Nashville, Tennessee on February 4, 1912, Richardson obtained his B.A. and M.A. degrees from the University of Illinois, and in 1937, his LL.B. from Howard University.

*Judge Pierce had been Deputy Commissioner of New York City Police Department.*

With the exception of one year (1938) when he served as a private attorney in Chicago, and another year (1943) when he was a senior attorney for the Office of Price Administration (OPA), Richardson was associated with Lincoln University as a professor of law and dean of the law school. He left Lincoln, in 1953, to accept an appointment from President Dwight D. Eisenhower to the U.S. Board of Parole, becoming its chairman the following year.

### AUBREY EUGENE ROBINSON JR.
### U.S. District Judge
### District of Columbia

Judge Robinson was appointed to the United States District Court for the District of Columbia on November 3, 1966, and entered on duty November 16, 1966. He received an A.B. degree from Cornell University in 1943, and an LL.B. degree from Cornell Law School in 1947. He served as a First Sergeant in the United States Army, from 1943-1946.

Prior to his appointment to the federal bench, Judge Robinson was an Associate Judge of the Juvenile Court for the District of Columbia, from 1965-1966. He is a member of the Judicial Conference Ad Hoc Committee on Court Facilities and Design and the District of Columbia Commission on Judicial Disabilities and Tenure.

From 1948 to 1965, Robinson practiced law in Washington, D.C. and acted on behalf of several black petitioners in civil rights cases.

In addition to serving on the federal bench, Robinson is a member of the Special Police Trial Board of the Washington, D.C. Police Department and of the Advisory Committee to the Special Project of the National Council on the Aging.

### SPOTTSWOOD W. ROBINSON III
### U.S. Circuit Judge
### District of Columbia Circuit

Judge Robinson was named Circuit Judge in 1966 by President Johnson, a promotion from his previous position of District Judge, a post to which he had been appointed in 1963.

Prior to becoming a judge, Robinson had served in the legal field for many years; first as a private attorney, then as faculty member, and ultimately as Dean of the Howard University Law School.

Robinson was born in Richmond, Virginia on July 26, 1916. He received his B.A. at Virginia Union University and his LL.B. from the Howard University Law School in 1939.

Judge Robinson was the Virginia representative of the NAACP Legal Defense and Educational Fund from 1948 to 1950, and later served for nine years as its southeast regional counsel. He was a member of the U.S. Commission on Civil Rights from 1961 to 1963.

### PAUL A. SIMMONS
### U.S. District Judge
### Western District of Pennsylvania

In 1978, Judge Simmons was appointed to the Western District of Pennsylvania, and was the first merit-selected federal judge in the history of that state. He was born on August 31, 1921 in Monongahela, Pennsylvania where he still resides.

Judge Simmons graduated with high honors from the University of Pittsburgh in 1946 and from Harvard Law School in 1949. While attending school, Judge Simmons worked in the construction industry and on the Pennsylvania Railroad. Following graduation from law school, he was a professor of law at South Carolina College Law School from 1949 to 1952, and at the North Carolina College of Law from 1952 to 1956. From 1956 to 1973, he practiced law in Washington County and the surrounding counties.

In 1973, he was appointed Judge of the Court of Common Pleas of Washington County, and in 1975 he was nominated by both the Democratic and Republican parties and elected to a full 10-year term to that court.

Over the years, Judge Simmons has been a member of various commissions and authorities, including the Pennsylvania Human Relations Commission, the Pennsylvania Minor Judiciary Education Board, and the Washington County Redevelopment Authority. He was also on the Founding Board of Directors of the Monongahela Valley United Health Services. Judge Simmons is a member of the Pennsylvania Bar Association, the American Judicature Society, and many other bar associations.

*Jack Edward Tanner was appointed U. S. District Judge in Washington in 1978.*

**JACK EDWARD TANNER**
**U.S. District Judge**
**Western District of Washington**

Judge Tanner was appointed U.S. District Judge for the Western District of Washington on May 19, 1978. He is a member of the Washington State Bar Association, the Loren Miller Law Club, the National Bar Association, the Board of Visitors of the University of Puget Sound Law School, the NAACP, and was a member of its National Board of Directors from 1962 to 1968.

**JOSEPH C. WADDY**
**U.S. District Judge**
**District of Columbia**

Joseph Waddy was appointed to the District Court bench in 1967, after lending his expertise in government operations to a number of advisory commissions.

Born in Virginia in 1911, Waddy received an A.B. degree from Lincoln University in 1935, and an LL.B. from Howard University Law School in 1938. He served as Associate Judge of the Domestic Relations Branch of the Municipal Court of the District of Columbia from 1962 to 1967. Prior to that time, he was a member of the Citizens Advisory Council to the District of Columbia Commissioners.

Since 1971, Judge Waddy has also served as a Commissioner of the National Conference of Commissioners on Uniform State Laws.

**JAMES L. WATSON**
**U.S. Customs Court Judge**

Judge Watson was born in New York City in 1922, the son of James S. Watson, the first black jurist elected in New York State.

Judge Watson was decorated for bravery in Italy in World War II, where he served with the 92nd Infantry Division. He graduated from Brooklyn Law School in 1951, served on the Board of Immigration Appeals, and in 1954 was elected to the New York State Senate. In 1963, he resigned from the Senate and was elected Judge of the Civil Court of New York City. In 1966, President Johnson named him to serve on the Customs Court.

**DAVID W. WILLIAMS**
**U.S. District Judge**
**Central District of California**

Judge Williams was appointed United States District Judge for the Central District of California on June 20, 1969. He is a graduate of Los Angeles Junior College, the University of California at Los Angeles, receiving an A.B. degree in 1934, and the University of Southern California Law School, receiving an LL.B. degree in 1937.

Prior to his appointment to the federal bench, Williams served as a Judge of the Los Angeles County Superior Court, from 1963-1969, and Judge of the Los Angeles Municipal Court, from 1956-1962. He was born in Atlanta in 1910.

## ROSTER OF BLACK JUDICIAL OFFICERS

*Courtesy of the Joint Center for Political Studies and the Judicial Council of the National Bar Association.

### Supreme Court of U.S.

**Hon. Thurgood Marshall**
Associate Judge
Supreme Court of the United States
1 First Street, N.E.
Washington, DC 20543

### U.S. Court of Appeals

**Hon. Harry T. Edwards**
District of Columbia Circuit
U.S. Courthouse
Third and Constitution Avenue, N.W.
Washington, DC 20001

**Hon. J. Jerome Farris**
Ninth Circuit
1908 34th. Avenue South
*Seattle, Washington 98014*

**Hon. Joseph Hatchett**
Eleventh Circuit
P.O. Box 10429
Tallahassee, FL 3230

**Hon. A. Leon Higginbotham, Jr.**
Third Circuit 15613
U.S. Courthouse
601 Market Street
Philadelphia, PA 19106

**Hon. Nathaniel Jones**
Sixth Circuit Room 541
U.S. Post Office and Courthouse
Cincinnati, OH 45202

**Hon. Amalya L. Kearse**
Second Circuit U.S. Courthouse
Room 1006 Foley Square
New York, NY 10007

**Hon. Damon Keith, Jr.**
Sixth Circuit
240 Federal Building
Detroit, MI 48226

**Hon. Theodore McMillian**
Eighth Circuit
1114 Market Street
St. Louis, MO 63101

**Hon. Lawrence W. Pierce**
2nd Circuit
U.S. Courthouse
Foley Square.
New York, N.Y. 10007

**Hon. Cecil F. Poole**
Ninth Circuit
Federal Building
450 Golden Gate Avenue
San Francisco, CA 94101

**Hon. Spottswood W. Robinson III**
I District of Columbia Circuit
U.S. Courthouse
Third & Constitution Ave.
N.W. Washington, DC 20001

### U.S. District Court

**Hon. William B. Bryant**
U.S. District Court for the District of Columbia
U.S. Courthouse
Third and Constitution Avenue, N.W.
Washington, DC 20001

**Hon. Clyde S. Cahill Jr.**
Missouri Eastern District
Room 812
1114 Market Street
St. Louis, MO 63101

**Hon. Robert L. Carter**
New York Southern District
U.S. Courthouse Foley Square
New York, NY 10007

**Hon. U. W. Clemon**
Alabama Northern District
305 Federal Courthouse
Birmingham, AL 35203

**Hon. Robert F. Collins**
Louisiana Eastern District C-465
U.S. District Courthouse
500 Camp Street
New Orleans, LA 70130

**Hon. Julian A. Cook Jr.**
Michigan Eastern District
Federal Building, Room 272
Detroit, MI 48226

**Hon. Richard C. Erwin**
North Carolina Middle District
P. O. Box 89
Greensboro, NC 27402

**Hon. Benjamin F. Gibson**
Michigan Western District
438 Federal Building
110 Michigan Street,
N.W. Grand Rapids, MI 49503

**Hon. James Giles**
Pennsylvania Eastern District
U.S. Courthouse, Room 8613
601 Market Street
Philadelphia, PA 19106

**Hon. Earl Gilliam**
California Southern District
940 Front Street
San Diego, CA 92189

**Hon. John Hargrove**
Maryland District
101 West Lombard Street
Baltimore, MD 21201

**Hon. Terry J. Hatter, Jr.**
California Central District
U.S. Courthouse
312 North Spring Street
Los Angeles, CA 90012

**Hon. Thelton E. Henderson**
California Northern District
450 Golden Gate Avenue
San Francisco, CA 94102

**Hon. Odell Horton**
Tennessee Western District
Federal Building
167 North Main
Memphis, TN 38103

**Hon. George Howard, Jr.**
Arkansas Eastern District
P. O. Box 349
Little Rock, AR 72203

**Hon. Joseph C. Howard**
Maryland District Court
U.S. Courthouse, Room 120
101 West Lombard Street
Baltimore, MD 21201

**Hon. Norma H. Johnson**
U.S. District Court for the District of Columbia
U.S. Courthouse
Third and Constitution Avenue,
N.W. Washington, DC 20001

**Hon. George N. Leighton**
Illinois Northern District 219
South Dearborn Street
Room 2156
Chicago, IL 60604

**Hon. Mary Johnson Lowe**
New York Southern District
U.S. Courthouse
Foley Square
New York, NY 10007

**Hon. Consuela B. Marshall**
California Central District
312 North Spring Street
Los Angeles, CA 90012

**Hon. Constance B. Matley**
Senior Judge
New York Southern District
U.S. Courthouse Foley Square
New York, NY 10007

**Hon. David S. Nelson**
U.S. District Court for Massachusetts
McCormack Post Office and Courthouse
Building Room 1525
Boston, MA 02109

**Hon. Barrington D. Parker**
U.S. District Court for the District of Columbia
U.S. Courthouse
Third and Constitution Avenue, N.W.
Washington, DC 20001

**Hon. James B. Parsons**
Senior Judge
Illinois Northern District 219

South Dearborn Street
Chicago, IL 60604

**Hon. John G. Penn**
U.S. District Court for the District of Columbia
3rd and Constitution Ave. N.W.
Washington, DC 20001

**Hon. Matthew J. Perry**
South Carolina District
P. O. Box 867
Columbia, SC 29202

**Hon. Aubrey E. Robinson Jr.**
Chief Judge
U.S. District Court for the District of Columbia
U.S. Courthouse
Third and Constitution Avenue, N.W.
Washington, DC 20001

**Hon. Paul A. Simmons**
Pennsylvania Western District
U.S. Post Office and Courthouse Building
6th Floor Pittsburg, PA 15219

**Hon. Jack E. Tanner**
Washington Western Districts
304 Post Office Building P.O. Box 2015
Tacoma, WA 98401

**Hon. Anna Diggs Taylor**
Michigan Eastern District
Federal Building, Room 235
Detroit, MI 48226

**Hon. Anne E. Thompson**
New Jersey District
U.S. Courthouse
402 East State Street
Trenton, NJ 08608

**Hon. Myron H. Thompson**
Alabama Middle District
P. O. Box 235
Montgomery, AL 36101

**Hon. Horace T. Ward**
Georgia Northern District
75 Spring Street, S.W.
Suite 2388
Atlanta, GA 30303

**Hon. George W. White**
Ohio Northern District
U.S. Courthouse
Cleveland, OH 44114

**Hon. Ann C. Williams**
Illinois Northern District
219 South Dearborn
Chicago, IL 60604

**Hon. David W. Williams**
California Central District 312
North Spring Street
Los Angeles, CA 90012

**Hon. Henry T. Wingate**
Mississippi Southern District
P. O. Box 22658
Jackson, MS 39205

### U.S. District Court (Term)

**Hon. Almeric L. Christian**
Chief Judge
U.S. Virgin Islands
Federal Building
P. O. Box 720
St. Thomas, VI 00801

### U.S. Customs Court

**Hon. James L. Watson**
U.S. Customs Court
One Federal Plaza
New York, NY 10007

### U.S. Court of Claims

**Hon. Reginald Gibson**
U.S. Court of Claims
717 Madison Place, NW
Washington, DC 20005

### U.S. Referees in Bankruptcy

**Hon. Rudolph Baxter**
Ohio Northern District
412 U.S. Courthouse
Cleveland, OH 44114

**Hon. Cornelius Blackshear**
New York Southern District
U.S. Courthouse
Foley Square
New York, NY 10007

**Hon. Franklin D. Burgess**
Washington Western District
P. O. Box 2214
Tacoma, WA 98410

**Hon. Charles N. Clevert**
U.S. District Court for Wisconsin
Eastern District
517 East Wisconsin Avenue
Milwaukee, WI 53202

**Hon. Marcia Cooke**
Michigan Eastern District
231 West LaFayette Blvd.
Detroit, MI 48226

**Hon. James Dooley**
U.S. District Court
California Central District 312
North Spring Street
Los Angeles, CA 90012

**Hon. Benjamin E. Franklin**
U.S. District Court for Kansas
Federal Building
812 North Seventh Street
P. O. Box 1339
Kansas City, KN 66117

**Hon. Ray R. Graves**
Michigan Eastern District
231 West LaFayette Blvd.
Detroit, MI 48226

**Hon. William J. Haynes Jr.**
Tennessee Middle District
649 U.S. Courthouse
Nashville, TN 37203

**Hon. Lynn V. Hooe Jr.**
Michigan Eastern District
231 West LaFayette Blvd.
Detroit, MI 48226

**Hon. Ivan L. R. Lemelle**
Louisiana Eastern District
500 Camp Street
New Orleans, LA 70130

**Hon. Louis Moore Jr.**
Louisiana Eastern District
500 Camp Street
New Orleans, LA 70130

**Hon. Grady L. Pettigrew Jr.**
U.S. District Court for Ohio Southern District
U.S. Courthouse
85 Marconi Boulevard
Columbus, OH 43215

**Hon. Thomas Rosemond**
Illinois Northern District
219 South Dearborn
Chicago, IL 60604
Hon. Albert A. Sheen
Virgin Islands
P. O. Box 720
St. Thomas, VI 00801

**Hon. Edward B. Toles**
U.S. District Court
Illinois Northern District
219 South Dearborn Street
Chicago, IL 60604

### U.S. Magistrates

**Hon. Joyce L. Alexander**
U.S. District Court for Massachusetts
932 Post Office—Courthouse
Boston, MA 02109

**Hon. Calvin Botley**
U.S. District Court
Texas Southern District
U.S. Courthouse
515 Rusk Avenue
Houston, TX 77208

**Hon. Arthur Burnett**
U.S. District Court
District of Columbia
U.S. Courthouse
Third and Constitution Avenue, N.W.
Washington, DC 20001

**Hon. William F. Hall Jr.**
U.S. District Court
Pennsylvania Eastern District
U.S. Courthouse, Room 5918
601 Market Street
Philadelphia, PA 19106

**Hon. Henry L. Jones**
U.S. District Court
Arkansas Eastern District
U.S. Courthouse
Little Rock, AR 72203

## STATE JUDICIARY

### District of Columbia

District of Columbia Court of Appeals
500 Indiana Avenue,
N.W. Washington, DC 20001

**Hon. Julia Cooper Mack**
**Hon. Theodore R. Newman Jr.**
**Hon. Hubert B. Pair**
Senior Judge
**Hon. William C. Pryor**
Chief Judge
**Hon. William S. Thompson**
Senior Judge
**Hon. Judith W. Rodgers**

Superior Court of the District of Columbia
500 Indiana Avenue,
N.W. Washington, DC 20001

**Hon. Iraline G. Barnes**
**Hon. Shellie F. Bowers**
**Hon. Harold H. Cushenberry Jr.**
**Hon. Herbert B. Dixon**
**Hon. William C. Garner**
**Hon. Eugene N. Hamilton**
**Hon. Susan R. Holmes**
**Hon. Henry H. Kennedy Jr.**
**Hon. George W. Mitchel**
**Hon. Luke C. Moore**
**Hon. Carlisle E. Pratt**
**Hon. Michael L. Rankin**
**Hon. Emmet Sullivan**
Senior Judge
**Hon. Robert S. Tignor**
**Hon. William S. Thompson**
**Hon. Ricardo M. Urbina**
**Hon. Annice M. Wagner**
**Hon. Reggie B. Walton**
**Hon. Paul R. Webber III**

## ALABAMA

### Supreme Court

**Hon. Oscar W. Adams Jr.**
Associate Justice
State Supreme Court
P.O. Box 218
Montgomery, AL 36101

### Circuit Court

**Hon. William M. Branch**
Greene County
P.O. Box 6526
Eutown, AL 35462

**Hon. Ralph D. Cook**
Jefferson County Courthouse Annex
Bessemer, AL 35020

**Hon. Cain Kennedy**
13th. Judicial District
Mobile County Court
House Mobile, AL 36602

**Hon. Richmond Pearson**
10th. Judicial District
Jefferson County Courthouse
Birmingham, AL 35263

**Hon. Charles Price**
Montgomery County
134 North Haardt Drive
Montgomery, AL 36105

### District Court

**Hon. Aubrey Ford**
Macon County District Court
Tuskegee, AL 36083

**Hon. Eddie Hardaway Jr.**
Sumter County
P. O. Box 9
Livingston, AL 34570

**Hon. Nathaniel Owens**
Calhoun County District Court
Anniston, AL 36202

**Hon. Jo Celeste Pettway**
Wilcox County
P. O. Box 549
Camden, NJ 36726

### Probate Court

**Hon. William McKinley Branch**
Greene County
P. O. Box 6526
Eutown, AL 35462

**Hon. Rufus C. Huffman**
Probate Court
Bullock County
P. O. Box 71
Union Springs, AL 36089

### Municipal Court

**Hon. Emery Anthony**
City Hall, Municipal Court
710 20th. Street North
Birmingham, AL 35203

**Hon. Michael Bellamy**
Phenix City Courthouse
1111 Broad Street
Phenix City, AL 36867

**Hon. Houston Brown**
City Hall
4543 Bessemer Super Highway
Roosevelt City, AL 35020

**Hon. Cecil Monroe**
P. O. Box 2446
Mobile, AL 36601

**Hon. Carole C. Smitherman**
Municipal Court, City Hall
710 20th. Street North
Birmingham, AL 35203

**Hon. Janice D. Spears**
P. O. Box 10427
Pritehard, AL 36610

### Recorder's Court

**Hon. Orzell Billingsley Jr.**
Recorder's Court
Masonic Temple Building
Roosevelt City, AL

**Hon. Peter A. Hall**
Recorder's Court
City Hall
Birmingham, AL 35203

**Hon. David H. Hood**
Brighton, AL

## ALASKA

None

## ARIZONA

### Superior Court

**Hon. Cecil Patterson**
Maricopa County
101 West Jefferson Street
Phoenix, AZ 85003

### Municipal Court

**Hon. Jean F. Williams**
Municipal Court Division 21
455 North 5th. Street
Phoenix, AZ 85004

## ARKANSAS

### Municipal Court

**Hon. Edwin Keaton**
Camden -Ouashita County
P.O. Box 524
Camden, AR 71701

### Juvenile Court

**Hon. Joyce Williams Warren**
Pulaski County
3201 West Roosevelt
Little Rock, AR 72204

## CALIFORNIA

### Courts of Appeal

***First Appellate District***
4154 State Building
Civic Center
San Francisco, CA 94104

**Hon. Clinton W. White**
Presiding Justice, Division Three

***Second Appellate District***
3580 Wilshire Boulevard
Room 301
Los Angeles, CA 90010

**Hon. Vaino Spencer**
District Two, Division One

**Hon. Leon Thompson**
**Hon. Arleigh Woods**
Associate Justice, Division Four

### Superior Court

***Central District***
111 North Hill Street
Los Angeles, CA 90012

**Hon. Gilbert Alston**
**Hon. David F. Cunningham**

**Hon. Stanley R. Malone Jr.**
**Hon. Albert D. Matthews**
**Hon. Billy G. Mills**
**Hon. Henry Nelson**
**Hon. H. Randolph Moore**
**Hon. Donald F. Pitts**

***South Central District***
200 West Compton Boulevard
Compton, CA 90220
**Hon. William Clay**
**Hon. Dion G. Morrow**

***Eastern District***
400 Civic Center Plaza
Pomona, CA 91766
**Hon. Charles E. Jones**
**Hon. Loren Miller Jr.**
**Hon. Florence Pickard**
**Hon. James Reese**
**Hon. Everett E. Ricks**
**Hon. Robert Roberson Jr.**
**Hon. Charles Scarlett**

***San Diego County***
200 West Broadway
San Diego, CA 92101
**Hon. Napoleon A. Jones Jr.**
**Hon. Alpha Montgomery**

***Alameda County***
1225 Fallon Street
Oakland, CA 94112
**Hon. Richard Bancroft**
**Hon. Donald P. McCullum**
**Hon. Wilmont Sweeney**
**Hon. Benjamin Travis**

***Sacramento County***
720 Ninth Street
Sacramento, CA 95814
**Hon. William K. Morgan**

***San Francisco County***
480 City Hall
San Francisco, CA 94102
**Hon. John Dearman**

***Stockton Judicial District***
222 East Weber Avenue
Room 200
Stockton, CA 95202
**Hon. John F. Cruikshank Jr.**

**Municipal Court**

Oakland-Piedmont Judicial District
600 Washington Street
Oakland, CA 94607
**Hon. James S. White**

***Bay Judicial District***
100-37th. Street
Room 202
Richmond, CA 94805
**Hon. George D. Carroll**

***Beverley Hills Judicial District***
9355 Burton Way
Beverley Hills CA
**Hon. Charles Boags**

***Compton Judicial District***
200 West Compton Blvd.
Compton CA 90220
**Hon. Hugo E. Hill**
**Hon. Xenophon F. Lang**

***Inglewood Judicial District***
1 Regent Street
Inglewood CA 90301
***Hon. Roosevelt F. Dorn***
***Hon. Roosevelt Robinson Jr.***

***Long Beach Municipal Court***
415 West Ocean Boulevard
Long Beach, CA 90802
***Hon. William Dunn***
***Hon. Marcus O. Tucker***

***Los Angeles Judicial District***
110 North Grand Avenue
Los Angeles, CA 90012
**Hon. Ernest L. Aubry**
**Hon. Glenette Blackwell**
**Hon. Candace Cooper**
**Hon. Giles B. Jackson**
**Hon. L. C. Nunley**
**Hon. Marion L. Obera**
**Hon. Harold J. Sinclair**
**Hon. Sherman W. Smith Jr.**
**Hon. Maxine Thomas**

***Central Judicial District***
Hall of Justice
Room C-10
San Rafael, CA 94903
**Hon. William H. Stephens**

***West Orange Judicial District***
8141-13th. Street
Westminster, CA 92638
**Hon. Marvin G. Weeks**

***Sacramento County***
720 Ninth Street,
Room 102
Sacramento, CA 94814
**Hon. Thomas G. Daugherty**

***Chino Division***
13260 Central Avenue
Chino, CA 91710
**Hon. Holly Graham**

***El Cajon Judicial District***
110 East Lexington Avenue
El Cajon, CA 92020
**Hon. Elizabeth Riggs**

***Southern Judicial District***
800 North Humbolt Street
San Mateo, CA 94401
**Hon. Phrasel L. Shelton**

**Quasi-Judicial Officials**

**Hon. James A. Braggs**

**Hon. Hugh E. MacBeth Jr.**

**Administrative Law Judge**

**Hon. Ivy G. Roberts**

## COLORADO

District Court
City-County Building
Denver, CO 80202
**Hon. Gilbert A. Alexander**
**Hon. James C. Flanigan**
**Hon. Raymond Jones**

**Municipal Court**

**Hon. Jerry L. Stevens**
15001 East Alamenda
Aurora, CO 80011

**Juvenile Court**

**Hon. Morris E. Cole**
Denver Juvenile Court
City-County Building
Denver, CO 80202

## CONNECTICUT

**Superior Court**

**Hon. Robert D. Glass**
300 Grand Street
Waterbury, CT 06720

**Hon. Leander C. Gray**
361 Sherman Avenue
New Haven, CT 0651

**Hon. Robert L. Lenister**
Senior Judge
123 Hoyt Street
Stamford, CT 06905

**Hon. L. Scott Melville**
Fairfield Judicial District
1061 Main Street
Bridgeport, CT 06604

**Hon. Flemming Norcott Jr.**
235 Church Street
New Haven, CT 06510

**Hon. Eugene Spear**
Fairfield Judicial Court
1061 Main Street
Bridgeport, CT 06610

**Hon. William B. Ramsey**
235 Church Street
New Haven, CT 06510

## DELAWARE

**Superior Court**

**Hon. Joshua Martin III**
Superior Courthouse
11th. and King Street
Wilmington, DE 19801

**Municipal Court**

**Hon. Leonard L. Williams**
1000 King Street
Wilmington, DE 19801

**Justices of the Peace**

**Hon. Lorin P. Hunt**
Wilmington, DE 19801

**Hon. Roslyn Toulson**
Wilmington, DE 19801

**Hon. Robert Handy**
Lewes, DE 19958

**FLORIDA**

**District Courts of Appeal**

**Hon. Wilkie D. Ferguson**
2001 Southwest 117th. Avenue
Miami, FL 33175

**Circuit Courts**

**Hon. Henry L. Adams Jr.**
Duval County Courthouse
Jacksonville, FL 32202

**Hon. Stephen P. Mickel**
Gainesville, FL 32601

**Hon. Ralph N. Person**
Miami, FL 33125

**Hon. Edward Rodgers**
Palm Beach County Courthouse
West Palm Beach, FL 33401

**Hon. James B. Sanderlin**
Clearwater, FL 33516

**Hon. Emerson R. Thompson Jr.**
Orange County Courthouse
Orlando, FL 32801

**Hon. Frank White**
St. Petersburg, FL 33701

**County Courts**

**Hon. Leo Adderly**
Dade County
North Miami, FL 33168

**Hon. Isaac Anderson**
Lee County
Ft. Meyers, FL 33901

**Hon. Perry A. Little**
Hillsborough County Courthouse
Tampa, FL 33610

**Hon. Calvin R. Mapp**
Dade County
Miami, FL 33150

**Hon. Leah A. Simms**
Dade County
Miami, FL 33125

**Hon. Thomas E. Stringer Sr.**
Hillsboro County
Tampa, FL 33602

**Hon. Zebedee Wright**
Broward County
Ft. Lauderdale, FL 33311

**GEORGIA**

**Superior Courts**

**Hon. William H. Alexander**
Fulton County
160 Pryor Street, S.W.
Atlanta, GA 30303

**Hon. Clarence Cooper**
Fulton County
160 Pryor Street, N.W.
Atlanta, GA 30303

**Hon. E. H. Gasden**
Eastern Judicial Circuit
Chatham County Courthouse
Savannah, GA 31402

**Hon.Isaac Jenrette**
Atlanta Judicial Circuit
136 Pryor Street, S.W.
Atlanta, GA 30303

**Court of Appeals**

**Hon. Robert Benham**
402 Judicial Building
Atlanta, GA 30334

**State Court**

**Hon. Thelma Wyatt Cummings**
Fulton County
160 Pryor Street, S.W.
Atlanta, GA 30303

**Hon. Albert L. Thompson**
Fulton County
160 Pryor Street, S.W.
Atlanta, GA 30303

**Probate Court**

**Hon. Edith Jacqueline Ingram**
Probate Court of Hancock County
718 New Street
Sparta, GA 31087

**Juvenile Court**

**Hon. Romae Turner Powell**
Juvenile Court of Fulton County
445 Capitol Avenue, S.W. Atlanta, GA 30312

**Municipal Courts**

**Atlanta**

**Hon. Edward Baety**
(Traffic Court)
104 Trinity Avenue, S.W.
Atlanta, GA 30303

**Hon. Juan Bayneum**
Magistrate
State Court
160 Pryor Street, S.W.
Atlanta, GA 30303

**Hon. Robert L. Burton**
Magistrate
Sanderville Highway
Route 1
Box 478
Sparta, GA 31087

**Hon. Clinton E. Deneaux**
165 Decatur Street, S.E.
Atlanta, GA 30305

**Hon. Andrew J. Hairston**
(Traffic Court)
104 Trinity Avenue, S.W.
Atlanta, GA 30305

**Hon. Michael Hancock**
(Recorder's Court)
3630 Camp Circle
Decatur, GA 30035

**Hon. Barbara Harris**
165 Decatur Street, S.E.
Atlanta, GA 30305

**Hon. Elmer Hopper**
Magistrate
Hancock County
P.O. Box 123
Sparta, GA 31087

**Hon. Howard Johnson**
Chief Judge
165 Decatur Street, S.E.
Atlanta, GA 30305

**Hon. Mereda D. Johnson**
Magistrate
Dekalb County
208 Church Street
Decatur, GA 30030

**Hon. Leah Sears-Collins**
(Traffic Court)
104 Trinity Avenue, S.W.
Atlanta, GA 30305

**HAWAII**

None

**IDAHO**

**District Court**

**Hon. Ronald Bruce**
District Court
P.O. Box 474
Rupert, ID 83350

**ILLINOIS**

**Appellate Court**
Daley Civic Center
Chicago, IL 60602

**Hon. Calvin C. Campbell**
**Hon. Glenn T. Johnson**
**Hon. Eugene Pineham**

**Circuit Court**
Cook County
Daley Civic Center
Chicago, IL 60602

**Hon. Clarence Bryant**
**Hon. William Cousins Jr.**
**Hon. Charles J. Durham**
**Hon. Charles Freeman**
**Hon. Marion W. Garnett**
**Hon. Sophia H. Hail**
**Hon. Arthur Hamilton**
**Hon. Richard A. Hudlin, IV**
**Hon. E.C. Johnson**
**Hon. Mark E. Jones**
**Hon. Sidney A. Jones Jr.**
**Hon. Carl McCormick**
**Hon. Howard M. Miller**
**Hon. Odas Nicholson**
**Hon. William E. Peterson**
**Hon. Maurice Pompey**
**Hon. Albert S. Porter**
**Hon. John W. Rogers**
**Hon. Earl Strayhorn**
**Hon. Lucia T. Thomas**
**Hon. Claude E. Whitaker**
**Hon. Willie Whiting**
**Hon. James M. Walton**

**Circuit Court Associate Judges**
Cook County
Daley Civic Center
Chicago, Illinois 60602

**Hon. Everette A. Branden**
**Hon. Lawrence Carroll**
**Hon. Chauncey Eskridge**
**Hon. Glen C. Fowlkes**
**Hon. Marvin E. Gavin**
**Hon. Calvin H. Hall**
**Hon. Evelyn F. Johnson**
**Hon. Wendell P. Marbly**
**Hon. Earle McCaskill**
**Hon. Adolphus D. Rivers**
**Hon. Howard T. Savage**
**Hon. Sherard W. Thomas**
**Hon. Milton S. Warton**
**Hon. William S. Wood**
**Hon. Robert R. Woolridge**
**Hon. Joseph W. Handy**

Downstate Illinois
12th Judicial Circuit
P.O. Box 417
Joliet, IL 60431

**Hon. James L. Harris**
**Hon. Blanche M. Manning**
**Hon. Milton Wharton**

20th Judicial Circuit
East St. Louis, IL 62203

**Hon. Clayton R. Williams**
3rd Judicial Circuit Alton, IL

## INDIANA

### Superior Court

**Hon. Webster L. Brewer**
Marion County City-County Building
Indianapolis, IN 46204

**Hon. James C. Kimbrough**
Lake County
2293 North Main Street
Crown Point, IN 46307

### Municipal Court

**Hon. Taylor Baker Jr.**
City-County Building
Indianapolis, IN 46204

**Hon. Clarence D. Bolden**
City-County Building
Indianapolis, IN 46204

**Hon. Charles Graddic**
City Court
910 Vermillion Street
Gary, IN 46403

## IOWA

### District Court

**District Court Magistrates**

**Hon. George L. Stigler**
Judicial Magistrate
First Judicial District
Black Hawk County Courthouse
Waterloo, IA

## KANSAS

### Court of Appeals

**Hon. Sherman A. Parks**
Statehouse Topeka,
KS 66612

### District Court

**Hon. Cordell D. Meeks Jr.**
29th. Judicial District
Wyandotte County Courthouse
Kansas City, KS 66101

**Hon. Robert Watson**
Sedgewick County
525 North Main Street
Wichita, KS 67203

## KENTUCKY

### Circuit Court

**Hon. William E. McAnulty**
**Hon. Benjamin F. Shobe**
30th. Judicial Circuit
3616 Breeland Avenue
Louisville, KY 40202

## LOUISIANA

### Court of Appeals

**Hon. Joan Bernard Armstrong**
District 1, Division G
4701 La Fon Drive
New Orleans, LA 70126

### District Courts

**Hon. Lionel Collins**
24th Judicial District Court
Jefferson Parish, Division L
New Gretna Court House
Gretna, LA 70053

**Hon. Yada Magee**
Civil District Court
421 Loyola Avenue
New Orleans, LA 70112

**Hon. Revius O. Ortique**
Civil District Court Orleans Parish,
Division H
421 Loyola Avenue
New Orleans, LA 70112

### Limited Trial Court Judges

***District Court Magistrate***
**Hon. Nils R. Douglas**
Criminal District Court
Parish of Orleans
2700 Tulane Avenue
New Orleans, LA 70112

***Juvenile Court***

**Hon. Ernestine Gray**
Juvenile Court For the Parish of Orleans
421 Loyola Avenue
New Orleans, LA 70112

### Commissioner

**Hon. Anis Russell**
Orleans Parish
421 Loyola Avenue
New Orleans, LA 70112

**Hon. Walter J. Wilkerson**
Orleans Parish
421 Loyola Avenue
New Orleans, LA 70112

### City Court

**Hon. Freddie Pitcher, Jr.**
E. Baton Rouge Parish
Division B
P.O. Box 1471
Baton Rouge, LA 70821

### Justices of the Peace

**Hon. Wesley B. Albert Sr.**
New Roads, LA 70760

**Hon. R. L. Belton**
Jonesboro, LA 71251

**Hon. Nolan Charles**
St. Martinville, LA 70582

**Hon. Lonnie Dempsey**
Plaquemine, LA 70764

**Hon. Clarence Drexler**
Franklin, LA 70538

**Hon. Isaac Garritt Jr.**
Vacherie, LA 70090

**Hon. Ellis Hall Sr.**
Edgard, LA 70049

**Hon. George Hamlin**
Gambling, LA 71245

**Hon. Charlie Harris Jr.**
New Roads, LA 70760

**Hon. Arthur L. Johnson**
Water Peoof, LA 71375

**Hon. Azadee Johnson**
Tallulah, LA 71282

**Hon. Frank E. Johnson**
Amite, LA 70422

**Hon. Melvin Johnson**
Chauvin, LA 70344

**Hon. Stanley G. Johnson Sr.**
Franklin, LA 70538

**Hon. Harrington La Brie**
Lebeau, LA 71345

**Hon. Edward E. Mason**
Arcadia, LA 71001

**Hon. Anadale L. Monconduit**
St. James, La 70086

**Hon. Francis Papillion**
Church Point, LA 70525

**Hon. Robert Perkins**
Conshatta, LA 71019

**Hon. James B. Williams**
Gibson, LA 70356

**Hon. Robert J. Williams Jr.**
Zachary, LA 70791

**Hon. Alexander Wright**
Sunshine, LA 70780

## MAINE

None

## MARYLAND

### Court of Appeals

**Hon. Harry A. Cole**
Court of Appeals Building
Annapolis, MD 21401

### Court of Special Appeals

**Hon. Robert M. Bell**
111 North Calvert Street
Baltimore, MD 21202

### Circuit Court

***Eighth Judicial Circuit***
Supreme Bench of Baltimore
City Courthouse
Baltimore, MD 21202

**Hon. Milton B. Allen**
**Hon. Solomon Baylor**
**Hon. Aries W. Davis**
**Hon. Clifton Gardy**
**Hon. Mable Horize Hubbard**
**Hon. Kennith Lanon Johnson**
**Hon. Daniel B. Mitchell**
**Hon. Thomas E. Noel**

***Seventh Judicial Circuit***
Prince George's County
Court House Upper
Marlboro, MD 20870

**Hon. G. R. Havey Johnson**
**Hon. James H. Taylor**

***Sixth Judicial District***
501 Courthouse Square
Rockville, MD 20850

**Hon. De Lawrence Beard**

### District Court

***District Court A***
5800 Wabash Avenue
Baltimore, MD 21215

**Hon. Askew Gatewood**
**Hon. Keith Matthews**
**Hon. David Young**

14757 Maine Street
Upper Marboro, MD 20772

**Hon. William Missouri**
**Hon. Sylvania Woods**

### Orphans Court

**Hon. David B. Allen**
Courthouse East
Baltimore, MD 21202

**Hon. Norma Lee Barkley**
Wicomico County
Courthouse
Salisbury, MD 21801

**Hon. Michael M. Lee**
Courthouse East
Baltimore, MD 21202

**Hon. Lucy B. Warr**
Prince George's County
Courthouse
Upper Marboro, MD 20772

## MASSACHUSETTS

### Appeals Court

**Hon. Frederick L. Brown**
New Courthouse
Pemberton Square
Boston, MA 02108

**Superior Court**
New Courthouse
Pemberton Square
Boston, MA 02108

**Hon. Harry J. Elam**
**Hon. Malcom Graham**
**Hon. James McDaniel Jr.**
**Hon. Joseph S. Mitchell**

### District Courts

***Third District Court of Eastern Middlesex***
40 Thorndike Street
Cambridge, MA 02141

**Hon. James W. Bailey**
**Hon. Marie Jackson**

**Hon. Baron H. Martin**
Wareham District Court
West Wareham, MA 02576

**Hon. Darrell L. Outlaw**
Dorchester and Suffolk Counties
510 Washington Street
Dorchester, MA 02124

**Hon. George A. Sheehy**
Springfield District Court
50 State Street
Springfield, MA 01103

***Roxbury District Court***
85 Warren Street
Roxbury, MA 02119

**Hon. Richard L. Banks**
**Hon. Julian T. Houston**

**Boston Municipal Court**
380 Old Court House
Boston, MA 02108

**Hon. Charles Ray Johnson**

### Juvenile Courts

***Bristol County Juvenile Courts***
**Hon. Ronald D. Harper**
26 North Sixth Street
New Bedford, MA 02740

***Boston Juvenile Court***
**Hon. Roderick Ireland**
Suffolk County Courthouse
Boston, MA 02108

### Housing Court

**Hon. John G. Martin**
Worcestor County
2 Main Street
Worcestor, MA 01618

## MICHIGAN

### Supreme Court

**Hon. Dennis W. Archer**
Associate Judge
State Supreme Court
144 LaFayette Avenue
Lansing, MI 48909

**Court of Appeals**
First Federal Building
Detroit, MI 48226

**Hon. Harold Hood**
**Hon. Myron H. Wahls**

**Circuit Courts**
Wayne County
City-County Building

Detroit, MI 48226

**Hon. Arthur M. Bowman**
**Hon. Charles S. Farmer**
**Hon. Claudia M. Marcom**
**Hon. Louis F. Simmons**
**Hon. Lucille Watts**

**Recorder's Court of Detroit**
The Frank Murphy
Hall of Justice
Detroit, MI 48226

***Criminal Division***

**Hon. Evelyn K. Cooper**
**Hon. George W. Crockett III**
**Hon. Robert L. Evans**
**Hon. Geraldine Bledsoe Ford**

**Hon. Samuel C. Gardner**
Chief Judge

**Hon. Henry L. Heading**
Recorder

**Hon. Donald L. Hobson**
**Hon. Beverly Anne Jasper**
**Hon. Vera Massey Jones**
**Hon. Warfield Moore Jr.**
**Hon. Dalton A. Roberson**
**Hon. James E. Roberts**
**Hon. Craig S. Strong**
**Hon. Edward M. Thomas**
**Hon. Leonard Townsend**

### Probate Court

**Hon. J. Robert Gragg**
Wayne County
1309 City-County Building
Detroit, MI 48226
Hon. Thomas E. Jackson

***Common Pleas Court of Detroit***
Room 1107
2 Woodward
Detroit, MI 48226

**Hon. John A. Murphy**

### District Courts

***36th. District Court***
421 Madison Avenue
Detroit, MI 48221

**Hon. Alex J. Allen Jr.**
**Hon. Thomas Bayles**
**Hon. Nancy Blount**
**Hon. Gerald Brock**
**Hon. Christopher Brown**
**Hon. Fredrick E. Byrd**
**Hon. Wendy Cooley**
**Hon. John Conzart**
**Hon. Daphne Means Curtis**
**Hon. Theresa Doss**
**Hon. Gershwin S. Drain**
**Hon. Prentis Edwards**
**Hon. Rufus Griffin**
**Hon. Leon Jenkins**
**Hon. Willie Lipscomb**
**Hon. Marion Moore**
**Hon. John Murphy**
**Hon. Elbert E. Nance Jr.**
**Hon. Denise Page Hood**
**Hon. Longworth Quinn Jr.**
**Hon. Adam Shakoor**
**Hon. Chris E. Stith**

***10th. District Court***
Marshall, MI

**Hon. Shelton C. Penn**

***54th. District Court***
Lansing City Hall
Lansing, MI 48933

**Hon. John W. Davis**
**Hon. Claude R. Thomas**

***Juvenile Detention***

**Hon. Adalle Jones**
**Hon. Eugene Terry**

***District Court Magistrates***

**Hon. Lawrence Chastang**
**Hon. Jimmylee Gray**
**Hon. Charles Hammon**
**Hon. Lorraine Roister**

***Quasi-Judicial Officers***

**Hon. Clinton Carter,**
Referee, Juvenile Division

**Hon. Frances Pitts,**
Referee

### Administrative Law Judges

***Michigan Workmen's Compensation Commission***
Detroit, MI 48226

**Hon. Thomas Burden**
**Hon. William B. Edward**
**Hon. Jacqueline Hall**
**Hon. Ivy Riley**
**Hon. Sharon Smith**
**Hon. Gerald Tilles**
**Hon. Steve Washington**

## MINNESOTA

### District Courts

**District Court**
Ramsey County
St. Paul, MN 55102

**Hon. Stephen L. Maxwell**

**District Court**
Hennepin County
Minneapolis, MN 55416

**Hon. Pamela G. Alexander**
**Hon. Michael J. Davis**
**Hon. William S. Posten**

## MISSISSIPPI

### Supreme Court

**Hon. Reuben Anderson**
Hinds County Courthouse
Jackson, MS 39201

### Circuit Court

**Hon. Fred L. Banks Jr.**
P. O. Box 327
Jackson, MS 39205

### Municipal Court

**Hon. Vicki Roach-Barnes**
P. O. Box 1495
Vicksburg, MS 39180
Hon. Barry W. Lord
P. O. Box 1661
Tupelo, MS 38802

**Hon. Oran Paige**
P. O. Box 17
Jackson, MS 39205

**Hon. Lille Blackman Sanders**
P. O. Box 555
Natchez, MS 39120

**Hon. Gwendolyn J. Thomas**
P. O. Box 932
Rosedale, MS 38769

**Hon. Kenneth J. Thomas**
P. O. Box 66
Rosedale, MS 38769

**Hon. Clell Ward**
P. O. Box 575
Greenville, MS 38701

### Justice Court

**Hon. Charlie Chamblins**
Fayette, MS 39069

**Hon. Clyde R. Chatman**
Jackson MS 39216

**Hon. Archie Cook**
Marks, MS 38646

**Hon. Bernard Crump**
Starkville, MS 39759

**Hon. Earnest Cunningham**
Holly Springs, MS 38635

**Hon. Jerry Fisher**
Lexington, MS 39095

**Hon. Debbie Gambiell**
Hattiesburg, MS 39401

**Hon. Edna H. Garner**
Port Gibson, MS 39150

**Hon. Larry Giles**
Yazoo City, MS

**Hon. Leroy Guire**
Fayette, MS 39069

**Hon. Jimmy S. Harris**
Woodville, MS 39669

**Hon. Johnny Hartzog**
Prentiss, MS 39474

**Hon. Irma L. Inge**
Mound Bayou, MS 38762

**Hon. Paul S. Johnson**
Clarksdale, MS 38614

**Hon. Daniel Lucas**
Port Gibson, MS

**Hon Spencer M. Nash**
Magnolia, MS 39652

**Hon. Shirley Neal**
Lexington, MS 39095

### Justices of the Peace

**Hon. Mabel Peterson**
Vicksburg, MS 39180

**Hon. A. J. Peyton**
Yazoo City, MS 39194

**Hon. Wilbert Robinson**
Canton, MS 39046

**Hon. Willie Scott**
Natchez, MS 39120

**Hon. Mary Toles**
Natchez, MS 39120

**Hon. George Walker**
Jackson, MS 39216

**Hon. Robert Ward**
Woodville, MS 39669

## MISSOURI

### Court of Appeals

**Hon. Fernando J. Gaiton Jr.**
Western District
1300 Oak Street
Kansas City, MO 64106

### Circuit Courts

*Circuit 22*
Civil Courts Building
12th. and Market Street
St. Louis, MO 63101

**Hon. Evelyn Marie Baker**
**Hon. Daniel T. Tillman**

### Circuit Court Associate Judges

**Hon. Henry Autrey**
St. Louis, MO 63103

**Hon. Michael Calvin**
St. Louis, MO

**Hon. Leonard Hughes III**
Kansas City, MO 64106

**Hon. Booker Shaw**
St. Louis, Mo 63101

### Municipal Courts

**Hon. Andrew Cain Jr.**
Howardville, MO

**Hon. Bernard Edwards**
St. Louis, MO 63103

**Hon. Leonard S. Hughes Jr.**
Kansas City, Missouri

**Hon. Thadeus Niemira**
St. Louis, MO 63103

## MONTANA

None

## NEBRASKA

### County Court

**Hon. Elizabeth D. Pittman**
Douglas County
17 Farnam, Hall of Justice
Omaha, NE 68102

## NEVADA

### District Court

**Hon. Addleliar D. Guy**
Department 11
200 East Carson
Las Vegas, NV 89101

**Hon. Earle W. White Jr.**
8th Judicial District
200 South Third Street
Las Vegas, NV 89155

## NEW HAMPSHIRE

### District Court

**Hon. Ivorey Cobb**
Colebrook District Court
Colebrook, NH 03576

## NEW JERSEY

### Superior Court

**Hon. Irwin B. Booker**
50 W. Market Street
Newark, NJ 07102

**Hon. Dennis Braithwaite**
1201 Bacharach Blvd.
Atlantic City, NJ 08401

**Hon. James H. Coleman Jr.**
Appellate Division
155 Morris Avenue
Springfield, NJ 07081

**Hon. Theodore Z. Davis**
Hall of Justice
Nickel Blvd.
Camden, NJ 08103

**Hon. Rudolph Hawkins**
2 Broad Street
Elizabeth NJ 07207

**Hon. Harry Hazelwood Jr.**
706 County Courts Building
Camden, NJ 07102

**Hon. Elliot Heard Jr.**
P. O. Box 797
Woodbury, NJ 08096

**Hon. Donald King**
Essex County Courthouse
Newark, NJ 07102

**Hon. Betty Lester**
470 Dr. Martin Luther King Blvd.
Newark, NJ 07102

**Hon. Samuel C. Scott**
595 Newark Avenue
Jersey City, NJ 07306

**Hon. Shirley Tolentino**
41 Gifford Avenue
Jersey City, NJ 07304

**Hon. William Walls**
Essex County Hall of Records
Newark, NJ 07102

### Municipal Courts

**Hon. Frances Lawrence Antonin**
769 Montgomery Street
Jersey City, NJ 07306

**Hon. David Brantley**
221 Freeway Drive
East Orange, NJ 27017

**Hon. Joseph M. Clark**
73 South Van Brunt Street
Englewood, NJ 07631

**Hon. Ronald J. Freeman**
309 Market Street
Camden, NJ 08102

**Hon. Beverly Giscombe**
221 Freeway Drive
East Orange, NJ 07018

**Hon. Derrick N. Hart**
Municipal Court Building
Freeway Drive
East Orange, NJ 07017

**Hon. Harvey C. Johnson**
Lawnside
228 Cooer Street
Camden, NJ 08102

**Hon. Golden E. Johnson-Burns**
Montclair
614 Central Avenue, Suite 17
East Orange, NJ 07018

**Hon. Clifford J. Minor**
31 Green Street
Newark, NJ 07102

**Hon. Chester A. Morrison**
31 Green Street
Newark, NJ 07102

**Hon. Carol P. Newton**
111 Broadway
Patterson, NJ 07505

**Hon. Freddie Pohill**
593 Lincoln Avenue
Orange, NJ 07050

**Hon. Joan Robinson-Gross**
325 Watchung Avenue
Plainfield, NJ 07060

**Hon. Paulette Sapp**
225 N. Clinton Avenue
Trenton, NJ 08607

**Hon. Marie White-Bell**
Municipal Complex-Salem Road
Willingboro, NJ 08046

**Hon. Renee Jones-Weeks**
31 Green Street
Newark, NJ 07102

**Hon. J. Clifton Wilkerson**
31 Green Street
Newark, NJ 07102

### Administrative Judges

**Hon. Philip N. Gumbs**
601 S. Atlantic Avenue
Aberdeen, NJ 07747

**Hon. Isaac G. McNatt**
14 Commerce Street
Newark, NJ 07102

**Hon. Thomas A. Penn**
185 Washington Street
Newark, NJ 07102

**Hon. August E. Thomas**
9 Quakerbridge Plaza
Mercervill, NJ 08625

### Administrative Law Judges

**Hon. Augustus Thomas**
88 East State Street
Trenton, NJ 08625

## NEW MEXICO

### Municipal Court

**Hon. Tommy Jewell**
P. O. Box 133
Albuquerque, NM 87103

## NEW YORK

### Court of Appeals

**Hon. Fritz W. Alexander**
100 Centre Street
New York, NY 10032

### Appellate Division

**Hon. Samuel L. Green**
50 Delaware Avenue
Buffalo, NY 14202

**Hon. Charles B. Lawrence**
45 Monroe Place
Brooklyn, NY 11201

**Hon. William C. Thompson**
54 Pierreport Street
Brooklyn, NY 11201

### Supreme Court

**Hon. Howard E. Bell**
100 Centre Street
New York, NY 10013

**Hon. Kenneth N. Browne**
125-01 Queens Blvd.
Kew Gardens, NY 11415

**Hon George D. Covington**
815 Grand Concourse
Bronx, NY 10451

**Hon. Reuben K. Davis**
Hall of Justice
Rochester, NY 14614

**Hon. David H. Edwards Jr.**
60 Centre Street
New York, NY 10007

**Hon. Elbert C. Hinkson**
851 Grand Concourse
Bronx, NY 10451

**Hon. Leroy B. Kellam**
114-73 176th Street
Jamaica, NY 11434

**Hon. Edith Miller**
165 West End Avenue
New York, NY 10023

**Hon. Franklin W. Morton Jr.**
360 Adams Street
Brooklyn, NY 11201

**Hon. Alfred S. Robbins**
28 Eddridge Avenue
Hempstead, NY 11550

**Hon. Jawn A. Sandifer**
60 Centre Street
New York, NY 10007

**Hon. Clifford A. Scott**
100 Centre Street
New York, NY 10013

**Hon. W. Eugene Sharpe**
125-01 Queens Blvd.
Queens, NY 11415

**Hon. James H. Shaw Jr.**
360 Adams Street
Brooklyn, NY 11201

**Hon. Kenneth L. Shorter**
60 Centre Street
New York, NY 10007

**Hon. George B. Smith**
60 Centre Street
New York, NY 10007

**Hon. Andrew Tyler**
60 Centre Street
New York, NY 10007

**Hon. Ivan Warner**
851 Grand Concourse
Bronx, NY 10451

**Hon. Albert P. Williams**
100 Centre Street
New York, NY 10013

**Hon. Joseph B. Williams**
360 Adams Street
New York, NY 10013

**Hon. Harold L. Wood**
111 Grove Street
White Plains, NY 10601

**Hon. Bruce M. Wright**
60 Centre Street
New York, NY 10007

***First District***
New York County
100 Centre Street
New York, NY 10013

**Hon. Fritz W. Alexander**
**Hon. Amos E. Bowman**
**Hon. Thomas Dickens**

**Hon. Edward R. Dudley**
Also assigned to Appellate Term, 1st Department

**Hon. David H. Edwards Jr.**

***First District, Bronx County***
851 Grand Concourse
Bronx, NY 10451

**Hon. Howard E. Bell**
**Hon. Andrew R. Tyler**

**Hon. Jawn A. Sandifer**
Also assigned to Dept. Administrative Judge of the Criminal Court of the City of New York

**Hon. Clifford A. Scott**
**Hon. George Bundy Smith**
**Hon. Oliver C. Sutton**
**Hon. Albert P. Williams**

***Second District, Kings County***
360 Adams Street
Brooklyn, NY 11201

**Hon. Thomas R. Jones**

**Hon. William C. Thompson**
Also designated Administrative Judge, 2nd District

***Second District, Kings County***
Civic Center, Montague Street
Brooklyn, NY 11201

**Hon. Charles B. Lawrence**
**Hon. Franklin W. Morton Jr.**
**Hon. James H. Shaw**

***Eighth District, Erie County***

**Hon. Samuel L. Green**
Buffalo, NY

***Ninth District, Westchester County***
111 Grove Street
White Plains, NY 10601

**Hon. Harold L. Wood**
**Hon. Joseph K. West**

***Tenth District, Nassau County***

**Hon. Alfred S. Robbins**
County Courthouse
Mineola, NY 11501

***Eleventh District, Queens County***
125-01 Queens Boulevard
Kew Gardens
Queens, NY 11415

**Hon. Kenneth N. Browne**
**Hon. W. Eugene Sharpe**

**Court of Claims**
111 Centre Street
New York, NY 10013

**Hon. Dorothy A. Cropper**

### Civil Court of the City of New York

*New York County*
111 Centre Street
New York, NY 11201

**Hon. Leland De Grasse**
**Hon. George M. Fleary**

744 Putnam Avenue
New York, NY 10021

**Hon. Wendell Levister**
**Hon. Milton Richardson**

**Hon. Kenneth L. Shorter**
Also Acting Supreme Court Justice

**Hon. Thomas V. Sinclair Jr.**
**Hon. Milton Tingling**
**Hon. Bruce M. Wright**

*Kings County*
141 Livingston Street
Brooklyn, NY 11201

**Hon. Thaddeus Owens**
Also Acting Supreme Court Justice

**Hon. John L. Phillips Jr.**
**Hon. George E. Wade**

*Queens County*
120-55 Queens Boulevard
Kew Gardens
Queens, NY 11415

**Hon. Richard B. Rutledge**
**Hon. Joscelyn E. Smith**

*Bronx County*

**Hon. Antonio Brandveen**
215 E. 161 Street
Bronx, NY 10451

**Hon. Hansel McGee**
851 Grand Concourse
Bronx, NY 10451

138-46 225th Street
Laurelton, NY 11413

**Hon. William Wallace III**
**Hon. Joscelyn Smith**

### Criminal Court of the City of New York

*New York County*
100 Centre Street
New York, NY 10013

**Hon. George D. Covington**
**Hon. William Davis**
**Hon. Lewis Douglas**

**Hon. Dennis Edwards Jr.**
Also Acting Supreme Court Justice

**Hon. L. Priscilla Hall**
**Hon. Leroy Kellam**

**Hon. William H. Logven**
Also Acting Supreme Court Justice

**Hon. Richard Lowe**
**Hon. Albert R. Murray**

**Hon. Milton L. Williams**
Also Acting Supreme Court Justice

**Hon. Livingston L. Wingate**

*Kings County*

**Hon. William H. Booth**
Also Acting Supreme Court Justice

120 Schermerhorn Street
Brooklyn, NY 11201

*Queens County*

**Hon. Claudius Matthews**
869 Linden Blvd.
Kew Gardens, NY 11415

**Hon. Wayne Scarbrough**
125-01 Queens Blvd.
Kew Gardens, NY 11415

*Bronx County*
851 Grand Concourse
Bronx, NY 10451

**Hon. Maurice Grey**
Also Acting Supreme Court Justice

**Hon. Alexander Hunter**
**Hon. Bernard Jackson**

### District Court

**Hon. Marquette L. Floyd**
Dennison Building, Vits Highway
Kauppauge, NY 11788

### City Courts

**Hon. Richard L. Baltimore, Jr.**
City Court of New Rochelle
900 Beaufort Place
New Rochelle, NY 10801

**Hon. Reuben K. Davis**
City Court of Rochester
Rochester, NY

**Hon. Reginald S. Matthews**
900 Sheridan Avenue
Bronx, NY 10475

**Hon. Hugh B. Scott**
50 Delaware Avenue
Buffalo, NY 14202

**Hon. Barbara M. Sims**
City Court of Buffalo
Buffalo, NY

**Hon. Bruce Tolbert**
1523 Central Park Avenue
Yonkers, NY 10710

**Hon. Wilbur P. Trammell**
50 Delaware Avenue
Buffalo, NY 14202

### Family Courts

*New York County*
60 Lafayette Street
New York, NY 10013

**Hon. Peggy Davis**
**Hon. Edith Miller**
**Hon. John F. Pollard**
**Hon. Phillip D. Roach**

**Hon. Joseph B. Williams**
Also designated Administrative Judge, Family Court, New York County

*Monroe County*

**Hon. Charles L. Willis (e)**
Civic Center Plaza
Rochester, NY 14614

*Bronx County*

**Hon. Elrich A. Eastman**
851 Grand Concourse
Bronx, NY 10451

*Kings County*
283 Adams Street
Brooklyn, NY 11201

**Hon. Claire T. Pearce (A)**
**Hon. Cesar H. Quinones**

*Queens County*

**Hon. Reginald S. Matthews**
89-14 Parsons Boulevard
Jamaica, NY 11432

### Housing Court

**Hon. Janice L. Bowman**
111 Centre Street
New York, NY 10013
Hon. Randolph Jackson
141 Livingston Street
Brooklyn, NY 11201

### Administrative Law Judges

**Hon. Milton B. Williams**
80 Centre Street
New York, NY 10007

## NORTH CAROLINA

### Supreme Court

**Hon. Henry E. Frye**
P. O. Box 1841
Raleigh, NC 27602

### Court of Appeals

**Hon. Charles L. Becton**
Ruffin Building
P. O. Box 888
Raleigh, NC 27602

**Hon. Richard C. Erwin**
P. O. Box 888
Raleigh, NC 27602

**Hon. Clifton Johnson**
Ruffin Building P. O. Box 888
Raleigh, NC 27602

**Hon. Arthur Lane**

### Superior Court

**Hon. James E. Beady Jr.**
325 Mayfair Drive
Winston-Salem, NC 27105

### District Courts

**Hon. Elreta Alexander**
Guilford County Courthouse
Greensboro, NC 27402

**Hon. Stafford G. Bullock**
Wake County Courthouse
Raleigh, NC 27611

**Hon. Karen Bethea Galloway**
3525 Mayfair Road
Durham, NC 27707

**Hon. George R. Greene**
P. O. Box 351
Raleigh, NC 27602

**Hon. Robert Harrell**
P. O. Box 7154
Ashville, NC 28807

**Hon. Roland Hayes**
P. O. Box 1411
Winston-Salem, NC 27102

**Hon. Orlando Hudson**
400 River Birch Road
Durham, NC 27705

**Hon. William K. Hunter**
P. O. Box Drawer T-5
Greensboro, NC 27402

**Hon. Jacqueline Morris-Goodson**
New Hanover Courthouse
Wilmington, NC 28401

**Hon. William G. Pearson**
126 Masondale Avenue
Durham, NC 27707

**Hon. Donald E. Ramseur**
1229 North Highland Street
Gastonia, NC 28052

**Hon. Herbert L. Richardson**
P. O. Box 1084
Lumberton, NC 28359

**Hon. Patricia Timmons-Goodson**
1677 Banburg Drive
Fayetteville, NC 28305

**Hon. T. Michael Todd**
Mecklenburg County Courthouse
Charlotte, NC 28202

**Hon. Terry Sherrill**
800 E. 4th Street
Charlotte, NC 28202

**Hon. Quinton Summer**
P. O. Box 1215
Rocky Mount, NC 27802

**Hon. Joseph Williams**
County Building
High Point, NC 27261

## NORTH DAKOTA

None

## OHIO

### Court of Appeals

**Hon. Leo A. Jackson**
3155 Ludlow Road
Shaker Heights, OH 44120

**Hon. Ira G. Turpin**
115 Central Plaza
Canton, OH 44702

### Court of Common Pleas

***Cuyahoga County***
Justice Center
1200 Ontario Street
Cleveland, OH 44113

**Hon. Lloyd O. Brown**
**Hon. Frederick M. Coleman**
**Hon. Leodis Harris**
**Hon. Stephanie Tubbs Jones**

***Lucas County***

**Hon. Charles J. Doneghy**
Lucas County Courthouse
Toledo, OH 43624

**Hon. Robert V. Franklin**
Adams and Erie Streets
Toledo, OH 43623

***Stark County***
Hon. Ira Turpin
Courthouse
Canton, OH 44702

***Montgomery County***

**Hon. Arthur O. Fisher**
303 W. 2nd Street
Dayton, OH 45402

### Referees

**Ramon Basie**
Domestic Relations Court
Cuyahoga County Court House
Cleveland, OH 44113

**Carol Buggs**
Juvenile Court
2163 East 22nd Street
Cleveland, OH 44115

**Lillian Greene**
Probate Court
Cuyahoga County Court House
Cleveland, OH 44113

**David Taylor**
Domestic Relations Court
Toledo, OH

### Municipal Courts

**Cleveland Municipal Court**
Justice Center
1200 Ontario Street
Cleveland, OH 44113

**Hon. Ronald B. Adrine**
**Hon. Lillian W. Burke**
**Hon. Jean M. Capers**
**Hon. C. Ellen Connally**

4034 Marlaine Drive
Toledo, OH 43606

**Hon. Sara J. Harper**
**Hon. Carl B. Stokes**
**Hon. George B. Trumbo**
**Hon. Robert Penn**

375 S. High Street
Columbus, OH 43215

**Hon. Arthur D. Jackson Jr.**
**Hon. Bush P. Mitchell**
**Hon. H. Alfred Glascor**

**Hon. Charles W. Fleming**
3058 Becket Road
Cleveland, OH 44113

**Hon. Clarence L. Gaines**
9909 Westchester Avenue
Cleveland, OH 44108

**Hon. Lloyd Haynes**
1849 5th Avenue
Youngstown, OH 44504

**Hon. Alice O. McCullum**
335 W. 3rd Street
Dayton, OH 45402

**Hon. James A. Pearson**
375 S. High Street
Columbus, OH 43215

**Hon. Joseph D Rhoulhac**
381 Sun Valley Drive
Ackron, OH 44313

**Hon. James R. Williams**
City-County Safety Building
217 S. High Street
Ackron, OH 44308

**Hon. Jack Sherman Jr.**
222 E. Central Parkway
Cincinnati, OH 45202

**Hon. Theodore Williams**
14340 Euclid
East Cleveland, OH 44112

## OKLAHOMA

### District Court

**Hon. Lynnell Anderson-Harkins**
321 W. Park Road Courthouse
Oklahoma City, OK 73102

**Hon. Charles L. Owens**
814 County Courthouse
Oklahoma City, OK 73102

**Major R. Wilson**
321 W. Park Road
Oklahoma City OK 73102

**Municipal Court**

**Hon. Albert V. Alexander**
Associate Municipal Judge
Oklahoma City, OK 73102

## OREGON

**Circuit Court**

**Hon. Mercedes F. Diaz**
1021 S. W. 4th Avenue
Portland, OR 97204

**Hon. Aaron Brown Jr.**
1021 S. W. 4th Avenue
Portland, OR 97204

**District Court**

**Hon. Aaron Brown Jr.**
County Court House
Portland, OR 97204

**Quasi-Judicial Officers**

**Hon. H. J. Belton Hamilton**
Hearings Examiner Social Security Department
1904 N. E. 45th Street
Portland, OR 97204

## PENNSYLVANIA

**Supreme Court**

**Hon. Robert N. C. Nix Jr.**
3 Penn Center
Philadelphia, PA 19107

**Superior Court**

**Hon. Justin M. Johnson**
330 Grant Street
Pittsburgh, PA 15219

**Commonwealth Court of Pennsylvania**

**Hon. Robert W. Williams**
392 City Hall
Philadelphia, PA 19107

**Common Pleas**

**Philadelphia County**
Philadelphia, PA 19107

**Hon. John L. Broxton**
**Hon. Matthew W. Bullock Jr.**
**Hon. Herbert R. Cain**
**Hon. Curtis C. Carson Jr.**
**Hon. Eugene H. Clark Jr.**
**Hon. Tama Meyers Clark**
**Hon. Charles L. Durham**
**Hon. Levon Gordon**
**Hon. Doris M. Harris**
**Hon. Kenneth S. Harris**
**Hon. Ricardo C. Jackson**
**Hon. Norman A. Jenkins**
**Hon. Julian F. King**
**Hon. Frederica Massiah-Jackson**
**Hon. Livingston Johnson**
**Hon. Theodore A. McKee**
**Hon. Lawrence W. Prattis**
**Hon. Harvey N. Schmidt**
**Hon. Henry R. Smith Jr.**
**Hon. Juanita Kidd Stout**
**Hon. Calvin T. Wilson**
**Hon. Charles Wright**

***Allegheny County***
Pittsburgh, PA 15219

**Hon. Thomas A. Harper**
**Hon. Henry R. Smith Jr.**
**Hon. J. Warren Watson**

***Montgomery County***
Morristown, PA 19494
**Hon. Horace A. Davenport**

***Delaware County***
Media, PA 19063
**Hon. Robert A. Wright**

**Municipal Court**

One East Penn Square Building
Philadelphia, PA 19107

**Hon. Lynwood F. Blount**
**Hon. Lydia Y. Kirkland**
**Hon. Ronald Merriweather**

**District Justice Court**

**Hon. Garland W. Anderson**
418 Avenue of the States
Chester, PA 19013

**Hon. William L. Brown Jr.**
418 Avenue of the States
Chester, PA 19013

**Hon. Helen Hull**
566 Brushton Avenue
Pittsburgh, PA 15208

**Hon. Dennis Schotzman**
7305 Mt. Vernon Street
Pittsburgh, PA 15208

**Hon. Edward A. Tibbs**
1200 Paulson Avenue
Pittsburgh, PA 15206

**Hon. Jacob H. Williams**
14 Wood Street
W. Penn Building
Pittsburgh PA 15222

**Hon. Louise B. Williams**
331 S. Franklin Street
Lancaster, PA 17602

**Quasi-Judicial Officers**

**Referee**

**Duane Darkins**
Workmen's Compensation
1510 State Office Building
Pittsburgh, PA 15222

## RHODE ISLAND

**District Court**

**Hon. Alton Wiley**
1 Dorrance Plaza
Providence, RI 02903

## SOUTH CAROLINA

**Supreme Court**

**Hon. Ernest A. Finney Jr.**
P. O. Box Drawer 1309
Sumter, SC 29151

**Court of Appeals**

**Hon. Jasper Marshall Cureton**
P. O. Box 11629
Columbia, SC 29211

**Circuit Court**

**Hon. E. Fields**
P. O. Box 428
Charleston, SC 29402

**Municipal Court**

**Hon. Cartrelle A. Brown**
P. O. Box 1190
Marion, SC 29571

**Hon. Merl F. Code**
22 W. Board Street
Greenville, SC 29601

**Hon. Franklin B. Goodwin Jr.**
P. O. Box 299
Santee, SC 29142

**Hon. Janie G. Goree**
P. O. Box 305
Carlisle, SC 29031

**Hon. Virgin Johnson**
P. O. Box 275
Gifford, SC 29923

**Hon. Arthur C. McFarland**
205 King Street
Charleston, SC 29401

**Hon. Veronica G. Small**
P. O. Box 1116
Charleston, SC 29402

**Hon. Joseph Thomas**
P. O. Box 147
Lynchburg, SC 29080

**Probate Court**

**Hon. Bernard R. Fielding**
2 Courthouse Square
Charleston, SC 29401

**Family Court**

**Hon. Harold R. Boulware**
5th Judicial Circuit
Route 1, Box 42
Irmo, SC 29603

**Hon. Willie T. Smith Jr.**
P. O. Box 757
Greenville, SC 29602

### Magistrate Courts

**Hon. Willie Lee Bethune**
205 Moorer Street
Manning, SC 29102

**Hon. Alvin Bligen**
P. O. Box 216
Edisto Island, SC 29438

**Hon. Albert Bradley**
Rt. 1, Box 191
Mayersville, SC 29104

**Hon. Nathan Brown**
P. O. Box 259
Pawleys Island, SC 29585

**Hon. Leroy Burgress Sr.**
Rt. 4, Box 200
Kingstree, SC 29556

**Hon. Graylon Charmichael**
Rt. 3, Box 1366
Marion, SC 29571

**Hon. Reuben B. Clark**
Rt. 2, Box 605
Pinewood, SC 29125

**Hon. Thelma Cook**
Fairfield County
Winnsboro, SC

**Hon. Eugene Cooper**
Rt. 1, Box 139
Caward, SC 29530

**Hon. Glen Davis**
5617 Bluff Road
Columbia, SC 29209

**Hon. Verbena DeLee**
Dorchester County
Ridgeville, SC 29477

**Hon. James Dingle**
P. O. Box 344
Manning, SC 29102

**Hon. Kenneth Edwards**
P. O. Box 61
Ravenel, SC 29470

**Hon. Rufus E. Ferguson**
P. O. Box 421
Fairfax, SC 29827

**Hon. Lennon Folk**
Rt. 1, Box 131-D
Ehrhardt, SC 29081

**Hon. Ulysses Frieson**
Drawer XX
City-County Complex
Florence, SC 29501

**Hon. Jonathan Garvin**
P. O. Box 1281
Ridgeland, SC 29936

**Hon. Jacob Gillens Sr.**
P. O. Box 188
Eutau, SC 29048

**Hon. Calvin C. Gore**
P. O. Box 723
Chester, SC 29706

**Hon. Aaron Harvey**
Charleston County
138 Spring Street
Charleston, SC 29403

**Hon. Bruster O. Harvin**
Rt. 2, Box 52
Lane, SC 29564

**Hon. Woodrow H. Hodges**
Rt. 3, Box 359
Canadys, SC 29433

**Hon. Clarence L. James**
Rt. 2, Box 297
Society Hills, SC 29593

**Hon. W. M. Jefferson**
P. O. Box 156
Mayesville, SC 29104

**Hon. John O. Johnston Sr.**
Charleston County
Route 1, Box 11
Adams Run, SC 29426

**Hon. Charles E. Jones**
P. O. Box 1871
Lexington, SC 35985

**Hon. Walter Jones**
1328 Huger Street
Columbia, SC 29201

**Hon. Eddie Kline**
Rt. 1, Box 256
Seabrook, SC 29940

**Hon. Leroy Linen**
1527 Main Road
Johns Island, SC 29455

**Hon. Lewis McNeil**
206 Brantford Lane
Greensville, SC 29605

**Hon. Charles D. Morris**
Rt. 1, Box 297
Nesmith, SC 29580

**Hon. Anthony O'Neil**
P. O. Box 941
Charleston, SC 29402

**Hon. Roosevelt Osborne**
217 Welsh Street
Camden, SC 29020

**Hon. Samuel Play**
5116 Fairfield Road
Columbia, SC 29201

**Hon. Cranston Pickney**
101 Ridge Street
St. George, SC 29477

**Hon. Delores Parcher**
P. O. Box 7
McClellenville, SC 29458

**Hon. William Sanders**
Rt. 2, Box 51
Rembert, SC 29128

**Hon. Hattie Sims**
Richland County
Route 1, Box 166-b
Hopkins, SC 29061

**Hon. Katherine Smalls**
P. O. Box 277
Huger, SC 29450

**Hon. Charles Snipes**
Rt. 2, Box 8
Ridgeville, SC 29472

**Hon. Benjamin Spells**
P. O. Box 1159
Holly Hill, SC 29059

**Hon. Jimmy Wilson Sr.**
Law Enforcement Center
Greenville, SC 29601

**Hon. Eddie A. Woods**
Rt. 2, Box 19-A
Greeleyville, SC 29056

**Hon. Harry Lee Wright**
Rt. 1, Box 246
Cross, SC 29436

**Hon. Ernest Yarborough**
Jasper County
Pineland, SC 29934

## TENNESSEE

### Circuit Court

***Shelby County***
140 Adams Avenue
Memphis, TN 38103

**Hon. George H. Brown Jr.**
**Hon. James E. Swearengen**
**Hon. Shepperson A. Wilbun**

***Davidson County***
609 Metropolitan Courthouse
Nashville, TN 37201

**Hon. Robert E. Lillard**

### Chancery Court

**Hon. Irvin H. Kilcrease Jr.**
401 Metro Courthouse
Nashville, TN 37201

### Criminal Court

**Hon. Arthur T. Bennett**
201 Poplar Avenue
Memphis, TN 37201

**Hon. Adolpho A. Birch Jr.**
609 Metropolitan Courthouse
Nashville, TN 37201

**Hon. Sterling Gray**
601 Metro Courthouse
Nashville, TN 37201

**Hon. H. T. Lockard**
201 Poplar Avenue
Memphis, TN 38103

**General Sessions Court**

**Hon. Bernice Donald**
201 Poplar Avenue
Memphis, TN 38103

**Hon. C. Anthony Johnson**
201 Poplar Avenue
Memphis, TN 38103

**Hon. Ira H. Murphy**
P. O. Box 26041
Memphis, TN 38124

## TEXAS

**Court of Appeals**

**Hon. Henry Doyle**
Associate Justice First Court of Civil Appeals
Civil Courts Building
Houston, TX 77002

**Hon. Ken Hoyt**
3715 Rosedale Street
Houston, TX 77004

**Criminal District Court**

**Hon. Larry W. Baraka**
600 Commerce Street
Dallas, TX 75202

**Hon. Clifford L. Davis**
300 W. Beeknap Street
Ft. Worth TX 76196

**Hon. Bonnie Fitch**
403 Caroline Street
Houston, TX 77002

**Hon. Maryellen Hicks**
400 Civil Court Building
Ft. Worth, TX 76196

**Hon. John W. Peavy Jr.**
1115 Congress
Houston TX 77002

**Hon. Thomas H. Routt**
301 San Jacinto
Houston, TX 77002

**Hon. Fred Tinsley**
600 Commerce Street Government Center
Dallas, TX 75202

**District Court**

**Hon. Alice Bonner**
80th District Court
Houston, TX

**Hon. Joan T. Winn**
191st District Court
Dallas, TX

**County Courts**

**Hon. Berlaind L. Brashear Jr.**
Criminal Court
Dallas County Courthouse
Dallas, TX

**Hon. Donald J. Floyd**
Jefferson County Courthouse
Beaumont, TX 77701

**Hon. James L. Muldrou**
Criminal Court at Law #6
Harris County
401 Caroline Street
Houston, TX 77002

**Hon. Benjamin Samples**
Bexar County Courthouse
San Antonio, TX 78205

**Municipal Courts**

**Hon. Robert Anderson**
1400 Lubbock Street
Houston, TX 77002

**Hon. Howard O. Banks**
2014 Main Street, Room 210
Dallas, TX 75201

**Hon. Gladys Bronsford**
1400 Lubbock Street
Houston, TX 77251

**Hon. Benjamin Durant**
P. O. Box 1562
Houston, TX 77251

**Hon. Charlye Farris**
Municipal Court
921 Seventh Street
Wichita Falls, TX 76301

**Hon. Maryellen Hicks**
Municipal Court
Municipal Courts Building
Ft. Worth, TX 76116

**Hon. Shirley Hunter**
P. O. Box 1562
Houston, TX 77251

**Hon. Gene Locke**
3303 Main Street
Houston, TX 77002

**Hon. Clarence McGowan**
Municipal Court
City Hall
San Antonio, TX

**Hon. Cleve Moten**
700 East Seventh Street
Austin, TX 78701

**Hon. Harriet Moore Murphy**
P. O. Box 2135
Austin, TX 78768

**Hon. William J. Rice Jr.**
1400 Lubbock Street
Houston, TX 77002

**Hon. Roy Smith**
Municipal Court
608 Fannin, Suite 2007
Houston, TX

**Hon. Fred L. Tinsley**
Municipal Court
7929 Brookriver Drive
Dallas, TX 75247

**Hon. Fran Totty**
1400 Lubbock Street
Houston, TX 77002

**Hon. Tad Wilson Jr.**
1400 Lubbock Street
Houston, TX 77002

**Justices of the Peace**

**Hon. George L. Allen**
414 S. Thornton Freeway
Dallas, TX 75203

**Hon. O. D. Baggett**
703 N. Pinkerton Street
Athens, TX 75751

**Hon. Betty Brock Bell**
1646 Old Spanish Trail
Houston, TX 77054

**Hon. Lewis C. Brazier**
614 Boston Place
Amarillo, TX 79107

**Hon. Cecil Bush**
4900 Fannin Street
Houston, TX 77004

**Hon. Jim Conley**
1814 South Na White Road
San Antonio, TX 78220

**Hon. Alexander Green**
5357 Cullen Boulevard
Houston, TX 77021

**Hon. Oneal Hunt**
Anderson County Courthouse
Palestine, TX 75801

**Hon. Quintin Jackson**
P. O. Box 250
Anahauc, TX 77514

**Hon. Hazel Lewis**
P. O. Box 834
Marlin, TX 76661

**Hon. Richard E. Scott**
3230 E. Martin Luther King Boulevard
Austin, TX 78721

**Hon. Clephas R. Steele Jr.**
414 South R. L. Thornton Freeway
Dallas, TX 75203

**Hon. Alphonza Williams**
2207 South Street
Marshall, TX 75670

**Hon. Arthur B. Williams**
Courthouse, 7th. and Lamar Streets
Wichita Falls, TX 76301

**Quasi-Judicial Officers**

***Master, Family District Court***
201Main Street
Houston, TX 77002

**Hon. Aldrinette Chapital**
**Hon. Francis Williams**
**Hon. Gladys R. Goffney**

**Hon. Craig Washington**
Master, Civil District Courts
Houston, TX 77002

#### Referees

**Hon. Bonnie Fitch**
Family District Court
Harris County Court
Houston, TX 77002

**Hon. Carolyn D. Hobson**
Criminal District Court
Houston, TX 77002

**Hon. Veronica Morgan**
Juvenile Court of Harris County
Family Law Center
Houston, TX 77002

### UTAH

#### Circuit Court

**Hon. Tyrone Midley**
2470 S. Redwood Road
West Valley City, UT 84119

### VERMONT

None

### VIRGIN ISLANDS

#### Territorial Court of the Virgin Islands

P. O. Box 70
St Thomas, VI 00801
**Hon. Ishmael A. Meyers**
**Hon. Verne A. Hodge**
**Hon. Alphonzo A. Christian**

RFD #2, P. O. Box 9000
St Croix, VI 00850
**Hon. Raymond L. Finch**
**Hon. Eileen R. Peterson**

### VIRGINIA

#### Supreme Court

**Hon. John Charles Thomas**
P. O. Box 1315
Richmond, VA 23219

#### Court of Appeals

**Hon. James W. Benton Jr.**
101 N. 8th. Street
Richmond, VA 23219

#### Circuit Court

**Hon. James Edward Sheffield**
City of Richmond,
Division I Courts Building
Richmond, VA 23219

**Hon. Melvin R. Hughes Jr.**
800 E. Marshall Street
Richmond, VA 23219

**Hon. Jerome James**
100 St. Paul Blvd.
Norfolk, VA 23510

#### District Courts

**Hon. Archie Elliot**
General District Court
Portsmouth, VA 23704

**Hon. George Harris**
Roanoke County Court, Main Street
Salem, VA 24153

**Hon. Joseph A. Jordan Jr.**
General District Court
811 East City Hall Avenue
Norfolk, VA 23510

**Hon. Thomas Monroe**
General District Court Courthouse
Arlington, VA 22201

**Hon. James A. Owerton**
Substitute Judge
General District Court
623 Effingham Street
Portsmouth, VA 23704

**Hon. William Stone**
Substitute Judge
General District Court
P. O. Box HB
Williamsburg, VA 23185

**Hon. I. Douglas Suggs**
Substitute Judge
General District Court
South Boston, VA

**Hon. Wilford Taylor Jr.**
P. O. Box 70
Hampton, VA 23669

**Hon. Phillip Walker**
Substitute Judge
General District Court
1715 25th Street
Hampton, VA

#### Juvenile and Domestic Relations District Courts

**Hon. Willard H. Douglas Jr.**
2000 Mecklenburg Street
Richmond, VA 23223

**Hon. Roland D. Ealy**
Substitute Judge
420 North First Street
Richmond, VA 23222

**Hon. Leonard W. Lambert**
Substitute Judge
2307 East Broad Street
Richmond, VA 23223

**Hon. Lester V. Moore Jr.**
800 East City Hall Avenue
P. O. Box 3608
Norfolk, VA 23514

### WASHINGTON

#### Superior Court

**Hon. Donald Haley**
King County Courthouse
Seattle, WA 98125

**Hon. Charles V. Johnson**
415 Randolph Avenue
Seattle, WA 98122

#### Municipal Court

Seattle Municipal Court
610 Third Avenue
Seattle, WA 98104
**Hon. Charles V. Johnson**
**Hon. Norma Smith**
**Hon. Herbert M. Stephens**

### WEST VIRGINIA

#### Circuit Court

**Hon. Herman Canady Jr.**
Kanawha County Courthouse
Judicial Annex
Charleston, WV 25301

**Hon. Booker T. Stephens**
8th. Judicial Circuit
66 Elkins
Welch, WV 24801

#### Magistrate Court

**Hon. Nancy Starks**
Magistrate Court
P. O. Box 3318
Charleston, WV 25333

#### Magistrate Court Kanawha County

**Hon. John Miller**
City Building South
Charleston, WV

#### Quasi-Judicial Officers

**Hon. William L. Lonesome**
Commissioner of Accounts
Kanawha County Probate Court
P. O. Box 241
Institute, WV 25112

### WISCONSIN

#### Circuit Court

**Hon. Harold B. Jackson Jr.**
10201 Watertown Plank Road
Wauwatosa, WI 53226

**Hon. Clarence R. Parrish**
3322 North 105th Street
Milwaukee County Court House
Milwaukee, WI 53222

**Hon. Russell Stamper**
821 W. State Street
Milwaukee, WI 53233

## ORGANIZATIONS RELATED TO THE LEGAL PROFESSION-PROVIDING PROGAMS, INFORMATION, ASSISTANCE OR GUIDANCE

Advocates for Basic Legal Equality Inc.
740 Spitzer Building,
Toledo, OH 43604
419/255-0814.

American Civil Liberties Union (ACLU)
132 West 43rd St.
New York, NY 10017
212/944-9800.

Arkansas Advocates for Children and Families
931 Donaghey Building
Little Rock, AR 72201.
1-5570.

Capital Legal Foundation
700 E Street, SE
Washington, DC 20003
202/546-5533.

Center for Constitutional Rights
853 Broadway, 14th Floor,
New York, NY 10003
212/674-3303.

Center for Law and Education
Six Appian Way, 3rd Floor
Cambridge, MA 02138
617/495-4666.

Center for Law and Social Policy
1616 P Street, NW, 3rd Floor,
Washington, DC 20036
202/328-5140.

Center for Law in the Public Interest
10951 W. Pico Blvd.
Los Angeles, CA 90064
213/470-3000.

Center on Social Welfare Policy and Law
95 Madison Avenue, Room 701
New York, NY 10016
212/679-3709.
-5797.

Children's Defense Fund
122 C Street NW
Washington, DC 20001
202/628-8787.

Colorado Coalition of Legal Services Programs
770 Grant Street, Suite 206
Denver, CO 80203
303/830-1551.

Colorado Lawyer' Committee
1441 18th Street, Suite 50
Denver, CO 80202
303/297-3115.

Community Development Legal Assistance Center
99 Hudson Street
New York, NY 10013
212/219-1800.

Harrison Institute for Public Law
Georgetown University Law Center
605 G Street, NW, Suite 401
Washington, DC 20001
202/624-8235.

Housing Advocates, Inc.
353 Leader Building
Cleveland, OH 44114
216/579-0575.

Immigration Law Clinic
Columbia University School of Law,
435 West 116th Street
New York, NY 10027
212/280-4291.

Juvenile Justice Law Clinic
Georgetown University Law Center,
605 G Street, NW, 3rd Floor
Washington, DC 20001
202/624-8205.

Lawyers Committee for Civil Rights Under Law (LCCRUL)
National Office
1400 I Street, NW, Suite 400
Washington DC 20005
202/371-1212.

Legal Action Center
19 West 44th Street
New York, NY 10036
212/997-0110.

Legal Services for the Elderly
132 West 43rd Street
New York, NY 10036
212/391-0120.

Michigan Legal Services
900 Michigan Building
220 Bagley
Detroit, MI 48226
313/964-4130.

Mid-Atlantic Legal Foundation
400 Market Street, 3rd Floor
Philadelphia, PA 19106
215/238-1367.

NAACP Legal Defense and Educational Fund
99 Hudson Street, 16th Floor
New York, NY 10013
212/219-1900.

National Bar Association
1225 11th Street, NW
Washington, D.C. 20001
202/842-3900.

National Coalition for the Homeless
105 East 22nd Street
New York, NY 10010
212/460-8110.

National Conference of Black Lawyers
12 West 119th Street
New York, NY 10026
212/864-4000.

National Committee Against Discrimination in Housing
733 15th St. NW, Suite 1026
Washington, DC 20005
202/783-8150.

National Employment Law Project Inc.
475 Riverside Drive, Suite 240
New York, NY 10115
212/870-2121.

National Health Law Program
2639 S. LaCienega Blvd.
Los Angeles, CA 90034
213/204-6010.

National Prison Project of the ACLU Foundation
1346 Connecticut Avenue NW, Suite 1031
Washington, DC 20036
202/331-0500.

National Senior Citizens Law Center
2025 M Street NW, Suite 400
Washington, DC 20036
202/887-5280.

New York Lawyers for the Public Interest Inc.
135 East 15th Street
New York, NY 10003
212/777-7707.

Northwest Labor and Employment Law Office
705 Second Avenue
Seattle, WA 98104
206/623-1590.

Project Justice and Equality
475 Broadway
Gary, IN 47402
219/883-0384.

Public Advocates Inc.
1535 Mission Street
San Francisco, CA 94103
415/431-7430.

Public Interest Law Center of Philadelphia
1315 Walnut Street, Suite 1600
Philadelphia, PA 19107
215/735-7200.

Southern Legal Counsel Inc.
115 North East 7th Avenue, Suite A
Gainesville, FL 32601
904/377-8288.

Southern Poverty Law Center
1001 S. Hull Street
Montgomery, AL 36104
205/264-0286.

Untapped Resources Inc.
60 First Avenue
New York, NY 10009.
212/532-4422.

Urban Legal Clinic
Rutgers University School of Law
15 Washington Street
Newark, NJ 07102
201/648-5576.

## TABLE 1: A STATISTICAL PROFILE

### Table 1 A

| State Judges[2] | Federal Court | Court |
|---|---|---|
| Total | 12,093 | 753 |
| Black American | 465 | 53 |
| Hispanic* | 150 | 24 |
| Asian or Pacific Islander | 77 | 3 |
| American Indian, Eskimo, Aleutian | 3 | 0 |

### Table 1 B

| Lawers[1] | |
|---|---|
| Total | 501,834 |
| Black American | 13,594 |
| Hispanic* | 8,930 |
| Asian or Pacific Islander | 3,737 |
| American Indian, Eskimo, Aleutian | 999 |

### Table 1 C

| Law school enrollment for 1987[3] | |
|---|---|
| Total | 123,198 |
| Black American | 6,028 |
| Hispanic* | 4,018 |
| Asian or Pacific Islander | 2,656 |
| American Indian, Eskimo, Aleutian | 499 |
| Other minority | 0 |

### Table 1 D

| Law Professors (full time) | |
|---|---|
| Total | 4,973 |
| All minorities | 306 |

* Hispanic includes Puerto Rican, Mexican and other Hispano Americans.

[1] U.S. Department of Commerce, Bureau of the Census, Detailed Occupation of the Civilian Labor Force by Sex, Race and Spanish Origin: 1980.
[2] The Success of Women and Minorities in Achieving Judicial Office: The Selection Process, Fund for Modern Courts, Inc., 1985.
[3] A Review of Legal Education in the United States, Fall 1987. Published by the American Bar Association, Section of Legal Education and Admissions to the Bar.

## TABLE 2: LYNCHINGS BY STATE AND RACE: 1882-1962

| State | Whites | Blacks | Total | State | Whites | Blacks | Total |
|---|---|---|---|---|---|---|---|
| Alabama | 48 | 299 | 347 | New Jersey | 0 | 1 | 1 |
| Arizona | 31 | 0 | 31 | New Mexico | 33 | 3 | 36 |
| Arkansas | 58 | 226 | 284 | New York | 1 | 1 | 2 |
| California | 41 | 2 | 43 | North Carolina | 15 | 85 | 100 |
| Colorado | 66 | 2 | 68 | North Dakota | 13 | 3 | 16 |
| Delaware | 0 | 1 | 1 | Ohio | 10 | 16 | 26 |
| Florida | 25 | 257 | 282 | Oklahoma | 82 | 40 | 122 |
| Georgia | 39 | 491 | 530 | Oregon | 20 | 1 | 21 |
| Idaho | 20 | 0 | 20 | Pennsylvania | 2 | 6 | 8 |
| Illinois | 15 | 19 | 34 | South Carolina | 4 | 156 | 160 |
| Indiana | 33 | 14 | 47 | South Dakota | 27 | 0 | 27 |
| lowa | 17 | 2 | 19 | Tennessee | 47 | 204 | 251 |
| Kansas | 35 | 19 | 54 | Texas | 141 | 352 | 493 |
| Kentucky | 63 | 142 | 205 | Utah | 6 | 2 | 8 |
| Louisiana | 56 | 335 | 391 | Vermont | 1 | 0 | 1 |
| Maryland | 2 | 27 | 29 | Virginia | 17 | 83 | 100 |
| Michigan | 7 | 1 | 8 | Washington | 25 | 1 | 26 |
| Minnesota | 5 | 4 | 9 | West Virginia | 20 | 28 | 48 |
| Mississippi | 40 | 538 | 578 | Wisconsin | 6 | 0 | 6 |
| Missouri | 53 | 69 | 122 | Wyoming | 30 | 5 | 35 |
| Montana | 82 | 2 | 84 | Total | 1,294 | 3,442 | 4,736 |
| Nebraska | 52 | 5 | 57 | | | | |
| Nevada | 6 | 0 | 6 | | | | |

No lynchings recorded as of July 19, 1963.

## TABLE 3: CAUSES OF LYNCHINGS CLASSIFIED: 1882-1962

| Year | Homicides | Felonious Assault | Rape | Attempted Rape | Robbery and Theft | Insult to White Persons | All Other Causes |
|---|---|---|---|---|---|---|---|
| 1882 | 54 | 0 | 33 | 0 | 16 | 0 | 10 |
| 1883 | 71 | 0 | 24 | 3 | 4 | 0 | 28 |
| 1884 | 62 | 0 | 36 | 0 | 10 | 0 | 103 |
| 1885 | 91 | 2 | 28 | 0 | 1 | 0 | 62 |
| 1886 | 70 | 1 | 32 | 0 | 8 | 0 | 27 |
| 1887 | 54 | 0 | 41 | 0 | 6 | 0 | 19 |
| 1888 | 62 | 0 | 31 | 0 | 3 | 4 | 37 |
| 1889 | 73 | 1 | 34 | 6 | 10 | 1 | 45 |
| 1890 | 35 | 0 | 31 | 2 | 5 | 0 | 23 |
| 1891 | 58 | 14 | 39 | 2 | 12 | 0 | 58 |
| 1892 | 93 | 3 | 49 | 12 | 15 | 1 | 57 |
| 1893 | 60 | 2 | 34 | 4 | 8 | 2 | 42 |
| 1894 | 75 | 1 | 37 | 12 | 5 | 1 | 61 |
| 1895 | 68 | 0 | 34 | 13 | 7 | 0 | 57 |
| 1896 | 39 | 6 | 35 | 6 | 6 | 0 | 31 |
| 1897 | 67 | 2 | 26 | 9 | 14 | 2 | 38 |
| 1898 | 68 | 7 | 15 | 6 | 8 | 2 | 14 |
| 1899 | 43 | 2 | 17 | 9 | 7 | 1 | 27 |
| 1900 | 43 | 5 | 21 | 16 | 7 | 1 | 22 |
| 1901 | 51 | 7 | 17 | 8 | 10 | 0 | 37 |
| 1902 | 37 | 6 | 18 | 12 | 2 | 0 | 17 |
| 1903 | 50 | 7 | 15 | 8 | 0 | 1 | 18 |
| 1904 | 37 | 1 | 15 | 7 | 0 | 2 | 21 |
| 1905 | 32 | 3 | 11 | 7 | 2 | 0 | 7 |
| 1906 | 25 | 7 | 16 | 10 | 2 | 1 | 4 |
| 1907 | 16 | 7 | 12 | 12 | 14 | 1 | 8 |
| 1908 | 35 | 8 | 15 | 14 | 3 | 1 | 21 |
| 1909 | 46 | 5 | 14 | 5 | 3 | 4 | 5 |
| 1910 | 41 | 3 | 18 | 5 | 4 | 2 | 3 |
| 1911 | 36 | 3 | 6 | 7 | 3 | 4 | 8 |
| 1912 | 34 | 2 | 11 | 3 | 4 | 3 | 6 |
| 1913 | 25 | 4 | 7 | 3 | 1 | 1 | 11 |
| 1914 | 31 | 9 | 6 | 1 | 2 | 1 | 5 |
| 1915 | 27 | 9 | 11 | 6 | 9 | 3 | 4 |
| 1916 | 21 | 7 | 3 | 9 | 8 | 2 | 4 |
| 1917 | 7 | 3 | 7 | 6 | 1 | 6 | 8 |
| 1918 | 27 | 3 | 10 | 6 | 5 | 2 | 11 |
| 1919 | 29 | 8 | 9 | 10 | 1 | 7 | 19 |
| 1920 | 23 | 9 | 15 | 3 | 0 | 3 | 8 |
| 1921 | 19 | 8 | 16 | 3 | 0 | 3 | 15 |
| 1922 | 15 | 5 | 14 | 5 | 4 | 2 | 12 |
| 1923 | 5 | 5 | 6 | 1 | 1 | 2 | 13 |
| 1924 | 4 | 2 | 5 | 2 | 0 | 3 | 0 |
| 1925 | 8 | 1 | 4 | 2 | 0 | 1 | 1 |
| 1926 | 13 | 3 | 2 | 3 | 1 | 1 | 7 |
| 1927 | 7 | 2 | 2 | 3 | 0 | 0 | 2 |
| 1928 | 5 | 2 | 3 | 0 | 0 | 0 | 1 |
| 1929 | 1 | 3 | 3 | 0 | 0 | 2 | 1 |
| 1930 | 5 | 0 | 8 | 2 | 3 | 0 | 3 |
| 1931 | 5 | 3 | 0 | 5 | 0 | 0 | 0 |
| 1932 | 1 | 2 | 1 | 1 | 0 | 1 | 2 |
| 1933 | 8 | 4 | 3 | 3 | 1 | 1 | 8 |
| 1934 | 2 | 2 | 2 | 4 | 1 | 3 | 1 |
| 1935 | 8 | 1 | 3 | 3 | 0 | 1 | 4 |

**TABLE 3 (CONT1NUED)**

| Year | Homicides | Felonious Assault | Rape | Attempted Rape | Robbery and Theft | Insult to White Persons | All Other Causes |
|---|---|---|---|---|---|---|---|
| 1936 | 1 | 0 | 3 | 3 | 0 | 1 | 0 |
| 1937 | 4 | 2 | 1 | 0 | 1 | 0 | 0 |
| 1938 | 3 | 0 | 1 | 0 | 0 | 1 | 1 |
| 1939 | 2 | 0 | 0 | 0 | 0 | 0 | 1 |
| 1940 | 0 | 0 | 0 | 1 | 0 | 1 | 3 |
| 1941 | 0 | 0 | 0 | 1 | 1 | 0 | 2 |
| 1942 | 1 | 1 | 0 | 3 | 0 | 0 | 1 |
| 1943 | 1 | 0 | 0 | 0 | 0 | 1 | 1 |
| 1944 | 2 | 0 | 0 | 0 | 0 | 0 | 0 |
| 1945 | 0 | 0 | 0 | 1 | 0 | 0 | 0 |
| 1946 | 0 | 1 | 0 | 0 | 2 | 0 | 3 |
| 1947 | 1 | 0 | 0 | 0 | 0 | 0 | 0 |
| 1948 | 0 | 0 | 0 | 0 | 1 | 0 | 1 |
| 1949 | 0 | 0 | 0 | 0 | 0 | 0 | 3 |
| 1950 | 0 | 0 | 0 | 0 | 0 | 0 | 2 |
| 1951 | 0 | 0 | 0 | 0 | 0 | 0 | 1 |
| 1952 | 0 | 0 | 0 | 0 | 0 | 0 | 0 |
| 1953 | 0 | 0 | 0 | 0 | 0 | 0 | 0 |
| 1954 | 0 | 0 | 0 | 0 | 0 | 0 | 0 |
| 1955 | 0 | 0 | 0 | 0 | 0 | 1 | 2 |
| 1956 | 0 | 0 | 0 | 0 | 0 | 0 | 0 |
| 1957 | 0 | 1 | 0 | 0 | 0 | 0 | 0 |
| 1958 | 0 | 0 | 0 | 0 | 0 | 0 | 0 |
| 1959 | 0 | 0 | 1 | 0 | 0 | 0 | 0 |
| 1960 | 0 | 0 | 0 | 0 | 0 | 0 | 0 |
| 1961 | 0 | 0 | 0 | 0 | 0 | 0 | 1 |
| 1962 | 0 | 0 | 0 | 0 | 0 | 0 | 0 |
| Total | 1,937 | 205 | 911 | 288 | 232 | 85 | 1,078 |

Compiled by the Department of Records and Research, Tuskegee Institute, Alabama.

*Lynch mobs killed more than 3,300 people between 1882 and 1903, and lynching of blacks continued to be savagely common as late as 1935. Even between 1935 and 1962, 60 blacks were lynched, but no more of these atrocities have been recorded since then.*

## TABLE 4: LYNCHINGS BY RACE AND YEAR: 1882-1962

| Year | Whites | Blacks | Total | Year | Whites | Blacks | Total |
|---|---|---|---|---|---|---|---|
| 1882 | 64 | 49 | 113 | 1923 | 4 | 29 | 33 |
| 1883 | 77 | 53 | 130 | 1924 | 0 | 16 | 16 |
| 1884 | 160 | 51 | 211 | 1925 | 0 | 17 | 17 |
| 1885 | 110 | 74 | 184 | 1926 | 7 | 23 | 30 |
| 1886 | 64 | 74 | 138 | 1927 | 0 | 16 | 16 |
| 1887 | 50 | 70 | 120 | 1928 | 1 | 10 | 11 |
| 1888 | 68 | 69 | 137 | 1929 | 3 | 7 | 10 |
| 1889 | 76 | 94 | 170 | 1930 | 1 | 20 | 21 |
| 1890 | 11 | 85 | 96 | 1931 | 1 | 12 | 13 |
| 1891 | 71 | 113 | 184 | 1932 | 2 | 6 | 8 |
| 1892 | 69 | 161 | 230 | 1933 | 4 | 24 | 28 |
| 1893 | 34 | 118 | 152 | 1934 | 0 | 15 | 15 |
| 1894 | 58 | 134 | 192 | 1935 | 2 | 18 | 20 |
| 1895 | 66 | 113 | 179 | 1936 | 0 | 8 | 8 |
| 1896 | 45 | 78 | 123 | 1937 | 0 | 8 | 8 |
| 1897 | 35 | 123 | 158 | 1938 | 0 | 6 | 6 |
| 1898 | 19 | 101 | 120 | 1939 | 1 | 2 | 3 |
| 1899 | 21 | 85 | 106 | 1940 | 1 | 4 | 5 |
| 1900 | 9 | 106 | 115 | 1941 | 0 | 4 | 4 |
| 1901 | 25 | 105 | 130 | 1942 | 0 | 6 | 6 |
| 1902 | 7 | 85 | 92 | 1943 | 0 | 3 | 3 |
| 1903 | 15 | 84 | 99 | 1944 | 0 | 2 | 2 |
| 1904 | 7 | 76 | 83 | 1945 | 0 | 1 | 1 |
| 1905 | 5 | 57 | 62 | 1946 | 0 | 6 | 6 |
| 1906 | 3 | 62 | 65 | 1947 | 0 | 1 | 1 |
| 1907 | 2 | 58 | 60 | 1948 | 1 | 1 | 2 |
| 1908 | 8 | 89 | 97 | 1949 | 0 | 3 | 3 |
| 1909 | 13 | 69 | 82 | 1950 | 1 | 1 | 2 |
| 1910 | 9 | 67 | 76 | 1951 | 0 | 1 | 1 |
| 1911 | 7 | 60 | 67 | 1952 | 0 | 0 | 0 |
| 1912 | 2 | 61 | 63 | 1953 | 0 | 0 | 0 |
| 1913 | 1 | 51 | 52 | 1954 | 0 | 0 | 0 |
| 1914 | 4 | 51 | SS | 1955 | 0 | 3 | 3 |
| 1915 | 13 | 56 | 69 | 1956 | 0 | 0 | 0 |
| 1916 | 4 | 50 | 54 | 1957 | 1 | 0 | 1 |
| 1917 | 2 | 36 | 38 | 1958 | 0 | 0 | 0 |
| 1918 | 4 | 60 | 64 | 1959 | 0 | 1 | 1 |
| 1919 | 7 | 76 | 83 | 1960 | 0 | 0 | 0 |
| 1920 | 8 | 53 | 61 | 1961 | 0 | 1 | 1 |
| 1921 | 5 | 59 | 64 | 1962 | 0 | 0 | 0 |
| 1922 | 6 | 51 | 57 | Total | 1,294 | 3,442 | 4,736 |

# THE BLACK VOTER AND ELECTED OFFICEHOLDER

**The Current Picture ■ Evolution of the Black Vote ■ Coverage of the Voting Rights Act ■ The Black Lobby ■ The Joint Center for Political Studies ■ The Voter Education Project ■ The Congressional Black Caucus ■ Biographies of Current Black Congressmen ■ Black Congressmen of the Past ■ Black Elected Officeholders at the State Level ■ Biographies of Elected State Executives ■ List of State Legislators ■ Black Mayors ■ Biographies ■ Past and Present Appointed Officials and Diplomats ■ Other Prominent Political Personages**

The decade of the 1980s has been one of major gains by blacks in virtually every aspect of political participation—in level of participation, the elective offices they hold, and in overall influence in the political system. Some obstacles to full participation by blacks remain, but the steady progress augers well for the future of the struggle for political equality.

Jesse Jackson's bold bid for the Democratic party's nomination for president in 1988 underscores the gains blacks have experienced as well as the remaining obstacles they face. The candidacy demonstrated the determination of African-Americans to participate on every level of political life; their capacity to mobilize their own considerable political power nationally; and the substantive depth and tactical brilliance in the political arena of which they are capable. At the same time it painfully demonstrated some of the barriers that blacks continue to face in the political arena because of their race.

Several blacks had been candidates for the presidential nomination of one of the two major political parties before, including Jackson in 1984. However, his 1988 race for the Democratic party's nomination was the first to move clearly beyond a symbolic gesture to become a genuinely serious bid for the Presidency. When the polls closed in California on June 23, ending the long battle for the Democratic party's nomination, Jackson had finished a strong second in a starting field of seven candidates. He had won 1,123 of the 3300 delegates (27 percent of the total), 6.7 million (29 percent) of the votes cast in party primaries, and a plurality in seven states and the District of Columbia. The accomplishment surprised even the most astute political observers, and may have permanently transformed national politics by making a black presidential candidate and a black president no longer inconceivable notions.

The Jackson presidential bid raised with new urgency the

*Michael Dukakis, the winner, and Jesse Jackson, runner-up, get together on the campaign trail.*

question of whether white Americans are willing to elect a candidate for president or vice president regardless of race. Since 1958 the Gallup Organization has asked the public each year in its opinion surveys whether they would vote for a qualified black as president, and has reported steadily increasing positive answers, from 35 percent in 1958 to 81 percent in 1983. In 1988, the public, for the first time, was faced with the question in concrete, not hypothetical terms. Their real responses are somewhat unclear, due to the complicating factors of partisanship, ideology, and Jackson's background as a minister and civil rights activist. However, the electorate as well as the news media displayed considerable hesitancy in accepting a black person as a viable presidential candidate.

In the primaries, Jackson made very strong showings in some states with relatively few black voters and even won Rhode Island. Yet, altogether, he received less than 15 percent of the white votes cast, even though he spent most of the campaign seeking the support of white voters. Throughout the campaign, virtually all commentators applauded Jackson's consistently brilliant performance as candidate and readily conceded that in most respects he towered over his opponents in the primary contests; yet they consistently questioned his real objectives, having dismissed the possibility of his election as president or vice president. In the face of success after success, journalists and political analysts kept asking "what does Jesse really want." Indeed, although race was only infrequently mentioned throughout the presidential campaign, many analysts saw race as the great unmentioned issue in the campaign. It influenced not only Jackson's presidential fortunes, but the campaign strategies of the two principal candidates as well. Thus, alongside the soaring political aspirations of blacks and their widening participation remains the reality that their race is an obstacle to achievement of the nation's highest political prize.

## Evolution of Black Suffrage

The evolution of black American suffrage has had a long and varied history—not only at the national level, but within the individual states as well. These problems have not been confined to the South but have been an issue in every corner of the country.

At the close of the Revolutionary War, more than 1 million of the 3,250,000 people (excluding Indians) living in the United States were not yet free. These included 600,000 black slaves; 300,000 indentured servants; and 50,000 convicts. Of the more than 2 million free Americans, only 120,000 could meet the voting requirements established by individual states at that time. Generally, these requirements took into consideration the following factors: sex, age, residence, morality (character), property, religion, status of freedom, and race.

In the two decades following the end of the Revolutionary War, various criteria were established for voting participation and many previously franchised individuals lost their privilege. Among those denied the vote were non-U.S. citizens, members of the military, paupers, and the mentally impaired, as well as blacks.

The wave of disenfranchisements stemmed in large measure from the failure of the Founding Fathers to agree as to who would be allowed to take part in the critical function of self-government.

The prevailing opinions generally fell into two categories: one embracing those who were in favor of the creation of a strong central government by individual citizens entitled from the very outset to take part through the responsible exercise of the franchise; the other advocating the maintenance of a stable government brought to power by a select group of men whose rank and education made them suitable arbiters of the new nation's initial political course. The latter group feared "mob rule," and sought to make the extension of the franchise subject to a program of massive popular education. This outlook tended to prevail, and it was decided to extend to the states themselves the right to choose their own electorate.

By 1800, eight states had revised their constitutions and three new states had been admitted to the Union. New constitutions had been put into effect in Georgia and New Hampshire, both of which abandoned their property qualifications in favor of tax paying requirements and also inserted specific provisions limiting the franchise to white males.

As appreciable numbers of blacks gained their freedom the situation deteriorated. Between 1792 and 1838, no less than nine states (generally those confined to the South and border areas) altered their constitutions to exclude blacks. Moreover, blacks were denied the ballot in every new state (except Maine) entering the Union between 1800 and 1861.

At the beginning of the Civil War, free black men were

"THE FIRST VOTE."—DRAWN BY A. R. WAUD.—[SEE NEXT PAGE.] (Harper's Weekly)

*Following the Civil War, blacks voted in large numbers in the South.*

permitted to vote on a par with their white counterparts in only five states: Maine, Massachusetts, New Hampshire, Rhode Island, and Vermont.

The Civil War shattered the pattern of disenfranchising blacks. Some 4 million slaves were suddenly transformed into citizens possessing the right to vote. The radical wing of the Republican party, led by Senator Charles Sumner of Massachusetts and Representative Thaddeus Stevens of Georgia, was committed to Negro enfranchisement, and to a strict and punitive program for the South as well.

The Reconstruction Act, which divided the former Confederate states into military districts, also called for new constitutional conventions elected by permanently enfranchised male delegates, regardless of race. Within three years, the right to vote had been legalized by the Fifteenth Amendment to the U.S. Constitution, a measure which had its particular impact on the South but was not without application in the North.

## Reconstruction and Backlash

Following the Civil War, blacks in the South voted in large numbers and elected many blacks to office. The degree of intelligence of black voters and the extent of integrity and competence of blacks elected during Reconstruction has been questioned by many historians in the past. However,

*Electioneering in the South as blacks sought public office.*

present-day reassessments indicate that the performance of Reconstruction blacks has been evaluated with a southern bias. Actually many Reconstruction blacks performed competently and with integrity.

The attempt to discredit black voters and office holders, according to the late Dr. William DuBois, reflected fear among many whites that blacks would earn a reputation for effective leadership. As DuBois once put it, "If there was one thing South Carolina feared more than bad Negro government it was good Negro government."

Such white self-interest and prejudice, plus the excesses of Reconstruction, eventually produced the backlash in the South which succeeded in undermining the Fifteenth Amendment and depriving blacks of the vote.

Perhaps the greatest force motivating the disenfranchisement of blacks was the threat posed to the Southern Democratic party by the possibility of a political alliance between the Populist Party and the Republicans. In such an alliance, it was believed that the black would hold the balance of power—a fact which induced most southern states to close ranks behind the concept of racial exclusion at the polls.

## Rise in Consciousness

Starting about 1940, blacks consistently have supported Democratic candidates for president. Previously, they tended to vote Republican. The Democratic majority support became an overwhelming majority in 1964, when blacks gave President Lyndon Johnson 94 percent of their votes. Since then blacks have cast at least 85 percent of their votes for Democratic candidates for president. While there has been significant change in black voting levels, the distribution of that vote by party has changed very little during the 1980s. This consistently massive support for one party is unique in the electorate and has made blacks a vital, though predictable part of the Democratic party's base of support. It has also placed them on the losing side of five of the six last presidential campaigns.

There was a sharp rise in black political consciousness during the 1960s, due in part to the enthusiasm generated by the Civil Rights Movement in the South and the community organization that was going on in the cities as part of the War on Poverty. The first major victories came in 1967 when Carl Stokes was elected mayor of Cleveland, Ohio, and Richard Hatcher took over City Hall in Gary, Indiana, as the nation's first black elected mayors of major cities. In both instances, it was organized black political strength that made victory possible.

In the early 1970s, black political participation became more sophisticated. The Voter Education Project was formed

*Nineteenth century cartoon: "Of course he wants to vote the Democratic ticket"*

in Atlanta with the express purposes of getting more blacks registered and assisting black candidates elected to political office in the South. The Joint Center for Political Studies in Washington, D.C., sponsored by Howard University and subsidized by the Ford Foundation, provided information of importance to black voters and to office holders and methods of distributing such information. The Lawyers Committee for Civil Rights Under Law, a national organization, offered assistance to lawyers involved in the litigating of matters related to various aspects of the political rights of groups and candidates. The Congressional Black Caucus was formed to lobby the view of blacks elected to the House of Representatives.

Other victories were also achieved, most notably Kenneth Gibson's election as Mayor of Newark in 1970, and Coleman Young and Maynard Jackson's elections as mayors of Detroit and Atlanta, respectively, in 1973.

Blacks climbed aboard the Jimmy Carter bandwagon early in 1976 and their 90% vote for him nailed down the Presidency for the Georgian. Blacks, quite reasonably, expected that their support would earn them some consideration from the Carter Administration, and it did. During his Administration, Carter appointed more black federal judges than all other Presidents combined, placed hundreds of blacks in key positions throughout his Administration, and backed domestic programs of special concern to blacks.

Personally responsive to black interests, Carter was also a pragmatist, and faced with the worsening economic picture, the growth of conservatism in the country, and his own declining popularity among the voters, his positions grew increasingly conservative, thus alienating some of his black support, which became critical of him.

A further sign of the growing black political maturity was evident in February 1980, during an election year, when the Black Leadership Forum took the initiative in calling together in Richmond, a National Conference on a Black Agenda for the Eighties. Other convenors were the National Council of Negro Women, the National Conference of Black Mayors, the National Black Caucus of State Legislators, and the Congressional Black Caucus. More than 1,000 blacks, representing over 300 organizations, gathered to formulate an agenda on domestic and international issues of special concern to blacks. With so many diverse groups taking part, there were fears that it would be impossible to hammer out such an agenda, but the Conference succeeded in achieving an unprecedented consensus on the broad issues with which

*Biased historians created the myth of illiterate blacks' corruption, as shown in this painting titled,* Southern Legislature During Carpetbagger Days.

*President Kennedy greets an NAACP delegation in the White house in 1962. He was the first president to declare that segregation was morally wrong.*

blacks should be concerned in the 1980s.

The agenda went far beyond the traditional civil rights concerns and advocated (1) domestic and foreign economic policies aimed at providing full employment opportunities and opportunities for development of black entrepreneurship; (2) reassessment of federal programs to improve the quality of education available to minorities, and provision of adequate financial assistance and health care for the needy; (3) curtailment of U.S. interaction with South Africa, and extension of a more equitable program of economic assistance to Caribbean countries; (4) steps by the government and political parties to mobilize the electorate and increase opportunities for full minority participation in the political process.

The nominating conventions of the two major parties had not been held yet but the major Democratic and Republican candidates were invited to address the Conference—Ronald Reagan, George Bush, President Carter, and Senator Edward Kennedy. Congressman John Anderson, the independent, was also invited. While each of the candidates sent observers, none attended, presumably because they might have been placed in the position of responding to the Conference agenda, which would not have been a politically feasible thing to do at that point in the campaign.

And even at that early point in the campaign, it was generally agreed that Carter was the front-runner, trailed by Kennedy, who was a popular favorite but lacked organized black support. Carter won 90% of the black vote in the general election that November, but went down to defeat in the Reagan landslide, bringing new problems for black political power. The Reagan Administration virtually ignored blacks. Only a handful of blacks, selected primarily because of their conservative leanings, were appointed to visible positions within the Administration. In addition, the Administration took several actions, including an ill-advised attempt to grant tax-exempt status to schools that discriminate because of race, demonstrating its lack of concern for blacks.

The Administration seemed perfectly willing to write off black political power as a force to be reckoned with until it was jolted by the gubernatorial election in 1981 in Virginia. The governor's office had been controlled by Republicans for nearly two decades, but the Republican candidate made the mistake of not endorsing the Voting Rights Act and of making subtle racial statements that angered the black electorate. As a result, the black electorate turned out in record number to hand the victory to the Democratic candidate, Charles Robb, a son-in-law of the late President Johnson.

This evidence of disenchantment with the Republican Party disturbed Republican leadership on two levels. First, while blacks generally vote Democratic, this is not always the case. Moderate Republicans have in fact done very well with black voters. Governor Dick Thornburg of Pennsylvania and Senators Charles Percy of Illinois, Charles Mathias of Maryland, and Jacob Javits of New York (before he was defeated in a primary election in 1980) have always done very well with black voters. Therefore, it was not that blacks would not vote Republican, it was more a matter of who they were voting for. This was clearly a sign that under the right circumstances, blacks could be attracted to the GOP. It made sense, therefore, for the Republicans to capitalize on this rather than writing off the black vote as a lost cause.

Second, the alienation of blacks from the Republican ranks worried its moderate faction, which did not want the party to become all white or to project a racist image. From a purely pragmatic position, the moderates argued that the party could not afford to write off the black vote, not if it ever intended to establish itself as the predominant party.

This line of thinking led to high-level meetings in the White House early in 1982 for the express purpose of mending fences with the black community. One of the first moves was to make several key black appointments of individuals who would relate to the black community—appointments the Reagan Administration had once vowed it would never make. The few appointments that Reagan made did little to assuage the apprehension that blacks had about the administration's agenda which appeared to be involved in dismantling previous civil rights gains and not enforcing current law. Consequently there was almost continuous acrimonious and adversarial tension between the administration and blacks in general. The appointment of a black, Clarence Pendelton, as commissioner of the U.S. Commission on Civil Rights was regarded by black leaders as a hostile act inasmuch as Pendelton demonstrated antagonism toward the very meaning of the Commission itself and at one point called for its abolition. In May of 1983 a group of prominent black Republicans warned the administration about a "vengeance vote" by blacks because of the social and economic policies that were perceived in the black community as callously indifferent. Despite the plea, the administration consequently reinforced the alienation of the black voter and in the elections of 1983, with the administration having a virtual lock on the election, no overtures whatsoever were extended to black leadership.

In 1983, a group of black political and civil rights leaders began exploring the possibility of a "black coalition for 1984" for the purpose of increasing voter registration and to inject the concerns of minorities into the Democratic campaign without endorsing any political candidate. The Rev. Jesse L. Jackson a participant at the meeting indicated that the groups decision made it likely that a black would enter the race. Mayor Richard Hatcher of Gary, Indiana, chairman of a committee exploring the possibility for a black presidential candidacy encouraged such a move at the annual Push convention in Atlanta which was seen as encouragement for a Jackson candidacy. With the support of a slim majority of the Congressional Black Caucus the candidacy of the Rev. Jackson became assured. While there was a concern that a Jackson candidacy could filter votes from white liberals in the primaries, the goal of garnering enough delegates through a black candidacy to have an impact on the Democratic convention's ultimate nominee and on the agenda of the party itself was accepted as worth the risk and the consequence. For blacks, despite the controversies created in their quest for political clout with the Jackson candidacy of 1984—Jackson never received the total support of black leadership, a number of whom were Mondale supporters—it had become time for greater political assertiveness and participation in the process at every level of government. In

*President Lyndon B. Johnson signs the historic Voting Rights Act of 1965. Third from the left is Senator Edward Brooke, to his right Senator Jacob Javits. To the President's right is Justice Brennan and Senator Walter Mondale.*

*Wendell Gunn, special assistant to President Ronald Reagan. In comparison to Richard Nixon and Jimmy Carter, few blacks received appointments to the Reagan Administration.*

the November election of 1984, blacks gave Walter Mondale, the Democratic Parties nominee against Ronald Reagan, 90% of their vote. Even as Reagan won in a spectacular landslide.

In 1988, blacks again voted overwhelmingly for Democrat, Michael Dukakis, giving him approximately 88 percent of their votes with only 11 percent for George Bush, the Republican winner, and less than 1 percent for black socialist candidate Lenora Fulani. The massive black support for the Democratic ticket held across all regions of the country and all age or socioeconomic segments of the black population. That support came in spite of widespread complaints by blacks that Dukakis had not cultivated ties to the black community, had not campaigned vigorously for black votes, and had bypassed Jesse Jackson in selecting his vice presidential candidate—after a very successful bid for the Democratic candidacy, Jackson came in as a strong second to Dukakis in a hotly contested nomination.

As a result of this lopsided Democratic party vote, newly elected president George Bush assumed the presidency with virtually no political debt to the black community. In the context of American politics this notable lack of support for the winner limits the black community's ability to demand the attention of the new president. Not surprisingly, this situation prompts renewed attention to a long standing dilemma that blacks face: can they be fully effective in national politics while remaining almost completely locked into one party? The dilemma is intensified by the growing concern among some analysts that the Democratic party's chances to win the presidency in the future might be hurt by the concentration of blacks and their growing influence in that party. This latter factor, while downplayed, was believed to be at the root of some of the opposition to the election of Ronald H. Brown, a black, as chairman of the Democratic National Committee in 1989.

In the years immediately ahead, blacks are likely to feel increasingly pressed to address this dilemma. Thus far, they have managed nothing more than mild grumbling about their misfortune for having been locked out of one party (the Republican) and taken for granted by the other (the Democrats). However, what kind of change is feasible and how to achieve it are not entirely clear. Some observers would simply encourage more blacks to vote for Republican candidates, but that might be impractical. Blacks have voted heavily for Democratic candidates because invariably that party and its candidates have been much more responsive to and supportive of issues that blacks regard as vital, than have the Republican party and its candidates. Significant change in the way blacks vote is likely to come about as the two parties begin to converge on the issues that are critical for them.

Such a convergence, and increased black support for the Republican party might be on the horizon for a number of reasons. One is that the country probably has just experienced what might have been the peak of conservative political influence for some time, and with the start of a Bush administration, we might be facing an era of more moderate pragmatic Republicanism, akin to the years of President Richard Nixon and Gerald Ford. In such circumstances, the Republican party could begin a credible outreach to the black voter by supporting policies that have been of particular importance to blacks.

Another reason why more blacks might support the Republican party in the future is the changing agendas of both the nation and the black community. For generations blacks have been preoccupied with the struggle for basic civil rights, and over the past two decades the Democratic party has been a strong ally in that cause. It led the struggles for the major civil rights legislation of the post-war era and advocated relatively aggressive enforcement of these policies. In addition, it initiated most of the major legislation aimed at improving social and economic opportunity and the overall quality of life for blacks. Although issues like civil rights remain vital and must be guarded, they are no longer the subject of intense political struggle. Even among blacks, they have been replaced at the top of the political agenda with issues of national and individual economic well-being in an increasingly competitive, complex global economy. Many of these economic issues are widely shared throughout the electorate and are matters with which the Republican party might be well positioned to deal.

Still another factor likely to facilitate change in black partisanship is the changing characteristics of the black population. As new age cohorts reach voting age and as more blacks reach middle class status, greater flexibility in partisanship appears likely. Three years of surveys of the black population by the Joint Center for Political Studies revealed a somewhat greater inclination among blacks under 30 to identify themselves as Republicans. In that survey, 59 percent of blacks over 50 years old identified themselves as "Strong Democrats" while only 37 percent of those under 30 did so. Moreover, blacks under 30 were more inclined to identify themselves as Republicans than were those over 30. Some analysts attribute this trend to the remoteness of the civil rights struggle. As these segments of the black population increase, and especially as we move away from the tumultuous years of the civil rights struggle, blacks are likely to find it easier to support a progressive Republican party.

President Bush might, therefore, find himself with a unique opportunity to build a bridge between portions of the black electorate and the Republican party. Such an opportunity is of considerable importance for the Republican party if it aspires to be a truly competitive, national party, not only in presidential elections, but in Congress, in the state houses, and city halls as well.

## Black Registration and Turnout

In 1988, the black voting-age population was 20.4 million, or 11.2 percent of the total voting age population. While a potentially powerful force in the electorate, blacks usually had not registered or voted at levels equal to those of whites, in part because many had been deliberately excluded from the electorate for nearly a century. This resulted in a wide participation gap between the races. Furthermore, between 1964 and 1980, overall participation declined by about 10 percentage points while the black-white gap remained largely unchanged. However, the 1980s has seen a significant upturn in participation. Black registration and voting recovered faster than that for whites, so that what was a 9.8 percentage point registration rate gap in 1968 declined to 3.3 percentage points in 1984. By the 1986 Congressional elections, the black-white registration gap had narrowed to just one percentage point. According to the Census Bureau, in the South, blacks were slightly more likely to be registered than whites, a dramatic turn-around in the region where blacks were widely denied the right to register just over two decades earlier. Preliminary data indicate that the registration level declined slightly for both races in 1988, but the gap between them remained largely unchanged. Thus, in 1988 blacks were a larger part of the registered electorate than at any time in the past, in both absolute and relative terms.

The trend in turnout followed the pattern for registration. What was an 11.5 percentage point gap in 1968 declined to only 5.6 percentage points in 1984 when a total of 10.29 million blacks voted. Voting falls off sharply in congressional election years for the entire electorate. However, it is still noteworthy that nationally the gap between black and white turnout was only 4 percentage points in 1986, and in the South that gap was only 1 point. In fact, when one looks at the youngest age cohort in the electorate for congressional elections, the 18 to 24 year-olds, black turnout equalled that for whites in 1982 and was well ahead in 1986.

Voting, like registration, declined in 1988, but the gap between the two groups remained largely unchanged. Analysts have suggested several likely reasons for the relative increase in black registration and turnout over the past 8 years, but three factors appear to have been especially important. One is the rise of conservative influence nationally, against which blacks rallied in the presidential election which even so culminated in the sweeping victory of ultra-conservative Ronald Reagan in 1980 and 1984. Like most other voters, blacks have tended to vote according to issues that insight their fears, and Ronald Reagan and his conservative political agenda evoked considerable fears among blacks, enough to send them to the polls in larger than usual numbers in both those elections.

A second factor involved black candidacies in several highly visible municipal elections. The 1983 Chicago mayoral election in which the late Harold Washington became the first elected black mayor of that city, was one such election, followed by others in Philadelphia and Baltimore, which captured the interest and support of blacks and became focal points for vigorous political mobilization. Finally, the two drama-filled campaigns by Jesse Jackson for the Democratic party's nomination for president appeared to electrify large segments of the black population and brought large numbers of young and previously disenchanted blacks into the electorate.

Registration and turnout apparently fell for blacks as for the rest of the electorate in 1988 in spite of Jackson's campaign. After eight years of President Reagan's conservative leadership and his persistent attacks on vital civil rights and social programs, blacks felt more relief than fear in the candidacy of Vice President George Bush. Moreover, the Democratic candidate, Governor Michael Dukakis, was largely unknown to blacks, made limited and belated efforts to appeal to them, and in the view of some analysts, failed to provide much motivation for blacks to turn out in large numbers. Even with the fall-off in 1988, blacks still approach the end of the decade as a formidable force in the electorate.

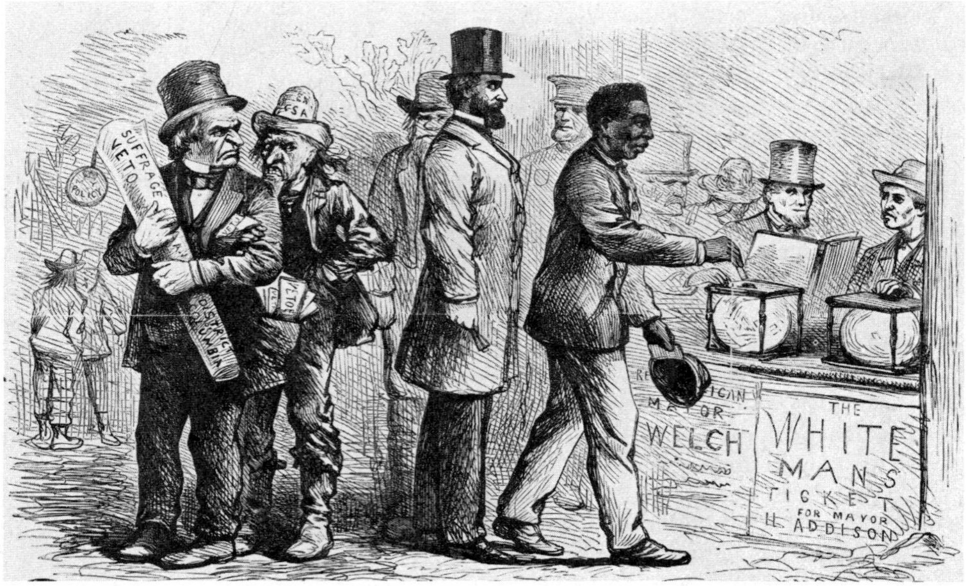


*The first black voters in the District of Columbia, in 1867, had to surmount entrenched white opposition to black suffrage.*

## BLACKS IN ELECTIVE OFFICE

Especially in presidential election years it is tempting to assess black political participation in terms of presidential politics. The critical question around which such assessments revolve is whether and to what extent did blacks influence the outcome of a particular presidential election. Yet, the political arena includes much more than the presidential election and in that larger arena, blacks have continued to do well. Throughout the 1980s the ranks of black elected officials continued a steady, if unspectacular growth. In some instances growth resulted from major new gains in efforts by blacks to eliminate electoral arrangements that diluted black voting power. In others it results from the overall increase in registration and turnout that has occurred over the past eight years. In still other cases gains are the result of progress by blacks in winning support from white voters in substantial numbers.

According to data from the Joint Center for Political Studies, as of January 1988, there were 6,829 black elected officials in the United States (Table 1). This represents a 2.2 percent increase over 1987 and continues an unbroken record of growth each year since 1970. Growth has occurred in every category of elective office, and in every region of the country. Although growth has been constant, the rate of that growth has slowed markedly in recent years, and blacks remain only about 1.5 percent of all elected officials.

### Members of Congress

Over the past five years, the number of blacks in Congress increased from 21 to 24 including Donald Payne, (D-NJ), who was elected in November 1988 to succeed the distinguished veteran Representative Peter Rodino. Perhaps the most noteworthy addition to the ranks of black members of Congress in recent years was Representative Michael Espy, elected from the 2nd District of Mississippi for the first time in 1986. He is the first black member of Congress from that state in this century. Representative Espy won for the first time in 1986 by a thin margin with only 10 percent of the district's white voters joining blacks in the majority black district to elect him. Two years later, Espy appears to have greatly solidified his position, winning over 60 percent of the votes cast and 40 percent of the white vote.

Representative Espy is one of 15 black members of Congress to be elected from majority-black districts. Two, Representatives Ron Dellums (D-CA) and Allan Wheat (D-KS) represent majority-white districts, while the remaining 8 represent districts in which blacks and Hispanics combine to form a voting majority.

In 1986, Veteran Representative Parren Mitchell of Baltimore retired from the House seat he occupied for 10 years. In the House of Representatives, Mitchell was widely known as a champion of minority business opportunity, and chaired the Sub-committee on Small Business of the House Commerce Committee. He was succeeded by Kweisi Mfume (D-MD).

Just as important as the steadily growing ranks of black members of Congress, is their growing seniority and with it, important leadership roles. There has been very little turnover among black members of Congress, as a result several now serve as chairpersons of major committees or subcommittees. Others are very senior members of key committees. In addition, Representative William Gray (D-PA) served as chairman of the powerful and prestigious Budget Committee between 1984 and 1988. Subsequently he was elected to the position of chairman of the Democratic Policy Committee, the first such leadership role held by a black member.

## State Officials

Blacks continue to make modest progress in winning state offices. Over the past five years the number of blacks holding statewide elective offices or seats in the state legislature grew from 389 to 410. Seven blacks hold statewide elected offices: Francis Borges, state treasurer, Connecticut; Roland Burris, comptroller, Illinois; Richard Austin, secretary of state, Michigan; L. Douglas Wilder, Lieutenant Governor, Virginia; d and Alexander Farrelly and Derek Hodge, governor and lieutenant governor, respectively, of the Virgin Islands.

Two blacks lost bids for governor: Democratic Los Angeles Mayor Tom Bradley lost for a second time in his bid to become governor of California, and Republican William Lucas lost his race for governor of Michigan.

Perhaps the most dramatic victory in a statewide race was that of Lieutenant governor A. Douglas Wilder of Virginia, the first such victory for a black person in the South in this century. Wilder is now the leading contender for the Democratic party's nomination for governor in 1989. In spite of achievements like Wilder's, the record for blacks in winning state-wide races remains disappointing. Few blacks have been able to mount major campaigns for state-wide offices, and very few have been successful. None have managed to win the governorship of a state aside from the Virgin Islands.

## Municipal Officials

The largest annual gains in the number of black elected officials have been at the municipal level where almost half (3,341) of all black elected officials serve. Of these, 2,621 serve as members of municipal governing bodies like city councils, 429 are judges of local courts, and 301 are mayors.

At the municipal level, mayors have been the most visible black political figures. Just over two decades ago, in 1986, Richard Hatcher of Gary, Indiana and Carl Stokes of Cleveland, Ohio, became the first elected black mayors of major cities. Other cities soon followed—Newark, New Jersey; Detroit, Michigan: Los Angeles, California; Atlanta, Georgia; and New Orleans, Louisiana all elected black mayors. In the 1980s, Chicago, Philadelphia, and Baltimore joined the ranks of cities with elected black mayors. This development more than any other underscores the growing political power of blacks.

To a great extent the growth in the number of black mayors in recent years reflects the increased concentration of blacks in central cities and their increased political participation. The high visibility of big city black mayors tends to overshadow the fact that the overwhelming majority of black mayors serve in very small municipalities. In fact only 28 are mayors of cities with populations over 50,000. The overwhelming majority of black mayors serve in jurisdictions with populations of 5,000 or less.

An interesting recent development has been a transition of power in several big cities from one black mayor to another. In New Orleans, Mayor Sidney Barthelemy succeeded two-term mayor Dutch Morial who was prohibited by law from seeking a third consecutive term. However, in Gary, Indiana and Newark, New Jersey, long-time incumbents were defeated by black challengers, while in Charlotte, North Carolina, incumbent mayor Harvey Gannt lost a close race to a white challenger. The big city black mayors with longest tenure in 1988 are Tom Bradley of Los Angeles and Coleman Young of Detroit, both of whom are expected to run successfully for reelection.

## Change and Challenges

Blacks clearly have not achieved full equality in the political arena. One indication of this is that blacks hold only 1.5 percent of all elective offices, and in no state does their representation in the legislature approach their proportion of the population. Yet, blacks continue in their steady march toward full and equal participation in politics, with substantial progress in virtually every area.

The level and character of black political participation must be viewed against the unique experience of the group. Most of the black population, concentrated in the South, were long deprived of the right to vote. Disenfranchised as slaves, and enfranchised briefly during the reconstruction period, states and localities throughout the South worked assiduously to deny to blacks the opportunity to vote, even though the 14th and 15th amendments to the constitution sought to provide that right. Official barriers like literacy tests imposed by state laws were augmented by party procedures like the white primary, and by terror inflicted by the white public to prevent blacks from voting. The Federal Courts invalidated the most flagrant of the barriers, but new ones quickly replaced them.

The Civil Rights Act of 1964, the Voting Rights Act of 1865, and subsequent amendments to these laws provided the bases for more than two decades of struggle for the right to vote and to hold elective office. That struggle has been painful and often frustrating, but gradually the barriers to participation have been eliminated. Few direct obstacles to political participation by blacks remain, witness to the steadily closing gap between black and white populations in levels of participation.

What remains are, first, subtle barriers to participation. Some are not directly related to race, but disproportionately affect blacks because of their socioeconomic circumstances. One of the most noteworthy such barriers is the currently tedious registration procedure. In spite of years of effort to simplify the process and eliminate the most burdensome features, registration remains more difficult and demanding on the individual than in almost any other democratic country in the world. Most researchers on the subject agree that individuals in the lower socioeconomic groups are the ones most severely hurt by demanding registration procedures.

A second kind of barrier involves racially discriminatory

districting arrangements that reduce the likelihood that black voters will elect candidates of their race to office. This has been accomplished with the racial gerrymander, in which black voters are either spread out over several districts, becoming a small minority in each or compacted into one or very few districts to confine their influence. As early as 1876, Mississippi created what was known as the "shoestring" congressional district that was 500 miles long and 40 miles wide to prevent the re-election of black congressman John R. Lynch. Several states soon adopted the strategy toward similar ends. In 1960, the courts invalidated the racial gerrymander in *Gomillion* v. *Lightfoot* [354 U.S. (1960)], but the practice persists. At-large or multi-member election arrangements also have been widely used to dilute black voting strength and reduce the number of blacks elected to public office.

In *White* v. *Regester* the courts ruled at-large elections unconstitutional on the ground that it dilutes the votes of blacks and Hispanics. However, the basis of evidence for a finding of unconstitutional vote dilution remained in dispute. In *Mobile* v. *Bolden* [446 U.S. (1980)] the Supreme Court addressed the issue by overturning a lower court decision on the ground that a plaintiff must show the intention of government to discriminate, not merely that the effect of its decision is discriminatory. Congress changed this "intent" standard by amending Section 2 of the Voting Rights Act in 1982. Four years later, the court revisited the issue in *Thornburgh* v. *Gingles* and then outlawed a system of multi-member districts on the ground that it unconstitutionally discriminated against blacks.

The third, and perhaps most formidable of the remaining obstacles are the attitudes of white Americans toward blacks as participants and especially as office holders. With rare exceptions the white electorate remains reluctant to vote for black candidates for public office. The overwhelming majority of blacks elected to public office rely on black voting majorities. This has been true in the large cities with black mayors; in many other municipal and state legislative races; in congressional races; and the Jackson candidacy further underscored the pattern.

There are indications of modest progress by blacks in winning the support of white voters. The victory of Lt. Governor Douglas Wilder in Virginia in 1985, and his almost certain selection by his party as its candidate for governor in 1989 is one example of such success. The sharp increase in white support for Representative Mike Espy received in his reelection bid—from 15 percent in 1986 to 40 percent in 1988—is another. The Wilder race and several similar races in recent years strongly suggest that blacks might make significant progress in winning white support with studied modification in traditional political styles, issue mix, and campaign strategies.

Most efforts by civil rights groups to expand voting rights in recent years have centered on eliminating at-large elections which, when combined with racial block voting, have been shown to deprive blacks of a fully effective ballot. Until recently, virtually all the court decisions, invalidating such at-large elections involved the South. Two recent developments have brought that campaign successfully into new areas. One is a Federal District Court decision in *McNeil* v. *City of Springfield* outlawing the at-large election system in Springfield, Illinois as discriminatory toward blacks, the first such decision outside the South. More recently the courts have made the same ruling in the election of judges to state courts. These decisions are sure to increase opportunities for the election of other blacks to public office.

A central concern for blacks is whether the recent developments in black politics mean increased influence in politics. While analysts may well disagree on this question, there is strong evidence of growing black influence in the political arena. That influence was perhaps most dramatically illustrated in the 1986 Congressional elections when they played a critical role in returning the Senate to Democratic control. It was this democratic majority, supported by blacks, which led to the defeat of President Reagan's nominee, Bork, to the Supreme Court. Several crucial votes in that confirmation decision were cast by Southern Senators who were direct beneficiaries of growing black voting power.

The growing influence is also evident in the national Democratic convention, in which blacks were a prominent and influential part of the leadership. Although Jackson failed to win the nomination, media attention focused upon his platform's agenda. To a much greater extent than at any other time in the past, blacks indeed helped to shape the national agenda.

Finally, while we usually look to the electoral arena in considering black political influence, appointive offices are also sources of considerable influence. It should be not be overlooked that in the closing years of the Reagan administration when dramatic changes were occurring in U.S.-Soviet relations and indeed across the entire international scene, a black man, General Colin Powell as the president's National Security Adviser was a key actor.

## THE BLACK LOBBY

Since the strengthening of black voting rights in the 1960s, a number of organizations have sought to aid and unite black voters, candidates, and officeholders.

Following are brief descriptions of some groups that have contributed significantly to the growing power of blacks in the American political process.

### The Congressional Black Caucus

Officially organized in 1971 when there were 12 black members of the House of Representatives, the Congressional Black Caucus is recognized as the single most important politically oriented black group operating at the national level. Its membership embraces all 24 black members of

Congress, when it speaks its voice is listened to, and it has earned high marks both for its commitment to black people and its progressive views.

Blacks have served in Congress since 1870, but it was not until 1969, when Congressman Charles Diggs (D. Mich.) called a meeting of the nine black members then serving in the House and proposed that they join together in a group, that there was an effort to establish a unified black presence on the Hill.

Out of this came the Democratic Select Committee, which sought to improve communication among black House members and between those members and the leadership of the House.

The structure was kept very informal, which limited its effectiveness. In 1970, Representative William Clay (D. Mo.) suggested that a different type of structure be created, and the idea fell on fertile soil. After some discussion on format and whether the continuing use of "Democratic" in the name might limit membership, the Congressional Black Caucus was created in 1971.

One of its first actions was to appoint a paid staff, something the Democratic Select Committee never had. A method of financing the CBC through an annual dinner was established, and an internal structure was set up consisting of a chairman, executive committee, and policy-oriented subcommittees.

Much of the visibility of the Caucus during the first year came from a series of hearings held around the country on health, education, black enterprise, the mass media, Africa, and racism. Searching for its proper role, the Caucus found itself involved in a number of activities including provision of casework services, gathering and dissemination of information, administrative oversight, articulation of the interests of specialized groups within the black community, and development of legislative proposals. Perhaps it was too broad an agenda for such a young group, for it could not devote enough attention to all these activities.

What also became evident was that while the members of the Caucus were tied together by mutual interests, each of its members was a personality within his or her own right, and as such, individual differences were bound to emerge. This was made evident when Caucus member Shirley Chisholm (D. N.Y.) sought the 1972 Democratic Presidential nomination and discovered that the Caucus was not totally in her corner. This destroyed the myth that the Caucus would always act as one, but at the same time it demonstrated that the Caucus was strong enough to withstand individual differences.

During the Nixon years, the Caucus spent much of its energies in attempting to preserve what remained of the War on Poverty programs and in fighting against the efforts of the President to impound funds for domestic programs. With such a limited agenda, questions were raised whether an elaborate mechanism like the Caucus was needed, and whether the activities in which it was involved might not be handled better by the individual members of Congress.

Through a series of retreats and evaluations, the Caucus stepped back and took a look at itself. This enabled it to focus on three strategies. The first involved strengthening efforts to get more favorable committee assignments for Caucus members. Such assignments are key elements in determining how influential a Representative can be, and the Caucus was successful in placing its members on all 22 of the standing committees in the House and on the three major ones, Rules, Ways and Means, and Appropriations in the 94th Congress. The second strategy involved targeting of Representatives from constituencies with high black representation for special lobbying efforts within Congress on such issues as the Home Rule Bill for the District of Columbia. This strategy met with mixed results because of the reluctance of some Caucus members and their staffs to violate existing Congressional mores, which frown on such a strategy. The third strategy was an expansion of the network of professional and academic advisors outside of Congress. These advisors are divided into groups, according to interests, and meet regularly with a Caucus member to discuss public policy issues and Congressional legislation. This has become an important CBC technique for gaining support and assistance for selected legislative priorities.

Over the years, the CBC has not hesitated to speak out on a variety of issues, regardless of which political party was in office. The present membership of the Caucus is all Democratic, but during his one term (1978-1980) Representative Melvin Evans, the nonvoting Republican delegate from the Virgin Islands, was a member. Former Republican Senator Edward Brooke, the lone black in the Senate during much of the Caucus' history, never chose to join.

When the Reagan Administration took office in 1981, the Caucus, like other black groups, found that its access to the White House was limited and its influence virtually nil. Nevertheless, the Caucus was one of the few organized voices raised in Congress against the sharp cutbacks in social service programs. The Caucus went even further and developed an alternative budget that earned from the Democratic Study Group the accolade of taking "the boldest step of any proposal being offered to the House to deal with the federal deficit and [offering] the largest and fairest tax cut of any of the proposals before the House."

While the Caucus has continued to enhance its role as an effective legislative mechanism, it has faced problems with funding since actions taken by the House in 1981 which imposed severe restrictions on Congressional caucuses receiving support and funding from non-Congressional sources. In essence, the restrictions said that if a Congressional caucus received any support from the House in the form of office space, furniture, telephone services, and the like, it could not receive outside funds. This remains crucial to the Caucus since, as an example, in 1980 it received $29,000 in donated Congressional services. In the same year, it raised 95% of its budget, or $550,000, from non-Congressional sources. While it is important that the Caucus keep its offices on Capitol Hill, it obviously cannot operate in the manner that it has without outside funding.

The Caucus maintains a 501(c) tax-exempt organization called the Congressional Black Caucus Foundation, which conducts legislative research and public policy analysis. Money can be raised through this entity but because of its tax-exempt status it cannot be involved in advocacy or lobbying, creating a problem for the Caucus, which still has to find an acceptable alternative.

The major fund-raising activity of the Caucus, its annual dinner, has become the single most important annual black political gathering. It has been enlarged so that it encompasses an entire weekend filled with workshops, brainstorming sessions, and speeches.

In assessing the accomplishments of the Caucus, Dr. Marguerite Ross Barnett, a political scientist at Columbia University, said:

*Ten years of CBC activity has produced an institutionalized organization with a number of experienced, senior legislators with good committee assignments and knowledge of the House and its membership. Translation of CBC potential into positive political realities will depend on a variety of factors, only some of which are in the direct control of the black members of Congress.*

The present chairman of the Caucus is Rep. Walter E. Fauntroy (nonvoting delegate, D.C.).

Address:
H2-344
House of Representatives Annex
Washington, D.C. 20515
Phone: (202) 255-1691

## The Joint Center for Political Studies

The Joint Center for Political Studies is the most important and authoritative source of information on black political participation in the country. It has been invaluable in enhancing the involvement of blacks in the political process by securing and analyzing data on blacks in the political arena.

The Center was established in 1970 with initial funding from the Ford Foundation. It was originally sponsored by Howard University and the Metropolitan Applied Research Center in New York City. The Center is now independent and is governed by a 10-member board headed by Wendell Freeland, an attorney from Pittsburgh.

The Center describes itself as a national nonprofit institution that conducts research on public policy issues of special concern to black Americans and promotes informed and effective involvement of blacks in the governmental process. The Center provides independent and nonpartisan analysis, publications, and outreach programs. One of its most valuable publications is its annual roster of elected black officials.

Though its basic emphasis remains on the political process, the Center has expanded its interests to include such areas as energy, community development, revenue sharing, crime, and regionalism, and has issued a number of valuable reports.

The Center has been headed since 1972 by Eddie N. Williams, President. Prior to joining the Center he served as the vice president for public affairs at the University of Chicago and director of the Center for Policy Study.

Funding for the Center is obtained through the Ford Foundation as well as other foundations and sources.

Address:
Suite 400
1301 Pennsylvania Ave., NW
Washington, D.C. 20004
Phone: (202) 626-3500

## Voter Education Project

The Voter Education Project came along at a time when there were the first faint glimmerings of hope that black political strength, which had been penned up so long in the South, might be unshackled. The Civil Rights Movement was on the march and one of its primary goals was to make it possible for black people to vote freely in the South. Already existing was the Southern Regional Conference, a biracial organization based in Atlanta that for many years had been involved in race relations.

The Council was the logical umbrella under which to place a concerted voter registration drive, and in 1961 the Council established the Voter Education Project, which was supported by all the major civil rights groups and endorsed by both the Republican and Democratic National Committees.

VEP's first director was Wiley A. Branton, who was later to become dean of the Howard University Law School. Its activities were limited to the 11 southern states. The programs conducted by the participating national and local agencies were designed to secure voter registration primarily, but in such a way as to gather reports which were submitted to VEP for analysis of methods and techniques used, the problems encountered, solutions developed, and results of the programs.

VEP contributed mightily to the effort which led to the passage of the 1965 Voting Rights Act. Through a combination of supporting locally initiated voter registration efforts and initiating its own voter registration drives, VEP assumed the major responsibility for fulfilling the promise of the 1965 Voting Rights Act. Overall in the South, more than a million black citizens became registered to vote between 1965 and 1969.

As more blacks were elected, VEP started to fulfill the vital function of informing black officeholders on the intricacies of vital issues and on techniques to obtain appropriations important to black voters. A result of this has been more new schools, paved streets, and police protection for many neglected black neighborhoods.

Branton was succeeded in 1965 by Vernon E. Jordan Jr., who left in 1970 to become head of the United Negro College Fund, and was replaced by John Lewis, the former executive director of the Student Non-Violent Coordinating Committee and a hero of the Selma to Montgomery March in 1965. Lewis resigned in 1977 and was succeeded by Vivian Malone Jones.

## THE BLACK CONGRESS

In 1989 there were 24 black members of Congress including a black nonvoting delegate from the District of Columbia serving in the 101st Congress—the largest number of blacks to serve in the House of Representatives at one time since Reconstruction.

Since the last edition of the *Negro Almanac* in 1982 nine new black members were elected; in 1983, Major Owens. (D-N.Y.), Edolphus Towns (D. N.Y.), Alan Wheat Jr.(D-Mo.), and Charles Hayes (D-Ill.); in 1987, Mike Espy (D-Miss.), Floyd Flake (D-N.Y.), John Lewis (D-Ga.), and Kweisi Mfume (D-Md.), and in 1988 Democrat Donald M. Payne became New Jersey's first black congressmen with his election to the congressional seat of the 10th district. Payne succeeded the then retiring Peter Rodino (D-N.J.) who had represented the 10th district since 1948. Mr. Payne had been a City Councilman in Newark.

Black members now constitute 5.5% of the total House membership of 435. They are all Democrats representing urban areas with only three coming from the South, although 53% of the nation's black population resides there. Most of the black members of Congress have been elected from districts with a majority, or nearly a majority of black voters, although Representatives Ronald V. Dellums, Mervyn M. Dymally, both, (D) of California, and Alan Wheat (D) of Missouri are exceptions to the rule with black populations in their districts of 24%, 36% and 20% respectively.

As the result of reapportionment following the 1980 Census—each Congressional district was adjusted so that each House member represents at least 510,000 people—some realignment of district boundaries has taken place. However, because of political considerations plus the desire not to come into conflict with the Voting Rights Act by reducing black congressional representation, it is generally felt that boundaries shifted were shifted in a manner to protect the incumbents.

The area of the greatest possible expansion of House membership for blacks is in the South, but the legislatures in these states have shown a reluctance to create districts in which blacks could win.

### Black Members Of The 101st Congress—1989

| Name | Party & State | District | Year |
|---|---|---|---|
| William L. Clay | (D-MO) | 1 | 1969 |
| Cardiss Collins | (D-IL) | 7 | 1973 |
| John Conyers | (D-MI) | 1 | 1965 |
| George W. Crockett | (D-MI) | 13 | 1980 |
| Ronald V. Dellums | (D-CA) | 8 | 1971 |
| Julian C. Dixon | (D-CA) | 28 | 1979 |
| Mervyn M. Dymally | (D-CA) | 31 | 1981 |
| Mike Espy | (D-MI) | 2 | 1987 |
| Walter B. Fauntroy | (D-DC) | At-Large | 1971 |
| Floyd Flake | (D-NY) | 6 | 1987 |
| Harold E. Ford | (D-TN) | 9 | 1975 |
| William H. Gray | (D-PA) | 2 | 1979 |
| Augustus F. Hawkins | (D-CA) | 29 | 1963 |
| Charles Hayes | (D-IL) | 1 | 1983 |
| Mickey Leland | (D-TX) | 18 | 1979 |
| John Lewis | (D-GA) | 5 | 1987 |
| Kweisi Mfume | (D-MD) | 7 | 1987 |
| Major Owens | (D-NY) | 12 | 1983 |
| Donald M. Payne | (D-NJ) | 10 | 1988 |
| Charles B. Rangel | (D-NY) | 16 | 1971 |
| Gus Savage | (D-IL) | 2 | 1981 |
| Louis Stokes | (D-OH) | 21 | 1969 |
| Edolphus Towns | (D-NY) | 11 | 1983 |
| Alan Wheat | (D-MO) | 5 | 1983 |

## BIOGRAPHIES OF CURRENT BLACK REPRESENTATIVES

### WILLIAM CLAY
### First District Missouri
### Elected 1969

William Clay, the first black man to represent the state of Missouri in the U.S. Congress, was born in 1931 in the lower end of what is now St. Louis' First District. Clay was educated locally and later took a degree in political science at St. Louis University, where he was one of four blacks in a class of 1,100. After serving in the Army until 1955, Clay became active in a host of civil rights organizations, including the NAACP Youth Council and CORE. During this time he worked as a cardiographic aide, bus driver, and insurance agent, but his heart had already surrendered to politics, at least judging from the number of demonstrations and picket lines he had joined.

In 1959, and again in 1963, Clay was elected alderman of the predominantly black 26th Ward. During his first term, he served nearly four months of a nine-month jail sentence for demonstrations at a local bank. Meanwhile, on the outside, the number of white-collar jobs held by blacks in St. Louis banks began a steady ascent from a low of 16 to a high of 700. In 1964, Clay stepped down from his alderman's post to run for Ward Committeeman, winning handily and being reelected in 1968.

Clay's election platform in 1969 included a number of progressive, even radical, planks. He advocated that all penal institutions make provisions for the creation of facilities in which married prisoners could set up house with their spouses for the duration of their sentences. He branded most testing procedures and diploma requirements, as well as references to arrest records and periods of unemployment, unnecessary obstacles complicating the path of a prospective employee. In his view, a demonstrated willingness to work and an acceptance of responsibility should be the criteria determining one's selection for a job.

Clay's last job before election to Congress was as race relations coordinator for Steamfitters Union Local 562. Subjected to considerable criticism from other St. Louis blacks who labeled the union racist, Clay pointed out that dramatic changes in the hiring practices of the union since he had joined it in 1966 were responsible for the employment of 30 black steamfitters in St. Louis—30 more than the union had previously put to work. Still, Clay conceded that the high-paying job had led him to reduce his active involvement with the civil rights struggle to some degree.

Clay's secure position in the First District, where blacks comprise 55% of the voters, allows him to express his militancy with little compromise, a factor which may have contributed to the fact that in 1972, he ran about 5% behind Senator McGovern in his district. However, Clay still received 64% of the vote and has obtained a seat on the House Education and Labor Committee, which was once chaired by a man Clay greatly admired, the late Adam Clayton Powell. He is currently chair of the Subcommittee on Labor Management Relations. He is also the ranking member of the Committee of Post Office and Civil Service and serves on the House Administration Committee.

Since 1969, when he was seated, Clay has sponsored more than 592 pieces of legislation including the Hatch Act Reform Bill, the City Earnings Tax bill, and the IRS Reform Bill. He is trustee on the Board of Directors for Tougaloo College, Benedict College and the Congressional Black Caucus Foundation.

He serves as the second ranking member of the Committee of Post Office and Civil Service, where he is Chairman of the Subcommittee on Postal Operations and Civil Service; he is fifth ranking member of the House Education and Labor Committee.

Since 1969, when he was seated, Representative Clay has sponsored 592 pieces of legislation including the Hatch Act Reform Bill, the City Earnings Tax Bill, and the IRS Reform Bill.

*After her husband's tragic death in an accident, Cardiss Colllins won election to succeed him in Congress.*

## CARDISS COLLINS
## Seventh District Illinois
## Elected 1973

Like many wives, Mrs. Cardiss Collins was immensely involved in her late husband's career as a U.S. Congressman. When a tragic accident in December 1972 took his life, she immediately qualified as a viable candidate to succeed him, and in 1973 won a special election to fill the unexpired term of her late husband, George, in the Seventh District in Illinois.

As a committee woman in Chicago's 24th Ward Regular Democratic Organization, Congresswoman Collins was no stranger to politics. She had been involved in the successful campaigns waged by her husband for the positions of committeeman and alderman of the 24th Ward and had worked on his campaigns for Congress, first in the Sixth and then in the Seventh District.

Mrs. Collins' District, located on the West Side of Chicago, remains largely loyal to the Democratic machine of Mayor Richard Daley, and still, in some areas, elects white aldermen who are supported by City Hall. In this sense, the District is unlike the South Side, which in 1973 supported Senator Charles Percy over the Democratic candidate.

With Daley's support behind her, Mrs. Collins received over 90% of the vote in the special election of 1973, in which she was chosen to fill her late husband's seat.

Some 55% of Congresswoman Collins' District is black, 22% is foreign born, and 17% Hispanic. She was unopposed in the 1988 elections.

Representative Collins is the first woman and the first black to chair the House Government Operations Subcommittee on Manpower and Housing, which has major oversight responsibility for the Department of Labor, the Department of Housing and Urban Development, ACTION, and the Community Services Administration. She later became chair of Government Operations Subcommittee on Government Activities and Transportation.

Recognizing her dedication and excellence, her colleagues in the Congressional Black Caucus elected her Chairwoman from 1978 to 1980. She had previously served the Caucus as Secretary during the 94th Congress and as Treasurer during the 95th. She was also the first woman and first black to hold the position of Whip-at-large for the House Democratic leadership.

## JOHN CONYERS JR.
## First District Michigan
## Elected 1965

Congressman John Conyers is a native of Detroit, where he was born on May 16, 1929. He received his B.A. and LL.B. degrees from Wayne State University, and served his political apprenticeship for three years as legislative assistant to Congressman John Dingell.

Before election to Congress, Conyers was a referee for the Michigan Workmen's Compensation Department and senior partner in the firm of Conyers, Bell and Townsend. He was general counsel for the Trade Union Leadership Council; a member of Local 900 of the United Auto Workers (UAW) and of Local 42 of the AFL-CIO. He also belonged to the Committee on Political Education in Michigan's 15th Congressional District.

In 1963, President Kennedy appointed Conyers to the National Lawyers Committee for Civil Rights Under Law, an organization designed to foster greater racial tolerance in the legal field. Conyers later served as a member of the Committee to Assist Southern Lawyers (CASL), and represented a number of clients who had been arrested in connection with alleged voter-registration irregularities throughout the South.

Conyers encountered far greater difficulty in gaining the Democratic nomination in Michigan's First Congressional District than in defeating his eventual Republican opponent, Robert Blackwell. Conyers won the primary election by a mere 45 votes, but, aided by his father, a trade unionist, and a group of dedicated volunteers, he then proceeded to trounce Blackwell, emerging with 84% of the total votes cast.

Conyers was co-sponsor of the Johnson Administration's Medicare program and a strong supporter of the 1965 Voting Rights Bill.

The Representative's District in Detroit reflects the rapid change that has transpired in so many cities. Between 1950 and 1970 the black population leaped from 5 to 70% of the total. However, the district is more affluent than most black districts in the United States and some observers have forecast that it will take a Republican turn.

However, neither President Nixon nor Conyers' Republican opponents were able to harvest more than 15% of the vote in the 1968, 1970, and 1972 elections and Conyers was so critical of Nixon that he appeared on the White House's "enemies list," which was revealed in 1973.

The first black man to serve on the House Judiciary Committee, Conyers participated in the impeachment hearings in 1974, at times taking the position that Democrats and Republicans alike were too cautious about confronting the White House's refusal to submit subpoena evidence.

*House Judiciary Committee member John Conyers took part in the impeachment inquiry that led to President Nixon's early retirement.*

*Ron Dellums, a member of Congress since 1971. He represents the district where the Black Panther Party originated.*

In 1980, John Conyers was reelected by 95% of the vote to his ninth term in the U.S. House of Representatives. The fifth ranking member of the Judiciary Committee, he chairs the Subcommittee on Criminal Justice and is a member on the Subcommittee on Crime. He also serves on the Subcommittee on Commerce, Consumer and Monetary Affairs, and Manpower and Housing of the Government Operations Committee.

Representative Conyers is a leader in the full employment movement and was a principal architect of the Humphrey-Hawkins Full Employment and Balanced Growth Act, which became law in 1978. He is a leading critic of federal budget priorities, particularly where this concerns the growth of military spending at the expense of domestic human resources programs and the subsidies awarded to business corporations.

In 1988, Conyers was reelected by 91% of the vote to his 19th term in the U.S. House of Representatives. He chairs the Government Operations Committee, and is a senior member of the Judiciary Committee where he sits on the Subcommittee on Civil and Constitutional Rights. He also serves on the House Small Business Committee and Speaker's Task Force on Minority Set-Asides.

## GEORGE W. CROCKETT JR.
## Thirteenth District Michigan
## Elected 1980

George W. Crockett Jr. was elected to Congress in 1980 from the 13th Congressional District of Michigan to fill the vacancy created by the resignation of Charles C. Diggs Jr. He is the ninth ranking member of the Committee on Foreign Affairs where he serves on the Africa and Western Hemisphere subcommittees. He is also on the Crime, Courts, Civil Liberties and the Administration of Justice subcommittees in the Judiciary Committee, and the Retirement Income and Employment subcommittee on the Select Committee on Aging. He is the fourteenth ranking member of the Committee on Foreign Affairs, seventeenth ranking member of the Small Business Committee, and serves on the Subcommittees on General Oversight, Export Opportunities, and Special Problems of Small Business. He is also a member of the Congressional Arts Caucus, the Congressional Auto Caucus, and the Executive Board of the Democratic Group.

After graduating from the University of Michigan Law School in 1934, Crockett began his legal practice in Jacksonville, Florida. He was admitted to the West Virginia Bar in 1935, the U.S. Supreme Court Bar in 1940, and the Michigan Bar in 1944.

In 1939, he was appointed as the first black lawyer with the U.S. Department of Labor and later became the senior attorney on employee lawsuits under the Fair Labor Standards Act. In 1943, President Roosevelt appointed him one of the first Fair Employment Practices Commission Hearing examiners.

George Crockett founded the International United Auto Workers Fair Employment Practices Department in 1944 and served both as its Director and as General Counsel to the UAW until 1946. From 1946 until 1966, Crockett was in private practice as a senior partner in the law firm Goodman, Crockett, Eden, and Robb. Crockett was elected judge of the Recorders Court in Detroit in 1966 and was reelected to a second term in 1972. In 1974, he became presiding judge of that same court. Following his retirement, he served as visiting judge for the Michigan Court of Appeals, and in 1980 he was acting corporation counsel for the city of Detroit.

## RONALD V. DELLUMS
## Eighth District California
## Elected 1971

An avowed "radical," Ronald Dellums represents one of America's more turbulent Congressional districts, one which combines the black population of Oakland's ghetto with the students and upper-income liberals of Berkeley. It was in this district that both the student movement of the 1960s and the Black Panther Party originated.

A product of the West Oakland ghetto and recipient of a master's degree in social work from the University of California at Berkeley, Dellums was employed prior to his election as a senior consultant to Social Dynamics, Inc., a

Berkeley-based enterprise which develops manpower and community organization programs on a national basis.

He was formerly director of an employment program of the San Francisco Economic Opportunity Council, a director at a Bay Area youth center and a community center, lecturer at San Francisco State College and the Graduate School of Social Work at the University of California at Berkeley, and sat on the Berkeley City Council. He served two years in the Marine Corps prior to entering his professional career.

In the Democratic primary of 1970, with only 22% of his district's population black, Dellums challenged the incumbent, Jeffrey Cohelan, a white man who, with strong backing from labor unions, had served 12 consecutive years in Congress. Dellums openly defended some Panther viewpoints and student demonstration tactics, positions that soon attracted considerable conservative opposition and money to defeat him. However, Dellums received 55% of the vote to defeat Cohelan in the primary and 57% in the November contest against the Republican nominee. He was reelected in November 1972, with 56% of the vote, 9% less than the percentage received in his district by Senator McGovern. But in 1974 the coalition which elected Dellums seemed firmly in control of the district.

He is the Chairperson of both the House Committee on the District of Columbia and the D.C. Subcommittee on Fiscal Affairs and Health.

*Julian Dixon has served in Congress since 1978.*

Dellums is also the tenth ranking member of the House Armed Services Committee, where he serves on the Research and Development Subcommittee. He also chairs the Armed Services Committee Panel dealing with problems on the Island of Vieques.

Representative Dellums is a former vice-chair of the Congressional Black Caucus, a member of its Executive Committee, and he now heads the Caucus Task Force on National Security and Foreign Policy issues. A former member of the Democratic National Committee, he is currently a national co-chair of the New Democratic Coalition. As a member of the Armed Services Committee, Dellums has aroused the ire of Republicans and Democrats alike with his charges that the military budget is bloated and that racism remains strong in the armed forces, despite claims by the Department of Defense that it has been eliminated. He has also stood against funding for the MX, Pershing II, Midgetman, B-1 Bomber, SDI (Strategic Defense Initiative), and was an original co-sponsor of the Nuclear Freeze Resolution. Dellums remains very much in the minority on the Committee, but his very presence there represents an important departure for black Congressmen, who formerly gravitated to such friendlier environments as the Education and Labor Committee.

In 1988, he was elected chair of the Congressional Black Caucus. He has also been a House leader in the effort to bring sanctions against South Africa, and was a staunch opponent of aid to the anti-communist rebels (contras) in Nicaragua.

Dellums is a firm believer in the twin concepts of participatory democracy and "Coalition Politics." In his judgment, when people begin to realize how and why they are being victimized and manipulated by those who control the real levers of power in this society, they will then be able to join together to form a new political majority—one which crosses racial, sexual, and economic barriers.

In his view, Congress is an institution that must be made aware of the forces at work for progressive social and economic change. In his efforts to jolt the House out of its institutional indifference to controversial issues, he has been willing to conduct extraofficial hearings to force "official" Washington to recognize the gravity of a particular situation. For example, he conducted personal investigations into U.S. war crimes in Indochina and the impact of Agent Orange and other toxic agents on the men and women who served in the Indochina theater of operations. In conjunction with the Congressional Black Caucus, he has conducted examinations on the extent of racism in the military and on various aspects of governmental lawlessness and bureaucratic indifference.

His major effort recently has been to fight for funding and counseling for AIDS victims and their families, and as chair of the D.C. Committee, for aid for the homeless.

### JULIAN C. DIXON
### Twenty-Eighth District California
### Elected 1978

Elected to the House of Representatives from the 28th Congressional District of California in 1978, Julian C.

Dixon serves on the powerful House Appropriations Committee as the 21st ranking member. In March 1980 he was selected Chairman of the Subcommittee on the District of Columbia, thus becoming the first freshman legislator in the history of Congress to chair a House Appropriations Subcommittee. Dixon also serves on the Appropriations Subcommittee on Foreign Operations and is chairman of House Committee Standards of Official Conduct, also referred to as the Ethics Committee. He is currently president of the Congressional Black Caucus Foundation.

Congressman Dixon's legislative priorities have focused on a wide array of issues ranging from domestic social concerns to African Caribbean affairs. Bills sponsored by Dixon have included the Civil Rights Amendments of 1979, which would prohibit discrimination on the basis of sexual orientation in housing, education, employment, and public accommodations; legislation to establish a Cabinet-level Department of Education; and a bill to provide federal assistance to victims of domestic violence.

Dixon opposed changes to the U.S. Civil Rights Commission during the Reagan years, and authored an amendment to bring the Commission into compliance with its original mandate as an independent fact finding agency. In 1983, he authored the first economic sanction measure against south Africa, which was signed into law during the 98th Congress. His bill required the U.S. to oppose loans by the International Monetary fund to any nation practicing apartheid.

His work on the Foreign Operations Subcommittee has succeeded in strengthening U.S. participation in the Sahel Development Program in West Africa and in the African Development Bank. Congressman Dixon has worked for the advancement of alternative forms of energy such as solar, biomass, and wind energy systems.

Dixon's efforts have also centered on issues affecting his own urban district. He was successful in obtaining a federal study of the Baldwin Hills area of Los Angeles—an area nationally recognized for its disastrous mudslides. As a member of the Congressional Olympic Task Force for the 1984 Olympics in Los Angeles, Representative Dixon has been a leading supporter of federal assistance for the games.

From 1973 until his election to Congress, Dixon represented the 49th Assembly District in the California State Assembly. In 1973, he was chairman of the Assembly Democratic Caucus, the first freshman ever elected to that post. He also chaired the Assembly Public Employees and Retirement Committee and was a member of the Committees on Criminal Justice, Ways and Means, and Education. His special assignments included chairman of the Select Committee on Juvenile Violence. In 1979 he received the "Outstanding Legislative Program" award from the National Council of Juvenile and Family Court Judges.

## MERVYN M. DYMALLY
## Thirty-First District California
## Elected 1980

Mervyn Dymally was elected in 1980 to serve as representative of the 31st Congressional District of California. He is the eleventh ranking member on the Foreign Affairs Committee, where he serves on the Asian and Pacific Affairs and International Operations Subcommittee. He is twelfth ranked on the Post Office and Civil Service committee, where he is chairman of the Census and Population Subcommittee. He chairs the Subcommittee on Judiciary and Education of the District of Columbia Committee. Dymally is also a member of the Democratic Study Group and serves as secretary/treasurer of the California Congressional Democratic Delegation.

Representative Dymally brings many years of experience and a deep concern for a broad range of people-oriented problems to the U.S. Congress. Prior to his election in 1980 he served four years as a California Assemblyman (1962-1966) and was elected to the California State Senate in 1966. During his eight years as State Senator, Dymally served as chair of the Senate Democratic Caucus and the committees on Social Welfare; Military and Veterans Affairs; Elections and Reapportionment; and the Subcommittee on Medical Education and Health Needs. He also headed the Senate Select Committee on Children and Youth; the Joint Committees on Legal Equality, and the Revision of the Election Code.

Dymally served as Lieutenant Governor of California from 1975 to 1979. In this capacity he headed the State Commission for Economic Development and the Commission of the Californias. He was a member of the Board of Regents of the University of California and the Board of Trustees of the State College and University system. Lieutenant Governor Dymally was responsible for organizing the Council on Intergroup Relations, the California Advisory Commission on Youth, and on Food and Nutrition.

Originally from Trinidad, West Indies, Dymally came to this country to attend Lincoln University in Jefferson City, Missouri.

## MIKE ESPY
## Second District Mississippi
## Elected 1986

Congressman Mike Espy became the first black congressman elected from Mississippi since Reconstruction when he wrested victory from incumbent Webb Franklin in 1986. Espy's reelection in 1988 demonstrated a resounding vote of support, as he carried all 22 counties in his district and received 66% of the total vote, including 40% of the white vote.

The Voting Rights Act contributed to his victory, as well. Mississippi's district lines were redrawn twice in the 1980s, which recreated western Mississippi's Second Congressional District into a largely black district.

It remains one of the nation's poorest districts which is why Espy's appointment to the House budget Committee and House Agriculture Committee have been important. His dual committee memberships have allowed him to protect programs such as farm programs, and Women, Infants and Children programs.

Espy was one of the few freshmen members of Congress to pass a major piece of legislation in the 100th Congress, the Lower Mississippi River Valley Delta Development Act,

*The Reverend Walter E. Fauntroy represents the District of Columbia in Congress, a district without home rule, hence, no vote. Fauntroy, however, does have a vote on committees and plays an active role with the Congressional Black Caucus.*

which will be an economic blueprint for a seven-state area in the Deep South. He also passed the National Catfish Day a subject of great importance to his constituents, 17,000 of whom work in the industry.

Espy sits on the House Select Committee on Hunger, and four subcommittees on the Agriculture Committee. He was also elected vice president of the 1986 House Democratic Class, and chairman of the House Democratic Freshman Class Budget Task Force.

He was born Nov. 30, 1953 in Yazoo City, Miss. He received a B.A. at Howard University in 1975 and a J.D. at the University of Santa Clara in 1978. Prior to his election, Espy was Assistant Secretary of State from 1980 to 1984, and Assistant Attorney General, and director of Mississippi Consumer Protection office from 1984-1985. Espy, who is married, is the grandson of one of the state's biggest landowners, who built 28 funeral homes and a hospital.

## WALTER E. FAUNTROY
## Congressman-Delegate District of Columbia
## Elected 1971

Congressman Walter E. Fauntroy, also pastor of Washington D. C.'s New Bethel Baptist Church, represents the District of Columbia. A Yale Divinity School alumnus, he was chairman of the Caucus task force for the 1972 Democratic National Committee and of the platform committee of the National Black Political Convention. Fauntroy was Washington, D.C. coordinator for the March on Washington for Jobs and Freedom in 1963, coordinator for the Selma to Montgomery march in 1965, and national coordinator for the Poor People's Campaign in 1969. He is also a Director of the Southern Christian Leadership Conference. As the district of Columbia does not have home rule, Fauntroy does not have a vote in Congress. However, he does have a vote on committees. Should the District be awarded statehood, or a corresponding status, Fauntroy would stand an excellent chance of being elected Governor. He has strong support from the city's overwhelmingly black population, especially the large population of black civil servants.

Since his election to Congress, he has continued to build a record of achievement by playing key roles in the mobilization of black political power. He is a member of the House Select Committee on Narcotics Abuse and Control and co-sponsored the 1988 $2.7 billion anti-drug bill. On Thanksgiving Eve in 1984, Fauntroy and two prominent national leaders launched the "Free South Africa Movement" (FSAM) with their arrest at the South African embassy. He serves as co-chair of the steering committee of the FSAM.

In the 95th Congress Fauntroy was a member of the House Select Committee on Assassinations and Chairman of its Subcommittee on the Assassination of Martin Luther King Jr. He is now the sixth ranking member of the House Banking, Finance, and Urban Affairs Committee and chairman of its Subcommittee on Domestic Monetary Policy. He is also the first ranking member of the House District Committee.

## FLOYD FLAKE
## Sixth District New York
## Elected 1986

Floyd Flake started his political career by winning a hotly contested primary and steamrolling through the general election, taking 78% of the vote, to become the first full-term black congressman from the 6th Congressional District. The seat was previously held for many years by Joseph Addabbo, who died of cancer in March 1986.

Flake is known in his Jamaica, Queens community as pastor of the powerful, 4,000-member Allen A.M.E. Church, which has built senior citizens homes and small businesses. As congressman, he has channeled his expertise into national issues by serving on the Banking, Finance and Urban Affairs Committee, Small Business Committee and on the Domestic Task Force of the Select Committee on Hunger.

Flake was born in Los Angeles, California on Jan. 30, 1945. He attended the public schools of Houston, Texas, through high school, and received a B.A. from Wilberforce

University. He also attended Payne Theological Seminary in Ohio from 1968 to 1970, and took graduate studies in business administration at Northeastern University in Boston, Mass. Flake is married and has four children.

## HAROLD FORD
## Ninth District Tennessee
## Elected 1974

In November 1974 Harold Ford, a 29-year-old Democratic member of the Tennessee House of Representatives, narrowly defeated the Republican incumbent, Dan Kuykendall, to win election to the U.S. House of Representatives. Ford won by 571 votes, 57,715 to 57,141 in a district which takes in most of the city of Memphis.

Elected in 1970 to the State House, Ford was selected majority whip by his fellow Democrats, the first freshman of that body, and probably the youngest to attain that post. While in the State House, Ford sponsored successful bills to regulate Tennessee's utility billing procedures to rehabilitate private housing.

Harold Ford's election to the U.S. Congress was bitter and racially polarized. Kuykendall had been a close ally of former President Nixon, a fact which along with inflation was a major issue in the campaign. Kuykendall, in addition, had sided with positions of the Congressional Black Caucus in only 10% of Congressional votes in 1973. Blacks comprise 47% of the district's population. Ford received some 12% of the white vote. In 1972, Kuykendall had defeated J. D. Patterson, Jr., a black, by nearly 19,000 votes.

The holder of a masters degree in Business Administration from Vanderbilt University, Ford managed a funeral home owned by his father prior to his election to the State House. Two brothers also won office in 1974, his brother John to the State Senate and Emmitt to the State House.

Reelected to his eighth term in 1988, Ford is the seventh ranking member on the House Ways and Means Committee and has served as chairman of the Subcommittee on Human Resources since 1982. He also is on the Select Committee on Aging.

In addition, Ford holds membership on the Congressional Arts Caucus, the Congressional Black Caucus, and the Congressional Caucus for Women's Issues. Because of his leadership in rafting a comprehensive Welfare Reform bill in the 101st Congress, Ford was named Child Advocate of the Year for 1987 by the Child Welfare League of America.

## WILLIAM H. GRAY III
## Second District Pennsylvania
## Elected 1978

William H. Gray III's election to Congress in 1978 is an extension of his long record of community service as pastor for eight years of Union Baptist Church in Montclair, New Jersey and, since 1972, of the 3,000-member Bright Hope Baptist Church in North Philadelphia.

As a representative in the 97th Congress, Gray remains active through assignments as the thirty-first ranking member of the Appropriations Committee, where he serves on the

*A new-comer to Congress in 1986, Flake is the first black representative from New York's Sixth Congressional District.*

Transportation and Foreign Operations Subcommittees; and sixth ranking member of the District of Columbia Committee, for which he chairs the Subcommittee on Government Operations and Metropolitan Affairs. In addition, Congressman Gray is vice-chair of the Congressional Black Caucus.

Gray's efforts in the civil rights field included the precedent-setting New Jersey Supreme Court case *Gray v. Serruto* , which ordered that financial damages be paid by those who discriminate on the basis of race in renting multi-family housing. The case later made civil rights history when it became part of a ruling by the U.S. Supreme Court.

During the 96th Congress, Representative Gray served on the House committees on Foreign Affairs, the Budget and the District of Columbia. He was elected secretary of the Congressional Black Caucus and was chosen by his freshman colleagues to represent them on the Leadership's Democratic Steering and Policy Committee.

As a member of the Foreign Affairs Committee in the 96th Congress, Bill Gray moved to increase U.S. visibility in Africa and to make our foreign aid more effective on that continent. He wrote the only new legislation by a freshman to be adopted by the 96th Congress. This legislation established the African Development Foundation, a new mechanism to deliver U.S. aid in a visible manner to the grassroots, village-level people of Africa. Gray also introduced legislation to increase the number of minorities and women in the U.S. Foreign Service and to assure equality in recruitment, promotion, and retention. His amendments to the Foreign Service Personnel Reform Act were adopted by the 96th Congress and signed into law by President Carter.

His work on the Foreign Affairs Committee and active advocacy of majority rule in Rhodesia led to his appointment as a U.S. representative at the inauguration of the government of Zimbabwe. President Carter appointed him to chair the United States/Liberia Presidential Commission, and more recently he headed a special mission to Liberia to begin talks with the government which took office after the 1980 coup. Gray also participated in Vice President Mondale's trade mission to Nigeria. Gray has continued to be a leading spokesman on African policy. In 1985 and 1986, he authored the House version of the anti-apartheid acts, which limited American financial support for apartheid. He also sponsored the emergency food aid bill for Ethiopia in 1984.

Domestically, he has pushed through measures which have provided $10 million to minority business owners who needed bonding assistance in the field of transportation and highway work. In 1983, he authored legislation requiring the U.S. Agency for International Development to include minority and women business owners, black colleges and minority private agencies in AID development assistance programs, a move which resulted in $300 million in AID contracts over three years to those concerns.

Gray received a BA from Franklin and Marshall College in 1963. He has been the senior minister at Bright Hope Baptist Church in North Philadelphia since 1972; he earned an MD from Drew Theological Seminary in 1966 and Masters in Theology from the Princeton Theological Seminary in 1970. He is married and has three sons.

As a member of the House Budget Committee in the 96th Congress, Bill Gray was deeply involved in the fight to preserve the human needs programs key to the survival of the poor, the elderly, and the minorities of this nation. He continues to be in the forefront of the fight to reorder Federal spending priorities.

Reelected to a sixth term in 1988, Gray captured the fourth highest leadership spot in the House of Representatives, as chair of the House Democratic Caucus. In that position, Gray helped the House Democrats to set priorities and plan strategies.

Gray continues to remain active as chairman of the Budget committee, and as a member of the Appropriations Committee, where he serves on the Foreign Operations and transportation subcommittees. He is also on the District of Columbia Committee, where he serves on the Fiscal Affairs and Health, Government Operations and Metropolitan Affairs subcommittees. In addition, he is vice-chair of the Congressional Black Caucus.

### AUGUSTUS F. HAWKINS
### Twenty-Ninth District California
### Elected 1963

Augustus Hawkins was born in Shreveport, Louisiana in 1907 and moved to California at the age of 12. He attended the universities of California and Southern California.

In 1934, when only 27, Hawkins was elected to the California State Assembly. He remained in the state legislature for 28 years, and on a few occasions came close to being elected speaker of the Assembly. During his 28-year tenure, he authored over 100 laws including minimum wage for women; a slum clearance and low-cost housing program; workmen's compensation for domestics; disability insurance; The Fair Housing Act; old age pension; child care centers; The Fair Employment Practices Act of 1959; and the 1961 Metropolitan Transit Authority Act. Eventually assuming the chairmanship of the Rules Committee, he also served as chairman of the Senate and Assembly Joint Legislative Organization Committee.

Under legislation he sponsored, racial designation was removed from all state documents such as driver's licenses and job orders. He was also instrumental in bringing about the appointment of the first California blacks as judges and as members of the highway patrol and of several state commissions.

Though less militant than younger members of the Black Caucus, Hawkins can be very forceful. In 1970, he was one of the Congressmen who discovered the "tiger cages" in the prisons of South Vietnam, a feat which increased his stature as an opponent of the war.

Hawkins holds an important post in Congress as Chairman of the Education and Labor Committee's Equal Employment Opportunities Subcommittee. His seat situated mainly in the Watts area of Los Angeles is considered safe. Some 54% of the residents are black, 21% Hispanic. In 1972, Hawkins received 84% of the vote.

For the 97th Congress, Representative Hawkins has been appointed chairman of the House Administration Committee. He also serves as chairman of the Joint Committee on the

*Representative Augustus Hawkins has been in Congress longer than any other member of the Congressional Black Caucus. He is co-author of the famed Humphrey-Hawkins bill.*

Library and as vice-chairman of the Joint Committee on Printing. Hawkins is first ranking member on the Committee on Education and Labor and is chairman of its Subcommittee on Employment Opportunities.

Representative Hawkins introduced three landmark pieces of legislation during the 93rd Congress: the Juvenile Justice and Delinquency Prevention Act; the Community Services Act; and the Civil Rights Act, Title VII Section amendment to the Equal Employment Opportunities Act.

In the 95th Congress, three other pieces of legislation sponsored by Hawkins became law: the CETA Amendments of 1978; the Youth Employment and Demonstration Projects Act; and the Pregnancy Disability Act. Hawkins witnessed the signing into law of the Humphrey/Hawkins Full Employment Act of 1978 which he began developing in 1974 with Senator Hubert H. Humphrey.

In the 96th Congress, Representative Hawkins introduced the Youth Act of 1980 to combat the disastrously high rate of unemployment among America's youth.

In recognition of Congressman Hawkins' outstanding contribution to education and labor issues, Lincoln University conferred an honorary degree of Doctor of Laws on him during its commencement exercises in May 1978.

Hawkins holds an important position in Congress as both chairman of the Education and Labor Committee, and the subcommittee on Elementary, Secondary and Vocational Education.

In 1986, Hawkins was reelected by 85% of the vote the highest in the California Congressional Delegation. In the 100th Congress (1987-88), he authored two more landmark pieces of legislation: the School Improvement Act, which reauthorized all major elementary and secondary education programs, and the Civil Rights Restoration Act, which strengthened four important civil rights laws.

### CHARLES A. HAYES
### First District Illinois
### Elected 1983

Congressman Charles Hayes was first elected to the U.S. House of Representatives in 1983 to fill the vacancy left by Chicago Mayor Harold Washington. Hayes was subsequently reelected in his own right.

To become congressman, Hayes retired as the International Vice President and Director of Region 12 of the United Food and Commercial Workers International Union. Hayes had been a union official since the 1940s, and is the first elected representative of rank-and-file trade unionists to serve in Congress.

He currently serves on the Elementary, Secondary and Vocational education and the Management Relations subcommittees of the Education and Labor Committee. He is also a member of the Small Business Committee and serves on the Procurement, Innovation and Minority Enterprises Development subcommittee.

In 1987, he introduced the "School Dropout Demonstration Assistance Act" which was signed into law as part of the School Improvement Act of 1987. The initiative provided some 450 million to various school districts for programs to encourage children to reenter school and complete their education.

Hayes was born Aug. 23, 1983, and raised in Cairo, Ill. He is married and has two daughters and two stepsons.

### MICKEY LELAND
### Eighteenth District Texas
### Elected 1978

Mickey Leland was elected to the House of Representatives in 1978 and was the freshman whip of the 96th Congress. Reelected in 1988, he is chairman of the Subcommittee on Postal Operations and Services and serves on the Compensation and Employee Benefits Subcommittee of the Post Office and Civil Service Committee. He is also chairman of the Select Committee on Hunger, and serves on three subcommittees of the Energy and Commerce Committee.

Congressman Leland was elected chairman of the Subcommittee on Postal Personnel and Modernization in 1980. He also serves on the Subcommittee on Census and Population, Subcommittee on Energy Conservation and Power, Subcommittee on Fossil and Synthetic Fuels, Subcommittee on Health and the Environment, and the Subcommittee on Manpower, Education, and the Judiciary.

Leland was a member of the Texas House of Representatives from 1972 to 1978. In 1976 he was selected to serve on the Democratic National Committee and was reelected in 1980. While attending the Memphis Midterm Conference of the National Democratic Party in 1978, he helped organize the National Black/Hispanic Democratic Coalition, on which he now serves as co-chair.

Leland was a member of the Democratic National Committee from 1976 to 1985 and served as chairman of the DNC's Black Caucus from 1982 to 1985. During 1985 and 1986, he also served as chairman of the Congressional Black Caucus for the 99th Congress.

He was born in Nov. 27, 1944 and attended school in Houston. He earned a bachelor of science degree from Texas Southern University in Houston in 1970. Prior to his election in 1978, Leland was a member of the Texas Legislature from 1973 to 1978. Leland is married and has one son.

### JOHN LEWIS
### Fifth District Georgia
### Elected 1986

John Lewis became Georgia's Fifth District representative in 1986 and was reelected by overwhelming majority to a second term in 1988. The campaign drew national attention, because Lewis had to defeat another black, Julian Bond, in a primary battle: Bond won more than 60% of the black votes, but Lewis captured 90% of the white votes.

In Congress, Lewis is a member of the Public works and Transportation Committee, and the House Interior and Insular Affairs Committee. He also serves on the Congressional Coalition of Soviet Jewry and the Democratic Congressional Campaign Committee.

Before his election to Congress, Lewis served on the Atlanta City Council, elected in 1981 and again in 1985.

In 1959 and 1960, Lewis was an active civil rights worker,

*A long-time civil rights activist in the South, Representative John Lewis was elected to Congress in 1986.*

helping to organize lunch counter sit-ins and later leading Freedom Rides. He was viciously beaten during such rides in Rock Hills, South Carolina and Montgomery, Alabama. He also played major roles in the March on Washington, the Student Non-Violent Coordinating Committee, and Selma-to-Montgomery march and the Mississippi Freedom Project. He later served in the Carter Administration at ACTION and as head of the Voter Education Project, to which he helped add 4 million minorities to the voter rolls. In 1981, he ran for a House seat vacated by Ambassador Andrew Young, but was unsuccessful.

Lewis was born the son of a sharecropper on Feb. 21, 1940 in Troy, Alabama. He attended public schools in Alabama, and earned a bachelor of arts degree in Religion and Philosophy from the Fisk University in Nashville. He is also a graduate of the American Baptist Theological Seminary. Lewis is married and has one son.

### KWEISI MFUME
### Seventh District Maryland
### Elected 1986

Congressman Kweisi Meume, a former Baltimore City councilman, won election in 1986, defeating two more widely known contenders. Meume, formerly named Frizzell Gray, also turned out to have political shortcomings: soon after his election, it was revealed that he had fathered five sons by four different women. The congressman admitted he had done so, as a youth, but that he had supported them. He earned continued public support by talking out against drug use and immoral behavior, and won reelection in 1988 with 87% of the vote.

Meume has seats on the Banking and Small business Committees, and also serves on the Select Committee on Hunger, on the Domestic Task Force.

Meume was born in Baltimore on Oct. 24, 1948. He earned a Bachelor of Urban Planning at Morgan State University in 1976 and Master of Arts from Joys Hopkins University in 1984. He later worked on presidential campaigns for Sen. Ted Kennedy and Jesse Jackson.

### MAJOR OWENS
### Twelfth District New York
### E lected 1982

Born June 28, 1936 in Memphis, Tennessee, Major Owens attended Morehouse College receiving a B. A. in 1956, and an M. S. in 1957 from Atlanta University. In 1982 he defeated Dr. Joseph Ceasar with 91% of the vote, replacing the distinguished Shirley Chisholm who retired from the 12th district seat. He currently serves on government committees for education, labor, employment, housing, government acitivities, and transportation.

Prior to this election, he served in the New York State Senate from 1975 to 1982 as representative from 17, a district newly created through reapportionment in Brooklyn.

In 1974, he was the Director of the Communication Media Library Program at Columbia University.

### DONALD M. PAYNE
### Tenth District New Jersey
### Elected 1988

In 1988, Donald M. Payne, a life-long resident of Newark and City Councilman, was elected the first black Congressman from New Jersey.

A graduate of Seton Hall University with a B.A. in Social Studies, Payne served as an executive with the Prudential Insurance Company as well as president of the the minority-owned computer forms manufacturer, Urban Data Systems, Inc. Payne was elected to the Essex County Board of Chosen Freeholders in 1972. He was selected as the Board's Director by his colleagues in 1977.

He was elected to the Newark Municipal Council in June, 1982 and re-elected in 1986. In June, 1988, he overwhelmingly won the Democratic nomination for the United States House of Representatives. In the November election, he won the seat with 86 percent of the vote.

Committed to community work, Payne worked as a teacher and with various youth-oriented activities. He was elected President of the YMCA's of the USA in 1970, serving as the first black president in that organization's history.

### CHARLES RANGEL
### Sixteenth District New York
### Elected 1970

Harlem-born Charles Rangel vaulted into the national spotlight in 1970 when he defeated Adam Clayton Powell for

Democratic nomination in New York's 18th Congressional District. Rangel's upset victory stirred hopes among black leaders that a grassroots political movement generated from within Harlem, rather than stemming from beyond the community, might result in the grooming of an energetic, capable, and untainted successor to the volatile and unpredictable Powell.

Born June 11, 1930, Rangel attended Harlem elementary and secondary schools before volunteering to serve in the U.S. Army during the Korean war. While stationed in Korea with the 2nd Infantry, he saw heavy combat and received the Purple Heart and the Bronze Star Medal for Valor, as well as U.S. and Korean Presidential citations. Discharged honorably as a Staff Sergeant, Rangel returned to finish high school (DeWitt Clinton in 1953) and to study at New York University's School of Commerce, from which he graduated in 1957. The recipient of a scholarship, Rangel then attended St. John's Law School, graduating in 1960.

After being admitted to the bar, Rangel earned a key appointment as Assistant U.S. Attorney in the Southern District of New York in 1961. For the next five years, he acquired legal experience as legal counsel to the New York City Housing and Redevelopment Board, as legal assistant to Judge James L. Watson, as associate counsel to the speaker of the N.Y. State Assembly, and as general counsel to the National Advisory Commission on Selective Service.

In 1966, Rangel was chosen to represent the 72nd District, Central Harlem, in the State Assembly. Since then, he has served as a member of, and secretary to, the New York State Commission on Revision of the Penal Law and Criminal Code.

In 1972, Rangel easily defeated Livingston Wingate in the Democratic primary and went on to an overwhelming victory in November as the candidate of the Democratic, Republican, and Liberal parties. In 1974 he was elected chairman of the Congressional Black Caucus.

In his first term, he was appointed to the Select Committee on Crime and was influential in passing the 1971 amendment to the drug laws that authorized the President to cut off all military and economic aid to any country that refused to cooperate with the United States in stopping the international traffic in drugs. In 1976, he was appointed to the Select Committee on Narcotics Abuse and Control. Rangel is regarded as one of the leading Congressional experts on the subject.

Representative Rangel served as chairman of the Congressional Black Caucus in 1974-1975 and was a member of the Judiciary Committee when it voted to impeach President Nixon. In 1975 he moved to the Ways and Means Committee, becoming the first black to serve on this committee. Two years later his colleagues in the New York Congressional delegation voted him the majority whip for New York State.

Now serving his ninth term in Congress, Rangel is the fourth ranking member of the Ways and Means Committee and chairs that Select Revenue Measures Subcommittee. he is also chairman of the Select committee on Narcotics Abuse and Control.

Blacks comprise 59% of the population in Rangel's district, Spanish-speaking Americans some 17%. His constituency also includes a long stretch of Central Park West and other white middle-class streets of New York's West Side.

*In 1988, Donald M. Payne became the first congressman ever to be elected from the State of New Jersey. He won the seat of retired congressman Peter Rodino after a hard fought primary campaign.*

### AUGUSTUS F. SAVAGE
### Second District Illinois
### Elected 1980

Augustus F. "Gus" Savage was elected in 1980 to the 97th Congress as Representative of Illinois' Second Congressional District. His election was a continuation of his many years of involvement in the civic and political life of Chicago and the Chicago publishing industry.

Savage is the tenth ranking member on the Public Works and Transportation Committee and eleventh ranking member of the Small Business Committee.

Savage has been outspoken in the Chicago community as a political activist, beginning in 1946 with his leading to victory the demonstrations for veterans' housing. He organized demonstrations to win the rights of blacks to be hired as department store clerks, to serve in downtown Chicago restaurants, to live in a middle-income housing development called Lake Meadows, to select school principals in their local areas, to have representation for the 2nd Ward on the City Council and to have a black candidate on the ballot for

Mayor of Chicago against former Mayor Michael Bilandic.

In 1950, Savage served as a full-time organizer for the Progressive Party. Thereafter he continued forward despite being subpoenaed into court in 1968 for supporting the Chicago Transit Workers strike, and jailed in 1970 for defending contracts of black home buyers. In 1979 he organized a community conference which enabled Mayor Byrne's transition team to hear the concerns and priorities of the citizens.

Awards that have been bestowed on Savage include the 1965 Independent Journalist of the Year; the City of Chicago Medal of Merit in 1976, by vote of the City Council; the Operation PUSH Award of Merit in 1976, for heroism in risking life to help save women being held as hostages during a robbery; the Businessman of the Year from *Dollars and Sense* magazine in 1978; in 1981 both the Freshman of the Year from the Evanston, Illinois NAACP, and the Presidential Award from the Cook County Bar Association.

Savage wrote the pamphlets "How to Increase the Power of the Negro Vote" in 1959 and "Political Power," in 1969.

*Louis Stokes, veteran representative from Cleveland, Ohio.*

## LOUIS STOKES
## Twenty-First District Ohio
## Elected 1969

The older brother of Cleveland's former mayor Carl Stokes, Congressman Louis Stokes skillfully engineered his 1968 victory by welding a successful coalition of ghetto poor and affluent suburbanites in the redrawn 21st Ohio Congressional District (Cleveland's East Side, Garfield Heights, and Newburgh Heights). Stokes garnered some 86,000 votes compared with only 31,000 for his black Republican opponent, Charles Lucas.

Stokes and Lucas had been allies after 1965, the year the Ohio legislature divided the 21st District in such a way that black voting strength was largely emasculated. Under such an arrangement, it would have been virtually impossible for a black Congressional candidate to capture a House seat. Lucas then brought suit before the U.S. Supreme Court protesting the gerrymander, and was joined by Stokes in arguing the case. The merits of their argument were so convincing that the Court instructed the legislature to shelve its original plan, whereupon the Ohioans hatched a new redistricting setup in which the black electorate formed 65% of the voting total. The victory severed the temporary alliance between Stokes and Lucas inasmuch as both were anxious to campaign for the opening.

A native of Cleveland, Stokes shined shoes and sold papers to earn money to help his widowed mother, Mrs. Louise Stokes, and his younger brother, Carl.

Stokes enlisted in the Army after finishing high school and used the GI Bill to finance higher education at Western Reserve University and the Cleveland-Marshall Law School. He later joined the NAACP as a crusading lawyer whose prominence in anti-discrimination lawsuits won him popular favor among the ghetto poor.

Congenial and experienced, Stokes has always impressed people with his ability to circulate comfortably among straitlaced businessmen as well as casual, street-wise billiard parlor habitues.

In 1970 and 1972, Stokes was reelected with some 80% of the district's vote and his seat is regarded as safe.

From 1972 to 1974, Stokes served as chairman of the Congressional Black Caucus.

Stokes was a member of the Select Committee to Conduct an Investigation and Study of the Circumstances Surrounding the death of President Kennedy and death of Dr. Martin Luther King Jr., and in 1977 Speaker Thomas P. "Tip" O' Neill appointed him chairman of this committee. On December 31, 1978 Stokes completed these historic investigations and filed with the House of Representatives 27 volumes of hearings, a Final Report, and Recommendations for Administrative and Legislative Reform.

Stokes was appointed to the House Committee on Standards of Official Conduct (Ethics Committee) in 1980 and early was elected its chairman.

Congressman Stokes has served two terms as chairman of the Congressional Black Caucus and is currently co-chairman of the Caucus Health Braintrust. He has been named by *Ebony* magazine as one of the 100 most influential black Americans each year since 1971, and at the 1980 Congressional Black Caucus Legislative Weekend Awards Program he was presented the William L. Dawson Award by his colleagues in the Caucus in recognition of his "unique leadership in the development of legislation."

He is currently the eight ranking member of the Appropriations Committee, and serves on three subcommittees, including District of Columbia, HUD-Independent Agencies, and Labor-Health and Human Services. He is also chairman of the permanent Select Committee on Intelligence, and was a member of the special committee which investigated the Iran-contra scandal.

## EDOLPHUS "ED" TOWNS
### Eleventh district New York
### Elected 1982

Formerly the first black deputy borough president in Brooklyn, Edolphus "Ed" Towns became one of the boroughs congressmen, with 90 percent of the vote, in 1982.

He is a member of the Public Works and Transportation Committee, the Government Operations Committee, and the Select Committee on Narcotics Abuse and Control.

Towns is a 1956 graduate of North Carolina A&T University and holds a master's degree in social work from Adelphi University. He served two years in the Army, and has taught in the New York City public schools, was program director for Metropolitan Hospital, and was assistant administrator at Beth Israel Hospital for 10 years. He has also served as professor at Medgar Evers College and Fordham University.

His political career began in 1972 when he was elected as Democratic State Committeeman in the 40th Assembly district.

Towns serves on executive boards of several organizations, including the American Red Cross, Kings County Boy Scouts, Share Our Strength and the Black Tennis Foundation . He is married and has two children.

## ALAN WHEAT
### Fifth District Missouri
### Elected 1982

Congressman Alan Wheat, elected in 1982, has the distinction of being a black office-holder voted in by a mostly white constituency. The son of an Air Force colonel and an Air Force officer himself, Wheat came to congress after distinguishing himself as an economist with the Department of Housing and Urban Development in Kansas City, and later as a state legislator.

In Congress, he was appointed to serve on the prestigious House Committee on Rules in 1982, becoming the third freshman congressman in history to be appointed to the Rules committee. He chairs the subcommittee on Government Operations and Metropolitan Affairs of the Committeement Service Task Force, and the Congressional Human Rights Caucus. He is vice-chairman of the Congressional Black Caucus.

Born in San Antonio on Oct. 16, 1951, Wheat was educated around the world with his military family. He received a Bachelor of Arts degree in economics from Grinnell College in Iowa in 1972. on the District of Columbia. He alsoserves on the Select Committee on Children, Youth and Families.

In 1987, Wheat was appointed to serve as Democratic whip for the 100th Congress. He is also a member of the Executive committee of the Democratic Study Group, the Congressional Caucus for Women's Issues, the Environmental and Energy Study Conference, the Federal Govern ment Service Task Force, and the Congeressional Black Caucus.

Born in San Antonio on October 16, 1951, Wheat was educated around the world with his military family. He received a Bachelor of Arts degree in economics from Grinnel College in Iowa in 1972.

*Elected in 1982, Representatives "Ed" Towns (left) of New York State and Alan Wheat of Missouri are future leaders in Congress.*

## CONTEMPORARY FORMER AFRICAN-AMERICAN CONGRESSMEN

African-American s have served as Congressional Representatives during three hisorical periods. These were the reconstructive period, the urbanization period, and, still in progress, a renewed civil rights legislative period.

### Reconstruction: 1870-1901

Between 1870 and 1901, 22 blacks, two Senators and 20 Representatives, served. All were from the South. Both Senators were from Mississippi. Of the Representatives, eight were from South Carolina, four were from North Carolina, three from Alabama, and one each from Florida, Georgia, Louisiana, Mississippi, and Virginia.

It is not surprising that these black legislators were expected to become a special breed of miracle worker seeking, wherever possible, to establish free public schooling, to abolish debtors' punishments, to extend voting rights—in short, to deliver to the black a host of privileges and rights long taken for granted by the white majority.

Some black legislators were party hacks; some were misguided idealists; some were unprincipled scoundrels. Yet, on the whole, black Congressmen were eager and willing public servants. The majority were not motivated solely by self-interest and political opportunism, nor did they approach government with an overweening desire for revenge against their southern oppressors.

The impact of these men on American history has not been enormous, yet they cannot be regarded merely as historical peculiarities. They were products of their age, but they also made their imprint on that age. With the triumph of white supremacist laws and evasions, the last of these men, George H. White of North Carolina, left Congress in 1901. By 1902 there was not a single black legislator on a national or state level.

### The Period of Urbanization: 1902-1965

The rapid emigration of blacks to the North eventually resulted in congressional districts with sufficient black voters to elect a few black legislators. The first was Oscar De Priest of Chicago, a Republican elected to the House in 1928. De Priest was defeated in 1934, during the Roosevelt landslide, by a black Democrat, Arthur Mitchell. During World War II William Dawson and Adam Clayton Powell, Jr. were elected, followed in the 1950s by Charles C. Diggs, who retired in 1980, and Robert N. C. Nix, who was defeated in 1978.

These men fought the long lonely battles for legislation to eliminate the poll tax and make lynching a federal crime. They were extremely important in Congress as a voice for the causes of blacks and as a bridge between blacks and white liberals, the alliance which was to win the civil rights victories of the 1960s.

### Legislation and Redistricting: 1965 to the Present

The present period, as noted, finds 16 blacks in the House of Representatives. Much of this achievement is attributable to the Voting Rights Act of 1965, which made possible the election of two black Representatives from the South, Barbara Jordan and Andrew Young, and the Supreme Court's requirements that the one man one vote dictum be applied by state legislatures so that cities be fairly represented.

Following is a list of former black Congressmen. All served in the House of Representatives unless otherwise indicated.

## BIOGRAPHIES

### EDWARD W. BROOKE
### Senator from Massachusetts
### Elected 1966

During his two terms in the U.S. Senate, Edward W. Brooke, the first black to be elected to that body since 1876, defied conventional political wisdom. In a state that was overwhelmingly Democratic and in which blacks constituted only 3% of the population, he was one of its most popular political figures and a Republican.

He first achieved statewide office in 1962 when he defeated Elliot Richardson to become Attorney General. He established an outstanding record in that post and in 1966 was elected to the Senate over former Massachusetts governor Endicott Peabody.

Born into a middle-class Washington, D.C. environment, Brooke attended public schools locally and went on to graduate from Howard. Inducted into an all-black infantry unit during World War II, Brooke rose to the rank of captain and was ultimately given a Bronze Star for his work in intelligence.

Returning to Massachusetts, Brooke attended the Boston University Law School, compiling an outstanding academic record and editing the *Law Review* in the process. After law school, he established himself as an attorney and also served as chairman of the Boston Finance Commission.

Brooke was later nominated for the attorney general's office, encountering stiff opposition within his own party. He eventually won both the Republican primary and the general election against his Democratic opponent.

Upon entering the national political scene, Brooke espoused the notion that the Great Society could not become a reality until it was preceded by the "Responsible Society." He called this a society in which "it's more profitable to work than not to work. You don't help a man by constantly giving him more handouts."

*Senator Edward Brooke, a popular two-term United States Senator (R) of Massachusetts, often visited the streets to get first-hand knowledge of his constituents' grievances.*

Brooke has also hastened to note that he is not merely "the first Negro this or the highest Negro that," but can likewise be described as "a Protestant in a Catholic state and a Republican in a Democratic state."

When first elected, Brooke strongly supported United States participation in the Vietnam War, though most black leaders were increasingly opposing it. However, in 1971 Brooke supported the McGovern-Hatfield Amendment which called for withdrawal of the United States from Vietnam.

As might be expected, matters of race rather than foreign affairs were to become Brooke's area of expertise. Reluctant and subdued, Brooke proceeded carefully at first, waiting to be consulted by President Nixon and loyally accepting the latter's apparent indifference to his views. However, as pressure mounted from the established civil rights groups and impatient black militants he decided to attack the Nixon policies. Brooke was roused into a more active role by the Administration's vacillating school desegregation guidelines, its "firing" of HEW official Leon Panetta, and the nominations to the Supreme Court of judicial conservatives Clement Haynsworth and G. Harrold Carswell.

In 1972 Brooke was reelected to the Senate overwhelmingly, even though Massachusetts was the only state not carried by his party in the Presidential election. While Brooke seconded the nomination of President Nixon at the 1972 Republican Convention, he became increasingly critical of the Nixon Administration. He also began to appear publicly at meetings of the Congressional Black Caucus, a group he had tended to avoid in the past. Brooke was considered a member of the moderate-to-liberal wing of the Republican Party.

He was defeated for his third term in the Senate in 1978 and returned to the private practice of law.

## YVONNE BRAITHWAITE BURKE
## Thirty-Seventh District California
## Elected 1973

Attorney and former California State Assemblywoman Yvonne Braithwaite Burke became the first black woman from California ever to be elected to the House of Representatives in November 1972.

Congresswoman Burke served in the state Assembly for six years prior to her election to Congress. During her final two years there, she was chairman of the Committee on Urban Development and Housing and a member of the Health, Finance and Insurance committees.

As a state legislator, Burke was responsible for enactment of bills providing for needy children, relocation of tenants and owners of homes taken by governmental action, and one which required major medical insurance programs to grant immediate coverage to newborn infants of the insured.

Burke was recently selected a fellow in the Harvard University Institute of Politics, which is part of the John F. Kennedy School of Government.

Prior to her governmental career, Burke was a practicing attorney, during which time she served as a Deputy Corporation Commissioner, a hearing officer for the Los Angeles Police Commissioner, and an attorney for the McCone

*Yvonne Burke was elected to the U.S. Congress in 1972.*

Commission, which investigated the Watts riots.

Burke's district, created in 1971 by the California legislature, contains low-and middle-income black and integrated neighborhoods plus some white suburban tracts and beach communities, including Venice, which is noted for its "counterculture" scene.

About 50% of the district's population is black, another 10% of Hispanic and Asian origin. In 1972 the district gave 64% of its vote to Burke, who was, at the time, Miss Braithwaite. She was married in 1972 and in 1973 became the first Congresswoman to give birth while in office, to a daughter, Autumn Roxanne Burke.

In 1978 Representative Burke resigned to run for Attorney General in California. She lost that race and has since been in the private practice of law although she remains prominent in California politics. She has also taken on a number of civic responsibilities including serving as a member of the University of California Board of Regents.

## SHIRLEY CHISHOLM
## Twelfth District New York
## Elected 1969

Representative Shirley Chisholm stunned a number of people early in 1982 when she announced that after almost 15 years in Congress she would not seek another term because of her desire to return to "a more private life." Her retirement brought an end to a political career that found her as well known nationally as she was in her home district, which encompasses the Bedford-Stuyvesant and Bushwick sections of Brooklyn.

Her decision was not a sudden one. She had been considering such a move for over a year and conceded that the defeat of many liberal lawmakers in the 1980 election and what she considered a growing conservatism in the country had played a part in her decision. At her leaving, she was a member of the all-important House Rules Committee and secretary of the House Democratic Caucus. Hers was one of the loudest voices raised in protest against the Reagan Administration's cutbacks in domestic programs.

Chisholm became the first black woman to sit in the House of Representatives in 1969. Her opponent for the seat was James Farmer, once the leader of CORE and an important figure in the Civil Rights Movement. Farmer allegedly sought to create a whisper campaign around the theme that black women had already exercised far too much influence on the fate of black communities and on the development of black self-assertiveness, but the issue, if it had any relevance at all, did not sway much opinion. Members of the newly created predominantly black and Puerto Rican 12th Congressional District chose the dynamic Chisholm over Farmer by a more than 3-1 margin.

Chisholm originally entered public life in response to local pleas for an honest, conscientious public servant in the New York State Assembly. While there, she sponsored the SEEK program, which offers students from minority groups

***New York's 12th District lost an exceptional representative when Shirley Chisholm decided not to seek reelection.***

the opportunity to obtain college-level training even if they do not yet have high school diplomas. She also introduced legislation to establish publicly supported daycare centers and to extend unemployment insurance to domestic workers.

Chisholm's decision to run for higher office was based in part on the continued appeals of people of her district, whose problems she knew because she had chosen to remain in Bedford-Stuyvesant rather than move on to more affluent surroundings.

Born Shirley St. Hill in 1926, Representative Chisholm is descended from West Indian immigrant laborers (her mother was a seamstress from Barbados and her father, a native of British Guiana, worked in a burlap factory). One of three sisters, she was sent to Barbados at the age of three to live with other immediate family members while her parents struggled to save money for the girls' education. At age 11, Shirley returned to Brooklyn, attending grade school and high school before earning a scholarship to pursue higher education. A graduate of both Brooklyn College and Columbia University, and holder of a masters in elementary education, Chisholm worked as a nursery school teacher, director of a daycare center, and consultant for the New York Department of Social Services before entering public life as a state representative in Albany.

After her election, Chisholm indicated her early preference for committee assignments which would reflect her interests and areas of expertise (education, labor management, and inner-city conditions in general) and take advantage of her experience in the social services. When saddled with a committee assignment in the area of agriculture, she openly balked at the idea, complaining outspokenly of the gross misuse of her talents.

Chisholm is a tough, tenacious crusader, whose belief in organization is almost as strong as her faith in the good will and basic decency of black people. Her efforts on their behalf dictate a practical and result-oriented philosophy which focuses on self-determination through the meaningful participation in the economic life of the nation. In her view, this means that black people need sound vocational education, access to higher learning, and sensible business counseling.

Though sympathetic with the goals of militants, she feels that they are often indisciplined and incapable of executing real change in a structured environment serving large numbers of people. She is, however, equally critical of the shallow thinking that produces appeals to law and order without placing equal emphasis on the theme of justice in American society.

In 1972, Representative Chisholm leaped to national prominence when she announced her candidacy for the Democratic Presidential nomination. She entered a large number of primaries and, though her share of the vote never exceeded 7%, she was regarded with the same respect as the white male candidates and was invited to join attempts to prevent the nomination of Senator McGovern.

However, Chisholm received only some 150 of 1,600 delegate votes at the Miami Convention, as a great many blacks supported McGovern or Senator Hubert Humphrey rather than Chisholm.

Chisholm has been the target of considerable criticism from black leaders and her constituents for her avid support of women's liberation. Of particular concern was a remark, attributed to her, to the effect that discrimination against women exceeds discrimination against blacks. Many blacks who agreed with the objectives of "women's lib" feel such views divert attention from the needs of blacks, men and women alike.

However, Chisholm was such a popular figure among her constituents that she continued to win her seat in each election by substantial margins.

## GEORGE W. COLLINS
## Illinois
## Elected 1970

George W. Collins had a brief, tragic career in Congress. Elected from the Seventh (Chicago West Side) District in 1970 and reelected in 1972, he died in an airplane crash in December, the same crash which killed Dorothy Hunt, wife of E. Howard Hunt, convicted Watergate conspirator.

Collins obtained his seat in 1970 as a result of redistricting in Illinois and the fear of the city's Democratic machine that it was losing support of Chicago's blacks. Mayor Richard Daley encouraged Representative Frank Annunzio, who had represented most of the district to seek election elsewhere, and handed the seat to Collins. Annunzio also won, in a new, white, blue-collar district, after reversing his opposition to anti-busing legislation.

Following his death, Collins was succeeded by his wife, Cardiss, who won a special election in 1973.

## CHARLES C. DIGGS
## Thirteenth District Michigan
## Elected 1954

Following his conviction for using funds from his federal payroll to pay personal bills and his sentencing to three years in prison, Congressman Charles C. Diggs, the senior black representative in the House, resigned in 1980. By resigning, Representative Diggs avoided what was certain to be a vote by his colleagues to expel him.

The resignation removed from Congress one of its most skilled and experienced members, who was particularly effective in his chairmanship of the House Foreign Affairs African Subcommittee.

Diggs was born in Detroit in 1922 and was educated there. In high school he compiled an outstanding academic record and excelled as a debater. Later, at the University of Michigan, Diggs won the university's oratorical championship. In 1942 he transferred to Fisk University in Nashville before being drafted into the Army Air Force where he was ultimately commissioned as a second lieutenant. He was honorably discharged in 1945.

Back in Detroit, Diggs enrolled at the Wayne State University School of Mortuary Science. At the same time, he was radio commentator on a program co-sponsored by the House of Diggs, the family business which has come to be the largest funeral home in Michigan.

Diggs entered politics in 1951 when he was elected to the

State Senate. Compiling a robust legislative record in civil rights, business, and labor relations, Diggs won the admiration of key figures in the Democratic party and by 1953 was in a position to run, though unsuccessfully for a seat on the Detroit Common Council.

In 1954, at the age of 28, Diggs upset the Democratic incumbent in a landslide primary victory and went on to win election to the House of Representatives. In Washington, he soon acquired a reputation as a diligent and shrewd watchdog of *de facto* discrimination in the armed forces and in federally sponsored programs in the South. Many positive acts by numerous Secretaries of Defense to reduce discrimination can be traced to Diggs.

In 1970, with the death of Congressman William L. Dawson and the defeat of Adam Clayton Powell, Diggs, at 48, became the senior black member of the House. In 1973 he was chosen chairman of the District of Columbia Committee, a position he occupied in addition to his chairmanship of the Foreign Affairs African Subcommittee.

Diggs' district existed entirely within the city of Detroit. It was about 67% black and contained some pockets of Polish and German ethnics. In each of his elections, Diggs faced only token opposition.

### MELVIN H. EVANS
### Virgin Islands
### Elected 1978

As the first elected governor of the U.S. Virgin Islands, and later as its non voting congressman in the House of Representatives, Dr. Melvin H. Evans has had two highly successful careers—one in the field of medicine and the other in the political arena. A native of the Virgin Islands, Dr. Evans graduated with honors from Howard University's College of Medicine and later took an advanced degree at the University of California at Berkeley.

He served in a number of medical posts both in the United States and in the Virgin Islands, where he was Commissioner of Health (1959-1967). He was a teaching fellow in Medicine at Howard (1948-1950), a senior assistant surgeon, U.S. Public Health Service (1948-1950), and a fellow in cardiology, Johns Hopkins Hospital (1956-1957). In 1969 he was appointed governor of the Virgin Islands and served until 1971 when he was elected to that post for four years.

In 1975 he was a representative of the State Department on a lecture tour that covered Sierra Leone, Liberia, Zambia, Tanzania, and Kenya. He engaged in the private practice of medicine from 1976 to 1978 when he was elected, as a Republican, to the 96th Congress where he served on the Committee of Armed Services, the Committee on Interior and Insular Affairs, the Committee on Merchant Marine and Fisheries, and the Congressional Tourism Caucus. During his one term in Congress Evans had the distinction of being the first, and as of 1981, the only Republican member of the Congressional Black Caucus.

*Parren Mitchell fought for the underdog.*

### BARBARA JORDAN
### Eighteenth District Texas
### Elected 1973

(See biography in this section, page 449.)

### PARREN J. MITCHELL
### Seventh District Maryland
### Elected 1971

Parren J. Mitchell was born in Baltimore in 1922. He received degrees from Morgan State (B.A.) and the University of Maryland (M.S.), and then became a professor of sociology at Morgan State.

Between 1965 and 1968 Mitchell worked as executive director of the Community Action Agency in Baltimore and as executive secretary with the Maryland Commission on Interracial Problems and Relations.

Mitchell is a member of the influential Democratic Policy and Steering Committee, a group which recommends legislative policy and strategy for the Democratic Caucus in the House.

Though Mitchell's district, which is entirely within the city of Baltimore, is 74% black and overwhelmingly Democratic, his seat is far from safe. In 1972 he was challenged in the primary by black supporters of the regular Baltimore Democratic Party and nearly defeated.

Representative Mitchell's family has long been prominent in politics and civil rights causes. His brother, Clarence, is head Washington lobbyist for the NAACP and his nephew, Clarence, ran for mayor of Baltimore in 1971.

In 1976, he attached to President Carter's $4 billion Public Works Bill an amendment that compelled state, county, and municipal governments seeking federal assistance to set aside 10% of each grant to retain minority firms as contractors, subcontractors, or suppliers. This amendment has led to more than $625 million (15%) going to legitimate minority firms.

Congressman Mitchell also introduced legislation which became Public Law 95-507 in 1978 which requires proposals from federal contractors to spell out goals for awarding contracts to minority subcontractors. This law potentially provides access to billions of dollars for minority businesses.

In the 97th Congress, Parren Mitchell served as chairman of the House Small Business Committee and as whip-at-large. He is a senior member of the House Banking, Finance, and Urban Affairs Committee and a member of the Joint Economic Committee. He is also chairman of the Subcommittee on Housing, Minority Enterprise and Economic Development of the Congressional Black Caucus.

He retired from office in 1986.

### ROBERT N. C. NIX
### Second District Pennsylvania
### Elected 1958

Born in Orangeburg, South Carolina in 1905, Robert Nix moved to New York and attended Townsend Harris Hall High School, a prep school with exceptionally high academic requirements. He went on to the Lincoln University and the University of Pennsylvania Law School. Having passed his bar examination, Nix became a special deputy attorney general for Pennsylvania (Escheats Division of the State Department of Revenue) from 1934 to 1936 and later was active in local Philadelphia politics.

Nix was elected in 1958 to fill the unexpired term of Congressman Earl Chudoff, and thus became the twenty-sixth black Congressman in United States history.

A long-time liberal, Nix was one of the first Congressmen to speak out in support of the Montgomery bus boycott. He was regarded by Speaker of the House Sam Rayburn Jr. as one of the most brilliant men he had ever known.

However, in the early 1970s, militant blacks charged Nix with indifference to U.S. involvement in Vietnam and to the problems of blacks in his district. He received only 47% of the vote in the 1972 Democratic primary, winning with a plurality over three other candidates. It was obvious then that Nix was likely to encounter ever-increasing challenges from other black Congressional aspirants in the coming years.

In 1978 Congressman Nix was defeated in the Democratic primary election by William Gray, who went on to win the general election.

### ANDREW YOUNG
### Fifth District Georgia
### Elected 1973

See biography in section on black mayors.

*Black members of the U.S. Congress during Reconstruction were (left to right) Senator Hiram Revels and Representatives Benjamin Turner, Robert DeLarge, Josiah T. Walker, Jefferson Long, Joseph M. Rainey and R. Brown Elliot.*

## AFRICAN-AMERICAN CONGRESSMEN OF THE PAST

### BLANCHE K. BRUCE
**Senator from Mississippi**
**1875-1881**

Blanche K. Bruce was born a slave in Farmville, Prince Edward County, Virginia on March 1, 1841. He received his early formal education in Missouri, where his parents had moved while he was still quite young, and later studied at Oberlin College in Ohio.

In 1868, Bruce settled in Floreyville, Mississippi. He worked as a planter and eventually built up a considerable fortune in property.

In 1870, Bruce entered politics and was elected sergeant-at-arms of the Mississippi Senate. A year later he was named assessor of taxes in Bolivar County. In 1872 he served as sheriff of that county and as a member of the Board of Levee Commissioners of Mississippi.

Bruce was nominated for the U.S. Senate from Mississippi in February 1874. Once elected he became an outspoken defender of the rights of minority groups, including the Chinese and Indians. He also investigated alleged election frauds and worked for the improvement of navigation on the Mississippi in the hope of increasing interstate and foreign commerce. Like Hiram Revels, Bruce also supported legislation aimed at eliminating reprisals against those who had opposed Negro emancipation.

After Bruce completed his term in the Senate, he was named Register of the U.S. Treasury Department by President James A. Garfield. Bruce held this position until 1885. In 1889 President Benjamin Harrison appointed him recorder of deeds in Washington, D.C. Seven years later, President William McKinley reappointed him to his former Treasury Department post as register.

Bruce died on March 17, 1898.

### RICHARD H. CAIN
**South Carolina**
**1873-1875; 1877-1879**

Richard Harvey Cain was born in 1825 in Greenbriar County, Virginia of free parents. While still young, he moved north to Ohio and, like many blacks of his day, found work on steamboats servicing the nation's major waterways.

At the age of 19 Cain became a preacher in Missouri for the Methodist Episcopal Church. Soon disillusioned, he returned to Ohio where he joined the African Methodist Episcopal (AME) Church, and was given a congregation in Iowa.

In the Civil War, Cain served as a minister and also helped publish a newspaper, *The Missionary Record*. In 1868, he was elected a state senator in South Carolina. Subsequently, he served South Carolina in the U.S. Congress, where he established a reputation for clean politics.

On his retirement from public life in 1880, Cain was named AME bishop of the Louisiana and Texas conference, and became president of Paul Quinn College in Waco, Texas. He died in 1887.

### HENRY P. CHEATHAM
**North Carolina**
**1889-1893**

Henry Plummer Cheatham was born in Henderson, North Carolina in 1857. He won his B.A. and M.A. degrees from Shaw University, and later studied law, although he did not enter practice.

Cheatham first entered public life as register of deeds for Vance County, North Carolina, serving in this post from 1884 to 1888. Thereafter, he was principal of the State Normal School at Plymouth, which was later incorporated into Elizabeth City State Teachers College.

In 1888, Cheatham ran successfully as a Republican candidate for the Second Congressional District of North Carolina. He won reelection in 1890, but was defeated in his try for a third term.

In 1901, Cheatham returned to North Carolina, settling in Oxford where he became superintendent of a black orphan asylum. He helped raise money for this institution, and served its interests unstintingly until his death in 1935.

### WILLIAM L. DAWSON
**Illinois**
**1943-1971**

William L. Dawson represented the First Congressional District of Illinois for 28 years, from 1943 to 1971.

Born in Albany, Georgia in 1886, Dawson received his early education locally and later graduated magna cum laude

*Blanche K. Bruce, a spokesman for minority rights.*

*President Harry S. Truman greets Representative William Dawkins. On the left, Truman's daughter Margaret.*

from Fisk University in Nashville. Interested at first in law, Dawson studied at Kent College before joining the U.S. Expeditionary Forces in 1917 as an officer. He saw combat with the 365th Infantry in the Argonne offensive, and was wounded and gassed while on the front lines.

At the end of the war, Dawson went back to law, completing his studies at Northwestern University and opening a practice in Illinois. After nine years as an attorney, he ran unsuccessfully as a Republican candidate for Congress in 1928. A year later, while serving as Republican State Committeeman in the First Congressional District, he was called upon to manage Judge John H. Lyle's mayoralty campaign.

Dawson's first political success came in 1935, when he was elected alderman. While serving on the City Council, he crossed party lines and became an avid supporter of President Franklin D. Roosevelt. In 1940, Dawson was elected Democratic committeeman from the Second Ward. Two years later he won a seat in the House of Representatives.

In 1944, Dawson was appointed assistant chairman of the Democratic National Committee, and he soon became the first black to be elected its vice chairman. He campaigned for President Harry S. Truman, whose surprise victory over Thomas E. Dewey was later attributed, at least in part, to the black electorate. He was thus able to see to it that, for the first time, blacks were invited in more than token numbers to the Inaugural Ball, a practice which has since been taken for granted.

Dawson occupied a number of key Congressional posts. During the 81st Congress, he was chairman of the House Committee on Expenditures in the Executive Department, and later became chairman of the Committee on Government Operations—considered to be among the most important on Capitol Hill.

Dawson retired in 1971, turning his seat over to Ralph Metcalfe. He died in 1972 at the age of 86.

## ROBERT C. DeLARGE
## South Carolina
## 1871-1873

Robert C. DeLarge was born a slave in 1842 in Aiken, South Carolina. He received what was for his day and race an above-average education and, during Reconstruction, became a successful farmer. Turning to politics, he served two years in the state legislature before being elected to Congress. The election, however, was marred by serious voting irregularities, and a Congressional Commission on Elections declared the seat vacant.

In 1873, his health failing, DeLarge was appointed a magistrate in the city of Charleston, a position he held until his death one year later.

## OSCAR De PRIEST
## Illinois
## 1929-1935

Oscar De Priest was the first black to win a seat in the U.S. House of Representatives in the twentieth century, and the first to be elected from a northern state.

Born in Florence, Alabama, De Priest moved to Kansas with his family at the age of six. His formal education there consisted of business and bookkeeping classes which he completed before running away to Dayton, Ohio with two white friends. By the year 1889 he had reached Chicago and become a painter and master decorator.

In Chicago, De Priest amassed a fortune in real estate and the stock market and in 1904 entered politics successfully when he was elected Cook County commissioner. In 1908, he was appointed an alternate delegate to the Republican National Convention and in 1915 became Chicago's first black alderman.

In 1928, he was a candidate for the post of Republican committeeman for the Third Ward, and a prospective delegate to the Republican National Convention. However, Martin B. Maddew, the Republican Congressman, died suddenly and De Priest waged a successful campaign for the vacant seat.

The unofficial spokesman for the 11 million blacks in the United States during this period, De Priest faced a formidable challenge, particularly since the country was undergoing a profound political and economic transformation during the Depression years. Though sincerely desirous of improving the Negro's lot, he found himself in a difficult partisan position and obliged to shift his support from Republican to Democratic candidates on the local level. On the national level, he usually voted with his party. In 1934 he was defeated by Arthur Mitchell, the first black Democrat elected to serve in Congress.

De Priest remained active in public life, serving from 1943 to 1947 as alderman of the Third Ward in Chicago. His final withdrawal from politics came about after a sharp dispute with his own party. De Priest returned to his real estate business, and he died in 1951.

### ROBERT B. ELLIOTT
### South Carolina
### 1871-1875

Robert. B. Elliott was born in Boston, to West Indian parents, in 1842. Much of his education was received abroad—first in the grammar schools of Jamaica, later in High Holborn Academy (London), and finally at Eton, from which he graduated with honors. While in England, he also studied the law.

Upon his return to the United States, Elliott became an editor with the *Charleston Leader,* was elected to the South Carolina Constitutional Convention, and in 1868 won a seat in the lower house of the state legislature.

Subsequently, he was elected to the 42nd U.S. Congress. After serving two terms, he retired to New Orleans where he practiced law until his death on August 9, 1884.

### JEREMIAH HARALSON
### Alabama
### 1875-1877

At one time considered the most influential black in Alabama, Jeremiah Haralson was born a slave in Muscogee County, Georgia in 1846. Haralson was basically self-educated. After Emancipation, he moved to Alabama where, in 1868, he was defeated in his first attempt to win a Congressional seat.

After his election in 1874 Haralson introduced several bills, but none was passed. Accused of fraud, he was forced to submit to a runoff election. He won with a safe majority.

An ardent defender of the principle of amnesty, Haralson encountered widespread opposition from Alabama party regulars, who accused him of trying to maintain too close a relationship with Jefferson Davis, the former president of the Confederate States of America. Among his chief opponents was James T. Rapier, the black Congressman whom he succeeded.

Defeated in the 1878 and 1884 elections, Haralson spent his last days in Colorado where he was killed in a hunting mishap.

### JOHN A. HYMAN
### North Carolina
### 1875-1877

Born a slave in 1840 near Warrenton, North Carolina, John A. Hyman was sold and sent to Alabama where he was forced to remain until the end of the Civil War.

In 1868, Hyman, who was self-educated, participated in the Constitutional Convention of North Carolina. Soon thereafter he was selected to the state legislature and served there for six years. In 1875 he won a seat in Congress, but he was not reelected. He remained in Washington, D.C. in a minor post with the Revenue Service until his death in 1891.

*(left) Robert C. DeLarge, successful planter and congressman. (above) Oscar DePriest, first black elected to Congress in 20th Century.*

*John Langston, politician and diplomat.*

## JOHN MERCER LANGSTON
**Virginia**
**1889-1891**

John Mercer Langston, U.S. Congressman from Virginia, was born in Virginia in 1829 of black, Indian, and English ancestry.

Upon the death of his father, Ralph Quarles, an estate owner, young Langston was emancipated and sent to Ohio, where he was given over to the care of a friend of his father. Langston spent his childhood there, attending private school in Cincinnati before graduating from Oberlin College in 1849. Four years later, after getting his degree from the theological department of Oberlin, he studied law and was admitted to the Ohio bar in 1854.

Langston began his practice in Brownhelm, Ohio. He was chosen in 1855 to serve as clerk of this township by the Liberty Party. During the Civil War, he was a recruiting agent for Negro servicemen, helping to raise such famed regiments as the 54th and 55th Massachusetts, and the 5th Ohio.

After the war, Langston served as inspector-general of the Freedmen's Bureau and as dean and vice president of Howard University. In 1877 he was named minister resident to Haiti and charge d'affaires to Santo Domingo, remaining in diplomatic service until 1885.

Soon after his return to the United States and to his law practice, he was named president of the Virginia Normal and Collegiate Institute. In 1888, he was elected to Congress from Virginia, but was not seated for two years until vote-counting irregularities had been investigated. He was defeated in his bid for a second term. In 1894 Langston wrote an autobiography, *From the Virginia Plantation to the National Capital.* (Eleven years earlier, he had published a volume of his speeches, *Freedom and Citizenship.)*

Langston died in 1897.

## JEFFERSON F. LONG
**Georgia**
**1869-1871**

Jefferson Franklin Long was born a slave in 1836 near Knoxville, Georgia. Primarily self-educated, he moved to Macon at an early age. There, he found work with a merchant tailor and eventually saved enough money to open a shop of his own.

At the close of the Civil War, Long rapidly rose to a position of influence within the local Republican party structure. Elected to the 41st Congress, he campaigned vigorously against the spread of lynch law in Georgia, for enforcement of the Fifteenth Amendment, and for universal suffrage in the District of Columbia.

Long retired in March 1871, returning to his prosperous tailoring business. He attended the Southern Republican Convention in Chattanooga in 1874, and also served as a delegate to the Republican National Convention of 1880.

He died in Macon in 1900.

## JOHN R. LYNCH
**Mississippi**
**1873-1877; 1881-1883**

The first black to preside over a national convention of the Republican party, Mississippi Congressman John R. Lynch

*John Lynch chaired the Republican Party's National Convention in 1884.*

was elected to the House of Representatives in 1873, 1875, and 1881.

Born a slave in Louisiana in 1847, Lynch attended evening classes in Natchez, Mississippi. In 1869, he was named a justice of the peace for Adams County, and elected to the Mississippi State Legislature where he ultimately served as speaker of the House.

From 1871 to 1889—a period which encompassed his Congressional service—Lynch was chairman of the Executive Committee of the Republican party. On three occasions he was a delegate to that party's national convention, and he presided over it in 1884.

In 1889, Lynch served under Benjamin Harrison as fourth auditor of the United States Treasury, but declined this same appointment when it was offered him four years later by Grover Cleveland. In 1896, he campaigned vigorously on behalf of Presidential candidate William McKinley, who showed his gratitude by naming him U.S. paymaster during the Spanish-American War.

Lynch retired to private law practice in 1911.

During his later years, he wrote two books: *The Facts of the Reconstruction* and *Some Historical Errors of James Ford Rhodes*. He died in Chicago in 1939.

## RALPH METCALFE
## Illinois
## 1971-1978

Ralph Metcalfe was born in Atlanta in 1910 and during the 1930s was famed as an Olympic track star who broke or equaled every sprint record between 40 and 220 yards. Metcalfe served in the Army in World War II and entered politics in 1949 when he was named Athletic Commissioner of Illinois.

Between 1954 and 1970, Metcalfe served on the Chicago City Council and was generally considered a loyal supporter of Mayor Richard Daley, a factor which played a role in his nomination and election to the seat held by the late William Dawson.

However, Metcalfe's positions had started to depart from those of the city's Democratic machine. His refusal, in 1972, to support the reelection of state's attorney Edward Hanrahan forced Daley to withhold his endorsement, a factor which led to the defeat of the man widely accused of leading a "cover-up" in the 1969 death of Fred Hampton, leader of the Illinois Black Panthers. Daley and Metcalfe also collided on the issue of police behavior, an ever-present problem that exploded in 1972 when some policemen allegedly beat up two black dentists who were friends of Metcalfe.

The Illinois First is the most solidly black (89%) and solidly Democratic district in the United States. By 1974, Metcalfe was widely acknowledged as the strongest political leader in the South Side, which is the largest black ghetto in the United States. He was reelected in 1976. His career ended with his death in 1978.

## THOMAS E. MILLER
## South Carolina
## 1889-1891

Born in Ferebeeville, South Carolina on June 17, 1849, Thomas Ezekiel Miller attended public schools in Charleston and Hudson, New York, before graduating from Lincoln University. He studied law, passed the bar in 1875, and set up private practice in Beaufort.

Miller held a number of local offices before being elected state senator in 1880. After an unsuccessful campaign for the lieutenant-governorship, Miller was elected for one term to the U.S. House of Representatives. In 1895, after having been chosen a member of the South Carolina Constitutional Convention, he became president of the State Colored College of Orangeburg, South Carolina, the first such institution for the higher education of blacks in the state.

He died in Charleston just before his eighty-ninth birthday, in 1938.

## ARTHUR W. MITCHELL
## Illinois
## 1934-1942

The 1934 victory of Arthur W. Mitchell, the first black Democrat ever elected to serve in Congress, was the first major shift in black voting sentiment in the United States since the days of Reconstruction. Conversely, Oscar De Priest, the man he defeated, was the last black Republican to serve in the House.

*Arthur W. Mitchell was the first black Democrat elected to the U.S. Congress.*

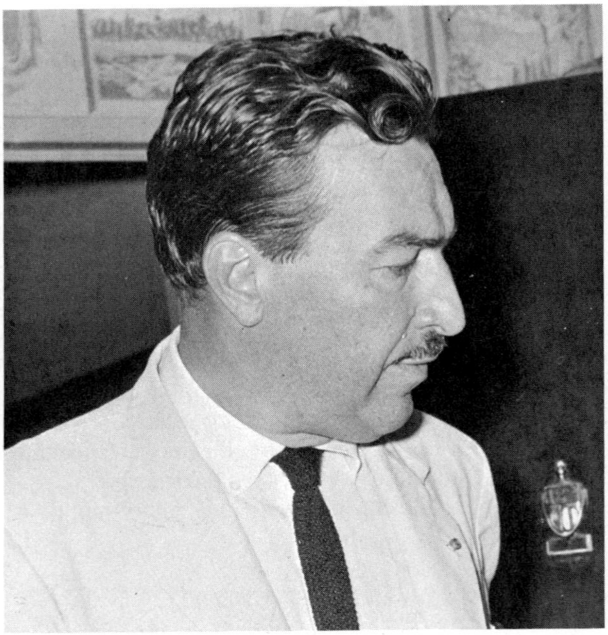

*Adam Clayton Powell Jr., eloquent, flamboyant, controversial—a legend in his own life time.*

Born to slave parents in 1883 in Chambers County, Alabama, Mitchell was educated at Tuskegee Institute and at Columbia and Harvard universities. By 1929, he had founded Armstrong Agricultural School in West Butler, Alabama, and become a wealthy landowner and a lawyer with a thriving practice in Washington, D.C. When he left the nation's capital that year, it was with the avowed purpose of entering politics and becoming a representative from Illinois.

Mitchell won Democratic approval only after Harry Baker (who had defeated him in the primary) died suddenly, leaving the nomination vacant. Aided by the overwhelming national sentiment for the Democratic party during this period, he unseated Oscar De Priest by the slender margin of 3,000 votes.

Mitchell's most significant victory on behalf of civil rights came, not in the legislative chamber, but in the courts. In 1937, Mitchell brought suit against the Chicago and Rock Island Railroad after having been forced to leave his first-class accommodations en route to Hot Springs, Arkansas, and sit in a "Jim Crow" car. He argued his own case before the Supreme Court in 1941, and won a decision which declared "Jim Crow" practices illegal.

A year later Mitchell retired from Congress and settled on his estate near Petersburg, Virginia, where he died in 1968 at the age of 85.

## GEORGE WASHINGTON MURRAY
### South Carolina
### 1893-1897

Long an advocate of free silver and a supporter of stronger federal election laws, George Washington Murray was born a slave in Rembert, South Carolina in 1853. He was left an orphan at Emancipation. Nonetheless, he acquired a substantial education, highlighted by his completion of two years of study at South Carolina University.

A teacher for some 14 years, Murray was chosen Republican party chairman for Sumter County in 1888. President Benjamin Harrison subsequently appointed him Customs Inspector for the port of Charleston. In 1893, he narrowly won a seat in Congress in a disputed election.

An exponent of industrial education, Murray sought to use his office in the promotion of better schooling opportunities for blacks in the South. He also induced Congress to print a list of those inventions which had been patented by blacks, neglecting to mention the fact that eight of these were for his own agricultural implements.

In 1895, Murray was given a leave of absence from his congressional duties for business and health reasons. A year later he was returned to the 54th Congress, this time by a margin of 2,000 votes.

Murray's political aspirations were dashed when he led a faction of dissident blacks in what proved to be an unsuccessful breakaway from the Republican ranks. Returning to Sumter County in 1897, he began a new career in real estate. He died in Chicago in 1926.

## CHARLES E. NASH
### Louisiana
### 1875-1877

Born in 1844 in Louisiana, Charles Edmund Nash earned his living as a bricklayer until his enlistment in the Union Army in 1863. A member of the famed *Chasseurs d'Afrique*, Nash lost a leg during the storming of Fort Blakely. After his discharge as a sergeant-major, he was named U.S. Inspector of Customs for his native state.

Elected to the 44th Congress, Nash failed in his bid for reelection. He thereupon became postmaster of a small Louisiana town. Soon after his retirement from this post he moved to New Orleans, where he died in 1913.

## JAMES E. O'HARA
### North Carolina
### 1883-1887

Born in New York City in 1844, James E. O'Hara first came to public office as an engrossing clerk for the North Carolina constitutional convention, then served a single term in the state legislature before going on to study law at Howard University. Admitted to the bar in 1873, he became one of six black delegates to the state constitutional convention two years later.

O'Hara first ran for Congress in 1878, but the seat was awarded to his adversary, William Hodges Kitchin. In 1882, however, he was successful—winning by a substantial majority.

Like most other black Reconstruction Congressmen, O'Hara placed the civil rights issue in the forefront of his legislative program. He managed to attach a rider to an interstate commerce bill, thereby sponsoring an amendment which guaranteed to all citizens equal accommodations. He also appended an anti-discrimination clause to the Pension Appropriation Bill. In 1884, O'Hara was renominated for his congressional post and won by a margin of 6,700 votes. However, O'Hara lost his bid for a third term, largely due to party dissension and the resurgence of the Democratic vote. Withdrawing from politics, he practiced law in New Bern, North Carolina, where he died in 1905.

### ADAM CLAYTON POWELL JR.
### New York
### 1945-1971

Adam Clayton Powell Jr. was a legend in his lifetime and one of the most controversial figures ever to grace American politics.

Born in 1908 to Mattie Fletcher and Adam Clayton Powell Sr., Adam Jr. was bred in New York City, attended high school there, and then went to Colgate University.

The young Powell launched his career as a crusader for reform during the depth of the Depression. He forced several large corporations to drop their unofficial bans on employing blacks and directed a kitchen and relief operation which fed, clothed, and provided fuel for thousands of Harlem's needy and destitute. He was instrumental in persuading officials of Harlem Hospital to integrate their medical and nursing staffs, helped many blacks find employment along Harlem's "main stem," 125th Street, and campaigned against the city's bus lines, which were discriminating against Negro drivers and mechanics.

When Powell Sr. retired from Abyssinian Baptist Church in 1937, his son, who had already served as manager and assistant pastor there, was named his successor.

In 1939, Powell served as chairman of the Coordinating Committee on Employment, which organized a picket line before the executive offices of the World's Fair in the Empire State Building and eventually succeeded in getting employment at the fair for hundreds of blacks.

Powell also sought better hospital, housing, and educational facilities for blacks.

Powell won a seat on the New York City Council in 1941 with the third highest number of votes ever cast for a candidate in municipal elections. In 1942, he turned to journalism for a second time (he had already been on the staff of the New York *Evening Post* in 1934), and published and edited the weekly *People's Voice,* which he called "the largest Negro tabloid in the world."

In 1945 Powell went to Washington, D.C. as the sole congressional representative of a community of 300,000, 89% of whom were black. Identified at once as "Mr. Civil Rights," he encountered a host of discriminatory procedures. He could not rent a room in downtown Washington, nor could he attend a movie in which his famed wife Hazel Scott had been starred. Within Congress itself, he was not authorized to use such communal facilities as dining rooms, steam baths, showers, and barber shops. Powell met these rebuffs head on by making use of all such facilities and insisting that his entire staff follow his lead.

As a freshman legislator, Powell engaged in fiery debates with arch-segregationists, fought for the abolition of discriminatory practices at U.S. military installations, and sought—through the controversial Powell amendment—to deny federal funds to any project where discrimination existed. (This amendment eventually became part of the Flanagan School Lunch Bill, making Powell the first black Congressman since Reconstruction to have legislation passed by both houses.)

Powell also sponsored legislation advocating federal aid to education, a minimum-wage scale, and greater benefits for the hard-core unemployed. He also drew attention to certain long-overlooked discriminatory practices on Capitol Hill itself, and in effecting their immediate elimination. It was Powell who first demanded that a Negro journalist be allowed to sit in the Senate and House press galleries, who introduced the first Jim Crow transportation legislation, and the first bill to prohibit segregation in the Armed Forces. At one point in his career, the *Congressional Record* reported that the House Committee on Education and Labor had processed more important legislation than any other major committee. In 1960, Powell, as senior member of this committee, became its chairman. He had a hand in the development and passage of such significant legislation as the Minimum Wage Bill of 1961, the Manpower Development and Training Act, the Anti-Poverty Bill, the Juvenile Delinquency Act, the Vocational Educational Act, and the National Defense Education Act. (In all, the Powell committee helped pass 48 laws involving a total outlay of 14 billion dollars.)

Powell also displayed considerable foresight in the cause of civil rights when he became the first Northerner of any race to endorse Lyndon Johnson for the presidency.

The flamboyant congressman, however, was accused of putting an excessive number of friends on the congressional payroll, of a high rate of absenteeism from congressional votes, and of excessive zeal for the "playboy's" life.

In 1967 the controversies and irregularities surrounding him led to censure in the House and a vote to exclude him from his seat in the 90th Congress. The House based its decision on the allegation that he had misused public funds and was in contempt of the New York courts due to a lengthy and involved defamation case which had resulted in a trial for civil and criminal contempt. Despite his exclusion, Powell was readmitted to the 91st Congress in 1968. In mid-1969, the Supreme Court ruled that the House had violated the Constitution by excluding him from membership, but left open the questions of his loss of 22 years seniority and the chairmanship of the Education and Labor Committee. Also unresolved were the $25,000 fine levied against him and the matter of back pay.

However, rather than return to Congress, Powell spent most of his time on the West Indian island of Bimini, where process servers could not reach him. But photographers did and the ensuing photos of Powell taking the sun on his boat while crucial votes were taken in Congress began to affect Powell in his home district. In 1970, he lost the Democratic primary and his seat to Charles Rangel by 150 votes. Powell's support had dwindled substantially, but it was a tribute to his popularity and achievement that Rangel required a majority of some 1,500 white voters in the district to defeat him. Powell then retired officially to Bimini, and on April 4, 1972, he died in Miami.

The controversy over Powell continues to rage after his death, and tends to follow racial lines. White supporters of the black cause praise his early achievements but feel that he was too difficult to work with. However, many blacks of all shades of the political spectrum defend him and many exult in the memory of his facility for defying the proprieties of the white establishment.

## JOSEPH H. RAINEY
## South Carolina
## 1869-1879

Joseph H. Rainey, the first black member of the House of Representatives, was born in 1832 in Georgetown, South Carolina. Drafted to work on Confederate fortifications in Charleston harbor during the Civil War, Rainey escaped to the West Indies and did not return until the close of the war in 1865.

In 1868, Rainey was elected as a delegate to the state constitutional convention and came to occupy a seat in the State Senate. A year later, he was elected to the House of Representatives, remaining in office until 1879.

In Congress, Rainey presented some 10 petitions for a civil rights bill which would have guaranteed blacks full constitutional rights and equal access to public accommodations. On one occasion, Rainey dramatized the latter issue by refusing to leave the dining room of a hotel in Suffolk, Virginia and by allowing himself to be forcibly ejected from the premises.

Rainey advocated passage of a bill to establish an American steamship line between the United States and Haiti, supported the rights of the Chinese minority in California, and became the first black to preside over the House of Representatives during a public debate—in this case, on a proposed bill to improve conditions on Indian reservations.

Upon his retirement from politics, Rainey was appointed a special agent for the U.S. Treasury Department in Washington, D.C. He served until 1881, after which he pursued banking and brokerage interests there.

In 1886 he returned to Georgetown, where he died in 1887.

## ALONZO J. RANSIER
## South Carolina
## 1873-1875

Born free in Charleston, South Carolina in 1834, Alonzo J. Ransier received a rudimentary education, and during his youth, worked as a shipping clerk. After serving as registrar of elections in 1865, Ransier attended South Carolina's first Republican convention the following year, and was commissioned to dispatch a memorandum to the U.S. Congress seeking federal protection for blacks.

In 1868, Ransier participated again in the South Carolina convention as a presidential elector and as chairman of the State Executive Committee. Two years later he was elected lieutenant governor of South Carolina, by a 33,000-vote plurality.

In Congress, Ransier became a key figure in the controversy over a "full and complete" civil rights bill. In addition, he advocated the extension of the presidential term to a period of six years, voted for the national tariff and against a salary increase for federal officials, and sought funds for the improvement of Charleston harbor.

Ransier failed to gain his party's nomination for a second term, returned to Charleston, and eventually became a day laborer for the city government. He died in 1882.

## JAMES T. RAPIER
## Alabama
## 1873-1875

Active in both the fields of politics and of labor, James T. Rapier was born in Florence, Alabama in 1837. Rapier's father, a successful planter, engaged a private tutor to educate his son, who later studied at Montreal College in Canada, the University of Glasgow in Scotland, and Franklin College in Nashville, Tennessee. Although reputedly trained as a lawyer, he never practiced.

In 1870, Rapier (by then a successful cotton planter) ran unsuccessfully as a candidate for secretary of state in Alabama.

Rapier later went to Montgomery as one of an enterprising group of reformers who sought to rewrite the state constitution so as to include provisions for universal suffrage and free public schooling. He then helped to form Alabama's first Republican party, and served as its vice-president before turning his attention to the field of labor. Urging urban workers and rural share-croppers to organize, Rapier was a key force in setting up Alabama's first black labor convention.

In 1872 Rapier won election to Congress by some 3,000 votes, and went to Washington where he worked for the passage of the 1875 Civil Rights Act.

Rapier's congressional career ended with the rapid rise of the Ku Klux Klan and the ascension to power of a Democratic bloc which came to control Alabama's politics. He died in Montgomery in 1882.

## HIRAM RHOADES REVELS
## Senator from Mississippi
## 1870-1871

Hiram Rhoades Revels, a native of North Carolina, was the first black to serve in the U.S. Senate. Revels was elected from his adopted state of Mississippi, and served for approximately one year, from February 1870 to March 1871.

Born in 1822, Revels was educated in Indiana and attended Knox College in Illinois. Ordained a minister in the African Methodist Church, he worked among black settlers in the Northwest Territory, and in the border states of Kentucky and Missouri before settling in Baltimore. There he served as a church pastor and school principal.

During the Civil War, Revels helped organize a pair of Negro regiments in Maryland, and in 1863 he went to St. Louis to establish a freedmen school and to carry on his work as a recruiter. For a year he served as chaplain of a Missis-

*A cartoon showing Senator Revels occupying Jefferson Davis's former seat. (right-rear) Rep. Robert Smalls was a crewman on the Confederate gunboat Planter.*

sippi regiment before becoming provost Marshall of Vicksburg.

Revels settled in Natchez at the end of the war, and was appointed alderman by the Union military governor of the state. He won the respect of his constituents for his alert grasp of important state issues and for his courageous support of legislation which would have restored voting and office-holding privileges to disenfranchised Southerners.

After leaving the senate, Revels was named president of Alcorn University near Lorman, Mississippi. In 1876 he became editor of the *South-Western Christian Advocate,* a religious journal.

Revels lived in Holly Springs during his last years, remaining active in religious work until his death on January 16, 1901.

### ROBERT SMALLS
### South Carolina
### 1875-1879;1881-1887

Robert Smalls of South Carolina served a longer period in Congress than any other black Reconstruction congressman. Born a slave in Beaufort, South Carolina in 1839, Smalls received a limited education before moving to Charleston with the family of his owner.

At the outbreak of the Civil War, Smalls became a Confederate member of the crew of the *Planter,* a transport steamer.

On the morning of May 13, 1862, Smalls smuggled his wife and three children on board, assumed command of the vessel, and sailed it into the hands of the Union squadron blockading Charleston harbor. Single-handedly, he was thus responsible for the freedom of his own family and for that of the 12 black crewmen.

His daring exploit led President Lincoln to name him a pilot in the Union Navy. He was also awarded a large sum of money for what constituted the delivery of war booty.

In December 1863, during the siege of Charleston, Smalls took command of the *Planter* and sailed it to safety—a feat for which he was promoted to captain, the only black to hold such a rank during the Civil War.

After the war, Smalls was elected to the South Carolina State Senate, serving there from 1868 to 1870. In 1875 he began a period of congressional service which was interrupted only by his defeat in the 1878 election. Smalls attributed his defeat to vote-counting irregularities at the polls; however, it is possible that an accusation made a year earlier to the effect that he had accepted a $5,000 bribe while a state senator had diminished his popularity. (Convicted at first, Smalls was eventually exonerated by Governor William Dunlap Simpson of South Carolina.)

An outstanding congressman, Smalls consistently supported a wide variety of progressive legislation, including a bill to provide equal accommodations for blacks in interstate travel and an amendment designed to safeguard the rights of children born of interracial marriages.

Beyond politics, Smalls showed an active interest in military affairs, serving from 1865 to 1877 as an officer in the South Carolina State Militia, where he rose to the rank of major-general.

Smalls died in 1916.

### BENJAMIN S. TURNER
### Alabama
### 1871-1873

Born a slave in 1825 in Halifax, North Carolina, Benjamin S. Turner was taken at an early age to Alabama where he was emancipated and then given the rudiments of a private education. As a young man, he served as tax collector of Dallas County and councilman in Salem before becoming a prosperous livery stable owner.

In September of 1870, having manifested a growing interest in politics, he was unanimously nominated by the Republican party for the Congressional seat from the 1st District of Selma, Alabama.

Although renominated in 1872, Turner was the victim of a split within his own party, which led to his defeat and eventual abandonment of politics.

He returned to his home in Alabama and resumed his former business activities. He died in 1894.

### JOSIAH T. WALLS
### Florida
### 1871-1877

The only black congressman from Florida, Josiah T. Walls was born free in Winchester, Virginia in 1842, received his early education in Florida, and was a successful farmer when the Civil War broke out.

Drafted into the Confederate Army, he served in an artillery battery until he was taken prisoner by Union forces. He joined the Northern army, and by the end of hostilities, had risen to the rank of sergeant-major.

Walls then returned to Florida and served a term as a member of the Florida legislature.

Elected to the U.S. Congress in 1871, he represented the state during the next five years, although his tenure was interrupted because of a contested election and the opposition of the governor.

As a congressman, Walls favored granting military support to insurgent Cubans in their revolt against Spain, which had introduced African slaves on the island's sugar and tobacco plantations, and had treated the original Indian inhabitants with great brutality.

His congressional career ended, Walls returned to life as a planter, although he remained in politics through his staunch advocacy of Rutherford B. Hayes for the presidency. When a severe frost one year almost ruined him financially, he accepted the post of superintendent of a farm on the campus of Tallahassee State College, remaining there until his death in 1905.

### HAROLD WASHINGTON
### First District Illinois
### Elected 1980

Harold Washington, a Democrat, was elected to Congress in 1980. As a freshman he became a member of the Committee on Education and Labor where he was the eighteenth ranking member; the Judiciary Committee where he ranked fourteenth; and the Committee on Government Operations where he ranked twenty-first. He also served on the Judiciary Subcommittee on Civic and Constitutional Rights, which had jurisdiction over the important Voting Rights Act that expired in August 1982, and the Subcommittee on Manpower and Housing. Congressman Washington served as secretary of the Congressional Black Caucus.

In addition to his committee assignments, Washington was a member of the Northeast-Midwest Congressional Coalition's Auto Task Force and the Congressional Steel Caucus. He also served on the Executive Board of the Federal Government Service Task Force.

After graduating from Northwestern University School of Law in 1952, Harold Washington was a practicing attorney until his appointment in 1954 as assistant city prosecutor for Chicago. He served for five years as arbitrator for the Illinois Industrial Commission, and in 1965 was elected to the Illinois House of Representatives where he served Chicago's 26th District until his election to the Illinois senate in 1977.

Washington was the founder and president of the Black Taxpayers Federation. He was also a member of the Boards of Directors of the Suburban Southern Christian Leadership Conference and the Mid-South Mental Health Association.

Representative Washington was a member of the Cook County, Illinois and National Bar Associations.

Washington left the house to run for mayor of Chicago Ill. and was elected. He died suddenly while mayor in 1987.

### GEORGE H. WHITE
### North Carolina
### 1897-1901

The last black congressman in the aftermath of Reconstruction, George H. White was born in Rosedale, North Carolina in 1852. After graduating from Howard in 1877, he taught school in his native state and studied law. Licensed in 1879 to practice in all state courts, he proved to be a brilliant lawyer, winning several cases against the best of his white colleagues.

In 1880 White entered politics—first as a member of the North Carolina House of Representatives, and four years later, as state senator. At the end of his two-year term, he was chosen state solicitor for the Second Judicial District.

While in Congress, White championed the cause of constitutional liberties and was particularly outspoken in denouncing lynching and mob law.

Once out of politics, White turned his energies to the establishment of an all-black residential community, eventually known as Whitesboro—after its founder—near Cape May in New Jersey. He later retired to law practice in Philadelphia where he died on December 28, 1918.

## BLACK MEMBERS OF CONGRESS—1870 TO 1989

The following list is that of all African-Americans who have served in the United States Senate or in the House of Representatives since blacks were able to achieve election to such office:

### SENATE

| | |
|---|---|
| Hiram R. Revel (R-Miss.) | 1870-1871 |
| Blanche K. Bruce (R-Miss.) | 1875-1881 |
| Edward W. Brooke (R-Mass.) | 1967-1979 |

### HOUSE OF REPRESENTATIVES

| | |
|---|---|
| Joseph H. Rainey (R-S.C.) | 1870-1879 |
| Jefferson F. Long (R-Ga.) | 1870-1871 |
| Robert B. Elliott (R-S.C.) | 1871-1874 |
| Robert C. DeLarge (R-S.C.) | 1871-1873 |
| Benjamin S. Tumer (R-Ala.) | 1871-1873 |
| Josiah T. Walls (R-Fla.) | 1871-1873 |
| Richard H. Cane (R-S.C.) | 1873-1875; 1877-1879 |
| John R. Lynch (R-Miss.) | 1873-1877; 1882-1883 |
| James T. Rapier (R-Ala.) | 1873-1875 |
| Alonzo J. Ransier (R-S.C.) | 1873-1875 |
| Jeremiah Haralson (R-Ala.) | 1875-1877 |
| John A. Hyman (R-N.C.) | 1875-1877 |
| Charles E. Nash (R. La.)1875-1877 | |
| Robert Smalls (R-S.C.) | 1875-1879 |
| James E. O' Hara (R-N.C.) | 1883-1887 |
| Henry P. Cheatharn (R-N.C.) | 1889-1893 |
| John M. Langston (R-Va.) | 1890-1891 |
| Thomas E. Miller (R-S.C.) | 1890-1891 |
| George W. Murray (R-S.C.) | 1893-1895; 1896-1897 |
| George W. White (R-N.C.) | 1897-1901 |
| Oscar DePriest (R-Ill.) | 1929-1935 |
| Arthur W. Mitchell (D-Ill.) | 1935-1943 |
| William L. Dawson (D-Ill.) | 1943-1970 |
| Adam C. Powell Jr. (D-N.Y.) | 1945-1967; 1969-1971 |
| Charles C. Diggs Jr. (D-Mich.) | 1955-80 |
| Robert N. C. Nix (D-Pa.) | 1958-78 |
| Augustus F. Hawkins (D-Calif.) | 1963- |
| John Conyers Jr. (D-Mich.) | 1965- |
| William L. Clay (D-Mo.) | 1969- |
| Louis Stokes (D-Ohio) | 1969- |
| Shirley Chisholm (D-N.Y.) | 1969-82 |
| George W. Collins (D-m.) | 1970-72 |
| Ronald V. Dellums (D-Calif.) | 1971- |
| Ralph H. Metcalfe (D-Ill.) | 1971-78 |
| Parren H. Mitchell (D-Md.) | 1971- |
| Charles B. Rangel (D-N.Y.) | 1971- |
| Walter E. Fauntroy (D-D.C.) | Del 1971- |
| Yvorme B. Burke (D-Calif.) | 1973-79 |
| Cardiss Collins (D-Ill.) | 1973- |
| Barbara C. Jordan (D-Tex.) | 1973-78 |
| Andrew Young (D-Ga.) | 1973-77 |
| Harold E. Ford (D-Term.) | 1975- |
| Julian C. Dixon (D-Calif.) | 1979- |
| William H. Gray (D-Pa.) | 1979- |
| Mickey Leland (D-Tex.) | 1979- |
| Melvin Evans (R-V.I.) Del | 1978-80 |
| Bennett McVey Steward (D-Ill.) | 1979-80 |
| George W. Crockete (D-Mich.) | 1980- |
| Mervyn M. Dymally(D-Calif.) | 1981- |
| Gus Savage (D-Ill.) | 1981- |
| Harold Washington (D-Ill.) | 1981-83 |
| Katie Hall (D-Ind.) | 1982-84 |
| Major Owens (D-N.Y.) | 1983- |
| Edolphus Towns (D-N.Y.) | 1983- |
| Alan Wheat (D-Mo) | 1983- |
| Charles Hayes (D-Ill.) | 1983- |
| Alton R. Waldon Jr. ( -N.Y.) | 1986- |
| Mike Espy (D-Miss.) | 1987- |
| Floyd Flake (D-N.Y.) | 1987- |
| John Lewis (D-Ga.) | 1987- |
| Kweisi Mfume (D-Md.) | 1987- |
| Donald M. Payne (D-NJ) | 1988- |

*Freedmen learning of their political rights.*

## BLACK ELECTED OFFICEHOLDERS AT THE STATE LEVEL

As of March 1989, 413 blacks occupied elected office at the state level. Of the 413, 308 were state representatives, 98 were state senators, and 7 held statewide office.The 413 state legislators held office in 43 states and the Virgin Islands. They comprise 5.5% of the 7,466 state legislators in the United States, a low figure when compared to the proportion of blacks who are eligible to vote, but more impressive than the total of blacks who occupy statewide elected office. The number of black state representatives has been growing slowly but steadily over the years. In 1982, 4.2% of state representatives were black while in 1971 only 2.2% were black.

At the statewide level, as of March 1989 blacks had not made any gains since 1981, and most who have made a run for state office have been turned back, the most notable exception being Lt. Governor L. Douglas Wilder (R) of Virginia who is seriously poised to become not only the first black governor in U.S. history but a governor in one of the states of the old confederacy.

In 1989, Illinois had the most black state senators with 7 , followed by Georgia with 6 and Alabama , Louisiana, Maryland with 5. Of the 50 states 36 had one or more state senators. Georgia had the most state representatives with 22, followed by Maryland and Mississippi with 21 and 20 respectively. Forty states, including Alaska, had at least one black state representative.

As of March 1989 there were seven blacks in administrative statewide office: Roland Burris, comptroller of Illinois; James Lewis, state treasurer of New Mexico; Richard Austin, secretary of state in Michigan; Alexander Farrelly, governor of the Virgin Islands; Derek Hodge, lieutenant governor of the Virgin Islands; Francisco Borges, treasurer of Connecticut; and L. Douglas Wilder , Lt. Governor of Virginia.

In 1980 the first black was elected to the Minnesota legislature, Randy Staten, and the first black woman to the Connecticut legislature, Carrie Perry.

Following are brief biographies of black statewide executives and a listing of blacks holding state administrative office as of June 1989.

### Elected State Officials

#### RICHARD H. AUSTIN
#### Secretary of State, Michigan
#### Elected 1970

Richard Austin began his four-year term as head of the Department of State in 1971, after winning statewide election by more than 300,000 votes. He succeeded James M. Hare, who had been secretary of state for 16 years. A Democrat, Austin had served as Wayne County auditor since his election to that post by more than 200,000 in 1966. He had also served as a delegate to Michigan's Constitutional Convention.

Austin was born in Alabama in 1913. His family moved to Pennsylvania in 1917. His father died in 1924 and his mother moved the family to Detroit the following year.

Austin worked while attending school to help his mother support the family, which included two brothers. His scholastic achievements and status as a track star won him a scholarship to Wayne University. However, family circumstances forced Austin to abandon the scholarship. Instead he sold and shined shoes and kept books in a shoe store while studying accounting at the Detroit Institute of Technology at night.

In 1941, Austin became Michigan's first black certified public accountant. He started his own accounting firm and over the years helped organize a number of other businesses, philanthropic foundations, and civic organizations, and has published articles on taxation and legislative apportionment.

Austin ran for mayor of Detroit in 1969. He led the field in the primary but lost the runoff by 6,000 votes, in a racially polarized election, to Roman Gribbs, Wayne County sheriff.

As secretary of state, Austin heads a department of 2,400 employees and over 250 branch offices who serve Michigan residents through the issuance of driver licenses and overseeing elections. In addition, Austin is keeper of the Great Seal and official records and archives of state government.

The secretary of state is the second in line of succession as governor of Michigan.

*State Treasurer of Connecticut, Francisco L. Borges.*

*Comptroller Roland Burris of Illinois.*

**FRANCISCO L. BORGES**
**State Treasure, Connecticut**
**Elected 1986**

Francisco L. (Frank) Borges was raised in New Haven, Connecticut, where he attended public schools. A graduate of the Millbrook School in Millbrook, New York, he received his Bachelor of Arts in Political Science from Trinity College in 1974 and his J.D. degree from the University of Connecticut School of Law in 1978.

Formerly an Associate Counsel with the Travelers Corporation in Hartford, Mr. Borges was elected city-wide to Hartford's Court of Common Council in 1981, where he distinguished himself as chairman of the Planning, Development and Zoning Committee and as a member of the Operations, Management and Budget Committee.

He was reelected in 1983 and served as Deputy Mayor of Hartford through 1985.

Mr. Borges was elected State Treasurer in November, 1986, and was sworn in as the state's 78th Treasurer on January 7, 1987.

An active member of the community, Mr. Borges serves on several state boards, commissions and committees, including the Banking, State Bond, and Finance Advisory commissions, the Connecticut Housing Finance Authority, the Connecticut Housing Authority, the Connecticut Development Authority, the Investment Advisory Council and the Family College Savings Plan Advisory Committee. He also serves as chairman of the Bridgeport Financial Review Board.

He is chairperson of Connecticut's Martin Luther King Jr. Holiday Commission and the Connecticut Coalition of Conscience, and in 1988 was chairman of the Government Division of the United Way/Combined Health Appeal's annual drive. In addition, Mr. Borges is a member of the Board of Trustees of the Museum of Art, Science and Industry in Bridgeport and of Trinity College and the Hartford Graduate Center, and serves on the Board of Regents of the University of Hartford.

Mr. Borges lives with his family in Hartford.

**ROLAND W. BURRIS**
**Comptroller, State of Illinois**
**Elected 1986**

A native of Centralia, Illinois, Roland W. Burris was born August 3, 1937. He received his B.A. degree in sociology from Illinois University and did postgraduate work at the University of Hamburg in Germany. Burris earned his law degree from Howard University in 1963. He has held various positions ranging from tax accountant to second vice president of Continental Illinois National Bank and Trust Company. In 1974 he was named one of ten outstanding business people, and in 1979 was one of the 100 most influential blacks in America compiled by Ebony magazine. In 1980 Burris received the Outstanding Alumnus Award from Howard University Law School alumni association.

**ALEXANDER A. FARRELY**
**Governor, U. S. Virgin Islands**
**Elected 1987**

Governor Alexander A. Farrelly, born on St. Croix., U. S. Virgin Islands December 29, 1923, attended St. Patrick's Parochial School. After he graduated from high school, he entered the U.S. Army attaining the rank of sergeant before his honorable discharge in 1946.

He graduated from St. John's College in New York City in 1951 with a Bachelor of Arts degree in History and Government and from St. John's University Law School with a Bachelor of Laws degree in 1954. In 1960, Farrelly entered Yale Law School and received his Masters of Laws degree. In 1962, was appointed by the U.S. Attorney General as Assistant U.S. Attorney for the District of the Virgin Islands.

In 1965, Farrelly became a judge of the Municipal Court of the Virgin Islands and in 1966 ran as a democrat and was elected Senator to the Seventh Legislature of the Virgin Islands. He was re-elected and served in the Eighth Legislature.

Farrelly is the first elected democrat to serve as Governor in the history of the U.S. Virgin Islands.

Farrelly, a widower with three children, is a devout Catholic and a member of the Holy Family Church where he is both a lay reader and president of the parish council.

**DEREK M. HODGE**
**Lieutenant Governor, U. S. Virgin Islands**
**Elected 1987**

Derek M. Hodge was born in Frederiksted, St. Croix, United States Virgin Islands, on October 5, 1941, and received both his elementary and secondary education at public schools in St. Croix. He attended Colegio San Justo in Puerto Rico (becoming fluent in Spanish), and Michigan State University, where he earned a Bachelor of Arts degree in Political Science.

In the early 1960s, Hodge was a teacher and instructor, first at Brooklyn College in New York City, then at the Elena Christian Junior High School and at the St. Thomas campus of the University of the Virgin Islands.

Later, Derek Hodge enrolled in the Georgetown University Law Center in Washington, D.C., from which he received his Juris Doctor degree in 1971. Following his graduation from law school, Hodge served as a law clerk to the former Judge of the District Court of the Virgin Islands, the Honorable Warren H. Young. Hodge was elected as the St. Croix District chairman of the Democratic Party and was the Party's unsuccessful candidate for governor in the 1982 elections.

In 1984, he was elected to the 16th Legislature and served as Senate President. In addition to his duties as President, Hodge was a member of the Legislature's standing committees on Conservation, Recreation & Cultural Affairs; Rules & Nominations; and Trade, Tourism & Industry.

Elected Lieutenant Governor of the Virgin Islands in November 1986 on a Democratic ticket and sworn into office on January 5, 1987.

His activities outside of law and politics include the V.I. National Guard, where he attained the rank of Captains Partners for Health, St. Croix, of which he is a past president; Chairman of the Board of St. Dunstan's Episcopal School; Rotary International; Boy Scout; and Little League.

Derek M. Hodge is married to the former Beatrice Neives, and is the father of two children.

## JAMES B. LEWIS
## State Treasurer of New Mexico
## Elected 1984

James B. Lewis was appointed New Mexico State Treasurer in December, 1985. In the following year, he was elected to a full term as Treasurer. He received 210,351 votes, more than any other opposed candidate, including the governor.

Lewis was born November 30, 1947 in Roswelll, New Mexico. He attended public school in Roswell, Albuquerque and Gallup New Mexico and went on to receive a B.S. degree in Education from Bishop College in Dallas, Texas in 1970. He served in the U.S. Army as a military policeman from 1970-1972. He then went on to hold such positions as Director of Administration for Public Service Careers for Barnalillo County; Consumer Advocate for Consumer Affairs Division; Investigator with White Collar Crime Section; and Director of Purchasing Division of the District Attorney's Office (Second Judicial District).

Lewis received an M.A. in Public Administration from the University of New Mexico in 1977 and a B.S. in Administration from the National Business College in Albuquerque in 1981.

In 1982, he was elected Bernalillo County Treasurer and was reelected to that position in 1984, receiving the greatest number of votes on the County Democratic ticket.

Lewis is a member of the National State Treasurer's Association as well as numerous other professional and civic organizations and was a nominee for National Outstanding Treasurers Award.

*Lt. Governor Lawrence Wilder of Virginia.*

## LAWRENCE DOUGLAS WILDER
## Lieutenant Governor Commonwealth of Virginia
## Elected 1985

Lawrence Wilder was elected Lieutenant Governor in November, 1985, the highest ranking elected black state official in the country and then made the decision four years later to run for governor of the state.

Born in Richmond, Wilder attended Virginia Union University where he received B.S. degree, and then a Juris Doctor degree from the Howard University Law School.

In 1969, he was elected the first black legislator to serve in the Virginia State Senate since Reconstruction. He was chairman of the Democratic Steering Committee and chairman of the Privileges and Elections, Transportation and Rehabilitation and Social Services Committees. After serving in the state senate for 15 years, Wilder's 1985 election victory was a surprise to many.

As a 58-year-old candidate for governor, Wilder was given an even chance of being a strong contender in the historic contest.

## ROSTER OF STATE LEGISLATORS

(With thanks to the Joint Center for Political Studies, Mr. Eddie Williams and Dr. Milton Morris, for this Roster and for their kind and considerate assistance in providing material for the entire scope of this section on the black voter.)

### ALABAMA

#### State Senators

**FIGURES, Michael A.**
Senator Dist. 33
2317 St. Stephens Rd.
Mobile, AL 36617

**HILLIARD, EarL F.**
Senator Dist. 20
1614 3rd Ave. N
Birmingham, AL 35203

**HORN, William Fred**
Senator Dist. 18
333 16th Ave. SW
Birmingham, AL 35211

**LANGFORD, Charles**
Senator Dist. 26
918 E. Grove St.
Montgomery, AL 36104

**SANDERS, Hank**
Senator Dist. 23
PO Box 1305
Selma, AL 36701

#### Representatives

**BLACK, Lucius Sr.**
Representative Dist. 67
PO Box 284
York, AL 36925

**BRYANT, Jenkins Jr.**
Representative Dist. 68
Rt. 1 Box 482
Newbern, AL 36765

**BUSKEY, James E**
Representative Dist. 99
2207 Barretts Lane
Mobile, AL 36617

**BUSKEY, John L**
Representative Dist. 77
1633 Robert C. Hatch Dr.
Montgomery, AL 36106

**CLARK, William**
Representative Dist. 98
711 S. Atmore Ave.
Prichard, AL 36611

**DAVIS, Pat**
Representative Dist. 58
9312 Sears Dr.
Birmingham, AL 35206

**ESCOTT, Sundra**
Representative Dist. 60
PO Box 8172
Birmingham, AL 35218

**GRAYSON, George**
Representative Dist. 19
3810 Melody Rd. NE
Huntsville, AL 358 11

**HOLMES, Alvin A.**
Representative Dist. 78
PO Box 6064
Montgomery, AL 36106

**KENNEDY, Yvonne**
Representative Dist. 103
1205 Glennon Ave.
Mobile, AL 36603

**McDOWELL, Bobbie W. G.**
Representative Dist. 56
2322 Dartmouth Ave.
Bessemer, AL 35050

**McLAIN, Edward**
Representative Dist. 57
3826 Troy Terr
Brighton, AL 35020

**MELTON, Bryant**
Representative Dist. 61
5003 4th Ave.
Tuscaloosa, AL 35405

**NEWTON, Demetrius**
Representative Dist. 53
PO Box 2525
Birmingham, AL 35202

**PERDUE, George**
Representative Dist. 54
2 Twelfth Ave. N
Birmingham, AL 35204

**REED, Thomas**
Representative Dist. 82
Drawer E E T
Tuskegee, AL Institute 36088

**ROGERS, John W.**
Representative Dist. 52
1424 18th St. SW
Birmingham, AL 35211

**SPRATT, Lewis G.**
Representative Dist. 59
3809 4th St. W
Birmingham, AL 35207

**THOMAS, James L.**
Representative Dist. 69
Rt. 1 Box 509
Lownesboro, AL 36752

### ALASKA

#### State Representatives

**FURNACE, Walter R.**
Representative Dist. 14B
7221 E. 22nd
Anchorage, AK 99510

### ARIZONA

#### State Senators

**WALKER, Carolyn A.**
Senator Dist. 23
Senate Wing
1700 W. Washington
Phoenix, AZ 85007

#### Representatives

**HAMILTON, Arthur M.**
Representative Dist. 22
House Wing
1700 W. Washington
Phoenix, AZ 85007

**KENNEDY, Sandra**
Representative Dist. 23
2333 E. Wier Ave.
Phoenix, AZ 85040

### ARKANSAS

#### State Senators

**JEWELL, Jerry**
Senator Dist. 24
1813 Pulaski St.
Little Rock, AR 72206

#### Representatives

**BROWN, Irma H.**
Representative Dist. 64
1920 S. Summit St.
Little Rock, AR 72202

**TOWNSEND, William H.**
Representative Dist. 63
1304 Wright Ave.
Little Rock, AR 72206

**WALKER, William**
Representative Dist. 62
1701 W. 20th
Little Rock, AR 72202

**WILKINS, Henry III**
Representative Dist. 82
303 N. Maple St.
Pine Bluff, AR 71601

### CALIFORNIA

#### State Senators

**GREENE, Bill**
Senator Dist. 29
State Capitol 4035
Sacramento, CA 95814

**WATSON, Diane E.**
Senator Dist. 28
4401 Crenshaw Blvd.
Los Angeles, CA 90043

#### Representatives

**BROWN, Willie L. Jr.**
Speaker of the Assembly
Dist. 17
State Capitol Rm 219
Sacramento, CA 95814

**HARRIS, Elihu M.**
Assembly Member Dist. 13
State Capitol #6031
Sacramento, CA 95814

**HUGHES, Teresa P.**
Assembly Member Dist. 47
State Capitol
Sacramento, CA 95814

**MOORE, Gwen**
Assembly Member Dist. 49
3731 Stocker St. #106
Los Angeles, CA 90008

**TUCKER, Curtis R.**
Assembly Member Dist.
PO Box 6500
Inglewood, CA 90306

**WATERS, Marine**
Assembly Member Dist. 48
7900 S. Central Ave.
Los Angeles, CA 90001

### COLORADO

#### State Senators

**GROFF, Regis F.**
Senator Dist. 33
2079 Albion St.
Denver, CO 80207

#### Representatives

**TANNER, Gloria T.**
Representative Dist. 7
2150 Monaco Pkwy
Denver, CO 80207

**WEBB, Wilma**
Representative Dist. 8
2329 Gaylord St.
Denver, CO 80205

**WILLIAMS, Sam**
Representative Dist.
PO Box 2159
Breckenridge, CO 80424

## CONNECTICUT

### Senators

**BARROWS, Frank D.**
Senator Dist. 2
38 Canterbury St.
Hartford, CT 06112

**DANIELS, John C. Jr.**
Senator Dist. 10
432 Norton Pkwy
New Haven, CT 06511

**MORTON, Margaret E.**
**Senator Dist. 23**
25 Currier St.
Bridgeport, CT 06607

### Representatives

**BAKER, Sheila**
Representative Dist. 124
25 Cowles St. #44
Bridgeport, CT 06607

**BEAMON, Reginald**
Representative Dist. 72
46 Catalina Dr.
Waterbury, CT 06704

**BROOKS, Walter S.**
Representative Dist. 95
102 Dewitt St.
New Haven, CT 06519

**COLEMAN, Eric**
Representative Dist. 1
77 Wintonbury Ave.
Bloomfield, CT 06002

**DYSON, William R.**
Representative Dist. 94
PO Box 2064
New Haven, CT 06521

**GILES, Abraham**
Representative Dist. 6
188 Cleveland Ave.
Hartford, CT 06120

## DELAWARE

### State Senators

**HOLLOWAY, Herman M. Sr.**
Senator Dist. 2
2008 Washington St.
Wilmington, DE 19802

### Representatives

**PLANT, Al O. Sr.**
Representative Dist. 2
523 Eastlawn Ave.
Wilmington, DE 19802

**SILLS, James H. Jr.**
Representative Dist. 3
502 E. 6th St.
Wilmington, DE 19801

## FLORIDA

### State Senators

**GIRARDEAU, Arnett E.**
Senator Dist. 7
26 E. 6th St.
Jacksonville, FL 32206

**MEEK, Carrie**
Senator Dist. 36
149 West Plaza #236
Miami, FL 33147

### Representatives

**BROWN, Corrine**
Representative Dist. 17
1707 N. Main St.
Jacksonville, FL 32206

**BURKE, James**
Representative Dist. 107
654 NW 62nd St. #100
Miami, FL 33150

**CLARK, Bill A.**
Representative Dist. 91
2200 NW 32 Terr
Lauderdale Lakes, FL 33313

**GAFFNEY, Donald**
Representative Dist. 16
P.O. Box 12496
Jacksonville, FL 32209

**HARGRETT, James Jr.**
Representative Dist. 63
2002 E. Emma
Tampa, FL 33610

**JAMERSON, Douglas "Tim"**
Representative Dist. 55
424 Central Ave. #904
St. Petersburg, FL 33701

**LAWSON, Al**
Representative Dist. 9
PO Box 3636
Tallahassee, FL 32301

**LOGAN, Willie F. Jr.**
Representative Dist. 108
PO Box 1036
Opa Locka, FL 33054

**REAVES, Jefferson Sr.**
Representative Dist. 106
3160 NW 48 Terr
Miami, FL 33142

**REDDICK, Alzo J.**
Representative Dist. 40
725 South Goldwyn Ave.
Orlando, FL 32805

## GEORGIA

### State Senators

**LANGFORD, Arthur Jr.**
Senator Dist. 35
1040 Gordon St. SW
Atlanta, GA 30310

**SCOTT, Albert J.**
Senator Dist. 2
PO Box 1704
Savannah, GA 3 1402

**SCOTT, David**
Senator Dist. 36
State Capitol Bldg. #126-A
Atlanta, GA 30334

**SHUMAKE, Hildred**
Senator Dist. 39
1103 Fair St.
Atlanta, GA 30314

**TATE, Horace E. Sr.**
Senator Dist. 38
621 Lilla Dr. SW
Atlanta, GA 30310

**WALKER, Eugene**
Senator Dist. 43
2231 Chevy Chase Lane
Decatur, GA 30032

### Representatives

**ALLEN, Roy L.**
Representative Dist. 127
1406 Law Dr.
Savannah, GA 31401

**BENN, Lorenzo**
Representative Dist. 38
579 Fielding Lane SW
Atlanta, GA 30311

**BISHOP, Sanford D. Jr.**
Representative Dist. 94
4129 Roman Dr.
Columbus, GA 31907

**BROOKS, Tyrone**
Representative Dist. 34
Station A - PO Box 11185
Atlanta, GA 30310

**BROWN, George M**
Representative Dist. 88
Richmond Co
PO Box 1114
Augusta, GA 30903

**CLARK, Betty J**
Representative Dist. 55
PO Box 17852
Atlanta, GA 30316

**DAVIS, Grace W**
Representative Dist. 29
260 Fulton St. SW
Atlanta, GA 30312

**HOLMES, Bob**
Representative Dist. 28
2421 Poole Rd. SW
Atlanta, GA 30311

**JOHNSON,**
Diane Harvey
Representative Dist. 123
POBox 5544
Savannah, GA 31414

**LUCAS, David E.**
Representative Dist. 102
448 Woolfolk St.
Macon, GA 31201

**MC KINNEY, James E.**
Representative Dist. 35
765 Shorter Terr NW
Atlanta, GA 30318

**RANDALL, William C.**
Representative Dist. 101
PO Box 121
Macon, GA 31202

**REDDING, Frank L. Jr.**
Representative Dist. 5O
2561 Creekwood Terr.
Decatur, GA 30030

**SINKFIELD, Georganna T.**
Representative Dist. 37
179 Tonawanda Dr. SE
Atlanta, GA 30315

**SMYRE, Calvin**
Representative Dist. 92
P.O. Box 181
Columbus, GA 31902

**STANLEY, LaNett**
Representative Dist. 33
712 Gary Rd. NW
Atlanta, GA 30318

**THOMAS, Mable**
Representative Dist. 31
PO Box 573
Atlanta, GA 30301

**THURMOND, Michael**
Representative Dist. 67
PO Drawer 1148
Athens, GA 30603

**WALKER, Charles W.**
Representative Dist. 85
1402 12th St.
Augusta, GA 30901

**WHITE, John**
Representative Dist. 132
PO Box 3506
Albany, GA 31706

**WILLIAMS, Juanita T.**
Representative Dist. 54
8 E. Lake Dr. NE
Atlanta, GA 30317

**YOUNG, Mary**
Representative Dist. 134
423 Holloway Ave.
Albany, GA 31705

## ILLINOIS

### Senators

**ALEXANDER, Ethel Skyles**
Senate Dist. 16
610 E. 61st St.
Chicago, IL 60637

**BROOKINS, Howard**
Senator Dist. 18
9453 S. Ashland #10
Chicago, IL 60620

**COLLINS-GRANT ,Earlean**
Senator Dist. 9
5943 W. Madison St.
Chicago, IL 60644

**HALL, Kenneth**
Senator Dist. 57
327 Missouri Ave. Rm. 222
East St. Louis, IL 62201

**JONES, Emil Jr.**
Senator Dist. 17
11357 S. Lowe Ave.
Chicago, IL 60628

**NEWHOUSE, Richard H**
Senator Dist. 13
1900 E. 71st St.
Chicago, IL 60649

**SMITH, Margaret**
Senator Dist. 12
130 E. Garfield Blvd
Chicago, IL 606 15

### Representatives

**BRAUN, Carol Moseley**
Representative Dist. 25
127 N. Dearborn #644
Chicago, IL 60602

**DAVIS, Monique**
Representative Dist. 36
9318 S. Green
Chicago, IL 60620

**FLOWERS, Mary E**
Representative Dist. 31
7017 S. Ashland
Chicago, IL 60636

**HUFF, Douglas**
Representative Dist. 19
3037 W. Warren Blvd.
Chicago, IL 60612

**JONES, Lovana S**
Representative Dist. 23
3634 S. Rhodes Rd.
Chicago, IL 60653

**LEFLORE, Robert Jr.**
Representative Dist. 15
2069 Stratton Bldg.
Springfield, IL 62706

**MORROW, Charles**
Representative Dist. 32
7605 S. Halsted
Chicago, IL 60620

**RICE, Nelson Sr.**
Representative Dist. 33
2074 Stratton Bldg.
Springfield, IL 62706

**SHAW, William**
Representative Dist. 34
2050 Stratton Bldg.
Springfield, IL 62706

**TURNER, Arthur L.**
Representative Dist. 18
2114 S. Pulaski Rd.
Chicago, IL 60623

**WHITE, Jesse C. Jr.**
Representative Dist. 8
300 W. Hill St.#714
Chicago, IL 60610

**WILLIAMS, Paul**
Representative Dist. 24
5344 S. Michigan
Chicago, IL 60615

**YOUNG, Anthony L.**
Representative Dist. 17
4525 W. Monroe St.
Chicago, IL 60624

**YOUNGE, Wyvetter**
Representative Dist. 113
1617 N. 46th St.
East St. Louis, IL 62205

## INDIANA

### State Senators

**CARSON, Julia M.**
Senator Dist. 34
2530 N. Park Ave.
Indianapolis, IN 46205

**MOSBY, Carolyn Brown**
Senator Dist. 3
328 Garfield St.
Gary, IN 46404

### Representatives

**BROWN, Charlie**
Representative Dist. 14
2021 Burr St. #103
Gary, IN 46406

**CRAWFORD, William A.**
Representative Dist. 51
3048 E. Fall Crk Pkwy N. Dr.
Indianapolis, IN 46205

**GOODALL, Hurley C.**
Representative Dist. 34
1905 Carver Dr.
Muncie, IN 47303

**HARRIS, Earl**
Representative Dist. 12
4114 Butternut St.
East Chicago, IN 46312

**ROGERS, Earline Smith**
Representative Dist. 14
3636 W. 15th Ave.
Gary, IN 46506

**SUMMERS, Joseph W**
Representative Dist. 51
3040 N. Capitol Ave.
PO Box 88060
Indianapolis, IN 46208

## IOWA

### State Senators

**MANN, Thomas Jr.**
Senator Dist. 43
4049 Lower Beaver Rd.
Des Moines, IA 50310

## KANSAS

### State Senators

**ANDERSON, Eugene**
Senator Dist. 29
PO Box 4598
Wichita, KS 67204

### Representatives

**CRIBBS, Theo**
Representative Dist. 89
1551 N. Minnesota
Wichita, KS 67214

**JUSTICE, Norman E.**
Representative Dist. 34
506 Washington Blvd.
Kansas City, KS 66101

**LOVE, Clarence C.**
Representative Dist. 35
2853 Parkview
Kansas City, KS 66104

## KENTUCKY

### State Senators

**POWERS, Georgia M.**
Senator Dist. 33
733 Cecil Ave.
Louisville, KY 40211

### Representatives

**HATCHER, E. Porter Jr.**
Representative Dist. 43
901 Southwestern Pkwy
Louisville, KY 40212

## LOUISIANA

### State Senators

**BAGNERIS, Dennis**
Senator Dist. 3
4945 Kendall St.
New Orleans, LA 70126

**JEFFERSON, William J.**
Senator Dist. 5
650 Poydras St. #1850
New Orleans, LA 70130

**JOHNSON, Jon D.**
Senator Dist. 2
5900 N. Roman St.
New Orleans, LA 70117

**TARVER, Gregory**
Senator Dist. 39
1104 Pierre Ave.
Shreveport, LA 71103

**TURNLEY, Richard Jr.**
Senator Dist. 14
2757 78th Ave.
Baton Rouge, LA 70807

### Representatives

**ALEXANDER, Avery C.**
Representative Dist. 93
2107 S. Claiborne
New Orleans, LA 70125

**BAJOIE, Diana E.**
Representative Dist. 91
PO Box 15168
New Orleans, LA 70175

**CARTER, Wilford D.**
Representative Dist. 34
1025 Mill St.
Lake Charles, LA 70601

**COPELIN, Sherman**
Representative Dist. 99
2016 Delery St.
New Orleans, LA 70117

**DELPIT, Joseph A.**
Representative Dist. 67
725 Lettsworth St.
Baton Rouge, LA 70802

**IRVIN, Melvin Jr.**
Representative Dist. 58
PO Box 905
Gonzales, LA 70737

**JACKSON, Alphonse Jr.**
Representative Dist. 2
3815 Lakeshore Dr.
Shreveport, LA 71109

**JETSON, Raymond A.**
Representative Dist. 61
4551 Gus Young Ave.
Baton Rouge, LA 70802

**JONES, Charles D.**
Representative Dist. 17
PO Box 3043
Monroe, LA 71201

**JONES, Charles R.**
Representative Dist. 96
2524 O'Reilly St.
New Orleans, LA 70119

**MORRELL, Arthur A.**
Representative Dist. 97

4925 Moore Dr.
New Orleans, LA 70122

**NEWMAN, Jewel J.**
Representative Dist. 63
PO Box 73547
Baton Rouge, LA 70807

**SINGLETON, Willie**
Representative Dist. 3
425 Abilene
Shreveport, LA 71106

**WARREN, Naomi White**
Representative Dist. 101
2804 Higgins Blvd.
New Orleans, LA 70127

## MARYLAND

### State Senators

**BLOUNT, Clarence W.**
Senator Dist. 41
4811 Liberty Heights Ave.
Baltimore, MD 21207

**BRAILEY, Troy F.**
Senator Dist. 40
2405 Baker St.
Baltimore, MD 21216

**IRBY, Nathan C. Jr.**
Senator Dist. 45
2800 E. Federal St.
Baltimore, MD 21213

**TROTTER, Decatur W.**
Senator Dist. 24
PO Box 1460
Landover, MD 20785

**WYNN, Albert R.**
Senator Dist. 25
8700 Central Ave. #306
Landover, MD 20785

### Representatives

**ANDERSON, Curtis**
Delegate Dist. 44
1664 N. Gate Rd.
Baltimore, MD 21218

**BOSTON, Frank D. Jr.**
Delegate Dist. 41
3738 Winterbourne Rd.
Baltimore, MD 21216

**CUMMINGS, Elijah**
Delegate Dist. 39
2225 St. Paul St.
Baltimore, MD 21218

**CURRIE, Ulysses**
Representative Dist. 25
7315 Calder Dr.
Capitol Heights, MD 20743

**DAVIS, Clarence**
Delegate Dist. 45
1628 E. 32nd St.
Baltimore, MD 21218

**DIXON, Richard N.**
Delegate Dist. 5
1224 Western Chapel Dr
New Windsor, MD 21776

**DOUGLASS, John W.**
Delegate Dist. 45
1535 E. North Ave.
Baltimore, MD 21213

**EXUM, Nathaniel**
Delegate Dist. 24
5611 Landover Rd.
Hyattsville, MD 20784

**FULTON, Tony**
Delegate Dist. 40
3501 Dennlyn Rd.
Baltimore, MD 21215

**HARRISON, Hattie N.**
Delegate Dist. 45
2503 E. Preston
Baltimore, MD 21213

**HUGHES, Ralph M.**
Delegate Dist. 40
2307 Braddish Ave.
Baltimore, MD 21216

**JONES, Christine Mill**
Delegate Dist. 26
3518 Everest Dr.
Hillcrest Heights, MD 20748

**KIRK, Ruth N.**
Delegate Dist. 39
516 North Charles St. #501
Baltimore, MD 21201

**LAWLAH, Gloria**
Delegate Dist. 26
3801 24th Ave.
Hillcrest, MD 20748

**MILLER, Juanita**
Delegate Dist. 25
90 Rowe Blvd.
Annapolis, MD 21401

**MONTAGUE, Kenneth C. Jr.**
Delegate Dist. 44
513 E. 39th St.
Baltimore, MD 21218

**MURPHY, Margaret H**
Delegate Dist. 41
315 Lowe Bldg.
Annapolis, MD 21401

**OAKS, Nathaniel T.**
Delegate Dist. 41
513 Normandy Ave.
Baltimore, MD 21229

**RAWLINGS, Howard P.**
Delegate Dist. 40
3502 Sequoia Ave.
Baltimore, MD 21215

**WOODS, Sylvania W. Jr.**
Delegate Dist. 24
7312 Barlowe Rd.
Landover, MD 20785

**YOUNG, Larry**
Delegate Dist. 39
516 N. Charles St. #501
Baltimore, MD 21201

## MASSACHUSETTS

### State Senators

**BOLLING, Royal Sr.**
Senator Dist. 2
State House #413-F
Boston, MA 02133

### Representatives

**FOX, Gloria**
Representative Dist. 7
7 Harold Park Apt. 2
Boston, MA 02119

**GRACE, Augusto F.**
Representative Dist. 23
Burlington Sch. Dist.
13 Skilton Lane
Burlington, MA 01803

**GRAHAM, Saundra M.**
Representative Dist. 28
State House #156
Boston, MA 02133

**HICKS, Shirley Owens**
Representative Dist. 6
115 Hazelton St.
Mattapan, MA 02126

**RUSHING, Byron**
Representative Dist. 9
State House
Boston, MA 02133

## MICHIGAN

### State Senators

**HOLMES, David S. Jr.**
Senator Dist. 4
124 State Capitol Bldg..
Lansing, MI 48909

**VAUGHN, Jackie III**
Senator Dist. 3
State Capitol
Lansing, MI 48909

### Representatives

**CLACK, Floyd**
Representative Dist. 80
3120 Helber
Flint, MI 48504

**HARRISON, Charlie J. Jr.**
Representative Dist. 62
State Capitol Bldg.
Lansing, MI 48909

**HOOD, Morris W. Jr.**
Representative Dist. 6
8872 Cloverlawn
Detroit, MI 48204

**HUNTER, Teola P.**
Representative Dist. 5
2688 Oakman Blvd.
Detroit, MI 48238

**KILPATRICK, Carolyn C.**
Representative Dist. 8
State Capitol Bldg.. Rm. 4
Lansing, MI 48909

**MURPHY, Raymond**
Representative Dist. 17
115-1/2 Capital Bldg.
Lansing, MI 48909

**SAUNDERS, Nelson**
Representative Dist. 7
17545 Santa Barbara
Detroit, MI 48221

**SMITH, Virgil C. Jr.**
Representative Dist. 10
19450 Gloucester
Detroit, MI 48203

**STALLWORTH, Alma G.**
Representative Dist. 4
19793 Sorrento
Detroit, MI 48235

**TERRELL, Ethel**
Representative Dist. 9
12219 Wooward Ave.
Highland, MI Park 48203

**WATKINS, Juanita**
Representative Dist. 16
555 Brush St., #2512
Lansing, MI 48226

**YOUNG, Joseph F. Sr.**
Representative Dist. 14
3449 Seminole
Detroit, MI 48214

**YOUNG, Joseph F. Jr.**
Representative Dist. 15
8570 E. Outer Dr.
Detroit, MI 48213

## MINNESOTA

### State Representatives

**JEFFERSON, Richard**
Representative Dist. 57B
1314 Washburn Ave. North
Minneapolis, MN 55411

## MISSISSIPPI

### State Senators

**ANDERSON, Douglas**
Senator Dist. 27
1340 Rockdale Dr.
Jackson, MS 39213

**HARDEN, Alice**
Senator Dist. 28
3247 Copperfield Dr.
Jackson, MS 39209

**Representatives**

**BLACKMON, Edward Jr.**
Representative Dist. 57
PO Drawer 568
Canton, MS 39046

**BUCKLEY, Horace L.**
Representative Dist. 70
735 Campbell St.
Jackson, MS 39203

**CALHOUN, Credell**
Representative Dist. 68
PO Box 3406
Jackson, MS 39207

**CLARK, Robert G.**
Representative Dist. 47
Box 179
Lexington, MS 39095

**CLARKE, Alyce**
Representative Dist. 69
1053 Arbor Vista Blvd.
Jackson, MS 39209

**ELLERBY, William M. Sr.**
Representative Dist. 110
4312 Raby Dr.
Moss Point, MS 39563

**ELLIS, Tyrone**
Representative Dist. 38
PO Box 892
Starksville, MS 39759

**FLAGGS, George Jr.**
Representative Dist. 55
417 Bellaire Circle
Vicksburg, MS 39180

**FRAZIER, Hillman T.**
Representative Dist. 67
2066 Queensroad Ave.
Jackson, MS 39213

**FREDERICKS, Isiah**
Representative Dist. 119
3500 Meadowlark Dr.
Gulfport, MS 39501

**GREEN, David**
Representative Dist. 96
Rt. 1 Box 152-A
Gloster, MS 39638

**HENDERSON, Clayton**
Representative Dist. 9
PO Box 469
Tunica, MS 38676

**HENRY, Aaron**
Representative Dist. 26
213 4th St.
Clarksdale, MS 38614

**KING, Leslie Darnell**
Representative Dist. 49
PO Box 27
Greenville, MS 38701

**ROBINSON, Walter Jr.**
Representative Dist. 63
PO Box 123
Bolton, MS 39041

**SCHOBY, Barney**
Representative Dist. 94
115 Florida Dr.
Natchez, MS 39120

**SHEPPARD, Charles**
Representative Dist. 85
PO Box 254
Lorman, MS 39096

**WALKER, Alfred L. Jr.**
Representative Dist. 41
1807 Martin Luther King Dr.
Columbus, MS 39701

**WATSON, Percy**
Representative Dist. 103
PO Box 1767
Hattiesburg, MS 39401

**YOUNG, Charles L.**
Representative Dist. 82
425 26th Ave.
Meridian, MS 39301

## MISSOURI

### State Senators

**BANKS, J. B.**
Senator Dist. 5
1442-A North Grand
St. Louis, MO 63106

**BASS, John F.**
Senator Dist. 4
4936 Maffitt Pl.
St. Louis, MO 63113

**CURLS, Phillip B. Sr.**
Senator Dist. 9
Senate Post Office
Capitol Building
Jefferson City, MO 65101

### Representatives

**BANTON, Steve**
Representative Dist. 94
929 St. Paul Rd.
Ellisville, MO 63021

**BLAND, Mary Groves**
Representative Dist. 43
6135 Indiana
Kansas City, MO 64130

**CARTER, Paula**
Representative Dist. 56
5935 Summit
St. Louis, MO 63147

**CLAY, William L. Jr.**
Representative Dist. 59
6136 Washington Blvd.
St. Louis, MO 63112

**DANIELS, Fletcher**
Representative Dist. 39
3537 Askew St.
Kansas City, MO 64128

**FORD, Louis H.**
Representative Dist. 58
1308 N. 16th St.
St. Louis, MO 63106

**GOWARD, Russell**
Representative Dist. 60
4015 Fair Ave.
St. Louis, MO 63115

**MCGEE, Jacqueline**
Representative Dist. 38
PO Box 31458
Kansas City, MO 64130

**SHELTON, 0. L.**
Representative Dist. 57
1803-A Cora St.
St. Louis, MO 63113

**THOMPSON, Vernon**
Representative Dist. 36
1330 Park
Kansas City, MO 64127

**TROUPE, Charles**
Representative Dist. 62
4512 Holly Pl.
St. Louis, MO 63115

**WALTON, Elbert A. Jr.**
Representative Dist. 61
8781 Jordan
St. Louis, MO 63147

## NEBRASKA

### State Senator

CHAMBERS, Ernest W.
**Senator Dist. 11**
3116 N. 24th ST
Omaha, NE 68110

## NEVADA

### State Senators

**NEAL, Joe**
Senator Dist. 4
304 Lance St.
North Las Vegas, NV 89030

### Representatives

**ARBERRY, Morse Jr.**
Assembly Member Dist. 7
425 Lass Cir.
North Las Vegas, NV 89030

**WILLIAMS, Wendell**
Assembly Member Dist. 6
2200 Canary Way
Las Vegas, NV 89106

## NEW HAMPSHIRE

### State Representatives

**LONG, Linda**
Representative Dist. 25
44 McKenna Dr.
Nashua, NH 03062

## NEW JERSEY

### State Senators

**LIPMAN, Wynona M.**
Senator Dist. 29
SO. Park Pl. #938
Newark, NJ 07101

**RICE, Ronald L.**
Senator Dist. 28
1101 S Orange Ave.
Newark, NJ 07106

### Representatives

**BROWN, Willie B.**
Assembly Member Dist. 29
375 Wainwright St.
Newark, NJ 0711 2

**BRYANT, Wayne R.**
Assembly Member Dist. 5
309 Market St.
Camden, NJ 08102

**BUSH, Stephanie**
Assembly Member Dist. 27
44 Greenwood Ave. Ste 103
East Orange, NJ 07017

**CHARLES, Joseph Jr.**
Assembly Member Dist. 31
490 Communipaw Ave.
Jersey City, NJ 07304

**MATHSON, Jackie R.**
Assembly Member Dist. 29
1072 Bergen St.
Newark, NJ 0711 2

**WATSON, John S..**
Assembly Member Dist. 15
Mercer Co.
224 W. State St.
Trenton, NJ 08608

## NEW YORK

### State Senate

**GALIBER, Joseph L.**
Senator Dist. 31
1967 Turnbull Ave.
Bronx, NY 10473

**JENKINS, Andrew**
Senator Dist. 10
109-43 Farmers Blvd.
St. Albans, NY 11412

**MONTGOMERY, Velmanette**
Senator Dist. 22
Comm. Sch. Dist. 13

195 Willoughby Ave.
Brooklyn, NY 11205

**PATERSON, David A.**
Senator Dist. 29
40 W. 135th St.
New York, NY 10037

### Representatives

**BOYLAND, William F.**
Assembly Member Dist. 55
1636 Pitkin Ave.
Brooklyn, NY 11212

**CLARK, Barbara**
Assembly member Dist. 33
120-56 224th St.
Queens, NY 11411

**DANIELS, Geraldine**
Assembly Member Dist. 70
163 W. 125th St.
New York, NY 10027

**DAVIS, Gloria**
Assembly Member Dist. 78
636 E. 169th St.
Bronx, NY 10456

**EVE, Arthur O.**
Assembly Member Dist. 141
1373 Fillmore Ave., 2nd Fl
Buffalo, NY 14211

**FARRELL, Herman D. Jr.**
Assembly Member Dist. 71
4060 Broadway
New York, NY 10032

**GANTT, David F.**
Assembly Member Dist. 133
196 Genesee St.
Rochester, NY 14611

**GREEN, Roger L.**
Assembly Member Dist. 57
300 Clermont Ave.
Brooklyn, NY 11205

**GREENE, Aurelia**
Assembly Member Dist. 76
1188 Grand Concourse #D
Bronx, NY 10456

**GRIFFITH, Edward**
Assembly Member Dist. 40
270 Broadway
Albany, NY 12248

**JENKINS, Cynthia**
Assembly Member Dist. 29
174-63 128th Ave.
Jamaica, NY 11434

**MARSHALL, Helen**
Assembly Member Dist. 35
Legislative Office Bldg. #619
Albany, NY 12248

**NORMAN, Clarence Jr.**
Assembly Member Dist. 43
845 Nostrand Ave.
Brooklyn, NY 11225

**PATTON, Barbara**
Assembly Member Dist. 18
208 N. Long Beach Ave.
Freeport, NY 11520

**SEABROOK, Larry**
Assembly Member Dist. 82
758 E. 217th St.
Bronx, NY 10467

**VANN, Albert**
Assembly Member Dist. 56
362 McDonough St.
Brooklyn, NY 11233

## NORTH CAROLINA

### State Senator

**HUNT, Ralph A.**
Senator Dist. 13
433 Pilot St.
Durham, NC 27707

**MARTIN, William N.**
Senator Dist. 31
PO Box 21363
Greensboro, NC 27421

**RICHARDSON, James F.**
Senator Dist. 33
1739 N. Brook Dr.
Charlotte, NC 28216

### Representatives

**BARNHILL, Howard C.**
Representative Dist. 60
2400 Newland Rd.
Charlotte, NC 28216

**BLUE, Daniel T. Jr.**
Representative Dist. 21
2541 Albermarle Ave.
Raleigh, NC 27610

**BURKE, Logan**
Representative Dist. 67
3410 Cumberland
Winston Salem, NC 27105

**CUNNINGHAM, W. Pete**
Representative Dist. 59
3121 W. Valleywood Pl.
Charlotte, NC 28216

**EDWARDS, Chancy R.**
Representative Dist. 17
1502 Boros Dr.
Fayetteville, NC 28303

**FITCH, Milton**
Representative Dist. 70
516 S. Lodge
Wilson, NC 27893

**FREEMAN, William M.**
Representative Dist. 62
502 Burton St.
Fuquay-Varina, NC 27526

**GIST, Herman C.**
Representative Dist. 26
442 Gorrell St.
Greensboro, NC 27406

**HARDAWAY, Thomas C.**
Representative Dist. 7
201 McDaniel St.
Enfield, NC 27823

**JERALDS, Luther R.**
Representative Dist. 17
319 Jasper St.
Fayetteville, NC 28301

**KENNEDY, Annie B.**
Representative Dist. 66
3727 Spaulding Dr.
Winston Salem, NC 27105

**LOCKS, Sydney A.**
Representative Dist. 16
PO Box 290
1600 Fairmont Rd.
Lumberton, NC 28358

**MICHAUX, Henry M. Jr.**
Representative Dist. 23
1722 Alfred St.
Durham, NC 27713

## OHIO

### State Senators

**BOWEN, William F.**
Senator Dist. 9
Statehouse
Columbus, OH 43215

**WHITE, Michael R.**
Senator Dist. 21
Ohio Senate State House
Columbus, OH 43216

### Representatives

**BEATTY, Otto Jr.**
Representative Dist. 31
970 Wellington Blvd.
Columbus, OH 43219

**JAMES, Troy Lee**
Representative Dist. 12
4216 Cedar Ave.
Cleveland, OH 44 103

**JONES, Casey C.**
Representative Dist. 45
355 Pinewood Ave.
Toledo, OH 43602

**MALLORY, William L.**
Representative Dist. 23
907 Dayton St.
Cincinnati, OH 45214

**MC LIN, C. J. Jr.**
Representative Dist. 36
1130 Germantown St.
Dayton, OH 45408

**MILLER, I. Ray**
Representative Dist. 29
Statehouse
Columbus, OH 43215

**RANKIN, L. Helen**
Representative Dist. 25
3461 Evanston Ave.
Cincinnati, OH 45207

**ROBERTS, Tom**
Representative Dist. 37
1739 Catalpa Dr.
Dayton, OH 45406

**SYKES, Vernon L.**
Representative Dist. 42
678 Garth Ave.
Akron, OH 44320

**THOMPSON, Ike**
Representative Dist. 14
899 E. 128th St.
Cleveland, OH 44 108

**WHALEN, Vermel**
Representative Dist. 16
16804 Glendale Ave.
Cleveland, OH 44128

## OKLAHOMA

### State Senators

**HORNER, Maxine**
Senator Dist. 11
PO Box 351
Tulsa, OK 74101

**MILES-LA GRANGE, Vicki**
Senator Dist. 48
4020 N. Lincoln Blvd.
Oklahoma City, OK 73105

### Representatives

**COX, Kevin**
Representative Dist. 97
5909 N. Terry
Oklahoma City, OK 73111

**ROSS, Don**
Representative Dist. 73
1520 N. Hartford St.
Tulsa, OK 74106

**WILLIAMS, Fredd**
Representative Dist.
1145 N. Page Ave.
Oklahoma City, OK 73111

## OREGON

### State Senators

**HILL, Jim**
Senator Dist. 16
4584 12th Pl. South
Salem, OR 97302

**MCCOY, William**
Senator Dist. 8
6650 N. Amherst St.
Portland, OR 97203

### Representatives

**CARTER, Margaret**
Representative Dist. 18
2948 NE l0th Ave.
Portland, OR 97212

## PENNSYLVANIA

### State Senators

**HANKINS, Freeman**
Senator Dist. 7
4075 Haverford Ave.
Philadelphia, PA 19104

**JONES, Roxanne**
Senator Dist. 3
3133 N. Broad St.
Philadelphia, PA 19132

**WILLIAMS, Hardy**
Senator Dist. 8
5137 Walnut St.
Philadelphia, PA 19139

### Representatives

**CARN, Andrew**
Representative Dist. 197
2015 N. 29th St.
Philadelphia, PA 19121

**EVANS, Dwight**
Representative Dist. 203
7174 0gontz Ave.
Philadelphia, PA 19138

**FATTAH, Chaka**
Representative Dist. 192
1845 N. 59th St.
Philadelphia, PA 19151

**HARPER, Ruth**
Representative Dist. 196
1427 W. Erie Ave.
Philadelphia, PA 19140

**HUGHES, Vincent**
Representative Dist. 190
5241 Chestnut St.
Philadelphia, PA 19139

**IRVIS, K. Leroy**
Representative Dist. 19
205 Tennyson Ave.
Pittsburgh, PA 15213

**LINTON, Gordon**
Representative Dist. 200
1521 E. Wadsworth Ave.
Philadelphia, PA 19150

**OLIVER, Frank L.**
Representative Dist. 195
Main Capitol Bldg.
1319 N. 29th St.
Philadelphia, PA 19121

**PRESTON, Joseph Jr.**
Representative Dist. 24
501 Larimer Ave.
Pittsburgh. PA 15206

**RICHARDSON, David P. Jr.**
Representative Dist. 201
South Office Bldg. #319
Harrisburg, PA 17120

**ROEBUCK, James R. Jr.**
Representative 188
435 S. 46th
Philadelphia. PA 19143

**WIGGINS, Edward A.**
Representative Dist. 186
1447 Point Breeze
Philadelphia, PA 19146

**WRIGHT, Robert C.**
Representative Dist. 159
1919 Providence Ave.
Chester, PA 19013

## RHODE ISLAND

### State Senators

**WALTON, Charles D.**
Senator Dist. 9
82 Homer St.
Providence, RI 02905

### Representatives

**CASTRO, George A.**
Representative Dist. 20
57 Carolina Ave.
Providence, RI 02905

**HERNANDEZ, John S.**
Representative Dist. 46
107 Chancer Dr.
North Kingtown, RI 02852

**LIMA, George**
Representative Dist. 83
64 Charles St.
East Providence, RI 02914

**METTS, Harold M.**
Representative Dist. 19
31 Tanner St.
Providence, RI 02907

**RICKMAN, Ray**
Representative Dist. 3
19 Pratt St.
Providence, RI 02906

## SOUTH CAROLINA

### State Senators

**FIELDING, Herbert U.**
Senator Dist. 42
PO Box 142
Columbia, SC 29202

**MATTHEWS, John W. Jr.**
Senator Dist. 39
PO Box 460
Bowman, SC 29018

**MITCHELL, Theo W.**
Senator Dist. 7
522 Woodland Way
Greenville, SC 29607

**PATTERSON, Kay**
Senator Dist. 19
6815 Gavilan Ave.
Columbia, SC 29203

### Representatives

**BLANDING, Larry**
Representative Dist. 66
PO Box 1446
Sumter, SC 29151

**BROWN, Joe E.**
Representative Dist. 73
1605 Frye Rd.
Columbia, SC 29203

**FABER, James**
Representative Dist. 70
PO Box 642
Eastover, SC 29044

**FERGUSON, Tee Sr.**
Representative Dist. 31
PO Box 151
Spartanburg, SC 29304

**FOSTER, Samuel R.**
Representative Dist. 49
Drawer 10072
Rock Hill, SC 29730

**GILBERT, Frank**
Representative Dist. 62
1523 Rocky Way Dr.
Florence, SC 29501

**GORDON, Benjamin Jr.**
Representative Dist. 101
PO Box 751
Kingstree, SC 29556

**MARTIN, Daniel E. Sr.**
Representative Dist. 111
117 Gordon St.
Charleston, SC 29403

**MC BRIDE, Frank E.**
Representative Dist. 74
2415 Pinehurst Rd.
Columbia, SC 29204

**SHELTON, Sarah V.**
Representative Dist. 23
312 Elder St. Extension
Greenville, SC 29607

**TAYLOR, Luther L. Jr.**
Representative Dist. 77
PO Box 3147
Columbia, SC 29230

**WASHINGTON, McKinley Jr.**
Representative Dist. 116
PO Box 247
Ravenel, SC 29470

**WHIPPER, Lucille**
Representative Dist. 109
PO Box 6203
Charleston, SC 29405

**WHITE, Juanita M.**
Representative Dist. 122
Rt. 1 Box 184-A
Hardeeville, SC 29927

**WILLIAMS, DeWitt**
Representative Dist. 102
PO Box 296
St. Stephen, SC 29479

## TENNESSEE

### State Senators

**DAVIS, Edward**
Senator Dist. 33
4924 Sagewood Dr.
Memphis, TN 38116

**FORD, John N.**
Senator Dist. 29
7 Legislative Plaza
Nashville, TN 37219

**WILLIAMS, Avon N. Jr.**
Senator Dist. 19
6 Legislative Plaza
Nashville, TN 37219

### Representatives

**DEBERRY, Lois M.**
Representative Dist. 91
Legislative Plaza #15
Nashville, TN 37219

**DIXON, Roscoe**
Representative Dist. 87
Legislative Plaza #17
Nashville, TN 37219

**DREW, Charles "Pete"**
Representative Dist. 15
1014 Weymouth Ln.
Knoxville, TN 37914

**JONES, Rufus E.**
Representative Dist. 86
War Memorial Bldg. #209
Nashville, TN 37219

**JONES, Ulysses Jr.**
Representative Dist. 98
2158 Piedmont
Memphis, TN 38108

**KING, Alvin M.**
Representative Dist. 92
1215 Tanglewood
Memphis, TN 38114

**LOVE, Harold M.**
Representative Dist. 54
4207 Drakes Hill Dr.
Nashville, TN 37218

**PRUITT, Mary**
Representative Dist. 58
1813 Hillside Ave.
Nashville, TN 37203

**ROBINSON, Clarence B.**
Representative Dist. 28
1909 E. 5th St.
Chattanooga, TN 37404

**TURNER, Larry**
Representative Dist. 85
752 W. Levi Rd.
Memphis, TN 38109

## TEXAS

### State Senators

**JOHNSON, Eddie Bernice**
Senator Dist. 23
6305 Elder Grove Dr.
Dallas, TX 75232

**WASHINGTON, Craig A.**
Senator Dist. 13
2323 Caroline #1000
Houston, TX 77004

### Representatives

**BLAIR, Fred**
Representative Dist. 110
210 W. Illinois
Dallas, TX 75224

**DELCO, Wilhelmina R.**
Representative Dist. 50
1805 Astor Pl.
Austin, TX 78721

**DUTTON, Harold V. Jr.**
Representative Dist. 142
PO Box 2910
Austin, TX 78769

**EDWARDS, Al**
Representative Dist. 146
PO Box 2910
Austin, TX 78769

**EVANS, Larry Q.**
Representative Dist. 147
P.O. Box 2910
Auston, TX 78769

**GIVENS, Ron**
Representative Dist. 83
PO Box 2910
Austin, TX 78769

**HUDSON, Samuel W. III**
Representative Dist. 100
2606 Martin L. King Blvd. #202
Dallas, TX 75215

**LARRY, Gerald H.**
Representative Dist. 111
2430 Marfa Ave.
Dallas, TX 75224

**PRICE, Albert J.**
Representative Dist. 22
3685 Blossom Dr.
Beaumont, TX 77701

**SUTTON, Lou Nelle**
Representative Dist. 120
11441 East Commerce St.
San Antonio, TX 78205

**THOMPSON, Garfield W.**
Representative Dist. 95
PO Box 50922
Ft. Worth, TX 76105

**THOMPSON, Senfronia**
Representative Dist. 141
10527 Homestead Rd.
Houston, TX 77016

**WILSON, Ron**
Representative Dist. 131
PO Box 2910
Austin, TX 78769

## VERMONT

### State Representative

**BROOKS, Francis K.**
Representative Dist. 5-1
27 Harrison Ave.
Montpelier, VT 05602

## VIRGINIA

### State Senators

**LAMBERT, Benjamin J. III**
Senator Dist. 9
3109 Noble Ave.
Richmond, VA 23222

**MILLER, Yvonne B.**
Senator Dist. 5
2315 Maltby Ave.
Norfolk, VA 23504

**SCOTT, Robert C.**
Senator Dist. 2
PO Box 251
Newport News, VA 23607

### Representatives

**CHRISTIAN, Mary T.**
Delegate Dist. 92
PO Box 1892
Hampton, VA 23669

**CUNNINGHAM, Jean**
Delegate Dist. 71
2607 E. Grace St.
Richmond, VA 23223

**EALEY, Roland D.**
Delegate Dist. 70
420 N. 1st St.
Richmond, VA 23219

**JONES, Jerrauld C.**
Representative Dist. 89
125 Saint Paul Blvd.
Norfolk, VA 23510

**MAXWELL, W. Henry**
Delegate Dist. 95
900 Shore Dr.
Newport News, VA 23607

**MELVIN, Kenneth R.**
Delegate Dist. 80
115 Yorkshire Rd.
Portsmouth, VA 23701

**ROBINSON, William P. Jr.**
Delegate Dist. 90
309 W Bute St.
Norfolk, VA 23510

## VIRGIN ISLANDS

### State Senators

**BELL, John A.**
Senator
PO Box 3737
Christiansted
St. Croix, VI 00820

**BROWN, Virdin**
Senator
PO Box 477
St. Thomas, VI 00801

**CANTON, Douglas**
Senator
PO Box 477
St. Thomas, VI 00801

**HANSEN, Alicia**
Senator
PO Box 477
St. Thomas, VI 00801

**O'BRYAN, James**
Senator
PO Box 501
St. Thomas, VI 00801

**O'CONNOR, Robert Jr.**
Senator
PO Box 477
St. Thomas, VI 00801

**RICHARDSON, Bingley**
Senator
PO Box 477
St. Thomas, VI 00801

**ROUSE, Ruby**
Senator
PO Box 865
Christiansted
St. Croix, VI 00820

**STRIDIRON, Iver**
Senator
PO Box 477
St. Thomas, VI 00801

**TORRB-JAMES, Alicia**
Senator
PO Box 477
St. Thomas, VI 00801

## WASHINGTON

### State Senators

**FLEMING, George**
Senator Dist. 37
1100 Lake Wash Blvd. S.
Seattle, WA 98144

**SMITHERMAN, Bill**
Senator Dist. 26
3408 N. Vassault St.
Tacoma, WA 98407

### Representative

**WINEBERRY, Jesse**
Representative Dist. 43
157 27th Ave.
Seattle, WA 98122

## WEST VIRGINIA

### StateRepresentatives

**MOORE, Ernest C.**
Delegate Dist. 18
PO Box 67
Thorpe, WV 24888

## WISCONSIN

### State Senators

**GEORGE. Gary R.**
Senator Dist. 6
3874 N. 42nd
Milwaukee, WI 53216

### Representatives

**COGGS, G. Spencer**
Representative Dist. 16
3732 N. 40 St.
Milwaukee, WI 53216

**COGGS, Marcia**
Representative Dist. 18
329 W. State Capitol
Madison, WI 53702

**WILLIAMS,.Annette Polly**
Representative Dist. 17
7 W. State Capitol
Madison, WI 53702

## WYOMING

### State Representative

**BYRD, Harriett Eliza**
Representative
Laramie Co.
6400 Antelope Ave.
Cheyenne, WY 82009

## BLACK MAYORS

As of March 1989 there were 304 black mayors in the United States, compared to 206 at the same time in 1982; 108 in 1974; and 80 in 1973. Of these 304 black mayors 244 are male and 60 are female. Black mayors, once a rare breed, have now become fixtures on the political landscape, though their total number is still comparatively small. The entities they serve range from small all-black towns such as Fairmount Heights, Maryland and Mound Bayou, Mississippi, to several of the nation's largest cities including Los Angeles, New Orleans, Washington, D.C., Atlanta, Detroit, Newark, and Gary.

A negative aspect for blacks, as far as mayors are concerned, was the loss of seven mayors in cities with populations of over 50,000; six lost reelection bids and one was recalled. The most significant defeat was in the city of Chicago where Eugene Sawyer, who replaced Harold Washington after Washington's sudden death, lost to Richard Daley a white and the son of former Cook County political boss Richard Daley. The situation which had currents of racial strife before and during the campaign has dissipated since Sawyer's defeat and the city seems to be waiting to see the direction of the new mayor. The five other defeats in mayoralty elections were as follows: in Saginaw, Michigan, Laurence D. Craford; in Charolotte, North Carolina, Harvey Gantt; in Tallahassee, Florida, Jack McLean; in Flint, Michigan, James A. Sharp; in West Palm Beach Florida, Samuel L. Thomas; and James W. Holley of Portsmouth Virginia was recalled.

*Richard Arrington Jr.; he became the Mayor of a city that fought change— Birmingham, Alabama.*

Along with their white counterparts they face the common problems afflicting many cities, particularly those in the older, more industrialized sections of the country, including changing population patterns, a decreasing industrial base, dwindling tax revenues, and increasing demands for social services. These problems were further exacerbated in the early 1980s by the Reagan Administration's New Federalism, which found the government reducing its flow of dollars to the cities.

While the realities of life put some constraints on what a mayor can do, regardless of whether he or she is black or white, the role of the black mayor continues to be important both symbolically and from a practical viewpoint. Political scientist Dr. Pearl Robinson of Tufts University has made this observation:

*Given the frequent setbacks that black elected officials face in federal and state legislative bodies where they are a distinct minority, local level executive offices hold far greater possibilities for forthright leadership. Under present conditions black political power in the United States is generally more viable as a grassroots phenomenon. Getting elected mayor is therefore a significant political milestone.*

One of the more interesting developments over recent years is that once blacks win office, competency more than race becomes the test for reelection.

Following are the biographies of a number of black mayors of major U.S. cities and,as well, mayors of some small cities of special interest.

### RICHARD ARRINGTON JR.
**Birmingham, Alabama**
**1980 Population: 284,413**
**Percentage Black: 55.6**
**Elected 1979**

One way of measuring how far the South has come from the tumultuous days of the 1960s when the Civil Rights Movement was in full flower is to take a look at Birmingham. If ever a city deserved the description "mean," it was Birmingham. If ever a city was so rigid that blacks and whites never mixed in public, not even in the state-owned liquor stores, where there was a door for the "Coloreds" and a door for the "Whites." The stock came from the same shelves and the money went into the same cash register, but a railing down the center separated the customers.

"Bull" Connor, the director of public safety, ruled Birmingham, or "Bombingham," as it was known among black people, with an iron fist. It was almost inconceivable that the city would ever change, but change it did in 1979 when Richard Arrington, a zoologist and a college professor, was elected mayor.

Arrington had not planned to run for mayor. After eight years as a member of the Birmingham City Council, and a member of two of its most important committees, he was looking to an appointment as president of one of two state colleges where the incumbents had announced plans to retire—Alabama A&M in Huntsville or Alabama State University in Montgomery.

Then came the shooting of 20-year-old Bonita Carter. She was shot three times in the back by a white policeman responding to a robbery call. The policeman claimed that he thought the unarmed woman was the shotgun-wielding bandit. A night of rioting that broke out was followed by a series of demonstrations. At the center was the white mayor who refused to fire the policeman, assigning him instead to a desk job.

Arrington says this incident "was important in my decision to run." He received the support of most blacks, but not the old-line black political leaders who warned that the time was not yet ripe. With limited financial backing—the figure has been put at $19,000—Arrington won 45% of the vote in the October primary, forcing a runoff in November. At this time a record 76% of the registered black voters turned out, giving him 98% of their vote, and white voters gave him 12% of theirs.

Arrington's inauguration was a symphony of irony. With him on the stand were former Alabama Governor George Wallace, once a leading apostle of segregation, as well as Robert Kennedy Jr., Ethel Kennedy, presidential aide Jack Watson, two other delegates from the Carter White House, both of Alabama's senators, Birmingham Congressman John Buchanan, and Arrington's two predecessors as mayor.

For the son of sharecroppers, Richard Arrington had made it in a big way. But success was nothing new to him.

Arrington started out to be a college professor. He earned his Ph.D. in invertebrate zoology from the University of Oklahoma. He began his teaching career as an assistant professor of biology at Miles College (Birmingham) in 1957. He was named a full professor at the college in 1966 and served as dean from 1967 to 1970. He then served as the fund raising executive director of the Alabama Center for Higher Education, a consortium of eight senior colleges in the state.

He did not neglect the civic side of life, serving as President, Board of Directors, Birmingham Urban League, and President, Board of Directors, Goodwill Industries, among other posts.

Arrington's political involvement began with his election to the Birmingham City Council where he served two terms. His philosophy during that time is summed up in a statement he made to a black magazine:

*I was told by the old-line black political leadership that I was going too far out on the limb, that you don't talk about things like police brutality. It didn't work out that way for me, because I was elected by an even bigger margin for my second four-year term. I was able to be independent because I wasn't depending on politics for a livelihood. If I wasn't reelected—well so what?*

Arrington's efforts to improve the lot of blacks and the poor in Birmingham have not met with city-wide approval and in his State of the City address in January of 1989 he called for a new bond referendum that has met with extensive resistance. Drug use in Birmingham has been extensive and 75% of all males arrested in that city have tested positive for drug use.

In 1986 he received a Doctor of laws degree from Livingston University and in May of 1988 he received the same honor from Woster College.

### THOMAS BARNES
### Gary, Indiana
### 1980 Population: 151,953
### Percentage Black: 70.8
### Elected 1987

Thomas V. Barnes won the mayoral primary race in Gary, Indiana, defeating Richard G. Hatcher, the nation's longest serving black Mayor of a major city.

Barnes, 50-years-old and an attorney who was a former Hatcher campaign worker, received 56 percent of the votes in a May, 1987 primary.

Born on July 23, 1936 in Marked Tree, Arkansas, Barnes received his B.S. degree from Purdue University and a JD Law degree from DaPaul University. A retired Army colonel who attended the U.S. Army Command and General Staff College, Barnes was elected Assessor of Calumet Township for three terms and previously worked as a Laborer for Inland Steel Company and a Caseworker for the Department of Public Welfare.

Barnes faced Republican Thaddeus Romanowski in the November general election and was victorious in that race.

### MARION S. BARRY
### Washington, D.C.
### 1980 Population: 637,651
### Percentage Black: 70.3
### Elected 1978

Marion S. Barry learned his politics the hard way—in the front ranks of the Civil Rights Movement and as an activist community organizer in the deepest part of the Washington, D.C., ghetto. When he announced in 1978 that he was running for mayor, there were few who gave him an outside chance to end up wearing the victor's crown. He wasn't part of the tightly knit black leadership group in the city—he was more of a free wheeling maverick who never hesitated to tilt against windmills. There seemed to be too many things going against him.

First, he was arrayed against two strong opponents, both black, who between them had most of the backing from the white and black establishment of the city. One of his opponents was the incumbent mayor, Walter E. Washington, a longtime fixture on the Washington scene who had been named in 1967 by President Lyndon B. Johnson as the

District Commissioner, under a reorganization plan for the District which called for replacement of the three-man governing board with a single official. This was the beginning of home rule for the District, which for many years had been under the thumb of Congress. Washington was the first person to hold the post, and he was reappointed by President Nixon in 1969 and 1973. When Washingtonians were able to vote for mayor in 1974, they elected Washington.

The second opponent, also a longtime fixture in Washington, was Sterling Tucker, who had for many years served as executive director of the Washington Urban League and in 1978 was serving as president of the City Council.

In the election, Washington and Tucker virtually canceled each other out since they were competing for the same universe of voters, and Barry won with 35% of the vote in the Democratic primary, which in heavily Democratic Washington ensured his win in the general election.

Mayor Barry was born in Itta Bena, Mississippi, in 1936. He received his undergraduate degree from LaMoyne College and an M.S.W. from Fisk University. He also took graduate work at the University of Kansas and the University of Tennessee. Barry was named the first national chairman of the Student Non-Violent Coordinating Committee in 1960, and moved to Washington in 1965 to take over as Washington director of SNCC. He soon became a familiar figure in the city as one of the principal movers in the civil rights movement.

Barry always had the ability to deal with the young and in 1967 he was a co-founder and chairman of an anti-poverty agency, Pride Economic Enterprises. Many of Pride's clients were "street dudes" to whom Pride provided an opportunity to work in jobs that paid them a wage and gave them self-respect. The program was highly successful. Barry severed his connection with Pride in 1970, and in 1972 he was elected president of the D.C. Board of Education. In 1975 he was elected to the City Council as a member-at-large. Barry is a Democrat.

During the late 80's particularly in 1988 and 89 Barry's character became an issue and with the increased drug problem in the D.C. area his popularity seems to be on the wane.

### SIDNEY BARTHELEMY
**New Orleans, Louisiana**
**1980 Population: 557,500**
**Percentage Black: 55**
**Elected 1986**

Nice guys don't always finish last as Sidney Barthelemy's critics realized after he won a record-setting landslide victory in the 1986 mayoral race of New Orleans. As Barthelemy said, "I want you to know that a nice guy can win—and can win big incidentally." His success maintains his consistent string of election victories and makes him the second black mayor of the city. Within his first year in office Barthelemy eliminated an inherited $30 million deficit, and was elected President of the National Association of Regional Councils (NARC), and to the Board of Directors of both the U.S. Conference of Mayors and National League of Cities. In 1988, he was named a vice chairman of the Democratic National Party.

Born in New Orleans in 1942, Sidney Barthelemy became the first black state senator since Reconstruction, in the 1974 election, and was twice elected councilman at large. During his eight years on the council he gained prominence for his congenial temperament.

Mr. Barthelemy, a Roman Catholic Creole, studied for 7 years for the priesthood earning an undergraduate degree in philosophy from St. Joseph Seminary in Washington, D.C. He later earned a master's degree in social work from Tulane University, and taught sociology at Xavier University where he also directed the Urbinvolve Project, which provides students with practical experience in city government. Among his many professional and career involvements, he served for two years as Director of the City Welfare Department.

He was honored as Outstanding Alumnus of Tulane University, and Social Worker of the Year by the Louisiana Chapter of the National Association of Social Workers for 1987, as well as the "American Freedom Award" from the Third Baptist Church of Chicago.

Mayor Barthelemy lives in Gentilly with his wife and three children Cherrie, Bridgette, and Sidney Jr.

### RONALD A. BLACKWOOD
**Mt.Vernon, New York**
**1980 Population: 66,713**
**Percentage Black: 48.7**
**Elected 1987**

Mayor Ronald A. Blackwood, 18th Mayor of the City of Mount Vernon, New York, was born in Kingston, Jamaica, and has been a resident of Mount Vernon for thirty-three years.

Mayor Blackwood became the first elected black Mayor in the history of New York State on January 25, 1985. He served as Acting Mayor in 1976 and was a member of the Mount Vernon City Council for fifteen years, serving as President four times. Mayor Blackwood was also a member of the Westchester County Board of Supervisors from 1968-1969 and a past president of the New York State Association of City Councils.

On November 3, 1987, Blackwood was reelected to a full four year term as Mayor of Mount Vernon.

As Chief Executive of the City of Mount Vernon, Mayor Blackwood serves as Chairman of the Board of Estimate and Contract, and the Urban Renewal and Industrial Development Agencies.

During his tenure as Mayor, Ronald A. Blackwood claims that he has:

Taken action to fight drugs and crime by establishing the Mayor's Task Force on Drugs, Crime and Blight.

Added new police and fire personnel, insuring a full complement for both departments.

Lowered the tax rate while improving City services.

Developed innovative programs to provide affordable housing for Mount Vernon families.

Attracted millions of dollars in State, Federal and private investment to improve housing city-wide.

Initiated an extensive beautification program in Mount Vernon, the first ever city-wide.

Developed an economic initiative plan to create new jobs.

Launched an ambitious recycling effort for the City of Mount Vernon.

On March 8, 1988, Mayor Blackwood received special recognition from the United States Department of Housing and Urban Development for outstanding achievements in promoting Minority Business Enterprise.

Mayor Blackwood is a member of the following organizations: United Way of Westchester/Putnam; N.A.A.C.P.; Rotary; Progressive Lodge No. 64 AFM; All Islands Association; Westchester 2000 Board of Directors; and Omega Psi Phi Fraternity

Mayor Blackwood attended Elizabeth Seton College and has a B.B.A. in Management from Iona College. His wife, Ann, is a teacher in the Mount Vernon School System and his daughter, Helen Marie, is a lawyer in New York City.

His motto: "Life is service, the one who progresses is the one who gives his fellow-beings a little more, a little better service."

### CHARLES E. BOX
**Rockford, Illinois**
**1980 Population: 139,712**
**Percentage Black: 13.2**
**Elected 1989**

Charles E. Box was elected the first black mayor of Rockford, Illinois in April, 1989. For eight years prior to his election, he served as the Legal Director and as City Administrator of Rockford. He practiced law between 1976 and 1981 as a member of the firm of Connolly, Oliver, Goddard, Coplan & Close.

Born in Rockland, he was a graduate of Dartmouth College in 1973 and the University of Michigan Law School in 1976. Box was active in civic, church and community organizations in Rockford and won all of the city's 14 wards even though the black population was only 15 percent.

### THOMAS BRADLEY
**Los Angeles**
**1980 Population: 2,966,763**
**Percentage Black: 17.0**
**Elected 1973**

A highly respected California Poll in 1981 reported that Los Angeles Mayor Thomas Bradley was the most popular politician in the state. This was quite an achievement for the son of a Texas sharecropper, but for Bradley, who has always been a super achiever, it was part of a pattern.

Elected as Los Angeles' first black mayor in 1973 with 56% of the vote; reelected in 1977 with 59.1% of the vote; returned for the third time in 1981 with 63.6% of the vote, Bradley has done extremely well in a city where the black population is only 17%. To the people of Los Angeles he is seen as a decent, conciliatory man who works behind the scenes while avoiding public confrontations, evenhandedly considering the interests of business, minority groups, and others.

Bradley, age seven, arrived in Los Angeles from Calvert, Texas with his family. He grew up in poverty, was a track star at high school, attended the University of California at Los Angeles on an athletic scholarship, and after graduation became a policeman. After 21 years on the force he retired as a lieutenant in 1960, having earned a law degree at night school. With the encouragement of friends, he ran for the City Council in 1963 and won.

In 1969, he ran for the post of mayor in a race that saw Sam Yorty, the incumbent—a talkative, combative, conservative Democrat—resort to blatant racism. Bradley, also a Democrat, was defeated but in 1973 he was back again and this time he won.

Bradley is regarded as one of the nation's most successful black political leaders. He has been credited with building confidence in Los Angeles, keeping racial conflicts in his city to a minimum in a time of rapid change in ethnic composition. He was a principal force in securing the 1984 Summer Olympic Games for Los Angeles while helping rebuild the downtown section without subsidies from local taxpayers.

In describing him, Warren M. Christopher, Deputy Secretary of State in the Carter Administration and a longtime California Democratic activist, said, "He has a sense of size and poise and dignity—maybe sturdiness is the best word."

Subsequent to his election to a third term, Bradley announced that he would run for governor of California in 1982.

### WILLIAM D. BURNEY JR.
**Augusta, Maine**
**1980 Population: 21,819**
**Percentage Black: 38**
**Elected 1988**

In November, 1988, Bill Burney was elected Mayor of Augusta, Maine and became the first black mayor in the state.

Born on April 23, 1951, Burney was a graduate of Cony High School in August before he attended Boston University School of Public Communication where he received a B.S. degree in 1973. He then attended the University of Maine Law School and received a Doctor of Jurisprudence in 1977.

He worked for two years as Project Manager of Housing Innovations in Boston before returning to Augusta to become Executive Director of Downstreet 82. He then joined the Maine State Housing Authority where he held several positions including Assistant Development Director for Housing Rehabilitation.

He was 37-years-old when he won election as mayor after holding the position of city council for the Third Ward. He was also the first black elected to that post.

*Ronald Blackwood was the first elected black mayor in New York State in the city of Mount Vernon.*

### JIM BUSBY
### Victorville, California
### 1980 Population: 14,220
### Percentage Black: 11
### Elected 1989

In February, 1989, Jim Busby was appointed Mayor—the first black to hold that post—by the City Council of Victorville, California.

Born in Houston, Texas on July 16, 1944, Busby attended Texas Southern University until he was drafted into the U.S. Navy during the Vietnam War.

After leaving the service, he joined TRW Space and Defense. During this time he received a B.S. degree in Business and completed his Masters in Business Management at the University of Redlands. He also completed Contract Law, Pricing and Proposal Management classes at the University of California, Los Angeles.

During his 22 years of employment at TRW, he worked on several major space programs.

In May, 1988, Busby was elected to the Victorville City Council and was soon named Mayor pro tem by his colleagues. His appointment followed the death of Mayor Jeff Goodwill in a traffic accident.

### CLAY DIXON
### Dayton, Ohio
### 1980 Population: 244,000
### Percentage Black: 30.9
### Elected1987

Richard Clay Dixon, a native Daytonian, graduated with an undergraduate a degree in industrial arts from Central State University, a master's degree in guidance and counseling from Xavier University of Cincinnati and a master's in education administration from the University of Cincinnati. Since his appointment as Commissioner in 1979 and Mayor in 1987, Richard Dixon has worked to upgrade Dayton's economic development efforts, reduce the city's unemployment rate through education and training programs—he is currently the Director of Dayton's Adult Basic Education program—and stabilize Dayton's neighborhoods through revitalization programs.

Toward these ends, Mayor Dixon, described as open to ideas, consensus-oriented, and collegial, actively participates in various organizations including, the Miami Valley Regional Planning Commission, Ombudsman, Board of Trustees; National League of Cities; U. S. Olympic Committee; and Jobs for Dayton Graduates, Board of Directors. He has worked as a consultant for Educational Testing Services in Princeton, New Jersey, and has served on the Princeton Park Advisory Council and the Northwest Priority Board. He is also a member of the Westmont Optimists; the Shriners; the Advisory Board of the Urban Youth Corps; the Energy Task Force; the National League of Cities; the National Advisory Council of Advanced Education; the State Advisory Board of Advanced Education; the Governor's Council on Ohio Job Training; and the U. S. Conference of Mayors Human Development Committee—Chairman of its Subcommittee on Human Services.

Mayor Dixon lives with his wife Judy, and their two children, Millie and Ricky, in Dayton, Ohio.

### LELIA SMITH FOLEY
### Taft, Oklahoma
### 1980 Population: 489
### Percentage Black: 88
### Elected 1973

Lelia Smith Foley became mayor of Taft, Oklahoma, a position which designated her the first black female mayor in the United States.

The town, which is virtually all-black with some 600 inhabitants, was the home of the young woman who took office on April 16, 1973.

The mother of five children, Ms. Foley was formerly a teacher aide and assistant director of the Taft Community Center. She was inspired to run for office after reading the book, "The Making of A black Mayor."

In 1974, Mayor Foley was voted one of the Ten Most Outstanding Young Women in American. She would remain in office through a period of 13 years.

**JAMES N. GARNER**
**Village of Hempstead, L.I., N.Y.**
**1980 Population: 40,404**
**Percentage Black: 57**
**Elected 1989**

James N. Garner became the first black mayor on Long Island in April, 1989. In a hotly contested race, Garner unseated the incumbent as well as a black candidate on the Democratic ticket.

A 44-year-old Republican, Garner was elected after a career in politics which began when he worked as a campaign manager for a former Hempstead trustee. Garner became a member of the Board in 1984 and was elected as a trustee in 1987.

Owner of Grand Central Exterminators, Garner was also a member of the Board of Trustees for Jackson Memorial AME Zion Church in Hempstead.

**WILSON GOODE**
**Philadelphia, Pennsylvania**
**1980 Population: 1.6 Million**
**Percentage Black: 42**
**Elected 1983**

W. Wilson Goode was elected the first black mayor of Philadelphia and re-elected to a second four-year term in November, 1987.

Born in North Carolina, he moved with his family to Philadelphia and attended Morgan State University where he received his undergraduate degree. He then spent two years as a Military Police lieutenant in the U.S. Army. Following his discharge, he earned a Master's Degree in Governmental Administration from the University of Pennsylvania's Wharton School.

He was nominated to the Public Utility Commission by Pennsylvania Governor Milton Shapp in 1978. Later that year, he was named Commission Chairman. In 1980, Goode was asked to serve as Philadelphia's Managing Director. He would later resign from that position to campaign for 16 hours a day to win the mayoral position.

A church deacon, Goode received some 12 honorary doctorate degrees from such institutions as The University of Pennsylvania, College of the Holy Cross and Hofstra University Law School.

**DOROTHY J. (Lee) INMAN**
**Tallahassee, Florida**
**1980 Population:**
**Percentage Black:**
**Elected 1988**

Dorothy J. Inman was elected Mayor pro tem of the Tallahassee City Commission in 1988 and became Mayor in 1989. A native of Birmingham, Alabama, she received her B.A. degree from Atlanta's Clark College in 1968 and went on to an internship at the University of Puget Sound in Tacoma, Washington.

She began an 18-year teaching career in 1968 at the San Antonio Independent School District in Texas and then went on to serve as a project administrator for the TORCH Project at Florida State University's Center for Policy Studies.

Ms. Inman was elected to the Tallahassee City Commission in 1986 and served there until her election as Mayor pro tem. She served on a number of educational advisory committees in Florida and received numerous awards for contributions to education and community service.

**CARL E. OFFICER**
**East St. Louis, Illinois**
**1980 Population: 55,200**
**Percentage Black: 95.6**
**Elected 1979**

The honorable Carl Edward Officer is the mayor of the City of East St. Louis, Illinois, the second most populous city in the southern Illinois region.

Elected by a 95% plurality in May 1979, Officer was confirmed by the U.S. Conference of Mayors as the youngest mayor of a major metropolitan city at that time.

Prior to entering the office of mayor, Officer was the deputy director of Drivers Services for the State of Illinois. He also served as the deputy coroner for St. Clair County.

Shortly after his inauguration, Mayor Officer, realizing that there is strength in unity, founded the Metro-East Conference of Black Mayors, Inc., an organization bringing together the mayors of the four other predominantly black municipalities that surround East St. Louis. He currently serves as president and chief spokesperson for that group.

Mayor Officer was recently selected as one of the future outstanding black leaders for the eighties by *Black Enterprise* magazine.

The youthful mayor holds membership in many professional and fraternal organizations. Included among them are the NAACP, Urban League, Jaycees, U.S. Conference of Mayors, and National Conference of Black Mayors.

**CARRIE PERRY**
**Hartford, Connecticut**
**1980 Population: 136,400**
**Percentage Black: 33.9**
**Elected 1987**

Inaugurated on December 1, 1987, Carrie Saxon Perry became the first black woman in New England to hold office as a mayor.

A life-long resident of Hartford, the Mayor was educated in the Hartford public schools and attended Howard University in Washington, D.C. where she pursued studies in English and Law. A community activist, Mayor Perry has been a social worker for the state of Connecticut, and administrator for the Community Renewal Team of Greater Hartford, Inc., and Executive Director of Amistad House, Inc.

Prior to her election as Mayor, Perry had been elected to four consecutive two-year terms as a State Representative from Hartford to the Connecticut General Assembly.

In her freshman year, the Mayor was appointed Assistant Majority Leader. A member of the Education Committee and the Finance, Revenue & Bonding Committee throughout her tenure at the Capitol, Mayor Perry also chaired the House Subcommittee on Bonding. As chair, the Mayor was instrumental in allocating funds for Hartford projects, and acquiring set-aside funds for minority contractors in the state. Committed to human rights, she was influential in convincing her colleagues to divest state funds linked to South Africa. Mayor Perry has also been an outspoken supporter of programs and litigation for quality education, job training, and programs to reduce high school drop-out rates, teenage pregnancies, and the high rate of infant mortality. It was the Mayor's initiative that franchised the homeless in Connecticut with the right to vote.

An alternate to the Democratic National Convention in San Francisco in 1984, the Mayor was a delegate pledged to the Presidential candidacy of Jesse Jackson in 1988. She is often asked to testify before Congressional hearings in Washington.

Profiled in various magazines including *Ebony* and *Essence,* Mayor Perry has also been the recipient of several awards.

## MELVIN R. PRIMAS JR.
## Camden, New Jersey
## 1980 Population: 84,910
## Percentage Black: 53
## Elected 1981

Mayor Melvin Randolph "Randy" Primas Jr. was born in Camden, New Jersey in August 1949, the second child of Yvonne and Melvin Primas Sr.

Spending his childhood years in East Camden and attending area elementary and junior high schools, he graduated in June 1967 from Woodrow Wilson High School. That fall, he was accepted to study economics and marketing at Howard University in Washington, D. C.

In August 1969, he married the former Bonita Wilson. (They have two sons.) A bachelor of arts degree was conferred upon Primas in May 1971, and three short months later the newly-graduated Primas was recruited as a marketing consultant for the Black People's Unity Movement, a fledgling self-help economic development agency which was destined to become one of the largest in the nation. He later became Vice President of Venture Development.

In May of 1973, at age 23, he was elected to the Camden City Council, as the youngest person ever elected to the council, and in 1978 was elected president of that body.

During the next six years, as a council member, Randy Primas sponsored and/or supported numerous pieces of progressive legislation destined to enrich the lives of Camden-ites.

Yet, there was still more to do for the city, and on May 12, 1981 Councilman Primas became Mayor Primas with a 55 percent mandate from a field of six candidates in the nonpartisan election. On July 1, Melvin R. Primas Jr. was confirmed as the first black mayor in the city's 151-year history, and was reelected to that office in May, 1985.

Mayor Primas serves as a member of the New Jersey State Planning Commission and the New Jersey Job Training Coordinating Council. He was also a superdelegate at the 1988 Democratic Convention in Atlanta. Numerous awards and honors have been bestowed upon him including Who's Who in American Politics, and Outstanding Achievement in Politics by the Congressional Black Caucus in 1981.

## KURT L. SCHMOKE
## Baltimore, Maryland
## 1980 Population: 786,775
## Percentage Black: 54.8
## Elected 1987

Kurt L. Schmoke was inaugurated Mayor of Baltimore on December 8, 1987. Mayor Schmoke grew up and attended public school in Baltimore. He graduated with honors from Baltimore City College high school, and in 1967 won the award as the top scholar-athlete in the City. Mayor Schmoke went on to receive his Bachelor of Arts degree from Yale University, studied at Oxford University as a Rhodes Scholar, and in 1976 earned his law degree from Harvard University.

After graduating from Harvard, Mayor Schmoke began his law practice with the Baltimore firm of Piper & Marbury, and shortly thereafter was appointed by President Carter as a member of the White House Domestic Policy staff.

In 1978, Mayor Schmoke returned to Baltimore as an Assistant United States Attorney where he prosecuted narcotics and white collar crime cases, among others. He later returned to private practice.

In November 1982, the Mayor was elected State's Attorney for Baltimore City, which is the chief prosecuting office of the City. As State's Attorney, he created a full time Narcotics Unit to prosecute all drug cases, and underscored the criminal nature of domestic violence and child abuse by setting up separate units to handle those cases.

Also while State's Attorney, Mayor Schmoke hired a community liaison officer to make sure that his office was being responsive to neighborhood questions and concerns.

In his inaugural address, Mayor Schmoke set the tone and future direction for his administration when he said that he wanted Baltimore to become known as "the city that reads." Since then, he has overseen the passage of the largest ever increase in the City's education budget, and in partnership with Baltimore businesses and community based organizations, Mayor Schmoke developed the Commonwealth Agreement and the College Bound Foundation. These programs will guarantee opportunities for jobs or for college to qualifying high school graduates. Also since taking office, Mayor Schmoke has begun major initiatives in housing, economic development and public safety.

Mayor Schmoke, in addition to being a prosecutor, has throughout his career worked to develop more effective criminal justice policies. He served on the Governor's Commission on Prison Overcrowding, the Maryland Criminal Justice Coordinating Council, and the Task Force to Reform the Insanity Defense.

In recognition of his commitment to excellence in education and his service to the community, Mayor Schmoke has received honorary degrees from several colleges and universities.

Throughout his career, Mayor Schmoke has been active in the civic and cultural life of the Baltimore community by serving as a member of numerous boards of trustees.

Mayor Schmoke, and his wife Patricia, an ophthalmologist, reside in Baltimore with their children, Gregory and Katherine.

### SHARPE JAMES
**Newark, New Jersey**
**1980 Population: 329,288**
**Percentage Black: 58.2**
**Elected 1986**

Sharpe James was elected Mayor of the City of Newark on May 13, 1986, and was sworn into office on July 1 of that year. Prior to becoming Mayor, James served for 16 years as a member of the Newark Municipal Council. James is the 35th person to be elected Mayor of New Jersey's largest city.

Mayor James gained nationwide attention by defeating the city's first black Mayor, Kenneth A. Gibson, who was seeking an unprecedented fifth term in office.

Having accumulated an impressive 16-year record as councilman of the South Ward and councilman-at-large, Mayor James has been a leader in the fight of New Jersey's cities for their fair share of federal and state funds. First elected to public office as South Ward councilman in 1970, Mayor James easily won re-election on the first ballot in 1974 and 1978, when he became the first public official in the city's history to run unopposed. He again made Newark history in 1982 when he won the post of councilman-at-large, becoming the first person to serve Newark as both a ward and at-large councilman.

Mayor James is the first councilman to be elected Mayor.

Born in Jacksonville, Florida, on February 20, 1936, Mayor James has lived most of his life in Newark, graduating from Miller Street School, Malcolm X Shabazz (then South Side) High School and with honors from Montclair State College. He holds a master's degree from Springfield College, where he received the 1961 Department of Physiology Award, and has done advanced study at Washington State, Columbia, and Rutgers Universities. In 1988 he was awarded an honorary Doctorate of Laws degree from Montclair State College.

An Essex County College professor for 18 years prior to his election, Mayor James was the first black to serve as department chairman and athletic director within the state college system. Mayor James has also served as vice-president and president of the Garden State Athletic Conference (GSAC). Mayor James is also a past recipient of the Montclair State College Distinguished Alumni Award.

Mayor James served with the U.S. Army in Europe and was a Newark public school teacher for seven years, coaching city, county, and state championship track and cross-country teams. He is also Newark's senior tennis champion and a former New Jersey State Tennis Association champion. A long-time community activist, Mayor James is the founder of Little City Hall, Inc. He is also a charter member and past president of the Organization of Negro Educators (ONE), and an executive of the Scholarship Assistance Guidance Association (SAGA).

He was co-chairman of Essex County and a delegate whip for Ted Kennedy for President in 1980. In addition, he served as 1988 state chairman of the Jesse Jackson for President Campaign and is former civil rights chairman for the Business and Industrial Coordinating Council, a volunteer aide to U.S. Senator Bill Bradley, and a member of the board of governors of the N.J. Historical Society. Presently he is a member of the board of the National League of Cities, committee member of the U.S. Conference of Mayors and locally serves on the executive committee of the Newark Collaboration Group.

In addition to his other accolades, Mayor James was named one of the nation's Ten Best-Dressed Men of 1987 by the Fashion Foundation of America.

Mayor James and his wife, Mary, have three sons: John, Elliott and Kevin. They live in Newark's South Ward

### WALTER R. TUCKER
**Compton, California**
**1980 Population: 81,286**
**Percentage Black: 74.8**
**Elected 1988**

In April of 1985, the people of Compton overwhelmingly returned Mayor Walter R. Tucker to office, the first black person ever re-elected as mayor in Compton.

Born in Taft, Oklahoma in 1924, Mayor Tucker has been a resident of Compton since 1957. A dentist and ordained minister, he has held public office for over 14 years serving as mayor, City Councilman, and Compton School Board Trustee. As mayor he is involved in ongoing negotiations and lobbying to ensure Compton's receipt of funds through H.P. 3129, a ports improvement bill.

The Mayor is a member of the Board of Directors of the National Conference of Black Mayors (NCBM); the California Council of Criminal Justice Planning; Chamber of Commerce; Independent Cities Association; NAACP; Los Angeles County Sanitation District, Board of Directors; and the Southern California Association of Governments (SCAG).

Mayor Tucker graduated from Los Angeles State College with a B. A., worked on his masters at the University of Southern California, and received a Doctor of Dental Surgery from Meharry Medical College.

### JAMES L. USRY
**Atlantic City, New Jersey**
**1980 Population: 40,199**
**Percentage Black: 50**
**Elected 1984**

James L. Usry was sworn in as Mayor of Atlantic City on

March 14, 1984. Prior to his election as Mayor, Mr. Usry was employed as Assistant Superintendent of Atlantic City Public Schools.

From 1952 through 1977 Mr. Usry held a number of positions within the Atlantic City school system including Junior High School Teacher, Principal, Director of Elementary Services and Director of School Community Services.

Born in Athens, Georgia, Usry served in the U.S. army in Africa and Italy in World War II, and from 1946 to 1951 was employed as a professional basketball player with the New York Rens and the Harlem Globetrotters.

In 1980, Mr. Usry became the President of the Atlantic City Congress of Community Organizations, an umbrella organization of local civic associations that was instrumental in bringing about the change of municipal government in Atlantic City. It was his involvement in the Congress that led to his decision to run for Mayor.

Mr. Usry has served on several Boards and been a member of a number of organizations including: Board of Directors Y.M.C.A.; Executive Board N.A.A.C.P.; Past Basileus Omega Psi Phi; and Board of Directors Midlantic Bank/South.

Mr. Usry has also been President Atlantic City Administrators Education Association; Member National Community School Education Association; Member Mayors Council on Youth, State of New Jersey; Commissioner Atlantic County Improvement Authority; Rutgers University Board of Governors; Casino Reinvestment Development Authority; the Board of Overseers Governor's School; the Governor's Council on New Jersey Outdoors; the National Advisory Council on Educational Research and Improvement; President of the National Conference of Black Mayors; President of the New Jersey Conference of Black Mayors; Member of New Jersey State Martin Luther King Jr. Commemorative Commission; and member, Board of Trustees, Lincoln University.

On March 31, 1984, the Mayor married the former LaVerne Young of Knoxville, Tennessee and New York City.

### LIONEL J. WILSON
**Oakland, California**
**1980 Population: 339,288**
**Percentage Black: 47.0**
**Elected 1977**

Oakland, which stood for a long time in the shadow of its larger, more famous sister city across the bay, San Francisco, has developed into a city with its own personality and style. With championship professional sports teams, a first-rate symphony orchestra, redevelopment, and a responsive daily newspaper, the Oakland Tribune, which has been revitalized under the editorship of a black journalist, Robert Maynard, Oakland is growing. Serving his second term as mayor is Lionel J. Wilson, who came to the city with his family from New Orleans when he was four years old, carved out a career for himself as a lawyer and then a judge, and capped it all by being elected mayor of Oakland in 1977 and being reelected in 1981.

Mayor Wilson, the first black man to govern the city, also has a number of other firsts to his credit. In 1960 Governor Edmund G. Brown Sr., appointed him to the Oakland Piedmont Municipal Court, making him the first black judge in Alameda County. He was serving as presiding judge of that court when Governor Brown elevated him to the Superior Court in 1964. He became presiding judge of the Alameda County Superior Court in 1973.

Wilson grew up in Oakland, the oldest of eight children, and attended public school there. He received his B.A. in Economics from the University of California at Berkeley in 1939, and then served overseas in World War II. After his honorable discharge, he earned his law degree in 1949 from the Hastings College of Law and began his law practice in Oakland.

His career on the bench was distinguished by his service as the chairman of Presiding Judges of California Superior Courts, four terms as the presiding judge of the Criminal Division of the Alameda County Superior Courts, and one year as the presiding judge of the Appellate Department of the Alameda County Superior Court. He was at that time the only black judge to serve as the presiding judge of a Superior Court in California, or of the Appellate Department of a Superior Court, and as chairman of Presiding Judges of California Superior Courts.

Mayor Wilson has also been active in community service, notably with the NAACP in both Berkeley and Oakland. Since his election he has served on the Board of Directors of the League of California Cities, various committees of the U.S. Conference of Mayors, and the National League of Cities. He was appointed by President Jimmy Carter to the U.S. Court of Patents and Appeals.

Mayor Wilson is married and the father of three sons, two of whom are graduates of the University of California at Davis School of Law.

### ANDREW YOUNG
**Atlanta, Georgia**
**1980 Population: 425,000**
**Percentage Black: 61.0**
**Elected 1981**

A leading civil rights activist, a congressman from Georgia, the U.S. ambassador to the United Nations, and mayor of the principal city in the South, Atlanta: this has been the career of Andrew Young, who came into national prominence nearly two decades ago and is probably as well known internationally as any living black American, save Muhammad Ali. Soft-spoken while eloquent, Young is widely admired for his incisive thinking and his willingness to speak his mind.

He was born in New Orleans in 1932, and received a B.S. degree from Howard University at 19 and a Bachelor of Divinity degree from Hartford Theological Seminary in 1955. He was ordained a minister in the United Church of Christ and then served in churches in Alabama and Georgia before joining the National Council of Churches in 1957. The turning point of his life came in 1961 when he joined

Reverend Martin Luther King and became a trusted aide and close confidante. He did much of the negotiating for the Southern Christian Leadership Conference and was respected for his coolness and rationality. He became executive vice president of SCLC in 1967 and remained with King until the latter's murder in 1968. During those years with SCLC Young also developed several programs including voter registration projects and other major civil rights drives.

In 1970, Young lost a bid for Congress when Fletcher Thompson, a white ultraconservative Republican, beat him by 20,000 votes in a campaign in which Thompson contended that Young sought the demise of Western Civilization. In 1972, however, the Fifth District in Atlanta was redistricted under court order and Thompson, who conceded that he had never met with one black group as a congressman, resigned to run unsuccessfully for the Senate.

Though large segments of the conservative white population had been removed from the Fifth, the race for Congress was not easy for Young. Blacks still comprised only 44% of the registered voters and Young's Republican opponent, Rodney Cook, was a more appealing candidate than Thompson. However, Young captured 23% of the white vote and 54% of the total vote to win by a margin of 8,000, even though Richard Nixon carried the district for president. Young was the first black representative to be elected from Georgia since Jefferson Long in 1870.

Thereafter, Young was elected with ease every two years. He was one of the most vocal supporters of his fellow Georgian Jimmy Carter's campaign for the Presidency in 1976. When Carter won, Young left his safe seat in Congress in 1977 to become America's ambassador to the United Nations.

His tenure there was marked by controversy as well as solid achievement. The controversy came because of his outspoken manner, which sometimes ruffled diplomatic feathers. His solid achievements were represented primarily in the tremendous improvement he fostered in relations between America and the Third World.

His career as a diplomat came to an end in 1979 when he met secretly with a representative of the Palestine Liberation Organization to discuss an upcoming vote in the United Nations. America had a policy that none of its representatives would meet with the PLO as long as it refused to recognize the right of Israel to exist as a state. When the news of Young's meeting leaked out, there was an uproar. Young had originally told the State Department that the meeting was by chance, but later he admitted that it had been planned.

Though the meeting had secured a vote in the United Nations that the United States wanted, the pressure mounted and Young tendered his resignation, which President Carter accepted. The incident badly strained black-Jewish relations because of the feeling within the black community that Jewish leaders were instrumental in Young's removal, a charge that they denied.

Young became a private citizen, but not for long. When Maynard Jackson was prevented by law from running for his third term of office as mayor of Atlanta in 1981, Young entered the race. Once again, it was not to be easy. He faced a black candidate and a strong white candidate and was forced into a runoff. Race entered the campaign when the outgoing mayor, himself a black, charged blacks who supported the white candidate, State Legislator Sidney Marcus, with "selling out" the civil rights movement.

Jackson's remarks were widely criticized, and it was feared that they would create a backlash against Young. However, he ended up winning 55% of the total vote. He won 10.6% of the white vote, compared to the 12% he had won in the primary, and 88.4% of the black vote, up from 61% earlier.

Young took office at a time when Atlanta was going through several economic and social problems. Its population was shrinking, the tax base stagnating, almost a quarter of the city's residents were below the poverty line, and the city was still shaken by the recent murders of 28 black youths and the disappearance of another—even though a man had been convicted of several of the murders.

The new mayor said on inauguration day: "We've gone through the strain and there have been no broken relationships and there will be none in the future."

Having been reelected until January of 1990 Young's plans for the future ( by law he can not run again for Mayor) appear to include preparations for a run for Governor of Georgia.

## COLEMAN YOUNG
**Detroit, Michigan**
**1980 Population: 1,203,339**
**Percentage Black: 63.1**
**Elected 1973**

In 1981 Coleman Young won his third term as mayor of Detroit, which surprised no one. By all odds one of the most popular mayors the Motor City has ever had, if not the most popular, Young won 65.8% of the votes cast. The vote was remarkable because even with the heavy unemployment in Detroit, caused by the difficulties of the automakers, a shortage of cash, and the drying up of funds that the city had received when Jimmy Carter was President, the voters returned Young to office.

Part of Young's support stemmed from a sense of revitalization which he breathed into Detroit and the confidence of the voters who believed that though things were rough, the mayor would persevere. A Democrat, and one of the earliest big-city mayors to come out for Jimmy Carter in 1976, Young had a very close relationship with the Carter Administration which proved helpful in securing funds for Detroit. Carter himself said, "There is no other mayor any closer to me than is Coleman Young."

The road leading to the front door of the White House was a along and often torturous one for Young. It started in Tuscaloosa, Alabama, where he was born in 1921. Young's family moved to Detroit's east side in 1926 after the Ku Klux Klan ransacked a neighborhood in Huntsville where his father was learning to be a tailor. In Detroit, he attended Catholic Central and then Eastern High School, graduating from the latter with honors. He had to reject a scholarship to the University of Michigan when the Eastern High School

Alumni Association, in contrast to policies followed with poor white students, declined to assist him with costs other than tuition.

Young entered an electrician's apprentice school at the Ford Motor Company, lost the only available electrician's job to a white man who scored much lower than he in tests, went to work on the assembly line, and soon engaged in underground union activities. One day a man Young describes as a company goon tried to attack him. Young hit him on the head with a steel bar and was fired.

Young then worked to integrate housing in Detroit's Sojourner Truth Housing Project until World War II. During the war he became a navigator in the Army Air Force and was commissioned a second lieutenant. Stationed at Freeman Field, Indiana, he demonstrated against exclusion of blacks from officers' clubs and was arrested along with 100 other black airmen, among them Thurgood Marshall, now an Associate Justice of the Supreme Court, and Percy Sutton, former president of New York's Borough of Manhattan. Young spent three days in jail. Shortly thereafter, the clubs were opened to black officers.

After the war, the future mayor of Detroit returned to his union organizing activities and in 1947 was named director of organization for the Wayne County AFL-CIO. However, the Union fired him in 1948 when he supported Henry Wallace, candidate of the Progressive Party, in the Presidential election. The Union regarded Wallace as a dupe of the Communist Party and supported Harry Truman.

Young managed a dry cleaning plant for a few years and then, in 1951, founded and directed the National Negro Labor Council. According to Young, the Council was way ahead of its time and successfully prevailed on Sears Roebuck & Co. and the San Francisco Transit System to hire blacks. However, the Council also aroused the interest of the House Un-American Activities Committee, which was then holding hearings around the country at which alleged Communists were required to produce names of people allegedly associated with the Party. Young, who denies he was ever a Communist, refused to name anyone. He emerged from the battle with his self-respect intact, but his Labor Council was placed on the Attorney General's subversive list, and in 1956 was disbanded. Says Young of the 1950s: "Anybody who was mentioned by any stool pigeon as being a Communist, lost their jobs. People were really scared." Charges that Young was a Communist were to be used against him, unsuccessfully, 21 years later in his mayoral campaign.

After working at a variety of jobs until 1961, Young won a seat on the Michigan Constitutional Convention. In 1962 he lost a race for state representative but became director of campaign organization for the Democratic gubernatorial candidate in Wayne County (Detroit). He sold life insurance until 1964 when, with Union support, he was elected to the State Senate. In the Senate, he was a leader of the civil rights forces, fighting among other things for low-income housing for people dislocated by urban renewal and for bars to discrimination in the hiring practices of the Detroit Police Force.

In 1969 Young sought to run for mayor but declined when a court ruled he would first have to resign his Senate seat. The black candidate in that race, Richard Austin, lost by 6,000 votes. However, in 1973 the Michigan Supreme Court declared that Young could run, and he won narrowly in a contest in which votes polarized according to race.

## ROSTER OF BLACK MAYORS

With thanks to the Joint Center for Political Studies and The National Conference of Black Mayors

### ALABAMA

**Arrington, Richard**
City Hall
710 North 20th Street
Birmingham, AL 35203
(205) 254-2000

**Bell, Joe**
Mosses
PO Box 296
Hayneville, AL 36040
(205) 563-9141

**Butler, Anthony S.**
City Hall
PO Box 157
Lisman, AL 36912
(205) 398-3889

**Carson, Rufus**
Franklin
Route 3, Box 882
Tuskegee, AL 36083
(205) 727-2111

**Daily, James**
PO Box 971
Emelle, AL 35459
(205) 652-7529

**Ford, Johnny L.**
Tuskegee Municipal Complex
101 Fonville Street
Tuskegee, AL 36083
(205) 727-2180

**Graham, C. J.**
PO Box 46
Gordon, AL 36343
(205) 522-3113

**Hayden, Andrew**
PO Box 201
Uniontown, AL 36786
(205) 628-2011

**Hopson, Charlie**
City Hall
PO Box 8
Akron, AL 35441
(205) 372-3148

**Huelett, John E.**
PO Box 365
Hayneville, AL 36040
(205) 548-2128

**Isaac, Jim, Jr.**
PO Box 126
Forkland, AL 36740
(205) 289-3032

**Jackson, Johnny**
White Hall
Route 1, Box 191-B
Hayneville, AL 36040
(205) 637-6378

**James, Fred**
City Hall
PO Box 93
North Courtland, AL 35618
(205) 637-6378

**Jimmar, Renita**
PO Box 308
Leighton, AL 35646
(205) 637-6378

**Kirkland, Diane**
Route 1, Box G24
Geiger, AL 35459
(205) 455-2811

**Knott, Perry**
PO Box 70
Wilmer, AL 36587
(205) 649-6883

**Landford, Larry**
4701 Gary Avenue
Fairfield, AL 35064
(205) 788-2492

**Manning, Levern**
Route 2
Carrollton, AL 35447
(205) 373-2068

**Madison, Essie B.**
McMullen
Route 2, Box 16-B
Aliceville, AL 35442
(205) 373-8959

**Powell, Lena**
Yellow Bluff
Route 3, Box 48
Pinehill, AL 36769

**Ollison, Robert L.**
PO Box 210
Beatrice, AL 36425
(205) 789-2540

**Reese, Mildred**
Route 1, Box 457
Ridgeville, AL 35954

**Sellars, Walter**
PO Box 733
Gordonville, AL 36040
(205) 563-7369

**Smith, Dorothy**
City Hall
PO Box 10
Hillsboro, AL 35643
(205) 637-2070

**Snow, Willie**
610 Park Avenue
Hobson City, AL 36201
(205) 831-0441

**Stovall, Mary K.**
PO Box 358
Hurtsboro, AL 36860
(205) 667-7771

**Thomas, Jewel**
3700 Main Street
Brighton, AL 35020
(205) 425-8943

**Tony, Alonzo**
640 Six Street
Madison, AL 35758
(205) 772-0151

**Walker, Esmar Jr.**
Union
PO Box 782
Eutaw, AL 35462
(205) 372-3202

**Ward, Elvin**
Town of Colony
Route 3, Box 48
Hanceville, AL 35077
(205) 287-1192

**Williams, Jimmie**
Old Memphis
Route 1, Box 213
Aliceville, AL 35442
(205) 373-8622

## ARKANSAS

**Barnes, George E.**
PO Box 62
Reed, AR 71670-0062
(501) 392-2610

**Barnes, George H.**
City Hall
PO Box 141
Wabbaseka, AR 72175
( 501) 766-4262

**Bowens, Emily**
Mitchellville
Route 1, Box 308
Dumas, AR 71639
( 501) 382-5172

**Brownlee, Christina**
Gilmore
PO Box 65
Gilmore, AR 72339
( 501) 343-2697

**Conely, Emmitt**
City Hall
PO Box 220
Cotton Plant, AR 72036
( 501) 459-2121

**Croft, Ira**
PO Box 300
Edmondson, AR 72332
(501) 735-6946

**Dillard, Jackie**
P.O Box 306
Alexander, AR 72072
( 501) 455-2585

**Dolphin, Randy**
Allport
Rt. 2, Box 39
England, AR 72046
(501) 275-3821

**Dolphin, Silas**
Lakeview
Route 1, Box 221 A
Helena, AR 72342
( 501) 827-6341

**English, Clarence**
General Delivery
Menifee, AR 72107
(5O1) 354-0898

**Feminster, Curtis**
PO Box 27
Huntington, AR 72940
(5O1) 928-5083

**Hendrix, Martha**
Route 1, Box 3271
Tollette, AR 71851
(5O1) 287-4336

**Jackson, Curly Lee**
Route 2, Box 283
Wilmar, AR 71675
(501) 469-5609

**Johnson, Evans, II**
Birdsong
Route 1, Box 66
Tyronza, AR 72386

**Johnson, Lloyd**
PO Box 17
Carthage, AR 7172S
(501) 254-2463

**Pulliam, Eddie**
PO Box 487
DeQueen, AR 71832
(5O1) 584-3445

**Sanders, Salina**
PO Box 10
Wilton, AR 71865
(501) 898-3230

**Smith, Lorraine D.**
PO Box 237
Wrightsville, AR 72183
(501) 897-4547

**Smith, Sherman**
PO Box 213
Earle, AR 72331
(501) 792-8909

**Whitaker, Willard**
Washington Street
PO Box 109
Madison, AR 72359
(501) 633-2174

**Wilburn, James Jr.**
300 H'wy 77 Bypass
Sunset, AR 72364
(501) 739-3528

**Williams, James**
610 Caddo Street
Arkadelphia, AR 71923
(501) 246-4211

**Wilson, John Lee**
PO Box 487
Haynes, AR 72341
(501) 633-4947

**Young, Elizabeth**
PO Drawer 6
LaGrange, AR 72352

**Young, Floyd Jr.**
611 Hickory Street
Hope, AR 71801

## CALIFORNIA

**Bostic, John B.**
2415 University Ave.
East Palo Alto, CA 94303
(415) 853-3101

**Bradley, Thomas**
City Hall
200 North Spring Street
Los Angeles, CA 90012
(213) 485-3311

**Levingston, George L.**
City Hall
PO Box 4046
Richmond, CA 94804

**McClair, Lance**
City Hall
PO Box 810
Seaside, CA 93955
(408) 899-6200

**Richards, Paul H. II**
City Hall
11330 Bullis Road
Lynwood, CA 90262
(213) 603-0220, Ext. 201

**Tucker, Walter**
205 S. Willowbrook
Compton, CA 90220
(213) 537-8008

**Vincent, Ed**
1 Manchester Boulevard
Inglewood, CA 90301
(213) 412-5300

**White, Billy R.**
1131 Menlo Oaks Drive
Menlo Park, CA 94025
(415) 858-3380

**Wilson, Lionel**
City Hall
14th & Washington Sts.
Oakland, CA 94612
(415) 273-3141

## CONNECTICUT

**Perry, Carrie S.**
City Hall
550 Main Street
Hartford, CT 06103
(203) 722-6610

## DISTRICT OF COLUMBIA

**Barry, Marion**
1350 Pennsylvania Ave., NW
Room 520
Washington, DC 20004
(202) 727-6319

## DELAWARE

**Fisher, Roger C.**
Town Office
PO Box 210
Laura, DE 19956
(302) 875-2277

**Wright, George C. Jr.**
PO Box 307
Smyrna, DE 19977
(302) 653-9231

## FLORIDA

**Anthony, Clarence**
South Bay

335 Southwest 2nd Ave.
South Bay, FL 33493
(305) 996-6751

**Benton, Derryl**
PO Drawer 68
Eustis, FL 32727-0068

**Ellis, Wallace E.**
PO Drawer A
Gretna, FL 32332
(904) 856-5257

**Flowers, Owen**
PO Box 1507
Haines City, FL 33844
(813) 422-3660

**Graham, John H.**
PO Box 58
White Springs, FL 32096
(904) 397-2310

**Larkins, Pat E.**
City Hall
101 South West First Ave.
Pompano Beach, FL 33061
(305) 786-4050

**McLean, Jack**
City Hall
300 South Adams
Tallahassee, FL 32301
(904) 599-8100

**Milton, Cedric E.**
Town of Welaka
PO Box H
Welaka, FL 32093

**Pittman, Isaac**
Jacob City
Route 3, Box 275A
Cottondale, FL 32431

**Ingram, Robert**
777 Sharazad Boulevard
Opa-Locka, FL 33054
(305) 688-4611

**Martin, Sadie**
801 East Haines St.
Plant City, FL 33566
(813) 752-3125

**Thompkins, Walter**
PO Box 527
Pierson, FL 32080
(904) 749-2661

**Vereen, Nathaniel**
PO Box 2163
Eatonville, FL 32751
(305) 647-0061

**Wallace, Otis**
404 West Palm Drive
PO Box 3001
Florida City, FL 33034

**Warmac, Freddie L.**
PO Box 23
Newberry, FL 32669
(904) 472-3748

**Williams, Clara K.**
PO Box 10682
Riviera Beach, FL 33404
(305) ~45-4000

## GEORGIA

**Bivens, Isaac**
PO Box 31
Harrison, GA 31035
(912) 552-7640

**Brown, Justine Thomas**
PO Box 82
Oliver, GA 30449
(912) 857-3163

**Carter, James**
PO Box 208
Woodland, GA 31836
(404) 674-2200

**Carter John L.**
PO Box 342
Greenville, GA 30222
(404) 672-4211

**Davis, Willie J.**
PO Box 436
Vienna, GA 31092
(912) 268-4744

**Deen, James E.**
PO Box 429
Alma, GA 31510
(912) 632-7363

**Gamble, Robert**
PO Box 151
Whitesburg, GA 30185
(404) 832-1184

**Grant, James**
City Hall
PO Box 125
Midway, GA 31320
(912) 884-3344

**Gresham, Emma**
PO Box 83
Keysville, GA 30816
(404) 547-3008

**Hollinshed, Samuel**
PO Box 194
Marshallville, GA 31057
(912) 967-2535

**Johnson, B. A.**
Wadley, GA 30477
(912) 252-1116

**Kent, Carrie**
PO Box 58
Walthourville, GA 31313
(912) 876-5383

**McIver, John M.**
PO Box 269
Riceboro, GA 31323
(912) 884-2986

**Mitchell, Donald**
Route 1, Box 1137
Woodbine, GA 31569
(912) 576-3211

**Mitchell, Douglas**
PO Box 180
Smithville, GA 31787
(912) 846-2101

**Myless, Coris**
City Hall
417 Pendleton Street
Waycross, GA 31501
(912) 287-2900

**Rivers, Felix Jr.**
108 Court Street
PO Box 6
Cuthbert, GA 31740

**Williams, Earl**
PO Box 1540
Thomasville, GA 31799
(912) 228-7673

**Williams, Thomas**
PO Box 7888
Buena Vista, GA 31803
(912) 649-7888

**Young, Andrew**
City Hall
68 Mitchell St., SW
Atlanta, Ga 30303
(404) 658-6100

## ILLINOIS

**Beck, Saul**
1343 Ellis Avenue
East Chicago Heights, IL 60411
(312) 758-3131

**Collins, Charles**
698 Burnham Drive
University Park, IL 60466
(312) 534-6451

**Davis, James**
City Hall
312 North 5th Street
Brooklyn, IL 62059
(618) 271-8424

**Echols Tyrone**
City Hall
Kline & Broadway Streets
Venice, IL 62090
(618) 884-6262

**Freelon, Joe**
115 South 5th Avenue
Maywood, IL 60193
(312) 344-1200

**Hamilton, John W.**
3327 W. 137th Street
Robbins, IL 60472
(312) 385-8606

**Haney, Napoleon**
Village of Hopkins Park
PO Box AK
Hopkins Park, IL 60944

**Harris, James C. Sr.**
Office of the Mayor
650 E. Phoenix Center Dr.
Phoenix, IL 60426
(312) 331-1455

**Johnson, David**
15320 Broadway
Harvey Municipal Center
Harvey, IL 60426
(312) 339-4200

**Loller, Zeb**
170 West 145th Street
Dixmoor, IL 60426
(312) 339-4200

**Miller, Evans**
16313 Kedzie Avenue
Markham, IL 60426
(312) 331-4905

**Mobley, Callie**
Villaae of Alorton
Alorton, IL 62207
(618) 271-4586

**Officer, Carl E.**
7 Collinsville Ave.
East St. Louis, IL 62201
(618) 482-6600

**Owens, Riley L. III**
City Hall
5800 Bond Avenue
Centreville, IL 62207
(618) 332-1021

**Sawyer, Eugene**
City Hall
121 North LaSalle Street
Room 507
Chicago, IL 60602

**Thompson, Bobby E.**
City of North Chicago
1850 Lewis Avenue
North Chicago, IL 60064

**Wade, Casey Jr.**
Route 6-Box 200A
Sun River Terrace, IL 60964
(815) 937-1219

## INDIANA

**Barnes, Thomas**
Municipal Building
401 Broadway
Gary, IN 46402
(219) 881-1301

## KANSAS

**Smothers, James**
1010 West 8th Street
Junction City, KS 66441
(913) 238-3103

## KENTUCKY

**Johnson, Arthur**
112 South Atkinson
Earlington, KY 42410
(502) 383-5364

## LOUISIANA

**Barthelemy, Sidney**
City Hall
Civic Center
New Orleans, LA 70112
(504) 586-4000

**Braxton Charles**
PO Box 140
Clarence, LA 71414
(318) 357-0440

**Brown, James W.**
200 Sparrow Street
Lake Providence, LA 71254
(318) 559-2942

**Harris Edward**
342 Brown Road
Richwood, LA 71202
(318) 322-2104

**Nora, Clemon, Jr.**
PO Box 258
Campti, LA 71411
(318) 476-3321

**Joseph, John W.**
City Hall
1711 Lawrence
Opelousas, LA 70570
(318) 948-2520

**Ludley, Richard**
PO Box 108
Grambling, LA 71245
(318) 247-6120

**Patrick, Julius**
PO Box 146
Boyce, LA 71409
(318) 443-5443

**Patterson, Dessie**
PO Box 995
South Mansfield, LA 71052
(318) 872-3917

**Shannon, George**
PO Box 125
Pleasant Hill, LA 71065
(318) 796-3680

**Smith, Peter**
Drawer G
Grand Coteau, LA 70541
(318) 662-5246

**Tobin, Leon**
Route 1, Box 40
Castor, LA 71016
(318) 576-3566

**Toussaint, Roosevelt**
PO Box 229
Natchez, LA 71456
(318) 352-1046

**Williams, Lawrence Jr.**
Office of the Mayor
PO Box 6
Napoleonville, LA 70390

**Wright, Charles**
PO Box 403
Maringouin, LA 70757
(318) 625-2600

**Wyche, Zelma**
City Hall
204 North Cedar St.
Tallulah, LA 71282
(318) 574-3157

## MARYLAND

**Anthony, Joseph S.**
3701 Lawrence Street
Colmar Manor, MD 20722-2099
(301) 277-4920

**Blackwell, Frank**
Town Hall
6301 Addison Road
Seat Pleasant, MD 20027
(301) 336-2600

**Coleman, Mary C.**
Town of Eagle Harbor
18407 Juniper Trail
Aquasco, MD 20608
(301) 888-1276

**Dodson, Vivian M.**
Town of Capitol Heights
One Capitol Heights Blvd.
Capitol Heights, MD 20743
(301) 336-0626

**Fletcher, James**
Municipal Building
8600 Glenarden Parkway
Glenarden, MD 20706
(301) 773-2100

**Gray, Robert R.**
717 60th Place
Fairmount Heights, MD 20027
(301) 925-8585

**Hall, Raymond A.**
4507 Church Street
North Brentwood, MD 20722
(301) 699-9699

**Nicholas, Julian C.**
Town of Highland Beach
PO Box 4206
Annapolis, MD 21403
(301) 268-6785

**Schmoke, Kurt**
City Hall
100 N. Holliday Street
Baltimore, MD 21202
(301) 396-3100

## MICHIGAN

**Bullet, Audrey**
Yates Township
PO Box 144
Idlewood, MI 49642
(616) 745-3940

**Childress, Leroy**
Webber Township
Route 1, Box 1042
Baldwin, MI 49304
(517) 754-6536

**Clark, Leon**
Buena Vista Townsnip
1160 South Outer Drive
Saginaw, MI 48601
(517) 776-1400

**Cook, Marcella**
Village of Vandalia
17809 Wood Street
Vandalia, MI 49094
(616) 476-2344

**Cradolph, Owen**
Calvin Township
64948 Wade Road
Cassopolis, MI 49031
(616) 476-2620

**Davis, Joseph Jr.**
City Hall
2121 Inkster Road
Inkster, MI 48141

**Hathaway, Mabel D.**
Charter Township of Royal Oak
Township Hall
21075 Wyoming Street
Ferndale, MI 48220
(313) 547-9800

**Kincaid, William**
58725 Havenridge
New Heaven, MI 48048
(313) 749-5301

**Moore, Walter**
450 Wide Track Dr., E.
Pontiac, MI 49031
(616) 476-2620

**Scott, Martha**
30 Gerald Ave.
Highland Park, MI 48203
(313) 252-0022/23

**Warren, Robert**
2724 Peck Street
Muskegon Heights, MI 49442
(616) 739-9302

**Young, Coleman**
1125 City County Building
Detroit, MI 48226
(313) 224-6340

## MISSISSIPPI

**Blackwell, Unita**
PO Box 188
Mayersville, MS 39113
(601) 873-6439

**Brown, Frank**
Town Hall
Beulah, MS 38726
(601) 759-6604

**Butler, Lawrence**
PO Box 7
Bolton, MS 39041
(601) 866-2221

**Cotton David**
PO Box 356
Tchula, MS 39169
(601) 235-5112

**Evers, Charles**
PO Box 10
Fayette, MS 39069
(601) 786-3682

**Gray, Robert D.**
PO Box 43
Shelby, MS 38774
(601) 398-7091

**Harris, Clifton**
PO Box 25
Arcola, MS 38722

**Holman, Jimmie Lee**
PO Box 315
Marks, MS 38646
(601) 326-3161

**Jackson, Louis**
4412 Danny St.
Moss Point, MS 39563
(601) 475-0300

**Jones, W. J.**
PO Box 23
Coahoma, MS 38617
(601) 358-4496

**Kyles, Sylvester Jr.**
PO Box 707
Shaw, MS 38773
(601) 754-3131

**LeFlore, Robert**
PO Box 188
Pace, MS 38764
(601) 723-6292

**Leggette Violet 0.**
PO Box 278
Gunnison, MS 38746
(601) 747-2213

**Lindsey, S. L.**
PO Box 250
Metcalfe, MS 38760
(601) 335-0212

**Lucas, Earl S.**
PO Box 680
Mound Bayou, MS 38748
(601) 741-2193

**Lucas, Maurice F.**

Route 1, Box R-29
Renova, MS 38732
(601) 843-8233

**Lyles, Marie**
PO Box 560
Crenshaw, MS 38621
(601) 382-5272

**Perkins, Helen**
PO Box 395
Hollandale, MS 38748
(601) 827-2241

**Pritchard, Daron**
PO Box 215
Edwards, MS 39066
(601) 852-5461

**Shanks, James**
PO Box 110
Jonestown, MS 38639
(601) 358-4328

**Smith Fannie**
PO Box 57
Falcon, MS 38628
(601) 382-7669

**Swearengen, James R.**
PO Box 163
Oakland, MS 38948
(601) 623-8980

**Thomas Johnny B.**
PO Box 90
Glendora, MS 38928
(601) 375-8262

**Trice J. Y.**
PO Box 370
Rosedale, MS
(601) 759-6813

**Tutwiler, Milton**
PO Box 151
Winstonville, MS 38781
(601) 741-2106

**Walker, Robert M.**
City Hall
PO Box 150
Vicksburg, MS 39180
(601) 636-3411

**Washington, James**
PO Box 185
Friars Point, MS 38631
(601) 383-2233

## MISSOURI

**Alexander, James E.**
Village of Upland Park
6390 Nature Bridge
St . Louis, MO 63121

**Brown, Zeke**
Penermon
Route 1
Essex, MO 63849
(314) 675-3657

**Clark, Theodore**
Village of North Lilbourn
PO Box 138
Lilbourn, MO 63862
(314) 688-2254

**Crawley, Darline**
City of Pagedale
1404 Ferguson
Pagedale, MO 63133
(314) 726-1200

**Dooley, Charlie**
City of Northwoods
4600 Oakridge Blvd.
St. Louis, MO 63121

**Ellis, Dairrel**
City of Homestown
PO Box 247
Wardell, MO 63879

**Humes, David**
City of Hayti Heights
PO Box 426
Hayti, MO 63851
(314) 359-2680

**Jenkins, Thomas**
1804 Kienlen Ave.
Wellston, MO 63133
(314) 38S-1015

**Johnson, Roosevelt**
Haywood City
258 Pine Street
Benton, MO 63771
(314) 471-3993

**Mays, Amos**
Village of Wilson City
PO Box 366
Wyatt, MO 63882

**Moore, Dorothy**
Village of Hillsdale
6428 Jesse Jackson Ave.
St. Louis, MO 63121

**O'Kain Roosevelt**
City of Pine Lawn
6250 Forest Avenue
Pine Lawn, MO 63120
(314) 261-5500

**Turner, Bernard**
City of Kinloch
5990 Monroe
Kinloch, MO 63140
(314) 521-3335

**Williams, Lottie**
City of Velda Village
2803 Maywood
Velda Village, MO 63121

**Williams, Warren**
Velda Village Hills
3501 Avondale
St. Louis, MO 63121
(314) 261-7221

**Wofford, Simon**
City of Howardsville
105 Howard Avenue
Howardville, MO 63869
(314) 688-2137

## NEW JERSEY

**Brooks, Bernard E.**
Municipal Green
812 Teaneck Road
Teaneck, NJ 07666
(201) 837-1706

**Brown, Robert L.**
29 N. Day Street
Orange, NJ 07050
(201) 266-4005

**Campbell, Doreatha**
Borough Hall
Salem Road
Willingboro, NJ 08046
(609) 877-2200

**Gaines, Walter**
Borough Hall
East Douglas Avenue
Lawnside, NJ 08045
(201) 547-6133

**Hatcher, John C., Jr.**
City Hall
44 City Hall Plaza
East Orange, NJ 07019
(201) 266-5151

**James, Sharpe**
City Hall - Room 200
920 Broad St.
Newark, NJ 07102
(201) 733-6400

**McGhee Samuel T.**
1548 Maple Avenue
Hillside, NJ 07205
(201) 547-3234

**Primas, Melvin**
City Hall
Camden, NJ 08101
(609) 757-7200

**Ramsey, James**
138 Grove Street
Montclair, NJ 07045
(201) 794-1400

**Taylor, Richard**
515 Watchung Avenue
Plainfield, NJ 07061
(201) 753-3310

**Usry, James**
City Hall
Room 707
1301 Bacharach Boulevard
Atlantic City, NJ 08401
(609) 347-5400

**Wanzer, Edward**
Second & Grant Avenue
Chesilhurst, NJ 08089
(609) 767-4135

## NEW YORK

**Blackwood, Ronald A.**
City Hall
Roosevelt Square
Mount Vernon, NY 10550
(914) 668-2200

**Jackson, Richard E.**
City Hall
840 Main Street
Peekskill, NY 10566
(914) 737-3400

## NEW MEXICO

**Gentry, Thomas**
PO Box 364
Corrales, NM 87048
(505) 987-0598

## NORTH CAROLINA

**Andrews, Milton**
PO Box 98
Railroad St.
Parmele, NC 27861
(919) 795-4242

**Beasley, Annie R.**
PO Box 305
Sharpsburg, NC 27878
(919) 446-9441

**Brown, Louis**
General Delivery
Navassa, NC 28404
(919) 371-9358

**Carter, Edward E.**
City of Greenville
PO Box 7207
Greenville, NC 27834
(919) 830-4420

**Clark, William**
PO Box 99
Cofield, NC 27922
(919) 358-8611

**Craige, Benjamin F. Jr.**
PO Box 338
East Spencer, NC 28039
(704) 636-7111

**Credle, Edward**
Route 1, Box 339
Mesic, NC 28515
(919) 745-4947

**Davis, Frank W. Sr.**
Dobbins Heights
PO Box 151
Hamlet, NC 28345
(919) 582-6002

**Dixon, Alfred**
Greenevers
Route 2, Box 331-E
Rose Hill, NC 28458
(919) 289-3078

**Dixon, Willie**
East Arcadia
Route 1, Box 273
Reigelwood, NC 28456
(919) 655-4388

**Frost William**
PO Box 870
Maysville, NC 28555
(919) 743-4441

**Greene Edith**
PO Box 327
Bolton, NC 28423
(919) 452-9945

**McRae, Emmett**
Rennert
Route 1, Box 42
Shannon, NC 28336
(919) 843-5755

**McRae, Geneva**
Town of Taylortown
PO Box 242
Pinehurst, NC 28374
(919) 295-1904

**Powell, Carolyn**
PO Box 1527
Princeville, NC 27886
(919) 823-1057

**Swindell, Charles S.**
PO Box 695
Enfield, NC 27823
(919) 445-3146

**Wilkins, E. V.**
Town of Roper
PO Box 217
Roper, NC 27970
(704) 793-5527

## OHIO

**Ayers, Timothy**
City Hall
76 East High Street
Springfield, OH 45502
(513) 324-7341

**Bailey, Bernard**
PO Box 320 B
Rendville, OH 43775
(614) 347-4571

**Dixon, Clay**
Municipal Building
PO Box 22
Dayton, OH 45401
(513) 443-3600

**Gray, Jennifer**
City Hall
1201 Stiffens Avenue
Lincoln Heights, OH 45215
(313) 733-5900

**Humphrey, James**
612 Park Street
Sidney, OH 45365
(513) 498-2335

**Hunter, Richard F. Sr.**
6860 Plainfield Road
Silverton, OH 45236
(513) 793-7980

**Lawson, Lawyer**
Village of Woodlawn
10141 Woodlawn Boulevard
Cincinnati, OH 45215
(513) 771-6130

**Miles, Vera M.**
Paulding Village
116 South Main
Paulding, OH 45879
(419) 399-3941

**Pittman, Darryl**
14340 Euclid Ave.
East Cleveland, OH 44112
(216) 681-5020

**Rainey, Sherlie**
27899 Chagrin Boulevard
Woodmere Village, OH 44122
Urbancrest, OH 43123
(216) 831-9511

**Shepherd, Veronika**
Administration Building
3492 First Avenue
Urbancrest, OH 43123
(614) 875-1279

## OKLAHOMA

**Banks, Leodus**
PO Box 538
1245. Mekusukey
Wewoka, OK 74884

**Brooks, James**
PO Box 25
Meridian, OK 73058
(405) 586-2282

**Bush, Marie**
PO Box 206
Clearview, OK 74835
(405) 786-2088

**Cherry, Albert**
PO Box 266
Boynton, OK 74422
(918) 472-3601

**Crisp, Ollie**
Grayson
Route 3, Box 552
Henryetta, OK 74437
(918) 652-3866

**Davis, Lelia Folley**
PO Box 101
Taft, OK 74463
(918) 683-5492

**Gay, James**
PO Box 1284
Tallahassee, OK 74466
(918) 483-8838

**Hogan Ogelia**
Town Hall
PO Box 147
Tatums, OK 73087

**Jones, Viola**
PO Box 657
Langston, OK 73050
(405) 466-2271 or 2276

**Lyons, Bobbie**
New Lima Gen. Delivery
New Lima, OK 74884
(405) 258-3909

**McClendon, Ruben**
PO Box 16
Rentiesville, OK 74459
(918) 473-5489

**Murell, Marilyn**
PO Box 189
Arcadia, OK 73007
(405) 235-0430

**Oliver, Lee**
Brooksville
Route 1, Box 151
Tecumseh, OK 74873
(405) 598-3497

**Richardson, Leroy**
3601 No. Maxwell Drive
Forest Park, OK 73121

**Thomas, Erma**
Summit
Route 4, Box 436C
Muskogee, OK 74401
(918) 687-8971

**Wilcots, Sam**
PO Box 975
Boley, OK 74829
(918) 667-9790

## PENNSYLVANIA

**Goode, W. Wilson**
Philadelphia City Hall
Room 215
Philadelphia, PA 19107
(215) 686-1776

**Fielding, Zelma**
PO Box 536
Lincolnville, SC 29484
(803) 873-3261

**Leake Willie**
5th Welsh Street
Chester, PA 19013
(215) 447-7700

**Reid Robert**
City Hall
60 West Emaus Street
Middletown, PA 17057
(717) 948-3050

**Robinson, Edward**
126 Pennsylvania Avenue
Yardley, PA 19067
(215) 493-6832

## SOUTH CAROLINA

**Carter, John**
PO Box 438
Gray Court, SC 29645
(803) 876-2581

**Cohen, Olivia**
PO Drawer 8
Fairfax, SC 29827

**Goodwin, Franklin B.**
PO Box 424-A
Santee, SC 29142
(803) 854-2152

**Goree, Janie B.**
PO Box 305
Carlisle, SC 29031
(803) 427-1505

**Grooms, Robert**
PO Box 267
Lamar, SC 29069
(803) 326-5551

**Holmes, William**
PO Box 551
Allendale, SC 29810
(803) 584-4619

**Inabinet, Curtis**
PO Box 104
Ravenel, SC 29470
(803) 889-3949

**Jefferson, Clifton**
PO Box 147
Lynchburg, SC 29080
(803) 437-2154

**Johnson, Carroll J.**
Town Hall
235 Main Street
Blackville, SC 29817

**Montgomery, Joe**
Atlantic Beach
PO Box 1425
No. Myrtle Beach, SC 29582
(803) 272-5287

**Risher, James, Jr.**
PO Box 189
Gifford, SC 29923
(803) 625-2712

**Robinson, Henry**
PO Drawer 8
Port Royal, SC 29935
(803) 524-5125

**Scott, Lewis**
Town Hall
PO Box 36
Eastover, SC 29044
(803) 353-2281

**Starkes-Parson, Hazel**
PO Box 56
Ridgeville, SC 29472
(803) 871-7960

**Wilson, Charlie B.**
PO Box 116
Sellers, SC 29592
(803) 752-5009

## SOUTH DAKOTA

**Williams, Leonard B.**
PO Box 278
Mitchell, SD 57301

### TENNESSEE

**Anderson, James**
Moores Station
Route 1, Box 133
LaRue, TX 75700
(214) 852-6185

**Bell, E. T.**
PO Box 7 354
Easton, TX 75641
(214) 643-3304

**Goudeau, Malcolm**
Ames
PO Box 1904
Liberty, TX 77575
( 409) 336-6236

**Leverett, Ronald**
PO Box 2809
Prairie View, TX 77445
(409) 857-3711

**McDaniel, Billy**
City Hall
210 Cedar Street
Hearne, TX 77859

**McKinney, Kevin**
114 North Lincoln Ave .
Jonesborough, TN 37659
(615) 753-3813

**Roberts, Billy**
PO Box 68
Cuney, TX 75759
(214) 876-4704

**Singleton, Leroy**
PO Box 68
Hempstead, TX 77445
(409) 826-3606

**Washington, Willie**
PO Box 245
Kerens, TX 75144
(817) 776-5543

**Wells, Billy**
PO Box 161
410 Tennessee Ave.
Bluff City, TN 37618
(615) 538-7414

**Zomalt, Ernest**
PO Box 700
Kendleton, TX 77451
(409) 532-8240

### VIRGINIA

**Davis, Lawrence**
801 Sophia St.
Fredericksburg,
(703) 371-3722
VA 22401

**Farley, Florence**
18 South Little Church Street
Petersburg, VA 23803
(804) 733-2323

**Kent, William A.**
PO Box 251
South Boston, VA 24594
(804) 572-3511

**Mizelle, Johnnie E.**
City Hall
PO Box 374
Suffolk, VA 23434
(804) 934-3111

**Rattley, Jessie**
City Hall
2400 Washington Avenue
Newport News, VA 23607
(804) 247-8888

**Taylor, Noel**
215 Church Avenue
Roanoke, VA 24017
(703) 981-2444

**West, Roy**
City Hall Room 201
900 East Broad Street
Richmond, VA 23219
(804) 780-4711

### WASHINGTON

**Jackson, Joe**
PO Box 293
Pasco, WA 99 301
(509) 545-3404

**TOTAL MAYORS - 305**
**FEMALE MAYORS - 60**
**MALE MAYORS -245**

### Black mayors of cities with populations over 50,000, 1988

| Name | Expires | City | Population | Black |
|---|---|---|---|---|
| Eugene Sawyer | 4/91 | Chicago, IL | 3,000,000 | 40.0 |
| Thomas Bradley | 7/89 | Los Angeles, CA | 2,996,763 | 17.0 |
| W. Wilson Goode | 12/91 | Philadelphia, PA | 1,588,220 | 40.2 |
| Coleman Young | 12/89 | Detroit, MI | 1,203 339 | 63.1 |
| Kurt Schmoke | 12/91 | Baltimore, MD | 786,775 | 54.8 |
| Marion Barry | 12/90 | Washington, DC | 637,651 | 66.6 |
| Sidney Barthelemy | 3/90 | New Orleans, LA | 557,482 | 55.3 |
| Andrew Young | 12/89 | Atlanta, GA | 425,022 | 66.6 |
| Sharpe James | 6/90 | Newark, NJ | 349,248 | 46.9 |
| Lionel J. Wilson | 6/89 | Oakland, CA | 339,288 | 46.9 |
| Richard Arrington | 12/91 | Birmingham, AL | 284,413 | 55.6 |
| Roy A. West | 6/88 | Richmond, VA | 219,214 | 51.3 |
| Richard C. Dixon | 12/89 | Dayton, OH | 203,371 | 37.0 |
| Lottie Shackelford | 12/88 | Little Rock, AR | 158461 | 32.2 |
| Thomas Barnes | 12/91 | Gary, IN | 151,953 | 70.8 |
| Jessie M. Rattley | 6/88 | Newport News, VA | 144,903 | 1.5 |
| Carrie Perry | 12/89 | Hartford, CT | 136,392 | 33.9 |
| Noel Taylor | 6/88 | Roanoke, VA | 100,247 | 22.0 |
| Edward Vincent | 11/90 | Inglewood, CA | 94,245 | 57.3 |
| Melvin Primas | 6/89 | Camden, NJ | 84 910 | 53.0 |
| Walter Tucker | 7/89 | Compton, CA | 81,286 | 74.8 |
| John Hatcher, Jr. | 12/89 | East Orange, NJ | 77,025 | 83.6 |
| Walter L. Moore | 12/89 | Pontiac, MI | 76,715 | 7.2 |
| George Livingston | 11/89 | Richmond, CA | 74,676 | 47.9 |
| Edna W. Summers | 4/89 | Evanston Township, IL | 73 706 | 21.4 |
| Ronald A. Blackwood | 12/9 | Mt. Vernon, NY | 66,713 | 48.7 |
| Carl E. Officer | 4/89 | East St. Louis, IL | 55,200 | 95.6 |
| Pat Larkins | 3/88 | Pompano Beach, FL | 52,618 | 17.2 |

## PAST AND PRESENT APPOINTED GOVERNMENT OFFICIALS AND REPRESENTATIVES

Black statesmen are now regularly considered for federal appointments to top-level diplomatic and administrative posts. This positive development is one of the fruits of the capable and skillful service rendered to the nation by the earlier black appointees who blazed a trail to the higher echelons of government. The biographies of several of these eminent men and women, both those still serving at high posts and retirees, are given here.

### CLIFFORD ALEXANDER JR.
**Former Associate Counsel to the President**
**Former Secretary of the Army**
**(appointed by Pres. Lyndon Johnson and Pres. Jimmy Carter)**

A native New Yorker, Clifford Alexander Jr. was appointed President Lyndon B. Johnson's Associate Special Counsel on August 25, 1965. He had previously served as the President's Deputy Special Assistant. In 1977 Alexander became the first black to lead the Army as its secretary. He was appointed to that post by President Jimmy Carter.

Born in 1933, Alexander graduated from Harvard University and then attended Yale Law School, where he was awarded an LL.B. At the age of 26, he became assistant district attorney of New York County, and two years later, executive director of the Hamilton Grange Neighborhood Conservation District in Manhattanville. After four years at this job, Alexander moved to HARYOU in 1963 as an executive program director.

After leaving his post with the EEOC, where he was under constant pressure from Republican Senators like Everett Dirksen who accused him of bullying reluctant employers into complying with federal guidelines for minority employment, Alexander entered private law practice and became a Harvard overseer. His function at Harvard was comparable to the one he was empowered to exercise while in the federal government, but in this case, he was actually involved in working out details with craft unions which were obliged to offer and implement concrete proposals for improving minority group employment opportunities. At Harvard, the pact worked out by Alexander related to "two live buildings" and involved 300 workers, some one-fifth of whom were black and Puerto Rican.

Alexander is currently in the private practice of law.

*Clifford Alexander (left) and Representative John Conyers at a conference on the EEOC.*

### MARY FRANCES BERRY
**Attorney, Government Official**
**(appointed by Pres. Jimmy Carter)**

Mary Frances Berry was born in 1938 and received her B.A. degree from Howard University in 1961 and her masters degree in 1962. In 1966, she received a Ph.D. from the University of Michigan and her J. D. from its law school in 1970. Berry was appointed Assistant Secretary of Education, U.S. Department of Health, Education and Welfare by President Jimmy Carter in 1977, and later became commissioner and vice chairman of the U.S. Commission on Civil Rights. She was "fired" from the Civil Rights Commission by President Ronald Reagan in 1983. In a compromise with Congress Berry was reinstated.

She currently is a professor of law and history at Howard University.

### MELVIN L. P. BRADLEY
**Government Official**
**(appointed by Pres. Ronald Reagan)**

Melvin L. P. Bradley was born in Texarkana, Texas and received his B.S. degree from Pepperdine University. He is a former assistant to the vice president of United Airlines and director of public relations. From 1973 to 1975, he was assistant to Governor Ronald Reagan of California as well as a member of Reagan's senior staff participating in cabinet meetings. Bradley served as senior advisor in President Reagan's office of OPD.

### ANDREW FELTON BRIMMER
**Former Member Federal Reserve Board**
**(appointed by Pres. Lyndon Johnson)**

Andrew Brimmer, an eminent black economist and teacher, was named to the Federal Reserve Board in 1966 by President Lyndon B. Johnson.

Born in Newellton, Louisiana on September 13, 1926, Brimmer was awarded a Ph.D. in economics by Harvard

University in 1957, having already done some of his graduate studies in India—both at the Delhi School of Economics and at the University of Bombay (1951-1952).

In 1955, after having spent a year at Harvard as a teaching fellow in economics, Brimmer joined the Federal Reserve Bank of New York as an economist—a post he surrendered in 1958 in order to become Assistant Professor of Economics at Michigan State University. In 1961, he joined the faculty of the Wharton School of Finance and Commerce, remaining there until his appointment to the position of Deputy Assistant Secretary of Commerce in May 1963.

His duties involved decisions relevant to the development of the American economy—duties which, under his later title as Assistant Secretary of Commerce, became broad enough to make him one of the key government spokesmen on such varied topics as balance of payments, tourist travel, and U.S. capital investment abroad. He was also in charge of the Bureau of Census and the Office of Business Economics, both of which provide valuable statistical data to the general public.

Aside from having taught at the University of California at Berkeley and at the City College of New York, Brimmer has published a number of books and monographs on his special field of interest, as well as several articles and reviews in some of the nation's leading economic journals. Perhaps his single most important project of 1964 was the research he contributed to the U.S. Supreme Court ruling on the constitutionality of the public accommodations sections of the Civil Rights Act.

Over the years, Brimmer has established himself as the most prominent black economist in the nation. It was natural, then, that he take an active stand pursuant to the Nixon Administration's stated policy of fostering black businesses and lending support to black entrepreneurs. Whereas many critics faulted Nixon for failing to provide a coordinated program of loans to black would-be entrepreneurs, Brimmer attacked the scheme on theoretical grounds, rather than for its organizational shortcomings. How, Brimmer asked, could most black businesses expect to be successful in the ghetto, where so much of the nation's black poor was concentrated? "Self-employment," Brimmer argued, "offers a low and rather risky payoff." In his view, blacks need more jobs as salaried managers and skilled craftsmen with major American companies, companies with the capital resources to command the attention of the national community.

Brimmer now heads his own consulting firm and teaches at Harvard's Graduate Business School.

## ROBERT L. BROKENBURR
## Former Alternate Delegate to the United Nations (appointed by Pres. Dwight Eisenhower)

For many years a lawyer, twice state senator from Indiana, and several times at different levels within the Indiana court system, Robert L. Brokenburr served as an alternate delegate to the U.N. General Assembly from 1955 to 1956.

A native of Phoebus, Virginia, Brokenburr was born on November 16, 1886. Educated initially in his hometown, he later attended Hampton Institute in Hampton, Virginia, receiving his B.A. in 1906. He completed his law studies at Howard in 1909.

## RALPH J. BUNCHE
## Former U.N. Undersecretary for Special Political Affairs (appointed by Pres. Harry Truman)

The first American black to win the Nobel Peace Prize, Ralph Bunche was an internationally acclaimed statesman whose record of achievement places him among the most significant American diplomats of the twentieth century. Bunche received the coveted award in 1950 for his role in effecting a cease fire in the Arab-Israeli dispute which threatened to engulf the entire Middle East in armed conflict.

Born in Detroit on August 7, 1904, Bunche graduated from UCLA in 1927 *summa cum laude* and with Phi Beta Kappa honors. A year later he received his M.A. in government from Harvard. Soon thereafter he was named head of the Department of Political Science at Howard University, remaining there until 1932 at which time he was able to resume work toward his doctorate from Harvard. (He later studied at Northwestern University, the London School of Economics, and Capetown University.)

*Ralph Bunche, with Iris King, mayor of Jamacia (West Indies). Dr. Bunche was the first African-American to win the Nobel Peace Prize.*

Before World War II broke out, Bunche did field work with the Swedish sociologist Gunnar Myrdal, author of the widely acclaimed *An American Dilemma*. During the war, he served initially as Senior Social Analyst for the Office of the Coordinator of Information in African and Far Eastern Affairs, and was then reassigned to the African section of the Office of Strategic Services. In 1942 he helped draw up the territories and trusteeship sections ultimately earmarked for inclusion in the United Nations charter.

But the single event which brought the name of Ralph Bunche into the international limelight occurred soon after his appointment in 1948 as chief assistant to Count Folke Bernadotte, U.N. mediator in the Palestine crisis. With the latter's assassination, Bunche was faced with the great challenge of somehow continuing cease fire talks between Egypt and Israel. After six weeks of intensive negotiations, Bunche worked out the now-famous "Four Armistice Agreements," which effected an immediate cessation of the hostilities between the two combatants. Once the actual cease fire was signed, Bunche received numerous letters and telegrams from many of the leading heads of state the world over, and was later accorded a hero's welcome upon his return to the United States.

Bunche died on December 9, 1971 after having served as the distinguished Undersecretary-General of the United Nations from 1955 to his retirement in October 1971.

### ARCHIBALD J. CAREY
### Former Alternate Delegate to the United Nations
### (appointed by Pres. Dwight Eisenhower)

Archibald Carey served as an alternate delegate to the United Nations from 1953 to 1956.

A native of Chicago and a graduate of John Marshall Law School, Carey presided for 19 years (1930-1949) as pastor of the Woodlawn A.M.E. Church in that city. Twice elected alderman from Chicago's Third Ward, Carey was on the Chicago city council for eight years, and later became an avid presidential supporter of Dwight D. Eisenhower, from whom he received his U.N. appointment. During the Eisenhower Administration, he was vice chairman of the President's Committee on Government Employment Policy.

Carey currently is a judge on the Supreme Court of Illinois.

### LISLE C. CARTER JR.
### Former Assistant Secretary, Department of Health, Education and Welfare (HEW)
### (appointed by Pres. Lyndon Johnson)

Lisle Carter was appointed Assistant Secretary of Health, Education and Welfare (HEW) by President Lyndon B. Johnson in 1966.

Born in New York City on November 18, 1925, Carter moved with his family to Barbados (British West Indies) and began his formal education there. On his return to New York in 1940, he enrolled at Cazenovia Seminary (Syracuse, New York) for one year of junior college before moving on to Dartmouth. In 1944, he received his B.A. in chemistry there, and after an interruption in his schooling caused by his induction into the Armed Forces, finally received an LL.B. from St. John's University School of Law in 1950.

From then until 1961, Carter combined his own law practice with the job of legal counsel for the National Urban League. Named Deputy Assistant Secretary in the Department of Health, Education and Welfare, he led a departmental team in 1962 through an inspection of health and educational conditions in 11 African countries. Later, he helped conduct a comprehensive survey aimed at ending discrimination in federally assisted programs. Before accepting his present post, Carter was a top aide to Sargent Shriver, Director of the Office of Economic Opportunity(OEO).

Currently he is president of the University of the District of Columbia in Washington, D.C.

### ARTHUR A. CHAPIN
### Former Director of Equal Employment Opportunity Department of Labor
### (appointed by Pres. John Kennedy)

Arthur Chapin's association with the Department of Labor dates back to 1961. Before accepting his federal assignment, Chapin had worked for many years at the state level as assistant to the president of the New Jersey CIO Council. He was concerned with civil rights legislation and minimum wage and unemployment compensation. He also served as a member of the New Jersey Committee on Housing, and of the State Wage Panel for restaurant employees.

While with the Labor Department, Chapin helped compile an annual *Directory of Negro College Graduates,* which aided business and industry in finding competent and qualified personnel. The directory enabled the Department to maintain close liaison with thousands of college graduates as well as numerous employment agencies.

### MERCER COOK
### Former Ambassador to Niger, Senegal, and Gambia
### (appointed by Pres. John Kennedy)

Dr. Mercer Cook, the first U.S. Ambassador to the Republic of Niger, also served as Ambassador to the West African nations of Senegal and Gambia.

Born in Washington, D.C. in 1903, Dr. Cook lived across the street from Duke Ellington during his childhood, and attended the famed Dunbar High School in the nation's capital, numbering among his classmates William H. Hastie (now a federal judge), Sterling Brown (noted literary critic and author), and Charles Drew (a pioneer in the development of blood plasma).

After receiving his B.A. from Amherst in 1925, Cook did graduate work at the University of Paris, and later acquired both his M.A. and Ph.D. degrees from Brown University. After a short stint in Haiti on an educational assignment, he returned to the United States to become professor of romance languages at Howard University, a post he held for the next 14 years.

Upon leaving Howard, Dr. Cook traveled widely, particularly in Africa. In 1963 he served briefly as an alternate delegate to the General Assembly of the United Nations.

Cook completed his diplomatic tour as ambassador to Senegal and Gambia in 1966. He returned to Howard University, where he became head of the Department of Romance Languages.

### PRESTON A. DAVIS
### Director of Small Business Affairs, U.S. Department of Agriculture
### (appointed by Pres. Jimmy Carter)

Preston A. Davis, director of Small Business Affairs of the U.S. Department of Agriculture, was born in Norfolk, Virginia. He received his B.S. degree in business administration from West Virginia State College in 1949 and his M.S.W. from George Washington University in 1974. Davis was appointed to his government position in 1979. Prior to that he worked in the Department of Agriculture for most of his career life. He was the first black to become a member of Kiwanis International Club and is the winner of the Purple Heart, the Bronze Star, and Army commendation medals as well as the Army Meritorious Service Award. Davis is author of *Firepower Chinese Communist Army* and *Signatures of Soviet Nuclear Missile Systems.*

### WILLIAM H. DEAN
### Former Chief of the African Unit, Division of Economic Stability and Development
### (appointed by Pres. Harry Truman)

William H. Dean was appointed chief of the African unit in the Division of Economic Stability and Development in 1949, and served in this capacity until his death in 1952.

Born in Lynchburg, Virginia on July 6, 1910, Dean graduated from Bowdoin College in Maine in 1930, and later attended Harvard on a fellowship. He received both his M.A. and Ph.D. degrees from this university in 1932 and 1938, respectively.

During the 1940s, Dean devoted his energies to a number of important posts in government, notably as a consultant to the National Resources Planning Board (1940-1942) and as a member of several technical missions to such places as Haiti, Libya, and the Virgin Islands (1944-1949). He also taught for a time at Atlanta University and City College of New York.

Dean committed suicide on January 9, 1952.

### EDWARD RICHARD DUDLEY
### Former Ambassador to Liberia
### (appointed by Pres. John Kennedy

Judge Edward R. Dudley is a justice of the Supreme Court of the State of New York. Born in South Boston, Virginia, he graduated from Johnson C. Smith University (B.S., 1932) and St. John's University Law School (1941). Admitted to the bar in 1941, he became U.S. Ambassador to Liberia (1948-1953) and started the first Point 4 program in Africa. After a term as Borough President of Manhattan (1961-1965), he was appointed an administrative judge of Criminal Court of New York City (1967) and an administrative judge of the New York Supreme Court (1971). Dudley is a life member of the NAACP and a trustee of the Fund for the City of New York.

*Arthur Chapin, former director of the EEOC.*

### ALFRED LEROY EDWARDS
### Former Deputy Assistant Secretary of Agriculture
### (appointed by Pres. John Kennedy)

In 1963 President John F. Kennedy appointed Alfred Edwards Deputy Assistant Secretary of Agriculture. Edwards became one of the key coordinators in the department's "Rural Renaissance" movement—a program aimed at reinvigorating those areas affected by a lack of real job opportunities, and the increasing migration of young people to the large cities.

In 1974 he was named Director of the Division of Research and Professional Business Administration, School of Business at the University of Michigan.

Born on August 9, 1920 in Key West, Florida, Edwards received a B.A. from Livingstone College in 1948, an M.A. in economics from the University of Michigan, and a Ph.D. from the University of Iowa in 1958.

Prior to becoming engaged in government service, Dr. Edwards was a faculty member of a number of leading universities. He also helped establish the University of Nigeria at Nsukka—arriving there with the first contingent of American teachers and administrators who were charged with the tremendous task of helping Nigeria organize and oversee the entire venture.

Essentially a social scientist, Dr. Edwards has tried to persuade qualified students to avail themselves of the many opportunities opening up in agriculture—a field which, he

*American representative to UNESCO Clarence Ferguson; he assisted in drafting the U.N. Statement on race.*

feels, has undeservedly been denied the status and importance currently due it.

### JAMES FARMER
### Former Assistant Secretary of Health, Education and Welfare
### (appointed by Pres. Richard Nixon)

For biography see Civil Rights section.

### CLARENCE CLYDE FERGUSON JR.
### Former Representative to the Economic and Social Council of the U.N.
### (appointed by Pres. Lyndon Johnson)

Clarence Ferguson was the U.S. Representative to the Economic and Social Council of the United Nations. He was also Deputy Assistant Secretary of State for African Affairs and prior to that U.S. Ambassador to Uganda.

Ferguson joined the Department of State as Special Coordinator for Relief to the Civilian Victims of the Nigerian Civil War with the personal rank of Ambassador in February 1969. Before coming into the Department of State, Ferguson was the Distinguished Professor of Law at Rutgers University Law School. He had previously served as the dean of Howard University Law School (1963-1969). During the Kennedy Administration, Ferguson was general counsel to the U.S. Commission on Civil Rights.

Ferguson was born November 4, 1924 in Wilmington, North Carolina. He served more than four years in the U.S. Army (1942-1946) in Europe and the Southwest Pacific Theaters. He earned a Battle Star for service with the Third Army in the Central European Campaign (1945).

Educated at Ohio State University, he graduated with High Distinction in Constitutional History in 1948 and was awarded his J.D. *cum laude,* from Harvard Law School in 1951.

Ferguson is a member of the Massachusetts and New York Bars and has practiced in both states. In 1954 and 1955 he was an assistant U.S. attorney for the Southern District of New York, having served previously as assistant general counsel to the Moreland-Act Commission to Investigate Harness Racing (1953-1954). From 1951 through 1955, Ferguson was associated as counsel to the firm of Baltimore, Paulson and Canudo, New York City, specializing in corporate and bankruptcy matters.

Ferguson was secretary and research director of the New Jersey State Commission to Study and Report on the Uniform Commercial Code, and author of New Jersey annotations on "Secured Transactions."

In 1952, he was appointed one of the U.S. representatives to the Western Hemisphere UNESCO Conference in Havana, Cuba. In 1963 and 1964 he served as U.S. alternate in the United Nations Sub-Commission on Prevention of Discrimination Against Minorities, and also as special legal advisor to the U.S. Mission to the United Nations. In April 1965, Ferguson was elected as U.S. expert to the United Nations Sub-Commission on Discrimination. He has also served as consultant to UNESCO on Human Rights (1965). Ferguson is one of the drafters of the UNESCO Statement on Race, 1967. He has headed many U.S. delegations to international conferences and meetings. He was also chairman of the Panel on Humanitarian Problems of International Law of the American Society of International Law.

Ferguson is a member of Phi Beta Kappa and several other honorary societies. In 1956 he was named Outstanding Young Man of New Jersey by the New Jersey Junior Chamber of Commerce. He has also served as chairman of the New Jersey Committee on Housing for the Aged and as civil rights consultant to Governor Nelson Rockefeller of New York from 1958 to 1964.

Ferguson was a member and treasurer of the East Orange Housing Authority; President of the Newark Rutgers Chapter of the American Association of University Professors, and was a member of the Committee on Racial Discrimination of the American Association of Law Schools. For two years he served on the Executive Committee of the American Association of Law Schools. At the present time, Ferguson is a member of numerous boards and advisory committees as well as consultant to many federal and international agencies. He currently is a member of the Executive Committee of the American Association of International Law as well as professor of law at Harvard Law School.

Ferguson is the author of six legal texts and more than 20 articles on constitutional and international law.

*Patricia Harris had a disinguished career under presidents Lyndon Johnson and Jimmy Carter.*

**ZELMA GEORGE**
**Former Alternate Delegate to the United Nations**
**(appointed by Pres. Dwight Eisenhower)**

Zelma George was appointed an alternate delegate to the Fifteenth General Assembly of the United Nations in 1960. Born in Hearne, Texas, Dr. George moved to Kansas with her family at an early age and later studied voice at the American Conservatory of Music in Chicago. She received an undergraduate degree from the University of Chicago and earned her doctorate in sociology from New York University.

George worked for a time as a probation officer for a juvenile court and then as dean of women at Tennessee State College. In 1955 she was appointed to the Defense Advisory Committee on Women in the Services, and four years later, under the auspices of the State Department, completed a three-month assignment in Southeast Asia, culminating in her attendance at the Pan Pacific and Southeast Asia Women's Assembly which took place in Singapore.

George is currently lecturing, writing, and performing consulting assignments for private business and government. She also serves as a committee member on Ethnic Heritage Studies Development Program Executive Committee.

**STEVE GLAUDE**
**Deputy Secretary of Housing and Urban Development**
**(appointed by Pres. George Bush)**

Prior to his appointment as Deputy Secretary of Housing and Urban Development, Steve Glaude was director of the National Association of Neighborhoods. He has also been Chairman of the board of the Capitol East Children's Center, a day-care facility in Washington, D. C. and has worked for the D. C. Association for retarded Citizens.

Mr. Glaude anticipates that "Bush's new black appointments represent a new vision."

**ERNEST GREEN**
**Former Assistant Secretary for Employment and Training, U.S. Department of Labor**
**(appointed by Pres. Jimmy Carter)**

Ernest Green was appointed Assistant Secretary for Employment and Training of the U.S. Department of Labor by President Carter in 1977. Green was born in 1941 and received his B.A. from Michigan State University in 1962 and his masters degree two years later. Prior to being appointed to the post by President Carter, Green was executive director of Recruitment Training Program and director of the Twentieth Century Fund on employment of black youth and apprenticeship.

**WENDELL WILKIE GUNN**
**Chief of Staff, Housing and Urban Development (HUD)**
**(appointed by Pres. George Bush)**

Wendell Wilkie Gunn operated his own financial management consulting firm of Gunn Associates in Stamford, Connecticut, prior to being appointed by President Bush as Chief of Staff of Housing and Urban Development in 1989. From 1982 to 1984, he served as special assistant to then President Reagan for international trade policy. Mr. Gunn has also been vice-president at Chase Manhattan bank and assistant treasurer of Pepsi Co. He is a member of the Joint Center for Political Studies' Economic Policy Task Force.

**PATRICIA ROBERTS HARRIS**
**Former Ambassador to Luxembourg**
**Former Secretary, Department of Health and Human Services**
**(appointed by Presidents John Kennedy and Jimmy Carter )**

As ambassador to Luxembourg, Patricia Harris was the first black woman to hold this diplomatic rank in U.S. history. Until President Ronald Reagan took office in 1980, Harris served as Secretary of the Department of Health and Human Services and also Secretary of Housing and Urban Development under President Jimmy Carter. She served in these positions from 1977 to 1981.

Born in Mattoon, Illinois, Harris attended elementary school in Chicago, and received her undergraduate degree from Howard University in 1945. After completing postgraduate work at the University of Chicago and at American University, she earned her doctorate in jurisprudence from George Washington University Law School in 1960.

Prior to her appointment, Harris had worked for the YWCA in Chicago (1946-1949), and also served as executive director for Delta Sigma Theta in Washington, D.C. An attorney and professor before she entered politics, Harris served under President John F. Kennedy as co-chairman of the National Women's Committee on Civil Rights and was later named to the Commission on the Status of Puerto Rico.

Harris was elected Permanent Chairman of the Democratic National Convention on June 27, 1972.

She died of cancer in March of 1985.

### ANDREW J. HATCHER
### Former Associate Press Secretary
### (appointed by Pres. John Kennedy)

In 1960, President John F. Kennedy named Andrew Hatcher as his associate press secretary—thus making him the first major black appointee of the New Frontier. Hatcher was the individual through whom many of the President's important news releases were made.

Born in Princeton, New Jersey in 1925, Hatcher attended Springfield College, graduating with a B.A. degree. During World War II he served for three years in the Army as a second lieutenant and, after his discharge, took a job with the San Francisco Sun-Reporter.

In 1960, Hatcher campaigned ardently for Kennedy's election to the presidency. Hatcher resigned after the assassination of the President, and held an executive position with a brewery company in New Jersey.

Hatcher is a business executive in New York City.

### CHESTER A. HIGGINS
### Former Assistant Chief of Public Affairs to the Secretary of the Army
### (appointed by Pres. Jimmy Carter)

Chester A. Higgins was born in 1917 and attended Kentucky State College for a year and Louisville Municipal College for two years. Higgins was general assistant to the first black commissioner of the Federal Communications Agency, Benjamin Hooks. Higgins has been a reporter and feature writer for the *Louisville Defender*, *Jet* magazine, *Ebony, a*nd *Tan*. Higgins served as assistant chief of public affairs to the office of Secretary of the Army in the Carter Administration. He is currently editor-in-chief of *Crisis* magazine, the official publication of the NAACP.

### JEROME HOLLAND
### Former U.S. Ambassador to Sweden
### (appointed by Pres. Richard Nixon)

Easily one of President Nixon's shrewdest political appointments, Jerome Holland is an experienced educator whose diplomatic skills often came into play mediating between insistent student radicals and adamant campus authorities. Convivial, articulate, and persuasive, Holland was appropriately discreet and notably confident in his ability to add to the "backlog of cooperation and friendship" which he felt characterized U.S.-Swedish relations. The estimate was perhaps a trifle optimistic in view of the Swedes' policy of granting asylum to U.S. deserters and aid to North Vietnam.

Holland resigned as Ambassador to Sweden in 1972 to become a member of the Board of Directors of the New York Stock Exchange, the first black ever elected to that body.

He currently serves on the boards of several large companies: AT&T, Chrysler Corporation, Continental Corporation, General Foods, Union Carbide, Federated Department Stores, Manufacturers Hanover Trust Company, New York Stock Exchange, Inc., and Zurn Industries, Inc.

### MELVIN HUMPHREY
### Director of the office of Small Business Development Unit, Department of Transportation
### (appointed by Pres. Ronald Reagan)

Melvin Humphrey was born in 1921 in St. Louis, Missouri. He received all of his degrees from the University of Illinois, acquiring a Ph.D. in 1955. Before his appointment by President Reagan to the Department of Transportation, Humphrey served as director of research for the Equal Employment Opportunity Commission and co-authored three textbooks: *Principles of Accounting, Principles of Economics, and Public Finance.* He also wrote *Black Experience Vs. Black Expectations EEOC 1977.* He has performed consulting services for private businesses and government and serves as a committee member on Ethnic Heritage Studies Development Program, executive committee.

### SAMUEL C. JACKSON
### Former Assistant Secretary, Department of Housing and Urban Development
### (appointed by Pres. Lyndon Johnson)

Samuel C. Jackson was appointed Assistant Secretary of Housing and Urban Development in 1969. At the time of his appointment he was the highest ranking black in federal government.

Born May 8, 1929 at Kansas City, Kansas, Jackson graduated from Washburn University with a B.A. and received an LL.B. from the same school in 1954.

Jackson was a member of the U.S. Equal Employment Opportunity Commission from 1965 to 1968 and headed the U.S. Housing Mission to Africa in 1971.

He is a member of the national board of directors and the legal committee of NAACP and is a past president of the Kansas chapter of the NAACP. Previously, Jackson served as deputy general counsel of the Kansas State Department of Welfare.

### HOWARD JENKINS JR.
### Member, National Labor Relations Board
### (appointed by Pres. John Kennedy)

Howard Jenkins Jr. was appointed by President John F. Kennedy in 1963 to a five-year term as a member of the National Labor Relations Board (NRLB)—the first black ever to serve with this federal government agency. Jenkins has been reappointed to serve as a member of the National Labor Relations Board by four presidents, Democrats and Republicans alike.

Born on June 16, 1915 in Denver, Colorado, Jenkins received his B.A. from the University of Denver in 1936 and soon thereafter became the first black to earn an LL.B. from the same institution. He was likewise the first black to be admitted to the Colorado bar.

After World War II (during which he had worked for the Office of Price Administration, the Denver War Labor Board, and the National Wage Stabilization Board), Jenkins taught labor and administrative law at Howard University for 10 years. In 1956, having completed a graduate program in law at New York University, he became an attorney for the Department of Labor. Over the years, he slowly climbed the rungs of this department's ladder, reaching the post of assistant commissioner in the Bureau of Labor Management Reports in 1962.

### BARBARA JORDAN
### Attorney, Educator, Former Congresswoman (appointed by Pres. Jimmy Carter)

Barbara Jordan's appointment to President Carter's Advisory Board on Ambassadorial Appointments marked her return to government service after she had resigned as U.S. Representative to the 95th Congress from Texas in 1976. A graduate of Boston University School of Law in 1959, the former Congresswoman served as an administrative assistant to the County Judge of Harris County in Texas. When she was elected to the State Senate, she became the first black to serve on that body since 1883.

In 1972, she was unanimously elected president pro tempore of the state senate and thus became the first black woman in the country ever elected to preside over a legislative body.

In the1972 election, Miss Jordan received more than 80% of the vote in both the primary and November elections to become, at 36, the first black woman elected to Congress from the South. In November she ran 16% ahead of Senator McGovern, a greater margin than that achieved by most other black Congressmen.

During her brief period in Congress Miss Jordan earned a reputation for being a shrewd legislator, who was more interested in results than rhetoric. Assigned to the House Judiciary Committe, she quickly became known as a strong and influential supporter of Peter Rodino, the Committee's Chairman and one of Congress' most learned authorities on the Constitution. Her understanding of the document and the ratification debates that occurred in the original 13 states emerged with great impact during the Judiciary Committee's debate on the impeachment of President Nixon, which Miss Jordan favored.

As a Congresswoman she was known to be totally devoted and attentive to the needs of her constituents. She was widely regarded as a "comer" in the Democratic Party, possibly as the most promising of all the black legislators. There was deep disappointment among Democrats nationally when she made her decision not to remain in political elective office. Over the past several years Miss Jordan has been ill. However, in 1988, desite her illness, she made public appearances to speak out against the re-election of Ronald Reagan.

### ROBERT WILSON KITCHEN, JR.
### Former Deputy Representative to the Economic and Social Council of the U.N. (appointed by Pres. Harry Truman)

Previously, Robert Kitchen was stationed in Washington, D.C., as Director of the Office of International Training in the Agency for International Development (AID) of the Department of State. He had been with AID and its predecessor organizations since 1952. Beginning as an administrative assistant in the Economic Development Mission to Liberia, Kitchen became acting director of that Mission, then economic advisor to the director of the International Cooperation Administration Mission to Pakistan, Pakistan Desk Officer, and in 1957 Chief of the Special Mission to the Sudan. Kitchen administered the first major AID program in Africa, the U.S. Mission to the Sudan, from 1958 to 1960. Following this assignment he became Special Assistant for Program and Policy in AID's Office of Development Finance and Private Enterprise.

Kitchen graduated from Morehouse College in 1943. He received his M.S. in business administration from Columbia University in 1946, did postgraduate work at American University, and received his LL.D. in industrial management and engineering from Chapman College in 1965. The following year Kitchen participated in the Department of

*Barbara Jordan raised an eloquent and effective voice while serving in the House of Representatives.*

*Jewel LaFontant was formerly deputy solicitor general of the United States.*

State's Senior Seminar on Foreign Policy, the most advanced training program in international affairs for principal officers of the department. Kitchen also holds the Department of State's Meritorious Service Award.

### CLINTON EVERETT KNOX
### Former Ambassador to Dahomey
### (appointed by Pres. Lyndon Johnson)

Clinton Knox, a career foreign service officer with more than 20 years experience, was appointed U.S. Ambassador to Dahomey in 1964.

A native of New Bedford, Massachusetts, Knox acquired his Ph.D. from Harvard in 1940. Having taught at Morgan State College for eight years, Knox joined the State Department at the close of World War II, doing research on Northern and Western Europe. In 1957, he was assigned to the NATO Defense College in Paris and subsequently became first secretary in the U.S. mission to NATO. Knox was later counselor and deputy chief of mission in the U.S. Embassy in Tegucigalpa, Honduras.

Knox has retired and is a member of the Diplomatic Consular Officers Association.

### JEWEL LAFONTANT
### Assistant Secretary of State for Refugee Affairs
### (Confirmation Pending)
### (appointed by Pres. Ronald Reagan and Pres. George Bush)

A senior partner in the law firm Vedder, Price, Kaufman and Kammholz, Jewel Lafontant's achievements include positions as Deputy Solicitor General in the U. S. Justice Department during the Nixon Administration and U. S. Representative to the United Nations. She has also been named to several boards and commissions of the federal government.

Born in Chicago, she took her B.A. at Oberlin College and her LL.D. at the University of Chicago (1946). Admitted to the Illinois Bar in 1947, she became a trial attorney for the Legal Aid Bureau (1947-1954), a member of the law firm of Rogers, Rogers and Strayhorn (1952-1954), and assistant U.S. attorney in Chicago (1955-1958), before taking a part-time position with a Chicago law firm in 1958. Her government service has included being a member of the Illinois Advisory Committee to the Commission on Civil Rights (1958-present), a legal advisor for the Inheritance Tax Division of Illinois (1962-1969), and a member of the U.S. Advisory Commission on International, Educational and Cultural Affairs (1969-present).

### WILLIAM LUCAS
### Assistant Attorney General for Civil Rights
### (Confirmation Pending)
### (appointed by Pres. George Bush)

A former county executive and sheriff of Wayne county, Detroit, William Lucas was nominated by President Bush as Assistant Attorney General for Civil Rights in 1989. He became a republican in 1986 during his unsuccessful bid for the governorship of Michigan. In his previous positions he had received the support of black voters, but in his campaign for governor which was backed by Reagan, he was vigorously opposed by prominent black Democrats and received little support of the black voters. His link to Reagan and his lack of experience in civil rights enforcement have made him a controversial black nominee.

### CHARLES H. MAHONEY
### Former Delegate to the United Nations
### (appointed by Pres. Dwight Eisenhower)

Charles H. Mahoney was the first black to become a permanent member of a U.S. delegation to the United Nations. Born in Decatur, Michigan on March 29, 1886, Mahoney received his B.A. from Fisk University and his LL.B. from the University of Michigan. An attorney for some 30 years, Mahoney was active in a number of civic and business enterprises in Michigan.

During his five-year U.N. tour (1954-1959), Mahoney was an important member of several committees, and also served on the Panel for Inquiry and Conciliation.

Mahoney died in Detroit on January 29, 1966.

### CARMEL CARRINGTON MARR
### Former Legal Advisor to the U.S. Mission to the United Nations
### (appointed by Pres. Harry Truman)

An experienced lawyer—particularly in matters pertaining to international law—Carmel Carrington Marr was appointed to the post of legal advisor to the U.S. Mission to the United Nations in 1953.

Apart from her specific duties, she was in close and constant contact with missions from other parts of the world, and served on a number of key committees of the U.N. General Assembly.

A native New Yorker, Marr is a graduate of Hunter College and holds an LL.B. degree from Columbia University.

In 1971, Marr was appointed to the Public Service Commission. She currently serves as a commissioner on the New York State Human Rights Appeal Board.

### FREDERICK D. McCLURE
### Presidential Assistant for Legislative Affairs
### (appointed by Pres. George Bush)

In January 1989, President Bush appointed Frederick McClure, a native of San Augustine Texas, as Assistant to the President for Legislative Affairs. Prior to his appointment, McClure had served as Government Affairs Staff Vice President of Texas Air Corporation, Special Assistant to President Reagan for Legislative Affairs, Associate Deputy Attorney General of the United States, and Legislative Director to former Texas Senator John Tower for whom he also served as Agricultural Assistant and State Office Director.

After receiving his Juris Doctor degree in 1981 from the Baylor University School of Law, McClure was a trial lawyer with the Houston firm of Reynolds, Allen and Cook. While in law school he was elected President of the Student Bar Association and was a member of the National Order of Barristers. McClure is also a director of the Texas Lyceum and the National Fraternity of Alpha Zeta.

Mr. McClure received his Bachelor of Science degree in agricultural economics from Texas A&M University in 1976, graduating summa cum laude. While at Texas A&M he served as Student Body President, was elected to Phi Kappa Phi, was a member of the Singing Cadets, and received the Brown-Rudder Outstanding Student Award. Since graduation he has remained active with various A&M related organizations.

In 1976, former President Ford appointed Mr. McClure as a White House intern.

A former National Secretary and Texas State President of the Future Farmers of America, he was appointed to the State Advisory Council for Technical-Vocational Education and has served as a member of the Real Estate Research Advisory Committee for the State of Texas since his appointment in 1979. McClure is a member of the American Council on Germany and Aero Club of Washington, D. C.

He lives in Falls Church, Virginia, with his wife Harriet and two children, Lauren and Frederick Jr.

### WADE HAMPTON McCREE
### Lawyer, Judge
### (appointed by Pres. Jimmy Carter)

Wade Hampton McCree was born in Des Moines, Iowa and following his graduation from Fisk University in 1941, he received his LL.B. Degree from Harvard Law School in 1944. He was admitted to the Michigan bar in 1948 at which time he practiced law in Detroit. In 1954, McCree became judge of the Michigan Circuit Court in Wayne County and in 1961 was named judge of the U.S. District Court for the Eastern Michigan District. In 1977, he was appointed solicitor general in the administration of President Jimmy Carter. McCree currently serves as solicitor general of the United States.

### DONALD F. McHENRY
### Former U.S. Permanent Representative to the United Nations
### (appointed by Pres. Jimmy Carter)

Donald F. McHenry was appointed U.S. Permanent Representative to the United Nations by President Jimmy Carter in 1979 following the resignation of Andrew Young. McHenry has studied, taught, and worked primarily in the fields of American foreign policy and international law and organizations. He joined the U.S. Department of State in 1963 and served for eight years in various positions related to U.S. policy in international organizations.

In 1971, while on leave from the Department, he was a visiting scholar at the Brookings Institution, Washington, D.C. and an international affairs fellow of the Council on Foreign Relations, New York. In 1973, after leaving the State Department, he joined the Carnegie Endowment for International Peace in Washington as director of Humanitarian Policy Studies. In 1976 he served as a member of President Carter's transition staff at the State Department prior to joining the U.S. Mission to the U.N.

During his career, Ambassador McHenry represented the United States in a number of international forums, and as the U.S. Representative on the U.N. Western Five Contact Group he was the chief U.S. negotiator on the question of Namibia.

McHenry was born in St. Louis, Missouri in 1936 and graduated from Illinois State University in 1957, receiving his masters degree two years later from Southern Illinois University. The former ambassador is on the Board of Trustees of the Ford Foundation, a governor of the American Stock Exchange, a director of the First National Boston Corporation, the Coca Cola Company, the International Paper Company, and a member of the Council on Foreign Relations. McHenry is currently university research professor of diplomacy and international affairs at Georgetown University.

### FRANK MONTERO
### Former Advisor to the U.S. Mission
### (appointed by Pres. Lyndon Johnson)

Frank Montero received his appointment as advisor to the U.S. Mission to the U.N. in 1962 after having served for almost 15 years as the assistant executive director of the National Urban League.

In addition to acting for a time as a special assistant to the late Adlai Stevenson, he represented the United States at the independence celebrations of Niger, Kenya, and Zanzibar, and as senior advisor on economic and social affairs for many of the specialized committees in the U.N. proper.

Born in New York City in 1912, Montero is a graduate of Howard University (1934) and holds graduate degrees from Columbia University (social administration) and New York University (public administration).

*President Dwight Eisenhower conferring with his administrative assistant E. Frederick Morrow.*

### E. FREDERIC MORROW
### Former Administrative Assistant to Pres. Eisenhower
### (appointed by Pres. Dwight Eisenhower)

When President Eisenhower named E. Frederic Morrow as his administrative assistant in 1955, this represented the first time in U.S. history that a black held an executive position on a presidential staff.

Born in Hackensack, New Jersey in April 1909, Morrow graduated from Bowdoin College and later received an LL.B. from the Law School at Rutgers University. In the interim period, he had been business manager of *Opportunity,* the official house organ of the National Urban League, Coordinator of Branches for the NAACP, and a major in the Armed Forces during World War II.

In 1952, after three years in the public affairs division of the Columbia Broadcasting System, he became part of Eisenhower's presidential campaign staff and traveled some 100,000 miles all over the country on behalf of the Republican nominee. The following year, he became Advisor on Business Affairs to the Secretary of Commerce and was in close liaison with Congress on all legislation affecting his department.

After six years of service with President Eisenhower (1955-1961), Morrow left Washington to become vice president of the African-American Institute—the largest privately endowed foundation in the United States. Its main function is to improve American economic and cultural relations with the nations of Africa.

Morrow is currently a vice president of the Bank of America's Department of Communications and Public Affairs in the New York City division.

### JOHN HOWARD MORROW
### Former Ambassador to Guinea
### (appointed by Pres. Dwight Eisenhower)

John Howard Morrow was appointed Ambassador to Guinea by President Dwight D. Eisenhower in 1959, and served in this post for the next two years.

A native of Hackensack, New Jersey, where he was born on February 10, 1910, Morrow received his B.A. from Rutgers and his M.A. and Ph.D. from the University of Pennsylvania. After some 25 years as a teacher, both on the high school and collegiate levels, Morrow was given his first political appointment in 1957 when President Eisenhower made him a member of the Commission on Government Security.

Since completing his assignment in Guinea, Morrow has served in several capacities: first as a member of the U.S. delegation to the U.N. General Assembly; then a vice chairman of a delegation on educational achievement which was posted off to Ethiopia; and, finally, as minister and permanent U.S. representative to UNESCO.

In 1963, he accepted a post with the Foreign Service Institute (Department of State, Washington, D.C.), which helps prepare promising candidates for careers overseas.

Morrow's brother, E. Frederic, once served as an administrative aide to President Eisenhower in the White House.

### JAMES M. NABRIT JR.
### Former Ambassador to the United Nations
### (appointed by Pres. Lyndon Johnson)

With his appointment on August 25, 1965 as an ambassador to the U.N., James M. Nabrit Jr. became the highest ranking black American to serve in any U.S. delegation to the world body.

Born in Atlanta on September 4, 1900, Nabrit received his early education in his home state, and later earned his B.A. from Morehouse. Drawn to the law at an early age, Nabrit set up his own practice in Houston, Texas in 1930, three years after having received his LL.B. from Northwestern University.

At once a specialist in civil rights, Nabrit participated in a number of historic cases tried before the Supreme Court, including one of the five cases connected with the monumental *Brown v. Board of Education* decision which outlawed segregation in U.S. public schooling.

During World War II, Nabrit was on both the Selective Service and Price Control boards. In 1954, he served as legal advisor to the Governor of the Virgin Islands and, later, was twice a delegate to the annual International Labor Conference held in Geneva, Switzerland.

Nabrit is president emeritus of Howard University and is an active attorney.

*Samuel Nabrit, Jr., President Johnson's Ambassador to the United Nations.*

### SAMUEL NABRIT
### Former Member, Atomic Energy Commission
### (appointed by Pres. Lyndon Johnson)

Dr. Samuel Nabrit is the first black to serve on the Atomic Energy Commission, having been appointed to this post in 1966 by President Lyndon B. Johnson.

Born on February 21, 1905 in Macon, Georgia, Nabrit moved with his family to Augusta, where he attended Walker Baptist Institute. Active in sports, he also edited the school newspaper and graduated as class valedictorian. He continued his education at Morehouse, earning his B.A. in 1925. That same year, he began his teaching career at Atlanta University as a biology instructor. (He later became dean of the graduate school of arts and sciences.) In 1932 he won the distinction of being the first black to earn a Ph.D. from Brown University. Dr. Nabrit taught at Columbia University in 1945, and then spent a year in Brussels doing research.

In 1956, he was appointed to a post on the National Science Board by President Dwight D. Eisenhower and during the Kennedy Administration, was made a special ambassador to Nigeria in West Africa.

He has been a marine biologist on the faculty of Texas Southern University. Dr. Nabrit is currently Executive Director of the Southern and National Fellowship Funds of the Council of Southern Universities (one of four black foundation heads in the nation). He served as president of Texas Southern University from 1955 to 1966. Dr. Nabrit is the brother of James M. Nabrit Jr., formerly the president of Howard University, who was named an Ambassador to the United States delegation to the United Nations in 1965.

### CONSTANCE "CONNIE" NEWMAN
### Director of the Office of Personnel Management
### (appointed by Pres. George Bush)

Culminating a career spanning 20 years of public affairs experience, Constance Newman was appointed in 1989 as Director of the Office of Personnel Management for the Bush administration. She served on Bush's presidential transition team as director of outreach, and was influential in the selection of several of the administration's black appointees.

Constance Newman's policymaking posts include director of Volunteers In Service To America (VISTA) from 1971 to 1973; Commissioner and Vice Chair of the Consumer Products Safety Commission from 1973 to 1976; and Assistant Secretary for regulatory programs at the Department of Housing and Urban Development from 1976 to 1977.

### ANNA PEREZ
### First Lady's Press Secretary
### (appointed by Pres. George Bush)

In 1989, Anna Perez was appointed as the First Lady's Press Secretary, the first black to hold this position. A native of New York City, Anna Perez has served as press aide to Senator Slade Gorton and most recently to Representative John Miller—both are republicans from Washington state. At one time she also published *Tacoma Facts,* a community newspaper in Washington state.

## JOSEPH PERKINS
### Deputy Assistant for Domestic Policy, Office of the Vice President (appointed by Pres. Ronald Reagan)

Joseph Perkins made a name for himself by writing conservative editorial pieces at the Wall Street Journal where he worked as an editorial writer for four and a half years, prior to his appointment as Deputy Assistant for Domestic Policy, Office of the Vice President. In a controversial article published in *Policy Review* magazine "Boom Time For Black America: The Middle Class Is Surging under Reagan," he asserted that the black middle class has thrived because of Reagan's policies.

Perkins graduated from Howard University's School of Communications.

## SAMUEL RILEY PIERCE
### Former Secretary of Housing and Urban Development (appointed by Pres. Ronald Reagan)

A man who was later to have a broad background in education and government, as well as in private industry, Samuel Pierce served as assistant to the Undersecretary of Labor from 1955 to 1956. Pierce was appointed in 1981 by President Ronald Reagan as Secretary of Housing and Urban Development.

Born in Glen Cove, New York on September 8, 1922, Pierce attended Cornell University where he received his B.A. in 1947 and his LL.B. in 1949. Three years later, he was awarded an LL.M. (in taxation) from New York University's School of Law.

From 1949 through 1955, he was first assistant district attorney for New York County and then assistant U.S. attorney for the Southern District of New York. Since 1958 Pierce has been a faculty member of the N.Y.U. Law School, served as a judge in the New York Court of General Sessions (1959-1961), and has become a partner in a prominent New York law firm.

## THOMAS E. POSEY
### Former Chief of the Labor and Industry Division, Agency for International Development (appointed by Pres. Dwight Eisenhower)

Dr. Thomas Posey is a former chief of the Labor and Industry Division of the Office of International Training within the Agency for International Development (AID).

A native of Washington, D.C., Posey received his B.A. in economics, monetary theory, and labor in 1923 from Syracuse University, and in 1926, his M.A. from the same school.

For the next 25 years he taught economics at West Virginia State College, taking time out, with the aid of a Rosenwald fellowship, to acquire his Ph.D. in 1948 from the University of Wisconsin. During these many years, he was active in the political life of his state, serving as a member of the West Virginia State Planning Board and as advisor to the West Virginia State Federation of Labor.

He also served as a consultant to the Fair Employment Practices Commission (1943), as Supervisory Industrial Economist with the Wage Stabilization Board (1951), and as an economic advisor for the Mutual Security Agency in Burma (1952).

*Samuel Pierce, President Reagan's Secretary of Housing and Urban Development.*

From 1954 to 1960, Dr. Posey served on foreign missions to the Philippines and to Turkey, where his duties involved him primarily with questions of labor productivity and industrial relations. Upon completion of a three-year term as a U.S. delegate to the U.N. Conference in Geneva on the Application of Science and Technology for the Benefit of the Less-Developed Areas of the World, Dr. Posey returned to the United States where he assumed his post with AID.

## CARL ROWAN
### Former Ambassador to Finland (appointed by Pres. Lyndon Johnson)

Carl Rowan has held two major diplomatic and administrative posts in his lifetime: one as Ambassador to Finland (1963), the other as Director of the United States Information Agency (USIA).

Born in Ravenscroft, Tennessee on August 11, 1925, Rowan studied for a year at Tennessee A&I in Nashville and, at the age of 19, became one of the first 15 blacks commissioned by the U.S. Navy during World War II. After the war, he received his B.A. from Oberlin College in Ohio, and later acquired an M.A. in journalism from the University of Minnesota.

Having established himself as a journalist and much-sought-after feature writer, Rowan soon turned his energies to the writing of full-length books. His first, *South of Freedom,* was based on many of his personal experiences, and was followed by *The Pitiful and the Proud* (1956) and *Go South in Sorrow* (1957). Three years later, he wrote *Wait Till Next Year*, a biography of the famous black baseball player Jackie Robinson.

*U.N. Representative Edith Sampson presents a Booker T. Washington memorial to Ambassador Entezam of Iran.*

Rowan returned to journalism after resigning from the USIA in July 1965. At present he writes a thrice-weekly column syndicated in a number of newspapers around the country. His commentaries are also heard on radio stations across the country. As he did in his Minneapolis *Tribune* days, Rowan covers more than just distinctly black stories. Only one in six columns is devoted to racial or civil rights topics.

## EDITH SAMPSON
### Former Alternate Delegate to the United Nations (appointed by Pres. Harry Truman)

The first black woman to be named to the United Nations, Edith Sampson served in this body from 1950 until 1953, first as an appointee of President Harry S. Truman and later during a portion of the Eisenhower Administration.

A native of Pittsburgh, Sampson acquired a Bachelor of Laws degree from the John Marshall Law School in Chicago in 1925, and two years later became the first woman to receive a Master of Laws from Loyola University.

A member of the Illinois bar since 1927, she was admitted to practice before the Supreme Court in 1934. During the 1930s, she maintained her own private practice, specializing particularly in domestic relations and in criminal law.

After her U.N. appointment, Sampson traveled around the world, often as a lecturer under State Department auspices. She was elected Associate Judge of the Municipal Court of Chicago in 1962. In 1978 she retired from Cook County Circuit Court.

Sampson died on October 7, 1979 at Northwestern Hospital in Chicago, Illinois.

## ELLIOTT PERCIVAL SKINNER
### Former Ambassador to Upper Volta (appointed by Pres. Lyndon Johnson)

Dr. Elliott Percival Skinner was appointed by President Lyndon B. Johnson to succeed Thomas S. Estes as Ambassador to Upper Volta, thus becoming the seventh black to hold such a major appointment within the Johnson Administration (the others being Mercer Cook, Patricia Harris, Clinton Knox, Dr. James Nabrit, Hugh Smythe, and Franklin Williams).

An assistant professor of anthropology at New York University, Dr. Skinner was born in 1924 in Port-of-Spain, Trinidad (West Indies), and received his early education in that city. He later acquired his B.A. from N.Y.U. and both his M.A. and Ph.D. degrees from Columbia. He teaches at Columbia University in New York City.

Skinner studied under a Whitney Fellowship in French West Africa from 1953 to 1955, and later continued his academic pursuits in French Guiana under a Ford Foundation Fellowship. A member of several professional associations, and an active participant in the work of the NAACP and the American Society of African Culture (AMSAC), Dr. Skinner has also written or co-authored a number of books, including *An Analysis of the Political Organization of the African People* (1957), *Christianity and Islam Among the Mossi* (1958), The *Mossi of the Upper Volta (*1964), and *A Glorious Age in Africa* (1965).

## HUGH H. SMYTHE
### Former Ambassador to Syria (appointed by Pres. Lyndon Johnson)

Hugh H. Smythe was a former Ambassador to Syria and also was a special advisor to the Senate Foreign Relations Committee, a member of the U.S. delegation to the Sixteenth U.N. General Assembly, and a State Department Research consultant. Smythe who lived in New York City, died in 1977 at the age of 63. He had been appointed Ambassador to Syria in 1965 by President Lyndon B. Johnson, a position he served in until 1967. That was the year that Smythe defied an order by the Syrian government to close the embassy in Damascus within 48 hours during a six-day war in that country.

Born in Pittsburgh in 1914, Smythe was educated locally and later received his B.A. and M.A. degrees from Virginia State College and Atlanta University, respectively. He also studied at Fisk and Chicago universities, and after World War II, won his Ph.D. in anthropology from Northwestern.

As a consequence of his ambassadorial appointment, Dr. Smythe was obliged to take a special leave of absence from Brooklyn College, where he was serving as a deputy chairman in the graduate division of the sociology department. His other governmental posts include lecturer at the Foreign Service Institute of the State Department (1961-1963), trainer of Peace Corps volunteers (1962-1963), and U.S. advisor to the National Research Council of Thailand.

Late in 1964, Smythe became chief consultant to Youth in Action, an organization falling under the Anti-Poverty Program. A year later, he participated in an orientation program designed to train Fulbright grantees bound for Southeast Asia.

## DR. LOUIS W. SULLIVAN
## Secretary of Health and Human Services
## (appointed by Pres.George Bush)

On March 1, 1989 Dr. Louis W. Sullivan was confirmed as Secretary of Health and Human Services by the Senate by a vote of 98 to 1, becoming the first African-American appointed to a cabinet position in the Bush Administration.

Essential in the development of the Morehouse School of Medicine as a separate entity from Morehouse College, Dr. Sullivan had served as professor of biology and medicine and as dean, director and founder of the medical education program at Morehouse College. In 1981, he was nominated as Morehouse School of Medicine's first dean and president.

Dr. Sullivan graduated from Morehouse College magna cum laude with a bachelor's of science degree in 1954, and went on to medical school at Boston University, graduating cum laude in 1958. He completed his internship at New York Hospital Cornell Medical Center, and his medical and general pathology residencies at Cornell Medical Center and Massachusetts General Hospital.

He then fulfilled two fellowships and served in a variety of positions with Harvard Medical School, Boston City Hospital, New Jersey College of Medicine, Boston University Medical Center, and the Boston Sickle Cell Center and others.

Described as a "distinguished and dedicated individual who makes things happen," Dr. Sullivan has led an academic and professional life of excellence. He has been involved in numerous educational, medical, scientific, professional, and civic organizations, advisory, consulting, research and academic positions, and has received many professional and public service awards. Dr. Sullivan's research and activities focus on hematology and he has authored and co-authored more than 60 publications on this and other subjects. He is also the founding president of the Association of Minority Health Professions.

## HOBART TAYLOR JR.
## Attorney
## (appointed by Pres. Lyndon Johnson)

Hobart Taylor Jr. was named director to the Export-Import Bank in 1965. In his government career, Taylor had previously served President Lyndon B. Johnson as an associate special counsel and had also been executive vice chairman of the President's Committee on Equal Employment Opportunity. He currently serves as general counsel in the law firm of Jones, Day, Reavis and Pogue in Washington, D.C.

Born in Texarkana, Texas, Taylor graduated from Prairie View College with a B.A., receiving his M.A. from Howard and his LL.B. from the University of Michigan. After a short period as a research assistant for the Chief Justice of Michigan's Supreme Court, he entered a Detroit law firm as a junior and, later, a full partner.

He sits on the board of directors of Aetna Life and Casualty Co., Great Atlantic and Pacific Tea Co., Standard Oil Co., Westinghouse Electric Corporation, and Eastern Airlines.

## GLORIA TOOTE
## Chairman, Merit System Procurement Board
## (appointed by Pres. Richard Nixon)

Gloria Toote received her J. D. degree from Howard Law School and also attended Columbia University Graduate Law School. She is a former member of the editorial staff of national affairs at *Time* magazine. Toote has practiced law in New York City since 1954. In 1971, she joined the Department of Housing and Urban Development as assistant secretary. She was chairperson of the Merit System Procurement Board in the Reagan Administration.

## EVERETT C. WALLACE
## Deputy Assistant Secretary, Fair Housing, HUD
## (appointed by Pres. Richard Nixon)

Everett C. Wallace was born in 1951 in Chicago. He received a B.A. degree from Northwestern University in 1973 and a J. D. from the same institution in 1976. He graduated with honors. Prior to his appointment to HUD, Wallace was legal assistant to the office of Senator Howard Baker and senior analyst and energy counsel to the U.S. Senate Budget Committee.

*Dr. Louis W. Sullivan, Secretary of Health and Human Services in the Bush administration.*

### JOSEPH P. WATKINS
**Associate Director in the White House Office of Public Liaison**
**(appointed by Pres. George Bush)**

In 1989, Joseph Watkins was appointed by President Bush as Associate Director in the White House Office of Public Liaison. Prior to his appointment, he was an assistant to the President of the University of Pennsylvania. Watkins, an ordained minister who lectures in churches, worked for Vice President Dan Quayle for three years while he was in the Senate.

In 1984, Mr. Watkins who has said he is a man dedicated to the people, ran unsuccessfully against incumbent Andy Jacobs Jr. in the 1986 race for the 10th district seat for Congress. He has attended and earned several degrees from prestigious colleges in the country including a master in arts in religious education from the University of Princeton's Theological Seminary. In 1983, he was listed as one of *Ebony Magazine's* 50 Young Leaders of the Future.

### GEORGE LEON-PAUL WEAVER
**Former Assistant Secretary of Labor for International Affairs**
**(appointed by Pres. John Kennedy)**

George Leon-Paul Weaver, a native of Pittsburgh, was named to the post of Assistant Secretary of Labor for International Affairs by President John F. Kennedy in 1961.

Born on May 18, 1912, Weaver attended Roosevelt University (at that time the YMCA School in Chicago) and the law school of Howard University.

Weaver has long been active in the labor movement, particularly in the areas of civil rights and international affairs. In 1941, for example, he joined the CIO as a member of the War Relief Committee, and within a year's time, was named assistant to the director of this organization's Civil Rights Committee. For the next 13 years, he continued to serve in both these capacities. In 1955 (the year of the AFL-CIO merger), he was appointed executive secretary of the new body's Civil Rights Committee.

Weaver was obliged to take occasional leaves of absence to handle a number of special government assignments with the International Confederation of Free Trade Unions, and with the National Security Resources Board. Traveling widely, he also was a member (during the mid-1950s) of various missions to the Far East and Southeast Asia. In 1957, he attended the conference of the International Labor Organization (ILO), and after participating the following year for a second time, was chosen assistant to the president of the International Union of Electrical, Radio and Machine Workers. At present, Weaver serves as a permanent representative to the ILO and as chairman of the U.S. delegation to its annual conference.

Weaver has received, among many other honors, the Eleanor Roosevelt Key for outstanding service to the world community.

In 1969, Weaver became a special assistant to the Director General of the United Nations International Labor Organization in Geneva, Switzerland.

### ROBERT WEAVER
**Former Secretary of Housing**
**(appointed by Pres. Lyndon Johnson)**

Robert Weaver became the first black appointed to a presidential cabinet when Lyndon B. Johnson named him to head the newly created Department of Housing and Urban Development (HUD) on January 13, 1966. Previously, Weaver had served as head of the Housing and Home Finance Agency (HHFA).

Robert Weaver was born on December 29, 1907 in Washington, D.C. where he attended Dunbar High School and worked during his teens as an electrician. Encountering discrimination when he attempted to join a union, he decided instead to concentrate on economics, and eventually received his Ph.D. in that field from Harvard University. (Weaver's grandfather, Dr. Robert Tanner Freeman, was the first black American to earn a doctorate in dentistry at Harvard.)

During the 1940s and 1950s, Weaver concentrated his energies on the field of education. (He had already been a professor of economics at the Agricultural and Technical College of North Carolina in Greensboro from 1931 to 1932.) In 1947 he became a lecturer at Northwestern University, and following this, a visiting professor at Teachers College, Columbia University and at the New York University School of Education. During this period, he was also a professor of economics at the New School for Social Research.

From 1949 to 1955 he was director of the Opportunity Fellowships Program of the John Hay Whitney Foundation; served as a member of the National Selection Committee for Fulbright Fellowships; was chairman of the Fellowship Committee of the Julius Rosenwald Fund, and a consultant to the Ford Foundation.

In 1955, Weaver was named Deputy State Rent Commissioner by New York's Governor Averell Harriman. By the end of the year, he had become State Rent Commissioner and the first black to hold state cabinet rank in New York. Still later, he served as vice chairman of the New York City Housing and Redevelopment Board, a three-man body which supervised New York's urban renewal and middle-income housing programs.

Weaver currently teaches in the Department of Urban Affairs at Hunter College in New York City.

### SAMUEL Z. WESTERFIELD
**Former Deputy Assistant Secretary for Economic Affairs, Bureau of African Affairs, Department of State**
**(appointed by Pres. Lyndon Johnson)**

Samuel Westerfield was named by President Lyndon B. Johnson in 1964 to the reactivated position of Deputy Assistant Secretary for Economic Affairs within the Bureau

*Franklin Williams at work at the United Nations.*

of African Affairs of the U.S. Department of State.

Born in Chicago in 1919, Westerfield received an A.B. in economics and political science from Howard University (1939), and later acquired both his M.A. and Ph.D. degrees in economics from Harvard. From 1940 to 1961, apart from a year spent as an economist with the War Labor Board and the United Auto Workers Union, he was actively engaged either in research projects or as a faculty member of such universities as Howard, West Virginia State, Lincoln, and Atlanta.

It was while holding the posts of professor of economics and dean of the school of business administration at the last of these institutions that Westerfield was appointed associate director of the debt analysis staff of the U.S. Treasury. He then became senior advisor to this department's Director of the Office of International Affairs, where he specialized in the economic problems facing the emerging nations of Africa and Latin America. While in this post, he served as a member of the U.S. delegation to the Inter-American Economic and Social Conference held in Mexico City in 1962.

### CLIFTON R. WHARTON
### Former Ambassador to Norway
### (appointed by Pres. Dwight Eisenhower)

Clifton Wharton's appointment as Ambassador to Norway in 1961 was the highlight of more than three decades as a foreign service officer of the U.S. government.

Born in Baltimore on May 11, 1899, Wharton received his appointment as ambassador the same year he was admitted to the Massachusetts bar. Three years later, he won his LL.M. from Boston University and the following year, accepted a post as a law clerk in the Department of State.

Wharton entered the U.S. foreign service in 1925, functioning as third secretary to Monrovia, Liberia. Over the next three decades, he held such posts as consul at Tananarive (Malagasy Republic), consul and first secretary to Lisbon (Portugal), and Minister to Rumania (1958). In this last post, he became the first black diplomat to head a U.S. delegation to a European country.

Wharton resigned from his Norway post in 1964.

Wharton is a chancellor of the State University of New York in Albany. In 1977 Wharton was appointed by President Jimmy Carter to the President's Commission on World Hunger. He serves on the board of directors of more than a dozen major American corporations.

### FRANKLIN H. WILLIAMS
### Former Ambassador to the United Nations; Ambassador to Ghana
### (appointed by Pres. Lyndon Johnson)

Franklin H. Williams occupied two top-echelon diplomatic posts during the Johnson Administration, one as U.S. Representative to the Economic and Social Council of the United Nations (1964-1965), and more recently, as U.S. Ambassador to Ghana.

Born in 1917 in Flushing, New York, Williams was educated in the city's public school system and later graduated from Lincoln University in Pennsylvania and from Fordham University Law School. After serving briefly as an assistant to Thurgood Marshall, then special counsel for the NAACP, Williams was sent to the West Coast, where he helped restructure the organization's branch offices in nine states.

A member of the bar in New York and California, Williams has often appeared before the U.S. Supreme Court, particularly in a number of cases involving fundamental constitutional rights. He was once assistant to Sargent Shriver, director of the Peace Corps.

Williams is now president of the Phelps-Stokes Fund and is a director of Consolidated Edison Company.

### HOWARD B. WOODS
### Associate Director of the United States Information Agency (USIA)
### (appointed by Pres. Lyndon Johnson)

Howard B. Woods was named Associate Director of the USIA in 1965, serving under Carl Rowan, who has since resigned from his post as head of this agency. Woods entered government service after a successful career in journalism, which included 16 years of experience as city editor and then executive editor of the *Argus*, one of the leading black newspapers in St. Louis, Missouri.

Born in Perry, Oklahoma on January 9, 1917, Woods began his journalistic apprenticeship at the age of 18 and worked for the next seven years with the St. Louis *Call*. In 1942 he acquired his first important journalistic post as St. Louis bureau chief of the Chicago *Defender*, a position he held through 1949.

His current position gives Woods considerable responsibility for USIA programs in the newly emerging countries of Africa, Asia, Latin America, and the Middle East.

## BLACKS APPOINTED TO KEY POSITIONS IN THE ADMINISTRATION OF PRESIDENT GEORGE BUSH

In a divergence from the traditional pattern, President Bush decided not to select an individual to advise the White House on how to deal with blacks, handle minority affairs or serve as a liaison to the black community. Instead he has named blacks to fulfil specialized White House roles, placing them in various key positions within the administration.

Foremost among these, Dr. Louis Sullivan was confirmed as Secretary of Health and Human services after controversial confirmation hearings questioned his equivocal stand on abortion and his acceptance of sabbatical leave pay from Morehouse College during his government tenure. Another controversial nominee includes William Lucas as Assistant Attorney General for Civil Rights, who became a republican in 1986 when he ran unsuccessfully for the governorship of Michigan. Due to his lack of experience in civil rights enforcement and his association with the Reagan agenda, few civil rights advocates are satisfied with his nomination. "We had hoped that the attorney general would have tried to pick someone who had some experience with civil rights litigation," said Julius Chambers, director council of the NAACP Legal Defense and Education Fund. During the Reagan administration, William Bradford Reynolds, who then headed the civil rights division, endeavored to undo many of the past civil rights gains.

Joseph Perkins, appointed Bush's Deputy Assistant for Domestic Policy Office of the Vice President, wrote "Boom Time For Black America: The Middle Class Is Surging under Reagan," in which he asserted that the black middle class has thrived because of Reagan's policies.

With appointments such as these, Bush's civil rights agenda and the administration's affect upon the black community remain obscure. Steve Glaude, the nominee for Deputy Secretary of Housing and Urban Development, anticipates that " Bush's new black appointments represent a new vision." However, the definition of that vision and the efficacy with which it may be implemented have yet to be determined.

**Steve Glaude**
Deputy Secretary of HUD

**Wendell Wilkie Gunn**
Chief of Staff, Housing and Urban Development (HUD)

**Jewel Lafontant (Confirmation Pending)**
Assistant Secretary of State for Refugee Affairs

**William Lucas (Confirmation Pending)**
Assistant Attorney General for Civil Rights

**Frederick D. McClure**
Assistant to the President for Legislative Affairs

**Constance "Connie" Newman**
Director of the Office of Personnel Management

**Anna Perez**
First Lady's Press Secretary

**Joseph Perkins**
Deputy Assistant for Domestic Policy, Office of the Vice President

**Leonard Spearman Jr.**
Personnel Office

**Dr. Louis Sullivan**
Secretary of Health and Human Services

**Kristen Taylor**
Director, Media Relations Staff

**Joe Watkins**
Associate Director in the White House Office of Public Liaison

## BLACKS APPOINTED TO EXECUTIVE LEVEL POSITIONS BY PRESIDENT RONALD REAGAN

**William Bell**
Chairman Equal Employ. Opportunity Council

**Benjamin Bobo**
Deputy Assistant Secretary R&D
Department of Housing and Urban Development

**Melvin Bradley**
Senior Advisor OPD

**Ted Britten**
Director, Office of International Affairs
Department of Housing and Urban Development

**Carlos Campbell**
Assistant Secretary for Economic Development
Department of Commerce

**Samuel Cornelius**
Deputy Director CSA

**Lawrence Davenport**
Assistant Director, Domestic Operations ACTION

**Thelma Duggin**
Deputy Special Assistant OP Liaison

**W. Antoinette Ford**
Assistant Administrator, Near East AID

**Claire Freeman**
Deputy Assistant Secretary, Planning and Evaluation
Department of Housing and Urban Development

**Thaddeus Garrett**
Special Assistant to the Vice President

**Rosslee Green-Douglass**
Director, Economic Impact
Department of Energy

**Clarence Hodges**
Assistant Director, Community Action CSA

**Melvin Humphrey**
Director, Office SBDU DOT

**Toye Lewis-Byrd**
Special Assistant OPD

**Stephanie Lee Miller**
Special Assistant
Department of Commerce

**Samuel Pierce**
Sec. Dep't. of Housing and Urban Development

**Wes Plummer**
Director, Civil Rights DOT

**Vincent Reed**
Assistant Secretary
Elementary and Secondary Education Deputy Special Assistant, Intergovernmental Affairs

**Harry Singleton**
Deputy Assistant Secretary, Congressional Relations Department of Commerce

**Daniel Smith**
Policy Analyst OPD

**Arthur Teele Administrator,**
Urban Mass Transit DOT

**John Tiller**
Special Assistant Department of State

**Clarence Thomas**
Assistant Secretary, Civil Rights
Department of Education

**Lennie Marie Tolliver**
Commissioner on Aging
Department of Health and Human Services

**Gloria Toote**
Chair Merit System Procurement Board

**Everett Wallace**
Deputy Assistant Secretary, Fair Housing
Department of Housing and Urban Development

**Armstrong Williams**
Congressional Liaison Department of Agriculture

**Bernice Williams**
Office SDBU Department of Housing and Urban Development

**Lance Wilson**
Special Assistant
Department of Housing and Urban Development

**Angela Wright**
Public Information, Africa AID

**Robert Wright**
Associate Administrator, MBESBA

## BLACKS APPOINTED TO KEY POSITIONS IN THE ADMINISTRATION OF PRESIDENT JIMMY CARTER

**Hon. Hank Aaron**
Member, President's Council on Physical Fitness and Sports

**Sam Frank Abram**
Member, Commission on Presidential Scholars

**O. Rudolph Aggrey**
Ambassador to Romania

**Clifford L. Alexander Jr.**
Secretary of the Army

**Marcus Alexis**
Member, Interstate Commerce Commission

**Ethel Allen**
Member National Commission on Neighborhoods

**William Allison**
Deputy Director, Community Services Organization

**Bernard A. Anderson**
Member, National Commission for Employment and Unemployment Statistics

**Betty Anderson**
Special Assistant to the Executive Director
Equal Employment Opportunity Commission

**Claud Anderson**
Federal Co-Chairman Coastal Plains Regional Commission

**Frank Anderson**
U.S. Marshall, Southern Indiana

**Joseph Anderson**
Special Assistant to the Secretary U.S. Department of Commerce

**Robert Anderson**
Administrator, Office of Comprehensive Employment Development U.S. Department of Labor

**Leon B. Applewhaite**
Member, Federal Labor Relations Authority

**Milele Archibald**
Special Assistant to the President Overseas Private Investment Corporation

**Ronald Arrington**
Special Assistant to the Commissioner
Equal Employment Opportunity Commission

**Ruth Banks**
Special Assistant to the Director
Office of Hearings and Appeals
U.S. Department of Interior

**Terry Banks**
Associate General Counsel
Federal Communications Commission

**Maurice Barboza**
Special Assistant to the Deputy Assistant Secretary for Legislation
U.S. Department of Health, Education and Welfare

**Maurice Bean**
Ambassador to Burma

**Mary Berry**
Assistant Secretary for Education U.S. Department of Health, Education and Welfare

**Shallie Bey Jr.**
Superintendent, U.S. Mint, Philadelphia

**Unita Blackwell**
Member, National Commission for the International Year of the Child

**William Blakey**
Deputy Assistant Secretary for Legislation U.S. Department of Health, Education and Welfare

**David Bolen**
Ambassador to the German Democratic Republic

**Shellie Bowers**
Superior Court Judge, District of Columbia

**Tom Bradley**
Member, National Commission on Air Quality

**Eddie Lee Brandon**
Member, National Commission for the International Year of the Child

**William Briggs**
Executive Assistant to the Chairman Commodities Futures Trading Commission

**William Broadwater**
Chief, Air Space and Traffic Rules Division U.S. Department of Transportation

**Benoit Brookens**
Special Assistant to the Deputy Assistant Secretary of State for Oceans and Fisheries Affairs

**Homer Broome Jr.**
Deputy Administrator Law Enforcement Assistance Administration

**Tyrone Brown**
Member Federal Communications Commission

**Hubert Bryant**
U.S. Attorney, Northern Oklahoma

**J. Jerome Bullock**
U.S. Marshall, District of Columbia

**James R. Burgess Jr.**
U.S. Attorney, Eastern Illinois

**Mr. John A. Burroughs**
Deputy Assistant Secretary of State for Equal Employment Opportunity

**Goler Butcher**
Assistant Administrator for the Bureau for Africa Agency for International Development

**James Byrd**
U.S. Marshall, Wyoming

**W. Beverly Carter**
Ambassador-at-Large, Office for Liaison with State and Local Governments

**Lisle Carter**
Member, President's Commission on Pension Policy

**William Cheatham**
Deputy Director of Program Review, Office of Civil Rights U.S. Department of Health, Education and Welfare

**Andrew Chisholm**
U.S. Marshall, South Carolina

**Almeric Christian**
Judge, District Court of the Virgin Islands

**William Clement Jr.**
Associate Administrator for Minority Small BusinessSmall Business Administration

**Maurice Clifford**
Member, Advisory Commission to the JFK Center

**Gayletha B. Cobb**
Special Assistant to the Assistant Administrator for Africa Agency for International Development

**Jewel Plummer Cobb**
Member, Board of Foreign Scholarships

**Lovida Coleman**
Special Assistant to the Deputy Attorney General
U.S. Department of Justice

**Robert Collins**
U.S. District Judge, Eastern District of Louisiana

**T. R. Coney**
U.S. Marshall, Southern District of Texas

**Julian Cook**
U.S. District Judge, Eastern District of Michigan

**Mr. Stoney Cooks**
Executive Assistant to the U.S. Ambassador to the United Nations

**William A. Cosby Jr.**
Member, National Commission for the International Year of the Child

**Jim Crawford**
Special Assistant to the Secretary U.S. Department of Housing and Urban Development

**Alonzo Crim**
Member, National Council on Educational Research

**Mr. George Dalley**
Deputy Assistant Secretary, Office of International and Organizational Affairs U.S. Department of State

**William Boone Darden**
Member, National Highway Safety Advisory Committee

**Ann Davis**
Member, Small Business Conference Committee

**Preston Davis**
Special Assistant to the Assistant Secretary for Administration U.S. Department of Agriculture

**Drew Days**
Assistant Attorney General, Civil Rights Division U.S. Department of Justice

**Anita Defrantz**
Member, President's Council on Physical Fitness and Sports

**Willi Delaney**
Special Assistant to the Director, Women's Bureau U.S. Department of Labor

**Bernadine Denning**
Director, Office of Revenue Sharing U.S. Department of the Treasury

**Dennis Derryck**
Deputy Assistant Director, Office of Policy and Planning Action

**Ruth Diggs**
President's Committee on Mental Retardation

**Anna Diggs-Taylor**
U.S. District Judge, Eastern District of Michigan

**Edwin Dorn**
Special Assistant to the Commissioner of Education U.S. Department of Health, Education and Welfare

**Fannie Dorsey**
Member, Federal Council on Aging

**L. C. Dorsey**
Member, National Advisory Council on Economic Opportunity

**Elwood Driver**
Member, National Transportation Safety Board

**Hazel M. Dukes**
Member, National Advisory Council on Economic Opportunity

**Willie Dean Durham**
U.S. Marshall, Western District of Tennessee

**Marion Wright Edelman**
Member, National Committee on the International Year of the Child

**Aubrey Edwards**
Special Assistant to the Deputy Assistant Secretary for Regulatory Functions and Interstate Land Sales Administration U.S. Department of Housing and Urban Development

**Harry Edwards**
Chairman of the Board National Railroad Passenger Corporation, AMTRAK

**Judy Ellis**
Special Assistant to the Vice Chairman Equal Employment Opportunity Commission

**Darryl Fagin**
Special Assistant to the U.S. Treasurer

**Francesta Farmer**
Director, Office of Interagency Coordination Equal Employment Opportunity Commission

**Marty Fleetwood**
Special Assistant to the Solicitor General

**Patsy Fleming**
Director, Inter-Governmental Affairs, Office of Civil Rights U.S. Department of Health, Education and Welfare

**Richard Fox**
Ambassador to Trinidad and Tobago

**Alfred W. Francis**
U.S. Marshall, Virgin Islands

**John Hope Franklin**
Member, Commission for International Education and Cultural Affairs

**Tina Garnett**
Special Assistant to the Assistant Administrator for Africa Agency for International Development

**Lucian Gatewood**
Special Assistant to the Assistant Secretary U.S. Department of Labor

**Gary D. Gayton**
Acting Administrator Urban Mass Transportation Administration

**Bryant George**
Director, Office of Pakistan and Nepal
Agency for International Development

**Kenneth Allen Gibson**
Member, President's Export Council

**Arleen Gilliam**
Executive Assistant to the Assistant Secretary U.S. Department of Labor

**Lamond Godwin**
Administrator, Office of National Programs U.S. Department of Labor

**Quinton Gordan**
Director, Office of Policy Development and Evaluation U.S. Department of Housing and Urban Development

**Michael Grace**
Special Assistant to the Deputy Assistant Attorney General (Antitrust) U.S. Department of Justice

**George Grant**
U.S. Marshall, Southern District of New York

**Donald S. Gray**
Director, Equal Opportunity (Military) U.S. Department of Defense

**Sandra Gray**
Assistant Commissioner, Office of Education U.S. Department of Health, Education and Welfare

**Ernest Green**
Assistant Secretary for Employment and Training U.S. Department of Labor

**Frederick Green**
Member, National Commission for the International Year of the Child

**Robert Lee Green**
Member, National Commission for the International Year of the Child

**Wallace Green**
Deputy Under Secretary U.S. Department of Interior

**Karl Gregory**
Member, Administrative Committee for Trade Negotiations

**Judy Griffin**
Executive Assistant to the Deputy Commissioner Bureau of Elementary and Secondary Education

**Mr. Evelio Grillo**
Executive Assistant to the Assistant Secretary for Human Development U.S. Department of Health, Education and Welfare

**Lani Guinier**
Special Assistant to the Assistant Attorney General for Civil Rights U.S. Department of Justice

**Gladys Gunn**
Member, Advisory Council on Women's Educational Programs

**Charles V. Hamilton**
Member, National Council on the Humanities

**Patricia Harris**
U.S. Department of Housing and Urban Development

**Hermene Hartman**
Member, Advisory Commission to the JFK Center

**Ulric St. Clair Haynes Jr.**
Ambassador to Algeria

**Alexis Herman**
Director, Women's Bureau U.S. Department of Labor

**Leon Higginbotham**
U.S. Circuit Judge, Third Circuit

**Chester Higgins**
Assistant Chief of Public Affairs Office of the Secretary of the Army

**Janet Hill**
Special Assistant to the Secretary of the Army

**Jesse Hill**
Member, Communications Satellite Corporation

**Matthew Holden Jr.**
Commissioner Federal Energy Regulatory Commission

**Meldon Hollis**
Special Assistant to the Assistant Secretary of Education U.S. Department of Health, Education and Welfare

**Anne Holloway**
Director, Washington Office of the Ambassador to the United Nations

**Carl Holman**
Member, National Council on the Humanities

**Carl Horton**
Special Assistant to the Associate Administrator Small Business Administration

**Joseph Howard**
U.S. District Judge, District of Maryland

**Gloria Hughes**
Special Assistant to the Assistant Secretary for Administra-

tion U.S. Department of the Treasury

**Teresa Hughes**
Member, National Student Loan Marketing Association

**G. William Hunter**
U.S. Attorney, Northern District of California

**Ira Hutchinson**
Deputy Director, National Park Service

**Alexis Jackson**
Associate Solicitor for General Law U.S. Department of the Interior

**C. Anthony Jackson**
Director, Program Development and the Office of Community Action Community Services Administration

**Maynard Jackson**
Member, National Commission on Neighborhoods

**Gilda Jacobs**
Special Assistant to the Director U.S. Office of Personnel Management

**Clarence James**
Member, Copyright Royalty Tribunal

**Carolyn Jefferson**
Congressional Liaison Officer, Office of Congressional Affairs U.S. Department of Commerce

**Howard Jenkins**
Member, National Labor Relations Board

**Elmima Johnson**
Special Assistant to the Commissioner, Office of Education U.S. Department of Health, Education and Welfare

**Vernon Johnson**
Assistant Secretary, Bureau of African Affairs U.S. Department of State

**Clara Stanton Jones**
Member, National Commission on Libraries and Information Science

**Franklin Jones**
General Counsel, Community Services Administration

**James Jones**
Member, Federal Service Impasses Panel

**Roosevelt Jones**
Executive Assistant to the Assistant Secretary for Community Planning and Development U.S. Department of Housing and Urban Development

**Thomas R. Jones**
Member, Interagency Commission on Emergency Medical Services

**William B. Jones**
Ambassador to Haiti

**James Joseph**
Under Secretary U.S. Department of the Interior

**Amalya Kearse**
U.S. Circuit Judge, Second Circuit

**Damon Keith**
U.S. Circuit Judge, Sixth Circuit

**Robert Kemp**
Executive Director, Interagency Council for Minority Business Enterprise

**Beverly King**
Special Assistant to the Director, Office of Civil Rights Environmental Protection Agency

**Colbert King**
Deputy Assistant Secretary for Legislative Affairs U.S. Department of the Treasury

**Howard King**
Deputy Director for Civil Rights U.S. Department of Transportation

**Crystal Kuykendall**
Member, National Advisory Council on Extension and Continuing Education

**Mr. Weldon Latham**
Deputy Assistant Secretary, Office of Fair Housing and Equal Opportunity U.S. Department of Housing and Urban Development

**Marjorie M. Lawson**
Member of the Board, JFK Center for the Performing Arts

**Lasalle D. Leffall**
Member, Advisory Commission to the JFK Center

**Ronald Le Flore**
Member, National Advisory Committee for Juvenile Justice and Delinquency Prevention

**Wilbert Le Melle**
Ambassador to Kenya

**Walter Leonard**
Member, Board of Visitors U.S. Naval Academy

**John Lewis**
Associate Director of Domestic and Anti-Poverty Operations, ACTION

**Rufus Lewis**
U.S. Marshall, Middle District of Alabama

**Lee A. Limbs Jr.**
U.S. Marshall, Arizona

**Bruce Llewellyn**
Director, Overseas Private Investment Corporation

**Mary Johnson Lowe**
U.S. District Judge, Southern District of New York

**Richard Lowe**
Special Assistant to the Vice Chairman Equal Employment Opportunity Commission

**Richard B. Lowe**
Deputy Inspector General U.S. Department of Health, Education and Welfare

**Gerald Lucas**
Special Assistant to the Assistant Secretary, Office of Administration U.S. Department of Commerce

**Myles Lynk**
Special Assistant to the Secretary U.S. Department of Health, Education and Welfare

**Benjamin Malcolm**
Vice Chairman and Commissioner U.S. Parole Commission

**Dorothy Mann**
Executive Assistant to the Deputy Director ACTION

**Mr. Richard Mapp**
Special Assistant to the Assistant Secretary for Housing U.S. Department of Housing and Urban Development

**Cora B. Marrett**
Member, President's Commission on the Accident at Three Mile Island

**Harry Marshall**
U.S. Marshall, Southern District of Illinois

**Walter Massey**
Member, National Science Board

**James W. Mayo**
Scientific Advisor to the Assistant Secretary for Energy Technology U.S. Department of Energy

**Benjamin Mays**
Member, President's Advisory Board on Ambassadorial Appointments

**William Mays**
Member, National Highway Safety Commission

**Andrew Metcalf**
U.S. Marshall, Western District of Michigan

**Ishmael Meyers**
U.S. Attorney, Virgin Islands

**Henry Michaux Jr.**
U.S. Attorney, Middle District of North Carolina

**Harriet Michel**
Director, Office of Community Youth Employment Program U.S. Department of Labor

**Michael Middleton**
Director, Office of Systemic Programs Equal Employment Opportunity Commission

**Albert Miller**
Deputy Under Secretary for Field Coordination U.S. Department of Housing and Urban Development

**George Miller**
Executive Assistant to the Assistant Secretary for Economic Policy
U.S. Department of the Treasury

**Sheila D. Minor**
Special Assistant to the Assistant Secretary for Fish, Wildlife and Parks U.S. Department of the Interior

**Steven Minter**
Member, National Commission for the International Year of the Child

**Tom Minter**
Deputy Commissioner of Elementary and Secondary Education U.S. Department of Health, Education and Welfare

**Beverly Mitchell**
Special Assistant to the Director of Congressional Liaison U.S. Department of Health, Education and Welfare

**Don Mitchell**
Member, Commission on Presidential Scholars

**Mr. George Mitchell**
Special Assistant to the Secretary U.S. Department of State

**Martha Mitchell**
Special Assistant to the Deputy Administrator Small Business Administration

**Alvin Moore**
Special Assistant to the Administrator Office of Comprehensive Employment Development U.S. Department of Labor

**Azie Taylor Morton**
Treasurer of the United States National Director of the U.S. Savings Bond Division

**Samuel L. Myers**
Member, Commission on Foreign Language and International Studies

**Noel Myricks**
Member, National Advisory Council on Extended and Continuing Education

**Carl McCarden**
Executive Assistant to the Assistant Secretary
U.S. Department of Housing and Urban Development

**Curtis McClinton**
Director, Office of Special Services Economic Development Administration

**Wade McCree**
Solicitor General

**Gabrielle McDonald**
U.S. District Judge, Southern District of Texas

**Donald F. McHenry**
Ambassador to the United Nations

**W. Philip McLaurin**
Member, National Advisory Commission on Economic Opportunity

**Theodore McMillian**
U.S. Circuit Judge, Eighth Circuit

**David Nelson**
U.S. District Judge, Massachusetts

**Mr. Edward Norton**
Acting General Counsel
U.S. Department of Housing and Urban Development

**Eleanor Holmes Norton**
Chair Equal Employment Opportunity Commission

**Revius Ortique**
Member, Legal Services Corporation

**Ernie Osborne**
Commissioner for Public Services and Human Development U.S. Department of Health, Education and Welfare

**Marian Palmer**
Executive Assistant to the General Manager of the New Community Corporation U.S. Department of Housing and Urban Development

**Amelia Parker**
Special Assistant, Office of Telecommunications Policy
U.S. Department of State

**Paul Parks**
Member, Advisory Council on Women's Educational Programs

**Franklin Payne**
U.S. Marshall, Eastern Missouri

**June Carter Perry**
Special Assistant to the Director for Public Affairs Community Services Administration

**Yvonne S. Perry**
Deputy Assistant Secretary
U.S. Department of Housing and Urban Development

**Marcella Peterson**
Assistant to Director
Office of Revenue Sharing

**Percy A. Pierre**
Assistant Secretary of the Army for Research, Development and Acquisition

**Anderson Pollard**
Member, President's Commission on Mental Retardation

**Ersa Poston**
Vice Chairman, Merit Systems Protection Board

**Johnnie Prothro**
Member, International Food and Agricultural Development Commission

**Albert Raby**
Intergovernmental Relations Officer ACTION

**M. Athalie Range**
Member, Board of Directors National Railroad Passenger Corporation

**Calvin Raullerson**
Assistant Administrator, Private Development Corporation Agency for International Development U.S. Department of State

**Inez Reid**
Deputy General Counsel for Regulations Review
U.S. Department of Health, Education and Welfare

**John Reinhardt**
Director, International Communication Agency

**Emmett John Rice**
Member, Board of Governors Federal Reserve System

**Lois D. Rice**
Member, Student Loan Marketing Association

**Archie Richardson**
Member, National Highway Safety Commission

**Tyree Richburg**
U.S. Marshall, Southern District of Alabama

**Wilson Riles**
Member, National Council on Educational Research

**Glen Robinson**
U.S. Marshall, Northern District of California

**Weldon Rougeau**
Director, Office of Federal Contract Compliance
U.S. Department of Labor

**Herman J. Russell**
Member, National Corporation for Housing Partnerships

**Bayard Rustin**
Member, President's Commission on the Holocaust

**Frederick A. Schenck**
Deputy Under Secretary U.S. Department of Commerce

**Basil Scott**
Member, National Highway Safety Commission

**Macler Shephard**
Member, National Commission on Neighborhoods

**Jake J. Simmons III**
Member, President's Commission on Personnel Interchange

**Paul A. Simmons**
U.S. District Judge, Western District of Pennsylvania

**Genevive C. Sims**
Special Assistant to the Vice Chairman Merit Systems Protection Board

**John B. Slaughter**
Assistant Director, National Science Foundation

**Constance Slaughter-Harvey**
Member, Commission on Presidential Scholars

**Edith Barksdale Sloan**
Member, Consumer Product Safety Commission

**J. Clay Smith**
Member, Equal Employment Opportunity Commission

**Otis Smith**
Administrative Conference of the United States

**Mabel M. Smythe**
Ambassador to Cameroon

**Renee Sprow**
Assistant to the Under Secretary of Defense for Acquisition Policy U.S. Department of Defense

**Vernon Stansbury**
Deputy Director, Bureau of Export Development U.S. Department of Commerce

**Allan A. Stephenson**
Acting Director, Office of Minority Business Enterprise U.S. Department of Commerce

**Mr. H. Patrick Swygert**
Special Counsel, U.S. Merit Systems Protection Board

**Jack Tanner**
U.S. District Judge, District of Washington

**Horace Tate**
Member, National Commission on Libraries and Information Sciences

**Quentin Taylor**
Deputy Administrator, Federal Aviation Administration
U.S. Department of Transportation

**Ethel Terry**
Special Assistant to the Federal Co-Chairman Coastal Plains Regional Commission

**Doris Thompson**
Director of Civil Rights Environmental Protection Agency

**John D. Thompson**
Member, Board of Directors Federal National Mortgage Association

**Elizabeth Thorton**
Special Assistant to the Commissioner
Equal Employment Opportunity Commission

**Terrance Todman**

Ambassador to Spain

**Margaret Triplett**
Special Assistant, Institute of Law Enforcement and Criminal Justice U.S. Department of Justice

**Benjamin M. Tucker**
Member, Advisory Committee to the JFK Center

**Sterling Tucker**
Assistant Secretary for Fair Housing and Equal Opportunity U.S. Department of Housing and Urban Development

**Howard J. Turner Jr.**
U.S. Marshall, Western District of Pennsylvania

**Art Varnado**
Special Assistant for Flight Standard Services Federal Aviation Administration U.S. Department of Transportation

**Shirley Verrett**
Member, Commission for the Preservation of the White House

**A. Maceo Walker**
Member, Small Business Conference Committee

**LeRoy Walker**
Member, President's Council on Physical Fitness and Sports

**Joan S. Wallace**
Assistant Secretary for Administration
U.S. Department of Agriculture

**John Waller**
Special Assistant to the Assistant Secretary for Employment and Training U.S. Department of Labor

**William Ware**
Director, Congressional Affairs Equal Employment Opportunity Commission

**Frank Washington**
Acting Chief of Policy and Rules Division, Broadcast Bureau Federal Communications Commission

**Warren Morton Washington**
Member, National Advisory Committee on Oceans and Atmosphere

**Barbara Watson**
Assistant Secretary for Consular Affairs
U.S. Department of State

**Paul Webber III**
Judge, District of Columbia Superior Court

**Togo West**
Special Assistant to the Secretary
U.S. Department of Defense

**Clifton Wharton**
Member, President's Commission on World Hunger

**Howard White**
Member, Corporation for Public Broadcasting

**DeWayne Wickham**
Special Assistant to the Assistant Secretary for Education U.S. Department of Health, Education and Welfare

**Eve Wilkins**
Special Assistant to the Chairman Equal Employment Opportunity Commission

**Bathrus Williams**
Member, Commission on Neighborhoods

**Dorothy Williams**
Special Assistant to the Deputy Assistant Secretary for Urban Affairs and Development
U.S. Department of Housing and Urban Development

**James F. Williams II**
Member of the Board of Regents National Library of Medicine

**James R. Williams**
U.S. Attorney, Northern District of Ohio

**Thomas Williamson Jr.**
Deputy Inspector General
U.S. Department of Energy

**Genevieve Wilson**
Member, Advisory Council on Juvenile Justice and Delinquency Prevention

**Margaret Bush Wilson**
Member, General Advisory Commission on Arms Control and Disarmament

**Judith Winston**
Executive Assistant to the Chairman
Equal Employment Opportunity Commission

**Jessie A. Woods**
Member, National Council on the Arts

**Josephine Worthy**
Member, Legal Services Corporation

**Patricia Worthy**
Deputy Assistant Secretary for Regulatory Functions, Interstate Land Sales
U.S. Department of Housing and Urban Development

**Cheryl Wright**
Special Assistant to the Secretary
U.S. Department of Housing and Urban Development

**Andrew Young**
U.S. Ambassador to the United Nations

**Jean C. Young**
Chairman, National Commission for the International Year of the Child

**Margaret Young**
Member, Board of Visitors, U.S. Military Academy

## BLACK AND MINORITY KEY WHITE HOUSE STAFF OF PRESIDENT JIMMY CARTER

**Elizabeth Abramowitz**
Assistant Director Domestic Policy Staff

**Raymone Bain**
Public Affairs Assistant
Office of Management and Budget

**Julia Dobbs**
Legal Deputy to Louis Martin

**Edna Draper**
Confidential Assistant to Hamilton Jordan

**James Dyke**
Special Assistant to the Vice President

**Christopher Edley**
Assistant Director
Domestic Policy Staff

**Nathaniel Fields**
Senior Policy Analyst
Office of Science and Technology

**Dianne Hampton**
Administrative Assistant to Louis Martin

**Gwendolyn Hemphill**
Secretary to Tim Kraft

**Marc Henderson**
Associate Press Secretary

**Cecelia Jakovich**
Special Assistant to the Deputy Appointments Secretary

**Ms. Elizabeth Lumpkin**
Press Aide

**Edward Maddox**
Staff Assistant
Advance Office

**Robert Malson**
Assistant Director
Domestic Policy Staff

**Louis Martin**
Special Assistant to the President

**Frederick McKinney**
Junior Staff Economist Council of Economic Advisors

**Valerie Pinson**
Special Assistant for Congressional Liaison

**Franklin Raines**
Associate Director Office of Management and Budget

**James Scott**
White House Fellow

**Ms. Pauline Schneider**
Staff Assistant Office of Intergovernmental Affairs

**Gerald Wallette**
Staff Assistant Presidential Personnel

**Franklin White**
Associate Director
Domestic Policy Staff

**Karen Zunig**
Deputy to Louis Martin

## OTHER PROMINENT POLITICAL PERSONAGES

Although elected only to state and local offices, certain black politicians have attained national reputations and influence as a result of their forceful and forward-looking legislative performances. Prominent among this promising group are the eight leaders sketched below. The biographies of many other local officeholders can be found in the section on Prominent Black Americans.

### JULIAN BOND
### State Legislator, Civil Rights Leader

Georgia State Senator Julian Bond, a bellwether of the new politics, continues to be a major force in the advance of civil rights. Articulate and dedicated to his principles, this young leader galvanized the desegregation of Atlanta lunch counters, led a successful insurgent delegation to the 1968 Democratic convention in Chicago, and became the first black American to be nominated for Vice President of the United States.

Born in Nashville to parents who are college educators and administrators, he attended a Quaker prep school and Morehouse College, where he took a philosophy course under Martin Luther King Jr. While at school he co-founded COHAR, the organization which began the desegregation of Atlanta lunch counters and eventually merged into SNCC in 1960. In his senior year, he quit college to work full time for the black weekly *Atlanta Inquirer* (ultimately as managing editor) and to become communications director of SNCC until 1965, when he won election to the Georgia House from Atlanta's 111th district.

*Julian Bond at the 1968 Democratic Convention.*

Objecting to Bond's outspoken opposition to the U.S. military adventure in Viet Nam, Georgia's other legislators refused to seat him for over a year, until the U.S. Supreme Court declared such exclusion unconstitutional. Because the state's regular Democratic organization systematically denied significant posts to blacks, Bond and fellow representative Ben Brown then led the insurgent Georgia Loyal National Democratic delegation to Chicago and won half of the state's 42 allotted seats. Bond was reelected as a representative in 1968 and as a state senator in 1974. He currently serves as a state senator of Georgia and is co-chairman of the Georgia Loyal National Democratic Delegation.

He has served as co-chairman of the National Conference for New Politics and is on the boards of the Delta Ministry Project of the National Council of Churches, the Robert F. Kennedy Memorial Fund, and the Martin Luther King Memorial Center.

Known as a hard working legislator and a responsive ombudsman, Bond is presently concentrating on voter organization. He is chairman of the Southern Elections Fund, an Atlanta-based group that supplies money and technical assistance to black candidates for public office in the South. Focusing on small towns, the fund has helped elect 407 blacks to office since 1969. Its goal, like Bond's, is to change politics in the South.

### RONALD H. BROWN
### Chairman of the Democratic National Committee

On February 10, 1989, Ronald H. Brown became the first black to head one of the country's major political parties, culminating a career consisting of more than 15 years of party service at all levels. He began as District leader in Mt. Vernon, NY in 1971, and his accomplishments include such positions as senior political advisor to the Dukakis-Bentson presidential campaign and 1988 Democratic Convention manager for Jesse Jackson.

Brown, a specialist in negotiation and compromise, advocates a stance diverging from the more traditional black political methods: "Well, you know, America happens to be a majority white country and if you are going to play a significant role as political leader in the broad sense, obviously you've got to attract votes, support, confidence and the esteem of the majority population."

Ronald Brown grew up in Harlem's Hotel Theresa—then a prestigious black hotel—where his father was manager. Both of his parents graduated from Howard University. After Hunter College Elementary School, a competitive New York public school for gifted children, and private high school, Brown became a popular leader at an all-white Middlebury College Vermont campus. While at Middlebury, Brown pledged the Sigma Phi Epsilon fraternity which consequently defied the organization's then racial barriers, eventually resulting in the repeal of fraternity exclusionary clauses.

After his college graduation and marriage to Alma Brown, he spent three years in Germany and Korea in the army, before starting his professional career at the Urban League in 1966, while attending law school at St. John's University in New York.

In 1973, he moved to Washington to become the spokesman for the Urban League, and then in 1979, became deputy manager of the presidential campaign of Sen. Edward M. Kennedy (D-Mass.)

After a brief tenure at a Senate Judiciary committee, Brown accepted a partnership at Patton, Blogs and Blow, a Washington lobbying law firm, and concurrently served the Democratic National Convention (DNC) from 1982 to 1985 as Deputy Chair, and as Chief Council and Chair, Task Force on Voting Rights and Voter Participation. Currently he remains a member of the DNC Executive Committee and is a member of the Bars of New York, the District of Columbia, and the United States Supreme Court. Brown was a fellow at the John F. Kennedy School of Government, Harvard in 1980, and his many achievements include Chairman, Senior Advisory Committee of the Institute of Politics, JFK School of Government; Trustee of Middlebury College; former Chair of Board of Trustees at the University of the District of Columbia; member of the U. S. National Commission to UNESCO; member of the Federal Home Loan Bank Board Advisory Committee; Middle East Representative on behalf of the National Urban League; and Legislative Chairman for the Leadership Council on Civil Rights.

## ALEXIS HERMAN
## Democratic National Committee Chief of Staff

Alexis Herman, once a social worker and guidance counselor, was in 1989 chosen as Chief of Staff under Ronald Brown, Chairman of the Democratic National Committee, and in 1988 named one of the 100 top outstanding business women in the U. S. She has also been listed by the American Chamber of Commerce as one of the 10 outstanding Young Women in America and selected as one of the 50 future leaders by *Ebony Magazine* and one of 10 women of the future for the 1980s by *Ladies Home Journal*.

Ms. Herman, president of her own professional management consulting firm A. M. Herman & Associates, serves Fortune 500 firms in developing management and organizational effectiveness plans. She worked in the administration of Jimmy Carter as Director of the Women's Bureau at the Department of Labor, and during her tenure there, served as White House Representative to the Organization of Economic Cooperation and Development Committee (OECD) in Paris, France. She was a founding member of the National Consumer Cooperative Bank Board and has worked in the General Election Campaigns of every Democratic presidential nominee since Jimmy Carter in 1976. Preceding her appointment to the Labor Department, Ms. Herman had been the National Director of the Minority Women Employment Program (MWEP) an outgrowth of a program she herself designed and implemented.

Ms. Herman, a graduate of Xavier University in Louisiana, has been contributing author to numerous magazine and journals and has lectured extensively throughout the U. S. and abroad.

She is presently affiliated with the National Commission on Working Women as Chair; the Vice President of the National Council on Negro Women; and Board of Directors of the District of Columbia Economic Development Finance Corp., and Adams National Bank of Washington, D. C.

## K. LEROY IRVIS
## State Legislator

Speaker of the Pennsylvania House of Representatives and minority leader, K. Leroy Irvis has been instrumental in the passage of much key legislation, including the state's controversial income tax law.

Born in Saugerties, New York, he is an alumnus of New

*Chairman of the Democratic National Committee, Ron Brown.*

York State Teachers College, New York University, and the University of Pennsylvania Law School. After serving as a civilian attache of the War Department's Aviation Training Division, he became Pennsylvania's assistant district attorney from 1957 to 1963 and a member of the NAACP's legal redress committee. Elected to the Pennsylvania House in 1958, he has coordinated Democratic legislative proposals as majority leader (1969-1970, 1970-1971) and minority whip (1967-1968, 1973—). Early in his career, Irvis had been a school teacher in Baltimore, a steel chipper in Pittsburgh, and a news correspondent for the *Pittsburgh Courier*.

Irvis is a member of the General State Authority Executive Board and a director of TRIAD, a member of Pennsylvania's Bicentennial Commission and a delegate to the Democratic national conventions of 1968 and 1972. As an attorney, he is a member of Federal, District, and all Pennsylvania courts. He is public relations secretary and a director of the Urban League of Pittsburgh, and a board member of Pittsburgh's Port Authority, United Black Frontiers, and the University of Pittsburgh.

### RICHARD H. NEWHOUSE
### State Legislator

Sent to the Illinois State Senate in 1966 as a Democrat from Chicago's 24th election district, Richard Newhouse has proved himself an energetic and responsive legislator.

Born in Louisville, Kentucky, he served in the World War II Air Force from 1943 to 1945, winning 12 battle stars as a staff sergeant in the 448th Signal Construction Unit. After the war he attended Boston University (B.S., 1950; M.S., 1952) and the University of Chicago (JD, 1960). In the state senate, he sits on the Appropriations, Education, Judiciary, and Welfare committees. He is founder and director of the Black Legislative Clearing House, a fellow of the Adlai Stevenson Institute, and serves on the Intergovernmental Relations Commission and the Council on the practicing lawyer in Chicago. He is a member of the American, Cook County, and Chicago bar associations.

A member of many civic groups, such as the National Urban Coalition, he has been singled out by his constituents to receive the "Best Legislator" award from both the Independent Voters of Illinois and the American Legion, and has been named "Outstanding Public Servant" by the Cook County Bar Association, and "Senator of the Year" by the Baptist Ministers Conference of Chicago.

### CECIL A. PARTEE
### State Legislator

Cecil A. Partee is treasurer for the City of Chicago and is a commissioner for the Department of Human Services and a member of the Democratic National Committee. He has been a member of the Illinois legislature since 1956, when he was first elected to the state's House of Representatives.

Born in Blytheville, Arkansas, Partee received a B.S. in business administration from Tennessee State University (1944) and a J.D. degree from Northwestern University

*Basil Paterson and Charles Rangel attend a Harlem community protest.*

(1946). After serving as an assistant state's attorney for Cook county from 1948 to 1956, he was elected to the state House in 1956, serving five consecutive terms there before being sent to the upper chamber in 1966. He was president pro tem of the senate from 1971 to 1973. He was a delegate to the Democratic National Convention in 1972.

In the nongovernmental sector, Partee is a senior partner in the Chicago law firm of Partee & Green and a member of the Cook County, State, American, and National bar associations. Active in many community drives, he belongs to the Chicago City Club, the Jane Dent Home, the NAACP, and the National Urban League. In 1969 he was named "Outstanding State Senator."

### BASIL A. PATERSON
### State Legislator

Progressive legislator Basil A. Paterson is a former New York State senator from New York City's 26th Senatorial District, and was the Democratic nominee for lieutenant governor in 1970. In addition to authoring many successful bills to improve educational quality, he was a leader in Senate battles for forward-looking social legislation and an opponent of the war in Southeast Asia. Paterson is currently Secretary of State of New York.

Born in New York City, Paterson is a graduate of St. John's College and Law School. He entered the general practice of law in 1952, and is currently a member of the law firm of Paterson, Michael & Murray. In 1964, he was elected president of the New York City branch of the NAACP, and the following year he was elected to the State Senate, where he has served on the Judiciary, Banking, Labor and Industry, Affairs of the City of New York, and Housing and Urban Development committees. He is ranking Democrat on the Joint Legislative Committee on Education Law, and a member of the joint committees on Mental Retardation and Physical Handicaps, and Conservation. He exercises an unusual amount of personal influence on the heavily Republican New York legislature.

Paterson has won many honors, including selection by the Eagleton Institute of Politics in 1967 as one of the two outstanding legislators in New York State. He has also won awards from Kappa Alpha Psi, Omega Psi Phi, and the Distinguished Service Award from the New York City Police Department. Paterson is currently New York State Secretary of State.

## PERCY SUTTON
## Former City Official, Political Leader

Percy Sutton is the former President of the Borough of Manhattan in New York City. While borough president, Sutton earned a national reputation for his skillful handling of urban problems. Now out of politics, Sutton is chairman of Inner City Broadcasting Company, which owns radio stations in New York City, Detroit, and California. Sutton's group is currently making plans to get into the cable television business with a franchise in Queens, New York. The group is also refurbishing the famed Apollo Theater in Harlem to present entertainment through cable television.

Born in San Antonio, Texas, he relocated to New York as a young man when southern recruiting officers rejected his World War II enlistment, and went on to win combat stars as a captain in Air Force intelligence. Studying on the GI Bill, he graduated from Brooklyn Law School in 1950 and was admitted to the New York bar in 1951. When the Korean conflict erupted, he rejoined the Air Force as a trial advocate judge.

Back in civilian life, Sutton opened his Harlem law firm in 1953 and served in a series of NAACP posts, becoming president of the New York Branch in 1961-1962, but he could make little headway with political leaders. In 1963, he and Charles Rangel formed the insurgent Harlem Democratic Club (now called the Martin Luther King Jr., Club) which has grown to over 1,000 volunteer workers. Elected to the New York State Assembly in 1964, Sutton united black representatives there into a power bloc that finally won major committee membership and was instrumental in the passage of such significant reform bills as the Wilson-Sutton Divorce Law and the legalization of abortion in New York State. Chosen to finish a vacated term as Manhattan's chief executive in September 1966, he twice won reelection by large majorities. As borough president, he increased citizen participation in government, cut costs through decentralization, and focused municipal attention on the roots of urban problems.

*Former New York Borough President Percy Sutton and Paul Gibson of American Airlines reviewing veteran's parade.*

Convinced that "black people must control elements in news media in order to liberate themselves, "Sutton formed the groups which purchased the *Amsterdam News*, the nation's second largest black newspaper, and radio station WLIB-AM. He is a national director of the Urban League and Operation Push, an advisor to Harlem Hospital, and a member of the boards of the American Museum of Natural History and the Museum of the City of New York.

# GROWTH AND DISTRIBUTION OF THE BLACK POPULATION

**Current Population Trends ■ Black Population in Colonial America ■ Regional Distribution ■ The Southern Exodus ■ Urbanization ■ The Decline of Black Farmers ■ The Beginnings of Deconcentration ■ The Suburbs and Large Cities ■ The 1990 Census ■ Selected Population Facts ■ Population Charts ■**

In the 1980s the nation's black population followed new patterns of redistribution established in the 1970s, including a movement away from central cities to the suburbs of metropolitan areas and a drift toward the southern region, particularly its metropolitan areas. The trend for blacks and whites to leave rural areas and small towns for metropolitan areas continues, although in the 1970s whites migrated away from metropolitan areas to the small towns and rural areas that make up nonmetropolitan America. This migration shift toward metropolitan suburban areas has been a major change in the movement of whites in the 1980s.

Perhaps as never before, blacks and whites are following broadly similar patterns of population redistribution. In the 1980s both groups have left rural areas and small towns for metropolitan areas, and within metropolitan areas both groups are increasingly suburbanized. Among blacks, the rate of suburbanization increased rapidly in the 1970s and has increased even more rapidly in the 1980s.

These trends do not mean that blacks and whites are moving to the same places or are coming to live in the same neighborhoods. Nor do they mean that the residential patterns of blacks and whites are necessarily "converging." Blacks are still more concentrated in central cities and in the South than are whites. Nevertheless, the directions of movement are similar: out of rural areas and small towns and out of central cities to suburbs. The migration of both groups to parts of the South increased for a while in the 1970s and early 1980s and later moderated, at least to southern states whose economies were strongly built around oil and gas and whose economic growth slowed by the mid-1980s.

Public policy and programs traditionally have emphasized problems of adjustment and accommodation of migrants to new surroundings, particularly those associated with the journey from the rural South to large cities of the North. The most pressing new challenges to policy may be with nonmigration and nonmigrants, persons who are left behind in southern "black belt" counties and other rural locations and in inner-city areas bypassed by economic growth and by more successful migrants. The growth and distribution of America's black population since colonial times lie as the background for these emerging concerns .

## BLACK POPULATION IN COLONIAL AMERICA

The beginning of America's black population is usually dated from the year 1619, when 14 or 20 blacks—historians are uncertain—landed in Jamestown, Virginia, from a Dutch man-of-war. These early black immigrants entered Virginia as indentured servants, as did many of their white counterparts, but within a short time the practice of enslaving newly arrived blacks spread its roots. By 1630, there were some 60 slaves in the American colonies, and when Virginia finally legalized slavery in 1662, the number of those condemned to lifetime servitude had reached 3,000.

In the 1680s, the colonies were beginning to flourish. The agrarian society demanded greater manpower to increase productivity, and this manpower was supplied by additional slave labor. By 1690, 70 years after the first importation of black slaves, there were 16,729 people at forced labor in the American colonies. Slavery had taken a firm hold on the economic life of the Southern colonies, but the importation of slaves increased rapidly. In 1700, there were 27,817 slaves in the colonies and, 10 years later, in the year 1710, this population had virtually doubled, to about 50,000. By 1740, the slave population reached 150,000. It was 326,000 in 1760; 462,000 in 1770, and 575,000 in 1780. From 1730 to 1800, the free black population grew at a slower rate than the slave population and by 1780 there was only one free black for every nine slaves.

### Growth of the Black Population

The first official census of the new government of the United States was taken in 1790, and 757,181 black people were counted. Not all were slaves. Nine percent, or some 59,557 blacks, had managed to acquire freedom. This group was beginning to become an important factor in the society in general. By 1790, most middle and eastern states—including Pennsylvania, Massachusetts, Connecticut, Rhode Island, New York, New Jersey, and the new Northwest Territory—had enacted legislation providing for gradual emancipation. Table 4 presents the results of the 1790 census.

The slave trade continued almost to the time of the Civil War. By 1860, there were almost 4 million black slaves in the United States, 90% of them in the South. The freedmen population, most of whom were in the North, numbered just short of half a million.

When the first national census was taken in 1790 blacks were nearly 19% of the nation's population. This figure means that as the Constitution was being ratified nearly one American in five was black. The proportion declined in subsequent decades but remained relatively high. Not until after the importation of slaves was stopped in the early 1800s did the proportion of blacks in the nation's population fall below 18% and begin to show steady and pronounced decline.

European immigration caused the white population to grow faster than the black population during the nineteenth and early twentieth centuries. Blacks declined as a proportion of the nation's population to a low point in 1930, when blacks made up just 9.7% of the U.S. population. Since 1930, however, the black population has grown faster than the national average, and by 1980 blacks made up 11.7% of the U.S. population. The rise in the percentage black since 1930 is the result of higher fertility among blacks than whites.

Blacks are likely to continue to increase faster than the national average, and therefore the proportion black in the total population is likely to continue to rise. One reason is that a momentum to future growth of the black population has been established as a result of higher-than-average fertility levels in the past. As a result of higher fertility in the past, the black population is somewhat younger than the white population and contains a slightly larger proportion of persons in the prime reproductive ages. A second reason is that for at least the next decade or two blacks are likely to continue to have higher age-adjusted fertility rates than whites (i.e., higher fertility even when differences in age composition are taken into account).

By 1980, the U.S. black population had grown to nearly 26.5 million, a figure higher than for many nations. The U.S.

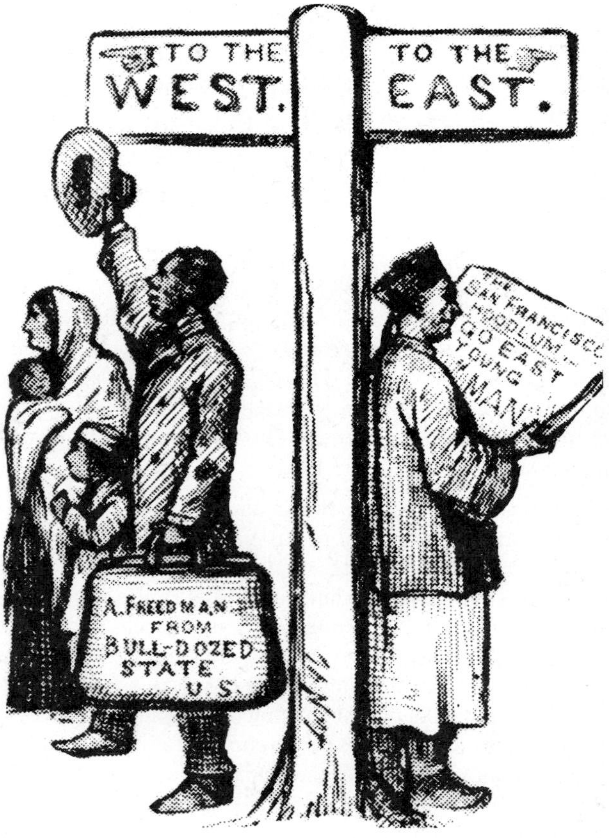


*A newspaper cartoon of the 1880s shows blacks heading west and Chinese heading east to escape racial persecution.*

## CHART 1. REGIONAL BLACK POPULATIONS AND SIX CITIES WITH LARGEST BLACK POPULATIONS

**In 1970 there were six cities in the United State with black populations of over one half million; at the last census in 1980 there were only five. Washington D.C. dropped below one half million with a loss of 16.6 % since the census of 1970, and from fifth to sixth position in cities having the largest black populations.**

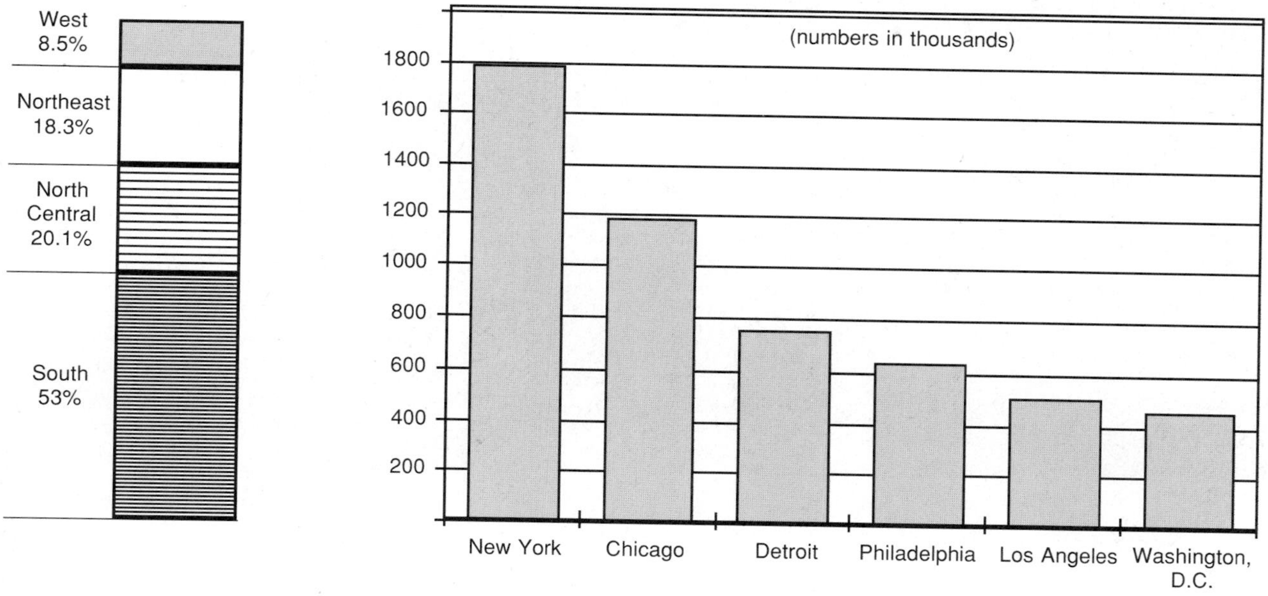


black population, for example, is slightly greater than the entire population of Canada. The only African nations with a black population that clearly exceeds the U.S. total of 26.5 million are Nigeria (with an estimated 1980 population of 77 million), Ethiopia (32 million), and Zaire (28 million).

In 1987, the black population of the U.S. was approaching 29,736,000, or about 12.2 percent of all Americans. The growth of the black population since the last census in 1980 is largely due to the excess of births over deaths, but like the white population, the black population has grown through immigration—legal as well as illegal. Streams of Asian and Hispanic migrants to the U.S. have been highly publicized, but black immigration has increased also. The Caribbean basin is one source of black immigration, with immigrants from Jamaica, Haiti, and other island nations entering the U.S. to look for work. The Mariel boatlift in 1980 also brought some blacks from Cuba. Political and economic conditions in Africa have given incentive to leave for other countries and may be associated with African students overstaying their student visas to work in the U.S. rather than return home. The size and effects of these sources of new population growth are speculative.

## CHART 2. POPULATION GROWTH RATES BY DECADE: 1900-1980

**Since the 1950s the population growth rates of both blacks and whites have been declining, but the white rate is declining more sharply and is now about three-fifths that of blacks.**

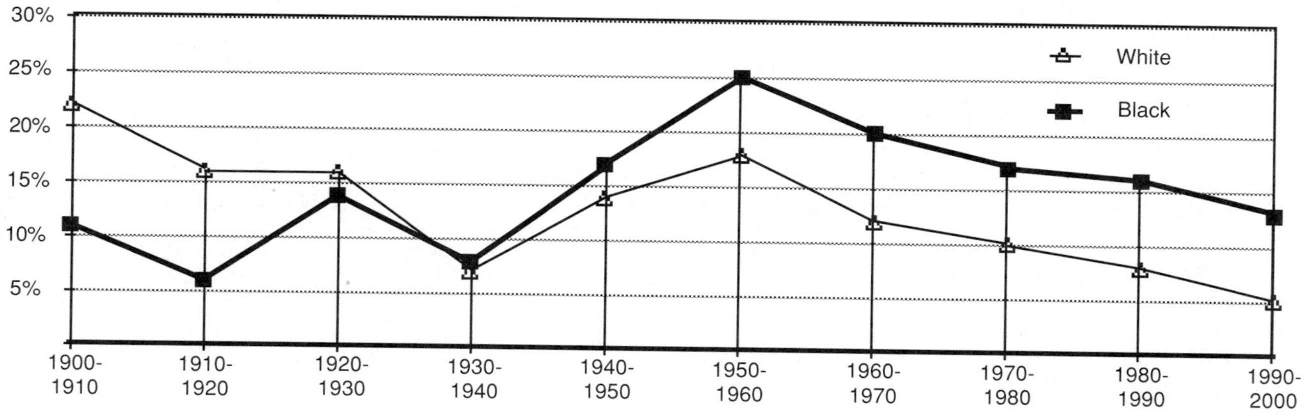


Source: Bureau of the Census    Figures for 1980-1990 and 1990-2000 are projected.

*The Vicksburg Wharf from which many blacks departed for the West in the Exodus of 1879-1881.*

## Regional Distribution

From 1790 until 1900, about 90 percent of all blacks resided in the South, mostly in rural areas. Even after the Civil War, the southern, rural character of the black population remained virtually intact and was not appreciably modified until the 20th century.

When the Emancipation Proclamation was signed, under 8 percent of blacks lived in the Northeast or Midwest. After the Civil War, the percent of the nation's blacks living in the Northeast fell slightly and rose in the Midwest. By 1900, only 10 percent of all blacks lived in these two northern regions. Migration from the South during this period was episodic.

An early exodus from the South occurred in the period 1879-1881 when some 60,000 blacks moved into Kansas. This spontaneous movement was made under difficult circumstances, by riverboat, railroad, deteriorated wagons, and on foot. The inmigration to Kansas created situations that strained the state, and several cities became refugee camps. The motivation behind this initial thrust to new lands was the need for social and economic freedom and the avoidance of political abuse. One of the towns created by this exodus was Nicodemus, which still exists as a small all-black community on the plains of Kansas.

Other movements of blacks out of the South and to the Midwest or Northeast have been chronicled, and although they often involved actions that were pioneering or even heroic and paved the way for other blacks to follow, the effects on the regional distribution of the total black population were small. By 1900, almost 90 percent of blacks still lived in the South. By the 1910-20 decade the percent of blacks living in the South began to fall significantly and the percent living in the Midwest or Northeast began to rise. By 1920, over 14 percent of blacks—more than one in seven—were Northerners. By 1930, more than 20 percent of blacks lived in the North, mostly in a few well-known enclaves in major cities.

The percent living in the North continued to rise and the percent living in the South continued to fall until around 1970. At that date about 39 percent of blacks were Northerners, 53 percent were Southerners, and about 7.5 percent lived in the West. These percentages are likely to change only modestly by the year 2000. The percent living in the North will probably fall slightly, and the percent living in the West should rise slightly. In the year 2000 about 37 percent of blacks are likely to live in the North, 53 percent in the South, and 10 percent in the West.

### CHART 3. DISTRIBUTION OF THE BLACK POPULATION

**Most of the black population lives in central cities although the black population living in the suburbs has been steadily increasing.**

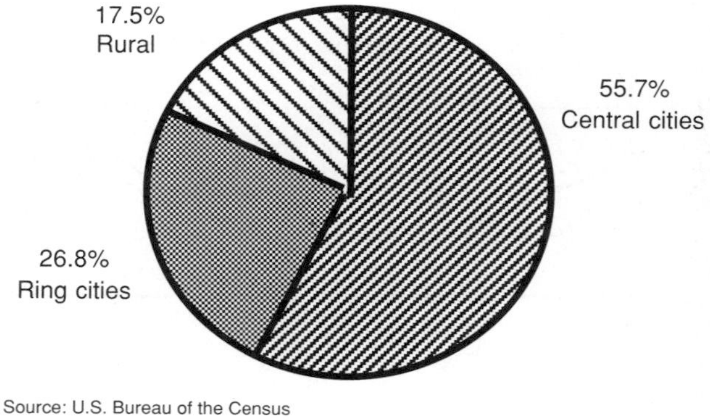


Source: U.S. Bureau of the Census

## The Southern Exodus

Historians and social scientists have long debated why blacks did not leave the South in larger numbers between the end of the Civil War and World War I. Virtually every migration stream is the product of both push and pull factors. Prejudice, discrimination, and a dearth of economic opportunities in the South would seem to have been the strong "push" factors needed to generate outmigration, and a somewhat more open society and the presence of jobs in the industrializing North should have provided the "pull" to establish a strong South-to-North migration stream. Some blacks were leaving the South during this period, typically following transportation routes directly northward from their state of birth, but the number moving north has always seemed smaller than what have been indicated by the combined push and pull forces.

Immigration may be one explanation for the relatively slow start of the southern exodus of blacks. As the North industrialized in the late nineteenth and early twentieth centuries, it generated a huge demand for labor, which was met in large part by massive immigration of Europeans. A great many of the urban factories were filled first by the Irish and German laborers in the nineteenth century and later by immigrants from Italy and southern and eastern Europe. Had northern industries not been able to meet their labor needs through immigration, they might have relied more on domestic sources, including southern blacks. There is substantial evidence that foreign migration can substitute for domestic migration, and this appears to have been the case in the United States in the late nineteenth and very early twentieth centuries.

As immigration to the United States was curtailed by World War I and restrictive legislation passed in the 1920s, blacks began to leave the South in larger numbers. As a consequence, the proportion of the nation's black population living in the South fell more rapidly during the 1910-1920 decade than during the entire period since emancipation.

Black outmigration from the South was reduced somewhat during the depression of the 1930s, but still the proportion of blacks living in the South fell. The greatest volume of outmigration of southern blacks occurred in the 1940-1950 decade and was instituted partly by mobilization during World War II. Therefore, the two world wars of the twentieth century provided a powerful impetus for blacks to leave the South.

During the 1940s, 1950s, and 1960s the net outmigration of blacks from the South totalled about 4.3 million persons. For many blacks this journey out of the South was also an uprooting from a rural, agricultural existence to life in big cities where jobs were in factories. The causes of this exodus were the push of limited opportunities of the rural South and the pull of a freer, but more competitive, life in the urban North. Mechanization of Southern agriculture after World War II decreased the demand for low-wage labor and gave further incentive to leave agricultural areas. The continued exodus of rural blacks decreased the supply of farm labor, thereby giving incentive for Southern farmers to mechanize further and adopt labor-saving methods.

The exodus of blacks from the South in the 30 years between 1940 and 1970 is one of the major migrations in American history. In volume it equals total Italian immigration to the United States during its peak, the 30-year period from the mid-1890s to the mid-1920s.

### CHART 4. POPULATION PROJECTIONS BY RACE 1990-2030.

**The Hispanic population is growing faster than the black population, due partly to an increase in Hispanic immigration. The white non-Hispanic population will continue to grow slowly and possibly start to decline after the year 2020.**

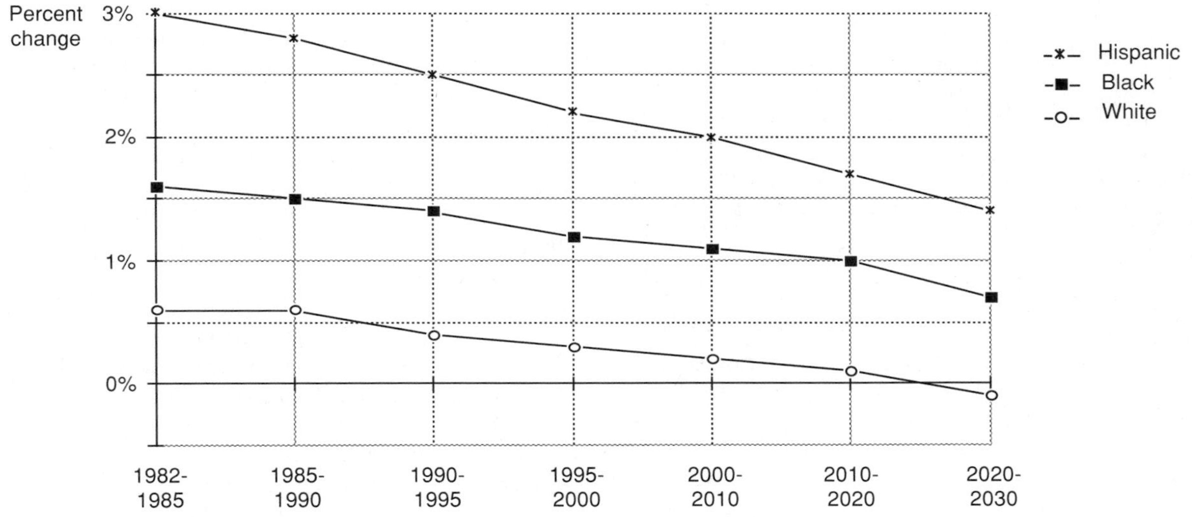


Source: U.S. Bureau of the Census

In the 1970s the exodus ended. Some blacks continued to leave the South, but others returned, and a few northern-born blacks—the children of earlier migrants—began to move to the South in response to jobs opening up and to a change in political and social relations in many parts of the region. In the early 1970s, about as many blacks were moving to the region as leaving it, and for the decade as a whole the South had net inmigration of blacks. A majority of blacks moving to the South were returnees—persons going back to their region of birth, but they were not necessarily going back to their roots, for about 7 out of every 10 were headed for one of the South metropolitan areas.

*"Pap" Singleton was the Moses of the movement of blacks west.*

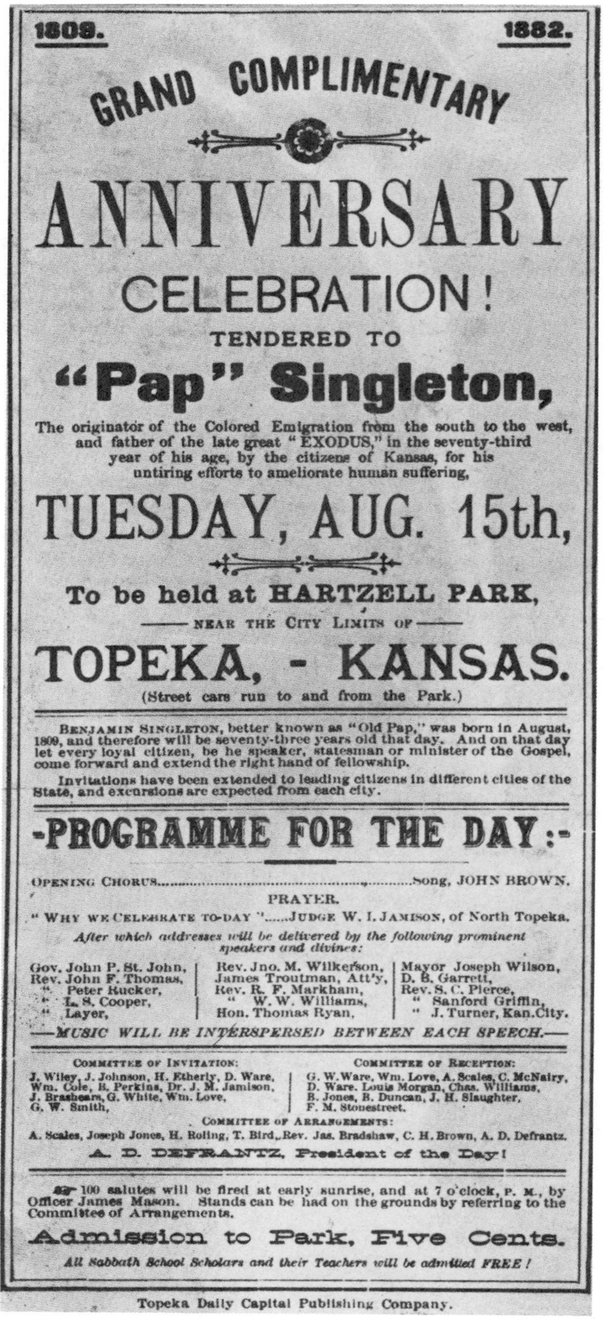


The volume of black migration to the South did not expand in the 1980s. By the mid-1980s economic growth in some areas of the South slowed, particularly locations with economies built around oil and gas. Other southern locations that had attracted new jobs in the 1970s had trouble holding on to them as a result of intensified foreign competition in textiles and other industries. The North had net outmigration of blacks in the 1980s, and the South and the West had net inmigration of blacks; but the volume of these flows essentially maintained levels established in the 1970s.

## Urbanization

The slow pace with which blacks left the South after emancipation was related to the fact that the black population was overwhelmingly rural and had limited access to information about opportunities in other regions. In 1880, about 13 percent of the black population lived outside cities or towns of 2,500 or greater population and therefore were classified as rural. About 28 percent of whites were rural at this date.

Urbanization of the white population was rapid in the late 1800s and early 1900s, and by 1920 a majority of whites were urban. This increase only partly reflects rural-to-urban migration, for much of it comes from massive immigration to the United States during this period. Immigrants overwhelmingly settled in cities, especially those arriving after 1900. Thus, the urbanization of the white population from 1880 to 1920 substantially reflects white immigrants settling in cites.

Urbanization of blacks consisted almost entirely of movement directly from rural areas to cities. By 1920, about 34 percent of blacks lived in urban areas, compared with 53 percent of whites. By this date, immigration had slowed and thereby slowed the increase in the percent of whites living in urban areas.

The urbanization of both blacks and whites was slowed during the Great Depression of the 1930s, when industrial jobs in northern cities disappeared. Many whites departed cities to return to farms they had left or to live with rural relatives. The urbanization of whites was reversed in the 1930s, and the percent of whites living in urban areas was somewhat lower in 1940 than in 1930. Blacks continued to urbanize during the 1930s.

Sometime around World War II a majority of the nation's black population came to live in urban areas. Urbanization of blacks was especially rapid in the 1940s, 1950s, and 1960s—precisely the period of greatest outmigration from the South. In 1940, just under one-half of blacks lived in urban areas; by 1960, 73 percent did so. The black rate of urbanization during this period was greater than that ever characterizing the white population.

By 1960, blacks were a more urban population than were whites. At that date 73 percent of blacks and 70 percent of

**CHART 5. PERCENTAGE OF POPULATION LIVING ON FARMS, BY RACE 1920-1987.**

**In 1920, almost half of the entire black population lived on farms, but by 1987 less than 1% of the black population was to be found on farms. In 1920, 99% of all black farm residents resided in the South as do virtually all of the less than 1% who still live on farms.**

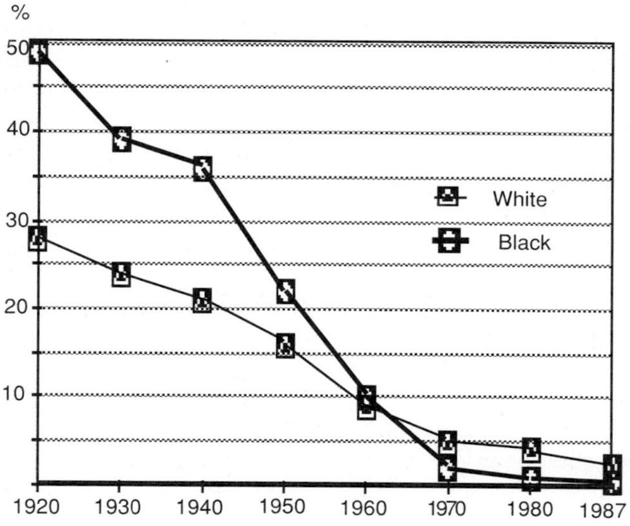


U.S. Bureau of the Census

whites were urban. Since then blacks have continued to urbanize, but as is shown later, by the 1970s the black urban population has increasingly come to live in the outer part—the suburbs—of urban settlements. The percent of blacks and whites who are technically urban (i.e., they live in urban places of 2,500 or more population or in the nearby suburbs of large cities) probably will not rise much more. By 1987, 86 percent of blacks and 71 percent of whites were urban by this measure.

## The Decline of Black Farmers

Continued rapid urbanization of the black population has been associated with spectacular decreases in the number of blacks living on farms. In 1920, about 49% of the black population lived on farms. Fifty years later only about 2% of the nation's black population resided on farms. In 1987, only 123,000 blacks in the entire nation lived on farms.

The decline in the farm population has been more precipitous for blacks than for whites. From 1920 to 1981, the black farm population fell by 96%, whereas the white farm population fell by 79%. Until the early 1960s blacks were much more dependent than whites on agriculture as a way of making a living, but in the last 20 years whites have become more likely than blacks to live on a farm. By 1987, only 2.4% of whites lived on farms, and only 0.4% of blacks did so.

Why has the black farm population fallen so rapidly? There are basically two types of forces at work. One is that the demand for farm labor has been falling as a long-term consequence of mechanization and changed farming techniques. At one time many blacks were employed as field hands in the harvesting of cotton, tobacco, and many other crops, but mechanization and shifts toward other agricultural products displaced workers and their families.

Another factor in the decline in the black farm population is the reduction in the number of black farm operators. In the 1930s, many black farm operators were tenants, but the consolidation of land holdings displaced many tenant farmers and all but forced their migration to cities. Few black farmers today are tenants, but of the small number of remaining black farmers, many operate under precarious economic conditions. According to the 1978 Census of Agriculture, black farmers, compared with white farmers, have a greater concentration of the elderly, farm smaller acreages, and have a lower dollar value of sales. In 1978, about 52% of black farmers were 55 years old or over (compared with 39% of white farmers). Only 11% of black farmers operated farms of 220 acres or more (compared with 35% of white farm operators), and only 3.5% of black farmers had agricultural sales of $100,000 or more (compared with 9% of whites).

These characteristics mean low incomes for black farm families. In 1978, the median income of black farm families was only about two-fifths that of white farm families. For the nation as a whole, black families tend to have incomes close to (but slightly below) three-fifths the median income of white families. Hence black-white income differences are greater on farms than off.

At one time, income differences between blacks and whites were strongly influenced by agricultural conditions. This was true when blacks were highly dependent on the agricultural sector of the economy. But today, since only 1% of blacks live on farms, the major influences on inequality between blacks and whites reflect conditions in the various nonagricultural sectors of the economy.

The black farm population has been almost exclusively a southern population. In 1920 nearly 99% of all black farm residents lived in the South, and in 1981 an estimated 99.5% of the few remaining black farm residents lived in the South. Among white farm residents, only 31% lived in the South in 1981.

## The Beginnings of Deconcentration

The urbanization of blacks from 1920 to 1970 represented population deconcentration, for not only were blacks leaving farms to go to cities but they were also especially attracted to relatively large cities that constituted the central portions of metropolitan areas. Along with urbanization, there developed a growing proportion of blacks living in central cities of metropolitan areas. The proportion of whites living in central cities has been falling for several decades, as large numbers of whites leave cities to move to the suburbs. But the proportion of blacks living in central cities has tended to increase.

In the 1970s, however, a turning point was recorded as the proportion of blacks living in central cities began to fall. This is an important development because it signifies that for the first time the number of blacks moving to the suburbs became large enough to significantly affect the overall distribution of the black population. The access of blacks to suburban residences is important for many reasons. One is simply that black suburbanization can further such ideals as open housing, freedom of movement, and the ability to choose a neighborhood that balances a family's income and its preferences and needs, such as aspirations for children's education.

Black suburbanization may be beneficial in other ways as well. Since so many jobs have been moving from cities to suburbs, a greater share of blacks living in suburbs might have long-term consequences for improving employment opportunities and occupational mobility. Finally, for many Americans a move to the suburbs has meant owning a home, a major form of wealth accumulation for middle-class families. Black households have been less likely than white households to own their own home, even when income and other socioeconomic characteristics are taken into account. A trend toward suburbanization might offer more blacks the opportunity to build equity in a home and thus might help to secure middle-class status and the transmission of that status across generations.

For many decades the proportion of blacks living in central cities of metropolitan areas went up, but from 1970 to 1980 it went down. By 1970, 58.2% of all blacks were living in central cities, but by 1980 the percentage had fallen to 55.7. This decline is small, but it signifies a break in a trend. For the first time, the black population in the suburbs grew more rapidly than the black population living in central cities. The black city population is continuing to grow—but not growing as rapidly as it did in the past and not as rapidly as the suburban black population.

## CHART 6. DISTRIBUTION OF POPULATION: PERCENT OF THE WHITE AND BLACK POPULATION BY AGE AND SEX, 1987

**The black population is increasing much faster than the white population. Between 1980 and 1987 the black population grew by 11.4%, but the white population grew by 5.7%, half the rate for blacks. The black population has a greater proportion of young people than does the white population.**

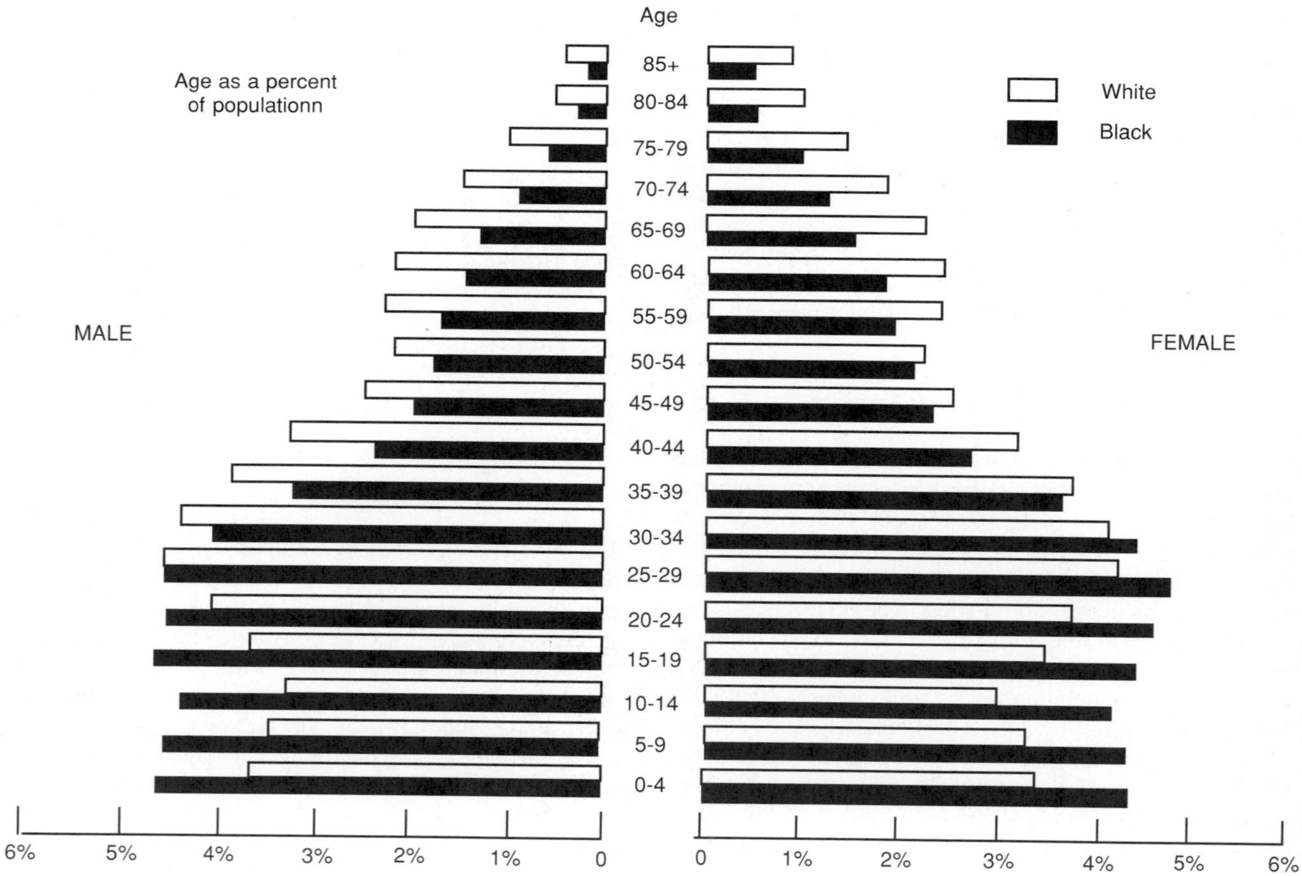


Source: U.S. Bureau of the Census.

## CHART 7. MEDIAN AGE OF BLACKS AND WHITES IN THE UNITED STATES, 1900-2000.

**Throughout the 20th century the black population has been younger than the white population. As shown below, the median age (half the population is older and half is younger) of the black population has been below that of whites primarily due to higher birth rates among blacks. For both blacks and for whites the baby boom from approximately 1948 through 1964 lowered the median age. By 2010 the median age should be close to 33 for blacks and 40 for whites.**

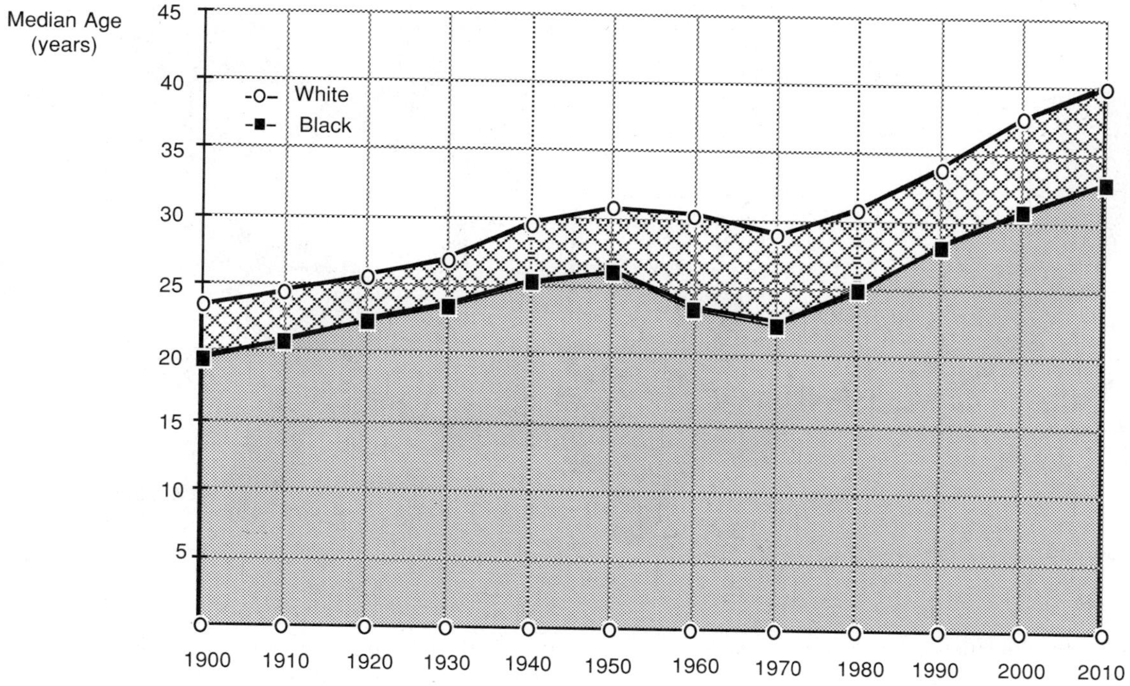


Source: U.S. Bureau of the Census.

## THE SUBURBS AND LARGE CITIES

### Racial Composition of Suburbs

The black population living in suburbs is growing faster than the white suburban population. Between 1970 and 1980 the total suburban population grew by 17.3% whereas the black population increased by 49.4%. In this way, a growing proportion of suburbanites was black. In 1970, blacks constituted 4.8% of all suburbanites, but by 1980 blacks were 6.1% of suburbanites. This change may seem small, but in the 1960s the proportion of blacks in the suburbs hardly changed at all.

As in previous decades, blacks constituted a growing proportion of central city residents. In 1960 blacks were 16.5% of all central city residents; by 1970 blacks were 20.6%, and by 1980 they constituted 23.4% of all central city residents. The growing proportion of blacks in central cities in the 1970s is the product of an absolute decline in the white population and continued growth of the black population (but at a lower rate than in earlier decades).

As central cities and suburban territory were becoming somewhat "blacker" in the 1970s, the territory beyond the suburbs was becoming "whiter." In the outermost suburban fringes (i.e., counties added to the fringes of metropolitan areas between 1970 and 1980), the proportion black fell between 1970 and 1980. In these "exurban" counties blacks made up 9.2% of the population in 1970 and 6.5% in 1980. Beyond these counties, in the residual nonmetropolitan territory, blacks also made up a declining share of the total population.

The overall picture is one of increased movement of blacks from central cities to suburban areas but not to rural areas or small towns that lie beyond the suburban fringe. Whites continue to leave cities for suburbs, but more whites are also moving to locations that lie well beyond the outermost limits of suburban expansion. Whites are not necessarily moving "back to the land," for there is no evidence of growth in the white farm population. But clearly more whites are choosing to live in rural locations even though many commute into cities or towns or otherwise depend on nonagricultural sources of employment.

The reasons for increased movement of blacks to suburbs are doubtlessly heterogeneous. On the one hand, open housing legislation and changing attitudes have contributed to opening

**CHART 8: TEN STATES WITH THE LARGEST BLACK POPULATION, YEAR 2000**
**( projections—numbers in thousands )**

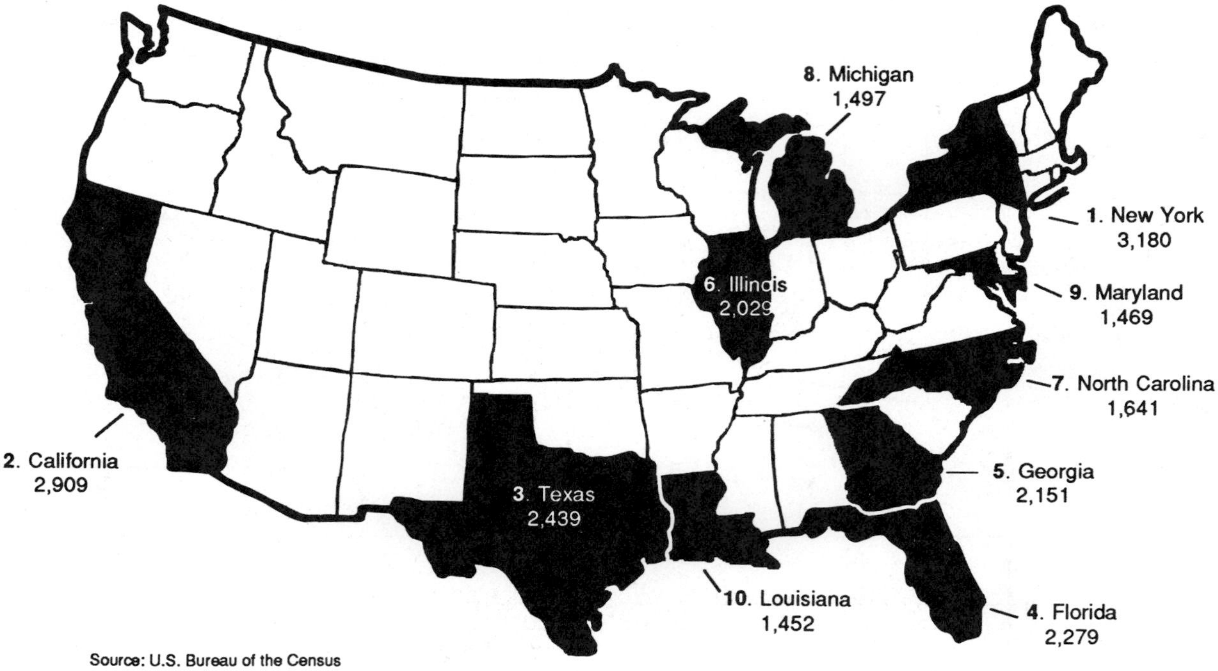


Source: U.S. Bureau of the Census

up the suburbs. On the other hand, there is simply an increase in the number of black families possessing middle-income status (even though both husband and wife may have to work), and families of middle-income status seek safety, good schools, large backyards, and the other considerations often cited by city-to-suburb movers in the past.

These new patterns of the 1970s were carried over into the 1980s, but comparisons of the two decades are affected by the fact that many new metropolitan areas have been recognized and many new counties have been added to existing metropolitan areas. These types of changes are reasonable since continued growth in a small nonmetropolitan city will eventually qualify it for designation as a metropolitan area. Similarly, as suburbanization spreads outward from existing metropolitan areas, boundaries have to be expanded as the character of nonmetropolitan counties is changed by tract homes, malls, and the other hallmarks of suburbanization.

Under the new sets of boundaries, the percent of blacks who live in suburbs has been rising, reaching almost 26 percent in 1988. The percent of blacks living outside metropolitan areas has continued to fall, to about 17 percent in 1988. A majority of blacks continue to live in central cities of metropolitan areas, but the new figures mean that blacks are increasingly a suburban population and continue to leave the small towns and rural areas of nonmetropolitan territory.

The shift of whites toward metropolitan territory in the 1970s was reversed in the 1980s. During the 1970s more whites left metropolitan areas than moved to them, and the percent of whites living in nonmetropolitan territory increased. In the 1980s, however, the percent of whites living in nonmetropolitan territory fell, as it did among blacks. Whites, however, are still somewhat more likely to live in small towns and rural territory than blacks.

## Individual Large Cities

In some large cities the black population began to decline in the 1970s. Of 14 cities with a black population of at least 200,000 in 1970, four experienced a decrease in the number of black residents between 1970 and 1980. After experiencing growing black populations for many decades, Philadelphia, Washington, D.C., Cleveland, and St. Louis registered losses of blacks between 1970 and 1980.

The transition of some of these cities from growth to decline in the number of blacks was dramatic. In Washington, D.C., the black population grew 30.6% in the 1960s but declined 16.6% in the 1970s. The black population of St. Louis grew 18.6% in the 1960s and then declined 18.8% in the 1970s. In Cleveland the black population grew 14.8% in the 1960s but declined 12.7% in the 1970s. These sudden reversals from growth to decline to some extent reflect the arrival of fewer blacks from rural areas, but most probably they are primarily the product of increases in rates of city-to-suburb moving. A black exodus, in addition to the white exodus of longer duration, helps explain why America's older cities generally lost population more rapidly in the 1970s than in the 1960s.

In all but two of the 14 cities the proportion black continued

**CHART 9: TEN STATES WITH THE LARGEST NUMBER INCREASE IN THE BLACK POPULATION, 1988-2000**
**( projections—numbers in thousands )**

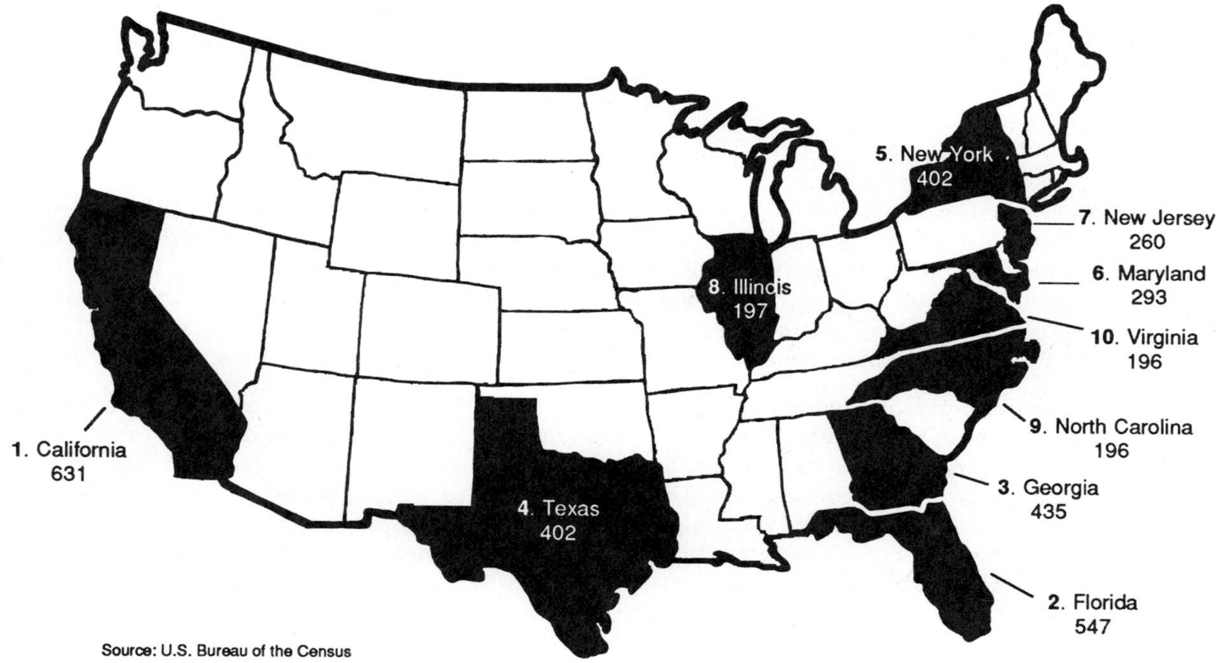


to increase, as it had in previous decades. The two exceptions were Washington, D.C. and Los Angeles. Washington, D.C. went from 71.1% black in 1970 to 70.3% black in 1980 (Table 6). The reason for the declining proportion black in Washington is simply that the non-black population declined somewhat less rapidly than the black population between 1970 and 1980, encouraging speculation that the non-black (mostly white) population of the nation's capital, after declining to less than 30% of the total, may finally be approaching a "hard core" of persons who have a reason for living in the city rather than the suburbs and will stay in the city.

The proportion black in Los Angeles went down for a different reason. The black population of Los Angeles grew in the 1970s, but the non-black population grew even faster, probably because of a rapid influx of Hispanics. In 1970, Los Angeles was 17.9% black, in 1980 blacks made up 17.0% of its population.

Of these 14 cities with the largest black concentrations, two—Washington, D.C. and Atlanta—had black majorities by 1970. By 1980 three more—Detroit, Baltimore, and New Orleans—were majority black. A number of smaller cities also had black majorities, but by 1980 five of the 11 largest cities in the nation were more than 50% black. Demographically speaking, a growing proportion black in the population of large cities has tended to be more the product of a white exodus rather than black immigration. That is, a growing proportion black in large cities since World War II has come about more as a result of the "abandonment" of cities by whites rather than a black "invasion." Blacks have not taken over cities so much as whites have deserted them.

### Where is Black Suburbanization Occurring?

The growing black suburban population is concentrated in, but is not limited to, a few large metropolitan areas. For the nation as a whole, the black population of the suburbs increased by about 800,000 in the 1960s and 1.8 million in the 1970s. The suburbs of the 14 cities with largest black populations accounted for 64% of the national growth of black suburban population in the 1960s but only 54% in the 1970s.

In the 1960s, Los Angeles was the major contributor to black suburbanization. It alone accounted for 15% of the nation's growth of black population in suburbs during that decade.

In the 1970s, Washington, D.C. emerged as the major contributor to black suburbanization. Its suburbs accounted for 12.5% of the national increase in the black suburban population between 1970 and 1980. Los Angeles dropped to second place. Its suburbs in the 1970s accounted for 8.8% of the national increase in black suburban population.

Atlanta was the third major contributor to black suburbanization in the 1970s. The number of blacks in suburban Atlanta grew only 11,000 in the 1960s, but 124,000 in the 1970s.

A puzzling phenomenon is the smaller black population

increase in New York City's suburbs in the 1970s than in the 1960s. The black population in the New York City suburbs grew 77,000 in the 1960s but only 68,000 in the 1970s. With a far larger black population than any other city in the country, New York City is the only one whose suburban black population grew less in the 1970s than the 1960s.

What is clear is that the growth of black population in the suburbs in the 1970s cannot be entirely accounted for by those cities that have the largest black populations. The fact that these cities accounted for a declining share of total black suburban population growth indicates that black suburbanization was more extensive in the 1970s than in the 1960s.

## THE 1990 CENSUS

The types of data shown above have not been fully updated since the last national headcount, the census of 1980. Intercensal updates for national individual subareas like states, cities, and counties depend upon having vital statistics (births and deaths) and other data (particularly migration statistics) according to racial classifications comparable to those used in the national censuses. However, such data are often not fully comparable. Not all states classify births and deaths by race in ways that are strictly comparable to census procedures. Migration is often a more important component of population than natural increase (the excess of births over deaths), and local-area migration data by race for the nation as a whole are almost nonexistent.

For these reasons local-area population updates by race are difficult to prepare and subject to large error. Moreover, whatever error that is present in such estimates cannot be fully evaluated until the next census comes along. The census in 1990 is important not only in terms of its coverage (see next section) but for purposes of assessing what has changed in individual cities, towns, and even neighborhoods.

### The Undercount

The provisional 1980 Census total of 26,488,218 blacks indicates significant coverage improvement for this group over 1970, according to Census Bureau officials. Comparisons with demographic estimates suggest that the 1980 undercount rate for blacks may be in the range of 4.5-5.5% compared to the estimated miss rate of 7.7% in 1970. In short, the Bureau feels that it may have achieved a 30-40% improvement in the undercount rate for blacks between 1970 and 1980. Similar analyses for other groups have not been completed, but there has been an increase for American Indians, Eskimos, and Aleutians, believed to have resulted from improved census taking and the greater likelihood in 1980 that the people would identify themselves in these categories.

**CHART 10. PROPORTION OF POPULATION 65 AND OVER, FOR BLACKS AND WHITES, 1900 TO 2010.**

**The black and white populations have both been aging. In 1900 only about 4% of whites and 3% of blacks were 65 years or over. Currently nearly 12% of whites are of that age group, as are 8% of blacks. By 2010 about 15% of whites and 10% of blacks will be 65 years or over.**

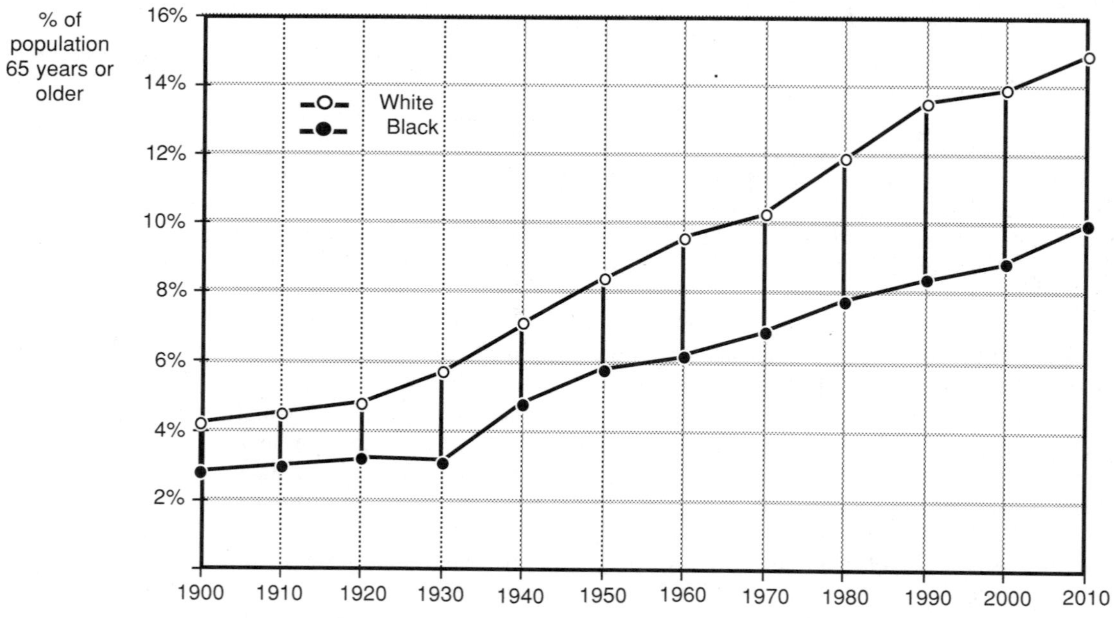


U.S. Bureau of the census

Several local jurisdictions, however, challenged the Census Bureau's figures and brought litigation seeking to force the Bureau to acknowledge far greater undercounts. A great deal, of course, is at stake in population figures in that financial aid from federal and state governments for many public services depends on a locality's population. Representation in the House of Representatives and state legislatures is also involved. Blacks are likely to lose representation when the areas they live in are undercounted. Some cities felt they had strong cases. In New York, for example, discrepancies between Census and city figures in city housing projects, which pointed to substantial undercounting, were presented. The courts, however, refused to reverse the Census Bureau.

Although the Census Bureau has prepared estimates of net undercount by race at the national level, there is no consensus regarding a method of allocating the national undercount to states, cities, counties, or other localities. However, the Census Bureau has begun to issue national population estimates that incorporate adjustments for undercount in 1980. For example, this section ("Growth and Distribution of the Black Population") reported that the resident black population of the U.S. in 1987 was estimated to be 29,736,000. This figure is consistent with 1980 census reports. But if adjustments are made for 1980 undercount and if black members of the U.S. armed forces serving overseas are included, the estimate of the nation's black population in 1987 rises to 31,589,000, or 12.8 percent of the total population.

## SELECTED FACTS

**Fact 1**

Since 1950 the population growth of both whites and blacks has been declining, however, the decline is much steeper for the white population. By the year 2000, the probability is that the black population of the U.S. will be rising at close to three times the rate of the white population even with both races in a declining mode.

**Fact 2**

Between 1980 and 1987, the black population grew by 11.4%, an annual growth rate of 1.5%. The white population grew by 5.7% during the same period, a growth rate of about .08% annually.

**Fact 3**

The U.S. has a population which consists of more older people than at any time in its history. In 1900 the black population, 65 or over was 3%, for whites it was 4%. In 1989, 8% of the black population was 65 or over while for whites it was 12%.

**Fact 4**

In 1987, and since 1950, most Americans lived in urban areas. About 86% of all blacks currently live in urban territory as do 71% of the white population. At the turn of the century, only 12% of the black population and 28% of the white population lived in urban areas

**Fact 5**

As of 1987 the median age of blacks was much younger than that of whites, 27.2 compared with 33.0 Persons of Spanish origin were still younger, with a median age of 25.2.

**Fact 6**

Of the 29,425,000 blacks in the U.S. in 1987, 13.837,000 were men and 15,588,000 were women.

**Fact 7**

In only five of the states do blacks have state populations of over 25%: Mississippi (35.3%), South Carolina(30.4%), Louisiana (29.4%), Georgia (26.8%), and Alabama (25.6%).

**Fact 8**

Seventy-two percent of Illinois' black population lives in Chicago, 74% of blacks in New York state live in New York City, and 64% of Michigan's blacks reside in Detroit.

**Fact 9**

States with the smallest proportions of blacks in their population were Montana and Vermont, each with about 0.2% blacks. Other states in which blacks comprised less than 1% of residents were Maine, Idaho, Wyoming, Utah, North Dakota, and South Dakota.

**Fact 10**

Over 50% of the total black population still resides in the South.

**Fact 11**

Blacks made up 30% of the population of the six cities in the United States that reported populations exceeding 1 million.

**Fact 12**

Five cities with populations exceeding 500,000 had fewer than 10% blacks. Five in the Far West are San Jose, 4.6%, Phoenix, 4.9%, San Diego, 8.9%, Seattle, 9.5%, and San Antonio, 7.3%. Fifty-four percent of San Antonio's population is Hispanic.

**Fact 13**

Four cities with populations exceeding 500,000 had more than 50% blacks: Washington D.C., 70.3%, Detroit, 63.1%, New Orleans, 55.3%, and Baltimore, 54.8%.

**Fact 14**

One of every 12 blacks in the United States lives in the West. In 1930, only one of every hundred lived in that part of the country.

**Fact 15**

Every Pacific and Mountain state except Alaska reported a larger Hispanic than black population. All in all, 18 states had more Hispanic than black residents. In New Mexico, Hispanics outnumber blacks by a ratio of 20 to 1.

**Fact 16**

There are about 7,096 black families in the U.S. There is an average of 3.52 persons in a black family.

**Fact 17**

One in every ninety-four whites living in the United States in 1987 was over 85 years of age compared with only one of every 165 blacks.

**Fact 18**

Metropolitan areas in which over 10% of the black population lived in the suburbs were all located in southern or border states. They were Memphis, where 21% of blacks lived in the suburbs, followed by Washington, D.C., Atlanta, New Orleans, and St. Louis.

**Fact 19**

In 1988 there were 32,500,000 Americans living in poverty, representing 13.5% of the total population. Of the total black population, 33.1% of blacks lived in poverty.

**Fact 20**

Poor black families are about four times more likely than poor white families to live in poverty areas. Almost half (45%) of black families with incomes under $10,000 live in poverty areas, compared to only one out of eight (12%) poor white families.

**Fact 21**

Middle-income whites live outside central cities more often than middle-income blacks. Three out of five (57%) of white families with incomes of $25,000 and over reside outside central cities, compared to 33% of black families with comparable income. However, 22% of middle-income blacks live in poverty areas, compared to 2% of middle-income whites.

**Fact 22**

Almost 50% of all black children live below the poverty line.

**Fact 23**

Median income for a black family, in 1987, was $18,098. For white families it was $32,274.

**Fact 24**

Middle-income and low-income black families continued to increase during the '80's. The proportion of black families with incomes under $10,000 edged up from 29% to 30% between 1979 and 1986. The proportion of black families with incomes over $25,000 rose from 34% to 36%. However, the proportion of middle-income white families fell from 62% to 61%, while low-income white families rose from 9% to lO%.

**Fact 25**

Black families often require an extra earner to have the same income as white families. Black families with three earners ($36,029) have about the same income as white families with two earners ($35,848). Black families with one earner ($13,116) have incomes lower than white families with no earners ($14,252).

**Fact 26**

There has been a dramatic shift in the number of married couples for both blacks and whites.

In 1978 fifty-five percent of black families reported they were a married couple living together, compared with 86% of white families. In 1987, only 42.2% of black families consisted of married couples, while for whites the number dropped to 78.7%.

**Fact 27**

Black women over 15 years of age accounted for only 6% of the nations' adult population, but 18% of all adults classified as living in poverty.

**Fact 28**

The proportion of blacks living in the District of Columbia declined between 1970 and 1980, but blacks made up some 90% of the population growth in the District's metropolitan area.

**Fact 29**

Rapid population shifts still occur. The town of Pagedale, Missouri, population 4,542, changed from 90% white to 84% black in 10 years.

**Fact 30**

Between 1920 and 1987, the population of black farmers plummeted from 49% of the total black population to less than 1/2 of 1%. Over 99% of all black farmers live in the South.

## TABLE 5. GROWTH OF SLAVERY IN THE COLONIES: 1630-1780

| Year | 1630 | 1640 | 1650 | 1660 | 1670 | 1680 | 1690 | 1700 |
|---|---|---|---|---|---|---|---|---|
| North | 10 | 427 | 880 | 1,162 | 1,125 | 1,895 | 3,340 | 5,206 |
| South | 50 | 170 | 720 | 1,758 | 3,410 | 5,076 | 13,389 | 22,611 |
| Total | 60 | 597 | 1,600 | 2,920 | 4,535 | 6,971 | 16,729 | 27,817 |
| Year | 1710 | 1720 | 1730 | 1740 | 1750 | 1760 | 1770 | 1780 |
| North | 8,303 | 14,091 | 17,323 | 23,958 | 30,222 | 40,033 | 48,460 | 56,796 |
| South | 36,563 | 54,748 | 73,698 | 126,066 | 206,198 | 285,773 | 411,362 | 518,624 |
| Total | 44,866 | 68,839 | 91,021 | 150,024 | 236,420 | 325,806 | 459,822 | 575,420 |

## TABLE 6. GROWTH OF SLAVE AND FREEDMAN POPULATION: 1790-1860

| Year | 1790 | 1800 | 1810 | 1820 |
|---|---|---|---|---|
| Slave | 697,624 | 893,602 | 1,191,362 | 1,538,022 |
| Free | 59,557 | 108,435 | 186,446 | 233,634 |
| Total | 757,181 | 1,002,037 | 1,377,808 | 1,771,656 |
| Year | 1830 | 1840 | 1850 | 1860 |
| Slave | 2,009,043 | 2,487,355 | 3,204,313 | 3,953,760 |
| Free | 319,599 | 386,293 | 434,495 | 488,070 |
| Total | 2,328,642 | 2,873,648 | 3,638,808 | 4,441,830 |

## TABLE 7. BLACK POPULATION BY STATE, CENSUS OF 1790

| State | Slaves | Free | Black Percentage of State's Population |
|---|---|---|---|
| Connecticut | 2,759 | 2,801 | 2.3 |
| Delaware | 8,887 | 3,899 | 21.6 |
| Georgia | 29,264 | 398 | 35.9 |
| Kentucky | 11,830 | 114 | 16.3 |
| Maryland | 103,036 | 8,043 | 34.7 |
| New Hampshire | 158 | 630 | .6 |
| New Jersey | 11,423 | 2,762 | 7.7 |
| New York | 21,324 | 4,654 | 7.7 |
| North Carolina | 100,572 | 4,975 | 26.8 |
| Pennsylvania | 3,737 | 6,537 | 2.4 |
| Rhode Island | 952 | 3,469 | 6.4 |
| South Carolina | 107,094 | 1,801 | 43.7 |
| Vermont | 17 | 255 | .2 |
| Virginia | 293,427 | 12,766 | 41.0 |
| Ohio Territory | 3,417 | 5,463 | 18.8 |
| Maine | None | 538 | .6 |

## TABLE 8. BLACK POPULATION GROWTH AND PERCENTAGE OF U.S. TOTAL: 1790-1987

| Year | Total Population | Black Population | Percentage |
|---|---|---|---|
| 1790 | 3,929,214 | 757,181 | 19.3 |
| 1800 | 5,308,483 | 1,002,037 | 18.9 |
| 1810 | 7,239,881 | 1,377,808 | 19.0 |
| 1820 | 9,638,453 | 1,771,656 | 18.4 |
| 1830 | 12,866,020 | 2,328,642 | 18.1 |
| 1840 | 17,169,453 | 2,873,648 | 16.1 |
| 1850 | 23,191,876 | 3,638,808 | 15.7 |
| 1860 | 31,443,790 | 4,441,830 | 14.1 |
| 1870 | 39,818,449 | 4,880,009 | 12.7 |
| 1880 | 50,155,783 | 6,580,793 | 13.0 |
| 1890 | 62,947,714 | 7,488,676 | 11.0 |
| 1900 | 75,994,775 | 8,833,994 | 11.6 |
| 1910 | 93,402,151 | 9,827,763 | 10.7 |
| 1920 | 105,710,620 | 10,463,131 | 9.9 |
| 1930 | 122,775,046 | 11,891,143 | 9.7 |
| 1940 | 131,669,275 | 12,865,518 | 9.8 |
| 1950 | 150,697,361 | 15,042,286 | 10.0 |
| 1960 | 179,323,175 | 18,871,831 | 10.5 |
| 1970 | 203,302,031 | 22,580,289 | 11.1 |
| 1980 | 226,504,825 | 26,488,218 | 11.7 |
| 1987 | 243,400,000 | 29,736,000 | 12.2 |

## TABLE 9. RESIDENT POPULATION, BY RACE AND SPANISH ORIGIN: APRIL 1, 1980*, AND APRIL 1, 1970

| United States | 1980 | 1970 | Percent Distribution 1980 | Percent Distribution 1970 |
|---|---|---|---|---|
| Total | 226,504,825 | 203,211,926 | 100.0 | 100.0 |
| White | 188,340,790 | 177,748,975 | 83.2 | 87.5 |
| Black | 26,488,218 | 22,580,289 | 11.7 | 11.1 |
| American Indian, Eskimo, and Aleut | 1,418,195 | 827,268 | 0.6 | 0.4 |
| Asian and Pacific Islander[1] | 3,500,636 | 1,538,721 | 1.5 | 0.8 |
| Other | 6,756,986 | 516,673 | 3.0 | 0.3 |
| Persons of Spanish origin | 14,605,883 | 9,072,602 | 6.4 | 4.5 |
| Persons not of Spanish origin | 211,898,942 | 194,139,324 | 93.6 | 95.5 |

Source: U.S. Bureau of the Census, 1980 Census of Population, Supplementary Report, PC80-SI-I; and 1970 Census of Population, Supplementary Report, PC(S1)-104.

[1] Asian and Pacific Islander groups such as Cambodian, Laotian, and Thai are included in the "other" race category. In sample tabulations, these groups will be included in the Asian and Pacific Islander category.

* Latest census report 1980

## TABLE 10. 1980 CENSUS POPULATION TOTALS FOR RACIAL AND SPANISH ORIGIN GROUPS IN THE UNITED STATES*

| United States | 1980 | 1970 | Percent Distribution 1980 | Percent Distribution 1970 |
|---|---|---|---|---|
| Total | 226,504,825 | 203,211,926 | 100.0 | 100.0 |
| White | 188,340,790 | 177,748,975 | 83.2 | 87.5 |
| Black | 26,488,218 | 22,580,289 | 11.7 | 11.1 |
| American Indian, Eskimo, and Aleut | 1,418,195 | 827,268 | 0.6 | 0.4 |
| Asian and Pacific Islander | 3,500,636 | 1,538,721 | 1.5 | 0.8 |
| Other | 6,756,986 | 516,673 | 3.0 | 0.3 |
| Persons of Spanish origin | 14,605,883 | 9,072,602 | 6.4 | 4.5 |
| Persons not of Spanish origin | 211,898,942 | 194,139,324 | 93.6 | 95.5 |

## TABLE 11. AGE OF THE RESIDENT POPULATION, BY RACE AND SPANISH ORIGIN: APRIL 1, 1980*

| Age | Total | White | Black | American Indian, Eskimo, and Aleut | Asian and Pacific Islander[1] | Other | Persons of Spanish Origin |
|---|---|---|---|---|---|---|---|
| All ages | 226,504,825 | 188,340,790 | 26,488,218 | 1,418,195 | 3,500,636 | 6,756,986 | 14,605,883 |
| Under 5 years | 16,344,407 | 12,631,197 | 2,435,915 | 149,003 | 293,470 | 834,822 | 1,662,792 |
| 5 to 9 years | 16,697,134 | 13,031,017 | 2,489,947 | 146,364 | 302,296 | 727,510 | 1,536,895 |
| 10 to 14 years | 18,240,919 | 14,460,283 | 2,672,908 | 155,731 | 279,849 | 672,148 | 1,474,837 |
| 15 to 19 years | 21,161,667 | 16,957,541 | 2,983,440 | 170,061 | 288,550 | 762,075 | 1,605,827 |
| 20 to 24 years | 21,312,557 | 17,283,385 | 2,724,355 | 148,985 | 320,129 | 835,703 | 1,585,651 |
| 25 to 34 years | 37,075,629 | 30,625,328 | 4,208,892 | 231,775 | 740,415 | 1,269,219 | 2,503,876 |
| 35 to 44 years | 25,631,247 | 21,584,367 | 2,708,418 | 153,226 | 497,583 | 687,653 | 1,566,200 |
| 45 to 54 years | 22,797,367 | 19,612,854 | 2,271,182 | 109,589 | 338,702 | 465,040 | 1,185,746 |
| 55 to 64 years | 21,699,765 | 19,210,785 | 1,907,335 | 78,673 | 227,808 | 275,164 | 775,274 |
| 65 to 74 years | 15,577,586 | 13,905,249 | 1,339,974 | 48,142 | 137,765 | 146,456 | 457,114 |
| 75 to 84 years | 7,726,826 | 6,994,079 | 586,991 | 20,794 | 60,215 | 64,747 | 202,841 |
| 85 years and over | 2,239,721 | 2,044,705 | 158,861 | 5,852 | 13,854 | 16,449 | 48,830 |
| Median age (years) | 30.0 | 31.3 | 24.9 | 23.0 | 28.6 | 22.8 | 23.2 |
| Percent Distribution | | | | | | | |
| All ages | 100.0 | 100.0 | 100.0 | 100.0 | 100.0 | 100.0 | 100.0 |
| Under 5 years | 7.2 | 6.7 | 9.2 | 10.5 | 8.4 | 12.4 | 11.4 |
| 5 to 9 years | 7.4 | 6.9 | 9.4 | 10.3 | 8.6 | 10.8 | 10.5 |
| 10 to 14 years | 8.1 | 7.7 | 10.1 | 11.0 | 8.0 | 9.9 | 10.1 |
| 15 to 19 years | 9.3 | 9.0 | 11.3 | 12.0 | 8.2 | 11.3 | 11.0 |
| 20 to 24 years | 9.4 | 9.2 | 10.3 | 10.5 | 9.1 | 12.4 | 10.9 |
| 25 to 34 years | 16.4 | 16.3 | 15.9 | 16.3 | 21.2 | 18.8 | 17.1 |
| 35 to 44 years | 11.3 | 11.5 | 10.2 | 10.8 | 14.2 | 10.2 | 10.7 |
| 45 to 54 years | 10.1 | 10.4 | 8.6 | 7.7 | 9.7 | 6.9 | 8.1 |
| 55 to 64 years | 9.6 | 10.2 | 7.2 | 5.5 | 6.5 | 4.1 | 5.3 |
| 65 to 74 years | 6.9 | 7.4 | 5.1 | 3.4 | 3.9 | 2.2 | 3.1 |
| 75 to 84 years | 3.4 | 3.7 | 2.2 | 1.5 | 1.7 | 1.0 | 1.4 |
| 85 years and over | 1.0 | 1.1 | 0.6 | 0.4 | 0.4 | 0.2 | 0.3 |

Source: U.S. Bureau of the Census, 1980 Census of Population, Supplementary Report, PC80-SI-I.

1 Asian and Pacific Islander groups such as Cambodian, Laotian, and Thai are included in the "other" race category. In sample tabulations, these Asian and Pacific Islander groups will be included in the Asian and Pacific Islander category.

* Latest census report 1980

## TABLE 12. BLACK POPULATION OF REGIONS, STATES AND BY AGE: 1980** AND 1990-2010

(numbers in thousands)

| Region division and State | All ages | Under 5 years | 5-13 years | 14-17 years | 18-24 years | 25-34 years | 35-44 years | 45-54 years | 55-64 years | 65-74 years | 75 and over | Median age |
|---|---|---|---|---|---|---|---|---|---|---|---|---|
| **United States** | 35,006 | 2,748 | 5,412 | 2,484 | 3,867 | 5,212 | 5,469 | 4,105 | 2,579 | 1,848 | 1,284 | 30.8 |
| **Regions & Divisions** | | | | | | | | | | | | |
| **Northeast** | 6,363 | 474 | 931 | 434 | 660 | 970 | 990 | 751 | 547 | 374 | 232 | 32.2 |
| New England | 702 | 56 | 109 | 51 | 79 | 111 | 109 | 78 | 53 | 35 | 22 | 30.3 |
| Middle Atlantic | 5,661 | 418 | 822 | 384 | 582 | 859 | 881 | 673 | 494 | 339 | 210 | 32.4 |
| **Midwest** | 6,542 | 528 | 1,042 | 456 | 720 | 977 | 995 | 749 | 475 | 359 | 241 | 30.3 |
| East North Central | 5,584 | 448 | 888 | 388 | 608 | 837 | 850 | 644 | 407 | 309 | 206 | 30.5 |
| West North Central | 958 | 80 | 154 | 68 | 112 | 140 | 145 | 105 | 68 | 50 | 36 | 29.6 |
| **South** | 18,546 | 1,460 | 2,895 | 1,348 | 2,081 | 2,712 | 2,919 | 2,182 | 1,301 | 946 | 702 | 30.5 |
| South Atlantic | 10,673 | 814 | 1,630 | 766 | 1,162 | 1,600 | 1,716 | 1,282 | 773 | 543 | 387 | 31.1 |
| East South Central | 3,354 | 274 | 543 | 247 | 390 | 463 | 514 | 375 | 221 | 178 | 148 | 29.8 |
| West South Central | 4,520 | 372 | 722 | 335 | 529 | 648 | 689 | 525 | 306 | 225 | 168 | 29.7 |
| **West** | 3,555 | 285 | 543 | 246 | 405 | 553 | 565 | 425 | 257 | 169 | 108 | 30.5 |
| Mountain | 432 | 34 | 66 | 30 | 54 | 71 | 70 | 49 | 28 | 18 | 11 | 29.4 |
| Pacific | 3,123 | 251 | 477 | 215 | 351 | 482 | 496 | 375 | 229 | 151 | 97 | 30.6 |
| **States:** | | | | | | | | | | | | |
| **New England** | | | | | | | | | | | | |
| Maine | 4 | (*) | (*) | (*) | (*) | (*) | (*) | (*) | (*) | (*) | (*) | (*) |
| New Hampshire | 10 | (*) | (*) | (*) | (*) | (*) | (*) | (*) | (*) | (*) | (*) | (*) |
| Vermont | 3 | (*) | (*) | (*) | (*) | (*) | (*) | (*) | (*) | (*) | (*) | (*) |
| Massachusetts | 327 | 26 | 50 | 24 | 38 | 51 | 50 | 36 | 24 | 16 | 12 | 30.2 |
| Rhode Island | 45 | 4 | 7 | 3 | 5 | 7 | 6 | 5 | 3 | 2 | 1 | 28.9 |
| Connecticut | 313 | 25 | 49 | 23 | 33 | 50 | 51 | 35 | 24 | 15 | 8 | 30.6 |
| **Middle Atlantic** | | | | | | | | | | | | |
| NewYork | 3,180 | 239 | 453 | 216 | 337 | 491 | 485 | 376 | 286 | 188 | 110 | 32.2 |
| NewJersey | 1,349 | 104 | 211 | 93 | 132 | 207 | 216 | 159 | 113 | 73 | 41 | 31.8 |
| Pennsylvania | 1,131 | 76 | 158 | 75 | 112 | 161 | 180 | 138 | 95 | 78 | 59 | 34.1 |
| **East North Central** | | | | | | | | | | | | |
| Ohio | 1,274 | 97 | 194 | 87 | 134 | 183 | 198 | 150 | 96 | 80 | 55 | 31.8 |
| Indiana | 513 | 42 | 83 | 35 | 56 | 74 | 79 | 58 | 38 | 29 | 20 | 30.5 |
| Illinois | 2,029 | 170 | 331 | 145 | 223 | 299 | 302 | 230 | 152 | 108 | 68 | 29.8 |
| Michigan | 1497 | 114 | 231 | 100 | 162 | 240 | 231 | 177 | 104 | 79 | 58 | 30.8 |
| Wisconsin | 273 | 25 | 49 | 21 | 32 | 41 | 39 | 29 | 17 | 12 | 6 | 27.1 |
| **West North Central** | | | | | | | | | | | | |
| Minnesota | 77 | 8 | 14 | 5 | 9 | 13 | 11 | 7 | 5 | 3 | 2 | 26.4 |
| Iowa | 58 | 5 | 9 | 4 | 7 | 8 | 9 | 6 | 4 | 3 | 2 | 28.6 |
| Missouri | 600 | 49 | 96 | 43 | 65 | 84 | 92 | 68 | 44 | 34 | 25 | 30.7 |
| North Dakota | 4 | (*) | (*) | (*) | (*) | (*) | (*) | (*) | (*) | (*) | (*) | (*) |
| South Dakota | 2 | (*) | (*) | (*) | (*) | (*) | (*) | (*) | (*) | (*) | (*) | (*) |
| Nebraska | 58 | 5 | 9 | 4 | 7 | 8 | 8 | 6 | 4 | 3 | 2 | 28.9 |
| Kansas | 158 | 13 | 25 | 11 | 22 | 24 | 23 | 16 | 10 | 8 | 5 | 28.3 |

## TABLE 12. BLACK POPULATION OF REGIONS, STATES AND BY AGE: 1980** AND 1990-2010 (CONTINUED)

(numbers in thousands)

| Region division and State | All ages | Under 5 years | 5-13 years | 14-17 years | 18-24 years | 25-34 years | 35-44 years | 45-54 years | 55-64 years | 65-74 years | 75 and over | Median age |
|---|---|---|---|---|---|---|---|---|---|---|---|---|
| **South Atlantic** | | | | | | | | | | | | |
| Delaware | 155 | 13 | 26 | 11 | 17 | 25 | 25 | 16 | 10 | 7 | 5 | 29.7 |
| Maryland | 1,469 | 100 | 208 | 103 | 148 | 229 | 257 | 195 | 117 | 71 | 41 | 32.9 |
| District of Columbia | 430 | 23 | 43 | 26 | 45 | 69 | 69 | 54 | 39 | 33 | 27 | 36.1 |
| Virginia | 1,332 | 90 | 189 | 90 | 143 | 201 | 218 | 165 | 103 | 79 | 56 | 32.9 |
| West Virginia | 45 | 3 | 6 | 3 | 5 | 6 | 7 | 5 | 4 | 4 | 4 | 36.1 |
| North Carolina | 1,641 | 115 | 241 | 116 | 191 | 241 | 258 | 198 | 119 | 92 | 72 | 31.5 |
| South Carolina | 1,170 | 89 | 181 | 85 | 132 | 166 | 187 | 143 | 81 | 59 | 47 | 30.9 |
| Georgia | 2,151 | 180 | 351 | 156 | 245 | 337 | 337 | 244 | 139 | 94 | 68 | 29.4 |
| Florida | 2,279 | 201 | 385 | 176 | 237 | 327 | 358 | 262 | 161 | 105 | 67 | 29.5 |
| **East South Central** | | | | | | | | | | | | |
| Kentucky | 294 | 23 | 44 | 21 | 40 | 42 | 44 | 32 | 20 | 17 | 13 | 29.6 |
| Tennessee | 887 | 65 | 130 | 61 | 101 | 128 | 144 | 110 | 62 | 48 | 38 | 31.7 |
| Alabama | 1,136 | 91 | 183 | 83 | 126 | 155 | 175 | 129 | 78 | 63 | 53 | 30.5 |
| Mississippi | 1,037 | 96 | 186 | 82 | 123 | 138 | 151 | 104 | 62 | 50 | 44 | 27.2 |
| **West South Central** | | | | | | | | | | | | |
| Arkansas | 398 | 36 | 71 | 32 | 46 | 51 | 55 | 40 | 24 | 21 | 21 | 27.5 |
| Louisiana | 1,452 | 124 | 243 | 114 | 167 | 190 | 215 | 169 | 101 | 73 | 55 | 29.2 |
| Oklahoma | 231 | 19 | 36 | 18 | 30 | 29 | 33 | 27 | 17 | 13 | 10 | 29.4 |
| Texas | 2,439 | 193 | 372 | 171 | 286 | 378 | 386 | 289 | 165 | 118 | 81 | 30.2 |
| **Mountain** | | | | | | | | | | | | |
| Montana | 2 | (*) | (*) | (*) | (*) | (*) | (*) | (*) | (*) | (*) | (*) | (*) |
| Idaho | 6 | (*) | (*) | (*) | (*) | (*) | (*) | (*) | (*) | (*) | (*) | (*) |
| Wyoming | 4 | (*) | (*) | (*) | (*) | (*) | (*) | (*) | (*) | (*) | (*) | (*) |
| Colorado | 156 | 11 | 21 | 10 | 19 | 27 | 27 | 19 | 11 | 7 | 4 | 31.4 |
| New Mexico | 34 | (*) | (*) | (*) | (*) | (*) | (*) | (*) | (*) | (*) | (*) | (*) |
| Arizona | 123 | 12 | 21 | 9 | 16 | 19 | 17 | 13 | 8 | 5 | 3 | 27.1 |
| Utah | 13 | (*) | (*) | (*) | (*) | (*) | (*) | (*) | (*) | (*) | (*) | (*) |
| Nevada | 94 | 7 | 14 | 6 | 1 | 16 | 17 | 12 | 6 | 3 | 2 | 30.4 |
| **Pacific** | | | | | | | | | | | | |
| Washington | 116 | 8 | 16 | 8 | 17 | 20 | 18 | 13 | 8 | 5 | 3 | 29.5 |
| Oregon | 50 | 4 | 8 | 3 | 5 | 7 | 8 | 7 | 4 | 2 | 2 | 31.9 |
| California | 2,909 | 234 | 446 | 202 | 319 | 444 | 463 | 351 | 216 | 142 | 92 | 30.8 |
| Alaska | 23 | (*) | (*) | (*) | (*) | (*) | (*) | (*) | (*) | (*) | (*) | (*) |
| Hawaii | 24 | (*) | (*) | (*) | (*) | (*) | (*) | (*) | (*) | (*) | (*) | (*) |

* Detailed age data are not shown for states where the total black population on April 1, 1980 was less than 25,000. The United States, region, and division totals include omitted states.

** Latest census 1980

## TABLE 13. AGE AND SEX STRUCTURE OF THE RESIDENT POPULATION OF THE UNITED STATES: APRIL 1, 1980*, AND APRIL 1, 1970

| Age and Sex | Population | | Percent Distribution | | Population Change, 1970-1980 | |
|---|---|---|---|---|---|---|
| | April 1, 1980 | April 1, 1970 | April 1, 1980 | April 1, 1970 | Number | Percent |
| **Both Sexes** | | | | | | |
| All ages | 226,504,825 | 203,235,298 | 100.0 | 100.0 | 23,269,527 | 11.4 |
| Under 5 years | 16,344,407 | 17,162,836 | 7.2 | 8.4 | -818,429 | -4.8 |
| 5 to 9 years | 16,697,134 | 19,969,056 | 7.4 | 9.8 | -3,271,922 | -16.4 |
| 10 to 14 years | 18,240,919 | 20,804,063 | 8.1 | 10.2 | -2,563,144 | -12.3 |
| 15 to 19 years | 21,161,667 | 19,083,971 | 9.3 | 9.4 | 2,077,696 | 10.9 |
| 20 to 24 years | 21,312,557 | 16,382,893 | 9.4 | 8.1 | 4,929,664 | 30.1 |
| 25 to 34 years | 37,075,629 | 24,922,511 | 16.4 | 12.3 | 12,153,118 | 48.8 |
| 35 to 44 years | 25,631,247 | 23,101,173 | 11.3 | 11.4 | 2,530,074 | 11.0 |
| 45 to 54 years | 22,797,367 | 23,234,790 | 10.1 | 11.4 | -437,423 | -1.9 |
| 55 to 64 years | 21,699,765 | 18,601,669 | 9.6 | 9.2 | 3,098,096 | 16.7 |
| 65 to 74 years | 15,577,586 | 12,442,573 | 6.9 | 6.1 | 3,135,013 | 25.2 |
| 75 to 84 years | 7,726,826 | 6,121,627 | 3.4 | 3.0 | 1,605,199 | 26.2 |
| 85 years and over | 2,239,721 | 1,408,136 | 1.0 | 0.7 | 831,585 | 59.1 |
| Median age (years) | 30.0 | 28.0 | | | | |
| **Male** | | | | | | |
| All ages | 110,032,295 | 98,926,204 | 100.0 | 100.0 | 11,106,091 | 11.2 |
| Under 5 years | 8,360,135 | 8,750,106 | 7.6 | 8.8 | -389,971 | -4.5 |
| 5 to 9 years | 8,537,903 | 10,175,283 | 7.8 | 10.3 | -1,637,380 | -16.1 |
| 10 to 14 years | 9,315,055 | 10,598,463 | 8.5 | 10.7 | -1,283,408 | -12.1 |
| 15 to 19 years | 10,751,544 | 9,641,372 | 9.8 | 9.7 | 1,110,172 | 11.5 |
| 20 to 24 years | 10,660,063 | 7,924,866 | 9.7 | 8.0 | 2,735,197 | 34.5 |
| 25 to 34 years | 18,378,764 | 12,225,584 | 16.7 | 12.4 | 6,153,180 | 50.3 |
| 35 to 44 years | 12,567,786 | 11,238,084 | 11.4 | 11.4 | 1,329,702 | 11.8 |
| 45 to 54 years | 11,007,985 | 11,206,753 | 10.0 | 11.3 | -198,768 | -1.8 |
| 55 to 64 years | 10,150,459 | 8,798,748 | 9.2 | 8.9 | 1,351,711 | 15.4 |
| 65 to 74 years | 6,755,199 | 5,440,350 | 6.1 | 5.5 | 1,314,849 | 24.2 |
| 75 to 84 years | 2,865,974 | 2,437,244 | 2.6 | 2.5 | 428,730 | 17.6 |
| 85 years and over | 681,428 | 489,351 | 0.6 | 0.5 | 192,077 | 39.3 |
| Median age (years) | 28.8 | 26.8 | | | | |
| **Female** | | | | | | |
| All ages | 116,472,530 | 104,309,094 | 100.0 | 100.0 | 12,163,436 | 11.7 |
| Under 5 years | 7,984,272 | 8,412,730 | 6.9 | 8.1 | -428,458 | -5.1 |
| 5 to 9 years | 8,159,231 | 9,793,773 | 7.0 | 9.4 | -1,634,542 | -16.7 |
| 10 to 14 years | 8,925,864 | 10,205,600 | 7.7 | 9.8 | -1,279,736 | -12.5 |
| 15 to 19 years | 10,410,123 | 9,442,599 | 8.9 | 9.1 | 967,524 | 10.2 |
| 20 to 24 years | 10,652,494 | 8,458,027 | 9.1 | 8.1 | 2,194,467 | 25.9 |
| 25 to 34 years | 18,696,865 | 12,696,927 | 16.1 | 12.2 | 5,999,938 | 47.3 |
| 35 to 44 years | 13,063,461 | 11,863,089 | 11.2 | 11.4 | 1,200,372 | 10.1 |
| 45 to 54 years | 11,789,382 | 12,028,037 | 10.1 | 11.5 | -238,655 | -2.0 |
| 55 to 64 years | 11,549,306 | 9,802,921 | 9.9 | 9.4 | 1,746,385 | 17.8 |
| 65 to 74 years | 8,822,387 | 7,002,223 | 7.6 | 6.7 | 1,820,164 | 26.0 |
| 75 to 84 years | 4,860,852 | 3,684,383 | 4.2 | 3.5 | 1,176,469 | 31.9 |
| 85 years and over | 1,558,293 | 918,785 | 1.3 | 0.9 | 639,508 | 69.6 |
| Median age (years) | 31.3 | 29.3 | | | | |

Source: 1980 and 1970 censuses.

* Latest census 1980

## TABLE 14. CENTRAL-CITY AND SUBURBAN MIGRATION

(numbers in thousands)

| | 1970-1975 | 1975-1980* |
|---|---|---|
| General Population | | |
| Central Cities | | |
| Inmigrants | 5,987 | 6,891 |
| Outmigrants | 13,005 | 13,237 |
| Net migration | -7,018 | -6,346 |
| Suburbs | | |
| Inmigrants | 12,732 | 13,628 |
| Outmigrants | 7,309 | 8,627 |
| Net migration | +5,423 | +5,001 |
| Blacks | | |
| Central cities | | |
| Inmigrants | 737 | 724 |
| Outmigrants | 980 | 1,163 |
| Net migration | -243 | -439 |
| Suburbs | | |
| Inmigrants | 827 | 1,123 |
| Outmigrants | 446 | 567 |
| Net migration | +381 | +556 |

## TABLE 15. METROPOLITAN AND NONMETROPOLITAN MIGRATION

(numbers in thousands)

| | 1965-1970 | 1970-1975 | 1975-1980* |
|---|---|---|---|
| General Population | | | |
| Metropolitan | | | |
| Inmigrants | 5,457 | 5,127 | 5,993 |
| Outmigrants | 5,809 | 6,721 | 7,337 |
| Net migration | -352 | -1,594 | -1,344 |
| Nonmetropolitan | | | |
| Inmigrants | 5,809 | 6,721 | 7,337 |
| Outmigrants | 5,457 | 5,127 | 5,993 |
| Net migration | +352 | +1,594 | +1,344 |
| Blacks | | | |
| Metropolitan | | | |
| Inmigrants | 452 | 463 | 469 |
| Outmigrants | 234 | 325 | 353 |
| Net migration | +218 | +138[a] | +116[a] |
| Nonmetropolitan | | | |
| Inmigrants | 234 | 325 | 353 |
| Outmigrants | 452 | 463 | 469 |
| Net migration | -218 | -138[a] | -116[a] |

[a] Difference from zero not statistically significant at the .05 level.

*Latest census 1980

## TABLE 16. INTERREGIONAL MIGRATION: 1965-1985

(numbers in thousands)

| Years | Northeast | Mid-West | South | West |
|---|---|---|---|---|
| General Population | | | | |
| 1965-1970 | | | | |
| Inmigrants | 1,273 | 2,024 | 3,142 | 2,309 |
| Outmigrants | 1,988 | 2,661 | 2,486 | 1,613 |
| Net migration | -715 | -637 | +656 | +696 |
| 1970-1975 | | | | |
| Inmigrants | 1,057 | 1,731 | 4,082 | 2,347 |
| Outmigrants | 2,399 | 2,926 | 2,253 | 1,639 |
| Net migration | -1,342 | -1,195 | +1,829 | +708 |
| 1975-1980 | | | | |
| Inmigrants | 1,106 | 1,993 | 4,204 | 2,838 |
| Outmigrants | 2,592 | 3,166 | 2,440 | 1,945 |
| Net migration | -1,486 | -1,173 | +1,764 | +893 |
| 1980-1985 | | | | |
| Inmigrants | 1,218 | 1,901 | 4,428 | 2,641 |
| Outmigrants | 2,240 | 3,426 | 2,531 | 1,992 |
| Net migration | -1,022 | -1,525 | +1,897 | +649 |
| Blacks | | | | |
| 1965-1970 | | | | |
| Inmigrants | 146 | 203 | 162 | 150 |
| Outmigrants | 110 | 111 | 378 | 61 |
| Net migration | +36 | +92 | -216 | +89 |
| 1970-1975 | | | | |
| Inmigrants | 118 | 150 | 302 | 153 |
| Outmigrants | 182 | 202 | 288 | 51 |
| Net migration | -64[1] | -52[1] | +14[1] | +102 |
| 1975-1980 | | | | |
| Inmigrants | 99 | 170 | 415 | 193 |
| Outmigrants | 274 | 221 | 220 | 163 |
| Net migration | -175 | -51[1] | +195 | +30[1] |
| 1980-1985 | | | | |
| Inmigrants | 127 | 197 | 413 | 213 |
| Outmigrants | 176 | 266 | 330 | 178 |
| Net migration | -49 | -69 | +83 | +35 |

[1] Difference from zero not statistically significant at the .05 level.

## TABLE 17. DISTRIBUTION OF THE TOTAL, BLACK, AND WHITE POPULATIONS IN CENTRAL CITIES, SUBURBS, AND NONMETROPOLITAN TERRITORY: 1960-1988

| | | Total % who live in — | | |
|---|---|---|---|---|
| | Population (1000s) metropolitan areas | Central cities of metropolitan areas | Suburbs of metropolitan areas | Outside metropolitan areas |
| All races | | | | |
| 1960 | 179,323 | 33.4% | 33.3% | 33.3% |
| 1970 | 203,212 | 31.4 | 37.2 | 31.3 |
| 1980 | 226,505 | 27.9 | 39.2 | 33.0 |
| (new series) | | | | |
| 1985 | 234,218 | 31.4 | 45.4 | 23.2 |
| 1986 | 236,335 | 31.2 | 46.0 | 22.9 |
| 1987 | 238,540 | 31.0 | 46.5 | 22.4 |
| 1988 | 240,684 | 30.9 | 46.8 | 22.3 |
| Black | | | | |
| 1960 | 18,872 | 52.5 | 15.0 | 32.5 |
| 1970 | 22,580 | 58.2 | 16.1 | 25.7 |
| 1980 | 26,488 | 55.7 | 20.5 | 22.8 |
| (new series) | | | | |
| 1985 | 28,250 | 58.7 | 23.5 | 17.8 |
| 1986 | 28,546 | 58.7 | 23.8 | 17.5 |
| 1987 | 28,945 | 58.0 | 24.5 | 17.5 |
| 1988 | 29,323 | 57.2 | 25.6 | 17.3 |
| White | | | | |
| 1960 | 160,451 | 31.2 | 35.4 | 33.4 |
| 1970 | 180,632 | 28.0 | 39.9 | 32.1 |
| 1980 | 200,017 | 24.2 | 41.7 | 34.2 |
| (new series) | | | | |
| 1985 | 199,038 | 27.2 | 48.6 | 24.2 |
| 1986 | 200,508 | 26.8 | 49.6 | 23.9 |
| 1987 | 201,947 | 26.7 | 49.8 | 23.4 |
| 1988 | 203,345 | 26.5 | 52.9 | 23.4 |

Notes: Data for 1960, 1970, and 1980 are from decennial censuses and hold constant the boundaries of metropolitan areas as of 1970. Data for 1985 and later are from the monthly Current Population Survey and reflect metropolitan-area boundaries adopted after the 1980 census. Data for 1985 were averaged over July through December; 1986 and 1987 data are annual averages; 1988 data were averaged through October. Data for "whites" in 1960, 1970, and 1980 include "other races." Data for 1985 and later exclude persons not in private households.

## TABLE 18. REGIONAL DISTRIBUTION OF THE BLACK POPULATION: 1850-1980

| | Percentage of Blacks Living in: | | | |
|---|---|---|---|---|
| Year | Northeast | North Central | South | West |
| 1850 | 4.1 | 3.7 | 92.1 | < 0.1 |
| 1860 | 3.5 | 4.1 | 92.2 | 0.1 |
| 1870 | 3.7 | 5.6 | 90.6 | 0.1 |
| 1880 | 3.5 | 5.9 | 90.5 | 0.2 |
| 1890 | 3.6 | 5.8 | 90.3 | 0.4 |
| 1900 | 4.4 | 5.6 | 89.7 | 0.3 |
| 1910 | 4.9 | 5.5 | 89.0 | 0.5 |
| 1920 | 6.5 | 7.6 | 85.2 | 0.8 |
| 1930 | 9.6 | 10.6 | 78.7 | 1.0 |
| 1940 | 10.6 | 11.0 | 77.0 | 1.3 |
| 1950 | 13.4 | 14.8 | 68.0 | 3.8 |
| 1960 | 16.0 | 18.3 | 59.9 | 5.8 |
| 1970 | 19.2 | 20.2 | 53.0 | 7.5 |
| 1980 | 18.3 | 20.1 | 53.0 | 8.5 |

Note: The Northeast consists of New England and the Middle Atlantic states of New York, Pennsylvania, and New Jersey. The North Central region consists of the Great Lakes states along with Missouri, Kansas, Iowa, Nebraska, and the Dakotas. The South is made up of all states south of the Mason-Dixon line (including the border states of Delaware, West Virginia, and Kentucky) and extends as far west as Texas and Oklahoma. The remaining states are in the West.

## TABLE 19. PERCENTAGE OF POPULATION LIVING IN URBAN TERRITORY: 1880-1980

| Year | Total Population | Blacks | Whites |
|---|---|---|---|
| 1880 | 26.3 | 12.9 | 28.3 |
| 1890 | 32.8 | 17.6 | 35.1 |
| 1900 | 37.3 | 20.5 | 39.7 |
| 1910 | 46.3 | 27.4 | 48.7 |
| 1920 | 51.4 | 34.0 | 53.4 |
| 1930 | 56.2 | 43.7 | 57.6 |
| 1940 | 56.5 | 48.6 | 57.5 |
| 1950 | 64.0 | 62.4 | 64.3 |
| 1960 | 69.9 | 73.2 | 69.5 |
| 1970 | 73.5 | 81.3 | 72.4 |
| 1980 | 73.7 | Not available | Not available |

Before 1950 "urban" meant everyone living in an incorporated place of 2,500 or greater population. After 1950 the urban total was expanded to include persons living in fairly dense suburban territory surrounding cities of 50,000 or greater population.

## TABLE 20. BLACK POPULATION CHANGE IN 14 CENTRAL CITIES AND THEIR SUBURBS, 1960-1980*

| | Black Population | Percent Change in Black Population | | Percent Black | | |
|---|---|---|---|---|---|---|
| Area | 1980 | 1960-70 | 1970-80 | 1960 | 1970 | 1980 |
| **Central Cities** | | | | | | |
| New York City | 1,784,000 | 53.3% | 7.0 | 14.0 | 21.2 | 25.2 |
| Chicago | 1,197,000 | 35.7 | 8.6 | 22.9 | 32.7 | 39.8 |
| Detroit | 759,000 | 37.0 | 14.9 | 28.9 | 43.7 | 63.1 |
| Philadelphia | 639,000 | 23.5 | -2.3 | 26.4 | 33.6 | 37.8 |
| Los Angeles | 505,000 | 50.4 | 0.3 | 13.5 | 17.9 | 17.0 |
| Washington, D.C. | 448,000 | 30.6 | -16.6 | 53.9 | 71.1 | 70.3 |
| Houston | 440,000 | 47.2 | 39.1 | 22.9 | 25.7 | 27.6 |
| Baltimore | 431,000 | 29.1 | 2.6 | 34.7 | 46.4 | 54.8 |
| New Orleans | 308,000 | 14.5 | 15.3 | 37.2 | 45.0 | 55.3 |
| Memphis | 308,000 | 31.6 | 26.9 | 37.0 | 38.9 | 47.6 |
| Atlanta | 283,000 | 36.8 | 12.1 | 38.3 | 51.3 | 66.6 |
| Dallas | 266,000 | 62.7 | 26.3 | 19.0 | 24.9 | 29.4 |
| Cleveland | 251,000 | 14.8 | -12.7 | 28.6 | 38.3 | 43.8 |
| St. Louis | 206,000 | 18.6 | -18.8 | 28.6 | 40.9 | 47.4 |
| **Suburbs (1970 definition)** | | | | | | |
| New York City | 285,000 | 55.5% | 31.4 | 4.8 | 5.9 | 7.6 |
| Chicago | 231,000 | 65.5 | 79.9 | 2.9 | 3.6 | 5.6 |
| Detroit | 128,000 | 26.1 | 32.5 | 3.7 | 3.6 | 4.5 |
| Philadelphia | 245,000 | 34.1 | 28.9 | 6.1 | 6.6 | 8.1 |
| Los Angeles | 398,000 | 105.0 | 65.7 | 3.6 | 6.2 | 9.6 |
| Washington, D.C. | 390,000 | 98.3 | 134.9 | 6.4 | 7.9 | 16.6 |
| Houston | 36,000 | 6.2 | 21.4 | 12.9 | 8.8 | 6.2 |
| Baltimore | 126,000 | 25.6 | 54.9 | 7.0 | 7.0 | 9.1 |
| New Orleans | 79,000 | 26.9 | 40.4 | 15.9 | 12.5 | 12.6 |
| Memphis | 37,000 | -34.8 | -18.4 | 40.2 | 31.7 | 21.0 |
| Atlanta | 179,000 | 23.5 | 222.4 | 8.5 | 6.2 | 14.2 |
| Dallas | 50,000 | 1.1 | 35.4 | 8.3 | 5.2 | 4.7 |
| Cleveland | 94,000 | 452.8 | 110.6 | 0.8 | 3.4 | 7.1 |
| St. Louis | 201,000 | 65.0 | 50.4 | 6.0 | 7.7 | 10.9 |

* Latest census 1980

## TABLE 21. CHANGING RACIAL COMPOSITION AND DISTRIBUTION OF POPULATION IN CITIES, SUBURBS, AND NONMETROPOLITAN AREAS: 1960-1980

| | United States | Central Cities of SMSAs[1] | Balance of SMSAs[1] | Fringe Counties[2] | Residual |
|---|---|---|---|---|---|
| | | Population | | | |
| All races | | | | | |
| 1960 | 179,323 | 59,947 | 59,648 | 3,214 | 56,514 |
| 1970 | 203,212 | 63,797 | 75,622 | 3,953 | 59,840 |
| 1980 | 226,505 | 63,111 | 88,737 | 5,342 | 69,314 |
| Black | | | | | |
| 1960 | 18,872 | 9,914 | 2,825 | 323 | 5,809 |
| 1970 | 22,580 | 13,140 | 3,630 | 326 | 5,484 |
| 1980 | 26,488 | 14,751 | 5,424 | 347 | 5,967 |
| | | Percentage Distribution | | | |
| All races | | | | | |
| 1960 | 100.0 | 33.4 | 33.3 | 1.8 | 31.5 |
| 1970 | 100.0 | 31.4 | 37.2 | 1.9 | 29.4 |
| 1980 | 100.0 | 27.9 | 39.2 | 2.4 | 30.6 |
| Black | | | | | |
| 1960 | 100.0 | 52.5 | 15.0 | 1.7 | 30.8 |
| 1970 | 100.0 | 58.2 | 16.1 | 1.4 | 24.3 |
| 1980 | 100.0 | 55.7 | 20.5 | 1.3 | 22.5 |
| | | Rates of Population Change (in percent) | | | |
| All races | | | | | |
| 1960-1970 | 13.3 | 6.4 | 26.8 | 23.0 | 5.9 |
| 1970-1980 | 11.5 | - 1.1 | 17.3 | 35.1 | 15.8 |
| Black | | | | | |
| 1960 1970 | 19.7 | 32.5 | 28.5 | 0.7 | - 5.6 |
| 1970-1980 | 17.3 | 12.3 | 49.4 | 6.6 | 8.8 |
| | | Percent Black | | | |
| 1960 | 10.5 | 16.5 | 4.7 | 10.1 | 10.3 |
| 1970 | 11.1 | 20.6 | 4.8 | 8.2 | 9.2 |
| 1980 | 11.7 | 23.4 | 6.1 | 6.5 | 8.6 |

1 Boundaries of Standard Metropolitan Statistical Areas (SMSAs) as of 1970 are used for all three dates.
2 Counties added between 1970 and 1980 to the fringes of SMSAs as defined in 1970.

## TABLE 22. BLACK POPULATION BY REGION AND STATE: 1970 AND 1980

| United States, Regions, Divisions, and States | 1980 | 1970 | 1980 (%) | 1970 (%) |
|---|---|---|---|---|
| **United States** | 26,488,218 | 22,580,289 | 11.7 | 11.1 |
| **Regions and Divisions** | | | | |
| **Northeast** | 4,848,786 | 4,344,153 | 9.9 | 8.9 |
| New England | 474,349 | 388,398 | 3.8 | 3.3 |
| Middle Atlantic | 4,374,237 | 3,955,755 | 11.9 | 10.6 |
| **North Central** | 5,336,542 | 4,571,550 | 9.1 | 8.1 |
| East North Central | 4,547,998 | 3,872,905 | 10.9 | 9.6 |
| West North Central | 788,544 | 698,645 | 4.6 | 4.3 |
| **South** | 14,041,374 | 11,969,961 | 18.6 | 19.1 |
| South Atlantic | 7,647,743 | 6,388,496 | 20.7 | 20.8 |
| East South Central | 2,868,268 | 2,571,291 | 19.6 | 20.1 |
| West South Central | 3,525,363 | 3,010,174 | 14.8 | 15.6 |
| **West** | 2,261,516 | 1,694,625 | 5.2 | 4.9 |
| Mountain | 268,660 | 180,382 | 2.4 | 2.2 |
| Pacific | 1,992,856 | 1,514,243 | 6.3 | 5.7 |
| **States** | | | | |
| **New England** | | | | |
| Maine | 3,128 | 2,800 | 0.3 | 0.3 |
| New Hampshire | 3,990 | 2,505 | 0.4 | 0.3 |
| Vermont | 1,135 | 761 | 0.2 | 0.2 |
| Massachusetts | 221,279 | 175,817 | 3.9 | 3.1 |
| Rhode Island | 27,584 | 25,338 | 2.9 | 2.7 |
| Connecticut | 217,433 | 181, 177 | 7.0 | 6.0 |
| **Middle Atlantic** | | | | |
| New York | 2,401,842 | 2,168,949 | 13.7 | 11.9 |
| New Jersey | 924,786 | 770,292 | 12.6 | 10.7 |
| Pennsylvania | 1,047,609 | 1,016,514 | 8.8 | 8.6 |
| **East North Central** | | | | |
| Ohio | 1,076,734 | 970,477 | 10.0 | 9.1 |
| Indiana | 414,732 | 357,464 | 7.6 | 6.9 |
| Illinois | 1,675,229 | 1,425,674 | 14.7 | 12.8 |
| Michigan | 1,198,710 | 991,066 | 12.9 | 11.2 |
| Wisconsin | 182,593 | 128,224 | 3.9 | 2.9 |
| **West North Central** | | | | |
| Minnesota | 53,342 | 34,868 | 1.3 | 0.9 |
| Iowa | 41,700 | 32,596 | 1.4 | 1.2 |
| Missouri | 514,274 | 480,172 | 10.5 | 10.3 |
| North Dakota | 2,568 | 2,494 | 0.4 | 0.4 |
| South Dakota | 2,144 | 1,627 | 0.3 | 0.2 |
| Nebraska | 48,389 | 39,911 | 3.1 | 2.7 |
| Kansas | 126,127 | 106,977 | 5.3 | 4.8 |
| **South Atlantic** | | | | |
| Delaware | 95,971 | 78,276 | 16.1 | 14.3 |
| Maryland | 958,050 | 699,479 | 22.7 | 17.8 |

continued

## TABLE 22. BLACK POPULATION BY REGION AND STATE: 1970 AND 1980 (CONTINUED)

| United States, Regions, Divisions, and States | 1980 | 1970 | 1980 (%) | 1970 (%) |
|---|---|---|---|---|
| District of Columbia | 448,229 | 537,712 | 70.3 | 71.1 |
| Virginia | 1,008,311 | 861,368 | 18.9 | 18.5 |
| West-Virginia | 65,051 | 67,342 | 3.3 | 3.9 |
| North Carolina | 1,316,050 | 1,126,478 | 22.4 | 22.2 |
| South Carolina | 948,146 | 789,041 | 30.4 | 30.5 |
| Georgia | 1,465,457 | 1,187,149 | 26.8 | 25.9 |
| Florida | 1,342,478 | 1,041,651 | 13.8 | 15.3 |
| **East South Central** | | | | |
| Kentucky | 259,490 | 230,793 | 7.1 | 7.2 |
| Tennessee | 725,949 | 621,261 | 15.8 | 15.8 |
| Alabama | 995,623 | 903,467 | 25.6 | 26.2 |
| Mississippi | 887,206 | 815,770 | 35.2 | 36.8 |
| **West South Central** | | | | |
| Arkansas | 373,192 | 352,445 | 16.3 | 18.3 |
| Louisiana | 1,237,263 | 1,086,832 | 29.4 | 29.8 |
| Oklahoma | 204,658 | 171,892 | 6.8 | 6.7 |
| Texas | 1,710,250 | 1,399,005 | 12.0 | 12.5 |
| **Mountain** | | | | |
| Montana | 1,786 | 1,995 | 0.2 | 0.3 |
| Idaho | 2,716 | 2,130 | 0.3 | 0.3 |
| Wyoming | 3,364 | 2,568 | 0.7 | 0.8 |
| Colorado | 101,702 | 66,411 | 3.5 | 3.0 |
| New Mexico | 24,042 | 19,555 | 1.8 | 1.9 |
| Arizona | 75,034 | 53,344 | 2.8 | 3.0 |
| Utah | 9,225 | 6,617 | 0.6 | 0.6 |
| Nevada | 50,791 | 27,762 | 6.4 | 5.7 |
| **Pacific** | | | | |
| Washington | 105,544 | 71,308 | 2.6 | 2.1 |
| Oregon | 37,059 | 26,308 | 1.4 | 1.3 |
| California | 1,819,282 | 1,400,143 | 7.7 | 7.0 |
| Alaska | 13,619 | 8,911 | 3.4 | 3.0 |
| Hawaii | 17,352 | 7,573 | 1.8 | 1.0 |

## TABLE 23. POPULATION INSIDE AND OUTSIDE SMSAS BY RACE: 1970 TO 1980*

| Metropolitan Status | All Races | White | Black | Other Races |
|---|---|---|---|---|
| **1980 Census** | | | | |
| Numbers | | | | |
| United States | 226,505 | 188,341 | 26,488 | 11,676 |
| Inside SMSAs | 169,405 | 138,044 | 21,474 | 9,887 |
| Inside central cities | 67,930 | 47,014 | 15,301 | 5,615 |
| Outside central cities | 101,475 | 91,029 | 6,173 | 4,272 |
| Outside SMSAs | 57,100 | 50,297 | 5,014 | 1,789 |
| Percent distribution | | | | |
| United States | 100.0 | 100.0 | 100.0 | 100.0 |
| Inside SMSAs | 74.8 | 73.3 | 81.1 | 84.7 |
| Inside central cities | 30.0 | 25.0 | 57.8 | 48.1 |
| Outside central cities | 44.8 | 48.3 | 23.3 | 36.6 |
| Outside SMSAs | 25.2 | 26.7 | 18.9 | 15.3 |
| Percent of total | | | | |
| United States | 100.0 | 83.2 | 11.7 | 5.2 |
| Inside SMSAs | 100.0 | 81.5 | 12.7 | 5.8 |
| Inside central cities | 100.0 | 69.2 | 22.5 | 8.3 |
| Outside central cities | 100.0 | 89.7 | 6.1 | 4.2 |
| Outside SMSAs | 100.0 | 88.1 | 8.8 | 3.1 |
| **1970 Census** | | | | |
| Numbers | | | | |
| United States | 203,302 | 177,749 | 22,580 | 2,973 |
| Inside SMSAs | 153,694 | 133,574 | 17,872 | 2,247 |
| Inside central cities | 67,850 | 53,100 | 13,546 | 1,204 |
| Outside central cities | 85,843 | 80,474 | 4,326 | 1,043 |
| Outside SMSAs | 49,608 | 44,175 | 4,708 | 725 |
| Percent distribution | | | | |
| United States | 100.0 | 100.0 | 100.0 | 100.0 |
| Inside SMSAs | 75.6 | 75.1 | 79.1 | 75.6 |
| Inside central cities | 33.4 | 29.9 | 60.0 | 40.5 |
| Outside central cities | 42.2 | 45.3 | 19.2 | 35.1 |
| Outside SMSAs | 24.4 | 24.9 | 20.9 | 24.4 |
| Percent of total | | | | |
| United States | 100.0 | 87.4 | 11.1 | 1.5 |
| Inside SMSAs | 100.0 | 86.9 | 11.6 | 1.5 |
| Inside central cities | 100.0 | 78.3 | 20.0 | 1.8 |
| Outside central cities | 100.0 | 93.7 | 5.0 | 1.2 |
| Outside SMSAs | 100.0 | 89.0 | 9.5 | 1.5 |
| **Change, 1970 to 1980** | | | | |
| Number | | | | |
| United States | 23,203 | 10,592 | 3,908 | 8,703 |
| Inside SMSAs | 15,711 | 4,469 | 3,602 | 7,640 |
| Inside central cities | 80 | 6,086 | 1,755 | 4,410 |
| Outside central cities | 15,631 | 10,555 | 1,847 | 3,229 |
| Outside SMSAs | 7,492 | 6,122 | 306 | 1,063 |
| Percent | | | | |
| United States | 11.4 | 6.0 | 17.3 | 292.8 |
| Inside SMSAs | 10.2 | 3.3 | 20.2 | 339.9 |
| Inside central cities | 0.1 | -11.5 | 13.0 | 366.3 |
| Outside central cities | 18.2 | 13.1 | 42.7 | 309.6 |
| Outside SMSAs | 15.1 | 13.9 | 6.5 | 146.6 |

Source: U.S. Department of Commerce, Bureau of the Census.
Numbers in thousands. SMSAs defined by Office of Management and Budget as of June 30, 1981.
*Latest census 1980

## TABLE 24. POPULATION BY RACE: 1980*

| United States, Regions, Divisions, and States | Total | White | Black | American Indian, Eskimo, and Aleut | | | |
|---|---|---|---|---|---|---|---|
| | | | | Total | American Indian | Eskimo | Aleut |
| **United States** | 226,504,825 | 188,340,790 | 26,488,218 | 1,418,195 | 1,361,869 | 42,149 | 14,177 |
| **Regions and Divisions** | | | | | | | |
| **Northeast** | 49,136,667 | 42,328,154 | 4,848,786 | 78,182 | 76,574 | 890 | 718 |
| New England | 12,348,493 | 11,585,633 | 474,549 | 21,597 | 21,108 | 277 | 212 |
| Middle Atlantic | 36,788,174 | 30,742,521 | 4,374,237 | 56,585 | 55,466 | 613 | 506 |
| **Midwest** | | | | | | | |
| North Central | 58,853,804 | 52,183,794 | 5,336,542 | 248,505 | 246,456 | 1,286 | 763 |
| East North Central | 41,669,738 | 36,138,962 | 4,547,998 | 105,881 | 104,520 | 834 | 527 |
| West North Central | 17,184,066 | 16,044,832 | 788,544 | 142,624 | 141,936 | 452 | 236 |
| **South** | 75,349,155 | 58,944,057 | 14,041,374 | 372,123 | 369,497 | 1,580 | 1,046 |
| South Atlantic | 36,943,139 | 28,647,762 | 7,647,743 | 118,656 | 117,386 | 772 | 498 |
| East South Central | 14,662,882 | 11,699,604 | 2,868,268 | 22,454 | 22,144 | 199 | 111 |
| West South Central | 23,743,134 | 18,596,691 | 3,525,363 | 231,013 | 229,967 | 609 | 437 |
| **West** | 43,165,199 | 34,884,785 | 2,261,516 | 719,385 | 669,342 | 38,393 | 11,650 |
| Mountain | 11,368,330 | 9,958,545 | 268,660 | 363,169 | 361,988 | 798 | 383 |
| Pacific | 31,796,869 | 24,926,240 | 1,992,856 | 356,216 | 307,354 | 37,595 | 11,267 |
| **States** | | | | | | | |
| **New England** | | | | | | | |
| Maine | 1,124,660 | 1,109,850 | 3,128 | 4,087 | 4,057 | 17 | 13 |
| New Hampshire | 920,610 | 910,099 | 3,990 | 1,352 | 1,297 | 41 | 14 |
| Vermont | 511,456 | 506,736 | 1,135 | 984 | 968 | 8 | 8 |
| Massachusetts | 5,737,037 | 5,362,836 | 221,279 | 7,743 | 7,483 | 129 | 131 |
| Rhode Island | 947,154 | 896,692 | 27,584 | 2,898 | 2,872 | 14 | 12 |
| Connecticut | 3,107,576 | 2,799,420 | 217,433 | 4,533 | 4,431 | 68 | 34 |
| **Middle Atlantic** | | | | | | | |
| New York | 17,557,288 | 13,961,106 | 2,401,842 | 38,732 | 38,117 | 330 | 285 |
| New Jersey | 7,364,158 | 6,127,090 | 924,786 | 8,394 | 8,176 | 130 | 88 |
| Pennsylvania | 11,866,728 | 10,654,325 | 1,047,609 | 9,459 | 9,173 | 153 | 133 |
| **East North Central** | | | | | | | |
| Ohio | 10,797,419 | 9,597,266 | 1,076,734 | 12,240 | 11,986 | 167 | 87 |
| Indiana | 5,490,179 | 5,004,567 | 414,732 | 7,835 | 7,681 | 107 | 47 |
| Illinois | 11,418,461 | 9,225,575 | 1,675,229 | 16,271 | 15,833 | 242 | 196 |
| Michigan | 9,258,344 | 7,868,956 | 1,198,710 | 40,038 | 39,702 | 208 | 128 |
| Wisconsin | 4,705,335 | 4,442,598 | 182,593 | 29,497 | 29,318 | 110 | 69 |
| **West North Central** | | | | | | | |
| Minnesota | 4,077,148 | 3,936,948 | 53,342 | 35,026 | 34,841 | 118 | 67 |
| Iowa | 2,913,387 | 2,838,805 | 41,700 | 5,453 | 5,367 | 59 | 27 |
| Missouri | 4,917,444 | 4,346,267 | 514,274 | 12,319 | 12,127 | 119 | 73 |
| North Dakota | 652,695 | 625,536 | 2,568 | 20,157 | 20,119 | 32 | 6 |
| South Dakota | 690,178 | 638,955 | 2,144 | 45,101 | 45,081 | 17 | 3 |
| Nebraska | 1,570,006 | 1,490,569 | 48,389 | 9,197 | 9,147 | 26 | 24 |
| Kansas | 2,363,208 | 2,167,752 | 126,127 | 15,371 | 15,254 | 81 | 36 |
| **South Atlantic** | | | | | | | |
| Delaware | 595,225 | 488,543 | 95,971 | 1,330 | 1,309 | 13 | 8 |
| Maryland | 4,216,446 | 3,158,412 | 958,050 | 8,021 | 7,823 | 113 | 85 |
| District of Columbia | 637,651 | 171,796 | 448,229 | 1,031 | 996 | 19 | 16 |

continued...

## TABLE 24. POPULATION BY RACE: 1980* (CONTINUED)

| United States, Regions, Divisions, and States | Total | White | Black | American Indian, Eskimo, and Aleut | | | |
|---|---|---|---|---|---|---|---|
| | | | | Total | American Indian | Eskimo | Aleut |
| Virginia | 5,346,279 | 4,229,734 | 1,008,311 | 9,336 | 9,093 | 156 | 87 |
| West Virginia | 1,949,644 | 1,874,751 | 65,051 | 1,610 | 1,555 | 37 | 18 |
| North Carolina | 5,874,429 | 4,453,010 | 1,316,050 | 64,635 | 64,519 | 57 | 59 |
| South Carolina | 3,119,208 | 2,145,122 | 948,146 | 5,758 | 5,666 | 70 | 22 |
| Georgia | 5,464,265 | 3,948,007 | 1,465,457 | 7,619 | 7,444 | 108 | 67 |
| Florida | 9,739,992 | 8,178,387 | 1,342,478 | 19,316 | 18,981 | 199 | 136 |
| **East South Central** | | | | | | | |
| Kentucky | 3,661,433 | 3,379,648 | 259,490 | 3,610 | 3,518 | 59 | 33 |
| Tennessee | 4,590,750 | 3,835,078 | 725,949 | 5,103 | 5,012 | 62 | 29 |
| Alabama | 3,890,061 | 2,869,688 | 995,623 | 7,561 | 7,483 | 50 | 28 |
| Mississippi | 2,520,638 | 1,615,190 | 887,206 | 6,180 | 6,131 | 28 | 21 |
| **West South Central** | | | | | | | |
| Arkansas | 2,285,513 | 1,890,002 | 373,192 | 9,411 | 9,346 | 48 | 17 |
| Louisiana | 4,203,972 | 2,911,243 | 1,237,263 | 12,064 | 11,950 | 59 | 55 |
| Oklahoma | 3,025,266 | 2,597,783 | 204,658 | 169,464 | 169,297 | 107 | 60 |
| Texas | 14,228,383 | 11,197,663 | 1,710,250 | 40,074 | 39,374 | 395 | 305 |
| **Mountain** | | | | | | | |
| Montana | 786,690 | 740,148 | 1,786 | 37,270 | 37,153 | 79 | 38 |
| Idaho | 943,935 | 901,641 | 2,716 | 10,521 | 10,418 | 76 | 27 |
| Wyoming | 470,816 | 447,716 | 3,364 | 7,125 | 7,088 | 27 | 10 |
| Colorado | 2,888,834 | 2,570,615 | 101,702 | 18,059 | 17,726 | 235 | 98 |
| New Mexico | 1,299,968 | 976,465 | 24,042 | 104,777 | 104,634 | 88 | 55 |
| Arizona | 2,717,866 | 2,240,033 | 75,034 | 152,857 | 152,610 | 138 | 109 |
| Utah | 1,461,037 | 1,382,550 | 9,225 | 19,256 | 19,158 | 81 | 17 |
| Nevada | 799,184 | 699,377 | 50,791 | 13,304 | 13,201 | 74 | 29 |
| **Pacific** | | | | | | | |
| Washington | 4,130,163 | 3,777,296 | 105,544 | 60,771 | 58,159 | 1,251 | 1,361 |
| Oregon | 2,632,663 | 2,490,192 | 37,059 | 27,309 | 26,587 | 407 | 315 |
| California | 23,668,562 | 18,031,689 | 1,819,282 | 201,311 | 198,095 | 1,734 | 1,482 |
| Alaska | 400,481 | 308,455 | 13,619 | 64,047 | 21,849 | 34,135 | 8,063 |
| Hawaii | 965,000 | 318,608 | 17,352 | 5,778 | 2,664 | 68 | 46 |

* Latest census 1980

## TABLE 25. 100 CITIES WITH THE LARGEST BLACK POPULATION, BY RANK: 1980*

| City Rank | Black Population | Percentage of Total Population | Total Population |
|---|---|---|---|
| 1 New York, NY | 1,784,124 | 25.2 | 7,071,030 |
| 2 Chicago, IL | 1,197,000 | 39.8 | 3,005,072 |
| 3 Detroit, MI | 758,939 | 63.1 | 1,203,339 |
| 4 Philadelphia, PA | 638,878 | 37.8 | 1,688,210 |
| 5 Los Angeles, CA | 505,208 | 17.0 | 2,966,763 |
| 6 Washington, D.C. | 448,229 | 70.3 | 637,651 |
| 7 Houston, TX | 440,257 | 27.6 | 1,594,086 |
| 8 Baltimore, MD | 431,151 | 54.8 | 786,775 |
| 9 New Orleans, LA | 308,136 | 55.3 | 557,482 |
| 10 Memphis, TN | 307,702 | 47.6 | 646,356 |
| 11 Atlanta, GA | 282,912 | 66.6 | 425,022 |
| 12 Dallas, TX | 265,594 | 29.4 | 904,078 |
| 13 Cleveland, OH | 251,347 | 43.8 | 573,822 |
| 14 St. Louis, MO | 206,386 | 45.6 | 453,085 |
| 15 Newark, NJ | 191,743 | 58.2 | 329,248 |
| 16 Oakland, CA | 159,234 | 46.9 | 339,288 |
| 17 Birmingham, AL | 158,223 | 55.6 | 284,413 |
| 18 Indianapolis, IN | 152,626 | 21.8 | 700,807 |
| 19 Milwaukee, WI | 146,940 | 23.1 | 636,212 |
| 20 Jacksonville, FL | 137,324 | 25.4 | 540,898 |
| 21 Cincinnati, OH | 130,467 | 33.8 | 385,457 |
| 22 Boston, MA | 126,229 | 22.4 | 562,994 |
| 23 Columbus, OH | 124,880 | 22.1 | 564,871 |
| 24 Kansas City, MO | 122,699 | 27.4 | 448,159 |
| 25 Richmond, VA | 112,357 | 51.3 | 219,214 |
| 26 Gary, IN | 107,644 | 70.8 | 151,953 |
| 27 Nashville-Davidson, TN | 105,942 | 23.3 | 455,651 |
| 28 Pittsburgh, PA | 101,813 | 24.0 | 423,938 |
| 29 Charlotte, NC | 97,627 | 31.0 | 314,447 |
| 30 Jackson, MS | 95,357 | 47.0 | 202,895 |
| 31 Buffalo, NY | 95,116 | 26.6 | 357,870 |
| 32 Norfolk, VA | 93,987 | 35.2 | 266,979 |
| 33 Fort Worth, TX | 87,723 | 22.8 | 385,141 |
| 34 Miami, FL | 87,110 | 25.1 | 346,931 |
| 35 San Francisco, CA | 86,414 | 12.7 | 678,974 |
| 36 Shreveport, LA | 84,627 | 41.1 | 205,815 |
| 37 Louisville, KY | 84,080 | 28.2 | 298,451 |
| 38 Baton Rouge, LA | 80,119 | 36.5 | 219,486 |
| 39 San Diego, CA | 77,700 | 8.9 | 875,504 |
| 40 Dayton, OH | 75,031 | 36.9 | 203,588 |
| 41 Mobile, AL | 72,568 | 36.2 | 200,452 |
| 42 Montgomery, AL | 69,765 | 39.2 | 178,157 |
| 43 Savannah, GA | 69,441 | 49.0 | 141,634 |
| 44 Flint, MI | 66,124 | 41.4 | 159,611 |
| 45 East Orange, NJ | 64,354 | 83.5 | 77,025 |
| 46 Tampa, FL | 63,835 | 23.5 | 271,523 |
| 47 Rochester, NY | 62,332 | 25.8 | 241,741 |
| 48 Jersey City, NJ | 61,954 | 27.7 | 223,532 |
| 49 Toledo, OH | 61,750 | 17.4 | 354,635 |
| 50 Compton, CA | 60,812 | 74.8 | 81,286 |

## TABLE 25. 100 CITIES WITH THE LARGEST BLACK POPULATION, BY RANK: 1980-(CONTINUED)

| City Rank | Black Population | Percentage of Total Population | Total Population |
|---|---|---|---|
| 51 Denver, CO | 59,252 | 12.1 | 491,396 |
| 52 Oklahoma City, OK | 58,702 | 14.6 | 403,213 |
| 53 Columbus, GA | 57,884 | 34.2 | 169,441 |
| 54 San Antonio, TX | 57,654 | 7.3 | 785,410 |
| 55 Inglewood, CA | 54,010 | 57.3 | 94,245 |
| 56 Chattanooga, TN | 53,716 | 31.7 | 169,565 |
| 57 Winston-Salem, NC | 52,968 | 40.2 | 131,885 |
| 58 East St. Louis, IL | 52,751 | 95.6 | 55,200 |
| 59 Akron, OH | 52,719 | 22.2 | 237,177 |
| 60 Macon, GA | 52,056 | 44.5 | 116,860 |
| 61 Greensboro, NC | 51,373 | 33.0 | 155,642 |
| 62 Little Rock, AR | 51,091 | 32.2 | 158,461 |
| 63 Durham, NC | 47,474 | 47.1 | 100,831 |
| 64 Portsmouth, VA | 47,185 | 45.1 | 104,577 |
| 65 Paterson, NJ | 47,091 | 34.1 | 137,970 |
| 66 Seattle, WA | 46,755 | 9.5 | 493,846 |
| 67 Hartford, CT | 46,186 | 33.9 | 136,392 |
| 68 Newport News, VA | 45,584 | 31.5 | 144,903 |
| 69 Camden, NJ | 45,008 | 53.0 | 84,910 |
| 70 Beaumont, TX | 43,270 | 36.6 | 118,102 |
| 71 Tulsa, OK | 42,594 | 11.8 | 360,919 |
| 72 Austin, TX | 42,118 | 12.2 | 345,496 |
| 73 Hampton, VA | 42,072 | 34.3 | 122,617 |
| 74 Trenton, NJ | 41,860 | 45.4 | 92,124 |
| 75 Raleigh, NC | 41,186 | 27.5 | 149,771 |
| 76 St. Petersburg, FL | 41,000 | 17.3 | 236,893 |
| 77 Kansas City, KS | 40,826 | 25.3 | 161,087 |
| 78 Long Beach, CA | 40,732 | 11.3 | 361,334 |
| 79 Columbia, SC | 40,391 | 40.7 | 99,296 |
| 80 New Haven, CT | 40,235 | 31.9 | 125,109 |
| 81 Youngstown, OH | 38,481 | 33.3 | 115,436 |
| 82 Orlando, FL | 38,390 | 29.9 | 128,394 |
| 83 Omaha, NE | 37,852 | 12.1 | 311,681 |
| 84 Phoenix, AZ | 37,682 | 4.9 | 764,911 |
| 85 Sacramento, CA | 36,866 | 13.4 | 275,741 |
| 86 Wilmington, DE | 35,858 | 51.1 | 70,195 |
| 87 Richmond, CA | 35,799 | 47.9 | 74,676 |
| 88 Albany, GA | 35,173 | 47.6 | 73,934 |
| 89 Mount Vernon, NY | 32,469 | 48.7 | 66,713 |
| 90 Charleston, SC | 32,318 | 46.5 | 69,510 |
| 91 Fort Lauderdale, FL | 32,225 | 21.0 | 153,256 |
| 92 East Cleveland, OH | 31,980 | 86.5 | 36,957 |
| 93 Chesapeake, VA | 31,510 | 27.6 | 114,226 |
| 94 Wichita, KS | 30,200 | 10.8 | 279,272 |
| 95 Bridgeport, CT | 29,898 | 21.0 | 142,546 |
| 96 Huntsville, AL | 29,535 | 20.7 | 142,513 |
| 97 San Jose, CA | 29,157 | 4.6 | 636,550 |
| 98 Prichard, AL | 29,129 | 73.7 | 39,541 |
| 99 Grand Rapids, MI | 28,602 | 15.7 | 181,843 |
| 100 Pontiac, MI | 28,532 | 37.2 | 76,715 |

* Latest census 1980

## TABLE 26. 100 CITIES WITH THE LARGEST BLACK POPULATION RANKED ACCORDING TO THE HIGHEST PROPORTION OF BLACKS: 1980*

| City Rank | Percentage of Total | City Rank | Percentage of Total |
|---|---|---|---|
| 1 East St. Louis, IL | 95.6 | 51 Greensboro, NC | 33.0 |
| 2 East Cleveland, OH | 86.5 | 52 Little Rock, AR | 32.2 |
| 3 East Orange, NJ | 83.5 | 53 New Haven, CT | 31.9 |
| 4 Compton, CA | 74.8 | 54 Chattanooga, TN | 31.7 |
| 5 Prichard, AL | 73.7 | 55 Newport News, VA | 31.5 |
| 6 Gary, IN | 70.8 | 56 Charlotte, NC | 31.0 |
| 7 Washington, D.C. | 70.3 | 57 Orlando, FL | 29.9 |
| 8 Atlanta, GA | 66.6 | 58 Dallas, TX | 29.4 |
| 9 Detroit, MI | 63.1 | 59 Louisville, KY | 28.2 |
| 10 Newark, NJ | 58.2 | 60 Jersey City, NJ | 27.7 |
| 11 Inglewood, CA | 57.3 | 61 Houston, TX | 27.6 |
| 12 Birmingham, AL | 55.6 | 62 Chesapeake, VA | 27.6 |
| 13 New Orleans, LA | 55.3 | 63 Raleigh, NC | 27.5 |
| 14 Baltimore, MD | 54.8 | 64 Kansas City, MO | 27.4 |
| 15 Camden, NJ | 53.0 | 65 Buffalo, NY | 26.6 |
| 16 Richmond, VA | 51.3 | 66 Rochester, NY | 25.3 |
| 17 Wilmington, DE | 51.1 | 67 Jacksonville, FL | 25.4 |
| 18 Savannah, GA | 49.0 | 68 Kansas City, KS | 25.3 |
| 19 Mount Vernon, NY | 48.7 | 69 New York, NY | 25.2 |
| 20 Richmond, CA | 47.9 | 70 Miami, FL | 25.1 |
| 21 Memphis, TN | 47.6 | 71 Pittsburgh, PA | 24.0 |
| 22 Albany, GA | 47.6 | 72 Tampa, FL | 23.5 |
| 23 Durham, NC | 47.1 | 73 Nashville-Davidson, TN | 23.3 |
| 24 Jackson, MS | 47.0 | 74 Milwaukee, WI | 23.1 |
| 25 Oakland, CA | 46.9 | 75 Fort Worth, TX | 22.8 |
| 26 Charleston, SC | 46.5 | 76 Boston, MA | 22.4 |
| 27 St. Louis, MO | 45.6 | 77 Akron, OH | 22.2 |
| 28 Trenton, NJ | 45.4 | 78 Columbus, OH | 22.1 |
| 29 Portsmouth, VA | 45.1 | 79 Indianapolis, IN | 21.8 |
| 30 Macon, GA | 44.5 | 80 Fort Lauderdale, FL | 21.0 |
| 31 Cleveland, OH | 43.8 | 81 Bridgeport, CT | 21.0 |
| 32 Flint, MI | 41.4 | 82 Huntsville, AL | 20.7 |
| 33 Shreveport, LA | 41.1 | 83 Toledo, OH | 17.4 |
| 34 Columbia, SC | 40.7 | 84 St. Petersburgh, FL | 17.3 |
| 35 Winston-Salem, NC | 40.2 | 85 Los Angeles, CA | 17.0 |
| 36 Chicago, IL | 39.8 | 86 Grand Rapids, MI | 15.7 |
| 37 Montgomery, AL | 39.2 | 87 Oklahoma City, OK | 14.6 |
| 38 Philadelphia, PA | 37.8 | 88 Sacramento, CA | 13.4 |
| 39 Pontiac, MI | 37.2 | 89 San Francisco, CA | 12.7 |
| 40 Dayton, OH | 36.9 | 90 Austin, TX | 12.2 |
| 41 Beaumont, TX | 36.6 | 91 Omaha, NE | 12.1 |
| 42 Baton Rouge, LA | 36.5 | 92 Denver, CO | 12.1 |
| 43 Mobile, AL | 36.2 | 93 Tulsa, OK | 11.8 |
| 44 Norfolk, VA | 35.2 | 94 Long Beach, CA | 11.3 |
| 45 Hampton, VA | 34.3 | 95 Wichita, KS | 10.8 |
| 46 Columbus, GA | 34.2 | 96 Seattle, WA | 9.5 |
| 47 Paterson, NJ | 34.1 | 97 San Diego, CA | 8.9 |
| 48 Hartford, CT | 33.9 | 98 San Antonio, TX | 7.3 |
| 49 Cincinnati, OH | 33.8 | 99 Phoenix, AZ | 4.9 |
| 50 Youngstown, OH | 33.3 | 100 San Jose, CA | 4.6 |

* Latest census 1980

# THE BLACK FAMILY

**Current Status ■ Overview ■ Family Organization ■ Stratification ■ Population Shortage of Eligible Black Males ■ Net Household Worth ■ Life Expectancy ■ Fertility Rates ■ Teenage Pregnancy ■ Child Support ■ Farm Population ■ Health ■ Housing ■ Budget Cuts and the Family—The Eighties ■ Assessment ■ Selected Facts on the Black Family ■ Family Charts ■ Family Tables**

By the end of 1987, some 20 years after President Lyndon Johnson declared his "war on poverty," poverty still remained one of America's more serious social problems, particularly for black Americans. In 1969, 32% of black Americans were living below a poverty level; in 1979, 31% of black Americans were living below a poverty level; and in 1987, at the height of President Ronald Reagan's six successive years of economic recovery and growth, 33.1% of black Americans were living below a poverty level. Of America's total population some 32,000,000 people were living at poverty levels, 21,000,000 were white (10.5% of the white population), 9,683,000 were black (33.1% of the black population). Forty-five percent of all black children lived below the poverty level, in 1987.

Poverty is most egregious in the urban ghettos of the central cities where three-fifths of America's blacks live. It is in these urban centers where housing, health care, transportation, education, insurance and police services are grossly insufficient, and where the cost of food and other staples are usually priced higher than in white areas.

In 1964, when President Lyndon Johnson signed the Economic Recovery Act he announced that the policy of the United States was "to eliminate the paradox of poverty in the midst of plenty." The War on Poverty started with great promise. In 1965, over $1.5 billion in federal funds was appropriated and, under the leadership of R. Sargent Shriver Jr., a variety of programs was soon helping the poor to organize in over 1,000 communities. However, the ebullience of the poor, with the young leading them, plus inevitable occurrences of confusion and extravagance, were soon to anger Congressmen and local officials. The result was increasing opposition from Congressmen and local officials and diminishing support from President Johnson himself. A typical situation: The Mississippi Congressional delegation was outraged by the civil rights activities of the Child Development Group, a pre-school development program which felt it within their realm to campaign for civil rights legislation.

In 1966 and 1967, Congress imposed numerous conditions and restrictions on its allocations to poverty programs.

However, anti-poverty efforts proceeded energetically. In 1966, Shriver announced that by means of income maintenance, job training and increased government services, 24 million of America's 36 million poor would be lifted out of the poverty bracket by 1972. The plan called for an outlay of $1.8 billion in 1967 rising to $6.7 billion in 1972, an increase that seemed modest and reasonable considering the expanding economy of the time. However, international and domestic political trends were to thwart these hopes.

In 1974, the Act was repealed and the consensus was that the program had failed. The premise behind President Johnson's program was that eradication of poverty could best come about if the poor became their own advocates at all governmental levels and through litigation—rather than through the perpetuation of dependence through government largesse. This approach, theoretically, was directed toward satisfying two deeply felt American traditions: the first, being that people should, if at all possible, be self-sufficient; and the second, that it is proper for competitive special interest groups to vie with one another for considerations of their interests among public officials. In effect, the poverty effort was to spawn and breed a poor people's lobby while providing direct aid to current needs.

The program was not specifically designed for blacks but for all poor and blacks stood to gain considerably in the overall effort. Programs of income maintenance, job training, and increased governmental services were designed to move 24,000,000 of the nations 36,000,000 poverty victims into a better standard of living. And although poverty programs were defined as a failed government attempt to legislate poverty out of existence there is much evidence that the program with all its short comings had more than a modest degree of success. The evidence of progress is as follows:

- Between 1959 and 1975, the median earnings ratio of black families increased relative to white families from .52 to .58.
- In some sections of the country, the earnings of young black families approached that of young white families.
- In 1972, in the North and West, black families with a head of family under 35 earned 93% as much as their white counterparts.
- Between 1965 and 1973, the proportion of black families earning less than $5000 in 1973 dollars dropped from 46% to 34%.
- Blacks in the United States, who comprise the world's ninth largest market with distinctive spending patterns, began to

**CHART 11. MEDIAN INCOME OF FAMILIES IN CURRENT AND CONSTANT DOLLARS**

**In 1970 the median income for black families was $6,279 while for white families it was $10,236; in 1986 the median income for black families was $17,604 while for white families it was $30,809. In terms of constant dollars the real income levels of both races has remained static indicating that the standard of living, for most people, has not increased since 1970.**

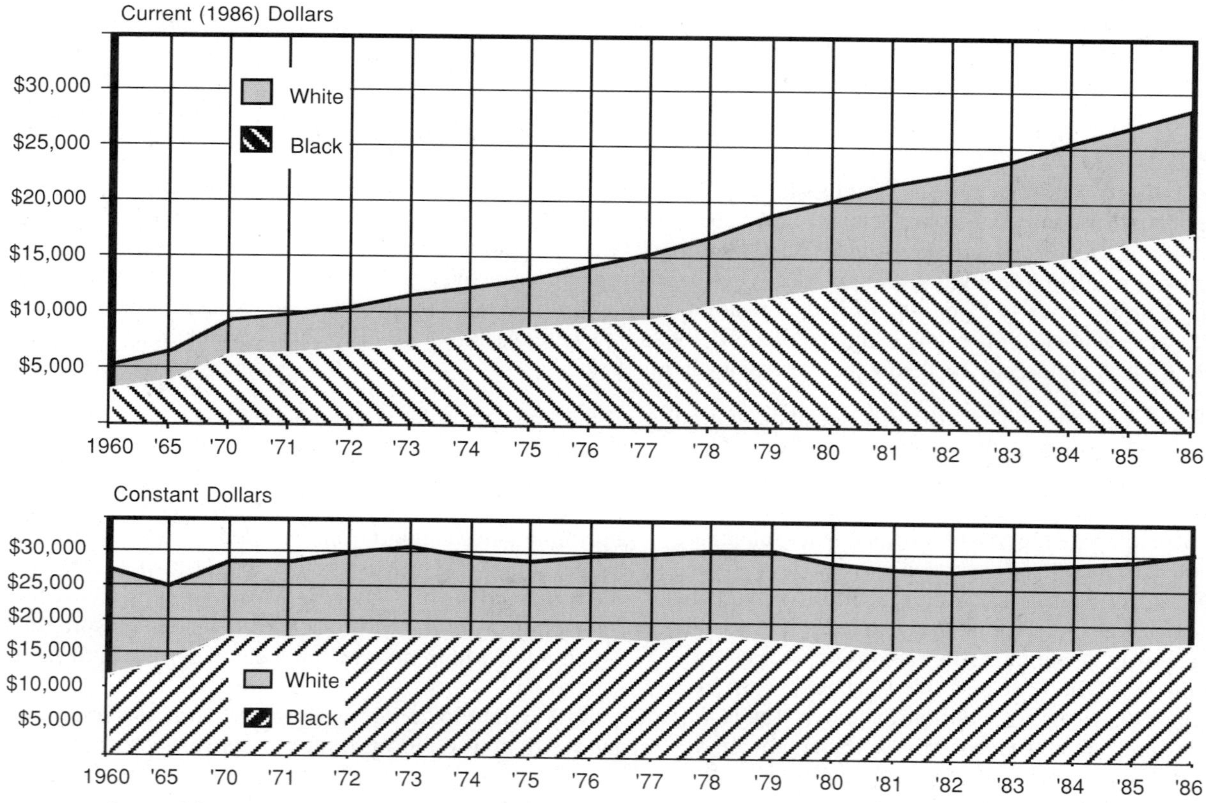


Source: U.S. Bureau of the Census

## CHART 12: SALARY GAP

**The gap in weekly earnings between black and white full time-workers increased from $49 in 1979 to $82 in1987.**

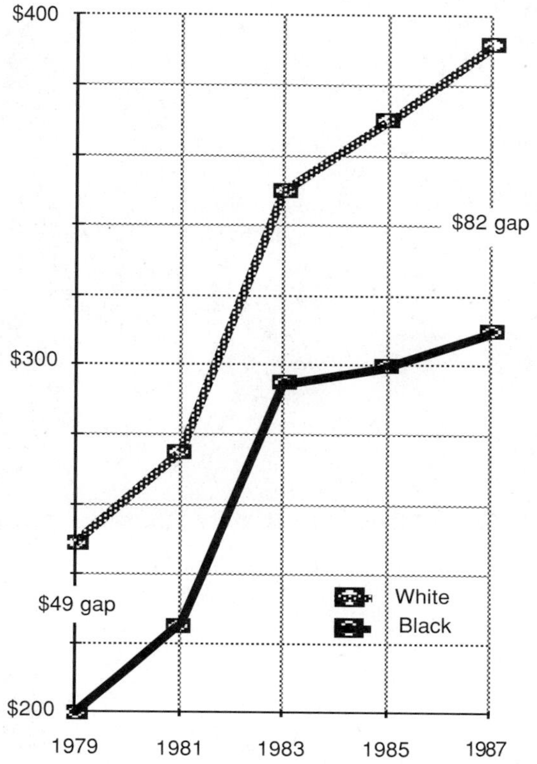


Source: *Newsweek.* March 7, 1988, p.24

emerge as a separate entity of significance to large segments of American business.

The major criticism of President Johnson's anti-poverty effort was related to the fears of local officials and leaders because of the increased activism of poor people who were using community programs as their base for increased political activities. There was as well evidence of fund misuse by a few community poverty program leaders. There was, however, no evidence that the program itself was failing and most money was being spent where it was intended to be spent. Two other problems emerged to plague anti-poverty efforts. Most crippling of all was escalation of the war in Southeast Asia. Congress was unwilling to vote funds for both the war against Communism there and the war against poverty at home. The nation's leadership gave priority to the former. There was at the time much negative media coverage of poverty programs and public opinion began to build against the entire concept of the program. Conservatives promised to cut budgets for welfare programs and ferret out the cheats. Such talk impressed the public. Liberal support for anti-poverty efforts, once energetic and hopeful, grew tentative and defensive.

Ironically, during the Nixon years and the Carter years there appeared to be a movement away from Johnson's thrust of eventual self-sufficiency and toward increasing direct aid. However, the direction during the Reagan era has been to drastically cut all programs, direct aid and self-help alike, the contention being that "all ships rise with the tide" and that economic expansion would move people out of poverty. If the Reagan philosophy was valid then blacks, during the successive years of economic growth, should have experienced improvements in income, poverty rates, labor market status, wealth, and business ownership, thereby reducing their dependency. Nonetheless, according to David Swinton in *The Economic Status of Black Americans* (The State of Black America 1989), "most standard indicators of economic life continue to record the highest levels of social inequality since the mid 1960s. There is no escaping the conclusion that a major impact of six years of Reagan administration leadership on the economy has been to increase racial inequality and exacerbate the economic difficulties of blacks." There were some gains made by blacks in the 60s and 70s, but such gains are now in a countertrend, for example:

- In 1970, the relative median black family income was $18,378, (constant dollars). In 1987, eighteen years later it is less at $18,098.
- In 1973, the median earnings of black families increased relative to white families and in 1987 demonstrated a significant decline.
- In 1972, in the North and West, black families with a head of family under 35 earned 93% as much as their white counterparts, the gap has now widened.
- The economic gains of the 60s and 70s in terms of a decrease in the earnings gap between black and white families have now increased at most levels.
- There has been some gain at the middle income range as a result of two incomes; yet it takes the earnings of three blacks in a family to achieve the median level of a white family with 2 earners.

The median annual wage for a black family of 4 in 1987 was $18,098 only $7,000 above the poverty level, and $14,176 below the $32,274 median annual wage for whites; black families are a lot closer to the poverty level than to the median wage for a white family. Only the upper third of black families fared well during the Reagan years, but it took more family earners than in white families to achieve the position. The richest 20% of all families ($52,910 and above) earned 43.7% of all the income generated in the United States while the poorest 20% ($14,450 and below) earned only 4.6% of all generated income in 1987.

Douglas G. Glasgow has indicated that there is a known black underclass of about 7 million individuals, living at marginal levels of subsistence—that figure may be conservative. Says Glasgow, "If we factor in all the unemployed; the discouraged worker population; the almost one million black men whose labor force status cannot be determined because they are missing from the census; blacks in prisons; the 3 million blacks hidden in hamlets in a host of small southern towns; and the new 'homeless' black poor, the size of the black underclass suggests a phenomenon of staggering magnitude. It is here in this underclass, where most social disorganization can be found, and amidst the disorganization there is much social disruption."

In The State of Black America 1987, Andrew Billingsley indicates that aside from a growing underclass, the signs of crisis in black family life are increasing, and he cites trends which define the crisis in twelve major areas. They are: (1) poverty, which undercuts the struggle for stability; (2) unemployment among black men, women, youth; (3) low family income among employed blacks; (4) decline in married couple families; (5) teenage pregnancy; (6) a growing underclass; (7) inadequate housing and homelessness; (8) less than adequate health care and greater health hazards; (9) school dropout rates; (10) incarcerated men (prisons have become black warehouses); (11) employment of the last resort has become the military. Billingsley's 12th sign of crisis, however, does not appear to be one of crisis but rather one of hope as (12) states "The black family continues to achieve despite overwhelming odds." Billingsley goes on to say that for black American family life in the 80s there are "rising levels of poverty, declining levels of income, rising levels of underemployment, declining levels of family stability, a rising underclass a struggling middle class, and a strong element of achieving families. These are the conditions of family life for America's largest minority..."

*Many black families are poor and struggle to stay together as a family.*

## OVERVIEW

The decade of the 1960s may have provided a brief respite from the trend toward economic decline for black families, but the now prevailing countertrends of the 70s and 80s have sharply eroded past advances. During the 1960s, black workers and their families made unprecedented economic gains. While the jobless rate for blacks declined from ten percent to six percent between 1960 and 1969, the total number of unemployed blacks fell from 787,000 to a 30-year low of 570,000. These record declines in joblessness occurred among black adults and teenagers. Moreover, while the number of black families in poverty fell from 1.9 million to 1.4 million between 1959 and 1969, the percent of black families in poverty plummeted from 48 percent to 28 percent. Similarly, while the number of black children in poor families fell from 5.0 million to 3.7 million during the 1960s, the percent of black children in poverty dropped from 66 percent to 40 percent.

The sharp decline in poor black families during the60's contributed to the remarkable growth in middle-class blacks. While the number of black families with incomes of $25,000 and over (in 1987 dollars) jumped from 515,000 to 1,641,000 between 1959 and 1970, the proportion of middle-income black families almost tripled from 12 percent to 33 percent. Thus, the racial gap in family income narrowed between 1959 and 1969, as the ratio of black to white median family income rose from 52 percent to 61 percent.

However, the 1970s and particularly the 1980s have severely whittled away at the overall economic progress achieved during the sixties. By 1983, the number of unemployed blacks jumped to 2.3 million, while their jobless rate soared to a record-high of 20 percent. Although the jobless rate for blacks declined to 12 percent by 1988, it is still double the jobless rate for blacks two decades ago—and one million more blacks are unemployed today. Moreover, while the unemployment rate for black adults rose from four percent to ten percent between 1969 and 1988, the jobless rate for black teenagers spiraled from 23 percent to 32 percent.

As might be expected, these sharp increases in joblessness resulted in marked rises in poverty among blacks during the 1970s and 1980s. While the number of black families in poverty jumped from 1.4 million to 2.1 million between 1969 and 1987, the percent of black families in poverty edged up from 28 percent to 30 percent. Similarly, while the number of black children in poor families rose from 3.7 million to 4.3 million between 1969 and 1987, the percent of black children in poor families increased from 40 percent to 45 percent.

Although two-parent black families had sharp declines in poverty during the 1970s, they experienced large increases in poverty during the 1980s. While the number of poor black families headed by women soared by 67 percent (from 737,000 to 1,234,000) between 1969 and 1979, the number of poor black couples fell by 22 percent (from 629,000 to 488,000). However, between 1979 and 1987, the growth in female-headed black families slowed to only 29 percent, while the number of poor two-parent black families rose by 14 percent.

While the number of middle-class black families continued to increase during the 70's and 80's, their rate of growth slowed. While the number of black families with incomes of $25,000 and over (in 1987 dollars) rose from 1.6 million to 2.2 million between 1970 and 1978, the proportion of middle-income black families increased from 33 percent to 38 percent. Although the number of middle-income black families continued to rise to 2.6 million by 1987, the proportion of middle-income black families fell to 36 percent. However, the most spectacular gains over the past two decades were experienced by upper-income blacks. While the number of black families with incomes of $50,000 and over more than doubled from 281,000 to 682,000 between 1970 and 1978, the proportion of upper-income black families jumped from six percent to ten percent.

Even with these increases, the overall economic gap between black and white families widened during the seventies and eighties. In 1969, the median income of black families relative to white families was 61 percent, by 1987 the ratio fell to 57 percent. While the racial gap narrowed among two-parent families (from 72% to 80%), it widened among single-parent families (from 61% to 59%). The strongest income gains relative to whites were achieved by two-parent black families with working wives, while the racial gap among couples without working wives remained relatively unchanged since 1969.

Moreover, the increased economic instability among black families led to social destabilization as well. While the number of black families headed by women doubled from 1.4 million to 3.1 million between 1969 and 1988, the proportion of black families headed by women soared from 28 percent to 44 percent. The surge in single-parent black families resulted from record-level rates of divorce and separation and sharp increases in out-of-wedlock births. While 2 out of 5 black births in 1970 were out-of-wedlock, over half of all black births today are out-of-wedlock. And, although out-of-wedlock birthrates declined among black teens during the 70's and 80's, black adolescents are still 4 times more likely than white adolescents to have babies out-of-wedlock.

Unprecedented levels of crime and gang violence also destabilized black families. With drug trafficking rampant in most inner city areas, drug-related homicides among blacks have reached record levels. Black families have also been disproportionately devastated by the declining stock of affordable housing due to abandonments, urban renewal, commercial development, gentrification and condominium conversions. Thus, homelessness soared to alarming levels among black families.

What are the major reasons for the marked erosion in the social and economic stability of black families over the past two decades? According to proponents of the "blaming the victim" thesis, joblessness, poverty and single-parent families among blacks are mainly caused by internal factors, such as "culture of poverty" values and "underclass" life-styles. Other scholars, however, contend that societal trends, including racism, are mainly responsible. Sociologist William

**CHART 13. HEAD OF HOUSEHOLD BY TYPE AND RACE: 1969, 1970, 1978 and 1986**

**A comparison of white and black married couples indicates that both groups have steep declines in the number of married couples; while the trend line for both groups is down it is much steeper for blacks. Because of the trend, both races have had large increases in females who head families.**

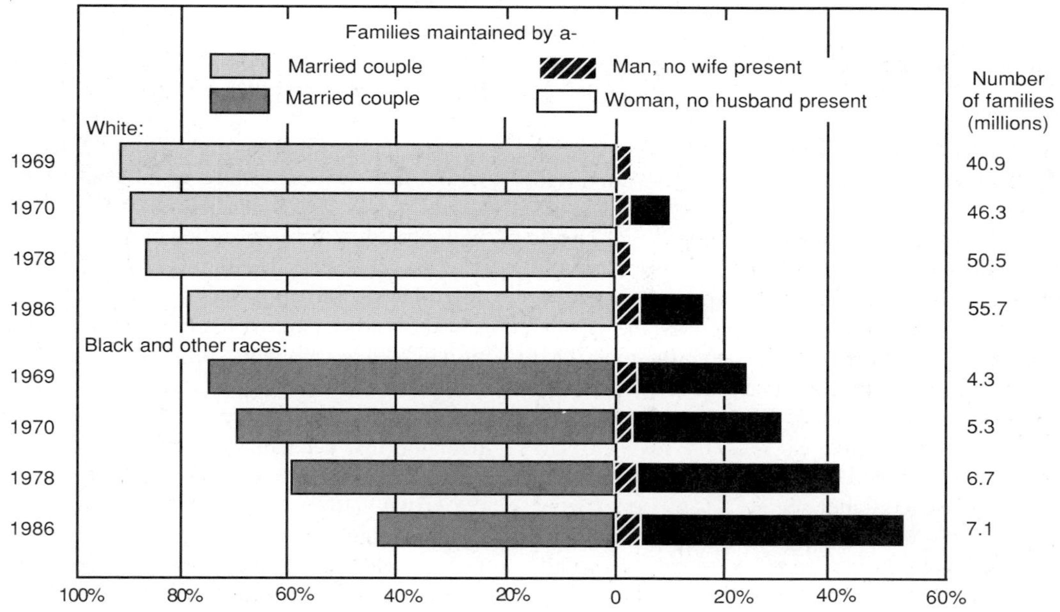

## CHART 14. MARITAL STATUS OF PARENTS IN ONE-PARENT FAMILY GROUP

**Only 48.55% of black females who are the head of a one-parent family group have ever been married; while about 82.9% of white females in a similar family structure had been married.**

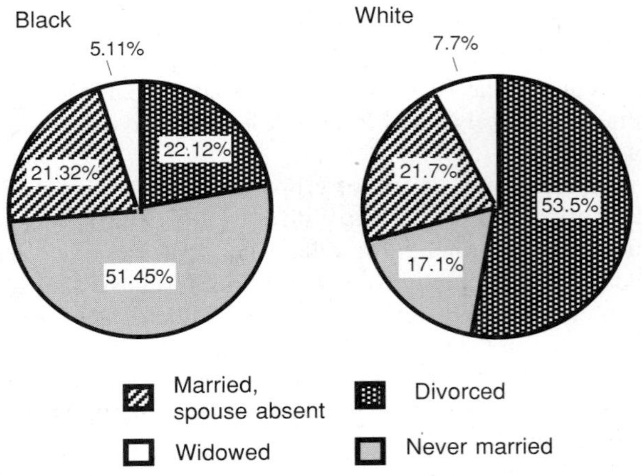


## CHART 15. CHILDREN'S LIVING ARRANGEMENTS

**Almost 60% of all black children live in one-parent families; only 40% live with both parents.**

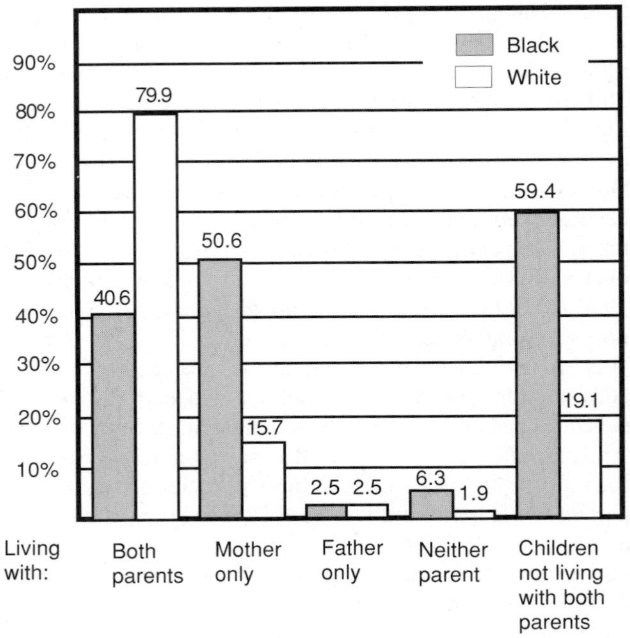


Wilson, for example, attributes the growth in the inner-city black poor to the exodus of jobs from inner-cities to the suburbs, industrial shifts from higher-paying manufacturing jobs to lower-paying service jobs and to stagnant economic growth as a result of periodic recessions.

It should be noted, however, that many of the social and economic dislocations during the '70's and '80's occurred among white families as well. While unemployment rates doubled among white workers, single-parent families rose about as fast among whites as among blacks. But the level of single-parent families did not remain as high among whites as among blacks, since white women had much higher remarriage rates than black women. Thus, the relative shortage of marriageable black men will continue to contribute to the instability of black families in the coming decades.

## FAMILY ORGANIZATION

### Number and Size of Families

Of the 9,797,000 black households in 1986, 6,921,000 or 70.6% were family households. Only 3,680,000 or 37.6% were married couples, significantly down from 53.3% married couples in 1970.

The number of female heads of the house grew, from 21.8% of the 1970 total to 29.3% of the 1986 total. Although the percentage of male heads of households increased as well, from 2.9% in 1970 to 3.8% in 1986, clearly the largest growth was in the numbers of homes headed by women. This can be attributed to the shortage of black males, separation and divorce rates, the early death of black males and the rate of out-of-wedlock parenthood.

Black households in 1986 averaged 2.90 persons each. This was larger than the greater society's 2.67 persons per household, but smaller than the 3.43-person Hispanic household. Black households were largest in the South, averaging 2.98 persons each, followed by the Midwest (2.91), Northeast (2.76) and the West (2.66). The majority of blacks—51%—still live in the South.

Most blacks and whites 15 years and older lived in some kind of family situation in 1986. The clear difference was that whites tended to live in nuclear arrangements (with spouse, white 58.5%; black 36%) while blacks tended to live with other relatives (extended families, white 24.1%; black 45.7%). The extended family arrangement among blacks and other people of color is considered to be both a cultural and economic adaptation. Only 12.2% of blacks and 11.5% of whites lived alone in 1986.

Black married couples are producing smaller families. The average size of married couple black families dropped over the last decade, from 4.13 persons in 1970 to 3.55 persons in 1986. In these nuclear black families, the majority—41.4%—in 1986 had no children under 18 years old. Little more than 23% had one such child, 19.6% had two minor children, 9.9% had three such children and 5.9% had four or more young children.

### Single-Parent Families

A February 1989 release from the Census Bureau reported that 54% of black children now lived in single-parent families, nine-tenths of which were headed by women.

This growth of one-parent families has been called "one of the most startling social developments of the past quarter century." Social scientists have blamed unrelenting poverty and the development of an underclass for this one-parent phenomenon. Poverty rates for female heads of households are much greater than for two-parent families. From 1980 to 1988, the number of children under age 18 who lived in single-parent homes increased across the board—from 46% to 54% among blacks, from 15% to 19% among whites, and from 21% to 30% among Hispanics. These figures are even more startling when viewed from 1960 to the present; in 1960, only 7% of white children and 22% of black children lived in single-parent homes. (Figures were not computed for Hispanics at that time).

Among blacks, the major reason given for the one-parent family was that the parent had never married (54%). The same reason applied to Hispanics (33%). Among whites, however, the chief cause of single-parent families was divorce (50%).

Although there is speculation about the reasons for the rise in single-parent families, exact causes are not known. With respect to blacks, most frequent factors are high unemployment among males, welfare assistance, and fewer marriages—even when the female is pregnant.

Divorce and separation rates, promiscuity, and fluctuating male economic fortunes account for much of this change in the larger society. Men who cannot secure and retain jobs find it very difficult to remain in family situations. It appears that social misfortunes experienced first by blacks—the lowest ranking group in status, esteem and opportunity in this country—may spread, and in time, become a more general condition. In this sense, the black condition can possibly be seen as a barometer of the nation's health. Further, there is much evidence that economic insecurity is disastrous to general psychological functioning, and even to one's physical health, while a sense of economic security adds significantly to general family stability.

## STRATIFICATION

As mentioned previously, David Swinton, in *Economic Status of Blacks 1987*, points out that close to one-third of the black population continues to be poor, and the poverty rate for blacks remains almost three times that of whites.

At the other end of the income range are an increased number of blacks who can be classified as upper middle class, with some individual blacks making impressive economic gains. Among these are the "Buppies"—black, urban, upwardly mobile professionals—who have benefited from education and employment opportunities, as well as the helping hands of parents and/or extended family members.

By 1986, 8.8% of black families had incomes of $50,000 or more, up from 4.7% in 1970. Some 12.4% of black families earned $35,000 to $49,999, compared with 11% in 1970. Although it often took two earners to achieve a comfortable living standard, by 1986, 21.2% of black families

### CHART 16. FAMILY STABILITY AND INCOME

**Families, both black and white, tend to remain stable as income increases. Below $20,000 about 50% of black families remain intact. Below $10,000 slightly under 30% of black families remain intact.**

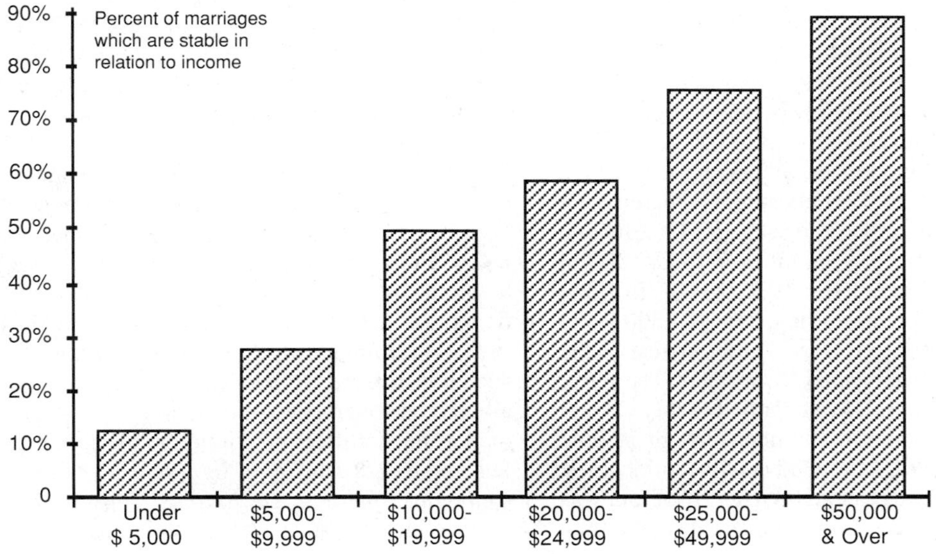

## CHART 17. MEDIAN INCOME FOR FAMILIES

**In every type of family structure, the income of black families remains behind that of their white counterparts. In 1987, median family income for black families was $18,098 while for white families it was $32,274.**

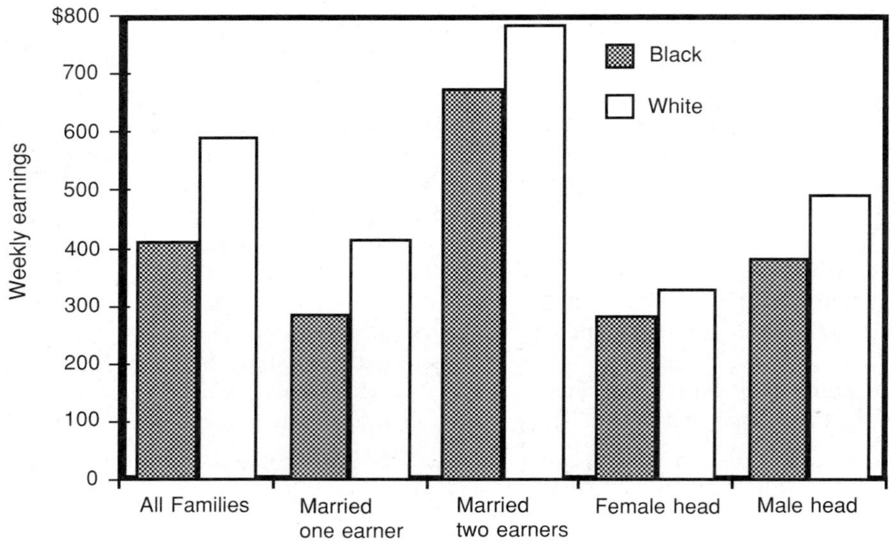


were earning more than $35,000 a year, up from 15.7% in 1970.

During the same time period, the number of black families in six middle to lower-middle class brackets dropped.

In 1970, 16.5% of black families had incomes in the $25,000 to $34,999 bracket. By 1986, that percentage had dropped to 14.7%. In the $20,000 to $24,999 bracket, the 11.1% in 1970 fell to 9.6% in 1986. This decline continued in succeeding brackets: in the $15,000 to $19,999 bracket, it dropped from 14.2% in 1970 to 10.7% in 1986; in the $12,500 to $14,999 bracket, it dropped from 7.9% in 1970 to 6.8% in 1986; in the $10,000 to $12,499 bracket, it fell from 7.8% in 1970 to 7.0% in 1986; and in the $7,500 to $9,999 bracket, it fell from 8.7% in 1970 to 7.8% in 1986. The bottom line was that in 16 years, the percentage of the black population earning these middle-class to lower-middle class salaries dropped from 66.2% to 56.6% in 1986.

Percentages of blacks in the lowest income groupings grew, as those in the mid-level groupings fell, indicating that as some blacks climbed the ladder, others slipped down a few rungs. In the $5,000 to $7,500 category, there was a slight decrease, from 8.5% in 1970 to 8.4% in 1986. But two other groups grew significantly: families in the $2,500 to $4,999 category grew from 6.4% in 1970 to 9.4% in 1986, and the percentage in the poorest group, under $2,500, grew from 3.2% in 1970 to 4.6% in 1986. These poorest of the poor were usually families headed by women. The term, "feminization of poverty," has been applied to them.

Thus, it is clear that while the number of high income black families increased, so did the number with low incomes. In 1986, when the poverty threshold for a family of four was $11,203, 30% of black families had incomes below $10,000.

The median income of black families in 1986 was $17,604, in white families $30,809, and in Hispanic families, $19,995. In most black families, both spouses, or the single adult person, were employed fully (not part-time) all year round, but even so, the median income of black families was well below that of the other two major ethnic/racial groups.

David Swinton and Bart Landry cite, as chronic conditions, the relative absence of wealth among black families, a relatively large debt burden as compared to white families, and an inability to maintain middle class status in the face of even short-term unemployment. In times of emergencies, more black than white families turn to banks, finance companies, relatives or friends for loans, large and small.

Black economic fortunes are dependent on the strength of the American economy, as well as the quality of black participation in it. If the level or character of black economic participation improves, black status can improve. The reverse is true, as well, as E. Franklin Frazier explained in the 1930s. Swinton believes that the key to releasing blacks from the lowliest economic positions rests in the formation of coalitions of blacks and whites which will develop strategies to improve both the economy and black positions in that economy. The need for this is clear as blacks have been twice as likely to be unemployed, even in the best of economic times. Economic downturns have had devastating effects on black families.

The prominent black scholar William J. Wilson, a sociologist at the University of Chicago, has made major, albeit controversial, contributions to the discussion of increasing stratification within the black population. In his 1978 book, *The Declining Significance of Race: Blacks and Changing American Institutions*, Wilson analyzed black societal changes since slavery's end, examining economic systems, laws, and state policies in each major economic period. Wilson concluded that prior to World War II, racial oppression and antagonism in the economic sector severely limited black opportunities. These factors, however, were reduced after the war, and especially after the 1960s, when state intervention was redesigned to promote racial equality and redress economic prejudices. Today, Wilson says, access to higher economic gains is based on educational criteria; gains made by blacks in the 1960s have translated into greater opportunities in the 1980s. The growing number of successful blacks, Wilson explains, is evidence that race is a factor of declining significance in American society.

Class, Wilson holds, not race, is the new divider. Social class divisions are growing within the black community as well as in the larger society. The plight of poor blacks, with their low-wage, temporary jobs or unemployment, and pervasive participation in welfare programs, is not solely a result of racism. Rather, Wilson argues, it has to do with economic class affiliation.

In 1987, Wilson continued his analysis in another book, *The Truly Disadvantaged- The Inner City, the Underclass and Public Policy*. In this work, he posed a very fundamental question: "Why have the social conditions of the urban underclass deteriorated so rapidly since the mid-1960s and especially since 1970?" There is no simple answer, he says, and explicitly exempts racism as a major factor. The true causes for the underclass woes are poor education, a paucity of employment opportunities for men, too few marriageable men, welfare-dependent homes, crime, drugs, and the isolation of the underclass from other, healthier segments of society. Further, Wilson notes as a major factor the departure of middle class and professional blacks—badly needed role models—from the ghetto.

Wilson does not believe that the problems of the growing black underclass can be solved with race-specific policies. He argues instead for universal programs of systemic reform: manpower training and education programs, an integration of social and economic policy, full-employment and so on. He is certain that a program's success depends on the availability of jobs in a given area, and urges the support and commitment of a broad constituency to implement full employment policies.

Wilson's *Truly Disadvantaged* received far more acceptance than his *Declining Significance of Race*, which was much disputed in the black community. Still, both works are very important analyses; neither can be overlooked by any serious student of race and class in the United States.

The lines of demarcation between the black middle class, the working class, and poor families are increasingly clear. There is controversy about the meaning and implications of these divisions, as well as who bears primary social responsibility for improving the plight of urban poor black families, now known as the underclass. How much responsibility rests with government? With the private sector? What should the underclass do? The black middle class? Society at large?

For a greater understanding of such questions, the following works are suggested: Douglas G. Glasgow, *The Black Underclass Poverty, Unemployment and Entrapment of Ghetto Youth*; William Julius Wilson, *The Truly Disadvantaged: The Inner City, the Underclass, and Public Policy*; Bart Landry, *The New Black Middle Class;* Reynolds Farley and Walter R. Allen, *The Color Line and the Quality of Life in America;* along with the National Urban League's annual assessment, *The State of Black America*. Additionally, the work of Harriet Pipes McAdoo and Joyce Ladner provides insight. This section of The Black Family has been influenced by such publications, as well as quantitative data from the U.S. Bureau of the Census.

## POPULATION SHORTAGE OF ELIGIBLE BLACK MALES

U.S. Census Bureau statistics show that the black population was 29,224,000 in 1986. It is expected to reach 31,148,000 of a total U.S. population of 250,410,000 by 1990, and become 35,129,000 by the turn of the century—or about 13% of the U.S. population of 268,266,000.

Black females will outnumber black males by 1,478,000 in 1990, and by 1,555,000 in the year 2000. Thus, individual preferences aside, the numbers alone indicate that it is not possible to match every black female of marriageable age with a same-race partner.

This excess of adult females over males has existed in the black population since 1840, although in the age group 14 years and younger there has consistently been more males than females. Black men, it turns out, often run into trouble as they approach adulthood.

In 1986, there were 102.9 males to every 100 females under 14 years old. As the groups aged, the number of males diminished: in the 14-24 age category, there were 97.7 males for every 100 females; in the 25-44 age group, there were 86.8 males per 100 females; in the 45-64 age group, there were only 81.7 males; and in the elderly group, 65 years and over, there were only 67 black males alive for every 100 females.

### Outmarriage

Marriage outside the race further reduces the number of black men available for marriage with black women. In 1987, there were 120,000 marriages composed of black husbands and white wives, and 33,000 cases where black husbands had wives who were of a race that was neither black nor white. In the same year, 61,000 black women were married to non-black husbands—53,000 marriages were with white men, and 8,000 were with non-whites. The net "loss" of marriageable black men for black women was 92,000.

### Incarcerated Black Men

The number of incarcerated black men further reduces the pool of available marriage partners. In 1985, there were 216,344 black male federal and state prisoners, compared to 136,893 such males detained in 1978. (The number of female black prisoners has also grown, from 6,483 in 1978 to 10,793 in 1985.)

## NET HOUSEHOLD WORTH

Racial differences are apparent upon examination of household net worth figures. In 1984, the net worth of holdings for black households was $3,397 as compared with $39,135 for white households. Proportionally fewer black than white households have interest earning assets, regular checking accounts, stocks and mutual funds, their own business or profession, motor vehicles, their own home, rental property, other real estate, or U.S. Savings Bonds, IRA or KEOGH accounts. These figures make it clear why most black families must borrow from others when financial difficulties occur; they have few resources of their own.

## LIFE EXPECTANCY

A December 1988 report from the National Center for Health Statistics revealed that life expectancy for blacks has declined for two successive years—1985 and 1986—while life expectancy for whites has continued to increase.

Until now, life expectancy has been increasing in the U.S. ever since records were kept. In 1900, the life expectancy was 47.6 for whites and 33 years for other races. By 1984, the numbers had risen to 75.3 for whites, and 69.7 for blacks. The 1985-1986 decline was the first time since 1962 that any race's life expectancy declined for two consecutive years, and the only time in this century when the life expectancy for blacks dropped while that for whites rose. Usually, the rates move in the same direction. For example, life expectancy rates for both races declined from 1979 to 1980 because of the effects of a severe influenza epidemic. Homicide was a chief cause for the drop in black life expectancy. One in 20 black men can expect to die in a homicide, according to Everett Lee, a demographer at the University of Georgia. In 1985 and 1986, there was a 15% increase in homicides among blacks, but only a 5% increase among whites. Some social theorists believe that the increasing numbers of blacks who are poor, and who are involved in drugs or other substance abuses, account for the rise in homicide rates.

Motor vehicle accidents also account for many black deaths. In 1985 and 1986, there was an 8% increase in the black motor vehicle deaths, compared with 4% for whites.

In addition, deaths from Acquired Immune Deficiency Syndrome (AIDS), pneumonia, and tuberculosis have increased disproportionately among blacks in the 1980s. Cancer, diabetes, hypertension, smoking, drug abuse and overeating also contributed to early deaths.

Infant mortality rates for blacks are more than double that of whites; however, that gap has not changed in the past few years and did not contribute to the widening gap of life expectancies in 1985 and 1986.

Suicide rates increased among white males, with 21.5 per

### CHART 18. LIFE EXPECTANCY

**For the first time since 1962 the life expectancy rate for blacks has declined for two consecutive years. In 1977 the life expectancy for blacks was 11 years less than that for whites; by1984 the gap had narrowed to a 5 year differential. In 1984 the life expectancy for blacks was 69.7; in 1985 it slipped to 69.5; and in 1986 it dipped once again to 69.4.**

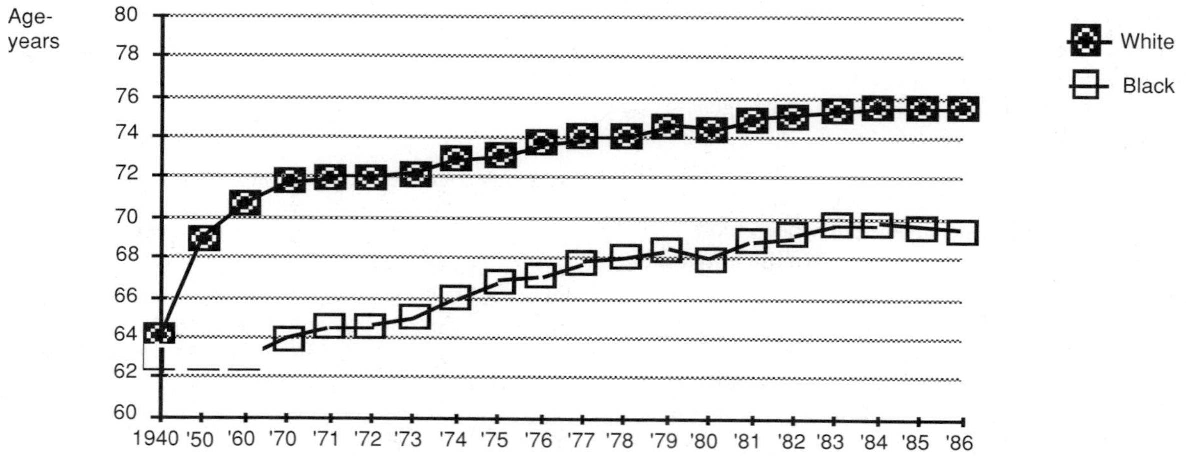

### CHART 19. ILLEGITIMATE BIRTHS

**The illegitimate birth rate for blacks is about 4.5 times greater than that of whites. In 1967 the rate was 6 times greater. The illegitimate birth rate for whites is up almost 100% since 1975. In the same time frame it was up 11% for blacks. Almost 60% of all births to black females are illegitimate.**

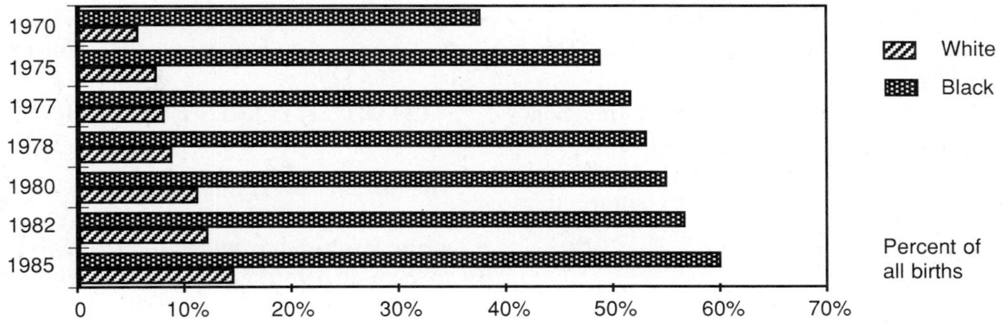


Source:U.S. Bureau of the Census.

100,000 in 1985, and among black males, with 10.8 per 100,000 in 1985. Females commit suicide considerably less often than males. From 1970 to 1985, the black female suicide rate declined from 2.6 to 2.1 per 100,000 population, and the white female rate declined from 7.1 to 5.6. The U.S. Department of Health and Human Services showed that 90% of young male suicide victims are white, and that the suicide rates for males 15-24 years old almost tripled between 1945 and 1985.

### FERTILITY RATES

Of 608,000 black births in 1985, 23% were to teenage mothers, and 60% to unwed mothers. This represents a continuous rise in unwed births from 37.6% in 1970. This factor is especially distressing to both the black community and to the society at large.

In terms of lifetime births expected by wives 18-34 years old, in 1986, 60% of black wives expected to have two or less children. Some 26.2% expected to produce three children, and 13.8% expected to produce four or more. Seventy percent of all women in this age group who had completed one year of college or more expected to have two or less children. The trend continued—married women and women with higher educations, usually expected to produce fewer children.

Infertility was not a major problem for currently married couples in 1982. Fifty-one percent were fertile. Among women aged 15-44, only 13% of these women were infertile. In 36% of the households, one of the spouses had undergone surgery to prevent conception.

### CHART 20. ORIGINS OF ONE-PARENT FAMILY STATUS, BY RACE

**Divorce is the predominant reason for single-parent families among whites; divorce is the second most prevalent reason in black single-parent families. Never having been married is the predominant reason for single-parent families among blacks. Both white and black single-parent families have approximately 21% of spouses absent.**

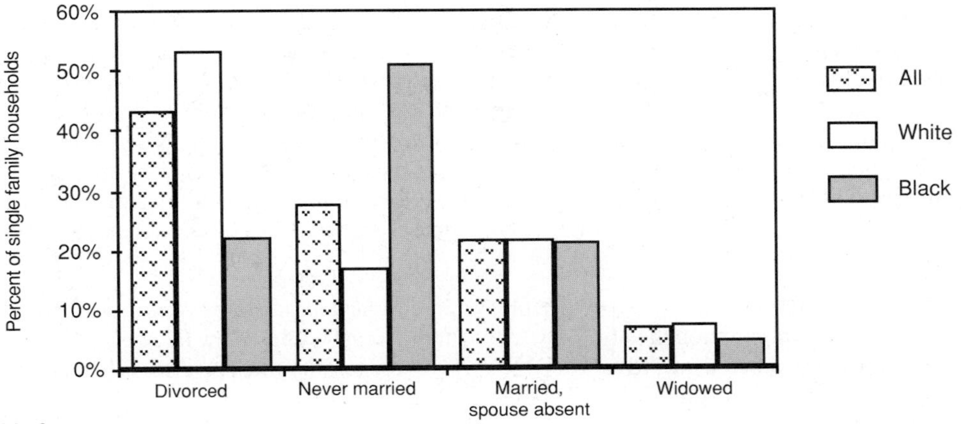


Source: U.S. Bureau of the Census.

## TEENAGE PREGNANCY

Teenage pregnancy is both a national problem and a black problem. In 1985 there were 477,705 births to mothers under 20 years of age. Of these births, 322,826 were to whites, 140,130 to blacks and 14,749 were to women of other groups. With respect to the mother' s marital status, 280,308 were unmarried and 197,397 were married. Unwed pregnancies among teenagers increased by 40% between 1970 and 1985, rising from 30% to 59%. In 1985, 78% of births to teens were first births, but 27% of black teen births were second children. This has caused great consternation in the black community as well as in the larger society.

Joyce Ladner has explained that the causes of teen pregnancy are too complex for simple explanation. The causes range from attempts to find emotional fulfillment, to symbolically achieving "womanhood," to ignorance of contraceptives. Marian Wright Edelman makes it clear that teen pregnancy is a special problem among poor and minority groups who usually have limited opportunities to offer their young people.

There are increased efforts to stem the tide of teenage pregnancy. The Children's Defense Fund has launched a multi-media campaign to enlighten the public, while black sororities, fraternities, churches and civil groups are actively working with youth to reduce pregnancies.

While the traditional and sensible solution to the problem is abstinence from premarital sex, contemporary lifestyles make it unlikely that most or all teenagers will successfully resist temptation. Sex is flaunted before them through television, movies, recorded music, dress styles, books and magazines. Therefore, sexually active teens are being urged to use contraceptive methods. Data show that more than one-half of white teens used contraception at first intercourse, but such precautions were taken by only a third of black teens. School-based comprehensive health clinics have proven effective in reducing birthrates and school dropout rates among teen mothers; however, such clinics have not been instituted without controversy. The sexual education of children is a hotly contested issue, with many parents opposing "value-free" instruction on such an important topic, while others feel that more education is crucial to avoiding sexually transmitted diseases and pregnancy.

### CHART 21. PERCENT OF FAMILIES HEADED BY FEMALES

**The number of families headed by women for all racial groups has been increasing dramatically. The rate for white women has increased from about 10% in 1974 to 26% in 1986. For black women the increase was from 40.2% in 1980 to 44% in 1986.**

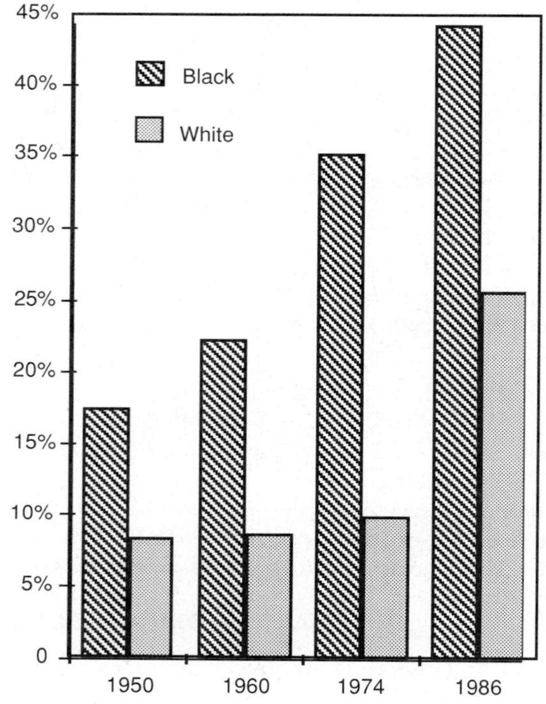


## CHILD SUPPORT

Unmarried teenage mothers are most likely to receive payments from Aid to Families with Dependent Children (AFDC) programs. Since black teen mothers are less likely than their white counterparts to be married, they therefore are proportionately more likely to receive AFDC funds. AFDC is the first recourse of unmarried women or married women with the husband absent to receive assistance money for their children's maintenance if no other funds are available. The second recourse for such women is the courts where the father is ordered by the court to pay child support. Court awarded child support is not only awarded to poor women but has always been a main support system for divorced or separated women with children. Court awarded child support has not been used extensively by the poor or unmarried until recently with the enactment of the Family Support Act of 1988, which gives federal, state and municipal agencies the ability to seek out absent fathers in order to force them to meet their legal obligations.

In 1985, there were about 2,310,000 black women eligible for child support from absent fathers although only 36.3% of these women received a court ordered award, and of the 839,000 women receiving a court award only 72% (473,000) actually received payment. Conversely 71% of white women in similar circumstance were awarded child support. The major reason for the low rate of court awarded child support is that paternity must be established before an award can be made.

The mean money income of black women who received

payments was $13,297, while mean child support was $1,754. Black women who did not receive child support payments had a mean monetary income of $10,477. Women who were not awarded payments had mean money income of $6,969—well below the poverty level.

There were 1,190,000 black women with incomes below the poverty level in 1985. Of that number, court ordered child support payments were awarded to 322,000 women, of whom only 54% or 174,000 actually received any funds. Their mean income award for child support was $1,085. About 868,000 of these poor women were not awarded payments. However, the data does not make it clear as to why so many eligible women are losing out on court awarded child support.

All of the above figures are presented here to illustrate the financial plight of children in families headed by single mothers. Since financial income is essential to providing decent housing, nutritious food, health care, and quality of life opportunities, clearly these mothers are having enormous problems caring adequately for their children.

Working mothers in metropolitan areas are having increasing problems providing housing for their families. In fact, the "working homeless" population is on the rise. Single mothers who's earned income is about $13,000-a-year, who work every day, cannot afford contemporary rents and are forced out of shared housing with extended family members because of restrictions on the number of occupants per unit. These families often end up in shelters with their children.

The female headed family is increasing dramatically, more than 50% of black families with children are headed by women and a similar trend is now emerging among white families. The majority of these families are poor or are in abject poverty. A part of the problem is related to women's mean earnings being far less than that of men, so fairness for women in terms of compensation for work would assist many families headed by women. This recycling of poverty portends an increase in the social ills that are known to accompany the poor and underprivileged of any race.

### Child Support Enforcement Program (CSE)

The Child Support Enforcement Program (CSE) seeks to ensure the collection of funds from an absent parent to support their children. In most cases, the absent parent is the father. The CSE program was established in 1975 as Part D of Title IV of the Social Security Act. It was amended in 1984, with a key provision that allowed wages to be withheld from salaries of parents who were not giving their court-ordered support.

As a result of the CSE program, some percentage of AFDC payments may be recovered through child support collections. In 1987, these recovery payments ranged from a high of 25.8% in Indiana to only 2.7% in Puerto Rico.

Each year since 1983 has shown an increase in recovery payments for AFDC and non-AFDC collections. Further information is available in the Child Support Enforcement Twelfth Annual Report to Congress for the period ending September 30, 1987, Volume I, U.S. Department of Health and Human Services, Office of Child Support Enforcement.

### Aid to Families with Dependent Children (AFDC)

In 1986 black families constituted about 41% of all AFDC families. About 40% were white, 14% were Hispanic, 2% were Asian and 1% were Native American, and 1% were of unknown race. Three of every five AFDC families in 1986 were members of minority races or ethnic groups.

While the number of recipient children paralleled those of families, but were not identical. White children constituted

**CHART 22. AFDC RECIPIENT CHILDREN BY AGE AND RACE: 1985-1986**

**About 55% of Aid to Families With Dependent Children goes to assist needy children who are below the age of 8. Approximately 42% of the recipients were black, 35% were white and 15% were Hispanic.**

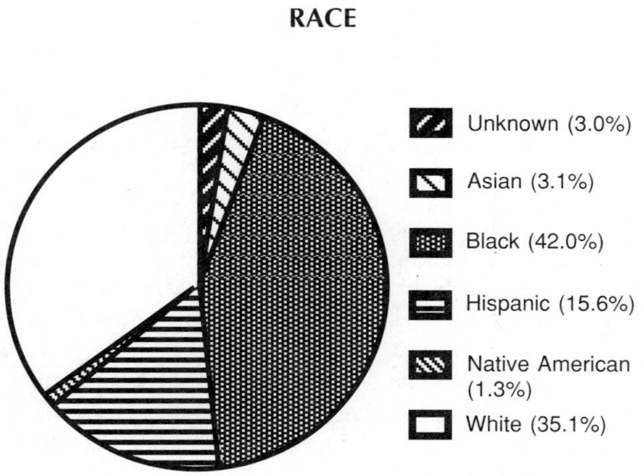


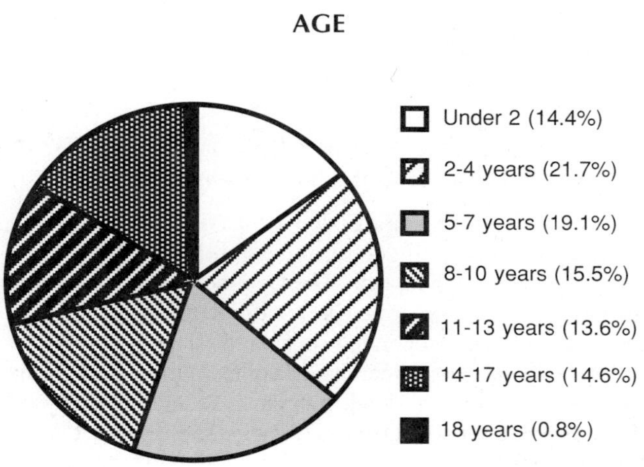

approximately 35% of recipients, black children about 42%. Hispanic children made up about 16%; Asian children, 3%; Native American children, 1.3%. The race of 3% was unknown.

In 1986, the average number of persons in an AFDC family increased slightly to 3.0 persons, with the average number of children per family being 2.0. Welfare families, therefore, are not as large as generally perceived.

Most AFDC families had been on the rolls fewer than three years in 1986. The median length of time since the most recent opening of the case was twenty-seven months. However, the number of families who had been on the rolls for five or more years increased to 26% in 1985, up from 23.5% in 1983.

The median age of AFDC children was seven years and one month in 1986, the same as in 1985. Only 11% were 15 years or more; 43% of children were under six years old in 1986.

The primary reason given for AFDC needs was that the children's parents had never married. This reason applied to 49% of recipient children in 1986. Children of separated or divorced parents declined to 36%. Children of deceased or incapacitated persons remained unchanged at about 2% and 3%, respectively.

Parents or stepparents constituted nearly all of the AFDC adult recipients—96%—while 2% were grandparents. Most of these adults were female; men accounted for only about 11% of the adult recipients in 1986.

The median age of these adults was 28.6 for women and 33.5 for men. About 7% of the mothers were teenagers, most of which were 18 or 19 years old. Thus, the AFDC rolls are not primarily populated by teenage mothers, as is the popular perception. About 13% of AFDC women were more than 40 years.

It is startling to see that in 59.7% of cases, the years of completed education by AFDC adult recipients is unknown.. Of the cases where the level of education is known, the average years were 10.8 in 1986. Thus, it appears that high school completion would assist AFDC adult recipients in their capacity for employment—a chronic problem among AFDC adults. Only 9% of men and 6% of women were employed in 1986.

*The numbers of black farmers have been steadily declining. By 1987 less than 1% of the black population resided on farms.*

An average AFDC family of one adult and two children received $382 a month, in addition to food stamps and Medicaid. The AFDC money, however, was the only cash income available to the family.

## FARM POPULATION

Black and other races farm population in 1970 was 938,000 or 9.7% of the entire farm population. By 1986, the minority numbers had dropped to 145,000 persons or 2.8%.

In 1982, the U.S. Commission on Civil Rights issued a comprehensive report that examined problems confronting black farmers. This report, "The Decline of Black Farming in America," also examined the condition that contributed to the loss of black-operated farmland. These conditions included racial discrimination, lack of institutional economic support, commercial lending practices, commodity and income supports, and tax structures geared to benefit large farm operations. The Commission acknowledged that all family farmers suffered the threat of displacement from their land, but that the black loss was two-and-a-half times the white loss rate. Their research found that almost 94% of the farms operated by blacks had been lost since 1920, and they predicted that there would be fewer than 10,000 black farmers in the U.S. by 1990.

Since the Commission's report was published, land values have escalated, and land speculators and developers have been successful in acquiring more black-owned land. This loss is irreversible.

# HEALTH

## Infant Mortality Rates/Maternal Death Rates

The black infant mortality rate has fallen dramatically from 44.3 per thousand live births in 1960 to 18.2 in 1985. Nonetheless, it remains about twice as high as the white rate of 9.3 in 1985. In like manner, the maternal death rate has fallen. In 1960, there were 103.6 maternal deaths per 100,000 live births among blacks, contrasted with 26.0 among whites. By 1985, the corresponding figures had dropped to 20.4 among blacks and 5.2 among whites—a great improvement due to improved prenatal care. Nonetheless, black women suffered four times as many maternal deaths as whites in 1985. Also, it remains true that black infant mortality rates in the U.S. strongly resemble those of Third World countries where preventive measures are much less available. In 1984, sixteen countries had better infant mortality rates than the United States, and all twenty-four countries listed had better rates than did blacks in the United States. These countries included Singapore and Cuba, which contain large populations of people of color and which are not thought of as being among the most affluent nations in the world.*

## Health Insurance

In 1985, 80.7% of black persons were covered by private or government health insurance; 56% of them by private carriers and 22% by Medicaid. Nineteen percent of black persons were not covered by health insurance in 1985. This compares with 12% of white persons not covered and 27% of Hispanics not covered. The extremely high costs of preventive health care and curative medicine indicate that every citizen needs to be covered by some kind of health insurance.

## Medicaid

In 1985, 22% of the black population, compared with 6.0% of the white population, was covered by Medicaid, thus making it possible for their families to receive health care. In numbers, this represents 6,349,999 blacks compared with 12,134,000 whites. Of these blacks, 54% had incomes below the poverty level, compared with 34% of whites. Nine percent of blacks and 3% of whites were poor, but had incomes above the poverty level.

## Immunizations

In 1985, fewer black than white, and fewer than half of black children aged 1-4 years old had been immunized against the childhood diseases of diphtheria, tetanus, polio, measles, rubella, and mumps. Although the proportions of blacks immunized against these diseases has improved, rising above 50% in the 5-14 year old group, still fewer proportions of blacks than whites have been immunized and sizeable proportions of blacks remain susceptible to these diseases because they have not been inoculated. Such an affluent society as this should guarantee every child immunization against these and any other preventable childhood diseases.

## AIDS

AIDS, the contemporary social plague, acutely concerns all American people. In 1987, 65% of AIDS victims were white, 23% blacks, and 12% Hispanic. From 1981-1987, a total of 37,481 AIDS cases had been reported. Of that number, most victims were male (37,741; 2,740 female).

## CHART 23. AIDS

**The number of AIDS cases per 1 million of the population is highest among blacks and other minorities. The reasons for such disproportionate numbers in minorities are unknown or speculative.**

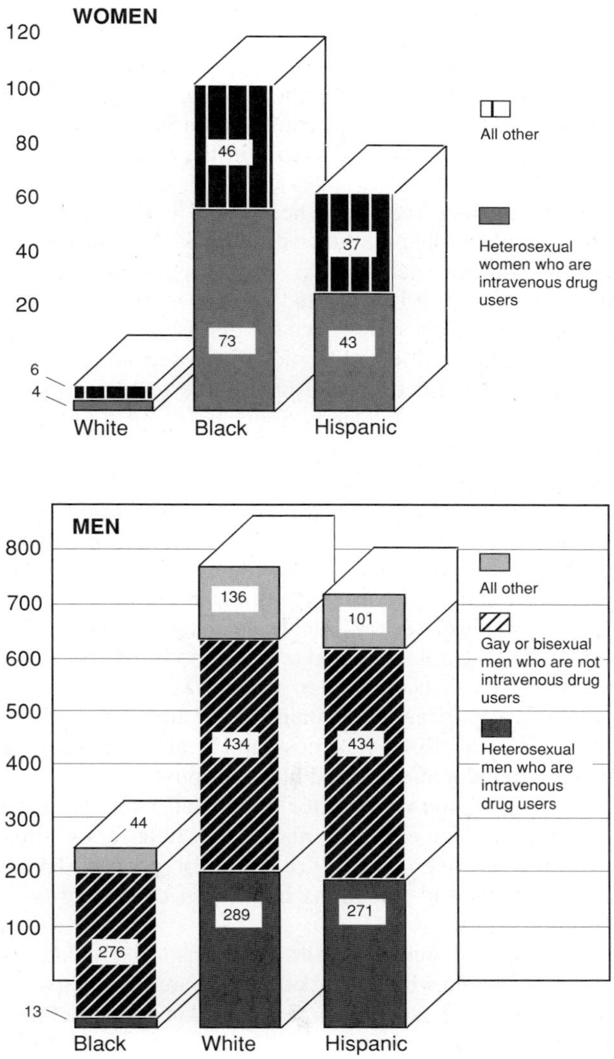


*National Center for Health Statistics: Health, United States, 1987. DHHS Pub. No. (PHS) 88-1232 Public Health Service. Wahsington. U. S. Government Printing Office, Mar. 1988. Table 19, P. 54.

There were 22,963 whites affected, 9,243 blacks, 4,908 Hispanics, and 367 "others." At this time we have no precise data on how many children have been affected because they were born to a mother or father with AIDS, or how many wives or husbands were infected by their spouses, thereby multiplying a personal problem into a family problem. We know that AIDS is spread via blood transfusions, though most common reasons are homosexual or heterosexual intercourse (especially anal intercourse), and use of infected needles for drug injection.

## Cancer

Five year relative survival rates for cancer in all body sites have been relatively constant in the white and black populations from 1974-1983. Fifty percent of whites and 38% of blacks, overall, survive at least five years after cancer has been diagnosed. Improvements are noted in survival rates of black and white men affected with prostrate cancer. Improvements are noted in survival rates for cancer of the bladder, as well.

## Sickle Cell Anemia

Sickle Cell Disease is an inherited affliction in which there is a defect in the hemoglobin. The presence of this defective or abnormal hemoglobin can cause distortion (sickling) of the red blood cells and a decrease in the number of these corpuscles.

Sickled red blood cells have been found in one of every 12 American blacks, but the active disease, SCA, occurs about once in 600 American blacks and once in every 1,200 American whites. It is estimated that about 50,000 persons in the United States suffer from the disease.

Other races are affected by sickle cell anemia. The trait and the anemia affect people from Southern India, Greece, Italy, Syria, Caribbean Islands, South and Central America, Turkey, and other countries.

The disease occurs as a result of the mating of two people, each of whom carries the gene for the sickling trait. The first symptoms usually appear in their child at about 6 months of age. Sickle cell anemia is diagnosed through a study of the blood of the patient microscopically and electrophoretically. This is a chronic disease and medical management is directed both toward the quiescent and active periods (crises) of the malady. "Crisis" occurs when the disease is active, and symptoms usually are fever, pain, loss of appetite, paleness of the skin, generalized weakness, and sometimes a striking decrease in the number of red blood corpuscles.

There is no known cure for sickle cell anemia. Good medical and home care may make it possible for children with the disease to lead reasonably normal lives. Complications and infections have been controlled with antibiotic drugs.

The source of sickle cell disease seems to be malarious countries. People with sickle cell disease are almost always immune to malaria, so it seems that the sickle cell is a defense mechanism against malaria.

Black people who intend to have children are advised to undergo blood tests to determine whether they are carriers of the sickle cell gene. Two such carriers should agree not to produce children, since half of the children will have the trait and one in four the anemia. There is only one chance in four that the child will be free of the disease.

Some jurisdictions, Washington, D.C., for example, have enacted laws mandating that newborns be screened for sickle cell anemia, along with other diseases. Newborns found to be afflicted can be cared for from birth, as a result of such legislation.

For further information see *The Sickle Cell Story* Published by the Howard University Center for Sickle Cell Disease, Washington, D.C. 20059.

## Alcohol, Marihuana, Cocaine

Addiction to, or heavy usage of, the above substances is a serious social problem in contemporary U.S. In 1985, 47.6 percent of blacks, 50.5 percent of Hispanics, and 61.8 percent of whites were alcohol users, with the heaviest usage in the Northeast and West. Considerably smaller proportions of each population used marihuana—13.2 percent of blacks, 7.4 percent of Hispanics, and 9.1 percent of whites. The heaviest usage was evident in the West and Northeast. Smaller still were percentages of current users of cocaine, 3.2 percent of blacks, 2.4 percent of Hispanics, and 3.0 percent of whites. Usage remained heaviest in the West and Northeast. The South has proportionately fewer users of alcohol, marihuana, and/or cocaine. While these percentages seem small, they represent large numbers of people. If the figures are accurate, and they may not be because of the difficulty in getting such statistics, it suggests that only small proportions of our population are creating social problems well out of proportion to their numbers, which appears somewhat unlikely. So much of street crime is attributed to drug sales and/or usage that it is difficult to accept the only available data as accurate.

## Death and Illness Caused by Unemployment

The high correlation between unemployment and indicators of stress has a more meaningful impact when translated into human terms. For example, studies have indicated that a 1% rise in unemployment will increase stroke, heart, and kidney disease deaths. How many people will actually be affected?

In 1970 unemployment rose 1.4% to 4.9%. This 1.4% increase has been sustained since that time. A 1% sustained rise in unemployment increases CVR disease deaths by a total comparable to 1.9% of all such deaths in the fifth year thereafter. The 1.4% rise in unemployment during 1970 increased total CVR disease deaths through 1975 by 2.7% (1.9% times 1.4). There were 979,180 CVR disease deaths in 1975. Therefore, 2.7%, or 26,440 CVR deaths, are directly attributable to the rise in unemployment during 1970.

In fact, the 1.4% rise in unemployment during 1970 is directly responsible for some 51,570 total deaths, including 1,740 additional homicides, 1,540 additional suicides, and

5,520 additional mental hospitalizations. These are not major portions of the total number of deaths, homicides, suicides, and mental hospitalizations which occurred during 1970 through 1975, but unlike most other factors which contributed to these statistics, rising unemployment can be readily avoided.

It should be noted that the further increases in unemployment since 1970 are now having an additional impact on individuals and society—an impact which is not in any fashion included in statistics. And this more recent rise in unemployment has been striking. From 1970 to 1976, almost 4 million additional men and women have been added to jobless rolls. By 1980 unemployment results in deaths and institutional admissions were almost three times larger than previously documented.

The low relative size of changes in these stress indicators due to unemployment fluctuations is not surprising. A bewildering variety of factors influence the mental and physical state of contemporary society—many of which are far more influential than jobless status alone. At the same time, the studies reveal that unemployment has a strikingly potent impact on society. Even a 1% increase in unemployment, for example, creates a legacy of stress, aggression, and illness affecting society long into the future. Studies reveal that it has a multiplier effect far exceeding the relative size of the unemployment rise.

The human tragedy alone of unemployment revealed is shocking—shocking enough to demand a persistent, priority effort by Washington policy planners to reduce unemployment and to keep it low, as well. At the same time, we can go further and attach specific monetary values to the human toll.

In instances of CVR disease, cirrhosis, suicide, homicide, and total mortality, appropriate dollar values include foregone incomes, adjusted for age and sex characteristics. In effect, illness and deaths attributed to unemployment reduce our nation's resources—our ability to produce goods and services. One good measure of this loss is the foregone income of deceased or ill workers. Direct medical costs for unemployment-related care should be included as well.

## HOUSING

### The Fair Housing Act

The Fair Housing legislation of 1968 has been weakly and unevenly enforced in the country and it has provided few remedies for those who have experienced discrimination. In 1988, the Fair Housing Law was amended to strengthen the enforcement capabilities of the previous 1968 legislation. Realtors had maintained their traditional steering practices; lending institutions and insurance agencies had continued their "red-lining" policies. These practices and others have determined to a very large extent where blacks lived and it was obvious that the Fair Housing Act of 1968 had not provided the relief anticipated. Housing choices continued to be closely related to skin color. High interest rates, inflated costs for dwellings, and economic adversity compounded the problem. For blacks who have below-average incomes, purchase of a home was almost impossible in the 1980s. Meanwhile, rental options declined in major cities like Washington, D.C., where apartments, rapidly converted to condominiums, sold at prices far beyond the means of all but the most affluent. The process called "gentrification," the return of whites to central cities, was under way in most major cities in 1982 and blacks were being pushed into the close-in deteriorating suburbs as a result. The Federal Fair Housing Law amendment of 1988 was designed to prohibit discrimination in the sale, rental or occupancy in housing and as well to prohibit discriminatory practices in real estate brokers' organizations multiple listing services, blockbusting and advertising.

### Housing Conditions

In 1985 (this was the latest governmental data available as of 1989 ) there were 88,425,000 occupied housing units in the United States. Of these, 63 percent were owner occupied, and 37 percent were occupied by renters (58,145,000 owners and 32,280,000 renters). Only 5,754,000, 7 percent, of these homes were of new construction, i.e., erected within the last four years. Mobile homes numbered 4,754,000 of the total, or 5 percent.

Severe physical problems were evident in 1,589,000 units (about 2 percent) and moderate physical problems were identifiable in 5,814,000 housing units (about 7 percent).

In terms of household characteristics 18,896,000 units, 21 percent, were occupied by the elderly (aged 65 and over); nineteen percent, 16,830,000, moved in the past year; and 14 percent, 12,550,000, were below the poverty level.

Black households numbered 9,903,000 of the total number of occupied units, or 11 percent. Hispanic households were 5,078,000, almost six percent of the total. More renters than home owners existed in both of these populations, the reverse of the majority group situation where more whites own than rent their dwelling places.

With respect to new construction (within the last four years) there were 441,000 black and 249,000 Hispanic new dwellings, 4 percent and 5 percent respectively—compared with 7 percent in the white population. Three percent each of blacks and Hispanics occupied mobile homes, compared with 5 percent of the white population.

Severe physical problems were evident in 540,000 black housing units (5 percent) and in 210,000 Hispanic units (4 percent), compared with only 2 percent of white. Moderate physical problems were identifiable in 1,667,000 black units (17 percent) and in 691,000 Hispanic housing units (14 percent), but only 7 percent of white dwellings.

Black elderly (65 years old and above) comprised 1,715,000 households (17 percent), compared with 21 percent of whites. On average blacks do not live as long as do whites. Some 2,034,000 (21 percent) of black households had moved in the past year—compared with 19 percent of white—and 3,336,000 black households were below the poverty level (34 percent) compared with 14 percent of white households. Blacks more than doubled the percentage of whites below the poverty level.

Hispanic elderly (65+) comprised 599,000 (12 percent). Twenty-five percent (1,283,000) had moved in the past year, and 1,341,000 (26 percent) were below the poverty level. In general, the Hispanic population is younger than the white population. The data show that Hispanics had moved more than blacks or whites, and that fewer of them fell below the poverty level than did blacks, but more of them were poor than were white.

Data show that blacks live in housing with the greatest deficiencies, that Hispanics are second worst in status, and that whites occupy housing with fewest proportions of deficiencies. Blacks and Hispanics had three or more times as many rat signs in the last three months as did whites, two to three times as many holes in floors, open cracks or holes in the interior, interior broken plaster or peeling paint, or exposed wiring. Twice as many blacks as whites have rooms without electrical outlets, and more Hispanics than whites face this problem.

The above described pattern generally holds with respect to overall condition of structures. Fewer blacks and Hispanics live in above-average to the best housing in terms of housing quality. More Hispanics than blacks, and more blacks than white, live in below average to worst quality structures.

## Housing Trends

Proportions of home ownership did increase among blacks from 1960 to 1975, though not markedly. In 1984, the black home ownership rate was 43.8%. In 1975, the black home ownership rate was 44%, compared with 42% in 1970 and 38% in 1960. These statistics tell only part of the tale; housing units occupied by blacks, whether as owners or tenants, were generally more overcrowded than those occupied by whites, this being especially true in the South. Further, more housing units occupied by blacks lack some or all plumbing facilities. This was as true in the 1980s as in the 1960s, particularly in the South.

Even in the more modern planned communities middle-class blacks face discrimination and racial epithets. These are mostly professional, well-educated and prosperous blacks who manifest all the attributes of cultivation and civility. In Columbia and Howard County, Maryland, for example racial, religious, and ethnic incidents increased in 1988. Columbia did not exist until the late 1960s, and began with a liberal bent which seems to be declining. County officials seem reluctant to address the concerns of blacks, apart from the workings of the county Office of Human Rights. Blacks, whites, Koreans, Chinese, and Jews are meeting to examine this county-wide problem, although blacks bear the brunt of the rising level of conflict. Planned communities, like their older counterparts, are showing signs of the "strains of age and change."

The legacy of the Reagan administration, regarding public housing, is long waiting lists of people who need housing, but about 70,000 units sitting empty because they are rundown and need renovation. Public housing is "the nation's greatest low-income resource," according to a National Housing Task Force Report. The Reagan administration cut housing programs by more than 70 percent during its eight years in office. The Bush administration began by asking for funding to aid the homeless and for tax incentives for urban enterprise zones, but President Bush did not ask for money for new public housing construction in his 1990 budget message. He did propose $1 billion for rehabilitation, a sharp drop by the already inadequate authorization of $1.6 billion.

Waiting lists are so long that more than 2/3 of all American cities have closed their lists to new applicants although the number of homeless and poorly housed continues to grow.

A National Housing Task Force Report proposes a "housing opportunities program" for development, renovation and conservation of low-income housing that would "induce substantial new funds and resources from state and local governments and the private sector.

### CHART 24. FAMILY HOME OWNERSHIP GAP

**About 67% of whites own their own home. For blacks the percent owning their own homes is about 43.5%, and for Hispanics it is about 39.6%. Discrimination in housing as well as economics plays a role in the disparity.**

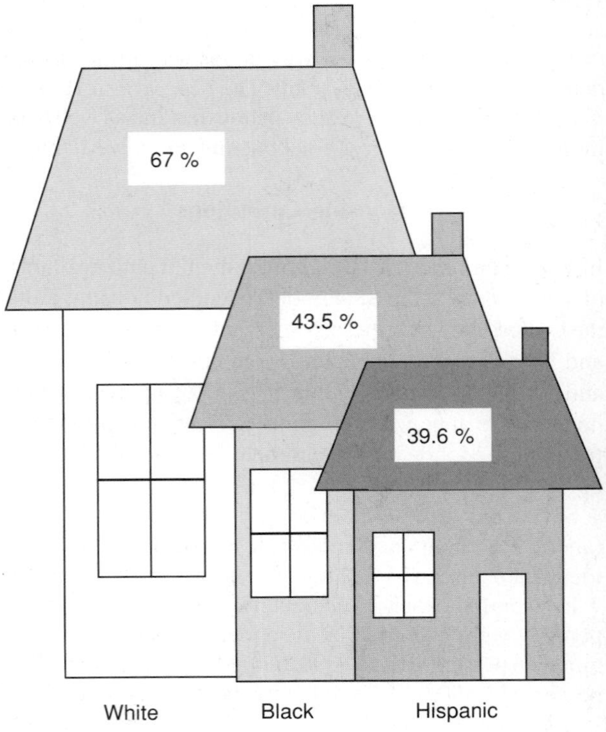

*Large portions of black families in central cities live in tenements like these.*

An analysis by University of Chicago researchers using 1980 Census data revealed that blacks are the only major ethnic minority in the U.S. that cannot find housing in well-integrated neighborhoods after receiving college degrees and attaining high incomes. Hispanic and Asian Americans, conversely, do find homes in well-integrated areas once they reach high education and income levels.

Nancy Denton and Douglas Massey, researchers, found that "no matter what their educational or occupational achievements and whatever their incomes, blacks are exposed to higher crime rates, less effective educational systems, higher mortality risks, more dilapidated surroundings and a poorer socioeconomic environment than white, simply because of the persistence of strong barriers to residential integration." Thus, black housing segregation remains in spite of high education and income.

Middle and high income blacks who have sought to join Holiday Spa health clubs have experienced discrimination. The Justice Department has found that this health club chain violated the civil rights of black applicants by seeking to discourage them from joining and by withholding from them more favorable financial terms offered to white applicants. Thus, income and education fail to guarantee blacks access to mainstream institutional arrangements that are taken for granted by whites in similar status.

In his article, "To Make Wrong Right: The Necessary and Proper Aspirations of Fair Housing," appearing in The State of Black America 1989, John 0. Calmore calls housing "the last major frontier in civil rights." He holds that in civil rights housing is the area in which progress has been slowest and the possibility of genuine change most remote. He describes the 1980s as the decade of radical fair housing retreat and says the 1990s will likely present the last chance for "fair housing."

Calmore says the housing crisis for blacks is reflected in terms of "unaffordability, unavailability, overcrowding, poor quality, forced displacement, and inequality." He explains that we must redirect efforts to improve life for poor blacks so that even if they must live under conditions of segregated housing it will not be deficient housing.

Calmore acknowledges that some suburban middle-class blacks have advanced in status and housing conditions/options, but still within relatively segregated areas. Current conditions were projected by the Kerner Commission's Report of the National Advisory Commission on Civil Disorders in 1968. Conditions are so bad now that the society has "moved very near to a point of division that is beyond uniting." Said the Kerner report, " Spatial equality must be provided by white Americans to right the historic wrong that has so long endured for black Americans." In effect, it was a demand to redress past and present wrongs.

### The Suburbs

Census data show that between 1970 and 1977 the number of blacks living in the suburbs increased approximately 34%. This city-to-suburb move included middle-income blacks who actively sought suburban residence as well as low-income blacks being displaced by "gentrification" in cities. The suburbs are, of course, predominantly white. Consequently, blacks who moved to the suburbs from 1974 to 1977 went into predominantly white neighborhoods, gradually integrating them.

A strong relationship was discernible between socioeconomic status of the mover and the suburb chosen. The higher-educated, higher-income blacks were more likely to move into predominantly white neighborhoods. Also, home ownership rates for recent black movers were greatest in white neighborhoods.

However, blacks were more likely than whites to be located at the lower end of the neighborhood's socioeconomic scale. In like manner, fewer blacks were to be found in very high-income tracts or tracts of high occupational status.

In 1982, blacks were not a significant force in the suburbs, since the actual number of blacks moving from central cities to suburbs is very small.

White flight in the suburbs has had the effect of creating and reinforcing *de facto* segregation in housing and schools in some suburban areas. Whites are moving from one suburban area to more affluent areas farther from the city, or at least from one suburban area to another. Prince Georges and Montgomery counties, in Maryland, are examples of suburban areas that have increasing pockets of *de facto* segregation in housing and public schools.

## BUDGET CUTS AND THE FAMILY—THE EIGHTIES

In 1981 and 1982, prospects for black families were dimmed by a series of budget cuts and proposed cuts of programs that over the years have provided poor families the wherewithal to obtain food, housing, medical care, and other essential products and services.

Though the administration promised to provide a "safety net" for the "truly needy" and that it would attack "weak claims rather than weak clients," millions of poor families have suffered. A substantial portion of these families have been black.

The services were affected two ways: through direct budget cuts and through allocation of much of the remaining funds via "block grants," which have weak provisions for the targeting, priorities, and accountability of appropriations.

Following are some of the cuts:

### Medicaid

One billion dollars has been cut from fiscal 1982 and a $2.1 billion cut proposed for fiscal 1983. Also, procedural cuts increase reductions about $900 billion further. Total reduction: $4 billion, or nearly 20%.

### Aid to Families with Dependent Children

For the 1982 budget $1 billion was cut from the original $7 billion fiscal 1981 budget. A further cut of $1.2 billion took place in 1983. Proposals aim to eliminate many programs within AFDC, such as emergency assistance.

### Food Stamps

$2.35 billion was cut from 1982, and $7 billion is projected in cuts for the years 1982-1984. The Children's Defense Fund estimates 1 million people would become completely ineligible for stamps and that 80% of the savings from cuts would come from funds of people below the poverty line. Placing food stamps on block grants is likely to result in further reductions. In the past, many local governmental jurisdictions with the authority to reject fully paid food stamp programs have done so. (The government program calls for a swap; the federal government to take over Medicaid, and the states AFDC and food stamps.)

### Health Services

In 1982, budget cuts for a series of successful health programs were made and more than 25% of such programs were seriously cut. Among these were: Community Health Centers, Migrant Health Centers, Family Planning, and several food, nutritional, and counseling programs for families and children. Forty community health centers had to close in 1981. The Reagan Administration proposed to abolish all these programs and replace them with block grants. In some cases, Congress rejected the government's requests, as with the Women's, Infant's, and Children's supplemental food plan, but funds for 1982 were cut 10% and the government plans a 35% reduction for 1983, with monies to be distributed through block grants.

Among other health services cut:

- School breakfast program, cut 20%, eliminating 400,00 children, 70% poor or near poor.

### CHART 25. AID TO FAMILIES WITH DEPENDENT CHILDREN (AFDC)

**Most public assistance goes to aid children. The average monthly AFDC stipend is $82.**

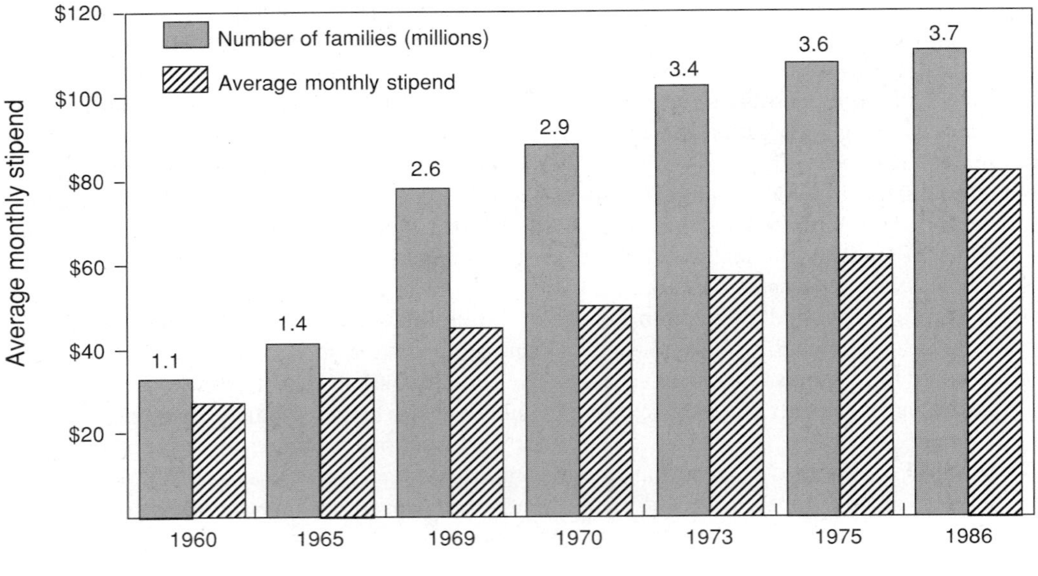

- School lunch, cut 30%, amounting to $1 billion.
- Child Care Food Program, also cut 30%, $130 million.
- Summer Food Program, cut 50%, with churches and religious organizations prohibited from participating.
- Special Milk Program, cut 80%.
- Title XX Day Care Services.

For 1983, further cuts were made for all but the school lunch program.

The Head Start Program survived relatively well but also was cut. The Reagan Administration at first accepted an increase proposed by Carter, from $820 million to $950 million, then cut back to $836 million. In 1983, proposals called for a $780 million appropriation, under block grants.

### Low-Income Energy Assistance

Appropriations were keyed at levels substantially below the Conference Report for the Windfall Profits Tax. As a result, appropriations in 1982 were off 40%, to $1.85 billion, and off 57% in 1982, to $1.75 billion.

## ASSESSMENT

Approximately one-third of black families are prospering in contemporary society. In general, these are married couples who are highly educated and who have benefited from the abolition of legal barriers to occupational access and housing availability. In most of these families there are two fully employed earners working year round. Many of them are second or third generation, even fourth generation college graduates who are beneficiaries of a heritage of education, motivation, and hard work. They continue to face attitude related barriers in many employment sectors as they seek to move up corporate or governmental hierarchies.

Another one-third of black families are holding themselves together and providing support systems for their young despite the obstacles they encounter. These are the hard-working families that have faced layoffs or termination as jobs have moved from cities to suburbs and out of the country. These are the men who once counted on employment in the automobile factories in Detroit, the steel mills in Gary and Pittsburgh, the tire and rubber factories in Youngstown, Ohio, and so on. Displacement and other such factors have made their economic status tenuous, but they struggle on to provide for themselves, their children, and grandchildren. The extended or augmented family structure is visible in many of these homes.

The final third are the families referred to as "underclass," or sometimes lower class, and they are filled with children. This group includes the poorest of the poor. A new Census Bureau report, released late in August 1988, states that in 1987 the poverty rate among blacks rose 2 percentage points to 33.1 percent, while 10.5 percent of white Americans lived in poverty, half a percentage point less than in 1986. This includes money income only. The poverty rate for children under 18 was 20 percent, and for female-headed households with no spouse present, 34.3 percent.

Andrew Billingsley's twelve major problems areas, listed earlier in this section which help define family crisis, need resolution if many black families are not to fall further and further behind. These are the families who need help because it is impossible for them alone to solve the structural and attitude related problems that are responsible for the condition. The society has not made a concerted effort to address and solve the structural problems such as unemployment, poverty, inadequate housing, and poor health care since President Lyndon Johnson's "War On Poverty" in the 60s.

Lisbeth B. Schorr urges the nation to stop recycling poverty. Her research, studying the results of 20 years of social programs that intervened positively in children's lives, provides evidence that there are social programs that work, and that we know why and how they work. She found: (1) early interventions are more effective and more economical than later interventions. For example, many Head Start programs have been successful; school based health clinics have reduced the rate of teenage child-bearing in St. Paul and in Baltimore; family support programs have reduced child abuse, neglect, and welfare dependence in New Haven, Elmira, and Washington State. (2) There were many common attributes in the programs with the greatest successes in reaching the most disadvantaged children and families; at bottom they provided intensive help in every way possible to these families. (3) Quick fixes and cheap short-cuts cannot meet the need. (4) Middle class models don't work for everyone. (5) Long-standing bureaucratic traditions must be changed if successful programs are to reach larger numbers of children.

Black families have been increasing their responsibility and involvement in local efforts to change their communities. It is evident that friendship networks have supplemented or supplanted the missing kinship networks, which were support systems in previous generations. Unrelated by blood ties, these young families are helping each other with baby-sitting, peer group relationships, and so on. They share time and tasks as their situations dictate. Because they moved away from their extended families as they sought employment opportunities, these young black adults have formed a friendship network substitute. Much community effort is being targeted toward teenage girls in an effort to reduce pregnancy rates. The Children's Defense Fund and other concerned groups have recommended that more efforts be exerted on teaching teenage boys sexual responsibility and alternative routes to manhood for those young men who find it through siring babies.

## SELECTED FACTS ON THE BLACK FAMILY

**Fact 1**

In 1986, there were 9,797,000 black households, with 6,921,000 being family households, 70.6 percent of the total.

**Fact 2**

Only 37.6 percent of these family households, 3,680,000, were married couples, visibly down from the 53.3 percent in 1970.

**Fact 3**

It is not possible to match every black female of marriageable age with a same-race partner in a lifetime monogamous marriage because there are more black women alive than men.

**Fact 4**

Black females will outnumber black males by 1,469,000 in 1989, by 1,478,000 in 1990, and by 1,555,000 in the year 2000. This excess of adult females over males has existed in the black population ever since 1840.

**Fact 5**

Outmarriage further reduces the number of black men available to black women for marriage. In 1987, there were 67,000 more outmarriages of black men to white women than of white men to black women, and 25,000 more outmarriages of black men to "other" ethnic or racial females than of "other" males to black women.

**Fact 6**

Female black householders accounted for 29.3 percent of black households in 1986, compared with 21.8 percent in 1970

**Fact 7**

In 1986 black male heads of households were 368,000, 3.8 percent of the total, compared with 2.9 percent in 1970.

**Fact 8**

The numbers and percentages of black families headed by women continue to grow. This is because of the shortage of black men, separation and divorce rates, early death of black men, and rate of out-of-wedlock parenthood.

**Fact 9**

Black households in 1986 were larger than households in general—2.90:2.67, but smaller than the 3.43 person Hispanic household.

**Fact 10**

Black households were largest in the South, followed by those in the Midwest, Northeast, and the West.

**Fact 11**

81.7 percent of black persons 15 years old and over lived in families of some kind in 1986, compared with 82.6 percent of white families.

**Fact 12**

The clear difference in family arrangements is that more whites than blacks lived in nuclear arrangements with spouses, and more blacks than whites lived with other relatives.

**Fact 13**

The extended family arrangement among blacks and other people of color is considered to be both a cultural and economic adaptation.

**Fact 14**

Married couple black families were smaller in size, 3.55 persons, in 1986 than in 1970, 4.13 persons.

**Fact 15**

50.6 percent of black children in 1986 lived with their mothers alone, up from 29.5 percent in 1970.

**Fact 16**

Fathers alone cared for 2.4 percent of their young children in 1986, compared with 2.3 percent in 1970, not much change.

**Fact 17**

In 1986, 6.3 percent of black children under 18 years old lived with neither parent, compared with 9.7 percent in 1970.

**Fact 18**

Social and economic stratification lines between black middle class, working class, and poor families are increasingly clear.

**Fact 19**

One-third of the black population is middle class, or upper middle class. These families usually are married couple units who are highly educated and who have benefited from the abolition of legal barriers to occupational access and housing availability. Usually both spouses are fully employed all year round.

**Fact 20**

Another one-third of black families are working class, and are holding themselves together and providing support systems for their young despite the obstacles they encounter, such as job layoffs or termination.

**Fact 21**

The lowest third of black families, increasingly known as the "underclass," are in crisis. They are the poorest of the poor. Most of these families are filled with children, who will grow up in poverty.

**Fact 22**

The term, "feminization of poverty," has been applied to the increasing numbers of poor families headed by women alone.

**Fact 23**

The term, "Buppies," has been applied to baby-boomers, young black upwardly mobile professionals, who are forming more prosperous middle class family units.

**Fact 24**

In 1986, 8.8 percent of black families had incomes of $50,000 or more, up from 4.7 percent in 1970.

**Fact 25**

While 11 percent of black families earned $35,000-$49,999 in 1970, in 1986 12.4 percent of black families were in this income bracket.

**Fact 26**

Fewer black families in 1986 than in 1970 were in these income categories: $25,000-$34,999; $20,000-$24,999; $15,000-$19,999; $12,500-$14,999; $10,000-$12,499; $7,500-$9,999. This drop occurred as the cost of living grew.

**Fact 27**

Percentages of blacks in the lowest income groupings grew, as those in the mid-level groupings fell. The lowest includes people who earned $7,499 or less in 1986. While 18 percent of blacks were in these low earning groups in 1970, 22.4 percent were there in 1986.

**Fact 28**

The average poverty threshold for a family of four was $11,203 in 1986, and 30 percent of black families had income below $10,000.

**Fact 29**

The median income of black families in 1986 was $17,604, in white families $30,809, and in Hispanic families $19,995.

**Fact 30**

Data released late in August 1988 by the U.S. Census Bureau stated that the median American family income was $30,853 in 1987. The cash income of the typical white family in 1987 dollars rose from $31,935 in 1986 to $32,274 in 1987. Hispanic families dropped 2 percent to $20,306, and black families dropped 0.8 percent to $18,098.

**Fact 31**

The Census Bureau reported that poverty among whites was reduced half a percentage point from 1987 to 1986; 10.5 percent of white Americans lived in poverty in 1987. The poverty rate increased among Hispanics 0.9 percent to 28.2 percent, and increased among blacks 2 percent to 33.1 percent.

**Fact 32**

The poverty line, total cash income for a family of four in 1987, was set at $11,611.

**Fact 33**

The newest Census data shows that poverty levels in 1987 are far higher than the 1978 rate of 11.4 percent, and that 8 million more Americans are poor. In 1987, 35.2 million Americans lived below the poverty line of $11,611.

**Fact 34**

One of every two young black children were poor in 1987.

**Fact 35**

The typical poor family fell lower in poverty in 1987 than in any year since 1960.

**Fact 36**

In the larger society the gap between rich and poor families is the greatest in forty years.

**Fact 37**

In 1987, the poverty rate for female headed households with no spouse present was 34.3 percent.

**Fact 38**

There is a relative absence of wealth among black families and a relatively large debt burden as compared with their white counterparts.

**Fact 39**

In 1984, the net worth of holdings for black households was $4,397 as compared with $39,135 for white households.

**Fact 40**

Life expectancy for blacks declined in two successive years, 1985 and 1986, while life expectancy for whites continued to increase. This is the first time since 1962 that any race's life expectancy has declined two consecutive years and the only time in this century that the life expectancy for blacks declined while that for whites rose.

**Fact 41**

Homicides were the chief causes of the black drop in life expectancy. One in 20 black men can expect to die from homicide.

**Fact 42**

In 1985 and 1986 there was an 8 percent increase in black motor vehicle deaths, compared with 4 percent for whites. Thus, motor vehicle accidents accounted for many black deaths.

**Fact 43**

Deaths from AIDS, pneumonia, and tuberculosis have increased disproportionately among blacks in the 1980s. Additional substantial death causes are diabetes, hypertension, drug abuse, and in the long run—smoking, and obesity due to overeating.

**Fact 44**

Many causes of death are not being overcome as rapidly for blacks as for whites. Cancer in its several forms is one of those death causes. Poverty among blacks means that many cannot afford preventive health care, or adequate medical treatment once a condition develops.

**Fact 45**

In 1985, 23 percent of all black births were to teenage mothers, and 60 percent to unwed mothers. This represents a continuous rise in unwed births from 37.6 percent in 1970.

**Fact 46**

In 1986, 60 percent of black wives expected to have two or less children, while 26.2 percent expected to produce three, and 13.8 percent expected to produce four or more.

**Fact 47**

Seventy percent of all college-educated black women expected to have two or less children. Thus, more highly educated and married black women usually expect to produce fewer children.

**Fact 48**

Infertility was not a major factor for married black couples; only 13 percent of the women were infertile.

**Fact 49**

Teenage pregnancy is a major black problem. Non-marital births among teenagers increased by 40 percent between 1970 and 1985; the proportion of teen births occurring outside of marriage has risen from 30 to 59 percent since 1970.

**Fact 50**

In 1985, 78 percent of births to teens were first births, but 27 percent of black teen births were repeats.

**Fact 51**

The Children's Defense Fund, black sororities and fraternities, are working with black teenagers to stem the tide of pregnancy.

**Fact 52**

School-based comprehensive health clinics have proven to be effective in reducing birthrates and school dropout rates among teen mothers.

**Fact 53**

Unmarried teenage mothers are likely to be dependent upon such public assistance programs as Aid to Families with Dependent Children (AFDC) for sustenance.

**Fact 54**

In 1985, only 36 percent of black women eligible for child support from absent fathers were awarded that support. Only 72 percent of those due actually received payments.

**Fact 55**

"Working homelessness" is on the increase in cities. Heads of households who earn \$5 to \$8 per hour cannot afford to pay urban rents. The average urban rent in mid-1988 is about \$662.00 a month, but workers cannot afford to pay more than \$450.00, and they have no accumulated funds for security deposits on apartments. Thus, mothers and their young children end up in shelters for the homeless even though the mothers are fully employed as fast food workers, nurses aides, domestic servants, and the like.

**Fact 56**

The black infant mortality rate has fallen dramatically, from 44.3 per thousand live births in 1960 to 18.2 in 1985. Yet it is about twice as high as the white rate, 9.3 in 1985.

**Fact 57**

The black maternal death rate has improved, as well. Improved prenatal care is a factor.

**Fact 58**

In 1984, sixteen countries had better infant mortality rates than the U.S., and 24 countries had better rates than those of blacks in the U.S. These countries included Japan, Singapore, and Cuba.

**Fact 59**

In 1985, 81 percent of blacks were covered by private or government health insurance. Nineteen percent of blacks were not covered, compared with 12 percent of whites and 27 percent of Hispanics.

**Fact 60**

The availability of Medicaid has been valuable to low income black, white, and Hispanic families, and has enabled them to have medical care.

**Fact 61**

In 1985, fewer than half of black children aged 1-4 years had been immunized against the childhood diseases. More than half of those in the 5-14-year-old group had been immunized, probably due to public school regulations.

**Fact 62**

In 1987, 65 percent of AIDS victims were white, 23 percent were black, and about 12 percent Hispanic. Most of these victims of the contemporary social plague were male.

**Fact 63**

Improvements have been noted in survival rates of black men affected with prostate cancer, and in survival rates for cancer of the bladder among black men and women.

**Fact 64**

Five year relative survival rates for cancer in all body sites have been relatively constant from 1974-83, with 38 percent of blacks surviving at least five years after cancer has been diagnosed.

**Fact 65**

Addiction to or heavy usage of alcohol, marihuana, and cocaine is a contemporary social problem. Heaviest use is documented for alcohol in 1985, with 47.6 percent of blacks addicted or heavy users, most of them in the Northeast and West. Considerably smaller proportions used marihuana heavily (13.2 percent) and still smaller were heavy users of cocaine (3.2 percent).

**Fact 66**

If addiction and heavy usage figures are accurate, they

suggest that small proportions of the population are creating social problems well out of proportion to their numbers. These problems include street crime and automobile accidents that are substance related.

**Fact 67**

Blacks and other races were 9.7 percent of the farm population in 1970, but only 2.8 percent in 1986. This land loss is irreversible.

**Fact 68**

Death rates per 100,000 population have improved for both black males and females from 1960-1985, though the gap remains between blacks and whites.

**Fact 69**

Death rates from homicide accounted for the largest proportions of black male deaths from 1970-1985.

**Fact 70**

More black females than males perish from diabetes.

**Fact 71**

Suicide rates increased from 8 per 100,000 in 1970 to 10.8 in 1985 among black males.

**Fact 72**

Females commit suicide considerably less than do males. From 1970 to 1985 the black female suicide rate declined from 2.6 to 2.1 per 100,000 population.

**Fact 73**

Some prominent black scholars, among them William J. Wilson, believe that race is of declining significance in determining the life chances of blacks today. Economic class affiliation is a more significant factor, according to their analyses.

**Fact 74**

The belief that race is of declining significance is based on the fact that since the end of World War II, and particularly since the 1960s, state intervention has been designed to promote racial equality and a more reciprocal relationship has existed between the polity and the economy. Educated, motivated, hard-working blacks have been increasingly successful in entering the mainstream of U.S. society since the 1960s. They form a middle class that is the largest that has existed among blacks in U.S. history.

**Fact 75**

Social conditions of the urban black underclass have deteriorated rapidly since 1970. Causes are the interaction of too few job opportunities for men, poor education, too few marriageable men, welfare-dependent homes, crime, drugs, and isolation of this underclass from other segments of society.

**Fact 76**

Wilson and other social theorists do not believe that the problems of the black underclass can be solved with race-specific policies. Therefore, universal programs of systemic reform are needed. These include manpower training and education programs, full employment, and integration of social and economic policy.

**Fact 77**

When one looks at children's figures, it is revealed that 42 percent of the children receiving AFDC funds are black, 35 percent are white, 16 percent are Hispanic, 3 percent Asian, and 1 percent Native American. The race of 3 percent of the children is unknown.

**Fact 78**

The average number of persons in an AFDC family in 1986 was 3.0, with 2.0 being the average number of children in the unit.

**Fact 79**

The median age of AFDC children was 7 years, 1 month in 1986. Only 11 percent were fifteen years old or older, and 43 percent of the children were under six years old.

**Fact 80**

Most AFDC families in 1986 had been on the rolls for fewer than three years. However those families who had been on the rolls for five or more years increased to 26 percent from 23-24 percent in 1983-1985.

**Fact 81**

The primary reason for deprivation, causing children to be AFDC recipients, is that their parents never were married.

**Fact 82**

In the cases where educational level is known, the years of education completed by AFDC adult recipients averages 10.8. Thus, if these adults could be helped to get a high school education or its equivalent they might become employable.

**Fact 83**

An average AFDC family of one adult and two children received $382.00 per month in 1986. They were also eligible for food stamps and for Medicaid.

**Fact 84**

The Child Support Enforcement Program (CSE) seeks to help needy families and save tax dollars. One facet of its operation is to collect funds from parents absent from the home; often this is the father. Some percentage of AFDC payments may be recovered through child support collections.

**Fact 85**

The poor are still poor even when noncash programs' benefits such as Medicare, Medicaid, food stamps, and housing subsidies are added to cash benefits. In 1986, counting cash benefits only, poverty rates were 31.1 percent for blacks, and 13.6 percent overall. Counting cash and noncash benefits, the rates declined to 11.6 percent overall, and 25.8 percent for blacks. For black children poverty rates declined from 43.1 percent to 35.8 percent when in-kind benefits were counted. For female-headed families with children, the poverty rate declined from 46 to 36.6 percent. Thus, the rate differences when in-kind benefits are counted are not nearly as much as some would have us believe. (Source: *The Washington Post*, 12/30/88, A 18.)

**Fact 86**

23 percent of the homeless are employed full time, but cannot afford the cost of housing in urban areas. (Source: NBC News, 1/18/89).

**Fact 87**

Crack, a highly addictive form of cocaine, has had a devastating effect on low-income urban black families. (Source: NBC News, 1/18/89).

**Fact 88**

In January 1989, a new medical report was released; information was reported by Robert J. Blendon of the Harvard School of Public Health in Boston. This report was prepared from a 1986 nationwide telephone survey of 10,130 representative U. S. residents. Regarding medical services and blacks, this report said:

A. One in 11 blacks reported not seeing a doctor for economic reasons, compared with one in 20 whites. In percentage terms, 9 percent of blacks compared with 5 percent of whites said their failure to get medical care was grounded in economic reasons.

B. On the average, blacks have a $1^1/_2$ times higher death rate than whites of the same age.

C. 32 percent of blacks, compared with 17 percent of whites, said they had not seen a doctor in the past year.

D. One in 10 blacks, compared with one in 6 whites, reported having a chronic or serious illness and had not seen a doctor in the past year.

E. Among blacks with high blood pressure, almost one-third had not had an annual blood pressure check, compared with less than one-fifth of whites.

F. Blacks were less likely than whites to have medical insurance coverage. Those who had such coverage were considerably less likely to be covered by a private insurance company—85.1 percent compared with 72.5 percent.

G. Blacks on Medicaid were 10 percent more likely than whites to live in a Southern or Southwestern state that has the least generous Medicaid benefits.

H. 50 percent of blacks, compared with 25 percent of whites, had used a hospital, clinic, emergency room or community health center for their last physician visit.

I. More blacks than whites were not satisfied with their last hospitalization, or their last visit to a doctor.

J. These researchers felt that the under supply of black physicians and physicians who are sensitive to minorities might also result in reduced opportunities for black medical care.

K. Blacks were almost twice as likely as whites to live in one-adult households, and were three times more likely to report problems getting to their doctors.

L. Fewer blacks than whites were included in medical studies published from 1984 through 1986.

M. These black-white differences persisted throughout all income groups.

## END NOTES

1. Charles V. Willie, "The Black Family: Striving Toward Freedom," in *The State of Black America 1988*, ed. Janet Dewart (New York: National Urban League, Inc., 1988), p. 78.

2. Examples of this literature are: Daniel Patrick Moynihan, *The Negro Family: The Case for National Action* (Washington, D.C.: U.S. Department of Labor, 1965); Lee Rainwater, "Crucible of Identity: The Negro Lower Class Family," Daedalus 95 (Winter 1966), pp. 172-216.

3. E. Franklin Frazier, *The Negro in the United States*. New York: MacMillan, 1949.

4. Reynolds Farley and Walter R. Allen, *The Color Line and the Quality of Life in America* (New York: Russell Sage Foundation, 1987), pp. 160-162.

5. Andrew Billingsley, *Black Families in White America*. Englewood Cliffs, N.J.: Prentice-Hall, 196.

6. *The World Almanac and Book of Facts 1988* (New York: World Almanac, 1987), pp. 808-809. 7. U.S. Bureau of the Census, Statistical Abstract of the United States: 1988 (108th edition.) Washington, D.C., 1987, Table 14, p. 14-8. *Statistical Abstract: 1988*, Table 16, p. 15. 9. Ibid.

10. E. Franklin Frazier came to this conclusion, using census data as his base.

11. *Statistical Abstract: 1988*, Table 18, p. 16.

12. *U.S. Bureau of the Census, Household and Family Characteristics: March 1987*, Current Population Reports, Series P-20, No. 424, U.S. Government Printing Office, Washington, D.C., 1988, Table 16, p. 94.

13. *Statistical Abstract: 1988*, Table 306, p. 175.

14. *Statistical Abstract: 1988*, Table 63, p. 47.

15. *Statistical Abstract: 1988*, Table 58, p. 44.

16. *Statistical Abstract: 1988*, Table 60, p. 45.

17. Ibid.

18 . *Statistical Abstract: 1988*, Table 63, p . 47 .

19 . Ibid., Table 67, p. 49 .

20. Ibid., Table 69, p. 5O . The 1970 figure is not available.

21. Andrew Billingsley, "Black Families in a Changing Society, " in *The State of Black America 1987*, ed . Janet Dewart (New York: National Urban League, Inc. ., 1987), p. 104 .

22 . Douglas G . Glasgow, *The Black Underclass: Poverty, Unemployment and Entrapment of Ghetto Youth* (San Francisco: Jossey-Bass, Inc., 1980); William Julius Wilson, *The Truly Disadvantaged: The Inner City, the Underclass,*

*and Public Policy* (Chicago: The University of Chicago Press, 1987); Bart Landry, *The New Black Middle Class* (Berkeley: University of California Press, 1987); Reynolds Farley and Walter Allen, op. cit.; *The State of Black America 1987*, op. cit.; *The State of Black America 1988*, op. cit.
23. Harriette Pipes McAdoo, ed., *Black Families* (Beverly Hills: Sage Publications, 1981); Harriette Pipes McAdoo and John Lewis McAdoo, *Black Children: Social, Educational, and Parental Environments* (Beverly Hills: Sage Publications, 1985), Joyce A. Ladner, "Black Teenage Pregnancy: A Challenge for Educators," *The Journal of Negro Education*, 56 (1987), 53-63.
24 . David Swinton, "Economic Status of Blacks 1987, " in *The State of Black America 1988*, ed. Janet Dewart (New York: National Urban League, Inc., 1988), pp. 129-152 .
25 U.S. Bureau of the Census, Current Population Reports, Series P-60, No. 157, *Money Income and Poverty Status of Families and Persons in the United States: 1986* (Advance Data from the March 1987 Current Population Survey), U.S. Government Printing Office, Washington, D.C., 1987, Table 3, p. 12.
2 6 . Ibid
2 7 . Ibid .
28. Swinton, op. cit., pp.141-142; Landry, op. cit., pp. 141-149.
29 . Landry, op. cit., pp. 153-156
30. Swinton, op. cit., pp. 151-152.
31. E. Franklin Frazier, *The Negro Family in the United States* (Chicago: University of Chicago Press, 1966 /1939.
32. Swinton, op. cit., pp. 151-152.
33. *Statistical Abstract of the United States:1988*, Table 728, p. 441.
34. *World Almanac*, p. 825.
35. *Statistical Abstract of the United States: 1988*, Tables 86 and 87, p. 62.
36. *Statistical Abstract of the United States: 1988*, Table 99, p. 67.
37. *Statistical Abstract of the United States: 1988*, Table 97, p. 66.
38. Kristin A. Moore, comp., "Facts at a Glance: 1987," (Washington, D.C.: Child Trends, Inc., 1987), p. 1.
39. Ibid.
40. Ibid.
41. Joyce Ladner, "Black Teenage Pregnancy: A Challenge for Educators, op. cit., pp. 54-55.
42. Marion Wright Edelman, "Address to the National Conference on Educating Black Children, in *Educating Black Children: America's Challenge*, eds. Dorothy S. Strickland and Eric J. Cooper (Washington, D.C.: Bureau of Educational Research, School of Education, Howard University, 1987), pp. 113-125.
43. Kristin A. Moore, op. cit., p. 2.
44. Joyce Ladner, op. cit., pp. 61-72.
45. Ibid.
46. Kristin Moore, op. cit., p. 2.
47. *Statistical Abstract of the United States: 1988*, Table 597, p. 358.
48. Mary Jordan, "A Steady Job But No Home," *The Washington Post, August 29, 1988*, Dl.
49. *Statistical Abstract of the United States: 1988*, Table 113, p. 75. 50. Statistical Abstract, Table 140, p. 92
51. *Statistical Abstract*, Table 579, p. 349.
52. *Statistical Abstract*, Table 168, p. 106.
53. *Statistical Abstract*, Table 170, p. 107.
54. *Statistical Abstract*, Table 176, p. 110.
55. *Statistical Abstract*, Table 181, p. 112.
56. *Statistical Abstract*, Table 1055, p. 608.
57. U.S. Commission on Civil Rights, *The Decline of Black Farming in America* (Washington, D.C.: 1982), p. III.
58. Ibid., p. 176, p. 4.
59. *Statistical Abstract*, Table 118, p. 78.
60 *Statistical Abstract*, Table 122, p. 81.
61. *Statistical Abstract*, Table 124, p. 82.
62. Ibid.
63. National Center for Health Statistics: *Health, United States, 1987*. DHHS Pub. No. (PHS) 88-1232. Public Health Service. Washington. U.S. Government Printing Office, Mar. 1988, p. 19.
64. Spencer Rich, "U.S. Family Income is up Slightly," *The Washington Post*, September 1,1988, Al; A6.
65. Ibid.
66. Andrew Billingsley, "Black Families in a Changing Society," op. cit., pp. 99-102.
67. Lisbeth R. Schorr, "Let's Stop Recycling Poverty," *The Washington Post*, August 7, 1988, B2.
68. Ibid.
69. U.S. Department of Labor, *Work Force 2000*
70. Tamara Henry, "Teaching Boys Sexual Responsibility Can Reduce Pregnancies, Study Says," *The Washington Post*, August 24, 1988, A9.
71. Charles V. Willie, op. cit., pp. 77-78.

Paraphrased from pp. 6-7 of the National Urban League's News Release dated January 20, 1989.

Sources: (l) Joyce Price, "blacks lag far behind whites in seeking medical service," *The Washington Times*, January 16, 1989, A5. (2) "Blacks Less Likely to Get Medical Advances," *Washington Post Health*, January 17, 1989, p. 11.

## TABLE 27. WHITE, BLACK AND HISPANIC HOUSEHOLDS BY TYPE: 1970 TO 1986

[As of March, except as noted. Based on Current Population Survey, except where noted; see headnote, table 56. See also *Historical Statistics, Colonial Times to 1970*, series A 320-334]

| | Number (1000's) | | | | | Percent Distribution | | | | |
|---|---|---|---|---|---|---|---|---|---|---|
| Characteristic | 1970 | 1975 | 1980 | 1985 | 1986 | 1970 | 1975 | 1980 | 1985 | 1986 |
| White | | | | | | | | | | |
| Total | 56,602 | 62,945 | 70,766 | 75,328 | 76,576 | 100.0 | 100.0 | 100.0 | 100.0 | 100.0 |
| Family households | 46,166 | 49,334 | 52,243 | 54,400 | 54,991 | 81.6 | 76.4 | 73.8 | 72.2 | 71.8 |
| Married couples | 41,029 | 42,951 | 44,751 | 45,643 | 45,924 | 72.5 | 68.2 | 63.2 | 60.6 | 60.0 |
| Male householder[1] | 1,038 | 1,257 | 1,441 | 1,816 | 1,956 | 1.9 | 2.0 | 2.0 | 2.4 | 2.6 |
| Female householder[1] | 4,099 | 5,126 | 6,052 | 6,941 | 7,111 | 7.2 | 8.1 | 8.6 | 9.2 | 9.3 |
| Nonfamily householder | 10,436 | 13,612 | 18,522 | 20,928 | 21,585 | 18.4 | 21.6 | 26.2 | 27.8 | 28.2 |
| Male householder | 3,406 | 5,038 | 7,499 | 8,608 | 9,013 | 6.0 | 8.0 | 10.6 | 11.4 | 11.8 |
| Female householder | 7,030 | 8,574 | 11,023 | 12,320 | 12,572 | 12.4 | 13.6 | 15.6 | 16.4 | 16.4 |
| Black | | | | | | | | | | |
| Total | 6,223 | 7,262 | 8,586 | 9,480 | 9,797 | 100.0 | 100.0 | 100.0 | 100.0 | 100.0 |
| Family households | 4,858 | 5,468 | 6,184 | 6,778 | 6,921 | 78.0 | 75.3 | 72.0 | 71.5 | 70.6 |
| Married couples | 3,317 | 3,343 | 3,433 | 3,469 | 3,680 | 53.3 | 45.0 | 40.0 | 36.6 | 37.6 |
| Male householder[1] | 181 | 211 | 256 | 344 | 368 | 2.9 | 2.9 | 3.0 | 3.6 | 3.8 |
| Female householder[1] | 1,358 | 1,915 | 2,495 | 2,964 | 2,874 | 21.8 | 26.4 | 29.1 | 31.3 | 29.3 |
| Nonfamily householder | 1,367 | 1,793 | 2,402 | 2,703 | 2,876 | 22.0 | 24.7 | 28.0 | 28.5 | 29.4 |
| Male householder | 564 | 791 | 1,146 | 1,244 | 1,412 | 9.1 | 10.9 | 13.3 | 13.1 | 14.4 |
| Female householder | 803 | 1,002 | 1,256 | 1,459 | 1,464 | 12.9 | 13.8 | 14.6 | 15.4 | 14.9 |
| Hispanic[2] | | | | | | | | | | |
| Total | 2,303 | NA | 3,684 | 4,883 | 5,213 | 100.0 | NA | 100.0 | 100.0 | 100.0 |
| Family households | 2,004 | NA | 3,029 | 3,939 | 4,205 | 87.0 | NA | 82.2 | 80.7 | 80.7 |
| Married couples | 1,615 | NA | 2,282 | 2,824 | 2,962 | 70.1 | NA | 61.9 | 57.8 | 56.8 |
| Male householder[1] | 82 | NA | 138 | 210 | 264 | 3.6 | NA | 3.7 | 4.3 | 5.1 |
| Female householder[1] | 307 | NA | 610 | 905 | 980 | 13.3 | NA | 16.8 | 18.5 | 18.8 |
| Nonfamily householder | 299 | NA | 654 | 944 | 1,006 | 13.0 | NA | 17.8 | 19.3 | 19.3 |
| Male householder | 150 | NA | 365 | 509 | 541 | 6.5 | NA | 9.9 | 10.4 | 10.4 |
| Female householder | 148 | NA | 289 | 435 | 465 | 6.4 | NA | 7.8 | 8.9 | 8.9 |

NA-Not available

[1]No spouse present

[2]Hispanic of any race

Source U.S. Bureau of the Census of Population: *1970, Persons of Spanish Origin,* PC(2)-1C; *Current Population Reports,* series p-20, No. 419 and earlier reports

# TABLE 28. FAMILIES, BY TYPE, SIZE OF METROPOLITAN AREA, RACE, AND HISPANIC ORIGIN OF HOUSEHOLDER: MARCH 1987

(Numbers in thousands)

| | | | | In MSA'S | | | | | | |
|---|---|---|---|---|---|---|---|---|---|---|
| | | | | MSA'S of 3,000 or more | | MSA'S of 1,000 to 2,999,999 | | MSA's With less than 1,000 | | |
| | Total | Central Cities | Ring | Central Cities | Ring | Central Cities | Ring | Central Cities | Ring | Not in MSA's |
| **Black families** | | | | | | | | | | |
| Total families | 7,096 | 4,101 | 1,749 | 1,391 | 374 | 1,304 | 660 | 1,406 | 715 | 1,245 |
| 2 persons | 2,335 | 1,464 | 496 | 469 | 107 | 500 | 174 | 495 | 215 | 375 |
| 3 persons | 1,874 | 1,096 | 481 | 368 | 98 | 333 | 219 | 395 | 163 | 297 |
| 4 persons | 1,431 | 774 | 413 | 282 | 107 | 239 | 148 | 254 | 159 | 243 |
| 5 persons | 764 | 422 | 190 | 151 | 34 | 121 | 70 | 149 | 87 | 152 |
| 6 persons | 362 | 182 | 93 | 60 | 17 | 55 | 36 | 67 | 40 | 87 |
| 7 or more persons | 331 | 163 | 76 | 62 | 11 | 55 | 14 | 46 | 52 | 91 |
| Age of members | | | | | | | | | | |
| Total families | 7,096 | 4,101 | 1,749 | 1,391 | 374 | 1,304 | 660 | 1,406 | 715 | 1,245 |
| With members: | | | | | | | | | | |
| Under 18 years | 4,811 | 2,739 | 1,227 | 917 | 260 | 857 | 453 | 964 | 514 | 845 |
| 18 to 64 years | 6,740 | 3,896 | 1,695 | 1,319 | 367 | 1,246 | 647 | 1,331 | 680 | 1,149 |
| 65 years and over | 1,093 | 620 | 214 | 243 | 35 | 158 | 83 | 219 | 96 | 259 |
| Total members | 24,978 | 14,002 | 6,275 | 4,842 | 1,303 | 4,406 | 2,284 | 4,755 | 2,688 | 4,700 |
| Under 18 years | 9,471 | 5,281 | 2,354 | 1,810 | 456 | 1,631 | 828 | 1,840 | 1,070 | 1,835 |
| 18 To 64 years | 14,009 | 7,880 | 3,641 | 2,705 | 805 | 2,556 | 1,354 | 2,619 | 1,481 | 2,488 |
| 65 years and over | 1,498 | 841 | 280 | 327 | 43 | 218 | 101 | 296 | 136 | 377 |
| Average per family | 3.52 | 3.41 | 3.59 | 3.48 | 3.49 | 3.38 | 3.46 | 3.38 | 3.76 | 3.77 |
| Under 18 years | 1.33 | 1.29 | 1.35 | 1.30 | 1.22 | 1.25 | 1.25 | 1.31 | 1.50 | 1.47 |
| 18 To 64 years | 1.97 | 1.92 | 2.08 | 1.94 | 2.15 | 1.96 | 2.05 | 1.86 | 2.07 | 2.00 |
| 65 years and over | 0.21 | 0.20 | 0.16 | 0.23 | 0.11 | 0.17 | 0.15 | 0.21 | 0.19 | 0.30 |
| **White families** | | | | | | | | | | |
| Total families | 55,676 | 14,141 | 27,957 | 3,130 | 4,645 | 3,948 | 10,284 | 7,063 | 13,028 | 13,578 |
| 2 persons | 23,490 | 6,395 | 11,183 | 1,374 | 1,699 | 1,820 | 4,202 | 3,201 | 5,282 | 5,912 |
| 3 persons | 13,123 | 3,376 | 6,547 | 713 | 1,090 | 917 | 2,406 | 1,746 | 3,051 | 3,200 |
| 4 persons | 11,783 | 2,667 | 6,334 | 618 | 1,080 | 726 | 2,289 | 1,322 | 2,964 | 2,783 |
| 5 persons | 4,905 | 1,116 | 2,655 | 272 | 510 | 317 | 935 | 526 | 1,209 | 1,135 |
| 6 persons | 1,614 | 389 | 846 | 89 | 170 | 111 | 315 | 189 | 361 | 379 |
| 7 or more persons | 761 | 198 | 394 | 63 | 96 | 57 | 138 | 78 | 160 | 169 |
| Age of members | | | | | | | | | | |
| Total families | 55,676 | 14,141 | 27,957 | 3,130 | 4,645 | 3,948 | 10,284 | 7,063 | 13,028 | 13,578 |
| With members: | | | | | | | | | | |
| Under 18 years | 27,961 | 6,908 | 14,262 | 1,516 | 2,483 | 1,905 | 5,156 | 3,486 | 6,623 | 6,791 |
| 18 To 64 years | 50,278 | 12,708 | 25,484 | 2,839 | 4,325 | 3,551 | 9,354 | 6,318 | 11,806 | 12,086 |
| 65 years and over | 10,745 | 2,868 | 5,093 | 706 | 738 | 804 | 1,829 | 1,357 | 2,525 | 2,785 |
| Total members | 174,235 | 43,300 | 89,053 | 9,834 | 15,369 | 12,071 | 32,515 | 21,395 | 41,168 | 41,882 |
| Under 18 years | 50,562 | 12,387 | 25,795 | 2,841 | 4,602 | 3,393 | 9,207 | 6,154 | 11,986, | 12,379 |
| 18 to 64 years | 106,757 | 26,412 | 55,293 | 5,944 | 9,640 | 7,413 | 20,413 | 13,055 | 25,240 | 25,052 |
| 65 years and over | 16,915 | 4,500 | 7,964 | 1,049 | 1,127 | 1,265 | 2,895 | 2,186 | 3,942 | 4,451 |
| Average per family | 3.13 | 3.06 | 3.19 | 3.14 | 3.31 | 3.06 | 3.16 | 3.03 | 3.16 | 3.08 |
| Under 18 years | 0.91 | 0.88 | 0.92 | 0.91 | 0.99 | 0.86 | 0.90 | 0.87 | 0.92 | 0.91 |
| 18 to 64 years | 1.92 | 1.87 | 1.98 | 1.90 | 2.08 | 1.88 | 1.98 | 1.85 | 1.94 | 1.85 |
| 65 years and over | 0.30 | 0.32 | 0.28 | 0.34 | 0.24 | 0.32 | 0.28 | 0.31 | 0.30 | 0.33 |

Source: U.S. Bureau of Commerce, Bureau of the Census, Current Population Reports, Series P-20 No. 424

## TABLE 29. NUMBER OF PERSONS, FAMILIES, AND UNRELATED INDIVIDUALS BELOW THE POVERTY LEVEL: 1986, 1985, 1983, AND 1978

(Numbers in thousands)

| Characteristic | 1986 | 1985 | 1983 | 1978 | 1986 minus 1985 |
|---|---|---|---|---|---|
| All persons | 32,370 | 33,064 | 35,303 | 24,497 | -694 |
| White | 22,183 | 22,860 | 23,984 | 16,259 | -677 |
| Black | 8,983 | 8,926 | 9,882 | 7,625 | 57 |
| Hispanic | 15,117 | 5,236 | 4,633 | 2,607 | -119 |
| Under 15 years | 11,018 | 11,110 | 11,863 | 8,192 | -92 |
| 15 to 24 years | 5,991 | 6,363 | 6,973 | 4,926 | -372 * |
| 25 to 44 years | 7,815 | 7,899 | 8,403 | 4,643 | -84 |
| 45 to 54 years | 1,886 | 1,911 | 2,053 | 1,639 | -25 |
| 55 to 59 years | 1,113 | 1,103 | 1,171 | 900 | 10 |
| 60 to 64 years | 1,071 | 1,222 | 1,215 | 964 | -151 * |
| 65 years and over | 3,477 | 3,456 | 3,625 | 3,233 | 21 |
| Northeast | 5,211 | 5,751 | 6,605 | 5,050 | -540 * |
| Midwest | 7,641 | 8,191 | 8,511 | 5,192 | -550 ** |
| South[1] | 3,106 | 12,921 | 13,504 | 10,255 | 185 |
| West | 6,412 | 6,201 | 6,682 | 4,000 | 211 |
| All related children under 18 years in families | 12,257 | 12,483 | 13,427 | 9,722 | -226 |
| White | 7,714 | 7,838 | 8,534 | 5,674 | -124 |
| Black | 4,039 | 4,057 | 4,273 | 3,781 | -18 |
| Hispanic[1] | 12,413 | 2,512 | 2,251 | 1,354 | -99 |
| All families | 7,023 | 7,223 | 7,647 | 5,280 | -200 |
| White | 4,811 | 4,983 | 5,220 | 3,523 | -172 |
| Black | 1,987 | 1,983 | 2,161 | 1,622 | 4 |
| Hispanic[1] | 1,085 | 1,074 | 981 | 559 | 11 |
| Married-couple families | 3,123 | 3,438 | 3,815 | 2,474 | -315 * |
| Male householder, no wife present | 287 | 311 | 268 | 152 | -24 |
| Female householder, no husband present | 3,613 | 3,474 | 3,564 | 2,654 | 139 |
| All unrelated individuals | 6,846 | 6,725 | 6,740 | 5,435 | 121 |
| Male | 2,536 | 2,499 | 2,641 | 1,824 | 37 |
| Female | 4,311 | 4,226 | 4,099 | 3,611 | 85 |

*Significant at the 95-percent confidence level.

**Signifioant at the 90-percent confidence level.

[1] Persons of Hispanic origin may be of any race.

Source: U.S. Department of Commerce, Bureau of the Census, Current Population Reports, Series P-60, No. 157.

## TABLE 30. FAMILY GROUPS WITH CHILDREN, BY TYPE, RACE AND HISPANIC ORIGIN OF HOUSEHOLDER OR REFERENCE PERSON: 1986

(Numbers in thousands)

| Subject | All family groups | | Family households | | Related subfamilies | | Unrelated subfamilies | |
|---|---|---|---|---|---|---|---|---|
| | Number | Percent | Number | Percent | Number | Percent | Number | Percent |
| All Races | | | | | | | | |
| Family groups with children | 33,939 | 100.0 | 31,670 | 100.0 | 1,883 | 100.0 | 386 | 100.0 |
| Two-parent groups | 25,010 | 73.7 | 24,630 | 77.8 | 353 | 18.7 | 27 | 7.0 |
| One-parent groups | 8,930 | 26.3 | 7,040 | 22.2 | 1,530 | 81.3 | 360 | 93.3 |
| Maintained by mother | 7,842 | 23.1 | 6,105 | 19.3 | 1,399 | 74.3 | 338 | 87.6 |
| Maintained by father | 1,088 | 3.2 | 935 | 3.0 | 131 | 7.0 | 22 | 5.7 |
| White | | | | | | | | |
| Family groups with children | 28,041 | 100.0 | 26,575 | 100.0 | 1,166 | 100.0 | 300 | 100.0 |
| Two-parent groups | 22,076 | 78.7 | 21,756 | 81.9 | 300 | 25.7 | 20 | 6.7 |
| One-parent groups | 5,964 | 21.3 | 4,818 | 18.1 | 866 | 74.3 | 280 | 93.3 |
| Maintained by mother | 5,070 | 18.1 | 4,040 | 15.2 | 771 | 66.1 | 259 | 86.3 |
| Maintained by father | 894 | 3.2 | 778 | 2.9 | 95 | 8.1 | 21 | 7.0 |
| Black | | | | | | | | |
| Family group with children | 4,772 | 100.0 | 4,059 | 100.0 | 641 | 100.0 | 72 | (B) |
| Two-parent groups | 2,022 | 42.4 | 1,997 | 49.2 | 23 | 3.6 | 2 | (B) |
| One-parent groups | 2,752 | 57.7 | 2,063 | 50.8 | 619 | 96.6 | 70 | (B) |
| Maintained by mother | 2,597 | 54.4 | 1,934 | 47.6 | 593 | 92.5 | 70 | (B) |
| Maintained by father | 155 | 3.2 | 129 | 3.2 | 26 | 4.1 | 0 | 0 |
| Hispanic* | | | | | | | | |
| Family groups with children | 3,043 | 100.0 | 2,755 | 100.0 | 246 | 100.0 | 42 | (B) |
| Two-parent groups | 2,057 | 67.6 | 1,987 | 72.1 | 64 | 26 | 6 | (B) |
| One-parent groups | 987 | 32.4 | 769 | 27.9 | 182 | 74 | 36 | (B) |
| Maintained by mother | 881 | 29.0 | 684 | 24.8 | 161 | 65.4 | 36 | (B) |
| Maintained by father | 106 | 3.5 | 85 | 3.1 | 21 | 8.5 | 0 | |

(B) Base less than 75,000

* May be of any race

Note: Family groups comprised family households, related subfamilies,and unrelated subfamilies.

Source: U.S. Department of Commerce, Bureau of the Census, *Current Population Reports,* Series P-20, No. 419, p. 9.

## TABLE 31. ONE-PARENT FAMILY GROUPS, BY RACE AND MARITIAL STATUS: 1970 TO 1986

(Numbers in thousands)

| Subject | 1986 | | 1980 | | 1970 | |
|---|---|---|---|---|---|---|
| | Number | Percent | Number | Percent | Number | Percent |
| All Races | | | | | | |
| One-parent family groups | 8,930 | 100.0 | 6,920 | 100.0 | 3,808 | 100.0 |
| Maintained by mother | 7,842 | 87.8 | 6,230 | 90.0 | 3,415 | 89.7 |
| Never married | 2,276 | 25.5 | 1,063 | 15.4 | 248 | 6.5 |
| Spouse absent | 1,724 | 19.3 | 1,743 | 25.2 | 1,377 | 36.2 |
| Separated | 1,506 | 16.9 | 1,483 | 21.4 | 962 | 25.3 |
| Divorced | 3,294 | 36.9 | 2,721 | 39.3 | 1,109 | 29.1 |
| Widowed | 546 | 6.1 | 703 | 10.2 | 682 | 17.9 |
| Maintained by father | 1,088 | 12.2 | 690 | 10.0 | 393 | 10.3 |
| Never married | 205 | 2.3 | 63 | 0.9 | 22 | 0.6 |
| Spouse absent* | 218 | 2.4 | 181 | 2.6 | 247 | 6.5 |
| Divorced | 571 | 6.4 | 340 | 4.9 | (NA) | (NA) |
| Widowed | 94 | 1.1 | 107 | 1.5 | 124 | 3.3 |
| White | | | | | | |
| One-parent family groups | 5,964 | 100.0 | 4,664 | 100.0 | 2,638 | 100.0 |
| Maintained by mother | 5,070 | 85.0 | 4,122 | 88.4 | 2,330 | 88.3 |
| Never married | 885 | 14.8 | 379 | 8.1 | 73 | 2.8 |
| Spouse absent | 1,129 | 18.9 | 1,033 | 22.1 | 796 | 30.2 |
| Separated | 972 | 16.3 | 840 | 18.0 | 477 | 18.1 |
| Divorced | 2,676 | 44.9 | 2,201 | 47.2 | 930 | 35.3 |
| Widowed | 380 | 6.4 | 511 | 11.0 | 531 | 20.1 |
| Maintained by father | 894 | 15.0 | 542 | 11.6 | 307 | 11.6 |
| Never married | 135 | 2.3 | 32 | 0.7 | 18 | 0.7 |
| Spouse absent* | 168 | 2.8 | 141 | 3.0 | 196 | 7.4 |
| Divorced | 513 | 8.6 | 288 | 6.2 | (NA) | (NA) |
| Widowed | 78 | 1.3 | 82 | 1.8 | 93 | 3 5 |
| Black | | | | | | |
| One-parent family groups | 2,752 | 100.0 | 2,114 | 100.0 | 1,148 | 100.0 |
| Maintained by mother | 2,597 | 94.4 | 1,984 | 93.9 | 1,063 | 92.6 |
| Never married | 1,355 | 49.2 | 665 | 31.5 | 173 | 15.1 |
| Spouse absent* | 546 | 19.8 | 667 | 31.6 | 570 | 49.7 |
| Separated | 510 | 18.5 | 616 | 29.1 | 479 | 41.7 |
| Divorced | 561 | 20.4 | 477 | 22.6 | 172 | 15.0 |
| Widowed | 133 | 4.8 | 174 | 8.2 | 148 | 12.9 |
| Maintained by father | 155 | 5.6 | 129 | 6.1 | 85 | 7.4 |
| Divorced | 47 | 1.7 | 43 | 2.0 | (NA) | (NA) |
| Widowed | 7 | 0.3 | 19 | 0.9 | 30 | 2.6 |

*Data for 1970 include divorced fathers.

NA Not available.

Note: Family groups comprise family households, related subfamilies and unrelated subfamilies.

Source: U.S. Department of Commerce, Bureau of the Census, *Current Population Reports*, Series P-20, No. 419.

## TABLE 32. RACE AND HISPANIC ORIGIN OF HUSBANDS AND WIFES: 1987

(Numbers in thousands)

| Subject | Total | Race of Wife | | | Origin of Wife | |
|---|---|---|---|---|---|---|
| | | White | Black | Other | Spanish Origin | Other Origin |
| | | | **All Married Couples** | | | |
| Race of husband | | | | | | |
| Total | 52,286 | 46,941 | 3 788 | 1 607 | 3 370 | 48,916 |
| White | 47,011 | 46,597 | 56 | 358 | 3,263 | 43,748 |
| Black | 3,828 | 121 | 3 674 | 33 | 66 | 3,762 |
| Other | 1,446 | 223 | 8 | 1,216 | 41 | 1,406 |
| Origin of husband | | | | | | |
| Total | 52,286 | 46,941 | 3,738 | 1,607 | 3,370 | 48,916 |
| Spanish origin | 3,253 | 3,171 | 52 | 30 | 2,766 | 487 |
| Other | 49,032 | 43,770 | 3,685 | 1,577 | 604 | 48,428 |
| | | | **Married-Couples Families** | | | |
| Race of husband | | | | | | |
| Total | 51,537 | 46,360 | 3,602 | 1,515 | 3,228 | 46,309 |
| White | 46,422 | 46,024 | 53 | 345 | 3,126 | 43,296 |
| Black | 3,754 | 120 | 3,601 | 33 | 63 | 3,692 |
| Other | 1,360 | 215 | 8 | 1,137 | 40 | 1,321 |
| Origin of husband | | | | | | |
| Total | 51,537 | 46,360 | 3,562 | 1,515 | 3,228 | 48,309 |
| Spanish origin | 3,113 | 3,037 | 49 | 28 | 2,639 | 474 |
| Other | 48 424 | 43,323 | 3,613 | 1,487 | 589 | 47,835 |
| | | | **Related Subfamilies** | | | |
| Race of husband | | | | | | |
| Total | 712 | 548 | 72 | 91 | 127 | 585 |
| White | 556 | 540 | 4 | 13 | 122 | 434 |
| Black | 70 | 1 | 69 | - | 4 | 66 |
| Other | 86 | 7 | - | 78 | 1 | 85 |
| Origin of husband | | | | | | |
| Total | 712 | 548 | 72 | 91 | 127 | 585 |
| Spanish origin | 123 | 117 | 4 | 2 | 112 | 11 |
| Other | 588 | 430 | 69 | 89 | 15 | 573 |
| | | | **Unrelated Subfamilies** | | | |
| Race of husband | | | | | | |
| Total | 37 | 33 | 4 | 1 | 15 | 22 |
| White | 33 | 33 | - | - | 15 | 18 |
| Black | 4 | - | 4 | - | - | 4 |
| Other | 1 | - | - | 1 | - | 1 |
| Origin of husband | | | | | | |
| Total | 37 | 33 | 4 | 1 | 15 | 22 |
| Spanish origin | 17 | 17 | - | - | 15 | 2 |
| Other | 20 | 16 | 4 | 1 | - | 20 |

Note: Persons of Spanish origin may be of any race.

Source: U.S. Department of Commerce, Bureau of the Census, Current Population Reports Series P-20, No. 424 Series P-20, No. 424.

## TABLE 33. LIVING ARRANGEMENTS OF PERSONS 15 YEARS OLD AND OVER, BY SELECTED CHARACTERISTICS: 1986

[Based on Current Population Survey which includes members of armed forces living off post or with families on post, but excludes other armed forces.]

| | | All Races[1] Percent living- | | | | White persons percent living- | | | Black persons percent living- | | |
|---|---|---|---|---|---|---|---|---|---|---|---|
| Age and sex | Total (1000's) | Alone | With spouse | With other relatives | With non-relatives | Alone | With spouse | With other relatives | Alone | With spouse | With other relatives |
| Total | 184,828 | 11.5 | 55.9 | 26.7 | 5.9 | 11.5 | 58.5 | 24.1 | 12.2 | 36.0 | 45.7 |
| 15-19 years old | 18,274 | .5 | 3.2 | 93.4 | 3.2 | .6 | 3.6 | 92.5 | .5 | 1.1 | 96.1 |
| 20-24 years old | 19,948 | 6.5 | 28.4 | 51.2 | 14.0 | 6.7 | 31.0 | 47.8 | 5.4 | 14.2 | 70.0 |
| 25-44 years old | 74,561 | 8.7 | 65.8 | 17.8 | 7.6 | 8.8 | 68.5 | 15.1 | 9.2 | 44.7 | 39.1 |
| 45-64 years old | 44,723 | 11.1 | 74.8 | 11.3 | 2.8 | 10.4 | 77.4 | 9.7 | 18.1 | 51.8 | 24.9 |
| 65 years old and over | 27,321 | 30.4 | 53.6 | 13.7 | 2.3 | 30.5 | 54.9 | 12.5 | 33.0 | 39.5 | 23.8 |
| 65-74 years old | 16,879 | 24.9 | 62.4 | 10.6 | 2.1 | 24.5 | 64.0 | 9.5 | 31.7 | 45.3 | 19.7 |
| 75 years old and over | 10,442 | 39.3 | 39.4 | 18.8 | 2.5 | 40.1 | 40.3 | 17.3 | 35.1 | 29.3 | 30.9 |
| Male | 88,474 | 9.4 | 58.4 | 25.1 | 7.1 | 9.1 | 60.7 | 23.2 | 12.2 | 40.4 | 39.1 |
| 15-19 years old | 9,183 | .5 | 1.5 | 95.1 | 2.9 | .5 | 1.7 | 94.8 | .3 | .2 | 97.0 |
| 20-24 years old | 9,788 | 7.0 | 21.3 | 56.7 | 14.9 | 7.4 | 23.3 | 54.0 | 5.5 | 10.8 | 71.6 |
| 25-44 years old | 36,911 | 10.7 | 64.6 | 15.1 | 9.6 | 10.6 | 66.6 | 13.3 | 12.6 | 47.7 | 29.5 |
| 45-64 years old | 21,320 | 9.0 | 80.4 | 7.1 | 3.4 | 8.1 | 82.4 | 6.5 | 18.1 | 62.0 | 11.9 |
| 65 years old and over | 11,272 | 14.9 | 75.3 | 7.2 | 2.5 | 14.3 | 76.7 | 6.7 | 23.3 | 59.9 | 11.9 |
| 65-74 years old | 7,440 | 12.7 | 79.2 | 5.7 | 2.4 | 11.8 | 80.4 | 5.4 | 23.0 | 64.0 | 9.9 |
| 75 years old and over | 3,832 | 19.2 | 67.9 | 10.2 | 2.7 | 19.0 | 69.5 | 9.2 | 24.0 | 51.7 | 16.0 |
| Female | 96,354 | 13.4 | 53.7 | 28.2 | 4.8 | 13.8 | 56.4 | 24.9 | 12.1 | 32.4 | 51.2 |
| 15-19 years old | 9,091 | .6 | 4.9 | 9.10 | 3.5 | .6 | 5.6 | 90.1 | .7 | 1.9 | 95.2 |
| 20-24 years old | 10,160 | 5.9 | 35.2 | 45.8 | 13.1 | 6.1 | 38.5 | 41.7 | 5.4 | 17.0 | 68.7 |
| 25-44 years old | 37,649 | 6.8 | 67.0 | 20.5 | 5.7 | 6.9 | 70.3 | 16.8 | 6.4 | 42.1 | 47.1 |
| 45-64 years old | 23,404 | 13.0 | 69.7 | 15.2 | 2.2 | 12.4 | 72.8 | 12.7 | 18.1 | 43.7 | 35.1 |
| 65 years old and over | 16,049 | 41.3 | 38.3 | 18.2 | 2.1 | 41.9 | 39.5 | 16.6 | 39.3 | 25.8 | 31.8 |
| 65-74 years old | 9,439 | 34.6 | 49.2 | 14.4 | 1.9 | 34.5 | 51.0 | 12.8 | 38.0 | 31.5 | 26.9 |
| 75 years old and over | 6,610 | 51.0 | 22.8 | 23.8 | 2.4 | 52.2 | 23.4 | 22.0 | 41.5 | 16.7 | 39.6 |

[1]Includes other races not shown separately

Source: US Bureau of the Census, *Current Population reports,* series P-20.

## TABLE 34. FAMILIES BY NUMBER OF OWN CHILDREN UNDER 18 YEARS OLD: 1970 TO 1986

[Except as noted, as of March, and based on Current Population Survey. See also *Historical Statistics, Colonial Times to 1970*, series A 353-358]

| Race and Year | Number of families (1000's) | Percent distribution by number of own children | | | | | | |
|---|---|---|---|---|---|---|---|---|
| | | All Families | none | 1 | 2 | 3 | 4 or more | average size of family |
| All Families[1] | | | | | | | | |
| 1970 | 51,586 | 100.0 | 44.1 | 18.2 | 17.4 | 10.6 | 9.8 | 3.58 |
| 1975 | 55,712 | 100.0 | 46.0 | 19.7 | 18.0 | 9.3 | 6.9 | 3.42 |
| 1980 | 59,550 | 100.0 | 47.9 | 20.9 | 19.3 | 7.8 | 4.1 | 3.29 |
| 1985 | 62,706 | 100.0 | 50.4 | 20.9 | 18.6 | 7.2 | 3.0 | 3.23 |
| 1986 | 63,558 | 100.0 | 50.2 | 21.0 | 18.7 | 7.2 | 2.7 | 3.21 |
| White Families | | | | | | | | |
| 1970 | 46,261 | 100.0 | 44.8 | 18.2 | 17.7 | 10.5 | 8.6 | 3.52 |
| 1975 | 49,451 | 100.0 | 47.2 | 19.4 | 18.0 | 9.2 | 6.2 | 3.36 |
| 1980 | 52,243 | 100.0 | 49.3 | 20.5 | 19.1 | 7.5 | 3.6 | 3.23 |
| 1985 | 54,400 | 100.0 | 51.8 | 20.5 | 18.3 | 6.8 | 2.6 | 3.16 |
| 1966 | 54,991 | 100.0 | 51.7 | 20.6 | 16.4 | 6.8 | 2.4 | 3.15 |
| Black Families | | | | | | | | |
| 1970 | 4,887 | 100.0 | 38.9 | 17.6 | 14.8 | 10.1 | 18.5 | 4.13 |
| 1975 | 5,498 | 100.0 | 36.8 | 22.0 | 17.0 | 10.6 | 13.6 | 3.90 |
| 1980 | 6,164 | 100.0 | 36.2 | 23.4 | 20.0 | 10.2 | 8.2 | 3.67 |
| 1985 | 6,778 | 100.0 | 42.6 | 23.3 | 19.6 | 9.0 | 5.5 | 3.60 |
| 1986 | 6,921 | 100.0 | 41.4 | 23.3 | 19.6 | 9.9 | 5.9 | 3.55 |
| Hispanic Families[2] | | | | | | | | |
| 1970[3] | 2,004 | 100.0 | 29.8 | 19.5 | 19.4 | 13.3 | 18.1 | (NA) |
| 1975 | 2,447 | 100.0 | 29.4 | 23.1 | 19.7 | 13.4 | 14.5 | (NA) |
| 1980 | 3,029 | 100.0 | 31.2 | 22.4 | 23.0 | 13.4 | 9.9 | 3.90 |
| 1985 | 3,939 | 100.0 | 33.9 | 22.9 | 22.0 | 12.2 | 8.9 | 3.88 |
| 1986 | 4,206 | 100.0 | 34.5 | 22.2 | 23.7 | 12.4 | 7.1 | 3.87 |

NA Not available [1] Includes other races, not shown separately. [2] Hispanic persons may be of any race. [3] As of April. Based on Census of Population
Source: U.S. Bureau of the census, U.S. Census of Population, 1970, and Current Population Reports, series P-20, No 149, and earlier reports.

## TABLE 35. CHILDREN UNDER 18 YEARS OLD, BY PRESENCE OF PARENTS: 1970 TO 1986

[Excludes persons under 18 years old who maintained households or family groups. It is possible that some of the sizeable increase in children living with never married mothers is the result of new and more definitive coding procedures introduced by the Census Bureau in 1982.]

| Race and Year | Number (1000's) | Both parents | Percent living with mother only: Total | Divorced | Married- spouse Absent | Single[1] | Widowed | Father only | Neither parent |
|---|---|---|---|---|---|---|---|---|---|
| All Races[2] | | | | | | | | | |
| 1970 | 69,162 | 85.2 | 10.8 | 3.3 | 4.7 | .8 | 2.0 | 1.1 | 2.9 |
| 1980 | 63,427 | 76.7 | 18.0 | 7.5 | 5.7 | 2.8 | 2.0 | 1.7 | 3.6 |
| 1985 | 62,475 | 73.9 | 20.9 | 8.5 | 5.4 | 5.6 | 1.5 | 2.5 | 2.7 |
| 1986 | 62,763 | 73.9 | 21.0 | 8.5 | 5.3 | 5.7 | 1.4 | 2.5 | 2.6 |
| White | | | | | | | | | |
| 1970 | 58,790 | 89.5 | 7.8 | 3.1 | 2.8 | .2 | 1.7 | .9 | 1.8 |
| 1980 | 52,242 | 82.7 | 13.5 | 7.0 | 3.9 | 1.0 | 1.7 | 1.6 | 2.2 |
| 1985 | 50,836 | 80.0 | 15.6 | 8.1 | 4.1 | 2.1 | 1.3 | 2.4 | 2.0 |
| 1986 | 50,931 | 79.9 | 15.7 | 8.2 | 4.1 | 2.3 | 1.2 | 2.5 | 1.9 |
| Black | | | | | | | | | |
| 1970 | 9,422 | 58.5 | 29.5 | 4.6 | 16.3 | 4.4 | 4.2 | 2.3 | 9.7 |
| 1980 | 9,375 | 42.2 | 43.9 | 10.9 | 16.2 | 12.8 | 4.0 | 1.9 | 11.9 |
| 1985 | 9,479 | 39.5 | 51.0 | 11.3 | 12.4 | 24.8 | 2.5 | 2.9 | 6.6 |
| 1986 | 9,532 | 40.6 | 50.6 | 11.1 | 12.0 | 24.9 | 2.6 | 2.4 | 6.3 |
| Hispanic[3] | | | | | | | | | |
| 1970[4] | 4,006 | 77.7 | (NA) | (NA) | (NA) | (NA) | (NA) | (NA) | (NA) |
| 1980 | 5,459 | 75.4 | 19.6 | 5.9 | 8.2 | 4.0 | 1.5 | 1.5 | 3.5 |
| 1985 | 6,057 | 67.9 | 26.6 | 7.3 | 11.1 | 6.5 | 1.7 | 2.2 | 3.3 |
| 1986 | 6,430 | 66.5 | 27.7 | 8.6 | 10.7 | 7.0 | 1.4 | 2.7 | 3.1 |

NA Not available. [1]Never married [2]Includes other races not shown separately.[3]Hispanic persons may be of any race
[4]All persons under 18 years old.
Source: U.S. Bureau of the Census, *Current Population Reports,* series P-20 No. 411and earlier and forthcoming reports

## TABLE 36. PERCENT MARRIED AND DIVORCED OF THE POPULATION BY SEX AND RACE: 1970 TO 1986

[Persons 18 years old and over. Excludes members of Armed Forces except those living off post or with their families on post.]

| Sex and Race | 1970 | 1975 | 1977 | 1979 | 1980 | 1982 | 1983 | 1984 | 1985 | 1986 |
|---|---|---|---|---|---|---|---|---|---|---|
| Percent married | | | | | | | | | | |
| Male[1] | 75.3 | 72.8 | 70.9 | 70.1 | 68.4 | 67.8 | 66.6 | 65.8 | 65.7 | 65.5 |
| White | 76.1 | 73.9 | 72.3 | 70.7 | 70.0 | 69.0 | 68.3 | 67.7 | 67.6 | 67.2 |
| Black | 66.5 | 62.7 | 59.6 | 57.6 | 54.6 | 53.5 | 52.2 | 50.6 | 50.7 | 51.7 |
| Female[1] | 68.5 | 66.7 | 65.3 | 63.5 | 63.0 | 61.9 | 61.4 | 60.8 | 60.4 | 60.5 |
| White | 69.3 | 68.0 | 66.7 | 65.2 | 64.7 | 63.7 | 63.3 | 62.8 | 62.7 | 62.4 |
| Black | 61.7 | 55.5 | 53.5 | 50.3 | 48.7 | 48.1 | 45.7 | 44.5 | 42.7 | 44.5 |
| Percent divorced | | | | | | | | | | |
| Male[1] | 2.5 | 3.7 | 4.5 | 4.7 | 5.2 | 5.7 | 5.8 | 6.1 | 6.5 | 6.6 |
| White | 2.4 | 3.6 | 4.4 | 4.5 | 5.0 | 5.7 | 5.7 | 6.0 | 6.4 | 6.6 |
| Black | 3.6 | 5.1 | 5.4 | 6.9 | 7.0 | 8.1 | 7.4 | 7.0 | 7.6 | 7.4 |
| Female[1] | 3.9 | 5.3 | 6.2 | 6.6 | 7.1 | 8.0 | 7.9 | 8.3 | 8.7 | 8.9 |
| White | 3.8 | 5.0 | 6.0 | 6.4 | 6.8 | 7.8 | 7.6 | 8.0 | 8.5 | 8.6 |
| Black | 5.0 | 7.5 | 8.8 | 9.3 | 9.5 | 10.3 | 10.5 | 11.0 | 11.0 | 11.6 |

[1]Includes other races, not shown separately.
Source: U.S. Bureau of the Census, Current Population Reports, series P-20, No. 418, and earlier reports.

## TABLE 37. MARITAL STATUS OF THE BLACK POPULATION: 1970 TO 1986

| Sex and Year | Number of persons (1000's) | | | | | Percent Distribution | | | | |
|---|---|---|---|---|---|---|---|---|---|---|
| | Total | Single | Married | Widowed | Divorced | Total | Single | Married | Widowed | Divorced |
| **Black** | | | | | | | | | | |
| Totals | | | | | | | | | | |
| 1970 | 12,972 | 2,668 | 8,310 | 1,427 | 567 | 100.0 | 20.6 | 64.1 | 11.0 | 4.4 |
| 1975 | 14,262 | 3,449 | 8,373 | 1,521 | 920 | 100.0 | 24.2 | 58.7 | 10.7 | 6.5 |
| 1980 | 16,638 | 5,070 | 8,545 | 1,627 | 1,396 | 100.0 | 30.5 | 51.4 | 9.8 | 8.4 |
| 1985 | 18,607 | 6,439 | 8,611 | 1,791 | 1,764 | 100.0 | 34.6 | 46.3 | 8.6 | 9.5 |
| 1986 | 18,940 | 6,439 | 9,036 | 1,830 | 1,837 | 100.0 | 34.0 | 47.7 | 8.6 | 9.7 |
| Male | | | | | | | | | | |
| 1970 | 5,898 | 1,435 | 3,944 | 307 | 212 | 100.0 | 24.3 | 66.9 | 5.2 | 3.6 |
| 1975 | 6,368 | 1,733 | 3,990 | 319 | 327 | 100.0 | 27.2 | 62.7 | 5.0 | 5.1 |
| 1980 | 7,416 | 2,540 | 4,051 | 308 | 517 | 100.0 | 34.3 | 54.6 | 4.2 | 7.0 |
| 1985 | 8,325 | 3,149 | 4,217 | 324 | 636 | 100.0 | 37.8 | 50.7 | 3.9 | 7.6 |
| 1986 | 8,501 | 3,155 | 4,391 | 328 | 626 | 100.0 | 37.1 | 51.7 | 3.9 | 7.4 |
| Female | | | | | | | | | | |
| 1970 | 7,074 | 1,233 | 4,366 | 1,120 | 355 | 100.0 | 17.4 | 61.7 | 15.8 | 5.0 |
| 1975 | 7,894 | 1,716 | 4,383 | 1,202 | 593 | 100.0 | 21.7 | 55.5 | 15.2 | 7.5 |
| 1980 | 9,222 | 2,530 | 4,494 | 1,319 | 878 | 100.0 | 27.4 | 48.7 | 14.3 | 9.5 |
| 1985 | 10,281 | 3,290 | 4,394 | 1,468 | 1,128 | 100.0 | 32.0 | 42.7 | 14.3 | 11.0 |
| 1986 | 10,441 | 3,284 | 4,645 | 1,301 | 1,211 | 100.0 | 31.5 | 44.5 | 12.5 | 11.6 |

Source: U.S. Bureau of the Census, Census of the population: 1970, PC(2)1C, Persons of Spanish Origin; Current Population Reports, series P-20, No. 418 and earlier reports; and unpublished data

## TABLE 38. LIFETIME-BIRTHS EXPECTED BY WIVES, 18-34 YEARS OLD-PERCENT DISTRIBUTION: 1975-1986

[Currently married women in the civilian noninstitutional population. Data limited to wives reporting on birth expectations. Based on Current Population Survey.]

| | Age | | | | Race | | | Years of School Completed | | |
|---|---|---|---|---|---|---|---|---|---|---|
| | Total[1] | 18-24 years | 25-29 years | 30-34 years | White | Black | Hispanic[2] | Not high school graduate | High school 4 years | College 1 year or more |
| Births Expected | | | | | | | | | | |
| **1975** | | | | | | | | | | |
| None | 4.8 | 4.1 | 4.9 | 5.2 | 4.9 | 3.0 | 3.2 | 2.7 | 4.2 | 7.0 |
| One | 10.9 | 11.2 | 11.7 | 9.8 | 10.8 | 10.7 | 10.6 | 11.0 | 11.4 | 10.1 |
| Two | 49.0 | 58.2 | 50.4 | 38.3 | 49.8 | 40.0 | 40.4 | 37.6 | 49.8 | 55.5 |
| Three | 23.2 | 19.4 | 23.3 | 26.8 | 23.3 | 22.4 | 25.2 | 25.0 | 24.3 | 20.0 |
| Four or more | 12.1 | 7.0 | 9.8 | 19.8 | 11.1 | 24.0 | 20.5 | 23.6 | 10.3 | 7.3 |
| **1980** | | | | | | | | | | |
| None | 5.9 | 4.9 | 5.5 | 7.0 | 6.0 | 4.0 | 2.8 | 2.6 | 5.6 | 7.7 |
| One | 13.3 | 12.8 | 13.2 | 13.6 | 13.2 | 14.4 | 9.4 | 11.7 | 14.4 | 12.4 |
| Two | 51.1 | 56.0 | 52.8 | 45.7 | 51.5 | 45.3 | 44.3 | 39.7 | 52.6 | 54.4 |
| Three | 20.5 | 19.1 | 20.3 | 21.8 | 20.4 | 22.2 | 24.2 | 26.7 | 19.7 | 18.8 |
| Four or more | 9.3 | 7.2 | 8.3 | 11.9 | 8.8 | 14.2 | 19.4 | 19.4 | 7.7 | 6.8 |
| **1986** | | | | | | | | | | |
| None | 4.7 | 2.9 | 4.5 | 5.9 | 4.8 | 2.8 | 2.5 | 2.5 | 4.3 | 6.0 |
| One | 12.2 | 11.6 | 10.9 | 13.9 | 12.0 | 14.8 | 11.9 | 12.0 | 13.3 | 11.1 |
| Two | 50.0 | 54.8 | 51.6 | 45.8 | 50.7 | 42.4 | 42.5 | 44.1 | 49.2 | 53.1 |
| Three | 23.1 | 21.4 | 23.6 | 23.6 | 22.9 | 26.2 | 23.4 | 24.3 | 23.4 | 22.3 |
| Four or more | 10.0 | 9.4 | 9.4 | 10.8 | 9.5 | 13.8 | 19.8 | 17.2 | 9.8 | 7.6 |

[1] Includes other races, not shown separately. [2] Hispanic persons may be of any race.
Source: U.S. Bureau of the Census, Current Population Reports, series P-20. No. 406, and earlier and forthcoming reports.

## TABLE 39. BIRTHS TO UNMARRIED WOMEN, BY RACE AND AGE OF MOTHER: 1960 TO 1985

[Beginning 1970, excludes births to nonresidents of U.S. Data for 1960-79 include estimates for States in which marital status data were not reported. Beginning in 1980, marital status is inferred from a comparison of the child's and parents surnames on the birth certificate for those States that do not report on marital status. No estimates included for misstatements on birth records or failures to register births.]

| Race and age of mother | 1960 | 1965 | 1970 | 1975 | 1980 | 1981 | 1982 | 1983 | 1984 | 1985 |
|---|---|---|---|---|---|---|---|---|---|---|
| | | | | Numbers in 1,000's | | | | | | |
| Total live births[1] | 224.3 | 291.2 | 398.7 | 447.9 | 665.7 | 686.6 | 715.2 | 737.9 | 770.4 | 828.2 |
| White | 82.5 | 123.7 | 175.1 | 186.4 | 320.1 | 337.1 | 355.2 | 370.9 | 391.9 | 433.0 |
| Black | (NA) | (NA) | 215.1 | 249.6 | 325.7 | 328.9 | 335.9 | 341.1 | 350.9 | 365.5 |
| Under 15 years | 4.6 | 6.1 | 9.5 | 11.0 | 9.0 | 8.6 | 8.7 | 8.8 | 9.1 | 9.4 |
| 15-19 years | 87.1 | 123.1 | 190.4 | 222.5 | 262.8 | 259.2 | 260.6 | 261.3 | 261.1 | 270.9 |
| 20-24 years | 68.0 | 90.7 | 126.7 | 134.0 | 237.3 | 246.9 | 257.5 | 265.6 | 279.2 | 300.4 |
| 25-29 years | 32.1 | 36.8 | 40.6 | 50.2 | 99.6 | 109.2 | 119.0 | 126.5 | 137.0 | 152.0 |
| 30-34 years | 18.9 | 19.6 | 19.1 | 19.8 | 41.0 | 45.3 | 49.6 | 53.9 | 59.3 | 67.3 |
| 35 years and over | 13.6 | 15.1 | 12.4 | 10.4 | 16.1 | 17.4 | 19.9 | 21.8 | 24.8 | 28.2 |
| | | | | Percent distribution | | | | | | |
| Total[1] | 100.0 | 100.0 | 100.0 | 100.0 | 100.0 | 100.0 | 100.0 | 100.0 | 100.0 | 100.0 |
| White | 36.8 | 42.5 | 43.9 | 41.6 | 48.1 | 49.1 | 49.7 | 50.3 | 50.9 | 52.3 |
| Black | (NA) | (NA) | 54.0 | 55.7 | 48.9 | 47.9 | 46.9 | 46.2 | 45.5 | 44.1 |
| Under 15 years | 2.1 | 2.1 | 2.4 | 2.5 | 1.4 | 1.3 | 1.2 | 1.2 | 1.2 | 1.1 |
| 15-19 years | 38.8 | 42.3 | 47.8 | 49.7 | 39.5 | 37.8 | 36.4 | 35.4 | 33.9 | 32.7 |
| 20-24 years | 30.3 | 31.1 | 31.8 | 29.9 | 35.6 | 36.0 | 36.0 | 36.0 | 36.2 | 36.3 |
| 25-29 years | 14.3 | 12.6 | 10.2 | 11.2 | 15.0 | 15.9 | 16.6 | 17.1 | 17.8 | 18.4 |
| 30-34 years | 8.4 | 6.7 | 4.8 | 4.4 | 6.2 | 6.6 | 6.9 | 7.3 | 7.7 | 8.1 |
| 35 years and over | 6.1 | 5.2 | 3.1 | 2.3 | 2.4 | 2.5 | 2.8 | 3.0 | 3.2 | 3.4 |
| | | | | Births to unmarried women as percent of all births in racial groups | | | | | | |
| Total[1] | 5.3 | 7.7 | 10.7 | 14.2 | 18.4 | 18.9 | 19.4 | 20.3 | 21.0 | 22.0 |
| White | 2.3 | 4.0 | 5.7 | 7.3 | 11.0 | 11.6 | 12.1 | 12.8 | 13.4 | 14.5 |
| Black | (NA) | (NA) | 37.6 | 48.8 | 55.2 | 56.0 | 56.7 | 58.2 | 59.2 | 60.1 |
| Birth rate[2] | | | | | | | | | | |
| Total[1] [3] | 21.6 | 23.5 | 26.4 | 24.5 | 29.4 | 29.6 | 30.0 | 30.4 | 31.0 | 32.8 |
| White[3] | 9.2 | 11.6 | 13.8 | 12.4 | 17.6 | 18.2 | 18.8 | 19.3 | 20.1 | 21.8 |
| Black[3] | (NA) | (NA) | 95,5 | 84.2 | 81.4 | 81.4 | 79.6 | 77.7 | 76.8 | 78.8 |
| 15-19 years | 15.3 | 16.7 | 22.4 | 23.9 | 27.6 | 28.2 | 28.9 | 29.7 | 30.2 | 31.6 |
| 20-24 years | 39.7 | 39.9 | 38.4 | 31.2 | 40.9 | 40.9 | 41.4 | 42.0 | 43.2 | 46 8 |
| 25-29 years | 45.1 | 49.3 | 37.0 | 27.5 | 34.0 | 34.7 | 35.1 | 35.6 | 37.0 | 39.8 |
| 30-34 years | 27.8 | 37.5 | 27.1 | 17.9 | 21.1 | 20.8 | 21.9 | 22.3 | 23.2 | 25.0 |

NA Not available. [1]Includes other races not shown separately. [2]Rate per 1,000 unmarried women (never-married, widowed and divorced) estimated. [3]Covers women aged 15-44 years.
Source. U.S. National Center for Health Statistics, *Vital Statistics of the United States*, annual; and unpublished data.

## TABLE 40. BIRTHS AND BIRTH RATES: 1960 TO 1985

[Births in thousands except where indicated. Beginning 1970 excludes births to nonresidents of U.S.]

| Item | 1960 | 1965 | 1970 | 1975 | 1980 | 1981 | 1982 | 1983 | 1984 | 1985 |
|---|---|---|---|---|---|---|---|---|---|---|
| Live Births[1] | 4,258 | 3,760 | 3,731 | 3,144 | 3,612 | 3,629 | 3,681 | 3,639 | 3,669 | 3,761 |
| Average annual percent change | .8 | -2.5 | -.2 | -3.4 | 3.4 | .5 | 1.4 | -1.1 | .8 | 2.5 |
| White | 3,601 | 3,124 | 3,091 | 2,552 | 2,899 | 2,909 | 2,942 | 2,904 | 2,924 | 2,991 |
| Black | 602 | 581 | 572 | 512 | 590 | 588 | 593 | 586 | 593 | 608 |
| Male | 2,180 | 1,927 | 1,915 | 1,613 | 1,853 | 1.660 | 1,688 | 1,866 | 1,879 | 1,928 |
| Female | 2,078 | 1,833 | 1,816 | 1,531 | 1,760 | 1,769 | 1,795 | 1,773 | 1,790 | 1,833 |
| Males per 1000 females | 104.9 | 105.1 | 105.3 | 105.4 | 105.3 | 105.2 | 105.1 | 105.2 | 105.0 | 105.2 |
| Age of mother | | | | | | | | | | |
| Under 20 years | 594 | 599 | 656 | 595 | 562 | 537 | 524 | 499 | 480 | 478 |
| 20-24 years | 1,427 | 1,337 | 1,419 | 1,094 | 1,226 | 1,212 | 1,206 | 1,160 | 1,142 | 1,141 |
| 25-29 years | 1,093 | 926 | 995 | 937 | 1,108 | 1,128 | 1,152 | 1,148 | 1,166 | 1,201 |
| 30-34 years | 688 | 529 | 428 | 376 | 550 | 581 | 605 | 625 | 658 | 696 |
| 35-39 years | 360 | 283 | 180 | 115 | 141 | 146 | 168 | 180 | 196 | 214 |
| 40 years or rnore | 97 | 86 | 53 | 28 | 24 | 25 | 26 | 27 | 28 | 29 |
| Birth rate per 1000 population | 23.7 | 19.4 | 15.0 | 14.6 | 15.9 | 15.8 | 15.9 | 15.5 | 15.5 | 15.8 |
| White | 22.7 | 18.3 | 17.4 | 13.6 | 14.9 | 14.8 | 14.9 | 14.6 | 14.5 | 14.8 |
| Black | 31.9 | 27.7 | 25.3 | 20.7 | 22.1 | 21.6 | 21.4 | 20 9 | 20 8 | 21.1 |
| Male | 24.7 | 20.3 | 19.4 | 15.4 | 16.8 | 16.7 | 16.7 | 16.4 | 16.3 | 16.6 |
| Female | 22.8 | 18.6 | 17.4 | 13.8 | 15.1 | 15.0 | 15.1 | 14.7 | 14.7 | 15.0 |
| Plural birth ratio[2] | 20.4 | 20.1 | [3]18.1 | 19.2 | 19.3 | 19.7 | 19.9 | 20.3 | 20.3 | 21.0 |
| White | 19.3 | 19.0 | [3]17.3 | 18.5 | 18.5 | 18.8 | 19.2 | 19.6 | 19.8 | 20.4 |
| Black | (NA) | (NA) | [3]22.8 | 23.1 | 24.1 | 24.7 | 24.1 | 24.5 | 24.2 | 25.3 |
| Birth rate per 1000 women[4] | 118.0 | 96.6 | 65.5 | 66.0 | 68.4 | 67.4 | 67.3 | 65.8 | 65.4 | 66.2 |
| White[4] | 113.2 | 91.4 | 84.1 | 62.5 | 64.7 | 63.9 | 63.9 | 62.4 | 62.2 | 63.0 |
| Blacks[4] | 153.5 | 133.2 | 115.4 | 87.9 | 88.1 | 85.4 | 84.1 | 81.7 | 81.4 | 82.2 |
| Age of mother | | | | | | | | | | |
| 10-14 years | .8 | .8 | 1.2 | 1.3 | 1.2 | 1.1 | 1.1 | 1.1 | 1.2 | 1.2 |
| 15-19 years | 89.1 | 70.5 | 68.3 | 55.6 | 53.0 | 52.7 | 52.9 | 51.7 | 50.9 | 51.3 |
| 20-24 years | 258.1 | 195.3 | 167.8 | 113.0 | 115.1 | 111.8 | 111.3 | 108.3 | 107.3 | 108.9 |
| 25-29 years | 197.4 | 161.6 | 145.1 | 108.2 | 112.9 | 112.0 | 111.0 | 108.7 | 108.3 | 110.5 |
| 30-34 years | 112.7 | 94.4 | 73.3 | 52.3 | 61.9 | 61.4 | 64.2 | 64.6 | 66.5 | 68.5 |
| 35-39 years | 56.2 | 46.2 | 31.7 | 19.5 | 19.8 | 20.0 | 21.1 | 22.1 | 22.8 | 23.9 |
| 40-44 years | 15.5 | 12.8 | 8.1 | 4.6 | 3.9 | 3.8 | 3.9 | 3.8 | 3.9 | 4.0 |
| 45-49 years | [5].9 | .8 | .5 | .3 | .2 | .2 | .2 | .2 | .2 | .2 |

NA Not available. [1]Includes other races, not shown separately.
[2]Per 1,000 live births. [3]1971. [4]Per 1,000 women, 15-44 years old in specified group.
[5]Rate computed by relating births to mothers 45 years old and over to women 45 to 49 years old.
Source: U.S. National Center for Health Statistics, *Vital Statistics of the United States*, annual; and unpublished data.

## TABLE 41. ABILITY TO BEAR CHILDREN OF CURRENTLY MARRIED COUPLES, BY AGE OF WIFE, NUMBER OF PRIOR BIRTHS, AND RACE

[Based on the National Survey of Family Growth]

| | Age of Wife | | | | Number of Prior Births | | | |
|---|---|---|---|---|---|---|---|---|
| | All women, 15-44 years | 15-24 years | 25-34 years | 35-44 years | 0 | 1 | 2 | 3 or more |
| Race and Fetility Status | | | | | | | | |
| All races[1] (1000) | 28,231 | 4,741 | 12,924 | 10,566 | 5,098 | 5,891 | 9,042 | 8,201 |
| Percent distribution: | | | | | | | | |
| Surgically sterile[2] | 38.9 | 7.2 | 31.6 | 62.0 | 9.9 | 17.7 | 46.9 | 63.3 |
| Infertile | 8.5 | 8.7 | 7.3 | 9.7 | 19.6 | 10.8 | 5.0 | 3.8 |
| Fecund | 52.6 | 84.1 | 61.0 | 28.3 | 70.5 | 71.5 | 48.1 | 32.9 |
| White (1000) | 25,195 | 4,323 | 11,457 | 9,414 | 4,678 | 5,254 | 8,107 | 7,156 |
| Percent distribution: | | | | | | | | |
| Surgically sterile[2] | 38.9 | 7.3 | 31.5 | 62.3 | 9.8 | 18.5 | 47.2 | 63.4 |
| Infertile | 8.1 | 8.0 | 7.0 | 9.6 | 19.1 | 10.1 | 4.7 | 3.4 |
| Fecund | 53.0 | 84.7 | 61.4 | 28.1 | 71.1 | 71.4 | 48.0 | 33.2 |
| Black (1000) | 2,130 | 328 | 1,025 | 778 | 252 | 410 | 678 | 790 |
| Percent distribution: | | | | | | | | |
| Surgically sterile[2] | 36.2 | 7.4 | 31.8 | 54.1 | 10.1 | 8.5 | 34.9 | 60.0 |
| Infertile[3] | 13.1 | 11.9 | 11.5 | 15.7 | 30.6 | 18.5 | 8.9 | [4]8.3 |
| Fecund[5] | 50.7 | 80.7 | 56.7 | 30.2 | 59.4 | 73.0 | 56.2 | 31.8 |

[1]Includes other races not shown separately. [2] Includes sterilization of the husband or wife. [3]Continuously married, had not used contraception, and had not become pregnant for at least 12 months before the date of interview. [4]Figure does not meet reliability standards. [5]Neither surgically sterile nor fertile.
Source: U.S. National Center for Health Statistics, Advance Data from *Vital and Health Statistics*, No. 104; and unpublished data.

## TABLE 42. PROVISIONAL STATISTICS: 1987

| | Number | | Rate* | |
|---|---|---|---|---|
| | 1986 | 1987 | 1986 | 1987 |
| Live births | 3,770,000 | 3,717,000 | 15.8 | 15.4 |
| Deaths | 2,085,000 | 2,089,000 | 8.7 | 8.6 |
| Natural increase | 1,685,000 | 1,628,000 | 7.1 | 6.8 |
| Divorces | 1,184,000 | 1,160,000 | 5.0 | 4.8 |
| Infant deaths | 39,400 | 38,300 | 10.5 | 10.3 |
| Population base (in millions) | 241.6 | 238.9 | | |

*Per 1000 population

Note: Rates are based on the 1980 Census of Population.

## TABLE 43. UNWANTED BIRTHS OF EVER- MARRIED WOMEN, 15-44 YEARS OLD: 1973 AND 1982

[Covers the birth experience to date of all ever-married women whether or not they gave children up for adoption. Based on the 1973 and 1982 National Survey of Family Growth.]

| | Number of children ever born (1,000's) | | Percent of children ever born | | | | | |
|---|---|---|---|---|---|---|---|---|
| | | | Wanted at conception | | | | Unwanted at conception | |
| | | | Total | | Mistimed | | | |
| Age and Race | 1973 | 1982 | 1973 | 1982 | 1973 | 1982 | 1973 | 1982 |
| All Races | 66,239 | 65,878 | 85.8 | 90.1 | 25.7 | 28.2 | 14.0 | 9.6 |
| 15-24 years | 5,763 | 4,843 | 91.8 | 93.6 | 41.7 | 46.8 | 8.1 | [2]6.4 |
| 25-34 years | 26,262 | 26,650 | 87.8 | 92.3 | 27.7 | 27.3 | 12.0 | 7.4 |
| 35-44 years | 34,214 | 34,385 | 83.2 | 86.0 | 21.5 | 26.2 | 16.6 | 11.7 |
| White | 57,012 | 55,497 | 88.4 | 92.1 | 25.5 | 27.7 | 11.4 | 7.7 |
| 15-24 years | 4,859 | 4,238 | 93.6 | 95.1 | 40.5 | 47.2 | 6.3 | [2]4.9 |
| 25-34 years | 22,760 | 22,314 | 90.0 | 94.1 | 27.2 | 26.7 | 9.9 | 5.6 |
| 35-44 years | 29,393 | 28,946 | 86.4 | 90.1 | 21.6 | 25.6 | 13.4 | 9.7 |
| Black | 8,634 | 8,467 | 68.0 | 77.5 | 27.4 | 32-2 | 31.5 | 21.8 |
| 15-24 years | 868 | 548 | 81.4 | 82.0 | 47.8 | 43.8 | 18.6 | [2]18.0 |
| 25-34 years | 3,239 | 3,491 | 72.1 | 82.3 | 31.0 | 33.9 | 27.3 | 17.5 |
| 35-44 years | 4,528 | 4,428 | 62.4 | 73.2 | 20.9 | 29.4 | 37.0 | 25.7 |

[1]Including other races not shown separately. [2]Figure does not meet standards of reliability or precision.
Source: U.S. National Center for Health Statistics, unpublished data.

## TABLE 44. INFANT, MATERNAL, AND NEONATAL MORTALITY RATES, AND FETAL MORTALITY RATIOS, BY RACE: 1960 TO 1985

[Deaths per 1,000 live births, except as noted. Beginning 1970, excludes deaths of nonresidents of U.S.]

| Item | 1960 | 1970 | 1975 | 1977 | 1979 | 1980 | 1981 | 1983 | 1984 | 1985 |
|---|---|---|---|---|---|---|---|---|---|---|
| Infant deaths[1] | 26.0 | 20.0 | 15.2 | 13.8 | 13.1 | 12.6 | 11.5 | 11.2 | 10.8 | 10.6 |
| White | 22.9 | 17.8 | 14.2 | 12.3 | 11.4 | 11.0 | 10.5 | 9.7 | 9.4 | 9.3 |
| Black and other | 43.2 | 30.9 | 23.5 | 21.1 | 19.8 | 19.1 | 17.3 | 16.8 | 16.1 | 15.8 |
| Black | 44.3 | 32.6 | 26.2 | 23.6 | 21.8 | 21.4 | 20.0 | 19.2 | 18.4 | 18.2 |
| Maternal deaths[2] | 37.1 | 21.5 | 12.3 | 9.6 | 9.6 | 9.2 | 7.9 | 8.0 | 7.8 | 7.8 |
| White | 26.0 | 14.4 | 9.1 | 7.7 | 6.4 | 6.7 | 6.3 | 5.9 | 5.4 | 5.2 |
| Black and other | 97.9 | 55.9 | 26.5 | 23.0 | 22.7 | 19.8 | 16.4 | 16.3 | 16.9 | 18.1 |
| Black | 103.6 | 59.8 | 31.3 | 29.2 | 25.1 | 21.5 | 20.4 | 18.3 | 19.7 | 20.4 |
| Fetal deaths[3] | 16.1 | 14.2 | 10.5 | 9.7 | 9.4 | 9.2 | 8.9 | 8.4 | 8.2 | 7.9 |
| White | 14.1 | 12.4 | 9.5 | 8.7 | 8.4 | 8.2 | 8.0 | 7.4 | 7.4 | 7.0 |
| Black and other | 26.8 | 22.6 | 15.2 | 14.7 | 13.8 | 13.4 | 12.7 | 12.2 | 11.5 | 11.3 |
| Neonatal deaths[4] | 18.7 | 15.1 | 10.9 | 9.5 | 8.9 | 8.5 | 7.7 | 7.3 | 7.0 | 7.0 |
| White | 17.2 | 13.8 | 10.4 | 8.7 | 7.9 | 7.5 | 7.1 | 6.4 | 6.2 | 6.1 |
| Black and other | 26.9 | 21.4 | 16.3 | 14.0 | 12.9 | 12.5 | 11.3 | 10.8 | 10.2 | 10.3 |
| Black | 27.8 | 22.8 | 18.3 | 16.1 | 14.3 | 14.1 | 13.4 | 12.4 | 11.8 | 12.1 |

[1]Represents deaths of infants under 1 year old, exclusive of fetal deaths. [2]Per 100,000 live births from deliveries and complications of pregnancy, childbirth, and the pueperium. Beginning 1979, deaths are classified according to the ninth revision of the *International Classification of Diseases;* for the earlier years classified according to the revision in use at the time. [3]Beginning 1970, includes only those deaths with stated or presumed period of gestational age not stated. [4]Represents deaths of infants under 28 days old, exclusive of fetal deaths.
Source: U.S. National Center for Health Statistics, *Vital Statistics of the United States*, annual; and unpublished data.

## TABLE 45. FETAL AND INFANT DEATHS—NUMBER AND PERCENT DISTRIBUTION: 1960 TO 1985

[State requirements for reporting of fetal deaths vary. Most States require reporting of fetal deaths of gestations of 20 weeks or more. There is substantial evidence that not all fetal deaths for which reporting is required are reported.]

| | Number | | | | | | Percent Distribution | | | | |
|---|---|---|---|---|---|---|---|---|---|---|---|
| | | Fetal deaths | | Infant deaths | | | Fetal deaths | | Infant deaths | | |
| | | | | Neonatal | | Post- | | | Neonatal | | Post- |
| Year | Total | Early[1] | Late[2] | Early[3] | Late[4] | neonatal[5] | Early[1] | Late[2] | Early[3] | Late[4] | neonatal[5] |
| 1960 | 179,353 | 16,496 | 51,984 | 71,125 | 8,608 | 31,140 | 9.2 | 29.0 | 39.7 | 4.8 | 17.4 |
| 1965 | 153,725 | 15,383 | 45,476 | 59,678 | 6,741 | 26,447 | 10.0 | 29.6 | 38.8 | 4.4 | 17.2 |
| 1970 | 127,628 | 17,170 | 35,791 | 50,821 | 5,458 | 18,388 | 13.5 | 28.0 | 39.8 | 4.3 | 14.4 |
| 1975 | 84,321 | 8,995 | 24,801 | 31,396 | 5,020 | 14,109 | 10.7 | 29.4 | 37.2 | 6.0 | 16.7 |
| 1976 | 81,376 | 9,200 | 23,911 | 29,497 | 5,090 | 13,678 | 11.3 | 29.4 | 36.2 | 6.3 | 16.8 |
| 1977 | 80,028 | 9,399 | 23,654 | 27,639 | 5,021 | 14,115 | 11.7 | 29.6 | 34.8 | 6.3 | 17.6 |
| 1978 | 76,246 | 10,013 | 22,288 | 26,607 | 5,011 | 14,327 | 12.8 | 28.5 | 34.0 | 6.4 | 18.3 |
| 1979 | 78,634 | 10,402 | 22,567 | 26,051 | 4,929 | 14,685 | 13.2 | 28.7 | 33.1 | 6.3 | 18.7 |
| 1980 | 78,879 | 10,754 | 22,599 | 25,492 | 5,126 | 14,908 | 13.6 | 28.7 | 32.3 | 6.5 | 18.9 |
| 1981 | 75,901 | 11,126 | 21,470 | 24,384 | 4,737 | 14,184 | 14.7 | 28.3 | 32.1 | 6.2 | 18.7 |
| 1982 | 75,095 | 11,028 | 21,666 | 23,706 | 4,629 | 14,066 | 14.7 | 28.9 | 31.6 | 6.2 | 18.7 |
| 1983 | 71,379 | 10,933 | 19,819 | 22,315 | 4,192 | 14,120 | 15.3 | 27.8 | 31.3 | 5.9 | 19.8 |
| 1984 | 69,679 | 10,963 | 19,136 | 21,566 | 4,125 | 13,889 | 15.7 | 27.5 | 31.0 | 5.9 | 19.9 |
| 1985 | 69,691 | 10,958 | 18,703 | 21,865 | 4,314 | 13,851 | 15.7 | 26.8 | 31.4 | 6.2 | 19.9 |

[1] 20-27 weeks gestation. [2] 28 weeks or more gestation. [3] Less than 7 days. [4] 7-27 days. [5] 28 days—11 months.
Source U.S. National Center for Health Statistics, *Vital Statistics of the United States,* annual.

## TABLE 46. LIVE BIRTHS BY RACE AND TYPE OF HISPANIC ORIGIN—SELECTED CHARACTERISTICS: 1985

[Represents live births. Excludes births to nonresidents of the U.S. Data are available on race of mother from all states, but data on Hispanic origin of mother are available from only 23 states and the District of Columbia. However, approximately 90 percent of all births to Hispanic mothers occur to residents of these 23 states.]

| | | | | Percent of Mothers beginning prenatal care during- | | |
|---|---|---|---|---|---|---|
| Race and Hispanic origin | Number of births (1000's) | Births to teenage mothers, percent of total | Births to unmarried mothers, percent of total | First trimester | Third trimester or no care | Percent of births with low birth weight[1] |
| Total | 3,761 | 12.7 | 22.0 | 76.2 | 5.7 | 6.8 |
| White | 2,991 | 10.8 | 14.5 | 79.4 | 4.7 | 5.6 |
| Black | 608 | 23.0 | 60.1 | 61.1 | 10.0 | 12.4 |
| American Indian | 43 | 19.1 | 40.7 | 60.3 | 11.5 | 5.9 |
| Asian and Pacific Islander[2] | 116 | 5.5 | 10.1 | 75.0 | 6.1 | 6.1 |
| Filipino | 21 | 5.8 | 12.1 | 77.2 | 4.6 | 6.9 |
| Chinese | 18 | 1.1 | 3.7 | 82.4 | 4.2 | 5.0 |
| Japanese | 10 | 2.9 | 7.9 | 85.8 | 2.6 | 5.9 |
| Hispanic origin[3] | 373 | 16.5 | 29.5 | 61.2 | 12.5 | 6.2 |
| Mexican | 243 | 17.5 | 25.7 | 59.9 | 12.9 | 5.8 |
| Puerto Rican | 35 | 20.9 | 51.1 | 58.3 | 15.5 | 8.7 |
| Cuban | 10 | 7.1 | 16.1 | 72.5 | 3.7 | 6.0 |

[1]Births less than 2.500 grams (5 lb. 8oz.). Includes races not shown separately, [3]Hipanic persons may be of any race. Includes other types, not shown separately.
Source: U.S. National Center for Health Statistics, unpublished data.

## TABLE 47. YEARS OF LIFE EXPECTED AT BIRTH

[Sources: National Center for Health Statistics]

| Year | Total | Total | | White | | | Black and other | | |
|---|---|---|---|---|---|---|---|---|---|
| | | Male | Female | Total | Male | Female | Total | Male | Female |
| 1920* | 54.1 | 53.6 | 54.6 | 54.9 | 54.4 | 55.6 | 45.3 | 45.5 | 45.2 |
| 1930 | 59.7 | 58.1 | 61.6 | 61.4 | 59.7 | 63.5 | 48.1 | 47.3 | 49.2 |
| 1940 | 62.9 | 60.8 | 65.2 | 64.2 | 62.1 | 66.6 | 53.1 | 51.5 | 54.9 |
| 1950 | 88.2 | 65.6 | 71.1 | 69.1 | 66.5 | 72.2 | 60.6 | 59.1 | 62.9 |
| 1955 | 69.6 | 66.7 | 72.6 | 70.5 | 67.4 | 73.7 | 63.7 | 61.4 | 66.1 |
| 1960 | 69.7 | 66.6 | 73.1 | 70.6 | 67.4 | 74.1 | 63.6 | 61.1 | 66.3 |
| 1965 | 70.2 | 66.8 | 73.7 | 71.0 | 67.6 | 74.7 | 64.1 | 61.1 | 67.4 |
| 1970 | 70.6 | 67.1 | 74.7 | 71.7 | 68.0 | 75.6 | 65.3 | 61.3 | 69.4 |
| 1971 | 71.1 | 67.4 | 75.0 | 72.0 | 68.3 | 75.8 | 65.6 | 61.6 | 69.8 |
| 1972 | 71.2 | 67.4 | 75.1 | 72.0 | 68.3 | 75.9 | 65.7 | 61.5 | 70.1 |
| 1973 | 71.4 | 67.6 | 75.3 | 72.2 | 68.5 | 76.1 | 66.1 | 62.0 | 70.3 |
| 1974 | 72.0 | 68.2 | 75.9 | 72.6 | 69.0 | 76.7 | 67.1 | 62.9 | 71.3 |
| 1975 | 72.6 | 66.8 | 76.6 | 73.4 | 69.5 | 77.3 | 68.0 | 63.7 | 72.4 |
| 1976 | 72.9 | 69.1 | 76.8 | 73.6 | 69.9 | 77.5 | 68.4 | 64.2 | 72.7 |
| 1977 | 73.3 | 69.5 | 77.2 | 74.0 | 70.2 | 77.9 | 68.9 | 64.7 | 73.2 |
| 1978 | 73.5 | 69.6 | 77.3 | 74.1 | 70.4 | 76.0 | 69.3 | 65.0 | 73.5 |
| 1979 | 73.9 | 70.0 | 77.6 | 74.6 | 70.8 | 78.4 | 69.8 | 65.4 | 74.1 |
| 1980 | 73.7 | 70.0 | 77.5 | 74.4 | 70.7 | 78.1 | 69.5 | 65.3 | 73.6 |
| 1981 | 74.2 | 70.4 | 77.8 | 74.8 | 71.1 | 78.4 | 70.3 | 66.1 | 74.4 |
| 1982 | 74.5 | 70.9 | 78.1 | 75.1 | 71.5 | 78.7 | 71.0 | 86.8 | 75.0 |
| 1983 | 74.6 | 71.0 | 78.1 | 75.2 | 71.7 | 78.7 | 71.1 | 67.2 | 74.3 |
| 1984 | 74.7 | 71.1 | 78.3 | 75.3 | 71.8 | 78.8 | 71.3 | 67.3 | 75.2 |
| 1985 | 74.7 | 71.2 | 78.2 | 75.3 | 71.8 | 78.7 | 71.2 | 67.2 | 75.2 |

*Data prior to 1940 for death registration states only.
Source: World Almanac, 1988, p 825

## TABLE 48. CURRENT USERS OF ALCOHOL, MARIHUANA, AND/OR COCAINE: 1985

| Substance and Age Group | Total[1] | Sex | | Race/Ethnicity | | | Region | | | |
|---|---|---|---|---|---|---|---|---|---|---|
| | | Male | Female | White[2] | Black[2] | Hispanic | North-east | North Central | South | West |
| | | | | [In percent] | | | | | | |
| Alcohol: Total | 59.2 | 67.9 | 51.2 | 61.8 | 47.6 | 50.5 | 66.1 | 64.8 | 47.2 | 65.0 |
| 12-17 years old | 31.5 | 33.7 | 29.0 | 34.6 | 21.3 | 22.8 | 33.5 | 33.5 | 26.1 | 36.0 |
| 18-25 years old | 71.5 | 78.4 | 64.5 | 75.8 | 57.8 | 58.0 | 76.6 | 77.8 | 64.5 | 68.9 |
| 26-34 years old | 70.0 | 79.8 | 60.6 | 72.2 | 65.9 | 65.5 | 78.7 | 75.1 | 58.3 | 72.5 |
| 35 years & older | 57.3 | 67.8 | 48.3 | 59.3 | 43.9 | 49.3 | 65.1 | 62.6 | 42.7 | 67.6 |
| Marihuana: Total | 9.4 | 12.3 | 6.8 | 9.1 | 13.2 | 7.4 | 10.2 | 9.5 | 8.0 | 10.9 |
| 12-17 years old | 12.3 | 13.2 | 11.2 | 13.2 | 8.2 | 9.9 | 13.3 | 11.6 | 8.8 | 17.1 |
| 18-25 years old | 21.9 | 26.5 | 17.0 | 22.2 | 24.1 | 14.8 | 19.6 | 23.1 | 21.5 | 22.8 |
| 26 34 years old | 16.8 | 22.4 | 11.4 | 16.9 | 22.8 | 10.1 | 18.0 | 17.0 | 15.2 | 17.7 |
| 35 years & older | 2.2 | 3.3 | 1.3 | 1.8 | 5.8 | 1.9 | 3.8 | 1.4 | 1.3 | 2.8 |
| Cocaine: Total | 2.9 | 3.9 | 2.0 | 3.0 | 3.2 | 2.4 | 3.5 | 2.6 | 1.4 | 5.2 |
| 12-17 years old | 1.8 | 2.0 | 1.4 | 1.8 | 1.1 | 2.7 | 2.7 | .8 | .5 | 3.3 |
| 18-25 years old | 7.7 | 9.0 | 6.2 | 8.0 | 6.5 | 6.4 | 7.5 | 8.2 | 3.9 | 12.7 |
| 26-34 years old | 6.1 | 8.6 | 3.8 | 6.6 | 5.6 | 2.7 | 6.6 | 4.7 | 3.6 | 11.4 |
| 35 years & older | .5 | .7 | .3 | .4 | 1.4 | .2 | 1.2 | .1 | .1 | .7 |

[1]Includes other races, not shown separately.[2] Non-hispanic.
Source: U.S. National Institute on Drug Abuse, Main findings From the 1985 *National Household Survey on Drug Abuse*

## TABLE 49. FEDERAL AND STATE PRISONERS, BY SEX AND RACE: 1978 TO 1985

| | Total | | | Male | | | Female | | | |
|---|---|---|---|---|---|---|---|---|---|---|
| Item | White | Black | Other | White | Black | Other | White | Black | Other | Unknown |
| 1978 | 157,208 | 143,376 | 3,283 | 151,534 | 136,893 | 3,090 | 5,674 | 6,483 | 193 | 2,735 |
| 1979 | 161,642 | 145,383 | 3,677 | 155,803 | 138,776 | 3,468 | 5,839 | 6,607 | 209 | 3,304 |
| 1980 | 169,274 | 150,249 | 3,853 | 163,083 | 143,700 | 3,677 | 6,191 | 6,549 | 176 | 5,319 |
| 1981 | 190,503 | 168,129 | 4,477 | 183,202 | 160,442 | 4,240 | 7,301 | 7,687 | 237 | 5,663 |
| 1982 | 214,741 | 189,610 | 5,262 | 206,167 | 180,844 | 4,990 | 8,574 | 8,766 | 272 | 4,749 |
| 1983 | 225,902 | 200,216 | 5,663 | 216,522 | 191,020 | 5,336 | 9,380 | 9,196 | 327 | 5,457 |
| 1984 | 239,428 | 209,673 | 6,654 | 229,323 | 199,692 | 6,250 | 10,105 | 9,981 | 404 | 6,687 |
| 1985 | 260,847 | 227,137 | 6,694 | 249,418 | 216,344 | 6,280 | 11,429 | 10,793 | 414 | 7,698 |

## TABLE 50. AIDS CASES REPORTED, BY PATIENT CHARACTERISTIC: 1981 TO 1987

[Provisional. For cases reported in the year shown.]

| | Number | | | | | | | Percent Distribution | | |
|---|---|---|---|---|---|---|---|---|---|---|
| Characteristics | Total | 1981-82 | 1983 | 1984 | 1985 | 1986 | 1987 | 1981-82 | 1985 | 1987 |
| Total | 37,481 | 941 | 2,098 | 4,461 | 8,249 | 12,929 | 8,783 | 100.0 | 100.0 | 100.0 |
| Age: | | | | | | | | | | |
| Under 13 years old | 497 | 13 | 34 | 47 | 127 | 169 | 107 | 1.4 | 1.5 | 1.2 |
| 13-29 years old | 7,998 | 214 | 467 | 972 | 1,716 | 2,770 | 1,859 | 22.7 | 20.8 | 21.2 |
| 30-39 years old | 17,468 | 440 | 949 | 2,130 | 3,877 | 6,026 | 4,046 | 46.8 | 47.0 | 46.1 |
| 40-49 years old | 7,807 | 204 | 454 | 935 | 1,710 | 2,645 | 1,859 | 21.7 | 20.7 | 21.2 |
| 50-59 years old | 2,745 | 65 | 164 | 314 | 620 | 950 | 632 | 6.9 | 7 5 | 7 2 |
| 60 years old and over | 966 | 5 | 30 | 83 | 199 | 369 | 280 | .5 | 2.4 | 3.2 |
| Sex: | | | | | | | | | | |
| Male | 34,741 | 879 | 1,941 | 4,189 | 7,669 | 11,922 | 8,141 | 93.4 | 93.0 | 92.7 |
| Female | 2,740 | 62 | 157 | 292 | 580 | 1,007 | 642 | 6.6 | 7.0 | 7.3 |
| Race/ethnic group: | | | | | | | | | | |
| White, non-Hispanic | 22,963 | 548 | 1,202 | 2,716 | 5,040 | 7,793 | 5,664 | 58 4 | 61.2 | 64 7 |
| Black, non-Hispanic | 9,243 | 260 | 559 | 1,117 | 2,076 | 3,245 | 1,966 | 27.7 | 25.2 | 22.7 |
| Hispanic | 4,908 | 127 | 310 | 610 | 1,071 | 1 768 | 1,022 | 13.5 | 13.0 | 11 7 |
| Other | 367 | 6 | 27 | 38 | 62 | 123 | 111 | .4 | .6 | .9 |
| Leading States: | | | | | | | | | | |
| New York | 10,889 | 466 | 875 | 1,589 | 2,504 | 3 794 | 1,661 | 49.5 | 30.4 | 18.9 |
| California | 8,784 | 189 | 489 | 1,031 | 1,982 | 2,656 | 2,437 | 20.1 | 24.0 | 27.8 |
| Florida | 2,553 | 68 | 153 | 314 | 552 | 840 | 626 | 7.2 | 6.7 | 7.1 |
| Texas | 2,512 | 20 | 88 | 251 | 486 | 939 | 728 | 2.1 | 5.9 | 8.3 |
| New Jersey | 2,211 | 64 | 137 | 280 | 471 | 773 | 486 | 6.8 | 5.7 | 5.5 |
| Illinois | 1,002 | 23 | 34 | 102 | 192 | 363 | 288 | 2.4 | 2.3 | 3.3 |
| Pennsylvania | 862 | 18 | 37 | 91 | 195 | 298 | 223 | 1.9 | 2.4 | 2 5 |
| Massachusettts | 799 | 13 | 33 | 87 | 165 | 279 | 222 | 1.4 | 2.0 | 2.5 |
| Georgia | 783 | 11 | 26 | 56 | 192 | 288 | 210 | 1.2 | 2.3 | 2.4 |
| Percent of total | 81.1 | 92.7 | 89.2 | 84.8 | 81.7 | 79.1 | 78 3 | (x) | (x) | (x) |

x Not applicable.
Source: U.S. Centers for Disease Control, Atlanta, GA. unpublished data

## TABLE 51. RATIO OF MALES TO FEMALES, BY AGE GROUP, 1920 TO 1986, AND BY RACE, 1986

[Represents number of males per 100 females. Total resident population]

| | 1920 (Jan. 1) | 1930 (Apr. 1) | 1940 (Apr. 1) | 1950 (Apr. 1) | 1960 (Apr. 1) | 1970 (Apr. 1) | 1980 (Apr. 1) | 1985 (July 1) | 1986 (July 1) Total[1] | White | Black |
|---|---|---|---|---|---|---|---|---|---|---|---|
| All ages | [2]104.1 | [2]102.5 | 100.7 | 98.6 | 97.1 | 94.8 | 94.5 | 94.8 | 94.9 | 95.5 | 90.1 |
| Under 14 years | 102.1 | 102.6 | 103.0 | 103.7 | 103.4 | 103.9 | 104.6 | 104.8 | 104.9 | 105.4 | 102.9 |
| 14-24 years | 97.3 | 98.4 | 98.9 | 98.2 | 98.7 | 98.7 | 101.9 | 102.2 | 102.3 | 102.9 | 97.7 |
| 25-44 years | 105.1 | 101.8 | 98.5 | 96.4 | 95.7 | 95.5 | 97.4 | 98.5 | 98.7 | 100.7 | 86.8 |
| 45-64years | 115.2 | 109.1 | 105.2 | 100.1 | 95.7 | 91.6 | 90.7 | 91.5 | 91.6 | 93.0 | 81.7 |
| 65 years and over | 101.3 | 100.5 | 95.5 | 89.6 | 82.8 | 72.1 | 67.6 | 67.9 | 68.1 | 68.0 | 67.0 |

[1] Includes other races not shown separately. [2] Includes "age not reported"
Source: U.S. Bureau of the Census, *U.S. Census of Population: 1930,* vol. II; *1940,* vol. II part 1, and vol. IV, part 1; *1950,* vol.II, part 1; *1960,* vol. I, part 1; *1970,* vol. I, part B; and *Current Population Reports,* series P-25, No. 1000.

## TABLE 52. MONEY INCOME OF FAMILIES—MEDIAN FAMILY INCOME IN CURRENT AND CONSTANT (1986) DOLLARS, BY RACE AND HISPANIC ORIGIN OF HOUSEHOLDER: 1960 TO 1986

| | Median income in Current dollars | | | | Median income in constant (1986) dollars | | | | Annual percent change of median income of All families | |
|---|---|---|---|---|---|---|---|---|---|---|
| Year | All families[1] | White | Black | Hispanic[2] | All families[1] | White | Black | Hispanic[2] | Current dollars | Constant dollars |
| 1960 | 5,620 | 5,835 | [3]3,230 | (NA) | 20,807 | 27,603 | 11,959 | (NA) | [4]4.9 | [4]2.9 |
| 1965 | 6,957 | 7,251 | [3]3,993 | (NA) | 24,176 | 25,198 | 13,876 | (NA) | 4.4 | 3.1 |
| 1970 | 9,867 | 10,236 | 6,279 | (NA) | 27,862 | 28,904 | 17,730 | (NA) | 7.2 | 2.9 |
| 1971 | 10,285 | 10,672 | 6,440 | (NA) | 27,845 | 28,893 | 17,435 | (NA) | 4.2 | .1 |
| 1972 | 11,116 | 11,549 | 6,864 | 8,183 | 29,134 | 30,269 | 17,990 | 21,447 | 8.1 | 4.6 |
| 1973 | 12,051 | 12,595 | 7,269 | 8,715 | 29,734 | 31,076 | 17,935 | 21,503 | 8.4 | 2.1 |
| 1974 | 12,902 | 13,408 | 8,006 | 9,540 | 28,687 | 29,812 | 17,801 | 21,211 | 7.1 | -3.1 |
| 1975 | 13,718 | 14,268 | 8,779 | 9,551 | 27,949 | 29,067 | 17,885 | 19,457 | 6.3 | -2.6 |
| 1976 | 14,958 | 15,537 | 9,242 | 10,259 | 28,811 | 29,926 | 17,801 | 19,760 | 9.0 | 3.1 |
| 1977 | 16,009 | 16,740 | 9,563 | 11,421 | 28,966 | 30,289 | 17,303 | 20,665 | 7.0 | .5 |
| 1978 | 17,640 | 18,368 | 10,879 | 12,566 | 29,647 | 30,870 | 18,284 | 21,119 | 10.2 | 2.4 |
| 1979 | 19,587 | 20,439 | 11,574 | 14,169 | 29,588 | 30,875 | 17,483 | 21,403 | 11.0 | -.2 |
| 1980 | 21,023 | 21,904 | 12,674 | 14,716 | 27,974 | 29,146 | 16,864 | 19,582 | 7.3 | -5.5 |
| 1981 | 22,388 | 23,517 | 13,266 | 16,401 | 26,991 | 28,352 | 15,993 | 19,773 | 6.5 | -3.5 |
| 1982 | 23,433 | 24,603 | 13,598 | 16,227 | 26,618 | 27,948 | 15,447 | 18,433 | 4.7 | -1.4 |
| 1983 | 24,674 | 25,837 | 14,561 | 16,930 | 27,155 | 28,435 | 16,025 | 18,632 | 5.3 | 2.0 |
| 1984 | 26,433 | 27,686 | 15,432 | 18,833 | 27,903 | 29,226 | 16,290 | 19,879 | 7.1 | 2.8 |
| 1985 | 27,735 | 29,152 | 16,786 | 19,027 | 28,269 | 29,713 | 17,109 | 19,393 | 4.9 | 1.3 |
| 1986 | 29,458 | 30,809 | 17,604 | 19,995 | 29,458 | 30,809 | 17,604 | 19,995 | 6.2 | 4.2 |

NA Not available. [1] Includes other races not shown separately. [2] Hispanic persons may be of any race.
[3] For 1960 and 1965, black and other races. [4] Change from 1955.
Source: U.S. Bureau of the Census, Current Population Reports, series P-60, No. 157, and unpublished data.

## TABLE 53. PERCENT OF CHILDREN IMMUNIZED AGAINST SPECIFIED DISEASES, BY AGE-GROUP: 1980 TO 1985

[Covers civilian noninstitutional population. Data are estimates from the Immunization Survey which is a supplemental questionaire submitted to a subsample of households interviewed for the Current Population Survey]

| | All Respondents | | | | | | | | | | Respondents Consulting Records,[1] | |
|---|---|---|---|---|---|---|---|---|---|---|---|---|
| | 1-4 Years Old | | | | | 5-14 Years Old | | | | | | |
| | | | 1985 | | | | | 1985 | | | 1985 | |
| Disease | 1980, total | 1984, total | Total | White | Black and other | 1980, total | 1984, total | Total | White | Black and other | 1-4 years old | 5-14 years old |
| Diphtheria-tetanus-pertussis[2] | 66.3 | 65.7 | 64.9 | 68.7 | 48.7 | 74.0 | 73.8 | 73.7 | 76.0 | 64.0 | 87.0 | 93.0 |
| Polio[2] | 58.8 | 54.8 | 55.3 | 58.9 | 40.1 | 70.0 | 70.2 | 69.7 | 72.6 | 57.5 | 75.7 | 88.4 |
| Measles | 63.5 | 62.8 | 60.8 | 63.6 | 48.8 | 71.0 | 73.5 | 71.5 | 73.6 | 62.6 | 76.9 | 87.6 |
| Rubella | 63.5 | 60.9 | 58.9 | 61.6 | 47.7 | 74.0 | 72.4 | 70.2 | 72.3 | 61.4 | 73.8 | 85.3 |
| Mumps | 56.6 | 58.7 | 58.9 | 61.6 | 47.0 | 63.2 | 70.9 | 71.6 | 73.6 | 63.2 | 75.5 | 87.1 |

[1] Data are based only on the 29 percent of white respondents and the 15 percent of black and other respondents who consulted records for some or all vaccination questions. [2] Three or more doses.
Source: U.S. Centers for Disease Control, Atlanta GA, *United States Immunization Survey,* annual.

## TABLE 54. MEDICAID—SELECTED CHARACTERISTICS OF PERSONS COVERED BY POVERTY STATUS: 1980 TO 1985

[In thousands except percent. Represents number of persons who were enrolled at any time in year shown. Person did not have to receive medical care paid for by Medicaid in order to be counted.]

| | | | | 1985 | | | | | | | |
|---|---|---|---|---|---|---|---|---|---|---|---|
| Poverty Status | 1980, total | 1983, total | 1984, total | Total[1] | White | Black | His-panic[2] | Under 15 | 15 to 44 | 45 to 64 | 65 and over |
| Persons covered, total | 18,966 | 19,286 | 19,348 | 19,204 | 12,134 | 6,349 | 2,724 | 7,213 | 7,437 | 1,838 | 2,716 |
| Below poverty level | 11,113 | 13,224 | 13,207 | 12,652 | 7,459 | 4,668 | 2,035 | 5,634 | 4,919 | 1,017 | 1,082 |
| Above poverty level | 7,854 | 6,062 | 6,141 | 6,552 | 4,675 | 1,681 | 689 | 1,579 | 2,518 | 821 | 1,634 |
| Percent of total population | 8.4 | 8.3 | 8.3 | 8.1 | 6.0 | 22.3 | 16.5 | 13.9 | 6.6 | 4.1 | 10.0 |
| Below poverty level | 39.1 | 38.7 | 40.4 | 39.7 | 34.0 | 53.7 | 42.7 | 51.6 | 36.6 | 24.5 | 32.1 |
| Above poverty level | 4.0 | 3.1 | 3.1 | 3.2 | 2.6 | 8 5 | 5.9 | 3.9 | 2.5 | 2.0 | 6.9 |

[1]Includes other races not shown separately. [2]Hispanic persons may be of any race.
Source: U.S. Bureau of the Census, *Current Population Reports.* series P-60 No. 155, and earlier reports.

## TABLE 55. HEALTH INSURANCE COVERAGE STATUS, BY SELECTED CHARACTERISTICS: 1985

[Data represents monthly averages for fourth quarter 1985. Government health insurance includes Medicare and military plans. Based on Survey of Income and Program Participation.]

| Characteristic | Health insurance covered | | | | | | | | | | |
|---|---|---|---|---|---|---|---|---|---|---|---|
| | | By Private or Government insurance | | | | | | By Government insurance | | | |
| | | | Private insurance | | | | | | | | |
| | Total | Total[1] | Total | Related to employment[2] | Covered by Medicaid | Not covered by health insurance | Total | Total[1] | Private | Covered by Medicaid | Not covered by health insurance |
| | Number (mil.) | | | | | | Percent | | | | |
| Total persons[3] | 235.5 | 204.2 | 180.1 | 147.1 | 17.2 | 31.3 | 100.0 | 86.7 | 76.5 | 7.3 | 13.3 |
| Male | 114.2 | 97.5 | 87.5 | 73.2 | 6.4 | 16.7 | 100.0 | 85.4 | 76.6 | 5.6 | 14.6 |
| Female | 121.4 | 106.8 | 92.6 | 73.8 | 10.8 | 14.6 | 100.0 | 88.0 | 76.3 | 8.9 | 12.0 |
| White | 200.1 | 175.2 | 159.3 | 129.9 | 10.1 | 24.8 | 100.0 | 87.6 | 79.6 | 5.0 | 12.4 |
| Black | 28.5 | 23.0 | 15.9 | 13.2 | 6.2 | 5.5 | 100.0 | 80.7 | 55.7 | 21.6 | 19.3 |
| Hispanic origin[4] | 14.2 | 10.4 | 7.8 | 7.0 | 2.3 | 3.8 | 100.0 | 73.0 | 55.2 | 15.9 | 27.0 |
| Under 16 years | 55.6 | 47.0 | 39.3 | 34.6 | 7.2 | 8.6 | 100.0 | 84.5 | 70.8 | 13.0 | 15.5 |
| 16-24 years | 34.6 | 27.2 | 24.4 | 19.0 | 2.6 | 7.4 | 100.0 | 78.6 | 70.7 | 7.5 | 21.4 |
| 25-34 years | 41.4 | 34.6 | 32.1 | 29.1 | 2.2 | 6.8 | 100.0 | 83.6 | 77.5 | 5.4 | 16.4 |
| 35-44 years | 32.1 | 28.6 | 26.8 | 24.4 | 1.3 | 3.5 | 100.0 | 89.1 | 83.4 | 4.1 | 10.9 |
| 45-54 years | 22.5 | 20.2 | 18.9 | 16.6 | .9 | 2.3 | 100.0 | 89.9 | 84.2 | 3.9 | 10.1 |
| 55-64 years | 22.1 | 19.6 | 18.0 | 14.6 | .8 | 2.6 | 100.0 | 88.5 | 81.3 | 3.7 | 11.5 |
| 65 years and over | 27.2 | 27.1 | 20.5 | 8.7 | 2.1 | .2 | 100.0 | 99.4 | 75.3 | 7.7 | .6 |
| Northeast | 50.7 | 46.1 | 41.3 | 34.3 | 3.8 | 4.6 | 100.0 | 90.9 | 81.4 | 7.5 | 9.1 |
| Midwest | 60.8 | 54.2 | 48.5 | 39.1 | 4.7 | 6.6 | 100.0 | 89.2 | 79.8 | 7.7 | 10.8 |
| South | 79.8 | 66.9 | 58.5 | 47.7 | 5.0 | 12.9 | 100.0 | 83.8 | 73.3 | 6.3 | 16.2 |
| West | 44.2 | 37.0 | 31.8 | 25.9 | 3.7 | 7.2 | 100.0 | 83.7 | 71.9 | 8.3 | 16.3 |

[1] Includes other Government insurance, not shown separately. [2] Related to current or prior employment of self or other family members. [3] Includes other races, not shown separately. [4] Hispanic persons may be of any race.

Source: U.S. Bureau of the Census, Current Population Reports, series P-70, No. 8 and unpublished data.

## TABLE 56. CHILD SUPPORT AND ALIMONY—SELECTED CHARACTERISTICS OF WOMEN: 1985

[Women as of spring 1986. Covers civilian noninstitutional population. Child support data are for women with own children under 21 years of age present from absent fathers. Alimony data are for ever-divorced and currently separated women. Based on Current Population Survey ]

| | | Current marital status | | | | | Race | | | Age (years) | | |
|---|---|---|---|---|---|---|---|---|---|---|---|---|
| Recipiency status of women | Units | Total[1] | Divorced | Married[2] | Single[3] | Separated | White | Black | Hispanic[4] | 18-29 years | 30-39 years | 40 and over |
| **All Women, total** | 1,000 | 8,808 | 3,045 | 2,322 | 2,009 | 1,363 | 6,341 | 2,310 | 813 | 2,887 | 3,614 | 2,307 |
| Payments awarded[5] | 1,000 | 5,396 | 2,492 | 1,904 | 370 | 587 | 4,476 | 839 | 342 | 1,288 | 2,547 | 1,561 |
| Percent of total | Percent | 61.3 | 81.8 | 82.0 | 18.4 | 43.1 | 70.6 | 36.3 | 42.1 | 44.6 | 70.5 | 67.7 |
| Due child support payment in 1985 | 1,000 | 4,381 | 2,179 | 1,416 | 303 | 453 | 3,651 | 657 | 282 | 1,089 | 2,182 | 1,110 |
| Received payment | 1,000 | 3,243 | 1,637 | 970 | 231 | 382 | 2,722 | 473 | 192 | 777 | 1,605 | 861 |
| Percent of due | Percent | 74.0 | 75.1 | 68.5 | 76.2 | 84.3 | 74.6 | 72.0 | 68.1 | 71.3 | 73.6 | 77.6 |
| Did not receive payment | 1,000 | 1,138 | 541 | 447 | 72 | 71 | 929 | 184 | 90 | 312 | 578 | 249 |
| Payments not awarded | 1,000 | 3,411 | 553 | 418 | 1,639 | 776 | 1,865 | 1,471 | 471 | 1,599 | 1,066 | 746 |
| Mean money income | | | | | | | | | | | | |
| Women received payments | Dollars | 14,776 | 16,778 | 13,512 | 9,675 | 12,642 | 15,052 | 13,297 | 11,505 | 10,886 | 15,513 | 16,913 |
| Mean child support | Dollars | 2,215 | 2,538 | 1,966 | 1,147 | 2,082 | 2,294 | 1,754 | 2,011 | 1,467 | 2,397 | 2,552 |
| Women did not receive payments | Dollars | 10,837 | 12,580 | 9,621 | (B) | (B) | 10,854 | 10,477 | 9,430 | 6,406 | 11,553 | 14,730 |
| Women not awarded payments | Dollars | 7,998 | 11,375 | 8,495 | 6,247 | 9,065 | 8,746 | 6,969 | 6,308 | 5,323 | 10,068 | 10,770 |
| **Women with incomes below the poverty level 1985, total** | 1,000 | 2,797 | 795 | 180 | 1,159 | 646 | 1,569 | 1,190 | 414 | 1,419 | 920 | 458 |
| Payments awarded[5] | 1,000 | 1,130 | 572 | 121 | 207 | 221 | 787 | 322 | 100 | 469 | 485 | 176 |
| Received payment in 1985 | 1,000 | 595 | 301 | 50 | 123 | 116 | 411 | 174 | 43 | 241 | 258 | 96 |
| Mean income from child support | Dollars | 1,383 | 1,522 | (B) | 900 | 1,503 | 1,463 | 1,085 | (B) | 963 | 1,674 | 1,649 |
| Did not receive payment | 1,000 | 310 | 198 | 31 | 40 | 41 | 221 | 83 | 31 | 128 | 147 | 35 |
| Payments not awarded | 1,000 | 1,668 | 223 | 59 | 952 | 425 | 782 | 868 | 314 | 951 | 435 | 282 |
| Alimony | | | | | | | | | | | | |
| **All women, total** | 1,000 | 19,156 | 8,000 | 7,381 | (x) | 2,610 | 16,039 | 2,766 | 1,196 | 2,817 | 5,678 | 10,662 |
| Payments awarded[5] | 1,000 | 2,803 | 1,368 | 1,015 | (x) | 261 | 2,539 | 220 | 132 | 216 | 618 | 1,969 |
| Received payments in 1985 | 1,000 | 616 | 443 | 52 | (x) | 120 | 559 | 44 | 29 | 62 | 195 | 358 |
| Mean income from alimony | Dollars | 3,733 | 3,975 | (B) | (x) | 3,083 | 3,858 | (B) | (B) | (B) | 3,200 | 4,365 |
| Did not receive payment | 1,000 | 225 | 161 | 37 | (x) | 26 | 193 | 25 | 13 | 45 | 75 | 106 |
| Payments not awarded | 1,000 | 16,354 | 6,632 | 6,346 | (x) | 2,348 | 13,500 | 2,546 | 1,064 | 2,601 | 5,060 | 8,693 |
| **Women with incomes below the poverty level in 1985, total** | 1,000 | 3,716 | 1,800 | 524 | (x) | 1,082 | 2,670 | 973 | 410 | 851 | 1,090 | 1,774 |
| Payments awarded | 1,000 | 434 | 247 | 55 | (x) | 93 | 378 | 49 | 35 | 86 | 111 | 237 |
| Percent of total | Percent | 11.7 | 13.7 | 10.5 | (x) | 8.6 | 14.2 | 5.0 | 8.5 | 10.1 | 10.2 | 13.4 |

B Base less than 75,000. x Not applicable. [1] Includes other items, not shown separately. [2] Remarried women whose previous marriage ended in divorce. [3] Never-married women. [4] Hispanic women may be of any race. [5] Includes women who were not supposed to receive payments in 1985, not shown separately.

Source: U.S. Bureau of the Census, *Current Population Reports,* series P-23, No. 152.

## TABLE 57. FARM POPULATION, BY CHARACTERISTICS: 1970 TO 1986

[1970 and 1980, April-centered five-quarter averages; 1985 and 1986 annual averages.]

| | Farm Population (1000) | | | | | | | Percent Distribution | | | |
|---|---|---|---|---|---|---|---|---|---|---|---|
| | 1969 definition | | 1974 definition | | | | | 1969 definition | 1974 definition | | |
| | | | | | 1986 | | | | | | |
| Characteristics | 1970 | 1980 | 1980 | 1985 | Total | Male | Female | 1970 | 1980 | 1985 | 1986 |
| Total | 9,712 | 7,241 | 6,051 | 5,355 | 5,226 | 2,733 | 2,493 | 100.0 | 100.0 | 100.0 | 100.0 |
| White | 8,775 | 6,828 | 5,714 | 5,195 | 5,081 | 2,654 | 2,427 | 90.4 | 94.4 | 97.0 | 97.2 |
| Black and other races | 938 | 413 | 337 | 160 | 145 | 79 | 66 | 9.7 | 5.6 | 3.0 | 2.8 |
| Under 15 years old | [1]2,490 | [1]1,391 | [1]1,146 | 1,100 | 1,047 | 551 | 496 | [1]25.6 | [1]18.9 | 20.5 | 20.0 |
| 15 years old and over | [2]7,222 | [2]5,851 | [2]4,905 | 4,255 | 4,179 | 2,182 | 1,997 | [2]74.4 | [2]81.1 | 79.5 | 80.0 |
| 15-19 years old | [3]1,316 | [3]926 | [3]790 | 456 | 436 | 229 | 207 | [3]13.6 | [3]13.1 | 8.5 | 8.3 |
| 20-24 years old | 502 | 502 | 444 | 381 | 350 | 194 | 156 | 5.2 | 7.3 | 7.1 | 6.7 |
| 25-34 years old | 770 | 735 | 606 | 640 | 654 | 355 | 299 | 7.9 | 10.0 | 12.0 | 12.5 |
| 35-44 years old | 1,061 | 862 | 712 | 687 | 648 | 331 | 317 | 10.9 | 11.8 | 12.8 | 12.4 |
| 45-64 years old | 2,452 | 1,892 | 1,607 | 1,342 | 1,369 | 701 | 668 | 25.2 | 26.6 | 25.1 | 26.2 |
| 65 years old and over | 1,122 | 934 | 746 | 747 | 723 | 372 | 351 | 11.6 | 12.3 | 13.9 | 13.8 |
| In labor force[4] | 4,293 | 3,682 | 3,139 | 2,853 | 2,865 | 1,797 | 1,068 | 59.4 | 64.0 | 67.1 | 68.6 |
| Employed, agriculture | 2,333 | 1,722 | 1,642 | 1,363 | 1,363 | 1,082 | 280 | 32.3 | 33.5 | 32.0 | 32.6 |
| Percent of labor force | 54.3 | 46.8 | 52.3 | 47.8 | 47.6 | 60.2 | 26.2 | (x) | (x) | (x) | (x) |
| Self-employed | 1,411 | 1,083 | 1,034 | 896 | 906 | 771 | 135 | 19.5 | 21.1 | 21.1 | 21.7 |
| Wage and salary workers | 395 | 344 | 326 | 318 | 318 | 265 | 52 | 5.5 | 6.6 | 7.5 | 7.6 |
| Unpaid family workers | 526 | 295 | 282 | 149 | 139 | 46 | 94 | 7.3 | 5.7 | 3.5 | 3.3 |
| Employed, nonagriculture | 1,878 | 1,853 | 1,415 | 1,402 | 1,418 | 673 | 745 | 26.0 | 28.8 | 32.9 | 33.9 |
| Self-employed | 159 | 210 | 161 | 159 | 158 | 97 | 61 | 2.2 | 3.3 | 3.7 | 3.8 |
| Wage and salary workers | 1,698 | 1,624 | 1,239 | 1,237 | 1,250 | 574 | 676 | 23.5 | 25.3 | 29.1 | 29.6 |
| Unpaid family workers | 21 | 19 | 16 | 7 | 10 | 2 | 8 | .3 | .3 | .2 | .2 |
| Unemployed | 82 | 106 | 82 | 88 | 85 | 41 | 43 | 1.1 | 17 | 21 | 2.0 |
| Not in labor force[4] | 2,929 | 2,169 | 1,766 | 1,402 | 1,314 | 385 | 929 | 40.6 | 36.0 | 32.9 | 31.4 |

x Not applicable. [1] Persons under 14 years old. [2] Persons 14 years old and over. [3] Persons 14-19 years old.

[4] Percent distribution by labor force status based on total population, 14 years old and over through 1980, and 15 years old and over beginning 1985.

Source: U.S. Bureau of the Census, Current Population Reports, series P-27, No. 60 and earlier reports; and unpublished data.

## TABLE 58. SELECTED HOUSING DEFICIENCIES

| | Overall U.S. Total and % | | Black Total and % | | Hispanic Total and % | |
|---|---|---|---|---|---|---|
| Rat signs in last 3 months | 4,539,000 | .05 | 1.829,000 | .18 | 749,000 | .15 |
| Holes in floors | 1,483,000 | .02 | 549,000 | .06 | 205,000 | .04 |
| Interior open cracks or holes | 5,572,000 | .06 | 1,535,000 | .16 | 638,000 | .13 |
| Interior broken plaster or peeling paint | 4,992,000 | .06 | 1,218,000 | .12 | 545,000 | .11 |
| No electrical wiring | 17,000 | .00019 | 7,000 | .0007 | - | - |
| Exposed wiring | 2,009,000 | .02 | 453,000 | .05 | 214,000 | .04 |
| Rooms without electrical outlets | 2,502,000 | .03 | 555,000 | .06 | 222,000 | .04 |

## TABLE 59. OVERALL OPINION OF STRUCTURE

| | Overall U.S. Total and % | | Black Total and % | | Hispanic Total and % | |
|---|---|---|---|---|---|---|
| 1 (worst) | 925,000 | .01 | 369,000 | .03 | 156,000 | .03 |
| 2 | 448,000 | .005 | 118,000 | .01 | 43,000 | .008 |
| 3 | 854,000 | .009 | 141,000 | .01 | 77,000 | .02 |
| 4 | 1,277,000 | .01 | 233,000 | .02 | 131,000 | .03 |
| 5 | 7,443,000 | .08 | 1,114,000 | .11 | 683,000 | .13 |
| 6 | 4,560,000 | .051 | 629,000 | .06 | 295,000 | .06 |
| 7 | 9,781,000 | .11 | 1,138,000 | .11 | 558,000 | .11 |
| 8 | 18,669,000 | .21 | 1,903,000 | .19 | 1,048,000 | .21 |
| 9 | 10,567,000 | .12 | 958,000 | .10 | 471,000 | .09 |
| 10 (best) | 33,415,000 | .38 | 3,241,000 | .33 | 1,576,000 | .31 |
| Not reported | 488,000 | .005 | 57,000 | .005 | 41,000 | .008 |

Note: Percentages do not add to 100 because of rounding.

| | | | |
|---|---|---|---|
| Worst half of housing | .12 | .19 | .21 |
| Best half of housing | .87 | .79 | .78 |

Worst half = categories 1 - 5 inclusive

Best half = categories 6 - 10 inclusive

# THE BLACK WORKER IN THE LABOR MOVEMENT

**Overview—The Eighties ■ A Brief History of Blacks and Organized Labor ■ Trends of the 1980s —Projections into 1990 ■ Selected Labor Facts ■ Labor Tables**

Black men and women have often found it to their advantage to belong to a labor union. In 1980, when union membership in the United States peaked at 20.1 million, blacks comprised about 12% of that membership, with 2.5 million members. With the black labor force at around 10.9 million, this meant that approximately 1 in 4 black wage and salary earners was a union member.

At this time, about one-third of organized black workers were concentrated in the automobile, steel and teamster unions. A substantial number of blacks also held white-collar occupations, especially clerical jobs, where black workers were more likely than whites to be union members.

Throughout the 1980s, the number of union members declined nationally, dropping by 1987 to 15.6 million, reflecting a loss of more than 5 million members. Blacks fared proportionately better than whites in this attrition: although black membership fell initially to 2,281,000 in 1983, it had stabilized by 1987 at 2,314,000—a net gain of 33,000 new members. By comparison, the number of white union members dropped steadily, from 13,604,000 in 1983 to 12,890,000 in 1987—a loss of 714,000 members. Black women garnered union positions more often than any other group, with 62,000 more black women employed in 1987 than in 1983.

From 1977 to 1987, the total number of employed wage and salary workers nationally increased by 22.3 million, from 81.3 million to 103.6 million by December 1987. More than 90% of these new jobs were white-collar occupations, with many of them within industry groups such as communications, public utilities, computers and financial services.

This massive increase of jobs tended to overshadow the simultaneous losses in bread-and-butter union jobs—as well as an attendant decline in union memberships.

The reasons for these changes in the country's economic

*Turpentine was produced by slave labor in this Old South Carolina camp.*

landscape were myriad. For example, government deregulation of the heavily unionized transportation industries in 1980 saw increased competition from nonunion firms—and forced labor cutbacks. The automobile industry was hit with competition from imports. The "smokestack" industries, a traditional barometer for union strength, stagnated or declined in the 1980s. A case in point is the United Steelworkers Union: in 1974, it had 1.3 million members. By 1988, that number had dropped to 700,000. Overall, the unionized industries, which were hard hit by the 1981-82 recession, did not fully rebound during the ensuing recovery. Instead, industries and services with low levels of unionization prospered.

However, much of the American labor movement continued to obstruct blacks, especially in the highly paid skilled jobs such as those in the building trades. Government, union, and employer programs, which encouraged minority hiring, made some inroads for blacks through affirmative action, but by the early 1980s the efforts had practically ceased. The end result was that "tokenism" existed in employer programs and blacks remained severely underrepresented.

In addition, blacks in many important unions continued to be locked into separate and unequal seniority systems that retarded their progress. Numerous consent decrees and court orders to employers and unions to alter discriminatory hiring and promotion practices, and compensate blacks for past inequalities seemed to be reaping satisfactory results by the late 1970s. However, the Reagan administration initiated an about-face in 1981 by relaxing laws governing affirmative action requirements for lucrative government contracts, and by declaring that preferential treatment could no longer be given to minorities and women.

As scarce as union jobs have become, they remain financially beneficial to blacks, although salary disparities continue to exist along race and gender lines.

In 1986, the median weekly earnings for nonunion white males was $407, and $275 for nonunion black males—a difference of $132. By comparison, white male union workers earned an average of $423 a week, while black male union workers earned $366—an average disparity of $57. Union women shared closer salary levels with white females earning an average weekly salary of $314 and black females earning $292—an average difference of $22.

Both black men and women earned more than their nonunion counterparts: union males averaged $91-a-week more than nonunion males; union females earned $56 more a week.

The American Federation of Government Employees union may be, representative of the state of unions in the late 1980s. For the first time in AFL-CIO history, a black man—indicative of the strong black presence in American unions—was elected president of a major union. In August 1988, AFGE Executive Vice President John Sturdivant won a hard fought contest over 12-year incumbent President Kenneth Blaylock. President Sturdivant faced major financial problems, however, with the 174,000-member union tottering on the brink of bankruptcy, he needed to organize approximately 3,000 new members a month to stay even due to the steady attrition in government employment.

## A BRIEF HISTORY OF BLACKS AND ORGANIZED LABOR

### The Early Years

The labor movement in the United States, as elsewhere, was born and nurtured on a mixture of fear and idealism. As a result, from its very inception, organized labor has been ambiguous toward minorities. On one hand, it has maintained the right of all working men and women to just wages, dignified working conditions, and job security. As such, "labor" has sought to help blacks attain a share of the nation's expanding wealth.

On the other hand, the predominantly white membership and leadership of unions have fueled the readiness of poor blacks to work for low wages and hindered the ability of skilled blacks to compete with whites for jobs in better

*Old drawings of a skilled black carpenter and a waiter.*

ambition.

Ironically, from their earliest days on these shores, many of the skills and trades in which blacks are now employed only as tokens were performed regularly, ably, and often brilliantly by free and slave blacks. This was especially so in the better paying construction trades, whose unions now train and admit blacks to only a minuscule degree. Throughout the seventeenth, eighteenth, and nineteenth centuries, blacks were prevalent, and often predominant, in the ranks of the carpenters, masons, ironworkers, and stonecutters who built the great mansions and government buildings that are now the pride of the South. Blacks also were conspicuous in the ranks of printers, coopers, tailors, and mechanics. In the 1830s, blacks comprised a majority of the carpenters in Charleston and a substantial portion of other skilled workmen in Atlanta, Philadelphia, New Orleans, and other cities.

But the organized efforts of whites to exclude blacks also dates back to early American history. In 1686, the legislature of the Carolinas was prevailed upon to enact a law excluding free blacks from trades. Laws enacted in many colonies and states in the eighteenth and nineteenth centuries forbade master workmen to teach black apprentices to read and write. Violence to exclude blacks from skilled and unskilled employment increased along with the arrival of white immigrants from Europe. In 1834 alone, there were riots in Trenton, Philadelphia, and Rochester.

The mad scramble for jobs created by the growth of the industrial revolution produced intense rivalry and competition between native-born whites and foreign-born whites for available jobs. In the early years of the craft or trade union movement, both these groups joined forces in propagating policies of racial exclusion—already part of the prevailing social climate of the United States. By the eve of the Civil War, many labor unions had formed nationally federated associations which incorporated these basic social attitudes as a matter of course.

After the war, black workers were encouraged by organizations like the National Labor Union (the first national federation of trade unions) to form their own counterpart unions within the framework of white-dominated federations. (In this way, the Colored National Labor Union came into being as an arm of the Republican party, falling into decline, however, with the panic of 1873 and the end of Reconstruction in 1877.)

For a brief period, the Noble Order of the Knights of Labor did attempt to maintain a labor organization which would include male and female, skilled and unskilled, and white and Negro workers. Organized in 1869, the Order grew rapidly until 1886, at which time it was in a position to boast of some 60,000 blacks among its more than 700,000 members. That year, however, May Day demonstrations in Chicago* and the Haymarket bombing caused both press and public alike to equate it with destructive anarchism and to brand it

*Pioneer black union organizer William S. Townsend, president of the United Transport Service employees.*

*Labor's major quest at the time was the eight-hour working day.

*Machinist Mike J. Farrell, a Knights of Labor delegate.*

and the Haymarket bombing caused both press and public alike to equate it with destructive anarchism and to brand it a social menace. Though it too had denounced the bombings, the Order itself was never able to recover from the bad publicity it received, nor live down the ominous nickname with which it was tagged—the "Black International."

## Attempts to End Discrimination

For the first three decades of the twentieth century, organized labor as a whole reflected the hostility of American society toward the black population. In so doing, the trade union movement seemed impotent to deal with the divide-and-conquer attitudes of employers.

However, at various intervals throughout the history of the labor movement attempts have been made to end discrimination and segregation. The tradition begun by the Knights of Labor was continued by the militant members of the International Workers of the World (I.W.W., or the "wobblies" as they were known) who went so far as to organize the underpaid and unskilled lumber workers in the South regardless of race. "Big Bill" Haywood, a leader of the I.W.W., refused to countenance segregated meetings of white and black workers in Louisiana even when joint meetings were prohibited by state law.

At its inception, the American Federation of Labor included as part of its credo the statement that "working people must unite and organize, irrespective of creed, color, sex, nationality or politics." But the AFL lacked the power and will to implement policies which counteracted the racist attitudes prevalent within its ranks. Thus it organized Negroes into separate locals, or affiliated them with central unions whenever they were refused admission on the basis of color.

During the whole dark chapter covering the period from the turn of the twentieth century to the 1930s, enlightened blacks, despite the rebuffs they had suffered, continued to recognize the potential usefulness of the labor movement to all American workers and its potential usefulness to blacks.

*"I carry on the title page of this magazine the union label,"* wrote W.E.B. DuBois in the *Crisis* magazine (1918), *"and yet I know, and everyone of my Negro readers knows, that the very fact that this label is there is an advertisement that no Negro's hand is engaged in the printing of this magazine."* DuBois added:

*Collective bargaining has undoubtedly raised modern labor from something like chattel slavery to the threshold of industrial freedom and in this advance of labor white and black have shared.*

## Progressivism in the CIO

With the Roosevelt era of the 1930s, and the passage of the Wagner Act, some leaders within the ranks of the AFL began to reject the discriminatory policies of the majority of the international union leaders. It became obvious to others that if the international unions continued to exclude blacks, employers would have little trouble in recruiting strikebreakers from the excluded class. Under the rising pressure of Negro protest, a number of AFL leaders launched a series of organizing campaigns in the mass-production industries, and ultimately formed the Congress of Industrial Organizations (CIO).

The resulting AFL-CIO rivalry caused a schism in the ranks of labor—one which led the CIO to concern itself primarily with the organization of the steel, auto, mining, packinghouse, and rubber industries, all of which employed large numbers of blacks. It has been said that no other CIO leader better understood "the importance of equalitarian racial policies for successful unionism than John L. Lewis of

the United Mine Workers." In this union, the common economic and occupational hardships endured by all minimized, although they did not totally eliminate, racial differences among members, even those in the South. Lewis' policies in this area were soon followed by Philip Murray, president of the steel workers, and Walter Reuther, head of the auto workers. CIO policies ultimately prompted Thurgood Marshall to declare that "the program (of this organization) has become a Bill of Rights for Negro labor in America."

These new unions broke sharply with traditional racial practices. Segregationist constitutions and bylaws were erased. Locals admitted blacks, and in a few cases, integrated seniority lines. Negroes were elected to executive positions within locals. Some new unions gave priority to lifting wage scales for low-paying jobs, most of which were filled by Negroes, and to training and upgrading "underemployed" black workers. One such union was the Transport Workers Union in New York, which negotiated substantial wage increases for change clerks and saw to the promotion of black workers to skilled, well-paying white-collar positions.

Unfortunately, such achievements were exceptions that proved the rule of discrimination throughout America's labor movement, especially in craft locals (e.g., cooks and electricians) and hall-oriented locals (e.g., seafarers and lumber and sawmill workers). In the South, the black's position in unions was actually weakened when, in reaction to the 1954 Supreme Court desegregation decision, segregationist groups formed alliances with union locals.

Far from being conducted in an aura of secrecy, the cooperation of Southern segregationists and union leaders was widely publicized. In many localities, notices appeared in local papers stating that the White Citizens Council or the Ku Klux Klan would be holding a meeting in a union hall.

In 1960, six years after the desegregation decision, the NAACP charged that the "Ku Klux Klan and White Citizen Council Forces, especially in Alabama, have moved into many local unions and made them, in effect, virtual extensions of segregationist organizations." Such union-segregationist alliances were apparent to Southern blacks who were understandably more concerned with the situation in their locality than with pro-civil rights declarations from national union headquarters. As a result, Southern blacks often voted in a bloc, in NLRB elections, against union certification. In some cases, black votes defeated major organizational campaigns. One such election, still discussed in union circles, was held at the South Wire Company, Carrollton, Georgia, where 45 Negro workers out of several hundred are believed to have voted en masse against certification of the International Brotherhood of Electrical Workers. The union lost by 8 votes. At the Savannah River Atomic Energy Project in Aiken, South Carolina, 600 black workers out of 3,100 tipped an election against certification of 17 metal trades.

## The Merger

It is against this background of erratic progress and racist reaction that the AFL and CIO merged in late 1955. The elimination of racism within unions was announced as a major goal of the new giant union. Its constitution pledged that the AFL-CIO would encourage all workingmen "without regard to race, creed, color or national origin or ancestry to share equally in the benefits of union organization." A Civil Rights Committee was established to achieve these goals.

This pledge was, of course, applauded by civil rights and liberal organizations. But five years later, in a report on racism within organized labor, the NAACP charged that "the national labor organization has failed to eliminate the broad pattern of racial discrimination and segregation," and that "efforts to eliminate discriminatory practices within trade unions have been piecemeal and inadequate and usually the result of protest."

There was considerable evidence to support these charges. Despite the exemplary declarations accompanying the merger, the AFL-CIO shortly thereafter admitted two unions, the Brotherhood of Locomotive Firemen and the Brotherhood

*Charleston dock workers organized a union of their own after the Civil War.*

*Trade unions which practiced black exclusion were a major target of protest groups throughout the country.*

of Railroad Trainmen, at a time when they had racist clauses in their constitutions.

The AFL-CIO also ignored defiance of state anti-discrimination orders by segregated locals. In April 1957, the New York State Commission against Discrimination ordered the merger of the all-white George N. Harrison Lodge and the all-black Friendship Lodges of the Brotherhood of Railway and Steamship Clerks. The white union disobeyed the order and the lodges remained segregated for several years.

The AFL-CIO also refrained from pressure or comment when member unions went to court to defend exclusion of blacks. In 1958, after elimination of a "Caucasian only" clause from its constitution, the Brotherhood of Locomotive Firemen and Enginemen successfully defended continued exclusion of blacks in a suit brought by Negro firemen in a Cincinnati Federal Court.

Leading black trade unionists observed that the AFL-CIO could expel unions for corruption or Communist ties, but not for violating civil right laws and policies.

Infighting between black and union leaders intensified in the late 1950s. The NAACP brought a number of suits under state fair employment practice laws to force admission of blacks to unions. Activists attacked labor's historic gods. In a scathing article in Commentary magazine, Herbert Hill, labor director of the NAACP, charged, with some telling evidence to support him, that Samuel Gompers, after struggling with some early idealism, became a racist who despised blacks and hated Asians. Hill also charged that the East St. Louis and Chicago black pogroms of 1917 and 1919 were incited and executed by white unionists who feared the use of Negro strike breakers, and that Gompers defended the rioters in a debate with Theodore Roosevelt.

The AFL-CIO promised it would try to eliminate discrimination from "within the house of labor." George Meany, president of the AFL-CIO, stated that discrimination only survived in the labor movement as a "bootleg product, sneaked in by subterfuge."

Meany added that those "that practice discrimination know that its days are numbered." But other leaders of the federation argued that it could not compel locals to adhere to the national union's egalitarian policies.

## The Civil Rights Alliance

Paradoxically, while black and union leaders were fighting one another over union racial practices, they were cooperating in support of state and federal civil rights legislation.

Black and union leaders were in part forced into an alliance because the only strong and consistent political support for each group stemmed from liberal Democrats.

Liberal Democrats favored civil rights legislation and such traditional union objectives as increases in the minimum wage and unemployment compensation, while Republicans and Southern Democrats generally opposed pro-labor and civil rights measures.

Republicans and Southern Democrats had achieved enactment of the Taft-Hartley Act, which increased the government's authority to prevent and end strikes. This same political alliance also combined to prevent cloture of filibusters against civil rights legislation.

Tensions between black and labor leaders were also diminished by the fact that black progress within labor unions was not really a major aim of civil rights leaders. The civil rights movement of the 1950s and early 1960s was far more intense about integration in schools, housing, transportation, and restaurants than in unions.

The reasons for this are complex. Civil rights leadership tended to rest in the hands of black and white professional men—lawyers, ministers, journalists, teachers. There was a tendency among them—perhaps a snobbish tendency—to despise blue-collar work both as a career and as a political issue. Perhaps this attitude was related to an association of blue-collar labor with slavery. At any rate, civil rights leaders of that time obviously felt it far more important for blacks to get degrees from colleges, houses in suburbs, and jobs in corporate suites than to soil their hands on railway engines or scaffolds, no matter how well such work paid.

Also, the immediate objectives of black leaders tended to be legalistic rather than economic. The thrust was for new legislation and constitutional interpretations that would provide legal sanction for equality and integration and would eventually, it was assumed, lead to good economic progress.

It was not until Malcolm X, a criminal who embraced Muslimism while in prison and went on to become a charismatic modern-day black leader, achieved notoriety that a "working man" was to obtain status among the postwar black generation.

Thus, though blacks were bitter about union exclusion, black leaders tended to take it easy on unions—in order to sustain their political alliance with unions and because civil rights advocates were really not all that interested in manual labor, skilled or unskilled.

The AFL-CIO leadership, however, was interested in blacks. The union leadership was not happy about its many surrenders and silences to segregationist affiliates. Many important unions were losing strength in the 1950s, both in terms of real numbers and comparative bargaining strength with employers.

Automation in the coal mines and the weak competitive position of coal vis-a'-vis other forms of power forced the United Mine Workers to accept massive layoffs and the closing of marginal pits. Organization in service industries was disappointingly slow, partly because of union racist policies. Corporations were acquiring bargaining strength via mergers and internal expansion. And the prospect of blacks again appearing in large numbers as scabs haunted labor leaders who had come up through the ranks to union leadership and who had long and clear memories of the days when Negro strike breakers received police protection in the mines of the Rocky Mountains and on the rails in Pennsylvania.

Also, a tinge of working-class socialist idealism survived, and still survives, amidst the guild exclusiveness and suburban conservatism of the labor movement. Some labor leaders find it easier to think of solidarity in terms of economic class than race, and of progress in terms of social legislation rather than political reaction.

*President John Kennedy greets black officials at the Centennial of the Emancipation Proclamation.*

This idealism was tempered by the McCarthyite red scare of the early 1950s and concern about Communist infiltration of unions. Walter Reuther of the auto-workers, had been a particular target of "witch hunters."

Thus it was that the 1950s ended on an eccentric note. Individual unions and locals were coolly excluding qualified blacks from good jobs and apprenticeships, while union and black leaders were cooperating in attempts to achieve legislation that would guarantee blacks the right to live, learn, vote, and work with whites, and on the same terms as whites.

## The 1960s—From Cooperation to Conflict

The 1960s saw profound changes within both the black and labor movements, with the two groups tending to pull in opposite directions. Blacks became more radical and assertive, labor more sluggish and cautious, with the end result that by 1970 the AFL-CIO and selected discriminatory unions were prime targets of both militant and moderate Negro groups.

Negro activity during the 1960s can be traced in terms of its changing targets and ways of exerting pressure.

From 1960 to 1964, the major objective remained civil rights legislation. The main target was Congress and the Kennedy and Johnson administrations. Pressure, however, was exerted more aggressively than during the 1950s, as blacks increasingly resorted to sit-ins, marches, and other forms of direct nonviolent confrontation.

The main target was the "business establishment," which black leaders of varying militancy felt had the financial and political muscle to effect rapid change.

From spring 1968 to the end of the decade, the period of conservatism and "law and order," the major objectives were economic progress, recognition of black ability and uniqueness, and protection of legislation and constitutional gains made since World War II. Major targets were unions which segregated or otherwise demeaned blacks.

While blacks were becoming more radical in the 1960s, the labor movement, as a whole, was becoming more conservative. As workers prospered, they moved to the suburbs or better urban residential areas where they lost interest in social reform, and saw blacks as a threat to their newfound middle-class status. Resistance to integration in unions, and other changes, became so firm by 1970 that A. H. Raskin, assistant editor and labor specialist of the *New York Times*, was to describe labor as "a static force in a chaotic society."

"A movement born as a voice of dissent," continued Raskin, "has become a mainstay of the status quo in a period when even the staidest institutions—educational, corporate, governmental—have felt obliged to take a look at all their most cherished precepts and scrap those made obsolete by changing technology and mores.

*A. Philip Randolph worked diligently for labor rights.*

## Blacks and Labor Elect Kennedy

Both black and union groups supported civil rights and pro-labor legislation and John F. Kennedy for president. Without an overwhelming black and labor vote, Kennedy would have been soundly defeated by Richard Nixon, who lost narrowly and only after some questionable vote counts in Chicago.

Cooperation at the policy-making level reached its high-water mark during the "1,000 days" of Kennedy and the first year or so of the Johnson administration.

Kennedy had promised strong civil rights legislation during his campaign, but by 1963 was clearly pessimistic of his chances of steering a strong bill through Congress. He was especially cynical about Congress's interest in enacting an equal employment opportunities requirement.

Labor historians credit George Meany with the eventual passage of equal opportunities provisions. Notes Raskin:

*The AFL-CIO itself was chiefly responsible for the inclusion of the equal employment opportunities requirement in the Civil Rights Act of 1964. When the original omnibus bill was drawn up in 1963, President Kennedy and Attorney General Robert F. Kennedy were both convinced that it would have trouble enough getting through Congress without a provision forbidding job discrimination by employers or unions. Their view would have prevailed if George Meany had not insisted that such a clause was essential. . . Through every phase of the long fight that followed on Capitol Hill, the AFL-CIO was a mainstay of the coalition that lobbied for a strong anti-bias law.*

Walter Reuther, then an AFL-CIO vice-president, was conspicuous in the 1963 March on Washington, as were the heads and memberships of other unions with large quantities of black members. Black labor leaders A. Philip Randolph and Cleveland Robinson were key organizers of the March.

During this period, blacks were progressing in such service-trades unions as the State, County and Municipal Employees and District 65 of the Retail, Wholesalers, Department Store Union. But in most unions, they were progressing slowly or not at all. Blacks were still excluded from the lucrative referral construction unions. And in large industrial unions, such as the steelworkers, blacks were usually consigned to menial jobs and deprived of seniority lines.

Little was achieved with state Fair Employment Practice Commissions. Although many states have FEP laws, their minuscule staffs and budgets confined the Commissions to slow case-by-case conciliation, where investigation of bias and enforcement of the laws were necessary to effect any real change in the job status of minorities.

The unions generally resisted integrationist pressures. AFL-CIO officials continued to protest that the national union lacked authority to interfere with locals. Negro leaders such as A. Philip Randolph chastised the national union and its Civil Rights Division for their indifferent progress in effecting integration.

## The Alliance Collapses

The union-civil rights alliance, strained at the best of times, disintegrated with the passage of civil rights legislation and the urban ghetto riots of 1964-1968.

However, black attention was focused elsewhere. Though

the urban ghetto riots of 1964-1968.

However, black attention was focused elsewhere. Though blacks continued to challenge discrimination in unions, the main targets of their fury were the police and white ghetto merchants. Their main sources of hope were the government and large corporations, whom blacks hoped would invest money and wield influence to erase employment, health, and housing problems. Thus black leaders made relatively little effort to challenge or work with unions.

White leaders who were seeking progress also displayed little interest in unions. For example, the National Advisory Commission on Civil Disorders (The Kerner Commission) was critical of unions and recommended steps to assure Negroes access to skilled jobs, but obviously regarded exclusion from unions as a lesser matter on the blacks' imposing list of grievances.

The government's response to the riots was to emphasize employment and training of poor blacks. The main responsibility for this was assigned to business. The Johnson administration set up the JOBS Program to subsidize recruiting and training of "hard core" ghetto residents and major corporations formed the National Alliance of Business to guide business in these activities. Unions were merely asked to cooperate and in many instances were granted the right to veto training programs which they felt threatened to glut a labor market. This veto power was, in effect, a continuation of a privilege unions had acquired over Department of Labor training programs earlier in the 1960s.

The reaction of unions to JOBS and NAB was erratic. The AFL-CIO pledged support to recruitment and training efforts. Support was forthcoming from many unions, particularly service industry unions with large numbers of minority-group members. Others were quick to exercise their vetoes.

## 1968-1970: Black Power Focuses on Unions

A number of ideological and practical factors served to divide blacks and unions during the final years of the sixties.

In the face of white backlash, unions tended to increase their resistance to integration. They maintained that this was necessary to prevent a massive defection by union voters from the Democratic Party to George Wallace. After the 1968 Presidential election union leaders claimed, though not for publication, that Wallace's vote in Northern cities, which generally ranged from 5 to 10%, would have been much larger if the unions had not stressed the low wages earned by workers in Wallace's home state of Alabama.

Whatever the case, there can be no doubt that Wallace won substantial support from Northern blue-collar whites.

Blacks and the AFL-CIO were also divided by varying positions on the Vietnam war. The AFL-CIO strongly supported the war while blacks, though fighting there in large numbers, tended to regard it as a racist conflict which was absorbing money needed to improve conditions in American cities.

The civil rights movement had also shifted strongly from its legal-legislative orientation to one of economic improvement. To be sure, court cases were abundant and many of them referred to the older issues of school and housing integration. But an increasing number were directed toward economic improvement, toward erasing bias by employers and unions.

## The New York Teachers Strike

One of the more significant labor disputes of the 1960s occurred in 1968 when a local of the United Federation of Teachers in New York City went out on strike, keeping more than 1 million children out of school for two months.

The UFT Strike protested the city's intention to decentralize its public schools and give control to community school boards. Such a program had been underway experimentally in three school districts, including the largely black Bedford Stuyvesant section of Brooklyn. When the school board overseeing the Bed-Stuy district appeared to be acting capriciously in the hiring and firing of teachers, union leader Albert Shanker called a strike—which lasted until the local school board's authority was diminished.

## The Charleston Hospital Strike

A large majority of American workers are not highly skilled or even industrial, but are employed in service jobs, many of

*The Newark Teachers' Union threatens to strike.*

which are menial, low-paying, and not unionized. Blacks are overrepresented in low-end service trades.

Thus the Charleston College Hospital Strike of 1969 assumes special significance. The strike, conducted by Local 1199 of the RDSWU, was cited by *Business Week* magazine as "a successful union-Negro alliance in which a fight for economic betterment is fused with a fight for racial dignity." The strike was provoked by the hospital's dismissal of 12 black workers. The union won recognition and reinstatement of the workers.

The strike also betrayed some of the conflict common between unions that have varying orientations to blacks. The AFL-CIO supported the strike, but some black union leaders charged that support from the national union was reluctant, tardy, and motivated solely by fear that Local 1199 would withdraw from the RDSWU, as Cleveland Robinson's distributive workers had done a few years earlier.

Nevertheless, the fact remains that the AFL-CIO did support the Charleston strikers and that, for all its internal bickering, organized labor was united on behalf of a group of low-paid service workers, most of them black.

Encouraged by success in Charleston, Local 1199 branched out to organize hospital and nursing homes in the East and Midwest. In the fall of 1969, it organized the Johns Hopkins Hospital in Baltimore and achieved more modest successes in Pennsylvania.

Coretta Scott King was a vocal supporter of the Charleston strike and in 1969 was named honorary chairman of the National Union of Hospital and Nursing Home Employees, the title under which Local 1199 expanded its efforts. The group enlisted the aid of local black and student leaders wherever it could, and staged dramatic demonstrations that harvested publicity and thwarted public services. In Charleston, the state police were called out to maintain order as pro-union demonstrations impeded hospital service, reduced the city's tourist and retail revenue, and produced 1,000 arrests. In Pittsburgh, Local 1199 staged a sit-in at the headquarters of the Mellon National Bank because a hospital trustee had an office there and the bank was a symbol of the "establishment."

In its readiness to frustrate public services on behalf of its aims, Local 1199 was something of a black power counterpart to the United Federation of Teachers in New York. In 1974, about three-fourths of the Local's members were minorities, about 65% were black.

In 1972, Local 1199 led a highly controversial strike against over 50 New York hospitals. The dispute was settled with a contract that brought the average weekly wage of orderlies, housekeepers, aides, and dietary employees to $210 with a minimum starting wage of $181. By 1974, Local 1199 had organized workers in 15 states with notable success in Philadelphia and Baltimore as well as New York.

## The Construction Workers

Unions, contractors, politicians and the unemployed have a stake in the lucrative construction industry, which was worth $168 billion in 1986. Construction jobs have long been among the highest paying in private industry. In 1986, the average hourly wage was $12.47, which was often accompanied by excellent fringe benefits in a union package. Training for jobs often required only a minimum of education.

During the nineteenth century, many of the skilled craftsmen were black, but since the unions gained tight control of the construction labor market in the early 1900s, blacks had been shut out. Today, despite 30 years of antidiscrimination legislation, ranging from executive orders to federal, state, and city laws, blacks still remain underrepresented in construction fields including asbestos workers, bricklayers, carpenters, cement masons, electrical workers, glaziers, ironworkers, lathers, operating engineers, painters, plasterers, plumbers, roofers, and sheet metal workers. Blacks had good reason to expect opposition in any reasoned attack they made on exclusive-skill unions, like construction locals.

Artificial scarcity had been created in the 1960s through restrictive apprentice programs and journeyman certifications, and construction unions enjoyed astronomical pay scales. Union plumbers in Philadelphia, for example, negotiated an annual minimum wage of $19,400. Such wages contributed to inflationary pay raises throughout the economy. The addition of black construction workers would reduce the scarcity and give blacks a piece of some well-paid action.

Also, construction unions found themselves in great demand: it was estimated in 1965 that 1,000,000 skilled construction men would have to be added to the labor force by 1975. Unfortunately, the Depression conscious construction unions worked effectively to minimize entrants into the field.

A number of provisions in federal and local law were instituted to require acceptance of blacks on government-supported construction projects. As Herbert Hill, then-Labor Director for the NAACP, remarked to the Senate Judiciary Committee in October 1969, the public share of the current dollar value of construction rose from 17% in 1947 to 34% in 1967. The government is very much in the construction business. And the construction industry is very dependent on government funds, he said.

The new emphasis on black history, reminding blacks that they were able craftsmen during slavery, may also have contributed to their decision to assault the skilled trades.

It should be said for the unions that economic gain has been a greater factor than racial bias in their exclusionist policies. By limiting the supply of officially qualified workers, they strengthened their position against any recession.

The AFL-CIO replied to black charges by repeating their assertion that national headquarters lacked the power to interfere with local unions, that blacks often failed to pass journeyman and apprenticeship qualification tests, and that under an AFL-CIO "Apprenticeship Outreach" program, the unions had trained 3,862 non-whites in construction trades in two years.

But essentially, 15 years after the highly touted Apprenticeship Outreach and other "hometown" plans were announced, it was found that nothing had been changed and the programs themselves hardly existed any longer. By years earlier and were finishing their training. No new trainees were accepted and the program was being phased out.

Discriminatory problems with black construction union members seemed to be perpetuated in two ways: the insistence of employers on hiring white union members, and reluctance of hiring hall bosses to dispatch black workers over whites.

Discriminatory practices are still maintained in the hiring halls of referral unions. Here, an employer puts in a request for a number of workers for a period of time, and the union dispatches the workers from their pool. Ideally, each union worker is rotated up a list until his or her name is called for a job. However, it has proven easy to get around rotation rules and blacks have been discriminated against in the white-dominated hiring halls.

A situation related to hiring halls triggered a violent melee in midtown Manhattan in July 1981. Construction opportunities had declined throughout the country in the late 1970s, but in New York City there was a booming hard-hat business. Since the 1960s, disgruntled blacks had been picketing construction sites where they had been excluded, but by the 1980s, demonstrations had become more violent. Groups such as Black Economic Survival were formed, and they bused dozens and sometimes hundreds of black and Hispanic workers from construction site to construction site to harass the workers and demand equal employment and the appointment of a "community coordinator" to ensure equal representation.

It was a confrontation like this that generated the July 20, 1981 riot in Manhattan where 325 riot police were needed to quell a violent demonstration during which some 800 unemployed blacks and Hispanics pitched battle with construction workers at two sites. The fighting raged briefly, with few serious injuries, although 25 workers and 12 police officers required hospitalization. Mayor Edward I. Koch denounced the violence but promised to investigate the allegations of violations of hiring laws. Several protestors were arraigned for assault, but no major action was taken.

A significant case for construction unions is pending in the Supreme Court. On October 19, 1981 the high court accepted a case on appeal from several groups of building contractors in Pennsylvania in order to decide who would be liable for damages in discrimination cases: the union or the contractor. A federal appeals court ruled that 1,488 contractors were jointly responsible with the International Union of Operating Engineers for the virtual absence of blacks in the state's construction business.

The case was first brought by a group of black construction workers, supported by the Pennsylvania state government, who sued both Local 542 of the Operating Engineers, which covers eastern Pennsylvania and all of Delaware, and the employers who patronized the hiring hall. At the time of the 1976 trial, 70% of the employers had never hired a black worker.

In their Supreme Court appeal, the employers and General Buildings Contractors argued that they should not be held liable for the union's discriminatory acts because under the terms of various collective bargaining agreements, they were prohibited from going beyond the hiring hall to employ workers directly. The contractors also argued that the Civil

**CHART 26. DECLINING UNION MEMBERSHIP**

**A myriad of changes in the country's economic landscape has produced a shift toward white-collar occupations and away from union jobs with a concurrent decline in union memberships.**

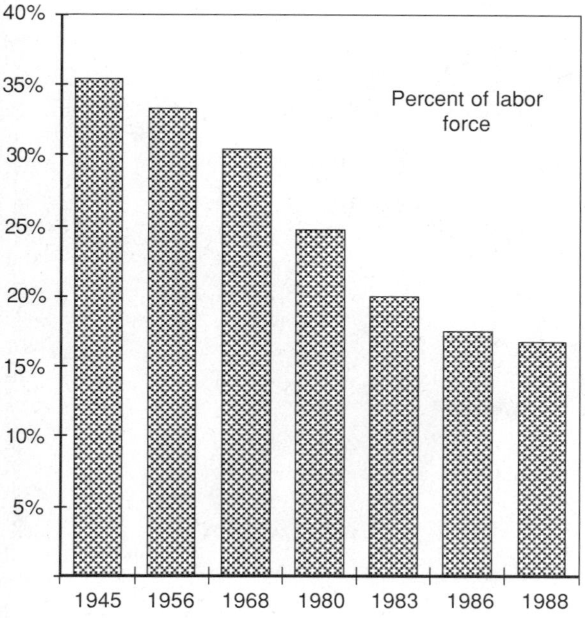


Source: Bureau of Labor Statistics

**CHART 27. DISPLACED WORKERS**

**The innumerable changes in the country's economy have also produced a shift from a primarily manufacturing economy towards a more service-oriented economy. Displacement of workers was an inevitable result of this.**

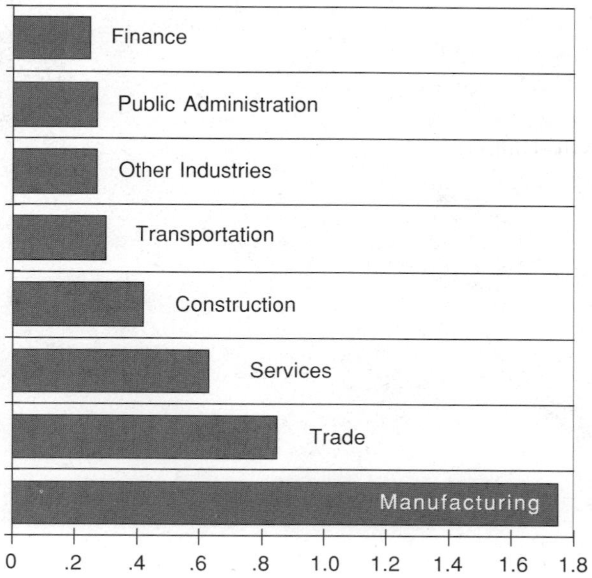


Source: Bureau of Labor Statistics

Rights Act of 1966 requires proof that discriminatory intent was present in order to establish a violation.

Following the Supreme Court ruling, a separate trial will be held to determine monetary damage and liability of the contractor and union for past discrimination.

## Pittsburgh, Chicago, and the "Philadelphia Plan"

In the early 1960s, blacks had demonstrated against hiring bias at construction sites in New York, Philadelphia and elsewhere. These earlier demonstrations were to pale before those which groups undertook in 1969 in Chicago, Pittsburgh, and other cities.

In the summer of 1969, the Pittsburgh Black Construction Coalition, an amalgam of skilled laborers and civil rights groups, blocked entrances to major construction projects for three days. The workers counter-demonstrated, some of them carrying "Wallace in '72" placards. The police were called upon to prevent violence.

In Chicago, also in the summer of 1969, the Chicago Coalition for United Community Action, a group of about 60 minority-group organizations ranging from the Southern Christian Leadership Conference to street gangs, halted work for several days on construction jobs valued at $100 million. The Coalition demanded 10,000 jobs for minorities and the easing of qualification requirements for minorities.

The Chicago & Cook County Building & Construction Trades Council, in a plan endorsed by George Meany, promised in January 1970 to "endeavor to obtain employment for 1,000 qualified journeymen" to be supplied by the Coalition, to accept workers of uncertain skills for 30-day probationary periods, and to expand information, recruiting, and training programs. In February the "agreement" awaited ratification by the unions and Coalition.

In response to rising pressure on construction unions, Secretary of Labor George Schultz in 1969 advanced the Philadelphia Plan, a program which would require builders receiving more than $500,000 in government funds to display a "good faith effort" toward hiring representative quotas of blacks to skilled jobs on all federally supported construction. The quotas would approximate the percentage of blacks resident in each city included in the plan.

George Meany, a number of Southern senators, and the U.S. Comptroller General opposed the Philadelphia Plan, some of them on the grounds that quotas are illegal under the Civil Rights Act of 1964. But Attorney General John Mitchell, who wielded considerable power in the government, declared the plan to be legal and Schultz stood by it. Black groups tended to support it, though they criticized the enforcement provisions as being too weak. At the start of 1970, the government was proceeding with the Philadelphia Plan and leaking word to the press that it would soon be expanded to 20 other cities.

However, the Philadelphia Plan, which one expert noted "came in with Nixon and left before him," did not reach more

*Coretta King speaks at workers' rally in Charleston, South Carolina.*

*Walter Reuther, president of the United Auto Workers, takes part in the massive Mother's Day 1969 march in support of the striking Hospital Workers Union.*

However, the Philadelphia Plan, which one expert noted "came in with Nixon and left before him," did not reach more than a few cities—certainly not 20—and dissipated within a few years.

### Nixon and the Building Trades: 1970-1974

By the early 1970s exclusion of blacks from the better building trades jobs became the major economic and symbolic issue in the efforts of blacks to attain a fair "piece of the action" from organized labor.

The electrical, plumbers, pipefitters, and other construction unions occupy a unique and powerful place in both organized labor and the American economy. In most construction work, unions, not employers, determine who is to be hired and who is to be trained in specific skills. This unusual authority has enabled individual locals to exclude almost anyone they chose from employment. It has also enabled them to maintain an artificial shortage of the labor supply, a shortage that strengthens their claims for high wages, wages that frequently exceed $24,000 a year. Inevitably, in such a situation, blacks are the last to be hired.

In 1970 and 1971, construction workers strengthened their position further when they supported President Nixon's Vietnam policies, going to the extent of attacking peace demonstrators in New York City. Nixon rewarded their support by donning, symbolically, a hard hat, appointing Peter Brennan of the New York Building & Construction Trades Council as his Secretary of Labor, and continuing with the coded rhetoric that promised a flaccid approach to enforcement of policies and procedures with which the government had pledged to increase the blacks' share of the lucrative construction union pie.

The administration had, broadly speaking, displayed two plans to increase black building-trades employment: the "hometown solution" and "Operation Outreach." The essence of the hometown approach was voluntary compliance with hiring and training goals approved by the Department of Labor. The Labor Department had two means of persuading unions to comply. They could offer the carrot of federal subsidies for training programs; and through the Office of Federal Contract Compliance, they could threaten to withdraw funds allocated to contractors for specific federal projects.

The results were dismal. Unions in some 90 cities undertook the hometown solution and none reached their goal. In 1974, the Department of Labor singled out 21 cities in which the voluntary goals were declared "mandatory." The report noted that in Boston only 28 craft and local placements had been achieved out of a goal of 121, in New Haven it was 2 out of 121, in Buffalo 4 out of 108, and in Dayton and Evansville, Indiana, none out of seven. Other cities such as Kansas City, Missouri, did better, but still fell far short of their originally unambitious goals.

In New York City in 1972, only 357 minorities were trained out of a goal of 1,000 and about 100 of these were previously involved in a Model Cities Training Program and thus served as "double statistics." In Chicago, fewer than 100 black workers had been hired, and many of them on a temporary basis. In Pittsburgh, few blacks were hired and the Internal Revenue Service found that hundreds of thousands of dollars in government subsidies for job training had been misappropriated.

*A heavy concentration of black workers fall under the term common laborer.*

Government funds to train minorities in the building trades were also provided an assortment of groups through "Operation Outreach." By 1973, after an expenditure of some $45 million, no reliable figures on the number of blacks trained had been released, but they were few, and again, provided no guarantees of actual employment.

A highly questionable aspect of the Outreach and other programs was their emphasis on apprentice programs. A labor expert at the Columbia University School of Social Work, Russell A. Nixon, estimates that about three fourths of people hired for skilled construction jobs receive training on the job rather than in apprentice programs. Thus the entire procedure of expensive apprentice programs, in which large sums of money for training are provided unions, have become suspect of corruption and political pork-barreling as well as nonproductiveness of jobs for minorities. In July 1974, the Equal Employment Opportunity Commission released figures detailing the results of building trades' hiring of minorities between 1969 and 1972 in some 2,615 locals (see Table 1). The results showed an overall increase of blacks in building trades from about 1,000,000 to 1,300,000 members during that three-year period. But black membership in the higher wage scale boilermakers, electrical workers, elevator constructors, ironworkers, plumbers and pipefitters increased very little, while it rose more rapidly in the lower paying trowel and miscellaneous trades and still more in the lowest paying laborer trades, where blacks comprise one fourth of the total. About three fourths of all blacks in construction trades work in the laborer jobs.

### Black Countermoves

Some black groups have attempted, with the limited funds at their disposal, to offer alternative sources of skilled building trades jobs. One such program is the National Association for the Advancement of Colored People's Afro-American Builders Association. This group organized black-owned construction companies in over 500 cities to employ over 3,000 black journeymen at an average annual wage of $10,000. Such efforts, productive for many blacks, cannot make up for the massive tokenism and unemployment of blacks resulting from the policies of construction unions and indulgence of these unions by the government.

### Blacks Challenge the Steel Union

The United Steelworkers, a union with 200,000 black members, has long helped legitimize bigoted hiring and promotion policies by incorporating, in labor management pacts, seniority, promotion, and job assignment policies that largely confine blacks to the most menial, uncomfortable, and poorest paying jobs. The NAACP studied and then challenged the steel union policies in the 1950s, but corrective action was inhibited by the union-black civil rights alliance of that era and the absence of laws providing for redress. But the Civil Rights Act of 1964 in its Title VII employment section, and President Johnson's 1965 Executive Order 11246 forbidding discrimination in companies holding government contracts, provided the government and courts with the legal means necessary to eliminate discriminatory practices. In 1971, a federal judge ruled that 80% of the blacks in the Bethlehem Steel plant in Lackawanna, New York were assigned to 11 departments which contained the hottest and dirtiest jobs in the place. In a rebuke to the union, the Court wrote that "seniority advantages are not indefeasibly vested rights, but mere expectation derived from a bargaining agreement subject to modification." The court also observed that "the Lackawanna Plant was a microcosm of classic job discrimination in the North" and that discriminatory contract provisions were embodied in nationwide master agreements negotiated by the United Steelworkers of America. The court ordered back pay to 1,600 workers.

Shortly thereafter another suit, filed by the Legal Defense Fund against the United Steel Company in an Alabama Federal Court, resulted in a decision permitting LDF to sue for back pay for all black workers in the plant.

Confronted with the possibility of 200,000 black, Hispanic, and woman steelworkers suing for back pay and integrated seniority lines, the companies and union sought a settlement.

*Thousands of unemployed workers demonstrate in Washington D.C. in 1983 hoping to move Congress to do something about jobs. The rally was organized by the National Unemployed Network.*

Fortunately for them, the Nixon administration was in the process of damping the enthusiasm of the Equal Employment Opportunity Commission. In April 1974 the EEOC, Departments of Labor and Justice, the employers and union agreed on a "consent decree" in which each black worker was to be awarded sums ranging from $250 to $775 in return for giving up their right to sue.

The settlement was a dramatic and significant acknowledgment of discrimination by both a giant industry and giant union. On August 18, 1975 nine steel companies agreed to sign consent orders to end racial discrimination against minorities and women by promising to comply with federal antidiscrimination laws and created a $31 million back pay fund.

According to the Justice Department, which had filed an initial discrimination suit in April 1974, the companies produced 73% of the nation's raw steel and employed 347,679 workers, 52,545 of whom were black, 7,646 Spanish-surnamed, and 10,175 women.

The consent order covered 245 steel plants in 25 states and affected 61,000 minority workers. But the agreement and the way it was negotiated have induced the NAACP and the Legal Defense Fund to challenge it in court. Herbert Hill of the NAACP Labor Department charges that the sums awarded to individuals are "anemic" and not a fraction of what workers would have earned if they had not been discriminated against, that punitive damages were not awarded, and that attorneys for the black workers were excluded from the negotiations. Especially shocking to Hill and others is a provision that the Justice Department will ally itself with the company and union in court against any worker who refuses back pay and sues, establishing a precedent in which future plaintiffs against the USW and steel companies will also have to take on the government.

Other unions have been quick to pick up the cue and try to buy off victims of discrimination with small settlements. One example: in May 1974 blacks and Chicanos who were suing the Pacific Intermountain Express Co. and the Teamsters Union were offered $500 if they signed a waiver of right to sue.

During the 1970s the federal government and Justice Department used "givebacks" to provide recompense to discriminated minority workers. A landmark civil rights case was decided on January 18, 1973 when the American Telephone and Telegraph Company agreed to give $15 million in back pay to 15,000 minority men and women who had suffered employment discrimination. AT&T also agreed to make a $23 million a year pay increase to 36,000 women and minorities who had been moved to higher-paying jobs without being credited with seniority gained in lower category jobs. In return for these actions, the EEOC agreed to drop its opposition to proposed AT&T rate increases, provided AT&T complied by January 1979.

Substantive action was taken after July 3, 1979, when the Supreme Court declined to review the case—thus allowing the lower court decisions to stand, and on January 17, 1979, the federal government reported to the federal district court that AT&T had given "substantial compliance" with the orders to end job discrimination. Of an estimated 980,000 national employees, the number of blacks employed rose from 10.6% in 1973 to 12% in 1979, and the percentage of blacks in management rose from 2.2% in 1973 to 5.5% in 1979.

Although the AT&T case was hailed as the largest job bias compensation at the time, union leaders noted that the award was still less than what employees would have earned if promoted earlier. The award also paled in comparison when the nine major steel companies were ordered to give $31 million in back pay in 1979.

The trucking industry was also challenged for its anti-black hiring and job discrimination tactics. On March 20, 1974 the Justice Department obtained a consent decree forcing seven national trucking companies to adopt a percentage hiring plan for blacks and Spanish-surnamed persons. The legal basis for the agreement was a discrimination suit filed the same day against the seven companies, 342 smaller truckers, the International Brotherhood of Teamsters, the International Association of Machinists, and the industry's collective bargaining organization, Trucking Employer's Inc. The decree directed that minorities be hired in 50% of vacancies that appeared in areas where less than 25% of the staff was black or Spanish-surnamed.

The seven companies included Arkansas Best Freight System, Inc., Ft. Smith, Arkansas; Branch Motor Express Co., New York City; Consolidated Freightways Inc., Menlo Park, California; I.M.L. Freight Inc., of Salt Lake City, Utah; Mason & Dixon Lines, Inc., Kingsport, Tennessee; Pacific Intermountain Express Co., Oakland, California; and Smith's Transport Corp., Staunton, Virginia.

Another discrimination case involved the Oklahoma City-based Lee Way Motor Freight Inc., which at one time employed only five blacks, eight Hispanics, and no women out of a long-distance trucking labor force of 820.

The company, a subsidiary of Pepsico, Inc., on January 10, 1980 reached a settlement in a job discrimination suit and agreed to pay $2.7 million to 82 black job applicants who were allegedly denied jobs because of race. The company also agreed to employ minorities in the sales and management fields, where no minorities had yet been hired.

Another giveback was authorized on April 13, 1981 when the EEOC reached agreement with the Alabama Power Co. requiring the utility to pay $2.2 million to blacks and women to settle discrimination complaints.

The case was initiated by the commission in 1974 as part of a program to pinpoint patterns of discrimination in industries and companies rather than individual complaints. Awards for the 1,350 maligned workers ranged from $50 to $11,350.

The company also agreed to step up recruitment, hiring, and promotion of blacks and women with affirmative action goals for five years.

The settlement of $1.7 million went for blacks in union or janitorial jobs.

The largest settlement without litigation in EEOC history occurred in October 1983, when General Motors agreed to provide $42 million to resolve discrimination against minorities and women in hiring, training and promotion opportunities. Included in the settlement was $15 million for educational endowments and scholarships. However, black auto workers appeared to be facing another, more subtle discrimination ploy by the end of the decade. A 1988 study by University of Michigan professors Robert Cole and Donald Deskins Jr. found that Japanese auto makers had been opening plants just outside commuting distances of areas with sizeable black populations.

The U.S. Census Bureau defines 29 miles as a reasonable commute. "If you look at most of these new plant ventures, they all seem to be between 20 and 30 miles away from a black cluster," said Prof. Deskins in an interview with the San Francisco Examiners. This practice was not restricted to foreign developers, the men added. "Industrial development specialists in state government report that they are often asked by American firms in a variety of industries to eliminate from consideration plant sites in counties with 30% or more black population."

## The Landmark Weber Case

The landmark 1977 Supreme Court ruling in the *Bakke* case, which held that educational institutions could take race into account when screening new employees or applicants—especially in order to remedy discrimination—was put to the test when Brian Weber, a white man from Gramercy, Louisiana, brought a suit against both his employer and his union to reclaim his job.

In 1974, the Kaiser Aluminum & Chemical Corporation and United Steelworkers of America agreed to establish a voluntary program to train minority workers for skilled positions at the Kaiser plants. Half the training positions were to go to blacks and half to whites.

At the Gramercy facility, where Weber, then 38, worked, there were 13 positions open for which Weber was a candidate. Seven positions went to blacks and six to whites, and Weber was rejected, although two of the black men accepted had less seniority than he did.

Weber filed a civil suit against the company, claiming that his rights, according to the 1964 Civil Rights Act, which forbids employment discrimination on racial grounds, had been violated.

Weber's position was initially upheld by the Federal District Court and the U.S. Fifth Circuit Court of Appeals based on Weber's argument that Kaiser Aluminum had maintained a nondiscriminatory policy since 1958. However, the Justice Department filed briefs declaring that there had been a racial bias at the Kaiser plants, and on December 11, 1978, the Supreme Court agreed to review the combined cases of *Kaiser Aluminum & Chemical Corporation v. Weber; U.S. v. Weber; and United Steelworkers of America v. Weber.*

"Reverse discrimination," the buzzword given to the landmark *Bakke* case, was also used with *Weber* when the case went to court on March 28, 1979. The largest crowd of spectators since the 1977 *Bakke* case was in attendance.

*Benjamin Hooks praised the Weber ruling as "the most important civil rights decision in recent history."*

Weber's lawyer argued long and hard, declaring, "You can't avoid discrimination by discriminating," but on June 27, 1979 the Supreme Court ruled that employers and unions could legally establish voluntary programs, including the use of quotas, to aid minorities and women in employment, turning back Weber's challenge.

NAACP Executive Director Benjamin Hooks praised the ruling as "the most important civil rights decision in recent history. . . Had we lost this case, the cause of affirmative action would have been set back ten years." AFL-CIO President George Meany called it a "victory for all who believe in racial justice and who are committed to private voluntary action to end discrimination."

## The Reagan Administration after Weber

The 1980s under the Reagan Administration saw the relaxing of affirmative action controls that had been built up so carefully during the 1960s and 1970s.

The ball started rolling in May 1981, when Republican Congressman Robert Walker of Pennsylvania introduced legislation that would bar the use of numerical quotas to increase the hiring or school enrollment of women or minorities. The bill, called the Equal Employment Opportunity Act, would have amended the Civil Rights Act of 1964 and reflected the views of the Reagan Administration on quotas. Specifically, the bill called for no timetables for integration and less affirmative action requirements on government contracts. Walker said his bill would cut away the paperwork. He noted that the previous requirements had been imposed by President Johnson's executive order, not constitutional amendment.

The bill, however, died in committee.

The same year, then Vice President George Bush was asked to head a special task force to investigate, among other things, affirmative action rules to be reviewed, including those to protect women, blacks, and other minorities from discrimination in hiring.

By August 25 the federal government had taken steps to relax antidiscrimination rules for federal contractors and ease requirements for remedial action. According to Secretary of Labor Raymond Donovan, this move would free three fourths of companies doing business with the federal government of the "burden" of paperwork. In past years, in order to be eligible for a federal contract, an employer would have to file extensive reports about its hiring practices. Under the federal proposal, which went into effect September 25, 1981 (it was filed in the Federal Register August 25, 1981) only businesses with more than 250 employees and a contract worth more than $1 million would have to file formal affirmative action documents. Previously, businesses with more than 50 employees and contracts worth at least $50,000 were subject to the requirements. The proposal was expected to affect 30 million workers and 200,000 contractors.

The action was further supplemented in September when the Justice Department said it would no longer try to remedy discrimination in employment by seeking preferential hiring. Justice Department Head William Brady Reynolds said that the Reagan Administration would enforce civil rights laws but would not tolerate strict preferences for minorities and women in hiring. Reynolds, who could have been quoting Brian Weber's defense attorney, described current practices as "meeting discrimination with discrimination."

The Reagan assault on affirmative action programs continues even after his departure as President; in 1989 a conservative Supreme Court, with a ideological majority due to Reagan appointees, is rehearing various cases related to such programs.

For further information on "Affirmative Action" see the Employment section and the section on Legal Status.

## TRENDS OF THE 1980s—PROJECTIONS INTO 1990

While economic conditions for many blacks have been improved since the 1960s civil rights struggles, many more black laborers remain locked in a state of economic distress and dependency, and the 1980s have brought conditions which have widened the gap between the more advanced black professionals and blacks who hold unskilled, low-wage jobs.

During the 1970s, both blacks and whites moved into more technical white-collar and professional jobs, with the proportion of black men growing slightly faster than the proportion of white men during the decade. In the 1980s, the ranks of blacks and whites in professional, managerial jobs swelled: at the beginning of the decade, 8% of blacks in the work force held such positions; by 1987, the percentage had grown to 13.1%. The percentage of white managers also grew, from 16% in 1980 to 25.9% in 1987. However, the majority of blacks took jobs that were concentrated in occupations at the lower end of the earnings scale, with heavy representation in health technology and counseling.

The largest economic advances were made by black women, who gained more jobs, and more significantly, attained virtual parity in earning power with white women. But the earnings of all women remained only slightly more than half that of men and thus remained an obstacle to hurdle.

Both white and black women were strongest in technical, sales and administrative support positions.

Prime blue-collar jobs, however, will continue to vanish. Union wages, in addition, are expected to drop, according to the Department of Labor. Already, due to pressure from foreign competitors, many unions, including the pace-setting United Steelworkers Union, have accepted contracts with lower wages. As a case in point, the United Food and Commercial Workers Union reported that their average hourly earnings were $7.13 in June 1988—a drop from the $7.74 reported in 1983.

New jobs will continue to flood the market, but they will be in service and manufacturing sectors, not heavy industry. The best of the new jobs will require more education, training and skills than the vanished jobs. Also, workers will not be expected to sign on to a job for life: Instead of offering long-term pension plans, companies may offer profit-sharing programs. Other signs of the times are health insurance plans paid by both the employee and employer, instead of solely by the employer. Wage increases may also be eschewed in favor of bonuses.

Also, from now on, a college degree is going to make a considerable difference for wage earners. In 1976, the Department of Labor noted, men aged 25-34 years old with a high school diploma had a median income of $24,000. Men of the same age with a college degree earned $28,000—a difference of only $4,000. Now, the department said, the median income of those with a high school diploma has fallen to $21,000 (adjusted for inflation) while the median earnings of college graduates has grown to $30,000.

According to the Bureau of Labor Statistics, employment in the services sectors is expected to rise from 17.3% of all jobs in 1973 to 22.9% in 1990—a total of 27 million service workers. On the other hand, the prospect for significant growth in the basic manufacturing industries, where large numbers of blacks held well-paying jobs, is quite small.

## CHART 28. OCCUPATIONS WITH THE LARGEST JOB GROWTH

(estimated growth over the next 10 year, 1989-1999)

**New jobs continue to expand the market, however growth has been in the service and technology sectors. The prospect for significant growth in the basic manufacturing industries, where large numbers of blacks held well-paying jobs, is quite small.**

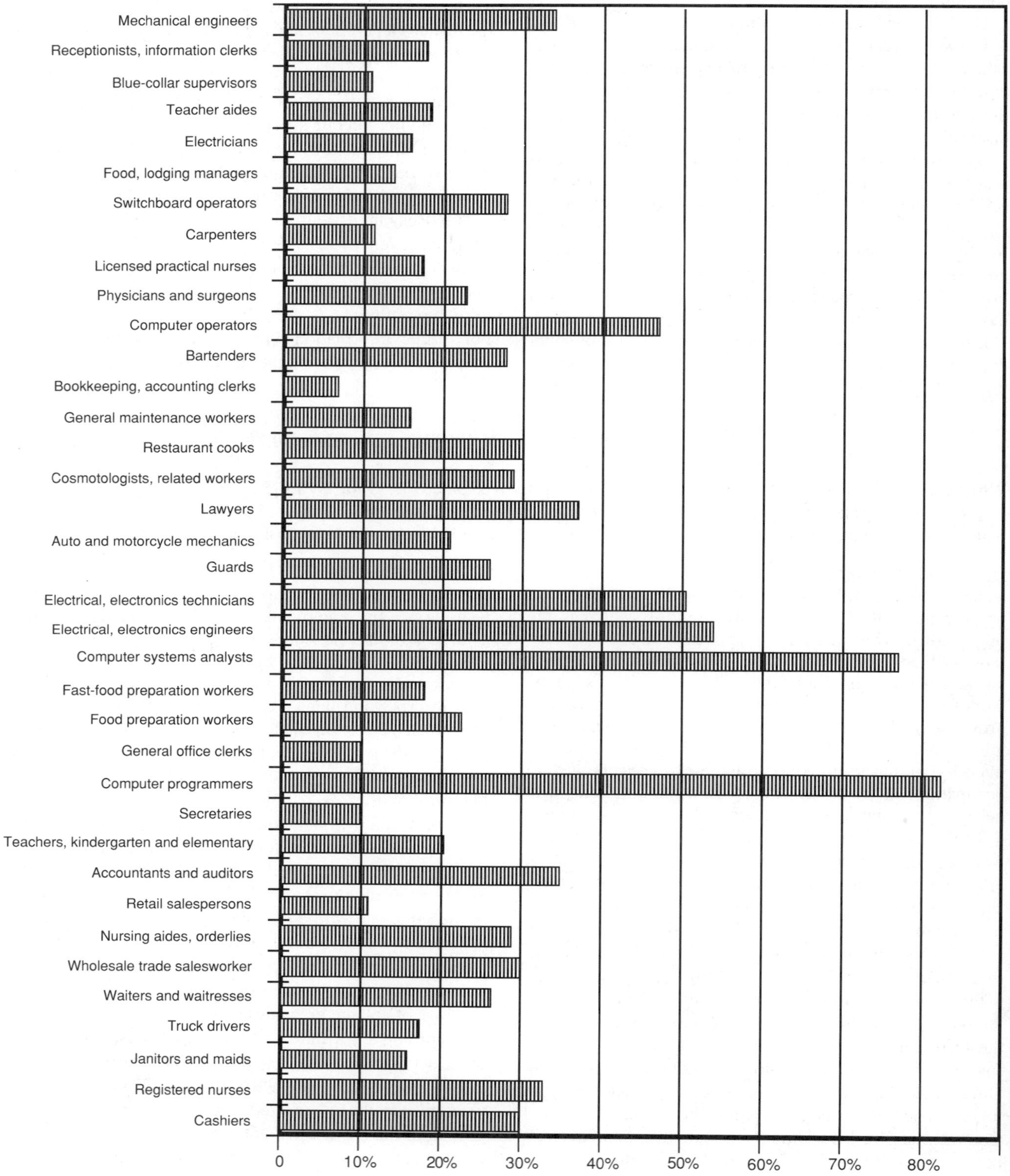

## SELECTED LABOR FACTS

**Fact 1**

The share of construction trade apprenticeships held by minorities increased from 10.6% in 1970 to 19.3% in 1980.

**Fact 2**

There are 1.2 million black civil servants in federal, state and local governments.

**Fact 3**

Nationally, in the 1985 work force, 24.5% of blacks worked as "operatives", 18.4% were service workers, 17.4% were office and clerical workers, and 10.9% were laborers. The highest concentration of black males was in the operatives category, while most black females were in the office and clerical workers category. Among white males, the highest concentrations were officials and managers (18.5%), operatives (18.8%), and craft workers (18.3%). The largest percentage of white females were clerical and office workers (32%).

**Fact 4**

Among construction trades in 1985, blacks comprised about 25% of the nation's 66,000 construction laborers. However, blacks comprised a much smaller percentage—12.5%—of construction craft workers, with only 13,538 blacks in a workforce of 169,888.

**Fact 5**

During the 1980s, black male union membership fluctuated, while the number of black female union members steadily swelled from 923,000 in 1983 to 985,000 by 1987. Roughly 1 out of 4 black women was a union member in 1987.

**Fact 6**

In 1970 blacks were underrepresented in the musicians union—comprising 3.7% of the total membership.

**Fact 7**

The referral union with the largest proportion of blacks was the Laundry and Dry Cleaning Union, in which blacks made up 55% of membership. Forty-two percent of longshoremen and warehousemen were black.

**Fact 8**

A black worker is more likely to be represented by a union than a white worker. In 1987, 22.6% or nearly a quarter of the 10.8 million blacks in the work force were union members. By comparison, white union members comprised only 16.3% or one-sixth of the 85.5 million white workforce.

**Fact 9**

In most industries, contract coverage for blacks exceeded that for whites. In durable goods manufacturing, for example, more than half of black workers, but less than two fifths of white workers, were covered by union contracts.

**Fact 10**

Black women in the labor force are more likely than black men to be represented by unions. Nearly one fifth of the nation's female union members are black, compared with only one eighth of male workers.

**Fact 11**

Black union members tend to be slightly younger than white union members. The median age for white male union members is 38, compared with 37 for blacks. Median ages for women are 34 for whites, 37 for blacks.

## CHART 29. TOTAL EMPLOYMENT OF THE TOP TEN INDUSTRIES

**Minority employment does not always correspond proportionately in terms of the total number of employees. Industries with the greatest number of employees do not necessary employ the greatest number of minority workers.**

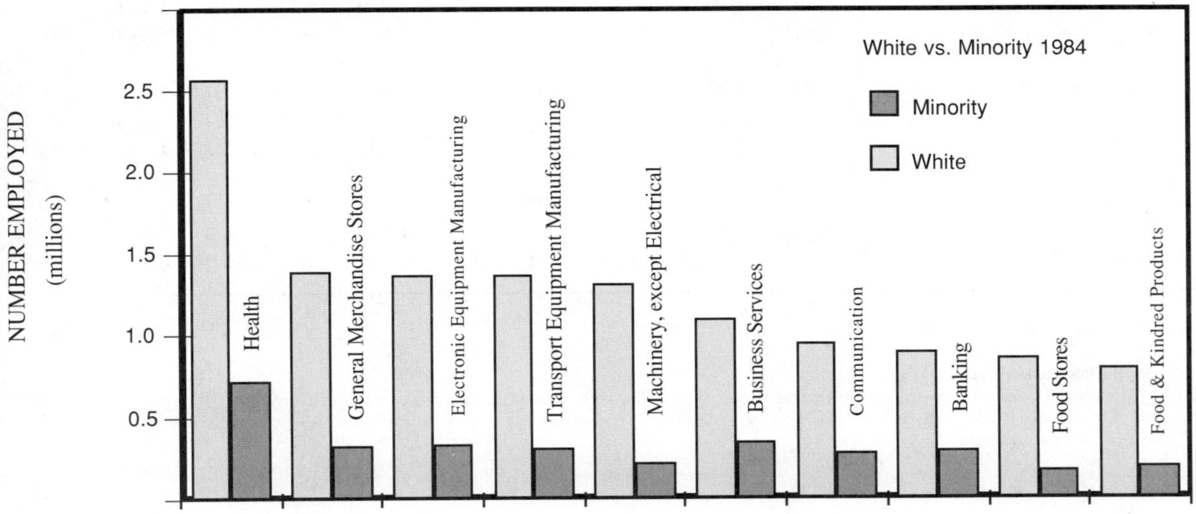

## TABLE 60. EMPLOYED WAGE AND SALARY WORKERS BY OCCUPATION, INDUSTRY, AND UNION AFFILIATION

(Numbers in thousands)

| | 1986 | | | | | 1987 | | | | |
|---|---|---|---|---|---|---|---|---|---|---|
| | | Members of unions[1] | | Represented by unions[2] | | | Members of unions[1] | | Represented by unions[2] | |
| Occupation and Industry | Total employed | Total | Percent of employed | Total | Percent of employed | Total employed | Total | Percent of employed | Total | Percent of employed |
| **Occupation** | | | | | | | | | | |
| Managerial and professional specialty | 22,492 | 3,328 | 14.8 | 4,213 | 18.7 | 23,378 | 3,512 | 15.0 | 4,286 | 18.3 |
| Technical, sales, and administrative support | 31,046 | 3,340 | 10.8 | 4,000 | 12.9 | 31,801 | 3,265 | 10.3 | 3,868 | 12.2 |
| Service occupations | 13,609 | 1,920 | 14.1 | 2,166 | 15.9 | 13,876 | 1,953 | 14.1 | 2,187 | 15.8 |
| Precision production, craft and repair | 11,455 | 3,268 | 28.5 | 3,489 | 30.5 | 11,567 | 3,132 | 27.1 | 3,364 | 29.1 |
| Operators, fabricators, and laborers | 16,554 | 5,012 | 30.3 | 5,288 | 31.9 | 16,920 | 4,956 | 29.3 | 5,234 | 30.9 |
| Farming, forestry, and fishing | 1,747 | 109 | 6.2 | 121 | 6.9 | 1,763 | 96 | 5.4 | 113 | 6.4 |
| **Industry** | | | | | | | | | | |
| Agricultural wage and salary workers | 1,437 | 35 | 2.5 | 41 | 2.9 | 1,469 | 33 | 2.2 | 37 | 2.5 |
| Private nonagricultural wage and salary workers | 79,091 | 11,051 | 14.0 | 12,165 | 15.4 | 80,993 | 10,826 | 13.4 | 11,850 | 14.6 |
| Mining | 822 | 144 | 17.5 | 157 | 19.1 | 782 | 143 | 18.3 | 153 | 19.5 |
| Construction | 4,959 | 1,092 | 22.0 | 1,158 | 23.4 | 5,052 | 1,060 | 21.0 | 1,123 | 22.2 |
| Manufacturing | 20,296 | 4,869 | 24.0 | 5,231 | 25.8 | 20,235 | 4,691 | 23.2 | 5,008 | 24.7 |
| Durable goods | 12,171 | 3,104 | 25.5 | 3,323 | 27.3 | 12,005 | 2,969 | 24.7 | 3,162 | 26.3 |
| Nondurable goods | 8,124 | 1,765 | 21.7 | 1,908 | 23.5 | 8,231 | 1,722 | 20.9 | 1,846 | 22.4 |
| Transportation and public utilities | 5,715 | 2,023 | 35.4 | 2,192 | 38.3 | 5,819 | 1,947 | 33.5 | 2,106 | 36.2 |
| Transportation | 3,142 | 1,077 | 34.3 | 1,144 | 36.4 | 3,274 | 1,051 | 32.1 | 1,113 | 34.0 |
| Communications and public utilities | 2,573 | 946 | 36.8 | 1,048 | 40.7 | 2,545 | 897 | 35.2 | 993 | 39.0 |
| Wholesale and retail trade | 19,839 | 1,425 | 7.2 | 1,554 | 7.8 | 20,401 | 1,440 | 7.1 | 1,572 | 7.7 |
| Wholesale trade | 3,768 | 282 | 7.5 | 309 | 8.2 | 3,935 | 330 | 8.4 | 359 | 9.1 |
| Retail trade | 16,071 | 1,144 | 7.1 | 1,245 | 7.7 | 16,466 | 1,110 | 6.7 | 1,213 | 7.4 |
| Finance, insurance, and real estate | 6,424 | 168 | 2.6 | 230 | 3.6 | 6,736 | 158 | 2.3 | 217 | 3.2 |
| Services | 21,036 | 1,329 | 6.3 | 1,643 | 7.8 | 21,965 | 1,387 | 6.3 | 1,673 | 7.6 |
| Government workers | 16,374 | 5,888 | 36.0 | 7,071 | 43.2 | 16,841 | 6,055 | 36.0 | 7,164 | 42.5 |

[1] Data refer to members of a labor union or an employee association similar to a union

[2] Data refer to members of a labor union or an employee association similar to a union as well as workers who report no union affiliation but whose jobs are covered by a union or an employee association contract.

NOTE: Data refer to the sole or principal job of full- and part-time workers. Excluded are self-employed workers whose businesses are incorporated although they technically qualify as wage and salary workers.

## TABLE 61. MEDIAN WEEKLY EARNINGS OF FULL-TIME WAGE AND SALARY WORKERS BY OCCUPATION, INDUSTRY, AND UNION AFFILIATION

| | 1986 | | | | 1987 | | | |
|---|---|---|---|---|---|---|---|---|
| Occupation and Industry | Total | Members of unions[1] | Non-unions | Represented by unions[2] | Total | Members of unions[1] | Represented by unions[2] | Non-union |
| **Occupation** | | | | | | | | |
| Managerial and professional specialty | $505 | $502 | $497 | $507 | $522 | $521 | $519 | $523 |
| Technical, sales, and administrative support | 320 | 404 | 397 | 309 | 332 | 413 | 407 | 319 |
| Service occupations | 223 | 356 | 350 | 201 | 234 | 375 | 370 | 209 |
| Precision production, craft and repair | 408 | 512 | 508 | 361 | 419 | 521 | 517 | 378 |
| Operators, fabricators, and laborers | 301 | 412 | 409 | 256 | 308 | 420 | 416 | 268 |
| Farming, forestry, and fishing | 217 | 356 | 350 | 209 | 217 | 373 | 369 | 210 |
| **Industry** | | | | | | | | |
| Agricultural wage and salary workers | 216 | ([3]) | ([3]) | 213 | 219 | ([3]) | ([3]) | 217 |
| Private nonagricultural wage and salary workers | 347 | 442 | 437 | 322 | 362 | 458 | 452 | 339 |
| Mining | 510 | 513 | 513 | 509 | 514 | 532 | 528 | 506 |
| Construction | 380 | 590 | 581 | 327 | 397 | 594 | 585 | 351 |
| Manufacturing | 380 | 417 | 417 | 359 | 389 | 426 | 424 | 370 |
| Durable goods | 405 | 432 | 433 | 390 | 413 | 448 | 447 | 398 |
| Nondurable goods | 332 | 390 | 389 | 312 | 344 | 399 | 396 | 322 |
| Transportation and public utilities | 477 | 511 | 508 | 430 | 482 | 519 | 516 | 432 |
| Transportation | 443 | 520 | 516 | 379 | 441 | 522 | 520 | 383 |
| Communications and public utilities | 499 | 502 | 498 | 501 | 515 | 516 | 512 | 520 |
| Wholesale and retail trade | 280 | 384 | 381 | 272 | 292 | 397 | 394 | 285 |
| Wholesale trade | 378 | 418 | 419 | 372 | 393 | 437 | 436 | 386 |
| Retail trade | 250 | 370 | 362 | 242 | 262 | 373 | 367 | 255 |
| Finance, insurance, and real estate | 352 | 348 | 357 | 352 | 373 | 363 | 369 | 373 |
| Services | 310 | 349 | 350 | 306 | 327 | 375 | 375 | 322 |
| Government workers | 409 | 449 | 442 | 375 | 424 | 475 | 470 | 388 |

[1] Data refer to members of a labor union or an employee association similar to a union.
[2] Data refer to members of a labor union or an employee association similar to a union as well as workers who report no union affiliation but whose jobs are covered by a union or an employee association contract.
[3] Data not shown where base is less than 50,000.
NOTE: Data refer to the sole or principal job of full-time workers. Excluded are self-employed workers whose businesses are incorporated although they technically qualify as wage and salary workers.

## TABLE 62. EMPLOYEES ON NONAGRICULTURAL PAYROLLS BY MAJOR INDUSTRY AND MANUFACTURING GROUP

(In thousands)

| Industry | 1984 | 1985 | 1986 | 1987P |
|---|---|---|---|---|
| Total | 94,496 | 97,519 | 99,610 | 102,105 |
| Total private | 78,472 | 81,125 | 82,900 | 85,042 |
| Goods-producing | 24,727 | 24,859 | 24,681 | 24,885 |
| Mining | 966 | 927 | 783 | 742 |
| Construction | 4,383 | 4,673 | 4,904 | 5,032 |
| Manufacturing | 19,378 | 19,260 | 18,994 | 19,112 |
| Durable goods | 11,505 | 11,490 | 11,244 | 11,235 |
| Nondurable goods | 7,873 | 7,770 | 7,750 | 7,876 |
| Service-producing | 69,769 | 72,660 | 74,930 | 77,219 |
| Transportation and public utilities | 5,159 | 5,238 | 5,244 | 5,377 |
| Wholesale trade | 5,555 | 5,717 | 5,735 | 5,797 |
| Retail trade | 16,545 | 17,356 | 17,845 | 18,259 |
| Finance, insurance, and real estate | 5,689 | 5,955 | 6,297 | 6,588 |
| Services | 20,797 | 22,000 | 23,099 | 24,136 |
| Government | 16,024 | 16,394 | 16,711 | 17,063 |

P = preliminary.
NOTE: Establishment survey estimates are currently projected from March 1986 benchmark levels. When more recent benchmark data are introduced, all unadjusted data from April 1986 forward are subject to revision.

## TABLE 63. AN OVERVIEW OF CHANGE EMPLOYMENT BY OCCUPATIONAL GROUP 1986 AND 2000 (MODERATE GROWTH PROJECTION)

| Major occupational group | 1986 | Projected, 2000 | Percent change, 1986-2000 |
|---|---|---|---|
| Total employment | 111,623,000 | 133,030,000 | 19.2% |
| Technicians and related support workers | 3,726,000 | 5,151,000 | 38.2 |
| Service workers, except private household workers | 16,555,000 | 21,962,000 | 32.7 |
| Salesworkers | 12,606,000 | 16,334,000 | 29.6 |
| Executive, administrative & managerial workers | 10,583,000 | 13,616,000 | 28.7 |
| Professional workers | 13,538,000 | 17,192,000 | 27.0 |
| Precision production, craft & repair workers | 13,924,000 | 15,590,000 | 12.0 |
| Administrative support workers including clerical | 19,851,000 | 22,109,000 | 11.4 |
| Operators, fabricators & laborers | 16,300,000 | 16,724,000 | 2.6 |
| Private household workers | 981,000 | 955,000 | -2.7 |
| Farming, forestry & fishing workers | 3,556,000 | 3,393,000 | -4.6 |

Source: Labor Department

## TABLE 64. TOTAL EEO-1 EMPLOYMENT AND PARTICIPATION RATES OF MINORITIES AND WOMEN, INDUSTRY DIVISION, U.S. SUMMARY, 1984

| | | Participation Rate Minority (percent) | | | | | | | | | | | |
|---|---|---|---|---|---|---|---|---|---|---|---|---|---|
| Industry division | Employment | Total | Total M | Total F | Black M | Black F | Hispanic M | Hispanic F | Asian; Pac. Islander M | Asian; Pac. Islander F | American In.*, Alaskan Total | |
| Total All Industries | 31,376,401 | 19.7 | 10.3 | 9.4 | 5.7 | 6.0 | 3.2 | 2.4 | 1.0 | 1.0 | .2 | .2 |
| Agriculture | 117,179 | 41.1 | 28.4 | 12.7 | 7.3 | 4.1 | 19.3 | 7.3 | 1.2 | 1.3 | .6 | .2 |
| Mining | 505,593 | 14.6 | 11.4 | 3.2 | 5.1 | 2.0 | 5.0 | .9 | .6 | ..3 | .7 | .1 |
| Construction | 471,306 | 18.7 | 16.7 | 2.0 | 9.1 | 1.1 | 6.2 | .7 | .7 | ..2 | .7 | .1 |
| Manufacturing | 12,995,704 | 18.7 | 11.4 | 7.3 | 6.6 | 4.5 | 3.5 | 2.0 | 1.1 | .7 | .3 | .1 |
| Durable goods | 7,821,987 | 17.6 | 11.6 | 6.0 | 6.4 | 3.4 | 3.6 | 1.8 | 1.3 | .7 | .3 | .1 |
| Non-durable goods | 5,173,717 | 20.4 | 11.1 | 9.3 | 6.9 | 6.1 | 3.2 | 2.3 | .7 | .6 | .3 | .2 |
| Transportation, communication and public utilities | 3,168,692 | 17.4 | 10.3 | 7.1 | 6.2 | 4.9 | 3.1 | 1.6 | .7 | .5 | .3 | .1 |
| Trade | 5,301,988 | 19.2 | 9.6 | 9.6 | 5.2 | 5.8 | 3.4 | 2.8 | .9 | .8 | .2 | .2 |
| Wholesale | 1,199,152 | 17.7 | 11.3 | 6.4 | 6.1 | 3.7 | 3.7 | 1.8 | 1.3 | .8 | .2 | .1 |
| Retail | 4,102,836 | 19.7 | 9.2 | 10.5 | 4.9 | 6.4 | 3.3 | 3.0 | .8 | .9 | .2 | .2 |
| Finance, Insurance and Real Estate | 2,497,733 | 19.6 | 5.8 | 13.8 | 3.1 | 8.5 | 1.6 | 3.4 | .9 | 1.7 | .1 | .2 |
| Services | 6,318,206 | 23.4 | 9.2 | 14.2 | 5.0 | 9.4 | 2.7 | 2.8 | 1.4 | 1.7 | .1 | .2 |

Sources; Employer Information Reports (EEO-l)
*Combined Male and Female for American Indian, Alaskan.

## TABLE 65. TOTAL EEO-1 EMPLOYMENT, BY POPULATION CLASS AND PERCENT DISTRIBUTION, BY SEX, U.S. SUMMARY, 1984

| | Employment 1984 (In thousands) | | | Employment as a Percent of total | |
|---|---|---|---|---|---|
| Population Class | Total Men & Women | Men | Women | Men | Women |
| Total, All Population Classes | 31,376 | 17,665 | 13,712 | 56.3 | 43.7 |
| White | 25,196 | 14,447 | 10,749 | 46.0 | 34.3 |
| Total Minority | 6,181 | 3,218 | 2,963 | 10.3 | 9.4 |
| Black | 3,668 | 1,799 | 1,869 | 5.7 | 6.0 |
| Hispanic | 1,756 | 1,018 | 739 | 3.2 | 2.4 |
| Asian, Pacific Islander | 634 | 327 | 307 | 1.0 | 1.0 |
| American Indian, Alaskan Native | 122 | 73 | 49 | .2 | .2 |

Source: Employer Information Reports (EEO-l) 1984

## TABLE 66. TOTAL EEO-1, 1984 EMPLOYMENT COMPARED TO 1980 CLF

| Population Class | 1984 EEO-1* Men | 1984 EEO-1* Women | CLF 1980 Census Men | CLF 1980 Census Women |
|---|---|---|---|---|
| | Total= 31,376,000 | | Total= 104,000,000 | |
| Total, All population classes | 56.3 | 43.7 | 57.4 | 42.6 |
| White | 46.0 | 34.3 | 47.7 | 34.3 |
| Total Minority | 10.3 | 9.4 | 9.7 | 8.3 |
| Black | 5.7 | 6.0 | 5.0 | 5.0 |
| Hispanic | 3.2 | 2.4 | 3.4 | 2.3 |
| Asian, Pacific Islander | 1.0 | 1.0 | .9 | .8 |
| American Indian, Alaskan Native | .2 | .2 | .3 | .2 |

Source: Employer Information Reports (EEO-l, 1984)
* Employment as a percentage of total

## TABLE 67. PERCENT BLACKS IN TOP 5 INDUSTRIES

| | Men | Women |
|---|---|---|
| Manufacturing | 6.6% | 4.5% |
| Service | 5.0% | 9.4% |
| Trade | 5.2% | 5.8% |
| Transportation | 6.2% | 4.9% |
| Finance | 3.1% | 8.5% |

## TABLE 68. TOTAL MINORITY EMPLOYMENT IN TOP 5 INDUSTRIES

| | Total Employment* | Total Minority | Percent Minority |
|---|---|---|---|
| Manufacturing | 12,996 | 2,469 | 19% |
| Service | 6,318 | 1,453 | 23% |
| Trade | 5,301 | 1,020 | 19% |
| Transportation | 3,168 | 538 | 17% |
| Finance | 2,498 | 499 | 20% |

* In Thousands

# BLACK CAPITALISM

**Trends In The 1980s ■ A Brief History ■ Nixon and "A Piece of the Action" ■ Carter's Changes ■ The Reagan Years ■ Large Highly Capitalized Black-Owned Corporations ■ Banking ■ Insurance ■ Outlook ■ Agriculture**

The 1982 Census Bureau survey of minority-owned businesses (the most recent available) indicates that as of 1982 the number of black-owned businesses totalled 339,239, up from 231,203 in 1977 and 187,600 in 1972. While the gross figures appear impressive, (a more than 80 percent increase in the total number of black-owned businesses between 1972 and 1982), it nonetheless indicates that in terms of numbers of new businesses in the over-all economy, blacks have barely been able to hold their own at about 3% of the total businesses in the United States.

Total receipts for black-owned businesses was $12.4 billion in 1982, up from $8.6 billion in 1977 and $5.6 billion in 1972. These figures in terms of raw numbers represent a seemingly large gain of 121%, however, when these figures are adjusted for inflation of the dollar the actual gross receipts represent a 9.6% decline in real value since 1972. In inflation adjusted dollars, receipts in 1982 were less that in 1972—$12.8 billion in 1972 as compared with $12.4 billion in 1982. This decline reversed a 7.9 percent increase in earnings between 1972 and 1977. Eighty nine percent of all black businesses in 1982 (300,608) had no paid employees, indicating that the trend of black ownership continues in the direction of very small business services. This represented a 57 percent increase from 1977. By contrast, firms with paid employees declined 3 percent to 38,631 in the same period.

The $12.4 billion aggregate receipts figure in 1982 may be broken down by major industry divisions, the sales for which are as follows: retail trade $4.1 billion; service $3.2 billion; construction $995 million; manufacturing $988 million; wholesale trade $859 million; transportation $795 million; finance $748 million; agriculture $129 million; mining $37 million; and miscellaneous $526 million.

Trends indicated in the 1982 census report do not vary substantially from the last reported trends in 1977. Black-owned buisinesses are mostly very small and do not appear to be doing very well, however, the larger well capitalized businesses are doing very well but represent a meger proportion of all black-owned businesses.

The general trends continue to be:

An increasing number of blacks owning their own businesses, but such businesses are very small and are likely to have gross receipts of $50,000 or less.

Most black-owned businesses are of a sole proprietorship nature and are mostly in service areas such as, auto mechanics, gas stations, barbering, beauty shops, food catering, neighborhood retail shops, and such diverse services as floor scraping and waxing to auto washing and rug installation.

There was a sharp decrease in the number of black-owned

*African-Americans, since early colonial times, have owned their own businesses. Most, however, have been small family service enterprises that required hard work and long hours. Today most black-owned businesses are in black neighborhoods such as the Reliable Shoe Repair Shop in Harlem.*

businesses with more than one employee. In 1977, this figure was trending up, it is currently trending sharply down with 89% of all black-owned businesses having no paid employees.

In 1977, there were 39,968 black-owned firms with paid employees of 164,177; in 1982 there were 38,631 black-owned firms with paid employees of 165,765 indicating a general lack of growth, or a trending decline for black-owned businesses as a whole.

There were 13,858,000 firms in the U.S. in 1982, of these 339,000 were owned by blacks. If there were a proportionate representation of blacks owning U.S. firms the number would be close to 1,400,000. The total number of employees in black businesses was 165,765 out of a total employment in U.S. businesses of 70,000,000. A 1984 census figure indicated that income for whites who owned a business was about five times greater than that of a black owning a business.

The Census Bureau's survey of minority-owned business is conducted only once during a five year period. Data Collected by the Bureau of Census in its 1987 survey will, in all probability, not be available until sometime in 1989. However, in 1985, Brimmer and Company, an economic and financial consulting firm based in Washington D.C., published a report in which it projects the growth of black-owned firms through 1990.

The report speculates that between 1985 and 1990 the tendency for black business activity to lag behind the economy will probably be checked. It estimates total sales for black-owned businesses in 1985 at $13.2 billion, 0.25 percent of all business sales, and representing 6.5 percent of the black consumer dollar. By 1990, it estimates that black-owned business receipts will have increased to $23.1 billion, 0.30 percent of all business receipts and representing 7.0 percent of the black consumer dollar. These income and market share improvements are expected to be accompanied by a net increase in the number of black entrepreneurs and by greater business diversification. Some claim that the Brimmer notions are over-optimistic for the 1990s.

The report also states that black-owned businesses will remain primarily dependent on the black consumer market which will come under increasing pressure from large white-owned corporations, and from businesses belonging to other ethnic groups: "The stage on which black businesses are competing is changing rapidly…As the income of black consumers increases, they are spending their money on a widening pattern of goods and services not supplied by black firms. Blacks are also moving to other parts of major cities and to the suburbs while black businesses remain concentrated primarily in the older neighborhoods..."

The report claims that even though ethnic demographics are changing—Asians, especially Koreans, are purchasing businesses in black neighborhoods formerly owned by Jews and Italians—the basic situation in which blacks do not own the majority of businesses catering to black consumers remains largely the same, and is not likely to change noticeably in the next few years.

## A BRIEF HISTORY

American blacks have owned businesses since their earliest days on these shores. In the seventeenth and eighteenth centuries, free blacks owned inns, construction, tailoring, farming, catering, and many other small businesses. In the nineteenth century, before the Civil War, some black firms grew sufficiently to hire several employees, black and white. One such was Henry Boyd, a furniture manufacturer in Cincinnati, who eventually had to give up his business because of numerous fires started by whites who resented his success. Another prewar black entrepreneur, William Wormley, had to abandon his riding stable in Washington, D.C., when it too was destroyed by fire.

Blacks have also succeeded as financial speculators in real estate and other ventures. In the late eighteenth century, a black barber in North Carolina, John Stanley, invested in plantations, accumulated wealth valued as high as $35,000, and used much of it to buy freedom for other blacks. Philadelphia blacks owned $250 thousand in property by 1814. New Orleans blacks owned property assessed at nearly $2.5 million in 1836. And in 1840, Cincinnati blacks owned more than $200 thousand in property. After the Civil War, blacks owned several banks and insurance companies and other enterprises, a factor that led to the formation in Boston in 1900 of the National Black Business League by Booker T. Washington. Some 400 blacks from over 30 states attended. By 1929, about 65,000 blacks were estimated by the League to own businesses in the United States.

After the abolition of slavery and on into the 1900s blacks steadily acquired relatively more capital and ventured into more entrepreneurial enterprises. Service enterprises, were a logical and popular area for blacks entering business. They served as an opportunity to provide personal services and employment to their own community as well as to acquire a piece of the growing business action in America. Bootblacking, barbering, catering services, funeral services, and later hairstyling and beauty culture became mainstays of the black business community. Reputedly the two wealthiest black women in America at the time, Madame C. J. Walker of Indianapolis, Ind. and Annie M. Malone of St. Louis, Mo., both amassed fortunes during this period from the manufacture and marketing of hair preparations for blacks (brand names such as "Poro," "Heroline," and "Black and White" ).

### Mutual aid and capitalism

As in so many other areas of black community development, the Church and other social bodies affiliated with the Church played a founding role in the development of structured mutual aid for Afro-Americans. The Free African Society, established in 1787 by Richard Allen (who founded the African Methodist Episcopal Church the same year, which is the oldest organization of any kind established by blacks in the United States) and Absalom Jones (who founded St. Thomas's Protestant Episcopal Church in 1794, and became the first black rector-priest of the Episcopal Church in America) was one of the earliest Afro-American organizations for mutual aid. Various antebellum church, fraternal and burial societies provided mutual aid to blacks as a sort of fringe benefit of membership. However, the formation of the first fully-fledged black insurance company did not take place until after the Civil War, when in 1884 more than 2000 representatives of these various quasi-insurance organizations met in Baltimore, Md., to discuss how best to improve mutual aid services to Afro-Americans. As a result of that conference, in 1893 the Southern Aid Society was charted in Richmond, Va. The company's creation is widely considered as the formal beginning of Afro-American Insurance.

*Neighborhood eateries similar to the* Hoochie Coochie Ribs and Things *in Harlem are often family-owned and operated.*

### Development of black-owned insurance companies and banks

By the turn of the century, large black insurance companies were well established. One of the leading companies of that period was Liberty life of Chicago. Its enterprising founder, Fred L. Gillespie, in establishing his company managed to sell $300 thousand in stock within the space of a year and a half—quite remarkable considering the social and economic pressures hampering black business progress at that period. Gillespie also played a founding role in the 1921 creation of the National Insurance Association, which consisted of 60 representatives of 13 black insurance companies.

Though banking among blacks began a good thirty years before the Civil War—free, wealthy blacks in cities such as New Orleans, New York and Philadelphia often underwrote black business ventures with their personal funds, or with funds entrusted to them by others—no formal black-owned banks existed until after the Civil War. After the Reconstruction (1865-1877) impetus for the development of black-owned banks grew when black churches and fraternities encountered difficulties in obtaining credit from white-owned banks. Another impetus came from black citizens who had difficulty opening deposit accounts, as many white-owned banks were reluctant the handle accounts for blacks. Also, with the slow but steady growth of black enterprise in general in what was tantamount to a segregated economy, it became imperative for blacks to own their own financial and funding institutions.

*Black-owned Citizens Savings Bank raises a new home office building in Nashville, Tennessee.*

### Growth since 1900

These various forces culminated in the establishment of more than a dozen black-owned banks by the turn of the century. The first was the True Reformers Bank, which was chartered in Virginia and began operating in April 1889. It was capitalized by $100 thousand and by the end of 1890 had deposits totalling $236 thousand. This growth in black owned banks, and as well, insurance companies and several other enterprises, led to the formation in Boston in 1900, as mentioned earlier in "Brief History" of the National Black Business League by Booker T. Washington.

By 1929, about 65,000 blacks were estimated by the League to own businesses in the United States. However, the climate in the United States has never been conducive to an abundance of black-owned businesses. A major factor in this was the massive immigration to American cities of whites from Europe. Often experienced in business and with sufficient capital and credit standing to start new businesses, these whites rather than blacks were able to start the ventures that grew with the cities. Indeed, whites more than blacks came to be the proprietors of the small retail businesses in neighborhoods where blacks settled, a factor that was to contribute to the racial tensions and violence of the 1960s.

The number and growth of black businesses were also affected, as most businesses in the United States have been, by the trend to concentration of fewer and bigger businesses in virtually every industry. The 1950 census reported that there were some 42,000 self-employed black men in businesses. By the 1960 census the number was down to 32,000.

The 1969 survey of minority-owned business enterprises reported 163,000 businesses, five times the number counted in 1960. However, a preponderance of the increase was attributable to a more thorough census rather than a pronounced increase in black capitalism.

## THE 1970S AND 1980S

### Nixon and "A Piece of the Action"

Following the riots of 1967, increasing attention was devoted to blacks who wished to own businesses. The Kerner Commission was created to understand the black communities civil unrest, its causes and likely remedies and in 1968 its report focused on the high rates of poverty and unemployment. One of the suggestions of the Kerner Commission was that the Federal Government get involved in fostering minority business development. A number of interracial advisory groups were established and various federally assisted programs were promulgated, most conspicuously through the Small Business Administration and the Department of

Commerce's Office of Minority Business Enterprise, and to a lesser extent through the Office of Economic Opportunity. Support of such efforts had been stressed in the 1968 Presidential campaign by Richard Nixon, when he noted repeatedly that the government should spend less on providing special aid to blacks, but that in the American tradition, blacks should have a chance to get "a piece of the action." Some blacks did receive a piece of the action, but the preponderance of manufacturing and service businesses in black communities remained white-owned.

Government support of minorities' businesses has also been hindered by red tape and confusion over jurisdiction between various agencies, such as the Small Business Administration and the Office of Minority Business Enterprise, the two major sources of aid to black businesses.

In 1968, the SBA initiated its 8(a) program which assured that a portion of all Federal Government contracts would be set aside for minority businesses, outside of the competitive bidding process. These programs which came to be known as 'set-asides' have helped many small black businesses, though over-all there has been much criticism and some doubt as to their overall impact.(see The Reagan Years this section) Minority businesses received an estimated $10.5 million in government contracts in 1968, in 1985 that figure had grown to $2.7 billion. There are currently 2,900 participants in the federal 8(a) program, 51 percent of which are black-owned firms. Another federally mandated 'Set Aside' business assistance program for minorities is the 1977 Public works employment Act, which stipulated that all contractors bidding for public works projects must assure that a minority subcontractor would receive at least 10 percent of the contract. The law also required every federal agency to set up an Office of Small and Disadvantaged Business Utilization which would facilitate the fullest possible use of minority businesses in the agency's purchase of goods and services. However, that program proved difficult to enforce. 'Set-Asides' have recently (1988) come under fire by the Reagan Administration.).

Government offices in the late 60s and early 70s were giving mixed signals about continued governmental help for minority businesses as they expressed concern over a reportedly high failure rate among minority businesses that received loans or other subsidies; however, at other times, without citing specific figures, OMBE declared the failure rate of minority businesses it supported to be at or below the national average.

## Carter's Changes

The Carter Administration generally supported efforts to strengthen black businesses. In 1978, the President signed PL 95-507, which required companies bidding for prime contracts with the government to submit a plan to subcontract to minority firms.

The law also required each federal agency to set up an Office of Small and Disadvantaged Business Utilization, to seek the fullest possible use of minority businesses in the agency's purchase of goods and services. Enforcement of this provision, however, was difficult and in 1980 such agencies as the Veteran's Administration and the Department of Defense had not established their OSDBU divisions.

In 1979, Carter replaced the troubled OMBE with the Minority Business Development Administration and tried to clarify the objectives and purview of the remaining agencies. MBDA was assigned the task of coordinating efforts to break new ground for minority businesses, especially for larger ventures and for businesses in fields where minorities have been under represented. Help for smaller businesses was left with the minority division of the Small Business Administration.

In 1982, these and other programs for minority business were still in place, but were weakened by the Reagan Administration's budget cuts and by opposition to affirmative steps to aid minorities. The President declared his support for the development and encouragement of minority business but put limitations on loan, development, and procurement programs and stated that government policy was to rely on the private sector.

*A black contractor, F. W. Eversley & Co., built this New York State Office building in Harlem, New York City, one of the few occasions when a minority construction firm has been the general contractor on a major public project.*

## The Reagan Years

The Reagan years have not been kind to many of the 'set-aside' programs. Administration budgetary cut-backs and its general philosophic opposition to affirmative action and minority aid programs has severely weakened their effectiveness. Also, in 1987 there were some judicial setbacks to the concept of 'set-asides' when federal judges ruled against two different local government set-asides. One of them was a dispute challenging the constitutionality of a Fulton County, Ga., requirement that bidders on a construction project for the county airport meet certain set-aside requirements. The federal district judge found for the plaintiffs, two Minnesota contracting firms, who lost out to a higher bidder despite their claim of good faith efforts to subcontract to qualified minority companies. The federal judge, J. Owen Forrester, found the Fulton County requirement unconstitutional on the grounds that its premise—that without 'set-asides' minority businesses would not have a fair opportunity to participate in government contracts had overlooked the existence of subtle forces pressing minority businesses, such as difficulties in raising financing, lack of adequate managerial and technical skills, and the state of the economy in general which constituted a kind of societal discrimination that is beyond the ability and authority of government to change.

Regardless of the Reagan Administration's *de facto* opposition, federal set-asides have not helped the growth of black enterprise as was their original intent. Critics contend that at best set-asides are dependency inducing charity and at worst characterized by favoritism, politics and fraud. Many contend that set-asides have in fact weakened the development of minority-owned businesses because of their arbitrary disregard for market forces which would usually ensure the survival of the fittest.

In 1979, an internal audit by the SBA revealed that as many as a third of the minority firms receiving 'set-asides' were actually ineligible. Many were front companies for white businesses, which were channeling billions of dollars worth of government contracts intended for minority businesses to white companies. In a nationally reported scandal which surfaced in 1985, involving bribery of public officials in order to secure government contracts, the now defunct Wedtech Corporation, a Bronx, N.Y. based defense contractor which received over $250 million in 'set-aside' federal contracts, exemplified for many all that is wrong with the 8(a) program.

In response to this widespread perception that the program is riddled with chicanery, in March 1987 a bipartisan reform bill was introduced into the House of Representatives which would raise the penalty for establishing "front" companies from $50 thousand to $500 thousand and the prison term from five to ten years. The bill would also raise the eligibility period for 8(a) companies from seven to nine years in an attempt to increase their chances of succeeding in the competitive market.

Many opponents of 'set-asides' claim that the protected business environment they have created for many black-owned businesses, have instead of building and strengthening the black business base, merely fostered a dependency mentality by black enterprise which has undermined its ability to compete in the larger and more lucrative free market. Many also claim a correlation between black enterprises' growing dependence on government set-asides and its shrinking sheer of the black consumer dollar. Black purchasing power has increased from $17.5 billion to $200 billion in the last 30 years, yet during the years 1969 through 1984 the portion of black disposable income secured by black-owned businesses dropped from 13.5 percent to 7 percent, a more than 50 percent reduction during a period

*Parks Sausage Company is one of the 100 largest black-owned businesses in the United States.*

that coincides with the growth of set-aside programs.

Currently white companies enjoy a virtual monopoly in providing goods that are purchased to a disproportionate extent by blacks, such as breakfast foods and cooking ingredients. Even more disturbing for black-owned growth is that white companies have made inroads into markets traditionally served by black-owned companies, such as black hair products—a $1 billion market for which Revlon and Alberto-Culver now claim more than a 50 percent share.

However, support for 'set-aside' programs is still generally very strong, and was bolstered by a report issued by the Senate Committee on small Business in may 1987 which stated that more than 70 percent of the 461 businesses that have "graduated" from 'set-aside' programs since 1980 are still in business and more than a 100 were ranked in the top 25 percent of minority-owned businesses. An 1989 Supreme Court ruling has put the entire future of affirmative action programs in doubt.

## Large Highly Capitalized Black-Owned Corperations

Though the 1982 Census Bureau survey may paint a somewhat gloomy picture of the state of black capitalism, it should be noted that in the years following the survey there have been some signs of a bettering of the relative position of black-owned businesses within the economy as a whole. At this point , however, it appears that the 'better' will apply mostly, if not solely, to the larger black-owned companies. The majority of black-owned businesses are small, usually sole proprietorships, sometimes referred to as "Mom and Pop" operations—megerly financed and with little growth potential and average receipts of about $50 thousand a year. The larger well financed black-owned corporations have always generally performed well, and the last five years have been relatively good.

*Henry Henderson of H. F. Henderson Industries.*

In 1986, *Black Enterprise* Magazine (a leading black-owned business publication) reported a 14.8 percent increase in receipts for the top 100 black corporations (*Black Enterprise* 100) during 1985. According to *Black Enterprise*, this growth not only surpassed the 1985 gross national product (GNP) growth rate (about 3.2% ) but far exceeded the growth rate of the Fortune 500 companies, which averaged 2.8 percent.

The 1988 *Black Enterprise* 100 indicates a continuing trend in the growing health of large black-owned companies and a growing sophistication by black business people in their methods of promoting expansion and growth. Mergers, acquisitions, leveraged buyouts and more innovative marketing are increasingly being used by black entrepreneurs as tools of quick growth. This spells a departure from the traditional mode of black entrepreneurism, which entailed building an enterprise over a lifetimes work. Many of the aforementioned tactics in the American business community are coming under increasing scrutiny and there is particular attention being given to leveraged buyouts as creating debt that is not essentially good for the economy, and the creation of high yield "junk" bonds that could cause investors serious trouble in the event of a recession.

Two recent notable feats of innovative acquisitions, breaking with black business tradition of single dimensional development, were the 1983 founding of TLC Group by Wall Street lawyer Reginald Lewis and the 1985 Acquisition of Philadelphia Coca Cola Bottling Co. by business executive J. Bruce Llewelyn and basketball star Julius "Dr. J" Erving.

In 1983, Lewis founded TLC group as a company that designed paper patterns for home sewing. A year later TLC Group acquired Mc Call Pattern Company (the number 2 pattern-maker company in the U.S.) for $20 million. To finance this transaction TLC administered a $22 million public bond offering—very rare for black-owned enterprises. In 1985, most of TLC's $60 million in sales was attributed to the McCall purchase. In 1987, in an even more audacious business deal, TLC Group orchestrated the sale of McCall for a reputed $95 million profit and followed up with a $985 million leveraged acquisition of Beatrice International Foods Inc., making TLC Group the largest black-owned company in U.S. history.

Likewise, in a move described as unprecedented in the soft drink industry, J. Bruce Llewelyn (the former head Fedco Foods, a black-owned New York based supermarket chain) and Julius Erving (an ex-Philadelphia 76ers basketball star) teamed up to acquire Philadelphia Coca Cola Bottling, making it the third largest black-owned company in America.

The 1988 *Black Enterprise* 100 lists TLC Beatrice International Holdings, Inc., Johnson Publishing Company, Inc., and Philadelphia Coca Cola Bottling Inc. as the top grossing U.S. black-owned companies during 1987, with sales of $1.8 billion, $201.5 million and $166 million respectively.

*Black Enterprise* reported sales of $4.1 billion in 1987 for industrial and service companies. Also, for the first time in its 16 year history, the *Black Enterprise* 100 included a list of auto dealers. This was due to a remarkable upswing in the performance of auto dealers generally and accounted for $2 billion plus in receipts for black-owned auto dealerships. The leaders of the *Black Enterprise* 100 Auto Dealers were Shack-Woods and Assoc., Dick Gidron Cadillac and Ford, Inc., and Baranco Pontiac-GMC Truck, Inc., with sales of $89 million, $52 million and $44.1 million respectively.

Black Enterprise also reported signs of an improving participation of blacks in manufacturing—a business area in which black enterprise has historically lagged—and also in new industries, such as computers and micro-chip engineering. Six manufacturing companies appeared on the 1988 *Black Enterprise* 100 accounting for $129.3 million in sales. The leading manufacturer was Bing Steel, Inc. of Detroit, with sales of $42.9 million in 1987. There were 9 companies in the computer and electronic engineering fields listed on the 1988 list, accounting for $281.3 million in sales. Many of these firms took advantage of the Federal requirement that the Pentagon extend 5 percent of its contracts to minority companies. Henderson Industries Inc., of New Jersey rang up sales of $42.3 million in 1987 (doubling its 1986 total) by dividing itself into two units, one of which focused purely on securing government contracts. Integrated Systems Analysis, Inc., which reported sales of $36.1 million, did so primarily by securing lucrative contracts to develop Navy combat systems.

Though government 'set-aside' contracts have benefited many black-owned companies in a variety of fields in overcoming the unique difficulties faced by both new and established companies, it is a controversial concept that is considered indispensable by some and at best a mixed blessing by others. (See Government and Black-owned businesses)

## Banking

U.S. banking as a whole has endured a rough period during the last five years as a result of bad foreign loans and domestic defaults. The stock market crash of October 1987 had an extremely bad effect on the earnings of black-owned banks. The combined effects of these three factors led to the closure of 184 commercial banks in 1987, a post-Depression record representing 1.3 percent of the nations 14,200 commercial banks. In the first quarter of 1988, forty-six commercial banks had failed. If this closure rate is sustained it will equal the 1987 post-Depression record. In 1987, there were 1,575 "problem banks" listed by the FDIC; this far surpassed the 369 listed in 1982.

Black-owned banks, of course, have not been immune to the vicissitudes of the overall economy, but on some levels they have fared relatively well. There are currently 36 black-owned commercial banks, down from 39 in 1986 (two failed and one was sold to white ownership). Their assets total $1.6 billion, with outstanding loans of $732 million. The top three black-owned banks during 1987, listed by Black Enterprise, are Seaway National Bank of Chicago, Freedom National Bank of New York, and Industrial Bank of Washington, with assets of $145.2 million, $124.5 million and $106.5 million respectively.

Though the loss of three black-owned banks in 1987 represented a disproportionate reduction (7.7 percent as compared with 1.3 percent for all commercial banks) the year did register a slight increase in both their assets and deposits—0.3 percent and 0.8 percent. Also, the recent performance of black-owned banks in general has been relatively good. According to the Sheshunoff Competitive Analysis Report, during 1986 (the most recent year for which figures are available) black-owned banks surpassed industry-wide performance in return on assets (ROA). Black-owned banks averaged 0.71 percent ROA, as compared with 0.63 percent for the industry as a whole.

Black-owned savings and loan institutions have had to do battle in a similarly hostile environment as their commercial counterparts. Over 500 thrifts have failed during this decade. In 1987, according to the Federal savings and Loan Insurance Corporation (FSLIC), thrifts as a whole lost a staggering $6.8 billion and deposits declined from $980.7 billion to $932.5 billion. Although no black-owned thrift folded in 1987, the three prior years saw at least one black-owned thrift close its doors every year. There are currently 32 black-owned savings and loan associations listed by *Black Enterprise*, which possess assets of $1.2 billion and deposits of $1.4 billion. The top three are Independence Federal Savings Bank (Washington D.C.), Family Savings and loan Association (Los Angeles), and Carver Federal savings Bank (New York City), with assets of $216.2 million, $182 million and $168.6 million respectively.

As with black-owned commercial banks, black-owned thrifts have performed relatively well in recent times. Although their assets fell 10.9 percent in 1987, in the same period deposits increased 18.3 percent and loans outstanding increased 5.9 percent. Their ability to stay afloat and even improve their performance slightly can mostly be attributed to two factors: First, ironically some benefit from last October's stock market crash was gained by thrifts in general. As wary and bitten investors licked their wounds and looked for more secure places in which to park their money, many turned to thrifts. Accord to the FSLIC, member institutions registered net withdrawals of $541 million in August 1987 and $1.6 billion in September. In the wake of the Stock Market collapse, FSLIC member thrifts have registered average monthly net deposits of $4.52 billion. The second factor is the conservative management, due to its much smaller deposit base, that has typified black-owned thrift administration. While the larger white-owned thrifts have gone after more adventurous real estate ventures, and

*Freedom National Bank is the first chartered, black-owned bank in Harlem.*

sometimes paid the price, black-owned thrifts have stuck with relatively less risky home mortgage loans.

All factors considered both black-owned commercial banks and savings and loan institutions have held there own, relatively speaking, in the sometimes hostile banking environment of this decade. Ironically, what has traditionally been considered one of their weaknesses, their smallness and fragile deposit base of low and middle income wage earners—conditions relatively foreign to white owned banks—may have endued them with a resilience and hunger which has served as a competitive edge in tough times.

### Insurance

In 1987 the total premium income for black-owned insurance companies dropped to $233 million, down from $234 million in 1986. The number of companies dropped by two to 32 in the same period. Total assets of black-owned insurance companies was $806.6 million in 1987 and total policies in force was $26.3 billion.

Similar to banking institutions, the insurance industry has endured a rough period in the last five years. For at least the last ten years the assets of insurance companies have increased at a slower rate than those of banks and thrift institutions. In addition, the fluctuating interest rates characteristic of the financial environment during the eighties has made life very difficult for all insurance companies. Unfortunately, unlike larger white-owned companies, which service polices worth on average $20 to $30 thousand, black-owned companies service policies worth on average $2 thousand.

The top three black-owned insurance companies listed on the *Black Enterprise* 100 list of insurance companies are North Carolina Mutual Life Insurance Company, Atlanta Life Insurance Company, and Golden State Mutual Life Insurance Company (Los Angeles), with assets of $216.3 million, $126.4 million and $119.2 million respectively.

### Outlook

The 1977 Census Bureau survey reported that the business ownership rate among ethnic minorities was as follows: Blacks 0.92 percent; Hispanics 1.95 percent; Asians 2.88 percent. The lagging entry rate of blacks into business is a vexing problem largely responsible for the community's low position on the economic totem pole. Succeeding waves of immigrant groups coming to America—Irish, Jewish, Italian—have been able to greatly improve their economic position within a relatively short period of time by creating small, tight-knit business communities and literally pulling themselves up by their own boot straps. Blacks, who arrived long before these groups, have been unable to do so. Admittedly, 250 years of slavery, in which blacks were conditioned into a dependence mentality, denied freedom of movement, education, and even a rudimentary familiarity with the free market system, has had a profound effect and may be largely responsible for blacks' poor affinity for enterprise.

"The Chinese are helping the Chinese, Cubans help Cubans, but blacks are helping everyone else. We have been conducting the most successful business boycott in American history—against ourselves," said public television host Tony Brown in a recent edition of *In* magazine. The statement highlights an essential factor in the sluggish development of black enterprise: poor loyalty on the part of black consumers to black merchants. Brown refers to a San Francisco survey that found that income circulates within the Chinese community five or six times before it leaves the ethnic enclave. The figure is four of five times for Jews. Black income, it found, leaves the community almost immediately.

One possible lasting effect of the "black experience"—in which they were constantly oppressed into second-class citizenship—is the exalted value blacks now place on social status as compared with economic status. Many blacks see professional careers as the ideal of success. Medicine, law, the Clergy and government positions serve as a magnet for the best and brightest black minds. These fields, while promoting a measure of social and economic success for black individuals, do little for the furtherance of the black community as a whole, as would successful black enterprise within the structure of the black community. Inner cities not only have 'white-flight' they have as well black-flight, as many successful black professionals (at times referred to as the black bourgeoisie) leave their old neighborhoods, taking their middle incomes with them, further undermining the economic development of their neighborhood businesses and their community at large. Brimmer and Company estimates that total money income for blacks will reach $332.3 billion by 1990, larger than the economy of many nations. It is clear that in order for black businesses to improve their relative position in the economy, and for the black community as a whole to improve its economic condition, a greater portion of black dollars must be spent on goods and services provided by black-owned businesses within the black community. One may speculate as to the reasons, psychological or social, for the reluctance on the part of blacks to support each other economically, but the fact remains that unless black enterprise finds a way to capture a bigger part of this market, possibly by more aggressive marketing or by a greater number of blacks founding their own enterprises, then the black community will have continued economic debilitation.

## Agriculture

The growth of the cotton industry and the westward expansion of the United States are the two historical factors which have largely determined the black's role in U.S. agriculture for more than three centuries. The Louisiana Purchase (1803) and the doctrine of Manifest Destiny (i.e., the inevitable expansion of the United States) instilled in most Southerners the belief that cotton would remain king as long as fertile land could be acquired by moving westward. By 1850, some 2.8 million slaves lived within the confines of the Cotton Kingdom, working on farms and plantations. Of these, some 1.8 million were engaged in the cultivation of cotton, with the remainder being used to raise tobacco, rice, and sugar cane.

After the destruction of the southern slave economy many blacks found themselves with freedom and few if any possessions. They lacked land and capital. Most were forced to return to work the very land from which they had been freed to work as hired laborers or farm tenants of some kind. Promises to distribute land to blacks weren't kept, and, though prices were low, blacks lacked the capital to buy it. By the turn of the century, most black farmers worked the land in one of the various forms of tenancy systems created at the time. Among these were sharecropping, share renting, cash renting, fixed renting and share-cash tenancy. Each of these tenancy systems was slightly different, but the common principle on which they all rested was the tenant's advance mortgaging of a percentage of his crop to the landowner or local merchant in return for food, shelter, tools and fertilizers. These tenant farmers and sharecroppers were forced to use credit until the crops were harvested and extremely high interest rates would leave little food or money after the debt was paid. The credit, with its exorbitant interest was provided by the white merchants and landowners, who also kept the accounts and did the bookkeeping for the semi-literate black farmers. Even with a bumper harvest and good farm prices the tenant would often find that he had just barely broken even, or that he was more deeply in debt to his creditor. This situation often led to debt peonage, under which many black tenants, could never extricate themselves from debt regardless of crop yield or prevailing prices, they were legally bound to work for their creditors until their debts were paid. This hold on the individual for debt amounted to involuntary servitude and was not found to be illegal until 1911 when the Supreme Court declared involuntary servitude for debt, unconstitutional. Even with the courts ruling the condition still persisted.

By 1880, blacks owned about 8% of all farms, had fewer acres of cropland than did white farmers, and were largely restricted to growing cotton by local merchants who financed them, and who regarded cotton as a safe crop that could be sold in the event of foreclosure. The fall in the price of cotton, from 29¢ a pound in 1868 to 5¢ in 1889, was especially hard on blacks.

Agricultural education also played a role in the relative success in the productivity of the black farms of this period. Hampton Normal and Agricultural Institute was founded at Hampton Va., in 1868. Its mandate was to teach selected young Afro-Americans to teach and lead their people. Its most eminent graduate was Booker T. Washington, who in 1881 founded Tuskegee Institute in Alabama, where from 1896 George Washington Carver served as a teacher and then director of agricultural research where he made major breakthroughs in the cultivation of soybeans, peanuts, sweet potato and cotton, which greatly improved and diversified the agrarian industry of the south.

The black farmers contribution to the nation's agricultural output, particularly from southern farms, may be gauged by their percent of the production of that areas principal crops. In 1909 these were: 52.7 percent of cotton, 28.5 percent of sweet potatoes, 28.2 percent of dry peas, 27.2 percent of peanuts, 19.2 percent of corn, 16.2 percent of tobacco, and 10.6 percent of potatoes. The estimated value of this yield was $373 million. It should be added that the 893 thousand blacks who worked on farms nationwide at this time represented only 14 percent of all American farmers.

The creation of small black-owned banks, plus a strong recovery of cotton prices, greatly aided blacks around the turn of the century. Between 1880 and 1911, 50 black lending institutions were created, and they played a great part in the growth of black farming. By 1910, 240,000 blacks owned their farms and comprised one sixth of all southern landowners. Another 670,000 blacks were tenant farmers, which was 40% of the tenant farmer population.

The boom was reversed in the early days of World War I, when cotton again plummeted, this time to 3¢ a pound, and help from private and government sources was largely

*These pickers of cotton could gather from one to three-hundred pounds per day.*

confined to white farmers. Most black lending institutions collapsed as a result of the depression in cotton. A few years later the boll weevil took a heavy toll of black farmers, few of whom could afford effective insecticides. Many black farm owners returned to tenancy.

A consequence of this depression was the first great urban migration of blacks. Between 1880 and 1910 only 79,000 southern blacks had moved north. Between 1910 and 1920 the number was 227,000, and between 1920 and 1930 it reached 440,000. The great majority of these migrants were sharecroppers or farm laborers.

Racial injustice and violence in rural areas accompanied and spurred the migration. Between 1900 and 1931, 345 of the South's 551 cotton-growing counties had at least one lynching, and 170 (31%) had 10 or more.

Within the tenant system, blacks were generally retarded by being denied renter or share tenant status, an improved position from which tenants could accumulate capital and emerge as landowners. In 1925, 71% of white tenants, but only 46% of blacks, were renters or share tenants.

The Depression of the 1930s brought extreme hardship to both white and black farmers. In 1934 the federal government began to take a hand in reorganizing the nation's agricultural system by providing cheap credit for farmers and helping them become landowners. This was done by purchasing heavily indebted plantations, which were subdivided into smaller farms suitable for one family. Many such plots were sold to former black tenants. In addition, the government put into effect certain crop acreage controls and a system of price supports designed to stabilize the market value of a variety of produce. However, there was little provision in aid programs to assure that monetary benefits would reach black farmers, and much of it was siphoned off by unscrupulous farm owners and local politicians.

Also, outreach programs of financial and technical aid were segregated and did little to help blacks. Black agents were often prevented from reaching black farmers who were tenants on white-owned land.

Dramatic shifts in black agriculture occurred after World War II. Tobacco became more important and by 1959, one sixth of all cigarette tobacco grown in the South was grown on black-operated farms. However, the decline of black agriculture after 1959 swept away both tobacco and cotton farmers. Between 1969 and 1979, the number of black cotton farms in the South declined an extraordinary 96%, the number of tobacco farms 77%, according to the agricultural census. Between 1970 and 1980, black farm population in the South fell at three times the rate of the white farm population (65 to 22%), and in 1980 blacks who remained as farm residents tended to be wage and salary workers rather than self-employed. The median income of black farm families in 1978 was $7,584 compared with $17,323 for their white counterparts. The unemployment rate of black farm workers was four times that of whites.

In the late 1970s and early 1980s, government policies seemed only to exacerbate the situation for black farmers. In 1982, the Civil Rights Commission reported that the number of black Farm Home Administration committee members in southern states had dropped enormously between 1979 and 1980 (see Table 14). Blacks also received a disproportionately small share of farm ownership, farm operating emergency, and soil and water loans.

The Commission concluded that the decline of black farms was especially unfortunate in that they had over the years been a force for stability and economic health for the communities near them.

Hope for rejuvenation rested largely with the Farm Home Administration, which was created to help the small farmer and lends some $6 billion per year. However, in 1982 the FMHA persisted in interpreting its mandate narrowly, much like that of a banking institution that must collect on its loans and that lacks jurisdiction to make loans for social purposes.

## TABLE 69. THE 100 LARGEST BLACK-OWNED INDUSTRIAL/SERVICE BUSINESSES IN THE UNITED STATES

( The business tables in this section provided through the courtesy of *Black Enterprise* Magazine. )

| Rank | Company | Location | Chief Executive | Year Started | Staff | Type of Business | 1987 Sales* |
|---|---|---|---|---|---|---|---|
| 1 | TLC BEATRICE INTERNATIONAL HOLDINGS, INC. | New York, New York | Reginald F. Lewis | 1983 | 20,365 | Processing & distribution of food products | 1,800.000 |
| 2 | JOHNSON PUBLISHING COMPANY, INC. | Chicago, Illinois | John H. Johnson | 1942 | 1,903 | Publishing,broadcasting, cosmetics & hair care products | 201.563 |
| 3 | PHILADELPHIA COCA-COLA BOTTLING CO., INC. | Philadelphia, Pennsylvania | J. Bruce Llewellyn | 1985 | 875 | Soft-drink bottling | 166.000 |
| 4 | H. J. RUSSELL & COMPANY | Atlanta, Georgia | Herman J. Russell | 1958 | 610 | Construction & communications | 141.902 |
| 5 | MOTOWN INDUSTRIES | Los Angeles, California | Berry Gordy | 1958 | 257 | Entertainment | 100.000 |
| 6 | SOFT SHEEN PRODUCTS, INC. | Chicago, Illinois | Edward G. Gardner | 1964 | 756 | Hair-care products manufacturer | 81.260 |
| 7 | TRANS JONES, INC./JONES TRANSFER COMPANY | Monroe, Michigan | Gary L. White | 1986 | 1,200 | Transportation services | 79.300 |
| 8 | SYSTEMS MANAGEMENT AMERICAN CORP. | Norfolk, Virginia | Herman E. Valentine | 1970 | 635 | Computer systems integration | 62.675 |
| 9 | THE MAXIMA CORPORATION | Rockville, Maryland | Joshua I. Smith | 1978 | 1,300 | Systems engineering & integration | 56.086 |
| 10 | M & M PRODUCTS COMPANY, INC. | Atlanta, Georgia | Cornell McBride | 1973 | 165 | Hair-care products manufacturer & distributor | 47.250 |
| 11 | DICK GRIFFEY PRODUCTIONS | Hollywood, California | Dick Griffey | 1975 | 97 | Entertainment | 43.875 |
| 12 | BING STEEL, INC. | Detroit, Michigan | David Bing | 1980 | 65 | Steel processing & distribution | 42.915 |
| 13 | H.F. HENDERSON INDUSTRIES, INC. | W. Caldwell, New Jersey | Henry F. Henderson, Jr. | 1954 | 100 | Process control & engineering systems | 42.275 |
| 14 | THE THACKER ORGANIZATION | Decatur, Georgia | Sandra J. Thacker | 1970 | 142 | Construction & engineering | 38.200 |
| 15 | THE BARFIELD COMPANIES | Ypsilanti, Michigan | John W. Barfield | 1955 | 760 | Manufacturer of auto parts; Janitorial services | 37.200 |
| 16 | CITY & SUBURBAN DISTRIBUTORS, INC. | Chicago, Illinois | C. Everett Wallace | 1985 | 85 | Beer distributor | 37.000 |
| 16 | COMMUNITY FOODS, INC. | Baltimore, Maryland | Oscar A. Smith, Jr. | 1970 | 370 | Retail foods | 37.000 |
| 18 | INTEGRATED SYSTEMS ANALYSIS, INC. | Arlington, Virginia | C. Michael Gooden | 1980 | 643 | Engineering & technical support services | 36.141 |
| 19 | JOHNSON PRODUCTS CO., INC. | Chicago, Illinois | George E. Johnson | 1954 | 285 | Hair-care products and cosmetics manufacturer | 33.875 |
| 20 | ESSENCE COMMUNICATIONS, INC. | New York, New York | Edward Lewis | 1969 | 102 | Magazine publishing & TV production | 31.147 |

*In millions of dollars, to nearest thousand. As of December 31, 1987. Prepared by BE Research. Audited by Mitchell/Titus & Co.

## TABLE 69. THE 100 LARGEST BLACK-OWNED INDUSTRIAL/SERVICE BUSINESSES IN THE UNITED STATES (CONTINUED)

( The business tables in this section provided through the courtesy of *Black Enterprise* Magazine. )

| Rank Company | Location | Chief Executive | Year Started | Staff | Type of Business | 1987 Sales* |
|---|---|---|---|---|---|---|
| 21 G & M OIL COMPANY, INC. | Baltimore, Maryland | Rudolph C. Gustus | 1963 | 39 | Petroleum products | 30.592 |
| 22 PRO-LINE CORPORATION | Dallas, Texas | Comer J. Cottrell | 1970 | 217 | Hair-care products manufacturer & distributor | 30.126 |
| 23 B.M.L. ASSOCIATES, INC. | Boston, Mass. | Bertram Lee | 1969 | 115 | Telecommunications | 30.000 |
| 24 GRIMES OIL COMPANY, INC. | Boston, Mass. | Calvin M. Grimes, Jr. | 1940 | 15 | Petroleum products distributor | 29.500 |
| 25 ADVANCED CONSUMER MARKETING CORP. | Burlingame, California | Harry W. Brooks, Jr. | 1984 | 284 | Computer systems integration; mail-order products | 29.374 |
| 26 WESTSIDE DISTRIBUTORS | South Gate, California | Edison R. Lara, Sr. | 1974 | 90 | Beer distributor | 28.668 |
| 27 PARKS SAUSAGE COMPANY | Baltimore, Maryland | Raymond V. Haysbert, Sr. | 1951 | 245 | Sausage manufacturer | 28.210 |
| 28 INNER CITY BROADCASTING CORP. | New York, New York | Percy E. Sutton | 1972 | 350 | Radio & TV broadcasting | 28.000 |
| 29 COMMONWEALTH HOLDING COMPANY, INC. | New York, New York | James H. Dowdy manufacturer | 1967 | 304 | Building materials | 26.340 |
| 30 HII CORPORATION | Boston, Mass. | Denis A. Blackett | 1966 | 130 | Construction & real estate development | 25.300 |
| 31 QUEEN CITY BROADCASTING, INC. | New York, New York | J. Bruce Llewellyn | 1985 | 125 | TV production | 24.000 |
| 32 RESTORATION SUPERMARKET CORPORATION | Brooklyn, New York | Ted Barnett | 1977 | 160 | Retail foods | 22.100 |
| 33 THE GOURMET COMPANIES | Atlanta, Georgia | Nathaniel R. Goldston III | 1975 | 1,227 | Food service & golf facilities management | 21.300 |
| 34 HILLS CAPITOL SECURITY, INC. | Sil. Spring, Maryland | Brandon T. Hill | 1972 | 861 | Security services | 21.000 |
| 35 BEAUCHAMP DISTRIBUTING COMPANY | Compton, California | Patrick L. Beauchamp | 1971 | 93 | Beer distributor | 20.657 |
| 36 BAY CITY MARINE, INC. | San Diego, California | David Lloyd | 1968 | 125 | Shipbuilding & repair | 20.600 |
| 37 ARGRETT ENTERPRISES, INC. | Flushing, New York | Joseph Argrette | 1977 | 400 | Highway construction | 19.500 |
| 38 COCOLINE CHOCOLATE COMPANY, INC. | Brooklyn, New York | Travers J. Bell, Sr. | 1974 | 75 | Chocolate manufacturer | 19.400 |
| 39 LAWSON NATIONAL DISTRIBUTING CO. | Chicago, Illinois | Daniel C. Lawson | 1979 | 81 | Assembly & distribution of transit vehicles | 19.176 |
| 40 MANDEX, INC. | Springfield, Virginia | Carl A. Brown | 1974 | 300 | Telecommunications | 18.888 |

*In millions of dollars, to nearest thousand. As of December 31, 1987. Prepared by BE Research. Audited by Mitchell/Titus & Co.

## TABLE 69. THE 100 LARGEST BLACK-OWNED INDUSTRIAL/SERVICE BUSINESSES IN THE UNITED STATES (CONTINUED)

( The business tables in this section provided through the courtesy of *Black Enterprise* Magazine. )

| Rank Company | Location | Chief Executive | Year Started | Staff | Type of Business | 1987 Sales* |
|---|---|---|---|---|---|---|
| 41 BRONNER BROTHERS | Atlanta, Georgia | Nathaniel Bronner, Sr. | 1947 | 500 | Hair-care products manufacturer | 18.200 |
| 42 AMERICAN DEVELOPMENT CORP. | N. Charleston, So. Carolina | W. Melvin Brown, Jr. | 1972 | 282 | Manufacturing & sheet-metal fabrication | 18.100 |
| 43 WILLIAM CARGILE CONTRACTOR, INC. | Cincinnati, Ohio | William Cargile III | 1956 | 85 | General construction & construction management | 17.500 |
| 44 EARL G. GRAVES, LTD. | New York, New York | Earl G. Graves | 1970 | 78 | Magazine publishing & radio broadcasting | 17.325 |
| 45 INPUT OUTPUT COMPUTER SERVICES, INC. | Waltham, Mass. | Thomas A. Farrington | 1969 | 210 | Computer software & systems integration | 17.000 |
| 46 DELTA ENTERPRISES, INC. | Greenville, Mississippi | Harold L. Hall | 1969 | 301 | Apparel, electronics & railroad products manufacturer | 16.000 |
| 47 TRUMARK, INC. | Lansing, Michigan | Carlton L. Guthrie | 1985 | 140 | Production of metal-stamping equipment | 15.600 |
| 48 ABBOTT PRODUCTS, INC. | Chicago, Illinois | Nelson Carlo | 1973 | 110 | Defense contracting | 15.500 |
| 49 KASS MANAGEMENT SERVICES, INC. | Oakland, California | Arthur B. Scott | 1975 | 400 | Food service management & janitorial supplier | 15.368 |
| 50 WATIKER & SON, INC. | Zanesville, Ohio | Al Watiker, Jr. | 1973 | 93 | Highway & bridge construction | 14.516 |
| 51 KEYS GROUP COMPANY | Detroit, Michigan | Brady Keys, Jr. | 1967 | 1,675 | Fast-food operation | 14.317 |
| 52 LE FONT ELECTRONICS CORPORATION | Bridgeport, Connecticut | Venoal M. Fountain, Sr. | 1983 | 120 | Manufacture of telecom-nications systems | 14.000 |
| 53 SENTINEL COMPUTER SERVICES | Oak Brook, Illinois | Gerald Guice | 1982 | 210 | Computer hardware maintenance | 12.761 |
| 54 ROYAL RIDGE MANAGEMENT COMPANY | Cleveland, Ohio | Ann F. Roberts | 1974 | 750 | Fast-food operation | 12.304 |
| 55 WILLIAMS & RICHARDSON CO., INC. | Detroit, Michigan | Eddie Williams, Sr. | 1980 | 50 | General contracting & construction management | 12.000 |
| 56 JAMES T. HEARD MANAGEMENT CORPORATION | Cerito, California | Lonear Heard | 1971 | 562 | Fast-food operation | 11.600 |
| 57 NBN BROADCASTING, INC. | New York, New York | Sydney L. Small | 1973 | 125 | Radio broadcasting | 11.500 |
| 58 TRUE TRANSPORT, INC. | Newark, New Jersey | Leamon M. McCoy | 1969 | 205 | Trucking & truck stop management | 10.600 |
| 59 LISMARK DISTRIBUTING COMPANY | St. Louis, Missouri | Clifton W. Gates | 1975 | 37 | Beer distributor | 10.376 |
| 60 ELLIS ENTERPRISES | Kenner, Louisiana | Zachary L. Ellis | 1974 | 117 | Building materials supplier; equipment rental | 10.216 |

*In millions of dollars, to nearest thousand. As of December 31, 1987. Prepared by BE Research. Audited by Mitchell/Titus & Co.

## TABLE 69. THE 100 LARGEST BLACK-OWNED INDUSTRIAL/SERVICE BUSINESSES IN THE UNITED STATES (CONTINUED)

( The business tables in this section provided through the courtesy of *Black Enterprise* Magazine. )

| Rank Company | Location | Chief Executive | Year Started | Staff | Type of Business | 1987 Sales* |
|---|---|---|---|---|---|---|
| 61 J. E. ETHRIDGE CONSTRUCTION, INC. | Fresno, California | John E. Ethridge | 1971 | 43 | General contracting | 10.000 |
| 61 PRECISION CONTRACTORS, INC. | Chicago, Illinois | Noah R. Robinson | 1981 | 86 | General construction | 10.000 |
| 63 POWERS & SONS CONSTRUCTION CO., INC. | Gary, Indiana | Mamon Powers, Sr. | 1967 | 60 | General construction | 9.858 |
| 64 MABIN CONSTRUCTION CO., INC. | Kansas City, Missouri | Joseph E. Mabin | 1980 | 57 | Highway construction | 9.701 |
| 65 PORTERHOUSE CLEANING & MAINTENANCE SERVICE CO., INC. | Edison, New Jersey | Bertha L. Griffin | 1973 | 500 | Janitorial maintenance & food service management | 9.000 |
| 66 MICHAEL ALAN LEWIS COMPANY | Milwaukee, Wisconsin | Wayne Embry | 1978 | 90 | Conversion & fabrication fiberboard & paper | 8.900 |
| 67 BURRELL COMMUNICATIONS GROUP | Chicago, Illinois | Thomas J. Burrell | 1971 | 105 | Advertising & public relations | 8.668 |
| 68 CARTER INDUSTRIAL SERVICES, INC. CARTER EXPRESS, INC. | Anderson, Indiana | Will J. Carter | 1976 | 150 | Repair of shipping containers; trucking | 8.085 |
| 69 CENTENNIAL ONE, INC. | Lanham, Maryland | Lillian H. Lincoln | 1975 | 850 | Building maintenance services | 7.990 |
| 70 BURNS ENTERPRISES | Louisville, Kentucky | Tommie Burns, Jr. | 1969 | 350 | Janitorial services & light manufacturing | 7.500 |
| 71 WENDY'S OF CHICAGO, INC. | Chicago, Illinois | Noah Robinson | 1983 | 367 | Fast-food operation | 7.200 |
| 72 HIGHBEAM BUSINESS SYSTEMS, INC. | East Orange, New Jersey | Henry E. Davis, Jr. | 1978 | 75 | Business equipment dealership | 6.100 |
| 73 UNIWORLD GROUP, INC. | New York, New York | Byron E. Lewis | 1969 | 75 | Advertising | 6.007 |
| 74 ATLANTIC BRANDS, INC. | Boston, | Paget T. Hodge | 1981 | 25 | Meat products Massachusetts | 6.000 |
| 74 3A INDUSTRIES, INC. | Seattle, Washington | Reginald S. Frye | 1972 | 80 | General & electrical contracting | 6.000 |
| 76 APEX CONSTRUCTION CO., INC. | Boston, Mass. | Jack E. Robinson | 1983 | 124 | General construction | 5.800 |
| 77 WHOLESALE ELECTRICAL DISTRIBUTION | Atlanta, Georgia | Clarence W. Robie | 1977 | 10 | Wholesale electrical distributor | 5.771 |
| 78 THE CHARISMA GROUP, INC. | New York, New York | Donald K. Harty | 1977 | 300 | Fast-food operation | 5.500 |
| 79 FASTAURANTS, INC. | Los Angeles, California | Ronald Smothers | 1974 | 200 | Fast-food operation | 5.301 |
| 80 BROADWAY-PAYNE, INC. | Baltimore, Maryland | Osborne A. Payne | 1973 | 225 | Fast-food operation | 5.000 |

*In millions of dollars, to nearest thousand. As of December 31, 1987. Prepared by BE Research. Audited by Mitchell/Titus & Co.

## TABLE 69. THE 100 LARGEST BLACK-OWNED INDUSTRIAL/SERVICE BUSINESSES IN THE UNITED STATES (CONTINUED)

( The business tables in this section provided through the courtesy of *Black Enterprise* Magazine. )

| Rank Company | Location | Chief Executive | Year Started | Staff | Type of Business | 1987 Sales* |
|---|---|---|---|---|---|---|
| 81 HIGHLAND CORPORATION | Cincinnati, Ohio | Norman Macon | 1983 | 7 | General construction contractor | 4.845 |
| 82 SHELLY'S OF DELAWARE, INC. | Wilmington, Delaware | Rodney W. Brown | 1967 | 26 | Construction, excavation & demolition | 4.700 |
| 83 DAVIS BROTHERS CONSTRUCTION, INC. | Richmond, Virginia | Melvin L. Davis | 1968 | 58 | General construction | 4.620 |
| 84 WGPR, INC. | Detroit, Michigan | George Mathews | 1975 | 63 | Radio & TV broadcasting | 4.500 |
| 85 CLIPPER INTERNATIONAL CORPORATION | Detroit, Michigan | Lionel Nicco-Annan | 1963 | 56 | Precision machining & metal fabrication | 4.374 |
| 86 SOUTHEASTERN ENTERPRISES, INC. | Groton, Connecticut | Aubrey J. Hamilton | 1973 | 270 | Janitorial services & food service management | 4.320 |
| 87 LANCE INVESTIGATION SERVICE, INC. | Bronx, New York | Ralph V. Johnson | 1961 | 300 | Security services | 4.228 |
| 88 CAMEO ELECTRONICS CO., INC. | Owing Mills, Maryland | Marilyn M. Rawlings | 1981 | 16 | Distributor of electronic components | 4.200 |
| 89 C.H. JAMES & COMPANY | Charleston, West Va. | Charles H. James II | 1883 | 21 | Wholesale food distributor | 4.031 |
| 90 PLATT CONSTRUCTION, INC. | Franklin, Wisconsin | Richard A. Platt | 1972 | 48 | General construction | 4.000 |
| 90 WEBSTER ENGINEERING CO., INC. | Dorchester, Mass. | Theodore Webster | 1977 | 24 | Demolition & excavation | 4.000 |
| 92 EVANBOW CONSTRUCTION CO., INC. | East Orange, New Jersey | Hamilton V. Bowser, Sr. | 1968 | 33 | Building construction & construction management | 3.760 |
| 93 THE BAR-PAT MANUFACTURING CO., INC. | Bridgeport, Connecticut | George M. Bellinger | 1970 | 49 | Manufacture of equipment & sheetmetal | 3.600 |
| 94 STEPCO OF SOUTH CAROLINA, INC. | Columbia, So. Carolina | Charles E. Stephenson III | 1980 | 150 | Fast-food operation | 3.500 |
| 94 DOVER GRAPHICS, LTD. | New York, New York | Ronald Brockett | 1970 | 30 | Promotional advertising | 3.500 |
| 96 ENGLEWOOD CONSTRUCTION CO. | Chicago, Illinois | Cleveland M. Chapman | 1973 | 47 | Highway construction | 3.286 |
| 97 ERNEST SPARKS SALES | Mt. Vernon, New York | Ernest Sparks | 1974 | 10 | Specialty & consumer promotions | 3.250 |
| 98 A. JAMES POINDEXTER, INC. | Dallas, Texas | Alonzo James Poindexter | 1983 | 130 | Fast-food operation | 3.200 |
| 99 ORIGINAL CONSTRUCTION CO., INC. | Detroit, | Joseph Walker Michigan | 1969 | 15 | General construction contractor | 3.177 |
| 100 D.L. & J. SERVICES, INC. | Cham'burg, Penn. | John L. Mills | 1978 | 200 | Custodial & salvage services | 3.124 |

*In millions of dollars, to nearest thousand. As of December 31,1987. Prepared by BE Research. Audited by Mitchell/Titus & Co.

## TABLE 70. THE 100 LARGEST BLACK-OWNED AUTO DEALERSHIPS IN THE UNITED STATES

( The business tables in this section provided through the courtesy of *Black Enterprise* Magazine. )

| Rank Company | Location | Chief Executive | Year Started | Staff | Type of Business | 1987 Sales* |
|---|---|---|---|---|---|---|
| 1 SHACK-WOODS & ASSOCIATES | Long Beach, California | William E. Shack, Jr. Timothy L. Woods | 1977 | 260 | Ford | 89.000 |
| 2 DICK GIDRON CADILLAC & FORD, INC. | Bronx, NY | Richard D. Gidron | 1972 | 200 | GM/Ford | 52.000 |
| 3 BARANCO PONTIAC-GMC TRUCK, INC. | Decatur, Georgia | Gregory T. Baranco | 1978 | 122 | GM | 44.127 |
| 4 PORTERFIELD WILSON PONTIAC-GMC TRUCK-MAZDA, INC. | Detroit, Michigan | Porterfield Wilson | 1970 | 76 | GM/Mazda | 42.700 |
| 5 AL BENNETT, INC. | Flint, Michigan | Al Bennett | 1979 | 120 | Ford | 40.944 |
| 6 SAM JOHNSON LINCOLN-MERCURY-MERKUR, INC. | Charlotte, North Carolina | Sam Johnson | 1977 | 73 | Ford | 38.697 |
| 7 GULF-FREEWAY DODGE, INC. | Houston, Texas | Richard L. Prophet, Jr. | 1985 | 85 | Chrysler | 35.987 |
| 8 LEADER LINCOLN-MERCURY-MERKUR, INC. | St. Louis, Missouri | Jesse Morrow | 1983 | 78 | Ford | 34.305 |
| 9 ROBINSON CADILLAC-VOLKSWAGON-LOTUS, INC. | E. Point, Georgia | Roosevelt V. Robinson | 1974 | 94 | GM/ VW | 34.211 |
| 10 BOB ROSS BUICK/MERCEDES/ GMC, INC. | Centerville, Ohio | Robert P. Ross | 1974 | 103 | GM/ Mercedes | 33.996 |
| 11 SOUTHSIDE FORD TRUCK SALES, INC. | Chicago, Illinois | Carl Statham | 1984 | 72 | Ford | 33.989 |
| 12 UNIVERSAL FORD, INC. | Richmond, Virginia | Bill Turner | 1983 | 82 | Ford | 32.869 |
| 13 BARRON CHEVROLET, INC. | Danvers, Massachusetts | Reginald Barron | 1984 | 78 | GM | 28.978 |
| 14 INNER HARBOR FORD, INC. | Baltimore, Maryland | John A. Minor | 1985 | 101 | Ford | 27.493 |
| 15 NORTHWESTERN DODGE | Ferndale, Michigan | Jesse J. Jones | 1980 | 89 | Chrysler | 27.321 |
| 16 COASTAL FORD, INC. | Mobile, Alabama | Del Dapremont, Jr. | 1984 | 95 | Ford | 27.200 |
| 17 DURYEA FORD, INC. | Brockport, New York | Jesse Thompson | 1985 | 73 | Ford | 27.100 |
| 18 PENINSULA PONTIAC, INC. | Torrance, California | Cecil B. Willis | 1979 | 45 | GM | 26.894 |
| 19 MEL FARR FORD, INC. | Oak Park, Michigan | Mel Farr | 1975 | 82 | Ford | 26.180 |
| 20 TEAM FORD, INC. | Sioux City, Iowa | Arthur P. Silva | 1986 | 80 | Ford | 26.000 |

*In millions of dollars, to nearest thousand. As of December 31, 1987. Prepared by BE Research. Audited by Mitchell/Titus & Co.

## TABLE 70. THE 100 LARGEST BLACK-OWNED AUTO DEALERSHIPS IN THE UNITED STATES (CONTINUED)

( The business tables in this section provided through the courtesy of *Black Enterprise* Magazine. )

| Rank Company | Location | Chief Executive | Year Started | Staff | Type of Business | 1987 Sales* |
|---|---|---|---|---|---|---|
| 21 R. H. PETERS CHEVROLET, INC. | Hurrican, West Virginia | R. H. Peters, Jr. | 1982 | 70 | GM | 25.500 |
| 22 FALKNER ENTERPRISES, INC. | Harvey, Illinois | Bobbie E. Falkner | 1983 | 105 | Chrysler | 25.000 |
| 23 SOUTH BOULEVARD CHRYSLER-PLYMOUTH, INC. | Charlotte, North Carolina | Omar S. Leatherman, Jr. | 1984 | 43 | Chrysler | 24.321 |
| 24 COLONIAL CADILLAC STERLING | Virginia Beach, Virginia | Ernest M. Hodge | 1985 | 65 | GM | 23.325 |
| 25 QUALITY FORD SALES, INC. | Little Rock, Arkansas | LeMon Henderson | 1986 | 52 | Ford | 23.200 |
| 26 AL JOHNSON CADILLAC-SAAB, INC. | Tinley Park, Illinois | Albert W. Johnson, Sr. | 1967 | 52 | GM/ Saab | 22.600 |
| 27 CONYERS RIVERSIDE FORD, INC. | Detroit, Michigan | Nathan G. Conyers | 1970 | 65 | Ford | 22.100 |
| 28 CHINO HILLS FORD, INC. | Chino, California | Timothy L. Woods | 1982 | 59 | Ford | 22.100 |
| 29 QUALITY FORD SALES INC. | Columbus, Georgia | Alan M. Reeves | 1987 | 71 | Ford | 21.953 |
| 30 METRO LINCOLN-MERCURY, INC. | Charlotte, North Carolina | Sam Johnson | 1983 | 50 | Ford | 21.063 |
| 31 ACE GOLDEN OLDSMOBILE, INC. | Port Richey, Florida | Robert C. Ambush | 1984 | 52 | GM | 21.047 |
| 32 WALTON BUICK-VOLKSWAGON, INC. | Medford, Massachusetts | Roland J. Walton | 1977 | 59 | GM/ VW | 20.701 |
| 33 POPE CHEVROLET, INC. | Modesto, California | Joseph N. Pope | 1986 | 90 | GM | 20.587 |
| 34 NORTH SEATTLE CHRYSLER-PLYMOUTH, INC. | Seattle, Washington | William E. McIntosh | 1985 | 62 | Chrysler | 20.500 |
| 35 REPUBLIC FORD, INC. | Republic, Missouri | Franklin D. Greene | 1983 | 49 | Ford | 20.482 |
| 36 ALLSTAR CHEVROLET, INC. | Elkridge, Maryland | Bob Davis | 1986 | 54 | GM | 20.459 |
| 37 BILL SCOTT ENTERPRISES, INC. | Syracuse, New York | William E. Scott | 1982 | 60 | GM | 20.335 |
| 38 JERRY WATKINS CADILLAC-GMC TRUCK, INC. | Winston-Salem, North Carolina | Jerry D. Watkins | 1983 | 47 | GM | 20.257 |
| 39 BROADWAY FORD, INC. | Edmond, Oklahoma | LeMon Henderson | 1983 | 55 | Ford | 20.000 |
| 40 SPALDING FORD-MERCURY, INC. | Griffin, Georgia | Alan M. Reeves | 1981 | 52 | Ford | 19.812 |

*In millions of dollars, to nearest thousand. As of December 31, 1987. Prepared by BE Research. Audited by Mitchell/Titus & Co.

## TABLE 70. THE 100 LARGEST BLACK-OWNED AUTO DEALERSHIPS IN THE UNITED STATES (CONTINUED)

( The business tables in this section provided through the courtesy of *Black Enterprise* Magazine. )

| Rank Company | Location | Chief Executive | Year Started | Staff | Type of Business | 1987 Sales* |
|---|---|---|---|---|---|---|
| 41 JIM BRADLEY PONTIAC-CADILLAC-GMC, INC. | Ann Arbor, Michigan | James H. Bradley, Jr. | 1973 | 61 | GM | 19.315 |
| 42 NORTH STAR DODGE CENTER | Brooklyn Center, Minnesota | John Reggans | 1986 | 58 | GM | 19.592 |
| 43 CAMPUS FORD, INC. | Okemos, Michigan | Windell Barron | 1986 | 77 | Ford | 19.000 |
| 44 LYNCHBURG FORD, INC. | Lynchburg, Virginia | James H. Mitchell | 1981 | 45 | Ford | 18.750 |
| 45 EMPIRE FORD, INC. | Spokane, Washington | Nathaniel D. Greene | 1986 | 62 | Ford | 18.726 |
| 46 EAST TULSA DODGE, INC. | Tulsa, Oklahoma | Henry Hill | 1986 | 48 | Chrysler | 18.667 |
| 47 PEYTON OLDS-CADILLAC-GMC, INC. | Alton, Illinois | Henry E. Peyton | 1978 | 30 | GM | 17.650 |
| 48 UNIVERSITY FORD OF PEORIA | Peoria, Illinois | James L. Oliver | 1985 | 72 | Ford | 17.567 |
| 49 ROYAL LINCOLN-MERCURY-MERKUR, INC. | Peoria, Illinois | C. Charles Royal, Sr. | 1986 | 41 | Ford | 17.485 |
| 50 FERNDALE HONDA INC. | Ferndale, Michigan | Barbara J. Wilson | 1983 | 24 | Honda | 17.300 |
| 51 TROPICAL FORD, INC. | Orlando, Florida | Hamilton W. Masey | 1985 | 75 | Ford | 17.029 |
| 52 LITTLE CHEVROLET, INC. | Roslyn Heights, New York | Clarence E. Little | 1984 | 32 | GM | 16.940 |
| 53 MISSION BLVD. LINCOLN-MERCURY, INC. | Hayward, California | Austin Chuks-Orji | 1986 | 52 | Ford | 16.930 |
| 54 HERITAGE LINCOLN-MERCURY, INC. | Hackensack, New Jersey | T. Errol Harper | 1983 | 32 | Ford | 16.929 |
| 55 SPRINGFIELD FORD/LINCOLN-MERCURY, INC. | Springfield, Tennessee | Bobbie Gene Johnson | 1982 | 52 | Ford | 16.696 |
| 56 LANDMARK FORD SALES, INC. | Fairfield, Ohio | Kenneth C. Younger | 1977 | 63 | Ford | 16.500 |
| 57 ALAN YOUNG BUICK, INC. | Fort Worth, Texas | Alan Young | 1979 | 66 | GM | 16.395 |
| 58 KEMPER DODGE, INC. | Cincinnati, Ohio | Paul C. Keels | 1986 | 34 | Chrysler | 16.204 |
| 59 BOB SMITH CHEVROLET, INC. | Louisville, Kentucky | Robert W. Smith | 1972 | 46 | GM | 16.170 |
| 60 RAY SYKES BUICK/ JEEP EAGLE, INC. | Kingwood, Texas | Raymond A. Aykes | 1984 | 52 | GM | 16.082 |

*In millions of dollars, to nearest thousand. As of December 31, 1987. Prepared by BE Research. Audited by Mitchell/Titus & Co.

## TABLE 70. THE 100 LARGEST BLACK-OWNED AUTO DEALERSHIPS IN THE UNITED STATES (CONTINUED)

( The business tables in this section provided through the courtesy of *Black Enterprise* Magazine. )

| Rank Company | Location | Chief Executive | Year Started | Staff | Type of Business | 1987 Sales* |
|---|---|---|---|---|---|---|
| 61 GEORGE HUGHES CHEVROLET | Freehold, New Jersey | George Hughes | 1978 | 31 | GM | 16.041 |
| 62 METROLINA DODGE, INC. | Charlotte, North Carolina | Reginald T. Hubbard | 1986 | 49 | Chrysler | 15.920 |
| 63 BOB JOHNSON CHEVROLET, INC. | Rochester, New York | Robert Johnson | 1981 | 65 | GM | 15.800 |
| 64 INDIAN SPRINGS FORD, INC. | Kansas City, Kansas | Roy S. Young | 1984 | 53 | Ford | 15.544 |
| 65 BANNISTER LINCOLN-MERCURY, INC. | Kansas City, Missouri | Sterling J. Stokes | 1983 | 75 | Ford | 15.308 |
| 66 GILLESPIE FORD, INC. | Gary, Indiana | Tom P. Gillespie, Jr. | 1980 | 60 | Ford | 15.047 |
| 67 SENTRY BUICK, INC. | Omaga, Nebraska | Gregory M. Williams | 1979 | 57 | GM | 15.000 |
| 68 NOBLE FORD-MERCURY INC. | Indianola, Iowa | Dimaggio Nichols | 1985 | 39 | Ford | 14.741 |
| 69 HARRELL CHEVROLET-OLDSMOBILE, INC. | Flat Rock, Michigan | Charles H. Harrell | 1983 | 25 | GM | 14.500 |
| 70 AURORA LINCOLN-MERCURY, INC. | Aurora, Colorado | Mel Farr | 1986 | 37 | Ford | 14.400 |
| 71 WEST COVINA LINCOLN | West Covina, California | Boyd Harrison, Jr. | 1986 | 47 | Ford | 14.349 |
| 72 MIKE BRANKER BUICK, INC. | Lincoln, Nebraska | Julian Michael Branker | 1985 | 55 | GM | 14.100 |
| 73 GORDON BUICK, INC. | Philadelphia, Pennsylvania | Darrell R. Gordon | 1972 | 29 | GM | 14.100 |
| 74 MARTIN OLDSMOBILE-CADILLAC, INC. | Bowling Green, Kentucky | Cornelius A. Martin | 1985 | 42 | GM | 14.100 |
| 75 DYERSBURG FORD, INC. | Dyersburg, Tennessee | George L. Mitchell | 1985 | 33 | Ford | 14.090 |
| 76 WESTFIELD FORD, INC. | Westfield, Massachusetts | Luther J. White | 1982 | 45 | Ford | 14.000 |
| 77 EL DORADO FORD/LINCOLN-MERCURY, INC. | El Dorado, Arkansas | Walter J. Catchings, Jr. | 1986 | 44 | Ford | 13.767 |
| 78 PUGET SOUND CHRYSLER-PLYMOUTH, INC. | Renton, Washington | Edward B. Fitzpatrick | 1986 | 47 | Chrysler | 13.343 |
| 79 AUBURN FORD/LINCOLN-MERCURY, INC. | Auburn, Alabama | Andrew L. Ferguson | 1985 | 34 | Ford | 13.189 |
| 80 PERRY LINCOLN-MERCURY, INC. | Montgomery, Alabama | Franklin D. Perry | 1985 | 42 | Ford | 13.003 |

*In millions of dollars, to nearest thousand. As of December 31, 1987. Prepared by BE Research. Audited by Mitchell/Titus & Co.

## TABLE 70. THE 100 LARGEST BLACK-OWNED AUTO DEALERSHIPS IN THE UNITED STATES (CONTINUED)

( The business tables in this section provided through the courtesy of *Black Enterprise* Magazine. )

| Rank Company | Location | Chief Executive | Year Started | Staff | Type of Business | 1987 Sales* |
|---|---|---|---|---|---|---|
| 81 R. L. DUKES OLDSMOBILE, INC. | Chicago, Illinois | Constance T. Dukes | 1971 | 40 | GM | 13.000 |
| 82 WOODRUFF OLDSMOBILE, INC. | Detroit, Michigan | James W. Woodruff | 1978 | 55 | GM | 12.977 |
| 83 UNIVERSAL FORD, INC. | Crosby, Texas | Curtis Franklin | 1986 | 51 | Ford | 12.902 |
| 84 FREEMAN MOTORS, INC. | Hopkinsville, Kentucky | Norman E. Freeman | 1986 | 58 | GM | 12.816 |
| 85 FRED JONES PONTIAC-GMC TRUCK, INC. | Brookfield, Wisconsin | Frederick E. Jones | 1984 | 53 | GM | 12.728 |
| 86 RAY WILKINSON BUICK-CADILLAC-ISUZU | Racine, Wisconsin | Raymond M. Wilkinson, Jr. | 1984 | 32 | GM/Isuzu | 12.211 |
| 87 MITCHELL OLDSMOBILE, INC. | Kansas City, Missouri | Emmitt W. Mitchell | 1982 | 50 | GM | 12.092 |
| 88 TONY MARCH BUICK | Hartford, Connecticut | Anthony March | 1985 | 40 | GM | 12.000 |
| 89 SHOALS FORD, INC. | Muscle Shoals, Alabama | Fred D. Lee, Jr. | 1986 | 47 | Ford | 11.845 |
| 90 CHANDLER LEE MOTORS, INC. | Southern Pines, North Carolina | Chandler Bancroft Lee | 1986 | 37 | GM | 11.691 |
| 91 PLAINFIELD LINCOLN-MERCURY-MERKUR, INC. | Grand Rapids, Michigan | George Timothy Turner | 1986 | 31 | Ford | 11.646 |
| 92 FAIRLANE FORD, INC. | Pottsville, Pennsylvania | James F. Delk, Jr. | 1985 | 36 | Ford | 11.317 |
| 93 HILLTOP FORD, INC. | Denison, Texas | Charles E. Bankston | 1986 | 35 | Ford | 11.047 |
| 94 PAT CARTER PONTIAC, INC. | Memphis, Tennessee | Patrick H. Carter, Jr. | 1981 | 49 | GM | 10.923 |
| 95 MEL FARR LINCOLN-MERCURY, INC. | Pontiac, Michigan | Mel Farr | 1986 | 27 | Ford | 10.831 |
| 96 BIAGAS PONTIAC-BUICK, INC. | Phoenixville, Pennsylvania | Edwin D. Biagas | 1985 | 25 | GM | 10.698 |
| 97 DAVIS BUICK-JEEP EAGLE, INC. | Battle Creek, Michigan | Richard O. Davis | 1984 | 37 | GM | 10.569 |
| 98 PITTSBURG FORD, INC. | Pittsburg, California | LaRoy S. Doss | 1974 | 35 | Ford | 10.239 |
| 99 ALLEGAN FORD-MERCURY SALES, INC. | Allegan, Michigan | Ed Weiss, Jr. | 1984 | 15 | Ford | 10.238 |
| 100 BARRINGTON DODGE, INC. | Barrington, Illinois | James W. Johnson, Jr. | 1986 | 25 | Chrysler | 10.061 |

*In millions of dollars, to nearest thousand. As of December 31, 1987. Prepared by BE Research. Audited by Mitchell/Titus & Co.

## TABLE 71. THE 36 LARGEST BLACK BANKS IN THE UNITED STATES

( The business tables in this section provided through the courtesy of *Black Enterprise* Magazine. )

| Rank Company | Location | Chief Executive | Year Started | Staff | Assets* | Deposits* | Loans* |
|---|---|---|---|---|---|---|---|
| 1 SEAWAY NATIONAL BANK OF CHICAGO | Chicago, Illinois | Walter E. Grady | 1965 | 155 | 145.26 | 2128.603 | 43.016 |
| 2 FREEDOM NATIONAL BANK OF NEW YORK | New York, New York | Louis Prezeau | 1964 | 114 | 124.519 | 100.300 | 48.182 |
| 3 INDUSTRIAL BANK OF WASHINGTON | Washington, D.C. | B. Doyle Mitchell | 1934 | 92 | 106.595 | 98.230 | 55.769 |
| 4 INDEPENDENCE BANK OF CHICAGO | Chicago, Illinois | Alvin J. Boute | 1964 | 98 | 106.077 | 92.358 | 44.863 |
| 5 CITIZENS TRUST BANK | Atlanta, Georgia | I. Owen Funderburg | 1921 | 130 | 105.836 | 95.562 | 39.505 |
| 6 FIRST INDEPENDENCE NATIONAL BANK OF DETROIT | Detroit, Michigan | Charles E. Allen | 1970 | 92 | 86.837 | 75.728 | 23.501 |
| 7 MECHANICS AND FARMERS BANK | Durham, North Carolina | Julla W. Taylor | 1908 | 100 | 84.197 | 74.806 | 40.855 |
| 8 FIRST TEXAS BANK | Dallas, Texas | William E. Stahnke | 1975 | 55 | 79.238 | 69.783 | 55.973 |
| 9 CITY NATIONAL BANK OF NEW JERSEY | Newark, New Jersey | Charles L. Whigham | 1973 | 36 | 68.098 | 62.943 | 14.463 |
| 10 CONSOLIDATED BANK AND TRUST COMPANY | Richmond, Virginia | Vernard W. Henley | 1903 | 68 | 61.587 | 56.075 | 33.550 |
| 11 TRI-STATE BANK OF MEMPHIS | Memphis, Tennessee | Jesse H. Turner, Sr. | 1946 | 60 | 55.620 | 49.775 | 26.606 |
| 12 FIRST BANK NATIONAL ASSOCIATION | Cleveland, Ohio | John H. Bustamante | 1974 | 64 | 53.155 | 43.096 | 38.748 |
| 13 BOSTON BANK OF COMMERCE | Boston, Massachusetts | Ronald A. Homer | 1982 | 47 | 50.767 | 47.454 | 37.644 |
| 14 HIGHLAND COMMUNITY BANK | Chicago, Illinois | George R. Brokermond | 1970 | 49 | 50.346 | 44.579 | 14.775 |
| 15 LIBERTY BANK AND TRUST COMPANY | New Orleans, Louisiana | Alden J. McDonald, Jr. | 1972 | 61 | 48.498 | 44.621 | 27.558 |
| 16 THE DOUGLASS BANK | Kansas City, Kansas | Donald D. Ford | 1983 | 33 | 35.839 | 33.283 | 11.337 |
| 17 CITIZENS SAVINGS BANK AND TRUST COMPANY | Nashvllle, Tennessee | Henry Hill, Jr. | 1904 | 39 | 32.417 | 30.437 | 18.719 |
| 18 THE HARBOR BANK OF MARYLAND | Baltimore, Maryland | Joseph Haskins, Jr. | 1982 | 27 | 32.293 | 29.513 | 17.354 |
| 19 COMMUNITY BANK OF LAWNDALE | Chicago, Illinois | Joyce K. Wade | 1977 | 44 | 24.954 | 22.551 | 9.541 |

* ln millions of dollars, to nearest thousand. Ranked by total assets as of December 31,1987. Prepared by BE Research. Audited by Mitchell/Titus & Co

## TABLE 71. THE 36 LARGEST BLACK BANKS IN THE UNITED STATES (CONTINUED)

( The business tables in this section provided through the courtesy of *Black Enterprise* Magazine. )

| Rank Company | Location | Chief Executive | Year Started | Staff | Assets* | Deposits* | Loans* |
|---|---|---|---|---|---|---|---|
| 20 NORTH MILWAUKEE STATE BANK | Milwaukee, Wisconsin | Charles L. Wallace | 1971 | 28 | 22.053 | 19.820 | 9.715 |
| 21 FIRST STATE BANK | Danville, Virginia | Sylvesta L. Jennings | 1919 | 16 | 21.811 | 16.795 | 9.923 |
| 22 ATLANTIC NATIONAL BANK | Norfolk, Virginia | Charles M. Reynolds, Jr. | 1971 | 36 | 21.538 | 20.304 | 13.064 |
| 23 PEOPLES NATIONAL BANK OF COMMERCE | Miami, Florida | Arthur J. Hill | 1982 | 18 | 21.190 | 19.526 | 6.652 |
| 24 GATEWAY NATIONAL BANK OF ST. LOUIS | St. Louis, Missouri | Gerard S. Hankins | 1966 | 29 | 19.873 | 18.790 | 11.199 |
| 25 GREENSBORO NATIONAL BANK | Greensboro, North Carolina | Robert S. Chiles, Sr. | 1971 | 26 | 18.653 | 17.276 | 9.572 |
| 26 VICTORY SAVINGS BANK | Columbia, South Carolina | Thomas E. Felder | 1921 | 18 | 18.045 | 16.037 | 8.456 |
| 27 THE CARVER STATE BANK | Savannah, Georgia | Robert E. James | 1927 | 27 | 16.838 | 15.096 | 9.227 |
| 28 AMERICAN STATE BANK | Portland, Oregon | Venerable F. Booker | 1969 | 12 | 15.945 | 13.766 | 4.353 |
| 29 SECURITY NATIONAL BANK | Shreveport, Louisiana | Frank Williams, Jr. | 1982 | 24 | 15.849 | 14.554 | 9.590 |
| 30 AMERICAN STATE BANK | Tulsa, Oklahoma | Leroy Thomas, Sr. | 1970 | 14 | 13.927 | 12.662 | 5.149 |
| 31 UNITED NATIONAL BANK | Fayetteville, North Carolina | Leonard Hedgepeth | 1976 | 12 | 11.565 | 10.006 | 7.837 |
| 32 HERITAGE NATIONAL BANK | Pittsburgh, Pennsylvania | Estella W. Smith | 1987 | 14 | 9.718 | 8.592 | 5.230 |
| 33 COMMONWEALTH NATIONAL BANK | Mobile, Alabama | Ronald E. Patterson | 1976 | 16 | 9.473 | 8.398 | 4.307 |
| 34 COMMUNITY BANK OF NEBRASKA | Omaha, Nebraska | Leon E. Evans, Jr. | 1973 | 15 | 8.799 | 7.951 | 5.253 |
| 35 MEDICAL CENTER STATE BANK | Oklahoma City, Oklahoma | Marian J. Humphrey | 1973 | 14 | 8.627 | 8.171 | 4.971 |
| 36 UNITY STATE BANK | Dayton, Ohio | Howard C. Smith | 1969 | 12 | 6.877 | 6.748 | 3,120 |

*In milllons of dollars, to nearest thousand. Ranked by total assets as of December 31,1987. Prepared by BE Research. Audited by Mitchell/Titus & Co

## TABLE 72. THE 32 LARGEST BLACK-OWNED SAVINGS AND LOAN INSTITUTIONS IN THE UNITED STATES

( The business tables in this section provided through the courtesy of *Black Enterprise* Magazine. )

| Rank Company | Location | Chief Executive | Year Started | Staff | Assets* | Deposits* | Loans* |
|---|---|---|---|---|---|---|---|
| 1 INDEPENDENCE FEDERAL SAVINGS BANK | Washington, D.C. | William B. Fitzgerald | 1968 | 70 | 216.212 | 151.376 | 174.484 |
| 2 FAMILY SAVINGS & LOAN ASSOCIATION | Los Angeles, California | Robert Bowdoin | 1948 | 70 | 182.000 | 143.000 | 147.000 |
| 3 CARVER FEDERAL SAVINGS AND LOAN ASSOCIATION | New York, New York | Richard T. Greene | 1948 | 80 | 168.694 | 149.123 | 123.964 |
| 4 FOUNDERS SAVINGS & LOAN ASSOCIATION | Los Angeles, California | Wayne Bradshaw | 1974 | 77 | 129.844 | 151.227 | 104.503 |
| 5 ILLINOIS SERVICE/FEDERAL S&L ASSOCIATION OF CHICAGO | Chicago, Illinois | Thelma J. Smith | 1934 | 40 | 104.561 | 101.263 | 76.247 |
| 6 BROADWAY FEDERAL SAVINGS & LOAN ASSOCIATION | Los Angeles, California | Elbert T. Hudson | 1946 | 54 | 91.974 | 83.242 | 72.487 |
| 7 CITIZENS FEDERAL SAVINGS BANK | Birmingham, Alabama | Louis J. Willie | 1957 | 35 | 60.478 | 54.038 | 41.170 |
| 8 UNITED FEDERAL SAVINGS & LOAN ASSOCIATION | New Orleans, Louisiana | Beverly N. Staes | 1964 | 40 | 54.485 | 44.782 | 38.786 |
| 9 FIRST FED. SAVINGS & LOAN ASSOC. OF SCOTLANDVILLE | Baton Rouge, Louisiana | Henry J. Stamper | 1956 | 21 | 44.026 | 39.711 | 32.428 |
| 10 MUTUAL FEDERAL SAVINGS & LOAN ASSN. OF ATLANTA | Atlanta, Georgia | Fletcher Coombs | 1925 | 18 | 35.547 | 31.191 | 26.397 |
| 11 ADVANCE FEDERAL SAVINGS & LOAN ASSOCIATION | Baltimore, Maryland | Winfred O. Bryson, Jr. | 1957 | 33 | 33.994 | 29.321 | 23.216 |
| 12 BERKLEY FEDERAL SAVINGS BANK | Norfolk, Virginia | Gary Roberson | 1913 | 20 | 33.300 | 25.000 | 23.000 |
| 13 BEREAN SAVINGS ASSOCIATION | Philadelphia, Pennsylvania | I. Maximilian Martin | 1888 | 19 | 31.727 | 27.919 | 17.342 |
| 14 TUSKEGEE FEDERAL SAVINGS & LOAN ASSOCIATION | Tuskegee, Alabama | Richard R. Harvey | 1894 | 16 | 29.287 | 26.806 | 24.394 |
| 15 PEOPLE'S SAVINGS & LOAN ASSOCIATION | Hampton, Virginia | John E. Coles | 1889 | 9 | 24.398 | 22.762 | 18.626 |
| 16 HOME FEDERAL SAVINGS BANK | Detroit, Michigan | Wilburn R. Phillips | 1947 | 18 | 22.893 | 21.224 | 17.271 |

*In millions of dollars, to nearest thousand. Ranked by total assets as of December 31, 1987. Prepared by BE Research. Audited by Mitchell/Titus & Co.

## TABLE 72. THE 32 LARGEST BLACK-OWNED SAVINGS AND LOAN INSTITUTIONS IN THE UNITED STATES (CONTINUED)

( The business tables in this section provided through the courtesy of *Black Enterprise* Magazine. )

| Rank Company | Location | Chief Executive | Year Started | Staff | Assets* | Deposits* | Loans* |
|---|---|---|---|---|---|---|---|
| 17 AMERICAN FED. SAVINGS & LOAN ASSOCIATION | Greensboro, North Carolina | J. Kenneth Lee | 1959 | 16 | 22.761 | 17.590 | 17.575 |
| 18 ENTERPRISE SAVINGS & LOAN ASSOCIATION | Long Beach, California | Cornell R. Kirkland | 1963 | 15 | 22.650 | 19.762 | 16.496 |
| 19 MUTUAL SAVINGS & LOAN ASSOCIATION | Durham, North Carolina | Ferdinand V. Allison, Jr. | 1921 | 12 | 22.494 | 18.803 | 19.126 |
| 20 STANDARD SAVINGS ASSOCIATION | Houston, Texas | Mack H. Hannah, Jr. | 1958 | 10 | 20.524 | 19.021 | 14.544 |
| 21 CONNECTICUT SAVINGS & LOAN ASSOCIATION | Hartford, Connecticut | John A. Hogan | 1968 | 11 | 19.823 | 14.121 | 16.481 |
| 22 COMMUNITY FED. SAVINGS & LOAN ASSN. OF TAMPA | Tampa, Florida | A. Leon Lowry, Sr. | 1967 | 10 | 12.549 | 13.184 | 9.313 |
| 23 DWELLING HOUSE SAVINGS & LOAN ASSOCIATION | Pittsburgh, Pennsylvania | Robert R. Lavelle | 1957 | 6 | 12.206 | 10.782 | 8.517 |
| 24 NEW AGE FEDERAL SAVINGS & LOAN ASSOCIATION | St. Louis, Missouri | Barbara J. Brown | 1915 | 9 | 12.037 | 11.532 | 9.250 |
| 25 COLUMBIA SAVINGS & LOAN ASSOCIATION | Milwaukee, Wisconsin | Thalia B. Winfield | 1924 | 9 | 10.879 | 9.551 | 8.532 |
| 26 STATE MUTUAL FEDERAL SAVINGS & LOAN ASSOCIATION | Jackson, Mississippi | Clinton Mayes, Jr. | 1955 | 12 | 10.800 | 10.300 | 8.300 |
| 27 WASHINGTON SHORES SAVINGS BANK, FSB | Orlando, Florida | John M. Hamilton | 1963 | 9 | 10.772 | 8.112 | 7.879 |
| 28 COMMUNITY FED. SAVINGS & LOAN ASSOCIATION | Newport News, Virginia | Thaddeus B. Holloman | 1957 | 10 | 9.240 | 9.690 | 7.529 |
| 29 IMPERIAL SAVINGS & LOAN ASSOCIATION | Martinsville, Virginia | William B. Muse, Jr. | 1929 | 5 | 7.241 | 6.755 | 4.356 |
| 30 IDEAL FEDERAL SAVINGS BANK | Baltimore, Maryland | E. Gaines Lansey | 1920 | 5 | 6.994 | 6.495 | 4.573 |
| 31 GULF FEDERAL BANK, FSB | Mobile, Alabama | Al Johnson | 1987 | 7 | 6.972 | 6.494 | 4.152 |
| 32 EQUITY FEDERAL SAVINGS BANK | Denver, Colorado | Earl M. West | 1954 | 5 | 3.365 | 3.353 | 2.663 |

*In milllons of dollars, to nearest thousand. Ranked by total assets as of December 31, 1987. Prepared by BE Research. Audited by Mitchell/Titus & Co

## TABLE 73. THE 32 LARGEST BLACK-OWNED INSURANCE COMPANIES IN THE UNITED STATES

( The business tables in this section provided through the courtesy of *Black Enterprise* Magazine. )

| Rank Company | Location | Chief Executive | Year Started | Staff | Assets* | Insurance in Force* | Premium Income | Net Invest-ment Income |
|---|---|---|---|---|---|---|---|---|
| 1 NORTH CAROLINA MUTUAL LIFE INSURANCE COMPANY | Durham | W. J. Kennedy III | 1898 | 897 | 216.357 | 9,841.512 | 72.825 | 13.178 |
| 2 ATLANTA LIFE INSURANCE COMPANY | Atlanta | Jesse Hill, Jr. | 1905 | 950 | 126.421 | 1,992.621 | 22.774 | 7,924 |
| 3 GOLDEN STATE MUTUAL | Los Angeles, California | Ivan J. Houston | 1925 | 925 | 119.229 | 5,218.248 | 38.054 | 9.431 |
| 4 UNIVERSAL LIFE INSURANCE COMPANY | Memphis, Tennessee | A. Maceo Walker, Sr. | 1923 | 800 | 66.327 | 690.978 | 21.617 | 4.885 |
| 5 SUPREME LIFE INSURANCE COMPANY OF AMERICA | Chicago, Illinois | John H. Johnson | 1921 | 342 | 58.954 | 2,587.993 | 17.872 | 2.122 |
| 6 CHICAGO METROPOLITAN MUTUAL ASSURANCE COMPANY | Chicago, Illinois | Anderson M. Schweich | 1927 | 190 | 54.474 | 2,687.016 | 14.405 | 1.774 |
| 7 BOOKER T. WASHINGTON INSURANCE COMPANY | Birmingham, Alabama | Louis J. Willie | 1932 | 175 | 34.033 | 726.693 | 10.203 | 1.907 |
| 8 MAMMOTH LIFE AND ACCIDENT INSURANCE COMPANY | Louisville, Kentucky | James P. King | 1915 | 175 | 29.101 | 304.770 | 3.984 | 2.112 |
| 9 THE PILGRIM HEALTH & LIFE INSURANCE COMPANY | Augusta, Georgia | Solomon W. Walker II | 1898 | 171 | 16.457 | 167.474 | 3.587 | 1.071 |
| 10 PROTECTIVE INDUSTRIAL INSURANCE CO. OF ALABAMA, INC. | Birmingham, Alabama | Virgil L. Harris | 1923 | 123 | 12.973 | 70.983 | 3.409 | .782 |
| 11 UNITED MUTUAL LIFE INSURANCE COMPANY | New York, New York | Arthur W. White | 1933 | 19 | 12.550 | 1,354.136 | 9.051 | .824 |
| 12 GOLDEN CIRCLE LIFE INSURANCE COMPANY | Brownsville, Tennessee | William D. Rawls, Sr. | 1958 | 75 | 7.365 | 20.994 | 1.545 | .671 |
| 13 AMERICAN WOODMEN'S LIFE INSURANCE COMPANY | Denver, Colorado | Lillie Anne Owens | 1966 | 37 | 6.168 | 304.684 | 1.009 | .232 |
| 14 WINNFIELD LIFE INSURANCE COMPANY | Natchitoches, Louisiana | Ben D. Johnson | 1936 | 25 | 5.958 | 51.231 | 1.897 | .366 |
| 15 CENTRAL LIFE INSURANCE COMPANY OF FLORIDA | Tampa, Florida | Lorenza P. Butler II | 1922 | 97 | 5.800 | 62.549 | 2.019 | .373 |
| 16 WILLIAMS-PROGRESSIVE LIFE & ACCIDENT INSURANCE CO. | Opelousas, Louisiana | Borel C. Dauphin | 1947 | 60 | 4.627 | 35.896 | 1.244 | .375 |

*In millions of dollars, to nearest thousand. Ranked by total assets as of December 31, 1987. Prepared by BE Research.

## TABLE 73. THE 32 LARGEST BLACK-OWNED INSURANCE COMPANIES IN THE UNITED STATES (CONTINUED)

( The business tables in this section provided through the courtesy of *Black Enterprise* Magazine. )

| Rank Company | Location | Chief Executive | Year Started | Staff | Assets* | Insurance in Force* | Premium Income | Net Invest-ment Income |
|---|---|---|---|---|---|---|---|---|
| 17 WRIGHT MUTUAL INSURANCE COMPANY | Detroit, Michigan | Wardell C. Croft | 1942 | 47 | 4.431 | 25.243 | .782 | .235 |
| 18 VIRGINIA MUTUAL BENEFIT LIFE INSURANCE CO., INC. | Richmond, Virginia | Daniel J. Mack | 1933 | 65 | 4.259 | 12.862 | .621 | .295 |
| 19 GERTRUDE GEDDES WILLIS LIFE INSURANCE COMPANY | New Orleans, Louisiana | Joseph O. Misshore, Jr | 1941 | 49 | 3.652 | 35.840 | 1.220 | .263 |
| 20 RELIABLE LIFE INSURANCE COMPANY | Monroe, Louisiana | Joseph H. Miller, Jr. | 1940 | 78 | 3.484 | 23.164 | 1.131 | .146 |
| 21 BENEVOLENT LIFE INSURANCE COMPANY, INC. | Shreveport, Louisiana | Granville L. Smith | 1934 | 96 | 2.557 | 16.913 | .731 | .152 |
| 22 NATIONAL SERVICE INDUSTRIAL LIFE INSURANCE COMPANY | New Orleans, Louisiana | Duplain Rhodes | 1940 | 45 | 2.257 | 12.907 | .648 | .106 |
| 23 MAJESTIC LIFE INSURANCE COMPANY, INC. | New Orleans, Louisiana | James V. Haydel, Sr. | 1947 | 20 | 2.117 | 10.105 | .389 | .161 |
| 24 SUPERIOR LIFE INSURANCE COMPANY | Baton Rouge, Louisiana | John K. Haynes | 1954 | 65 | 1.375 | 10.250 | .695 | .088 |
| 25 VALLEY LIFE INSURANCE GROUP | Phoenix, Arizona | Lincoln J. Ragsdale | 1958 | 10 | 1.203 | 4.661 | .306 | .074 |
| 26 AMERICAN TRUST LIFE INSURANCE COMPANY | Birmingham, Alabama | Earl F. Hilliard | 1932 | 8 | 1.124 | 3.980 | .066 | .044 |
| 27 LIGHTHOUSE LIFE INSURANCE COMPANY | Shreveport, Louisiana | Bunyan S. Jacobs, Sr. | 1949 | 100 | 1.035 | 13.026 | .524 | .054 |
| 28 RHODES LIFE INSURANCE COMPANY OF LOUISIANA | New Orleans, Louisiana | Duplain Rhodes | 1927 | 26 | .952 | 4.430 | .241 | .049 |
| 29 RHODES LIFE INSURANCE COMPANY OF ALABAMA | Mobile, Alabama | Duplain Rhodes | 1949 | 14 | .755 | 1.900 | .223 | .295 |
| 30 PEOPLE'S PROGRESSIVE BURIAL INSURANCE COMPANY | Rayville, Louisiana | Marion Gundy Hill | 1936 | 21 | .411 | 4.257 | .189 | .030 |
| 31 PEOPLES ASSURED FAMILY LIFE INSURANCE COMPANY | Jackson, Mississippi | James A. Stewart III | 1985 | 110 | .195 | 5.480 | .096 | .012 |
| 32 UNITY LIFE INSURANCE COMPANY | Jackson, Mississippi | Clare Harvey Collins | 1978 | 18 | .157 | 1.694 | .197 | .005 |

*In millions of dollars, to nearest thousand. Ranked by total assets as of December 31, 1987. Prepared by BE Research.

## TABLE 74. BLACKS IN THE AMERICAN ECONOMY, 1984, 1985, AND 1990

| Category | 1984 | 1985 | 1990 |
|---|---|---|---|
| U.S. Population (Thousands) | | | |
| Total | 235,303 | 238,648 | 249,731 |
| White | 200,876 | 203,237 | 210,964 |
| Black | 28,416 | 29,107 | 31,452 |
| Other races | 6,011 | 6,304 | 7,315 |
| Black as percent of total | 12.1 | 12.2 | 12.6 |
| Gross National Product ($ Billions) | | | |
| Current dollars | 3,662.8 | 3,902.7 | 5,752.0 |
| Real GNP (1972 Dollars) | 1,639.3 | 1,686.0 | 1,981.8 |
| Money income ($ Billions) | | | |
| Total | 2,415.7 | 2,575.3 | 3,775.8 |
| White | 2,177.3 | 2,312.6 | 3,345.3 |
| Black | 182.4 | 202.7 | 332.3 |
| Other races | 56.0 | 60.0 | 98.2 |
| Black as per cent of total | 7.6 | 7.9 | 8.8 |
| Business sales ($ Billions) | | | |
| Total sales | 4,911.0 | 5,225.3 | 7,701.4 |
| Black businesses | 12.8 | 13.2 | 23.1 |
| Black as per cent of: | | | |
| Total Sales | .261 | .253 | .300 |
| Black Money Income | 7.03 | 6.52 | 6.95 |

Source: Calculations and estimates by Brimmer & Company, Inc. Basic data from U.S. Department of Commerc

# EMPLOYMENT, UNEMPLOYMENT, AND THE LABOR FORCE



The decade from 1978 to 1988 was a rocky one for black workers in the United States. From the prosperous heights of 1978, black employment and well being plummeted with the nation's economic health during the back-to-back recessions of 1980 and 1981-82. The net effect of these recessions was to produce the most severe economic decline since the depression of the 1930s. For many, it was not until 1988 that earlier levels of prosperity were matched. Although the black population shared in the nation's economic recovery, significant disparity persisted between black and white participation.

Since blacks tend to be the last to be hired and the first to be fired, the economic decline of the early 1980s fell heavily upon the black worker, erasing the gains of many years during the 1970s. Specifically, the median family income of black families fell to 55.2% of the level of white families in 1982 from 61.3% in 1978. By 1986, black median family income had only recovered to 57.1% of the level for white families, well below the 1978 figure. In addition, the ratio of black unemployment to white unemployment, which had, fallen as low as 1.8 to 1 during the late 1970s, increased to over 2.5 to 1 during the early 1980s. Even as late as 1987 it remained as high as 2.45 to 1.

Both the 1980 recession and the 1981-82 recession were caused by the tight money/high interest rate policies of the Federal Reserve Bank under the leadership of Paul Volker, its Chairman. The stated purpose of these policies was to arrest the high levels of inflation, which did in fact peak in 1979-80. These policies brought severe hardships to the labor force, and black workers in particular. In 1982, when national unemployment peaked at 9.7% black unemployment was 18.9%. Black unemployment did not peak until 1983 when it reached 19.5%, representing 2.2 million unemployed black workers. Teenage black unemployment rose to 38.6% during the early 1980s. The unemployment picture for blacks was even bleaker when discouraged long-term unemployed and part-time workers unable to find full-time work were added. Unemployment then exceeded 25% for black adults and 55% for black teenagers.

By 1988 the situation had improved significantly. In June 1988, the national unemployment rate fell to 5.3%. This was the lowest level in 14 years. In the black community, the number of employed blacks rose from 9.2 million (49% of the working age population) in 1982 to 11.5 million (56%) in 1988.

The black unemployment rate hit a low of 10.8% in May of 1988, but was still more than double the rate for whites. Total unemployment rose slightly in the fall of 1988 to 5.6%. This increase was reflected in black joblessness which rose to a rate of 11.3% in September of 1988.

While the unemployment rates had returned to the low levels of 1978, the poverty level in 1988 remained higher than the 1978 figure of 11.4%. In 1988, 32.5 million Americans or 13.5% of the population lived in poverty (which was measured as a cash income of $11,611 or less for a family of four in 1987). Disparity by race was still plainly evident. Among white Americans, 10.5% lived in poverty. For blacks the poverty rate was more than triple—33.1%. (The poverty data is based upon cash income only. If non-cash benefits such as Medicaid, food stamps and housing assistance are included the poverty rates would be lower. (See the section on Income and Earnings.) These figures are confirmed by the income statistics. In 1987 the typical white family had an income of $32,274, while the typical black family had an income of only $18,098.

The increase in poverty rates was part of an important phenomenon of the 1980s; the increase in both rich and poor families at the expense of a shrinking middle class. The proportion of white families with incomes below $10,000 (constant 1986 dollars) increased from 9.2% in 1978 to 10.2% in 1986. For black families the comparable increase was from 27.4% to 30.2%. Over the same period, the proportion of white families with incomes above $35,000 (constant 1986 dollars) increased from 41.7% to 42.6%. The corresponding change for black families was from 20.3% to 21.2%. While the decline of the middle class has been true for both blacks and whites, the burden of this phenomenon has fallen primarily on the blacks since there were only half the proportion of high income black families. One common misconception is that lower income and higher unemployment for blacks is the result of lower levels of education. This is not the case. By 1979, the median years of school completed by members of the labor force was 12.7 for whites and 12.3 for blacks. Furthermore, a 1986 study of unemployment by B. J. Tidwell compared the unemployment rates for blacks and whites grouped by levels of education. The analysis, based upon data for March of 1984, shows that the greater the level of education, the greater the disparity between black

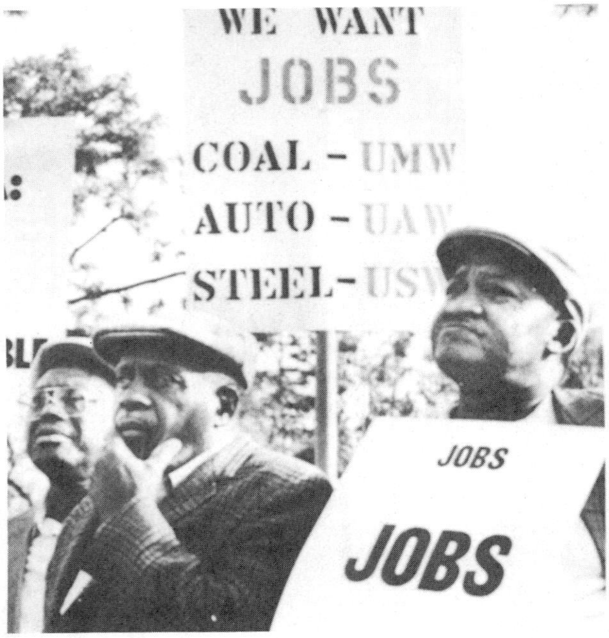


*In September, 1982 the jobless rate climbed above 10% for the total population. Demonstrators marched near the White House demanding jobs.*

and white unemployment. Specifically, for those with four or more years of college, the ratio of black to white unemployment was 2.42 to 1. For those with 1-3 years of high school the ratio was 1.80 to 1 and for those with no high school the ratio fell to 1.30 to 1.

A major problem for blacks was that the recessions of the early 1980s most adversely affected jobs in industries and skills where blacks had made the most progress. Also, a continuing influx of aliens, many of whom were willing to work for less than the legal minimum, swelled the ranks of those seeking unskilled labor, traditionally the province of many blacks. Jobs in the public sector, the employer of more than half of the nation's black college graduates, were also cut back as a result of the Reagan Administration's drive to reduce the role of all areas of the government, except the military. Blacks were also employed at a disproportionately high rate in industries adversely affected by foreign trade. Policies pursued by the Federal Reserve Bank significantly increased the value of the dollar relative to other currencies between 1979 and 1985. The result of this was to create a trade deficit in excess of $150 billion per year, and cause the closure of many U.S. factories which could not compete with low cost imports. Beginning in mid-1985, the government pursued a policy of reducing the relative value of the dollar. By 1988, the value of the dollar had been reduced significantly. However, the trade deficit remained stubbornly high.

Skilled jobs in which blacks had attained notable strides during the 1970s, were being erased by automation and relocation of factories. The job market relentlessly shifted its orientation to higher technology skills that few displaced blacks were in a position to obtain. The private sector did little to offer training or job upgrading. The federal government under the Reagan Administration sought to reduce government job training and affirmative action programs that had done much to lift the status and self-sufficiency of blacks during the previous 20 years. The above statistics speak for themselves in demonstrating the impact of the policies of the Federal Reserve and the Reagan Administration upon the relative status of the black worker.

## MAJOR TRENDS OF THE 1970s AND EARLY 1980s

Notable among the developments of the 1970s were:

The ratio of black to white unemployment rates remained above 2 to 1 for most of the 1970s, and in February 1982 was 2.225 to 1.

Teenage unemployment for blacks was above the 30% level throughout most of the decade and averaged over 40% in 1981. Unemployment of black youths rose sharply, nearly doubling for black men between the ages of 20 and 24.

The labor force participation rate of white women increased substantially, from 42% to 52%, while the rate of black women increased only slightly from 50% to 53% and did not change after 1978.

The racial gap in completed school years narrowed. In 1979, the median number of years completed by members of the labor force was 12.7 for whites and 12.3 for blacks.

Reversing a trend, unemployment of black Vietnam veterans declined to a point in 1981 which was lower than the rate for black non-veterans. Unemployment of the white Vietnam era veterans remained higher than for white non-veterans.

The proportion of blacks employed in professional, technical, mechanical, and administrative jobs increased at a faster rate than it increased for whites, but blacks remained underrepresented in these positions.

Employment of blacks in upper-level jobs by firms with more than 100 employees increased. Between 1966 and 1978, the proportion of blacks in professional positions more than tripled and the proportion of black managers almost doubled.

Notable developments by the end of the 1980s

The 2 to 1 ratio of black to white unemployment remained about the same by December 1987, although fewer persons of both races were out of work.

Teenage unemployment for blacks remained high, with almost 35% of the 16- to 19-year-olds, and nearly 22% for 20-to 24-year-olds unable to find employment.

Black women continued to surpass white women in numbers of unemployed, employment in low-paying jobs, and poverty-level income.

One-third of black families earned middle-class incomes between $20,000 and $50,000. Black middle-class jobs are concentrated in three areas: government posts, manufacturing jobs, and staff positions in the private sector.

The number of discouraged workers— persons who want to work but do not look for jobs because they believe they cannot find any— declined to 900,000 by the end of 1987, the lowest point since 1979.

The number of discouraged black workers fell from 464,000 in 1984, when 1 in 3 job seekers did not look for work because they believed they could not find a job, to 237,000 in 1988, with about 1 in 5 job seekers discouraged.

### Unemployment as an Issue

Long before unemployment rates became part of America's economic literature, blacks comprised a disproportionate share of people who could not find work. Throughout their history in the colonies and the United States, blacks were consistently displaced by white immigrants from trades in which they specialized, and relegated by employers, unions, and laws to unskilled and strikebreaking "scab" jobs.

### CHART 30. LABOR FORCE PARTICIPATION OF BLACKS.

**Blacks comprise about 11% of the total labor force, however, their share of unemployment—being unemployed for long time periods and other problems—is disproportionate to the general population.**

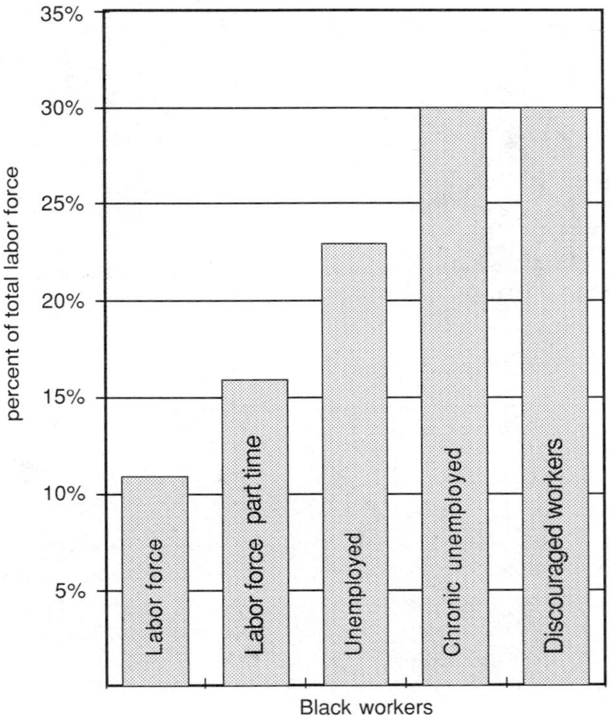

This unemployment and underemployment of blacks thwarted the rise of a skilled black artisan and entrepreneurial class after the Civil War and hindered the integration of blacks and the acceptance of black leaders in important positions in American life.

The relationship of unemployment to discrimination, and also to family instability, was of great concern to W. E. B. DuBois, who spurred and sponsored studies of the problem in the late nineteenth and early twentieth centuries. However, unemployment was only one of many matters which preoccupied the eminent scholar and the NAACP, which he helped found in 1910. The NAACP was more concerned with furthering the legal and political position of blacks than boosting their economic status. Leadership in efforts to help blacks contend with unemployment fell largely to the Urban League, which sought to find work for blacks who had moved to cities.

Progress was slow and retarded by the depression of the thirties, during which unemployment rates commonly exceeded one-third of the black and one-fourth of the white working force.

## Employment and World War II

With the outbreak of World War II, the economic scene changed drastically from competition for employment among workers to a need for full utilization of the nation's work force in rapidly expanding industries. However, resistance to employing blacks remained entrenched, especially in skilled trades. In 1941, with the nation gearing for war, Asa Philip Randolph, founder of the Brotherhood of Sleeping Car Porters, developed plans for a march on Washington by some 100,000 blacks. The objective was to increase employment opportunities in defense plants, which were largely confining blacks to menial service jobs, such as janitors. The NAACP declared its support of Randolph's march. An intense behind-the-scenes struggle ensued in Washington between those who urged action for blacks on the basis of manpower needs and fairness, and those who advocated minimal action so as not to divide the country in a time of crisis.

Historians still debate whether Randolph could have made

**CHART 31. UNEMPLOYMENT RATES (ANNUAL AVERAGES),1948-1988 (ABOVE) AND RATIO OF BLACK TO WHITE UMEMPLOYMENT, 1948-1988 (BELOW).**

**During periods of recession the unemployment rate for blacks rises disproportionately sharper than that for whites. The unemployment ratio between blacks and whites has been at least 2 to 1 since 1948. This ratio increases substantially during periods of recession and has been as high as 2.5 as recently as 1987. The last available figure was 2.2 in 1988.**

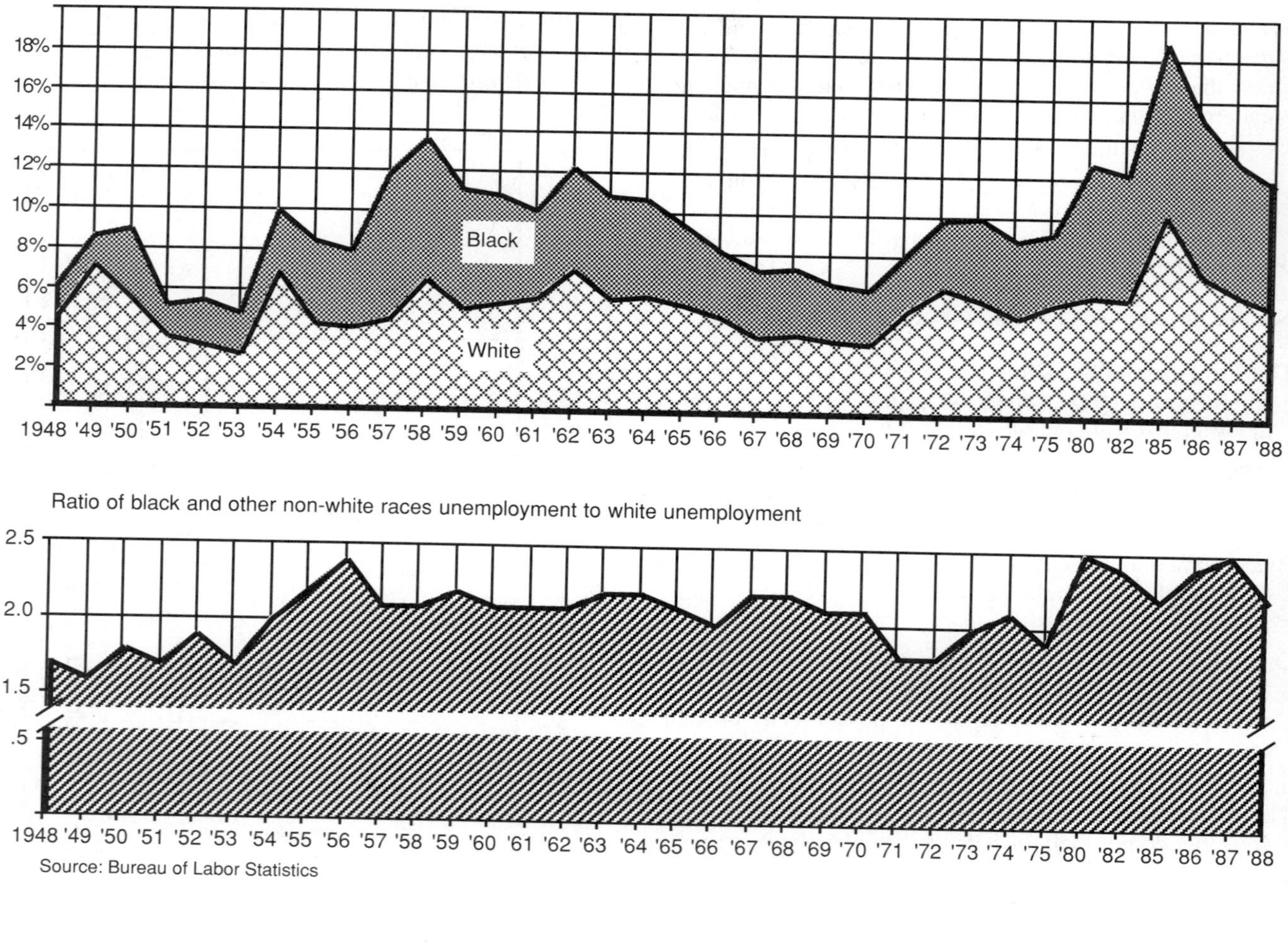


Source: Bureau of Labor Statistics

the march come off, but Roosevelt respected the articulate labor leader enough to fear it. On June 25, 1941, a week before the march's scheduled date, FDR signed Executive Order 8802, which forbade discrimination in government and defense job hiring and established a Fair Employment Practices Commission to enforce the order. This was the first of antidiscrimination orders that were to be issued periodically into the 1960's and the first significant step by the government to reduce discrimination in the hiring of minorities.

Roosevelt's order of course did not eliminate discrimination, but did reduce it, and it set a precedent for ensuing governmental action against employment barriers.

### Discrimination after World War II

Improving the job situation for blacks aroused increasing attention during the 1950s and 1960s and by 1970 was the principal aim of public officials and businessmen interested in reducing racial tensions.

The growing concern regarding black unemployment and underemployment reflected a significant change in America's approach to racial problems. In the early 1960s, efforts to ease the burdens of blacks were based on the ideal of integration and directed toward a variety of issues—housing, education, welfare, and constitutional justice as much as employment. Response to the integration ideal peaked with the passage of the Civil Rights Act in 1964, and thereafter subsided before the shock waves from ghetto riots and the sudden intensity of black nationalism. Following the violent urban disturbances in the summer of 1967, the nation's "establishment" decided that it was urgent to get blacks "off the streets and into jobs." Integration was debated in political arenas as an unworkable liberal theory that benefited only a minute proportion of blacks. Racial peace and racial justice, it was decided, depended on obtaining jobs for the "hard core," the black who was abandoned, despised, and unemployed in squalid neighborhoods in large cities. Actually, as the National Advisory Commission on Racial Disorders was to reveal, employed blacks were as prone to riot as the unemployed. Nevertheless, the emphasis turned to jobs.

As a result, scores of federally assisted manpower programs and thousands of diverse, publicly supported training and placement ventures on the state and local levels were set up. Urban-based service industries such as banks and public utilities intensified efforts to recruit and train black and Spanish-speaking employees.

The government programs provided businesses with incentives to employ people whose abilities and job motivation were unproven. The incentives took the form of subsidies to businesses for on-the-job training and referrals of prospective employees who were located and trained at public expense.

These programs reflected a change of approach to employers; a change from pressure to blandishment by public officials charged with the responsibility of bettering the black employment situation. Earlier efforts to rectify the employment status of blacks relied largely on legal and monetary pressure. Employers who discriminated against blacks were threatened with court action or denial of government contracts. In the late 1960's, the emphasis shifted to aiding employers who agreed to hire "under qualified" minorities.

### Title VII and the EEOC

Aside from the Johnson Administration's War on Poverty actions in the early 1960s, there was there was little significant fair employment legislation on the federal level until the Civil Rights Act of 1964. Title VII of this Act prohibited discrimination on the part of employers and unions who have more than 25 employees or members and who are involved in interstate commerce. Title VII also established the Equal Employment Opportunities Commission to mediate disputes and identify patterns of deliberate and systematic discrimination. As set up, EEOC could refer discrimination cases to the Attorney General, who, in turn, could bring them before a three-judge federal court. The EEOC was also empowered to refer cases of discrimination to the Office of Federal Contract Compliance, which could press businesses dealing with the government to adhere to fair employment practices.

Title VII of the Civil Rights Act of 1964 not only outlawed discrimination in employment but contained an extremely important provision that was scarcely noticed at the time. The law granted courts the power to award fees to attorneys for plaintiffs who successfully sued employers and unions that discriminated. This encouraged lawyers to undertake the arduous and highly detailed leg and legal work essential to proving discrimination.

Until 1972, this provision attracted little attention from the legal profession. EEOC lacked the power to sue. President Nixon was pursuing a "southern strategy" and wooing the "silent majority" with thinly veiled hints that civil rights laws and court decisions would not be enforced. There was little expectation that the Justice and Labor Department divisions empowered to act against unfair employers would do so.

However, the EEOC was strengthened during the 1967-1972 years of Nixon's first term. EEOC's annual budget was raised from $12 million to $42 million and its staff from 250 to 2,500. Critics of Nixon contend that his increasing EEOC's staff and budget were meaningless in the face of its power to do little more than argue and attempt out-of-court conciliation agreements, enforced by voluntary compliance. However, in 1972, with EEOC weak and saddled by a backlog of 60,000 cases, Congress granted EEOC the power to take cases to court, though it refused the agency power to issue cease and desist orders. Nixon signed the bill.

The 1972 Law also granted EEOC power to bring "Pattern and Practice" suits, starting in March 1974. Pattern and Practice suits usually consist of large class actions against large employers and unions whose hiring, promotion, and seniority policies have been systematic in nature.

These suits could involve hundreds of millions, perhaps even billions of dollars in compensation to employees for past "patterns and practices" of discrimination.

The cause of equal rights in employment was also

strengthened by the growing expertise and public support of the women's movement for equal rights. This brought more money, legal talent, and political muscle to equal employment ranks.

However, few felt the EEOC would act forcefully. Skeptics pointed out that other government agencies, such as the Interstate Commerce Commission and the Federal Power Commission, had strong regulatory powers but somehow had become allies of the very businesses they were supposed to regulate. It was assumed this would occur with the EEOC.

At the time the 1972 Law was passed, EEOC's chairman was William Brown III, a black man with life-long Republican ties and a staunch advocate of the conciliatory approach. It was thus a surprise when Brown, in 1972, developed a "tracking system" which in effect committed EEOC, in cooperation with private "public interest" lawyers, to taking on major corporate violators of equal employment laws. As a part of this approach, EEOC issued some $400,000 in legal contracts among such groups as the Lawyers' Committee For Civil Rights Under Law, and subsidized equal employment legal clinics in major law schools.
Previously filed suits were pursued and new suits were filed. Most actions were undertaken by civil rights groups, such as the Legal Defense Fund, NAACP, The Lawyers' Committee for Civil Rights Under Law, and the National Organization of Women.

The response of most businesses and unions was to sue for peace. It would have been possible for these defendants to drag out cases for several years, but few wanted the publicity and many felt that favorable agreements would become harder to attain under future national administrations.

## Reparations and the Telephone Case

The first major company to sign an agreement was the American Telephone & Telegraph Company, the largest employer in the United States. In a 1973 consent decree between EEOC, the Labor Department, and AT&T, the telephone company agreed to pay $15 million in reparations and to allocate $23 million each year to raise the pay of blacks, other minorities, and women to that of the company's white male employees. AT&T also agreed to institute an affirmative action program to increase and improve opportunities for minorities and women. In return, EEOC dropped all pending charges against AT&T.

The settlement was controversial. Critics felt that the company, whose annual profits are some $2.5 billion, owed and could have afforded more. They noted that no employee, under the agreement, would receive back pay of more than $400. EEOC had estimated the actual loss in wages to AT&T minorities at $500 million per year for the eight years preceding the settlement, or a total of $4 billion, not $23 million.

Supporters of the pact emphasized the symbolic and precedent-setting importance of having America's largest business admit, if only implicitly, to charges of bias and to its responsibility to compensate employees for it, however inadequately.

Supporters of the agreement also pointed out that barely two weeks before the agreement was signed, a weaker deal, involving no back pay or substantial affirmative action policy, was very nearly executed between AT&T and the General Services Administration, under President Johnson's Executive Order 11246. This arrangement, which had the support of the Nixon Administration, would have derailed the stronger EEOC settlement, granted no reparations at all, and introduced only a modest affirmative action program. But Chairman Brown personally intervened, and under threat of massive publicity about a sellout of blacks and women, the administration capitulated to the extent of the accord that was reached.

## Other Suits

Following the AT&T agreement, precedent-setting decisions were won in suits against the Detroit Edison and New York Telephone companies, with the judge in the Detroit Edison case granting back pay, retroactive from 1973 to 1965 plus punitive damages and forward pay. In 1974, expectations in legal circles were that the court would award several hundred thousand dollars, perhaps a million dollars, in attorney's fees to the lawyers who sued Detroit Edison. Unlike AT&T, Detroit Edison had adopted a hard-line defense.

Within months of the AT&T agreement, EEOC filed over 80 suits, almost all against such powerful and prestigious companies as General Electric and General Motors. These suits, plus the victories against AT&T, Detroit Edison, and steel makers and unions (see the section on unions) frightened the business community, much of which considered itself vulnerable to the bad publicity and high costs of class action litigation. Brown's presence as head of EEOC was considered a further threat, for despite his solid Republican credentials, he was doing little to restrain the enthusiasm of his staff in their quest to correct current and historic wrongs inflicted on minority workers. And his support of Nixon in the 1972 Presidential election had been tepid.

In the 1973, with the nation's attention on Watergate, the Administration quietly announced that in January 1974, Brown would be replaced by John Powell Jr. Brown did not learn of his dismissal until he read it in the *Washington Post*.

The agreement that was reached between the government and the steel companies in 1974 was considered weaker because of Brown's pending absence and the presence in the negotiations of the Justice and Labor departments whose involvement followed their exclusion from such cases in the 1972 EEOC Act. A key point in the steel agreement was a provision precluding future suits by requiring workers to execute releases.

## Equal Opportunity and the Carter Years

Affirmative action in employment progressed during the Presidential term of Jimmy Carter (1977-1981), though the government never became the activist Carter's earlier stance for equal opportunity had promised.

One serious problem was the immense backlog of cases that besieged EEOC. In April 1976, during the final year of the Ford Administration, EEOC's backlog passed 130,000. By 1978, despite increases in the staff, it reached 340,000, with cases generally requiring two to seven years to resolve.

To reduce this burden, Commissioner Eleanor Holmes Norton cut back efforts to consolidate complaints into class action suits and pressed the parties involved to resolve the issues among themselves. The net result of this was that the Commission increasingly confined its best efforts to a few selected cases in the hope that favorable resolution of these would have a ripple effect for blacks among the nation's employers.

This approach had it successes. The very potential of activity by EEOC and the presence of a national administration at least partially committed to affirmative action had a positive effect on employers. Black employment in firms reporting to EEOC during the seventies rose at a significantly greater rate than did the total growth of jobs in these firms, especially in craft and service jobs. The proportion of blacks hired also rose faster in professional and technical fields.

Also encouraging were Supreme Court decisions rejecting "reverse discrimination" challenges brought by whites. Two of the most important suits sought to have the Court reverse voluntary agreements between employers and groups championing the cause of minorities.

In July 1978, the Court rejected a challenge brought by the Communications Workers of America to the EEOC-AT&T agreement. And in June 1979, the Court upheld a voluntary affirmative action plan in the Weber Decision, (see Labor section) when by a vote of 5 to 2 it declared that an employer can legally give preference to blacks to eliminate racial imbalance in skilled crafts traditionally filled almost exclusively by whites. The Kreps Case (see Legal section) was another victory for supporters of affirmative action. Other Court decisions, however, weakened EEOC by limiting some of its enforcement authority and the award of attorneys' fees and back pay.

### Discrimination in Public Employment

In 1972, amendments to Title VII empowered the EEOC to investigate and try to conciliate complaints of discrimination against state and local governments. Additionally, the Justice Department was empowered to sue on behalf of individuals or groups of public service employees or to remedy "pattern and practice" discrimination in specific locations.

In response to suits brought under these amendments, courts have ruled that public service employment tests which have a racially discriminatory impact are unlawful unless they can be shown to have a demonstrable relationship to job performance. In addition, suits against police and fire departments have brought forth specific numerical goals for hiring minority personnel. Among successful cases were suits against the Boston and Akron fire departments, the San Francisco and Bridgeport, Connecticut police departments, the entire city of Montgomery, Alabama, and the Alabama State Highway Patrol.

**CHART 32. UNEMPLOYMENT RATES BY SEX, AGE, AND RACE (ANNUAL AVERAGES), 1988.**

**In every age group or sex group the unemployment rate for blacks is at least twice that of whites. The most disproportionate rates are found among teenage females and those in their early twenties, here the unemployment rate is close to three times that of similar white groups.**

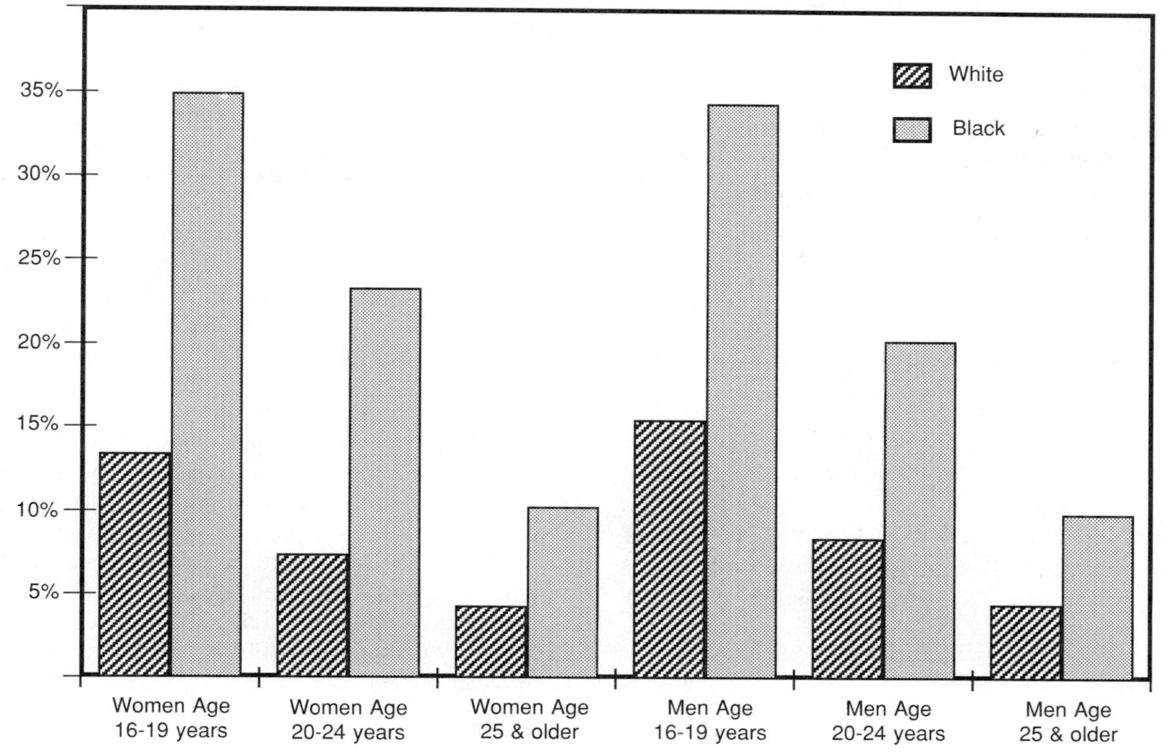

This pattern of success continued throughout the 1970s and into 1980 with victories involving police and fire departments in Chicago, Cincinnati, New York, and Los Angeles. In the New York case, the Supreme Court refused to overturn a lower court decision requiring that one-third of police to be hired be black or Hispanic. Los Angeles was required to pay $2 million in back wages to victims of discrimination by its police department and to hire blacks, women, and Hispanics in proportion to their participation in the city's labor force.

### Reagan and Affirmative Action

Opposition to affirmative action intensified during the 1970s. Some opponents, many of them erstwhile liberals who had supported the civil rights movement, maintained that affirmative action was bad for the moral and the morality of its recipients. A few blacks such as Thomas Sowell endorsed this stance. Others asserted that government activity to effect equality was a wrongful imposition on individuals and only served to exacerbate discrimination and tension between the races. Affirmative action even caused a rift in the black-Jewish alliance, as the latter did not know how their minority status would be affected by quotas in schools and jobs.

Proponents of these views rallied behind Ronald Reagan in the Presidential campaign of 1980, and by the fall of 1981, the Reagan Administration had issued a series of sweeping proposals that threatened to erase most of the gains of the last two decades.

In its first year, the administration announced that it would:

End use of quotas and numerical goals in hiring and promotion.

End timetables and other detailed plans for hiring and promotion of minorities by companies that had yet to comply fully with previous affirmative action commitments.

Eliminate government class action lawsuits and require that cases be brought by individuals.

Seek a reversal of the Weber Decision, which the government contended discriminated unfairly against whites, and thus discourage or terminate voluntary agreements among employers, unions, and minorities.

Recommend a standard of "intent" rather than "effect" in determining the merits of discrimination cases. Intent, of course, is more difficult to prove.

Despite their weakened position within the government, civil rights proponents marshalled a response. In a report titled *Civil Rights in the 1980s: Dismantling the Process of Discrimination*, the Civil Rights Commission endorsed quotas that "select qualified minorities and women according to designated ratios or percentages for limited periods of time."

In May 1982, President Reagan appointed Clarence Thomas as chairman of the Equal Employment Opportunity Commission, replacing Eleanor Holmes Norton.

Under the Reagan Administration, top priorities for the EEOC were to overhaul management of the agency, and to clear the huge backlog of cases accrued from 1972 to 1981. By fiscal year (FY) 1983, all Title VII charges from before January 1979 had been dealt with.

**CHART 33. COMPARISON OF TEENAGE AND ADULT UNEMPLOYMENT.**

**The 1987 ratio of black to white unemployment varied by age and sex groups. The greatest ratio among adult women at about 2.6 and teenagers at 2.5. For adult males it was 1.8.**

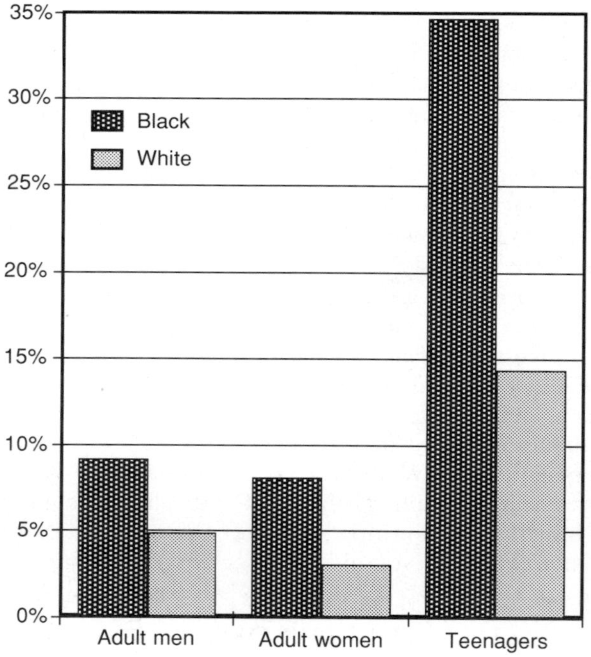


Meanwhile, the President dismissed Civil Rights Commission Chairman Arthur Fleming, effectively disbanding the six-member commission. In 1983, the commission was reconstituted as the U. S. Commission on Civil Rights, with half of the appointments made by the president, and half by Congress. President Reagan appointed Clarence Pendleton Jr., a black, as commission chairman.

The number of Title VII discrimination cases brought to the EEOC grew, with 56,425 in FY 1980 to more than 66,000 in FY 1985. The EEOC opted to give these new cases fuller investigations, and by 1984 had 35% of its staff working on such "full" investigations.

Actual litigation of cases also rose, due to more comprehensive reviews and an increased caseload for staff attorneys. Some 358 cases were litigated in FY 1980, and by FY 1986, a record 526 court actions were filed. Monetary awards (primarily back pay) also increased, from $20.9 million in FY 1980 to more than $46 million in FY 1986.

Although there had been concern about a Reagan Administration prohibition on class action suits, this appeared to be largely unfounded. While the number of class action suits declined from FY 1980 to FY 1982, from FY 1983 on, class action suits comprised more than half of all the suits brought into court. Notable victories included a 1983 class action suit against General Motors in which GM agreed to provide $42 million to resolve alleged discrimination against minorities and women in hiring, training, and promotion; and in 1985, Burlington Northern, in which $10 million in back pay was awarded to victims of discrimination.

A controversial Supreme Court decision was made in 1984, in the case of Firefighters v. Stotts. The court ruled that a court may not order a company to lay off more senior employees in favor of less senior employees on the basis of race in order to preserve a certain racial mix, if there is a valid, preexisting seniority system.

The decision was applauded by Chairman Pendleton, who called it a "nail in the coffin of discriminatory affirmative action programs." Others denounced it. NAACP executive director Benjamin Hooks, for example, called the decision "a complete abandonment of this nation's affirmative action policy... and an affront to black Americans."

During 1986 and 1987, the Supreme Court examined five additional affirmative action cases in 1986 and 1987 but issued opinions with mixed messages. Hence, the fate of affirmative action programs remained unclear for a period of time.

At the core of the debate over affirmative action was whether strict numerical quotas were needed to combat racial discrimination, or whether numerical or percentage "goals" set "in good faith" were sufficient.

The federal government itself could not agree. The Department of Labor favored the setting of "good faith" goals; however, the Justice Department issued a study which showed that the DOL had applied its "good faith" hiring of federal contractors in an uneven fashion, and actually promoted discrimination. In 1985, the White House came under fire when it was revealed that it had considered a plan to "free" federal contractors from meeting numerical goals in hiring of women and minorities. The plan, which was not implemented, would have affected some 30,000 companies doing an estimated $1090 billion a year in business with the federal government.

During the Reagan years, the U.S. Commission on Civil Rights and the EEOC were routinely criticized for their actions. Civil rights groups, liberal and other Congressional leaders argued that the agencies were backing off past commitments.

In 1984, the EEOC officially renounced the use of racial quotas as a means to correct job discrimination, infuriating civil rights activists. In 1986, following a Supreme Court decision which at least seemed to back affirmative action, the EEOC announced that it would resume the use of quotas. Chairman Thomas responded at the time with, "The Supreme Court has ruled, and as far as I'm concerned, that's that."

In 1986, the Commission on Civil Rights refused to approve a report urging a one-year halt of programs in which some federal contracts were "set aside" for minority contractors. Although the Reagan Administration had indicated its support for such "set asides," which directed about $8 billion a year to minority businesses, Chairman Pendleton had strongly supported the cessation of such programs. Mr. Pendleton's resignation was immediately called for by another member of the commission.

By the end of the Reagan Administration in 1988, affirmative action seemed to have been confirmed. In June 1988, the Supreme Court, which now consisted of three Reagan appointees as well as the elevation of William Rehnquist as Chief Justice, ruled unanimously in Watson v. Fort Worth Bank & Trust, that employees need not prove intentional discrimination by employers. Instead, the court said, employees may use statistical evidence as demonstrable proof that minorities or women have been underrepresented in the workplace.

In June 1988, Commission Chairman Pendleton died of an apparent heart attack in San Diego. He was replaced by William Allen, a black college professor appointed to the commission in 1987. Chairman Allen was expected to be less combative than Mr. Pendleton, but was viewed as "yet another right wing ideologue" by liberal activists, according to Ralph Neas, the executive director of the Leadership Conference on Civil Rights. (As of late 1988, Mr. Allen's future as chairman was undecided: President-elect George Bush could replace him with someone else, at which time Mr. Allen would resume his role as commission member.

## Black Immigrants

The elimination of ethnocentric quotas in 1965 encouraged immigration from the West Indies. Not counting Cubans, the number of West Indians entering the United States as permanent residents rose from 44,500 in the 1950s to 263,000 in the 1960s and 304,000 between 1971 and 1977. These numbers were swelled by what is estimated to be a still larger group of illegal aliens from the Caribbean, their number exceeding 500,000.

Black immigrants settled mostly in the northeast, particularly New York City, where in 1977 they comprised about 20% of the city's black population.

In the mid-seventies, nearly 10% of legal black immigrants in New York City held professional and technical jobs compared with 8% for indigenous blacks. By a 19% to 15% difference, a greater proportion of immigrants were employed craftsmen and by 58% to 33%, indigenous blacks were more likely to hold jobs below the level of craftsmen.

There was, however, considerable downward mobility among black immigrants, especially for those who occupied managerial jobs in their countries of origin. White immigrants experienced similar difficulties but were more likely than blacks to regain lost occupational status.

A two-year study commissioned by the Ford Foundation and released in January 1988 indicated that while immigration into the U.S. has continued unabated, it has had "little adverse impact on the natives."

Instead, "the greatest job impact typically was felt by other immigrants," said the study, which was conducted by the National Bureau of Economic Research.

There have been "modest adverse impacts" on the employment and wages of workers who are the closest substitutes for immigrants," the study said, "but little if any impact on young black and Hispanic-Americans, who are likely to be the next closest substitutes."

The study showed that from 1959 to 1971, nearly 40% of all immigrants came to the U.S. from Europe. From 1971 to 1981, the European percentage dropped to 17%, while the percentage from Asia rose to more than 37%. The main reason for immigration was for family unification rather than economic opportunity.

### Undocumented Aliens

Only a small portion of the immigrants during the 1970s were black. A much larger group, numbering from 3 million to 5 million, and the vast majority of them in the country illegally, entered the United States from all parts of the world. The largest numbers came from Latin America, mostly from Mexico, and from China, Korea, Eastern and Southeastern Europe.

By the mid-seventies, millions of the "undocumented aliens" were employed in low-paying, sweatshop-type jobs, most frequently in restaurants and garment manufacturing shops and on farms.

In the Los Angeles area, 65% of the restaurants inspected by the state between 1978 and 1980 were breaking wage laws. A Labor Department survey of Chicago restaurants found 91% underpaying workers. In garment shops wages of $1 an hour and less were commonplace.

As Congressman Harold Washington of Illinois noted: "The mere presence of a large number of aliens depresses wages generally and forces unskilled blacks to take dirtier, lower-paying jobs."

Undocumented black immigrants were found working in demeaning conditions as migrant farm labor. In 1980, it was revealed that black migrant farm workers, both American and West Indian, were victims of peonage and enslavement on farms in East Coast states between Connecticut and Florida. The Department of Justice appointed an Involuntary Servitude Coordinator and by the end of 1981 had won ten convictions for involuntary servitude and peonage in six cases it prosecuted. The Department conceded that these cases only scratched the surface.

In 1981, President Reagan proposed granting legal status to all aliens who had entered the country prior to 1980, and instituting heavy fines for employers who knowingly hire illegal aliens. The hope was that legal status would reassure exploited aliens to assert their rights. Meanwhile, their prevalence was having an adverse effect on the nation's blacks, who worried that illegal aliens would swell the job market and take their jobs.

### Vietnam Veterans

During the 1970s, black Vietnam veterans improved their position within the work force. In 1981, black veterans of the Vietnam era between the ages of 25 and 39 had a lower unemployment rate than nonveterans, 10.5% compared with 12%. Their rate, however, was considerably higher than the rate for white veterans (5.8%) and white nonveterans (5.6%).

An alarming by-product of these figures was a sharp rise in unemployment rates between 1979 and 1981 for veterans

**CHART 34. FEWER JOBS FOR HIGH SCHOOL DROPOUTS.**

**The high school drop out rate has been on an increase and at the same time most newly created jobs require at least a high school proficiency level. It is said that 9 out of 10 jobs in Baltimore require a high school education.**

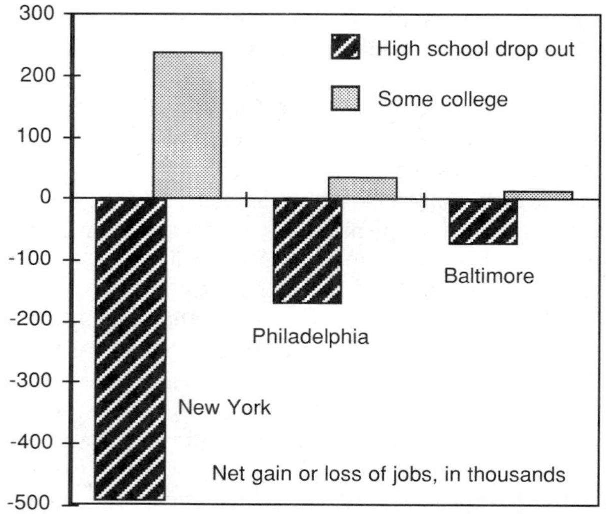


Source: University of North Carolina

of both races, 46% for blacks, 66% for whites. Increases for nonveterans were higher for both races.

By 1987, these unemployment figures had fallen along with the national jobless rate.

By 1986, some 56,000 black Vietnam veterans, or 10% of the black workforce aged 30 to 44 years, could not find work. By the next year, that number had dropped to 50,000 or 9.3% of the workforce.

Among white Vietnam vets during the same period, 259,000 or 4.8% of the workforce, were jobless. Again, that number dropped to 238,000 or 4.5% by 1987.

Unemployment for nonveterans during 1986 was 12.2% for blacks, or 200,000 out of 1.6 million workers. This fell in 1987 to 9.9%, or 173,000 out of a 1.7 million workforce. Among white nonveterans, unemployment was 4.7% in 1986, or 716,000 out of a 15.1 million workforce. The next year, this too fell, to 4.1% or 658,000 out of a 15.9 million workforce.

### Youth Unemployment—a Persistent Problem

The employment situation of young blacks between the ages of 16 and 24 deteriorated in the 1970s, and hit its lowest point in the 1981-82 recession

For teenagers between 16 and 19, this continued a long-term trend that first appeared in the recession of 1958. For older youths, however, the decline was startling. Unemployment of non-white men between 20 and 24 rose from 12.6% in 1973 to 24.3% in 1981. The 1981 rate for black males was 26.5%.

The difficulties young blacks encountered were

### CHART 35. TEENAGERS SEEKING WORK.

**While most young workers do find jobs of sorts, there is a sizable proportion of youth that have been unable to find work and an ever greater number that can find work only occasionally. Consequently, 68.3% of white teens and only an astonishingly low 40.1% of black teens worked the entire year.**

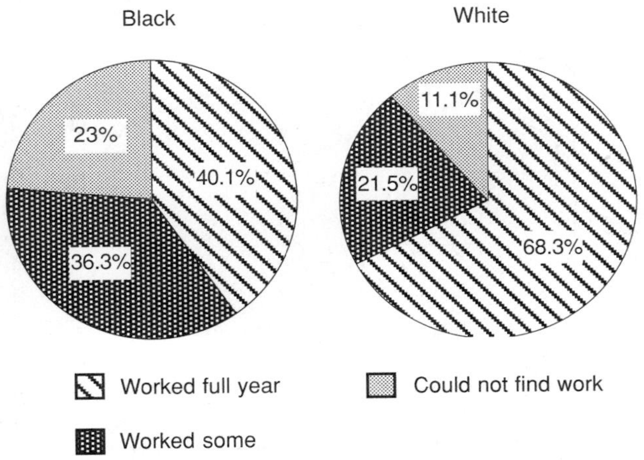


underscored by a tendency for their unemployment rates to remain high after the rest of the labor force has recovered from a recession. The jobless rate for blacks between 16 and 24, for example, was higher in 1978 than in the pre-recession year of 1974. The white rate had dropped.

Another notable trend of the 16-24 groups was the declining labor force participation rate of young black men after the mid-seventies and of young black women after 1978.

By the end of 1987, a total of 1.3 million teenagers aged 16-19, the equivalent of 16.9% of the national workforce, was unemployed. More than 1.4 million young adults, age 20-24, or 9.7% of the workforce, also were jobless.

Black teenagers and youths again were disproportionately reflected in these figures: 312,000 or 34.7% of black 16- to 19-year-olds, and 397,000 or 21.8% of black 20- to 24-year-olds were out of work at the end of 1987.

Among whites, by 1987, 995,000 or 14.4% of 16- to 19-year-olds, and 1 million or 8% of 20- to 24-year-olds were jobless.

Unemployment was most tenacious among black teens. In 1982, at the height of the recession, 396,000 black 16- to 19-year-olds couldn't find work. In 1987, that number had only dropped by 84,000, to 312,000. Blacks in the 20- to 24-year-old group fared better: their jobless number dropped by a third, from a peak of 591,000 in 1983 to 396,000 in 1987.

By comparison, the number of white unemployed teens, aged 16-19, fell from 1.5 million in 1982 to 995,000 in 1987. The number of white unemployed 20- to 24-year-olds fell from 1.7 million in 1982 to 1 million in 1987.

In poverty areas throughout the United States, black teen unemployment remained around 40% in the late 1980s.

Several explanations have been advanced for the stubborn severity of youth unemployment.

Economic changes have markedly reduced the need for unskilled and semiskilled workers, and intensified the demand for people with advanced technological skills. Such skills require school degrees and training available to few blacks.

These and other so-called structural trends have been international in scope. Unemployment rates of teenagers and youths have risen sharply in most industrialized nations.

In the United States, such structural changes combined with rising youth unemployment have sparked concern that a major long-term problem has been brewing and that disadvantaged youths, unable to obtain the necessary training and work experience, will come to form a chronically unemployed underclass far more widespread and resistant to economic upturns than the underclass that grew during the 60s and 70s.

Blacks can be expected to suffer disproportionately under such conditions, and in fact, as the youth unemployment figures testify, they already are. (In such countries as Sweden and the United Kingdom, minorities also have suffered disproportionately, though not to the same degree as blacks in the United States; see FACTS.)

In the United States, rising minimum wages were also blamed for higher teenage and youth joblessness. The Urban League challenged this view, noting that the average wage paid teenagers was below the legal minimum anyway, an indication that the minimum was substantially ignored where young people are concerned and not an important hindrance to hiring them.

Another view attributed increases in youth unemployment to a higher rate of black school dropouts between 16 and 24. However, in 1977, 54% of this age group had graduated from high school and another 17% had gone to college. Also, significantly, in 1977 white high school dropouts between 16 and 24 had a lower unemployment rate than 16- to 24-year-old blacks with some college education (16.7% versus 21.4%).

In 1986, a study entitled "The Black Youth Employment Crisis" was released. It was based on a 1979-1980 National Bureau of Economic Research survey of young, black men living in poverty areas of major American cities, and edited by Harvard professor Richard Freeman and Henry Holzer of the University of Chicago. The study showed that there was no single cause for joblessness in young black men. Instead, factors such as crime, drug and alcohol abuse, and performance on the job, i.e., absenteeism, played major roles.

Crime was singled out as possibly the most important element in chronic unemployment. Quite simply, it was easier to make money, and lots of it, through illegal means, such as drug dealing, than by working an 8-hour shift at minimum wage. Some 32% of the youths interviewed in the NBER survey believed they could earn more from criminal "street" activity than legitimate work. One-fourth of the income reported in the survey was indicated as coming from criminal activity. Adding to the belief that crime does pay was the perception that there was little chance of being arrested, convicted, or sent to jail, the study found.

Growing up in a welfare family also was significant. The study found that unemployment among 19- to 24-year-olds whose families did not receive public assistance, nor live in public housing was 28% in 1979. Unemployment among those from the same age group who came from families on welfare rose to 43.8%. Youths from families who lived both on public assistance and in public housing experienced an unemployment rate of 52%. The problem, Freeman and Holzer wrote, was that "the current welfare system, lacking programs or incentives to promote employment, is doing nothing to correct joblessness."

On the positive side, the survey found that when black youths were surrounded by family members who worked, had "good" attitudes, and went to church, the youths developed stronger, healthier, long-term career desires.

Nationally, the job market strongly favored teen workers by the end of 1982. The number of minimum-wage, entry-level jobs, especially in the booming service industry, continued to grow. Meanwhile, the number of 16- to 19-year-olds steadily dropped, from 16.7 million in 1979 to 14.5 million in 1986. Thus, the demand for entry-level and minimum wage employees far exceeded the pool of typical applicants. With demand so high, many teenagers were able to pick and choose their place of employment, and in many cases opted for those jobs which paid more than minimum wage, which ranged, state by state, from the federally-mandated low of $3.35 to as much as $4.25 in 1988. In many places, entry-level jobs carried $5 and $6 hourly wages.

In 1988, the $3.35 minimum wage was subject of hot debate. A bill in Congress proposed raising it to $5.05. There was argument that employers didn't mind paying to train employees at the lower minimum wage, but if they were going to pay more, they would expect the employee to have certain basic skills. A state employment manager in Vermont noted that even people who "flip hamburgers or sell french fries" should know how to read and calculate a bill; such employees also need to know how to deal with the public and be punctual about hours. Others cited studies which showed that each 10% increase in the minimum wage reduces the hiring of teenagers by 10%.

A study released in November of 1988 by the Commission on Work, Family and Citizenship, warned that the "forgotten half" of American youth who do not go to college, some 20 million 16- to 24-year-olds, would fall into "economic limbo" if not helped. Most of these youths were white, the study said, but an increasing share were black. The "economic limbo" was defined as unemployment, part-time work and poverty wages. The commission called on the government to commit $5 billion a year for the next 10 years to enlarge Head Start, the Job Training Partnership Act, the Job Corps and Chapter I program for remedial education for disadvantaged children.

The wealth of job opportunities was expected to permeate inner city neighborhoods, favorably affecting black teens. However, it was also anticipated that there would be fewer wage increases among those jobs. Inner-city teens also faced the reality that most entry-level jobs were in non-metropolitan areas, which necessitated commuting time and expenses for them.

**CHART 36. TEENAGE UNEMPLOYMENT RATES BY RACE AND HISPANIC ORIGIN.**

**Since the 1930s, the unemployment to population ratios between black and white youth have become increasingly disproportionate, reaching a peak in 1982 during the recession. The gap, while trending down (1988), still remains very great.**

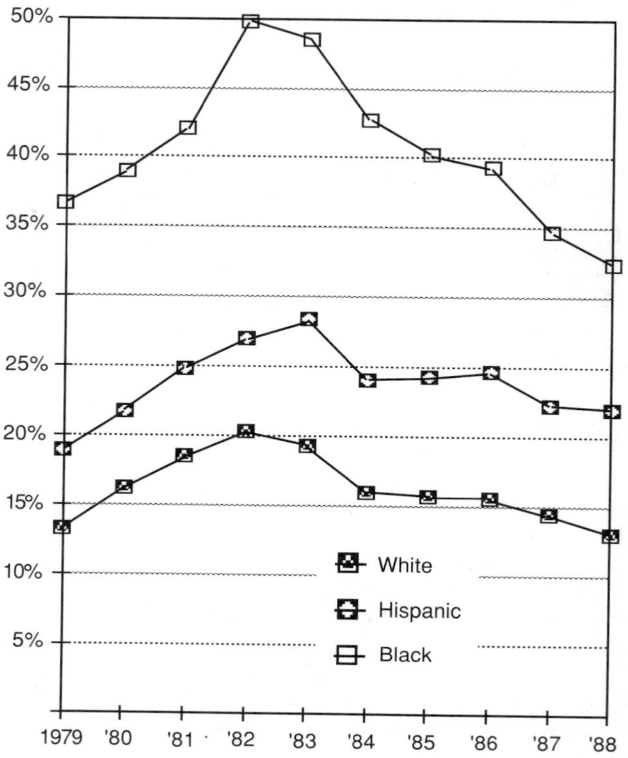


Still, there was some optimism that with the booming American economy and the sheer abundance of jobs in the United States, 21 million new jobs were projected by the year 2000, the chronic unemployment problems among teenagers, and black teens in particular, could at least be assuaged.

## Jobs Programs

During the depression of the 1930s, and again in the 1960s, the Federal government led efforts to reduce unemployment through an assortment of training and employment activities, identified until the 1970s as "manpower programs."

The Manpower Development and Training Act of 1962 was the first of many legislative measures intended to serve as a base for federal support and activity in job training and placement. Originally designed to retrain workers displaced by technological advances, the MDTA's focus was changed to serve inner-city youth during the 1960s. Among programs operating under MDTA's banner were the Job Corps, Apprenticeship Outreach Program, and the Neighborhood Youth Corps. Blacks comprised a substantial portion of participants in these programs, for example, between 40 and 50% in New York City during the late 1960s. Some blacks,

*Unemployment among black youth has historically been high. Jobs that are available for black youth are usually at minimum wage in places such as fast food restaurants.*

however, were concerned that minorities were more frequently assigned to classrooms than to actual work-experience instruction.

Advocates of federal activity programs cited substantial reduction in unemployment rates of young blacks and proclaimed MDTA's programs a success. But some conservatives branding them inefficient, indulgent, and corrupt, and also aided by racial backlash and the nation's disillusionment with the Vietnam War, were able in 1968 to elect Richard Nixon.

### Nixon and "New Federalism"

After 1969, the proportion of blacks enrolled in Department of Labor programs dropped from more than 50% to 40% in 1973. Also in 1973, blacks comprised only 26% of enrollees in the JOBS Program.

These trends stemmed from Nixon's emphasis on a "new federalism" under which programs were shifted from federal to local control, with the federal government earmarking monies, or "block grants," for community development and other projects. The vehicle for this was the Comprehensive Employment and Training Act (CETA) of 1973. By 1975, with Gerald Ford President, the Department of Labor handled only $460 million of CETA's $2.05 billion budget.

Under CETA, the political claims of individual communities frequently replaced the needs of the disadvantaged, thus reducing services for locations with the greatest need. In addition, local communities occasionally overlooked the needy in their allocations. Also, continuing a pattern noticeable during the sixties, blacks tended to be assigned to classroom rather than on-the-job programs.

### Carter and CETA

In 1976, Jimmy Carter campaigned on a pledge to increase help for minorities and in 1977 restored much of CETA's emphasis to the disadvantaged and increased its overall budget. In 1978, CETA's peak year, outlays were $5.8 billion, with over 3.5 million people served, a substantial number of them black. Blacks, however, were not always well represented in apprentice activities focusing on development of higher skills. During the first six months of 1979, only 17% of apprentices in training programs were minorities.

During Carter's years, the public came to regard inflation as a more serious problem than unemployment and to accept higher levels of unemployment as normal. Provisions of the Humphrey-Hawkins full employment bill were diluted. The mid-seventies objective of a 3% unemployment maximum was quietly abandoned as a 6% rate came to be regarded as reasonable and proper.

### The Reagan Approach

CETA was a major issue in the 1980 Presidential campaign, with champions of governmental jobs activity clearly on the defensive. The public, fatigued and frightened by high living costs and exaggerated anecdotes of coddled welfare cheats, increasingly blamed government activity as the source of economic instability.

Elected on promises to cut taxes, eliminate waste in government, and balance the budget, President Ronald Reagan and his advisors soon unleashed an awesome attack on CETA that caught its defenders in despair and disarray. By 1982, CETA's funds had been cut to $2 billion.

In some areas, cuts were especially devastating. In East St. Louis, Illinois, an impoverished area, with some two-thirds of its black labor force unemployed, CETA funds for 1982 were cut from $2.3 million to $65,000.

Reagan's proposed alternative to these cuts was to induce a spirit of volunteerism among businesses and individuals, in which training and placement of the disadvantaged would reside in the hands of the private sector. Private generosity, claimed the President, would in the long run achieve more for minorities than the government programs of the past twenty years.

Actually, the private sector had often been involved in

employment programs, notably in the JOBS (Job Opportunities in the Business Sector) program launched in 1967, and the Opportunities Industrialization Centers of America, founded in 1964 by the Reverend Leon Sullivan. By 1970, 80,000 disadvantaged persons had been hired under JOBS, and OIC soon became a national institution operating in some 100 cities. However, government was deeply involved in these programs. JOBS was a joint venture between the Department of Labor and the National Alliance of Businessmen, and OIC received some 85% of its budget from national, state, and local governments.

In 1978, President Carter signed into law the Private Sector Initiative Program, which claimed to have served some 60,000 individuals in fiscal 1980, 25,000 of them minorities. PSIP was intended to coordinate CETA with the private sector through councils of representatives from business, industry, labor, community organization, and educational institutions.

## The Reagan Cuts

For fiscal year 1982, the Reagan Administration eliminated:

80% of the funding for the Youth Employment Demonstration Projects Act

20% from the Summer Youth Program

All funding for the Youth Conservation Corps (CETA Title VIII)

All funding for the Public Service Employment Program, which in 1981 helped over 500,000 people

64% of the funding for Title III of CETA, which helped displaced homemakers, the elderly, migrants, and welfare recipients

27% of the funding for Title XX of the Social Security Act, which subsidized daycare centers for low- and moderate-income working parents.

The continuing legislation under which most of these cuts were passed permitted further cuts of 6% and more.

As of March 1982, the Administration proposed for fiscal 1983 to eliminate:

The Summer Youth Employment Program, the only source of jobs for poor youths during the summer (fiscal 1982 funding was $674 million)

Many of the tax exemptions on unemployment insurance

The Work Incentive Program (WIN), which provided jobs for welfare recipients

The total employment and training budget proposed for 1983 was to be $2.4 billion (compared with $8.9 billion for CETA in 1980) of which $1.8 billion was to be earmarked for a private sector program to replace CETA.

By the spring of 1982 the outlines of two plans to reduce unemployment appeared. One would grant tax credits to companies establishing or expanding businesses in impoverished areas which would be labeled "enterprise zones." This approach received a sympathetic hearing from blacks, but by the spring of 1982, little was expected of it. Representative Charles Rangel of New York was dubious of its prospects on the grounds that corporate taxes under the Reagan Administration would be so low or nonexistent that further tax credits would be redundant. Others pointed out that businesses did little to avail themselves of earlier tax credit programs, notably the WIN Program of 1972 and New Jobs Tax Credit Program of 1977.

The second Reagan weapon requested businesses voluntarily to devote a portion of their profits to training and placement of disadvantaged people. In early 1982, a Presidential Task Force on Private Sector Initiative was seeking ways to persuade businesses to cooperate but skeptics pointed out that even massive cooperation would cover only a small portion of the loss sustained by the CETA cuts. Total corporate philanthropic contributions in 1979 were $2.3 billion, mostly to higher education. More than this was cut from CETA alone in 1981, and more than $10 billion from other programs serving the disadvantaged.

Private industry already had been unable to fill the gap in jobs erased by budget cuts. Only 180,000 of the 535,000 people in eliminated CETA-PSE Projects found employment within a month of their release. Most of these jobs were in state and local government. A year later, one-third of the 535,000 remained out of work.

In March 1982, the Administration proposed a program under which $1.8 billion in block grant money would be granted, via states, to private industry councils to set up job training programs. Local business leaders, through the councils, would have decision-making authority. Training would focus on young members of welfare families between the ages of 16 and 25. Businesses would be compensated for their training costs. Ten percent of the funds could be used to train displaced workers in new skills.

The plan also called for $387 million to continue the Jobs Corps at a reduced level. And $200 million would be provided to train special target groups, such as Indians and migratory workers.

Secretary of Labor Raymond Donovan conceded the venture would do little to affect the nation's unemployment rate, but emphasized that despite the $53 billion CETA had spent during its existence, unemployment of minority youths had risen from 28 to 40%. Critics of the proposal charged it was inadequate and that no stipends had been suggested to cover living costs of the welfare youths during training periods. In 1980, CETA programs reached some 3 million people, 40% of whom received stipends.

The Jobs Corps program, which received $617 million in 1985, came under fire for several years. The Office of Budget Management recommended its elimination, while others, including conservative Sen. Orrin Hatch of Utah argued for its continuation as a valuable program "designed to give youth the chance to learn lifetime skills." Something of a compromise was reached in 1986, when six of the so-called "worst" centers were closed to save money. The closings eliminated 1,200 training positions, about 3% of the 40,000 slots for teens, with an estimated savings of $20

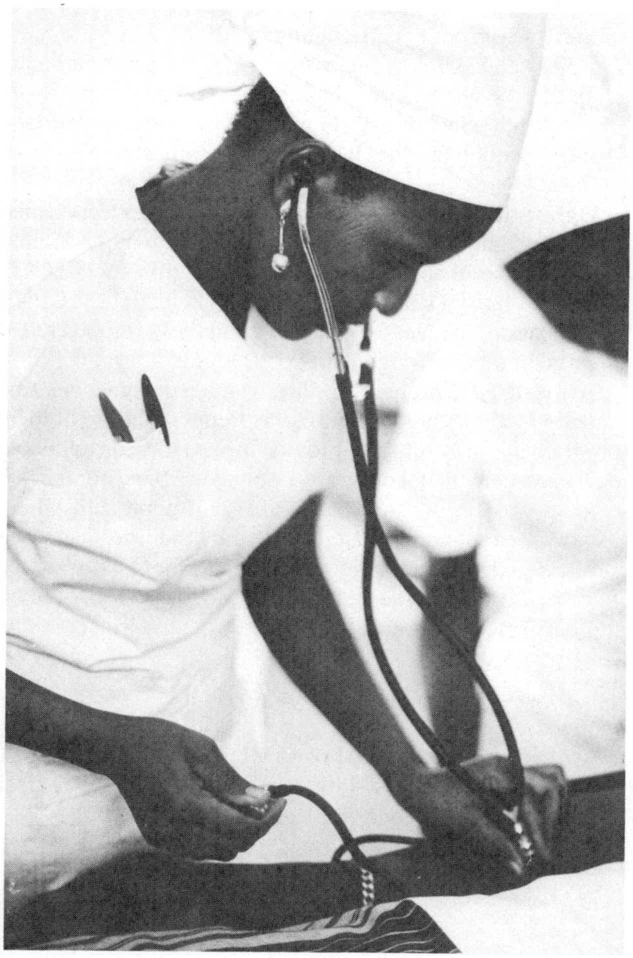

*Black women have made enormous strides in gaining access into many skilled technical occupations.*

million.

By 1988 and the end of the Reagan Administration, there were 107 Job Corps centers with a national enrollment of 40,544. The current budget was $716 million.

## Working Women

The seventies was a decade of progress and problems for working black women. On one hand, black women moved in large numbers from menial service employment into white-collar professional and clerical work. The declining proportion of black domestic servants was especially dramatic, from 1 in 12 of the female black working population in 1970 to 1 in 38 in 1979.

On the other hand, many black women continued to be segregated into low-paying dead-end jobs.

The number of working black women increased steadily from about 3.7 million in 1970 to 5.6 million in 1987.

The percentage of black women in the labor force, while stagnating during the mid-1980s, had reached 53% by 1987. The percentage of working white women was slightly lower, at 52.8%.

Unemployment among young women had dropped by 1987. Among white females, aged 16- to 24 -years, joblessness dropped from a high of 1.3 million in 1982, to 896,000 in 1987. Among black females in the same age bracket, unemployment dropped from 459,000 in 1983 to 363,000 in 1987.

Examined by percentages, however, white women fared better. The jobless rate for white women of all ages, which peaked at 8.3% in 1982, fell to 5.2% in 1987. For black women, the highest jobless rate of 18.6% in 1983 fell to 13.2% in 1987.

For young black women, aged 16- to 24- years, the jobless rate continued to be about three times that of young white women: in 1982-83, black joblessness was at 36.7% as compared to white joblessness of 13.8%. By 1987, those rates had dropped to 27.1% and 9.5%, respectively.

The number of women entering the work force grew steadily, regardless of marital status. The highest percentage of working white women were single. The highest percentage of working black women were married with spouse present.

Women continued to have lower median hourly earnings than men, with black women earning slightly lower than white women. In 1987, a white man earned $7.93 as compared to $6.74 of a black man. A white woman earned $5.62, as compared to $5.40 for a black women.

The percentage of working mothers was high among both races. In March 1984, 63% of black mothers with children under 18 were in the labor force. Among white mothers, the percentage was 60%. Among black mothers who had children under the age of 17 but not as young as 6, 70% were employed. Among white mothers in the same category, only 60% were working. Regarding those mothers with children under the age of 6, more than half were employed: 57% of black mothers, and 52% of white mothers.

There has been some improvement in the occupational status of employed black women. Between 1970 and 1988, black women increased their representation in many professional and technical jobs, including accountant, nurse, dietitian, therapist, engineering and science technician, and vocational and educational counselor. Limited progress has been made in both the numbers and proportions of black women in sales, management and administration, and administrative support positions. Of the 5.6 million black women employed in 1987, 1.4 million were government workers.

An unresolved dilemma continued to confront single mothers on welfare. If they accepted a job at minimum wage of $3.35, they often lost social service benefits for food, housing, and health care. Nor could they lift themselves above the poverty level: a minimum wage earned during a 40-hour week, 52-weeks a year, only amounted to $6,968. This was $431 below the poverty line for a family head with one dependent and about $4,644 below the line for a family of four.

Although the 1986 tax reform removed about 6 million workers from the tax rolls, it was unlikely to bring them out of poverty. A proposed hike in the minimum wage to $4.65 an hour, to be phased in over 3 years, was approved by committees in both the Senate and the House in early 1989. The Bush Administration countered with a proposal to keep $3.35 an hour as a six-month "training wage," which could be raised to as high as $4.25. The president threatened to veto any maximum minimum wage that exceeded $4.25 an hour.

Neither figure, however, brings a single-earner family of four out of poverty. Even without taxes taken out, a full time, 40-hour-a-week job at $4.65 an hour equals a take home pay of $9,672. A full time, 40-hour-a-week job at $4.25 nets $8,840. The poverty level for a family of four was $11,611 in 1987.

From 1965 to 1980, labor force participation of white women over age 16 increased by nearly 1 million per year, to approximately 39 million, and their participation rate grew from 42 to 52.8%. During the same period, the participation rate of black women grew from 49 to 53%. By 1984, unmarried women headed half of all black families with children, compared with less than 20% for white families.

Participation of black women in the labor force was markedly higher in two-parent families (64 vs. 53% for whites), while white participation was higher in one-parent families headed by a women (66 vs. 56%). (Participation by Hispanic women was considerably lower than that of white or black women.) In 1977, unemployment of single black women heading families was 22%, three times the white rate of 7%.

During the 1970's, single mothers were underrepresented in training and placement programs. Single women of both races comprised 56% of the population eligible for CETA in 1977, but only 44% of its enrollees. Their highest CETA participation rate was 46% in 1978 and they were excluded in large numbers from on-the-job training.

An obstacle to progress by disadvantaged women was the paucity of child care facilities, plus frequent failure of local program administrators to provide information on available day care centers to program applicants. The number of centers was limited by the block grant approach, which usually meant that the cost of child care facilities had to be subtracted from the training and placement allocations. Statistics in the early seventies indicated that 15% of welfare mothers interested in obtaining jobs were rejected by the

**CHART 37. COMPARISON OF WHITES AND BLACKS BY OCCUPATION GROUPS.**

**Blacks are much less likely than whites to be in managerial, professional, technical or sales positions. Blacks outnumber whites disproportionately in low level service occupations, where less skills are required. The one area where blacks do well proportionately is in health related technical positions.**

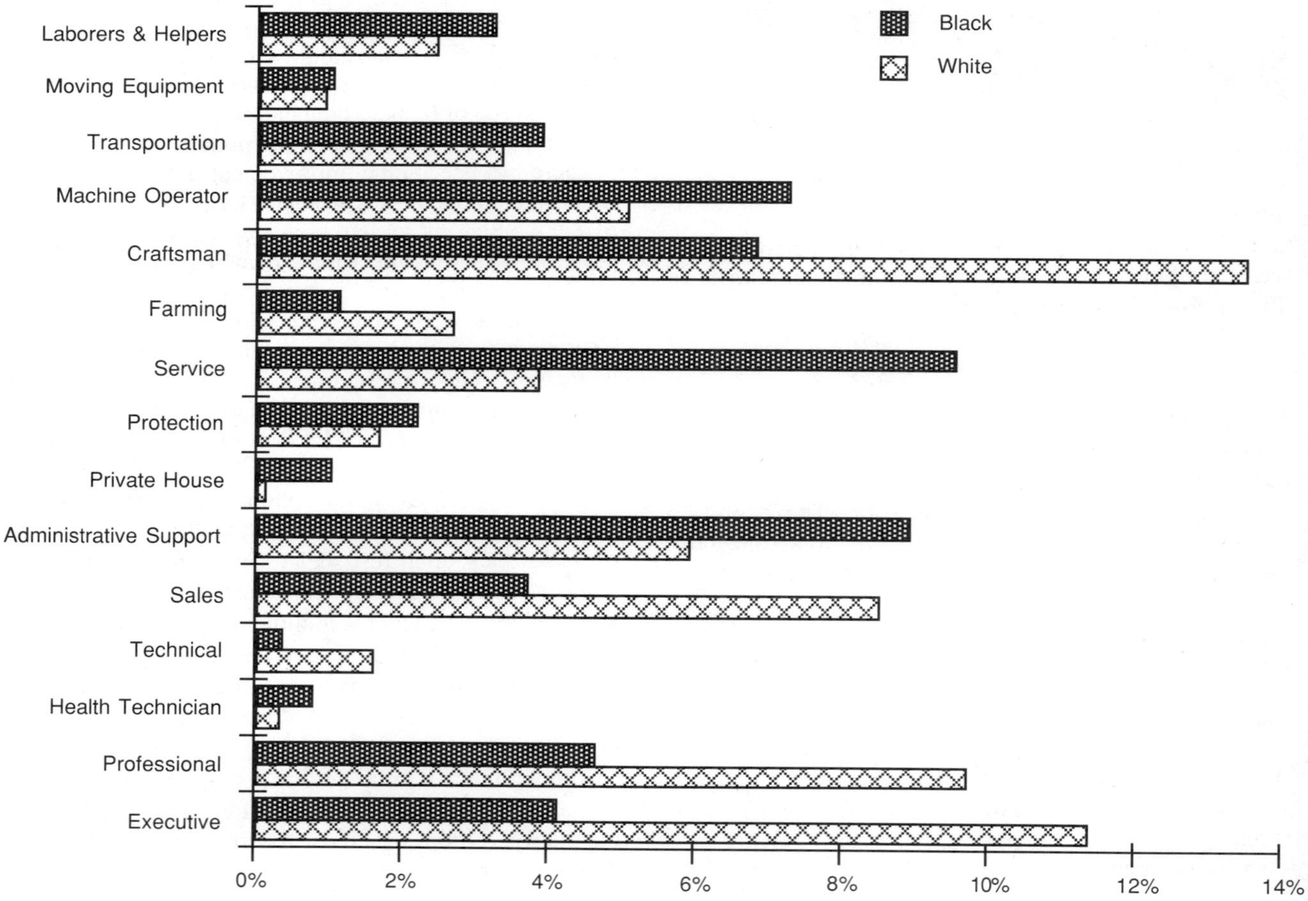

WIN Program or not referred to it because child care facilities were not available for them. Further guarantees of child care for WIN graduates were limited to 30 to 90 days after a parent ended training or obtained employment, as a result, many welfare mothers who successfully completed the program had to leave their jobs to care for their children.

The administration's budget of 1982 cut child care funds before previous levels. In January 1982, it was estimated that 150,000 families would lose federally funded child care services previously provided under Title XX of the Social Security Act. In 1980, 750,000 persons received subsidized child care services under this provision.

### Occupations

Blacks attained considerable job upgrading in the 1970s. By the end of the decade, the proportion of black men employed in craft jobs increased from 15% to 18%, while it remained at 21% for white men. The proportion of black women employed in white-collar work rose from 23% to 29%, while remaining stable at 36% for white women.

In 1978, in companies with 100 or more employees, the proportions of blacks employed in white-collar jobs had more than doubled the 1966 rate, though progress has diminished since 1973.

Also, though they remained severely underrepresented, the proportion of black men and women engaged in professional, technical, managerial, and administrative jobs increased so that 1 black worker in 7 occupied such a position by 1980. In 1981, approximately 9% of the nation's teachers, stenographers, and construction craft workers were black.

By 1987, the percentage of black workers surpassed that of whites in service occupations, and also among operators, fabricators, and laborers. Black women were strongest in the service occupations, which included jobs in health fields, cleaning and building services, and food preparation. Black men were heavily represented in transportation and material moving occupations.

Black men and women were also strong in technical, sales, and administrative support positions, particularly in postal services.

**CHART 38. INDUSTRY PARTICIPATION FOR BLACKS AND WHITES**

**The figures here are not proportional but rather actual numbers to demonstrate trends within an industry. For example, in the largest area of employment, manufacturing, in the 1975 to 1984 period the number of blacks increased. As the American service economy increases, the trend is for whites to move in the direction of occupational improvement while blacks fill in the gaps left by whites.**

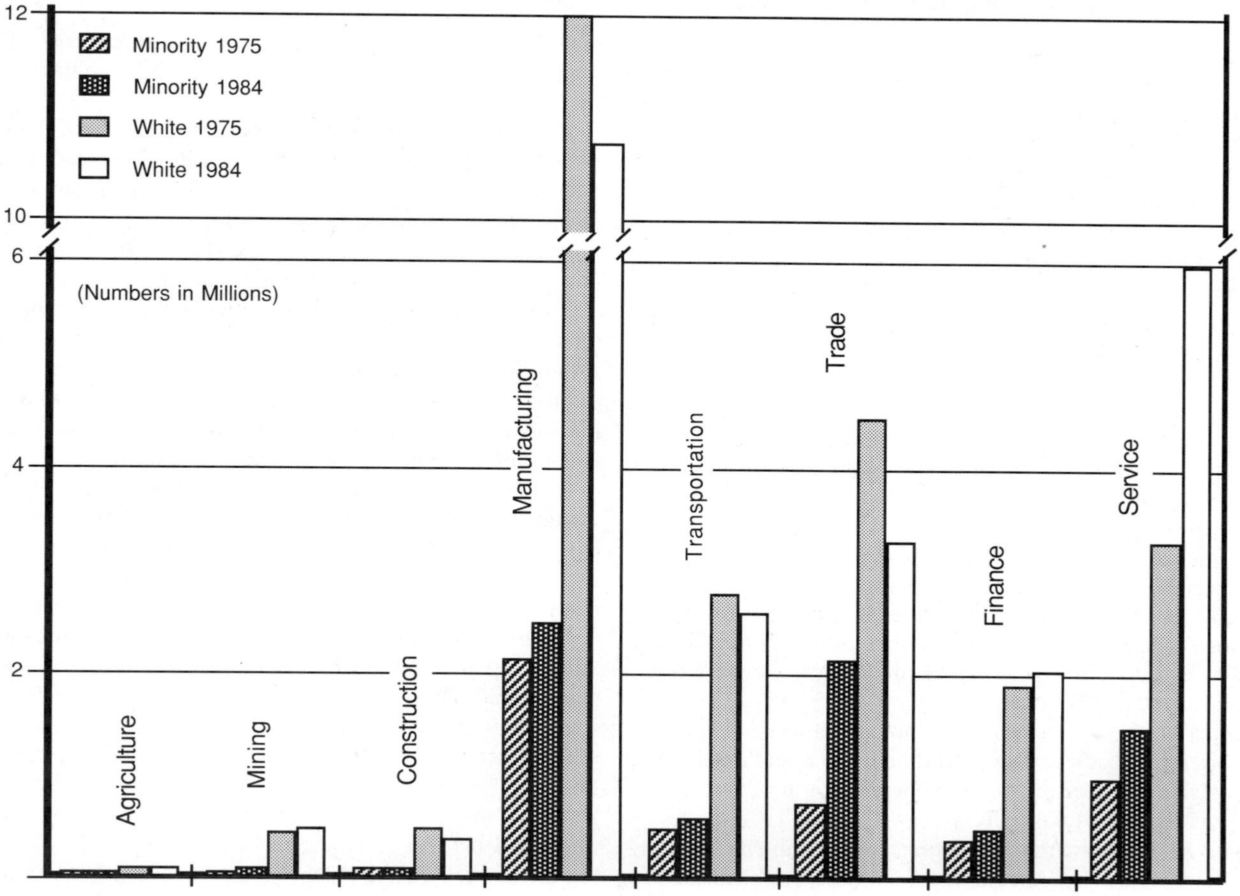

Some 1.7 million or more than 15% of the black adult labor force was employed in managerial and professional specialty jobs by 1987.

Such gains, however, left blacks far short of an equity position, and access to upper-level executive professional standing. A symptom of the limited access of blacks to such areas appears in the large proportion of black college graduates employed in government—in 1980, 74% for black women college grads and 58% for men.

### Trade-Sensitive Employment

In 1975, non-whites comprised 11.5% of the workforce in industries most adversely affected by international trade and only 7.4% of persons in the 20 most favorably affected industries.

The problems of minorities in such industries relate closely to structural problems reviewed earlier. Industries competing favorably include computers, oil field machinery, aircraft equipment, engines and parts, electronic components, and others that employ a high proportion of scientists and engineers. Only three of the 20 trade-enhanced industries employed more than 7% minorities in 1975. These were logging, plywood, and sawmills. However, in 11 of the 20 adversely affected industries, 10% or more of the workforce was non-white. The greatest proportion of minorities was employed in steel and motor vehicles, 14% in each of 1975. In 1981, according to the Department of Labor, blacks alone comprised 13.4% of employees in the troubled automobile industry. In March 1982, unemployment in that industry was 21% and there was also a high rate of discouraged workers.

The automobile industry suffered in the recession of the early 1980s, but underwent considerable recovery. Employment in the industry was 805,000 in 1987, as against 793,000 in 1981. Black employment there was 13.2%.

At the start of 1982, long-range prospects were not propitious. The recession and government retreats from affirmative action reduced incentives for industry and universities to take positive steps. Black enrollment in medical and law schools had leveled off in the late seventies after earlier increases. And, as noted, few blacks had been trained for the increasingly complex technological skills that industry was demanding. Indeed, there was a shortage of skilled whites for many of these areas.

## THE FUTURE

Between 1980 and 1990, the black labor force was expected to increase by double the rate of the white labor force. Between 1985 and 1995, the black growth rate is expected to triple the white rate. By the year 2000, it was estimated that 80% of new entrants into the workforce would be women minorities or immigrants.

Confronted by profound changes in the nation's economic and political climate, the coming generation of black workers will require a full measure of the perseverance and courage that distinguished the efforts of their predecessors. An estimated 3 out of 4 jobs in the future will require some education beyond high school.

At the same time, by the 1990s, jobs were expected to be so plentiful that chronic problems such as black and youth unemployment would at last be defeated. The job demand will be "enormous," Labor Secretary William Brock said in 1986, "and the demand for people with skills is going to be high."

The way Americans work is expected to change dramatically, with the dramatic transition from manual skills to skills requiring reasoning and communicating. In the future, for instance, less than 5% of the workforce will work on assembly lines.

From 1979 to 1987, an estimated two million manufacturing jobs were lost. Periods of rebound, such as in July 1988 when 70,000 new manufacturing jobs were created, were followed by losses, such as in August and September 1988, when a total of 27,000 jobs were lost. Overall, the massive job losses were viewed as permanent.

Other declining occupations included those related to factories, railroads, textiles and shoe leather, and machines in general. The need for stenographers was expected to drop 40% by the end of the century.

The fastest-growing occupations will be in the skilled labor areas, such as paralegal work, computer and electronics technicians and analysts, and medical technicians. The greatest number of jobs, however, will remain in the semi-skilled labor areas of service.

Since 1982, during the 6-year so-called "Reagan Recovery" period, some 16.8 million more new jobs were created than were lost. More than half of these were in occupations where the average pay is $22,000 or more, falling into categories as managerial, professional, craft and repair. Only 7% of the new jobs were listed in "low-pay" categories.

Critics, however, refuted this "good news," claiming that many of the new jobs carried small wages when compared to the high-paying jobs lost in the "smokestack manufacturing industries. An oft-used case-in-point was that a man who lost his job in a steel mill and now worked in a fast- food restaurant could hardly be considered better off.

A study prepared for the Joint Economic Committee of Congress in the fall of 1988 showed a $10,000-a-year gap existed between jobs in declining industries, such as steel and mining, and jobs in the growth industries, such as restaurants and health services.

The average wage for workers in declining industries was $26,193 plus $6,194 in benefits, or a total of $32,387, the study found. The average wage in the new jobs was $21,983 a year, $19,154 in wages plus $2,829 in health, pension and other benefits, including employer contributions to Social Security. Hence, the average difference was $10,404 a year.

Part of the gap was due to a difference in hourly wage rates: in 1987, for example, the average hourly wage in a retail trade job was $6.07, whereas the average wage in a

*Many skilled airplane mechanics and other aircraft technicians, now working in commercial industry, were trained while in military service.*

restaurant was $4.39 an hour.

A more significant factor was that jobs in manufacturing and other retreating industries usually offered overtime opportunities with an average work week of 40.4 hours. Jobs in the expanding areas of the economy had an average work week of only 32.7 hours, the report said.

Not all the shifts were negative. For example, the report noted that the low-paying apparel and textile industry and private household services declined sharply this decade while financial brokerage firms with high-paying jobs were expanding rapidly.

With the advancement of computers and machinery into the workplace, American businesses were revamping their personnel. In numerous manufacturing companies, lost jobs were not rank-and-file, but white-collar positions deemed superfluous. For instance, when Philip Morris Companies, Inc. took over General Foods Corp. in 1988, they set an agenda to eliminate 2,000 middle manager jobs, and consolidated a number of vice president jobs into three division president positions. Another position commonly phased out in many companies, including General Motors Corp., was that of the "production manager," who essentially stood guard on those working the line. Instead of remaining unemployed, the majority of these displaced managers applied their skills in the more lucrative fields of finance, insurance, and real estate.

The greatest problem facing workers of the 1990s is not a lack of jobs, but a lack of skills needed to do those jobs. "The questions is, do we have in place the systems, the processes, to provide those skills? And the answer is, really, no," Secretary Brock said in 1986. Faced with a huge deficit, the federal government has cut back in retraining programs. Businesses in 1986 were already spending $40 billion a year on training and retraining. However, it was already apparent that this wouldn't be enough to account for the skill shortages which were predicted to appear by 1990. In the end, the nation's educational system, particularly public schools, was being eyed with concern, as being the weakest component in the nation's economy.

## SELECTED FACTS

**Fact 1**

The number of unemployed whites declined by over 500,000 between 1975 and 1980. But the number of unemployed blacks increased by more than 200,000.

**Fact 2**

Between 1975 and 1981, the proportion of unemployed whites decreased by 15%, while the percentage of unemployed black men rose by 5%.

**Fact 3**

Unemployment of minorities is also more severe for blacks than whites in England. In 1977-1978, Asians and West Indians born in Britain suffered an 11% rate, compared

## CHART 39. FASTEST GROWING AND FASTEST SHRINKING FIELDS

**Projected trends indicate that maximum job growth will take place in services that require a high degree of skill such as in computers and data processing, health, and legal and finance. The fastest declining areas are in manufacturing, mining and certain transportation industries where the numbers of blacks working have been rising.**

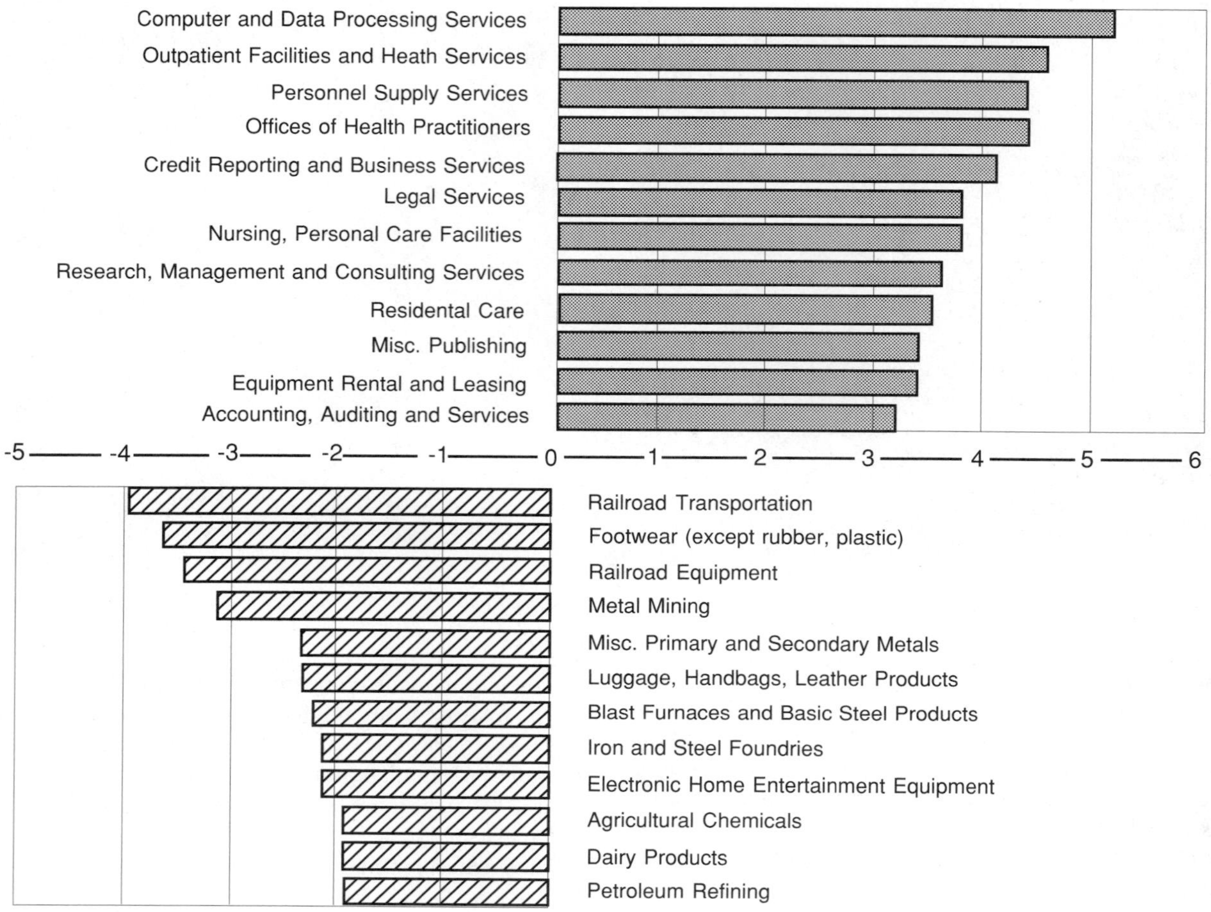


to 7% for people of white ethnic origin. Approximate unemployment figures in the United States for those years were 6% for whites, 13% for non-whites.

**Fact 4**

In 1980, 70% of unemployed blacks had never received unemployment insurance.

**Fact 5**

Blacks have a higher ratio of teenage to adult unemployment than either whites or Hispanics. The ratios in 1980: blacks 3.2, whites 2.9, Hispanics 2.6.

**Fact 6**

In recent years whites have tended more than blacks to hold extra jobs. In 1973, 5% of each group held two or more jobs, but by 1978 only 3% of blacks were multiple job holders, compared with 5% of whites.

**Fact 7**

In March 1978, according to Labor Department figures, there were 626,000 never-married white women heading families, compared with 642,000 black women. Of these, 7.1% of the whites and 22.6% of the black women were unemployed.

**Fact 8**

Black women tend to hold jobs longer than white women, by 3.6 to 2.6 median years. The median tenure of white men exceeds that of black men by 4.6 to 3.7 years. Tenure rates are about the same for men under 45 regardless of race.

**Fact 9**

Members of the black labor force are more likely than white workers to return to school after age 35. In 1978, 2.1% of blacks over 35, compared with 1.8% of whites, were attending high school, college, or trade school.

**Fact 10**

Between 1959 and 1981, the percentage of employed blacks with white-collar jobs rose from 14 to 40%, and the number of blacks in this area rose from 0.95 to 4.5 million. Conversely, the number of blacks estimated to be working on farms dropped from 2.8 to 1.4 million.

**Fact 11**

In 1979, the unemployment rate of black high school graduates no longer enrolled in school was 24%, compared with only 9.6% for whites and 9.7% for Hispanics of the same status. The rates for students enrolled in college: 23% for blacks, 13% for Hispanics, 8% for whites.

**Fact 12**

56% of black male college graduates and 72% of female college graduates are employed in public service.

**Fact 13**

Between 1975 and 1980 whites accounted for 64% of the increase in working-age population and received 75% of the new jobs. Blacks comprised 15% of the population and received 10% of the new jobs.

**Fact 14**

In 1978 blacks displayed slightly greater job stability than whites; 74% of blacks employed had been on the job a year or more, compared with 72% for whites and 66% for Hispanics.

**Fact 15**

Unemployment of black youth tends to be of longer duration than for whites or Hispanics. In 1979, 50% of all unemployed black teenagers had been out of work over five weeks compared with 40% for whites and 37% for Hispanics.

**Fact 16**

At the end of 1981, the ratio of black to white unemployment was more than 2 to 1 in every major category. The ratio for adult black men to white men was 2.06, for adult women, 2.13, and for teenagers of both sexes, 2.35 to 1. In the summer of 1981 the unemployment ratio of blacks to whites in the 16-19 age group was nearly 3 to 1.

**Fact 17**

The labor force participation rate of black women is higher than that of white women, 53 to 52 in December 1981. The reverse is true with men where the rate of whites exceeds blacks, 79 to 74%, and among teenagers of both sexes where 57% of whites but only 37% of blacks belong to the labor force.

**Fact 18**

In the fourth quarter of 1981, 30.5% of the black unemployed had been out of work 15 or more weeks, compared with 23% of the white unemployed and 19% of jobless Hispanics.

**Fact 19**

In 1979, at the senior high school level, about one-third of blacks, one-fifth of Hispanics, and one-seventh of whites were unemployed.

**Fact 20**

The percentage of black grammar school dropouts in the labor force has declined drastically since 1959, when 53% of

**CHART 40. EARNINGS DECLINE FOR MALE WORKERS.**

**A. The median earnings for full-time year-round workers, in terms of 1986 dollars, is on the decline. There has been a $3,000 decline in purchasing power between 1973 and 1986.**

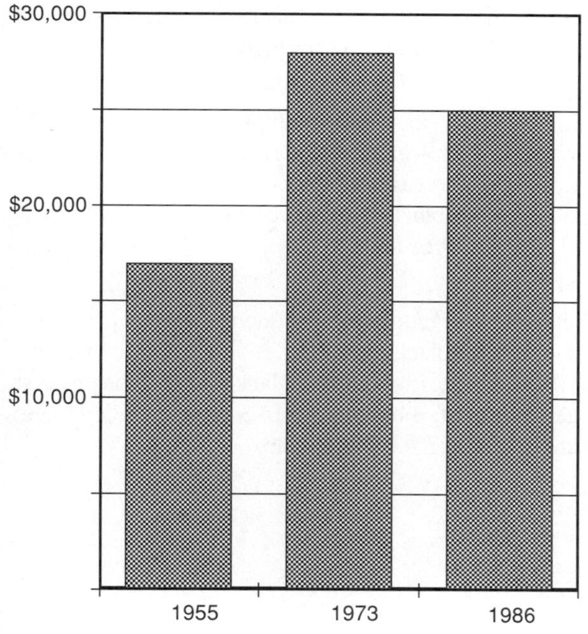


**B. For male workers at the youngest age level the average deline in earnings is greatest. The age group 25-34 also shows a marked decline. Only at the 45-54 age group is there a modest gain.**

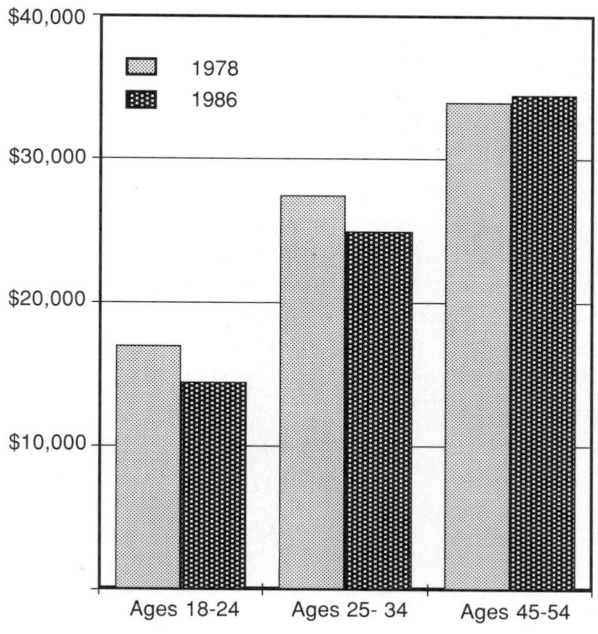

black civilian workers had completed less than eight years of school. In 1979, grammar-school dropouts comprised only 15% of the labor force.

**Fact 21**

In 1959 the median number of school years attained by whites in the labor force exceeded that of blacks by 12.2 years to 8.6. By 1979, the lead of whites was much smaller, 12.7 to 12.3. However, the proportion of college graduates remains heavily on the side of whites. In 1959, it was 10 to 4% in favor of whites; in 1979, 18 to 9%.

**Fact 22**

Black women who are college graduates have a substantially higher labor force participation rate than their white counterparts, 81 to 68%. The rates for both black and white men are about 89%.

**Fact 23**

Black unemployment generally runs higher than for any of the nation's three most populous Hispanic groups. For example, in the third quarter of 1981, the unemployment figure for blacks was 15.9, compared with 13.7 for residents of Puerto Rican origin, 9.4 for Mexicans, and 9.2 for Cubans.

**Fact 24**

Between the third quarter of 1980 and the third quarter of 1981, unemployment of blacks increased 1% while it declined more than 1% each for the three largest Hispanic groups.

**Fact 25**

Blacks comprise only about one-ninth of the labor force, but nearly one-third of discouraged workers.

**Fact 26**

Blacks experience periodic unemployment at a greater rate than whites. In 1979, only 59% of black men compared with 67% of white men worked the full year at full-time jobs. About one-fourth of all black workers, compared with only one-seventh of white workers, were unemployed during that year.

**Fact 27**

In one-parent families maintained by women, black children are less likely than white children to have mothers in the labor force by 66 to 57%.

**Fact 28**

In 1981, black children, by 59 to 53%, were more likely than white children to have mothers working or seeking work. The difference was especially pronounced in two-parent families, where 64% of black children compared with 52% of white children have mothers in the labor force. Hispanic children were less likely than white or black children to have working mothers.

**Fact 29**

In 1979, 36% of black high school graduates under age 24 were unemployed, compared with 17% Hispanics and 13% whites.

**Fact 30**

In every area of residence—central cities, suburbs, and nonmetropolitan—the participation rate, in the labor force, of men of Hispanic origin was higher than either white or black men. But in each area the participation rate for Hispanic women was lower than for white or black women.

**Fact 31**

In central cities in 1980, the labor force participation rate of black women (52.5) was higher than it was for white women (51.6). However, by 69 to 77%, the rate for black men was lower than the rate for white men.

**Fact 32**

A black worker is more likely to be represented by a union than a white worker. In 1980, blacks comprised 11.8% of the nation's work force but 14.7% of workers represented by unions. Hispanics were also represented in greater proportion, comprising 5.4% of the labor force and 6.1% of union membership.

**Fact 33**

In most industries, contract coverage for blacks exceeded that for whites. In durable goods manufacturing, for example, more than half of black workers, but less than two-fifths of white workers, were covered by union contracts.

**Fact 34**

Black women in the labor force are more likely than black men to be represented by unions. Nearly one-fifth of the nation's female union members are black, compared with only one-eighth of male workers.

**Fact 35**

Black union members tend to be younger than white union members. The median age for white male union members is 38 years, compared with 37 for blacks. The median age for women is 37.5 for whites, 37 for blacks.

**Fact 36**

Ratios of black to white unemployment rose sharply above their 25-year averages in 1981 for all age groups under 35. The sharpest increase was for women between 20 and 24, where the average black-white ratio since 1954 was 2.3 to 1. In 1981, it was 2.9 to 1.

**Fact 37**

In 1981, the average duration of unemployment for whites was 13 weeks, for blacks 16 weeks. Median duration was 8.1 weeks for blacks, 6.7 for whites. Black men had the greatest average length of joblessness, 18.3 weeks on average, compared with 14.7 for white males.

## TABLE 75. EMPLOYED CIVILIANS BY DETAILED OCCUPATION, SEX, RACE, AND HISPANIC ORIGIN

(Numbers in thousands)

| Occupation | 1987 | | | |
|---|---|---|---|---|
| | | Percent of total | | |
| | Total employed | Women | Black | Hispanic origin |
| Total, 16 years and over | 112,440 | 44.8 | 10.1 | 6.9 |
| Managerial and professional specialty | 27,742 | 44.3 | 6.2 | 3.7 |
| Executive, administrative, and managerial | 13,316 | 37.9 | 5.6 | 3.6 |
| Officials and administrators, public administration | 474 | 41.6 | 9.6 | 3.9 |
| Financial managers | 462 | 43.8 | 3.9 | 3.5 |
| Personnel and labor relations managers | 127 | 53.0 | 4.0 | 3.4 |
| Purchasing managers | 100 | 27.8 | 7.6 | 3.1 |
| Managers, marketing, advertising, public relations | 444 | 27.4 | 3.0 | 2.3 |
| Administrators, education and related fields | 516 | 48.5 | 9.9 | 3.7 |
| Managers, medicine and health | 154 | 59.9 | 6.9 | 3.1 |
| Managers, properties and real estate | 397 | 43.8 | 4.6 | 6.5 |
| Management-related occupations | 3,577 | 48.4 | 7.4 | 3.7 |
| Professional specialty | 14,426 | 50.1 | 6.7 | 3.5 |
| Architects | 135 | 12.6 | 2.2 | 7.2 |
| Engineers | 1,731 | 6.9 | 3.5 | 2.6 |
| Mathematical and computer scientists | 685 | 34.1 | 6.7 | 2.5 |
| Natural scientists | 388 | 24.1 | 2.4 | 2.7 |
| Health diagnosing occupations | 793 | 16.5 | 3.0 | 4.5 |
| Health assessment and treating occupations | 2,148 | 86.3 | 7.7 | 2.9 |
| Teachers, college and university | 661 | 37.1 | 4.6 | 3.1 |
| Teachers, except college and university | 3,587 | 73.6 | 9.4 | 3.9 |
| Counselors, educational and vocational | 191 | 59.5 | 14.0 | 5.2 |
| Librarians, archivists and curators | 219 | 81.8 | 6.8 | 2.6 |
| Social scientists and urban planners | 316 | 48.7 | 5.8 | 2.7 |
| Social, recreation, and religious workers | 980 | 46.6 | 12.5 | 5.6 |
| Lawyers and judges | 707 | 19.7 | 3.4 | 2.0 |
| Writers, artists, entertainers, and athletes | 1,858 | 45.9 | 4.7 | 3.9 |
| Technical, sales, and administrative support | 35,082 | 64.7 | 8.8 | 5.6 |
| Technicians and related support | 3,346 | 48.6 | 8.5 | 3.9 |
| Health technologists and technicians | 1,142 | 84.3 | 13.8 | 3.5 |
| Engineering and related technologists technicians | 896 | 17.1 | 4.9 | 5.4 |
| Science technicians | 204 | 31.5 | 7.5 | 3.0 |
| Technicians, except health, engineering, science | 1,104 | 40.2 | 6.0 | 3.2 |
| Sales occupations | 13,480 | 48.0 | 6.0 | 5.3 |
| Supervisors and proprietors | 3,572 | 31.8 | 4.3 | 4.4 |
| Sales representatives, finance, business services | 2,330 | 40.1 | 3.5 | 3.4 |
| Sales representatives,commodities, except retail | 1,544 | 17.1 | 2.5 | 4.2 |
| Sales workers, retail and personal services | 5,973 | 68.5 | 8.9 | 6.8 |
| Sales-related occupations | 60 | 67.8 | 2.3 | 4.0 |
| Administrative support, including clerical | 18,256 | 80.0 | 11.0 | 6.2 |
| Supervisors | 723 | 56.9 | 11.3 | 5.2 |
| Computer equipment operators | 914 | 66.0 | 14.1 | 6.2 |
| Secretaries, stenographers, and typists | 5,004 | 98.1 | 8.4 | 5.2 |
| Information clerks | 1,371 | 90.0 | 8.8 | 7.6 |

Continued...

Source: U.S. Department of Labor, Bureau of Labor Statistics

## TABLE 75. EMPLOYED CIVILIANS BY DETAILED OCCUPATION, SEX, RACE, AND HISPANIC ORIGIN (CONTINUED)

(Numbers in thousands)

| Occupation | 1987 | | | |
|---|---|---|---|---|
| | Total employed | Percent of total | | |
| | | Women | Black | Hispanic origin |
| Records processing occupations, except financial | 844 | 80.9 | 15.8 | 6.7 |
| Financial records processing | 2,469 | 90.9 | 6.0 | 4.7 |
| Duplicating, mail and other office machine operators | 69 | 64.7 | 20.3 | 5.6 |
| Communications equipment operators | 225 | 91.8 | 19.9 | 6.1 |
| Mail and message distributing occupations | 961 | 34.7 | 19.8 | 7.7 |
| Material recording, scheduling, and distributing clerks | 1,709 | 39.9 | 13.3 | 8.1 |
| Adjusters and invegtigators | 897 | 73.0 | 12.0 | 5.5 |
| Miscellaneous administrative support | 3,071 | 84.9 | 12.7 | 6.9 |
| Service occupations | 15,054 | 60.6 | 17.4 | 9.1 |
| Private household | 934 | 96.3 | 22.6 | 12.8 |
| Protective service | 1,907 | 14.2 | 16.6 | 5.8 |
| Firefighting and fire prevention | 221 | 2.0 | 7.4 | 5.3 |
| Police and detectives | 717 | 11.4 | 15.1 | 5.2 |
| Guards | 809 | 21.5 | 21.7 | 6.9 |
| Service occupations, except private household and protective service | 12,213 | 65.2 | 17.1 | 9.3 |
| Food preparation and service occupations | 5,204 | 62.4 | 12.7 | 9.1 |
| Health service occupations | 1,873 | 89.8 | 25.5 | 7.0 |
| Cleaning and building service occupations | 2,886 | 41.7 | 24.2 | 12.9 |
| Personal service occupations | 2,249 | 81.3 | 11.2 | 7.2 |
| Precision production, craft, and repair | 13,568 | 8.5 | 7.3 | 8.0 |
| Mechanics and repairers | 4,445 | 3.4 | 7.3 | 7.0 |
| Construction trades | 5,011 | 1.9 | 7.1 | 7.7 |
| Extractive occupations | 161 | 3.3 | 3.7 | 9.1 |
| Precision production occupations | 3,951 | 22.8 | 7.9 | 9.4 |
| Operators, fabricators, and laborers | 17,486 | 25.8 | 15.2 | 10.8 |
| Machine operators, assemblers, and inspectors | 7,994 | 41.2 | 14.9 | 12.5 |
| Fabricators, assemblers, and hand working occupations | 1,877 | 32.9 | 12.2 | 11.8 |
| Production inspectors, testers, samplers, and weighers | 861 | 51.0 | 14.5 | 9.3 |
| Transportation and material moving occupations | 4,712 | 8.4 | 14.8 | 7.6 |
| Motor vehicle operators | 3,489 | 10.1 | 14.8 | 7.9 |
| Transportation occupations, except motor vehicles | 194 | 1.9 | 8.1 | 3.4 |
| Material moving equipment operators | 1,029 | 3.8 | 16.1 | 7.7 |
| Handlers, equipment cleaners, helpers, and laborers | 4,779 | 17.1 | 16.0 | 11.1 |
| Helpers, construction and extractive occupations | 170 | 5.2 | 14.3 | 13.3 |
| Construction laborers | 766 | 3.2 | 16.1 | 13.9 |
| Production helpers | 71 | 21.5 | 14.5 | 20.1 |
| Freight, stock, and material handlers | 1,696 | 16 9 | 15 9 | 81 |
| Garage and service station related occupations | 257 | 7.1 | 10.5 | 8.7 |
| Vehicle washers and equipment cleaners | 214 | 15.4 | 20.0 | 12.3 |
| Hand packers and packagers | 306 | 64.8 | 13.7 | 15.7 |
| Laborers, except construction | 1,251 | 18.3 | 17.5 | 11.6 |

Continued...

Source: U.S. Department of Labor, Bureau of Labor Statistics

## TABLE 75. EMPLOYED CIVILIANS BY DETAILED OCCUPATION, SEX, RACE, AND HISPANIC ORIGIN (CONTINUED)

(Numbers in thousands)

| Occupation | 1987 | | | |
|---|---|---|---|---|
| | | Percent of total | | |
| | Total employed | Women | Black | Hispanic origin |
| Farming, forestry, and fishing | 3,507 | 15.8 | 6.5 | 13.2 |
| Farm operators and managers | 1,317 | 4.9 | 1.4 | 1.5 |
| Other agricultural and related occupations | 2,013 | 17.1 | 9.6 | 21.6 |
| Forestry and logging occupations | 104 | 5.9 | 17.1 | 2.6 |
| Fishers, hunters, and trappers | 73 | 9.1 | 1.0 | 6.3 |

Source: U.S. Department of Labor, Bureau of Labor Statistics

## TABLE 76. EMPLOYED CIVILIANS BY INDUSTRY, SEX, RACE, AND HISPANIC ORIGIN

(Numbers in thousands)

| Industry | 1987 | | | |
|---|---|---|---|---|
| | | Percent of total | | |
| | Total employed | Women | Black | Hispanic origin |
| Total, 16 years and over | 112,440 | 44.8 | 10.1 | 6.9 |
| Agriculture | 3,208 | 20.7 | 5.1 | 12.4 |
| Mining | 818 | 15.0 | 3.8 | 6.7 |
| Construction | 7,456 | 8.9 | 7.2 | 7.2 |
| Manufacturing | 20,935 | 32.8 | 10.3 | 8.2 |
| Durable goods | 12,478 | 27.0 | 8.7 | 7.3 |
| Nondurable goods | 8,456 | 41.4 | 12.6 | 9.4 |
| Transportation, communications, and other public utilities | 7,880 | 26.9 | 13.3 | 6.0 |
| Wholesale and retail trade | 23,392 | 47.4 | 8.0 | 7.1 |
| Wholesale trade | 4,580 | 28.0 | 5.8 | 7.0 |
| Durable goods | 2,525 | 26.6 | 4.8 | 5.8 |
| Nondurable goods | 2,054 | 29.6 | 6.9 | 8.5 |
| Retail trade | 18,812 | 52.2 | 8.5 | 7.2 |
| Finance, insurance, and real estate | 7,763 | 59.3 | 7.9 | 5.7 |
| Services | 35,743 | 61.6 | 11.6 | 6.2 |
| Foresty and fisheries | 192 | 20.3 | 3.5 | 5.9 |
| Public administration | 5,246 | 41.1 | 14.6 | 5.7 |

Source: U.S. Department of Labor, Bureau of Labor Statistics

## TABLE 77. EMPLOYED CIVILIANS BY OCCUPATION, RACE, AND SEX

(Percent distribution)

| Occupation and race | Total | | Men | | Women | |
|---|---|---|---|---|---|---|
| | 1986 | 1987 | 1986 | 1987 | 1986 | 1987 |
| White | | | | | | |
| Total, 16 years and over (thousands) | 95,660 | 97,789 | 53,785 | 54,647 | 41,876 | 43,142 |
| Total, percent | 100.0 | 100.0 | 100.0 | 100.0 | 100.0 | 100.0 |
| Managerial and professional specialty | 25.2 | 25.7 | 25.7 | 25.9 | 24.6 | 25.3 |
| Technical, sales, and administrative support | 31.9 | 31.6 | 20.3 | 20.2 | 46.7 | 46.1 |
| Service occupations | 12.2 | 12.2 | 8.5 | 8.5 | 17.0 | 16.8 |
| Precision production, craft, and repair | 12.6 | 12.5 | 20.7 | 20.6 | 2.3 | 2.3 |
| Operators, fabricators, and laborers | 14.7 | 14.7 | 19.8 | 19.7 | 8.2 | 8.2 |
| Farming, forestry, and fishing | 3.3 | 3.3 | 4.9 | 4.9 | 1.2 | 1.2 |
| Black | | | | | | |
| Total, 16 years and over (thousands) | 10,814 | 11,309 | 5,428 | 5,661 | 5,386 | 5,648 |
| Total, percent | 100.0 | 100.0 | 100.0 | 100.0 | 100.0 | 100.0 |
| Managerial and professional specialty | 14.7 | 15.1 | 12.8 | 13.1 | 16.7 | 17.2 |
| Technical, sales, and administrative support | 27.0 | 27.4 | 15.9 | 16.2 | 38.3 | 38.7 |
| Service occupations | 22.9 | 23.1 | 17.6 | 18.2 | 28.3 | 28.0 |
| Service, except private household & protective | 18.3 | 18.5 | 13.4 | 13.7 | 23.2 | 23.3 |
| Precision production, craft, and repair | 9.3 | 8.8 | 16.0 | 15.5 | 2.6 | 2.0 |
| Operators, fabricators, and laborers | 23.9 | 23.5 | 34.0 | 33.3 | 13.7 | 13.7 |
| Farming, forestry, and fishing | 2.1 | 2.0 | 3.7 | 3.6 | .4 | .4 |

Source: U.S. Department of Labor, Bureau of Labor Statistics

# TABLE 78. EMPLOYED CIVILIANS BY SELECTED SOCIAL AND ECONOMIC CATEGORIES, RACE, AND HISPANIC ORIGIN

(In thousands)

| Category | Total | | White | | Black | | Hispanic origin | |
|---|---|---|---|---|---|---|---|---|
| | 1986 | 1987 | 1986 | 1987 | 1986 | 1987 | 1986 | 1987 |
| **Characteristic** | | | | | | | | |
| Total (all civilian workers) | 109,597 | 112,440 | 95,660 | 97,789 | 10,814 | 11,309 | 7,219 | 7,790 |
| Men | 60,892 | 62,107 | 53,785 | 54,647 | 5,428 | 5,661 | 4,428 | 4,713 |
| Women | 48,706 | 50,334 | 41,876 | 43,142 | 5,386 | 5,648 | 2,791 | 3,077 |
| **Occupation** | | | | | | | | |
| Managerial and professional specialty | 26,554 | 27,742 | 24,134 | 25,107 | 1,594 | 1,712 | 923 | 1,018 |
| Executive, administrative, and managerial | 12,642 | 13,316 | 11,649 | 12,200 | 658 | 741 | 466 | 509 |
| Professional specialty | 13,911 | 14,426 | 12,485 | 12,907 | 936 | 972 | 457 | 509 |
| Technical, sales, and administrative support | 34,354 | 35,082 | 30,497 | 30,949 | 2,923 | 3,099 | 1,812 | 1,969 |
| Technicians and related support | 3,364 | 3,346 | 2,953 | 2,914 | 277 | 283 | 134 | 130 |
| Sales occupations | 13,245 | 13,480 | 12,168 | 12,295 | 750 | 806 | 646 | 713 |
| Administrative support, including clerical | 17,745 | 18,256 | 15,377 | 15,740 | 1,896 | 2,010 | 1,032 | 1,126 |
| Service occupations | 14,680 | 15,054 | 11,685 | 11,916 | 2,480 | 2,614 | 1,298 | 1,369 |
| Private household | 981 | 934 | 721 | 703 | 235 | 211 | 127 | 120 |
| Protective service | 1,787 | 1,907 | 1,487 | 1,558 | 268 | 316 | 99 | 111 |
| Service, except private household and protective | 11,913 | 12,213 | 9,478 | 9,655 | 1,977 | 2,087 | 1,071 | 1,139 |
| Precision production, craft, and repair | 13,405 | 13,568 | 12,083 | 12,262 | 1,009 | 996 | 1,031 | 1,083 |
| Mechanics and repairers | 4,374 | 4,445 | 3,959 | 4,028 | 318 | 324 | 302 | 312 |
| Construction trades | 4,924 | 5,011 | 4,497 | 4,582 | 349 | 354 | 366 | 387 |
| Other precision production, craft, and repair | 4,108 | 4,112 | 3,627 | 3,652 | 342 | 318 | 363 | 384 |
| Operators, fabricators, and laborers | 17,160 | 17,486 | 14,107 | 14,340 | 2,583 | 2,659 | 1,795 | 1,890 |
| Machine operators, assemblers, and inspectors | 7,911 | 7,994 | 6,462 | 6,498 | 1,167 | 1,195 | 956 | 1,001 |
| Transportation and material moving occupations | 4,564 | 4,712 | 3,847 | 3,934 | 641 | 699 | 344 | 360 |
| Handlers, equipment cleaners, helpers, and laborers | 4,685 | 4,779 | 3,798 | 3,909 | 776 | 765 | 494 | 528 |
| Construction laborers | 743 | 766 | 619 | 627 | 112 | 123 | 105 | 106 |
| Other handlers, equipment cleaners, helpers, laborers | 3,942 | 4,013 | 3,179 | 3,282 | 665 | 641 | 389 | 422 |
| Farming, forestry, and fishing | 3,444 | 3,507 | 3,154 | 3,214 | 224 | 229 | 360 | 461 |
| **Major industry and class of worker** | | | | | | | | |
| Agriculture | | | | | | | | |
| Wage and salary workers | 1,547 | 1,632 | 1,397 | 1,467 | 120 | 128 | 292 | 339 |
| Self-employed workers | 1,447 | 1,423 | 1,395 | 1,370 | 33 | 34 | 36 | 54 |
| Unpaid family workers | 169 | 153 | 165 | 149 | 2 | 2 | 2 | 5 |
| Nonagricultural industries | | | | | | | | |
| Wage and salary workers | 98,299 | 100,771 | 85,157 | 86,983 | 10,308 | 10,769 | 6,484 | 6,972 |
| Government | 16,342 | 16,800 | 13,364 | 13,662 | 2,468 | 2,590 | 862 | 961 |
| Private industries | 81,957 | 83,970 | 71,792 | 73,321 | 7,840 | 8,179 | 5,622 | 6,012 |
| Private households | 1,235 | 1,208 | 914 | 915 | 291 | 265 | 149 | 143 |
| Other industries | 80,722 | 82,762 | 70,878 | 72,407 | 7,549 | 7,915 | 5,474 | 5,869 |
| Self-employed workers | 7,881 | 8,201 | 7,311 | 7,586 | 347 | 369 | 392 | 401 |
| Unpaid family workers | 255 | 260 | 235 | 233 | 4 | 7 | 13 | 18 |
| **Full-and part-time status**[1] | | | | | | | | |
| Full-time schedules | 88,789 | 91,251 | 77,332 | 79,133 | 8,875 | 9,342 | 5,957 | 6,469 |
| Part-time for economic reasons | 5,588 | 5,402 | 4,523 | 4,378 | 904 | 861 | 568 | 579 |
| Part-time for noneconomic reasons | 15,221 | 15,788 | 13,806 | 14,278 | 1,036 | 1,106 | 694 | 742 |

[1] Employed persons "with a job but not at work" are distributed according to whether they usually work full or part time. NOTE: Detail for the above race and Hispanic-origin groups will not sum to totals because data for the "other races" group are not presented and Hispanics are included in both the white and black population groups.

Source: U.S. Department of Labor, Bureau of Labor Statistics

## TABLE 79. EMPLOYMENT STATUS OF THE CIVILIAN NONINSTITUTIONAL POPULATION IN POVERTY AND NONPOVERTY AREAS BY RACE

(Numbers in thousands)

| | Total United States | | | | Metropolitan areas | | | | Nonmetropolitan areas | | | |
|---|---|---|---|---|---|---|---|---|---|---|---|---|
| | Poverty areas | | Nonpoverty areas | | Poverty areas | | Nonpoverty areas | | Poverty areas | | Nonpoverty areas | |
| Employment status, & race | 1986 | 1987 | 1986 | 1987 | 1986 | 1987 | 1986 | 1987 | 1986 | 1987 | 1986 | 1987 |
| Total | | | | | | | | | | | | |
| Civilian noninstitutional population | 26,529 | 27,554 | 154,058 | 155,199 | 17,761 | 18,382 | 122,180 | 123,937 | 8,768 | 9,172 | 31,878 | 31,262 |
| Civilian labor force | 15,043 | 15,643 | 102,793 | 104,222 | 9,969 | 10,340 | 82,695 | 84,423 | 5,073 | 5,302 | 20,098 | 19,799 |
| Percent of population | 56.7 | 56.8 | 66.7 | 67.2 | 56.1 | 56.3 | 67.7 | 68.1 | 57.9 | 57.8 | 63.0 | 63.3 |
| Employed | 13,013 | 13,842 | 96,585 | 98,599 | 8,533 | 9,070 | 77,975 | 80,068 | 4,480 | 4,771 | 18,610 | 18,531 |
| Unemployed | 2,029 | 1,801 | 6,207 | 5,623 | 1,437 | 1,270 | 4,720 | 4,355 | 593 | 531 | 1,487 | 1,268 |
| Unemployment rate | 13.5 | 11.5 | 6.0 | 5.4 | 14.4 | 12.3 | 5.7 | 5.2 | 11.7 | 10.0 | 7.4 | 6.4 |
| Men, 20 years & over | 12.3 | 10.3 | 5.2 | 4.7 | 13.3 | 11.3 | 4.9 | 4.5 | 10.4 | 8.5 | 6.4 | 5.6 |
| Women, 20 years & over | 11.9 | 10.2 | 5.4 | 4.7 | 12.4 | 10.7 | 5.1 | 4.5 | 10.8 | 9.0 | 6.9 | 5.6 |
| Both sexes, 16 - 19 years | 32.4 | 28.6 | 16.2 | 15.1 | 35.1 | 28.7 | 15.9 | 14.5 | 26.9 | 28.4 | 17.6 | 17.4 |
| Men | 32.1 | 28.9 | 17.0 | 16.0 | 35.0 | 29.3 | 16.6 | 15.6 | 26.4 | 28.0 | 18.2 | 17.7 |
| Women | 32.7 | 28.3 | 15.5 | 14.0 | 35.2 | 28.0 | 15.1 | 13.3 | 27.4 | 28.9 | 17.0 | 17.0 |
| Not in labor force | 11,486 | 11,911 | 51,265 | 50,977 | 7,791 | 8,042 | 39,485 | 39,514 | 3,695 | 3,869 | 11,780 | 11,463 |
| White | | | | | | | | | | | | |
| Civilian noninstitutional population | 15,804 | 16,652 | 139,628 | 140,306 | 9,309 | 9,943 | 109,595 | 110,807 | 6,495 | 6,709 | 30,033 | 29,499 |
| Civilian labor force | 9,098 | 9,614 | 92,703 | 93,676 | 5,283 | 5,693 | 73,750 | 74,988 | 3,815 | 3,921 | 18,953 | 18,688 |
| Percent of population | 57.6 | 57.7 | 66.4 | 66.8 | 56.8 | 57.3 | 67.3 | 67.7 | 58.7 | 58.4 | 63.1 | 63.4 |
| Employed | 8,157 | 8,776 | 87,504 | 89,013 | 4,695 | 5,154 | 69,896 | 71,478 | 3,461 | 3,622 | 17,608 | 17,536 |
| Unemployed | 942 | 838 | 5,199 | 4,663 | 588 | 539 | 3,853 | 3,510 | 354 | 299 | 1,345 | 1,152 |
| Unemployment rate | 10.3 | 8.7 | 5.6 | 5.0 | 11.1 | 9.5 | 5.2 | 4.7 | 9.3 | 7.6 | 7.1 | 6.2 |
| Men, 20 years & over | 9.6 | 8.1 | 4.9 | 4.4 | 10.3 | 8.8 | 4.5 | 4.2 | 8.6 | 7.0 | 6.2 | 5.4 |
| Women, 20 years & over | 9.2 | 7.4 | 5.0 | 4.3 | 9.9 | 8.1 | 4.6 | 4.0 | 8.3 | 6.4 | 6.5 | 5.3 |
| Both sexes, 16 - 19 years | 23.7 | 21.4 | 14.8 | 13.7 | 25.9 | 21.9 | 14.3 | 12.9 | 20.7 | 20.6 | 16.9 | 16.8 |
| Men | 24.0 | 22.4 | 15.5 | 14.7 | 25.6 | 23.7 | 15.0 | 14.0 | 21.7 | 20.2 | 17.3 | 17.1 |
| Women | 23.4 | 20.2 | 14.2 | 12.7 | 26.2 | 19.7 | 13.6 | 11.7 | 19.6 | 21.1 | 16.5 | 16.5 |
| Not in labor force | 6,706 | 7,038 | 46,925 | 46,630 | 4,026 | 4,250 | 35,845 | 35,819 | 2,680 | 2,789 | 11,080 | 10,811 |
| Black | | | | | | | | | | | | |
| Civilian noninstitutional population | 9,760 | 9,878 | 10,229 | 10,474 | 7,783 | 7,732 | 8,837 | 9,130 | 1,977 | 2,146 | 1,392 | 1,343 |
| Civilian labor force | 5,416 | 5,468 | 7,238 | 7,525 | 4,316 | 4,264 | 6,366 | 6,662 | 1,100 | 1,204 | 873 | 863 |
| Percent of population | 55.5 | 55.4 | 70.8 | 71.8 | 55.5 | 55.2 | 72.0 | 73.0 | 55.6 | 56.1 | 62.7 | 64.2 |
| Employed | 4,397 | 4,572 | 6,418 | 6,737 | 3,504 | 3,566 | 5,652 | 5,965 | 893 | 1,006 | 765 | 772 |
| Unemployed | 1,019 | 896 | 821 | 788 | 812 | 699 | 714 | 697 | 207 | 198 | 107 | 91 |
| Unemployment rate | 18.8 | 16.4 | 11.3 | 10.5 | 18.8 | 16.4 | 11.2 | 10.5 | 18.8 | 16.4 | 12.3 | 10.5 |
| Men, 20 years & over | 17.5 | 14.9 | 9.6 | 8.4 | 18.0 | 15.6 | 9.8 | 8.4 | 15.9 | 12.4 | 8.3 | 7.7 |
| Women, 20 years & over | 15.8 | 14.3 | 9.8 | 9.7 | 15.3 | 13.9 | 9.4 | 9.6 | 17.9 | 15.5 | 13.3 | 10.6 |
| Both sexes, 16 - 19 years | 45.0 | 40.3 | 34.4 | 30.4 | 45.2 | 38.1 | 34.9 | 30.8 | 44.2 | 47.4 | 30.8 | 27.8 |
| Men | 44.2 | 40.6 | 35.2 | 30.3 | 46.2 | 38.6 | 35.5 | 30.4 | 37.4 | 46.4 | 33.5 | ([1]) |
| Women | 45.9 | 40.0 | 33.5 | 30.7 | 44.2 | 37.7 | 34.4 | 31.3 | ([1]) | 48.5 | ([1]) | ([1]) |
| Not in labor force | 4,345 | 4,410 | 2,990 | 2,949 | 3,467 | 3,468 | 2,471 | 2,468 | 877 | 942 | 520 | 480 |

[1] Data not shown where base is less than 35,000.

Source: U.S. Department of Labor, Bureau of Labor Statistics

# TABLE 80. EMPLOYED CIVILIANS BY INDUSTRY, RACE, AND OCCUPATION

(In thousands)

| Industry and race | 1987 | | | | | | | | | | | | |
|---|---|---|---|---|---|---|---|---|---|---|---|---|---|
| | | Managerial and professional specialty | | Technical, sales, and administrative support | | | Service | | | Operators, fabricators and laborers | | | |
| | Total employed | Executive, administrative, and managerial | Professional specialty | Technicians and related support | Sales | Administrative support, including clerical | Private household | Other service[1] | Precision production, craft, and repair | Machine operators, assemblers, and inspectors | Transportation and material moving | Handlers, equipment cleaners, helpers and laborers | Farming, foresty, and fishing |
| **White** | | | | | | | | | | | | | |
| Agriculture | 2,986 | 66 | 61 | 24 | 21 | 97 | - | 15 | 35 | 8 | 39 | 17 | 2,605 |
| Mining | 766 | 119 | 77 | 27 | 13 | 82 | - | 7 | 248 | 18 | 134 | 38 | 2 |
| Construction | 6,805 | 883 | 118 | 50 | 67 | 433 | - | 26 | 3,952 | 86 | 450 | 723 | 16 |
| Manufacturing | 18,107 | 2,192 | 1,538 | 625 | 671 | 2,190 | - | 286 | 3,550 | 5,401 | 650 | 942 | 63 |
| Durable goods | 10,980 | 1,349 | 1,056 | 444 | 281 | 1,269 | - | 163 | 2,509 | 3,060 | 335 | 458 | 55 |
| Nondurable goods | 7,127 | 843 | 482 | 180 | 390 | 921 | - | 123 | 1,041 | 2,340 | 315 | 483 | 7 |
| Transportation and public utilities | 6,622 | 776 | 412 | 224 | 279 | 1,733 | - | 197 | 1,116 | 95 | 1,427 | 352 | 11 |
| Wholesale and retail trade | 20,741 | 1,760 | 387 | 89 | 8,739 | 2,157 | - | 3,630 | 1,399 | 263 | 797 | 1,481 | 38 |
| Wholesale trade | 4,179 | 464 | 69 | 34 | 1,675 | 760 | - | 34 | 312 | 116 | 414 | 286 | 16 |
| Retail trade | 16,562 | 1,296 | 318 | 55 | 7,064 | 1,397 | - | 3,597 | 1,087 | 146 | 383 | 1,196 | 22 |
| Finance, insurance, and real estate | 6,932 | 1,751 | 170 | 126 | 1,755 | 2,691 | - | 220 | 123 | 13 | 8 | 19 | 56 |
| Services | 30,518 | 3,721 | 9,545 | 1,572 | 736 | 5,200 | 703 | 5,758 | 1,627 | 586 | 389 | 302 | 377 |
| Private households | 921 | 3 | 7 | 5 | 1 | 8 | 703 | 72 | 9 | 1 | 7 | 18 | 87 |
| Other service industries | 29,597 | 3,718 | 9,538 | 1,567 | 735 | 5,193 | - | 5,687 | 1,618 | 585 | 382 | 284 | 290 |
| Professional services | 19,581 | 2,041 | 8,458 | 1,278 | 120 | 3,725 | - | 3,102 | 346 | 141 | 213 | 80 | 77 |
| Public administration | 4,311 | 931 | 598 | 179 | 14 | 1,156 | - | 1,072 | 212 | 28 | 38 | 35 | 47 |
| **Black** | | | | | | | | | | | | | |
| Agriculture | 164 | 1 | 3 | 1 | - | - | - | - | 3 | 3 | 4 | 3 | 146 |
| Mining | 31 | 4 | 2 | 2 | - | 6 | - | - | 7 | - | 6 | 3 | - |
| Construction | 533 | 28 | 5 | 4 | 3 | 18 | - | 6 | 266 | 8 | 55 | 138 | 3 |
| Manufacturing | 2,154 | 63 | 54 | 35 | 25 | 230 | - | 67 | 315 | 985 | 148 | 215 | 17 |
| Durable goods | 1,088 | 34 | 37 | 19 | 7 | 112 | - | 31 | 179 | 484 | 82 | 87 | 15 |
| Nondurable goods | 1,066 | 29 | 17 | 16 | 18 | 118 | - | 35 | 136 | 501 | 66 | 129 | 2 |
| Transportation and public utilities | 1,051 | 54 | 28 | 22 | 19 | 352 | - | 59 | 125 | 19 | 261 | 110 | 2 |
| Wholesale and retail trade | 1,864 | 99 | 11 | 5 | 626 | 175 | - | 482 | 102 | 34 | 119 | 207 | 4 |
| Wholesale trade | 264 | 15 | 2 | 3 | 44 | 48 | - | 6 | 21 | 18 | 61 | 44 | 1 |
| Retail trade | 1,600 | 83 | 9 | 1 | 582 | 127 | - | 477 | 81 | 16 | 58 | 163 | 3 |
| Finance, insurance, and real estate | 611 | 95 | 11 | 6 | 69 | 338 | - | 51 | 19 | 6 | 3 | 5 | 9 |
| Services | 4,133 | 263 | 773 | 184 | 56 | 644 | 211 | 1,540 | 134 | 129 | 90 | 69 | 42 |
| Private households | 266 | - | 2 | 1 | - | 1 | 211 | 29 | 1 | - | 2 | 2 | 16 |
| Other service industries | 3,867 | 262 | 771 | 183 | 56 | 643 | - | 1,510 | 133 | 129 | 88 | 66 | 26 |
| Professional services | - | 180 | 710 | 164 | 14 | 476 | - | 978 | 40 | 32 | 60 | 15 | 11 |
| Public administration | 767 | 134 | 85 | 25 | 8 | 247 | - | 197 | 25 | 11 | 14 | 15 | 6 |

1 Includes protective service, not shown separately.

Source: U.S. Department of Labor, Bureau of Labor Statistics

## TABLE 81. EMPLOYMENT STATUS OF THE CIVILIAN NONINSTITUTIONAL POPULATION BY SEX, AGE, RACE, AND HISPANIC ORIGIN

(Numbers in thousands)

| | Total | | White | | Black | | Hispanic origin | |
|---|---|---|---|---|---|---|---|---|
| Employment status, sex, and age | 1986 | 1987 | 1986 | 1987 | 1986 | 1987 | 1986 | 1987 |
| Total | | | | | | | | |
| Civilian noninstitutional population | 180,587 | 182,753 | 155,432 | 156,958 | 19,989 | 20,352 | 12,344 | 12,867 |
| Civilian labor force | 117,834 | 119,865 | 101,801 | 103,290 | 12,654 | 12,993 | 8,076 | 8,541 |
| Percent of population | 65.3 | 65.6 | 65.5 | 65.8 | 63.3 | 63.8 | 65.4 | 66.4 |
| Employed | 109,597 | 112,440 | 95,660 | 97,789 | 10,814 | 11,309 | 7,219 | 7,790 |
| Unemployed | 8,237 | 7,425 | 6,140 | 5,501 | 1,840 | 1,684 | 857 | 751 |
| Unemployment rate | 7.0 | 6.2 | 6.0 | 5.3 | 14.5 | 13.0 | 10.6 | 8.8 |
| Not in labor force | 62,752 | 62,888 | 53,631 | 53,669 | 7,335 | 7,359 | 4,268 | 4,327 |
| Men 16 years and over | | | | | | | | |
| Civilian noninstitutional population | 85,798 | 86,899 | 74,390 | 75,189 | 8,956 | 9,128 | 6,106 | 6,371 |
| Civilian labor force | 65,422 | 66,207 | 57,217 | 57,779 | 6,373 | 6,486 | 4,948 | 5,163 |
| Percent of population | 76.3 | 76.2 | 76.9 | 76.8 | 71.2 | 71.1 | 81.0 | 81.0 |
| Employed | 60,892 | 62,107 | 53,785 | 54,647 | 5,428 | 5,661 | 4,428 | 4,713 |
| Unemployed | 4,530 | 4,101 | 3,433 | 3,132 | 946 | 826 | 520 | 451 |
| Unemployment rate | 6.9 | 6.2 | 6.0 | 5.4 | 14.8 | 12.7 | 10.5 | 8.7 |
| Not in labor force | 20,376 | 20,692 | 17,173 | 17,410 | 2,583 | 2,642 | 1,158 | 1,208 |
| Women 16 years and over | | | | | | | | |
| Civilian noninstitutional population | 94,789 | 95,853 | 81,042 | 81,769 | 11,033 | 11,224 | 6,238 | 6,496 |
| Civilian labor force | 52,413 | 53,658 | 44,584 | 45,510 | 6,281 | 6,507 | 3,128 | 3,377 |
| Percent of population | 55.3 | 56.0 | 55.0 | 55.7 | 56.9 | 58.0 | 50.1 | 52.0 |
| Employed | 48,706 | 50,334 | 41,876 | 43,142 | 5,386 | 5,648 | 2,791 | 3,077 |
| Unemployed | 3,707 | 3,324 | 2,708 | 2,369 | 894 | 858 | 337 | 300 |
| Unemployment rate | 7.1 | 6.2 | 6.1 | 5.2 | 14.2 | 13.2 | 10.8 | 8.9 |
| Not in labor force | 42,376 | 42,195 | 36,458 | 36,258 | 4,752 | 4,717 | 3,110 | 3,119 |

NOTE: Detail for the above race and Hispanic-origin groups will not sum to totals because data for the "other races" group are not presented and Hispanics are included in both the white and black population groups.

Source: U.S. Department of Labor, Bureau of Labor Statistics

## TABLE 82. EMPLOYMENT STATUS OF THE CIVILIAN NONINSTITUTIONAL POPULATION BY RACE, SEX, AND AGE, SEASONALLY ADJUSTED

(Numbers in thousands)

| Employment status, race, sex, and age | 1986 | 1987 | | | | |
|---|---|---|---|---|---|---|
| | Dec | Jan | Mar | June | Sept | Dec |
| White | | | | | | |
| Civilian noninstitutional population[1] | 156,111 | 156,313 | 156,561 | 156,930 | 157,242 | 157,552 |
| Civilian labor force | 102,474 | 102,669 | 102,836 | 103,150 | 103,357 | 103,907 |
| Percent of population | 65.6 | 65.7 | 65.7 | 65.7 | 65.7 | 66.0 |
| Employed | 96,544 | 96,749 | 97,074 | 97,698 | 98,069 | 98,779 |
| Employment-population ratio[2] | 61.8 | 61.9 | 62.0 | 62.3 | 62.4 | 62.7 |
| Unemployed | 5,930 | 5,920 | 5,762 | 5,452 | 5,288 | 5,128 |
| Unemployment rate | 5.8 | 5.8 | 5.6 | 5.3 | 5.1 | 4.9 |
| Both sexes, 16 to 19 years | | | | | | |
| Civilian labor force | 6,777 | 6,878 | 6,862 | 6,786 | 6,836 | 6,970 |
| Percent of population | 57.0 | 57.8 | 57.5 | 56.7 | 57.2 | 58.6 |
| Employed | 5,750 | 5,840 | 5,813 | 5,842 | 5,857 | 6,021 |
| Employment-population ratio[2] | 48.4 | 49.1 | 48.7 | 48.8 | 49.0 | 50.6 |
| Unemployed | 1,027 | 1,038 | 1,049 | 944 | 979 | 949 |
| Unemployment rate | 15.2 | 15.1 | 15.3 | 13.9 | 14.3 | 13.6 |
| Men | 15.8 | 16.1 | 16.8 | 14.8 | 15.1 | 14.9 |
| Women | 14.5 | 14.0 | 13.7 | 13.0 | 13.4 | 12.3 |
| Black | | | | | | |
| Civilian noninstitutional population[1] | 20,152 | 20,187 | 20,249 | 20,341 | 20,426 | 20,508 |
| Civilian labor force | 12,706 | 12,807 | 12,853 | 12,892 | 13,028 | 13,215 |
| Percent of population | 63.1 | 63.4 | 63.5 | 63.4 | 63.8 | 64.4 |
| Employed | 10,968 | 10,995 | 11,072 | 11,238 | 11,421 | 11,605 |
| Employment-population ratio[2] | 54.4 | 54.5 | 54.7 | 55.2 | 55.9 | 56.6 |
| Unemployed | 1,738 | 1,812 | 1,781 | 1,654 | 1,607 | 1,610 |
| Unemployment rate | 13.7 | 14.1 | 13.9 | 12.8 | 12.3 | 12.2 |
| Both sexes, 16 to 19 years | | | | | | |
| Civilian labor force | 849 | 850 | 864 | 856 | 929 | 948 |
| Percent of population | 39.6 | 39.6 | 40.1 | 39.5 | 42.8 | 43.7 |
| Employed | 538 | 517 | 544 | 570 | 643 | 631 |
| Employment-population ratio[2] | 25.1 | 24.1 | 25.2 | 26.3 | 29 6 | 29.1 |
| Unemployed | 311 | 333 | 320 | 286 | 286 | 317 |
| Unemployment rate | 36.6 | 39.2 | 37.0 | 33.4 | 30.8 | 33.4 |
| Men | 36 2 | 36.5 | 36.1 | 31.4 | 31.5 | 33.5 |
| Women | 37.1 | 42.3 | 38.0 | 35 4 | 30 0 | 33.4 |

[1] The population figures are not adjusted for seasonal variation.
[2] Civilian employment as a percent of the civilian noninstitutional population.

Source: U.S. Department of Labor, Bureau of Labor Statistics

# TABLE 83. EMPLOYED CIVILIANS BY SEX, AGE, RACE, AND HISPANIC ORIGIN

(In thousands)

| Sex and age | Total | | White | | Black | | Hispanic origin | |
|---|---|---|---|---|---|---|---|---|
| | 1986 | 1987 | 1986 | 1987 | 1986 | 1987 | 1986 | 1987 |
| Total, 16 years and over | 109,597 | 112,440 | 95,660 | 97,789 | 10,814 | 11,309 | 7,219 | 7,790 |
| 16 to 19 years | 6,472 | 6,640 | 5,792 | 5,898 | 536 | 587 | 430 | 474 |
| 16 to 17 years | 2,622 | 2,736 | 2,386 | 2,468 | 183 | 203 | 146 | 149 |
| 18 to 19 years | 3,850 | 3,905 | 3,406 | 3,431 | 353 | 385 | 284 | 325 |
| 20 to 24 years | 13,790 | 13,524 | 12,027 | 11,748 | 1,429 | 1,421 | 1,231 | 1,273 |
| 25 years and over | 89,335 | 92,276 | 77,841 | 80,143 | 8,849 | 9,301 | 5,558 | 6,043 |
| 25 to 54 years | 75,011 | 77,771 | 65,011 | 67,241 | 7,654 | 8,023 | 5,008 | 5,453 |
| 55 years and over | 14,324 | 14,506 | 12,830 | 12,900 | 1,196 | 1,277 | 550 | 588 |
| Men, 16 years and over | 60,892 | 62,107 | 53,785 | 54,647 | 5,428 | 5,661 | 4,428 | 4,713 |
| 16 to 19 years | 3,323 | 3,381 | 2,966 | 2,999 | 278 | 304 | 254 | 266 |
| 16 to 17 years | 1,352 | 1,393 | 1,225 | 1,252 | 96 | 109 | 82 | 81 |
| 18 to 19 years | 1,971 | 1,988 | 1,741 | 1,747 | 182 | 195 | 172 | 188 |
| 20 to 24 years | 7,250 | 7,058 | 6,340 | 6,150 | 732 | 728 | 773 | 777 |
| 25 years and over | 50,319 | 51,668 | 44,478 | 45,499 | 4,417 | 4,629 | 3,402 | 3,666 |
| 25 to 54 years | 41,912 | 43,136 | 36,853 | 37,817 | 3,799 | 3,957 | 3,053 | 3,314 |
| 55 years and over | 8,407 | 8,532 | 7,624 | 7,681 | 619 | 671 | 348 | 353 |
| Women, 16 years and over | 48,706 | 50,334 | 41,876 | 43,142 | 5,386 | 5,648 | 2,791 | 3,077 |
| 16 to 19 years | 3,149 | 3,260 | 2,825 | 2,900 | 259 | 283 | 176 | 206 |
| 16 to 17 years | 1,270 | 1,343 | 1,160 | 1,216 | 87 | 93 | 64 | 69 |
| 18 to 19 years | 1,879 | 1,917 | 1,665 | 1,684 | 171 | 190 | 112 | 137 |
| 20 to 24 years | 6,540 | 6,466 | 5,687 | 5,598 | 696 | 693 | 458 | 496 |
| 25 years and over | 39,016 | 40,609 | 33,363 | 34,644 | 4,432 | 4,672 | 2,156 | 2,376 |
| 25 to 54 years | 33,099 | 34,635 | 28,158 | 29,424 | 3,855 | 4,066 | 1,955 | 2,141 |
| 55 years and over | 5,916 | 5,974 | 5,206 | 5,219 | 577 | 606 | 202 | 235 |

NOTE: Detail for the above race and Hispanic-origin groups will not sum to totals because data for the "other races" group are not presented and Hispanics are included in both the white and black population groups.

Source: U.S. Department of Labor, Bureau of Labor Statistics

## TABLE 84. EMPLOYMENT STATUS OF THE CIVILIAN NONINSTITUTIONAL POPULATION BY AGE, SEX, AND RACE

(Numbers in thousands)

| Age, sex, and race | December 1987 | | | | | | | | | | |
|---|---|---|---|---|---|---|---|---|---|---|---|
| | Civilian noninsti-tutional popula-tion | Civilian labor force | | | | | Not in labor force | | | | |
| | | Total | Percent of popula-tion | Employed | Unemployed | | Total | Keeping house | Going to school | Unable to work | Other reasons |
| | | | | | Number | Percent of labor force | | | | | |
| **White, all** | | | | | | | | | | | |
| 16 years and over | 157,552 | 103,443 | 65.7 | 96,639 | 4,804 | 4.6 | 54,109 | 25,129 | 7,164 | 2,342 | 19,474 |
| 16 to 19 years | 11,903 | 6,587 | 55 3 | 5,761 | 826 | 12.5 | 5,316 | 340 | 4,629 | 23 | 324 |
| 20 to 24 years | 15,554 | 12,149 | 78.1 | 11,414 | 735 | 6.0 | 3,406 | 1,177 | 1,710 | 83 | 435 |
| 25 to 54 years | 85,450 | 71,206 | 83 3 | 68,370 | 2,834 | 4.0 | 14,244 | 10,385 | 799 | 800 | 2,259 |
| 55 to 64 years | 19,127 | 10,616 | 55 5 | 10,284 | 332 | 3.1 | 8,510 | 4,487 | 16 | 485 | 3,523 |
| 65 years and over | 25,519 | 2,886 | 11.3 | 2,809 | 77 | 2.7 | 22,633 | 8,741 | 11 | 949 | 12,932 |
| Men | | | | | | | | | | | |
| 16 years and over | 75,497 | 57,555 | 76.2 | 54,729 | 2,826 | 4.9 | 17,942 | 456 | 3,703 | 1,300 | 12,484 |
| 16 to 19 years | 5,993 | 3,358 | 56.0 | 2,855 | 503 | 15.0 | 2,634 | 20 | 2,421 | 13 | 180 |
| 20 to 24 years | 7,604 | 6,306 | 82.9 | 5,876 | 430 | 6.8 | 1,298 | 21 | 963 | 60 | 254 |
| 25 to 54 years | 42,268 | 39,881 | 94.4 | 38,225 | 1,655 | 4.1 | 2,387 | 151 | 312 | 545 | 1,379 |
| 55 to 64 years | 9,052 | 6,226 | 68.8 | 6,037 | 189 | 3.0 | 2,826 | 97 | 6 | 295 | 2,429 |
| 65 years and over | 10,581 | 1,784 | 16.9 | 1,735 | 49 | 2 8 | 8,796 | 168 | 1 | 385 | 8,242 |
| Women | | | | | | | | | | | |
| 16 years and over | 82,055 | 45,888 | 55.9 | 43,910 | 1,978 | 4.3 | 36,167 | 24,673 | 3,461 | 1,043 | 6,990 |
| 16 to 19 years | 5,910 | 3,229 | 54.6 | 2,906 | 323 | 10.0 | 2,682 | 319 | 2,208 | 10 | 144 |
| 20 to 24 years | 7,950 | 5,843 | 73.5 | 5,538 | 305 | 5.2 | 2,108 | 1,157 | 747 | 23 | 181 |
| 25 to 54 years | 43,182 | 31,325 | 72.5 | 30,145 | 1,179 | 3.8 | 11,857 | 10,234 | 487 | 255 | 880 |
| 55 to 64 years | 10,074 | 4,390 | 43.6 | 4,247 | 143 | 3 3 | 5,684 | 4,390 | 10 | 190 | 1,094 |
| 65 years and over | 14,938 | 1,102 | 7.4 | 1,074 | 28 | 2.5 | 13,837 | 8,573 | 9 | 564 | 4,691 |
| **Black, all** | | | | | | | | | | | |
| 16 years and over | 20,508 | 13,127 | 64.0 | 11,631 | 1,496 | 11.4 | 7,381 | 2,761 | 1,550 | 677 | 2,393 |
| 16 to 19 years | 2,169 | 860 | 39.6 | 575 | 285 | 33.2 | 1,309 | 96 | 1,123 | - | 91 |
| 20 to 24 years | 2,553 | 1,841 | 72.1 | 1,514 | 327 | 17.8 | 712 | 278 | 253 | 31 | 151 |
| 25 to 54 years | 11,305 | 9,059 | 80.1 | 8,224 | 835 | 9.2 | 2,245 | 1,243 | 172 | 266 | 565 |
| 55 to 64 years | 2,103 | 1,111 | 52.8 | 1,067 | 44 | 4.0 | 992 | 415 | 2 | 158 | 416 |
| 65 years and over | 2,378 | 256 | 10.8 | 251 | 5 | 1.8 | 2,122 | 729 | - | 222 | 1,170 |
| Men | | | | | | | | | | | |
| 16 years and over | 9,200 | 6,466 | 70.3 | 5,716 | 750 | 11.6 | 2,734 | 98 | 733 | 371 | 1,534 |
| 16 to 19 years | 1,067 | 440 | 41.2 | 285 | 154 | 35.1 | 627 | 6 | 571 | - | 51 |
| 20 to 24 years | 1,162 | 917 | 79.0 | 760 | 158 | 17.2 | 244 | 16 | 108 | 18 | 103 |
| 25 to 54 years | 5,066 | 4,415 | 87.1 | 4,011 | 404 | 9.1 | 649 | 31 | 54 | 174 | 392 |
| 55 to 64 years | 947 | 558 | 58.9 | 527 | 31 | 5.5 | 389 | 18 | - | 95 | 276 |
| 65 years and over | 958 | 134 | 14.0 | 132 | 3 | 2.1 | 823 | 27 | - | 84 | 712 |
| Women | | | | | | | | | | | |
| 16 years and over | 11,308 | 6,661 | 58.9 | 5,915 | 746 | 11.2 | 4,647 | 2,663 | 817 | 307 | 860 |
| 16 to 19 years | 1,102 | 420 | 38.1 | 289 | 131 | 31.2 | 682 | 90 | 552 | - | 40 |
| 20 to 24 years | 1,391 | 923 | 66.4 | 754 | 169 | 18.3 | 468 | 262 | 145 | 13 | 48 |
| 25 to 54 years | 6,239 | 4,644 | 74.4 | 4,213 | 431 | 9.3 | 1,596 | 1,212 | 118 | 92 | 173 |
| 55 to 64 years | 1,156 | 553 | 47.8 | 539 | 13 | 2.4 | 603 | 397 | 2 | 63 | 140 |
| 65 years and over | 1,420 | 121 | 8.5 | 119 | 2 | 1.6 | 1,299 | 702 | - | 138 | 458 |

1 Data not shown where base is less than 75,000

Source: U.S. Department of Labor, Bureau of Labor Statistics

## TABLE 85. UNEMPLOYMENT RATES OF U.S. WORKERS BY RACE, 1969 - 1988

(Percent unemployed)

| Year | Blacks | Whites | B/W ratio |
|---|---|---|---|
| 1969 | 6.4% | 3.1% | 2.1 |
| 1970 | 8.2 | 4.5 | 1.8 |
| 1971 | 9.9 | 5.4 | 1.8 |
| 1972 | 10.0 | 5.1 | 2.0 |
| 1973 | 9.6 | 4.3 | 2.2 |
| 1974 | 10.5 | 5.0 | 2.1 |
| 1975 | 14.8 | 7.8 | 1.9 |
| 1976 | 14.0 | 7.0 | 2.0 |
| 1977 | 14.0 | 6.2 | 2.3 |
| 1978 | 12.8 | 5.2 | 2.5 |
| 1979 | 12.3 | 5.1 | 2.4 |
| 1980 | 14.3 | 6.3 | 2.3 |
| 1981 | 15.6 | 6.7 | 2.3 |
| 1982 | 18.9 | 8.6 | 2.2 |
| 1983 | 19.6 | 8.4 | 2.3 |
| 1984 | 15.9 | 6.5 | 2.4 |
| 1985 | 15.1 | 6.2 | 2.4 |
| 1986 | 14.5 | 6.0 | 2.4 |
| 1987 | 13.0 | 5.3 | 2.5 |
| 1988 | 11.8 | 4.7 | 2.5 |

Source: U.S. Department of Labor, Bureau of Labor Statistics

## TABLE 86. UNEMPLOYED PERSONS BY DURATION OF UNEMPLOYMENT, RACE, AND HISPANIC ORIGIN

(Numbers in thousands)

| | Total | | White | | Black | | Hispanic origin | |
|---|---|---|---|---|---|---|---|---|
| Weeks of unemployment | 1986 | 1987 | 1986 | 1987 | 1986 | 1987 | 1986 | 1987 |
| Duration | | | | | | | | |
| Total, 16 years and over | 8,237 | 7,425 | 6,140 | 5,501 | 1,840 | 1,684 | 857 | 751 |
| Less than 5 weeks | 3,448 | 3,246 | 2,629 | 2,468 | 712 | 671 | 391 | 358 |
| 5 to 14 weeks | 2,557 | 2,196 | 1,906 | 1,621 | 574 | 509 | 264 | 215 |
| 15 weeks and over | 2,232 | 1,983 | 1,605 | 1,412 | 554 | 504 | 202 | 178 |
| 15 to 26 weeks | 1,045 | 943 | 772 | 684 | 235 | 224 | 100 | 93 |
| 27 weeks and over | 1,187 | 1,040 | 834 | 728 | 319 | 281 | 103 | 86 |
| Average (mean) duration, in weeks | 15.0 | 14.5 | 14.5 | 14.0 | 17.1 | 16.4 | 13.2 | 12.7 |
| Median duration, in weeks | 6.9 | 6.5 | 6.6 | 6.2 | 7.9 | 7.6 | 6.1 | 5.6 |
| Percent distribution | | | | | | | | |
| Total unemployed | 100.0 | 100.0 | 100.0 | 100.0 | 100.0 | 100.0 | 100.0 | 100.0 |
| Less than 5 weeks | 41.9 | 43.7 | 42.8 | 44.9 | 38.7 | 39.8 | 45.6 | 47.6 |
| 5 to 14 weeks | 31.0 | 29.6 | 31.0 | 29.5 | 31.2 | 30.2 | 30.6 | 28.6 |
| 15 weeks and over | 27.1 | 26.7 | 26.1 | 25.7 | 30.1 | 29.9 | 23.6 | 23.8 |
| 15 to 26 weeks | 12.7 | 12.7 | 12.6 | 12.4 | 12.8 | 13.3 | 11.7 | 12.4 |
| 27 weeks and over | 14.4 | 14.0 | 13.6 | 13.2 | 17.3 | 16.7 | 12.0 | 11.4 |

NOTE: Detail for the above race and Hispanic-origin groups will not sum to totals because data for the "other races" group are not presented and Hispanics are included in both the white and black populations.

Source: U.S. Department of Labor, Bureau of Labor Statistics

## TABLE 87. UNEMPLOYMENT RATES BY SEX, AGE, RACE, AND HISPANIC ORIGIN

(Civilian workers)

| Sex and age | Total | | White | | Black | | Hispanic origin | |
|---|---|---|---|---|---|---|---|---|
| | 1986 | 1987 | 1986 | 1987 | 1986 | 1987 | 1986 | 1987 |
| Total, 16 years and over | 7.0 | 6.2 | 6.0 | 5.3 | 14.5 | 13.0 | 10.6 | 8.8 |
| 16 to 19 years | 18.3 | 16.9 | 15.6 | 14.4 | 39.3 | 34.7 | 24.7 | 22.3 |
| 16 to 17 years | 20.2 | 19.1 | 17.6 | 16.7 | 43.0 | 39.7 | 28.1 | 27.7 |
| 18 to 19 years | 17.0 | 15.2 | 14.1 | 12.7 | 37.2 | 31.6 | 22.9 | 19.5 |
| 20 to 24 years | 10.7 | 9.7 | 8.7 | 8.0 | 24.1 | 21.8 | 12.9 | 10.6 |
| 25 years and over | 5.4 | 4.8 | 4.8 | 4.2 | 10.5 | 9.5 | 8.8 | 7.1 |
| 25 to 54 years | 5.7 | 5.0 | 5.0 | 4.4 | 11.1 | 10.1 | 8.8 | 7.2 |
| 55 years and over | 3.9 | 3.3 | 3.6 | 3.0 | 6.2 | 5.3 | 7.9 | 6.1 |
| Men, 16 years and over | 6.9 | 6.2 | 6.0 | 5.4 | 14.8 | 12.7 | 10.5 | 8.7 |
| 16 to 19 years | 19.0 | 17.8 | 16.3 | 15.5 | 39.3 | 34.4 | 24.5 | 22.2 |
| 16 to 17 years | 20.8 | 20.2 | 18.4 | 17.9 | 41.4 | 39.0 | 28.5 | 28.2 |
| 18 to 19 years | 17.7 | 16.0 | 14.7 | 13.7 | 38.2 | 31.6 | 22.4 | 19.3 |
| 20 to 24 years | 11.0 | 9.9 | 9.2 | 8.4 | 23.5 | 20.3 | 13.0 | 10.2 |
| 25 years and over | 5.4 | 4.8 | 4.7 | 4.2 | 10.9 | 9.4 | 8.7 | 7.2 |
| 25 to 54 years | 5.6 | 5.0 | 4.9 | 4.5 | 11.4 | 9.9 | 8.7 | 7.3 |
| 55 years and over | 4.1 | 3.5 | 3.8 | 3.2 | 7.3 | 6.3 | 8.2 | 6.8 |
| Women, 16 years and over | 7.1 | 6.2 | 6.1 | 5.2 | 14.2 | 13.2 | 10.8 | 8.9 |
| 16 to 19 years | 17.6 | 15.9 | 14.9 | 13.4 | 39.2 | 34.9 | 25.1 | 22.4 |
| 16 to 17 years | 19.6 | 18.0 | 16.7 | 15.5 | 44.6 | 40.5 | 27.6 | 27.1 |
| 18 to 19 years | 16.3 | 14.3 | 13.6 | 11.7 | 36.1 | 31.7 | 23.6 | 19.9 |
| 20 to 24 years | 10.3 | 9.4 | 8.1 | 7.4 | 24.7 | 23.3 | 12.9 | 11.4 |
| 25 years and over | 5.5 | 4.8 | 4.9 | 4.1 | 10.1 | 9.6 | 8.8 | 6.9 |
| 25 to 54 years | 5.9 | 5.1 | 5.1 | 4.3 | 10.9 | 10.3 | 9.1 | 7.2 |
| 55 years and over | 3.6 | 3.0 | 3.4 | 2.8 | 5.0 | 4.3 | 6.9 | 4.9 |

NOTE: Detail for the above race and Hispanic-origin groups will not sum to totals because data for the "other races" group are not presented and Hispanics are included in both the white and black populations.

Source: U.S. Department of Labor, Bureau of Labor Statistics

## TABLE 88. EMPLOYED CIVILIANS IN NONAGRICULTURAL INDUSTRIES BY SEX, AGE, AND RACE 1987

(In thousands)

| Sex, age, and race | Mining | Con-struction | Manufacturing: Total | Manufacturing: Durable goods | Manufacturing: Non-durable goods | Trans-portation and public utilities | Wholesale and retail trade | Finance, insurance, and real estate | Services[1] | Public admin-istration |
|---|---|---|---|---|---|---|---|---|---|---|
| **Total** | | | | | | | | | | |
| 16 years and over | 818 | 7,456 | 20,935 | 12,478 | 8,458 | 7,880 | 23,392 | 7,763 | 34,527 | 5,246 |
| 16 to 19 years | 10 | 317 | 496 | 241 | 255 | 135 | 3,418 | 220 | 1,446 | 77 |
| 20 to 24 years | 47 | 1,008 | 2,158 | 1,224 | 934 | 678 | 3,932 | 1,063 | 3,782 | 350 |
| 25 to 54 years | 678 | 5,323 | 15,600 | 9,412 | 6,189 | 6,140 | 13,438 | 5,483 | 24,670 | 4,103 |
| 55 years and over | 83 | 809 | 2,681 | 1,601 | 1,080 | 926 | 2,606 | 1,017 | 4,629 | 717 |
| **White** | | | | | | | | | | |
| Men | | | | | | | | | | |
| 16 years and over | 660 | 6,183 | 12,338 | 8,072 | 4,285 | 4,882 | 10,872 | 2,856 | 11,739 | 2,614 |
| 16 to 19 years | 7 | 274 | 282 | 153 | 129 | 77 | 1,473 | 54 | 539 | 27 |
| 20 to 24 years | 36 | 854 | 1,223 | 775 | 448 | 378 | 1,709 | 257 | 1,227 | 139 |
| 25 to 54 years | 545 | 4,385 | 9,150 | 6,051 | 3,109 | 3,795 | 6,425 | 2,015 | 8,097 | 2,072 |
| 55 years and over | 72 | 670 | 1,673 | 1,092 | 581 | 632 | 1,265 | 531 | 1,875 | 376 |
| Women | | | | | | | | | | |
| 16 years and over | 106 | 622 | 5,770 | 2,908 | 2,862 | 1,741 | 9,869 | 4,077 | 17,858 | 1,697 |
| 16 to 19 years | 1 | 25 | 152 | 65 | 87 | 41 | 1,551 | 147 | 715 | 34 |
| 20 to 24 years | 6 | 72 | 662 | 317 | 345 | 191 | 1,704 | 677 | 2,012 | 132 |
| 25 to 54 years | 90 | 459 | 4,218 | 2,164 | 2,055 | 1,341 | 5,492 | 2,822 | 12,972 | 1,282 |
| 55 years and over | 9 | 66 | 736 | 361 | 375 | 167 | 1,121 | 431 | 2,158 | 249 |
| **Black** | | | | | | | | | | |
| Men | | | | | | | | | | |
| 16 years and over | 22 | 504 | 1,320 | 758 | 562 | 734 | 985 | 219 | 1,333 | 372 |
| 16 to 19 years | - | 12 | 34 | 13 | 21 | 11 | 150 | 4 | 76 | 4 |
| 20 to 24 years | 2 | 61 | 123 | 65 | 58 | 64 | 212 | 32 | 178 | 33 |
| 25 to 54 years | 19 | 366 | 1,014 | 584 | 430 | 566 | 536 | 158 | 911 | 292 |
| 55 years and over | 2 | 65 | 148 | 96 | 52 | 93 | 88 | 26 | 169 | 42 |
| Women | | | | | | | | | | |
| 16 years and over | 9 | 30 | 834 | 330 | 504 | 317 | 879 | 392 | 2,534 | 395 |
| 16 to 19 years | 1 | 2 | 17 | 4 | 12 | 3 | 160 | 12 | 73 | 9 |
| 20 to 24 years | - | 4 | 84 | 30 | 54 | 33 | 203 | 69 | 254 | 35 |
| 25 to 54 years | 8 | 23 | 677 | 273 | 404 | 262 | 458 | 297 | 1,880 | 321 |
| 55 years and over | - | 1 | 56 | 22 | 34 | 19 | 58 | 15 | 326 | 29 |

1 Excludes private households.

Source: U.S. Department of Labor, Bureau of Labor Statistics

## TABLE 89. WORK-SEEKING INTENTIONS OF PERSONS NOT IN THE LABOR FORCE AND WORK HISTORY OF THOSE WHO INTEND TO SEEK WORK WITHIN THE NEXT 12 MONTHS BY SEX, AGE, AND RACE

(In thousands)

| Work-seeking intentions, work history, and sex | Total | | Age | | | | | | Race | | | |
|---|---|---|---|---|---|---|---|---|---|---|---|---|
| | | | 16 to 24 years | | 25 to 59 years | | 60 years and over | | White | | Black | |
| | 1986 | 1987 | 1986 | 1987 | 1986 | 1987 | 1986 | 1987 | 1986 | 1987 | 1986 | 1987 |
| Total | | | | | | | | | | | | |
| Do not intend to seek work | 52,691 | 53,095 | 5,798 | 5,842 | 16,727 | 16,757 | 30,165 | 30,496 | 45,778 | 45,937 | 5,509 | 5,583 |
| Intend to seek work in the next 12 months | 10,216 | 9,850 | 5,403 | 5,301 | 4,167 | 3,927 | 646 | 623 | 7,889 | 7,809 | 1,940 | 1,743 |
| Never worked | 1,696 | 1,657 | 1,548 | 1,476 | 145 | 178 | 1 | 2 | 1,113 | 1,136 | 487 | 452 |
| Last worked over 5 yrs ago | 1,295 | 1,174 | 60 | 45 | 1,047 | 932 | 188 | 199 | 913 | 902 | 339 | 239 |
| Last worked 1 to 5 yrs ago | 2,157 | 1,979 | 628 | 562 | 1,291 | 1,223 | 237 | 195 | 1,654 | 1,545 | 410 | 364 |
| Worked during previous 12 months | 5,069 | 5,040 | 3,166 | 3,218 | 1,684 | 1595 | 219 | 227 | 4,207 | 4,227 | 705 | 688 |
| Men | | | | | | | | | | | | |
| Do not intend to seek work | 16,806 | 17,155 | 2,330 | 2,385 | 2,911 | 3,112 | 11,565 | 11,657 | 14,357 | 14,604 | 2,007 | 2,048 |
| Intend to seek work in the next 12 months | 3,966 | 3,975 | 2,555 | 2,606 | 1,102 | 1,050 | 309 | 319 | 3,109 | 3,178 | 673 | 660 |
| Never worked | 750 | 736 | 736 | 710 | 15 | 27 | - | - | 505 | 523 | 201 | 180 |
| Last worked over 5 yrs ago | 252 | 276 | 12 | 9 | 190 | 172 | 50 | 94 | 173 | 185 | 58 | 80 |
| Last worked 1 to 5 yrs ago | 698 | 625 | 105 | 182 | 379 | 343 | 4 | 101 | 533 | 482 | 126 | 110 |
| Worked during previous 12 months | 2,266 | 2,338 | 1,609 | 1,705 | 520 | 509 | 137 | 124 | 1,897 | 1,989 | 289 | 289 |
| Women | | | | | | | | | | | | |
| Do not intend to seek work | 35,884 | 35,941 | 3,469 | 3,457 | 13,816 | 13,645 | 18,600 | 18,837 | 31,421 | 31,333 | 3,502 | 3,535 |
| intend to seek work in the next 12 months | 6,251 | 5,875 | 2,849 | 2,696 | 3,064 | 2,876 | 338 | 304 | 4,780 | 4,631 | 1,267 | 1,083 |
| Never worked | 946 | 920 | 813 | 766 | 131 | 151 | 1 | 2 | 608 | 613 | 286 | 272 |
| Last worked over 5 yrs ago | 1,043 | 899 | 49 | 36 | 856 | 760 | 138 | 103 | 740 | 717 | 281 | 159 |
| Last worked 1 to 5 yrs ago | 1,459 | 1,354 | 430 | 382 | 914 | 879 | 115 | 94 | 1,121 | 1,063 | 284 | 254 |
| Worked during previous 12 months | 2,803 | 2,702 | 1,557 | 1,512 | 1,163 | 1,086 | 83 | 104 | 2,310 | 2,238 | 416 | 398 |

Source: U.S. Department of Labor, Bureau of Labor Statistics

## TABLE 90. UNEMPLOYMENT IN FAMILIES BY TYPE OF FAMILY, RACE, HISPANIC ORIGIN, AND PRESENCE OF EMPLOYED FAMILY MEMBERS

(Numbers in thousands)

| Type of family, and race | 1986 | | | | | 1987 | | | | |
|---|---|---|---|---|---|---|---|---|---|---|
| | | With unemployment | | | | | With unemployment | | | |
| | | | Percent of families | | | | | Percent of families | | |
| | Total families | Total | With no employed person in family | With at least one employed person in family | With at least one person in family employed full time | Total families | Total | With no employed person in family | With at least one employed person in family | With at least one person in family employed full-time |
| **Total** | | | | | | | | | | |
| Total families | 63,518 | 5,780 | 30.0 | 70.0 | 60.1 | 64,178 | 4,970 | 29.0 | 71.0 | 62.4 |
| With children under 18 | 31,608 | 3,441 | 32.1 | 67.9 | 57.7 | 31,504 | 3,030 | 31.7 | 68.3 | 60.0 |
| Married-couple families | 50,625 | 4,014 | 20.7 | 79.3 | 69.1 | 50,833 | 3,449 | 19.2 | 80.8 | 72.2 |
| With children under 18 | 24,246 | 2,426 | 19.6 | 80.4 | 70.0 | 24,069 | 2,128 | 18.5 | 81.5 | 72.7 |
| Families maintained by women | 10,450 | 1,450 | 53.0 | 47.0 | 37.7 | 10,703 | 1,239 | 54.2 | 45.8 | 36.6 |
| With children under 18 | 6,412 | 896 | 62.9 | 37.1 | 27.3 | 6,446 | 790 | 63.9 | 36.1 | 28.7 |
| Families maintained by men | 2,444 | 316 | 43.0 | 57.0 | 47.8 | 2,642 | 282 | 38.3 | 61.7 | 54.6 |
| With children under 18 | 950 | 119 | 55.5 | 44.5 | 36.1 | 989 | 112 | 55.4 | 44.6 | 40.2 |
| **White** | | | | | | | | | | |
| Total families | 54,832 | 4,405 | 27.2 | 72.8 | 62.5 | 55,299 | 3,722 | 25.8 | 74.2 | 65.3 |
| With children under 18 | 26,469 | 2,594 | 27.9 | 72.1 | 61.3 | 26,350 | 2,229 | 27.3 | 72.7 | 63.9 |
| Married-couple families | 45,740 | 3,351 | 20.8 | 79.2 | 68.8 | 45,817 | 2,852 | 19.3 | 80.7 | 72.0 |
| With children under 18 | 21,502 | 2,002 | 19.4 | 80.6 | 69.8 | 21,327 | 1,741 | 18.3 | 81.7 | 72.8 |
| Families maintained by women | 7,182 | 829 | 49.2 | 50.8 | 40.3 | 7,402 | 674 | 49.0 | 51.0 | 40.8 |
| With children under 18 | 4,212 | 499 | 57.3 | 42.7 | 31.3 | 4,242 | 403 | 59.0 | 41.0 | 31.6 |
| Families maintained by men | 1,910 | 224 | 40.9 | 59.1 | 50.2 | 2,080 | 196 | 40.3 | 59.7 | 52.6 |
| With children under 18 | 755 | 93 | 52.7 | 47.3 | 38.7 | 781 | 85 | 61.2 | 38.8 | 35.3 |
| **Black** | | | | | | | | | | |
| Total families | 6,975 | 1,206 | 41.1 | 58.9 | 50.2 | 7,082 | 1,078 | 40.9 | 59.1 | 51.4 |
| With children under 18 | 4,103 | 738 | 47.5 | 52.5 | 44.8 | 4,124 | 688 | 46.7 | 53.3 | 46.9 |
| Married-couple families | 3,547 | 534 | 20.0 | 80.0 | 70.4 | 3,592 | 468 | 19.0 | 81.0 | 72.6 |
| With children under 18 | 1,908 | 335 | 19.8 | 80.2 | 71.3 | 1,901 | 301 | 18.9 | 81.1 | 72.4 |
| Families maintained by women | 2,983 | 589 | 59.1 | 40.9 | 33.4 | 3,039 | 533 | 61.4 | 38.6 | 31.5 |
| With children under 18 | 2,029 | 378 | 70.9 | 29.1 | 22.2 | 2,051 | 367 | 70.5 | 29.5 | 25.4 |
| Families maintained by men | 445 | 83 | 50.0 | 50.0 | 39.3 | 451 | 77 | 31.6 | 68.4 | 60.5 |
| With children under 18 | 166 | 26 | ([1]) | ([1]) | ([1]) | 172 | 20 | ([1]) | ([1]) | ([1]) |

1 Data not shown where base is less than 60,000.

Source: U.S. Department of Labor, Bureau of Labor Statistics

## TABLE 91. PERSONS NOT IN THE LABOR FORCE BY REASON, RACE, AGE, AND SEX

(In thousands)

| | Total | | Age | | | | | | Sex | | | |
|---|---|---|---|---|---|---|---|---|---|---|---|---|
| | | | 16 to 24 years | | 25 to 59 years | | 60 years and over | | Men | | Women | |
| Reason and race | 1986 | 1987 | 1986 | 1987 | 1986 | 1987 | 1986 | 1987 | 1986 | 1987 | 1986 | 1987 |
| White | | | | | | | | | | | | |
| Total not in labor force | 53,631 | 53,669 | 8,194 | 8,089 | 17,952 | 17,669 | 27,485 | 27,910 | 17,173 | 17,410 | 36,458 | 36,258 |
| Do not want a job now | 49,369 | 49,455 | 6,681 | 6,636 | 15,703 | 15,422 | 26,986 | 27,399 | 15,705 | 15,931 | 33,664 | 33,524 |
| Current activity: | | | | | | | | | | | | |
| Going to school | 4,886 | 4,923 | 4,287 | 4,302 | 584 | 609 | 17 | 13 | 2,486 | 2,503 | 2,400 | 2,420 |
| Ill, disabled | 3,288 | 3,386 | 110 | 116 | 1,556 | 1,642 | 1,623 | 1,630 | 1,759 | 1,750 | 1,529 | 1,636 |
| Keeping house | 23,475 | 22,862 | 1,364 | 1,268 | 11,119 | 10,781 | 10,990 | 10,813 | 303 | 357 | 23,172 | 22,505 |
| Retired | 14,043 | 14,629 | - | - | 352 | 374 | 13,691 | 14,257 | 9,192 | 9,363 | 4,851 | 5,266 |
| Other activity | 3,677 | 3,655 | 920 | 950 | 2,092 | 2,016 | 665 | 686 | 1,965 | 1,958 | 1,712 | 1,697 |
| Want a job now | 4,262 | 4,213 | 1,513 | 1,451 | 2,250 | 2,248 | 501 | 511 | 1,468 | 1,479 | 2,794 | 2,734 |
| Reason for not looking: | | | | | | | | | | | | |
| School attendance | 986 | 1,016 | 820 | 805 | 162 | 206 | 4 | 5 | 503 | 518 | 483 | 498 |
| Ill health, disability | 602 | 649 | 57 | 53 | 405 | 450 | 139 | 145 | 310 | 340 | 292 | 309 |
| Home responsibilities | 977 | 932 | 231 | 207 | 713 | 682 | 34 | 43 | - | - | 977 | 932 |
| Think cannot get a job | 770 | 693 | 166 | 162 | 450 | 389 | 154 | 140 | 300 | 279 | 470 | 414 |
| Other reasons[1] | 927 | 923 | 239 | 224 | 520 | 521 | 170 | 178 | 355 | 342 | 572 | 581 |
| Black | | | | | | | | | | | | |
| Total not in labor force | 7,335 | 7,359 | 1,998 | 2,025 | 2,662 | 2,643 | 2,676 | 2,691 | 2,583 | 2,641 | 4,752 | 4,717 |
| Do not want a job now | 5,982 | 6,075 | 1,416 | 1,491 | 1,978 | 1,987 | 2,588 | 2,597 | 2,158 | 2,210 | 3,824 | 3,865 |
| Current activity: | | | | | | | | | | | | |
| Going to school | 1,006 | 1,035 | 902 | 920 | 102 | 115 | 2 | - | 489 | 496 | 517 | 540 |
| Ill, disabled | 694 | 814 | 23 | 39 | 354 | 425 | 315 | 350 | 342 | 395 | 353 | 419 |
| Keeping house | 2,228 | 2,161 | 230 | 251 | 1,071 | 1,025 | 927 | 885 | 70 | 77 | 2,158 | 2,084 |
| Retired | 1,305 | 1,344 | - | - | 25 | 27 | 1,281 | 1,317 | 813 | 822 | 492 | 521 |
| Other activity | 748 | 721 | 261 | 281 | 426 | 395 | 63 | 45 | 444 | 420 | 304 | 301 |
| Want a job now | 1,353 | 1,284 | 580 | 535 | 686 | 657 | 88 | 94 | 424 | 431 | 929 | 852 |
| Reason for not looking: | | | | | | | | | | | | |
| School attendance | 374 | 333 | 313 | 277 | 59 | 56 | 1 | - | 166 | 159 | 208 | 174 |
| Ill health, disability | 216 | 188 | 24 | 18 | 153 | 132 | 40 | 37 | 84 | 72 | 132 | 116 |
| Home responsibilities | 284 | 295 | 85 | 99 | 194 | 192 | 5 | 5 | - | - | 284 | 295 |
| Think cannot get a job | 297 | 294 | 100 | 90 | 172 | 173 | 25 | 32 | 112 | 127 | 185 | 167 |
| Other reasons[1] | 182 | 174 | 58 | 51 | 108 | 104 | 17 | 20 | 62 | 73 | 120 | 100 |

[1] Includes small number of men not looking for work because of "home responsibilities."

Source: U.S. Department of Labor, Bureau of Labor Statistics

## TABLE 92. EMPLOYMENT STATUS OT MALE VIETNAM-ERA VETERANS AND NONVETERANS BY AGE, RACE, AND HISPANIC ORIGIN

(Numbers in thousands)

| | Veterans | | | | | | Nonveterans | | | | | |
|---|---|---|---|---|---|---|---|---|---|---|---|---|
| | White | | Black | | Hispanic origin | | White | | Black | | Hispanic origin | |
| Employment status and age | 1986 | 1987 | 1986 | 1987 | 1986 | 1987 | 1986 | 1987 | 1986 | 1987 | 1986 | 1987 |
| Total 30 to 44 years | | | | | | | | | | | | |
| Civilian noninstitutional population | 5,616 | 5,406 | 609 | 588 | 265 | 253 | 16,163 | 17,053 | 1,893 | 2,006 | 1,640 | 1,812 |
| Civilian labor force | 5,402 | 5,168 | 573 | 529 | 243 | 239 | 15,464 | 16,298 | 1,663 | 1,768 | 1,528 | 1,691 |
| Employed | 5,156 | 4,944 | 522 | 479 | 224 | 221 | 14,739 | 15,701 | 1,472 | 1,612 | 1,389 | 1,582 |
| Unemployed | 246 | 223 | 51 | 50 | 19 | 19 | 725 | 596 | 191 | 156 | 139 | 109 |
| Unemployment rate | 4.5 | 4.3 | 9.0 | 9.4 | 7.6 | 7.9 | 4.7 | 3.7 | 11.5 | 8.8 | 9.1 | 6.4 |
| 30 to 34 years | | | | | | | | | | | | |
| Civilian noninstitutional population | 910 | 676 | 129 | 133 | 56 | 59 | 7,451 | 7,770 | 892 | 895 | 755 | 804 |
| Civilian labor force | 872 | 646 | 122 | 121 | 51 | 58 | 7,149 | 7,460 | 785 | 800 | 698 | 764 |
| Employed | 808 | 594 | 107 | 100 | 47 | 50 | 6,800 | 7,166 | 697 | 714 | 628 | 715 |
| Unemployed | 64 | 51 | 15 | 21 | 4 | 8 | 349 | 295 | 88 | 86 | 70 | 48 |
| Unemployment rate | 7.3 | 8.0 | 12.1 | 17.1 | ([1]) | ([1]) | 4.9 | 4.0 | 112 | 10.7 | 10.0 | 6.3 |
| 30 to 39 years | | | | | | | | | | | | |
| Civilian noninstitutiona populationl | 2,556 | 2,152 | 299 | 240 | 123 | 91 | 5,081 | 5,485 | 567 | 659 | 480 | 548 |
| Civilian labor force | 2,464 | 2,061 | 283 | 215 | 111 | 86 | 4,855 | 5,229 | 503 | 588 | 448 | 498 |
| Employed | 2,355 | 1,984 | 255 | 198 | 101 | 80 | 4,640 | 5,055 | 427 | 546 | 405 | 466 |
| Unemployed | 108 | 77 | 28 | 17 | 10 | 7 | 215 | 173 | 76 | 42 | 43 | 33 |
| Unemployment rate | 4.4 | 3.7 | 9.9 | 7.8 | 9.4 | 7.9 | 4.4 | 3.3 | 15.1 | 7.2 | 9.6 | 6.6 |
| 40 to 44 years | | | | | | | | | | | | |
| Civilian noninstitutional population | 2,150 | 2,577 | 181 | 216 | 86 | 102 | 3,632 | 3,798 | 434 | 452 | 405 | 460 |
| Civilian labor force | 2,066 | 2,461 | 169 | 193 | 81 | 95 | 3,461 | 3,609 | 375 | 379 | 382 | 429 |
| Employed | 1,993 | 2,366 | 160 | 180 | 77 | 91 | 3,300 | 3,481 | 348 | 352 | 355 | 401 |
| Unemployed | 73 | 95 | 9 | 12 | 4 | 4 | 161 | 128 | 27 | 28 | 26 | 28 |
| Unemployment rate | 3.5 | 3.9 | 5.1 | 6.5 | 4.6 | 4.6 | 4.7 | 3.5 | 7.1 | 7.3 | 6.9 | 6.5 |

[1] Data not shown where base is less than 60,000.

NOTE: Male Vietnam-era veterans are those who served in the Armed Forces between August 5, 1964 and May 7, 1975. Nonveterans are men who never served in the Armed Forces; published data are limited to those 30 to 44 years of age the group that most closely corresponds to the bulk of the Vietnam-era veteran population Detail for the above race and Hispanic-origin groups will not sum to totals because data for the "other races" group are not presented and Hispanics are included in both the white and black population groups.

Source: U.S. Department of Labor, Bureau of Labor Statistics

## TABLE 93. PERSONS AT WORK IN NONFARM OCCUPATIONS BY SEX AND FULL- OR PART-TIME STATUS

(Numbers in thousands)

| | December 1987 | | | | | | | | |
|---|---|---|---|---|---|---|---|---|---|
| | | | | On full-time schedules | | | | | |
| Occupation and sex | Total at work | On part time for economic reasons | On voluntary part time | Total | 40 hours or less | 41 to 48 hours | 49 hours or more | Aver. hours total at work | Aver. hours, workers on full-time schedules |
| Total, 16 years and over[1] | 107,049 | 4,900 | 15,242 | 86,908 | 55,117 | 11,571 | 20,219 | 39.3 | 43.7 |
| Managerial and professional specialty | 27,739 | 503 | 2,579 | 24,657 | 13,493 | 3,163 | 8,002 | 42.5 | 45.3 |
| Technical, sales, and administrative support | 34,873 | 1,195 | 6,328 | 27,350 | 18,613 | 3,346 | 5,392 | 37.9 | 42.8 |
| Service occupations | 14,720 | 1,526 | 4,272 | 8,922 | 6,346 | 1,009 | 1,567 | 33.5 | 42.7 |
| Precision production, craft, and repair | 12,909 | 581 | 438 | 11,890 | 7,475 | 1,874 | 2,542 | 41.8 | 43.5 |
| Operators, fabricators, and laborers | 16,808 | 1,095 | 1,625 | 14,088 | 9,191 | 2,181 | 2,717 | 39.8 | 43.5 |
| Men, 16 years and over[1] | 57,816 | 2,160 | 4,525 | 51,131 | 28,846 | 7,260 | 15,026 | 42.3 | 45.2 |
| Managerial and professional specialty | 15,426 | 226 | 736 | 14,463 | 6,786 | 1,846 | 5,831 | 45.4 | 47.2 |
| Technical, sales, and administrative support | 12,350 | 270 | 1,160 | 10,919 | 5,826 | 1,546 | 3,547 | 42.6 | 45.6 |
| Service occupations | 5,886 | 420 | 1,230 | 4,236 | 2,806 | 517 | 913 | 36.8 | 43.9 |
| Precision production, craft, and repair | 11,818 | 526 | 322 | 10,970 | 6,830 | 1,731 | 2,409 | 42.1 | 43.6 |
| Operators, fabricators, and laborers | 12,337 | 718 | 1,076 | 10,543 | 6,597 | 1,619 | 2 326 | 40.7 | 44.1 |
| Women, 16 years and over[1] | 49,233 | 2,739 | 10,717 | 35,777 | 26,271 | 4,312 | 5,193 | 35.8 | 41.6 |
| Managerial and professional specialty | 12,313 | 276 | 1,842 | 10,194 | 6,707 | 1,317 | 2,170 | 38.8 | 42.7 |
| Technical, sales, and administrative support | 22,524 | 925 | 5,168 | 16,431 | 12,787 | 1,799 | 1,845 | 35.4 | 40.9 |
| Service occupations | 8,834 | 1,106 | 3,042 | 4,686 | 3,539 | 492 | 654 | 31.3 | 41.5 |
| Precision production, craft, and repair | 1,091 | 56 | 115 | 920 | 645 | 143 | 133 | 38.9 | 42.2 |
| Operators, fabricators, and laborers | 4,471 | 377 | 550 | 3,545 | 2,593 | 561 | 391 | 37.5 | 41.6 |

[1] Excludes farming, forestry, and fishing occupations

Source: U.S. Department of Labor, Bureau of Labor Statistics

## TABLE 94. CIVILIAN LABOR FORCE AND UNEMPLOYMENT RATES OF PERSONS 25 TO 64 YEARS OLD BY EDUCATIONAL ATTAINMENT AND RACE, MARCH OF 1973, 1979, AND 1985

| Educational attainment | 1973[1] | 1979 | 1985 |
|---|---|---|---|
| **Civilian labor force** | | | |
| Black | | | |
| Total: Number (thousands) | 7,224 | 7,327 | 9,157 |
| Total: Percent | 100.0 | 100.0 | 100.0 |
| Less than 4 years high school. | 48.0 | 37.1 | 26.2 |
| High school: 4 years only | 31.8 | 36.6 | 39.5 |
| College: 1 to 3 years | 9.5 | 15.2 | 19.2 |
| 4 years or more | 10.6 | 11.0 | 15.0 |
| White | | | |
| Total: Number (thousands) | 57,177 | 65,853 | 76,739 |
| Total: Percent | 100.0 | 100.0 | 100.0 |
| Less than 4 years high school. | 28.8 | 20.2 | 14.7 |
| High school: 4 years only | 40.7 | 40.2 | 40.7 |
| College: 1 to 3 years | 13.4 | 17.4 | 19.1 |
| 4 years or more | 17.0 | 22.2 | 25.6 |
| **Unemployment rates** | | | |
| Black | | | |
| Total: Percent | 5.5 | 8.2 | 12.0 |
| Less than 4 years high school. | 6.3 | 9.9 | 15.3 |
| High school: 4 years only | 5.9 | 8.7 | 13.0 |
| College: 1 to 3 years | 4.2 | 6.2 | 10.6 |
| 4 years or more | 2.2 | 3.7 | 5.4 |
| White | | | |
| Total: Percent | 3.3 | 3.8 | 5.3 |
| Less than 4 years high school. | 5.2 | 6.4 | 10.5 |
| High school: 4 years only | 3.0 | 3.8 | 6.1 |
| College: 1 to 3 years | 2.7 | 3.0 | 3.9 |
| 4 years or more | 1.7 | 1.9 | 2.1 |

[1] Data are for black and other minority races.

Source: U.S. Department of Labor, Bureau of Labor Statistics

## TABLE 95. INCIDENCE OF POVERTY AMONG PERSONS WITH UNEMPLOYMENT, INVOLUNTARY PART-TIME WORK, AND LOW EARNINGS BY RACE, 1979-84

| Race and year | With unemployment | | With involuntary part time employment | | Low earners | |
|---|---|---|---|---|---|---|
| | Number | Percent in families below the poverty level | Number | Percent in families below the poverty level | Number | Percent in families below the poverty level |
| Black | | | | | | |
| 1979 | 2,880 | 31.3 | 1,533 | 29.1 | 678 | 32.6 |
| 1980 | 3,352 | 35.0 | 1,841 | 30.1 | 702 | 30.9 |
| 1981 | 3,703 | 36.2 | 2,081 | 31.1 | 669 | 31.5 |
| 1982 | 4,096 | 38.6 | 2,180 | 31.9 | 474 | 32.5 |
| 1983 | 3,640 | 43.7 | 2,046 | 36.0 | 464 | 32.7 |
| 1984 | 3,473 | 40.0 | 2,016 | 32.5 | 450 | 37.2 |
| White | | | | | | |
| 1979 | 15,168 | 11.0 | 9,693 | 10.8 | 4,140 | 20.6 |
| 1980 | 17,506 | 14.0 | 10,866 | 12.8 | 4,330 | 23.1 |
| 1981 | 19,140 | 15.7 | 12,223 | 14.2 | 4,443 | 25.8 |
| 1982 | 21,730 | 17.1 | 13,555 | 15.8 | 4,008 | 29.6 |
| 1983 | 19,549 | 19.0 | 12,530 | 16.5 | 3,859 | 29.9 |
| 1984 | 17,461 | 18.1 | 12,077 | 15.0 | 3,886 | 30.5 |

Source: U.S. Department of Labor, Bureau of Labor Statistics

## TABLE 96. PERCENT OF EMPLOYED PERSONS WHO WORK PART TIME FOR ECONOMIC REASONS BY AGE, SEX AND RACE, 1985 ANNUAL AVERAGES

| Age and sex | Black | White |
|---|---|---|
| Total, 16 years and over | 8.7 | 4.8 |
| 16-19 years | 19.7 | 11.5 |
| 20 years and over | 8.1 | 4.4 |
| 20-24 years | 14.4 | 7.4 |
| 25 years and over | 7.1 | 3.9 |
| 25-54 years | 7.0 | 3.9 |
| 55 years and over | 7.4 | 3.9 |
| Men, 16 years and over | 8.0 | 3.9 |
| 16-19 years | 20.1 | 11.2 |
| 20 years and over | 7.4 | 3.5 |
| 20-24 years | 14.5 | 7.1 |
| 25 years and over | 6.1 | 3.0 |
| 25-54 years | 6.1 | 3.0 |
| 55 years and over | 6.2 | 2.9 |
| Women, 16 years and over | 9.4 | 6.0 |
| 16-19 years | 19.4 | 11.8 |
| 20 years and over | 8.9 | 5.6 |
| 20-24 years | 14.3 | 7.9 |
| 25 years and over | 8.1 | 5.2 |
| 25-54 years | 7.9 | 5.1 |
| 55 years and over | 8.9 | 5.4 |

Source: U.S. Department of Labor, Bureau of Labor Statistics

## TABLE 97. FULL-TIME AND PART-TIME EMPLOYMENT AS A PERCENT OF TOTAL EMPLOYMENT BY AGE, SEX, AND RACE, 1985 ANNUAL AVERAGES

| Age and sex | Full time | | Part time | |
|---|---|---|---|---|
| | Black | White | Black | White |
| Total, 16 years and over | 84.0 | 82.4 | 16.0 | 17.6 |
| 16-19 years | 39.5 | 39.0 | 60.5 | 61.0 |
| 20 years and over | 86.4 | 85.3 | 13.6 | 14.7 |
| 20-24 years | 76.4 | 79.0 | 23.6 | 21.0 |
| 25 years and over | 88.0 | 86.3 | 12.0 | 13.7 |
| 25-54 years | 90.2 | 88.1 | 9.8 | 11.9 |
| 55 years and over | 74.7 | 77.2 | 25.3 | 22.8 |
| Men, 16 years and over | 88.1 | 90.2 | 11.9 | 9.8 |
| 16-19 years | 42.3 | 43.5 | 57.7 | 56.5 |
| 20 years and over | 90.6 | 92.9 | 9.4 | 7.1 |
| 20-24 years | 78.1 | 83.6 | 21.9 | 16.4 |
| 25 years and over | 92.7 | 94.3 | 7.3 | 5.7 |
| 25-54 years | 93.9 | 96.4 | 6.1 | 3.6 |
| 55 years and over | 85.6 | 84.4 | 14.4 | 15.6 |
| Women, 16 years and over | 79.9 | 72.4 | 20.1 | 27.6 |
| 16-19 years | 36.4 | 34.2 | 63.6 | 65.8 |
| 20 years ant over | 82.1 | 75.2 | 17.9 | 24.8 |
| 20-24 years | 74.6 | 73.9 | 25.4 | 26.1 |
| 25 years and over | 83.3 | 75.4 | 16.7 | 24.6 |
| 25-54 years | 86.5 | 77.1 | 13.5 | 22.9 |
| 55 years and over | 63.5 | 66.3 | 36.4 | 33.7 |

Source: U.S. Department of Labor, Bureau of Labor Statistics

## TABLE 98. DURATION OF UNEMPLOYMENT BY RACE, 1985 ANNUAL AVERAGES

| Duration | Black | | White | |
|---|---|---|---|---|
| | Men | Women | Men | Women |
| Total unemployed: | | | | |
| Number (in thousands) | 951 | 913 | 3,426 | 2,765 |
| Percent | 100.0 | 100.0 | 100.0 | 100.0 |
| Less than 5 weeks | 33.4 | 43.3 | 38.7 | 48.9 |
| 5 to 14 weeks | 29.7 | 30.5 | 30.3 | 30.0 |
| 15 weeks and over | 36.9 | 26.2 | 31.0 | 21.1 |
| 15 to 26 weeks | 14.8 | 11.7 | 13.7 | 10.1 |
| 27 weeks and over | 22.1 | 14.5 | 17.3 | 11.0 |
| Average (mean) duration | 20.3 | 14.8 | 17.4 | 12.1 |
| Median duration | 8.5 | 5.6 | 7.8 | 5.3 |

Source: U.S. Department of Labor, Bureau of Labor Statistics

## TABLE 99. EMPLOYMENT STATUS OF PERSONS 16 TO 24 YEARS OLD BY SCHOOL ENROLLMENT AND LEVEL OF EDUCATIONAL ATTAINMENT, OCTOBER 1985

(Numbers in thousands)

| Enrollment status and race | Civilian population | Civilian labor force | Employment-population ratio | Unemployment rate |
|---|---|---|---|---|
| Black | | | | |
| Total, 16 to 24 years | 4,795 | 2,686 | 38.7 | 30.9 |
| Enrolled in school | 1,999 | 653 | 21.4 | 34.4 |
| High school | 1,230 | 308 | 14.4 | 42.6 |
| College | 770 | 345 | 32.6 | 27.1 |
| Full-time students | 631 | 223 | 23.3 | 33.9 |
| Part-time students | 139 | 122 | 74.8 | 14.5 |
| Not enrolled in school | 2,796 | 2,033 | 51.0 | 29.8 |
| School completed: | | | | |
| Less than 4 years in high school | 716 | 373 | 30.9 | 40.9 |
| High school: 4 years | 1,590 | 1,232 | 54.7 | 29.5 |
| College: 1 to 3 years | 392 | 344 | 68.1 | 22.3 |
| 4 years or more | 98 | 84 | 70.4 | 17.2 |
| White | | | | |
| Total, 16 to 24 years | 28,577 | 19,972 | 62.1 | 11.2 |
| Enrolled in school | 12,660 | 6,401 | 45.0 | 11.1 |
| High school | 5,961 | 2,552 | 35.2 | 17.8 |
| College | 6,699 | 3,849 | 53.6 | 6.6 |
| Full-time students | 5,645 | 2,879 | 47.4 | 7.1 |
| Part-time students | 1,054 | 969 | 87.3 | 5.0 |
| Not enrolled in school | 15,917 | 13,571 | 75.7 | 11.2 |
| School completed: | | | | |
| Less than 4 years in high school | 3,437 | 2,460 | 54.5 | 23.9 |
| High school: 4 years | 8,546 | 7,432 | 78.5 | 9.8 |
| College: 1 to 3 years | 2,524 | 2,312 | 85.9 | 6.3 |
| 4 years or more | 1,409 | 1,367 | 92.4 | 4.8 |

Source: U.S. Department of Labor, Bureau of Labor Statistics

## TABLE 100. EMPLOYMENT STATUS OF THE CIVILIAN NONINSTITUTIONAL POPULATION IN POVERTY AND NONPOVERTY AREAS BY RACE

(Numbers in thousands)

| | Total United States | | | | Metropolitan areas | | | | Nonmetropolitan areas | | | |
|---|---|---|---|---|---|---|---|---|---|---|---|---|
| | Poverty areas | | Nonpoverty areas | | Poverty areas | | Nonpoverty areas | | Poverty areas | | Nonpoverty areas | |
| Employment status, and race | 1986 | 1987 | 1986 | 1987 | 1986 | 1987 | 1986 | 1987 | 1986 | 1987 | 1986 | 1987 |
| Total | | | | | | | | | | | | |
| Civilian noninstitutional population | 26,529 | 27,554 | 154,058 | 155,199 | 17,761 | 18,382 | 122,180 | 123,937 | 8,768 | 9,172 | 31,878 | 31,262 |
| Civilian labor force | 15,043 | 15,643 | 102,793 | 104,222 | 9,969 | 10,340 | 82,695 | 84,423 | 5,073 | 5,302 | 20,098 | 19,799 |
| Percent of population | 56.7 | 56.8 | 66.7 | 67.2 | 56.1 | 56.3 | 67.7 | 68.1 | 57.9 | 57.8 | 63.0 | 63.3 |
| Employed | 13,013 | 13,842 | 96,585 | 98,599 | 8,533 | 9,070 | 77,975 | 80,068 | 4,480 | 4,771 | 18,610 | 18,531 |
| Unemployed | 2,029 | 1,801 | 6,207 | 5,623 | 1,437 | 1,270 | 4,720 | 4,355 | 593 | 531 | 1,487 | 1,268 |
| Unemployment rate | 13.5 | 11.5 | 6.0 | 5.4 | 14.4 | 12.3 | 5.7 | 5.2 | 11.7 | 10.0 | 7.4 | 6.4 |
| Men, 20 years & over | 12.3 | 10.3 | 5.2 | 4.7 | 13.3 | 11.3 | 4.9 | 4.5 | 10.4 | 8.5 | 6.4 | 5.6 |
| Women, 20 years & over | 11.9 | 10.2 | 5.4 | 4.7 | 12.4 | 10.7 | 5.1 | 4.5 | 10.8 | 9.0 | 6.9 | 5.6 |
| Both sexes, 16 to 19 years | 32.4 | 28.6 | 16.2 | 15.1 | 35.1 | 28.7 | 15.9 | 14.5 | 26.9 | 28.4 | 17.6 | 17.4 |
| Men | 32.1 | 28.9 | 17.0 | 16.0 | 35.0 | 29.3 | 16.6 | 15.6 | 26.4 | 28.0 | 18.2 | 17.7 |
| Women | 32.7 | 28.3 | 15.5 | 14.0 | 35.2 | 28.0 | 15.1 | 13.3 | 27.4 | 28.9 | 17.0 | 17.0 |
| Not in labor force | 11,486 | 11,911 | 51,265 | 50,977 | 7,791 | 8,042 | 39,485 | 39,514 | 3,695 | 3,869 | 11,780 | 11,463 |
| White | | | | | | | | | | | | |
| Civilian noninstitutional population | 15,804 | 16,652 | 139,628 | 140,306 | 9,309 | 9,943 | 109,595 | 110,807 | 6,495 | 6,709 | 30,033 | 29,499 |
| Civilian labor force | 9,098 | 9,614 | 92,703 | 93,676 | 5,283 | 5,693 | 73,750 | 74,988 | 3,815 | 3,921 | 18,953 | 18,688 |
| Percent of population | 57.6 | 57.7 | 66.4 | 66.8 | 56.8 | 57.3 | 67.3 | 67.7 | 58.7 | 58.4 | 63.1 | 63.4 |
| Employed | 8,157 | 8,776 | 87,504 | 89,013 | 4,695 | 5,154 | 69,896 | 71,478 | 3,461 | 3,622 | 17,608 | 17,536 |
| Unemployed | 942 | 838 | 5,199 | 4,663 | 588 | 539 | 3,853 | 3,510 | 354 | 299 | 1,345 | 1,152 |
| Unemployment rate | 10.3 | 8.7 | 5.6 | 5.0 | 11.1 | 9.5 | 5.2 | 4.7 | 9.3 | 7.6 | 7.1 | 6.2 |
| Men, 20 years & over | 9.6 | 8.1 | 4.9 | 4.4 | 10.3 | 8.8 | 4.5 | 4.2 | 8.6 | 7.0 | 6.2 | 5.4 |
| Women, 20 years& over | 9.2 | 7.4 | 5.0 | 4.3 | 9.9 | 8.1 | 4.6 | 4.0 | 8.3 | 6.4 | 6.5 | 5.3 |
| Both sexes, 16 to 19 years | 23.7 | 21.4 | 14.8 | 13.7 | 25.9 | 21.9 | 14.3 | 12.9 | 20.7 | 20.6 | 16.9 | 16.8 |
| Men | 24.0 | 22.4 | 15.5 | 14.7 | 25.6 | 23.7 | 15.0 | 14.0 | 21.7 | 20.2 | 17.3 | 17.1 |
| Women | 23.4 | 20.2 | 14.2 | 12.7 | 26.2 | 19.7 | 13.6 | 11.7 | 19.6 | 21.1 | 16.5 | 16.5 |
| Not in labor force | 6,706 | 7,038 | 46,925 | 46,630 | 4,026 | 4,250 | 35,845 | 35,819 | 2,680 | 2,789 | 11,080 | 10,811 |
| Black | | | | | | | | | | | | |
| Civilian noninstitutional population | 9,760 | 9,878 | 10,229 | 10,474 | 7,783 | 7,732 | 8,837 | 9,130 | 1,977 | 2,146 | 1,392 | 1,343 |
| Civilian labor force | 5,416 | 5,468 | 7,238 | 7,525 | 4,316 | 4,264 | 6,366 | 6,662 | 1,100 | 1,204 | 873 | 863 |
| Percent of population | 55.5 | 55.4 | 70.8 | 71.8 | 55.5 | 55.2 | 72.0 | 73.0 | 55.6 | 56.1 | 62.7 | 64.2 |
| Employed | 4,397 | 4,572 | 6,418 | 6,737 | 3,504 | 3,566 | 5,652 | 5,965 | 893 | 1,006 | 765 | 772 |
| Unemployed | 1,019 | 896 | 821 | 788 | 812 | 699 | 714 | 697 | 207 | 198 | 107 | 91 |
| Unemployment rate | 18.8 | 16.4 | 11.3 | 10.5 | 18.8 | 16.4 | 11.2 | 10.5 | 18.8 | 16.4 | 12.3 | 10.5 |
| Men, 20 years and over | 17.5 | 14.9 | 9.6 | 8.4 | 18.0 | 15.6 | 9.8 | 8.4 | 15.9 | 12.4 | 8.3 | 7.7 |
| Women, 20 years& over | 15.8 | 14.3 | 9.8 | 9.7 | 15.3 | 13.9 | 9.4 | 9.6 | 17.9 | 15.5 | 13.3 | 10.6 |
| Both sexes, 16 to 19 years | 45.0 | 40.3 | 34.4 | 30.4 | 45.2 | 38.1 | 34.9 | 30.8 | 44.2 | 47.4 | 30.8 | 27.8 |
| Men | 44.2 | 40.6 | 35.2 | 30.3 | 46.2 | 38.6 | 35.5 | 30.4 | 37.4 | 46.4 | 33.5 | ([1]) |
| Women | 45.9 | 40.0 | 33.5 | 30.7 | 44.2 | 37.7 | 34.4 | 31.3 | ([1]) | 48.5 | ([1]) | ([1]) |
| Not in labor force | 4,345 | 4,410 | 2,990 | 2,949 | 3,467 | 3,468 | 2,471 | 2,468 | 877 | 942 | 520 | 480 |

[1] Data not shown where base is less than 35,000.

Source: U.S. Department of Labor, Bureau of Labor Statistics

# INCOME, EARNINGS, AND INCIDENCE OF POVERTY

**Overview ■ Key Economic Forces and Policies ■ Recessions ■ Inflation ■ Federal Budget Cuts ■ Gramm-Rudman-Hollings Act ■ Income Taxes ■ Welfare Reform ■ Income and Poverty Trends ■ Earnings ■ Family Income ■ Poverty ■ Child Care ■ Child Support ■ Public Assistance ■ Income ■ Social Security ■ Noncash Benefits ■ Net Worth and Assets ■ Taxes ■ Future Economic Outlook ■ Selected Facts**

During his Presidential campaign in 1984, Ronald Reagan repeatedly asked the American people to judge his performance in that office by their response to the following question, "Were your economic circumstances at the end of the Reagan administration better or worse than they were at the beginning?" While most whites reported some improvement in their situation during the Reagan era, the overwhelming majority of blacks perceived little or no progress. This negative assessment of the '80's by blacks is supported by a host of government and non-government data.

As a result of the devastating recession of 1981-82, unemployment among blacks soared between 1980 and 1983 from 14 percent to 20 percent—the highest jobless rate for blacks since the Great Depression of the '30's. Although the jobless rate for blacks by 1988 (12%) was slightly less than their rate in 1980 (14%), there were just as many blacks unemployed (1.5 million) in 1988 as there were eight years earlier. The proportion of blacks in poverty in 1987 was as high (33%) as it was in 1980. Further, 1.1 million more blacks were poor in 1987 (9.7 million) than in 1980 (8.6 million). Similarly, the proportion of black children in poverty was higher in 1987 (45%) than in 1980 (42%). There were also 400,00 more poor black children in 1987 than in 1980.

Unemployment and poverty also rose among whites during the '80's. However, whites were able to recover more quickly than blacks. Consequently, the earnings, unemployment and income gaps between blacks and whites were wider by the end of the Reagan administration than at the beginning. For example, the ratio of black to white unemployment rates increased from 2.3 to 2.5 between 1980 and 1988. Similarly, the ratio of black to white family income fell from 57 percent to 56 percent between 1979 and 1987.

These and other data reveal significant erosion of black economic progress during the '80's. What economic trends and social policies contributed to this retrogression? What were the key earnings, income and poverty trends among blacks during the Reagan era? Which segments of the black community were hit hardest and which segments continued to make important economic gains? What is the economic outlook for blacks during the 1990s under the new administration of President George Bush? These and related questions will now be addressed in detail.

## KEY ECONOMIC FORCES AND POLICIES

### Recessions

The preeminent economic trend during the early 1980s was the back-to-back recessions of 1980 and 1981-82. The first slump occurred during the last year (1980) of the Carter administration and the second—and most severe—occurred during the first two years (1981-82) of the Reagan administration. Although the 1980 recession lasted for only seven months, unemployment among blacks rose by 234,000 between 1979 and 1980, while rising by 1.2 million among whites.

Blacks and whites were more acutely affected by the 18-month recession of 1981-82. Unemployment among blacks increased by 719,000 between 1980 and 1983, raising their jobless rate from 14.3% to 19.5% while unemployment among whites increased by 2.2 million, raising their jobless rate from 6.3% to 8.4%.

### Inflation

At the same time that the nation was being hit by back-to-back recessions, it was being battered by double-digit inflation. Studies consistently reveal that black and low-income families are more acutely affected by inflation than white and middle-income families. Although each of the administrations—Nixon, Ford, Carter and Reagan—promised not to place the burden of fighting inflation on the backs of the unemployed, the four recessions between 1970 and 1982 were induced by government fiscal and monetary policies and were not "natural disasters." Traditionally, the Federal Reserve Board (the "Fed") tried to stem inflation by keeping interest rates within pre-determined ranges, while permitting the money supply to expand more freely. But these restrictive fiscal policies created the recessions of 1970-71 and 1974-75.

Although the inflation rate fell from 13.3% to 12.4% between 1979 and 1980, it was still at an alarming rate of 8.4% when Ronald Reagan was inaugurated as President in January 1981. With the appointment of Volker in 1978, the Fed changed its policies. It was now determined to control growth in the money supply and allow interest rates to seek their own level of equilibrium. More restrictive targets were set on the money supply and interest rates were permitted to rise unfettered. The tight monetary policies that led to soaring interest rates also caused the 1980 and 1981-82 recessions.

### Federal Budget Cuts

On February 18, 1981, President Reagan unveiled his Economy Recovery Plan which pledged to: (1) cut personal taxes by 30% over the next three years; (2) increase tax incentives for businesses; (3) raise defense spending 17% annually between 1980 and 1984; (4) hold nondefense spending to annual increases of only 1% after 1981; (5) shift the major responsibility for administering and funding major social programs for the poor to state and local governments;

*Address unknown.*

(6) eliminate burdensome federal regulations on businesses; (7) sharply reduce inflation; (8) spur job growth; and (9) achieve a balanced budget by 1984.

Although Congress refused to reduce government funding of social programs for the poor to the levels requested by Mr. Reagan, the President succeeded in obtaining sizeable cuts. By FY (fiscal year) 1985, Congress enacted the following reductions in annual expenditures: (a) AFDC by $1.4 billion to $8.4 billion; (b) food stamps by $2.0 billion to $12.5 billion; (c) low-income energy assistance by $0.2 billion to $1.1 billion; (d) child nutrition by $1.4 billion to $10.9 billion; (e) Medicaid by $0.7 billion to $24.2 billion; (f) compensatory education by $0.8 billion to $3.3 billion; and (g) Job Corps by $.05 billion to $.65 billion.

The Reagan administration sought the total elimination of the Community Services Block Grant (CSBG) and the Work Incentive (WIN) program for employable welfare recipients. Congress only reduced FY 1985 funding for CSBG by $0.3 billion to $0.4 billion and reduced funding for WIN by $0.2 billion to $0.3 billion. However, Congress did accede to the administration's request to totally eliminate the Public Service Employment program, one of the most effective components of CETA. Since blacks comprise between 25%-45% of the participants in most programs for the poor, they were

**CHART 41. MEDIAN INCOME FOR BLACK AND WHITE FAMILIES 1960-1986**

**The median family income for black families in 1986 was $17, 328 while for white families it was $30,869. Although the dollar gap between black and white has increased the purchasing power has maintained a fairly constant ratio.**

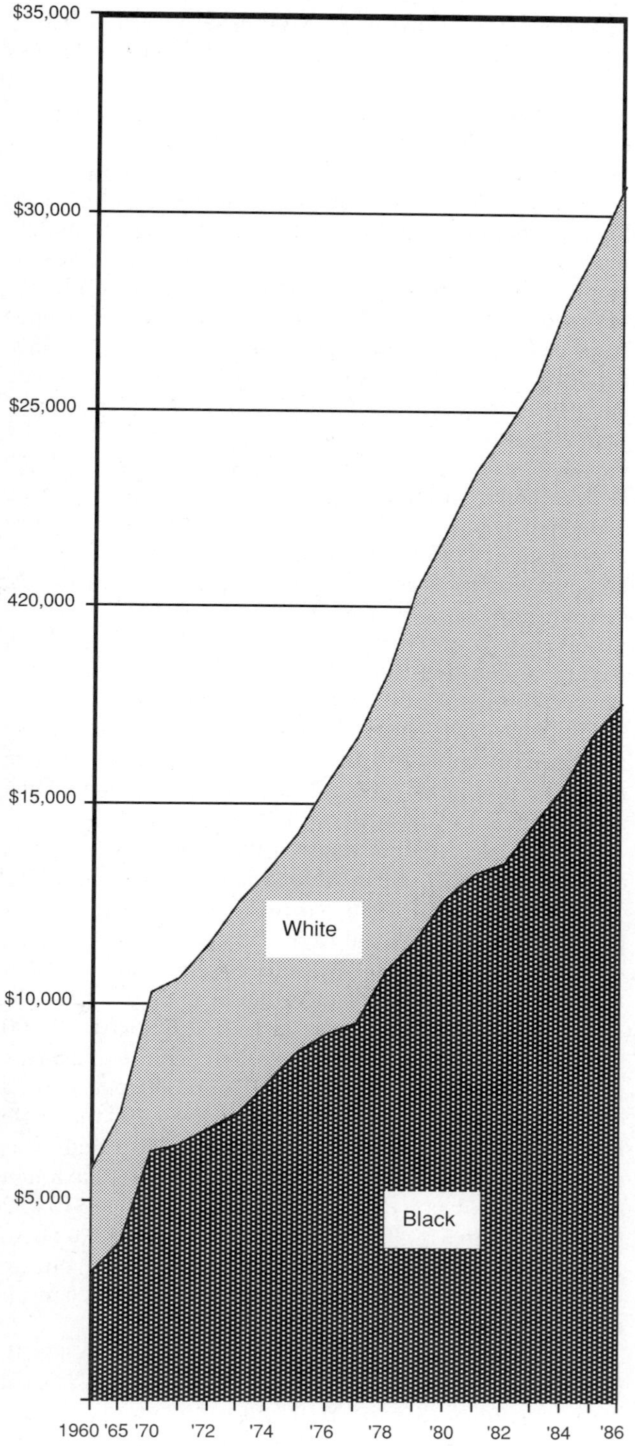


disproportionately affected by these sharp budget cutbacks.

Most of the cuts in the programs for the poor were achieved by tightening eligibility requirements for the working poor and reducing the value of cash and non-cash benefits for the poor who continued to receive assistance. For example, the OBRA cuts in 1981 removed between 400,000-500,000 working poor families (about 11%-14% of the total AFCDC case load) from the welfare rolls and eliminated about one million persons from the food stamp program due to more stringent eligibility criteria. About 300,000 working poor families that remained on AFDC experienced sharp reductions in cash and in-kind benefits thereby decreasing work incentives—these families could receive more assistance without working. According to a 1987 report prepared by the Physician Task Force on Hunger in America, the number of Americans experiencing hunger and malnutrition rose to 20 million, largely because of the $7 billion and $5 billion cuts, respectively, in the food stamps and school lunch programs between 1981 and 1985.

One might assume that President Reagan's policies of excluding the working poor from its safety net for "the truly needy" had the positive side-effect of retargeting funds to the non-working poor. Evaluations of those budget cuts (by such groups as the Children's Defense Fund, the Center on Budget and Policy Priorities, etc.) revealed that savings from those reductions were not used to increase the purchasing power of the non-working poor who remained on the public assistance rolls. Consequently, even "the truly needy"

**CHART 42. FAMILY INCOME IN CURRENT AND CONSTANT DOLLARS**

**In terms of constant dollars the median income for both white and black families has not gained ground since 1979. Since 1979 the median family income for black families has remained at about 57% that of whites.**

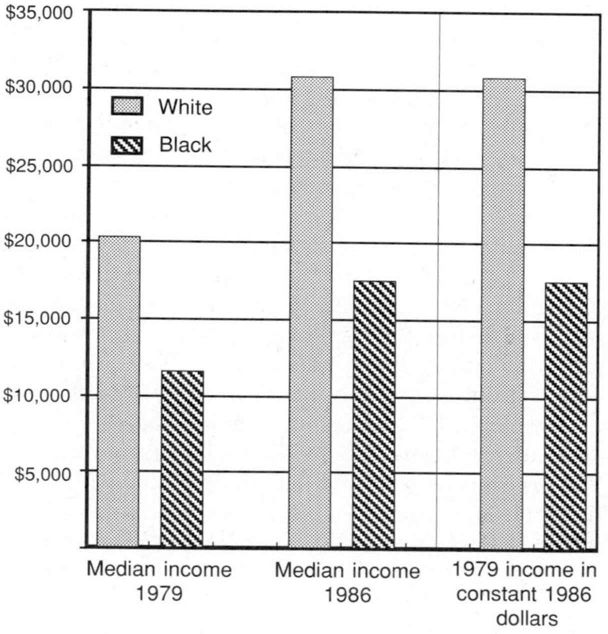

experienced sharp declines in their living standards as a result of the drastic cuts in cash and non-cash programs for the poor.

Those who list President Reagan's successes will include among them his reducing personal income taxes which from a tax point of view somewhat helped the working poor, increasing tax incentives for corporations, increasing defense spending, obtaining federal deregulation, slowing the rate of spending for social welfare programs (excluding social security), and reducing annual increases in consumer prices from 13.5% to 4.3% between 1980 and 1984. It should be noted that the reduction in inflation was primarily due to Fed policies and was achieved at a high cost in terms of unemployment lost productivity, huge budget deficits and a major imbalance in the U. S. foreign trade position. It should also be noted that the price borne by the less fortunate had to be extremely painful in coping with the daily problems of everyday living.

Although employed workers in the U.S. increased by six million between 1980 and 1984, unemployed workers also rose by one million. Not only did Reagan fail to achieve a balanced budget by 1984, but the sharp tax cuts and deep recession caused the budget deficit to soar from $74 billion to $185 billion between FY 1980 and FY 1984.

## Gramm-Rudman-Hollings Act

Since the President's economy recovery policies increased rather than decreased the budget deficit, Congress enacted the Balanced Budget and Emergency Deficit Control Act (more popularly known as "Gramm-Rudman-Hollings" or GRH) in 1985 to force the President and Congress to agree on annual federal budgets that would reduce the deficit from $172 billion in FY 1986 to zero by FY 1991. The GRH Act mandated automatic across-the-board cuts ("sequesters") of the same magnitude in "controllable" domestic programs whenever the deficit for the upcoming year was projected by the Congressional Budget Office and the Office of Management and Budget to exceed the GRH ceiling by $10 billion or more. The target year for a balanced budget was later changed to fiscal year 1994.

Programs exempted from these across-the-board cuts included: Social Security, interest on the federal debt, the earned income tax credit, AFDC, Medicaid, food stamps, WIC (WIC abbreviation for Women Infants Children, an AFDC childrens nutritional program related to a work incentive program), other child nutrition programs, and community health centers. Moreover, although the base budget for "indexed" programs (e.g., government pensions, etc.) with cost-of-living adjustments ("COLAS") were exempt from across-the-board reductions, automatic increases in the COLA's could be reduced or frozen.

On July 7, 1986, the U.S. Supreme Court upheld an earlier 1986 decision by a special three-judge panel of the U.S. District Court that declared the across-the-board "sequestration" progress to be unconstitutional, since it violated the principle of separation of powers. The Court ruled that the GRH Act conferred upon the Comptroller General executive powers that could not constitutionally be exercised by an officer removable by Congress. The deficit ceilings of the GRH Act continue to be binding—minus the automatic across-the-board cuts. Blacks and low-income groups are expected to bear the brunt of automatic budget reductions.

## Income Taxes

Blacks were also disproportionately affected by increasing tax burdens during the '70's and '80's. This was primarily due to increases in payroll taxes for Social Security. This tax is regressive in two ways. First the rate is the same regardless of income. Second, income above a fixed amount (increased in most years) is exempt from this tax thereby lowering the effective tax rate for higher income families. Together with income tax "bracket creep" resulting from inflation, a significant portion of the total tax burden was shifted from high income families and corporations to low and middle income wage earners. The combined payroll taxes of employees and employers rose from 3.00% to 15.51% between 1950 and 1988. The proportion of federal revenues from payroll taxes more than tripled from 12% to 38% between 1950 and 1983. The total tax rates (i.e., both income and payroll taxes) for families of poor at the poverty level jumped from 4.9% to 16.5% between 1955 and 1983, while the rates for near-poor families soared from 4.5% to 18.3%. Because of the erosion in the personal exemption and standard deduction by inflation during the first half of the '70's, more poor families not only paid income taxes, but paid much larger payroll taxes as well. To correct for those inequities, the Earned Income Tax Credit (EITC) was enacted in 1975 to: (a) restore poor families to their earlier status of not paying any income taxes, and (b) refund a portion of the Social Security payroll tax to working poor families.

The value of the personal exemption, standard deduction and the EITC continued to be eroded by double-digit inflation. (Thus, the tax burden for families of four at the poverty level rose from 1% to 10% between 1975 and 1985.

To restore the progressiveness of the income tax, Congress enacted comprehensive tax reform legislation in 1986. The Tax Reform Act of 1986, not only markedly raised the thresholds of the personal exemption, standard deduction and EITC, but indexed them, for the first time, to insure that they are kept abreast of rising inflation.

The personal exemption was raised from $1,080 to $2,000 by 1989, while the standard deduction (for non-itemizing tax payers) was increased (from $3,670) to $5,000 for a married couple filing jointly and (from $2,480) to $4,400 for single household heads by 1988. The maximum EITC credit was raised from $550 to $800 for 1987, while the maximum eligible family income was raised from $11,000 to $15,432 for 1987 and to $18,500 for 1988. It is expected that about four million working poor families (one-fourth of whom are black) will be removed form the income tax rolls as a result of the 1986 legislation.

Other key provisions of the 1986 Tax Reform Act included: (a) setting a separate standard deduction for families headed by single parents; (b) reducing the number of tax brackets for individual taxpayers to two rates of 15% and 28%; (c) increased taxes on capital gains; (d) elimination of most tax shelters, and strict limits on those that remain; (e) a more comprehensive minimum tax (including a minimum tax on corporations for the first time); (f) retroactive repeal of the investment tax credit. Certain provisions are likely to have a disproportionate negative impact on the economic well-being of blacks: (a) reducing the deductibility of charitable contributions; and (b) reducing tax incentives for investing in the creation and rehabilitation of low-income housing.

In general, blacks pay about the same proportion of their income for taxes as whites in comparable income brackets. For example, among households with annual incomes between $10,000-$19,999, blacks paid 13% of aggregate income in taxes and whites paid 12%. Similarly, among households with annual incomes of $50,000 or more, blacks paid 28% of aggregate income in taxes and whites paid 30%.

Poor blacks are less likely than poor whites to pay taxes. Over half (55%) of poor blacks paid taxes in 1986, compared to two-thirds (69%) of poor whites. Payroll taxes (40%) and property taxes (25%) accounted for the bulk of the taxes paid by poor blacks. Only about one-tenth of poor blacks paid federal (6%) or state (11%) incomes taxes. Payroll (44%) and property (39%) taxes also comprised most of the taxes paid by poor whites. Only one-tenth of poor whites paid either federal (9%) or state (14%) income taxes. The Welfare Reform Act of 1986 is expected to remove about 4 million poor families from the income tax rolls by 1988.

### Welfare Reform

According to conventional wisdom, the growth in one-parent black families over the past two decades was mainly due to an "overgenerous" welfare system. Yet, many studies reveal that double-digit inflation eroded the value of welfare benefits markedly, since most states failed to raise AFDC needs and payment standards to fully reflect inflation. Both liberals and conservatives agreed that the current welfare system needed to be overhauled radically, since it was only maintaining families in poverty.

After extensive deliberations and compromises, Congress enacted the Family Support Act of 1988. This Act contains several provisions to help welfare recipients to achieve economic self-sufficiency: (a) the ineffective WIN (Work Incentive) program was replaced by JOBS (Job Opportunities and Basic Skills Training)—a comprehensive education, training and employment program; (b) States must guarantee child care for welfare mothers required to participate in JOBS; (C) child care and Medicaid coverage must be extended for 12 months for the families of recipients who leave welfare rolls due to employment, and (d) there is a mandated extension of the AFDC-Unemployed Parent (AFDC-UP) program to all 50 states.

Certain omissions from the 1988 Family Support Act are likely to have disparate adverse effects on poor black families: (a) it does not mandate increases in AFDC benefit levels; (b) it does not set national minimum AFDC needs and payment standards; (c) it allows newly-participating states the option of limiting participation in their AFDC-UP programs for six months; and (d) it fails to assign high priority to enhancing the employability of low-income and young noncustodial fathers.

Congress should be commended for making the AFDC-UP program mandatory for all 50 states. Since AFDC-UP was established in 1961 as an optional program, only about half of the states (none in the South) participated in it. However, thousands of poor two-parent black families may still not be able to benefit form the 1988 legislation because of very restrictive eligibility standards.

Poor two-parent black families—especially those headed by young fathers—are disparately "screened out" by eligibility criteria that require AFDC-UP recipients to: (a) have long-term and stable work histories; (b) be eligible for unemployment insurance; and (c) not be disqualified for UI benefits. Such insensitive criteria explain why only 25% of poor two-parent black families received AFDC-UP in 1984, compared to 40% of poor two-parent white families.

**CHART 43. SOURCES OF INCOME FOR BLACK FAMILIES, 1986**

**More than half of poor black families have some income that is earned even though their reliance is on other sources to meet basic subsistence expenses.**

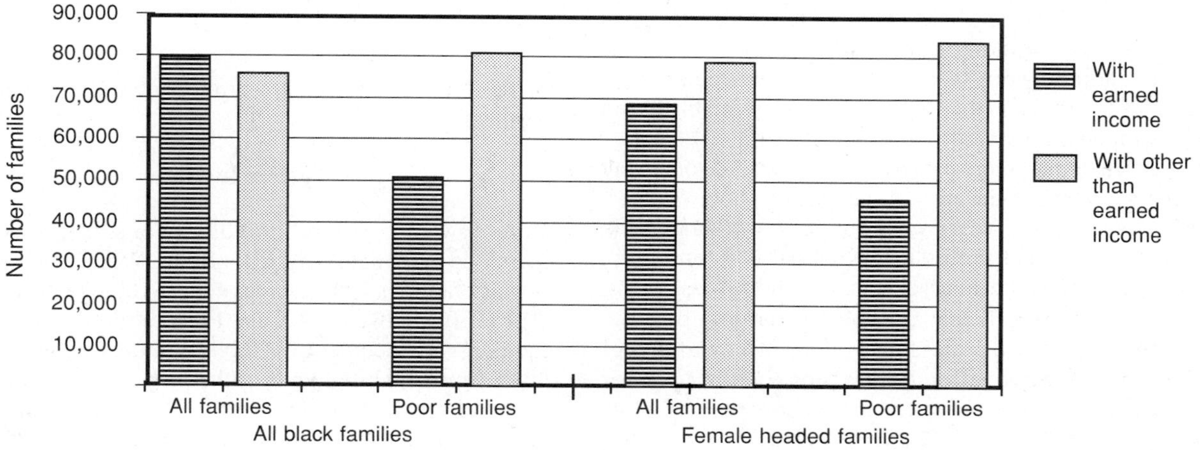

## INCOME AND POVERTY TRENDS

What have been the major earnings, income and poverty trends among blacks during the 1980s? Which segments of the black population have been affected most and least by the economic forces and policies during the Reagan administration?

Employment Status: The back-to-back recessions of the '80's led to declines in the labor force participation (LFP) rates of family heads, regardless of race, and increases in their unemployment rates. While the LFP rates of white family heads decreased form 79% to 76% between 1979 and 1987, the LFP rates of black family heads fell more sharply from 73% to 68%. However, although the LFP rates of male family heads declined over that eight-year span, the LFP rates of female family heads rose. While the LFP rates of black male family heads declined from 79% to 75%, the LFP rates of black female family heads increased form 54% to 58%. Similar LFP patterns occurred between male and female white family heads.

The unemployment rates of white family heads increased from 3.3% to 4.7% between 1979 and 1987, while those of black family heads jumped from 8.4% to 10.5%. Thus, black heads of families were more than twice as likely as white family heads to be unemployed. Black women heading families experienced sharper increases in unemployment than any other heads of families.

### Earnings

While all workers experienced declines in their real (i.e., adjusted for inflation) weekly earnings during the '80's, black workers experienced sharper declines than white workers. The real weekly earnings of white workers fell by 2% between 1979 and 1986. The real weekly earnings of black workers decreased by 5% over the same period. Consequently, the earnings gap between black and white workers widened. In fact, the ratio of black to white weekly earnings feel from 82% to 79% between l979 and 1986.

The gap in annual earnings between black and white workers also widened during the '80's. Among all workers, while the earnings ratio between black and white men declined from 66% to 64% between 1979 and 1986, the earnings ratio between black and white women dropped from 98% to 94%. Among year-round, full-time workers, the earnings ratio between black and white men edged down from 71% to 69%, and the earnings ratio between black and white women fell markedly from 95% to 91%.

In certain employment categories blacks fared somewhat better than average but were still significantly below whites. For example, among year-round, full-time workers, black, male executives and professionals earned 68% and 76%, respectively, of white male executives and professionals. One interesting note is that in 1986 the earnings of black female executives and professionals equaled the earnings of white female executives and professionals. On the other hand, black, male sales workers earned only 66% of white male sales workers, and the earnings of black, female sales workers were 82% of the earnings of white female sales workers.

### CHART 44. BLACK MEDIAN FAMILY INCOME AS A PERCENTAGE OF WHITE, 1964-1986

**The average black family take home pay is only $56 for each $100 taken home by the average white family. Although this ratio rose above 60% in 1969-1970, it has since declined.**

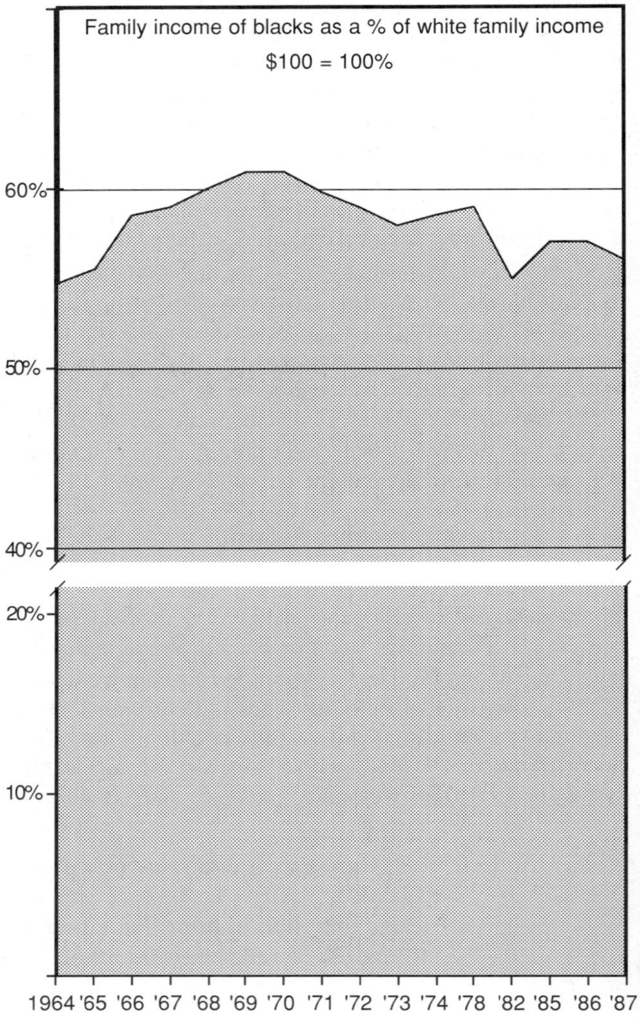


### Family Income

Both low-income and middle-income black families increased in number during the 1980s. While the proportion of black families with incomes under $10,000 edged up from 29% to 30% between 1979 and 1986, the proportion of black families with incomes of $25,000 or more rose form 34% to 36%. Among white families, the proportion with incomes under $10,000 edged up from 9% to 10%. In contrast, the proportion of white families with incomes of $25,000 or more edged down from 62% to 61%.

When the median income of families in 1979 is converted to 1986 dollars to adjust for inflation, black families had somewhat higher increases in purchasing power than white families over that seven-year span. Among all family heads, the real median income of black families rose by 0.7%, while the real income of white families fell by 0.2%. These gains of black families relative to white families are largely due to the higher proportion of working wives among black than white couples.

In 1979, 59% of black married couples had working wives, compared to only 48% of white married couples. By 1986, 65% of black married couples had working wives, compared to 54% of white married couples. Consequently, while the real income of couples with working wives increased by 3% among blacks between 1979 and 1986, it increased by 2% among whites. On the other hand, couples without working wives experienced declines in real income, regardless of race. In fact, both black and white couples without working wives experienced declines of 4% in their real income between 1979 and 1986. Female-headed families among blacks and whites experienced the sharpest declines in real income, 10% and 9%, respectively.

The overall income gap between black and white families remained at 57% between 1979 and 1986. However, the racial income gap narrowed among married couples, but widened among single parent families. While the income ratio of black couples to white couples rose from 77% to 80%, the income ratio between black and white female-headed families edged down from 60% to 59%. Two-earner black couples made gains in narrowing the racial income gap with whites. One-earner black couples fell further behind. The income ratio of black to white couples with working wives edged up from 81% to 82% between 1979 and 1986, while the income ratio of black to white couples without working wives edged down from 64% to 63%.

Yet, white families now have more earners in their families than black families. Not only did the proportion of white families with two or more earners jump from 53% to 57% between 1970 and 1979, but it continued to rise to 58% by 1986. Among black families, however, the proportion with two or more earners fell from 54% to 47% between 1970 and 1979 and remained at 47% by 1986. Thus, black families require an extra earner to have the same income as white families. For example, black families with three earners ($36,029) had about the same income as white families with two earners ($35,848) in 1986.

## Poverty

The percent of black individuals and families below the official poverty level remained unchanged during the '80's. The proportion of black individuals in poverty held at 31% between 1979 and 1986. However, the proportion of black children in poverty rose from 41% to 43%. Only the black elderly experienced a sharp drop in poverty (from 36% to 31%) between 1979 and 1986. The proportion of poor black families remained at 28% over that seven-year span. At the

### CHART 45. DISTRIBUTION OF FAMILY INCOME

**The top 20% of families in the highest income bracket recieved 43.5% of the total income generated in the U.S. during the year 1985, the highest percent ever recorded. The 3 lowest family income groups, 60% of all families, received but 32.4% of total generated income, the lowest level ever recorded. The chart demonstrates a dramatic disparity in the growth of incomes for the rich, in comparison to both the middle class and the poor.**

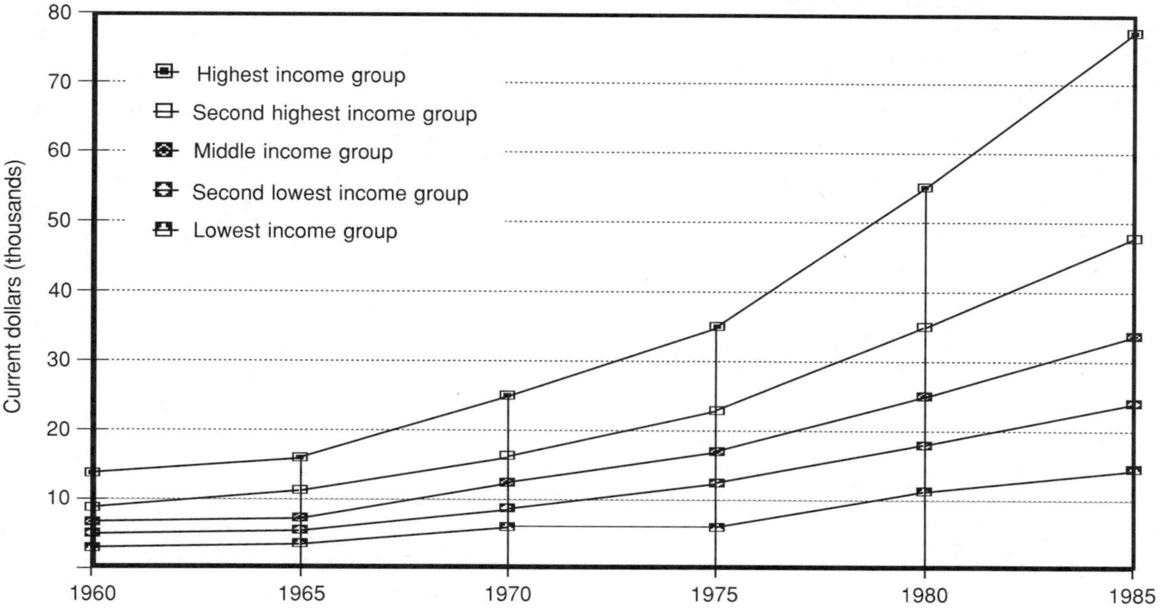


Source: Scientific America, May 1987, a study by Lester C. Thurow

same time the proportion of female-headed black families in poverty edged up from 49% to 50%.

The number of blacks in poverty rose sharply during the '80's. The number of poor black individuals increased from 8.0 to 9.0 million between 1979 and 1986; The number of poor black families rose from 1.7 to 2.0 million and the number of poor black children increased from 3.7 to 4.0 million. Thus, there were 2 million more poor blacks and 0.3 million more poor black children in 1986 than there were in 1969.

The official poverty statistics sharply understate the actual extent of economic deprivation among blacks. While 9.0 million blacks were poor in 1986 based on the official poverty level, using the more accurate 125% of the official poverty standard*, the total number of blacks in poverty would rise to 11.1 million. Similarly, the number of black children in poverty would increase from 4.0 to 4.8 million. Using the 125% criterion, the poverty rates for all blacks in 1986 would rise form 31% to 39%, while the poverty rates for all black children would increase from 43% to 51%.

***The government-established official poverty level is an arbitrary point which says little about the actual poverty of a person in terms of daily needs.**

## CHART46. FEMINIZATION OF POVERTY

**The feminization of poverty has been increasing steadily over the years. At the lower levels of income there is a predomination of women headed families; this applies to women regardless of race.**

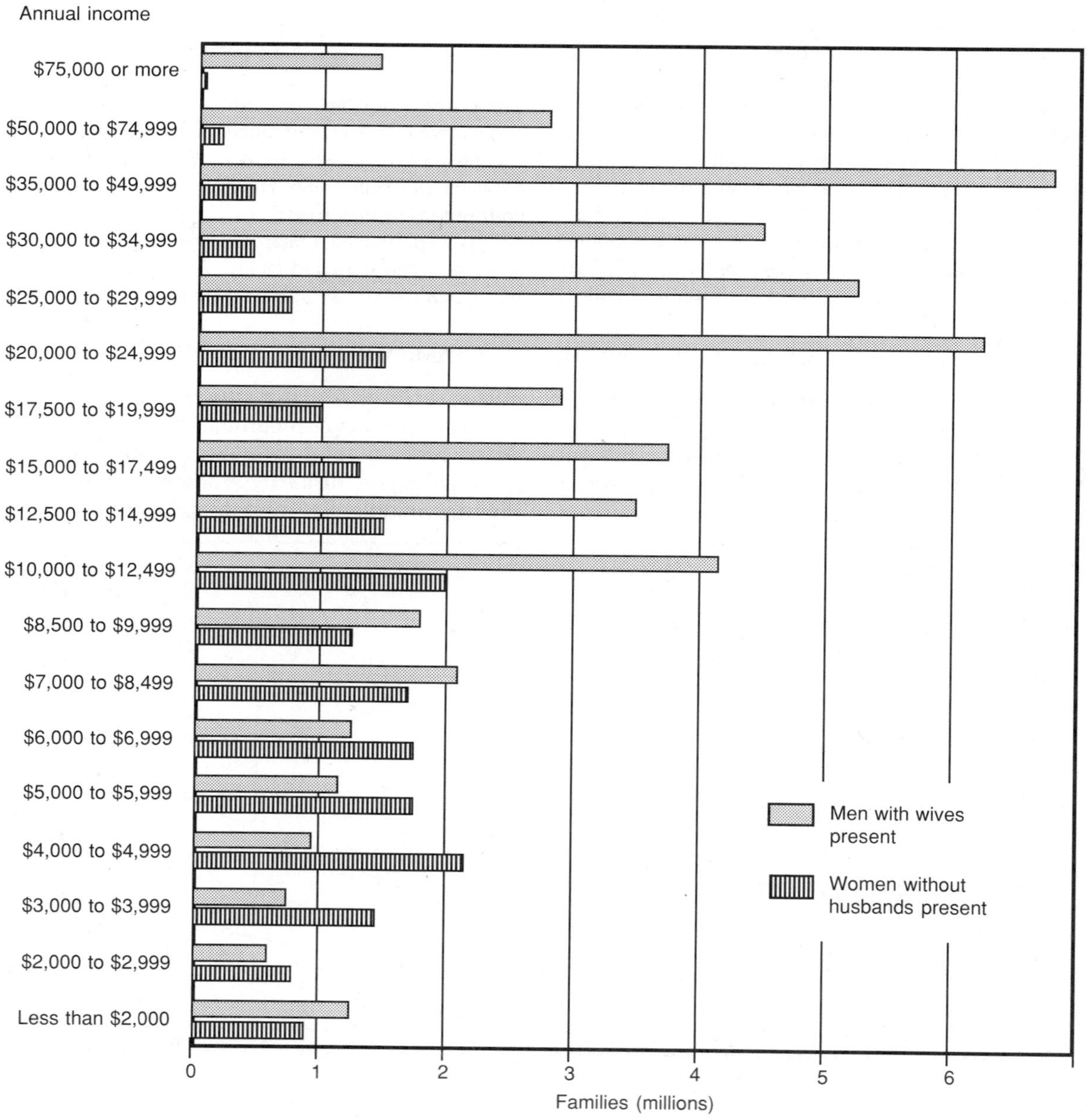

## CHART 47. NEWLY CREATED JOBS AND PAY RATES IN HIGH, MEDIUM AND LOW PAYING JOBS

**Between 1963 and 1979 there was a greater proportion of new jobs created in the middle and upper pay ranges than during the 1979-1985 time period. The trend is for newly created jobs to be in lower and middle ranges of pay, indicating a downward bias in general incomes for the future.**

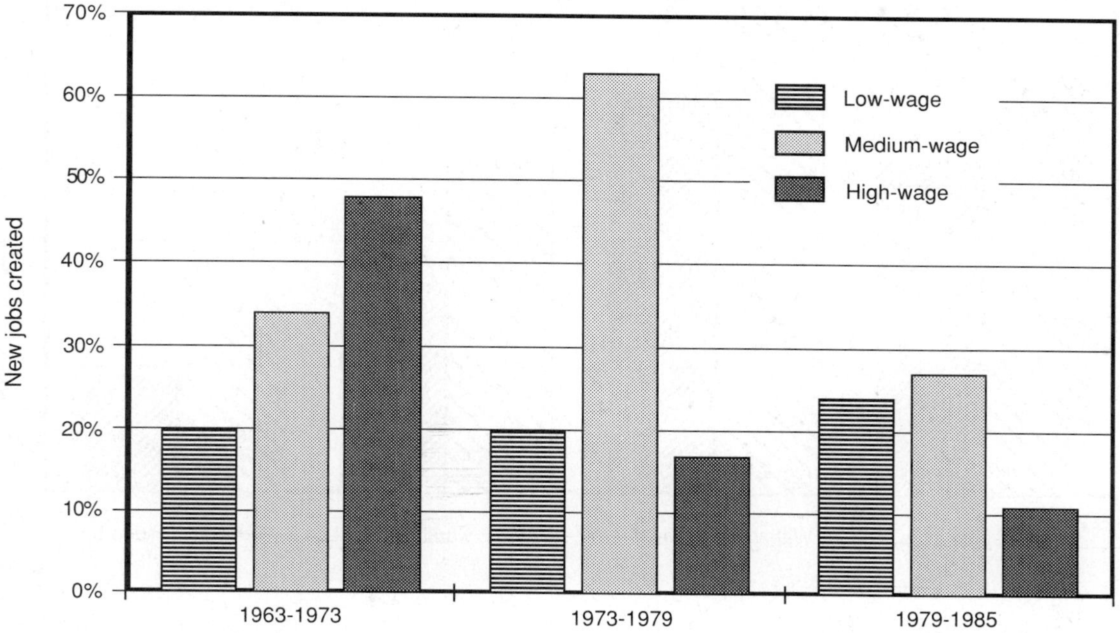


Three out of four (75%) poor blacks live in metropolitan areas, and six out of ten (57%) poor blacks live in central cities. Poor black children are more highly concentrated in central cities than poor elderly. Three out of five (57%) black children live in central cities, compared to one out of two (48%) poor blacks 65 years and over. Moreover, 61% of poor blacks in female-headed families reside in central cities, compared to only 4% of poor blacks in two-parent families. Regionally, 71% of poor elderly blacks reside in the south, compared to 59% of poor black children.

A major impediment to the economic progress of blacks is the residential segregation of the majority (57%) of central city blacks to poverty areas. While one-third (33%) of all black families live in the poverty areas of central cities, three-fifths of central city blacks reside in poverty areas. In contrast, only 4% of all white families—and 16% of central city white families—live in poverty areas.

### Child Care

The need for child care increased markedly during the '70's and '80's because of the surge in the labor force participation of mothers in one-parent and two-parent families. The labor force participation rate rose from 56% to 70% among black wives with children under 18 years old, between 1970 and 1984. At the same time the LFP rate among black women heading families rose from 53% to 62%. Mothers of pre-school children also entered the labor force in record numbers. The LFP rates of black wives with children under age 6 jumped from 50% to 72% between 1970 and 1984. Black, working mothers are more likely to rely on relatives for child care than white, working mothers. Almost half (44%) of black working mothers rely on kin for child care, compared to only one-fourth (24%) of white working mothers.

Black working mothers are more likely to be in poverty than white working mothers, whether they are wives or single parents. One-fifth (21%) of black mothers who worked in 1986 were poor, compared to only one-tenth (8%) of white working mothers. And, 39% of black single mothers who worked were poor, compared to 25% of white single mothers. Even black mothers who worked full time in 1986 were twice (15%) as likely to be poor as white mothers who worked full time (7%).

### Child Support

Although black single mothers have a greater need for child support than white single mothers, they are less likely to receive it. Only 36% of black single mothers received child support awards in 1985. Twice as many (71%) white single mothers were awarded child support. Since child support accounts for only about one-sixth of the total income of single mothers, regardless of race, many of them remain in poverty—even when they receive child support payments regularly.

## CHART 48. MEDIAN INCOME OF MARRIED FAMILIES

**Married couples with working wives have the highest median income while families headed by women have the lowest median income. Married couples with working wives have median incomes close to three times that of females who head families.**

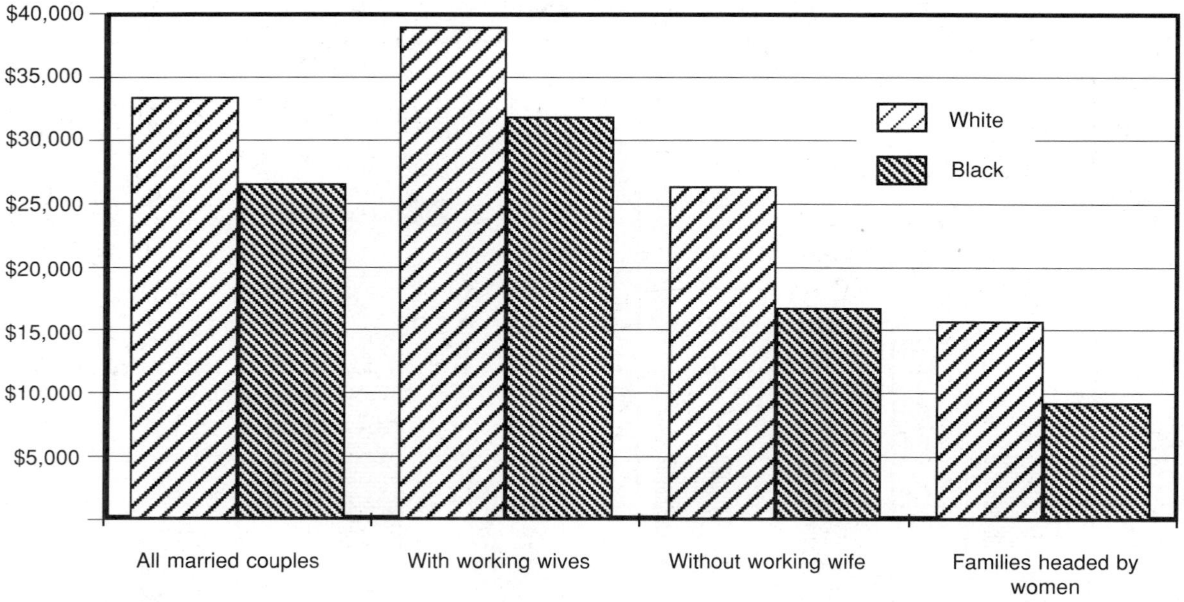


High rates of unemployment among black noncustodial fathers contribute to the low child support payments received by black single mothers. The failure to establish paternity for out-of-wedlock children is the major reason for the low rates of court-ordered child support awards. To facilitate the collection of child support for low-income single mothers, the Family Support Act of 1988 strengthens state efforts to establish paternity, to locate nonsupporting parents, and to institute automatic withholding of the wages of noncustodial fathers—even when they were not in arrears. Since low-income fathers often pay higher proportions of their income for child support than middle-income fathers, the Act also urges more equitable court guidelines.

### Public Assistance

Contrary to popular belief, the proportion of black families on welfare declined throughout most of the '70's and '80's. The largest increases occurred partly as a result of the 1970-71 recession. Between 1969 and 1973, the proportion of all black families receiving welfare rose from 18% to 25%, while the proportion of poor black families on welfare jumped from 35% to 57%. By the first year of the Reagan administration, the proportion of all black families on welfare fell to 22%. The proportion of poor black families on welfare dropped to 52%. The proportion of poor black families receiving welfare remained at 52% by 1986. However, the proportion of all black families on welfare plummeted to 18%—back to its level in 1969.

The removal of about 400,000 working poor (black and white) families from the welfare rolls as a result of the AFDC budget cuts in 1981 contributed to the decline in the number of black families on welfare during the 1980s. For example, the proportion of all female-headed black families on welfare fell from 42% to 37% between 1981 and 1986.

Public assistance comprises only a small fraction of the total income received by black families each year, whether poor or not. Although 18% of all black families received cash public assistance in 1986, welfare accounted for only 3% of the total aggregate income of all black families. Similarly, while half (52%) of poor black families received public assistance, welfare comprised only one-third of the total aggregate income of poor black families. Finally, while 37% of black families headed by women received cash public assistance in 1986, welfare accounted for only one-tenth of their aggregate income.

### Income

Earnings are the predominant source of income for most black families. Eight out of ten (80%) black families had income from earnings in 1986, as did seven out of ten (69%) families headed by black women. Half (51%) of all poor black families and half (46%) of poor black families headed by women had earnings income in 1986.

Earnings accounted for 84% of the aggregate income of all black families and for 74% of the aggregate income of all black families headed by women in 1986. However, earnings comprised only 40% of the aggregate income of all poor black families and only 34% of the aggregate income of poor black families headed by women in 1986.

## Social Security

Although one-fifth of all black families receive income from social security, this source accounts for less than one-tenth of the aggregate income of black families. One-fifth (21%) of all black families and one-fifth (19%) of all black families headed by women received social security in 1986. Yet, social security comprised only 6% of the aggregate income of all black families and only 7% of the aggregate income of black families headed by women in 1986.

As to be expected, elderly women heading families are more likely to receive social security than non-elderly female family heads. Nine out of ten (91%) black families headed by women 65 years and over received social security in 1986, compared to only 13% and 3% of black families headed by women age 25-64 and under age 25, respectively. Social security accounted for only one-third (34%) of the aggregate income of black families headed by elderly women, and for only 5% and 1%, respectively, of the aggregated income of families headed by women age 25-64 and under 25.

Although elderly persons living alone or not with relatives receive social security to the same extent as elderly persons heading families, the former are more dependent on social security for their income than the latter. Almost 93% of all black families headed by persons 65 years and over received social security in 1986. Approximately 89% of all black unrelated individuals who were 65 years and over were totally dependent on social security. But three-fourths (74%) of black, elderly, unrelated individuals relied on social security for over half of their total income in 1986, compared to half (48%) of black families headed by elderly persons.

Poor elderly persons, whether in families or not, are more dependent on social security than the non-poor aged. While over eight out of ten poor black elderly family heads (87%) and poor unrelated elderly individuals (84%) received social security in 1986, social security accounted for over half of the income of two-thirds (67%) poor black families headed by the elderly and of eight out of ten (81%) poor black unrelated elderly individuals. In contrast, less than half (43%) of non-poor black unrelated elderly individuals relied on social security for over half of their income in 1986.

*Streching a dollar by buying at thrift shops is a necessity for many families.*

## Noncash Benefits

On average, blacks receive higher levels of government cash and noncash benefits for the poor. This is the result of their higher rates of poverty. However, whites continue to comprise the bulk of the participants in those programs. For example, whites account for about six out of ten recipients of public assistance, public or subsidized housing, reduced-price school lunches, food stamps and Medicaid. Blacks comprised about one-third of the recipients of these programs.

Poor black families headed by women receive a disproportionate level of noncash government benefits. Over half of black families headed by women receive Medicaid, food stamps and school lunches, compared to about one-fourth of all black families. Over three-fourths of poor black families headed by women participate in these three in-kind programs for the poor, compared to six out of ten of all poor black families.

Although black families are often portrayed as "overdependent" on government aid, sizeable numbers of low-income blacks receive none of those benefits. In fact, half of all poor black families receive no cash public assistance. Half do not receive either Medicaid or food stamps. Three-fifths are not recipients of either public or subsidized housing.

Many conservative analysts contend that government statistics overstate the actual extent of poverty in America, since they are based solely on cash public assistance and exclude in-kind benefits. In response to such criticism, the Census Bureau began issuing experimental annual data on noncash benefits from 1979. These data reveal that at least half of the poor receive none of the in-kind benefits for the poor. They also show that poverty among blacks remains at high levels—even after noncash benefits are included.

Poverty among blacks in 1987 only changed from 33% to 27% when the value of food stamps, housing subsidies and Medicaid was factored in. Even when in-kind benefits were "cashed out," poverty among blacks surged from 22% to 27% between 1979 and 1987—faster than the rise in the official poverty rates for blacks over that eight-year span from 31% to 33%.

Several studies revealed that fewer low-income families were lifted out of poverty by these programs at the end of the Reagan administration than at its beginning. Clearly, this resulted from the disproportionate Federal budget cuts in programs for the poor. While 16% of black families were lifted from poverty by cash entitlement programs (e.g., public assistance, unemployment compensation and social security) in 1979, only 9% of black families were able to move out of poverty as a result of these government benefits.

### Net Worth and Assets

Official income statistics understate the economic gap between the rich and poor in America. To clarify the picture the Census Bureau began collecting periodic data on wealth by race. In 1984, black households had a median net worth ($3,397) that was only 9% that of white households ($39,135). The net worth of white households with monthly incomes of $4,000 or more ($128,237) was twice as large as the net worth of black households with monthly incomes of $4,000 or more ($58,758).

Two-thirds of the total net worth of white households consists of homes. Interest-earnings deposits account for 15% and business equity 11%. Three-fourths of the total net worth of black households consists of homes. Rental property accounts for another 12%. The primary assets of black households are: homes (65%), motor vehicles (65%), interest-earning deposits (44%) and regular checking accounts (32%). Similarly, the primary assets of white households are: motor vehicles (89%), interest-earning deposits (75%), homes (67%) and regular checking accounts (57%).

### Future Economic Outlook

The economic well-being of blacks during the 1990s will depend heavily on the state of the economy. Despite the current record-level budget deficit, most economists do not forecast a recession for 1989, but many anticipate a "mild" recession during 1990. The Labor Department projects two "mild" recessions by the year 2000. Historically, all recessions—however mild—have had disproportionate adverse effects on black workers and their families.

Moreover, with inflation beginning to creep upward, there is a strong likelihood that the Federal Reserve Board may raise interest rates to such an extent that another recession may be induced. Because of President Bush's repeated pledge not to raise taxes to reduce the budget deficit, there is a possibility that programs for the poor may, once again, bear the brunt of federal deficit-reduction initiatives.

The economic status of most blacks will be affected markedly by the quantity and quality of jobs that are created during the 1990s. There is much debate about the quality of the millions of jobs created during the 1980s. It is clear, however, that many high paying manufacturing jobs, where blacks had achieved success, were last due to the erosion of the U. S. Trade position. In their place, came low paying retail and service jobs.

Last but not least are the demographic factors. These bode well for the black worker. The "baby bust" of the 1970s is now reaching working age. This means substantially slower growth in the labor force over the next 10 years as compared to the past 25 years. Continued growth in the economy implies a better level of success and security for all workers at the margins, including blacks.

## EARNINGS AND INCIDENCE OF POVERTY
## SELECTED FACTS

**Fact 1**

While the real median weekly earnings of white men fell by 6% between 1979 and 1986, those of black men declined by 10%. However, the real earnings of white women rose by 4% over that seven-year span, while the real earnings of black women remained about the same.

**Fact 2**

The earnings gap between black and white workers widened between 1979 and 1986. While the median weekly earnings ratio between black and white men decreased from 76% to 73%. The earnings ratio between black and white women declined fnom 93% to 89%.

**Fact 3**

Black and white families experienced similar declines in their real earnings. Real median weekly earnings fell by 5% among white families between 1979 and 1986, and real earnings declined by 6% among black families. Similarly, real earnings fell by 3% and 4%, respectively, among families headed by black and white women.

**Fact 4**

Real earnings fell more sharply among married couples without working wives than among couples with working wives. Real median weekly earnings fell by 1% among two-earner white families between 1979 and 1986. It plummeted by 13% among one-earner white families. While real earnings edge up by 1% among two-earner black families, it dropped by 10% among one-earner black families.

**Fact 5**

While all black male workers had annual mean earnings that were 64% of all white male workers in 1986, black males who worked year-round, full-time earned 69% of comparable white males. Black and white women both had about half the earnings of white male workers.

**Fact 6**

The gap in annual earnings between black and white workers also widened during the '80's. The earnings ratio between black and white men declined from 66% to 64% between 1979 and 1986. Among year-round, full-time

## CHART 49. ANNUAL MEAN EARNINGS OF YEAR-ROUND, FULL-TIME WORKERS BY OCCUPATION, SEX AND RACE: 1986

**Black male full-time workers have mean earnings that are 64% of the earnings their white counterpart. For black and white females mean earnings are almost equal (b/w ratio 95%).**

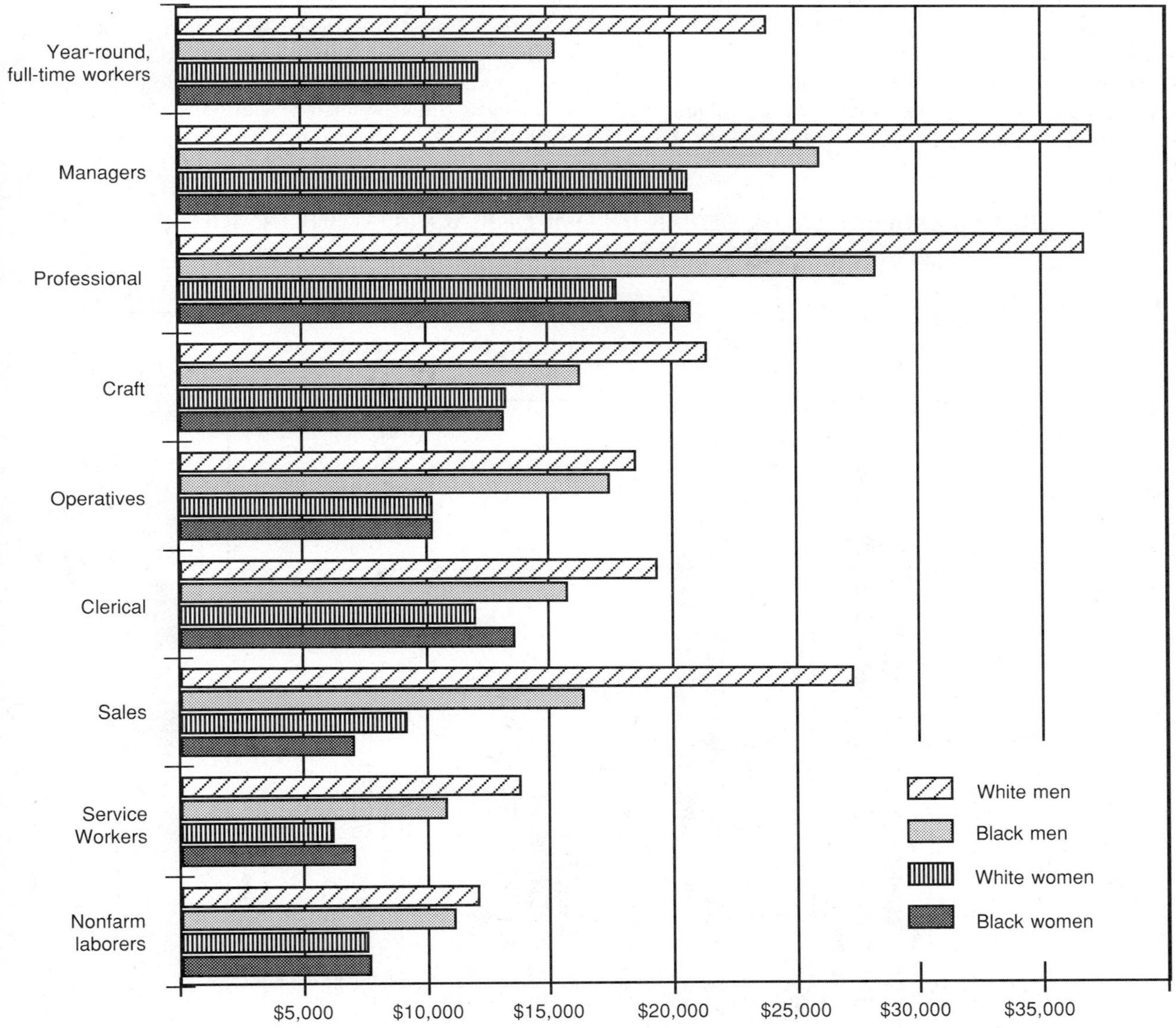


workers, the earnings ratio between black and white men edged down from 71% to 69%. The earnings ratio between black and white women also fell from 95% to 91%.

**Fact 7**

Among year-round, full-time workers, black male professionals earn three-fourths (76%) of white male professionals. Black male sales workers only earn two-thirds (66%) of white male sales workers. While black female professionals earn 61% of white male professionals, black female sales workers earn only 40% of white male sales workers.

**Fact 8**

Service workers have the lowest earnings among black men and women, while professionals have the highest earnings. Among year-round, full-time workers, black male service workers earn only half (51%) of black male professionals, while black female service workers earn only 46% of black female professionals.

**Fact 9**

Unemployment rose sharply among black and white family heads after 1979, due to the back-to-back recessions of 1980 and 1981-82. The number of unemployed heads of black families rose by 48% (from 335,000 to 496,000) between 1979 and 1986. The number of jobless heads of white families also increased by 48% (from 1.3 to 2.0 million). The number of unemployed black husbands rose by 22% between 1979 and 1986. The number of unemployed white husbands rose by 50%. Unemployed black women heading families soared by 72% over that time span. Joblessness among white female heads of families increased by 40%.

**Fact 10**

Unemployment rates increased among the heads of both black and white families between 1979 and 1986. Joblessness among white husbands increased from 3.0% to 4.3%. Unemployment among black husbands jumped from 6.2% to 7.0%. The jobless rate of white female family heads rose from 7.0% to 7.7%. Unemployment among black female family heads soared from 12.9% to 16.5%.

**Fact 11**

Middle-income and low-income black families continued to increase during the '80's. The proportion of black families with incomes under $10,000 edged up from 29% to 30% between 1979 and 1986. The proportion of black families with incomes over $25,000 rose from 34% to 36%. However, the proportion of middle-income white families fell from 62% to 61%, while low-income white families rose from 9% to 10%.

**Chart 50. RATIO OF GROSS MEDIAN INCOME OF BLACK TO WHITE FAMILIES BY REGION OF RESIDENCE: 1969-1987**

**The gap between black and white family income levels is widening, in every region of the country particularly the North-Central region**

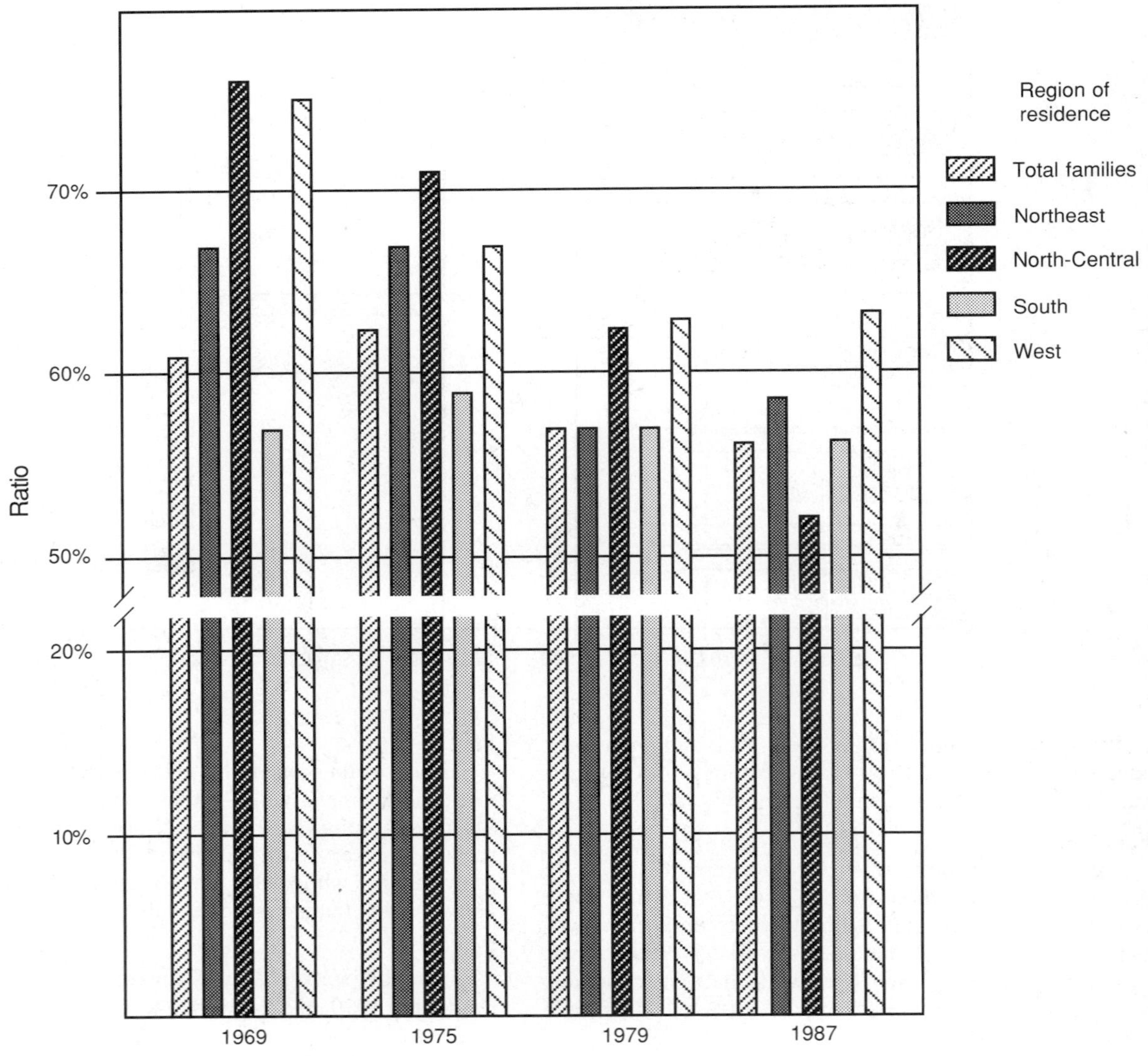

**Fact 12**

The proportion of middle-income ($25,000 & over) black families rose from 32% to 36% between 1970 and 1986. The proportion of low-income (under $10,000) black families increased from 27% to 30%. The proportion of middle-income white families went from 59% to 61% between 1970 and 1986. The proportion of low-income white families remained at 10% over that 16-year span.

**Fact 13**

The income gap between black and white families widened markedly during the '70's. It remained largely unchanged during the '80's. The income ratio of black to white families fell from 61% to 57% between 1969 and 1979. It was still at 57% by 1986.

**Fact 14**

The racial income gap narrowed between black and white married couples. It widened slightly between black and white single parent families. The income ratio of black to white husband-wife families rose from 77% to 80% between 1979 and 1986. The income ratio between black and white female-headed families edged down from 60% to 59%.

**Fact 15**

Two-earner black couples made strong gains in narrowing the gap with whites. One-earner black couples made little or no progress. The income ratio of black to white couples with working wives increased from 77% to 81% between 1969 and 1979, and continued to rise to 82% by 1986. However, while the income ratio of black to white couples without working wives rose from 62% to 64% between 1969 and 1979, it fell to 63% by 1986.

**Fact 16**

When changes in family income are adjusted for inflation, the real incomes of black and white families, as a whole, barely kept even with the cost of living during the '80's. The real gross income of black families only rose by 1% between 1979 and 1986. The real income of white families had no gain in purchasing power.

**Fact 17**

Real income increased sharply among black and white couples, but declined markedly among black and white single-parent families. Real income among black and white couples rose by 5% and 2%, respectively, between 1979 and 1986. Real income among black and white families headed by women dropped from 10% and 9%, respectively.

**Fact 18**

Two-parent black families continue to have more working wives than two-parent white families. The proportion of white couples with working wives rose from 48% to 54% between 1979 and 1986. The proportion of black couples with working wives increased from 59% to 65%. (Table 8)

**Fact 19**

But white families now have more multiple earners than blacks. The proportion of white families with two or more earners jumped from 53% to 57% between 1970 and 1979. It continued to rise to 58% in 1986. Among black families, however, the proportion with two or more earners fell from 54% to 47% between 1970 and 1979. It remained at 47% in 1986.

**Fact 20**

Black families often require an extra earner to have the same income as white families. For example, black families with three earners ($36,029) have about the same income as white families with two earners ($35,848). Black families with one earner ($13,116) still have incomes lower than white families with **no** earners ($14,252).

**Fact 21**

The proportion of blacks in poverty remained virtually unchanged during the '80's. The proportion of poor black families remained at 28% between 1979 and 1986. The proportion of poor female-headed black families edged up from 49% to 50%. The proportion of poor black individuals remained at 31% between 1979 and 1986. The proportion of

**CHART 51. CONSTANT DOLLARS AND NET WORTH**

**In constant dollars, poor people and middle income people are losing net worth while the net worth at higher income levels is rapidly expanding.**

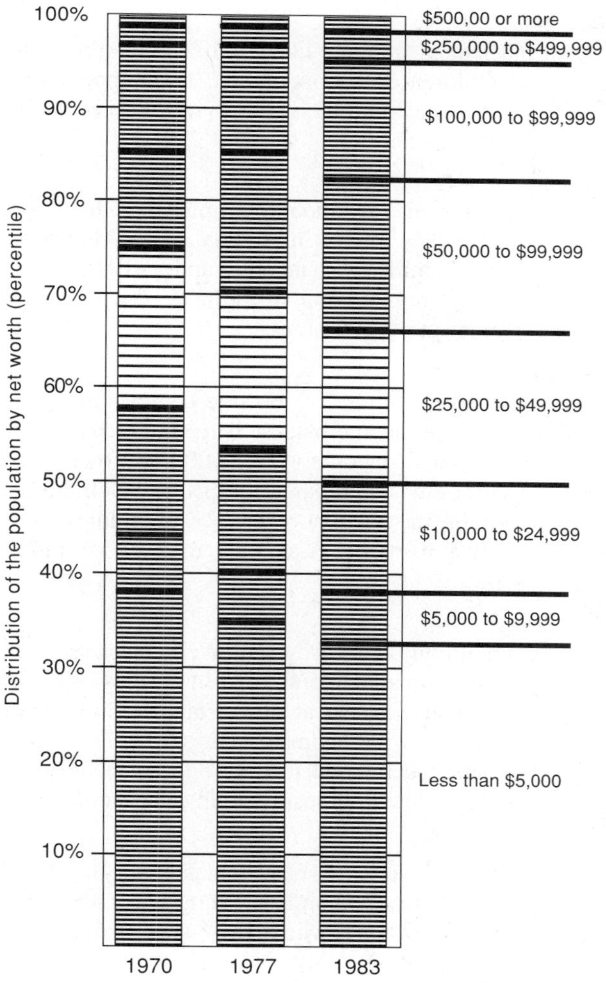

black children in poverty increased from 41% to 43%. Only the black elderly experienced a sharp drop in poverty (from 36% to 31%) between 1979 and 1986.

**Fact 22**

The number of blacks in poverty increased sharply during the '80's. Poor black persons rose from 8.0 to 9.0 million between 1979 and 1986. Poor black families increased from 1.7 to 2.0 million. Poor black children increased from 3.7 to 4.0 million.

**Fact 23**

Based on the official poverty level, 9.0 million blacks were poor in 1986. If the more reasonable 125% of the official poverty level is used, the number of poor blacks rises to 11.1 million. Similarly, the number of poor black children increases from 4.0 to 4.8 million. Using the 125% standard, the poverty rate for all blacks would rise from 31% to 39%, and the rate for black children would increase from 43% to 51%.

**Fact 24**

Three out of five (57%) poor black children live in central cities, compared to one out of two (48%) poor blacks 65 years and older. Also, 61% of poor blacks in female-headed families reside in central cities, compared to only 43% of poor blacks in two-parent families.

**Fact 25**

Poor black aged are more likely to live in the South than poor black children. Seven out of ten (71%) of poor elderly blacks reside in the South. This compares with six out of ten (59%) poor black children.

**Fact 26**

Poor black families are about four times more likely than poor white families to live in poverty areas. Almost half (45%) of black families with incomes under $10,000 live in poverty areas. Only one out of eight (12%) poor white families resides in poverty areas.

**Fact 27**

Middle-income whites live outside central cities more often than middle-income blacks. Three out of five (57%) white families with incomes of $25,000 and over reside outside central cities, compared to 33% to black families with comparable income. However, 22% of middle-income blacks live in poverty areas, compared to 2% of middle-income whites.

**Fact 28**

Three out of four poor (74%) central city blacks reside in poverty areas, compared to only two out of five (39%) poor whites who also live in central cities. Four out of ten central city black families with incomes of $25,000 or more reside in poverty areas, compared to only one out of ten (8%) middle-income white families living in central cities.

**Fact 29**

Only one out of four (24%) black female family heads who worked full-time were poor in 1986. Three out of four (76%) black female family heads who did not work at all that year were classified as poor. Only 6% of black husbands who worked full-time were poor in 1986, compared to 29% of black husbands who did not work that year.

**Fact 30**

Four-tenths (37%) of black working mothers with children under age 18 were poor in 1986. The figure drops to only one-tenth (11%) for black working mothers who were wives. However, 14% of white working mothers were poor, compared to 7% of white working mothers who were wives.

**Fact 31**

Almost half (44%) of black working mothers rely on relatives for child care. This is almost double the level (24%) for white working mothers.

**Fact 32**

About 36% of black single mothers received child support awards in 1985. Twice as many (71%) white single mothers were awarded child support. Three-fourths (75%) of white single mothers who were due child support payments received them, about the same as (72%) of black single mothers.

**Fact 33**

The proportion of black single mothers with child support awards rose from 34% to 36% between 1981 and 1985. The proportion of white single mothers with child support awards went from 69% to 71% during that time.

**Fact 34**

The proportion of black families on welfare declined from 22% to 18% between 1979 and 1986. The proportion of black female-headed families receiving public assistance fell from 41% to 37%. The proportion of poor black families on welfare remained at 52% between 1979 and 1986. The proportion of poor black female-headed families on welfare edged down from 65% to 63%.

**Fact 35**

Approximately 37% of black families headed by women were on welfare in 1986. Public assistance accounted for only one-tenth of their aggregate income. Although half of poor black families were on welfare, public assistance accounted for only one-third of their aggregate income.

**Fact 36**

Earnings accounted for 84% of the aggregate income of all black families in 1986. Earnings comprised only 40% of the aggregate income of all poor black families. Earnings accounted for 74% of the aggregate income of female-headed black families. They comprised only 34% of the aggregate income of poor female-headed black families.

**Fact 37**

Two-thirds (67%) of women under age 25 heading black families were on welfare in 1986. Only 36% of black, female family heads between the ages of 25-64 were on welfare. Public assistance comprised only one-tenth (9%) of their aggregate income. Three-fourths (73%) of black female family heads between the ages of 25-64 had income from earnings. This compares to only half (52%) for women under age 25 heading black families.

**Fact 38**

Blacks comprise one-tenth of the 37.6 million total recipients of Social Security in 1986. Blacks account for one-fifth (21%) of the 3.3 million children receiving Social Security.

**Fact 39**

Blacks comprise only 8% of all retired workers receiving Social Security benefits in 1986. They make up 16% of all disabled workers receiving Social Security.

**Fact 40**

Two-thirds (67%) of black families headed by poor elderly persons rely on Social Security for over half of their total income. Less than half (43%) of the black families headed by non-poor aged rely on social security for half of their income.

**Fact 41**

Black retired workers ($407) received monthly social security benefits in 1986 that were 82% of those received by white retired workers ($496). Black disabled workers ($434) received social security benefits that were 87% of those received by white disabled workers ($500).

**Fact 42**

The overwhelming majority of the recipients of government benefits for the poor are white, not black. Whites account for 67% of Medicaid recipients, 65% of food stamps beneficiaries, 63% of the recipients of public or subsidized housing, 63% of reduced-price school lunches, 62% of welfare recipients, and 54% of all SSI (Supplemental Security Income) beneficiaries.

**Fact 43**

Blacks comprise one-third of the recipients of public assistance (35%), public or subsidized housing (34%), reduced-price school lunches (33%), food stamps (32%) and Medicaid (30%) and one-fourth of the recipients of SSI.

**Fact 44**

About one-fourth of all black households receive Medicaid (25%), public or subsidized housing (24%), and food stamps (22%). About half (49%) of all black households with school-age children receive reduced-price school lunches. Half of all black households headed by women receive Medicaid (50%) and food stamps (46%). Two in five (38%) are public or subsidized housing recipients, and 64% receive reduced-price school lunches.

**Fact 45**

Two out of every five black households below the official poverty level do not receive benefits from Medicaid (43%) or food stamps (43%). About three fifths (61%) of poor black households are not recipients of public or subsidized housing. One-fourth of poor female-headed black households do not receive Medicaid (26%) or food stamps (24%), and half (49%) of them are not recipients of public or subsidized housing.

**Fact 46**

Black households had a median net worth ($3,397) only one-tenth (9%) the net worth ($39,135) of white households in 1984. The median white household has 12 times the net worth of the median black household. White households with monthly income of $4 000 or more have a median net worth ($128,237). This is only twice as large as the net worth ($58,758) of black households with monthly incomes of $4,000 or more.

**Fact 47**

The primary assets of black households are (proportion of households with such assets): homes (65%), motor vehicles (65%) interest-earning deposits (44%); and regular checking accounts (32%). The primary assets of white households are motor vehicles (89%), interest-earning deposits (75%), homes (67%) and regular checking accounts (57%).

**Fact 48**

Two-thirds of the total net worth of white households consist of homes. Interest-earning deposits are 15% of net worth, and business equity is 11%. Three-fourths of the total net worth of black households consist of homes and rental property represents about 12%.

**Fact 49**

Blacks paid one-fifth (19%) of their $201 billion aggregate gross income in federal, state and local taxes in 1986. Whites paid one-fourth (23%) of their $2,476 billion aggregate gross income in taxes.

## TABLE 101. EARNINGS OF ALL WORKERS BY OCCUPATION, SEX AND RACE, 1986

A. Annual median earnings of all workers

| Occupation | White men | Black men | White women | Black women |
|---|---|---|---|---|
| All Workers | $ 23,912 | $ 15,384 | $ 12,248 | $ 11,571 |
| Exec, Mgrs | 37,063 | 26,074 | 20,664 | 20,922 |
| Professionals | 36,726 | 28,341 | 17,840 | 20,752 |
| Technicians | 26,622 | 20,852 | 16,641 | 14,812 |
| Sales | 27,351 | 16,392 | 9,224 | 7,097 |
| Clerical | 19,440 | 15,744 | 11,973 | 13,570 |
| Craft | 21,424 | 16,281 | 13,294 | 13,196 |
| Machine Operatives | 18,526 | 17,519 | 10,265 | 10,353 |
| Transport Operatives | 19,895 | 15,110 | 8,545 | 12,404 |
| Handlers & Laborers | 12,160 | 11,207 | 7,670 | 7,760 |
| Service | 13,865 | 10,883 | 6,264 | 7,067 |

B. Ratio of earnings of other workers to white male workers

| Occupation | White men | Black men | White women | Black women |
|---|---|---|---|---|
| All Workers | 100 | 64 | 51 | 48 |
| Execs, Mgrs | 100 | 70 | 56 | 56 |
| Professionals | 100 | 77 | 49 | 57 |
| Technicians | 100 | 78 | 63 | 56 |
| Sales | 100 | 60 | 34 | 26 |
| Clerical | 100 | 81 | 62 | 70 |
| Craft | 100 | 76 | 62 | 62 |
| Machine Operatives | 100 | 95 | 55 | 56 |
| Transport Operatives | 100 | 76 | 43 | 62 |
| Handlers & Laborers | 100 | 92 | 63 | 64 |
| Service | 100 | 78 | 45 | 51 |

Source: U.S. Commerce Department, Bureau of the Census

## TABLE 102. EARNINGS OF FULL-TIME WORKERS BY OCCUPATION, SEX AND RACE, 1986

A. Annual mean earnings of year-round, full-time workers

| Occupation | White men | Black men | White women | Black women |
|---|---|---|---|---|
| All workers | $ 29,581 | $ 20,295 | $ 18,075 | $ 16,478 |
| Execs, Mgrs | 40,413 | 27,279 | 23,788 | 22,734 |
| Professionals | 41,202 | 31,326 | 24,186 | 25,114 |
| Technicians | 30,482 | 23,981 | 20,539 | 17,329 |
| Sales | 32,714 | 21,607 | 16,178 | 17,044 |
| Clerical | 24,229 | 19,980 | 10,987 | 11,505 |
| Craft | 25,654 | 20,961 | 18,342 | 17,887 |
| Machine Operatives | 21,827 | 20,466 | 13,964 | 13,247 |
| Transport Operatives | 24,287 | 17,476 | 15,234 | — |
| Handlers & Laborers | 19,017 | 16,993 | 13,693 | — |
| Service | 20,023 | 15,855 | 10,987 | 11,505 |

B. Ratio of earnings of other workers to white male workers

| Occupation | White men | Black men | White women | Black women |
|---|---|---|---|---|
| All workers | 100 | 69 | 61 | 56 |
| Execs, Mgrs | 100 | 68 | 59 | 61 |
| Professionals | 100 | 76 | 59 | 61 |
| Technicians | 100 | 79 | 67 | 57 |
| Sales | 100 | 66 | 49 | 40 |
| Clerical | 100 | 82 | 67 | 70 |
| Craft | 100 | 82 | 71 | 70 |
| Machine Operatives | 100 | 94 | 64 | 61 |
| Transport Operatives | 100 | 72 | 63 | — |
| Handlers & Laborers | 100 | 89 | 72 | — |
| Service | 100 | 79 | 55 | 57 |

Source: U.S. Commerce Department, Bureau of the Census

## TABLE 103. MEDIAN INCOME OF FAMILIES BY RACE, 1969-1986

(In current dollars)

| All families | 1969 | 1979 | 1986 |
|---|---|---|---|
| Black | $ 5,999 | $ 11,574 | $ 17,604 |
| White | 9,794 | 20,439 | 30,809 |
| B/W ratio | 61% | 57% | 57% |
| All married couples | | | |
| Black | 7,329 | 16,801 | 26,583 |
| White | 10,241 | 21,754 | 33,426 |
| B/W ratio | 72% | 77% | 80% |
| Wives in labor force | | | |
| Black | 9,132 | 20,524 | 31,949 |
| White | 11,884 | 25,236 | 38,972 |
| B/W ratio | 77% | 81% | 82% |
| Wives not in labor force | | | |
| Black | 5,611 | 11,574 | 16,766 |
| White | 9,109 | 18,158 | 26,421 |
| B/W ratio | 62% | 64% | 63% |
| Families headed by women | | | |
| Black | 3,341 | 6,865 | 9,300 |
| White | 5,500 | 11,432 | 15,716 |
| B/W ratio | 61% | 60% | 59% |

Source: U.S. Bureau of the Census

## TABLE 104. EMPLOYMENT STATUS OF FAMILY HEADS BY RACE, 1979-1987

| A. Number of family heads in civilian labor force | | | | |
|---|---|---|---|---|
| | Black family heads | | White family heads | |
| Number in labor force (thousands) | 1979 | 1987 | 1979 | 1987 |
| All family heads | 4,015 | 4,732 | 39,763 | 41,725 |
| Male heads | 2,731 | 2,997 | 36,101 | 37,112 |
| Female heads | 1,283 | 1,735 | 3,661 | 4,614 |
| **B. Labor force participation rates of family heads** | | | | |
| Labor force participation rates | 1979 | 1987 | 1979 | 1987 |
| All family heads | 73 | 68 | 79 | 76 |
| Male heads | 79 | 75 | 81 | 78 |
| Female heads | 54 | 58 | 62 | 64 |
| **C. Number of unemployed family heads** | | | | |
| Number unemployed (thousands) | 1979 | 1987 | 1979 | 1987 |
| All family heads | 335 | 496 | 1,327 | 1,970 |
| Male heads | 170 | 209 | 1,072 | 1,613 |
| Female heads | 166 | 286 | 255 | 357 |
| **D. Percent of family heads who were unemployed** | | | | |
| Percent unemployed | 1979 | 1987 | 1979 | 1987 |
| All family heads | 8.4 | 10.5 | 3.3 | 4.7 |
| Male heads | 6.2 | 7.0 | 3.0 | 4.3 |
| Female heads | 12.9 | 16.5 | 7.0 | 7.7 |

Source: U.S. Commerce Department, Bureau of the Census

## TABLE 105. MEDIAN WEEKLY EARNINGS OF WORKERS BY RACE AND SEX, 1979-1986

| Workers | 1979 | 1986 | Percent Change[1] 1979-86 |
|---|---|---|---|
| All workers | $ 244 | $ 358 | - 3 % |
| Black | 204 | 291 | - 5 % |
| Men | 233 | 318 | - 10 % |
| Women | 174 | 263 | 0 |
| White | 249 | 370 | - 2 % |
| Men | 306 | 433 | - 6 % |
| Women | 187 | 294 | + 4 % |

Ratio of Black to White Median Weekly Earnings

| Workers | 1979 | 1986 |
|---|---|---|
| All workers | 82 | 79 |
| Men | 76 | 73 |
| Women | 93 | 89 |

[1] Change in 1986 constant dollars.
Source: U.S. Department of Labor, Bureau of Labor Statistics

## TABLE 106. FAMILY MEDIAN INCOME IN CONSTANT 1986 DOLLARS BY RACE, 1979-1986

| | Working heads | | | Year-round, full-time | | |
|---|---|---|---|---|---|---|
| Family structure | 1979 | 1986 | Percent change 1979-86 | 1979 | 1986 | Percent change 1979-86 |
| Total families | | | | | | |
| Black | 17,483 | 17,604 | + 0.7 | 28,169 | 28,690 | + 1.8 |
| White | 30,875 | 30,809 | - 0.2 | 37,281 | 38,413 | + 3.0 |
| Married couples | | | | | | |
| Black | 25,378 | 26,583 | + 4.7 | 32,535 | 34,179 | + 5.1 |
| White | 32,859 | 33,426 | + 1.7 | 38,531 | 40,375 | + 4.8 |
| Couples with working wives | | | | | | |
| Black | 31,002 | 31,949 | + 3.1 | 35,767 | 37,679 | + 5.3 |
| White | 38,119 | 38,972 | + 2.2 | 41,111 | 42,957 | + 4.5 |
| Couples without working wives | | | | | | |
| Black | 17,483 | 16,766 | - 4.1 | 26,308 | 24,304 | - 7.6 |
| White | 27,428 | 26,421 | - 3.7 | 34,879 | 35,521 | + 1.8 |
| Families headed by women | | | | | | |
| Black | 10,370 | 9,300 | -10.3 | 17,322 | 17,985 | + 3.8 |
| White | 17,268 | 15,716 | - 9.0 | 23,218 | 23.353 | + 0.6 |

## TABLE 107. FAMILY INCOME IN CONSTANT 1986 DOLLARS BY RACE, 1979-1986

| | Black families | | White families | |
|---|---|---|---|---|
| Family Income | 1979 | 1986 | 1979 | 1986 |
| Total families[1] | 6,184 | 7,096 | 52,243 | 55,676 |
| Percent | 100 | 100 | 100 | 100 |
| Under $10,000 | 29 | 30 | 9 | 10 |
| Under $2,500 | 3 | 5 | 1 | 2 |
| 2,500-4,999 | 7 | 9 | 1 | 2 |
| 5,000-7,499 | 9 | 8 | 3 | 3 |
| 7,500-9,999 | 9 | 8 | 4 | 4 |
| $10,000-24,999 | 37 | 34 | 29 | 29 |
| 10,000-12,499 | 8 | 7 | 4 | 5 |
| 12,500-14,999 | 7 | 7 | 4 | 5 |
| 15,000-19,999 | 13 | 11 | 11 | 10 |
| 20,000-24,999 | 9 | 10 | 10 | 10 |
| $25,000 & over | 34 | 36 | 62 | 61 |
| 25,000-34,999 | 15 | 15 | 21 | 19 |
| 35,000-49,999 | 13 | 12 | 22 | 21 |
| 50,000 & over | 7 | 9 | 19 | 22 |
| Median income | $ 17,483 | $ 17,604 | $ 30,875 | $ 30,809 |

[1] Numbers in thousands.
Source: U.S. Commerce Department, Bureau of the Census

## TABLE 108. MEDIAN FAMILY INCOME BY NUMBER OF EARNERS AND RACE, 1979-1986

A. Median income of all families

| | 1979 | | | 1986 | | |
|---|---|---|---|---|---|---|
| Number of earners | Black | White | B/W ratio | Black | White | B/W ratio |
| All families | $ 11,509 | 20,492 | 56 | 17,328 | 30,869 | 56 |
| No earners | 4,296 | 8,523 | 50 | 5,798 | 14,252 | 41 |
| One earner | 9,059 | 16,714 | 54 | 13,116 | 24,026 | 55 |
| Two earners | 18,231 | 23,080 | 79 | 27,694 | 35,848 | 77 |
| Three earners | 22,906 | 29,995 | 76 | 36,029 | 45,251 | 80 |
| Four or more | 27,618 | 36,881 | 75 | 43,345 | 67,037 | 76 |

B. Median income of families with year-round, full-time working heads

| | 1979 | | | 1986 | | |
|---|---|---|---|---|---|---|
| Number of earners | Black | White | B/W ratio | Black | White | B/W ratio |
| All families | $ 18,627 | 24,684 | 75 | 28,751 | 38,400 | 75 |
| No earners | — | — | — | — | — | — |
| One earner | 11,647 | 19,781 | 59 | 17,321 | 28,725 | 60 |
| Two earners | 20,891 | 24,642 | 85 | 31,864 | 38,921 | 82 |
| Three earners | 25,561 | 31,516 | 81 | 40,906 | 47,693 | 86 |
| Four or more | 29,385 | 38,545 | 76 | 47,012 | 59,569 | 79 |

## TABLE 109. NUMBER AND PERCENT OF BLACKS AND WHITES BELOW DIFFERENT POVERTY LEVELS, 1986

| | Below 100% of poverty level | | Below 125% of poverty level | | Percent | |
|---|---|---|---|---|---|---|
| Family status | Number[1] | Percent | Number[1] | Percent | Under 100% | Under 125% |
| **White** | | | | | | |
| Total persons | 22,183 | 100 | 30,685 | 100 | 11 | 15 |
| 65& over | 2,689 | 12 | 4,602 | 15 | 11 | 18 |
| In families | 16,393 | 74 | 22,609 | 74 | 9 | 13 |
| Under 18 | 7,714 | 35 | 10,077 | 33 | 15 | 20 |
| Children under 6 | 3,004 | 14 | [2] | [2] | 17 | [2] |
| In male-headed families | 10,222 | 46 | 15,063 | 49 | 7 | 10 |
| In female-headed families | 6,171 | 28 | 7,546 | 25 | 31 | 37 |
| Children under 18 | 3,522 | 16 | 4,132 | 13 | 46 | 54 |
| Children under 6 | 1,311 | 6 | [2] | [2] | 60 | [2] |
| Unrelated individuals | 5,198 | 23 | 7,414 | 24 | 19 | 27 |
| 65 & over | 1,827 | 8 | 3,078 | 10 | 22 | 37 |
| **Black** | | | | | | |
| Total persons | 8,983 | 100 | 11,169 | 100 | 31 | 39 |
| 65 & over | 722 | 8 | 1,043 | 9 | 31 | 45 |
| In families | 7,401 | 82 | 9,240 | 83 | 30 | 37 |
| Children under 18 | 4,039 | 45 | 4,811 | 43 | 43 | 51 |
| Children under 6 | 1,441 | 16 | [2] | [2] | 45 | [2] |
| In male-headed families | 1,928 | 21 | 2,938 | 26 | 13 | 20 |
| In female-headed families | 5,473 | 61 | 6,302 | 56 | 54 | 52 |
| Children under 18 | 3,251 | 36 | 3,622 | 32 | 67 | 75 |
| Children under 6 | 1,194 | 13 | [2] | [2] | 71 | [2] |
| Unrelated individuals | 1,431 | 16 | 1,757 | 16 | 39 | 47 |
| 65 & over | 449 | 5 | 596 | 5 | 54 | 72 |

[1] Numbers in thousands.
[2] Data are not available for children under age 6.
Source: U.S. Commerce Department, Bureau of the Census

## TABLE 110. DISTRIBUTION OF POOR BLACKS BY REGION OF RESIDENCE, 1986

| | | Region of residence (numbers in thousands) | | | |
|---|---|---|---|---|---|
| Family status | Total Percent | North-East | North-Central | South | West |
| Total poor | 100 | 13 | 21 | 60 | 6 |
| 65 & over | 100 | 14 | 12 | 71 | 4 |
| In families | 100 | 12 | 22 | 60 | 5 |
| Children under 18 | 100 | 12 | 23 | 59 | 6 |
| Children under 6 | 100 | 12 | 23 | 58 | 7 |
| In male-headed families | 100 | 9 | 16 | 70 | 4 |
| In female-headed families | 100 | 14 | 24 | 57 | 6 |
| Children under 18 | 100 | 13 | 25 | 56 | 6 |
| Children under 6 | 100 | 12 | 24 | 57 | 7 |
| Unrelated individuals | 100 | 15 | 19 | 57 | 9 |
| 65 & over | 100 | 15 | 16 | 65 | 4 |

## TABLE 111. DISTRIBUTION OF POOR BLACKS BY AREA OF RESIDENCE, 1986

| | | Inside metropolitan area (numbers in thousands) | | | |
|---|---|---|---|---|---|
| | | | Central cities | | |
| Family status | Total percent | Total | Inside | Outside | Outside metropolitan areas |
| Total poor | 100 | 75 | 57 | 18 | 25 |
| 65 & over | 100 | 66 | 48 | 18 | 34 |
| In families | 100 | 75 | 57 | 18 | 25 |
| Children under 18 | 100 | 76 | 57 | 18 | 24 |
| Children under 6 | 100 | 77 | 59 | 18 | 23 |
| In male-headed families | 100 | 63 | 43 | 20 | 37 |
| In female-headed families | 100 | 79 | 61 | 17 | 21 |
| Children under 18 | 100 | 79 | 61 | 17 | 21 |
| Children under 6 | 100 | 78 | 61 | 17 | 22 |
| Unrelated individuals | 100 | 78 | 61 | 17 | 22 |
| 65 & over | 100 | 69 | 53 | 15 | 31 |

## TABLE 112. POVERTY AREA RESIDENCE OF BLACK AND WHITE FAMILIES BY INCOME, 1986

(Percent)

| Family income | Total U.S. | Inside central cities: Total | Poverty areas: Inside | Poverty areas: Outside | Outside central cities | Non-metro-areas |
|---|---|---|---|---|---|---|
| Black | | | | | | |
| All families | 100 | 58 | 33 | 25 | 25 | 18 |
| Under $10,000 | 100 | 61 | 45 | 16 | 17 | 22 |
| Under $5,000 | 100 | 59 | 46 | 13 | 18 | 23 |
| 5,000-9,999 | 100 | 64 | 44 | 20 | 16 | 21 |
| 10,000-24,999 | 100 | 57 | 33 | 23 | 23 | 21 |
| 25,000 & over | 100 | 56 | 22 | 34 | 33 | 11 |
| 50,000 & over | 100 | 51 | 14 | 37 | 42 | 7 |
| White | | | | | | |
| All families | 100 | 25 | 4 | 21 | 51 | 24 |
| Under $10,000 | 100 | 31 | 12 | 18 | 33 | 36 |
| Under $5,000 | 100 | 31 | 13 | 18 | 31 | 38 |
| 5,000-9,999 | 100 | 30 | 12 | 19 | 35 | 35 |
| 10,000-24,999 | 100 | 26 | 6 | 20 | 43 | 31 |
| 25,000 & over | 100 | 24 | 2 | 22 | 57 | 19 |
| 50,000 & over | 100 | 24 | 1 | 23 | 64 | 12 |

Source: U.S. Commerce Department, Bureau of the Census

## TABLE 113. PERCENT OF BLACK FAMILIES AND INDIVIDUALS WHO ARE POOR, 1969-1986

| Year | Black families: All families | Black families: Male-headed | Black families: Female-headed | Black individuals: All persons | Black individuals: All children | Black individuals: All elderly[1] |
|---|---|---|---|---|---|---|
| 1986 | 28 | 12 | 50 | 31 | 43 | 31 |
| 1985 | 29 | 13 | 51 | 31 | 43 | 32 |
| 1984 | 31 | 15 | 52 | 34 | 46 | 32 |
| 1983 | 32 | 16 | 54 | 36 | 46 | 36 |
| 1982 | 33 | 16 | 56 | 36 | 47 | 38 |
| 1981 | 31 | 16 | 53 | 34 | 45 | 39 |
| 1980 | 29 | 14 | 49 | 33 | 42 | 38 |
| 1979 | 28 | 13 | 49 | 31 | 41 | 36 |
| 1975 | 27 | 14 | 50 | 31 | 41 | 36 |
| 1973 | 28 | 15 | 53 | 31 | 41 | 37 |
| 1971 | 29 | 17 | 54 | 33 | 41 | 39 |
| 1969 | 28 | 18 | 53 | 32 | 40 | 50 |

[1] Persons 65 years and older.

# TABLE 114. PERCENT POOR OF FAMILY HEADS BY WORK EXPERIENCE AND RACE, 1986

A. Percent poor of family heads by sex of head

| Work experience | Black family heads | | | White family heads | | |
|---|---|---|---|---|---|---|
| | Family heads | Male heads | Female heads | Family heads | Male heads | Female heads |
| All family heads | 28 | 12 | 50 | 9 | 6 | 28 |
| Worked last year | 16 | 8 | 32 | 6 | 5 | 18 |
| 50-52 weeks | 8 | 5 | 16 | 3 | 3 | 8 |
| Work full-time | 12 | 6 | 24 | 5 | 4 | 12 |
| 50-52 weeks | 7 | 4 | 13 | 3 | 3 | 6 |
| Did not work | 56 | 29 | 76 | 18 | 11 | 46 |

B. Working women who are poor by work experience and race

| Work experience | Black working women | | | White working women | | |
|---|---|---|---|---|---|---|
| | Working mothers | Working wives | Female heads | Working mothers | Working wives | Female heads |
| All working wives | 37 | 11 | 60 | 14 | 7 | 41 |
| Worked last year | 21 | 6 | 39 | 8 | 4 | 25 |
| 50-52 weeks | 11 | 3 | 20 | 4 | 2 | 11 |
| Worked full-time | 15 | 4 | 28 | 7 | 4 | 17 |
| 50-52 weeks | 7 | 2 | 15 | 3 | 2 | 8 |
| Did not work | 70 | 27 | 95 | 25 | 14 | 84 |

C. Working mothers who are poor by age of children by race

| Age of children | Black working mothers | | | White working mothers | | |
|---|---|---|---|---|---|---|
| | Working mothers | Working wives | Female heads | Working mothers | Working wives | Female heads |
| Under age 18 | 37 | 11 | 60 | 14 | 7 | 41 |
| Under age 6 only | 39 | 7 | 67 | 15 | 8 | 57 |
| Under age 6 and 6-17 children | 46 | 14 | 80 | 18 | 11 | 63 |
| 6-17 only | 32 | 11 | 51 | 11 | 6 | 31 |

Source: U.S. Commerce Department, Bureau of the Census

## TABLE 115. CHILD CARE ARRANGEMENTS OF WORKING MOTHERS BY RACE, 1984-1985

| Child care arrangements | Black working mothers | White working mothers |
|---|---|---|
| Total children[1] | 1,782 | 9,262 |
| percent | 100 | 100 |
| By father | 11 | 24 |
| Self-care | 3 | 4 |
| By relatives | 44 | 24 |
| In own home | 26 | 11 |
| Outside home | 18 | 13 |
| By non-relatives | 17 | 27 |
| In own home | 3 | 7 |
| Outside home | 14 | 20 |
| Formal care | 25 | 20 |
| Day care | 17 | 12 |
| Nursery school | 8 | 8 |

[1] Number of children under age 15 in thousands.

Source: U.S. Commerce Department, Bureau of the Census

## TABLE 116. CHILD SUPPORT PATTERNS BY RACE, 1981-1985

A. Percent of single mothers with child support awards

| Single mothers | Total number[1] | Percent with awards 1981 | 1983 | 1985 |
|---|---|---|---|---|
| All mothers | 8,808 | 59 % | 58 % | 61 % |
| White | 6,341 | 69 % | 67 % | 71 % |
| Black | 2,310 | 34 % | 34 % | 36 % |

B. Percent of support payments due that were received

| Single mothers | Total Due[1] | Percent receiving payments 1981 | 1983 | 1985 |
|---|---|---|---|---|
| All mothers | 4,381 | 72 % | 76 % | 74 % |
| White | 3,651 | 73 % | 77 % | 75 % |
| Black | 657 | 67 % | 69 % | 72 % |

C. Mean child support payment received

| Single mothers | 1981 | 1983 | 1985 | Percent change[2] 1981-1985 |
|---|---|---|---|---|
| All mothers | $ 2,106 | $ 2,341 | $ 2,215 | - 11 % |
| White | 2,180 | 2,475 | 2,294 | - 11 % |
| Black | 1,640 | 1,465 | 1,754 | - 10 % |

[1] Numbers in thousands in 1985.
[2] Percent change in constant 1985 dollars.

Source: U.S. Commerce Department, Bureau of the Census

## TABLE 117. SOURCES OF BLACK FEMALE-HEADED FAMILY INCOME BY AGE OF HEAD, 1986

A. Percent of female-headed families with different types of income

(All black families headed by women)

| Type of income | All families | Under 25 yrs | 25-64 yrs | 65 + yrs |
|---|---|---|---|---|
| Total families[1] | 2,967 | 306 | 2,408 | 253 |
| With earnings income | 69 | 52 | 73 | 53 |
| Other than earnings | 79 | 86 | 76 | 98 |
| Social security | 19 | 3 | 13 | 91 |
| Supplemental Security income (SSI) | 10 | 4 | 8 | 39 |
| Public assistance | 37 | 67 | 36 | 15 |
| Other transfers | 9 | 4 | 9 | 11 |
| Property income | 20 | 8 | 21 | 22 |
| Pensions | 25 | 20 | 25 | 29 |

B. Percent of poor female-headed families with different income

(Poor black families headed by women)

| Type of income | All families | Under 25 yrs | 25-64 yrs | 65 + yrs |
|---|---|---|---|---|
| Total families[1] | 1,488 | 250 | 1,165 | 74 |
| With earnings income | 46 | 41 | 48 | 30 |
| Other than earnings | 84 | 87 | 83 | 97 |
| Social security | 14 | 2 | 12 | 86 |
| Supplemental Security income (SSI) | 9 | 2 | 8 | 42 |
| Public assistance | 63 | 77 | 62 | 19 |
| Other transfers | 4 | 3 | 5 | 4 |
| Property income | 5 | 2 | 6 | 10 |
| Pensions | 20 | 16 | 20 | 22 |

[1] Numbers in thousands.

## TABLE 118. SOURCES OF BLACK FEMALE-HEADED FAMILY INCOME BY AGE OF HEAD, 1986

A. Percent distribution of aggregate income of female-headed families

(All black families headed by women)

| Type of income | All families | Under 25 yrs | 25-64 yrs | 65 + yrs |
|---|---|---|---|---|
| Total percent | 100 | 100 | 100 | 100 |
| With earnings income | 74 | 56 | 78 | 44 |
| Other than earnings | 26 | 44 | 22 | 56 |
| Social security | 7 | 1 | 5 | 34 |
| Supplemental Security income (SSI) | 3 | 3 | 2 | 8 |
| Public assistance | 10 | 35 | 9 | 3 |
| Other transfers | 1 | 1 | 1 | 2 |
| Property income | 2 | 1 | 1 | 2 |
| Pensions | 4 | 4 | 4 | 8 |

B. Distribution of aggregate income of poor female-headed families

(Poor black families headed by women)

| Type of income | All families | Under 25 yrs | 25-64 yrs | 65 + yrs |
|---|---|---|---|---|
| Total families[1] | 100 | 100 | 100 | 100 |
| With earnings income | 34 | 22 | 38 | 18 |
| Other than earnings | 66 | 78 | 62 | 82 |
| Social security | 11 | — | 9 | 55 |
| Supplemental Security income (SSI) | 5 | 2 | 5 | 14 |
| Public assistance | 43 | 67 | 42 | 7 |
| Other transfers | 2 | 1 | 2 | 1 |
| Property income | 1 | 2 | — | — |
| Pensions | 5 | 5 | 5 | 6 |

[1] Numbers in thousands.

## TABLE 119. PERCENT OF BLACK FAMILIES RECEIVING PUBLIC ASSISTANCE, 1969-1986

| Year | All black families | | | Poor black families | | |
|---|---|---|---|---|---|---|
| | All families | Male-headed | Female-headed | Poor families | Male-headed | Female-headed |
| | | | (Percent on welfare) | | | |
| 1986 | 18 | 5 | 37 | 52 | 19 | 63 |
| 1985 | 19 | 5 | 39 | 52 | 16 | 65 |
| 1984 | 20 | 6 | 39 | 52 | 22 | 63 |
| 1983 | 21 | 6 | 40 | 52 | 21 | 65 |
| 1982 | 20 | 6 | 40 | 50 | 21 | 62 |
| 1981 | 22 | 6 | 43 | 52 | 22 | 66 |
| 1980 | 21 | 7 | 41 | 52 | 23 | 64 |
| 1979 | 22 | 7 | 41 | 52 | 19 | 65 |
| 1975 | 22 | 7 | 47 | 54 | 21 | 70 |
| 1973 | 25 | 10 | 55 | 57 | 25 | 75 |
| 1971 | 25 | 12 | 54 | 53 | 29 | 70 |
| 1969 | 18 | 10 | 38 | 35 | 21 | 50 |

## TABLE 120. SOURCES OF BLACK FAMILY INCOME BY POVERTY STATUS, 1986

A. Percent of families receiving different types of income

| Type of income | All black families | | Black families headed by women | |
|---|---|---|---|---|
| | All families | Poor families | All families | Poor families |
| Total families[1] | 7,096 | 1,987 | 2,967 | 1,488 |
| With earnings income | 80 % | 51 % | 69 % | 46 % |
| Other than earnings | 76 | 81 | 79 | 84 |
| Social security | 21 | 19 | 19 | 14 |
| Supplemental Security income (SSI) | 7 | 11 | 10 | 9 |
| Public assistance | 18 | 52 | 37 | 63 |
| Other transfers | 13 | 7 | 9 | 4 |
| Property income | 35 | 7 | 20 | 5 |
| Pensions | 23 | 17 | 25 | 20 |

B. Percent distribution of aggregate black family income

| Type of income | All black families | | Black families headed by women | |
|---|---|---|---|---|
| | All families | Poor families | All families | Poor families |
| Total Percent | 100 | 100 | 100 | 100 |
| With earnings income | 84 | 40 | 74 | 34 |
| Other than earnings | 16 | 60 | 26 | 66 |
| Social security | 6 | 15 | 7 | 11 |
| Supplemental Security income (SSI) | 1 | 6 | 3 | 5 |
| Public assistance | 3 | 33 | 10 | 43 |
| Other transfers | 2 | 3 | 1 | 2 |
| Property income | 2 | 1 | 2 | 1 |
| Pensions | 4 | 4 | 4 | 5 |

[1] Numbers in thousands.

## TABLE 121. NUMBER OF CURRENT SOCIAL SECURITY RECIPIENTS BY RACE, 1986

| Social security recipients | Total | White | Black | Percent black |
|---|---|---|---|---|
| Total Number[1] | 37,636 | 33,304 | 3,563 | 10 % |
| Men | 13,974 | 12,491 | 1,202 | 9 |
| Women | 20,377 | 18,360 | 1,685 | 8 |
| Children | 3,285 | 2,453 | 676 | 21 |
| Under age 18 | 2,650 | 1,932 | 577 | 22 |
| Disabled, 18 & over | 551 | 461 | 78 | 14 |
| Students, age 18-21 | 84 | 60 | 21 | 25 |
| Retired workers & dependents | 26,474 | 23,965 | 2,040 | 8 |
| Retired workers | 22,939 | 20,764 | 1,793 | 8 |
| Wives and husbands | 3,085 | 2,862 | 163 | 5 |
| Children | 451 | 338 | 84 | 19 |
| Disabled workers & dependents | 3,979 | 3,159 | 688 | 17 |
| Disabled workers | 2,719 | 2,198 | 440 | 16 |
| Wives and husbands | 299 | 246 | 42 | 14 |
| Children | 961 | 715 | 206 | 21 |
| Survivors of deceased workers | 7,157 | 6,157 | 834 | 12 |
| Widows and widowers | 4,924 | 4,484 | 379 | 8 |
| Widowed mothers and fathers | 352 | 266 | 67 | 19 |
| Children | 1,873 | 1,399 | 387 | 21 |
| Parents | 9 | 7 | 1 | 11 |
| Special age-72 beneficiaries | 24 | 23 | 1 | 4 |

[1] Numbers in thousands.

## TABLE 122. SOCIAL SECURITY SHARE OF BLACK ELDERLY INCOME, 1986

| A. Share of income of black elderly heads of families | | | | |
|---|---|---|---|---|
| Social security Share of income | Total | Nonpoor | Poor | Percent poor |
| Total Families[1] | 0.9 | 0.7 | 0.2 | — |
| Percent | 100 | 100 | 100 | 22 % |
| No social security | 7 | 5 | 13 | 43 |
| Some social security | 93 | 95 | 87 | 21 |
| Under one-fourth | 20 | 25 | 5 | 6 |
| One-fourth to one-half | 25 | 28 | 14 | 13 |
| One-half to three-fourths | 20 | 20 | 21 | 23 |
| Three-fourths or more | 28 | 23 | 46 | 36 |

| B. Share of income of black elderly unrelated individuals | | | | |
|---|---|---|---|---|
| Social security Share of income | Total | Nonpoor | Poor | Percent poor |
| Total Families[1] | 0.8 | 0.4 | 0.4 | — |
| Percent | 100 | 100 | 100 | 54 % |
| No social security | 11 | 6 | 16 | 74 |
| Some social security | 89 | 94 | 84 | 51 |
| Under one-fourth | 5 | 10 | 1 | 9 |
| One-fourth to one-half | 10 | 19 | 3 | 14 |
| One-half to three-fourths | 20 | 21 | 19 | 52 |
| Three-fourths or more | 54 | 45 | 62 | 62 |

[1] Numbers in millions.

Source: U.S. Commerce Department, Bureau of the Census

## TABLE 123. SOCIAL SECURITY SHARE OF WHITE ELDERLY INCOME, 1986

A. Share of income of white elderly heads of families

| Social security Share of income | Total | Nonpoor | Poor | Percent poor |
|---|---|---|---|---|
| Total families[1] | 9.2 | 8.7 | 0.5 | — |
| Percent | 100 | 100 | 100 | 5 % |
| No social security | 7 | 6 | 15 | 12 |
| Some social security | 93 | 94 | 85 | 5 |
| Under one-fourth | 23 | 24 | 4 | 1 |
| One-fourth to one-half | 28 | 30 | 6 | 1 |
| One-half to three-fourths | 22 | 22 | 17 | 4 |
| Three-fourths or more | 20 | 18 | 59 | 16 |

B. Share of income of white elderly unrelated individuals

| Social security Share of income | Total | Nonpoor | Poor | Percent poor |
|---|---|---|---|---|
| Total Families[1] | 8.3 | 6.4 | 1.8 | — |
| Percent | 100 | 100 | 100 | 22 % |
| No social security | 5 | 4 | 12 | 47 |
| Some social security | 95 | 96 | 88 | 21 |
| Under one-fourth | 10 | 13 | 1 | 2 |
| One-fourth to one-half | 22 | 27 | 5 | 5 |
| One-half to three-fourths | 22 | 24 | 15 | 15 |
| Three-fourths or more | 40 | 33 | 67 | 37 |

[1] Numbers in millions.

Source: U.S. Commerce Department, Bureau of the Census

## TABLE 124. AVERAGE MONTHLY SOCIAL SECURITY BENEFITS BY RACE, 1986

| Social security recipients | Total | White | Black | B/W ratio |
|---|---|---|---|---|
| Retired workers | $ 489 | $ 496 | $ 407 | 82 |
| Men | 550 | 559 | 457 | 82 |
| Women | 420 | 427 | 356 | 83 |
| Disabled workers | 487 | 500 | 434 | 87 |
| Men | 538 | 552 | 476 | 86 |
| Women | 384 | 390 | 359 | 92 |
| Widowed mothers & fathers | 339 | 358 | 283 | 79 |
| Nondisabled widows & widowers | 444 | 453 | 351 | 77 |
| Surviving children | 338 | 357 | 284 | 79 |

## TABLE 125. RECIPIENTS OF CASH AND IN-KIND BENEFITS BY RACE, 1985-1986

| Cash and noncash benefits | Total number[1] | Percent | White | Black |
|---|---|---|---|---|
| Means-tested cash aid [2] | | | | |
| Public assistance | 4,240 | 100 | 62 | 35 |
| Supplemental security income (SSI) | 4,269 | 100 | 54 | 25 |
| Other cash aid[2] | | | | |
| Social security | 37,636 | 100 | 88 | 10 |
| Means-tested noncash aid [3] | | | | |
| Medicaid | 8,178 | 100 | 67 | 30 |
| Food stamps | 6,779 | 100 | 65 | 32 |
| Reduced price school lunches | 5,752 | 100 | 63 | 33 |
| Public or subsidized housing | 3,799 | 100 | 63 | 34 |
| Other in-kind aid [3] | | | | |
| Employee group health | 50,804 | 100 | 88 | 10 |
| Employee pension plan | 38,983 | 100 | 87 | 10 |
| Medicare | 21,833 | 100 | 89 | 10 |
| Regular school lunches | 11,772 | 100 | 87 | 10 |

[1] Numbers in thousands.
[2] Cash aid data for 1986.
[3] Noncash aid data for 1985.

## TABLE 126. NUMBER AND PERCENT OF BLACK HOUSEHOLDS RECEIVING NONCASH BENEFITS, 1985

A. Black household recipients by poverty status

| Noncash benefits | All black households Number[1] | All black households Percent | Poor black households Number[1] | Poor black households Percent |
|---|---|---|---|---|
| Total households | 9,797 | 100 | 2,935 | 100 |
| with children 5-18 | 3,916 | 40 | 1,397 | 48 |
| Renter-occupied | 5,436 | 55 | 2,168 | 74 |
| Means-tested benefits | | | | |
| Medicaid | 2,486 | 25 | 1,666 | 57 |
| Food stamps | 2,162 | 22 | 1,687 | 57 |
| Reduced price school lunches | 1,904 | 49 | 1,118 | 80 |
| Public or subsidized housing | 1,284 | 24 | 848 | 39 |
| Other in-kind benefits | | | | |
| Employee group health | 4,897 | 50 | 333 | 11 |
| Enployee pension plan | 4,015 | 41 | 211 | 7 |
| Medicare | 2,127 | 22 | 770 | 26 |
| Regular school lunches | 1,160 | 30 | 79 | 6 |

B. Black female-headed household recipients by poverty status

| Noncash benefits | All female-headed households Number[1] | All female-headed households Percent | Poor female-headed households Number[1] | Poor female-headed households Percent |
|---|---|---|---|---|
| Total households | 2,874 | 100 | 1,452 | 100 |
| with children 5-18 | 1,955 | 68 | 1,116 | 77 |
| Renter-occupied | 1,960 | 68 | 1,175 | 81 |
| Means-tested benefits | | | | |
| Medicaid | 1,439 | 50 | 1,079 | 74 |
| Food stamps | 1,323 | 46 | 1,103 | 76 |
| Reduced price school lunches | 1,256 | 64 | 902 | 81 |
| Public or subsidized housing | 737 | 38 | 598 | 51 |

[1] Numbers in thousands.

## TABLE 127. NUMBER AND PERCENT OF WHITE HOUSEHOLDS RECEIVING NONCASH BENEFITS, 1985

A. White household recipients by poverty status

| | All white households | | Poor white households | |
|---|---|---|---|---|
| Noncash benefits | Number[1] | Percent | Number[1] | Percent |
| Total households | 76,576 | 100 | 8,707 | 100 |
| with children 5-18 | 22,122 | 29 | 2,838 | 33 |
| Renter-occupied | 25,559 | 33 | 5,068 | 58 |
| Means-tested benefits | | | | |
| Medicaid | 5,465 | 7 | 2,976 | 34 |
| Food stamps | 4,431 | 6 | 3,109 | 36 |
| Reduced price school lunches | 3,616 | 16 | 1,738 | 61 |
| Public or subsidized housing | 2,390 | 9 | 1,164 | 23 |
| Other in-kind benefits | | | | |
| Employee group health | 44,652 | 58 | 1,132 | 13 |
| Employee pension plan | 33,993 | 44 | 513 | 6 |
| Medicare | 19,401 | 25 | 2,659 | 31 |
| Regular school lunches | 10,296 | 47 | 430 | 8 |

B. White female-headed household recipients by poverty status

| | All female-headed households | | Poor female-headed households | |
|---|---|---|---|---|
| Noncash benefits | Number[1] | Percent | Number[1] | Percent |
| Total households | 7,111 | 100 | 1,950 | 100 |
| with children 5-18 | 3,759 | 52 | 1,331 | 68 |
| Renter-occupied | 3,371 | 47 | 1,713 | 88 |
| Means-tested benefits | | | | |
| Medicaid | 1,746 | 25 | 1,189 | 61 |
| Food stamps | 1,536 | 22 | 1,231 | 63 |
| Reduced price school lunches | 1,377 | 37 | 886 | 67 |
| Phblic or subsidized housing | 613 | 18 | 444 | 26 |

[1] Numbers in thousands.

## TABLE 128. NET WORTH OF HOUSEHOLDS BY TYPE OF ASSETS AND RACE, 1984

A. Percent of households owning various assets by race

| Type of assets | Total | White | Black |
|---|---|---|---|
| Total households[1] | 86,790 | 79,343 | 9,509 |
| Motor vehicles | 86.8 % | 88.5 % | 65.0 % |
| Interest-earning deposits | 71.8 | 75.4 | 43.8 |
| Own home | 64.3 | 67.3 | 65.0 |
| Regular checking accounts | 53.9 | 56.9 | 32.0 |
| Stocks & mutual fund shares | 20.0 | 22.0 | 5.4 |
| IRA or Keogh accounts | 19.5 | 21.4 | 5.1 |
| U.S. savings bonds | 15.0 | 16.1 | 7.4 |
| Own business or profession | 12.9 | 14.0 | 4.0 |
| Other real estate | 10.0 | 10.9 | 3.3 |
| Rental property | 9.8 | 10.1 | 6.6 |
| Other interest-earning assets | 8.5 | 9.4 | 2.1 |
| Mortgages | 2.9 | 3.3 | 0.1 |
| Other assets | 3.5 | 3.9 | 0.7 |

B. Percent distribution of total net worth by type of asset

| Type of assets | Total | White | Black |
|---|---|---|---|
| Total net worth | 100.0 | 100.0 | 100.0 |
| Own home | 41.3 | 40.5 | 64.7 |
| Interest-earning deposits | 14.4 | 14.7 | 6.8 |
| Equity in own business | 10.3 | 10.5 | 6.7 |
| Rental property | 9.0 | 8.6 | 12.4 |
| Stocks & mutual fund shares | 6.8 | 7.1 | 0.8 |
| Motor vehicles | 6.0 | 5.9 | 11.1 |
| Other real estate | 4.4 | 4.4 | 2.4 |
| Other interest-earning assets | 3.1 | 3.2 | 0.7 |
| IRA or Keogh accounts | 2.2 | 2.2 | 0.9 |
| Checking accounts | 0.6 | 0.6 | 0.9 |
| U.S. savings bonds | 0.5 | 0.5 | 0.2 |

[1] Numbers in thousands.

## TABLE 129. NET WORTH OF HOUSEHOLDS BY RACE, 1984

A. Median net worth of households by race

| Monthly household income | White | Black | W/B ratio |
|---|---|---|---|
| Total households | 39,135 | 3,397 | 11.5 |
| Less than $ 900 | 8,443 | 88 | 96.0 |
| $ 900-1,999 | 30,714 | 4,218 | 7.3 |
| $ 2,000-3,999 | 50,529 | 15,977 | 3.2 |
| $ 4,000 or more | 128,237 | 58,758 | 2.2 |

B. Distribution of households by net worth and race

| Total net worth | White | Black |
|---|---|---|
| Total households[1] | 75,343 | 9,509 |
| Percent | | |
| Less than $1 | 8 | 30 |
| $ 1-4,999 | 14 | 24 |
| $ 5,000-24,999 | 19 | 21 |
| $ 25,000-99,999 | 36 | 21 |
| $ 100,000 & over | 23 | 4 |
| Median net worth | 39,135 | 3,397 |
| Mean net worth | 86,332 | 20,241 |

[1] Numbers in thousands.

## TABLE 130. FAMILIES WITH MARRIED COUPLES BY INCOME AND RACE, 1986

| | Black families | | White families | |
|---|---|---|---|---|
| Family income | Number of Families[1] | Percent Couples | Number of Families[1] | Percent Couples |
| Total Families | 7,096 | 53% | 55,676 | 83% |
| Under $5,000 | 994 | 13% | 1,947 | 42% |
| $5,000 - 9,999 | 1,146 | 28% | 3,747 | 60% |
| $10,000 - 19,999 | 1,734 | 50% | 10,409 | 76% |
| $20,000 - 24,999 | 678 | 59% | 5,513 | 81% |
| $25,00 - 49,999 | 1,921 | 76% | 21,793 | 89% |
| $50,000 & over | 624 | 89% | 12,267 | 95% |

[1] Numbers in thousands
Source: U.S. Bureau of the Census

## TABLE 131. HOUSEHOLD TAX-PAYING PATTERNS BY RACE AND POVERTY STATUS, 1986

A. Aggregate income before and after taxes by race

| Annual household income | Black households Before taxes | Black households After taxes | Black households Percent taxes | White households Before taxes | White households After taxes | White households Percent taxes |
|---|---|---|---|---|---|---|
| Total Income[1] | 200.7 | 152.7 | 19 % | 2,476.2 | 1,898.9 | 23 |
| Under $5,000 | 5.6 | 5.2 | 7 | 13.0 | 11.6 | 11 |
| $ 5,000-9,999 | 12.8 | 11.9 | 7 | 62.5 | 58.1 | 7 |
| $ 10,000-19,999 | 35.3 | 30.8 | 13 | 240.2 | 210.3 | 12 |
| $ 20,000-24,999 | 20.5 | 17.1 | 17 | 167.7 | 140.3 | 16 |
| $ 25,000-34,999 | 37.8 | 30.6 | 19 | 390.5 | 315.3 | 19 |
| $ 35,000-49,999 | 41.6 | 32.8 | 21 | 556.3 | 431.4 | 23 |
| $ 50,000 & over | 47.5 | 34.3 | 28 | 1,046.1 | 731.9 | 30 |
| $ 75,000 & over | 16.3 | 11.0 | 33 | 496.6 | 322.1 | 35 |

B. Percent of poor households paying various taxes

| Type of taxes | Total | White | Black |
|---|---|---|---|
| Total Poor[2] | 11,217 | 7,988 | 2,906 |
| Percent | 100 | 100 | 100 |
| No taxes paid | 35 | 31 | 45 |
| One or more taxes | 65 | 69 | 55 |
| Federal income taxes | 8 | 9 | 6 |
| State income taxes | 13 | 14 | 11 |
| FICA payroll taxes | 43 | 44 | 40 |
| Federal retirement | 1 | 1 | 1 |
| Property taxes | 35 | 39 | 25 |

[1] Numbers in billions.
[2] Numbers in thousands.

# THE FEDERAL GOVERNMENT AND ASSISTANCE PROGRAMS

**The Reagan Changes ■ Federal Aid—A Brief History ■ Federal Assistance and Minorities ■ The Nixon Years ■ Ford and Carter ■ Specific Programs of Importance to Blacks ■ Federal Assistance Programs**

Drastic cuts in federal assistance programs were enacted in 1981 and more cuts were on the drawing board during the budget debates of spring 1982 and through the remainder of the Reagan Years. The spur to these cuts was a revolutionary change in the philosophy and policies of government. The philosophy of the Reagan Administration held that government activity on behalf of the poor was unproductive for its intended recipients, a dangerous economic burden for the nation to carry and morally questionable in and of itself. The administration also contended that cuts in assistance programs were necessary to increase military expenditures and to control a spiraling national debt that was expected to exceed $100 billion for the coming (1983) fiscal year.

As a result, funding for many programs was reduced significantly. Among affected programs were: Food Stamps, Aid to Families with Dependent Children, Medicaid, Energy Assistance, and The Job Corps.*

State and local programs were also affected adversely by cuts in federal aid. Declining tax revenues due to the recession and reductions in business, corporate and property taxes have also affected state and local programs.

## Federal Aid—A Brief History

The concept of federal aid to underprivileged groups and individuals came slowly to the United States, which has traditionally valued the virtues of individual initiative and volunteerism, and has distrusted expansion of government's size and influence. The spur to such government activity was provided by the Great Depression and the magnetism of Franklin Delano Roosevelt, who became president in 1933. The cost-cutting economies of the Hoover Administration that preceded Roosevelt had failed to help the poor and unemployed or reverse the economic decline. The theories of British economist John Maynard Keynes suggested that the answer to economic depression was not for government to save money, but to stimulate its circulation and thus produce demand for goods and services. Roosevelt and his advisors felt that government spending to boost the economy was entirely compatible with America's prevailing doctrine of private enterprise and set out to press through Congress a great variety of programs that provided employment and direct monetary aid to large numbers of people who were unemployed or impoverished.

This approach was so popular it was soon embraced in

* See Sections on unemployment, income-earnings, and family for more specific details on reductions in federal aid.

fact, though not in theory, by many of Roosevelt's political opponents, and federal assistance programs expanded during the Truman and Eisenhower administrations that followed.

## Federal Assistance and Minorities

Many of these programs, however, were criticized by minorities for not recognizing their underprivileged position and singling them out for special aid. Indeed, though blacks and other minorities benefited greatly from Roosevelt's "New Deal" efforts, administration of government aid often discriminated against them, especially during the 1930s in much of the aid to farmers in the South. Later in the 1950s, many blacks also charged that too much direct aid and tax relief incentives were directed to businesses and affluent citizens rather than to people with low incomes.

The concept of federal aid for disadvantaged groups reached a peak in the early 1960s, spurred in large measure by the recognition of Presidents Kennedy and Johnson that very large pockets of poverty existed in cities and rural areas, especially among minorities.

Kennedy encountered strong opposition from Congress, in his federal aid, as well as civil rights efforts, but many of his proposals were enacted during his administration, and following his assassination, under President Johnson.

The number of blacks participating in federally aided job programs multiplied at least fivefold between 1964 and 1969, and poverty programs started during the Kennedy and Johnson presidencies were aiding an increasing number of people.

Decentralization involved the use of some 10,000 job training subcontractors, a step which according to the U.S. Civil Rights Commission increased the possibilities for discrimination in specific programs and decreased the possibility of adequate policing of non-discrimination rules by federal agencies. Personnel to enforce anti-discrimination laws in federal programs was sparse and rarely spurred to action by the Administration. The basis of a "Southern Strategy" emphasized white ethnics and suburban areas where the black population is small.

Though job training of blacks was deemphasized it remains important. In 1973, the percentage of blacks enrolled in federally assisted job training programs still constituted twice the official percentage of the nation's unemployed.

As noted in the Income and Earnings section, aid to blacks under various poverty programs has also decreased. The one area in which aid has increased since 1968 is "black capitalism," which is discussed elsewhere in this book.

## The Nixon Years

The enrollment of blacks in federally assisted employment programs began to recede in 1969, during the first term of President Nixon, and did so steadily every year through 1973. Between 1971 and 1973, the only program in which the percentage of black enrollees increased was the Work Incentive Program, a program that is geared primarily to the reduction of the welfare rolls. Between 1972 and 1973, the percentage of blacks enrolled in all programs dropped from 45% to 40%. The drop in black enrollees was most apparent

*Government assistance for education has, until now, been a bipartisan effort.*

in the JOBS program, from 43% to 26% in the two-year period.

Major reasons for the decline of black enrollment were the decentralization of training and assistance programs, and the Nixon Administration's increased emphasis on aid to groups other than disadvantaged minorities.

Upon taking office in January 1975, Gerald Ford blamed much of the nation's economic ills on federal assistance programs. Said the President:

"We have been self-indulgent ....for decades we have been voting ever-increasing levels of government benefits ....adding so many new programs....that their cost increases every year....because the number of people eligible for benefits increases." He then suggested that present programs be restrained and no new programs be added except in the field of energy.

## Ford and Carter

A key area in which President Ford suggested cuts was the Food Stamp Program. In specific terms, he proposed an increase in the cost people would pay for the stamps so that the great majority of recipients of this aid would be required to pay more for food than they had previously.

The government's rationale for proposing this cut was twofold. First, the cost of the program had increased greatly, from $250 million annually in fiscal 1969 to over $4 billion in fiscal 1975, despite the fact that a great many families eligible for the benefits had not made use of them. In addition, many economists felt that food stamps contributed to large increases in food costs; that they were responsible for as much as half the rise of food prices between 1973 and 1975.

These economists suggested that a more efficient way to help poor people was via increases of direct welfare payments rather than with food stamps. This suggestion actually appeared in the 1975 Economic Report to the President.

However, the status quo was to remain. The Administration was in no mood to grant increases in welfare payments and Congress was of no mind to saddle large blocs of voters with increases in food stamp costs. So, for the time being at least, the food stamp program survived without cuts or a substitute. But cutbacks in other federal aid were extensive—especially in areas of health and education—and in the summer of 1975 there was little prospect of restoration or increases in the near future.

With cutbacks at the federal level, many state and local governments faced severe financial strains with a result that they were often unable to produce "matching" funds which would enable them to take advantage of federal money that was available.

The election of Jimmy Carter in 1976 brought a respite to the cutbacks. Notable increases in CETA, Food Stamps, and other major programs were enacted. As his term progressed, however, Carter felt increasing pressures to cut back and in many areas did so. But his premise that the federal government had a duty to help the impoverished and unemployed, remained intact and became an issue in the 1980 presidential campaign, when Ronald Reagan opposed Carter. Though Reagan's view carried the day, few expected the massive cuts of social programs the newly elected president was to propose and pursue successfully through an acquiescent Congress. In this area, the administration's objectives and accomplishments dwarfed those of such earlier opponents of government aid as Nixon and Ford.

The administration suggested three alternatives to federal activity. One was to transfer a sizeable portion of responsibility and funds to state and local governments. Another was to ask private businesses and business groups to undertake and direct activities such as job training. Yet another was to seek to replace government aid with volunteer contributions of money and time from individuals, business, religious and social groups.

## Specific Programs of Importance to Blacks

Of the hundreds of federal aid programs available, the Negro Almanac believes the following are of special importance to blacks. We have based our selection on each program's orientation in helping people who need economic assistance, growth and development, greater job skills, or educational direction. We have also sought to list those programs with specific orientation to blacks or minorities.

In some programs, support is provided directly to individuals. More often, however, funds are channeled

*Many people who are old and poor have no where to turn except to government.*

through political subdivisions or public or private nonprofit corporations with further criteria stipulated as to the specific beneficiaries of funds.

For further information about the eligibility requirements of specific programs or on their uses or restrictions, one should contact the office of the agency listed under the "Eligibility" classification in the ensuing list.

### A Caution

All individuals and groups applying for any form of assistance are urged first to inquire as to the specific information forms and documents that they must submit. This is especially important with regard to programs aiding low income individuals such as The Food Stamp Program where extensive red tape often causes long and unproductive waiting periods. Adequate preparation can improve one's chances of qualifying and lessen the number and duration of trips to agency offices.

Also, due to the unsettled focus of the new Bush Administration there is a wait and see climate as to what the attitude will be toward federal assistance programs, such as those listed here. The continuity of programs listed in the following pages and the appropriation figures listed with them cannot be guaranteed.

## FEDERAL ASSISTANCE PROGRAMS

NOTE: Budget cuts may have substantially reduced the indicated budget figure for many programs though they remain in force.

### Low to Moderate Income Rural Housing Loans

**Agency**: Department of Agriculture

**Program Number:** 10.410

**Types of Assistance**: Guaranteed/insured loans are provided to assist rural families obtain decent, safe and sanitary dwellings and related facilities.

**Uses**: Loans may be used to build, repair or purchase housing, sewage disposal facilities or a site on which to build them. In 1973, 116,700 loans totaling $1.7 billion were granted.

**Restrictions**: Dwellings for people with low or moderate income must be modest in design and cost. Applicant must be without sufficient funds to provide facilities on their own or obtain credit on reasonable terms from another source.

### Related Programs of Interest (Housing)

10.411 RURAL HOUSING SITE LOANS
Aids public or private nonprofit corporations to acquire or

*Poverty is not confined to inner cities, as is the popular view, but is dispersed in many rural areas of the country as well.*

develop land to be subdivided as building sites and sold on a nonprofit basis to low and middle income families. The limit is $100,000 unless approval for a greater sum is granted by The National Farm Home Administration Office.

10.417 VERY LOW INCOME HOUSING REPAIR LOANS
Seeks through loans to give very low income rural home owners the means to make minor repairs essential to safety and health.

10.420 RURAL SELF-HELP HOUSING TECHNICAL ASSISTANCE
Aims to provide financial support for technical assistance to needy low income families to carry out mutual self help efforts in rural areas. Support is provided through political subdivisions or nonprofit corporations. Funds can't be used to buy land or building materials or to hire people for construction work. The idea is to pay for the technical expertise and some of the office and administrative expenses.

ELIGIBILITY FOR 1O.410 1O.411 1O.417 1O.420
Contact State or local office of the Farmers Home Administration or write The Administrator, Farmers Home Administration, Washington, D.C. 20250.

### Extension Service

**Agency**: Department of Agriculture

**Program Number**: 10.500

**Types of Assistance:** Educational programs in the areas of agricultural production and marketing, rural development, youth development and home economics.

**Uses:** The Extension Service program seeks to benefit farmers, producers, marketing firms, community organizations, homemakers, youth in general and 4 H Club members to benefit from technical developments and research in the areas of farming, nutrition, home management, family development, parent education, leadership development and career guidance.

The program has considerable potential for black farmers and land grant colleges, but according to 1970 reports of the Civil Rights Commission, blacks have been receiving a disproportionately small share of the funds appropriated. Total projected appropriations for fiscal 1975 were $176 million.

**Restriction:** By law, grants are made only to designated land grant institutions in the State and are administered by the Director of the State Extension Service.

**Eligibility:** Contact Extension Service, Department of Agriculture, Washington, D.C.

### Food Administration

**Agency:** Department of Agriculture

**Program Number**: 10.550

**Types of Assistance**: The government gives away surplus food, primarily to needy families and schools, also to institutions.

**Uses**: To improve the diets of school children, the elderly, and needy individuals and the quality of food provided by charitable institutions.

To increase the market for food acquired via surplus food and price support programs. For fiscal 1975, assistance projected was about $500 million in food donations, only $2 million in formula grants.

**Restrictions**: Vary from state to state. State, federal, and local distributing agencies are designated by the government of each state. Food may not be sold, exchanged, or otherwise disposed of without permission from the U.S. Department of Agriculture. Beneficiaries must be certified by local welfare officials as having inadequate income and resources. However, the beneficiary may be employed, unemployed, pensioned, or on strike.

**Eligibility**: Contact local or regional Food and Nutrition Service of the Department of Agriculture or the Food Distribution Division, Food and Nutrition Service, Department of Agriculture, Washington, D.C. 20250.

### Food Stamps

**Agency:** Department of Agriculture

**Program Number**: 10.551

**Type of Assistance**: Government subsidies for the purchase of food, plants that produce food, and garden seeds in amounts up to 30% of income.

**Uses:** Mainly for low income families. Some elderly people may use stamps to pay for home delivered or institutional meals. Alcoholics and drug addicts may use stamps to pay for meals provided by programs they have enrolled in. In Alaska, recipients may use stamps to buy hunting and fishing equipment.

**Restrictions:** Families must live in an area that has the program and be unemployed, part-time employed, working for low wages, living on small pensions, or deemed eligible by local welfare officials. As a rule, able-bodied adults must meet a work registration requirement.

**Eligibility:** It is estimated that only one-third of the nation's families that are eligible for stamps use them, mainly because they are not aware of the many deductions that may be taken from their income. Some of these deductions include alimony, child support, a dependent's education. For information contact the Food and Nutrition Service Regional Office or their headquarters, Department of Agriculture, Washington, D.C.

**Related Programs of Interest**

10.552 SPECIAL FOOD SERVICE PROGRAM FOR CHILDREN
Known as the "non school food program," this program

*There is a Special Food Service Program for needy non school-age children.*

seeks primarily to aid handicapped children and children from low income families that are receiving care in an institution. Aid is channeled through public and nonprofit institutions such as day care centers, settlement houses, recreation centers, and day camps. To be approved, institutions must operate a nonprofit food service for all children regardless of race, color, or national origin. In 1973 195,000 school children participated in the year-round program and 1,175,000 in the summer program.

10.553 SCHOOL BREAKFAST PROGRAM
Any public or private school that is exempt from income tax may receive aid which is intended to provide free or reduced price breakfasts for children who are deemed to be eligible by school officials.

10.554 NONFOOD SERVICE ASSISTANCE FOR SCHOOL SERVICE PROGRAMS (EQUIPMENT PROGRAM)
The objective is to provide funds for equipment and storage facilities to schools in low income areas so they can establish, maintain, and expand food services. Seventy-five to 100% of the cost of equipment is given. Recipients must agree to participate in the National School Lunch and/or Breakfast Program.

10.555 NATIONAL SCHOOL LUNCH PROGRAM
Seeks to provide lunch in schools for poor children of high school age and under. It is similar to the Breakfast Program 10.553.

10.556 SPECIAL MILK PROGRAM FOR CHILDREN
The government reimburses money to schools for expenses incurred in starting and expanding distribution of fluid milk to children. Public and nonprofit schools and child care institutions are eligible, but they must agree to operate the program without regard to race, color, or national origin.

10.557 SPECIAL SUPPLEMENTAL FOOD PROGRAM—FOR WOMEN, INFANTS, AND CHILDREN
This program has two principal objectives—to provide food to pregnant or lactating women identified as nutritional risks and to collect and evaluate data to identify the medical benefits of the program. Funds are provided to local public and nonprofit health service agencies which must provide health services free or at reduced cost to residents of a low income area.

ELIGIBILITY FOR PROGRAMS 10.552, 10.553, 10.554, 10.555, 10.556
Contact the Director, Child Nutrition Division, Food and Nutrition Service, Department of Agriculture, Washington, D.C. 20250 or the regional office of the Food and Nutrition Service of the U.S. Department of Agriculture.

ELIGIBILITY FOR PROGRAM 10.557
Food Distribution Division, Food and Nutrition Service, Department of Agriculture, Washington, D.C. 20250, or the Regional Office of the Food and Distribution Service.

### Youth Conservation Corps

**Agency:** Department of Agriculture

**Program Number:** 10.661

**Type of Assistance:** Employment of male and female teenagers between the ages of 15 to 18 in conservation work on public lands.

**Uses:** All States, virtually all territories, and many local and municipal governments are eligible for grants or sub-grants. The program seeks to achieve a racial mix and to bypass the personnel requirements for full-time employment of the local or state authority that carries out the program. As such it is an opportune source for brief employment of teenagers.

**Restrictions:** No one can be employed in this program for more than 90 days per year.

**Eligibility:** Contact State Foresters or Directors of Departments of Natural Resources or the Forest Service Division of Manpower and Youth Conservation Programs of the Department of Agriculture, 12th St. and Independence Avenue S.W., Washington, D.C. 20250.

### Minority Business Enterprise (OMBE)

**Agency:** Department of Commerce Program Number: 11.800

**Type of Assistance:** Grants, counseling, and research contracts, usually ranging in size from $100,000 to $350,000, are given to nonprofit organizations for channeling to an existing or potential business that is owned or controlled by one or more persons who is disadvantaged from cultural, racial, or chronic economic circumstance or background. As defined by OMBE, such persons include, but are not limited to, "Negroes, Puerto Ricans, Spanish-speaking Americans, American Indians, Aleuts, Eskimos and Orientals."

**Uses:** This program supports a broad range of efforts to aid minorities and develop minority businesses. The businesses can include universities and trade associations as well as financial institutions and corporations. In addition, OMBE coordinates federal assistance programs for minorities, assists development of state and local programs, and conducts pilot projects designed to overcome special problems of minority businessmen.

**Restrictions:** Federal minority business programs have been widely criticized for supporting too many small businesses that could not succeed competitively without continuing and expensive support. As such, the government is increasingly stressing aid to larger minorities' businesses and demanding ever-increasing portents of success before committing its support.

**Eligibility:** Contact Regional or Local Office of the Office of Minority Business Enterprise or the Assistant Director, Administration and Field Operation Division, Office of Minority Business Enterprise, Department of Commerce, Washington, D.C. 20230.

### Health Care of Children and Youth

**Agency:** Department of Health and Human Services

**Program Number:** 13.218

**Type of Assistance:** Grants to state health agencies for the promotion of health services for low income families. Uses: Screening, diagnosis, treatment, correction of defects, and aftercare, both medical and dental.

Funds may not be used for purchase or construction of buildings.

**Eligibility:** Contact Regional Health Administrator, Department of Health and Human Services Regional Office or Associate Bureau Director for Maternal & Child Health, Bureau of Community Health Services, Room 12-05, Parklawn Building, 5600 Fishers Lane, Rockville, Maryland 20852.

13.217 FAMILY PLANNING PROJECTS
Grants made to state health agencies to provide persons from low income families with family planning advice, contraceptive supplies, and counseling, plus diagnostic and treatment centers for infertility.

13.224 HEALTH SERVICES DEVELOPMENT PROJECT GRANTS
Funds to be allocated to public or non-profit private agencies, institutions, or organizations that, in accordance with plans of the state comprehensive health planning agency, propose to improve the accessibility of health care to low income families.

12.230 INTENSIVE INFANT CARE PROJECTS
Grants available to state health agencies, agencies of political subdivision of the state, and to any other public or nonprofit agency or institution to provide first year health care to infants from low income families.

13.232 MATERNAL & CHILD HEALTH SERVICES
Grants made to state health agencies to reduce infant mortality and improve health of mothers and children in areas suffering from severe economic distress.

13.234 MATERNITY AND INFANT CARE PROJECTS
Grants available to health agencies of states, political subdivisions, and nonprofit organizations to provide diagnostic and specialist consultation to vulnerable low income women early in pregnancy. The aim is to reduce the incidence of mental retardation and other handicapping child-bearing conditions.

ELIGIBILITY FOR 13.217
Contact Regional Health Administrator, Department of Health and Human Services, or Associate Bureau Director for Family Planning Services, Health Services, Department of Health and Human Services, Rockville, Maryland.

ELIGIBILITY FOR 13.224
Contact Regional Health Administrator, Department of

Health and Human Services or Associate Bureau Director for Neighborhood Health Centers, Room 12A-56, Parklawn Building, 56 Fishers Lane, Rockville, Maryland 20852.

ELIGIBILITY FOR 13.230, 13.232 AND 13.234
Contact Regional Health Administrator, Department of Health and Human Services or Associate Bureau Director, Maternal and Child Health Services, Bureau of Community Health Service, Room 12-05, Parklawn Building, 5600 Fishers Lane, Rockville, Maryland 20852.

### Drug Abuse Community Service Programs

**Agency:** Department of Health and Human Services

**Program Number:** 13.235

**Type of Assistance:** Grants given to community mental health centers, affiliates of a community mental health center, or a public or private nonprofit agency located in an area that has no community mental health center. Provides salaries for personnel and services, inpatient, outpatient, intermediate (halfway house or partial hospitalization), 24-hour emergency service, community-wide consultation, and education services.

**Uses:** To reach, treat, and rehabilitate drug addicted and drug dependent persons through community based services.

**Eligibility:** National Institute on Alcohol, Drug Abuse and Mental Health Administration, 11400 Rockville Pike, Rockville, Maryland 20852.

### Migrant Health Grants

**Agency:** Department of Health and Human Services Program Number: 13.246

**Type of Assistance:** Grants to public or private nonprofit agency.

**Uses:** Establishment and operation of family health service clinics to raise health status of migratory seasonal farm workers and their families. Included are: medical care to prevent or treat illness, nursing services, sanitation services, health education, training of migrants to be health aides, and coordination of services between areas and states along the same migrant stream.

**Eligibility:** Contact Regional Health Administrator or Associate Bureau Director, Migrant Health, Bureau of Community Health Services, Room 7-22, Parklawn Building, 5600 Fishers Lane, Rockville, Maryland 20852.

### National Health Service Corps

**Agency:** Department of Health and Human Services

**Program Number:** 13.258

**Type of Assistance:** Provision of specialized health personnel to areas having critical shortages of such personnel. Applicants must be state or local health agencies, public or nonprofit private health organizations.

*Health Manpower Education Initiative Awards recruit minority students.*

**Uses:** To provide medical, dental, nursing, psychiatric, and paramedical services to anyone within the designated area wishing it at reasonable or no cost.

Assignment and designation of personnel will be partly based upon the availability of the Service's personnel to provide the services requested.

13.261 FAMILY HEALTH CENTERS
Grants available to public or private nonprofit agencies to develop health maintenance and treatment services to low income and poor people in areas with scarce health services. Funds are not to be used for services which are paid for by Medicaid, Medicare, or union health plans.

ELIGIBILITY FOR 13.258 AND 13.261
Contact Regional Health Administrator or National Health Service Corps Program Director or National Health Service Corps, Health Services Administration, Parklawn Building, 5600 Fishers Lane, Rockville, Maryland.

*Several maternal and child health services are funded by the federal government.*

13.430 EDUCATIONALLY DEPRIVED CHILDREN—STATE ADMINISTRATION
Funds available to state or outlying area to improve and expand educational programs for disadvantaged children through administrative assistance to state and local educational agencies.

13.431 EDUCATIONALLY DEPRIVED CHILDREN IN STATE-ADMINISTERED INSTITUTIONS SERVING NEGLECTED OR DELINQUENT CHILDREN
Grants to state agencies directly responsible for providing free public education in state institutions for neglected or delinquent children or adult correctional institutions. Services proposed must supplement, not supplant those normally provided with State or local funds.

13.433 FOLLOW THROUGH
Grants to communities with full year Headstart or similar program and the resources to provide Follow Through's range of services.

ELIGIBILITY FOR 13.420 AND 13.431
Contact Division of Education for the Disadvantaged, Office of Compensatory Education Programs, Bureau of School Systems, Office of Education, 7th and D Streets, S.W., Washington, D.C. 20202.

ELIGIBILITY FOR 13.433
Contact Follow Through Division, Office of Compensatory Education Programs, Bureau of School Systems, Office of Education, 7th and D Street, S.W., Washington, D.C. 20202.

### Special Services for Disadvantaged Students in Institutions of Higher Education

**Agency:** Department of Health and Human Services Program Number: 13.482

**Type of Assistance:** Grants to accredited institutions of postsecondary education.

**Uses:** Funds to provide assistance to low income and physically handicapped students enrolled or accepted for enrollment to initiate, continue, or resume postsecondary education.

Monies cannot be used to staff ethnic studies programs, building or outfitting tutorial or media centers, or duplicate services available through vocational rehabilitation, medicare or medicaid.

**Eligibility:** Director of Higher Education, Department of Health and Human Services Regional Office or Division of Student Support and Special Programs, Bureau of Postsecondary Education, Office of Education, 400 Maryland Avenue, S.W., Washington, D.C. 20202
689-1

#### Related Programs of Interest

13.488 TALENT SEARCH
Grants to institutions of higher education, including those with vocational and career education programs, to enable them to provide educational opportunity to young people bypassed by traditional educational procedures offering them options for continuing their education.

13.492 UPWARD BOUND
Grants to institutions of higher education, including those with vocational and career education programs to carry out Upward Bound Projects which are developed to generate skill.

13.501 VOCATIONAL EDUCATION WORK STUDY
Grants to state boards for vocational education to be used for assisting economically deprived, full-time vocational education students, aged 15-20, to remain in school by providing part-time employment with public employers.

13.502 VOCATIONAL EDUCATION INNOVATION
Grants and contracts to State boards for vocational education, local educational agencies, public and private agencies and organizations to develop, establish and operate occupational education programs as models for vocational education programs as models for academic, socioeconomic or other handicaps.

ELIGIBILITY FOR 13.488, 13.492
Director of Higher Education, Department of Health and Human Services Regional Office or Division of Student

Support and Special Programs, Bureau of Postsecondary Education, Office of Education, 400 Maryland Avenue, S.W., Washington, D.C. 20202.

ELIGIBILITY FOR 13.501
Contact Director, Division of Vocational and Technical Education, Center for Adult, Vocational, Technical and Manpower Education, Office of Education, Washington, D.C. 20202.

ELIGIBILITY FOR 13.502
Contact Regional Office, Department of Health and Human Services or Director, Division of Research and Demonstration Bureau of Occupational and Adult Technical Education, Office of Education, Washington, D.C. 20202.

### Educationally Deprived Children—Special Grants for Urban and Rural Schools

**Agency:** Department of Health and Human Services Program Number: 13.511

**Type of Assistance:** Grants to eligible districts, based on state-conducted comprehensive survey of areas with highest concentration of children from low income areas.

**Uses:** Emphasis for preschool and elementary school programs to meet the special educational needs of deprived children.

#### Related Programs of Interest

13.512 EDUCATIONALLY DEPRIVED CHILDREN SPECIAL INCENTIVE GRANTS
Incentive grants to state educational agencies to be used to provide an incentive for increases in state and local funding for elementary and secondary education which meets the needs of educationally deprived children.

ELIGIBILITY FOR 13.511 AND 13.512
Contact Division of Education for the Disadvantaged, Office of Compensatory Educational Programs, Bureau of School Systems, Office of Education, 7th and D Streets, S.W., Washington, D.C. 20202.

### Emergency School Aid Act—Basic Grants to Local Educational Agencies

**Agency:** Department of Health and Human Services

**Program Number:** 13.525

**Type of Assistance:** Grants to elementary and secondary local educational agencies for plans to eliminate, reduce, or prevent the isolation of minority group students in their schools.

**Uses:** Plans requesting funds must make available the following: remedial services, supplemental staff, teacher aids and training, guidance and counseling, curriculum development, career education, interracial activities, community activities, support services, planning, and minor remodeling.

**Eligibility:** Contact Emergency School Aid Director, Office of Education, Department of Health and Human Services Regional Office or Associate Commissioner, Office of Equal Educational Opportunity Programs, Bureau of School Systems, Office of Education, 400 Maryland Avenue, S.W., Washington, D.C. 20202.

#### Related Programs of Interest

13.526 EMERGENCY SCHOOL AID ACT—PILOT PROGRAMS
Grants to local educational agencies to assist them in eliminating, reducing, or preventing minority group isolation. Focus will be on districts having either a minimum of 15,000

*Project Head Start operates over 13,000 Child Development Centers for preschool youngsters.*

minority students or a minority enrollment of at least 50%.

13.527 EMERGENCY SCHOOL AID ACT—METROPOLITAN AREA PROJECTS
Grants to local educational agencies involved in establishing and maintaining integrated schools, developing a plan to reduce minority group isolation in a Standard Metropolitan Statistical Area, or planning integrated educational parks.

13.529 EMERGENCY SCHOOL AID ACT—SPECIAL PROGRAMS AND PROJECTS
Grants to nonprofit organizations to conduct programs which support local educational agencies' efforts to meet special problems incident to desegregation, to encourage voluntary integration, or to aid schoolchildren in overcoming the educational disadvantages of minority group isolation.

13.530 EMERGENCY SCHOOL AID ACT—EDUCATIONAL TELEVISION
Grants to public or private nonprofit agencies with expertise in the development of television programming which has positive cognitive and affective value and presents multi-ethnic children's activities. Purpose is to overcome educational disadvantages of minority group isolation.

13.532 EMERGENCY SCHOOL AID ACT—SPECIAL PROGRAMS
Grants to local educational agencies and supporting public organizations which will conduct activities to help children overcome the educational disadvantages of minority group isolation.

13.533 RIGHT TO READ—ELIMINATION OF ILLITERACY
Grants to public or non-public school districts which will plan and implement reading and teacher training practices designed to increase functional literacy so that by 1980, 99% of those 16 years of age and 90% of those over 16 will be functionally literate.

ELIGIBILITY FOR 13.526, 13.527, 13.529, 13.530 AND 13.532
Contact Associate Commissioner, Officer of Equal Educational Opportunity Programs, Bureau of School Systems, Office of Education, 400 Maryland Avenue, S.W., Washington, D.C. 20202.

ELIGIBILITY FOR 13.533
Contact Office of Education, Department of Health and Human Services Regional Office or National Right To Read Office, Office of Education, 400 Maryland Avenue, S.W., Washington, D.C. 20202.

### Educational Opportunity Centers

**Agency:** Department of Health and Human Services

**Program Number:** 13.543

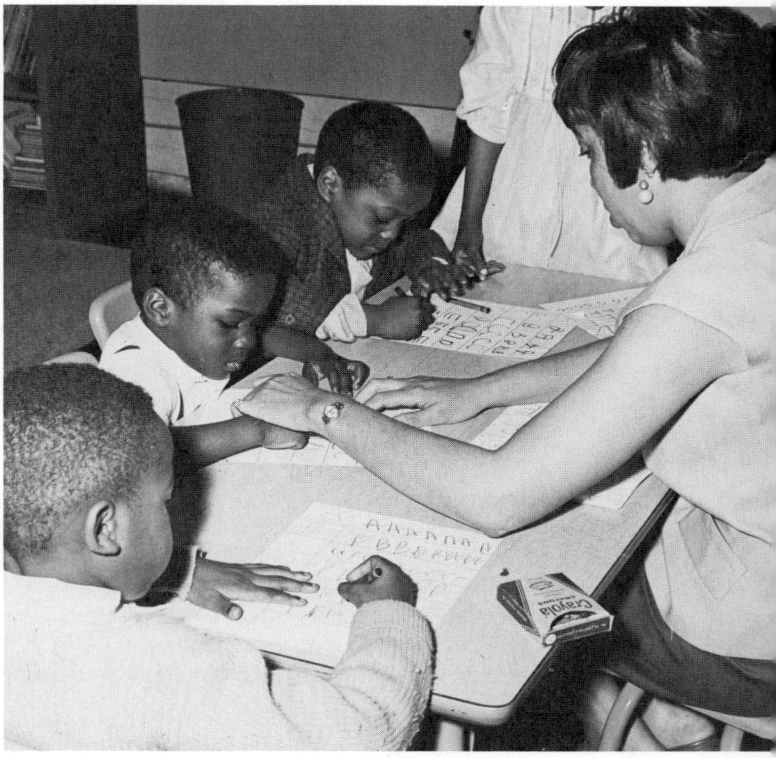

*There is a government sponsored "Right to Read" program.*

**Type of Assistance:** Grants to institutions of higher education including those with vocational and career education programs, and in exceptional cases, secondary and secondary vocational schools.

**Uses:** Funds to be provided for setting up services to facilitate entry into postsecondary educational programs, particularly for low income students.

**Eligibility:** Contact Director of Higher Education, Department of Health and Human Services Office or Division for Student Support and Special Programs, Bureau of Postsecondary Education, Office of Education, 400 Maryland Avenue, S.W., Washington, D.C. 20202.

### Child Development—Head Start

**Agency:** Department of Health and Human Services

**Program Number:** 13.600

**Type of Assistance:** Grants and contracts to public or private nonprofit agencies.

**Uses:** Funds for provision of educational, nutritional, and social services to preschool children of poor families, so that they enter school on equal terms with the less deprived children. Programs involve parents in activities of their children.

Head Start Programs are primarily for children from age 3 to age of entrance into the school system.

**Eligibility:** Contact Regional Program Director, Office of Child Development, Office of Human Development, Department of Health and Human Services or Office of Child Development, Head Start, Office of Human Development, Department of Health and Human Services, P.O. Box 1182, Washington, D.C. 20013.

### Civil Rights Compliance Activities

**Agency:** Department of Health and Human Services

**Program Number:** 13.602

**Type of Assistance:** Investigation of complaints made by anyone who feels discriminated against in the provision of federal funds or services due to race, color, or national origin.

**Uses:** Enforcement of Title VI of Civil Rights Act of 1964, which prohibits Federal funds for programs that discriminate as to race, color, or national origin. This program has been extended to include anti-sex discrimination provisions.

To ensure that beneficiaries of major programs receive services without discrimination or segregation, the Office of Civil Rights investigates and takes corrective steps to assure equal opportunity.

**Eligibility:** Contact Civil Rights Directors, Department of Health and Human Services Regional Offices or Director, Office for Civil Rights, Office of the Secretary, Department of Health and Human Services, Washington, D.C. 20201.

### Youth Development Delinquency Prevention

**Agency:** Department of Health and Human Services

**Program Number:** 13.610

**Type of Assistance:** Grants to federal, state, local public, or private nonprofit agencies. Private agencies must be in existence at least two years before applying.

**Uses:** To develop and implement coordinated youth service systems for the prevention of delinquency.

**Eligibility:** Contact Office of Assistant Regional Director for Human Development or Commissioner, Office of Youth Development, Office of Human Development, Department of Health and Human Services, Washington, D.C. 20201.

### Social and Rehabilitation Service

**Agency:** Department of Health and Human Services

**Program Number:** 13.707

**Type of Assistance:** Grants to states, District of Columbia, Puerto Rico, Virgin Islands, and Guam.

**Uses:** To establish, extend, and strengthen services provided by state and local public welfare programs for development of preventive and protective services which will preclude neglect, abuse, exploitation, or delinquency of children.

Monies can be used for costs of personnel, licensing of, and standard setting for child caring agencies, assisting with costs of foster care, day care, homemaker services, return of runaway children and adoptive placement of children.

**Eligibility:** Contact Regional Community Services, Officials of Social and Rehabilitative Service or Director, Division of Child and Family Services, Community Services Administration, Social and Rehabilitative Service, Department of Health and Human Services, 330 C Street, S.W., Washington, D.C. 20201.

### Medical Assistance Program

**Agency:** Department of Health and Human Services

**Program Number:** 13.714

**Type of Assistance:** Grants to state and local welfare agencies.

**Uses:** Financial assistance to States for payments of medical assistance on behalf of cash assistance recipients.

Services include: in and out patient hospital services, laboratory and x-ray, skilled home nursing, home health for persons over 21, family planning, physicians and early periodic screening, diagnosis and treatment for individuals under 21.

State and local welfare agencies must operate under government-approved state plan.

**Eligibility:** Contact Regional Commissioner, Medical Services Administration, Social and Rehabilitative Service or Commissioner, Medical Services Administration, Social and Rehabilitative Services, Department of Health and Human Services, 330 C Street, S.W., Washington, D.C. 20201.

### Work Incentives Program—Child Care—Employment Related Supportive Services

**Agency:** Department of Health and Human Services

**Program Number:** 13.748

**Type of Assistance:** Grants to state welfare agencies.

**Uses:** To furnish community resources to help persons receiving aid to families with dependent children become self-supporting by providing necessary child care and supportive services to registrants and participants in WIN and other man-power programs.

**Eligibility:** Contact Regional Commissioner, Regional Coordination Committee, Social and Rehabilitation Service or Administrator, Social and Rehabilitation Service, Department of Health and Human Services, Washington, D.C. 20201.

### Public Assistance—Maintenance Assistance

**Agency:** Department of Health and Human Services Program Number: 13.761

**Type of Assistance:** Grants to state and local welfare

agencies operating under approved Health and Human Services State Plan.

**Uses:** Financial aid to families with dependent children, emergency welfare assistance, assistance to repatriated U.S. nationals. In Guam, Virgin Islands, and Puerto Rico funds are to provide aid to the aged, blind, and permanently disabled.

Direct money payments by states covers costs for food, shelter, clothing, and other necessary items for daily living and payments for care of specified children in foster homes or institutions.

**Eligibility:** Individuals should contact local welfare agency. States should contact Regional Office, or Chief, Office of Public Information, Social and Rehabilitation Service, Department of Health and Human Services, Washington, D.C. 20201.

## Blood Diseases and Resources Research

**Agency:** Department of Health and Human Services

**Program Number:** 13.839

**Type of Assistance:** Project and research grants to any nonprofit organization engaged in biomedical research. In certain cases individuals may qualify for fellowship, award or research grant.

**Uses:** To further the development of blood resources and promote research on blood diseases including Sickle Cell Disease.

Funds can support salaries, equipment, supplies, travel, and patient hospitalization as required for performance of research.

**Eligibility:** Contact Director, Division of Blood Diseases, National Heart and Lung Institute, Bethesda, Maryland 20014.

## Interest Subsidy—Acquisition and Rehabilitation of Homes for Resale to Lower Income Families

**Agency:** Department of Housing and Urban Development

**Program Number:** 14.104

**Type of Assistance:** Insured loans, direct payments for specified use to private nonprofit and public organizations.

**Uses:** Loans may be used to finance, purchase, and rehabilitate housing for resale to low income families.

Purchasers of these homes must be families, handicapped persons or single persons 62 and older whose incomes fall within specified limits.

**Eligibility:** Production Information: contact Director, Multifamily Underwriting Division, Housing Production and Mortgage Credit, Federal Housing Authority, Department of Housing and Urban Development, Washington, D.C. 20410. For Management Information: contact Director, Office of Loan Management, Housing Management, Department of Housing and Urban Development, Washington, D.C. 20410.

*The Department of Housing and Urban Development was empowered to fund the clearance of slums.*

### Related Programs of Interest

14.105 INTEREST SUBSIDY HOMES FOR LOWER INCOME FAMILIES
Guaranteed/insured loans and direct payments for specified use to families, handicapped persons, or single persons 62 and older whose income and assets fall within certain limits. Loans can be used to finance purchase of single-family or 2-family units or units in a multifamily dwelling which has been constructed or rehabilitated under FHA within 2 years prior to application for assistance.

14.106 INTEREST SUBSIDY PURCHASE OF REHABILITATED HOMES BY LOWER INCOME FAMILIES
Guaranteed/insured loans, direct payments for specified use to finance purchase of single-family or 2-family units or units in multifamily dwelling which has been rehabilitated by a nonprofit sponsor.

14.120 MORTGAGE INSURANCE HOMES FOR LOW AND MODERATE INCOME FAMILIES
Guaranteed/insured loans to make home-ownership more readily available to families displaced by urban renewal as well as low and moderate income families. Loans may be

used for purchase of proposed or existing low cost 1 to 4 family housing or the rehabilitation of such housing.

ELIGIBILITY FOR RELATED PROGRAMS OF INTEREST
Contact nearest local Housing and Urban Development Area Office or Director, Single Family Underwriting Division, Housing Production and Mortgage Credit, Federal Housing Authority Department of Housing and Urban Development, Washington, D.C. 20410.

### Public Housing—Home-Ownership for Low Income Families

**Agency:** Department of Housing and Urban Development

**Program Number:** 14.147

**Type of Assistance:** Project grants and direct loans to local housing authorities, authorized public agencies, or Indian tribal organizations.

**Uses:** To provide housing purchase opportunities for low income families by crediting amount budgeted for routine maintenance performed by tenants to family equity accounts. When family income reaches the point where permanent financing for the unit can be obtained or when equity account equals unamortized debt and closing costs, ownership passes to family.

The program was suspended in January 1973 pending comprehensive evaluation of subsidized housing.

**Eligibility:** Contact Director, Publicly Financed Housing Division, Housing Production and Mortgage Credit, Department of Housing and Urban Development, Washington, D.C. 20410.

### Related Program of Interest

14.148 PUBLIC HOUSING LEASED
Project grants to local housing authorities, authorized public agency, or Indian tribal organizations providing annual contributions which permit local public agency to provide decent, safe, sanitary housing for low income families at rents they can afford to pay.

**Eligibility:** Contact Director, Publicly Financed Housing Division, Housing Production and Mortgage Credit, Department of Housing and Urban Development, Washington, D.C. 20410.

### Rent Supplements—Rental Housing for Low Income Families

**Agency:** Department of Housing and Urban Development

**Program Number:** 14.149

**Type of Assistance:** Direct payments for specified use to nonprofit, cooperative, builder-seller, investor-sponsor, and limited distribution mortgagors.

**Uses:** To supplement partial payments of families within income limits prescribed for admission to public housing. Assistance covers the difference between tenants' payments and market rental, but may not exceed 70% of market rental.

Persons 62 years or older, physically handicapped, living in substandard housing and certain military personnel are also eligible to receive benefits.

**Eligibility:** Production Information: Contact Director, Multifamily Underwriting Division, Housing Production and Mortgage Credit, Federal Housing Administration, Department of Housing and Urban Development, Washington, D.C. 20410.

### Equal Opportunity in Housing

**Agency:** Department of Housing and Urban Development

**Program Number:** 14.400

**Type of Assistance:** Investigation and conciliation of complaints.

**Uses:** Any individual may file a complaint with HUD or may file suit in Federal or local court seeking injunctive relief, actual damages and not more than $1,000 in punitive damages together with court costs and reasonable attorney fees.

Individuals are assured an equal opportunity to choose housing suited to their needs and financial ability in the area in which they desire to live without discrimination because of race, color, religion, or national origin.

Training and technical assistance has been provided to many state agencies as well as a training film for use in housing discrimination matters.

**Eligibility:** Contact Assistant Regional Administrator for Equal Opportunity in Department of Housing and Urban Development Regional Office or Assistant Secretary for Equal Opportunity, Department of Housing and Urban Development, Washington, D.C. 20410.

### General Research and Technology Activity

**Agency:** Department of Housing and Urban Development

**Program Number:** 14.506

**Type of Assistance:** Project and research grants to public and/or private profit and nonprofit organizations.

**Uses:** Funding for research related to national housing needs, evaluation of existing housing and community development programs, and improving the environment.

**Eligibility:** Contact Assistant Secretary for Policy Development and Research, Department of Housing and Urban Development, 441 7th Street, S.W., Washington, D.C. 20410.

### Public Housing—Modernization of Projects

**Agency:** Department of Housing and Urban Development

**Program Number:** 14.607

**Type of Assistance:** Direct loans to local housing authorities operating federally assisted public housing projects.

**Uses:** Loans may be used for upgrading low rent housing projects which, because of condition, location, or outmoded management policies, adversely affect the quality of living of the tenants. The program must provide for the involvement of tenants in plans for rehabilitation.

**Eligibility:** Contact Area Director, Department of Housing and Urban Development Area Office or Office of Housing Programs, Assistant Secretary for Housing Management, Department of Housing and Urban Development, Washington, D.C. 20413.

### National Historic Landmarks

**Agency:** U.S. Department of Interior

**Program Number:** 15.912

**Type of Assistance:** Provision of specialized services to anyone—individual, government, or corporate body—who is owner of property.

**Uses:** To study, identify, recognize honorifically, and encourage preservation of nationally significant historic properties.

National Historic Landmarks are selected by the National Survey of Historic Sites and Buildings. Theme studies recently completed or currently underway include sites associated with nineteenth Century Architecture, Political and Military Affairs 1865-1900 and Black History, Science and Invention and Literature, Drama and Music.

**Eligibility:** Contact Director, National Park Service, U.S. Department of Interior, Washington, D.C. 20240.

### Desegregation of Public Education

**Agency:** Department of Justice

**Program Number:** 16.100

**Type of Assistance:** Provision of specialized services to parent or group of parents in case of public schools, to individual or his parents in the case of public college; to applicant for employment or employee of an educational agency.

**Uses:** To provide equal education for children regardless of race, color, religion, sex, or national origin. To investigate, negotiate, and litigate allegations of employment discrimination by educational agencies.

**Eligibility:** Contact Chief, Education Section, Civil Rights Division, United States Department of Justice, Washington, D.C. 20530.

### Equal Employment Opportunity

**Agency:** Department of Justice

**Program Number:** 16.101

**Type of Assistance:** Provision of specialized services. Uses: To enable Attorney General to sue to enjoin discrimination in employment by state and local government agencies enforce nondiscrimination in employment provisions of Executive Order 11246, as amended, regarding government contractors and subcontractors.

**Eligibility:** Contact Chief, Employment Section, Civil Rights Division, U.S. Department of Justice, Washington, D.C. 20530.

### Equal Enjoyment of Public Accommodations

**Agency:** Department of Justice

**Program Number:** 16.102

**Type of Assistance:** Provision of specialized services.

**Uses:** To provide equal access to all establishments offering public accommodations without regard to race, color, religion, or national origin.

The Justice Department may go to court for an injunction or other order prohibiting discrimination.

**Eligibility:** Contact Chief, Voting and Public Accommodations Section, Civil Rights Division, U.S. Department of Justice, Washington, D.C. 20530.

### Fair Housing

**Agency:** Department of Justice

**Program Number:** 16.103

**Type of Assistance:** Provision of specialized services.

**Uses:** To provide freedom from discrimination on basis of race, color, religion, or national origin in connection with sale, rental, or financing of housing by filing suit alleging such discrimination in appropriate federal or state court.

**Eligibility:** Contact Chief, Housing Section, Civil Rights Division, U.S. Department of Justice, Washington, D.C. 20530.

### Protection of Voting Rights

**Agency:** Department of Justice

**Program Number:** 16.104

**Type of Assistance:** Provision of specialized services to all U.S. citizens old enough to vote.

**Uses:** To provide protection of individual's right to register and vote in all local, state or federal elections without discrimination on account of race or color.

The 1970 amendments suspend the use of literacy and other tests in all states and counties not previously covered by 1965 Act, set forth uniform standards regarding duration for residency requirements and absentee registration and balloting in Presidential elections, and lower to 18 the minimum age for voting in federal elections.

**Eligibility:** Contact Chief, Voting and Public

Accommodations Section, Civil Rights Division, U.S. Department of Justice, Washington, D.C. 20530.

### Desegregation of Public Facilities

**Agency:** Department of Justice

**Program Number:** 16.105

**Type of Assistance:** Provision of specialized services to individuals.

**Uses:** Attorney General may bring suit for an injunction for discrimination on account of race, color, religion, or national origin in operation of public facilities.

**Eligibility:** Contact Director, Office of Institutions and Facilities, Civil Rights Division, U.S. Department of Justice, Washington, D.C. 20530.

### Community Relations Service

**Agency:** Department of Justice Program Number: 16.200

**Type of Assistance:** Advisory services and counseling to any person, group, community, or state or local governmental unit seeking to alleviate conditions caused by discrimination based on race, color, or national origin.

To assist in developing programs and in directing available public and private resources to alleviate problems in the minority community.

**Eligibility:** Contact regional or local office or Community Relations Service, U.S. Department of Justice, Washington, D.C. 20530.

### Veterans Re-employment Rights

**Agency:** Department of Labor

**Program Number:** 17.102

**Type of Assistance:** Advisory services and counseling, investigation of complaints, dissemination of technical information to persons (including reservists and national guardsmen) who have served on active duty or training duty for Armed Forces, or persons who have applied for enlistment or been inducted but were found not qualified.

**Uses:** To assist veterans of the Armed Forces, reservists, National Guardsmen, rejected persons, and examinees in securing reinstatement with their employers, the crediting of seniority, and other benefits to which the individual is entitled.

**Eligibility:** Contact nearest Department of Labor, Labor Management Services Administration Regional or Area Office or Office of Veterans Re-employment Rights, U.S. Department of Labor, Washington, D.C. 20216.

### Apprenticeship Outreach

**Agency:** Department of Labor

**Program Number:** 17.200

**Type of Assistance:** Project grants and research contracts to local organizations.

**Uses:** To seek out qualified applicants from minority groups and assist them in entering apprenticeship programs.

Funds may not be used to subsidize trainees while they are in training programs.

Apprenticeship Information Centers are located in selected State employment offices to provide easily accessible sources of information.

**Eligibility:** Contact Director, Office of National Programs, Manpower Administration, U.S. Department of Labor, Washington, D.C. 20213.

### Employment Service

**Agency:** Department of Labor

**Program Number:** 17.207

**Type of Assistance:** Project grants, advisory services, and counseling, provision of specialized services to state employment security agencies to place persons in employment.

**Uses:** General services including outreach, interviewing, testing, counseling, and referral.

Special services for veterans, with preferential treatment

*The Apprenticeship Outreach program subsidizes trainees.*

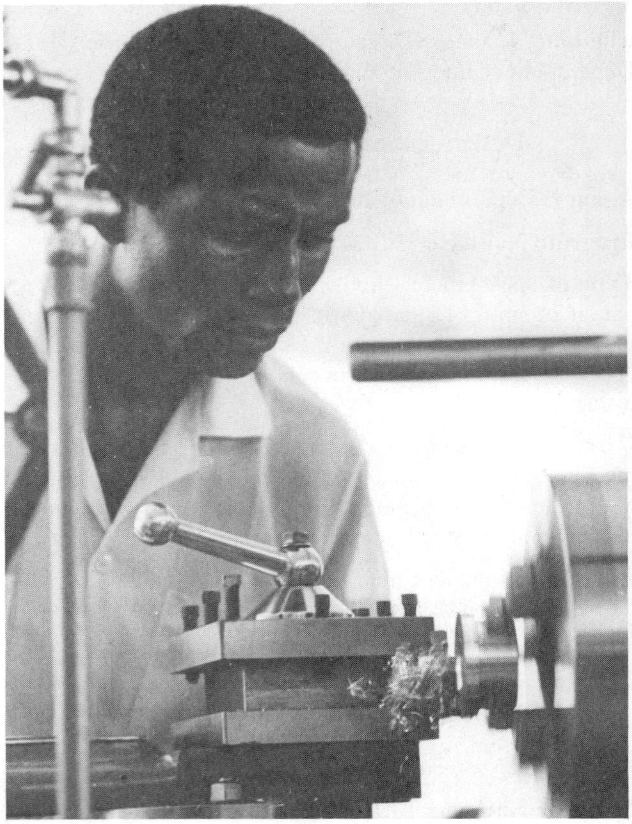

of disabled. The Employment Service emphasizes service to the poor, unemployed and underemployed, handicapped by race, age, lack of education, and assists them by supportive services, job research, and development.

Among services to youth are the Summer Employment Program designed to give priority to disadvantaged youth to enable their return to school, and the recruitment, screening, and referral of young people for manpower training programs.

Special services are provided to inmates and former inmates of correctional institutions by making available placement, employment counseling and testing services.

**Eligibility:** Contact nearest office of State Employment Security Agency or Director, Program and Management Services staff, U.S. Employment Service, Manpower Administration, U.S. Department of Labor, Washington, D.C. 20213.

### Job Opportunities in the Business Sector (Jobs)

**Agency:** Department of Labor

**Program Number:** 17.212

**Type of Assistance:** Direct payment for specified use, training advisory services and counseling to private profit or nonprofit companies.

**Uses:** To enable employers to hire and train disadvantaged individuals in entry level jobs and to upgrade present employees for jobs of higher responsibility.

**Eligibility:** Contact Regional Manpower Administration Office or Director, Office of National Programs, Manpower Administration, U.S. Department of Labor, 601 D Street, N. W., Washington, D.C. 20213.

### Operation Mainstream

**Agency:** Department of Labor

**Program Number:** 17.223

**Type of Assistance:** Project grants to private nonprofit national organizations with emphasis on establishing projects in rural areas or towns.

**Uses:** To provide work training and employment activities, with necessary supportive services for chronically unemployed poor older workers.

Job opportunities may involve management, development and conservation of parks, highways, and recreational areas of federal, state, and local governments; rehabilitation of other community facilities and provision of social, health, and educational services to the poor.

**Eligibility:** Contact Director, Office of National Programs, Manpower Administration, U.S. Department of Labor, 607 D Street, N. W., Washington, D.C. 20213.

### Work Incentives Program and Incentives (WIN)

**Agency:** Department of Labor

**Program Number:** 17.226

**Type of Assistance:** Project grants to state employment service agencies.

**Uses:** To move men and women and out-of-school youth age 16 or older from AFDC rolls into employment through training, social services, and job placement.

Services include placement or on-the-job training, work orientation, basic education, skill training, work experience to improve employability, and placement in public service employment.

Employers hiring individual under the WIN program are eligible to receive 20% tax credit on first 12 months salary paid to the individual.

**Eligibility:** Contact local office of State employment service or Director, Office of Work Incentive Programs, Office of Manpower Development Programs, Department of Labor, Washington, D.C. 20213.

### National On-the-job Training

**Agency:** Department of Labor

**Program Number:** 17.228

**Type of Assistance:** Project grants to national organizations.

**Uses:** To provide occupational training for unemployed and underemployed persons who cannot otherwise obtain appropriate full-time employment.

Funds may be used for reimbursement of instructors, administrative costs, supplies, supplementary classroom education, trainee allowances, and supportive services.

Approximately 23,500 job placements have resulted from this program.

**Eligibility:** Contact Director, Office of National Programs, Manpower Administration, U.S. Department of Labor, 601 D Street, N. W., Washington, D.C. 20213.

### Migrant Workers

**Agency:** Department of Labor

**Program Number** 17.230

**Type of Assistance:** Project grants to federal, state, and local government agencies, private profit and nonprofit organizations, or migrant organizations.

**Uses:** To help migrant and seasonal farm worker families find economically viable alternatives to agricultural labor.

Among services are relocation assistance, occupational training, education, health services, job development, and placement.

**Eligibility:** Contact Director, Office of National Programs, Manpower Administration, U.S. Department of Labor, 601 D Street, N. W., Washington, D.C. 20213.

*For migrant workers there are programs to help them find economically viable alternatives to agricultural labor.*

### Comprehensive Employment and Training Programs (CETA)

**Agency:** Department of Labor

**Program Number:** 17.232

**Type of Assistance:** Formula grants to units of state and local general government with populations of more than 100,000, and consortia consisting of general local government at least one of which has a population of 100,000 or more.

**Uses:** Funds for assistance to provide training or employment opportunities for low income, unemployed, or underemployed persons.

**Eligibility:** Contact Regional Manpower Office or Manpower Administration, U.S. Department of Labor, 601 D Street, N. W., Washington, D.C. 20213.

### Equal Employment Opportunity by Federal Contractors

**Agency:** Department of Labor

**Program Number:** 17.301

**Type of Assistance:** Investigation of complaints, dissemination of technical information to any individual employed by federal contractors or in federally involved construction who feels he has been the subject of discrimination.

**Uses:** To provide equal opportunity in the performance of Federal contracts and subcontracts. To set policy, monitoring and evaluating the compliance of Federal contractors and subcontractors.

**Eligibility:** Contact Director, Officer of Federal Contract Compliance, Employment Standards Administration, U.S. Department of Labor, Washington, D.C. 20210.

### Minimum Wage and Hour Standards

**Agency:** Department of Labor

**Program Number:** 17.303

**Type of Assistance:** Advisory services and counseling,

investigation of complaints to and by any covered employee, who unless specifically exempt, must be paid in accordance with applicable monetary standards.

**Uses:** To provide standards protecting wages of working persons by requiring a minimum hourly wage rate. Overtime pay and equal pay for men and women performing the same or substantially equal work is provided for.

**Eligibility:** Contact nearest office of Employment Standards Administration or Assistant Secretary, Employment Standards Administration, U.S. Department of Labor, Washington, D.C. 20210.

### Consumer Credit Protection

**Agency:** Department of Labor

**Program Number:** 17.306

**Type of Assistance:** Advisory services and counseling, investigation of complaints by any person whose earnings have been subjected to garnishment.

**Uses:** To provide restrictions on the amount of an employee's wages or salary which may be garnisheed, that is, beginning January 1, 1975, if an individual's weekly disposable earnings were $84 or less only the amount in excess of $63 could be garnisheed.

Under no circumstances may an employee be discharged from his employment by reason of garnishment for any one indebtedness.

**Eligibility:** Contact local office of Employment Standards Administration or Assistant Secretary, Employment Standards Administration, U.S. Department of Labor, Washington, D.C. 20210.

### Farm Labor Contractor Registration

**Agency:** Department of Labor

**Program Number:** 17.308

**Type of Assistance:** Provision of specialized services, project grants to states and state employment service agencies.

**Uses:** To assure more equitable treatment for migrant agricultural workers. Program provides for contractual arrangements between the contractor and the migrant worker. Requires that the contractor obtain motor vehicle liability insurance and that he insure migrant worker and his personal property against injury or damage arising from automobile accident.

Any person who, for a fee either for himself or on behalf of another person, recruits, solicits, hires, furnishes, or transports ten or more migrant workers must register under the Farm Labor Contractor Registration Act.

**Eligibility:** Contact State Employment Office, nearest Employment Standards Administration Office or Assistant Secretary, Employment Standards Administration, U.S. Department of Labor, Washington, D.C. 202 10.

### Federal Employment for Disadvantaged Youth—Part Time

**Agency:** Civil Service Commission

**Program Number:** 27.003

**Type of Assistance:** Federal employment for students accepted for or enrolled in secondary school or institution of higher learning who maintain acceptable school standing and need their job earnings to stay in school.

**Uses:** To give disadvantaged youth, 16-21 part time employment with federal agencies which will allow them to continue their education. Work week consists of 16 hours during school year and 40 hours during extended vacation periods.

#### Related Program of Interest

27.004 FEDERAL EMPLOYMENT FOR DISADVANTAGED YOUTH—SUMMER
Federal Employment for disadvantaged youth, ages 16-21, with federal agencies, Economic criteria must be met.

Minimum wage rate is paid and no special skills or experience are required.

**Eligibility:** Contact Civil Service Commission Regional office or Office of Youth Employment Programs, Manpower Sources Division, Bureau of Recruiting and Examining, U.S. Civil Service Commission, Washington, D.C. 20415.

### Clearinghouse Services, Civil Rights and Sex Discrimination Complaints

**Agency:** Commission on Civil Rights

**Program Number:** 29.001

**Type of Assistance:** Dissemination of technical information, investigation of complaints.

**Uses:** To further opportunities for minority group members and women utilizing federal programs. Commission investigates complaints of devices to deny equal protection under the laws in voting, employment, housing, education, and administration of justice.

**Eligibility:** Contact nearest regional or local office or United States Commission on Civil Rights, Washington, D.C. 20425.

### Job Discrimination—Investigation and Conciliation of Complaints

**Agency:** Equal Employment Opportunity Commission
Program Number: 30.001

**Type of Assistance:** Investigation of complaints by any aggrieved party or individuals knowing of discriminatory practices.

**Uses:** To provide for enforcement of federal prohibition against discrimination in employment based on race, color, religion, sex, or national origin.

Complaints are received, investigated, and conciliated by EEOC. Enforcement can be sought through the courts.

**Eligibility:** Contact any EEOC field office or Director, Office of Voluntary Programs, Equal Employment Opportunity Commission, 1800 G Street, N. W., Washington, D.C. 20506.

### Related Programs of Interest

30.002 JOB DISCRIMINATION—SPECIAL PROJECT GRANTS
Project grants and contracts with official state and local antidiscrimination agencies to increase their capability to combat employment discrimination.

30.003 JOB DISCRIMINATION—TECHNICAL ASSISTANCE
Advisory services and counseling to employees, labor unions, employment agencies, educational institutions, state and local governments to assist them in bringing their employment practices into voluntary compliance with the law and limit their liabilities to class action suits.

**Eligibility:** For 30.001 or 30.002. Contact any EEOC field office or Director, Office of State and Community Affairs, Equal Employment Opportunity Commission, Room 1229-C, 1800 G Street, N. W., Washington, D.C. 20506.

## Promotion of the Humanities—Fellowships in Selected Fields

**Agency:** National Foundation on the Arts and the Humanities

**Program Number:** 45.107

**Type of Assistance:** Project grants to citizens of the U.S. or native residents of its territorial possessions who have completed their professional training and are at an early point in their careers.

**Uses:** To be used for projects in historical, social, or cultural studies of American ethnic minorities and in the interrelationships between human values and science and technology.

**Eligibility:** Contact Director, Division of Fellowships, National Endowment for the Humanities, Washington, D.C. 20506.

## Economic Opportunity Loans for Small Business

**Agency:** Small Business Administration

**Program Number:** 59.003

**Type of Assistance:** Direct loans, guaranteed/insured loans, advisory services, and counseling to people with low incomes who have been denied the opportunity to acquire adequate business financing through normal lending channels or reasonable terms.

**Uses:** For management assistance and loans up to $50,000 with maximum maturity of 15 years to socially or economically disadvantaged persons for small businesses.

Communications media, nonprofit enterprises, speculation in property, lending or investment enterprises, and financing of real property are excluded.

**Eligibility:** Contact Director of Financing, Small Business Administration, 1441 L Street, N. W., Washington, D.C. 20416.

### Related Programs of Interest

59.006 MINORITY BUSINESS DEVELOPMENT—PROCUREMENT ASSISTANCE
Specialized services are provided to black Americans, American Indians, Spanish Americans, Oriental Americans, Eskimos and Aleuts, as well as others, to insure their participation as owners of businesses in a normal competitive environment. Authority of Small Business Act to enter into procurement contracts with other federal agencies is utilized.

**Eligibility:** Contact Office of Business Development, Small Business Administration, 1441 L Street, N. W., Washington, D.C. 20416.

59.007 MANAGEMENT AND TECHNICAL ASSISTANCE FOR DISADVANTAGED BUSINESSMEN
Project grants to public or private organizations having capability to provide management and technical assistance to existing or potential businessmen who are economically or socially disadvantaged or located in areas of high concentration of unemployment.

**Eligibility:** Contact Director of Management Assistance, Small Business Administration, 1441 L Street, N. W., Washington, D. C. 20416

59.011 SMALL BUSINESS INVESTMENT COMPANIES
Direct loans, guaranteed insured loans, advisory services, and counseling to any chartered small business investment company with combined paid-in-capital and paid-in surplus of not less than $150,000 having qualified management and giving evidence of sound operations. MEBIC investment policy is directed toward providing assistance which will contribute to a well balanced national economy by making it easier to become the owner of small business concerns by individuals who have been disadvantaged by social or economic reasons.

**Eligibility:** Contact Associate Administrator, Small Business Administration, 1441 L Street, N. W., Washington, D.C. 20416.

59.019 MINORITY VENDORS PROGRAMS
Specialized services provided to minority firms which manufacture goods or perform services purchased by the

**Eligibility:** Contact Associate Administrator, Small Business Administration, 1441 L Street, N. W., Washington, D.C. 20416.

59.019 MINORITY VENDORS PROGRAMS
Specialized services provided to minority firms which manufacture goods or perform services purchased by the nation's business community.

Small retail businesses which do not, by definition, provide product or service to major corporations are excluded from this program.

**Eligibility:** Contact Minority Vendors Program Field Representative in Regional Office or Assistant Administrator for Minority Enterprises, Small Business Administration, Minority Vendors Program, 1441 L Street, N. W., Washington, D.C. 20416.

COMPREHENSIVE EMPLOYMENT AND TRAINING PROGRAMS
CETA was designed to provide job training and employment opportunities for economically disadvantaged, unemployed, and underemployed persons to enable them to increase future earnings and secure self-sustaining, unsubsidized employment.

For CETA activities, prime sponsors (usually units of State or local government with a population of 100,000 or more) are responsible for developing programs responsive to local needs; these sponsors have wide discretion with regard to program design. The range of services provided includes classroom and on the-job training, basic and remedial education, testing, job referral and development, work experience, and supportive social services. Sponsors may provide these services directly or indirectly through contracts or sub-grants with such organizations as State Employment Security Agencies (SESA's), vocational agencies, schools, community groups, labor organizations, or private businesses. Prime sponsors are responsible for monitoring and evaluating programs to determine that local needs are met.

SYNOPSIS OF THE COMPREHENSIVE EMPLOYMENT AND TRAINING ACT, AS AMENDED IN 1978

### Title I, Administrative Provisions

Organizational and general provisions applicable to the entire act; consolidates the procedures for planning, reporting, auditing, and other administrative requirements; authorized appropriations generally for fiscal years 1979-1982.

### Title II, Comprehensive Employment and Training Services

Authorizes comprehensive work and training activities. Authorizes institutional and on-the-job training, work experience, job search assistance, and supportive services in title II B and C. Also contains a separate counter structural public service employment program in title II D, with new jobholders limited to economically disadvantaged persons who have been unemployed 15 of the last 20 weeks or who are receiving or are part of a family receiving welfare benefits.

### Title III, Special National Programs and Activities

Authorizes special target group programs for Indians and other Native Americans, migrant and seasonal farm workers, ex-offenders, older workers, displaced homemakers, women, and the handicapped. Continues programs of research and development, technical assistance, and labor market information.

### Title IV, Youth Programs

Authorizes Job Corps residential training program, summer youth employment program, and youth programs first authorized by the Youth Employment and Demonstration Projects Act of 1977, except the Young Adult Conservation Corps, which is in title VIII.

### Title V, National Commission for Employment Policy

Authorizes an advisory commission with members to be appointed by the President.

### Title VI, Public Service Employment Program

Authorizes a counter-cyclical public service employment program. Participation is limited to unemployed persons who have been without work for 10 of the last 12 weeks and have family incomes at or below the Bureau of Labor Statistics' lower living standard level or have received public assistance 10 of the last 12 weeks.

### Title VII, Private Sector Initiative Program

Authorizes a demonstration of alternative approaches to obtaining greater involvement of private sector in employment and training of the disadvantaged. Establishes Private Industry Councils with representatives from industry, business, organized labor, community based organizations, and educational institutions to participate with prime sponsors in improving access for all CETA participants to private sector jobs.

### Title VIII, Young Adult Conservation Corps

Authorizes year-round corps open both to disadvantaged and non-disadvantaged youth, 16 to 23 years old, for conservation work in national parks, forests, and other public lands.

## TABLE 132. TITLE II-A PROGRAMS FOR DISADVANTAGED ADULTS AND YOUTH: ENROLLMENTS, TERMINATIONS, AND END-OF-QUARTER ON-BOARD ENROLLEES, OCT. 1983 THROUGH JUNE 1986

| Time Period | Title II-A Enrollments | Title II-A Terminations | On-Board at End-of-Quarter[1] |
|---|---|---|---|
| JTPA Transition Year | | | |
| October-December 1983 | 212,700 | 53,100 | 159,600 |
| January-March 1984 | 202,500 | 95,100 | 267,000 |
| April-June 1984 | 170,600 | 202,100 | 235,500 |
| Total | 585,800 | 350,300 | |
| Program Year 1984 | | | |
| July-September 1984 | 173,500 | 110,400 | 298,600 |
| October-December 1984 | 162,300 | 118,300 | 342,600 |
| January-March 1985 | 203,400 | 131,500 | 414,500 |
| April-June 1985 | 168,700 | 219,100 | 364,100 |
| Total | 708,000 | 579,300 | |
| Program Year 1985 | | | |
| July-September 1985 | 195,100 | 140,600 | 418,600 |
| October-December 1985 | 178,500 | 128,100 | 469,000 |
| January-March 1986 | 213,600 | 142,000 | 540,600 |
| April-June 1986 | 165,700 | 246,700 | 459,600 |
| Total | 752,900 | 657,400 | |

[1]On-Board estimates presented here should be treated with caution. Comparisons of JTLS Title II-A data for PY 1985 to administrative information obtained through the JTPA Annual Status Reports (JASR) have revealed that the JTLS estimate for terminations in PY 1985 was approximately 15 percent lower than that obtained from the JASR. This, compounded by similar discrepancies in previous years, leads to a PY 1985 JTLS "on-board" estimate that is 66 percent higher than the JASR figure, Reasons for the difference continue to be examined by DOL and Census Bureau staff. Source: U.S. Department of Labor, Employment and Training Administration, Office of Strategic Planning and Policy Development, Division of Performance Management and Evaluation .

JTPA: Job Training Partnership Act
JTLS: Job Training Longitudinal Survey

# TABLE 133. TITLE II-A PROGRAMS FOR DISADVANTAGED ADULTS AND YOUTH: SELECTED CHARACTERISTICS OF ENROLLEES IN THE TRANSITION PERIOD AND IN PROGRAM YEARS 1984 AND 1985 AND OF PROGRAM ELIGIBLES IN 1985

| | Enrollees | | | |
|---|---|---|---|---|
| Characteristic | Transition period Oct 1983 - Jun 1984 | PY 1984 Jul 1984 - Jun 1985 | PY 1985 Jul 1985 - Jun 1986 | JTPA eligibles[1] 1985 |
| Total enrollees/eligibles | | | | |
| Number | 585,800 | 708,000 | 752,900 | 39,401,000 |
| Percent | 100 | 100 | 100 | 100 |
| Sex | | | | |
| Male | 51 | 48 | 47 | 44 |
| Female | 49 | 52 | 53 | 56 |
| Minority status | | | | |
| White (excluding Hispanics) | 53 | 55 | 55 | 63 |
| Black (excluding Hispanics) | 31 | 31 | 32 | 23 |
| Hispanic | 12 | 10 | 10 | 11 |
| Other | 4 | 4 | 3 | 3 |
| Age at enrollment | | | | |
| 18 and younger | 18 | 20 | 22 | 19 |
| 19 - 21 | 20 | 20 | 20 | 19 |
| 22 - 54 | 60 | 56 | 55 | 81 |
| 55 and older | 2 | 3 | 3 | 81 |
| Economic status | | | | |
| Economically disadvantaged | 95 | 93 | 92 | 77[2] |
| Receiving AFDC at application | 17 | 21 | 21 | 16 |
| Receiving public assistance (Including AFDC) at application | 37 | 42 | 40 | 48 |
| Education status | | | | |
| School dropout | 28 | 27 | 27 | 51 |
| Student (H.S. or less) | 11 | 13 | 14 | 51 |
| High School graduate or more | 61 | 60 | 59 | 49 |
| Barriers to employment | | | | |
| Limited English | 4 | 3 | 3 | NA |
| Handicapped | 7 | 9 | 10 | NA |
| Offenders | 9 | 8 | 8 | NA |
| Displaced Homemakers | 4 | 4 | 4 | NA |

[1] Based on Current Population Survey (CPS) for March 1986.

Source: U.S Department of Labor, Office of Strategic Planning and Policy Development, Division of Performance Management and Evaluation (JTLS Data) and CPS March 1986.

## TABLE 134. PROGRAMS FOR DISADVANTAGED ADULTS AND YOUTH: SELECTED CHARACTERISTICS OF ALL TERMINEES IN PROGRAM YEARS 1984 AND 1985

| Characteristic | Percent of Terminees in: PY 1984 July 1984 - June 1985 | PY 1985 July 1985 - June 1986 |
|---|---|---|
| Total Terminees | | |
| Number | 579,300 | 657,400 |
| Percent | 100 | 100 |
| Sex | | |
| Male | 49 | 48 |
| Female | 51 | 52 |
| Minority Status | | |
| White (excluding Hispanics) | 55 | 54 |
| Black (excluding Hispanics) | 31 | 32 |
| Hispanic | 11 | 11 |
| Other | 4 | 4 |
| Age at Enrollment | | |
| 18 or younger | 20 | 22 |
| 19-21 | 21 | 21 |
| 22-54 | 56 | 54 |
| 55 and older | 3 | 3 |
| Economic Status | | |
| Economically Disadvantaged | 94 | 93 |
| Receiving AFDC at Application | 21 | 20 |
| Receiving Any Public Assistance (Including, AFDC) at Application | 42 | 41 |
| Education Status | | |
| School Dropout | 27 | 27 |
| Student (H.S. or less) | 12 | 15 |
| High School Graduate or more | 61 | 58 |
| Handicapped | 9 | 10 |

Source: U S. Department of Labor, Office of Strategic Planning and Policy Development Division of Performance Management and Evaluation

## TABLE 135. TITLE II-A PROGRAMS FOR DISADVANTAGED ADULTS AND YOUTH: SELECTED CHARACTERISTICS OF TERMINEES WHO ENTERED EMPLOYMENT IN PROGRAM YEARS 1984 AND 1985

| | Percent of Terminees Entering Employment in: | |
|---|---|---|
| Characteristic | PY 1984<br>July 1984 - June 1985 | PY 1985<br>July 1985 - June 1986 |
| Total terminees entering employment | | |
| Number | 370,500 | 407,700 |
| Percent | 100 | 100 |
| Sex | | |
| Male | 52 | 49 |
| Female | 48 | 51 |
| Minority satus | | |
| White (excluding Hispanics) | 58 | 58 |
| Black (excluding Hispanics) | 28 | 28 |
| Hispanic | 10 | 10 |
| Other | 3 | 3 |
| Age at enrollment | | |
| 18 or younger | 15 | 14 |
| 19-21 | 21 | 21 |
| 22-54 | 61 | 61 |
| 55 and older | 3 | 3 |
| Economic status | | |
| Economically disadvantaged | 94 | 92 |
| Receiving AFDC at application | 18 | 17 |
| Receiving any public assistance (Including AFDC) at application | 38 | 37 |
| Education status | | |
| School dropout | 25 | 25 |
| Student (H.S. or less) | 8 | 7 |
| High School graduate or more | 68 | 67 |
| Handicapped | 8 | 8 |

Source. U.S. Department of Labor, Office of Strategic Planning and Policy Development, Division of Performance Management and Evaluation

## TABLE 136. TITLE II-B SUMMER YOUTH EMPLOYMENT AND TRAINING PROGRAMS: TOTAL PARTICIPANTS AND SELECTED CHARACTERISTICS SUMMARY, 1986 SUMMER PROGRAM (OCT. 1, 1985 - SEPT. 30, 1986)[1]

| Number/Characteristic | 1986 Summer Program |
|---|---|
| Total participants | |
| Number | 748,101 |
| Percent | 100 |
| Cost per participant | $1,021 |
| Sex | |
| Male | 51 |
| Female | 49 |
| Minority status | |
| White (excluding Hispanic) | 32 |
| Black (excluding Hispanic) | 43 |
| Hispanic | 20 |
| Other | 4 |
| Age at enrollment | |
| 14- 15 | 34 |
| 16- 17 | 40 |
| 18 - 21 | 26 |
| Education status | |
| School dropout | 6 |
| Student | 81 |
| H.S. graduate or equivalent and above | 13 |
| Barriers to employment | |
| Single head of household with dependent under 18 | 3 |
| Limited English language proficiency | 10 |
| Handicapped | 11 |

[1] Characteristics data was not collected for the JTPA Summer Program until the 1986 summer
Source: U.S Department of Labor, Employment and Training Administration, Office of Information, Resources Management.

## TABLE 137. JTPA TITLE III PROGRAMS FOR DISLOCATED WORKERS: DISTRIBUTION OF ELIGIBLE DISLOCATED WORKERS AND NEW ENROLLEES IN PROGRAM YEARS 1984 AND 1985

| Characteristic | Eligible Displaced Workers | JTPA Title III New Enrollees | |
|---|---|---|---|
| | | PY 1984 | PY 1985 |
| **Eligibles/enrollees** | | | |
| Estimated total | 5,091,100[1] | 97,000 | 95,600 |
| Percent | 100 | 100 | 100 |
| **Sex** | | | |
| Male | 65 | 62 | 59 |
| Female | 35 | 38 | 41 |
| **Minority status** | | | |
| White (excluding Hispanic) | 81 | 70 | 72 |
| Black (excluding Hispanic) | 12 | 21 | 19 |
| Hispanic | 6 | 7 | 7 |
| Other | 2 | 2 | 1 |
| **Age** | | | |
| 21 and younger | 2[2] | 6 | 5 |
| 22 - 44 | 62 | 74 | 72 |
| 45 - 54 | 36 | 15 | 15 |
| 55 and over | 36 | 6 | 8 |
| **Education** | | | |
| School dropout | 25 | 19 | 19 |
| Student (H.S. or less) | 25 | 1 | 1 |
| High School graduate or equivalent (no post H.S.) | 75 | 52 | 55 |
| Post High School | 75 | 28 | 26 |

[1] As defined by the Bureau of Labor Statistics (BLS), U.S. Department of Labor, this estimate represents persons with tenure of three or more years who lost or left a job between January 1979 and January 1984 due to plant closings or moves, slack work, or the abolishment of their positions or shifts.

[2] The BLS data for this category represent 20- and 21-year-olds only.

Source: U.S. Depanment of Labor, Employment and Training Administration. Office of Stategic Planning and Policy Development. (JTLS data for PY 1985, publisbed in November 1986. Note that JASR data differs somewhat from these proportions.)

## TABLE 138. TITLE III PROGRAMS FOR DISLOCATED WORKERS: PROPORTIONS OF TERMINATIONS AND TERMINEES WHO ENTERED EMPLOYMENT, SELECTED CHARACTERISTICS, PROGRAM YEARS 1984 AND 1985

| Characteristic | All Terminations | | Entered Employment | |
|---|---|---|---|---|
| | PY 1984 | PY 1985 | PY 1984 | PY 1985 |
| Total | | | | |
| Number | 80,100 | 83,700 | 52,300 | 56,700 |
| Percent | 100 | 100 | 100 | 100 |
| Sex | | | | |
| Male | 65 | 58 | 64 | 58 |
| Female | 35 | 42 | 36 | 42 |
| Minority status | | | | |
| White (excluding Hispanics) | 75 | 71 | 75 | 73 |
| Black (excluding Hispanics) | 18 | 20 | 17 | 19 |
| Hispanic | 6 | 7 | 6 | 6 |
| Other | 2 | 2 | 2 | 2 |
| Age | | | | |
| 21 and younger | 6 | 5 | 6 | 6 |
| 22 - 44 | 74 | 72 | 74 | 72 |
| 45 - 54 | 14 | 15 | 15 | 15 |
| 55 and older | 6 | 8 | 5 | 7 |
| Education | | | | |
| School dropout | 20 | 20 | 16 | 19 |
| Student (H.S. or less) | 1 | 1 | 1 | 1 |
| High School graduate or equivalent (no post H.S.) | 52 | 54 | 54 | 54 |
| Post High School | 27 | 25 | 30 | 26 |
| Reason for termination | | | | |
| Entered employment | 65 | 68 | 100 | 100 |
| Returned to school | 1 | 1 | — | — |
| Other positive termination | 1 | 1 | — | — |
| Non-positive termination | 33 | 31 | — | — |

Source: U.S. Department of Labor, Employment and Training Administration, Office of Strategic Planning and Policy Development (JTLS Data for PY 1985).

## TABLE 139. COMPARISON OF SELECTED CHARACTERISTICS OF TITLE III JTPA PARTICIPANTS, UNEMPLOYED DISLOCATED WORKERS AS OF JANUARY 1984, AND TITLE II-A JTPA PARTICIPANTS

JTPA; Job Training Partnership Act

| | Percent of Participants | | |
|---|---|---|---|
| Characteristic | Title III | Unemployed Dislocated Workers a/o Jan. 1984[2] | Title II-A[3] |
| **Age** | | | |
| Under 55 | 92 | 80 | 97 |
| Age 55 and over | 8 | 20 | 3 |
| **Educational level** | | | |
| Less than High School | 22 | 32 | 39 |
| High School graduate or more | 78 | 68 | 61 |
| **Sex** | | | |
| Male | 60 | 69 | 48 |
| Female | 40 | 31 | 52 |
| **Race[1]** | | | |
| White | 69 | 79 | 54 |
| Minorities | 31 | 21 | 46 |

[1] Hispanics are included as minorities in Title III statistics, but in the CPS data, they may be included in the totals for either race.
[2] From the supplement to the January 1984 CPS.
[3] From the U.S. Department of Labor, Job Training Longitudinal Survey, August 1985.
Source: U.S. Department of Labor, Employment and Training Administration.

## TABLE 140. DISTRIBUTION OF TITLE IIA ENROLLEES IN EACH INITIAL PROGRAM ASSIGNMENT BY SELECTED CHARACTERISTICS: PARTICIPANTS NEWLY ENROLLED IN JTPA DURING PY 1985 (JULY 1985 - JUNE 1986) AND PY 1984 (JULY 1984 - JUNE 1985)

| | Initial Program Assignment and Time Periods | | | | | | | | | | | |
|---|---|---|---|---|---|---|---|---|---|---|---|---|
| | Total | | CT[2] | | OJT[3] | | JSA[4] | | WE[5] | | Other services | |
| Selected characteristics | PY 85 | PY 84 | PY 85 | PY 84 | PY 85 | PY 84 | PY 85 | PY 84 | PY 85 | PY 84 | PY 85 | PY 84 |
| Total enrollees (thousands) | 752.9 | 708 | 282.4 | 270 | 168 | 158.7 | 164.4 | 149.7 | 56.5 | 57.1 | 81.6 | 72.5 |
| Sex | | | | | | | | | | | | |
| Male | 47 | 48 | 39 | 38 | 56 | 59 | 53 | 53 | 49 | 50 | 47 | 48 |
| Female | 53 | 52 | 61 | 62 | 44 | 41 | 47 | 47 | 51 | 50 | 53 | 52 |
| Minority status | | | | | | | | | | | | |
| White (excluding Hispanic) | 55 | 55 | 49 | 50 | 65 | 67 | 52 | 51 | 53 | 56 | 57 | 57 |
| Black (excluding Hispanic) | 32 | 31 | 36 | 35 | 22 | 20 | 34 | 35 | 33 | 30 | 33 | 33 |
| Hispanic | 10 | 10 | 11 | 11 | 10 | 10 | 11 | 11 | 9 | 8 | 7 | 6 |
| Other | 3 | 4 | 3 | 4 | 3 | 3 | 4 | 3 | 5 | 6 | 2 | 4 |
| Age at enrollment | | | | | | | | | | | | |
| Younger than 19 | 22 | 20 | 19 | 16 | 9 | 9 | 16 | 15 | 54 | 57 | 45 | 38 |
| 19-21 | 20 | 20 | 22 | 21 | 21 | 21 | 19 | 19 | 19 | 20 | 17 | 19 |
| 22-29 | 28 | 29 | 29 | 32 | 36 | 37 | 29 | 29 | 14 | 12 | 18 | 19 |
| 30-44 | 23 | 23 | 25 | 25 | 27 | 26 | 26 | 25 | 9 | 9 | 12 | 17 |
| 45-54 | 4 | 4 | 4 | 4 | 5 | 4 | 5 | 6 | 3 | 2 | 4 | 4 |
| 55 and older | 3 | 3 | 2 | 2 | 3 | 2 | 4 | 5 | 1 | 1 | 4 | 3 |
| Economically disadvantaged | 92 | 93 | 92 | 94 | 91 | 93 | 91 | 92 | 94 | 94 | 91 | 95 |
| Unemployment compensation claimant at application | 7 | 9 | 7 | 9 | 9 | 10 | 8 | 12 | 3 | 2 | 6 | 7 |
| Participant did not work during the 26 weeks prior to application | 52 | 54 | 57 | 57 | 41 | 42 | 53 | 55 | 61 | 67 | 53 | 58 |
| Handicapped | 10 | 9 | 10 | 8 | 7 | 7 | 9 | 9 | 17 | 15 | 17 | 13 |
| Veteran at application | 9 | 9 | 7 | 7 | 13 | 14 | 12 | 11 | 3 | 3 | 7 | 8 |
| Receiving public assistance at application | | | | | | | | | | | | |
| AFDC | 21 | 21 | 28 | 28 | 12 | 14 | 18 | 18 | 22 | 23 | 20 | 21 |
| Cash public assistance (AFDC, General, Refugee, SSI) | 28 | 28 | 35 | 35 | 17 | 18 | 26 | 25 | 30 | 29 | 26 | 27 |
| Food stamps | 31 | 31 | 36 | 35 | 25 | 27 | 30 | 27 | 33 | 35 | 28 | 31 |
| Any public assistance (cash and/or noncash) | 40 | 42 | 47 | 48 | 31 | 33 | 38 | 38 | 46 | 47 | 39 | 42 |
| Adult welfare[1] | 16 | 17 | 21 | 23 | 12 | 13 | 17 | 16 | 8 | 7 | 9 | 10 |
| Other adult assistance | 10 | 10 | 9 | 10 | 12 | 12 | 10 | 10 | 6 | 6 | 6 | 9 |
| Youth (age < 22) | 15 | 15 | 16 | 15 | 6 | 8 | 11 | 11 | 33 | 34 | 24 | 23 |
| Education status | | | | | | | | | | | | |
| School dropout | 27 | 27 | 29 | 29 | 25 | 26 | 28 | 26 | 19 | 21 | 26 | 23 |
| Student (H. S. or less) | 14 | 13 | 10 | 8 | 4 | 3 | 9 | 10 | 50 | 51 | 36 | 32 |
| High School graduate or equivalent (no post H. S.) | 42 | 43 | 44 | 46 | 51 | 50 | 43 | 44 | 21 | 20 | 29 | 33 |
| Post High School | 17 | 17 | 17 | 17 | 21 | 20 | 19 | 21 | 10 | 8 | 9 | 12 |

[1] Receiving AFDC, General Assistance and/or Refugee Assistance and at least 22 years of age at enrollment. [2] CT: Classroom training [3] OJT: On -the-job training [4] JSA: Job search assistance [5] WE: Work experience

# PERSPECTIVES ON BLACK EDUCATION

**Current Status ■ Victories and Defeats ■ Chronology of Educational Developments ■ Scholarships, Loans, and Awards ■ Elementary and Secondary Education Act ■ Higher Education Act of 1965 ■ The Higher Education Amendments of 1968 ■ Vocational Education ■ Civil Rights Institutes ■ National Defense Education Act ■ Blacks in Higher Education ■ Employment in Higher Education ■ Predominantly Black Colleges and Universities in the United States ■ Community and State Colleges with Black Administrative Heads ■ Education Films ■ Education Facts ■ Education Charts and Tables**

Every society provides for the socialization of youth in those areas of knowledge, abilities, values and attitudes deemed essential for its continued development. Preparing for the 21st Century society, the school is second only in importance to the home as a socializing agency. Without the developmental contributions it is supposed to promote, young people find it almost impossible to cope with the complex, highly competitive, urban-industrial society which now prevails. This is especially there for urban black children, usually poverty-stricken, whose families do not provide the educational assets available in affluent homes. The longer many black-children stay in school, the farther they fall behind in scholastic achievement. They rely upon the school for the development of competency in the English language, for facility in handling qualitative relationships, for understanding the physical and social world of which they are a part, and in large measure, for the development of attitudes toward self and society which contribute to effective living.

At the present time, most urban black-children for whom the school does not propagate these developments simply do not make it. Unable to compete within the normal channels of social interactivity, they fall prey to anti-social influences which prevail in the world around them, i.e. drugs, the streets and the ghetto, thus becoming a part of the growing population of educational "aliens" whose life patterns foil the realization of their own potential, pose dependency or worse for the community, and pass on to their own offspring an outlook no more hopeful than their own.

Black efforts to attain equality in education produced notable successes in the 1970s and early 1980s. However, since that time the school has been besieged with problems; high drop-out rate, teenage pregnancy, drug and alcohol abuse, discipline, teenage unemployment, computer illiteracy and desegregation issues. Public schools for the most part, failed to educate the black youngsters.

The Reagan Administration, in what Dr. Kenneth Clark termed a "functional repeal of the *Brown vs The Board of Education Decision,*" proposed and supported a series of measures that eliminated effective means for integration and forwarded families and institutions that wished to segregate.

## VICTORIES AND DEFEATS

Contrasts of success and failure by black students were especially evident in reports on the achievement levels of black pupils. Referring to education in inner cities, the Urban League reported in 1981 that black students "continue to lag two, even five years behind national norms." A study by the National Assessment of Educational Progress, a federally funded, state-administered program designed to measure student performance in a variety of subjects, found black high school sophomores and seniors lagging behind whites in vocabulary, math, reading, science, and civics.

However, the same tests also revealed that blacks were closing the gap when 1980 figures were compared with those of 1970. For subjects other than writing, the average difference between black and white nine-year-olds fell from about 17 percentage points in 1970 to 10-11 percentage points by 1980. For 13-year-olds, blacks closed the gap markedly in all subjects except mathematics, from 17-18 points in 1970 to 12-13 points in 1980. The analysis also indicated that improvements for nine-year-old black children were mirrored in their performance at age 13, when the same children were tested four years later.

The crucial question to blacks was whether such progress can continue to a point where no gap exists. A provocative view on this matter was advanced by Professor Lyle Jones of North Carolina University, a director of the National Assessment study. Professor Jones contended that black children have progressed primarily because programs under the Compensatory Education Programs of the Elementary and Secondary Education Act stimulated a climate of hope. The support provided pupils and schools by these programs gave black children a sense that the country cared about their future.

*Kenneth Clark calls the Reagan policy a "functional repeal of the Brown decision."*

### The Threat

The climate of hope for black children, however, was chilled in 1981 and 1982 by proposals that threatened both blacks and the public school system itself. Among these were:

- Tuition tax credits for parents earning up to $75,000 annually who send their children to private schools.
- Stripping lower federal courts of the power to order busing as a remedy for segregation if children involved were to be transported more than 5 miles or longer than 15 minutes.
- Elimination of efforts to desegregate entire school districts.
- Cuts in funding for Public Education Programs.

According to Kenneth Clark, such policies would accelerate the white middle class's flight from public schools and result in a racial caste system in education, with whites attending private schools and public schools reserved for rejected blacks.

While these and other measures were receiving serious Administration and Congressional support, aid to public education by the federal government, and many local jurisdictions as well, was being cut.

The cuts were not as severe as President Reagan wanted, however. For fiscal 1982, the Administration sought cuts amounting to about 25% but succeeded in obtaining only 10%, from $14 billion to $12.7 billion. For fiscal 1983, the President again requested slashes of about 25%, to $9.6 billion. As of May 1982, this plan was encountering strong opposition in Congress and there was some chance that the 1983 education budget would not be reduced at all.

### The Quality Issue

While most blacks regarded integration as vital, increasing concern was expressed over the quality of education their children received. Throughout the 1970s, schools in the major urban areas were beset by violence, vandalism, under financing, and the fear, hostility, and low expectations of teachers and administrators. Rigidity and over specialization in public education also disturbed blacks.

Bernard Watson wrote in *The State of Black America, 1982,*

*The need is not just a matter of lowering or raising standards but to allow enough flexibility and humanity to permeate*

*(above) Students on the front steps of Tuskegee Institute, a college that was created for blacks so that they could achieve a higher education. (below) African-Americans in Boston demonstrating their support for a Court-ordered busing program.*

*both the schools and public policies that shape them so that students can be viewed as individuals who have the ability and motivation to use their minds constructively and create their own ways. Unfortunately, the types of policies and instructional practices that treat students as automatons or fragmented entities to be parceled out to specialists and remediators are most intensively applied to minority students and to the children of poverty.*

Blacks also continued to suffer from negative perceptions of their ability to learn. The Urban League noted in *The State of Black America, 1980*, that an entire lexicon of phrases and terms such as "culturally deprived," "deficit model," "psychology of the streets," "welfare dependence," "maternal dominance," and others had been created to justify assertions that learning and excellence were beyond the reach of blacks and that they therefore should be content to accept inferior facilities and instruction as "adequate."

Though attention was focused on the poor quality of northern urban schools, inferior education apparently persisted in rural black areas of the South. In 1981, a report by the Southern Regional Council found schools in 34 predominantly black counties in Georgia and Alabama to be inferior. The Council reported that schools were better where mandatory state and federal standards were imposed or where blacks comprised a majority of the school board.

In support of this view, the Commission quoted psychologist William Ryan:

*When drinking fountains were desegregated no one expected the water quality to improve; when lunch counters were desegregated the hamburgers and cokes didn't taste any better... And no one expected black kids in desegregated swimming pools to start swimming faster, or preachers in desegregated churches to preach more eloquently. Segregation itself unjustly inflicts pain and suffering on black people. Desegregation is designed to stop that particular source of hurt; that's a good enough goal.*

In November 1981, the U.S. Commission on Civil Rights urged that the quality issue not be used as an argument for or against integration. The Commission noted that there is strong evidence integration improves the quality of education, but added that the point of desegregation was not to improve the quality of education but to erase the caste implications of color.

## The Current Status of Desegregation

In 1954, less than 1% of black students in the South attended schools with white children. By 1968, 20% of black students in the South attended schools that were more than 50% white, and by 1978, 44% did so. Nationally, in 1978, 38% of black students were in schools that contain more than 50% whites in the student body. These figures underscore two points: desegregation has progressed, and a great deal more remains to be achieved.

Integration has been delayed in many areas by lengthy litigation over various plans. In 1981, Chicago's school

*(Left) Arthur Benezet, opponent of slavery and teacher of black youth in colonial America. (above) Many states had laws prohibiting the education of blacks; here black youngsters are turned away at the school door.*

system remained largely segregated, despite a series of violations cited by courts since 1964. A similar pattern existed in New York City, which was also cited frequently between 1977 and 1982 for not using enough black teachers. Desegregation litigation is usually lengthy. Frequently, one case can involve 25 written opinions, 10 years, and cost the disputing parties a million dollars, before a final decision is reached and invoked.

Prolonged battles were also fought over the issue of metropolitan integration, that is, integrating a city's schools with those of its nearby suburbs. Orders and agreements for metropolitan integration of schools went into effect in St. Louis and Kansas City, Missouri, in 1981 but in early 1982 were still the subject of litigation.

Busing is rarely a logistical problem in metropolitan plans, and in fact is sometimes reduced. This was the result in Charlotte-Mecklenburg County, North Carolina, an integrated school district of 550 square miles with 84,000 pupils. The desegregation plan there actually required less busing than had been required before desegregation. The reason: city-suburb boundaries frequently separate schools that differ racially but are not far apart.

In a survey conducted by the U.S. Commission on Civil Rights of 16 desegregated districts, only 11 showed increases in transportation costs and in no case did transportation costs rise more than 2%.

## Education Prior to 1861

Many Africans who came to the English colonies in 1619 as indentured servants were previous residents of West Africa, which had had a brilliant cultural and educational heritage. The West African Empire of Ghana, which became the Empire of Mali, was mentioned by Arab sources in A.D. 800. Timbuktu and Gao were prominent cultural centers of the Moslem world for 300 years. A school system was established by Emperor Askia Mohammed Toure, ruler of Songhay from 1493 to 1512. Black students and others in the Moslem world looked to the University of Sankore at Timbuktu as a major institution of higher learning. Accomplished scholars taught law, history, medicine, and literature, including the works of Plato and Aristotle.

Early supporters of the black in the United States were masters who desired to increase the economic efficiency of their labor supply, sympathetic persons who wished to help the oppressed, and zealous missionaries who taught slaves English so that they might learn the principles of the Christian religion. The Church of England, which founded the Society for the Propagation of the Gospel in Foreign Parts, was instrumental in teaching reading, prayers, and catechism to blacks and Indians of the colonies. Other religious groups such as the Quakers advocated education of blacks. Two patterns of education emerged: instruction by religious groups and emphasis on occupational training.

Early black education met great difficulties. Alexander Garden, Commissioner of North and South Carolina and the Bahamas, wrote of insuperable educational problems relating to age, race, and language, and suggested in 1740 that only those born in the colonies and under the age of 10 be educated. South Carolina, for instance, received most of her slaves directly from Africa during the eighteenth century. Over 100,000 black people were imported directly to South Carolina and Georgia prior to 1808. Charleston served as a direct point of landing by ships sailing from Africa. Many masters observed that slaves could be more useful if they acquainted themselves with the language and customs of the colonies rather than African customs and speech.

In spite of statutes which prohibited education of blacks, progress was made in urban areas. The growth of the American city made possible the contact of blacks with many people, affording an opportunity to embrace Western civilization. Many slaves became mechanics, clerks, overseers. Mulattoes, protected from the rigors of the slave codes, helped fellow blacks learn to read and write. Urban blacks had further advantage in their opportunity to attend well-regulated Sunday schools which, though cloaked with the purpose of instructing blacks in the Christian religion, permitted, in many cases, the teaching of reading and writing.

Free blacks in Charleston and other metropolitan areas

established societies and organizations devoted to the cause of black education. One of the earliest was the Brown Fellowship Society organized in 1790, which had as its purpose the construction and maintenance of schools for black children. Others established in Charleston were the Humane and Friendly Society (1802), the Minors Moralist (1803), and the Unity and Friendship Society. Benevolent societies of free blacks advanced the cause of education until 1830-1835 when stringent laws were passed by state legislatures limiting education of blacks—because of slave uprisings led by Denmark Vesey and Nat Turner.

The Principles of the Rights of Man, which preceded the Revolution of 1776, affected the thinking of many Americans, white and black. As early as 1787, Prince Hall, a free black and Boston property owner, petitioned the city to establish schools for black children equal in quality to those for whites. The increase in free blacks in the North and South provided pressure for more education. In 1829, Congressmen and Washington citizens founded the African Education Society with the avowed object of giving blacks academic, mechanical, and agricultural skills. Whites feared that slaves would read the literature of the French and Haitian revolutions and writings of abolitionists. Prudence Crandall met mob resistance in trying to integrate her Canterbury, Connecticut girls' school. In spite of discouragements, black schools continued to function. In 1842 a school for Negro and Indian boys was opened in Ohio by Augustus Wattles of the American Anti-Slavery Society and Samuel Emlen, a Quaker.

Although general education for blacks had been forbidden in the South and limited in the North, many schools had been established by 1861 (see Chronology).

## Educational Efforts of the Civil War Period

The Civil War successfully removed legal prohibitions against the education of the black and freed some 4,000,000 persons. As Union armies penetrated the South, blacks looked to the federal government for help, refuge, and education. In May 1863, the War Department established a Bureau of Colored Troops with schools devoted to the training of commanders of black regiments. The idea of using the army as a training school for freedmen was voiced by Representative John Hickman of Pennsylvania. Declaring that the rebellion would not have broken out if poor whites and colored people of the South had been better educated, he introduced a bill on January 27, 1863, to increase the number of "colored" regiments to 300. Although Congress defeated the proposal, the idea that the army could serve as a potential school for blacks gained many supporters. Congress later declared that proceeds from rebel property were to be used to establish a system of education in the South provided that education taught that liberty was the fundamental principle of the government of the United States, and that education was available to all persons without regard to race, sex, or color.

Lincoln was well aware of his educational responsibilities

*Black women took the initiative in attending schools established by the Freedmen's Bureau. Often such schools were burned down; however, they were rebuilt quickly.*

*At the end of the Civil War, public lectures by U.S. Army speakers informed black freedmen of their new status and rights.*

to blacks. As a member of the House of Representatives, he declared on January 10, 1849, that blacks should be apprenticed and educated in the District of Columbia. Later, on August 5, 1863, he expressed his concern to General Nathaniel Banks in Louisiana that provision be made for the education of young blacks. The Proclamation of Amnesty and Reconstruction said that states must include provisions for education for freedom in order to be restored to the Union. Lincoln further showed his interest in the education of blacks by signing a bill on June 25, 1864, providing schools for black children in the District of Columbia.

Many opposed the education of blacks. In April 1860, Jefferson Davis declared that he was opposed to the use of tax money to put black and white children on the same level. Southerners feared genuine education for poorer people, black or white. Davis declared that "colored" people had already been educated by means of regular and systematic work, language, and the religion of a civilized country. On March 18, 1863, Secretary of War Stanton appointed an American Freedman's Inquiry Commission to investigate the conditions of the black population. Robert Dale Owen of Indiana, Colonel James McKay of New York, and Samuel Howe of Massachusetts traveled along the Eastern seaboard and reported that black refugees were very concerned about schools for their children and religious instruction for themselves. In Alexandria, Virginia, one of the first acts of freed blacks was to establish schools at their own expense. Many declared, however, that they still wished the presence and teaching of educated whites.

Four stages mark the attitude of the federal government toward the black during the first two years of the Civil War: (1) the black was ignored; (2) the black was declared contraband; (3) the Second Confiscation Act provided that the Army could receive blacks and take them from masters; (4) Emancipation Proclamation and Federal Guardianship.

Congress was concerned that an immense black population without education could not use freedom wisely. With Union victories, the aid of northern philanthropy was sought to provide funds for experiments in mass education of freedmen. General Frederick Augustus Mitchel, Commander of the Department of the South, epitomized the feeling of the times when he said to a black congregation:

*There is a new time coming for you colored people, a better day is dawning for you oppressed and downtrodden blacks. If now you are unwilling to help yourselves, nobody will be willing to help you. I believe the good God will lift you up to a higher level than you have yet occupied, so that you and your children may become educated and industrious citizens.*

Hundreds of schools were founded in "colored" regiments, contraband camps, towns, and plantations. That a public school system for blacks appeared in the South prior to the establishment of the Freedman's Bureau and with little available money is one of the wonders of American history.

An important experiment in black education took place in the Sea Islands, located between Charleston and Savannah on the Atlantic seaboard. This includes St. Helena, Port Royal, Morgan, Paris, Ladies, and Phillips islands. Lesser islands including Folly, James and others in Georgia are known collectively as "Port Royal." Possession of these islands by General Thomas W. Sherman was accomplished in November of 1861 when contraband camps were established at Hilton Head, South Carolina. Classes for pupils six to 15 years of age were organized in Beaufort, the largest town in the area, by the Reverend Peck of Massachusetts and Reverend French of New York. Black teachers supervised educational activities but were hampered by lack of funds and supplies. General Sherman divided the territory into districts and asked Congress for help in meeting administrative and educational problems of the black population. Congress failed to act, but sympathetic attention was received from relief societies in Philadelphia, New York, and Boston.

The first was known as the Educational Commission and later became the New England Freedmen's Aid Society, organized in Boston on February 7, 1862. Its object was the intellectual improvement of persons released from slavery and promotion of education among blacks. Supporters included Edward Everett Hale, Samuel Cabot, Charles Barnard, William Lloyd Garrison, and William Cullen Bryant. New York City organized the National Freedmens Relief Association on February 20, 1862. This was followed by the Port Royal Relief Committee, later known as the Pennsylvania Freedmens Relief Association, founded in Philadelphia on March 3, 1862. Many societies confederated in 1863 to form the United States Commission for the Relief of the National Freedmen, which, in 1865, became the American Freedmans Aid Union.

General Saxton in the Department of the South declared that black children showed as much aptitude and learning as the average of children in the North and were eager to learn to read and write. Numerous and orderly schools were established in which classes were often held with teachers dispensing clothing and food from their own pocket. Cotton barns, sheds, tents, were utilized. School farms were organized and the profits used for educational purposes. Desks were often boards thrown across chairs. However, yellow fever and smallpox caused hardship and even death among pupils and teachers alike. By March 1863, Port Royal had 30 schools with 40 teachers and an enrollment of over 3,000 children from eight to 12 years of age. *Hillard's Second Primary Reader* and *Wilson's Second Reader* were among the 36,000 books sent by northern agencies to the South.

The Port Royal experiment destroyed the myth of the ineducability of blacks.

Elsewhere, in North Carolina and Virginia, General Benjamin Butler laid the foundations of a labor and educational system in the area. By March 1865, school attendance for 5-14 year olds was made compulsory. General Ulysses Grant and Chaplain John Eaton in the Department of Tennessee and the State of Arkansas allowed teachers from relief societies to assume a multiplicity of duties. "Schools for Negroes" had been prohibited by municipal law in Memphis. By 1865, however, 51 schools with 105 teachers and 7,360 pupils were engaged in carrying out a humane educational policy. The Department of the Gulf under the direction of General Nathaniel Banks created Boards of Education with the power to levy taxes to defray educational expenses for the contrabands of Louisiana. School commenced at 8:45 and ended at 2:30, with teachers receiving a remuneration of 65 dollars per month. Black soldiers had their own schools which were supervised by black officers and chaplains.

Statistics show that by the summer of 1865, South Carolina had 10,000 pupils, 48 schools, 76 teachers, of whom 24 were black. Additional data include Georgia, with 3,603 pupils, 69 schools, 69 teachers of whom 43 were black; Florida with 1,900 pupils, 30 schools and 19 teachers; Arkansas with 10 schools, 19 teachers, 1,393 pupils; Mississippi with 31 schools, 50 teachers, and 3,396 pupils; Western Tennessee with 56 teachers, 4,095 pupils; and Alabama with 13 schools, 30 teachers, and 1,620 pupils.

## Education Since the Civil War

The Congress, on July 16, 1865, passed a bill which made education an authorized function of the Bureau of Refugees, Freedmen, and Abandoned Lands (Freedmen's Bureau, which came into existence on March 3, 1865). General Oliver Otis Howard was appointed Commissioner of the Bureau and announced his intention of furthering black education by working with benevolent societies in dispensing aid. Later, Howard University was named in honor of this commissioner who, with John M. Langston, a black lawyer graduate of Oberlin College and Inspector-General of schools, worked to establish educational facilities for blacks. The influence of the Bureau declined after 1870 and ceased in 1874.

A decade after the Civil War, the character of the educational program for blacks had changed for the following reasons:

1. State education authorities began to take over administration of schools.
2. Disagreement on the question of segregation of the races.
3. Controversy as to whether schools should be purely educational or parochial.

Churches withdrew support from national organizations and established denominational societies. This proved helpful to blacks in that many permanent institutions which later became senior colleges were established. Lack of general public support led to the establishment of private funds such as the Peabody and John F. Slater funds (see Chronology). Cooperation between philanthropic organizations and denominational societies made possible the growth of higher education for blacks, especially in the South.

Successful efforts to establish educational institutions were usually those that made no attempt at integration. The Supreme Court declared in 1883 that the Fourteenth Amendment enjoined states, not individuals, from discrimination. The decision of 1896 holding that separate and equal facilities for blacks was constitutional provoked controversy for many years. In 1899 the Court ruled that Richmond County, Georgia, could operate white schools, although there were no schools for black children. It was not until 1954 that the doctrine of "separate but equal" was declared unconstitutional, thus ending the legality of segregated facilities.

Not all black Americans had sought integration. Booker T. Washington, speaking to the Atlanta Exposition in 1895, gained white support by arguing that education would enable blacks to maintain a separate society while advancing the progress of the nation as a whole. On the other hand, William Edward Burghardt DuBois, a founder of the NAACP, demanded total equality, declaring that black schools were generally inferior to white ones.

Between 1900 and 1930, black teachers earned $100-400 per year, compared with $200-900 for their white counterparts. Segregated schools were not providing education equal to that of white schools. It was not until the Depression that federal interest in black education increased. The Civilian Conservation Corps and the National Youth Administration helped educate many blacks. Mary McLeod Bethune, who helped create Bethune-Cookman College in Florida, directed the National Youth Administration's Division of Negro Affairs. More than 600,000 black students participated in educational activities; 60,000 blacks gained occupational skills in work-study programs, 200,000 were trained by the Civilian Conservation Corps for employment in forestry and related fields. Federal projects enabled black artists to pursue their vocation. Well-known WPA intellectuals included Langston Hughes, Charles Wright, Ralph Ellison, and Richard Wright.

## Mid-Twentieth Century Progress

By 1970, progress was apparent. But the ultimate aim of excellent and nonsegregated education for all the schools in the United States had not been achieved. The National Guard was continually used to control public defiance of attempts to desegregate schools. Southern states enacted 145 laws between 1954 and 1958 to protect segregation. New Rochelle, New York, was ordered to integrate its schools, which had been segregated by pattern of attendance areas. Berkeley, California effected an integrated school plan. Dr. Harvey Scribner, a white educator and former Superintendent of Schools for Teaneck, New Jersey, sought educational change and innovation by creating a central integrated six-grade school which was successfully put into operation in an all-white suburb. Elsewhere, integration was met with sit-ins, demonstrations, and boycotts, though in a number of places it was put into effect quietly and successfully. Black mothers demonstrated in Chicago, New York, and elsewhere in the nation against poor educational conditions and *de facto* segregation. In New York, Intermediate School 201 became a center of controversy concerning integration, local responsibility, and quality education. Community control became a rallying cry and black people tried to gain control of the educational institutions which affected them.

The federal government advanced the cause of the black by initiating legislation such as Title I of the Elementary and Secondary Education Act of 1965 and Title IV of the Civil Rights Act of 1964, outlawing discrimination in the use of federal funds for educational projects. Title IV made funds available for institutions engaged in desegregation. New problems for black people arose. Between May and September 1965, over 660 black teachers were displaced for reasons relating to integration. By 1966, 5,000 black teachers had been adversely affected.

Shifts in housing patterns imposed *de facto* resegregation. *De facto* segregation results from residential housing patterns and does not violate the constitution. By contrast, *de jure* segregation arises by law or by the deliberate act of school officials and is unconstitutional. In 1955 (*Briggs* v. *Elliott* ) a District Court held that the Constitution does not require integration. It merely forbids the use of governmental power to enforce segregation. In 1966, another court pointed out that this doctrine had been used to justify techniques for perpetuating school segregation. In 1969, the Fourth Circuit Court of Appeals invalidated the *Briggs* v. *Elliott* dictum. Thus in 1970 a California state court ordered the Los Angeles school board to establish a virtually uniform racial balance throughout its 711 square-mile district with 775,000 children in 561 schools.

In 1968, 55 school districts submitted acceptable plans under Title VI. Of the 35,815 black students in these districts, 31,089 (86.8%) attended schools of predominantly white enrollment. This compared with the 23.4% desegregation figure nationally, the 18.4% figure for 11 southern states, and the 10.5% figure for Alabama, Georgia, Louisiana, Mississippi, and South Carolina—the Deep South. In 1969, more than 200 Title VI "acceptable" plans called for completed desegregation in the school year 1969-1970, and over 100 called for "substantial desegregation."

Leon Panetta, former director of the Office for Civil Rights, interpreted the data as follows:

*With the aid of thousands of cooperating state and local school officials who submitted raw data, we can see a stark portrayal of ethnic isolation in schools. Whether a child is isolated with his own or other minorities, he is still likely to suffer educationally as a result of this segregation according to numerous education studies.*

*to numerous education studies.*

In a regional study of black segregation, for example, it was shown that there was a great variation in the number of blacks attending 100% minority schools, from six heavily industrial northern states, where 15.4% of the blacks attended 100% minority schools, to six border states and the District of Columbia, where 25.2% of the blacks attended 100% minority schools, to five deep southern states, where 81.9% of the blacks attended 100% minority schools. (This last figure is based on 431 districts in five states out of 4,477 districts in 17 southern and border states.)

The years 1969-1970 saw the percentage of blacks in white schools double.

## Nixon's Views Change

President Nixon declared in March 1970 that there was a constitutional mandate that dual school systems and other forms of *de jure* segregation be totally eliminated. School boards were requested to act in good faith and formulate plans of desegregation which best suited their needs. To obtain the benefits of integration without depriving the child of his neighborhood school, it was suggested that a portion of a child's educational activities be shared with children from other schools. Many experts considered integration a vital aid to educating the disadvantaged. James S. Coleman, author of the 1966 study on educational equality, called for massive programs to aid blacks in the 1970s.

Among new educational ideas advocated were after-school schools and "voucher systems" in which parents, black and white, can "buy" the kind of education they choose in a "market" that would generate the establishment of a variety of innovative schools. Integration and availability of educational opportunity for black and white is the ultimate goal.

*In Macon, Georgia, a protest rally against integration is held at the home of the Federal judge who issued the Court order.*

In the first week of 1970, then-Secretary of Health, Education and Welfare Robert Finch announced that school districts implementing voluntary desegregation plans were making "significant and effective progress" in providing equal educational opportunity. It was difficult to reconcile this report with the 23.4% nationwide figure of black students enrolled in predominantly white public elementary and secondary schools. Some 61% of black students were shown to be isolated in 95-100% minority schools. Some 43.3 million students were represented by the ethnic data collected by the HEW Office for Civil Rights.

The Nixon administration's support of integration was waning, as the President committed himself increasingly to a "Southern Strategy," designed to appeal to Southerners and ethnics who feared the incursion of blacks and were particularly aroused by the prospect of school children being bused to achieve integration. "Busing" soon became a code word around which fretful and racist whites rallied, providing the now-discredited ex-President with the means to undercut in the 1972 election, possible third-party opposition from Governor George Wallace on the right, and support of many traditionally northern Democrat labor and middle-class voters in the center and on the left.

By the end of 1973, Congress was seriously considering strong anti-busing legislation and actual promulgation of a constitutional amendment to obviate busing for thepur-poses of integration.

While this was going on, however, major integration decisions were being made in the Supreme Court.

## Integration and the "Burger Court"

The Supreme Court in *Swann* v. *Charlotte-Mecklenburg Board of Education* (1971) called on lower courts to make every effort to achieve the greatest possible degree of actual desegregation taking into account the practical realities of the situation. "The Constitutional command to desegregate does not mean that every school in every community will always reflect the racial composition of the school system as a whole," declared Chief Justice Burger. In *Keyes* v. *School District No. 1 Denver, Colorado* (June 1973) the Supreme Court emphasized that the differentiating factor between *de jure* and *de facto* segregation is *purpose* or *intent* to segregate and demanded that the School Board prove that it had not intentionally effected a policy that created or maintained segregation in the core city schools. Again in *Lau* v. *Nichols* (January 1974) the Court affirmed that minority children may not be denied a meaningful opportunity to participate in the public educational program and cited Section 601 of the Civil Rights Act of 1964, which bans discrimination based "on the grounds of race, color, or national origin in any program or activity receiving federal financial assistance."

## The Detroit Decision

On July 25, 1974, the Supreme Court of the United States declared in the *Detroit* case that integration could not be achieved by linking city schools with those of the surrounding suburbs. An integration plan involving more than one school district could be justified only if discriminatory acts in one district produced segregation in the other, or where district lines had been deliberately drawn to separate the races. The 5 to 4 *Detroit* case ruling reversed a decision of the U.S. District Court of Appeals for the Sixth Circuit (Cincinnati, December 8, 1972), which upheld a plan to link Detroit's 185,000 black pupils with the 53 suburban school districts in Oakland, Wayne, and Macomb counties surrounding the City of Detroit. The integration plan approved by Federal Judge Stephen Roth on September 27, 1971, would have affected 780,000 children.

Dr. Kenneth B. Clark, head of the Metropolitan Applied Research Corporation, and Nathaniel B. Jones, chief legal counsel for the NAACP, stated that the Detroit ruling in no way excused the larger school systems to "evade the constitutional requirement that schools be desegregated." Michigan's Governor William Milliken stated that busing was "superficial and counterproductive" and hailed the Detroit decision as a "victory for reason." Although Detroit parents, black and white, were divided on the busing issue, many stated their preference for neighborhood schools and agreed with Chief Justice Burger when he stated that "no single tradition in public education is more deeply rooted than local control over the operation of schools." Others argued that busing would have meant less crowded classrooms, greater variety of courses, and better educational facilities.

## Desegregation and Violence

In spite of court decisions, desegregation efforts were hampered by violence, racial hostility, segregated housing patterns, and tradition of neighborhood schools, especially in Baltimore, Los Angeles, Boston, and Phoenix. Two hundred leaders of anti-busing groups gathered in Pontiac, Michigan (March 1972) and made plans to march to Washington to protest busing policies. Earlier, 10 school buses had been dynamited in protest against a court order to bus one-third of Pontiac's 24,000 students. Virginians protested the ruling of U.S. District Judge Robert R. Merhige Jr., later overturned in a higher court, which ordered the merger of Richmond schools with those of two surrounding counties. Thousands drove in a motorcade to protest the plan which would mix city black children with suburban white children.

In Atlanta (July 1973), a "compromise" plan left 83 of the city's 141 schools all black while increasing the number of desegregated schools by eight. Half of the schools' administrative posts were to be filled by blacks. NAACP's Roy Wilkins condemned the plan and suspended the Atlanta chapter after learning that the proposal had been worked out between the school board and Lonnie King, a black Atlanta businessman who was president of the Atlanta NAACP. Wilkins argued that the precedent established by the compromise was dangerous in view of the fact that Atlanta had long been considered an example of enlightened leadership in race relations.

Whites in South Boston boycotted schools and stoned buses carrying black children in September 1974, despite pleas for peace by Mayor Kevin White and Senator Edward Kennedy. However, most of Boston's whites and blacks accepted the city's busing plan with little protest.

## Federal Activity

Funds to reduce racial isolation were granted under the Emergency Assistance Program begun in 1971 and the Emergency School Aid Act (Title VII of the Education Amendments of 1972). ESAA funds are used to encourage voluntary elimination, reduction, or prevention of minority group isolation. For example, students placed in educationally unjustifiable ability groupings that resulted in classroom segregation were reassigned. Black principals who had been

*Irate mothers shout their disapproval of Senator Edward Kennedy for his support of desegregation.*

demoted when schools desegregated were restored to their positions, and black teachers who lost jobs as schools desegregated were rehired. In one five-state region of HEW, school districts in 1974 made commitments to hire 500 black teachers to correct discriminatory attrition during the years of desegregation.

In *Adams* v. *Richardson* (U.S. Court of Appeals, District of Columbia; June 12, 1973), HEW's Office of Civil Rights was asked to move faster in enforcing Title VI of the Civil Rights Act of 1964 by taking appropriate action to end segregation in public educational institutions receiving federal funds. In Baltimore (June 1974), the city argued that withholding federal money in the absence of an acceptable desegregation plan was unfair because scattering the minority of white students (comprising less than 30% of total student population) evenly through the school system would lead to a departure from the city of white lower-middle-income families who wished to preserve their neighborhood schools.

## The Carter Years

Busing and other forms of affirmative action remained the primary issues during President Carter's term (1977-1980). While most public attention focused on the *Bakke* case, a number of other important matters were fought in the courts, Congress, and regulatory agencies.

In 1979, the Supreme Court reaffirmed its previous support of busing to integrate schools. Prolonged battles were fought between the Department of Health, Education and Welfare and school boards in such cities as Chicago, Cleveland, and Pittsburgh over the validity of various integration plans and complaints against school boards for not executing integration plans that had been ordered by courts or agreed to voluntarily. By 1982, the status of Chicago's school system remained unresolved.

All in all, desegregation remained halting and tentative and of lesser significance as urban school systems became predominantly black and Hispanic. This flaw was compounded by the reluctance of courts to order and enforce inter-district and metropolitan remedies. Consequently, to many blacks, busing became a pointless shifting of bodies rather than a positive step toward the education and integration of their children.

Conflict over busing persisted on many fronts. In California, voters approved a referendum to prohibit busing except where segregation could be shown to be intentional. A similar proposition was approved in the State of Washington, where voters outlawed busing, even when it was voluntary. Both of these laws were challenged in the courts with the outcome uncertain by the spring of 1982. A lower court found the Washington law unconstitutional. The state appealed to the Supreme Court and was supported by the U.S. Department of Justice in a switch from the government's previous opposition to the measure.

The strongest assaults on busing were undertaken in Congress. Shortly before his term expired, President Carter vetoed a bill with an anti-busing rider that would prohibit the Justice Department from bringing court cases to require busing to integrate schools. The measure was reintroduced after the inauguration of Ronald Reagan in 1981. Civil rights groups vowed to contest any such measures in the courts.

There were many pros and cons to the actions of the Carter Administration. Blacks generally applauded its initiative in establishing a separate Department of Education and Carter's refusal to accept the more extreme attacks on integration. He was criticized, however, for not taking firmer stands on monetary and moral support for public education and its integration.

## The Views of The Reagan Administration

The Reagan Administration's unprecedented shifts in federal educational policy in the past decade, have been major factors in the decline of educational equality as we see today. The Reagan Administration has neglected its responsibilities to blacks and other minorities in assuring compliance with affirmative action legislation and minority policy issues that are of national importance. These shifts have forced states to assume increased responsibility for financing education and enforcing desegregation. As a result the federal government has played a decidedly lesser role in education.

In its first edition for 1985, Time Magazine offered an observation that is helpful in understanding the black perspective on the Reagan Administration:

"But in Reagan's America... there has been a fundamental shift in values. From the beginning, American sentiment has been in tension between the values of freedom and equality. Under President Roosevelt, and for several generations thereafter, the official American inclination has been toward equality. In Reagan's America, the value of freedom has asserted itself, sometimes at the expense of the gentler instincts."

The National Urban League "The State of Black America 1985" reported, the Reagan Administration's philosophy, at least as perceived by many blacks, favors the federal government removing itself from any activity that would foster equality, leaving fate to correct any imperfections that might exist in the society. When you are already equal, that type of approach may be acceptable. But when you are still struggling with an unequal status, this is a most difficult pill to swallow.

The beginning of the Reagan era coincides with limited enforcement of civil rights laws. In 1983, the U. S. Supreme Court, in *Bob Jones University v. IRD*, authorizes the denial of tax exempt status to an institution that practices racial discrimination. In *Wygant* v. *Jackson Board of Education*, the U. S. Supreme Court, in 1986, declares that preferences to minority teachers at the expense of white teachers, bias racial preferences in employment. *Fiddick* v. *School Board of Norfolk* allowed the first school district to end-court ordered busing. Congress passed, over President Reagan's veto, the Civil Rights restoration of the effectiveness of four Civil Rights Statutes that prohibit discrimination in federally assisted programs, including Title IX of the Education Amendments of 1972, enforcement of which was limited by the Supreme Court's Grove City College decision.

## CHRONOLOGY OF BLACK EDUCATION

**1634** French Catholics are instrumental in providing instruction for laborers in Louisiana. The French and Spanish had liberal attitudes toward slaves. Many were respected for their worth and given privileges as freemen. Estevanico, an enlightened slave sent by Niza, the Spanish adventurer, to explore Arizona, was a favored servant of this class. French Jesuits, among them missionary Paul LeJeune, promote educational opportunities for blacks.

**1685** Virginia laws prohibiting slaves from attending Quaker meetings for the purpose of instruction are denounced by the Reverend Morgan Goodwyn in a sermon preached in Westminster Abbey, London.

**1695** Reverend Samuel Thomas of Goose Creek Parish, South Carolina, instructs blacks in reading and writing. Enlisting community support, he is able to educate many blacks in his parish.

**1700** A monthly meeting for blacks is established by William Penn. Penn advocated the emancipation of slaves so they might have the opportunity for improvement. Many colonists were teaching slaves and free blacks.

**1701** Chief Justice Sewall of Massachusetts publishes an anti-slavery pamphlet, The Sewall pamphlet represented the first direct attack on slavery in New England. One of the few Puritans to espouse the black cause, Sewall urged emancipation and education. Earlier, Cotton Mather and other Massachusetts Puritans made efforts to organize black people when they founded the Society of Negroes in 1693. Later, in 1717, Mather began an evening school for Indians and blacks.

**1701** The Church of England organizes the Society for the Propagation of the Gospel in Foreign Parts for the purpose of converting and educating black slaves. Although merchants and other vested interests pressured religious groups in America to sanction slavery, the churches endorsed policies of Christianization, which proved to be the first great step in providing educational opportunity for blacks. Dr. Thomas Bray, sent to Maryland by the Bishop of London in 1669, exerted a profound influence in the conversion and education of blacks.

**1704** Catechizing school at Trinity Church in New York City is founded under the direction of Elias Neau. Instruction was given regularly at this church until 1712, when blame for a local slave uprising was attributed by some masters to Neau's work. While enrollment was temporarily curtailed, instruction continued until the middle of the century, despite Neau's death in 1722.

**1724** A document encouraging the Christian education of Indian, black, and mulatto children is circulated in Virginia. The document stated that slaves should be educated and that baptized children who understood the Christian religion should receive exemption from taxes until the age of 18.

**1728** Nathaniel Piggott announces that he is opening a school for "instruction of Negroes in reading, catechizing, and writing."

**1738** Moravians establish a mission exclusively for blacks. A mission for blacks was established by the Moravian brethren at Bethlehem, Pennsylvania. A painting of some converts prior to 1747 shows, among others, two blacks, Johannes of South Carolina and Jupiter of New York.

**1743** A school for black youths opens in Charlestown, South Carolina. Mr. Garden's school for training black youths opened in Charlestown, in September 1743. Supported almost entirely by the people of Charlestown, the school exerted a profound influence throughout the province. Individual missionaries saw an earnest desire among black parents to have their children instructed. Fifty-five children were taught during the day and 15 adults in the evening. Mr. Bray died in 1756.

**1745** French Code Noire makes it incumbent upon masters to enlighten their slaves in order that they might grasp the principles of Christianity.

**1747** Presbyterians begin religious instruction of blacks in Virginia. In 1740, Hugh Bryan, a wealthy Presbyterian, showed interest in the education of blacks and by 1755 was operating a school for slaves.

**1749** Reverend Thomas Bacon preaches four sermons in Talbot County, Maryland, declaring that next to one's children, slaves enjoyed certain rights, including the right to knowledge and enlightenment.

**1750** Anthony Benezet opens an evening school for Philadelphia blacks in his home. Quakers made the most conscientious efforts to fight slavery and educate blacks, permitting them to attend Quaker meetings in the face of great opposition. After teaching blacks in his home for 20

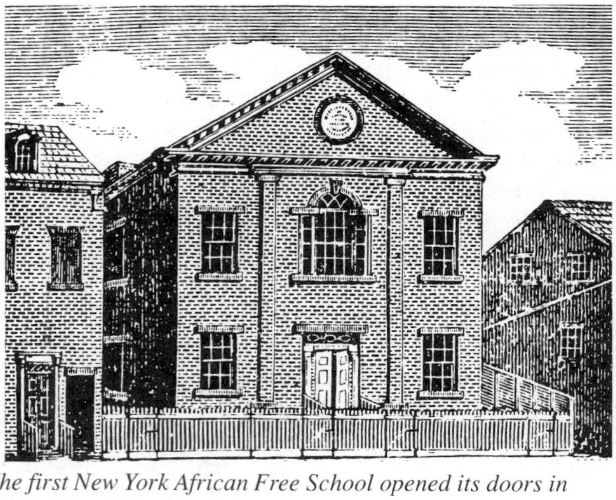

*The first New York African Free School opened its doors in 1787. School No. 2 is shown here.*

years, Benezet opened a free school for them in Philadelphia under Moses Patterson. Upon Benezet's death, money he left was used for the continuation of the school, known thereafter as Benezet House. Benezet, a French Protestant persecuted on account of his religion, had moved from France to England and later to Philadelphia. He declared that he had "found among Negroes a variety of talents as amongst a like number of whites." Besides fighting for the amelioration of the condition of blacks, he published some of America's first textbooks and urged religious equality.

**1751** Society for the Propagation of the Gospel sends Joseph Ottolenghi to convert and educate blacks in Georgia. Ottolenghi, a convert from Judaism and a native of Italy, arrived in Georgia in July 1751. He "promised to spare no pains to improve the young children" and asked God's blessings on his educational efforts, which included reading and religious instruction to blacks. He became so successful and influential in the colonies that he was later elected a member of the Georgia Assembly and remained a member till 1765.

**1773** Benjamin Rush advocates the abolition of the slave trade and urges the education of blacks. In *An Address to the Inhabitants of the British Settlements of America upon Slave keeping,* Benjamin Rush, a Philadelphia physician of Quaker parentage, was in contact with the most enlightened men of his time, and by persuasive argument, advanced the black cause.

**1774** Benjamin Franklin opens a school for blacks. While students of government were exposing the inconsistency of slaveholding among a people contending for political liberty, and men like Samuel Webster, James Swan, and Samuel Hopkins were attacking slavery on economic grounds, Benjamin Franklin, Jonathan Boucher, and Dr. Rush were devising plans to educate slaves for freedom. Benjamin Franklin associated with friends of blacks and was made president of the Abolition Society of Philadelphia, which in 1774 founded a successful school for blacks.

**1777** New Jersey begins educating black children. By 1801, schools are in operation in Salem, Burlington, and Trenton.

**1787** New York African Free School is established by the Manumission Society. Beginning with 40 students, it encountered opposition, but grew when New York required masters to teach the children of slaves to read Scripture. By 1820 more than 500 black children were enrolled.

**1788** New Jersey passes an act making the teaching of slaves to read compulsory under a penalty of five pounds.

**1791** Thomas Jefferson writes to Benjamin Banneker, a black mathematician and astronomer. Jefferson declared that he wished to see blacks improve their condition and stated that lack of progress was due to the degraded condition of the black man in Africa and America. Writing the Declaration of Independence, he had in mind the rights of blacks as well as whites, and declared that blacks had a natural right to education and freedom. He advocated the training of slaves in industrial and agricultural schools to equip them for a higher station in life.

**1794** American Convention of Abolition Societies expresses hope that freedmen would participate in the battle for civil rights as fast as they gained their education.

**1798** A school for black children is established in the home of Primus Hall, a prominent Boston black.

**1800-1830** Individual schools for blacks are developed by churches, slaveholders, and free blacks. Despite legal restrictions in the South, many blacks did receive some education from their masters and in small clandestine private schools in the new nation. In 1820, for example, Boston opened an elementary school for blacks. In the District of Columbia, George Bell, Nicholas Franklin, and

*Atttorneys Robert Morris and Charles Sumner began the fight against exclusion of blacks from Boston's schools in 1849. Although their test case lost, Massachusetts passed a law in 1855 which admitted blacks into the public school system.*

Moses Liverpool, former slaves, built the first schoolhouse for blacks in 1807. Unsuccessful, it opened again in 1818 under the direction of the Resolute Beneficial Society, an association of free people of color. Catholics vied with Quakers in admitting blacks to parochial schools.

During these years, a few blacks were beginning to attend colleges. (In 1826, Edward A. Jones graduated from Amherst and John Russwurm received his degree from Bowdoin. They were the first two black college graduates in the United States.)

In Philadelphia (1804), African Episcopalians found a school at the church of the free people of color who are organized by this time. Eleven of the 16 schools in Philadelphia in 1822 were taught by teachers of African descent. In 1830, one-fourth of the 1,200 black children in the schools of that city paid for their instruction, where as in 1825 only 250 students were in attendance.

**1830-1860** Educational opportunities for blacks are curtailed due to a rising fear of the increasing power of slaves. This was precipitated by the fear aroused in the white population after the slave insurrection led by Nat Turner in Virginia in 1831. "Black Codes" were then enacted in several states to keep the black "in his place" by denying him access to educational facilities of any kind.

**1831** Vocational education for black youth is proposed by a black convention. The First Annual Negro Convention was held in Philadelphia June 6-11, 1831. Delegates attended from New York, Pennsylvania, Delaware, Maryland, and Virginia. The idea was suggested by Samuel Cornish in 1827 and taken up by the Reverend S. A. Jocelyn, an anti-slavery white minister from New Haven. Vocational education for black youth was discussed at this and ensuing conferences held in Philadelphia, New York, and Rochester. The conference declared that colleges and high schools were needed where youth could be instructed in the manual labor system and the arts of civilized life. Money was raised for a school in New Haven, but the citizens objected and declared that "the founding of colleges for colored people was a dangerous undertaking."

**1834** Prudence Crandall is imprisoned and mobbed at Canterbury, Connecticut. Reaction to the education of blacks was manifest when Prudence Crandall, a young Quaker who had established a boarding school at Canterbury, tried to enroll Sarah Harris, a black girl, at her institution. When whites objected, she advertised for young women of color. Imprisonment and violence resulted.

**1840** Blacks attend school with whites in Wilmington, Delaware.

**1842** A school for black and Indian boys opens in Ohio. Augustus Wattles, agent of American Anti-Slavery Society, and Samuel Emlen, New Jersey philanthropist, open Emlen Institute for Negro and Indian Boys, in Mercer County, Ohio. The school specialized in the teaching of agricultural and skilled crafts.

**1848** A black industrial training school opens in Philadelphia at the House of Industry. By 1851, Sarah Luciana was teaching 70 youths at the training school and at the Sheppard School, another industrial institution. Other schools in operation were the Corn Street Unclassified School (1849), the Holmesburg Unclassified

*The Penn School for black children on St. Helena Island, South Carolina, was established and operated by Quakers after the Civil War.*

School (1854), and the Home for Colored Children (1859). By this date there were 1,031 pupils in the black public schools of Philadelphia; 748 in the charity schools; 211 in the benevolent schools; 331 in private schools. In all, 2,231 were in attendance, whereas 10 years earlier there were only 1,643. Besides supporting these institutions, the blacks of Philadelphia maintained many small schools and a system of lyceums and debating clubs, one of which had a library of 1,400 volumes.

**1849** *Roberts* v. *City of Boston.* Robert Morris, a prominent black lawyer, and Charles Sumner argued that segregation hurts white and black children alike. The suit was filed in Boston by Benjamin F. Roberts on behalf of his daughter, Sarah, who had applied under the Equal Education Act of 1845 to attend a white school closer to her home. The court ruled against Sumner and a local ordinance providing for the separate education of the races was upheld. During the next six years, however, public opinion persuaded the Massachusetts legislature to repudiate the court. This was accomplished in 1855 by a law which forbade distinction of race, color, or religion for purposes of admission into the state's public schools.

**1852** Students in the North become converted to the doctrine of equality in education through the efforts of President C. B. Storrs of Western Reserve College, Hudson, Ohio. By 1852 black students had attended the Institute of Easton, Pennsylvania; the Normal School of Albany, New York; Bowdoin College, Brunswick, Maine; Rutland College, Vermont; Jefferson College, Pennsylvania; Athens College, Athens, Ohio; Franklin College, New Athens, Ohio; and Hanover College, near Madison, Indiana. Blacks had taken courses at the Medical School of New York, the Castleton Medical School in Vermont, the Berkshire Medical School in Pittsfield, Massachusetts, the Rush Medical School in Chicago, the Eclectic Medical School in Philadelphia, the Homeopathic College of Cleveland, and the Medical School of Harvard University. Black preachers had been educated at the Theological Seminary of Charlestown, South Carolina. Vocational schools were abundant. Statistics of 1850 and 1860 show that there was an increase in the number of black mechanics, especially in Philadelphia, Cincinnati, Columbus, the Western Reserve, and Canada. But this was probably due to the decreasing prejudice of the local white mechanics toward black artisans fleeing from the South rather than to formal industrial training.

**1855** The Massachusetts legislature enacts a law providing that no distinction be made on account of race, color, or religion, in admitting scholars to public schools.

**1864** The Civil War sees mass education of blacks. The Christian Commission sponsored 50 teachers who taught blacks in the Union Army. Chaplains also taught black troops. By the war's end, 20,000 had been taught to read.

**1865** The Freedman's Bureau is founded under General Oliver O. Howard. The Bureau was created by Congress on March 3, 1865, to cooperate with benevolent and religious societies in the establishment of schools for blacks. John Mercer Langston, black lawyer, and Inspector General of Schools in the Bureau, reported in August 1869 the existence of many good schools for blacks. By 1870, the Freedmen's Bureau operated over 2,600 schools in the South with 3,300 teachers educating 150,000 students.

*Noon recess at the primary school for freedmen, Vicksburg, Misissippi.*

*A typical classroom in one of the early colleges associated with the United Negro College Fund.*

Four thousand schools were in operation prior to the abolition of the Bureau.

**1865-1871** Several predominantly black institutions of higher learning are established. During these years, a number of important black institutions of learning were founded, including Virginia Union and Shaw University (1865); Fisk University and Lincoln Institute (1866); Talladega College, Augusta (Georgia) Institute, Biddle University, Howard University, and Scotia Seminary (1867); Tougaloo College (1869); and Alcorn College and Benedict College (1871). Many of these colleges have changed their names since their founding.

**1867** Establishment of the Peabody Fund. The two million dollar Peabody Fund was established for promotion and encouragement of intellectual, moral, and industrial education among the young of the more destitute portions of the southern and southwestern states.

**1872** Alcorn College becomes the first black land grant college. This was made possible under the Morrill Act of 1862, which provided federal land grant funds for higher education. It was the Morrill Act of 1890, however, which provided that funds for black education be distributed on a "just and equitable basis." Such legislation, however, also served to strengthen the doctrine of "separate but equal," with the result that the 17 southern states maintained colleges which came to be known as "Negro land grant colleges."

**1897** In Washington, D.C. the American Negro Academy is founded. Organized on March 5, 1897, by the Reverend Alexander Crummell, black theologian and educator, the Academy has five stated objectives: (1) defense of the black against vicious assaults; (2) publication of scholarly work; (3) fostering higher education among blacks; (4) formulation of intellectual tastes; (5) promotion of literature, science, and art.

Crummell's father was a prince and son of a West African tribal chief (Temme tribe). Crummell himself first conceived the idea of an American Negro Academy while a student at Cambridge University, England. The Academy was the first body in America to bring together black scholars from all over the world. The general purpose of the organization was to foster scholarship and culture in the black race and encourage budding black genius. In March 1897, the year of McKinley's inauguration, celebrated black scholars and writers assembled in the Lincoln Memorial Church and organized into a brotherhood of scholars. In attendance was Dunbar, the poet; DuBois, the sociologist; Scarborough, the Greek scholar; Miller, the mathematician; Grimke, the theologian; Cromwell, the historian; and many other noted educators. At Crummell's death on September 12, 1908, DuBois was elected president and stated that those with higher education must take responsibility for uplifting the black race. Many brilliant papers were published, which are still today the best discussion on Negro suffrage and southern disfranchisement.

**1900** The New York legislature, under the governorship of Theodore Roosevelt, passes an act providing that no one should be denied admittance to any public school on account of race, color, or previous condition of servitude.

**1902** The General Education Board is founded and supported by John D. Rockefeller. Funds from this organization aided black education materially in such categories as endowment, scholarships, teacher training, and industrial education.

**1908** Founding of the Anna T. Jeanes Fund. The Jeanes Fund sponsored the Jeanes Teacher Program to improve the quality of instruction in rural black schools.

**1908** *Berea College* v. *Kentucky.* A Kentucky law had made segregation mandatory. At issue was whether a private college had the right to teach blacks and whites together. The Supreme Court ruled, on technical grounds, against the college.

**1913** The Julius Rosenwald Fund is founded. The Fund provided grants for constructing schools. By 1932, more than 5,000 school buildings in 883 counties of 15 states had been built under Rosenwald sponsorship.

**1932** Publication of the *Journal of Negro Education.* This organ, published at Howard University, has done much to improve educational opportunities for blacks and to democratize education in general.

**1954** *Brown* v. *Board of Education.* This decision by the U.S. Supreme Court declared segregation in public schools to be unconstitutional. It was based on the theory that "the segregation of children in public schools solely on the basis of race, even though the physical facilities and other tangible factors may be equal, deprives children of the minority group of equal educational facilities." (For fuller discussion see "review" and Supreme Court section.)

**1957** The Little Rock crisis. After a federal court ordered desegregation in Little Rock, Arkansas, Governor Orval Faubus called out the Arkansas National Guard to prevent nine black students from entering Central High School. As a result, President Eisenhower dispatched U.S. troops to Little Rock to enforce the court order, and ultimately federalized the Arkansas National Guard as well.

**1961** New Rochelle: *The Lincoln School Case.* In this case, Federal District Court Judge Irving A. Kaufman ruled that the New Rochelle Board of Education had deliberately created and maintained Lincoln as a racially segregated school. Judge Kaufman ordered the Board to present a plan to desegregate the predominantly black school at all levels. This case marked the first court decision against *de facto* segregation in the North.

**1964** The Civil Rights Act is passed. This act placed further legal restrictions on discrimination in education.

**1965** The Elementary and Secondary School Education Act is passed. This act provides funds under Title I for promoting racial integration in the public schools of the United States.

**1966** Federal judge orders Lowndes County school districts to desegregate. Federal District Court Judge Frank M. Johnson, Jr. directed the Lowndes County, Alabama school board to install a sweeping desegregation order. All grades

*President John F. Kennedy meets with the Presidents of United Negro Colleges.*

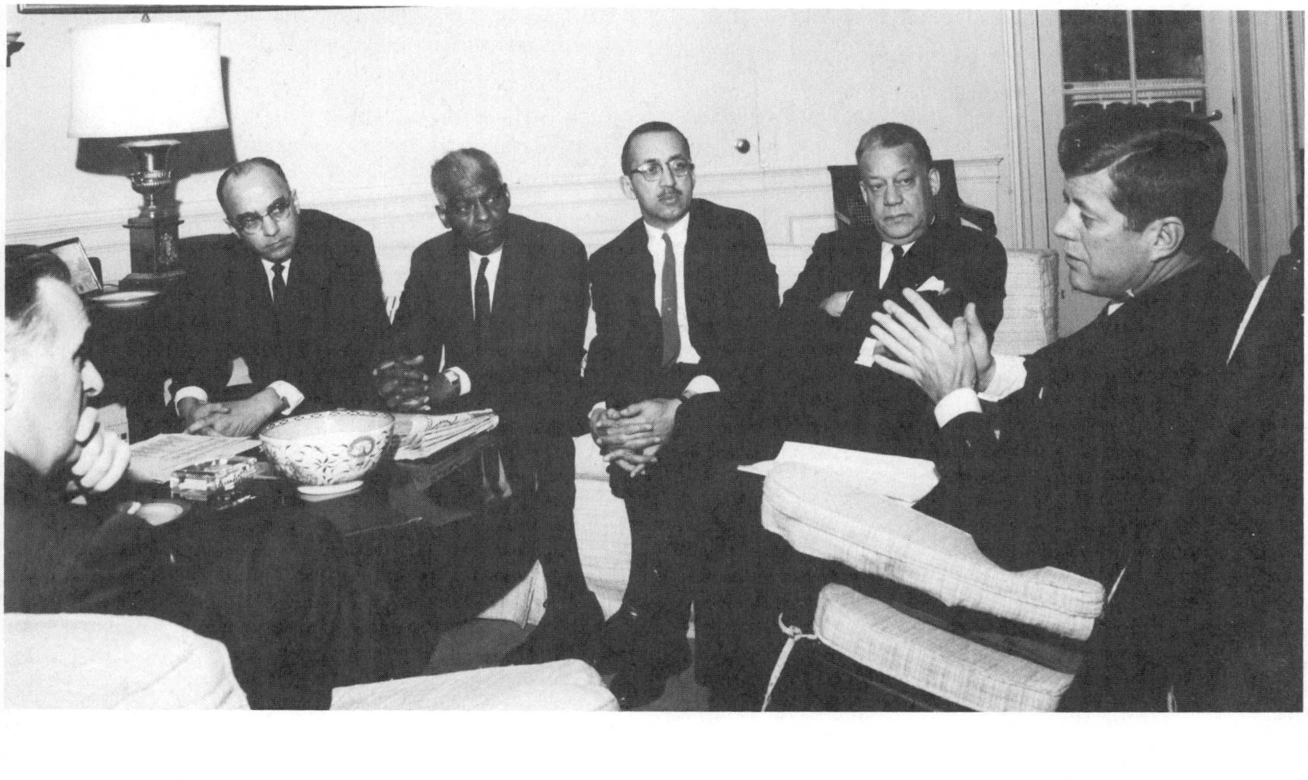

*Neighborhood control of education was the goal of the Ocean Hill-Brownsville Demonstration.*

were ordered desegregated within two years. A free choice transfer system to any school was to be effected and all black teachers integrated.

**1966** The teaching profession continues to appeal to black students despite the emphasis on the need to diversify careers. Secretary of Labor Willard Wirtz declared that two-thirds of all black college students are preparing to teach and that many of these students should be preparing for careers other than in education in order to fill positions that are finally becoming available to black applicants.

**1966** The Kennedy plan for urban ghettos. Senator Robert F. Kennedy called for eradication of huge central city ghettos and criticized the deliberate location of public housing in ghettos. To help desegregate schools, he urged a program for boarding children in the suburbs.

**1966** The *Chester School* case. The Court of Common Pleas of Dauphin County, Pennsylvania, decides the *Chester School* case. The court upholds the order by the Pennsylvania Human Relations Commission that the Chester school board stop assigning black teachers and clerks only to all-black schools, and that the board cease refusing to assign white teachers to a predominantly black school. The court rejects two contentions: (1) that it has authority to act against *de facto* segregation and (2) that the school board has engaged in extensive gerrymandering.

**1966** The *Tometz* case against the Waukegan school board. State Circuit Court Judge Philip W. Yaeger of Illinois rejects a Waukegan school board motion to dismiss the *Tometz* case filed against it by a group of black parents.

**1966** A Detroit suburb agrees to integrated textbooks. The school board of Inkster, Michigan, a Detroit suburb, signs a contract with Local 1068 of the American Federation of Teachers agreeing that effective education must be integrated education. Only integrated textbooks are to be used in reading and social studies classes.

**1966** Prince Edward County school board is found guilty of contempt. The U.S. Circuit Court of Appeals for the Fourth Circuit finds the Prince Edward County, Virginia school board guilty of contempt of court for illegally distributing state funds to be used for tuition in private schools so as to avoid desegregation.

**1966** Plaquemine Parish, Louisiana is desegregated. The public schools of Plaquemine Parish, Louisiana are ordered by a federal district court to desegregate six of 12 grades through a free choice plan.

**1966** Integration in Fayette, Mississippi. In Fayette, Mississippi, 13 black children are enrolled in two formerly all-white schools as a result of an agreement between the school board and the state NAACP headed by Charles Evers.

**1966** The integration question is raised at I.S. 201 in Harlem. A community movement in East Harlem calls upon the school board to integrate the new intermediate school I.S. 201 or place its management under effective community control.

**1967** Civil Rights Commission releases an important study. The U.S. Commission on Civil Rights releases its study, Racial Isolation in the Public Schools, made in response to a November 1965 request by President Johnson.

**1967** The *Girard College* case. Girard College in

Philadelphia does not have to admit blacks under the state's Public Accommodations Act, according to a ruling by the U.S. Court of Appeals for the Third Circuit. This part of the opinion thus reverses an earlier ruling by Federal District Court Judge Joseph S. Lord III.

**1967** The Court of Appeals declares that southern states are obliged to foster integration. The U.S. Court of Appeals for the Fifth Circuit endorses an earlier ruling that six southern states have an affirmative responsibility to integrate their public schools. In April, the U.S. Supreme Court declines to delay the implementation of the Court of Appeals' order. A federal court strikes down an Alabama law against the HEW desegregation guidelines as a violation of the Constitutional supremacy of Congressional legislation.

**1967** Final ruling on the *Tometz* case by the Illinois Supreme Court. The Illinois Supreme Court holds unconstitutional the Armstrong law and thus reverses the earlier *Tometz* ruling. The statute, enacted in 1963, required school boards to redistrict attendance boundaries periodically to reduce segregation and prevent further segregation. The state high court finds the law to be arbitrary and unreasonable and in violation of the equal protection clause of the Fourteenth Amendment.

**1967** The Supreme Court upholds a Court of Appeals ruling in *Oklahoma City Dowell* case. The U.S. Supreme Court refuses to review a Tenth Circuit Court of Appeals decision in the *Oklahoma City Dowell* case, thus leaving intact a District Court order of September 5, 1965. The 1965 order called for sweeping changes in school organization; the attendance areas of various schools were to be merged to promote desegregation; a child in a racial majority would be permitted to transfer to a school in which he was in a racial minority; faculties were to be desegregated by 1970 so that the racial composition in each school approximated the system-wide composition (plus or minus a 10% tolerance).

**1968** There is a racial imbalance in Massachusetts, the District of Columbia, and Lansing. The Massachusetts racial imbalance law withstands attack before the U.S. Supreme Court. The statute, which requires a school board to take action whenever a school's enrollment exceeds 50% nonwhite, is unsuccessfully challenged as unconstitutional by Boston school authorities. The Supreme Court rules that the suit failed to raise a substantial federal question. In the District of Columbia, the Board of Education reports on plans to effectuate the court's ruling in *Hobson v. Hansen.* Plans are submitted to the court regarding the reduction of racially imbalanced student bodies and faculties; measures include attendance boundary changes and busing. New teachers are assigned to achieve racial balance. Discussions are held with suburban school officials about attendance of District students in schools outside the city. The Ingham County Circuit Court rules that the Lansing school board can change attendance boundaries to bring about racial balance.

**1968** A rise in the population of black students is recorded at predominantly white colleges in North Carolina. Between 1963 and 1967, the percentage of black students in predominantly white colleges and universities increases from 0.4 to 1.6%, according to the North Carolina Board of Higher Education.

**1968** "One man, one vote" is applied to school board election. The U.S. Supreme Court holds that the "one man, one vote" rule must be applied to elections of school boards and other local agencies. "Units with general governmental powers over an entire geographic area," ruled the court, "must not be apportioned among single-member districts of substantially unequal population."

**1968** The Supreme Court rules on "open enrollment" or "freedom of choice." The Supreme Court rules unanimously that "freedom of choice" desegregation plans (called "open enrollment" in the North) must promise significant progress before being approved. Desegregation plans that result in no substantial change of segregation will be rejected. School boards are given the affirmative responsibility of finding realistic plans. The Supreme Court explicitly limits its ruling to southern and border states that had permitted legal segregation before 1954.

**1968** In its final ruling, the State Supreme Court reverses its earlier ruling in the *Tometz* case. At issue was the 1963 Illinois Armstrong Act which required school districts to change or revise school attendance areas to prevent or end segregation. In its 1967 ruling, the court invalidated the law, holding that race could not properly be a consideration in attendance area revision. Now, however, it determines that the "issue here is whether the constitution permits, rather than prohibits, voluntary state action aimed toward reducing and eventually eliminating *de facto* school segregation. The Armstrong Act was thereupon found to be constitutional."

**1968** Deliberate segregation is unearthed in South Holland. Legal proceedings continued in the federal complaint of deliberate segregation against School District No. 151 in South Holland, Illinois. In a deposition, Superintendent Charles B. Watts stated he was present when a school board member acknowledged that race was taken into account in locating the site of two schools. Federal attorneys introduced evidence showing that a white school board member had been allowed to enroll his children in a white school.

**1968** The right of an experimental school district—Ocean Hill-Brownsville Demonstration School District—to transfer or dismiss teachers becomes the central issue in a continuing confrontation between the United Federation of Teachers and black parents constituting the majority of the district's governing board.

**1968** In May, in its final ruling of the *Girard* case, the U.S. Supreme Court refused to review a lower court ruling that ended a 120-year-old practice of exclusion of black boys from Girard College, a free boarding school in Philadelphia. Four weeks later, numerous black mothers brought their youngsters to register for entrance in September.

**1968** U.S. Circuit of Appeals declines to rule on "freedom of choice." The Fifth U.S. Circuit Court of Appeals refused to strike down 42 freedom of choice plans in four southern states. It ordered federal district courts in the states to determine by November 4 how effective the plans were. The court defined an effective plan as one that produces integration of faculties, staff, facilities, transportation, and school activities along with integration of students.

**1968** The U.S. Justice Department intervenes against the Ku Klux Klan. The U.S. Department of Justice filed suit against a Ku Klux Klan chapter in Crenshaw County, Alabama, charging interference with a court-ordered "free choice desegregation plan." The Klan, according to federal complaint, intimidated black parents into withdrawing their children from white schools.

**1968** Busing begins in South Holland, Illinois. Federal court-ordered desegregation takes effect in South Holland, Illinois without incident in September. Nine-tenths of the white enrollment as of June reentered the desegregated schools. About 800 pupils equally divided between black and white were bused daily.

**1968** A federal panel in Illinois refuses to rule on per-pupil expenditure disparities between school districts. A three-man federal court panel in Illinois refused to rule unconstitutional large per-pupil expenditure disparities between school districts in the state. One suburb spent $1,283 per high school student, another $919. Plaintiffs contended state laws permitting such disparities violated the equal protection clause of the Fourteenth Amendment. Without doubt, ruled the panel, the educational potential of each child should be cultivated to the utmost and the poorer districts should have more funds, but the allocation of public revenues is a basic policy decision, more appropriately handled by a legislature than a court.

**1969** Integration pressure is applied to Los Angeles school district. Lawsuit filed in Los Angeles Superior Court asking that the Inglewood Unified School District be ordered to eliminate *de facto* segregation in school district number 17. The board allegedly refuses even to adopt a policy statement committing the district to integration.

**1969** Citizens move to bar the erection of a *de facto* segregated high school in Muncie, Indiana. Black citizens filed suit in federal court, Muncie, Indiana, to bar construction of a high school in an all-white area. The suit charged that the resulting exclusion of black children from the new facility would be in violation of their constitutional rights to equal educational opportunities.

**1969** Mt. Vernon elementary schools are desegregated. The State Supreme Court of New York upholds a state order to desegregate the Mt. Vernon elementary schools.

**1969** Pennsylvania is directed to achieve greater integration of schools of higher learning. Pennsylvania was directed by the Department of Health, Education and Welfare to desegregate its public colleges and universities. Pennsylvania, H.E.W. charged, "is operating a system of higher education that is segregated on a statewide basis." The state's only predominantly black school, Cheyney State, enrolls 85% black students, which amount to more than 4.5 times the number of blacks in all other 13 state colleges combined.

**1970** HEW's office for Civil Rights issues a memorandum, "Discrimination and Denial due to National Origin." The memorandum reports that states and districts continue to institute practices that discriminate against Spanish-speaking Americans, violating their Title VI of the Civil Rights Act of 1964, which forbids the discriminatory use of national origin as well as race or color. School districts are warned: "where the inability to speak or understand the English language excludes national origin minority group participation in the education program... the districts must take affirmative steps to rectify the language deficiency in order to open its instructional program to these students."

**1971** Lower courts are urged to support integration. The Supreme Court called upon lower courts to make every effort to achieve the greatest possible degree of desegregation based on practical realities of local situations. (*Swann v. Charlotte-Mecklenburg Board of Education.*)

**1972** New York Regents back busing. New York State Board of Regents backed the use of "judicious and reasonable busing to achieve school integration."

**1972** Justice Department lawyers oppose Nixon. In the Justice Department, 95 lawyers publicly expressed opposition to President Nixon's anti-busing legislation.

**1973** Denver is challenged to disprove *de facto* segregation. The Supreme Court emphasized that the differentiating factor between *de jure* and *de facto* segregation is *purpose* or *intent* to segregate and demanded that Denver School Board prove that it had not intentionally effected a policy that created or maintained segregation in the core city schools.(*Keys v. School District #1 Denver, Colorado.*)

**1974** The Court affirmed that minority children may not be denied a meaningful opportunity to participate in public educational programs and cited section 601 of the Civil Rights Act of 1964 which bans discrimination based on the grounds of "race, color or national origin in any program or activity receiving federal financial assistance." (*Lau* v. *Nichols.* )

**1974** HEW is pressed to enforce desegregation. HEW's Office of Civil Rights is urged to move faster in enforcing Title VI of Civil Rights Act of 1964 by taking action to end segregation in public education institutions receiving federal funds. (*Adams* v. Richardson. )

**1974** A Detroit Metropolitan integration plan is defeated. In the *Detroit* case, in a 5 to 4 ruling, the Supreme Court reversed a District court plan to link Detroit's 185,000 black students with the 53 suburban school districts surrounding the City of Detroit.

*Racial violence flared in the schools after courts ordered Boston desegregation in 1974.*

**1974** Boston opposes integration. The city of Boston resisted a court order to desegregate public schools, succumbing to white demonstrations.

**1974** James A. Harris becomes NEA president. The National Education Association, the nation's largest professional organization, elected James A. Harris, a black schoolteacher from Des Moines, Iowa, as its president.

**1974** Senator Edward Kennedy is prevented from speaking out on Boston desegregation issue. Senator Edward Kennedy of Massachusetts was driven from a speaker's platform by jeers and egg-throwing, while urging whites to accept the desegregation guidelines established for the Boston school system.

**1975** The Civil Rights Commission cites laxity in the enforcement of civil rights laws in education. In a report made public on January 22, the U.S. Civil Rights Commission accused the federal government of failing to enforce the civil rights laws as they apply to education. Singled out for criticism was the Department of Health, Education and Welfare.

**1975** In a report issued March 11, the U.S. Commission on Civil Rights recommended that the federal government withhold federal aid from schools that fail to comply with desegregation directives within a 90 day period.

**1975** Justice Department charges segregation in Mississippi Colleges. The U.S. Department of Justice charged that Mississippi's 25 state colleges and universities were illegally segregated. The charge was submitted to the U.S. District Court in Aberdeen.

**1975** Dr. James S. Coleman, a prominent black educator, issued a study entitled Recent Trends in School Integration. The core of the study concluded that integration efforts in the United States have failed and that modification of approaches was needed.

**1975** U.S. Justice Department files a suit against a Detroit suburb charging segregation. The Justice Department filed suit in federal court charging Ferndale, a Detroit suburb, of operating a racially segregated school system. The suit, taken on behalf of the Office of Revenue Sharing, is the first of its kind.

**1976** Black conservatives led by Thomas Sowell attack busing and affirmative action programs as ineffective and charge that government efforts in this direction benefit lawyers and government officials advocating busing more than the black children the policy is supposed to serve.

**1976** Integrationists have mixed feelings about the election of Jimmy Carter to the Presidency. While they prefer him to outgoing President Gerald Ford, they feel he has been lukewarm in his support of integration.

**1977** Leaders of the National Association for the Advancement of Colored People accuse several northern political leaders of abandoning support for strong measures against school districts that evade integration.

**1977** Joseph Califano, Secretary of Health, Education and Welfare, blames an anti-desegregation mood in Congress for a slowdown in integration efforts.

**1977** A survey by the National Urban League indicates that 45% of blacks interviewed, while favoring integration, believe that an equal say in control of schools is more important.

**1978** The U.S. Civil Rights Commission charges that large areas of the South have still failed to integrate their schools.

**1978** By a 5 to 4 vote, the Supreme Court rules that Alan Bakke, a young white man, is entitled to admission to the University of California because the university's affirmative action program for minorities discriminated against him. However, the Court also holds that college admission affirmative action programs are constitutional.

**1979** Stronger federal enforcement of civil rights laws are stated as a prerequisite. The civil rights commission charges that segregation remains most severe in the northeastern states and North Carolina. The remedy, it declares, is stronger enforcement of civil rights laws and Congressional action to enforce the Department of Health, Education and Welfare's power to order busing.

**1979** A sharp decline in black high school dropouts is reported by the Census Bureau, from 35% in 1968 to 24% in 1976. The white rate remained stable at 14%.

**1979** The Supreme Court sustains busing as a means to desegregate entire school systems when the policies of local officials result in a racial imbalance in parts of the system.

**1979** The formation of a cabinet level Department of Education is assured by a narrow 5-vote margin in the House of Representatives. The first year's budget is to be $14 million.

**1979** Signs of trouble in university black studies programs surface, as Harvard's administration recommends its Afro-American Studies Department be downgraded. Russell Adams, a Howard University professor, reports that the number of college-level black studies programs has dropped from about 600 in 1961 to 250 in 1975.

**1979** In Topeka, Kansas, Linda Brown joins other parents in bringing an action against the Topeka school system on the grounds that it remains segregated 25 years after her historic victory in *Brown v. Board of Education.*

**1980** Supreme Court Justices Powell, Stewart, and Rehnquist express concern that school busing induces white flight to the suburbs.

**1980** In separate decisions involving Cleveland, Ohio, and New Castle, Delaware, the Supreme Court supports busing as a means to end segregation. The Justice Department presses for speedier desegregation in Chicago. However, attempts to include suburban schools in Houston and St. Louis plans are rejected.

**1980** A "Black College Day" attended by 20,000 black students is held in Washington, D.C. Its purpose is to mobilize the public to support historic black colleges, which have suffered since desegregation opened the predominantly white colleges to blacks. Tony Brown, a black writer, contends that 70% of blacks attending "white" colleges do not graduate. Meanwhile, the Justice Department contends that university systems in Texas, Louisiana, and North Carolina are segregated.

**1980** Ronald Reagan is elected president. During his campaign he advocated elimination of the Department of Education, elimination of busing to achieve integration, and deep cuts in federal aid to education.

**1981** A series of actions to curb busing are undertaken on several fronts. The House and Senate vote to forbid the Justice Department to use busing for integration in any but the most limited circumstances; anti-busing steps, of questionable constitutionality, are also proposed to limit the Supreme Court's power to order busing; and anti-busing constitutional amendments are proposed.

**1981** Drastic cuts in federal aid to education programs are included in the Reagan budget which Congress approves and the President signs. Cuts run the gamut from the preschool Head Start program to the Pell loans for college students.

**1981** The Justice Department announces it will no longer sue to desegregate entire school districts when only a part of a district discriminates. Instead, litigation is to concentrate on individual schools that discriminate. System-wide suits had become a major weapon of integrationists and had been upheld by the Supreme Court.

**1982** A storm erupts as the Administration reverses its 11-year policy of denying tax exempt status to private schools and colleges that discriminate racially. Stunned by the force of broad-based opposition to its stand, the government refers the matter to Congress and the Supreme Court but defends its action as one of necessary restraint on the powers of an administrative agency.

**1982** Civil rights lawyers assail the Justice Department's approval of a Chicago desegregation plan that relies extensively on voluntary student transfers.

**1982** Governor Carey of New York criticizes medical schools for a 46% drop in enrollment of minorities since 1976.

**1982** Efforts to eliminate the Department of Education appear to have failed as bipartisan Congressional support rallies around the beleaguered agency.

**1983** The U. S. Supreme Court, in *Bob Jones University* v. *IRS*, authorizes the denial of tax-exempt status to an institution that practices racial discrimination.

**1984** In *Grove City College* v. *Bell*, the U. S. Supreme Court rules that the financial-aid office of Grove City College is the only part of the institution subject to federal laws protecting women against discrimination because that office is the only part of the college receiving federal funds.

**1984, March 29** Dr. Benjamin E. Mays, a national civil rights education figure died in Atlanta, Ga., at age 89. He had served as president of Atlanta's Morehouse College from 1940 to 1967, and often said that one of his greatest honors was teaching and advising the late Dr. Martin Luther King, Jr., who was a student there. Raised on a farm, Dr. Mays attended college in 1916, and eventually earned a doctorate from the University of Chicago. He gained international renown as an educator and lecturer while dean of the Howard University Divinity School, from 1934-1940. During his career, he received 45 honorary degrees in law, divinity and the humanities.

**1984, April 14** In order to consolidate community support, Federal Judge Henry Woods orders the merger of the mostly black Little Rock School District with the mostly white North Little Rock and Pulaski County Districts in Arkansas. the judge cited the Little Rock District's inability to pass a property tax in five years as an indication that white voters were unwilling to support a mostly black school district. The case is to be heard by the Court of Appeals.

**1986** In February, Federal District Judge Jack Tanner rules that the state of Washington must pay $482 million over 6 years to bring the pay of 35,000 state workers—mostly women—up to the level of jobs of similar difficulty and worth held by most men. The ruling is the first major triumph for women fighting for "comparable worth."

**1985, May 2** the Ford Foundation announces it will give $9 million in fellowships for doctoral studies by blacks and minorities.

**1985, August 1** By a vote of 9 to 4, Dr. Laval S. Wilson, 47, becomes Boston school system's first black superintendent. His duties include overseeing a student population that is

48% black, 28% white, and 24% other minorities, and which has seen racial discord for more than a decade.

**1985, August 31** The Justice Department announces it no longer requires actual tabulations as proof that the court-ordered school desegregations have been met. Instead, the department says, school districts may be released from such obligations if they can demonstrate that they have "fully and in good faith" abided by measures outlined in the desegregation plan.

**1985, December 11** A group of black educators, politicians and community leaders form "The Select Committee on the Education of Black Youth." The committee's goal is to reduce dropout rates and increase college attendance of black youth. They offer an alternative curriculum for public school students, called "Foundation for Learning," which stresses reading, writing, and speaking skills.

**1986, January 1** In Congress, the House Committee on Government Operations criticizes the Reagan Administration in its handling of civil rights complaints against schools and colleges. The report recommended that federal anti-discrimination agencies insist that colleges do more than offer "good faith" efforts to correct previous racial imparities. The report, based on investigations and hearings by the Subcommittee on Intergovernmental Relations, cited as an example of the refusal of the Education Department's Office of Civil Rights to impose a mandatory cessation of federal funding to school districts and colleges which were found discriminatory in their treatment of blacks, women and handicapped persons.

**1986, February** Amendments to the Higher Education Act authorize the Ronald E. McNair Post-Baccalaureate Achievement Program and the Special Child Care Services for Disadvantaged College Students Program.

**1986, February 6** Federal judges in Richmond, Va., uphold a lower-court decision to end court-ordered busing in Norfolk, Va. The decision was seen as reflecting the Reagan Administration's proposal that if school districts demonstrated "good faith" efforts to desegregate, they would be allowed to choose alternatives to busing, as long as resegregation was not a result, Proponents argued that busing was driving whites from the city's public schools. Opponents protested that the decision threatened a 30-year effort to integrate the nation's public school system, and promised to seek an injunction from the Supreme Court.

**1986, April 23** National Education Association President Mary Futrell declares that the current levels of finances are insufficient to bring needed reform to public schools. Her announcement is buttressed by a NEA report that shows a 7.1% increase in school funding in the 1985-85 school year — far below the 20% to 25% increase needed for reform.

**1986, April 24** A general mood in America to apply economic sanctions against South Africa places black college officials in a financial quandary. Many of the companies which fund black institutions also have operations in white-ruled South Africa. If the black colleges divest themselves economically from those companies, they clearly stand to lose much more than other, better-financed institutions.

**1986, June** *Wygant* v. *Jackson Board of Education*, the U. S. Supreme Court in June declares unconstitutional a Jackson, Mich. school board plan for laying off teachers that gives preference to minority groups. In their decision, however, the Justices reject the broad position that the Constitution bars governments from using any racial preferences in employment that, at the expense of whites, benefit members of minority groups who are not personally the victims of discrimination.

**1986, June 16** The Supreme Court denies the injunction requested by black parents in Norfolk, Va., which would prevent the cessation of busing. The case, however, remains eligible for consideration on the high court's docket in the fall.

**1986, July 4** In Richmond, Va., a 25-year-old school desegregation case requiring busing ends when a federal judge finds no vestiges of state-sanctioned segregation in the school system.

**1986, October 7** The famous Brown v. Board of Education of Topeka, Kansas lawsuit is reopened by the original plaintiff and others. They contend that the defendant has neither fully integrated their schools as mandated, nor eradicated elements which permitted racial separation in previous years. Instead, said Richard Jones, a lawyer for the plaintiffs, the school board has approved racially divisive school boundaries, and has allowed white parents to circumvent desegregation efforts through school attendance alternatives.

**1986, November 3** The U. S. Supreme Court in *Riddick* v. *School Board of Norfolk* allows Norfolk to become the first school district in the U. S. to end court-ordered busing of elementary school pupils. At the same time, the Court, in *Board of Education of the Oklahoma City Public Schools* v. *Dowell*, lets stand a U. S. Circuit Court of Appeals ruling in Denver in June 1985 that blocked Oklahoma City's plan to end busing. Although the rulings appear contradictory, the likely result is that school districts will follow Norfolk and try to abandon busing plans.

**1986, November 4** The Norfolk, Va., and an Oklahoma, OK., school desegregation cases are declined for review by the Supreme Court without explanation. The decision meant that busing would end in Norfolk, Va. The second case involved a bid by the Oklahoma City School Board to end busing of students in grades 1 through 4. Observers felt the Supreme Court, by declining to accept these cases, was choosing to leave the decisions in local disputes to lower courts rather than set a national standard.

**1986, December 14** A federal district court judge dismisses a 26- year-old desegregation case in Chattanooga, Tenn., ruling that the local board of education has successfully complied with orders to integrate students and faculty. However, James Mapp, a black real estate agent who initiated the suit in 1960, maintained that some schools continued to have a student body of entirely one race, even though blacks compose 51.6% of the school system's 23,700 students.

**1987, April 1** The United Negro College Fund and the National Institution of Independent Colleges and Universities release a study which finds that black students are bearing the brunt of federal cut backs. The Findings were based on a survey of the nation's 57 historically black private colleges.

**1987, April 9** College Board President Donald Stewart decries the Reagan Administration's efforts to cut federal aid to college students, although he praised the president's Education Secretary William Bennett for calling for more coherence and rigor in college curriculums.

**1987, April 27** Hunter College anthropologist Johnetta Cole is named president of Spelman College in Atlanta, Ga. She also succeeds Donald Stewart as president of the College Board.

**1987, April 29** Billionaire John Kluge donates $25 million to Columbia University in New York for a new aid program for minority students. The funds will allow the university to offer financial aid to more than 60 Kluge Presidential Scholars who are chosen annually by the university provost.

**1987, May 20** The U.S. Commission on Civil Rights releases a report validating the role of desegregation plans, such as busing, in improving racial balances in public schools. The report notes, however, that white enrollment in public schools declined during the same period.

**1987, May 22** The House of Representatives approves a sweeping education bill, called the School Improvement Act, which will affect a majority of the nation's elementary and secondary school children. The Act consolidates 14 programs and renews them until 1993, and is estimated to add $780 million to current budget projections for the programs.

**1987, August 7** The NAACP Legal Defense and Educational Fund faults the Department of Education for failing to enforce desegregation in higher education systems in Arkansas, Florida, Georgia, Oklahoma and Virginia.

**1987, September 17** A federal district judge orders increases in property and income taxes to pay for improvements in the Kansas City, Mo., school system. One such improvement was the creation of magnet schools, designed to attract students from suburban and private schools elsewhere in the city.

**1987, September 23** Scholastic Aptitude Test results show that black students are making gains nationwide; however, College Board assessments find that the overall average school scores of black students have remained unchanged for the third year in a row.

**1987, September 25** Howard University in Washington, D.C. celebrates its 120th anniversary. The university, created by a congressional act in 1867, opened with a single building and four students.

**1987, October 4** In a follow up from a report issued in January 1986, the House Committee on government Operations finds that Virginia and nine other Southern states have not eliminated racial discrimination in their colleges and universities. The report cited disparities between black and white enrollment and retention rates, shortages of black faculty members and low minority enrollment in graduate and professional schools.

**1987, December 11** William Pratt of D. C. Superior Court ruled in Adams vs. Bennett that the so-called "Adams" decision is no longer enforceable. The Office of Civil Rights is required to obtain desegregation plans from 18 states with vestiges of *de jure* segregation.

**1988, February 17** A New York Times article finds that colleges and universities are finding it difficult not only to recruit black students, but to keep them on their rolls.

**1988, April 1** University of Maryland at College Park Chancellor Dr. John B. Slaughter announces his resignation in favor of accepting the post of president at Occidental College, a small, private college in Los Angeles. Dr. Slaughter was the first black to hold a high administrative position at the prestigious Maryland university.

**1988, April 25** the Supreme Court, in a 5-4 decision, decides to review a pivotal (1976) decision prohibiting private schools from discriminating on the basis of race.

**1988, August 16** Bishop College in Dallas, Texas, which was founded by freed slaves and was once the largest college west of the Mississippi, closes its doors after 108 years. The college reportedly owed more than $12 million to creditors.

**1988, September 16** Racial discussions consume residents of Hillside, N.J., a suburb of Newark. The 22,000-member community is at odds over a new plan to achieve racial balance in elementary schools where some two-thirds of the students are minorities.

**1988, October** Congress passes, over President Reagan's veto, the Civil Rights Restoration Act of 1987, which restores the effectiveness of four civil rights statutes that prohibit discrimination in federally assisted programs, including Title IX of the Education Amendments of 1972, enforcement of which was limited by the Supreme Court's *Grove City College* decision.

**1988, November 4** Actor Bill Cosby and wife, Camille, donate $20 million to Spelman College in Atlanta, Ga., the prestigious black women 's college. The contribution is the single largest gift ever made to a black college. Cosby said he made the donation with the hope of encouraging others to support black learning institutions, which are seriously underfunded.

**1988, December 27** Fifteen years atter court-ordered busing touched off violent opposition and "white flight" from the city, Boston approves a new plan to save its troubled public school system. The plan will allow parents to select a school closer to home, in order to reduce the lengthy bus rides of their children.

## SCHOLARSHIPS, LOANS, AND AWARDS

### Scholarships Primarily for Black Students

The importance of scholarships for blacks becomes evident when one considers the rising cost of a college education in the United States and the fact that education often provides the sole basis for the advancement of the black in our highly complex and industrialized society. The inverse relationship that exists between high college costs and low family incomes among blacks makes urgent the need for financial aid to students in predominantly black colleges.

This need is being met by an increasing number of scholarships, work-study programs, and loans. Scholarships are generally obtained from the following principal sources: colleges and universities; corporate philanthropy; religious groups; and federal, state, and local government agencies.

Below is a list of scholarship programs which are granted predominantly to black students. A guide which includes scholarships available to all students is published by the Scholarship Information Center of the University of North Carolina YMCA-YWCA, and can be ordered from the University of North Carolina YMCA-YWCA Human Relations Committee, Chapel Hill, North Carolina 27514. The annotated items which open this section are followed by a less detailed, but more comprehensive, listing of additional scholarship and loan sources. These have been provided courtesy of the United Negro College Fund, Research Division.

**National Achievement Scholarship Program for Outstanding Negro Students.** *Eligibility:* High school seniors. *Where valid:* Anywhere. *Restrictions:* None. *Value:* Two hundred four-year $1,000-6,000 scholarships. *How to apply:* Through high school principal or write to: National Achievement Scholarship Program, 990 Grove Street, Evanston, IL 60201. *Basis of award:* Need and scholarship. *Deadline:* Apply very early. By December 10 of year *before* entry into college.

**National Scholarship Service and Fund for Negro Students (Supplementary Scholarship Fund).** *Eligibility:* High school seniors. *Where valid:* Any regionally accredited, (state or city) degree-granting, INTERRACIAL institution at which campus facilities are extended equally without regard to race. *Restrictions:* Must have been counseled by organization. *Value:* Unspecified number, up to $600 per year. Renewable—Twice Only. *How to apply:* Write early in Junior Year to: NSSFNS, 6 East 82nd Street, New York, NY 10028. *Basis of awards:* Need, scholastic record, extracurricular activities, staff interviews, SAT tests. *Deadline:* Early in senior year for final applications.

**North Carolina College at Durham $1,000 Student Scholarships.** *Eligibility:* High school graduating seniors. *Where valid:* North Carolina College only.

*Commencement exercises.*

*Restrictions:* SAT score of at least 1000. *Value:* Several $1,000 grants available. Renewable. *How to apply:* Chairman of Committee on Financial Assistance to Students, North Carolina College at Durham, Box 601, Durham, NC. *Basis of awards:* SAT score of 1000 and good high school records. *Deadline:* May 1.

**Herbert Lehman Education Fund.** For Negroes at recently desegregated colleges in the Deep South. Apply Herbert Lehman Education Fund, 10 Columbus Circle, Suite 2040, New York, NY 10019.

**Martin DePorres Foundation.** For Philadelphia Catholics planning to attend nearby Catholic colleges. Apply M. H. McCloskey III, 2050 Suburban Station Building, Philadelphia 3, PA.

Minority Groups Scholarship Program. (Endowed by Rockefeller Fund). *Eligibility:* High school senior. *Where valid:* Any of seven specified colleges or universities. *Restrictions:* Must be member of minority group (Negro, Mexican, Oriental in the United States). *Value:* Determined by individual college. *How to apply*: Admissions Office of particular member college. *Basis of award:* Exceptional academic drive, leadership potential, financial need. *Deadline:* Unannounced.

**Polytechnic Institute of Brooklyn, New York.** *Eligibility:* High school seniors. *Where valid:* Polytechnic Institute of Brooklyn, New York. *Restrictions:* None. Priority given to southern blacks. For students interested in electrical engineering. *Value:* Remedial course work in summer if needed. Full tuition and maintenance for three or more students. *How to apply:* Have principal write to Polytechnic Institute requesting information. *Basis of award:* Need and scholarship. Interest in electrical engineering. *Deadline:* None.

**Eleanor Roosevelt Scholarship Program.** For students who have been actively involved in the civil rights movement. Apply CORE Scholarship, Education and Defense Fund, Inc., 150 Nassau Street, New York, NY 10038. The CORE Fund grants scholarships of up to $1,500 to cover tuition and living costs for a period of one year. Scholarships are awarded twice a year—in the spring and fall.

**Alfred P. Sloan Foundation.** *Eligibility:* High school seniors , high school juniors . *Where valid:* Ten major black colleges and universities. Restrictions: Male students only. *Value:* For juniors: Two summers remedial instruction at listed schools (Dillard University, New Orleans; Morehouse College, Atlanta). Will be granted scholarship for four years on completion of courses. For seniors: four-year grants to any of 10 schools. About 60 in number. *How to apply:* For juniors: United Negro College Fund, 22 East 54th Street, New York, NY 10022. For seniors: Apply to listed colleges. *Basis of awards:* Need. *Deadline:* Ideally in spring.

**Ralph E. Smith Freedom Scholarships.** *Eligibility:* High school seniors. *Where valid:* Macalester College, St. Paul, Minnesota. Restrictions: Three white and three Negro awards yearly. *Value:* Four-year scholarships, maximum value $2,000 yearly. *How to apply:* Make application to Macalester and request consideration for Ralph E. Smith Freedom Scholarships. *Basis of awards:* (1) leadership, (2) scholarship, (3) desire to work toward humanitarian goals in the tradition of the American way of life. *Deadline:* March 1.

**Texas Southern University School of Business, Houston, Texas Scholarships.** *Eligibility*: High school senior. *Where valid:* Texas Southern University only. *Restrictions:* None, interest in business career. Fifteen four-year full payment grants. *How to apply:* Have guidance counselor write to Texas Southern University. *Basis of awards:* Recommendations of principal and high school counselor, results of CEB and American College Testing Program examinations. *Deadline:* March 31.

**United Negro College Fund.** *Eligibility*: High school seniors and college undergraduates. *Where valid:* Any of 42 listed southern Negro colleges and universities. *Restrictions:* None. *Value:* The Fund grants money to the listed schools who then make the funds available to entering students. (In 1965, the goal was over $5,000,000.) *How to apply:* Apply to the Director of Admissions at the college or university listed. *Basis of award:* Set by each college or university. Need is certainly taken into consideration. *Deadline:* Unspecified

**John Hay Whitney Fund.** The "Opportunity Fellowships" of this fund are open to citizens from a number of diverse racial and cultural backgrounds, including Negroes. Candidates under 35 are given decided preference. Awards range to a maximum of $3,000, and are governed by the need of the candidate, as well as the nature of the program he desires to undertake. They are limited to a full year of serious graduate study. For further information (or applications), write the John Hay Whitney Foundation, 111 West 50th Street, New York, NY 10020

## Scholarships With No Racial Criteria

**Cooperative College Development Program.** Established with the assistance of the Alfred P. Sloan Foundation in 1965, the Cooperative Development Program extends its services to 23 southern Negro colleges and universities. The program assists member colleges in making presentations to industry, government, private foundations, and other potential sources of funds.

**Lever Brothers.** This organization provides 51 renewable $500 scholarships (one in each state and the District of Columbia) for study in the pharmaceutical field. Through the National Merit Program, Lever Brothers also contributes to graduate fellowships for blacks who wish to pursue a career in management. For more information, contact state pharmaceutical associations or Public Relations Department, Lever Brothers, 390 Park Avenue, New York, NY.

**National Merit Scholarship Corporation.** Established by the Ford Foundation and the Carnegie Foundation of New York in 1955, the National Merit Scholarship Corporation awards about 1,600 scholarships each year to high school students who qualify both on the National Merit Scholarship Qualifying Test, given in the spring, and the Scholastic Aptitude Test, given in the autumn, and who then pass the third and final phase of competition, where the criteria are outstanding grades, extracurricular activities, and leadership qualities. Winners receive up to $1,500 per year, depending on financial need, and may enroll in the school of their choice. For information, write Mr. Edward Smith, Executive Vice President, National Merit Scholarship Corporation, 990 Grove Street, Evanston, IL.

**Pulitzer Free Scholarship Committee.** This committee awards 10 four-year scholarships at $250 per year to male New York high school students. In addition, it awards graduate fellowships to a number of institutions participating in the program. For more information, contact Pulitzer Free Scholarship Committee, 105 Low Library, Columbia University, New York, NY.

**Radio Corporation of America.** The institutions (white and Negro) participating in the Radio Corporation of America program offer 34 undergraduate scholarships at $800 per year in various fields. In addition, RCA awards 11 fellowships for graduate study in electrical engineering, physics, electronics, dramatic arts, and journalism. The stipend is $2,100 with a supplementary $900 to a married graduate student with dependent children. An additional $500 may be made available for summer work.

## General Scholarship Aid

**Alcoa Foundation Scholarship Fund**
Pittsburgh
Pennsylvania

**Alpha Chi Rho Educational Foundation Inc.**
225 Lafayette Street
New York, NY 10012

**American Baptist Convention**
152 Madison Avenue
New York, NY
*Conditions:* Student must attend Baptist college

**American Machine and Foundry Company**
261 Madison Avenue
New York, NY 10016

**American Schools and Colleges Association**
30 Rockefeller Plaza
New York, NY 10020
*Conditions and Limits:* 1,200 scholarships to New York and New Jersey graduates Candidates must have worked during high school and shown scholastic and essay-writing ability.

**ASARCO Foundation**
120 Broadway
New York, NY

**George F. Baker Trust**
2 Wall Street
New York, NY 10005

**Bell Foundation, Inc.**
Buffalo, NY
*Conditions and Limits:* 2 tuition scholarships (Erie County Technical institute and Niagara University).

**Boy's Club of America**
171 First Avenue
New York, NY 10017
*Conditions and Limits:* Those Interested in Boy's Club career

**Campe (Ed. Lee & Jean) Foundation**
U.S. Trust Company of New York
New York, NY 10005

**Celanese Corp. of America**
522 Fifth Avenue
New York, NY 10036

**College Scholarship Service(CEEB)**
Princeton, NJ
Booklet: Sponsored scholarship programs using College Board Service

**Cook (Wm. J.) Fund Scholarships**
Chicago Community Trust
10 South La Salle Street
Chicago, IL 60603

**Cornell Club of Buffalo**
92 Pearl Street
Buffalo, NY
*Conditions:* For students wishing to attend Cornell

**Dedombrowski (G. Louise Robinson) Charitable Trust**
Simpson, Tatcher, Baetlett
120 Broadway
New York, NY 10005

**The Dillon Fund**
c/o Sherman and Sterling
20 Exchange Place
New York, NY 10005

**Dolan Foundation**
Edward Joy Company
905 Canal Street
Syracuse 3, NY

**Education Funds, Inc.**
10 Dorrance Street
Providence 3, RI
Up to $2,500 per year Renewable: Any educational expenses; no tests

**Elks National Foundation Scholarship Plan**
Chairman Elks National Foundation
16 Court Street
Boston, MA (142)
High school seniors in upper five per cent of their class. $700 to $1,500 annually

**Field Foundation, Inc.**
250 Park Avenue
New York, NY 10017

**Fischbach Foundation, Inc.**
454 Madison Avenue
New York, NY 10022

**Foresight Foundation, Inc.**
30 East 71st Street
New York, NY 10021

**Friedman Foundation, Inc.**
250 West 57th Street
New York, NY 10017

**The Fund for Theological Education, Inc.**
163 Nassau Street
Princeton, NJ 08540

**General Motors College Scholarship Plan**
**General Motors Corporation**
General Motors Building
Detroit 2, MI
(350) High school seniors
Up to $2,000 annually

**Generoso Pope Scholarship Awards**
Columbus Citizens Committee, Inc.
136 West 52nd Street
New York, NY

**Grant (Ulysses S.) Scholarship Foundation**
New Haven, CT

**Green Foundation**
167-10 Hillside Avenue
Jamaica 32, NY

**Greenspan (The Henry) Foundation**
469 Seventh Avenue
New York, NY
10018

**Hirsch Memorial Foundation, Inc.**
350 Fifth Avenue
New York, NY

**Honig (Ely) Memorial Scholarship Fund**
Angelo Fabrics Company, Inc.
1407 Broadway New York, NY
Fashion Industry

**Insurance Federation of New York**
116 Nassau Street
New York, NY 10038
Essay Contest determines winner of scholarship

**International Supreme Council of World Masons**
1775 West Forest Avenue
Detroit, MI

**Interracial Scholarship Committee of Greater Hartford**
Hartford Foundation for Public Giving
621 Farmington
Hartford 5, CT
*Conditions:* Hartford residents.

**J. R. S. Foundation, Inc.**
530 Fifth Avenue
New York, NY 10036

**Jephson Educational Trust**
c/o Chase Manhattan Plaza
New York, NY 10005

**Jones (W. Alton) Foundation, Inc.**
70 Pine Street
New York, NY 10005

**Kiwanis Club of New York**
Hotel Lexington
New York, NY 10017

**Knights of Columbus Scholarships**
New York State Council
486 Park Avenue
Yonkers, NY

**Knights Templar Educational Foundation, Foundation Committee**
Division of New York
71 West 23rd Street, Room 1527
New York, NY 10010

**Levy (Adele R.) Fund, Inc.**
100 Park Avenue
New York, NY 10017

**Levy (Jacob) Foundation, Inc.**
1440 Broadway New York, NY

**Littauer Foundation, Inc.**
345 East 46th Street
New York, NY 10017

**Lutheran Scholarships**
National Lutheran Council
50 Madison Avenue
New York, NY 10010
Graduate Students in social work

**Wheat Ridge Foundation**
Scholarship Office
2590 Devon, East

Des Plaines, IL
*Conditions:* Lutheran students preparing careers in Lutheran Welfare Service

**Marcus Foundation, Inc.**
1410 Broadway
New York, NY 10018

**Mazer (The Abraham) Family Fund**
477 Madison Avenue
New York, NY 10022

**McCormick Foundation**
5 Broadway
New York, NY 10004

**McGregor Fund**
2486 First National Building
Detroit 26, MI

**McMillin Foundation, Inc.**
435 East 52nd Street
New York, NY

**Mercy College**
Detroit, Ml

**Muehlstein Foundation, Inc.**
60 East 42nd Street
New York, NY 10017

**National Council of Boy Scouts of America**
New Brunswick, NJ 08903
A summary of colleges and universities that offer scholarships for boy scouts.

**National Honor Society Scholarships**
1201 Sixteenth Street, N.W.
Washington, D.C.
*Conditions:* (225 high school seniors who are National Honor Society members. $500 to $5,000 for four years

**National Merit Scholarships**
National Merit Scholarship Corporation
1580 Sherman Avenue
Evanston, IL
*Conditions:* 750 high school seniors in upper five per cent of their class. $100 to full tuition for four years.

**National Methodist Scholarships**
Department of Student Loans & Scholarships
P. 0. Box 871
Nashville, TN 37202
*Conditions:* Outstanding Methodist students in Methodist colleges.

**National Presbyterian College Scholarships**
Office Education Loan for Scholarships
Board of Christian Education United Presbyterian Church in the U.S.A.
425 Witherspoon Building
Philadelphia, PA 19187
*Conditions:* Up to $1,000 to qualified members of Presbyterian church enrolled in Presbyterian colleges.

**National Restaurant Association**
Educational Director
1530 North Lakeshore Drive
Chicago, IL 60610
*Conditions:* 5 scholarships at $1,000 each to persons entering the field of Food Service Administration

**National Scholarship Fellowship Program of YMCA**
Program of YMCA Personnel Services
National Council of YMCA
291 Broadway
New York, NY 10007
*Conditions:* Full time graduate professional study to prepare for YMCA work.

**New York City—Board of Higher Education**
Superintendent of Schools
10 Livingston Street
Brooklyn, NY

**New York State Funeral Directors Association**
369 Lexington Avenue
New York, NY 10017

**New York State Regents College Scholarship**
State Education Department
Regents Exam and Scholarship Center
Albany 1, NY
17,000 high school seniors who are residents of New York State. $250 to $750 annually.

**Jessie Smith Noyes Foundation**
205 East 42nd Street
New York, NY 10017
*Conditions:* Undergraduates with the exception of freshmen. Range from $500 to $1,500 with 2% interest after graduation.

**Azalia P. Oberg Foundation, Inc.**
Thomas & Thomas
504 Broadway, Room 1016
Gary, IN

**P.E.O. Educational Fund**
Executive Office
Mt. Pleasant, IA
*Conditions:* Women students

**Procter and Gamble Company Scholarship Program**
P. 0. Box 599
Cincinnati, OH
*Conditions:* Full tuition plus allowance for books, fees, supplies renewable up to four years. No restrictions.

*Students in class at Brooklyn College, part of the New York City College system.*

**Revlon Foundation, Inc.**
666 Fifth Avenue
New York, NY 10019

**Henry Warren Roth Educational Fund**
Henry Warren Roth
University of Pittsburgh
Pittsburgh, PA
*Conditions:* All undergraduates; range from $500 to $1,500 maximum 4% interest after graduation.

**Rothschild Fund, Inc.**
470 Park Avenue, South
New York, NY 10016

**Royal A. & Mildred D. Eddy Student Loan Fund**
Eddy Student Loan Fund
Thomas & Thomas
504 Broadway, Room 1016
Gary, IN
$1,500 annually
*Conditions:* No restrictions other than financial need; no tests; no deadline.

**S & H Foundation National Scholarship Program**
Educational Testing Service
Princeton, NJ
*Conditions*: High school seniors Up to $1,000 renewable for four years

**Sandy Hill Foundation**
27 Allen Street
Hudson Falls, NY

**Scholarship Foundation, Inc.**
120 East End Avenue
New York, NY

**Scott Fund, Inc.**
Five Quaker Center
Scarsdale, NY

**Schepp Leopold Foundation**
551 Fifth Avenue
New York, NY 10017

**Sloan (Alfred P.) Foundation**
630 Fifth Avenue
New York, NY 10020
*Conditions*: 150 scholarships awarded to juniors and seniors in participating schools. Range from $200 to $2,400.

**Society of Exploration Geophysicist**
Scholarship Committee Shell Building
Tulsa, OK 74119
*Conditions*: Scholarships for persons interested in a career as a geophysicist.

**Social Research Foundation, Inc.**
345 Park Avenue
New York, NY 1002

**Henry Strong Educational Foundation**
50 South LaSalle Street
Chicago, IL

**Student Opportunity Scholarships**
475 Riverside Drive, Room 1140
New York, NY 10027

**Telluride Association**
Ithaca, NY
*Conditions:* Students to attend Cornell

**Tiffany Foundation**
1083 Fifth Avenue
New York, NY 10028

**Vocational Advisory Service**
23 East 26th Street
New York, NY 10010

**Weisberg Foundation, Inc.**
29 Cooper Road
Scarsdale, NY

**Western Golf Association**
Golf, Illinois
*Conditions*: Four year scholarships to qualified caddies

**Westinghouse Science Talent Search**
Westinghouse Electric Corporation
East Pittsburgh, PA
*Conditions:* 40 high school seniors in top 10% of their class. $250 to $7,500 for four years.

**White Scholarship Fund**
73 Main Street
Cooperstown, NY

**Woike Foundation, Inc.**
1775 Broadway
New York, NY 10019

**Woodrow Wilson National Fellowship Foundation**
Box 642 Princeton, NJ
*Conditions*: 1,000 fellowships for first year graduate students interested in college teaching careers.

## Business And Industry Scholarship Sources

(Courtesy United Negro College Fund)

**Association of American Railroads**
59 East Van Buren
Street Chicago, IL

**Atlantic Refining Company**
260 South Broad Street
Philadelphia, PA

**Boston Insurance Company**
87 Kilby Street
Boston, MA

**Brown and Sharpe Manufacturing Company**
Providence, RI

**Bryant Chucking Grinder Company**
Springfield, VT

**Buckeye Pipe Line Company**
30 Broad Street
New York, NY

**Bulova Watch Company, Inc.**
Bulova Park
Flushing, NY

**Chance Vought Aircraft, Inc.**
P. 0. Box 5907
Dallas, TX

**Chicago Title & Trust Foundation**
Chicago, IL

**Chubb Foundation**
90 John Street
New York, NY 10038

**Climas Molybdenum Company**
Langeloth, PA

**Cummins Engine Company, Inc.**
Columbus, IN

**Fairchild Aircraft Division**
Hagerstown, MD

**Firestone Tire & Rubber Company**
1200 Firestone Parkway
Akron, OH

**Fisher Scientific Company**
717 Forbes Street
Pittsburgh, PA

**Food Fair Stores, Inc.**
2223 East Allegheny Avenue
Philadelphia, PA

**Ford Motor Company**
Central Building American Road
Dearborn, MI

**Fruehauf Trailer Company**
c/o Frank Strick Foundation
1335 Glenbrook Road
Huntingdon Valley, PA

**General Dynamics Corporation**
445 Park Avenue
New York, NY

**General Electric Company**
Schenectady, NY

**General Motors Corporation**
3044 West Grand Boulevard
Detroit, MI

**Goodbody & Company**
115 Broadway New York, NY

**Goodrich, B. F. Company**
Akron, OH

**Greenfield Tap & Die Corporation**
Greenfield, MA

**Gruman Engineering Company**
Bethpage, NY

**Greenwall, Susan Foundation**
Holmdel, NJ

**Gulf Oil Company**
Pittsburgh, PA

**Handcraft Company, Inc.**
Princeton, WI

**Handy & Harman**
82 Fulton Street
New York, NY

**Hood Dairy Foundation**
500 Rutherford Avenue
Boston, MA

**Hunt, C. Howard Pen Company**
7th & State Streets
Camden, NJ

**Imperial Coal Company**
Johnstown, PA

**Inland Steel Company**
38 South Dearborn Street
Chicago, IL

**International Business Machines Corporation**
590 Madison Avenue
New York, NY

**Joanna Cotton Mills**
Joanna, SC

**Johnstown Coal and Coke Company**
Johnstown, PA

**Jones & Laughlin Steel Corporation**
3 Gateway Center
Pittsburgh, PA

**Joy Manufacturing Company**
Henry W. Oliver Building
Pittsburgh, PA

**Katz Underwear Company**
Honesdale, PA

**Luria Engineering Company**
1745 Easton Avenue
Bethlehem, PA

**Mayer, Oscar & Company**
Madison, WI

**McCormick & Company**
414 Light Street
Baltimore, MD

**Mead Corporation**
Dayton, OH

**Merck & Company, Inc.**
Rahway, NJ

**National Starch Products Company**
270 Madison Avenue
New York, NY

**Niles-Bement-Pond Company**
West Hartford, CT

**Norfolk & Western Railway Company**
Roanoke, VA

**North American Aviation, Inc.**
International Airport
Los Angeles, CA

**Northern Illinois Gas Company**
c/o National Merit Scholarship Corporation
1580 Sherman Avenue
Evanston, IL

**Ohio Boxboard Company**
Rittman, OH

**Ohio Oil Company**
539 South Main Street
Findlay, OH

**Ohmite Manufacturing Company**
Skokie, IL

**Outboard Marine Corporation**
Evinrude Motors
Milwaukee, WI

**Pan American Petroleum Corporation**
c/o National Merit Scholarship Corporation
1580 Sherman Avenue
Evanston, IL

**Paragon Oil Company**
2100 Hunters Point Avenue
Long Island City, NY

**Pennsylvania Power & Light Company**
901 Hamilton Street
Allentown, PA

**Pennsylvania Railroad**
1617 Pennsylvania Boulevard
Philadelphia, PA

**Pennsylvania Salt Manufacturing Co.**
Three Penn Center
Philadelphia, PA

**Phelps Dodge Corporation**
300 Park Avenue
New York, NY

**Philip Morris**
100 Park Avenue
New York, NY

**Philips Petroleum Company**
Adams Boulevard
Bartlesville, OK

**Pitney-Bowes, Inc.**
Walnut & Pacific
Stanford, CT

**Pittsburgh Plate Glass Company**
632 Fort Duquesne Boulevard
Pittsburgh, PA

**Pratt & Whitney Company, Inc.**
Charter Oak Boulevard
West Hartford, CT

**Public Service Electric & Gas Company**
Newark, NJ

**Pullman Company**
11024 South Michigan Avenue
Chicago, IL

**Purolator Products, Inc.**
970 New Brunswick Avenue
Rahway, NJ

**Riegel Paper Corporation**
Box 170, Grand Central Station
New York, NY

**Riegel Textile Corporation**
Box 170, Grand Central Station
New York, NY

**Riverside Memorial Chapel**
180 West 76th Street
New York, NY

**Rockefeller Center, Inc.**
50 Rockefeller Plaza
New York, NY

**Sante Fe Foundation, Inc.**
Chicago, IL

**Schlumberger Well Surveying Corporation**
P. 0. Box 2175
Houston, TX

*Many African-American adults are taking advantage of college general studies courses.*

**Standard Oil Company of New Jersey**
30 Rockefeller Plaza
New York, NY

**Standard Oil Company of Ohio**
c/o Foundation of Independent Colleges
4554 Starret Road
Columbus, OH

**Superior Tube Company**
Norristown, PA

**Time-Life**
Time & Life Building
New York, NY

**UARCO, Inc.**
141 West Jackson Boulevard
Chicago, IL

**United Aircraft Corporation**
East Hartford, CT

**United States Industries, Inc.**
250 Park Avenue
New York, NY

**Van Raalte Company**
417 Fifth Avenue
New York, NY

**Victor Adding Machine Company**
3900 N. Rockwell Street
Chicago, IL

**Visking Corporation**
6733 West 65th Street
Chicago, IL

**West Chemical Products, Inc. (Marcuse Fund)**
c/o National Merit Scholarships Corp.
1580 Sherman Avenue
Evanston, IL

**Western Union Telegram Company**
60 Hudson Street
New York, NY

**William Manufacturing Company**
Gallia & Murray Street
Portsmouth, OH

**Wings Shirt Company, Inc.**
4 West 33rd Street
New York, NY

**Young & Rubicam, Inc.**
285 Madison Avenue
New York, NY

**Schmidt, Christian**
3965 Germantown Avenue
Philadelphia, PA

**Shatterproof Glass Corporation**
c/o William B. Chase Foundation
4815 Cabot Avenue
Detroit, MI

**Standard Oil Company of Indiana**
910 South Michigan Avenue
Chicago, IL

## Federal Financial Aid

**Division of Student Financial Aid**
U.S. Office of Education
Washington, D.C. 20202
(Request publication OE-55001:65)

**National Defense Education Act of 1958:**
*Conditions:* Loans may not exceed $1,000 per year or $5,000 for all years to any student.

**Students Loans for High Education—Title II**
*Conditions:* For the college where student is enrolled or has been accepted.

## Architecture and Engineering

**The American Institute of Architects**
110 Pearl Street
Buffalo 2, NY
*Conditions:* One scholarship for student interested in architecture as a career.

**The Cooper Union (For the Advance of Science and Art)**
Director of Admissions
The Cooper Union
Cooper Square
New York, NY 10003
*Conditions:* Scholarships valued at $1,500 to $2,000 per year. Competitive—scholarships in Art, Architecture, Engineering and Science.

**Antioch-Niagara Frontier Council**
116 Hartwell Road
Buffalo 16, NY
*Conditions:* 2 scholarships, from $400 to $800 in engineering.

Director Polytechnic Institute of Brooklyn
*Conditions:* Students wishing to graduate in electrical engineering, especially those from Southern Negro high schools. All tuition and maintenance costs.

**Union Carbide Education Fund**
270 Park Avenue
New York, NY 10017
*Conditions:* Engineering scholarships at 35 engineering colleges and universities.

## Journalism and Drama

**The Newspaper Fund**
P. 0. Box 300
Princeton, NJ 08540
*Conditions:* List of nearly $700,000 in scholarships offered by schools and departments of Journalism.

**William Randolph Hearst Foundation**
3rd and Market Streets, Suite 1018
San Francisco, CA 94103
*Conditions:* Grants for study to undergraduate journalism students range from $75 to $100 each month.

**Abbott (George) Educational Foundation Inc.**
630 Fifth Avenue
New York, NY 10020
*Conditions:* Students with talent in dramatic playwriting willing to attend the University of Rochester.

## Medical and Allied Professions

**American Dental Association**
Council of Dental Education
222 East Superior
Chicago, IL 60611

**American Association of Dental Schools**
840 North Lakeshore
Drive Chicago, IL 60611

**American Medical Association**
Education & Research Foundation
535 North Dearborn Street
Chicago, IL 60610
*Conditions:* Loans: Students admitted to approved medical schools.

*Chemistry class at Dillard in the 1950's.*

**Association of American Medical Colleges**
2530 Ridge Avenue
Evanston, IL
*Conditions:* Brochure: For sources of financial aid to medical students.

**Bergen Foundation**
6536 Sunset Boulevard
Hollywood 28, CA
*Conditions:* Loans: Nurses training.

**Beta Chi Inc.**
1211 Leeds Street
Utica, NY
*Conditions:* One scholarship of $500 for a girl to attend any accredited hospital school of nursing.

**Bureau of State Services (Community Health)**
U.S. Department of Health, Education, and Welfare
Washington, D.C. 20201
(Request publication 1154)
*Conditions:* Person enrolled or accepted for enrollment as full-time students in an accredited school of nursing having a loan fund under the Act. Students may borrow up to $1,000 an academic year.

**Bureau of State Services (Community Health)**
U.S. Department of Health, Education, and Welfare
Washington, D.C. 20201
(Request publication 1347)
*Conditions:* Persons enrolled or accepted as full-time students in a school which has a loan fund under the Act. Establishes student loans funds, for students pursuing a degree in medicine, dentistry, optometry, or osteopathy. May obtain loans of up to $2,000 a year.

**COSTEP**
Surgeon General U.S. Public Health Service
Washington, D.C.
Att: Office of Personnel
*Conditions:* For juniors and seniors in health related fields and students in programs of engineering and science.

**The Health Profession Educational Assistance Act of 1963: The Health Professions Student Loan Program—PTA.**
*Conditions:* Institution where student is enrolled or has been accepted.

**National Institute of Health**
Division of Research Grants
U.S. Public Health Service
Bethesda, MD 20014
*Conditions:* Undergraduate and graduate training grants.

**Navy Nurse's Corps Candidate Program**
Nearest U.S. Navy Recruiting Station
*Conditions: Open to students for junior and senior years in an accredited college or* nursing school. Provide for tuition, salary, and/or allowance benefits.

**Nurse Training Act of 1964: Nursing Student Loan Program**
*Conditions:* Institution where student is enrolled or has been accepted.

**National League for Nursing**
10 Columbus Circle
New York, NY 10019
*Conditions:* Scholarships for persons interested in nursing.

**Reyngolds Foundation, Inc.**
Polikoff & Clarehen
11 West 42nd Street
New York, NY 10036
*Conditions:* Students of medical and social sciences.

**The Surgeon General**
Department of Army
Washington, D.C. 20315
*Conditions:* Scholarships for dietetic therapeutics fields under the Army.

## Veterans

**AMVETS National Foundation**
P.O. Box 6038
Mid-City Station
Washington 5, D.C.
*Conditions:* Children whose fathers are deceased or totally disabled as a result of military service.
$2,000 total for four years.

**War Orphans Education Program**
Local Veterans Administration Office
*Conditions:* Children of servicemen who died in U.S. Armed Forces, must be between ages 18-23. $110 monthly.

## Miscellaneous Professions

**The Kroger Company**
1014 Vine Street
Cincinnati, OH
*Areas:* Freshman scholarships for students majoring in Agricultural and Home Economics at land grant colleges in the Midwest and South.

**Sears, Roebuck Foundation**
Apply to Dean of Land Grant College in home state.
*Areas:* Scholarships for male agricultural students and female home economics students.

**The Ralston Purina Fellowships**
Ralston Purina Company
Education Department
St. Louis, MO 63102
*Areas:* Scholarships for training in animal husbandry.

**Allstate Foundation**
10 Columbus Circle
New York, NY 10009
*Areas:* Scholarships for driver education to high schoolteachers.

**National Board of Civil Air Patrol**

Civil Air Patrol
Ellington Air Force Base
TX
*Areas:* Undergraduate and graduate scholarships awarded to Civil Air Patrol members.

**Institute of Food Technology**
176 West Adams Street
Chicago, IL 60603
*Areas:* Scholarships range from $300 to $1,000.

**Council of Hotel, Restaurant, and Institutional Education**
Statler-Hall Ithaca, NY 14858
*Areas:* Summary of financial aid available to students pursuing courses of study leading to a career in hotel, restaurant, and institutional work.

**Abraham & Strauss Scholarships**
*Areas:* Executive scholarships annually for students to combine on-the-job training and studies in retailing at Adelphi College, City College, Hofstra College, Long Island University, and New York University.

**National Commission for Social Work Careers**
345 East 46th Street
New York, NY 10017
*Areas:* Handbook of graduate scholarships in the field of social work.

**Public Inquiry Branch**
U.S. Department of Health, Education & Welfare
Washington, D.C. 20201
*Areas:* Undergraduate college students and graduate students training for teaching. Provides for scholarships of up to $800 to $1,000 based on need and academic standing in high school.

## Student Counseling Services

**College Admission Assistance Center**
41 East 65th Street
New York, NY
($20.00 service fee)

**College and Career Consultants YWCA**
New York, NY

**National Scholarships Service and Fund for Negro Students**
6 East 82nd Street
New York, NY

**New York City Board of Education Bureau of Guidance**
110 Livingston Street
Brooklyn, NY

**Masons**
2775 W. Forest Avenue
Detroit, MI

**Alfred P. Sloan Foundation**
630 Fifth Avenue
New York, NY 10020

**The Dillon Fund**
c/o Shearman & Sterling
20 Exchange Place New York, NY 10005

**American Baptist Convention**
(in order to attend Baptist College)
152 Madison Avenue
New York, NY

**George F. Baker Trust**
2 Wall Street
New York, NY 10005

**Jephson Educational Trust**
c/o Chase Manhattan Bank
1 Chase Manhattan Plaza
New York, NY 10005

**McGregor Fund**
2486 First National Building
Detroit, MI

**National Scholarship Service & Fund for Negro Students**
6 East 82nd Street
New York, NY 10028

**Omega Psi Phi Fraternity**
3104 13th Street, N.W.
Washington, D.C.

**Rockefeller Foundation Scholarship Aid**
Duke University, Durham, North Carolina
Emory University, Atlanta, Georgia
Tulane University, New Orleans, Louisiana
Vanderbilt University, Nashville, Tennessee
For disadvantaged graduates of Southern high schools. Tuition varies.

**Rockefeller Foundation Scholarship Aid for Negro Students**
Antioch College, Yellow Springs, Ohio
Carleton College, Northfield, Minnesota
Grinnell College, Grinnell, Iowa
Oberlin College, Oberlin, Ohio
Occidental College, Los Angeles, California
Reed College, Portland, Oregon
Swarthmore College, Swarthmore, Pennsylvania
High school juniors—Tuition for four years.

**The Eleanor Roosevelt Scholarship Program CORE Scholarship Education & Defense Fund, Inc.**
150 Nassau Street, Room 312
New York, NY 10038
Students who have actively been involved in efforts to eliminate racial prejudice and discrimination and to secure legal rights for persons of all races. Up to $2,000 annually.

**Roosevelt University**
3430 S. Michigan Avenue Chicago, IL
Negro and Indian students wishing to study in the college of Business Administration, $1,500 per year.

## Financial Aid for Spanish-Speaking Students

**ASPIRA Agency Scholarships**
137 West 72nd Street
New York, NY

**Barnard College**
New York, NY 10027
2 scholarships (Spanish speaking)

**Board of Home Missions**
287 Fourth Avenue
New York, NY
Four scholarships

**Mercy College**
Detroit, MI
Catholic Puerto Rican students.

**Miami University**
Oxford, OH
Conversational classes

**New York Puerto Rican Scholarship Fund, Inc.**
250 Church Street
New York, NY
Competitive

**St. Laurence University**
Canton, NY

**St. Mary of the Woods College**
St. Mary of the Woods
Indiana

Southern Illinois University
Cardonale, IL

**University of Arizona**
Tucson, AR
10 scholarships of $360 each.

**University of Chattanooga**
Chattanooga, TN
Scholarships available in return for help in conversational classes.

**University of New Mexico**
Albuquerque, NM
Scholarship and stipend for tuition, board and room.

## General Loans

**Beans Foundation**
2 Broadway
New York, NY 10004
*Grants and Loans:* Students attending colleges and universities

**Central Scholarship Bureau, Inc.**
819 West Monument St.
Baltimore 1 MD
*Limit:* $750

**Insured Tuition Plan**
38 Newbury St.
Bosyon, 16 MA
*Loans:* No restrictions on school location

## Additional Sources of Financial Aid

**Catholic Scholarships for Negroes, Inc.**
Mrs. Roger L. Putnam
224 Union Street
Springfield, MA 01105

**The Fund for Theological Education, Inc.**
163 Nassau Street
Princeton, NJ 08540

**Howard University Foreign Service Grant**
Howard University
Washington, D.C.

**Minority Groups Scholarship Program**
Write to:
Antioch College, Yellow Springs, Ohio
Carleton College, Northfield, Minnesota
Grinnell College, Grinnell, Iowa
Oberlin College, Oberlin, Ohio
Occidental College, Los Angeles, California
Reed College, Portland, Oregon
Swarthmore College, Swarthmore, Pennsylvania

**Polytechnic Institute of Brooklyn, NY**
Electrical Engineering (priority given to southern Negroes for remedial courses).

**Ralph L. Smith Freedom Scholarships Macalester College**
St. Paul, Minnesota

**Student Opportunity Scholarships**
Room 1140
475 Riverside Drive
New York, NY 10027

**Texas Southern University School of Business**
Houston, TX

**Home Guidance Counselor**
Catholic Scholarships for Negroes
254 Union Street
Springfield, MA

**Elks National Foundation**
Chairman Scholarship Awards
16 Court Street Boston, MA

**Field Foundation Inc.**
250 Park Avenue
New York, NY 10017

**International Supreme Council of World St. Mary's College**
Notre Dame, IN
One scholarship for black girl, competitive.

**Ralph L. Smith Freedom Scholarships**
Macalester College
St. Paul, MI

**Texas Southern University**
Houston, TX
107 high school juniors Tuition and fees for four years.

**Texas Southern University School of Business Home**
Guidance Counselor Houston, TX

**John Hay Whitney Foundation**
11 West 50th Street
New York, NY 10020
Graduate work in the Creative Arts Minority groups solicit. Range from $1,000 to $3,000/ year.

*President Lyndon B. Johnson added many federally sponsored school programs to provide better environments for learning and for physical and emotional health.*

## ELEMENTARY AND SECONDARY EDUCATION ACT

The passage of the Elementary and Secondary Education Act of 1965 served notice of the intention of the federal government to assume direct responsibility for providing all children—particularly the disadvantaged—with quality education. The five key provisions of the act can be summarized as follows:

### Title I. *Opportunity for the Disadvantaged*

This title provides funds to school districts under state plans approved by the U.S. Office of Education. During the first year of the program, Congress appropriated 775 million dollars to individual states and school districts. Each local public school is eligible to receive half the average current school expenditure per child in the state, multiplied by the number of school-age children in the district whose families earn less than $2,000 annually.

Funds may be used to benefit both public and nonpublic school children through such arrangements as dual enrollment, educational media centers, mobile education centers and equipment, and educational radio and television. They may also be used for broadened health programs, school breakfasts, guidance and counseling, in-service teacher training, additional teaching personnel, curriculum development, pre-school training and special audio-visual aids and other equipment.

Title I funds are in the form of 100% grants to state educational agencies which then allocate money to school districts according to a formula established by Congress.

### Title II. *School Library and Instructional Resources*

Under Title II, Congress has authorized 100 million dollars for school library aid. Funds may be used to purchase textbooks, library books, periodicals, documents, tapes, records, physical facilities, equipment, and for administration and financing. (Under present estimates, Title II funds are expected to add about $2 per pupil annually for each of the nation's 47 million school children.) Funds are allocated under state plans on the basis of public and nonpublic elementary and secondary school populations.

Administrative plans under this title require the approval of the U.S. Office of Education. They must spell out criteria for fund use and provide assurance that materials will be available on an equitable basis *for all children.* Materials are loaned to privates school pupils, and remain the property of the designated public agency.

Since the needs and requirements of each state vary, uniform plans are not mandatory.

### Title III. *Supplementary Educational Centers*

This title is designed to help local school districts relate research to practice through the support of supplementary centers and services. These must seek to improve the quality of education by providing services *not now available* to the children within a given community, such as psychological testing, audiovisual aids, radio and television, programmed materials, etc.

Congress appropriated 75 million dollars for Title III Supplementary centers for fiscal 1966. Services are available to public and nonpublic pupils on a nonsectarian basis.

### Title IV. *Educational Research*

Under this title, Congress has appropriated 100 million dollars over a five-year period in an effort to improve the depth of U.S. educational research. The money is being used to construct and equip national and regional research facilities, including educational laboratories. These laboratories are regionally based, and work in such areas as basic research, curriculum development and teacher training.

### Title V. *Strengthening State Education Agencies*

Under this title, Congress has appropriated 17 million dollars for the first year of a five-year program designed to strengthen state education departments. (Title V provides unmatched federal grants for the first two years, and then calls for matching state grants of from 33 to 50% of the federal total.)

Two kinds of grants—basic and experimental—are authorized under this title. Eighty-five percent of the funds must be used for basic administrative improvements, with the remainder earmarked for experimental projects. Provision has also been made under Title V for the exchange of personnel between the U.S. Office of Education and state education departments in order to establish a better understanding of programs and problems.

## THE HIGHER EDUCATION ACT OF 1965

The Higher Education Act of 1965 sought to "strengthen the educational resources of our colleges and universities and to provide financial assistance for students in post-secondary and higher education. "In short, this act seeks to take advantage of the skills and knowledge of the university by, in effect, putting the university to work toward solving the problems of the community. The first five titles of the act may be summarized as follows.

### Title I. *Community Service and Continuing Programs*

Title I authorized the appropriation of 25 million dollars in fiscal 1966 for community service and continuing education programs. The programs, set up by the states, place special emphasis on solving problems in urban and suburban areas. Each participating state has chosen an existing agency or institution to carry out this title. This agency, through a federally approved plan, has established guidelines for giving federal funds to qualifying colleges and universities.

### Title II. *College Library Assistance and Library Training and Research*

Title II provided grants to colleges and universities for library materials such as books, periodicals, documents, magnetic tapes and phonograph records. These grants sometimes double and triple the funds available for library development in small and poorly supported colleges.

### Title III. *Strengthening Developing Institutions*

Under this title, 55 million dollars has been provided to carry out cooperative programs and set up national teaching fellowships for developing institutions. Seventy-eight percent of the money goes to four-year colleges; the remaining 22% to two-year colleges.

To be eligible, institutions must meet the following requirements.

1. Admit as regular students only high school students, or the equivalent.
2. Award a bachelor's degree or provide a two-year program creditable toward such a degree, or a two-year technical program.
3. Be accredited, or be making reasonable progress toward reaching this status.

### Title IV. *Student Assistance*

Title IV establishes educational opportunity grants and provides federally subsidized student loans. Seven million dollars has been authorized for these grants in the 1966-1967 school year. Colleges themselves administer the grants, select the eligible students, and decide on the size of individual grants.

### Title V. *Teacher Programs*

Title V is aimed at improving the caliber and increasing the number of America's teachers, with a view toward thus increasing the educational opportunity offered America's elementary and secondary school children. It also establishes the National Teacher Corps (NTC), providing fellowships for graduate study. Members of the NTC are often used to visit impoverished school districts, and supplement the teaching force there.

## THE HIGHER EDUCATION AMENDMENTS OF 1968

Amendments to the Higher Education Act constitute the most comprehensive aid-to-education package to take effect since the Elementary and Secondary Education Act of 1965. These amendments not only extend through 1971 such key legislation as the National Defense Education Act, but also create six new higher education programs, including Special Services for Disadvantaged Students, Cooperative Education and Education for the Public Service. As a whole, the amendments broaden the search for talented and ambitious youths from the preschool to the Ph.D. level. The five amendments can be summarized as follows.

### Title I. *Student Assistance*

Student assistance has several features which can be characterized under a number of appropriate headings. The Educational Opportunity Grant Program increases maximum student grants from $800 to $1,000 a year. The federal government is still paying interest charges on loans to borrowers in college or in their deferment period. The College Work-Study Program allows students to work more than 15 hours per week during the summer, with 80% of salary being paid by the federal government. Under Cooperative Education, grants are authorized to plan and develop programs which alternate full-time study with full-time employment. The National Defense Student Loan Program permits teachers in low-income schools to cancel up to 100% of their loans.

### Title II. *Amendments to Other Provisions of the Higher Education Act*

Other amendments to HEA offer assistance to college libraries, to junior colleges, to state educational authorities recruiting teachers and teacher aides, sharing faculty, and improving graduate programs. The Law School Clinical Experience Program (Title 9) will pay up to 90% of the cost of establishing clinical experience projects at accredited law schools.

### Title III. *Amendments to Provisions of the National Defense Education Act*

The NDEA amendments include those which provide 7,500 new fellowships per year, offer short-term training sessions for guidance counselors, and extend, without change, language development.

### Title IV. *Amendments to the Higher Education Facilities Act*

New legislation appended to the HEFA authorizes federal interest grants to help cover the cost of nonfederal financing of construction, and makes student health facilities eligible for building funds. These apply to both graduate and undergraduate facilities.

### Title V. *Miscellaneous Amendments*

The HEA amendments extend the life of Section 12 of the National Foundation on the Arts and Humanities Act and the International Education Act of 1966. These amendments also specify instances in which Federal assistance can be cut off, to wit: when a student is convicted of a serious crime involving force or seizure of a campus facility which denies the majority access to the institution.

## VOCATIONAL EDUCATION

### Vocational Education Act (P.L. 88-210)

Funds are available for state vocational education programs for persons in high school, for persons who have completed or left high school, for persons who are unemployed or underemployed, and for persons who have academic, socioeconomic, or other handicaps that prevent them from succeeding in regular vocational education programs. Residential vocational schools, work-study programs, teacher-training, and research programs are included in the provisions of this Act. School systems interested in knowing more about this resource should contact their state education agency. Additional information may be obtained from the Division of Vocational and Technical Education, Bureau of Adult and Vocational Education, Office of Education, Washington, D.C. 20202.

### Aid to Technical and Vocational Education (Formerly NDEA, Title VIII, P.L. 85-864, as amended by P.L. 88-210)

Grants are available to states for the development of area vocational education programs in scientific or technological fields. These programs are designed to train persons for employment as highly skilled technicians in recognized occupations requiring scientific knowledge in fields necessary for the national defense. Provision can be made for retraining and refresher courses for adults in such fields as electronics and industrial chemistry. School systems interested in knowing more about this resource should contact their state education agency. Additional information may be obtained from the Division of Vocational and Technical Education, Bureau of Adult and Vocational Education, Office of Education, Washington, D.C. 20202.

## CIVIL RIGHTS INSTITUTES

### Civil Rights Act of 1964, Title IV (P.L. 88-352)

Title IV provides funds to colleges and universities to conduct institutes for school personnel, grants to the school boards for in service training and the employment of advisory specialists, and technical assistance, including consultants, to enable schools to deal more effectively with educational problems caused by desegregation. Further information may be obtained from the Equal Educational Opportunities Program, Office of Education, Washington, D.C. 20202.

## NATIONAL DEFENSE EDUCATION ACT

### Loans to Students in Institutions of Higher Learning, Title II (P.L. 85-864, as amended by P.L. 88-665)

Undergraduate and graduate students at American colleges and universities may obtain loans under this Title to pursue their higher education. Students receiving loans who become full-time teachers in public or other nonprofit elementary or secondary schools or institutions of higher education may have up to 50% of their loans canceled. Additional information may be obtained from the Director, Division of Student Financial Aid, Bureau of Higher Education Programs, Office of Education, Washington, D.C. 20202.

*A teacher helps his students with a geometry problem.*

### Grants to Strengthen Subject Areas, Title III (P.L. 85-864, as amended by P.L. 88-665)

Matching grants to states are available for the purpose of strengthening education in elementary and secondary schools in the critical subjects of science, mathematics, history, civics, geography, modern foreign language, English, and reading. This is accomplished through federal grants and loans for the acquisition of laboratory and other special equipment and through federal grants for state programs of supervisory and related services in those subjects. School systems interested in knowing more about this resource should contact their state education agency. Additional information may be obtained from the Division of Program Operations, Bureau of Elementary and Secondary Education, Office of Education, Washington, D.C. 20202.

### Guidance, Counseling, and Testing, Title V (P.L. 85-864, as amended by P.L. 88-865)

State education agencies may receive matching grants under this Title to establish and maintain elementary and secondary school programs of testing, guidance, and counseling. These programs are designed for the early identification of students with outstanding aptitude. School systems interested in knowing more about this resource should contact their state education agency. Additional information may be obtained from Division of Program Operations, Bureau of Elementary and Secondary Education, Office of Education, Washington, D.C. 20202.

### Institutes for Advanced Study, Title XI (P.L. 88-865)

Funds are available to institutions of higher education to conduct institutes for advanced study in order to improve the qualifications of individuals engaged in the teaching of disadvantaged youth. Short-term or regular session institutes may be held; usually summer programs predominate. The law defines such youth as those who are "culturally, economically, socially, and educationally handicapped." An institute may focus on teachers whose students are rural, urban, migrant, Indian, non-English speaking, and so forth. Additional information may be obtained from the Division of Educational Personnel Training, Bureau of Elementary and Secondary Education, Office of Education, Washington, D.C. 20202.

### Captioned Films for the Deaf (P.L. 85-505, as amended by P.L. 87-715)

Under this Act a service of films is available to provide cultural and educational experiences and to promote educational advancement for the deaf. The Act also supports research in the use and production of these films and for training persons in this area. Additional information may be obtained from Director, Captioned Films for the Deaf Branch, Division of Research Training and Dissemination, Bureau of Research, Office of Education, Washington, D.C. 20202.

### National Technical Institute for the Deaf (P.L.89-36)

The National Technical Institute for the Deaf will provide a residential vocational school for postsecondary training of deaf youth for employment in high skill jobs. Additional information may be obtained from Phillip Des Marias, Office of the Secretary, Department of Health, Education, and Welfare, Washington, D.C. 20201.

*Federally sponsored "Double Discovery" program at Columbia University.*

# BLACKS IN HIGHER EDUCATION

## College Participation Rates

For the past several years the American Council on Education, Office of Minority Concerns has issued a status report on minorities in higher education and virtually all the material presented in this piece on college participation rates is from their annual report.

Although there is a greater number of blacks graduating from high school there is a lower percentage of these young people enrolling in college.

In 1976, the "enrolled-in-college" participation rates for white, black, and Hispanic high school graduates were nearly equal. However, during the late 1970s and the early 1980s, as the number of white high school graduates began to decline and the number of black and Hispanic graduates continued to increase, the gap in their relative "enrolled-in-college" participation rates widened. Between 1977 and 1986, the participation rate for white 18-to-24-year-old high school graduates was consistently higher than that for blacks and Hispanics. Since the "enrolled-in-college" participation rate for both blacks and Hispanics in this age range has dropped, while it has increased some-what for whites, the gap between rates for whites and these two minority group has increased.

College participation trends for white 18-to-24-year-old high school graduates show that, despite declines in the number of white high school graduates in this age group, whites maintained an "enrolled-in-college" participation rate ranging from a low of 31.1% in 1978 to 34.4% in 1985. Between 1976 and 1986, the white participation rate increased from 33% to 34.1%. The "enrolled-in-college" rate for high school graduates was slightly higher for white men than for white women.

The "enrolled-in-college" participation rate for black 18-to-24-year-olds ranged from a high of 33.4% in 1976 to a low of 26.1% in 1985. This participation rate showed some improvement between 1985 and 1986, rising to 28.6% . In 1986, the participation rate for black female high school graduates was 29.3%, compared to 27.8% for their black male counterparts. However, for nine of the 11 most recent years for which data are available, black men in this age range had a higher "enrolled-in-college" participation rate than black women.

Between 1976 and 1986, the 18-to-24-year-old Hispanic population increased by 62%, by far the largest population increase for any racial or ethnic group in this age cohort. The number of 18-to-24-year-old Hispanic high school graduates increased by nearly 75%. However, as the size of this population and the number of high school graduates increased, its "enrolled-in-college" participation rate actually declined, from 35.8% in 1976 to a low of 26.9% in 1985. As with blacks, this participation rate rebounded in 1986, to 29.4%. The decline in the "enrolled-in-college" participation rate was more severe for Hispanic men, who dropped from a high of 39.7% in 1976 to 29.0% in 1986. Hispanic women in this age cohort had an "enrolled-in-college" participation rate that varied greatly (from a high of 33.1% in 1976 to a low of 24.8% in 1978). Their rate was 29.9% in 1986. Until 1984, Hispanic men generally had higher "enrolled-in-college" rates than Hispanic women; since then, however, Hispanic women have maintained higher participation rates.

An analysis of the "attended-college" participation rates for high school graduates by race and ethnicity reflects the same general pattern; whites consistently have the highest rate, followed by blacks and Hispanics, with a slight widening between the rates for whites and minorities. Between 1976 and 1986, the "attended-college" participation rate for whites increased from 53.5% to 55.3%, compared to a decline from 50.4% to 47.4% for blacks, and a corresponding decline from 48.9% to 45% for Hispanics. As with the "enrolled-in-college" rates, the "attended-college" rates for the three groups were closer to being equal in the mid-1970s. Since that time, this rate has improved for whites but declined for blacks and Hispanics. Between 1985 and 1986, there was some improvement in the "attended- college" rate for blacks, increasing from 43.8% to 47.4%. Conversely, Hispanics experienced a slight drop, from 46.7% to 45%, while whites remained stable at 55.3%.

## General Enrollment Trends—1976-1988

Despite predictions of enrollment declines in higher education, enrollment in the nation's colleges and universities has increased. In 1986, enrollment in higher education reached an all-time high of 12.5 million students. Between 1976 and 1986 (the latest year for which enrollment figures are available through the National Center for Education Statistics), total enrollment in higher education increased 13.8%, from just under 11 million students. The enrollment of older students, women, and minorities contributed to this increase. Gains were evident at the undergraduate and graduate levels.

Enrollment increases were fairly evenly distributed between public and independent institutions. Public colleges and universities increased 12.5% in enrollment, while independent institutions netted a gain of nearly 18.5%. Throughout the decade, public institutions accounted for close to 80% of total enrollment.

Two-year colleges showed more growth than their four-year counterparts. Total enrollment in two-year colleges increased 20.5% (from 3.9 million students in 1976 to 4.7 million in 1986). Four-year institutions experienced a 10.1% enrollment gain. The increased enrollment in two-year institutions changed their proportional representation from 35 to 37% of the total enrollment in higher education.

During this same period (1976-1986), enrollment distribution by gender was reversed. In 1976, women accounted for 47.3% of total college enrollment, while men made up 52.7%. By 1986, women represented 53% of the total.

## Trends Between 1984 and 1986

Between 1984 and 1986, enrollment in higher education increased. In 1986, total enrollment increased 2.2% over 1984. During this period, enrollment at public institutions grew from 9.5 million to 9.7 million (a gain of 2.8%). Enrollment at independent institutions stayed relatively stable. Women comprised 53% of college enrollment and continued to enroll in higher education in larger numbers than did men. While male enrollment did not change much, increasing by only 0.4% during this period, there was a 3.7% increase in female enrollment. Graduate enrollment increased nearly 7% and professional school enrollment declined 3.2%. Total enrollment at two-and four-year institutions increased 3.3% and 1.5%.

## Minority Enrollment Trends

Between 1984 and 1986, the enrollment of minorities (non-Hispanic blacks, Hispanics, Asians, and American Indians) in higher education increased by 7.6 percent. As a group, minorities have continued to increase in college enrollment since racial and ethnic figures were first reported in 1976. This increase has been fueled mainly by the increased enrollment of Asians and Hispanics. These gains, although significant and encouraging, must be viewed in a context of the overall participation-in-college rates of minorities and the degree completion rates of each group, both of which are less favorable for blacks and Hispanics than for whites.

In 1984, minority enrollment was just under 2.1 million students (17.1% of total college enrollment). As of 1986, these figures had increased to 2.2 million students (17.9% of total enrollment). During this period, Hispanics led in enrollment gains, increasing by 16.6%. Asians followed closely with a 14.9% gain. Enrollment gains for American Indians were less dramatic (7.1%). In 1986, black enrollment increased by only 0.5% from 1984. Black enrollment in 1984 was 2.8% below the 1980 peak of 1.1 million students. When enrollment figures for minorities are considered as a whole, enrollment increases for Asians and Hispanics mask the earlier declines and the current stagnation in black enrollment.

Since the number of blacks enrolling in college did not change much between 1984 and 1986, while total enrollment in higher education increased, the black share of total enrollment declined from 8.8% in 1984 to 8.6% in 1986. The black share of college enrollment in 1976 was 9.4%, which was an all-time high. It should be noted that the proportion of whites enrolling in higher education also declined, from 80.2% in 1984 to 79.3% in 1986.

Increases in minority enrollment between 1984 and 1986 were larger at public colleges and universities than at independent institutions (8.8% versus 2.1%). With a gain of 18.2%, Hispanics showed the greatest gain in public institutions, followed by Asians. Asian enrollment increased 15.2%. Hispanic enrollment gained 6.3% in independent institutions, while blacks experienced a loss of 2.6%. American Indian enrollment increased 9.7% at public institutions but remained stable at independent institutions. As a result of these changes, minorities increased their share of the enrollment in public colleges and universities from 17.9% in 1984 to 19% in 1986, and inched upward from 14 to 14.2% at independent institutions.

Women made significant gains in both numbers and relative proportion of college enrollment during the last decade. Asian and Hispanic women made the greatest gains, followed by American Indian women and black women.

Between 1984 and 1986, enrollment for black women increased by less than 1%, which was considerably below that of women of other racial and ethnic groups. For black men, the trends were even more dismal.

During the decade between 1976 and 1986, black men experienced the only enrollment decline among minorities (-7.2%). Between 1984 and 1986, the downward slide of black male enrollment appears to have levelled off (-0.2%). White men also experienced a loss in enrollment (-0.9%). For all men, the enrollment declines of black and white men were offset by the gains of Asian and Hispanic men, 13.8 and 15%, respectively. American Indian men made moderate gains, with a 5.3% increase between 1984 and 1986.

Enrollment trends between 1976 and 1984 show that minorities enrolled in two-year institutions in higher proportions than their white counterparts. This trend continued between 1984 and 1986. In 1984, 46.1% of minorities who were enrolled in college attended two-year institutions, compared to 35.8% of whites. Within two years, minority enrollment in two-year colleges increased 8.9%,

*A mathematics class in a modern black college.*

resulting in 46.7% of minorities attending two-year institutions. In 1986, whites enrolled in two-year institutions in about the same proportion as they did in 1984 (36.1%). As in prior years, American Indian (56.7%) and Hispanic students (55.3%) attended two-year colleges more frequently than other minority groups. This compares to 41.5% for Asians and 43.1% for blacks.

With a 17.5% increase in Asian enrollment and a 13% increase in Hispanic enrollment, total enrollment of minorities climbed 6.3% in four-year institutions between 1984 and 1986. American Indian enrollment in four-year colleges and universities increased 5.3% during this period. Blacks were the only group that moved downward in four-year enrollments. In 1984, 617,000 blacks were enrolled in four-year institutions; by 1986 the number of black students had dropped by 2,000.

At the undergraduate level, total enrollment increased from 10.6 million students in 1984 to 10.8 million in 1986 (a gain of 1.8%). In 1986, undergraduates accounted for 86% of total enrollment. After declining by 33,000 students between 1980 and 1984, there was little change in black undergraduate enrollment between 1984 and 1986. Hispanics and Asians both gained 14.9% in undergraduate enrollment, while American Indians experienced a 7.7%increase.

## College Completion Rates

Hispanics and blacks who entered college completed it at a much lower rate than whites, according to *High School and Beyond*, a longitudinal study of 1980 high school seniors. The data of that study showed that by spring 1986, 44.9% of all students who entered a public four-year college and 51.9% of all those who entered an independent institution had received their bachelor's degree. However, six years after entrance into a public four-year institution, only 25.6% of Hispanics and blacks had received a B.A. The equivalent rate for whites was 48%.

The corresponding completion rates for independent institutions were slightly higher. Nearly 56% of the whites who entered an independent college or university completed their degree within six years. The completion rate for blacks was 28.5%, slightly higher than that of Hispanics at 26.8%. The discrepancy in the completion rates reported here between whites and blacks and Hispanics is exacerbated by the fact that more white students attended a four-year college full-time directly after high school than did blacks or Hispanics. Consequently, they were more likely to finish their bachelor's degree within the six years than students who postponed their college entrance, attended a two-year college, or attended college part-time.

Other data from *High School and Beyond* show that 71% of the black 1980 high school graduates, 66% of the Hispanics, and 65% of the American Indians who entered postsecondary education by 1982 left by 1986 without a bachelor's degree. These figures were much lower for Asians and whites; 47% of the Asians and 55% of the whites did not receive a B.A. degree. (These figures include students who entered post-secondary education without the intention of obtaining a four-year degree.)

Both sets of data show lower college completion rates for blacks and Hispanics than for whites. The study underscores the need to increase both the enrollment of underrepresented minorities in higher education and efforts to retain them through college graduation.

## Graduate and Professional School Enrollment

From 1984 to 1986, total graduate enrollment grew by 90,000 students, from 1.3 million in 1984 to an all-time high of 1.4 million in 1986. Minorities accounted for 11.6% of graduate enrollment in 1986, compared to 10.5% in 1984. Enrollment trends for this two-year period reveal gains for all racial and ethnic groups except American Indians, who maintained approximately the same enrollment level. Between 1984 and 1986, black graduate enrollment increased by 5,000 students (a gain of 7.5%). This brought graduate enrollment for this group back to the 1976 level of 72,000, which was its highest. However, blacks continued to constitute only 5% of total graduate enrollment.

Hispanics and Asians repeated their undergraduate patterns at the graduate level. Hispanics gained 43.8% in graduate enrollment, which increased their relative share of graduate enrollment from 2.4% in 1984 to 3.2% in 1986. Asians gained 16.2% in the number of students attending graduate school. In 1986, Asians represented 3% of graduate enrollment.

Total enrollment in professional schools declined 2.9% between 1984 and 1986, with 278,000 students enrolled during the earlier period and 270,000 students enrolled in 1986. This decline was caused by enrollment losses of white students. In 1986, the representation of whites in professional schools remained above 85%, down from a high of 90.1% in 1976. Minority enrollment in professional schools was 13.2% in 1986, up from 11.4% in 1984. While blacks and Hispanics increased in professional school enrollment by approximately 1,000 students each, Asians gained an additional 2,000 students. Professional school enrollment for American Indians remained at approximately 1,000 students, a representation of only 0.4%.

## Blacks in Predominantly White Colleges

A concern of the 1970s was that blacks were not progressing significantly in the quality of education available to them. A spur to this concern was the large number of blacks in two-year colleges which did not offer full university or advanced degrees and offered little instruction in the sciences and advanced technology. In 1978 these two-year schools enrolled more than half of all black freshmen entering universities for the first time.

Blacks enrolled in predominantly white colleges encountered a variety of difficulties, ranging from racist incidents and decline of black studies programs to a reversal of the small advances blacks had achieved in gaining admission to professional schools. Black retention rates in major universities have been low. In September 1980, at Black College Day in Washington, D.C., journalist Tony Brown asserted that seven of ten blacks attending predominantly white colleges do not graduate.

The percentage of black men and women receiving masters degrees declined during the late 1970s, as did the proportion of black men receiving bachelor's degrees. Greatest gains in these areas were recorded by Americans of Asian descent and nonresident aliens. As a group, women of all races showed the greatest increases in doctoral and first professional degrees.

In 1981, the American Bar Association reported that the proportion of blacks enrolled in accredited law schools had declined during the previous six years, from 4.7 to 4.4%. The problem stemmed as much from economic difficulties as from direct racism. In 1979, the American Medical Association reported a decline in medical school enrollment of lower-income students, largely as a result of a decline in government scholarships. The Bakke decision has also had an effect. Though it did not outlaw affirmative action, it did remove pressure from universities to seek black students for medical and other professional schools.

Overt discrimination remained a factor in some universities. In the late 1970s and early 1980s the government charged several states with failing to meet federal college desegregation standards. In the final days of the Carter Administration, cut offs in federal aid to state universities in Delaware, South Carolina, Pennsylvania, West Virginia, Alabama, Florida, Missouri, and Kentucky were considered, but Reagan's Secretary of Education, Terrel Bell, decided to avoid confrontation and reopen negotiations. Texas and North Carolina were also accused of failing to desegregate their public universities properly.

Troubling incidents occurred at both the administrative and student levels in some private universities. Especially disconcerting was a 1980 draft review of admissions policies at Harvard that compared black students unfavorably with other ethnic groups and questioned whether "elite universities" such as Harvard should compete strongly for black students. Harvard was also one of many universities to curtail its black studies program. In 1979, a study released by Professor Russell Adams of Howard stated that between 1961 and the mid-1970s, the number of black studies programs offered by colleges and universities dropped from 600 to 250.

Integrationists were especially concerned to have Harvard, long regarded as the epitome of liberalism, retreat in its programs and attitudes. The response of many blacks was that many elite white institutions were cliquish, exclusive cultures with an environment and methods of instruction that were frequently divorced from both reality and black experience.

## EMPLOYMENT IN HIGHER EDUCATION

Employment in higher education has expanded. In 1985, there were nearly 17% more full-time positions in academics than ten years earlier. The majority of this growth has been concentrated in nonfaculty positions. Nonfaculty positions grew by 20.5%, compared to 9.4% for faculty positions. While minorities benefited from this expansion, as demonstrated by a 34.3% increase in their full-time employment in higher education, their gains were greater in nonfaculty positions and in low-ranking faculty positions than in tenured faculty or administration positions. As of 1985, blacks, Hispanics, and American Indians continued to be grossly underrepresented on faculties and in college administrations.

Half of the workforce in higher education was female in 1985, up from 46% in 1975. Women held 59% of full-time nonfaculty positions, 35.1% of all administrative positions, and 27.5% of the full-time faculty positions. Women made their greatest proportional gain at the administrative level, rising from a representation of 23% in 1975. The number of women in full-time administrative positions nearly doubled between 1975 and 1985. In general, minority women made more gains in higher education employment than minority men.

Despite a 32.9% increase in the number of full-time faculty positions held by minorities between 1975 and 1985, as a group they made little progress in increasing their relative share. In 1975, minorities held 8.3% of the full-time faculty positions, and by 1985 their share had increased to 10%. With an increase from 2.2% to 3.9%, Asians were the only group to net a significantly larger share of full-time faculty positions.

Throughout this decade, there was little change in the relatively small number of black faculty or in their respective distribution among faculty ranks. Of all racial and ethnic groups, blacks had the smallest gain in full-time faculty positions. Between 1975 and 1985, they increased 2.7% in faculty positions, compared to 7.3% for whites, 27.9% for Hispanics, 48.2% for American Indians, and 95.7% for Asians. A higher proportion of black appointments were in the lower faculty ranks when compared to whites or Asians. In both 1975 and 1985, only 2.2% of the full-time full professorships were held by blacks, compared to 3.8% and 5.3% of the assistant professorships, and 5.6% of the instructor and lecturer positions.

Despite the aforementioned increases in Hispanic and American Indian faculty, their participation in faculty positions remained extremely low during this period. As with black faculty, Hispanic and American Indian faculty were more concentrated in instructor and lecturer positions than in professorships. In 1985, Hispanics and American Indians made up only 1.1% and 0.2% of the professorships. They comprised a slightly higher percentage of the associate and assistant professorships, while holding 2.3% and 0.6% of the instructor and lecturer positions in higher education.

In 1985, Asians continued to make gains in their faculty participation at all ranks. Of all minority groups, they held the most full professorships (3.7% in 1985, up from 1.9% ten years earlier). They were also more evenly distributed throughout different faculty ranks than other minority groups. Although Asians have made gains in faculty participation, their overall tenure rate was well below the national average. It should be further noted that according to one researcher, American-born Asians are still underrepresented in faculty positions, and that they are outnumbered ten to one by foreign-born Asians. Asian women also are underrepresented in faculty ranks at all levels.

Between 1975 and 1985, the tenure rate and the number of tenured faculty increased significantly. In 1985, 71.1% of faculty were tenured, compared to 64.3% in 1975. This rate was slightly higher for white faculty (72%). During this period, the disparity between the tenure rate for white faculty and for minority faculty remained conspicuous. In 1985, the tenure rates for blacks and Asians were 61.7 and 61.2%. Hispanics had the highest tenure rate of all minorities at 67.1%, followed by American Indians at 64.9%.

Minorities made larger gains in higher education administration than on faculties. In 1985, 11.6% of the college administrators were minorities, compared to 9.2% in 1975. Blacks represented 7.6% of the administrative staff, Hispanics 2%, Asians 1.5%, and American Indians 0.4%. Minority women made more dramatic gains in their number of administrative positions than did minority men.

Again, black men's progress was behind that of other groups. Although they gained 14% in their number of administrative positions, they declined slightly in participation rate from 4.7% in 1975 to 4.2% in 1985.

## Historic Black Colleges

For almost a century, the major resource for educating blacks at the college level was the "Historic Black Colleges" (HBCs) which are to be found in some 19 states, mostly in the South. Most HBCs were founded to teach former slaves after the Civil War, but the oldest, Cheyney State in Pennsylvania, was founded in 1837. The newest, Valley State College in Mississippi, was founded in 1950.

Sixteen of the colleges were founded in the nineteenth century as land grant colleges or later given this status to conform with federal requirements that benefits of land grant programs be available to both blacks and whites. A majority were founded as state colleges, often with significant black leadership. Elizabeth City State University, for example, was created in 1891 by a bill introduced into the North Carolina legislature by Hugh Cale, a black legislator from Pasquotank County. In 1871, when Alcorn A&M College was officially opened for Mississippi's black citizens, Hiram R. Revels, the first black elected to the U.S. Senate, resigned his seat to become the college's first president. Alcorn originated as Oakland College, a school for the education of white males.

Thirteen of the colleges were initially organized under private auspices, generally with gifts from both black and white individuals and groups. The soldiers and officers of the 62nd U.S. Colored Infantry gave $5,000 to provide funds for Lincoln University's incorporation in Missouri and are credited with the college's founding and eventual financing. Fort Valley State College was established in 1895 by leading local white and black citizens and was generously supported by gifts from Miss Anna T. Jeanes of Philadelphia. Albany State College in Georgia was begun as the Albany Bible and Manual Training Institute, receiving financial support from the Hazard family of Newport, Rhode Island, as well as from concerned local philanthropists. Financial problems led some private colleges to seek state support, and they became public institutions.

In 1964, over 51% of all blacks in college were still enrolled in the historically black colleges and universities. By 1970 the proportion was 28%, and by fall 1978, 16.5%. As recently as 1977, 38% of all blacks receiving baccalaureate degrees earned their degrees at an HBC. In the four-year college sector (other than universities), the proportion of blacks in HBCs was 32.8. Many HBCs have experienced increased enrollment of white students.

## Enrollment at Historically Black Colleges and Universities

According to data from the National Association for Equal opportunity in Higher Education (NAFEO) and the National Center for Education Statistics, enrollment at Historically black Colleges and Universities (HBCUs) peaked in 1980, with over 222,000 students enrolled. By 1986, total enrollment in HBCUs dropped to 213,093 (-4.0%). In 1987, enrollment in HBCUs took a slight upturn and increased to just over 217,000.

HBCUs have experienced greater losses in black enrollment than other institutions. However, they continue to enroll a significant share of the total black college population. HBCUs' share of black college enrollment declined slightly from 1976. Despite the decline, these institutions still enrolled 16.8% of the nearly 1.1 million black college students in 1986. HBCUs enrolled less than 2.0% of the 12.5 million students in higher education. Meanwhile, black enrollment in other institutions peaked in 1982 at 924,000, then declined to 904,404 in 1986. Enrollment figures for 1987 indicate that HBCUs are gradually recouping some of their losses.

According to NAFEO's 1987 Fall Enrollment Survey, 83.7% of the total enrollment at HBCUs was black, compared to 87.6% in 1976. Since 1980, the proportion of students from other races and ethnic groups attending HBCUs has remained fairly stable, at around 12.0%. White enrollment at HBCUs peaked in 1984, with nearly 23,500 students enrolled. In 1987, with an enrollment of 23,225, white students represented 10.7% of the enrollment at HBCUs. The majority of these students are enrolled at five HBCUs which have over 5O% white enrollment.

Collectively, Asians, Hispanics, and American Indians represented less than 2% of the total enrollment at HBCUs in 1987. Since 1976, both Hispanics and American Indians have gradually increased their enrollment at HBCUs. Despite some losses between 1984 and 1986, Hispanic enrollment in HBCUs increased 54.2% between 1980 and 1987. However, in actual numbers of students, the gain was much less dramatic: only 558 students. During this same period,

American Indian enrollment increased by 119 students after declining between 1982 and 1984. Asians followed the same pattern as whites; their participation peaked in 1984, then declined to 1,187 by 1987.

## New Black Colleges

Throughout the 1970s, another group of institutions emerged, the newer predominantly black colleges (NPBCs). The number of NPBCs has increased in the last decade along with the increase in the number of black students in higher education. In 1978, there were 60 institutions whose total and full-time enrollments were more than 50% black. The large black enrollment at these institutions, 77% of which are two-year colleges, can be attributed largely to their location in major urban areas, where they provide educational opportunities to black students who may be unable to attend another type of institution and who may be forced or choose to live at home. This group of colleges enrolled nearly 13% of all blacks in higher education in the fall of 1978. A recent follow-up study of freshmen who entered two-year institutions indicates that although three out of four community college freshmen intended to get the baccalaureate degree, only one in four actually did so.

The NPBCs must constantly assure that their mission fits into the overall goal of attaining equity for blacks in higher education. In 1980 close to 20% of the freshmen in all two-year colleges came from families with annual incomes lower than $10,000. Fifty-five percent of the freshmen at HBCs came from families with incomes lower than $10,000.

Historically black colleges and universities are also facing challenges. Having been the primary providers of higher education opportunities for blacks when traditionally white institutions refused to open their doors, HBCs were constantly under pressure during the 1970s to justify their continued existence. Arguments that access now existed for blacks to attend predominantly white institutions were used to undermine the need for the continued existence of the HBCs. A landmark court decision, *Adams* v. *Richardson,* in 1969 reinforced the *Brown* decision and previous court cases which applied to desegregation of higher education institutions. That decision was intended to eradicate the "vestiges of dual systems of higher education" in states that had previously operated segregated systems of higher education. Unfortunately, it created a host of problems for the black colleges and universities by diverting public and private support and promising students from HBCs.

In 1981, President Reagan issued an Executive Order (12320) intending to show his Administration's commitment to the HBCs. This Executive Order, like one before it issued by Jimmy Carter, was intended to increase the flow of federal funds to these institutions. President Reagan's Order calls on the private sector to do their share. However, there was no noticeable increase in funding.

In the spring of 1982, the Congress cut aid to education and student loan programs. Blacks had a great deal at stake in the outcome. Further cuts would seriously reduce the number of low-income students who could attend college and blacks would be affected disproportionately. Some 90% of all black students in traditionally black colleges come from families with low income and aid from either the federal government or the State is necessary for many students to stay in college or to begin; in predominantly white colleges some 50% of all black students need some assistance to begin or stay in college. During the Reagan years, in terms of constant dollars, aid to education declined by 29%.

*The beautiful campus of Atlanta University in Atlanta, Georgia.*

## TRADITIONALLY AND PREDOMINANTLY BLACK COLLEGES AND UNIVERSITIES IN THE UNITED STATES

[with a few indicated exceptions]

| Institution | Address | President | Jr/Sr | PubPriv |
|---|---|---|---|---|
| Alabama A & M University | Normal, Al 35762 | Dr. R. D. Morrison | Sr | Pub |
| Alabama State University | Montgomery, Al 36101 | Dr. Robert L. Randolph | Sr | Pub |
| Albany State College | Albany, GA 31705 | Dr. Billy C. Black | Sr | Pub |
| Alcorn A & M College | Lorman, MS 39096 | Dr. Walter Washington | Sr | Pub |
| Allen University | Columbia, S C 29204 | Dr. David W. Williams | Sr | Priv |
| Arkansas Baptist College | Little Rock, Ar 72200 | Dr. J. C. Oliver | Sr | Priv |
| Atlanta Junior College[a] | Atlanta, GA | Dr. Edwin A. Thompson | Jr | Pub |
| Atlanta University | Atlanta, GA 30314 | Dr. Thomas Cole, Jr. | Sr | Priv |
| Barber-Scotia College[a] | Concord, NC 28025 | Dr. Tyrone L. Burkette | Sr | Priv |
| Benedict College[a] | Columbia, SC 29204 | Dr. Marshall C. Grigsby | Sr | Priv |
| Bennett College[a] | Greensboro, NC 27420 | Dr. Glortia J. R. Scott | Sr | Priv |
| Bethune-Cookman College[a] | Daytona Beach, FL 32015 | Dr. Oswald P. Bronson | Sr | Priv |
| Bishop College[a] | Dallas, TX 75241 | Dr. Harry S. Wright | Sr | Priv |
| Bowie State College | Bowie, MD 20715 | Dr. Rufus L. Barfield | Sr | Pub |
| Central State University | Wilberforce, OH 45384 | Dr. Lionel H. Newsom | Sr | Pub |
| Cheyney State College | Cheyney, PA 19319 | Dr. Luther Burse (Interim) | Sr | Pub |
| Chicago State University | Chicago, IL 60628 | Dr. Benjamin H. Alexander | Sr | Pub |
| Chicago Theological Seminary[b] | Chicago, IL | Dr. Charles S. Rooks | | |
| Chaflin College[a] | Orangeburg, SC 29115 | Dr. Oscar A. Rogers Jr. | Sr | Priv |
| Clark College[a] | Atlanta, GA 30314 | Dr. Thomas Cole Jr. | Sr | Priv |
| Clinton Jr. College | Rock Hill, SO 29730 | Dr. S. V. Moreland | Jr | Priv |
| Coahoma Jr. College | Clarksdale, MS 38614 | Dr. McKinley C. Martin | Jr | Pub |
| College of the Virgin Island | St. Thomas, Virgin Island 00801 | Dr. Lawrence C. Wanlass | Sr | Pub |
| Compton College | Los Angeles, CA 90221 | Dr. Abel B. Sykes Jr. | Jr | Pub |
| Concordia College | Selma, AL 36701 | Dr. Julius Jenkins | Jr | Priv |
| Choppin State College | Baltimore, MD 21216 | Dr. Calvin W. Burnett | Sr | Pub |
| Daniel Payne College | Birmingham, AL 35212 | Dr. Daniel T. Grant | Sr | Priv |
| Delaware State College | Dover, DE 19901 | Dr. Luna I. Mishoe | Sr | Pub |
| Detroit Institute of Technology | Detroit, MI 48201 | Dr. Dewey F. Barich | Sr | Pub |
| Dillard University[a] | New Orleans, LA 70122 | Dr. Samuel Du Bois Cook | Sr | Priv |
| Dist. of Col. Teachers College | Washington, D.C. 20009 | Dr. Paul P. Cooke | Sr | Pub |
| Edward Waters College | Jacksonville, FL 32209 | Dr. Cecil W. Cone | Sr | Priv |
| Elizabeth City State University | Elizabeth City, NC 27909 | Dr. Marion D. Thorpe | Sr | Pub |
| Essex County College | Newark, NJ 07102 | Dr. J. Harry Smith | Jr | Pub |
| Fayetteville State University | Fayetteville, NC 28301 | Dr. Charles Lyons, Jr. | Sr | Pub |
| Federal City College | Washington, D.C. 20005 | Dr. Wendell P. Russell | Sr | Pub |
| Fisk University | Nashville, TE 37203 | Dr. Henry Powder | Sr | Priv |
| Florida A & M University | Tallahassee, FL 32307 | Dr. Walter L. Smith | Sr | Pub |
| Florida Memorial College[a] | Miami, FL 33054 | Dr. Willie C. Robinson | Sr | Priv |
| Fort Valley State College | Fort Valley, GA 31030 | Dr. Cleveland Pettigrew | Sr | Pub |
| Friendship Jr. College | Rock Hill, SC 29730 | Dr. Charles W. Petress | Jr | Priv |
| Grambling College | Grambling, LA 71245 | Dr. Joseph B. Johnson | Sr | Pub |
| Hampton Institute | Hampton, VA 23368 | Dr. William R. Harvey | Sr | Priv |
| Howard University | Washington, D.C. 20001 | Dr. James E. Cheek | Sr | Priv |
| Huston-Tillotson College[a] | Austin, TX 78702 | Dr. Joseph T. McMillian | Sr | Priv |
| Interdenominational Theological | CenterAtlanta, GA 30314 | Dr. James H. Laston | Sr | Priv |
| Jackson State College | Jackson, MS 39217 | Dr. James A. Peoples Jr. | Sr | Pub |
| Jarvis Christian College[a] | Hawkins, TX 75765 | Dr. Julius F. Nimmons | Sr | Priv |
| Johnson C. Smith University[a] | Charlotte, NC 28208 | Dr. Robert L. Albright | Sr | Priv |
| Kennedy-King College | Chicago, IL 60621 | Dr. Maceo T. Bowie | Jr | Pub |
| Kentucky State University | Frankfort, KY 40601 | Dr. W. A. Butts | Sr | Pub |

## TRADITIONALLY AND PREDOMINANTLY BLACK COLLEGES AND UNIVERSITIES IN THE UNITED STATES

[with a few indicated exceptions ) continued

| Institution | Address | President | Jr/Sr | PubPriv |
|---|---|---|---|---|
| Kittrell College | Kittrell, NC 27544 | Dr. John A. Middleton | Jr | Priv |
| Knoxville College[a] | Knoxville, TN 36921 | Dr. Joe L. Boyer | Sr | Priv |
| Lane College | Jackson, TE 38301 | Dr. Alex A. Chambers, Jr. | Sr | Priv |
| Langston University | Langston, OK 73050 | Dr. Ernest L. Holloway | Sr | Priv |
| LeMoyne-Owen College[a] | Memphis, TE 38126 | Dr. Irving P. McPhail | Sr | Priv |
| Lincoln University | Jefferson City, MO 65101 | Dr. Walter C. Daniel | Sr | Pub |
| Lincoln University | Lincoln PA 19352, | Dr. Niara Sudardasa | Sr | Priv |
| Livingstone College[a] | Salisbury, NC 28144 | Dr. Ozell K. Beatty | Sr | Priv |
| Lomax-Hannon College | Greenville, AL 36037 | Dr. D. M. Montgomery | Jr | Priv |
| Los Angeles S.W. College | Los Angeles, CA 90047 | Dr. W. J. Longmire | Jr | Pub |
| Malcolm-King: | | | | |
| Harlem College Extension | NYC, NY 10035 | Dr. Mattie Cook | Jr | Priv |
| Malcolm X College | Chicago, IL 60612 | Dr. E. Aikin | Jr | Pub |
| Manhattan Community College[b] | NY, NY | Dr. Augusta Kappner | Jr | Pub |
| Manhattanville College[b] | Purchase, NY | Dr. Harold Delaney | Sr | Priv |
| Mary Allen Jr. College | Crockett, TX 75835 | Dr. Ira L. Clark | Jr | Priv |
| Mary Holmes College | West Point, MS 39773 | Dr. Joseph A. Gore | Jr | Priv |
| Martin Tech Institute[b] | Williamston, NC 27892 | Dr. E. M. Hunt | Jr | Pub |
| Medgar Evers Community College | Brooklyn, NY | Dr. Richard D. Trent | Jr | Pub |
| Meharry Medical College | Nashville, TN 37208 | Dr. Lloyd C. Elam | Prof | Priv |
| Michigan State University[b] | East Lansing, MI | Dr. Clifton R. Wharton | Sr | Pub |
| Miles College[a] | Birmingham, AL 35208 | Dr. Leroy Johnson | Sr | Priv |
| Mississippi Industrial College | Holly Springs, MS 38635 | Dr. Theodore R. Debro | Sr | Priv |
| Mississippi Valley State College | Itta Bena, MS 38941 | Dr. Joe L. Boyer | Sr | Pub |
| Mobile State (see S. D. Bishop) | | | | |
| Morehouse College[a] | Atlanta, GA 30314 | Dr. Leroy Kieth, Jr. | Sr | Priv |
| Morgan State College | Baltimore, MD 21239 | Dr. Earl Richardson | Sr | Priv |
| Morris College | Sumter, SC 29150 | Dr. Luns C. Richardson | Sr | Priv |
| Morris Brown College[a] | Atlanta, GA 30314 | Dr. Calvert H. Smith | Sr | Priv |
| Morristown College | Morristown, TN 37814 | Dr. Charles Wade | Jr | Priv |
| Natchez Jr. College | Natchez, MS 39120 | Dr. William C. Boykins | Jr | |
| Norfolk State College | Norfolk, VA 23504 | Dr. Harrison B. Wilson | Sr | Pub |
| North Carolina A & T State Univ. | Greensboro, NC 27411 | Dr. Edward Fort | Sr | Pub |
| North Carolina Central University | Durham, NC 27707 | Dr. Albert N. Whiting | Sr | Pub |
| Oakwood College[a] | Huntsville, AL 35806 | Dr. Benjamin F. Reaves | Sr | Priv |
| Olive-Harvey College | Chicago, IL 60628 | Dr. Nathaniel P. Tillman, Jr. | Jr | Pub |
| Paine College[a] | Augusta, GA 30901 | Dr. Julius A. Scott | Sr | Priv |
| Palmer College | Columbia, SC 29201 | Dr. Raymond P. Carson | Jr | Priv |
| Paul Quinn College[a] | Waco, TX 76704 | Dr. Warren W. Morgan | Sr | Priv |
| Philander Smith College[a] | Little Rock, AR 72202 | Dr. Alvin I. Thomas | Sr | Priv |
| Prairie View A & M College | Prairie View, Texas 77445 | Dr. Alvin I. Thomas | Sr | Pub |
| Prentiss N & I Institute | Prentiss, MS 39474 | Dr. Sidney James | Jr | Priv |
| Rust College[a] | Holly Spring, MS 38565 | Dr. William A. McMillan | Sr | Priv |
| Saint Augustine's College[a] | Raleigh, NC 27602 | Dr. Prezell R. Robinson | Sr | Priv |
| Saint Paul's College[a] | Lawrenceville, VA 23868 | Dr. Robert L. Satcher | Sr | Priv |
| Savannah State College | Savannah, GA 31404 | Dr. Wendell G. Rayburn | Sr | Pub |
| S. D. Bishop State Jr. College | Mobile, AL 36603 | Dr. Sanford D. Bishop | Jr | Pub |
| Selma University | Selma, AL 36701 | Dr. M. C. Cleveland, Jr. | Sr | Priv |
| Shaw College at Detroit[a] | Detroit, MI 48202 | Dr. Talbert D. Shaw | Sr | Priv |
| Shaw University | Raleigh, NC 27602 | Dr. Stanley H. Smith | Sr | Priv |
| Shorter College | Little Rock, AK 72114 | Dr. Oley L. Griffin | Jr | Priv |
| Simmons University | Louisville, KY 40210 | Dr. William L. Holmes | Sr | Priv |

## TRADITIONALLY AND PREDOMINANTLY BLACK COLLEGES AND UNIVERSITIES IN THE UNITED STATES

[with a few indicated exceptions]

| Institution | Address | President | Jr/Sr | PubPriv |
|---|---|---|---|---|
| South Carolina State College | Orangeburg, SC 29115 | Dr. M. Maceo Nance Jr. | Sr | Priv |
| Southern University[a] | Baton Rouge, LA | Dr. Jesse Stone | Sr | Pub |
| Southwestern Christian College | Terrell, TX 75160 | Dr. Jack Evans | Jr | Priv |
| Spelman College[a] | Atlanta, GA 30314 | Dr. Sohnnetta B. Cole | Sr | Priv |
| Stillman College[a] | Tuscaloosa, AL 35401 | Dr. Cordell Wynn | Sr | Priv |
| Theodore A. Lawson State Jr. College | Birmingham, AL 35228 | Dr. Leon Kennedy | Jr | Pub |
| Talladega College[a] | Talladega, AL 35160 | Dr. Joseph E. Thompson | Sr | Priv |
| Tennessee State University | Nashville, TN 37203 | Dr. Frederick S. Humphries | Sr | Pub |
| Texas College[a] | Tyler, TX 75701 | Dr. David H. Johnson | Sr | Priv |
| Texas Southern University | Houston, TX 77004 | Dr. Leonard H. 0. Spearman | Sr | Pub |
| Tougaloo College[a] | Tougaloo, MS 39174 | Dr. Adib A. Shakir | Sr | Priv |
| Tuskegee Institute[a] | Tuskegee Institute, AL 36088 | Dr. Benjamin Payton | Sr | Priv |
| University of Arkansas | Pine Bluff, AR 71601 | Dr. Lloyd V. Hackley | Sr | Pub |
| University of Maryland (Eastern Shore) | Princess Anne, MD 21853 | Dr. William P. Hytche | Sr | Pub |
| Utica Jr. College | Utica, MS 39175 | Dr. J. Louis Stokes | Jr | Pub |
| Virginia College | Lynchburg, VA 24501 | Dr. Langford Hankins | Jr | Priv |
| Virginia State College | Petersburg, VA 23803 | Dr. Thomas M. Law | Sr | Pub |
| Virginia Union University[a] | Richmond, VA 23220 | Dr. Sidakas Simmons | Sr | Priv |
| Voorhees College[a] | Denmark, SC 29042 | Dr. Leonard E. Dawson | Sr | Priv |
| Washington Technical Institute | Washington, D.C. 20008 | Dr. Cleveland L. Dennard | Jr | Pub |
| Wayne County Community College | Detroit, MI 48201 | Dr. Ronald J. Temple | Jr | Pub |
| Westfield State College[b] | Westfield, MA | Dr. Robert L. Randolph | | |
| Wilberforce University[a] | Wilberforce, OH 45384 | Dr. John L. Anderson | Sr | Priv |
| Wiley College[a] | Marshall, TX 75670 | Dr. David Beckley | Sr | Priv |
| Winston-Salem State University | Winston-Salem, NC 27102 | Dr. Harold D. Covington | Sr | Pub |
| Xavier University[a] | New Orleans, LA 70125 | Dr. Norman C. Francis | Sr | Priv |

a United Negro College Fund member institutions
b Black enrollment high though not known as a traditionally black school.
For further information contact United Negro College Fund, Inc., 55 East 52nd Street, New York, N.Y. 10022, (212)Pl 1-0700.

## COMMUNITY AND STATE COLLEGES WITH BLACK ADMINISTRATIVE HEADS

Bronx Community College
Bronx, New York
Dr. Roscoe C. Brown Jr., President

California State University
Fullerton, California
Dr. Jewel Plummer Cobb, President

City College of New York
New York City
Dr. Bernard Harleston, President

Essex County College
Newark, New Jersey
Dr. Zachery Yamba, President

Harris-Barber College
Raleigh, North Carolina
Charles R. Stone, President

Indian Valley Colleges
Novato, California
Constance M. Carroll, President

Manhattan Community College
New York City
Dr. Augusta Kappner, President

Malcolm-King Harlem Extension College
New York City
Mattie Cook, President

Maricopa Community College District
Phoenix, Arizona
Dr. Charles A. Green, President

Medgar Evers College
Brooklyn, New York
Dr. Richard D. Trent, President

Medical College of Pennsylvania
Philadelphia, Pennsylvania
Dr. Maurice C. Clifford, President

Metropolitan State University
St. Paul, Minnesota
Reatha King, President

University of the District of Columbia
Washington, D.C.
Dr. Lisle C. Carter Jr., President

Wayne County Community College
Detroit, Michigan
Ronald J. Temple, President

## EDUCATIONAL FILMS WITH BLACK THEMES

The following list was compiled under the direction of Wendell Wray, Director, North Manhattan project, Countee Cullen Branch, New York Public Library, and William Sloan, librarian of the NYPL's film division. Their kind permission makes possible its reproduction here. The films are ideal for classroom or community use.

**Africa:** An Introduction: Stresses the climate and geography of all parts of Africa. Shows the ruins of great civilizations, nomads in North Africa, desert oasis, life in the markets, places of worship, large cities, etc. 1972. *BFA*. (18 min.)

**An African Community:** The Masai: Illustrates the dependence of the nomadic Masai of East Africa on the land, their adaptation to their environment, their tribal interdependence, and the roles of men, women, and different age groups. A good pictorial record; the commentary is superficial. Produced by Frank Gardonyi and Clifford Janoff, 1969. Bailey-Film Associates. (17 min)

**African Girl—Malobi:** Presents the experiences of Malobi, a lO-year-old girl of the Ibo tribe of Nigeria. There are scenes of the tribe building homes in the traditional way, her grandfather carving furniture, and Malobi attending school. Directed by Michael Hagopian. 1960. *Atlantis Productions*. (11 min)

**AFRICAN VILLAGE LIFE** (series title): **Annual Festival of the Dead:** Follows the annual ceremony of the Dogon tribe of Mali, Africa, near the Niger River in the interesting and unusual festival they hold for those who died during the year. Produced by Julien Bryan. 1968 (14 min)

**Daily Life of the Bozo:** Exciting photography, without narration, but with effects and music recorded on the spot, offers an honest picture of the daily life of the Bozo tribe in Mali, near the Niger River. Photography by Hermann Schlenker. Produced by Julien Bryan. 1967. (15 min.)

**Fishing on the Niger River:** A careful depiction of fishing on the Niger River by members of the Bozo Tribe of Mali. Natural sounds of the people at work provide the background; no narration. Photography by Hermann Schlenker. Produced by Julien Bryan. 1967. (17 mm)

**Herding Cattle:** Records the activities of the Peul Tribe of Mali, as the men and young boys skillfully lead a herd of cattle across the Niger River. Sound background is recorded on the spot. Photography by Hermann Schlenker. Produced by Julien Bryan. 1967 (7 min.) *Series by International Film Foundation.*

**Anansi the Spider:** A folk tale from the Ashanti tribe retold in delightful abstract animation using African designs and brilliant colors to account for a troublesome spider and the origin of the moon. By Gerald McDermott. 1969. *Landmark Educational Media, Inc.* (10 min.)

**Ancient Games:** Rafer Johnson and Bill Toomey compete in a reconstruction of the Olympic games of ancient Greece. Script by Erich Segal. 1973. *ABC Media Concepts*. (28 min.)

**Black African Heritage:** The Congo: Aspects of the land culture of the Congo, featuring wildlife, arts and crafts, and tribal dances. Narrated by Julian Bond. Directed and filmed by Eliot Elisofon. 1972 (55 min.)

**Black American Dream Black:** leaders reveal that today Black Power seems to be all things to all men. Includes interviews with Stokely Carmichael and Jesse Jackson. Produced by BBC-TV. 1973. *Time- Life*. (65 min.)

**Black and White In South Africa:** An objective appraisal of the policy of apartheid and its background in the Union of South Africa. Produced by the National Film Board of Canada. Commonwealth of Nations series. 1958. *McGraw-Hill* (30 min.)

**The Black Cop:** Explores the attitudes of blacks toward black policemen, and the views of black policemen themselves. Includes interviews with police officers in New York and Los Angeles. Written and produced by Kent Garrett, for NET's Black Journal. 1969. *NET*. (15 min.)

**The Black G.I. :** A probing exploration of the attitudes of black G.I.s serving in Vietnam. Reveals their concern about discrimination in service clubs and in promotional opportunities, about white Americans teaching racial epithets to Vietnamese, and about problems affecting blacks in the United States. Produced, written, and directed by Kent Garrett, for NET's Black Journal. 1970. *NET*. (54 min.)

**Black on Black:** Martin Luther King: Dr. Martin Luther King explains his philosophy on nonviolence, how he favors not riots but massive civil disobedience and wants his people to organize, learn, and earn rather than "burn baby, burn." Ends with his moving speech from the night before his death. 1970. Time-Life. (54 min.)

**Black Panthers:** Journalistic record of Oakland, California Black Panthers. Discussions by Huey Newton, Bill Brandt, Bobby Seale, Stokely Carmichael, and Mrs. Eldridge Cleaver. By Agnes Varda. 1969. *Grove Press*. (26 min.)

**Black Power:** Juxtaposition of widely varying opinions and comments by Malcolm X, Eldridge Cleaver, Floyd McKissick, Martin Luther King, and others, as they view the problems and prospects of the black movement generally and the concept of black power specifically. 1969. Reaction Films (15 min.)

**Blue Dashiki:** Jeffrey and His Neighbors: A little boy on Chicago's South Side works at odd jobs in order to earn the money to buy a beautiful blue dashiki. A film without words that should appeal to all ages. A film by Maclovia, 1969. *Encyclopedia Britannica Educational Corporation*. ( 14 min.)

**The Blues:** Shows the music and some of the instruments of several country-blues singers including Sleepy John Estes, Memphis Willie B., and J. D. Short. A low-budget film in which the visuals are not synchronized with the sound. Produced by noted blues authority Samuel X. Charters. 1963. Brandon. (2 1 min.)

**The Blues Maker:** Shows country-blues singer Fred McDowell singing and discussing his music, interspersed with scenes of rural Mississippi. Written and directed by Christian Garrison. Made by the Dept. of Educational Film Production, Univ. Extension, Univ. of Mississippi. 1969. *Univ. of Miss*. (14 min.)

**BODY AND SOUL**
**Part 1: Body:** History of the Negro's breakthrough in the world of sports, from Jesse Owen up to the Mexico City Olympics. Stresses the fact that few blacks have attained positions as coaches or managers; and raises the question of a black boycott of professional sports as a means of correcting this inequity. Produced by *CBS News*. 1968. (25 min.)

**Part 2: Soul:** Explains how the frustration and depression of the American Negro gave rise to spirituals, revival music, jazz, the blues, and soul music. Produced by CBS News. 1968. (25 min.)
Booker T. Washington: Covers the early years of Booker T. Washington and highlights the founding of Tuskegee Institute. 1972. *BFA*. (11 min.)

**Boy of Central Africa :** Vincent Chisembwa, a teenage woodcarver from Zambia, is shown in daily life with his family: the girls fix their hair, grandfather carves, friends play instruments and make canoes, the women gather peanuts. Interesting picture of village life, but commentary is superficial. A Kevin Duffy Production, 1969. *Bailey-Film Associates* (14 min.)

**Discovering American Folk Music:** Singers trace the variations of folksongs from British and African origins. "The Unfortunate Rake" becomes "Streets of Laredo." "St. James Infirmary" even funny modern version on the death of a telephone lineman. Includes black treatments of traditional songs and handclapping patterns. 1969. *BFA*. (22 min.)

**Discovering the Music of Africa:** A master drummer of Ghana demonstrates various African instruments and describes their uses. Traditional dances are also seen. A studio-made film with excessively artificial lighting. Informative, but not outstanding cinematically. Produced by Bernard Wilets. *Bailey-Film Associates*. (22 min.)

**Frederick Douglass:** An iconographic treatment of the life of ex-slave, abolitionist, and national political figure Frederick Douglass. 1972. For children. (9 min.)

**DuBois Dedication:** A report on the dedication of DuBois Park in Great Barrington, Mass. in October 1969, honoring the late author W. E. B. DuBois. Includes some of the speeches of Ossie Davis and Julian Bond, and interviews with other participants. Narrative by Ossie Davis. By Samuel B. Holmes. 1970. *Samuel B. Holmes* (8 min.)

**East Africa:** Reports on the physical geography, agriculture, handicrafts, commerce, industry, and social customs in Kenya, Uganda, and Tanganyika. Emphasizes the importance of education in the development of the diverse East African population. 1962. *Encyclopedia Britannica Films*. (21 min.)

**Fabulous Harlem Globetrotters:** A humorous and quickly paced demonstration of the dexterity of this famous basketball team. *Blackhawk*. (9 min.)

**Family of Ghana:** A somewhat dated but still moving documentary of the people who live on the coast of Ghana and make their living from the sea. Conflict between the old ways and the new is represented between the father and his son. Produced by the National Film Board of Canada. Directed by Julian Biggs. *National Film Board of Canada*. 1958. McGraw-Hill (30 min.)

**Felicia :** Filmed in her home, school, and neighborhood in Watts, California, teenager Felicia is shown observing the area as it was in the spring of 1965, just before the Watts riots. Directed by Trevor Greenwood and produced by Stuart Roe. 1965. *University of California*. (13 min.)

**First World Festival of Negro Arts:** Pictures scenes of the first World Festival of Negro Arts held at Dakar in 1966, showing music, dance, sculpture, painting, and the reciprocal influences of Negro art and culture in relation to the modern Western World. A pedestrian presentation of an important subject. U.S. release, 1969. *Contemporary/McGraw-Hill* (20 min.)

**For All My Students:** A thought-provoking and moving study of the particular problems and rewards of teaching Negro high school students. Filmed at Ravenswood High School in East Palo Alto, California. Teaching methods are examined, as are students' feelings about what is wrong with their school, their teachers, and themselves; and the doubts, convictions, frustrations, and satisfactions of the teachers are expressed. A student-made film by Bonnie Sherr under a grant from the U.S. Office of Education. Supervision by George C. Stoney. *University of California*. (36 min.)

**Four Women:** Young women dance to Nina Simone's interpretations of the song "Four Women." Directed by Ilanga Witt. Danced and filmed by students of the Harlem Preparatory School. 1971. (7 min.)

**Gabriella and Selena :** A live action film based on the book by Peter Desbarats. Two middle-class girls about eight years old, one white, one black, change identities and homes for the evening and find that they've been fooled by the parents into eating things and doing jobs that both of them hate. Suitable for children (older). *BFA*. (13 min.)

**Game:** A candid, nonsensational documentary study of a black prostitute and her pimp in New York City who openly discuss their way of life. The film includes primarily interviews and street scenes, with one brief encounter with a "client." By Jon and Abby Child. 1972. (40 min.)

**The Game:** Black and Puerto Rican teenagers act out their lives in a series of games which depict their situations in a New York City ghetto. A powerful and moving film. Produced by Roberta Hodes in association with Mobilization for Youth. 1967. *Grove Press*. (17 min.)

**Goodbye and Good Luck:** A black ex-G.I. returns from Vietnam and is confronted with various black power activists. He is forced to question his reasons for having served in the military and what he wants to do in the future. Technically poor, but important subject content. Produced by William Jersey. 1967. *NET*. (30 min.)

**Harlem Wednesday:** Paintings and sketches by American artist Gregorio Prestopino are colorfully arranged and backed with a vibrant jazz score by Benny Carter to evoke the activities and mood of a Wednesday in Harlem. Directed by John Hubley and Faith Elliot, 1959. *Brandon*. (10 min.)

**Al Stacey Hayes:** Portrait of a black high school senior in Shelby, Mississippi and his efforts in voter registration drives. Vividly depicts the generation gap between young black southerners and their parents and grandparents. By Joel A. Levitch, 1969. *Jason Films*. (28 min.)

**Heritage in Black:** Panorama of the history and contributions of black people to the United States from the Revolution to present times. c. 1969. *Encyclopaedia Britannica*. (27 min.)

**HISTORY OF THE NEGRO IN AMERICA (series title):**
Part 1: 1619-1860: Out of Slavery: The development of the slave trade and the growth of slavery from the ancient world to colonial times and on through the Revolution is depicted in stills, prints, and drawing. Narrated by James Earl Jones. 1965. (17 min.)

**Part 2: 1861-1877:** Civil War and Reconstruction: Traces the causes and effects of two critical periods in U.S. history, the Civil War and Reconstruction, and indicates how the Emancipation Proclamation, Thirteenth, Fourteenth, and Fifteenth amendments sought to protect and preserve the Negro's newly won freedom. Made from still pictures. 1965. (20 min.)

**Part 3: 1877-Today:** Freedom Movement: Portrays the post-Reconstruction flight of the Negro, the problems of segregation, Negro heroism in World War I and II, and the advances made in the area of civil rights since 1950; uses stills, prints, drawings, and film footage. Narrated by James Earl Jones. 1965. *McGraw-Hill*(20 min.)

**HISTORY OF THE NEGRO PEOPLE (series title):**
**Part 1. Heritage of the Negro:** Explores the heritage of the Negro by examining the civilization and achievements of ancient Africa and their significance to the American Negro today. Produced by *NET*. 1965. (30 min.)

**Part 2. Negro and the South:** Interviews Negroes (a teacher, a mechanic, and a minister), and whites (a mayor, a sheriff, and a judge) of Mississippi, to depict the "Southern way of life." Produced by *NET*. 1965. (30 min.)

**Part 3. Slavery:** Based on actual testimony of former slaves, tells of the tragic and sometimes humorous experiences of life in the Old

South and depicts the liberation of slaves by the Yankee troops. Uses Negro spirituals to help tell the story. Produced by *NET*. 1965. (30 min.)

**Part 4. Brazil:** The Vanishing Negro: Depicts the interracial experiences of the Negro in Brazil and stresses that they differ markedly from the experiences of North American Negroes. Produced by *NET*. 1965. (30 min.)

**Part 5. Free at Last:** Uses dramatic readings from the works of Frederick Douglass, Booker T. Washington, W. E. B. DuBois, and Marcus Garvey to trace the history of the American Negro from emancipation to the end of World War 11. Produced by *NET*. 1965. (30 min.)

**Part 6. Omowale:** The Child Returns Home: Pictures author John Williams, a Mississippi-born black, on an odyssey to Africa to explore his ancestral roots and the relationship of the American Negro to Africa and the Africans. Produced by *NET*. 1965. (30 min.)

**Part 7. New Mood:** Reviews the civil rights struggle of 1955-1965 and traces the impact of the new Negro militancy on both white and Negro Americans. Produced by *NET*. 1965. (30 min.)

**Part 8. Our Country, Too:** Explores the inner world of the American black: values, attitudes, and impressions of life through interviews at such places as an African rite in Harlem, a black debutante ball, the office of a black newspaper, and a black-owned radio station. Produced by *NET*. 1965. (30 min.)

**Part 9. Future and the Negro:** Presents a panel discussion on the subject of the Negro's future. Discusses the economic plight of the Negro in the United States and in black nations and emphasizes the racism felt to be deeply ingrained in people throughout the world. Produced by *NET*. 1965. (75 min.)

**House on Cedar Hill:** Events in the life of Frederick Douglass, the runaway slave who became an editor, orator, and statesman, are presented with skill and sensitivity, through historical documents, period drawings, photographs, and mementos found in the Douglass House in Washington, D.C. Written and directed by Carlton Moss. 1953. *Contemporary/McGraw- Hill*(30 min.)

**The Hunters:** A starkly beautiful documentary on the bushmen of the Kalahari Desert in Southwest Africa where continued existence depends entirely upon a man's skill and stamina as a hunter. Produced by the Film Study Center of the Peabody Museum, Harvard University. Directed by John Marshall in collaboration with Robert Gardner. 1958. *Contemporary/McGraw-Hill* (72 min.)

**The Hurdler:** Biographical account of Dr. Charles Drew, the research physician who discovered the value of blood plasma in transfusions and set up the first Blood Bank in the United States during World War 11. The forced comparison between a hurdler and Drew's life lessens the effectiveness of the film for some audiences. Narrated by Ossie Davis. 1969. *New York Times/Arno Press*. (16 min.)

**I Am Somebody:** A moving record of the 113-day strike by members of Local 1199B of the National Union of Hospital and Nursing Home Employees, in Charleston, S.C. during the spring of 1969. Most of the strikers were black women, and the film follows their struggle for decent wages, improved working conditions, respect and dignity. Directed by Madelyn Anderson. 1970. *Contemporary*. (28 Min.)

**I Have A Dream:** The biography of Martin Luther King made from newsreel footage of the civil rights movement during the 1950s and 1960s. Reveals his dedication to the movement and to the principles of nonviolence. Bailey-Film Associates (35 min.)

**In Search of a Past:** Three young Afro-American students visit Africa to study their racial and cultural origins and compare similarities and differences with the situation in the United States. Produced by CBS News. 1968. *Bailey-Film Associates*. (2 films; each 26 min.)

**In the Company of Men:** Documents the role playing and sensitivity training of hardcore unemployed blacks and white foremen—techniques implemented to establish communication between these two groups in a large General Motors assembly plant in Georgia. A film by *William Greaves*. 1969. William Greaves. (52 min.)

**Interview with Bruce Gordon:** Bruce Gordon, a 23-year-old black civil rights leader, talks of his own beliefs and hopes, the lot of the black in America, and the civil rights movement. A Harold Becker production. 1963. *Harold Becker*. (17 min.)

**J. T. :** Just before Christmas, a lonely Harlem boy steals a radio and hides in an abandoned building. There he finds a sick cat, which he nurtures back to health and develops a sense of responsibility in the process. Presented in CBS Children's Hour; stereotyped characterizations may bother some adults. Written by lane Wagner; directed by Robert Young; produced for CBS-TV, 1969. *Carousel Films*. (51 min.)

**Jackie Robinson:** A graphic biography of the life of the famous ballplayer, the first black to play in the major leagues. From the television program Biography; produced by David Wolper, 1965. *Sterling*. (26 min.)

**James Weldon Johnson:** An attractive biography of the famous black poet, coupled with a stunning visual treatment of the best known of his poems, "The Creation." (18 min.)
Jeffries-Johnson 1910: Historical film footage and photographs retell the story of the boxing match between Jack Johnson and Jim Jeffries (the "great white hope"). Produced by *Bill Kimberlin*. 1972. (21 min.)

**The Late Show:** A young black American cleans and assembles a rifle while watching the late show on television in this brief social commentary. A British Film Institute production. 1971. (12 min.)

**Lay My Burden Down**: An important document on the economic and educational plight of black tenant farmers of the southern United States. Directed by Jack Willis for National Educational Television. 1966. *Indiana University*. (60 min.)

**Legend of Mark Twain:** The world of author Samuel Clemens (Mark Twain) is recreated through photographs and scenes along the Mississippi near his Hannibal, Missouri home, an old Edison newsreel of Twain, and Twain's own words. Also included are dramatic scenes based on *Huckleberry Finn* and *The Jumping Frog of Calaveras County*. 1967. (32 min.)

**Malcolm X:Struggle for Freedom:** Filmed during his trip to Europe and Africa, just three months before his assassination in the United States, Malcolm X discusses racial and other social ills of our age. Directed by Lebert Bethune. 1964. *Grove Press*. (22 1 min.)

**Martin Luther King Jr.:** Still photographs and newsreel clips make up this short biography of the famed black civil rights leader. 1972. (10 min.)

**Martin Luther King: The Man and the March:** A documentary of the late Martin Luther King Jr.'s "Poor People's March." Shows Dr. King conferring with aides, speaking at rallies, and traveling as he solicits support for and develops the operational details of the march. Indicates the methods used by his aides to create interest and support on a local level and with other ethnic groups. Produced by Public Broadcast Laboratory of *NET*. 1968. *Indiana University*. (83 min.)

**Martin Luther King Jr.: A Man of Peace:** The film centers on Dr. King receiving the Nobel Peace Prize and his work in the Southern Christian Leadership Conference. King explains his philosophy of achieving racial equality through the use of nonviolence. Provides a look at the man, the minister, the father, and the leader of the civil rights movement. Produced by Walter Schwimmer, Inc. 1964. j *Journal Films*. (30 min.)

**Martin Luther King Jr.: From Montgomery to Memphis:** Excellent use of newsreel footage to cover the major events in Martin Luther King's civil rights struggles from the Montgomery bus boycotts through Memphis. *Bailey-Film Associates*. (27 min.)

**A Mask for Me, A Mask for You :** A lonely little boy finds his way to the Watts Towers Art Center and finds companionship and satisfaction in creating masks and other art projects. Poor sound track, but some good visuals. 1969. *Universal Educational & Visual Arts*. (16 min.)

**Memory of John Earl:** A black teenager refuses to submit to rude treatment by a white storekeeper, and is chased and threatened with a gun by some rednecks. Powerful re-creation of an actual incident in the life of the young filmmaker, John McFadden. Produced 1968. *Youth , Film Distribution Center*. (6 min.)

**Migrant:** A study of migrant workers, including many blacks and Chicanos, in Florida. Reveals problems of housing, sanitation, working conditions, schooling, and racial discrimination. 1970. Marten Car, Dir. *NBC* (52 min.)

**Move:** Black children in third-and fourth-grade classes in Washington, D.C. learn to make animated films. Role playing is used to create the stories and sound tracks, then simple crayon pictures are drawn in sequence on paper and animated. Three short, finished films are included. By Vilma Berarducci. 1971. (16 min.)

**My Childhood:** A distinctive two-part film: part one is on Hubert Humphrey; part two, which may be used separately, is on the early years of James Baldwin. Brilliantly directed by Arthur Barron. Produced by Metromedia Television. 1964. *Benchmark Films*. (51 min.)

**The Negro and the American Promise:** Dr. Martin Luther King, Jr., Malcolm X, Dr. Kenneth Clark, and James Baldwin discuss their motivations, doctrines, methods, goals, and place in the American Negro's movement for social and racial equality. *Indiana University*. (60 min.)

**Nene de la Ruta Mora:** A small boy, Nenen, from the village of Loiza Aldea, meets the "vejigante" (bogeyman) who takes him to the Fiesta de Santiago, celebrated annually by Puerto Ricans. The film shows the African and Spanish influence present in the culture. In Spanish. *Quality Film Labs*. (23 min.)

**Nigeria: Giant in Africa:** The vastness of the country and the diverse nature of its 40 million people are stressed in this carefully documented study of the culture and geography of Nigeria. The history of the country is told through early prints and newsreel footage. Produced for the National Film Board of Canada by Ronald Dick. 1960. *McGraw-Hill*(52 min.)

**No Harvest for the Reaper:** A documentary which describes how a group of black farm workers, recruited in Arkansas to work on farms in Long Island, get trapped in a system that keeps them perpetually in debt. Growers and processors are interviewed and the labor camps and working conditions are shown. Produced by NET. 1968. *Indiana University*. (59 min.)

**No Vietnamese Ever Called Me Nigger:** Three black G.I.s discuss their experiences in Vietnam, the racism that exists in the armed

*Scene from the educational film,* No Harvest for the Reaper.

forces, and their dissatisfaction with life in the United States upon their return. This is intercut with scenes of a black Anti- Vietnam War protest march. By David Loeb Weiss. 1969. *Bob Maurice Paradigm*. (68 min.)

**Now Is The Time:** Chronicles the history of the American black through emergence from the slave state over 300 years ago to 1968 where rights and equal status are demanded. Combines the sounds and rhythms of the violence of race riots with folk, rock, and hymnal music and the works of Langston Hughes, Countee Cullen, James Baldwin, Malcolm X, and Stokely Carmichael. Produced by WCAU-TV, Philadelphia. 1967. *Carousel Films*. (36 min.)

**The Nuer:** The Nuer, a tribe of Ethiopia and the Sudan, are depicted in this beautifully photographed and detailed study. 1970. (75 min.)

**OF BLACK AMERICA (series title):**
**Black History: Lost, Stolen or Strayed:** Bill Cosby reviews the achievement of Negroes which our history books have omitted and shows how Negroes have been denied recognition of their contributions to American culture. Produced by *CBS News*. 1968. (2 films, each 27 min.)

**Black World:** A worldwide panel discussion in which Mike Wallace interviews prominent blacks of many countries to reveal their social and cultural problems and their reactions to current racial and political problems. Produced by CBS News. 1968. (2 films, each 26 min.)

**Portrait in Black and White:** By means of a public opinion poll, the film explores the attitudes of blacks and whites toward each other, and the misconceptions and prejudices of each group. Produced by *CBS News*. 1968. (2 films, each 27 min.)

**The Heritage of Slavery:** Traces the history of the Emancipation and explains the freed slave and his descendants; also shows the debilitating effect of slavery on the nation's social and economic life. Produced by *CBS News*. 1968. (2 films, each 26 min.)

**The Black Soldier:** Surveys the black American's participation in U.S. wars, from the Revolution to the Vietnamese conflict. Produced by CBS News. 1968. (25 min.)

**People Who Fix Things:** A black airplane mechanic, a young man who repairs musical instruments, and a tree surgeon—three workers with special repair skills—talk about the satisfaction of fine craftsmanship and why they enjoy their service jobs. Directed by Paul Boorstin. 1971. (19 min.)

**People Who Make Things:** A glimpse into the working lives of three people who are excited by and take pride in their creative skills; a young woman who designs and constructs huge wooden dolls, a young black man who is an apprentice cake decorator, and a man who works in a custom car shop.

**Phyllis and Terry:** Life in one of New York's ghettos as experienced by two Negro teenagers. Completely improvised, the film lets Phyllis and Terry display their wit and outspoken friendship against a background of a city neighborhood. Directed by Eugene and Carol Marner. 1965. Center for Mass Communications of Columbia University. (35 min.)

**The Professionals: Basketball:** Interviews famous basketball stars and team members including Wilt Chamberlain, then of the Philadelphia 76ers, and Jerry West of the Los Angeles Lakers, and shows them in action. Produced by *Warner Brothers-Seven Arts*. (30 min.)

**Prudence Crandall:** Depicts the life of nineteenth-century New England schoolteacher Prudence Crandall, who tried to open an integrated girls' school against legal and social opposition. One of the Profiles in Courage television series. For older children. Produced by Robert Saudek Associates. 1964 *Robert Saudek* (50 min.)

**Rafer Johnson Story:** Relates the story of Olympic decathlon champion Rafer Johnson, his early life, and his eventual triumph as one of the most honored athletes in the world. Produced by David Wolper Productions. 1964. *Sterling* (55 min.)

**A. Phillip Randolph:** Biography of the black labor leader who succeeded in gaining recognition for Pullman Car Porters' Union. Includes newsreel footage and an interview in which Mr. Randolph recalls his confrontations with Roosevelt and Kennedy and speaks of his continuing struggle for job equality for black Americans. Rediscovery Productions. 1971.(10 min.)

**River Nile:** An exploration in rich color of the course of the Nile River. Describes the civilizations that have flourished on its banks throughout history. Narrated by James Mason. Produced by Lou I. Hazam for NBC News. Photographed by Guy Blanchard. Directed by Ray Garner. 1962. McGraw-Hill (52 min.)

**The Seasons Change:** A report on the events surrounding the 1968 Democratic National Convention in Chicago, with emphasis on the civil rights issues involved in the interaction of police, demonstrators, and bystanders. Includes interviews with demonstrators, reporters, bystanders, convention delegates, police officials, supporters of Mayor Daley, Rennie Davis, Tom Hayden, Allen Ginsberg, Dick Gregory, Jay Miller of the American Civil Liberties Union, and others, intercut with scenes of the violence which occurred. By William Jersey. 1968. (60 min.)

**Sit In:** A highly dramatic news analysis of the sit-in movement as it occurred in Nashville at the beginning of the sixties. The very objectivity of the film confirms the courage of the students in the face of intransigence. An NBC White Paper produced by Al Wasserman. Narrated by Chet Huntley. 1961. McGraw-Hill (54 min)

**Some of My Best Friends Are White:** A provocative examination of America's racial problem as discussed from the point of view of the middle class Negro involving his acceptance by society and the future of his children growing up in white suburbia. A BBC-TV production. Produced by Michael Latham. 1967. *Robeck*. (30 1 min.)

**Something to Build On:** A survey of new college possibilities for black students, including a review of innovative programs, scholarship, and loan information throughout the country. A Chamba Production, directed by St. Claire Bourne. 1971. (29 min.)

**Still a Brother:** Inside the Negro Middle Class: Documents the economic, social and personal life of America's black middle-class, constituting approximately 25% of the black population. Through conversations with prominent Negroes and a study of various trends in behavior, examines the conflict between the middle-class black's personal aspirations and his commitment to the general black movement. Narrated by Ossie Davis. Produced by William Greaves and William Brance. 1967. *McGraw-Hill* (90 min.)

**A Story, A Story:** A beautifully executed animation of the book by Gail Haley. Anasi, a hero of African folklore, uses his wits to win a box of stories from the sky god. Narrated in the rich, West Indian accent of John Akar. (10 min.)
Street of the Flower Boxes: Documents the efforts of a young boy and the people on his block to change a slum neighborhood into a more attractive and humane environment. *NBC Educational Enterprises*. (48 min.)

**Sunday on the River:** A sensitive and poetic documentary in which members of a Harlem social club take an excursion boat trip on the Hudson River. In an atmosphere of quiet relief the Sunday tourists picnic and play, enjoying to the full their limited escape from cramped city quarters. Traditional Negro songs sung by George Tipton. Produced by Gordon Hitchens and Ken Resnick. 1961 *Hitchens*. (26 min.)

**Tauw:** A day in the life of a young African, the eldest son of a poor family, as he tries to find employment and to deal with the tensions in his family created by hunger, the breakdown of old tribal ways, and a society in transition. Filmed in Dakar, Senegal. By Ousmane Sembene. 1970. (27 min.)

**The Tenement:** A vivid and moving cross section of a Chicago slum dwelling and of the people who inhabit it. Their despair, their feeling, and their delicate hopes are expressed in their own words. Produced by CBS News. 1967. Carousel (40 min.)

**A Time for Burning:** Cinema verite account of a young minister's attempt and failure, to lead his congregation to taking one small step toward integration and intergroup relations in his church in Omaha. Made by William Jersey and Barbara Connell, for the Lutheran Film Associates. 1966. *Contemporary/ McGraw-Hill* (58 min.)

**Time of the Horn :** A small black boy finds an old horn and imagines he is a great trumpeter. Has a fine jazz background. By Russell Merritt. *Journal Films* (7 min.)

**Troublemakers:** A moving *cinema verite'* account of an unsuccessful attempt by the Students for a Democratic Society and the people of a Newark, New Jersey ghetto neighborhood to improve the living conditions of the community. Made by Robert Machover and Norman Fruchter. 1966. *Blue Van Films.* (54 min.)

**220 Blues:** Sonny is a star high school track man, a good candidate for a college athletic scholarship, and promising future architect. His values are challenged by Larry, another young black student, who is militant and determined to make Sonny choose a side. A study of awakening racial awareness, this is an open-ended, unresolved film intended to open discussions of issues raised. Directed by Richard Gilbert. 1970. (23 min.)

**Veronica:** Intimate portrait of a black teenager in New Haven, Connecticut. Veronica Glover is a pretty, popular girl who finds herself torn between the demands of black classmates and her efforts to understand and be herself. Produced, directed, and edited by Pat Powell; photographed by Roger Murphy. 1969. *Jason Films* (28 min.)

**The Way It Is:** Documents the efforts of a New York University team of teachers and educators to redesign teaching methods and establish new ones in a ghetto Junior High School in Williamsburg, Brooklyn. Actual footage of classroom activity, which is often shocking and seemingly unbelievable, shows how it "really is." 1967. *Indiana University.* (58 min.)

**The Weapons of Gordon Parks:** The story of the internationally known Negro Life magazine photographer seen at work, in his home, with his family, and on the streets of Harlem, as part of his past life is recreated. An inspiring and moving photographic essay. Directed by Warren Forma. 1967. *Contemporary/ McGraw-Hill* (28 min.)

**Willis Reed: Center Play:** Willis Reed demonstrates some of the basketball techniques that have made him famous. *Schloat Productions.* (2 parts, 10 min.)

## DISTRIBUTORS

Atlantis Productions, Inc.
894 Sheffield Place
Thousand Oaks, California 91360

Bailey-Film Associates
11559 Santa Monica Boulevard
Los Angeles, California 90025

Harold Becker
295 Fifth Avenue
New York, New York 10016
(212) 689-6160

Blue Vun Films
28 West 31st Street
New York, New York 10001
(212) 524-4570

Brandon Films Inc.
221 West 57th Street
New York, New York 10019
(212) 246-4868

Carousel Films Inc.
1501 Broadway
New York, New York 10036
(212) 279-6734

Center for Mass Communications
of Columbia University
440 West 11Oth Street
New York, New York 10025
(212) 865-2000, ext 16

Contemporary/McGraw-Hill Films
330 West 42nd Street
New York, New York 10036
(212) 971-3333

Encyclopaedia Britannica
Educational Corporation
180 East Post Road
White Plains, New York 10601
(914) 949-4142

William Greaves Production, Inc.
254 West 54th Street
New York, New York 10019
(212) 586-7710

Grove Press Cinema 16 Library
80 University Place
New York, New York 10003
(212) 677-2400

Gordon Hitchens
838 West End Avenue
New York, New York 10025
(212) 749-1652

Indiana University
Audio-Visual Center
Bloomington, Indiana 47401

International Film Foundation, Inc.
Julien Bryan, Executive Director
475 Fifth Avenue
New York, New York 10017
(212) 685-4998

Jason Films
2621 Palisade Avenue
Riverdale, New York 10463
(212) 884-7648

Journal Films
909 West Diversey Parkway
Chicago, Illinois 60614

Landmark Educational Media
1600 Broadway
New York, New York 10019
(212) 581-1090

McGraw-Hill (see Contemporary/
McGraw-Hill)

NET (see Indiana University)

New York Times Library Services Dept.
229 West 43rd Street
New York, New York 10036
(212) 556-1234

Paradigm Films
2248 Broadway
New York, New York 10024
(212) 799-7543

Quality Film Laboratories, Inc.
450 West 56th Street
New York, New York 10019
(212) 586-4912

Reaction Films/Intext
Scranton, Pennsylvania 18515

Peter M. Robeck & Company, Inc.
230 Park Avenue
New York, New York 10017
(212) 689-2687

Robert Saudek Assoc.
630 Fifth Avenue

New York, New York 10020
(212) 581-1070

Sterling Educational Films
241 East 34th Street
New York, New York 10016
(212) 683-6300

Universal Education & Visual Arts
221 Park Avenue South
New York, New York 10003
(212) 777-6600

University of California Extension
Media Center
Film Distribution
2223 Fulton Street
Berkeley, California 94720

Warner Brothers-Seven Arts
666 Fifth Avenue
New York, New York 10019
(212) 986-1717

Youth Film Distribution Center
4 West 16th Street
New York, New York 10011
(212) 989-7265

## THE CURRENT STATUS OF BLACK PUBLIC EDUCATION

### School Enrollment

In the Fall 1987, 58.4 million Americans were enrolled in public elementary and secondary schools. At the elementary level, enrollment declined about 3 percent between 1981 and 1985 but began to increase in 1986. Secondary enrollment, which started to decrease in 1976, is projected to begin rising again in 1991. Population changes affected elementary school enrollment differently for whites and blacks. The proportional decline in the number of black students was smaller than that for whites, mainly because the overall population decline was less for blacks. Between 1970 and 1986, white elementary enrollment dropped 24 percent, but only 11 percent for blacks. Since 1970, the year of the highest elementary school enrollment, the proportional decline in black elementary school enrollment was smaller than that for whites because the proportional population decline was less for blacks than for whites. Both groups experienced decreases in birth rates, but the rate for blacks remained higher than that for whites. From 1970 to 1986, white elementary school enrollment declined by 24 percent and black enrollment declined by 11 percent. Different trends are projected for the future size of each group. Because of likely continued higher fertility rates among blacks, the increase in the elementary school-age population will be proportionately greater for blacks than for whites. According to latest population projections, from 1986 to

**CHART 52. PERCENTAGE OF ADULTS COMPLETING FOUR YEARS OF HIGH SCHOOL OR MORE: 1950 TO 1986**

**The proportion of black adults who have completed high school has more than tripled between 1950 and 1986**

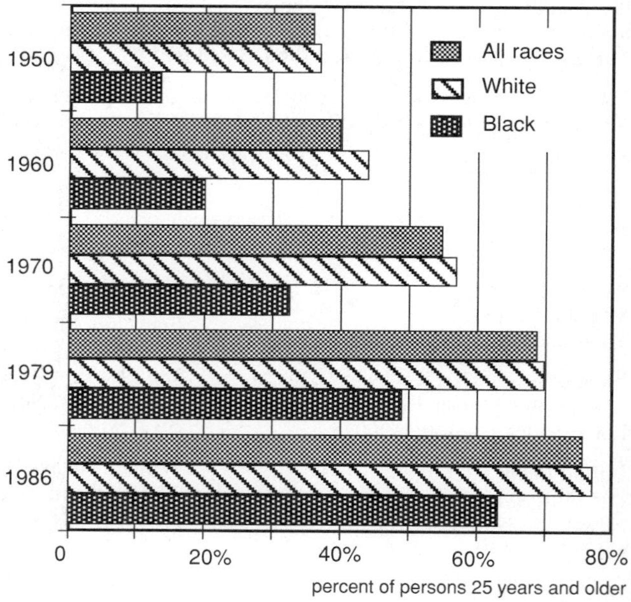


**CHART 53. MEDIAN SCHOOL YEARS COMPLETED**

**In 1960 the median of school years completed for blacks was 8.0 while for whites it was 10.9, a difference of three years. In 1986 the gap had dwindled to a third of a year.**

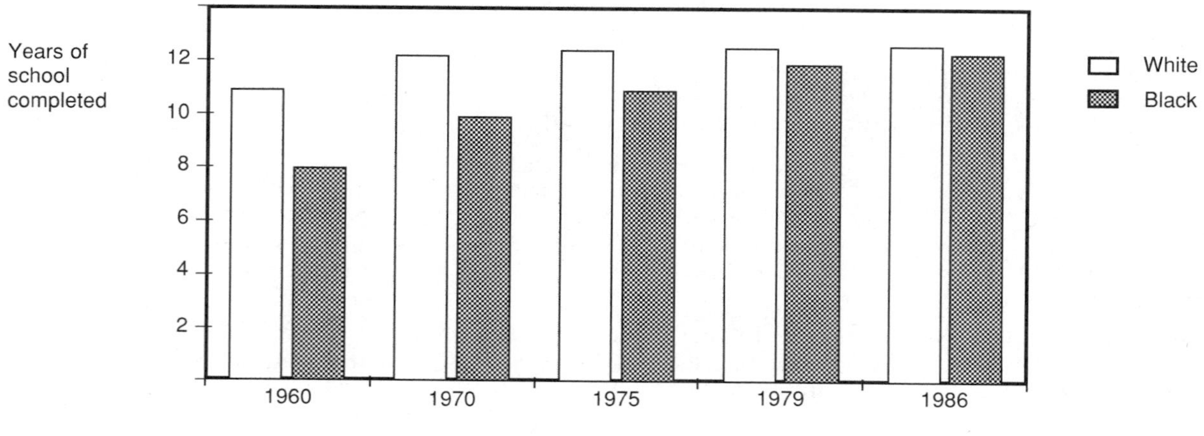

### CHART 54. HIGH SCHOOL COMPLETION RATES WOMEN, AGES 20 TO 24, BY RACE 1976 TO 1986

### CHART 55. HIGH SCHOOL COMPLETION RATES MEN, AGES 20 TO 24, BY RACE 1976 TO 1986

**While more young blacks are finishing high school the percentage of black high school graduates attending college is on the decline.**

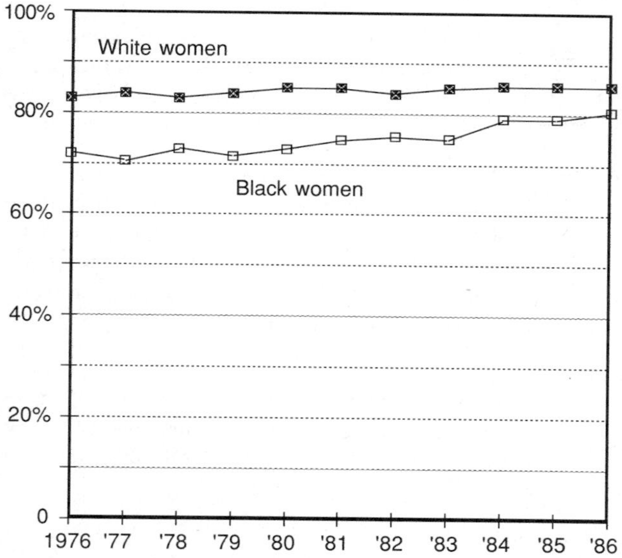


Source: Bureau of the Census

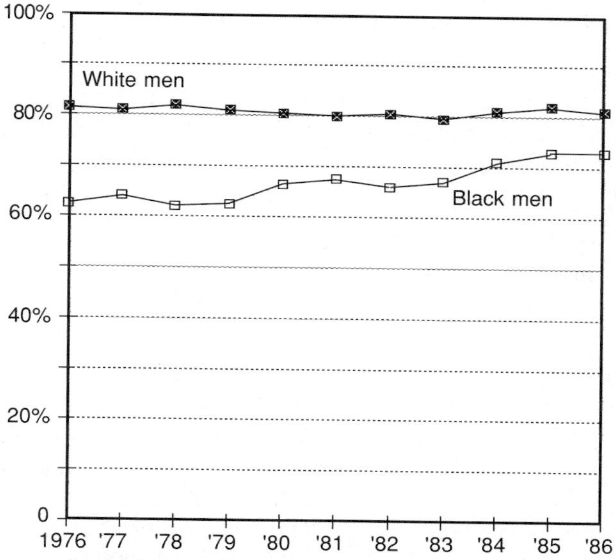


Source: Bureau of the Census

1998 (projected to be the next peak year for the elementary school age population), the white population 6 to 13 years old will rise by 14 percent but the black population will increase by 24 percent. By 1998, when the elementary school-age population reaches a new peak of 31 million, there will be a new all-time-high number of black elementary school-age children. The size of the black population 6 to 13 years old will be about 15 percent larger than in the last peak year, 1970. For whites, the new peak will be about 12 percent lower than the 1970 figure. Even with the greater proportional increase among blacks than whites, blacks will increase only slightly as a proportion of the total population in the age group, from 15.6 in 1986 to 16.7 in 1998 (they were 13.6 percent in 1970). For further data on population trends see population projections in Population Section.

### Educational Attainment

Educational attainment in 1986 reached a peak level for both black and white students while declining for Hispanics. Though the white level of students graduating from high school is at an all time high of 83.6% it is only up about 2% from 1971 levels, however since 1971 the percent of black students graduating from high school is up over 14% as 76.4% completed high school in 1986. The proportion for blacks was not statistically different from the 1986 level, but both the 1986 and 1987 years were higher than previous years.

Differences between the total number of white and black persons having completed high school have been decreasing over the past several years. While 77 percent of white adults have completed high school, 63.4 percent of blacks completed high school. In 1971, there was a 20% difference in the number of students completing high school, but in 1986 the figure had dropped to 8%.

### CHART 56. HIGH SCHOOL COMPLETION RATES AGES 18 TO 24, BY RACE/ ETHNICITY 1976 TO 1986

**More black females graduate from high school than do black males.**

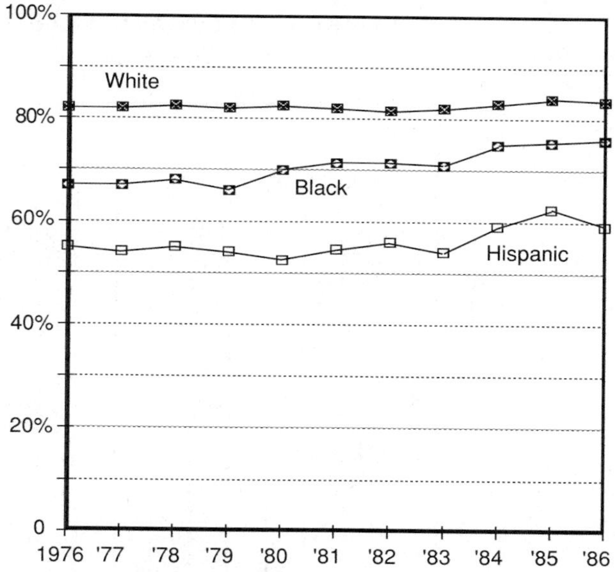


Source: Bureau of the Census

## EDUCATION FACTS

**Fact 1**
Forty-four percent of public schools in the Northeast and Midwest were classified in 1978 as racially isolated, that is, over 90% minority. In the South less than one fourth (24%) were racially isolated, and in the west only 18%.

**Fact 2**
Approximately three of every five blacks over 25 years of age who live in the West, North Central, and Northeast have graduated from high school. In the South, however, only two in every five blacks over 25 are high school graduates.

**Fact 3**
In central cities over 20% of white students are enrolled in private schools, compared with only 9% of blacks. However, the proportion of blacks in public schools has more than tripled since 1970.

**Fact 4**
In the nation as a whole, blacks comprise 16% of the public school population but only 10% of pupils enrolled in programs for the talented and gifted. In the South 27% of the school population and only 12% of students in such programs are black. In the Northeast and Midwest, however, the proportion of blacks in such programs is about the same as their overall rate of public school enrollment.

**Fact 5**
A larger proportion of black than white high school seniors are enrolled in high school vocational training programs. The difference is most marked in home economics, where 3.5% of black seniors and less than 1% of whites are enrolled.

**Fact 6**
In 1978 blacks more than whites were subject to disciplinary actions in high school. Blacks constituted 16% of enrollment but 28% of expulsions, suspensions, and recipients of corporal punishment.

**Fact 7**
Blacks in the labor force have closed the racial gap in the number of school years completed. In 1959, only 16% of blacks and 32% of whites in the work force had completed high school. In 1979, 40% of whites and 37% of black workers were high school graduates.

**Fact 8**
The proportion of whites in the work force who have college degrees remains more than twice that of black workers. In 1959, the ratio was 10% white, 4% black; in 1979, it was 18% white and 9% black.

**Fact 9**
In June 1980, 26% of black high school seniors were enrolled in CETA work programs, compared with only 5.4% of whites. In cooperative education, however, the proportions were closer, 12.6% black, 9.7% white.

**Fact 10**
Black high school students were less likely than whites or

### CHART 57. ATTENDED-COLLEGE PARTICIPATION RATES FOR 14- TO - 24- YEAR- OLDS BY RACE/ ETHNICITY, 1976 TO 1986

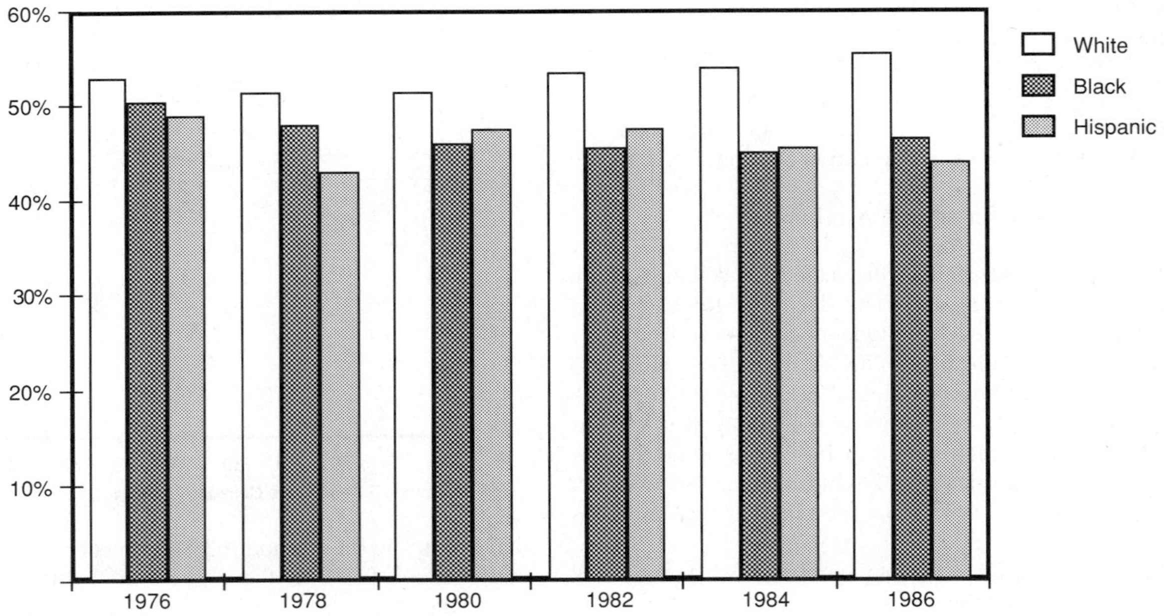


Source: Bureau of the Census

Hispanics to be employed in the private sector. The figures for seniors: blacks 35%, Hispanics 43%, whites 58%.

**Fact 11**

In 1976, more than three times as many doctoral level degrees were conferred on nonresident aliens as on black citizens of the United States.

**Fact 12**

In 1976, approximately one-fifth of black students pursuing professional programs were enrolled in HBCs.

**Fact 13**

Black colleges continue to be the predominant source of professional degrees in many areas of the South. Meharry Medical College conferred 96% of the dentistry and 92% of the medical degrees awarded blacks in Tennessee. Texas Southern conferred two-thirds of all law degrees awarded blacks in Texas, and Howard 92% of the dentistry and 84% of the medical degrees awarded blacks residing in the District of Columbia.

**Fact 14**

Black college students are more likely than whites to suffer from withdrawal of financial aid. In 1974, the college dropout rate for blacks receiving financial aid was 24%, but it was 46% for blacks receiving no aid. For whites, the rates were 21% when aid was received, 29% for whites without aid.

**Fact 15**

A child walking to or from school is three times more likely to be injured in an accident than a child who is being bused.

**Fact 16**

In 1976, 50% of the children in the United States were being bused to school. Only 3.5%, however, were being bused for desegregation purposes.

**Fact 17**

Segregation often required more busing than integration, because blacks were frequently bused past white schools. After desegregation in Tennessee, the number of students transported declined by 20,000 and the number of miles traveled by 1,900,000 per school year. In Georgia, 14,000 more students were bused, but miles traveled dropped by 474,000 per school year.

**CHART 58. HIGH SCHOOL GRADUATES AMONG POPULATION 25 YEARS OLD AND OVER, BY REGION AND RACIAL/ETHNIC GROUP, 1979-1987**

**The largest discrepancy between black and white high school graduates is in the South where some 25% fewer blacks are high school graduates.**

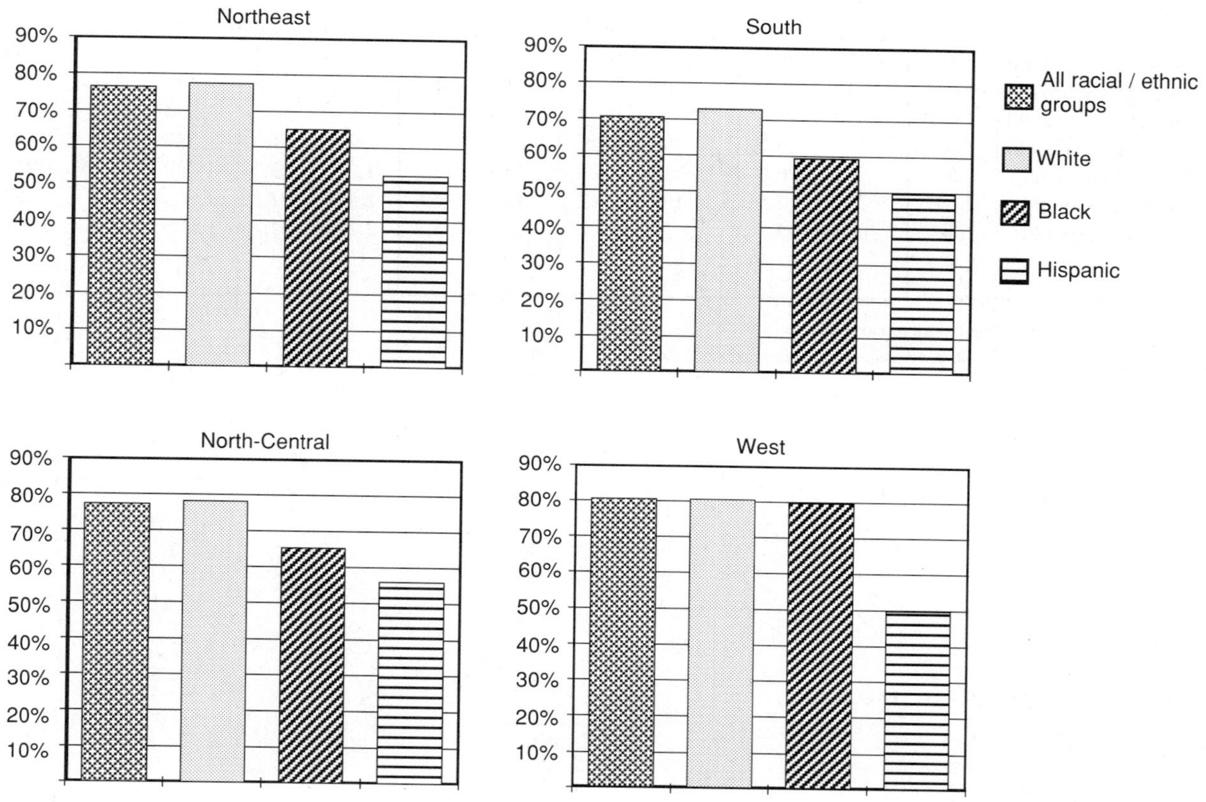

## TABLE 141. ENROLLMENT STATUS FOR PERSONS 3 TO 34 YEARS OLD BY AGE, SEX, AND RACE: OCTOBER 1986

(Numbers in thousands. Civilian noninstitutional population.)

| | | Enrolled in school | | | | | | Not enrolled in school | | | | | |
|---|---|---|---|---|---|---|---|---|---|---|---|---|---|
| | | Total | | Below college level[1] | | In college | | Total | | High school graduate | | Not high school graduate | |
| Age, sex, and race | Population | Number | Percent | Number | Percent | Number | Percent | Number | Percent | Number | Percent | Number | Percent |
| White | | | | | | | | | | | | | |
| Both sexes | 99,698 | 47,267 | 47.4 | 38,324 | 38.4 | 8,943 | 9.0 | 52,431 | 52.6 | 40,581 | 40.7 | 11,850 | 11.9 |
| 3 and 4 years old | 5,867 | 2,296 | 39.1 | 2,296 | 39.1 | - | - | 3,570 | 60.9 | - | - | 3,570 | 60.9 |
| 5 and 6 years old | 5,799 | 5,524 | 95.3 | 5,524 | 95.3 | - | - | 275 | 4.7 | - | - | 275 | 4.7 |
| 7 to 9 years old | 8,223 | 8,162 | 99.3 | 8,162 | 99.3 | - | - | 60 | 0.7 | - | - | 60 | 0.7 |
| 10 to 13 years old | 10,504 | 10,417 | 99.2 | 10,417 | 99.2 | - | - | 87 | 0.8 | - | - | 87 | 0.8 |
| 14 and 15 years old | 5,806 | 5,677 | 97.8 | 5,668 | 97.6 | 9 | 0.2 | 129 | 2.2 | - | - | 129 | 2.2 |
| 16 and 17 years old | 6,072 | 5,587 | 92.0 | 5,408 | 89.1 | 179 | 2.9 | 485 | 8.0 | 91 | 1.5 | 394 | 6.5 |
| 18 and 19 years old | 5,825 | 3,192 | 54.8 | 669 | 11.5 | 2,523 | 43.3 | 2,633 | 45.2 | 1,940 | 33.3 | 693 | 11.9 |
| 20 and 21 years old | 6,090 | 2,042 | 33.5 | 55 | 0.9 | 1,987 | 32.6 | 4,048 | 66.5 | 3,175 | 52.1 | 873 | 14.3 |
| 22 to 24 years old | 10,093 | 1,759 | 17.4 | 32 | 0.3 | 1,728 | 17.1 | 8,334 | 82.6 | 6,926 | 68.6 | 1,408 | 13.9 |
| 25 to 29 years old | 18,054 | 1,589 | 8.8 | 49 | 0.3 | 1,540 | 8.5 | 16,465 | 91.2 | 14,066 | 77.9 | 2,400 | 13.3 |
| 30 to 34 years old | 17,365 | 1,021 | 5.9 | 43 | 0.2 | 977 | 5.6 | 16,344 | 94.1 | 14,383 | 82.8 | 1,961 | 11.3 |
| Black | | | | | | | | | | | | | |
| Both sexes | 16,752 | 8,556 | 51.1 | 7,418 | 44.3 | 1,138 | 6.8 | 8,196 | 48.9 | 5,761 | 34.4 | 2,435 | 14.5 |
| 3 and 4 years old | 1,075 | 411 | 38.2 | 411 | 38.2 | - | - | 664 | 61.8 | - | - | 664 | 61.8 |
| 5 and 6 years old | 1,156 | 1,100 | 95.2 | 1,100 | 95.2 | - | - | 56 | 4.8 | - | - | 56 | 4.8 |
| 7 to 9 years old | 1,551 | 1,548 | 99.8 | 1,548 | 99.8 | - | - | 3 | 0.2 | - | - | 3 | 0.2 |
| 10 to 13 years old | 2,036 | 2,016 | 99.0 | 2,016 | 99.0 | - | - | 20 | 1.0 | - | - | 20 | 1.0 |
| 14 and 15 years old | 1,117 | 1,079 | 96.6 | 1,077 | 96.4 | 2 | 0.2 | 38 | 3.4 | - | - | 38 | 3.4 |
| 16 and 17 years old | 1,090 | 1,015 | 93.2 | 998 | 91.6 | 17 | 1.6 | 75 | 6.8 | 23 | 2.1 | 52 | 4.7 |
| 18 and 19 years old | 1,048 | 518 | 49.4 | 211 | 20.1 | 306 | 29.3 | 530 | 50.6 | 374 | 35.7 | 156 | 14.9 |
| 20 and 21 years old | 1,044 | 268 | 25.7 | 29 | 2.8 | 239 | 22.9 | 776 | 74.3 | 587 | 56.2 | 189 | 18.1 |
| 22 to 24 years old | 1,573 | 261 | 16.6 | 5 | 0.3 | 256 | 16.3 | 1,311 | 83.4 | 1,039 | 66.1 | 272 | 17.3 |
| 25 to 29 years old | 2,641 | 197 | 7.5 | 18 | 0.7 | 180 | 6.8 | 2,444 | 92.5 | 1,963 | 74.3 | 481 | 18.2 |
| 30 to 34 years old | 2,422 | 143 | 5.9 | 5 | 0.2 | 137 | 5.7 | 2,280 | 94.1 | 1,775 | 73.3 | 504 | 20.8 |

1 Includes nursery school, kindergarten, and grades 1 to 12.

Source: U.S.Department of Commerce, Bureau of the Census

## TABLE 142. ENROLLMENT RATES FOR PERSONS 3 TO 34 YEARS OLD BY AGE, RACE, AND REGION: OCTOBER 1986

(Numbers in thousands. Civilian noninstitutional population.)

| Age and race | U.S. enrollment | | Northeast enrollment | | Midwest enrollment | | South enrollment | | West enrollment | |
|---|---|---|---|---|---|---|---|---|---|---|
| | Number | Percent | Number | Percent | Number | Percent | Number | Percent | Number | Percent |
| All races | 58,153 | 48.2 | 11,794 | 49.2 | 14,247 | 48.0 | 19,958 | 47.7 | 12,155 | 48.3 |
| 3 and 4 years old | 2,813 | 38.9 | 626 | 46.1 | 667 | 36.7 | 934 | 38.6 | 586 | 35.9 |
| 5 and 6 years old | 6,917 | 95.3 | 1,271 | 96.9 | 1,722 | 95.0 | 2,368 | 95.1 | 1,556 | 94.6 |
| 7 to 13 years old | 22,988 | 99.2 | 4,424 | 99.0 | 5,585 | 99.2 | 8,227 | 99.3 | 4,751 | 99.2 |
| 14 to 17 years old | 13,868 | 94.9 | 2,845 | 96.2 | 3,331 | 95.6 | 4,912 | 93.2 | 2,780 | 95.8 |
| 18 to 24 years old | 8,456 | 31.9 | 1,980 | 36.0 | 2,129 | 32.7 | 2,650 | 28.6 | 1,697 | 32.5 |
| 25 to 34 years old | 3,111 | 7.4 | 648 | 7.7 | 813 | 7.8 | 866 | 6.1 | 785 | 8.7 |
| White | 47,267 | 47.4 | 10,071 | 48.5 | 12,305 | 47.2 | 14,672 | 46.8 | 10,218 | 47.6 |
| 3 and 4 years old | 2,296 | 39.1 | 542 | 47.3 | 568 | 36.0 | 688 | 38.7 | 498 | 36.4 |
| 5 and 6 years old | 5,524 | 95.3 | 1,052 | 97.5 | 1,464 | 94.6 | 1,731 | 95.0 | 1,277 | 94.5 |
| 7 to 13 years old | 18,580 | 99.2 | 3,758 | 99.0 | 4,833 | 99.3 | 5,957 | 99.2 | 4,031 | 99.3 |
| 14 to 17 years old | 11,264 | 94.8 | 2,437 | 96.2 | 2,895 | 95.9 | 3,586 | 92.5 | 2,346 | 95.8 |
| 18 to 24 years old | 6,994 | 31.8 | 1,718 | 35.7 | 1,868 | 32.6 | 2,010 | 28.7 | 1,398 | 31.3 |
| 25 to 34 years old | 2,609 | 7.4 | 564 | 7.6 | 678 | 7.2 | 700 | 6.4 | 668 | 8.6 |
| Black | 8,556 | 51.1 | 1,423 | 63.2 | 1,603 | 52.0 | 4,810 | 50.0 | 720 | 52.4 |
| 3 and 4 years old | 411 | 38.2 | 60 | 35.6 | 78 | 37.0 | 225 | 38.3 | 48 | 44.2 |
| 5 and 6 years old | 1,100 | 95.2 | 180 | 93.3 | 222 | 97.1 | 602 | 95.3 | 97 | 93.9 |
| 7 to 13 years old | 3,564 | 99.3 | 565 | 99.0 | 642 | 98.7 | 2,069 | 99.6 | 287 | 100.0 |
| 14 to 17 years old | 2,094 | 94.9 | 357 | 96.0 | 379 | 93.6 | 1,211 | 95.0 | 146 | 95.1 |
| 18 to 24 years old | 1,047 | 28.6 | 190 | 32.7 | 191 | 28.2 | 563 | 26.8 | 103 | 33.5 |
| 25 to 34 years old | 340 | 6.7 | 71 | 9.0 | 89 | 9.8 | 140 | 4.7 | 39 | 9.5 |

Source: U.S.Department of Commerce, Bureau of the Census

## TABLE 143. LEVEL OF ENROLLMENT FOR PERSONS 3 TO 34 YEARS OLD, BY CONTROL OF SCHOOL, RESIDENCE, AND RACE: OCTOBER 1986

(In thousands. Civilian noninstitutional population. )

| Sex, control of school, | Enrolled below college level | | | | | | Enrolled in college (year) | | | |
|---|---|---|---|---|---|---|---|---|---|---|
| residence, and race | Total | Nursery school | Kinder-garten | Grades 1 to 6 | Grades 7 and 8 | Grades 9 to 12 | Total | 1 and 2 | 3 and 4 | 5 or more |
| **White** | | | | | | | | | | |
| All areas | | | | | | | | | | |
| Total | 38,324 | 2,144 | 3,161 | 16,523 | 6,238 | 11,259 | 8,943 | 4,632 | 2,882 | 1,429 |
| Public | 32,508 | 601 | 2,589 | 14,432 | 4,658 | 10,229 | 6,821 | 3,750 | 2,126 | 946 |
| Private | 5,815 | 1,543 | 572 | 2,091 | 580 | 1,030 | 2,122 | 882 | 757 | 483 |
| Metropolitan | | | | | | | | | | |
| Total | 28,672 | 1,707 | 2,417 | 12,165 | 3,872 | 8,510 | 7,349 | 3,728 | 2,408 | 1,213 |
| Inside central city | 9,181 | 693 | 819 | 4,050 | 1,204 | 2,514 | 2,815 | 1,289 | 918 | 608 |
| Public | 7,315 | 195 | 624 | 3,363 | 991 | 2,142 | 2,118 | 1,043 | 682 | 392 |
| Private | 1,866 | 398 | 195 | 688 | 213 | 372 | 697 | 246 | 235 | 216 |
| Outside central city | 19,492 | 1,114 | 1,598 | 8,115 | 2,668 | 5,997 | 4,534 | 2,439 | 1,490 | 605 |
| Public | 16,552 | 249 | 1,302 | 7,107 | 2,390 | 5,503 | 3,337 | 1,932 | 1,038 | 367 |
| Private | 2,940 | 865 | 296 | 1,008 | 277 | 494 | 1,197 | 507 | 452 | 238 |
| Nonmetropolitan | | | | | | | | | | |
| Total | 9,652 | 436 | 744 | 4,358 | 1,366 | 2,748 | 1,594 | 904 | 474 | 216 |
| Public | 8,642 | 156 | 663 | 3,962 | 1,277 | 2,584 | 1,367 | 775 | 405 | 186 |
| Private | 1,010 | 280 | 81 | 395 | 89 | 164 | 227 | 128 | 70 | 29 |
| **Black** | | | | | | | | | | |
| All areas | | | | | | | | | | |
| Total | 7,418 | 315 | 647 | 3,292 | 1,034 | 2,130 | 1,138 | 648 | 383 | 108 |
| Public | 6,973 | 200 | 600 | 3,140 | 994 | 2,040 | 896 | 530 | 300 | 65 |
| Private | 445 | 115 | 47 | 153 | 40 | 91 | 242 | 117 | 83 | 42 |
| Metropolitan | | | | | | | | | | |
| Total | 5,894 | 274 | 517 | 2,580 | 815 | 1,708 | 980 | 558 | 322 | 99 |
| Inside central city | 4,155 | 186 | 363 | 1,827 | 582 | 1,197 | 692 | 380 | 239 | 74 |
| Public | 3,897 | 138 | 338 | 1,721 | 655 | 1,145 | 537 | 318 | 178 | 41 |
| Private | 258 | 48 | 25 | 106 | 27 | 51 | 155 | 62 | 61 | 33 |
| Outside central city | 1,739 | 88 | 154 | 753 | 233 | 511 | 288 | 179 | 84 | 25 |
| Public | 1,599 | 35 | 141 | 716 | 224 | 483 | 209 | 129 | 63 | 18 |
| Private | 140 | 52 | 12 | 37 | 9 | 29 | 78 | 50 | 21 | 7 |
| Nonmetropolitan | | | | | | | | | | |
| Total | 1,524 | 41 | 130 | 713 | 219 | 422 | 168 | 89 | 61 | 8 |
| Public | 1,478 | 26 | 121 | 703 | 215 | 412 | 160 | 84 | 60 | 6 |
| Private | 48 | 15 | 9 | 9 | 4 | 10 | 9 | 6 | 1 | 2 |

Source: U.S.Department of Commerce, Bureau of the Census

## TABLE 144. ENROLLMENT STATUS OF PRIMARY FAMILY MEMBERS 3 TO 34 YEARS OLD BY EDUCATIONAL ATTAINMENT OF FAMILY HOUSEHOLDER, LEVEL AND CONTROL OF SCHOOL, AND RACE: OCTOBER 1986 (WHITE)

(Numbers in thousands. Civilian noninstitutional population. Excludes persons in families in which the householder is a member of the Armed Forces. Also excludes family members who are family householders and family members who are married, spouse present.)

| Level and control of school, enrollment status, sex, and race | Years of school completed by family householder | | | | | | | |
|---|---|---|---|---|---|---|---|---|
| | | Elementary school | | | High school | | College | |
| | Total | 0 to 4 years | 5 to 7 years | 8 years | 1 to 3 years | 4 years | 1 to 3 years | 4 years |
| **White** | | | | Percent Distribution | | | | |
| All family members | 100.0 | 2.5 | 3.9 | 4.1 | 11.0 | 38.1 | 18.0 | 22.4 |
| Enrolled | 100.0 | 2.1 | 3.5 | 3.4 | 9.9 | 37.0 | 19.1 | 25.1 |
| Nursery school and kindergarten | 100.0 | 1.5 | 2.7 | 2.2 | 8.9 | 38.5 | 19.7 | 26.6 |
| Public | 100.0 | 2.3 | 4.2 | 3.3 | 11.9 | 42.4 | 18.0 | 17.8 |
| Private | 100.0 | 0.4 | 0.3 | 0.6 | 4.3 | 32.4 | 22.2 | 39.8 |
| Elementary 1 to 8 years | 100.0 | 2.4 | 4.2 | 3.6 | 10.9 | 37.8 | 18.5 | 22.6 |
| Public | 100.0 | 2.7 | 4.5 | 3.7 | 11.7 | 38.6 | 18.1 | 20.6 |
| Private | 100.0 | 0.1 | 1.7 | 2.2 | 5.4 | 32.5 | 20.9 | 37.2 |
| High school, 1 to 4 years | 100.0 | 2.4 | 3.2 | 4.1 | 10.1 | 38.1 | 18.9 | 23.3 |
| Public | 100.0 | 2.6 | 3.4 | 4.1 | 10.5 | 38.8 | 19.1 | 21.5 |
| Private | 100.0 | 0.4 | 1.3 | 3.7 | 6.2 | 31.0 | 17.3 | 40.2 |
| College, full- time | 100.0 | 0.5 | 1.3 | 1.7 | 6.3 | 29.0 | 21.2 | 40.0 |
| Public | 100.0 | 0.6 | 1.5 | 2.0 | 6.2 | 30.3 | 22.9 | 36.7 |
| Private | 100.0 | 0.2 | 1.0 | 1.1 | 6.5 | 25.7 | 16.7 | 48.8 |
| College, part- time | 100.0 | 1.5 | 4.5 | 5.3 | 8.7 | 33.7 | 23.8 | 22.6 |
| Public | 100.0 | 1.5 | 4.8 | 5.8 | 8.3 | 34.0 | 23.1 | 22.6 |
| Private | 100.0 | 1.8 | 2.7 | 1.8 | 10.9 | 31.8 | 28.2 | 22.7 |
| Not enrolled: | | | | | | | | |
| 3 to 13 years old | 100.0 | 2.4 | 4.9 | 3.7 | 13.9 | 42.6 | 17.2 | 15.3 |
| 14 to 34 years old | 100.0 | 4.2 | 5.7 | 7.6 | 14.1 | 41.3 | 13.7 | 13.4 |
| Not high school graduate | 100.0 | 11.9 | 11.5 | 12.2 | 22.6 | 29.2 | 8.7 | 3.9 |
| 14 to 24 years old | 100.0 | 11.3 | 10.5 | 11.5 | 24.1 | 30.3 | 8.8 | 3.6 |
| 25 to 34 years old | 100.0 | 13.7 | 14.1 | 14.3 | 18.6 | 26.2 | 8.3 | 4.7 |
| High school graduate | 100.0 | 2.2 | 4.2 | 6.4 | 11.9 | 44.4 | 15.0 | 15.8 |
| No college | 100.0 | 2.6 | 5.4 | 8.2 | 14.3 | 48.6 | 11.8 | 9.1 |
| College 1 to 3 years | 100.0 | 2.0 | 2.3 | 3.1 | 8.8 | 39.2 | 23.1 | 21.5 |
| College 4 years or more | 100.0 | 0.8 | 1.0 | 2.7 | 4.4 | 31.5 | 19.0 | 40.5 |

Source: U.S. Department of Commerce, Bureau of the Census

## TABLE 145. ENROLLMENT STATUS OF PRIMARY FAMILY MEMBERS 3 TO 34 YEARS OLD BY EDUCATIONAL ATTAINMENT OF FAMILY HOUSEHOLDER, LEVEL AND CONTROL OF SCHOOL, AND RACE: OCTOBER 1986 (BLACK)

(Numbers in thousands. Civilian noninstitutional population. Excludes persons in families in which the householder is a member of the Armed Forces. Also excludes family members who are family householders and family members who are married, spouse present.)

| | Years of school completed by family householder | | | | | | | |
|---|---|---|---|---|---|---|---|---|
| | | Elementary school | | | High school | | College | |
| Level and control of school, enrollment status, sex, and race | Total | 0 to 4 years | 5 to 7 years | 8 years | 1 to 3 years | 4 years | 1 to 3 years | 4 years |
| **Black** | | | | Percent Distribution | | | | |
| All family members | 100.0 | 4.0 | 6.7 | 5.1 | 24.5 | 37.7 | 15.0 | 7.0 |
| Enrolled | 100.0 | 2.8 | 5.6 | 4.1 | 23.8 | 39.0 | 16.9 | 7.8 |
| Nursery school and kindergarten | 100.0 | 3.3 | 5.0 | 4.1 | 20.7 | 39.9 | 17.3 | 9.8 |
| Public | 100.0 | 4.0 | 5.4 | 4.6 | 22.0 | 41.3 | 16.0 | 6.6 |
| Private | 100.0 | - | 3.1 | 1.2 | 14.2 | 33.3 | 23.5 | 25.3 |
| Elementary, 1 to 8 years | 100.0 | 2.7 | 5.3 | 3.8 | 24.4 | 40.8 | 16.3 | 6.7 |
| Public | 100.0 | - | 5.4 | 3.8 | 25.0 | 40.7 | 16.3 | 6.0 |
| Private | 100.0 | - | 1.6 | 4.2 | 12.0 | 42.9 | 16.8 | 22.5 |
| High school, 1 to 4 years | 100.0 | 2.8 | 6.4 | 4.9 | 26.3 | 35.7 | 16.3 | 7.7 |
| Public | 100.0 | 2.9 | 6.4 | 5.0 | 26.9 | 35.0 | 16.5 | 7.3 |
| Private | 100.0 | - | 6.0 | 2.4 | 11.9 | 52.4 | 10.7 | 16.7 |
| College, full- time | 100.0 | 2.4 | 6.1 | 3.5 | 17.0 | 35.5 | 21.7 | 13.9 |
| Public | 100.0 | 3.1 | 6.3 | 2.4 | 15.7 | 38.2 | 20.5 | 13.8 |
| Private | 100.0 | - | 5.1 | 7.3 | 21.2 | 26.3 | 25.5 | 14.6 |
| College, part- time | 100.0 | 2.0 | 8.2 | 9.2 | 18.4 | 36.7 | 21.4 | 3.1 |
| Public | 100.0 | 2.4 | 8.4 | 9.6 | 21.7 | 31.3 | 22.9 | 3.6 |
| Private | (B) | (B) | (B) | (B) | (B) | (B) | (B) | (B) |
| Not enrolled: | | | | | | | | |
| 3 to 13 years old | 100.0 | 4.4 | 3.8 | 5.2 | 25.4 | 40.9 | 12.8 | 7.7 |
| 14 to 34 years old | 100.0 | 7.8 | 11.2 | 7.9 | 26.3 | 32.8 | 9.7 | 4.3 |
| Not high school graduate | 100.0 | 10.4 | 13.3 | 10.8 | 35.7 | 22.0 | 6.2 | 1.3 |
| 14 to 24 years old | 100.0 | 11.0 | 7.5 | 12.0 | 37.7 | 23.4 | 7.9 | 0.8 |
| 25 to 34 years old | 100.0 | 9.5 | 26.1 | 8.6 | 32.0 | 19.4 | 2.7 | 2.7 |
| High school graduate | 100.0 | 6.8 | 10.3 | 6.8 | 22.6 | 36.9 | 11.1 | 5.4 |
| No college | 100.0 | 6.8 | 11.5 | 7.1 | 25.1 | 36.1 | 10.3 | 3.1 |
| College, 1 to 3 years | 100.0 | 7.8 | 8.3 | 6.0 | 14.0 | 39.0 | 13.3 | 11.5 |
| College, 4 years or more | 100.0 | 2.4 | 1.2 | 5.9 | 24.7 | 38.8 | 14.1 | 11.8 |

Source: U.S. Department of Commerce, Bureau of the Census

## TABLE 146. ENROLLMENT STATUS FOR PERSONS 3 TO 34 YEARS OLD BY RESIDENCE, AGE, AND RACE: OCTOBER 1986 (WHITE)

(Numbers in thousands. Civilian noninstitutional population.)

| | | Enrolled in school | | | | | | Not enrolled in school | | | | | |
|---|---|---|---|---|---|---|---|---|---|---|---|---|---|
| | | Total | | Below college level[1] | | In college | | Total | | High school graduate | | Not high school graduate | |
| Age, residence, and race | Population | Number | Percent | Number | Percent | Number | Percent | Number | Percent | Number | Percent | Number | Percent |
| **White** | | | | | | | | | | | | | |
| Metropolitan | | | | | | | | | | | | | |
| Total | 76,395 | 36,021 | 47.2 | 28,672 | 37.6 | 7,349 | 9.6 | 40,373 | 62.8 | 31,637 | 41.4 | 8,736 | 11.4 |
| Inside central city | 27,134 | 11,996 | 44.2 | 9,181 | 33.8 | 2,815 | 10.4 | 15,139 | 66.8 | 11,448 | 42.2 | 3,691 | 13.6 |
| 3 & 4 years old | 1,644 | 649 | 42.0 | 649 | 42.0 | - | - | 896 | 68.0 | - | - | 895 | 68.0 |
| 5 & 6 years old | 1,524 | 1,434 | 94.1 | 1,434 | 94.1 | - | - | 90 | 6.9 | - | - | 90 | 6.9 |
| 7 - 9 years old | 2,078 | 2,062 | 99.2 | 2,062 | 99.2 | - | - | 16 | 0.8 | - | - | 16 | 0.8 |
| 10 - 13 years old | 2,337 | 2,311 | 98.9 | 2,311 | 98.9 | - | - | 26 | 1.1 | - | - | 26 | 1.1 |
| 14 & 15 years old | 1,294 | 1,266 | 97.8 | 1,259 | 97.3 | 7 | 0.5 | 28 | 2.2 | - | - | 28 | 2.2 |
| 16 & 17 years old | 1,406 | 1,278 | 90.9 | 1,223 | 87.0 | 56 | 3.9 | 128 | 9.1 | 20 | 1.4 | 108 | 7.7 |
| 18 & 19 years old | 1,663 | 812 | 61.9 | 179 | 11.4 | 633 | 40.6 | 761 | 48.1 | 632 | 34.0 | 219 | 14.0 |
| 20 & 21 years old | 1,730 | 669 | 32.9 | 20 | 1.2 | 649 | 31.7 | 1,161 | 67.1 | 861 | 49.8 | 300 | 17.3 |
| 22 - 24 years old | 3,116 | 630 | 20.2 | 12 | 0.4 | 617 | 19.8 | 2,486 | 79.8 | 1,982 | 63.6 | 604 | 16.2 |
| 26 - 29 years old | 6,685 | 638 | 11.2 | 25 | 0.4 | 613 | 10.8 | 5,047 | 88.8 | 4,213 | 74.1 | 834 | 14.7 |
| 30 - 34 years old | 4,858 | 348 | 7.2 | 6 | 0.1 | 341 | 7.0 | 4,510 | 92.8 | 3,839 | 79.0 | 670 | 13.8 |
| Outside central city | 49,261 | 24,026 | 48.8 | 19,492 | 39.6 | 4,534 | 9.2 | 25,235 | 51.2 | 20,190 | 41.0 | 5,045 | 10.2 |
| 3 & 4 years old | 2,818 | 1,199 | 42.6 | 1,199 | 42.6 | - | - | 1,619 | 57.4 | - | - | 1,619 | 57.4 |
| 5 & 6 years old | 2,857 | 2,761 | 96.6 | 2,761 | 96.6 | - | - | 96 | 3.4 | - | - | 96 | 3.4 |
| 7 - 9 years old | 3,973 | 3,947 | 99.3 | 3,947 | 99.3 | - | - | 26 | 0.7 | - | - | 26 | 0.7 |
| 10 - 13 years old | 5,384 | 5,348 | 99.3 | 5,348 | 99.3 | - | - | 36 | 0.7 | - | - | 36 | 0.7 |
| 14 & 15 years old | 3,038 | 2,963 | 97.5 | 2,961 | 97.5 | 2 | 0.1 | 76 | 2.5 | - | - | 76 | 2.5 |
| 16 & 17 years old | 3,219 | 2,986 | 92.8 | 2,892 | 89.9 | 93 | 2.9 | 233 | 7.2 | 58 | 1.8 | 175 | 6.4 |
| 18 & 19 years old | 2,924 | 1,713 | 68.6 | 310 | 10.6 | 1,403 | 48.0 | 1,211 | 41.4 | 917 | 31.3 | 296 | 10.1 |
| 20 & 21 years old | 3,038 | 1,131 | 37.2 | 21 | 0.7 | 1,110 | 36.6 | 1,906 | 62.8 | 1,649 | 61.0 | 367 | 11.8 |
| 22 - 24 years old | 4,764 | 788 | 16.6 | 12 | 0.2 | 776 | 16.3 | 3,976 | 83.6 | 3,376 | 70.8 | 601 | 12.6 |
| 26 - 29 years old | 8,646 | 702 | 8.1 | 16 | 0.2 | 687 | 7.9 | 7,943 | 91.9 | 6,981 | 80.8 | 962 | 11.1 |
| 30 - 34 years old | 8,601 | 488 | 5.7 | 25 | 0.3 | 463 | 5.4 | 8,113 | 94.3 | 7,310 | 85.0 | 802 | 9.3 |
| Nonmetropolitan | | | | | | | | | | | | | |
| Total | 23,303 | 11,245 | 48.3 | 9,652 | 41.4 | 1,594 | 6.8 | 12,057 | 51.7 | 8,943 | 38.4 | 3,114 | 13.4 |
| 3 & 4 years old | 1,505 | 448 | 29.8 | 448 | 29.8 | - | - | 1,057 | 70.2 | - | - | 1,057 | 70.2 |
| 5 & 6 years old | 1,418 | 1,328 | 93.7 | 1,328 | 93.7 | - | - | 90 | 6.3 | - | - | 90 | 6.3 |
| 7 - 9 years old | 2,171 | 2,154 | 99.2 | 2,154 | 99.2 | - | - | 18 | 0.8 | - | - | 18 | 0.8 |
| 10 - 13 years old | 2,783 | 2,759 | 99.1 | 2,759 | 99.1 | - | - | 25 | 0.9 | - | - | 25 | 0.9 |
| 14 & 15 years old | 1,473 | 1,448 | 98.3 | 1,447 | 98.2 | 1 | - | 25 | 1.7 | - | - | 25 | 1.7 |
| 16 & 17 years old | 1,447 | 1,324 | 91.5 | 1,293 | 89.3 | 31 | 2.1 | 124 | 8.5 | 13 | 0.9 | 111 | 7.7 |
| 18 & 19 years old | 1,337 | 667 | 49.9 | 180 | 13.5 | 487 | 36.4 | 670 | 60.1 | 491 | 36.7 | 179 | 13.4 |
| 20 & 21 years old | 1,323 | 342 | 25.9 | 14 | 1.0 | 328 | 24.8 | 981 | 74.1 | 765 | 57.8 | 216 | 16.3 |
| 22 - 24 years old | 2,214 | 342 | 16.4 | 7 | 0.3 | 334 | 15.1 | 1,872 | 84.6 | 1,570 | 70.9 | 302 | 13.7 |
| 25 - 29 years old | 3,724 | 249 | 6.7 | 9 | 0.2 | 240 | 6.4 | 3,475 | 93.3 | 2,871 | 77.1 | 604 | 16.2 |
| 30 - 34 years old | 3,907 | 185 | 4.7 | 12 | 0.3 | 173 | 4.4 | 3,722 | 95.3 | 3,234 | 82.8 | 488 | 12.5 |

[1] Includes nursery school, kindergarten, and grades 1 to 12.

Source: U.S.Department of Commerce, Bureau of the Census

## TABLE 147. ENROLLMENT STATUS FOR PERSONS 3 TO 34 YEARS OLD BY RESIDENCE, AGE, AND RACE: OCTOBER 1986 (BLACK)

(Numbers in thousands. Civilian noninstitutional population. For meaning of symbols, see text)

| | | Enrolled in school | | | | | | Not enrolled in school | | | | | |
|---|---|---|---|---|---|---|---|---|---|---|---|---|---|
| | | Total | | Below college level[1] | | In college | | Total | | High school graduate | | Not high school graduate | |
| Age, residence, and race | Population | Number | Percent | Number | Percent | Number | Percent | Number | Percent | Number | Percent | Number | Percent |
| **Black** | | | | | | | | | | | | | |
| Metropolitan | | | | | | | | | | | | | |
| Total | 13,629 | 6,873 | 50.4 | 6,894 | 43.2 | 980 | 7.2 | 6,755 | 49.6 | 4,875 | 35.8 | 1,880 | 13.8 |
| Inside central city | 9,724 | 4,847 | 49.8 | 4,155 | 42.7 | 692 | 7.1 | 4,878 | 50.2 | 3,424 | 35.2 | 1,453 | 14.9 |
| 3 & 4 years old | 628 | 243 | 38.7 | 243 | 38.7 | - | - | 385 | 61.3 | - | - | 385 | 61.3 |
| 5 & 6 years old | 670 | 640 | 95.5 | 640 | 95.5 | - | - | 30 | 4.5 | - | - | 30 | 4.5 |
| 7 - 9 years old | 867 | 864 | 99.6 | 864 | 99.6 | - | - | 3 | 0.4 | - | - | 3 | 0.4 |
| 10 - 13 years old | 1,117 | 1,108 | 99.1 | 1,108 | 99.1 | - | - | 10 | 0.9 | - | - | 10 | 0.9 |
| 14 & 15 years old | 621 | 598 | 96.3 | 598 | 96.3 | - | - | 23 | 3.7 | - | - | 23 | 3.7 |
| 16 & 17 years old | 595 | 544 | 91.5 | 536 | 90.2 | 8 | 1.3 | 51 | 8.5 | 19 | 3.2 | 31 | 5.3 |
| 18 & 19 years old | 614 | 281 | 45.7 | 123 | 20.0 | 158 | 25.7 | 334 | 54.3 | 242 | 39.4 | 92 | 14.9 |
| 20 & 21 years old | 636 | 175 | 27.5 | 23 | 3.6 | 152 | 23.9 | 462 | 72.5 | 339 | 53.2 | 123 | 19.3 |
| 22 - 24 years old | 1,007 | 193 | 19.1 | 4 | 0.4 | 189 | 18.7 | 815 | 80.9 | 635 | 63.1 | 180 | 17.8 |
| 25 - 29 years old | 1,574 | 116 | 7.3 | 12 | 0.8 | 104 | 6.6 | 1,459 | 92.7 | 1,161 | 73.8 | 297 | 18.9 |
| 30 - 34 years old | 1,395 | 88 | 6.3 | 5 | 0.4 | 82 | 5.9 | 1,307 | 93.7 | 1,028 | 73.7 | 280 | 20.1 |
| Outside central city | 3,904 | 2,027 | 51.9 | 1,739 | 44.5 | 288 | 7.4 | 1,878 | 48.1 | 1,451 | 37.2 | 427 | 10.9 |
| 3 & 4 years old | 254 | 112 | 44.3 | 112 | 44.3 | - | - | 141 | 55.7 | - | - | 141 | 55.7 |
| 5 & 6 years old | 264 | 246 | 93.1 | 246 | 93.1 | - | - | 18 | 6.9 | - | - | 18 | 6.9 |
| 7 - 9 years old | 362 | 362 | 100.0 | 362 | 100.0 | - | - | - | - | - | - | - | - |
| 10 - 13 years old | 458 | 453 | 98.9 | 453 | 98.9 | - | - | 5 | 1.1 | - | - | 5 | 1.1 |
| 14 & 15 years old | 268 | 263 | 98.1 | 261 | 97.4 | 2 | 0.7 | 5 | 1.9 | - | - | 5 | 1.9 |
| 16 & 17 years old | 270 | 257 | 95.2 | 248 | 91.9 | 9 | 3.3 | 13 | 4.8 | 4 | 1.4 | 9 | 3.4 |
| 18 & 19 years old | 269 | 143 | 53.1 | 53 | 19.9 | 90 | 33.2 | 126 | 46.9 | 93 | 34.6 | 33 | 12.3 |
| 20 & 21 years old | 213 | 57 | 26.6 | 2 | 1.0 | 55 | 25.6 | 156 | 73.4 | 124 | 58.0 | 33 | 15.3 |
| 22 - 24 years old | 296 | 38 | 12.8 | - | - | 38 | 12.8 | 258 | 87.2 | 219 | 73.7 | 40 | 13.4 |
| 25 - 29 years old | 636 | 56 | 8.8 | 1 | 0.2 | 55 | 8.6 | 580 | 91.2 | 516 | 81.1 | 64 | 10.1 |
| 30 - 34 years old | 615 | 40 | 6.5 | - | - | 40 | 6.5 | 574 | 93.5 | 496 | 80.7 | 79 | 12.8 |
| Nonmetropolitan | | | | | | | | | | | | | |
| Total | 3,123 | 1,683 | 53.9 | 1,524 | 48.8 | 158 | 5.1 | 1,441 | 46.1 | 886 | 28.4 | 555 | 17.8 |
| 3 & 4 years old | 194 | 56 | 28.9 | 56 | 28.9 | - | - | 138 | 71.1 | - | - | 138 | 71.1 |
| 5 & 6 years old | 222 | 215 | 96.7 | 215 | 96.7 | - | - | 7 | 3.3 | - | - | 7 | 3.3 |
| 7 - 9 years old | 322 | 322 | 100.0 | 322 | 100.0 | - | - | - | - | - | - | - | - |
| 10 - 13 years old | 461 | 455 | 98.8 | 455 | 98.8 | - | - | 6 | 1.2 | - | - | 6 | 1.2 |
| 14 & 15 years old | 228 | 218 | 95.7 | 218 | 95.7 | - | - | 10 | 4.3 | - | - | 10 | 4.3 |
| 16 & 17 years old | 225 | 215 | 95.2 | 214 | 94.8 | 1 | 0.4 | 11 | 4.8 | - | - | 11 | 4.8 |
| 18 & 19 years old | 164 | 94 | 57.4 | 35 | 21.2 | 59 | 36.2 | 70 | 42.6 | 38 | 23.3 | 32 | 19.3 |
| 20 & 21 years old | 195 | 37 | 18.9 | 4 | 2.1 | 33 | 16.8 | 158 | 81.1 | 124 | 63.9 | 33 | 17.2 |
| 22 - 24 years old | 269 | 31 | 11.4 | 1 | 0.5 | 29 | 11.0 | 238 | 88.6 | 186 | 68.9 | 53 | 19.6 |
| 25 - 29 years old | 431 | 26 | 5.9 | 4 | 1.0 | 21 | 5.0 | 406 | 94.1 | 286 | 66.3 | 120 | 27.8 |
| 30 - 34 years old | 412 | 15 | 3.6 | - | - | 15 | 3.6 | 398 | 96.4 | 252 | 61.0 | 146 | 35.4 |

1 Includes nursery school, kindergarten, and grades 1 to 12.

Source: U.S.Department of Commerce, Bureau of the Census

## TABLE 148. ENROLLMENT STATUS IN 1985 FOR PERSONS 14 TO 24 YEARS OLD BY EDUCATIONAL ATTAINMENT, AGE, AND RACE: OCTOBER 1986

(Numbers in thousands. Civilian noninstitutional population.)

| | | Not enrolled October 1986 | | | Enrolled in college, October 1986 | | |
|---|---|---|---|---|---|---|---|
| Age, years of school completed, and race | Population | Enrolled, October 1985 | Not enrolled, October 1985 | Enrolled, October 1986 | Enrolled, October 1985 | Not enrolled, October 1985 | Enrolled below college, October 1986 |
| **White** | | | | | | | |
| Both sexes | 33,886 | 3,271 | 12,357 | 18,257 | 5,595 | 831 | 11,831 |
| 14 and 15 years old | 5,806 | 86 | 43 | 5,677 | 4 | 5 | 5,668 |
| 16 and 17 years old | 6,072 | 293 | 192 | 5,586 | 170 | 8 | 5,408 |
| 18 and 19 years old | 5,825 | 1,276 | 1,357 | 3,192 | 2,330 | 193 | 669 |
| 20 and 21 years old | 6,090 | 632 | 3,415 | 2,043 | 1,771 | 217 | 55 |
| 22 to 24 years old | 10,093 | 984 | 7,350 | 1,759 | 1,320 | 407 | 32 |
| Years of school completed: | | | | | | | |
| Elementary, 8 years or less | 4,520 | 167 | 830 | 3,523 | - | - | 3,523 |
| High school: | | | | | | | |
| 1 year | 3,664 | 135 | 616 | 2,913 | - | - | 2,913 |
| 2 years | 3,651 | 96 | 782 | 2,774 | - | - | 2,774 |
| 3 years | 3,493 | 137 | 734 | 2,622 | - | - | 2,622 |
| 4 years | 10,361 | 1,442 | 6,854 | 2,065 | 1,622 | 443 | |
| College: | | | | | | | |
| 1 year | 2,743 | 300 | 808 | 1,635 | 1,490 | 145 | - |
| 2 years | 2,306 | 340 | 767 | 1,198 | 1,111 | 87 | - |
| 3 years | 1,227 | 98 | 131 | 998 | 924 | 74 | - |
| 4 years | 1,658 | 490 | 787 | 381 | 314 | 67 | - |
| 5 years or more | 263 | 67 | 49 | 147 | 133 | 14 | - |
| **Black** | | | | | | | |
| Both sexes | 5,870 | 608 | 2,122 | 3,141 | 712 | 109 | 2,320 |
| 14 and 15 years old | 1,117 | 28 | 10 | 1,079 | 2 | - | 1,077 |
| 16 and 17 years old | 1,090 | 50 | 24 | 1,015 | 14 | 3 | 898 |
| 18 and 19 years old | 1,048 | 270 | 260 | 517 | 291 | 15 | 211 |
| 20 and 21 years old | 1,044 | 133 | 643 | 268 | 199 | 40 | 29 |
| 22 to 24 years old | 1,573 | 127 | 1,184 | 262 | 206 | 51 | 5 |
| Years of school completed: | | | | | | | |
| Elementary, 8 years or less | 861 | 38 | 98 | 725 | - | - | 725 |
| High school: | | | | | | | |
| 1 year | 734 | 19 | 145 | 570 | - | - | 570 |
| 2 years | 678 | 21 | 147 | 510 | - | - | 510 |
| 3 years | 753 | 41 | 198 | 514 | - | - | 514 |
| 4 years | 1,766 | 311 | 1,186 | 270 | 206 | 64 | - |
| College: | | | | | | | |
| 1 year | 460 | 76 | 137 | 246 | 226 | 20- | |
| 2 years | 319 | 51 | 117 | 161 | 140 | 11 | - |
| 3 years | 168 | 21 | 45 | 102 | 94 | 8 | - |
| 4 years | 112 | 26 | 49 | 36 | 34 | 2 | - |
| 5 years or more | 19 | 4 | - | 15 | 12 | 3 | - |

Source: U.S.Department of Commerce, Bureau of the Census

## TABLE 149. YEAR OF HIGH SCHOOL GRADUATION FOR PERSONS 16 TO 34 YEARS OLD BY EDUCATIONAL ATTAINMENT, ENROLLMENT STATUS, AND RACE: OCTOBER 1986

(Numbers in thousands. Civilian noninstitutional population.)

| | Number | | | | | | | Percent distribution | | | | | | |
|---|---|---|---|---|---|---|---|---|---|---|---|---|---|---|
| | Year of high school graduation | | | | | | | Year of high school graduation | | | | | | |
| | | | | | 1981 or earlier | | | | | | | 1981 or earlier | | |
| Enrollment status, year of college, years of school completed, and race | Total | 1986 | 1983 to 1985 | 1982 | Under 26 years old | 26 to 28 years old | 29 to 34 years old | Total | 1986 | 1983 to 1985 | 1982 | Under 26 years old | 26 to 28 years old | 29 to 34 years old |
| **White** | | | | | | | | | | | | | | |
| Both sexes | 49,515 | 2,342 | 7,787 | 3,069 | 8,712 | 9,367 | 18,239 | 100.0 | 100.0 | 100.0 | 100.0 | 100.0 | 100.0 | 100.0 |
| Enrolled in college | 8,934 | 1,300 | 3,331 | 886 | 1,294 | 933 | 1,190 | 18.0 | 55.5 | 42.8 | 28.9 | 14.9 | 10.0 | 6.5 |
| First year | 2,474 | 1,284 | 562 | 82 | 167 | 168 | 210 | 5.0 | 54.8 | 7.2 | 2.7 | 1.9 | 1.8 | 1.2 |
| Second year | 2,149 | 11 | 1,474 | 126 | 178 | 165 | 195 | 4.3 | 0.5 | 18.9 | 4.1 | 2.0 | 1.8 | 1.1 |
| Third year | 1,534 | 2 | 840 | 178 | 208 | 125 | 181 | 3.1 | 0.1 | 10.8 | 5.8 | 2.4 | 1.3 | 1.0 |
| Fourth year | 1,348 | 3 | 442 | 332 | 272 | 138 | 161 | 2.7 | 0.1 | 5.7 | 10.8 | 3.1 | 1.4 | 0.9 |
| Fifth year | 743 | - | 12 | 157 | 256 | 141 | 177 | 1.5 | - | 0.2 | 5.1 | 2.9 | 1.5 | 1.0 |
| Sixth year or higher | 686 | - | 1 | 10 | 212 | 197 | 266 | 1.4 | - | - | 0.3 | 2.4 | 2.1 | 1.5 |
| Not enrolled | 40,581 | 1,042 | 4,454 | 2,183 | 7,418 | 8,434 | 17,049 | 82.0 | 44.5 | 57.2 | 71.1 | 85.1 | 90.0 | 93.5 |
| Years of school completed: | | | | | | | | | | | | | | |
| High school, 4 yrs. | 22,607 | 1,025 | 3,551 | 1,330 | 4,107 | 4,547 | 8,046 | 45.7 | 43.8 | 45.6 | 43.3 | 47.1 | 48.5 | 44.1 |
| College: | | | | | | | | | | | | | | |
| 1 year | 3,471 | 7 | 446 | 252 | 635 | 629 | 1,501 | 7.0 | 0.3 | 5.7 | 8.2 | 7.3 | 6.7 | 8.2 |
| 2 years | 4,260 | 3 | 349 | 251 | 825 | 869 | 1,963 | 8.6 | 0.1 | 4.5 | 8.2 | 9.5 | 9.3 | 10.8 |
| 3 years | 1,249 | - | 42 | 69 | 221 | 319 | 599 | 2.5 | - | 0.5 | 2.2 | 2.5 | 3.4 | 3.3 |
| 4 years | 6,423 | 7 | 58 | 270 | 1,412 | 1,528 | 3,147 | 13.0 | 0.3 | 0.7 | 8.8 | 16.2 | 16.3 | 17.3 |
| 5 years or more | 2,571 | - | 7 | 11 | 219 | 542 | 1,793 | 5.2 | - | 0.1 | 0.3 | 2.5 | 5.8 | 9.8 |
| **Black** | | | | | | | | | | | | | | |
| Both sexes | 6,897 | 390 | 1,256 | 441 | 1,242 | 1,253 | 2,314 | 100.0 | 100.0 | 100.0 | 100.0 | 100.0 | 100.0 | 100.0 |
| Enrolled in college | 1,136 | 141 | 425 | 113 | 182 | 113 | 162 | 16.5 | 36.2 | 33.8 | 25.6 | 14.7 | 9.0 | 7.0 |
| First year | 345 | 138 | 114 | 12 | 22 | 33 | 27 | 5.0 | 35.4 | 9.1 | 2.7 | 1.8 | 2.6 | 1.2 |
| Second year | 301 | 3 | 197 | 20 | 39 | 15 | 26 | 4.4 | 0.8 | 15.7 | 4.5 | 3.1 | 1.2 | 1.1 |
| Third year | 193 | - | 88 | 24 | 32 | 17 | 32 | 2.8 | - | 7.0 | 5.4 | 2.6 | 1.4 | 1.4 |
| Fourth year | 190 | - | 24 | 54 | 47 | 25 | 39 | 2.8 | - | 1.9 | 12.2 | 3.8 | 2.0 | 1.7 |
| Fifth year | 46 | - | 3 | - | 28 | 8 | 8 | 0.7 | - | 0.2 | - | 2.3 | 0.6 | 0.3 |
| Sixth year or higher | 61 | - | - | 2 | 14 | 15 | 30 | 0.9 | - | - | 0.5 | 1.1 | 1.2 | 1.3 |
| Not enrolled | 5,761 | 249 | 830 | 328 | 1,060 | 1,141 | 2,152 | 83.5 | 63.8 | 66.1 | 74.4 | 85.3 | 91.1 | 93.0 |
| Years of school completed: | | | | | | | | | | | | | | |
| High school, 4 yrs | 3,632 | 236 | 645 | 220 | 667 | 693 | 1,171 | 52.7 | 60.5 | 51.4 | 49.9 | 53.7 | 55.3 | 60.6 |
| College: | | | | | | | | | | | | | | |
| 1 year | 556 | 8 | 117 | 48 | 92 | 100 | 192 | 8.1 | 2.1 | 9.3 | 10.9 | 7.4 | 8.0 | 8.3 |
| 2 years | 689 | 5 | 50 | 37 | 136 | 141 | 319 | 10.0 | 1.3 | 4.0 | 8.4 | 11.0 | 11.3 | 13.8 |
| 3 years | 257 | - | 11 | 9 | 71 | 51 | 114 | 3.7 | - | 0.9 | 2.0 | 5.7 | 4.1 | 4.9 |
| 4 years | 515 | - | 7 | 14 | 87 | 126 | 281 | 7.5 | - | 0.6 | 3.2 | 7.0 | 10.1 | 12.1 |
| 5 years or more | 112 | - | - | - | 7 | 30 | 75 | 1.6 | - | - | - | 0.6 | 2.4 | 3.2 |

Source: U.S.Department of Commerce, Bureau of the Census

## TABLE 150. HIGH SCHOOL COMPLETION RATES AND ENROLLED-IN-COLLEGE PARTICIPATION RATES FOR 18-TO-24-YEAR-OLD HIGH SCHOOL GRADUATES IN INSTITUTIONS OF HIGHER EDUCATION BY RACE/ETHNICITY, 1976 TO 1986

| | Total Population | High school Graduates | High school Completion rate[a] (Percentages) | Enrolled in College[b] | Enrolled in College Participation rate (Percentages) |
|---|---|---|---|---|---|
| | (numbers in thousands) | | | | |
| Total Populatlon | | | | | |
| 1976 | 26,919 | 21,677 | 80.5 | 7,181 | 33.1 |
| 1977 | 27,331 | 22,008 | 80.5 | 7,142 | 32.5 |
| 1978 | 27,647 | 22,309 | 80.7 | 6,995 | 31.4 |
| 1979 | 27,974 | 22,421 | 80.1 | 6,991 | 31.2 |
| 1980 | 28,130 | 22,745 | 80.8 | 7,226 | 31.8 |
| 1981 | 28,965 | 23,343 | 80.6 | 7,575 | 32.5 |
| 1982 | 28,846 | 23,291 | 80.7 | 7,678 | 33.0 |
| 1983 | 28,580 | 22,988 | 80.4 | 7,477 | 32.5 |
| 1984 | 28,031 | 22,870 | 81.6 | 7,591 | 33.2 |
| 1985 | 27,122 | 22,349 | 82.4 | 7,537 | 33.7 |
| 1986 | 26,512 | 21,766 | 82.1 | 7,397 | 34.0 |
| White | | | | | |
| 1976 | 23,119 | 19,046 | 82.4 | 6,276 | 33.0 |
| 1977 | 23,430 | 19,292 | 82.3 | 6,209 | 32.2 |
| 1978 | 23,650 | 19,526 | 82.6 | 6,077 | 31.1 |
| 1979 | 23,895 | 19,614 | 82.1 | 6,119 | 31.2 |
| 1980 | 23,975 | 19,786 | 82.5 | 6,334 | 32.0 |
| 1981 | 24,486 | 20,123 | 82.2 | 6,548 | 32.5 |
| 1982 | 24,206 | 19,944 | 82.4 | 6,593 | 33.1 |
| 1983 | 23,899 | 19,644 | 82.2 | 6,464 | 32.9 |
| 1984 | 23,347 | 19,374 | 83.0 | 6,526 | 33.7 |
| 1985 | 22,632 | 18,917 | 83.6 | 6,501 | 34.4 |
| 1986 | 22,008 | 18,280 | 83.1 | 6,239 | 34.1 |
| Black | | | | | |
| 1976 | 3,316 | 2,238 | 67.5 | 748 | 33.4 |
| 1977 | 3,387 | 2,287 | 67.5 | 722 | 31.6 |
| 1978 | 3,451 | 2,340 | 67.8 | 695 | 29.7 |
| 1979 | 3,511 | 2,356 | 67.1 | 696 | 29.5 |
| 1980 | 3,555 | 2,480 | 69.8 | 688 | 27.7 |
| 1981 | 3,779 | 2,680 | 70.9 | 749 | 27.9 |
| 1982 | 3,872 | 2,743 | 70.8 | 767 | 28.0 |
| 1983 | 3,865 | 2,741 | 70.9 | 742 | 27.1 |
| 1984 | 3,863 | 2,885 | 74.7 | 786 | 27.2 |
| 1985 | 3,716 | 2,809 | 75.6 | 734 | 26.1 |
| 1986 | 3,665 | 2,801 | 76.4 | 801 | 28.6 |
| Hispanic[c] | | | | | |
| 1976 | 1,551 | 862 | 55.6 | 309 | 35.8 |
| 1977 | 1,609 | 880 | 54.7 | 277 | 31.5 |
| 1978 | 1,672 | 935 | 55.9 | 254 | 27.2 |
| 1979 | 1,754 | 968 | 55.2 | 292 | 30.2 |
| 1980 | 1,963 | 1,054 | 53.7 | 315 | 29.9 |
| 1981 | 2,052 | 1,144 | 55.8 | 342 | 29.9 |
| 1982 | 2,000 | 1,153 | 57.7 | 337 | 29 2 |
| 1983 | 2,025 | 1,110 | 54.8 | 349 | 31 4 |
| 1984 | 2,017 | 1,212 | 60.0 | 362 | 29.9 |
| 1985 | 2,223 | 1,396 | 62.8 | 375 | 26.9 |
| 1986 | 2,513 | 1,506 | 59.9 | 443 | 29.4 |

(a) The number of high school graduates was calculated by adding the number of individuals in this age group enrolled in college as of October of that year and the number of high school graduates not enrolled in college; these rates include individuals who enrolled in college without receiving a high school diploma or a GED. Several states do not require entering junior college students to have a diploma or GED. Therefore, these high school completion rates wlll be slightly higher than figures that do not include this relatively small population.

(b) Totals differ from those shown in other tables. These figures came from sample surveys of households rather than surveys of institutions of higher education. The Current Population Survey samples are derived from the decennial census of the U.S. population.

(c) Hispanics may be of any race.

Source: U.S. Department of Commerce, Bureau of the Census, *Current Population Peports*, Series P-20, various years.

Source: U.S.Department of Commerce, Bureau of the Census

## TABLE 151. TOTAL ENROLLMENT IN INSTITUTIONS OF HIGHER EDUCATION BY TYPE OF INSTITUTION AND RACE/ETHNICITY OF STUDENT BIENNIALLY, FALL 1976 TO FALL 1986[a]

Percentage distribution of total enrollment

| Type of Institution and race /ethnicity of student | 1976 | 1978 | 1980 | 1982 | 1984 | 1986 |
|---|---|---|---|---|---|---|
| All Institutions | 100.0 | 100.0 | 100.0 | 100.0 | 100.0 | 100.0 |
| White, non-Hispanic | 82.6 | 81.9 | 81.4 | 80.7 | 80.2 | 79.3 |
| Total minority | 15.4 | 15.9 | 16.1 | 16.6 | 17.0 | 17.9 |
| Black, non-Hispanic | 9.4 | 9.4 | 9.2 | 8.9 | 8.8 | 8.6 |
| Hispanic | 3.5 | 3.7 | 3.9 | 4.2 | 4.4 | 5.0 |
| Asian | 1.8 | 2.1 | 2.4 | 2.8 | 3.2 | 3.6 |
| American Indian | 0.7 | 0.7 | 0.7 | 0.7 | 0.7 | 0.7 |
| Nonresident alien | 2.0 | 2.3 | 2.5 | 2.7 | 2.7 | 2.7 |
| Four-year Institutions | 64.7 | 64.1 | 62.6 | 61.7 | 63.0 | 62.6 |
| White, non-Hispanic | 54.6 | 53.7 | 51.9 | 50.9 | 51.5 | 50.7 |
| Total minority | 8.5 | 8.7 | 8.7 | 8.7 | 9.2 | 9.6 |
| Black, non-Hispanic | 5.5 | 5.4 | 5.2 | 4.9 | 5.0 | 4.9 |
| Hispanic | 1.6 | 1.7 | 1.8 | 1.8 | 2.0 | 2.2 |
| Asian | 1.1 | 2.1 | 1.3 | 1.6 | 1.8 | 2.1 |
| American Indian | 0.3 | 0.3 | 0.3 | 0.3 | 0.3 | 0.3 |
| Nonresident alien | 1.6 | 1.8 | 2.0 | 2.2 | 2.3 | 2.3 |
| Two-year Institutions | 35.3 | 35.9 | 37.4 | 38.3 | 37.0 | 37.4 |
| White, non-Hispanic | 28.0 | 28.2 | 29.4 | 29.8 | 28.7 | 28.6 |
| Total minority | 6.9 | 7.2 | 7.4 | 8.0 | 7.9 | 8.4 |
| Black, non-Hispanic | 3.9 | 3.9 | 3.9 | 3.9 | 3.7 | 3.7 |
| Hispanic | 1.9 | 2.0 | 2.1 | 2.3 | 2.4 | 2.8 |
| Asian | 0.7 | 0.9 | 1.0 | 1.3 | 1.4 | 1.5 |
| American Indian | 0.4 | 0.4 | 0.4 | 0.4 | 0.4 | 0.4 |
| Nonresident alien | 0.4 | 0.5 | 0.5 | 0.5 | 0.4 | 0.4 |

[a] Includes estimates for nonresponse and underreporting. Details may not add to total because of rounding.
Source: U.S. Department of Education, Center for Education Statistics, *Trends in Minority Enrollment in Higher Education, Fall 1976-Fall 1986* (Washington D.C.: Office of Education Research and Improvement, April 1988

Source: Minorities in Higher Education, Status Report 1988s

## TABLE 152. UNDERGRADUATE ENROLLMENT IN HIGHER EDUCATION BY RACE/ETHNICITY BIENNIALLY, FALL 1976 TO FALL 1986[a]

(numbers in thousands)

| Race/Ethnicity of Student | 1976 | 1978 | 1980 | 1982 | 1984 | 1986 | Percentage Change 1984-1986 |
|---|---|---|---|---|---|---|---|
| Total | 9,520 | 9,757 | 10,560 | 10,875 | 10,610 | 10,797 | 1.8 |
| White, non-Hispanic | 7,827 | 7,946 | 8,556 | 8,749 | 8,484 | 8,552 | 0.8 |
| Total minority | 1,550 | 1,642 | 1,797 | 1,907 | 1,911 | 2,041 | 6.8 |
| Black, non-Hispanic | 950 | 975 | 1,028 | 1,028 | 995 | 995 | 0.0 |
| Hispanic | 357 | 388 | 438 | 485 | 495 | 569 | 14.9 |
| Asian | 173 | 206 | 253 | 313 | 343 | 394 | 14.9 |
| American Indian | 70 | 72 | 79 | 82 | 78 | 84 | 7.7 |
| Nonresident alien | 142 | 169 | 208 | 220 | 216 | 204 | -5.6 |
| **Race/Ethnicity of Student** | **1976** | **1978** | **1980** | **1982** | **1984** | **1986** | |
| | | | (percent distribution) | | | | |
| White, non-Hispanic | 82.2 | 81.4 | 81.0 | 80.5 | 80.0 | 79.2 | |
| Total minority | 16.3 | 16.8 | 17.0 | 17.5 | 18.0 | 18.9 | |
| Black, non-Hispanic | 10.0 | 10.0 | 9.7 | 9.4 | 9.4 | 9.2 | |
| Hispanic | 3.7 | 4.0 | 4.1 | 4.5 | 4.7 | 5.3 | |
| Asian | 1.8 | 2.1 | 2.4 | 2.9 | 3.2 | 3.6 | |
| American Indian | 0.7 | 0.7 | 0.7 | 0.8 | 0.7 | 0.8 | |
| Nonresident alien | 1.5 | 1.7 | 2.0 | 2.0 | 2.0 | 1.9 | |

(a) Includes estimates for nonresponse and underreporting. Details may not add to total because of rounding.
Source: U.S. Department of Education, Center for Education Statistics, *Trends in Minority Enrollment in Higher Education, Fall 1976-Fall 1986* (Washington, D.C.: Office of Educational Research and Improvement, April 1988).

Source: Minorities in Higher Education, Status Report 1988

## TABLE 153. ENROLLMENT IN HISTORICALLY BLACK COLLEGES AND UNIVERSITIES (HBCUs) BY RACE/ETHNICITY, FALL 1976 TO FALL 1987

| Race/Ethnicity | 1976 | 1980 | 1982 | 1984 | 1986 | 1987 | Percentage 1986-1987 | Percentage 1976-1987 |
|---|---|---|---|---|---|---|---|---|
| Number of HBCUs | 105 | 102 | 100 | 104 | 104 | 100 | | |
| Total | 212,120 | 222,220 | 216,570 | 216,050 | 213,093 | 217,367 | 2.0 | 2.5 |
| Black, non-Hispanic | 185,820 | 185,780 | 177,000 | 175,110 | 176,596 | 182,019 | 3.1 | -2.0 |
| White, non-Hispanic | 18,390 | 21,480 | 23,040 | 23,450 | 22,651 | 23,225 | 2.5 | 26.3 |
| Asian | 610 | 1,340 | 1,050 | 1,350 | 1,237 | 1,187 | -4.0 | 94.6 |
| Hispanic | 460 | 1,030 | 1,070 | 1,560 | 1,485 | 1,588 | 6.9 | 245.2 |
| American Indian | 180 | 400 | 570 | 240 | 552 | 519 | -6.0 | 187.2 |
| Nonresident alien | 6,660 | 12,200 | 13,840 | 14,340 | 10,572 | 8,829 | -16.5 | 32.6 |

Note: Details may not add to total because of rounding.
Source: Hill, Susan T., *The Traditionally Black Institutions of Higher Education, 1860 to 1982* (Washington, D.C.: Government Printing Office, 1984); National Association for Equal Opportunity Research Institute, staff analysis of the U.S. Department of Education, Office of Civil Rights unpublished data, fall 1984,1986, and 1987.

Source: Minorities in Higher Education, Status Report 1988

## TABLE 154. GRADUATE ENROLLMENT IN HIGHER EDUCATION BY RACE/ETHNICITY BIENNIALLY, FALL 1976 TO FALL 1986[a]

(numbers in thousands)

| Race/Ethnicity of Student | 1976 | 1978 | 1980 | 1982 | 1984 | 1986 | Percent Change 1984-1986 |
|---|---|---|---|---|---|---|---|
| Total | 1,221 | 1,219 | 1,250 | 1,235 | 1,344 | 1,434 | 6.8 |
| White, non-Hispanic | 1,030 | 1,019 | 1,030 | 1,002 | 1,087 | 1,132 | 4.1 |
| Total minority | 119 | 120 | 125 | 123 | 141 | 166 | 17.7 |
| Black, non-Hispanic | 72 | 68 | 66 | 61 | 67 | 72 | 7.5 |
| Hispanic | 22 | 24 | 27 | 27 | 32 | 46 | 43.8 |
| Asian | 21 | 24 | 28 | 30 | 37 | 43 | 16.2 |
| American Indian | 4 | 4 | 4 | 5 | 5 | 5 | 0.0 |
| Nonresident alien | 73 | 80 | 94 | 108 | 115 | 136 | 18.3 |

Percentage Distribution

| Race/Ethnicity of Student | 1976 | 1978 | 1980 | 1982 | 1984 | 1986 |
|---|---|---|---|---|---|---|
| Total | 100.0 | 100.0 | 100.0 | 100.0 | 100.0 | 100.0 |
| White, non-Hispanic | 84.3 | 83.6 | 82.4 | 81.1 | 80.9 | 78.9 |
| Total minority | 9.8 | 9.8 | 10.0 | 10.0 | 10.5 | 11.6 |
| Black, non-Hispanic | 5.9 | 5.6 | 5.3 | 4.9 | 5.0 | 5.0 |
| Hispanic | 1.8 | 1.9 | 2.2 | 2.2 | 2.4 | 3.2 |
| Asian | 1.7 | 2.0 | 2.2 | 2.5 | 2.8 | 3.0 |
| American Indian | 0.4 | 0.4 | 0.4 | 0.4 | 0.4 | 0.4 |
| Nonresident alien | 6.0 | 6.6 | 7.5 | 8.8 | 8.6 | 9.5 |

[A] Includes estimates for nonresponse and underreporting. Details may not add to total because of rounding.
Source: U.S. Department of Education, Center for Education Statistics, *Trends in Minority Enrollment in Higher Education, Fall 1976-Fall 1986* (Washington, D.C.: Office of Educational Research and Improvement, April 1988).

Source: U.S.Department of Commerce, Bureau of the Census

## TABLE 155. PROFESSIONAL SCHOOL ENROLLMENT IN HIGHER EDUCATION BY RACE/ETHNICITY BIENNIALLY, FALL 1976 TO FALL 1986[(a)]

(numbers in thousands)

| Race/Ethnicity of Student | 1976 | 1978 | 1980 | 1982 | 1984 | 1986 | Percentage Change 1984-1986 |
|---|---|---|---|---|---|---|---|
| Total | 244 | 255 | 277 | 278 | 278 | 270 | -2.9 |
| White, non-Hispanic | 220 | 229 | 248 | 246 | 243 | 230 | -5.3 |
| Total minority | 21 | 22 | 26 | 29 | 32 | 36 | 12.5 |
| Black, non-Hispanic | 11 | 11 | 13 | 13 | 13 | 14 | 7.7 |
| Hispanic | 5 | 5 | 7 | 7 | 8 | 9 | 12.5 |
| Asian | 4 | 5 | 6 | 8 | 9 | 11 | 22.2 |
| American Indian | 1 | 1 | 1 | 1 | 1 | 1 | 0.0 |
| Nonresident alien | 3 | 3 | 3 | 3 | 3 | 4 | 33.3 |

Percentage Distribution

| Race/Ethnicity of Student | 1976 | 1978 | 1980 | 1982 | 1984 | 1986 |
|---|---|---|---|---|---|---|
| Total | 100.0 | 100.0 | 100.0 | 100.0 | 100.0 | 100.0 |
| White, non-Hispanic | 90.1 | 89.8 | 89.5 | 88.5 | 87.4 | 85.2 |
| Total minority | 8.6 | 8.6 | 9.5 | 10.4 | 11.4 | 13.2 |
| Black, non-Hispanic | 4.6 | 4.3 | 4.6 | 4.7 | 4.8 | 5.2 |
| Hispanic | 1.9 | 2.0 | 2.4 | 2.5 | 2.9 | 3.4 |
| Asian | 1.7 | 2.0 | 2.2 | 2.9 | 3.4 | 4.2 |
| American Indian | 0.5 | 0.4 | 0.3 | 0.4 | 0.4 | 0.4 |
| Nonresident alien | 1.3 | 1.2 | 1.0 | 1.1 | 1.2 | 1.5 |

(a) Includes estimates for nonresponse and underreporting. Details may not add to total because of rounding.

Source: U.S. Department of Education, Center for Education Statistics, *Trends in Minority Enrollment in Higher Education, Fall 1976-Fall 1986* (Washington D.C.: Office of Educational Research and Improvement, April 1988.)

Source: U.S.Department of Commerce, Bureau of the Census

## TABLE 156. TENURED AND NON-TENURED FACULTY IN HIGHER EDUCATION BY RACE/ETHNICITY 1975, 1983, AND 1985

| Race/Ethnicity | 1975 | | 1983 | | 1985 | | Percentage Change | | |
|---|---|---|---|---|---|---|---|---|---|
| | Number | Percent | Number | Percent | Number | Percent | 1975-1983 | 1983-1985 | 1975-1985 |
| Total | 363,101 | 100.0 | 365,739 | 100.0 | 366,666 | 100.0 | 0.7 | 0.3 | 1.0 |
| Tenured | 233,498 | 64.3 | 258,136 | 70.6 | 260,541 | 71.1 | 10.6 | 0.9 | 11.6 |
| Non-tenured | 129,603 | 35.7 | 107,603 | 29.4 | 106,125 | 28.9 | -17.0 | -1.4 | -18.1 |
| White | 335,401 | 100.0 | 332,906 | 100.0 | 330,403 | 100.0 | -0.7 | -0.8 | -1.5 |
| Tenured | 219,160 | 65.3 | 237,501 | 71.3 | 237,861 | 72.0 | 8.4 | 0.2 | 8.5 |
| Non-tenured | 116,241 | 34.7 | 95,405 | 28.7 | 92,542 | 28.0 | -17.9 | -3.0 | -20.4 |
| Black | 14,740 | 100.0 | 13,954 | 100.0 | 15,036 | 100.0 | -5.3 | 7.8 | 2.0 |
| Tenured | 7,045 | 47.8 | 8,746 | 62.7 | 9,282 | 61.7 | 24.1 | 6.1 | 31.8 |
| Non-tenured | 7,695 | 52.2 | 5,208 | 37.3 | 5,754 | 38.3 | -32.3 | 10.5 | -25.2 |
| Hispanic | 4,831 | 100.0 | 5,714 | 100.0 | 6,011 | 100.0 | 18.3 | 5.2 | 24.4 |
| Tenured | 2,599 | 53.8 | 3,814 | 66.7 | 4,032 | 67.1 | 46.7 | 5.7 | 55.1 |
| Non-tenured | 2,232 | 46.2 | 1,900 | 33.3 | 1,979 | 32.9 | -14.9 | 4.2 | -11.3 |
| Asian | 7,354 | 100.0 | 12,287 | 100.0 | 13,882 | 100.0 | 67.1 | 13.0 | 88.8 |
| Tenured | 4,281 | 58.2 | 7,454 | 60.7 | 8,500 | 61.2 | 74.1 | 14.0 | 98.6 |
| Non-tenured | 3,073 | 41.8 | 4,833 | 39.3 | 5,382 | 38.8 | 57.3 | 11.4 | 75.1 |
| American Indian | 775 | 100.0 | 878 | 100.0 | 1,334 | 100.0 | 13.3 | 51.9 | 72.1 |
| Tenured | 413 | 53.3 | 621 | 70.7 | 866 | 64.9 | 50.4 | 39.5 | 109.7 |
| Non-tenured | 362 | 46.7 | 257 | 29.3 | 468 | 35.1 | -29.0 | 82.1 | 29.3 |

Note: Figures exclude faculty who are in non-tenure earning positions. These figures are therefore less than full-time faculty figures which include faculty in non-tenure earning positions.
Details may not add to total because of rounding.
Source: U.S. Equal Employment Opportunity Commission, "EE0-6 Higher Education Staff Information" surveys, 1975, 1983, and 1985.

Source: Minorities in Higher Education, Status Report 1988

## TABLE 157. FULL-TIME ADMINISTRATORS IN HIGHER EDUCATION BY RACE/ETHNICITY AND SEX 1975, 1983, AND 1985

| Race/Ethnicity and Sex | 1975 Number | 1975 Percent | 1983 Number | 1983 Percent | 1985 Number | 1985 Percent | Percentage Change 1975-1983 | Percentage Change 1983-1985 | Percentage Change 1975-1985 |
|---|---|---|---|---|---|---|---|---|---|
| Total | 96,924 | 100.0 | 117,486 | 100.0 | 124,374 | 100.0 | 21.2 | 5.9 | 28.3 |
| Male | 74,650 | 77.0 | 79,340 | 67.5 | 80,676 | 64.9 | 6.3 | 1.7 | 8.1 |
| Female | 22,274 | 23.0 | 38,146 | 32.5 | 43,698 | 35.1 | 71.3 | 14.6 | 96.2 |
| White | 88,054 | 90.8 | 105,420 | 89.7 | 109,972 | 88.4 | 19.7 | 4.3 | 24.9 |
| Male | 68,551 | 70.7 | 72,126 | 61.4 | 72,204 | 58.1 | 5.2 | 0.1 | 5.3 |
| Female | 19,503 | 20.1 | 33,294 | 28.3 | 37,768 | 30.4 | 70.7 | 13.4 | 93.7 |
| Black | 6,801 | 7.0 | 8,362 | 7.1 | 9,446 | 7.6 | 23.0 | 13.0 | 38.9 |
| Male | 4,566 | 4.7 | 4,727 | 4.0 | 5,203 | 4.2 | 3.5 | 10.1 | 14.0 |
| Female | 2,235 | 2.3 | 3,635 | 3.1 | 4,243 | 3.4 | 62.6 | 16.7 | 89.8 |
| Hispanic | 1,203 | 1.2 | 2,040 | 1.7 | 2,490 | 2.0 | 69.6 | 22.1 | 107.0 |
| Male | 906 | 0.9 | 1,386 | 1.2 | 1,598 | 1.3 | 53.0 | 15.3 | 76.4 |
| Female | 297 | 0.3 | 654 | 0.6 | 892 | 0.7 | 120.2 | 36.4 | 200.3 |
| Asian | 600 | 0.6 | 1,234 | 1.1 | 1,920 | 1.5 | 105.7 | 55.6 | 220.0 |
| Male | 413 | 0.4 | 790 | 0.7 | 1,279 | 1.0 | 91.3 | 61.9 | 209.7 |
| Female | 187 | 0.2 | 444 | 0.4 | 641 | 0.5 | 137.4 | 44.4 | 242.8 |
| American Indian | 266 | 0.3 | 430 | 0.4 | 546 | 0.4 | 61.7 | 27.0 | 105.3 |
| Male | 214 | 0.2 | 311 | 0.3 | 392 | 0.3 | 45.3 | 26.0 | 83.2 |
| Female | 52 | 0.1 | 119 | 0.1 | 154 | 0.1 | 128.8 | 29.4 | 196.2 |

Note: Details may not add to total because of rounding.
Source: U.S. Equal Employment Opportunity Commission, "EE0-6 Higher Education Staff Information" surveys, 1975, 1983, and 1985.

Source: Minorities in Higher Education, Status Report 1988

## TABLE 158. FULL-TIME FACULTY IN HIGHER EDUCATION BY RACE/ETHNICITY AND SEX 1975, 1983, AND 1985

| Race/Ethnicity and Sex | 1975 Number | 1975 Percent | 1983 Number | 1983 Percent | 1985 Number | 1985 Percent | Percentage Change 1975-1983 | Percentage Change 1983-1985 | Percentage Change 1975-1985 |
|---|---|---|---|---|---|---|---|---|---|
| Total | 446,830 | 100.0 | 485,739 | 100.0 | 488.799 | 100.0 | 8.7 | 0.6 | 9.4 |
| Male | 336,362 | 75.3 | 356,579 | 73.4 | 354.213 | 72.5 | 6.0 | -0.7 | 5.3 |
| Female | 110,468 | 24.7 | 129,160 | 26.6 | 134,586 | 27.5 | 16.9 | 4.2 | 21.8 |
| White | 409,947 | 91.7 | 440,505 | 90.7 | 439,767 | 90.0 | 7.5 | -0.2 | 7.3 |
| Male | 312,293 | 69.9 | 326,171 | 67.1 | 320,969 | 65.7 | 4.4 | -1.6 | 2.8 |
| Female | 97,654 | 21.9 | 114,334 | 23.5 | 118,798 | 24.3 | 17.1 | 3.9 | 21.7 |
| Black | 19,746 | 4.4 | 19,571 | 4.0 | 20,283 | 4.1 | -0.9 | 3.6 | 2.7 |
| Male | 10,894 | 2.4 | 10,541 | 2.2 | 11,053 | 2.3 | -3.2 | 4.9 | 1.5 |
| Female | 8,852 | 2.0 | 9,030 | 1.9 | 9,230 | 1.9 | 2.0 | 2.2 | 4.3 |
| Hispanic | 6,323 | 1.4 | 7,456 | 1.5 | 8,087 | 1.7 | 17.9 | 8.5 | 27.9 |
| Male | 4,573 | 1.0 | 5,240 | 1.1 | 5,683 | 1.2 | 14.6 | 8.5 | 24.3 |
| Female | 1,750 | 0.4 | 2,216 | 0.5 | 2,404 | 0.5 | 26.6 | 8.5 | 37.4 |
| Asian | 9,763 | 2.2 | 16,889 | 3.5 | 19,104 | 3.9 | 73.0 | 13.1 | 95.7 |
| Male | 7,830 | 1.8 | 13,677 | 2.8 | 15,323 | 3.1 | 74.7 | 12.0 | 95.7 |
| Female | 1,933 | 0.4 | 3,222 | 0.7 | 3,781 | 0.8 | 66.7 | 17.3 | 95.6 |
| American Indian | 1,051 | 0.2 | 1,308 | 0.3 | 1,558 | 0.3 | 24.5 | 19.1 | 48.2 |
| Male | 772 | 0.2 | 950 | 0.2 | 1,185 | 0.2 | 23.1 | 24.7 | 53.5 |
| Female | 279 | 0.1 | 358 | 0.1 | 373 | 0.1 | 28.3 | 4.2 | 33.7 |

Note: Includes full-time faculty who are in non-tenure earning positions, tenured faculty, and faculty who are non-tenured, but in positions which lead to consideration for tenure.
Details may not add to total because of rounding.
Source: U.S. Equal Employment Opportunity Commission, "EE0-6 Higher Education Staff Information" surveys, 1975, 1983, and 1985.

Source: Minorities in Higher Education, Status Report 1988

# BLACKS IN COLONIAL AND REVOLUTIONARY AMERICA

**The Colonial Period ■ First Settlements ■ New England ■ Slave Codes ■ Early Black Soldiers ■ Divergence of European and American Interests (1763-1770) ■ The Boston Massacre ■ Road to Revolution (1770-1775) ■ The War of Independence (1775-1783) ■ Black Military Service ■ A Chronology of Black Participation in the American Revolution ■ Biographies of Black Patriots**

In 1776, delegates from 13 North American colonies declared themselves independent from the constraints and control of foreign rule and stepped dramatically onto the world stage with one of history's most articulate pronouncements of the right of all to life, liberty, and the pursuit of happiness. With such resolute humane beliefs, one question still now nags at the minds of many; How could people so moved to self-sacrifice and passion on the basis of such "self-evident"— "unalienable"— "truths" sanction the enslavement of fellow human beings.

For an answer, one might look back to ancient Greece, which like many nations since was able in its codes and conscience to reconcile the contradiction between democracy and slavery. For the America of 1776, the answer was over a century and a half in the making, starting in 1607 when a band of 107 settlers who had survived a hazardous four-month sea voyage chose a site 30 miles up the James River and settled in what was to become Jamestown, Virginia. In 1620, the Pilgrims landed in Massachusetts. Both groups, and others that followed, lacked the quantity and quality of manpower to cope with the labor and military demands of their newly founded wilderness settlements and so resorted to the use of black indentured servants. Twenty such servants were landed and pressed into service in Jamestown in 1619 and by 1638, at the latest, a substantial number were brought to Boston.

From these early days of the seventeenth century, the ideals of liberty and equality that were to ennoble the Declaration of Independence and the peculiar institution of slavery that was to trouble many of that Declaration's framers unfolded side by side.

### The Common Goal

Although the early colonies were founded for such different purposes as a refuge for religious rebels (Rhode Island) or the trading outpost of a London stock company (Virginia), the majority of colonists shared a goal. They had come seeking some variety of freedom—be it religious, political, or economic. The Pilgrims were the first of many groups who came in search of religious freedom. The armies of poor who broached American shores were seeking freedom to work their way out of the misery into which Europe's feudal structure had consigned them. Merchants, whose self-interest was soon to mint America's dominant laissez-faire values, were to carry the flag of freedom into enterprise and trade.

Not all the passengers crossing the Atlantic, of course, traveled for idealistic purposes. Many came to impose Old World privileges on the new territory, others thought solely of accumulating wealth without regard for human values.

And the black man was brought in chains.

## First Settlements

As the mother of the colonies, Virginia became a model for later settlements (a role subsequently played by Massachusetts in the North) giving many local events far-reaching importance. Self-government took its first steps here. Although Jamestown began as a commercial venture equipped and financed by a company of London merchants, and which was eventually taken over by the authoritarian Stuart king, the settlers acquired a large measure of control over their local affairs through an annually chosen representative assembly, the House of Burgesses, which first met in July 1619.

These early rulers of Virginia were not eager to enslave the black, and when in the 1640's they finally decided to do so, they wished to restrict slavery's use and growth. There were a variety of reasons for this, but fear of the bravery and military prowess of blacks was among the foremost. Thus the first black born in the colonies, William Tucker, owned a birthright of freedom shared by all settlers. By 1650 there were only some 300 blacks in all of Virginia.

Ironically, it was the very competence and strength of blacks that were to doom them, for Virginia suffered serious manpower shortages that were exacerbated by expirations of indentured servant contracts. Once free of legal bonds to work for others, these people, both white and black, sought the promises of prosperity and freedom that were developing in the colonies.

Attempts to enslave the Indians failed, largely due to their existence on the continent as unified communities able to fight for their freedom, avoid capture, or escape. The black man, who could be brought in chains from distant lands and enslaved for life, offered an obvious, tragic, solution.

Court cases of the early 1650's show that black servants were being sold for life servitude. Reversing English common law, the House of Burgesses decreed in 1661 that children born in the colonies would be bound or free depending on the status, not of their fathers, but of their mothers.

Slavery in the New World was also to be fostered by political pressures from the Old. In the late seventeenth century, the Royal African Company emerged as a powerful influence in the English Court and Parliament. The company's most profitable commodity was slaves. Pressures were soon asserted from London on New World colonies to develop attitudes, economies, and laws conducive to the acceptance of slaves. The Company's influence was even effective in Pennsylvania where William Penn revealed a willingness to accept the institution despite complaints from his fellow Quakers.

The success of the Royal African Company was also to have the effect of attracting New England shippers to the lucrative slave trade. In 1696, when the RAC's monopoly on the West African trade was broken, New England sea captains were quick to become part of the massive slave

*The first black immigrants to the British colonies entered Jamestown, Virginia as indentured servants in 1619, but later arrivals were condemned to slavery.*

*A female slave being branded as punishment for a minor offense.*

*Puritan Governor William Bradford's Bible.*

incursions there.

While slavery was growing, so was the freedom of the individual settler. The filigree of navigable waterways feeding Chesapeake Bay encouraged the dispersal of tobacco plantations and other farms. In this way, the English yeoman, who returned to a central village every night, was succeeded by the American farmer, whose isolated homesteads became the steppingstones of independence.

## New England

The Puritans, whose shiploads of settlers began arriving at Salem and Boston in 1629 and 1630, worked hard to build a civil government that would emblazon their spiritual beliefs. By making certain that all shares in their Massachusetts Bay Company were purchased by inhabitants, they became the first colony not under the control of a board of directors in England. Although church and state worked hand in glove, they were not merged. The Puritans suspected power and whoever held it. This led them to devise a well-defined system of checks and balances. "Let all the world learn to give mortal men no greater power than they are content they shall use—for use it they will," said the preacher John Cotton, words to be heeded by the United States Constitutional Convention a century and a half later. In these and similar ways the church pressed the movement for a government of law. It was the minister at Watertown, for example, who first (1632) warned his flock that it was wrong to pay taxes to which they had not consented.

The Puritans believed that the congregation of each church should be subject to no higher authority. Within a decade nearly thirty churches, each with a town around it, were scattered through the Bay Colony, New Haven, Connecticut, and Plymouth. Many of these "hivings-out" were the result of irreconcilable differences regarding religious matters. Minister Roger Williams, a quiet and gentle person, was one of the most rebellious thinkers of the age. He wondered aloud whether the King had any right to give the colonists land that already belonged to the Indians, argued for complete separation of church and state, and claimed that freedom of worship must be absolute. When Plymouth finally expelled him in 1635, he wintered among the Rhode Island Indians and bought land from them for his own colony.

Despite their zeal for independence, few Puritans were fond of democracy. A Calvinist notion categorizing people into 2 groups, either God's blessed saints or the rest of mankind, cushioned their acceptance of slavery. Massachusetts Bay was the first colony to recognize this institution legally, in a document ironically entitled the *Body of Liberties* of 1641. Evidence exists that a Puritan owned black slaves in the 1620s. Also, by 1638, when the first shipment of black slaves is believed to have reached that colony, the enslavement of Indians had already begun, with Indian villages sometimes destroyed on slender pretexts for the purpose of taking captives into bondage. Indian children under 12 were sold as late as 1706. The only New England colony to prohibit slavery was Roger Williams' Rhode Island, in its law of 1652. Unfortunately, that singular statute was openly violated.

### Slave Codes and the Right to Bear Arms

The majority of early settlers were soldier-farmers. The growth of a plantation economy in the South, however, soon resulted in a different policy for incoming blacks. Realizing that armed slaves might try to restore their birthright by violence, Virginia relieved all blacks of their military obligations and created an all-white militia as early as 1636. The question of whether blacks should be allowed to bear arms was destined, as we shall see, to be a major problem right through the Revolution. It was here in Virginia that the first "No" was recorded.

For the next 90 years or so, white Virginians found ample persuasion to continue their exclusionist policy, every time a slave fled into the forest there to join and be assimilated by the Indians, or every time a settlement was threatened by a slave revolt—such as the 1663 rebellion nipped in the bud in Gloucester, Virginia, and the bloody uprising at Stone, South Carolina, which resulted in the deaths of 30 whites and many more slaves. Virginia's rules reaffirmed the repressive measures they had adopted to avert racial revolution.

These stern measures were drawn up in Slave Codes that were much the same throughout the South. Slaves could not own property, carry arms, or leave their plantations without a written pass. Murder, rape, and arson were punishable by death; lesser offenses by maiming, branding, or whipping. Similar codes prevailed in the North. A large slave revolt in New York City in 1712, and public paranoia about an unproven conspiracy in 1741, were employed as justification for laws and repression as severe as those found in the South. While similar laws were on the books in Pennsylvania, the blacks there had much more freedom because of the influence of the Quakers. The situation differed somewhat in New England, where the slave codes generally reflected Old Testament law, so that slaves never wholly lost their legal status as persons, and enjoyed many more rights than elsewhere in the colonies.

### The Early Black Soldier

Despite their fears, settlers under siege eventually started to enlist blacks to fight beside whites. Records of King William's War (1689-1697) show that one of the first to fall in Massachusetts was "an Naygro of Colo. Tyng," slain at Falmouth. During Queen Anne's War (1702-1713), whenever levies of the white colonists failed to meet their quota, blacks were drafted and sent against the French and their Indian allies. Many armed blacks fought at Fort William Henry in New York. Those who were slaves sought freedom as their payment; those who were already free sought the wider benefits of added land and cash payments.

By 1723, Virginia saw fit to reverse its policy of excluding blacks from recruitment in the militia. In 1747, the South Carolina Company made slaves eligible for enlistment in the territorial militia according to a quota system. For every three white men in any company, one black man could be added—the 3:1 ratio abating fears of insurrection. Later, blacks were to fight for the British in the French and Indian War.

*Much of the work on colonial docks was done by slaves.*

## THE DIVERGENCE OF EUROPEAN AND AMERICAN INTERESTS: 1763-1770

### Aftermath of the French and Indian War

The signing of the Peace of Paris on February 10, 1763, brought the French and Indian War to a close by giving Canada, Florida, and all of North America east of the Mississippi to victorious Britain. This enormous booty strained Britain's capacity to govern.

Western Indians reacted violently to Britain's replacement of France as the dominant power in their areas. Chief Pontiac, who hated the British, attacked Fort Detroit in May 1763, beginning the largest Indian uprising in American history. London's response was a Proclamation which forbade settlers from migrating into the Indian lands west of the Appalachians, and which provided for stationing a 10,000-man British army in the colonies. General Amherst handled the war badly for Britain and there were several massacres on both sides before Pontiac buried the hatchet in July 1766.

Settlers and speculators refused to honor the Proclamation Line along the Appalachian crest. Washington, one of many eminent men involved in land schemes, is known to have remarked that such a good opportunity would not be repeated. Fortunately a new treaty line was negotiated. However, the British still felt it necessary to tighten their reins on the colonies.

To deal with these financial burdens, Prime Minister Grenville introduced the Revenue Act of 1764, which provided for a duty on molasses and contained several new trade restrictions, among them a provision that all imports from Europe and the East Indies must be routed through England. Colonists complained that the taxes would be used to support a British army in America which had failed to protect their frontiers and which contained no colonial officers. All the colonies filed protests against the Act, New York taking an irreconcilable stand against any form of Parliamentary taxation whatsoever.

Meanwhile, much of the New England clergy was registering strong negative reactions to the Archbishop of Canterbury's plan to graft the Anglican hierarchy to America. Their sermons, John Adams later remarked, did as much as anything to arouse the people's doubts about the constitutional authority of Parliament over the colonies.

### The Stamp Act

On February 6, 1765, the Prime Minister presented a proposal for duties on American stamps. The Stamp Act suggestion was especially significant because it would establish Parliament's right to levy an internal tax on the colonies. The first colonial reaction to the plan flared in the Virginia House of Burgesses where a young member, Patrick Henry, called for "no taxation without representation." Massachusetts' legislature tried to convey calm, calling for delegates from all the colonies to meet in New York City, but riots broke out and the homes of stamp distributors were ransacked.

In Boston, blacks played a significant role in protests against the Act.

When the New York meeting convened in October, the delegates acknowledged Parliament's right to legislate for the colonies, but denied it had the right to tax them in any way. This Stamp Act Congress marked the first time

*Boston patriots tossed British tax stamps onto bonfires.*

*British tax stamps.*

*Panicky British troops opened fire on a crowd of demonstrators led by runaway slave Crispus Attucks, who became the first patriot to die for American freedom in the Boston Massacre.*

representatives from all the colonies assembled for their own purposes. By November 1, when the stamps were slated to go on sale, there was hardly a distributor in the colonies who had not resigned his post. Business proceeded without stamps. In 1766, when it became clear the enforcement would out cost the levies to be raised, Parliament repealed the Stamp Act. However, more tax proposals were to follow.

## The Townshend Acts

In July 1767, Parliament passed the three Townshend Acts. The first Act imposed customs duties on a large variety of items that America had to import from Britain; the second beefed up the customs service watching American ports; the third threatened to suspend the New York assembly for its refusal to provide room and board for British soldiers according to the Quartering Act of 1765. American reaction was generally temperate. Philadelphia's John Dickinson penned 12 articles which invoked legal precedents to argue against Parliament's right to tax the colonies. In Massachusetts, the assembly approved a circular letter to all the colonies written by Sam Adams. Although Adams was moderate in this instance, British reaction was harsh. The assembly was ordered to disband when it refused to rescind the letter. Then, on June 10, 1768, customs officers began a clean-up campaign by seizing John Hancock's ship *Liberty*

*Patrick Henry stood in the Virginia House of Burgesses to demand "no taxation without representation".*

for bond violations. Within a few days, the officers had been driven back to their warships by angry mobs. London responded by sending two regiments of regulars.

### The Boston Massacre

Although the redcoats behaved reasonably well, and Parliament saw fit to lift all the customs duties except the tax on tea, the presence of troops gradually enflamed the citizens. Violence erupted on a cold, wet night—March 5, 1770. A crowd of angry towns people started throwing snowballs and ice at a British soldier who had been accused of hitting a boy with his rifle butt. A nearby squadron rushed to the soldier's rescue, and someone began ringing the fire bell. Bostonians came running to the scene, violence and confusion escalated, and—possibly in panic, or possibly because they thought they heard an order to shoot—the British fired upon and killed five of the crowd. Among the dead was a leader of the protest, Crispus Attucks, a big man, said to be of terrifying looks, 47 years old, of black and Indian extraction, probably a runaway slave, perhaps a drifter, and clearly a man of courage and commanding presence. In the trial that followed, lawyer John Adams defended the soldiers with the argument that the rioters, including Attucks, were rabble. Though the soldiers were exonerated, having acted under intense provocation, the "Boston Massacre" fevered popular resentment towards the British. As Adams was to say later, in words now inscribed on the Crispus Attucks monument in Boston Common: "On that night the foundation of American independence was laid."

## THE ROAD TO REVOLUTION: 1770-1775

### A Festering Quiet: 1770-1773

On the day British troops were firing into the Boston mob, Parliament was moving to repeal the Townshend Acts, except the tax on tea. The concessions pacified many colonists, but Samuel Adams, Patrick Henry, and Thomas Jefferson went to work on forming the Committee of Correspondence, which soon became a revolutionary communications network. A Tory pamphleteer was eventually to acknowledge the effectiveness of the Committee by labeling it "the foulest, subtlest, and most venomous serpent ever issued from the egg of sedition."

### Trouble over Tea

To save the East India Company from a bankruptcy that might have been disastrous for the Empire, the Crown gave that company's wholesalers the right to sell directly to American consumers, free of all duties and customs in England and subject to only a threepenny tax in America. These advantages enabled the company to sell its tea more cheaply than its competitors. In addition, many American merchants were denied opportunities to sell the company's tea, as English favorites were instead awarded such grants. Immediately, American merchants of every commodity from wine to hardware demanded that the ports be closed to ships bearing the tea. In Boston, the royal governor insisted that the ships be unloaded. On the night of December 16, 1773, a band of men disguised as Indians, including John Hancock and Sam Adams, swarmed aboard the tea ships and dumped 45 tons of it into the harbor.

The British were outraged. Moderates who had been sympathetic to the colonies were compromised, and in 1774 the British closed the port of Boston and demanded that Boston citizens compensate the East India Company. The Committees of Correspondence reacted with a call for unity and dispatched Paul Revere, an express rider for the Committee, southward with a message seeking solidarity from other colonies.

*At the Boston Tea Party, a band of patriots dumped 45 tons of British tea into the harbor.*

### The Intolerable Acts

While the colonies were in agitation over the Boston blockade, Lord North (the British Prime Minister) launched a full-scale reform movement. His Intolerable Acts provided for quartering troops in Massachusetts towns, transferring military murder trials to England, and eviscerating the liberties from Massachusetts' charter. Still another act gave Quebec territorial rights as far south as the Ohio River. When Virginia called for a general congress, all the colonies quickly agreed to meet in Philadelphia in September 1774.

### The First Continental Congress

The Congress that met in Philadelphia represented every shade of American opinion, but the intense feelings prevailing in the colonies tipped the balance of power toward radical elements. Britain's coercive acts had transferred the people's attention from economic to political grievances, and here the radicals were at home. Long discussions and animated addresses served to clarify American ideals and to give them a cutting edge they would not lose even in the heat of battle. The Congress resolved to disregard the Intolerable Acts and to deny Parliament's claim to tax the colonies. And the 12 separate and often jealous colonies managed to unite on a program to boycott British goods.

Perhaps even more significant, liberty was becoming a watchword. The doctrine that God created all men equal and endowed them with "natural" rights that neither laws nor men could remove swept through the towns, farms, factories, and salons of the colonies. Inevitably much of this philosophy reached blacks, the few who were free and many of the 500,000 who were not.

### Reactions to Slavery

Many colonists were so preoccupied with their struggle against the British that they failed to notice the incompatibility between the philosophy that all men owned a right to freedom and the belief that some men could justly be enslaved. Others were too concerned with their personal affairs to bother with the matter. Still others embraced a doctrine which contended that blacks were "biologically inferior" and thus not entitled to considerations granted other humans. Though disproven by scientists as early as the eighteenth century, the "biological" justification for oppression was eagerly grasped by many. "Biological racism" was to re-emerge in the nineteenth century as a sanction for the European conquest of Africa and in the twentieth century to serve as an excuse for Hitler's racist policies.

Other colonists, however, regarding slavery as a blight on the colonist's cause, were seriously troubled. Many of these people avoided the subject for reasons of expediency. They feared, with reason, that to make an issue of slavery could destroy the fragile unity the colonies had achieved. Even though in the 1770s, with the cotton gin still to be invented (1794), the dependence of the Southern economy on slave labor was in decline. Still others sought to blame the British entirely for slavery. Jefferson was to do this in his condemnation of slavery that was removed from the *Declaration of Independence*.

But there were also men and women who were ready to accept the colonists' responsibility and fight for the freedom of all people. One of them, James Otis of Massachusetts, declared in a tone reflective of the rational approach of his era: "The colonists are by law of nature free born... as indeed all men are, white or black. Does it follow that 'tis right to enslave a man because he is black?"

In a quieter vein, Abigail Adams wrote to husband John, who wavered on the subject of slavery, that it was "iniquitous... to fight ourselfs for what we are daily robbing and plundering from those who have as good a right to freedom as we have."

Such words reached the ears and eyes of a great many blacks, with two significant effects. Slaves in New England began to sue for their freedom and large numbers of blacks joined the militia.

### Blacks Sue for Freedom

A Massachusetts slave, Caesar Hendrick, took his master to court in 1773, arguing that he was enslaved against his will and deprived of his natural right to liberty. He was upheld by an all-white jury which freed him and ordered his master to pay reparations, court costs, and damages.

Despite this encouraging lead, few blacks were able to follow suit. Proceedings were complicated and expensive. It was not possible to take a freedom suit to the courts in order to liberate a large number of slaves—each case had to be considered separately.

Still, for a time the climate appeared to favor elimination of slavery. In his *Summary of the Rights of British America*

*Slave codes provided for the public burning of slaves who attacked their masters.*

*Black minutemen Lemuel Hayes and Peter Salem helped drive the British back from Concord bridge, where the "shot heard round the world" sparked the American Revolution.*

(1774), Thomas Jefferson stated abolition was favored by the colonies. Shortly thereafter, the Continental Congress' *Articles of Association* proposed the end of the slave trade and a boycott of all nations participating in it. And though fear of blacks was intense in the South—where four Georgia whites were killed in a slave revolt—many Southerners also favored abolition.

## The Outbreak of Hostilities

On the night of April 18, 1775, 700 British troops received orders to march secretly to Concord, 18 miles away, to destroy colonial stockpiles there and to arrest John Hancock and Sam Adams. Learning of their plan, Paul Revere rode out to warn the countryside. The British hope of surprise was destroyed as church bells clanged in every village through which they passed. The troops reached Lexington as the sun rose, to find Minutemen awaiting them on the Common. Here the first skirmish took place. The British fought on to Concord bridge, where "the shot heard round the world" was fired, but by now Minutemen were pouring in from all directions. The regulars were forced to retreat under punishing rifle fire. Before they could regain the safety of Boston, 273 were killed or wounded. The colonists' casualties were 95 killed or wounded.

## Black Patriots

Black men participated in the earliest battles of the Revolution. Lemuel Haynes, a gifted speaker who would become a prominent Congregationalist minister after the war, was one of many black Minutemen who defended Concord bridge. At his shoulder was Peter Salem, who had been granted his freedom to enlist. Other black men who fought in the American ranks on that first day include Pomp Blackman, Caesar and John Ferrit (father and son), Prince Estabrook (one of the wounded at Lexington), and Samuel Craft. A few weeks later, Haynes joined Primas Black and Epheram Blackman in the celebrated capture of Fort Ticonderoga, as members of Ethan Allen's Green Mountain Boys.

*The first great battle of the war was at Bunker Hill where two black soldiers, Salem Poor and Peter Salem, earned commendations for leadership and valor.*

The next important military engagement was the Battle of Bunker Hill (also known as Breed's Hill). The British managed to drive the Americans from their commanding position, but at a fearful cost to their regulars. When British Major John Pitcairn climbed the breastworks to shout out "The day is ours!"—a gesture not only foolhardy but premature—a black rifleman named Peter Salem shot him through, and he fell. The rifleman was honored by his companions and presented to General Washington for his feat. Salem Poor, another black combatant, was singled out for special commendation. Officers' reports to the General Court of Massachusetts praised Poor for his high standard of leadership and courage throughout the battle, making him the first acknowledged black military heroin in American history. Other black freedom fighters at Bunker Hill were Barzillai Lew, a seasoned veteran who had seen combat during the French and Indian War as a Massachusetts enlistee in 1760, and Cuff Whittemore, a Minuteman from Arlington. Titus Coburn, Charlestown Eads, and Sampson Taylor also fought, and Caesar Brown was one of those who gave his life that day.

Recognition that blacks could serve their country as citizens as well as soldiers was also forthcoming in 1775, when America's first abolitionist organization was formed in Philadelphia, the Pennsylvania Society for the Abolition of Slavery.

However, the courage of black fighting men and the zeal of principled whites were soon to be swept aside in the movement to exclude blacks from the armed services. Before this was to happen, the Congress was called back into session.

## The Second Congress

Most of the same faces showed up when Congress convened again on May 10, 1775, but the mood was different. George Washington, now wearing the buff blue uniform of the Virginia militia, was chosen commander-in-chief of the embryonic Continental Army, then forming around Boston. Nevertheless, loyalty to the mother country did not die

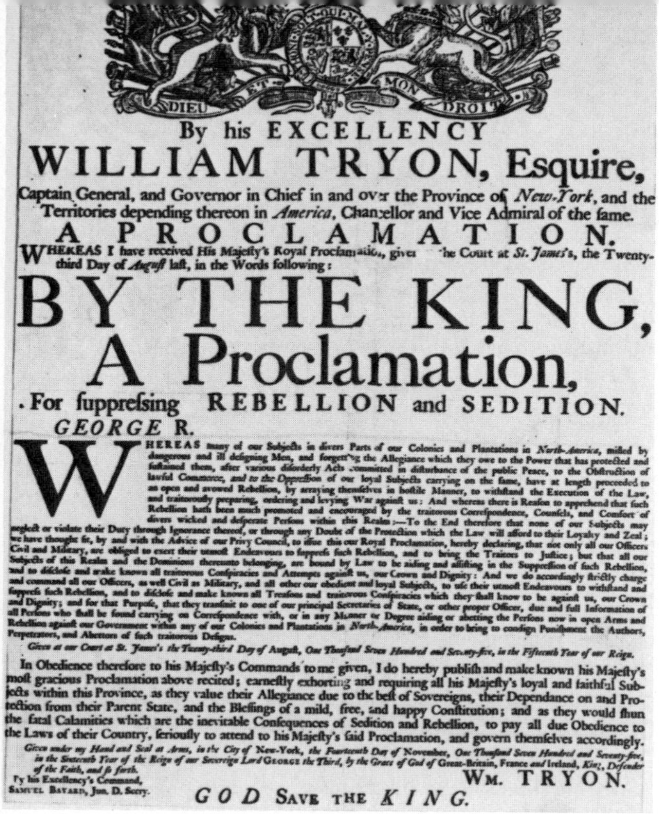

DIEU ET MON DROIT

By his EXCELLENCY

WILLIAM TRYON, Esquire,

Captain General, and Governor in Chief in and over the Province of *New-York*, and the Territories depending thereon in *America*, Chancellor and Vice Admiral of the ſame.

A PROCLAMATION.

WHEREAS I have received His Majeſty's Royal Proclamation, given at the Court at *St. James's*, the Twenty-third Day of *Auguſt* laſt, in the Words following:

BY THE KING,

A Proclamation,

For ſuppreſsing REBELLION and SEDITION.

*GEORGE* R.

WHEREAS many of our Subjects in divers Parts of our Colonies and Plantations in *North-America*, miſled by dangerous and ill deſigning Men, and forgetting the Allegiance which they owe to the Power that has protected and ſuſtained them, after various diſorderly Acts committed in diſturbance of the public Peace, to the Obſtruction of lawful Commerce, *and to the Oppreſsion* of our loyal Subjects carrying on the ſame, have at length proceeded to an open and avowed Rebellion, by arraying themſelves in hoſtile Manner, to withſtand the Execution of the Law, and traitorouſly preparing, ordering and levying War againſt us: And whereas there is Reaſon to apprehend that ſuch Rebellion hath been much promoted and encouraged by the traitorous Correſpondence, Counſels, and Comfort of divers wicked and deſperate Perſons within this Realm:—To the End therefore that none of our Subjects may neglect or violate their Duty through Ignorance thereof, or through any Doubt of the Protection which the Law will afford to their Loyalty and Zeal; we have thought fit, by and with the Advice of our Privy Council, to iſſue this our Royal Proclamation, hereby declaring, that not only all our Officers Civil and Military, are obliged to exert their utmoſt Endeavours to ſuppreſs ſuch Rebellion, and to bring the Traitors to Juſtice; but that all our Subjects of this Realm and the Dominions thereunto belonging, are bound by Law to be aiding and aſſiſting in the Suppreſsion of ſuch Rebellion, and to diſcloſe and make known all traitorous Conſpiracies and Attempts againſt us, our Crown and Dignity: And we do accordingly ſtrictly charge and command all our Officers, as well Civil as Military, and all other our obedient and loyal Subjects, to uſe their utmoſt Endeavours to withſtand and ſuppreſs ſuch Rebellion, and to diſcloſe and make known all Treaſons and traitorous Conſpiracies which they ſhall know to be againſt us, our Crown and Dignity; and for that Purpoſe, that they tranſmit to one of our principal Secretaries of State, or other proper Officer, due and full Information of all Perſons who ſhall be found carrying on Correſpondence with, or in any Manner or Degree aiding or abetting the Perſons now in open Arms and Rebellion againſt our Government within any of our Colonies and Plantations in *North-America*, in order to bring to condign Puniſhment the Authors, Perpetrators, and Abettors of ſuch traitorous Deſigns.

*Given at our Court at St. James's the Twenty-third Day of Auguſt, One Thouſand Seven Hundred and Seventy-five, in the Fifteenth Year of our Reign.*

In Obedience therefore to his Majeſty's Commands to me given, I do hereby publiſh and make known his Majeſty's moſt gracious Proclamation above recited; earneſtly exhorting and requiring all his Majeſty's loyal and faithful Subjects within this Province, as they value their Allegiance due to the beſt of Sovereigns, their Dependance on and Protection from their Parent State, and the Bleſsings of a mild, free, and happy Conſtitution; and as they would ſhun the fatal Calamities which are the inevitable Conſequences of Sedition and Rebellion, to pay all due Obedience to the Laws of their Country, ſeriouſly to attend to his Majeſty's ſaid Proclamation, and govern themſelves accordingly.

*Given under my Hand and Seal at Arms, in the City of* New-York, *the Fourteenth Day of November, One Thouſand Seven Hundred and Seventy-five, in the Sixteenth Year of the Reign of our Sovereign Lord* GEORGE *the Third, by the Grace of God of* Great-Britain, France *and* Ireland, *King, Defender of the Faith, and ſo forth.*

WM. TRYON.

By his Excellency's Command,
SAMUEL BAYARD, Jun. D. Secry.

*GOD* SAVE THE *KING*.

*Although the British king called for all loyal subjects to put down the rebellion, the announcement of the Declaration of Independence was greeted with cheers by freedom-loving black and white Americans.*

easily. Moderates, who wished to send an olive branch to the King, remained powerful over the next year, but they were buffeted by events, among them Washington's attack on Canada, following Ethan Allen's offensive tactics, as well as the British Parliament's Prohibitory Act, which made it clear that all branches of British government were united in coercing the colonies into submission. Tom Paine's *Common Sense* urged that people who would be free of tyranny must be willing to attack the tyrant. It is ridiculous, Paine said, that a continent should be ruled by an island. The hiring of German mercenaries and the burning of New England towns fueled Congressional resentment. Finally, on June 7, 1776, Richard Henry Lee of Virginia introduced the resolution for independence.

## The Declaration of Independence

While Congress pressed toward a final vote on separation from Britain, Thomas Jefferson was given the responsibility of declaring America's independence to the world. In true American fashion, he did not simply declare, he defined—for the world, for Americans, and for his own conscience. Like no nation before it, America came into being through a process in which its founders were constantly clarifying their principles.

The document Jefferson wrote enumerated the grievances which made the colonies repudiate British rule, and more profoundly, the ideals on which the colonists based their assertion of independence.

Although the ideals Jefferson cited were not new, he used them in a new way, not as a basis for philosophical speculation but to define man and to set down "natural laws" which he felt forbade human bondage.

## The War of Independence: 1775-1783

The American Revolution was in many ways a revolutionary kind of war—a people's war. There was no central objective to be captured which could signal victory. America's strength did not center in any one colony or city but was scattered the length of the continent. While most eighteenth-century wars were fought by professionals, a large part of America's people would see action in this one. Washington's Continental Army never topped the 17,000 mark, but estimates are that over 400,000 men served in it over the course of the war, mostly for short-term enlistments.

## The Movement to Disarm Blacks

Conflict about whether to allow slaves, or even free black men, to bear arms was a pernicious undercurrent of the war. Despite their prowess in early battles, the blacks' welcome in the army was short-lived.

On May 29, 1775, the Massachusetts Committee of Safety, reflecting John Adams' anxiety to strengthen ties with the southern colonies, proclaimed that the enlistment of slaves "was inconsistent with the principles that are to be supported, and reflect[s] dishonor on the colony."

Men who had already risked their lives in the American cause could no longer pass muster because they were slaves.

Even Salem Poor, a hero of Bunker Hill, was nearly drummed out of the army until his masters emancipated him so that he could continue to fight. Shortly, however, all black enlistments were frozen. On July 9, 1775, the adjutant general of the Continental Army, Horatio Gates, issued an order from Washington's headquarters stating that recruiting officers were no longer to accept "any stroller, Negro, or vagabond."

Southern delegates to the second Continental Congress were still unsatisfied however, so intense was their fear of uprisings by the enormous slave populations of certain states. In South Carolina, slaves outnumbered whites, and neighboring Georgia had a population that was at least 40% slave. To minimize all risk of slaves becoming armed, South Carolina's Edward Rutledge introduced a measure in the Congress proposing that all blacks, bond or free, be discharged from the Continental Army. Although the proposal was rejected, Gen. Washington's own council of war two weeks later decided to terminate all black enlistments, a ban which Congress formalized into law on October 13, 1775. The protest of colonial generals like John Thomas, who argued that blacks made just as good soldiers as whites and that many black troops had already "proved themselves brave" in action, went unheeded. Thus, as 1775 drew to a close, it had become extremely difficult for any black to join the revolutionary forces at any level.

While the Congress' decision was clearly political, designed to keep the South from running to the British camp, its wisdom remains debatable. When the Earl of Dunmore, royal governor of Virginia, assessed the situation, he placed his colony under martial law, and on November 7, 1775, issued a proclamation offering freedom to all "indentured servants, Negroes, or others" able and willing to bear arms "for more speedily reducing the Colony to a proper sense of their duty to His Majesty's crown and dignity." The news spread through the countryside like wildfire. Blacks, showing a great willingness to fight and die if necessary for freedom, flocked to Dunmore's "Ethiopian Regiment" at the rate of 100 fugitive slaves a week. Stepped-up continental patrols could not staunch the flow of manpower, and by December 1, Lord Dunmore had over 100 trained black troops. Ironically, this crisis was brought to an end only by the loyalty to America of an unidentified black man, posing as a runaway slave, who fed Lord Dunmore false reports and lured him into a disastrous attack on Norfolk, Va. Severely beaten, Dunmore's troops had to fall back to his ships and were never again able to establish a fixed camp on the mainland to which slaves could desert.

Shortly after Dunmore's defeat, Washington listened to the protests of a group of black veterans, and reversing his policy, ordered recruiting officers to begin accepting the re-enlistments of free blacks who had already served. On January 16, 1771, Congress approved this decision, but insisted that no new black volunteers were to be accepted.

The difficulty of raising enough white troops to meet the demands of war eventually eroded America's exclusionist policy. Local militias unable to fill their muster rolls won quiet agreement from recruiting boards and reluctant slave owners to accept free blacks as substitutes for those white men who could afford to buy their way out and wished to do so. As the war progressed, these arrangements came to involve slaves, who were declared free (compensation being awarded to the master) provided they enlist. Rhode Island passed the first slave enlistment act on February 2, 1778, raising a regiment that participated gallantly in many important battles. In 1780, Maryland became the only Southern state to enroll slave troops. Slave conscripts were at first assigned to combat-support functions, but in the heat of battle, with little time to debate the fine points of status, slaves were often armed. As a result of the longer terms for which blacks often enlisted, many of America's seasoned veterans in the latter years of the war for independence turned out to be the black troops who had been denied the right to bear arms until the situation became desperate.

## The Tide Turns: 1777

British General Howe planned for the brunt of his forces to capture Pennsylvania, while part of his army was dispatched north, where General Burgoyne, attacking from Canada, would coordinate a three-pronged squeeze on Albany. While Howe had little difficulty, the British campaign in the north was a disaster. After a season of determined fighting and clever ruses, the colonials captured Burgoyne's force of 5,000 men at Saratoga. The victory boosted American morale and convinced France of the colonists' ability to win. French officers led by the Marquis de Lafayette were soon to be sent to help Washington, a step that was to be a turning point in the war. But the French could offer Washington little help in the brutal winter of 1777-1778.

Once again Washington had pitted his forces against the strongest part of the British Army with dire results. As Howe wintered comfortably in captured Philadelphia, Americans froze, starved, and deserted at Valley Forge. The men lacked warm clothing and shoes. While farmers sold barrels of flour and pork to the speculators in Philadelphia, the Continentals drank soup "full of burnt leaves and dirt."

It is known that the Valley Forge Army averaged about 54 blacks in each of its seven brigades. Their importance grew during this terrible winter, when their desertion rate was considerably lower than that of white Patriots.

## Black Participation

Blacks made some political progress in 1777. Vermont became the first state to abolish slavery, and the Connecticut legislature passed a measure granting equal pay to white and black soldiers. Connecticut also provided for the formation of a fighting company of 55 slaves, as prohibitions against enlisting slaves were becoming a dead letter in Washington's mind.

Rhode Island's military situation—4,000 slaves along with unfulfilled manpower quotas—cried out for black recruitment. The state had already given the nation one black hero, Prince Whipple, a daring participant in the capture of a British general. To Washington, with the war entering a third bitter year, with manpower short, and with victory

*Guerrilla commander Marion invites a captured British officer to dine with his famous volunteers.*

*(left) Lord Dunsmore mustered the first black regiment for Britain. (above) Adjutant General Gates barred blacks from the Continental Army in 1775.*

more important than the fears of slave owners, exclusion of black men, slave or free, was becoming a wasteful indulgence.

Tacitly bypassing his own standing order, Washington endorsed a Rhode Island plan which called for slaves serving in its forces to be freed and their owners to be reimbursed by the state (which would be ultimately paid by Congress). As in Connecticut, the same pay scale was to apply equally to white and black troops.

The plan paid off handsomely. In the Battle of Rhode Island (August 1778) a regiment of 125 blacks, 95 of them slaves, held its ground against three concerted British-Hessian attacks, thus enabling six brigades of American troops to make a successful retreat with all their equipment. The resistance of the black regiment earned the admiration of friend and foe alike. Barely past the recruit stage, they had inflicted casualties of 6:1 on the professionals who fought for the British. Many of the same blacks were to fight later at Ponts Bridge, in New York.

## The War in the South

After 1778, British efforts in the North were limited to blockade and local raiding operations. The significant fighting was now in the South where, with Tory and Indian support Britain hoped to reestablish control. In a brief winter campaign, 1778-1779, British troops occupied Savannah and threatened South Carolina. Washington chafed at the situation. Lafayette believed enlistment of only a few thousand slaves could wrest most of the South from the British.

In an attempt to obtain the cooperation of South Carolina, Washington dispatched his former aide de camp, Lieutenant Colonel John Laurens, a handsome 22-year-old native of the state and a deeply convinced abolitionist, to try to persuade the state legislature to permit enlistment of slaves. Though South Carolina could barely raise 200 able-bodied white soldiers, and Charleston was clearly endangered, political leaders there still threatened to go over to the British if Washington insisted on arming their slaves. Frustrated and disappointed, Laurens wrote Washington that reason had

*Private Edward Hector, Artillery.*

*The American Navy grew into a respected fighting force during the Revolution, relying often on the skill of black pilots and crewmen.*

been "drowned by the howlings of a triple-headed monster, in which prejudice, avarice, and pusillanimity were united."

On May 12, 1780, Charleston fell, and an army of 5,000 American troops and 300 cannon were surrendered to the British. South Carolina's fate appeared sealed, its only hope lying with the persistent daring raids of such guerrilla commanders as Francis Marion ("The Swamp Fox") and Thomas Sumter. For nearly a year after the surrender, British General Cornwallis, harassed by these raids, tried to force the elusive Americans to stand and fight against his larger, better-equipped army. He did not succeed.

## Blacks in the Navy

The navies of the Chesapeake Bay states, Maryland and Virginia, did not fail to capitalize on the experience and skill of the black pilots who had long been operating small craft in bay waters and river inlets. The best-known slave pilot during the war was Caesar, owned by Carter Tarrant. Caesar was at the wheel of the *Patriot* when it took possession of the *Fanny*, a British brig. In 1789, Caesar was set free. Some years later a parcel of land was awarded to his daughter in Ohio, as a reward for his services.

*The British sent many captured slaves to the West Indies.*

Another black naval hero was James Forten, who joined the navy at 14. He was taken prisoner by the British while serving as powder boy on the *Royal Lewis*. Forten became friends with the ship captain's son and was invited to accompany him back to England, where a life of wealth and aristocratic privilege awaited. Forten's answer to this suggestion was, "I am a prisoner here for the liberties of my country. I never, NEVER shall prove a traitor to her interests."

Black prisoners rarely were considered eligible for exchange. Usually they were sent to the West Indies and sold in the slave market. Transferred to a British prison ship, Forten made plans to escape by hiding himself in a chest. At the last moment, however, he relinquished his hiding place to Daniel Brewton, who he thought would be more valuable to the American cause. Brewton publicly praised Forten's heroism when he got to Philadelphia. Forten himself was eventually to become a renowned abolitionist and civic leader.

## Blacks and the British Forces

American loyalists lobbied against the use of black troops by His Majesty's armies. The recruitment of blacks was further undercut by a dandyish atmosphere pervading the royal forces. It was fine for rebellious colonials to use blacks, red men, and the like, but the British Army was too gentlemanly and disciplined to employ such rabble in any but menial capacities. As it turned out, the British refusal to arm slaves in the South sealed the Crown's fate in the war, for victories were badly needed below the Potomac to counter American successes in the North, and the only source of manpower was slaves.

*Many blacks volunteered for hazardous spying missions behind enemy lines.*

## The Fortification of Virginia

In 1781, England's General Cornwallis, feeling secure after victories in North Carolina, decided he could move the war to Virginia. Traveling overland from Charleston, Cornwallis' forces lived off the countryside, supplied by blacks who foraged successfully despite Cornwallis' stripping them of arms. Reaching Virginia in May, the British dug in around Yorktown and Portsmouth with the help of 1,000 black laborers. As they had throughout their Southern campaigns, the British made superior use of the blacks in supportive capacities.

The brutality of the British to their black men clearly manifest itself in an outbreak of smallpox. Underclothed and underfed, an "immense number of Negroes," in the words of a British commander on the scene, "died in the most miserable manner" to be, as another British officer suggested, "strewn about rebel plantations" for the purposes of spreading the plague.

In the Continental Army, on the other hand, blacks were serving in military capacities.

## Spies, Couriers, and Guides

Black men assumed many key intelligence roles during the war, especially in the Virginia campaign. The most famous slave spy was named James, the property of William Armistead, and so sometimes referred to as James Armistead. He served under Lafayette in 1781. James' reports from the enemy base at Portsmouth won such high praise from the French general that the Virginia legislature gave James his freedom. Thirty-three years later, in 1819, James was awarded, by a vote of the legislature, a $40,000 annual pension for life. When Lafayette returned to America, in 1824, he remembered to look up James—who was by then calling himself James Lafayette.

Saul Mathews, another slave spy who operated in Virginia during the Cornwallis operation, completed many missions behind British lines, returning with detailed information regarding enemy movements, thereby enabling Continental strategists to form effective battle plans. Some ten years after the close of the war Mathews petitioned for, and was awarded, his freedom.

## Yorktown

The climax of the war for independence came at Yorktown. Cornwallis was trapped in his fortifications by the sudden appearance of a French fleet of 20 warships under Admiral de Grasse. Learning the news in New York, Washington speedily slipped past the main British army in Philadelphia and turned up outside Yorktown. Cornwallis had no choice but to surrender, which he did on October 19, 1781.

Though fighting was to continue for months, and the British were to linger on beyond that, the defeat at Yorktown marked the end of British power south of Canada. After Yorktown, all Britain's efforts were concentrated on getting her troops home safely and negotiating peace. The Americans had won their independence and would soon draft the Constitution.

## Blacks after Yorktown

The fortunes of blacks following Yorktown varied enormously. Hundreds of slaves freed to fight and labor on both sides, were re-enslaved by conquering American and French officers. The French returned some slaves but many were kept to meet a diversity of fates. Some found freedom in the North, a few in France, and many were sold into slavery in the West Indies.

The British kept many slaves behind their lines. When the royal ships departed, the evacuees included slaves of owners who had remained loyal to the Crown, black captives, and ex-slaves who had been promised freedom for their wartime help. A few slaves who had fought with the British waged guerrilla warfare from the Georgia and South Carolina swamps until their defeat in 1786.

In the States, most of the slaves who had served in the armed forces were freed, though deceitful and occasionally successful attempts were made to re-enslave them. The country was already beginning to polarize. Slaves belonging to loyalist owners were generally freed in the North but not in the South. Economic factors were probably conclusive. The North, with new trading opportunities developing, had little reason to keep slaves, but the South felt a need for

*The unjust laws of Lord North inflamed Americans and intensified their resistance.*

slaves to replace wartime losses and to harvest the cotton which was becoming its dominant crop.

The force of ideology, however, should not be dismissed. Abolitionist convictions grew stronger in the North. The Philadelphia Society, whose anti-slavery activities had been suspended during the war, resumed operations. Pennsylvania's program of gradual abolition went into effect. Finally, in 1783, Massachusetts ended slavery and granted the vote to black taxpayers. The road to the future was now charted.

## The American Victory

America's victory was formally sealed by the Treaty of Paris in 1783. America had won a victory in a war of revolution unlike any other. The American Revolution, as writer Hannah Arendt was to put it some 200 years later, "succeeded where all others were to fail, namely, in founding a new body politic stable enough to survive the onslaught of centuries to come."

By the end of the revolutionary struggle, America's feet were planted firmly on the world stage. By word and arms, a new nation had carved itself out of the wilderness.

*French General Lafayette, shown with his orderly, pressed George Washington to create black regiments.*

## A CHRONOLOGY OF BLACK PARTICIPATION IN THE AMERICAN REVOLUTION

**1770, March 5** Panicky British troops open fire on a crowd of protesters apparently led by runaway slave Crispus Attucks. Attucks is the first of five patriots to die for freedom in what history remembers as the Boston Massacre.

**1770, March 12** The Massachusetts *Gazette* publishes Paul Revere's celebrated engraving of the Boston Massacre, which inflames American resentment of Britain.

**1770, June 28** Quaker Anthony Benezet opens the first nonsegregated school for black and white children in Philadelphia.

**1770, October 24** Lawyer John Adams defends Capt. Preston, whose troop committed the Boston Massacre, holding Crispus Attucks responsible for the bloodshed. Preston is found innocent, but colonial public opinion now leans strongly toward revolution.

**1772, June 9** A black man named Aaron participates in the burning of the British revenue cutter *Gaspee* off the coast of Rhode Island.

**1772, June 22** Slavery is abolished in England by the Mansfield decision, which further states that any slave brought to the British Isles must be freed.

**1773, January 6** Blacks petition the governor of Massachusetts for equal rights and for an end to slavery. Two weeks later a follow-up petition with more signatures is sent to the Massachusetts assembly.

**1773, February 17** In Pennsylvania, the slave trade is stifled by the imposition of a 20 pounds sterling tax on every imported slave.

**1773, March 13** Jean Baptiste Point du Sable, a black trader, founds the first permanent settlement on the present site of Chicago, Illinois.

**1773, April 5** White ministers Samuel Hopkins and Ezra Stiles enroll free black John Quaumino and slave Bristol Yamma in a radical program to train blacks for missionary work in Africa.

**1773, April 20** Slaves petition the Massachusetts legislature to be allowed to earn money to buy their freedom.

**1773, July 5** The Lord Mayor of London presents a copy of *Paradise Lost* to Phillis Wheatley, the black American poet.

**1773, November** Massachusetts slave Caesar Hendricks takes his master to court "for detaining him in slavery." The all-white jury frees Hendricks and awards him damages.

**1773, November 6** Quaker merchant Moses Brown of Rhode Island voluntarily frees his slaves.

**1774, March 8** The Massachusetts General Assembly passes a measure prohibiting the importation of slaves, but is unexpectedly suspended by the royal governor on the following day.

*The capture of Fort Ticonderoga, in which Lemuel Hayes and two other black fighting men took part.*

**1774, May 27** Massachusetts blacks send a petition to royal Governor General Thomas Gage, denouncing slavery as evil and destructive of natural rights.

**1774, September 7** Abigail Adams, in a letter to her husband John, writes: "It always appeared a most iniquitous scheme to me to fight ourselfs for what we are daily robbing and plundering from those who have as good a right to freedom as we have."

**1774, October 2** The Continental Congress votes for discontinuance of the slave trade after December 1, 1774.

**1774, October 26** Massachusetts blacks enlist in the Minuteman companies being organized by the Committee of Safety.

**1774, November 2** Slaves revolt in St. Andrew's Parish, Georgia.

**1775, March 8** Thomas Paine publishes his first essay, "African Slavery in America," which denounces slavery, calls for abolition, and demands that blacks be given land in payment for long years of slavery.

*Black rifleman Peter Salem stopped a British charge at Bunker Hill by picking off an enemy major.*

**1775, March 10** Daniel Boone's expedition sets out for Kentucky guided by an aged black slave.

**1775, April** As war becomes imminent, Maryland slave owners petition Governor Robert Eden for arms and ammunition to put down possible slave uprisings.

**1775, April 14** America's first Abolition Society elects as officers Benjamin Franklin and Benjamin Rush.

**1775, April 18** The midnight rides of Paul Revere and William Dawes alert the Minutemen, many of whom are black volunteers, that the British are coming.

**1775, April 19** Black American Minutemen fighting in the first battles of the Revolution at Lexington and Concord include Peter Salem, Lemuel Haynes, Pompy____, Prince _, Prince Estabrook (wounded), Pomp Blackman (at both battles), Cato Stedman, Cato Boardman, Cuff Whitmore, and Cato Wood.

**1775, April 24** Minuteman Salem Poor hurries to enlist in Captain Simon Edgel's Framingham company, which later sees action at Bunker Hill.

**1775, May 1** Lemuel Haynes and two other black volunteers in Ethan Allen's Green Mountain Boys take part in America's first aggressive military action, the capture of Fort Ticonderoga.

**1775, May 3** Seasot___ and Pharaoh___ enlist in Colonel Seamman's "Regiment on Foot." They too, will fight on Bunker Hill.

**1775, May 29** The Massachusetts Committee of Safety suddenly prohibits the enlistment of slaves as "inconsistent with the principles that are to be supported, and reflecting dishonor on this colony."

**1775, June 16** Colonel William Prescott of the Massachusetts militia leads his regiment, which contains many black veterans of Lexington and Concord, to the top of Bunker Hill, where they prepare for a British attack.

**1775, June 17** Black soldiers distinguish themselves at the Battle of Bunker Hill. Among the day's heroes are Salem Poor, Barzillai Lew, Cuff Whitmore, and Peter Salem, who is credited with shooting British major John Pitcairn. Two of America's 100 dead are free black men.

**1775, July** Virginia opens the militia to all free male persons; an unforeseen consequence is that many slaves manage to pass themselves off as free, and sign up.

**1775, July 3** Prince Hall founds the first lodge of black Freemasons in Boston.

**1775, July 9** Horatio Gates, the adjutant general of the new American army (distinct from state militias), orders recruiting officers not to enroll any "stroller, negro, or vagabond."

**1775, August 3** Connecticut brigantine *Minerva* signs on two black marines, Peter ___and Gist ____.

**1775, August 18** White pilot and well-to-do slave owner Jerry ______, of South Carolina, is hanged for supplying weapons to slaves and advising them to join the British.

**1775, September 26** The Continental Congress hears, but rejects, South Carolinian Edward Rutledge's proposal to discharge all blacks, free or slave, from the army.

**1775, October 8** Bowing to Southern pressures, General Washington's council of war decides to exclude blacks from the Continental Army.

**1775, October 13** Congress legalizes the General's resolution barring blacks from the army.

**1775, October 14** Congress authorizes the Continental navy, in which black sailors, both free and slave, serve from the very beginning.

**1775, October 24** General John Thomas protests to John Adams that it is a mistake for the army to reject black soldiers, many of whom "have proved themselves brave" in action.

**1775, November 7** The Earl of Dunmore, Virginia's royal governor, issues his famous proclamation offering freedom to slaves who will desert their rebel masters and join the British army.

**1775, November 10** South Carolina authorizes the hiring of slaves to build fortifications, with payment to be made to their masters.

**1775, November 23** Southern newspapers mount a bitter attack on Lord Dunmore's call for blacks to enlist in British troops.

**1775, November 25** Slaves are reported to be flocking to join Lord Dunmore's regiments where they are not only welcomed to serve but promised freedom after the war.

**1775, December 1** Nearly 300 runaway slaves in Virginia have joined Lord Dunmore's forces. They are officially dubbed the "Ethiopian Regiment."

**1775, December 5** Salem Poor's extraordinary bravery at the battle of Bunker Hill is praised by 14 officers who send a petition on his behalf to the General Court of Massachusetts.

**1775, December 8** A patriotic black American posing as a runaway slave dupes Dunmore into believing that Norfolk's Great Bridge is inadequately guarded.

**1775, December 9** Dunmore attacks the Great Bridge with 600 troops and is badly defeated. He is forced to flee to his ships, where the "Ethiopian Brigade," gradually devastated by disease, never takes part in another major encounter.

**1775, December 13** The Virginia Convention publishes a broadside offering to pardon runaway slaves if they will promptly return from Lord Dunmore's brigade. Slaves captured in battle will be sold to the West Indies.

**1775, December 30** After listening to the protests of free black veterans, General Washington reverses his policy and orders recruiting officers to accept their enlistments. He also promises to ask Congress to reconsider the question of allowing blacks to serve.

**1776, January 1** General Washington writes to John Hancock, president of the Continental Congress, to press for a decision allowing the enlistment of free black soldiers.

**1776, January 16** Granting General Washington's request, the Congress approves the re-enlistment of free black veterans but insists that no new black volunteers are to be accepted.

**1776, January 18** South Carolina's Council of Safety sends out a militia captain with 34 Catawba Indians on a scouting patrol to catch runaway slaves.

**1776, January 22** Negro Jack is one of 15 privates from West Hartford who join the army invading Canada.

**1776, January 23** Adopting the exclusionist policies of the central government, Massachusetts bans blacks, Indians, and mulattos from serving in its militia.

**1776, February 28** General Washington invites poet Phillis Wheatley to Cambridge headquarters to thank her for a poem in his honor.

**1776, March** Free black Scipio Fayerweather refuses to join the British in their evacuation of Boston despite reprisals in which they tear down his house.

**1776, March 17** In New York City, Captain Benjamin Egbert's 59-man company contains 11 black soldiers.

**1776, March 26** Congress resolves to draft Indians.

**1776, April** South Carolina authorizes the death penalty for slaves who defect to join the British.

**1776, April 6** Congress bans the importation of slaves into the 13 colonies.

**1776, April 13** Two fugitive slaves attempting to join a British man-of-war are captured by the Virginia navy and hung "as an example to others."

**1776, April 23** To prevent black defections to the British force in the area of Charleston, S.C., General R. H. Lee orders all blacks who can fight to be "secured immediately and sent up to Norfolk."

**1776, May** Surriname Wanton and Loushir_____ are two black sailors aboard the U.S. brig *Cabot* when it captures a British merchantman. Because they are slaves, their 120 pounds share of the booty is given to their owner.

**1776, June** Spain joins France as an ally of America bringing black troops from Louisiana into the combat. These troops include militia companies of free blacks and slaves commanded by black officers of the line.

**1776, June** Virginia navy pilot Minny _______, a slave volunteer, is killed attempting to board an enemy vessel in the Rappahannock River.

**1776, June 17** Thomas Hubey is hanged for conspiracy against General Washington, after his plot was exposed by black serving girl Phoebe Francis.

**1776, July 4** The *Declaration of Independence* is adopted in Philadelphia, but only after voting out Thomas Jefferson's sharp condemnation of the slave trade as "cruel war against human nature itself, violating its most sacred rights of life and liberty."

**1776, July 23** Major Thomas Price tells the Maryland Council of Safety that he has seen the bodies of dead blacks washed ashore from Lord Dunmore's ships, where an epidemic is ravaging the troops.

**1776, August 6** Lord Dunmore finally gives up and sails for the West Indies. The best black troops remaining from the "Ethiopian Regiment" sail for Sandy Hook where they will fight in the principal British army.

*American Militia uniforms in 1782: Massachusetts (left) and New Jersey.*

*Black casualties were heavy when the outnumbered Americans were driven from Long Island in 1776.*

**1776, August 12** Georgia assigns black pilots to patrol state waterways and seacoast.

**1776, August 27** Black casualties are heavy in Washington's defeat at the Battle of Long Island.

**1776, September 16** At the Battle of Harlem Heights, a major skirmish in Washington's withdrawal to Valley Forge, many black militiamen see action.

**1776, September 22** The British hang Nathan Hale as an American spy. The hangman is 15-year old loyalist slave, Bill Richmond, who in later years becomes Europe's heavyweight boxing champion.

**1776, October 10** The U.S. Cavalry is formed, but few blacks see service in this elite branch. An exception is free black John Banks of Goochland, Va., who rides for two years in Theodorick Bland's regiment.

**1776, December 3** Silas Deane urges Americans to stir up slave rebellions in Jamaica, but his plan is not implemented.

**1776, December 17** Congress gives General Washington specific authority to raise troops. The quotas he levies on the various states finally lead to the general acceptance of black enlistments, eventually including slaves.

**1776, December 25** Washington makes his famous midnight crossing of the icy Delaware. Many black soldiers are in the boats, including Prince Whipple and Oliver Cromwell.

**1776, December 26** American troops, including many black militiamen, earn an important victory in the Battle of Trenton.

**1777** Cato Carlile and Scipio Africanus, freeborn blacks from New England coastal towns, enlist for service under Captain John Paul Jones. The navy welcomes black men who know the sea, whether they are free or slave.

**1777, January 13** A black petition to end slavery is sent to the Massachusetts House of Representatives, arguing that every principle which impelled America to break with England also pleads for abolition. Signers include Prince Hall.

**1777, April** Black pilot Dick___ is hired by the Maryland state navy.

**1777, April 9** John Jay urges that New York's Constitution abolish slavery.

**1777, May 2** The Connecticut legislature officially considers recruiting slaves, votes against it, but finally permits drafted men to supply black substitutes for their army service.

**1777, May 6** Virginia moves to prevent slaves from enlisting as though they were free by making it mandatory for a black man to have a certificate of freedom from the

*The hangman at Nathan Hale's execution was Bill Richmond, a fifteen-year-old black American, who fought with the British. Richmond later became heavyweight champion of England.*

county judge before he can sign up.

**1777, May 12** Several blacks sail on the frigate *Boston*, including Cato Austin, number one gunner on the starboard watch.

**1777, June** Moved by a black petition, Massachusetts drafts a bill abolishing slavery, but the measure is tabled by John Adams' deft behind-the-scenes politicking for fear that it would imperil friendly relations with Southern states.

**1777, June 7** Ty, the best-known black American fighting for the British, leads a raiding party of 20 black and white troops in the capture of two American captains and some stock.

**1777, July 2** Vermont, not one of the original 13 states, becomes the first U.S. territory to abolish slavery.

**1777, July 9** Black commando Tack Sisson spearheads a daring raid to capture British Major General Richard Prescott from his own headquarters.

**1777, August 4** Reflecting the bigotry of some American commanders, General Philip Schuyler complains of the high number of black soldiers in his reinforcements as a disgrace to American arms. However, this army shortly wins the great victory over Burgoyne at Saratoga.

**1777, September** Ty, the feared black commando working for the British, is mortally wounded in his squad's attack on the house of Captain Joshua Hardy.

**1777, September 5** Virginia legislators are alarmed by the continued flight of slaves to join British forces, yet they will not allow slaves to enlist on the American side.

**1777, September 10** Many black veterans see action in the Battle of Brandywine, including Samuel Charlton, Oliver Cromwell, John Frances (wounded), and artillery man Edward Hector, who risks his life to keep the enemy from capturing an ammunition wagon.

**1777, October 4** Samuel Charlton, a 17-year-old slave enlisted as his master's substitute, is one of the black soldiers fighting in the daring attack on the British at Germantown.

**1777, October 22** Black and white troops stand firm to repel a British attack on Delaware River's Fort Mercer.

**1777, October 23** A Hessian officer's diary reads: "The Negro can take the field instead of his master, and therefore no regiment is to be seen in which there are not Negroes in abundance, and among them are able-bodied and strong fellows."

**1777, November** Connecticut's largest vessel, the *Oliver Cromwell,* carries five black marines in its patrol of the Lesser Antilles and the Azores.

**1777, November 15** The Articles of Confederation, which govern the states during the Revolution, are adopted. The document makes no reference to black people.

**1777, December 11** Washington begins his retreat to Valley Forge. Many soldiers will desert during this terrible winter, but black troops less than whites.

**1778, January 1** Rhode Island's two battalions are severely depleted at Valley Forge. General James Varnum proposes to Washington that the state be allowed to meet its quota by raising a slave-soldier regiment, and Washington agrees.

**1778, January 19** With the Southern colonies reluctant to use blacks as soldiers, General Washington suggests to Maryland, Virginia, and the Carolinas that blacks be employed in combat-support functions.

**1778, February 2** Rhode Island passes the first slave enlistment act, which provides that slaves who serve for the duration of the war will be declared free and grants them the same pay and bounties as whites.

**1778, February 23** The organization of Rhode Island's black 1st Regiment officially begins.

**1778, April** Massachusetts passes an act legalizing the enlistment of blacks, but turns down artillery captain Thomas Kench's proposal to raise a black regiment.

**1778, April** Black civil rights leader Prince Hall enlists at Medford, Mass., receiving a bounty of $100.

**1778, June 8** Georgia's Council of Safety empowers Colonel Andrew Williamson to hire or impress black laborers to repair state roads.

**1778, June 28** At Monmouth courthouse, the last great battle in the North, 700 black troops fight under General Washington in an attack that rattles the main core of the British army.

**1778, July 28** The newly recruited, black 1st Rhode Island Regiment is sent out on a planned combat-support mission as one of its first assignments.

**1778, July 29** Admiral D'Estaing's French fleet arrives at Newport, R.I., to coordinate a land-sea attack against the British.

**1778, August** Names on Northern muster roles show that black soldiers are bearing arms in exchange for their freedom. One Connecticut regiment includes Jeffery Liberty, Pomp Liberty, Sharp Liberty, Cuff Liberty, Dick Freedom, Ned Freedom, Cuff Freedom, Peter Freeman, Jube Freeman, and Prinnis Freeman.

**1778, August 10** A hurricane forces Admiral D'Estaing to seek refuge in Boston harbor, leaving General Sullivan to face a much stronger British force on Rhode Island. Part of Sullivan's command is the new black regiment.

**1778, August 11** In the Battle of Rhode Island, Colonel Greene's raw First Regiment of 125 black soldiers holds the lines against four hours of British-Hessian assaults, enabling the entire American army to escape a trap.

**1778, August 24** Muster rolls show 775 black troops in the Continental army; 148 are serving in General Samuel Parson's brigade.

**1778, November 4** French Admiral D'Estaing sails from Boston for the West Indies to recruit blacks.

**1778, December 10** John Jay, an advocate of black rights, is elected president of the Continental Congress.

**1778, December 29** The British capture Savannah, Ga., thanks to aged slave guide Quamino Dolly, who volunteers to lead them through a heavy swamp to the undefended rear of the American position.

**1779, February** After taking Savannah and Augusta, General Henry Clinton's army is joined by large numbers of runaway slaves who, barred from joining Georgia's militia, have defected to the British in order to fight for their freedom.

**1779, February 16** Freed to enlist as his master's substitute, artillery man Abner Dabney of Georgia shows "bravery and fortitude" in the Battle of Kettle Creek, while sustaining a broken thigh.

**1779, March** At the head of a "half-white and half-black army," Bernardo Galvez, Spanish governor of Louisiana, drives the British from the Mississippi Valley.

**1779, March 14** Alexander Hamilton urges Congress to allow slaves to enlist, reminding them that "the contempt we have been taught to entertain for the blacks, makes us fancy many things that are founded neither in reason nor experience."

**1779, March 16** Henry Laurens writes Washington that the British could be driven from Georgia if the American forces were strengthened by 3,000 blacks from South Carolina.

**1779, March 29** Congress urges South Carolina and Georgia to immediately enlist 3,000 black soldiers. This so incenses the privy council of South Carolina that it recommends withdrawing from the Revolution.

**1779, May 11** A black petition to end slavery is sent to the general assembly of Connecticut.

**1779, May 12** An unidentified black civilian provides American general William Moultrie with detailed information about surprise British troop deployments.

**1779, May 18** Massachusetts frees six black sailors captured from the British, provided they enlist in the state navy.

**1779, May 26** South Carolina stubbornly rejects a Congressional proposal to form a black militia, even though Charleston is threatened and the state can barely raise 750 white men for active duty—partly because so many citizens have to remain at home to prevent their slaves from revolting or deserting to the British.

**1779, June** Admiral D'Estaing enlists both white and black slaves in the West Indies.

**1779, June 30** To recruit blacks for the British army, General Clinton proclaims that rebel "Negroes who reach the British lines are free."

**1779, July 2** General Horatio Gates, now impressed by black fighting men, writes a letter on behalf of runaway slaves who "assist us in securing our freedom at the risk of their own lives."

**1779, July 15** Black spy Pompey________ brings the information which General Anthony Wayne then uses to storm Stony Point, N.Y.

**1779, August** Black trader Jean Baptiste Point du Sable is arrested by royal troops in Wisconsin for his anti-British sentiments.

**1779, September 14** South Carolina's naval commissioners issue orders for the recruiting of black seamen.

**1779, September 23** The Father of the American Navy, John Paul Jones in the *Bonhomme Richard*, whose crew includes free black seamen, defeats the *Serapis* in the Atlantic.

**1779, October 9** Admiral D'Estaing's 3,600-strong army, including 545 black troops from Santo Domingo, is beaten back from an ill-advised attack on Savannah, but the black unit holds off a British counterattack, preventing a rout.

**1779, November** The army from Louisiana, containing a majority of black troops and several black officers, captures Mobile and Pensacola; six black officers are decorated for bravery.

**1779, November 12** Blacks petition the New Hampshire legislature to outlaw slavery.

**1779, December 7** Papers for the Virginia navy's *Tempest* show four blacks aboard. It is probable that at least 140 black seamen served on the state fleet during the war.

**1779, December 9** Eighteen-year-old Jabez Olly enlists in Captain Rufus Lincoln's company of the 7th Massachusetts Regiment as a drummer, a typical assignment for black soldiers.

**1780, February 9** Paul Cuffe and six other free black residents of Massachusetts petition the legislature demanding the right to vote since they pay taxes. The case is eventually decided in their favor.

**1780, February 26** Concerted British forces attack Charleston, S.C., which the state legislature would rather leave inadequately defended than protect by arming blacks.

**1780, March** Writing from Charleston, General Benjamin Lincoln alerts Washington that the enlistment of slaves is

*The battle of Rhode Island, where the first black American regiment took the field.*

necessary for the safety of the town, but the South Carolina assembly will not consent.

**1780, March 1** Pennsylvania becomes the first state to pass a measure abolishing slavery, though emancipation is to be gradual.

**1780, April 1** The British encircle Charleston in a steel ring made possible by using blacks in combat-support functions more extensively than anywhere else in the war.

**1780, May 12** Charleston surrenders to the British, who dispatch patrols of blacks and noncommissioned officers to dismount and remove the captured guns.

**1780, May 17** The British army that has conquered Charleston, South Carolina's largest city, is swelled by runaway slaves.

**1780, June 1** Connecticut organizes a 52-man black company, which fights as a separate unit until November 1782.

**1780, June 3** British commander-in-chief Clinton proclaims freedom to fugitive slaves of rebel masters, provided they serve the British faithfully till the end of the war.

**1780, July** The Hospital Department in Virginia signs on a black woman slave, promising to pay her master a fixed rate as long as she is employed. This practice of hiring slaves for combat-support functions is common.

**1780, July 9** After twice debating freedom petitions pressed by slaves, the New Hampshire legislature postpones further deliberations "to a more convenient opportunity."

**1780, August 16** Black wagonners and laborers participate on both sides as the British crush the Americans at Camden, S.C.

**1780, September 3** Henry Laurens, who has strongly advocated creation of black regiments in the South, falls captive to the British.

**1780, October** Maryland authorizes slave enlistments, the only Southern state to do so during the Revolutionary War.

**1780, October 19** Pennsylvania prohibits the importation of slaves.

**1780, November 22** In an effort to secure more white volunteers, the Virginia legislature considers a bill to give a slave to every new recruit, but the measure is rejected.

**1780, November 28** James Madison tries to convince the

*Revolutionary flagship* The Bonhomme Richard, *whose crew numbered several blacks, won America's first great naval victory over the British man-of-war* Serapis.

Virginia assembly to liberate certain slaves for enlistment, but slave-owner opposition is inflexible.

**1781** Slave Cuffee______, pilot of Virginia Commodore Richard Barron's ship, dies of wounds received at the wheel.

**1781** James Forten, not yet 15 years old, enlists as a powderboy on the Pennsylvania privateer *Royal Lewis*.

**1781** Military dispatches praise black Jupiter, who "saved four guns during the time the enemy was in Richmond."

**1781** In one of the best-executed operations of the war, the largely black army of Louisiana takes control of Florida.

**1781, January 18** Many black veterans fight in the strategic victory at Cowpens, S.C., which is often considered the best-executed American battle of the war.

**1781, February 5** General Cornwallis gives the order that blacks are not to be armed under any circumstances.

**1781, March 20** New York passes a law freeing slaves whose masters allow them to enlist. The masters are to receive a compensation of 500 acres per emancipation.

**1781, March 25** Richard Barnes in Maryland writes to Governor Lee of Virginia describing, with great concern, the favorable reaction of blacks to the sight of British ships in the area.

**1781, March 27** Lafayette takes James Armistead into his service as a spy.

**1781, April** Quok Walker brings a freedom suit against his master on the basis of Massachusetts' constitution, which states that "all men are born free and equal." Walker eventually wins his freedom.

**1781, May 4** Rhode Island's black regiment suffers heavy casualties at Point Bridge, N.Y., in a futile attempt to save the life of its commanding officer, Colonel Greene.

*Long before leading the black revolution in Haiti, King Henri Christophe was a teenage soldier at the Battle of Savannah.*

*Relying heavily on black labor, the British encircled Charleston in a steel ring.*

*The "old swamp fox" Francis Marion and his guerrillas; they hit the British behind their lines. Many blacks fought with the "fox."*

**1781, May 9** Jefferson appeals to the Virginia legislature to at the very least draft slaves into the army as laborers. However, the legislature will go no further than petitioning masters to lease out their bondsmen.

**1781, May 10** The Maryland legislature decrees that all free black men are eligible for the draft.

**1781, June** Smallpox, aggravated by unsanitary conditions, kills great numbers of blacks laboring for the British.

**1781, June** Virginia slave Saul Matthews, an American spy, returns with crucial information about British defenses and, that very night, leads the successful raid which forces Cornwallis to abandon his strong position at Portsmouth, Va.

**1781, July 4** Black troops make up one-fourth of the army assembled at White Plains headquarters.

**1781, July 13** British General Leslie conceives a plan to use the corpses of 700 black smallpox victims to spread the disease around rebel plantations.

**1781, July 20** Petitioning for a force of 400 black troops, Lafayette writes to Washington: "Nothing but a treaty of alliance with the Negroes can find us dragoon horses, and it is by this means the enemy have so formidable a cavalry."

**1781, August 13** Black patriot Nicholas______, of Kent County, Del., rides to Dover to give the alarm that the British are coming.

**1781, September 6** At the Battle of Groton Heights the fierce tenacity of hugely outnumbered Americans infuriates the ultimately victorious British into killing their captives, including black orderly Jordan Freeman, who had speared the British major in hand-to-hand fighting, and black volunteer Lambo Latham.

**1781, September 8** Fort Griswold surrenders to the British following heavy casualties to its garrison, which included many black soldiers.

**1781, October 1** The Virginia schooner *Patriot* is taken by the British. Among the many black crewmen made prisoner is veteran James Ranger.

**1781, October 6** The American army begins the climactic siege of Cornwallis at Yorktown. Blacks serve on both sides but are generally restricted to laboring roles for the British.

**1781, October 19** Slave James Robinson wins a gold medal at the Battle of Yorktown, where Cornwallis' defeat marks the end of Britain's major war effort.

**1781, October 22** Visiting Lafayette's camp, defeated General Cornwallis is surprised to find that his chief black spy is really an American double agent. Although unidentified, the black man is probably James Armistead.

**1781, December 9** Rhode Island's skillful General Nathanael Green is dispatched to the Southern theater, where he bluntly tells South Carolina's governor that slave enlistments are necessary to protect the state's territory.

**1782, February 25** Instead of arming blacks, South Carolina offers a slave bounty to each new white recruit.

**1782, May 19** Describing South Carolina's refusal to allow blacks to bear arms, Laurens writes Washington that the voice of reason was "drowned by the howlings of a triple-headed monster, in which prejudice, avarice and pusillanimity were united."

**1782, July 21** 5,000 fugitive slaves chose to leave with the

British as they evacuate Savannah, Ga.

**1782, August** Caesar Perry ranks first in a Massachusetts list of noncommissioned officers and privates entitled to length of service honors. Many black soldiers in the 1st Rhode Island Regiment served for five consecutive years.

**1782, November 10** Furnished with troop information by a black who has lived with the Shawnee tribe, General G. R. Clark routs Indian-loyalist forces at Piqua.

**1782, November 16** Many of 3,500 Virginians conscripted to level the works at Yorktown are blacks.

**1782, November 20** A preliminary peace agreement is signed in Paris, but the British fail to comply with the provision to return fugitive slaves to their rebel masters.

**1782, December 16** The British evacuation of Charleston, S.C., is completed; 5,327 escaped slaves leave with them to be resettled in Jamaica, St. Lucia, Halifax, East Florida, and England.

**1783, April 19** War is over, Congress declares. More than 5,000 blacks have served in the American forces, and another 1,000 have borne arms for the British.

**1783, June 13** Rhode Island's black regiment is disbanded at Saratoga, N.Y.

**1783, October** Virginia puts up for sale most of the state-owned slaves in its navy when it disbands that force. The few retained to man the state's two remaining vessels, such as Joseph Ranger, William Bush, and Jack Knight, are given their freedom in 1789.

**1783, October 20** The Virginia legislature forbids the re-enslavement of black veterans who had been promised freedom for their military service.

**1783, November 29** For the final evacuation of British subjects from New York City, the British commissioners compile a detailed list of evacuees, which includes 2,722 blacks.

**1783, December 4** For his retirement banquet and farewell to his officers, General Washington chooses New York City's Fraunces Tavern, a famous black-owned restaurant.

**1784, February 13** Rhode Island's assembly legislates that all children of slaves born after March 1, 1784 shall be born free.

**1784, April 4** Despite efforts by his former master to re-enslave him, honorably discharged Ned Griffin is guaranteed his freedom by the South Carolina legislature.

**1784, April 22** Jefferson draws up an ordinance for the government of the Northwest Territory, which recommends the exclusion of slavery.

**1784, September 1** Peter Williams, who later becomes one of the founders of the AME Zion Church in New York, is freed from his loyalist master.

**1784, November 20** General Lafayette writes a letter commending James Armistead's services to the Continental army; Virginia's state legislature eventually buys Armistead his freedom.

*John Hancock presented this flag to Boston's black regiment, which called itself the "Bucks of America."*

# BLACK PATRIOTS IN THE ERA OF THE AMERICAN REVOLUTION

## CRISPUS ATTUCKS
## Patriot
## c. 1723-1770

Crispus Attucks, a runaway slave, holds the place of honor in the American Revolution as "the first to defy, the first to die." He earned this honor on March 5, 1770, the night of the infamous Boston Massacre, when British troops fired into an unruly crowd of Bostonians, killing five of them. Many historians cite this incident as the beginning of the war for independence.

The most widely accepted account of what Attucks did that night was given by John Adams during the subsequent trial of the British soldiers. According to what Adams told the jury, Attucks undertook "to be the hero of the night; and to lead this army with banners, to form them in the first place in Dock Square, and march them up to King Street with their clubs." When the crowd reached the soldiers, it was Attucks who "had hardiness enough to fall in upon them, and with one hand took hold of a bayonet, and with the other knocked the man down." At this point the panicked soldiers fired, and in the echoes of their volley, as five men fell dying to the wintry street, the seeds of the American Revolution were sown.

As a runaway slave, Crispus Attucks seems to have taken the first step for independence in more than one way. Certainly, no account of the American struggle for freedom would be complete without remembering his heroic dedication to liberty.

## SAMUEL CHARLTON
## Soldier
## 1760-1843

Samuel Charlton was enlisted in the American forces by his master when he was only 16 or 17 years old. Like many other black men, he was ordered to take his master's place in the fighting. Despite this wartime service, he went back to slavery when the war was over and was not liberated until his master's will freed all his slaves and provided Charlton with a special pension.

Charlton saw action at the battles of Brandywine, Germantown, and Monmouth. Historians estimate that of the 15,000 troops at Monmouth—Washington's historic attack on the British evacuating Philadelphia—700 were black. Many of these men were veterans of the terrible winter at Valley Forge, when cold, hunger, and inadequate clothing thinned the ranks of the patriots. Records from this desperate point in American history show that black men deserted at a lower rate than whites.

When Charlton was freed, he and his wife moved to New York City, where he lived for the rest of his life.

## OLIVER CROMWELL
## Soldier
## 1753-1853

Oliver Cromwell served in the American revolutionary forces for 6 years and 9 months, much longer than most of the

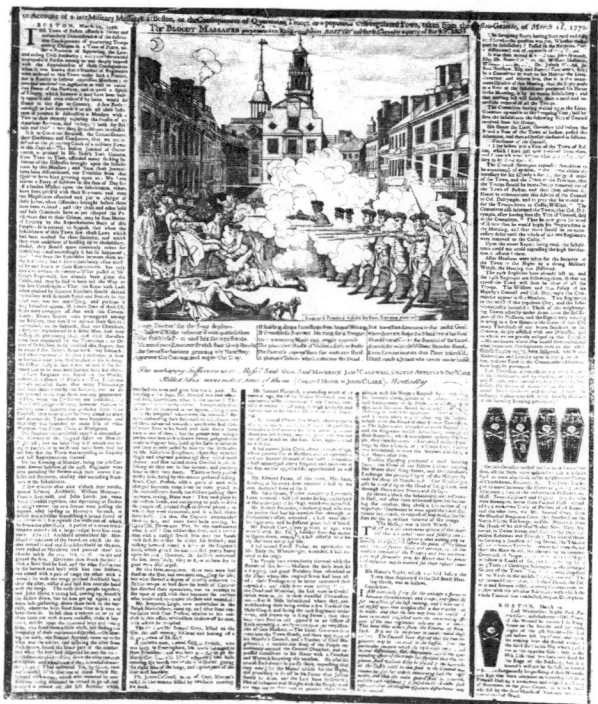

*Contemporary newspapers headlined the massacre in Boston with Paul Revere's famous engraving.*

*Protestor Crispus Attucks was among those slain in the Boston Massacre.*

*Many black veterans fought in the strategic victory at Cowpens, South Carolina, which is often considered the best executed American battle of the war.*

patriots, and saw action in many important battles. Besides being present at the surrender of Cornwallis at Yorktown, he was one of the valiant soldiers who crossed the Delaware River with Washington on Christmas night in 1776.

Born in Columbus, N.J., Cromwell enlisted in the Second New Jersey Regiment, under the command of Colonel Israel Shreve. He participated in the battles of Trenton and Princeton in 1776-1777, Brandywine in 1777, Monmouth in 1778, and Yorktown in 1781. When he was discharged he was awarded an Army pension of $96 a year in recognition of his honorable service. He settled on a farm in his native state and, after raising a large family, lived to be 100 years old.

## WILLIAM FLORA
## Soldier, Business Leader
## 1755-1820

Long after his comrades had retreated into the fort at Norfolk, Va., William Flora stood his ground on the Great Bridge, defending it against the British attack of December 9, 1776. His bravery is credited with sparking an American victory that eventually forced the British to withdraw from Norfolk. Born in Portsmouth, Va., he was one of the 1,000 free blacks in that colony at the outbreak of the Revolution. Although the British governor tried to win the support of the black population, Flora was among the leaders of the majority who joined the American side. After the war, he received the standard 100-acre land bounty and became a successful livery stable operator. When the War of 1812 broke out, he quickly leaped to his country's defense once more, enlisting as a marine on a gunboat.

## JORDAN FREEMAN
## Soldier
## ?-1781

Like the majority of black infantrymen, orderly Jordan Freeman was assigned to noncombative battle-support functions. When the chance to fight came at the Battle of

*Lemuel Haynes interrupted his preparations for the ministry to bear arms for America.*

*Black infantryman Jordan Freeman killed the British commander at the battle of Groton Heights.*

Groton Heights, however, he fought valiantly and gave his life in one of the fiercest combats of the Revolution.

The Battle of Groton Heights took place on September 6, 1781, when a British force under traitor Benedict Arnold was sent to capture the port of New London. Although victory was impossible, the hugely outnumbered Americans put up a terrible resistance. Jordan Freeman was in the thick of the action. When the British stormed the fortifications, it was Freeman who met the British major in vicious hand-to-hand fighting and speared him fatally. British casualties were so high in this battle that when they finally triumphed, they madly bayoneted their captives. Dying alongside Freeman was Lambo Latham, another black orderly who had insisted on volunteering for that day's fighting. The courage of these men stands as an undying example of the mettle of the majority of unknown black infantrymen.

## LEMUEL HAYNES
## Minuteman, Clergyman
## 1753-1833

Lemuel Haynes was the son of a black father and a white mother. Deserted by his mother, he was brought up by Deacon David Rose of Granville, Mass. Extraordinarily precocious, he began writing adult sermons while still a youngster, but his preparation for the ministry was interrupted by the advent of the Revolution. Answering Paul Revere's midnight call to arms, he fought in the war's first battle at Lexington on April 19,1775. He joined the regular forces and served with Ethan Allen's Green Mountain Boys at the capture of Fort Ticonderoga.

After the war he became pastor of the Congregational Church of Middle Granville, and in 1786, he transferred to Torrington, Conn., becoming the first black minister of a church with a white congregation. Famous as a sermon writer, he served as a pastor in Vermont and New York until his death in 1833.

## EDWARD HECTOR
## Soldier
## c. 1744-1834

One of the few black men to serve in the artillery regiments, Edward Hector was a private in Captain Hercules Courtney's company of the Third Pennsylvania Artillery. After enlisting

*James Armistead Lafayette, one of America's intelligence agents.*

*Heeding the command not to fire "until you see the whites of their eyes," Peter Salem shot British Major Pitcairn at the Battle of Bunker Hill.*

in March 1777, he served valorously in the Battle of Brandywine, where he had charge of an ammunition wagon. The Americans were forced to retreat, and the order was given to abandon the wagons to the enemy. Hector courageously disobeyed the order, and not only brought his team, wagon, and cargo to safety, but stopped a few times on the field of battle to gather up weapons that had been cast away by fleeing soldiers. Nevertheless, Hector became one of the forgotten veterans of the Revolution. The Pennsylvania legislature refused to award him a pension for his service and did not see fit to grant him any recompense until 1833, when he was sent a $40 donation.

### AGRIPPA HULL
### Soldier
### c. 1759-?

Agrippa Hull, a free-born black man from Massachusetts, enlisted at the age of 18. He served for six years, four of them under General Tadeusz Kosciuszko. Assigned to a unit of military surgeons, he assisted at many field operations and amputations. After his discharge, he returned to the Massachusetts town of Stockbridge, where he was a respected citizen.

### PRINCE HALL
### Fraternal Leader, Civil Rights Activist
### 1735-1807

Prince Hall, the founder of black Freemasonry, was one of America's first civil rights leaders. Born in the British West Indies, he migrated to Boston as a young man and rose to become an influential member of the black community there. In January 1777, he was the prime force behind a black petition sent to the Massachusetts House of Representatives, arguing that every principle which impelled America to break with England pleaded for immediate abolition of slavery. Although small in stature, Hall enlisted in the Medford militia and served in the armed forces during the Revolution. After the war, he obtained a charter from Masons in England for African Lodge Number 459, which is the oldest black fraternal organization in America. True to the ideals of Freemasonry, Hall was dedicated to helping his fellowmen. He was self-educated and had a high regard for schooling. As early as 1787, he lobbied for the organization of schools for black children in Boston. Another important petition drawn up under his leadership was the 1788 document which raised a public outcry against the kidnapping and sale into slavery of free blacks. Until his death, Hall remained a notable citizen of Massachusetts, where he was a property owner with full voting rights. Many Masonic lodges celebrate September 7 as Prince Hall Day.

### JAMES ARMISTEAD LAFAYETTE
### American spy

Although born a slave, James Armistead was willing to risk his life behind enemy lines collecting information for the American cause. The many valuable reports he furnished the

*The romanticized painting of the surrender of British General Cornwallis to General Washington pays tribute to the major contributors of the American victory.*

Marquis de Lafayette enabled the French commander to check the troop advances of British General Cornwallis, setting the stage for Washington's 1781 victory at Yorktown, which crushed the Crown's North American empire south of Canada. In recognition of these services, Armistead was granted his freedom by the Virginia legislature in 1786. It was not until 1819, however, that Virginia finally thought to award him a pension of $40 a year along with a grant of $100. He adopted the surname "Lafayette" in honor of his former commander who, on an 1824 trip to the United States, did not fail to pay him a visit.

## BARZILLAI LEW
### Soldier
### 1743-1793

Adventurous Barzillai Lew was the son of a free father who had immigrated to Massachusetts from Haiti. A cooper by trade, he joined Captain Thomas Farrington's volunteers for nine months of combat during the French and Indian wars of the 1760s. When the evolution broke out, he enlisted in May 1775, and saw action at the Battle of Bunker Hill and the siege of Boston. He continued to serve for the full six years of hostilities as a soldier and a fifer. Because of his courage and seasoned skills, this veteran was chosen for many daring guerrilla assignments in New England.

## SAUL MATTHEWS
### Soldier, Spy

Born a slave in Virginia, Saul Matthews won his freedom for "many essential services rendered to the Commonwealth during the... war." Although he had joined the American forces as a rifleman, his most memorable exploit was as a spy. To dislodge British General Cornwallis from his control of Portsmouth, the Americans desperately needed information about his fortifications. Matthews penetrated enemy lines, carefully collected the necessary data, and led a successful raiding party against the British on the very night of his return. So many British prisoners were taken that Cornwallis was forced to abandon his strong position.

## SALEM POOR
### Soldier

Salem Poor was a member of a predominantly white Massachusetts regiment, who distinguished himself so gallantly in the Battle of Charleston in 1775 that 14 officers sent a petition on his behalf to the General Court of Massachusetts. The petition says, in part: "Salem Poor of Col. Frye's Regiment... behaved like an Experienced officer, as well as an Excellent Soldier... We would only begg leave to Say in the Person of this Negro Centers a Brave and gallant Soldier. The reward due to so great and Distinguished a caracter, We Submit to the Congress." Poor went on to serve at Valley Forge and White Plains.

### JOSEPH RANGER
### Seaman

Joseph Ranger, a free black man, enlisted in Virginia's navy in 1776 and served on four of her ships of war during the Revolution. He was crewman of the *Jefferson* when the British exploded it during a James River combat. Undaunted, he joined the *Patriot*, on which he served until a defeat shortly before Yorktown ended with the whole crew being taken prisoner. After the end of hostilities, Ranger continued to serve on Virginia ships until the last of them was retired in 1787. His 11-year term of enlisted service is apparently one of the longest on record for the American revolutionary forces. Following his discharge, he received a land grant of 100 acres and a pension of $96 per year for life.

### JAMES ROBINSON
### Soldier
### 1753-1868

The story of James Robinson's life exemplifies the bad treatment received by many black veterans of the Revolution. Although he was promised his freedom for serving in the American army, and despite the fact that he won a gold medal for military valor at Yorktown, James Robinson's reward was to be sold down the river into the harsh slavery of the deep South. This came about because his master died, and the heirs refused to honor the promise of freedom. Although predictably Robinson should have been bitter and resentful, when war broke out again in 1812, he gallantly answered Andrew Jackson's call for riflemen at the Battle of New Orleans. When the fighting was over, Robinson once more returned to a life of slavery on a cotton plantation. He never gave in, however. Although condemned to servitude, he lived to be 115 years old and, when the Emancipation Proclamation was finally written, he was there to hear it's announcement. This extraordinary man, who had twice fought for American freedom, was able to live the last years of his life as a free citizen.

### PETER SALEM
### Soldier
### ?-1816

Peter Salem was one of the patriots who manned the breastworks at Bunker Hill on June 17, 1775. According to contemporary accounts, he was the marksman who shot British Major Pitcairn dead when he leapt on the wall and claimed victory. Because he was a slave, Salem was almost drilled out of the army shortly after that feat when the Congress decided to use only free men in the Continental Army. However, his owners, the Belknaps of Framingham,

*This famous picture of Washington crossing the Delaware shows Prince Whipple manning the first starboard oar.*

*The victorious American Colonial Army.*

gave him his freedom so that he could continue to fight. He was one of the many black soldiers who served valiantly in the cause of freedom for all Americans.

### TACK SISSON
**Soldier**

Commando Tack Sisson participated in many raids behind enemy lines in New England. His most famous exploit was the daring capture of British Major General Prescott in his own headquarters, and the subsequent escape with his prize through enemy lines. This high-ranking abduction was necessary to bait a prisoner exchange for captured American Major General Charles Lee. The colonel in charge of the Rhode Island militia hand-picked a squadron of 44 men, and he and Sisson were among the three commandos who finally crept to the British general's quarters, subdued a sentry, broke down the door, and captured their quarry. They returned through the sentries without any problems and the operation was a complete success, although, as the *London Chronicle* reported, the British general had been carried off "without his breeches."

### CAESAR TARRANT
**Ship Pilot**
**1755-1796**

Caesar Tarrant was one of a number of knowledgeable black pilots spawned by the Chesapeake Bay waterways whose skills were put to service for the American Revolution. A Virginia slave, Tarrant served in that state's navy for over four years, until his bark, the Patriot, was captured just before the battle of Yorktown. He is known to have been at the helm during a famous sea encounter with a British privateer. When the war was over, the Virginia legislature emancipated Tarrant for his services. He became a wealthy landowner.

### PRINCE WHIPPLE
**Soldier**

One of George Washington's most loyal comrades-in-arms was Prince Whipple, a black man born in Amabon, Africa. History claims that Whipple was sent to America as a child to get an education, but was sold into slavery on his arrival in Baltimore. In any event he succeeded in joining the Continental forces as a body guard to General Whipple of New Hampshire, whose name he took, and served in many of General Washington's campaigns. After enduring the hardships of the retreat from Long Island, he was one of the soldiers to have the privilege of being in the boat with Washington during the famous Christmas night crossing of the Delaware. This event is commemorated in Emanuel Gottlieb Leutze's inspiring painting of the event. Prince Whipple is buried in North Cemetery, Portsmouth, N.H.

# BLACK SERVICEMEN AND THE MILITARY ESTABLISHMENT

**The Nation's Wars ■ A Chronology of Military Events ■ Black Congressional Medal of Honor Winners ■ Black Graduates of the U.S. Military Academy ■ Black Graduates of the U.S. Naval Academy ■ Black Graduates of the U.S. Air Force Academy ■ Black Cadets Enrolled at the Service Academies ■ Black Armed Forces Brass ■ Outstanding Military Figures**

The experience of settling America, and the burden of defending it, have been shared by people of many continents. Black men, too, have built the nation, forged its destiny in peace, and defended it in war. They began serving America long before the nation had come into being and have fought long and honorably in every major American conflict.

As in other areas of American life, the black man in the military establishment has been subject to discriminatory treatment and second-class status. In the Revolutionary War, he achieved parity with the white patriot only because conditions were too desperate to impose artificial barriers between men in the field; in the War of 1812, he excelled on land and sea when emergency conditions required his involvement; during the Civil War, he was a pawn until his importance was recognized by both sides and he was thrust into the heat of battle, often without adequate preparation and with the added risk of being slaughtered by a vengeful enemy.

The black soldier fought on America's frontier at the close of the nineteenth century, developing great camaraderie with white counterparts of the same hardy and robust breed. Even in Cuba, during the Spanish-American War, much of this mutual respect for each other's combat prowess was in evidence between the four black regiments and Teddy Roosevelt's "Rough Riders." In both world wars, however, a cumbersome and often insensitive military bureaucracy imposed conditions which created class divisions between the men and so contributed to the systematic demoralization of most black forces. Blacks sought to fight alongside white men, but were summarily rejected—often on the uninformed grounds that they possessed no military tradition worthy of recognition. With the coming of integration in 1948, black men widened their role in combat and support functions, often exhibiting a sense of pride in personal excellence and sometimes cultivating a framework of exclusivity. Today, both trends are in evidence: the constant policing by the military itself of placement and promotion opportunities, and the dynamic drive by young black men to express their manhood even before considering questions of involvement with whites. Whatever the merits of these policies and attitudes, one thing remains indisputable: black men have served with valor and distinction in all of America's wars, and have come away with a substantial share of its major citations and decorations.

## THE FIRST BLACK SOLDIERS

### The American Revolution (1775-1781)

American blacks fought in most major battles of the Revolutionary War including Lexington and Concord, Bunker Hill, Trenton, Long Island, Savannah, Valley Forge, and Yorktown. In the most serious prewar clash between the Americans and the British, the Boston Massacre of 1770, one of the five colonists who fell was runaway slave Crispus Attucks. Attucks was in the vanguard of marchers protesting the general presence of British "occupation" forces in Boston and a specific incident involving the alleged beating of an unruly youth by a British "lobster-back."

After war broke out in 1775, General George Washington at first moved to bar all black enlistments in the Continental Army but was forced to modify his stand as soon as the British governor of Virginia, Lord Dunmore, promised to free all blacks who would desert their masters and fight for the British Crown. Washington then recommended that free blacks be allowed to enlist in the Continental Army, although many of the 5,000 who eventually saw combat were in reality slaves who passed muster because of the difficulty recruiters encountered in meeting their monthly quotas.

Blacks served in a variety of capacities—as spies, as pilots, as infantrymen, and as laborers, cooks, and teamsters. Some blacks were with the Minutemen at Lexington and Concord; others wintered with Washington at Valley Forge, crossing the Delaware with him enroute to surprising the Hessians quartered at Trenton. Two blacks—Peter Salem and Salem Poor—were singled out for gallantry at the Battle of Bunker Hill in 1775. Lemuel Haynes, a minister, served at Lexington and with the Ticonderoga expedition. All told, between 8,000 and 10,000 blacks served in the colonial armies of the Revolution. Statistics are available for some states including Massachusetts (572 blacks); Virginia (250 blacks); Rhode Island (one all-black battalion and hundreds of other blacks scattered through "white" regiments); Connecticut (49 blacks in the 2nd Company, Third Regiment); New Hampshire (almost every black of military age); Maryland (780 blacks in one regiment, others in mixed ranks); New York (two battalions of blacks as of 1780); New Jersey and Pennsylvania (mixed battalions).

Blacks serving in the Revolutionary Navy were generally ordinary seamen or orderlies, but not a few were pilots, especially in the coastal patrol boats of the individual states.

(For a more detailed account see the section on Blacks in Colonial and Revolutionary America.)

### The War of 1812

On a June morning in 1807, the British man-of-war Leopard attacked the U.S. Navy's Chesapeake, killing three men and wounding 18 others in a skirmish outside Norfolk harbor. British officers then boarded the Chesapeake and threw irons on four alleged Royal Navy deserters, among them three black seamen, Daniel Martin, William Ware, and John Strachan. Impressment of U.S. seamen was one of the issues which culminated in the War of 1812, a conflict waged primarily at sea. Its most celebrated battle—the Battle of New Orleans—was fought after a peace treaty had been signed in Ghent, Belgium.

The most famous naval figure associated with the war is Oliver Hazard Perry, who requested reinforcements for a projected battle at Lake Erie in 1813, and was appalled when his immediate superior, Commodore Isaac Chauncey, sent him a parcel of "blacks, soldiers, and boys." The word used to describe the reinforcements: "motley."

Chauncey, in his turn, was irritated at his subordinate's sharp criticism, though his reply is subdued and philosophical:

*I have yet to learn that the color of the skin or the cut and trimmings of the coat can affect a man's qualifications or usefulness. I have fifty blacks on board this ship and many of them are my best men; and these people you call soldiers have been to sea from two to seventeen years; and I presume you will find them as good and useful as any men on board your vessel.*

Perry changed his appraisal once the "motley" brigade proved itself under fire. They seemed, in his words, "absolutely insensible to danger," despite the far-from-ideal circumstances under which they had served. The lack of fresh water, for example, had been particularly critical on board ship, impairing the health of many and causing widespread discomfort.

Nathaniel Shaler of the schooner Governor Tompkins registered similar approval of the combat prowess of one of his crew members during a subsequent sea engagement. One man, according to Shaler,

*The British Navy boarded U.S. ships to take American sailors to serve the Crown; both black and white sailors were taken.*

*ought to be registered in the book of fame, and remembered with reverence as long as bravery is considered a virtue. He was a black man, by the name of John Johnson. A twenty-four-pound shot struck him in the hip, and took away all the lower part of his body. In this state, the poor brave fellow lay on the deck, and several times exclaimed to his shipmates: "Fire away, my boys; no haul a color down." The other was also a black man, by the name of John Davis, and was struck in much the same way. He fell near me, and several times requested to be thrown overboard, saying he was only in the way of others.*

*"When America has such tars, she has little to fear from the tyrants of the ocean."*

The most famous land battle of the war found Old Hickory, Andrew Jackson, so hard pressed for troops that he was forced to issue a call for black recruits in a letter to Louisiana's Governor Claiborne. Jackson declared:

*They must be either for us, or against us. Distrust them and you make them your enemies, place confidence in them, and you engage them by every dear and honorable tie to the interest of the country, who extends to them equal rights and privileges with white men.*

His address to the "Free Colored Inhabitants" of Louisiana is far more exalted in tone.

*As sons of freedom, you are now called upon to defend our most inestimable blessing. As Americans, your country looks with confidence to her adopted children for a valorous support, as a faithful return for the advantages enjoyed under her mild and equitable government. As fathers, husbands and brothers, you are summoned to rally around the standard of the eagle, to defend all which is dear in existence...*

*To every noble-hearted, generous freeman of color, volunteering to serve during the present contest with Great Britain, and no longer, there will be paid the same bounty in money and lands, now received by the white soldiers of the United States, viz. one hundred and twenty-four dollars in money, and one hundred and sixty acres of land ...*

*Due regard will be paid to the feelings of freemen and soldiers. You will not, by being associated with white men in the same corps, be exposed to improper comparisons or unjust sarcasm. As a distinct, independent battalion or regiment, pursuing the path of glory, you will, undivided, receive the applause and gratitude of your countrymen.*

Given the era, "feelings" could hardly be expected to hold much weight among brusque frontiersmen of the Jackson breed. Still, they had been brought up by the general himself, apparently out of regard for a code of chivalry which had some relevance among southern gentlemen. Such chivalry, however, was not the primary concern when it came to the matter of the men's pay which was held up by some

*Black sailors fought in every sea engagement of the War of 1812. Shown here is the Battle of Lake Erie.*

*General Andrew Jackson issued an urgent call for black recruits for the Battle of New Orleans, a victory in which black riflemen played an important role.*

subordinate. Outraged, Jackson quickly ordered that the men be paid whether they were "white, black, or tea."

Applause and gratitude held little appeal for the average Southerner who had participated in the glorious victory over the British. After all, what value could there be in according to the black man a share of the triumph? Surely, it might cause him to feel a dangerous sense of importance even as it dramatized his undeniable competency with combat weapons in a critical situation. Thus the annual New Orleans parade commemorating the event afforded blacks little opportunity to feel that they had played a part in this significant chapter of American military history. Ironically, the next time black drummer boy Jordan B. Noble marched through the streets of town was in 1862—the year Union troops took possession of New Orleans. Noble had wanted to stay in service. But he was declared ineligible in the aftermath of an 1820 General Order which stated: "No Negro or Mulatto will be received as a recruit of the Army."

## THE CIVIL WAR (1861-1865)

The Crispus Attucks incident (the Boston Massacre), the Chesapeake-Leopard debacle, the John Brown Raid—all have a common denominator as skirmishes which portended the arrival of full-scale war in these United States.

By 1859 slavery had so aroused the indignation of black and white activists (compromises had kept the agitation in check, but the Dred Scott decision of 1857 had added fuel to the flames of the cause) that there seemed little chance to avoid an armed showdown over the issue. White abolitionist John Brown was never one to wait for a battle, however. Crucial to his strategy was the element of surprise and the prospect of guerrilla warfare. On October 16, 1859, Brown and a band of 21 men—five of them black—seized the arsenal at Harpers Ferry and held it for a few precious hours until federal troops commanded by Robert E. Lee forced him to fight. Brown's capture did not appease the outraged South, which interpreted the very gesture as symptomatic of the North's alleged willingness to attempt the forcible overthrow of slavery. Relatively few abolitionists would ever publicly advocate such a posture since they realized that the more explicit they became, the more they increased the risk of publicizing the struggle as racial rather than sectional.

Those hanged alongside Brown at Charleston in December 1859 included Dangerfield Newby, a runaway slave; John A. Copeland, a North Carolinian; Sheridan Leary, a harness maker and a freedman; and Shields Green, a sailor from South Carolina. (Black Green died alongside white Brown.) One of the five, Osborne Perry Anderson, escaped death, only to write his memoirs and eventually to serve in the Union Army.

Once the South determined to bring the issue to the battlefield, it was not, as is often implied, an appreciably weaker foe than the North. In arms and materiel, yes, but not in the coherence of its aims and the passion of its defenders. The South knew at once what the stakes were; the North was, conversely, ambiguous and equivocal.

None realized the indecisiveness of the North better than Lincoln, a man whose demonstrated moral aversion to slavery should suffice to prove the efficacy of his intentions. It is well to remember, however, that Lincoln came to abolition by guarded states, not in one grand, uninterrupted movement. Originally he argued containment of slavery, that is, prevention of its spread to the Western Territories. For those touched by its blight, he proposed resettlement in Africa, mainly out of a genuine realization that little hope existed for a reconciliation of the races in the South. Compensation of the slaveowner was an unsavory part of this proposed course of action, a gesture embraced by Lincoln mainly in keeping with his stated objective of "preserving the Union."

Political considerations aside, however, there was clearly little resolve cementing the fighting men of the North in their approach to the war. Lincoln issued an initial order calling for 75,000 volunteers—whites only. Black frontiersman Jacob Dodson came forward with an offer to raise 300 black volunteers to defend Washington, D.C. Over 100 Wilberforce students followed suit by attempting to join Union forces. These and all other gestures of black support were rejected for political reasons.

As in the Revolutionary War, however, military concerns soon became the overriding issue. The South could put the black man to use tilling the soil and performing other functionary labors which freed the white gentry to fight the war. The North had no such ready-made class to provide a similarly needed service.

Blacks themselves held the answer. Would they remain loyal to their immediate oppressors, those who, however benevolent, owned them outright, or would they seek refuge in another territory which might potentially alter their condition? For obvious reasons, the risk was worth taking. The black tide of humanity soon flowing into Union lines volunteered to do teamster work, to build roads and fortifications, to forage for units in the field, to load weapons, to serve as personal valets—whatever was needed to guarantee de facto freedom. By the summer of 1861, Lincoln had gone so far as to instruct Union commanders not to return such fugitive slaves to their place of origin. Pressure was already mounting to plug up all the military loopholes that were making victory dubious.

In 1862, one of the "contraband" (this was the name applied to black refugees entering Union lines, a name usually applied to materiel) brought in a Confederate gunboat he had sailed out of Charleston harbor at dawn's early light. Robert Smalls was declared a hero, and declared himself and his family free men. There was compensation, too, for the singular deed of valor in the form of prize booty from the U.S. Senate.

Elsewhere, some white generals sought to obtain a clear directive from Washington, D.C. on the possible use of black fighting men. "Black Dave" Hunter raised the First South Carolina Volunteers but was unable to requisition the necessary equipment and uniforms to incorporate the group properly. Jim Lane of Kansas, an abolitionist and Free Soiler who later became a U.S. senator, cut through the mass of red tape by organizing the First and Second Regiments of Kansas Colored Volunteers. Being frontier soldiers, they were perhaps less preoccupied with the formal regalia of their station. They had two brief and successful skirmishes with the enemy—one at Clay County, Mississippi, the other at the Osage River in Bates County, Missouri. "They fought like tigers," said one Confederate observer. Still another Union commander was comparatively quick to realize the virtues of "Africa." The word "Africa" is extracted from General Ben Butler's own quote in which he professed willingness to "call on Africa to intervene "and confidence that he would not "call in vain." The First Regiment Louisiana Native Guards were mustered into the U.S. Army on September 27, 1862. They fought under the impressive name *Chasseurs D'Afrique*.

By January 1, 1863, it was clear that the nation was at a historic crossroads. The Union was torn asunder, its armies unable to bring the rebellious South to heel. It would be presumptuous to claim that the Emancipation Proclamation changed all of this; but it would be equally foolish to see no

*An escaped slave in the Union Army, from an 1860s Harpers drawing.*

connection between the Union victory and the freedom promised slaves by the document. Lincoln's edict not only pronounced the dread word "freedom" but also paved the way for black participation in the conflict—not as support units, but as fighting men.

Three years, the recruiting order stated, not three months as Lincoln's first summons had dictated.(three year enlistments rather than the original three months call—originaally it was believed it would take but a few months to defeat the South) By the summer of 1863, Mayor George Stearns of Medford, Massachusetts, reported, somewhat obtusely, that "colored men" were beginning "to understand they gain nothing by standing off but if they would gain their rights and secure protection at the hands of government they

*This black battalion was ambushed by "rebels and bloodhounds" in South Carolina.*

must rally at its call." The implication that blacks were hanging back, waiting for whites to get the job done, is not only insulting, it is woefully inaccurate. Dodson and the Wilberforce students were among those who knew otherwise.

Word from Massachusetts read as follows:

*Massachusetts now welcomes you to arms as her soldiers. She has but a small colored population from which to recruit. She has full leave of the General Government to send one regiment to the war, and she has undertaken to do it. Go quickly and help fill up this first colored regiment from the North. I am authorized to assure you that you will receive the same wages, the same rations, the same equipment, the same protection, the same treatment, and the same bounty secured to white soldiers....*

Thus the 54th and the 55th took the banner of the U.S. Army and marched into South Carolina to face the entrenched legions of Fort Wagner in July 1863. Even after the Union batteries had pummeled the fort in an effort to soften it up for an infantry attack, it was virtually unscathed and ready for the onslaught. "Forward Fifty-Fourth! For God and Governor Andrew," regimental commander Robert Gould Shaw bellowed to his men. The men charged into withering barrages of small-arms fire, held ranks, and reached the outer parapet before Shaw fell. A few feet away lay black standard bearer William H. Carney, Company C, shot several times. Carney managed to drag himself to safety, the colors always held aloft. Miraculously, he got back, but over 1,500 of his comrades didn't. His regiment alone lost more men than all the Confederate forces combined.

Battles in which black casualties were high were numerous throughout the war. At Port Hudson, Louisiana, in May 1863, 600 men were left dead on the battlefield after what amounted to near suicidal charges against the enemy. The First and Third Louisiana Negro Regiments, raised in New Orleans, were the primary units involved in the engagement. Of them, General Nathanael Banks said:

*The highest commendation is bestowed upon them by all officers in command... [The] history of this day proves conclusively... that the Government will find in this class of troops effective supporters and defenders.*

Elsewhere up the Mississippi, at Miliken's Bend, the 9th Louisiana, the 11th Louisiana, and the 1st Mississippi were attacked by Confederate troops further spurred by the knowledge that their adversaries were black troops. Untrained troops who relied on instinct to survive, they prevented the Confederates from realizing their objective, and once again proved what one eyewitness put into words.

*Tauntingly it has been said that Negroes won't fight. Who says it... when the Battle of Milliken's Bend finds its place among the heroic deeds of this war?... [The] freed slaves will fight.*

They fought, too, at the Battle of Olustee in Florida where, according to one press report,

*the First North Carolina and the Fifty-fourth Massachusetts... did admirably. The First North Carolina held the positions it was placed in with great tenacity, and inflicted heavy losses on the enemy... The Fifty-fourth sustained the reputation they had gained at Fort Wagner, and bore themselves like soldiers throughout the battle.*

Perhaps it was combat fatigue that triggered the upsurge of a new issue: equal pay for equal risks. The black units which had been recruited on the basis of Union slogans promising "the same wages" as all other campaigners had begun to protest shortly after the Fort Wagner struggle. Their pleas had been reasonable and subdued; their arguments logical and persuasive. "[Are] we soldiers," they asked, "or are we laborers? We have done a soldiers duty. Why can't we have a soldiers pay?"

Among their supporters were such prominent Bostonians as Oliver Wendell Holmes and Charles Eliot Norton and such capable field commanders as General Ben Butler, who was appalled at the logic of paying white soldiers an extra $3.50 a month as a clothing allowance when "the colored man fills an equal space in the ranks while he lives, and an equal grave when he falls." It was not until 1864 that the Army Appropriation Act finally succeeded in obliterating the invidious racial distinction which institutionalized separate pay ledgers.

This was the year of one of the most infamous and demoralizing combat episodes of the war, the brutal Fort Pillow Massacre. The few black survivors of the bloody affair were unanimous in their condemnation of the fighting practices of Confederate forces. Their butchery not only increased Union casualties at the close of the day but bore ugly testimony to the hysteria and hatred gripping certain elements of the Confederacy. Only desperate men could have clubbed wounded soldiers, burned them alive, or impaled them on buildings and trees. Hospital patients were sabered to death in their beds; women and children were slain without quarter by men either gone berserk or so furious with rage that hardly a shred of reason or compassion prevailed. Though the massacre was condemned after an official inquiry, no concrete measures were taken to impose a severe penalty on the officers who had somehow permitted, or even justified, the bloodshed.

Another key battle of the war in which black soldiers were subjected to undue pressure and risk occurred at the crater near Petersburg, Virginia, in the summer of 1864. The military objective of the battle was to destroy a small fort protecting Confederate lines. Union General Ambrose Burnside ordered his men to dig a tunnel under the fort, lay explosive mines in the excavation, and blow up the obstruction. The strategy then called for an assault wave to engage the enemy. Black troops, originally singled out to lead the attack, were withdrawn in an eleventh-hour gesture by General Grant himself. After mines were detonated, leaving a gigantic crater in the middle of the battlefield, three white divisions made a rush at the enemy, but they were unable to reach the lines and forced to seek refuge in the crater itself. Exposed and immobilized, they were virtual sitting ducks for Confederate sharp-shooters.

Black reserve troops were immediately summoned to the rescue, but were soon slowed down in their spirited advance by demoralized white troops. Still, they formed a tiny beachhead at the crest of the crater, hanging on tenaciously until they too were forced to retreat. By this time, however, they found themselves lodged between white Union and white Confederate forces. The results of this impasse were disastrous. Panic-stricken Union troops fired wildly into the ranks of their black comrades, even as well-disciplined Confederate forces took full advantage of the desperate plight of the black troops. A Union colonel reported:

*The bravest [white troops] lost heart and men who distrusted Negroes vented their feelings freely. Some colored men... found a worse fate than death in the charge... white men bayoneted blacks who fell into the crater.*

The Battle of Nashville, fought in December 1864, was one of the few engagements in which the coordinated efforts of both black and white troops resulted in the effective repulsion of Confederate forces. Union General James B. Steedman explained:

*All, white and black, nobly did their duty as soldiers and*

*The charge of the 22nd Negro Regiment, Petersburg, Virginia, June 16, 1864. Painted by Andre Castaigne.*

*evinced cheerfulness and resolutions, such as I have never seen excelled in any campaign of the war in which I have borne a part.*

Overall, the extent of black participation in the war can be tabulated with reasonable accuracy, both in terms of the kinds of units in which they were enrolled and the geographical distribution of such troops. Besides the 186,000 combat troops, there were more than 200,000 members of so-called service units. Of the combat troops, nearly 100,000 were mustered into service through the federal government, with the remainder being raised through state levy. Regionally, there were some 34,000 soldiers from the New York-New England area, including Pennsylvania and New Jersey. An additional 12,000 came from the West, including its territories. Over 45,000 came from border states, which Lincoln had feared he would lose and whose loyalty and manpower proved to be valuable adjuncts to the Union victory. Over 93,000 were raised in the rebellious states of the South, which might have done well to utilize black manpower, had it been possible.

Organizationally, black units were subdivided into 120 combat infantry regiments (close to 100,000 men), seven cavalry regiments (over 7,000 men), 12 heavy artillery regiments (over 12,000 men), and 10 companies of light artillery with over 1,300 men. These men saw combat in more than 200 battles classified either as full-scale engagements or minor skirmishes.

All told, one out of every four Union navy men—29,511 in all—was black. They fulfilled a variety of roles on vessels engaged in coastal blockades and in pursuit craft activity, hunting down enemy privateers and gun runners. Black river and harbor pilots were among the best operating in the states. Others served as gunners, loaders, coal heavers, stewards, and firemen. On the docks, black men were equally active as laborers unloading supplies and other equipment. Blacks served aboard the *Kearsage* when she destroyed the *Alabama*, aboard the *Monitor* on its famed engagement with the *Merrimac*, and aboard Farragut's flagship in the Battle of Mobile Bay.

On the very day of Lee's surrender to Grant at Appomattox, black Union troops were still under fire on other battlegrounds, serving under such commanders as General Birney and General Sherman. Black soldiers were complemented by some 200,000 black civilians employed by the Union Army as laborers, cooks, teamsters, and in other support functions.

Four black sailors won Congressional Medals of Honor for valor in combat conditions. (For full details, see the list of winners elsewhere in this section.)

## The Confederate "Experiment"

Not all black participants in the war served with Union forces. Indeed, as hostilities ground to a close, the South searched desperately for some last-ditch measure to stave off defeat. In agonizing frustration, some southern authorities entertained the notion of arming slaves, rationalizing this proposed policy by claiming that many blacks would still regard the South as their homeland, and so fight to save it from "foreign" encroachment, while others would follow their masters out of fear or personal loyalty.

On at least one occasion, the South gave at least momentary consideration to a formal proposal to recruit slaves. The proposal was made by General Pat Cleburne, an Irish supporter of the Confederacy, who broached the subject at a meeting of senior officers in 1864. Since every slave, in Cleburne's view, was a potential free man, he constituted an ever-present source of rebellion within the Confederacy itself, as well as an instant collaborator with Union troops. What had been a source of southern strength at the outset of the war was now "one of our chief sources of weakness." Cleburne proposed that the South turn slavery from weakness to strength again, by boldly and resolutely promising freedom to all slaves who would enlist.

*A rifle company of black Union troops.*

*When the Union called upon blacks to enlist, enlist they did. Here black recruits are taught the use of the minnie rifle.*

His proposal was signed by three other generals and a handful of lower-echelon officers from his own command, but the high command listened in stunned silence, never giving formal approval. "I will not attempt to describe my feelings," one Confederate officer later wrote, "on being confronted with a proposal so startling in its character, so revolting to Southern sentiment, Southern pride and Southern honor... If this thing is once openly proposed to the Army, the total disintegration of that Army will follow in a fortnight." Such quotation gives some indication as to the intensity of feeling against the utilization of armed slaves to aid the Southern cause. Dejectedly, General Cleburne put away his proposal. The war ground on as before.

Although no formal consent was given, there is some evidence that on an informal basis, rather than as a Confederate policy, slaves were at times used in combat. However, the number of slaves and freed black men in combat units was totally insignificant in numbers.

No definitive record exists to determine just how many black soldiers fought on the side of the Confederacy during the Civil War. Most who were readied for combat, however, were freedmen rather than slaves. The latter were generally engaged in construction work on roads, fortifications, and canals. They were also regarded as the "Army of the Soil," workers whose primary function was to tend and harvest the crops which helped feed an army in the field.

The largest of the black units was the First Louisiana Volunteer Regiment, also known as the Native Guards and consisting of nearly 1,000 men. The volunteers had answered Governor Moore's call to arms, issued on March 21, 1862:

*The Governor and Commander-in-Chief, relying implicitly upon the loyalty of the free colored people of this city and state... calls upon them to maintain their organization and be prepared for such orders as may be transmitted to them.*

There were at the time in New Orleans some 13,000 or so free blacks, many of them direct descendants of men who had fought with Andrew Jackson during the War of 1812. Many were educated men of property, even slaveowners themselves, who felt that emancipation and a Union victory would only bring an end to their privileged status.

The fate of the First Louisiana Militia remains shrouded in mystery, however. There is no report of their having followed regular Confederate troops out of the city when it was evacuated following the triumphant entry of the Union Forces in the spring of 1862. Four months later, in August to be exact, General Ben Butler reorganized the Native Guards and recruited them for the Federal side.

There may have been no more than 150 soldiers in the 15 other black militia units serving throughout the country. This figure remains dubious, however. It is based on the muster roll of a Mississippi militia unit with 12 black infantrymen. Many more are known to have served in the defense of Richmond toward the close of the war, and presumably were also present in numbers greater than 12 in the First South Carolina Volunteer Regiment. One black officer, a Colonel Gregg (regiment unknown), surrendered his life on the battlefield of Fredericksburg.

An 1862 issue of Harpers' Magazine provides full insight into the scope of black activity during the war:

*The works before Charleston, commenced late in 1860, were mainly thrown up by large gangs of negroes [sic] from the plantations, and by free negroes [sic] of Charleston, of whom 150 in a single day offered their services to the Governor of South Carolina. In April the Lynchburg Republican proposed "three cheers for the patriotic free Negroes of Lynchburg," of whom seventy had "tendered their services to the governor to act in whatever capacity may be assigned them in defense of the state." It was triumphantly announced that all the fortifications required for the harbor of Norfolk could be erected by the voluntary labor of negroes [sic] In June the Legislature of Tennessee passed an act authorizing the governor to receive into the military service of the state all male free persons of color between the ages of fifteen and fifty; and if a sufficient number did not volunteer they were to be impressed. The Southern newspapers of 1861 were full of accounts of colored volunteers. One told of a grand display, held November 23 at New Orleans, where 28,000 troops were reviewed, among whom was a "regiment composed of 1400 free colored men." The works of Manassas Junction were mainly thrown up by the slaves of the neighboring planters. In February, 1862, the Virginia House of Delegates passed a bill ordering the enlistment of free colored persons for six months. On the 10th of March, Mr. Foote declared in the Confederate Congress that, when Nashville was surrendered, 1000 or 1500 slaves had been called out and employed on the fortifications. In November, Governor Brown of Georgia, called for slaves to complete the fortifications of Savannah; if these were not voluntarily tendered a levy would be made upon every planter in the state of one slave out of five, which would give a working force of 15,000. Subsequent to this time still more stringent measures were taken to bring negroes [sic] into the Confederate service.*

It was not until July 17, 1862 that Congress authorized President Lincoln to employ "persons of African descent" in the naval and military service of the United States. On August 15, 1862, President Davis bitterly denounced "two at least of the generals of the United States" for exciting servile insurrection, and "arming and training slaves for warfare against their masters, citizens of the Confederacy." Clearly, however, from the evidence at least, it was a case of military charges and propaganda.

By the spring of 1865, the Confederates, poised upon the abyss of defeat, again broached the subject of arming slaves. Again Harpers' Magazine reported the particulars with unfailing accuracy:

*In September, 1864, the Governor of Louisiana urged upon the Secretary of War that the time had come to put into the army every able-bodied negro [sic] as a soldier. "I would," he said, "free all able to bear arms, and put them into the field at once." In his message in November Mr. Davis discussed the question. It was to be viewed, he said, "solely in the light of policy and our domestic economy." Late in February, 1865, Lee strongly urged the employment of negroes [sic] as soldiers. "I think," he said, "the measure not only important, but necessary. I do not think our white population can supply the necessities of a long war. I think those who are employed should be freed. It would not be just or wise to require them to remain as slaves." An impressment or draft he thought would not bring out the best class; he would rather call upon those who are willing to come, with the consent of their owners.*

An Act of Congress was ultimately passed (the margin of victory was a lone vote)which empowered the Confederacy to experiment with the idea of using slaves on a limited scale and granting them freedom for their efforts. Critics regarded the motion as an admission of despair to foreign observers, an abandonment of the very principles for which the Confederacy was ostensibly fighting, a gesture which would further demoralize their own white forces, and a decision which would remove too much needed black manpower from the fields. Though the matter remained academic, the stipulations of the enactment are intriguing and revealing:

1. Pay and rations the same for both white and black troops.
2. A quota from each state "not exceeding 300,000 troops to be raised irrespective of color."
3. Eligibility for no more than 25% of the male slaves of any state.
4. "Nothing in this act shall be construed to authorize a change in the relation [between master and slave]."

The last condition was, of course, logically impossible, the desperately incongruous act of a faltering enemy seeking vainly to preserve its ebbing life by arming its natural enemy.

*Mustered out black volunteers rejoin their loved ones in Little Rock, Arkansas.*

## CIVIL WAR BATTLES ENGAGED IN BY THE UNITED STATES COLORED TROOPS (USCT)

Black soldiers played a major role in the Civil War. Nearly 200,000 black combat troops fought in the Union Army, and one of every four men in the Union Navy was black. Blacks saw action in all sections of the country and in all types of warfare. Some of the more significant battles in which they participated are listed below.

Amite River
Appomattox Court House
Arkansas River
Ash Bayou
Ashepoo River
Ashwood Landing
Athens
Barrancas
Bayou Bidell
Bayou Boeuf
Bayou Macon
Bayou St. Lewis
Bayou Tensas
Bayou Tunica
Bermuda Hundreds
Berwick
Big Creek
Big River
Big Springs
Black Creek
Black River
Boggs' Mill
Boyd's Station
Boykin's Mills
Bradford Spring
Brawley For
Brice's Crossroads
Brigsen Creek
Brush Creek
Bryant's Plantation
Cabin Creek
Cabin Point
Camden
Cedar Keys
Chapin's Farm
Charleston
Chattanooga
City Point
Clarkesville
Clinton
Coleman's Plantation
Columbia
Concordia Bayou
Cow Creek
Cox's Bridge
Dallas
Dalton
Darbytown Road
David's Bend
Decatur
Deep Bottom
Deveraux Neck
Drewry's Bluff
Dutch Gap
East Pascagoula
Eastport
Fair Oaks
Federal Point
Fillmore
Floyd
Fort Adams
Fort Anderson
Fort Blakely
Fort Brady
Fort Burnham
Fort Donelson
Fort Gaines
Fort Gibson
Fort Jones
Fort Pillow
Fort Pocahontas
Fort Smith
Fort Taylor
Fort Wagner
Franklin
Ghent
Glasgow
Goodrich's Landing
Grand Gulf
Gregory's Farm
Haines' Bluff
Hall Island
Harrodsburg
Hatcher's Run
Helena
Henderson
Holly Springs
Honey Hill
Hopkinsville
Horse Head Creek
Indian Bay
Indian Town
Indian Village
Island Mound
Island No. 76
Issequena County
Jackson
Jacksonville
James Island
Jenkin's Ferry
John's Island
Johnsonville
Jones' Bridge
Joy's Ford
Lake Providence
Laurence
Little Rock
Liverpool Heights
Madison Station
Magnolia
Marengo
Mariana
Marion
Marion County
McKay's Point
Meffleton Lodge
Memphis
Milliken's Bend
Milltown Bluff
Mitchell's Creek
Morganzia
Moscow Station
Mound Plantation
Mount Pleasant Landing
Mud Creek
Murfreesboro
Nashville
Natchez
Natural Bridge
New Kent Court House
New Market Heights
Olustee
Owensboro
Pass Manchal
Palmetto Ranch
Petersburg
Pierson's Farm
Pine Barren Creek
Pine Barren Ford
Pine Bluff
Plymouth
Point Lookout
Point of Rocks
Point Pleasant
Poison Springs
Port Hudson
Powhatan
Prairie d'Anne
Pulaski
Raleigh
Rector's Farm
Richland
Richmond
Ripley
Roache's Plantation
Rolling Fork
Rooseville Creek
Ross Landing
Sabine River
Salkehatchie
Saltville
Sand Mountain
Sandy Swamp
Scottsboro
Sherwood
Shipwith's Landing
Simpsonville
Smithfield
South Tunnel
Spanish Fort
St. John's River
St. Stephens
Steamer *Alliance*
Steamer *Chippewa*
Steamer *City Belle*
Steamer *Lotus*
Suffolk
Sugar Loaf Hill
Sulphur Branch
Swift Creek
Taylorsville
Timber Hill
Town Creek
Township
Trestle
Tupelo
Vicksburg
Vidalia
Wallace Ferry
Warsaw
Waterford
Waterloo
Waterproof
White Oak Road
White River
Williamsburg
Wilmington
Wilson's Landing, Wharf
Yazoo City
Yazoo Expedition

*The black 10th Cavalry, along with the black 9th Cavalry, patrolled the high plains of the Old West for over fifty years and played a major role in the pacification of the territories.*

## LATER WARS

### Indian Wars on the Frontier

At the close of the Civil War, several USCT regiments remained on active duty for a time, but Congress later authorized the creation of only two regular regiments of cavalry (the 9th and the 10th) and two of infantry (the 24th and the 25th). Known to the Indians as "Buffalo Soldiers," they served on isolated posts located in Texas and the Southwest—building roads, stringing telegraph wire, escorting groups crossing Indian territory, and scouting hostile tribes as well. During this period, 12 blacks won Congressional Medals of Honor for bravery in combat. (See Black Congressional Medal of Honor section for names and units.)

The first action between black troopers and Indians came 40 miles east of Fort Hays, Kansas in September 1867 when 40 troopers on duty protecting workers of the Kansas Pacific Railroad engaged 300 Cheyenne; the last action of black troopers and Indians was likewise the last armed fight between the U.S. Army and the Indian on this continent and took place on January 9, 1918 between Troop E of the 10th Cavalry and a well-armed band of Yaqui Indians 25 miles west of Nogales, Mexico, in Bear Valley, Arizona. Between these years the black soldiers on the American frontier played important roles in General Phillip Sheridan's campaign against the Cheyennes and Arapahoes and in subduing the Apache uprisings of the Southwest led by Victorio, Mangus Colorado, and Geronimo.

The most famous Indian uprising punctuating those years occurred at the Little Big Horn in the Dakota Territory between June 25 and 26, 1876. This is one of history's most

*A "Buffalo Soldier", the name given to black troopers by the Indians.*

frightfully memorable battles, largely because it resulted in the extermination of three whole U.S. battalions, led by Colonel George Armstrong Custer, at the hands of Sioux and Cheyenne Indians. It is not generally known that a black cavalryman by the name of Isaiah Dorman fought and fell at the Little Big Horn.

Originally an interpreter and scout, Dorman was an escaped slave who made his way into Indian territory and lived there for some years before taking an Indian wife. The "black white man," as the Indians called him, was trusted by them even though he worked for the white man. It would seem that he enjoyed the role of intermediary between the U.S. government (represented by the cavalry) and the Sioux nation (represented by an explosive mixture of volatile young chiefs and their more reluctant elders).

While reconnoitering the area through which Custer had decided to ride, Dorman detected various signs of a hostile Indian presence. His warnings were communicated to Custer, who paid as little heed to them as he paid to his War Department orders to avoid an armed confrontation. He led his men—Dorman among them—right into the trap the Indians had laid.

Dorman was one of those who fell. He was found on the battlefield by a bevy of Sioux women whose custom it was to circulate among the wounded, stripping them of arms and valuables. He was not scalped, according to one version of the story, because Sitting Bull himself intervened once he had learned his old friend was among the day's victims. Seeing that it was too late to save him, the chief then requested that he be spared from the customary ritual of mutilation designed, in Indian eyes, to prevent the victim from passing into the spirit world as a "whole man."

Although battles such as these tend to etch themselves into the public consciousness, it is well to remember that the glamorous or adventurous aspects of frontier life were generally far outweighed by the prosaic and uneventful routine of garrison or escort duty.

No chronicler of the West has captured the authentic flavor of life in these regiments more dramatically than author/illustrator Frederic Remington. In much of his writing, Remington recreates the up-front aura of the 10th Cavalry—not a stately, majestic, spruced-up lot of men suited for parades and other ceremonial gestures, but a rough-and-ready detail of "old soldiers who know what it is all about, this soldiering." The all-black 10th, Remington tells us, "never had a soft detail since it was organized," and was composed exclusively of "good horses and hardy men, divested of military fuss." Remington respected men such as these, for he knew that it was they who were best equipped to grapple with the rigors of the frontier and to subdue "the great strange stretches of the high plains." The soldiers "in the colored regiments" were all veterans with several years of frontier life behind them, men who could never be replaced, men whose like would "never come again." The artist admired the obvious physical equipment of the black cavalrymen—fellows who were "great chested, broad shouldered (and) bull-necked," ideally built to contend with the rigors of the strenuous life.

The sociological significance of the passing of the frontier may have been lost on the men themselves but was of primary concern to the artist observer. Remington not only correctly identified the signs of encroaching civilization but captured its essential flavor with note worthy sensitivity and unmistakable sympathy for the meritorious service of the Army regular.

*The black 9th Cavalry in formation at Fort Robinson, Nebraska.*

*10th Cavalry trooper taking a drink on the trail.*

*The country through which we were then operating was howling wilderness; it is now traversed by railroads and covered with villages and farms. Children at play unwittingly trample the grass over the graves of soldiers who gave their lives that they might live and thrive, and communities throughout the West generally send representatives to Congress some of whom, in the peace and plenty of their comfortable homes, fail to recognize, in Washington, the hardships, privations, and sacrifice of life suffered by the army, before their prosperity could be possible or the lives of their constituents assured.*

*In this the simple duty of soldiers was performed, and no credit is claimed, but should not the record of past deed such as these accompanied by the prosperity that has followed, at least guarantee a more generous feeling for the army by all citizens, more especially by those who are called upon to support it?*

## The Spanish-American War (1898)

It was the jingoistic Spanish-American War which roused the nation to reconsider the status of its black frontier regiments. The diary of a black sergeant of the 25th Infantry, Frank Pullen, suggests the hardships which the unit had undergone at its duty stations in Minnesota and, later, the Dakotas and Montana:

*This gallant regiment of colored soldiers served eighteen years in that climate, where, in winter, which lasts five months or more, the temperature falls as low as 55 degrees below zero, and in summer rises to over 100 degrees in the shade and where mosquitoes rival the Jersey breed.*

Considering the isolation, drudgery, and discomfort the

*Troop H, 10th Cavalry, Spanish-American War.*

troops had undergone, it is not surprising that they reacted with unvarnished enthusiasm when news reached them that they were to embark for Cuba to avenge the sinking of the Maine.

Despite the ostensible importance of their patriotic mission, the men were at times subjected to considerable harassment and to humiliating affronts. They were jeered at whistle stops in southern towns; they were not only given separate quarters on government transport ships, but officially forbidden to socialize in any manner with white troops while enroute to their destinations; they ate in separate sections of the mess hall, which they entered only after white troops were all seated; they took their morning coffee alone after their white counterparts were finished.

Despite these indignities, black soldiers fought spiritedly and with great determination during the brief encounter. One white Southerner who saw them in action commented: "Of all the men I saw fighting, there were none to beat the 10th Cavalry and the colored infantry, and I don't mind saying so." Rough Rider Frank Knox, a cohort of Theodore Roosevelt's, promised that many of the black cavalry men who had rushed up San Juan Hill would "live in my memory forever."

Roosevelt, on the other hand, recalled incidents in which black troopers had allegedly shown a tendency to "drift to the rear." In a magazine article, he described his stalwart intercession at crucial points to prevent mass desertions but neglected to take into account the possibility that orders from actual battle zones may have governed the men's behavior. As it turned out, Sergeant Preston Holliday of the 10th Cavalry later explained that black soldiers were often ordered to the rear to remove casualties or to stock up on rations, water, and other supplies. Other white Rough Riders backed the sergeant, although they did not command the same audience Roosevelt addressed.

As in other wars, conflicting white opinions concerning the calibre of black troops determined, to a large degree, their overall deployment and combat effectiveness. Individual heroes like Private T. C. Butler of the 25th Infantry and Sergeant Major Edward L. Baker of the 10th Cavalry (as well as six other Medal of Honor winners) distinguished themselves in combat at El Cavey, Santiago, and San Juan Hill, but the mass of black men who tried desperately to participate in the conflict were discouraged, delayed, or rejected.

In the South, National Guard units did not accept black volunteers. Elsewhere volunteer regiments found the War Department in Washington, D.C. sluggish in responding to their pleas for active involvement. Among the state militias which were eventually raised pursuant to Congressional authorization were the 9th Ohio (a unit commanded by former West Pointer Charles Young), the 3rd Alabama Infantry, the 3rd North Carolina Infantry, the 6th Virginia, the 23rd Kansas, the 8th Illinois, two infantry companies

*Heroic charge of black regulars near Santiago, Cuba, during the Spanish-American War. The regiments participating were the 9th and 10th Cavalry and the 24th and 25th infantry.*

*Black infantry units in action during the Spanish-American War, at Las Gusimas.*

from Indiana, and Company L of the 6th Massachusetts (otherwise an all-white regiment).

Officer promotions during the war were scanty, although some black men were advanced on the basis of combat heroism. In most cases, however, few command positions were meted out to black officers at the head of regimental-sized units. There was also a distinct reluctance on the part of American authorities to utilize black troops as part of the overall occupying force on the island after hostilities ended.

Significantly, some black critics of the war pointed to it as little more than an exercise in American imperialism, and saw black involvement in it as a double tragedy. In the view of historian Kelly Miller, blacks were in the awkward position of being subject to a form of domination at home which they themselves imposed on people fighting for liberation in Cuba and the Philippines.

## World War I (1917-1918)

When the United States declared war on Germany on April 6, 1917, the call went out for thousands of black volunteers to help supply the war zones in France and Germany. Segregated in the draft and in a lone officer's training camp, and allowed at first to volunteer only as laborers in the Army and as servants in the Navy, blacks were assigned to the American Expeditionary Force, serving as stevedores, road builders, wood choppers, railroad hands, mechanics, grave diggers—in short, as cogs in the war machinery.

Black combat troops were organized into two divisions (the 92nd and the 93rd), each composed of four regiments. The 92nd consisted of the 365th to 368th regiments, and the 93rd was made up of the 369th to 372nd regiments. The most famous of the regiments was unquestionably the "Fighting

*A famous regiment in World War I was the black "Fighting 369th," which remained on the front lines for 191 consecutive days without losing a trench or surrendering one prisoner.*

369th," an outgrowth of the old 8th Illinois, and a contingent well-stocked with New Yorkers. This unit landed at Brest, France in the spring of 1918, went into action in the Champagne sector, and remained on the front lines for 191 consecutive days without losing a trench, retreating an inch, or surrendering a prisoner. The unit was awarded the Croix de Guerre by the appreciative French.

Two members of the 369th showed particular valor in combat and became the most celebrated black heroes of the war. Privates Henry Johnson, an Albany, New York, redcap, and Trenton, New Jersey resident Needham Roberts, while on forward observer duty, were suddenly overrun by a sizable band of German infiltrators. Though wounded, Roberts held the enemy at bay for a time by lobbing hand grenades into their midst. Low on supplies and losing strength, Roberts was soon overwhelmed by the Germans. While Roberts was being dragged off to German lines, Johnson rushed the enemy with a bolo knife, creating such a diversion and inflicting so many casualties that he managed single-handedly to disperse the invaders. The next morning, four German bodies were found, and Unit Commander William Hayward praised the "two brave Colored boys" who had fought "like tigers at bay." The French added their approval by nominating the men for the nation's highest military honor, the Croix de Guerre.

The other three black regiments were also brigaded with the French. The 370th saw action north of the Oise-Aisne canal; the 371st and the 372nd regiments helped defend the Meuse-Argonne front and earned the Croix de Guerre (with Palm) for their efforts.

The 92nd Division, left under American command, fared badly in comparison to its sister unit—largely because of familiar taunts by southern commanders that the troops were badly motivated, cowardly, and a detriment to overall morale. As a result, the unit saw little action at the front.

The behind-the-scenes racial arrangements of U.S. military officials were not disclosed until *Crisis* correspondent W. E. B. DuBois uncovered a blatantly discriminatory document which explored the "official" U.S. position on the use and status of black troops.

Young black officer candidates were not aware of these disturbing policies when they pleaded so earnestly with Washington congressmen for the creation of a training camp. The Des Moines, Iowa camp which finally came into existence, graduated hundreds of junior officers, among them Charles Houston, later dean of Howard University's Law School. Houston's experiences in France led him to exclaim: "There [is] no sense of dying in a world ruled by them. German prisoners were kinder than our white American comrades."

After the famous parade up Fifth Avenue which marked the triumphant return of the 369th to Harlem, Dr. DuBois served notice on America that returning black servicemen meant to realize full equality under the law as first-class citizens:

*We stand again to look America squarely in the face. It lynches... it disfranchises... it insults us... We return fighting. Make way for Democracy! We saved it in France, and by the great Jehovah, we will save it in the U.S.A.*

## World War II (1941-1945)

World War II blasted its way onto the American scene on the

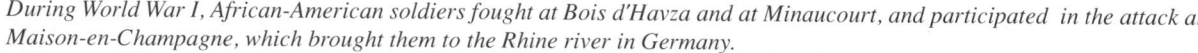

*During World War I, African-American soldiers fought at Bois d'Havza and at Minaucourt, and participated in the attack at Maison-en-Champagne, which brought them to the Rhine river in Germany.*

infamous morning of December 7, 1941, when Japanese fighters flew over Pearl Harbor and rained a hail of bombs and bullets on the slumbering U.S. naval base there. Among the battle vessels sunk or reduced to helpless hulks was the U.S.S. *Arizona*, the ship on which black messman Dorie Miller was routinely going about his duties collecting laundry when the ear-splitting sounds of battle sirens and exploding shells rent the air. Miller rushed up on deck, and instantly hauled his wounded captain to safety. Moments later, he sprung into action behind an anti-aircraft gun he had never been trained to operate. Firing calmly and accurately, he brought down four Zero fighter planes before the cry to abandon ship was heeded by all survivors.

On May 7, 1942, messman Dorie Miller was cited for bravery by Fleet Admiral Chester Nimitz, who decorated him with a Silver Star and so acknowledged the nation's debt to a black man of "extraordinary courage." The medal did not bring with it an instant promotion, or a transfer to a line of duty which might have been more in keeping with Miller's demonstrated aptitudes or preferences. After returning from a trip back to Harlem, where he drummed up support for U.S. war bonds, Miller was assigned to the *Liscome Bay*, which went down in the Pacific on November 25, 1944, with no survivors.

There seems little doubt that the treatment accorded black servicemen was a contributing factor to the severe disillusionment gripping elements of the black community with the announcement of war. Dr. DuBois, for example, sensed instantly that blacks would continue to face the double burden of defending a nation abroad even as that nation, by virtue of its domestic policies, had not yet assured all of its citizens equal protection under the Constitution. Both Bayard Rustin and Elijah Muhammad were conscientious objectors during the war; Rustin on pacifist grounds and Muhammad in consequence of his religious separatism.(Muhammad was indicted for pro-Japanese sympathies in 1942.)

Still, most black civilians rallied to the side of the nation, endorsed the war effort, and sought to make a vital contribution to it. In the case of air cadet Yancy Williams, that endorsement involved a fearless insistence on the right of prospective black airmen to join the Air Force as fighter pilots, not merely ground jockeys or maintenance personnel. Williams, a Howard graduate, threatened a lawsuit, whereupon the Air Force quickly succumbed to the pressure of adverse publicity and opened its Jim Crow training facility at Tuskegee Institute.

The Navy, however, was equally lax in withdrawing the restrictions under which black sailors were forced to serve until pressure from the White House overturned existing policies of apathy and neglect. By the summer of 1942, some trainees in segregated camps and schools were receiving instructions as gunner's mates, petty officers, quartermasters, and coxswains. Despite these gestures, by 1945 the Navy was still operating under a *de facto* quota system which kept someone out of every 20 black seamen in the messman's branch.

The most important branch of the military complex remained the Army, however. Here, by the end of 1942, it was apparent that there was widespread reluctance to utilize black combat forces abroad. One unit of black engineers had been sent to Liberia to prepare landing strips for anticipated combat missions over North Africa, but War Plans Chief Dwight D. Eisenhower was frankly doubtful that large blocks of black troops could be indiscriminately assigned to overseas duty in Europe. In the Pacific theater, Generals Douglas MacArthur and Millard F. Harmon responded more to manpower needs than to an anticipated maze of social roadblocks and circumspect pressures. "Please disabuse yourself," wrote MacArthur to Washington, "of any idea that I might return these troops after your decision to dispatch them."

*General Benjamin O. Davis Sr. with General George Patton reviewing positions in the field.*

Black troops of the 93rd Division later fought at Bougainville and the Treasury Islands, and joined MacArthur in a historic moment of triumph and national glory when the Philippines were retaken in October 1944. By then, black marines had helped win the Battle of Saipan, and black engineers had pitched in to build the Burma Road on the Asian mainland. Black aviation engineers had built runways and landing strips in New Caledonia, the point of origin for the Air Force escort bombers that struck the Japanese in the crucial Battle of the Coral Sea, fought in 1942.

The 92nd also saw combat overseas, although its record was by far the most controversial of all black fighting units. General Benjamin O. Davis, the Army's first black general, joined the unit overseas in Italy, where he shot a propaganda film entitled Teamwork in an effort to prepare the American public for the advent of black combat troops on the European firing line. Great Britain's crusty and indomitable leader Winston Churchill, on hand to offer words of encouragement, was followed by dozens of white correspondents sent to improve public relations. Perhaps the most transparent public relations episode was the "battlefield promotion" invented by General Mark Clark to demonstrate the vital combat role already being played by the 92nd when it had not in fact taken its positions on the Gothic Line. General Clark rashly promoted First Lieutenant Charles F. Gandy of Washington, D.C., as a gesture to allay black criticism of the promotion policies in effect for black officers. Clark simply plucked the captain's bars off one of his white staff members and placed them on the shoulders of a man he had designated, clairvoyantly it seemed, as one who ought to be made visible.

Other problems of morale, level of training, and competence were simply overlooked by the high command of the 92nd. There were some initial combat successes, largely against light resistance along Highway 12 enroute to the foothills of the Apennines. Once in the mountains, however, the 92nd faltered badly. Some ran, some hesitated, some advanced sluggishly and without any combat crispness and determination. Still, there were contingents which engaged the enemy aggressively and fought earnestly to capture key objectives. Mass frustration, mismanagement, and confusion keynoted the experience as a whole, however. Lieutenant Colonel Marcus Ray, a black officer, conceded he was "heartsick," but was emphatic in denying the 92nd was "a complete failure as a combat unit."

Other black units performed many missions without any stigma of controversy. General Eisenhower, watching a black battalion charge the beach at Normandy, commended the troops for carrying out their mission "with courage and determination." General George S. Patton found the all-black 761st Tank Battalion worthy of fighting in his select company. "I would never have asked for you," he told them bluntly, "if you weren't good." The men were good enough to be on hand for the German capitulation in Austria.

At the Battle of the Bulge, Germany's last-ditch attempt to drive a wedge into Allied lines, black troops were called into action on an emergency basis to help withstand a ferocious Nazi assault. General Lanham commented that he had "never seen soldiers who have performed better in combat." Again, neither proficiency nor praise was sufficient to override rigid patterns of segregation. The "heroes" were returned to their all-black units as soon as the crisis passed.

The 99th Pursuit Squadron remains the most glamorous black unit associated with World War II. Commanded by Colonel Benjamin O. Davis, this unit had flown over 500 combat missions and more than 3,000 sorties against the Germans by the summer of 1944. After being attached to the 332nd Fighter Group, the record of the unit grew even more impressive. By the spring of 1945, it boasted of nearly 1,600 combat missions and over 15,000 sorties. It destroyed

*Colonel Benjamin O. Davis Jr., commanding officer of the 99th Pursuit Squadron.*

Messerschmitts in the air and on the ground, and terrorized enemy shipping as well in the role of the roving marauder.

Neither the Navy nor the Marines could boast of such an accomplished unit. The Merchant Marine, on the other hand, had recruited some 24,000 black members, most of whom had had ample opportunity to win their spurs in a relatively unencumbered and desegregated environment. Eighteen Liberty ships were actually named for black men, including the S.S. *Frederick Douglass* and the S.S. *Robert L. Vann.*

Pressure mounted in the wake of World War II to continue to break down the most onerous patterns of racial segregation and to assure blacks—both in and out of service—the opportunity to make professional progress commensurate with their ability.

Blacks could point to impressive statistics as a testimonial to their unflagging commitment to the war effort. Three million had registered for service; 700,000 had served in the Army, 165,000 in the Navy, 5,000 in the Coast Guard, 17,000 in the Marines, and 4,000 in the WAVES and WACS.

Despite the record, recognition was not forthcoming until pressure was applied. In June 1948, A. Philip Randolph made extensive preparations to urge blacks to resist induction into a segregated Armed Forces. His League for Nonviolent Civil Disobedience against Military Segregation threatened to cause heavy embarrassment to the Truman Administration.

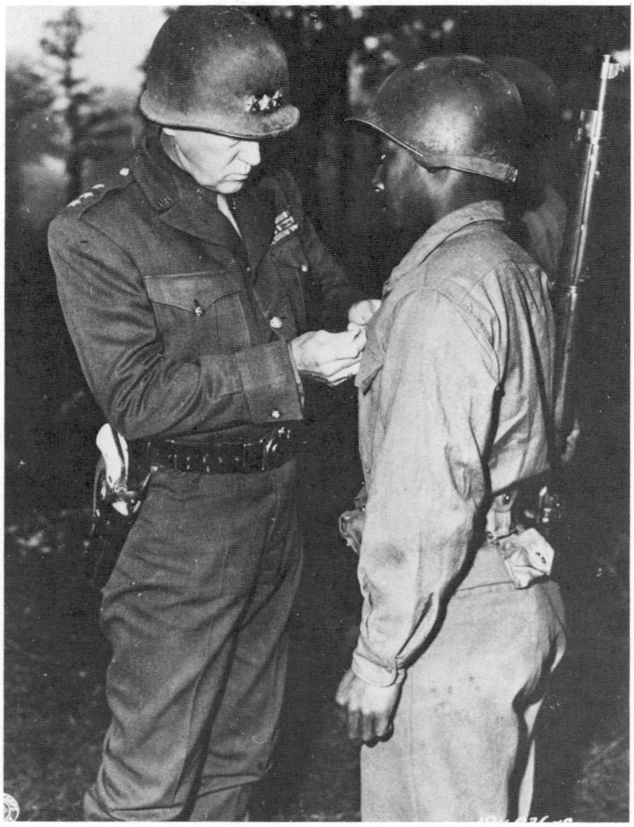

*General Patton pins a silver star on a member of the all-black 761st tank battalion.*

After studying the situation carefully, President Truman decided not only to issue Executive Order 9981 barring segregation in the Armed Forces, but also to appoint a blue-ribbon panel to study equality of treatment and opportunity throughout the Armed Forces. The resulting group, the Fahy Committee, still found considerable evidence of unconscionable manipulation in the training patterns of black enlisted men, but reported that segregation was largely a thing of the past in the Army, Navy, Marines, and Air Force. Remnants of all-black units were to surface one last time before being officially doomed to oblivion in the Korean War.

## Korea

On June 25, 1950, North Korean forces, armed with Soviet weapons, ripped across the 38th parallel, driving hard for the Republic of Korea (ROK) capital at Seoul. Seventeen days after the Korean bombshell burst, the men of the 24th Infantry Regiment, a unit which, for all of its 81 years, had been composed entirely of black combatants, landed in Korea from Japan. The 24th entered the grim fighting against an enemy which had all but routed the ROK army and forced them into one strategic retreat after another. It was a somber beginning. Then, on July 22, 1950, the *New York Times* reported that the important railhead city of Yech'on had been recaptured by attacking black American soldiers of the 24th Infantry. And the *New York Daily News* headlined: "Negroes Gain 1st Korea Victory." Thus remnants of an all-black unit were credited with the first victory for U.N. forces in Korea.

Despite this initial success, terrible controversy surrounded the performance of many black fighting units during the war. As in other wars, criticism of black units was sometimes unduly harsh. In January 1951, NAACP counsel Thurgood Marshall was dispatched to Japan to investigate the conditions surrounding court-martial proceedings involving 32 blacks convicted of violating the 75th Article of War. Of the 32, half had been sentenced to death or life imprisonment, and the remainder anywhere from 10 to 50 years. After examining the trial records, Marshall found that several of the deliberations which had resulted in the conferral of life sentences had lasted less than an hour. Four life sentences had been issued in a space ranging from 42 to 50 minutes, hardly time for the observance of court formalities and the presentation of adequate arguments.

Later interviews with the prisoners uncovered other germane facts. One soldier had actually been in an Army hospital at the time he was accused of being absent without leave; another had falsified his age in order to enlist, and was not yet 18 at the time of his conviction; four others were found guilty of cowardice even though they were doing mess duty behind the battle lines at the time of their alleged disappearance. Five other men had been placed on trial in the aftermath of a confused withdrawal during which they had become separated from their unit. An examination of the trial testimony showed that the captain who testified against them had given three different versions of what happened on the night in question. Despite these discrepancies, the captain was promoted to major, and the five men were convicted of being AWOL. In all, 32 black GIs had been sentenced to imprisonment for criminal behavior as opposed to only two whites. Moreover, many of the convicted blacks, though accused of the same offense as the convicted whites, had been given far stiffer penalties.

From Japan, Marshall went on to Korea, where he conducted many interviews with infantrymen who claimed that their officers frequently berated them and made no effort whatsoever to disguise their contempt for "nigger troops." Marshall concluded his investigation by maintaining that the frequency of such episodes not only contributed to the high rate of casualties but also encouraged the practice of scapegoating—the habit of blaming black troops for every conceivable combat snafu.

Marshall's findings offered convincing proof that many blacks were being accused by, and tried before, officers who held them in the kind of prejudicial contempt which made legal justice a virtual impossibility. The NAACP gathered enough evidence to reverse many of the court-martials entirely and to lighten sentences in the majority of other cases. It also succeeded in drawing renewed attention to the numerous instances of combat heroism by blacks.

Two black infantrymen received Congressional Medals of Honor, both of them awarded posthumously. Private William H. Thompson, one of the designees, had manned a machine-gun nest single-handedly and remained at his post until his buddies withdrew to safety. Sergeant Cornelius H. Charlton, the other medal winner, had led three valiant attacks up an enemy-held hill, and though wounded, somehow continued to fire until the enemy emplacement under attack was destroyed.

Private Edward O. Cleaborn was honored by an official ceremony in his home town of Memphis, Tennessee, for covering the withdrawal of his comrades, including wounded buddies, while under fire on a ridge near the town of Kuri. Cleaborn's parents, presented with the Distinguished Service Cross, were told how their son had wiped out the Communist machine-gun crews threatening Company A of the 24th. He had mowed down enemy infiltrators which had outflanked the platoon, staying at his post and pumping his weapon until it grew hot enough to burn his hand. Everyone had made it back... except Private Cleaborn.

Lieutenant Harry Sutton was so conspicuous in fighting off a Communist breakthrough at Hungnam beachhead in December 1950 that the ridge he and his black infantry platoon had defended came to be known as "Sutton's Ridge." Sutton was later killed by Communist machine-gun fire while fighting in the Suwon sector, and thus never got to wear his Silver Star back home.

Among the black heroes who survived the rigors of combat were Lieutenant Ellison Wynn, acting commander of Company B, 9th Infantry Regiment. When dawn broke after a night attack, Lieutenant Wynn, out of ammunition, threw rocks and C-ration cans at scores of charging Chinese troops attempting to overrun his position near the Yalu River. Wynn was thus able to cover the retreat of 34 men, losing only four.

Sergeant Arthur Dudley, holder of a Distinguished Service Cross, was known to his war-weary senior officers on the line as "the best damn squad leader in Korea." The head of an international and interracial squad consisting of three

*Three Mustang fighter pilots in Korea.*

KATUSAs (Koreans attached to the U.S. Army), and four Americans (one of them black), Dudley personally accounted for 53 enemy dead while under fire with the 19th Regiment. He had received his DSC for heroism displayed at the Battle of Ch'angyong, near the Naktong River, early in August 1950.

By the end of the Korean War, deactivation and reorganization had proceeded throughout the various military echelons. All black infantry units were discontinued, their men redistributed elsewhere. The 9th and 10th Cavalries were reconstituted as the all-black 509th and 510th Tank Battalions, and white replacements soon filtered into them. Statistics showed that only 88 all-black concentrations were still identifiable within the Army's structure, and 95% of black personnel were serving in integrated units. These included units stationed in Alaska and Australia, along with the Orient. Only in Europe and the United States did a few pockets of segregation remain.

## Vietnam

During the brief period of cease-fire which intervened between the end of the Korean War and the intensification of the conflict in Vietnam, the Kennedy Administration proceeded energetically with a program designed to ferret out the remaining vestiges of discrimination in the Armed Forces. President Kennedy, speaking through his Secretary of Defense Robert McNamara, impressed upon the military establishment the need for fostering friendship and equal opportunity for black servicemen, both on and off base. By 1965, however, it was apparent that the nation was no longer on a peacetime footing. Statistics released by the Department of Defense showed that almost 15% of the infantrymen serving in Vietnam were black. Added to these were 5.1% of the Navy, 8.9% of the Marine Corps, and 8.3% of the Air Force. The grand total: 9.3% of the Armed Forces.

The figures, and the war itself, generated tremendous controversy in the black community. In 1965 Malcolm X claimed that the U.S. government was "causing American soldiers to be murdered every day, for no reason at all." Two years later, Martin Luther King Jr., reminded the American public that "the Negro" had always managed to become a "100% citizen in warfare," but was always reduced to a "50% citizen on American soil." The most famous defector from the ranks was heavyweight champion Muhammad Ali, who declared himself a conscientious objector on religious grounds as a Black Muslim. Ali was convicted of violating the Selective Service Act, and stripped of his championship as well. Ali was vindicated by the Supreme Court in1970.

Still, most young blacks were willing to answer the draft board's call when it came. Private First Class Milton Olive, 19, of Chicago, was typical of the young black men who risked, and sometimes lost their lives in arduous battle far from the familiar sounds of home. Olive was blown to bits by an exploding grenade on which he had fallen to save the lives of his comrades, and posthumously awarded the Congressional Medal of Honor. By mid-1969, nine other blacks had joined Olive as recipients of the medal: Captain Riley L. Pitts, First Lieutenant Ruppert L. Sargent, Sergeant Rodney M. Davis, Sergeant Matthew Leonard, Sergeant

*The Second Infantry in action near the Chongchon River in Korea.*

Donald R. Long, SP5 Lawrence Joel, SP5 Clarence E. Sasser, SP5 Dwight H. Johnson, and PFC James Anderson Jr.

Like Olive, many perished in combat. For Sergeant Davis, the end came in Quahg Nam on September 6, 1968 when, like Olive, he threw himself on a live grenade to protect his comrades.

Black servicemen stationed in Vietnam saw duty in hazardous combat zones and in the full spectrum of support functions. They could be found patrolling the Mekong Delta, advising the South Vietnamese Army at Pleiku, repairing jet planes on aircraft carriers in the Gulf of Tonkin (or flying them over Hanoi), joining the gruelling sieges (as at the Citadel of Hue after the Tet Lunar New Year offensive) or the bloody fights (as at Hill 875, Dakto), wading across the treacherous rice paddies, and slashing through the barely penetrable bamboo thickets. Black men in the ranks were unloading ships, digging latrines, driving trucks, servicing warplanes, and walking mountain ranges, even as black desk men and strategists were planning battles, practicing international law, and running press centers, to name but a few of their diversified assignments.

According to *New York Times* reporter Thomas Johnson, officers in the Military Assistance Command said that the 173rd Airborne Brigade, a crack outfit with heavy black representation, was "the best performing unit in Vietnam." In elite combat units like these, one out of every four combat troops was a black man; elsewhere in Vietnam's battle zones, the ratio fell to one out of every five men apt to see action. This same ratio prevailed among the Army's front-line supervisors (ranging in rank from PFC to Master Sergeant).

Until General Davis retired (to become Cleveland's Public Safety Director) two of the 1,342 admirals and generals in the U.S. military establishment were black. General Davis was last assigned to deputy command of MacDill Air Force Base in Florida after serving as full commander of the 13th Air Force in the Philippines, and prior to that, in a Korean headquarters assignment. The other was Lieutenant General Frederic E. Davison, appointed Brigadier General in July 1968, and named deputy commanding officer of the 199th Infantry Brigade in Vietnam. He was the highest ranked of 35 black senior officers in the U.S. Army at the time of his promotion.

By 1969, it had become apparent that many young black combat troops were beginning to exhibit the same trends toward racial separatism that had characterized the behavior of white troops. Experience quickly showed that such efforts at racial elitism, spawned no doubt by the constancy of rejection on the part of white troops, constituted a dangerous menace to the peace and well-being of all concerned. The primary cause of the difficulty was the unwillingness of the biased white GI to accept black troops. The more obvious manifestation of the problem was reflected in the black GI's contempt for his intransigent white counterpart.

At Fort Bragg, North Carolina, in the summer of 1969, for instance, racial unrest flared into a full-fledged brawl when 35 black troops at an enlisted men's club squared off with a squad of about 25 white MPs. The club was described as a voluntarily segregated meeting place for black soldiers who, like their white counterparts, had opted for exclusivity in their after-hours leisure and recreation. Such a withdrawal, thought to be harmless enough on the surface, allowed young men to lock up their assorted complaints, nourish their private rages, and magnify their gnawing grievances and suspicions. Though the Bragg incident had no tragic outcome, it afforded unmistakable evidence that a base camp could be transformed into gangland turf as soon as two militantly uncompromising factions found an explosive

*A search and destroy mission in Vietnam, where the U.S. infantry was 13 percent black.*

*Viet Cong flags taken by Marines of the 1st Division after brief firefight.*

issue around which to rally.

The violence which erupted at the Marine base in Kaneohe, Hawaii, bore some similarities to the Bragg fisticuffs, although the rumble on the island centered on more readily discernible discriminatory trends, such as inequities in military discipline and punishment, as well as unjust favoritism involving promotions. The black-power salute rendered by a group of black leathernecks brought the series of provocations to a flash point, resulting in a donnybrook which left 16 injured and three hospitalized.

At Camp Lejeune, North Carolina, one white Marine died in the aftermath of an interracial brawl whose origins were not immediately apparent. Even before the incident, however, an Ad Hoc Committee on Equal Treatment and Opportunity had outlined some of the more deliberate practices which could lead to racial confrontations, including *de facto* segregation in housing, bars, and barber shops. Still, the Committee had not proceeded beyond the warning-and-advice stage by the time the tragedy struck.

The Marine Corps responded, several weeks later, with a directive which restated the integration policies of the Corps, ordered all officers and men to observe them, and added a pair of human touches which might have been amusing if the situation had not become so serious:

1. Natural haircuts, with certain minimal modifications, would henceforth be allowed.
2. Black-power salutes would be permitted so long as they were intended as greetings between "brothers" and not in defiance of the Corps.

The Army quickly realized that orders regarding haircuts and ghetto salutes were not substantive enough measures to prevent further outbreaks. This was communicated to Washington officials, who began to formulate a preliminary blueprint for easing the conflicts and preventing their escalation. Structural reform was clearly required, and the Department of Defense offered concrete proposals to clear

*A black paratrooper crosses a native-built bridge in Kontum Province in Vietnam.*

the air and improve the racial climate within the military establishment. Implicit in its formula was the assumption that the Armed Services could not merely quarantine the problems of the civilian community with a stern and inflexible mandate. Instead, the Armed Services would have to face up to every vestige of bias which both raw recruits and seasoned commanders had inherited from civilian life. Such defects would have to be dissected in special indoctrination courses and mandatory biracial councils on such problems as housing, recreation, officer-soldier relationships and promotion opportunities.

With such vigorous and affirmative action, the Armed Services sought to overcome the failures which rank-and-file violence underscored and to recover its acknowledged position as a stalwart leader in the fight to achieve integration in American life.

## BLACK SERVICEMEN IN THE 1970S

Between 1970 and 1975, major issues facing blacks in the armed forces were:

1. Continuing interracial tensions between black and white personnel, often resulting in disproportionate punishment of black servicemen.
2. Widespread application to blacks of administrative "other-than-honorable" discharges.
3. The use of coded discharges, in which numbers printed on separation papers alluded to presumed be havior and personality problems of individual serv icemen.
4. Unequal application of military justice.

In 1972, the Defense Department issued "The Search for Military Justice," the formal report of a special task force set up by Defense Secretary Melvin Laird. The report "affirmed that vestiges of discrimination remain in the military system," and went on to prove that blacks and Hispanics are involved in more disciplinary incidents than Caucasians and are punished more severely. Cited as major causes of inequities in military justice were :

1. Societal racism and preservice factors such as educa tion and language disadvantages.
2. Mistrust and suspicion of and by people in command.
3. Coerced induction in lieu of civilian jail terms.
4. Heavy assignment of blacks into combat and service units and deficient training and use of blacks in tech nically skilled assignments.

### Discharges and Punishment

In 1972. blacks comprised about 13% of discharged servicemen but received 33% of the dishonorable discharges, 21% of bad conduct discharges, 16% of undesirable discharges, and 20% of general discharges.

According to the National Association for the Advancement of Colored People, over one-third of the discharges of minorities for Vietnam era veterans have been dishonorable, bad conduct, or less than honorable.

A count of military prisoners in Germany in 1971 showed that the proportion of black prisoners ranged from 40 to 50%, or more than three times the percentage of black servicemen stationed there. More than three-fifths of prisoners convicted for willful disobedience or assault were black.

Blacks also received a higher proportion than Caucasians of Article 15, or "Company Punishment." Article 15 of the Uniform Code of Military Justice allows company commanders to impose non judicial punishment for various infractions. Article 15s have traditionally served two somewhat contrasting purposes. They are a compromise mechanism to reduce the severity of a punishment and mark on a serviceman's record, roughly similar to plea bargaining in civilian courts. And they are a means for junior officers to act against enlisted men with relatively little chance that unfair actions exercised under the Article will come to the attention of higher authorities.

In many units, Article 15 punishment was often used by company level officers to discourage blacks from military

*Basic training for new Army recruits—learning to heave a grenade.*

career ambitions or reenlistments, in contradiction to the policies of the Defense Department and many higher officers. The problem was compounded by the traditional service policy of leaving maximum discretion in disciplinary action to commanders at the company or battalion level.

### Administrative Discharges

Although not widely known, a whole gamut of discharges exists between the "honorable" and "dishonorable" extremes. These are known as administrative discharges and are given for a variety of official reasons ranging from "the good of the service" to "unsuitability" and "unfitness." Although some of these discharges are classified as honorable, the majority have fallen into "general" and "undesirable" categories. According to the NAACP, in Europe in the early 1970s blacks received about 45% of all discharges issued below the "honorable" category. Though servicemen could appeal these and were entitled to counsel, fear and a paucity of legal knowledge prevented all but a few from doing so. And often, less than honorable discharges were accepted by individual servicemen as an alternative to unexpired stockade terms or to a court martial and the likelihood of incarceration.

*Anti-aircraft shoulder-launched "Smart" missile, part of the modern "technical" army.*

Less than honorable discharges can have the effect of branding a person for life, affecting career, earning ability, relations with civilian law enforcement agencies, and receipt of veterans' benefits. Though such discharges can be appealed, the appeal mechanism has been cumbersome and very few appeals have succeeded—only 5% by estimate of the NAACP.

Upper echelons of the Armed Forces have moved to reduce abuses. All-volunteer military service is in great part dependent on the enlistments, hopes, and positive attitudes to military service among minorities of all education levels. The Marine Corps has announced its intention to recruit at least 100 black officers annually. The Air Force wishes to raise its proportion of black officers. To do this and obtain enough enlisted personnel the services must improve their reputation among blacks, a reputation tarnished by inequities in military justice and assignments, and the Vietnam War, where a disproportionate number of blacks were killed in a venture unpopular with great segments of black, and white, Americans.

### Attempts to Improve Conditions— The 1960s to The 1980s

In 1962, President John Kennedy reestablished the Committee on Equal Opportunity in the Armed Forces, and the body was asked to look into the general problem of equal opportunity for Armed Forces members and their families. The major findings of the report were:

1. Black advancements in the military since 1949 were meager, and much remained to be done to achieve equality of opportunity.
2. Blacks in the military and their families were suffer ing daily humiliation and degradation in communi ties near bases at which they were compelled to serve.
3. No one in the military was charged with the respon sibility to listen to equal opportunity complaints.
4. Installation commanders lacked specific directives to guide them in dealing with off-base discrimination and, in fact, did not view this as a military command responsibility.

The major outcome of the report was a directive, "Equal Opportunity in the Armed Forces," which:

1. Created within the Office of the Secretary of Defense a Civil Rights Office.
2. Established, as policy, the responsibility of military commanders to oppose discriminatory practices af fecting military personnel and their families and to foster equal opportunity for them, both in the military and in surrounding communities.
3. Authorized procedures for use of the off-limits sanc tions in matters involving discrimination.
4. Directed the military services to issue the necessary regulations and orders to implement equal opportunity.

*Navy Petty Officer Karl Graham checks a radar sensor control panel.*

The findings of "The Search for Military Justice" were underscored in 1972 by serious interracial battles aboard two Navy ships, the *Kitty Hawk* and *Constellation*, incidents in which the overwhelming number of servicemen blamed and detained were minorities. Blacks fought the case, with the NAACP undertaking legal proceedings. In December 1973, all convictions were reversed.

In January 1974, the Secretary of Defense eliminated coded discharges, which had labeled many ex-servicemen, often on the basis of supposition or rancor rather than fact, as homosexuals, drug users, or generally unstable.

The Defense Department ruling also entitled blacks who had been discharged to scratch out or otherwise conceal the code numbers on their separation papers. The NAACP declared this to be unsatisfactory and demanded that administrative discharges be eliminated. They also sought to have veterans with coded discharges guaranteed the right to full veteran's benefits.

However, for all the very serious problems, the position of blacks in the services seems to be improving. And in many ways, military life is less discriminatory than civilian life.

Vast changes have begun to occur in the military—especially in the status of the black officer. Current attention to affirmative action has led the military to develop programs for the black serviceman. And in the 1980s, increasing numbers of women are joining the military, working side by side with men in all aspects of military life. Women are being trained as pilots and navigators on noncombat aircraft. But even in the 1980s there is evidence of discrimination and racism in all branches of the military. Despite glowing reports of plans of affirmative action by the branches of service, such organizations as the NAACP and the American Civil Liberties Union have criticized the military's steps in meeting that plan.

In the late sixties and the early seventies, there was a rash of incidents within the military in which black servicemen experienced the type of harassment they considered racial. The NAACP contacted the Defense Department and pressed for a general investigation, which resulted in affirmative action policies by all branches of the military. Those racial incidents seemed to have abated by the mid 1970s and the early part of 1980—when a black, Clifford Alexander, was Secretary of the Army. However, with the change of administration, there was a downgrading of affirmative action and the mechanisms that had been put into place in an attempt to curb the racist policies within the armed services.

The NAACP points to one incident that occurred on February 19, 1982 in the Phillips Building, Headquarters U.S. Army Engineer Division, Europe, in Frankfurt, Germany. The NAACP said that it had received reports that an Equal Employment Opportunity Officer, identified as Mrs. Patsy Moore, had been observed in full regalia of the Ku Klux Klan, visiting several division offices of the U.S. Army Engineers in Europe.

In a letter to Percy A. Pierre, Acting Secretary of the Army, Samuel Wright, the NAACP's Armed Forces Director, said, "An EEOC officer represents a unique position in our military services as elsewhere, seeking to redress inequality because of race that crops up in our American society and cultural structure. In view of her obvious adherence to the basic tenets of the KKK philosophy by her outrageous conduct, we respectfully demand an inquiry into this entire matter for appropriate action by the Army. Such action would, of course, include removal of Mrs. Moore from her EEOC position, if this incident is verified."

In 1979, the American Civil Liberties Union charged the Navy with what it termed "widespread discrimination" against blacks and other minority members seeking to enter the service. John Shattuck, director of the A.C.L.U.'s Washington office, said that the recruitment policies of the Navy excluded qualified black youth instead giving preference to whites who were not as qualified. Statistically, the Navy has had the lowest percentage of blacks and other minorities in its enlisted and officer ranks. In 1978, the Navy had 8.6% of blacks in comparison to 26.3% in the Army, 17.6% in the Marines, and the Air Force with 13%. However, in a statement following Shattuck's charge, the Navy denied the allegation, stating that its "policy was to ensure that all racial groups have an equal opportunity for advancement. Equal opportunity in the Navy has improved through various management initiatives."

A report by the A.C.L.U. called "The White Man's Navy: Keeping the Blacks Out," compiled by the organization's director, William Olds, said, "Getting minorities into the

Navy has been mind-boggling for Navy recruiters. A member of the Navy, based in Maryland, said only about 10 percent of blacks in his particular recruitment zone was able to enter the Navy in 1978 despite the fact that all were qualified and had passing grades on the qualification test. He observed that he had never seen a "White Charlie' or a "White Bravo' rejected."("Alphas," "Charlies," and "Bravos" represent military jargon for A, B, and C scores.)

## BLACK SERVICEMEN IN THE 1980S

In assessing its affirmative action plan for fiscal year 1980, all branches of the military said that they were continuing their commitment to full equality or all members.

The United States Air Force said that commanders are responsible for managing its equal opportunity and treatment programs. The USAF said that during 1980 commanders continued to implement sound career development programs which provide Air Force people the opportunity to progress regardless of their race, creed, sex, national origin, or age. The Air Force said that it made excellent progress in increasing its numbers of minorities and women. The number of minority officers rose 9.6% over fiscal year 1979. Officer end strength increases included 435 blacks, 157 Hispanics, and 85 minorities. Minority enlisted force representation increased by 3%. Enlisted end strength increases included 2,294 blacks, 359 Hispanics, and 505 other minorities.

The Air Force said that its ROTC scholarships are used to procure the best qualified applicants to meet pilot, navigator, missile, technical, doctor, and nurse requirements. The Air Force said that it awarded scholarships to as many qualified minority and women officer candidates as possible through central scholarship selection boards.

The U.S. Army, in its affirmative action report, said that minority officer recruitment is being expanded to include appointments in specialty and professional areas, and the U.S. Military Academy has instituted long-range innovative programs to assist in meeting and sustaining goals in the years ahead. The Army's report also pointed out that although minority chaplains continue to be underrepresented, the accessions for all minorities are increasing. To recruit more minority chaplains, the Office of the Chief of Chaplains is planning to take measures to ensure chaplain visits to church conferences and seminars in the proximity of their installations to actively solicit qualified candidates.

The report of the U.S. Navy noted that its 1980 demographics continued to show an increase in minority representation. The Navy said that its officer programs to increase minority representation are centered on the Naval Academy Preparatory School (NAPS) and the Broadened Opportunity for Officer Selection and Training (BOOST) efforts to prepare potential candidates for the rigors of college-level academic work. The Navy said that it met its 60% goal of minority students at BOOST and continues to strive toward a 50% goal at NAPS. On discrimination complaints, the Navy said that the number of complaints reviewed within various Navy headquarters had increased during 1979. The report noted that initial monitoring of cases concerning sexual harassment indicated the existence of this form of discriminatory practice in the force. The Navy said that initiatives to address these issues started through the use of training materials and aides to inform personnel of their rights to seek redress. During fiscal year 1980, the Navy chartered a Minority Officer Accession Study to recommend initiatives necessary to achieve the fiscal year 1985 end strength goal. The study concluded that the potential pool of eligible minorities is limited in terms of low Scholastic Aptitude Test scores and the preponderance of backgrounds in nontechnical fields. Sixteen initiatives were recommended to increase minority officer accessions. The initiatives included increasing minority affairs advisor billets at the U.S. Naval Academy from two to six, establishing a fifth NROTC unit on a predominantly black college campus, and expanding contact with minority colleges or universities, counselors, students, and organizations.

In 1983, the Navy met a key goal of ensuring that 12%of its recruits were black—a ratio that reflected the American population. The percentage of blacks in the Navy has since grown to 15%. Even so, a Navy inquiry conducted in June 1988 revealed that a widespread and subtle bias continued to exist against black and Hispanic sailors. The report, ordered by the Chief of Naval Operations, found that while there

*Drill instructor Hackett, a combat veteran and a representative of the modern Marine Corps.*

were few overt racial incidents in recent years, there was evidence that minority seamen were given lower marks on evaluations, passed over for promotions and allowed to remain undertrained. Minorities were given lower prestige positions. The inquiry made 75 recommendations for change, all of which were accepted by chief of Naval Operations Admiral Carlisle A. H. Trost. In conducting the study and making the entire study public, the Navy has demonstrated forthrightness and sincerity in its efforts to eliminate discrimination.

In assessing its affirmative action plan for 1980, the U.S. Marine Corps said that minorities increased by approximately 1% of the total enlisted population for a total of 30.7%, and minority officer strength remained the same at 5.8% with an increase among black officers and a slight decrease among Hispanic officers. The Marine Corps said that the readily apparent area of concern is the disproportionately low number of minority officers, both male and female, when compared to the minority population within the enlisted force. The report pointed out that its program to provide equitable distribution of minorities within occupational fields continues to show success. Mental group test classification scores used to determine school eligibility were reduced by 10 points for high school graduates. The Marine Corps noted that its goal is to attain a representation of minorities and women in each occupational field comparable to its composition of minorities and women in the total grade structure.

## Changes

Changes made in the military during the 1980s were:

1. Racial integration was carried further in the military, especially the Army, than most American institutions.
2. More women in both the commissioned and enlisted ranks joined the military.
3. Over a fifteen year period since 1972, the percent age of active-duty personnel who are black showed a steady increase.
4. Blacks constitute a large portion of the nation's volunteer army. About 400,000 blacks are enlisted in the Army.
5. Blacks joined the military as a means of escaping the nation's poor communities and because of their inability to find employment.

The military is one of the few sectors in American society which has had to, because of necessity, open its doors to black Americans. Therefore the military has been in the vanguard in the arena of race relations.

Racial integration was advanced in the military more readily since the armed forces can regulate behavior better than civilian institutions. The military has set up programs in race relations, appointed interracial counselors and desegregated housing and recreational facilities.

In the 1980s, blacks are attracted to the military because of what has been described as the "push-pull factor"—the push of unemployment and the pull of benefits. Black enlisted personnel found that the military offered them job training and education that they couldn't get anywhere else. Many had no high school diplomas.

A report, "Military Service Effects for Minority Youth" which looked at 15 years of America's all-volunteer armed forces concluded that:

1. Minority youths had equal opportunity in the armed forces with respect to pay, promotion, career oppor tunity, and job satisfaction.
2. Discharged soldiers became successful in the civilian labor market as veterans.
3. Enlistees tended to have jobs in the military that had a lower income potential in civilian life.

The United States Army redesigned its personnel policies in order to attract quality recruits and included such incentives as $18,000 a year for up to four years in college and a commission through the Reserve Officers Training Corps.

The black attrition rate was cut by the incentives and more blacks enlisted for a second tour and for career service than did whites.

In the 1980s, blacks comprised 28.2 percent of the total enlisted Army force, while black women numbered 44.5 percent of enlisted women.

Blacks serving active-duty in the United States Marines went from below 15 percent in 1972 to about 20 percent in 1987. Blacks in the Air force rose slightly upwards from 10 percent in 1972 to about 14 percent in 1987. Navy active-duty personnel went from 5 percent in 1972 to about 11 percent in 1987.

The all-volunteer army forces relied more heavily on blacks and poor whites than the draft-era military which means that should the United States become involved in a major conflict, the burden of battle and casualties would fall in the early stages on minorities.

Such was the case during the Vietnam conflict from 1965-1966 when there were heavy black casualties due to the disproportionate numbers of blacks in the infantry and artillery.

The conclusion that opportunities for blacks are better in the military than in civilian fields is disputed by the National Association for the Advancement of Colored People. The civil rights organization contended that opportunities are no better in the military than in the private sector because few blacks hold policy-making jobs in either.

Recruiting blacks as officers has been difficult in the 1980s with industry, law schools and the professions seeking able young black men and women and offering higher salaries than the military.

Blacks were commissioned into the United States Army as second lieutenants basically because of their enrollment into Army ROTC programs at historically black colleges. Because of that trend, there is only one black General in the United States Marine Corp., one Colonel, 28 Lieutenant Colonels, 128 Majors, 280 Captains, 263 First Lieutenants, 140 Second Lieutenants and 112 Warrant Officers. Of those, there are 47 black women officers in the Marines.

## A CHRONOLOGY OF MILITARY EVENTS (1770-1989)

**1770, March 5** Crispus Attucks, "a mulatto fellow about 27 years of age... 6 feet 2 inches high, short, curled hair, his knees nearer together than common," is the first to fall in the "Boston Massacre."

**1775, May 20** The Hancock and Warren Committee decides to use free blacks in the conflict but rejects slaves.

**1775, June 17** Peter Salem, a former slave in Framington, Massachusetts, becomes a hero of the day at Bunker Hill by shooting British Major Pitcairn, the officer who had ordered the British to fire on the Minutemen at Lexington.

**1775, July 9** George Washington directs colonial recruiters not to enlist "any deserter from the ministerial army, nor any stroller, black or vagabond or person suspected of being an enemy to the liberty of America."

**1775, November 7** The British Colonial Governor of Virginia, John Murray, Earl of Dunmore, seeks to recruit blacks for the loyalist cause. His recruits become known as "Dunmore's Ethiopian Regiment."

**1776, January 16** The Continental Congress accepts a December 30, 1775 proposal from Washington for the enlistment of free blacks. During the war approximately 5,000 blacks serve in the Colonial Army.

**1776, April 15** John Martin, becomes the first black Marine, enlisted for service in the Continental brig *Reprisal*.

**1776, December 25** Blacks Prince Whipple and Oliver Cromwell cross the Delaware with Washington. By this time more blacks are serving among white units than fighting in separate units. Many are "substitutes" for whites. One separate unit distinguishes itself. It includes men from Massachusetts who proudly call themselves "The Bucks of America."

**1778, August 29** At the Battle of Rhode Island, an all-black regiment from Connecticut "distinguishes itself by deeds of desperate valor" against German mercenaries fighting for the British.

**1779, July 15** Pompey Lamb, posing as a vegetable vendor, aids materially in the capture of Stony Point by General Anthony Wayne. Spies and saboteurs like Lamb were active in many roles and on many fronts during the war.

**1807, June 22** The American man-of-war *Chesapeake* is captured by the British frigate *Leopard* in one of the key skirmishes that led to the War of 1812. Three black sailors are among those impressed aboard the British vessel.

**1813, September 12** Captain (later Commodore) Oliver Hazard Perry wins a decisive victory against the British in the Battle of Lake Erie. The Commander reverses earlier criticisms regarding the possible effectiveness of black sailors.

**1814, September 21** General Andrew Jackson calls on all black citizens to enlist in the defense of New Orleans.

**1814, December 23-24** "The Battle of Chalmette Plains or the Battle of New Orleans." Black troops hold a strategic position in Jackson's defense force and contribute materially to the crushing defeat of the British. After the black troops and others have some trouble collecting their pay, Jackson angrily writes: "Receive my orders for the payment of the necessary muster roll without inquiring whether the troops are white, black or tea."

**1846, May 13** Few blacks see combat during the Mexican War. It is largely a war supported by the South and West and thus chiefly a white man's affair. Blacks who do participate go mostly as personal servants.

**1856, October 18** The first black is listed on Navy muster rolls as sailmaker.

**1861, June 28** The Tennessee Legislature authorizes the enlistment of free blacks between 15 and 50 years of age. Many southern blacks work on fortifications, and through their labor on plantations, help feed the bulk of the Confederate force. There are occasional all-black units in the early years of the war, but almost every Confederate regiment has its share of blacks who accompany white masters into battle and occasionally see action.

**1861, August 6** The Confiscation Act declares that property used in direct or indirect acts against the Union are lawful prizes of war. Slaves who fit this category are considered free.

**1862, May 9** General David "Black Dave" Hunter, holding captured South Carolina territory, begins to enlist blacks. This is the first organized attempt to use black manpower for combat duty in the War. By August, however, military pressures force Hunter to disband his "First South Carolina Volunteers."

**1862, May 12** Robert Smalls, a black pilot, takes the Confederate Transport CSS *Planter* out of Charleston harbor and delivers her to the Union Squadron. Smalls is later named Captain of the *Planter*.

**1862, July 16** Congress authorizes the enlistment of blacks "for the purpose of constructing entrenchments, of performing camp service, or any war service for which they may be found competent." The Enlistment Act, signed the next day, provides that whites with the rank of private should receive $13 a month and $3.50 for clothing, but blacks of the same rank are to receive $7 and $3, respectively. Pay is not equalized until 1864.

**1862, October 28** The First Kansas Colored Volunteers, the first official all-black unit in the Civil War, fights a victorious skirmish at Island Mound, Missouri.

**1863, January 1** President Abraham Lincoln formally issues the Emancipation Proclamation.

**1863, January 13** The first Kansas Colored Volunteers are formally mustered.

*Blacks served as crewmen aboard the Union warship* Monitor *during the Civil War. About 25% of the sailors in the Union Navy were black.*

**1863, May 22** The Bureau of Colored Troops is established by the War Department. Union black troops are organized into 165 regiments of light and heavy artillery, cavalry, infantry and engineers. They are called "United States Colored Troops."

**1863, May 27** During the attack on Port Hudson, the First Louisiana Native Guards fight valiantly, despite heavy losses. Captain Andre Cailloux distinguishes himself with a heroic death at the head of his men.

**1863, October 2** Dr. A. T. Angusta is appointed surgeon of the 17th Regiment, U.S. Colored Volunteers. He is said to be the first commissioned black medical officer.

**1863, December 25** Robert Blake wins the Navy Medal of Honor for distinguished service aboard the USS *Marblehead.*

**1864, June 19** Joachim Pease wins the Navy Medal of Honor for gallant conduct aboard the USS *Kearsage* near Cherbourg, France.

**1864, August 4** William Brown, James Mifflin, and John Lawson win the Navy Medal of Honor for heroic acts aboard a Union gunboat during the battle of Mobile Bay.

**1865, March 13** A black enlistment bill is passed in the South. The action, originally initiated in 1864, comes too late to affect the outcome of the war.

**1865, March 17** Aaron Anderson wins the Navy Medal of Honor for heroic action aboard the USS *Wyandank* at Mattox Creek, Virginia.

**1865, April 9** Surrender at Appomattox.

**1866, July 28** The 9th and 10th all-black Cavalry Regiments are formed under provisions of an Act of Congress. The 38th, 39th, 40th and 41st Infantry Regiments are also formed.

**1869, March 3** A consolidation of the 38th and 41st makes the 24th all-black Infantry Regiment. A consolidation of the 39th and 40th makes the 25th all-black Infantry Regiment. The four regiments, mostly staffed by white officers, patrol the plains and participate in the opening of the western frontier in the late nineteenth century.

**1872, September 21** The first black, John H. Conyers, is admitted to the U.S. Naval Academy.

**1872, December 26** Joseph Noil the wins Navy Medal of Honor for a daring rescue at sea aboard the USS *Powhatan* off Norfolk.

**1877, June 15** Henry O. Flipper is the first black to graduate from West Point. Other black graduates follow in 1887 (John H. Alexander) and 1889 (Charles Young). A fourth, B. O. Davis Jr., completed his training at the Point in 1936.

**1898, February 11** Daniel Atkins wins the Navy Medal of Honor for gallant conduct aboard the USS *Cushing*.

**1898, July 20** Robert Penn wins the Navy Medal of Honor for heroic action aboard the USS *Iowa* off Santiago de Cuba.

**1906, August 13** One man is killed and several are wounded in Brownsville, Texas after racial disturbances involving black infantry men of the 25th. When the men of the 25th refuse to identify those who participated in the violence, President Theodore Roosevelt takes extreme action and dishonorably discharges three whole companies. The Senate, in 1908, upholds his action in the "Brownsville Affair."

**1917, March 25** The District of Columbia National Guard is called up to help protect the nation's capital and black units are included, reluctantly.

**1917, March 28** "The Bulletin #35 Incident." General C. L. Ballou, commander of the 92nd Division, in response to

*Henry Jones (left) and Needham Roberts, two American soldiers who served in France in WWI, received from France the highest decoration, the Croix De Guerre, for heroism.*

discrimination against a black NCO at a theater in Kansas, orders "all colored members . . . [to] refrain from going where their presence will be resented . . . The sergeant is guilty of the greater wrong in doing anything, no matter how legally correct."

**1917, May 1** The Central Committee of Negro College Men is set up at Howard University to prove the willingness of blacks to fight.

**1917, May 12** Black leaders succeed in getting a black officer's training base at Des Moines, Iowa. The camp opens on June 15.

**1917, May 18** Passage of a Selective Service Act greatly increases black participation in the Expeditionary Force.

**1917, July 5** Registration Day. Some 700,000 blacks register for the draft.

**1917, October 5** Secretary of War Newton D. Baker announces the appointment of Emmett J. Scott, secretary to Booker T. Washington, as Special Assistant to the Secretary of War serving as "confidential adviser in matters affecting the interests of the 10 million blacks of the United States and the part they play in connection with the present war." Scott remains in the position until June 1919.

**1917, October 24** The 92nd Division, an all-black unit, is formed.

**1917, December 27** The 369th Infantry Regiment of the 93rd arrives in Brest, the first black unit overseas. After training, they move up to the fighting front in April of 1918. Fighting with the French, they create an enviable record. In 191 days of front line action, the regiment never loses a man, a trench or a foot of ground, Soon the 369th is known to the Germans as the "Hell Fighters."

**1918, May 15** "The Battle of Henry Johnson." When rifle fire fails to stop advancing Germans and his fellow sentry, Needham Roberts, has been captured, Henry Johnson attacks the enemy with his bolo knife, freeing his friend and forcing the Germans into retreat. Both he and Roberts receive the highest French military award, the Croix de Guerre—the first Americans of the war to do so.

**1918, August 7** A document is circulated among the French entitled "Secret Information Concerning Black-American Troops." It describes the necessity for separating blacks and whites. The 92nd division, at the front, finds itself confronted with German propaganda aimed at undermining black loyalty to a country which enjoins them to fight for rights abroad they still do not have at home.

**1918, September 26** The 368th Infantry Regiment of the 92nd begins a mission against the enemy which ends in confusion and disorder. Despite honorable records of the

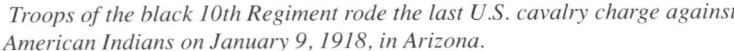

*Troops of the black 10th Regiment rode the last U.S. cavalry charge against American Indians on January 9, 1918, in Arizona.*

majority of black units, this incident is offered by many in the military and the white press as proving black inability to survive combat pressure. Secretary of War Baker later makes the following statement: "The circumstances disclosed by a detailed study of the situation do not justify the highly colored accounts which have been given of the troops in the action, and they afford no basis at all for any of the general assumptions with regard to the action of colored troops in this battle and elsewhere in France."

**1919, February 17** The famed 369th marches up Fifth Avenue to Harlem through cheering crowds. The celebration over, most black units are quickly disbanded except for the four permanent regiments. Finally, as blacks and whites fresh from the service compete for jobs, increased racial friction occurs. By year's end, some 25 race riots have breached the peace.

**1923, July 12** A War Department directive provides for use of blacks in emergencies—and then only on a limited scale. The letter adds: "No Negro troops are to be mobilized in the state of Texas." Military policy becomes even more specific in 1938 with the recommendation that blacks be accepted in proportion to the general population—at that time about 9% of the total.

**1939, September 11** West Virginia State College is granted the right to establish the first black Civilian Pilot Training Program approved in peacetime.

**1940, September 16** Congress passes a Selective Training and Service Act containing the following antidiscrimination clause: "In the selection and training of men under this Act, and in the interpretation and execution of the provisions of this Act, there shall be no discrimination against any person on account of race or color." The 10% quota system is not regarded as discriminatory.

**1940, September 27** With U.S. entry into the war more and more probable, President Franklin D. Roosevelt receives a delegation of three blacks, Walter White, A. Philip Randolph, and T. Arnold Hill, concerning utilization of black manpower in the war effort.

**1940, October 9** With Roosevelt's initials, Assistant Secretary of War Robert Patterson issues a memo declaring the initial policy on the use of black troops: segregation as usual. "It has been proven satisfactory over a long period of years and to make changes would produce situations destructive to the morale and detrimental to the preparations for national defense."

**1940, October 25** Colonel B. O. Davis Sr., veteran of the Spanish-American War, becomes the first black general officer.

**1940, November 1** The Office of the Civilian Aide to the Secretary of War in matters of black rights is established for William H. Hastie, dean of Howard University Law School. This is a position similar to the one occupied by Emmett Scott during World War I. Hastie holds the office until February 1943. Colonel Campbell Johnson, black head of Reserve Officer Training at Howard University, is made special aide to draft director Lewis B. Hershey.

**1941, February 10** The first all-black officered regular Army Infantry Regiment (366th) is activated.

**1941, March 21** A 99th Fighter squadron of black aviators is activated.

**1941, May 1** The first black Signal Unit (275th Cons. Co.) is activated.

**1941, June 1** The first black Tank Battalion (758th) is activated.

**1941, July 1** Integrated Officers' Candidate Schools open, the first major step toward an integrated Army.

**1941, July 19** Inaugural ceremonies are held at Tuskegee Institute, beginning black air training, which culminates in the 99th squadron.

**1941, July 25** President Roosevelt issues Executive Order 8802 forming the FEPC.

**1941, December 7** The Japanese attack Pearl Harbor. Black mess steward Dorie Miller mans a machine gun during the attack and downs four Japanese fighters, winning a Navy Cross.

**1942, February 6** The first black military police battalion (730th) is activated.

**1942, March 7** First black pilots complete training and are commissioned into the Air Corps. Included among them is West Point graduate B. O. Davis Jr., son of the Army's first black general.

**1942, March 24** The first black numbered Station Hospital (25th) is activated.

**1942, April 7** Secretary of Navy Frank Knox initiates a policy calling for acceptance of blacks in the general

*Black soldiers of the American Army in action in France during World War I.*

service in the Navy and Reserves of the Marine and Coast Guard.

**1942, April 14** The first black officer is commissioned into the Coast Guard: Ensign Joseph C. Jenkins, a graduate of the Coast Guard Academy.

**1942, May 15** The 93rd Infantry Division is activated.

**1942, June 1** The Marine Corps begins the enlistment of blacks at the Marine Training Center, Camp Lejeune, North Carolina. The Navy, too, begins to accept blacks in positions other than the stewards branch.

**1942, July 20** With the formation of the Women's Army Auxiliary Corps (WAC), black women are accepted with whites.

**1942, August 24** Colonel B. O. Davis Jr., takes command of the newly formed 99th Squadron.

**1942, October 13** The 332nd all-black Fighter Group is activated, joining the 99th.

**1942, October 15** The 92nd Division is activated.

**1942, November 13** Leonard Roy Harmon wins the Navy cross for extraordinary action aboard the USS San Francisco in the Solomon Islands.

**1942, December 5** Executive Order 9279 requires all services to accept recruits through the Selective Service System. The order portends a greater percentage of blacks in service.

**1943, February 19** Truman K. Gibson Jr., succeeds William H. Hastie as Civilian Aide. Gibson, Assistant since November 1940, officially becomes Civilian Aide in September 1943, and stays in the position until November of 1945.

**1943, February 28** The Navy makes a decision to induct blacks into all branches of the service according to their percentage of the total population, 10%. The announcement is made next month.

**1943, April 16** The 1st Marine Depot company was the first black unit to be sent overseas in World War II.

**1943, April 24** The 99th arrives in North Africa at Oued N'ja, is moved to Fardjourna and attached to the 33rd Fighter Group.

**1943, June 1** The third black air unit, the 477th Bomb Group, is activated.

**1943, June 12** William Pinckney is awarded the Navy Cross for heroism while serving aboard the USS *Enterprise* during the Battle of Santa Cruz Islands.

**1943, June 20** Race tension explodes in the most serious race riot of the war in Detroit. The cause is largely black exclusion from the huge military efforts which are lucrative to civilian defense workers.

**1943, July 2** Black pilots see action over Italy, and down their first aircraft.

**1943, August 31** USS *Leonard Roy Harmon* is commissioned as the first vessel named for a negro.

**1943, November 12** Dorie Miller is lost at sea and presumed dead. He was awarded the Navy Cross for heroic actions during the attack on Pearl Harbor.

**1944, January 3** The 332nd enters the European theater.

**1944, January 27** The 99th distinguishes itself over the Anzio-Nettuno beachhead. Eight confirmed hits are scored. The black air units, especially the 99th, go on to establish an outstanding combat record. Numerous black pilots will win the Distinguished Flying Cross by the end of the war.

**1944, February 23** The Navy Department announces that two anti-submarine vessels being commissioned will be manned by all-black crews. The two all-black vessels, the USS *Mason* and the *PC-1253*, will only have one black officer aboard between them.

**1944, March 17** Thirteen blacks become the first group to be commissioned as Naval officers.

**1944, March 20** The first Naval vessel with a predominantly black crew is commissioned as the USS *Mason* at the Boston Naval Shipyard.

**1944, April 14** *PC-1264* is commissioned at the Navy Yard, New York City, as the second naval vessel with a predominantly black crew of officers and men.

**1944, May 1** Charles F. Anderson becomes the first black in the Marine Corps to be promoted to Sergeant Major, the highest noncommissioned rank among enlisted men.

**1944, May 20** Secretary of the Navy Forrestal orders all naval vessels to be integrated. A group of 25 preselected ships are thoroughly briefed before the blacks arrive in August.

**1944, June 6** D-Day. The 320th Negro Anti-aircraft Barrage Balloon battalion helps with the landing.

**1944, July 3** The 99th is attached to the 332nd.

*Major Charity Adams reviews her WAC troops during World War II.*

**1944, July 8** In an attempt to partially remedy the cause of most racial incidents still breaking out in service, the War Department forbids racial discrimination in recreation and transportation facilities on all Army stations. Serious riots occur at Fort Bragg, Camp Robinson, Camp Davis, Camp Lee, and Fort Dix.

**1944, August 9** The "Port Chicago Mutiny." After an ammunition explosion at the docks near San Francisco on July 17, black stevedores, some of them with advanced technical training, refuse to return to work. They are then brought to trial and sentenced to 8-15 years hard labor. Thurgood Marshall appeals the case and wins an acquittal in January of 1946.

**1944, October 19** Black women are notified they will be admitted into the WAVES. The first are sworn in on November 13 and the first WAVE officers graduate from training at Smith College on December 21.

**1944, December 26** The Germans strike back at the Allies, creating a bulge in the broad advancing force. A directive is issued by Lieutenant General John C. H. Lee for black volunteers to be integrated by platoons into the white units fighting in the area. The move succeeds but does not usher in a new policy.

**1945, January 31** The "Bulge" is neutralized. Most officials still refuse to recognize the Bulge Experiment as any kind of precedent, but rather simply as a successful special case.

**1945, February 7** During a planned attack on the German Gothic Line on the Cinquale Canal, elements of the all-black 92nd Division reportedly fall back in a disordered retreat and are accused of "melting away" in the face of enemy resistance. "Failure" is again trotted out as proof of the black's inability to endure combat pressure. Segregation continues to evade exposure as the real culprit.

**1945, March 8** The first black nurse is sworn in to the Navy Nurse Corps in New York City. She is Phyllis Mae Dailey.

**1945, March 24** The 332nd stages a raid over Berlin and later receives a Distinguished Unit Citation for its bravery.

**1945, April 13** The Navy lifts all restrictions on the number and type of auxiliary vessels to which black personnel can be assigned.

**1945, July 23** An urgent appeal goes out "to qualified women to join with the two Negro commissioned officers and the 54 enlisted WAVES in playing an active part in a speedy victory."

**1945, August 25** Reviewing the Bulge Experiment, General George C. Marshall agrees that the results of the integrated force should be regarded as a special case and not lead to premature judgments.

**1945, October 4** Secretary of War Robert P. Patterson sets up the Gillem Board to study the use of black manpower in the armed forces.

**1945, October 17** The 332nd returns triumphantly to the U.S.

*Benjamin O. Davis Sr. became the first black general in the U.S. Army in 1940.*

**1945, November 10** The first black Marine officer, Frederick C. Branch, is commissioned a second lieutenant in the Marine Corps Reserve.

**1946, January 2** Lieutenant Colonel Marcus H. Ray, fresh from the Italian campaign, becomes Civilian Aide, a post he holds until July 1947.

**1946, February 27** Secretary of the Navy James V. Forrestal announces: "Effective immediately, all restrictions governing the types of assignments for which Negro Navy personnel are eligible are hereby lifted. Henceforth, they shall be eligible for all types of assignments in all ratings in all activities and all ships of the Naval Services."

**1946, March 4** The Gillem report calls for the continuation of the 10% quotas and is released as "War Department Circular 124" on April 27, 1946.

**1946, June 23** The first group of 31 black officers are integrated into the Regular Army.

**1946, December 5** Executive Order 9808 establishes the President's Commission on Civil Rights.

**1947, March 15** Ensign John W. Lee is the first black officer to be transferred into the Regular Navy.

**1947, October 29** The Office of Civilian Aide is transferred to the Office of the Secretary of Defense. James C. Evans officially begins his duties in this post in January, 1948.

**1948, February 2** President Truman issues a Civil Rights message to Congress which states: "During the recent war

Lieutenant General Benjamin O. Davis, Jr. takes command of U.N./U.S. forces in Korea.

Wesley A. Brown, who in 1949 became the first African-American to graduate from the U.S. Naval Academy.

and in the years since its close we have made much progress toward equality of opportunity in our armed services without regard to race, color, religion or national origin. I have instructed the Secretary of Defense to take steps to have remaining instances in the armed services eliminated as rapidly as possible. The personnel policies and practices of all the services in this regard will be made consistent."

**1948, February 12** The first black nurse is integrated into the Regular Army Nurse Corps.

**1948, April 1** The *New York Times* announces that A. Philip Randolph has formed a Committee against Jim Crow in the Military Service and Training. The group threatens mass civil disobedience and a black boycott of the draft.

**1948, June 9** The first black doctor is integrated into the Regular Army Medical Corps.

**1948, June 23** The Republican Party platform states "We are opposed to the idea of racial segregation in the armed forces of the United States."

**1948, July 1** ROTC units are established at Morgan State University, Florida A & M, and Southern University, predominantly black schools.

**1948, July 1** The first blacks are augmented into the Regular Marine Corps.

**1948, July 15** The Democratic Party platform states: "We call upon the Congress to support our President [to guarantee] the right of equal treatment in the service and defense of our nation."

**1948, July 17** A. Philip Randolph impresses on President Truman the "bipartisan mandate to end military segregation."

**1948, July 25** Training centers for blacks and whites are established at Fort Riley, Kansas and Fort Ord, California.

**1948, July 26** President Truman issues Executive Order 9981, setting up a Committee to study Equality of Treatment and Opportunity in the Armed Services (the Fahy Committee).

**1948, October 23** The Navy commissions and assigns to duty its first black aviator, Ensign Jessie Brown.

**1949, April 6** Secretary of Defense Louis Johnson directs the Secretaries of the Army, Navy, and Air Force to examine their personnel practices in line with Executive Order 9981.

**1949, April 28** Now under the Defense Department the title Civilian Aide is changed to Civilian Assistant to the Secretary of Defense. James C. Evans still occupies the position.

**1949, June 1** The 332nd Fighter Wing is deactivated at Lockbourne Air Force Base and integrated into the Regular Air Force throughout the world. Integration seems to proceed more smoothly within the military than with the civilian community.

**1949, June 3** Wesley A. Brown of Washington, D.C. graduates from the U.S. Naval Academy, the first black in its history.

**1949, June 7** The Secretary of Defense approves of the Department of Navy's policies under Executive Order 9981.

**1949, June 23** Secretary of the Navy Francis Matthews

declares: "It is the policy of the Navy Department that there shall be equality of treatment and opportunity for all persons in the Navy and Marine Corps without regard to race, color, religion or national origin."

**1949, September 30** A nondiscriminatory job policy is adopted by the Army. All school courses are opened to blacks.

**1949, October 1** New Army Secretary Gordon Gray issues orders abolishing black quotas.

**1950, January 16** The Department of the Army promulgates Special Regulations 600-629-1, "Utilization of Negro Manpower," and declares its new policy: Blacks with special skills will be "assigned to any . . . unit without regard for race or color."

**1950, March 27** Quotas in Army enlistments are officially abolished.

**1950, May 22** The Report of the President's Committee on Equality of Treatment and Opportunity in the Armed Services (Fahy Committee), "Freedom to Serve," is issued.

**1950, July 20** The first United States victory in Korea is won by the all-black 24th Infantry Regiment.

**1950, October 20** The 9th and 10th Cavalry are converted into the 509th and 510th black Tank Battalions and integrated with white units on March 7, 1952 and December 31,1953 respectively. The 25th Infantry is broken into smaller units and integrated with white units during early 1951 and 1952.

*A naval reservist photographer's mate first class answers recruiting station phone.*

**1950, December 4** Ensign Jesse L. Brown becomes the first black to win the Navy's Distinguished Flying Cross for heroic action over Korea.

**1951, June 21** In Korea, the first black since the Spanish American War is posthumously awarded the Medal of Honor.

**1951, July 21** The Army makes its first cautious press release concerning its integration plans. They announce that the 24th Infantry Regiment will be broken up and that plans are underway to integrate the Far Eastern Command.

**1951, July 26** The Department of the Army announces plans for the complete racial integration of the Far Eastern Command. Integration has, however, already existed to a greater or lesser extent for some time in Korea.

**1951, October 1** The 24th Infantry Regiment is deactivated and its personnel are integrated into white units. Much of the 24th is already spread out among white units in Korea.

**1951, November 1** The Draft Form of Project Clear (three volumes), "Utilization of Negro Manpower in the Army," is issued. It clearly shows that an integrated force is effective, even much more effective than a segregated service.

**1952, April 1** Plans for racial integration throughout the Army's European Command are announced. Meanwhile, the Air Force has been at work and now announces complete integration of its personnel.

**1952, October 1** The first black Marine pilot, Frank E. Petersen Jr., is commissioned a second lieutenant and receives his wings.

**1953, August 20** Secretary of the Navy Robert Anderson directs the elimination of segregation in all facilities at Naval shore installations.

**1954, January 12** The Secretary of Defense Charles Wilson announces that "the operation of all school facilities located on military installations shall be conducted without segregation on the basis of race or color."

**1954, May 17** The Supreme Court hands down its historic decision on the unconstitutionality of school segregation. The armed forces already had moved to break down segregationist practices.

**1954, June 11** The Secretary of Defense provides a program "to familiarize contracting officers" with the Department's policies on discrimination. On paper, at least, integration is finally a general policy within the military establishment.

**1966, February 1** Thomas D. Parham Jr., becomes the first black chaplain to attain the rank of Captain.

**1967, September 1** Minority Officer Recruiting Effort (MORE) is established at the Navy Bureau of Personnel, Washington, D.C.

**1968, May 19** First Naval Reserve Officer Training Corps is established at Prairie View A&M.

**1968, August 21** The Medal of Honor is posthumously awarded to the first black Marine recipient, PFC James Anderson Jr.

**1969, January 24** A report released in Saigon by the Army contends that "all indications point to an increase in racial tensions" in the Army. Insufficient numbers of black junior officers and disproportionately heavy punishment for black soldiers are cited as the major causes.

**1970, May 17** Prairie View A&M (Texas) University NROTC commissions the first group of 11 Naval Reserve Ensigns and two Marine Corps second lieutenants.

**1970, December** Seven black soldiers petition the Secretary of Army to investigate bias against black soldiers stationed in Germany.

**1970, December 17** Chief of Naval Operations Admiral E. R. Zumwalt issues Z-66, a directive outlining specific actions to be taken by all U.S. Naval Personnel to ensure equal opportunity.

**1971, February 8** Secretary of the Navy John Chafee announces that a destroyer escort would be named in honor of Ensign Jesse L. Brown, the first black naval aviator.

**1971, March 15** Defense Secretary Laird announces a program to end discrimination in the Armed Forces. Included are mandatory race relations classes in basic training and a Defense Department Race Relations Institute to train teachers of race relations.

**1971, April 28** Captain Samuel L. Gravely is selected to become the U.S. Navy's first black admiral.

**1971, May 13** Three blacks are among 80 colonels promoted to Brigadier General. This raises the number of black generals to four. The Air Force has one black general and on June 2 Navy Captain Samuel L. Gravely is named the first black admiral.

**1971, June 3** Representative Shirley Chisholm charges that racial tension between Germans and black soldiers stationed in Germany is critical.

**1971, June 13** Twenty airmen are injured in a racial clash at Sheppard Air Force Base, Texas. On June 24, similar conflicts erupt at Travis Air Force Base, California.

**1971, July 24** Twelve high-ranking military officers are reprimanded and transferred for failure to comply with Defense Department race relations policies.

**1971, September 1** The Defense Department announces that blacks now comprise 10% of the nation's forces in Vietnam and that this percentage is greater than the percentage of black soldiers being killed in action. In 1969 blacks accounted for 8.5% of the soldiers and over 13% of the deaths.

**1972, September 28** The first black to complete 30 years of service as a Marine, Sergeant Major Edgar R. Huff, retires.

**1972, October and November** Interracial skirmishes involving over 100 crewmen break out on the ships *Kitty Hawk* and *Constellation*.

**1973, May 21** Daniel James Jr., named Lieutenant General, becomes the highest ranking black in the Armed Forces.

**1973, June** Secretary of Army Robert F. Froehlke orders a reversal of all the discharges without honor imposed on

*Searching a village for Viet Cong. African-Americans served in every area of the Vietnam War. At the height of the war one in every seven U.S. servicemen killed in battle was black.*

167 black soldiers of the 25th Infantry Regiment in 1907, following the riots in Brownsville, Texas. Records of all the men were cleared.

**1974, February** Captain Gerald Thomas becomes the second black Rear Admiral in U.S. Navy history and is assigned to Pacific Destroyer Squadron 9.

**1974, April 19** The first permanent Marine Corps facility to be named for a black Marine, Camp Johnson, at Camp Lejeune, North Carolina, is dedicated to the memory of Sergeant Major Gilbert H. "Hashmark" Johnson, USMC (Ret.)

**1974, June and July** Forty-three black sailors refuse to report to the U.S. *Midway*, charging racial bias, long hours, and mistreatment aboard their aircraft carrier. This is the second ship-jumping incident aboard the *Midway* in two years.

**1974 July** The Reverend Alice Henderson, a black woman, is commissioned a chaplain in the U.S. Army, becoming the only female chaplain, black or white, in the country's armed forces.

**1974, July** Five black women are among the group of 15 women who become the first female cadets at the U.S. Merchant Marine Academy at Kings Point, New York.

**1974, July** Brigadiers Julius W. Becton, 47, and Harry W. Brooks Jr., 45, are promoted to the rank of Major General in the U.S. Army.

**1974, November** Jill Brown becomes the first black woman to qualify as a pilot in the U.S. armed forces. Brown is in the Navy.

**1975, May** Lieutenant Donna P. Davis becomes the first black woman physician in the Naval Medical Corps.

**1975, August** General Daniel "Chappie" James Jr., becomes Commander-in-Chief of the North American Air Defense Command (NORAD) on the same day that he is promoted to the first black four-star general in U.S. military history.

**1976, May 6** Midshipman First Class Mason C. Reddix Jr., of San Antonio becomes the first black in the history of the U.S. Naval Academy to earn the highest midshipman's rank. Midshipman First Class Derwood C. Curtis of Chicago is named Regimental Commander.

**1976, June 7** Edward Scarborough, a member of the Defense Manpower Commission, says that a report about the military written for the Commission by Kenneth J. Coffey and Frederick J. Reeg suppressed evidence of racial discrimination in all four major services. Scarborough says that the report showed that Armed Service recruiting policies were "racially motivated" but he says those findings did not appear in the final report.

**1976, June 19** A hearing is issued by the military manpower subcommittee of the House Armed Services Committee into the Marine Corps recruitment and training practices. Harry Hiscock, a former Marine private, one of the witnesses, tells of harsh treatment at the hands of drill instructors.

**1976, July 1** Two former Marine recruiters testify before a House Armed Services Subcommittee that they were ordered to limit the number of blacks they took into the corps.

**1976, August 1** Veteran Columbia, South Carolina NAACP lawyer Matthew J. Perry Jr. is confirmed by the Senate as a judge in the U.S. Court of Military Appeals in Washington. He is the first civil rights lawyer in the South to gain a judicial position during the Ford Administration.

**1976, September 2** The Army reorganizes part of its college scholarship program in an attempt to double the number of black officers in the ROTC within 10 years.

**1976, December 6** The Marine Corps begins pretrial hearings for three black Marines who face charges stemming from a November 13, 1976 incident. The alleged assailants had attacked a group of white marines holding a party because they thought the party was a meeting of Marine Ku Klux Klan members.

**1977** Togo West becomes the first black sworn in as Navy General Counsel.

**1977** Clifford Alexander Jr. becomes the first black Secretary of the Army. He has a budget of $28.8 billion and supervises over 1.3 million Army regulars and others. He also supervises 370,000 civilian employees.

**1977, September 25** A report by the Rand Corporation terms the volunteer military a success while conceding that the percentage of black enlisted men had risen from about 8 in 1960 to approximately 16 at the present. The report contends that the proportion of enlisted blacks would have increased by about the same amount under the draft.

**1977, November 15** Dr. John White, an assistant secretary of defense, says that more than 40% of the recruits for the volunteer armed forces were being discharged before completion of their first term. He said the discharge rate was more than twice what it had been during the draft era and among the factors he cited were lack of literacy, medical problems, financial hardships, and poor performance. White said that blacks accounted for 20% of new enlistees in fiscal 1977, up from 2% from fiscal 1976.

**1978** Majors Frederick D. Gregory and Gulon S. Bluford, along with Dr. Ronald McNair, begin training as astronauts.

**1978, February 2** Federal contracts totaling $240 million are earmarked for the nation's minority business sector for defense purposes in fiscal year 1979.

**1978, March 16** General Daniel "Chappie" James, the first black four-star general is buried. General James had earned more than 24 awards and commissions. Representative Louis Stokes (D. Ohio) urges legislation to construct a memorial to James at Alabama's Tuskegee Institute where the general received his wings.

**1978, June 1** The Black Panthers of World War II receive the Distinguished Presidential Unit citation award for "courageous and professional actions." The honor was presented to retired Army Lieutenant Colonel Charles

Gates, president of the 761st Tank Battalion Association, by Army Secretary Clifford Alexander Jr. during a ceremony at Fort Meyer, Virginia.

**1978, June 29** Brigadier General Harvey Williams is denied entry to a disco in Bonn, Germany until someone mentions his rank. Williams said after the incident that American GIs "of all races, but primarily black" are turned away at doors of 10 nightspots in the German capital.

**1978, August 3** W. Graham Claytor Jr., Secretary of the Navy, says the Supreme Court's controversial *Bakke* decision "leaves the legality of Navy affirmative action programs, both military and civilian, unchallenged."

**1978, August 15** Army Chief of Staff General Bernard W. Rogers writes that "black soldiers receive disproportionate numbers of punitive discharges, are overrepresented in confinement facilities and are charged with more serious offenses per 1,000 soldiers than white soldiers." At the same time an internal Army study of equal opportunity claims that there has been "significant progress" in race relations in the Army.

**1978, August 24** U.S. Navy Captain Richard E. Williams is the first black to assume duties as Commander of Air Wing Four at the Naval Air Station in Corpus Christi, Texas.

**1978, November** The Army drafts a plan aimed at young college-bound men that would reduce some enlistments to two years from three and offer a better GI bill. Army officials deny that the plan is aimed at changing the racial composition of the Army by attracting whites. Blacks compose about 30% of the Army, which numbers 770,000.

**1978, December 6** The Pentagon reports that the percentage of black soldiers in the Army's enlisted ranks doubled over the past eight years.

**1979, January 4** Lieutenant General Julius W. Becton is sworn in as commanding general of headquarters, VLL Corps, in Frankfort, Germany. The command includes two infantry divisions and one German Panzer division.

**1979, February 8** Army Secretary Clifford Alexander promotes five blacks to the rank of general. Those promoted by Alexander are Arthur Holmes, an ordnance officer; John Michael Brown, a West Point graduate attached to the infantry; Colon Powell, an infantry officer; John Forte, an air defense artillery officer; and Edward Honor of the transportation corps.

**1979, April 1** Lieutenant Colonel Reginald Jones becomes the first black munitions staff officer in the Munitions and Missile Division in the U.S. Air Force in Washington, D.C.

**1979, April 12** Former POW Air Force Colonel Fred Cherry claims the Air Force failed to safeguard against the misspending of his wages while he was a prisoner of war. The U.S. Court of claims rules that the Air Force had allowed the colonel's wife, whom he divorced, to squander his military pay.

**1979, April 27** Frank E. Petersen of the U.S. Marine Corps becomes the first black Brigadier General in the Marine Corps. General Petersen is the Director, Facilities and Senior Division, Installations and Logistics Department Headquarters, Marine Corps, Washington, D.C.

**1979, June 15** The U.S. Navy is charged with widespread discrimination against blacks and other minorities. John Shattuck, Washington Director of the American Civil Liberties Union, states that the Navy uses a quota system restricting minority access to the Navy by giving preference to whites having the same or fewer qualifications than blacks.

**1979, July 5** Army Assistant Secretary Percy Pierre is praised on Capitol Hill "for presenting to Congress the most readable and honest presentation on the needs of the Army." The report, which involves military needs against a background of Soviet build-up, is also credited with "pulling no punches because the Army admits its failures, refuses to portray the Russians as 10 feet tall, and provides examples which clearly explain military needs."

**1979, July 23** Deputy Assistant Secretary of Defense for Equal Opportunity M. Kathleen Carpenter says she believes there is "a new racism" appearing in the military. Carpenter says it is a form of backlash from affirmative action programs.

**1979, August 2** Representative Ronald V. Dellums (D. Calif.), vice chairperson of the Congressional Black Caucus

*Nineteen-year-old Lance Corporal Felicia A. Lynch, part of the new Marine Corps.*

and a member of the House Armed Services Committee, says the 17-member CBC strongly opposes the reinstitution of the military draft during peacetime.

**1979, August 17** Master Chief Boatswain's Mate Jesse J. Holloway becomes the first chief petty officer of the Pacific Fleet.

**1979, August 29** The Navy announces that all ship and shore commanders have been ordered to use their full powers to "deal effectively with racist activity."

**1979, September 20** Bill Daniels, an Oakland, California civilian Army employee who is an amputee, is among a trio of people receiving the title of Handicapped Employees of the Year.

**1979, November** Second Lieutenant Marcella A. Hayes becomes the first black woman pilot in the U.S. armed forces. She is only the fifty-fifth woman out of 48,000 officers to graduate from the Army Aviation School in Fort Rucker, Alabama.

**1980, March** General Hazel W. Johnson becomes the first black woman promoted to the rank and position of Brigadier General, Chief of the U.S. Army Nurse Corps. Brigadier General Johnson received her Ph.D. from Catholic University in Washington, D.C.

**1980, May 28** Lieutenant Vincent K. Brooks becomes the first black West Point cadet to hold the post of "Captain of the Cadets."

**1980, December** Ensign Brenda Robinson becomes the first black female aviator in the U.S. Navy assigned to the Fleet Logistics Support Squadron Forty in Norfolk, Virginia.

**1981, March 23** A New York-based research team for the Veterans Administration releases a study stating that Vietnam veterans suffer from "significantly more" emotional, social, educational, and job-related problems than do military veterans who did not serve in Vietnam. The study shows that unemployment among black Vietnam veterans was more than three times as high as for white Vietnam veterans.

**1982, February 19** The NAACP calls on Acting Secretary of the Army Percy A. Pierre to investigate the complaint against an Equal Employment Officer, Mrs. Patsy Moore, who was said to have been wearing the full regalia of the Ku Klux Klan while visiting several division offices of the U.S. Army Engineers in Europe.

**1982, February 24** A major Pentagon study discloses that while white recruits score a bit below the general white population, black and Hispanic recruits score significantly above the general black and Hispanic populations.

**1982, April 29** Twelve black American veterans of the 761st Tank Battalion who helped liberate Paris during World War II are honored in that city. The twelve were the first all black group to see action in the war.

**1982, May 15** The highest ranking black in the U.S. Air Force, Maj. Gen. Titus Hall is forced into early retirement over allegations that he showed favoritism toward blacks under his command.

**1982, July 3** Studies by the Brookings Institution and a panel assembled by the Atlantic Council urge a return to the draft in order to get more middle class whites into uniform. The Brookings study pointed out that the rising percentage of blacks in the Army in particular raised social and military questions while the Atlantic Council report

*Field exercises of the allied and American forces in Germany. The exercise called "Autumn Forge" is an annual event.*

was concerned more with numbers of men than their race.

**1982, July 4** Two reports that contend that the Army has too many black soldiers and that they might not execute their duties as well in action against black civilians in domestic disorders or against black soldiers in an enemy Army is disputed by Lt. Gen. Maxwell Thruman, U.S. Army Personnel Chief.

**1982, August 25** About 800 Marines of the 32nd Marine Amphibious Unit (MAU) land in Beirut as part of a multinational peacekeeping force to oversee evacuation of Palestine Liberation Organization (PLO) guerillas.

**1982, September 10** Evacuation of the PLO is completed and the 32nd Marine Amphibious Unit is ordered out of Beirut by the President of the United States.

**1982, September 26** The 32nd Marine Amphibious Unit is redeployed to Beirut in the wake of the assassination of Lebanese President-elect Bashir Gemayel.

**1982, September 26** The role of blacks in aviation is depicted in an exhibit called "Black Wings, The American Black in Aviation" at the National Air and Space Museum in Washington.

**1983, May 18** Angela Dennis of Arkansas becomes one of two first black women to graduate from the United States Coast Guard Academy in New London, Connecticut.

**1983, June 23** Names of the Army's first black unit which was formed in Massachusetts in 1867 are added to the list of soldiers memorialized at the Boston Commons.

**1983, October 25** U.S. Marines land on the island of Grenada to restore order and democracy and to safeguard the lives of approximately 1,000 Americans citizens who were living on the island.

**1983, November 2** Elements of the 82nd Airborne Division arrive in Grenada to relieve the Marines.

**1984, January 4** Democratic Presidential candidate Jesse Jackson wins the release of Navy Lt. Robert O. Goodman Jr. from Syrian captivity.

**1984, October 29** Former slave, Sgt. Brent Woods, a Congressional Medal of Honor winner is laid to rest with full military honors in Somerset, Kentucky 78-years after his death and more than a century following his service in the Indian wars. Woods died in 1906 and his body was in an unmarked grave in the black section of Somerset.

**1985, February 24** Libyan strongman Col. Muammar Qaddafi, speaking at a Nation of Islam International Savior's Day convention in Chicago calls on black Americans to immediately leave the military and fight with his support for an independent black state.

**1985, February 25** Blacks in Chicago with military backgrounds denounce Libyan leader Col. Muammar Qaddafi's call for U.S. blacks to leave the military service.

**1985, February 26** The White House accuses Libyan dictator Col. Muammar Qaddafi of encouraging racism and sedition against the U.S. Government in his call for black Americans to quit the military and fight for an independent state.

**1985, February 26** Nation of Islam Minister Louis Farrakhan rejects call the by Libyan leader Col. Muammar Qaddafi for black soldiers to lead an armed struggle against the United States Government. Stated Farrakhan: "We cannot entertain the thought of armed struggle unless we have exhausted all of the means that are open to us for our advancement."

**1985, July 28** Dr. Edwin Dorn, a defense analyst with the Joint Center for Political Studies and Dr. Alvin Schexnider, an Associate Dean of Virginia Commonwealth University in Richmond, Virginia tells conferees at the National Urban League Conference in Washington, D.C. that blacks should widen their role in military matters.

**1986, April 7** Sgt. Kenneth Terrance Ford of Detroit is killed in a nightclub bombing in Berlin. The bombing was blamed on Arab extremists.

**1986, April 21** Northwestern University Sociologist Charles Moskos states in an article in Atlantic Magazine that blacks have been more successful moving up the career ladder into leadership positions in the armed forces than in any other major segment of U.S. society.

**1986, May 22** Black soldiers known as the "Hellfighters of Harlem" who served in the 369th infantry in France are honored at a reception at New York's 369th Armory.

**1986, June 28** Army Sgt. Kenneth Ford's family is awarded his Purple Heart following his death by a terrorist bombing in a West Berlin nightclub two months earlier.

**1986, November 21** Kevin Nesmith, a freshman at the Citadel which is a state-supported military academy in Charleston, South Carolina withdraws from school after a group of white cadets dressed as the Ku Klux Klan barged into his room with a lighted paper cross uttering racial slurs.

**1986, November 24** Thirty cadets at the Citadel meet with the Rev. Jesse Jackson to discuss racial problems at the institution.

**1986, December 9** Three cadets at the Citadel are suspended after a second incidence of harassment is reported.

**1987, October 1** Lt. Gen. Andrew P. Chambers becomes commander of the Third Army at Fort McPherson, Georgia.

**1987, November 16** Lt. Gen. Colin Powell is profiled in a Time Magazine article shortly after becoming National Security Advisor under President Ronald Reagan.

**1988, October 9** The U.S. Army announces that it will review records of World War One heroes to determine whether any were denied high honors because of their race.

**1988, October 31** Noted lecturer and theologian Dr. Norman L. Wagner of Youngstown, Ohio who is host of a weekly television worship program "Dr. Norman L. Wagner and The Power of Pentecost," is selected by the U.S. Department of Defense to become the host of the first black worship service to air on the Armed Forces Radio and Television Network.

## BLACK MILITARY HEROES

In view of the absence of racial identification of many military records dating from the Civil War, it is difficult to determine how many black servicemen have been awarded the Medal of Honor. By pinpointing a number of segregated units in which blacks served until World War II, however, the editors of this volume have been able to verify the names of 46 blacks who have won this coveted award since it was instituted during the Civil War. The Department of Defense is at present compiling a definitive list of all black CMH recipients. According to the preliminary information gathered by this agency, 46 black soldiers have won the medal: 16 in the Civil War; 14 in the Indian wars; 5 in the Spanish-American War; 2 during the Korean Conflict; and 11 in the Vietnamese War. Of the 8 winners in the Navy, 5 were honored for their exploits during the Civil War, 1 for a feat of peacetime bravery (1872), and 2 in the Spanish-American War.

Pending further research, the following list is offered to our readers, along with biographical data where available.

### ARMY

#### Civil War (1861-1865)

##### 1863

**Sergeant William H. Carney,** *Company C. 54th Massachusetts Colored Infantry.* Born in New Bedford, Massachusetts, Carney was the first black to win the Congressional Medal of Honor. He was cited for valor on June 18, 1863 during the Battle of Fort Wagner, South Carolina, in which he carried the colors and led a charge to the parapet after the standard bearer had been felled by rifle fire. During this battle, Carney was twice severely wounded. His medal was issued on May 23, 1900.

*Sergeant William H. Carney, first African-American to be awarded the Congressional Medal of Honor.*

##### 1864

**Private William H. Barnes,*** *Company C, 38th U.S. Colored Troops.* Born in St. Mary's County, Maryland.

**First Sergeant Powhatan Beaty,*** *Company G, 5th U.S. Colored Troops.* Born Richmond, Virginia.

**First Sergeant James H. Bronson,*** *Company D, 5th U.S. Colored Troops.* Born in Indiana County, Pennsylvania.

**Sergeant-Major Christian A. Fleetwood,*** *4th U.S. Colored Troops.* Born in Baltimore, Maryland.

**Private James Gardiner,*** *Company I, U.S. Colored Troops.* Born Gloucester, Virginia.

**Sergeant James H. Harris,*** *Company B, 38th U.S. Colored Troops.* Born in St. Mary's County, Maryland.

**Sergeant Alfred B. Hilton,*** *Company H, 4th U.S. Colored Troops.* Born in Harford County, Maryland.

**Sergeant-Major Milton M. Holland,*** *5th U.S. Colored Troops.* Born in Austin, Texas.

**Corporal Miles James,*** *Company B, 36th U.S. Colored Troops.* Born in Princess Anne County, Virginia.

**First Sergeant Alexander Kelly,*** *Company F, 6th U.S. Colored Troops.* Born in Pennsylvania.

**First Sergeant Robert Pinn,*** *Company I, 5th U.S. Colored Troops.* Born in Stark County, Ohio.

**First Sergeant Edward Radcliff,*** *Company C, 38th U.S. Colored Troops.* Born in James County, Virginia.

**Private Charles Veal,*** *Company D, 4th U.S. Colored Troops.* Born in Portsmouth, Virginia.

**Sergeant-Major Thomas Hawkins,*** *6th U.S. Colored Troops.* Born in Cincinnati, Ohio, Hawkins was cited for valor in the Battle of Deep Bottom, Virginia on July 21, 1864. He was credited with the rescue of his regimental colors from the enemy. His medal was issued on February 8, 1870.

**Sergeant Decatur Dorsey,*** *Company B, 39th U.S. Colored Troops.* Born in Howard County, Maryland, Dorsey was cited for valor in the Battle of Petersburg, Virginia, on July 30, 1864. When his regiment was driven back to Union lines, he carried the colors and rallied the men in his unit. His medal was issued on November 8, 1865.

* These 13 men won their awards for valior during the Battle of New Market Heights on September 29, 1864. With the exception of Sargent James Harris, all were awarded their citations on April 16, 1865.

### Indian Wars (1870-1890)

**Sergeant Emanuel Stance,** *Troop F, 9th U.S. Cavalry.* Born in Carroll County, Louisiana, Stance was cited for valor in the Battle of Kickapoo Springs, Texas. An outstanding Indian scout, he was awarded his medal on June 28, 1870.

**Corporal Clinton Greaves,** *Troop C, 9th U.S. Cavalry.* Born in Madison County, Virginia, Greaves was cited for valor in the Battle of Florida Mountain, New Mexico, on June 24, 1877. His medal was issued on June 26, 1879.

**Sergeant Thomas Boyne,** *Troop C, 9th U.S. Cavalry.* Born in Prince George's County, Maryland. Boyne was cited for bravery in action during two New Mexico battles in 1879. His medal was issued on January 6, 1882.

**Sergeant John Denny,** *Troop B, 9th U.S. Cavalry.* Born in Big Flats, New York, Denny was cited for removing a wounded comrade to a place of safety while under heavy fire in Las Animas Canyon, Mexico, on September 18, 1879. His medal was issued on November 27, 1894.

**Sergeant Henry Johnson,** *Troop D, 9th U.S. Cavalry.* Born in Boynton, Virginia, Johnson was cited for valor in the Battle of Milk River, Colorado, on October 25, 1879. While under heavy fire, he fought his way to a creek to bring water to the wounded. His medal was issued on September 22, 1890.

**Sergeant George Jordan,** *Troop K, 9th U.S. Cavalry.* Born in Williamson County, Tennessee, Jordan was cited for bravery in two battles: one at Fort Tulersu, New Mexico, on May 14,1880; the other at Carrizo Canyon, New Mexico, on August 12, 1881.

**Sergeant Thomas Shaw,** *Troop K, 9th U.S. Cavalry.* Born in Covington, Kentucky, Shaw was cited for valor in Carrizo Canyon, New Mexico, on August 12, 1881. He forced the enemy back after holding his ground in a dangerous position. His medal was issued in December, 1890.

**First Sergeant Moses Williams,** *Troop I, 9th U.S. Cavalry.* Born in Carroll County, Pennsylvania, Williams was cited for valor in the Battle of Cuchillo Negro Mountains, New Mexico, on August 16, 1881. His medal was issued on November 12, 1896.

**Private Augustus Walley,** *Troop I, 9th U.S. Cavalry.* Born in Reisterstown, Maryland, Walley was cited for bravery in action in the Battle of Cuchillo Negro Mountains, New Mexico, on August 16, 1881. His medal was issued on October 1, 1890.

**Sergeant Brent Woods,** *Troop B, 9th U.S. Cavalry.* Born in Pulaski, Kentucky, Woods was cited for valor in New Mexico on August 19, 1881. His medal was issued on July 12, 1894.

**Sergeant Benjamin Brown,** *Company C, 24th Infantry Regiment.* Born in Virginia, Brown won his award nipping an attempted robbery in Arizona on May 11, 1889. His medal was issued on February 19, 1890.

**Corporal Isaiah Mays,** *Company B, 24th Infantry Regiment.* Born in Carter's Bridge, Virginia, Mays was cited for gallantly stopping an attempted robbery in Arizona on May 11, 1889. Like Brown, he was awarded his medal on February 19, 1890.

**Corporal William O. Wilson,** *Troop I, 9th U.S. Cavalry.* Born in Hagerstown, Maryland, Wilson was cited for bravery in the Sioux campaign of 1890. His medal was issued on September 17, 1891.

**Sergeant William McBryar,** *Troop K, 10th U.S. Cavalry.* Born in Elizabeth, North Carolina, McBryar was cited for bravery in an engagement against Apache Indians in Arizona on March 7, 1890. His medal was issued on May 15, 1890.

### Spanish-American War (1898)

**Private Dennis Bell,*** *Troop H, 10th U.S. Cavalry.* Born in Washington, D.C.

**Private Fitz Lee,*** *Troop M, 10th U.S. Cavalry.* Born in Dinwiddie County, Virginia.

**Private William H. Thompkins,*** *Troop G, 10th U.S. Cavalry.* Born in Paterson, New Jersey.

**Private George Wanton,*** *Troop M, 10th U.S. Cavalry.* Born in Paterson, New Jersey.

**Sergeant-Major Edward L. Baker,** *Band,* 10th *U.S. Cavalry.* Born in Laramie County, Wyoming, Baker was cited for bravery in the under-fire rescue operation of a wounded comrade in Santiago, Cuba, on July 1, 1898. His medal was issued on July 3, 1902. Promoted to Lieutenant.

*Cited for bravery at Tayabacoa, Cuba. They received their medals on June 23, 1899.

### Korean War (1950-1953)

**Pfc. William Thompson,** *Company M, 24th Infantry.* Born in Brooklyn, New York, Thompson was the first black to win the CMH since the Spanish-American War. He lost his life on August 6, 1950 after fighting off the enemy single-handedly during a withdrawal operation. The medal was awarded in June 1951.

**Sergeant Cornelius Charlton,** *Company C, 24th Infantry.* Born in the Bronx, New York, Charlton was the second black to win the Congressional Medal of Honor in Korea. On June 2, 1951, he was killed while leading a platoon attack on a Communist-held ridge. The medal was awarded on February 12, 1952.

### Vietnam (1965-1973)

**PFC Milton L. Olive III,** *Company B, 503rd Infantry, 173rd Airborne Brigade.* While participating in a search-and-destroy operation in the vicinity of Phu Coung on October 22, 1965, PFC Milton Olive saved the lives of his fellow soldiers by falling on a live grenade and absorbing the shock of its blast with his body. Olive was cited for conspicuous gallantry by the President of the United States at the White House on Thursday, April 21, 1966, at which time the Medal was awarded posthumously to his parents. Born in Chicago on November 7, 1946, Olive attended parochial school in his native city and later went to Saints Junior College High School for three years. He took basic combat training at Fort Knox, Kentucky, and also attended a number of service schools. During his service tour, he won the Combat Infantryman Badge, the Armed Forces Expeditionary Medal, and the Purple Heart with an Oak Leaf Cluster. Olive died a few weeks before his twentieth birthday.

**PFC James Anderson Jr.,** *Company F, 2nd Battalion, 3rd Marine Division.* Like PFC Olive before him, James Anderson Jr. reacted instantaneously to danger "with complete disregard for his own personal safety," grabbing a live grenade thrown into the midst of his platoon, pulling it to his chest and curling around it as it exploded. The shock was so great that other Marines received shrapnel wounds from the fragmentation. Anderson was killed instantly. The highly decorated soldier (he had won the Purple Heart and several service medals) was a native of Los Angeles, California, where he was born January 22, 1947.

**Sergeant First Class Webster Anderson,** *Battery A, 2nd Battalion, 320th Artillery, 101st Airborne Division.* Complete disregard for his personal safety and the ability to function in an exemplary fashion while under fire earmarked Sergeant Anderson for the Medal of Honor, presented him by President Nixon at the White House on November 24, 1969. Anderson, a native of Winnsboro, South Carolina, entered the U.S. Army on September 11, 1953.

**Sergeant First Class Eugene Ashley Jr.,** *Company C, 5th Special Forces Group [Airborne], 1st Special Forces.* Born in Wilmington, North Carolina, on October 12, 1931, Ashley was killed in action during an attempted rescue operation at Camp Lang Vei in Vietnam. Ashley lost his life while being carried from the summit of the hill from which he and his men had dislodged the enemy. He was killed by an artillery shell.

**PFC Oscar P. Austin,** *Company E, 2nd Battalion, 1st Marine Division.* On February 23, 1969, PFC Oscar P. Austin threw himself on an enemy grenade to protect an injured Marine, and later was mortally wounded when he lunged in front of a fallen comrade who was exposed to enemy rifle fire. Austin was cited for "inspiring initiative and selfless devotion to duty." A native of Nacogdoches, Texas, Austin was born January 15, 1948. He completed high school in Phoenix, Arizona, and joined the Marine Corps in April 1968. Austin had won other medals, including the Purple Heart, before being designated a Medal of Honor winner.

**Sergeant Rodney M. Davis,** *Company B, 1st Battalion, 1st Marine Division.* During a heavy battle in Quang Nam Province (Republic of Vietnam), Sergeant Rodney M. Davis and his platoon were pinned down by mortars, heavy automatic and small arms fire. Unable to withstand the enemy assault, the Marines were lodged in a trench and in danger of being overrun by the enemy. A grenade lobbed in from close range landed in the trench, threatening the lives of the entire unit.

*The parents of Milton Olive accept his posthumous Medal of Honor from President Lyndon Johnson.*

Sergeant Davis "instantly" threw himself upon it in what was described as "a final valiant act of complete self-sacrifice." Davis died September 6, 1967. Born in Macon, Georgia, in 1942, he had enlisted in the Corps on August 31, 1961.

**PFC Robert H. Jenkins,** *Company C, 3rd Reconnaissance Battalion, 3rd Marine Division.* PFC Robert H. Jenkins was killed in action on the morning of March 5, 1969 while occupying a defense position south of the DMZ. Jenkins and his comrade constituted a two-man fighting emplacement manning a machine gun. When a North Vietnamese grenade was thrown into their midst, Jenkins seized his comrade, shielding him from the full impact of the explosion. He died later of injuries sustained on the scene. Born June 1, 1948, Jenkins was a graduate of Central Academy High School in Palatka, Florida. He enlisted in the Marines in 1968.

**Specialist Six Lawrence Joel,** *HQ & HQ Company, 1st Battalion [Airborne] 503rd Infantry, 173rd Airborne Brigade.* One of the earlier winners of the Medal of Honor, Specialist Joel was cited for "gallantry and intrepidity at the risk of his life above and beyond the call of duty" while serving as a medical aidman in a combat operation on November 8, 1965. Despite his own wounds, Joel left his cover to minister to several fallen comrades, giving them plasma, pain killers, and other necessary medication while under a continuous barrage. Joel, a native of Winston-Salem, North Carolina, was born February 22, 1928.

**PFC Ralph H. Johnson,** *Company A, 1st Reconnaissance Battalion, 1st Marine Division.* As part of a 15-man reconnaissance patrol deep in enemy territory, PFC Ralph H. Johnson was manning an observation post on Hill 146 when a heavily armed, platoon-sized Vietnamese force attacked his position. A grenade tossed into the three-man fighting hole occupied by Johnson and two comrades threatened the lives of all until Johnson flung himself on the device, absorbing its shattering fragments. Johnson was killed in action on March 5, 1968, less than a year after he had enlisted in the Regular Marine Corps. Johnson was born in Charleston, South Carolina, January 11, 1949.

**Specialist Five Dwight Hal Johnson,** *Company B, 1st Battalion, 69th Armor, 4th Infantry Division.* Climbing fearlessly out of his disabled tank, Johnson, armed only with a .45 caliber pistol, engaged the heavily armed enemy and killed several North Vietnamese. After running out of ammunition, he returned to his tank, where he grabbed a submachine gun before braving yet another enemy barrage. Johnson also rescued comrades and killed several North Vietnamese at close range. A native of Detroit, Michigan, Johnson is a graduate of Northwestern High School. He was born May 7, 1947.

**Private First Class Garfield M. Langhorn,** *Troop C, 7th Squadron [Airmobile] 17th Cavalry, 1st Aviation Brigade.* A radio operator, Langhorn lost his life after falling on a grenade thrown into the midst of a group of wounded men he was helping rescue during a helicopter mission. Born in 1948 in Cumberland, Virginia, Langhorn attended Riverdale High School before being inducted into service in 1968.

**Platoon Sergeant Matthew Leonard,** *Company B, 1st Battalion, 16th Infantry, 1st Infantry Division.* Sergeant Leonard was awarded the Medal of Honor in 1967 for "conspicuous gallantry and intrepidity in action" during combat operations near Suoi Da in Vietnam. Surviving numerous assaults and several gunshot wounds, Leonard showed remarkable "fighting spirit" and qualities of "heroic leadership." Leonard is a native of Eutaw, Alabama, and was born on November 26, 1929.

**Sergeant Donald Russell Long,** *Troop C, 1st Squadron, 4th Cavalry, 1st Infantry Division.* Sergeant Long was killed in action during an attack on his troop by a Viet Cong regiment on June 30, 1966. Long abandoned the relative safety of his armored personnel carrier and exposed himself to withering enemy fire while carrying the wounded to evacuation helicopters. He was killed by an exploding grenade whose shock he absorbed with his body. Born August 27, 1939, Long was a native of Blackfork, Ohio.

**Captain Riley Leroy Pitts,** *Company C, 2nd Battalion, 27th Infantry, 25th Infantry Division.* Captain Pitts died in Vietnam on October 31, 1967 after leading an airmobile assault in the vicinity of Ap Dong. The captain risked his life when a grenade which he had lobbed against the entrenched enemy rebounded off the dense jungle foliage and threatened to explode in the midst of his men. Pitts fell on the grenade but, miraculously, it failed to explode. He was later mortally wounded during an exchange of gunfire with the enemy. Captain Pitts, a native of Fallis, Oklahoma, was born October 15, 1937.

**Lieutenant Colonel Charles Calvin Rogers,** *1st Battalion, 5th Artillery, 1st Infantry Division.* Rogers is the highest ranking black officer to have received the Medal of Honor while on active duty in Vietnam. Rogers served in the embattled country from November 1967 to November 1968, and was cited for exceptional gallantry while on duty with the 1st Infantry Division. Despite several wounds, Colonel Rogers rallied the beleaguered men of a fire support base which was in danger of being overrun by a numerically superior enemy, and prevented it from being captured. Rogers' citation singled out his "relentless spirit of aggressiveness, conspicuous gallantry and intrepidity in action."

**First Lieutenant Ruppert L. Sargent,** *HQ & HQ Company, 3rd Battalion, 60th Infantry, 9th Infantry Division.* Lieutenant Sargent died in action on March 15, 1967.

**Specialist Five Clarence Eugene Sasser,** *HQ & HQ Company, 3rd Battalion, 60th Infantry, 9th Infantry Division.* Medical aidman Clarence E. Sasser was awarded the Medal of Honor in recognition of his heroic efforts, under fire, on behalf of wounded comrades stranded in an exposed rice paddy. Sasser himself was wounded, but stayed at his post for several hours tending others. Born September 12, 1947 in Chenango, Texas, Sasser is a graduate of Marshal High School in Angleton, Texas.

**Staff Sergeant Chester Sims,** *Company D, 2nd Battalion [Airborne] 501st Infantry, 101st Airborn Division.* Squad leader Sims distinguished himself in action on February 21, 1968 while his company was engaged in a furious assault of a heavily fortified enemy position. While advancing his unit, Sims heard the unmistakable noise of a concealed booby trap and unhesitatingly hurled himself on the device, absorbing its shock with his body. Vice President Agnew presented the medal posthumously at the White House on December 21, 1969. Sims, a native of Port Saint Joe, Florida, was born June 18, 1942.

**First Lieutenant John E. Warren Jr.,** *Company C, 2nd Battalion [Mechanized], 22nd Infantry, 25th Infantry Division.* The bravery of Lieutenant Warren cost him his life in Vietnam on January 14, 1969. Warren and his men were moving through a rubber plantation to join a friendly unit when they were set upon by a well-fortified enemy. The lieutenant maneuvered his men to within six feet of the enemy bunker, at which point a grenade was thrown into their midst. Warren fell on the grenade and saved three others. A native of Brooklyn, New York, Lieutenant Warren was born November 16, 1946.

*John Lawson received the U.S. Naval Medal of Honor for heroism in the Battle of Mobile Bay, August 5, 1864.*

## NAVY

### Civil War

**Aaron Anderson,** *Landsman.* Anderson served on board the USS *Wyandank* during a boat expedition up Mattox Creek, on March 17, 1865. Participating with a boat crew in the clearing of Mattox Creek, Anderson carried out his duties courageously in the face of a devastating fire which cut away half the oars, pierced the launch in many places, and cut the barrel of a musket being fired at the enemy. (General Order 59, June 22, 1865.)

**Robert Blake,** *Contraband.* He was on board the U.S. Steam Gunboat *Marblehead* off Legareville, Stono River, on December 25, 1863, in an engagement with the enemy on John's Island. Serving the rifle gun, Blake, an escaped slave, carried out his duties bravely throughout the engagement which resulted in the enemy's abandonment of positions, leaving a caisson and one gun behind. (General Order 32, April 16,1864.)

**William Brown,** *Landsman.* Born 1836, Baltimore. Accredited to Maryland. He was on board the USS *Brooklyn* during its successful attacks against Fort Morgan rebel gunboats and the ram *Tennessee* in Mobile Bay on August 5, 1864. Stationed in the immediate vicinity of the shell whips which were twice cleared of men by bursting shells, Brown remained steadfast at his post and performed his duties in the powder division throughout the furious action which resulted in the surrender of the prize Southern ram *Tennessee* and in the damaging and destruction of batteries at Fort Morgan. (General Order 45, December 31, 1864.)

**John Lawson, *Landsman.*** Born 1837. Accredited to Pennsylvania. Lanson was on board the flagship USS *Hartford* during its successful attacks against Fort Morgan, rebel gunboats and the rebel ram *Tennessee* in Mobile Bay on August 5, 1864. Wounded in the leg and thrown violently against the side of the ship when an enemy shell killed or wounded the six-man crew at the shell whip on the berth deck, Lawson, upon regaining his composure, promptly returned to his station, and although urged to go below for treatment, steadfastly continued his duties throughout the remainder of the action. (General Order 45, December 31, 1864.)

**James Mifflin,** *Engineer's Cook.* Born 1839, Richmond. Accredited to Virginia. He was on board the USS *Brooklyn* during its successful attacks against Fort Morgan, rebel gunboats and the Southern ram *Tennessee* in Mobile Bay on August 5, 1864. Stationed in the immediate vicinity of the shell whips which were twice cleared of men by bursting shells, Mifflin remained steadfast at his post and performed his duties in the powder division throughout the furious action which resulted in the surrender of the prize rebel ram *Tennessee* and in the damaging and destruction of batteries at Fort Morgan. (General Order 45, December 31, 1864.)

**Joachim Pease,** *Seaman.* Born Long Island, New York. Accredited to New York. He served as a seaman on board the USS *Kearsarge* when that vessel destroyed the *Alabama* off Cherbourg, France, June 19, 1864. Acting as loader on the No. 2 gun during this bitter engagement, Pease exhibited marked coolness and good conduct and was highly recommended by his divisional officer for gallantry under fire. (General Order 45, December 31, 1864.)

### Interim (1871 to 1898)

**Daniel Atkins,** *Ship's Cook, First Class.* Born 1867, Brunswick. Accredited to Virginia. Atkins was on board the USS *Cushing* on February 11, 1898. Showing gallant conduct, Atkins risked his life as he attempted to save the life of Ensign Joseph C. Breckenridge, U.S. Navy, who fell overboard at sea from that vessel on that date. (General Order 489, May 20, 1898.)

**Joseph B. Noil,** *Seaman.* Born 1841, Nova Scotia. Accredited to New York. Serving on board the USS *Powhatan* near Norfolk, December 26, 1872, Noil saved Boatswain J. C. Walton from drowning.

### Spanish-American War

**Robert Penn,** *Fireman First Class.* Born October 10, 1872, City Point. Accredited to Virginia. On board the USS *Iowa* off Santiago de Cuba, July 20, 1898. Performing his duty at the risk of serious scalding at the time of the blowing out of the manhole gasket on board the vessel, Penn hauled the fire while standing on a board thrown across a coal bucket one foot above the boiling water which was still flowing from the boiler. (General Order 501, December 14, 1898.)

## BLACK GRADUATES OF U.S. MILITARY ACADEMY (1877-1988)

**Class of 1877**

Flipper, Henry O.

**Class of 1887**

Alexander, John H.

**Class of 1897**

Young, Charles W.

**Class of 1936**

Davis, Benjamin O. Jr.

**Class of 1941**

Fowler, James, D.

**Class of 1943**

Davenport, Clarence M.
Tresville, Robert B. Jr.

**Class of 1944**

Francis, Henry M.

**Class of 1945**

Davis, Ernest J. Jr.
Rivers, Mark E. Jr.

**Class of 1946**

McCoy, Andrew A. Jr.

**Class of 1949**

Howard, Edward B.
Smith, Charles L.

**Class of 1950**

Carlisle, David K.
Green, Robert W.

**Class of 1951**

Brown, Norman J.
Robinson, Roscoe Jr.
Wainer, Douglas F.
Woodson, William B.
Young, James R. Jr.

**Class of 1953**

Corprew, Gerald
Hughes, Bernard C.
Worthy, Clifford

**Class of 1954**

Lee, Ronald B.
Robinson, Hugh G.
Turner, LeRoy C.

**Class of 1955**

Batchman, Gilbert R.
Brown, John M.
Cassells, Cyrus C. Jr.
Hamilton, John M. Jr.
Olive, Lewis C. Jr.

**Class of 1956**

Blunt, Robert R.

**Class of 1957**

Bradley, Martin G.
McCullom, Cornell Jr.

**Class of 1958**

Brunner, Ronald S.

**Class of 1959**

Baugh, Raymond C.
Kelley, Wilbourne A. III

**Class of 1960**

Dorsey, Ira

**Class of 1961**

Brown, Reginald J.
Quinn, Kenneth L.

**Class of 1962**

Gorden, Fred A.

**Class of 1963**

Banks, Edgar Jr.
Handcox, Robert C.
Ivy, William L.
Jackson, David S.

**Class of 1964**

Miller, Warren F. Jr.
Ramsay, David L.

**Class of 1965**

Anderson, Joseph B.
Conley, James S.
Hester, Arthur C.
Jenkins, Harold A. Jr.

**Class of 1966**

Cox, Ronald E.
Davis, Thomas B. III
Ramsay, Robert B.

**Class of 1967**

Fowler, James D. Jr.
Whaley, Bobby G.

**Class of 1968**

Copeland, Rene G.
Flowers, Ernest Jr.
Garcia, Victor
Howard, James T.
Jordan, Larry R.
Martin, John T. III
Outlaw, LeRoy B.
Robinson, Benny L.
Rotie, Wilson L. Jr.
Tildon, Ralph B.

**Class of 1969**

Cooper, Cornelius M. Jr.
Cousar, Robert J. Jr.
Groves, Sheridon H.
Hackett, Jerome R.
Minor, James A. Jr.
Steele, Michael F.
Tabela, Francis E.
Williams, Michael M.

**Class of 1970**

Mason, Robert E.
Morgan, Roderick H.
Price, Willie J.
Reid, Trevor A.
Robinson, Bruce E.
Steel, Gary R.
Thomas, Kenneth L.

**Class of 1971**

Anderson, Edgar
Brice, David L.
Dedmond, Tony L.
Edwards, Joe F.
Freeman, Robert E.
James, Kevin T.
Plummer, William W.

**Class of 1972**

Burns, Cornelius
Mension, Danny L.
Squires, Percy

**Class of 1973**

Adams, Jesse B.
Bell, Richard Jr.
Bivens, Courtland II
Bonner, Garland C.
Christopher, Clyde J.
Coats, Charles S. Jr.
Coleman, Frederick D.
Crisp, William Ira
Edwards, Lawrence D.
Ferguson, Mercer E.
Fountain, Foster F. III
Gains, Michael B.
Jenkins, Gil S.
Johnson, Edward C. Jr.
Lewis, Brett H.
Martin, Edwin L.

*Henry O. Flipper (right) was the first African-American to graduate from West Point (class of 1877). Ten years later, John H. Alexander became the second African-American to graduate from the Point (class of 1887).*

Moore, William I.
Perry, William H.
Robinson, Lenwood Jr.
Rowe, Dennis W.
Sayles, Andre H.
Sutton, Lloyd I.
Topping, Gary E.
Twitty, Theophlise K.

**Class of 1974**

Anderson, Gary J.
Banks, Allan A.
Best, Marshall
Braxton, Maceo
Bryant, Albert
Chachere, Ernest G.
Elmore, Terry E.
Fowler, David L.
Helton, Dwight A.
Holmes, Keith B.
Hughes, Samuel J. III
Hunter, Joseph
Jones, Harvey D. Jr.
King, Jimmie D.
Lewis, Kevin M.
Lynch, Myron C.
Mallory, Phillip L.
Reid, Ronny E.
Sample, Allen L.
Spaulding, Milton C.
Taylor, Theodore R.
Topping, Gerald W.
Wallace, Michael D.
Wheeler, Clayton R.

**Class of 1975**

Anderson, D. T.
Armstong, B. M.
Austin, L. J. III
Benn, J. F. Jr.
Boddie, O. B. Jr.
Bradley, R.
Briggs-Hall, M. A.
Brown, A. B. Jr.
Byrd, J. E.
Cheese, R. A.
Dupree, D.W.
Dyer, A. G.
Hanford, C. B.
Harris, D. L.
Harris, J. W. III
Hicks, J. E.
Johnson, E. A. Jr.
Johnson, R. E.
Jones, J. D. III
Jordan, N. C.
Lewis, S. J.
Maney, E. K.
Mooney, D.L.
Peters, V. M.
Pinkney, R. M.
Shaw, E. E. Jr.
Smith, M. L.
South, C. H. Jr.
Taylor, P. L. III
Thigpen, W. L.
Williams, D. L.
Williams, J. P.

**Class of 1976**

Alexander, M. A.
Austin, C. W.
Bivins, D. K.
Brown, J. L.
Chase, R. P.
Collins, L. C.
Crecy, W. G.
Crocker, V. B.
Crofton, W. T.
Dixon, M. L.
Elam, A.
Fields, G.
Floyd, J. N.
Grammer, J. K.
Hayes, A. B.
Hicks, P. L.
Jett, S. A.
Johnson, R. L.
Little, L. L.
Louis, V. D.
Lullen, J. J.
McKenzie, C.
Miles, H. A.
Morgan, E. R.
Owens, J. F.
Perry, M. J.
Pruitt, W. H.
Ricks, S. J.
Shelton, L. E.
Simpson, P. R.
Sims, K. E.
Slate, L. K.
Smith, M. A.
White, M. A.
Whitlock, W. P.
Williams, H. M.

**Class of 1977**

Belcher, Gerald J.
Beverly, Raymond N.
Butler, Cranson A.
Carson, Ivory D.
Chapman, Reginal K.
Clark, Edward D.
Clay, James
Collins, Vincent R.
Daily, Anthony B.
Eugene, Bernhard G.
Howell, Mitchell A.
Jackson, Arthur D.
Jones, Curtis L.
Lewis, Brett A.
Lunsford, Joseph M.
Lynem, Joseph P.
McFadden, Reginald
Miott, Rory Q.
Mitchell, Robert L.
Mosby, William E.

Pace, Gerald D.
Peebles, Darrell
Ross, James L.
Sanders, Carl E.
Scott, Kenneth L.
Scriber, Phillip H.
Taliaferro, Jerry
Terry, William R.
Thompson, Terrance
Vaughn, James A.
Washington, Donald
Williams, Calvin
Wilson, Alfred A.
Wilson, Michael B.

**Class of 1978**

Adams, D. C.
Allen, C. D.
Alston, L. M.
Bassa, R. L.
Beatty, W. D.
Bastick, T. P.
Bowman, Q. V
Bulls, H. E.
Cade, B. D.
Carter, R. L.
Clark, M. C.
Collins, T. W.
English, M. A.
Ford, S. H.
Fore, H. R.
Fry, D. L.
Grant, R. A.
Hall, M. H.
Hamilton, W.
Hargrove, P. H.
Harris, C. A.
Herndon, H. E.
Hollingsworth, J.
Holman, S. E.
Johns, O. H.
Johnson, H. E.
Jourdan, L. T.
King, G.
Landry, P. G.
Lewis, D. G.
Mallory, R. P.
Martin, Q. R.
Miles, F. M.
Mingilton, M. D.
Mitchell, C.
Mobley, D. L.
Moseley, D. L.
Moseley, M. M.
Moye, M. D.
Nixon, W. J.
Owens, C. D.
Ouslley, G. M.
Pilgrim, C. F.
Price, W. W.
Scribner, C. F.
Seaton, M. J.
Smith, C.
Taylor, T. T.
White, W. L.
Wilson, K. H.
Winton, G. J.
Young, V. J.

**Class of 1979**

Adams, William D.
Ash, Toney L.
Austin, Michael D.
Balom, Curtis II
Beasley, Michael D.
Bonds, Marcus B.
Brannon, Gregory K.
Brooks, Leo A.
Brundidge, Clennie
Bullard, Edward J.
Clark, David C.
Clemons, Edward F.
Darlington, Loyd
Deramus, Lawrence D.
Fowlkes, Essex
Fuller, Duane E.
Gordon, Robert L.
Griffin, Wesley B.
Hall, Kevin L.
Hardrick, Harold S.
Hooper, Charles W.
Howard, Maroc L.
Hughes, Bernard C.
Jackson, Stanley M.
Jennings, Tony O.
Macklin, Philip D.
McCall, James T.
McKissick, Isaac V.
Miller, Kevin L.
Mitchell, Chris T.
Oliver, Joseph P.
Petit, Jules G.
Pettus, Carlous T.
Sears, Walter A.
Sledge, Nathanial H.
Sobers, Arthur A.
Staten, Michael U.
Stewart, John
Tabler, Anthony D.
Taylor, Clarence E.
Traylor, Jimmie L.
Veney, David W.
Walter, Clifford S.
Wilkerson, Joseph W.
Williams, C. Jr.
Williams, James I.
Williams, Thomas
Willis, Michael B.
Yancey, David T.
Yeldell, Anthony L.

**Class of 1980**

Beans, Michael K.
Bland, Andrew R.
Brooks, Vincent K.
Dallas, Joy S.
Dennis, Daryl C.
Ellerbe, Michael D.
Gayle, Michael D.
Gillis, Reginald R.
Grace, Karl F.
Grayer, Curtis A.
Harrington, W. D.
Hervey, George A.
Hilliard, John F.
Jones, Ernest W.
Jones, Jeffery
Laney, Mark N.
Mattingly, John A.
Mays, George S.
Miles, Lloyd
Perdue, Rodney
Rivers, Eddie L.
Robinson, Hugh G.
Scott, James C.
Shepherd, Gilbert
Sledge, William T.
Stephens, Gregory B.
Strode, Tollie
Turner, Henry C.
Walter, Priscilla

**Class of 1981**

Bland, Melvin H.
Britton, Randy A.
Cook, Jeffrey S.
Cooper, Kieth L.
David, James E.
Davis, Archie L.
Delahoussaye, P. J.
Evans, Leroy M.
Freeman, Thomas
Gates, James A.
Gibson, Byron J.
Grady, Norman M.
Graham, David G.
Green, Emmett F.
Hall, Kimetha G.
Harris, Daryl E.
Hembrey, James E.
Hill, James B.
Hines, Curtis T.
Jackson, Christopher H.
Johnson, Hiram N.
Lambright, Michael
Luster, Robert A.
Lyons, Dereck E.
Mazyck, Alphonse F.
Miner, Michael D.
Peterson, Darryl W.
Petty, James E.
Pittard, Dana J.
Polite, Anita M.
Porter, Ronald A.
Pullen, Harvey L.
Reid, Carlton B.
Shields, Robert L.
Somersall, Paul O.
Streets, Kevin A.
Stroud, Andrew B.
Taylor, John J.
Thompson, Kevin S.
Topping, Kenneth L.
Turrentine, Larry C.
Webb, Anthony V.
Wilkins, Stephen M.
Williams, Eddie E.
Williams, Michael G.
Wilson, Duane K.

**Class of 1982**

Almore, Arthur
Austin, Stanley
Bell, Oliver
Bennett, Jerry L.
Bland, Christopher
Boston, Stephen
Boutte, Brian M.
Buchanan, Mickey
Callahan, Dennis
Cofield, William
Coleman, Joseph
Dabney, Harold
Dodson, Walter
Dunn, James F.
Goodwin, Michael
Grammer, Nadja
Hackney, John K.
Hargraves, William
Harris, David D.
Heard, Lance
Hervey, Cardell Jr.
Hollifield, Rodney
Johnson, Chris
Jones, Emmett
Jones, Kermit
Knotts, Lester
Lowry, William I.
Malloy, Brian
Miller, Cliff
Miller, Marlon
Mosby, Stewart

Perry, Benjamin II
Powell, Webster
Pullen, Harvey L.
Skinner, Eugene
Spencer, Michael
Terry, Gary L.
Thomas, David L.
Wilkins, David
Williams, Gary
Wilmer, Archie III
Wynder, Allen

**Class of 1983**

Alexander, William
Allen, Clinton O.
Allen, William T.
Babers, Charles R.
Bell, Jonathon A.
Blow, Jerry
Brinkley, Marc A.
Cary, Richard J.
Copeland, Anthony
Crumlin, Michael A.
Crutcher, Charlie
Daniel, Jeffrey A.
Davis, Alfrazier J.
Fitzgerald, Gregory
Foster, Steven P.
Gates, Willie E.
George, Marc C.
Hamilton, Marcus K.
Hayes, Morris G.
Hooper, Marc
Hopson, Mark J.
Jackson, Julius H.
Jackson, Libby Ann
Johnson, Christine
Johnson, Regina
Lighthall, Donnell
McCall, Vincent D.
McFadden, Willie J.
Morgan, Thomas Jr.
Neason, Clarence Jr.
Newkirk, Bryan T.
Oakes, Patrick B.
Poinsette, Kenneth
Porter, John
Pruitt, Larry H.
Ridgeley, Raymond
Rodriguez, Anthony
Stubblefield, Lavern
Thompson, James A.
Thomas, Johnny F.
Vaughn, John K.
Walker, Gerald J.
Williams, Cardell
Williams, Darryl A.
Williams, Michael

**Class of 1984**

Alsberry, Dennis M.
Armstrong, Bryan J.
Baldwin, Cleophas
Banks, Robert C. Jr.
Bradley, Sherry J.
Boyd, Daniel O.
Brooks, Alfred L.
Brown, Kenneth
Brown, Marvin C. Jr.
Celestan, Gregory J.
Cobb, Alma J.
Cuerington, Andre M.
Delphin, Julie A.
Dow, Thurman E.
Dunham, Andrea M.
Gales, Byron E.
Gamble, Eddie L.
Gardner, Kelvin G.
Gaston, Angela M.
Gordon, Paul G.
Grayer, Gerren S.
Green, Kent M.
Harris, William C. III
Hinton, Robert C.
Howard, Rory J.
Jefferson, William H.
Johnson, Derek
Johnson, Derek V.
Johnson, Faith A.
Jones, Kevin
Lambert, Alexander L.
McCloud, William P.
McNair, Kerry V.
Mickens, Stanley, V.
Morgan, Gregory L.
Myers, Cynthia L.
Myhand, Rickey C.
Newsome, Earl
Oatis, Demetrius C.
Oliver, Ernest M.
Peterson, Paul M.
Reever, Darryl K.
Rhodes, Robert E.
Richardson, Ricky W.
Robinson, Bruce E.
Rogers, Beverly Y.
Shaw, Everett M.
Sistrunk, Thomas M. III
Smith, Daryl G.
Smith, Troy L.
Sparkman, Gary N.
Steele, Marcus E.
Tai, Neville P.
Thomas, Fern J.
Tunnell, Harry D.
Waters, Anthony J.
Watford, Roslyn A.
White, Ronald O.
Wilson, Henry L.
Wilson, Tee Gee

**Class of 1985**

Adams, Reginald O.
Abins, Elton D.
Allen, Michael C.
Allen, Reginald M.
Asberry, Herman III
Augustine, Harvey III
Banks, Daniel T.
Babers, Alex L. III
Baisden, Michael K.
Baptiste, Martin W.
Barring, Troy A.
Bishop, Gary P.
Black, Aurelia L.
Blount, Anthony, L.
Bowling, Anthony
Brown, James B.
Bryant, Vincent D.
Carr, Angela D.
Carroll, Catherine L.
Clark, Geoffrey R.
Clark, Michelle
Collins, Michael L.
Corbett, Carl D.
Corbett, Jeffrey C.
Curry, Clarence W.
Dallas, Jeffrey B.
Davis, Amah A.
Devore, Matthew A.
Eberhart, Jimmie L.
Edmond, Pamela
Gary, Michael W.

*Lieutenant Vincent K. Brooks, the first African-American cadet to hold the post of Captain of Cadets (class of 1980).*

Gaston, Patrick B.
Gilbreat, Byron J.
Giles, Edward E.
Goodly, Timothy W.
Greenhouse, Paul S.
Griffin, Eric S.
Griffin, Oliver C. II
Hamilton, Marvin C.
Harris, Charles H.
Harris, Mark C.
Harrison, Ora E.
Holiday, Herschel S.
Hollingsworth, Jarvis
Hood, Brian M.
Hope, Charles J.
Horton, Michael P.
Jacobs, Ronald
Jackson, Samuel D. J.
Johnson, Calvin V.
Johnson, Mark D.
Johnson, Mark S.
Jones, Leon Jr.
Jones, Melvin Jr.
Jones, Luis D.
Jordan, Jansen J.
King, Rhonda H.
Labee, Kevin A.
Ladson, Gary L.
Lane, Charles B.
Lawson, John
Lipscomb, Racheaud
Lockett, Philip W.
Lowery, Veronica A.
Madden, Vernard C.
Manzy, Tyrone J.
Marshall, Jacqueline Y.
McCloud, Jamie L.
McDow, William E.
McKeloy, William K.
McLoyer, Bryford G. Jr.
Milburn, Dwayne S.
Moore, Kevin D.
Morris, John S.
Myers, Robert T.
Newsome, Mike
Otey, Francoise Y.
Owens, Ronald Jr.
Patrick, Bruce A.

**Class of 1986**

Anderson Frank, H. III
Ashley, Ricanthony R.
Atkins, John T.
Bazemore, Cleavland D.
Boykin, Oswald S. III
Bradford, Richard L.
Calloway, Dennis L.
Champion, Wendell M.
Childs, J.
Collins, Michelle L.
Cooke, Berkeley E.
Cooper, Byron W.
Costen, Wanda M.
Crenshaw, Cynthia D.
Davis, Sharri J.
Davis, Tania L.
Day, Richard A.
Drisdale, Leighton S.
Edwards, Keevin B.
Ellis, Michael D.
Erkins, Phyllis R.
Etheredge, Tod S.
Farley, John H.
Fleming, Lorie N.
Gaines, Eric Allen
Garland, Paul W.
Gibbs, Marilyn Marie
Gilchrist, Thomas C. Jr.
Grandberry, Walter L. III
Greene, Terrance M.
Harris, Marc D.
Hemmans, Eve R.
Henderson, Michael A.
Holliday, Guy D.
Huggins, Kevin L.
Hylton, Anthony C.
Johnson, Beverly D.
Kennedy, Frank M.
Lane, Sherman H.
Lipscome, Racheau D.
Loche, George E.
Lokett, Robert F.
McKelvy, Kevin W.
McKnight, Balvin A.
McLeod, Craig M.
Mixon, Laurence M.
Monroe, Dexter B.
Motley, Edward T.
Mount, Edward J. Jr.
Noble, William F. Jr.
Pearson, Pamela D.
Phillips, Elliott O. Jr.
Pope, Danita
Purnell, Lavon R.
Richardson, Clifford
Scott, Gordon A.
Searcy, William III
Smith, Eugene D.
Smith, Frederica S.
Smith, Michael D.
Stephens, Stephanie L.
Tafares, David A.
Tolson, Todd Fitzgerald
Turner, Karen A.
Ward, William E.
Washington, Valerie L.

*Graduation day at West Point.*

Whale, George L.
White, James S. Jr.
Williams, Antonio
Williams, Charles E. Jr.
Williams, Thearon M.

**Class of 1987**

Allen, Lawrence C.
Andrus, James A.
Armstrong, Michael A.
Austin, Valarie R.
Banks, Bernard B.
Bembry, Lisa L.
Benjamin, Robert E. Jr.
Bennett, Benjamin M.
Biggins, Larry D.
Billington, Courtney L.
Blackwell, Darren C.
Bidiford, Kurt A.
Boston, James E.
Brown, Deanna Y.
Campbell, Terrance D.
Cephas, John W.
Croskey, Joseph P. II
Cunningham, Walter L. Jr.
Downey, Eric R.
Fleece, David H.
Forchion, Preston L. II
Fore, Aaron B.
Fullwood, Reginald Jr.
Gilkey, Paula E.
Greaux, Keith D.
Hall, Katrina D.
Harmon, Jonathan P.
Harrison, Karl Desmond
Hope, Nathaniel D.
Hunter, Yvette N.
Jackson, Charles J. Jr.
Jackson, Roderic C.
James, David L.
Johnson, Anthony J.
Johnson, Nathan Jr.
Jones, Clarence C. Jr.
Jones, Kim L.
Jones, Michael
Kegler, Michael A.
King, Reginald
Kyle, George M.
Lampley, William T.
Lewis, Ronald F.
Long, Sean T.
Matthews, George N.
McGriff, Sammie L. II
McKenzie, Pearline V.
Morris, Stephen A. R.
Morrison, Rickey M.
Nelson, Wendell L.
Polanco, Miguel A.
Pollard, Stephanie L.
Riley, Nicola I.
Rivera, Franklin D.
Sampson, Kenneth C. Jr.
Sanders, William A.
Santos, Michael C.
Shannon, Joyce M.
Smith, Irving III
Smith, Maria Y.
Smith, Monica L.
Smith, Paolo F.
Solomon, Norman E.
Steptoe, Ronald J.
Suggs, Michael L.
Tatum, Vernon L.
Tuggle, Eric A.
Turner, Eric C.
Turner, Keven
Turner, Michael E.
Washington, Paul L. Jr.
Wells, Robert L.
White, Benjamin M.
White, Timothy M.
Williams, Charlene C.
Williams, Daniel E.
Williams, Ila N.
Williams, Rufus B. III
Willis, Dale Costello II
Wright, Benny L.
Young, Cheryl L.

**Class of 1988**

Adams, Kevin H.
Allen, Gregory J.
Barnes, Russell
Barsella, Michael K.
Bernard, Deanna L.
Bond, Richard K. K.
Branch, Gary D.
Brown, James E. III
Brown, Kerk B.
Bruns, Eric B.
Burrus, Norvin D.
Campbell, Hugh S.
Carroll, Alvin B.
Carson, Brian A.
Clark, Ronald P.
Cook, Chris T.
Crawforo, Tory J.
Cushon, Albert K.
Duncan, Gary V.
East, Michael O.
Evans, Arnold B.
Frye, Walter D. E.
Gano, Sean K.
Gray, Delvakia
Hall, Jo L.
Ham, Linwood Q. Jr.
Hamilton, David M.
Hamilton, Karlton.
Harris, Robert D.
Hinds, Sidney R. D. I.
Hodge, Clifford A.
Hopkins, Dennis C.
Hotnit, Colin E.
Hunter, Ian P.
Jackson, Archie III
Jean-Louis, Davis E. Jr.
Jefferson, Raymond M.
Jenkins, Gregory M.
Johnson, Charlie Jr.
Magee, Christopher H.
Masters, Monte M.
McClendon, Kelvin D.
Michael, Stephen L. A.
Miller, Gregory J.
Nelson, John H.
Nichols, Ernest III
Nutter, Frederick I.
Oliver, Eddie III
Overton, David S. III
Patin, Michelle J.
Porter, Torrance J.
Reeves, Kevin R.
Sanks, Warren C.
Saulny, Edward D.
Settles, Monica R.
Smith, Kevin L.
Stall, Worth W. S.
Sumter, Darren J.
Toomer, Jeffery K.
Tuggle, Sherise L.
Turner, Morris A.
Webb, Benjamin E.
Wells, Leonard E.
Williams, Charles H.
Woodberry, John L.

**Class of 1989**

Alston, Roy E.
Bell, Michael, D.
Bowman, George F. Jr.
Boyd, Eearnest E.
Campbell, Ronald L.
Carter, Tyno B.
Cheek, Tonya L.
Cleveland, Jeffrey C.
Crenston, Everton M.
Crosland, Telita
Davis, Ron
Dcosta, Joseph
Drake, Jonathan T.
Fletcher, Antonio M.
Fowler, Christopher D.
Freaell, James E. Jr.
Gadson, Gregory D.
Gardener, Randie A.
George, Oliver C.
Gibson, Kenneth C.
Gourrier, Troy M.
Gwynn, Adolphus R.
Hall, Arthur L. III
Handy, Eric D.
Hargrow, Cynthia
Harris, David K.
Hemmans, John M. Jr.
Hines, Calvin L.
House, Mark D.
Hutchinson, Jeffrey W.
Jackson, Anthony T.
Jackson, Corwin F.
Jamison, Selwyn R.
Jarmon, Thad P.
Johnson, Frank R. Jr.
Jones, Trudy O.
Lacey, Jonathan R.
Lattimer, Todd L.
Lee, Algustus W. Jr.
Lewis, John W. Jr.
Lilly, Gerald E.
Loggins, Mark L.
Maddox, Lisa M.
Mathis, Douglas D.
McGlothian, Jonathan T.
McRae, William E.
Montgomery, Damon G.
Nero, David M.
Parker, Melvin F.
Parker, Steven L.
Patterson, Anne S.
Peterson, Byron D. II
Phillips, Mark A.
Powell, Darius A.
Ramsey, Carl D.
Rayfield, John C.
Reed, Joseph O. III
Roddy, Gene E.
Sampson, Kenton C.
Singleton, Tamara G.
Smith, Melody D.
Stubblefield, Lolita M.
Wallace, Vincent M.
Waller, Aaron K. Jr.
Wellington, Deborah A.
White, Charles W. Jr.
Williams, Maurice L.
Williams, Robert L. Jr.
Williamson, Russell M.
Wilson, Isaiah III

## BLACK GRADUATES OF U.S. NAVAL ACADEMY (1949-1988)

**Class of 1949**

Brown, W. A.

**Class of 1952**

Chambers, L. C.

**Class of 1953**

Taylor, R. R.

**Class of 1954**

Raiford, J. D.

**Class of 1955**

Gregg, L. P.

**Class of 1956**

Baudit, H. S.
Sechrest, E. A.

**Class of 1957**

Jamison, V. L.
Slaughter, K. W.

**Class of 1958**

Fennell, G. M. Jr.

**Class of 1959**

Bruce, M. D.
Bush, W. S. III
Clark, M. E.
Powell, W. E.

**Class of 1961**

Byrd, W. Z.
Johnson, M. Jr.
Shelton, J. A.

**Class of 1962**

Jackson, J. T.
McCray, D.

**Class of 1963**

Newton, R. C.

**Class of 1964**

Jones, W. C.
McDonald, J. F. Jr.
Prout, P. M.
Thomas, B. F.

**Class of 1965**

Carter, S. J. Jr.
Grayson, F. F. Jr.
Reason, J. P.

**Class of 1967**

Huey, C. W.
Tzomes, C. A.

**Class of 1968**

Bolden, C. F. Jr.
Clark, W. S. Jr.
Lucas, R. G.
Simmons, D. F.

**Class of 1969**

Carr, E. F.
Jones, F. E.

**Class of 1970**

Freeman, J. B.
Greene, E. L.
Henry, B. A.
Roberts, M. C.
Watson, A. J.
Williams, L. V.

**Class of 1971**

Collier, C. M.
Porter, J. F.
Shaw, H. M. Jr.

**Class of 1972**

Burnette, E. A.
Coleman, A. B.
Crump, W. L. Jr.
Jones, N. M.
Keaser, L. W.
Lovely, E.
Mason, M. T.
McMillian, J. A.
Rucks, C. H.
Smith, E. M.
Staton, E. M.
Tindall, J. S.

**Class of 1973**

Calhoun, L. W.
Caliman, K. H.
Campbell, J. H.
Evans, W. G.
Faust, H. L.
Jackson, J. E.
Jones, L. W.
Kennard, W. M.
Samuels, R. G.
Shockley, R. L.
Watts, R. D.
Young, E. C.

**Class of 1974**

Corpin, O. D.
Dunn, K. D.
Jolly, E. L
Kirk, F. L.
Minor, T. E.
Montgomery, D.
Rasin, S. E.
Robinson, C.
Tate, J. D.

**Class of 1975**

Ardine, J. E.
Baily, C. E.
Everet, W. M.
Graves, B. E.
Grover, R. O.
Hampton, M. L.
Hargrove, C.
Harris, W. M.
Jackson, D. E.
Jackson, J. T.
Lawson, H.
Merrell, W.
Miller, K. E.
Montgomery, W. J.
Nollie, T. C.
Robinson, J. W.
Russell, D.
Washington, M. B.
Watson, L. J.
Williams, R. B.
Willis, C. J.

**Class of 1976**

Bass, R. G.
Boyd, C. C. Jr.
Brown, C. A.
Clark, A. W. Jr.
Cole, C.
Curtis, D. C.
Davis, N. Jr.
Dennis, J. I.
Ellis, R. L.
Epps, J. B.
Ford, E. Jr.
Franklin, D. W.
Giron, B. A.
Halton, E. S.
Harris, W. J.
Hicks, G. R.
Holmes, E. I.
Howard, R.
Jenkins, G.
Lassiter, I. W.
Leonard, K. E.
Liscomb, J. C.
Littlejohn, G. A.
Miles, D. A.
Mitchell, R. I
Moore, G.
Owens, I. H.
Paulding, O.
Payton, L. Jr.
Pritchett, R. R.
Queen, G. A.
Reddix, M. C.
Sears, W. T.
Sharperson, C. H.
Smith, J. B. Jr.
Sparks, J. E. Jr.
Stevens, M. K.
Walton, D. F.
Woumnm, E. D.

**Class of 1977**

Adair, S. A.
Almeida, J. M.
Anderson, K.
Bonner, D. R.
Booker, C. B.
Booker, R. L.
Brinkly, R. W.
Bruce, P. J.
Burns, M. W.
Byrd, G. L.
Caeser, J. S.
Caldwell, R. L.
Campbell, A. L.
Clay, J. L.
Cook, D.
Davis, P. L. E.
Deane, L. E.
Dory, C. E.
Ellison, W. L. Jr.
Faulkner, R. M.
Floyd, M. L.
Foster, A. P.
Franklin, D. E.
Freeman, D. W.
Garcia, B.A.
Gilmore, E. J.
Goodrum, R. A.
Graham, D. F.
Gray, S. G.
Hallman, C.
Handy, C. D.
Hardy, J. T. Jr.
Harrington, J.
Hill, M. L.
Hithon, C. J.

Ivey, C. G.
Jackson, L. Jr.
Lee, S. Jr.
Lockett, K. V.
Lockley, J.
Long, A. IV
McNair, E. R.
McNeil, R. A.
Mitchell, R. V.
Nacoste, P. J.
Ray, D. D.
Rogers, M. L.
Roxe, M. V.
Sapp, J. K.
Sawyer, G. R.
Schoolfield, D. J.
Seldon, R. W.
Smith, J. W.
Station, G. V.
Trass, K. R.
Tucker, M.
Turner, E. A.
Valentine, J.
Washington, V. L.
Wright, E. J.

**Class of 1978**

Abernethy, T. S.
Anderson, D. E.
Andre, C. A.
Bramlett, L.
Carter, B. W.
Cato, A. M.
Cook, D.
Crawford, T.
Dyer, M. A.
Fields, M. H.
Flanagan, G.
Goodman, R. O. Jr.
Guillory, V. G.
Haney, C. E. D.
Harris, B. F.
Johnson, M. R.
Johnston, M. R.
Jones, S. E.
Jubert, G. A.
King, M. E.
Knight, R. L.
Marchant, B. F.
Meadows, F. J.
Miller, L. E.
Moore, C. E.
Mosley, E. K.
Newby, L. D.
Perry, C. A.
Peterson, J. C. Jr.
Prince, L. O. Jr.
Reddick, M. P. Jr.
Redvict, P. C.
Robinson, W. I.
Saddler, M. R.
Scott, R. W.
Sears, M. E.
Stallings, J. B.
Taylor, R. R.
Thompson, L. B.
Williams, A.
Williams, M. G. Jr.
Winns, A. L.
Wood, D. L.
Woods, H. M.
Wray, K. L.
Young, O. W.

**Class of 1979**

Adams, J. Jr.
Allen, M. T.
Ballard, W. W.
Beam, D. A.
Berry, E. C.
Brooks, S. E.
Burrell, A. K.
Cousin, D. G.
Darring, P. L.
Gibson, M. A.
Green, N. B.
Jackson, K. L.
Johnson, A. J. Jr.
Johnson, M. D.
Jones, H.
Jones, L. H. Jr.
Jones, S. A.
Lewis, W. D.
Martin, W. B.
Massie, W. R.
McCoy, L. J.
McKenzie, S. S.
Miller, A. B.
Monroe, G. A.
Norgrove, K. E.
Smith, A. R.
Wilder, C. R.
Wise, J. E.
Womack, K.
Woodward, C. C. Jr.

**Class of 1980**

Atkins, M.
Barnhill, L.
Bradley, E.
Brown, G. V.
Burks, L. J.
Carmichael, B.
Character, D.
Clark, C. B.
Clark, I. R. Jr.
Coker, M. Jr.
Colvin, J. T.
Cooper, S. L.
Cornish, B. F.
Dancy, J. G.
Daniel, F.
Dennis, D. C.
Figgins, R. L.
Gay, E. L.
Grooms, B. E.
Hodge, R. R.
Jackson, B. K.
Jiles, A. W.
Johnson, R.
Johnson, R.
Josia, A. H.
Mack, T. A.
Manns, E.
McCauley, L. H.
Meyers, C. L.
Mines, J. L.
Minor, I. L.
Mosley, A. S.
Nemecek, R. A.
Paul, W.
Raymond, D. K.
Shorts, V.
Smith, B. E.
Smith, V. C.
Sneed, M.
Thompson, C.
Thornton, C.
Trass, R. E.
Vonlipsey, R. K.
Walker, J. L.
White, T.

*Midshipman Donna Hazard, graduate of the U.S. Naval Academy at Annapolis (class of 1982).*

Williams, N.
Wilson, C. A.

**Class of 1981**

Abernathy, R.
Bailey, P. E.
Barnes, A. P.
Brownlee, E.
Butler, R. A.
Coker, T.
Curry, B.
Denkler, G.
Evans, W. T.
Gainer, C.
Green, L. R.
Gross, K. J.
Harness, K. N.
Herrod, A. L.
Howard, A. M.
Jackson, B. D.
Jackson, R. C. III
Knock, J. A.
Lee, F. A.
McCree, V.
McElroy, D. M.
Mines, G.
Nixon, M.
Oliver, B. C.
Pace, G. H.
Perez, M. C.
Reaves, J. C.
Redden, S. D.
Ricks, D. L.
Roberts, W.
Swoope, A. M.
Taylor, R. L.
Thomas, A. A.
Tolbert, K. C.
Ware, R. E.
Weems, R. A.

**Class of 1982**

Banks, M. E.
Baptiste, B.
Batchlor, C. D.
Bates, A. Y.
Baugh, K. A.
Bennett, D. C. Jr.
Butts, W. S.
Carodine, C. K.
Cole, P.
Davis, N. M.
Dixon, D. S.
Ferrell, T. J.
Gay, W. H. Jr.
Goodson, E. H.
Gray, A. M.
Hayes, S. K. Jr.
Hazzard, D. M.
Howard, M. J.
Leisch, J. K.
Malcolm, M. W.
McLain, J. S.
Meyers, E. A.
Morris, M. J.
Nobles, W. E. Jr.
Odom, A. A.
Palmer, D. K.
Parker, C. T.
Reagans, E. Jr.
Rogers, W. F. III
Simons, J. M.

*Lieutenant Roger Isom (left) and Lieutenant Kennon Artis (right) chosen as role models for the entire Naval Corps of Cadets. They were also the first African-Americans to be chosen as role models at the Naval Academy (class of 1988).*

Terrell, W. A.
Tondu, J. L.
Watson, R. K.
Wiggins, C. A.
Williams, A.
Winbush, N. W. C. II

**Class of 1983**

Alexander, Catherine D.
Barclift, Michael R.
Battle, John Clayborne
Bedell, Kevin Fredric
Blackwell, Jacqueline
Blake, James A.
Butler, Christopher L.
Carter, George R.
Clark, Jerome A.
Coles, James R. III
Crockett, Jerry M.
Crozier, Wilbur V.
Deberry, Dennis
Edmondson, Michael J.
Fears, George M.
Finley, Julian G.
Gatson, Darryl K.
Hale, Kevin T.
Hester, Gina L.
Hicks, Warren T.
Hundley, Herbert
Jackson, Eric K.
Jackson, Stephen M.
James, Kenneth A.
Jones, Eugene W.
Key, Kevin D.
Lakins, Darryl D.
Mackay, Leo Sidney Jr.
Martin, Robert C.
McClusky, Kenneth W.
McCoy, Angelo A.
McNeil, Franklin N. Jr.
Miller, Kevin L.
Mitchell, Troy M.
Moore, Richard A.
Outing, Donald A.
Posey, Brian W.
Raines, Clinton Jr.
Roane, Elmer W. Jr.
Robinson, Russell L.
Rupp, John
Scissum, Adolph C.
Smith, Henry C.
Smith, Leonard Jr.
Thames, Tyrone M.
Tyree, William D. III
Wallington, Joseph T.
Waye, Reginald B.
Williams, Joseph E. Jr.
Williams, Leo W. II
Williams, Yolanda Y.
Wilson, Joe David Jr.
Wilson, Kenneth
Wrice, Jesse Edward Jr.

**Class of 1984**

Abbott, Denise M.
Andrews, Jeffrey A.
Andrews, Tae Wan
Baker, Beverly M.
Brown, Conrad N. Jr.
Brown, Jeffrey D.
Chambers, Cliffton D.
Clayton, Eric V.
Curbeam, Robert L. Jr.
Darden, Ronald K.
Davis, Christopher D.
Davis, Jacqueline R.
Fegan, Frederick M.
Flaggs, Moreatha Y.
Fortune, Idean J. II
Gaines, Leonard S.
Hosch, Willie H.
Howard, James H.
Howard, Kevin T.
Hudson, Derek D.
Jones, Michael L.
Kizzee, Carlos P.
Law, Leitia L.
Manning, Cameron A.
Marshall, Lawrence E.
McDonald, Ronald K.
McKinney, Billy L.
Neal, Sherman E.
Newhouse, Darryl B.
Nixon, Randall L.
Parrish, Demetrius J. Jr.
Peoples, Gerald K.
Price, Lenny F.
Rasbury, Stanley O.
Shepherd, Michael A.
Skinner, Steven G.
Smith, David H.
Smith, Jonathan J.
Stephens, Carla R.
Stevens, Monica
Taylor, James Jr.
Tillman, Willard Jr.
Turner, Jean-Francois
Walton, Terrance B.
Wilson, Joslyn G. Jr.
Wilson, Woodrow III
Wright, Darin C.

**Class of 1985**

Adams, Thomas L. III
Adkins, Lemonte A.
Alexander, Lewis B. Jr.
Atkinson, David
Betton, Christopher R.
Biggs, Jeffrey S.
Bryan, Curtis E. Jr.
Burke, Christopher K.
Bugg, Lois
Bush, Rani D.
Coleman, Austin H.
Daniel, Jeffrey A.
Davis, Bruce G.
Dejoie, Bertel J.
Dillard, Mark V.
Figgins, Gerald D.
Flowers, Michael L.
Gex, Geoffrey D.
Graham, Michael R.
Greenwood, Michael D.
Hacker, Bruce L.
Harris, Paul Jr.
Henry, Frederick D.
Hines, Joseph E.
Johnson, Dreste M.
Jones, Warren R. Jr.
Keyes, Warren F.
Maddox, Mario R.
Marsh, Laurence A.
McCallum, N.
McKinney, Roberta V.
Melvin, Barry S.
Mills, Charlie H. III
Mimms, Bernard F.
Moore, David J.
Moore, Michael T.
Morant, Kevin
Nolan, Charles H. Jr.
Parham, Thomas D. III
Phelps, Peter M.
Phillip, Lester U.
Pierce, Carlton
Pleasant, Mervin A. III
Rhoe, Reginald M.
Richmond, Phillip P.
Studevan, Colin C.
Wallace, EricK.
Williams, Byron A.
Williams, Steven C.

**Class of 1986**

Allen, Averett M.
Allen, Michael A.
Atkinson, Craig A.
Brown, Kevin J.
Bustamante, George A.
Carpenter, Jerry A.
Carroll, John W. III
Dampier, Louis H.
Dixon, Derrick L.
Echols, Eddie L. Jr.
Edwards, Douglas T.
Ellison, Arron S.
Gray, Robert L.
Harris, Linzell L.
Hines, Joseph E.
Hubbard, Bryan D.
Jackson, Edward K.
Jones, Marius B.
Jordan, Anthony D.
Lupton, Michael F.
Maye, Larry
McDonald, Johnath L.
McElroy, Terry S.
McMichael, Gregory
McQueen, Eric S.
Pierce, Ivan C. III
Poinsette, Raymond M.
Powers, Zack Jr.
Reed, James D.
Reitan, Paula J.
Smith, Thomas M.
Stallings, Herry
Thames, Joseph R.
Thompkins, Geselle D.
Totty, Earl Jr.
Turner, Ingrid M.
Wade, Spencer A.
Wakefield, Bryce E.
Wells, Royce A.
Wharton, Richard G. Jr.
Williams, Daniel J.
Williams, Gregg B. K.
Williams, Michael
Williams, Robert
Wilson, Jesse A.
Wright, Grover L. Jr.

**Class of 1987**

Bond, Phillip S.
Campbell, Nicholas
Cooke, Rabon E.
Council, George H.
Curry, Sean C.
Dove, John C. Jr.
Fennell, David A.
Fletcher, Kirklin C.
Flewellen, Demetrius L.
Fuller, John V.
Garrett, Stephen C.
Gary, Francesca, D.
Harris, Ronald J.
Hawkins, Albert W.
Higgs, Ronald L. Jr.
Hollinger, Anthony
Johnson, Christopher E
Lindsey, Dwayne

Littlejohn, Stuart M.
Magee, Edward O. Jr.
Malloy, Terence P.
Manhertz, Carey M.
McBeth, Vincent D.
Merritt, Howard F.
Miles, Mary A.
Moore, Wallace F.
Nickels, Trent D.
Rideau, Errol E. Jr.
Robinson, David M.
Robinson, Joycelin
Ross, Wendell
Smith, Michael K.
Tyner, Jerry D.
Vaughn, Leroy D.
Watkins, Daryl V.
Wilson, John G.

**Class of 1988**

Albritton, David J.
Artis, Kennon A.
Bennett, Dawn L.
Brown, Curtis L.
Brown, Patrick W.
Bryant, Richard R.
Clausell, David A.
Dismuke, Jerry B.
Dupree, John C. Jr.
Fisher, William R. Jr.
Grayson, Roger S. IV
Greene, Michael R.
Hall, Myron L.
Hitt, David A.
Irby, Curtis M.
Isom, Roger G.
Jones, Mark W.
Mann, Charisse M.
Owens, James K.
Payton, Howard Jr.
Preer, Cassondra L.
Richardson, Claude E.
Richmond, Rosalind J.
Saunders, Troy
Simmons, Gregory L.
Smith, Darryl L.
Sparrock, Rober C.
Stephens, Truman Jr.
Stokes, Andre E.
Tabb, Michael E.
Trigg, Christopher F.
Union, Craig D.
Wallace, Vernon L.
Williams, Glenn N.
Williams, Varanda K.
Wingo, Harry M. Jr.
Wright, Anthone R.
Wright, Matice J.
Yeldell, Harold S.

**Class of 1989**

Adams, Charlton P.
Alexander, Randy E.
Anderson, Darryl C.
Archer, Luther Jr.
Barber, Michael R.
Billingslea, Willie D.
Britton, Brian J.
Campbell, Kevin B.
Campbell, Marvin G.
Casey, David P.
Clay, Orin B.
Cornwall, Harold R.
Duvall, John A. III
Edwards, Dondi
Fuller, Derek A.
Garvin, Derrick E.
Gay, Riccardio D.
Gilbert, Aaron E.
Glasper, Eddie L. Jr.
Green, Christina R.
Griffin, Patrick S.
Grimes, Kenneth R.
Hammond, Terrence E.
Harris, Krista
Hinton, Pierre R. Jr.
Holland, Monica K.
Horton, Anthony C.
Howard, Reginald M.
Jones, Robert J.
Jones, Ronald F.
Jordan, Carl C.
Leflore, Michael R.
Lemieux, Tawayla M.
Mann, James A.
Martin, Eugene T. III
Mathis, Gerald H. Jr.
Mills, Don A.
Moore, Charles L. Jr.
Muse, Roland S.
Peltier, Albert R.
Phillilps, Timothy B.
Powers, Patrick J.
Prather, Craig S.
Sawyer, Michael E.
Simmons, Jeffrey W.
Simmons, William E. Jr.
Smith, Calvin F.
Smith, Joseph A.
Snead, William B.
Spencer, Yessic C. III
Stephenson, Donna M.
Triplett, William M.
Tucker, Barbara D.
Turner, Derric T.
Wade, Joseph F.
Warren, Jay A.
Willie, Clarence E. Jr.
Wingfield, Theodore V. II
Womack, Carol J.
Woodson, John K.

*Three P-51 Mustangs on mission in Italy during WWII, flown by the distinguished, but segregated, all-black fighter group of the 15th Air Force. Since the creation of the Air Force Academy, African-Americans have been part of every graduating class.*

## BLACK GRADUATES OF THE U.S. AIR FORCE ACADEMY (1963-1988)

**Class of 1963**

Bush, Charles V.
Payne, Isaac
Sims, Roger B.

**Class of 1964**

Gregory, Frederick D.

**Class of 1965**

Beaman, Arthur L.
Plummer, Bentley V.
Thomas, Charles A.
Wiley, Fletcher H.

**Class of 1967**

Cunningham, Thomas L.

**Class of 1968**

Ecung, Maurice
Gibson, Samuel B.
Groves, Weldon K.
Moore, Francis M.
Thompson, James E.

**Class of 1969**

Hopper, John D.
Howland, Walter T.
Little, Kenneth H.
Love, James E.
Spooner, Richard E.
Stevenson, Kenneth E.

**Class of 1970**

Arnold, Harry
Battles, Dorsey
Bowie, Harold V.
Bryant, Robert S.
Elliot, Norman L.
Jones, Reuben D. Jr.
Key, George
Mohr, Dean B. Jr.

**Class of 1972**

Bassa, Paul Jr.
Harrison, Booker
Henderson, Clyde R.
Jones, Raymond J.
McDonald, Michael
Meredith, Keith S.
Nelson, Michael V.
Parks, Reginald D.
Rhaney, Mahlon C. Jr.
Ross, Joseph D. Jr.
Rucker, Raymond I. Jr.
Slade, John B. Jr.

**Class of 1973**

Abraham, Robert E.
Baker, Richard A.
Bolton, Robert M.
Butler, Ernest E. Jr.
Childress, Charlie Jr.
Dunn, Arther L.
Gilbert, Robert L.
Harrison, Herbert A.
Hodges, Rudnaldo
Lewis, Gerald E.
Mitchell, David L.
Mitchell, Joseph R. Jr.
Mitchell, Orderia F.
Stallworth, Charles E.
Thompson, William L.
Way, Spencer Jr.

**Class of 1974**

Berry, William M. III
Bryant, Frederic B. Jr.
Caldwell, Richmond H. Jr.
Collins, Dennis F.
Crenshaw, Ronald L.
Hairston, Carlton P.
Lockette, Emory W. Jr.
McAlpin, Sherman E.
Murphy, Franklin
Robinson, Neal T.
Scott, Darryl A.
Smith, Clarence D. Jr.
Tarleton, Gadson J. III
Timberlake, Marion A.
Walker, Philip E.
Watson, Ronald W.
Webb, Lance C.

**Class of 1975**

Benjamin, Philip G. II
Bready, Alvin
Cason, Wilbert Jr.
Cosby, Willie J. III
Crenshaw, Larry D.
Franklin, George E. Jr.
Graves, Jeffrey C.
Hargrove, Julius L.
Kendall, Phillip L.
Osborne, William B.
Roberts, Randy W.
Smith-Harrison, Leon I.
Whitley, Kenneth L.
Williams, Douglas L. II

**Class of 1976**

Allen, Calvin L.
Benton, Jimmie L.
Butler, Michael W.
Campbell, Stephen C.
Correia, Stanley C.
Crosley, Hilton C.
Dantzler, Willie C.
Dorman, Glenn A.
Felder, Lloyd R.
Franklin, William H.
Gandy, Edward R. Jr.
Garner, Larry E.
Gray, Robert M.
Hoyes, Michael B.
Johnson, Anthony R.
Kyle, Gary A.
Levell, Edward A.
Macklin, Winfred H. Jr.
Manson, Harold C.
Miller, Michael P.
Norris, Johnnie E. Jr.
Palms, Wilfred G. R.
Pannell, Garland J.
Powers, Ahart W.
Reed, Raymond Jr.
Ross, Dave M.
Williams, Gregory
Williams, John F.
Williams, Mark R.
Williams, Roderick M.

**Class of 1977**

Adams, Craig F.
Bailey, Zachery E.
Balancierre, Milton G. III
Clegg, Robert S.
Cosby, Ricky Joe
Crafton, Wilson D. Jr.
Cromer, DeJuan
Cross, Michael A.
Gipson, Anthony
Grady, Walter A.
Johnson, Sterling
Jones, Clarence D.
Jones, Daryl L.
Lee, Williams C.
Lyle, Harron V.
McReynolds, James C. Jr.
Parker, Thomas G.
Peters, Burnett W. III
Ratchford, Monroe J.
Robinson, Vernon L. III
Scott, Lynn M.
Shropshire, Theodore V.
Singletery, James
Smith, Gregory F.
Wallace, Frank L.
Wells, Kennard R.
White, Kenneth R.

**Class of 1978**

Allen, Martin W.
Clemons, Russell
Clethen, Eric L.
Cooper, Gary Lee
Cox, Andrew H.
Crowe, Lelvin Jr.
Dean, Garry C.
Drake, Ricky J.
Ghiden, Reginald
Gilmore, Samuel L.
Gravatt, Wayne K.
Harrison, Oliver
Hawkins, Michael
Henderson, Herbert
Hicks, John E.
Holder, Livingston L.
Lankford, Morgan
Lawrence, Michael
Lee, Lyman Anthony
Mason, Linwood Jr.
Mills, Raymond G.
Moye, Arthur L.
Rice, Edward A.
Richardson, Anthony
Shaw, William J.
Simons, James T.
Stewart, Moses Jr.
Temple, David J.
Woodfork, Isaac K.
Wrenn, Mark L.

**Class of 1979**

Allen, Travis L. Jr.
Alston, Stephen M.
Austin, Christopher L.
Belt, James M.
Blake, Gregory N.
Bordenave, Paul B. Jr.
Brown, Al C.
Brundidge, Gregory L.
Colvin, James T. Jr.
Donald, Edward G.
Dubose, Ted
Duvalle, Reginald A.
Faulkner, Paul E.
Francois, Frank Jr.
Gilchrist, Lenue Jr.
Hall, Richard P.
Harris, Junious L. III
Holmes, Reginald C.
Jones, Vernon D.
Leonard, Steven D.

*Directing traffic at the Air Force Academy Tower in Colorado.*

Maxwell, Richard P.
Mitchell, Verner D.
Murry, Curtis R.
Osler, Benjamin F.
Pate, Walter R. Jr.
Pearson, Ricardo
Petterson, Hernes J. Jr.
Pointer, Ronald L.
Ramirez, Juanito E.
Rayfield, William L. II
Robinson, Eddie
Sawyer, Willis E. Jr.
Smith, Gregory L.
Sowards, Mark A.
Thomas, Michael A.
Warner, Curt E.
Watkins, Steven D.
Williams, Asa R.

**Class of 1980**

Adams, Daniel S. Jr.
Alexander, David L. III
Ball, Shelby G.
Batts, Stephen M.
Benjamin, Gail F.
Benjamin, Vaughn P. Jr.
Benn, Mack III
Best, James H.
Burrell, Hugh F.
Campbell, Jeffrey O.
Campbell, Patrick E.
Desbordes, David A.
Floyd, Kevin S.
Fortson, Michael L.
Glenn, Michael L.
Gray, Ronald P.
Gunn, Willie A.
Harris, Andre W.
Hill, Walter B.
Jones, William Jr.
Knuckles, Gwendolyn
Lester, Thomas Jr.
Mack, Oscar Jr.
Mallory, Patrick A.
Marshall, Brian
Payton, Timothy J.
Robinson, Thomas E. Jr.
Ross, Michael D.
Saxon, Frank IV
Sears, Alvin D.
Strickland, Robert H. Jr.
Turman, Beverly C.
Upshur, Robert A. Jr.
Walters, Donald E.
Warr, Dartanian
White, Michael P.
Woodland, Paul S.

**Class of 1981**

Anderson, Alan K.
Andrews, Dale
Blount, Robert Jr.
Brooks, Frank K. Jr.
Burks, Eric S.
Butler, Craig A.
Campbell, Andre K.
Carroll, Marvin D.
Clark, David A.
Cloud, Albert T. Jr.
Coleman, Clarence J. C. Jr.
Cox, Michael A.
Dennis, Sheldon
Derry, Heyward Jr.
Dismuke, Theophus D.
Dortch, Joseph
English, Nelson W.
Evans, Adolphus Jr.
Garvin, Eric D.
Griffin, Drees C.
Guess, James Allen Jr.
Gunter, Gurnie C. Jr.
Handy, Dexter R.
Harris, Timothy A.
Hasty, Thomas J. III
Ingram, Mark E.
Jenkins, Craig M.
Johnson, Ernest J. Jr.
Jones, Reginald L.
Knight, Gregory G.
Manning, Kelvin M.
Perry, Phillip L.
Phillips, Charles E. Jr.
Richardson, Ernest I.
Rosier, Isaac Jr.
Silas, Michael O.
Smith, Kenric

Stevens, Cecil D. Jr.
Stewart, Alfred J.
Stewart, Freddie Jr.
Streeter, Xavier L.
Wallace, Everton R.
Wright, Robert F.

**Class of 1982**

Bankole, Cullen R.
Barnes, Marion E. II
Berry, Carson C.
Bizzell, William A.
Buchanan, Julia M.
Christian, Nathaniel D.
Craft, Raymond Jr.
Davis, Earl Q.
Davis, Elton D.
Davis, Michael N.
Duncan, Marc B.
Francisco, Raymond A.
Graham, Nancy F.
Hamilton, Gregory J.
Hill, Larry D.
Hithe, Troy A.
Howard, Richard N. II
Hunigan, Kirk A.
Jackson, Antoine
Jackson, Johnny L.
Jackson, Walter L. Jr.
James, George F. III
Jarrell, Allen K.
Johnson, Jonnie
Johnson, Thomas L.
Jones, Daryl P.
Jones, Jerome S.
Lewis, Gregory L.
Lofton, Victor E.
Mack, Lin A.
Maize, Robert D.
Maragh, Vivet V.
Mason, John R. Jr.
Moragne, Jeffrey A.
Payne, Glenn R.
Richards, Thomas L.
Riles, Jeffrey M.
Roath, Anthony S.
Robinson, Kenneth L.
Shelton, Cynthia
Singletery, Rodney
Smith, Elva D.
Smith, James E.
Smith, Kathryn L.
Stevenson, Martha
Stevenson, Mary
Temple, Alan J.
West, Steven A.
White, Alex Jr.
Williams, Billy W.
Williams, Darryl A. C.
Williams, Edward L.
Willis, Cynthia
Wolters, Tod D.

**Class of 1983**

Aikens, Johnny III
Anderson, Nicole P.
Babers, Alonzo C.
Bland, Othello Jr.
Brisbon, Harris L.
Brown, Virginia G.
Bullock, Jay P.
Cannon, Kevin A.
Carter, Norris E.
Cephas, Earl F.
Childress, Iris R.
Collins, Brian D.
Corbett, Dorian I.
Davis, Howard D. Jr.
Dooley, Bryan P.
Evans, Quintin A.
Ford, Apryl A.
Gibbs, Gregory C.
Glover, Kendall R.
Gobern, Alexis M. Jr.
Gore, Kevin A.
Gould, Patrick A.
Grant, Cecil A. Jr.
Graves, Ronald E.
Hall, Nathaniel C.
Harris, Charles H. Jr.
Harris, Johnnie C. Jr.
Head, Robert L. Jr.
Hockaday, Cleophas S. Jr.
Holloway, Theodore P.
Holmes, Stewart E. Jr.
Hudson, Tony D.
Hunter, Raymond A.
Johnson, Roger E.
Johnson, Steven B.
Jones, Charles D.
Jones, Herbert H. Jr.
Lewis, Errol I.
Lofton, Ricky O.
McCray, Cleveland R.
McDaniel, Donald A.
Moore, Kyle R.
Moreland, Carol L.
Peart, Michael A.
Peterson, Eugene G. Jr.
Pratt, Bryan P.
Richardson, Derrick M.
Robinson, Donovan O.
Rogers, John F. III
Samuda, Eric F.
Sears, Emanuel O.
Simmons, Richard I.
Simpson, Dorothy E.
Singleton, Harold L. Jr.
Smith, Donald R.
Sullivan, Konda H.
Tingman, Kenneth R.
Valentine, Lee A.
Veal, Kenny
Washington, Erwin V.
Williams, Bernard S. Jr.
Williams, Troy M.
Wilson, Jahn D.
Winston, Moses B.
Yancy, Daniel M.

**Class of 1984**

Aiken, Charles H. Jr.
Allen, Cheryl A.
Aubert, Steven F.
Aycock, Kent D.
Baker, Herman L. Jr.
Banks, Melody C.
Barrant, Winston I.
Best, Leonard Jr.
Bethea, Mark I.
Billups, Aundra E.
Boyd, Robin D.
Bradley, Dave W.
Burke, John C.
Calderon, Joseph P.
Callahan, Mark A.
Chatman, Cleophus D.
Clark, Andrea D.
Clark, Warren H.
Collins, Colleen A.
Conway, Norphesia G.
Crews, Alfred Jr.
Cross, Clarice
Dawson, Jay W.
Dieudonne, Carl H.
Dixon, Charles I.
Drew, Benjamin A. Jr.
Dugue, Brett A.
Dulaney, Keith L.
Elliott, Grady N.
Eubanks, James C. Jr.
Fisher, Christopher S.
Foster, Derek C.
Freeman, Myron
Glass, George C.
Glass, Robert C. Jr.
Gomes, Marie E.
Goodman, Anthony L.
Greer, Byron L.
Griffis, Craig E.
Hamilton, Caleb L.
Hargrove, Reginald P.
Harris, William J. Jr.
Haynes, Victor C.
Healy, Steven J.
Hill, Douglas E.
Hill, Prince A.
Hood, Charles M. III
Hurst, Thurston L.
Jackson, Ingrid M.
Johnson, David C.
Johnson, Stephen T.
Jones, Marvin E.
Joseph, Garland R.
King, Konrad
Leblanc, Stewart M.
Lewis, Randy
Major, Derrick S.
Malone, Michael L.
Marshall, Gregory
Martin, Mark A.
McClary, Wayne H.
McGlotten, Douglas L.
Milteer, Michael N.
Milton, Elbert Jr.
Moore, Lee
Myers, Chris A.
Owens, John E.
Paige, Clive A.
Petteway, Malcolm
Phanord, Bettina A.
Phifer, Julia C.
Prince, John H.
Randall, Ivan T.
Reaves, Irving W.
Revels, Allen R.
Ross, Hubert A.
Rozier, David E
Rucker, Sharon L.
Sanders, Samuel T.
Scott, Lamont G.
Scott, Leon C. Jr.
Seals, Regan W.
Sheppard, Gwendolyn M.
Smith, Eugenio R.
Smith, Susan E.
Smith, Marcel R.
Strong, Crystal L.
Suber, Craig J.
Tann, Martin C.
Taylor, John D.
Thom, Maxie C.
Thomas, Andre L.
Thomas, Michael J.
Tucker, Wade L.
Valentine, Fred L. Jr.
Westbrook, James B.
Wickliffe, Carlton P.
Wigfall, James E.
Williams, Anthony
Williams, Daniel E.
Williams, David H.

Williams, Douglas
Williams, Horace L.
Willis, Cedric C.

**Class of 1985**

Abram, Dorera J.
Adkins, Thomas A.
Allen, Marc L.
Anderson, Jerry D.
Baker, Robert K.
Banks, Kenneth
Barnes, Glenn D.
Barnum, Usher L.
Baylor, William L. III
Bessellieu, Susan P.
Black, Michael B.
Blackmon, Elihu R.
Boswell, Anthony O.
Boyd, Randy D.
Bridgers, Matthew X.
Brown, Gerald Q.
Brown, Regina J.
Brown, William C.
Broussard, Kerri L.
Burns, Bennie L.
Butler, Derrick D.
Byrd, Edward L.
Cameron, Von M.
Carter, Miguel A.
Cleaves, Chevalier P.
Corns, Toi V.
Dawkins, Keith A.
Devane, Mark W.
Dixon, Kevin W.
Dobbs, Deric K.
Dorsey, Alfred M.
Douglas, Robert H.
Durante, Paris A.
Eady, Monica J.
Evans, Kenneth C.
Evans, Robert A.
Ferrell, Melodi L.
Fields, Mark K.
Foster, Nagaila
Garrett, Gerald B.
Gest, Robert IV
Gibbs, Gregory L.
Gilmore, Robert E.
Gilyard, Reginald H.
Gordon, Eric L.
Gould, Evelyn J.
Graham, Anterro A.
Grant, Karl A.
Griffith, Rodney N.
Griggs, Gordon J.
Harris, Philecia L.
Harris, Wanda D.
Harvey, Dwight E.
Hatchett, Danielle L.
Hayes, Jesse D.
Hines, Hugh L.
Hodge, Nicole C.
Holsey, Reginald C.
Hussain, Kobir
Ivory, James C.
Jackson, Larry D.
Jackson, Reginald W.
James, Thomas M.
Johnson, Ellis
Jones, Charles E. Jr.
Jones, William A
Jordan, Jonathon D.
Kelley, Russell V.
Larkins, Charles G.
Lesane, Jonathan
Luster, Maurice
Mason, Gerald M.
Mayes, Bobby L.
McClary, Carl W.
McElhannon, Neal B.
McKnight, Ivan S.
Mills, Johnny R.
Modesty, Ronald K.
Moore, Vernon L.
Mooreland, Christopher J.
Morton, Clarence R.
Nixon, Kevin M.
Paige, Clive A.
Patterson, Edward A.
Perry, David F. D.
Philpotts, Gregory
Pickett, Marquis D.
Randolf, Mark J.
Richardson, Darrell
Ross, Anthony D. Jr.
Ross, Arthur Jr.
Russell, Frank E. II
Sampson, Rodney N.
Scott, Alton J.
Simmons, Cedric D.
Sisson, Michael A.
Smith, Ronald G.
Sowell, Michael T.
Stewart, Dennis J.
Street, Christopher L.
Streeter, Charles A.
Thomas, Douglas
Timberlake, Douglas
Ussery, Harold A.
Walker, Gary L.
Walton, James D.
Washington, Joyce D.
Washington, Robert
Weathersby, George
Wiggins, Joseph Jr.
Williams, Albert H.
Williams, Frank Q.
Williams, Jeffrey D.
Woods, Robert A. Jr.
Wright, Wanda A.

**Class of 1986**

Armstrong, Merrill F.
Batts, Alan L.
Beaufils, Igor F.
Brooks, Christopher L.
Brown, Euyene A. Jr.
Bumpus, Wllliam M.
Burfict, Samuel
Caldwell, David A.
Calhoun, Paul R. Jr.
Carter, Don D.
Chambers, Victor B.
Chandler, George E. II
Christie, Ricrlard W.
Clark, Rlchard M.
Clay, Byron K.
Cook, Raynard J.
Dennis, Warren D.
Eddins, Timothy L.
Flournory, Martin L.
Golden, Northan F.
Goldsmith, Stafford R.
Graves, Johnnie J.
Green, Curtis L.
Greenlea, Willie V.
Harrison, Arcolar R.
Hawkins, Bruce W. Jr.
Horton, Andre M.
Hudson, Derrick K.
Huguley, Harold III
Ingram, Henry O. Jr.
Johnson, Deborah L.
Johnson, Theron E.
Lopes, John A.
Love, Ricky A.
Lowman, Leon Jr.
Martin, Carl R.
Mayfield, Leon C.
McClean, Scott D.
McCullough, Vanessa
McDonald, Maurice
Montgomery, Ronald
Moreland, Christopher
Norris, Kenneth J.
Payne, Manuel A.
Pickett, Marquis D.
Roberts, Sanford E. II
Robinson, Bobby L. II
Rodgers, Rickey S.
Saulny, Stanley M. Jr.
Scott, Todd J.
Simon, Daryl R.
Smith, Courtney L.
Speight, Joel S.
Stukes, Joaquin D.
Thompson, Ivan G.
Tillman, Antonio W.
Toliver, Renea L.
Veazie, Christopher
Vickers, John F.
Waters, Denise Y.
White, Patricia I.
Wilburn, Joe N.
Williams, Albert C. II
Williams, Calvin B.
Williams, John A.
Wilson, Bryawn E.
Wilson, Nathaniel J. Jr.
Wood, Yolandea M.
Wright, Michael W.
Wright, Paul W.

**Class of 1987**

Abbott, James E. Jr.
Abercrombie, D. II
Allen, James T.
Auzenne, Joshua P.
Benovil, Marie A.
Branche, Michael C.
Broussard, Byron K.
Brown, Billy Bob Jr.
Brown, Donald L.
Brown, Lucy A.
Brown, Terrence A.
Brundidge, Lawrence
Butler, Rhett L.
Campbell, Gregory A.
Clewis, Robert V. I.
Coffey, Lavanson C.
Day, Robert E. Jr.
Dingle, Levenchi L.
Eaton, Howard E. III
Elmore, Carson A.
Evans, Patricia
Fisher, Wayne A.
Fitch, Linda G.
Flournoy, Shawn R.
Fortson, Myron K.
Gray, James R. III
Harris, Darrin W.
Harris, John H.
Holman, Lillian P.
Holmes, Joseph A.
Homer, LeRoy W. Jr.
Honesty, Carlos L. II
Houston, Anthony M.
Howard, Walter G.
Hunter, Eric J.
Jeffcoat, James T.
Johnson, Kymberli S.
Jones, Alaln Louis M.

Jones, Elijah A. III
Jones, Tracy A.
Jordan, Eric A.
Lewis, Brenda S.
Mallette, Frank E.
Martin, Kevin C.
Moore, Carolyn A.
Moore, Dennis K.
Morris, Michele R.
Nelson, James R. W.
Ringold, Lloyd E. Jr.
Shedd, WIlliam K.
Shines, Franklin P. Jr.
Smith, Rudolph A. Jr.
Taylor, John W. Jr.
Toliver, Michael K.
Turner, Edward E.
Turner, Kenneth J.
Veney, Samuell R.
Weeks, Alexander Jr.
Willoughby, Robert
Wilson, Stacey A.
Wilson, William J.

**Class of 1988**

Adkins, George C.
Aiken, Mark G.
Barbosa, Jorge Pedro.
Boyd, Marcus A.
Brown, Cheryl L.
Brown, Earl D. Jr.
Brown, Harold D. Jr.
Burroughs, Louis M.
Butler, Jeffrey T.
Cherry, Sophella E.
Cole, PhiIbert A. Jr.
Crain, Jeffery K.
Davis, Darrel T.
Davis, John C.
Dixon, Lisa M.
Emmert, Patrick R.
Glenn, Darryl L.
Grant, Roger H.
Graves, Erik L.
Griggs, Linda M.
Haley, David L.
Hammond, Michael
Haynes, Kerby II
Hicks, Malcolm W.
Hodges, Chiquita J.
Horner, Dawn M.
Hunt, Jeffrey R.
Jackson, Linwood J.
Jenkins, Eric R.
Johnson, Clarence Jr.
Jones, Roy Vicente J.
Kelley, James A.
Lewis, Raymond K.
Miller, Michael A.
Mims, Avery D.
Minter, Darrell C.
Mitchell, Terence B.
Moore, Jonathan N.
Murphy, Ricky R.
Newton, Maurice A.
Nicholson, Anthony
Preston, Lisa J.
Profit, Michael K.
Roberts, Quinton D.
Roberts, Stephen P.
Speight, Calvin B.
Taylor, Ellery R.
Thomas, Michael
Turk, Roy C. Jr.
Walker, Christopher S. W.
Walker, Michael D.
Washington, Anthony
Weaver, Nichole V.
Whittaker, Emily A.
Williams, Amanda O.
Williams, Noel F.
Williams, Richard A.
Wilson, Darryl L.
Wilson, Dwayne L.
Wilson, Terrence V.

**Class of 1989**

Acker, Lawyer L. III
Anderson, Matthew T.
Barr, Lafayette A.
Bell, Javier L.
Booker, Al
Booth, Charles A.
Braxton, Eric M.
Burtley, Bryan M.
Carothers, Alexander
Clark, Trevor M.
Cochran, David V.
Cochran, Gregory E.
Copeland, Thomas J.
Dabney, Dennis P.
Darey, Roland M. Jr.
Earle, Stephen M.
Ervin, Harry L. Jr.
Ewing, Shawnie R.
Finn, Karen A.
Franklin, Gregory D.
Garrett, Ronald P.
Golden, Tracey M.
Haith, Andre B.
Henry, Joseph E. III
Hughes, Kevin J.
Jackson, Cedric B.
Johnson, Steven M.
Jones, Kelly C.
Keasley, Dawn D.
King, Kevin W.
LaSure, Anthony M.
Levy, Karl Andrew
Lewis, Andre A.
Lewis, Richard L. Jr.
Lockwood, Michael
Mason, Thomas Ja. Jr.
McMilian, Michelle
Murray, Ivan D.
O'Neal, Phillio G.
Phillips, Keith L.
Reed, Randall
Roberson, Anthony J.
Roberts, Karl
Robinson, Burtis B.
Rosser, Robert B.
Singleton, James F.
Stephens, Michael J.
Toliver, David
Turman, Oliver L.
Ware, Ramon D.
Warrior, Steven K.
Washington, L.
Watson, Pernell B.
Williams, Lunnon D.
Williams, Timothy .
Young, Dirk L.

*An Air Force enlisted crewman, the usually unsung heart of the Air Force, receives the Flying Cross and the Silver Star. In this Air Force photo he is referred to simply as Sergeant Mack of Spring Lake N.C. Sergeant Mack is congratulated by Air Force Chief of Staff, General John F. McConnell. In the center is Captain Joseph E. Glenn of Fayetteville, N.C. Both the General and the Captain are fully identified.*

## BLACK ARMED FORCES BRASS

### BRIGADIER GENERAL ROBERT BRADSHAW ADAMS
**Director of Resources and Management, Office of the Deputy Chief of Staff for Logistics, United States Army, Washington, D.C.**

General Adams was born in Buffalo, New York. He received a BBA degree in accounting/auditing from Canisius College and BBA and MBA degrees in automated data processing from George Washington University. During his 25-year career in the U.S. Army, General Adams has been Finance Officer of the 23rd Infantry Division and was later Finance Officer of the 196th Infantry Brigade in Vietnam; Commandant, U.S. Army Institute of Administration, Fort Benjamin Harrison, Indiana; Deputy Commander for Integration, U.S. Army Administration Center, Fort Benjamin Harrison, Indiana; and Assistant Comptroller for Resource Policy and Financial Planning, Office of the Comptroller of the Army, Washington, D.C. He has received the Bronze Star Medal, the Legion of Merit with two oak leaf clusters, the Meritorious Service Medal with an Oak Leaf Cluster, and the Army Commendation Medal with an oak leaf cluster.

### BRIGADIER GENERAL CLARA LEACH ADAMS-ENDER
**Chief, Army Nurse Corps, Office of the Surgeon General Falls Church, Virginia**

General Adams-Ender was born in Willow Springs, North Carolina. She received her Bachelor of Science degree in Nursing from North Carolina A&T State University in Greensboro, North Carolina and her Master of Science in Medical Surgical Nursing from the University of Minnesota. General Adams-Ender also received her MMAS degree in Military Science from the United States Army Command and General Staff College.

General Adams-Ender has served as Inspector General, Headquarters, United States Army Health Services Command, Fort Sam Houston, TX; Assistant Chief and later Chief, Department of Nursing, 97th General Hospital, United States Army Europe; Chief, Nurse Recruiting, United States Army Recruiting Command, Fort Sheridan, Illinois; Chief, Department of Nursing, Walter Reed Army Medical Center, Washington and Special Assistant to the Chief, Army Nurse Corps, Office of the Surgeon General, Falls Church, VA. She has been awarded the Meritorious Service Medal with three Oak Leaf Clusters, the Army Good Conduct Medal and the Expert Field Medical Badge.

### BRIGADIER GENERAL WALLACE CORNELIUS ARNOLD
**Commanding General, First Reserve Officer Training Corps Region, Fort Bragg, North Carolina**

General Arnold was born in Washington, DC and received his Bachelor of Science degree in Industrial Education from Hampton Institute and his Master of Arts degree in Personnel Management and Administration from George Washington University.

General Arnold has served as Director of Personnel, J-1/ Inspector General, United States European Command; Commander, 69th Air Defense Artillery Brigade, 32nd Army Air Defense Command, United States Army Europe; Inspector General, VII Corps, United States Army Europe; Military Assistant, Office, Under Secretary of the Army, Washington, DC; Computer Systems Software and Analysis Officer, Functional Systems Division, Office, Assistant Chief of Staff for Automation and Communications, United States Army, Washington, DC.; Student, Naval War College, Newport, Rhode Island; Commander, 3rd Battalion, 61st Air Defense Artillery, 3rd Armored Division, United States Army Europe; and Personnel Management Officer, Air Defense Artillery Branch, Officer Personnel Directorate, United States Army Military Personnel Center, Alexandria, Va.

He has been awarded the Legion of Merit with an Oak Leaf Cluster, the Bronze Star Medal with an Oak Leaf Cluster, the Meritorious Service Medal with four Oak Leaf Clusters, the Army Commendation Medal with an Oak Leaf Cluster and the Parachutist Badge.

### BRIGADIER GENERAL JULIUS WESTLEY BECTON Jr.
**Deputy Commanding General U.S. Army Training Center, Infantry, Fort Dix, N.J.**

General Becton began his service career when he was called to active duty in July 1944, from the Air Corps Enlisted

*Chief, Army Nurse Corps, Brigadier General Clara Leach Adams-Ender.*

*Brigadier General Julius Westley Becton Jr.*

Reserve, which he joined in 1943. He attended the Infantry Officer Candidate School at Fort Benning, Georgia, and graduated in 1945.

His assignments include Commanding Officer, Second Squadron, Seventh Cavalry, 101st Airborne Division, United States Army, Vietnam. His medals and awards are the Silver Star with Oak Leaf Cluster, Legion of Merit with Oak Leaf Cluster, Distinguished Flying Cross, Bronze Star Medal with Oak Leaf Cluster, five awards of the Air Medal with V Device, Army Commendation Medal with Oak Leaf Cluster, Purple Heart with Oak Leaf Cluster, Combat Infantry Badge (2d Award), and the Parachutist Badge.

### BRIGADIER GENERAL JAMES T. BODDIE Jr.
### Deputy Director for Operations, National Military Command Center, Organization of the Joint Chiefs of Staff, Washington, D.C.

General Boddie was born in 1931 in Baltimore and received his bachelors degree from Howard University. He is a graduate of the Academic Instructors School and Squadron Officer School, both located at Maxwell Air Force Base, Alabama. He received his commission through the Air Force Reserve Officers Training Corps program and was awarded the Convair Aviation Association Award for his outstanding accomplishments as a cadet. In June 1965 General Boddie joined the 4453rd Combat Crew Training Wing, Davis-Monthan Air Force Base, Arizona, where he flew and instructed in F-4s. In October of the following year he volunteered for combat duty in Southeast Asia and was assigned to the 559th Tactical Fighter Squadron, Cam Ranh Bay Air Base, Republic of Vietnam. General Boddie is a command pilot with more than 4,000 hours in jet fighter aircraft. His military decorations and awards include the Legion of Merit, Distinguished Flying Cross, Meritorious Service Medal with two oak leaf clusters, Air Medal with 13 oak leaf clusters, Air Force Commendation Medal, Air Force Outstanding Unit Award ribbon with three oak leaf clusters and "V" device, Combat Readiness Medal and the National Defense Service Medal.

### MAJOR GENERAL DELANO BRAILSFORD
### Commanding General, United States Army Armament, Munitions and Chemical Command, Rock Island, Illinois

General Brailsford was born in Burkeville, Texas and received his bachelor of science degree in Biology from Prairie View A&M University and his master of science degree in Bacteriology from Iowa State University. He was commissioned a Second Lieutenant in the United States Army through the ROTC.

His major duty assignments have included Deputy Chief, Special Operations Division, Executive Officer, Deputy Commander, United States Army Biological Laboratories, Fort Detrick, Maryland; Chief, Academic Operations Division, Deputy Director of Instruction, United States Army Chemical Center and School, Fort McClellan, Alabama; Assistant Project Manager for Logistics, Assistant Development Project Officer for Select Ammunition, Chief, Systems Evaluation Officer, Deputy Chairman for Operations, Division Air Defense Gun Source Selection Board, and Chief, Program Management Office, United States Army Armament Research and Development Command, Dover, New Jersey; Commander, 101st Ordnance Battalion, 60th Ordnance Group. VII Corps, United States Army Europe; Deputy Commander, Kaiserslautern Army Depot, United States Army Europe; Commanding General, 59th Ordnance Brigade, United States Army Europe and Deputy/Commanding General, United States Army Armament Research and Development Center, Picatinny Arsenal, Dover, New Jersey.

General Brailsford's decorations and honors include the Legion of Merit, the Bronze Star Medal, the Meritorious Service Medal with four Oak Leaf Clusters, the Army Commendation Medal as well as the Parachutist Badge.

### BRIGADIER GENERAL ELMER T. BROOKS
### Commander of the 381st Strategic Missile Wing, McConnell Air Force Base, Kansas

A native of Washington, D.C., General Brooks received a bachelor of arts degree in zoology from Miami University of Ohio and was commissioned through the Air Force Reserve Officers Training Corps. He received a master of science degree from George Washington University. General Brooks has served in Houston as a flight control technologist for Gemini and Apollo space missions at the National Aeronautics and space Administration's Manned Spacecraft Center. He was also vice commander of the 381st Missile Wing, a Titan II intercontinental ballistic missile unit at McConnell Air Force Base. He assumed command of that wing in January 1979.

His awards include the Defense Superior Service Medal

with one oak leaf cluster, Meritorious Service Medal with one oak leaf cluster, and the Joint Service Commendation Medal.

### BRIGADIER GENERAL HARRY WILLIAMS BROOKS Jr.
### Assistant Division Commander, U.S. Army 2nd Infantry Division, 8th Army

General Brooks was commissioned a Second Lieutenant in 1949 through Officer Candidate School. He earned a B.S. from the University of Omaha in business administration.

During his career he was assigned Commanding Officer, Second Battalion, 40th Artillery, 199th Infantry Brigade, Vietnam; Special Assistant to Deputy Commanding Officer, 199th Infantry Brigade, Vietnam; Commanding Officer, 72d Field Artillery Group, Europe; and Army Director of Equal Opportunity Programs, Office of the Deputy Chief of Staff for Personnel, Washington, D.C.

He has been awarded the Legion of Merit with Oak Leaf Cluster, Bronze Star Medal with Oak Leaf Cluster, Meritorious Service Medal, seven awards of the Air Medal and the Army Commendation Medal.

### BRIGADIER GENERAL LEO AUSTIN BROOKS
### Commanding General, United States Army Troop Support Agency, Fort Lee, Virginia

General Brooks was born in Washington, D.C. and received his B.S. degree in music education from Virginia State College and his M.S. in financial management from George Washington University. During his 26 years in the U.S. Army, General Brooks' assignments have been Assistant for Budget and Congressional Coordinators, Office, Deputy Chief of Staff for Logistics, Washington, D.C.; Deputy Secretary of the General Staff, U.S. Army Materiel Command, Washington, D.C.; Commander, 13th Corps Support Command, Fort Hood, Texas, and Director of Industrial Operations, Fort Hood, Texas. He has received the Legion of Merit with two oak leaf clusters, the Army Commendation Medal with an oak leaf cluster, the Bronze Star Medal, the Meritorious Service Medal, and the Joint Service Commendation Medal.

### BRIGADIER GENERAL COVERDALE BROWN Jr.
### Deputy Commandant, U.S. Army War College, Carlisle Barracks, Pennsylvania

General Brown was born in New Orleans and received his bachelor of arts degree in history from West Virginia State College and his master of arts degree in government from Indiana University. He has been Commander of the 519th Military Intelligence Battalion, 525th Military Intelligence Group in Vietnam; Deputy Chief, Soviet/East European Division; Directorate for Estimates and later Chief, Ground Forces/Mutual Balanced Forced Reduction Branch, Soviet-Warsaw Pact Division; Directorate for Intelligence Research, Defense Intelligence Agency, Washington, D.C.; Deputy Chief of Staff for Intelligence, U.S. Army Forces Command, Fort McPherson, Georgia; and Assistant Vice Director for Estimates and Deputy Vice Director for Foreign Intelligence, Defense Intelligence Agency, Washington, D.C.

General Brown has received the Meritorious Service Medal with an oak leaf cluster, the Joint Service Commendation Medal, the Army Commendation Medal, and the Master Parachutist Badge.

### MAJOR GENERAL JOHN MITCHELL BROWN
### Deputy Commanding General III Corps and Fort Hood, Texas

General Brown was born in Vicksburg, Mississippi and received his bachelor of science degree in engineering from the U.S. Military Academy. He received his MBA degree in comptrollership from Syracuse University and attended the advanced management program at the University of Houston. General Brown has been Commander, 1st Battalion, 87th Infantry, 8th Infantry Division, U.S. Army in Europe; Executive to the Comptroller of the Army in Washington, D.C.; Assistant Chief of Staff Comptroller, U.N. Command, U.S. Forces Korea, and the Eighth U.S. Army; and Assistant Division Commander, 2nd Infantry Division, Korea.

He has received the Legion of Merit, the Bronze Star Medal, the Meritorious Service Medal, the Army Commendation Medal with two oak leaf clusters, the Combat Infantryman Badge, the Parachutist Badge, and the Ranger Tab.

### MAJOR GENERAL WILLIAM E. BROWN Jr.
### Commander of the 17th Air Force

General Brown was born in the Bronx, New York. He received a bachelor of science degree from Pennsylvania State University and has acquired graduate credits toward a masters degree in systems management from the University of Southern California. He also attended the Harvard Business School's advanced management program. General Brown was stationed at McGuire Air Force Base in New Jersey for seven years. During his stay, he flew the F-84 Thunderjet, the F-86D, and the F-102 Delta Dagger with the 2nd and 332nd Fighter-Interceptor Squadrons and the New York Air Defense Sector. He is a command pilot with more than 4,900 flying hours.

General Brown's decorations and awards include the Legion of Merit with two oak leaf clusters, the Distinguished Flying Cross with one oak leaf cluster, the Air Medal with four oak leaf clusters, the Air Force Commendation Medal with two oak leaf clusters, the Purple Heart, the Air Force Outstanding Unit Award, the Combat Readiness Medal, and the Republic of Korea Presidential Unit Citation.

### BRIGADIER GENERAL CUNNINGHAM CAMPBELL BRYANT
### The Adjutant General, District of Columbia National Guard, Washington, D.C.

General Bryant entered the enlisted reserve at Howard University in 1942 as an Army ROTC cadet. He was called to active duty in 1943 and was commissioned as a Second Lieutenant after completing Infantry Officer Candidate

*Major General Delano Brailsford.*

School at Fort Benning in 1944.

He served as Company Commander with the 317th Combat Engineer Battalion and the 92d General Service Regiment. After he was released from active duty in 1949, he remained in the U.S. Army Reserve until 1954.

He has been awarded the Bronze Star Medal, Army Commendation Medal, Purple Heart, Army of Occupation Medal (Germany), World War II Victory Medal, National Defense Service Medal, European-African Middle Eastern Campaign Medal with two stars, American Campaign Medal, and the Combat Infantry Badge.

### MAJOR GENERAL CHARLES DAVID BUSSEY
### Deputy Chief of Staff for Personnel, United States Army Materiel Command, Washington, DC

General Bussey was born in Edgefield, South Carolina and received his bachelor of science degree in English from North Carolina Agricultural and Technical State University, Greensboro, North Carolina; his masters degree in Journalism from Indiana University and a master of science degree in Communications Science from Shippensburg State College.

He has also attended The Infantry School, basic and advanced courses, the Armed Forces Staff College and the United States Army War College. General Bussey was commissioned a Second Lieutenant in the United States Army through the ROTC.

General Bussey's assignments include Commander, Company A, 1st Battalion, 5th Calvary, 1st Calvary Division, Korea; Assistant Professor of Military Science, Junior ROTC, Indianapolis Public Schools, Indianapolis, Indiana and Professor of Military Science and Senior Army Instructor, Junior ROTC, Indianapolis Public High Schools, Indianapolis, Indiana.

General Bussey has received the Distinguished Service Medal, the Legion of Merit with an Oak Leaf Cluster, the Bronze Star Medal with an Oak Leaf Cluster, the Meritorious Service Medal with two Oak Leaf Clusters, the Air Medal, the Army Commendation Medal with two Oak Leaf Clusters, the Combat Infantryman Badge and the Parachutist Badge.

### BRIGADIER GENERAL MELVIN LEON BYRD
### Commanding General, United States Army Materiel Command-Europe

General Byrd was born in Suffolk, Virginia and received his BA degree in Accounting from Howard University and his MBA degree in Business Administration from Babson College.

He was commissioned a Second Lieutenant through the ROTC in 1959. His assignments have included Logistics Staff Officer, Materiel Management Division, Office of the Deputy Chief of Staff for Logistics; Commander, 702nd Maintenance Battalion, 2nd Infantry Division, Korea; Inspector General, Assistance Division, United States Army Inspector General Agency; Deputy Director for Joint Actions, Plans, Force Structure and Systems Directorate, Office of the Deputy Chief of Staff for Logistics; Commander, Division Support Command, 82nd Airborne Division, Fort Bragg, North Carolina and Commander, United States Army Electronics Materiel Readiness Activity, Vint Hill Farms Station, Warrenton, Virginia.

General Byrd has received the Bronze Star Medal with two Oak Leaf Clusters, the Meritorious Service Medal with two Oak Leaf Clusters, the Air Medal, Combat Infantry and the Senior Parachutist Badges.

### BRIGADIER GENERAL SHERIAN GRACE CADORIA
### Deputy Commanding General, Total Army Personnel Agency, Alexandria, Virginia

General Cadoria was born in Marksville, Louisiana and received her bachelor of science degree in Business Education from Southern University A&M College and a masters degree in Social Work from the University of Oklahoma.

Her assignments include Administrative Officer, Provost Marshal's Office, United States Army, Vietnam; Protocol Officer, Qui Nhon Support Command, Vietnam; Chief, Personnel Division/Adjutant, United States/Army Ordnance Center and School, Aberdeen Proving Ground, Maryland; Instructor, Officer Education and Training Branch, United States Army Women's Army Corps Center and School, Fort McClellan, Alabama; Commander, First Region, United States Army Criminal Investigation Command, Fort George Meade, Maryland; Chief, Law Enforcement Division, Human Resource Development Directorate, Office of the Deputy Chief of Staff for Personnel, United States Army, Washington, DC and Director, Manpower and Personnel Directorate, Organization of the Joint Chiefs of Staff, Washington, DC.

*Major General Sheridan Grace Cadoria.*

General Cadoria's honors and decorations include the Defense Superior Service Medal, the Legion of Merit, the Bronze Star Medal with two Oak Leaf Clusters, the Meritorious Service Medal with an Oak Leaf Cluster, the Air Medal and the Army Commendation Medal with three Oak Leaf Clusters.

### BRIGADIER GENERAL ROSCOE CONKLIN CARTWRIGHT
**Assistant Division Commander, U.S. Army 3rd Infantry Division, Europe**

In 1942, General Cartwright was commissioned a Second Lieutenant through Officer Candidate School. He served as Commanding Officer, 108th Artillery Group, Pacific-Vietnam; Deputy Commanding Officer, U.S. Army Support Command, Cam Ranh Bay; Chief, Budget and Five-Year Defense Program, Coordination Division, Manpower and Forces Directorate, Office of the Assistant Chief of Staff for Force Development, Washington, D.C.; and Director of Management Review and Analysis, Office of Comptroller of the Army, Washington, D.C.

He was awarded the Legion of Merit with oak leaf cluster, Bronze Star Medal with two oak leaf clusters, Meritorious Service Medal, three awards of the Air Medal and the Army Commendation Medal with two oak leaf clusters.

General Cartwright died December 1974 in an air crash in Virginia.

### LIEUTENANT GENERAL ANDREW PHILLIP CHAMBERS
**Deputy Commanding General, United States Army Forces Command/Commanding General, Third United States Army, United States Army Forces Command, Fort McPherson, Georgia**

Major Chambers was born in Bedford, Virginia and received his B.S. from Howard University and his M.S. from Shippensburg State College. During his 26 years in the military, General Chambers' assignments have included Deputy Commander, 1st Brigade, 8th Infantry, 8th Infantry Division, Europe; Deputy Director and later Director, Equal Opportunity Programs, Office, Deputy Chief of Staff for Personnel, Washington, D.C.; Director, Personnel, Inspector General, Pacific Command, Camp H. M. Smith, Hawaii; and Assistant Division Commander, 1st Cavalry Division, Fort Hood, Texas.

He has received the Defense Superior Service Medal, the Legion of Merit, the Soldier's Medal, the Bronze Star Medal with V device, the Meritorious Service Medal with an oak leaf cluster, the Air Medal, the Army Commendation Medal with two oak leaf clusters, the Combat Infantryman Badge, and the Senior Parachutist Badge.

### BRIGADIER GENERAL THOMAS E. CLIFFORD
**Deputy Commanding General, 17th AF, Ramstein, Germany**

General Clifford was commissioned as a member of the ROTC at Howard University in March 1949. Later he was an all-weather jet pilot with the 5th Fighter Interceptor Squadron, McGuire AFB a fighter pilot attached to the 449th Interceptor Squadron in Alaska, and then with the 437th at Oxnard Air Force Base.

He was weapons training officer and flight commander, 329th Fighter Interceptor Squadron, George Air Force Base, California; and management analyst, U.S. Air Forces.

He has been awarded the Legion of Merit with oak leaf cluster and Air Force Commendation Medal with one oak leaf cluster.

### MAJOR GENERAL RUFUS CROMARTIE
**Commanding General, United States Army Criminal Investigation Command, Falls Church, Virginia**

Colonel Cromartie was born in Wabasso, Florida. He received his bachelor of science degree in social science from Florida A&M University and his master of science in education/guidance and counseling from the University of Dayton. Colonel Cromartie, during his military career, has been Commander, 503rd Military Police Battalion, Fort Bragg, North Carolina; Provost Marshal, 82nd Airborne Division, Fort Bragg; Special Assistant to the Commanding General, U.S. Army Criminal Investigation Command, Falls Church, Virginia; and Commander, First Region, U.S. Army Criminal Investigation Command, Fort Meade, Maryland.

Colonel Cromartie has received the Bronze Star Medal with an oak leaf cluster, the Meritorious Service Medal with two oak leaf clusters, the Army Commendation Medal with an oak leaf cluster, and the Parachutist Badge.

*Major General Eugene R. Cromartie.*

### MAJOR GENERAL JERRY RALPH CURRY
### Deputy Assistant Secretary of Defense (public affairs), Washington, D.C.

A native of McKeesport, Pennsylvania, General Curry received his BE degree in general education from the University of Nebraska-Omaha and his master of arts degree in international relations from Boston University. He obtained his Ph.D. in religious theology from Luther Rice Seminary. General Curry has been Commander of the 2nd Battalion, 30th Infantry, 3rd Infantry Division (mechanized), U.S. Army in Europe; Commander, 3rd Brigade, 8th Infantry Division (mechanized), U. S. Army, Europe; Deputy Commanding General, U.S. Army Military District of Washington, Washington, D.C.; Assistant Division Commander, 4th Infantry Division (Mechanized), Fort Carson, Colorado; and Commanding General, U. S. Army Test and Evaluation Command, Aberdeen Proving Ground, Maryland.

General Curry has received the Legion of Merit with an oak leaf cluster, the Bronze Star Medal, the Meritorious Service Medal with an oak leaf cluster, Air Medals, the Army Commendation Medal with two oak leaf clusters, the Navy Commendation Medal, the Combat Infantryman Badge, the Parachutist Badge, and the Master Army Aviator Badge.

### MAJOR GENERAL FREDERICK ELLIS DAVISON
### Commanding General, 8th Infantry Division, U.S. Army, Europe

General Davison entered Howard University in Washington, D.C., in 1934 and earned B.S. and M.S. degrees in zoology and chemistry. While earning his baccalaureate degree, he completed Army ROTC and was commissioned a Second Lieutenant in the Infantry Reserve in 1939.

During his career he was assigned as Chief, Reserve Forces Division, Office Deputy Under Secretary of the Army, Washington, D.C.; and Commanding Officer, Third Training Brigade, U.S. Army Training Center, Air Defense.

His awards include the Distinguished Service Medal, Legion of Merit with oak leaf cluster, Bronze Star Medal, forty-nine awards of the Air Medal, Army Commendation Medal with two oak leaf clusters, and Bronze Star Medal (infantryman's) Badge, Second Award.

### BRIGADIER GENERAL DONALD JOSEPH DELANDRO
### Deputy, The Adjutant General for Administrative Systems and Executive Director, Military Postal Service, the Adjutant General Center, U.S. Army, Washington D.C.

General Delandro is a native of New Orleans. He received his bachelor of science degree in business administration from Southern University A&M College and his MBA degree from the University of Chicago. His assignments during his 24-year career in the U.S. Army have included Adjutant General, 23rd Infantry Division (America), Vietnam; Executive Officer, Weapons Systems Analysis Directorate, Office, Assistant Vice Chief of Staff, Washington, D.C.; Chief of Staff, U.S. Army Military Personnel Center, Alexandria, Virginia; and Chief of Staff, U.S. Army Recruiting Command, Fort Sheridan, Illinois. Among the decorations and badges General Delandro has received are the Legion of Merit with an oak leaf cluster, the Bronze Star Medal, the Meritorious Service Medal, the Air Medal, the Joint Service Commendation Medal, and the Army Commendation Medal with an oak leaf cluster as well as the Parachutist Badge.

### BRIGADIER GENERAL OLIVER WILLIAMS DILLARD
### Deputy Chief of Staff for Intelligence, Headquarters, U.S. Army Forces Command, Fort McPherson, Georgia

General Dillard began his service career in 1945 when he was inducted into the U.S. Army. He was accepted into the Infantry Officer Candidate School at Fort Benning, Georgia, and was commissioned a Second Lieutenant in 1947.

His first three years of duty as a commissioned officer consisted of various assignments within the 365th Infantry Regiment, which was involved in basic training of recruits. His assignments also include Assistant Professor of Military Science at A & T College, Greensboro, North Carolina, Commanding Officer, 5th Combat Support Training Brigade, Fort Dix, New Jersey; Director of Intelligence Support.

He has been awarded the Silver Star, Legion of Merit with two oak leaf clusters, Bronze Star Medal with oak leaf cluster, Army Commendation Medal with oak leaf cluster, Purple Heart, Combat Infantryman's Badge, and the Vietnamese Army Distinguished Service Order (2d class).

### LIEUTENANT GENERAL HENRY DOCTOR Jr. The Inspector General, United States Army, Washington, D.C.

General Doctor, born in Oakley, South Carolina, was commissioned a Second Lieutenant through the Army ROTC following graduation in 1954 with a bachelor of science degree in general agriculture from South Carolina State College. He also received his master of arts degree in counseling and psychological services from Georgia State University. General Doctor's assignments have included Commander, 1st Battalion, 29th Infantry, 197th Infantry Brigade, Fort Benning, Georgia; Chief, Modern Volunteer Army Control Group, U.S. Army Infantry Center, Fort Benning, Georgia; Director of Enlisted Personnel Management, U.S. Army Military Personnel Center, Alexandria, Virginia; and Assistant Division Commander, 24th Infantry Division, Fort Stewart, Georgia.

He has been awarded the Legion of Merit, the Bronze Star Medal, the Meritorious Service Medal, the Air Medal, the Army Commendation Medal with three oak leaf clusters, and the Combat Infantryman Badge.

### BRIGADIER GENERAL ARCHER L. DURHAM Commander of the 76th Airlift Division, Military Airlift Command, Andrews Air Force Base, Maryland

General Durham was born in 1932 in Pasadena, California. He received a bachelor of science degree in political science from Utah State University in 1960 and a master of science degree in international affairs from the George Washington University in Washington, D.C. in 1975. General Durham began his military career in 1953 as an aviation cadet and in April 1954 received his commission and pilot wings at Laredo Air Force Base, Texas. In July 1977 he took command of the 1606th Air Base Wing, Kirtland Air Force Base, New Mexico, a position he held until February 1979. He next served as commander of the 436th Military Airlift Wing at Dover Air Force Base, Delaware, until February 1980. He is a command pilot with more than 6,000 flying hours.

His military decorations and awards include the Legion of Merit with one oak leaf cluster, Meritorious Service Medal with one oak leaf cluster, and the Air Force Commendation Medal with one oak leaf cluster.

### BRIGADIER GENERAL ALONZO L. FERGUSON Commander, 21st North American Air Defense Command Region at Hancock Field, New York; Commander, 21st Aerospace Defense Command Region, and Commander, 21st Air Division, Air Defense Component of the Tactical Air Command

General Ferguson began active duty in 1952 after completion of flight and jet training. Born in Washington, D.C., General Ferguson graduated from Howard University with a bachelor of science degree in psychology. General Ferguson served at Headquarters Tactical Air Command, Langley Air Force Base, Virginia as chief of the weapons systems branch under the deputy for operations from January 1968 to July 1971. General Ferguson returned to South Korea in 1974 and in March 1975 was named Vice Commander of the 355th Tactical Fighter Wing at Davis-Monthan Air Force Base, Arizona.

His military decorations and awards include the Silver Star with one oak leaf cluster, the Legion of Merit, the Defense Meritorious Service Medal, Meritorious Service Medal with one oak leaf cluster, the Air Medal with 13 oak leaf clusters, and the Air Force Commendation Medal with one oak leaf cluster.

### BRIGADIER GENERAL JOHNNIE FORTE Jr. Director of Personnel, J-1 Inspector General, U.S. European Command

General Forte was born in New Boston, Texas and received his bachelor of science degree in political science from Prairie View University and his master of science in public administration from Auburn University. General Forte has been commander, 41st Civil Affairs Company, Civil Operations and Rural Development Support, U.S. Military Assistance Command in Vietnam; Commander, 4th Battalion, 61st Air Defense Artillery, 4th Infantry Division (Mechanized), Fort Carson, Colorado; and Liaison Officer to the U.S. Air Force, Europe, U.S. Army Europe Liaison Group, Ramstein Air Force Base, Germany.

General Forte has received the Legion of Merit with the oak leaf cluster, the Meritorious Service Medal, the Army Commendation Medal with two oak leaf clusters, the Air Force Commendation Medal, and the Aircraft Crewman Badge.

### MAJOR GENERAL ROBERT CLARENCE GASKILL Deputy Director, Defense Logistics Agency, Cameron Station, Alexandria, Virginia

General Gaskill is a native of Yonkers, New York. He received his bachelor of arts degree in business administration from Howard University and his MBA degree also in business administration from George Washington University. He was commissioned a Second Lieutenant through the Army ROTC program. His assignments during his 28-year career have been Commanding General, 1st Support Brigade, U.S. Army, Europe; Commanding General, Letterkenny Army Depot, Chambersburg, Pennsylvania; Deputy Commanding General, 21st Support Command, U.S. Army, Europe; Deputy Commandant, U.S. Army War College, Carlisle Barracks, Pennsylvania.

He has received the Legion of Merit, the Meritorious Service Medal, and the Army Commendation Medal each with an oak leaf cluster.

### BRIGADIER GENERAL FRED AUGUSTUS GORDEN Commandant of Cadets, United States Military Academy, West Point, New York

General Gorden, born in Anniston, Alabama, is a graduate of the United States Military Academy with a bachelor of science degree in Military Science and a master of arts degree from Middlebury College in Foreign Language Literature.

General Gorden was commissioned a Second Lieutenant in the United States Army through the United States Military Academy.

His assignments include Commander, Battery C, 2nd Battalion, 320th Artillery, 1st Brigade, 101st Airborne Division, United States Army, Vietnam; Executive Officer, 1st Battalion, 15th Field Artillery, 2nd Infantry Division, Korea; Commander, 1st Battalion, 15th Field Artillery, 2nd Infantry Division, Korea; Commander, 1st Battalion, 8th Field Artillery, 25th Infantry Division, Schofield Barracks, Hawaii; Executive Officer, Office of the Chief of Legislative Liaison, United States Army, Washington, D.C.; Director, Inter-American Region, Office of the Assistant Secretary of Defense (International Security Affairs), Washington, D.C.; and Assistant Division Commander, 7th Infantry Division, Ford Ord, California.

General Gorden's commendations and honors are the Defense Distinguished Service Medal, the Bronze Star Medal with "V" Device and an Oak Leaf cluster, the Legion of Merit, the Meritorious Service Medal, the Air Medal, Army Commendation Medal with an Oak Leaf cluster, the Parachutist Badge and the Ranger Tab.

### REAR ADMIRAL SAMUELL. GRAVELY Jr.
### Commander, Cruiser Destroyer Flotilla Two

Admiral Gravely enlisted in the U. S. Naval Reserve in 1942. He transferred from the Reserve to the U.S. Navy in 1955.

He has been Assistant Battalion Commander, Naval Training Center, Great Lakes; Communications Officer, Electronics Officer, and later Executive Officer and Personnel Officer of the USS PC 1264 submarine chaser; Communications Watch Officer, Fleet Training Group, Norfolk, Virginia; Assistant to the Officer in Charge for Recruiting, Naval Recruiting Station; and Officer Procurement, Washington, D.C.

He has been awarded the Meritorious Service Medal, Navy Commendation Medal (with Gold Star and Combat V), Korean Presidential Unit Citation Ribbon, Naval Reserve Medal, American Campaign Medal, World War II Victory Medal, National Defense Service Medal (with Bronze Star), China Service Medal, Korean Service Medal (with two Bronze Stars), U.N. Service Medal, Armed Forces Expeditionary Medal, Vietnam Service Medal (with four Bronze Stars), and Republic of Vietnam Campaign Medal (with device).

### BRIGADIER GENERAL EDWARD GREER
### Deputy Commanding General, U.S. Army Training Center, Engineer, Fort Leonard Wood, Missouri

General Greer was commissioned through the Army ROTC in 1948 from West Virginia State College. He was born in Gary, West Virginia.

His assignments include Commanding Officer, First Battalion, Seventh Artillery, U.S. Army, Pacific-Korea; Author-Instructor, Department of Command, U.S. Army Command and General Staff College, Fort Leavenworth, Kansas; Deputy Commander, XXIV Corps Artillery, U.S. Army, Pacific-Vietnam; Commanding Officer, 108th Artillery Group, U.S. Army, Pacific-Vietnam; and Assistant Director, Directorate for Reserve Forces, Plans, Programs and Budgets, Office, Assistant Secretary of Defense, Washington, D.C.

His medals and awards are the Silver Star, Legion of Merit with oak leaf cluster, Bronze Star Medal with oak leaf cluster, Air Medal, Joint Service Commendation Medal, and Army Commendation Medal with oak leaf cluster.

### BRIGADIER GENERAL ARTHUR JAMES GREGG
### Deputy Director of Supply and Maintenance, for Logistics, U.S. Army, Washington, D.C.

General Gregg was born in Florence, South Carolina. He attended St. Benedict's College, Atchison, Kansas, and earned a B.S. degree in business administration. He was commissioned a Second Lieutenant through Officer Candidate School in 1950.

His assignments include Commanding Officer 96th Quartermaster Battalion, Fort Riley, Kansas; Commanding Officer, Nahbollenbach Army Depot, U.S. Army, Europe; and Director of Troop Support, Office, Deputy Chief of Staff for Logistics, U.S. Army.

He has been awarded the Legion of Merit with oak leaf cluster, Meritorious Service Medal, Joint Service Commendation Medal, and Army Commendation Medal with two oak leaf clusters.

*Commander, Cruiser Destroyer Flotilla Two, Rear Admiral Samuel Gravely, Jr.*

*Major General Titus C. Hall, Commander of the Lowery Technical Training Center, Lowery Air Force Base, Colorodo.*

### BRIGADIER GENERAL DAVID M. HALL
### Deputy Chief of Staff, Comptroller, Air Force Logistics Command, Wright-Patterson Air Force Base, Ohio

General Hall was born in 1928 in Gary, Indiana where he graduated from Roosevelt High School. He earned a bachelors degree in business administration from Howard University, Washington, D.C. and a masters degree in educational sociology from the Agricultural and Technical State University of North Carolina, Greensboro. General Hall was assigned to the Air Force Accounting and Finance Center, Denver, in September 1967. He was chief of the Computer Operations Division in the Directorate of Data Automation until 1969 when he joined a software development division as an analyst-programmer. In March 1971 he was assigned to Scott Air Force Base, Illinois, where he became chief of the Computer Operations Division for Military Airlift Command headquarters, and in March 1972 he became the assistant for social actions in the office of the Deputy Chief of Staff for Personnel at Scott. General Hall became the deputy base commander for Scott Air Force Base in May 1974 and base commander in February 1975.

His military decorations and awards include the Legion of Merit, Meritorious Service Medal with one oak leaf cluster, and the Air Force Commendation Medal with one oak leaf cluster.

### MAJOR GENERAL JAMES REGINALD HALL Jr.
### Commanding General, 4th Infantry Division (Mechanized), Fort Carson, Colorado

General Hall was born in Anniston, Alabama and received a B.A. degree in political science from Morehouse College in Atlanta and an M.S. degree in public administration from Shippensburg State College in Pennsylvania. His assignments have included Personnel Management Officer, Infantry Branch, Officer Personnel Directorate, Office of Personnel Operations in Washington, D.C.; Commander 1st Battalion, 9th Infantry, 2nd Infantry Division, Korea; Chief, Army Wide Test Branch, Skill Progression Directorate; and later Executive Officer, Office, Deputy Chief of Staff for Training and Schools, U.S. Army Training and Doctrine Command, Fort Monroe, Virginia; Commander, 4th Regiment, U.S. Corps of Cadets, U.S. Military Academy, West Point; Commander, 197th Infantry Brigade, Fort Benning, Georgia; and Secretary, U.S. Army Infantry School, Fort Benning, Georgia.

His awards and decorations include the Legion of Merit, the Bronze Star Medal, Meritorious Service Medal with the oak leaf cluster, Army Commendation Medal with oak leaf cluster, the Combat Infantryman Badge, and the Parachutist Badge.

### MAJOR GENERAL TITUS C. HALL
### Commander of the Lowry Technical Training Center, Lowry Air Force Base, Colorado

General Hall entered active duty with the U.S. Air Force in 1942 after he received his bachelor of science degree in electrical engineering from Tuskegee Institute, Alabama. A native of Pflugerville, Texas, General Hall also earned a masters degree in systems engineering from the University of Southern California in 1971. The General attended basic navigator flying school at Ellington Air Force Base, Texas, and advanced bombing and navigation school at Mather Air Force Base, California, from March 1956 to January 1958. General Hall became chief avionics engineer for the B-1 strategic manned bomber at Headquarters Aeronautical Systems Division, Wright-Patterson Air Force Base, Ohio, in March 1972. General Hall became deputy for systems, now reconnaissance and electronic warfare systems, Headquarters Aeronautical Systems Division, Wright-Patterson Air Force Base, in July 1978. He is a master navigator with 4,000 flying hours in the FB-111s, EF-111s, F-4G Wild Weasels, and the U.S. Navy A-7Ds. His military decorations and awards include the Distinguished Service Medal, Legion of Merit, Distinguished Flying Cross, Bronze Star Medal, Meritorious Service Medal with one oak leaf cluster, and the Air Medal with two oak leaf clusters.

### MAJOR GENERAL JAMES FRANK HAMLET
### Commanding General, U.S. Army 4th Infantry Division (Mechanized), Fort Carson, Colorado

General Hamlet was born in Alliance, Ohio. A student at Tuskegee Institute in Alabama when he enlisted in the U.S. Army in 1942, he was commissioned a Second Lieutenant in 1944 through Officer Candidate School.

His career has been marked by command and staff officer assignments at all levels of command. A senior aviator and qualified parachutist, he has extensive combat experience,

*Brigadier General Robert Alonzo Harleston, Assistant Inspector General, Department of Defense.*

including three years of combat command time in Vietnam.

General Hamlet's assignments include Chief, Doctrine and Systems Division, U.S. Army Combat Development Command Combat Arms Group, Fort Leavenworth, Kansas; and Commanding Officer, Eleventh Aviation Group, First Cavalry Division, U.S. Army Vietnam.

He has been awarded the Distinguished Service Medal, Legion of Merit with two oak leaf clusters, Distinguished Flying Cross, Soldier's Medal, Bronze Star Medal with oak leaf clusters, 49 awards of the Air Medal, Army Commendation Medal with three oak leaf clusters, and the Combat Infantryman Badge.

### BRIGADIER GENERAL ROBERT ALONZO HARLESTON
### Assistant Inspector General for Inspections, United States Army Element, Office of the Secretary of Defense, Washington, D.C.

General Harleston was born in Hempstead, New York and is a graduate of Howard University with a bachelor of arts degree in Accounting, a master of science degree from the Michigan State University in Police Science and Administration and a Juris Doctorate from Georgetown University Law Center. He was commissioned a Second Lieutenant in the United States Army through the ROTC.

General Harleston's assignments include Commander, Hawaii Armed Forces Police Detachment, Fort DeRussy, Hawaii; Provost Marshall, 179th Military Police Detachment, United States Army, Vietnam; Commander, Area Confinement Facility, 532nd Military Police Company, Fort Dix, New Jersey; Action Officer, Correction Branch, Office of the Deputy Chief of Staff for Personnel, Washington, D.C.; Chief, Assistance Division, later Executive to The Inspector General, Office of The Inspector General, United States Army, Washington, D.C. and Chief, Law Enforcement Division, Human Resources Development Directorate, Office of the Deputy Chief of Staff for Personnel, United States Army, Washington, D.C.

His commendations and honors are the Legion of Merit, the Army Commendation Medal and the Bronze Star Medal all with an Oak Leaf cluster; the Meritorious Service Medal, Air Medals and the Joint Service Commendation Medal.

### BRIGADIER GENERAL CHARLES ALFONSO HINES
### Director, Manpower, Plans and Budget and Force Integration, Office of the Deputy Chief of Staff for Personnel, United States Army, Washington, D.C.

General Hines was born in Washington, D.C. and graduated from Howard University with a bachelor of science degree in Physical Education, a master of science degree in Police Science from Michigan State University, a master of science degree in Military Science from the United States Army Command and General Staff College and a PhD degree in Psychology from Johns Hopkins University. He was commissioned a Second Lieutenant in the United States Army through the ROTC.

General Hines assignments include Commander, 521st Military Police Company (Service), Fort Belvoir, Virginia; Instructor, Military Police Science and Administration Division, United States Army Military Police School, Fort Gordon, Georgia; Chief, Criminal Intelligence Program, later Operations Officer, and later Chief, Criminal Information Division, United States Army Criminal Investigation Command, Washington, D.C.; Commander, 14th Military Police Group and Provost Marshall, VII Corps, United States Army, Europe and Director, Officer Personnel Management Directorate, United States Total Army Personnel Agency, Alexandria, Virginia.

His commendations and honors are the Legion of Merit and the Army Commendation Medal both with an Oak Leaf cluster, the Bronze Star Medal, the Meritorious Service Medal with five Oak Leaf clusters and the Parachutist Badge.

### BRIGADIER GENERAL ARTHUR HOLMES Jr.
### Director of Readiness, U.S. Army Materiel Development and Readiness Command, Alexandria, Virginia

General Holmes was born in Decatur, Alabama and received a B.S. degree in chemistry from Hampton Institute in Hampton, Virginia. He received an MBA degree from Kent State University. General Holmes also attended the Field

Artillery School's basic course, The Ordnance School's advanced course, the U.S. Army Command and General Staff College, and the U.S. Naval War College. His assignments have included Commander, 724th Maintenance Battalion, 24th Infantry Division, Fort Riley, Kansas; Chief, Materiel Program Coordination Section, later Chief, Weapons and Combat Vehicles Section, Materiel Analysis Branch, Materiel Acquisition Directorate, Office, Deputy Chief of Staff for Logistics, U.S. Army, Washington, D.C.; Commander, 62nd Maintenance Battalion, U.S. Army, Qui Nhon Support Command, Vietnam; Commander, Division Support Command, 1st Infantry Division (mechanized) Fort Riley, Kansas; and Executive to the Secretary of the Army, Washington, D.C.

He has received the Legion of Merit, the Bronze Star Medal, the Meritorious Service Medal with oak leaf cluster, the Joint Service Commendation Medal, and the Army Commendation Medal with two oak leaf clusters.

### LIEUTENANT GENERAL EDWARD HONOR
### Director, J-4, Organization of the Joint Chiefs of Staff, Washington, D.C.

General Honor was commissioned a Second Lieutenant through the Army ROTC in 1954 from Southern Uni- versity A&M College where he received a B.A. degree in education. He was born in Melville, Louisiana. General Honor has been Commander, 36th Transportation Battalion, U.S. Army Cam Ranh Bay Support Command, Vietnam; Assistant Chief of Staff, Security, Plans and Operations, U.S. Army Cam Ranh Bay Support Command, Vietnam; Chief, Transportation Service Branch, Transportation Division, Office Deputy Chief of Staff for Logistics, U.S. Continental Army Command, Fort Monroe, Virginia; Commander, Military Traffic Management Command, Transportation Terminal Group-Europe, Rotterdam, Netherlands; and Director for Plans, Doctrine, and Systems, U.S. Army Materiel Development and Readiness Command, Alexandria, Virginia.

He has received the Legion of Merit with three oak leaf clusters, the Bronze Star Medal, the Meritorious Service Medal, and the Army Commendation Medal all with an oak leaf cluster, and the Joint Service Commendation Medal.

### MAJOR GENERAL CHARLES EDWARD HONORE
### Deputy Commanding General, Fifth United States Army, Fort Sam Houston, Texas

General Honore was born in Baton Rouge, Louisiana and graduated from Southern University Agriculture and Mining College with a bachelor of arts degree in Geography and a master of science degree in Administration from George Washington University. He was commissioned into the United States Army as a Second Lieutenant through the ROTC.

General Honore's assignments include Deputy Military Senior Advisor, Military Region 3, United States Military Assistance Command, Vietnam; Commander, 2nd Battalion, 64th Armor, 3rd Infantry Division (Mechanized), United States Army, Europe; Commander, Headquarters Command, Fort Polk, Louisiana; Commander, 1st Brigade, 5th Infantry Division (Mechanized), Fort Polk, Louisiana; Chief, United States Army Readiness Group, Los Alamitos, California; Deputy Chief of Staff for Support, Central Army Group, Europe and Assistant Division Commander, 3rd Infantry Division (Mechanized), United States Army, Europe.

His commendations and honors include the Legion of Merit, the Bronze Star Medal, the Meritorious Service Medal with an Oak Leaf cluster, the Air Medal, the Army Commendation Medal and the Combat Infantryman Badge.

*Lieutant General Edward Honor.*

### BRIGADIER GENERAL BENJAMIN LACY HUNTON
### Commander, U.S. 97th Army Reserve Command, Fort Meade, Maryland

General Hunton was commissioned a Second Lieutenant, Infantry, through Army ROTC upon graduation from Howard University in 1940, and entered active duty in 1942. He was assigned to the 368th Infantry Regiment, the Infantry School and Assistant Professor of Military Science at Howard University. He was released from active duty in August 1949.

During his Army Reserve status he served as Battalion Commander, 428th Infantry Regiment; Battalion Commander, Executive Officer, and Commander, 317th Infantry Regiment, 80th Infantry division; and upon redesignation of the unit to 80th Division (training), he became Commander, First Brigade.

General Hunton's present civilian occupation is Assistant Director, Education and Training, U.S. Bureau of Mines, Department of Interior, Washington, D.C.

### BRIGADIER GENERAL AVON C. JAMES
### Director of Computer Resources, Office of the Comptroller of the Air Force, Headquarters U.S. Air Force, Washington, D.C.

General James was born in Hampton, Virginia and earned his bachelors degree from Morgan State University in 1951. General James was assigned in July 1972 as a computer systems staff officer with the Automatic Data Processing Equipment Selection directorate at Hanscom Air Force Base, Massachusetts. In July 1973 he was assigned as Chief of Staff, Electronic Systems Division, Air Force Systems Command at Hanscom Air Force Base. In June 1978 General James was assigned as the First Deputy Commander for Data Automation, Headquarters Air Force Communications Command, Scott Air Force Base, Illinois.

His military decorations and awards include the Legion of Merit with one oak leaf cluster, Meritorious Service Medal, the Air Force Commendation Medal with one oak leaf cluster, and the Air Force Organizational Excellence Award.

### BRIGADIER GENERAL CHARLES B. JIGGETTS
### Director, Communications and Data Processing, J-6, Pacific Command, Camp H. M. Smith, Hawaii

General Jiggetts was born in Henderson, North Carolina and received a bachelor of arts degree in political science from Howard University, Washington, D.C. In the fall of 1971, General Jiggetts was assigned as the Military Assistant to the Director of the Office of Telecommunications Policy, Executive Office of the President of the United States. In July 1974 he became Vice Commander of the Northern Communications Area of the Air Force Communications Service. He became Commander of that unit in July 1976.

His military decorations and awards include the Distinguished Service Medal, Legion of Merit with one oak leaf cluster, Bronze Star Medal, Meritorious Service Medal, Joint Service Commendation Medal, and the Air Force Commendation Medal.

### BRIGADIER GENERAL HAZEL WINIFRED JOHNSON
### Chief, Army Nurse Corps, Office of the Surgeon General, U.S. Army, Washington D.C.

General Johnson was born in West Chester, Pennsylvania and received her bachelor of science degree in nursing from Villanova University, her master of arts degree in nursing education from Columbia University, and her Ph.D. in educational administration from Catholic University. General Johnson's assignments during her 22 years in the military have included Project Officer, Development Branch, Materiel Development Division, Surgical Directorate, U.S. Army Medical Research and Development Command, Washington, D.C.; Dean, Walter Reed Army Institute of Nursing, Walter Reed Army Medical Center, Washington, D.C.; Chief Nurse, U.S. Army Medical Command, Korea; and Special Assistant to the Chief, Army Nurse Corps, Washington, D.C.

General Johnson has been awarded the Legion of Merit, the Meritorious Service Medal, and the Army Commendation Medal with an oak leaf cluster.

### BRIGADIER GENERAL JULIUS FRANK JOHNSON
### Commander, Third Brigade, Third Infantry Division, United States Army Europe

General Johnson is a native of Fort Leavenworth, Kansas and received his bachelor of science degree in social science from Lincoln University. He also earned his MD degree in counseling psychology from Lincoln.

General Johnson was commissioned a Second Lieutenant through the ROTC in 1964.

His assignments have included Assistant Professor of Military Science, Lincoln University; Commander, Mobile Security Training Team, Field Training Command, United States Military Advisory Group, Military Assistance Command Vietnam; Personnel Management Officer, Officer Personnel Management Division, United States Military Personnel Center, Alexandria, Virginia; Commander, Second Battalion, 36th Infantry, Third Armored Division, United States Army Europe; Director of Operations, Armed Forces Inaugural Committee, Fort Lesley J. McNair, Washington, D.C.; and Executive Officer, Office of the Deputy Chief of Staff for Development, Engineering and Acquisition, United States Army Materiel Command, Alexandria, Virginia.

General Johnson's decorations and medals include the Silver Star, the Bronze Star Medal with two Oak Leaf Clusters, the Defense Meritorious Service Medal, the Meritorious Service Medal, the Air Medal, Army Commendation Medal with an Oak Leaf Cluster; Combat Infantry and the Air Assault Badge.

### BRIGADIER GENERAL WALTER FRANK JOHNSON III
### Chief, Medical Service Corps/Director, Health Care Operations, United States Army, Falls Church, Virginia

General Johnson is a native of Charleston, South Carolina and graduated from West Virginia State College with a bachelor of science degree in Zoology and a master of arts degree in Political Science from the University of Missouri.

He was commissioned into the United States Army as a Second Lieutenant through the ROTC.

General Johnson's assignments include Plans Officer, later Chief, Force Structure Branch, Plans and Operations Division, Health Care Operations Directorate, Office of The Surgeon General, United States Army, Washington, D.C.; Commander, 2nd Medical Battalion, 2nd Infantry Division, Korea; Assistant Executive Officer, Office of The Surgeon General, United States Army, Washington, D.C.; Executive to The Surgeon General, United States Army, Washington, D.C.; and Executive to the Surgeon General/Chief, Medical Service Corps, Office of The Surgeon General, United States Army, Washington, D.C.

His commendations and honors are the Legion of Merit, the Meritorious Service Medal and the Army Commendation Medal all with an Oak Leaf cluster; the Bronze Star Medal, the Senior Parachutist and the Expert Field Medical Badges.

### MAJOR GENERAL JAMES RICHARD KLUGH
### Assistant Deputy Chief of Staff for Logistics, Office of the Deputy Chief of Staff for Logistics, Washington, D.C.

General Klugh, a native of Greenwood, South Carolina received a bachelor of science degree in Chemistry from South Carolina State College and a master of science in Public Administration from Shippensburg State College. He was commissioned a Second Lieutenant in the United States Army through the ROTC.

General Klugh's assignments include Assistant Headquarters Commandant, 7th Infantry Division, United States Army, Europe; Program Analysis Officer, Program Coordinating Branch, United States Army Chemical Corps School, Fort McClellan, Alabama; Commander, 502nd Supply and Transport Battalion, 2nd Armored Division, Fort Hood, Texas; Chief of Staff, United States Army Tank Automotive Command, Warren, Michigan; Commander, Dugway Proving Ground, Utah; Deputy Commander for Training Development, United States Army Logistics Center, Fort Lee, Virginia; Deputy Commanding General, Chemical Materiel, United States Army Armament, Munitions and Chemical Command/Commanding General, United States Army Chemical Research and Development Center, Aberdeen Proving Ground, Maryland; and Deputy Chief of staff for Personnel, United States Army Materiel Command, Alexandria, Virginia.

His honors and decorations are the Legion of Merit and the Army Commendation Medal both with two Oak Leaf clusters, the Meritorious Service Medal with an Oak Leaf cluster, Air Medals and the Parachutist Badge.

### MAJOR GENERAL JAMES FRANKLIN MCCALL
### Director, Army Budget, Office of the Comptroller, United States Army, Washington, D.C.

General McCall received his B.S. degree in economics from the University of Pennsylvania and was commissioned a Second Lieutenant through the OCS at the university in 1958. He was born in Philadelphia and received an MBA degree in comptrollership from Syracuse University. General McCall has served as a Military Assistant, Office of the Assistant Secretary of the Army (Financial Management) in Washington, D.C.; Commander, 1st Battalion 31st Infantry, 2nd Infantry Division, Eighth Army, Korea; Commander, 4th Training Brigade, U.S. Army Armor School, Fort Knox, Kentucky; and Chief, Procurement Programs and Budget Division, Materiel Plans and Programs Directorate, Office of the Deputy Chief of Staff for Research, Development, and Acquisition, U.S. Army, Washington, D.C.

His decorations and badges include the Parachutist Badge, the Combat Infantry Badge, Meritorious Medal, the Legion of Merit with an oak leaf cluster, and Air Medals. He also received the Army Commendation Medal with an oak leaf cluster.

### LIEUTENANT GENERAL EMMETT PAIGE Jr.
### Commanding General, United States Army Information Systems Command, Fort Huachuca, Arizona

General Paige received his B.A. degree in business administration from the University of Maryland and an MBA in public administration from Pennsylvania State University. General Paige was born in Jacksonville, Florida and during his career has been awarded the Legion of Merit with two oak leaf clusters, the Bronze Star Medal, the Joint Service Commendation Medal, the Meritorious Medal, and the Army Commendation Medal.

He has been Commander, 361st Signal Battalion, 1st Signal Brigade, U.S. Army Strategic Communications Command-Vietnam; Staff Officer, Voice Networks Branch, Operations Directorate, Defense Communications Agency, Washington, D.C.; Commander, 11th Signal Group, U.S. Army Communications Command, Fort Huachuca, Arizona; and Commanding General, U.S. Army Communications Research and Development Command, Fort Monmouth, New Jersey.

*Lieutenant General Frank E. Peterson.*

### MAJOR GENERAL JULIUS PARKER Jr. Commanding General, United States Army Intelligence Center/Commandant, United States Army Intelligence School, Fort Huachuca, Arizona

General Parker was born in New Braunfels, Texas and received a B.S. degree in biology and chemistry from Prairie View A&M University and an M.S. degree in public administration from Shippensburg State College. He was commissioned a Second Lieutenant in 1955 from Prairie View through the school's ROTC program. General Parker has served as a Combat Intelligence Staff Officer, later Chief, Ground and Special Systems Branch, Doctrine and Systems Division, later Ground Surveillance Officer, Tactical Surveillance and Reconnaissance Branch, Doctrine and Surveillance Division, Office, Assistant Chief of Staff for Intelligence, U.S. Army, Washington, D.C.; Strategic Research Analyst, Strategic Studies Institute, U.S. Army War College, Carlisle Barracks, Pennsylvania; Commander, 501st Military Intelligence Group, U.S. Army Intelligence and Security Command, Korea; and Executive to the Assistant Chief of Staff for Intelligence, Washington, D.C.

He has received the Parachutist Badge, the Combat Infantry Badge, the Purple Heart, the Army Commendation Medal with an oak leaf cluster, the Meritorious Service Medal with three oak leaf clusters, the Air Medal, and the Bronze Star Medal with V device and with an oak leaf cluster.

*Lieutenant General Colin Luther Powell, former National Security Advisor to President Ronald Reagan.*

### LIEUTENANT GENERAL FRANK E. PETERSEN, USMC Commanding General, Marine Corps Combat Development Command, Quantico, Virginia

He is currently by date of aviator designation the senior ranking aviator in the U.S. Marine Corps and the U.S. Navy with respective titles of "Silver Hawk" and "Grey Eagle". His date of designation as an aviator also precedes all other aviators in the U.S. Air Force and Army.

Brigadier General Frank E. Petersen was born March 2, 1932 in Topeka, Kansas, and graduated from Topeka High School in 1949. He attended Washburn University in Topeka and received his B.A. degree from George Washington University in 1967. He completed his masters degree in 1973 at that university. He began flight training through the Naval Aviation Cadet Program at the Naval Air Station in Pensacola, Florida, and at Corpus Christi, Texas. In October 1952 he was designated a Naval Aviator and commissioned a Second Lieutenant in the Marine Corps Reserve. During the Korean conflict, in 1953, he flew 60 combat missions and was awarded the Distinguished Flying Cross and the Air Medal with one silver star denoting five subsequent awards. His decorations and medals include the Legion of Merit with Combat V, the Distinguished Flying Cross, Meritorious Service Medal, Air Medal with Numeral 14, Purple Heart, Combat Action Ribbon, Presidential Unit Citation, Korean Service Medal with two bronze stars, Vietnam Service Medal with two bronze stars, and United Nations Service Medal.

### LIEUTENANT GENERAL COLIN LUTHER POWELL National Security Advisor, The White House, Washington, D.C.

General Powell's assignments include Military Assistant to the Secretary of Defense, Office of the Secretary of Defense, Washington, D.C.; Commanding General, V Corps, United States Army, Europe; APO New York; and Deputy Assistant to the President for National Security Affairs, The White House, Washington, D.C. General Powell has also served as Assistant Chief of Staff in Vietnam; Commander, 2nd Brigade, 101st Airborne Division (Air Assault) Fort Campbell, Kentucky, and Commander, 1st Battalion, 32nd Infantry, 2nd Infantry Division, Eighth Army.

General Powell was born in New York City, received his B.S. degree in geology from City University, and his MBA degree from George Washington University. General Powell was commissioned a Second Lieutenant through the ROTC in 1958.

He received the Defense Superior Service Medal, the Legion of Merit with an oak leaf cluster, the Bronze Star Medal, the Soldiers Medal, the Purple Heart, the Parachutist Badge, the Ranger Tap, and the Joint Service Commendation Medal.

### MAJOR GENERAL WINSTON D. POWERS
**Deputy Chief of Staff for Communications, Electronics and Computer Resources for the North American Air Defense Command and U.S. Aerospace Defense Command at Peterson Air Force Base, Colorado; Chief, Systems Integration Office, Aerospace Defense Center**

General Powers was born in New York City and earned his bachelor of arts degree from McKendree College, Illinois. General Powers attended graduate school at the George Washington University and completed the Industrial College of the Armed Forces. In 1974, General Powers returned to Korea as commander of the 2146th Communications Group and director of communications-electronics for the 314th Air Division at Osan Air Base. General Powers became deputy director of telecommunications and command and control resources, Office of the Assistant Chief of Staff, Communications and Computer Resources, Headquarters U.S. Air Force in September 1975. He became the director in 1978. He is a master navigator with more than 4,000 flying hours.

His military decorations and awards include the Meritorious Service Medal with two oak leaf clusters, the Air Medal with one oak leaf cluster, the Air Force Commendation Medal, the Presidential Unit Citation emblem, and the Outstanding Unit Award ribbon.

### BRIGADIER GENERAL BERNARD P. RANDOLPH
**Director of Space Systems, and Command, Control and Communications, Office of the Deputy Chief of Staff, Research, Development and Acquisition, Headquarters U.S. Air Force, Washington, D.C.**

A native of New Orleans, General Randolph received his bachelor of science degree in chemistry from Xavier University of Louisiana in New Orleans. He also earned the bachelor (*magna cum laude)* and master of science degrees in electrical engineering from the University of North Dakota, Grand Forks, through the Air Force Institute of Technology program in 1964 and 1965, respectively. In July 1980, General Randolph became Vice Commander of the Warner Robins Air Logistics Center, Robins Air Force Base, Georgia.

His military decorations and awards include the Legion of Merit with one oak leaf cluster, Bronze Star Medal, the Meritorious Service Medal, the Air Force Commendation Medal, and the Presidential Unit Citation emblem.

### BRIGADIER GENERAL HUGH GRANVILLE ROBINSON
**Division Engineer, U.S. Army Engineer Division Southwestern, Dallas, Texas**

General Robinson was born in Washington and received a B.S. degree in military science from the U.S. Military Academy and an M.S. degree in civil engineering from the Massachusetts Institute of Technology. General Robinson has been Executive Officer, 45th Engineer Group, U.S. Army, Pacific-Vietnam; Staff Officer, Regional Capabilities Branch, War Plans Division, Plans Directorate, Office, Deputy Chief of Staff for Military Operations, U.S. Army, Washington, D.C.; Commander, 3rd Regiment, U.S. Corps of Cadets, U.S. Military Academy, West Point; and District Engineer, U.S. Army Engineer District, Los Angeles, California. His decorations and badges include the Joint Service Commendation Medal, the Parachutist Badge, the Presidential Service Badge, the Army Commendation Medal with an oak leaf cluster, along with the Legion of Merit and the Bronze Star Medal both with oak leaf clusters.

### MAJOR GENERAL JACKSON EVANDER ROZIER Jr.
**Deputy Chief of Staff for Logistics, United States Army, Europe and Seventh Army, APO New York**

General Rozier was born in Richmond, Virginia and earned his B.S. degree in educational administration from Morgan State University in Baltimore. He received his M.A. degree also in educational administration from Howard University in Washington, D.C. His assignments have included Personnel Management Officer and Executive Officer, U.S. Army Military Personnel Center, Alexandria, Virginia; Commander, 801st Maintenance Battalion, 101st Airborne Division (Air Assault), Fort Campbell, Kentucky; and Commander, Division Support Command, 8th Infantry Division (mechanized), U.S. Army, Europe.

He has received the Meritorious Service Medal and the Army Commendation Medal both with the oak leaf cluster and the Parachutist Badge.

### BRIGADIER GENERAL FRED CLIFTON SHEFFEY
**Operations and Maintenance Resources, Office of Deputy General Staff for Logistics, Department of the Army Headquarters**

During the past 10 years, General Sheffey has been Chief, Clothing and Textile Materiel Section, Supply Branch, Quartermaster Division, 3rd Logistical Command, U.S. Communications Zone, Europe; Assistant Division Supply Officer, 4th Infantry Division, Fort Lewis, Washington; Executive Officer, 4th Supply and Transport Battalion, 4th Infantry Quartermaster Battalion, Fort Lewis, Washington; Commanding Officer, 266th Quartermaster Battalion, later 266th Supply and Service Battalion, Fort Lewis, Washington, and later U.S. Pacific-Vietnam; Logistical Plans Officer, later Chief, Plans and Policy Branch, G-4 Section, U.S. Vietnam, U.S. Pacific-Vietnam; Chief, Facilities Branch.

He has been awarded the Legion of Merit with two oak leaf clusters, Bronze Star Medal, Army Commendation Medal, Purple Heart, and Combat Infantry Badge.

### BRIGADIER GENERAL ALONZA EARL SHORT Jr.
**Commanding General United States Army Information Systems Engineering Command/Program Manager, Army Information Systems, Fort Huachuca, Arizona**

General Short is a native of Greenville, North Carolina and is a graduate of Virginia State University with a bachelor of science degree in Industrial Arts and a MBA degree in Business Administration from New York Institute of Technology.

He was commissioned a Second Lieutenant in the United States Army through the ROTC.

General Short's assignments include Academic Plans Officer, Armed Forces Staff College, Norfolk, Virginia; Deputy Program Manager, Secure Voice Division, Defense Communications Agency, Washington, D.C.; Commander, 3rd Signal Brigade, Fort Hood, Texas; Chief of Staff, 7th Signal Command, Fort Ritchie, Maryland; Commander, United States Army Information Systems Engineering Installation Activity/Project Manager, Defense Communications Systems, Army, Fort Monmouth, New Jersey and Deputy Commanding General/Deputy Program Manager, Army Information Systems, United States Army Information Systems Engineering Command, Fort Belvoir, Virginia.

His commendations and honors are the Legion of Merit, the Bronze Star and the Meritorious Service Medals both with an Oak Leaf cluster, the Parachutist and the Air Assault Badges.

### MAJOR GENERAL ISAAC DIXON SMITH
### Deputy Chief of Staff for Personnel, United States Army, Europe and Seventh Army, APO New York

General Shuffer was commissioned a Second Lieutenant in 1943 through Officer Candidate School. During his tour of duty he was assigned as Commanding Officer Second Battalion, Second Infantry, Fort Devens, Massachusetts; Assistant for Continuity of Operations Plans, Office, Assistant Secretary of Defense, Washington, D.C.; and Commanding Officer, 193d Infantry Brigade, U.S. Army Forces Southern Command, Fort Kobbe, Canal Zone.

He has been awarded the Silver Star with two oak leaf clusters, Legion of Merit with two oak leaf clusters, Bronze Star Medal with V device and two oak leaf clusters, five awards of Air Medal, Army Commendation Medal, Purple Heart, Combat Infantryman's Badge with the third award, and the Parachutist Badge.

### BRIGADIER GENERAL ISAAC DIXON SMITH
### Commanding General, U.S. Army Second Reserve Officer Training Corps Region, Fort Knox, Kentucky

General Smith was born in Wakefield, Louisiana and received his B.S. degree in agriculture from Southern University. He earned his M.A. degree in public administration from Shippensburg State College. General Smith has been Commander, 8th Battalion, 4th Artillery, XXIV Corps Artillery, U.S. Army in Vietnam; Commander, 2nd Battalion, 75th Field Artillery, 36th Field Artillery Group, V Corps Artillery, U.S. Army, Europe; Special Assistant to the Commander, Third Reserve Officer Training Corps Region, Fort Riley, Kansas; and Chief, Reserve Forces Division, Office of the Assistant Secretary of the Army, Washington, D.C.

He has received the Silver Star, the Legion of Merit with an oak leaf cluster, the Bronze Star Medal, and the Army Commendation Medal with two oak leaf clusters.

### MAJOR GENERAL JOHN HENRY STANFORD
### Commanding General, Military Traffic Management Command, Washington, D.C.

General Stanford was born in Darby, Pennsylvania and received his bachelor of arts degree in Political Science from Pennsylvania State University and his master of science degree in Personnel Management/Administration from Central Michigan University.

He was commissioned in the United States Army as a second lieutenant through the ROTC.

General Stanford's assignments include Platoon Leader, Company D, 2nd Air Reconnaissance Battalion, 36th Infantry, 3rd Armored Division, United States Army Europe; Commander, 40th Transportation Company, 15th Quartermaster Battalion, 6th Quartermaster Group, United States Army Europe; Fixed Wing Army Aviator, 55th Aviation Company, Eighth United States Army Korea; Fixed Wing Aviator, 73rd Aviation Company, Eighth United States Army Vietnam; Chief, Electrical Section, United States Army Transportation School, Fort Eustis, Virginia; Executive Assistant to the Special Assistant to the Secretary of Defense, Office of the Secretary of Defense, Washington, D.C.; Commander, Military Traffic Management Command, Western area, Oakland Army Base, Oakland, California and Deputy Commander for Research and Development, United States Army Aviation Systems Command, St. Louis, Missouri.

His decorations and honors include the Defense Distinguished Service Medal, Defense Superior Service Medal, the Legion of Merit with an Oak Leaf cluster, the Distinguished Flying Cross, Bronze Star Medal with "V" Device and four Oak Leaf clusters, the Meritorious Service Medal with an Oak Leaf cluster, the Air Medals, Army Commendation Medal with three Oak Leaf clusters, the Expert Infantry Badge, the Parachutist Badge, Master Army Aviator Badge and the Ranger Tab.

### BRIGADIER GENERAL LUCIUS THEUS
### Special Assistant for Social Actions, Directorate of Personnel Plans, Deputy Chief of Staff, Personnel, Headquarters U.S. Air Force, Washington, D.C.

General Theus entered the Army Air Corps in December 1942, as a private. In January, 1946 he was commissioned as a Second Lieutenant. He has served as squadron adjutant, Tuskegee Army Air Field, Alabama; Base Statistical Control Officer, Lockbourne Air Force Base, Ohio; Commander of the Statistical Control Flight and Depot Statistical Control Officer, Erding Air Depot, Germany; and Chief of the Materiel Logistics Statistics Branch, Office of the Deputy Chief of Staff, Comptroller, Headquarters U.S. Air Force, Washington, D.C.

His military decorations and awards include the Legion of Merit, Bronze Star Medal, Air Force Commendation Medal with oak leaf cluster, Air Force Outstanding Unit Award

Ribbon, Good Conduct Medal, and the Republic of Vietnam Commendation Medal.

### REAR ADMIRAL GERALD E. THOMAS
### Commander Cruiser-Destroyer Group FIVE

Born in Natick, Massachusetts, Gerald Thomas became a member of the Naval Reserve Officers Training Corps Unit during his student days at Harvard, and upon graduation in 1951 was commissioned Ensign. While attached to the cruiser *Worcester,* as a lieutenant in November 1955, he studied Russian at the Defense Language Institute and qualified as a Russian interpreter, after which he served at the National Security Agency, Fort Meade, Maryland. His first command was in 1962 aboard the USS *Impervious,* an ocean mine sweeper then operating in the western Pacific.

His major permanent duty assignments have been Assistant Head, College Training Programs Section, Bureau of Naval Personnel; student, Naval War College; commanding officer, USS *Bausell*; executive officer, NROTC, Prairie View College; commander, Destroyer Squadron NINE.

Admiral Thomas' medals and awards include the Meritorious Service Medal, the Navy Commendation Medal with Combat "V', the Navy Occupation Service Medal with Europe Clasp, the National Defense Service Medal with Bronze Star, the Armed Forces Expeditionary Medal (Vietnam), and the Vietnam Service Medal with two Bronze Stars.

### MAJOR GENERAL AUGUSTINE HOFFMAN WALLER
### Commanding General, 8th Infantry Division (Mechanized), APO New York

General Waller was born in Baton Rouge, Louisiana and received a bachelor of science degree in Agriculture from Prairie View A&M University and a master of science degree in Public Administration from Shippensburg State University.

General Waller was commissioned a Second Lieutenant in the U.S. Army through the ROTC.

General Waller's commendations and honors are the Defense Superior Service Medal, the Bronze Star Medal with an Oak Leaf cluster, the Meritorious Service Medal with three Oak Leaf clusters, Air Medals, the Army Commendation Medal and the Master Parachutist Badge.

### BRIGADIER GENERAL CHARLES EDWARD WILLIAMS
### Commanding General, United States Army Engineer Division, North Atlantic, New York, New York

General Williams was born in Wedgeworth, Kansas and received a bachelor of science degree in Biology from Tuskegee Institute in Tuskegee, Alabama and an MBA degree in Business Administration from Atlanta University.

General Williams was commissioned a second lieutenant in the United States Army through the ROTC.

His assignments include Commander, Headquarters and Headquarters Company, 70th Engineer Battalion (Combat), 937th Engineer Group (Combat), 101st Airborne Division, Fort Campbell, Kentucky; Aviation Officer, Headquarters, 18th Engineer Brigade, United States Army, Vietnam.

General William's honors and decorations include the Legion of Merit with two Oak Leaf Clusters, the Distinguished Flying Cross, the Bronze Star with an Oak Leaf Cluster, the Meritorious Service Medal with an Oak Leaf Cluster, Air Medals with "V" Device, Air Medals, Army Commendation Medal with "V" Device and the Senior Army Aviation Badge.

### BRIGADIER GENERAL EDWARD WILLIAMS
### Commanding General, United States Army Engineer Division, North Atlantic, New York, New York

General Williams, born in Wedgeworth, Alabama was commissioned into the United States Army as a Second Lieutenant through the ROTC. A graduate of Tuskegee Institute with a bachelor of science degree in Biology, General Williams received an MBA degree in Business Administration from Atlanta University.

His assignments include Commander, Headquarters and Headquarters Company, 70th Engineer Battalion (Combat), 937th Engineer Group (Combat), 101st Airborne Division, Fort Campbell, Kentucky; Aviation Officer, Headquarters, 18th Engineer Brigade, United States Army, Vietnam; Commander, 3rd Battalion, Training Brigade, United States Army Engineer Center, Fort Belvoir, Virginia.

General Williams' decorations and honors include Legion of Merit with two Oak Leaf clusters, the Distinguished Flying Cross, the Bronze Star and the Meritorious Service Medals both with Oak Leaf clusters, the Air Medal with "V" Device, Air Medals, the Army Commendation Medal with "V" Device and the Senior Army Aviation Badge.

### MAJOR GENERAL HARVEY DEAN WILLIAMS
### Commanding General, U.S. Army Readiness and Mobilization Region III and Deputy Commanding General, First U.S. Army, Fort Meade, Maryland

General Williams was born in Whiteville, North Carolina and received his B.A. degree in political science from West Virginia State College and his M.S. degree in international relations from George Washington University. His assignments have included Commander, 1st Battalion, 92nd Artillery, I Field Force, U.S. Army Pacific-Vietnam; Military Advisor, U.S. Arms Control and Disarmament Agency, Washington, D.C.; Commander, U.S. Army Garrison, Fort Myer, Virginia; and Commanding General, VII Corps Artillery, U.S. Army, Europe.

His commendations and awards include the Legion of Merit, the Bronze Star Medal with an oak leaf cluster, the Army Commendation Medal with three oak leaf clusters, along with Air Medals.

## OUTSTANDING MILITARY FIGURES

*Ensign Jesse L. Brown, a hero of the Korean War. Winner of the Distinguished Flying Cross, Ensign Brown was killed during the action which won him the medal.*

### ENSIGN JESSE L. BROWN
### 1926-1950

Jesse L. Brown was the first black American to become a naval aviator and the first black naval officer to be killed in action during the Korean War.

Born in Hattiesburg, Mississippi, he attended Ohio State University. In October 1948, he qualified as an aviator and became the first black man to wear the Navy wings. When the Korean War broke out he entered the combat as a pilot with the 32nd Fighter Squad and quickly rose to section leader. For his daring attacks on enemy transportation facilities and military installations at Wonsun, Songjin, and Sinanju, he earned the Air Medal. On December 4, 1950, he was dispatched to fly close air support for the marines fighting near Chosin Reservoir. As he repeatedly returned to strafe enemy positions, his low-flying craft was hit by hostile fire and almost immediately crashed. He died in the wreckage. Ensign Brown was posthumously awarded the Distinguished Flying Cross for his exceptional courage, airmanship, and devotion to duty.

In 1973, he became the first black man to have a naval vessel named in his honor. The USS *Jesse L. Brown,* Commissioned at the Boston Naval Yard, is a new type of destroyer escort.

### LIEUTENANT GENERAL BENJAMIN O. DAVIS Jr.
### 1912-

Described by a former instructor as "the closest thing to a model cadet I ever saw," General Benjamin O. Davis rose to become the highest ranking black military man in the United States.

Born in Washington in 1912, Davis was educated in Alabama (his father taught military science at Tuskegee), and later, in Cleveland, where he graduated as president of his class with one of the highest scholastic averages in the city.

Davis attended Western Reserve University and the University of Chicago before accepting an appointment to the U.S. Military Academy in 1932. Davis survived the silent treatment as a cadet, and graduated 35th in his class of 276.

After serving in the infantry for five years, he transferred to the Army Air Corps in 1941 and was among the first six black air cadets to graduate from the Advanced Army Flying School in 1942.

As Commander of the 99th Fighter Squadron (and later commander of the all-black 332nd Fighter Group), Davis flew 60 missions in 224 combat hours during World War II, winning several medals, including the Silver Star.

Davis became a Lieutenant General in 1965 and closed out his career as deputy commander of the U.S. Strike Command at McDill Air Force Base in Tampa, Florida. In civilian life, Davis worked briefly in the administration of Cleveland's black mayor Carl Stokes, resigning after a policy dispute.

*General Benjamin Davis Sr. pins the Distinguished Flying Cross on his son Colonel Benjamin Davis Jr. in Italy, WWII.*

*General Daniel "Chappie" James, Korean War ace, became the first black four-star general in American history.*

## BRIGADIER GENERAL BENJAMIN OLIVER DAVIS Sr. 1877-1970

Benjamin Oliver Davis Sr., was the first black American to become a general in the U.S. Army. He deserves exceptional recognition for his distinguished 50-year military career, which began with the Spanish-American War. Promoted to Brigadier General in 1940, he supervised the World War II progress of integration policy in the European military theater.

Born in the nation's capital, General Davis graduated from Howard University and joined the army during the emergency of 1898. At the end of that war with Spain, he reenlisted in the 9th Cavalry and was made Second Lieutenant in 1901. Black promotions were rare in those years, but Davis rose through the officer's ranks until he was made a full Colonel in 1930. During that time, in addition to his military commands, he was a professor of military science and tactics at Wilberforce and Tuskegee universities, military attache to Liberia, and instructor of the 372nd Infantry of the Ohio National Guard. After his promotion to Brigadier General and his service in World War II, he became an assistant to the inspector general in Washington, D.C. until his retirement in 1948.

Among General Davis' many awards and decorations are the Distinguished Service Medal, the Bronze Star Medal, the Grade of Commander of the Order of the Star of Africa, from the Liberian government, and the French Croix de Guerre with Palm. General Davis died on November 26, 1970.

## LIEUTENANT HENRY O. FLIPPER 1877-1940

The first black officer to graduate from West Point and the first to be assigned to a command position in a black unit after the Civil War, Henry O. Flipper was the victim of a controversial court-martial proceeding which cut short the career of one of the most promising black military men to wear the uniform of an American soldier.

Flipper was not defeated by the debacle, however. He went on, as a civilian, to become a notable figure on the American frontier—as a mining engineer and consultant and later, as a translator of Spanish land grants.

Flipper tried on many occasions to vindicate himself, befriending such prominent Washington officials as Senator A. B. Fall of New Mexico. When Fall became Secretary of the Interior, Flipper became his assistant until the infamous Teapot Dome affair severed their relationship.

Flipper returned to Atlanta at the close of his mining career, living with his brother, an AME bishop, until his death in 1940. His quest to remove the stain of "conduct unbecoming an officer and a gentleman" remained unfulfilled to his dying day, partly because certain records which might shed light on the situation are not yet open for public scrutiny.

*Admiral Nimitz awards the Navy Cross to Dorie Miller for heroism at Pearl Harbor. Miller was later killed in action in the South Pacific in 1943.*

## GENERAL DANIEL JAMES Jr.
## 1920-1978

Appointed Commander of NORAD on August 29, 1975, Daniel "Chappie" James was the first black four-star general in U.S. military history. Before coming to this post, he had been a flying ace in the Korean War, had served as Deputy Secretary of Defense, and was Vice Commander of Military Airlift Command.

Born on February 11, 1920 in Pensacola, Florida, he attended Tuskegee Institute, where he took the Army Air Corps program and was commissioned a Second Lieutenant in 1943. During the Korean War, James flew 101 combat missions in F-51 and F-80 aircraft. After the war, he performed various staff assignments until 1957, when he graduated from the Air Command and Staff College at Maxwell Air Force Base, Alabama. In 1966, he became Deputy Commander for Operations of the 8th Tactical Fighter Wing stationed in Thailand, before promotion to Commander of the 7272nd Flying Training Wing at Wheelus Air Force Base in Libya.

James became a Brigadier General in 1970, a Lieutenant General in 1973, and a Four-Star General in 1975. He has received numerous civilian awards. His military awards include Legion of Merit with one oak leaf cluster, Distinguished Flying Cross, Air Medal with 10 clusters, Distinguished Unit Citation, Presidential Unit Citation, and Air Force Outstanding Unit Award. General James was widely known for his speeches on Americanism and patriotism. One citation he received reads in part: "fighter pilot with a magnificent record... and eloquent spokesman for the American Dream we so rarely achieve."

He died of a heart attack at the age of 58 in Colorado Springs, February 25, 1978. General James had suffered from a heart condition and had retired from the Air Force for medical reasons earlier that month.

## HENRY JOHNSON
## 1897-1929

A member of the 15th National Guard of New York, which became the 369th Infantry, Henry Johnson was probably the most famous black soldier to have fought in World War I.

The 369th itself was the first group of black combat troops to arrive in Europe. After a summer of training, the group saw action at Champagne and fought its way to the Rhine River in Germany, receiving the Croix de Guerre from the French government. Johnson and another soldier (Needham Roberts) were the first Americans to receive this French medal for individual heroism in combat.

During a night skirmish, Johnson fought off an entire German patrol single-handedly, rescuing his wounded comrade from almost certain capture in the process. He personally accounted for four dead, a host of wounded, and a virtual stockpile of abandoned equipment. Wounded himself, he lost a shin bone and had several broken bones in one of his feet.

Johnson was cited by the French as a "magnificent example of courage and energy." He was later promoted to sergeant.

## DORIE MILLER
## 1919-1943

A messman aboard the USS *Arizona,* Dorie Miller had his first taste of combat at Pearl Harbor on December 7, 1941, when he manned a machine gun and brought down four Japanese planes.

Born on a farm near Waco, Texas in 1919, Miller was the son of a sharecropper and grew up to become star fullback on the Moore High School football team in his native city. At 19, he enlisted in the U.S. Navy, and was nearing the end of his first hitch at the time of the Pearl Harbor attack.

For his heroism, Miller was awarded the Navy Cross, which was conferred by Admiral Chester W. Nimitz, the Commander in Chief of the Pacific Fleet.

He remained a messman during the hostilities, serving aboard the aircraft carrier *Liscome Bay* and being promoted to Mess Attendant Third Class. He was killed in action in the South Pacific in December of 1943. Miller was commended for "distinguished devotion to duty, extreme courage, and disregard of his personal safety during attack."

Miller was one of several "noncombatant" blacks who distinguished themselves for heroism during combat. Others included Leonard Roy Harmon of the USS *San Francisco*; William Pinckney of the USS *Enterprise,* and Elbert H. Oliver of the USS *Intrepid.* Harmon and Pinckney were awarded the Navy Cross; Oliver, the Silver Star.

## COLONEL CHARLES YOUNG
## 1864-1922

Charles Young saw his first major combat during the Spanish-American War, less than 10 years after he had become the third black to have graduated from the U.S. Military Academy at West Point.

Born on March 12, 1864 in Mayslick, Kentucky, Young moved to Ripley, Ohio with his parents at an early age. Having finished high school, he taught for a time until winning an appointment to West Point in 1884. Upon graduation, Young was commissioned a Second Lieutenant in the 10th Cavalry, an all-black unit. In 1894 he became a military instructor at Wilberforce University in Ohio, and with the outbreak of the Spanish American War, was reassigned to the 9th Ohio Regiment, which was transferred to Cuba.

After the war Young served in the Philippines and in Haiti, and also in the Mexican campaign of 1915, where he commanded a squadron of the 10th Cavalry which rescued a group of ambushed white soldiers near Parral, Mexico. Declared physically unfit for service overseas in World War I, Young rode on horseback from his home in Xenia, Ohio to Washington, D.C. where, to no avail, he protested the decision of the War Department to retire him from active duty.

Five days before the Armistice, however, Young was ordered to Camp Grant in Illinois to take charge of trainees. Sent to Liberia after completing this assignment, Young helped organize the army there.

He died in 1922 of a fever contracted while he was on furlough in Nigeria, and was buried with full military honors at Arlington National Cemetery in Virginia.

## TABLE 159. BLACK SERVICEMEN AND WOMEN ON ACTIVE DUTY AROUND THE WORLD (JANUARY1988)

| Service | Officers (%) | Enlisted (%) | Total (%) |
|---|---|---|---|
| Army | 11,080 (10.2) | 199,200 (29.9) | 210,280 (27.2) |
| Navy | 2,508 (3.5) | 77,580 (15.2) | 80,088 (13.7) |
| Marine Corps | 939 (4.7) | 37,031(20.7) | 37,970 (19.1) |
| Air Force | 5,749 (5.4) | 85,102 (17.2) | 90,851(15.1) |
| Total | 20,276 | 398,913 | 419,189 |

* Includes Commissioned and Warrant Officers.

## TABLE 160. DISTRIBUTION OF BLACKS BY PERCENTAGE WITHIN EACH SERVICE (JANUARY 1988)

| Service | Officers | Enlisted | Year |
|---|---|---|---|
| Army | 10.2 | 29.9 | 87 |
| Navy | 3.5 | 15.2 | 87 |
| Marine Corps | 4.7 | 20.7 | 87 |
| Air Force | 5.4 | 17.2 | 87 |

## TABLE 161. STATISTICS ON BLACK COMMISSIONED AND WARRANT OFFICERS (JANUARY 1988)

| Grade (Army, Air Force, Marine) | Number (Percentage) | | | | |
|---|---|---|---|---|---|
| | Grade (Navy) | Army | Navy | Air Force | Marines Corps |
| General | Admiral | 28 (?) | 5 (?) | 4 (?) | 1 (?) |
| Colonel | Captain | 223 (4.7) | 28 (0.7) | 126 (2.2) | 8 (1.2) |
| Lieutenant Colonel | Commander | 513 (4.5) | 99 (1.3) | 236 (1.9) | 26 (1.6) |
| Major | Lieutenant Commander | 1,370 (8.0) | 427 (3.2) | 844 (4.3) | 126 (3.9) |
| Captain | Lieutenant | 4,552 (13.3) | 860 (3.7) | 3,133 (7.4) | 269 (4.5) |
| First Lieutenant | Lieutenant (JG) | 2,089 (12.5) | 446 (4.5) | 805 (5.3) | 248 (5.6) |
| Second Lieutenant | Ensign | 1,067 (12.6) | 459 (4.2) | 601 (5.4) | 137 (5.4) |
| Warrant Officer | Warrant Officer | 1,238 (8.3) | 184 (6.3) | 0 | 124 (8.7) |
| Total Officers and Percentages | | 11,080 (10.2) | 2,508 (3.5) | 5,749 (5.4) | 939 (4.7) |

## TABLE 162. STATISTICS ON BLACK ENLISTED PERSONNEL (NUMBER AND PERCENT OF BLACK PERSONNEL IN EACH GRADE)

| Grade | Army | Navy | Air Force | Marine Corps |
|---|---|---|---|---|
| E-9 | 1,423 (31.5) | 247 (5.5) | 661 (12.8) | 221 (15.3) |
| E-8 | 3,789 (24.4) | 483 (4.8) | 1,431 (14.4) | 702 (17.8) |
| E-7 | 14,245 (26.9) | 2,060 (6.3) | 6,592 (16.9) | 1,837 (19.6) |
| E-6 | 32,711 (36.7) | 9,069 (10.9) | 10,743 (18.2) | 3,535 (22.7) |
| E-5 | 44,959 (37.1) | 14,838 (14.3) | 21,010 (18.4) | 6,091 (24.6) |
| E-4 | 55,293 (29.5) | 16,805 (15.1) | 22,236 (18.3) | 7,025 (20.7) |
| E-3 | 23,277 (24.1) | 18,027 (20.5) | 16,035 (16.4) | 11,194 (19.5) |
| E-2 | 12,422 (23.4) | 8,383 (19.1) | 3,913 (14.1) | 3,981 (19.4) |
| E-l | 11,081 (24.4) | 7,668 (20.4) | 2,481 (12.8) | 2,445 (20.8) |
| Total Enlisted | 199,200 (29.9) | 77,580 (15.2) | 85,102 (17.2) | 37,031 (20.7) |

# THE BLACK AMATEUR AND PROFESSIONAL ATHLETE

**Baseball ■ Basketball ■ Football ■ Boxing ■ Track and Field ■ Golf ■ Horse Racing ■ Tennis ■ Wrestling ■ Outstanding Black Athletes**

Historically, the 1987-88 professional football season provided a long-sought breakthrough for blacks in the sports world — perhaps the milestone of the entire decade. However, the season began in turmoil. After a highly publicized debate between owners and their players over the rights of free agency, the players voted to assemble outside the stadiums at games and practice times during what would become a nasty three-week strike. The conflict soured even more when the league brought in replacement teams to play in the place of the vocal strikers. Gene Upshaw, a retired player who was executive director of the NFL Players Association held a high profile position in both the negotiation process and media attention as a spokesman for the players. When the strike was settled, teams struggled to regain momentum lost during the weeks of inactivity.

When the post-season playoffs began, two of the three black quarterbacks in the league were prominent. Warren Moon of the Houston Oilers and Randall Cunningham of the Philadelphia Eagles lost out, but Doug Williams of the Washington Redskins moved ahead toward the world championship.

On January 24, 1988, the Redskins were one of the teams that took the field on Super Bowl Sunday. And before one of the consistently largest sports audiences in the world, the veteran Williams directed his team to a lopsided 42-10 win over the Denver Broncos. It was a spirited come-from-behind victory and the impressive statistics generated by Williams were rewarded as an MVP-winning performance.

The game brought back memories of Joe Gilliam in Super Bowl VIII and instilled unparalleled pride to elated observers. Skeptics had long held that blacks were incapable of providing the leadership to direct the offense of a winning professional team. A veteran with several years under his belt, Williams had come back after leaving the game with a knee injury and convincingly silenced those skeptics, setting a Super Bowl record with four touchdown passes in the process.

And when training season began for the new season several months later, Randall Cunningham was in the unusual position of being challenged for his starting job at Philadelphia by another black, Don McPherson, who had been drafted after leading Syracuse University's Orangement to its best season in decades.

Yet, accomplishments like these and others brought a new level of public scrutiny to the black professional athlete.

As the decade of the 1980s came to a close, one fact remained. As in the past, it was still relatively easy to excel in the arenas by just allowing those natural athletic gifts to be used. Still, this new generation of athletes labored under a need to live up to the expectations of cynical fans and often hyper-critical journalists who were quick to judge them overpaid after one sub-par performance. In time, it became increasingly clear that athletic talent alone would not be enough to ensure a successful pro career.

Some college stars were turning pro and gaining astronomical contracts worth millions of dollars. They were often gaining status as the highest paid athletes in their sport. That status occasionally brought unreasonable pressure from owners and fans expecting a consistently high level of performance for the team's investment.

A few college stars became known as "the franchise," a dubious honor since the weight of success or failure of an entire team was placed on their shoulders. When Georgetown basketball star Patrick Ewing was drafted by the New York Knicks, such was the case.

Success also made these athletes targets for exploitation by the unscrupulous, who often led unseasoned young men and women from backgrounds of relative innocence into various forms of corruption. Targeted athletes were often on the news pages and in celebrity columns as much as on the sports pages. Product endorsement contracts were awarded to a selected few, bringing more attention, celebrity status — and more temptation — to those instant millionaires.

And there was another dark side to the sports increasingly stalked by tragedy. Drugs began to take a heavy toll among high school, college and professional athletes despite warnings and campaigns aimed at prevention. In some cases, otherwise bright careers were abruptly ended.

Michael Ray Richardson became the first active NBA player to be banned from the league for drug use and public attention became riveted on the depth of the problem. In time, New York Giants All-Pro linebacker Lawrence Taylor would miss part of the 1986-87 season due to drug use. Then, Mets star pitcher Dwight Gooden checked himself into a drug treatment program following a series of highly publicized and seemingly inexplicable incidents.

Len Bias was a University of Maryland basketball All-American who had been drafted by the Boston Celtics when he succumbed to a drug overdose. Cleveland Browns player Don Rogers died under similar circumstances shortly thereafter and there was hope that the deaths would have a deterring effect. Yet, as drug testing continued and became the norm, several others would be suspended for drug use. One of those was Lawrence Taylor, who was again removed from the Giant's active roster on the eve of the 1988-89 season.

Finally, the decade was notable for public statements made by two personalities in the sports world about the role of blacks in sports.

Al Campanis, an executive with the Los Angeles Dodgers organization, was ultimately fired after suggesting that blacks did not qualify to be managers of pro baseball teams. His remarks set off a fire storm and after meetings with leaders like Jesse Jackson, baseball commissioner Peter Ueberroth conceded that baseball did have problems and set in process a drive to bring more blacks into managing and front office positions throughout the major leagues.

Then, longtime CBS Sports commentator Jimmy the Greek also found himself out of a job when he made highly objectionable remarks during an interview about blacks being historically bred to be successful in the sports world.

In sum, the 1980s brought new achievements in sports for blacks, but there were still issues to be dealt with before they would feel accepted as full participants in the world of athletic competition. One of the most oft heard goals as blacks looked to the 1990s, was for blacks to achieve ownership of a major league sports franchise.

## THE EARLY DAYS

### Baseball

The first black major league baseball player was not Jackie Robinson but probably Bud Fowler, who played for a Newcastle, Pennsylvania, team in 1872. In 1884, Moses Fleetwood Walker, a bare-handed catcher and graduate of Oberlin College, played for Toledo in the old major league American Association. However, in the 1880s, as segregation was becoming established as a way of life, these and other blacks were increasingly excluded from major league play, continued to the minor leagues, and gradually eased out.

In the early 1900s, John McGraw, the great manager of the New York Giants, tried three times with short-lived success to bring black ball players on to his team. They were represented as American "Indians" but soon were exposed and McGraw was forced to release them. The men were Charles Grant and Jose Mendez, pitchers, and Andrew Foster, a pitching coach who had taught Christy Mathewson. In 1925 a black Latin, Ramon Herrera, played for the Boston Red Sox. Perhaps unknown, other blacks "passed" successfully during the 1888-1946 period.

Blacks and whites did, however, play openly against one another. Starting in 1884, blacks organized their own teams and then their own leagues. To these teams came some of the great, unheralded baseball players of all time: George Stovey, Josh Gibson, Oscar Charleston, and of course Satchel Paige, and in the 1940s, to the Kansas City Monarchs, Jackie Robinson.

In the 1920s, pitcher Smokey Jo Williams and his team, the Lincoln Giants, shut out the National League champion Philadelphia Phillies 1 to 0 in an exhibition game in New York after the World Series. Henceforth, no more exhibition games between whole major league teams and black teams were permitted. But individuals of both races did play beside and against one another, especially in Winter Baseball in the Caribbean, where blacks excelled. Black professional baseball teams blossomed at the turn of the century. In the 1920s, a black professional baseball league was formed primarily through the efforts of Andrew "Rube" Foster, a black baseball pitcher who in 1905 had won 51 of 55 games. The "Negro National League" had franchises in Indianapolis, Kansas City, Chicago, Detroit and St. Louis. Several years later, a "Negro American League" was established and an all-black world series was annually held.

*Josh Gibson, the greatest hitter in Negro League's history, was voted to Cooperstown in 1972.*

## Basketball

The basketball color line was broken in 1951 with the signing of Chuck Cooper by the Boston Celtics. Cooper was the son of Charles Cooper, who was a superstar on the all-black Harlem Renaissance pro basketball team. The Harlem Renaissance, or the Rens, as it was called, was founded in 1923 and was widely considered the best basketball team of its time. They usually had to hold the score down to maintain spectator interest. The Rens record: 1,588 won, 239 lost. Another great all-black basketball team still going strong is the Harlem Globetrotters. The Globetrotters started to play in the early 1920s as The Savoy Big Five.

## Football

The breaking of the modern day color line in pro football occurred shortly after World War II when a goodly number of black players were recruited by the pro teams. In its early days, around the turn of the century, pro football utilized black ball players and many colleges had black players on their rosters from the time of the sport's inception. William H. Lewis from Harvard University was, in 1892, the first black all-American. One of the early great black pro football players was Henry McDonald, who played for the Rochester Jeffersons and later the Akron Giants. Fritz Pollard, another all-time great in pro football, was playing at about the same time as McDonald. Around 1930, the recruiting of blacks for pro football ceased and in major league pro football there were no black athletes until after World War II.

## Black Coaches

In professional sports, blacks began receiving head coaching assignments in the 1950s and those assignments increased several-fold during the following three decades.

In baseball, John Buck O'Heil became a coach of the Chicago Cubs in 1962. In years to follow, others like Elston Howard would coach for teams like the New York Yankees.

In 1975, Frank Robinson — the only player to win the MVP Award in the National and American Leagues — became the first black manager of the Cleveland Indians. Robinson was named manager again in 1981, as Maury Wills — who had set the base-stealing record — made his debut as manager of the Seattle Mariners. Robinson would return again as a replacement manager for the struggling Baltimore Orioles, in 1988, and then have his contract extended for an additional season.

In 1966, Bill Russell was named coach of basketball's Boston Celtics. After guiding the team to national championship status, the talented former center retired to sports broadcasting. In 1974, he returned to coaching with the Seattle Supersonics and would later coach the Sacramento Kings.

In 1975, blacks were coaching at five of the National Basketball Association franchises. Russell was at Seattle, Ray Scott at Detroit, Al Attles at San Francisco, K.C. Jones at Washington and Lenny Wilkins in Portland. Willis Reed would also join the ranks as head coach of the New York Knicks.

Jones moved to the Boston Celtics and when he announced his retirement in 1988, he had guided the team to the playoffs after having won two championships in previous seasons. At that time, other NBA coaches included Don Chaney at Houston, Wes Unseld at Washington, and Willis Reed, who had been named head coach of the New Jersey Nets. While pointing out that the number of assistant coaches in the National Football League had grown from 14 in 1980 to 41 at the end of the 1987-88 season, Commissioner Pete Rozelle stressed the goal to have the league hire its first black head coach. By that time, the Toronto Argonauts of the Canadian Football League had hired former Green Bay Packers star and San Diego Chargers assistant coach Willie Wood as their head coach.

On the college level, there were a number of outstanding players including John Thompson, who coached the Big East at Georgetown as well as the 1988 U.S. Olympic basketball squad and John Chaney of Temple, who was named Coach of the Year by the U.S. Basketball Writers Association after the 1987-88 season.

## THE BLACK IN MODERN PROFESSIONAL BASEBALL

On April 10, 1947, Jackie Robinson broke the color barrier in modern major league baseball. He immediately excelled and was named rookie of the year. And as the Brooklyn Dodgers went on to win six league pennants, Robinson continued as a mainstay of the team, soon being cited as the league MVP.

Since that first historic season, a host of black baseball players in major league baseball have followed as stars in the Robinson tradition. Don Newcombe, Roy Campanella, Elston Howard, Monty Irvin, and Larry Doby are among the score of pioneers whose achievements were later complemented by a new breed of superstar who made an impact on professional baseball with precedent-setting entries on the record books.

While Jackie Robinson complained of his treatment by some fans, the crowds who cheered the great American summer pastime, 30 years later, paid little attention to the racial background of the player. For more often than not, black players were giving those fans more than enough to cheer about. By the 1970s, blacks were on the roster of every team in the league and were joined in increasing numbers by talented players from Puerto Rico, the Dominican Republic, Venezuela, and other parts of Latin America. Among the stars who excelled were Hank Aaron, who became the all-time home run leader; Lou Brock, who set an all-time single season mark for stealing bases with 118; Willie Mays, acclaimed as baseball's greatest center fielder; and Frank Robinson, the only player to win the MVP award in both the National and American leagues.

For their efforts in winning, scoring, batting, base stealing, and RBI titles, blacks became regular participants in the most valuable player selections as well as being designated to play in the annual all-star games. Soon several, including Robinson, Mays, and even the Negro League's outstanding player Satchel Paige, were voted into the Baseball Hall of Fame.

Some of the highlights for blacks of the 1980s occurred when Reggie Jackson hit his 400th home run and Dave Winfield, Eddie Murray, and Dwight Gooden consecutively replaced each other as baseball's highest paid players. (Although Orel Hertzhizer later succeeded Dwight Gooden in monetary terms.)

During the summer of 1981, 50 former players from the Negro Baseball League met for a reunion in Ashland, Kentucky and provided fascinating commentary on the role of blacks in one of America's great pastimes.

Contrary to the previous decade, no team dominated during the World Championship series. The St. Louis Cardinals won the Series in 1982 and the Baltimore Orioles were victors in 1983. In 1984, the Detroit Tigers won and in 1985, the Kansas City Royals were the champs. The New York Mets won a long-sought title in 1986 and the Minnesota

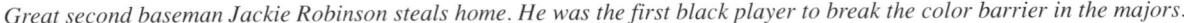

*Great second baseman Jackie Robinson steals home. He was the first black player to break the color barrier in the majors.*

Twins were the surprise winners in 1987.

The decade was marked by the retirement of Reggie Jackson in 1987, and the induction of Willie Stargell, an outstanding player with the Pittsburgh Pirates, into the Baseball Hall of Fame. Another unusual story involved all-around collegiate star Bo Jackson who was drafted by the Kansas City Royals and went on to play as a rookie. The multi-talented athlete caused quite a stir when he went on to play professional football as a running back with the Oakland Raiders.

Major league baseball endured two strikes during the 1980s. The first, in 1981, lasted seven weeks and resulted in 713 canceled games. In August 1985, the players walked out again, but this time for only three days.

When the 1988 season was on the verge of beginning, New York Yankee Dave Winfield found himself in a familiar controversy over a book about his career, especially his tenuous relationship with team owner George Steinbrenner.

Yet, even in the midst of controversy, black players continued to excel. Rickey Henderson set a record in the American League for base stealing while Vince Coleman set a new record in the National League. Players like Dwight Gooden and Darryl Strawberry of the New York Mets excelled as Rookies of the Year and continued to remain impressive in ensuing seasons, but like all too many, found public fascination about their personal lives a continued distraction.

A lot about baseball was changing in the major leagues, and young black players were quickly learning that it was one thing to break into professional baseball and another to remain on top of their game when everything from team ownership to the rules themselves was changing from season to season.

The two big stories of 1981 involved a chubby, 20-year-old rookie from Mexico who provided such inspiration for the Los Angeles Dodgers that they won their first World Series in years, and a 50-day strike that resulted in 714 canceled games, a split season, and the greatest feeling of disaffection baseball fans had ever experienced.

For Fernando Valenzuela, his major league debut would result in being honored with the Cy Young Award. For the New York Yankees, who won their fourth division title, there was disappointment when their fortunes against the Dodgers proved to be just the reverse of the 1978 season.

And while Dave Winfield was not a hero of the World Series, both he and Reggie Jackson performed admirably during the season as just two among several black players who exhibited formidable batting power. Veterans like Rod Carew, Ken Singleton, and George Foster managed to maintain their hitting stride of previous seasons, as did Amos Otis, Ben Ogilvie, and Andrew Dawson.

A rookie on the Montreal Expos, Tim Raines, made an early impression as he built up an impressive record for stealing bases. (Montreal was a contender during the close of the season playoffs.)

And while blacks distinguished themselves with their batting prowess throughout the major leagues, pitchers like Jim Bibby and Rudy May were to influence the outcome of individual games during the course of the season.

During the summer, on a nostalgic note, 50 former players of the Negro Baseball League met for a reunion in Ashland, Kentucky and provided fascinating commentary on the role of blacks in one of America's great pastimes. From the groundwork they laid and the contributions blacks made in 1981, there was a general consensus that the future bode well for blacks in major league baseball.

As the 1980s decade came to a close, Bill White a former major league All-Star was named the new president of the National League. As he assumed his position in early 1989, he became the highest ranking black executive in the history of professional sports.

White had played 14 years in the majors with the New York and San Francisco Giants, the St. Louis Cardinals and the Philadelphia Phillies, batting over .300 four times and playing in six All-Star games before he began a career as a broadcaster for the New York Yankees for 18 years.

The league reportedly had considered two other blacks, former deputy commissioner of the National Basketball Association Simon Gourdine and Bristol Myers executive Gilroye Griffin Jr. for the position as well.

As the 1989 season began, two players—Dwight Gooden of the New York Mets and Kirby Puckett of the Minnesota Twins—received multi-million dollar contracts which ranked among the highest in professional sports.

*Hank Aaron, in baseball's Hall of Fame*

## 1989 NATIONAL LEAGUE ROSTER OF MINORITY PLAYERS

**Atlanta Braves**
Jose L. Alvarez - P
German Jimenez - P
Ron E. Gant - IF
Lonnie Smith - OF

**Chicago Cubs**
Shawon Dunston - IF
Andre Dawson - OF
Rafael Palmeiro - OF
Angel Salazar - IF

**Cincinnati Reds**
David Concepcion - IF
Eric Davis - OF
Ken Griffey - OF
Barry Larkin - IF
Luis Quinones - IF

**Houston Astros**
Juan Agosto - P
Joaquin Andujar - P
Kevin Bass - OF
Rafael Ramirez - IF
Gerald Young - OF

**Los Angeles Dodgers**
Mike Davis - OF
Alfredo Griffin - IF
Ramon Martinez - P
Jesse Orosco - P
Alejandro Pena - P
Tony Phillips - OF
Mario Soto - P
Willie Randolph - IF
Franklin Stubbs - IF
John Shelby - OF
Fernando Valenzuela - P

**Montreal Expos**
Hubert Brooks - OF
Andres Galarranga - IF
Dennis Martinez - P
Otis Nixon - IF
Timothy Raines - OF
Luis Rivera - IF
Pascual Perez - P

**New York Mets**
Dwight Goooden - P
Darryl Strawberry - OF
Mookie Wilson - OF

**Philadelphia Phillies**
Philip Bradley - OF
Joaquin Gutierrez - IF
Milt Thompson - OF

**Pittsburgh Pirates**
Rafael Belliard - IF
Barry Bonds - OF
Gary Redus - OF

**San Diego Padres**
Roberto Alomar - IF
Tony Gwynn - OF
Carmelo Martinez - OF
Benito Santiago - IF
Garry Templeton - IF

**San Francisco Giants**
Kevin Mitchell - IF
Donell Nixon - OF
Jose Uribe - IF
Jeffrey Leonard - OF

**St. Louis Cardinals**
Vince Coleman - OF
Curt Ford - OF
Pedro Guerrero - IF
Willie McGee - OF
Terry Pendleton - IF
Ozzie Smith - IF

## 1989 AMERICAN LEAGUE ROSTER OF MINORITY PLAYERS

**Baltimore Orioles**
Jose Bautista - P
Eddie Murray - IF
Al Newman - OF
Oswaldo Peraza - P

**Boston Red Sox**
Dennis Boyd - P
Ellis Burks - OF
Jim Rice - OF
Lee Smith - P

**California Angels**
Chili Davis - OF
Devon White - OF

**Chicago White Sox**
Aarold Baines - OF
Daryl Boston - OF
Ozzie Guillen - IF
Melido Perez - P
Gary Redus - OF

**Cleveland Indians**
Joe Carter - OF
Julio Franco - IF
Mel Hall - OF
Willie Upshaw - IF
Reggie Williams - OF

**Detroit Tigers**
Guillermo Hernandez - P
Larry Herndon - OF
Chet Lemon - OF
Dwayne Murphy - OF
Luis Salazar - IF
Lou Whitaker - IF

**Kansas City Royals**
Bo Jackson - OF
Danny Tartabull - OF
Israel Sanchez - P
Frank White - IF
Willie Wilson - OF

**Milwaukee Brewers**
Juan Castillo - IF
Teddy Higuera - P
Jeff Leonard - P
Juan Nieves - OF

**Minnesota Twins**
Juan Berenguer - P
German Gonzalez - P
Kirby Puckett - OF

**New York Yankees**
Luis Aguayo - IF
Jesse Barfield - OF
Cecilio Guante - P
Rickey Henderson - OF
Charlie Hudson - P
Rafael Santana - IF
Gary Ward - OF
Claudell Washington - OF
Dave Winfield - OF

**Oakland Athletics**
Don Baylor - OF
Ken Griffey - OF
Jose Canseco - OF
Dave Henderson - OF
Dave Parker - OF
Luis Polonia - OF
Dave Stewart - P

**Seattle Mariners**
Darnell Coles - OF
Henry Lotto - OF
Mario Diaz - IF
Rey Quinones - IF
Harold Reynolds - IF

**Texas Rangers**
Jose Guzman - P
Ruben Sierra - OF

**Toronto Blue Jays**
George Bell - OF
Manny Lee - IF
Lloyd Moseby - OF
Fred McGriff - IF

## RECORD SETTERS IN BASEBALL

### Black Batting Champions (National League)

| Player | Year | Avg. |
|---|---|---|
| Jackie Robinson, *Bklyn.* | 1949 | .342 |
| Willie Mays, *N.Y. Giants* | 1954 | .345 |
| Hank Aaron, *Mil.* | 1956 | .328 |
| Hank Aaron, *Mil.* | 1959 | .355 |
| Roberto Clemente, *Pitt.* | 1961 | .351 |
| Tommy Davis, *L.A.* | 1962 | .346 |
| Tommy Davis, *L.A.* | 1963 | .326 |
| Roberto Clemente, *Pitt.* | 1964 | .339 |
| Roberto Clemente, *Pitt.* | 1965 | .329 |
| Matty Alou, *Pitt.* | 1966 | .342 |
| Roberto Clemente, *Pitt.* | 1967 | .357 |
| Rico Carty, *Atl.* | 1970 | .366 |
| Billy Williams, *Chi.* | 1972 | .333 |
| Ralph Garr, *Atl.* | 1974 | .353 |
| Bill Madlock, *Chi.* | 1975 | .354 |
| Bill Madlock, *Chi.* | 1976 | .339 |
| Dave Parker, *Pitt.* | 1977 | .338 |
| Dave Parker, *Pitt.* | 1978 | .334 |
| Bill Madlock, *Pitt.* | 1982 | .341 |
| Willie McGee, *St.L.* | 1985 | .353 |
| Tim Raines, *Mont.* | 1986 | .354 |
| Tony Gwynn, *S.D.* | 1987 | .369 |
| Tony Gwynn, *S.D.* | 1988 | .313 |

### Black Batting Champions (American League)

| Player | Year | Avg. |
|---|---|---|
| Tony Oliva, *Minn.* | 1964 | .323 |
| Tony Oliva, *Minn.* | 1965 | .321 |
| Frank Robinson, *Balt.* | 1966 | .316 |
| Rod Carew, *Minn.* | 1969 | .332 |
| Alex Johnson, *Cal.* | 1970 | .329 |
| Tony Oliva, *Minn.* | 1971 | .337 |
| Rod Carew, *Minn.* | 1972 | .318 |
| Rod Carew, *Minn.* | 1973 | .350 |
| Rod Carew, *Minn.* | 1974 | .364 |
| Rod Carew, *Minn.* | 1975 | .359 |
| Rod Carew, *Minn.* | 1977 | .388 |
| Rod Carew, *Minn.* | 1978 | .333 |
| Willie Wilson, *K.C.* | 1982 | .332 |

*Willie McCovey, 1969 National League home run champion.*

*George Foster batting during 1976 World Series.*

### Black Home Run Champions (National League)

| Player | Year | Total |
|---|---|---|
| Willie Mays, *N.Y. Giants* | 1955 | 51 |
| Hank Aaron, *Mil.* | 1957 | 44 |
| Ernie Banks, *Chi.* | 1958 | 47 |
| Ernie Banks, *Chi.* | 1960 | 41 |
| Orlando Cepeda, *S.F.* | 1961 | 46 |
| Willie Mays, *S.F.* | 1962 | 49 |
| Willie McCovey, *S.F.* | 1963 | 44 |
| Willie Mays, *S.F.* | 1964 | 47 |
| Willie Mays, *S.F.* | 1965 | 52 |
| Hank Aaron, *Atl.* | 1966 | 44 |
| Hank Aaron, *Atl.* | 1967 | 39 |
| Willie McCovey, *S.F.* | 1968 | 36 |
| Willie McCovey, *S.F.* | 1969 | 45 |
| Willie Stargell, *Pitt.* | 1971 | 48 |
| Willie Stargell, *Pitt.* | 1973 | 44 |
| George Foster, *Cinn.* | 1977 | 52 |
| George Foster, *Cinn.* | 1978 | 40 |
| Andre Dawson, *Chi.* | 1987 | 49 |
| Darryl Strawberry, *N.Y.* | 1988 | 39 |

### Black Home Run Champions (American League)

| Player | Year | Total |
|---|---|---|
| Larry Doby, *Cleve.* | 1952 | 32 |
| Larry Doby, *Cleve.* | 1954 | 32 |
| Frank Robinson, *Balt.* | 1966 | 49 |
| Dick Allen, *Chi.* | 1972 | 37 |
| Reggie Jackson, *Oak.* | 1973 | 32 |
| Dick Allen, *Chi.* | 1974 | 32 |
| Reggie Jackson, *Oak.* | 1975 | 36 |
| George Scott, *Mil.* | 1975 (tie) | 36 |
| Jim Rice, *Bos.* | 1977 | 39 |
| Jim Rice, *Bos.* | 1978 | 46 |
| Reggie Jackson, *N.Y.* | 1980 | 41 |
| Eddie Murray, *Balt.* | 1981 | 22 |
| Reggie Jackson, *Cal.* | 1982 | 39 |
| Jesse Barfield, *Tor.* | 1986 | 40 |

*Baseball immortal Willie Mays collected over 3,250 hits in 22 seasons.*

### Black Most Valuable Player Awards (National League)

| Player | Team | Year |
|---|---|---|
| Jackie Robinson | Bklyn. Dodgers | 1949 |
| Roy Campanella | Bklyn. Dodgers | 1951 |
| Roy Campanella | Bklyn. Dodgers | 1953 |
| Willie Mays | N.Y. Giants | 1954 |
| Roy Campanella | Bklyn. Dodgers | 1955 |
| Don Newcombe | Bklyn. Dodgers | 1956 |
| Hank Aaron | Mil. Braves | 1957 |
| Ernie Banks | Chi. Cubs | 1958 |
| Ernie Banks | Chi. Cubs | 1959 |
| Frank Robinson | Cinn. Reds | 1961 |
| Maury Wills | L.A. Dodgers | 1962 |
| Willie Mays | S.F. Giants | 1965 |
| Roberto Clemente | Pitt. Pirates | 1966 |
| Orlando Cepeda | St.L. Cardinals | 1967 |
| Bob Gibson | St.L. Cardinals | 1968 |
| Willie McCovey | S.F. Giants | 1969 |
| Joe Morgan | Cinn. Reds | 1975 |
| Joe Morgan | Cinn. Reds | 1976 |
| George Foster | Cinn. Reds | 1977 |
| Dave Parker | Pitt. Pirates | 1978 |
| Willie Stargell | Pitt. Pirates | 1979 |
| Willi McGee | St.L. Cardinals | 1985 |
| Andre Dawson | Chi. Cubs | 1987 |

### Black Most Valuable Player Awards (American League)

| Player | Team | Year |
|---|---|---|
| Elston Howard | N.Y. Yankees | 1963 |
| Zoilo Versalles | Minn. Twins | 1965 |
| Frank Robinson | Balt. Orioles | 1966 |
| Vida Blue | Oak. Athletics | 1971 |
| Dick Allen | Chi. White Sox | 1972 |
| Reggie Jackson | Oak. Athletics | 1973 |
| Rod Carew | Minn. Twins | 1977 |
| Jim Rice | Bos. Red Sox | 1978 |
| Don Baylor | Cal. Angeles | 1979 |
| Willie Hernandez | Det. Tigers | 1984 |

### Black Runs-Batted-In Leaders (National League)

| Player | Year | Total |
|---|---|---|
| Monte Irvin, *N.Y. Giants* | 1951 | 121 |
| Hank Aaron, *Mil.* | 1957 | 126 |
| Ernie Banks, *Chi.* | 1958 | 129 |
| Ernie Banks, *Chi.* | 1959 | 143 |
| Hank Aaron, *Mil.* | 1960 | 126 |
| Orlando Cepeda, *S.F.* | 1961 | 142 |
| Tommy Davis, *L.A.* | 1962 | 153 |
| Hank Aaron, *Mil.* | 1963 | 130 |
| Hank Aaron, *Atl.* | 1966 | 127 |
| Orlando Cepeda, *St.L.* | 1967 | 111 |
| Willie McCovey, *S.F.* | 1968 | 105 |
| Willie McCovey, *S.F.* | 1969 | 126 |
| Willie Stargell, *Pitt.* | 1973 | 119 |
| George Foster, *Cinn.* | 1976 | 121 |
| George Foster, *Cinn.* | 1977 | 149 |
| George Foster, *Cinn.* | 1978 | 120 |
| Dave Winfield, *S.D.* | 1979 | 121 |
| Dave Parker, *Cinn.* | 1985 | 125 |
| Andre Dawson, *Chi.* | 1987 | 137 |

### Black Runs-Batted-In Leaders (American League)

| Player | Year | Total |
|---|---|---|
| Larry Doby, *Cleve.* | 1954 | 126 |
| Frank Robinson, *Balt.* | 1966 | 122 |
| Dick Allen, *Chi.* | 1972 | 113 |
| Reggie Jackson, *Oak.* | 1973 | 117 |
| Lee May, *Balt.* | 1976 | 109 |
| Larry Hisle, *Minn.* | 1977 | 119 |
| Jim Rice, *Bos.* | 1978 | 139 |
| Don Baylor, *Cal.* | 1979 | 139 |
| Cecil Cooper, *Minn.* | 1980 | 122 |
| Eddie Murray, *Balt.* | 1981 | 81 |
| Hal McRae, K.C. | 1982 | 133 |
| Cecil Cooper, *Mil.* | 1983 | 126 |
| Jim Rice, *Bos.* | 1983 | 126 |

### Blacks in Baseball Hall of Fame

| Player | Team |
|---|---|
| Hank Aaron | Atlanta Braves |
| Ernie Banks | Chicago Cubs |
| Lou Brock | St. Louis Cardinals |
| Roy Campanella | Brooklyn Dodgers |
| Roberto Clemente | Pittsburgh Pirates |
| Bob Gibson | St. Louis Cardinals |
| Monte Irvin | New York Giants |

| Player | Team |
|---|---|
| Juan Marichal | Giants, Dodgers |
| Willie Mays | Giants, Dodgers |
| Willie McCovey | Giants, Padres |
| Sachael Paige | Cleveland Indians |
| Frank Robinson | Reds, Baltimore |
| Jackie Robinson | Brooklyn Dodgers |
| Billy Williams | Chicago Cubs |

## THE BLACK IN PROFESSIONAL BASKETBALL

The first black man to play as a professional in the National Basketball Association (NBA) was Chuck Cooper, a forward who signed a contract with the Boston Celtics in 1951. He remained with the team for six years. Former Harlem Globetrotters star Nat "Sweetwater" Clifton joined the pro ranks later in 1951, playing with the New York Knicks. Within the decade, many of the top players in both leagues were black. Bill Russell, K. C. Jones, and Sam Jones were in Boston; Ray Felix and Willie Naulls were in New York; and Elgin Baylor starred in Minneapolis.

### The 1960s

By 1964, most NBA teams had five or six black players, all accomplished athletes contributing to their respective squads as they were called upon.

The incomparable Wilt Chamberlain, for instance, soon held virtually every scoring record. In fact, he scored an incredible 100 points in a game against the Knicks on March 2, 1962 and repeated the feat again before he retired.

As the decade progressed, new players joined the ranks. Kareem Abdul-Jabbar, the New York City teen who, as an outstanding player at UCLA, led his team to three NCAA championships, signed with the Milwaukee Bucks. During the 1969-1970 season, the Bucks ranked second in a division known for its tough standards.

Other outstanding players included Elvin Hayes, who won the NBA scoring title in his rookie year. Willis Reed, with the Knicks, would win the MVP Award twice within a 10-year period.

### The 1970s

In the 1970s black representation grew even more substantial. During the 1973-1974 season, Bob McAdoo of the Buffalo Braves stood out. In only his second season, he scored 2,261 points and rolled up a 30.6-point scoring average, both tops in the league. The towering center so established himself as an excellent rebounder with a 15.1 average, third highest in the NBA.

Other outstanding players were Jabbar of the Bucks (later the Los Angeles Lakers), who would become a dominant force as center and the central force of his teams. Two other ranking centers in the league were Hayes with the Washington Bullets and Nate Thurmond with the Chicago Bulls.

Julius Erving was the top player of the New York Nets of the American Basketball Association (ABA) during the 1973-1974 season (before it merged into the NBA later in the decade). Nicknamed "Dr. J." and "The Doctor," he was the league's top scorer with 2,299 points, averaging 27.4 points per game. George McGinnis of the Indiana Pacers was another top scorer of the ABA during the decade.

During the 1974-1975 season, the dominance of black players continued as four of the top five players in the three categories of scoring, rebounding, and assists were black. The top NBA scorer was again McAdoo, the top rebounder was Wes Unseld, and the top play maker, Kevin Porter. Both Unseld and Porter played in Washington.

NBA directly from high school, Wayne Embry became the first black general manager of an NBA team.

### The 1980s

As the decade began, another powerful center had come to dominate the league. Kareem Abdul-Jabbar had steadily

*Patrick Ewing of the New York Knickerbockers is a future inductee into basketball's Hall of Fame. His acquisition has given new life to a struggling team .*

grown to become a phenomenal star with the Los Angeles Lakers. His contributions through the year led the team to victory as the NBA champs on May 16, 1980 as they defeated the Philadelphia 76ers. When the final game was played, Abdul-Jabbar was injured and rookie guard Earvin (Magic) Johnson incredibly substituted at center, contributing 42 points and being named MVP for the tournament.

In defeating the 76ers, the Lakers faced off against Julius Erving, fast becoming a perennial basketball superstar. With solid, exciting play, he continued to be one of the major attractions in pro sports.

*The all-around play of Earvin Johnson has given him the name "Magic." The concensus is that he is among the very best of those who have ever played the game of basketball.*

In the following year, the Boston Celtics took the NBA crown with Cedric Maxwell walking away with MVP honors as the east coast team defeated the Denver Rockets. And in 1982, Kareem Abdul-Jabbar led the Lakers in regaining the crown.

Abdul-Jabbar would be awarded the league MVP trophy six times before the decade more than any other player. He announced his retirement to take place after the end of the 1988-89 season.

Another legend, Julius Erving of the Philadelphia 76ers also announced his retirement after a total of 16 years, 11 at Philadelphia and five additional years between the Virginia Squires and the New York Nets of the former American Basketball Association.

Centers would prove to be among the most regarded players in the league. Manute Bol, for instance, a 7'6" player from the African nation of Sudan was not only the tallest player on his team, the Washington Bullets, but also in the entire league.

Another highly valued player was David Robinson, a 7'1" graduate of the Naval Academy who signed an eight year, $26 million contract with the San Antonio Spurs, even as he signed on for active duty as a Navy officer and began his active duty assignment after the government refused to allow a waiver granting him the right to play immediately.

The faces in the coaching ranks continued to change with the fortunes of their respective teams. Veteran Bill Russell was released as coach of the Sacramento Kings during the 1987-88 season and appointed vice president in charge of basketball operations. Back on the east coast, K.C. Jones announced his retirement as head coach of the Boston Celtics after leading the team to two championships. At that time, Wes Unseld, a Hall of Famer, was coaching the Washington Bullets.

The league continued to expand as two new teams, the Charlotte Hornets and the Miami Heat, joined the NBA at the beginning of the 1988-89 season.

There were literally scores of outstanding players during the decade, such as Michael Jordon of the Chicago Bulls and Patrick Ewing of the New York Knicks, who went on after rookie of the year seasons to become full-fledged stars in subsequent seasons. The league became a source of fascination as the Celtics and the Lakers came to be near-annual contenders for pro basketball's championship crown.

Fighting remained an issue of concern as emotionally charged players—both in the pro and college ranks—found calls for increasingly stronger penalties for the growing violence on the playing court.

In 1989, K.C. Jones and Lenny Wilkens were elected to the Basketball Hall of Fame along with William (Pop) Gates, who played with the New York Renaissance and other teams during basketball's barnstorming years in the 1930s and 1940s.

In all of the professional sports, basketball remained a showcase for black talent with a consistently large number of players per team and coaches on the sidelines.

## 1989 NBA ROSTER OF MINORITY PLAYERS

### Atlanta Hawks
John Battle
Antoine Carr
Cliff Levingston
Mike McGee
Glenn Rivers
Wayne Rollins
Spud Webb
Dominique Wilkins
Gus Williams
Kevin Willis

### Boston Celtics
Darren Daye
Dennis Johnson
Reggie Lewis
Robert Parish
Sam Vincent

### Chicago Bulls
Gene Banks
Artis Gilmore
Horace Grant
Michael Jordan
Charles Oakley
Scottie Pippen
Brad Sellers
Sedale Threatt

### Cleveland Cavaliers
John Bagley
Tyrone Corbin
Brad Daugherty
Ron Harper
Phil Hubbard
Kevin Johnson
Keith Lee
Johnny Newman
Mel Turpin
John Williams

### Dallas Mavericks
Mark Aguirre
Rolando Blackman
James Donaldson
Derek Harper
Sam Perkins
Roy Tarpley

### Denver Nuggets
Alex English
Lafayette Lever
Maurice Martin
Andre Moore
Calvin Natt
Otis Smith
Darrell Walker

### Detroit Pistons
Freddie Banks
William Bedford
Adrian Dantley
Joe Dumars
Sidney Green
Vinnie Johnson
Rick Mahorn
Dennis Rodman
John Salley
Isiah Thomas

### Golden State Warriors
Joe Barry Carroll
Eric Floyd
Perry Moss
Purvis Short
Larry Smith
Chris Washburn
Jerome Whitehead

### Houston Rockets
Buck Johnson
Allen Leavell
Cedric Maxwell
Rodney McCray
Dirk Minniefield
Akeem Olajuwon
Robert Reid
Ralph Sampson

### Indiana Pacers
Vern Fleming
John Long
Reggie Miller
Churck Person
Walker Russell
Wayman Tisdale
Herb Williams

### Los Angeles Clippers
Benoit Benjamin
Earl Cureton
Quintin Dailey
Larry Drew
Lancaster Gordon
Marques Johnson
Norm Nixon
Darnell Valentire
Rory White
Reggie Williams
Mike Woodson

### Los Angeles Lakers
Kareem Abdul-Jabbar
Adrian Branch
Michael Cooper
A.C. Green
Magic Johnson
Wes Matthews
Byron Scott
Billy Thompson
Mychal Thompson
James Worthy

### Milwaukee Bucks
Terry Cummings
Winston Garland
John Lucas
Sidney Moncrief
Paul Pressey

### New Jersey Nets
James Bailey
Otis Birdsong
Darryl Dawkins
Dennis Hopson
Albert King
Dwayne Washington
Buck Williams
Ray Williams
Leon Wood
Orlando Woolridge

### New York Knickerbockers
Paul Cummings
Patrick Ewing
Gerald Henderson
Mark Jackson
Jawann Oldham
Louis Orr
Rory Sparrow
Trent Tucker
Kenny Walker
Gerald Wilkins

### Philadelphia 76ers
Charles Barkley
Maurice Cheeks
Kenny Green
Roy Hinson
Cliff Robinson
Andrew Toney
David Wingate

### Phoenix Suns
Alvan Adams
Rafael Addison
Walter Davis
James Edwards
Armon Gilliam
Larry Nance
Bernard Thompson

### Portland Trail Blazers
Sam Bowie
Kenny Carr
Clyde Drexler
Kevin Duckworth
Ken Johnson
Caldwell Jones
Fernando Martin

### Sacramento Kings
Franklin Edwards
Ed Pinckney
Johnny Rogers
Derek Smith
Kenny Smith
Reggie Theus
Otis Thorpe

### San Antonio Spurs
Greg Anderson
Walter Berry
Nate Blackwell
Johnny Dawkins
Anthony Jones
Johnny Moore
Ed Nealy
Alvin Robertson

### Seattle Supersonics
Dale Ellis
Clemon Johnson
Eddie Johnson
Curtis Kitchen
Alton Lister
Maurice Lucas
Xavier McDaniel
Derrick McKey
Olden Polynice
Kevin Williams

### Utah Jazz
Thurl Bailey
Dell Curry
Rickey Green
Darrell Griffith
Karl Malone

### Washington Bullets
Michael Adams
Tyrone Bogues
Manute Bol
Dawrin Cook
Derrick Dowell
Frank Johnson
Jeff Malone
Moses Malone
Jay Vincent
Duane Washington

## RECORD SETTERS IN BASKETBALL

### Black NBA Rebounding Leaders

| Player | Year | Rebounds |
|---|---|---|
| Maurice Stokes, *Roch.* | 1956-1957 | 1256 |
| Bill Russell, *Bost.* | 1957-1958 | 1564 |
| Bill Russell, *Bost.* | 1958-1959 | 1612 |
| Wilt Chamberlain, *Phil.* | 1959-1960 | 1941 |
| Wilt Chamberlain, *Phil.* | 1960-1961 | 2149 |
| Wilt Chamberlain, *Phil.* | 1961-1962 | 2052 |
| Wilt Chamberlain, *S.F.* | 1962-1963 | 1946 |
| Bill Russell, *Bost.* | 1963-1964 | 1930 |
| Bill Russell, *Bost.* | 1964-1965 | 1878 |
| Wilt Chamberlain, *Phil.* | 1965-1966 | 1943 |
| Wilt Chamberlain, *Phil.* | 1966-1967 | 1957 |
| Wilt Chamberlain, *Phil.* | 1967-1968 | 1952 |
| Wilt Chamberlain, *L.A.* | 1968-1969 | 1712 |
| Elvin Hayes, *S.D.* | 1969-1970 | 1386 |
| Wilt Chamberlain, *L.A.* | 1970-1971 | 1493 |
| Wilt Chamberlain, *L.A.* | 1971-1972 | 1572 |
| Wilt Chamberlain, *L.A.* | 1972-1973 | 1526 |
| Elvin Hayes, *Wash.* | 1973-1974 | 1463 |
| Bob McAdoo, *Buff.* | 1974-1975 | 1155 |
| Kareem Abdul-Jabbar, *L.A.* | 1975-1976 | 1383 |
| Kareem Abdul-Jabbar, *L.A.* | 1976-1977 | 1090 |
| Truck Robinson, *N.O.* | 1977-1978 | 1288 |
| Moses Malone, *Hous.* | 1978-1979 | 1444 |
| Moses Malone, *Hous.* | 1980-1981 | 1180 |
| Moses Malone, *Hous.* | 1981-1982 | 1188 |
| Moses Malone, *Phil.* | 1982-1983 | 1194 |
| Moses Malone, *Phil.* | 1983-1984 | 950 |

### Black NBA Scoring Leaders

| Player | Year | Pts. | Avg |
|---|---|---|---|
| Wilt Chamberlain, *Phil.* | 1959-1960 | 2707 | 37.9 |
| Wilt Chamberlain, *Phil.* | 1960-1961 | 3303 | 38.4 |
| Wilt Chamberlain, *Phil.* | 1961-1962 | 4029 | 50.4 |
| Wilt Chamberlain, *S.F.* | 1962-1963 | 3586 | 44.8 |
| Wilt Chamberlain, *S.F.* | 1963-1964 | 2948 | 36.5 |
| Wilt Chamberlain, *Phil.* | 1964-1965 | 2534 | 34.7 |
| Wilt Chamberlain, *Phil.* | 1965-1966 | 2649 | 33.5 |
| Dave Bing, *Det.* | 1967-1968 | 2142 | 27.1 |
| Elvin Hayes, *S.D.* | 1968-1969 | 2327 | 28.4 |
| Lew Alcindor, *Mil.* | 1970-1971 | 2596 | 31.7 |
| Kareem Abdul-Jabbar, *Mil.* | 1971-1972 | 2822 | 34.8 |
| Nate Archibald, *K.C.-O* | 1972-1973 | 2719 | 34.0 |
| Bob McAdoo, *Buff.* | 1973-1974 | 2261 | 30.6 |
| Bob McAdoo, *Buff.* | 1974-1975 | 2831 | 34.5 |
| Bob McAdoo, *Buff.* | 1975-1976 | 2427 | 31.1 |
| George Gervin, *San Ant.* | 1977-1978 | 2232 | 29.2 |
| George Gervin, *San Ant.* | 1978-1979 | 2365 | 29.6 |
| George Gervin, *San Ant.* | 1979-1980 | 2585 | 33.1 |
| Adrian Dantley, *Utah* | 1980-1981 | 2452 | 30.7 |
| George Gervin, *San Ant.* | 1981-1982 | 2551 | 32.3 |
| Alex English, *Den.* | 1982-1983 | 2326 | 28.4 |
| Adrian Dantley, *Utah* | 1983-1984 | 2418 | 30.6 |
| Bernard King, *N.Y.* | 1984-1985 | 1809 | 32.9 |
| Dominique Wilkins, *Atl.* | 1985-1986 | 2366 | 30.3 |
| Michael Jordan, *Chi.* | 1986-1987 | 3041 | 37.1 |

### Black NBA Assist Leaders

| Player | Year | Assists |
|---|---|---|
| Oscar Robertson, *Cinn.* | 1960-1961 | 690 |
| Oscar Robertson, *Cinn.* | 1961-1962 | 899 |
| Guy Rodgers, *S.F.* | 1962-1963 | 825 |
| Oscar Robertson, *Cinn.* | 1963-1964 | 868 |
| Oscar Robertson, *Cinn.* | 1964-1965 | 861 |
| Oscar Robertson, *Cinn.* | 1965-1966 | 847 |
| Guy Rodgers, *Chi.* | 1966-1967 | 908 |
| Wilt Chamberlain, *Phil.* | 1967-1968 | 702 |
| Oscar Robertson, *Cinn.* | 1968-1969 | 772 |
| Lenny Wilkens, *Sea.* | 1969-1970 | 683 |
| Norm Van Lier, *Cinn.* | 1970-1971 | 832 |
| Nate Archibald, *K.C.-O* | 1972-1973 | 910 |
| Kevin Porter, *Wash.* | 1974-1975 | 650 |
| Don Watts, *Sea.* | 1975-1976 | 661 |
| Don Buse, *Ind.* | 1976-1977 | 685 |
| Kevin Porter, *N.J.* | 1977-1978 | 837 |
| Kevin Porter, *Det.* | 1978-1979 | 1099 |
| Michael Ray Richardson, *N.Y.* | 1979-1980 | 832 |
| Kevin Porter, *Wash.* | 1980-1981 | 734 |
| Johnny Moore, *San Ant.* | 1981-1982 | 762 |
| Magic Johnson, *LA.* | 1982-1983 | 829 |
| Magic Johnson, *LA.* | 1983-1984 | 875 |

*Oscar Robertson holds the record for most assists in a career.*

## THE BLACK IN PROFESSIONAL FOOTBALL

### The 1970s

In the 1970s, outstanding black players excelled at virtually every offensive and defensive position. For the first time, quarterback James Harris of the Los Angeles Rams was consistently successful as a week-to-week starter and helped to overcome the stereotype of black signal callers performing erratically and failing under pressure.

During the 1974 season, Harris, who graduated from fabled Grambling College, was the NFC's second leading passer. Two years later he would capture the crown in that category.

Quarterbacking was an important concern among observers who watched numerous blacks excel at college, and then fail or not be allowed to try out in that position. With responsibility for leading the offense, gaining acceptability and respectability in that position was a crucial goal for those outstanding college players and their supporters.

In time, Joe Gilliam joined the Pittsburgh Steelers and performed admirably as a backup quarterback for a team that would claim the Super Bowl title in unprecedented fashion. In 1978, Doug Williams became an offensive outstanding players as he quarterbacked an expansion team, the Tampa Bay Buccaneers, to contender status within three years. By that time, Vince Evans had become a successful backup signal caller with the Chicago Bears.

During the decade, blacks virtually dominated the year-end statistics in pass receiving, rushing, and for a time, scoring. While these records on offense continued to fall, there were notable achievements by blacks on the defensive teams as well.

Linemen anchored defensive lines and made vital contributions to team efforts in the secondary areas as well. Each year new players were joining the NFL and making their reputations in short order. Within time, half of all the active players in the league were black.

Soon the Football Hall of Fame gave recognition to a number of blacks, including all-pro Willie Davis of the Green Bay Packers, Herb Adderly of the Packers and Dallas Cowboys, Jim Brown of the Cleveland Browns, Roosevelt Brown of the New York Giants, David (Deacon) Jones of the Rams, San Diego Chargers, and Washington Redskins, Lenny Moore of the Baltimore Colts, and Gale Sayers of the Chicago Bears.

And each year new collegiate wonders would join the ranks. George Rogers, a star at the University of South Carolina, became the seventh black in a row to win the coveted Heisman Trophy in 1980. And while Rogers was excelling as a rookie with the New Orleans Saints, Marcus Allen of USC became the 1981 winner, the eighth black honored with college football's most coveted individual award.

### The 1980s

In January, the Pittsburgh Steelers had won an unprecedented fourth Super Bowl victory by defeating the Los Angeles Rams in the fifteenth championship contest.

*Chuck Foreman, #44 Minnesota, "Offensive Player of the Year" 1976.*

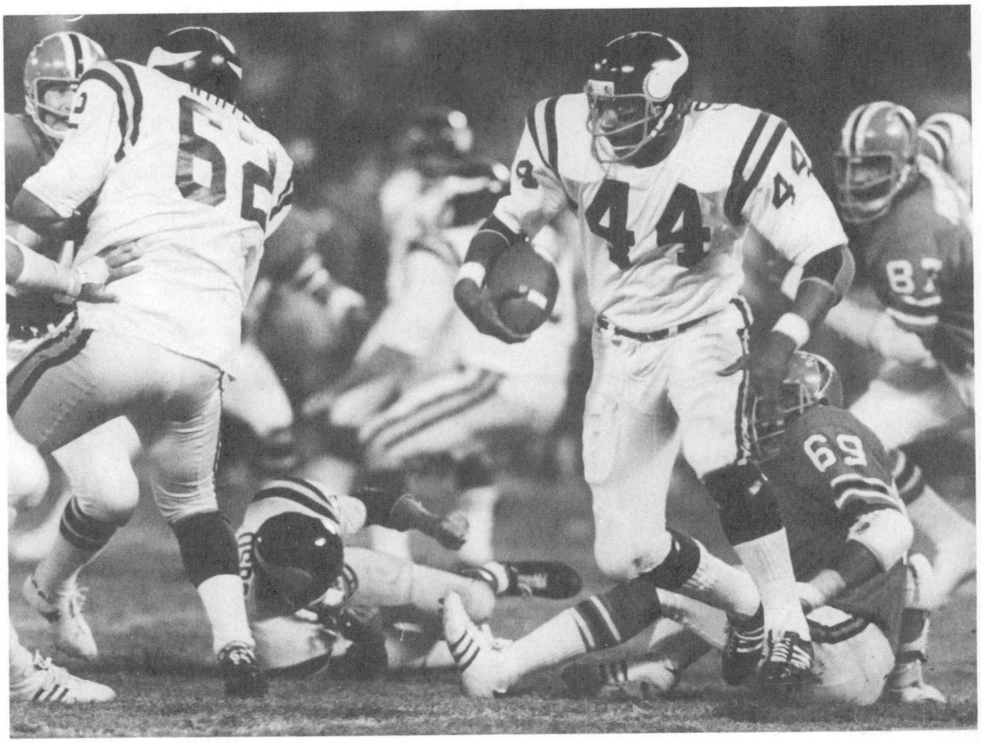

*Walter Payton, living proof that you can be a gentleman and a magnificient athlete with a winning attitude.*

When the season started that fall, the Steelers were plagued by injuries and got off with a series of four losses before changing to winning ways. At Buffalo, a young runner named Joe Cribbs was providing the kind of excitement not seen since the retirement of O. J. Simpson. The Philadelphia Eagles also appeared strong, with receiver Harold Carmichael contributing substantially each week. At Atlanta, a back named William Andrews and a receiver named Wallace Francis combined for a tremendous offensive threat.

As the season drew to a close, the Eagles beat the Minnesota Vikings 42-7, as the playoff series began. Oakland overcame the Cleveland Browns 14-12, and the Dallas Cowboys defeated Atlanta 30-27. In the final game, the Buffalo Bills were vanquished by the San Diego Chargers. In the next competition, Oakland and Philadelphia moved up as contenders in Super Bowl XV.

As the final score indicated, Oakland overwhelmed the Eagles, with quarterback Jim Plunkett throwing for three touchdowns. While the offensive line was credited with giving Plunkett the time he needed, Cliff Branch, who caught two of the TD passes, and Kenny King, who caught the third—a record 80-yard pass—were certainly heroes that day. Rod Martin, a defensive outstanding player, was also singled out for praise after catching three interceptions—another Super Bowl record—to aid the Raiders in their second world championship.

Other outstanding players during the 1980-1981 season were Earl Campbell, the Houston Oiler who led the league in rushing; John Jefferson, who was the leading receiver with 1,340 yards and 13 touchdowns; and Tony Dorsett of the Cowboys, who rushed for 160 yards in a single game. Veterans Chuck Muncie, Wilbert Montgomery, Billy Sims, and Mike Pruitt all provided excitement and solid offensive statistics throughout the season.

The San Francisco 49ers defeated the Cincinnati Bengals in Super Bowl XVI, as two teams who had never reached the championships played to a 26-21 decision. The game marked the culmination of a season in which the two ultimate contenders were praised most for the talent of their respective quarterbacks and the strategy of their coaches.

However, a number of black players were instrumental in bringing the West Coast team its first victory. Earl Cooper caught a crucial touchdown pass, and Dwight Hicks was on the receiving end of an intercepted pass that helped to bring about the Bengal's downfall.

During the playoffs, preceding the championship game, Doug Williams quarterbacked his team into contention while several heroes produced playoff opportunities for the New York Giants and Jets, in a rare outburst of spirited play for the second major story of the season.

Among the perennial offensive outstanding players, during the season, were Walter Payton in Chicago, Earl Campbell in Houston, Tony Dorsett in Dallas, and Chuck Muncie in San Diego.

The decade began with the Pittsburgh Steelers winning an unprecedented fourth Super Bowl victory by defeating the Los Angeles Rams in the 14th championship contest. The following season was highlighted by the accomplishments of Earl Campbell, the Houston Oiler who led the league in rushing and John Jefferson, who was the leading receiver with 1,340 yards and 13 touchdowns. That year, the Oakland Raiders defeated the Philadelphia Eagles in the Super Bowl as Kenny King caught a record 80-yard pass, and Rod Martin set another Super Bowl record with three interceptions. In Super Bowl 16, the 49ers did benefit in their first Super Bowl victory, with Earl Cooper catching a crucial touchdown pass and Dwight Hicks providing an interception that helped bring about the Bengal's downfall.

Early in the decade, the Bert Bell Memorial Trophy honoring the outstanding rookie was presented to Lawrence Taylor, Marcus Allen and Eric Dickerson, who would all continue to distinguish themselves in the seasons to come.

During the next four years, the 49ers would win the Super Bowl again in 1985 while the Washington Redskins were winners in 1983 and then again in 1987. In between, the Los Angeles Raiders were winners in 1984, with Marcus Allen winning MVP honors for setting a Super Bowl record of 191 yards rushing and two touchdowns. The Chicago Bears won the top trophy in 1986 for the first time since 1983, with defensive outstanding player Richard Dent being named MVP.

Life in the NFL could be fraught with uncertainty, however, and even top players like Tony Dorsett, who became the sixth all-time leading rusher of the Dallas Cowboys and Eric Dickerson, another consistently strong runner, found themselves on the trading block to new teams.

Professional football continued to reel from a high number of injuries, particularly to quarterbacks at the beginning of the 1988-89 season, as the league searched for ways to limit the often permanent and career-threatening problems often caused by overly aggressive players.

During the decade, Walter Payton of the Chicago Bears, retired as the NFL's all-time leading rusher, and Alan Page, a former defensive lineman for the Bears and the Minnesota Vikings was inducted into the Hall of Fame.

When the San Francisco 49ers achieved victory in Super Bowl XXIII in January, 1989, wide receiver Jerry Rice was named the games Most Valuable Player after setting a record for 11 receptions and 215 yards.

Within weeks, three other former black players—Willie Wood, a defensive back with the Green Bay Packers, Art Shell, a right tackle for the Los Angeles Raiders and Mel Blount, a former member of the Pittsburgh Steelers—were announced as new members of the Football Hall of Fame.

## REPRESENTATIVE ROSTER OF MINORITY PLAYERS IN THE NATIONAL FOOTBALL LEAGUE

### Atanta Falcons

Stacey Bailey - WR
Greg Brown - DE
Aundrey Bruce - LB
Bobby Butler - CB
Reggie Camp - DE
Scott Case - CB
Charles Dimry - CB
Floyd Dixon - WR
Mike Haynes - WR
Jessie Hester - WR
Houston Hoover - G
Gene Lang - T
Aubrey Matthews - WR
Robert Moore - S
James Primus - RB
Mike Reid - LB
Gerald Riggs- RB
John Settle - RB
Elbert Shelley - S
Sylvester Stamps - RB
Joel Williams - LB

### Buffalo Bills

Howard Ballard - T
Cornelius Bennett
Chris Burkett - WR
Leonard Burton - T
Carl Byrum - RB
Shane Conlon - LB
Wayne Davis - CB
Ronnie Harmon - RB
Trumaine Johnson - WR
Keith McKeller - TE
Andre Reed - WR
Robb Riddick - WR
Butch Rolle - TE
Leon Seals - DE
Leonard Smith - RB
Thurmon Thomas - RB

### Chicago Bears

Neal Anderson - RB
Wendell Davis - WR
Richard Dent - DE
Maurice Davis - S
Dave Duerson - S
Dennis Gentry - WR
Al Harris - LB
Vestee Jackson - CB
Troy Johnson - LB
Dante Jones - LB
Dennis McKinnon - WR
Emory Moorehead - TE
Ron Morris - WR
William Perry - DT
Mickey Pruitt - S
Mike Richardson - CB
Thomas Sanders - RB
Mike Singletary - LB
Lemuel Stinson - CB
David Tate - CB
Calvin Thomas - RB

### Cincinnati Bengals

Leo Barker - LB
Lewis Billups - CB
James Brooks - RB
Eddie Brown - WR
Cris Collinsworth - WR
Rodney Holman - TE
Stanford Jennings - RB
Tim McGee - WR
Eric Thomas - CB
Leon White - LB
Reggie Williams - LB
Ickey Woods - RB

### Cleveland Browns

Anthony Blaylock - CB
Stephen Braggs - CB
Earnest Bryner - RB
Hanford Dixon - CB
Dave Grayson - LB
Carl Hairston - DE
Mark Harper - CB
Will Hill - CB
Mike Johnson - LB
Marlon Jones - DE
Reggie Langhorne - WR
Kevin Mack - RB
Gerald McNeil - WR
Frank Minnifield - CB
Ozzie Newsome - TE
Michael Perry - DE
Darryl Sims - DE
Webster Slaughter - WR
Derek Tennell - TE
Van Waiters - LB
Brian Washington - S
Clarence Weathers - WR
Felix Wright - S

### Dallas Cowboys

Ray Alexander - WR
Bill Bates - S
Kevin Brooks - DT
Thornton Chandler -
Darryl Clack - RB
Garry Cobb - LB
Doug Cosbie - TE
Mike Downs - S
Kelvin Edwards - WR
Everett Gay - WR
Manuel Hendrix - CB
Michael Irvin - WR
Jim Jeffcoat - DE
Ed Jones - DE
Eugene Lockhart - LB
Kelvin Martin - WR
Tim Newsome - RB
Nathaniel Newton - G
Billy Owens - S
Sean Scott - LB
Herschel Walker - RB
Everson Walls - CB
Robert Williams - CB
Charles Wright - CB

### Denver Broncos

Ken Bell - RB
Tyrone Braxton - S
Michael Brooks - LB
Jeremiah Castille - CB
Kevin Clark - S
Tony Dorsett - RB
Freddie Gilbert - DE
Sam Graddy - WR
Mark Haynes - CB
Mark Jackson - WR
Vance Johnson - WR
Rulon Jones - DE
Clarence Kay - TE
Kevin Mack - RB
Mike Harden - CB
Kevin Guidry - CB
Simon Fletcher - DE
Orson Mobley - TE
Ricky Nattiel - WR
Randy Robbins - S
Dennis Smith - S
Andre Townsend - DE
Gerald Wilhite - RB
Sammy Winder - RB

### Detroit Lions

Jerry Ball - NT
Bennie Blades - CB
Carl Bland - WR
Pat Carter - TE
Raphel Cherry - S
Jessie Clark - RB
Mike Cofer - LB
Keith Ferguson - DE
Dennis Gibson - LB
Curtis Green - DE
James Griffin - S
Jerry Holmes - CB
Garry James - RB
George Jamison - LB
Gary Lee - WR
Tony Paige - RB
Carl Painter - RB
Shelton Robinson - LB
Reggie Rogers - DE
Ray Roundtree - WR
Chris Spielman - LB
Bobby Watkins - CB
William White - CB
Butch Woolfolk - RB

### Green Bay Packers

Dave Brown - CB
Kenneth Davis - RB

Burnell Dent - LB
Phillip Epps - WR
Nate Hill - DE
Norman Jefferson - CB
Perry Kemp - WR
Mark Lee - CB
Larry Mason - RB
Gary Richard - CB
Walter Stanley - WR
Sterling Sharp - WR
Keith Woodside - RB

**Houston Oilers**

Robert Banks - DE
Keith Bostic - S
Steve Brown - CB
Domingo Bryant - S
Ray Childress - DE
Cris Dishman - CB
Willie Drewrey - WR
Curtis Duncan - WR
Eric Fairs - LB
Ernest Givins - WR
Leonard Harris - WR
Alonzo Highsmith - WR
Drew Hill - WR
Kenn Johnson - S
Richard Johnson - CB
Sean Jones - DE
Bruce Davis - T
Walter Johnson - LB
William Fuller - DE
Calvin Loveall - CB
Robert Lyles - LB
Warren Moon - QB
Allen Pinkett - RB
Mike Rozier - RB
Eugene Seale - LB
Spencer Tillman - RB
Lorenzo White-RB

**Indianapolis Colts**

Harvey Armstrong - NT
Roy Banks - WR
Albert Bentley - RB
Bill Brooks - WR
Johnie Cooks - LB
Eugene Daniel - CB
Eric Dickerson - RB
Randy Dixon - T
Chris Goode - CB
Jon Hand - DE
Chris Hinton - G
Orlando Lowry - LB
Clifton Odom - LB
Freddie Robinson - S
Craig Swoope - S
Donnell Thompson - DE
Willie Tullis - CB
Clarence Verdin - WR
George Wonsley - RB
Terry Wright - S
Joe Cribbs - RB

**Kansas City Chiefs**

Carlos Carson - WR
Deron Cherry - S
Darrell Colbert - WR
Kenny Gamble - RB
Greg Hill - CB
Keyvan Jenkins - RB
Sidney Johnson - CB
Albert Lewis - CB
Stephone Paige - WR
Aaron Pearson - LB
J.C. Pearson - CB
Alfredo Roberts - TE
Kevin Ross - CB

**Los Angeles Raiders**

Marcus Allen - RB
Eddie Anderson - S
Tim Brown - WR
Mervyn Fernandez - WR
Willie Gault - WR
Rory Graves - T
Mike Haynes - CB
James Lofton - WR
Howie Long - DE
Terry McDaniel - CB
Reggie McKenzie - LB
Dennis Price - CB
Steve Smith - RB
Stacey Toran - S
Rod Martin - LB
Jerry Robinson - LB
Malcolm Taylor - T
Lionel Washington - CB

**Los Angeles Rams**

Willie Anderson - WR
Greg Bell - RB
Henry Ellard - WR
Jerry Gray - CB
Gaston Green - RB
LeRoy Irvin - CB
Gary Jeter - DE
Damone Johnson - TE
Johnnie Johnson - S
Buford McGee - RB
Anthony Newman
Vince Newsome - S
Jackie Slater - T
Aaron Cox - WR

**Miami Dolphins**

Fred Banks - WR
Woody Bennett - RB
Mark Clayton - WR
Ron Davenport - RB
Mark Duper - WR
High Green - LB
Lorenzo Hampton - RB
William Judson - CB
Don McNeal - CB
James Pruitt - WR
Reggie Roby - P
Rodney Thomas - CB
Reyna Thompson - CB
Jarvis Williams - S

**Minnesota Vikings**

Alfred Anderson - RB
Anthony Carter - WR
Darrell Fullington - S
Darryl Harris - RB
John Harris - S
Wymon Henderson - S
Issaic Holt - CB
Hassan Jones - WR
Carl Lee - CB
Darrin Nelson - RB
Allen Rice - RB
Reggie Rutland - S
Jesse Solomon - LB
Scott Studwell - LB

**New England Patriots**

Marvin Allen - RB
Jim Bowman - S
Ray Clayborn - CB
Reggie Dupard - RB
Russ Francis - TE
Irving Fryar - WR
Earnest Gibson - CB
Darryl Holmes - S
Craig James - RB
Roland James - S
Tim Joran - LB
Ronnie Lippett - CB
Sammy Martin - WR
Stanley Morgan - WR
Johnny Rembert - LB
Andre Tippett - LB
Brent Williams - DE
Bob Perryman - RB
John Stephens - RB

**New Orleans Saints**

Gene Atkins - S
Robert Clark - WR
James Geathers - DE
Antonio Gibson - S
Mel Gray - RB
Craig Heyward - RB
Lonzell Hill - WR
Dalton Hilliard - RB
Rickey Jackson - LB
Vaughan Johnson - LB
Milton Mack - CB
Eric Martin - WR
Rueben Mayes - RB
Brett Perriman - WR
Pat Swilling - LB
Jim Wilks - DE

**New York Giants**

George Adams - RB
Ottis Anderson - RB
Carl Banks - LB
Harry Carson - LB
Maurice Carthon - RB
Mark Collins - CB
Eric Dorsey - DE
Andy Headen - LB
Byron Hunt - LB
Pepper Johnson-LB
Terry Kinard - S
Lionel Manuel - WR
Leonard Marshall - DE
George Martin - DE
Joe Morris - RB
Odessa Turner
Adrian White - S
Sheldon White - DB
Perry Williams - CB

**New York Jets**

Marion Barber - RB
Troy Benson - LB
John Booty - CB
K.D. Dunn - TE
James Hasty - CB
Johnny Hector - RB
Carl Howard - CB
Bobby Humphrey - CB
Reggie McElroy - T
Erik McMillan - S
Freeman McNeil - RB
Al Toon - WR
Jo Joe Townsell - WR
Wesley Walker - WR
Terry Williams - CB

**Philadelphia Eagles**

Eric Allen - CB
Jerome Brown - DT
Keith Byars - RB

Cris Carter - WR
Byron Evans - LB
Eric Everett - CB
Jimmie Giles - TE
Michael Haddix - RB
Wes Hopkins - S
Keith Jackson - TE
Izel Jenkins - CB
Dwayne Jiles - LB
Reggie Singletary - T
Anthony Toney - RB
Andre Waters - S
Reggie White - DE
Roynell Young - CB
Shawn Beals - WR
Randall Cunningham - QB
Clyde Simmons - DE

**Phoenix Cardinals**

Anthony Bell - LB
Carl Carter - CB
Travis Curtis - S
Roy Green - WR
Don Holmes - WR
Ricky Hunley - LB
Ernie Jones - WR
Tony Jordon - RB
E.J. Junior - LB
Tony Jordan - LB
Cedric Mack - CB
Stump Mitchell - RB
Ricky Moore - RB
Todd Peat - G
Reggie Phillips CB
J.T. Smith - WR
Lonnie Young - S
Earl Ferrell - RB
Leonard Smith - S
Tim McDonald - CB

**Pittsburgh Steelers**

Rodney Carter - RB
Joe Clinkscales - WR
Everett Thomas - S
Lorenzo Freeman - NT
Preston Gothard - TE
Larry Griffin - CB
Delton Hall - CB
Earnest Jackson - RB
Aaron Jones - DE
Greg Lee - CB
Louis Lipps - WR
Charles Lockett - WR
Dwight Stone - RB
Weegie Thompson - WR
Warren Williams - RB
Rod Woodson - CB

**San Diego Chargers**

Curtis Adams - RB
Gary Anderson - RB
Roy Bennett - CB
Gill Byrd - CB
Leonard Coleman - S
Jeffrey Dale - S
Jamie Holland - WR
Lionel James - RB
Tyrone Keys - DE
Anthony Miller - WR
Elvis Patterson - CB
Lee Williams - DE

**San Francisco 49ers**

Dwaine Board - DE
Chet Brooks - CB
Wes Chandler - WR
Roger Craig - RB
Doug DuBose - RB
Don Griffin - CB
Calvin Nicholas - WR
Bubba Paris - T
Jerry Rice - WR
Keena Turner
Jeff Fuller - S
Larry Roberts - DE
Eric Wright

**Seattle Seahawks**

Tommie Agee - RB
Brian Blades - WR
Jeff Bryant - DE
Raymond Butler - WR
Ken Clarke - DT
Bobby Joe Edmonds - RB
Jacob Green - DE
Dwayne Harper - CB
Mel Jenkins - CB
M.L. Johnson - LB
Rufus Porter - LB
Alvin Powell - G
Eugen Robinson - S
Curt Warner - RB
John T. Williams - RB
Mike Wilson - T
Tony Woods - LB

**Tampa Bay Buccaneers**

Mark Carrier - WR
Sidney Coleman - LB
Reuben Davis - DT
Donnie Elder - CB
Bobby Futrell - CB
Odie Harris - CB
William Howard - RB
Roderick Jones - CB
Calvin Magee - TE
Ricky Reynolds - CB
Mark Robinson - S
Jeff Smith - RB
Gene Taylor - WR
James Wilder - RB

**Washington Redskins**

Anthony Allen - WR
Reggie Branch - RB
Kelvin Bryant - RB
Gary Clark - WR
Brian Davis - CB
Darryl Grant - DT
Darrell Green - CB
Anthony Jones - TE
Dexter Manley - DE
Wilbur Marshall - L
Art Monk - WR
Ricky Sanders - WR
Timmy Smith - RB
Johnny Thomas - DB
Clarence Vaughn - S
Alvin Walton - S
Doug Williams - QB

*The greatest offensive back in football history—Jimmy Brown.*

## RECORD SETTTERS IN FOOTBALL

### Black NFC Rushing Leaders

| Player | Year | Yards |
|---|---|---|
| Jim Brown, *Cleve.* | 1957 | 942 |
| Jim Brown, *Cleve.* | 1958 | 1527 |
| Jim Brown, *Cleve.* | 1959 | 1329 |
| Jim Brown, *Cleve.* | 1960 | 1257 |
| Jim Brown, *Cleve.* | 1961 | 1408 |
| Jim Brown, *Cleve.* | 1963 | 1863 |
| Jim Brown, *Cleve.* | 1964 | 1446 |
| Jim Brown, *Cleve.* | 1965 | 1544 |
| Gale Sayers, *Chi.* | 1966 | 1331 |
| Leroy Kelly, *Cleve.* | 1967 | 1205 |
| Leroy Kelly, *Cleve.* | 1968 | 1239 |
| Gale Sayers, *Chi.* | 1969 | 1032 |
| Larry Brown, *Wash.* | 1970 | 1125 |
| John Brockington, *G.B.* | 1971 | 1105 |
| Larry Brown, *Wash.* | 1972 | 1216 |
| John Brockington, *G.B.* | 1973 | 1144 |
| Lawrence McCutcheon, *L.A.* | 1974 | 1109 |
| Walter Payton, *Chi.* | 1976 | 1390 |
| Walter Payton, *Chi.* | 1977 | 1852 |
| Walter Payton, *Chi.* | 1978 | 1395 |
| Walter Payton, *Chi.* | 1979 | 1610 |
| Walter Payton, *Chi.* | 1980 | 1460 |
| George Rogers, *N.O.* | 1981 | 1674 |
| Tony Dorsett, *Dallas* | 1982 | 745 |
| Eric Dickerson, *L.A.* | 1983 | 1808 |
| Eric Dickerson, *L.A.* | 1984 | 2105 |
| Gerald Riggs, *Atl.* | 1985 | 1719 |
| Charles White, L.A. | 1987 | 1374 |

### Black AFC Rushing Leaders

| Player | Year | Yards |
|---|---|---|
| Cookie Gilchrist, *Buff.* | 1962 | 1096 |
| Clem Daniels, *Oak.* | 1963 | 1098 |
| Cookie Gilchrist, *Buff.* | 1964 | 981 |
| Paul Lowe, *S.D.* | 1965 | 1121 |
| Jim Nance, *Bost.* | 1966 | 1458 |
| Jim Nance, *Bost.* | 1967 | 1216 |
| Paul Robinson, *Cinn.* | 1968 | 1023 |
| Floyd Little, *Den.* | 1970 | 901 |
| Floyd Little, *Den.* | 1971 | 1133 |
| O.J. Simpson, *Buff.* | 1972 | 1251 |
| O.J. Simpson, *Buff.* *All-time NFL record* | 1973 | 2003 |
| Otis Armstrong, *Den.* | 1974 | 1407 |
| O.J. Simpson, *Buff.* | 1975 | 1817 |
| O.J. Simpson, *Buff.* | 1976 | 1503 |
| Earl Campbell, *Hous.* | 1978 | 1450 |
| Earl Campbell, *Hous.* | 1979 | 1697 |
| Earl Campbell, *Hous.* | 1980 | 1434 |
| Earl Campbell, *Hous.* | 1981 | 1376 |
| Freeman McNeil, *N.Y.* | 1982 | 786 |
| Curt Warner, *Sea.* | 1983 | 1446 |
| Earnest Jackson, *S.D.* | 1984 | 1179 |
| Marcus Allen, *L.A.* | 1985 | 1759 |
| Eric Dickerson, *Ind.* | 1987 | 1288 |

### Black NFC Scoring Leaders

| Player | Year | Points |
|---|---|---|
| Jim Brown, *Cleve.* | 1958 | 108 |
| Lenny Moore, *Balt.* | 1964 | 120 |
| Gale Sayers, *Chi.* | 1965 | 132 |
| Leroy Kelly, *Cleve.* | 1968 | 120 |
| Chuck Forman, *Minn.* | 1975 | 132 |
| Billy Sims, *Det.* | 1980 | 96 |
| Wendell Tyler, *L.A .* | 1982 | 78 |
| Mark Moseley, *Wash.* | 1983 | 161 |

### Black AFC Scoring Leaders

| Player | Year | Points |
|---|---|---|
| Gene Mingo, *Den.* | 1962 | 137 |
| O.J. Simpson, *Buff.* | 1975 | 138 |
| Earl Campbell, *Hous.* | 1980 | 78 |
| Marcus Allen, *L.A.* | 1982 | 84 |

*Timmy Brown holds the game record for most touchdowns scored from kickoff returns.*

## Black NFC Receiving Leaders

| Player | Year | Catches |
|---|---|---|
| Bobby Mitchell, *Wash.* | 1962 | 72 |
| Charley Taylor, *Wash.* | 1966 | 72 |
| Charley Taylor, *Wash.* | 1967 | 70 |
| Clifton McNeil, *S.F.* | 1968 | 71 |
| Dick Gordon, *Chi.* | 1970 | 71 |
| Harold Jackson, *Phil.* | 1972 | 62 |
| Harold Carmichael, *Phil.* | 1973 | 67 |
| Claude Young, *Phil.* | 1974 | 63 |
| Chuck Forman, *Minn.* | 1975 | 73 |
| Drew Pearson, *Dall.* | 1976 | 50 |
| Ahmad Rashad, *Minn.* | 1977 | 51 |
| Rickey Young, *Minn.* | 1978 | 88 |
| Ahmad Rashad, *Minn.* | 1979 | 80 |
| Earl Cooper, *S.F.* | 1980 | 83 |
| Roy Green, *St.L.* | 1983 | 78 |
| Charlie Brown, *Wash.* | 1983 | 78 |
| Earnest Gray, *N.Y.* | 1983 | 78 |
| Art Monk, *Wash.* | 1984 | 106 |
| Roger Craig, *S.F.* | 1985 | 92 |
| J.T. Smith, *St.L.* | 1987 | 91 |

*Washington Redskins' Doug Williams in college days.*

## Black AFC Receiving Leaders

| Player | Year | Catches |
|---|---|---|
| Lionel Taylor, *Den.* | 1962 | 77 |
| Lionel Taylor, *Den.* | 1963 | 78 |
| Lionel Taylor, *Den.* | 1965 | 85 |
| Marlin Briscoe, *Buff.* | 1970 | 57 |
| Lydell Mitchell, *Balt.* | 1974 | 72 |
| Lydell Mitchell, *Balt.* | 1975 | 60 |
| Reggie Rucker, *Balt.* | 1976 | 60 |
| MacArthur Lane, *K.C.* | 1977 | 66 |
| Lydell Mitchell, *Balt.* | 1978 | 71 |
| JoeWashington, *Balt.* | 1979 | 82 |
| Kellen Winslow, *S.D.* | 1980 | 89 |
| Kellen Winslow, *S.D.* | 1981 | 88 |
| Kellen Winslow, *S.D.* | 1982 | 54 |
| Ozzie Newsome, *Cleve.* | 1984 | 89 |
| Lionel James, *S.D.* | 1985 | 86 |
| Al Toon, *N.Y.* | 1987 | 68 |

*Tony Dorsett, who spent most of his career with the Dallas Cowboys, was traded to the Denver Broncos.*

## THE BLACK IN PROFESSIONAL BOXING

The black prize fighter has been active in America for well over two centuries. In fact, the first American heavyweight contender was a black, Tom Molineaux, a Virginia slave. Molineaux lost two championship fights against the English titleholder, Tom Crib, in 1810 and again 1811.

With the advent of the twentieth century, the black boxer came to occupy a place of ever-growing importance in American ring annals, particularly after Jack Johnson, regarded by many as the greatest fighter of all time, won the heavyweight championship of the world in 1908.

By the 1930s, blacks were challenging for supremacy in other divisions as well. Henry Armstrong had become featherweight, lightweight, and welterweight champion of the world—the first and only fighter to hold three titles at once. Joe Louis had already been world heavyweight champion for almost 10 years when Ray Robinson took the welterweight crown at the end of 1946. Robinson moved up to the middleweight championship in the 1950s, and came close to taking the light-heavyweight title from Joe Maxim, losing only after wilting in the heat at Yankee Stadium in 1952.

Throughout most of this era (in fact, for all but five years since 1937), blacks have retained the heavyweight championship of the world. Although there have been many champions in all divisions, we are listing the records of only the heavyweight titleholders, along with those of Henry Armstrong and Ray Robinson, two of the greatest black champions in other divisions.

Certainly the most prominent figure in the past two decades was Muhammad Ali (who boxed first under the name Cassius Clay). Winner of the heavyweight boxing title three times, Ali continued to challenge contenders even after his third loss, succumbing to a younger Trevor Berbick in a bout in the Bahamas in December 1981. He was then on the verge of his fortieth birthday.

After winning the Olympic gold medal in 1960, Ali turned pro and defeated reigning champ Sonny Liston. Over the next 20 years, he was at the center of attention as he lost the title after refusing to register for the draft. Of course, he then went on to win it twice more.

Even while Ali remained in the picture, a host of strong competitors came into focus. George Foreman and Joe Frazier were among those who faced Ali in the ring. Larry Holmes, 1968 Olympic gold medalist, and Leon Spinks, 1976 gold medal winner, both fought Ali during the decade.

*The first American heavyweight contender was Tom Molineaux, a Virginia slave, who fought two championship bouts against English titleholder Tom Crib, in 1810 and 1811.*

*Sugar Ray Robinson won this classic battle with Gene Fullmer by KO in round 5 (top). "The Brown Bomber," Joe Louis (right).*

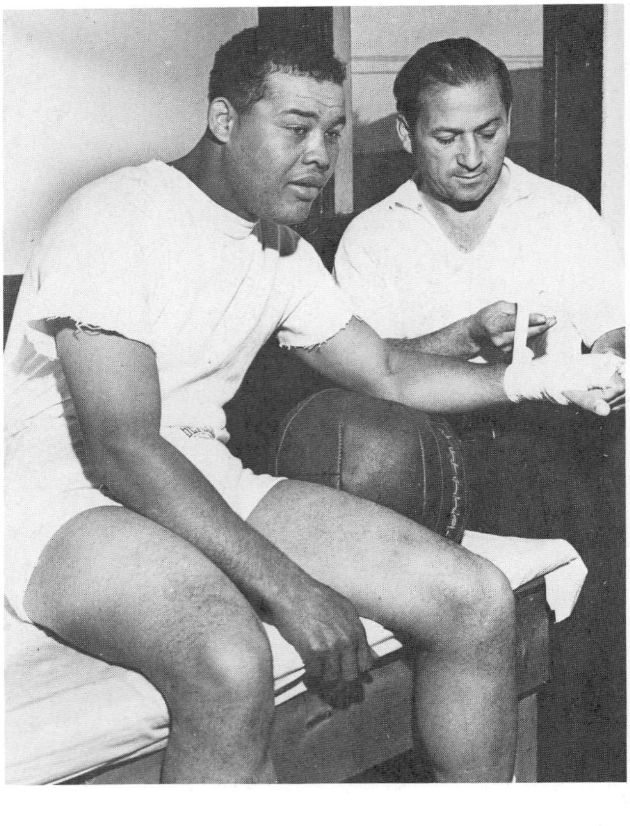

In 1981, Foreman preceded Ali in an unsuccessful comeback bid.

In another interesting turnabout, Ed "Too Tall" Jones left a successful pro football career as a defensive end with the Dallas Cowboys to try a career in boxing. Within a year he returned to the Cowboys.

Sugar Ray Leonard, a 1976 Olympic gold medal winner as a light welterweight, then turned pro, ultimately winning the title after facing Roberto Duran. Later, boxing against Thomas Hearns, the WBA champ, he was victorious in a highly publicized match which made him the undisputed champ in that weight class.

## 1980s

As the decade progressed following Ali's retirement, no boxer would dominate the fight world with his consistency. In fact, there was a fragmentation of the title as numerous governing bodies including the World Boxing Council, the World Boxing Association, the International Boxing Federation, the United States Boxing Association, the North American Boxing Federation and the European Boxing

Union all naming their own champions.

In fact, by 1988, the only title holders generally accepted were in the heavyweight (Mike Tyson) and Cruiserweight (Evander Holyfield) divisions.

Early in the decade, WBC champ Sugar Ray Leonard would knockout WBA champ Thomas Hearns in the 14th round of a spirited bout to become the undisputed welterweight champ. Hearns was the first fighter to win the title in four different weight classes.

Leonard soon announced a highly publicized retirement but would enter the ring twice more as an active fighter, surprising many observers since he had a serious eye injury. When he faced WBA champ Michael Spinks in 1987, he would achieve a controversial split decision after a tough 15-round bout.

No fighter would dominate headlines like Michael Tyson. A tough youngster from Brooklyn, who after training under one of boxing's legendary managers, channeled his awesome strength to become the youngest heavyweight champ ever in 1986, winning the title at the age of 20. When Larry Holmes decided to return from retirement in February of 1988, Tyson dominated the fight until victory in the fourth round. He then beat challenger Tyrell Bibbs with a knockout in seven rounds. Later, he would face off against Michael Spinks in Atlantic City and walk away with a $22 million purse after defeating his generally praised competitor in 91 seconds.

Before Tyson could complete plans for his next bout, however, he would become embroiled in a controversial battle with his manager Bill Cayton with promoter Don King and building magnate Donald Trump joining in the battle. Then, after a highly publicized street confrontation with former opponent Mitch Green, Tyson and his actress wife, Robin Givens would hold headlines and magazine covers for months as their ill-fated marriage ended up in a nasty divorce battle.

(The following records are reprinted here through the courtesy of Nat Fleischer and *Ring* magazine.)

## BLACK BOXING CHAMPIONS (ALL DIVISIONS)

*Current heavyweight champ, Mike Tyson.*

### Heavyweight

| Name | Years Held |
|---|---|
| Jack Johnson | 1908-1915 |
| Joe Louis | 1937-1949 |
| Ezzard Charles | 1949-1951 |
| Jersey Joe Walcott | 1951-1952 |
| Floyd Patterson | 1956-1959; 1960-1962 |
| Sonny Liston | 1962-1964 |
| Muhammad Ali (Cassius Clay) | 1964-1967; 1974-1978 |
| Joe Frazier | 1970-1973 |
| George Foreman | 1973-1974 |
| Ken Norton (WBC) | 1978 |
| Larry Holmes (WBC) | 1978 |
| John Tate (WBA) | 1979 |
| Mike Weaver (WBA) | 1980 |
| Michael Dokes (WBA) | 1982 |
| Tim Witherspoon (WBC) | 1984 |
| Pinklon Thomas (WBC) | 1984 |
| Greg Page (WBA) | 1984 |
| Tony Tubbs (WBA) | 1985 |
| Michael Spinks (IBF) | 1985 |
| Tim Witherspoon (WBA) | 1986 |
| Trevor Berbick (WBC) | 1986 |
| Mike Tyson (WBC) | 1986 |
| James (Bonecrusher) Smith (WBA) | 1986 |
| Mike Tyson (WBA) | 1987 |
| Mike Tyson (WBA) (WBC) (IBF) | 1988 |

### Light Heavyweight

| Name | Years Held |
|---|---|
| Battling Siki | 1922-1923 |
| John Henry Lewis | 1935-1939 |

| | |
|---|---|
| Archie Moore | 1952-1961 |
| Harold Johnson | 1961-1963 |
| Jose Torres | 1965-1966 |
| Dick Tiger | 1966-1968 |
| Bob Foster | 1968-1975 |
| Marvin Johnson (WBC) | 1978 |
| Matthew Saad Muhammad (WBC) | 1979 |
| Eddie Mustava Muhammad (WBA) | 1980 |
| Michael Spinks (WBA) | 1981 |
| Michael Spinks (WBA) | 1981 |
| Dwight Braxton (WBC) | 1981 |
| Michael Spinks (WBC) | 1983 |
| Marvin Johnson(WBA) | 1986 |
| Thomas Hearns WBC) | 1987 |
| Virgil Hill (WBA) | 1987 |
| Sugar Ray Leonard (WBC) | 1988 |
| Virgil Hill (WBA) | 1988 |
| Charles Williams (IBF) | 1988 |

### Middleweight

| Name | Years Held |
|---|---|
| Tiger Flowers | 1926-1931 |
| Gorilla Jones | 1931-1932 |
| Sugar Ray Robinson | 1951;1951-1952;1955-1957; 1957; 1958-1960 |
| Randy Turpin | 1951 |
| Dick Tiger | 1962-1963; 1965-1966 |
| Emile Griffith | 1966-1967 |
| Marvin Hagler | 1980 |
| Sugar Ray Leonard (WBC) | 1987 |

### Welterweight

| Name | Years Held |
|---|---|
| Joe Walcott | 1901-1904; 1904-1906 |
| Young Jack Thompson | 1931 |
| Henry Armstrong | 1938-1940 |
| Sugar Ray Robinson | 1946-1951 |
| Johnny Bratton | 1951 |
| Kid Gavilan | 1951-1954 |
| Johnny Saxton | 1954-1955; 1956 |
| Virgil Akins | 1958-1960 |
| Benny Kid Paret | 1960-1961 |
| Emile Griffith | 1963-1966 |
| Curtis Cokes | 1966-1969 |
| Jose Napoles | 1969-1970; 1971 |
| Sugar Ray Leonard (WBC) | 1981 |
| Thomas Hearns (WBA) | 1981 |
| Sugar Ray Leonard (WBA) | 1981-1982 |
| Mark Breland (WBA) | 1987 |

### Lightweight

| Name | Years Held |
|---|---|
| Joe Gans | 1901-1908 |
| Henry Armstrong | 1938-1939 |
| Beau Jack | 1942-1944 (New York) |
| Bob Montgomery | 1944-1947 (New York) |
| Ike Williams | 1945-1947 (NBA); 1947-1951 |
| Jimmy Carter | 1951-1952;1952-1954; 1954-1955 |
| Wallace Bud Smith | 1955-1956 |
| Joe Brown | 1956-1962 |
| Livingstone Bramble (WBA) | 1984 |

### Featherweight

| Name | Years Held |
|---|---|
| George Dixon | 1890-1892 |
| Kid Chocolate | 1932- 1934 (New York) |
| Henry Armstrong | 1937-1938 |
| Chalky Wright | 1941-1942 |
| Sandy Saddler | 1948-1949; 1950-1957 |
| Hogan Kid Bassey | 1957-1959 |
| Davey Moore | 1959-1963 |

### Bantamweight

| Name | Years Held |
|---|---|
| George Dixon | 1890-1892 |
| Panama Al Brown | 1929-1935 |
| George Pace | 1940 |
| Harold Dade | 1947 |
| Jimmy Carruthers | 1953-1954 |

## TITLE BOUTS OF BLACK CHAMPIONS

### Muhammad Ali

| | |
|---|---|
| February 25,1964 | |
| Sonny Liston, Miami Beach | KO 7 |
| May 25, 1965 | |
| Sonny Liston, Lewiston, Maine | KO 1 |
| November 22, 1965 | |
| Floyd Patterson, Las Vegas | KO 12 |
| March 29, 1966 | |
| George Chuvalo, Toronto | W 15 |
| May 21, 1966 | |
| Henry Cooper, London | KO 6 |
| August 6, 1966 | |
| Brian London, London | KO 3 |
| September 10, 1966 | |
| Karl Mildenberger, Frankfurt | KO 12 |
| November 14, 1966 | |
| Cleveland Williams, Houston | KO 3 |
| February 6, 1967 | |
| Ernie Terrell, Houston | W 15 |
| March 22, 1967 | |
| Zora Folley, New York | KO 7 |
| March 8, 1971 | |
| Joe Frazier, New York | L 15 |

October 29, 1974
George Foreman, Kinshasa, Zaire — KO 8
March 24, 1975
Chuck Wepner, Cleveland — KO 15
May 16, 1975
Ron Lyle, Las Vegas — KO 11
June 30, 1975
Joe Bugner,Malaysia — W 15
October 1, 1975
Joe Frazier, Manila — KO 14
February 20, 1976
Jean-Pierre Coopman, San Juan — KO 5
April 30, 1976
Jimmy Young, Landover, Md. — W 15
May 25, 1976
Richard Dunn, Munich — KO 5
September 28, 1976
Ken Norton, New York — W 15
May 16, 1977
Alfredo Evangelista, Landover, Md. — W15
September 29, 1977
Ernie Shavers, New York — W 15
February 15, 1978
Leon Spinks, Las Vegas — L 15
September 15, 1978
Leon Spinks, New Orleans — W 15
October 2, 1980
Larry Holmes, Las Vegas — KO by 11

### Henry Armstrong

*(Fought early in career as Melody Jackson. Won 58 out of 62 amateur bouts.)*

October 29, 1937
Petey Sarron, New York — KO 6
May 31, 1938
Barney Ross, Long Island City, N Y — W 15
August 17, 1938
Lou Ambers, New York — W 15
November 25, 1938
Ceferino Garcia, New York — W 15
December 5, 1938
Al Manfredo, Cleveland — KO 3
*(Won welterweight title. Relinquished featherweight)*
August 22, 1939
Lou Ambers, New York — L 15
December 11, 1939
Jimmy Garrison, Cleveland — KO 7
October 4, 1940
Fritzie Zivic, New York — L 15
January 17, 1941
Fritzie Zivic, New York — KO by 12

### Joe Brown

August 24, 1956
Wallace (Bud) Smith, New Orleans — W 15
February 13, 1957
Wallace (Bud) Smith, Miami Beach — KO 11
June 19, 1957
Orlando Zulueta, Denver — KO 15
December 4, 1957
Joe Lopes, Chicago — KO 11
May 7, 1958
Ralph Dupas, Houston — KO 8
July 23, 1958
Kenny Lane, Houston — W 15
February 11, 1959
Johnny Busso, Houston — W 15
June 3, 1959
Paolo Rosi, Washington, D.C. — KO 8
December 2, 1959
Dave Charnley, Houston — KO 5
October 28, 1960
Cisco Andrade, Los Angeles — W 15
April 18, 1961
Dave Charnley, London — W 15
October 28, 1961
Bert Somodio, Quezon City — W 15

*Muhammad Ali, possibly the best heavyweight ever, shown here with the title belt.*

April 21, 1962
Carlos Ortiz, Las Vegas — L 15

*(Brown retired in the mid-1960s.)*

### Ezzard Charles

June 22, 1949
Joe Walcott, Chicago — W 15
August 10, 1949
Gus Lesnevich, New York — KO 7
October 14, 1949
Pat Valentino, San Francisco — KO 8
August 15, 1950
Freddy Beshore, Buffalo — KO 14
September 27, 1950
Joe Louis, New York — W 15
December 5, 1950
Nick Barone, Cincinnati — KO 11
January 12, 1951
Lee Oma, New York — KO 10
March 7, 1951
Joe Walcott, Detroit — W 15
May 30, 1951
Joey Maxim, Chicago — W 15
July 18, 1951
Joe Walcott, Pittsburgh — KO by 7
June 5, 1952
Joe Walcott, Philadelphia — L 15
June 17, 1954
Rocky Marciano, New York — L 15
September 17, 1954
Rocky Marciano, New York — KO by 8

*(Charles announced his retirement from the ring on 12/1/56)*

### George Foreman

January 22, 1973
Joe Frazier, Kingston, Jamaica — KO 2
September 1, 1973
Joe (King) Roman, Tokyo, Japan — KO 1
March 26, 1974
Ken Norton, Caracas, Venezuela — KO 2
October 29, 1974
Muhammad Ali, Kinshasa, Zaire — KO by 8

### Bob Foster

March 24, 1968
Dick Tiger, New York N.Y. — KO 4
January 22, 1969
Frankie DePaula, New York N.Y. — KO 1
May 24, 1969
Andy Kendall, West Springfield, Mass. — KO 4
April 4, 1970
Roger Rouse, Missoula, Mont. — KO 4
June 27, 1970
Mark Tessman, Baltimore Md. — KO 10
November 18, 1970
Joe Frazier, Detroit — KO by 2
*(Heavyweight title fight)*
March 2, 1971
Hal (T.N.T.) Carroll, Scranton, Pa. — KO 4
April 24, 1971
Ray Anderson — W 15
October 29, 1971
Tommy Hicks, Scranton, Pa. — KO 8
December 16, 1971
Brian Kelly, Oklahoma City Ok. — KO 3
April 7, 1972
Vincente Rondon, Miami Beach Fl. — KO 2
June 27, 1972
Mike Quarry, Las Vegas Nev. — KO 4
September 26, 1972
Chris Finnegan, London — KO 14
August 21, 1973
Pierre Fourie, Albuquerque New Mexico — W 15
December 1, 1973
Pierre Fourie, Johannesburg S.A. — W 15
June 17, 1974
Jorge Ahumada, Albuquerque, N.M. — D 15

*(Foster retired as champion on 9/16/74. He had a final record of 51-6-1 and never lost to a light heavyweight, all his losses coming at the hands of heavyweights.)*

### Joe Frazier

March 4, 1968
Manuel Ramos, New York — TKO 2
December 1, 1968
Oscar Bonavena, Philadelphia — W 15
June 23,1969
Jerry Quarry, New York — TKO 7
February 16, 1970
Jimmy Ellis, New York — TKO 5
*(Wins Undisputed Official Title)*
November 18, 1970
Bob Foster, Detroit — KO 2
March 8, 1971
Muhammad Ali, New York — W 15
January 15, 1972
Terry Daniels, New Orleans — KO 4
May 25, 1972
Ron Stander, Omaha — KO 5
January 22, 1973
George Foreman, Kingston, Jamaica — KO by 2

### Emile Griffith

April 1, 1961
Benny Paret, Miami Beach — KO 13
*(Won welterweight title)*
June 3, 1961
Gaspar Ortega, Los Angeles — KO 12
September 30, 1961
Benny Paret, New York City — L 5
March 24, 1962
Benny Paret, New York City — KO 2
*(Paret died ten days later from injuries suffered in this fight)*
July 13, 1962
Ralph Dupas, Las Vegas — W 15

| | |
|---|---|
| December 8, 1962 | |
| Jorge Fernandez, Las Vegas | KO 9 |
| March 21, 1963 | |
| Luis Rodriguez, Los Angeles | L 15 |
| June 8, 1963 | |
| Luis Rodriguez, New York City | W 15 |
| September 22, 1964 | |
| Brian Curvis, London | W 15 |
| March 30, 1965 | |
| Jose Stable, New York | W 15 |
| December 10, 1965 | |
| Manuel Gonzalez, New York | W 15 |
| April 25, 1966 | |
| Dick Tiger, New York City | W 15 |
| *(Won middleweight title and had to relinquish)* | |
| July 13, 1966 | |
| Joey Archer, New York | W 15 |
| January 23, 1967 | |
| Joey Archer, New York | W 15 |
| April 17, 1967 | |
| Nino Benvenuti, New York | L 15 |
| September 29, 1967 | |
| Nino Benvenuti, New York | W 15 |
| March 4, 1968 | |
| Nino Benvenuti, New York | L 15 |
| October 18, 1969 | |
| Jose Napoles, Los Angeles | L 15 |
| *(Welterweight title fight)* | |
| September 25, 1971 | |
| Carlos Monzon, Buenos Aires | KO by 14 |
| *(Middleweight title fight)* | |
| June 2, 1973 | |
| Carlos Monzon, Monte Carlo | L 15 |
| *(Middleweight title fight)* | |

*Jimmy Ellis lies flat on his back after being knocked down by Joe Frazier in fourth round of championship match.*

## Larry Holmes

| | |
|---|---|
| June 9, 1978 | |
| Ken Norton, Los Vegas | W 15 |
| *(Won WBC Heavyweight Title)* | |
| November 10, 1978 | |
| Alfredo Evangelista, Las Vegas | KO 7 |
| *(Retained WBC Heavyweight Title)* | |
| March 23, 1979 | |
| Osvaldo Ocasio, Las Vegas | KO 7 |
| *(Retained WBC Heavyweight Title)* | |
| June 22, 1979 | |
| Mike Weaver, New York | KO 12 |
| *(Retained WBC Heavyweight Title)* | |
| September 28, 1979 | |
| Earnie Shavers, Las Vegas | KO 11 |
| *(Retained WBC Heavyweight Title)* | |
| February 3, 1980 | |
| Lorenzo Zanon, Las Vegas | KO 6 |
| *(Retained WBC Heavyweight Title)* | |
| March 31,1980 | |
| Leroy Jones, Las Vegas | KO 8 |
| *(Won Vacant World Heavyweight Title)* | |
| July 7, 1980 | |
| Scott LeDoux, Bloomington | KO 7 |
| *(Retained World Heavyweight Title)* | |
| October 2, 1980 | |
| Muhammad Ali, Las Vegas | KO 11 |
| *(Retained World Heavyweight Title)* | |
| April 11, 1981 | |
| Trevor Berbick, Las Vegas | W 15 |
| *(Retained World Heavyweight Title)* | |
| June 12, 1981 | |
| Leon Spinks, Detroit | KO 3 |
| *(Retained World Heavyweight Title)* | |
| November 6,1981 | |
| Renaldo Snipes, Pittsburgh | KO 11 |
| *(Retained World Heavyweight Title)* | |
| November 9, 1984 | |
| James Smith, Las Vegas | KO 12 |
| *(Retained WBC Heavyweight Title)* | |
| September 21, 1985 | |
| Michael Spinks, Las Vegas | L 15 |
| January 22, 1988 | |
| Mike Tyson, Atlantic City | KO 4 |

## Jack Johnson

| | |
|---|---|
| December 26, 1908 | |
| Tommy Burns, Sydney | W 14 |
| May 19, 1909 | |
| P. Jack O'Brien, Phil. Pa. | ND 6 |
| June 30, 1909 | |
| Tony Ross, Pitt. Pa. | ND 6 |
| September 9, 1909 | |
| Al Kaufman, San Francisco | ND 10 |
| October 16, 1909 | |
| Stanley Ketchel, Colma, Ca. | KO 12 |

| | |
|---|---|
| July 4, 1910 | |
| James J. Jeffries, Reno, Nevada | KO 15 |
| July 4, 1912 | |
| Jim Flynn, Las Vegas | W 9 |
| November 28, 1913 | |
| Andre Spoul, Paris | KO 2 |
| June 27, 1914 | |
| Frank Moran, Paris | W 20 |
| April 5, 1915 | |
| Jess Willard, Havana, Cuba | KO by 26 |

*(Died June 10, 1946, Raleigh, North Carolina)*

*Jack Johnson, first black heavyweight champion.*

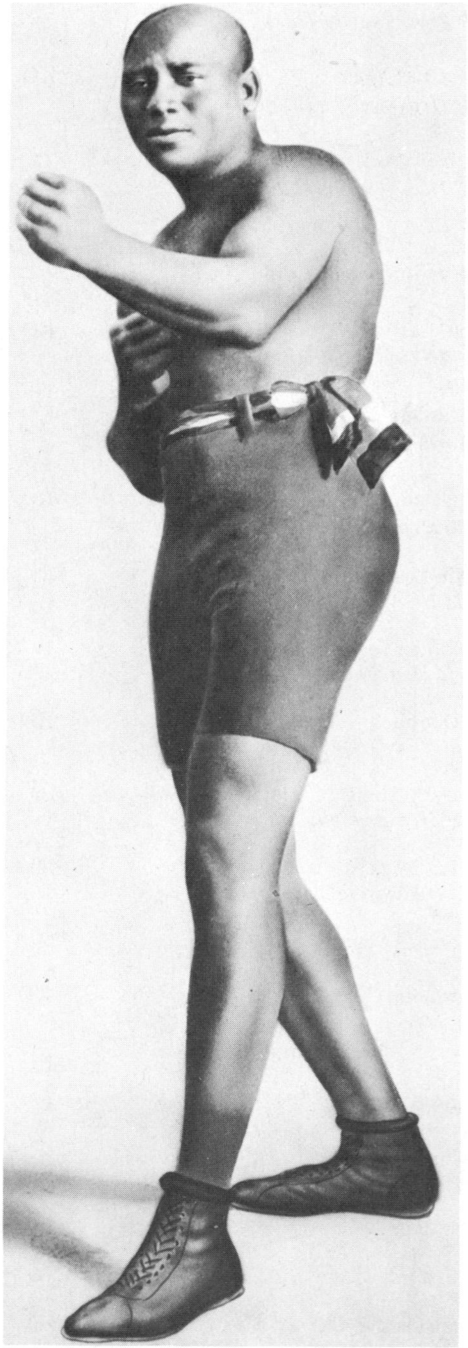

## Sonny Liston

| | |
|---|---|
| September 25, 1962 | |
| Floyd Patterson, Chicago | KO 1 |
| *(Won World Heavyweight Championship)* | |
| July 22, 1963 | |
| Floyd Patterson, Las Vegas | KO 1 |
| *(World Heavyweight Title)* | |
| February 25, 1964 | |
| Cassius Clay, Miami Beach | KO by 7 |
| May 25, 1965 | |
| Cassius Clay, Lewiston, Maine | KO by 1 |

*(Liston was found dead in his home in 1971)*

## Joe Louis

| | |
|---|---|
| June 22, 1937 | |
| James J. Braddock, Chicago | KO 8 |
| August 30, 1937 | |
| Tommy Farr, New York | W 15 |
| February 23, 1938 | |
| Nathan Mann, New York | KO 3 |
| April 1, 1938 | |
| Harry Thomas, Chicago | KO 5 |
| June 22, 1938 | |
| Max Schmeling, New York | KO 1 |
| January 25, 1939 | |
| John Henry Lewis, New York | KO 1 |
| April 17, 1939 | |
| Jack Roper, Los Angeles | KO 1 |
| June 28, 1939 | |
| Tony Galento, New York | KO 4 |
| September 20, 1939 | |
| Bob Pastor, Detroit | KO 11 |
| February 9, 1940 | |
| Arturo Godoy, New York | W 15 |
| March 29, 1940 | |
| Johnny Paychek, New York | KO 2 |
| June 20, 1940 | |
| Arturo Godoy, New York | KO 8 |
| December 16, 1940 | |
| Al McCoy, Boston | KO 6 |
| January 31, 1941 | |
| Red Burman, New York | KO 5 |
| February 17, 1941 | |
| Gus Dorazio, Phil. Pa. | KO 2 |
| March 21, 1941 | |
| Abe Simon, Detroit | KO 13 |
| April 8, 1941 | |
| Tony Musto, St. Louis | KO 9 |
| May 23, 1941 | |
| Buddy Baer, Washington, D.C. | W disq. 7 |
| June 18, 1941 | |
| Billy Conn, New York | KO 13 |
| September 29, 1941 | |
| Lou Nova, New York | KO |
| January 9, 1942 | |
| Buddy Baer, New York | KO 1 |
| *(Donated purse to Naval Relief Fund)* | |
| March 27, 1942 | |

Abe Simon, New York KO 6
*(Donated purse to Naval Relief Fund)*
June 19, 1946
Billy Conn, New York KO 8
September 18, 1946
Tami Mauriello, New York KO 1
December 5, 1946
Jersey Joe Walcott, New York W 15
June 25, 1948
Jersey Joe Walcott, New York KO 11
*(Louis announced his retirement as undefeated world heavyweight champion on March 1, 1949)*
September 27, 1950
Ezzard Charles, New York L 15
*(Final record 68-3 with 54 by KO. Elected to Boxing Hall of Fame in 1954.)*

## Jose Napoles

April 18, 1969
Curtis Cokes, Los Angeles KO 13
June 29, 1969
Curtis Cokes, Mexico City KO 10
October 18, 1969
Emile Griffith, Los Angeles W 15
February 15, 1970
Ernie Lopez, Los Angeles KO 15
December 3, 1970
Billy Backus, Syracuse KO by 4
June 4, 1971
Billy Backus, Los Angeles KO 8
December 14, 1971
Hedgemon Lewis, Los Angeles W 15
March 28, 1972
Ralph Charles, London KO 7
June 10, 1972
Adolph Pruitt, Monterrey, Mex. KO 2
February 28, 1973
Ernie Lopez, Los Angeles KO 7
June 23, 1973
Rober Menetrey, Grenoble W 15
September 22, 1973
Clyde Gray, Toronto W 5

## Floyd Patterson

November 30,1956
Archie Moore, Chicago KO 5
July 29, 1957
Tommy Jackson, New York KO 10
August 22, 1957
Pete Rademacher, Seattle KO 6
August 18, 1958
Roy Harris, LosAngeles KO 12
May 1, 1959
Brian London, Indianapolis KO 11
June 26, 1959
Ingemar Johansson, New York KO by 3
June 20, 1960
Ingemar Johansson, New York KO 5
March 13, 1961
Ingemar Johansson, Miami Beach KO 6
December 4, 1961
Tom McNeeley, Toronto KO 4

*Floyd Patterson, the first fighter to win back the world heavyweight championship.*

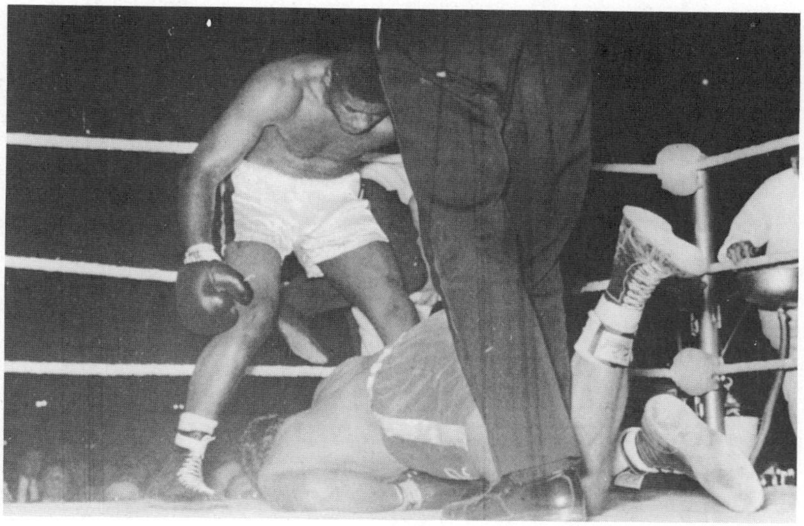

| | |
|---|---|
| September 25, 1962 | |
| Sonny Liston, Chicago | KO by 1 |
| *(Lost World Heavyweight Title)* | |
| July 22, 1963 | |
| Sonny Liston, Las Vegas | KO by 1 |
| November 22, 1965 | |
| Muhammad Ali, LasVegas | KO by 12 |
| September 14, 1968 | |
| Jimmy Ellis, Stockholm | L 15 |
| *(WBA heavyweight title fight)* | |

## Ray Robinson

*(Won Golden Gloves featherweight title in 1939 and lightweight title in 1940 in New York and in intercity competition. Engaged in 85 amateur bouts. Had 69 KOs [40 in firstround ]). Boxed as Walker Smith.)*

| | |
|---|---|
| December 20, 1946 | |
| Tommy Bell, New York | W 15 |
| *(Won Vacant World Welterweight Title)* | |
| June 24, 1947 | |
| Jimmy Doyle, Cleveland | KO 8 |
| December 19, 1947 | |
| Chuck Taylor, Detroit | KO 6 |
| June 28, 1948 | |
| Bernard Docusen, Chicago | W 15 |
| July 11, 1949 | |
| Kid Gavilan, Philadelphia | W 15 |
| June 5, 1950 | |
| Robert Villemain, Philadelphia | W 15 |
| August 9, 1950 | |
| Charley Fusari, Jersey City | W 15 |
| August 25, 1950 | |
| Jose Basora, Scranton | KO 1 |
| October 26, 1950 | |
| Carl Olson, Philadelphia | KO 12 |
| February 14, 1951 | |
| Jake La Motta, Chicago | KO 13 |
| July 10, 1951 | |
| Randy Turpin, London | L 15 |
| September 12, 1951 | |
| Randy Turpin, New York | KO 10 |
| March 13, 1952 | |
| Carl (Bobo) Olson, San Francisco | W 15 |
| April 16, 1952 | |
| Rocky Graziano, Chicago | KO 3 |
| June 25, 1952 | |
| Joey Maxim, New York | KO by 14 |
| December 9, 1955 | |
| Carl (Bobo) Olson, Chicago | KO 2 |
| May 18, 1956 | |
| Carl (Bobo) Olson, Los Angeles | KO 4 |
| January 2, 1957 | |
| Gene Fullmer, New York | L 15 |
| May 1, 1957 | |
| Gene Fullmer, Chicago | KO 5 |
| September 23, 1957 | |
| Carmen Basilio, New York | L 15 |
| March 25, 1958 | |
| Carmen Basilio, Chicago | W 15 |
| January 22, 1960 | |
| Paul Pender, Boston | L 15 |
| June 10, 1960 | |
| Paul Pender, Boston | L 15 |
| December 3, 1960 | |
| Gene Fullmer, Los Angeles | D 15 |
| March 4, 1961 | |
| Gene Fullmer, Las Vegas | L 15 |

## Michael Tyson

| | |
|---|---|
| November 22, 1986 | |
| Trevor Berbick, Las Vegas | W 2 |
| March 7, 1987 | |
| James Smith, Las Vegas | W 12 |
| May 30, 1987 | |
| Pinklon Thomas, Las Vegas | KO 6 |
| August 1, 1987 | |
| Tony Tucker, Las Vegas | W 15 |
| January 22, 1988 | |
| Larry Holmes, Atlantic City | KO 4 |
| March 20, 1988 | |
| Tony Tubbs, Tokyo, Japan | KO 2 |
| June 27, 1988 | |
| Michael Spinks, Atlantic City | KO 1 |
| February 25, 1989 | |
| Frank Bruno, Las Vegas | W 5 |

## Jersey Joe Walcott

| | |
|---|---|
| December 5, 1947 | |
| Joe Louis, New York | L 15 |
| June 25, 1948 | |
| Joe Louis, New York | KO by 11 |
| June 22, 1949 | |
| Ezzard Charles, Chicago | L 15 |
| March 7, 1951 | |
| Ezzard Charles, Detroit | L 15 |
| July 18, 1951 | |
| Ezzard Charles, Pittsburgh | KO 7 |
| June 5, 1952 | |
| Ezzard Charles, Philadelphia | W15 |
| September 23, 1952 | |
| Rocky Marciano, Philadelphia | KO by 13 |
| May 15, 1953 | |
| Rocky Marciano, Chicago | KO by 1 |

*(Walcott retired to become a parole officer and a referee)*

## Mike Weaver

| | |
|---|---|
| March 31, 1980 | |
| John Tate, Knoxville KO | 15 |
| *(Won WBA Heavyweight Title)* | |
| October 28, 1980 | |
| Gerrie Coetzee, Bophuthatswana | KO 13 |
| *(Retained WBA Heavyweight Title)* | |
| October 3, 1981 | |
| James (Quick) Tillis, Rosemont, Ill. | W 15 |

## THE BLACK IN TRACK AND FIELD

The number of black athletes with achievements in track and field is voluminous, so a number of lists containing the names of black World, and American record holders has been compiled. Biographies of outstanding black performers in track and field will be found in the last subsection of this sports section.

### World, Track and Field Records Held by American Blacks

| Event<br>Athlete | Time, Height, or Distance | Year |
|---|---|---|
| **1,600 m relay** | | |
| Otis Davis | | |
| (3 white teammates) | 3:02.2 | 1960 |
| **120 yard high hurdles** | | |
| Lee Calhoun | 13.2 | 1960 |
| **110 m high hurdles** | | |
| Lee Calhoun | 13.2 | 1960 |
| **100 yard dash** | | |
| Bob Hayes | 9.1 | 1963 |
| **1 mi relay** | | |
| Kent Bernard | | |
| Wendell Mottley | | |
| Edwin Roberts | 3:02.8 | 1966 |
| **220 yard with turn** | | |
| Tommie Smith | 20.0 | 1966 |
| **220 yard straightaway** | | |
| Tommie Smith | 19.5 | 1966 |
| **440 yard relay** | | |
| Earl McCullough | | |
| O.J. Simpson | | |
| Lennox Miller | | |
| Lee Evans | 38.6 | 1966 |
| **100 yard dash** | | |
| Charlie Greene | 9.1 | 1967 |
| Jim Hines | 9.1 | 1967 |
| **800 meter relay** | | |
| Lee Evans | | |
| Tommie Smith | | |
| Vince Matthews | | |
| Ron Freeman | 1:22.1 | 1967 |
| **120 yard high hurdles** | | |
| Earl McCullough | 13.2 | 1967 |
| **110 meter high hurdles** | | |
| Earl McCullough | 13.2 | 1967 |
| **1,600 meter relay** | | |
| Ron Freeman | | |
| Lee Evans | | |
| Vince Matthews | | |
| Larry James | 2:56.1 | 1968 |
| **400 meter relay** | | |
| Charlie Greene | | |
| Mel Pender | | |
| Ronnie Ray Smith | | |
| Jim Hines | 38.2 | 1968 |

*Bob Hayes races to victory in the 100-meter semi-finals at Tokyo; his time was 9.9.*

*Jackie Joyner-Kersee makes her javelin throw during heptathlon competition at the Seoul Olympics.*

| Event<br>Athlete | Time, Height,<br>or Distance | Year |
|---|---|---|
| **200 meters with turn** | | |
| Tommie Smith | 19.8 | 1968 |
| **400 meter dash** | | |
| Lee Evans | 43.8 | 1968 |
| **100 meter dash** | | |
| Jim Hines | 9.9 | 1968 |
| Ronnie Ray Smith | 9.9 | 1968 |
| Charlie Greene | 9.91 | 1968 |
| **Long jump** | | |
| Bob Beamon | 29' 2-1/2" | 1968 |
| **1600 meter relay** | | |
| Ron Freeman | | |
| Larry James | | |
| Lee Evans | | |
| Lennox Yearwood | 2:56.1 | 1968 |
| **200 meter dash** | | |
| Tommie Smith | 19.8 | 1968 |
| **High jump** | | |
| Bob Beamon | 7' 1-1/2" | 1968 |
| **120 yard high hurdles** | | |
| Erv Hall | 13.2 | 1969 |
| Willie Davenport | 13.2 | 1969 |
| **110 meter high hurdles** | | |
| Willie Davenport | 13.2 | 1969 |
| **100 yard dash** | | |
| John Carlos | 9.1 | 1969 |
| **440 yard run** | | |
| Curtis Mills | 44.7 | 1969 |

*Jesse Owens, who infuriated Adolf Hitler in the 1936 Olympics.*

| Event<br>Athlete | Time, Height,<br>or Distance | Year |
|---|---|---|
| **440 yard run** | | |
| Edwin Roberts | 44.5 | 1971 |
| Wendell Mottley | 44.5 | 1971 |
| John Smith | 44.5 | 1971 |
| **120 yards, 36 hurdles** | | |
| Rod Milburn | 13.0 | 1971 |
| **100 meter dash** | | |
| Eddie Hart | 9.9 | 1972 |
| **400 meter relay, 2 turns** | | |
| Larry Black | | |
| Gerald Tinker | | |
| Robert Taylor | | |
| Eddie Hart | 38.2 | 1972 |
| **Long jump** | | |
| Randy Williams | 27' 1/2" | 1972 |
| **400 meter run** | | |
| Vince Matthews | 44.7 | 1972 |
| **110 meter hurdles** | | |
| Rod Milburn | 13.2 | 1972 |
| **400 meter hurdles** | | |
| Edwin Moses | 47.13 | 1972 |
| **110 meter hurdles** | | |
| Renaldo Nehemiah | 12.93 | 1972 |
| **110 meter hurdles** | | |
| Renaldo Nehemiah | 12.93 | 1981 |
| **400 meter hurdles** | | |
| Edwin Moses | 47.02 | 1983 |
| **400 meter relay** | | |
| Graddy | | |
| Brown | | |
| Smith | | |
| Lewis | 37.83 | 1984 |
| **Triple jump** | | |
| Willie Banks | 58' 11-1/2" | 1985 |
| **1600 meter relay** | | |
| Everett | | |
| Lewis | | |
| Robinzine | | |
| Reynolds | 2: 56.16 | 1988 |
| **400 meters** | | |
| Butch Reynolds | 43.29 | 1988 |

*Evelyn Ashford, gold medalist in 4 x 400 relay, 1988 Olympics.*

## Track and Field Records Held by American Black Women

| Event<br>Athlete | Time, Height,<br>Distance | Year |
|---|---|---|
| **Running high jump** | | |
| Mildred McDaniel | 59' 9-1/2" | 1956 |
| **200 meter dash** | | |
| Wilma Rudolph | 22.9 | 1960 |
| **shot put** | | |
| Earlene Brown | 54' 9" | 1960 |
| **Discus throw** | | |
| Earlene Brown | 176' 10-1/2" | 1960 |
| **100 meter dash** | | |
| Wilma Rudolph | 11.3 | 1960 |
| **100 meter dash** | | |
| Wilma Rudolph | 11.2 | 1961 |
| **400 meter relay** | | |
| Willye White | | |
| Ernestine Pollards | | |
| Vivian Brown | | |
| Wilma Rudolph | 44.3 | 1961 |
| **80 meter low hurdles** | | |
| Rosie Bonds | 10.8 | 1964 |
| **Running broad jump** | | |
| Willye White | 246 | 1964 |
| **4 x 110 yard relay** | | |
| Mattline Render<br>(with three others) | 44.7 | 1971 |
| **4 x 440 yard relay** | | |
| Iris Davis | | |
| Cheryl Toussaint | | |
| Gale Fitzgerald<br>(with one other) | 3:38.8 | 1971 |
| **200 meter dash** | | |
| Evelyn Ashford | 21.83 | 1979 |
| **100 meter dash** | | |
| Evelyn Ashford | 10.90 | 1981 |

| Event<br>Athlete | Time, Height,<br>or Distance | Year |
|---|---|---|
| **100 meter dash** | | |
| Florence Griffith Joyner | 10.49 | 1988 |
| **200 meters** | | |
| Florence Griffith Joyner | 21.34 | 1988 |

### Track and Field Achievements of Black U.S. Olympic Team Members

| Place<br>Athlete | Year | Event | Place, time or dist. |
|---|---|---|---|
| **St. Louis,** | **1904** | | |
| George C. Poag | | 200 m hurdles | 3rd |
| George C. Poag | | 400 m hurdles | 3rd |
| **London,** | **1908** | | |
| J. B. Taylor (3 white teammates) | | 1,600 m relay | 1st—3:29.4 |
| **Paris,** | **1924** | | |
| Dehart Hubbard | | Long jump | 1st—24' 5-1/8" |
| Edward Gourdin | | Long jump | 2nd—23' 10" |
| **Los Angeles,** | **1932** | | |
| Eddie Tolan | | 100 m dash | 1st—10.3[a] |
| Ralph Metcalf | | 100 m dash | 2nd—10.3 |
| Eddie Tolan | | 200 m dash | 1st—21.2 |
| Ralph Metcalfe | | 200 m dash | 3rd—21.5 |
| Edward Gordon | | Long jump | 1st—25' 3/4" |
| **Berlin,** | **1936** | | |
| Jesse Owens | | 100 m dash | 1st—10.3[b] |
| Ralph Metcalfe | | 100 m dash | 2nd—10.4 |
| Jesse Owens | | 200 m dash | 1st—20.7[c] |
| Matthew Robinson | | 200 m dash | 2nd—21.1 |
| Archie Williams | | 400 m run | 1st—46.5 |
| James DuValle | | 400 m run | 2nd—46.8 |
| John Woodruff | | 800 m run | 1st—1:52.9 |
| Fritz Pollard Jr. | | 110 m hurdles | 3rd—14.4 |
| Cornelius Johnson | | High jump | 1st—6' 7-15/16"[c] |
| Jesse Owens | | Long jump | 1st—26' 5-5/16"[a] |
| Jesse Owens (team)<br>Ralph Metcalfe | | 400 m relay | 1st—39.8 |
| **London,** | **1948** | | |
| Harrison Dillard | | 100 m dash | 1st—10.3 |
| Norwood Ewell | | 100 m dash | 2nd—10.4 |
| Norwood Ewell | | 200 m dash | 1st—21.1 |
| Mal Whitfield | | 400 m run | 3rd—46.9 |
| Willie Steele | | Long jump | 1st—25' 8" |
| Herbert Douglass | | Long jump | 3rd—25' 3" |
| Lorenzo Wright | | Long jump | 4th—24' 9" |
| Lorenzo Wright (team)<br>Harrison Dillard<br>Norwood Ewell | | 400 m relay | 1st—40.6 |
| Mal Whitfield (team) | | 1,600 m relay | 1st—3.10.4 |
| Audrey Patterson | | 200 m dash | 3rd—25.2 |
| Alice Coachman | | High jump | 1st—5' 6-1/8" |
| **Helsinki,** | **1952** | | |
| Andrew Stanfield | | 200 m dash | 1st—20.7 |
| Ollie Matson | | 400 m run | 3rd—46.8 |
| Mal Whitfield | | 400 m run | 6th—47.8 |
| Mal Whitfield | | 800 m run | 1st—1:49.2[c] |
| Reginald Pearman | | 800 m run | 6th |
| Harrison Dillard | | 110 m hurdles | 1st—13.7[c] |
| Jerome Biffle | | Long jump | 1st—24' 10" |
| Meredith Gourdine | | Long jump | 2nd—24' 8-1/8" |
| Harrison Dillard (team)<br>Andrew Stanfield<br>Ollie Matson | | 400 m. relay | 1st—40.1 |
| Bill Miller | | Javelin | 2nd—237 |
| Milton Campbell | | Decathlon | 2nd—6,975 pts. |
| Mae Faggs | | 100 m dash | 6th |
| Barbara Jones (team) | | 400 m relay | 1st—45.9[a] |
| **Melbourne,** | **1956** | | |
| Andrew Stanfield | | 200 m dash | 2nd—20.7 |
| Charles Jenkins | | 400 m run | 1st—46.7 |
| Arnold Sowell | | 800 m run | 4th—1:48.3 |
| Lee Calhoun | | 110 m hurdles | 1st—13.5 |
| Charles Dumas | | High jump | 1st—6’11-1/4"[c] |
| Gregory Bell | | Long jump | 1st—25' 8-1/4" |
| Willye White | | Long jump | 2nd—19' 11-3/4" |
| Ira Murchison (team)<br>Leamon King | | 400 m relay | 1st—39.5[c] |
| Charles Jenkins (team)<br>Lou Jones | | 1,600 m relay | 1st—3:04.8 |
| Milton Campbell | | Decathlon | 1st—7,937 pts. |
| Rafer Johnson | | Decathlon | 2nd—7,587 pts. |
| Mildred McDaniel | | High jump | 1st—5’ 9-1/4"[a] |
| Margret Matthews (team)<br>Isabelle Daniels<br>Mae Faggs<br>Wilma Rudolph | | 400 m relay | 3rd—44.9 |
| **Rome,** | **1960** | | |
| Les Carney | | 200 m dash | 2nd—20.6 |
| Lee Calhoun | | 110 m hurdles | 1st—13.8 |
| WillieMay | | 110 m hurdles | 2nd—13.8 |
| Hayes Jones | | 110 m hurdles | 3rd—14 |
| Otis Davis | | 400 m run | 1st—44.9 |
| John Thomas | | High jump | 3rd—7' 1/4" |
| Ralph Boston | | Long jump | 1st—26' 7-3/4"[c] |
| Irv. Roberson | | Long jump | 2nd—26' 7-1/4" |
| Ira Davis | | Triple jump | 4th—53' 11" |
| Otis Davis (team) | | 1,600 m relay | 1st—3:02.2 |
| Rafer Johnson | | Decathlon | 1st—8,392pts.[c] |
| Earlene Brown | | Shot put | 3rd—53' 10-1/4" |
| Wilma Rudolph | | 100 m dash | 1st—11 |
| Wilma Rudolph | | 200 m dash | 1st—24 |
| Martha Judson (team)<br>Lucinda Williams | | | |

| Place / Athlete | Year | Event | Place, time or dist. |
|---|---|---|---|
| Barbara Jones | | | |
| Wilma Rudolph | | 400 m relay | 1st—44.5[b] |
| **Tokyo,** | **1964** | | |
| Robert Hayes | | 100 m dash | 1st—9.9[a] |
| Henry Carr | | 200 m dash | 1st—20.3 |
| Paul Drayton | | 200 m dash | 2nd—20.5 |
| Hayes Jones | | 110 m hurdles | 1st—13.6 |
| Robert Hayes (team) | | | |
| Paul Drayton | | | |
| Richard Stebbins | | 400 m relay | 1st—39.0[b] |
| John Thomas | | High jump | 2nd—7' 1-3/4" |
| John Rambo | | High jump | 3rd—7' 1" |
| Ralph Boston | | Long jump | 2nd—26' 4" |
| Ira Davis | | Triple jump | 5th—52' 1-1/4" |
| Wyomia Tyus | | 100 m dash | 1st—11.4 |
| Edith McGuire | | 100 m dash | 2nd—11.6 |
| Marilyn White | | 100 m dash | 3rd—11.6 |
| Edith McGuire | | 200 m dash | 1st—23 |
| Wyomia Tyus (team) | | | |
| Edith McGuire | | | |
| Willye White | | | |
| Marilyn White | | 400 m relay | 2nd—43.9 |
| Rosie Bonds | | 80 m hurdles | 8th—10.8 |
| Eleanor Montgomery | | High jump | 8th—5' 7-1/4" |
| Willye White | | Long jump | 12th—19' 8-1/4" |
| Earlene Brown | | Shot put | 12th—48' 6-1/4" |
| **Mexico City,** | **1968** | | |
| Jim Hines | | 100 m dash | 1st—9.9 |
| Charles Greene | | 100 m dash | 3rd—10.0 |
| Tommie Smith | | 200 m dash | 1st—19.8 |
| John Carlos | | 200 m dash | 3rd—20.0 |
| Lee Evans | | 400 m run | 1st—43.8 |
| Larry James | | 400 m run | 2nd—43.9 |
| Ron Freeman | | 400 m run | 3rd—44.4 |
| Willie Davenport | | 110 m hurdles | 1st—13.3 |
| Ervin Hall | | 110 m hurdles | 2nd—13.4 |
| Jim Hines (team) | | | |
| Charlie Greene | | | |
| Mel Pender | | | |
| Ronnie Ray Smith | | 400 m relay | 1st—38.2 |
| Wyomia Tyus (team) | | | |
| Barbara Ferrell | | | |
| Margaret Bailes | | | |
| Mildrette Netter | | 400 m relay | 1st—42.8 |
| Lee Evans (team) | | | |
| Vince Matthews | | | |
| Ron Freeman | | | |
| Larry James | | 1,600 m relay | 1st—2:56.1 |
| Edward Caruthers | | High jump | 2nd—7' 3-1/2" |
| Bob Beamon | | Long jump | 1st—29' 2-1/2" |
| Ralph Boston | | Long jump | 3rd—26' 9-1/4" |
| Wyomia Tyus | | 100 m dash | 1st—11.0 |
| Barbara Ferrell | | 100 m dash | 2nd—11.1 |
| Madeline Manning | | 800 m run | 1st—2:00.9 |
| **Munich,** | **1972** | | |
| Robert Taylor | | 100 m dash | 2nd—10.24 |
| Larry Black | | 200 m dash | 2nd—20.19 |
| Vince Matthews | | 400 m run | 1st—44.66 |
| Wayne Collett | | 400 m run | 2nd—44.8 |
| Rod Milburn | | 100 m hurdles | 1st—13.24[a] |
| Eddie Hart (team) | | | |
| Robert Taylor | | | |
| Larry Black | | | |
| Gerald Tinker | | 400 m relay | 1st—38.19 |
| Randy Williams | | Long jump | 1st—27' 1/4" |
| Arnie Robinson | | Long jump | 3rd—26' 4" |
| Jeff Bennett | | Decathlon | 3rd—7,974pts |
| Wayne Collett | | 400m dash | 2nd—44.80 |
| Cheryl Toussain (team) | | | |
| Mable Fergerson | | | |
| Madeline Manning | | 1600 m relay | 2nd—3:25.2[b] |
| **Montreal,** | **1976** | | |
| Millard Hampton | | 200 m dash | 2nd—20.29 |
| Dwayne Evans | | 200 m dash | 3rd—20.43 |
| Fred Newhouse | | 400 m run | 2nd—44.40 |
| Herman Frazier | | 400 m run | 3rd—44.95 |
| Willie Davenport | | IIO m hurdles | 3rd—13.38 |
| Edwin Moses | | 400 m hurdles | 1st—47.64 |
| Millard Hampton (team) | | | |
| Steve Riddick | | | |
| Harvey Glance | | | |
| John Jones | | 400 m relay | 1st—38.33 |
| Herman Frazier (team) | | | |
| Benny Brown | | | |
| MaxieParks | | | |
| Fred Newhouse | | 1600 m relay | 1st—2:58.7 |
| Arnie Robinson | | Long jump | 1st—27' 4-3/4" |
| Randy Williams | | Long jump | 2nd—26' 7-1/4" |
| James Butts | | Triple jump | 2nd—56 '8-1/2" |
| Rosalyn Bryant (team) | | | |
| Shelia Ingram | | | |
| Pamela Jiles | | | |
| Debra Sapenter | | 1600 m relay | 2nd—3:22.8 |
| **Moscow,** | **1980** | | |
| (U.S. does not attend, boycott by President Carter) | | | |
| **Los Angeles,** | **1984** | | |
| Carl Lewis | | 100 m dash | 1st—9.9 |
| Sam Graddy | | 100 m dash | 2nd—10.19 |
| Carl Lewis | | 200 m dash | 1st—19.80[b] |
| Kirk Baptiste | | 200 m dash | 2nd—19.96 |
| Alonzo Babers | | 400 m run | 1st—44.27 |
| Antonio McKay | | 400 m run | 3rd—44.71 |
| Earl Jones | | 800 m run | 3rd—1:43.83 |
| Roger Kingdom | | 110 m hurdles | 1st—13:20 |
| Greg Foster | | 110 m hurdles | 2nd—13:23 |
| Edwin Moses | | 400 m hurdles | 1st—47.75 |
| Danny Harris | | 400 m hurdles | 2nd—48.13 |

| **Place** **Year** Athlete | Event | Place, time or dist. |
|---|---|---|
| Sam Graddy (team) | | |
| Ron Brown | | |
| Calvin Smith | | |
| Carl Lewis | 400 m Relay | 1st—37.83[a] |
| Sunder Nix (team) | | |
| Roy Armstead | | |
| Alonzo Babers | | |
| Antonio McKay | 1600 m Relay | 1st—2:57.91 |
| Michael Carter | shot put | 1st—21.09 m |
| Carl Lewis | Long jump | 1st—8.54 m |
| Al Joyner | Triple jump | 1st—17.26m |
| Mike Conley | Triple jump | 2nd—17.18m |
| Evelyn Ashford | 100 m dash | 1st—10.97[b] |
| Alice Brown | 100 m dash | 2nd—11.13 |
| Valerie Brisco-Hooks | 200 m dash | 1st—21.81[b] |
| Florence Griffith | 200 m dash | 2nd—22.04[b] |
| Valerie Brisco-Hooks | 400 m run | 1st—48.83 |
| Chandra Cheeseborough | 400 m run | 2nd—49.05 |
| Kim Gallagher | 800 m run | 2nd—1:58.63 |
| Benita Fitzgerald-Brown | 100 m hurdles | 1st—12.84 |
| Kim Turner | 100 m hurdles | 2nd—12.88 |
| Judi Brown | 400 m hurdles | 2nd—55.20 |
| Valerie Brisco-Hooks (team) | | |
| Chandra Cheeseborough | | |
| Lillie Leatherwood | | |
| Sherri Howard | 1600 m relay | 1st—3:18.29[b] |
| Jackie Joyner | Heptathlon | 2nd—6,385pts. |
| Patrick Ewing | Men's basketball | 1st |
| Vern Fleming | | |
| Michael Jordan | | |
| Sam Perkins | | |
| Alvin Robertson | | |
| Wayman Tisdale | | |
| Leon Wood | | |
| Cathy Boswell | Women's basketball | 1st |
| Teresa Edwards | | |
| Janice Lawrence | | |
| Pamela McGee | | |
| Cheryl Miller | | |
| Lynette Woodard | | |
| **Seoul S. Korea, 1988** | | |
| Carl Lewis | 100 m dash | 1st—9.92 |
| Calvin Smith | 100 m dash | 2nd |
| Joe DeLoach | 200 m dash | 1st—19.75 |
| Carl Lewis | 200 m dash | 2nd |
| Steve Lewis | 400 m run | 1st—43.87 |
| Butch Reynolds | 400 m run | 2nd |
| Danny Everett | 400 m run | 3rd |
| Roger Kingdom | 110 m hurdles | 1st—12.98 |
| Tonie Campbell | 400 m hurdles | 3rd |
| Andre Phillips | 400 m hurdles | 1st—47.19 |
| Edwin Moses | 400 m hurdles | 3rd |
| Butch Reynolds (team) | | |
| Steve Lewis | | |
| Antonio McKay | | |
| Danny Everett | 1600 m relay | 1st—2:56.16 |
| Carl Lewis | Long jump | 1st—28' 7-1/4" |
| Mike Powell | Long jump | 2nd |
| Larry Myricks | Long jump | 3rd |
| Flo Griffith Joyner | 100 m dash | 1st—10.54 |
| Evelyn Ashford | 100 m dash | 2nd |
| Flo Griffith Joyner | 200 m dash | 1st—21.34 |
| Sheila Echols (team) | | |
| Flo Griffith Joyner | | |
| Evelyn Ashford | | |
| Alice Brown | 400 m relay | 1st—41.98 |
| Jackie Joyner-Kersee | Long jump | 1st—24' 3-1/2" |
| Jackie Joyner-Kersee | Heptathlon | 1st—7,291pts |
| Denean Howard-Hill (team) | | |
| Valerie Brisco | | |
| Diane Dixon | | |
| Flo Griffith-Joyner | 1600 m relay | 2nd |
| Kim Mitchell | 800 m run | 3rd |
| Andrew Maynard | Boxing-l heavy | 1st |
| Ray Mercer | Boxing-heavy | 1st |
| Kennedy McKinney | Boxing-bantam | 1st |
| Riddick Bowe | Boxing-super heavy | 2nd |
| Roy Jones | Boxing-middle | 2nd |
| Kenny Monday | Wrestling-freestyle | 1st |
| Nate Carr | Wrestling-freestyle | 3rd |
| Zina Garrison | Tennis-doubles | 1st |
| Zina Garrison | Tennis-singles | 3rd |
| Tom Goodwin | Baseball | 1st |
| Ty Griffin | | |
| Cindy Brown | Women's basketball | 1st |
| Vicky Bullett | | |
| Cynthia Cooper | | |
| Teresa Edwards | | |
| Jennifer Gillom | | |
| Bridgette Gordon | | |
| Katrina McCLain | | |
| Teresa Weatherspoon | | |
| Willie Anderson | Men's basketball | 3rd |
| Stacey Augmon | | |
| Vernell Coles | | |
| Jeff Grayer | | |
| Hsersey Hawkins | | |
| Danny Manning | | |
| J.R. Reid | | |
| Mitch Redmond | | |
| David Robinson | | |
| Charles D. Smith | | |
| Charles E. Smith | | |

[a] Olympic and world record.
[b] Olympic record.
[c] World record.
[d] World record, disallowed,wind.

## THE BLACK GOLFER

In the late 1960s, golfers Lee Elder and Pete Brown began to challenge Charlie Sifford as the most successful black pro playing on the PGA circuit. Sifford was the first black golfer to win admission to the Professional Golfers Association. His most successful money-winning year was 1967, when he earned $57,000, largely on the heels of a spectacular triumph in the Hartford Open. This occurred a full 10 years after he had become the first black man to capture a nation-wide tournament, the Long Beach Open in which he defeated Eric Monti in a sudden-death playoff.

Sifford slipped to $33,000 in 1968, the year Lee Elder made a rush at top prize money in the American Classic at Akron, Ohio. Playing against one of the all-time greats, Jack Nicklaus, Elder finished the course at 8 under par, for 280. A sudden death playoff, carried on nationwide television, pitted him against Nicklaus, whom he played stroke for stroke until the fifth hole, at which point Elder missed a putt and had to settle for a little over $12,000, rather than first-prize money of $25,000. Still, by year's end, Elder finished the tour with earnings of more than $31,000.

Another up-and-coming black golfer, Pete Brown, was the third leading black money winner in 1968 with some $8,300. Brown came from nowhere, three years later to capture the San Diego Open, winning $30,000 in a sudden-death playoff against Britain's Tony Jacklin.

The top woman golfer, at least judging from her numerous national titles over the past decade, is Ethel Funches, who won the 1968 championship at Lanston Golf Course in Washington, D.C. Althea Gibson, the former tennis great, tried golfing for a while, but performed indifferently, winning only $2,700 in 1968.

On April 22, 1974 Lee Elder won a sudden-death playoff against Peter Oosterhuis at the Monsanto Open in Pensacola, Florida. Elder's victory thus made him the first black to qualify for the 1975 Masters Tournament. In April 1975, Elder did play in the Masters but failed to make the second-round cut.

During the 1980s, Calvin Peete won 12 tournaments as a pro as he and a young newcomer, Jim Thorpe remained the only two blacks on the circuit. Their careers flourished some 14 years after Elder won his first PGA event as a pro.

*Charles Sifford, a top pro-golfer and the first black to be admitted to the Professional Golfers Association (PGA).*

## THE BLACK IN HORSE RACING

From the time of the first running of the Kentucky Derby in 1875 until 1911, the last year a black jockey (Jess Conley) rode in the event, black riders were featured performers in the gala pageantry which surrounded the annual Churchill Downs classic. No less than 11 black jockeys have won a total of 15 Kentucky Derbies in the history of the event. The race was every bit as glamorous and thrilling in its early days as it is now; audiences were as tense and as animated; the clubhouse, the grandstand, the lawns, the flower beds, the track itself were all meticulously and irreproachably prepared for the rush of excitement that was to grip thousands of on lookers for the race's few, but unforgettable, moments. The stable scene was dominated not only by black jockeys, but by black trainers, exercise riders, grooms, and stableboys, a whole cadre of skilled black race track people without whom the glorious and magical atmosphere of uproarious and suspenseful competition would never have developed. These were men more preoccupied with the attraction of sport than with the blandishments of money. They cherished the moment; they loved the horses; victory inspired them, even as defeat crushed them. Two great black jockeys towered over their contemporaries: Isaac Murphy (the Colored Archer) and Jimmy Winkfield.

Except for Murphy (three-time winner of the Derby) and Winkfield (twice winner of the same racing classic), few of the early black jockeys who once dominated the riding end of the sport are known to the public. One of the reasons is that jockeys were not generally identified in the programs of the

*Before the turn of the century most professional jockeys were black, several years later the black jockey had virtually disappeared.*

early days. Another is that, as the sport was transformed into a big business with staggeringly lucrative purses for owners and high annual income for jockeys, black aspirants were gradually phased into the more menial aspects of turf life, shunted aside by a base professionalism which completely undercut their long and distinguished association with the sport.

Winkfield might possibly have competed with Murphy for top honors as the leading black jockey of all time, but the wiry little Kentuckian left the United States to ride in Europe, where he won such prominent races as the Polish Derby, the Grand Prix de Baden, the Emperor's Purse, the Moscow Derby, and the Russian Derby. At the time of the Russian Revolution, he was reportedly making $100,000 a year, but was forced to flee to France in the wake of the upheaval. Winkfield continued to race on the Continent, winning several important races in France, Italy, and Spain. In 1930, after amassing a total of 2,600 winners on tracks all over the globe, Winkfield retired, built a stable near Paris, and bred a string of successful race horses until he was driven out by the Nazis in World War II. In 1953, Winkfield returned to Maisons-Lafitte, and was able to remodel his stable and remain in business.

Winkfield was not the first black man to win the derby. That feat was accomplished by Oliver Lewis, who rode his mount (Aristides) to victory in the first running of the event in 1875, during which 14 of the 15 starters in the race were ridden by black mounts.

In recent years, the best-known black jockey has been Bob McCurdy, a native of Atlantic City. McCurdy posted over 100 victories in 1963, and earned over $60,000 at his profession. He also won the jockey championship at the Garden State park meet with 27 wins. He is the first black man to ride at Tropical Park, Florida. Interviewed regarding the potential for black jockeys in the business today, McCurdy claims "the sport is wide open for Negroes now." McCurdy will succeed, says George Howell, "because he has had a good upbringing."

Still, as late as 1967, the *New York Times* wrote: "In recent years, Negro jockeys could be counted on the fingers of one hand."

**Black Winners of the Kentucky Derby (1875-1895)**

| Jockey | Mount | Year |
|---|---|---|
| Oliver Lewis | Aristides | 1875 |
| Billy Walker | Baden Baden | 1877 |
| Barrett Lewis | Fonso | 1880 |
| Babe Hurd | Apollo | 1882 |
| Isaac Murphy | Buchanan | 1884 |
| Erskine Henderson | Joe Cotton | 1885 |
| Isaac Lewis | Montrose | 1887 |
| Isaac Murphy | Riley | 1887 |
| Isaac Murphy | Kingman | 1891 |
| Alonzo Clayton | Azra | 1892 |
| James Perkins | Halma | 1895 |

## THE BLACK TENNIS PLAYER

The most outstanding black tennis stars have been Arthur Ashe and Althea Gibson. Miss Gibson, winner of both the Wimbledon and U.S. championships in 1957 and 1958, while in her early thirties, was the first black athlete to win a major tennis title. At that time, Arthur Ashe was a teenager who was playing in the semifinals of the under-15 division of the National Junior Championships, which he won in 1960 and 1961. Ashe's most successful year on the court was in 1968 when, as a member of the U.S. Davis Cup Team, he guided the United States to its first championship in five years. Ashe won every match in the Cup preliminaries, showing particularly impressive form against Premjit Lall and Ramanathan Krishnan of India. The United States thus qualified to play Australia, and Ashe, despite an ailing elbow, won the opening match against Ray Ruffels in four sets. He did not play again until the final match, by which time the U.S. had already clinched the crown. (Ashe lost the final to Bill Bowery, 2-6, 6-3, 11-9, 8-6.)

Even more impressive was Ashe's sensational showing in the U.S. Open Tournament, a competition featuring the world's best players, regardless of professional or amateur standing. Ashe, an amateur, defeated Tom Okker of Holland in a grueling five-set match, thus earning his rightful plaudits as the world's top amateur player. Ashe won other tournaments that year, including the U.S. amateur title. Ashe became a pro tennis player in the early 1970s, and became one of the top money winners on the tour. After cardiac surgery ended Ashe's playing career, he became the captain of the U.S. Davis Cup team.

There has been a long tradition of "black" tennis much the same as has existed in baseball. One black player, Jimmie McDaniel, once played U.S. Singles champion Don Budge, and was easily defeated by him, although inexperience and lack of opportunity to play in championship competition were clearly factors influencing the outcome. The first black to play in the U.S. Lawn Tennis Singles Championships, Dr. Reginald S. Weir, did not appear until 1948.

Two talented young women from Houston would be the next to make an impact on the world of professional tennis.

*Zina Garrison, one of the top players in women's tennis.*

In 1988, Zina Garrison upset #2 seeded Martina Navratilova in the U.S. Open quarterfinals. The first black to rank in the top 10 since women's pro tennis tour began in 1971, Garrison had earned more than $1.5 million in prize money. Ranked #8 in the world, she went on to win a gold medal in the Seoul Summer Olympics with her doubles partner, Pam Shriver.

Garrison, 24, was named International Tennis Federation's Junior of the Year after winning the 1981 Wimbledon and U.S. Open junior titles. After turning pro, she was ranked in the top 12 for the next five years.

Lori McNeil, ranked #11 in the world, was the first black women's singles semi-finalist in the 1987 U. S. Open, after having played on the pro circuit for four years.

*Arthur Ashe lofts the Wimbledon Cup after decisively winning the men's singles final in the English classic.*

## THE BLACK IN WRESTLING

Relatively few blacks have claimed world championships in professional wrestling, but this sport is not without its black participants. Jack Claybourne, one of the earlier successful black pro wrestlers, did lay claim to the black world's heavyweight title by pinning Rufus Jones in 1943. Seven years later, Don Blackman was reported to be the only black to hold a world's wrestling title, that of light-heavyweight champion. Woody Strode, the football star turned Hollywood actor, was also active for a time as a wrestler, as were Bobo Brazil, Shag Thomas, Frank James, and "Black Panther" Mitchell. Black women also perform in this sport from time to time.

## MISCELLANEOUS SPORTS

Other competitive sports which deserve some mention include swimming and bowling, although blacks have not achieved prominence in either of these.

A National Negro Bowling Association was established in Detroit in 1939, two years before the first black bowling alley was opened in Cleveland. By the early 1960s, J. Wilbert Sims had won for himself a solid reputation as a topflight black bowler, but his performance could not be matched by too many other black bowlers. Clearly "separate competition" has contributed in part to the black's "separate development" in this sport.

Swimming exhibits a similar pattern, inasmuch as it had been difficult for blacks to find suitable recreational facilities in which to develop their skills. Lack of good coaching, the difficulty in finding standard-sized pools nearby, and the consequent inability to develop a systematic method of training are all related factors which must be taken into account in any attempted evaluation of the black's performance in swimming.

Hockey is another sport in which blacks have not yet come to the fore. At the present time, there is only one black in pro-hockey, despite the fact that some blacks have managed to play minor league hockey. Again, access to the facilities, as well as cost of the equipment, must be cited as contributory factors for the lack of participation.

Only one black, Cicero Murphy, has ever competed for the world's billiards championship. Murphy defeated his first rival in the 1965 playoffs by a 150-32 count, and lost to his second opponent, 150-105. Murphy seems destined to win permanent rating among the world's best in this sport.

Blacks are notably absent in any large numbers from a host of other sports which are conventionally associated with higher-income groups, including boating, big-game hunting, fishing, and even camping.

*Cicero Murphy, ranking competitor for the world billiard championship.*

# OUTSTANDING BLACK ATHLETES

## HANK AARON
### Baseball

Hank Aaron hit more home runs than anyone else in the history of major league baseball. He attained this plateau with his second home run of the 1974 season, a shot which marked his 715th career round-tripper and thus broke the previous record of 714 which had been held by the immortal Babe Ruth. At the advanced age of 40, Aaron finished that season with 20 homers and brought his career mark to a total of 733, a record to which he added 22 more to complete his career with a total of 755.

Born in Mobile, Alabama on February 5, 1934, Aaron played sandlot ball as a teenager. He then played for a team called the Black Bears, but soon thereafter, signed a $200-per-month contract with the Indianapolis Clowns of the Negro American League. He began as a shortstop and went 10-for-11 in a doubleheader on his first day.

He was purchased by the Boston Braves in June of 1952, and proceeded to hit .336 at Eau Claire of the Northern League. The following season, playing for Jacksonville, his .362 average led the South Atlantic League. This led to a promotion to the Braves, then based in Milwaukee, and the beginning of his brilliant major league career in 1954.

In his second big league season, he hit .314, socked 27 homers, and drove in 106 runs, numbers which were to become routine for Aaron in the years ahead.

He enjoyed perhaps his finest season in 1957, when he was named Most Valuable Player and led his team to a world championship. His stats that year included a .322 average, 44 homers, 132 runs batted in, and 118 runs scored.

Over his career, Aaron has won a pair of batting titles and hit over .300 in 12 seasons. He won the home run and RBI crowns 4 times apiece, hit 40 or more homers 8 times, and hit at least 20 for 20 consecutive years, a National League record. In addition, he was named to 20 consecutive all-star teams.

In November 1974, after playing for Atlanta since 1966, Aaron was traded to the present Milwaukee franchise (now the Brewers), enabling him to finish his career in the city where he began and which became a home town to him.

In January 1982, Aaron received 406 of 415 votes from the Baseball Writers Association as he was elected into the Baseball Hall of Fame. While some observers complained that his election should have been unanimous, it was still an overwhelming tribute to a man who held some 13 major league records in an outstanding career.

## KAREEM ABDUL-JABBAR
### Basketball

A dominant force in professional basketball, Kareem Abdul-Jabbar was named the Most Valuable Player of the NBA for six seasons. An outstanding player with the Los Angeles Lakers during many of their most memorable seasons, Jabbar, born Ferdinand Lewis Alcindor, Jr., at 7' 1/2" tall, was easily the most sought after high school basketball player during the 1960s, particularly after he established a New York City record of 2,067 points and 2,002 rebounds in leading Power Memorial High School to three straight schoolboy championships. Power won 95 and lost only six during Lew Alcindor's years with the team; 71 of these victories were consecutive.

Taller than Wilt Chamberlain at the time of his entrance to UCLA, Jabbar combined great height with catlike moves and a deft shooting touch to lead UCLA to three consecutive NCAA Championships. Twice, as a sophomore and a senior, he was chosen the top collegiate player in the country. He finished his career at UCLA as the ninth all-time collegiate scorer, accumulating 2,325 points in 88 games for an average of 26.4 points per game. After leading UCLA to its third consecutive NCAA title, Jabbar signed a contract with the Milwaukee Bucks of the NBA calling for $1.4 million.

*Hank Aaron—he broke Babe Ruth's lifetime home run record.*

In his rookie season, 1969-1970, he wasted little time showing any doubters that he was worth every penny of it by leading the Bucks, a recently established expansion club, to a second place finish in the Eastern Division, only a few games behind the division winners—the New York Knickerbockers. Jabbar won personal acclaim for his outstanding play in the 1970 NBA All-Star game, combining with the Knicks' Willis Reed to lead the East to victory. After being voted Rookie of the Year, he went on to win the scoring championships in 1971 and 1972. He was one of the keys to the Bucks' world championship in 1971. In 1973, he finished second in scoring with a 30.2 point average, but he had become dissatisfied with life in Milwaukee. At the end of the 1974-1975 season he was traded to the L.A. Lakers.

A serious person both on and off the court, Abdul-Jabbar is a convert to the Hanafi Muslims. Greatly influenced by the life and struggles of Malcolm X, he believes that the Islamic religion (as distinct from the nationalistic Black Muslims) and determined effort have much to offer for a good life.

Abdul-Jabbar announced that he would retire after the 1988-89 season, one year after the Lakers had won back-to-back World Championships.

*Kareem Abdul-Jabbar, the NBA's all-time leading scorer.*

## MUHAMMAD ALI
### Boxer

Heavyweight champ for the second time, Muhammad Ali (born Cassius Clay) is recognized as one of the great figures in ring history.

Born in Louisville, Kentucky, he started boxing because he thought it was "the quickest way for black people to make it." After winning the 1960 Olympic gold medal as light-heavyweight, he turned pro. He also turned Black Muslim, although the sect strongly disapproves of boxing, and changed his name in 1963.

In February 1964, Ali won the world heavyweight championship by KO'ing Sonny Liston. Nine successful title defenses followed before Ali's famous war with the Army began. Refusing to serve in the Armed Forces (1967), Ali maintained that it was contrary to Muslim tenets. He also remarked: "I ain't got nothing against them Viet Congs." Stripped of his title and banned from boxing in the United States, Ali faced prison, but he refused to back down and was finally vindicated by the Supreme Court in 1970. Coming back to the ring after a 3 1/2 year layoff, he worked his way up for another title shot. Biggest matches along the way were Superfights I and II against Joe Frazier in which Ali suffered his first loss, and, in a return match, evened the score.

Few fans gave Ali a chance against Champ George Foreman when they met in Zaire on October 30, 1974. A 4-1 underdog at ring time, Ali amazed the boxing world by using his brains and speed to exhaust and then KO his stronger, six-years-younger opponent. After regaining the crown, Ali KO'd Chuck Wepner and Ron Lyle, and decisioned Joe Bugner. His earnings for 1975, as of July, were over $6,000,000.

In December of 1981, Muhammad Ali entered the ring in a bout against Canadian heavyweight Trevor Berbick. It was a rare occasion where not many besides those at the Bahamas site paid much attention as Ali lost in a decision—his second defeat (the previous being at the hands of Larry Holmes) in two years. It was an inauspicious end to a career for a fighter who had won the heavyweight title three times.

Ali, fast approaching his 40th birthday, had resisted suggestions that he not venture into the ring against younger and stronger fighters. Still, after 20 years, it was obviously difficult for the man who had been called champ and so dominated the sport that he had become one of the great figures in ring history. A popular talk show guest and even star of a movie about his life, *The Greatest,* Ali was named Athlete of the Decade for the 1970s by the Associated Press.

As he gets older Ali's personal dedication to helping black people everywhere becomes increasingly more generous, and he now places special emphasis on setting a good example for black youth.

## HENRY ARMSTRONG
### Boxer

The only fighter ever to hold three titles at the same time is Henry Armstrong, who accomplished this feat on August 17, 1938, when he added the lightweight championship to the featherweight and welterweight titles which he had won earlier.

Armstrong was born on December 12, 1912 in St. Louis, and orphaned five years later. One of 13 children, he managed not only to get through eight grades, but to graduate from Vashon High School as well.

In 1929, while fighting under the name of Melody Jackson, he was knocked out in his professional debut in Pittsburgh.

Within two weeks, however, he had won his first fight, and for the next eight years he learned his trade from coast to coast, fighting all comers until he was finally given a shot at the featherweight title on October 20, 1937. Armstrong defeated Petey Sarron, knocking out a champion who had never before been off his feet.

Less than a year later, on May 31, 1938, Armstrong picked up his second title with a decision over welterweight champion Barney Ross. Within three months he copyrighted his own triple crown, winning a decision over lightweight champion Lou Ambers.

Inducted into the Black Athletes Hall of Fame in 1975, Armstrong is now a minister living in Norwood, Missouri.

## ARTHUR ASHE
### Tennis

Arthur Ashe was named captain of the U.S. Davis Cup team in 1981. Inactive as a competition player after suffering a heart attack in 1979, Ashe had been not only the world's leading black professional tennis star for nearly a decade but on the professional circuit as well. In a sport traditionally closed to blacks because of its private-club setting and the financial cost involved, Ashe rose to be the No. 1 amateur tennis player in America in the late 1960s before turning pro. Twice ranked as the number one player in the world, Ashe was winner at various times of Wimbledon, the Australian Open, the U.S. Open, the U.S. Clay Court Championships, and the World Championship Tennis Tournament.

Ashe was a former president and active member of the board of directors of the Association of Tennis Professionals, and a co-founder of the National Junior Tennis League. Late in his career, he also served as a television sports commentator.

Born in 1943 in Richmond, Virginia, Ashe learned the game at the Richmond Racket Club, which had been formed by local black enthusiasts. Dr. R. W. Johnson, who had also served as an advisor and benefactor to Althea Gibson, sponsored Ashe's tennis career, spending thousands of dollars and a great deal of time with him.

By 1958, Ashe reached the semifinals in the under-15 division of the National Junior Championships. In 1960 and 1961, he won the Junior Indoors Singles title. Even before he finished high school, he was ranked 28th in the country.

In 1961, Ashe entered UCLA on a tennis scholarship. Since then, on the way to winning the U.S. Amateur Tennis Championship and the U.S. Open Tennis Championship, in addition to becoming the first black man ever named to a Davis Cup Team, Ashe beat most of the world's top players. Tennis great Pancho Gonzales, known as having one of the fastest serves in tennis said, "He has the fastest service since mine."

In 1975, Ashe had to be recognized as one of the world's great tennis players having defeated Jimmy Connors at Wimbledon as well as taking the World Championship Tennis (WCT) singles title over Bjorn Borg. At Wimbledon he defeated Connors 6-1, 6-1, 5-7, 6-4.

After quadruple bypass heart surgery in 1980, Ashe retired from active tennis activity. He began writing a nationally syndicated column and contributed monthly articles to Tennis magazine. He is the author of a tennis diary, "Portrait in Motion" and his autobiography, "Off the Court." In addition, he compiled the historical work, *A Hard Road to Glory: A History of the African-American Athlete*.

Ashe is also the author of the book *Advantage Ashe* .

## ELGIN BAYLOR
### Basketball

The owner of a National Basketball Association team once made a serious offer to trade his entire team for Elgin Baylor of the Lakers, and was quickly turned down! The Laker star is rated among the top three or four players who ever played basketball, his proneness to injury not withstanding.

Born in 1936 in Washington, D.C., Baylor first became an all-American while attending Spingarn High School. He and R. C. Owens (later a professional football star) then joined forces to lead the College of Idaho to a 23-4 record. When Baylor transferred to Seattle University, he became an all-American as the team won 45 out of 54 games over the next two years, losing to Kentucky in the 1958 NCAA finals.

In 1959 Baylor made a sensational professional debut. He was the first rookie to be named Most Valuable Player in the All Star Game. That same year, he was named to the All-League team, and set a scoring record of 64 points in a single game. After five years as a superstar, Baylor ripped off part of his kneecap during a 1965 playoff game against the Bullets. Constant work brought him back to competitive

*Elgin Baylor, considered one of basketball's all-time great pros.*

form, but he never reached his former greatness. His career point total of 23,149 is fourth highest in NBA history, and his field goal average of 27.4 is second. His best year was 1961-1962, when he averaged 38.2 points a game. When he retired in 1968, Baylor had made the All-Pro first team nine times and had played eight consecutive All-Star games.

Inducted into the Black Athletes Hall of Fame in 1975, Baylor is now assistant coach of the Utah Jazz.

## LOU BROCK
### Baseball

Lou Brock, who led the National League in bats, runs score and bases stolen in 1967 was the only black to be inducted into the Hall of Fame whose career began in the 1960s. In 1968, he led the league in doubles, tripes and stolen bases.

In 1974, he stole 118 bases, passing the record set by Maury Wills. Brock is first on the all-time list with stolen bases, breaking the record on August 29, 1977. He was also first in total World Series stolen bases with 14.

A native of Eldorado, Arkansas, Brock was a left-handed and a power hitter. He played for 19 years and his career included appearances in three World Series.

## JIM BROWN
### Football

A Football Hall of Fame honoree, Jim Brown is still acknowledged by some observers to be the greatest offensive back in the history of football. In many circles, he is viewed as the best all-around athlete since the legendary Jim Thorpe.

Brown was born February 17,1936 on St. Simon Island, Georgia, and moved to Manhasset, Long Island at the age of seven. At Manhasset High School he became an outstanding competitor in baseball, football, track and field, basketball, and lacrosse. At graduation, he had a choice of 42 college scholarships, as well as professional offers from both the New York Yankees and the Boston Braves.

Brown chose Syracuse University, where his athletic prowess gained him national recognition. An All-American performer in both football and lacrosse, he turned down the opportunity to compete in the decathlon at the 1956 Olympics because it would have conflicted with his football schedule. When he graduated from Syracuse in 1957, he spurned a three-year $150,000 offer to become a professional fighter.

Brown's 1957 entry into professional football with the Cleveland Browns was emblematic of the manner in which he would dominate the game in the decade to come. He led the league in rushing; paced Cleveland to a division championship; and was unanimously named Rookie of the Year.

Thereafter, Brown broke rushing and scoring records in both single season and lifetime totals, and he was All-League fullback virtually every season. His records include most yards gained, lifetime 12,312, and most touchdowns, lifetime 106. He was voted Football Back of the Decade for 1950-1960.

Brown announced his retirement in the summer of 1966, deciding to devote his time to a budding movie career, and to the improvement of black business. He has made several films, including *Rio Conchos, The Dirty Dozen, Ice Station Zebra, Year of the Cricket, The Split, The Riot,* and *100 Rifles*. In addition to his movie-making activities, he is president and founder of the Negro Industrial and Economic Union, an organization that arranges financing for black businessmen and provides business expertise.

## ROY CAMPANELLA
### Baseball

The only black baseball star to be named Most Valuable Player for three separate years is Roy Campanella, who won this coveted title in 1951, 1953, and 1955. He is also a member of the Baseball Hall of Fame.

Campanella, the fourth black to establish himself in the modern major leagues, was born in Philadelphia in 1921, and began playing semi-pro baseball 15 years later with the Bacharach Giants. In time, he became part of the hectic life of black professional baseball, touring the states in buses with the Baltimore Elites during the summer, and playing Latin American ball in winter.

In 1945, Campanella turned down the opportunity to become the first black in the major leagues when he mistakenly understood Branch Rickey's offer to be a contract with a rumored black team in Brooklyn. A few days later, he learned from Jackie Robinson that the offer had involved the possibility of playing with the Brooklyn Dodgers of the National League.

In 1946, Campanella was signed by the Dodgers, and along with pitcher Don Newcombe, assigned to their Nashua, New Hampshire team. Two years later, Branch Rickey delayed Campanella's debut with the Dodgers by deciding instead to break the color barrier of the American Association, specifically at St. Paul.

Before the year was out, however, Campanella was brought up to Brooklyn. Over the next eight years, the Dodger star played with five National League pennant winners, and one world championship team. He played on seven consecutive National League All-Star teams (1949-1955).

In January of 1958, Campanella's career as a player was ended by an automobile accident which left him paralyzed, and confined to a wheel chair. Today, he remains active in the game as a sports commentator.

In March 1975, he was inducted into the Black Athletes Hall of Fame in Las Vegas, Nevada.

## WILT CHAMBERLAIN
### Basketball

Elected to the Basketball Hall of Fame in 1979, Wilt Chamberlain is ranked as the greatest offensive player in the history of the sport. He led the NBA in scoring from 1959 to 1967, and held the single game record of 100 points, a feat he achieved twice.

Chamberlain was born in Philadelphia on August 21, 1936. By the time he entered high school, he was already 6'11", two inches short of his present height.

Unlike most men this tall, Chamberlain is strong, agile,

and fast. He has run a 47-second quarter-mile, put a 16-pound shot 55 feet, and high-jumped 6 feet 10 inches. When he graduated from high school, he had his choice of 77 major colleges, and 125 smaller ones. He chose Kansas University, but left after his junior year with two years of All-American honors behind him. He then played with the Harlem Globetrotters before joining the Philadelphia Warriors of the NBA in 1959.

Although dominating the sport with the Philadelphia 76ers (1959-1967), and with the Los Angeles Lakers (1968-1972), Chamberlain was a member of only two championship teams, Philadelphia (1961) and Los Angeles (1972). For his gargantuan effort in defeating the Knicks in the latter series, including playing the final game with both hands painfully injured, he was voted MVP. At the start of the 1974 season, he jumped the Lakers to become player-coach of the San Diego Conquistadors (ABA) for a reported $500,000 contract.

Wilt Chamberlain holds most major basketball records, such as: for single games, most points (100); most field goals made (36); most free throws (28); most rebounds (55). His career records are: most rebounds (23,924); highest scoring average (30.1); most points (31,419); most field goals made (12,681); most free throws attempted (11,862).

## ROBERTO CLEMENTE
## Baseball

Roberto Clemente was one of the greatest major league baseball players of all time. A devout student of physical condition, he excelled in every facet of the game, and following 18 big league seasons, seemed capable of playing forever. On December 31, 1972, however, while heading a relief mission for earthquake victims in Nicaragua, his plane crashed shortly after takeoff from San Juan, Puerto Rico, ending his life and career at the age of 38. A fund to continue the relief effort was established in his name.

Born in Carolina, Puerto Rico on August 18, 1934, Clemente was signed by the Brooklyn Dodgers and shipped to their Montreal farm club in 1954. He was drafted by the Pittsburgh Pirates in the off-season and quickly established himself as a major leaguer the following year.

He hit .311 in 1956, but didn't come into his own until the 1960s. His batting averages speak for themselves: .351 in '61, .339 in '64, .329 in '65, .317 in '66, .357 in '67, .345 in '69, .352 in '70, .341 in '71, and .312 in '72.

Clemente also proved himself as an outstanding World Series performer, hitting a combined .362 for the 1960 and 1971 fall classics. His .414 against the Baltimore Orioles in '71 deserves more than honorable mention, especially remembering that he was 37 at the time.

Overall, he won 4 batting titles and was named to 12 All-Star teams. In addition, he earned the league's Most Valuable Player Award in 1966. He achieved his 3,000th base hit, coincidentally, with the final hit of his career.

In the spring of 1973, Clemente was voted into the Hall of Fame in a special election by the Baseball Writers Association of America. His lifetime batting average was .317. In 1975, he was posthumously inducted into the Black Athletes Hall of Fame.

## ERIC DICKERSON
## Football

After a stellar season with Southern Methodist University, Dickerson was drafted by the Los Angeles Rams and set a rushing record as a rookie with 1,808 yards. One year later, in 1984, he broke O.J. Simpson's single season rushing record, running for 2,007 yards. A power runner, Dickerson was able to set the new record after the 15th game in the season.

He would later move on to the Indianapolis Colts, where again he became one of the regular outstanding players on their offensive team.

## LEE ELDER
## Golf

Lee Elder became the first black to play in the coveted Masters Golf Tournament in Augusta, Georgia in 1975. Although he missed the cut that time, he knew he'd be back. Born in Washington, D.C. in 1935, Elder picked up golf as a 15-year-old caddie in Dallas. After his father's death during World War II, Elder moved his mother to Los Angeles, where he met and traveled with the famed black golfer Ted Rhodes. While learning from Rhodes he was drafted by the Army where he was allowed to sharpen his skills as captain of the golf team at Fort Lewis, Washington. In 1960, after his discharge, he taught at the Langston Golf Course. In 1962, he debuted as a pro, winning the United Golf Association (a black organization) National Title. He debuted in the PGA in November 1967 in the Cajun Classic of New Orleans, finishing one stroke out of the money. Prior to his participation on the PGA tour Elder had done 17 years on the Negro tour (participating in close to 50 tournaments). In 30 tournaments as a PGA rookie (1968), Elder earned $38,000 (40th on PGA list of money-winners). Elder was the first black pro to reach $1 million in earnings.

## JULIUS ("DR. J") ERVING
## Basketball

One of the most exciting players in professional basketball, Julius Erving invariably brings crowds to their feet with such moves as leaping from the foul line to slam dunk the ball. An outstanding player with the Philadelphia 76ers, after several seasons with the New York Nets, Erving was scoring champ and Most Valuable Player of the ABA three times. Between his combined seasons with the two teams, he became the thirteenth player to score 20,000 points.

Born in Hempstead, Long Island, on February 22, 1950, Erving was raised by his mother, who worked as a domestic after his father deserted the family. Throughout a childhood in low-income housing he was always confident he could do something with his life if he stuck to his goals. "I saw that basketball could be my way out and I worked hard to make sure that it was."

As a player at Roosevelt High School, Erving made the All-County and All-Long Island teams while keeping a scholastic average in the 80s. At graduation he chose the

University of Massachusetts from many athletic scholarships. Dropping out after junior year, he hired the services of a management firm and signed a $500,000 contract for four years with the Virginia Squires of the ABA. Voted Rookie of the Year in 1972, he renegotiated his contract and eventually landed with the Nets for $2.8 million for four years.

In his first season with the Nets (1973), he led the league in scoring for the second consecutive year and paced his team to the ABA championship. Although bothered by tendonitis in 1974, he had another great year, but the Nets were eliminated in the early rounds of the playoffs. After being traded to the 76ers, Erving became a favorite with Philadelphia fans. He led the 76ers to the NBA championship finals in 1982.

*Julius Erving sails to the hoop for a fourth quarter basket.*

*Sand flies as Lee Elder blasts out of a trap on his way to winning the Monsanto Open.*

## ALTHEA GIBSON
### Tennis

Black participation in the world of tennis is so rare that Althea Gibson's rise to the top is truly one of America's more remarkable success stories. In a sport which is traditionally developed on the more affluent private club circuit, she became the most accomplished female player in the world after learning to play paddle tennis on a play street in Harlem.

Born in Silver, South Carolina on August 25, 1927, Miss Gibson was raised in Harlem. After her paddle tennis days, she entered and won the Department of Parks Manhattan Girls' Tennis Championship. In 1942, she began to receive professional coaching at the interracial Cosmopolitan Tennis Club, and a year later, won the New York State Negro Girls Singles Title. In 1945 and 1946, she won the National Negro Girls Singles championship, and in 1948, began a decade of domination of the same title in the Women's Division.

A year later Miss Gibson entered Florida A & M, where she played tennis and basketball for the next four years. In 1950, she was runner-up for the National Indoor Championship, and that same year became the first black to play at Forest Hills.

The following year she became the first black to play at Wimbledon. In 1957 she won the Wimbledon singles crown, and teamed with Darlene Hard to win the doubles championship as well. When she returned to New York, she was greeted by a ticker-tape parade in recognition of her position as the best woman tennis player in the world.

Since then, Miss Gibson has engaged in public relations work with a bakery firm.

## BOB GIBSON
### Baseball

Bob Gibson has won more games than anyone else in the history of the St. Louis Cardinals. Despite numerous injuries and ailments throughout his career, he has proven himself as one of the game's top performers.

Born in Omaha, Nebraska on November 9, 1935, Gibson began as a basketball player with the Harlem Globetrotters. He soon turned to baseball, however, and after attending Creighton, signed with the Cardinals in 1957. Following an apprenticeship in the minor leagues, he spent his first full season with the big club in 1961.

He went on to lead his team to pennants in 1964 and 1967, and was instrumental in both World Series victories.

His best year, however, was 1968. He was named Most Valuable Player, led the Cardinals to another pennant, and earned the Cy Young Award, posting a 22-9 record and an incredible 1.12 earned run average, a mark which stands as the lowest for a performance of no less than 200 innings. He also struck out a record 17 batters in a World Series game.

Gibson's other career achievements include a 21-win season and a pair of 19-win performances, a major league record of 8 years with 200 or more strikeouts, a record 7 consecutive World Series victories, a no-hitter (8/14/71), a second Cy Young Award, over 2,900 strikeouts, 55 shutouts, a 4-strikeout inning, and 8 All-Star appearances. At the end of 1973, he had boosted his won-lost record to 237-151, for a lifetime percentage of .611.

He also boasts a hitting prowess which includes 22 career home runs, an impressive statistic for a pitcher, and is the only hurler with two World Series homers to his credit.

## HARLEM GLOBETROTTERS
### Basketball

The most widely known black team in the world is the Harlem Globetrotters, whose comic brand of basketball has captivated audiences around the globe.

The original Globetrotters, formed in the 1927-1928 basketball season by Abe Saperstein, traveled to local engagements by automobile. The present-day Globetrotters are really three separate troupes playing simultaneously in different parts of the world under the name "Harlem Globetrotters."

The Globetrotters have become more an entertainment package than an athletic team, playing against familiar opponents who travel with them and follow the script. But the athletic ability of the group has always been there when needed. Such stars as Sweetwater Clifton and Wilt Chamberlain went from the Globetrotters to stardom in the

*The Harlem Globetrotters have astounded fans the world over with their amazing feats of basketball wizardry.*

National Basketball Association. Other stars have included Reece "Goose" Tatum, and dribbling sensation Marcus Haynes. The current lead clown is Meadowlark Lemon.

The Globetrotters played before the largest audience to see a basketball game when 75,000 fans jammed into Berlin's Olympic Stadium.

## MARVIN HAGLER
### Boxer

"Marvelous" Marvin Hagler, the clean-shaven, left-handed middleweight is known as an aggressive and determined fighter. A native of Newark, New Jersey, he won the 1973 National AAU middleweight championship. He moved to Brockton, Massachusetts and soon won the World title, defeating Alan Minter in a September 27, 1980 bout.

A prolific fighter, Hagler had fought some 64 fights by the end of 1984, and had never been knocked out. During that time, he had defended his title on 10 occasions. One of his most memorable fights came when he successfully defeated Thomas Hearns, keeping the undisputed middleweight championship.

Three years later, on April 6, 1987, Hagler faced off against Sugar Ray Leonard at Caesar's Palace for what was billed as "The Super Fight." Hagler was guaranteed $12 million and Leonard received $11 million minimum. The event attracted a huge audience as boxing remained the third most-watched professional sport on television, among blacks, after wrestling and professional basketball.

## BOB HAYES
### Track Football

Known as the "world's fastest human," Olympic sprint champion Bob Hayes became one of professional football's most dazzling performers as a split end and flanker back for the Dallas Cowboys of the National Football League. However, it is his track achievements that remain most impressive.

Hayes still holds the world record for the 100 yard dash, 9.1 seconds, a mark he set on June 21, 1963. At the 1964 Olympics in Tokyo, Hayes came away with two gold medals for victories in the 100 meter dash and the 400 meter relay.

Born on December 20, 1942, in Jacksonville, Florida Hayes played football in high school and later attended all-black Florida A & M. He first captured the national track spotlight in 1961 by equaling the then world record of 9.3 seconds for the 100. Two years later, he set his own long-standing record at the National AAU championships in St. Louis, Missouri.

After finishing college, Hayes signed to play football with the Dallas Cowboys. In 14 games he caught 46 passes for 1,003 yards and 12 touch-downs. In 1965 he led the league in TD pass receptions (12) and average yardage per reception (21.8). He was leading TD pass receiver again in 1966, and punt yardage return leader (276) in 1967. Continuing to be one of the reasons for the Cowboy's dominance of the NFL's Eastern Division, he played in the 1971 and 1972 Superbowls.

*Reggie Jackson, baseball's "Mr. October."*

Now retired from sports, Hayes is associated with the consolidated Wig Corp. of Dallas, Texas.

## THOMAS HEARNS
### Boxer

Thomas "Hit Man" Hearns was a tough and feared welterweight who was born in Memphis, Tennessee. He won his first 17 bouts by knockouts. In fact, 30 of his first 32 were won that way. On August 2, 1980, he defeated Pipino Cuevas and won the WBA title in a second round knockout.

One year later, he faced off against Sugar Ray Leonard in a bid to unify the world title, but lost in a 14th round TKO.

Hearns remained active and won the WBC junior middleweight title, defeating Wilfredo Benitez in December, 1982. Two years later, he unified the world junior middleweight title in a second-round knockout of WBA champion Roberto Duran. At the end of that year, he lost to Marvin Hagler in a challenge to take over the undisputed middleweight championship.

After gaining 10 pounds, Hagler moved up a class and knocked out Dennis Andries to win the WBC Light heavyweight title.

Ultimately Hearns would remain a special fighter for the Memphis native was the first boxer to win the title in four different weight classes.

**RICKEY HENDERSON**
**Baseball**

Henderson was one of baseball's outstanding players who achieved a consistently high stolen-base record season after season. By the end of the 1984 season, he had reached a total of 493. In the 1982 season, he broke all-time career leader Lou Brock's single season record of 118 by making 130 steals.

The Yankee outfielder continued his top performances, excelling as a hitter and defensive player as well.

**REGGIE JACKSON**
**Baseball**

Because of his outstanding performance in the early fall, Reggie Jackson became known as "Mr. October." During his years with the Oakland Athletics and New York Yankees, Jackson captured or tied 13 World Series records to become baseball's greatest record holder for the fall classic. Reggie Jackson ranks among baseball's crop of players with proven superstar ability. His temperament, long reported to be as explosive and dynamic as his skill with the bat, gave him the drive to reach the top.

Born in Wynecote, Pennsylvania, he followed his father's encouragement to become an all-around athlete in Cheltenham High School, where he ran the 100 in 9.7, starred at halfback, and batted .550. An outstanding football and baseball collegian at Arizona State U, he left after sophomore year to join the Athletics (then located in Kansas City), having been passed over by the New York Mets' draft because, it is rumored, he was considered too hot to handle.

In 1968, his first full season, he hit 29 homers and batted in 74 runs, but made 18 errors and struck out 171 times, the second worst seasonal total in baseball history. He hit 49 homers in 1969, but feuding over money with owner Charlie Finley led to a bad year in 1970. Playing winter ball that year under Frank Robinson's managership seemed to get Jackson back on the track. His performance continued to improve, and in 1973 he batted .293, led the league in home runs (32), RBIs (117), and slugging average (.531), and won the MVP.

While with the Oakland Athletics, Jackson participated in helping the team go to three straight World Series, 1972, 1973, and 1974. Oakland won each of the championships and Jackson was named series MVP in 1973. Later, with the New York Yankees, Jackson was again prominent as the Yankees participated in the series of 1977, 1978, and 1981. In 1977, he was named series MVP after hitting five home runs, three in the crucial sixth and deciding game.

The first of the big money free agents, Jackson hit 144 homers, drove in 461 runs, and boosted his total career home runs to 425 while with the Yankees for five seasons. In January 1982, after an often stormy tenure, he signed with the California Angels.

Jackson retired as an active player in 1987, and has occasionally been hired as a commentator on baseball broadcasts. He has also devoted more time to his collection of antique cars.

**EARVIN "MAGIC" JOHNSON**
**Basketball**

One of the most exciting players to dominate the league in the 1980s, Johnson helped to guide Michigan State to an NCAA title when he was only a sophomore.

He went on to join the Los Angeles Lakers and as a 6' 9" inch guard, displayed an uncanny ability to handle the ball and provide lightning-speed assists to his teammates. Within five years, the Lakers had won two NBA titles and in 1981 Johnson was rewarded with a 25-year, $25 million contract, the largest total sum in team-sports history.

**JACK JOHNSON**
**Boxer**

Jack Johnson, the first black heavyweight champion, won the crown from Tommy Burns in Sydney, Australia on December 26, 1908. Nat Fleischer, the editor of *Ring* magazine and a foremost boxing authority, has said: "After years devoted to the study of heavyweight fighters, I have no hesitation in naming Jack Johnson as the greatest of them all. He possessed every asset."

Johnson was born in Galveston, Texas in 1878, the son of a school janitor. He was so tiny as a boy that he was nicknamed "Li'l Arthur," a name that stuck with him throughout his career. As a young man, he "hoboed" around the country, making his way to Chicago, Boston, and New York, and learning the fighting trade by working out with veteran professionals whenever he could. When he finally got his chance at the title, he had already been fighting for nine years and had lost only three of some 100 bouts.

With his victory over Burns, Johnson became the center of a bitter racial controversy, as the American public clamored for the former white champion, Jim Jeffries, to come out of retirement and recapture the crown. When the two fought on July 4, 1910 in Reno, Nevada, Johnson knocked out Jeffries in the fourteenth round.

In 1913, Johnson left the United States because of legal entanglements. Two years later he defended his title against Jess Willard in Havana, Cuba and was knocked out in the twenty sixth round. His career record was 107 wins, 6 losses.

In 1946, Johnson died in an automobile crash in North Carolina. He was inducted into the Boxing Hall of Fame in 1954.

**RAFER JOHNSON**
**Track and Field**

Rafer Johnson holds the Olympic record (set in 1960) for points scored in the decathlon, considered to be the toughest test of all-around athletic ability in the world of sports.
The decathlon consists of 10 events (Greek: deka means 10, athlos means contest) designed to test strength, speed, and agility under the most grueling of conditions. The events are the 100-meter dash, the broad jump, the shot put, the high jump, the 400-meter run, the 100-meter hurdles, the discus

*Rafer Johnson set the Olympic decathlon record in 1960.*

throw, the pole vault, the javelin toss, and the 1,500-meter run. Only an athlete with a considerable combination of athletic skills and endurance can compete in such a formidable event.

Johnson was born in Hillsboro, Texas, on August 18, 1935, and competed in his first decathlon in 1954 while attending UCLA, where he was president of the student body.

In spite of a knee injury in the 1956 Olympics at Melbourne, Australia, Johnson competed in the event, and finished second to Milt Campbell, another American black who was the first of his race to win an Olympic decathlon.

Competing in Moscow in 1958, Johnson shattered the world record with a total of 8,302 points. Two years later, at the Olympics in Rome, Johnson won the decathlon gold medal with another record-breaking performance, amassing 8,392 points to gain recognition as "the greatest all-around athlete in the world." He is now a director of the Kennedy Foundation.

## CHARLIE JOINER
### Football

In 1984, Charlie Joiner set a record as the all-time NFL leader in receptions with 657 catches. A member of the San Diego Chargers, he played on a team with two other outstanding receivers, Kellen Winslow and John Jefferson. All three were able to break the 1,000-yard mark during the early 1980s.

A star at Grambling, the wide receiver had joined the pro ranks in 1969, and played until 1987 when he retired after playing 239 games. During his career, he caught 750 passes for a total of 12,146 yards and 65 touchdowns. He remained with the Chargers organization as a receiver's coach.

## MICHAEL JORDAN
### Basketball

A star at the University of North Carolina, Michael Jordan played on the 1984 U.S. Olympic basketball team and was named College Player of the Year for the 1983-84 season.

As a rookie, Jordan was named to the All-Star Team during the 1985 season. A dazzling ball-handler and popular favorite during the league's slam-dunk competitions, Jordan during the 1986-87 season, became the second NBA player in history to score more than 3,000 points in a single season. That season, he also set another record when he scored 18 consecutive points in a game against the New York Knicks. Jordan was the league's individual scoring champ during the 1986-87 season and the 1987-88 season. He was also named the NBA's Most Valuable Player at the end of the 1987-88 season.

## FLORENCE GRIFFITH JOYNER
### Track

They called her "Flo Jo" and few American athletes caught the imagination of the American public prior to the 1988 Olympics like Florence Griffith Joyner. She was acknowledged as the fastest woman in the world and when she won the 100 meter and 200 meter sprints as well as being a part of two medal-winning relay teams, she satisfied the hopes of her growing legion of fans.

Married to 1984 Olympic gold medalist Al Joyner, Griffith went about seating worlds records and capturing the eye of an admiring media with her colorful fingernails and hooded bodysuits that set her apart in the competition.

Born in Los Angeles, she started in track at an early age and decided to attend Cal State-Northridge. She later transferred with her coach Bobby Kersee when he moved to UCLA, and soon excelled to win a silver medal in the 1984 Olympics.

She left the world of track for a while to work for a bank, but soon was drawn back with an even greater desire to excel. On the verge of the 1988 Olympics, she was the subject of cover stories in both sports and general interest magazines.

## LEROY KELLY
### Football

Leroy Kelly was a dominant force throughout his playing days in the National Football League. Never considered a finesse player, his ability to eat up opposing defenders, along with yardage, earned him acclaim as one of the league's most powerful running backs.

Born in Philadelphia on May 20, 1942, Kelly attended Morgan State University before joining the Cleveland Browns in 1964. Following two years as apprentice to the great Jim Brown, he became a regular, and soon thereafter, began to prove his star ability.

After leading the league in average yardage on punt returns (15.6) in 1965, he achieved back to back rushing titles in 1967 and 1968, amassing over 1,200 yards each season. His 1968 season made him the third three-time 1,000-yard gainer in NFL history, and he also led in scoring with 20 TDs, a feat seldom accomplished.

Kelly was an All-Pro selection from 1966 through 1969, and at the end of his 10-year career, ranked fourth on the National Football League's all-time rushing list with a career mark of 7,274 yards.

He is now a member of Base Enterprises in Los Angeles, a TV producing company.

## JACKIE JOYNER-KERSEE
### Track

Often touted as the world's greatest female athlete in the late 1980s, Jackie Joyner-Kersee won two gold medals in the 1988 Olympics in Seoul. As the first place winner in the long jump and the heptathlon, she climaxed a brilliant career of achievements.

The only woman to gain more than 7,000 points in the heptathlon four times, she set a world record for the grueling two-day event with 7,215 points at the Olympic trials prior to the competition itself.

Working closely with husband and coach, she was required to prepare for the seven events which test strength, speed and precision.

A native of East St. Louis, Illinois, she studied previous outstanding woman athletes and soon teamed with her husband to pursue her dreams of success in the field of competition. Prior to winning the 1988 gold, she participated in the 1984 Olympics and came away with a silver medal for the heptathlon despite a torn hamstring muscle.

## SUGAR RAY LEONARD
### Boxer

In 1981, Sugar Ray Leonard was named Athlete of the Year by ABC-TV's Wide World of Sports and Sportsman of the Year by *Sports Illustrated* magazine.

Just 25 years old, the 1976 Olympic gold medal winner was the undisputed professional welterweight champion. After his Olympic victory, Leonard had embarked on a professional boxing career in 1977 and proceeded to win 25 fights, 16 of them by knockouts, while losing none.

Before a Las Vegas crowd on November 30, 1979, Leonard KO'd Wilfredo Benitez to win the welterweight crown for the first time. In June 1980, he fought Roberto Duran in Montreal. The purse for that fight was $9.5 million—the largest in boxing history—and Leonard lost by decision. In a climactic November rematch—this time with a purse of $7 million—Leonard won the title back in a New Orleans bout as Duran quit in the eighth round, claiming stomach cramps.

Then, as a two-time World Boxing Council champ, he faced off against Thomas Hearns, the tough World Boxing Association and became the undisputed welterweight champ with a fourteenth-round TKO.

Besides being a talented athlete, Leonard was praised for his sportsmanlike demeanor and his wise business sense, which some observers felt would set a pattern for the boxer of the 1980s. This young multi-millionaire, and close companion to his wife and son, is both a colorful personality and outstanding image for his profession.

Leonard had undergone surgery for a detached retina and retired in 1984 following the Hearns bout. He worked as a commentator for HBO cable but then surprised the boxing world with a decision to return to training and fighting. He achieved a controversial split decision after a tough 15-round bout with Marvin Haggler in 1987, and when many thought he was finished, he declared his intentions to enter the ring again. In 1989, Leonard will fight Thomas Hearns in a rematch.

## CARL LEWIS
### Track and Field

In the 1984 Olympics in Los Angeles, Carl Lewis became the first athlete, since Jesse Owens in 1936, to win four gold medals in Olympic competition. He was victor in the lOO-meter dash, the 200-meter dash, the long jump and the lOO-meter relay.

An often controversial track and field performer, the New Jersey native went into the 1984 competition with the burden of tremendous expectations as the result of intense pre-Olympics publicity. He did not set any Olympic records, even as a gold medalist and found that his public image and statements were often the subject of public concern.

Lewis went to the 1988 Olympics in Seoul, hoping to duplicate his four gold medal wins, and was the subject of widespread interest as he faced off against his arch-rival Canadian Ben Johnson.

Lewis did win gold medals in the long jump and the 100-meter dash, but the latter prize came only after Ben Johnson was disqualified following the race when he tested positive for steroid use. Lewis did win a silver medal in the 200-meter dash as well.

## JOE LOUIS
### Boxer

Joe Louis held the heavyweight championship longer than anyone else (11 years, eight months, and seven days), and defended it more often than any other heavyweight champion. His 25 title fights were more than the combined total of the eight champions who preceded him.

*Carl Lewis won four gold medals at the 1984 Olympics.*

Born in a sharecropper's shack in Chambers County, Alabama in 1914, Louis moved to Detroit as a small boy. Taking up boxing later as an amateur, he won 50 out of 59 bouts (43 by knockout) before turning professional in 1934. He quickly gained a reputation in the Midwest and in 1935 came East to meet Primo Carnera, the former champion who was then staging a comeback. Louis knocked out Carnera in six rounds, and earned his nickname, "The Brown Bomber."

After knocking out ex-champion Max Baer, Louis suffered his lone pre-championship defeat at the hands of Max Schmeling, the German title holder who knocked him out in the twelfth round. Less than a month later, Louis knocked out another former champion, Jack Sharkey, in three rounds. After defeating a number of other challengers, he was given a title fight with Jim Braddock on June 22, 1937. He stopped Braddock in the eighth round, and began the long championship reign that was to see him defending his crown as often as six times in six months (1941), and battering Schmeling to the canvas in one round in their 1938 return bout.

One of Louis' greatest fights was his 1941 come-from-behind thirteenth-round-knockout of Billy Conn. After winning a disputed decision over Joe Walcott in 1947, Louis knocked out the Jersey challenger six months later, and then went into retirement.

His later comeback attempts against the likes of Ezzard Charles and Rocky Marciano were unsuccessful.

Joe Louis died April 12, 1981 at the age of 67.

## WILLIE MAYS
### Baseball

In his 21 seasons with the Giants, Willie Mays hit more than 600 home runs. Besides being a solid hitter, Mays also has been called the game's finest defensive outfielder and perhaps its best baserunner as well.

Born in Fairfield, Alabama on May 6, 1931, Mays made his professional debut on July 4, 1948, with the Birmingham Black Barons. He was signed by the Giants in 1950 and reached the major leagues in 1951, in time to become the National League's Rookie of the Year with 20 home runs, 68 RBIs, and the sensational fielding which contributed to his team's pennant victory.

After two years in the Army, Mays returned to lead the Giants to the World Championship in 1954, gaining recognition as the league's Most Valuable Player for his 41 homers, 110 RBIs and .345 batting average.

After the Giants moved to San Francisco, Mays continued his phenomenal home run hitting, and led his team to a 1962 pennant. A year later, *Sport* magazine named him "the greatest player of the decade." He won the MVP award again in 1965, after hitting 52 home runs and batting .317.

Traded back to the New York National League team (the Mets) before the 1972 season, he continued to play outfield and first base. At the end of the 1973 season, his records included 2,992 games (3rd on the all-time list), 3,283 hits (7th), and 660 home runs (3rd).

Willie Mays is one of only seven ballplayers to have hit four home runs in one game. In addition, he was the only black member of the living all-time baseball team, selected in 1969 by the Baseball Writer's Association of America. After acting as a coach for the Mets, Mays left baseball to pursue a business career. He was elected to the Baseball Hall of Fame in 1979.

## JESSE OWENS
### Track and Field

The track and field records Jesse Owens once set have all been eclipsed, but his reputation as one of the first great athletes with the combined talents of a sprinter, low hurdler, and broad jumper has hardly diminished with the passing of time.

Born on September 12, 1913 in Danville, Alabama, Owens moved to Ohio at an early age. The name "Jesse" derived from the way a teacher pronounced his initials, "J. C." In 1932, while attending East Technical High School in Cleveland, Owens gained national fame with a 10.3 clocking in the 100-meter dash.

Two years later, Owens entered Ohio State University, and for the next four years made track history, becoming universally known as "The Ebony Antelope." While competing in the Big Ten Championships at Ann Arbor, Michigan on May 25, 1935, Owens had what has been called "the greatest single day in the history of man's athletic

*Willie Mays, on offense or defense, an all time great.*

achievements." In the space of about 70 minutes, he tied the world record for the 100-yard dash and surpassed the world record for five other events, including the broad jump, the 220-yard low hurdles, and the 220-yard dash.

In 1936, at the Berlin Olympics, Owens won four gold medals, at that time the most universally acclaimed feat in the history of the games. When Adolf Hitler refused to present him with medals he had won in the various competitions, Owens' fame became even more widespread as a result of the publicity.

## SATCHEL PAIGE
### Baseball

Long before Jackie Robinson broke the color barrier of "organized baseball," Satchel Paige was a name well-known to the general sports public. As the outstanding performer in "Negro baseball," Paige had become a legendary figure whose infrequent encounters with major league players (he defeated Dizzy Dean in a 1-0 game in 1933, and four years later, was called "the best pitcher I ever faced" by Joe DiMaggio) added considerable laurels to his athletic reputation.

Paige was born in Mobile, Alabama in September 1904, and began playing semi-pro ball while working as an iceman and porter. In the mid-1920s, he became a professional with the Birmingham Black Barons, and later, while playing at Chattanooga, acquired the nick-name "Satchel" because of his "Satchel-sized feet."

For the next two decades, Paige compiled a phenomenal record. In 1933, he won 31 games and lost four. The following year, he pitched for a Brunswick, North Dakota team which reportedly took 104 out of 105 games, with Paige himself starting a total of 29 games over a one-month span. Along with Josh Gibson and other black stars, Paige, also dominated winter ball in Latin America during the 1930s.

In 1942, Paige led the Kansas City Monarchs to victory in the Negro World Series, and four years later he helped them to the pennant by allowing only two runs in 93 innings, a performance which included a skein of 64 straight scoreless innings.

In 1948, when he was brought up to the major leagues, Paige was well past his prime, but he still was able to contribute six victories in Cleveland's pennant drive. Four years' later, while pitching for the St. Louis Browns, he was named to the American League All-Star squad.

Up until the 1969 baseball season, Paige was primarily active on the barnstorming circuit with the Harlem Globetrotters and a host of other exhibition teams. It was in 1969 that the Atlanta Braves, in an attempt to make Paige eligible for baseball's pension plan, signed him to a one-year contract as coach.

Satchel Paige died in June 1982.

## WALTER PAYTON
### Football

When Walter Payton retired as a running back for the Chicago Bears, he had become the National Football League's all-time leading rusher, breaking a long-held record by Jim Brown.

He was the only runner to set an all-time rushing record for college conference and then repeat that achievement as a professional. A graduate of Jackson State in Mississippi, Payton played his entire career in Chicago and was able to savor in the team's success as well as still achieve while the team floundered.

Nicknamed "Sweetness," he broke O.J. Simpson's single game rushing record after gaining 275 yards during a game with the Vikings in 1977. Seven years later, he beat Jim Brown's career rushing record of 12,312 yards as the Bears played the New Orleans Saints.

A true gentleman and team-oriented player, Payton gained the respect of both his teammates and opponents during a distinguished career.

## PELE
### Soccer

The undisputed all-time king of world soccer is Edson Arantes do Nascimento, known to his fans as Pele. He has led his Santos (Brazil) Football Club to five South American championships and two world championships (1962, 1963), and has sparked the Brazilian National Team's first World Cup victory (1958) and its defense of the title (1962). In international competition, he has maintained an awesome

*Oscar Robertson drives for the hoop and the second highest point total in NBA history.*

average of nearly a goal a game.

Born in Tres Coracoes, Brazil, on October 23, 1940, Pele began playing soccer as a youngster. His father had been a minor league soccer player besides working as a civil servant. At 15 Pele left the provinces, and his $2 a month job as a shoemaker's apprentice, and within a year he had won a starting berth on the major league Santos team.

Famous for his speed and ball control, Pele has performed many remarkable feats. In the 1962 defense of the World Cup in Lisbon, Portugal, he scored three goals and passed for two others in Brazil's 5-2 triumph.

Pele's private life is quiet and serious. Concerned with setting a good example for youth, he refuses to do cigarette or alcohol commercials. In response to U.S. interviewers he said, that despite being married to a white woman, he has "never been faced with any kind of race problems....In Brazil no one thinks that way."

Pele, soccer's all-time goal leader with a total of 1,281 points in 22 years, was the highest paid player in any professional sport, receiving $4.75 million for two years—about 100 games—with the New York Cosmos. He retired and became a good-will ambassador for the sport, appearing in the feature film *Victory* with Sylvester Stallone.

## WILLIS REED
### Basketball

After seven seasons with the New York Knicks—which included two world championships and several playoff berths—Willis Reed returned to the team as head coach during the 1977-1978 season. His debut proved to be quite a challenge and he stayed with the team only until the beginning of the following season. By the 1981-1982 season he decided to return to coaching, this time on the college level at Creighton University.

A native of Louisiana, Reed spent his boyhood picking cotton around his hometown of Bernice, where he was born in 1943. He attended Grambling College, where he was discovered by Red Holzman, then the Knicks' chief scout.

Reed led the Knicks in scoring and rebounding on his way to becoming Rookie of the Year in 1965. As he matured, he captured rave notices from opposing centers who admired his shooting prowess and jarring "picks." In 1970, when the Knicks won their first title, Reed was voted three separate MVP awards: one for the regular season, one for the All-Star game, and one for the playoffs. Particularly memorable was his astonishing comeback after being injured in the fifth game of the playoffs against the Los Angeles Lakers. With Reed sidelined, Chamberlain dominated the sixth game and the Lakers romped to a 135-113 victory. In the seventh and deciding game, Reed took the floor, his mobility seriously impaired by his injured leg and hip, and scored the first two baskets of the night. The Knicks won the game handily and took the title back to New York.

At 6'9" and 240 pounds, Reed is not at all big for a center. However, he was named to the All Star team his first seven seasons. He missed the 1972 season because of knee trouble. Able to return in 1973 after operations, he captained the Knicks to their second title and won the playoff MVP. Unfortunately, continued knee problems ended his career.

Reed active in a number of business ventures, including a basketball camp and a farm in Louisiana, returned to active coaching when he was hired by the New Jersey Nets during the 1987-88 season.

## OSCAR ROBERTSON
### Basketball

Standing 6' 5", Oscar Robertson is remembered as the best "small man" in professional basketball, particularly in view of his outstanding scoring and playmaking ability. Averaging 25.7 points a game, he ended up as the second leading scorer in NBA history, with a point total of 26,710.

Born on November 29, 1938 in Charlotte, Tennessee, Robertson is the great-grandson of Marshall Collier, an ex-slave who died in 1954 at the age of 116, allegedly the oldest person in the United States at that time. The Robertsons moved to Indianapolis when Oscar was three. As soon as he and his brothers were old enough, they began playing basketball at the local YMCA. Oscar's oldest brother, Baily, later played briefly for the Harlem Globetrotters.

At Crispus Attucks High School, Robertson led his team to the first unbeaten season in Indiana history, a 45-game winning streak, and two consecutive state championships. He was All-State for three years, broke numerous individual scoring records, and was named a high school All-American. In addition to starring on the baseball and track teams, Robertson also was a member of the National Honor Society.

At the University of Cincinnati, Robertson became the nation's leading scorer as a sophomore, then went on to set 14 major collegiate records while leading his team to 89 wins in 98 games.

As a professional with the Cincinnati Royals, he became the game's leading backcourt scorer. He holds the records for highest assist average in the season, 11.5 in 1964-1965, and for most assists in a career: 9,887. While second to Chamberlain in free throws attempted, he ranks first in free throws made. Three times MVP (1961, 1964, and 1969), Robertson was traded to the Milwaukee Bucks, becoming a key part of the 1970-1971 championship team.

He is now a TV sports announcer.

### FRANK ROBINSON
### Baseball

Frank Robinson was baseball's first black major league manager. Named to the head post of the Cleveland Indians in October of 1974, he lost none of the calm control that carried him through 18 consistently good seasons as a player. On the first day of the 1975 season he put himself into the lineup as designated hitter and boomed career home run 575.

Robinson left the Indians, but was hired for a new manager's position with the San Francisco Giants during the 1981 season. At season's end, his contract was extended an additional two years. In January 1982, he was voted into the Baseball Hall of Fame.

Born in Beaumont, Texas in 1936, Robinson moved with his family to Oakland, California at the age of five. During his teens, he was a football and baseball star at McClyronds High School (which also produced Bill Russell, Vada Pinson, and Curt Flood). After graduation in 1953, he signed with the Cincinnati Reds.

In his first year of professional ball, Robinson batted .348 and led Ogden, Utah to the Pioneer League pennant. The following year, he batted .336 in the Sally League.

In 1956, he made a smash debut in the major leagues, hitting 38 homers and winning Rookie of the Year honors. Over the next eight years, he hit 259 homers and had 800 RBIs, an outstanding record, but one which was often underpublicized, playing in the shadow of such greats as Willie Mays and Hank Aaron.

In 1961, Robinson was named Most Valuable Player for leading Cincinnati to the National League pennant. Five years later, Robinson won the American League's Triple Crown and became the first player to win the MVP in both leagues. By the end of the 1973 season, he had hit .297 in 2,432 games with 2,614 hits, 1,639 runs, and 1,613 RBIs.

Robinson was hired as manager of the Orioles during one of the team's worst losing streaks in the late 1980s, and then signed on to continue with the team for the following season.

*Frank Robinson, baseball's first black manager, led the Baltimore Orioles to pennant and World Series victories in 1966.*

## JACKIE ROBINSON
## Baseball

Jackie Robinson's pioneer efforts in breaking the color barrier in organized baseball not only opened the door for other black players, but for black athletes in all major American sports.

Robinson's importance, however, can never be limited to the sociological feat which he performed. It was solely on the basis of his meritorious baseball playing that he was named, on July 3,1962, to the Hall of Fame in Cooperstown, New York.

Born in Cairo, Georgia, on January 31, 1919, Robinson was raised in Pasadena, California. At UCLA he gained all-American honorable mention as a halfback, but he left college in his junior year to play professional football for the Los Angeles Bulldogs. After serving as an Army lieutenant during World War II, Robinson returned to civilian life with the hope of becoming a physical education coach. To achieve this, he felt he had to make a name for himself, and for this reason decided to spend a few seasons in black baseball.

In 1945, while he was playing with the Kansas City Monarchs, Branch Rickey of the Brooklyn Dodgers assigned him to the Montreal Royals, the team's top farm club, where he was to be groomed for a career in the majors.

On April 10, 1947, the Dodgers announced that they had purchased Robinson's contract and the following day he began his major league career. When he retired in 1956, he had compiled an outstanding record as a hitter, fielder, and base-stealer.

During a 10-year career, he hit .311 in 1,382 games with 1,518 hits, 947 runs, 273 doubles, and 734 RBIs. He stole home 19 times, once in World Series play. He won the National League's Most Valuable Player award in 1949, and played on six National League pennant winners, as well as one world championship team.

After retirement, Robinson became a bank official, president of a land development firm, and a director of programs to combat drug addiction. He died on October 24, 1972 in Stamford, Connecticut.

## "SUGAR RAY" ROBINSON
## Boxer

Sugar Ray Robinson is often labeled the greatest fighter pound-for-pound in the history of boxing.

Born Walker Smith, in Detroit on May 3, 1920, he took the name Robinson from the certificate of an amateur boxer whose identity enabled him to meet the age requirements for getting a match in Michigan. The "Sugar" came from his having been dubbed "the sweetest fighter."

As a 10-year-old boy, Robinson had watched a Detroit neighbor, Joe Louis, train for an amateur boxing career. When Robinson moved to New York two years later, he began to spend most of his time at local gyms in preparation for his own amateur career.

After winning all 89 of his amateur bouts and the 1939 Golden Gloves featherweight championship as well, he turned professional in 1940 at Madison Square Garden, fighting for the first time on a card headlined by the Fritzie Zivic-Henry Armstrong fight. (Armstrong, Robinson's idol, lost the fight.) A year later, Robinson himself decisioned Zivic, and three months after that, knocked him out.

After several years of being "the uncrowned king of the welterweights," Robinson beat Tommy Bell in an elimination title bout in December 1946. He successfully defended the title for five years, and on February 14, 1951, took the middleweight crown from Jake LaMotta.

In July 1951, he lost the title to Randy Turpin, only to win it back two months later. Retiring for a time, Robinson subsequently fought a series of exciting battles with Carl "Bobo" Olsen, Carmen Basilio, and Gene Fullmer before retiring permanently, on December 10, 1965, with six victories in title bouts to his credit—more than any other fighter in history.

Founder of the Sugar Ray Robinson Youth Foundation for underpriveleged children, Robinson suffered from diabetes, hypertension and Alzaheimer's disease in his elder years.

One month shy of his 68th birthday, Robinson died of apparent natural causes at the Brotman Medical Center in Culver City, CA on April 12, 1989. Over his career, he had won 174 of 201 professional bouts, including titles in three weight classes.

## WILMA RUDOLPH
## Track and Field

Wilma Rudolph is the only American woman runner ever to win three gold medals in the Olympic Games. Her performance is all the more remarkable in light of the fact that she had double pneumonia and scarlet fever as a young child and could not walk without braces until age 11.

Born on June 23, 1940, in St. Bethlehem, Tennessee, she soon moved with her family to Clarksville, the town in which she grew up. At an early age, she survived an attack of double pneumonia and scarlet fever, but was left with the use of her right leg only. Through daily leg massages administered in turn by different members of her family, she progressed to the point where, at the age of eight, she was able to walk only with the aid of a special left shoe. Three years later, however, she discarded the shoe, and began joining her brother in backyard basketball games.

At Burt High School in Clarksville, while a sophomore, Miss Rudolph broke the state basketball record for girls. As a sprinter, she was undefeated in all her high school track meets.

In 1957, she enrolled at Tennessee State University and began to set her sights for the Olympics in Rome three years later. In the interim, she gained national recognition in collegiate meets, setting the world record for 200 meters in July 1960.

In the Olympics, she earned the title of the "World's Fastest Woman" by winning gold medals for the 100-meter dash, the 200-meter dash (Olympic record), and for anchoring the 400-meter relay (world record). She was named by the Associated Press as the U.S. Female Athlete of the Year for 1960, and also won United Press Athlete of the Year honors.

She is assistant director of athletics for the Mayor's Youth Foundation in Chicago.

## BILL RUSSELL
### Basketball

Bill Russell, who led the Boston Celtics to 11 titles, 8 in a row, is regarded as the finest defensive basketball player in the game's history. The 6' 10" star is also the first black to coach and play for a National Basketball Association team. His style of play is credited with revolutionizing basketball.

Russell was born on February 12, 1934, in Monroe, Louisiana. The family moved to Detroit when he was nine. Two years later, after his mother died, they continued on to Oakland. There, at McClyronds High School (the starting point for numerous black professional athletes), Russell proved to be an awkward but determined basketball player who eventually received a scholarship to the nearby University of San Francisco.

In college, Russell came into his own, in his sophomore year becoming the most publicized athlete on the West Coast. Over the next two years, his fame spread across the nation as he led his team to 60 consecutive victories (a collegiate record) and two straight NCAA titles.

The Celtics had never won the title before Russell's arrival, but since his specialties ( defense in general, a great shot blocker and offensive as well as defensive rebounding ) were added to their arsenal, they became the most successful team in the history of professional sports, winning the world championship eight years in a row. Russell himself was named Most Valuable Player on five separate occasions (1958, 1961-1963, 1965).

After the 1968-1969 season, having led the Celtics to their eleventh NBA crown, Russell retired as both coach and player. The move had its impact on the team, for the next season (1969-1970) the Celtics failed to make the playoffs for the first time in a good many years. The NBA's Most Valuable Player five times, Russell is the NBA leader in career minutes (40,726) and second in career rebounds (21,721).

After retirement, Russell was a color commentator on NBC-TV's NBA Game of the Week. In 1974, he returned to active basketball, accepting a lucrative contract to be head coach and general manager of the Seattle Supersonics. That year, he was inducted into the Basketball Hall of Fame.

Russell left active basketball for a time, and returned once again to active coaching with the Sacramento Kings. Then during the 1987-88 season he was moved to a new position as a team Vice President.

## GALE SAYERS
### Football

Gale Sayers was an All-Pro running back with the Chicago Bears from 1965 to 1971, during which time he was considered football's greatest offensive weapon. In 1965, the 200-pound 22-year-old Sayers combined great speed and agility with explosive power to capture Rookie of the

*Wilma Rudolph won the 1960 Olympic gold medals for the 100 meter run, 200 meter run, and 400 meter relay.*

Year Honors in the National Football League in what was surely the most remarkable debut in professional football. Not only did Sayers win the scoring title, but in the process, he also broke the league scoring record with 22 touchdowns (including six in one game).

Sayers was born in Wichita, Kansas and moved to Omaha, Nebraska in 1952. At the University of Kansas, he earned All-American honors and received $50,000 for signing with the Bears.

A dazzling runner from scrimmage, he was also adept at punt and kickoff returns and showed pass-catching and pass-throwing ability. In 1966, having set the scoring standard the

*Gale Sayers, a great career cut short by injury.*

previous year, Sayers led the league in rushing with 1,231 yards. In 1968, en route to one of his best years ever, Sayers suffered a crippling knee injury. During the off season, there was much speculation as to whether Sayers would ever be able to play again. In the 1969 season, Sayers not only played but led the league in rushing as well, with 1,032 yards.

In March 1975, accepting his nomination to the Black Athletes Hall of Fame from O. J. Simpson, he asked today's black stars to "drop back down and give young black athletes wise counsel about the pitfalls of professional sports."

## CHARLES SIFFORD
### Golf

Charlie Sifford started caddying at the age of nine in his hometown of Charlotte, North Carolina. As a 13-year-old, Sifford won a Charlotte tournament for caddies. In the late 1930s, he moved to Philadelphia where it was somewhat easier for a black golfer to gain access to a golf course.

From 1947 to 1953, Sifford worked between matches as a private golf instructor and sometime chauffeur and valet to singer Billy Eckstine, who later offered Sifford the financial support he needed to keep playing golf. From 1953 on he won the Negro National title six times. In the late fifties, Charlie got to play in a few tournaments on the PGA tour. On the tour in 1967, Sifford earned $57,000. In 1968, he added $33,000 more from competing on the tour. In 1968, he won the first PGA tournament of the year, the Los Angeles Open, copping the $20,000 first prize. The victory was his second major one (he had earned $20,000 in 1967 while winning the Hartford Open).

## O. J. SIMPSON
### Football

Orenthal J. Simpson may have been the finest running back in pro football. Nicknamed "The Juice," he holds rushing records for most yards in a single game and most yards in a single season.

Born in San Francisco on July 9,1947, Simpson began his football days at the University of Southern California, culminating with a Heisman Trophy in 1968. A year prior to that, he was a member of the relay team which set a world record of 38.6 seconds in the 440-yard run. A year after graduation, ABC Sports voted him College Player of the Decade.

He signed with the Buffalo Bills in 1969, and three years later achieved his first rushing title, gaining over 1,200 yards.

Then came his record-breaking 1973 season. On opening day, he rushed for 250 yards against the New England Patriots, breaking the record of 247 yards held by Willie Ellison. He gained an astonishing 2,003 yards for the entire season, surpassing the previous mark of 1,863 yards held by Jim Brown. In addition, he scored 12 touchdowns, averaged 6 yards per carry, and had more rushing yardage than 15 of the other NFL clubs. He was named Player of the Year and won the Jim Thorpe Trophy.

Recently retired from football, O. J. has begun a movie career with feature parts in *The Towering Inferno* and *The Klansman*, and he also works for ABC-TV sports.

## WILLIE STARGELL
### Baseball

Willie "Pops" Stargell joined the Pittsburgh Pirates in 1962 after a tumultuous career in the minor leagues, enduring racial harassment. He played his entire career in Pittsburgh, lasting 21 seasons.

Stargell, who spent 12 years playing in the outfield, led the National League with home runs in 1971, hitting 48 for a batting average of .295. In 1973, he led the league in doubles with 43, in home runs with 44 and in home-run percentage with 8.4. In addition, he was tops with RBI's with 119 and a hitting average of .646.

When the Pirates made it to the World Series in 1979, Stargell led the team to victory. Overall, he had 12 hits and scored seven runs, driving seven others. He batted .400 during the series.

Inducted into the Hall of Fame in 1987, Stargell was named a coach with the Atlanta Braves.

## LAWRENCE TAYLOR
## Football

Named an outstanding rookie in his first season with the New York Giants, Lawrence Taylor was soon heralded as one of the league's top linebackers. A fierce tackler and defensive team leader, Taylor was at the top of his game when the Giants won the Super Bowl in 1986, and was a consistent leader in sacks during a career often marred with off-the-field problems.

## MARSHALL W. TAYLOR
## Bicycling

Marshall W. "Major" Taylor became America's first black world bicycle champion in 1899. Born in Indianapolis, the son of a coachman, he worked at a bicycle store part-time as a teen-ager. After attending his first race, his boss suggested that Major enter a couple of races. To their surprise, he won a lO-mile race and proceeded to compete as an amateur.

By the time he was 16, he went to work in a factory owned by a former champion, and with his new boss's encouragement, competed in races in Canada, Europe, Australia and New Zealand.

During nearly 16 years of competition, he won numerous championships and set several world records. Years after he retired, he met President Theodore Roosevelt, who told him that he had followed his career with admiration.

## MIKE TYSON
## Boxer

In November, 1986, at the age of 20, Mike Tyson entered a ring with Trevor Berbick. By virtue of his victory, he became the youngest man ever to hold the heavyweight championship title.

His career seemed to be on the verge of unparalleled greatness, as he defeated challenger after challenger during the next two years.

He appeared to be at the height of his career by 1988 when he faced off against Michael Spinks in Atlantic City, and after only 91 seconds, walked away with victory and a $22 million purse.

Soon, however, Tyson entered into a bitter battle with his manager Bill Cayton over his finances, and soon thereafter became the subject of sustained press coverage when he and his wife, actress Robin Givins, became embroiled in a bitter divorce battle. Just when it seemed that he was back on the road to returning to the ring, he left training for his next fight to be with his estranged wife, leaving dismayed observers to wonder whether his life outside of the ring would ultimately bring his career to an end.

## PAUL WARFIELD
## Football

From his first year in the league, Paul Warfield combined speed with great hands, to baffle defenses, and lead him to All-Pro recognition in four of his first seven seasons.

Born in Warren, Ohio on November 28, 1942, Warfield attended Ohio State University.

In 1964, his first year with the Cleveland Browns, he caught 52 passes, good for 920 yards and 9 touchdowns. Similar seasons followed. In 1968, he made 50 receptions, gained 1,067 yards, and scored 12 touchdowns. A year later, he posted 42 catches, gained 886 yards, and recorded 10 scores.

Warfield was traded to the Miami Dolphins in 1970, and the following year had another outstanding season (43/996/11). In addition, he went on to help the Dolphins to three consecutive Super Bowl appearances. At the end of the 1974 season, Warfield jumped from Miami to sign a seven-figure contract with the Memphis Southmen of the World Football League.

## BILL WHITE
## National League President

In early 1989, Bill White was named to become the first black president of the National League. The distinction also made the 55-year-old former player and broadcaster the first black to head any major league sports position.

White began his career with the New York Giants in 1952, and spent several years as a major league player with stints on the St. Louis Cardinals and the Philadelphia Phillies. He retired in 1969, and in 1971 joined Phil Rizzuto and Frank Messer on the New York Yankee broadcast team.

In addition to the slugging first baseman, the league also considered such other blacks as Simon Gourdine, a former deputy commissioner of the National Basketball Association and Gil Griffin, the vice president of labor relations for Bristol Myers.

## DAVE WINFIELD
## Baseball

During the 1980s, Winfield remained one of the league's consistently top power hitters. His season batting was .265 when it was at its lowest. After eight years with the San Diego Padres, he signed the largest baseball contract in history up until that time, $13 million for 10 years with the New York Yankees.

While he continued to excel on the field and in the community as head of the Dave Winfield Foundation, he became an active participant in the on-going public disputes between players and their boss, team owner George Steinbrenner. The dispute became personal when Winfield wrote his biography at the beginning of the 1988 season, and then became embroiled in an angry exchange over whether the Yankee organization was making pledged donations to his foundation.

## OTHER NOTABLE BLACK BASEBALL PLAYERS

| Name | Position | Born | Name | Position | Born |
|---|---|---|---|---|---|
| Tommie Agee | of | 1942 | Jim Ray Hart | 3b | 1941 |
| Dick Allen | 1b | 1942 | George Hendrick | of | 1949 |
| Felipe Alou | of | 1935 | Willie Horton | of | 1942 |
| Jesus Alou | of | 1943 | Elston Howard | c | 1929 |
| Matty Alou | of | 1938 | Monte Irvin | of | 1919 |
| Dusty Baker | of | 1949 | Ferguson Jenkins | of | 1943 |
| Gene Baker | if | 1918 | Alex Johnson | of | 1942 |
| Dan Bankhead | p | 1924 | Cleon Jones | of | 1942 |
| Sammy Bankhead | if | 1905 | Buck Leonard | 1b | 1907 |
| Ernie Banks | ss | 1931 | Dave Lopes | 2b | 1946 |
| Earl Battey | c | 1935 | Juan Marichal | p | 1937 |
| Johnny Beckwith | of | 1902 | Carlos May | of | 1948 |
| James "Cool Papa" Bell | of | 1905 | Lee May | 1b | 1943 |
| Paul Blair | of | 1944 | John Mayberry | 1b | 1950 |
| Vida Blue | p | 1949 | Al McBean | p | 1938 |
| Bobby Bonds | of | 1946 | Willie McCovey | 1b | 1938 |
| Chet Brewer | p | 1902 | Hal McRae | of | 1946 |
| Johnny Briggs | of | 1944 | Willie Montanez | 1b | 1948 |
| Lou Brock | of | 1939 | Joe Morgan | 2b | 1943 |
| Gates Brown | of | 1939 | Manny Mota | of | 1938 |
| Ollie Brown | of | 1944 | Tony Oliva | of | 1940 |
| Ray Brown | p | 1903 | Al Oliver | of | 1946 |
| Willard Brown | of | 1921 | Amos Otis | of | 1947 |
| Billy Bruton | of | 1929 | Tony Perez | 1b | 1942 |
| Bert Campaneris | ss | 1942 | Vada Pinson | of | 1938 |
| Jose Cardenal | of | 1943 | Juan Pizarro | p | 1937 |
| Leo Cardenas | ss | 1938 | Floyd Robinson | of | 1936 |
| Rod Carew | 2b | 1945 | Manny Sanguillen | c | 1944 |
| Rico Carty | of | 1939 | George Scott | 1b | 1944 |
| Dave Cash | 2b | 1948 | Ken Singleton | of | 1947 |
| Cesar Cedeno | of | 1951 | Reggie Smith | of | 1945 |
| Orlando Cepeda | 1b | 1937 | Charlie Spikes | of | 1951 |
| Donn Clendenon | 1b | 1935 | Willie Stargell | of | 1941 |
| Nate Colbert | 1b | 1946 | Luis Tiant | p | 1940 |
| Wes Covington | of | 1932 | Bobby Tolan | of | 1945 |
| Willie Crawford | of | 1946 | Quincy Troupe | c | 1922 |
| Mike Cuellar | p | 1937 | Bob Veale | p | 1935 |
| Tommy Davis | of | 1939 | Zoilo Versalles | ss | 1940 |
| Willie Davis | of | 1940 | Leon Wagner | of | 1934 |
| Larry Doby | of | 1924 | Bob Watson | of | 1946 |
| Al Downing | p | 1941 | Bill White | 1b | 1934 |
| Dock Ellis | p | 1945 | Roy White | of | 1943 |
| Curt Flood | of | 1938 | Billy Williams | of | 1938 |
| Andy "Rube" Foster | p | 1879 | Earl Williams | 1b | 1948 |
| Ralph Garr | of | 1945 | Maury Wills | ss | 1932 |
| Josh Gibbon | c | 1911 | Don Wilson | p | 1945 |
| Tony Gonzalez | of | 1936 | Earl Wilson | p | 1935 |
| Tommy Harper | of | 1940 | Jimmy Wynn | of | 1942 |

## OTHER NOTABLE BLACK FOOTBALL PLAYERS

| Name | Position | Born |
|---|---|---|
| Herb Adderly | DB | 1939 |
| Lem Barney | CB | 1946 |
| Bill Bell | T | 1909 |
| Bobby Bell | LB | 1942 |
| Elvin Bethea | DE | 1946 |
| Verlon Biggs | DE | 1942 |
| Emerson Boozer | RB | 1943 |
| John Brockington | RB | 1949 |
| Bob Brown | DT | 1940 |
| Larry Brown | RB | 1947 |
| Timmy Brown | RB | |
| Willie Brown | CB | 1941 |
| Fred Carr | LB | 1946 |
| Charlie Cowan | T | 1938 |
| Curley Culp | DT | 1946 |
| Clem Daniels | RB | |
| Earl Edwards | DE | 1946 |
| Carl Eller | DE | 1942 |
| Chuck Foreman | RB | 1949 |
| John Gilliam | WR | 1945 |
| Cornell Green | DB | 1940 |
| Joe Greene | DT | 1947 |
| L.C. Greenwood | DE | 1947 |
| Roosevelt Grier | DB | |
| Cedrick Hardman | DE | 1949 |
| Franco Harris | RB | 1950 |
| Calvin Hill | RB | 1947 |
| Winston Hill | T | 1942 |
| Claude Humphrey | DE | 1944 |
| Harold Jackson | WR | 1946 |
| Roy Jefferson | WR | 1944 |
| Jimmy Johnson | CB | 1938 |
| Ron Johnson | RB | 1948 |
| Walter Johnson | DT | 1943 |
| Deacon Jones | DB | |
| Dick "Night Train" Lane | RB | |
| Willie Lanier | LB | 1945 |
| Floyd Little | RB | 1942 |
| Larry Little | G | 1945 |

| Name | Position | Born |
|---|---|---|
| Carl "Spider" Lockhart | DB | 1943 |
| John Mackey | TE | |
| Jim Marshall | DE | 1938 |
| Reggie McKenzie | G | 1950 |
| Lenny Moore | RB | |
| Mercury Morris | RB | 1947 |
| Alan Page | DT | 1945 |
| Jim Parker | T | 1934 |
| Woody Peoples | G | 1943 |
| Don Perkins | RB | 1938 |
| Joe "The Jet" Perry | RB | 1927 |
| Fritz Pollard | RB | 1895 |
| Jethro Pugh | DT | 1944 |
| Mel Renfro | CB | 1942 |
| Paul Robeson | RB | 1898 |
| Dave Robinson | | |
| Paul Robinson | RB | 1947 |
| Charlie Sanders | TE | 1946 |
| Art Shell | T | 1947 |
| Paul Smith | DT | 1945 |
| Ron Smith | DB | 1943 |
| Matt Snell | RB | |
| Bruce Taylor | CB | 1948 |
| Charley Taylor | WR | 1942 |
| Lionel Taylor | WR | |
| Otis Taylor | WR | 1942 |
| DuaneThomas | RB | 1947 |
| Gene Upshaw | G | 1945 |
| Gene Washington | WR | 1947 |
| Warren Wells | WR | 1944 |
| Charley West | RB | 1899 |
| Ernie Wheelwright | RB | 1939 |
| Freeman White | WR | 1943 |
| Travis Williams | RB | 1946 |
| Willie Williams | DB | 1942 |
| Bill Willis | G | 1928 |
| Rayfield Wright | T | 1945 |
| Tank Younger | RB | 1921 |

## OTHER NOTABLE BLACK BASKETBALL PLAYERS

| Name | Position | Born |
|---|---|---|
| Nate Archibald | G | 1948 |
| Dick Barnett | G | 1936 |
| Dave Bing | G | 1943 |
| Austin Carr | G | 1948 |
| Phil Chenier | G | 1950 |
| Wayne Embry | C | 1937 |
| Walt Frazier | G | 1945 |
| Artis Gilmore | C | 1948 |

| Name | Position | Born |
|---|---|---|
| Hal Greer | G | 1936 |
| Elvin Hayes | C | 1945 |
| Spencer Haywood | F | 1949 |
| Lou Hudson | G | 1944 |
| Lucious Jackson | F | 1941 |
| Sam Jones | F | 1933 |
| Bob Lanier | C | 1948 |
| Bob Love | F | 1942 |

| Name | Position | Born |
|---|---|---|
| Bob McAdoo | C | 1951 |
| George McGinnis | F | 1950 |
| Earl Monroe | G | 1944 |
| Nate Thurmond | C | 1941 |
| Wes Unseld | F | 1946 |
| Chet Walker | F | 1940 |
| Jo Jo, White | G | 1946 |
| Sidney Wicks | F | 1949 |
| Lenny Wilkens | G | 1937 |

## OTHER NOTABLE BLACK TRACK AND FIELD STARS

| Name | Born |
|---|---|
| Dave Albritton | 1918 |
| Johnny Borican | 1918 |
| Ralph Boston | 1940 |
| Earlene Brown | 1935 |
| Frank Budd | 1925 |
| John Carlos | 1946 |
| Alice Coachman | 1921 |
| Josh Culbreath | 1935 |
| Willie Davenport | 1943 |
| Harrison Dillard | 1923 |
| Howard P. Drew | 1890 |
| Eddie Hart | 1948 |
| Jimmy Hines | 1946 |
| DeHart Hubbard | 1899 |
| Cornelius Johnson | 1918 |
| Ralph Metcalfe | 1910 |
| Rod Milburn | 1950 |
| Ira Murchison | 1933 |
| Mel Pender | 1937 |
| Tommie Smith | 1944 |
| John Thomas | 1941 |
| Edward Tolan | 1911 |
| Mal Whitfield | 1921 |
| Johnny "Longjohn" Woodruff | 1917 |

## OTHER NOTABLE BLACK BOXERS

| Name | Division | Born |
|---|---|---|
| Henry Aldridge | middleweight | 1946 |
| Paul Armstead | lightweight | 1937 |
| Hogan "Kid" Bassey* | bantamweight | 1932 |
| Joe Brown *lightweight | | |
| Panama Al Brown* | bantamweight | 1904 |
| Ezzard Charles* | heavyweight | |
| Curtis Cokes* | welterweight | 1939 |
| Jimmy Ellis* (WBA) | heavyweight | 1944 |
| Zora Folley | heavyweight | |
| George Foreman* | heavyweight | 1949 |
| Bob Foster* | light heavyweight | |
| Joe Frazier* | heavyweight | 1944 |
| Joe Gans* | lightweight | 1874 |
| George Godfrey | heavyweight | 1853 |
| Emile Griffith* | middleweight | 1938 |
| Beau Jack* | lightweight | 1921 |
| Peter Jackson | heavyweight | 1861 |
| Harold Johnson* | light heavyweight | |
| Doug Jones | heavyweight | |
| Sam Langford | heavyweight | 1886 |
| John Henry Lewis* | light heavyweight | 1914 |
| Sonny Liston* | heavyweight | |
| Eddie Machen | heavyweight | |
| Tom Molineaux | heavyweight | 1784 |
| Bob Montgomery* | lightweight | 1919 |
| Archie Moore* | light heavyweight | |
| Davey Moore* | featherweight | |
| Jose Napoles* | welterweight | |
| Ken Norton | heavyweight | |
| Benny "Kid" Paret* | welterweight | |
| Floyd Patterson* | heavyweight | |
| Luis Rodriguez* | welterweight | 1937 |
| Joe "Sandy" Saddler* | featherweight | 1926 |
| Johnny Saxton* | welterweight | |
| Battling Siki* | light heavyweight | 1897 |
| Bob Smith | heavyweight | 1840 |
| Ernie Terrell* (WBA) | heavyweight | 1935 |
| Mervine Thompson | heavyweight | 1869 |
| Dick Tiger* | light heavyweight | 1929 |
| Bob Travers | heavyweight | 1836 |
| Gil Turner | middleweight | 1928 |
| Jersey Joe Walcott* | heavyweight | 1914 |
| Cleveland Williams | heavyweight | |
| Ike Williams* | lightweight | 1923 |
| Harry Wills | heavyweight | 1889 |
| Jackie Wilson* | featherweight | 1909 |
| Chalky Wright* | featherweight | 1917 |

*Denotes champion.

# BLACK WRITERS, SCHOLARS, AND POETS

**Present Issues ■ The Harlem Renaissance ■ Activism ■ Outstanding Literary Figures**

In the wake of the civil rights "revolution" of the 1960s, the voices of black Americans were being raised and heard as never before, and major publishing houses became eager to put into print the expressions of black writers. For a time, the reading public expressed active interest in the many previously ignored black themes and perspectives, but such interest was relatively short-lived. Toward the end of the 1970s, black writers were discovering that white-owned publishing houses were becoming increasingly inaccessible.

Many black writers instead began to write books for children and for young people using African or Afro-American settings. Black writers found that the market for young people was far better than that for black adult books.

However, black poets and novelists have continued to publish books of poetry and novels dealing with the black problem in today's society. Black playwrights have also written and had many of their contemporary plays produced on stage, and a few blacks have written in the area of science fiction. Books by such authors as Richard Wright and Zora Neale Hurston have been revived and there were bio-bibliographies, autobiographies, and biographies written about many of the black writers.

One of the more important developments in black writing was the emergence of the black woman. Black women received further recognition through the white feminist movement and through publishing houses that were sympathetic to women.

Perhaps the biggest trend in black writing has been the Alex Haley *Roots* syndrome. The resounding success of *Roots* stimulated great interest in Africa and black genealogy and history. Many books of family genealogy have been written and published. Such historical novels and plays as *The Chaneysville Incident* and *The Brownsville Raid* were written, all of which perhaps had been greatly stimulated by the *Roots* phenomenon. Many books on the history of blacks in the various sections of the Middle West, the Far West, the South, and the North were published, mainly by noncommercial or university presses. The authors of these books were black as well as white writers.

## The Issue

The issue that permeates the writings of all members of acknowledged minorities, be they Eskimoes, Jews, Rosicrucians, or blacks, is whether to try in their writings to further the particular cause of their group or, through observation and self-expression, to help illuminate the universal human condition. Though the two goals are not always mutually exclusive, few writers can avoid a commitment to one position or the other at some point during their career.

The great problem faced by the black writer to this day, and especially before the Renaissance of the 1920s, was that he was not allowed a choice. Literary dominion in the United States—the establishment of publishers, editors, critics, and professors—has been lodged in the hands of whites, whose tastes determined the authors who were to be published, promoted, and praised. Until the 1920s, these people, often innocently, left no room for those blacks who chose to write in the black idiom.

Much of the early literature produced by American blacks (as with Phillis Wheatley) was merely imitative of the general literature of the time, its racial facet being the attempt to exhibit the writer's intrinsic effort as sufficient refutation of the belief that the black was an inherently inferior creature. Other early works were little more than pious tracts written to assure the masters that the servants wanted nothing more than to serve in religious humility, as in the case of Jupiter Hammon. In contrast to these, however, there was also a long succession of autobiographical narratives by former slaves who chose to attack the existing system in an attempt to force "White America" to look into the human face of "Negro America."

From the post-Reconstruction period to the decade of the 1920s, much of American black literature was an attempt to show the general public that blacks could be as respectably middle class in outlook and ideals as whites. If much of "Negro America" was unable to afford the creature comforts of such an environment, it could still produce literary commentaries which would at least show a people happily laughing at their assigned lot.

It was in the 1920s that black literature made a sharp change of direction, removing itself once and for all from polite and strait laced conventions and its grinning, dancing, ingratiating manner. With the emergence of the "Harlem School" came a sense of racial pride which expressed itself in earthy, realistic terms—the protests of both the black and white establishments not withstanding.

## Self-Expression and the Renaissance

Oddly, despite acclaim for many authors and poets of the Harlem Renaissance, black writers were never considered part of American literature, or at best were viewed as a distant phase of it. Blacks could, as Willard Motley and Frank Yerby were to do, write as individual observers without reference to their racial interests or background. But despite the integrationist political stance of leading American publishers and critics, black writers were never regarded as

*Richard Wright drew on his personal experience to dramatize racial injustice.*

part of the nation's overall intellectual fabric and, absurdly, anthologies of black writing were frequently selected, edited, and prefaced by whites.

The cause of this, rather than blatant prejudice, was a kind of parochial racism, particularly found in the English departments of universities, which found it hard to accept writers who did not follow in the hallowed Dryden to T. S. Eliot tradition which tended to emphasize exquisiteness of language and to derogate the unabashed self-expression which was the hallmark of the Harlem School.

Renaissance self-expression had emerged in large measure because the moralizing writings of blacks prior to this era had failed to reach white consciences and abate racism. Much of this writing by Douglass, DuBois, and James Weldon Johnson was of excellent caliber and truly reflected the experience of blacks. However, it remained for Alain Locke to stress to blacks of post-World War I America that whites were not really paying much attention, and that the time had come for blacks to cease propagandizing and reach into themselves to express their suffering through art rather than pamphleteering. Thus, though they did not abrogate interest in the black cause, the political objectives of Renaissance writers were largely beneath the surface. Grievances and objectives were not spelled out. Readers were encouraged to draw their own conclusions.

The ideology of self-expression was underscored by Ralph Ellison, when he noted: "If *Invisible Man* is free from ideological penalties suffered by Negroes in this country, it is because I tried to the best of my ability to transform these elements into art."

*Alain Locke defined the aims of the black artists of the Harlem Renaissance.*

### Wright and Activism

This view was not seriously challenged until 1940 when, with economic depression still present and world war brewing, Richard Wright appeared as an important writer and declared that with racism still rampant in the United States, "art for art's sake" was an indulgence that blacks could not afford. And Claude McKay, who had been a harbinger of the Renaissance, expressed fierce and direct protest in his poem "If We Must Die."

Wright, however, was no separatist. A strong theme in his writing was that the black was part of an American culture which in turn rejected him. As such, though politically radical, Wright's literary efforts coincided with much of the ideology of the civil rights movement of the 1950s and 1960s.

The militancy and violence of the 1960s shaped not only new leaders of the black cause but a new breed of activist writer who, far from belonging to an established black intellectual elite, wrote of the passions and experiences that emerge from people in direct conflict with society. Much leading black literature of the late 1960s came from men bred in the conflicts of streets and prisons. Foremost among these writers were Eldridge Cleaver, George Jackson, Ron , and Malcolm X. Imamu Baraka had also been involved in bouts with the law.

By the 1970s, black writers had achieved a position of respect in the American intellectual scene even if they, and black critics, still remained outsiders. Black studies faculties at universities added to this stature, though many were being eliminated by 1975.

The writers reviewed in this section have been included for their historical and/or aesthetic importance. In this limited space, the list can only be representative, although it can serve as a vital springboard for developing a greater understanding of the contributions made by the American black writer, both to the mainstream and to the tributaries of the American literary experience.

There have been some deaths over the years of quite a few black writers and scholars: James Baldwin, John O. Killens, Owen Dodson, Sterling A. Brown, Charles T. Davis, Chester Himes, Rayford W. Logan, Julian Mayfield, George Kent, J. Saunders Redding and Charles H. Wesley. Some died too early; some were quite old.

There are several first novel or first non-fiction writers who are not included here. Also not here are many children's books by black writers. The new writers and scholars here were either inadvertently overlooked in the previous edition or have become prominent and now cannot be left out. They include Houston A. Baker Jr., Cyrus Cofter, Lenwood Davis, Charles T. Davis, Henry Louis Gates Jr., Donald Gibson, Vincent Harding, Charles Johnson, Audre Lorde, David Levering Lewis, Gloria Naylor, Thomas Sowell, August Wilson, Charles V. Willie and Jay Wright.

The updating shows that the writers and scholars by and large have continued to write books of poetry, essays, novels, short stories, biographies, plays and sociological and historical works. There must be many books that black authors were not able to get published. But some writers, like Toni Morrison and Alice Walker, have won Pulitzer Prizes and have published books that were best sellers. Others just below the top have produced novels that had good sales especially the paperback editions. There have been more black women novel writers in the current period than black men, if we leave out Samuel R. Delany's many science fiction novels. But the men writers have held their own with the various non-fiction works.

## MAJOR BLACK LITERARY FIGURES

### RAYMOND ANDREWS
**Novelist**
**1934**

Born in Madison, Georgia, Raymond Andrews left his sharecropper farm home at 15, to live, work, and attend high school at night in Atlanta. After graduation, he served in the U.S. Air Force (1952-1956) and attended Michigan State University before moving to New York City where he worked in a variety of jobs: airline reservations clerk, hamburger cook, photo librarian, proofreader, inventory taker, mail room clerk, messenger, air courier dispatcher, and bookkeeper. And all the while he was writing.

His first novel, *Appalachee Red* (1978), set in the black

neighborhood of a northern Georgia town called Appalachee, was widely acclaimed. In the view of the reviewer for the *St. Louis Globe Democrat,* it marked the literary debut of a significant modern American novelist of the stature of a Richard Wright or James Baldwin. The following year Raymond Andrews was the first recipient of the annual James Baldwin Prize presented by The Dial Press at a ceremony attended by Baldwin.

Andrews' second work, *Rosiebelle Lee Wildcat Tennessee: A Novel* (1980), chronicled the 40-year reign in Appalachee, beginning in 1906, of the spiritual and temporal leader of the black community there. And like his previous novel, it was illustrated by his brother Benny.

His third novel titled *Baby Sweets* (1984), is also published by Dial Press and illustrated by his brother Benny.

Raymond Andrews lives in New York City with his wife, Heidi, a classical singer from Switzerland, and their two cats.

### MAYA ANGELOU
### Writer, Poet, Actress
### 1928

Born in St. Louis, Maya Angelou spent her formative years shuttling between that city, a tiny, totally segregated town in Arkansas, and San Francisco where she realized her ambition of becoming that city's first Negro streetcar conductor.

In the 1950s, she studied dancing with Pearl Primus in New York, later appearing as a nightclub singer in New York and San Francisco. She worked as an editor for *The Arab Observer,* an English-language weekly published in Cairo; lived in Accra, Ghana, where under the black nationalist regime of Kwame Nkrumah she taught music and drama; and studied cinematography in Sweden. She became a national celebrity in 1970 with the publication of *I Know Why the Caged Bird Sings,* the first volume of her autobiography, which detailed her encounters with southern racism and a pre-pubescent rape by her mother's lover.

*Maya Angelou, a writer, a poet, and nominated for an Emmy for her acting.*

In 1971, she produced *Just Give Me a Cool Drink of Water 'fore I Die: The Poetry of Maya Angelou;* in 1975, *Oh Pray My Wings Are Gonna Fit Me Well* (poetry); in 1979, *And Still I Rise* (poetry); and in 1983, *Shaker Why Don't You Sing?* (poetry). In 1977, she was nominated for an Emmy award for her portrayal of Nyo Boto in the television adaptation of the best-selling novel *Roots.*

Three more volumes of her autobiography have been published: *Gather Together in My Name* (1974); *Singin' and Swingin' and Gettin' Merry Like Christmas* (1976); and *The Heart of a Women* (1981). In 1986, (paperback in 1987) *All God's Children Need Traveling Shoes* was published. She is now co-authoring with Dorothy I. Height, president of the National Council of Negro Women, Height's autobiography to be published by Warner Books early in 1990.

The extravagantly tall, multi-talented Angelou lives in Winston-Salem, North Carolina with her husband, Paul DeFeu.

### HOUSTON A. BAKER JR.
### Critic, Scholar
### 1943-

Born in Louisville, Kentucky, he graduated from Howard University Phi Beta Kappa, and received his master's and doctoral degrees from the University of California at Los Angeles. He taught English at Yale University and the University of Virginia. He is now the Albert M. Greenfield Professor of Human Relations at the University of Pennsylvania.

The author of many essays in books and magazines, Baker's books are: (editor) *Black Literature in America* (1971); (editor) *Twentieth Century Interpretations of Native Son* (1972); *Long Black Song: Essays in Black American Literature and Culture* (1972); *A Many Colored Coat of Dreams: The Poetry of Countee Cullen* (1974); *Singers of Daybreak: Studies in Black American Literature* (1975, 1983); (editor) *A Dark and Sudden Beauty: Two Essays in Black American Poetry by George Kent and Stephen Henderson* (1977); (editor) *Reading Black: Essays in the Criticism of African Caribbean and Black American Literature* (1978); *Blues, Ideology and Afro-American Literature: A Vernacular Theory* (1984); *Afro-American Poetics: Revisions Of Harlem and the Black Aesthetic* (1988); and *Modernism and the Harlem Renaissance* (1987,1989). Baker has also published three volumes of poetry, the last one titled *Blues Journeys Home* (1985). He is editing a book about a black professor at Howard University who impressed him and steered him into literature.

*James Baldwin with Bayard Rustin at a press conference where they urge President Kennedy to send troops into Alabama after a series of racial incidents in the state.*

### JAMES BALDWIN
### Novelist, Essayist, Playwright
### 1924-1987

James Baldwin is one of the most widely quoted black writers of the past two decades.

Born in New York City, Baldwin turned to writing after an early career as a boy preacher in Harlem's storefront churches. He attended Frederick Douglass Junior High School in Harlem and later graduated from DeWitt Clinton High School, where he was editor of the school magazine. Three years later, he won a Eugene Saxton Fellowship, which enabled him to write full-time. Now a resident of France, since leaving the United States, Baldwin has also been a resident of Turkey.

Baldwin's first novel, *Go Tell It on the Mountain,* was published in 1953, receiving good critical notices. Two years later, his first collection of essays, *Notes of a Native Son,* again won favorable critical acclaim. This was followed, in 1956, by the publication of his second novel, *Giovanni's Room,* set in Paris. His second collection of essays, *Nobody Knows My Name,* brought him into the literary spotlight and established him as a major voice in American literature.

In 1962, *Another Country*, Baldwin's third novel, was a critical and commercial success. A year later, he wrote *The Fire Next Time*, an immediate best-seller and already regarded as one of the most brilliant essays written in the history of the black protest.

Since then, two of Baldwin's plays, *Blues for Mister Charlie* and *The Amen Corner*, have been produced on the New York stage, where they achieved modest success.

His novel *Tell Me How Long The Train's Been Gone* was published in 1968. Baldwin himself regards it as his first "grown-up novel," but it has generated little enthusiasm among critics.

Much to the distress of his public, Baldwin then entered an extended fallow period, and the question of whether he had stopped writing was widely debated. After a silence of several years, he published the 1974 novel *If Beale Street Could Talk.* In this work, the problems besetting a ghetto family, in which the younger generation is striving to build a life for itself, are portrayed with great sensitivity and humor. Baldwin's skill as a novelist is evident as he sets and solves the difficult problem of conveying his own sophisticated analyses through the mind of his protagonist, a young woman. To many critics, however, the novel lacks the undeniable relevance and fiery power of Baldwin's early polemical essays.

Baldwin's other works include *Going to Meet the Man* (short stories); *No Name in the Street; One Day When I Was Lost;* a scenario based on Alex Haley's *The Autobiography of Malcolm X; A Rap on Race* with Margaret Mead; and *A Dialogue* with Nikki Giovanni. He is one of the rare authors who works well alone or in collaboration. Other books by Baldwin are *Nothing Personal* (1964) with photographs by Richard Avedon; *The Devil Finds Work* (1976), about the movies; his big sixth novel *Just Above My Head* (1979); and *Little Man, Little Man: A Story of Childhood* (1977). He has written 16 books including the book for children, and has co-authored three others. There are six books about Baldwin's life and writings including a reference guide and bibliography.

*Just Above My Head,* published in 1979, dealt with the intertwined lives from childhood to adulthood of a gospel singer, his brother, and a young girl who is a child preacher. The next year Baldwin's publisher announced *Remember This House,* described as his "memoirs, history and biography of the civil rights movement" interwoven with the biographies of three assassinated leaders: Martin Luther King Jr. Malcolm X, and Medgar Evers. Meanwhile, in his lectures Baldwin appears to remain pessimistic about the future of race relations.

His last two books were *The Evidence of Things Not Seen* (1985) about the killing of 28 black youths in Atlanta, Ga. in the early 1980s; and *The Price of the Ticket: Collected Non-fiction 1948-1985* (1985).

Baldwin spent most of his life in France. In 1986, the French government made him a commander of the Legion of Honor, France's highest civilian award. Since 1984, he had been a Five College professor in the W.E.B. Dubois Department of Afro-American Studies at the University of Massachusetts at Amherst. He died at his home in France, on November 30, 1987, at the age of 63. The Five College community held a memorial service for him at the University of Massachusetts on December 16, 1987. The great special number (Winter 1987) of *The Massachusetts Review* on

Baldwin has a selection of the tributes and remarks by Baldwin's friends and colleagues at the memorial plus many other writings by, and interviews with, black writers.

The statement by 48 black writers and critics deploring Toni Morrison's failure, up to that time, to win the Pulitzer Prize or the National Book Award (N.Y. Times Book Review, Jan. 24, 1988) was accompanied by a letter from June Jordan and Houston A. Baker Jr. which stated that Baldwin, who had just died, "never received the honor of these Keystones to the canon of American literature: the National Book Award and Pulitzer Prize: never." At his death, Baldwin was working on a book about Martin Luther King Jr.

The books about Baldwin are: Fern M. Eckman's *The Furious Passage of James Baldwin* (1967); Kenneth Kinnamon's edited *James Baldwin: A Collection of Critical Essays* (1973); Therman B. O'Daniel's edited *James Baldwin: A Critical Evaluation* (1977); Louis H. Pratt's *James Baldwin* (1978); Fred L. and N.V. Standley's *James Baldwin: A Reference Guide*; and Trudie Harris's *Black Women in the Fiction of James Baldwin.*; plus scores of essays and reviews on Baldwin and his writings in many books and magazines. Two black Florida A&M University professors are collecting the many interviews with Baldwin for a book to be published by University Press of Mississippi. And David Leeming and David Baldwin (James' brother) are compiling Baldwin letters, manuscripts, notes, photos, audio and video tapes for a forthcoming authorized biography of James Baldwin by David Leeming to be published by A. A. Knopf. James Campbell had been commissioned, in 1988, by the publishing house Faber and Faber in London to write a biographical study of Baldwin.

## IMAMU AMIRI BARAKA (Leroi Jones)
### Poet, Playwright, Essayist
### 1934

(For Biography see Civil Rights Section.)

## LERONE BENNETT JR.
### Historian
### 1928

Lerone Bennett Jr. is often referred to as the "resident historian" of the Johnson Publishing Company, publisher of *Ebony, Jet,* and *Ebony Jr.*

Bennett was born in Clarksdale, Mississippi, and was educated in the public school system of Jackson, where he worked on his high school paper and edited the local Negro Weekly, *The Mississippi Enterprise.* At Morehouse College in Atlanta he was editor of the student newspaper and, after graduation, became a reporter and later city editor of the *Atlanta Daily World.*

Bennett joined Johnson in 1953, and worked as associate editor of *Jet* and *Ebony* before being named the latter's first senior editor in 1960.

His books include *Before the Mayflower: A History of Black America* (1962); *The Negro Mood And Other Essays* (1964); *What Manner of Man* (a biography of Martin Luther King published in 1964); *Confrontation, Black and White* (1965); *Black Power, U.S.A., The Human Side of Reconstruction 1867-1877* (1967); *Pioneers in Protest* (1968); *The Challenge of Blackness* (1972); *The Shaping of Black America* (1974); and *Wade in the Water: Great*

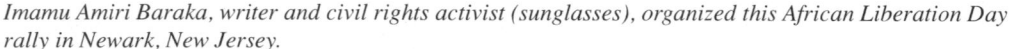

*Imamu Amiri Baraka, writer and civil rights activist (sunglasses), organized this African Liberation Day rally in Newark, New Jersey.*

*Moments in Black History* (1979). Bennett received the Literature Award from the American Academy of Arts and Science in 1978. He also co-authored with John H. Johnson, *Succeeding Against the Odds: The Autobiography of John H. Johnson* (1989).

In 1969, he published a revised and enlarged edition of *Before the Mayflower: A History of Black America.* Also in 1982, Bennett published the fifth revised and enlarged edition of this very popular history. He is also a lecturer and teacher of black history.

### JOHN W. BLASSINGAME
### Historian

A professor of history for many years at Yale University, he is the editor of *New Perspectives on Black Studies* (1973); the author of *Black New Orleans: 1860-1880* (1973); the co-editor with Mae G. Henderson and Jessica M. Dunn of *Antislavery Newspapers and Periodicals* (5 vols., 1980-1984); and earlier he wrote *Frederick Douglass: The Clarion Voice* (1976). He is the author of *The Slave Community: Plantation Life in the Antebellum South* (1972); editor of *Slave Testimony: Two Centuries of Letters, Speeches, Interviews and Autobiographies* (1976); and author with Mary F. Berry of *Long Memory: The Black Experience in America* (1981). Blassingame is also editing the 14 volumes of the Frederick Douglass papers—15,000 documents of speeches, debates, interviews, editorials, essays, poems, and correspondence. The first book of the series *The Frederick Douglass Papers: Series One (Speeches, Debates and Interviews)*, Volume I, *1841-46* was published in 1979 by Yale University Press.

### ARNA BONTEMPS
### Poet, Novelist, Anthologist
### 1902-1973

Arna Bontemps was one of the most productive black writers of the twentieth century. Born in Alexandria, Louisiana and raised in California, Arna Bontemps received his B.A. degree from Pacific Union College in Angwin in 1923. The next year, his poetry first appeared in *Crisis* magazine, the NAACP periodical edited by Dr. W. E. B. DuBois. Two years later, *Golgotha Is a Mountain* won the Alexander Pushkin Award, and in 1927, *Nocturne at Bethesda* achieved first honors in the *Crisis* poetry contest. *Personals,* Bontemps collected poems, was published in 1963.

In the late 1920s, Bontemps decided to try his hand at prose, and over the next decade produced such novels as *God Sends Sunday* (1931); *Black Thunder* (1936); and *Drums at Dusk* (1939).

His books for young people include *We Have Tomorrow* (1945); and *Story of the Negro* (1948). Likewise of literary merit are such children's books as *Sad-Faced Boy* (1937); and *Slappy Hooper* (1946). He edited *American Negro Poetry* and two anthologies, with Langston Hughes among others.

Bontemps also served for many years as the chief librarian at Fisk University in Nashville, Tennessee.

In 1968, he completed the editing of a volume of children's poetry. Other publications have been *One Hundred Years of Negro Freedom* (1961); *Anyplace But Here* (published in 1966 in collaboration with Jack Convoy); *Black Thunder* (1968 reprint); *Great Slave Narratives* (1969); *The Harlem Renaissance Remembered: Essays* (1972, 1984); and *The Old South.* He also edited several anthologies. In 1978, Charles H. Nichols edited the *Arna Bontemps/Langston Hughes Letters, 1925-1967,* selected correspondence of two of the most important black U.S. writers from the Harlem Renaissance to the 1960s—an event in black belles-lettres. Robert E. Fleming's *James Weldon Johnson and Arna Wendell Bontemps: A Reference Guide* was published in 1979. A revised updated, expanded edition of *American Negro Poetry* was published in 1974 after Bontemps's death.

### DAVID BRADLEY
### Novelist
### 1950

Born in Bedford, Pennsylvania, Bradley grew up in a rural area. His father, a minister who had attended the University of Pittsburgh and New York University and wrote several books on the history of the Methodist church, was most responsible for Bradley's interest in writing. When he was nine years old, he wrote a play, *Martian Thanksgiving,* which was performed by his Cub Scout troop. Bradley entered the University of Pennsylvania in 1968, and majored in English and creative writing, preparing for a writing career. While an undergraduate he wrote the novel *South Street*, published in 1975, about the black underclass on South Street in Philadelphia. He rejected the civil rights struggle for power of the 1960s by his black fellow students at the university. Believing that blacks were powerless with no way of getting any power, he gravitated to the powerless underclass on South Street. After graduating from college, Bradley's postgraduate research in American history at the University of London sent him back to the story he had heard in Bedford about the 13 escaped slaves who asked to be killed rather than recaptured, and the 13 unmarked graves discovered by his mother. His fourth version of this big novel about those runaway slaves was finally published in the spring of 1981 as *The Chaneysville Incident.* The book received many glowing reviews, and in 1982, was selected as one of the six novels or books of short stories nominated for the second annual P.E.N./Faulkner Award for fiction. His novel won the award. Bradley is a professor of English at Temple University in Philadelphia.

### WILLIAM STANLEY BRAITHWAITE
### Poet, Critic
### 1878-1962

In the early part of his career, it was not generally known that William Stanley Braithwaite was black although his name was familiar to many readers through his book reviews for the *Boston Transcript,* and such books of poetry as *Lyrics of Life and Love* (1904), and *The House of Falling Leaves* (1908).

The prolific Arna Bontemps.

In 1950 Gwendolyn Brooks became the first black writer to win a Pulitzer Prize.

From 1913 to 1929, Braithwaite published an annual *Anthology of Magazine Verse* which brought before the public many of the works of such noted American poets as Edgar Lee Masters, Vachel Lindsay, and Carl Sandburg long before they were ever published in book form.

Braithwaite's other books include *The Book of Elizabethan Verse* (1906), *The Book of Georgian Verse* (1908); *The Book of Restoration Verse* (1909); his *Selected Poems* (1948); and a biography of the famous Bronte literary family in England. *The William Stanley Braithwaite Reader,* edited by Philip Butcher, was published in 1972.

The recipient of the NAACP's Spingarn Medal in 1918, Braithwaite spent most of his later years in education, serving notably as professor of creative literature at Atlanta University.

## BENJAMIN BRAWLEY
### Literary, Historian
### 1882-1939

Although he wrote a number of poems and short stories, the major portion of Benjamin Brawley's work was in the field of literary and social history.

Brawley was born in Columbia, South Carolina and educated at Morehouse College, the University of Chicago, and Harvard. He later taught at Morehouse, Shaw, and Howard.

His books include *A Short History of English Drama* (1921); *A New Survey of English Literature* (1925); *The Negro Genius* (1937), a biography of Paul L. Dunbar; *A Short History of the American Negro;* and *Negro Builders and Heroes* (1937). The latter was written two years before his death.

## GWENDOLYN BROOKS
### Poet
### 1912

Gwendolyn Brooks is one of many blacks to win Pulitzer Prizes in various fields. (Duke Ellington was nominated for the Pulitzer Prize in music in 1965 but was turned down amid controversy and resignation of judges.) Miss Brooks received this prestigious award in 1950 for *Annie Allen,* a volume of her poetry which had been published a year earlier.

Miss Brooks was born in Topeka, Kansas, moved to Chicago at an early age, and was educated there, graduating from Wilson Junior College in 1936.

She had her first taste of ghetto life during her first job as secretary to a "spiritual advisor" who sold "lovedrops." Although unfamiliar with these conditions from her native environment, she was nonetheless alert enough to realize that they could offer her much in the way of unique material for her writing.

In 1945, she completed a book of poems, *A Street in Bronzeville,* and was selected by *Mademoiselle* as one of the year's 10 most outstanding American women. She was made a fellow of the American Academy of Arts and Letters in 1946, and received Guggenheim Fellowships for 1946 and 1947.

In 1949, she won the Eunice Tietjen Prize for Poetry in the annual competition sponsored by *Poetry* magazine. She was poet laureate of the state of Illinois.

Her other books include a collection of children's poems, *Bronzeville Boys and Girls* (1956); a novel, *Maud Martha* (1953); and two books of poetry, *The Bean Eaters* (1960); and *Selected Poems* (1963). She has also written *In the Mecca; Riot; The World of Gwendolyn Brooks; Report from Part One: The Autobiography of Gwendolyn Brooks; Family Pictures; Beckonings; Aloneness; Primer for Blacks;* and *To Disembark.*

Her poems and stories have also been published in magazines and two anthologies *Soon, One Morning;* and *Beyond the Angry Black.* She has edited *A Broadside Treasury* and *Jump Bad, A New Chicago Anthology.* George Kent, a black professor of English at the University of Chicago, was writing a biography of Gwendolyn Brooks with access to her notebooks, but he died some years ago. However, D. H. Melhem's *Gwendolyn Brooks: Poetry and the Heroic Voice* was published in 1986 by University Press of Kentucky. This doctoral dissertation is a critical study of Brooks's work by a white woman critic and poet. Another book is R. Baxter Miller's *Langston Hughes and Gwendolyn Brooks: A Reference Guide* (1979)

## CLAUDE BROWN
### Author
### 1927

Claude Brown's claim to literary fame rests largely on his best-selling autobiography *Manchild in the Promised Land,* which was published in 1965 when its author was 28.

The book is the story of Brown's life in Harlem and, in the process, becomes a highly realistic documentary of life in the ghetto. It tells of Brown's escapades with the Harlem Buccaneers, a "bopping gang," and of his later involvement with the Forty Thieves, an elite stealing division of this same gang.

After attending the Wiltwyck School for emotionally disturbed and deprived boys, Brown returned to New York, was later sent to Warwick Reform School three times, and eventually made his way downtown to a small loft apartment near Greenwich Village. Changing his style of life, Brown finished high school and went on to graduate from Howard University in 1965.

Brown began work on his book in 1963, submitting a manuscript of some 1,500 pages which was eventually cut and reworked into the finished product over a two-year period. Brown completed law school in the late 1960s and is now practicing in California. In 1976, he published *The Children of Ham* about a group of young blacks living as a family in a condemned Harlem tenement, begging, stealing, and doing whatever is necessary to survive.

## STERLING BROWN
### Poet, Critic
### 1901-1989

In the period immediately following the Harlem Renaissance, Sterling Brown received favorable attention for *Southern Road*, a volume of poetry published in 1932 (reprinted in 1974). In contrast to the urban environment of the Harlem school, Brown drew his material from the rural South.

Born in Washington, D.C., Brown was educated at Williams College and Harvard. Except for brief periods during which he served as visiting lecturer at the New School for Social Research, Vassar, and at the University of Minnesota, he spent his entire teaching career at Howard University except for his first three years at other black colleges. He retired many years ago.

In the 1930s, Brown received a Guggenheim Fellowship and the following year published two works: *The Negro in American Fiction,* and *Negro Poetry and Drama* in 1937 (both reprinted in 1969). He was one of the three editors of *The Negro Caravan* (1941, 1969), authored many magazine articles, and in 1974 published *The Last Ride of Wild Bill,* a book of poetry. In 1980, The Collected Poems of Sterling Brown, edited by Michael S. Harper, was published and was co-winner of the Anisfield-Wolf Award for 1980.

There are two books about Brown and his work: *Sterling A. Brown: A/UMUM Tribute* , published in 1976 by the Black History Museum UMUM Committee of Philadelphia with many tributes and memoirs, some of his poems and essays and a 13-page bibliography of writings by and about Brown; The other book is Joanne V. Gabbin's *Sterling A. Brown: Building The Black Aesthetic Tradition* (1985), the first full-length study of Brown's life and works. He was involved in the Federal Writer's Project. Brown had been writing his memoirs and he had often said that he wanted to bring out a new updated edition of *The Negro Caravan.* But other editors will have to take over his projects which he left uncompleted when he died January 13, 1989, at the age of 87.

*Claude Brown's life story forms the basis for* Manchild in the Promised Land.

*Ed Bullins has captured wide audiences with* The Taking of Miss Jenny.

He lived in Washington, D.C. Darry Pinckney's *"The Last New Negro"* (*N.Y. Review of Books*, Mar. 16, 1989) was written about Brown after his death.

**WILLIAM WELLS BROWN**
**Novelist, Dramatist**
**1815-1884**

Williams Wells Brown was the first American black to publish a novel, the first to publish a drama, and the first to publish a travel book.

Born a slave in Lexington, Kentucky and taken to St. Louis as a young boy, Brown worked for a time in the offices of the *St. Louis Times,* and then took a job on a riverboat in service on the Mississippi. In 1834, Brown fled to Canada, taking his name from a friendly Quaker whom he met there. While working as a steward on Lake Erie ships, he educated himself and became well known as a public speaker. In 1849, he went to England and Paris to attend the Peace Congress, remaining abroad for five years.

His first published work, the *Narrative of William H. Brown,* went into three editions within eight months. A year later, a collection of his poems was published, *The Anti-Slavery Harp,* and in 1852 his travel book *Three Years in Europe* appeared in London.

Brown's *Clotel, or the President's Daughter,* a melodramatic novel about miscegenation, was first published in London in 1853. As the first novel by an American black (it subsequently went through two revisions), its historical importance transcends its aesthetic shortcomings.

Brown's other books include the first Negro drama *The Escape, or a Leap for Freedom* (1858); *The Black Man: His Antecedents, His Genius, and His Achievements* (1863); *The Negro in the American Rebellion: His Heroism and Fidelity* (1867); and *The Rising Son* (1874). Two important books about Brown are William E. Farrison's *William Wells Brown: Author and Reformer* (1969); and Jean F. Yellin's *The Intricate Knot: Black Figures in American Literature 1776-1863* (1972).

**ED BULLINS**
**Dramatist, Essayist, Poet**
**1935**

Ed Bullins was born in Philadelphia and grew up in Los Angeles. Bullins is a writer of drama, and one of the founders of the Black Arts/West in the Fillmore District of San Francisco. He patterned this experiment after the Black Arts Repertory Theater School in Harlem, which was founded and directed by Imamu Baraka and is active in analyzing the black experience in America. In 1977, when *Daddy,* the sixth play in his "20th-Century Cycle" opened at the New Federal Theatre in New York's Henry Street Settlement, Bullins in an interview with the *New York Times* foresaw black theatrical producers taking plays to cities with large black populations and spreading out unless something happens to kill the economy. A leader of the black theater movement and creator of more than 50 plays, he has yet to have a play produced on Broadway.

Bullins' main themes are the violence and tragedy of drug abuse and the oppressive life style of the ghetto. He presents his material in a realistic and naturalistic style. From 1965 to 1968 he wrote *The Rally; How Do You Do; Goin' a Buffalo; Clara's Old Man; The Electronic Nigger;* and *In The Wine Time.* He has also produced *The Fabulous Miss Marie.*

He has been a creative member of Black Arts Alliance, working with Baraka in producing films on the West Coast.

Bullins has been connected with the New Lafayette Theater in Harlem where he was a resident playwright. His books are *Five Plays; New Plays from the Black Theatre* (editor); *The Reluctant Rapist; The New Lafayette Theatre Presents; The Theme Is Blackness; Four Dynamite Plays; The Duplex; The Hungered One: Early Writings;* and *How Do You Do: A Nonsense Drama.*

**PHILIP BUTCHER**
**Essayist, Scholar**
**1918**

Philip Butcher was born in Washington, D.C., and attended Howard University where he received an A. B. in 1942 and an M. A. in 1947. He pursued his education at Columbia University where he was awarded a Ph.D. in 1956.

After serving in the U.S. Army during World War II, he received fellowships from the General Education Board (1948) and from the John Hay Whitney Foundation (1951).

The works of Philip Butcher can be found in *Opportunity, Phylon, Journal of Negro History, CLA Journal, Shakespeare*

*Quarterly,* and *The American Literary Realism.* His essays present vital analyses of, and key insight into, the works of major American writers.

His two books on George W. Cable were published by Columbia University Press and Twayne Publishers. He edited The *William Stanley Braithwaite Reader,* which was published in 1972, and *The Ethnic Image in Modern American Literature* (1984). He also edited *The Minority Presence in American Literature* (1977).

### CHARLES WADDELL CHESNUTT
**Novelist**
**1858-1932**

Charles Waddell Chesnutt was the first black writer to deal with the race question from the Negro's point of view.

Born in Cleveland, Ohio, in 1858, Chesnutt moved to North Carolina with his family at the age of eight. Largely self-educated, he was admitted to the Ohio bar in 1887, the same year in which his first story, *"The Gophered Grapevine,"* was published in the *Atlantic Monthly.* This was followed in 1899 by two collections of his stories, *The Conjure Woman* and *The Wife of His Youth.*

His first novel, *The House Behind the Cedars* (1900), dealt with a young girl's attempt to "pass" for white. A year later, *The Marrow of Tradition* examined the violence of the post-Reconstruction period. His final novel, *The Colonel's Dream,* was published in 1905 and typified Chesnutt's basically ingratiating approach to his art, one which the writers of the Harlem School were later to reject. Chesnutt also wrote a biography, *Frederick Douglass.* There has been a great revival of interest in Chesnutt in recent years with the publication of six or more books about him. Two of these books are Sylvia Lyons Render's edited *The Short Fiction of Charles W. Chesnutt* (1982) and William L. Andrews's *The Literary Career of Charles W. Chesnutt (1981)*

### ALICE CHILDRESS
**Playwright, Novelist, Actress**
**1920**

Born in Charleston, South Carolina, she studied acting at the American Negro Theatre and attended Radcliffe Institute from 1966 to 1968 through a Harvard University appointment as a scholar-writer. Her plays are *Florence* (one-act play); *Gold Through the Trees; Just a Little Simple* (based on Langston Hughes' *Simple Speaks His Mind* ); *Trouble in Mind; Wedding Band; Wine in the Wilderness;* and *When the Rattlesnake Sounds: A Play about Harriet Tubman.* Childress also edited *Black Scenes* (1971), excerpts from plays in the Zenith series for children. Her other books are *Like One of the Family: Conversations from a Domestic's Life* (1956); *A Hero Ain't Nothing but a Sandwich* (1973) (novel); and *A Short Walk* (1979), a novel. Childress' play *Trouble in Mind* won the Obie Award in 1956 as the best original off-Broadway production. Her book *Rainbow Jordan* for young people was published in 1982. She wrote, in the 1980s, a play based on the life of the black woman comedian Jackie (Moms) Mabley (see performing arts section). The play was produced in New York City.

### JOHN HENRIK CLARKE
**Essayist, Editor, Anthologist**
**1915**

Born in Union Springs, Alabama in 1915, Clarke spent most of his early youth in Columbus, Georgia. Since 1933, Clarke has been a resident of New York City, for the most part in Harlem. He has written for a number of magazines and newspapers, among them *Black World, Negro History Bulletin, New York Amsterdam News,* and *The Pittsburgh Courier.* Clarke was a co-founder of the *Harlem Quarterly* in 1950, and since 1962, has been an associate editor of *Freedomways.* Since 1974, he has been a professor in Black Studies at Hunter College, New York City. His specialty is African history, but he also teaches Afro-American history.

Some of the books edited by Clarke include *Harlem: A Communication in Transition* (1964, 1970); *Harlem U.S.A.* (1965, 1971); *American Negro Short Stories* (1966); *William Styron's Nat Turner, Ten Black Writers Respond* (1968); *Malcolm X: The Man and His Times* (1969); and *Marcus Garvey and the Vision of Africa* (1973). Other books edited by Clarke are Harlem (short stories, 1970); *Slave Trade and Slavery* (1970) with Vincent Harding; *Pan-Africanism and the Liberation of Southern Africa: A Tribute to W. E. B. DuBois* (1978); and *Dimensions of the Struggle Against Apartheid, A Tribute to Paul Robeson* (1979).

### ELDRIDGE CLEAVER
**Author, Civil Rights Leader**
**1935**

(For Biography see Civil Rights section.)

### CYRUS COLTER
**Novelist**
**1910-**

Cyrus Colter, a master story teller, was born in Indiana. He became a lawyer in Chicago in 1940 and was appointed to state and federal jobs. He is the author of four novels: *River of Eros* (1972, 1973); *The Hippodrome* (1973); *A Chocolate Soldier* (1988); and *Night Studies* (1982). He also wrote *The Beach Umbrella* (1970, 1971) short stories and *The Amoralists & Other Tales:Collected Stories* (1988). His work has been published in anthologies and magazines, and he has received several literary awards including the Iowa School of Letters Award.

### JOSEPH SEAMON COTTER SR.
**Poet**
**1861-1949**

Though he did not, in his youth, attend school past the third grade, Joseph Seamon Cotter, Sr. achieved distinction during his lifetime as a poet—primarily in the dialect idiom. Cotter's earliest work, *A Rhyming* (1895), was followed in later years by the prize-winning *"Tragedy of Pete,"* which was awarded an Opportunity Prize during the Harlem Renaissance. His *Collected Poems* appeared in 1938. Cotter published seven other books.

*Countee Cullen was a leading figure in the Harlem Renaissance.*

Born at Bardstown, Kentucky, Cotter worked in various odd jobs during his youth and became a school teacher in Louisville after he returned to his schooling at the age of 22. His poetry reflects more than 50 years' experience as a teacher, and is a dynamic mixture of the storytelling art, the young man's thirst for racial leadership, and the tutor at work. His dialect poetry is mindful of Paul Laurence Dunbar at his best, although Cotter tends to be more racially critical than his more famous peer.

## JOSEPH SEAMON COTTER JR.
### Poet
### 1895-1919

Young Joseph Seamon Cotter, Jr. followed in his father's footsteps as a poet, although he enjoyed the benefit of collegiate training at Fisk University in Nashville. Sickly, Cotter was forced to abandon the school in his second year after contracting tuberculosis. His only distinguished work, *The Bank of Gideon,* a thin volume of only 30 pages, was published in 1918, shortly before his death.

## COUNTEE CULLEN
### Poet
### 1903-1946

Countee Cullen was one of the leading figures in the Harlem Renaissance.

Born Countee Porter on May 30, 1903 in Baltimore, he was orphaned at an early age and adopted by Reverend Frederick Cullen, pastor of New York's Salem Methodist Church. At New York University, Cullen won Phi Beta Kappa honors and was awarded the Witter Bynner Poetry Prize. In 1925, while still a student at New York University, Cullen completed *Color*, a volume of poetry which received the Harmon Foundation's first gold medal for literature two years later.

In 1926, he earned his M.A. at Harvard and a year later finished both *The Ballad of the Brown Girl* and *Copper Sun.* This was followed in 1929 by *The Black Christ,* written during a two-year sojourn in France on a Guggenheim Fellowship. In 1927, he edited *Caroling Dusk: An Anthology of Verse by Negro Poets.* The book was reprinted in 1972.

Upon his return to New York City, Cullen began a teaching career in the public school system. During this period, he also produced a novel, *One Way to Heaven* (1932); *The Medea and Other Poems* (1935); *The Lost Zoo* (1940); and *My Lives and How I Lost Them* (1942, 1971).

In 1947, a year after his death, Cullen's own selections of his best work were collected in a volume published under the title *On These I Stand.*

His second wife Mrs. Ida Cullen Cooper died in New York City on May 3, 1986.

Two books about Cullen and his work are Blanche Ferguson's Countee Cullen and the Negro Renaissance (1966) and Margaret Perry's A Bio-Bibliography of Countee Cullen, 1903-1946 (1971).

## ARTHUR P. DAVIS
### Essayist, Scholar
### 1904

Arthur P. Davis was born in Hampton, Virginia. He received his Ph.D. from Columbia University in 1942. He has served as a college professor at North Carolina College (1927-1928) and at Virginia Union (1929-1944).

Davis is most noted for co-editing *The Negro Caravan* (1941) with Sterling A. Brown and Ulysses Lee. He published a book based on his doctoral dissertation, called *Isaac Watts: His Life and Works* (1943).

A leading critic of Negro literature, many of Davis' essays can be found in *Phylon, Common Ground,* and *Opportunity.* His most famous essays have been analyses of works by Phillis Wheatley, Langston Hughes, Countee Cullen, and writers of the Harlem Renaissance. He recently retired as an English teacher from Howard University where he had been a professor since 1944.

Davis is the editor, with Saunders Redding, of *Cavalcade, Negro American Writing from 1760 to the Present,* published in 1971. A new edition of this anthology was published in 1983. His book *From the Dark Tower: Afro-American Writers 1900 to 1960* was published in 1974.

## CHARLES T. DAVIS
### Professor, Critic
### 1918?-1981

Charles T. Davis was born at Hampton University, Va. He earned degrees from Dartmouth College, the University of Chicago, and New York University. He also taught at New York University, Princeton University, and Pennsylvania State University, and was visiting professor at Harvard University, Rutgers University and Bryn Mawr. He received a Rockefeller Foundation fellowship of $10 to $20,000 to study the early development of the Afro-American literary tradition. Davis had been professor of English and chairman of Afro-American studies at Yale University for many years before he died on March 25, 1981, at the age of 62.

His books are *Walt Whitman's Poems* (1955) edited by Davis and Gay Wilson Allen; *Selected Early Peoms and Letters of Edwin A. Robinson* edited by Davis; Lucy Larcom's *A New England Girlhood* edited by Davis; a section by Davis on modern poetry in *American Literary Scholarship* (1963); *On Being Black: Writings by Afro-Americans from Frederick Douglass to the Present* (1970) edited by Davis and Daniel Walden; *Richard Wright: A Primary Bibliography* (1982) by Davis and Michel Fabre; *The Slave's Narrative* edited by Davis and Henry Louis Gates Jr.; and his last book *Black Is The Color of the Cosmos: Essays on Afro-American Literature and Culture, 1942-1981* (1984).

## LENWOOD G. DAVIS
### Bibliographer, Writer
### 19-?

Having received his undergraduate and master's degrees in history from North Carolina Central University and Doctorate in history from Carnegie-Mellon University, Davis has taught at several colleges. He is now associate professor of history at Winston-Salem State University.

Davis has compiled more than seventy-eight bibliographies mostly as booklets and is the author of a dozen or more books. These are *I Have a Dream: The Life and Times of Martin Luther King Jr.* (1973); *The Black Woman in American Society: A Selected Annotated Bibliography* (1975); *The Black Family in the United States: A Selected Bibliography of Annotated Books, Articles and Dissertations on Black Families in America* (1978); *Sickle Cell Anemia: An Annotated Bibliography* (1978); *Black Artists in the United States: An Annotated Bibliography* (1980) with Janet L. Sims; *Marcus Garvey: An Annotated Bibliography* (1980) also with Janet L. Sims; *Black Aged in the United States* (1980) and *Black Athletes in the United States: A Bibliography* (1981) both with Belinda S. Daniels; *A Paul Robeson Research Guide: A Selected, Annotated Bibliography* (1982); *The Ku Klux Klan: A Bibliography* (1984) with Janet L. Sims; *Black-Jewish Relations in the United States, 1752-1984: A Selected Bibliography* (1984); *A Bibliographical Guide to Black Studies Programs in the United States: An Annotated Bibliography* (1985) with George H. Hill; *Religious Broadcasting, 1920-1983: A Selectively Annotated Bibliography* (1984) and *Blacks in the American Armed Forces 1776-1983: A Bibliography* (1984) both with George H. Hill; *Joe Louis: A Bibliography of Articles, Books, etc.* (1983) and *Malcolm X: Selected Bibliography* (1984) both with Marsha L. Moore.

Davis said that he started compiling these bibliographies to provide sources for his students who said that they could not find material to write papers on various subjects and individuals. See Richard Newman's *Black Access: A Bibliography of Afro-American Bibliographies* (1984) for a listing of Davis's bibliographical booklets and pamphlets. Also, see the *Bulletin of Bibliography* for September 1985 for a bibliography of Davis's works.

## MARTIN R. DELANY
### Essayist, Author
### 1812-1885

Most of Martin R. Delany's writing was concerned with the search for identity and self-realization. Delany, a native of Charlestown, Virginia, was widely read and traveled, and developed in his lifetime a dynamic and expressive black power ethic.

One of Delany's first serious ventures was to trace his lineage to the African chieftains whom he believed were his actual forefathers. Delany pursued formal education with resolve and vigor once his parents had escaped from Virginia to western Pennsylvania. He eventually studied medicine at Harvard University Medical School and while a practicing physician in Pittsburgh, was instrumental in putting down a cholera epidemic there.

Prior to the outbreak of the Civil War, Delany led an investigation into the Niger Valley in West Africa, later publishing an official report of his explorations in a study which contained specific recommendations for black repatriation. During the war itself, Delany served as a medical officer, rising to the rank of major. Reconstruction found him active in politics, albeit unsuccessfully.

Retirement enabled him to prepare his most ambitious work, *Principles of Ethnology* (1879). His best-known work, however, remains a political tract entitled *The Condition, Elevation, Emigration and Destiny of the Colored People of the United States, Politically Considered* (1852). He also wrote the novel *Blake, or the Huts of America* published in 1859; reprinted in 1970. *Search for a Place* by Delany and Robert Campbell was resurrected and published in 1869. It is the *Official Report of the Niger Valley Exploring Party* (1861).

Two books about Delany are Dorothy Sterling's *The Making of an Afro-American: Martin Robison Delany* (1969); and Victor Ullman's *Martin Delany: The Beginning of Black Nationalism* (1971).

Delaney died in Xenia, Ohio, home of Wilberforce University.

## SAMUEL R. DELANY
### Science Fiction Writer
### 1942

Born in Harlem, and a published writer at the age of 19, Delany has been a prolific writer of science fiction, novelettes,

Major Martin R. Delany penned an early political analysis of race.

Paul Laurence Dunbar introduced the nation to black dialect in formal poetry.

and novels. His first book was *The Jewels of Aptor* (1962); followed by *Captives of the Flame* (1963); *The Towers of Toron* (1964); *City of a Thousand Suns* (1965); *The Ballad of Beta-2* (1965); *Babel-17* (1966); *Empire Star* (1966); *The Einstein Intersection; Out of the Dead City* (1968); and *Nova* (1968). *Babel-17* and *The Einstein Intersection* both won Nebula Awards from the Science Fiction Writers of America, as have his short stories *"Aye, and Gomorrah"* and *"Time Considered as a Helix of Semi-Precious Stones,"* which also won a Hugo Award at the World Science Fiction Convention at Heidelberg. Delany co-edited the speculative fiction quarterly *Quark, Nos. 1, 2, 3, 4* with his wife, National Book Award winning poet Marilyn Hacker. It was published by Popular Library in New York. The Delanys have a daughter. He also wrote, directed, and edited the half-hour film *The Orchid*. In 1975, Delany was Visiting Butler Chair Professor of English at the State University of New York at Buffalo.

His novels and short stories of the 1970s are *Diftglass: Tales of Speculative Fiction* (1971); and *The Fall of the Towers trilogy* (1971); *Captives of the Flame; The Tower of Toron;* and *City of a Thousand Suns*. He has also published *The Tides Lust* (1973); and *Tales of Neveryona*. *Dhalgren* (1975) is the major novel of this brilliant young writer, published when he was 32 years old. His last three books are the novel *Triton* (1976); *Empire: A Visual Novel* with Howard V. Chaykin; and *Heavenly Breakfast: An Essay on the Winter of Love* (1979), an autobiographical look back by Delany of his youthful adventures of the winter and spring of 1967-1968. *Galaxy* magazine has called Delany "the best science fiction writer in the world." Michael W. Peplow and Robert S. Bravard's *Samuel R. Delany: A Primary and Secondary Bibliography* was published in 1980.

Other later books by this prolific author are *Distant Stars* (1981); *Stars in My Pocket Like Grains of Sand* (1984); *The Splendor and Misery of Bodies of Cities* (1985); *Flight from Neveryona* (1985); *Neveryon* a(1986); and *The Bridge of Lost Desire* (1988). His non-fiction includes: *The Jewel-Hinged Jaw; The American Shore*; *Starboard Wine; The Straits of Messina (1988);* and *The Motion of Light in Water* (autobiography) (1988).

Delany is in *Who's Who in Science Fiction* (1976) compiled by Brian Ash, and also in Seth McEvoy's Samuel R. Delany (1984).

He has been appointed a professor of comparative literature at the University of Massachusetts at Amherst.

## OWEN DODSON
### Dramatist, Poet, Novelist
### 1914-1983

Poet/dramatist Owen Dodson's most ambitious work revolves about the Father Divine legend and is, with pun-like intent, entitled *The Divine Comedy*. The play was produced at the Yale University Theatre in 1938.

A native of Brooklyn, Dodson attended Bates College and went on to earn a Master of Fine Arts degree from Yale. His alma mater also presented Dodson's *The Garden of Time*. Success in university theater led to the play's later appearances at predominantly black universities throughout the South.

Dodson later went into teaching at the Atlanta University complex, although he was commissioned to write a play about the Amistad Mutiny, a shipboard slave uprising in the 1840s. His traditional and experimental verse and short stories were published in several quarterlies and anthologies. He has now retired after many years at Howard University.

His books are: *Powerful Long Ladder* (1946) (poetry); *Boy at the Window* (1951) (novel), reprinted in paperback with the title *When Trees Were Green* ; *Come Home Early Child* (1977) (novel); and his short story *The Summer Fire* which won The Paris Review prize when published there in 1956; also reprinted in *Come Out The Wilderness* (1965) edited by L. M. Schulman; and lastly, *The Confession Stone* (1970).

Dodson also has poetry in James Van Der Zee's *The Harlem Book of the Dead* (1979) Also James V. Hatch wrote *Owen Dodson: Excerpts from a Biography in Progress* (The Massachusetts Review, Winter 1987).

Dodson died June 21, 1983, in New York City at the age of 68.

## W. E. B. DUBOIS
## Critic, Editor, Scholar, Author, Civil Rights Leader
## 1868-1963

(For biography see Civil Rights Section.)

## PAUL LAURENCE DUNBAR
## Poet
## 1872-1906

The first black poet to gain a national reputation in the United States, Paul Laurence Dunbar was also the first to use Negro dialect within the formal structure of his work.

Born of former slaves in Dayton, Ohio, Dunbar went to work as an elevator operator after graduating from high school. His first book of poetry, *Oak and Ivy,* was privately printed in 1893 and was followed by *Majors and Minors,* which appeared two years later. Neither book was an immediate sensation, but there were enough favorable reviews in such magazines as Harper's to encourage Dunbar in the pursuit of a full-fledged literary career. In 1896, Dunbar completed *Lyrics of a Lowly Life*, the single work upon which his subsequent reputation was irrevocably established.

Before his untimely death in 1906, Dunbar had become the dominant presence in the world of American Negro poetry. His later works included *Lyrics of Love and Laughter* (1903); *Lyrics of Sunshine and Shadow* (1905); and *Complete Poems*, published posthumously in 1913. This last work contains not only the dialect poems which were his trademark, but many poems in conventional English as well. The book has enjoyed such enormous popularity that it has, to this day, never gone out of print. He also published four novels including *The Sport of Gods* and *The Uncalled,* and four volumes of short stories. There are several biographies of Dunbar.

## RALPH ELLISON
## Novelist, Essayist
## 1914

Ralph Ellison's critical and artistic reputation rests largely on a single masterpiece, his first and only novel, *Invisible Man*. Acclaimed by virtually all who have read it, the novel was given the National Book Award for fiction in 1952. It had been years in the making, and its success heralded the emergence of a major writing talent.

Ellison was born in Oklahoma City, Oklahoma and came to New York City in the late 1930s, after having studied music at Tuskegee Institute for three years. At first interested in sculpture, he turned to writing after coming under the influence of T. S. Eliot's poetry, and as a direct consequence of his friendship with Richard Wright.

In 1955, the American Academy of Arts and Letters awarded Ellison the *Prix de Rome*, which enabled him to live and write in Italy for a time. Since then, he has lectured at New York University and at Bennington College, and has been writer-in-residence at Rutgers University.

His second published work was *Shadow and Act*, a book of essays which appeared in 1964. Excerpts from his second novel have been published in several literary journals. There are three books of essays on him and his novel.

He has retired as Albert Schweitzer Professor of Humanities at New York University (1970-1980) in New York City, and in 1974, was awarded an honorary Doctor of Letters degree by Harvard University.

The thirtieth anniversary edition of *Invisible Man* with a new introduction by Ellison was published in 1982.

Elected to the National Institute of Arts and Letters and the American Academy of Arts and Letters, Ellison was the subject of a *New Yorker* magazine profile in 1976. He received the Medal of Freedom from President Richard M. Nixon in 1969, and an honorary Doctor of Letters degree from Wesleyan University in June 1980 "for his insight into the role of the artist in American culture." There was a Ralph Ellison Festival at Brown University in November 1979. Michael S. Harper and John Wright edited *A Ralph Ellison Festival*, *The Carleton Miscellany* (Vol. 18, No. 3, Winter 1980) with three essays by Ellison and other essays by literary critics. The Ralph Ellison County Library was named for Ellison in Oklahoma City, Okla. in 1975. (See Jervis Anderson's long profile of Ellison's going to the Oklahoma territory for the naming of the library in *The New Yorker*, Nov. 22, 1976). He won the new Langston Hughes Medallion given by the City College of the City University of New York in April 1984 "for contributions to arts and letters" (on the 20th anniversary of the publication of his book Shadow and Act in 1964). President Ronald Reagan gave him the National Medal of Arts in the 1980s.

Ellison lost a 365-page manuscript of an uncompleted novel in a fire at his country place in November 1967. He is now completing his novel for publication and presumably a collection of his short stories. His third book and second book of essays and speeches, *Going To The Territory* (1986, 1987), was hailed as highly literate essay writing although some reviewers disagreed with some of his opinions. Ellison's writings are in many literary anthologies and collections and there are chapters about his work in scores of books as well as masters theses and thirty or more doctoral dissertations on him as a writer.

Some books other than the three books of essays mentioned above about Ellison and his work are Jacqueline Covo's *The Blinking Eye: Ralph Waldo Ellison and His American, French, German and Italian Critics, 1952-1971* (1974), updated by a checklist of Ellison criticism, 1972-1978 in *Black American Literature Forum* (Summer 1978); Robert G. O'Meally's *The Craft of Ralph Ellison* (1980); Alan Nadel's *Invisible Criticism: Ralph Ellison and the American Canon* (1988); Robert N. List's *Daedalus in Harlem : The Joyce-Ellison Connection* (1982); Kimberly W. Benston's edited *Speaking for You: Ralph Ellison's Cultural Vision* (1986); Michael S. Harper and Robert B. Stepto's edited *Chant of Saints: A Gathering of Afro-American Literature, Art and Scholarship* (1979); and M. Thomas Inge et al. (editors ) *Black American Writers: Bibliographical Essays II: Richard Wright, Ralph Ellison, James Baldwin and Amin Baraka* (1975).

## MARI EVANS
### Poet

A poet first noticed in the early 1960s, Mari Evans is noted for her ability to jolt her readers with the beauty of blackness.

Born in Toledo, Ohio, she studied at the University of Toledo. In 1963, her poetry was published in *Phylon, Negro Digest*, and *Dialog*. Two years later she was awarded a John Hay Whitney Fellowship.

One of her better known works is probably *The Alarm Clock,* which deals with the rude awakening of the black American to the white "Establishment." It captures and summarizes the scene of the sixties in the United States.

Miss Evans has been employed as a television producer-director. She also teaches at Purdue University in Indiana.

Her books are *I Am A Black Woman;* and Where Is All the Music?; *Black Women Writers (1950-1980): A Critical Evaluation* (1984) edited by Evans, covering fifteen black women poets, novelists, and playwrights; and her book *Nightstar: Poems From 1973-1978* (1982), published by the Center for Afro-American Studies, University of California, Los Angeles; *J. D.; I Look at Me; Singing Black; The Day They Made Benani;* and *Jim Flying High;* 5 books which were written for children. Her poems appear in over 40 textbooks and anthologies.

## RONALD L. FAIR
### Novelist

Ronald L. Fair was born in Chicago in 1932. He spent two years at a local business college and was a court reporter from 1955 to 1966. He published his first novel, *Many Thousand Gone*, in 1965; and his second novel, *Hog Butcher*, in 1966 which was reprinted in 1975 in paperback with the new title *Cornbread, Earl and Me*, the name of the film made from the novel. Since then, he has taught at Columbia College in Chicago, at Northwestern University, and at Wesleyan University in Connecticut. Fair's third book, *World of Nothing*, consisting of two novellas, was published in several anthologies and magazines. His third novel, *We Can't Breathe,* published in 1971, is an autobiographical work about Fair's growing up in a black ghetto. He has lived in Europe since 1971. Winner of a Guggenheim Fellowship, he published *Rufus*, a book of poems, in Germany in 1976.

## JESSIE REDMON FAUSET
### Novelist
### 1886-1961

Jessie Redmon Fauset was one of the last mainstays of the so-called traditional school of Negro literature. Written in a genteel style, her novels deal primarily with middle-class blacks and are in sharp contrast to the work produced by the young writers of the Harlem School who sought to capture the stark realism of life in the Negro ghetto.

An editor of *Crisis*, Miss Fauset often championed the works of the young writers, even though their direction ran counter to her own. She herself was a prolific Renaissance novelist, publishing four books over a ten-year span: *There is Confusion* (1924); *Plum Bun* (1928); *The Chinaberry Tree* (1931); and *Comedy American Style* (1933).

*Ralph Ellison, a writer of numerous essays, has to date written only one novel,* Invisible Man, *which critics call a masterpiece.*

## ELTON C. FAX
**Illustrator, Writer**
**1909**

Elton Fax stands among America's leading fine artists and illustrators. He is also a noted essayist. Both his drawings and his writings reflect a proud interest in the African legacy of the American black.

Born in Baltimore, he graduated from Syracuse University (B.F.A., 1931). He taught at Claflin University from 1935 to 1936, and was an instructor at the Harlem Community Art Center from 1938 to 1939. His work has been exhibited at the Baltimore Art Museum in 1939; the American Negro Exposition in 1940; the Metropolitan Museum of Art; and Visual Arts Gallery in New York in 1970. Examples of his work hang in some of the nation's best university collections, including Texas Southern, the University of Minnesota, and Virginia State University.

Some notable artworks by Fax include: *Steelworker;* and *Ethiopia Old & New*.

Publications by Fax include *Africa Vignettes; Garvey; Seventeen Black Artists;* and *Black Artists of the New Generation. The Portfolio Black and Beautiful* features his art work, and he has written *Hashar,* about the life of the people of Soviet Central Asia and Kazakhstan.

Other books by Fax are *Contemporary Black Leaders*; *Through Black Eyes: Journeys of a Black Artist to East Africa nd Russia; Elyuchin* (about the Azerbaijan, Armenia and Georgia republics); and *Soviet People as I Knew Them* , with many photographs. *Hashar, Elyuchin, and Soviet People as I Knew Them* are all in the Impressions of the USSR Series.

## RUDOLPH FISHER
**Novelist, Short Story Writer**
**1897-1934**

Rudolph Fisher was born in Washington, D.C. and raised in Providence, Rhode Island. He attended Brown University and Howard Medical School. He came to New York to study biology at Columbia University's College of Physicians and Surgeons and then went on to specialize in roentgenology.

"The City of Refuge," Fisher's first short story, was written while he was still in medical school and depicted Harlem life during the 1920s. It was subsequently reprinted in the anthology *The Best Short Stories of 1925*.

Fisher's two novels, *The Walls of Jericho* (1928) and *The Conjure Man Dies* (1932), never became as popular as his short stories. Other short stories by Fisher are "Ringtail," "High Yaller," "The Promised Land," and "Miss Cynthie."

## CHARLOTTE L. FORTEN
**Author, Poet**
**1837-1914**

A member of the distinguished Forten family (her grandfather James served in the Revolutionary War), Charlotte Forten attended school in Salem, Massachusetts, winning early honors for her poetry while at Higginson Grammar School. She was unable to obtain an education in her native city of Philadelphia because of race.

Her education prepared her for a career in teaching, which she pursued until the Civil War when she served as an agent with the Freedmen's Aid Society at Port Royal, St. Helena Island, off South Carolina.

Her best-known writing was comprised of a series of articles entitled *Glimpses of New England,* which was published in the *National Anti-Slavery Standard.* Other articles on life in the Sea Islands were printed in *Atlantic Monthly,* a publication which gave her widespread circulation. *The Journal of Charlotte Forten,* edited by Roy Allen Billington, was published in 1961.

Though her work is by no means lasting literature, it is important for the exposure Miss Forten gave to racial prejudice in antebellum New England in a middle-class atmosphere, and for her equally relevant characterization of the Sea Islands.

## JOHN HOPE FRANKLIN
**Historian**
**1915**

Black history has had no more scholarly spokesman in the last two decades than John Hope Franklin, whose classic analysis of American history and the blacks place in it, *From Slavery to Freedom* (1947), is ranked in the company of the most authoritative studies of the period. It has gone through many editions and is still in print.

A native of Rentiesville, Oklahoma, Franklin graduated from Fisk University in 1935, and later received his M.A.

*In the work of John Hope Franklin, there is an analysis of the role of African-Americans in American history.*

and Ph.D. degrees from Harvard. Since then, he has taught at Howard, Fisk University, Alabama State Teachers College, and Brooklyn College and has received Rosenwald and Guggenheim Fellowships for research.

In addition to numerous articles in professional journals, Franklin has an impressive list of full-length book credits, including *The Free Negro in North Carolina, 1790-1860* (1943); *The Civil War, Diary of James Ayers* (1947); *Reconstruction After the Civil War* (1961); *The Emancipation Proclamation* (1963); *The Negro in Twentieth Century America* (1967); *Color and Race* (1968); *An Illustrated History of Black Americans; Racial Equality in America;* and *A Southern Odyssey: Travelers in the Antebellum North.* His long-awaited book *George Washington Williams: A Biography* (1985) won the Clarence L. Holte Literary Prize in 1986.

Franklin, who had retired as a professor of History at the University of Chicago, co-edited with August Meier, *Black Leaders of the Twentieth Century* (1982), a volume in the Blacks in the New World series (general editor is August Meier). Franklin was the editor of the Negro American Biographies and Autobiographies series for the University of Chicago Press in the 1960s and 1970s.

Franklin is now teaching constitutional history at Duke University Law School, Durham, N.C. In 1987, he came to Washington, D. C., and read a speech before the Senate Committee holding hearings against Judge Bork's confirmation as a Supreme Court justice.

## E. FRANKLIN FRAZIER
**Historian, Sociologist**
**1894-1962**

Once chairman of Howard University's sociology department, E. Franklin Frazier is best remembered for his controversial book *Black Bourgeoisie,* in which he expounded the theory that the black middle class was isolating itself from the problems of marginal or poverty-stricken blacks. He was an authority on the black family among other subjects.

Born in Baltimore in 1894, Frazier graduated from Howard in 1916 and received his Ph.D. from the University of Chicago in 1931. Three years later, he began a 25-year period in the sociology department of Howard, interrupting his tenure there on occasion to teach at Columbia, New York University, and other universities.

In 1940, and again the following year, Frazier was a Guggenheim fellow in Brazil and the West Indies. He became president of the American Sociological Society in 1948, and a year later was named Chairman of UNESCO's committee of experts on race. Later he served as chief of UNESCO's Applied Science Division in Paris.

Frazier died at George Washington University Hospital after a long illness. He had retired from Howard in 1959. His books include *The Negro Family in the United States; The Negro in the United States; The Negro Church in America;* and *The Free Negro Family and Race; and Culture Contacts in the Modern World.*

*Pulitzer Prize winner Charles Fuller.*

## CHARLES FULLER
**Playwright**
**1939**

He became "stagestruck" in his high-school days when he went to the Old Walnut Street Theater in his native Philadelphia, and saw a Yiddish play starring Molly Picon and Menasha Skulnik. Fuller didn't understand a word of it, "but it was live theater, and I felt myself responding to it."

In 1959, Fuller entered the Army and served in Japan and South Korea, after which he attended Villanova University and La Salle College. While Fuller was working as a housing inspector in Philadelphia, the McCarter Theater in Princeton, New Jersey produced his first play. The theme was intermarriage, and its creator is quick now to tag it "one of the world's worst interracial plays." However, during this time he met members of The Negro Ensemble Company, and in 1974 he wrote his first play for them, *In the Deepest Part of Sleep.* "I decided then that I wanted to do something bigger and beyond myself, something historical, that would stand outside normal black theater. I wanted to open up black theater so that it couldn't be labeled that easily." For NEC's tenth anniversary Fuller wrote *The Brownsville Raid* about the black soldiers who were dishonorably discharged on President Teddy Roosevelt's orders in 1906 after a shoot-out in Brownsville, Texas. The play was a hit and Fuller followed it a few seasons later with *Zooman and the Sign*, a melodrama that won two Obie awards.

*A Soldiers Play,* which won a Pulitzer Prize in 1982, is his fourth play for The Negro Ensemble Company. This drama dealing with a murder set in a backwater New Orleans Army camp in 1944, opened NEC's fifteenth anniversary season in 1981 with a long run and was hailed by the *New York Times* as "tough, taut and fully realized." *A Soldiers Play* became *A Soldier's Story* when it was produced as a film in 1984 by Columbia Pictures. Fuller wrote the screenplay and black actor Howard E. Rollins Jr. was the film's star.

After several years, the Negro Ensemble Company of New York presented Fuller's two-act play *Sally*, about southern slaves and the Civil War, at the First National Black Arts Festival in Atlanta, Georgia, from July 29 to August 7, 1988. Douglass Turner Ward directed and acted in the play which was also presented as the opening work in the Company's new season in New York beginning in October 1988. Fuller's second play *Prince,* in a cycle of five new plays tracing the history of Black America from the Civil War to the turn of the century, will be produced in the fall of 1989 by the Company. The other three plays are to be produced in the 1990s. Theater reviewers found some problems of drama craftsmanship and characterization in *Sally,* the first play of the series when it was produced in Atlanta.

The recipient of the Guggenheim Foundation Fellowship, the Rockefeller Foundation, and the National Endowment for the Arts and CAPS Fellowships in playwrighting, Fuller describes himself as a playwright who happens to be black, rather than a black playwright.

## ERNEST J. GAINES
### Novelist, Short Story Writer
### 1933

Although Ernest J. Gaines had written three novels and many short stories, it was not until 1968 and the publication of *Bloodline*, a book of short stories, that he began to receive considerable attention.

Gaines was born on a plantation in Louisiana. He moved to California in 1949 where he did his undergraduate study at San Francisco State College. In 1959, he received the Wallace Stegner Fellowship in creative writing. The following year he was awarded the Joseph Henry Jackson Literary Award.

His first novel to be published was *Catherine Carmier* (1964). Other novels by Gaines are *Of Love and Dust* (1967); *Barren Summer* (completed in 1963 but never published); *The Autobiography of Miss Jane Pittman* (1971); *A Warm Day in November* (for young people); and *In My Father's House* (1978). The 1974 television production of *The Autobiography of Miss Jane Pittman* with Cicely Tyson boosted his reputation quite a bit. Gaines's latest work is the novel *A Gathering of Old Men* published in 1983.

## HENRY LOUIS GATES JR.
### Professor, Critic

Gates, a young MacArthur Foundation Award winner, is W. E. B. DuBois professor of literature at Cornell University. Earlier, he was a professor at Yale University. Several years ago, Gates established that Harriet Wilson, the author of the 1859 novel *Our Nig*, was a black woman and brought out a new edition of the novel. *Our Nig* thus became the first novel by a black U. S. woman instead of Frances E. W. Harper's *Iola Leroy*, or *Shadows Uplifted,* published in 1892. Jean Fagan Yellin also recently established that Harriet Jacobs, the author of *Incidents in the Life of a Slave Girl* (1861), was a black woman and brought out a new edition of the book published by Harvard University Press with a photograph of the author. Frances E. W. Harper and Harriet Jacobs (but not Harriet Wilson) are included in The Schomburg Library of Nineteenth-Century Black Women Writers (30 vols.) edited by Henry Louis Gates Jr.

Gates has written essays and book reviews for *Southern Review, N. Y. Times Book Review, Critical Inquiry, Representations* and other periodicals. He has three essays in Afro-American Literature: *The Reconstruction of Instruction* (1979), edited by Dexter Fisher and Robert B. Stepto. Recently he has published *The Signifying Monkey: Theory of Afro-American Literary Criticism* (1988) and *Figures in Black: Words Signs and the "Racial" Self* (1987). He also edited *Black Literature and Literary Theory* and *The Slave's Narrative* with Charles T. Davis. Gates is also editing *The Norton Anthology of Afro-American Literature* to be published in the future.

*Ernest J. Gaines, novelist and short story writer*

## ADDISON GAYLE JR.
**Professor, Writer**
**1932**

Born in New York City, Gayle obtained a bachelors degree from City College of the City University of New York in 1964, and a master's degree from the University of California at Los Angeles in 1965. He was a lecturer in English at C. C. N. Y. from 1965 to 1969, and has been a professor of English at Bernard Baruch College in the City University from 1969 to the present.

Gayle wrote many articles and essays during the 1960s and 1970s for *Negro Digest* (*later Black World*), *CLA Journal, Phylon* and other magazines. His Books are: (editor) *Black Expression: Essays By and About Black Americans in the Creative Arts* (1969, 1970); (editor) *The Black Aesthetic* (1971, 1972); (editor) *Bondage, Freedom and Beyond: The Prose of Black Americans* (1971); *Oak and Ivy: A Biography of Paul Laurence Dunbar* (1971); *Claude McKay: The Black Poet at War* (1972); *The Black Situation* (1970, 1972); *The Way of the New World: The Black Novel in America* (1975); *Wayward Child: A Personal Odyssey* (1977); and *Richard Wright: Ordeal of a Native Son* (1980). His essays are in anthologies of Black writers such as *Black Literature in America* (Baker) and *New Black Voices* (Chapman).

*Nikki Giovanni is a successful young author who often reads her poetry on TV.*

## DONALD B. GIBSON
**Professor, Writer**

Gibson is professor of English at Rutgers College, Rutgers University, New Brunswick, New Jersey. His writings have been published in many journals and books. His critical books are *The Fiction of Stephen Crane*; and *The Politics of Literary Expression: A Study of Major Black Writers.* (1981); Gibson edited the well-known *Five Black Writers: Essays on Wright, Ellison, Baldwin, Hughes and LeRoi Jones* (1970); and *Modern Black Poets: A Collection of Critical Essays* (1973).

## NIKKI GIOVANNI
**Poet**
**1943**

Nikki Giovanni was born in Knoxville, Tennessee. She studied at Fisk University and at the University of Pennsylvania. Her first book of poetry, *Black Feeling, Black Talk,* published in the mid-1960s, was followed by *Black Judgment* in 1968. These two were combined as *Black Feeling, Black Talk, Black Judgment* in 1970.

In 1974, her poems were to be found in many black literature anthologies and she had also become a media personality through her TV appearances where she read her poetry. Many of her poems were put to soul or gospel music accompaniment. One such recording is *Truth Is on Its Way.*

Giovanni is a prolific author. Her other books are *Re-creation; Spin a Soft Black Song; Night Comes Softly: Anthology of Black Female Voices; My House; Gemini: An Extended Autobiographical Statement; Ego Tripping and Other Poems for Young People; A Dialogue (with James Baldwin);* and *A Poetic Equation: Conversations Between Nikki Giovanni and Margaret Walker.* (There is a second edition of this work (1983) with a new piece by Giovanni putting the book in historical perspective.) Wilberforce University in Xenia, Ohio, gave her an honorary Doctor of Humanities degree in 1972 when she was 28 years old. Later books by Giovanni are *The Women and the Men: Poems* (1975); *Cotton Candy on a Rainy Day* (1978); and *Vacation Time, a collection of poems for children* (1980) which was dedicated to her son, Tommy. Her last book is *Those Who Ride the Night Winds* (1984).

In 1981, a newspaper reporter noted that Giovanni, one of the premiere black revolutionary poets of the 1960s, appeared to have shed all trace of the angry, bitter radical. Explaining her transformation, Giovanni said, "One winds down. We've touched on every sore that anybody in the world ever had and I think we ought to do some healing. I'm not downgrading anger, but how long can you stay angry?"

Besides writing and lecturing, today Giovanni is also a volunteer in the Cincinnati public schools system where she teaches poetry.

*Alex Haley, author of the TV bockbuster* Roots, *with his wife stand before the marker of his boyhood home in Tennessee.*

## SHIRLEY GRAHAM
## Biographer
## 1907-1977

Born in Indianapolis, Indiana, Miss Graham received her B.A. degree in 1934 at Oberlin College, and her M.A. from the same institution a year later. While at Oberlin, she wrote and composed her first musical play, *Tom-Tom,* which was produced in 1932. She then studied music in Paris for years, and later taught at Morgan State and Tennessee State universities.

During a short stint with the Chicago Federal Theatre, she directed, designed, and composed for *Little Black Sambo* (1937) and created *The Swing Mikado* (1938). In 1941, while she was a Rosenwald Fellow at the Yale University Drama School (1938-1941), her play *Dust to Earth* was produced there. A later work, *Elijah's Raven,* was produced in Cleveland.

In 1944, in collaboration with George Lipscomb, she published her first biography for young people, *Dr. George Washington Carver, Scientist.* A year later she wrote *Paul Robeson, Citizen of the World,* and in 1949 completed *The Story of Phillis Wheatley.*

Miss Graham received a Guggenheim grant in 1947 and a year later won the Julian Messner Award for *There Was Once A Slave.* In 1950, *Your Most Humble Servant,* a biography of Benjamin Banneker, won the Anisfield-Wolf prize.

She married W. E. B. DuBois in the 1950s and went to Ghana with him in 1961. She lived in Cairo, Egypt, until her death. Her other books are *Booker T. Washington; His Day Is Marching On: A Memoir of W. E. B. DuBois; Gamal Abdel Nasser: Son of the Nile; Zulu Heart,* a novel; *Jean Baptiste Pointe Du Sable, Founder of Chicago; The Story of Pocahontas; Julius K. Nyerere: Teacher of Africa;* and *DuBois: A Pictorial Biography* (1978).

## ALEX HALEY
## Journalist, Novelist
## 1921

The author of the widely acclaimed novel *Roots* was born in Ithaca, New York and reared in Henning, Tennessee. The oldest of three sons of a college professor father and a mother who taught grade school, Haley graduated from high school at 15 and attended college for two years before enlisting in the U.S. Coast Guard as a messboy in 1939.

A voracious reader, he began writing short stories while working at sea, but it took eight years before small magazines began accepting some of his stories. He still likes to write in a boat at sea.

By 1952, the Coast Guard had created a new rating for Haley, Chief Journalist, and he began handling U.S. Coast Guard public relations. In 1959, after 20 years of military service, he retired from the Coast Guard and launched a new career as a freelance writer. He eventually became an assignments writer for *Reader's Digest* and moved on to *Playboy* where he initiated the "Playboy Interviews" feature.

One of the personalities Haley interviewed was Malcolm X—an interview that inspired Haley's first book, *The Autobiography of Malcolm X* (1965). Translated into eight languages, the book has sold over 6 million copies.

Pursuing the few slender clues of oral family history told him by his maternal grandmother in Tennessee, Haley spent the next 12 years traveling three continents tracking his maternal family back to a Mandingo youth, named Kunta Kinte, who was kidnaped into slavery from the small village of Juffure, in The Gambia, West Africa. During this period, he lectured extensively in the United States and in Great Britain on his discoveries about his family in Africa, and wrote many magazine articles on his research in the 1960s and the 1970s. He received several honorary doctor of letters degrees for his work.

The book *Roots*, excerpted in *Reader's Digest* in 1974 and heralded for several years, was finally published in the fall of 1976 with very wide publicity and reviews. In January 1977, ABC-TV produced a 12-hour series based on the book, which set records for the number of viewers. With cover stories, book reviews, and interviews with Haley in scores of magazines and many newspaper articles, the book became the number one national best-seller, sold in the millions, and was published as a paperback in 1977. *Roots* became a phenomenon. It was serialized in the *New York Post* and the *Long Island Press*. Instructional packages, lesson plans based on *Roots* and other books about *Roots* for schools were published along with phonograph records and tapes of Haley and *Roots*. He quickly became a multimillionaire.

All of this stimulated interest in Africa and in black genealogy. The U.S. Senate passed a resolution paying tribute to Haley and comparing *Roots* to *Uncle Tom's Cabin* by Harriet Beecher Stowe in the 1850s. The book got all sorts of awards, including the National Book Award for 1976 special citation of merit in history and a special Pulitzer Prize in 1976 for making an important contribution to the literature of slavery. Haley received more honorary doctorates from colleges and universities. There was criticism of the errors in *Roots*, and then there was a 1977 lawsuit brought by Margaret Walker Alexander charging that *Roots* plagiarized her novel *Jubilee;* Harold Courlander also filed a suit charging that *Roots* plagiarized his novel *The African*. Courlander received a settlement said to be hundreds of thousands of dollars after several passages in *Roots* were found to be almost verbatim from *The African*. Haley claimed that researchers helping him had given him this material without citing the source.

Haley received the NAACP's Spingarn Medal for 1977 for Roots. Four thousand deans and department heads of colleges and universities throughout the country in a survey conducted by *Scholastic Magazine* selected Haley as America's foremost achiever in the literature category. (Dr. Martin Luther King Jr. was selected in the religious category.) The ABC-TV network presented another series, *Roots: The Next Generation*, in February 1979 (also written by Haley). *Roots* had sold almost 5 million copies by December 1978 and had been reprinted in 23 languages. Haley later with Norman Lear produced a TV series about his childhood in Henning. His next book is supposed to be *My Search for Roots*, or *How I Wrote Roots*, but from newspaper reports his plans may have changed. *Presence Africaine* magazine had a special issue (Fall 1978) on *Roots*. There are also two related books, David L. Wolper and Quincy Troupe's *The Inside Story of TV's Roots* (1978) and Leslie A. Fiedler's *The Inadvertent Epic: From Uncle Tom's Cabin to Roots* (1979).

In 1988, Haley had done a promotional tour for a novella titled *A Different Kind of Christmas* (published by Doubleday for Christmas) about slave escapes in the 1850s. This book is total fiction without any characters from the book *Roots*. He had also been promoting a drama, *Roots: The Gift*, a 2-hour television program shown in December 1988. Haley's story outline for this screenplay by D. M. Eyre Jr. is about two key characters from *Roots* who are involved in a slave break for freedom on Christmas Eve.

Haley has moved from California to Knoxville, Tenn. His book *Henning, Tennessee*, about his home town when he was a boy, will be published in September 1989. He is also writing a biography of Madam C. J. Walker and another TV story with *Roots* characters for Thanksgiving in 1989.

## JUPITER HAMMON
**Poet**
**1720?-1800?**

Hammon was the first black to be published in America. *An Evening Thought, Salvation by Christ, with Penitential Cries* appeared in 1761, when Hammon was a slave belonging

*Lorraine Hansberry, her plays entertain and stimulate the mind.*

to a Mr. Lloyd of Long Island, New York.

Due to his fondness for preaching, the major portion of Hammon's poetry is religious in tone, and is usually dismissed by critics as being of little aesthetic value because of its pious platitudes, faulty syntax, and forced rhymes. Hammon's best-known work is a prose piece, *An Address to the Negroes of the State of New York,* delivered before the African Society of New York City on September 24, 1786. This speech was published the following year and went into three editions.

## LORRAINE HANSBERRY
**Dramatist**
**1930-1965**

The artistic reputation of Lorraine Hansberry rests largely on the success of her first play, *A Raisin in the Sun*, which was awarded the New York Drama Critics Circle Award for the year 1959. (Miss Hansberry was the first black to win this award, but August Wilson much later won this award three times with his plays.)

Born in Chicago, Miss Hansberry studied art at Chicago's Art Institute, the University of Wisconsin, and, finally, in Guadalajara, Mexico.

*Middleton Harris ferrets out the secrets of black history.*

She wrote *Raisin* while living in New York's Greenwich Village, having conceived it after reacting distastefully to what she called "a whole body of material about Negroes. Cardboard characters. Cute dialect bits. Or hip-swinging musicals from exotic scores." It opened on Broadway on March 11, 1959, at a time when it was generally held that all plays dealing with Negroes were "death" at the box-office. Produced, directed, and acted by blacks, it was later made into a successful movie starring Sidney Poitier. It was then converted to *Raisin,* a musical which won a Tony Award in 1974.

Her second Broadway play, *The Sign in Sidney Brustein's Window,* dealt with "the western intellectual poised in hesitation before the flames of involvement." Shortly after its Broadway opening, Miss Hansberry succumbed to cancer on January 12, 1965 in New York City.

Her books, in addition to the two published plays, are *To Be Young, Gifted and Black; The Movement: Documentary of a Struggle for Equality* (text); and *Les Blancs: The Collected Last Plays of Lorraine Hansberry.*

Books about her and her work include Anne Cheney's *Lorraine Hansberry* (1984) Catherine Scheader's *They Found A way: Lorraine Hansberry* (1978) for young people; Margaret B. Wilkenson of the University of California, Berkeley, is writing a literary biography of Lorraine Hansberry. There was also a special issue of *Freedomways* magazine (Fourth Quarter, 1979) devoted to Lorraine Hansberry with an extensive bibliography. Her play *Raisin in the Sun* continues to be produced by theater companies and on television. Another doctoral dissertation was completed on her plays in 1986.

## VINCENT HARDING
**Historian, Theologian**

Harding is a native of New York City and a graduate of the City University of New York and Columbia University School of Journalism. He also has a master of arts degree and a doctor of philosophy degree in history from the University of Chicago. He worked full-time in the southern-based black freedom movement in the early 1960s, before becoming chairperson of the Department of History and Sociology at Spelman College, Atlanta, Ga. In 1968, Harding became director of the Martin Luther King Jr. Memorial Center in Atlanta, Ga. and the coordinator of the nationally televised CBS "Black Heritage" series. He was one of the organizers of the Institute of the Black World in Atlanta, Ga., and in 1969 became its first director and later chairperson of the Institute's board. He has been on the faculty of the Iliff School of Theology at the University of Denver in Denver, Colorado for some years. Before that he was on the faculty of Pendle Hill, a Quaker study center near Philadelphia. He has lectured widely in the United States on black history, religion and social issues, and his writings have been published in many newspapers, magazines and books.

His books are *Must Walls Divide?, The Other American Revolution* (1980); *Slave Trade and Slavery* (with John H. Clarke) (1970); and *There Is a River: The Black Struggle for Freedom in America* (1981, 1983), an eloquent highly acclaimed intellectual history of the slavery period. *There Is a River* won the Clarence L. Holte Literary Prize ($10,000) for 1984. Earlier, Harding received a $15,000 Rockefeller Foundation Fellowship in the Humanities to aid him in writing *There Is a River.*

### FRANCES E. W. HARPER
### Poet, Abolitionist
### 1825-1911

Frances Ellen Watkins Harper was born in Baltimore of free parents, and orphaned a few years later. She attended a school for free Negroes conducted by her uncle, William Watkins, interrupting her formal education at the age of 13 to find employment as a nursemaid.

While she was still in her teens, Miss Harper's poetry and prose were published in a volume called *Autumn Leaves.* Her biggest commercial success came in Philadelphia in 1854, when she published Poems on Miscellaneous Subjects, which sold 10,000 copies in its first five years.

Her next work, *Moses, A Story of the Nile,* appeared in 1869. Three years later, she completed *Sketches of Southern Life,* which is notable for its attempt to recreate the speech of American Negroes while avoiding dialect. Her other books of poetry are *Poems* (1871, 1895, 1900); *Atlanta Offering; Effie Alton; Eventide; Forest Leaves; Idylls of the Bible; The Sparrow's Fall. Iola Leroy: On Shadows Uplifted* is a novel.

### MICHAEL S. HARPER
### Poet
### 1938

Michael S. Harper was born in Brooklyn, New York, but lived for many years in California. He studied creative writing at the Iowa University Writers' Workshop and has published poems in the magazines *Poetry, Southern Review, Quarterly Review of Literature, Negro Digest, December,* and others. He has been writer-in-residence, visiting lecturer, and associate professor of English at several colleges. Since 1974, Harper has been an associate professor of English at Brown University, Providence, Rhode Island. His books of poetry are *Dear John, Dear Coltrane: Poems* (1970); *History Is Your Own Heartbeat; Photographs; Negatives; History as Apple Tree; Song: I Want a Witness; Debridement; Poems; Nightmare Begins Responsibility* (1974); and *Images of Kin: New and Selected Poems* (1977). His latest book of poetry is *Healing Song for the Inner Ear* (1985). He and Robert B. Stepto edited two issues of *The Massachusetts Review* (Autumn, Winter, 1977) which became the book *Chant of Saints: A Gathering of Afro-American Literature, Art and Scholarship* (1979).

### MIDDLETON A. "SPIKE" HARRIS
### Historian
### 1910-1977

Born and schooled in New York City, Middleton A. Harris' early formal education began at P. S. 9 in Brooklyn and continued through Brooklyn's Manual Training High School and the Manhattan Textile High School. He later attended Howard University, graduating with a degree in sociology.

After college, Harris became a social worker, directing numerous youth groups before joining the City of New York as a parole officer. During World War II, "Spike" served as social director for the American Red Cross in the South Pacific.

Curiosity about his family beginnings started Harris on his lifelong quest for his own origins and for the largely buried elements of black history. Like Joel Rogers, Harris realized that the history of his people was dispersed and would require intensive research. Thus he wrote letters to government officials, conducted investigations of records in local courthouses, and relentlessly followed every lead. Over the years, Harris was able to accumulate a vast personal collection of memorabilia, mementos, tokens, souvenirs, and diversified keepsakes germane to the history of blacks.

Harris' personal library of rare books, graphics, audiovisual materials, and duplicates of government records relative to the history of the black provides a treasure trove for scholars. Some of this material is now in the Schomburg Collection in New York City. As President of Negro History Associates, Harris had successfully assumed responsibility for generating interest in what he calls the "lost pages of our national history." He dedicated four historical plaques in Manhattan which pertain to episodes involving black contributions or achievements.

Harris is also the author of a unique guidebook of Manhattan Island as seen from the vantage point of a black observer. The book, *A Negro History Tour of Manhattan,* contains several startling, revealing, and intriguing facts and incidents. *The Black Book,* edited by Middleton Harris, Morris Levitt, Roger Furman, and Ernest Smith was published in 1974. At the time of his death Harris was working on a book, yet unpublished, titled *The Black Man and the Sea.*

### JAMES HASKINS
### Writer
### 1941

James Haskins was a public school teacher in New York City in the late 1960s. His first book, *Diary of a Harlem School Teacher* (1970, 1979), resulted from this experience. He then began to write and edit books for children and adults. They were *Profiles of Black Power; A Piece of the Power: Four Black Mayors; Black Manifesto for Education; Jokes from Black Folks; Religious;* and *From Lew Alcindor to Kareem Abdul Jabbar* (1972). In 1974, Haskins was teaching at the Experimental College at Staten Island Community and Manhattanville Colleges. His other works are *Pinckney Benton Stewart Pinchback; The Psychology of Black Language* (with High F. Butts); *Adam Clayton Powell: Portrait of a Marching Black; Jobs in Business and Office; Witchcraft, Mysticism and Magic in the Black World; Ralph Bunche: A Most Reluctant Hero; Babe Ruth and Hank Aaron: The Home Run Kings; The War and the Protest: Viet Nam and Resistance;* and *Profiles in Nonviolence.*

From 1975 to the present, Haskins has devoted full time to

writing mostly for young people and children, sometimes in collaboration. He has written *The Creoles of Color of New Orleans; Fighting Shirley Chisholm; The Picture Life of Malcolm X; Dr. J: A Biography of Julius Erving; The Story of Stevie Wonder; Children Have Rights Too; The Consumer Movement; Your Rights, Past and Present; Pele: A Biography; Teen-Age Alcoholism; Aging in America: The Great Denial; A Time To Win: The Story of the Kennedy Foundation's Special Olympics for the Mentally Retarded; Always Movin' On: The Life of Langston Hughes; The Cotton Club* (now a film); *Scott Joplin; James Van Der Zee: The Picture Takin' Man; The Life and Death of Martin Luther King, Jr.;* and *I'm Gonna Make You Love Me: The Story of Diana Ross.* A few other earlier titles by Haskins not listed here make him the author of 36 to 40 books.

Later books by probably the most prolific of all the black writers including Frank Yerby (although many have errors and other signs of haste) are *The Long Struggle: The Story of American Labor; Voodoo & Hoodoo; The Quiet Revolution: The Struggle for the Rights of Disabled Americans; The Child Abuse Help Book; Katherine Dunham; The Guardian Angels*; *The New Americans: Cuban Boat People; New Americans: Vietnamese Boat People; Street Gangs: Yesterday & Today; Sugar Ray Leonard*; *Donna Summer: An Unauthorized Biography; Black Theater in America; Nat King Cole; The Cotton Club* (1984 second edition); *Lena Horne and Lena: A Personal & Professional Biography of Lena Horne; Space Challenger: The Story of Guion Bluford*; *Diana Ross: Star Supreme; Leaders of the Middle East; Break Dancing; About Michael Jackson; The Statue of Liberty: America's Proud Lady; Black Music in America: A History Through Its People; Mabel Mercer: A Life; Queen of the Blues*: *A Biography of Dinah Washington*; *Count Your Way Through China*; *Count Your Way Through Japan*; *Count Your Way Through Russia*; *Count Your Way Through the Arab World; Corazon Aquino*; *The Sixties Reader*; *The Magic Johnson Story*; and *Bricktop and Mr. Bojangles: The Biography of Bill Robinson.* The Bulletin of Bibliography for September 1985 has a bibliography of Haskins.

## ROBERT E. HAYDEN
### Poet
### 1913-1980

Poet Robert E. Hayden, a graduate of Wayne University, who was chief researcher on Negro history and folklore for the Federal Writers Project in 1936, later went on to do advanced work in English, play production, and creative writing at the University of Michigan. While there, he won the Jule and Avery Hopwood Prize for poetry twice. Hayden also completed radio scripts and a finished version of a play about the Underground Railroad, *Go Down Moses.*

His first book of poems, *Heart-Shape in the Dust,* was published in 1940 shortly before he assumed the music and drama critic function for the *Michigan Chronicle.* He taught at Fisk University from 1946 to the early 1970s, and later at the University of Michigan. His works include *The Lion and the Archer* (with Myron O'Higgins); *A Ballad of Remembrance; Selected Poems; Words in the Mourning Time;* and *The Night-Blooming Cereus.* He edited *Kaleidoscope: Poems by American Negro Poets;* and *Afro American Literature: An Introduction* (with David J. Burrows and Frederick R. Lapsides). His other books are *Figure of Time; Angle of Ascent: New and Selected Poems;* and *American Journal* (poems). In 1975, the Academy of American Poets elected him its Fellow of the Year, and in 1976, he was awarded the Grand Prize for Poetry at the First World Festival of Negro Arts in Dakar, Senegal. From 1976 to 1978, he served as Consultant in Poetry at the Library of Congress. He was a professor of English at the University of Michigan at the time of his death February 25, 1980.

There are two books about Hayden and his works: John Hatcher's *From the Auroral Darkness: The Life and Poetry of Robert Hayden* (1984), published in England, available from George Ronald Books, St. Louis MO; and Pontheolla T. Williams's *Robert Hayden: A Critical Analysis of His Poetry* (1987). Also, the Bulletin of Bibliography for September 1985 has a bibliography of Hayden.

## GEORGE H. HILL
### Professor, Writer

Hill is director of the Institute of Research and a media instructor at Los Angeles Southwest College. Accredited by the public Relations Society of America, he has a doctorate in communications and masters degrees in humanities, religious information, and business administration.

Hill was issue editor for two numbers of the *Bulletin of Bibliography* (June and September 1985) on black studies

*Chester Himes; his forte was satire.*

with a later issue to be on black women. His books are: *Black Media in America: A Resource Guide and Bibliography* (1984); *Airwaves to the Soul: The Influence and Growth of Religious Broadcasting in America; Blacks in the American Armed Forces, 1776-1983: A Bibliography (1984)* with Lenwood G. Davis; *Religious Broadcasting, 1920-1983: A Selectively Annotated Bibliography* (1984) also with Lenwood G. Davis; *Black Business and Economic Conditions, 1900-1983: A Bibliography* (1985); *Jessie Louis Jackson—From Country Preacher to Presidential Candidate: A Bibliography* (1985) with Janet Sims-Wood; *Michael Joe Jackson: A Bio-Bibliography* (1985); *Civil Rights Leaders and Organizations: A Bibliography* (1985); *Blacks on Television: A Selectively Annotated Bibliography* (1985) with Sylvia Saverson Hill; *Ebony Images: Black Americans and Television* (1984); *Blacks & Public Relations, 1934-1985: A Bibliography* (1984); *Black Radio in Chicago, Los Angeles and New York, 1925-1985: A Sixty Year Bibliography* (1985); and *A Bibliographical Guide to Black Studies Programs in the United States: An Annotated Bibliography* (1985) with Lenwood G. Davis. Hill also is director of Daystar Publishing Co. in Carson, CA.

*Langston Hughes, a major American writer.*

## CHESTER HIMES
## Novelist
## 1909-1984

Chester Himes began his career as a writer of popular material, and later moved to biting satiric fiction.

Born in Jefferson City, Missouri, Himes was educated at Ohio State University, had lived in France and in Spain.

In 1945, he completed his first novel *If He Hollers Let Him Go,* the story of a black working in a defense plant. His second book, *The Lonely Crusade* (1947), was set in similar surroundings.

Since then, Himes wrote many other books: *The Third Generation* (1954); *Cotton Comes to Harlem* (1965); and *Pinktoes* (1965). More recently, he published *The Quality of Hurt: The Autobiography of Chester Himes;* and *Black on Black: Baby Sister and Selected Writings.*

Himes suffered a stroke which had confined him to a wheelchair. He had lived with his wife in Alicante, Spain, and in 1977, they came to New York for the publication of the concluding volume of his autobiography *My Life of Absurdity.* At that time in answer to a question about his work habits, he told a reporter: "I do a little writing after breakfast and I think about what I would write if I had the strength."

Himes died in Spain in November 1984, at the age of 75. A prolific author of almost 20 books, several of his popular novels are being reprinted posthumously in hard and paperback editions. Books about Himes are James Lundquist's *Chester Himes* (1976); and Edward Margolies's *Which Way Did He Go? The Private Eye in Dashiell Hammett, Raymond Chandler, Chester Himes and Ross MacDonald* (1982).

## GEORGE MOSES HORTON
## Poet
## 1797-1883?

George Moses Horton was born in slavery in North Carolina. While working as a janitor at the University of North Carolina, Horton wrote light verse for some students in exchange for spending money.

Some of his early poems were printed in the newspapers of Raleigh and Boston. When Horton published his first book of poems in 1829, he entitled it *The Hope of Liberty* in the belief that profits from its sales would be sufficient to pay for his freedom. His hopes did not materialize, however, with the result that he remained a slave until the coming of Emancipation. This book was reprinted in 1837 under the title *Poems by a Slave.*

In 1865, he published *Naked Genius,* a poem containing many bitter lines about his former condition which are in sharp contrast to the conformist verse of earlier black poets. Richard Walser's *The Black Poet* written about Horton was published in 1967.

## LANGSTON HUGHES
## Poet, Novelist, Playwright, Journalist
## 1902-1967

Langston Hughes belongs in the ranks of the major American writers of the twentieth century.

Born in Joplin, Missouri, Hughes moved to Cleveland at the age of 14, graduated from Central High School, and spent a year in Mexico before studying at Columbia University. After roaming the world as a seaman and writing some poetry as well, Hughes returned to the United States, winning the Witter Bynner Prize for undergraduate poetry while attending Lincoln University, later his alma mater (1928). Two years later, he received the Harmon Award, and in 1935, with the help of a Guggenheim Fellowship, traveled to Russia and Spain.

The long and distinguished list of Hughes' prose works includes *Not Without Laughter* (1930), a novel; and *The Big Sea* (1940); and *I Wonder as I Wander* (1956), his autobiography. To this must be added such collections of poetry as *The Weary Blues* (1926); *The Dream Keeper* (1932); *Shakespeare in Harlem* (1942); *Fields of Wonder* (1947); *One Way Ticket* (1947); and *Selected Poems* (1959).

Hughes was also an accomplished song lyricist, librettist, and newspaper columnist. Through his newspaper columns, he created Jesse B. Simple, a Harlem character who saw life on the musical stage in *Simply Heavenly*. There are also several volumes of the Simple Columns.

Throughout the 1960s, Hughes edited several anthologies in an attempt to popularize black authors and their works. Some of these are *An African Treasury* (1960); *Poems from Black Africa* (1963); *New Negro Poets: U.S.A.* (1964); and *The Best Short Stories by Negro Writers* (1967). Published posthumously were, *The Panther and the Lash: Poems of Our Times* (1969); and *Good Morning Revolution: Uncollected Writings of Social Protest*. Hughes wrote many plays, including *Emperor of Haiti;* and *Five Plays by Langston Hughes*. *Mulatto* was produced on Broadway in the 1930s. He also wrote gospel song plays such as *Tambourines to Glory; Black Nativity;* and *Jericho—Jim Crow*.

In tone and spirit, Hughes remained a poet with a twist of gray humor. Sadness, rather than anger, seemed his primary emotion. There are many books about Hughes written for adults and children since his death in 1967. Some of these are R. Baxter Miller's *Langston Hughes and Gwendolyn Brooks: A Reference Guide* (1979); Alice Walker's *Langston Hughes, American Poet* (1974), for children; Kenneth P. Neilson's *The World of Langston Hughes' Music: A Bibliography of Musical Settings of Langston Hughes' Work with Recordings and Other Listings* (1982); *Langston Hughes' Block* (1978); Faith Berry's *Langston Hughes: Before and Beyond Harlem* (1983); Therman B. O'Daniel (editor) *Langston Hughes: Black Genius, A Critical Evaluation (*1971); and Arnold Rampersad's *The Life of Langston Hughes: Vol. I*; *1902-1941: I, Too, Sing America*; *Vol. II*; and *1941-1967: I Dream a World* (1986, 1988). This two-volume work was commissioned by the executor of the Langston Hughes estate, George Houston Bass, after Arna Bontemps, who was to write the biography, died. Vol. I won for Rampersad the Clarence L. Holte Award in 1988. Another book about Hughes is Charles H. Nichols (editor) *Arna Bontemps-Langston Hughes Letters, 1925-1967* (1980). There is also the large, beautiful 1984 edition of *The Sweet Flypaper of Life* with photographs by Roy DeCavava and text by Langston Hughes. This book was published originally in 1955 and reprinted in 1967.

### ZORA NEALE HURSTON
### Novelist, Folklorist
### 1903-1960

Once placed in "the front rank of American writers" for her mastery of folklore, Zora Neale Hurston was born and raised in an all-black town in Florida (Eatonville), an experience that left a deep imprint on her later literary efforts.

After traveling north as a maid with a Gilbert and Sullivan company, she acquired her education at Morgan State, Howard, and Columbia. While at Howard, under Alain Locke's influence, she became a figure in the Negro Renaissance, publishing short stories in *Opportunity* and serving with Langston Hughes and Wallace Thurman on the editorial board of the magazine *Fire*.

In 1934, *Jonah's Gourd Vine* was published after her return to Florida. Her more important novel, *Their Eyes Were Watching God,* appeared three years later and then *Moses; Man of the Mountain* (1939), was followed in 1948 by *Seraph on the Suwanee*. Her other three works are two books of folklore and her autobiography. They are *Mules and Men* (1935); *Tell My Horse* (1938); and *Dust Tracks on a Road* (1942), her autobiography which was reprinted in 1985 with a new introduction and with the several altered or expunged chapters restored.

Toward the end of her life, Miss Hurston was a drama instructor at the North Carolina College for Negroes in Durham. She died in obscurity and poverty on January 28, 1960. Since then, six of her works have been reprinted with new introductions and Alice Walker edited *A Zora Neale Hurston Reader*. These books plus two books about Hurston and her works constitute a Hurston revival. Robert Hemenway's *Zora Neale Hurston: A Literary Biography* (1977) is the most widely known.

### CHARLES JOHNSON
### Novelist, Professor

A young professor of English at Indiana University, Johnson has written three novels: *Faith and the Good Thing* (1974); *Oxherding Tale* (1982); and *The Sorcerer's Apprentice* (1985). His latest book is *Being and Race: Black Writing since 1970* (1988), an analysis of some of the major contemporary black writers such as Toni Morrison, Alice Walker, Paule Marshall, Ntozake Shange, Ishmael Reed, Clarence Major, Gloria Naylor and others including himself.

### FENTON JOHNSON
### Poet
### 1888-1958

Fenton Johnson was born in Chicago in 1888, and received his formal education there, in the public school system and at the University of Chicago. In 1914, Johnson completed his first volume of poetry, *A Little Dreaming,* followed in 1916 by *Visions of the Dusk;* and *Songs of the Soil*. Johnson's prose works include *Tales of Darkest America* (1920) and a book of short stories.

His last work, *The Daily Grind: 42 W.P.A. Poems*, was listed in 1963 in the *Paul Breman Heritage Series* but was never published.

### GEORGIA DOUGLAS JOHNSON
**Poet**
**1886-1966**

Georgia Douglas Johnson was born in Atlanta and educated at Atlanta University and at the Oberlin Conservatory in Ohio.

Initially, she was interested in musical composition, but gradually she turned toward lyric poetry. After teaching school in Alabama, she moved to Washington, D.C. with her husband, who had been appointed as Recorder of Deeds by President William Howard Taft. While in the nation's capital, she too engaged in government work while completing such books as *The Heart of a Woman* (1918); *Bronze* (1922); *An Autumn Love Cycle* (1928); and *Share My World*, published in 1962.

### JAMES WELDON JOHNSON
**Poet, Lyricist, Civil Rights Leader**
**1871-1938**

Like DuBois, black intellectual James Weldon Johnson played a vital role in the civil rights movement of the twentieth century—as poet, teacher, critic, diplomat, and NAACP official. Johnson is perhaps most often popularly remembered as the lyricist for *Lift Every Voice and Sing*, the poem which is often referred to as the black national anthem.

*Poet and diplomat James Weldon Johnson wrote "Lift every Voice and Sing."*

Born in 1871 in Jacksonville, Florida, Johnson was educated at Atlanta and Columbia Universities. His career included service as a school principal, a lawyer, and a diplomat (U.S. Consul at Puerto Cabello, Venezuela, and later, in Nicaragua). From 1916 to 1930, he was a key policy maker of the NAACP, eventually serving as the organization's executive secretary.

In his early days, Johnson's fame rested largely on his lyrics for popular songs, but in 1917 he completed his first book of poetry, *Fifty Years and Other Poems*. Five years later, he followed this with *The Book of American Negro Poetry*, and in 1927, he established his literary reputation with *God's Trombones*, a collection of seven folk sermons in verse. Over the years, this work has been performed countless times on stage and television.

In 1930, Johnson finished *St. Peter Relates an Incident of the Resurrection* , and three years later, his lengthy autobiography *Along This Way*.

Johnson died in 1938 following an automobile accident in Maine.

### JUNE JORDAN
**Poet, Novelist**
**1936**

Born in Harlem of parents from Jamaica, West Indies, June Jordan attended Barnard College and the University of Chicago. She has been married and has a son. She has taught Afro-American literature, English, and writing at several colleges and universities and was co-founder and co-director of The Voice of the Children, Inc., a creative workshop. Her poems have been published in many magazines, newspapers, and anthologies. She received a Rockefeller Grant in creative writing for 1969. Her books for children and young people are *Fannie Lou Hamer* (1972); *His Own Where* (1971), her first novel nominated for the National Book Award; *Who Look at Me* (1969); *Dry Victories* (1972); *New Room, New Life* (1974); and *The Voice of the Children: Writings by Black and Puerto Rican Young People* (1970, 1974), edited by Jordan and Terri Bush. Her books for adults are *Soulscript* (1970), edited by Jordan; *Some Changes* (1971); *New Days: Poems of Exile and Return* (1973); *Things That I Do in the Dark: Selected Poems* (1976); and *Passion: New Poems 1977-1980* (1980). Another book by Jordan is *On Call: Political Essays* (1985), her second book of political writings. There is also a study of Jordan and her writings in *Woman Poet—The East* (1984). She has been a professor of English at the State University of New York, Stonybrook for several years.

### WILLIAM MELVIN KELLEY
**Novelist**
**1937**

William Melvin Kelley's first novel, *A Different Drummer* (1962), was widely acclaimed for its provocative theme and imaginative development. The story concerns the mass exodus of the black inhabitants of an imaginary Southern state.

Born in New York City, Kelley is a graduate of the Fieldston School and of Harvard, where he studied under Archibald MacLeish and John Hawkes. He has won the Dana Reed Literary Prize and the Rosenthal Foundation Award of the National Institute of Arts and Letters. He was author-in-residence at New York State University College at Geneseo.

In 1964, a collection of his stories appeared under the title *Dancers on the Shore*. The following year his second novel was published, *A Drop of Patience*. *Dem,* a surrealistic fantasy, was published in 1967. His fourth novel, *Dunsford Travels Everywhere,* was published in 1970. He now lives with his family in Paris, France.

### JOHN OLIVER KILLENS
### Novelist
### 1916-1987

John Oliver Killen's first novel, *Youngblood* (1954), dealt with life in a southern black family, a theme which Killens knew well, having been born into just such an environment in Macon, Georgia.

Killens studied at three black colleges what was then the Terrell Law School, at Columbia, and at New York University. From 1936 to 1942, and again in 1946 after completing his military service, Killens worked with the National Labor Relations Board in Washington, D.C.

After serving as head of the Harlem Writers' Workshop, Killens second novel, *And Then We Heard the Thunder,* was published in 1963. Prior to that, he had written the script for *Odds Against Tomorrow,* a film which starred Harry Belafonte in 1959. He has taught creative writing at Fisk, Columbia, and Howard Universities.

Killens' book of essays, *Black Man's Burden,* appeared in 1965. His later works are *Sippi* (1967), a novel; the film script for the film *Slaves* (1969); *The Cotillion* (1971), a novel; and *The Trial Record of Denmark Vesey* (1970); *Great Gittin' Up Morning* (1972), a biography of Denmark Vesey; and *A Man Ain't Nothin' But A Man: The Adventures of John Henry* (1975). He lived with his family in Brooklyn, New York, and taught writing at Medgar Evers College in Brooklyn.

Killens's first two novels *Youngblood* (1982) and *And Then We Heard the Thunder* (1984) have been reprinted by the University of Georgia Press and the Howard University Press Library of Contemporary Literature respectively. Killens died October 27, 1987, in New York City at the age of 71. A memorial service was held at Bethany Baptist Church, Brooklyn, New York on Jan. 16, 1988. His works were translated into at least a dozen languages. Killens's final work *Great Black Russian : A Novel on the Life and Times of Alexander Pushkin* is being published posthumously by Wayne State University Press, Detroit, Michigan. Killens visited the Pushkin Festival in the Soviet Union and waged a long "campaign" to get this novel published.

*Julius Lester, the essayist as provocateur.*

### JULIUS LESTER
### Essayist, Critic, Novelist
### 1939

Julius Lester, a forceful advocate of the black militant movement, is the author or editor of *Look Out, Whitey! Black Power's Gon' Get Your Mama; To Be A Slave; Revolutionary Notes; Black Folktales; Search for the New Land; The Seventh Son; The Thought and Writings of W. E. B. DuBois; Long Journey Home: Stories from Black History; Two Love Stories; The Knee High Man and Other Tales;* and *Who I Am.*

*To Be A Slave* (1968) was the 1968 Newbery Medal runner-up. His writings have appeared in *The Village Voice, The Guardian, The Movement, Broadsides, Liberator,* and *Sing Out.* In addition, Lester has made records for Vanguard Records. His reviews appear frequently in the pages of the *New York Times.* His autobiography, *All Is Well,* was published in 1976. *This Strange New Feeling* (1982) is a compilation of love stories of newly freed slaves.

A professor of Afro-American studies at the University of Massachusetts, Amherst, his conversion to Judaism and his treatment of James Baldwin, Jesse Jackson and civil rights in his latest book *Lovesong: Becoming a Jew* (1987) led the Department of Afro-American Studies at the University to ask that Lester be reassigned to another department. Lester was reassigned to another department and is currently professor of Judaic and Near Eastern studies at the University of Massachusetts. *Do Lord Remember Me* (1985) is a recent novel by Lester. Several of Lester's books were written for young people.

## DAVIS LEVERING LEWIS
### Historian
### 1936

Born in Little Rock, Arkansas, he received a masters degree from Columbia University in 1958, and a doctorate in French History from the London School of Economics and Political Science, University of London in 1962. He taught modern French History at several colleges during the 1960s and 1970s, and is now Martin Luther King Jr. professor of history at Rutgers University. Lewis received grants to write books during the 1960s and 1970s from the American Philosophical Society and the Social Science Research Council. In 1986, he received a Guggenheim Foundation fellowship award to write *The Life and Times of W. E. B. DuBois*. Lewis's books are *Martin Luther King, A Critical Biography* (1971, 1978); *Prisoner of Honor: The Dreyfus Affair* (1973); *The public Image of Henry Ford: An American Folk Hero and His Company* (1975); *District of Columbia: A Bicentennial History; Washington, D. C. : The Fight for Freedom at Home and Abroad; When Harlem Was in Vogue* (1981, 1982, 1989); and *The Race To Fashoda: European Colonialism and African Resistance in the Scramble for Africa* (1987, 1988). Lewis' illustrated 7-page essay "Harlem's First Shining," was published in *Modern Maturity* (Feb.-Mar. 1989).

## C. ERIC LINCOLN
### Religionist, Sociologist
### 1924

Born in Athens, Alabama, C. Eric Lincoln graduated from Le Moyne College, received a masters degree from Fisk University, a bachelor of divinity from the University of Chicago, a masters in education and a doctorate of divinity from Boston University, and did post doctorate study.in divinity. Lincoln has taught and lectured at many colleges and universities. He was professor of religion and sociology and chairman of the Department of Religion & Philosophy Studies at Fisk University and adjunct professor of. Ethics & Sociology in the School of Divinity, Vanderbilt University. Now he is a professor of religion and culture at Duke University.

Lincoln has written many books, magazine and newspaper articles. His books are: *The Black Muslims in America* (1961, 1972); *My Face Is Black* (1964); *Sounds of the Struggle* (1967); *The Negro Pilgrimage in America* (1967); *Is Anybody Listening?* (1968); (editor) *A Profile of Martin Luther King Jr.* (1970, 1984); *The Black Americans* (1969); *The Black Church Since Frazier* (1974); *The Black Experience in Religion* (1974); *Readings in Black Religion* (1974); *A Pictorial History of Black Americans* (1968, 1974, 1983) with Langston Hughes and Milton Meltzer. He is editor of the C. Eric Lincoln Series in Black Religion (6 books, 1970-1973) and author of *Race, Religion and the Continuing American Dilemma* (1984 ); and *The Avenue, Clayton City* (1988) his first novel.

## ALAIN LEROY LOCKE
### Critic
### 1886-1954

Alain Leroy Locke shares the spotlight—along with Benjamin Brawley and Sterling Brown—as a critic and chronicler of the Harlem Renaissance.

Locke was born in Philadelphia and educated at Harvard, and as a Rhodes scholar, at Oxford. He served for many years as chairman of the philosophy department at Howard University, but his main contribution to American culture lies in his efforts to make the public aware of the Negro's aesthetic achievements, from the art and artifacts of Africa to the poetry and novels of the American writer.

In 1925, Locke edited *The New Negro,* a volume which sought to define the aims of the black artists then in the full flush of the Harlem Renaissance. Consisting of the representative work of a number of young black writers, this anthology served notice of the existence of a new literary self-image for the Negro, founded partly on an uncompromising demand for equal rights.

Locke's championing of the new writers who had outgrown what he called "the pathetic overcompensation of a group inferiority complex," helped promote a number of outstanding literary works written by blacks during the postwar period.

Locke died in 1954 while in the midst of collecting material for what he hoped would be his greatest contribution to American letters. This work, later completed by Margaret Just Butcher, is entitled *The Negro in American Culture* (1956). His other works are *The Negro and His Music; Negro Art: Past and Present;* and *The Negro in Art*. Eugene C. Holmes, retired professor of philosophy at Howard University, died before he completed the biography of Locke that he was writing. Russell J. Linnemann has edited *Alain Locke: Reflections on a Modern Renaissance Man* (1982). *The Bulletin of Bibliography* for June 1985 has a bibliography of Locke's writings. Leonard Harris has edited *The Philosophy of Alain Locke: Harlem Renaissance and Beyond* (1988). All five of Locke's books were reprinted in the 1960s and 1970s.

## RAYFORD W. LOGAN
### Historian
### 1897-1982

Rayford W. Logan is a native of Washington, D.C., where he received a public school education prior to attending Harvard and Williams College.

During World War I, Logan served abroad with the 372nd Infantry of the segregated 93rd Division, a unit which was brigaded with French troops overseas. After the war, Logan went into teaching, first at Virginia Union University, then at Atlanta University, and last at Howard. While there, he became an assistant to Carter Woodson in the Washington-based Association for the Study of Negro Life and History. In this capacity, he contributed numerous articles to a variety of scholarly and popular periodicals, edited *The Attitude of the Southern White Press Toward Negro Suffrage, 1932-1940* (1940), and wrote a study entitled *The Diplomatic Relations of the United States with Haiti, 1776-1891* (1941). Logan has written numerous other books since then, including *The Negro in the United States* (1957); *The Betrayal of the Negro from Rutherford B. Hayes to Woodrow Wilson* (1965); *The American Negro* (with Irving S. Cohen); and Howard University: *The First Hundred Years 1867-1967.* He was editing with Michael R. Winston the *Dictionary of American Negro Biography* (1982) when he became ill and died in November, 1982, at the age of 85. Winston completed the editing of the *Dictionary*. As the publication of this book was delayed over about ten years, Logan wrote from a fourth to a third of the hundreds of biographies in the *Dictionary* when many of his jointly-written-with-others biographies did not materialize. Earlier, Philip Sterling and Logan wrote *Four Took Freedom: The Lives of Harriet Tubman, Frederick Douglass, Robert Smalls and Blanche K. Bruce* (1967), illustrated by Charles White for children in the Zenith Series. Logan also edited *W. E. B. DuBois: A Profile* (1971). His book, *The Struggle for Universal Human Rights* (1983), was published after his death.

### AUDRE LORDE
**Poet, Teacher**
**1934**

Audre Lorde was born in New York City, educated at Hunter College with a masters in library science from Columbia University; was poet-in-residence at Tougaloo College; taught at Lehman College, Bronx; and is now teaching at John Jay College, CCNY. She received a National Endowment for the Arts grant for poetry and a Cultural Council Foundation grant also for poetry. Her books of poetry are *Cables to Rage* (1970); *The First Cities* (1968); *From a Land Where Other People Live* (1973); *Coal* (1968); *The New York Head Shop and Museum* (1974); *Between Ourselves* (1976); *The Black Unicorn* (1978); *Chosen Poems-Old and New* (1982); *Zami: A New Spelling of My Name* (1982); *Sister/Outsider: Essays & Speeches* (1984); *Lesbian Poetry: An Anthology* (1982); and *Woman Poet—The East* (1984). The last two books have poetry and a study of Audre Lorde respectively. Lorde's poetry has been published in many anthologies, magazines and lesbian books and periodicals\

### CLARENCE MAJOR
**Poet, Novelist**
**1936**

Clarence Major, although born in Atlanta, Georgia, was essentially a product of the elementary and high school system of Chicago where his family had moved shortly after his birth. He attended the Art Institute of Chicago and later studied English and journalism. His poems, short stories, and essays have been published in many magazines and anthologies. He was an associate editor of *Umbra* magazine and was a contributing editor of *The Journal of Black Poetry* (the magazine no longer exists). In 1974, he was living in New York City and taught literature and creative writing at Sarah Lawrence College. Major has been a visiting writer at many colleges and universities. He has written or edited many books—three novels and a novelette: *All-Night Visitors* (1969); *No* (1973); *Reflex and Bone Structure* (1975); and *Emergency Exit* (1980); *The New Black Poetry* (anthology); *Dictionary of Afro-American Slang*; and five books of poetry: *Swallow the Lake; Symptoms and Madness; Private Line; The Cotton Club;* and *The Syncopated Cakewalk*. Major has also written *The Dark and Feeling: Black American Writers and Their Work* (1974) and his latest novel is *Such Was The Season* (1987).

### PAULE MARSHALL
**Novelist, Short Story Writer**
**1929**

Paule Marshall was born in Brooklyn, New York, and graduated from Brooklyn College as a Phi Beta Kappa. In Barbados (the birthplace of her parents) she wrote her first novel, *Brown Girl, Brownstones* (1959, reprinted twice in 1970 and also in 1981), which deals with the dislocation one

*Short story specialist James A. McPherson.*

experiences in moving from the tropics to the cruel reality of a home in Brooklyn.

Marshall is also the author of *Soul Clap Hands and Sing* (1961) which is a collection of four short stories or novellas set in Brazil, Barbados, British Guiana, and Brooklyn. Her big novel, entitled *The Chosen Place, The Timeless People*, was published in 1969. Recently she has written *Merle*, a novella adapted from *The Chosen Place, The Timeless People*. Her fourth book, *Praisesong For The Widow* (1982) is also a novel. Her short stories have been published in many anthologies and magazines, and *Reena and Other Stories* (Feminist Press, 1984), is a collection of Marshall's short fiction. She has received both the Guggenheim and the Ford Foundation fellowships. Marshall also wrote an autobiographical essay in "The Making of a Writer" series in the *New York Times Book Review*, January 9, 1983.

## JULIAN MAYFIELD
### Novelist, Essayist, Editor
### 1928-1984

Julian Mayfield was born in Greer, South Carolina, and at the age of 10 moved with his family to Washington, D.C. Upon completing high school, he served in the Army in the Pacific. At the conclusion of World War II he attended Lincoln University in Pennsylvania. As with many other artists, he was employed in a myriad of unrewarding jobs. He acted in the Broadway play *Lost in the Stars* and in the film *Up Tight*.

Mayfield spent many years in Africa, Europe, and the Caribbean. Much of his work can be found in the *Puerto Rico World Journal*, *The African Review in Accra*, *Commentary*, *The New Republic*, *The Nation*, *Negro Digest*, and *Freedomways*.

His novels include *The Hit* (1957); *The Long Night* (1958); and *The Grand Parade* (1961). His works have been translated into French, Japanese, Czech, and German. He was a teaching fellow at Cornell University and by 1974 was living in Guyana. He edited *Ten Times Black* (short stories) in 1972. He has been a writer-in-residence at several colleges, including Howard University in Washington, D. C. (his home town) from 1978 until his death on October 20, 1984, at the age of 56. His novel, *The Long Night* was made into a film in 1976 by Woodie King Jr., and was shown at the Black Film Center/Archives Festival at Indiana University in June 1985.

## CLAUDE McKAY
### Poet
### 1890-1948

Claude McKay is generally regarded as the herald of the Harlem Renaissance.

Born the son of a farmer in Jamaica (then British West Indies), McKay began writing early in life. Two books of his poems, *Songs of Jamaica* and *Constab Ballads*, were published just after he turned 20. In both, he made extensive use of the Jamaican dialect known as patois.

In 1913, McKay came to America to study agriculture at Tuskegee Institute and at Kansas State University, but his interest in poetry induced him to move to New York City, where he published his work in small literary magazines.

McKay then made a trip abroad, visiting England. While there, he completed a collection of lyrics entitled *Spring in New Hampshire*. When he returned to the United States, he became associate editor of *The Liberator* under Max Eastman. In 1922, he completed *Harlem Shadows*, a landmark work during the Harlem Renaissance period.

McKay then turned to the writing of such novels as *Home to Harlem* (1928), *Banjo* (1929), and four other books including an autobiography and a study of Harlem. The Passion of Claude McKay: *Selected Prose and Poetry 1912-1948* edited by Wayne Cooper, was published in 1973. McKay traveled extensively abroad before returning to the United States, where he died. His final work, *Selected Poems*, was published posthumously in 1953.

During World War II, when Winston Churchill addressed a joint session of the U.S. Congress in an effort to enlist American aid in the battle against Nazism, the climax of his oration was his reading of the famous poem *If We Must Die*, which is taken from a stirring poem originally written by McKay to assail lynchings and mob violence in the South. McKay's *Trial by Lynching* (1967), edited and translated stories, and his *The Negroes in America* (1979 or 1980), edited and translated from the Russian language, have also been published. Many of his books or works have been reprinted since his death: *Home to Harlem; Banana Bottom; Banjo* (1970); *A Long Way From Home* (1970); *Songs of Jamaica and Constab Ballads* bound together as *The Dialect Poems of Claude McKay; Harlem: Negro Metropolis* (1972), and *Selected Poems of Claude McKay* (1971). Also, recently Wayne F. Cooper completed a study *Claude McKay: Rebel Sojourner in the Harlem Renaissance* (1987).

## JAMES ALAN McPHERSON
### Short Story Writer
### 1943

James McPherson, born in Savannah, Georgia, received his B.A. degree in 1965 from Morris Brown College in Atlanta, a law degree from Harvard University in 1968, and an M.F.A. degree from the University of Iowa in 1969. He has taught writing at several universities, presently at the University of Iowa, and is a contributing editor of *Atlantic Monthly*. His short stories have appeared in several magazines. *Hue and Cry*, a collection of short stories published in 1969, was highly praised by Ralph Ellison. A Guggenheim Fellow in 1972-1973, McPherson's second book of short stories, *Elbow Room*, was published in 1977 and was given the Pulitzer Prize for fiction in 1978. He taught fiction writing for several years at the University of Virginia in Charlottesville. McPherson was one of the three black writers who in 1981, with Elma Lewis, was awarded five-year grants by the McArthur Foundation of Chicago for exceptional talent. His grant was $192,000. After this happened, he left the University of Virginia with his wife and son to keep to his privacy.

## KELLY MILLER
## Historian
## 1863-1939

A voice of reason and scholarship, Kelly Miller was one of the major black spokesmen and teachers of the early twentieth century. His thoughtful essays analyzed racial problems in terms of their global development, the potency and promise of the black race, and viable solutions. For Miller, who devoted his life to teaching, the surest release from the house of bondage was by the road of education.

Born in Winnsboro, South Carolina, during the Civil War, he worked his way through school, graduating from Howard University in 1886, studying postgraduate mathematics and physics at Johns Hopkins (1887-1889), and eventually earning from Howard his A.M. (1901) and LL.D. (1903) degrees. After a short stint teaching in the public schools of Washington, D.C., he joined Howard's faculty, where he was to remain for most of his academic career, serving variously as professor of mathematics, chairman of the department of sociology, dean of the junior college, and dean of the College of Arts and Sciences. In addition to his collegial responsibilities, he published many important essays, became the first black academician to write a regular column for the black press, and helped W. E. B. DuBois edit the journal *Crisis*.

In the face of prevailing pessimism about race relations, Miller emphasized the great capacity for progress the black race had shown in the 50 years since emancipation. Literacy had increased enormously, a managerial and professional class was crystallizing, property ownership had swelled, and the masses' need for self-expression and self-government had given birth to the unique socio-religious institution of the black church. Armed with the belief that no people in world history had made such great advances in so brief a span, and convinced of the inherently democratizing effect of American institutions, Miller proclaimed certainty that the black race would eventually assume its rightful position of equality in the United States. Unlike DuBois, who felt that color would always single blacks out for prejudicial treatment, Miller held that the evolution of similar behavior patterns would obviate the importance of physical differences.

Miller's major publications were *Race Adjustment* (1903); *Out of the House of Bondage* (1917); *History of the World War and the Important Part Taken by the Negroes* (1919); and *The Everlasting Stain*(1924).

His drama (with music added) about black people moving uptown in New York City and living in Harlem, *Tell Pharaoh*, was produced at Holy Trinity Episcopal Church on East 88th St. in Manhattan, in April 1986, for a 4-day run to raise funds for several charities. Micki Grant, Graham Brown, Nora Cole, La Tanya Richardson (director) and others participated.

## LOFTEN MITCHELL
## Dramatist
## 1919

Raised in the Harlem of 1920s, Loften Mitchell first began to write as a child, creating scripts for backyard shows he and his brother put on. After completing junior high school, he decided to enroll at New York Textile High because he had been promised a job on the school newspaper there. But Mitchell soon realized that he needed the training of an academic high school, and with the help of one of his teachers, transferred to DeWitt Clinton.

Graduating with honors, Mitchell found a job as an elevator operator and a delivery boy to support himself while he studied play writing at night at the City College of New York. However, he met a professor from Talladega College in Alabama who helped him win a scholarship to study there. He graduated with honors in 1943, having won an award for the best play written by a student.

After two years of service in the Navy, Mitchell enrolled as a graduate student at Columbia University in New York. A year later, he accepted a job with the Department of Welfare as a social investigator and continued to go to school at night. During this time, he wrote one of his first successful plays, *Blood in the Night,* and in 1957 he wrote *A Land Beyond the River,* which had a long run at an off-Broadway theater and was published as a book.

The following year Mitchell won a Guggenheim award, which enabled him to return to Columbia and write for a year. Since then, he has written a new play, *Star of the Morning,* the story of Bert Williams, famous black entertainer.

In 1967, Mitchell published a study entitled *Black Drama,* the story of the American Negro in the theater. His other books are *Tell Pharaoh,* a play; and *The Stubborn Old Lady Who Resisted Change* (1973), a novel; and *Voices of the Black Theatre* (1976). Mitchell also wrote the books for the Broadway musicals *Ballads for Bimshire* (1963); *Bubbling Brown Sugar* (in the 1970s); as well as a 1979 musical, *Cartoons for a Lunch Hour*.

## TONI MORRISON
## Novelist, Editor
## 1931

Born in Lorain, Ohio, she received a B.A. degree from Howard University in 1953 and an M.A. from Cornell in 1955. After working as an instructor in English and the humanities at Texas Southern University and Howard University, Morrison eventually became a senior editor at Random House in New York City. Morrison has been responsible for the publication of many books by blacks at Random House: Middleton Harris' *The Black Book*, which she edited, and books by Toni Cade Bambara and others. In 1971-1972, she was also an associate professor at the State University of New York at Purchase. Formerly married, she has two sons. Her first novel, *The Bluest Eye*, was published in 1970. Her second novel, *Sula,* was published in 1974 and won a 1975 Ohioana Book Award. Morrison's third novel, *Song of Solomon* (1977), was very widely reviewed and received the 1978 award in literature of $3,000 from the American Academy and Institute of Arts and Letters. Her fourth novel, *Tar Baby* (1981) was even more widely reviewed. *Newsweek* magazine's front cover story on Morrison's life and writings called her the best of the black writers today. She was elected to the American Institute of Arts and Letters in 1981 and gave the keynote address at the

American Writers' Congress in New York City in the fall of that year. Barbara Christian's *Black Women Novelists* (1980) has a section on her first three novels; and there is an interview with Morrison in Michael S. Harper and Robert B. Stepto's *Chant of Saints: A Gathering of Afro-American Literature, Art and Scholarship* (1979). She has written the story for the musical *Storyville*, which is about jazz music originating in the brothels of New Orleans.

After *Song of Solomon* won the National Book Critics Circle Award for 1970, and *Tar Baby* reached best seller status, Morrison became Albert Schweitzer Professor of the Humanities at the State University of New York at Albany, after 20 years as a senior editor for Random House. She had written the lyrics or story for the musical New Orleans (formerly Storyville), a New York Public Theater workshop production and also a screenplay of her novel *Tar Baby*. Then her drama, *Dreaming Emmett*, about the black 14-year-old youth killed in Mississippi in the 1950s, commissioned by the New York State Writers Institute at SUNY-Albany and directed by Gilbert Moses, was produced at the Market Theater in Albany beginning January 4, 1986. Morrison, teaching writing, says she writes good dialogue that it's theatrical and moves.

Morrison's fifth novel *Beloved* was published in 1987. A historical novel, it received rave reviews. Then after the death of James Baldwin on November 30, 1987, without his ever winning the Pulitzer Prize or the National Book Award, 48 black writers and critics issued a statement deploring Toni Morrison's failure up to that time, to win either the Pulitzer Prize or the National Book Award. A letter by two of the writers recounted Baldwin's failure as well. (New York Times Book Review, January 24, 1988). But her novel *Beloved*, about the agonizing remembrances of a former slave in post-Civil War Ohio, was awarded the Pulitzer Prize for fiction on March 31, 1988. *Beloved* was a finalist for the National Book Critics Circle Award and was one of the three contenders for the Ritz Hemingway prize in Paris, from which no winner emerged. This novel by Morrison was also a finalist for the National Book Award for 1987, but it did not win there either.

Morrison also was one of the seven artists to receive the New York City Mayor's Awards of Honor for Art and Culture in May 1988. Since the Spring of 1989, she has been teaching as a full professor with an endowed chair at Princeton University where her courses encompass creative writing, African studies and women's studies (Lisa W. Foderaro's "Big Name on Campus", *New York Times Education Life* Section 4A, August 7, 1988).

There is a 27-page conversation between Gloria Naylor and Toni Morrison in *The Southern Review* (Vol. 21, No. 3, July 1985), a number devoted entirely to Afro-American writing. Also, Nellie Y. McKay edited *Critical Essays on Toni Morrison* (1988).

## WILLARD MOTLEY
**Novelist**
**1912-1965**

Because most of his work dealt with poor whites on Chicago's West Side, it was not generally known that Willard Motley was black.

Born in a middle-class Chicago neighborhood, Motley wrote his first book, *Knock on Any Door*, in 1947. One of the first naturalistic novels to deal with the problem of juvenile delinquency, it enjoyed enormous commercial success before being made into a Hollywood film starring Humphrey Bogart.

In 1951, Motley completed *We Fished All Night*, an attempt to describe the impact of World War II on three young Chicagoans. Seven years later, a sequel to his first novel was published under the title *Let No Man Write My Epitaph*, also made into a movie.

Motley died of gangrene in Mexico City on March 4, 1965, a year before his last novel, *Let Noon Be Fair*, was published. Jerome Klinkowitz edited *The Diaries of Willard Motley*, published in 1978.

## ALBERT MURRAY
**Essayist, Novelist**
**1916**

Born in Nokomis, Alabama, Albert Murray received a B.A. from Tuskegee Institute and an M.A. from New York University and has completed additional study at several other universities. He has been a visiting professor and a lecturer at many universities since he retired from the U.S. Air Force as a major some years ago. Murray's short stories and essays are found in numerous anthologies of black writing. His first book was *The Omni-Americans: New Perspectives on Black Experience and American Culture* (1970). *This was followed by South to a Very Old Place* (1972); then, *The Hero and the Blues* (1973), a collection of the Paul Anthony Buck lectures (ninth series) at the University of Missouri, Columbia. His fourth book was a novel, *Trainwhistle Guitar* (1974), the first part of a trilogy of novels to be published. Murray's biggest book was *Stomping the Blues* (1976), a profusely illustrated discussion of the aesthetic values of blues music, how these values originated and the blues developed as an art in the black communities. His writings on Duke Ellington's music have also been published elsewhere. *Stomping the Blues* was reprinted in the Vintage Book series. Murray has lived with his wife and daughter in New York City for many years. He has influenced many young black writers such as Stanley Crouch of the *Village Voice* newspaper, Jervis Anderson of *The New Yorker* magazine, and many others.

Murray worked in interviewing, writing and researching Count Basie's life for several years before his death, whenever Basie had time off from performing. The result was the book *Good Morning Blues: The Autobiography of Count Basie* (1985) as told to Albert Murray.

## GLORIA NAYLOR
**Novelist**
**1950**

Gloria Naylor was born in New York City and still lives there. She received a B.A. in English from Brooklyn College and a M. A. in Afro-American studies from Yale University. She has taught writing and literature at George Washington University, New York University and Boston University. In

1983, she won the American Book Award for first fiction for her novel *The Women of Brewster place,* later in 1988 produced on television. Her second novel was *Linden Hills* published in 1985. Her third novel *Mama Day* (1988) was written with the aid of a grant from the National Endowment for the Arts. In 1988, Naylor was awarded a Guggenheim Fellowship. There is a 27-page conversation between Gloria Naylor and Toni Morrison in *The Southern Review* (Vol. 21, No. 3, July 1985), a number devoted entirely to Afro-American writing. In 1988, Naylor was also named a judge, along with J. Anthony Lukas, of the Book-of-the-Month Club. Earlier in February 1986, she wrote several "Hers" columns for the *New York Times.*

### WILLIAM C. NELL
### Historian, Journalist
### 1816-1874

The most important contribution of William C. Nell to American military history is his *The Colored Patriots of the American Revolution* (1855), a factual, vividly descriptive account of the role played by blacks in the wars in 1776 and 1812.

Though he had little formal education, Nell struggled impressively to improve his condition, and eventually came to be a close friend of William Lloyd Garrison, with whom he was closely associated in the publication of *The Liberator*. Other abolitionists associated with Garrison encouraged Nell in his writing, and two of them, Wendell Phillips and Harriet Beecher Stowe, contributed introductions.

Nell not only documented rare and underpublicized events of the Revolutionary War and the War of 1812, but also painstakingly sifted his sources to separate fact from hearsay. His account of the Boston Massacre is particularly helpful in understanding the full implication of the event—both when it happened and generations later.

*Gordon Parks holds world class honors in four artistic fields, photographer, composer, author and director.*

### GORDON PARKS
### Photographer, Composer, Author, Director
### 1912

Gordon Parks, long acclaimed internationally as a photographer, has recently become a leading producer of black films. He is also a composer (First Concerto for Piana and Orchestra) and novelist (The Learning Tree).

Born in Fort Scott, Kansas, Parks moved to St. Paul, Minnesota, and attended high school there for a time while engaging in a variety of odd jobs. Having chosen photography as a career in 1937, Parks went to Chicago, where he became closely associated with the South Side Community Art Center.

A one-man exhibit of his work eventually led to a Rosenwald Fellowship, after which he accepted a government assignment in the Overseas Division of the Office of War Information.

After World War II, Parks made a number of documentaries for a large New Jersey oil firm, and was later taken on as a staff photographer for *Life.* Since then, he has traveled widely, lived abroad, and captured a number of impressive awards, including Magazine Photographer of the Year (1961), the Newhouse Award from Syracuse University, and NAACP's Spingarn Award in 1972.

Parks also has won awards for his writing. His subject matters include such diverse topics as Black Muslims, Paris of the 1920s, and the plight of all oppressed peoples in U.S. ghettos. His music has been performed in New York, Venice, and Philadelphia.

In addition to *The Learning Tree,* Parks has written an autobiography entitled *A Choice of Weapons* (1965). For National Educational Television, he has produced three documentaries which focus on ghetto life. In 1968, he was the director of the motion picture version of *The Learning Tree.*

His other movies have included *Shaft* and its sequel *Shaft's Big Score, Super Cops,* and *Leadbelly.*

In 1968, his book *A Poet and His Camera* was published. In 1978, he published *Flavio,* the story of a Rio de Janeiro slum child who had become famous because of an earlier picture essay which Parks had done for *Life* magazine. In 1977, with three partners, he gained control of *Essence,* the largest magazine for black women, to prevent the magazine from falling into the hands of whites.

Parks, in 1988, was one of 12 recipients of the National Medal of Arts from President Ronald Reagan at the White House.

Also in 1988, "Gordon Parks: Moments Without Proper Names" was presented on the public television station in New York City examining the life and career of this modern day Renaissance man. Harlem School of the Arts gave Parks an award also in 1988. Earlier he gave some of his photographs to the Schomburg Center in Harlem. Parks has recently had one or two major exhibits of his photographs in New York City and elsewhere.

His other books are *Whispers of Intimate Things* (1971); *Born Black* (1971); *In Love* (1971); *Moments Without Proper Names* (1975); *To Smile in Autumn: A Memoir* (1979); and *Shannon: A Novel* (1983) a story of an Irish man with a black buddy in the immigrant Irish struggle for a place in New York City just before World War I. A section from Parks' diary or journal was published in the twice a year magazine *Antaeus 61: Journals, Notebooks & Diaries* (1988).

*The Reverend Daniel A. Payne, author of* The History of the A.M.E. Church.

## DANIEL A. PAYNE
## Historian, Educator
## 1811-1893

Education and expansion of the Negro church were the two activities which occupied most of Daniel Payne's professional career, although he found time late in life to record his experiences in a number of valuable publications.

Born in Charleston, South Carolina, Payne was educated at the school of the Miner's Moralist Society in his native city and later at the Gettysburg Lutheran Seminary. Payne ran a private school for blacks in antebellum Charleston until 1835—the year a state law against schools for Negro children was passed. Forced to close down, he moved to Philadelphia where he established a similar operation.

During the Civil War, after urging President Lincoln to sign a bill emancipating slaves in the District of Columbia, Payne urged the African Methodist Episcopal Church to purchase Wilberforce. Payne served as president of the school for some 16 years.

In retirement, Payne turned to writing. His most important full-length work is *The History of the A.M.E. Church* (1891). He also wrote *Recollections of Seventy Years* (1888).

## ANN PETRY
## Novelist, Short Story Writer
## 1911

Ann Petry was born in Old Saybrook, Connecticut, where her father was a druggist. After graduating from the College of Pharmacy at the University of Connecticut, she went to New York where she found employment as a social worker and newspaper reporter, studying creative writing at night.

Her early short stories appeared in *Crisis* and *Pylon*. In 1946, after having received a Houghton Mifflin Fellowship, she completed and published her first novel, *The Street*. This was followed by *Country Place* (1947); and *The Narrows* (1953). She then wrote *The Drugstore Cat; Harriet Tubman; Tituba of Salem Village; Legends of Saints;* and a fourth book for children and young people. *Miss Muriel and Other Stories* (1971) is for adults. Her earlier novels are being reprinted.

## BENJAMIN QUARLES
## Historian
## 1904

A specialist in military history, Benjamin Quarles has done extensive research on the Revolutionary and Civil wars and has produced two full-length books dealing with the blacks' role in these conflicts.

Born in Boston, and educated in the public schools there, Quarles has also studied at Shaw University in North Carolina and at the University of Wisconsin. He had taught for many years at Dillard University in New Orleans and at Morgan State University in Baltimore, and served as an associate editor of the *Journal of Negro History*. He retired from teaching some years ago.

The recipient of Rosenwald Fellowships and the University of Wisconsin President Adams Fellowship in Modern History, Quarles has completed a number of books on Negro history and life, including full-length studies of Frederick Douglass and Abraham Lincoln.

His books are *Frederick Douglass* (1948); *Lincoln and the Negro* (1962); *The Negro in the Civil War* (1953); *The Negro in the American Revolution* (1961); *The Negro in the Making of America* (1964); *Black Abolitionists;* and *Allies for Freedom: Blacks and John Brown.* He has edited *Blacks on John Brown; Frederick Douglass* (Great Lives Observed Series); *The Black American: A Documentary History,* with Leslie H. Fishel Jr.; and *Narrative of the Life of Frederick Douglass.* His essays and lectures have been published over the years in *Daedalus*, the *Proceedings of the American Antiquarian Society*, by the Howard University Department of History and in other publications. These essays and lectures are pulled together in *Black Mosaic: Essays in Afro-American History and Historiography* (1987)

### J. SAUNDERS REDDING
### Critic, Scholar
### 1906-1988

J. Saunders Redding has written a number of perceptive appraisals of black literature, completed a novel, an autobiography, and several volumes of history.

Born in Wilmington, Delaware, Redding received his undergraduate and graduate degrees from Brown University where he won Phi Beta Kappa honors. In 1944, he received the Mayflower Award for the best book by a resident of North Carolina. A 1945-1946 Guggenheim Fellowship enabled him to take a leave from his teaching position at Hampton Institute in Virginia.

Redding's books are *To Make a Poet Black* (1939); *No Day of Triumph* (1942); *Stranger and Alone* (1950); *They Came in Chains* (1950); *On Being Negro in America* (1951); *An American in India* (1955); *The Lonesome Road* (1958); and *The Negro.*

In recent years, Redding has assumed several prominent and important educational and consulting assignments. His reviews on black historical, cultural, and scholarly themes have often appeared in the *New York Times.* He is the editor with Arthur P. Davis of *Cavalcade: Negro American Writing from 1760 to the Present* (1971); and earlier *Reading for Writing* (1952) with Ivan E. Taylor. He retired in 1975 as a professor at Cornell University's College of Arts and Sciences where he was the first black professor when hired in 1970. In 1949, when Redding was a visiting professor at Brown University, his alma mater, he was the first black Ivy League faculty member. He was a member of the Phi Beta Kappa Society at Brown University as an undergraduate in the 1920s. Later Redding was a member of the editorial board of *The American Scholar*, the Society's national quarterly from 1951 to 1963 and he returned to the board in 1970. (See longtime *American Scholar* editor Hiram Haydn's *Words &Faces* [1974].) In 1983, a new edition of Redding and Davis's anthology *Cavalcade* was published in two volumes. Redding died March 2, 1988 at his home in Ithaca, N. Y., at the age of 81.

*Called brilliant and imaginative, novelist Ishmael Reed has lived up to early plaudits.*

### ISHMAEL REED
### Novelist, Poet
### 1938

Powerfully imaginative Ishmael Reed is one of America's most promising young novelists, with a great ability to create characters with ideas.

Born in Chattanooga, Tennessee, he grew up in Buffalo, New York, learned to write in New York City, and wised up in Berkeley, California, where he now lives and teaches at the university. His first volume of poetry published in the United States, *Conjure* (1972), was nominated for the National Book Award, as was his third novel, *Mumbo Jumbo* (1972). He has also published *Chattanooga,* a second volume of poetry, and four other novels: *The Free-lance Pallbearers; Yellow Back Radio Broke Down; The Last Days of Louisiana Red*, which appeared in 1974; and *Flight to Canada* (1976).

Reed edited the breakthrough anthology *19 Necromancers from Now* and *The Yardbird Reader,* Volume I. His poetry has appeared in numerous anthologies and magazines, including *The Poetry of the Negro, The New Black Poetry, The Norton Anthology, Cricket,* and *Scholastic* magazine. *His Shrovetide in Old New Orleans* (1978) is a collection of essays.

Reed has published two novels in the 1980s, *The Terrible Twos* (1982), a political satire; and *Reckless Eyeballing* (1987), a farce in which the sinister Flower Phantom punishes feminists for defaming black manhood. Both novels were re-issued in paperback in 1988 by Atheneum Publishers. Reed's two books of essays, editorials, and book reviews for this period are *God Made Alaska for the Indians: Selected Essays* (1983); and *Writin' Is Fightin': Thirty-Seven Years of Boxing on Paper* (1988). Reed's eighth novel, *The Terrible Threes,* was published in 1989. Also, Elizabeth A. and Thomas A. Settle have written *Ishmael Reed: A Primary and Secondary Bibliography* (1982).

### JOEL A. ROGERS
**Historian**
**1880-1966**

For more than 50 years, Joel A. Rogers was one of the foremost black historians and journalists in the United States.

Born in Jamaica, West Indies, Rogers came to the United States in 1906. Originally a journalist, he covered Haile Selassie's coronation as Emperor of Ethiopia in 1930, and five years later, became the first black war correspondent in U.S. history by reporting the Italo-Ethiopian War for the *Pittsburgh Courier.*

Rogers was a member of the American Geographical Society and the Academy of Political Science. He was the author of numerous newspaper and magazine articles and wrote an illustrated feature ("Your History") for the *Pittsburgh Courier*. His books are *From Superman to Man* (1917); *As Nature Leads* (1919); *World's Greatest Men of African Descent* (1931); *Real Facts About Ethiopia* (1935); *Sex and Race* (3 vols.,1940-1944); *World's Great Men of Color* (2 vols., 1947, 1972); *Nature Knows No Color Line;* and *Africa's Gift to America.*

Although the work of Joel Rogers has at times been challenged for the accuracy of its documentation and interpretation, it is nonetheless impressive when one considers that Rogers was conducting much of his research at a time when black historians were very rare in the United States.

Rogers continued to work on a number of manuscripts until his death in New York City in January 1966.

### DAVID RUGGLES
**Author**
**1810-1849**

David Ruggles probably gained his most lasting fame for aiding Frederick Douglass' escape from slavery, however, he is worthy of recognition in his own right.

Described as a jack-of-all-trades, Ruggles seems to have been a self-educated activist who was involved with the ministry, opened a reading room in New York exclusively for Negroes, served as Secretary of the Committee of Vigilance of New York, ran a magazine, deluged the press with antislavery letters, and somehow found time to be proprietor of a spa.

His books are both polemical in tone and somewhat effusive, but they give considerable evidence of the man's unbounded enthusiasm and debating excellence. His books include *The "Extinguisher" Extinguished, or David M. Reese, M.D.; Used Up* (1834); and *An Antidote for a Poisonous Combination Recently Prepared by a "Citizen of New York," alias Dr. Reese.*

### SONIA SANCHEZ
**Poet, Playwright**
**1934**

Sonia Sanchez was born in Birmingham, Alabama. She studied at New York University and Hunter College in New York City. She is married to Etheridge Knight, a black writer of poetry and fiction. She has taught at San Francisco State College and is now teaching in the Black Studies Department of Temple University in Philadelphia. Her plays are published in the special black drama number of *The Drama Review* (Summer 1968), and in *New Plays from the Black Theatre* (1969) edited by Ed Bullins. Her poems have been published in many magazines and anthologies. Books written or edited by her are six volumes of poetry: *Homecoming* (1969); *We a Badd DDD People* (1970); *It's a New Day; A Blues Book for Blue Black Magical Women; Love Poems* (1975); and *I've Been a Woman;* two anthologies edited by her: *Three Hundred and Sixty Degrees of Blackness Comin at You, An Anthology of the Sonia Sanchez Writers Workshop at Countee Cullen Library in Harlem* (1971); and *We Be Word Sorcerers: 25 Stories by Black Americans* (1974). In 1975, she was working on another book, *Behind the Bamboo Curtain,* an account of her recent visit to the Peoples' Republic of China. She has also written *A Sound Investment* (1978), a collection of short stories.

### GEORGE S. SCHUYLER
**Journalist, Author**
**1895-1977**

George S. Schuyler was born in Providence, Rhode Island in 1895. Educated in the Syracuse public schools, Schuyler served as a first lieutenant in World War I and returned to civilian life as a newspaperman for such publications as the *Pittsburgh Courier, Crisis, Opportunity,* and *The Nation.*

Schuyler graduated into fiction as his style matured, publishing a novel, *Black No More* (1931), and a slave account entitled *Slaves, Today: A Story of Liberia* (1931). Other sketches and short stories appeared in Harlem publications which highlighted the work of black writers before the onset of the Depression. Schuyler drew heavily from his military experience (he was in the U.S. Army from 1912 to 1920), and from various odd jobs to create the setting and mood for his various vignettes. His autobiography, *Black and Conservative,* was published in 1966; Michael W. Peplow's George S. Schuyler appeared in 1980.

### NATHAN ALEXANDER SCOTT JR.
**Critic, Professor**
**1925**

Nathan A. Scott Jr. is a critic of modern literature who has written extensively on the relationships between the literary and religious imagination.

Born in Cleveland, Scott attended the University of Michigan and the Union Theological Seminary in New York. He received his Ph.D. from Columbia University at the age of 24. He later became Chairman of the Theology and

Literature Field of the Divinity School at the University of Chicago.

Scott's essays are noted for their diversity and quality. His works have appeared frequently in journals such as *Review of Metaphysics* and *Christian Century,* as well as *Saturday Review* and *The Kenyon Review*. Scott Jr.'s essays have also been published in many books edited by other writers: H. J. Mooney Jr. and T. F. Staley (editors) *The Shapeless God: Essays on Modern Fiction* (1968), and others.

In addition to his teaching, lecturing, and essays, Scott has written or edited many books: *Rehearsals of Discomposure: Alienation and Reconciliation in Modern Literature* (1952); *Modern Literature and the Religious Frontier* (1958); *Samuel Beckett* (1965); *The Broken Center: Studies in the Theological Horizon of Modern Literature* (1966); *Craters of the Spirit: Studies in the Modern Novel* (1968); *Forms of Extremity in the Modern Novel; Adversity and Grace; Negative Capability; The Poetry of Civic Virtue: Eliot, Malraux, Auden;* the essay on Black Writing in the *Harvard Guide to Contemporary American Writing* (1980), edited by Daniel Hoffman; and *Three American Moralists: Mailer, Bellow, Trilling*.

## NTOZAKE SHANGE
## Playwright, Poet, Novelist
## 1948

Born in Trenton, New Jersey, Ntozake Shange graduated from Barnard College and received her masters degree from the University of Southern California. She studied Afro-American dance and gave many poetry readings in California. Shange taught at Sonoma College in California. Her play *For Colored Girls Who Have Considered Suicide When the Rainbow is Enuf,* a choreopoem, was first produced in California after her dance-drama *Sassafrass* was presented in 1975. *For Colored Girls* showed real talent and was later produced in New York City where it had a long run before going on the road. Other works by Shange that have been produced on the stage are *Spell #7; A Photograph: Lovers in Motion;* and *Boogie Woogie Landscapes. For Colored Girls* has been published twice as a book and Shange's book *Three Pieces* (1981) contains *Spell #7, A Photograph: Lovers in Motion,* and *Boogie Woogie Landscapes.* Her other books are *Sassafrass, Cypress & Indigo* (1983), a novel; and *A Daughter's Geography* (1983) and *From Okra to Greens* (Coffee House Press, 1984), both collections of poetry. Earlier she published *Nappy Edges* (1979), also a book of poetry. Her second novel *Betsey Brown* was published in 1985. *See No Evil: Prefaces & Accounts, 1976-1983* was published in 1984. There is an interview with Shange in *The Massachusetts Review,* (Winter 1987). *Betsey Brown* rewritten by Shange as a drama, with music by the jazz trumpeter and composer Baikida Carroll, opened the American Music Theater Festival in Philadelphia with a two-week run (March 25-April 8, 1989)

*William Grant Still chronicled the Underground Railroad.*

## THOMAS SOWELL
## Economist, Author

Thomas Sowell, a leader of the black conservatives, is an economist and a senior fellow at the Hoover Institution, Stanford University, California. Sowell is the author of many books: *Black Education: Myths and Tragedies; Ethnic America: A History; Knowledge and Decisions; Marxism; Education; A Conflict of Visions: Ideological Origins of Political Struggles; Compassion vs. Guilt; The Economics and Politics of Race and Civil Rights: Rhetoric or Reality?*

*Liberty Tree Catalog,* a right-wing, ultra-conservative California publication, lists many of Sowell's books with annotations along with the books of the other ultra-conservative economists: F. A. Hayek, Ludwig Von Mises, Milton Friedman and Peter T. Bauer. Also listed in the catalog are the works of another black conservative professor, Walter Williams: *All It Takes Is Guts* ( a collection of his syndicated newspaper columns) and *The State Against Blacks*. These ultra-conservatives want to get rid of the federal tax system and abolish public schools, among other things.

## WILLIAM GRANT STILL
## Journalist, Editor
## 1821-1902

William Grant Still was the nineteenth century's foremost chronicler of the Underground Railroad, having compiled numerous case histories involving fugitive slaves. Perhaps the most harrowing and revealing escapade involved an encounter with a man who turned out to be his brother—an escapee from Alabama. That episode strengthened Still's resolve to keep records on as many slaves as possible. Still

*Jean Toomer led the novel beyond literary realism.*

kept these records from 1850 to 1860, and in 1872 compiled a thick volume entitled *Underground Railroad Records.*

Still himself was born free, only because his parents had escaped separately from Maryland's eastern shore to New Jersey. The young man was frequently involved in forwarding passengers to safety in Canada, and also aided survivors of the Harpers Ferry debacle to escape from Virginia. In 1861, Still organized a social, civil, and statistical clearinghouse to collect and preserve historical materials relating to blacks. Some 20 years later, he founded the first YMCA branch for Negroes. He engaged in civil rights and welfare work until his death.

### ELLEN TARRY
### Author
### 1906

Ellen Tarry's service as the "Story Lady" of Friendship House, a Catholic community center in Harlem, brought her into close contact with the actual person who served as the model for "Hezekiah Horton," the character she created in the book of the same name. This same character appears in *The Runaway Elephant,* which was enthusiastically received by critics and public alike at its publication in 1950.

*The Runaway Elephant* was illustrated by cartoonist Oliver Harrington, whose "Bootsie" is one of the best-known cartoon characters in the black press.

Born in Birmingham, Alabama, Miss Tarry was educated in a Southern convent school and converted to Catholicism. Later a journalist in the South and in New York, she began her work in Harlem in 1929, becoming associated with Catherine De Hueck, founder of Friendship House; she went on to establish a similar institution in Chicago. During World War II she served as a staff member of the National Catholic Community Service.

Her books include *Katherine Drexel* (1958); *Martin de Porres* (1963); and *Young Jim: The Early Years of James Weldon Johnson* (1967). Her autobiography *The Third Door* was published in 1955. Tarry's most recent book, *The Other Toussaint* (1981), a biography of Pierre Toussaint, traces this post-revolutionary black's life from Haiti to New York where he became hairdresser to most of the great society ladies of that era.

### LUCY TERRY
### Poet
### 1730-1821

Lucy Terry is generally considered to be the first black poet in America. In a ballad which she called "Bars Fight," she recreated an Indian massacre which occurred in Deerfield, Massachusetts in 1746 during King George's War. (Although of little poetic value, "Bars Fight" has been hailed by some historians as the most authentic account of the massacre.)

A semi-literate slave in the household of Ensign Ebenezer Wells, she won her freedom and was married to a freed man named Prince. The Prince house served as a center for young people who gathered to listen to their hostess's storytelling. Lucy Terry was a strong woman who argued eloquently for her family's rights in several cases. See *Black Woman: A Fictionalized Biography of Lucy Terry Prince* (1973) by Bernard and Jonathan Katz.

### HOWARD THURMAN
### Author
### 1900-1981

Almost all of Howard Thurman's considerable writing has centered on religious themes and been printed in such publications as *Christian Century, The World Tomorrow, The Southern Workman, Christendom, The Journal of Religion,* and *Religion and Life. With Head and Heart: The Autobiography of Howard Thurman* (1979) along with other achievements, Thurman won the religious award in the Ebony American Achievement Award for 1979.

He was co-founder of the Interracial Interdenominational Fellowship Church of San Francisco. In 1978, Ebony magazine published an article titled "Howard Thurman: 20th Century Holy Man." He died in his home in San Francisco in 1981.

Born in Florida and educated at the Florida Baptist

Academy (later Florida Normal Institute), Thurman later received collegiate training at Morehouse and Rochester Theological Seminary, the Oberlin Divinity School, and Haverford. In 1935, Thurman led a "pilgrimage of friendship" of students of religion to colleges in Burma, India, and Ceylon. Later, he was pastor and religious advisor at Oberlin, Morehouse, and Howard. He was also professor of Christian theology at Howard. His many books include *The Negro Spiritual Speaks of Life and Death; Deep River; The Luminous Darkness; The Inward Journey; Disciplines of the Spirit;* and an essay called *Why I Believe There Is a God.* Writings about Thurman include Luther E. Smith Jr.'s *Howard Thurman: The Mystic As Prophet* (1982) and a special issue of *Debate & Understanding* magazine (Spring 1982) devoted to Thurman, published at the M. L. King Jr. Center, Boston University.

## WALLACE THURMAN
## Novelist, Playwright
## 1902-1934

Death claimed Wallace Thurman not long after he had produced two of his major works, a play, *Harlem* (1929), and a novel, *The Blacker the Berry,* published the same year. His other major literary effort was *Infants of the Spring*, published in 1932.

Born in Salt Lake City, Utah and educated at the University of Southern California, Thurman served on the editorial staffs of *The Messenger,* and of Macaulay Publishing Company. He was also involved in a pair of short-lived magazine ventures, *Fire* and *Harlem. The Blacker the Berry* and *Fire* have been reprinted.

## MELVIN B. TOLSON
## Poet
## 1898-1966

Born in Moberly, Missouri, educated at Fisk, Lincoln, and Columbia Universities, Tolson had been a contributor to many newspapers and to publications such as *Arts Quarterly* and *American Poets.* The recipient of several prizes from state and local organizations, he has also won the National Poetry Contest for his poem "Dark Symphony." *Rendezvous with America*, published in 1944, was his first volume of poetry. In 1951, *Poetry* magazine presented him with the Bess Hokim Award for a poem called "Foe."

To date, his best-known work is probably *Libretto for the Republic of Liberia* (1953). Another of his narrative poems, *Harlem Gallery*, was published in 1965 as a book. He taught for many years at Langston University in Oklahoma. Tolson's *A Gallery of Harlem Portraits* was published posthumously in 1979, edited by Robert M. Farnsworth. Farnsworth also edited *Caviar and Cabbage: Selected Columns by Melvin B. Tolson from the "Washington Tribune", 1937-1944* (1983). Farnsworth has also published a biography titled *Melvin B. Tolson (1898-1966): Plain Talk and Poetic Prophecy* (1984). Mariann Russell has written *Melvin B. Tolson's Harlem Gallery: A Literary Analysis* (1981) and Joy Flasch's *Melvin B. Tolson* (1972) is in *Twayne U.S. Authors Series.*

## JEAN TOOMER
## Novelist, Poet
## 1894-1967

Jean Toomer's *Cane,* published in 1923, has been called one of the three best novels ever written by an American black—the others being Richard Wright's *Native Son* and Ralph Ellison's *Invisible Man.* According to Columbia University critic Robert Bone, "Cane is by far the most impressive product of the Negro Renaissance."

A mixture of poems and sketches, *Cane* was written during that period in which most black writers were reacting against earlier "polite" forms by creating works marked by literary realism. Toomer even went beyond this realm to the threshold of symbol and myth, using a "mystical" approach which is much more akin to the contemporary mood than it was to the prevailing spirit of his own day. *Cane* sold only 500 copies on publication, and was still little known until it was reprinted recently with new introductions. A lot has been written about Toomer and *Cane* in recent years including a *Cane* casebook.

Born in Washington, D.C. in 1894, Toomer was educated for law at the University of Wisconsin and City College of New York before he turned to writing. His transcendental bent is said to have stemmed in part from his early study under Gurdjieff, the Russian mystic.

Toomer also published quite a bit of poetry. Darwin T. Turner edited *The Wayward and The Seeking: A Collection of Writings by Jean Toomer* (1974), a book of his poetry, short stories, dramas, and autobiography. Other books about Toomer and his writings are Therman O'Daniel (editor) *Jean Toomer: A Critical Evaluation* (1985), over 40 essays of the most thorough, up-to-date scholarship on Toomer; Robert B. Jones and Margery Toomer Latimer (editors) *The Collected Poems of Jean Toomer* (1988), 55 poems; and Nellie Y. McKay's *Jean Toomer, Artist: A Study of His Literary Life and Work, 1894-1936* (1984, 1987)

## DARWIN T. TURNER
## Critic, Scholar
## 1931

Born in Cincinnati, Ohio, and very precocious, Turner obtained a bachelor's degree from the University of Cincinnati in 1947, at the age of 16, with Phi Beta Kappa honors; also a masters degree from the same university in 1949, and a doctorate from the University of Chicago in 1956. He taught at several black colleges during the 1950s and 1960s, and later was visiting professor at several white universities. Turner has been professor of English and director of the Afro-American Studies Program at the University of Iowa from 1972 to the present. He was general editor of the Arno Press Afro-American Culture Series (1969) and the Charles E. Merrill Co.'s African/Afro-American Series (1970).

Turner's writings are: (editor) *A Guide to Composition* (1960); (editor) *Standards for Freshman Composition* (1961);

*Kidnapped into slavery, Gustavus Vassa lived to become a spokesman for abolition.*

*Escaped slave Samuel R. Ward had to flee the United States because of his fiery speechmaking.*

*Katharsis* (poetry) (1964); (co-editor) *Images of the Negro in America* (1965) with Jean M. Bright; *One Last Word* (poetry) (1964); (editor) *Afro-American Writers* (1970); (editor) *Black American Literature: Essays, Fiction, Poetry, Drama* (4 vols, 1969); (editor) *Black Drama in America: An Anthology* (1971); *In a Minor Chord: Three Afro-American Writers and Their Search for Identity* (1971); (editor) *Responding: Five* (1973) with Philip Thompson; (editor) *Voices from the Black Experience: African and Afro-American Literature* (1972) with others; and (editor) *The Wayward and the Seeking: A Collection of Writings by Jean Toomer* (1974). Turner has also published essays in many books, anthologies and magazines edited by others, and essays in several encyclopedias.

## GUSTAVUS VASSA
## Author
## c. 1745- c. 1801

Gustavus Vassa was born in 1745, in Benin, in Southern Nigeria. At the age of 11, he was kidnapped and shipped to the New World as a slave. His masters included a Virginia plantation owner, a British officer, and a Philadelphia merchant from whom he eventually purchased his freedom.

Vassa then settled in England where he worked diligently for the elimination of slavery. He even went so far as to present a petition to Parliament calling for its abolition.

His autobiography, *The Interesting Narrative of the Life of Oloudah Equiano, or Gustavus Vassa,* was published in London in 1789 and went through five editions in the next five years. It is regarded as a highly informative account of the evils of slavery as it affected both master and slave.

Vassa died around 1801. *Equiano's Travels* has also been published recently.

## ALICE WALKER
## Poet, Novelist
## 1944

Alice Walker was born in Eatonton, Georgia, has lived in Mississippi, and in 1974 moved to New York City. She was educated at Spelman College, Atlanta, Georgia, and at Sarah Lawrence College, Bronxville, New York.

Her short stories and poems have been published in *Freedomways, Essence,* and other magazines and anthologies. She has been writer-in-residence and teacher at Jackson State College and Tougaloo College in Mississippi and is a prolific writer. Her first book was poetry entitled *Once,* published in 1968. Her second book, published in 1970, was a novel, *The Third Life of Grange Copeland.* A second book of poetry, *Revolutionary Petunias & Other Poems,* was published in 1973. She also wrote *In Love and Trouble: Stories of Black Women* (1973); *Langston Hughes, American Poet* (1974), for children; *Meridian* (1976), a novel; *Good Night, Willie Lee, I'll See You in the Morning* (1979), poetry; and *You Can't Keep A Good Woman Down* (1981), short stories.

Walker edited *A Zora Neale Hurston Reader* published in 1980. David Bradley's "Novelist Alice Walker: Telling the Black Woman's Story" (*New York Times Magazine*, Jan. 8,

1984) says that she left New York City in 1979 to live and write in California. Walker told Bradley that Zora Neale Hurston had become her model.

Her book *In Love & Trouble: Stories of Black Women* (1973) won the American Academy and Institute of Arts and Letters' Rosenthal Award. *Revolutionary Petunias and Other Poems* (1973) was nominated for the National Book Award and was given the Lillian Smith Award. She has received the Merrill Fellowship for Writing, the National Endowment for the Arts Grant, the Radcliffe Institute Fellowship and other honors. In 1983 , her third novel *The Color Purple* (1982) won the American Book Award in the hardcover category and also the Pulitzer Prize. The book was reviewed negatively by black men and some women reviewers for its degrading depiction of black men. *The Color Purple* became a best seller in hard and paperback. It was released in 1985 as a film. Blacks debated vehemently over it, with many black women defending the film as accurate, and other black women and men condemning the movie and the book's distortions of black history, and failure to deal with the socioeconomic conditions of the period. Alice Walker became a very wealthy woman.

Her other later books are *In Search of Our Mothers' Gardens: Womanist Prose* (1983); *Horses Make the Landscape Look More Beautiful* (1984), a book of poems; *To Hell With Dying* (1987), a book for children; *Living By The Word: Selected Writings, 1973-1987* (1988), a book of essays; and her fourth novel *The Temple of My Familiar* (1989), which was both panned and praised and was a Book-of-the-Month Club featured alternate.

## DAVID WALKER
**Pamphleteer**
**1785-1830**

David Walker is something of a mystery, both as a literary figure and as a man. His fame rests exclusively on a small but explosive pamphlet which circulated clandestinely through the antebellum South and "rumored" slave uprisings as the only possible solution to the black problem. The full title of Walker's work is *Walker's Appeal in Four Articles Together With A Preamble to the Colored Citizens of the World, But in Particular and Very Expressly to Those of the United States* (1829).

Born of a free mother and a slave father, Walker left his native North Carolina while in his teens, and settled in Boston, where he earned a living as a dealer in old clothes. After his Appeal was published, his life was threatened, but he refused to flee to Canada and seek anonymity. Instead, he vowed to fight on. He died shortly thereafter, in circumstances which led many abolitionists to believe that he had been murdered. The blacks of Boston believed him a true martyr to their cause.

## MARGARET WALKER
**Poet, Novelist**
**1915**

Margaret Walker was born on July 7, 1915 in Birmingham, Alabama, and received her early education in Alabama, Louisiana, and Mississippi. She earned her B.A. from Northwestern University and her M.A. from the University of Iowa (1940).

In 1942, Miss Walker published *For My People* and two years later was awarded a Rosenwald Fellowship for creative writing. She has taught English and literature at Livingston College in North Carolina, at West Virginia State College, and at Jackson State College in Mississippi. Her novel appeared in 1966 and is entitled *Jubilee. For My People* was reprinted in 1969. Her other works are *Prophets for a New Day; How I Wrote Jubilee; October Journey;* and *A Poetic Equation: Conversations Between Nikki Giovanni and Margaret Walker.* June 17, 1976, was proclaimed Margaret Walker Alexander Day by the mayor of her native Birmingham.

Her book, Richard Wright: Daemonic Genius (1988), which she had been working on for many years has finally been published after a change of publishers. She knew Richard Wright in Chicago. Also, a second edition of *A Poetic Equation: Conversations Between Nikki Giovanni and Margaret Walker* (1983) has been published. Margaret Walker was honored at the eighth annual Langston Hughes Festival at City College, New York in April 1983.

## ERIC WALROND
**Essayist, Short Story Writer**
**1898-1966**

Eric Walrond was born in Georgetown, Guyana, came to Harlem in 1918, and studied at Columbia University and The City College of New York while he held several odd jobs. He became associate editor of *The Negro World* in 1923.

Two years later he wrote an essay entitled *"On Being Black"* which was published in *The New Republic* and brought him a measure of attention from the literary world.

*Tropic Death,* his first and only book, was published in 1926. It is a collection of stories depicting the contrast between the natural beauty of the American tropics and the poverty, disease, and death of its inhabitants. Walrond lived for many years in London, where he died in 1966.

## SAMUEL RINGGOLD WARD
**Author**
**1817-1864**

Primarily a serious orator, although his writing was laced with much humor and satire, Samuel Ringgold Ward published only one full-length book in his lifetime, *The Autobiography of a Fugitive Negro* (1855).

An escapee from slavery, Ward was raised in New York, where he was sufficiently educated to teach school and become a preacher. He soon extended his involvements to include the antislavery cause and was eventually forced to flee to Canada because of his fiery speech making on behalf of fugitive slave Jerry McHenry. Ward remained an active lecturer in Canada and England. He died in Jamaica during the Civil War. His book was reprinted in 1968 by Arno Press.

*The frontispiece from a book of Phillis Wheatley's poems. The artist is thought to be Scipio Moorehead.*

### CHARLES H. WESLEY
### Historian
### 1891-1987

Charles H. Wesley, president from 1942 until 1965 of Wilberforce University and Central State University (1947-1965), both in Ohio, was one of America's major black historians.

Born in Louisville, Kentucky, Wesley studied at Fisk, Howard, Harvard, Yale, Columbia, and the Guilde International in Paris. Among his many awards were scholarships from Yale (1913) and Harvard (1920-1921), and a Guggenheim Fellowship (1930-1931).

Wesley served as professor and dean of Howard. He is the author of such works as *Negro Labor in the United States, 1850-1925; A Study in American Economic History* (1927); *Richard Allen, Apostle of Freedom* (1935); *The Collapse of the Confederacy* (1937); and *The Negro in the Americas* (1940).

His most recent works include *Neglected History* (1965); *In Freedom's Footsteps* (1968); *The Quest For Equality* (1968); and *Henry Arthur Callis: Life and Legacy* (1977). For several years Wesley was director of the Association for the Study of Afro-American Life and History.

Wesley married for a second time in the 1970s. His second wife is Dorothy B. Porter, librarian, bibliographer, the author or editor of quite a few books and curator emerita of Howard Unviersity's Moorland-Spingarn Collection. Wesley's last book is *The History of the National Association of Colored Women's Clubs: A legacy of Service* (1984) published when he was 92 years old. He had earlier written histories of his Alpha Phi Alpha Fraternity, Sigma Pi Phi Fraternity, and the Elks and the Masons (the first black fraternity), of Ohio; *Negro Americans in the Civil War* (1967) with Patricia Romero and other books. Wesley died August 16, 1987, a few months before his 96th birthday of December 2.

### PHILLIS WHEATLEY
### Poet
### 1753?-1784

Born in Senegal, Phillis Wheatley was brought to the United States as a slave and received her name from Mrs. Susannah Wheatley, the wife of the Boston tailor who had bought Phillis.

Miss Wheatley received her early education in the household of her master. Her interest in writing stemmed from her reading of the Bible and the classics under the guidance of the Wheatley's daughter, Mary.

In 1770, her first poem was printed under the title *A Poem by Phillis, A Negro Girl on the Death of Reverend George Whitefield.* Her book *Poems on Various Subjects: Religious and Moral* was published in London in 1773. After a trip to England for health reasons she later returned to the United States, and was married. She published the poem *Liberty and Peace* in 1784, shortly before her death. Most of the old books of her poems, letters, and memoirs about her life were reprinted in the late 1960s and early 1970s. Two books about her are Julian D. Mason Jr.'s *The Poems of Phillis Wheatley* (1966); and William H. Robinson's *Phillis Wheatley, A Biography* (1981). Robinson also compiled and published *Phillis Wheatley: A Bio-Bibliography* (1981).

Although George Washington was among her admirers (she had once sent him a tributary poem, which he graciously acknowledged), her poetry is considered important today largely because of its historical role in the growth of American Negro literature. In its style and thematic preoccupations, Miss Wheatley's poetry reflects Anglo-Saxon models, rather than her African heritage. It is nevertheless, a typical example of the verse manufactured in a territory—the British colonies—not yet divorced from its maternal origins.

### WALTER WHITE
### Journalist, Novelist
### 1893-1955

Walter White, who could have passed for white, chose instead to identify with his black ancestry, and ultimately came to be the most ardent protagonist in the fight to stamp out lynching in America, particularly after World War I. His most famous work was *Rope and Faggot:A Biography of Judge Lynch* (1929).

Born in Atlanta, and educated in that Georgia city as well as in New York, White worked as secretary of the National Association for the Advancement of Colored People

*Controversial independent thinker John Williams.*

*Carter Woodson, pioneer in the analysis of the history of African-Americans.*

(NAACP). He completed his most important study after two years as a Guggenheim Fellow. This work stood alongside two earlier novels, *Fire in the Flint* (1924) and *Flight* (1926). White's other work appeared in the leading periodicals of the day, including *Harper's, The Nation,* and *New Republic.* White was awarded a Spingarn Medal in 1937 in recognition of his tireless efforts on behalf of all black Americans.

His other books are *A Rising Wind* (1945); his autobiography *A Man Called White* (1948); and *How Far The Promised Land?* (1955).

Margaret Perry's *The Harlem Renaissance: An Annotated Bibliography and Commentary* (1983) includes White in works by and about 20 individual authors. Also, Edward E. Waldron produced *Walter White and the Harlem Renaissance* (1979).

## JOHN EDGAR WIDEMAN
**Novelist**
**1941**

John Wideman was born in Washington, D.C. and educated at the University of Pennsylvania and at Oxford University where he was a Rhodes Scholar. Rhodes Scholars are selected because of their excellence in more than one field. Wideman was an outstanding basketball player and scholar at the University of Pennsylvania. He attended the University of Iowa Writers' Workshop and was associate professor of English at the University of Pennsylvania. Wideman has been professor of English at the University of Wyoming for some years.

His first novel, *A Glance Away,* was published in 1967 when he was 26 years old. His second novel, *Hurry Home,* was published in 1970. Wideman's third novel is *The Lynchers* (1973). His novels have always received enthusiastic reviews by the literary critics. Wideman is also a reviewer of black novels and books about black literature and music for the *New York Times Book Review.* In 1981, he published two paperback books: *Hiding Place,* a novel based on his family history; and *Damballah,* related short stories about his family history. His other later books are *Brothers and Keepers* (1984), about his brother in prison for life for committing a crime; the novel *Reuben* (1987, 1988); and the novel *Sent For You Yesterday* (1983, 1988), a part of the Homewood (section of his home town Pittsburgh) trilogy with *Hiding Place* and *Damballah. Sent For You Yesterday* won the P. E. N./ Faulkner Award for fiction given in 1984. Wideman is now a professor of English at the University of Massachusetts at Amherst.

*Vanity Fair* magazine (Feb. 1989) has a story about Wideman's family. His son Jake Wideman, 18 years old, one of his three children, has confessed to two murders. This is reminiscent of Wideman's brother who committed a crime early in his life as a youth.

## GEORGE WASHINGTON WILLIAMS
### Historian
### 1849-1891

George Washington Williams was the writer of a pair of definitive works on the black experience in the Civil War and the period stretching from the Jamestown landing to the end of Reconstruction. Williams' major works are *The History of the Negro Race in America from 1619-1880* (1883); and *A History of the Negro Troops in the War of the Rebellion* (1888).

A native of Bedford Springs, Pennsylvania, Williams enlisted in the Union Army at the age of 14, served through the war, and went on to become a lieutenant-colonel in the Mexican army. After the fall of Maximilian, he moved west, serving in several Indian campaigns on the frontier. Later he attended Howard University and Newton Theological Seminary, the latter after he had decided on a career in the ministry. His career eventually reached into journalism (he conducted two newspapers), into law (he practiced in Ohio), and into politics (he served in the Ohio state legislature and as Minister to Haiti). Williams subsequently became interested in the Congo and entered the service of the Belgian government. He died in England while still in the service of Leopold II, the Belgian King.

John Hope Franklin's biography *George Washington Williams: A Biography* (1985) won the Clarence L. Holte Literary Prize in 1986.

## JOHN A. WILLIAMS
### Novelist
### 1925

John A. Williams was born in Jackson, Mississippi but grew up in Syracuse, New York. Educated locally, he also took both his undergraduate and graduate degrees at Syracuse University.

His first novel, *The Angry Ones*, was published in 1960, and was followed within a year by a second offering, *Night Song*. In 1962, Williams wrote the text for *Africa: Her History, Lands and People*. That same year, he won the Roman Fellowship of the American Academy in Rome, the unanimous choice of the jury here. The award, however, was rescinded by officials in Rome in an unprecedented action, which caused considerable controversy.

Williams wrote *Sissie* (1963); and *This Is My Country Too* (1965). He has written or edited many other books: *Beyond the Angry Black* (1966); *The Man Who Cried I Am* (1967); *The Most Native of Sons; Captain Blackman; Sons of Darkness, Sons of Light; Flashbacks: A Twenty-Year Diary of Article Writing;* and *Mothersill and the Foxes*.

In 1970, Williams published a controversial work in which he lamented the alleged "failure" of Dr. Martin Luther King Jr. The book, *The King God Didn't Save*, professed to be an objective appraisal of the life and work of the slain civil rights leader. His seventh novel is *Click Song* (1982), about racism in the publishing industry. Williams' other works include *West Virginia and The Captains of Industry* (1976); and *Y'bird* (1978). One of Williams's best, highly acclaimed novels, *The Man Who Cried I Am* which seemed to be based on the life of Richard Wright, was reprinted in 1984. *The Most Native of Sons* is also subtitled *A Biography of Richard Wright* (1970). Also, Gilbert H. Muller and John A. Williams authored *The McGraw-Hill Introduction to Literature*, a huge, 800-page book in 1984. *The Junior Bachelor Society*, a novel about the black middle class, was published in 1976. Williams's first novel, *The Angry Ones* (1960) was reprinted by Chatham Bookseller in the 1970s with the new title *One for New York*. He had been a Distinguished Professor of English at LaGuardia Community College of the City University of New York for many years. Now he is teaching at Rutgers University at Newark, N. J.

## CHARLES V. WILLIE
### Social scientist
### 1927

Charles Willie was born in Dallas, Texas, graduated from Morehouse College, got a master's degree from Atlanta University and a Ph. D. from Syracuse University in 1957. He has taught or lectured at the State University of New York, the Harvard Medical School, Syracuse University and at the Graduate School of Education, Harvard, as professor of education and urban studies where he has remained since 1974.

Willie's books are *Church Action in the World* (1969); *The Family Life of Black People* (1970); *Black Students in White Colleges* (1972) with Arline McCord; *Racism and Mental Health* (1973) with others; *Oreo* (1975); *Black Colleges in America: Challenge, Development, Survival* (1979) with Ronald R. Edmonds (editors); *Caste and Class Controversy* (1980); *The Ivory and Ebony Towers* (1980); *Black/Brown/White Relations: Race Relations in the 1970s* (1981); *A New Look at Black Families* (1981); and *Race Mixing in the Public Schools* (1981). Willie was made a Phi Beta Kappa at Morehouse College in 1972. He has received two honorary degrees from divinity schools and other awards. He was president of the Eastern Sociological Society and on the Social Science Research Council's executive committee.

## AUGUST WILSON
### Playwright
### 1945

August Wilson was born in 1945, and now lives in St. Paul, Minnesota.

Although black playwright Charles Fuller is now writing a cycle of five plays tracing the history of black Americans from the Civil War to 1900—*Sally* and *Prince* are the first two of the series— black playwright August Wilson is farther along in his cycle of plays about black history. The first of Wilson's plays, with their panoramic sweep, was *Ma Rainey's Black Bottom* about the 1920s. First produced at the Yale Repertory Theater and directed by Lloyd Richards, then brought to New York, the play was the New York Drama Critics Circle's best new play in 1985. Wilson's next play *Fences*, about the 1930s, 1940s, and 1950s, was the best new play in 1987 for the New York Drama Critics Circle, after first being produced at the Yale Repertory Theater. Wilson's third play produced in New York, *Joe Turner's Come and Gone* also started at the Yale Repertory Theater and was named the best new play in 1988 by the New York Drama Critics Circle. *Joe Turner's Come and Gone* is about 1911 and the earlier period of black migration from the South, sharecropping and being dispossessed; about a search for cultural roots and identity in a dark and distant past to the psychic burden of years of slavery.

In 1986, Wilson was one of ten writers to win the Whiting Writer's Awards of ten tax-free checks for $25,000 each. The awards were established in 1985 by the Whiting Foundation to reward "exceptionally promising, emerging talent." In 1988, Yale University gave Wilson an honorary degree. Wilson's *Joe Turner* opened in Boston before coming to New York. It was produced in 1987 by the Seattle Repertory Theater. *Fences* was also produced in San Francisco in 1987.

## CARTER G. WOODSON
### Historian
### 1875-1950

Carter Woodson was for many years, along with W. E. B. DuBois, the main voice in American Negro historiography.

Born in New Canton, Virginia, Woodson attended Berea College, the University of Chicago, Harvard, and the Sorbonne in Paris. He and others organized the Association for the Study of Negro Life and History in 1915.

In 1921, Woodson organized Associated Publishers in order to produce textbooks and other supplementary material on blacks, which, at the time, were not readily accepted by most publishers. A year later, he retired from academic life to become Director of the Association for the Study of Negro Life and History, and continued as editor of the *Journal of Negro History,* started in 1916. (Woodson had taught at the elementary and high school level, and served as Dean of the School of Liberal Arts of Howard University.)

*George Washington Williams wrote two definitive works on African-Americans which cover the time span from the first arrivals at Jamestown in 1619 through the Civil War.*

Many of Woodson's books have become the foundations upon which contemporary historians have based their own research. These include *The Education of the Negro Prior to 1861* (1915); *A Century of Negro Migration* (1918); *The Negro in Our History* (1922); *The Rural Negro* (1930); *The Miseducation of the Negro; The Mind of the Negro; History of the Negro Church;* and *The African Background Outlined.*

Woodson started Negro History Week in 1926. Now it has become Black History Month (February). Also, Sister Anthony Scally has compiled the book Carter G. Woodson: A Bio-Bibliography (1985), the first book-length bibliography of Woodson's writings, with over 800 entries annotated plus an accurate chronology of Woodson's life.

Woodson died in Washington, D.C. on April 3, 1950.

## JAY WRIGHT
### Poet, Playwright
### 1935

Born May 25, 1935 in Albuquerque, New Mexico, Wright studied at several universities. He was living in Penicuik, Scotland in the 1970s, but now lives in Piermont, New Hamshire. He has been poet-in-residence at several predominantly black colleges. He was in 1986 the recipient of a 5-year MacArthur Fellowship. Earlier, he was awarded the Hodder Fellowship in playwriting at Princeton University (1970-1971), an Ingram Merrill Foundation award (1974), and a Guggenheim Fellowship (1974, 1975). Highly praised by the critics Harold Bloom, John Hollander and others, his works are *Dimension of History*; *Death as History* (1967); *The Homecoming Singer* (1971); *Soothsayers and Omens* (1977); *The Double Invention of Komo* (1980); *Explications/Interpretations* (1984) in the Callaloo Poetry Series; and *Selected Poems of Jay Wright* (1987) edited by Robert B. Stepto with an afterword by Harold Bloom. Wright's poems have been published in several anthologies, in *Callaloo* and other journals. Finally, he wrote *Elaine's Book* (1988) written originally as a birthday gift for his wife's sister.

## RICHARD WRIGHT
### Novelist
### 1908-1960

The work of Richard Wright is still used as the yardstick by which black novelists in America are measured. It was Wright who, in the 1940s, set the standard for a whole generation of prose writers, including Ralph Ellison and James Baldwin.

Born on a plantation near Natchez, Mississippi, Wright drew on his personal experience to dramatize racial injustice and its brutalizing effects. In 1938, under the auspices of the WPA Illinois Writers Project, Wright published *Uncle Tom's Children,* a collection of four novellas based on his Mississippi boyhood memories. The book won an award for the best

*Richard Wright's novel* Native Son *was produced for the stage by Orson Welles. Pictured here is Canada Lee in the Broadway success.*

work of fiction by a WPA writer, and Wright received a Guggenheim Fellowship.

Two years later, *Native Son*, a novel of Chicago's Negro ghetto, further enhanced Wright's reputation. A Book-of-the-Month Club choice, it was later a successful Broadway production under Orson Welles' direction and was filmed in South America with Wright himself in the role of Bigger Thomas. He published *12 Million Black Voices* in 1941.

In 1945, Wright's largely autobiographical *Black Boy* was selected by the Book-of-the-Month Club and went on to become a second best-seller.

Wright later moved to Paris where he continued to write fiction and nonfiction including *The Outsider* (1953); *Black Power* (1954); *Savage Holiday* (1954,1965); *The Color Curtain* (1956); *The Long Dream* (1958); *Lawd Today* (1963); *Eight Men* (1961); *White Man Listen* (1957); and *American Hunger* (1977), a continuation of Wright's autobiographical work *Black Boy*.

Wright died on November 28, 1960. There are over a dozen adult books about Wright, two casebooks on *Native Son*, a children's book, and a critical pamphlet in a writers series. These include a *Richard Wright Reader* (1978); Addison Gayle Jr.'s *Richard Wright: Ordeal of a Native Son* (1980); Charles T. Davis and Michel Fabre's *Richard Wright: A Primary Bibliography* (1982); and Margaret Walker's *Richard Wright: Daemonic Genius* (1988), a portrait of the man and a critical look at his work.

## FRANK YERBY
## Novelist
## 1916

Frank Yerby, a commercially successful writer, has published over 30 novels which have sold more than 20 million copies and earned for their author a gross amount in excess of 10 million dollars.

Born in Augusta, Georgia in 1916, Yerby studied at Fisk University and the University of Chicago, and taught briefly at Florida A&M and Southern University before moving to Detroit in 1942 to work in a wartime assembly plant.

His early work often dealt with significant social issues such as race. In 1944, for example, *Harper's* published his short story "Health Card," which won a special O. Henry award. Later, after studiously researching the ingredients of popular fiction, Yerby turned his talent to the creation of swashbuckling costume novels which were an immediate success.

In 1949, he published *The Foxes of Harrow*, soon to become a best-seller and a successful movie as well. His commercial successes then became an annual occurrence: *The Vixens* (1947); *The Golden Hawk* (1948); *Pride's Castle* (1949); *Floodtide* (1950); *A Woman Called Fancy* (1951); *The Saracen Blade* (1952); and many others.

Yerby has lived in Europe since 1952. His other books: *The Old Gods Laugh; An Odor of Sanctity; Goat Song;* and *The Dahomean*, are departures from the "costume motif." He has himself expressed a desire to create literature of greater substance. Yerby's recent books are *The Girl from Storyville: A Victorian Novel* (1972); *The Voyage Unplanned* (1974); *Tobias and the Angel* (1975); *A Rose for Ana Maria* (1976); *Fair Oaks* (1977); *Hail the Conquering Hero* (1978); *The Darkness at Ingraham's Crest: A Tale of the Slaveholding South* (1979). His latest book is *Devil Seed* another novel, his 31st about San Francisco during the Gold Rush of the 1850s.

## AL YOUNG
## Poet, Novelist
## 1939

Born in Ocean Springs, Mississippi, Al Young is the son of a professional musician and auto worker. Young attended the University of Michigan, studied creative writing at Stanford University, and received a B.A. degree from the University of California at Berkeley in 1969. A musician and a teacher of writing, his works are *Dancing Poems* (1969); *Snakes* (1970), a novel; *The Song Turning Back into Itself* (1971), poetry; *Earth, Air, Fire and Water* (1971), poetry; *Who Is Angelina?* (1974), a novel; *Geography of the Near East* (1976), poetry; *Sitting Pretty* (1976), a novel; *Ask Me Now* (1981), a novel; *The Blues Don't Change; New and Selected Poems* (1981); and *Bodies and Souls: Musical Memoirs* (1982); *Seduction By Light* (1988) a novel; *Things Ain't What They Used to Be* (1987), a collection of musical memoirs; and *Kinds of Blue* (1984), autobiographical essays by Young.

## NOTABLE BLACK PLAYWRIGHTS

| Name | Dates |
|---|---|
| Garland Anderson | 1886-1939 |
| Marita Bonner | 1905 |
| Theodore Browne | 1910 |
| Hazel Bryant | |
| Ben Caldwell | |
| Steve Carter | |
| Bob Cole | |
| N. R. Davidson | 1940 |
| Philip Hayes Dean | |
| Tom Dent | |
| Val Ferdinand | 1947 |
| J. E. Franklin | |
| Ruth Gaines-Shelton | 1873 |
| Neil Harris | |
| Abraham Hill | |
| Errol Hill | |
| J. Leubrie Hill | 1873-1916 |
| Adrienne Kennedy | 1931 |
| Lew Leslie | 1890-1963 |
| William MacKey | 1861-1918 |
| William Marshall | 1924 |
| John Matheus | 1887-1935 |
| May Miller | |
| Ron Milner | 1938 |
| Barbara Molette | |
| Alice D. Nelson | 1875-1958 |
| Thomas D. Pawley | 1917 |
| Louis Peterson | 1922 |
| Lennox Raphael | 1940 |
| Alex Rogers | |
| John M.Ross | |
| Ruth Gaines Shelton | 1849-1891 |
| Jesse Shipp | 1859-1934 |
| Wole Soyinka | |
| Eulalie Spence | 1894 |
| Evan Walker | |
| Joseph Walker | 1935 |
| Richard Wesley | 1935 |
| Edgar White | 1947 |
| Vantile Whitfield | |
| Frank Wilson | 1886-1956 |
| Marvin X | |

## OTHER NOTABLE BLACK WRITERS

| Name | Craft | Dates |
|---|---|---|
| George Leonard Allen | Poet | 1905-1935 |
| Samuel Allen | Poet, essayist | 1917 |
| Jervis Anderson | Novelist | |
| Russell Atkins | Poet | 1926 |
| William Attaway | Novelist | 1912 |
| Kofi Awoonor | Poet | |
| Toni Cade Bambara | Poet, educator | |
| Gwendolyn B. Bennett | Poet | 1902 |
| Hal Bennett | Novelist | 1930 |
| James Boggs | Essayist | 1919 |
| Donald Bogle | Poet | |
| John H. Bracey Jr. | Writer | 1941 |
| Jonathan Brooks | Poet | 1904-1945 |
| James E. Campbell | Poet | 1860-1905 |
| Catherine Cater | Novelist | 1918 |
| Ocania Chalk | Writer | |
| William Calvin Chase | Journalist, editor | 1854 |
| Marcus Christian | Poet | 1900 |
| Leslie M. Collins | Poet | 1914 |
| Cyrus Coltee | Writer | 1910 |
| Orde Coombs | Poet | |
| Waring Cuney | Poet, musician | 1906 |
| Margaret Danner | Poet | 1915 |
| Frank Marshall Davis | Poet | 1905 |
| Clarissa Delaney | Poet | 1901-1927 |
| William Demby | Novelist | 1922 |
| Alfred A. Duckett | Journalist | 1918 |
| James A. Emanuel | Poet | 1921 |
| Julia Fields | Poet | 1938 |
| Nick Aaron Ford | Editor, critic | 1904 |
| Timothy T. Fortune | Editor, pamphleteer | 1855-1928 |
| Hoyt W. Fuller | Journalist | 1927 |
| Addison Gayle Jr. | Critic, essayist | 1932 |
| Dick Gregory | Satirist, social activist | 1932 |
| Yvonne Gregory | Writer | 1919 |
| Angelina W. Grimke | Poet, teacher | 1880-1958 |
| Rosa Guy | Novelist | 1925 |
| Warren Halliburton | Author, educator | 1924 |
| Charles V. Hamilton | Author, educator | 1929 |
| Donald Jeffrey Hayes | Poet | 1904 |
| Calvin Hernton | Essayist | 1932 |
| Frank Hercules | Novelist | 1917 |
| Leslie Pinckney Hill | Author | 1880-1960 |
| Carl W. Hines Jr. | Poet | 1940 |
| M. Carl Holman | Poet, journalist | 1919 |
| Frank Horne | Poet | 1899 |
| Alton Hornsby Jr. | Editor | |
| Kristin Hunter | Novelist | 1931 |
| Lance Jeffers | Writer | 1919 |
| Ted Joans | Poet, artist | 1928 |

**OTHER NOTABLE BLACK WRITERS** (continued )

| Name | Craft | Dates |
|---|---|---|
| Charles Johnson | Novelist | |
| Charles Spurgeon | Editor | 1895-1956 |
| Gayle Jones | Author, playwright | 1949 |
| George E. Kent | Critic | 1920 |
| Etheridge Knight | Poet | 1931 |
| Don L. Lee | Editor, poet | 1942 |
| John Lovell Jr. | Author, educator | 1907 |
| Naomi Long Madgett | Poet | 1923 |
| Sharon Bell Mathis | Novelist | 1937 |
| Louise Meriwether | Author | |
| Pauli Murray | Poet, lawyer | 1910 |
| Walter Dean Myers | Author | 1937 |
| Larry Neal | Poet | 1937 |
| Effie Lee Newsome | Author, poet | 1885 |
| Gloria C. Oden | Poet | 1923 |
| Earl Ofari | Writer | 1945 |
| Myron O'Higgins | Poet | 1918 |
| Roi Ottley | Journalist | 1906-1960 |
| Lindsay Patterson | Editor | |
| Raymond Patterson | Poet | 1929 |
| Oliver Pitcher | Poet, actor | 1923 |
| Dudley Randall | Poet | 1914 |
| T. J. Reddy | Novelist | |
| Eugene B. Redmond | Poet | |
| Clayton Riley | Writer | 1935 |
| Conrad Kent Rivers | Poet | 1933 |
| Carolyn M. Rodgers | Poet | |
| Charlemae H. Rollins | Author, bibliographer | 1897 |
| Gil Scott-Heron | Poet, musician | 1949 |
| Ann Allen Shockley | Editor | |
| Rev. William J. Simmons | Biographer | 1849-1890 |
| William Gardner Smith | Novelist, journalist | 1926-1974 |
| Thomas Sewell | Writer | 1930 |
| Anne Spencer | Poet, librarian | 1882 |
| Robert Staples | Writer | 1942 |
| Darwin T. Turner | Critic,editor | 1931 |
| Charles Enoch Wheeler | Writer | 1909 |
| James M. Whitfield | Writer | 1830-1870 |
| George W. Williams | Historian, legislator | 1849-1891 |
| Lucy Ariel Williams | Writer | 1905 |
| Charles V. Willie | Writer | 1927 |
| Charles Wright | Novelist | 1932 |
| Bruce M. Wright | Writer | 1918 |
| Jay Wright | Author, poet | 1935 |

# THE BLACK ARTIST

**Black Artists In America—A Brief Review ■ Black Museums and Galleries ■ Black Exhibitions and Mainstream Art Institutions ■ Black Artist Organizations And Movements ■ Outstanding Black Artists**

*The constructive lessons of African art are among the soundest and most needed of art creeds today. They offset with equal force the banalities of sterile, imitative classicism and the superficialities of literal realism. They emphasize intellectually significant form, abstractly balanced design, formal simplicity, restrained and unsentimental emotional appeal. Moreover, Africa's art creed is beauty in use, vitally rooted in the crafts, and uncontaminated with the blight of the machine. Surely the liberating example of such art will be as marked an influence in the contemporary work of Negro artists as it has been in that of the leading modernists: Picasso, Modigliani, Matisse, Epstein, Lipchitz, Brancusi and others too numerous to mention.* (Alain Locke, Professor of Philosophy, Howard University, 1931)

This comment, by one of America's foremost art critics over 40 years ago, during the height of the Harlem Renaissance, underscores the problems and promise encountered by blacks interested in expanding their artistic skills throughout their history in the United States. The substantial contributions of black artists have been achieved against numerous obstacles. Foremost among these obstacles are:

Blacks in the western world and also Europe were long cut off from the artistic heritage of Africa, a heritage now known for enormous achievements as far back as the fifteenth century. As Locke points out, "the liberating example" of African art was used by white Europeans long before American blacks.

From colonial days to the present, black talent has been encouraged and recognized on a very limited basis by reigning art establishments and connoisseurs of the United States, though some white institutions, such as the Rosenwald Fund in the early twentieth century, did subsidize promising blacks.

Themes and expressions of black life, whether they relate to slave, sharecropper, or ghetto life, have rarely been regarded as prime moneymakers by leading merchants and curators of the art world.

Few blacks attained the economic security of leisure essential to creativity and patronage of artists.

### Early European Art

The fact that blacks could excel in Euro-American art forms was firmly established in seventeenth-century Spain by the success of Juan de Pareja, a slave, apprentice, and pupil of the great master Velasquez. Many of Pareja's works were of such a quality that they were mistakenly accepted as Velasquez' own and hung in the great museums and mansions of western Europe. Today, Pareja's paintings, properly credited to him, hang in the Dulwich Gallery in London, the Prado in Madrid, the Munich Gallery, and the Hermitage in Leningrad. Pareja's talent was recognized in his lifetime and in 1652 he was manumitted by King Philip IV.

Another well-known seventeenth-century black artist, Sebastian Gomez, a servant of Murillo, was discovered painting secretly at night in his master's studio after Murillo's pupils had departed. Gomez was made a pupil of the master and eventually, known as The Mulatto of Murillo, became famous for paintings and murals in Seville.

Although Pareja and Gomez were black artists, their genius was nurtured in a European setting and tradition. Cut off from their African heritage, they naturally worked in the same style and format as their white contemporaries. Their paintings were devoted to the religious themes and aristocratic portraits desired by the art world of that historical era.

## BLACK ARTISTS IN AMERICA—A BRIEF REVIEW

### Blacks in Early America

The only eighteenth-century Afro-American artist in Colonial America to have been recorded was Scipio Morehead. Morehead's artistic endeavors appear to have been aided by two prominent women who lived in Boston where he was a slave. One was the wife of his clergyman master, Reverend John Morehead, who was a patron of the arts, and the other, poet Phillis Wheatley, who was herself a slave. Morehead's style has been reported to have been in keeping with the period—classically allegorical, resembling the work of Romney and Reynolds, British masters of the era. Although no major work is known to have survived, it is believed that the small portrait of Phillis Wheatley is by Morehead's hand.

It is certain that there were other black artists and craftsmen that went unrecorded in the eighteenth century, but fortunately

*From the folk art collection of Abby Aldrich Rockefeller, a watercolor entitled* The Old Plantation *by an unknown eighteenth-century artist.*

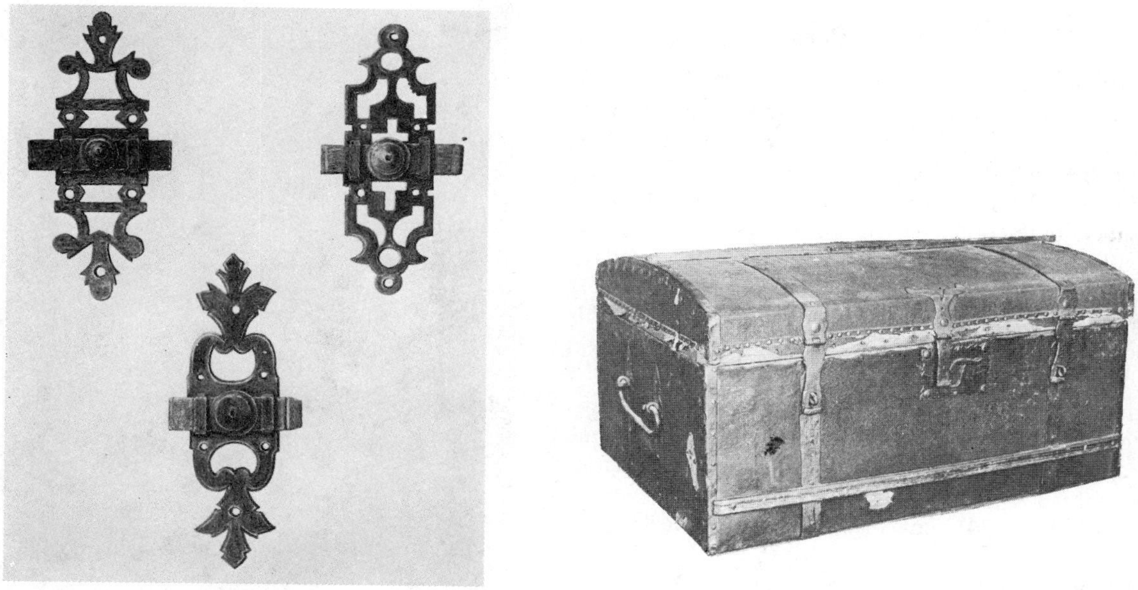

*Among examples of fine craftsmanship produced by slave labor are these brass locks and hinges.*

as scholars have more of a desire to understand the nature and development of the American culture a more multi-ethnic pattern is beginning to emerge with the basic foundation being Western European, African and American Indian. Records show that skilled blacks interested in buying their freedom worked as sign painters, silversmiths, cabinet and coach makers, ornamentalists and shipwrights. Eugene Warbourg, for example, a black sculptor from New Orleans, became well known for his ornamental gravestones and eventually went to study in Europe. Bill Day, a celebrated carpenter of his day, who owned slaves in his shop, has recently gained recognition for his interior designs as well as his furniture.

Much colonial iron work and metal work on eighteenth-century mansions, churches, and public buildings was created and executed by blacks and occasionally reached heights that can be classified as fine art. But as with a watercolor entitled *The Old Plantation*, the artists and the artisans are not known.

## Nineteenth Century

The black presence in nineteenth-century art is better documented. Blacks able to overcome the immense obstacles to their performance and recognition included Duncanson, Simpson, Bannister, Johnston, Douglass Bowser, Edmonia Lewis, Tanner, Harper, and Meta Warwick Fuller.

These talents generally performed in the prevailing fashion of American art at the time, which was to copy the styles and techniques then popular in Europe. Many, among whom were two women sculptors Lewis and Fuller, went to Europe to study, attained recognition, and eventually settled there.

Many black artists attempting to escape the classical tradition into which they were confined, painted themes closer to their heritage and existence. Some fine portraits of black freedmen were painted by talented but obscure black artists in the rural South during the period from 1870 into the early part of this century. Henry Tanner's paintings of the 1880s and Meta Fuller's sculptures of peasant blacks stem from this unheralded school of black art.

*Meta Vaux Warrick Fuller's bronze* Water Boy, *in the National Archives, Washington, D.C.*

### Twentieth Century

From 1900 to the 1920s, black artists continued to work in the stilted, imitative styles of the late-nineteenth century. However, in 1913, the now famous New York Armory Show of European cubist and modernist painters swept the art world into a totally different direction, which in retrospect bears traces of important African influences. Even so, it was not until after World War I that twentieth-century trends in art and respect for the African idiom and negritude began to manifest itself in the paintings of black America. Out of this period came Archibald Motley, Palmer Hayden, Malvin Gray Johnson, Laura Wheeler Waring, and W. E. Scott.

Karamu House, a center for cultural activities in the arts, was founded in 1915 in Cleveland. From this center came such artists as Hughie Lee-Smith, Zell Ingrams, Charles Sallee, Elmer Brown, William E. Smith, and George Hulsinger. In 1924, the Amy Spingarn Awards were established. Three years later, in 1927, the Harmon Foundation was established by philanthropist William E. Harmon to aid Afro-American artists. The foundation offered financial awards and exhibitions and encouraged the growth of art education programs in many black institutions throughout the country. The Harmon Foundation was to become one of the major organizations involved in the perpetuation and presentation of Afro-American art in the United States, and which continued to exist until the mid-1960s. Howard University established its first art gallery, under the directorship of James V. Herrings, in 1930.

The 1930s brought the depression and the Works Progress Administration. Black artists abandoned by the white philanthropists of the 1920s were rescued by the W.P.A. Aaron Douglas, Augusta Savage, Charles Alston, Hale

Modern Science in Medicine, *Charles Alston's heroic mural, was executed in the 1930's for Harlem Hospital.*

*Art and black militancy in the 1960's—a mood, an explosion of emotion, a philosophical exposition, a celebration of the people.*

Woodruff, and Charles White created murals and other works for public buildings under this program. In 1939, the Baltimore Museum Show, the first exhibition of black artists to be held in a southern region, presented the works of Richmond Barthe, Malvin Gray Johnson, Henry Bannarn, Florence Purviance, Hale Woodruff, Dox Thrash, Robert Blackburn, and Archibald Motley.

The Harlem Art Center and The Chicago South Side Community Art Center also began with the W.P.A.

The search for a black identity and the expression of black militancy were the most pervasive themes of black art in the 1950s and 1960s. Emotions could not always be contained on canvas, channeled into familiar forms, or exhibited in traditional settings. Art literally took to the streets of the ghetto to meet with, appeal to, and celebrate the people, as was richly illustrated in Chicago and Detroit murals. Artists also demonstrated an abiding preoccupation with social themes. Black art had become their vehicle to champion the cause of the "people." Others felt that art should be separated from politics and remain an expression of the individual not necessarily with reference to race. The two views occasionally clashed, producing dissension among black artists, but also contributing to the vitality and diversity of black art.

*Artists Mel Edwards* (left) *and Vincent Smith at the opening exhibition of The Studio Museum in Harlem.*

## BLACK MUSEUMS AND GALLERIES

The 1960s was an era which saw a great many radical changes in both the social and the cultural aspects of the United States. Afro-Americans throughout the country were demanding political and social recognition. Afro-Americans added cultural recognition to those demands. No longer satisfied with the limited support of such philanthropic organizations as the Harmon Foundation, these artists looked for alternative forms of exposure. The result of their demands was an outpouring of galleries, community art centers, and community art galleries and programs established within the major art museums around the country.

In New York City, the *Acts of Art Gallery*, established in 1969 by Nigel Jackson, a former artist turned administrator, and his wife, provided exhibition space for contemporary artists. A not-for-profit organization, the gallery was dedicated to promoting these artists and providing them with the opportunity to attract collectors interested in their work. The gallery exhibitions included the works of such artists as James Denmark, Dinga McCannon, Frank Wimberly, Ann Tanksley, Don Robertson, Lloyd Toomes, Lois Mailou Jones, Jo Butler, Robert Threadgill, and Faith Ringgold. Largely because of the politically volatile period, but also because of the gallery's aggressive action policy, the *Acts of Art Gallery,* in 1971 became the center for the controversial 'Whitney Rebuttal Show.'

*The Studio Museum In Harlem* began in 1969 under the direction of Edward Spriggs. Set up as a place for artists who needed working space, it eventually branched out into a cultural center where the artists could display their work, meet other artists and art supporters, and hold concerts, panel discussions, and other art related activities. *The Studio Museum In Harlem* had become, by 1972, the cultural center of New York for the Afro-American community. Important retrospectives were presented including the works of Palmer Hayden, Hale Woodruff, Beauford Delaney, Bob Thompson and James Van Der Zee. Also at the Studio Museum the Lewis H. Michaux book Fair took place for three years (1976-1979) under the direction of Special Program Coordinator David Jackson. Lewis Michaux was a legend in the world of book selling, because he established a bookstore on 125th Street and Lenox Avenue which became a landmark for people from around the world who were interested in literature of or about Afro-Americans, Africans, Caribbeans, and South Americans. The store opened in 1930 and continued to exist for the next 44 years. It was called *The National Memorial African Book Store*.

While under the directorship of Edward Spriggs, the museum began the special holiday celebration KWANSA, a time during which the museum opened its doors to the entire neighborhood to share in dancing, singing, and eating with the artists. Dancer Chuck Davis would come to lead off the dancing, ending with the whole room filled with guests in the center of the floor dancing.

By 1980, the museum had grown out of its two-floor loft space and moved into an old office building on 125th Street and 7th Avenue. The new space provided the museum with additional exhibition galleries, larger office areas, and space for its growing collection and the artist-in-residence program. In 1977, during this period of growth for the museum, a new director Mary Campell Schmidt, took over the operations of the institution. In 1988, she was appointed commissioner of the Department of Cultural Affairs in New York.

*Just Above Midtown Gallery* was the first organization to move into the gallery district in New York City. Established in 1976, it set up its operation base in a modest space on 57th Street in midtown Manhattan. Under the directorship of Linda Bryant, the organization presented many of the leading contemporary artists of the 1970s including David Hammons, Senga Nengudi, Randy Williams and Howardina Pindell. Placing the African-American artists in direct competition with the mainstream American artists was the objective of Bryant, her board, and her artists. No longer could art critics refuse to review these works because they could not get to Harlem or Queens, or Brooklyn . But the cost of running a gallery took its tole and in order to continue operations Bryant was forced to turn the gallery into a not-for-profit organization, adding educational programs for young artists, music concerts, performance programs, slide reviews and lectures.

By the end of 1979, *Just Above Midtown* moved from 57th Street to a larger space on Franklin Street in the Tribeca section of New York, changed its name to the *Just Above Midtown/Downtown Alternative Art Center*, and opened its doors to the vanguard, new-wave artists.

*The Schomburg Center for Research in Black Culture* of The New York Public Library is one of the most widely used research facilities in the world devoted to the preservation of materials on black life. The Center's collections first won international acclaim in 1926 when the personal collection of the distinguished black scholar and bibliophile, Arthur A. Schomburg, was added to the Division of Negro Literature, History and Prints of the 135th Street Branch of The New York Public Library. Schomburg's collection included over 5,000 volumes, 3,000 manuscripts, 2,000 etchings and paintings and several thousand pamphlets. He served as the curator in the Negro Division from 1932 until his death in 1938. Renamed in his honor in 1940, the collection grew steadily through the years. In 1972 it was designated as one of the Research Libraries of The New York Public Library and became *The Schomburg Center for Research in Black Culture*. Today, the Schomburg Center is the guardian of collections including over 5 million items, and provides services and programs for constituents from the United States and abroad.

The *Cinque Gallery,* another New York gallery, was the concept of three distinguished artists, Romare Bearden, Norman Lewis, and Ernest Crichlow. The gallery which opened in 1969 was named after the famous African prince Cinque, who in 1839 led a successful revolt aboard the slave ship Amistad, won his freedom, and returned to Africa. It was the wish of Bearden, Crichlow, and Lewis to establish an exhibition space specifically for young Afro-American artists who needed to learn the process of being a professional artist. However, by the end of the 1970s it was decided that the gallery doors be opened to all new and emerging artists regardless of age.

The *Weusi Ya Nambe Yasana Gallery*, also in New York, was one of the few cooperative community galleries to come out of the late 1960s. Housed in a brownstone in Harlem, the gallery was established to present the art work of its members. Headed by Ademola Olagebefola, the other members included Otto Neals, Kay Brown, and Jean Taylor. Genesis II was one of the alternative profit-making galleries that emerged out of the 1960s. Like many of its kind, the gallery functioned out of the dealer's apartment to cover the cost of overhead expenses. The dealer would invite his or her clients to come view the works in a living environment , so that they might better appreciate the art work. Also, at these gatherings, clients had the opportunity to meet other collectors as well as meet the artist and talk in detail about the work. The concept proved valuable for many African-American artists who needed to develop supporting collectors and to establish a real market for their work.

*The New Muse* in Brooklyn began in the late 1960s, offering the African-American Brooklyn community the same kinds of art programs presented at the *Studio Museum*. In addition to the art programs, *The New Muse* also offered lessons in jazz with bassist Reggie Workman, who headed the program.

*The Store Front Museum* in Queens was established to satisfy the artistic needs of its community. Offering art classes in painting and drawing, its focus leaned more toward the performing arts, dancing and drama.

*The Benin Gallery* opened its doors in 1976. Director Edward Sherman operated the gallery as a non-profit tax exempt corporation so that the public in Harlem would have a gallery to call its own. Located at 2366 Adam Clayton Powell Jr., Boulevard, in the St. Nicholas Historic District, the gallery focused on photography.

In Washington, D.C., the *Museum of African Art*, formerly known as the *Frederick Douglass Institute*, was established in 1964 and until 1984 existed in a Victorian row house on Capitol Hill, nestled in the shadow of the Supreme Court. The house had belonged to Frederick Douglass, a former slave who became an advisor to President Lincoln. In 1984, the museum was moved to the *Smithsonian Institute* and the house was singularly devoted to early Afro-American art and memorabilia and continues to he known as the *Frederick Douglas Institute*. The museum, which was established to promote and familiarize Americans with the artistic heritage of Africa, today includes a large and extensive collection devoted exclusively to African art and culture. The collection, one of the largest and most diverse of its kind in the United States, consists of some 65,000 works—traditional carvings, musical instruments, and textiles with particular emphasis on works from Nigeria, Ghana, Liberia, the Ivory Coast, and Zaire. In the transition, the Smithsonian has also acquired the Eliot Elisofon Photographic Archives, which contains some 150,000 slides and motion pictures available to the public.

*The Hatch-Billops Studio* began in New York in 1968 as an organization designed to present multi-ethnic plays, performances and exhibitions. By 1973, the studio began collecting third world memorabilia. Based on the understanding that no one will protect your history or present your history the way you do, the collection became incorporated in 1975. Camille Billops and her husband Jim Hatch began taping the history of some black theatre artists. Today the collection houses more than 604 taped interviews, and panel and media events of, about, or by artists. There are well over 10,000 slides and 3,000 books, clipping, files, letters, memorabilia, programs, photographs, drawings, scrapbooks, and videotapes. This collection is one of the most complete reference centers focusing on Afro-American art—visual, literary, and theatrical. It is a collection available to artists, scholars, and students.

Galleries and Museums for Afro-American artists were developing throughout the country. In Los Angeles, Dr. Samella Lewis, a painter, art historian, and professor at Claremont College, founded the *Contemporary Craft Center.* In 196t, Alonzo and Dale Davis established and directed the *Brockman Galleries Productions*, a nonprofit gallery showing contemporary African-American art and the work of other minority artists.

In Chicago, the *Du Sable Museum* was established in 1961 under the directorship of Margaret Burroughs to provide the South Side community with an art center. The museum grew out of an art center that was established under the Work-Progress Administration during the depression period. Some of the artists presented there include Charles White, Elizabeth Catlett, Gordon Parks, Rex Gorleigh, William McBride Jr., and Eldzier Cortor.

On the East Coast, in Boston, the museum of the *National Center of Afro-American Artists*, begun in 1969 under the curatorship of Edmond Gaither, is a multi-media art center featuring dance, theater, visual arts, film, and educational programs.

*The Smith-Mason Gallery Museum* located in Washington, D.C. is a four-story Victorian house established in 1968 to present its permanent collection, which features paintings, sculptures and graphics of Afro-American and Caribbean artists. The works remain on permanent display.

## BLACK EXHIBITIONS AND MAINSTREAM ART INSTITUTIONS

During the late 1960s and early 1970s, leading mainstream museums responded to the demands being made by Afro-American artists to open their doors and hire Afro-American scholars as curators and administrators. At the time of the intensive demonstrations, Kynastan McShine, a young West Indian who had already established his reputation as a strong curator at the Jewish Museum, moved on to become the Assistant Curator of Painting and Sculpture at The Museum of Modern Art.

Howardena Pindell had just begun her career at the Museum of Modern Art as the Assistant Curator of Drawings and Prints, would later move on to become the Associate Curator of Drawings and Prints, and would in 1980 resign from that

*The Jacob Lawrence Exhibition at the Whitney Museum in 1974 opened with a gala, drawing Raymond Saunders, Dorothy White, Haywood Rivers, Ed Clark, Camille Billops, Joe Overstreet, Benny Andrews, Louise Parks, Bob Blackburn, Romare Bearden, Norman Lewis, Herbert Gentry, and Vincent Smith, among others*

position to pursue her career as an artist. However, this progress was not satisfactory to the artists who demonstrated and wrote letters demanding that jobs be made available to black art historians. In 1968, Gylbert Coker became the first Afro-American to be hired at the Guggenheim Museum in an administrative trainee position. She later went on to work at the Museum of Modern Art as a cataloguer in the museum's registration department. In 1976 she received the Rockefeller Fellowship in Museum Education, and spent one year at the Metropolitan Museum of Art. The following year she became the curator of *The Studio Museum In Harlem* where she set up their registration department and organized such important exhibitions as The Bob Thompson Exhibition and the Hale Woodruff Retrospective, before leaving to pursue a career as a freelance critic and curator. In 1980 and again in 1982, Coker co-directed *Art Across the Park* an outdoor exhibition created by the artist Davis Hammons. The project was so popular that several groups in New York tried to copy the concept. It was the first large scale exhibit that openly encouraged all artists to take part—it was in this exhibition that the term *multi-ethnic* was coined.

The second Afro-American to work at the Guggenheim in an administrative position was Cheryl McClenny. She went on to direct the Museum Collaborative Programs for the City of New York and in 1978 she became an administrator with the National Endowment for the Arts in Washington, D.C. In 1980, she was appointed director of the Philadelphia Museum of Art.

From the Whitney Museum's Museum Studies Program came Faith Weaver and Horace Brockington. Faith Weaver went on to teach American Art History at the School of Visual Arts. Brockington gained recognition for his exhibition *Another Generation* for The Studio Museum In Harlem in 1978, which set the stage for Afro-American Abstraction, presented two years later at P.S. 1 an alternative art center. Also, the Brooklyn Museum opened its Community Gallery and hired Henri Ghent, who began to produce some very important exhibitions, including several Afro-American exhibitions, which were sent to Europe.

The largest community program existed in the Metropolitan Museum of Art in New York City. There, people like Randy Williams, Florence Hardney, Dolores Wright, Cathy Chance, and Lowery Sims actively presented the art works of Afro-American and other minority artists to the Metropolitan Museum's audience. By 1977, Lowery Sims was made the museum's first Afro-American assistant curator within the museum's Twentieth-Century Department, under the curatorial guidance of Henry Geldzahler. Today, she is the Associate curator under William Lieberman.

Dr. Regina Perry was invited by the Metropolitan Museum of Art in 1976 to produce an exhibition called *Selections Of Nineteenth-Century Afro-American Art*. It was an exhibition which highlighted, for the first time, many early Afro-American portrait painters and landscape artists, and it even made attempts to document some important slave artifacts and put them into an aesthetic rather than sociological perspective. Also in 1976, Lowery Sims put together an exhibition of selected works by twentieth-century Afro-American artists from the museum's collection for the Bedford-Stuyvesant Restoration Corporation. Three years later, in 1979 Sims mounted another exhibition of Afro-American paintings from the twentieth-century collection. This time the exhibition was inside the Metropolitan Museum.

The Newark Museum of Art in New Jersey held its first black exhibition back in 1944. The exhibition included the works of Richmond Barthe, Romare Bearden, and William Edmonson. Thirty years later, in 1974, the museum presented its second Afro-American art exhibit Black Artists: Two Gernerations. The curator was Paul Waters.

## BLACK ARTIST ORGANIZATIONS AND MOVEMENTS

Black artist organizations have been portals through which many black artists entered the art world, whether their personal forums were to be in storefronts or established galleries.

In 1953, a group of artists and art educators primarily from Florida and Georgia met in Florida A&M College. This meeting, whose guest speaker was Hale Woodruff, sparked the beginning of the *National Conference Of Artists*. This auspicious beginning was sponsored by Florida A&M's Art Department, which was at that time headed by Dr. Samella Lewis. The purpose of the gathering was to establish a national organization which would address itself to the needs of black artists. In 1954, a second meeting was held at Lincoln University in Jefferson City, Missouri. Those present were Samella Lewis, James Parks, James Porter, Hayward Oubre, Margaret Burroughs, Jimmy Mosley, Venola Seals Jennings, F.L. Spellman, Phillip Hampton, Marion Perkins, Juanita Moulon, Eugene Jesse Brown, and Bernard Gross. By 1959, at a meeting at Atlanta University, the N.C.A. had been established as a viable organization of art educators, historians, and arts interested in stimulating and promoting black artists in the United States.

*Spiral*, a New York-based organization, was active between 1963 and 1966. Its gallery-meeting place was housed on Christopher Street on the lower west side of Manhattan. The first exhibition was held in 1965. A membership of 15 included Romare Bearden, Reginald Gammon, Emma Ammos, Charles Alston, Hale Woodruff, Richard Mayhew, Al Hollingsworth, Calvin Douglass, Merton Simpson, Earl Miller, Felrath Hines, Norman Lewis, Perry Ferguson, William Majors, and James Yeargans. In 1966, it officially closed its doors when it was dispossessed.

*Art West Associated*, founded in Los Angeles in the early 1960s, is a conference of southern California artists. Its founder and director, Ruth Waddy, has co-edited two volumes on black art published by Contemporary Crafts of Los

Angeles.

*Art West Associated North*, a sister organization to A.W.A., was organized by Evangeline Montgomery in Berkeley, California. Ms. Montgomery has been the black art consultant to the *Oakland Museum of Art* and *Rainbow Sign* of Berkeley.

In 1968, a group of black artists joined efforts to form an organization called *AFRI-COBRA*, an acronym for African Commune of Bad Relevant Artists. As stated in its tenets, art is to serve the people. In an attempt to fulfill this aim, art must have specific colors, style, form, and intent. The original members were Jeff Donaldson, a painter and now chairman of the art department at Howard University, Wadsworth Jarrell, and Gerald Williams. Carolyn Mims Lawrence, Barbara Jones Hogu, Frank Smith, Howard Mallory, Napoleon Henderson, and Nelson Stevens joined later.

In New York in 1968, the Black *Emergency Cultural Coalition* gained prominence when it formed to protest the Whitney Museum's exclusionary show "American Artist of the 1930s". BECC charged that the Whitney exhibition excluded notable black artists who had painted during the thirties. Led by Henri Ghent, Vivian Browne, and Faith Ringgold, a counter exhibition involving some fifty-two artists from all over the country was presented. Entitled "Invisible Artists: 1930" the exhibition was mounted at the Studio Museum of Harlem.

In 1969, BECC picketed the Metropolitan Museum, which was staging the "Harlem On My Mind" exhibition, a large multimedia show, which many believe misrepresented the Harlem community.

Following the Metropolitan Museum protest, the critical attention of the BECC turned again to the Whitney. Deciding that it had not responded to its original protest, the Coalition formed a picket line on the sidewalk surrounding the museum and demanded full participation for black artists in the museum's exhibitions. As a result, several blacks were included in subsequent annuals, and in 1971 the first black art exhibition at the Whitney, "Contemporary Black Art in America," was held. However, a rebuttal show was held again, this time at *Acts of Art Gallery*, for the Whitney had failed to include blacks on the curatorial level, a necessary step in the selection of works slated for exhibition.

During the early 1970s, the BECC developed art programs in correctional institutions throughout New York State, an innovation soon adopted elsewhere in the nation.

In 1971, a New York-based organization, the *Where We At Together Black Women,* was developed as an art collective. Co-founded by Dinga McCannon, Kay Brown, and Faith Ringgold, the organization was created in an attempt to provide black women artists an opportunity to exhibit and sell their work. During this period there was a white women's liberation movement developing, but most black women artists found themselves removed from that organizations philosophies, believing that their problems as black women and as artists were specific. In the end the organization produced their own catalogues, curated their own exhibits, and slowly developed a history for themselves. At this time the membership included: Dinga McCannon, Kay Brown, Faith Ringgold, Iris Crump, Carole Blank, Gerri Crooks, Mai Mai Leabua, Onnie Millar, Ann Tanksley, Carol Byard, Viola Burley, Doris Kane, Charlotte Richardson, Pat Davis, and Gylbert Coker.

*The National Conference of Artists held its second annual meeting in 1954, convening (from left to right) Jimmy Mosley, Samella Lewis, F. Spellman, Phillip Hampton, Venola Jennings, Juanita Moulon, James Porter, Eugene Brown and Hayward Oubre.*

## Workshops

In 1949, *The Printmaking Workshop* of New York, under the direction of its founder, Bob Blackburn, opened its doors to provide working space for printmakers. In 1971, it was incorporated as a non-profit printmaking studio for work in lithography, etching, relief and photo-processes. *The Workshop,* besides providing space for artists, has also printed the work of such artists as Norman Lewis, Eldzier Cortor, Vivian Browne, Camille Billops, Benny Andrews, Romare Bearden, Charles Alston, Ernest Crichlow, and many, many, more. Through an environment which fosters creativity and experimentation, the *Workshop* is committed to serving artists of differing cultural and ethnic backgrounds, and to provide them with oportunities to pursue their own work supported by an established institution. It achieves this goal through the programs it offers and by maintaining low-

*Robert Blackburn, a printmaker of exceptional talent, spends as much time as possible working with novices as well as artists of renown such as Romare Bearden, Elizabeth Catlett, Camille Billops and Betye Saar. Here Blackburn inspects a student's proof at the printmaking workshop.*

cost facilities. *The Workshop*, a magnet for third-world and minority artists that reflects Mr. Blackburn's warmth and encouraging personality, remains a haven for artists "to turn out prints for the love of it" and to do anything from experimental hodgepodge to polished pieces.

The original Children's Art Carnival was initiated in the garden of the *Museum of Modern Art* under a tent during the summer of 1942. It was a means of introducing parents to the fact that the Museum of Modern Art had an art school for children which operated during the school year. During President John F. Kennedy's term of office, his wife, Jacqueline, requested that a replica of the Children's Art Carnival be sent to the World's Fair in Brussels, Belgium to serve as an example of quality art education provided for better schools. The concept was so well received the Museum of Modern Art decided that a site should be found for this new Carnival project. In 1969 a space was provided by the Harlem School of the Arts. It was a large open garage on St. Nicholas Avenue.

The Carnival's activities focus on the needs of individual youngsters. Providing students with vehicles for expressing themselves, the Carnival staff has developed tools to help the teachers better understand their students. The Carnival is designed to provide service for preschool-age children up to high school youngsters, as well as the handicapped. The Carnival offers free classes, which include painting, puppetry, clay and 3-D construction, printmaking, and photography.

Kamoinge Workshop was organized by photographer Roy DeCarava in 1963 out of a need to communicate and share the photographic dialogue flowing throughout the black community, a dialogue not being shared at that time within "the" photography circle. It ended in 1966. However, through this organization's work, a book, The Black Photographer's Annual, was produced to showcase the work of many black photographers. Its first edition was published in 1973; the second in 1974; the third in 1978; and its fourth and final edition was produced in 1980. Publication ended when funds no longer existed.

## Spray Can Graffiti

In 1972, in New York City, black and Hispanic teenagers combined the paint spray can and street pride into a colorful art form, "wall graffiti," which at the time of this writing is embroiled in heated artistic and political controversy.

The content of wall graffiti has often been no more than the name of a street gang or the nickname of the individual painter and the name or number of the street on which he lives, or to which he gives his loyalty. On the other hand, the paintings can be as extravagant as a scene with cartoon characters and lavishly flamboyant lettering. Towards the end of the 1970s and well into the 1980s this graffiti style became so popular its value increased. Several of the young street artists were welcomed into the mainstream art world making a few famous for a short period and promoting one young artist, Jean-Michel Basquiat, into a super-star. Basquiat became an instant success, and was taken on by the Mary Boon Gallery in New York. His work was promoted all over the world. —His graffiti guerrillas street name was SAMO ( as in Same Old Shit)—As he made the transition from street murals to paintings, drawings, and sculpture, his works began to challenge the European idea of the "primitive". His disciples were Dubuffet and Twombly. He wanted to give his heroes the black face of his history. He lived for a short time, dying at the age of twenty-seven

There were also mainstream artists who took on the graffiti style and made it their own such as artists like Keith Herring and galleries like the Paula Cooper Gallery that opened their doors to this new and defiant art. Choreographer Twyla Tharp choreographed a ballet for the Joffrey Company, "Deuce Coupe," showing dancers moving against a background provided by boys painting with spray cans on ceiling-hung sheets of paper.

## OUTSTANDING BLACK ARTISTS

### Black Artists of the Eighteenth, Nineteenth, and Early Twentieth Centuries

#### JOHN JAMES AUDUBON (Also known as JEAN RABINE, JEAN-JACQUES FORGERE)
**Painter**
**1785-1851**

**Some Notable Works:** *Portrait of Henri De Gallon; Portrait of John Cleives Simms*

John James Audubon was the son of a French merchant sea captain and planter and his Afro-Caribbean mistress. Born on April 26, 1785, in Les Cayes (now Aux Cayes) in the French colony of Saint-Dominique (now Haiti), Audubon was taken to his father's home in France, Coueron, near Nantes, along with his half-sister following the death of his mother. He was six years old. After a suitably discreet period of time, both he and his sister were formally adopted by the captain's legal wife, Anne Moynet.

As a youngster in France, Audubon began to collect his bird specimens and draw, receiving a basic education during the French Revolution. In the summer of 1803, to escape conscription into Napoleon's army and to acquire business training, Audubon was sent to Mill Grove, his father's farm near Philadelphia. Living the life of a young dandy, he met Lucy Bakewell, the daughter of a nearby plantation owner. They married five years later in 1808 and moved to Kentucky to establish a general store at the falls of the Ohio River. For a brief period Audubon painted portraits of frontier gentry, gave art lessons, and worked as a taxidermist. Later he began to travel down the Mississippi River in search of specimens to draw. He and his family lived in New Orleans for a time, and then Audubon took his bird drawings and sailed for England, where his work was appreciated; it was then that he published *The Birds of America*.

#### EDWARD MITCHELL BANNISTER
**Painter**
**1828-1901**

**Some Notable Works:** *After the Storm; Sabin Point; Driving Home the Cows; Pleasant Pastures; Narragansett Bay; Swale Land; Sad Memories*

Born in Nova Scotia, Bannister was the son of a West Indian father and Afro-American mother. Both parents died when he was very young. Bannister moved to Boston in the early 1850s, where he learned to make solar plates and worked as a photographer.

Influenced by the Barbizon style popular at this time, Bannister's paintings convey his own love of the quiet beauty of nature and his pleasure in picturesque scenes with cottages, cattle, dawns, sunsets, and small bodies of water.

In 1871, Bannister moved from Boston to Providence,

*Detail of Bannister's* Driving the Cows Home *1818*

Rhode Island, where he lived until his death. He was the only nineteenth-century Afro-American artist who did not travel to Europe to study art, believing that he was an American and that he wished to paint as an American. Bannister became one of the most outstanding artists in Providence in the 1870s and 1880s, and in 1880 was to become one of seven founders of the Providence Art Club, which later became known as the Rhode Island School of Design.

### ROBERT DUNCANSON
### Painter
### 1817-1872

**Some Notable Works:** *Portraits: William and Freeman Cary; Nicholas Longworth; The Berthelets of Detroit; Bishop Payne; Murals at Taft Museum; Romantic Landscape*

Robert Duncanson was the son of an Afro-American mother and a Scottish-Canadian father. Born in upstate New York, he was to spend much of his childhood in Canada. At some point in his youth, he and his mother moved to Mt. Healthy, Ohio, where in 1840 the Western Freedman's Aid Society, an anti-slavery group, raised funds to send him to Glasgow, Scotland, where he could study art. Returning to Cincinnati three years later, Duncanson turned to the local newspaper where he advertised as the proprietor of a daguerreotype studio. Even though he seemed to have been gaining a reputation as a painter, he continued to work at his daguerreotype until 1855, when he began to devote all of his time to his painting. Like many landscape artists of this time, Duncanson traveled around the United States drawing his compositions from the images of nature before him. In 1853, he made his second trip to Europe—this time to visit Italy, France, and England.

It is interesting to note that Duncanson was active during and after the Civil War, yet with the exception of his painting of Uncle Tom and Eva, Duncanson made no attempts to present the turmoil that was taking place within America or the social pressures that he experienced. In September 1872, Duncanson, while at the height of his success, suffered a severe mental breakdown and ended his life on December 21 in the Michigan State Retreat in Detroit.

*Robert S. Duncanson, America's first black studio artist, painted the Hudson River scene mural in 1848.*

### MINNIE EVANS
### Painter
### 1892

**Some Notable Work:** *Design Made at Airlie Garden*

Minnie Eva Jones was born on December 1, 1892 in a log cabin in Long Creek, Pender County, North Carolina. In 1893, she moved with her mother, grandmother, and great-grandmother to Wilmington, North Carolina, where she spent her childhood. In 1908 she married Julis Evans, the body servant of Mr. Pembroke Jones.

Minnie Evans began to draw in 1935, working with crayon, pencil, and ink, on the backs of discarded stationery. In 1961, Evans was given her first exhibition at the Little Gallery in Wilmington, which was followed by her first New York exhibition "The Lost World of Minnie Evans" in 1966 at the Church of the Epiphany and at St. Clement's Episcopal Church. Also in 1966, Evans began to make collages, covering her earlier drawings with oil paint and ink and pencil. Her work was exhibited in 1969 at the Davison Art Center, Wesleyan University, in Middletown, Connecticut. Her first European exhibition was held in 1970 in the Portal Gallery in London, and in 1975 Evans was given a one-person exhibition at the Whitney Museum of American Art.

### META VAUX WARRICK FULLER
### Sculptor
### 1877-1968

**Some Notable Works:** *The Awakening of Ethiopia; Richard B. Harrison; The Talking Skull; John*

Meta Vaux Warrick Fuller was born in 1877 in Philadelphia and educated at the school of Industrial Art and the Pennsylvania Academy. Her interest in sculpture led her to study with Charles Grafly and then with Rodin at the Academie Colarossi in Paris.

In 1903 and again in 1904, her group, entitled *The Wretched* (considered by most experts to be her masterpiece)was exhibited at the Paris Salon. In 1910, most of her works were destroyed by fire, but her subsequent efforts were exhibited by the Harmon Foundation and the Boston Art Club, among others.

Today her work can be found in the Cleveland Museum. She died in 1968 at the age of 90.

### WILLIAM HARPER
**Painter**
**1873-1910**

**Some Notable Works:** *Autumn Landscape; Afternoon at Montigny; Landscape; An Autumn Day in France*

William Harper was born in 1873 in Canada, and died 37 years later in Mexico City, at a time when many critics already considered his work superior to Henry Ossawa Tanner's.

Harper was a protege of Tanner, and along with him, came to be regarded as one of the truly significant American black painters of the nineteenth century.

### ISAAC HATHAWAY
**Sculptor, Ceramicist**
**1871-?**

**Some Notable Works:** *Busts of Frederick Douglass, Booker T. Washington and Paul Dunbar; Memorial Coins of Booker T. Washington and George Washington Carver*

Isaac Hathaway's major works are portrait busts, the most famous of which are those of Frederick Douglass, Paul Laurence Dunbar, and Booker T. Washington. He was also commissioned by the U.S. Mint to design the memorial coins issued in honor of Booker T. Washington and George Washington Carver.

Born in Lexington, Kentucky in 1871, Hathaway studied in the Art Department of the New England Conservatory of Music and the Ceramics Department of Pittsburgh Normal College. One of America's outstanding ceramicists, he was for many years head of the Ceramics Department at Alabama State Teachers College in Montgomery.

### JULIEN HUDSON
**Painter**
**Active 1831-1844**

**Some Notable Works:** *Self—Portrait; Colonel Jean Michel Fortier Jr.*

Julien Hudson was a native of New Orleans. He studied in Paris and upon his return to New Orleans taught art and portrait painting. On December 3, 1831 Hudson published a notice in the New Orleans *Courier* announcing his return from Paris and advertising his services as a portrait painter to the ladies and gentlemen of New Orleans. Although there are only two known works by Hudson, both are dated and signed.

### MAY HOWARD JACKSON
**Sculptor**
**1877-1931**

**Some Notable Works:** *Busts of Paul Laurence Dunbar; Dean Kelly Miller of Howard University, Francis J. Grimke; Head of a Negro Child*

Born in 1877 in Philadelphia (the same year and place as fellow sculptor Meta Vaux Warrick Fuller), Mrs. Jackson was educated at J. Liberty Tadd's Art School in her native city, and at the Pennsylvania Academy. She had her own art studio in Washington, D.C. from 1902 until her death in 1931.

Executing busts of famous people remained her forte, although after 1914 she became preoccupied with the production of black thematic sculpture.

Mrs. Jackson's work has been exhibited at the National Academy of Design, the New York Emancipation Exposition, and the National Academy of Art in New York City.

In addition to lecturing and exhibiting, Mrs. Jackson taught sculpture at Howard University for several years.

### JOSHUA JOHNSTON
**Painter**
**c. 1765-1830**

**Some Notable Works:** *Portrait of a Cleric; In the Garden; Benjamin Franklin and Son*

The best known black portrait artist of the eighteenth and early nineteenth centuries was Joshua Johnston, from Baltimore. Over the years, researchers have uncovered some two dozen of his paintings. It is believed that Johnston, who was active in Baltimore, was probably manumitted because he is listed in the Baltimore Directories between 1769 and 1824 as a "free house-holder of colour, portrait painter," with a studio in various central locations.

It is believed that Johnston may have been a former slave of Charles Wilson Peale, the artist who is also known for having started a drawing school in Maryland in 1795, a school which was to encourage the development of the Pennsylvania Academy in Philadelphia, or he may have seen examples of Peale's work and begun to copy his style. It is

*A work by the best-known black portrait painter of the nineteenth century, Joshua Johnston.*

also possible that Johnston had seen the work of Peale's son Rembrandt Peale and studied his style as well.

One could call Johnston a primitive painter, probably for the most part self-taught. His work had a quaint simplicity, honesty, and charm. He depicted subjects with enormous warmth and sensitivity. The gentle qualities of Johnston demonstrate themselves most readily in *Portrait of a Cleric*, his only known black subject.

## EDMONIA LEWIS
### Sculptor
### 1845-1890

**Some Notable Works:** *Hiawatha; The Marriage; Hagar in the Wilderness; Madonna and Child; Forever Free; The Death of Cleopatra*

Edmonia Lewis was America's first black woman artist and also the first of her race and sex to be recognized as a sculptor.

Born in 1845 in upstate New York, she was the daughter of a Chippewa Indian mother and a free black father. From 1859 to 1863, under the patronage of a number of abolitionists, she was educated at Oberlin College, the first American college to admit women on a nonsegregated basis.

After completing her schooling, Miss Lewis moved to Boston where she studied with Edmund Brackett and did a bust of Colonel Robert Gould Shaw, the commander of the first black regiment raised in the state of Massachusetts during the Civil War.

In 1865 she moved to Rome, where she soon became prominent. Returning to the United States, she fulfilled many commissions, including a bust of Henry Wadsworth Longfellow which was executed for the Harvard College Library.

Her works are fine examples of the neoclassical sculpture that was fashionable in her lifetime.

Miss Lewis is believed to have died in Rome in 1890.

*Edmonia Lewis created* Hagar in the Wilderness.

## SCIPIO MOORHEAD
### Artist
### c. 1773-?

**Some Notable Work:** *Phillis Wheatley, engraving from* Poems on Various Subjects, Religious and Moral.

Recognition is given Scipio Moorhead as a symbolic gesture to all the unknown blacks who contributed to the American art scene. There are today no known works by Moorhead in existence and of course no way of evaluating his place among artists. Memory of him is preserved primarily by the slave poet Phillis Wheatley, who dedicated a poem "To S.M., a Young African Painter, on Seeing His Works." In a penciled note of the 1773 edition of Miss Wheatley's *Poems on Various Subjects, Religious and Moral*, she identifies S.M. as "Scipio Moorhead, Negro servant to the Rev. John Moorhead of Boston whose genius inclined him that way."

The talent of Scipio Moorhead was initially recognized and cultivated by Sarah Moorhead, wife of the Reverend, a teacher of art and an expert in drawing techniques, japanning, and painting on glass. It is possible Scipio painted the unsigned portrait of Phillis Wheatley that was used as a frontispiece for several of her works.

## PATRICK REASON
### Artist-Engraver
### 1817-1852

**Some Notable Works:** *De Witt Clinton (engraving); Granville Sharp (engraving); Am I Not a Man and a Brother? (engraving copy); Treadmill in Jamaica (illustrations)*

At the age of 13 in the year 1830, Patrick Reason designed the frontispiece for Charles Andrew's *History of the African Free Schools*. Through the patronage of abolitionist organizations, Reason was apprenticed to a white engraver and subsequently became an independent engraver and draftsman himself.

*Patrick Reasons demonstrated artistic talent as a young lad and learned his craft as an engraver through apprenticeship; two examples of his mature work are the engravings shown here, copperplates of* Henry Bibb *(above)* and *(below)* DeWitt Clinton.

For many years, Reason was actively involved in the abolitionist movement and much of his work was designed as propaganda for abolitionist organizations.

## WILLIAM SIMPSON
### Painter
### 1818-1872

**Some Notable Works:** *Portrait of Bishop J. W. Loguen, Portrait of Carolina E. S. Loguen*

William Simpson was a prolific painter in Boston around the 1860s, but only two works that he produced are available to us today, both at the Howard University Art Gallery in Washington, D.C. The paintings reveal enormous competence and general artistic sensibility.

Born in Buffalo, New York in 1818, Simpson became the apprentice of Matthew Wilson around 1854 and worked with him some six years before moving on to Boston, where he lived until his death.

## HENRY OSSAWA TANNER
### Painter
### 1859-1937

**Some Notable Works:** *Daniel in the Lions' Den; He Healed the Sick; Christ Walking on the Water; Flight into Egypt; Lions in the Desert; The Disciples on the Road to Bethany; The Sabot Makers; Banjo Lesson*

Alain Locke has called Henry Ossawa Tanner the leading talent of the "journeyman period" of black American art. Born in Pittsburgh in 1859, Tanner chose painting rather than the ministry as a career, overcoming the strong objections of his father, an African Methodist Episcopal bishop. After attending the Pennsylvania Academy of Fine Arts, he taught at Clark University in Atlanta, supplementing his salary by working as a photographer. Some of Tanner's most compelling work—such as *The Banjo Lesson* (1890)—was produced during this period, with Tanner himself emerging as the most promising black artist of his day.

In 1891, however, Tanner abandoned black subject matter and left the United States for Paris, where he concentrated on religious themes. In 1896, his *Daniel in the Lion's Den,* a mixture of realism and mystical symbolism, won honorable mention at the Paris Salon. The following year, the French government purchased his *Resurrection of Lazarus.*

In 1900, Tanner received the Medal of Honor at the Paris Exposition and the Lippincott Prize.

Tanner died in 1937.

## EUGENE WARBOURG
### Sculptor
### 1825-1867

**Some Notable Works:** *Bust of John Bason Brown; Le Pecheur; Le Premier Baiser*

Born a freeman in New Orleans, Eugene Warbourg, a stonemason by trade, shared a workshop with his brother Daniel, also a stonemason. Eugene demonstrated a strong talent for

*Henry Tanner was able to depict scenes of the human condition with a sensitivity that touched an empathetic bond with the viewer.*

sculpturing and received his formal training from a French artist of the vicinity called Gabriel. He was so successful that in 1852 jealousy and economic rivalry caused him to leave the United States for Europe where he stayed until his death. His best known American work is that of John Young Mason, a marble bust now at the Virginia Historical Society in Richmond.

### A. B. WILSON
### Painter
### (active 1840-1848)

**Some Notable Work:** *Portrait of Bishop Payne*

Not much is known about A. B. Wilson except that he was the son of a member of the Bethel A. M. E. Church in Philadelphia. His one known painting is the group portrait of Bishop Payne and his family, which is an unusual narrative with an angel floating above. A portrait of John Cornish, a lithographic copy, is more conventional, still the sensitivity of the religious and social philosophies of both images reveal the intensity of the individual.

*Henry Tanner, the most respected black artist of his time.*

## BLACK ARTISTS OF THE HARLEM RENAISSANCE

### RICHMOND BARTHE
**Sculptor**
**1901-1989**

**Some Notable Works:** *Singing Slave; Maurice Evans; Lot's Wife; Henry O. Tanner*

Born in 1901 in Bay St. Louis, Mississippi, Barthe was educated at the Art Institute in Chicago from 1924 to 1928. He studied under Charles Schroeder and Albin Polasek. Barthe's first love was painting, but it was through his experiments with sculpture that he began initially to gain critical attention in 1927. His first commissions were busts of Henry Ossawa Tanner and Toussaint L'Ouverture. The acclaim resulting from them led to a one-man show in Chicago and a Rosenwald Fellowship for study in New York City.

Barthe's work has been exhibited at several major American museums, including the Metropolitan Museum of Art in New York City. In 1946, he received the first commission given to a black for a bust slated in New York University's Hall of Fame. A year later he was one of a committee of 15 artists chosen to help modernize the sculpture in the Catholic churches of the United States.

Barthe held membership in the National Academy of Arts and Letters. He died March 6, 1989 at his home in Pasadena California at the age of 88.

### WILLIAM E. BRAXTON
**Painter**
**1878-1932**

**Some Notable Works:** *Figural Study; Seascape; Portraits of Ira Aldridge; Alexander Pushkin; D'Artagnan*

Born in Washington, D.C. where he received his early education, Braxton came to New York where he studied art at Adelphi College. He never attained financial success and so worked at many jobs. Early in his life he was an office boy, later he became a valet, and still later a Pullman porter. Braxton is considered the first American black to work as an expressionist painter. His major work was probably *Figural Study*, which is now in the Schomburg collection.

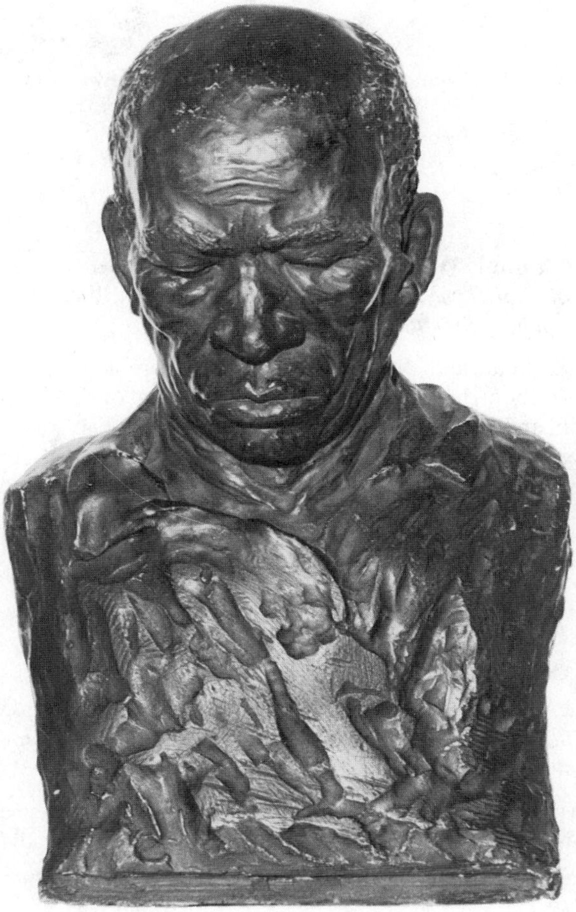

*The poignant, powerful touch of Richmond Barthe is exemplified in these two sculptures.*

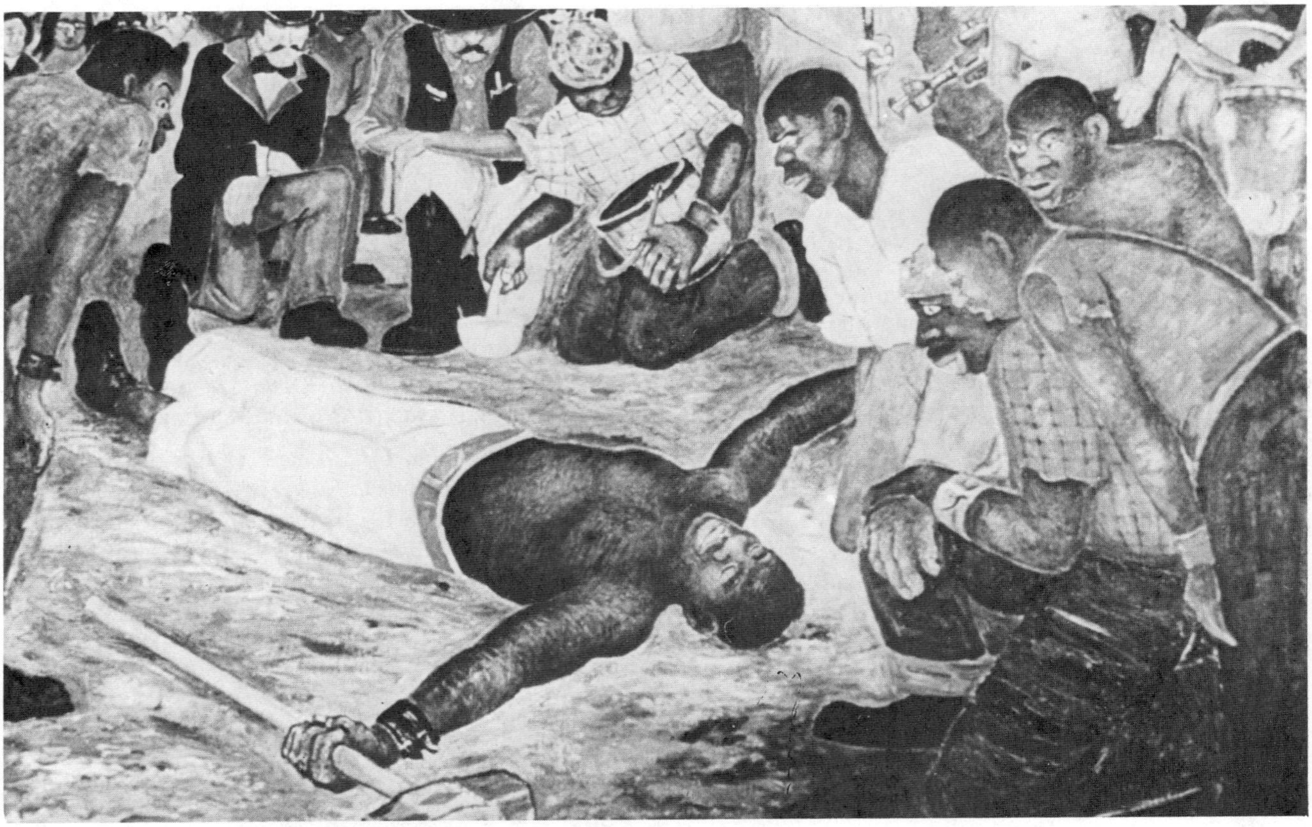

Died Wid His Hammer in His Hand *from Palmer Hayden's* John Henry Series.

### ALLAN ROHAN CRITE
**Painter, Illustrator**
**1910**

**Some Notable Works:** *Beneath the Cross of St. Augustine; City of God; Tyre Jumping; Book Illustrations; Were You There; These Spirituals*

Born in Plainfield, New Jersey in 1910 where he attended public school, he attended the Boston Museum of Fine Arts School and later the Massachusetts School of Art at Boston University. He completed works for the M. I. T. chapel, for Grace Church in Martha's Vineyard, and Holy Cross Church in Morrisville, Vermont among many others.

### AARON DOUGLAS
**Painter**
**1899-1988**

**Some Notable Works:** *Murals in the Countee Cullen Branch of the New York City Public Library; Illustrations in books by Cullen, James Weldon Johnson, Alain Locke, Langston Hughes; Alexander Dumas; Marion Anderson*

Born in Topeka, Kansas in 1899, Aaron Douglas has achieved considerable eminence as a muralist, illustrator, and academician.

As a young man, Douglas studied at the University of Nebraska, Columbia University Teachers College, and l'Academie Scandinave in Paris. He has had one-man exhibits at the universities of Kansas and Nebraska and has also exhibited in New York at the Gallery of Modern Art. In 1939, Douglas was named to the faculty of Fisk and later became head of its Department of Art Education.

### ALICE GAFFORD
**Painter**
**1886**

**Some Notable Work:** *Tea Party*

Mrs. Alice Gafford is among the pioneer black artists who have worked in the Los Angeles area for several generations.

Born in Kansas in 1886, Mrs. Gafford studied at the Otis Art Institute, at UCLA, and with private tutors. Mrs. Gafford is a member of several local art associations and has exhibited her work all over the United States. It is today represented in several private collections.

### PALMER C. HAYDEN
**Painter**
**1893-1973**

**Some Notable Works:** *Southern Scenes and City Streets Series; John Henry Series*

Palmer Hayden painted sophisticated landscapes and street scenes, gentle and humorous portraits, satirical caricatures, and canvases protesting the plight of blacks in the United

States.

Hayden was born in Widewater, Virginia and served in the Army during World War I, after which he studied at Boothbay Colony, Maine, under Asa G. Randall and in 1925 at Cooper Union in New York City, where he earned his bread and canvas by house cleaning and washing windows. At the first Harmon Exhibit of African American Art in 1926, he was awarded the Gold Medal. He then studied in Paris and Boston, returning to the United States in 1933, the year in which he received the Rockefeller award in art.

### MALVIN GRAY JOHNSON
### Painter
### 1896-1934

**Some Notable Works:** *Self Portrait; Turkeys at Roost; Portrait of a Soldier; Meditation*

Johnson was born in Greensboro, North Carolina in 1896. He is noted especially for the pictures made in Brightwood, Virginia in the late summer of 1934. Along with Hale Woodruff, he was one of the first black artists to incorporate modern concepts of cubism in his paintings.

### SARGENT JOHNSON
### Sculptor
### 1888-1967

**Some Notable Works:** *Sammy; Esther; Golden Gate Exposition Aquatic Park murals; Forever Free*

Sargent Johnson, who three times won the Harmon Foundation's medal as the outstanding artist of his race in the nation, worked in stylized idioms, heavily influenced by the art forms of Africa, in sculpture, mural bas-reliefs, metal sculpture, and ceramics.

Born in Boston, he studied at the Worcester Art School and moved west to the San Francisco Bay area in 1915, where his teachers were Beniamino Bufano and Ralph Stackpole. He exhibited at the San Francisco Artists Annual, 1925-1931; Harmon Foundation, 1928-1931, 1933; Art Institute of Chicago, 1930; Baltimore Museum, 1939; American Negro Exposition, Chicago, 1940. He was the recipient of numerous awards and prizes.

From the beginning of his career he spoke of his sculpture as an attempt to show the "natural beauty and dignity of the pure American Negro" and wished to present "that beauty not so much to the white man as to the Negro himself. Unless I can interest my race, I am sunk."

### WILLIAM H. JOHNSON
### Painter
### 1901-

**Some Notable Works:** *Booker T. Washington; Young Man in Vest; Descent from the Cross; On a John Brown Flight*

William H. Johnson has been a pioneer black modernist whose ever-developing work has gone from abstract expressionist landscape and flower studies, influenced by Van Gogh, to studies of black life in America, and finally to abstract figure studies in the manner of Rouault.

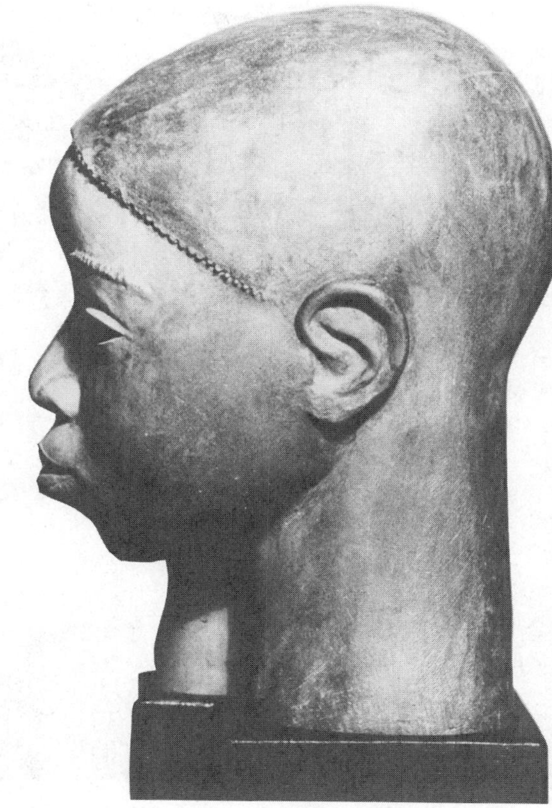

*Sargent Johnson stated that he attempted to show the "natural beauty and dignity of the pure American Negro."*

Born in Florence, South Carolina, he studied at the National Academy of Design; Cape Cod School of Art, under Charles Hawthorne; southern France, 1926-1929; Denmark and Norway, 1930-1938. Exhibits include Harmon Foundation (Gold Medal in 1929); Aarlins, Denmark, 1935; Baltimore Museum, 1939; American Negro Exposition, Chicago, 1940. He produced one-man shows in Copenhagen, in 1935, and at the Artists Gallery, New York, in 1938.

### LOIS MAILOU JONES
### Painter
### 1905

**Some Notable Works:** *Old Street in Montmartre; Jennie; Speracedes; Series; Paris, Haiti, Africa*

Lois Mailou Jones, a multifaceted artist who first gained recognition in the world of fashion with her textile designs and fashion illustrations, later turned to working in oils and watercolors, presenting a variety of figurative images that covered her interpretation of the Caribbean, Africa, Europe, and the United States.

Born in Boston, Lois Mailou Jones studied at the High School of Practical Arts and then went on to the Boston Museum School of Fine Arts and the Designers School. In 1930, Jones became a professor at Howard University, where she taught courses in design and watercolor painting.

*Archibald Motley's* Chicken Shack

### ARCHIBALD MOTLEY
### Painter
### 1891-1980

**Some Notable Works:** *The Jockey Club; The Plotters; Parisian Scene; Black Belt*

Archibald Motley touched on many topics and themes in his work but none was more gratifying to him than his candid depictions of black Americans.

Born in New Orleans, Motley's artistic talent was apparent by the time he attended high school. His father wanted him to become a doctor, but Archibald insisted on art and began formal education at the Art Institute of Chicago, earning his subsistence by working as a day laborer. During this time Motley came in contact with the driftwood, scavengers, and hustlers of society, who are now immortalized in his street scenes.

In 1928, Motley had a one-man show at the New Galleries in downtown New York and became the first artist, black or white, to make the front page of the *New York Times*.

### JAMES A. PORTER
### Art Historian, Painter
### 1905-1970

**Some Notable Works:** *On a Cuban Bus; Portrait of F. A. as Harlequin; Dorothy Porter; Nude*

James A. Porter is a painter of considerable scholarship, famous both for his original works and for his studies. Born in Baltimore, he studied at Howard University (B.S.); Art Students League, New York; Sorbonne; and New York University (M.A.). He has enjoyed numerous travel grants enabling him to study African and European art at firsthand.

Among his ten one-man shows are Port-au-Prince, Haiti, 1946; Dupont Gallery, Washington, D.C., 1949; and, Howard University, 1965. His works are in the collections of Howard University; Lincoln University, Missouri; Harmon Foundation; IBM; and others. He is the author of the classic *Modern Negro Art* (1943), and numerous articles.

He was a delegate to the UNESCO Conference on Africa, Boston, 1961 and to the International Congress of African Art and Culture, Salisbury, Southern Rhodesia, 1962. Since 1953 he has been chairman of the Department of Art, and director of the Gallery of Art at Howard University.

In 1965, at the twenty-fifth anniversary of the founding of the National Gallery of Art, he was named "one of America's Most Outstanding Men of the Arts."

### AUGUSTA SAVAGE
### Sculptor
### 1900-1962

**Some Notable Works:** *Lift Every Voice and Sing; The Chase; Black Women; Lenore, Gamin*

A leading sculptor who emerged during the Negro Renaissance, Augusta Savage was one of the artists represented in the first all-black exhibition in America, sponsored by the Harmon Foundation at International House in New York

City. In 1939 her symbolic group piece *Lift Every Voice and Sing*was shown at the New York World's Fair Community Arts Building.

Miss Savage was born in Florida, studied at Tallahassee State Normal School, at Cooper Union in New York City, and in France as the recipient of Carnegie and Rosenwald fellowships. She was the first black to win acceptance in the National Association of Women Painters and Sculptors.

## WILLIAM EDOUARD SCOTT
## Painter
## 1884

**Some Notable Works:** *Haitian Man; Blind Sister Mary; Mexican Scene*

William Edouard Scott was born in Indianapolis in 1884 and studied at the Art Institute in Chicago between 1904 and 1908. He later went on to Paris, where he studied at the Julien and Colossi academies and privately under Henry O. Tanner.

In 1907, at the age of 23, Scott won first prize for a mural at the Chicago Shakespeare Festival and went on to a series of successful exhibitions in the United States and a Harmon Gold Medal in 1927. In 1931, he visited Haiti on a Rosenwald Fellowship to paint "Negro types" of the island. It was there that whatever inhibitions Scott had, faded and he reached the peak of his originality and brilliance of expression. Upon his return to the United States he painted numerous murals in public buildings throughout the country.

## LAURA WHEELER WARING
## Artist, Educator
## 1887-1948

**Some Notable Works:** *Alonzo Aden; W. E. Burghardt DuBois; James Weldon Johnson; Mother and Daughter*

Born in 1887 in Hartford, Connecticut, this portrait painter and illustrator received her first training at the Pennsylvania Academy of Fine Arts, where she studied for six years. In 1914, she won the Cresson Memorial Scholarship, which enabled her to continue her studies at the Academie de la Grande Chaumiere in Paris.

Mrs. Waring returned to the United States as an art instructor at Cheyney State Teachers College in Pennsylvania, eventually becoming head of the art department there. Her work, particularly portraits, has been exhibited at several leading American art galleries. In 1927, she received the Harmon Award for achievement in fine art. Mrs. Waring with Betsy Graves Reyneau completed a set of 24 repaintings of a variety of their works titled *Portraits of Outstanding Americans of Negro Origin* for the Harmon Foundation in the 1940s.

Mrs. Waring was also the director in charge of the black art exhibits at the Philadelphia Exposition in 1926 and was a member of the national advisory board of Art Movements, Inc.

She died in 1948.

## HALE WOODRUFF
## Painter, Muralist
## 1900-1979

**Some Notable Works:** *Ancestral Remedies; The Little Boy; The Amistad Murals*

Hale Woodruff's paintings have been largely modernist landscapes and formal abstractions, but he has also done rural Georgia scenes evocative of the "red clay" country.

Born in 1900 in Cairo, Illinois, Woodruff is a graduate of the John Herron Art Institute in Indianapolis. Encouraged by a bronze award in the 1926 Harmon Foundation competition, Woodruff went to Paris to study at both the Academie Scandinave and the Academie Moderne, as well as with Henry Ossawa Tanner.

In 1931, he became art instructor at Atlanta University and five years later accepted a similar post at New York University. In 1939, he was commissioned by Talladega College to do *The Amistad Murals*, an episodic depiction of a slave revolt.

In 1948, Woodruff teamed up with Charles Alston to work on the Golden State Mutual Life Insurance Company Murals in California, which presented the contribution of Afro-Americans to the history of the development of California. Woodruff's last mural assignment came in 1950 when he developed the series of mural panels for Atlanta University entitled "The Art of the Negro."

Hale Woodruff died in 1979 after creating a body of works with styles that moved from the figurative, to the Impressionistic period of his Paris experience, to a brief exploration of the cubist visual concepts, to moving comfortably into the abstract style. With all of these stylistic developments, Hale Woodruff also became one of America's strongest mural painters.

*Sensitive portrayals of the human condition were found in W.E. Scott's paintings.*

## BLACK ARTISTS FROM THE DEPRESSION THROUGH WORLD WAR II

### CHARLES ALSTON
### Painter, Sculptor, Muralist
### 1907-1972

**Some Notable Works:** *Frederick Douglass* (1968); *Nobody Knows* (1966); *Blues Song* (1958); *Blues with Guitar and Bass* (1957); *Sons and Daughters* (1966); *School Girl* (1958)

It is the murals of painter Charles Alston that has established his reputation and insured his fame as a black American artist of importance.

Born in Charlotte, North Carolina in 1907, Alston studied at Columbia University in New York, receiving B.A. and M.A. degrees. He was later awarded several fellowships and grants to launch his painting career.

Alston's paintings and sculpture are in such collections as those of IBM and the Detroit Museum. His murals depicting the history of medicine adorn the facade of Harlem Hospital in New York. Alston is a member of the National Society of Mural Painters.

### WILLIAM ARTIS
### Sculptor
### 1914

**Some Notable Work:** *Head of a Girl* (1933)

William Artis, one of the first black Americans to achieve recognition for his work in ceramics, is now a professor of art at Mankato State College.

Born in Washington, North Carolina, he studied at Alfred University and later at Syracuse University under Ivan Nestrovic. Among the major national shows in which his works have been exhibited are the Harmon Foundation exhibitions, the surveys of Afro-American art at the Albany Institute of History and Art in 1945, and the City College of New York in 1967. The largest collection of his work is at Atlanta University; he is also represented at Howard University, Fisk University, Chadron State College, the National Portrait Gallery of the Smithsonian Institution, the Joslyn Art Museum, Omaha; and the IBM collection, Chicago.

### ROMARE BEARDEN
### Painter, Collagist
### 1914-1988

**Some Notable Works:** *Street Corner; He Is Arisen; The Burial*

Romare Bearden was born in Charlotte, North Carolina. His family moved to Pittsburgh and later to Harlem. Bearden studied with George Grosz at the Art Students League and later, on the G.I. Bill, went to Paris where he met Matisse, Joan Miro, and Carl Holty. A product of the new generation of Afro-Americans who had migrated from the rural areas of the South to the urban cities of the North, Bearden's work reflected the era of industrialization. His would become the visual images that would reflect the city life, the music—jazz—the city people. Bearden's earlier works belonged to the school of Social Realism, but after his return from Europe his images became more abstract.

In the 1960s, Bearden changed his approach to his picture-making and began to make collages, soon becoming one of the best known collagists in the world. His images are

*Hale Woodruff's famous mural memorializes the early contributions of blacks to the growth of California, from exploration and colonization through settlement.*

haunting montages of his memories of past experiences, of stories told to him by other people. They are for Bearden "an attempt to redefine the image of man in terms of the black experience."

### JOHN BIGGERS
### Painter
### 1924

**Some Notable Works:** *Cradle; Mother and Child; The Contributions of Negro Women to American Life and Education*

John Biggers has been a leading figure in Social Realism as a painter, sculptor, printmaker, and teacher, and an outstanding surrealistic muralist as well.

Born in Gastonia, North Carolina in 1924, Biggers has derived much of his subject matter from the contributions made by blacks to the development of the United States.

While teaching at Texas Southern University, Biggers has become a significant influence on several young black painters.

### MARGARET BURROUGHS
### Painter, Sculptor
### 1917

**Some Notable Works:** *Mexican Landscape; Head; Black Queen; Two Girls*

Margaret Burroughs brings her formidable talents as painter, sculptor, educator, writer, illustrator, and graphic artist to bear upon the situations of the black and of the artist in America.

Born in St. Rose Parish, Louisiana, she studied at Chicago Normal School; Art Institute of Chicago (B.A. , M.A.E.); Teachers' College, Columbia University; Northwestern University; and in Mexico City. She is a founder of the Museum of Negro History, Chicago; The South Side Community Art Center, Chicago; and the National Conference of Artists.

Her numerous exhibitions include American Exposition, Chicago, 1940; San Francisco Civic Museum, 1949; Market Place Gallery, New York, 1950; House of Friendship, Moscow, 1967; Elmhurst College, 1970. Her work can be found in the collections of Howard University; Alabama State Normal; Atlanta University; DuSable Museum of African-American History, Chicago; Johnson Publishing Company; and the Oakland Museum.

### WILLIAM CARTER
### Painter, Muralist
### 1909

**Some Notable Works:** *Missouri Snow; Clouds Over Kuilock; Small Town Dandy; Hermits; Demi-Monde; Portrait of Rev. Joseph Branham*

Muralist William Carter was one of the leading black painters active during the early 1940s, a comparatively productive period for blacks in American art.

Born in Missouri in 1909, Carter received his education at the Art Institute of Chicago and the University of Illinois. Though he is primarily known as a muralist, Carter is equally adept on canvas.

*Alston's California mural focuses on the post-Civil War period. Blacks participated in all the state-building activities, as well as in their own struggle against racist discrimination.*

## ELDZIER CORTOR
**Painter, Educator**
**1915**

**Some Notable Works:** *Day Clean; Vision of Sunset; Oak Table; The Woman; Environment; The Merchants*

Born in Chicago in 1915, Cortor received his art education at Chicago Art Institute, Institute of Design, Columbia University, and Pratt Graphic Art Center.

## ERNEST CRICHLOW
**Painter, Illustrator**
**1914**

**Some Notable Works:** *Young Boy; The White Fence; The Domestic; Lend Me Your Hand; Young Hand;* Illustrations for *Two is a Team* (1945); *Corrie and Yankee* (1959)

The black child has never been more effectively employed as subject matter than in the work of Ernest Crichlow. Although adolescence and motherhood are often recurring themes in Crichlow, it is through his portrayal of the touching simplicity of children that he has made his most memorable contribution.

Crichlow was born in 1914 in New York City, and received art instruction at New York University and the Art Students League.

In the 1930s, he worked on Federal art projects in North Carolina and New York and exhibited in many galleries, among them the Harlem Community Art Center and Federal Gallery in New York. Crichlow has taught art at Shaw and other universities and is a founder of the Cinque Gallery in New York City.

## BEAUFORD DELANEY
**Painter**
**1910-1979**

**Some Notable Works:** *Greene Street; Yaddo; Head of a Poet; Snow Scene*

Born in Knoxville, Tennessee, Beauford Delaney was described by his elder brother Samuel as a "remarkably dutiful child." His father, the Reverend Samuel Delaney, and his mother, Delia Johnson Delaney, understood and recognized Beauford Delaney's artistic talent, as well as that of his brother Joseph, and when the time came they encouraged them in the development of their skills. For Beauford Delaney, recognition came by way of an elderly white artist of Knoxville, Lloyd Branson. Branson gave him lessons and after a time urged him to go to a city where he might study and come into contact with the art world.

In 1924, Beauford Delaney went to Boston to study at the Massachusetts Normal School, later studying at the Copley Society, where he took evening courses while working full-time at the South Boston School of Art. From Boston, Delaney moved on to New York, swept up, like many artists during this period, by the Harlem Renaissance.

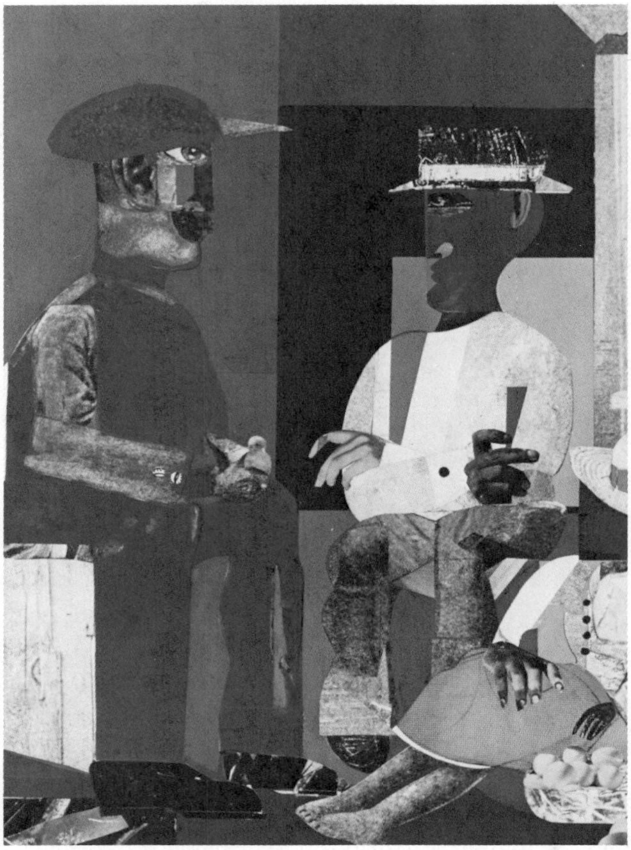

*Romare Bearden's collage* Eastern Barn.

It was in New York that Delaney took on the life of a bohemian, living in the village in coldwater flats. Much of his time was spent painting the portraits of the personalities of the day, such as Louis Armstrong, Ethel Waters, and Duke Ellington. In 1938, Beauford Delaney gained national attention when *Life Magazine*, in an article on "negroes," featured a photograph of him surrounded by a group of his paintings at the annual outdoor exhibition in Washington Square in New York. In 1945, Henry Miller wrote the essay "The Amazing and Invariable Beauford Delaney," which was later reprinted in *Remember to Remember*. The essay describes Delaney's bohemian lifestyle in New York during the 1940s and 1950s.

The fifties was the era of Rome. Every artist in New York saw Rome as the "New Paris" and rushed off to study and absorb its culture. Delaney, receiving money from a young benefactor, also rushed off to Rome. Taking the *Ile de France*, he sailed to Paris, next visiting Greece, Turkey, Northern Italy—but somehow he never got to Rome. Returning to Paris for one more visit, Delaney began to paint, make new friends, and create a new social life filled with the famous and the soon-to-be-famous, like James Baldwin, who at that time had not yet become a famous novelist. Paris was to become Beauford Delaney's home, and he would live out his life in that city.

By 1961, Delaney was producing paintings at such an intense rate that the pressure began to wear upon his strength, and he suffered his first mental collapse. Confined to a clinic in Vincennes, his dealer and close friends began to organize Delaney's life, hoping to help relieve some of the pressure, but it was of little use. For the rest of his life, Delaney was to continue to suffer repeated breakdowns, and by 1971 was back in a sanitarium, where he was to remain until his death in 1979.

Beauford Delaney's numerous exhibitions included Artists Gallery, New York in 1948; Roko Gallery, New York, 1950-1953; Museae d'Art Moderne, Paris, 1963; American Negro Exposition, Chicago, 1940; and Newark Museum, 1971. His work can be found in the collections of the Whitney Museum of American Art, New York, the Newark Museum, New Jersey, and the Morgan State College in Baltimore, Maryland.

## JOSEPH DELANEY
### Painter
### 1904

**Some Notable Works:** *Portraits: Eartha Kitt; Chester A. Arthur III; Eleanor Roosevelt; Tallulah Bankhead*

Joseph Delaney's art celebrates the personal. His portraits, many of which have been executed on sidewalks, record the expressions of momentary contact with other human beings.

Born in Knoxville, Tennessee, he did considerable drawing on his own before enrolling in the Art Students League in 1930 and eventually studying with Thomas Hart Benton, George Bridgeman, and Alexander Brooke. From 1932 to 1971, he exhibited work and did portraits on the sidewalks of New York, in Washington Square Park, Prospect Park, two World's Fairs, museums, and galleries. In 1968, he taught at Vermont Academy under a grant from the Ford Foundation. He has had one-man shows at McClung Museum Gallery, University of Tennessee, 1970; and The Studio Museum, Harlem, 1971.

Delaney says that his doing portraits was a natural result of talking with interested people and sitting out on the street during the Washington Square Outdoor Art Shows.

*Author-illustrator Elton Fax at work in his studio.*

## WILLIAM EDMONSON
### Sculptor
### 1882-?

**Some Notable Works:** *Choir Girls; Lion; Sculpture of Animal*

William Edmonson was a stonecutter, self-taught in sculpture.

Born in Davidson County, Kentucky, he supported himself as a stonemason until the late 1930s. His work was discovered by Mrs. Meyer Dahl-Wolfe, who has an extensive private collection, and who brought it to the attention of the Museum of Modern Art. In an exhibition of self-taught artists, his work was received extremely well. In May 1938, he had a one-man exhibit at the museum. Private collectors and museums have purchased his few sculptures, which are vigorously executed original primitives.

## ELTON FAX
### Illustrator, Writer
### 1909

(information on Fax as a writer appears in the section on writers)

**Some Notable Works:** *Steelworker; Ethiopia Old & New; Contemporary Black Leaders; Through Black Eyes*

Elton Fax stands among America's leading fine artists and illustrators. He is also a noted essayist. Both his drawings and his writings reflect a proud interest in the African legacy of the American black.

Born in Baltimore, he graduated from Syracuse University (B.F.A., 1931). He taught at Claflin University from 1935 to 1936, and was an instructor at the Harlem Community Art Center from 1938 to 1939. His work has been exhibited at the Baltimore Art Museum, 1939; American Negro Exposition, 1940; the Metropolitan Museum of Art; and Visual Arts Gallery, New York, 1970. Examples of his work hang in some of the nation's best university collections, including Texas Southern, the University of Minnesota, and Virginia State University.

Publications by Fax are *Africa Vignettes; Garvey; Seventeen Black Artists;* and *Black Artists of the New Generation. The Portfolio Black and Beautiful* features his art work, and he has written *Hashar,* about the life of the peoples of Soviet Central Asia and Kazakhstan.

*A Contempary Collage by Ronald Joseph*

## FRED FLEMISTER
**Painter**
**1916**

**Some Notable Works:** *Man with a Brush* (1950); *The Mourners* (1952); *Self Portrait* (1945)

Fred Flemister was born in Atlanta. He studied at Morehouse College and under Hale Woodruff at Atlanta University, 1935-1939; and he was a scholarship student at John Herron Art Institute, Indianapolis, 1940-1941. Before his Army service, he was for a time an instructor in art at Atlanta University.

His exhibits have been seen at the Albany Institute of History and Art, 1945; Xavier University, 1963; City College of New York, 1967; and Smith College Museum of Art. His work is represented in the Atlanta University Collections.

## RONALD JOSEPH
**Painter**
**1910**

**Some Notable Works:** *Card Players; Park Avenue Market; Mood* (1941); *Backstage* (1941); *Introspect* (1937) *Family Group*

Ronald Joseph is considered by many to be America's foremost black abstract artist.

Born in St. Kitts, British West Indies, he moved to Harlem with his adoptive parents between 1920-1921. During the Depression he took various jobs to earn a living, including running an elevator, all the while drawing and painting. Eventually he was able to abandon these odd jobs when he became involved in the WPA murals project. Around this time he also belonged to the Harlem Artists Guild.

After the war, Joseph received the Rosenwald Fellowship and the G. I. Bill of Rights Scholarship concurrently. He studied art for two years in Peru (1945-1947) under the Rosenwald Fellowship, and then took two years in Paris under the G. I. Bill. In 1956, he left for Europe, disappointed in the lack of receptivity of his work in the U.S., and has lived in Brussels for the last 33 years.

His exhibitions include Harlem Art Center, 1938, 1939; Baltimore Museum, 1939; American Negro Exposition, 1940; Library of Congress, 1940; and City College of New York, 1967.

Joseph's work receives a great deal of attention from his contemporaries. It is particularly important in terms of the development of black consciousness, and has recently been studied against the backdrop of militancy in the arts.

## JACOB LAWRENCE
**Painter**
**1917**

**Some Notable Works:** *The Life of Toussaint L'Ouverture* (41 panels-1937); *The Life of Harriet Tubman* (40 panels-1939); *The Negro Migration Northward in World War* (60 panels-1942).

Born in 1917 in Atlantic City, New Jersey, Jacob Lawrence received his early training at the Harlem Art School and the American Artist School. His rise to prominence was ushered in by his painting of several series of biographical panels commemorating important episodes in Afro-American history. A narrative painter, Lawrence creates the "philosophy of Impressionism" within his work. Capturing the essential meaning behind the natural appearance of a historical moment or personality, Lawrence creates a formal series of several dozen small paintings which relate the course of a particular historic event in American history, such as *The Migration Series* ("...and the Migrants kept coming"), which traces the migration of the Afro-American from the South to the North, or the discussion on the course of a man's life (e.g., Toussant L'Ouverture and John Brown).

Jacob Lawrence is a visual American historian. His paintings record the Afro-American in trade, theater, mental hospitals, and neighborhoods, or running in the Olympic races. Lawrence's works are found in such collections as the Metropolitan Museum of Art, Museum of Modern Art, and Whitney Museum of American Art.

## NORMAN LEWIS
### Painter
### 1909-1979

**Some Notable Works:** *Arrival and Departure, 1963; Heroic Evening*

Norman Lewis was born in New York City in 1909. Lewis studied at Columbia University. He also studied under Augusta Savage, Raphael Soyer, Vaclav Vytacil, and Angela Streater. During the Great depression he taught art through the Federal Art Project from 1936-39 at the Harlem Art Center. He received the Carnegie International Award in Painting in 1956 and has had several one-man shows at the Willard Gallery in New York. As one of the American artists to develop the Abstract movement in the United States Lewis has participated in many group shows throughout the country in such institutions as the Whitney Museum of American Art, the Metropolitan Museum of Art, and the Art Institute of Chicago.

*Jacob Lawrence's* Tombstones.

## MARION PERKINS
### Sculptor
### 1908-1961

**Some Notable Work:** *Mother and Child* (1956)

Marion Perkins' sculpture was the art at which he excelled, but it was just one of his creative talents, which included painting, the writing of poetry and plays, and teaching.

Born in Marche, Arkansas, he received his secondary education in Chicago, but in art he was largely self-taught. His early sculptures were worked on while he tended a newspaper stand on Chicago's South Side. He later studied privately with Simon Gordon, and the two men became close friends.

Perkins exhibited at the Art Institute of Chicago; American Negro Exposition, 1940; Xavier University, 1963; and Rockland College, Illinois 1965.

As artist in residence at Jackson State College in Mississippi, Perkins founded a scholarship fund for art students at that college, which is where much of his sculpture can be seen today.

*Mood study of Jacob Lawrence, considered one of America's finest artists.*

*Primordial themes and forms, Horace Pippin's* Buffalo Hunt.

## HORACE PIPPIN
**Painter**
**1888-1946**

**Some Notable Works:** *John Brown Goes to a Hanging; Flowers with Red Chair; The Den; The Milk Man of Goshen; Dog Fight Over the Trenches*

Horace Pippin is known as a major primitive painter and has been ranked in the company of Henri Rousseau as a self-taught artist.

Pippin was born in 1888 in West Chester, Pennsylvania, and painted steadily from 1920 until his death in 1946. Among his most vivid portrayals on canvas are the battle scenes which he remembered from his own experience in World War I, during which he was wounded and partially paralyzed.

Pippin's work was discovered in the late 1930s. From that time on, he was championed by many critics as the finest black painter in America.

## CHARLES SEBREE
**Painter, Illustrator, Theater Designer**
**1914**

**Some Notable Works:** *The Clown;* Illustrations for Countee Cullen's book *The Lost Zoo; Harlem Saltimbanques*

Charles Sebree was born in Madisonville, Kentucky. He studied at the Art Institute of Chicago and worked for the Easel Division of the Illinois Federal Art Project (1936-1938).

He has exhibited at the International Watercolor Society, 1935; American Negro Exposition, Chicago, 1940; Institute of Modern Art, Boston, 1943; City College of New York, 1967; James A. Porter Gallery, 1970; and others. Among the collections in which his work is represented are those of the Renaissance Society; University of Chicago; Thornton Wilder; National Archives; and the New York Public Library Schomburg Art Collection.

## DOX THRASH
**Painter, Printmaker**
**1893**

**Some Notable Works:** *Mary Lou; Harmonica Blues; Surface Mining*

Dox Thrash is co-inventor of the graphic technique of the carborundum print, which facilitates combination plates.

Born in Griffin, Georgia, he studied art through a correspondence course till 1908; at the Art Institute of Chicago under Seyffert, Naughton, and Poole, 1919-1922; and under Earl Horton of Graphic Sketch Club, Philadelphia.

His exhibitions include Graphic Sketch Club, 1933, 1934, 1935; New York World's Fair, 1939, 1940; American Negro Exposition, 1940; Newark Museum, 1970; and James A. Porter Gallery, 1970. His work is represented in the National Archives.

## BILL TRAYLOR
**Painter**
**1854-1947**

**Some Notable Works:** *Turkeys; Horse-Man; He Smells a Cow*

Bill Traylor was born a slave in 1854 on the George Traylor plantation near Benton, Alabama. Freed in 1864, Traylor chose to remain a farmer on the plantation, where he was to spend most of his life. By the late 1930s, Traylor was alone and without work. Living in the back room of the Ross-Clayton Funeral Home, a "Negro" funeral parlor, Traylor, in order to earn a living, began to draw on bits of scrap paper he found in the streets. His works were soon discovered by a white dealer in Montgomery, Alabama. He was given his first one-person exhibition at New South, an art center in Montgomery, in 1940, and in a brief time he gained national attention.

In 1942, Traylor's works were exhibited at Fieldston School in New York. Traylor's surreal world belongs to that of Mark Twain, Walt Whitman, and Zora Neal Hurston. His images, abstract ideas of life and reality, never imitate natural forms but create new ones. His mules, cats, dogs, and men and women meeting under the street lights were created in a folk idiom that was as un-self-conscious and spontaneous as an old spiritual. It spoke of the simple country life-the custom and the daily activities.

During World War II, Traylor lived with his children in Detroit, Washington, and possibly elsewhere as well. It was during this time that he had a leg amputated because of gangrene. Traylor returned to Montgomery and Monroe Street in 1946, where he once again slept from place to place, ending up sleeping regularly in a shoe repair shop. In 1947 he moved into his daughter's home in Montgomery, where he died.

*Bill Traylor was born a slave in 1854. He began drawing when he was approximately 82. His first New York Exhibit took place when he was 88 years old.*

### CHARLES WHITE
### Painter
### 1918

**Some Notable Works:** *Let's Walk Together; Frederick Douglass Lives Again; Women; Gospel Singer*

Charles White is an eminent exponent of social art. His paintings have used as their subject matter the notable achievements of famous American blacks as well as the suffering of the lowly and the anonymous.

White was born in 1918 in Chicago, and was influenced as a young boy by Alain Locke's critical review of the Harlem Renaissance: *The New Negro.*

At the age of 23,White won a Rosenwald Fellowship which enabled him to work in the South for two years, during which time he painted a celebrated mural depicting the black's contribution to American democracy. It is now the property of Hampton Institute in Virginia.

The bulk of White's work is done in black-and-white, a symbolic motif which he feels gives him the widest possible purview.

### ELLIS WILSON
### Painter
### 1899

**Some Notable Works:** *Lunch Hour; Field Workers; Four Sisters; Marchande*

Ellis Wilson is a chronicler of Afro-American history.

Born in Mayfield, Kentucky, he studied at the Art Institute of Chicago. He was awarded the Charles S. Peterson Prize in Fine Arts for his African poster, and won a Guggenheim Fellowship in 1944.

His exhibitions include Harmon Foundation; Atlanta University; Detroit Museum; New York World's Fair, 1939; Contemporary Arts, New York, 1948, 1951; and James A. Porter Gallery, 1970. His work is represented in various museums and private collections, including the Schomburg Collection of the New York Public Library.

### JOHN WILSON
### Painter, Printmaker, Educator
### 1922

Some Notable Works: *Roxbury Landscape* (oil, 1944); *Trabajador* (print, 1951); *Child with Father* (graphic, 1969)

John Wilson is both an extremely versatile and fecund artist as well as possessor of considerable erudition.

Born in Boston, he studied at Boston Museum of Fine Arts; Fernand Leger School, Paris; The Institute Politecnico, Mexico City; and others. He has been a teacher at Boston Museum, Pratt Institute, and is currently at Boston University.

His very numerous exhibits include Albany Institute, 1945; Library of Congress National (and International) Print Exhibit(s); Smith College; Carnegie Institute; and American International College, Springfield, Massachusetts, 1971, one-man. Wilson's work is represented in the collections of the Museum of Modern Art; Schomburg, New York; Department of Fine Arts, French Government; Atlanta University; and Bezalel Museum, Jerusalem.

## BLACK ARTISTS: WORLD WAR II TO THE PRESENT

### BETTY BLAYTON-TAYLOR
**Painter, Sculptor, Teacher, Administrator**
**1937**

**Some Notable Works:** *State of Mind; Being and Becoming I, II, III*

Betty Blayton-Taylor is active as artist, teacher, lecturer, and arts administrator. She is the president and founding director of The Children's Art Carnival in Harlem, originally sponsored by the Museum of Modern Art. She was on of the founder of The Studio Museum in Harlem and is an active member of the Board of Directors of the Printmakers Workshop in New York City. She has been an art consultant on the Board of "Kids Magazine," and was a member of the Commission for Cultural Affairs for six years. She is now a Member of the Arts and Business Council.

In 1984, Ms. Blayton-Taylor was named "Empire State Woman of the Year in Arts" and received the Governor's Award.

Born in Williamsburg, Virginia, she received her bachelor of Fine Arts degree with Honors from Syracuse University. She has also studied at the Art Students League and with sculptors Arnold Prince and Munoru Niizuma, and has completed courses in Art Education and Educational Psychology at City College of New York.

Ms. Blayton-Taylor has exhibited her work at the Riverside Museum and Staten Island Museum in New York; the San Francisco Museum of Art; the Boston Museum of Art; High Museum of Art in Atlanta; the Minneapolis Institute of Art, Everson Museum of Art in Syracuse, the Capricorn Gallery, and others.

Her works are included in many private as well as permanent collections such as The Studio Museum in Harlem and the Metropolitan Museum of Art in New York City.

Betty Blayton-Taylor has been a subject of ABC-TV "Like It Is," Channel 13's "Ruth Bowman on the Arts," German Television, and several radio programs. She is also included in a film documentation of five blacks artists, entitled "Five" in addition to numerous books and articles.

She has been an adjunct professor at City College of New York, and has lectured extensively. Ms. Blayton-Taylor has also participated as Artist-in-Residence on several college campuses including Brown, Tugaloo, Fiske, and Virginia State University at Norfolk.

### TINA ALLEN
**Sculptor**
**1957**

**Some Notable Works:** *A. Philip Randolph, Boston; Marcus Garvey; Firechief Wesley Williams.*

Following a nationwide search and selection proces administered by Urban Arts, Inc. Tina Allen was awarded the commission to memorialize A. Philip Randolph in a bronze sculpture of the black labor leader and civil rights activist. "I'm building monuments to great black achievers," Ms. Allen says, which includes Marcus Garvey and Firechief Wesley Williams, and she's booked to work on Dr. Charles Drew and Thelonious Monk.

Allen, who has studied sculpture and painting in New York at The School of Visual Arts and Pratt Institute, and in Italy at the University of Venice, has also worked on her M. Ed. at the University of South Alabama. She has created sculptures for a wide range of public and private collections in North America and abroad, including those of the Pratt Institute, New York's Afro-American Museum, The Schomburg Collection, and Essence Communications. Her pieces can also be found on the sets of "Hill Street Blues", "A Different World" and The Eddie Murphy movie "Harlem Nights". Her work encompasses the spectrum of African American thoughts and images.

Along with numerous awards, Ms. Allen's work has been the subject of Entertainment Tonight, Black Entertainment Television, the Mc Creary Report, In Focus, and Urban Update in Boston, as well included in various T. V. and radio shows, and magazine and newspaper articles.

*Tina Allen has poured her enormous talents into sculpture that memorializes the achievements of blacks.*

*Camille Billops; her creations are bold, imaginative and at times, whimsical.*

She is also affiliated with teaching and professional associations.

### TOYCE ANDERSON
**Painter, Mixed Media**
**1950**

Toyce Anderson was born in New York in 1950. He studied at Ohio University and Pratt Institute. He has exhibited at P.S.I in 1985 and the Henry Street Gallery in 1984 and his work is in the collection of the Smithsonian Institute in Washington D.C.

### BENNY ANDREWS
**Painter, Mixed Media**
**1930**

**Some Notable Work:** *The Family, 1965; The Invisible Man.*

Born in Madson, Georgia on November 13, 1930, Andrews studied at Fort Valley State College in Georgia and later at the University of Chicago. He received his BFA degree in 1958 at the Art Institute of Chicago. During his career he taught at New York School of Social Research, New York City University, and Queens College in New York. His works have appeared in exhibitions around the country including the Boston Museum of Fine Arts, The Martha Jackson Gallery in New York, the University of Wisconsin in Milwaukee and more. Andrews' works are in such collections as the Joseph H. Hirshhorn Collection, the Wisconsin State University, the Museum of Modern Art and the Museum of African Art in Washington, D.C. Benny Andrews has been awarded the John Hay Whitney Fellowship in 1965-66, the Dorne Professorship at Bridgeport University, the New York State Council Creative Arts Program Award in 1971, and the Atlanta University Negro Art Collection Award for "Educational Arts," in 1971.

### CAMILLE BILLOPS
**Ceramic Sculptor**
**1933**

**Some Notable Works:** *Tenure; Black American; Portrait of an American Indian* (all 3 ceramic sculptures); *Year after Year* (painting)

A sculptor of note in the art and retailing world, Camille Billops was born in California, graduated from California State College in 1960, and then studied sculpture on the West Coast under a grant from the Huntington Hartford Foundation. In 1960, she had her first exhibition at the African Art Exhibition in Los Angeles, followed in 1963 by an exhibit at the Valley Cities Jewish Community Center in Los Angeles. In 1966 she participated in a group exhibition in Moscow. Since then, her multifaceted artistic talents, which include poetry, book illustration, and jewelry making, have earned the praise of critics throughout the world, particularly in Ceylon and Egypt, where she has lived and worked.

Billops has also taught extensively. In 1975, she was active on the faculties of the City University of New York and Rutgers State University, New Jersey. In addition, she has conducted special art courses in the New York City jail (the Tombs) and in 1972 lectured in India for the United States Information Service on black American artists. Also, she participated in an exhibit at the New York Cultural Center in 1973.

*Blackburn's massive figures convey towering strength.*

## ROBERT BLACKBURN
**Printmaker**
**1921**

**Some Notable Works:** *Boy with Green Head; Negro Mother*

Robert Blackburn was born in New York City. He studied at the Harlem Workshop, the Art Students League, and the Wallace Harrison School of Art. His exhibits include Art of the American Negro, 1940; Downtown Gallery, New York; Albany Museum; Contemporary Art of the American Negro, 1966; and numerous print shows in the United States and Europe. His work is represented in the Library of Congress, the Brooklyn and Baltimore museums, and the Atlanta University Collections. He is a member of the art faculty of Cooper Union.

Along with his other accomplishments, in 1949, he founded The Printmaking Workshop as an artist-run cooperative. In 1971, it was incorporated as a non-profit printmaking studio for work in lithography, etching, relief and photo-processes. The Workshop, a magnet for third-world and minority artists that reflects Mr. Blackburn's warmth and encouraging personality, remains a haven for artists "to turn out prints for the love of it" and to do anything from experimental hodgepodge to polished pieces. In 1988, Bob Blackburn and the Printmaking Workshop were given the Governor's Art Award for making "a significant contribution to the cultural life of New York State."

*Elizabeth Cattlett's* Woman Resting *on exhibit at the Bronx Museum in 1989.*

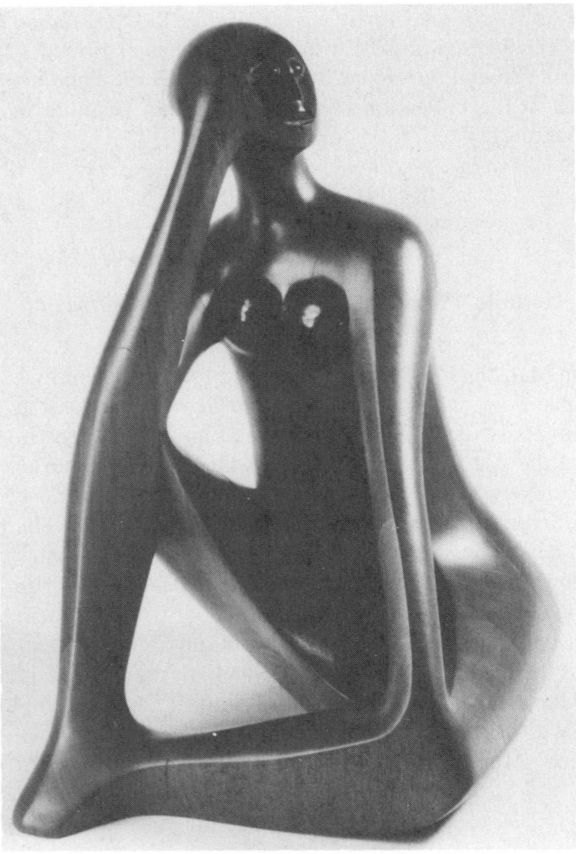

### FRANK BOWLING
**Painter**
**1936**

**Some Notable Works:** *Mel Edwards Decides*, 1969; *Where is Lucienne?*, 1970; *Stations Of The Cross From St. Johns Street, New Amsterdam: Nos. 1&2.*

Born in Guyana in 1936 Frank Bowling studied at the Chelsea School of Art in England and later at the London University, the Slade School and Royal College of Art. Moving to the United States he began teaching art history at Massachusetts College of Art.

Bowling exhibited at the Grabowski Gallery in London in 1962 where he received a one person show. He was one of many artists in the First World Festival Of Negro Art in Dakar, Senegal in 1966. He was among the selected few blacks to appear in the Whitney Museum of American Art in 1966 and again in 1971. His work was also exhibited at the Boston Museum of Fine Arts in 1970. One of his works is owned by the Whitney Museum of American Art. Bowling was awarded the Guggenheim Fellowship in 1967, and the Grand prize, for the First World Festival of Negro Art in 1966.

### VIVIAN BROWNE
**Painter**
**1929**

**Some Notable works:** *Two Men*; *The Dance*; *View Of The Window*.

Born in Laural, Florida in 1929 Vivian Browne came to New York where she studied at Hunter College, receiving both her BFA and her MFA. From there, she went to Teachers College at Columbia and later the New School for Social Research and New York University. She also studied at the Art Students League and Pratt Institute. Browne is a teacher at Rutgers University and was the co-director and organizer of the Lever House Annual. She was also the coordinator of "Black Artists of the 1930's" an exhibition presented at the Studio Museum in Harlem.

Vivian Browne was awarded the Huntington Hartford Fellowship in 1964 and the National Association of Business and Professional Negro Women in 1965. Her works have been exhibited throughout the country.

### NANETTE CARTER
**Printer**
**1954**

Nanette Carter was born in Columbus Ohio in 1954. She received her BA in 1976 from Oberlin College and her MFA from Pratt Institute in 1978. She also studied at L'Accademia di Belle Arti in Perugia Italy in 1975.

Her works have been exhibited at the Cinque Gallery in New York in 1985, N'Namdi in Detroit, Michigan in 1986, the Association of American Artist in 1986, the Wenniger Gallery in 1987, and June Kelly Gallery in 1987.

### ELIZABETH CATLETT
**Sculptor, Painter**
**1919**

**Some Notable Works:** *Black Unity* (1968); *Target Practice* (1970); *Mother and Child* (1972); *Woman Resting* (1981)

The granddaughter of North Carolina slaves, Elizabeth Catlett was raised in the Northwest Washington, D.C. district. As a young woman she attempted to gain admission into a then all-white art school, Carnegie Institute of Technology in Pittsburgh, Pennsylvania. She was refused entry and instead went to Howard University, and graduated as an honor student in 1937. In 1940, she went on to study at the University of Iowa, where she became the first of their students to receive an M.F.A.

Her exhibition history dates back to 1937 and includes group and solo presentations at all the major American art museums as well as institutions in Mexico City, Moscow, Paris, Prague, Tokyo, Beijing, Berlin and Havana. Catlett's public sculpture can be found in Mexico City; Jackson, Miss.; New Orleans; Washington, D.C. and New York. Her work is represented in the permanent collection of over 20 museums throughout the world. The artist resides in Cuernavaca, Mexico.

Catlett accepted teaching positions at various black colleges in order to earn a living, but by 1946 she had moved to Mexico, where she eventually settled. Always a promoter of human struggle—visually concerned with the recording of economic, social, and political themes—Catlett became involved with the Civil Rights Movement so deeply that it contributed greatly to her philosophy of life and art. Between 1941 and 1969, Catlett won eight prizes and honors, four in Mexico and four in America.

### DANA CHANDLER
**Painter**
**1941**

**Some Notable Works:** *Fred Hampton's Door; Martin Luther King Jr. Assassinated; Death of Uncle Tom; Rebellion '68; Dynamite; Death of a Bigot; The Golden Prison*

Dana Chandler is one of the most visible, outspoken, and provocative black painters on the American scene. Chandler's huge, colorful black power murals are spotted throughout the ghetto area of Boston, a constant reminder of the resolve and determination manifested by the new breed of young black urban dwellers—proud and even scornful.

"All this stuff whites are buying," Chandler says, "tells the black man a lot about where the white community is at, namely, nowhere."

Chandler's easel works are bold and simple. One, The Golden Prison, shows a black man with a yellow and red striped flag "because America has been yellow and cowardly in dealing with the black man." Another, *Freddie Hampton's Door*, shows a bullet-splintered door replete with a stamp of U.S. government approval.

Born in Lynn, Massachusetts, Chandler received his B.S. from the Massachusetts College of Art in 1967.

## BARBARA CHASE-RIBOUD
**Sculptor**
**1939**

**Some Notable Works:** *Monuments to Malcolm X; The Bullfighter; The Ultimate Sound*

Born in Philadelphia in 1939, Barbara Chase-Riboud received her BFA at Temple University in Philadelphia in 1957 followed by her studies at Yale where she received her MFA in 1960, after which she moved to Paris where she continues to live. Her works are recognized internationally and she has participated in such events as the First Spoleto Festival in 1958, the First World Festival of Negro Art in Dakar, Senegal in 1966, and L'Oeil ecoute, Festival of Avignon. Her works are in the collections of the Museum of Modern Art in New York City, the Bertha Schaefer Gallery in New York, the Newark Museum in New Jersey, and Philadelphia Art Alliance. She has had one person exhibitions at the Betty Parsons Gallery in New York in 1972, the Salon de Mai in Paris in 1971-72, and Le Cadron Solaire in Paris in 1966. Chase-Riboud has been awarded the John Hay Whitney Foundation Fellowship in 1957-58, the Philadelphia Art Alliance Purchase Prize in 1957 and the National Endowment for the Arts Award.

## EDWARD CLARK
**Painter**

**Some Notable Works:** *The Big Egg; Vetheuil, Summer 1968; Vetheuil, Fall 1968; Paris Rose; Calm Force*

Edward Clark is an adherent of the 1950s "action school" of painting whose philosophical and psychological view of painting holds that it is a purely visual experience whose primary constituent elements are nothing but color and movement.

Born in New Orleans, he studied at the Art Institute of Chicago and L'Academie de la Grand Chaumiegre. His one-man shows include Gallery Creuze, Paris, 1966; Brata Gallery, New York, 1958; United States Embassy, Paris, 1969; Prince Street Gallery, New York, 1971; and South Houston Gallery, New York, 1974. His work has also been shown at the Modern Museum, Tokyo and Kyoto; Boston Museum of Fine Arts, 1970; and the University of Texas, 1970.

Clark has resided alternately in Paris and New York. His search for the best method to express movement extending beyond the limits of the canvas has led him to a prolonged exploration of the dynamics of the ellipse.

## ROBERT COLESCOTT
**Painter**
**1925**

Robert Colescott was born in California in 1925. He received his BA in 1949 from the University of California and later his MA in 1952 from the same university. In 1953, Colescott studied in Paris with Fernand Leger. His exhibitions include The Whitney Museum of American Art Biennial in 1983, The Hirshorn Museum and Sculpture Garden in Washington D.C. in 1984, and the Institute of Contemporary Art at the University of Pennsylvania in 1985. His work is in the collections of The Metropolitan Museum of Art, The Seattle Art Museum, The Oakland Art Museum, the Portland Art Museum and the University of Mass.

## EMILIO CRUZ
**Painter**
**1938**

**Some Notable Work:** *Silver Umbrella.*

Emilio Cruz was born in New York in 1938. His education includes work at the Art Students League in 1955. Cruz has exhibited at the Anita Shapolsky Gallery in 1986, The Studio Museum in Harlem in 1987, the Portland Museum of Art in 1987, and the Rhode Island School of Design in 1987. His work is in the Hirshhorn Museum and Sculpture National Gallery of Art, the Albright-Knox Gallery, the Museum of Modern Art, The Freedom National Bank, The Brooklyn Museum of Art, and the Studio Museum in Harlem.

## JOHN DOWELL
**Painter**
**1941**

**Some Notable Works:** *Tomorrow's Solo; Tune Break Away; To Open Time*

Born in Philadelphia and educated in Seattle, Dowell moved back to Philadelphia to teach and work. As full professor of printmaking and chairman of the department at Tyler School

*Melvin Edwards'* Mjuju, *one of many depictions of oppression in his* Lynch Fragment *series.*

of Art, Dowell divides his time between the running of his classroom and his own artwork. In 1976, Dowell formed the Visual Arts Ensemble, which consists of a saxophone, cello, percussion, and Dowell at the piano. The group has traveled throughout Europe and the United States performing many of Dowell's paintings and watercolors. Influenced by East Asian art forms, from which the musical sounds are improvised, the group dissects, plucks, and hammers out the visual forms.

### MELVIN EDWARDS
### Sculptor
### 1937

**Some Notable Work:** *Harlem Group #2 Windows.*

Born in Houston, Texas in 1937, Melvin Edwards studied at the Los Angeles County Institute and later went on to receive his BFA from the University of Southern California. His works have been exhibited in the Santa Barbara Museum of Art in 1965, the Richard Corey Gallery in Chicago in 1966, the Walker Art Center in Minn. in 1968, the Andrew Dickson White Museum of American Art in 1970, and the Wright State University in Dayton, Ohio in 1972. Edwards works are in the Los Angeles Co. Museum of Art, Chase Manhattan Bank in New York, the Museum of Modern Art, and the Long Beach Museum in California.

### SAM GILLIAM
### Painter

**Some Notable Works:** *Watercolor 4* (1969); *Herald* (1965); *Carousel Change* (1970); *Mazda* (1970); *Plantagenets Golden* (1984)

Mississippi-born Sam Gilliam produces hanging canvases which are laced with pure color pigments rather than shades or tones. The artist bunches these pigments in weird configurations on drooping, drapelike canvases, giving the effect, in the words of *Time Magazine*, of "clothes drying on a line." His canvases are said to be "like nobody else's, black or white."

Gilliam took his M.A. from the University of Louisville, and was awarded National Endowment of Humanities and Arts Grants. He has had one-man and group shows at the Washington Gallery of Modern Art; Jefferson Place Gallery; Adams-Morgan Gallery in Washington, D.C.; the Art Gallery of Washington University, St. Louis, Missouri; the Speed Museum, Louisville; the Philadelphia Museum of Art; the Museum of Modern Art; the Phillips Collection and Corcoran Gallery of Art, both in Washington, D.C.; the San Francisco Museum of Art; the Walker Art Center, Minneapolis and the Whitney Museum of American Art. He is represented in the permanent collection of over 45 American museums.

Gilliam has also been represented in several group exhibitions, including the First World Festival of Negro Arts in Dakar, Senegal (1966), "The Negro in American Art" at UCLA (1967), and the Whitney Museum's American Art Annual (1969).

In 1968, 1969, and 1970 his work was displayed in one-man shows at Washington, D.C.'s Jefferson Place, and in 1971 he was featured in a one-man show at New York City's Museum of Modern Art.

In 1980, Sam Gilliam was commissioned, with 13 other artists, to design an art piece for installation in the Atlanta, Georgia Airport Terminal, one of the largest terminals in the world and the first to install contemporary artwork on its walls for public viewing.

### DAVID HAMMONS
### Painter
### 1939

**Some Notable Works:** *America the Beautiful* (1969); *American Hang-Up* (1970); *Injustice Case* (1970); *Pray for America* (1969)

Born in Springfield, Illinois, the youngest of 10 children in a family on welfare, David Hammons passed the home of Abraham Lincoln every day on his way to school, and somehow derived from this experience an abiding preoccupation with the American flag, a recurring theme in his early

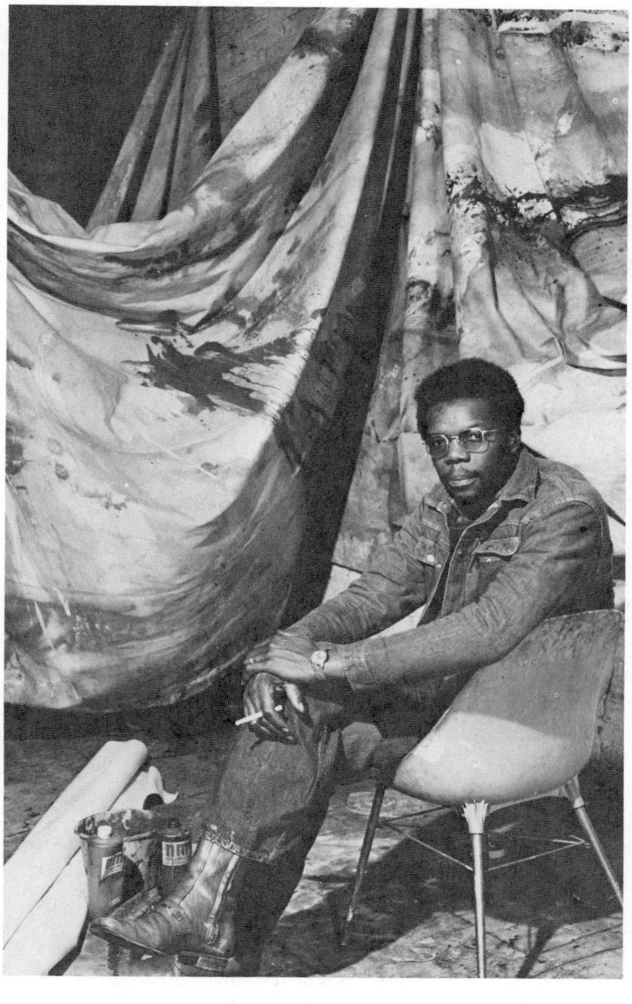

*Sam Gilliam's works are often bold and brilliant blazes of color on unusual canvases.*

Extending Horizontal Form *typifies Richard Hunt's interest in spatial concepts*

*The paintings of David Hammons are a militant outcry against oppression.*

work. From the flag, Hammons went on to incorporate the Spade into his visual constructions. Hair, wire, eggs, found objects, recycled objects—Hammons finds no need to purchase art supplies, believing that art is the product of the mind and not of the store.

Art critic John Perreault identified Hammons as "a very active new energy source." As an artist, he works to use andcommunicate his background and his life within his work. In 1980, Hammons was identified as one of the artists to watch in the 1980s. His installation work in such exhibitions as Afro-American Abstraction, presented at P.S. 1 in New York, and a window installation for the New Museum in New York, both done in 1980, and a group installation done at the Studio Museum of Harlem brought David Hammons into the art world as one of America's top young artists.

## RICHARD HUNT
### Painter, Sculptor
### 1935

**Some Notable Works:** *Man on a Vehicular Construct* (1956); *Arachve* (1956); *Linear Spatial Theme* (1962); *The Chase* (1965); *Arching* (1986)

Richard Hunt was born in Chicago and began his formal career after studying at the School of the Art Institute of Art School of Detroit, Society of Arts and Crafts, and John Huntington Polytechnic Institute. He also studied under Sarkis Sarkisian.Smith's works have been exhibited at the Association of American Artists Galleries in 1943, the Western Michigan University in Kalamazoo, MI in 1977, the June Kelly Gallery in 1987 and the National Headquarters of the Urban League in 1988. His work is in such collections as Standard Oil of Ohio, Cleveland Ohio, Atlanta

University in Atlanta GA, New Jersey State Museum in Chicago, where he received a number of awards.

After graduating in 1957, Hunt was given the James Nelson Raymond Traveling Fellowship. He later taught at the School of the Art Institute of Chicago and at the University of Illinois. From 1962 to 1963, he pursued his craft while under a Guggenheim Fellowship.

Hunt's solo presentations have appeared at the Cleveland Museum of Art; Milwaukee Art Center; Museum of Modern Art; Art Institute of Chicago; Springfield Art Museum, Mass.; Indianapolis Museum of Art and a U.S.I.S.-sponsored show throughout Africa which was organized by the Los Angeles Museum of African American Art. Hunt sits on the board of Governors at the School of the Art Institute of Chicago and the Skowhegan School of Painting and Sculpture, is a Commissioner at the National Museum of American Art, Washington, D.C. and serves on the Advisory Committee at the Getty Center for Education in the Arts, Malibu.

### DANIEL JOHNSON
**Painter**
**1938**

**Some Notable Works:** *Homage to Rene D'Harnoncourt; Yesterday; Death of Tarzan; Eve; Study for a Church Altar; Big Red; Wendell*

Though a native of the Los Angeles Watts ghetto, Daniel Johnson does not attribute his creative instincts to his color. Instead, he believes that questions of race "are frivolous" and "have nothing to do with the consciousness of people who attempt to make art."

His own works, seen in prominent display at Manhattan's French & Co. in 1970, are painted sculptures which have already sold for upwards of $3,500. Critic Margit Rowell says of his work: "The sensation of a temporal, even acoustical experience—for which one was unprepared and which is intangible—is perhaps the most unsettling aspect of one's first encounter" with Johnson's work. Otherwise, the visual impact is one of strict sobriety—the total absence of extraneous forms and preoccupation.

Johnson holds a B.F.A. from Chouinard Art Institute (1960). He has befriended, or studied with, such giants as Larry Rivers, Willem de Kooning, and Alberto Ghouls. In 1961, he was awarded the Stanton Fellowship, and within two years, he was touring the South collecting common objects for constructions. By 1966, he was fully involved in developing the technique of using high polishes for surface-painted wood.

### HUGHIE LEE-SMITH
**Painter**
**1925**

**Some Notable Works:** *Portrait of a Sailor; Old Man and Youth; Waste Land; Little Diana; Aftermath*

Hughie Lee-Smith was born in 1915 in Eustis, Florida. He studied at Wayne State University where he received his B.S. degree. He later attended the Cleveland Institute of Art where he was awarded the Gilpin Players Scholarship; the Trenton, New Jersey, and Howard University in Washington, D.C. During WWII Lee-Smith served in the U.S. Navy from 1943 through 1945.

Hughie Lee-Smith has received more than a dozen important prizes, including the Founders Prize of the Detroit Institute of Arts (1953) and the Emily Lowe Award (1957). He is a member of Allied Artists of America, the Michigan Academy of Arts, Sciences & Letters, and the Artists Equity Association.

### JAMES LITTLE
**Painter**
**1952**

James Little was born in Tennessee in 1952. He received his B.F.A. degree at the Memphis Academy of Art in 1974 and later attended the Syracuse University in New York State. His works have been exhibited at the Albright Knox Art Gallery in Buffalo, New York in 1983, the Museum of Art in Pennsylvania State University in 1985, and the Harris Brown Gallery in Mass., in 1986.

### EDWARD LOVE
**Sculptor**
**1936**

**Some Notable Works:** *Genisis; All My Fathers*

Edward Love was born in 1936 in Los Angeles California. He studied at Los Angeles City College and later went to the University of Southern California and California State College at Los Angeles and finally to the University of Uppsala in Sweden. Love exhibited his works in Uppsala Sweden in 1968, again in the exhibition Black Focus in Reston Virginia in 1969, Howard University, and the Smith-Mason Gallery in Washington D.C. in 1971.

### ALVIN LOVING
**Painter**
**1935**

**Some Notable Works:** *Time Trip One; Untitled,1970*

Alvin Loving was born in Detroit in 1935. Loving studied at the University of Illinois in Champaign where he received his BFA in 1963 and at the University of Michigan where he gained his MFA in 1965. As an artist he participated in the "Afro-American Art After 1950" exhibition at Brooklyn College in 1969 and in 1971 he was exhibiting his work at the Whitney Museum. Loving won a teaching fellowship at the University of Michigan in 1963, and another teaching fellowship at the Rackham School of Graduate Studies at the University of Michigan in 1964.

### RICHARD MAYHEW
**Painter**
**1924**

**Some Notable Works:** *West* (1965); *Field* (1950); *Thorn Bush*

Richard Mayhew's oils have earned wide critical respect.

His awards include John Hay Whitney Fellowship, 1958; MacDowell Colony Foundation, 1958; Ingram Merrill Foundation Grant, 1960; National Institute of Arts and Letters Grant, 1965; and Benjamin Altman Award, National Academy of Design, 1970.

Born in Amityville, New York, he studied at the Brooklyn Museum School. Among his very numerous exhibitions have been the American Academy of Arts and Letters; Boston Museum; Brooklyn Museum; Museum of Modern Art; Whitney Museum; and in 1974, a one-man show at the Midtown Gallery, New York. Some of the collections which include his works are Albion College, Michigan; Brooklyn Museum; Whitney Museum; Olsen Foundation, Connecticut; Evansville Museum; and New York University.

### GERALDINE MCCULLOUGH
**Sculptor**
**1928**

**Some Notable Works:** *Bessie Smith; View from the Moon; Toad Hall Front; Atomic Rose; Phoenix*

Geraldine McCullough's steel and copper abstraction "Phoenix" won the George D. Widener Gold Medal at the 1964 exhibition of the Pennsylvania Academy of Fine Arts. In capturing this award, her name was added to a roster of distinguished artists who have already won the same honor, including Jacques Lipchitz and Theodore Roszak. Of further note was the fact that this had been her first showing in a major national exhibition.

A native of Arkansas, McCullough has lived in Chicago since she was three and is a 1948 graduate of the Art Institute there.

### EARL MILLER
**Painter**
**1930**

**Some Notable Works:** *Tone Poems with Two Blue Squares; Accordion Flyer; American Flyer; Steller*

Among the most talented new Afro-American artists exhibiting in America since 1950 is Earl Miller, born in Seattle in 1930.

Miller studied in the United States until 1957, first at Pratt Institute in Brooklyn (1954-1956), later at the Art School of the Brooklyn Museum (1956), and finally at the Art Students League. He also attended the Akademie der Bildenden Kunste in Munichin 1963.

Miller has had several one-man exhibits, notably at New York's Phoenix Gallery (1961) and the Town Hall in Marbella, Spain (1962). In 1968 and 1969, he was among those featured at the American Greetings Gallery, the Lever House, the Museum of Modern Art, and Brooklyn College, all in New York.

### CLARENCE MORGAN
**Painter**
**1950**

**Some Notable Works:** *Upper Volta; Linear Notation; Neon Juke*

Clarence Morgan grew up in Philadelphia, where he received his B.A. at the University of Pennsylvania. In 1978 Morgan took on the role of art instructor at East Carolina University. There he stresses the importance of color, form, composition, and their position in space, principles that he

Stellar, *acrylic on canvas, by Earl Miller.*

adheres to in the development of his own work.

Morgan's visual style is a layering process which produces paintings heavy with noisy rhythms rising and falling across the surface. Personal and intimate, both in scale and content, these works, like those of artists Howardena Pindell and Betye Saar, involve a selective and intuitive eye that searches, gathers, and accumulates the materials which ultimately provide the energy of the works. His exhibitions include "Small Works" at New York University and "Paper in Particular" at Columbia College in Columbia, Missouri, both in 1980.

## NORMA MORGAN
## Painter, Engraver

**Some Notable Works:** *Storm over Hawort Moor* (painting); *Glen in Badenoch* (engraving)

Norma Morgan is a well-known younger New York artist, at home with both traditional and abstract themes. Much of her work has been inspired by travels through remote areas in England and Scotland, and she is especially drawn to subjects, whether natural objects or people, which show their struggle with the forces of erosion.

Born in New Haven, Connecticut, she attended the Hans Hoffman School of Fine Art and the Art Students League. She has taken part in many invitational and touring exhibitions.

Her engravings are represented in the collections of the Philadelphia Museum, the Library of Congress, the American Federation of Arts, Washington's National Gallery of Art, the Victoria and Albert Museum in London, the Glasgow Museum, and such private collections as those of Nelson Rockefeller and Ruth Ford.

## SENGA NENGUDI
## Painter-Sculptor
## 1943

**Some Notable Works:** *R.S.V.P. XIII; Ritual Chant; Inside Out*

Born in Chicago, Illinois, Senga Nengudi has always been interested in the process of art. During her early development stages—school at the California State University, the Waseda University in Tokyo, Japan and then back to California State University for her masters degree—Nengudi was more concerned with the process than the final result. First she created images made by filling vinyl bags with water, thereby developing a loose, flowing rhythm. Later she switched to filling the bags with mud, creating an art form that was more earthy in texture but was too difficult to install and move. One of the pieces from this series was exhibited in "8 Black Artists" in Geneva, Switzerland.

From this point, Nengudi moved on to working with nylon body stockings, which allowed her to draw upon her knowledge of weight, stretch, and balance. Filling the stockings with sand, Senga Nengudi had found a substance that allowed her to control and distribute the weight of her pieces without destroying the images' naturalness. Her more recent works have concerned themselves less with the final piece itself and more with the performance of the piece. Working with artists Frank Marane and Maren Hassinger, Nengudi has developed a series of performance pieces that have been presented in California.

## HAYWOOD OUBRE
## Painter

**Some Notable Work:** *Colorwheel* (1962)

Hayward Oubre explores the properties of color within the framework of scientific research.

He attended Dillard University, New Orleans (M.F.A.), and went on to teach art at Tuskegee Institute, Alabama; Florida A&M University, Tallahassee; and Alabama State College, Montgomery. He is currently chairman of the Art

*Norma Morgan's engraving,* David in the Wilderness.

Department at Winston-Salem University, North Carolina.

His works have been exhibited at Atlanta University, Georgia; Walker Art Center, Minneapolis; Isaac Delgado Museum, New Orleans; Art Directions Gallery, New York; and Southern Illinois University, Carbondale.

## JOSEPH OVERSTREET
**Painter**
**1934**

**Some Notable Works:** *The New Jemima* (1964); *Justice, Faith, Hope, and Peace* (1968); *Indian Sun* (1969)

Born in Conehatta, Mississippi in 1934, Joe Overstreet studied at the California School of Arts and Crafts and participated in "New Black Artists," seen at the Brooklyn Museum in 1969.

Overstreet's canvases have of late eschewed racial themes to concentrate instead on vivid color and original configuration. Thus many of his abstractions are based on a medley of African and Indian colors. When they are exhibited, the canvases are often held in place by guy wires.

Overstreet's work is equally memorable when it deals with racial subject matter; noteworthy are *Jazz in 4/4 Time* (oil on canvas) and *Keep on Keeping On* (oil on canvas).

## HOWARDENA PINDELL
**Painter**
**1943**

**Some Notable Works:** *Memory Test; Inflation; You Have a Friend at Chase; Lake Lilies for Kim; East-West: Waterfall* (1983)

Born in Philadelphia, Howardena Pindell received her education at Boston University and Yale University. She first gained national recognition for her artistic skills in 1969 with the exhibition "American Drawing Biennial XXIII" at the Norfolk Museum of Arts and Sciences in Virginia. By the mid-1970s, Pindell's work began appearing in such exhibitions as "Eleven Americans in Paris," Gerald Piltzer Gallery, Paris, 1975; "Recent Acquisitions; Drawings," Museum of Modern Art, New York, 1976; and "Pindell: Video Drawings," Sonja Henie Onstad Foundation, Oslo, Norway, also in 1976.

Around this same time, Howardena Pindell began to travel around the world as a guest speaker. Some of her lectures included "Current American and Black American Art: A Historical Survey" at Madras College of Arts and Crafts, Madras, India, 1975; and "Black Artists, U.S.A.," Academy of Art, Oslo, Norway, 1976.

Her work is part of the permanent collection in over 30 museums including the Brooklyn Museum, High Museum in Atlanta, Newark Museum, Fogg Museum in Camgridge, Mass., Whitney Museum of American Art, Museum of Modern Art and Metropolitan Museum of Art. Howardena Pindell has received two National Endowment for the Arts Fellowships and a Guggengeim Fellowship. She is professor of Art at the State University of New York at Stony Brook.

## ROBERT REID
**Painter**
**1924**

**Some Notable Works:** *Mid-west Landscape #2, Falling Figure #3*

Robert Reid was born in Atlanta, Georgia in 1924. Reid studied at Clark College in Atlanta from 1941-43, the Art Institute of Chicago between 1943-43 and the Parson School of Design in New York between 1948-50. Reid then went on to teach at the Rhode Island School of Design. His exhibitions traveled across the country and included such institutions as Minneapolis Institute of Arts in 1968, the Studio Museum in Harlem, 1968-69, the Whitney Museum in 1971, the Newark Museum, in New Jersey in 1971, the University of Iowa, 1971-72 and the US Information Center in Washington D.C.in 1971.

*Howardena Pindell's* East-West: Waterfall, *a montage of acrylic, tempera, gouache and post cards.*

### FAITH RINGGOLD
**Painter**

**Some Notable Works:** *The Flag Is Bleeding; Flag for the Moon; Die Nigger; Mommy & Daddy; Soul Sister*

Committed to a revolutionary perspective both in politics and in aesthetics, Faith Ringgold is a symbolic expressionist whose stark paintings are acts of social reform directed toward educating the consciousness of her audience. Her most intense focus has been upon the problematic of being black in America. Her works highlight the violent tensions which tear at American society, including the discrimination suffered by women.

Born in Harlem in 1934, she was raised by parents who took care to make sure that she would enjoy the benefits of a good education. She attended the City College of New York, receiving her B.S. in 1955 and her masters in Fine Arts in 1959.

Her boldly political work has been well-received and widely shown. She has had several one-person shows, the first in 1968, and her paintings are included in the collections of the Chase Manhattan Bank, New York City; the Museum of Modern Art; the Bank Street College of Education, New York City; and Melvin Van Peebles.

In 1972, Ringgold became one of the founders of the Women Students and Artists for Black Liberation, an organization whose principal goal is to make sure that all exhibitions of black artists give equal space to paintings by men and women. In line with her interest in sexual parity, she has donated a large mural depicting the roles of women in American society to the Women's House of Detention in Manhattan.

Aesthetically, she believes that "black art must use its own color black to create its light, since that color is the most immediate black truth." Her most recent paintings have been an attempt to give pictorial realization to this vision.

### BETYE SAAR
**Painter, Sculptor**
**1926**

**Some Notable Works:** *The Vision of El Cremo; Africa; The View from the Sorcerer's Window.*

Betye Saar was born in California in 1926. She went to college, got married, and raised her children—all the while creating artwork, images built upon discarded pieces of old dreams, postcards, photographs, flowers, buttons, fans, and ticket stubs. Her motifs range from the fetish to the everyday object. In 1978, Saar was one of a select group of American female artists to be discussed in a documentary film entitled *Spirit Catcher: The Art of Betye Saar*. It appeared on WNET/13 in New York as part of "The Originals: Women in Art" series. Her exhibitions include an installation piece especially designed for the Studio Museum of Harlem in 1980, and several one-person exhibitions at the Monique Knowlton Gallery in New York in 1981.

*Faith Ringgold's "Aunt Edith" from the family of women mask series.*

### RAYMOND SAUNDERS
**Painter**
**1934**

**Some Notable Works:** *Doctor Jesus, Icons And Gods*

Raymond Saunders was born in 1934. He studied at the Carnegie Institute of Technology from 1950-53, the Pennsylvania Academy of Fine Arts from 1953 to 1955, the University of Pennsylvania from 1954 to 1957 and back to the Carnegie Institute of Technology where he received his BFA in 1960, and the California College of Arts and Crafts where he received his MFA in 1961. Saunders received the Cresson European Travelling Scholarship in 1956 and the Prix de Rome in 1964. His first one-man exhibition was at the Pittsburgh Playhouse in 1953 and he later participated in "The Portrayal of the Negro in American Paintings" in 1967, the Forum Gallery and "New Voices-15 New York Artists," New York, 1968. His work is represented in the collections of the Whitney Museum of American Art, Howard University and the Addison Gallery of American Art.

### SKUNDER (ALEXANDER BOGHOSSIAN)
**Painter**
**1937**

Skunder is the first Ethiopian whose paintings have been purchased by the Museum of Modern Art in New York, and the first African to have a work hanging in the Museae d'Art Moderne in Paris.

Born in Addis Ababa, he took second prize at the National Art Exhibition, 1955, and received a scholarship to study abroad. After two years in London he went on to study at the Ecole des Beaux Arts and La Grande Chaumiegre in Paris, as well as with leading artists.

His exhibitions include London Contemporary Arts Society, 1956; Merton Simpson Gallery, New York, 1961; Biennale de Sao Paolo, Brazil, 1967; and Contemporary Art of Africa, Montgomery, Alabama, 1969. Skunder is presently Artist-in-Residence at Howard University.

### VINCENT SMITH
**Painter**
**1929**

**Some Notable Works:** *Repairing a Bombed Church; Peace and Freedom Party; Molotov Cocktail; The People Cry Out; Sharecropper's Shack; Black Family*

Vincent Smith, born in 1929, belongs to the social commentary school of artists—those who explore themes relating to the rise of black militancy and the aspirations of black youth.

A native of Brooklyn, Smith studied at the Art Students League (1953) and continued his training at the Brooklyn Museum School of Art. In 1957, he received a John Hay Whitney Fellowship.

Smith has exhibited widely in the East and has even had several one-man shows.

### BOB THOMPSON
**Painter**
**1937-1966**

**Some Notable Works:** *Ascension to the Heavens; Untitled Diptych; The Dentist* (1963); *Expulsion and Nativity* (1964)

The death of Bob Thompson took from the black art world one of its outstanding painters, a man who had studied extensively here in the United States and also traveled widely in Europe and North Africa, living in Paris (1961-1962), Ibiza (1962-1963), and Rome (1965-1966).

Born in Louisville, Kentucky, Thompson studied at the Boston Museum School in 1955 and later spent three years at the University of Louisville. In 1960, Thompson participated in a two-person show at Zabriskie Gallery and two years later received a John Hay Whitney Fellowship.

For the next several years, Thompson had several one-man exhibitions in such leading U.S. cities as New York and Chicago. His work was also seen in Spain. He died in Rome at the age of 29.

Thompson's work is in several permanent collections around the country, including the Chrysler Museum in Provincetown, Massachusetts. In 1970, Thompson's work was featured in the Afro-American Artist exhibition at the Boston Museum of Fine Arts.

### CLIFTON WEBB
**Painter-Sculptor**
**1950**

**Some Notable Works:** *Landscape; The Raft; A Closer Connection*

Born in New Orleans on August 7, 1950, Webb was raised in Baton Rouge, Louisiana. Involved with the inner relationship of African people and Afro-American people, Webb approaches his interest in African art forms through a shared sense of musical order. His objects are often arranged in a polyrhythmic structure emphasizing the individuality of the various items used within the total work. Webb's synthesizing of African and Meso-American sensations through the use of raw materials provides an element of fetishisism, eccentricity, and kinetic energies that makes his works both funky and magically endowed.

### JACK WHITTEN
**Painter**
**1939**

**Some Notable Works:** *Psychic Square 1; First Frame* (1971)

Painter Jack Whitten was born in Bessemer, Alabama in 1939, and studied at Tuskegee Institute and Southern University in Baton Rouge, Louisiana before coming North to receive his B.F.A. degree from Cooper Union in New York.

Whitten, who teaches at Pratt Institute, received a Whitney Fellowship in 1964. His second one-man show was given at the Allan Stone Gallery in February 1970. He was also represented in the 1969 Whitney Museum of American Art Annual.

# OUTSTANDING BLACK PHOTOGRAPHERS

## MICHELL AGINS
**Photographer**
**1956**

**Principal Subjects:** *Journalism*

Born in 1956, she had an early interest in photography and art. John Tweedle, photographer of the Chicago Daily News became her mentor. She studied at Loyola University, worked part-time at the Chicago Daily News, and landed a job at Encore Magazine at the same time she was free-lancing for the New York Times and Newsweek.

In 1974, she returned to Chicago intent on finishing school, entered Rosary College and majored in communication and science. In 1983 she was hired as the mayor's photographer. She also became the first black female to join the International Photographers of the Motion Picture and Television Industries Union. Also a member of Chicago Association of Black Journalists, the National Association of Black Journalists, and Chicago Press Photographer Association

She had been the official photographer to Mayor Harold Washington, Chicago before his untimely death in 1987.

## JULES ALLEN
**Photographer**
**1947**

**Principal Subjects:** *Film, Art*

In 1978, Jules Allen established himself in the New York art world with a two-man exhibition shared with Frank Stewart at *The Studio Museum of Harlem*. In 1979, his work appeared in a group photography exhibition at Gallery 22. For Allen, photography provides the means to document the unique esthetics of African Americans. Light and form are his poetry, and Allen captures the different ways in which black people take pictures.

Jules Allen also worked as a production photographer for the play *For Colored Girls Who Have Considered Suicide When the Rainbow Is Enuf* in Rio de Janeiro, Brazil, and was the co-producer and assistant cameraman for the film *Americans in Havana, Cuba.*

## WINIFRED HALL ALLEN
**Photographer**
**Active 1930s**

**Principal Subjects:** *Journalism*

Born in Jamaica, West Indies Winifred Hall Allen moved to New York City at the age of 18 and worked for William Woodard in his photo studio in Harlem. She also attended the New York Institute of Photography. After graduating she took over the Woodard Studio when Woodard decided to move to Chicago. Later changing the name of the studio to the Winifred Hall Photography Studio. Like James Van Der Zee, Allen was a photo journalist and much of her work provides us with another biography of Harlem of the 1930s.

## HANSEN AUSTIN
**Photographer**
**1910-**
**Active 1930s to the present**

**Principal Subjects:** *Street Scenes, Portraits*

Austin began his career in photography in the Virgin Islands, his birthplace. Clair Taylor, the Islands' official photographer in the early 1920s taught him photography basics. In 1928, Austin moved to New York City where he took assorted jobs such as messenger, elevator operator, and musician. He was also a musician of sorts and played the drums in the local clubs of Harlem. Later, during the WPA years, he joined the musicians' union which enabled him to play with larger bands in clubs out of the city. During the WPA years Austin studied art and began to become more involved with photography. During World War II, Austin joined the Navy where he learned combat/war photography. He was given the rank of photographer's mate, 2nd class, and he worked with the Office of War Information in 1945.

After the war, Hansen moved back to Harlem to set up the studio on West 135th Street. He is noted for his photographs

*A Ball and Thomas portrait of an unidentified man.*

of the churches, professional schools, organizations, personalities and events in Harlem, and his collection of over 20,000 photographs was recently donated to the Schomburg Center for Research in Black Culture. His work has appeared in the *Amsterdam News*, *New York Age*, *African Express*, and *People's View*

His work is in the following collections: Austin Hansen, private collection and the

Schomburg Center for Research in Black Culture, New York, New York.

## JOHN B. BAILEY
## Photographer

**Principal Subjects:** *Portraits*

He was active in Boston, Mass. in the 1840s, and is recognized for having taught J.P. Ball of Cincinnati.

## JAMES PRESLEY BALL (J.P.)
## Photographer
## 1825-1905
## Active in Cincinnati, Helena, Montana and Seattle, Washington.

**Principal Subjects:** *Portraits, Scenes of African-American Life*

He began photography in 1845. That same year he opened a daguerrean gallery in Cincinnati. The following year he became an itinerant craftsmen because the gallery work had failed. He traveled to Pittsburgh, Pa. and Richmond, Va. earning enough money to return in 1847 in order to open another gallery in Cincinnati. Ball's Daguerrean Gallery of the West. Exhibited in his gallery was a 600-picture panorama of "Negro Life" in the Ohio, Susquehanna and Mississippi Rivers. He went into partnership with Alexander Thomas, and the name of the business was changed to Ball and Thomas. However, the partnership was dissolved several years later and Ball began to work with his son.

In the early 1870s, J.P. Ball and Son moved west to Helena, Montana. As opposed to his portrait work of whites in Cincinnati, most of his subjects were of blacks in the Helena area.

## CARY BETH CRYOR
## Photographer
## 1947

**Principal Subjects:** *Film*

Born in Baltimore, Maryland in 1947, she received her B.S. in art education from Morgan State University in 1969; and her M.F.A. from Pratt Institute in photography in 1971. She worked for three years in the film industry as a film editor and worked on the movie Claudine.

She took her own photographs of the birth of her child in 1979. Currently she is the Associate Professor of art at Coppin State College in Baltimore.

## BILLIE LOUISE BARBOUR DAVIS
## Photographer
## 1906-1955

**Principal Subjects:** *Landscapes, Portraits*

Billie Louise Barbour Davis was born in Kansas City Missouri in 1906. She was a graduate of Sargeant College, now known as Boston University. She married Collis Davis. The couple moved to Hampton, Va. around 1930 where they took positions at the Hampton Institute. Davis became interested in photography while at Hampton Institute and took up courses with the photo division there. Davis specialized in portraits and landscapes. Later her work was to become influenced by Edward Weston with her cloud studies.

## LENORE DAVIS
## Photographer

**Principal Subjects:** *Journalism*

Lenore Davis grew up in New York City and graduated from the School of Visual Arts. She exhibited at the Kodak Camera Club in Rochester and at the Women's Inter-art Center in Manhattan.

In August 1973, she was featured as the Art Direction Magazine's "Up and Coming Photographer" of the month. In 1983, she traveled to Thailand where she photographed the surrender of the communist insurgents and sympathizers to the Thai commander-in-chief. She is currently the staff reporter for the New York Post.

## ROY DECARAVA
## Photographer
## 1919

**Principal Subjects:** *Portraits, Urban Scenes*

Roy DeCaravа is an urban man. His existence in New York City prepared him for his destined work as a photographer. He began as a commercial artist in 1938 by studying painting at Cooper Union. This was followed by classes at the Harlem Art Center from 1940-1942, where he concentrated on painting and printmaking. By the mid-1940s, he began to use photography as a convenient method of recording ideas for his paintings. In 1958, DeCarava gave up his commercial work and became a full-time freelance photographer. Edward Steichen, a very important photographer at this time, began to study his work and suggested that he apply for a Guggenheim Fellowship. Winning the award allowed DeCarava the financial freedom to take his pictures and tell his story. One of DeCarava's photographs from this body of work appeared in Steichen's exhibition "Family of Man" at the Museum of Modern Art. Later, Langston Hughes worked with DeCarava to create the book *Sweet Flypaper of Life*.

DeCarava has worked as a photographer for Sports Illustrated and currently teaches photography at Hunter College, New York.

DeCarva's work can be found in many important collections throughout the country, among them: Andover Art Gallery, Andover-Phillips Academy, Massachusetts; Art Institute of Chicago, Chicago, Illinois; Atlanta University, Atlanta,

Georgia; Belafonte Enterprises, Inc., New York; Center for Creative Photography, University of Arizona, Arizona; *The Corcoran Gallery of Art*, Washington, D.C.; *Harlem Art Collection*, New York State Office Building, New York; *Lee Witkin Gallery*, New York; Menil Foundation, Inc., Houston, Texas; Metropolitan Museum of Fine Arts, Houston Texas; The Museum of Fine Arts, Houston, Texas; Museum of Modern Art, New York; Olden Camera, New York; Joseph E. Seagram & Sons, Inc., New York;

*Sheldon Memorial Art Gallery*, University of Nebraska, Nebraska.

### BARBARA DUMETZ
### Photographer

**Principal Subjects:** *Commercial*

Born in Charleston, West Virginia, she grew up in Detroit and moved to New York after graduating from Fisk University in 1969. From there she moved to California where she enrolled in a three-year program in commercial photography at the Art Center College of Design in Los Angeles. She began to do free-lance work in 1973.

### MIKKI FERRILL
### Photographer
### 1937

**Principal Subjects:** *Journalism*

Mikki Ferrill studied at the Art Institute of Chicago where she majored in Design. Born in Chicago, in 1937, Ferrill met Chicago photographer Ted Williams, and through his class discovered an interest in photography. Other members of the class included Roy Lewis, Bill Grant, and Chester Sheard. She was the only woman and the only beginner. In 1967, after completing William's class, she moved to Mexico, where she worked as a free-lance foreign correspondent. She returned to the U.S. in 1970. Her credits include published work in the *Times*, *Ebony*, and *Jet*. Her work has been exhibited at the *Sheppard Gallery* in Chicago, the South Side Community Art Center in Chicago; Lincoln Center in New York City; MOMA in S.F. and the Black Photographer's Annual Traveling Exhibition in the U.S.S.R.

### FRANCIS GRICE
### Photographer
### Active during 1850s

**Principal Subjects:** *People*

Born in Port-au-Prince, Haiti, Francis Grice was active during 1855 as a photographer and daguerrotypist.

### INGE HARDISON
### Photographer
### Active 1950s-1960s

**Principal Subjects:** *People*

A native of Portsmouth, Va., Hardison studied painting, sculpture, and photography at the Art Student's League in New York City. During the 50s, she worked as a free-lance photographer. She was also the Founding member of the Black Academy of Arts and Letters.

### ELISE FORREST HARLESTON
### Photographer
### 1891-1971
### Active 1919-1920s

**Principal Subjects:** *Portraits*

Elise Forrest Harleston enrolled in September 1919 at the E. Brunel School of Photography in New York City where she was one of two students to attend the photography school. She was the only female student. In 1921, following her completion she enrolled at Tuskegee Institute in Alabama. There she took graduate courses with C.M. Battey who was head of the Photography Division.

She married Edwin Harleston in Charleston South Carolina and together they opened a studio of painted portraits in 1922. She would photograph the sitters and he would work directly from the photos to create the portraits.

### FRANK HARRIS
### Photographer
### Birth around 1875
### Active in Philadelphia 1900-1930s

**Principal Subjects:** *Portraits, Street Scenes*

Harris had one of the largest studios in Philadelphia owned by an African American. He photographed social clubs, cornerstone layings, and the people of Philadelphia (both black and white). His photographs are in the private collection of Betty Lawrence, Philadelphia, Pennsylvania and in the Schomburg Center for Research in Black Culture, New York, New York.

### VERA JACKSON
### 1912

**Principal Subjects:** *Journalism*

Born in Wichita, Kansas in 1912, Vera Jackson moved to California after her mother died. There her family bought a farm. In 1930, she graduated from Corona High School, and in 1931, married Vernon Jackson. In 1936, she enrolled in a government sponsored photography program and learned to use the Speed Graphic and other cameras. Her teachers were George Manuel and Frank Wiggins. She also worked for the free-lance photographer Maceo Sheffield as his printer. He worked for The California Eagle where she was later hired by the editor Charlotta A. Bass as staff photographer

### LOUISE JEFFERSON
### Photographer

Born in Washington D.C., she studied at Hunter College. From 1942-1960, she was the art director and production assistant for Friendship Press, the publication art of the National Council of Churches. She is the consultant for the Gallery of Modern Art in New York. Her works have been exhibited at the Baltimore Museum of Art, the African

American Institute, the Schomburg Center for Research in Black Culture, the New York Public Library, and New York Bank for Savings. Her awards include a ULSL government Certificate of Recognition for Outstanding Achievement, and a Ford Foundation Fellowship Special Award.

### JULES LION
**Photographer**
**1810-1866**

**Principal Subjects:** *Architectural Studies, Portraits*

Born in Paris, France in 1810, Jules Lion was originally a lithographer. Lion was active in photography in the 1840s to 1860s. His work concentrated on New Orleans architecture and portraits of its leaders and people. He moved from Paris to New Orleans in 1837 and lived and worked there until his death in 1866. He is credited with introducing the daguerreotype to New Orleans. By 1840, he appears to have been fairly well established in the business of making pictures. He was also a successful painter, exhibiting his work at the Exposition of Paris in 1833, and awarded the honorary mention for his lithograph "Affut Aux Canards". In 1841, he and an M. Canova, another artist, founded an art school and from 1852 to 1865 he was listed as a professor of drawing at the college of Louisiana.

### LOUISE MARTIN
**Photographer**
**1914**

**Principal Subjects:** *Portraits, Commercial Photos*

Born in Brenham Texas in 1914, she graduated from Denver University where she earned a degree in photography. In 1946, she became the proprietor of the Louise Martin Art Studio, a portrait and commercial studio in Houston. She later opened the Louise Martin School of Photography in 1973 also in Houston, Texas. She was the only black photographer, male or female to become a member of the Southwestern Photography Convention in 1952. She later joined the Professional Photographers of America, the Texas Professional Photographers Association, the Southwestern Professional Photographers of Texas and the Business and Professional Women's Association.

### ROBERT MCNEIL
**Photographer**
**Active in Washington D.C. in 1930s**

**Principal Subjects:** *Portraits*

McNeill is noted for his photographs of the Roosevelt administration, particularly the "Black Cabinet," and the National Youth Administration, a work incentive program headed by Mary McCloud Bethune. A graduate of the New York Institute of Photography, he was appointed photographic consultant for the Works Progress Administration.

His work is in the following collections: Library of Congress, Washington, D.C.; National Archives and Records Service, Washington, D.C.; and the Schomburg Center for Research in Black Culture, New York, New York.

### GORDON PARKS
**Photographer, Composer, Author, Director**
(see writers section)

### PHILLDA RAGLAND-NJAU
**Photographer**
**1919**

**Principal Subjects:** *Portraits*

Born in Plainfield, New Jersey in 1939, Ragland-Njau became the first black woman photographer to be sent on an overseas mission assignment by the United Presbyterian Church. At 29, she was the manager of production for the filmstrip and photography section of the Commission on Ecumenical Missions and Relations—the Overseas Department of the United Presbyterian Church in the United States.

Her assignment occurred during the height of the civil rights movement. Many of her works were published in *Ebony*, *Jet*, and *Popular Photographer*.

She received her M.A. from Columbia University. In 1970, she was named New Jersey State's one of the most outstanding young women in America. Her husband, Elimo Njau, an East African mural painter, invited her to join the East African International Arts Program, which sponsored two art centers, one in Tanzania and the other, *Paayapaa Art Gallery*, in Nairobi, Kenya. She lives in East Africa and has, since 1974, been working exclusively with the overall program of the *Kibo Art Gallery* in Tanzania.

*A photo of Oprah Winfrey, by Gordon Parks, on the set of* The Color Purple.

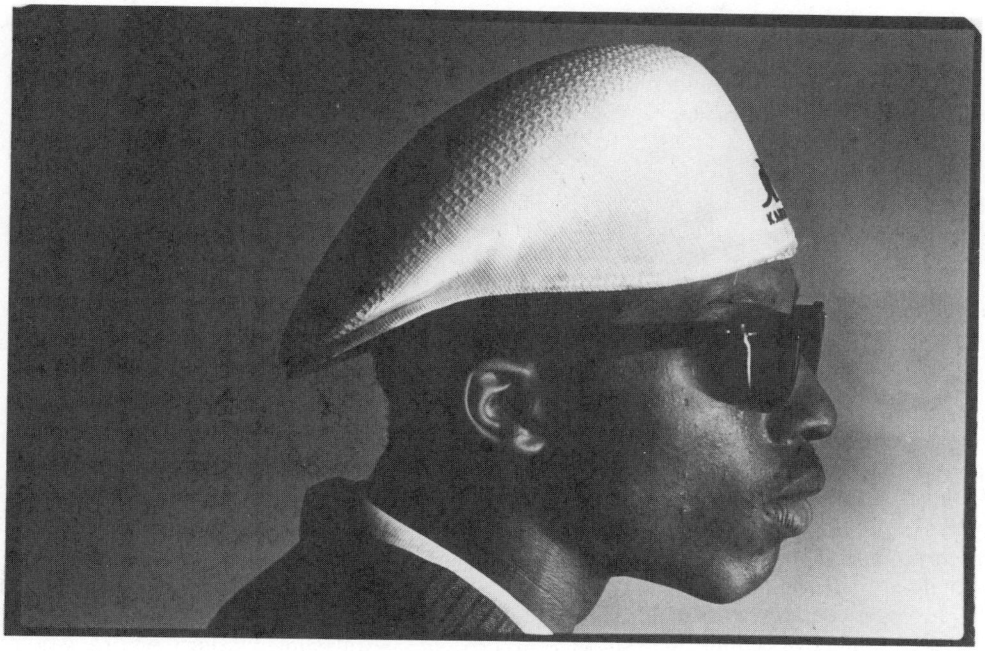

Jammin',
*by Coreen Simpson.*

### RICHARD SAMUEL ROBERTS
### Photographer
### 1881-1930
### active in Fernandina, Florida, and Columbia, South Carolina, 1920s 1930s

**Principal Subjects:** *Portraits, Group Portraits*

Roberts began the study of photography through correspondence courses and through his reading of photography books. With the assistance of his wife, Wilhelmina, Roberts opened his first studio in his home in Fernandina, Florida. Later Roberts moved to Columbia, South Carolina, and opened a larger studio in mid-city. A photographer by day Roberts worked at night as a custodian in a post office in Columbia. He advertised that his studio took superior photographs by day or by night. "To those who desire photographs made of parents and grandparents but can't persuade them to visit the studio, we say... Leave them at home. They probably love their home surroundings. Engage us to make that sitting at home. We will respond with pleasure."

The couple travelled throughout the state of South Carolina during the 1920s and 1930s, photographing church groups, schools, and community organizations. Roberts operated the *Roberts' Studio* until his death in 1936.

His work is in the following collections: Schomburg Center for Research in Black Culture, New York, New York; Wilhelmina Wynn, private collection, New York, New York; and Carolinian Library, Columbia, South Carolina.

### WILHELMINA PEARL SELENA ROBERTS
### 1887-1976
### Active 1920s-1930s

**Principal Subjects:** *Children's Portraits*

Married Richard Roberts (see preceeding biography) in 1902. Later, they left Florida to make their home in Columbia, South Carolina. She learned the basic skills of photography from her husband. Her specialty was portraits of children. Because of her interest and knowledge of fabric and her sensitivity towards detail she often contributed a touch of class to the appearance of her children by developing a special style to their clothing.

### ESLANDA CARDOZA GOODE ROBESON
### 1896

**Principal Subjects:** *Artistic Statements*

Eslanda Robeson, wife of Paul Robeson, was born in Washington, D.C. in 1896. She earned her B.S. in Chemistry at Columbia University. Robeson began studying photography in London while married to Paul Robeson. At first she used her photography for her scientific work and anthropological field-work. Her photos reveal philosophical ideas, a view of worldly political problems, and deep human compassion. The Robesons were friends with the Carl Van Vechtens and Carl talked a great deal about philosophy. Also in 1939, she met and became friends with photographer Edward Steichen after he made the well-known photo of Paul as The Emperor Jones.

### HARRY SHEPHERD
### Birth around 1850s
### Active in St. Paul, Minnesota, 1880s

**Principal Subjects:** *Portraits and scenes at and of Tuskegee Institute*

Shepherd opened his first portrait gallery in 1887. Shepherd advertised that "his patrons are among all classes—from the millionaires to the day wage worker." In 1888 Shepard had three studios.

Shepherd won first prize (a gold medal) at the 1891

Minnesota State Fair, and he exhibited photographs of the Tuskegee Institute at the Paris Exposition in 1900. Shepherd was one of the few black members of the National Photographers Association of America at the turn of the century.

### COREEN SIMPSON
### Photographer
### 1940

**Principal Subjects:** *Journalism, People*

Born in 1942, in New York City, she has worked as a free-lance photographer for the *New York Amsterdam News*, *The Village Voice*, *Black Enterprise*, *Encore*, and *Essence*. Her photos have appeared in the book "Harlem on my Mind" which originated at the Metropolitan Museum of Art back in 1976 and was released in 1979. She has had one-person exhibits at the Brooklyn Museum of Art, the *Addison Green Gallery*, and the *Tompkins Square Gallery* in New York City, and was associate curator of photography at the Studio Museum of Harlem and staff photographer. Her work is included in the Harlem State Office Building Collection, the International Center for Photography, the James Van Der Zee Institute, and the Schomburg Center for Research in Black Culture.

In 1982, she began working in the medium of design for fashion jewelry. The noted designer Carolina Herrerra, who exhibited Ms. Simpson's necklaces along with her own collection, said of the designs, "each piece is more magnificent than the last. " She has also designed a special collection of necklaces for Bloomingdales in New York City.

### MONETA SLEET JR.
### Photographer
### 1926

**Principal Subjects:** *Journalism*

Moneta Sleet was born February 14, 1926, in Owensboro, Kentucky. His career as a photographer began when his parents gave him a box camera. He continued his interest in photography through high school and then at Kentucky State College under Dr. John Williams, a family friend who was dean of the college and an accomplished photographer. After service in World War II Sleet returned to the United States where Dr. Williams offered him an opportunity to set up a photography department at the Maryland State College. This was in 1948. By 1950, Sleet had moved to New York where he obtained a master's degree in journalism. In 1969, Moneta Sleet was to become the first black American to win a Pulitzer Prize in photography. Although employed by a monthly magazine, Ebony, he was eligible for the award because his photograph of Coretta Scott King at her husband's funeral was used by a wire service and published in daily newspapers throughout the country.

Sleet also was awarded a Citation for Excellence from the Overseas Press Club of America, awards from the National Urban League (1969), and the National Association of Black Journalists (1978). His work has appeared in several group exhibitions at museums, including, in New York City, the Studio Museum in Harlem and Metropolitan Museum of Art. In 1970, a solo exhibition was held at the City Art Museum of St. Louis and another one at the Detroit Public Library.

### MARVIN AND MORGAN SMITH
### Photographers
### 1910
### Active New York, 1930s-1950s

**Principal Subjects:** *Harlem street scenes, portraits of authors, poets, performing and visual artists, historians, educators, and political figures.*

Twin brothers Marvin and Morgan Smith were prolific photographers in Harlem in the 1930s and 1940s. Their studio, located near the Apollo Theater on 125th Street, was frequented by performing artists, writers, historians and others of the Harlem community. Their cameras captured the Lindy Hoppers in the Savoy Ballroom and Easter Sunday in Harlem as well as the political rallies, street corner preachers, and the breadlines during the Depression.

Marvin, also a successful painter during the WPA, worked as a photographer's mate, 3rd class and as Chief Photographer's mate in the Navy in World War II. He was the first black American to attend the Naval Air Station School of Photography and Motion Pictures at Pensacola, Florida. His paintings won 2nd prize in the Federal Art Exhibit in 1934 and 3rd prize in the Art Exhibit in 1940.

Lindy Hoppers *by Marvin Smith.*

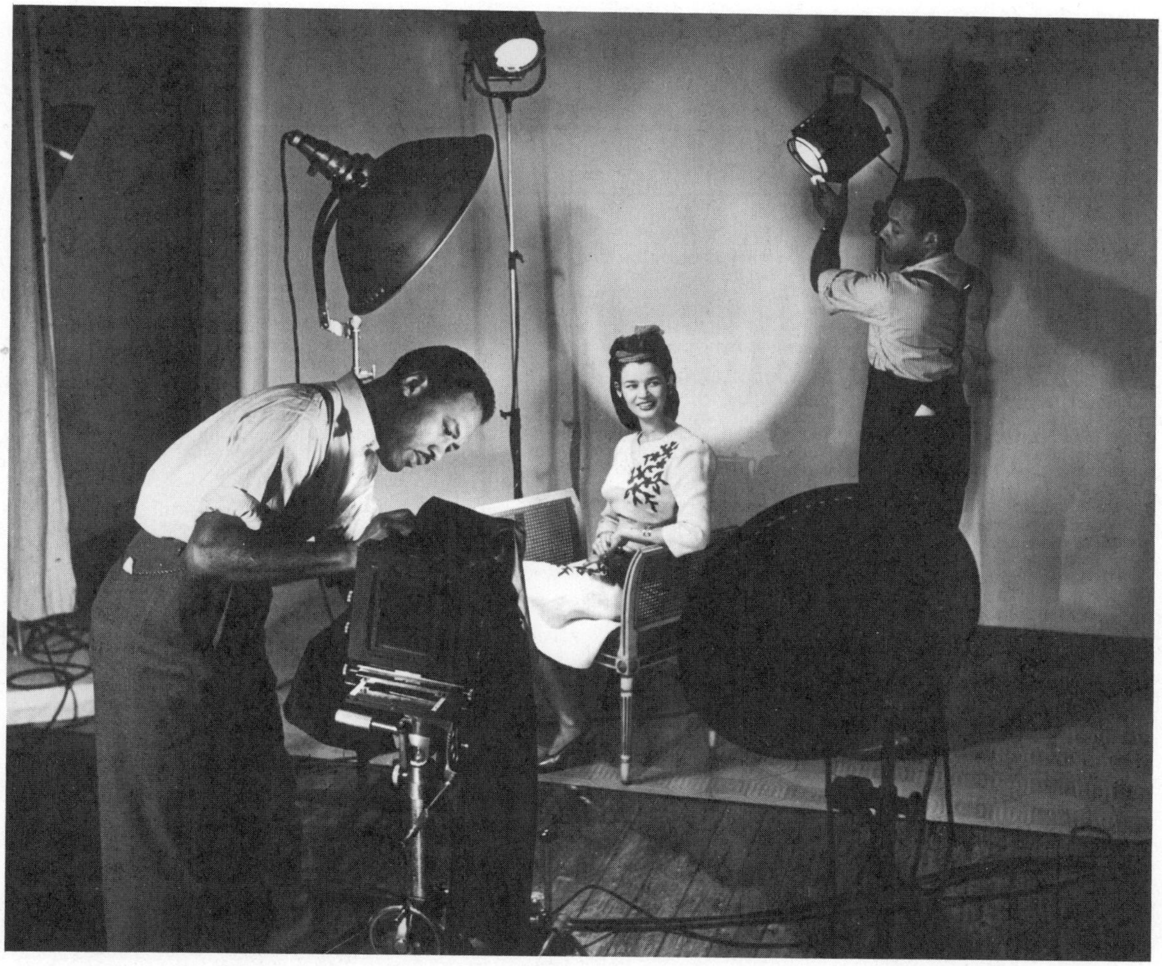

*Marvin and Morgan Smith setting up in their studio, around 1940.*

During the WPA Art Program, Morgan assisted muralist Vertis Hayes doing the murals at Harlem Hospital Nurses' residence. In 1937, his photographs of a little boy playing paddle ball won first prize in the *Herald Tribune* contest.

The Smiths studied art in France in 1950-1952, formed a newspaper picture service, and did pictorial editorials of Harlem and its leaders for the Urban League, *Ebony, Pittsburgh Courier, Crisis, Our World, Opportunity*, and *Travel Guide*. During, the 1950s, the Smith twins also worked as sound and recording engineers for local TV stations. Their photographs have been included in Claude McKay's *Harlem Metropolis, 1940*.

Over 30 photographs were included in an exhibit at the Schomburg Center's exhibition in 1982 entitled "Black Dance in Photographs, from the mid-19th Century to the Present", and 15 photographs were part of Tom Beck's 1982 exhibition entitled "Blacks in Labor 1850-1950" at the University of Maryland library. In 1982 an organization in New York comprised of contemporary photographers, *The International Black Photographers*, honored the twins for their excellence and contributions to photography.

The Smiths donated 2,000 of their photographs to the Schomburg Center's Photography Collection.

## ELNORA TEAL
### Photographer
### Active 1919-1960s

**Principal Subjects:** *Studio Portraits*

Elnora Teal was raised in Houston, Texas. She learned photography from her husband, Arthur Chester Teal, a photographer. Together they opened up the Teal Studio which was located in downtown Houston. She worked out of that studio while her husband worked out of a second studio on Dowling Street. Her work was of a high quality and she had an instinctive eye for portrait work.

## JAMES VAN DER ZEE
### Photographer
### 1886-1983

**Principal Subjects:** *Life in Harlem, Portraits*

James Van Der Zee was born on June 29, 1886, in Lenox, Massachusetts. His parents had moved there from New York in the early 1880s after serving as maid and butler to Ulysses S. Grant, who then resided at 34th Street in New York City. The second of six children, James grew up in a family filled with creative people. Everybody painted, drew, or played an instrument, so it was not considered out of the ordinary when, upon receiving a camera in 1900, Van Der Zee became interested in photography.

By 1906, Van Der Zee moved to New York, married, and took on odd jobs to support his new and growing family. In 1907, they moved to Phoetus, Virginia, where he worked in the dining room of the Hotel Chamberlin in Old Point Comfort, Virginia. During this time he worked as a photographer on a part-time basis. In 1909 he returned to New York.

By 1915, Van Der Zee had his first photography job as assistant in a small concession in the Gertz Department Store in Newark, New Jersey. With the money he saved from this job he was able to open his own studio in 1916, on 135th Street. World War I had begun and many young soldiers came to the studio to have their pictures taken. Over the course of a half-century, James Van Der Zee would record the visual history of Harlem. His subjects include Marcus Garvey, Daddy Grace, Father Divine, Joe Louis, Madame Walker, and many more.

In 1969, the exhibition "Harlem On My Mind," produced by Thomas Hoving, then director of the Metropolitan Museum of Art, brought James Van Der Zee international recognition.

## AUGUSTUS WASHINGTON
### Photographer
### 1820-?

**Principal Subjects:** *Portraits*

His father, an ex-slave, and Asian mother lived in Trenton New Jersey where he was born. Well educated by the time he had reached his teens, he had become influenced by anti-slavery readings and abolitionist meetings. His political interests were reflected in his photographs. He took portraits of W.L. Garrison and other abolitionists.

He had a brief career as a teacher in Brooklyn, New York and from there he moved to Hartford, Connecticut in 1843, where he opened a daguerreotype studio to help finance his college education at Kimball Union Academy and later at Dartmouth College in Hanover, New Hampshire. In 1847, he opened a second daguerreotype shop in Hartford, Ct. but soon left to travel. By 1850, he was back from his travels and working again. Both his studios apparently were successful.

In early 1854, he immigrated to the African Colony of Liberia where he worked as a teacher, photographer, farmer and store proprietor.

*James Van Der Zee captured, in photo, the character of Harlem in the 30s. This photo is titled* Couple in Racoon Coats.

## OTHER NOTABLE ARTISTS

| Name | Craft | Dates |
|---|---|---|
| Ron Adams | Painter | 1934 |
| Emma Amos | Painter | 1938 |
| Dorothy Atkins | Painter, sculptor | 1936 |
| Casper Banjo | Sculptor | |
| Malcolm Bailey | Painter, illustrator | 1947 |
| Jene Ballentine | Painter, architect | 1942 |
| Henry W. Bannard | Painter | 1910 |
| Cleveland Bellow | Painter | 1946 |
| Arthur Berry | Sculptor | 1923 |
| Eloise Bishop | Painter | 1921 |
| Betty Blayton | Painter, sculptor | 1937 |
| Gloria Bohanon | Painter | 1941 |
| Shirley Bolton | Painter | 1942 |
| David P. Bradford | Painter | 1937 |
| Peter Bradley | Painter | 1940 |
| Arthur L. Britt | Painter (abstract) | 1934 |
| Grafton Tyler Brown | Painter | 1841-1918 |
| Fred Brown | Painter (abstract) | 1941 |
| Henry Brownlee | Painter | 1940 |
| Margaret Burroughs | Painter, sculptor, illustrator | 1917 |
| Nathaniel Bustion | Painter | 1942 |
| Sheryle Butler | Designer | 1947 |
| Arthur Carraway | Painter | 1927 |
| William Carter | Painter | |
| Bernie Case | Painter | 1939 |
| Yvonne Catchings | Painter | |
| Mitchell Caton | Muralist | 1930 |
| George Clach | Sculptor | |
| Claude Clark | Painter | 1914 |
| Edward Clark | Painter | 1926 |
| Floyd Coleman | Painter | 1937 |
| Donald F. Coles | Painter | 1947 |
| Dan Concholar | Painter | 1939 |
| Eldzier Cortor | Painter | 1915 |
| Marva Cremer | Painter | 1942 |
| Doris Crudup | Painter | 1933 |
| Iris Crump | Sculptor | 1933 |
| William Curtis | Painter | 1939 |
| Emilio Cruz | Painter | 1938 |
| Alonzo Davis | Painter | 1942 |
| Bing Davis | Painter | 1937 |
| Dale Davis | Painter | 1945 |
| Charles C.Dawson | Painter | 1889 |
| Avel de Knight | Painter | 1933 |
| Murray De Pillars | Painter | |
| Robert R. d'hue | Painter | 1917 |
| Kenneth Dickerson | Painter | 1935 |
| David Diskill | Painter | 1931 |
| Jeff Donaldsen | Painter | |
| David Driskell | Painter | 1931 |
| Eugenia V. Dunn | Painter | 1918 |
| Eugene Eda | Painter, muralist | 1939 |
| William Edmonson | Sculptor | 1882 |
| Marion A. Epting | Painter | 1940 |
| Frederick J. Eversley | Sculptor | 1941 |
| Cyril Fabio | Sculptor | 1921 |
| Kenneth Falana | Painter | 1940 |
| William M. Farrow | Painter | 1885 |
| John Farrar | Painter | 1927 |
| Tom Feelings | Painter | 1933 |
| Allan R. Freelon | Painter | 1895 |
| Ibibio Fundi | Sculptor | 1929 |
| Reginald Gammon | Painter | 1921 |
| Herbert Gentry | Painter | 1921 |
| William Giles | Painter | 1930 |
| Robert Glover | Collage artist, painter | 1941 |
| Rex Gordeigh | Painter | 1902 |
| Robert H. Green | Painter (abstract) | |
| Donald O. Greene | Painter | 1940 |
| Stephen Greene | Painter | 1918 |
| Eugene Grigsby | Painter | 1918 |
| Henry Gridgell | Craftsman | 1826-1895 |
| Ron Griffin | Sculptor | 1938 |
| Wes Hall | Painter | 1934 |
| Phillip J. Hampton | Painter | 1922 |
| Edward A. Harleston | Painter | 1882 |
| John T. Harris | Painter | 1908 |
| Bob Heliton | Photographer | 1934 |
| Dion Henderson | Painter | 1941 |
| William Henderson | Painter | 1943 |
| Ernest Herbert | Painter (abstract) | 1932 |
| Felrath Hines | Painter | 1918 |
| Alvin Hollengsworth | Painter | 1931 |
| Humbert Howard | Painter | 1915 |
| Julien Hudson | Painter c. | 1830 |
| Howard Humbert | Painter | 1915 |
| Bill Hutson | Painter | 1936 |
| Suzanne Jackson | Painter | 1944 |
| Walter Jackson | Sculptor | 1940 |
| Daniel Lorne Johnson | Sculptor | 1938 |
| David Johnson | Painter | 1938 |
| Benjamin Jones | Painter | 1941 |
| Henry B. Jones | Painter | 1889 |
| Tonnie Jones | Sculptor | |
| Jack Jordan | Sculptor | 1925 |
| Cliff Joseph | Painter | 1922 |
| Ronald Joseph | Painter | 1910 |
| Paul Keene | Painter | 1920 |
| Gwendolyn Knight | Painter, sculptor | |
| Compton L. Kolowole | Painter | 1931 |
| Doyle Lane | Ceramicist | 1953 |

| Name | Craft | Dates |
|---|---|---|
| Raymond Lark | Painter | 1939 |
| James Lewis | Painter | 1923 |
| Larry Lewis | Painter | 1927 |
| Samella S. Lewis | Painter | |
| Tom Lloyd | Sculptor | 1929 |
| Juan Logan | Painter | 1940 |
| Juan Logan | Sculptor | 1946 |
| Willie F. Longshore | Painter | 1933 |
| Edward Loper | Painter | 1916 |
| David Mann | Painter | 1927 |
| Lloyd McNeill | Painter | 1936 |
| Leon Meeks | Painter | 1940 |
| Earl Miller | Painter | 1930 |
| Ron Moore | Painter | 1944 |
| Isaac Nommo | Painter | 1940 |
| William Pajaud | Painter | 1925 |
| Denise Palm | Painter | 1951 |
| James Dallas Parks | Painter, printmaker, sculptor | |
| Robert S. Pious | Painter, illustrator | 1908 |
| Larry Potter | Painter | |
| Leslie Price | Painter (abstract) | 1945 |
| Nancy E. Prophet | Sculptor | 1890 |
| William Pryor | Painter | 1949 |
| Noah Purifoy | Sculptor | 1917 |
| Roscoe Reddix | Painter | 1933 |
| Jerry Reed | Painter | 1949 |
| John Rhoden | Sculptor | 1918 |
| Gary A. Rickson | Painter, muralist | 1942 |
| Haywood Rivers | Painter | 1922 |
| Joseph Ronald | Painter | |
| Raymond Saunders | Painter | 1934 |
| Christopher Shelton | Sculptor | 1933 |
| Thomas Sills | Painter | 1914 |
| Jewel Simon | Painter, sculptor | 1911 |
| Walter Simon | Painter | 1916 |
| Merton D. Simpson | Painter | 1928 |
| Alvin Smith | Painter | 1933 |
| Arthur Smith | Jeweler | 1923 |
| Thelma J. Streat | Painter | 1912 |
| Rod Taylor | Sculptor | 1932 |
| Alma W. Thomas | Painter | 1896 |
| Lovett Thompson | Sculptor | |
| Roberta Thompson | Painter | 1928 |
| Russ Thompson | Painter | 1922 |
| Charlene Tull | Painter | 1945 |
| Les Twiggs | Painter | 1934 |
| Alfred Tyler | Painter, drawing | 1933 |
| Anna Tyler | Painter (abstract) | 1933 |
| Bernard Upshur | Painter, woodcuts | 1936 |
| Florestee Vance | Painter | 1940 |
| Ruth G.Waddy | Painter | 1909 |
| William Walker | Painter, muralist | |
| Carole Ward | Sculptor | 1943 |
| James Watkins | Painter | 1925 |
| Richard Waytt | Painter | 1955 |
| James L. Wells | Painter | 1902 |
| Jack White | Sculptor | 1940 |
| Walter Williams | Painter | 1920 |
| William T. Williams | Painter | 1942 |
| Ed Wilson | Sculptor | 1925 |
| Fred Wilson | Sculptor | 1932 |
| Stanley Wilson | Sculptor | 1947 |
| Estella Wright | Sculptor | |
| Charles Young | Painter | 1930 |
| Milton Young | Painter (abstract) | 1935 |

## OTHER NOTABLE PHOTOGRAPHERS

| Name | Dates of activity |
|---|---|
| John B. Bailey | active in Boston 1840s |
| Thomas Ball | active in Cinn. 1850s |
| Johnnie Mae Bomar | active 1940s-1950s |
| Alberta H. Brown | active 1930s-1940s |
| Benjamin Higgins | active in N.Y.born 1853 |
| Harvey Husband | active in Louisville 1880s |
| Anne Elizabeth Jackson | active1940s |
| Andrew F. Jackson | active in Dayton 1880s |
| John W. Johnson | active in Wilkesbarre, PA 1880s |
| W. H. Lawson | active in Louisville, 1880s |
| Henry E. Lee | active in Chicago, 1880s-1890s |
| Fern Logan | 1945 |
| John R. Lynch | 1847-1939 |
| Julia Jones | 1940 |
| Dora Miller | active 1940s-1950s |
| J. W. Miller | active in Mexico, Missouri 1880s |
| G. W. Minter | active in Kansas City, KA 1880s |
| Thestus Myzell | active in San Francisco, 1880s |
| F. R. Perryman | active in Chicago, 1880s |
| Elizabeth "Tex" Williams | active 1940s-1970s |
| Joycer Wilson | active 1940s |
| Ethel Worthington | active 1940s |
| Adine Williams | active 1936-present |
| Akili-Casundria Ramsess | 1942 |
| W.H. Ross | active in Sacramento, CA 1870s |
| Fannie J. Thompson | active in Memphis 1880s |
| Leah Ann Washington | 1942 |

# INVENTORS AND SCIENTISTS

**Anonymity and Achievement ■ Biographies of Outstanding Scientific Pioneers ■ NASA Astronauts and Scientists ■ Black Scientific Organizations ■ List of Inventions by Blacks**

America's earliest black scientists and inventors are buried in the anonymity that concealed their contributions prerevolutionary America. While Bannaker's eighteenth-century successes in time pieces and urban planning are known and applauded, numerous achievements of seventeenth- and eighteenth-century blacks in architecture, agriculture, and masonry cannot be identified. Thus, while it is increasingly recognized that blacks had a significant impact on the design and construction of plantations and public buildings in the South, and that rice farming in the Carolinas might not have been possible without blacks, the individuals who spearheaded these accomplishments remain unknown.

Prior to the Civil War, in one of history's most absurd bureaucratic fiats, slaves could neither be granted patents nor assign patents to their masters. The theory behind this was that since slaves were not citizens they could not enter into contracts with their owners or the government. As a result, the efforts of slaves were dismissed or, if accepted, credited entirely to their masters. One can only speculate on the part blacks played in significant inventions they are known to have worked on. One such area of speculation concerns the grain harvester of Cyrus McCormick. Jo Anderson, one of McCormick's slaves, is believed to have played a major role in the creation of the McCormick harvester, but available records are insufficient to determine the degree of Anderson's importance in the invention.

The inventions of free blacks were, however, recorded. The first black granted a patent was probably Henry Blair's 1834 seed planter patent. But again, records fail the historian, for the race of patent-seekers was rarely noted. Blair may well have had numerous predecessors. Other black inventions were not patented for various reasons, as was the case with ice cream, invented by Augustus Jackson of Philadelphia in 1832.

The Reconstruction era unleashed the creativity that had been suppressed in blacks. Between 1870 and 1900, though some 80% of black adults in the United States were illiterate, blacks were awarded several hundred patents. Notable among these were the shoe last (Jan Matzeliger, 1883); a machine for making paper bags (William Purvis, 1884); assorted machinery-lubricating equipment (Elijah McCoy, from 1872); an automatic railroad car coupler (Andrew Beard, 1897); and the synchronous multiplex railroad telegraph (Granville Woods, 1888).

The contributions of black scientists are better known than those of black inventors, partly because of the recognition awarded George Washington Carver, an agricultural scientist who, incidentally, refused to patent his inventions. However, it is not widely known, as this section reports, that black scientists contributed enormously to the development of blood plasma, open heart surgery, and cortisone, all vital ingredients of modern health care.

The achievements of black inventors and scientists of the mid-twentieth century have been increasingly obscured by reasons more complex than blatant racial prejudice. An important element is the replacement of the individual inventor by government and corporate research and development teams. Individuals, whatever their race, receive less recognition. Thus it is that creators of such devices as the computer, television, heart pacers, and lasers are relatively obscure while such names as Bell, Edison, and Marconi are imparted to every school child.

It is difficult to ascertain exactly how many black inventors and scientists have received patents in the recent past. We have gathered a few and have included them in the inventors patent list.

In recent years, there have been an increasing number of black students demonstrating an interest in science, and even more so since the death of Major Robert H. Lawrence America's first black astronaut. Therefore, black colleges in the 1980s have been advancing their curriculums in science and technology. Within the collegiate walls, students both black and white have begun training for future orbital flights. Already, African-American scientists and engineers are an integral part of NASA. African-American scientists and engineers of the corporate world and academia also play a substantial role in the development of solid state devices, high-powered and ultra fast lasers, hypersonic flight, and elementary particle science. These developments augur well indeed for the future increased impact of this under-recognized and under-rewarded group.

African-American engineers employed at NASA in managerial, as well as research positions, have and are making considerable contributions. However, government research [contracted or direct] work often renders individual recognition inconspicuous as it is frequently done in groups or in teams. Moreover, there are patent holders who are very reluctant to admit to having patents because of the security nature of their work.

African-American manufacturing and servicing firms in various computer and engineering areas are springing up and beginning to grow. For a variety of reasons, several exist that do not receive coverage in *Black Enterprise* , a magazine that explores black business in the United States.

Academia has more African-American science and technology faculty members, college presidents, and school of engineering deans today, in 1989, than there were eight years ago. Many of these academia are serving in the country's majority institutions.

America, as it faces the twenty-first century is confronted with a major challenge in science and technology from European and Asian nations. At stake are world leadership, maintenance of our position as a world super power, jobs for our citizens and the future standard of living for all Americans. The challenge has to be met in the elementary and secondary schools, and as of now it appears that our schools have not kept pace with the challenge. It is a problem that needs confrontation at the national level and a reshoring of public education at all levels.

## BIOGRAPHIES OF OUTSTANDING SCIENTIFIC PIONEERS

### GEORGE E. ALCORN
### Solid State Physicist

George Alcorn established himself as a good student and athlete while attending H.S. He had received a four-year academic scholarship from Occidental College in L.A. where he majored in physics. He received his degree with honors while earning 8 letters in basketball and football. In nine months, in 1963, he was able to complete a masters degree in nuclear physics at Howard University. During the summers of 1962 and 1963, he worked as a research engineer for the Space Division of North America Rockwell. His work involved computer analysis of trajectories and orbital mechanics for missiles [Titan I and II, Saturn IV, and the Nova].

In 1965, he earned his doctorate from Howard University in atomic and molecular physics. In the summers of 1965 and 1966, he did research on negative ion formation under a NASA grant.

He has produced innovations in the semiconductor industry. He holds 8 patents in the US and Europe. Among his eminent achievements are: adaptation of chemical ionization mass spectrometers for the detection of amino acids and development of other experimental methods for planetary life detection; work on secret projects concerning missile reentry and missile defense; the design and building of space instrumentation, atmospheric contaminant sensors, magnetic mass spectrometers, various mass analyzers; development of new concepts in magnet design and invention of a new type of high x-ray spectrometer. He also likes to teach complex science and math to diverse student populations.

### HAROLD AMOS
### Bacteriology

Dr. Amos had been with Harvard Medical School since 1954. He is Maude & Lillian Presly Professor of Microbiology and Molecular Genetics since 1975, as well as chairperson of the department.

He has had many prestigious grants and has produced much significant research through the years.

He earned his B. S. degree from Springfield College and a masters and doctorate from Harvard University.

## ARCHIE ALEXANDER
**Engineer**
**1887-1958**

Born in Ottumwa, Iowa, Archie Alexander graduated from the University of Iowa with a Bachelor of Science in 1912. Although advised by the head of the University to avoid a career in engineering because of racial prejudice, Alexander persisted and gained recognition. After working for a bridge construction firm for a time, he founded his own business, and in the next 11 years completed contracts amounting to $4,500,000. One of his most satisfying jobs was the construction of a million-dollar heating plant for his alma mater, using tunnels running under the Iowa River. In 1945, this institution awarded him an honorary degree.

## BENJAMIN BANNEKER
**Inventor, Mathematician, Almanac-Maker**
**1731-1806**

Benjamin Banneker's mechanical inventiveness led him, in 1761, to construct what was probably the first clock made in America—a wooden "striking" clock so accurate that it kept perfect time and struck each hour unfailingly for more than 20 years.

Born in Ellicott, Maryland of a free mother and slave father, who ultimately purchased his own freedom, Banneker himself was considered free and thus able to attend an integrated private school, where he secured the equivalent of an eighth-grade education.

His aptitude in mathematics and knowledge of astronomy enabled him to predict the solar eclipse of 1789. Within a few years, he began publishing an almanac which contained tide tables, data on future eclipses, and a listing of useful medicinal products and formulas. This almanac was the first scientific book written by a black American, and it appeared annually for more than a decade.

Banneker's major reputation, however, stems from his service as a surveyor on the six-man team which helped lay out the blueprint for Washington, D.C. When the chairman of the committee, Major L'Enfant, abruptly resigned and returned to France with his plans, Banneker's precise memory enabled him to reproduce the plans in their entirety.

## ANDREW J. BEARD
**Inventor**
**c. 1850-1910**

In 1897, Andrew J. Beard received $50,000 for an invention which has since prevented the death or maiming of countless railroad men.

While working in an Alabama railroad yard, Beard had seen men lose hands, even arms, in accidents occurring during the manual coupling of railroad cars. The system in use involved the dropping of a metal pin into place when two cars crashed together. Men were often caught between cars and crushed to death during this split-second operation.

Beard's invention, (patent # 594,059) called the "Jenny Coupler," was an automatic device which secured two cars by merely bumping them together.

## HENRY BLAIR
**Inventor**
**c. 1804-1860**

On October 14, 1834, Henry Blair of Maryland was granted a patent for a corn-planting machine, and two years later, a second patent for a similar device used in planting cotton.

In the registry of the Patent Office, Blair was designated "a colored man"—the only instance of identification by race in these early records. Since slaves could not legally obtain patents, Blair was evidently a free man and is probably the first black inventor to receive a U.S. patent.

Benjamin Banneker's
PENNSYLVANIA, DELAWARE, MARY-
LAND, AND VIRGINIA
ALMANAC,
FOR THE
YEAR of our LORD 1795;
Being the Third after Leap-Year.

PHILADELPHIA:
Printed for WILLIAM GIBBONS, Cherry Street

***Benjamin Banneker, America's first black scientist, helped plan Washington, D.C.***

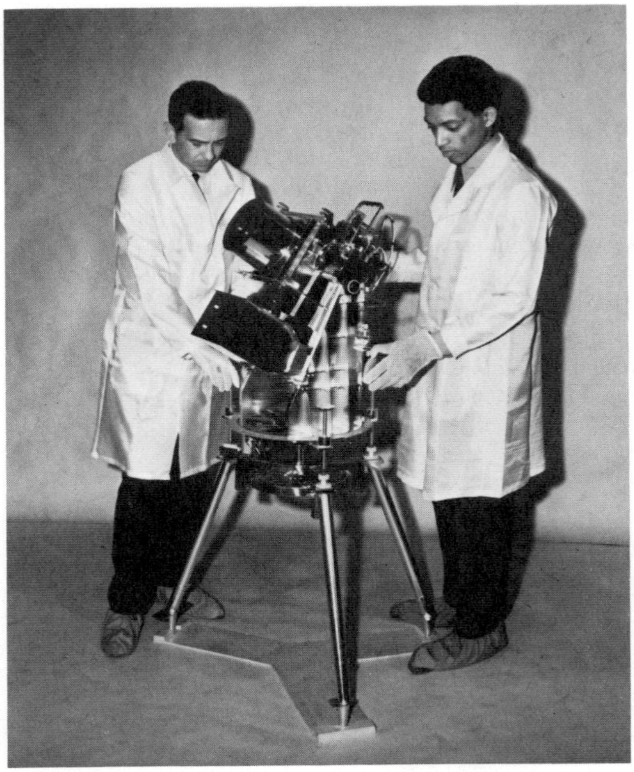

*Dr. George Carruthers (right) designed this lunar surface ultraviolet camera spectograph for Apollo 16.*

## OTIS BOYKIN
### Inventor
### 1920

Otis Boykin's career began as a laboratory assistant testing automatic controls for airplanes. Boykin invented a wide range of electronic devices, one of them a type of resistor now used in many computers, radios, television sets, and other electronically controlled devices. He also developed a control unit for artificial heart stimulators, a variable resistor used in guided missiles, small components such as thick-film resistors for computers, a burglar-proof cash register, and a chemical air filter. His innovations have been used both in the military and commercially. Presently, several products with Boykin components are used worldwide.

## GEORGE E. CARRUTHERS
### Physicist
### 1940

Dr. George Carruthers is one of the two naval research laboratory people responsible for the Apollo 16 lunar surface ultraviolet camera/spectrograph, which was placed on the lunar surface in April 1972. It was Carruthers who designed the instrument while William Conway adapted the camera for the lunar mission. The spectrographs, obtained from 11 targets, include the first photographs of the ultraviolet equatorial bands of atomic oxygen that girdle the earth.

Carruthers, born and raised on Chicago's south side, built his first telescope at the age of 10. He received his Ph.D. in physics from the University of Illinois in 1964, the same year that he started employment with the Navy. Carruthers is the recipient of the National Aeronautical Space Agency (NASA) Exceptional Scientific Achievement medal for his work on the ultraviolet camera/spectrograph.

## GEORGE WASHINGTON CARVER
### Agricultural Scientist
### 1864-1943

George Washington Carver devoted his life to research projects connected primarily with southern agriculture. The products he derived from the peanut and the soybean revolutionized the economy of the South by liberating it from an excessive dependence on cotton.

Born a slave in Diamond Grove, Missouri, Carver was only an infant when he and his mother were abducted from his owner's plantation by a band of slave raiders. His mother was sold and shipped away, but her son was ransomed by his master in exchange for a race horse.

At the age of 13, Carver was already on his own. By working as a farm hand, he managed to obtain a high school education. He was admitted as the first black student of Simpson College, Indianola, Iowa. He then attended Iowa Agricultural College (now Iowa State University) where, while working as the school janitor, he received a degree in agricultural science in 1894. Two years later he received a masters degree from the same school and became the first black to serve on its faculty. Within a short time his fame spread, and Booker T. Washington offered him a post at Tuskegee.

He held three patents:

| | | |
|---|---|---|
| 01/ 06/25 | #1.552, 176 | Cosmetics |
| 01/09/25 | #1, 541, 478 | Paint & Stain & Process |
| 06/14/27 | #1, 632, 365 | Process & production, Paint |

From the peanut, he derived 300 products; from the sweet potato 100 different products. He revolutionized the southern agricultural economy by showing how these many products could be made from the peanut. By 1938, peanuts had become a $ 200 million industry and a chief product of Alabama.

Dr. Carver never patented most of the many discoveries he made while at Tuskegee, saying "God gave them to me, how can I sell them to someone else?" In fact, in 1938 he donated over $30,000 of his life's savings to the George Washington Carver Foundation and willed the rest of his estate to the organization so his work might be carried on after his death.

Carver is buried alongside Booker T. Washington. His epitaph reads: "He could have added fortune to fame, but caring for neither, he found happiness and honor in being helpful to the world."

## W. MONTAGUE COBB
### Physician, Teacher, Medical Editor
### 1903

For 51 years Dr. Cobb was a member of the Howard University Medical School faculty. Therefore, thousands of medical and dental students have studied under his directions. At Howard, he built a collection of over 600 documented skeletons and a comparative anatomy museum in the gross anatomy laboratory.

As editor of the Journal of the National Medical Association for 28 years, he developed a wide range of scholarly interests manifest by the nearly 700 published works under his byline in fields of medical education, anatomy, physical anthropology, public health and medical history.

He was the first African-American elected to the presidency of the American Association of Physical Anthropologists and served as the chairman of the anthropology section of the American Association for the Advancement of Science. Among his many scientific awards is the highest award given by the American Association of Anatomists. For 31 years he has been a member of the Board of Directors of the NAACP and served as the President of the Board for many years.

He has received many honorary degrees, earned a B. A. from Amherst College, an M.D. from Howard University and a doctorate from Western Reserve.

## JOHNNETTA COLE
### Anthropology

Before becoming the first women and the seventh president of Spelman College, Dr. Cole was professor of Anthropology and director of the Latin & Caribbean Studies program at Hunter College. Prior to that in 1982-83, she was Hunter's first Russell Sage professor. She has edited *Anthology for the Eighties: Introductory Readings* and *All American Women: Lines That Divide, Ties That Bind*. Her essays on gender and race appear in several anthologies.

She received her B.A. in sociology from Oberlin College and her Ph. D. in Anthropology from Northwestern University. She taught at several universities before coming to Hunter College in 1982.

## DAVID N. CROSTHWAIT JR.
### Engineer
### 1898-1976

Some of David Crosthwait's inventions and patents include the automatic water feeder, 1920; automobile indicator, 1921; thermostat-setting apparatus, 1928; vacuum heating system, 1929; and the vacuum pump, 1930.

Born in Nashville, Tennessee, Crosthwait attended high school in Kansas City and went on to receive a B.S. and M.S. in engineering from Purdue University.

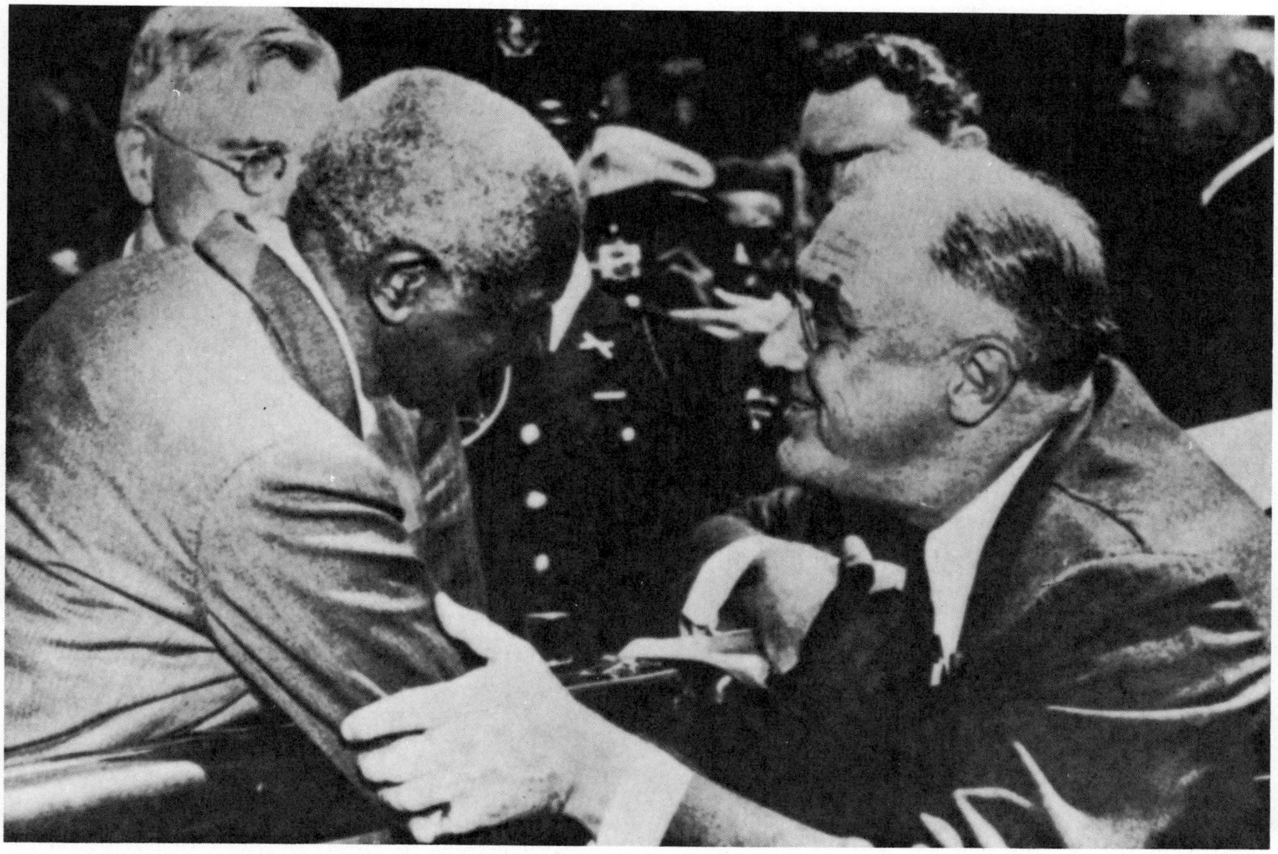

*George Washington Carver was the most prominent black agricultural scientist of his day.*

As a supervisor with the firm C. A. Durham of Michigan City, Indiana, Crosthwait designed and diagnosed heating systems and installations.

In his capacity as consultant and technical advisor to utility companies of metropolitan areas, Crosthwait helped develop the method and apparatus for heating the 70-story Radio City Music Hall in New York City.

He had at least 34 patents and 80 foreign ones relating to the design, installation, testing and servicing of power plants heating and ventilating systems

## ULYSSES GRANT DAILEY
## Surgeon
## 1885-1961

Ulysses Grant Dailey served for four years (1908-1912) as surgical assistant to Dr. Daniel Hale Williams, founder of Provident Hospital and noted heart surgeon.

Born in Donaldsonville, Louisiana, Dailey graduated in 1906 from Northwestern University Medical School, where he was appointed a demonstrator in anatomy. He later studied in London, Paris, and Vienna and in 1926 set up his own hospital and sanitarium in Chicago. His name soon became associated with some of the outstanding achievements being made in anatomy and surgery.

For many years an associate editor of the *Journal of the National Medical Association,* Dr. Dailey traveled around the world in 1933 under the sponsorship of the International College of Surgeons, of which he was a Founder Fellow.

In 1951 and again in 1953, the U.S. State Department sent him to Pakistan, India, Ceylon, and Africa. A year later he was named honorary consul to Haiti.

## CHARLES DREW
## Physician
## Blood Plasma Researcher
## 1904-1950

Using techniques already developed for separating and preserving blood, Dr. Drew pioneered further into the field of blood preservation and organized procedures from research to a clinical level. [This lead to the founding of blood banks as war was imminent]

Born in Washington, D.C., Drew graduated from Amherst College in Massachusetts, where he received the Messman Trophy for having brought the most honor to the school during his four years there. He was not only an outstanding scholar but the captain of the track team and a star halfback on the football team.

After receiving his medical degree from McGill University in 1933, Drew returned to Washington, D.C., to teach pathology at Howard. In 1940, while taking his D.Sc. degree at Columbia University, he wrote a dissertation on "banked blood" and soon became such an expert in this field that the British government called upon him to set up the first blood bank in England.

During WW.II, Dr. Drew was appointed director of the American Red Cross blood donor project. Later, he served as chief surgeon at Freedmen's Hospital in Washington, D.C. as well as Professor of Surgery at Howard University Medical School from 1941-1950.

He was killed in an automobile crash.

*Dr. Charles R. Drew developed the preserving technique for blood transfusions.*

*Frederick Jones stands in front of a refrigerated food truck based on his patents.*

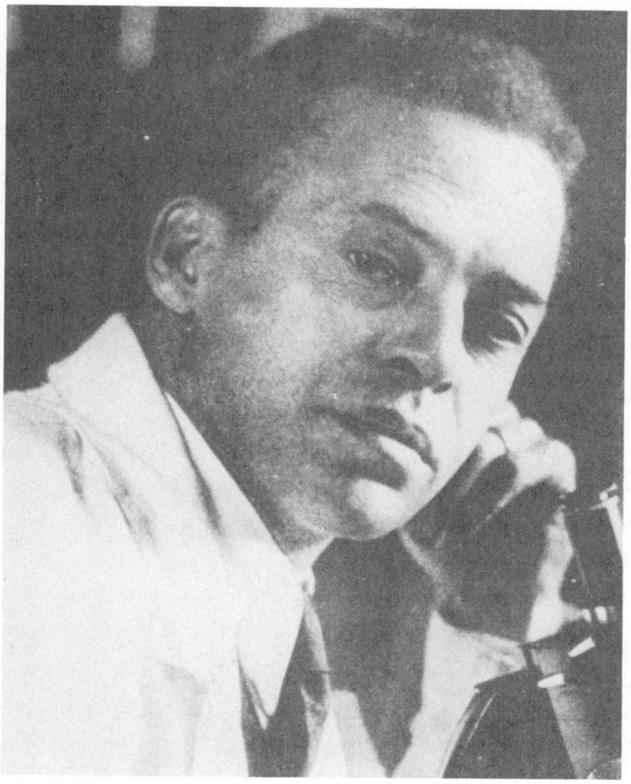

*Dr. Julian is credited with 86 patents. Some of his research helped to create derivative drugs used by sufferers of arthritis and glaucoma.*

**MEREDITH GOURDINE**
**Physicist**
**1929**

Dr. Meredith Gourdine was born in New Jersey and grew up on the streets of Harlem and Brooklyn. From his ideas in the field of electrogasdynamics (EGD), Dr. Gourdine built a million-dollar corporation, and through his manufacturing firm he found a successful method to use the principles of EGD to convert gas to electricity for everyday use. Dr. Gourdine attended Cornell University and received his Ph.D. in engineering science from California Institute of Technology. While a student at Cornell, Dr. Gourdine entered the Olympic competition in Helsinki, Finland as a broad jumper, missing first place by 4 centimeters.

**HENRY A. HILL**
**Chemist**
**1915-1977**

Dr. Hill hailed from Missouri. He earned his B.S. from Johnson C. Smith University in 1936 and his Ph.D. from MIT in 1942.

After considerable research in the areas of polymer chemistry and fabric flammability he became an authority.

He founded and became president of Riverside Laboratories in 1961. The firm did consulting in organic chemistry—particularly resins, plastics and rubber.

As an active member of the American Chemical Society [ACS] for 38 years, he became the president in 1977 when the organization was approximately 101 years old, with 110, 000 members. He presided over the northeast section in 1963 as chairman, and represented the NE section on the society 's national council for many years. He also served on the Board of Directors beginning in 1971.

In 1968, President Lydon B. Johnson appointed Dr. Hill to the National Commission on Product Safety.

**LLOYD AUGUSTUS HALL**
**Chemist**
**1894-**

As the chief chemist and director of research for Griffith Laboratories of Chicago, Lloyd Hall discovered curing salts for the preserving and processing of meats, thus revolutionizing the meat-packing industry. He has more than 100 patents registered for processes used in the manufacturing and packing of food products, especially meat and bakery products.

An honor graduate in science from East High School of Aurora, Illinois, Hall received a B.S. in pharmaceutical chemistry from Northwestern University. He continued his training with graduate work at the University of Chicago and University of Illinois and then embarked on his unique and fruitful career.

**WILLIAM A. HINTON**
**Medical Scientist**
**1883-1959**

Long one of the world's authorities on venereal disease, Dr. William A. Hinton is responsible for the development of the Hinton test, a reliable method for detecting syphilis. He also collaborated with Dr. J. A. V. Davies on what is now called the Davies-Hinton test for the detection of this same disease.

Born in Chicago, Hinton graduated from Harvard in 1905. In 1912, he finished his medical studies in three years at Harvard Medical School. For three years after graduation, he was a voluntary assistant in the pathological laboratory at Massachusetts General Hospital. This was followed by eight years of laboratory practice at the Boston Dispensary and at the Massachusetts Department of Public Health. In 1919, Dr. Hinton was appointed lecturer in preventive medicine & hygiene at Harvard Medical School where he served for the 34 years. In 1949, he was the first person of color to be granted a professorship there.

In 1931, at the Boston dispensary, Hinton started a training school for poor girls so that they could become medical technicians. From these classes of volunteers grew one of the country's leading institutions for the training of technicians.

Though he lost a leg in an automobile accident, Dr. Hinton remained active in teaching and at the Boston Dispensary Laboratory, which he directed from 1916 to 1952.

He died in Canton, Massachusetts.

## SHIRLEY ANN JACKSON
### Physicist

In 1973, physicist Jackson was the first African-American woman in the US to earn a Ph.D. in Physics which she was awarded from MIT.

Her activism on campus increased the black enrollment to almost 100 graduate students many of whom have received their doctorates. Since Dr. Jackson's graduation, she has been active at MIT and is a member of their board of trustees.

Since 1976, she has worked at Bell Laboratories in theoretical solid state physics. In the mid 1970's, she was visiting scientist at the European Organization for Nuclear Research in Geneva. In 1982, she lectured at NATO International Advanced Study Institute in Belgium.

Currently she is employed at Bell Labs in N.J. where she now specializes in solid or condensed state physics. She is studying and seeking to explain the behavior of physical systems at and below the molecular level.

Dr. Jackson is a native of Washington, D.C. She graduated valedictorian of her class from Roosevelt H.S.

## KATHERINE JOHNSON
### Aerospace Technologist
### 1918

Katherine Johnson was born in West Virginia and is an aerospace technologist at the National Aeronautics and Space Administration's Langley Research Center in Hampton, Virginia. Ms. Johnson was a pioneer in the study of new navigation procedures to determine more practical ways to track manned and unmanned space missions. Because of her work she was the recipient of the Group Achievement Award presented to NASA's Lunar Spacecraft and Operations Team. Ms. Johnson has also analyzed data gathered by tracking stations around the world during the lunar orbital missions—the moon shots.

## FREDERICK McKINLEY JONES
### Technician
### 1892-1961

In 1935, Frederick McKinley Jones built the first automatic refrigeration system for long haul trucks. Later, the system was adapted to various other carriers including railway cars and ships.

Previously, foods were packed in ice so slight delays led to spoilage. Jones's new method instigated a change in eating habits and patterns of the entire nation and allowed for the development of food production facilities in almost any geographic location.

Jones was born in Cincinnati. His mother died when he was a boy and he moved to Covington, Kentucky, where he was raised by a priest until he was 16. When he left the rectory, Jones worked as a pin boy, mechanic's helper, and finally, as chief mechanic on a Minnesota farm. He served in World War I, and in the late 1920s, his mechanical fame spread when he developed a series of devices to adapt silent movie projectors into talkies.

Jones also developed an air conditioning unit for military

*Dr. Samuel L. Kountz, an international leader in transplant surgery.*

field hospitals, a portable x-ray machine, and a refrigerator for military field kitchens.

During his life, a total of 61 patents were issued in Jones's name.

## PERCY JULIAN
### Chemist
### 1898-1975

Percy L. Julian was better known years ago than he is today despite the fact that he has a total of 86 patents—some as sole inventor and others shared. Some of Dr. Julian's research helped to create derivative drugs which were used by sufferers of arthritis. Currently, while the drug does give relief it is a drug of last resort inasmuch as the side effects are many, some of which could be serious.

Born in Montgomery, Alabama, Julian attended DePauw University in Greencastle, Indiana. He graduated Phi Beta Kappa and was valedictorian of his class after having lived during his college days in the attic of a fraternity house where he worked as a waiter.

For several years, Julian taught at Fisk and Howard universities, as well as at West Virginia State College, before attending Harvard and the University of Vienna.

In 1935, Julian synthesized the drug physostigmine, which is used today in the treatment of glaucoma.

He later headed the soybean research department of the Glidden Company and then formed Julian Laboratories in order to specialize in the production of sterols, which he extracted from the oil of the soybean. The method perfected by Dr. Julian in 1950 eventually lowered the cost of sterols to less than 20 cents a gram, and ultimately enabled millions of people suffering from arthritis to obtain relief through the use of cortisone, a sterol derivative.

In 1953, after being Director of Research for the Gliddens Co., he founded his own company, The Julian Institute in Franklin Park Ill. and another in Mexico. Years later, the Institute was sold to Smith Klein and French.

The Chemistry and Mathematics building at De Pauw University is named for him.

### ERNEST E. JUST
### Biologist
### 1883-1941

E.E. Just was a biologist who theorized and pulled together concepts and research [descriptive and experimental].of cell life and metabolism. In so doing, he became a pioneer investigator of egg fertilization, artificial parthenogenesis, and cell division. In 1939, his book *The Biology of the Cell Surface* was published. Many of his ideas and statements have only recently been confirmed. Moreover, he trained an entire generation of biologists who sought his help while he worked at the Marine Biological Laboratory, in Woods Hole, Massachusetts.

Born in Charleston, South Carolina, Just received his B.A. with high honors from Dartmouth and his Ph.D. from the University of Chicago. He began teaching at Howard University and by 1912 had become professor of zoology.

A member of Phi Beta Kappa, Just received the Spingarn Medal in 1914 and served as associate editor of *Physiological Zoology, The Biological Bulletin,* and *The Journal of Morphology.* He wrote two books and more than 60 papers on his field and served as vice-president of the American Society of Zoologists.

### SAMUEL L. KOUNTZ
### Surgeon
### 1930-1981

Dr. Samuel L. Kountz was an international leader in transplant surgery. He performed 500 kidney transplants, believed to be the most performed by any physician at that time. Dr. Kountz was head of surgery at the Downstate Medical Center and chief of general surgery at Kings County Hospital Center, both in Brooklyn, New York. Born in Lexa, Arkansas, he graduated third in his class at the Agricultural, Mechanical and Normal College of Arkansas in 1952. He pursued graduate studies at the University of Arkansas, earning a degree in chemistry. Senator J. W. Fulbright, who he met while a graduate student, advised him to apply for a scholarship to medical school. Kountz won the scholarship on a competitive basis and was the first black to enroll at the University of Arkansas Medical School in Little Rock. Dr. Kountz was responsible for finding out that large doses of the drug methylprednisolone could help reverse the acute rejection of a transplanted kidney. The drug was used for a number of years in the standard management of kidney transplant patients.

In 1964, working with Dr. Roy Cohn, one of the pioneers in the field of transplantation, Dr. Kountz made medical history by transplanting a kidney from a mother to a daughter—the first transplant between humans who were not identical twins. At the University of California in 1967, Dr. Kountz worked with other researchers to develop the prototype of a machine which is now able to preserve kidneys up to 50 hours from the time they are taken from the body of a donor. The machine, called the Belzer Kidney Perfusion Machine, was named for Dr. Folkert O. Belzer, who was Dr. Kountz's partner. Dr. Kountz died in 1981 after a long illness contracted on a trip to South Africa in 1977. The illness was never diagnosed and Dr. Kountz remained brain-damaged until the time of his death.

### LEWIS HOWARD LATIMER
### Inventor, Draftsman, Engineer
### 1848-1928

Lewis Howard Latimer was employed by Alexander Graham Bell to make the patent drawings for the first telephone, and later went on to become chief draftsman for both the General Electric and Westinghouse companies.

Born in Chelsea, Massachusetts, on September 4, 1848, Latimer enlisted in the Union Navy at the age of 15, and began studying drafting upon completion of his military service. In 1881, he invented a method of making carbon filaments for the Maxim electric incandescent lamp which he patented. He also supervised the installation of electric light in New York, Philadelphia, Montreal, and London for the Maxim-Weston Electric Company. In 1884, he joined the Edison Company.

### THEODORE K. LAWLESS
### Dermatologist
### 1892-1971

Theodore K. Lawless, one of the leading skin specialists in the United States, was born in Thibodeaux, Louisiana. He was educated at Talladega College in Alabama and at Kansas, Columbia, and Harvard universities before receiving his M.D. from Northwestern.

From 1924 until 1941, Lawless taught at the Northwestern School of Medicine and did special research in Vienna, Freiburg, and Paris, where he made valuable contributions to the scientific treatment of syphilis and leprosy.

The dermatology clinic at the Beilinson Hospital Center for Israel was erected largely through his efforts, and bears his name, as does a chapel at Dillard University in New Orleans.

In 1929, Lawless won the Harmon Award in medicine, and he was later awarded the Spingarn Medal (1954).

### ROBERT H. LAWRENCE JR.
### Pilot-Scientist
### 1935-1967

Air Force Major Robert H. Lawrence Jr. was the first black astronaut to be appointed to the Manned Orbiting Laboratory. Lawrence was a native of Chicago, and while still in elementary school he became a model airplane hobbyist and

*Dr. Arthur C. Logan was highly involved in the civil rights movement of the 60s.*

a chess enthusiast. Lawrence became interested in biology during his high school days at Englewood High School in Chicago. As a student at Englewood, Lawrence excelled in chemistry and track, placing top in the 440 and 880. When he graduated, he placed in the upper 10% of the class.

Lawrence entered Bradley University, joining the Air Force Reserve Officer's Training Corps and attaining the rank of lieutenant colonel, the second highest ranking cadet at Bradley. Lawrence was commissioned a second lieutenant in the U.S. Air Force in 1956, and soon after, received his bachelors degree in chemistry. Following a stint at an air base in Germany, Lawrence entered Ohio State University through the Air Force Institute of Technology as a doctoral candidate. At Ohio State, Lawrence earned a number of A's in courses such as nuclear chemistry, photochemistry, chemical kinetics, advanced inorganic chemistry, and thermodynamics.

Major Lawrence's career came to an end in 1967 when his F-104D Starfighter jet crashed on a runway in a California desert.

## ARTHUR C. LOGAN
### Physician-activist
### 1909-1973

Dr. Arthur Logan was born at Tuskegee Institute, Alabama in 1909. As a boy of 10 his parents moved to New York City where he received his middle school and high school education. After attending Williams College, in Williamstown, Massachusetts he went to medical school and received his M.D. degree from Columbia University College of Physicians and Surgeons in 1934. Wanting to work among his people, Dr. Logan interned at Harlem Hospital and had been affiliated, in one form or another with the hospital for the rest of his life.

During his many years of medical service to Harlem residents and others, Dr. Logan also headed NYC's Council Against Poverty in 1965 at the request of Mr. Robert. F Wagner, the former mayor of the City.

He was a Board Member of the City's Health & Hospital Corporation, a long time activist in the civil-rights movement, and a strong supporter of a wide range of community causes. He also contributed a great deal of time and effort to bring about their social realization. He was active with the National Urban League, The NAACP Legal Defense Fund and was an intimate friend of Dr. Martin Luther King, Whitney Young and Roy Wilkens. His home in New York was often a meeting place for the greats of the civil rights revolution of the 60s.

As a physician, Dr. Logan had many notable African-American patients, especially in the entertainment field.

Before he died, a hospital on Convent Avenue in Harlem was renamed for him as it was undergoing renovations to serve an underserved community in terms of private hospital care.

## MILES VANDAHURST LYNK
### Physician and Attorney
### 1871-1956

Dr. Miles Vandahurst Lynk, M.D., Esq., was born on June 3, 1871 near Brownsville, Tennessee. He was founder, editor, and publisher of the first black medical journal, the *Medical and Surgical Observer,* first published in December 1892. It ran for 18 months. At the age of 19, Dr. Lynk first received his M.D. degree from Meharry Medical College. Dr. Lynk was one of the organizers of the first black national medical association. The organization later became the National Medical Association. He also founded and was president of the School of Medicine at the University of West Tennessee.

## WALTER E. MASSEY
### Theoretical Physicist

He was the 1987 president-elect of the American Association for the Advancement of Science [AAAS], the largest general science organization in the country, first established in 1848. He served on the AAAS Board of Directors from 1981-1985. He is the first African-American scientist to serve as its president.

As vice president for research at the University of Chicago, Dr. Massey oversees Argonne National Laboratory for the University which operates a lab for the federal government. He serves on two committees of the National Science Foundation and on the Board of Trustees of Brown University and the Chicago Museum of Science and Industry.

Always interested in math, Massey states that when he became a student at Morehouse University at age 16, he was not well prepared. However, very good teachers and an especially committed physics teacher insured his preparedness for physics. He then began to see physics as an exciting way to use math as a means to better understand the physical world.

In 1966, he earned his doctorate in physics from Washington University in St. Louis, Missouri. He then received a joint appointment at Argonne National Lab and the University of Illinois. He shifted to Brown University in Providence, R.I. eventually becoming professor and dean of the college. While there, he was the originator and director of the Inner City Teachers of Science program, which trained science teachers in urban schools.

In 1979, he returned to Argonne as its director , a post he held until 1982, when he became vice president for research at the university.

Dr. Massey holds six honorary degrees and belongs to numerous professional organizations.

Despite his heavy scientific responsibilities, he gives vital time and effort to his community .

## JAN MATZELIGER
### Inventor
### 1852-1889

The shoe-lasting machine invented by Jan Matzeliger not only revolutionized the shoe industry but also made Lynn, Massachusetts, the "shoe capital of the world."

Born in Paramaribo, Dutch Guiana, Matzeliger found employment in the government machine works at the age of 10. Eight years later, he immigrated to the United States, settling in Philadelphia, where he worked in a shoe factory. He later moved to New England, settling permanently in Lynn.

*The shoe-lasting machine invented by Jan Matzeliger cut American shoe prices in half and doubled wages.*

The Industrial Revolution had by this time resulted in the invention of machines to cut, sew, and tack shoes, but none had been perfected to last a shoe. Seeing this, Matzeliger lost little time in designing and patenting just such a device, one which he refined over the years to a point where it could adjust a shoe, arrange the leather over the sole, drive in the nails, and deliver the finished product—all in one minute's time.

Matzeliger's patent was subsequently bought by Sydney W. Winslow, who established the United Shoe Machine Company. The continued success of this business brought about a 50% reduction in the price of shoes across the nation, doubled wages, and improved working conditions for millions of people dependent on the shoe industry for their livelihood.

Between 1883 and 1891, Jan received 5 patents on his inventions, all which contributed to the shoe making revolution. His last patent was issued in September 1891, two years posthumously.

Matzeliger died when only 37, long before he had the chance to realize a share of the enormous profit derived from his invention. He never received any money. Instead, he was issued stock in the company which did not become valuable until after his death.

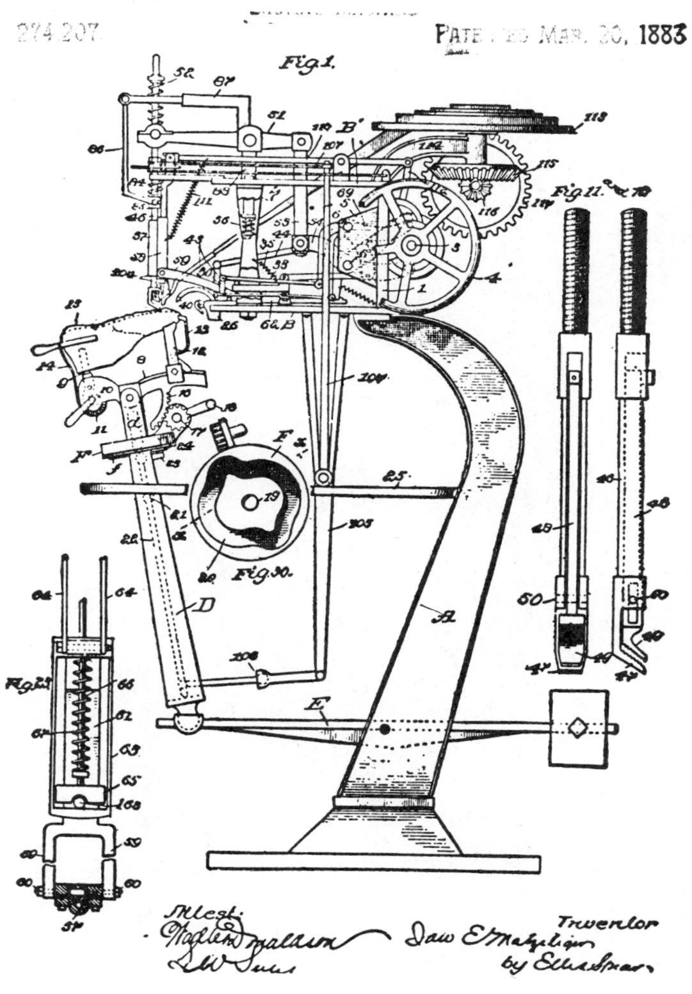

## WALTER McAFEE
### Theoretical physics, Math

As the highest ranking scientist at Fort Monmouth's Army Electronics Research and Development Command [ERADCOM], Dr. Mc Afee has had a fruitful 42 year career! He was senior scientist and scientific advisor to ERADCOM. In 1971, he was the first African-American civilian to attain the super grade [GS 16] in the Army. He retired in 1986.

His work covered a wide range of areas such as radar sighting, minimum detectable signal and radar range, radar coverage, radar cross-sections, antennas and propagation, nuclear weapons effects, designing and outfitting a lab for nuclear radiation studies, high-altitude nuclear explosions, passive sensing, and quantum optics and laser holography.

A highlight of his early career occurred through his participation in and his contribution to Project Diana, man's first radar contact with the moon in January 1946. This was a team project.

## ELIJAH McCOY
### Inventor
### 1844-1928?

Elijah McCoy's inventions were primarily connected with the automatic lubrication of moving machinery. Perhaps his most valuable design was the "drip cup," a tiny container filled with oil whose flow to the essential moving parts of heavy-duty machinery was regulated by means of a "stopcock." The drip cup was a key device in perfecting the overall lubrication system used in large industry today.

Born in Canada, McCoy moved to Ypsilanti, Michigan, after the Civil War, and over the next 40 years, acquired some 57 patents for devices designed to streamline his automatic lubrication process.

## W. DELANO MERIWETHER
### Research Hematologist
### 1943

Dr. W. Delano Meriwether is a clinical and research hematologist who has studied leukemia and sickle cell anemia. Dr. Meriwether is also known for his athletic prowess and is an award-winning sprinter. Born in Nashville, Tennessee, Meriwether attended Michigan State University on an academic scholarship. He left Michigan State after three years, and became the first black to enroll at Duke University School of Medicine in Durham, North Carolina. At Duke, Dr. Meriwether studied on a National Medical Fellowship from the Sloan Foundation.

Dr. Meriwether joined the Baltimore Cancer Research Center in 1969 as a clinical associate, and for a year he worked with young leukemia patients and researched the effects of experimental drugs on leukemic mice. Dr. Meriwether took up running, in evenings on a high school

*Both the gas mask and the traffic light were invented by Garrett Morgan. An early version of his gas safety helmet is shown.*

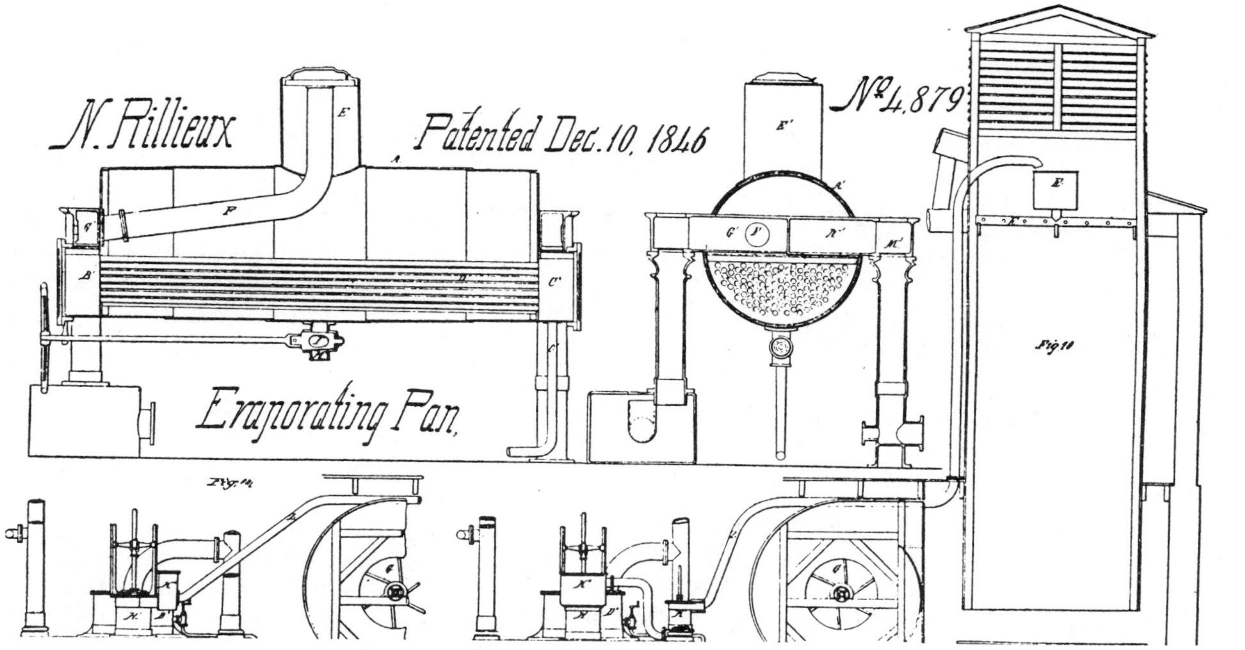

*Mechanical genius Norbert Rillieux invented the evaporating pan which revolutionized many industries, starting with sugar-refining*

track, to keep his mind off the tragedy of leukemia. In 1973, Dr. Meriwether received a White House Fellowship and was assigned to the Department of Health, Education and Welfare as a special assistant. He went on fact-finding missions to the Sahel drought area of the sub-Sahara, to South Africa, and to the Soviet Union. At the end of his year's assignment he became special assistant to Assistant Secretary for Health Dr. Theodore Cooper. He spent most of his time working on federal nutrition programs until he was appointed in 1976 director of the national swine flu immunization program.

## JAMES W. MITCHELL
**Chemist**

James W. Mitchell, an outstanding chemist, is best known for his contributions and achievements in advancing the accuracy of trace element analyses. For his research, Mitchell received the 1981 Percy L. Julian Outstanding Research Award.

A native of Durham, North Carolina, Mitchell is head of the Analytical Chemistry Department at Bell Laboratories in Murray Hill, New Jersey. In his research, Mitchell found techniques for identifying extremely small quantities of trace elements and contaminants in high-purity materials. He also worked on processes for producing ultra-high-purity chemicals.

Mitchell received his B.S. degree in chemistry from North Carolina Agriculture and Technical State University in Greensboro, North Carolina, and a Ph.D. in analytical chemistry from Iowa State University. He has published a number of articles and is co-author of *Contamination Control in Trace Element Analysis*.

## GARRETT A. MORGAN
**Inventor**
**1877-1963**

The value of Garrett Morgan's "gas inhalator" was first acknowledged during a successful rescue operation of several men trapped by a tunnel explosion in the Cleveland Waterworks, some 200 feet below the surface of Lake Erie. During the emergency, Morgan, his brother, and two other volunteers—all wearing inhalators—were the only men able to descend into the smoky, gas-filled tunnel, and save several workers from asphyxiation.

Orders for the Morgan inhalator soon began to pour into Cleveland from fire companies all over the nation, but as soon as Morgan's racial identity became known, many of them were canceled. In the South, it was necessary for Morgan to utilize the services of a white man to demonstrate his invention. During World War I the Morgan inhalator was transformed into a gas mask used by combat troops.

Born in Paris, Kentucky, Morgan moved to Cleveland at an early age. His first invention was an improvement on the sewing machine which he sold for $150. In 1923, having established his reputation with the gas inhalator, he was able to command a price of $40,000 from the General Electric Company for his automatic traffic signal.

Morgan died in Cleveland, the city which had awarded him a gold medal for his devotion to public safety.

## NORBERT RILLIEUX
**Inventor**
**1806-1894**

Norbert Rillieux's inventions were of great value to the sugar-refining industry. The method formerly used called for gangs of slaves to ladle boiling sugarcane juice from one kettle to another—a primitive process known as "The Jamaica Train."

In 1845, Rillieux invented a vacuum evaporating pan (a series of condensing coils in vacuum chambers) which reduced the industry's dependence on gang labor and helped manufacture a superior product at a greatly reduced cost. The first Rillieux evaporator was installed at Myrtle Grove Plantation, Louisiana, in 1845. In the following years, factories in Louisiana, Cuba, and Mexico converted to the Rillieux system.

A native of New Orleans, Rillieux was the son of Vincent Rillieux, a wealthy engineer, and Constance Vivant, a slave on his plantation. Young Rillieux's higher education was obtained in Paris, where his extra ordinary aptitude for engineering led to his appointment at the age of 24 as an instructor of applied mechanics at L'Ecole Centrale. Rillieux returned to Paris permanently in 1854, securing a scholarship and working on the deciphering of hieroglyphics.

When his evaporator process was finally adopted in Europe, he returned to inventing with renewed interest—applying his process to the sugar beet. In so doing, he cut production and refining costs in half.

Rillieux died in Paris on October 8, 1894, leaving behind a system which is in universal use throughout the sugar industry, as well as in the manufacture of soap, gelatin, glue, and many other products.

## HILYARD R. ROBINSON
**Architect**

Robinson was trained in architecture at the University of Pennsylvania, the Columbia University School of Architecture, and the University of Berlin.

In 1926, his design was chosen for the historic restaurant in the Henry Hudson Hotel in Troy, New York. In 1927, he received the first, second, and fourth prizes offered by the professional journal *Architecture*.

Robinson was responsible for organizing and conducting the slum housing survey in the District of Columbia in 1933. He was professor of architecture and chairman of the department at Howard University for 13 years. In 1934, he was appointed consulting architect to the National Capitol Advisory Committee and senior architect for the United States Suburban Resettlement Administration.

The $1.8 million Langston Public Works Administration Housing Project for Negroes was his most outstanding project. In 1940, he completed the Alabama Avenue S. E. government housing project and collaborated with Paul R. Williams in the design of the men's dormitory at Howard University.

## LEWIS TEMPLE
**Inventor**
**1800-1854**

The toggle harpoon invented by Lewis Temple so improved the whaling methods of the nineteenth century that it more than doubled the catch for this leading New England industry.

Little is known of Temple's early background, except that he was born in Richmond, Virginia, in 1800, and had no formal education. As a young man he moved to New Bedford, Massachusetts, then a major whaling port.

Finding work as a metal smith, Temple modified the design of the whaler's harpoon, and in the 1840s, manufactured a new version of the harpoon which allowed lines to be securely fastened to the whale. Using the "toggle harpoon," the whaling industry soon entered a period of unprecedented prosperity.

Temple, who never patented his harpoon, died destitute.

## ROBERT A. THORNTON
**1899-1984**
**Physics, Math**

Thornton was a 1922 Howard University graduate with a B.S. in Math and physics, a 1925 M.S. graduate of Ohio State University, and received a Ph.D. from the University of Minnesota in 1956. He did post graduate work at Princeton with Albert Einstein.

His professional career spanned 65 years and 9 universities, the last being Dean of the School of Science and professor of physics at San Francisco State University from 1956 to 1969. The physical science building is named in his honor.

## DANIEL HALE WILLIAMS
**Surgeon**
**1856-1931**

A pioneer in open heart surgery, Daniel Hale Williams was born in Holidaysburg, Pennsylvania. His father died when he was 11, and his mother deserted him after apprenticing him to a cobbler. He later worked as a roustabout on a lake steamer and as a barber before finishing his education at the Chicago Medical College in 1883.

Williams opened his office on Chicago's South Side at a time when Chicago hospitals did not allow black doctors to use their facilities. In those days, operations were often performed on kitchen tables in tenements scattered through the Black Belt. Dr. Williams helped put an end to this practice by founding Provident Hospital, in 1891,which was open to patients of all races.

At Provident Hospital in 1893, Dr. Williams performed the operation upon which his later fame rests. On July 10 of

*The toggle harpoon, invented by Lewis Temple, doubled the whaling catch of nineteenth-century New England.*

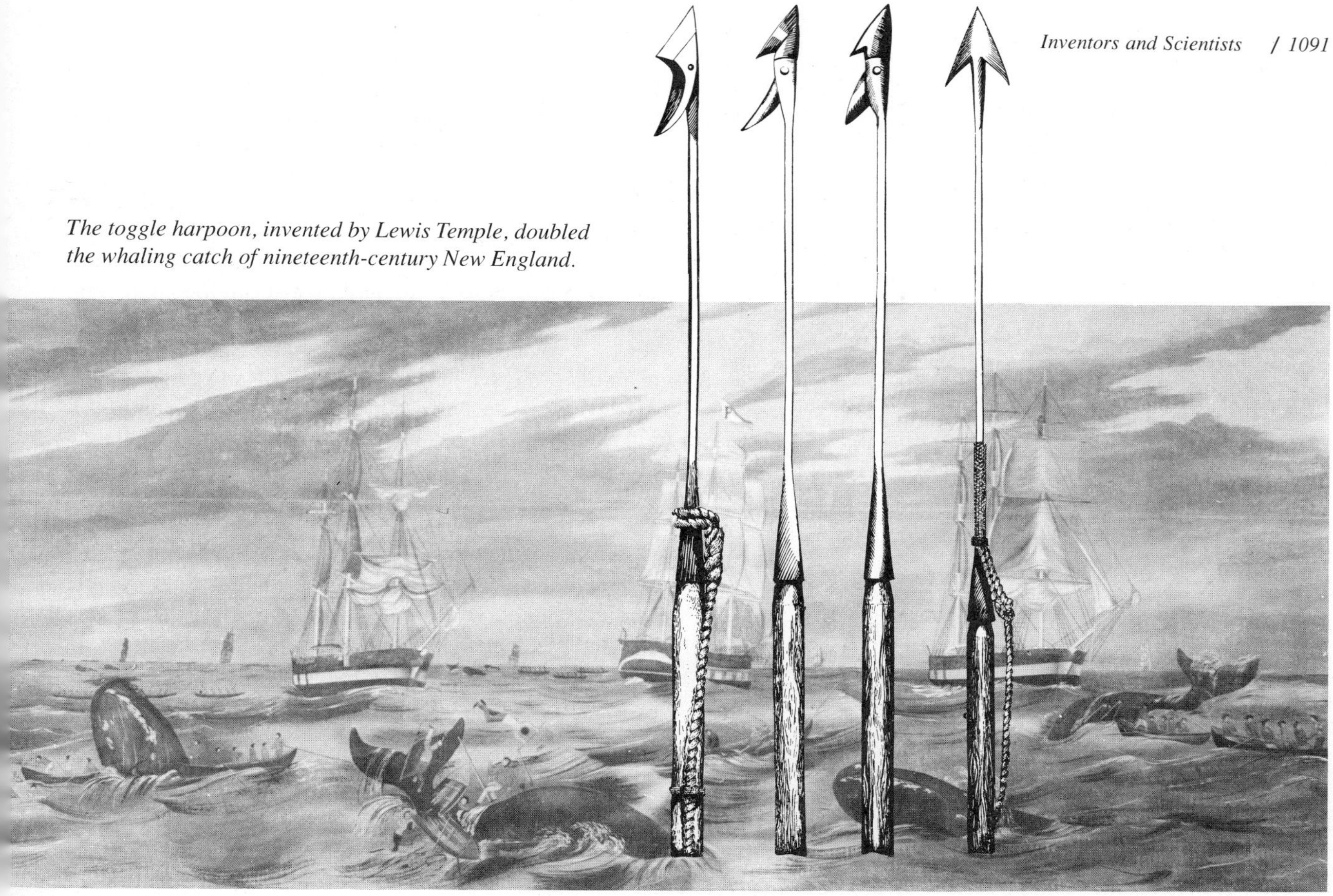

that year, a patient was admitted to the emergency ward with a knife wound in an artery lying a fraction of an inch from the heart. With the aid of six staff surgeons, Williams made an incision in the patient's chest and operated successfully on the artery.

The operation performed by Williams was an astonishing feat. The doctor began by making a six-inch incision and detaching the fifth rib from the breastbone, so he could settle down to work through a 2 X 1.5-inch opening. After securing the left internal mammary artery, he inspected the heart, noting instantly that the pericardium had been punctured by the knife. The heart muscle, too, had been nicked, but the wound here was not serious enough to require suturing or stitching. Dr. Williams then repaired the pericardium, sutured the chest opening, and completed the momentous operation.

For the next four days, the patient, James Cornish, lay near death, his temperature far above normal and his pulse dangerously uneven. An encouraging rally then brought him out of immediate danger, terminating the crisis period. Three weeks later, minor surgery was performed by Dr. Williams to remove fluid from Cornish's pleural cavity. After recuperating for still another month, Cornish fully recovered and was able to leave the hospital, scarred but cured.

An uproar of publicity greeted Dr. Williams' later announcement that his heart surgery had been successful. Much of it was negative, in the sense that skeptics doubted that a black doctor could engineer such a significant breakthrough. Unaffected by the notoriety, Williams continued a full-time association with Freedmen's Hospital, which he headed, prior to the founding of Provident Hospital.

Dr. Williams died in 1931 after a lifetime devoted to his two main interests—the NAACP and the construction of hospitals and training schools for black doctors and nurses.

At the first convention of the American Board of Surgery in 1913, he was inducted into its Fellowship.

## O. S. (OZZIE) WILLIAMS
**Aeronautical Engineer**
**1921**

O. S. (Ozzie) Williams was the first black person to be hired by Republic Aviation, Inc., as an aeronautical engineer. He graduated from NYU's College of Engineering with a bachelors & a masters in aeronautical engineering. Later he joined Greer Hydraulics, Inc., where he became a group project engineer and helped develop the first airborne radar beacon for locating crashed aircraft. Williams, a specialist in small rocket engine design, was also associated with the Reaction Motors Division of Thiokol Chemical Corporation. Williams joined Grumman International in 1961, and was in charge of developing and producing the control rocket systems that guided lunar modules during moon landings.

During the Appollo Space Program, he was the engineer manager responsible for developing the Lunar Module's reaction control rocket system.

## PAUL R. WILLIAMS
### Architect
### 1894

Paul R. Williams is a renowned architect of the environmentalist school which seeks to fuse homes to a closer feeling and relationship with their surroundings.

Born in Los Angeles, Williams graduated from Polytechnic High School and studied at the University of Southern California. He was certified as an architect in 1915 and worked in the office of a landscape architect.

Early in his career Williams conceived many fine civic and institutional buildings in the young, booming city of Los Angeles, including the Shriner Auditorium and the First Methodist Church. Movie stars and moguls observing Williams's talent then engaged his services to build many of their elaborate dwellings.

Commissioned by the national convention of Disabled American Veterans in 1952, he designed the memorial at Pearl Harbor that was known as the

Grave of the Unknown Sailor.

## GRANVILLE T. WOODS
### Inventor
### 1856-1910

During his lifetime, Granville Woods obtained some 50 patents, including one for an incubator which was the forerunner of present machines capable of hatching 50,000 eggs at a time.

*Inventor Granville Woods obtained some 50 patents.*

Born in Columbus, Ohio, Woods attended school until he was 10. He was first employed in a machine shop, and continued to improve his mechanical aptitude by working on a railroad in 1872, in a rolling mill in 1874, and later by studying mechanical engineering at college. In 1878, Woods became an engineer aboard the *Ironsides,* a British steamer, and within two years was handling a steam locomotive on the D&S Railroad.

In 1887, Woods patented the most advanced of his many inventions—the Synchronous Multiplex Railway Telegraph. This device was designed to avert accidents by keeping each train informed of the whereabouts of the train immediately ahead or following it by enabling communication between stations from moving trains.

Woods marketed this product, and others which followed, through his own company. A perusal of the patent files in Washington, D.C., shows Woods to have been an extremely prolific inventor. In the 20-year span between 1879 and 1899, no less than 23 separate inventions bear his name. In 1887 alone, he registered seven separate inventions with the Patent Office, all of them connected with the ingenious railway communications system he devised.

Woods died in New York City.

## LOUIS TOMPKINS WRIGHT
### Physician Surgeon, Medical Researcher
### 1891-1952

Dr. Louis Tompkins Wright, one of the country's outstanding surgeons and medical researchers, is known for the first extensive study of the intradermal method of smallpox vaccination, the design of a special brace for patients with head and neck injuries, the first use of chlortetracycline, a new antibiotic, on humans, and the use of drugs to treat cancer patients.

Dr. Wright was born in LaGrange, Georgia, and was a graduate of Harvard Medical School. In 1928, Dr. L.T Wright made major efforts to open for negro doctors the doors to integrated professional activity in the voluntary hospital structure of NYC. He was Director of Surgery at Harlem Hospital 1928-1939 and 1943-1952, and was responsible for the racial integration of the Hospital.

Dr. Wright was also an important force in the American Civil Rights movement and served many years as Chairman of the National Board of Directors of the NAACP.

In the late thirties, he became the second black surgeon to be awarded a Fellowship in the American College of Surgeons. He also became a diplomat of the American Board of Surgery by competitive examination after he was unsuccessful in securing admission as a founding member.

He was the first black person to be appointed to the staff of New York Hospital and in 1939 was also the first black to be elected to a fellowship in the American College of Surgeons.The last two paragraphs give inconsistent conflicting data

Posthumously, he was made Emeritus Director of Surgery of Harlem Hospital in 1972.

## BLACK ASTRONAUTS AND SCIENTISTS WITH THE NATIONAL AERONAUTICS AND SPACE ADMINISTRATION (NASA)

### Astronauts

#### GUION S. BLUFORD JR.
#### Air Force Lt. Colonel, NASA Astronaut

Born in Philadelphia, Pennsylvania, Col. Bluford received a B.S. degree in Aerospace Engineering from Pennsylvania State University and an M.S. and Ph.D. in Aerospace Engineering from the Air Force Institute of Technology.

Col. Bluford graduated from Penn State University in 1964 as a distinguished Air Force ROTC graduate. He then proceeded to pilot training at Williams Air Force Base, Arizona, where he received his pilot wings in January, 1965. Immediately following, he went to F-4C combat training in Arizona and Florida. In 1967, he served as a T-38 pilot and in 1971 as an executive support officer to the Deputy Commander of Operations at Sheppard Air Force Base.

Upon graduating from the Air Force Institute of Technology in 1974, he was assigned to the Wright-Patterson Air Force Base, as a Staff Development Engineer. He served as Deputy for the Aeromechanics Division and as Branch Chief of the Aerodynamic and Air-frame Branch Laboratory. He has written and presented several scientific papers in the area of computational fluid dynamics.

Col. Bluford was selected as an astronaut candidate by NASA in January 1978. He completed a l-year training and evaluation period in 1979, and served as a mission specialist on Shuttle Flight Number 8 in 1983.

Bluford was the first African-American to fly in space and did so in August 1983, after a Cuban of African descent had been in a USSR space ship. Bluford flew as a mission specialist whose primary responsibility was the deployment of a satellite from Challenger's cargo bay.

His second space mission involved a cooperative mission with the Germans, and a German astronaut was on board. Lt. Col. Bluford spent many months in Germany working with German scientists in preparation for the mission. Bluford speaks fluent German.

#### CHARLES F. BOLDEN, JR.
#### Marine Corps Major, NASA Astronaut
#### 1946

Charles F. Bolden Jr. Received a B.S. degree in Electrical Science from the United States Naval Academy and an M.S. degree in Systems Management from the University of Southern California.

Major Bolden began his career as a second lieutenant in the U.S. Marine Corps. In 1970, he underwent flight training and became a naval aviator. In 1973, he flew more than 100 sorties while assigned in Thailand. Upon return to the United States, Bolden began a tour as a Marine Corps selection and

*Four of the astronauts in NASA's Space Shuttle Program are (from left to right) Col. Guion S. Bluford, Jr., Dr. Ronald E. McNair, Col. Frederick D. Gregory, and Lt. Col. Charles F. Bolden, Jr.*

*Astronuaut Mae C. Jemison M.D.*

recruiting officer. In 1979, he graduated from the U.S. Naval Test Pilot School, and was assigned to the Naval Test Aircraft Directorates. He has logged more than 2,600 hours flying time including 2,300 hours in jet aircraft.

Major Bolden was selected as an astronaut candidate by NASA in May 1980, and in July 1981 completed a l-year training and evaluation program—making him eligible for assignment as a pilot on future space shuttle flight crews.

## FREDERICK D. GREGORY
## Air Force Colonel, NASA Astronaut

Gregory received a B.S. degree from the United States Air Force Academy in 1964, and also holds an M.S. degree in Information Systems from George Washington University.

From 1971 until 1977, Gregory was research/engineering test pilot for the Air Force at Wright-Patterson Air Force Base and for NASA at Langley Research Center. He has flown more than 40 different types of military and civilian aircraft including gliders. He has logged over 4,100 hours flight time and holds an FAA commercial and instrument certificate for single-and multi-engine and rotary aircraft. He has authored several papers in the areas of aircraft handling qualities and flight controllers.

Colonel Gregory was selected as an astronaut candidate by NASA in 1978 and is now eligible for assignment as a pilot on future space shuttle flight crews. He has received many military awards and is a member of several military and civilian organizations. He has been assigned to Shuttle Flight No. 18 as a pilot.

## MAE C. JEMISON M.D.
## NASA Astronaut, First Black Woman Candidate

This 30-year-old physician, general practioner is one of 15 candidates chosen from 2,000 qualified applicants. She considers this candidacy a great challenge.

Mae Jemison attended Morgan Park High school in Chicago. In 1977, she graduated from Stanford University with majors in chemical engineering and Afro-American Studies. After graduating from Cornell Medical school in 1981, she interned in Los Angeles.

In 1983 she worked as a staff physician in the Peace Corp in Sierra Leone for two and a half years.

## RONALD E. MCNAIR
## NASA Astronaut
## 1950-1986

A graduate of North Carolina A & T State University with a B.S. degree in Physics, McNair also received a Doctor of Philosophy in Physics from Massachusetts Institute of Technology. He was presented an honorary Doctorate of Laws from North Carolina A & T in 1978.

Dr. McNair was selected as an astronaut candidate by NASA in January 1978. He was working in optical physics in 1978 when he was selected to train as an astronaut. In August 1979, he completed a one-year training and evaluation period that made him eligible for assignment as mission specialist on space shuttle flight crews. He has presented papers in the areas of lasers and molecular spectroscopy, and has given many presentations in the United States and Europe. He was the second African-American to orbit the earth on a NASA Mission.

Despite the rigorous training in the NASA program, he taught karate at a church, played the saxophone and found time to talk to young people.

Dr. McNair was aboard the flawed shuttle Challenger which exploded shortly after lift-off from Cape Kennedy and plunged into the waters off the Florida coast in January 1986. The shuttle had a crew of seven persons , including two women, a mission specialist and a teacher-in-space participant.

### Black Scientists And Specialists With NASA

## HARRISON ALLEN JR.
## Chemical Engineer

A graduate of Cleveland State University, Mr. Allen received a Bachelor of Science degree in Chemical Engineering. He has also done graduate work at Case Western Reserve University.

Allen is the Technology Utilization Officer at the Lewis Research Center where he has specialized in the fields of high energy fuels, supersonic combustion, and solid rocket ignition. He has written many technical papers and holds a U.S. patent on the ignition of solid propellant rocket motors.

### LEWIS E. ANDREWS
### Mathematics and Chemistry

A graduate of Alabama A & M University with a B.S. degree in Mathematics and Chemistry, Andrews also received an M.S. degree in Systems Management from the University of Southern California.

Andrews began his career in the field of environmental management as a space scientist at NASA's Marshall Space Flight Center where he conducted research and managed studies on natural environmental parameters for space flight missions. He is currently an environmental manager at NASA Headquarters. His duties include managing NASA activities under the National Environmental Policy Act, Executive Order 12088, and various environmental conservation laws and regulations.

Andrews has received several honors and was recently selected to attend the Office of Personnel Management Executive Seminar at Oak Ridge, Tennessee.

### DR. ALBERT C. ANTOINE
### Chemistry

Dr. Antoine received his B.S. degree from the City College of New York in 1946 and was awarded his doctorate in Chemistry from Ohio State University in 1953.

Dr. Antoine joined the NASA Lewis Research Center staff in 1954. He has conducted research on the synthesis of high-energy fuels for jet aircraft, the physical properties and combustion characteristics of rocket fuels, and the thermodynamic properties of alkali-metal liquid amalgams. He served as project manager involving basic investigations of batteries. He was also responsible for a program to evaluate instruments designed for identifying and measuring organic constituents in airborne particulate matter. Dr. Antoine is presently responsible for the characterization of jet fuels. He is a member of the American Chemical Society and is listed in American Men of Science.

### RUTH P. BLAIR
### Management technician

Ruth Blair graduated from Loyola University, in New Orleans, LA, where she received a degree in Business Administration,

Mrs. Blair also studied at Dillard University. A native of New Orleans, Blair began working with NASA as a management technician at the Marshall Space Flight Center in 1964. She was selected for participation in the Specialty Training for Entry Professionals Program (STEP) as a program analyst in 1975. Ruth works as a contract specialist, a position which she acquired through Marshall's Professional Intern Program in 1976.

*Lawrence J. Caw at the Advanced Fighter Technology Integration Mission Adaptive Wing Research Program.*

### LONNIE BLOCKER
### Mathematics and Chemistry

Received a Bachelor of Science degree in Mathematics/ Chemistry from Bethune-Cookman College in Daytona Beach, FL in 1963. Mr. Blocker also received a Master of Commercial Science degree in General Management in 1969 from Rollins College, Winter Park, FL.

Blocker began working for NASA as a technical management specialist at Kennedy Space Center in 1963. He is currently working as an aerospace technologist in the Design Engineering Directorate at Kennedy Space Center where he coordinates design engineering policies, plans, and procedures, and also the development, coordination, and maintenance of the STS/Cargo facility, systems, and equipment baseline.

He is active in the community and has received several awards for his civic accomplishments.

### CHARLES A. BROWN
### Aeronautical Engineering

Charles Brown received an Associate degree in Engineering Drafting from Franklin University (Columbus, Ohio) and a B.S. degree in Aeronautical Engineering from Tri-State University (Indiana). He has also received an M.B.A. degree from Golden Gate University.

Brown joined NASA in 1977 as a Data System Engineer at the Dryden Flight Research Facility. Presently he serves as Shuttle Facilities Manager where his responsibilities include the technical management and coordination of the activation and validation of shuttle facility systems, conducting major tests, and the development and maintenance of shuttle facilities operational schedules.

### LAWRENCE J. CAW
### Mathematics and Physics

A graduate of Wichita University in Kansas, in 1962, with a B.A. degree in Mathematics and Physics, Mr. Caw has done graduate work at UCLA and USC in Aerospace Engineering, Mathematics, Computer Science, and Business Management.

Born in Wichita, Kansas, Caw joined NASA's Dryden Flight Space Research Facility in 1962 as a simulation engineer. Since then, he has worked as a computer operations engineer, a flight test engineer, and a manager for the Advanced Fighter Technology Integration Mission Adaptive Wing Research Program.

### HENRY J. CLARKS III
### Systems Engineering

Henry Clarks III was born in Charenton, Louisiana, received his B.S. in Electronics from Southern University, and his MSA in Management Engineering from George Washington University. He has done post-graduate work at George Washington University and Virginia Polytechnic Institute in Systems Engineering. He was selected as a NASA Headquarters nominee to attend the Graduate School of Business Administration at Harvard University.

At NASA, he is responsible for the development and negotiations of launch agreements with domestic and international customers for expendable launch vehicle launchings of communications satellites, and for assisting in the development of agreements for similar Space Shuttle launchings. His customers include Italy, Japan, Canada, etc. He has received numerous awards including NASA's Outstanding Performance, Superior Accomplishment, and Sustained Superior Performance awards.

### KATHERINE L. CLINTON
### Electrical Engineer

A graduate of Albany State College, Albany, Georgia, Katherine Clinton has also done graduate work at Florida Institute of Technology.

Mrs. Clinton is an electrical engineer at the Kennedy Space Center in the Electrical Systems Branch of the Experiments Processing Division. Her responsibilities include the development of mission dependent ground application software for the Spacelab Payload Checkout Unit and for the High Data Rate Mix Interface Test System/ Experiment Checkout Equipment Processor (HITS/ECEP). She also acts as a liaison for the experimenters for the resolution of technical problems that may arise. Mrs. Clinton is the first black female engineer hired at Kennedy Space Center.

### DR. CHRISTINE MANN DARDEN
### Aerospace Engineer

Christine Darden, graduated from Hampton Institute with a B.S. degree in mathematics, and received a Master of Science degree in mathematics from Virginia State College. She has done extensive graduate work at the University of Virginia and the College of William and Mary, and was recently awarded a Doctor of Science degree in Mechanical Engineering at George Washington University.

Ms. Darden joined NASA in 1967 as a data analyst at the Langley Research Center. She is now an aerospace engineer in the high-speed aerodynamics division. Darden is the author of several technical papers and is a member of Langley's Exchange Council. She is a member of the American Institute of Aeronautics and Astronautics (AIAA) and is an officer in the Hampton Roads Chapter of the National Technical Association (NTA).

### DR. JULIAN M. EARLS
### Radiation Physics

A graduate of Norfolk State College with a B.S. degree in Physics, Dr. Earls also holds an M.S. in Physics from the University of Rochester, an M.S. in Environmental Science, and a Ph.D. in Radiation Physics from the University of Michigan.

A native of Portsmouth, Va., Dr. Earls joined NASA at the Lewis Research Center in 1965. In 1968, became head of the Health Physics Section, becoming one of the youngest managers in NASA's history. Dr. Earls is also an adjunct professor at Cuyahoga Community College and Cleveland

State University, and has received numerous awards for academic and professional excellence. Among these are: honored by Ohio House of Representatives for contributions to the community and the state, 1974; former president of the National Technical Association; and Distinguished Young Black American, 1973.

In 1979, Dr. Earls was selected by NASA to attend the program for management development at Harvard Business School. He is currently Chief of the Health, Safety and Security Division at Lewis Research Center.

### NETTIE D. FAULCON
### Engineer

An honor graduate of Norfolk State College with a B.S. degree in Physics, Faulcon also received a Master of Science degree in Engineering from George Washington University in 1978.

Faulcon began with NASA as a co-op student in 1967 at the Langley Research Center, where she received training in various divisions. In 1970, she joined the professional staff as an aerospace technologist assigned to the Instrument Research Division. In this position she performs research in acoustic and structural dynamics instrumentation, using a mini-computer centered system. Faulcon has authored several technical papers and is a member of the National Technical Association (N.T.A.). She is also listed in Who's Who in the South and Southwest, 1980.

### CLYDE FOSTER
### Mathematics and Chemistry

A 1954 graduate of Alabama A & M University with a B.S. degree in Mathematics and Chemistry, Clyde Foster has also done post-graduate work in Mathematics at Alabama A & M University and the University of Alabama.

A native of Birmingham, Alabama, Foster joined NASA in 1960 as a computer specialist when the Marshall Space Flight Center was created. He has served as a mathematics instructor in the Center's Computation Laboratory and is currently the Director of the Center's Equal Opportunity Office. He is very active in his community of Triana, Alabama, where he has served as Mayor for many years. Foster has received numerous citations and awards. Among his NASA awards are the Apollo Achievement Award and the Commendation Achievement Award.

### JOSEPH FULLER
### Physics and Mathematics

Joseph Fuller has a B.S. degree in Physics and Mathematics from Texas Southern University and an M.B.A. from the University of Houston.

Fuller joined the Johnson Space Center as a flight controller, working on mission planning and operations for Gemini, Apollo, and Skylab. In 1975, he went to the Headquarters in the Administrator's office as a staff assistant. In 1977, he became Shuttle Spacelab Payloads Project Manager at the Goddard Space Flight Center, where he was responsible for managing the development, integration, and operations of Spacelab missions. Since April 1979, Fuller has held the position of Tiros Project Manager. He is responsible for developing and placing into operation the National Oceanic and Atmospheric Administration polar orbiting meteorological satellite system. He was recently promoted to the position of Deputy Director, Applications Directorate.

### ISAAC T. GILLAM IV
### Mathematics

Isaac Gillam IV received a B.A. degree in mathematics from Howard University, and first joined NASA in 1963 as a resources management specialist. In 1966, he was appointed Assistant Program Manager for the Delta Launch Vehicle, and then became Delta Program Manager in 1968. He was appointed Program Manager of Small Launch Vehicles and International Projects in 1973. Gillam has also held the position of Director of Shuttle Operations at Dryden Flight Research Center . In November 1977, he became Acting Director and later Director of Dryden Flight Research Center. Among his numerous awards, Gillam received NASA's highest award, the Distinguished Service Medal. He is currently the Assistant Associate Administrator for policy in the office of Space Flight at NASA Headquarters.

### YVETTE B. GILMORE
### Psychology

Yvette Gilmore was born in Washington, D.C., but reared primarily in Richmond, Virginia. She attended Howard University where she earned both the bachelors and masters degrees in psychology. Mrs. Gilmore currently works as an employee development specialist at NASA Headquarters. Her primary role is that of Coordinator of the Headquarters Upward Mobility Program. This includes identifying and staffing upward mobility positions, working with employees in the development of individual development plans, and providing career counseling services. Additional functions include the development and coordination of training programs for the Presidential Management Interns, Veteran's Readjustment Appointees, and student employees.

Mrs. Gilmore began her career with NASA in 1971 when she was hired as a student aide. After completing this tour of duty she was given a permanent appointment and was later selected for the Headquarters Personnel Intern Program. Mrs. Gilmore worked in most of the areas of personnel and was elected to a permanent assignment in employee development about 3 years ago.

### CARL E. GRANT
### Economics and Business

Carl Grant received a B.S. degree in Economics and Business Administration from the University of Detroit. He completed an Executive Development Program at the Federal Executive Institute, in Charlottesville, Va.

Grant was appointed to the position of NASA Director of Personnel in 1976. He works at NASA Headquarters where he is responsible for personnel program administration agency wide.

### DR. CURTIS M. GRAVES
### Business Administration.

Dr. Graves graduated from Texas Southern University, receiving a B.A. degree in Business Administration. He has also been awarded two honorary Doctorate degrees, one from Union Baptist Bible College in Houston, Texas and the other from the University of Texas-San Antonio. Before coming to NASA Headquarters, he was Managing Associate and Director of Continuing Education for the National Civil Service League in Washington, D.C. He also served six years as a member of the Texas House of Representatives. Graves has also worked for two Houston newspapers serving as editor for one and advertising manager of the other. Graves is the Deputy Director of Public Affairs for Academic Services at NASA Headquarters. In this capacity, he is responsible for all the agency's contacts with the various levels of the academic community and the learning public.

### NORMAN T. GRIER
### Mathematics and Physics

A 1956 graduate of Clark College (Atlanta, Ga.) with a B.S. degree in Mathematics and Physics, Norman Grier earned an M.S. degree in Physics from Case Western Reserve University in 1968.

Grier was the recipient of the G. W. Taylor Award at Clark for maintaining the highest average in math. He has authored approximately 30 technical papers and is the recipient of a NASA recognition award for contribution to the Plasma Interaction Experiment Satellite Team. He works at the NASA Lewis Research Center in Cleveland, Ohio.

### JAMES L. HARRIS
### Mathematics and Administration

James Harris received a Bachelor of Science degree in Mathematics from Virginia State College, a Master of Science degree in Mathematics from the College of William and Mary, and a Master of Science degree in Administration from George Washington University.

Harris joined NASA in 1965 at the Langley Research Center as a mathematician. He spent one year at NASA Headquarters in Washington, D.C., as a management intern in NASA's Career Development Program. In his current position in the analysis and computer division, Harris assists in the fiscal and technical management of the Central Computer Complex.

### JESSIE J. HARRIS
### Sociology

Jessie Harris received a B.A. in Sociology from Virginia Union University, Richmond, Va., and has been awarded a Masters Degree in Social Work by Virginia Commonwealth University. Harris appears in Who's Who in American Colleges and Universities and is a member of the Alpha Kappa Alpha Sorority.

Harris joined NASA Headquarters in 1978 as Resources Management Specialist in the Office of Management Operations, Institutional Operations Division. She is responsible for the analyses necessary for the budgeting and control of resources, both manpower and funding, for two of NASA's largest field Centers.

### DR. PHILIP E. HODGE
### Physical Chemistry

A Magna Cum Laude graduate of West Virginia State College, with a B.S. degree in Mathematics and Chemistry, Hodge also holds a Ph.D. in Physical Chemistry from Case Western Reserve University.

He joined NASA in 1976 at the Lewis Research Center, and works as a research physical chemist in the Surface Protection Branch of the installation. His position involves research on ceramic coatings for turbine vanes and blades. Hodge is a member of the National Technical Association, Inc., and in 1979, shared an IR-100 award for his work on a Corrosion Resistant Ceramic Thermal Barrier Coating. In 1980, Dr. Hodge was selected to participate in NASA's Career Development Program for future executives at NASA Headquarters.

### MARY W. JACKSON
### Mathematics and Physical Science

A graduate of Hampton Institute with a B.S. degree in Mathematics and Physical Science, Ms. Jackson is currently doing graduate study in public administration at Golden Gate University.

*Clyde Foster, recipient of many scientific awards.*

Ms. Jackson joined NASA's Langley Research center in 1951 as a research mathematician and worked in the installation's computer section and the compressibility research division. She entered the Center's Engineer-in-Training career development program, and in 1958, qualified as an aeronautical engineer. Her engineering position (1958-1978) involved boundary-layer research studies. Jackson now serves as Federal Women's Program Manager in the Office of Equal Opportunity Programs. In this position, she plans, develops and implements programs to assure equitable consideration of women in job placement, training and advancement. She serves as the Center's representative in outreach programs focusing on greater effectiveness in women's programs. She is listed in the 1975-79 editions of Community Leaders and Noteworthy Americans, was featured in *Ebony* Magazine's Special Issue "The Black Woman," August 1977, and is a member of the National Technical Association, Inc.

## DR. HARRIETT G. JENKINS
## Assistant Administrator for Equal Opportunity Programs

Dr. Jenkins earned a B.A. degree in Mathematics from Fisk University, an M.A. in Education and a Doctorate of Education in Policy, Planning and Administration from the University of California at Berkeley, and she completed the Advanced Management Program of Harvard Business School.

During her distinguished professional career, Dr. Jenkins served for 19 years as a public school educator in Berkeley California, before reaching the post of Assistant Superintendent for Instruction. She has been a leading participant in many activities on human rights, education and public administration. She has been an expert on matters of desegregation and integration of schools and on in-service programs for teachers.

Dr. Jenkins has been with NASA since 1974. In 1977, NASA honored Dr. Jenkins with that agency's highest award, the Distinguished Service Medal. She received the Civil Service Commissioners' Award for Distinguished Service for her work in the Personnel Management Project and Federal Government Reorganization Project. In 1978, she was honored by the Montgomery County Branch of the NAACP in their salute to women for her contributions to the betterment of humankind in the struggle for social equality. She received the 1979 Affirmative Action Award for excellence in management, leadership and public service from the Long Island Chapter of the American Society of Public Administration at C. W. Post Center, Long Island University. In 1980, Dr. Jenkins received the Presidential Rank for Meritorious Executive for sustained accomplishment in the Senior Executive Service, and also received NASA's Outstanding Leadership Medal in 1981.

## JAMES L. JENNINGS
## Mathematics and Physics

A graduate of Alabama A & M University, where he received a B.S. degree in Mathematics and Physics, Jennings has also earned a Master of Business Administration from Alabama

*Philip E. Hodge Ph.D. is a research physical chemist.*

A & M, and a Master of Administrative Science from the University of Alabama at Huntsville.

Jennings began his career with NASA as a co-op student in 1967 at the Marshall Space Flight Center. In 1975, he spent one year at NASA Headquarters in the Career Development Program. Jennings has held several positions at the Marshall Space Flight Center in the Computer Services Office and the Comptroller's Office. He now serves in the Kennedy Space Center Comptroller's Office as Chief of the Shuttle Operations Resources Management Branch where his responsibilities are to provide advice, consultation, and staff assistance in the preparation and analysis of financial affairs and management of resources.

He is a member of the National Technical Association, Inc.

## DR. PATRICIA COWINGS JOHNSON
## Psychology

A graduate of the State University of New York at Stony Brook, Dr. Cowings received a B.A. degree in Psychology. She was also awarded an M.A. and a Ph.D. in Psychology from the University of California at Davis.

Born in New York City, Dr. Cowings initially joined NASA in 1971 at the Ames Research Center, working as a research assistant and then a research psychologist in its Summer Student Program. She is presently a research psychologist in the Biomedical Research Division. In this capacity she is currently engaged in research directed toward documenting autonomic manifestations associated with the onset of motion sickness. She has received several honors and awards and has authored numerous publications on autonomic responses and motion sickness.

### ROBERT B. LEE III
### Atmospheric Science and Physics

Robert Lee III received a B.S. degree in Physics from Norfolk State College, and holds a Masters degree in Engineering Physics from the University of Virginia. He has also attended George Washington and Old Dominion Universities for advanced studies in atmospheric science and physics.

In 1964, Lee joined NASA as a co-op student at the Langley Research Center. He joined Langley's professional staff in 1966, doing research related to material science and space optics. He is currently serving as the center's Equal Opportunity Officer. Lee has received a Langley Special Achievement Award as well as the National Urban League Achievement Award under the Black Executive Exchange Program.

### DR. IRENE D. LONG
### Aerospace Medicine,

After receiving a B.S. degree in Biology from Northwestern University in 1973, Dr. Irene Long went on to pursue a medical degree from the St. Louis School of Medicine. Fulfilling a childhood dream to go into aerospace medicine, Dr. Long enrolled into the Wright State University School of medicine—this time receiving a M.S. degree in Aerospace Medicine.

A native of Cleveland, Ohio, Dr. Long joined NASA in 1981 as part of a residency program at Ames Research Center in Mountainview, Ca. In her present capacity as Chief of the Research Support Branch at NASA's Kennedy Space Center, Dr. Long oversees the research which deals with life science experiments in support of physiology of weightlessness. In addition, Dr. Long has plans for researching problems of calcium loss and changes in the red blood cell volume of space travelers.

Looking forward to future travels in space as a medical officer, Dr. Long encourages other blacks to pursue the areas of science and technology.

### ELSIE BEATRICE MCGOWAN
### Mathematics and Management

A graduate of New Mexico Highlands University in Las Vegas, New Mexico, with a B.S. degree in Mathematics, McGowan also received an M.B.A. degree in Management from Pepperdine University in Malibu, California.

Ms. McGowan started her career with NASA in 1964 as a mathematics aide at the Dryden Flight Research Center in Edwards, California. Two and one-half months later she became a computer programmer. From 1973 to 1975, she served as Computer Operations Project Engineer. Her success led her to the position of Flight Data Processing System Project Engineer responsible for planning, designing, developing and testing the Center's Flight Data Processing System. She then became system's analyst in charge of the Dryden microfiche system. Before beginning her present position as computer systems engineer, she served a year as systems engineer responsible for the integrity of the data pipeline for several research projects. McGowan is a member of the American Management Association and Women in Business.

### HERBERT E. PEETE
### Mechanical Engineering

Herbert Peete received a B.S. degree in Mechanical Engineering from North Carolina A & T State University. He is a mechanical systems engineer in the Propellants and Gases Branch at the NASA Kennedy Space Center, in Florida. He is responsible for servicing the space shuttle propulsion subsystems with nypergol propellants and high pressure gases required to support space flight.

### JAMES S. RABY
### Electrical Engineer

James Raby received a B.S. degree in Electrical Engineering from Illinois Institute of Technology, and has done graduate work at San Jose State and Stanford Universities.

Born in Chicago, Illinois, Raby joined NASA at the Ames Research Center in 1959, working on computer systems for motion based flight simulators. As a branch chief, he supervises a team of engineers in the division of advanced motion simulators and computer systems technology. He has authored several papers describing real-time software systems for digital computers.

### LONNIE REID
### Mechanical Engineer

Lonnie Reid received a B.S. degree in Mechanical Engineering from Tennessee State University and an M.S. degree in Mechanical Engineering from the University of Toledo.

Mr. Reid is the head of the Small Compressor Section, Fluid System Components Division. He joined Lewis Research Center in 1961, and since has specialized in fluid flow and compressor aerodynamics. He is responsible for planning and developing research projects to improve the design and performance of small axial and centrifugal compressors.

### DR. RAYMOND E. ROSE
### Aerospace Engineer

Dr. Rose received his B.S. in 1951 from the University of Kansas and his M.S. and Ph.D. in 1956 and 1966, respectively, from the University of Minnesota; all in Aerospace Engineering. He was a Research Fellow at the University of Minnesota from 1962 to 1966, and a Research Scientist to Project Staff Engineer/Supervisor at Honeywell from 1966 to 1976.

Dr. Rose joined NASA Headquarters in 1976 and is now Program Manager, General Aviation, in the Subsonic Aircraft Office. Dr. Rose was honored as the 1980 recipient of NASA's Space-Ship Earth Award for the many years he has worked to encourage disadvantaged young people to improve and educate themselves, especially for careers in science and engineering. Before joining NASA, he did research involving advanced helicopter aerodynamics, and studies of the shock-swallowing concept for aircraft supersonic air data sensing and supersonic parachute stability. He has a patent on a supersonic air data sensor that uses this principle and has authored or co-authored more than 20 technical publications. He is a member of Sigma Gamma Tau, Sigma Tau, and Tau Beta Pi honorary engineering societies, and is listed in American Men and Women of Science.

### LAWRENCE W. RUCKER
### Business Administration

Lawrence Rucker attended Syracuse University and Golden Gate University where he received his M.S. degree in Business Administration.

Rucker is the Director of the Procurement Division for NASA's Dryden Flight Research Facility, in Edwards, California. He is responsible for planning and directing the Center's procurement and supply program. Prior to joining NASA, Rucker served as Deputy Chief of Procurement and Chairman of the Procurement Committee at Edwards Air Force Base. Rucker recently served as a consultant to the Defense Intelligence Agency on Procurement Authority, Organizational Structure, Personnel and other areas. He is also the author of several technical papers on procurement and contracts.

### JAMES 0. SCALES
### Mechanical Engineer

James Scales received a B.S. degree in mechanical engineering from Prairie View A & M University and has done graduate work in engineering and management at UCLA, USC, and the University of Houston.

Scales joined NASA in 1962 at the Dryden Flight Research Facility, and performed stability and control analysis of the X-15 research aircraft. He has worked at Johnson Space Center on flight mission simulations for all transportation spaceflights of the Gemini through Skylab programs. As an aerospace engineer, he has served as instructor for astronaut training on spaceflight missions and vehicle systems. Currently, he is a systems engineering manager for space transportation system simulations responsible for technical performance of JSC's simulator contract.

### JEANETTE A. SCISSUM
### Mathematics And Computer Science

Jeanette Scissum received a B.S. degree in Mathematics and Science and an M.S. degree in Mathematics from Alabama A & M University, and has done graduate work in computer science at Michigan State University.

As a computer systems analyst at NASA Headquarters, Scissum is responsible for analyzing and directing overall approaches and standards for development and implementation of NASA management information and technical support systems. Scissum appeared in the 1973 issue of Who's Who among Women in America, and in 1974 was presented the NASA Equal Employment Opportunity Award for exceptional contributions to equal employment opportunity at the Marshall Space Flight Center. She is a member of the National Technical Association.

### JAMES A. SMITH
### Mathematics And Systems Management

A graduate of Tennessee State with a B.S. degree in Mathematics, James Smith also received an M.S. degree in Systems Management from Florida Institute of Technology.

Smith began a career with NASA in 1963 as a technical management specialist at the Kennedy Space Center. In 1966, he became resources management specialist and subsequently, Chief of Information Systems, Resources Management Section. He came to NASA Headquarters in 1977 as Director of the Functional Analysis Division, where he made plans for improvement of the NASA Institutional Management Process. Presently, Smith is Chief of the Resources Management Branch in the Office of Management. He is a member of the National Technical Association.

### CARRINGTON H. STEWART
### Electrical Engineer

A graduate of Prairie View A & M University, with a B.S. degree in Electrical Engineering, Stewart also holds a masters degree in Electrical Engineering from the University of Houston.

Stewart began work at the Johnson Space Center in 1962 as a development engineer in electro-acoustics. Since that time, he has served as a project engineer in Apollo and Skylab, and is responsible for the design, development, and testing of Orbiter audio system. At present, he is an aerospace engineer and holds two U.S. patents for electronic designs. He was selected to spend one year at NASA Headquarters in the Agency's Career Development program for future executives. He is a member of the National Technical Association.

### INELLIA F. SULLIVAN
### Business Education

A graduate of Alabama A & M University with a B.S. degree in Business Education, Ms. Sullivan was born in Huntsville, Alabama.

In 1968, Sullivan joined NASA as a secretary at the Marshall Space Flight Center. She was selected for an administrative position through the Specialty Training for Entry Professionals Program (STEP) in 1975. Sullivan is an administrative officer for a large technical laboratory and is responsible for developing management techniques and controls in order to provide an effective and responsive administrative management program.

### PHYLLIS D. STOVALL TANKSLEY
### Mathematics

Phyllis Tanksley was born in Galveston, Texas, and attended Dominican College where she was Freshman and Sophomore

Class President and President of Alpha Mu Gamma Honor Society. In 1975, she transferred to Texas A & M University where she received a B.S. in Mathematics and was named outstanding and distinguished student.

Miss Stovall began at NASA's Johnson Space Center as a junior co-op in 1973, joined the Co-op Program in 1974, and became a permanent employee in the Program Operations Office in 1978. She is presently involved in the Engineering Evaluations Office as an electromagnetic interference analyst. Her position also involves circuit and lightning analysis. She is a member of the National Technical Association.

### HAROLD PERRY WASHINGTON
### Aerospace Engineer

Harold Washington graduated from Virginia Union University with a B.S. degree in Mathematics. Washington joined the NASA staff in 1957 as an aerospace engineer. In 1972, he was Branch Chief of the Aeronautical Engineering Division at the Dryden Flight Research Facility. Presently he holds the position of Deputy Chief of the Aeronautical Engineering Division. He has written several technical papers and has received many achievement awards.

### DONALD L. WOOD
### Electrical Engineer

A graduate of Howard University with a B.S. degree in Electrical Engineering, Wood is also pursuing graduate work in Electrical Engineering at George Washington University.

Wood joined NASA in 1975 as an electronics engineer. Since that time, Wood has planned, conducted, and analyzed the ground support system for satellites whose missions entailed communication, meteorological, and astronomical studies. Wood is now working as an electrical systems engineer for the Space Telescope satellite program at the Goddard Space Flight Center.

## OTHER NOTABLE BLACK INVENTORS AND SCIENTISTS

| Name | Occupation | Dates |
|---|---|---|
| Dr. William Harry Barnes | Medical | 1887-1945 |
| Charles W. Buggs | Microbiologists | NA |
| Charles F. Baxter | Scientist | 1927- |
| Jesse F. Berry | Engineer | 1932- |
| Max J. Bond, Jr. | Architect | 1935- |
| Edward A. Bouchet | Physicist | 1852-1918 |
| Herman Russell Branson | Scientist | 1914- |
| John L. Carter | Physicist | NA |
| Ernest Coleman | Physics | 1942- |
| Dr. lloyd M. Cooke | Chemistry | NA |
| Samuel Dixon Jr. | Electronics engineer | NA |
| Annie Easley | Energy Research | 1932- |
| Lloyd Noel Ferguson | Chemist | 1918- |
| Solomon C. Fuller | Neurologist | 1872-1953 |
| William A. Guillory Ph.D. | Chemist | NA |
| James Harris Green | Scientist | NA |
| James Harris | Nuclear Chemist | 1932- |
| James Henderson | Scientist | 1917- |
| Henry Aaron Hill | Scientist | 1915- |
| Dr. William A. Hinton | Medical | 1883-1959 |
| Defield T. Holmes | Scientist | NA |
| Jaquelyne J. Jackson Ph.D. | Medical sociology | NA |
| William Jackson Ph.D. | Physical Chemist | NA |
| Dr. Rebecca Lee | Physician | 1833- |
| Robert P. Madison | Architect | 1923- |
| Huey Perry Malone | Engineer | 1935- |

| Name | Occupation | Dates |
|---|---|---|
| Julia M. Martin | Chemist | 1924- |
| Samuel P. Massie, Jr. | Scientist | 1919- |
| Caldwell McCoy | Energy Research | 1933- |
| Louis W. Roberts | Physicist | 1913- |
| Dr. John Sweat Rock | Physician | 1825-1866 |
| David W. Robinson | Scientist | 1933- |
| Elijah Saunders | Cardiologist | 1934- |
| Dr. Roland Scott | Pediatricks | NA |
| Barnard Smith | Physicist | NA |
| Aubre de L. Maynard | Physician | NA |
| Walter T. Mc Afee | Theoretical physicist | NA |
| Dr. John B. Slaughter | Engineer | NA |
| Dr. James McCune Smith | Medical | 1813-1865 |
| Vertner W. Tandy | Architect | 1885 |
| Julius H. Taylor | Physicist | 1914- |
| Lawnie Taylor | Physicist | NA |
| Moddie Daniel Taylor | Scientist | 1942-1976 |
| James Tyson Tildon | Scientist | 1931- |
| Virgil G. Trice, Jr. | Nuclear Researcher | 1926- |
| Charles H. Turner | Entomologist | 1861-1923 |
| Dr. Arthur B.Walker, Jr. | Applied physics Astronomy | NA |
| William L. Wade, Jr. | Chemist | NA |
| John Lewis Wilson | Architect | 1898- |
| Dr. Jane Cooke Wright | Surgeon | 1919- |
| Ronald E. Zanders | Engineer | 1933- |

## BLACK SCIENTIFIC ORGANIZATIONS

**American Association of Blacks in Energy**
James Caldwell (Secretary)
1429 Larimer Square
Denver, CO 80802
*Chairman:* Rufus McKinney, Washington, DC
*Founded*: 1977
*Purpose:* To insure that black Americans and other minorities gain their adequate share of representation and participation in the development and implementation of this nation's activities involving energy.
*Membership:* 300; open to managerial and professional employees of energy-related businesses, trade associations and government agencies; consultants, educators, and students in related disciplines who support the purposes of the association.
*Dues:* $25; $50 Gold Star Sustaining

**Association of Third World Anthropologists (ATWA)**
Department of Sociology-Anthropology
Morgan State University
Baltimore MD 21239
*Presidents (joint):* Dr. Mario Zamora, Williamsburg, VA; Dr. Stefan Goodwin, Baltimore, MD
*Founded:*1977
*Purpose:* To make anthropology more sensitive and responsive to the views and needs of Third World peoples; to make anthropology less prejudiced against Third World peoples by making it less ethnocentric in its use of language, paradigms, and conceptual grids; to genuinely incorporate Third World professionals into its organizations and their perspectives into the mainstream of its literature.
*Membership:* 110 (on every continent except Australia); open to all anthropologists and specialists in cognate disciplines interested in achieving the purposes or objectives.
*Dues:* $26 institutional; $15 fellows and associates; $10 students; Gratis by special request to limited numbers of overseas persons unable to pay.
*Publications:* The *ATWA Research Bulletin*—quarterly

**Atlanta Council of Black Professional Engineers**
148 International Boulevard, Suite 448
Atlanta, GA 30303
*President:* Calvin Espy, Atlanta, GA
*Founded:*1976
*Purpose:* To develop an awareness in the black community of the opportunities available in engineering.
*Membership:* 75; open to practicing engineers and technicians.
*Publications: Atlanta Council of Black Professional Engineers*—quarterly

**Los Angeles Council of Black Professional Engineers**
Federal Building
Los Angeles, CA 90053
*President:* Sylvia Weatherford, Torrence, CA
*Founded:*1969
*Purpose:* To promote an interest in, recruit, and retain minorities in academic and professional careers in engineering. This objective is accomplished through the Council's committees on youth motivation, college relations, summer work exposure, newsletter, special projects, planning and operations, pan-African committee, and its Mathematics-Engineering Science Achievement (MESA) center.
*Membership:* 200; open to engineering, mathematics, and computer science professionals
*Dues:* none
*Publications:* newsletter—monthly

**National Conference of Black Political Scientists**
Department of Political Science
Morgan State University
Baltimore, MD 21239
*President:* Dr. Elsie Scott, Washington, DC
*Founded:* 1971
*Purpose:* To bring black political scientists together to maximize their role in the liberation of black people; to promote the study of political science with particular reference to the black experience; to reflect on the proper means by which political scientists can approach the study of politics with a view toward enriching the black experience; to facilitate the solving of professional problems that are unique to black political scientists.
*Membership:* 300; open to any political or social scientists and others interested in the political life and liberation of black people and who pay the requisite dues for a given year.
*Dues:* $20 per year
*Publications: Journal of Political Repression*—quarterly

**National Dental Association**
Mrs. Rubye C. Porter, Administrator
5506 Connecticut Avenue, NW, Suite 24
Washington, DC 20015
*President:* Dr. Elisha Richardson, Nashville, TN
*Founded:*1913
*Purpose:* To promote the interests of dentistry in general and of minority dentists in particular; to represent the interests of the minority population with respect to health care, especially dental care.
*Membership:* 2,000+; open to dentists and four affiliated groups: The Auxiliary of NDA, The National Dental Hygienists Association (NDHA). The National Dental Assistants Association (NDAA), and The Student National Dental Association (SNDA).
*Dues:* $125 per year
*Publications: NDA Quarterly;* and a bimonthly newsletter

**National Organization for the Professional Advancement of Black Chemists and Chemical Engineers**
Dr. Clarence Tucker
Polaroid Corporation
1265 Main Street
Waltham, MA 02154
*President:* Dr. James H. Porter, Cambridge, MA
*Founded*: 1972
*Purpose:* To develop programs to assist blacks in realizing their full potential in the fields of chemistry and chemical engineering.
*Membership:* 700; open to persons who support and are willing to attain the objectives of the organization; full membership—a bachelors or advanced degree in chemistry or the equivalent; associate membership—all others.
*Dues:* $35 full membership; $15 associate membership; no dues student membership
*Publications:* Newsletter—quarterly; proceedings of national meetings—annually

**National Society of Black Engineers**
317 Clermont Avenue
Brooklyn, NY 11205
*Chairperson:* Carolynn Cooper, Brooklyn, NY
*Founded:* 1971
*Purpose:* To promote black scholastic achievement; to insure the completion of a degree in a science or engineering program once a student has entered the university; to promote the social standing of the black student in the sciences and engineering; to establish and maintain tutorial programs for college, high school, and junior high school students; to provide college, high school, and junior high school students with proper engineering counseling; to assist in job placement; and to strive toward a better understanding among all engineers regardless of race, creed or color.
*Membership:* 4,000 (approximately); open to undergraduate and graduate students in engineering or applied science; junior membership open to junior high and high school students; auxiliary memberships are available to professional engineers and corporations.
*Dues:* Exempt, honorary and junior members; $1,500 corporate membership; $25 senior associate; $12 associate; $3 affiliate and member
*Publications:* Newsletter—three times a year; national conference proceedings—yearly; technical conference proceedings—yearly

**National Society of Black Physicists**
Dr. Shirley Jackson
Bell Laboratories
600 Mountain Avenue
Murray Hill, NJ 07974
*President:*Dr. Shirley Jackson
*Founded:* 1978
*Purpose:* To promote the professional well-being of black physicists within the scientific community and within society at large, and to develop and support efforts to increase opportunities for and the number of blacks in physics.
*Membership:* About 50; open to persons who have a Ph.D. in physics and/or are employed as professional physicists, or are currently matriculating toward a doctoral degree in physics.
*Dues:* $20
*Publications:* Newsletter published periodically; proceedings of annual meeting.

**Organization of Black Scientists, Inc.**
P.O. Box 8715
Washington, DC 20011
*President:* Dr. Franklin Hamilton, Atlanta, GA
*Founded:* 1971
*Purpose:* To identify, provide, and administer research and educational goals of black scientists.
*Membership:* 600 (with local chapters in several cities); open to anyone active in natural sciences or mathematics and who will further the objectives of the organization.
*Dues:* $10
*Publication:* Newsletter

## OTHER ASSOCIATIONS OF / FOR RACIAL & ETHNIC MINORITY SCIENCE, ENGINEERING AND HEALTH PROFESSIONALS

[Abstracted from MESHWORK, Office of Opportunities in Science, American Association for the Advancement of Science, Washington, D.C.]

**American Association of Blacks in Energy [AABE]**
Founded 1977
Mary Helen Thompson, Exec. Dir.
1220 L St. N.W. Suite 605
Washington, DC 20005
Has bimonthly *Energy News*

**American Psychological Association [APA]**
Board of Ethnic and Minority Affairs
Attn: Joe Martinez
1200 Seventeenth St. N.W.
Washington, D.C. 20036.
Room 311.

**American Indian Science and Engineering Society [AISES]**
Founded 1977
Norbert S. Hill Jr.
Exec. Dir. 13110
College Avenue Suite 1506
Boulder, CO 80302
Publishes AISES *Winds of Change*, quarterly.

**Arizona Council of Black Engineers Founded 1981**
Attn: Public relations Committee
P. O. Box 21163
Phoenix, AZ 85036-1163
[602] 990-522330
Publishes Newsletter, bimonthy.

**Asian American Psychological Association**
Founded1974
Herbert Z. Wong, Exec. Dir.
Richmond Area Multiservices, Inc.
San Francisco, CA 94121
[415] 668-5955
Publishes *Journal of Asian American Psychological Assoc.*

**Association of American Indian Physicians [AAIP]**
Founded 1971
Tery Hunter, Exec. Dir.
10015 South Pensylvania, Bld.G
Oklahoma City, OK 73159
[405] 692-1202
Publishes AAIP Quarterly News

**Association of Black Sociologists**
Founded1969
Dr. Lena Wright-Myers
Dept. Sociology, Jackson State Univ.
Jackson, MI 39217
[601] 968-2591
Publishes *The Black Sociogists Newsletter* quarterly.

**Association of Native American Medical Students**
Founded 1972
Attn: Steeve Barse, Program Coordinator
c/o Assoc. Of Amer. Indian Physicians
10015 South Pennsylvania , Blg. G
Oklahoma, OK 73159

**Association of Third World Anthropologists [ATWA]**
Founded 1977
Prof. Zamora,Dept. Of Anthropology, College of William & Mary
Williamsburg, VA 23185
[804] 2253-4341
Publishes *The ATWA Research Bulletin* biannually

**Association of Puerto Ricans in Science and Engineeering**
Founded1982
Dr. Pedro Barbosa, Pres.
P.O. Box 1725
Washington, DC 20013

**Association of Social and Behavioral Scientists**
Founded 1935
c/o Dr. Evonne Bueford, Exec. Sec.
Fort Valley State College,
Fort Valley, GA 31030
[912] 825 6446
Publishes *Journal of Social & Behavioral Sciences* 4x/yr
Newslettter *From the Desk of the Exec. Sec.* quarterly.

**Atlantic Council of Black Professional Engineers**
Founded 1976
Anthony George, Chairman Bd. of Directors
1401 Peachtree St. N.E. Suite 120
Atlanta, GA 30309
[404] 894-2444
Publishes *Atlanta Council of Black Professonal Engineers* , quarterly

**Los Angeles Council of Black Professional Engineers**
Founded 1969
Larry Mc Elroy Exec. Dir.
611 South Catalina St. Suite 307
E.Los Angeles, CA 90005
[213] 384-2337
Publishes LACBPE Newsletter, bimonthly

**National Association of Black Professional Engineers**
Founded 1976
6406 Georgia Ave. N.W.
Washington, DC 20012
[202] 291-3550
Membership consists of Engineering Firms
Publishes NABCE

**National Association of Black Psychologists**
Founded 1968
Dr.Halford Fairchild, Pres.
P.O. Box 55999
Washington, DC 20040
[202] 722-0808
Publishes Newsletter, Quarterly

**National Association of Black Geologists and Geophysicists**
Founded 1981
c/o Millicent Mc Caskill Prg Chair.
P.O. Box 720157
Houston, TX 77272
[713] 778-7128
Publishes Newsletter, bimonthly

**National Black Nurses Association, Inc. [NBNA]**
Founded 1971
P.O. Box. 18358
Boston, MA 02118
Publishes NBNA Newsletter , quarterly, Journal NBNA, biannually

**National Conference Of Black Political Scientists**
Founded 1971
c/o Dept of Policital Science
Albany State College, Albany, GA
[912] 430-4600
Publishes Newsletter, quarterly

**National Economic Association**
Founded 1975
c/o Dr. Gus T. Ridgel
Vice Pres. for Academic Affairs, Southern Univ.
Southern Univ. Branch Post Office
Baton Rouge, LA 70813
[504] 771 5150

**National Dental Association**
Founded 1913
Sharon Mc Millan, Mgr.
5506 Connecticut Ave., N. W. Suite 24
Washington, DC 20015
[202] 244-7555

**National Institute Of Science [NIS]**
Founded 1943
Arthur C. Washington, Exec. Sec.
P.O. Box 2784
Prairie View A & M Univ.
Prairie View, TX 77445
[409] 857-2315

**National Organization For The Professional Advancement Of Black Chemists And Chemical Engineers**
[NOBCHE]
Founded 1973
Dr. Clarence Tucker, Chair of Exec. Bd.
8 Longmeadow Rd.
Westboro , MA 01581
[617] 684-4682
Publishes Newsmagazine, quarterly

**National Medical Association**
Founded1895
William Garret, Exec. Vice Pres. & Dir.
1012 10th St. N.W.
Washington, DC 20001
[202] 347-1985
Publishes *JNMA*, monthly, NMA Newsletter

**National Society Of Black Engineers**
Founded 1975
Florida Morehead Exec. Dir.
344 Commerce St.
Alexandria, VA 22314
[703] 549 -2207
Publishes *NSBE*, 5x/yr. and preceedings of National Meetings annually

**National Network Of Minority Women In Science [MWIS]**
Founded 1978
Patricia A. Boulware, Coordinator
Office of Opportunities in Science
Amer. Assoc. for the Advancement of Science
1333 H St. N.W.
Washington, DC 2000
[202] 326-6674

**National Pharmaceutical Association**
Founded 1947
James N. Tyson, Exec. Dir.
Howard University
College of Pharmacy
2300 4th Street, N.W.
Washington, DC 20059
[202] 636-6530
Publishes *Journal of National Pharmaceutical Association*

**National Society Of Allied Health**
Founded 1978
Mrs. E. Atkinson, Exec. Dir.
P.O. Box 2815
Washington, DC 20013
[202] 636-7565
Publishes Newsletter, Journal biannually

**National Technical Association**
Founded1926
P.O. Box 27787
Washington, DC 20036-7787
[202] 829-6100
Publishes *NTA Journal* 4x/yr.
Student chapters exists in many areas.

## ADDITIONAL SCIENCE RELATED ORGANIZATIONS

**American Institute Of Architects [Minority Resources Committee]**
1735 NY Avenue, N.W.
Washington, DC 20006

**American Society For Engineering Education**
Ms. Barbara Ramey
NY, NY
[212] 293-7080

**Association Of The Study Of Afro-American Life & History**
1407 14th St, N.W.
Washington, D.C. 20005
[202] 667-2822.

**Black Psychiatrists Of America**
P. O. Box 370659
Decatur, GA 30037
[203] 236-2320

**Coalition Of Black Trade Unionists**
P.O. Box 73055
Washington, DC 20056-3055
[202] 644-1203.

**National Action Council For Minorities In Engineering**
3 West 35 St.
NY, NY 10001
[212]-279-2626

**The National Association Of Black Counselors**
c/o Prof. Rebecca Cutler
Brooklyn College
Graduate Guidance & Counseling Prgm.
11409 James Hall
Bedford and Ave H
Brooklyn, N Y 11210

**National Association Of Black Manufacturers**
1910 K St. N.W.
Washington, DC 20006.
[202] 785-5133.

**National Association Of Minority Contractors [NAMC]**
318 Massachuetts Av. N.E.
Washington, DC 20002
(202) 347-8259

**National Association Of Minority Engineers Program Administrators [NAMEPA]**
3200 S. Washburn Ave.
P.O. Bx # 1
Chicago, IL 60616

**National Alliance Of Third World Journalists**
P.O. Box 43208
Washington, DC 20010

**National Association Of Health Services Executives [NAHSE]**
1101 14th St. N.W.
10th Fl.
Washington, DC 20005.
[202] 289-1030

**National Black Association For Speech, Language & Hearing**
P.O. Box 06154
Cleveland, OH 44106
[216] 751-9302

**National Black Child Development Institute**
1463 Rhode Island Ave., N.W.
Washington, DC 20005
[202] 387-1281

**National Center For The Advancement Of Blacks In The Health Professions**
P.O. Box 21121 Detroit, MI 48221
[313] 342-1522

**National Consortium For Graduate Degrees For Minorities In Engineering, Inc. [GEM]**
P.O. Box 537
Notre Dame IN 46556
[219] 239-7183

**National Economic Association**
Att. Dr. Gus Ridgel
Southern University
Baton Rouge, LA

**National Optometric Association**
2850 S. Indiana Ave.
Chicago, IL 60616T
[312] 326-2929

**National Patent Law Association**
P.O. Box 8700
Washington, DC 20011

**National Pharmaceutical Association**
Howard University
P.O. Box 934
Washington, DC 20059
[202] 636-7960

**National Podiatry Association**
2115 Vann Ness Ave.
San Francisco, CA 94109

**New York Association Of Black Psychologists, Inc.**
P.O. Box 1764
NY, NY 10027
[212] 857-4280

**New York Black Nurses Association, Inc.**
P. O. Box 3635
Grand Central Station
NY, NY 10017

**The New York Association Of Black Psychologists, Inc.**
P.O. Box 1764
NY, NY 10027

**Society Of Women Engineers [Minority Concerns Committee]**
United Engineering Center
Rm. 305
345 E. 47 Street
NY, NY 10017

**Student National Medical Association**
Pres. Ms. Cassandra Tribble
1012 10th St. N.W.
Washington, DC 20001
[202] 371-1616

## INVENTIONS BY BLACKS 1834-1900[a]

(Some later inventions through 1989 are included.)

| Inventor | Invention | Date | Patent |
|---|---|---|---|
| Abrams, W. B. | Hame attachment | Apr. 14, 1891 | 450,550 |
| Allen, C. W. | Self-leveling table | Nov. 1, 1898 | 613,436 |
| Allen, J. B. | Clothes line support | Dec. 10, 1895 | 551,105 |
| Ancker Johnson, Betsy | Signal Generator | Nov. 22, 1966 | 3,287,659 |
| Ashbourne, A. P. | Process for preparing coconut for domestic use | June 1, 1875 | 163,962 |
| Ashbourne, A. P. | Biscuit cutter | Nov. 30, 1875 | 170,460 |
| Ashbourne, A. P. | Refining coconut oil | July 27, 1880 | 230,518 |
| Ashbourne, A. P. | Process of treating coconut | Aug. 21, 1877 | 194,287 |
| Bailes, William | Ladder scaffold-support | Aug. 5, 1879 | 218,154 |
| Bailey, L. C. | Combined truss and bandage | Sept. 25, 1883 | 285,545 |
| Bailey, L. C. | Folding bed | July 18, 1899 | 629,286 |
| Bailiff, C. O. | Shampoo headrest | Oct. 11, 1898 | 612,008 |
| Ballow, W. J. | Combined hatrack and table | Mar. 29, 1898 | 601,422 |
| Bayliss, R.G. & D.D. Emrick | Encapsulation Process & Its product | Feb 2, 1971 | 3, 565, 818 |
| Barnes, G. A. E. | Design for sign | Aug. 19, 1889 | 29,193 |
| Beard, A. J. | Rotary engine | July 5, 1892 | 478,271 |
| Beard, A. J. | Car-coupler | Nov. 23, 1897 | 594,059 |
| Becket, G. E. | Letter box | Oct. 4, 1892 | 483,525 |
| Bell, L. | Locomotive smoke stack | May 23, 1871 | 115,153 |
| Bell, L. | Dough kneader | Dec. 10, 1872 | 133,823 |
| Benjamin, L. W. | Broom moisteners and bridles | May 16, 1893 | 497,747 |
| Benjamin, M. E. | Gong and signal chairs for hotels | July 17, 1888 | 386,286 |
| Binga, M. W. | Street sprinkling apparatus | July 22, 1879 | 217,843 |
| Blackburn, A. B. | Railway signal | Jan. 10, 1888 | 376,362 |
| Blackburn, A. B. | Spring seat for chairs | Apr. 3, 1888 | 380,420 |
| Blackburn, A. B. | Cash carrier | Oct. 23, 1888 | 391,577 |
| Blair, Henry | Corn planter | Oct. 14, 1834 | |
| Blair, Henry | Cotton planter | Aug. 31, 1836 | |
| Blue, L. | Hand corn shelling device | May 20, 1884 | 298,937 |
| Bluford, Sr. G. S. | Artillery Ammunition Training Round | Feb. 13, 1951 | 2, 541, 025 |
| Booker, L. F | Design rubber scraping knife | Mar. 28, 1899 | 30,404 |
| Boone, Sarah | Ironing board | Apr. 26, 1892 | 473,653 |
| Bowman, H. A. | Making flags | Feb. 23, 1892 | 469,395 |
| Brooks, C. B. | Punch | Oct. 31, 1893 | 507,672 |
| Brooks, C. B. | Street-sweepers | Mar. 17, 1896 | 556,711 |
| Brooks, C. B. | Street-sweepers | May 12, 1896 | 560,154 |
| Brooks, Hallstead and Page | Street-sweepers | Apr. 21, 1896 | 558,719 |
| Brown, Henry | Receptacle for storing and preserving papers | Nov. 2, 1886 | 352,036 |
| Brown, L. F. | Bridle bit | Oct. 25, 1892 | 484,994 |
| Brown, O. E. | Horseshoe | Aug. 23, 1892 | 481,271 |
| Brown & Latimer | Water closets for railway cars | Feb. 10, 1874 | 147,363 |
| Bluford, Sr. G. S. | Artillery Ammunition Training Round | Feb. 13, 1951 | 2, 541, 025 |
| Bundy, R. | Signal Generator | Jan. 26, 1960 | 2, 922, 924 |
| Burr, J. A. | Lawn mower | May 9, 1899 | 624,749 |
| Burr, W. F. | Switching device for railways | Oct. 31, 1899 | 636,197 |
| Burwell, W. | Boot or shoe | Nov. 28, 1899 | 638,143 |
| Butler, R. A. | Train alarm | June 15, 1897 | 584,540 |
| Butts, J. W. | Luggage carrier | Oct. 10, 1899 | 634,611 |
| Byrd, T. J. | Improvement in holders for riens for horses | Feb. 6, 1872 | 123,328 |
| Byrd, T. J. | Apparatus for detaching horses from carriages | Mar. 19, 1872 | 124,79 |

[a] In cases where an inventor has patented several variations on the same basic invention, a composite entry has been devised.

| Inventor | Invention | Date | Patent |
|---|---|---|---|
| Byrd, T. J. | Improvement in neck yokes for wagons | Mar. 19, 1872 | 124,790 |
| Byrd, T. J. | Improvement in car couplings | Dec. 1, 1874 | 157,370 |
| Campbell, W. S. | Self-setting animal trap | Aug. 30, 1881 | 246,369 |
| Cargill, B. F. | Invalid cot | July 25, 1899 | 629,658 |
| Carrington, T. A. | Range | July 25, 1876 | 180,323 |
| Carter, W. C. | Umbrella stand | Aug. 4, 1885 | 323,397 |
| Carruthers, Geo. R. | Image Converter for Dect. Electromagnetic etc. | Nov. 11, 1969 | 3, 478,216 |
| Carter, J.L. & M. Weiner & R.J. Youmans | Distributed pulse forming network for magnetic modulator | Sept. 16, 1986 | 4,612,455 |
| Certain, J. M. | Parcel carrier for bicycles | Dec. 26, 1899 | 639,708 |
| Cherry, M. A. | Velocipede | May 8, 1888 | 382,351 |
| Cherry, M. A. | Street car fender | Jan. 1, 1895 | 531,908 |
| Church, T. S. | Carpet beating machine | July 29, 1884 | 302,237 |
| Clare, O. B. | Trestle | Oct. 9, 1888 | 390,752 |
| Coates, R. | Overboot for horses | Apr. 19, 1892 | 473,295 |
| Cook, G. | Automatic fishing device | May 30, 1899 | 625,829 |
| Coolidge, J. S. | Harness attachment | Nov. 13, 1888 | 392,908 |
| Cooper, A. R. | Shoemaker's jack | Aug. 22, 1899 | 631,519 |
| Cooper, J. | Shutter and fastening | May 1, 1883 | 276,563 |
| Cooper, J. | Elevator device | Apr. 2, 1895 | 536,605 |
| Cooper, J. | Elevator device | Sept. 21, 1897 | 590,257 |
| Cornwell, P. W. | Draft regulator | Oct. 2, 1888 | 390,284 |
| Cornwell, P. W. | Draft regulator | Feb. 7, 1893 | 491,082 |
| Cralle, A. L. | Ice-cream mold | Feb. 2, 1897 | 576,395 |
| Creamer, H. | Steam feed water trap | Mar. 17, 1895 | 313,854 |
| Creamer, H.[a] | Steam trap feeder | Dec. 11, 1888 | 394,463 |
| Cosgrove, W. F. | Automatic stop plug for gas oil pipes | Mar. 17, 1885 | 313,993 |
| Darkins, J. T. | Ventilation aid (variation) | Feb. 19, 1895 | 534,322 |
| Davis, I. D. | Tonic | Nov. 2, 1886 | 351,829 |
| Davis, W. D. | Riding saddles | Oct. 6, 1896 | 568,939 |
| Davis, W. R., Jr. | Library table | Sept. 24, 1878 | 208,378 |
| Deitz, W. A. | Shoe | Apr. 30, 1867 | 64,205 |
| Dickinson, J. H. | Pianola | NA 1899 | NA |
| Dixon Jr. S. & T. R. AuCoin & R.J. Malik | Monolithic planar doped barrier limiter | Mar. 31, 1987 | 4,654, 609 |
| Dixon Jr. S. & R.J. Malik | Monolithic planar doped barrier subharmonic mixer | Jan. 7, 1986 | 4,563, 773 |

[a] Creamer also patented five steam traps between 1887 and 1893.

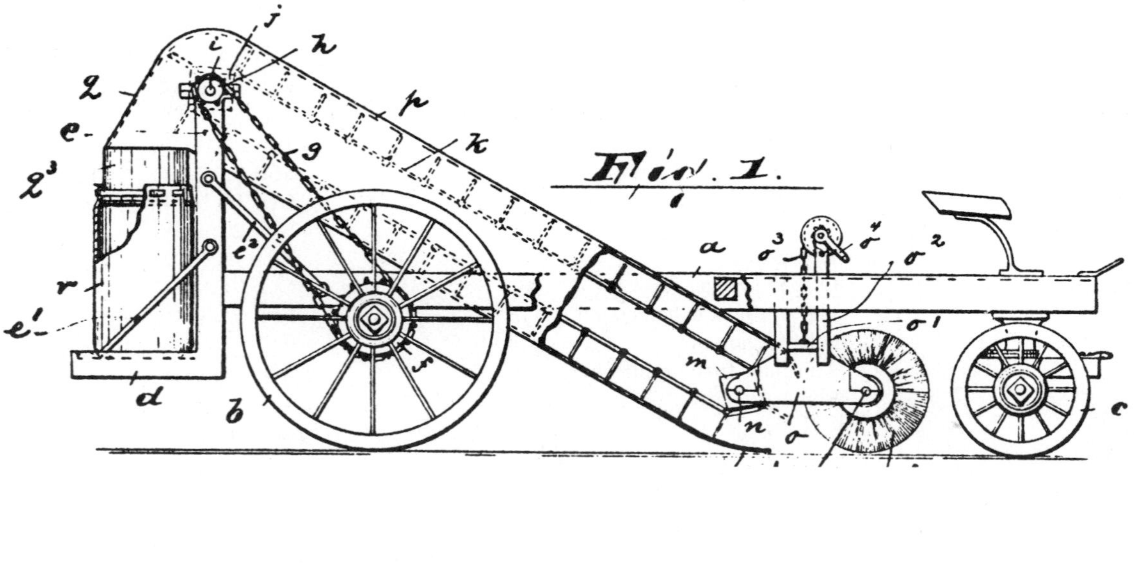

| Inventor | Invention | Date | Patent |
|---|---|---|---|
| Dorsey, O. | Door-holding device | Dec. 10, 1878 | 210,764 |
| Dorticus, C. J. | Device for applying coloring liquids to sides of soles or heels of shoes | Mar. 19, 1895 | 535,820 |
| Dorticus, C. J. | Machine for embossing photo | Apr. 16, 1895 | 537,442 |
| Dorticus, C. J. | Photographic print wash | Apr. 23, 1875 | 537,968 |
| Dorticus, C. J. | Hose leak stop | July 18, 1899 | 629,315 |
| Downing, P. B. | Electric switch for railroad | June 17, 1890 | 430,118 |
| Downing, P. B. | Letter box | Oct 27, 1891 | 462,093 |
| Downing, P. B. | Street letter box | Oct. 27, 1891 | 462,096 |
| Dunnington. J. H. | Horse detachers | Mar. 16, 1897 | 578,979 |
| Edmonds, T. H. | Separating screens | July 20, 1897 | 586,724 |
| Elkins, T. | Dining, ironing table, and quilting frame combined | Feb. 22, 1870 | 100,020 |
| Elkins, T. | Chamber commode | Jan. 9, 1872 | 122,518 |
| Elkins, T. | Refrigerating apparatus | Nov. 4, 1879 | 221,222 |
| Evans, J. H. | Convertible settees | Oct. 5, 1897 | 591,095 |
| Faulkner, H. | Ventilated shoe | Apr. 29, 1890 | 426,495 |
| Ferrell, F. J. | Steam trap | Feb. 11, 1890 | 420,993 |
| Ferrell, F. J.[a] | Apparatus for melting snow | May 27, 1890 | 428,670 |
| Fisher, D. | Joiners' clamp | Apr. 20, 1875 | 162,281 |
| Fisher, D. C. | Furniture castor | Mar. 14, 1876 | 174,794 |
| Flemming, F., Jr. | Guitar (variation) | Mar. 3, 1886 | 338,727 |
| Forten, J. | Sail control(described in Mass. Newspaper) | 1850 | |
| Goode, Sarah E. | Folding cabinet bed | July 14, 1885 | 322,177 |
| Gourdine, M.C. | Electrogas dynamic mtd & Apparatus | June 10, 1969 | 3, 449, 667 |
| Grant, G. F. | Golf tee | Dec. 12, 1899 | 638,920 |
| Grant, W. | Curtain rod support | Aug. 4, 1896 | 565,075 |
| Gray, R. H. | Bailing press | Aug. 28, 1894 | 525,203 |
| Gray, R. H. | Cistern cleaners | Apr. 9, 1895 | 537,151 |
| Gregory, J. | Motor | Apr. 26, 1887 | 361,937 |
| Grenon, H. | Razor stropping device | Feb. 18, 1896 | 554,867 |
| Griffin, F. W. | Pool table attachment | June 13, 1899 | 626,902 |
| Gunn, S. W. | Boot or shoe (variation) | Jan. 16, 1900 | 641,642 |
| Haines, J. H. | Portable basin | Sept. 28, 1897 | 590,833 |
| Hale, Wm. | An improvement in aeroplanes | Apr. 7, 1925 | 1, 563, 278 |
| Hall, Lloyd A. | Manuf. stable dry papain composition | March 15, 1949 | 2, 464,200 |
| Hall, Lloyd A. | Asphalt emulsion & manuf. thereof | Oct. 18, 1932 | 1, 882, 834 |
| Hall, Lloyd A. | Sterilizing foodstuff | Feb 8, 1938 | 2, 107, 697 |
| Hall, Lloyd A. | Puncture sealing composition & manuf thereof | Sept. 5, 1944 | 2, 357,650 |
| Hammonds, J. F. | Apparatus for holding yarn skeins | Dec. 15, 1896 | 572,985 |
| Harding, F. H. | Extension banquet table | Nov. 22, 1898 | 614,468 |
| Harper, Solomon | Electric Hair Treatment | Aug. 5, 1930 | 1, 772,002 |
| Harper, Solomon | Thermostatic Control Hair Curlers | Aug. 8, 1953 | 2, 648, 757 |
| Harper, S. | Thermostatic Controlled Fur etc | Aug. 11, 1953 | 2, 711, 095 |
| Hawkins, J. | Gridiron | Mar. 26, 1845 | 3,973 |
| Hawkins, R. | Harness attachment | Oct. 4, 1887 | 370,943 |
| Headen, M. | Foot power hammer | Oct. 5, 1886 | 350,363 |
| Hearness, R. | Detachable car fender | July 4, 1899 | 628,003 |
| Hilyer, A. F. | Water evaporator attachment for hot air registers | Aug. 26, 1890 | 435,095 |
| Hilyer, A. F. | Registers | Oct. 14, 1890 | 438,159 |
| Holmes, E. H. | Gage | Nov. 12, 1895 | 549,513 |
| Hunter, J. H. | Portable weighing scales | Nov. 3, 1896 | 570,553 |
| Hyde, R. N. | Composition for cleaning and preserving carpets | Nov. 6, 1888 | 392,205 |
| Jackson, B. F. | Heating apparatus | Mar. 1, 1898 | 599,985 |

[a] Ferrell also patented eight valves between 1890 and 1893.

| Inventor | Invention | Date | Patent |
|---|---|---|---|
| Jackson, B. F. | Matnx drying apparatus | May 10, 1898 | 603,879 |
| Jackson, B. F. | Gas burner | Apr. 4, 1899 | 622,482 |
| Jackson, H. A. | Kitchen table (variation) | Oct. 6, 1896 | 569,135 |
| Jackson, W. H. | Railway switch | Mar. 9, 1897 | 578,641 |
| Jackson, W. H. | Railway switch | Mar. 16, 1897 | 593,665 |
| Jackson, W. H. | Automatic locking switch | Aug. 23, 1898 | 609,436 |
| Johnson, D. | Rotary dining table | Jan. 15, 1888 | 396,089 |
| Johnson, D. | Lawn mower attachment | Sept. 10, 1889 | 410,836 |
| Johnson, D. | Grass receivers for lawn mowers | June 10, 1890 | 429,629 |
| Johnson, I. R. | Bicycle frame | Oct. 10, 1899 | 634,823 |
| Johnson, P. | Swinging chairs | Nov. 15, 1881 | 249,530 |
| Johnson, P. | Eye protector | Nov. 2, 1880 | 234,039 |
| Johnson, W. | Egg beater | Feb. 5, 1884 | 292,821 |
| Johnson, W. | Velocipede | June 20, 1899 | 627,335 |
| Johnson, W. A. | Paint vehicle | Dec. 4, 1888 | 393,763 |
| Johnson, W. H. | Overcoming dead centers | Feb. 4, 1896 | 554,223 |
| Johnson, W. H. | Overcoming dead centers | Oct. 11, 1898 | 612,345 |
| Jones, F. M. | Ticket dispensing machine | June 27, 1939 | 2,163,754 |
| Jones, F. M. | Air conditioning unit | July 12, 1949 | 2,475,841 |
| Jones, F. M. | Two-cycle gasoline engine | Nov. 28, 1950 | 2,523,273 |
| Jones, F. M. | Starter generator | July 12, 1949 | 2,475,842 |
| Jones, F. M,[a] | Thermostat and temperature control system | Feb. 23, 1960 | 2,926,005 |
| Jones & Long | Caps for bottles | Sept. 13, 1898 | 610,715 |
| Joyce, J. A. | Ore bucket | Apr. 26, 1898 | 603,143 |
| Julian, Hubert | Airplane safety device | May 24,1921 | 1, 379,264 |
| Julian, Percy L. | Preparation of Cortisone | Aug. 10, 1954 | 2,752, 339 |
| Julian, P.C.et al. | Recovery of sterols | Oct 22, 1940 | 2,718, 971 |
| Latimer, L. H. | Lamp Fixture | Aug. 10, 1910 | 968, 787 |
| Latimer, L. H. | Manufacturing carbons | June 17, 1882 | 252,386 |
| Latimer, L. H. | Apparatus for cooling and disinfecting | Jan. 12, 1886 | 334,078 |
| Latimer, L. H. | Locking racks for hats, coats, and umbrellas | Mar. 24, 1896 | 557,076 |
| Latimer & Nichols | Electric lamp | Sept. 13, 1881 | 247,097 |
| Latimer & Tregoning | Globe support for electric lamps | Mar. 21, 1882 | 255,212 |
| Lavalette, W. | Printing press (variation) | Sept. 17, 1878 | 208,208 |
| Lee, H. | Animal trap | Feb. 12, 1867 | 61,941 |
| Lee, J. | Kneading machine | Aug. 7, 1894 | 524,042 |
| Lee, J. | Bread crumbing machine | June 4, 1895 | 540,553 |
| Leslie, F. W. | Envelope seal | Sept. 21, 1897 | 590,325 |
| Lewis, A. L. | Window cleaner | Sept. 27, 1892 | 483,359 |
| Lewis, E. R. | Spring gun | May 3, 1887 | 362,096 |
| Linden, H. | Piano truck | Sept. 8, 1891 | 459,365 |
| Littlc, E. | Bridle-bit | Mar. 7, 1882 | 254,666 |
| Loudin, F. J. | Sash fastener | Dec. 12, 1892 | 510,432 |
| Loudin, F. J. | Key fastener | Jan. 9, 1894 | 512,308 |
| Love, J. L. | Plasterers' hawk | July 9, 1895 | 542,419 |
| Love, J. L. | Pencil sharpener | Nov. 23, 1897 | 594,114 |
| Marshall, T. J. | Fire extinguisher (variation) | May 26, 1872 | 125,063 |
| Marshall, W. | Grain binder | May 11, 1886 | 341,599 |
| Martin, W. A. | Lock | July 23, 1889 | 407,738 |
| Martin, W. A. | Lock | Dec. 30, 1890 | 443,945 |
| Matzeliger, J. E. | Mechanism for distributing tacks | Nov. 26, 1899 | 415,726 |
| Matzeliger, J. E. | Nailing machine | Feb. 25, 1896 | 421,954 |
| Matzeliger, J. E. | Tack separating mechanism | Mar. 25, 1890 | 423,937 |
| Matzeliger, J. E. | Lasting machine | Sept. 22, 1891 | 459,899 |
| McCoy, E. | Lubricator for steam engines | July 2, 1872 | 129,843 |
| McCoy, E. | Lubricator for steam engines | Aug. 6, 1872 | 130,305 |

[a] Jones also patented multiple devices related to gas engines and temperature control between 1939 and 1960.

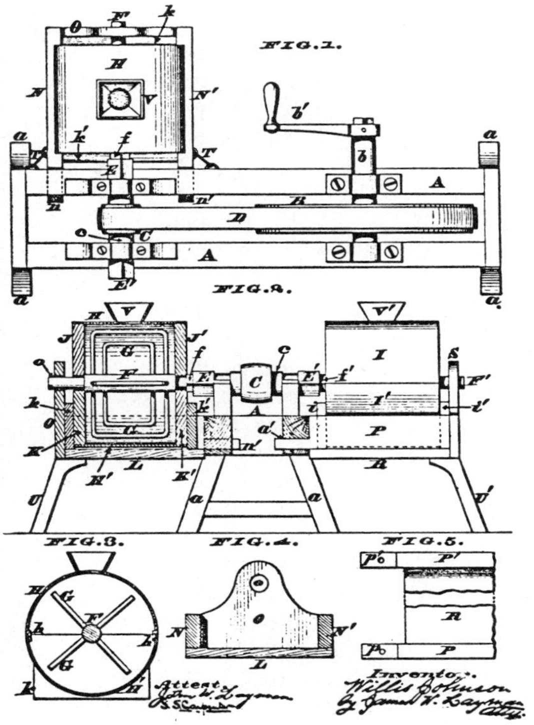


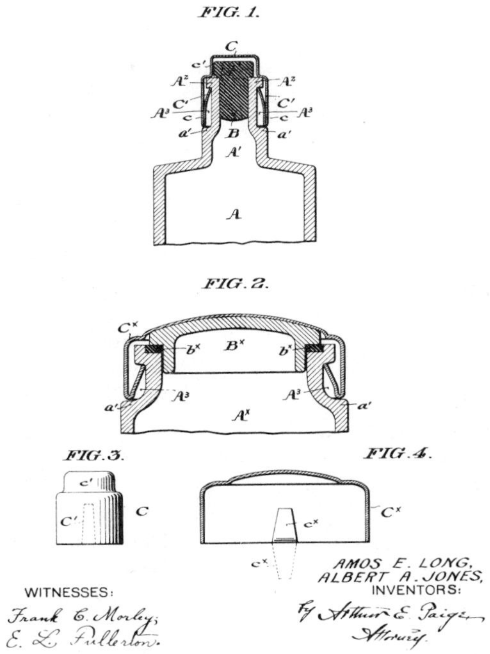


| Inventor | Invention | Date | Patent |
|---|---|---|---|
| McCoy, E. | Steam lubricator | Jan. 20, 1874 | 146,697 |
| McCoy, E. | Ironing table | May 12, 1874 | 150,876 |
| McCoy, E. | Steam cylinder lubricator | Feb. 1, 1876 | 173,032 |
| McCoy, E. | Steam cylinder lubricator | July 4, 1876 | 179,585 |
| McCoy, E. | Law sprinkler design | Sept. 26, 1899 | 631,549 |
| McCoy, E. | Steam dome | June 16, 1885 | 320,354 |
| McCoy, E. | Lubricator attachment | Apr. 19, 1887 | 361,435 |
| McCoy, E. | Lubricator for safety valves | May 24, 1887 | 363,529 |
| McCoy, E. [a] | Drip cup | Sept. 29, 1891 | 460,215 |
| McCoy & Hodges | Lubricator | Dec. 24, 1889 | 418,139 |
| McCree, D. | Portable fire escape | Nov. 11, 1890 | 440,322 |
| Mendenhall, A. | Holder for driving reins | Nov. 28, 1899 | 637,811 |
| Miles, A. | Elevator | Oct. 11, 1887 | 371,207 |
| Mitchell, C. L. | Phoneterism | Jan 1, 1884 | 291,071 |
| Mitchell, J. M. | Check row corn planter | Jan 16, 1900 | 641,462 |
| Moody, W. U. | Game board design | May 11, 1897 | 27,046 |
| Morehead, K. | Reel carrier | Oct. 6, 1896 | 568,916 |
| Murray, G. W. | Combined furrow opener and stalk-knocker | Apr. 10, 1894 | 517,960 |
| Murray, G. W. | Cultivator and marker | Apr. 10, 1894 | 517,961 |
| Murray, G. W. | Planter | June 5, 1894 | 520,887 |
| Murray, G. W. | Cotton chopper | June 5, 1894 | 520,888 |
| Murray, G. W. | Fertilizer distributor | June 5, 1894 | 520,889 |
| Murray, G. W. | Planter | June 5, 1894 | 520,891 |
| Murray, G. W. | Planter and fertilizer distributor reaper | June 5, 1894 | 520,892 |
| Murray, W. | Attachment for bicycles | Jan 27, 1891 | 445,452 |
| Nance, L. | Game apparatus | Dec. 1, 1891 | 464,035 |
| Nash, H. H. | Life-preserving stool | Oct. 5, 1875 | 168,519 |
| Newson, S. | Oil heater or cooker | May 22, 1894 | 520,188 |

[a] *In addition, McCoy held 16 different patents for lubricators designed between 1873 and 1899.*

| Inventor | Invention | Date | Patent |
|---|---|---|---|
| Nichols & Latimer | Electric lamp (variation) | Sept. 13, 1881 | 247,097 |
| Nickerson, W. J. | Mandolin and guitar attachment for pianos | June 27, 1899 | 627,739 |
| O'Conner & Turner | Alarm for boilers | Aug. 25, 1896 | 566,612 |
| O'Conner & Turner | Steam gage | Aug. 25, 1896 | 566,613 |
| O'Conner & Turner | Alarm for coasts containing vessels | Feb. 8, 1898 | 598,572 |
| Outlaw, J. W. | Alarm for coasts containing vessels | Feb. 8, 1898 | 598,572 |
| Outlaw, J. W. | Horseshoes | Nov. 15, 1898 | 614,273 |
| Perryman, F. R. | Caterers' tray table | Feb. 2, 1892 | 468,038 |
| Perry, John Jr & Hunger, H.F. | Biochem Fuel Cell | Nov. 8, 1966 | 3, 284, 239 |
| Peterson, H. | Attachment for lawn mowers | Apr. 30, 1889 | 402 189 |
| Phelps, W. H. | Apparatus for washing vehicles | Mar. 23, 1897 | 579,242 |
| Pickering, J. F. | Air ship | Feb. 20, 1900 | 643,975 |
| Pickett, H. | Scaffold | June 30, 1874 | 152,511 |
| Pinn, T. B. | File holder | Aug. 17, 1880 | 231,355 |
| Polk, A. J. | Bicycle support | Apr. 14, 1896 | 558,103 |
| Prather, Al. G.B. | Man powered glider aircraft | Feb. 6, 1973 | 3, 715, 011 |
| Pugsley, A. | Blind stop | July 29, 1890 | 433,306 |
| Purdy, W. | Device for sharpening edged tools | Oct. 27, 1896 | 570,337 |
| Purdy, W. | Design for sharpening edged tools | Aug. 16, 1898 | 609,367 |
| Purdy, W. | Device for sharpening edged tools | Aug. 1, 1899 | 630,106 |
| Purdy & Peters | Design for spoons | Apr. 23, 1895 | 24,228 |
| Purdy & Sadgwar | Folding chair | June 11, 1889 | 405,117 |
| Purvis, W. B. | Bag fastener | Apr. 25, 1882 | 256,856 |
| Purvis, W. B. | Hand stamp | Feb. 27, 1883 | 273,149 |
| Purvis, W. B. | Fountain pen | Jan. 7, 1890 | 419,065 |
| Purvis, W. B. | Electric railway (variation) | May 1, 1894 | 519,291 |
| Purvis, W. B. | Magnetic car balancing device | May 21, 1895 | 539,542 |
| Purvis, W. B. | Electric railway switch | Aug. 17, 1897 | 588,176 |
| Queen, W. | Guard for companion ways and hatches | Aug. 18, 1891 | 458,131 |
| Ray, E. P. | Chair supporting device | Feb. 21, 1899 | 620,078 |
| Ray, L. P. | Dust pan | Aug. 3, 1897 | 587,607 |
| Reed, J. W. | Dough kneader and roller | Sept. 23, 1884 | 305,474 |
| Reynolds, H. H. | Window ventilator for railroad cars | Apr. 3, 1883 | 275,271 |
| Reynolds, H. H. | Safety gate for bridges | Oct. 7, 1890 | 437,937 |
| Reynolds, R. R. | Nonrefillable bottle | May 2, 1899 | 624,092 |
| Rhodes, J. B. | Water closets | Dec. 19, 1899 | 639,290 |
| Richardson, A. C. | Hame fastener | Mar. 14, 1882 | 255,022 |
| Richardson, A. C. | Churn | Feb. 17, 1891 | 466,470 |
| Richardson, A. C. | Casket-lowering device | Nov. 13, 1894 | 529,311 |
| Richardson, A. C. | Insect destroyer | Feb. 28, 1899 | 620,363 |
| Richardson, A. C. | Bottle | Dec. 12, 1899 | 638,811 |
| Richardson, W. H. | Cotton chopper | June 1, 1886 | 343,140 |
| Richardson, W. H. | Child's carriage | June 18, 1889 | 405,599 |
| Richardson, W. H. | Child's carriage | June 18, 1889 | 405,600 |
| Richey, C. V. | Car coupling | June 15, 1897 | 584,650 |
| Richey, C. V. | Railroad switch | Aug. 3, 1897 | 587,657 |
| Richey, C. V. | Railroad switch | Oct. 26, 1897 | 592,448 |
| Richey, C. V. | Fire escape bracket | Dec. 28, 1897 | 596,427 |
| Richey, C. V. | Combined hammock and stretcher | Dec. 13, 1898 | 615,907 |
| Rickman, A. L. | Overshoe | Feb. 8, 1898 | 598,816 |
| Ricks, J. | Horseshoe | Mar. 30, 1886 | 338,781 |
| Ricks, J. | Overshoes for horses | June 6, 1899 | 626,245 |
| Rillieux, N. | Sugar refiner (evaporating pan) | Dec. 10, 1846 | 4,879 |
| Robinson, E. R. | Electric railway trolley | Sept. 19, 1893 | 505,370 |
| Robinson, E. R. | Casting composite | Nov. 23, 1897 | 594,386 |
| Robinson, J. H. | Lifesaving guards for locomotives | Mar. 14, 1899 | 621,143 |
| Robinson, J. H. | Lifesaving guards for street cars | Apr. 25, 1899 | 623,929 |
| Robinson, J. | Dinner pail | Feb. 1, 1887 | 356,852 |
| Romain, A. | Passenger register | Apr. 23, 1889 | 402,035 |

| Inventor | Invention | Date | Patent |
|---|---|---|---|
| Ross, A. L. | Runner for stops | Aug. 4, 1896 | 565,301 |
| Ross, A. L. | Bag closure | June 7, 1898 | 605,343 |
| Ross, A. L. | Trousers support | Nov. 28, 1899 | 638,068 |
| Ross, J. | Bailing press | Sept. 5, 1899 | 632,539 |
| Roster, D. N. | Feather curler | Mar. 10, 1896 | 556,166 |
| Ruffin, S. | Vessels for liquids and manner of sealing | Nov. 20, 1899 | 737,603 |
| Russell, L. A. | Guard attachment for beds | Aug. 13, 1895 | 544,381 |
| Sampson, G. T | Sled propeller | Feb. 17, 1885 | 312,388 |
| Sampson, G. T. | Clothes drier | June 7, 1892 | 476,416 |
| Scottron, S. R. | Adjustable window cornice | Feb. 17, 1880 | 224,732 |
| Scottron, S. R. | Cornice | Jan. 16, 1883 | 270,851 |
| Scottron, S. R. | Pole tip | Sept. 21, 1886 | 349,525 |
| Scottron, S. R. | Curtain rod | Aug. 30, 1892 | 481,720 |
| Scottron, S. R. | Supporting bracket | Sept. 12, 1893 | 5O5,008 |
| Shanks, S. C. | Sleeping car berth register | July 21, 1897 | 587,165 |
| Shewcraft, Frank | Letter box | Detroit, Mich. | |
| Shorter, D. W. | Feed rack | May 17, 1887 | 363,089 |
| Smith , B. & L.E. Branovich, & G.L. Freeman | Mtd. or preparing nonlaminating anisotropic Boron Nitride | Oct. 1, 1985 | 4, 544, 535 |
| Smith, J. W. | Improvement in games | Apr. 17, 1900 | 647,887 |
| Smith, J. W. | Lawn sprinkler | May 4, 1897 | 581,785 |
| Smith, J. W. | Lawn sprinkler | Mar. 22, 1898 | 601,065 |
| Smith, P. D. | Potato digger | Jan. 21, 1891 | 445,206 |
| Smith, P. D. | Grain binder | Feb. 23, 1892 | 469,279 |
| Snow & Johns | Liniment | Oct. 7, 1890 | 437,728 |
| Spears, H. | Portable shield for infantry | Dec. 27, 1870 | 110,599 |
| Spikes, R. B. | Combination milk bottle opener and bottle cover | June 29, 1926 | 1,590,557 |
| Spikes, R. B. | Method and apparatus for obtaining average samples and temperature of tank liquids | Oct. 27, 1931 | 1,828,753 |
| Spikes, R. B. | Automatic gear shift | Dec. 6, 1932 | 1,889,814 |
| Spikes, R. B. | Transmission and shifting thereof | Nov. 28, 1933 | 1,936,996 |
| Spikes, R. B. | Self-locking rack for billiard cues | around 1910 | not found |
| Spikes, R. B. | Automatic shoeshine chair | around 1939 | not found |
| Spikes, R. B. | Multiple barrel machine gun | c1940 | not found |
| Standard, J. | Oil stove | Oct. 29, 1889 | 413,689 |
| Standard, J. | Refrigerator | July 14, 1891 | 455,891 |
| Stewart, E. W. | Punching machine | May 3, 1887 | 362,190 |
| Stewart, E. W. | Machine for forming vehicle seat bars | Mar. 22, 1887 | 373,698 |
| Stewart, T. W. | Mop | June 13, 1893 | 499,402 |
| Stewart, T. W. | Station indicator | June 20, 1893 | 499,895 |
| Stewart & Johnson | Metal bending machine | Dec. 27, 1887 | 375,512 |
| Sutton, E. H. | Cotton cultivator | Apr. 7, 1878 | 149,543 |
| Sweeting, J. A. | Device for rolling cigarettes | Nov. 30, 1897 | 594,501 |
| Sweeting, J. A. | Combined knife and scoop | June 7, 1898 | 605,209 |
| Taylor, B. H. | Rotary engine | Apr. 23, 1878 | 202,888 |
| Taylor, B. H. | Slide valve | July 6, 1897 | 585,798 |
| Temple, L. | Toggle harpoon | 1848 | |
| Thomas, S. E. | Waste trap | Oct. 16, 1883 | 286,746 |
| Thomas, S. E. | Waste trap for basins, closets, etc. | Oct. 4, 1887 | 371,107 |
| Thomas, S. E. | Casting | July 31, 1888 | 386,941 |
| Thomas, S. E. | Pipe connection | Oct. 9, 1888 | 390,821 |
| Toliver, George | Propeller for vessels | Apr. 28, 1891 | 451,086 |
| Tregoning & Latimer | Globe supporter for electric lamps | Mar. 21, 1882 | 255,212 |
| Walker, Peter | Machine for cleaning seed cotton | Feb. 16, 1897 | 577,153 |
| Walker, Peter | Bait holder | Mar. 8, 1898 | 600,241 |
| Waller, J. N. | Shoemaker's cabinet or bench | Feb. 3, 1880 | 224,253 |
| Washington, Wade | Corn husking machine | Aug. 14, 1883 | 283 173 |
| Watkins, Isaac | Scrubbing frame | Oct. 7, 1890 | 437,849 |

| Inventor | Invention | Date | Patent |
|---|---|---|---|
| Watts, J. R. | Bracket for miners' lamp | Mar. 7, 1893 | 493,137 |
| West, E. H. | Weather shield | Sept. 5, 1899 | 632 385 |
| West, J. W. | Wagon | Oct. 18, 1870 | 108 419 |
| White, D. L. | Extension steps for cars | Jan. 12, 1897 | 574,969 |
| White, J. T. | Lemon squeezer | Dec. 8, 1896 | 572,849 |
| Williams, Carter | Canopy frame | Feb. 2, 1892 | 468,280 |
| Williams, J. P. | Pillow sham holder | Oct. 10, 1899 | 634,784 |
| Winn, Frank | Direct acting steam engine | Dec. 4, 1888 | 394,047 |
| Winters, J. R. | Fire escape ladder | May 7, 1878 | 203,517 |
| Winters, J. R. | Fire escape ladder | Apr. 8, 1879 | 214,224 |
| Woods, G. T. | Steam boiler furnace | June 3, 1884 | 299,894 |
| Woods, G. T. | Telephone transmitter (variation) | Dec. 2, 1884 | 3,088,176 |
| Woods, G. T. | Apparatus for transmission of messages by electricity | Apr. 7, 1885 | 315,368 |
| Woods, G. T. | Relay instrument | June 7, 1887 | 364,619 |
| Woods, G. T. | Polarized relay | July 5, 1887 | 366,192 |
| Woods, G. T. | Electromechanical brake | Aug. 16, 1887 | 368,265 |
| Woods, G. T. | Telephone system and apparatus | Oct. 11, 1887 | 371,241 |
| Woods, G. T. | Electromagnetic brake apparatus | Oct. 18, 1887 | 371,655 |
| Woods, G. T. | Railway telegraphy | Nov. 15, 1887 | 373,383 |
| Woods, G. T. | Induction telegraph system | Nov. 29, 1887 | 373,915 |
| Woods, G. T. | Overhead conducting system for electric railway | May 29, 1888 | 383,844 |
| Woods, G. T. | Electromotive railway system | June 26, 1888 | 385,034 |
| Woods, G. T. | Tunnel construction for electric railway | July 17, 1888 | 386,282 |
| Woods, G. T. | Galvanic battery | Aug. 14, 1888 | 387,839 |
| Woods, G. T. | Railway telegraphy | Aug. 28, 1888 | 388,803 |
| Woods, G. T. | Automatic safety cut-out for electric circuits | Jan. 1, 1889 | 395,533 |
| Woods, G. T. | Automatic safety cut-out for electric circuits | Oct. 14, 1889 | 438,590 |
| Woods, G. T. | Electric railway system | Nov. 10, 1891 | 463,020 |
| Woods, G. T. | Electric railway supply system | Oct. 31, 1893 | 507,606 |
| Woods, G. T. | Electric railway conduit | Nov. 21, 1893 | 509,065 |
| Woods, G. T. | System of electrical distribution | Oct. 13, 1896 | 569,443 |
| Woods, G. T. | Amusement apparatus | Dec. 19, 1899 | 639,692 |
| Wormley, James | Lifesaving apparatus | May 24, 1881 | 242,091 |

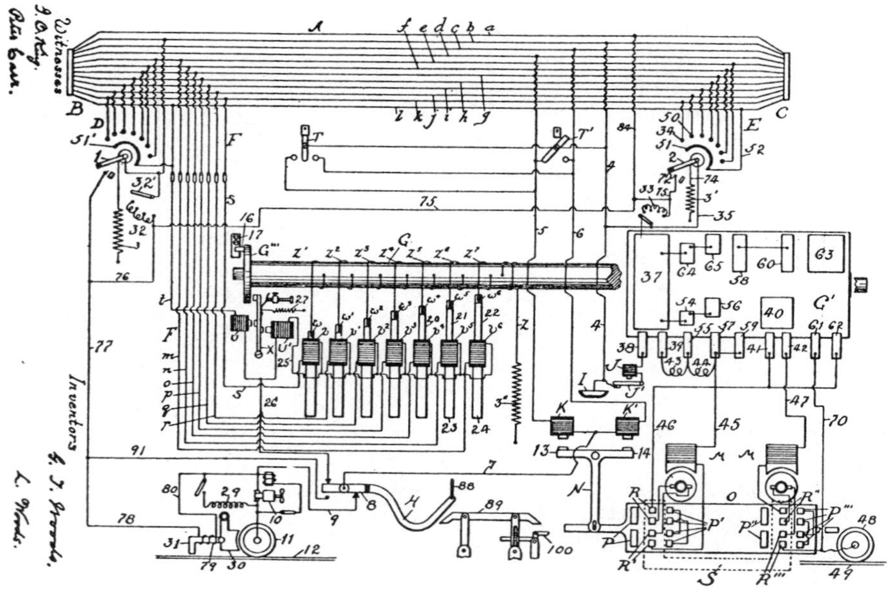

# THE BLACK ENTERTAINER IN THE PERFORMING ARTS

**Early American Theater ■ Blackface and Minstrelsy ■ Post-Civil War Theater Groups ■ Serious Drama ■ The Renaissance ■ The 1930s to the Present ■ Outstanding Black Entertainers ■ Plays By and About Blacks ■ Other Black Entertainers**

The black contribution to the world of American entertainment has been powerful, personal, and profound. The black presence has been felt to a degree far greater than could normally be expected, given the clear population minority blacks represent and the barely peripheral place which American society often provides them. Nonetheless, much of what the world at large considers uniquely American in the performing arts can be traced directly to black performers and their heritage. For more than a century, the most formidable obstacle faced by black entertainers was that they were often excluded—both as spectator and participant—from those public places of entertainment which are the logical training ground for any performer. Nevertheless, from the earliest days of slavery, entertainment was one of the few avenues of expression open to blacks.

In the book *Black Magic,* Langston Hughes and Milton Meltzer document that the "first stage for the captive Africans was the open deck of a slave ship. There, on the way to the Americas, blacks in chains, when herded up on deck for exercise, were forced to sing and dance in the open air for the amusement of the crew." After reaching the southern plantations, the African traditions, rhythms, and dances that had survived the cultural transplantation mixed with a developing folk tradition to form the basis for black American entertainment. Drawings, paintings, and patches of oral history depict the rich folklore which provided virtually the only entertainment and means of self-expression for black slaves.

As singers, dancers, or bones players, slaves were often called upon to perform for their masters and, if talented enough, were even hired out by them to entertain others. Numerous newspaper advertisements for slave entertainers of the antebellum period can be found in *Readings in Black American Music* by Eileen Southern. Best remembered of the slave entertainers is Blind Tom, a talented pianist, whose many concerts in the United States and Europe won fame for himself and profit for Colonel Bethune, his owner. Blind Tom's story has been dramatized by Theodore Ward in the musical *Charity.*

Slaves also used the medium of religious songs (considered "safe" by the masters) to express their dissatisfaction with their lot. In this fashion, *Go Down Moses, Oh Freedom, God's Gonna Cut You Down,* and many other spirituals have become part of the vast oral tradition created by the black musical artist. After the Civil War, the Fisk Jubilee Singers extended the realm of the Negro spiritual to the international arena by going on a tour of Europe with "Negro" music as the basis of their repertoire.

*Tribal music and dances, kept alive on colonial plantations, gradually blended into Afro-American culture.*

### European Traditions

While blacks were beginning to build up Afro-American culture in the fields and slave shacks of plantations, the American theater was still growing from European roots. This cultural lag showed itself in a peculiar, unnatural conception of blacks on the stage.

From the role of the black magus in the medieval plays to *Othello* on the Elizabethan stage, the black was most often presented as the "noble Moor." Shakespeare himself believed that Moors were Negroes, even without scientific verification. His investiture of Othello with the alleged personal attributes and moral characteristics of "the Negroes" of Elizabethan England was by no means accidental, nor was it even an unusual dramatic license for Shakespeare.

*Othello* was followed, in 1696, by *Oroonoko,* a tragedy in five acts written by Thomas Southerne. The hero was an African prince stolen from Angola during the reign of Charles II and sold as a slave in the West Indies. The "noble Moor" image was dying, fading into another stereotype. On stage, Oroonoko had black skin and woolly hair, spoke in the stilted blank verse of the period, and showed more traits assignable to the buffoon than to an African prince.

Another stage black of dubious authenticity was Mungo, slave hero of the comic opera *The Padlock.* The stage role was at least played by an Englishman who had studied the manners and dialect of the black man he was trying to impersonate. However, the writing reflected little real contact with any black cultural context. The result was that Mungo was a further step in the development of the lowly stereotype. This stereotype was given a powerful expression in the character Friday, in *Robinson Crusoe*, who is portrayed as having no options other than remaining a low-born savage or becoming a contented, ignorant servant.

This poor fellow was the chief black image imported to the American theater. Apparently the first black character in an American play appeared in *The Disappointment or, The Force of Credulity* in 1767. The character, a comic stereotype, was named "Raccoon." From these beginnings the history of blacks in the American theater can be viewed as a progression throughout two centuries from stereotypical to realistic portrayals.

### Early American Theater

In the United States, references to the black actor are rare in any setting prior to 1821. A unique handbill of "The African Company," at "The Theatre in Mercer Street, in the rear of the 1 Mile Stone, Broadway," refers to two dramatic offerings: *Tom and Jerry* and *Obi, or Three Fingered Jack.* These are believed to be the only traces of a company of black amateurs who played in New York about 1820 or 1821.

During the same epoch New York City was host to the foundation of the African Grove Theatre. Little is known about the origins of this important theater. One Henry Brown wrote *King Shotaway,* generally recognized as the first drama by a black man in the United States. Brown is also credited with founding the African Grove. This black-operated theater was one of only four theaters (the other three were white operated) that existed in New York City before 1830. During the early 1820s, this house presented regular performances by the famous tragedians James Hewlitt, from the West Indies, and Ira Aldridge. Unfortunately, hostile white audiences, segregated into the back of the auditorium, caused disturbances that eventually forced the theater to close. By 1824, Ira Aldridge, one of the great Shakespearean actors of the nineteenth century, had gauged there was no future for his talents in the Americas and left for

*White minstrels caricatured blacks and black music in the period from 1830 to 1860. From left are George Christy, Charley White, and T. D. Rice (the original "Jim Crow").*

Europe, where he enjoyed a highly successful career, his most memorable role being Othello, for which he received numerous royal awards.

### Blackface and Minstrelsy

Comic roles were the forte of the white-turned-black actor. In 1823, at the Globe Theatre in Cincinnati, Edwin Forrest played a black in a farce called *The Tailor in Distress,* singing and dancing, and winning the praise from a black onlooker that he was indeed "nigger all over." Other eminent American actors who donned blackface include "Sol" Smith and Bernard Flaherty. In 1850, when Edwin Booth was 17, and a year after his debut at the Boston Museum, he gave a performance with a friend at the courthouse in Belair, Maryland. Along with selections from *Richelieu* and *Julius Caesar,* they also sang, with blackened faces, a number of Negro melodies, "using appropriate dialogue," as Mrs. Asia Booth Clarke records in the memoirs of her brother. Ralph Keeler was among the most prominent of the stage Negroes of later years. His *Three Years a Negro Minstrel,* first published in the *Atlantic Monthly* for July 1869, is instructive reading, and gives an excellent idea of the wandering minstrel of that period.

Thomas D. Rice, though not the originator, was the man who made so-called Ethiopian minstrelsy popular on both sides of the Atlantic. The history of "Jim Crow Rice," as he was affectionately called for many years, was recounted with particular vividness in the columns of the *New York Times*, June 5,1881. In back of the Louisville theater was a livery stable kept by a man named Crow. The actors could look into the stable yard from the windows of their dressing rooms and were fond of watching the movements of an old and decrepit slave who was employed by the proprietor to do odd jobs. The slave, who called himself Jim Crow, was physically deformed—the right shoulder was drawn up high, and the left leg was stiff and crooked at the knee. As he walked with his painful, but at the same time ludicrous, limp, he was in the habit of crooning an old tune, to which he had applied words of his own. At the end of each verse he gave a peculiar step, "rocking de heel" in the manner that has since become so general among the long generations of his delineators. The words of his refrain were as follows:

*Wheel about, turn about*
*Do jis so,*
*An' ebery time I wheel about*
*I jump Jim Crow.*

Rice closely watched this unconscious performer, and recognized in him a character entirely new to the stage. He wrote a number of verses, quickened and slightly changed the air (made up exactly like the original), and appeared before a Louisville audience, which reportedly went mad with delight, recalling him on the first night at least 20 times. And so Jim Crow, reinforcing the image of the black buffoon, jumped into the dramatic pantheon.

Rice aside, the first band of black minstrels was organized in the boarding house of Mrs. Brooks, in Catherine Street, New York, late in the winter of 1842, consisting of "Dan" Emmet, "Frank" Brower, "Billy" Whitlock, and "Dick" Pelham. They opened at the Chatham Theatre, New York, on February 17, 1843, and later toured other American cities before going on to Europe. Not until after the Civil War did black performers begin appearing regularly in minstrel shows, and then usually under the supervision of white managers.

What the review of minstrelsy indicates is that, although much credit was due to the minstrel, the basic popularity was dependent on the black melody he introduced and on the characteristic bones, banjo, and tambourine upon which he accompanied himself. It was certainly the song, not the singer, which once moved Thackeray to write:

*Talanted black performers, like the Canadian Jubilee Singers, were internationally famous in the last century.*

*I heard a humorous balladist not long since, a minstrel with wool on his head and an ultra-Ethiopian complexion, who performed a Negro ballad that I confess moistened these spectacles in a most unexpected manner. I have gazed at thousands of tragedy queens dying on the stage and expiring in appropriate blank-verse, and I never wanted to wipe them. They have looked up, be it said, at many scores of clergymen without being dimmed; and behold, a vagabond with a corked face and a banjo sings a little song, strikes a wild note, which sets the heart thrilling with happy pity.*

Despite Joel Chandler Harris' contention that he'd never seen a banjo in the hands of a black on any of the plantations of middle Georgia, there is much evidence of the instrument's popularity. George Washington Cable, in a pre-Civil War work, quotes a popular Creole ditty in which "Musieu Bainjo" is mentioned in every line. Maurice Thompson says the banjo is a common instrument among the field hands in North Georgia, Alabama, and Tennessee, and describes a rude banjo manufactured by its "dusky" performer out of a flat gourd, strung with horsehair. In Jefferson's *Notes on Virginia,* printed in 1784, the following statement is worthy of note:"In music they [the blacks] are more generally gifted than the whites with accurate ears for tune and time, and they have been found capable of imagining a small catch." In a footnote, Jefferson adds: "The instrument proper to them is the banjar, which they brought hither from Africa."

### Post-Civil War Theater Groups

After the war, blacks formed their own groups, among them the Charles Hicks Georgia Minstrels and Lew Johnson's Plantation Minstrel Company. These groups copied their white counterparts' style of blackened face with red and white lines around the mouth. Audiences were usually segregated—whites on one side, blacks on the other. The important thing, however, was that black people had finally achieved a tenuous access to the American stage. Among the best known of these black minstrels was William C. Handy, who joined the W. A. Mahara Minstrels in 1896.

Female choruses were added to the previously all-male shows before the turn of the century. An example was *The Creole Show* (1891). When Bob Cole's *A Trip to Coontown* combined music with plot line in 1898, the black American musical was born. Cole worked with Sissieretta Jones in conceiving *Black Patti's Troubadours,* which toured widely to great acclaim. *Clorindy—The Origin of the Cakewalk,* with book by Paul Laurence Dunbar and music by Will Marion Cook, was a smash hit at New York's Casino Roof Garden.

These black minstrel shows flourishing in the mid- and late 1800s, usually carried bands consisting of only four instruments: tambourine, bones, fiddle, and banjo. These were the first black theater orchestras. At the beginning of this century black bands frequently traveled with carnivals, tent shows, and vaudeville companies. At the turn of the century and into the 1920s and 1930s black pit orchestras were popular as was black theater. This situation changed in the 1940s and 1950s when black musicians were employed in the theater only occasionally, and then only under pressure.

### Ragtime

The ragtime musical took a long stride closer to Broadway. In the shows of the Williams and Walker Company, this novel style of music flashed across the New York stage. Of all the Williams and Walker shows, from *Sons of Ham* through *Abyssinia* and *Bandanna Land,* the most successful was *In Dahomey*, which featured the work of Will Marion Cook, Paul Laurence Dunbar, and Jesse Shipp. This show toured both the United States and Europe following its first production in 1903.

The first decade of this century saw the hey-day of black musicals and vaudeville. Minstrelsy disappeared from the professional circuit. Unfortunately, George Walker's ill health led to the dissolving of the company. Bert Williams left to join the Follies in 1911. When Walker died a year later, another epoch in black theater history ended.

The cakewalk, the dance that had become an American craze by the turn of the century, was derived from the blacks' "chalk-line" walk, which they had presented at the 1876 celebration of the Centennial of American Independence in Philadelphia.

## Serious Drama

Besides the wealth of light musicals, the early 1900s witnessed the beginnings of serious black theater. The first attempts met with little public support. Scott Joplin wrote an opera, *Treemonisha*, in 1915, but could not find a producer, although friends backed it for a one-night run. In the 1970s when the musical score for *The Sting* was adapted from his compositions and *Treemonisha* became a hit on Broadway, Joplin finally received his due. The themes of lynching and racial injustice were addressed by Angela Grimkea's *Rachel* in a 1916 NAACP production. Although the play received attention and sparked controversy, the production was not a success.

On April 5, 1917, the production of three one-act plays by poet Ridgely Torrance, with music conducted and performed by blacks, marked "the first time anywhere in the United States for black actors in the dramatic theater to command the serious attention of the critics, the general press, and public."

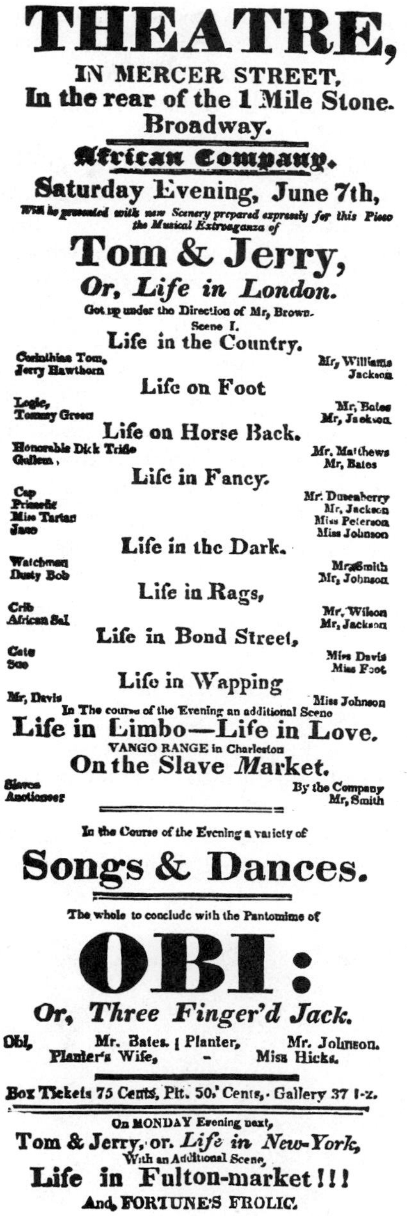


## The Renaissance

During World War I, small houses kept alive the spirit of black theater, preparing the way for the great Renaissance of the 1920s when hundreds of theaters sprang up all around the country. Some were simple movie houses which offered live entertainment at intermission; others were tent shows nostalgically clinging to the minstrel tradition. Many of them were eventually organized into the T.O.B.A. (Theatre Owners Booking Association), which operated into the beginning of the Great Depression. With member theaters across the country, including the Howard in Washington, D.C. and the Booker T. in St. Louis, T.O.B.A. provided work for many black actors and performers.

Harlem's Lafayette Theatre first received wide notice for its 1915 production of Miller and Lyles' *Darkydom*. In 1919, Anita Bush joined with Charles Gilpin to form the Lafayette Players, a touring company which enjoyed many successes. A year later Gilpin became famous for his creation of the role of Brutus Jones in Eugene O'Neill's *Emperor Jones*, and Bush went on to form her own stock company.

Russell and Rowena Jelliffe, white social workers devoted to integrated theater, founded Cleveland's Karamu Theatre in 1916.

## The Twenties

The "Negro" or "Harlem" Renaissance, which reached its peak in the 1920s, was an era of general harvest in black arts. This was the time of Howard philosopher Alain Locke's "New Negro" movement. Carter Woodson founded the Association for the Study of Negro Life and History, and throughout the nation artists' groups, theater groups, and writers' workshops came together, gelled, and produced. Every aspect of theater was touched by the energies of the Renaissance.

The early 1920s saw the growth and success of the Ethiopian Art Players, founded in Chicago. In 1923, this company brought the production of Willis Richardson's *Chip Woman's Fortune* to New York City. Two years later, Garland Anderson's *Appearances* became the first full-length drama by a black playwright to reach Broadway.

From the ragtime rhythms of the Williams and Walker era came musicals which imaginatively combined jazz and ragtime themes. The team of Miller and Lyles, starting at the Lafayette Theatre, joined with Noble Sissle and Eubie Blake. Together, they created *Shuffle Along*, one of the most popular shows in American theater since 1900. In 1921, *Shuffle Along* came to the Howard Theatre in Washington, D.C., for two weeks, then opened at the 63rd Street Theatre in New York City, and went on to become an international success. Josephine Baker was catapulted to stardom in a cast full of notables, including Florence Mills and Caterina Jarboro on stage and William Grant Still and Hall Johnson in the orchestra. All became famous in their own right.

With the success of this production, a new genre was adopted, and other shows followed the style and format of *Shuffle Along*. Sissle and Blake went on to produce *Chocolate Dandies;* Miller and Lyles came out with *Runnin' Wild, Keep Shufflin'*, and *Rang Tang*.

In 1924, Paul Robeson opened in O'Neill's *All God's Chillun Got Wings*. A controversy ensued, but the play had its clear effect: Rose McClendon, Abbie Mitchell, Jules Bledsoe, and Frank Wilson were cast in white playwright Paul Green's *In Abraham's Bosom,* which won the Pulitzer Prize.

The twenties was a great period for black musicals. Lew Leslie's *Blackbirds of 1928* starred the famous singer and dancer Bill Robinson. *Blackbirds of 1929* had music by Eubie Blake. Across the country the Renaissance spirit was manifest in many community-oriented productions.

Harlem was an oasis of black theater. The Crescent Theatre, the Lincoln Theatre, as well as the Lafayette and the Harlem Experimental Theatre in 1928, preceded and encouraged the Negro Art Theatre, Harlem Community Players, and the Dunbar Garden Players.

Elsewhere in America, W.E.B. DuBois had founded the Krigwa Players, sponsored by *Crisis* magazine, with member groups in various cities. The Krigwa players mostly performed one-act plays. Among great playwrights they produced were Georgia Douglass Johnson, Willis Richardson, and Eulalie Spence.

Richardson and May Miller were invited by Carter Woodson to write plays for Negro History Week, which was organized in part by playwright and educational theater proponent Randolph Edmonds. Richardson eventually published *Plays and Pageants from the Life of the Negro,* and with May Miller (Sullivan), *Negro History in Thirteen Plays*.

In sum, the creative energy of the Renaissance fed three very positive developments: the creation of the new musicals, the growth of black drama, and the expansion of the historical-educational theater movement.

## THE 1930S TO THE PRESENT

### The Thirties

In the early 1930s, there was a brief reversion. Black professional theater work was limited to stereotyped roles in plays and films by white writers, such as *Green Pastures* by Marc Connelly. By the middle of the decade, however, black theater was reasserting itself. Langston Hughes' *Mulatto* went to Broadway with Rose McClendon in the lead. Hall Johnson's musical *Run Little Chillun* was well received. In 1935, Dick Campbell joined forces with Rose McClendon to form the Negro People's Theatre, which enjoyed some early successes but came unstuck after the death of McClendon. Many of the members moved on to the Negro Unit of the Federal Theatre Project.

*Sensational Florence Mills, acclaimed as the leading black entertainer of her time.*

Founded under the sponsorship of the Works Progress Administration (WPA), the Negro Unit became the primary source of employment for black theater workers. The Lafayette Theatre was the core of the East Coast movement, with shows such as Orson Welles' *Macbeth,* cast in a Haitian setting. Other productions included William Dubois' *Haiti,* Frank Wilson's *Walk Together, Children,* and *Meek Moses,* and Rudolph Fisher's *The Conjure Man Dies*. In California, Clarence Muse directed Hall Johnson's *Run Little Chillun,* and in Seattle, the Federal Theatre performed Theodore Browne's *Natural Man*. When Congress cut off federal funds in 1939, the work stopped.

Independent community theaters fought for their lives during the Depression. The Harlem Suitcase Theatre was one. Founded by Langston Hughes and Louise Patterson in 1937, it opened with Hughes' *Don't You Want To Be Free?* This theater lasted just two years. Hughes then sought to spread his idea of a Negro People's Theatre by founding the New Negro Theatre (1939) in Los Angeles.

Dick Campbell and Muriel Rahn formed the Rose McClendon Players in the late 1930s. The group variously featured Canada Lee, Dooley Wilson, Frederick O'Neal, Ossie Davis, Ruby Dee, and Maxwell Glanville. Early productions included *Goodbye Again* by Arthur Kobers and *Having a Wonderful Time*. Moving to the 124th Street Library basement, the Rose McClendon Workshop Theatre opened officially in 1939 with Abram Hill's *On Strivers' Row*. The show was a big hit and has been revived frequently.

## The Forties

The American Negro Theatre (ANT) was formed in Harlem in 1940 by Abram Hill, Frederick O'Neal, and former members of the McClendon Players. ANT produced Hill's *On Strivers' Row* and *Walk Hard,* Theodore Brown's *Natural Man,* and Owen Dodson's *The Garden of Time.* Subsequently, Hill adapted *Anna Lucasta* for ANT presentation. The cast included Hilda Simms, Fred O'Neal, Alice Childress, Alvin Childress, and Earle Hyman. By the time *Anna Lucasta* reached Broadway in 1944, where it was destined to remain nearly three years, the cast variously included the talents of Canada Lee, Ossie Davis, Ruby Dee, and Frank Silvera. Despite its apparent success and support, ANT survived only a few years, the stresses of World War II playing a large part in its downfall.

Paul Robeson's portrayal of Othello, in the longest run a Shakespearean play has ever received in America, is often considered the peak of his prodigious career. Theodore Ward, one of America's leading playwrights, came out with two dramas in the late forties. His *Big White Fog* was produced as part of the Negro Playwrights' Company, and featured Canada Lee. In 1947, his *Our Lan'* reached the Broadway stage, but the script had been fatally watered down by director Eddie Dowling, and the play never received the acclaim it deserved.

By the end of the decade, many black actors and writers were among the casualties of the "Red Scare." The blacklisting of Paul Robeson and Canada Lee epitomized the outrage.

*Canada Lee in the Broadway hit* Anna Lucasta.

***Paul Robeson as the Emperor Jones.***

## The Fifties

These years are noted for the formation of small production companies and for little black activity on Broadway. But between the Committee for the Negro in the Arts, founded in 1951, and Lorraine Hansberry's award-winning *Raisin in the Sun* in 1959, many worthy productions were staged.

William Branch's *Medal for Willie* had its first production (1951) by the Committee. The play had a successful run, but elicited controversial reactions from both whites and blacks. Branch himself was inducted into the Army the day after the show opened. An earlier production of the Committee, Alice Childress' *Just a Little Simple*, adapted from Langston Hughes' *Simple Speaks His Mind* columns, opened at the Club Baron in the fall of 1950, but had only a short run.

Two companies successful in this period were Roger Furman's Negro Art Players and the Group formed by Maxville Glanville and Julian Mayfield. Both came to the stage in 1952. The Negro Art Players did such productions as Furman's *The Quiet Laughter,* T. Williams' *Mooney's Kids Don't Cry,* and Charles Griffin's *Oklahoma Bearcat.* Mayfield and Glanville opened with one-acts: *A World Full of Men* and *The Other Foot* by Mayfield, and Ossie Davis' *Alice in Wonder.* In 1953 Davis rewrote this one-act into *The Big Deal,* presented at the New Playwrights Theatre.

Louis Peterson's *Take a Giant Step* reached Broadway in 1953 with Frederick O'Neal, Pauline Meyers, Frank Wilson, and Louis Gossett's debut. Though favorably reviewed, the production suffered from empty seats and shortly died. It was revived three years later, off-Broadway, with Bill Gunn, Beah Richards, and Godfrey Cambridge.

In downtown Manhattan, the Greenwich Mews Theatre helped black theater survive the fifties. William Branch's *In Splendid Error* had a 1954 showing. The same year saw a production of Alice Childress' *Trouble in Mind,* starring Clarice Taylor and Hilda Simms. In 1957, Loften Mitchell's *Land Beyond the River* ran nearly a year, featuring, at various times, Diana Sands, Charles Griffin, Ivan Dixon, Douglas Turner Ward, and Roscoe Lee Brown.

Lorraine Hansberry's tragically short career flowered in 1959 when *Raisin in the Sun* reached New York after several small northeastern productions. The cast eventually included Ossie Davis, Diana Sands, Ruby Dee, and Sidney Poitier. Hansberry was awarded the Drama Critics' Circle Award.

## The Sixties

These years were a complex, uneven, and fertile period for black drama. A curious and tragic ambivalence affected both the artist and the actor, for the success of being courted in public by the foundations was played out against the backdrop of aborted lives and insufficient social change.

At the onset of the 1960s, black playwright Loften Mitchell reflected on the situation of his peers with some optimism, noting that such fellow playwrights as William Branch, Alice Childress, Louis Peterson, Theodore Ward, Langston Hughes, Gertrude Jeanette, Harold Holifield, Charles Sebree, and Lorraine Hansberry were either in production or the beneficiaries of critical acclaim. Within six years, the burst of promise had shriveled into despair. Lorraine Hansberry was dead after her second play, *The Sign in Sidney Brustein's Window,* had opened to mixed reviews; William Branch's *Wreath for Udomo* was performed successfully in Cleveland, but found little sympathy on the English stage; Alice Childress withdrew her *Trouble in Mind* when she grew disillusioned over hot-then-cold producers; Julian Mayfield's *417* found few dedicated backers; Louis Peterson suffered a heart attack and needed six months to recuperate. Loften Mitchell, though he produced *Tell Pharaoh* and *Ballad of the Winter Soldiers*, had become mistrustful. The difficulties were not strictly racial, but they were not totally divorced from racial alienation either.

The early sixties, swelling to the climax of the Civil Rights movement, had been a time of idealism and activism. *Fly Blackbird,* with book by James V. Hatch and music by C. Bernard Jackson, gives a lively musical portrayal of this era. The cast opening at the Metro Theatre in Los Angeles in 1961 included Micki Grant, Josie Dotson, Thelma Oliver, Camille Billops, George Takei, and Russ Ellis. The New York run, adding Avon Long to the cast, opened in 1962 to critical acclaim and won the Obie Award for best musical off-Broadway. Though it was not financially rewarding, Ossie Davis' 1961 *Purlie Victorious* was another of the era's optimistic hits.

By the time Adrienne Kennedy's *Funnyhouse of a Negro* opened at the Circle-in-the-Square (1963), integrationist ideals had begun to surrender to more nationalist politics, such as those eloquently dramatized by Imamu Amiri Baraka (then LeRoi Jones) and his Black Arts Theatre. Based in Harlem, because of a felt need to reside in the black community in order to speak truthfully about blacks, the theater went public with *Experimental Death #1* and quickly made a name for itself. Baraka's classic *Dutchman* went on to win an Obie and has had several revivals; *The Toilet* and *The Slave* also earned widespread recognition and acclaim, though white reviewers were stunned by the playwright's vehemence. In the late sixties, Baraka founded radical Spirit House in Newark's ghetto and continued to carry out his cultural ideals within the framework of that city's political struggles. By 1975, however, Baraka had abandoned his black nationalism for a political perspective oriented along class rather than color lines. In 1982, he was teaching history at the State University of New York's Stony Brook campus.

Another black big name to gather impact during the sixties was James Baldwin, whose angry plays appalled some white theatergoers. His *Amen Corner,* first produced at Howard University in 1954, was picked up by Frank Silvera's Theatre for Being on the West Coast in the early sixties. The play struggled to Broadway in 1965, with a brilliant lead played by Beah Richards, but ran for less than three months. *Blues for Mister Charlie*, opening in New York under the direction of Burgess Meredith and starring Diana Sands, Al Freeman Jr., and Rip Torn, also had an acclaimed but limited Broadway run.

Langston Hughes was another big name prominent during this period, but his was an idiom reflecting wit and wisdom rather than rage and rebuttal. He had a number of successes on and off Broadway.

There were more disappointments than surprises in the late sixties. Childress' *Wedding Band* went unproduced, as did much of the work of Mitchell. Along came Howard Sackler with a play called *The Great White Hope,* an ideal vehicle for James Earl Jones in the role of the first black heavyweight champion, Jack Johnson. The play was a success, though in the words of Mitchell, it did not have "one well-constructed scene." It was followed by the lusitanic *Big Time Buck White* which not even Muhammad Ali could save.

Other controversial plays which spanked the white public exposed racism both historically and in contemporary terms. They took their raps, though this did not in any way alter their efficacy. Among those included in this category are *Slave Ship* (Imamu Amiri Baraka), *Ceremonies in Dark Old Men* (Lonnie Elder), and *No Place to be Somebody* (Charles Gordone).

The abrasive spirit of the 1960s focused on the tensions building in American society. If it did not resolve them, it at least exposed them.

## Black Theater Companies

Aided by grants from the Ford Foundation, playwright Ed Bullins and artistic director Robert Macbeth founded the New Lafayette Theatre in 1966. Toward the goal of developing a successful theater for black people in their own community, the New Lafayette produced the works of Baraka,

Milner, Neil Harris, Marvin X, Richard Welsley, Martie Charles, Milburn Davis, and Bullins, to name but a few. Workshops in all aspects of the theater provided rich training for young people. *Black Theatre Magazine*, which published a total of six issues over the course of the theater's existence, was the first national periodical to devote itself exclusively to black theater. Unfortunately, the group ran out of funding in the early seventies, and the doors of the New Lafayette closed.

Douglas Turner Ward, actor-turned-playwright, had two one-acts: *Days of Absence* and *Happy Ending*, produced at the St. Marks Playhouse in 1966. Winning two Obies for them (writing and acting), Ward gave impetus to an entire movement which culminated in the formation of the foundation-sponsored Negro Ensemble Company (NEC).

### Black Theater Across the Nation

The success of black companies has not been limited to New York. The Free Southern Theatre was founded in 1963 by Gilbert Moses, John O'Neal, and Doris Derby. Making its base in Jackson, Mississippi, the group produced the plays of Tom Dent, Val Ferdinand, and Gilbert Moses. In New Orleans, the group's affiliate, Blkartsouth, adhered to the traditions of the Krigwa, New Lafayette, and Spirit House Movements. *Nkombo* was the quarterly published by the group. California's Inner City Cultural Center was founded in the late sixties and involved such diverse activities as touring dance groups and a local travel service. Inner City sponsored a repertory company which produced many plays of note. Other theaters formed around the country included Marvin X and Ed Bullins' Black Arts/West in San Francisco and Woodie Kings' Concept-East Theater in Detroit.

The late sixties also saw the resurgence of the black educational theater movement, which was begun in the early 1900s by Dr. Carter Woodson and Dr. Randolph Edmonds, then chairman of the drama department at Florida A&M University.

### The Seventies

By the early 1970s there were more than 60 black community theaters functioning throughout the United States. In 1970, the Negro Ensemble Company's production of *River Niger* moved to Broadway, attracting large audiences. In 1971, Melvin Van Peebles had two musicals running simultaneously on Broadway, *Ain't Supposed to Die a Natural Death* and *Don't Play Us Cheap*. In 1972, critic Howard Thompson, writing in the *New York Times*, described *A Revival; Change! Love Together! Organize!* as "impressive, vivid and often gripping"; it was the initial regularly scheduled offering of a major production by the National Black Theater located in Harlem and partly supported by the National Endowment for the Arts. Reviewing *Black Visions*, four playlets by Sonia Sanchez, Neil Harris, and Richard Wesley, presented by Joseph Papp at the storefront annex to the Public Theater in New York, both *Time* and *Newsweek* magazines commented on the "new" black theater. T. E. Kalem in the May 1, 1972 issue of *Time* wrote:

*Current plays written by blacks about blacks display strange and interesting aspects of the prickly pride of the outcast. They almost brazenly embrace some of the least admirable notions about blacks held by many whites—that they can be lazy, foulmouthed, deadbeats addicted to alcohol, gambling, and promiscuity. Another aspect of black drama is that it bears a surprising relationship to the class-conscious plays of the '30s. The manner is naturalistic. The tone is hortatory. The focus is not on individuals but on a downtrodden group undergoing a consciousness-raising exercise.*

Jack Kroll in the April 17, 1972 issue of *Newsweek* wrote:

*The American black man, from slavery on, has always been trapped in reality, and his art, especially his music, has always been the most brilliant example in Western culture of redeeming the time... The new black theater continues this tradition, but it goes beyond redeeming the time, and begins to shape a new time, a time that has always been hinted and heralded in the rhythms of American black art. In* Black

*Fats Waller's music and a very talented cast received the coveted Tony Award for* Ain't Misbehavin', *a smash Broadway success. (left to right:) Ken Page, Charlaine Woodard, Nell Carter, Armelia McQueen, Andre De Shields, and Luther Henderson (at the piano).*

Visions *one can see in microcosm the answer to the perennial black question, "What's happening?"*
*What's happening is that the growing number of remarkable people—writers, actors, directors, designers and a remarkable number of people who combine these roles—are engaged in an extraordinary attempt to hold the mirror up to the unnature of the American black man's life... The new black theater is preparing for transformation by insisting on reality. From this strong base, hopefully it will, as the brilliant black director Robert Macbeth says, "be moved on by the swell of reality" into a theater that has a chance to be unique for its mixture of esthetic form and social power.*

Throughout the 1970s, there were notable black successes on Broadway as well as many Off-Broadway productions. In 1974, *Sizwe Banzi Is Dead* by Athol Fugard, a white South African, opened to critical acclaim on Broadway. Its stars, black actors John Kani and Winston Ntshona, both won Tony Awards. In 1975, *The Wiz,* the black musical version of the children's classic *The Wizard of Oz,* opened on Broadway, with a book by William F. Brown and music and lyrics by Charles Smalls. In 1976, poet Ntozake Shange's verse play For *Colored Girls Who Have Considered Suicide When the Rainbow Is Enuf* moved from Joseph Papp's Public Theatre to Broadway where it had the greatest success of any serious black play since Lorraine Hansberry's *A Raisin in the Sun* in 1959. In the same year, 1976, there was the musical *Bubbling Brown Sugar* by Loften Mitchell (with Rosetta LeNoire) with music by Duke Ellington, Eubie Blake, Cab Calloway, and others and *Your Arms Too Short to Box with God* conceived and directed by Vinnette Caroll with music and lyrics by Alex Bradford and Micki Grant.

In 1978, Ain't Misbehavin, conceived and directed by Richard Maltby Jr., with most of the music and lyrics by Fats Waller (who died in 1943), opened on Broadway, winning the New York Drama Critics Circle Award and the Tony Award as best musical. *Timbuktu,* based on the musical *Kismet,* opened the same year starring Eartha Kitt. Also in 1978, *Eubie*, a tribute to the great Eubie Blake, opened on Broadway.

In the mid-1970s, a television production about the black experience became an American phenomenon. The American Broadcasting Company's dramatization of Alex Haley's book *Roots* on eight consecutive evenings was viewed by an estimated 130 million people and on seven evenings ranked among the Top Ten in all-time TV ratings. Other television productions followed, including Cicely Tyson's award-winning performance in "The Autobiography of Miss Jane Pittman,"; Leslie Uggams and Olivia Cole in "Backstairs at the White House,"; Tyson in "A Woman Called Moses,"; and, of course, "Roots: The Next Generation."

As the new decade began Samm-Art Williams' play *Home,* produced by the Negro Ensemble Company during the 1979-80 season, won a Drama Desk Award and moved to Broadway where it was nominated for two Tony Awards.

*The versatile Gregory Hines and sultry Judith Jamison in a scene from the Broadway hit, Duke Ellington's Sophisticated Ladies.*

## The Eighties

In 1980, Athol Fugard's *A Lesson from Aloes* moved from the Yale Repertory Theater to Broadway where it was nominated for a Tony Award as best play and won the New York Drama Critics Circle Award as best play of 1980.

In the spring of 1982 Broadway had four long-running black musicals, one black drama, and a famous black actor doing Shakespeare. *Dreamgirls,* a smash hit loosely based on the singing group The Supremes, won 13, 1982 Tony Award nominations; *Lena Horne, The Lady and Her Music* was a highly acclaimed one-woman performance which had won a special Tony Award in 1981; Duke Ellington's *Sophisticated Ladies* was described by the *New York Times* as "a stroke of genius"; *Waltz of the Stork* was Melvin Van Peebles' new comedy musical which he wrote, directed, and acted in; *Master Harold ...and the Boys*, by Athol Fugard, had moved from the Yale Repertory Theater in New Haven were it had been highly praised to the Lyceum Theatre on Broadway where it was nominated for three Tony Awards; and James Earl Jones was appearing in *Othello*.

At the same time off-Broadway, the Negro Ensemble Company was presenting *A Soldier's Play* by Charles Fuller, which won a 1982 Pulitzer Prize; and *One Mo' Time*, written and directed by Vernel Bagneris, was still at the Village Gate. And there were other black productions off-Broadway.

While dramas were not as successful in sustaining audiences, musical plays continued to draw audiences over a sustained period of time.

Gospel music in particular was a strong draw with such productions as *Mama, I Want to Sing* drawing grass roots audiences as well as regular theatregoers for a run of over five years. Other plays like *Amen Corner* and *Don't Get God Started* were not able to continue for such a long time, but brought new audiences, including busloads from New York area churches to Broadway—many for the first time.

*The Tap Dance Kid* and *Black and Blue* were two musical presentations featuring talented dancers which also found audiences and popularity among theatergoers. Another musical, *Sarafina*, with rousing compositions and a story line focused on the South African apartheid problem, also gained a loyal and sustained following. In the drama realm, the Pulitzer Prize winning *Fences* by August Wilson was an acclaimed drama which was well received by critics and seasoned theatregoers.

*From left to right, Charles Brown, James Earl Jones, Mary Alice and Ray Aranha in August Wilson's Broadway hit* Fences.

## OUTSTANDING BLACK ENTERTAINERS

### ALVIN AILEY
### Dancer, Choreographer

Alvin Ailey, founder of the Alvin Ailey American Dance Theatre, has won international fame as both dancer and choreographer.

Ailey studied dancing after graduating from high school where he was a star athlete. With a short stint in college behind him, he formed his own dance group in 1961 and began giving four concerts annually. A year later, the Ailey troupe made an official State Department tour of Australia, receiving accolades throughout the country. One critic called it "the most stark and devastating theatre ever presented in Australia."

After numerous appearances as a featured dancer with Harry Belafonte and others, Ailey performed in a straight dramatic role with Claudia McNeil in Broadway's *Tiger, Tiger Burning Bright*.

In 1965, Ailey took his group on one of the most successful European tours ever made by an American dance company. In London it was held over six weeks to accommodate the demand for tickets, and in Hamburg it received an unprecedented 61 curtain calls.

A German critic called this performance "a triumph of sweeping, violent beauty, a furious spectacle. The stage vibrates. One has never seen anything like it."

During the mid-seventies Ailey, among his other professional commitments, devoted much time to creating special jazz dance sequences for America's Bicentennial celebration.

*Ira Aldridge stands among the great nineteenth-century Shakespeareans.*

### IRA ALDRIDGE
### Actor
### 1807-1867

Ira Aldridge was one of the leading Shakespearean actors of the nineteenth century. Although he was denied the opportunity to exhibit his talent to the American public, the fame which he won abroad is more than enough to establish him as one of the landmark figures in the annals of international theater.

Aldridge's origins are obscure. Some accounts give his birthplace as Africa; others name Bel-Air, Maryland; still others list New York City. His birth date ranges from 1804 to 1807. It seems clear that he attended the African Free School in New York until he was around 16, at which time he left home.

His early dramatic training centered around the African Grove Theatre in New York in 1821. His first role was in *Pizarro*, and he subsequently played a variety of small roles in classical productions before accepting employment as a steward on a ship bound for England.

After studying briefly at the University of Glasgow in Scotland, Aldridge went to London in 1825, appearing in the melodrama *Surinam, or a Slave's Revenge*. For the next eight years, he toured the provinces learning his craft. When he finally appeared in London's Theatre Royal in 1833, his Othello was acclaimed as brilliant by the critics. For the next three decades he toured the continent with great successes, appearing before several members of European royalty.

Aldridge died in Lodz, Poland, on August 7, 1867. He is honored by a tablet housed in the New Memorial Theatre in Stratford-upon-Avon, England.

### DEBBIE ALLEN
### Actress/Director

A talented performer who impressed audiences with her energy on stage, Debbie Allen soon developed as a respected choreographer and the most talented black woman working as a television director in the 1980s.

A cum laude graduate of Howard University, Debbie began her career on the Broadway stage in the chorus line of the hit musical, *Purlie*. She then portrayed Beneatha in the Tony and Grammy Award winning musical, *Raisin*. Her other early stage roles were in the national company of *Guys and Dolls* and the drama, *Anna Lucasta,* performed for the New Federal Theatre at the Henry Street Settlement.

Soon, she was selected to star in an NBC pilot, *3 Girls*, and then appeared on other TV hits like *Good Times* and *The Love Boat.* At this time, her talent as a choreographer was noted and she worked on such projects as television's *Midnight Special* as well as two films, *The Fish That Saved Pittsburgh* and *Under Fire.*

The year of 1982 was a pivotal one for the Houston-born actress/singer/dancer. She appeared in the film, *Ragtime* and the television series, *Fame* as well as the Joseph Papp television special, *Alice at the Palace.* Debbie also starred in dance sequence during the Academy Awards Ceremonies.

Her career continued to advance with roles in the miniseries, *Roots: The Next Generation* and the television special, *Ben Vereen... His Roots.* She also appeared on stage again in *Ain't Misbehavin* and a revival of *West Side Story*, for which she was nominated for a Tony Award and won a Drama Desk Award.

As each season passed on *Fame*, she became more involved as a choreographer and soon was directing episodes of the series on a regular basis. In time, she was selected by the producers of the television sitcom, *A Different World* to become director of the series. In another acknowledgment of her stature as a performer and creative talent, she starred in her first television special during the 1988-89 season.

### EDDIE (ROCHESTER) ANDERSON
### Comedian
### 1906-1977

For many years Eddie Anderson was the only black performing regularly on a network radio show. As the character Rochester on the Jack Benny program, he became one of the most widely known black American entertainers.

Anderson was born in Oakland, California in 1906, the son of Big Ed Anderson, a minstrel performer, and Ella Mae, a tightwire walker. During the 1920s and early 1930s, Anderson traveled throughout the Middle and Far West singing, dancing, and clowning in small clubs. On Easter Sunday, 1937, he was featured on Benny's radio show in what was supposed to be a "one-shot" appearance, but Anderson was such a hit that he quickly became a regular on the program.

Anderson is best known for his work with Benny (in television, as well as on radio), but he also appeared in a number of movies, including *Star Spangled Rhythm* and *Cabin in the Sky.*

Anderson made a point of staying out of public view. He made a rare public appearance when he attended the funeral of his longtime friend Jack Benny in 1974. Anderson died on February 28, 1977 at the age of 71.

### PEARL BAILEY
### Singer

With her easy style and impromptu wit, Pearl Bailey has starred as singer, actress, author, and United Nations representative during her long career.

Born March 29, 1918 in Newport News, Virginia, she moved to Philadelphia with her family in 1933. She began to sing at small clubs in Scranton, Pennsylvania and in Washington, D.C. before becoming the vocalist for Cootie Williams and later for Count Basie. In 1941 she had her first successful New York engagements at the Village Vanguard and the Blue Angel, and during World War II she toured with the U.S.O. Bailey made her New York stage debut in 1946 in *St. Louis Woman,* for which she won a Donaldson Award as the year's most promising new performer.

In 1952, in London she married drummer Louis Bellson, who is white. He now acts as her musical conductor and they continue to tour in many parts of the world. They have two adopted children, Tony and Dee Dee.

*Eddie "Rochester" Anderson with Ethel Waters in the the movie* Pinky.

During the 1950s Bailey appeared in the movies *Carmen Jones* and *Porgy and Bess* and on Broadway in *House of Flowers*. In the 1950s and 1960s, she was a recording artist, nightclub headliner, and television performer. In 1967, she received a special Tony Award for her starring role on Broadway in *Hello, Dolly* and in 1968 she published her autobiography, *The Raw Pearl*.

In the 1970s, she was named a special adviser to the United States Mission to the United Nations. In 1976, she had another book published, *Hurry Up, America, And Spit,* a collection of prose, poetry, and letters. That same year she did the movie *Norman, Is That You?* with Redd Foxx, appeared in Washington, D.C. in *Something To Do,* a musical saluting the American worker, and received an award from the Screen Actors Guild for Outstanding Achievement in Fostering the Finest Ideals of the Acting Profession. Georgetown University made her an honorary doctor of Human Letters in 1977, and in 1978 she enrolled as a student at Georgetown stating that she wanted to prepare for a career in teaching.

In January 1980, she did a one-night concert at Radio City Music Hall in New York. In 1981 she was the voice of the cartoon character "owl" in the Disney movie *The Fox and the Hound.* The movie was described as "a story of two friends who didn't know they were supposed to be enemies" and it also aptly describes Bailey's long involvement in furthering human understanding and international relations.

## JOSEPHINE BAKER
**Chanteuse, Stage Star**
**1906-1975**

A legend in her own time, and one of America's foremost entertainment expatriates, Josephine Baker first became an internationally famous variety show dancer and a celebrated music hall star in Paris during the 1920s. From then on she continued to win applause for her polished performances,

*Josephine Baker at the Casino de Paris in 1931.*

her supple, lithe dance movements, and her sultry and engaging voice. By today's standards, her material would be considered only mildly risque; in the context of her time, however, it was considerably more bold and shocking.

Born in St. Louis on June 3, 1906, Baker received little formal education, first leaving school at the age of eight to supplement the family income by working as a kitchen helper and baby-sitter. While still in elementary school, she took a part-time job as a chorus girl, a job she repeated at age 17 in Noble Sissle's musical comedy *Shuffle Along,* which played Radio City Music Hall in 1923. Her next show was *Chocolate Dandies*, followed by a major dancing part in La Revue *Neggre*, an American production that introduced *le jazz hot* to Paris in 1925.

Baker later left the show to create her most sensational role, that of the "Dark Star" of the Follies Bergegre. At the height of her act, she appeared topless on a mirror, clad only in a protective waist shield of rubber bananas. The spectacular dance made her an overnight star and a public figure with a rabid following. In true "star" tradition, she catered to her fans and to her success by adopting such flamboyant eccentricities as walking pet leopards down the Champs Elysees.

In 1930, after completing an around-the-world tour, she made her debut as a singing and dancing comedienne at the Casino de Paris. Critics called her a "complete artist, the perfect master of her tools." In time, she ventured into films, starring alongside French idol Jean Gabin, and into light opera, performing in *La Creole*, an operetta about a Jamaican girl.

During World War II, she served first as a Red Cross volunteer, and later did underground intelligence work through an Italian Embassy attache. After the war, the French government decorated her with the Legion of Honor. She returned to the entertainment world, regularly starring at the Follies Bergegre, appearing on French television, and going on still another lengthy international tour.

In the early 1950s, Josephine Baker earned another reputation—not as a lavish and provocative entertainer but as a warm-hearted and devoted friend of humanity. She used her fortune to adopt and tutor a group of orphaned babies of all races, retiring from the stage in 1956 to devote all her time to her "rainbow family." Within three years, however, her "experiment in brotherhood" had taken such a toll on her finances that she was forced to return to the footlights, starring in *Paris, Mes Amours*, a musical based in part on her own fabled career.

Baker survived numerous financial crises without a public hint of despair, or audible groans of discouragement. Illness hardly managed to slow down or otherwise deter her indomitable spirit. Through her long life, she retained her most noteworthy stage attributes—an intimate, subdued voice, coupled with an infectiously energetic and vivacious manner.

Baker died in Paris on April 12, 1975, after opening a gala show to celebrate her fiftieth year in show business.

*Playing a Jewish angel in The Angel Levine, Harry Belafonte glares past Milo O'Shea at a skeptical Zero Mostel.*

**SHIRLEY BASSEY**
**Singer**
**1937**

Shirley Bassey's melodious voice and dynamic style make her one of the best female vocalists ever to come out of England. While her recordings are excellent, her most exciting work is done in live performances before nightclub and concert audiences.

Born in Cardiff, Wales, she was raised in the run-down Tiger Bay section and taught herself to sing by listening to the radio. She had to leave school in her early teens to help support her family. Her first singing job was in the chorus of a touring show, *Memories of Al Jolson*. She continued picking up spots in small clubs and minor shows until the success of her 1956 single "Banana Boat Song" turned the spotlight on her. The next few years brought such hits as the English version of "Climb Ev'ry Mountain" and "As Long as He Needs Me." Coming to the United States in 1961, she opened with a sensational performance in New York's Persian Room and went on to a successful tour.

Her versatility as a singer has enabled her to broaden out from ballads to include folk-rock and soul songs in her repertoire. In 1965, she sang the title theme from the movie *Goldfinger*. Her U.S. concerts have been very well received by both audiences and critics. Among her more recent hits are "Shirley Bassey Is Really Something," "Something Else," "I Capricorn," "Diamonds Are Forever," and "Never, Never, Never."

**HARRY BELAFONTE**
**Singer**

Although he has not made a film, appeared on television, or had a hit record in years, Harry Belafonte's performances are still standing room only around the world.

Born March 1, 1927 in New York City, he moved to the West Indies at the age of eight and returned at 13 to New York where he attended high school. In 1944 he joined the Navy. After his discharge, while working as a janitor, he became interested in drama. He studied acting at Stanley Kubrick's Dramatic Workshop and also with Erwin Piscator at the New School for Social Research in New York City where his classmates included Marlon Brando and Walter Matthau. A successful singing engagement at The Royal Roost, a New York jazz club, led to other engagements around the country. But Belafonte, dissatisfied with the music he was performing, returned to New York, opened a restaurant in Greenwich Village, and studied folk singing. He first appeared as a folk singer in the 1950s and "helped give folk music a period of mass appeal" according to John S. Wilson in a 1981 *New York Times* article. During his performances at the Palace Theater in New York, Belafonte had audiences calypsoing in the aisles.

Belafonte produced the first integrated musical shows on television, which won two Emmy Awards and resulted in his being fired by the sponsor. The famous incident in which white British singer Petula Clark touched his arm while singing a song caused a national furor in pre-civil rights

America. When Dr. Martin Luther King marched in Montgomery, Alabama and Washington, D.C., Harry Belafonte joined him and brought along a large contingent of performers. Touring in the stage musical *Three for Tonight* in which he also had appeared on Broadway, Belafonte was forced to flee in the middle of a performance in Spartanburg, South Carolina and be rushed to the airport in the mayor's car when word came that the Klu Klux Klan was marching on the theater.

Belafonte also appeared on Broadway in John Murray Anderson's *Almanac*, and his movies include *Carmen Jones, The Angel Levine, Odds against Tomorrow, Buck and the Preacher, Uptown Saturday Night, Island in the Sun, and The World, the Flesh, and the Devil.*

In the 1960s and early 1970s, he appeared on television and in nightclubs. In 1968 he substituted for Johnny Carson as host of "The Tonight Show." In 1970 he did an ABC-TV special, "Harry and Lena," with Lena Horne, and also appeared with her at Caesar's Palace in Las Vegas.

In the 1980s, coming out of what *Ebony* magazine in a 1981 article described as a self-imposed semi-seclusion, he appeared in his first dramatic role on television in the NBC-TV presentation of "Grambling's White Tiger." In 1981 Columbia Records released his first album in seven years, "Loving You Is Where I Belong," mostly ballads. In April 1981, he began a 7½-month tour of the United States, Europe, and Australia which he described as cleaning up unfulfilled commitments so that he could devote himself daily to developing outlets in the third world for black and minority group artists who, after finding acceptance in the 1970s in this country in the wake of the civil-rights movement, are now being bypassed by motion pictures, the recording industry, and the theater. He also is planning to turn his full attention to other projects such as getting black plays and black actors into American regional theaters.

Belafonte and his wife, Julia, who is white, live in a cooperative apartment in a Manhattan building which he purchased many years ago when he was denied another apartment because of his race. They were married in 1957 and have two children, David, a sound engineer, and Gina, a college student. Belafonte has two other daughters from a previous marriage, Shari, an actress, and Adrienne, a weaver in West Virginia.

## CHUCK BERRY
**Singer**

A proficient guitarist and pioneer in the field of rock'n'roll, Chuck Berry was another artist whose music influenced an entire generation, including many of the artists who attempted to emulate his performances.

Born on October 18, 1926, Berry learned the guitar as a teen-ager, but had problems early and throughout his life with the law. He was in reform school from 1944 to 1947 for attempted robbery. He then went to work on the assembly line at General Motors Fisher Body plant and studied hairdressing and cosmetology in night school.

In 1952, he formed a trio with drummer Ebby Harding and pianist Johnnie Johnson, his keyboard artist on and off and on for the next three decades. Within three years, the trio had become a top club band in the St. Louis area. In time, Berry met Muddy Waters in Chicago and the head of Chess records. Soon, Berry had his first Top Ten hit, "Maybellene."

In short succession, he had recorded a string of hits including *School Day, Rock & Roll Music, Sweet Little Sixteen*, and *Johnny B. Goode*. With his famous duckwalk, Berry was popular on the concert circuit during the 1950s. He also appeared in such films as *Rock, Rock, Rock, Mister Rock and Roll* and *Go, Johnny, Go*.

He had problems with the law in 1959 and spent time in federal prison for hiring an underage teen-ager to work in his St. Louis nightclub. After his release, he found that his music was being incorporated into the repertoire of many of the British groups who visited the United States and became popular.

He wrote and recorded one more million seller in 1972, *My Ding-a-Ling*, but only performed sporadically in the ensuing years while problems with the law continued to crop up from time to time.

Ultimately, he would be honored by the Rock 'n' Roll Hall of Fame for his contributions to the world of one of Americas most distinctive forms of music.

## JAMES HUBERT "EUBIE" BLAKE
**Musician-Composer**

Eubie Blake was born in Baltimore, the son of former slaves, on February 7, 1883, the last of 10 children and the only one to survive beyond two months. His mother worked as a laundress, his father as a stevedore. One day in 1888, as a child of five, he strayed from his mother's side while she was shopping in downtown Baltimore and disappeared into a musical instrument store that had an organ displayed just inside the entrance, climbed on the organ stool, and fingered the keys.

The store manager insisted on placing a $75.00 organ in the Blake home for 25¢ a week. Young James played so well, he started taking piano lessons with the renowned teacher Margaret Marshall. The following year he was taught musical composition by Llewelyn Wilson, who at one time conducted an all-black symphony orchestra sponsored by the city of Baltimore.

At 17, Blake started playing piano professionally. In 1915, Sissle and Blake, together with Miller and Lyles, created one of the pioneers of black shows, *Shuffle Along*, which was produced on Broadway. "I'm Just Wild About Harry" was one of the hits of this show. The show was produced again on Broadway in 1952. Eubie Blake and Noble Sissle sold their first song, "It's All Your Fault," to Sophie Tucker in 1915 and her introduction of the song started them on their way.

In the early 1930s, Blake collaborated with Andy Razaf and wrote the musical score for Lew Leslie's *Blackbirds*. Out of this association came the hit *Memories of You*.

During World War II Blake was appointed musical conductor for the United Services Organizations (USO)

Hospital Unit. In 1946 he announced his "retirement" and proceeded to enroll in New York University, completing a course, "The Schillinger System of Composition," a method of composing based on higher mathematics, although he had never finished grade school.

In 1966, Blake attended a concert given by a young black girl at Baltimore's Peabody Conservatory of Music. In 1890, the conservatory color bar was so rigid they objected to his carrying his mother's laundry bundles past their building. Three years later, Blake recorded a two-record album entitled *The Eight-Six Years of Eubie Blake.*

In 1973, Biograph issued a two-record set of all his known available piano rolls, "Eubie Blake: Blues and Rags" and "Eubie Blake, 1921, Vol. 2." Later he put out two disks on his own label, "Eubie Blake, Rags to Classics" and "Eubie Blake and His Friends." From 1973 through 1981 he performed in concerts in this country and abroad. In 1976, New World Records issued a new album of songs from *Shuffle Along*. In 1978, the Broadway show *Eubie* opened, a tribute to him featuring 24 of his songs. In the spring of 1981 he made his first appearance on cable TV, taped during his February 1981 concert at Carnegie Hall in New York, where he headlined an evening of jazz greats. That concert also produced a record album and a video disk cassette.

Eubie Blake has received honorary doctorates from numerous colleges and universities. For many years his most frequently requested song was "Charleston Rag," which he composed in 1899 and which had to be written down by someone else because he could not then read music. Among his most famous songs were "How Ya' Gonna Keep 'Em Down on the Farm," "Love Will Find a Way," and "You're Lucky to Me."

Blake's first wife, Avis, died in 1939 after 31 years of marriage. In 1945, he married Marion Taylor, who now acts as his agent and manager.

Though known as the master of ragtime, Blake has always most loved the music of the masters. In the intimacy of his Brooklyn studio, Blake rarely plays music of the type with which the world reveres him.

Several thousand people attended concerts at the Shubert Theatre and St, Peters Lutheran Church, celebrating Blake's 100th birthday on February 8, 1983. Mayor Koch honored Blake and a congratulatory message from President Reagan was read.

Five days later, Blake died.

## JAMES BLAND
### Composer
### 1854-1911

James Bland was an accomplished minstrel comedian, but his fame rests largely on his work as a composer of more than 600 popular songs.

Born in Flushing, New York on October 22, 1854, Bland moved to Washington, D.C. at an early age. His father, Allan M. Bland, one of the country's earliest Negro college graduates, had been appointed an examiner in the U.S. Patent Office there.

*James Brown, the "God Father of Soul."*

Bland himself attended Howard University, studying music and beginning to create his own tunes. His more famous songs include "Carry Me Back to Old Virginny," "Oh, Them Golden Slippers," and "In the Evening by the Moonlight."

More than a quarter of a century after his death, when "Carry Me Back to Old Virginny" was recommended by the Virginia Conservation Committee to become the official state anthem, many people were surprised to learn that the song had actually been written by Bland, and not by Stephen Foster, as was popularly believed. In January 1940, it became the official state anthem.

Bland died of pneumonia on May 5, 1911.

## JAMES BROWN
### Singer

James Brown is America's leading exponent of big-beat "soul" music, a highly personal blending of blues and gospel forms with a driving beat.

Brown was born in 1934 and raised in Augusta, Georgia. He formed his own group, which was discovered during a recording session in a Macon, Georgia radio station in 1956.

He first appeared at the Apollo Theater in New York's Harlem in 1959 and has since appeared there more than 25 times.

With a style made up of frenzied wails and intricate, speedy dance steps, Brown rose to the top of the rock field. Annoyed by the fact that the American public was neglecting its native "down home" music while embracing its synthetic British imitations, Brown organized his own troupe to tour the country with the "genuine article." With a 40-man ensemble known as "The James Brown Show," he played on the road for 340 days in 1965 and grossed over a million dollars. He drew crowds of 11,000 in Los Angeles; 15,000 in Annapolis, Maryland, and 27,000 in Atlanta. Estimates of future earnings ran as high as $3,000,000 annually.

His hit songs include *Please, Please, Please, It's a Man's World,* and *I Feel Good.*

In 1968, Brown toured military bases in the Pacific for the USO. He also came under attack for his endorsement of President Nixon. Brown, who has been called "The Godfather of Soul," records for Polydor Records. At one time he owned five radio stations. In 1980, he appeared in the movie Blues Brothers. In 1981 and 1982, he was touring his show across the country. Brown continued to tour throughout the ensuing years, both around the United States as well as abroad. Problems with his marriage and confrontations with law authorities resulted in his arrest and finally, in 1989, he was sentenced to six years in jail after being prosecuted for fleeing police on a high-speed chase through two states.

## OSCAR BROWN JR.
**Composer, Singer**
**1926**

The many talents of Oscar Brown Jr. make it necessary to view him as both a creative artist working behind the scenes and a dynamic interpreter delivering original and highly innovative "up-front" material to beguiled, and often enraptured, audiences.

Brown's talents first achieved nationwide recognition in the early 1960s. *Time Magazine* characterized him as "the best new entertainer" in show business "since Belafonte" in 1962, quoting *Ebony Magazine,* which viewed him as a "hip Negro folk poet," and Lorraine Hansberry, who called him "a startling genius."

Brown subsequently demonstrated the full measure of his jazz, folk music, and blues talents in the off-Broadway musical *Joy. New York Times* critic Clive Barnes called composer/singer Brown "an artist of great merit" and "a major talent."

Brown, a native of Chicago, was born in 1926. He first gained a reputation as a jazzman playing Mister Kelly's there in the 1950s.

## JOHN BUBBLES
**Singer, Dancer**

Song-and-dance man John Bubbles was born in 1902 in Louisville and, at the age of seven, teamed with a fellow bowling alley pinboy, Ford (Buck) Washington, in what was soon to become one of the top vaudeville acts in show business. Throughout the 1920s and 1930s, Buck and Bubbles played the top theaters in the country at salaries of up to $1,750 a week.

The two appeared in several films, including Cabin in the Sky. Bubbles captured additional fame as Sportin' Life in the 1935 version of Porgy and Bess. After Buck's death in 1955, Bubbles virtually disappeared from show business until 1964 when he teamed up with Anna Maria Alberghetti in a successful nightclub act. Since then, he has made numerous appearances with Johnny Carson, toured Vietnam with Bob Hope, and released several successful records.

In 1979, at the age of 77 and partially crippled from a 1967 stroke, he recreated his characterization of "Sportin' Life" for a one-night show entitled *Black Broadway* at Avery Fisher Hall of New York's Lincoln Center. The show was repeated in 1980 for a limited engagement at Town Hall in New York. In the fall of 1980, Bubbles received the Lifetime Achievement Award from the American Guild of Variety Artists and a Certificate of Appreciation from New York presented by Mayor Koch at City Hall. At that time he was living in Los Angeles.

## HARRY T. BURLEIGH
**Composer**
**1866-1949**

Of Harry T. Burleigh, Alain Locke has said: "More than any other single person, Mr. Burleigh as arranger, composer, and baritone soloist played the role of a path breaking ambassador of Negro music to the musically elect." Burleigh's pioneer work in introducing Negro spirituals on the concert stage and his transcription of songs which had been previously transmitted only orally constitutes a major contribution to the field of American music.

Burleigh was born in Erie, Pennsylvania on December 2, 1866, the grandson of a blind slave who had been dismissed by his Maryland owners when he was unable to work. Burleigh's mother, a college graduate, supported the family after her husband's death by working as the janitor of a local school.

Singing in several choirs in Erie, Burleigh was urged to seek a scholarship to the National Conservatory of Music, one which he ultimately received with the aid of composer Edward MacDowell's mother. In 1900, he joined the choir of Temple Emanu-El in New York, the first Negro to have sung in that synagogue, one of the nation's largest. He was, for some 53 years, soloist at St. George's Episcopal Church in New York City, and received the NAACP Spingarn Medal in 1917 for "excellence in creative music."

Burleigh's concert tours included appearances before numerous presidents and members of royalty. In addition to his arrangements of such spirituals as "Deep River" and "Were You There," he composed 250 original songs.

## ANITA BUSH
**Singer, Actress**
**1883-1974**

Anita Bush was busily involved in the theater during her early childhood. Her father was the tailor for the Bijou, a large neighborhood theater in Brooklyn, and Anita would carry the costumes to the theater for him, thus giving her a backstage view of performers and productions. Her singing/acting career took off full swing while she was in the chorus of the Williams and Walker Company from 1903 to 1909. With Williams and Walker, she performed in such hits as

*Godfrey Cambridge shows off his comic flair.*

*Abyssinia* and In *Dahomey*, which had a successful European tour. When the group split up in 1909, she went on to form the Anita Bush Stock Company, which included her own show of chorus girls, plus such greats as Charles Gilpin and Dooley Wilson, with whom she also worked as part of the founding group of the Lafayette Players. Bush died February 16, 1974.

## CAB CALLOWAY
### Bandleader, Singer

During the 1930s Cab Calloway was one of the best known black entertainers in the United States.

Calloway was born on Christmas Day in 1907 in Rochester, New York. At the age of 22, he was already being booked in New York's famous Cotton Club, a unique musical feat considering the number of well-known musicians active during this era. Calloway's band alternated with the Duke Ellington Orchestra at the Cotton Club throughout the 1930s. It was during this period that Calloway wrote and recorded the song which became an enormous international success and his personal theme song, "Minnie the Moocher."

Calloway has been featured along with his band in such movies as *Big Broadcast, International House,* and *Stormy Weather*.

Since 1948 he has worked with small groups and has also been seen in such shows as the Broadway revival of *Porgy and Bess* in 1950, in which he played the part of Sportin' Life. In the 1960s Calloway appeared with Pearl Bailey on Broadway in *Hello Dolly.*

Also a talented composer, his compositions include "St. James Infirmary," "Lady With a Fan," and "That Man's Here Again."

In the mid-seventies Calloway appeared in a nostalgic review called *Cotton Club* and in 1980 at Town Hall in a Tribute to the Big Bands.

Calloway also appeared at Belmont Park, the Brooklyn Academy of Music, various night spots, and in a one-night performance when his daughter, Chris Calloway, opened an engagement in New York in 1981. In 1976, the book *Of Minnie the Moocher and Me* by Cab Calloway and Bryant Robbins was published. It is an autobiography and documentary collage of remembrances of former employees, friends, and children. Calloway also published a pamphlet, *Hipster's Dictionary*. Calloway will probably always be remembered as "the Hi-De-Ho Man," and he calls himself the ultimate practitioner of "jive."

## GODFREY CAMBRIDGE
### Comedian, Actor
### 1933-1976

Godfrey Cambridge gained considerable distinction both as a comedian and as an actor. Born in New York, Cambridge was raised in Harlem and attended grammar school in Nova Scotia while living there with his grandparents. His parents had emigrated from British Guiana. After finishing his schooling in New York at Flushing High School and Hofstra College, he began to study acting.

Cambridge made his Broadway debut in *Nature's Way,* and was featured in *Purlie Victorious,* both on stage, and later on screen. He has also appeared off-Broadway in *Lost in the Stars, Take a Giant Step*, and *The Detective Story*. He won the Obie award for the 1960-1961 season's most distinguished off-Broadway performance in The *Blacks.*

As a comedian, he appeared on the Jack Paar show, the Johnny Carson show, and many other variety hours. His material, drawn from the contemporary racial situation, was often presented in the style associated with the new wave of black comedians.

Cambridge has also performed dramatically on many television series. In 1965 he starred in the stock version of *A Funny Thing Happened on the Way to the Forum.*

One of Cambridge's most memorable roles was as the star of a seriocomic Hollywood film offering, *The Watermelon Man*. In it the comedian played a man who turns color overnight, a transformation which not only shocks his friends, but leaves his movie wife (Estelle Parsons) somewhat baffled. The action turned on Cambridge's zesty and unhesitating approach to the role.

During the mid-seventies Cambridge appeared to be in semi-retirement, making few public appearances.

Cambridge was a compulsive eater who once weighed 300 pounds. In 1974, he moved with his wife, Audrey, to Ridgefield, Connecticut, where they were the first blacks and targets for racial harassment. Godfrey Cambridge died at the age of 43 in California on November 29, 1976. He was stricken on a Warner Brothers set where he was playing the role of Ugandan dictator Idi Amin in the television film "Victory at Entebbe."

## DIAHANN CARROLL
### Singer, Actress

The stunning Diahann Carroll, the first black ingenue to star in a long-running network television series, has had a diversified career in films, on stage, in nightclubs, and in the recording industry. Her most important dramatic role on live stage came in 1962 when she played opposite Richard Kiley in *No Strings*.

Carroll was born in the Bronx, the daughter of a subway conductor and a nurse. She joined the Abyssinian Baptist Church choir as a Tiny Tot, and at the age of 10, won a Metropolitan Opera scholarship. Singing lessons held little appeal to her, however, so she continued her schooling at the High School of Music and Art, a "wonderful, beautiful oasis in my life." As a concession to her parents, she enrolled at New York University, where she was to be a sociology student, but stage fever led her to an appearance on a television talent show netting her $1,000. A subsequent appearance at the Latin Quarter launched her professional career.

In 1954, Carroll appeared in *House of Flowers,* winning favorable press notices as a refreshing personality "with a rich, lovely, easy voice." In that year, she also appeared in a film version of *Carmen Jones,* as Myrt.

Movie and television appearances kept her busy until 1958, the year she was slated to appear as an Oriental in Richard Rodgers' *Flower Drum Song*. The part did not materialize, however, largely due to Carroll's height and makeup problems.

Three years later, Rodgers cast her in *No Strings* as a high-fashion model playing opposite a hesitant and troubled Pulitzer Prize author. The show was not a smashing success, but Carroll's performance received good notices.

In the late 1960s, Miss Carroll was cast as lead in the television series *Julia* in which she played a nurse and war widow. Carroll won a Tony for her performance in the Broadway production *No Strings*. Some of her films include *Porgy and Bess, Goodbye Again, Paris Blues*, and in 1974, *Claudine* with James Earl Jones, a serious comedy in which she played a mother struggling to raise children in Harlem, a role for which she was nominated for an Academy Award.

Following the death of her husband in 1981, she was making only occasional appearances. She lives in California.

## VINETTE CARROLL
### Actress

Unlike many of her contemporaries who started young, Vinette Carroll didn't decide upon a career in the theater until the age of 25. Coming from a science-oriented family, Carroll had first intended to enter the field of psychology. As her life progressed, she went from part-time acting classes at the New School to two years of stock work, during which time she worked hard at developing the theatrical tools for expressing "the things I was feeling in my gut."

Born in New York City, Vinette Carroll lived in Jamaica, West Indies from the age of three until she was 11. She earned a B.A. in psychology from Long Island University, an M.A. in psychology from New York University, and had completed all of the course work for a Ph.D. at Columbia University.

As an actress she won an Obie for her performance in the play *Moon on the Rainbow Shawl* and an Emmy for the TV special "Beyond the Blues." She played Sojourner Truth in the CBS television special "We the Women" and appeared in the movies, *One Potato, Two Potato, Up the Down Staircase,* and *Alice's Restaurant.*

Moving beyond acting to become artistic director of the Urban Arts Corps, she conceived and directed the award-winning musical *Don't Bother Me, I Can't Cope,* which reached Broadway in 1972. Her next Broadway musical was *Your Arm's Too Short to Box with God,* which opened December 1976, and the same year, with Micki Grant, *I'm Laughin' but I Ain't Tickled.*

*Nat "King" Cole ruled the airwaves with his silken voice.*

*The ubiquitous Bill Cosby, stand-up comic, actor, TV personage, and supersalesman.*

## NAT "KING" COLE
## Singer, Pianist
## 1919-1965

The style and smooth delivery of Nat "King" Cole made him one of the most imitated singers ever produced in American popular music. His death from cancer in 1965 came after he had already enjoyed many successful years at the top of his profession.

Cole was born on March 17, 1919, in Montgomery, Alabama (the family name was Coles, but Cole dropped the "s" when he formed the *King Cole Trio* years later). When he was five, the family moved to Chicago, and he was soon playing piano and organ in the church where his father served as minister. While attending Phillips High School, Cole formed his own band, and also played with small combos, including one headed by his brother Edward, a bassist.

In 1936, Cole joined the touring company of *Shuffle Along*. When it folded in Los Angeles, he found work in small clubs there. In 1937, *The King Cole Trio* was formed quite by accident when the drummer in his quartet failed to appear for a scheduled performance. That same year, Cole made his singing debut when a customer insisted he sing "Sweet Lorraine" (a number he later recorded with great success).

Cole's first record was made in 1943. It was his own composition ("Straighten Up and Fly Right"), and sold more than 500,000 copies. Over the years, one hit followed another in rapid succession—*Paper Moon, Route 66, I Love You for Sentimental Reasons, Chestnuts Roasting on an Open Fire, Nature Boy, Mona Lisa, Too Young, Pretend, Somewhere Along the Way, Smile,* and many others.

Cole died in 1965, from cancer, at the height of his career and shortly after he finished the celebrated movie *Cat Ballou.*

## BILL COSBY
## Comedian

Bill Cosby is the most successful performer and businessman in the United States. By 1989, his annual income was estimated at $57 million a year. After becoming the first black to star in a prime time series *I Spy* and winning three Emmy Awards, he catapulted to phenomenal success in a number of areas.

He was star and creator of the consistently top-rated *The Cosby Show*, for five seasons, author of two best-selling books, *Fatherhood* and *Time Flies* and a performer at the top rooms in Las Vegas where he earned $500,000 a week. He also won top fees as a commercial spokesman for Jell-O and Coca Cola.

Cosby also made headlines when he and his wife donated $20 million to Spelman College in Atlanta.

A native of Philadelphia, Cosby dropped out of high school to become a medic in the Navy, obtaining his diploma while in service. On becoming a civilian, he entered Temple University, where he played football and worked evenings as a bartender.

While doing this work, he began to entertain the customers with his comedy routines and, encouraged by their reception, left Temple in 1962 to pursue a career in show business. He began by playing small clubs around Philadelphia and New York's Greenwich Village. Within two years he was playing the top nightclubs around the country and making television appearances on the Johnny Carson (he acted as guest host during Carson's absence), Jack Paar, and Andy Williams shows.

In the 1970s, he appeared regularly in nightclubs in Las Vegas, Tahoe, and Reno and did commercials for such sponsors as Jell-O, Del Monte and Ford. In 1980, he did a comedy concert at Carnegie Hall in New York. From 1969 until 1972 he had his own TV series, *The Bill Cosby Show*. He has recorded more than 27 albums and has received five Grammy Awards. He appeared in such films as *Uptown Saturday Night, Let's Do It Again, A Piece of the Action,* and the award-winning television movie "To All My Friends On Shore."

In 1975, Random House published his book, *Bill Cosby's Personal Guide to Tennis or Don't Lower the Lob, Raise the Net*. For several years he was involved in educational television with the Children's Television Workshop. He returned to college, spending five years at the University of Massachusetts earning a masters degree and then a doctorate in education in 1977 when he was 39 years old. He had received his bachelors degree from Temple University.

Cosby and his wife, Camille, live in rural New England with their five children.

## RUPERT CROSSE
### Actor
### 1928-1973

Actor Rupert Crosse's most important film role was as Ned McCaslin, the black companion of Steve McQueen in the uproarious screen adaptation of William Faulkner's Pulitzer Prize-winning novel, *The Reivers.* Crosse was nominated for an Academy Award as best supporting actor for his outstanding performance.

Born in Nevis, British West Indies, Crosse moved to Harlem at an early age, but returned to Nevis at the age of seven, after the death of his father. Reared by his grandparents and strongly influenced by his grandfather, a schoolmaster, Crosse received a solid education before returning to the United States, where he attended Benjamin Franklin High School. He later worked at odd jobs before spending two years in service in Germany and Japan.

Once out of service, Crosse renewed his educational pursuits, finishing high school and entering Bloomfield College and Seminary in New Jersey. Though he intended to become a minister, it was obvious from the jobs he held—machinist, construction worker, and recreation counselor—that his career plans were not yet definite.

Crosse subsequently enrolled at the Daykarhanora School for the stage, studying the acting craft and appearing in the Equity Library Theatre off-Broadway production *Climate of Eden.* He then transferred to John Cassavetes' workshop, where he helped create *Shadows,* winner of a Venice Film Festival Award. Crosse's first Hollywood role was in a Cassavetes movie, *Too Late Blues.* Other film credits are *The Wild Seed* and *Ride in the Whirlwind.*

Stage credits are also numerous, including appearances in *Sweet Bird of Youth, The Blood Knot,* and *Hatful of Rain.* Television viewers have seen Crosse in "Dr. Kildare," "I Spy," and "The Man from U.N.C.L.E.," as well as several other series. Crosse's big film break came in 1968 during an appearance at an Actors Studio production of *Echoes* at UCLA.

The actor had the ability to play American black roles and to interpret various African and West Indian characters. An ardent Yoga enthusiast and a practitioner of karate, Crosse believed his hobbies and experience broadened his ability to feel comfortable with a wide variety of roles.

Rupert Crosse died of cancer on March 5, 1973 at the age of 45 at his sister's home in Nevis, West Indies.

## OSSIE DAVIS, RUBY DEE
### Acting Team

The Ossie Davis-Ruby Dee husband and wife team has won notable accolades in the American theater. Acting together or separately, the Davises have also performed successfully on television, in movies, and in cabarets.

Davis grew up in Waycross, Georgia, and attended Howard University in Washington, D.C., where Dr. Alain Locke suggested he try for an acting career in New York. After completing service in the Army, he landed his first role in 1946 in *Jeb,* the play in which he met Dee. (Two years later, they were married.)

After appearing in the movie *No Way Out,* Davis won Broadway roles in *No Time for Sergeants, Raisin in the Sun,* and *Jamaica.* In 1961, he and Dee starred in *Purlie Victorious,* which Davis himself had written. Two years later, they repeated their roles in the movie version, Gone Are the Days.

Davis' other movie credits include The *Cardinal* and *Shock Treatment.* He has also written a number of TV scripts, and has acted on such television series as "The Defenders," "The Nurses," and "East Side, West Side."

He also directed such films as *Cotton Comes to Harlem* and *Black Girl.* His play *Escape to Freedom: A Play about Young Frederick Douglass* had its debut at Town Hall in New York and later was published by Viking Junior Books.

Ruby Dee was born in Cleveland but grew up in Harlem, taking her undergraduate training at Hunter College in New York. In 1942, she appeared in *South Pacific* with Canada Lee, and five years later met Ossie Davis while they were both playing in *Jeb.*

Her movies include *No Way Out, Edge of the City, Raisin in the Sun,* and *The Balcony.* She has appeared often on network television.

In 1965, she was the first black actress to appear in major roles at the American Shakespeare Festival in Stratford, Connecticut. She wrote a musical satire *Take It from the Top,* in which she appeared with her husband in a showcase run at the Henry Street Settlement Theatre in New York in 1979.

*The complete entertainer, Sammy Davis Jr., sings a sermon in* Sweet Charity,

Ossie Davis and Ruby Dee were involved in the civil rights struggle long before it became a "fashionable" cause. In 1970, they received the Frederick Douglass Award from the Urban League and in 1975 Actors Equity presented them with the Paul Robeson Citation "for outstanding creative contributions both in the performing arts and in society at large."

As a team they recorded several talking story albums for Caedmon. In 1974, they produced "The Ruby Dee/Ossie Davis Story Hour," which was sponsored by Kraft Foods on more than 60 stations of the National Black Network. Together they founded the Institute of New Cinema Artists to train selected youths for jobs in films and television, and then founded The Recording Industry Training Program to develop jobs in the music industry for disadvantaged youths.

In 1981, Alcoa funded a television series on the Public Broadcasting System titled "With Ossie and Ruby" using guests to provide an anthology of the arts. The show began its second season in the spring of 1982.

Ossie Davis and Ruby Dee live in a large house in New Rochelle, in New York's Westchester County. They have two daughters, a son, and a grandson born in May 1982.

## SAMMY DAVIS JR.
## Singer, Dancer, Comedian, Actor

Sammy Davis Jr. is often called "the world's greatest entertainer" (a title which attests to his remarkable versatility as singer, dancer, actor, mimic, and musician).

Davis was born in New York City on December 8, 1925, and four years later was appearing in vaudeville with his father and "uncle" in the Will Mastin Trio. In 1931, Davis made his movie debut with Ethel Waters in *Rufus Jones for President,* and followed this with an appearance in *Season's Greetings.*

Throughout the 1930s, the Will Mastin Trio continued to play vaudeville, burlesque, and cabarets. In 1943, Davis entered the Army and served for two years writing, directing, and producing camp shows. After his discharge, he rejoined the trio, which in 1946 cracked the "big-time" club circuit with a successful Hollywood engagement.

Davis recorded a string of hits ("Hey There," "Mr. Wonderful," "Too Close for Comfort") during his continued climb to the top of show business. In November 1954, he lost an eye in an automobile accident, but this did not in any way interfere with his career. He scored a hit in his first Broadway show *Mr. Wonderful* (1956), and later repeated this success in *Golden Boy.*

In 1959, he played Sportin' Life in the movie version of *Porgy and Bess.* Other Davis movies include *Oceans 11* and *Robin and the Seven Hoods.* In 1966, his autobiography *Yes, I Can* was a best seller, and he starred in his own network television series.

In 1968, the National Association for the Advancement of Colored People awarded him its Spingarn Medal. In the 1970s Davis appeared in films, television, and nightclubs. In 1972, he was involved in a controversy over his support of Richard Nixon attested by a famous photograph of Nixon hugging Davis at the 1972 Republican Convention. In 1974, Davis renounced his support of Nixon and Nixon's programs. In the same year his TV commercials for Japan's Suntory Whiskey won the grand prize at the Cannes Film Festival, and the National Academy of TV Arts and Sciences honored him for his unique contributions to TV.

In 1975, he became host of an evening talk and entertainment show. In 1980, he marked his fiftieth anniversary as an entertainer and the Friars Club honored him with its Annual Life Achievement Award.

Davis has been married three times. His first marriage was in 1959 to singer Loray White. He married his second wife, actress Mai Britt, in 1961 and she is the mother of his three children. In 1970 he married dancer Altovise Gore.

## KATHERINE DUNHAM
## Dancer , Choreographer

Katherine Dunham has for many years been one of the leading exponents of primitive dance in the world of modern choreography. She has used her training in anthropology and her study of primitive rituals from tropical cultures to create unique dance forms which blend native qualities with sophisticated Broadway stage settings.

Born in Chicago on June 22, 1910, Dunham attended the University of Chicago, where she majored in anthropology. With the aid of a Rosenwald Fellowship, she was able to visit the Caribbean and Brazil to further her research in her chosen field.

In the 1930s, she founded the Dunham Company using Dunham techniques. She has been called the mother of Afro-American dance.

In 1940, she appeared in *Cabin in the Sky*, a musical for which she had done the choreography. She later toured the United States with her own dance group, and after the war, also played to enthusiastic audiences in Europe.

Among her best-known choreographic pieces are *Bhahiana* and *Burrell House.* Under the pseudonym Kaye Dunn, Dunham has written several articles and books on primitive dance.

On January 15, 1979 (Martin Luther King's Birthday) at Carnegie Hall in New York she received the 1979 Albert Schweitzer Music Award, and selections from her dance repertory from 1938 to 1975 were staged. In recent years she founded a free school to teach her dance techniques in East St. Louis. Dunham is married to stage designer John Pratt.

## GAIL FISHER
## Actress

Gail Fisher won the Emmy Award from the Academy of Television Arts and Sciences and garnered four additional Emmy nominations for her co-starring role as Peggy Fair, secretary to Mike Connors, in the CBS-TV series "Mannix."

Fisher was born in Potters Crossing, New Jersey—often referred to as "the worst rural slum on the eastern seaboard." Gail's father, a carpenter, died when she was two, leaving her mother $8.45.

*Roberta Flack, a major force in contemporary music.*

In 1960, Fisher appeared in the first Ford Grant production performed by the San Francisco Actors' Workshop and drew rave reviews for her role in *The Rocks Cried Out,* which lasted for three months. In 1961, she became the first black to do a national TV commercial with lines.

In 1967, the producers of the TV show "Mannix" chose Gail to play the Peggy Fair role. "I read for the part five times and got it," she said before adding, "Peggy replaced a bank of computers and a man to make room for me in the show." It appears as though the move was beneficial to all parties. Gail has received the producer's nod for Emmy consideration every season, and the series, after Fisher joined it, grew in the ratings.

Gail's penchant is for creative expression, be it painting, decorating or lyric writing. She is also known to be one of Hollywood's finest pool players.

In 1982, she was appearing on the television series "General Hospital," a daytime "soap."

Fisher has been married several times and has two daughters.

## ROBERTA FLACK
## Singer

During the early 1970s Roberta Flack rose from a musical cult figure in Washington to become one of the most popular female singers in the world. Her two smash singles—"First Time Ever I Saw Your Face" and Norman Gimbel's beautiful "Killing Me Softly With His Song"—established her as a major force in contemporary music.

Roberta Flack was born in Asheville, North Carolina, and as a child moved with her family to Richmond and then to Arlington, Virginia. Her family was musical, her mother playing church organ and her father the piano in what Roberta calls "A primitive Art Tatum style."

Roberta entered Howard University on a scholarship at 15, graduating three years later with a B.A. in music education. She accepted teaching jobs in Farmville, North Carolina, then later in Washington, D.C. and then took a part-time job accompanying opera singers at a restaurant in the Georgetown section of Washington. She also directed an amateur production of *Aida.* In 1967, after three years with the D.C. school system, she decided to try a music career.

In 1967, Roberta started a regular singing gig at Mr. Henry's Pub in Washington. Word of her talent soon spread and many entertainers who were in Washington would make it a point to see her. Les McCann was so impressed that he brought Roberta to Atlantic Records where she recorded her first album called *First Take.* Roberta's first smash single "The First Time Ever I Saw Your Face" was taken from this album. She quickly followed up with another success, "Killing Me Softly With His Song" and a hit album *Quiet Fire.*

Roberta Flack handles a wide variety of contemporary material with a soulful and mellow-smooth personal style that transcends categorization. The flexibility and purity of her delivery has produced a star who promises more in years to come.

## REDD FOXX
## Comedian

Redd Foxx's most famous role was Fred Sanford, the junkman on the popular NBC-TV series "Sanford and Son," which began in 1972. It was considered to be the second most popular role on television (the first being Archie Bunker). As a result Foxx became one of the highest paid actors in show business. In 1976, it was reported that he was earning \$25,000 per half-hour episode plus 25% of the producer's net profit.

Coincidentally, Sanford is actually Foxx's family name. He was born John Elroy Sanford in St. Louis and both his father and his brother are named Fred. As a boy he concocted a washtub band with two friends and played for tips on street corners, earning as much as \$60 a night. At 14, Foxx and the band moved to Chicago. The group broke up in World War II. Foxx moved to New York, worked as a rack pusher in the garment district, but persevering, began to find entertainment spots in night clubs and on the black vaudeville circuit. While in New York he played pool with a hustler named Malcolm Little, who was to change his name to Malcolm X.

In the early 1950s Foxx tried Hollywood. He had a brief stint with the Dinah Washington Show, but mostly survived by combining vaudeville and sign painting.

His comedy act was X-rated adult entertainment, which limited his bookings. His first real success came in 1955 when he began to record party records. He made more than 50 of them which sold over 20 million copies. His television career was launched in the 1960s with guest appearances on The Today Show, The Tonight Show, and others. He also began to appear in the Las Vegas nightclubs. Throughout the long run of "Sanford and Son," Foxx was in disputes with his producer over money. Originally he was not receiving a percentage of the show's profits, so he sat out several episodes resulting in a breach of contract suit filed by the producers. There were also racial undertones with Foxx referring to himself as a "tuxedo slave" and pointing to white stars who owned a percentage of their shows. Eventually he broke with the show and with NBC. He then signed a multimillion dollar, multiyear contract with ABC, which resulted in a disastrous comedy variety hour which he quit on the air in October 1977.

He has also done a TV situation comedy "My Buddy" for ABC-TV which he wrote and starred in, and served as executive producer. In 1978, ABC filed a breach of contract suit. In 1979, Foxx was back at NBC planning a sequel to "Sanford and Son."

Foxx had done a movie for MGM in 1976, *Norman, Is That You?* He continued his appearances in nightclubs in Las Vegas and New York. He also had a deal with CBS Inc., which in 1981 was suing him for a second time, allegedly to recover advances not paid back. In 1979 a book, Redd Foxx, B.S., was published. It is comprised of a collection of chapters written by his friends.

In 1973, Foxx received the Entertainer of the Year Award from the National Association for the Advancement of Colored People. In 1974, he was named police chief of Taft, Oklahoma, an all-black village of 600 people. He also was running a Los Angeles nightclub to showcase aspiring young comedians, both black and white. Foxx also did numerous prison shows, probably more than any other famous entertainer, and he paid for the shows out of his own pocket.

*Redd Foxx achieved national attention with his* Sanford and Son *TV series.*

*Aretha Franklin is a warm and natural performer.*

## ARETHA FRANKLIN
### Singer

The uncontested modern queen of "Soul," Aretha Franklin is a vigorous and talented performer who reigns over the pop music field. She has already reached the magic figure of one million sales on several singles and long-playing albums, all of which are characterized by a lively and pulsating rhythm and a compelling, infectious beat. Some of her music stems straight from the openly emotional jubilant gospel choir tradition in which her father, Reverend C. L. Franklin, was immersed during his evangelical years in Memphis and Detroit. She is, however, equally capable of delivering a warm blues number or a rhythmically explosive solo reminiscent of her mentor, Ray Charles. Whatever the music calls for, her style radiates a relaxed natural honesty that critics regard as an admirable trademark.

Born in 1942, Franklin moved to Detroit at the age of two, and grew up teaching herself the gospel songs and piano accompaniment which were to form the basis of her early career. Her success on the gospel circuit inspired her to test the pop music field, but she was only modestly successful until 1966, when she signed a contract with Atlantic Records, a company specializing in rhythm and blues performers.

Franklin has had 21 gold records and has won 10 Grammy Awards. One of the secrets of her astonishing success was the breakthrough which black music itself was finally achieving. Much of it had been copied and adulterated by white artists familiar with its driving rhythms and throbbing vitality. When Franklin came along, black artists were finally beginning to be appreciated nationally as the originators and prime interpreters of such music. In the words of one observer, it no longer needed to be "manicured" or "sanitized."

In 1976, Aretha Franklin made her first European tour. That same year, cheering and foot-stomping crowds greeted her at a performance at Lincoln Center in New York City. In 1981, she did a concert series at the City Center in New York.

In 1980, she signed with a new record label, Arista. Her highly successful album "Aretha" came out in 1981, launching the popular single release "United Together" followed by "What a Fool Believes" and "Can't Turn You Loose."

Franklin appeared in the Universal film *The Blues Brothers* in 1980. Franklin had been married to her manager, Ted White in the 1960s. In 1978 she married actor Glynn Turman.

## AL FREEMAN JR.
### Actor

Al Freeman Jr. has won recognition for his many roles in the theater and motion pictures. His title role, portrayal in the television film "My Sweet Charlie" earned him an Emmy Award nomination.

Freeman was born in San Antonio, Texas, the son of late pianist Al Freeman Sr., and Lottie Coleman Freeman. After attending primary schools there, Freeman continued his education in Ohio, then moved to the West Coast to study law at Los Angeles City College. Encouraged by fellow students to audition for a campus production, he decided to change his major to theater arts when he returned to college following a tour of duty with the Army in Germany.

He did radio shows and appeared in little theater productions in the Los Angeles area before performing in his first Broadway play, *The Long Dream.* Other Broadway credits include *Golden Boy, Blues for Mr. Charley, Look to the Lilies, The Dozens, Medea, Tiger, Tiger Burning Bright, Conversations at Midnight, The Long Dream,* and *Kicks and Company.*

Off-Broadway Freeman worked in *The Premise, Trumpets of the Lord, The Slave, Great McDaddy,* and *Measure for Measure* and *Troilus and Cressida* for the New York Shakespeare Festival. He has also done more than a dozen feature films including *Dutchman, Finian's Rainbow, The Lost Man, The Detective,* and *Castle Keep.*

Freeman has appeared in such TV series as "The Defenders," "The FBI," "Naked City," and is featured as Lt. Ed Hall in ABC's daytime drama "One Life to Live," estimated to have a 25% black audience. He also appeared on TV in Norman Lear's "Hot l Baltimore."

## MARVIN GAYE
### Singer 1939-1984

Marvin Gaye was one of Motown's most talented and respected singers, whose often troubled life ended in tragedy. Born on April 2, 1939 in Washington, D.C., Marvin, the son of an Apostolic minister, started singing at the age of three in church. He also learned to play the organ soon thereafter.

After serving in the Air Force, he returned home and started singing in groups including the Rainbows. In 1957, he formed his own group, the Marquees and cut a single, *Wyatt Earp* for the Okeh label. One year later, Harvey Fequa heard the group and hired them to become the latest version of his ensemble, the Moonglows. Gaye was part of the group who recorded *Mama Loocie* and other songs on the Chess label in 1959.

By the 1960s, the group was touring widely and heard by Berry Gordy Jr. while performing at a club in Detroit. Marvin was soon signed on the Motown label and then married Gordy's sister Anna. Initially, he was a session drummer who played on all the early hits by Smokey Robinson and the Miracles.

After three records, Gaye's first hit was *Stubborn Kind of Fellow* in 1962. Over the next 10 years, he would enjoy more than 20 hits while working with all of the label's top producers.

A second phase of his career began in 1971 with the album, *What's Going On,* which dealt with issues of life. Within two years, another album, *Let's Get It On* revealed an emphasis on eroticism.

In 1982, Gaye signed with Columbia Records, having divorced his wife and decided to leave Motown. His first album, *Midnight Love* produced the Grammy-winning single, *Sexual Healing* which he sang live at the Grammy broadcast, and in 1983, in a rare concert appearance at Radio City Music Hall. On April 1, 1984, he died during a violent confrontation with his father.

## CHARLES GILPIN
### Actor
### 1878-1930

Charles Gilpin has been described by Margaret Just Butcher as "the first modern American Negro to establish himself as a serious actor of first quality."

Gilpin was born in Virginia in 1878, and after a brief period in school, began work as a printer's devil. In 1890, he began to travel with vaudeville troupes, a practice he continued for two decades, working as a printer, elevator operator, prizefight trainer, and porter during long interludes of theatrical unemployment.

From 1911 to 1914, he toured with a group called the Pan-American Octette, and in 1914 he had a bit part in *Old Ann's Boy.* Two years later he organized and managed the Lafayette Theatre Company, one of the earliest black stock companies in New York.

After Eugene O'Neill saw Gilpin in *Abraham Lincoln,* he was chosen to play the lead in *Emperor Jones,* the role in which he starred from 1920 to 1924. (In 1921, he was named winner of the NAACP Spingarn Award for his theatrical accomplishment.)

Gilpin lost his voice in 1926 and was forced to earn his living once again as an elevator operator. He died in 1930.

*Charles S. Gilpin, the dean of serious black American actors.*

## DANNY GLOVER
### Actor

By the late 1980s, Danny Glover had become one of the most versatile and respected actors working.

A native of San Francisco, who was born in 1947, he attended San Francisco State University and trained at the Black Actors Workshop of American Conservatory Theatre

He went on to appear in many stage productions including "Island," "Macbeth," "Sizwe Banzi is Dead" and New York productions of "Suicide in B Flat, " "The Blood Knot" and "Master Harold . . . and the Boys, " which won a Theatre World Award . "

His feature film roles included appearances in *Chu Chu and the Philly Flash, Iceman, Escape From Alcatraz, Witness, Places in the Heart, The Color Purple, Lethal Weapon* and *Bat-21*.

On television, he appeared in the hit series, *Hill Street Blues*, such miniseries as *Chief s* and *Lonesome Dove* and other projects including *Many Mansions, Face of Rage, A Place at the Table, Mandela* and *A Raisin in the Sun*.

## WHOOPI GOLDBERG
### Actress/Comedienne

While remaining popular on the concert circuit with her one-woman show, Whoopi Goldberg became one of the most active black film actresses of the late 1980s.

She was born in Manhattan's Chelsea district on November 13, 1949 and began performing at the age of eight at the children's program at Hudson Guild and Helen Rubeinstein Children's Theatre. After trying her hand at theatre, improvisation and chorus bit parts on Broadway (*Jesus Christ Superstar, Pippin* and *Hair*), she moved to San Diego in 1974 and appeared in repertory productions of *Mother Courage*, and *Getting Out*.

Soon, she joined the Black St. Hawkeyes Theatre in Berkeley as a partner with David Schein and then went solo to create *The Spook Show*, working in San Francisco and later touring the United States and Europe.

In 1983, he work caught the attention of Mike Nichols, who created and directed her Broadway show a year later. She made her film debut in *The Color Purple*, winning an NAACP Image Award as well as a Golden Globe Award.

Her other film credits include *Jumpin' Jack Flash, Burglar, Fatal Beauty, The Telephone, Homer and Eddie, Clara's Hea*r and *Beverly Hills Brats*.

On television, she starred in *Whoopi Goldberg on Broadway?, Carol, Carl, Whoopi and Robin, Funny, You Don't Look 200* and hosted *Comedy Tonight*. She received an Emmy nomination for her guest appearance on an episode of *Moonlighting* and was a founding member of the Comic Relief benefit shows.

## LOUIS GOSSETT, JR.
### Actor

As the tough drill sergeant in the film, *An Officer and a Gentleman*, Louis Gossett, Jr. won an Academy Award and became one of the few blacks to be so recognized by the motion picture industry .

*Academy Award winner Louis Gossett Jr.*

Born in Brooklyn on May 27, 1936, Gossett began acting at the age of 17 when a leg injury prevented him from pursuing his first love at the time—basketball. In 1953, he won out over 445 contenders for the role of a black youngster in *Take A Giant Step* and won a Donaldson Award as Best Newcomer of the Year.

While performing in *The Desk Set* in 1958, he was drafted by the pro basketball New York Knicks, but decided to remain in theatre. Ultimately, he would appear in more than 60 stage productions including such places as *Lost in the Stars, A Raisin in the Sun, The Blacks* and *Murderous Angels*.

On television, he played characters roles in such series as *The Nurses, The Defenders and East Side, West Side*. In 1977, he won an Emmy for his performance in the acclaimed mini-series, *Roots* He also starred in such films as *Skin Game*, *The Deep*, *Iron Eagle* and *Iron Eagle II*.

In 1989, he starred in his own television series, *Gideon Oliver*.

## ARSENIO HALL
### Actor/TV Talk Show Host

Arsenio Hall is the first black to host a nationally-broadcast weekly television talk show.

The Cleveland native, who was born in 1960, started his professional career as a standup comic, making the rounds of clubs where he honed his presentation. In time, he would appear on television specials as well as tour with noted musical performers.

Hall was selected as a guest-host of Fox Television's "Joan Rivers Show" when Rivers left and soon won over both studio and television audiences. When the show concluded, he went on to star with Eddie Murphy in the movie, "Coming To America" and then was hired by Paramount to be the host of his own show.

Within weeks after the show premiered in 1989, Hall had again built a solid audience following, particularly with young viewers and provided the most substantial competition existing shows had ever faced.

## RICHARD B. HARRISON
### Actor
### 1864-1935

Richard B. Harrison is one of the few actors to gain national prominence on the basis of one role, a feat which he accomplished with his characterization of "De Lawd" in *Green Pastures*.

Harrison was born in Canada in 1864 and moved to Detroit as a young boy. There he worked as a waiter, porter, and handyman, using whatever money he could save to attend the theatrical offerings playing in town. After studying drama in Detroit, he made his professional debut in Canada in a program of readings and recitations.

For three decades he entertained black audiences with one-man performances of *Macbeth, Julius Caesar,* and *Damon and Pythias*, as well as with poems by Shakespeare, Poe, Kipling, and Paul Laurence Dunbar. In 1929, while serving on the faculty of North Carolina A&T as a drama instructor, he was chosen for the part in *Green Pastures*.

When he died in 1935, Harrison had performed as "De Lawd" 1,656 times. His work had won him the 1930 Spingarn Medal and several honorary degrees as well.

## JIMI HENDRIX
### Singer
### 1942-1970

Jimi Hendrix was one of the most influential electric guitarists in the era of ever-changing rock and roll during the 1960s.

Born in Seattle, Washington on November 27, 1942, Hendrix taught himself to play the guitar as a teen-ager by listening to records by artists ranging from Muddy Waters to Chuck Berry. He played in high school bands before enlisting into the army in 1959.

In 1961, he began working as a pickup guitarist and by the time he moved to New York City in 1964, had played behind Sam Cook, B.B. King, Little Richard, Jackie Wilson, Ike and Tina Turner and Wilson Pickett. While in New York, he played the club circuit with King Curtis, the Isley Brothers and others.

In 1965, Hendrix organized his own band, Jimmy James and the Blue Flames. A member of the group, the Animals, took him to London where the Jimi Hendrix Experience was

*Gregory Hines relaxes during the filming of* Taps.

created. The group's first single, "Hey Joe" was a hit as well as the song, "Purple Haze." After becoming a hit in England, Hendrix came back to the U.S. in 1967, appearing at the Monterey Pop Festival.

His second American tour would prove problematic as audiences responded coolly to his performance. The Experience soon disbanded after internal dissension and Hendrix formed the Electric Sky Church and appeared at the Woodstock Festival. His last concert was at the Isle of Wight Festival in August, 1970.

Hendrix died a month later, reportedly from the inhalation of vomit following barbiturate intoxication. Suicide was not ruled out by the coroner's report, but evidence suggested that the death was an accident.

## GREGORY HINES
### Actor/Dancer

After a distinguished career as a talented tap dancer, Gregory Hines made an unusual transition to dramatic actor.

Hines began dancing with his brother Maurice under the instruction of tap dancer Henry LeTang. When Gregory was five, the brothers became professionals and were known as the Hines Kids. As they appeared in nightclubs and theatres around the country, they were able to get advice from dance legends like "Honi" Coles, Sandman Sims, the Nicholas Brothers and Teddy Hale.

As teenagers, they became known as the Hines Brothers and when Gregory was 18, they were joined by their father, Maurice Sr. on drums and became known as Hines, Hines and Dad. They performed internationally and appeared on *The Tonight Show* but eventually, Gregory tired of the touring and moved to California where he formed a jazz-rock band, Severance.

In time, he moved back to New York and landed a role in *The Minstrel Show*. He would later appear in such Broadway musicals as *Eubie*, *Comin' Uptown* and *Sophisticated Ladies* as well as feature films including *The Cotton Club*, *White Nights*, *Running Scared* and *Off Limits*.

On television, he appeared in the series, *Amazing Stories* and the special *Motown Returns to the Apollo*, earning an Emmy nomination. When not appearing in films or television, he toured internationally with a solo club act. *Gregory Hines*, his first solo album, was released by CBS/Epic in 1988. The album was produced by Luther Vandross, who teamed with Gregory for a single, *There's Nothing Better Than Love*, which reached number one on the R&B charts in 1987.

Hines starred in the 1989 Tri-Star film, *Tap* with Sammy Davis Jr. and not only acted and danced, but sang as well.

## GEOFFREY HOLDER
### Actor, Dancer, Choreographer, Director, Costume Designer, Writer, Painter

Geoffrey Holder is an artistic man for all seasons. He also is an imposing presence, 6 feet, 6 inches tall, handsome, with a shaved head.

Born in Trinidad, he left school to become the costume designer for his brother's dance troupe, which he took over in 1948 leading the dancers, singers, and steel band musicians through a series of successful small revues to the Caribbean Festival in Puerto Rico where they represented Trinidad. His appearances with his troupe in the mid-1950s were so popular that he is credited with launching the calypso vogue.

Early in his career he appeared in New York as a featured dancer in *House of Flowers*, later dancing with the Metropolitan Opera and as a guest star on many television shows. He also appeared in many TV dramas and in the films *Live and Let Die*, a James Bond adventure, and *Dr. Doolittle*, the children's classic starring Rex Harrison.

He received two Tony Awards in 1976 as director and as costume designer for the Broadway show *The Wiz*, the all-black adaptation of *The Wizard of Oz*. In 1978, he directed and choreographed the successful Broadway musical *Timbuktu*.

He is the recipient of a Guggenheim Fellowship for painting and his impressionist paintings have been shown in galleries such as the Corcoran in Washington, D.C. Holder also has written two books. *Black Gods, Green Islands* is a retelling of West Indian legends and Geoffrey Holder's *Caribbean Cookbook* is a collection of recipes which he also illustrated.

He appeared in the film *Annie*, based on the hit Broadway musical, playing Punjab, a character from the original comic strip. In early 1982, he was planning a new project, *A Voodoo Tragedy*, the story of Elektra, which he proposed to direct, costume, choreograph, and film in Haiti.

Holder is married to the ballet dancer Carmende Lavallade. They have one son, Leo.

## LENA HORNE
### Singer, Actress

Lena Horne has been called the most beautiful woman in the world, an opinion which has been no small factor in the continued success of her stage, screen, and nightclub career

Born on June 30, 1917, in Brooklyn, she joined the chorus line at the Cotton Club in 1933, and then left to tour as a dancer with Noble Sissle's orchestra. She was given a leading role in *Blackbirds of 1939*, but the show folded quickly, whereupon she left to join Charlie Barnett's band as a singer. She made her first records (including the popular "Haunted Town") with Barnett.

In the early 1940s she worked at New York's Cafe Society Downtown, and from there went to Hollywood where she was the first black woman ever to sign a term contract in films.

Her films include *Panama Hattie* (1942), *Cabin in the Sky* (1943), *Stormy Weather* (1943), and *Meet Me in Las Vegas* (1956). In 1957, she took a break from her nightclub schedule to star in her first Broadway musical, Jamaica.

Her most popular recordings include "Stormy Weather," "Blues in the Night," "The Lady Is a Tramp," and "Mad about the Boy."

In the 1970s, Lena Horne was appearing in nightclubs and

concerts, but her greatest recent success was on Broadway. On May 12, 1981 Lena Horne opened a one-woman show called *Lena Horne: The Lady and Her Music*. It was a critical and box-office success. Although it opened too late to qualify for the Tony Award nominations, the show was awarded a special Tony at the June ceremonies. In December of that year she received New York City's highest cultural award, The Handel Medallion.

Horne was married for 23 years to Lennie Hayton, a white composer, arranger, and conductor, who died April 24, 1971. She had been married previously at a young age to Louis Jones, with whom she had two children. Her son, Edwin, died at the age of 29 in 1970 of a kidney ailment. She also has a daughter, Gail Lumet, and grandchildren.

An extremely generous and gracious woman, Horne has devoted much time quietly and unobtrusively in the interest of many humane causes.

*The lovely Lena Horne, song stylist extraordinaire.*

## EDDIE HUNTER
**Vaudevillian**
**1888-1974**

Eddie Hunter, star of vaudeville, got his start as an elevator operator in a building frequented by the great tenor Enrico Caruso. Hunter had been writing comedy parts on the side and Caruso encouraged and helped him. By 1923, Hunter's show *How Come,* a musical revue, reached Broadway.

Hunter performed himself in the majority of the shows he wrote. *Going to the Races*, produced at the Lafayette Theatre in Harlem, had Hunter and his partner live on stage, interacting with a movie of themselves flashed on the screen. Hunter considered this show one of his best. As one of the principal performers in *Blackbirds*, he toured Europe in the late twenties. His show *Good Gracious* also toured Europe.

Depicting himself as "the fighting comedian, "Hunter developed a reputation for his struggle against racial discrimination in the performing arts. He frequently told the story about Phoenix, Arizona, where the male members of the show were forced to sleep in the theater where they were performing; accommodations for blacks simply did not exist at the time. In contrast, Hunter characterized his European receptions as being generally free of prejudice. There, he felt he received the respect and recognition due him.

By 1923, Hunter had a full recording contract with Victor Records. His recordings have included "It's Human Nature to Complain," "I Got," and "My Wife Mamie." Shortly thereafter, he suspended his singing career to begin traveling with a new show he had developed. But when talking movies came into being, time and the public ran out on people like Eddie Hunter and the types of shows he produced. Vaudeville was dying, if not already dead. Eddie Hunter retired from show business and entered the real estate business in the 1930s.

Hunter lived in Harlem, where he managed over 20 buildings. He died there in 1974 at the age of 86.

## EARLE HYMAN
**Actor**

When Earle Hyman made his debut in Eugene O'Neill's *Emperor Jones* in Oslo, Norway, he became the first American to perform a title role in a Scandinavian language. Hyman had originally become acquainted with Norway during a European trip made in 1957. He had planned to spend only two weeks in the Scandinavian country, but found himself so enchanted with it that he all but forgot the rest of Europe.

When he returned to New York, he resolved at once to learn Norwegian, and for practice, began to study the role of Othello (which he was doing for the Great Lakes Shakespeare Festival of 1962) in that language. By sheer coincidence, the director of *Den Nationale Scene* Theatre of Bergen, Norway, invited him to play Othello there in the spring of the following year, a performance which marked Hyman's first success in the Norwegian theater.

Two years later Hyman returned to Norway to play *Emperor Jones* for a different theater company, and was greeted with high critical acclaim for his portrayal; he stayed for six years. Due to the interest of the Norwegian people in his life, Hyman has been the subject of several radio broadcasts and numerous television interviews. He still spends six months each year in Scandinavia playing "Othello" and other classical roles. A bronze bust of the actor as Othello has been erected

*Al Watts, Rex Ingram (center, wearing hat), Georgette Harvey, Leigh Whipper, Jack Carter, and Edna Thomas in a scene from the movie* Stevedore.

in the Norwegian theater where Hyman performed, and he has also been presented with an honorary membership in the Norwegian Society of Artists, the third foreigner and first American to be so honored.

Born in North Carolina in 1926, Hyman began his acting career with the American Negro Theatre in New York, after which he appeared in eight Broadway productions and over 100 television programs. He is also a five-year veteran of the American Shakespeare Festival at Stratford, Connecticut.

His many on and off-Broadway credits include *Mister Johnson, Waiting for Godot, No Time for Sergeants, St. Joan* (with Diana Sands at Lincoln Center), Lorraine Hansberry's *Les Blancs*, Edward Albee's *Lady from Dubuque,* and the black version of Eugene O'Neill's *Long Day's Journey into Night* (at the Public Theatre in 1981). In the mid-1970s he also appeared on a daytime "soap" "Love of Life."

### REX INGRAM
### Actor
### 1895-1969

A major movie and radio personality of the 1930s and 1940s, Rex Ingram was born in 1895 aboard the *Robert E. Lee,* a Mississippi riverboat on which his father was a stoker. He attended military schools where he displayed an interest in acting.

After working briefly as a cook for the Union Pacific Railroad and as head of his own small window-washing business, Ingram gravitated to Hollywood where in 1919 he appeared in the original Tarzan film. Roles in such classics as *Lord Jim, Beau Geste, King Kong, Green Pastures* and *Huckleberry Finn* followed. During the late twenties and early thirties, Ingram also appeared prominently in legitimate theater in San Francisco. In the late thirties, he was to star in daytime radio soap operas and in WPA theater. This launched a distinguished career in New York on the legitimate stage and in television, which was to last into the 1960s. In 1957, he played Pozzo in *Waiting for Godot.* During this period, he appeared periodically in motion pictures, his last role being in *Your Cheating Heart* in 1964.

### MAHALIA JACKSON
### Gospel Singer
### 1911-1972

The rich contralto of Mahalia Jackson—with its great range and singular control—has no equal in performing the original compositions of "gospel," a unique musical form produced by the style of worship prevalent in many black churches.

Mahalia Jackson was born in New Orleans on October 26, 1911. She was acquainted with the records of Bessie Smith and other blues singers, but at home her preacher father confined the family's listening habits to strictly religious music.

She moved to Chicago at 16 and joined the Salem Baptist choir, saving enough from her work as a hotel maid to open her own beauty shop. In 1934 she made her first record, "*God Gonna Separate the Wheat from the Tares,*" but she did not achieve national fame until 1945 with "Move On Up a Little Higher," which ultimately sold over a million copies.

Over the next few years, her fame was even greater in Europe than at home. In 1950, however, she gave a highly successful concert at Carnegie Hall in New York City. After that, she had several hit records and has made guest appearances on major television shows.

Her best-known record albums include "Bless This House," "Sweet Little Jesus Boy," and "The World's Greatest Gospel Singer."

Jackson died on January 27, 1972 ending a career that brought traditional gospel music to huge audiences through her truly remarkable voice and presentation. At the time of her death Jackson had been devoting much time to civil rights causes.

## MICHAEL JACKSON
### Singer

No other performer has had a greater impact on a generation of teenagers and children than Michael Jackson.

Having suggested a possible retirement from active performing after a triumphant, record-breaking world tour encompassing part of 1988 and 1989, Jackson had set a number of impressive career accomplishments for those who kept records by that juncture in his professional life.

Born on August 29, 1958, in Gary, Indiana, Michael was the fifth of nine children. Both of his parents, Katherine and Joe Jackson influenced the entire family musically. After singing at home, the youngsters began performing in public in the mid-1960s. When he was only five-years-old, Michael had left the bongos and had become the group's lead singer.

From talent contests and small-money jobs around Gary, the group began to appear at the Apollo in New York City and the Uptown in Philadelphia. They were discovered at the Apollo by Diana Ross and were soon signed by Berry Gordy to the Motown label. Their first single, *I Want You Back* was released in November, 1968. A series of hits followed and the group captured huge, enthusiastic audiences when they toured.

A television special and an animated cartoon series followed and soon Michael recorded his first album, *Got to Be There*. The group was able to keep its teen fans and build a new audience with disco fans with their new albums, *Get It Together* and *Dancing Machine*.

In 1975, the group moved to Epic Records where they recorded another series of successful albums. In the summer of 1976, the group starred in *The Jacksons,* a CBS musical/variety television show. Michael appeared two years later in the Motown/Universal film, *The Wiz* and then collaborated with the film's music director Quincy Jones on Michael's first debut album on Epic, *Off the Wall*. The album sold 5 million copies in the U.S. alone as well as 2 million more abroad.

In the summer of 1981, the Jacksons made their most successful concert tour ever. The show was recorded on a double album with narration by Michael. At that time, he also sang, *Someone in the Dark* on a story book about the movie, ET: *The Extra-Terrestrial.*

Michael's abilities as a composer and co-producer were much in evidence with the album, *Thriller*, in which he again collaborated with Quincy Jones. The album was the best-selling work in 1983 and the largest seller in CBS history.

Jackson was soon rewarded with literally scores of music industry awards and was honored in addition for his philanthropy to causes he supported. His work with Lionel Richie resulted in the tune, *We Are The World,* which was recorded by a score of top artists to benefit the Ethiopian drought relief fund.

*Teenage idol and supershowman, Michael Jackson.*

While considered by some to be eccentric, Jackson continued to produce popular tunes and work more and more in the video field with top producers and directors. His greatest work remained on the stage where critics and fans alike, found him one of the most exciting performers of the generation which so admired him. And many observers wondered after that record-breaking world tour that lasted nearly a year, what would be the next step in his spectacular career.

## JUDITH JAMISON
### Dancer

Judith Jamison, the leading dancer of the interracial Alvin Ailey Dance Theater, emerged in the 1970s as the first black superstar of American dance.

Tall, fluid, and spirited, Jamison portrays a wide gamut of black roles, many of which have been especially choreographed for her by Ailey, including two roles in "Cry," a 20-minute solo depicting the nobility and suffering of black women in which Jamison plays both a slave and black queen. Her talent for comedy is portrayed in her famous "parasol" role in "Revelations."

Born in Philadelphia, Jamison started to study dance at the age of six and was discovered in her early twenties by choreographer Agnes De Mille, who felt her spontaneity should be encouraged. Notes the great dancer: "Being on stage is the second most uninhibited thing I do. I turn myself totally inside out. I am preoccupied with the audience. I'm trying to turn them on, not the critics or the other dancers."

In the 1980s, Jamison scored a great success on Broadway in *Sophisticated Ladies,* a musical featuring the music of Duke Ellington.

## JAMES EARL JONES
### Actor

James Earl Jones is one of the most prominent black actors in the United States today, having starred in a variety of Shakespearean roles as well as a number of contemporary avant-garde theatrical productions.

Jones (whose actor father Robert Earl Jones was featured in the movie *One Potato, Two Potato*) was born in Tate County, Mississippi, and raised by his grandparents on a farm near Jackson, Michigan. He turned to acting after a brief period as a premedical student at the University of Michigan (from which he graduated cum laude in 1953) and upon completion of military service with the Army's Cold Weather Mountain Training Command in Colorado.

After drifting to New York, Jones studied at the American Theatre Wing, making his off-Broadway debut in 1957 in *Wedding in Japan.* Since then, he has appeared in more than 30 plays on and off Broadway, including *Sunrise at Campobello, The Cool World, The Blacks, The Blood Knot,* and *Anyone, Anyone.* Jones holds a number of awards, including the 1961 Obie and the 1961-1962 Daniel Blum Theatre World Award.

Jones' progress as an actor was, in a sense, slow and deliberate, rather than meteoric, until he portrayed Jack Jefferson in the Broadway smash hit *The Great White Hope.* The play, based on the life of Jack Johnson, the first black heavyweight champion, invariably reminded audiences of the career of Muhammad Ali. In 1969, Jones received the Tony Award for the best dramatic actor in a Broadway play, and the Drama Desk award for one of the best performances of the 1968-1969 New York season.

In the 1970s, Jones was appearing in roles traditionally performed by white actors. Among the performances was King Lear and an award-winning performance as Lenny in Steinbeck's *Of Mice and Men.*

In 1978, Jones appeared in the highly controversial *Paul Robeson,* a one-man show on Broadway. Many leading blacks advocated a boycott of the show because they said it did not measure up to the man himself. However, critics gave the show high praise.

In 1980, Jones starred in Athol Fugard's *A Lesson from Aloes,* which was a top contender for a Tony Award that year. He also appeared in the Yale Repertory Theater Production of *Hedda Gabler.* In the spring of 1982, he co-starred with Christopher Plummer on Broadway in *Othello* in a production acclaimed as one of the best ever done of the Shakespearean tragedy.

Among his films have been *Dr. Strangelove* and *River Niger.* He was the screen voice of Darth Vader in *Star Wars* and its sequel *The Empire Strikes Back,* and he made the horror movie, *Red Tide* and the adventure *Conan the Barbarian.* On television he portrayed author Alex Haley in "Roots: The Next Generation," and narrated documentaries for the Public Broadcasting System. In 1977 he was reported to command $200,000 for his performance in a movie.

In 1976, Jones was elected to the Board of Governors of the Academy of Motion Picture Arts and Sciences. In 1979, New York City presented him with the "Mayor's Award of Honor for Arts and Culture." He received an honorary Doctorate of Humane Letters from the University of Michigan in 1971 and the Michigan Club of New York Man of the Year Award in 1976.

Jones has a home in Pawling, New York. In March 1982, he married his *Othello* co-star, white actress Cecilia Hart.

## QUINCY JONES
### Composer

Quincy Jones is a prolific composer who has developed a long-standing relationship with film-making while working with many of the top recording artists in his lifetime.

Born in Chicago in 1934, Jones grew up in Seattle, Washington and became interested in music after meeting Ray Charles when the budding singer was 16-years-old. Later, while attending the prestigious Berklee College of Music, Jones made his professional debut as a trumpeter with the Lionel Hampton Big Band. His real love, however, was writing music and he worked under the instruction of Nadia Boulanger.

In 1961, he joined Mercury Records, becoming the first black vice president of a white record company. While there, his reputation as a producer grew. During this time, Jones wrote the score for several films, including the television mini-series, *Roots.*

He also wrote the music for the Oscar-nominated film, *The Color Purple,* which he also co-produced. Among his hits were the single, *Killer Joe* and the albums *Body Heat, Walking in Space, Mellow Madness* and *Smackwalker Jack.*

His success as a producer include such musical hits as

*Courtney Vance (left) and James Earl Jones in* Fences.

George Benson's *Give Me The Night* and Michael Jackson's *Thriller,* which sold 38 million copies. Jones was the conductor for the hit, *We Are The World* and has been nominated for Grammy and Oscar Awards on several occasions.

## GLADYS KNIGHT AND THE PIPS
### Recording Artists

Gladys Knight and the Pips, an Atlanta-based family group, performed for more than three decades and recorded many of the popular music hits of the 1960s and 1970s.

Gladys was born on May 28, 1944 in Atlanta and like her parents, sang in church choirs. Before she was five, she was touring churches with the Morris Borwn Choir. At age seven, she won a grand prize on the *Ted Mack Amateur Hour*, which led to several television appearances. The Pips were formed in 1952 on Gladys' older brother Merald's birthday after Gladys arranged an impromptu singing group to entertain the family.

The group toured nationally with Jackie Wilson and Sam Cooke before Gladys was 13, but their 1957 recording debut with Brunswick Records was not a success. In 1961, the group recorded its first r&b Top Twenty hit, *Every Beat of My heart*. The group, composed of Merald, William Guest and Edward Patten resorted to singing studio backups in the early 1960s when Gladys had a baby. When they were signed as a guest act on the Motown touring revue, they soon joined the label and recorded such hits as *I Heart It Through The Grapevine*, *Friendship Train* and *If I Were Your Woman.*

The group decided to leave Motown in 1973 and when they joined Buddah Records, their *Imagination* album as well as three singles, *I've Got To Use My Imagination, Midnight Train to Georgia* and *Best Thing That Ever Happened To Me* became , at that time became their biggest hits selling over 1,000,000 records, and, as they say in the trade, went gold.

They performed in the movie soundtrack to *Claudine* and Gladys made her acting debut in the movie, *Pipe Dreams.* While continuing to perform, the group was not allowed to record together for three years because of a contract dispute but they did reunite again in 1980 and recorded *About Love* on the Columbia label, which was produced by Ashford and Simpson. During this time, Gladys Knight and the Pips continued to perform in concerts as well as on stage in major theatre settings.

## HUDDIE (LEADBELLY) LEDBETTER
### Folk Singer
### 1888-1949

A legendary figure in the history of American entertainment is Huddie Ledbetter, known widely as "Leadbelly." The violence of Ledbetter's personal life sometimes tends to obscure the major contribution he made to the folk music revival in the United States.

Ledbetter was born in Mooringsport, Louisiana in 1888, and raised in Texas where he learned to play accordion and guitar. From 1903 until 1917, he worked in the Louisiana-Texas area. In 1918 he was jailed for murder under the name

*The ever popular recording artists, Gladys Knight and the Pips.*

*Huddie Ledbetter, better known as "Leadbelly", his songs were mixed with sweet music and raw wit.*

Walter Boyd. Seven years later he was pardoned, but in 1930 he was jailed again for attempted homicide and this time served four years in prison. (There seems to be no basis for the legend that Ledbetter was freed by the Governor of Louisiana because "he played the sweetest 12-string guitar in the whole wide world.")

Discovered by folklorist Alan Lomax, Ledbetter recorded for the Library of Congress and played numerous nightclub engagements during the 1940s. In 1949 he toured France successfully, and during this period, began to spark a general interest both at home and abroad in American folk music. Some of his songs, such as "On Top of Old Smoky" and "Irene Good Night," became commercial successes when recorded by others.

He died in New York City on December 6, 1949.

### CANADA LEE
### Actor
### 1907-1951

Canada Lee is best known for his work in the 1941 Broadway version of *Native Son,* in which he played Bigger Thomas, and for his performance in the 1952 film *Cry the Beloved Country.*

Lee was born in Manhattan on May 3, 1907. After studying violin as a young boy, he ran off to Saratoga with the intention of becoming a jockey. Failing in this, he returned to New York and began a boxing career. By 1926 he had turned professional after winning 90 out of 100 fights, including the national amateur lightweight title.

Over the next few years he won 175 out of some 200 fights against such top opponents as Jack Britton and Vince Dundee. In 1933, a detached retina brought an end to his ring career. (He had acquired his name when a ring announcer could not pronounce his real name—Lee Canetaga.)

In 1934, Lee was a struggling musician when he successfully auditioned at the Harlem YMCA for his first acting role in a WPA production of *Brother Mose.*

In 1941, Orson Welles, who had met him in the production of the Federal Theatre's Negro *Macbeth,* chose him to play Bigger Thomas in the stage version of Richard Wright's famed novel *Native Son. New York Times* critic Brooks Atkinson called him "a superbly imaginative player."

In 1944 Lee served as narrator of a radio series called "New World Comin'," the first such series devoted to the race question. That same year, he also appeared in Alfred Hitchcock's film *Lifeboat,* and in the Broadway play *Anna Lucasta.*

Lee died in 1951.

### JACKIE (MOMS) MABLEY
### Comedienne
### 1897-1975

Although she was virtually unknown to the general public, Jackie (Moms) Mabley was a favorite of black audiences for almost half a century. Late in her life her comedy record albums made her "an overnight success almost 50 years in show business."

Mabley was born Loretta Mary Aiken in North Carolina, and entered show business as a teenager when the team of Buck and Bubbles gave her a bit part in a vaudeville skit called *Rich Aunt from Utah.*

With the help of comedienne Bonnie Bell Drew, Mabley developed a monologue, and was soon being booked on the black vaudeville circuit. Influenced by such teams as Butterbeans and Susie, she developed her own comic character, that of a world-weary old woman in a funny hat and droopy stockings, delivering her gags with a mixture of sassy folk wisdom and sly insights. Her first big success came in 1923 at Connie's Inn in New York.

Her first record album "Moms Mabley at the U.N." was a commercial success, and was followed by "Moms Mabley at the Geneva Conference." In 1962 she made her Carnegie Hall debut on a program with Cannonball Adderley and Nancy Wilson. Her subsequent record successes made her the favorite of a new generation.

Moms Mabley died May 23, 1975 at the age of 78 in White Plains (New York) Hospital. She had lived in Greenburgh, New York and was survived by five children.

### JOHNNY MATHIS
### Singer

Records and nightclub engagements have combined to establish Johnny Mathis as one of the most successful pop

*Johnny Mathis cutting a recording.*

singers. Mathis was born in San Francisco on September 30, 1935, and won an athletic scholarship to San Francisco State College, where he set a high-jump record. In 1935, while watching a friend perform in a San Francisco nightclub, he answered a request to sing, and was discovered by the club's owner. He was soon signed to a recording contract and begin to tour the nightclub circuit.

In 1958 he sang the title song and was featured in the movie *A Certain Smile*. Since then, he has made countless television appearances and is one of the few singers on the current scene whose appeal is not limited to members of a single age group.

His biggest hits include "Chances Are," "It's Not For Me to Say," and "Twelfth of Never."

Mathis has more than 50 gold and platinum albums and singles. His "Greatest Hits" album stayed on the Billboard best seller charts for a record 490 weeks. In 1978, almost 23 years after his first record was released, he had the number one pop single for the first time, "Too Much, Too Little, Too Late" (with singer Deniece Williams ). Mathis continues to tour the world doing concerts and nightclubs. He also has done television specials. He lives in the Hollywood Hills in California.

## HATTIE McDANIEL
**Actress**
**1898-1952**

The first black to win an Oscar was Hattie McDaniel, who received the Motion Picture Academy's highest award in 1940 as the year's best supporting actress in *Gone with the Wind.*

McDaniel was born on June 10, 1898 in Wichita, Kansas and moved to Denver, Colorado as a child. After singing on Denver radio as an amateur for some time, she entered vaudeville professionally, and by 1924, was a headliner on the Pantages circuit.

By 1931, she had made her way to Hollywood where, after a slow start (during which she supported herself as a maid and washer woman), she gradually began to get more movie roles. *Judge Priest, The Little Colonel,* and *Showboat* were some of the movies in which she appeared, along with *Saratoga* and *Nothing Sacred*. Her portrayal of a "mammy" figure in *Gone with the Wind* is still regarded as a kind of definitive interpretation of this role.

In addition to her movie roles, she also had ample success on radio during the 1930s, particularly as Hi-Hat Hattie. She followed this in the 1940s in the title role of the very successful *Beulah* series.

McDaniel died on October 26, 1952.

## FLORENCE MILLS
**Stage Performer**
**1895-1927**

When Florence Mills died in New York City in November of 1927, she had been acclaimed as the leading black entertainer of her time. As a singing and dancing comedienne, she had become a star not only on Broadway but in London and Paris as well.

Mills was born in Washington, D.C. on January 25, 1895, and made her debut there at the age of five in *Sons of Ham.* In 1903, the family moved to Harlem, and in 1910 she joined her sisters in an act known as The Mills Trio. She later appeared with a group called The Panama Four. (One of its members was Ada "Bricktop" Smith.)

In 1920, she appeared in *Shuffle Along*, a prototype among Negro musicals, and her success led to a long engagement at The Plantation, a New York night spot. After a successful appearance in London, she returned to the United States in 1924 to star in From Dixie to Broadway, the show in which she sang the song that became her trademark, I'm Just a *Little Blackbird Lookin' for a Bluebird*. Later, her own Blackbirds revue was a great success in London and Paris.

Mills returned to the United States in 1927. Exhausted by her work abroad, she entered the hospital on October 25 for a routine appendectomy, and died suddenly a few days later.

## ABBIE MITCHELL
**Singer, Actress**
**1884-1960**

Most celebrated as a concert artist, Abbie Mitchell also displayed her versatility in the areas of serious acting and light musical comedy. At the age of 13, she came to New York City from Baltimore, joining Will Marion Cook's Clorindy Company, and later, achieving her first real success with the Williams and Walker Company.(Mitchell married Cook while still in her teens and bore him a son, Mercer, now a diplomat in Africa.)

By 1923, Mitchell had performed in nearly every European country, and returned home to give the first of her many voice concerts in the United States at the Mother A.M.E. Zion Church in New York.

Mitchell also performed with many opera companies and acted in several plays, including *Stevedore* in 1934 and

*Coquette* with Helen Hayes. She also headed the voice department at Tuskegee Institute for three years.

She died in 1960 after a long illness.

### MELBA MOORE
### Singer, actress

With her powerful voice, polychrome personality, and wide range of singing styles, Melba Moore has become one of the brightest new stars in the international entertainment world.

Born in New York City, daughter of singer Melba "Bonnie" Smith and jazz saxophonist Teddy Hill, she spent her early years in Harlem and the rest of her childhood in a middle-class part of Newark, New Jersey. This mixture of backgrounds has contributed much to the unique range of her personality. After graduating from Montclair State Teachers College, she taught elementary school music for a year and began working her way into show business doing lounge work and some background voice sessions for recording companies. She successfully auditioned for the Broadway opening of *Hair* in 1968, and in her 18-month stint with the show, went up the rungs from ordinary tribe member to female lead. In 1970, she created the musical role of Lutiebelle in Purlie, where she received rave reviews and rousing ovations for her rendition of I *Got Love*. She also won the Antoinette Perry Award for best supporting actress in a musical, and the New York Critics Award, and the Drama Desk Award for best actress in a musical.

In 1978, she appeared on Broadway in the musical *Timbuktu*. In 1981, she did Inacent Black, a comedy with music, on Broadway. She has had straight acting roles in two movies, *Pigeons* and *Lost in the Stars*. On television she guest starred on talk and variety shows, played Harriet Tubman in the 1976 ABC-TV series *The American Woman: Portraits in Courage*, and won both the Emmy and the Peabody Award for the PBS Children's series *Big Blue Marble*. She was the first black artist to be featured in a one-woman concert at the Metropolitan Opera House in New York, has appeared in concert around the world, and has done many nightclub engagements.

She recently has been involved in producing her own record albums. In 1980, Moore introduced her new sportswear line "500 Francs for Melba Moore," designed, she said, for "a better fit for black women who tend to be smaller waisted and wider hipped."

### EDDIE MURPHY
### Actor/Comedian

By the late 1980s, Eddie Murphy had become the most successful black working in the movie industry. His rise to prominence had come at a rapid pace.

He was a little-known stand-up comedian when he made his first appearance on the late-night television show, *Saturday Night Live*. He made a memorable impression and within three years was being hailed as a major new star based on his work in the hit films, *48 Hours* and *Trading Places*.

A multi-million dollar contract with Paramount Pictures followed and along with his best-selling debut comedy album, *Eddie Murphy*, and in the words of fellow performer Dan Aykroyd, "Eddie's on his way to becoming an industry."

Eddie was born on April 3, 1961 in the Bushwick section of Brooklyn, the son of a New York City policeman and amateur comedian. As a youngster, he did imitations of cartoon characters and began preparing comic routines with impressions of Elvis Presley, Jackie Wilson, Al Green and the Beatles as he grew older.

He attended Roosevelt Junior-Senior High School in Long Island and hosted a talent show at the Roosevelt Youth Center before beginning to call local talent agents to secure bookings at Long Island nightclubs.

After his success with the first two Paramount films, he starred in *Beverly Hills Cop* and its sequel, *Beverly Hills Cop II*, which were two of the major box office hits of the decade. A concert film, *Raw* followed as well as an effort at light-hearted fantasy, *The Golden Child*.

Murphy was also responsible for the successful comedy, *Coming To America* and was invited as a regular guest on television talk shows, including two Barbara Walters specials. He made plans to produce his first television show by 1989 and began to work on a film project with Richard Pryor.

Murphy has grown to become an industry phenomenon, often collaborating with a group of young comic talents known in the industry as "The Black Pack."

*Dan Aykroyd and Eddie Murphy trade places in the comedy with a twist,* Trading Places.

## CLARENCE MUSE
### Actor
### 1889-1979

Perhaps best known for his film acting, Clarence Muse was also successful as a director, playwright, and actor on the legitimate stage.

Born in Baltimore, Muse's parents came from Virginia and North Carolina, and his grandfather from Martinique. After studying law at Dickinson University in Pennsylvania, Muse sang as part of a hotel quartet in Palm Beach, Florida. A subsequent job with a stock company took him on tour through the South with his wife and son. Coming to New York, he barely scraped a living together, mostly performing as a vaudevillian.

After several plays with the now-famous groups of The Lincoln Theatre and The Lafayette Players in Harlem, and then a Broadway stint in *Dr. Jekyll and Mr. Hyde,* where white roles were played by blacks in white-face creating quite a controversy, Muse had established himself as an able actor and singer.

His first movie role was in *Hearts in Dixie,* produced at the William Fox Studio, in which Muse played the role of a 90-year-old man. Later he returned to the stage for the role of a butler in the show called *Under the Virgin Moon.* After Muse wrote the theme song, the title was changed to his *When It's Sleepy Time Down South.* Both the song and the show were hits. Muse recalls six encores on opening night.

When the Federal Theatre Project in Los Angeles presented Hall Johnson's *Run Little Chillun,* Clarence Muse directed the show. After a successful run for two years, Muse adapted *Way Down South* for the screen.

During his career he appeared in 219 films and was at one time one of the highest paid black actors, often portraying faithful servant "Uncle Tom" characters. His last film was *Black Stallion* in 1979. He also appeared over the years in concerts and on radio.

Muse died October 13, 1979, the day before his ninetieth birthday. He lived in Perris, California on his Muse-a-While Ranch. He was survived by his third wife, Irene, a son and a daughter.

In October 1980, he was the subject of a segment of the PBS series *Western Exposure—Clarence Muse: Black Star of the Silver Screen.*

## FREDERICK O'NEAL
### Actor

Frederick O'Neal is the first black to hold the position of President of Actor's Equity. The honor of leading his profession's union is a fitting tribute to his long years of service to the American theater as both actor and teacher.

O'Neal was born August 27, 1908 in Brookville, Mississippi. After his father's death in 1919, he moved with his family to St. Louis, finishing high school there, and then appearing in Urban League dramatic productions.

In 1927, with the help of some friends in St. Louis, O'Neal founded the Ira Aldridge Players, the second Negro acting group in America. For the next 10 years, he played in 30 of its productions. In 1937, he came to New York, and three years later helped found the American Negro Theatre. Today, its alumni include such established stars as Sidney Poitier, Earle Hyman, Harry Belafonte, Ruby Dee, Ossie Davis, and Hilda Simms.

O'Neal himself starred in *Anna Lucasta,* and was later featured in *Take a Giant Step, The Winner,* and several other stage productions. In the 1944-1945 season, he won the Derwent Award and the Drama Critics Award for the best supporting performance by an actor on Broadway.

His films include *Pinky* and *The Man with the Golden Arm.* He has also appeared on several TV dramatic and comedy shows.

Devoting full time to Actor's Equity, O'Neal was in 1970 elected International President of the Associated Actors and Artists of America, the parent union which included all of the show business performers' unions. He became president and chairman of the board of the Schomburg Corporation to raise money to conserve and preserve materials in the center, to solicit material, and to work toward construction of a new building. He was a member of the New York State Council on the Arts, President of the Catholic Interracial Council, chairman of the AFL-CIO Civil Rights Committee, and vice president of the A. Philip Randolph Institute. In 1980, he received the National Urban Coalition's Distinguished Trade Unionist Award.

## GORDON PARKS
### Photographer, Composer, Author, Director

Gordon Parks, long acclaimed internationally as a photographer, has recently become a leading producer of black films. He is also a composer (First Concerto for Piano and Orchestra) and novelist (The Learning Tree).

Born in Fort Scott, Kansas, Parks moved to St. Paul, Minnesota, and attended high school there for a time while engaging in a variety of odd jobs. Having chosen photography as a career in 1937, Parks went to Chicago, where he became closely associated with the South Side Community Art Center.

A one-man exhibit of his work eventually led to a Rosenwald Fellowship, after which he accepted a government assignment in the Overseas Division of the Office of War Information.

After World War II, Parks made a number of documentaries for a large New Jersey oil firm, and was later taken on as a staff photographer for *Life.* Since then, he traveled widely, lived abroad, and captured a number of impressive awards, including Magazine Photographer of the Year (1961), the Newhouse Award from Syracuse University, and NAACP's Spingarn Award in 1972.

Parks also has won awards for his writing. His subject matter has included such diverse topics as Black Muslims, Paris of the 1920s, and the plight of all oppressed peoples in U.S. ghettos. His music has been performed in New York, Venice, and Philadelphia.

In addition to *The Learning Tree,* Parks has written an autobiography entitled *A Choice of Weapons* (1965). For

National Educational Television, he has produced three documentaries which focus on ghetto life. In 1968, he was the director of the motion picture version of *The Learning Tree*.

His other movies have included *Shaft* and its sequel *Shaft's Big Score, Super Cops,* and *Leadbelly*.

In 1968, his book *A Poet and His Camera* was published. In 1978, he published *Flavio,* the story of a Rio de Janeiro slum child who had become famous because of an earlier picture essay which Parks had done for *Life* magazine. In 1977, with three partners, he gained control of *Essence,* the largest magazine for black women, to prevent the magazine from falling into the hands of whites.

## SIDNEY POITIER
### Actor

In 1965 Sidney Poitier became the first black to win an Oscar for a starring role, receiving this award for his performance in *Lilies of the Field*. Seven years earlier, Poitier had been the first black actor nominated for the award for his portrayal of an escaped convict in *The Defiant Ones*.

Poitier was born on February 20, 1927 in Miami, but moved to the Bahamas with his family at a very early age. At 15, he returned to Miami, later riding freight trains to New York City, where he found employment as a dishwasher. With the coming of Pearl Harbor, he enlisted in the Army and served on active duty for four years.

*The first black male to win an Academy Award, Sidney Poitier.*

Back in New York, he auditioned for the American Negro Theatre, but was turned down by director Frederick O'Neal. After working diligently to improve his diction, Poitier was accepted in the theater group and received acting lessons in exchange for performing backstage chores.

In 1950, he made his Hollywood debut in *No Way Out,* and followed this with successful appearances in *Cry the Beloved Country* (1952), *Red Ball Express* (1952), *Go, Man, Go* (1954), *Blackboard Jungle* (1956), *Goodbye, My Lady* (1956), *Edge of the City* (1957), *Band of Angels* (1957), *Something of Value* (1957), and *Porgy and Bess* (1959), among others.

Poitier starred on Broadway in 1959 in Lorraine Hansberry's award-winning *Raisin in the Sun,* and repeated this success in the movie version of the play in 1961.

His notable recent films include *To Sir with Love* and *Heat of the Night* in 1967, *Guess Who's Coming to Dinner* with Spencer Tracy and Katherine Hepburn in 1968, *Buck and the Preacher* in 1972 and *A Warm December* in 1973 in both of which he acted and directed, *Uptown Saturday Night* in 1974 for the now defunct First Artists Company (which he had formed with Barbra Streisand, Paul Newman and Steve McQueen), and *A Piece of the Action* in 1977. In 1978 he directed Richard Pryor and Gene Wilder in *Stir Crazy*.

Poitier spent two years writing his memoirs. *This Life* was published by Knopf in 1980. In 1981, Citadel Press published The Films of Sidney Poitier by Alvin H. Marill.

Poitier has six daughters, four from his first marriage to Juanita Hardy and two from his second marriage to Joanna Shimkus, in 1976.

After years of inactivity, Poitier made two films, *Little Nikita* and *Shoot To Kill,* which were both released in 1988.

In 1989, he was honored with the Pioneer Award at the Black Oscar Nominees Dinner and was later cited at another dinner in New York highlighting his achievements and contributions to the motion picture industry over a period of some three decades.

## CHARLEY PRIDE
### Country Singer

Charley Pride is the most prominent and successful black performer in the field of country music.

Born in the small cotton town of Sledge, Mississippi on March 18, 1938, Pride was part of a large family of Baptists who joined his siblings working in the cotton fields at the age of five. His primary entertainment was listening to the Grand Ole Opry from Nashville on Saturday nights. Charley loved spending hours in front of the radio and learned all the lyrics of his favorite performers.

Hoping to escape from his dreary life in the cotton fields, he began to pursue a career in professional baseball as a teenager. He also bought a guitar and set out to first become a baseball great, and then turn to singing as a career.

When he was 17, he left home for Memphis and played for Detroit, Birmingham and Memphis in the Negro American League. After two years in the service, he returned to the league, ultimately retiring after a dispute over pay. Pride moved to Montana to play with a semi-pro team and even unsuccessfully tried out with the California Angels. Still in

Montana, he worked in a mining firm while performing at night.

He was eventually signed to a long-term contract by Chet Atkins of RCA Victor in Nashville and he cut his first record, *Snakes Crawl in the Night*. His career took off and he received a Grammy nomination in 1966 for Best Country and Western Male Vocal Performance. In 1967, he made his first appearance at the Grand Ole Opry. Soon, *The Best of Charley Pride* and *Country Charley Pride* had turned gold. In fact, 9 of his 21 albums did. He appeared on numerous television specials and won two Grammy Awards in 1971.

Pride performs in 70 or more concerts a year and is a partner in three music publishing houses. While satisfied with the success of his career, he still maintains a strong love for baseball, working out with the Texas Rangers and the Milwaukee Brewers during their spring training camps.

## RICHARD PRYOR
### Comedian, Actor, Writer

"Pryor: Hollywood's Hottest Star" was the headline in a New York newspaper in the spring of 1982. Pryor was starring in two movies simultaneously running in New York, *Live on the Sunset Strip* and *Some Kind of Hero*, both of them taking in millions of dollars at the box office. His movie fee was said to be $3,000,000 plus more than a third of the gross profit. This was the same Richard Pryor who in June 1980 lay near death for six weeks in the Sherman Oaks (California) Burn Center after an accident in which he had turned himself into a flaming torch.

In June 1981, he was on the cover of People magazine and the movie he had been making at the time of the accident, *Bustin' Loose*, became a hit.

Before his accident his life had been filled with violence, fights, lawsuits, drugs, and alcohol. After his recovery he was said to be a changed man.

In an interview with Ernie Johnston Jr., former managing editor of the *New York Amsterdam News* soon after his release from the hospital, Pryor told Johnston, "What is good is getting high on energy. I get high on myself now and I really like Richard. Dope is for dopes," he said in the interview.

Richard Franklin Lennox Thomas Pryor III was born in Peoria, Illinois in 1940. His grandmother owned a bar and brothel and both his parents worked there. Nonetheless, he was strictly brought up, going to church and to parochial school until his family's profession was discovered. He transferred to public school where his long history of being in trouble began.

His interest in show business began when he was seven while sitting in on drums at Peoria's famous Door Club and watching impromptu performances by Louis Armstrong, Count Basie, and Duke Ellington. His first professional job was at a small club in Canada followed by his first New York job at The Wha? coffee house (when he was hired, he had only 33 cents in his pocket). An appearance on the Ed Sullivan Show led to his first movie, *The Busy Body*, in 1966 followed by *Wild in the Streets*. His movie *Stir Crazy* was one of the top ten grossers in Hollywood history.

*Max Julien explains his success as a Mack to Richard Pryor in* The Mack.

Pryor also is a writer and creator of comedy. His work as a writer on the Lily Tomlin specials resulted in two Emmy Awards. He collaborated with Mel Brooks in putting together *Blazing Saddles*, for which he received the American Writers Guild Award and The American Academy of Humor Award.

It was Pryor who created the role of Piano Man in *Lady Sings the Blues*, starring Diana Ross as Billie Holliday. His first Grammy was for *Craps after Dark* in 1971. In 1974 he won a Grammy for his album *That Nigger's Crazy* and in 1976 another Grammy for the album *Bicentennial Nigger*. He also had a nightclub act in the late 1970s. By 1980, four of his comedy albums were gold.

Pryor moved to the island of Maui in Hawaii to seek more privacy, but has remained active making films. He starred in *Bustin Loose* in 1981, *The Toy* in 1982, *Some Kind of Hero*, also in 1982, *Brewsters Millions* in 1985, *Critical Condition* in 1987, *Moving* in 1988 and *See No Evil, Hear No Evil*, a 1989 release.

He had made plans by that time to join Eddie Murphy in a film, *Harlem Nights*, which the two comedians would star in together.

Pryor has been married several times and has four children.

## LOU RAWLS
### Singer

Lou Rawls has remained a classy, elegant singer with a strong baritone voice and an ability to reach audiences ranging from those in sophisticated nightclubs to those who frequent livelier settings.

Louis Allen Rawls was born in Chicago on December 1, 1936, the son of a Baptist minister. When his father left the family and his mother moved to the west coast, Lou remained home and was raised by his grandmother. He attended the Greater Mount Olive Baptist Church and joined the junior choir when he was seven. When he was 14, he joined the gospel quintet, the *Chosen Gospel Singers*. After a stint in the army, he became part of *The Pilgrim Travelers* with Sam Cooke and others.

The group recovered after a serious highway accident and was soon singing in Los Angeles. There, Rawls made the transition to secular music, first doing solo gigs in small coffee houses and clubs. Within a year, he performed in a Dick Clark Show at the Hollywood Bowl and had taken on acting roles in such television series as *Bourbon Street Beat* and *77 Sunset Strip* as well as appearing on Steve Allen's late night show on ABC.

In 1961, Rawls signed a recording contract with Capitol Records. His album, *Lou Rawls Live* went gold, selling more than a million copies and winning his first Grammy in 1967. In 1975, now signed with Philadelphia International Records, he recorded his first gold single, *You'll Never Find Another Love Like Mine* and an album, *All Things in Time,* which became a platinum seller.

In time, his agent Norman Brokaw, negotiated a contract with Anheuser-Busch and Rawls voice and face became identified with Budweiser beer in television, radio and print advertising.

In 1979, he launched the Lou Rawls Parade of Stars to benefit the United Negro College Fund, which has continued as an annual telethon for that cause. He continued to be a mainstay on television as well as on stage, always attired—by his own rule—impeccably and performing flawlessly.

## OTIS REDDING
### Singer 1941-1967

Otis Redding was a singer well-known for his husky voice and energetic stage performances.

As a youth, Redding was influenced by Little Richard and Sam Cooke. Born on September 9, 1941, Redding took odd jobs around the south and then worked as a chauffeur and part-time singer for Johnny Jenkins and the Pinetoppers. While driving Jenkins to Memphis for an audition with the Stax record label, he decided to audition himself. One of the songs he sang, *These Arms of Mine* won him a contract and when released, was a hit on the r&b charts. As he went out on tour, Redding became the most popular performer on the so-called chitlin circuit next to James Brown.

Redding wrote many of his own hits including *Sittin on the Dock of the Bay* and *I've Been Loving You Too Long*. Among albums, his *Dictionary of Soul* is considered one of the best examples of the Memphis soul sound.

Redding also collaborated with other singers, participating in an album together with Carla Thomas and producing Authur Conley's *Sweet Soul Music.*

Redding appeared at the Monerey Pop Festival and won over a much broader audience. However, on December 10, 1967, Redding and four members of his backup band were killed when their chartered plane crashed into a Wisconsin lake. His greatest hit, *The Dock of the Bay,* was a success that soared to the top of the charts in early 1968, unknown to the co-author and performer of the song.

## WILLIS RICHARDSON
### Playwright

The great playwright Angelina Grimkea taught at the Washington, D.C. high school attended by Willis Richardson. Upon seeing a school production of one of her plays, Richardson commented to a friend that he could write a better play than that, and within a year he had set about the task. Alain Locke and Montgomery Gregory liked Richardson's work and suggested he send it to W. E. B. DuBois at *Crisis,* which was sponsoring plays and productions. *Crisis* promptly accepted and produced Richardson's *Chip Woman's Fortune* along with Oscar Wilde's *Salome*. In 1923, *Chip Woman's Fortune* became the first drama by a black writer to reach Broadway.

In 1930, Dr. Carter Woodson, who had founded the Association for the Study of Negro Life and History, and was sponsoring a national Negro History Week, asked Richardson to edit a book of plays about black history. The result was *Plays and Pageants for the Life of the Negro,* 12 plays, including Richardson's own *The King's Dilemma* and *The House of Sham,* both one-acts for children. In 1935, Richardson collaborated with May Miller (Sullivan), poet and sometimes playwright, to write *Negro History in Thirteen Plays,* using some materials provided by Dr. Woodson.

Willis Richardson, who was 84 years old in 1974, has written nearly 30 one-act plays and almost a dozen three-acts. Besides *Chip Woman's Fortune,* perhaps his most famous, there are *The Broken Banjo, The Amateur Prostitute, Flight of the Natives, The Visiting Lady,* and *Joy Rider.* Throughout his career, Richardson has devoted himself to portrayals of the lives and history of blacks in America, as well as actively participating in the black theater movement in and around Washington, D.C. Of the many groups he worked with, his mutual endeavors with Carter Woodson and the Howard Theatre are the most noteworthy.

Active in a theatrical career which in itself would mean full-time commitment to more average talent, Richardson spent over 40 years of his life as a full-time employee of the Government Engraving Office.

## LITTLE RICHARD
### Singer/Actor

One of the most flamboyant and sometimes controversial performers in the world of rock 'n' roll, Little Richard remained a popular performer when his career in movies blossomed.

Born on Christmas Day, 1932 in Macon, Georgia, Richard Penniman grew up in a devout Seventh Day Adventist family. He sang gospel and learned to play the piano at a local church. After begin ejected from his home at the age of 13 (he claimed because of his homosexuality), he moved in with a white family and performed in their Macon nightclub.

In 1951, Penniman won a contract with RCA after playing in an Atlanta radio audition. Over the next two years, he recorded such tunes as *Every Hour* and *Get Rich Quick* and then moved to Houston where he began to record on the Peacock label. He also toured small black nightclubs,

*The flamboyant rock 'n' roller, Little Richard.*

performing mostly blues since his rock numbers were not well received.

After sending a demo tape to Specialty Records in Los Angeles, Little Richard entered a recording studio in 1955 and recorded *Tutti Frutti*. The single sold over 3 million copies by 1968 and had a lasting impact on rock music. Richard would record 36 tunes for Specialty, seven of which turned gold. He also appeared in three early rock 'n' roll movies. In 1957, at the height of his career, he retired and entered Oakwood College in Huntsville, Alabama where he received a BA degree and was ordained a minister in the Seventh Day Adventist Church.

By 1964, he had returned to rock after a failed attempt to gain major audiences on the evangelical circuit with his gospel recordings. He did not achieve much success until the 1970s and soon returned to the church again — renouncing rock'n'roll, drugs and his homosexuality.

He did continue to perform and was often invited to make television appearances such as on *The Tonight Show*, and *The 1982 Grammy Awards* telecast on the Oscar presentations.

He was cast in a major role in the movie, *Down and Out in Beverly Hills* and soon was expressing plans to enter the acting field in a major way, perhaps with his own television show.

All the time, he maintained his unique persona of performing with a loud falsetto voice while playing the piano and adorning himself in mascara-coated eyelashes and a high pompadour. He became an outspoken critic of many in the music field who he claimed had stolen his music and never given him credit for his contributions as "the king of rock 'n' roll."

## LIONEL RICHIE
## Singer

A talented composer and popular contemporary balladeer, Lionel Richie became one of the more popular singers to reach cross-over audiences during the 1980s. A broad variety of musical influences would be reflected in his music.

Lionel B. Richie Jr. was born in 1949 in Tuskegee, Alabama. As a child, he taught himself to play piano by imitating his grandmother. While growing up, he had learned to play a saxophone received from an uncle. After graduating from high school, he enrolled in Tuskegee Institute and soon joined a group called the Commodores. While studying at Tuskegee, the group performed on weekends and summers. They met a Motown executive while appearing in New York City and were signed to be the opening act for the Jackson Five's 1971 European Tour. They returned and signed a recording contract with Motown.

By 1976, the group had three gold albums as well as one platinum album. In time, Richie became the group's primary composer and lead singer. In 1978, the Commodores were ranked the top R&B group by *Rolling Stone, Billboard* and *Cashbox*.

Richie's career outside of the group was flourishing as he wrote *Lady*, for Kenny Rogers, and *Endless Love* for Diana Ross. In 1982, he released his first solo album, *Lionel Richie* and received his first Grammy after 11 nominations. His first solo tour in 1983 was a tremendous success and set the way for a busy career including his work in creating the tune, *We Are The World* with Michael Jackson.

## PAUL ROBESON
## Actor, Singer
## 1898-1976

Paul Robeson earned worldwide fame in a variety of roles— as athlete, actor, singer, and scholar. Born in Princeton, New Jersey on April 9, 1898, Robeson is the son of a runaway slave who put himself through Lincoln University and later became a Presbyterian minister.

Robeson entered Rutgers on a scholarship, and won a total of 12 letters in track, football, baseball, and basketball. In 1917 and again in 1918, he was named all-American by Walter Camp, who later called him "the greatest defensive end that ever trod the gridiron." In addition to his athletic exploits, his academic ability gained him Phi Beta Kappa honors in his junior year.

In 1923, Robeson won a law degree from Columbia, financing his schooling by playing professional football. While at Columbia, Robeson was seen by Eugene O'Neill in an amateur play. After making his professional debut in *Taboo* (1922), Robeson appeared in O'Neill's *All God's Chillun Got Wings* and *Emperor Jones*.

Called upon to whistle in the latter play, Robeson sang instead, and his voice met with instant acclaim. In 1925, he made his concert debut with a highly successful program of all-Negro music. He went on to such stage successes as *Show Boat, Porgy,* and *Othello*. (When he did *Othello* in 1943 in New York, his ovation was called "one of the most prolonged

*Paul Robeson plays a porter who becomes a potentate in the classic film* The Emperor Jones.

and wildest... in the history of the New York theatre.")

A world traveler in the Soviet Union, Asia, and Europe, Robeson spoke several languages, including Chinese, Russian, Gaelic, and Spanish.

Robeson's political affiliations at times tended to attract even more publicity than his artistic career. In 1950, for instance, he was denied a passport after refusing to sign an affidavit as to whether or not he had ever belonged to the Communist Party. Eight years later, the U.S. Supreme Court ruled that the refusal to sign such an affidavit was not valid grounds for denial of a passport. Robeson subsequently settled in London, making a number of trips to the continent (and to the U.S.S.R. as well) before returning to the United States in 1963.

Robeson died January 23, 1976 in Philadelphia, Pennsylvania.

## BILL (BOJANGLES) ROBINSON
### Dancer
### 1878-1949

Throughout his long career on stage and in movies, Bill Robinson was known as the "King of Tap Dancers."

Robinson was born on May 25, 1878 in Richmond, Virginia and, being orphaned early, was raised by his grandmother, a former slave. By the time he was eight, he was earning his own way dancing in the street for pennies and working as a stable boy.

In 1887, he toured the South in a show called *The South Before the War* and, the following year, moved to Washington, D.C. where he began working as a stable boy. By 1896, he had teamed up with George Cooper in vaudeville. This act had success on the Keith circuit until the slump of 1907 caused it to fold. Robinson returned to Richmond to work as a waiter, and a year later was discovered by a theatrical manager who soon had him working as a cabaret and vaudeville headliner.

In 1927, he starred on Broadway in *Blackbirds,* and in 1932 he had top billing in *Harlems Heaven,* the first all-Negro talking movie. Later, he scored a Hollywood success teaching his famous stair dance to Shirley Temple in *The Little Colonel.* Robinson made 14 movies, including *The Littlest Rebel, In Old Kentucky, Rebecca of Sunnybrook Farm, Stormy Weather,* and *One Mile from Heaven.*

Robinson died on November 25, 1949.

## SMOKEY ROBINSON
### Singer/Composer

Smokey Robinson is one of the most prolific performers and songwriters to have ever worked for Motown Records.

Born in Detroit in 1940, Robinson formed the Miracles while still in high school. In 1957, he met producer Berry Gordy and soon convinced Gordy to form a record company. The company, Tamla (now a division of Motown), recorded its first hit with the Miracles' 1960 single, *Shop Around.*

Many other hits followed, including *You Really Got a Hold on Me, Ooh Baby Baby, Tears of a Clown, Tracks of My Tears* and *I Second That Emotion.* During this time, Robinson also wrote songs for Motown artists such as Mary Wells, the Temptations and Marvin Gaye.

In 1971, Robinson left the Miracles to become a Motown vice president. Ten years later, however, Robinson's love ballad, *Being With You* won over a newer generation and he succeeded as a solo performer.

In 1989, Robinson's biography, *Smokey: Inside My Life* was released, chronicling the singer's 30 years of performing as well as the highs and lows of his life away from the stage.

## DIANA ROSS and The SUPREMES
### Actress, Singer

As lead singer with The Supremes, Diana Ross was part of one of the most popular singing groups in musical history. More recently, she's been on her own, garnering raves from critics, college students and night-club goers. Born in Detroit, Diana Ross grew up in a low-rent housing project where she played baseball, sewed her own clothes, and sang with girl friends after school. When she was 14 and had failed to win a singing role in a school musical, she and two friends, Mary Wilson and Florence Ballard, decided to form a musical group of their own. In 1960, in their senior year in high school, the three were hired by Motown Records to sing background and play record hops with Marvin Gaye and Mary Wells.

After finishing high school, the trio was named The Supremes and went on tour with the Motor Town Revue.

*Diana Ross (right), Cindy Birdsong (left), and Mary Wilson—The Supremes—one of the top recording groups of the sixties.*

Their first record to make the charts was *Let Me Go the Right Way*. Then, *Where Did Our Love Go?* reached number one on the national charts. Over a period of 10 years, The Supremes had 15 consecutive smash hit singles, and at one point had five consecutive records in the number one position on the charts.

In 1969, Diana Ross decided she was ready to go out on her own. She appeared on the television special *Like Hep* and stole the show from such veteran performers as Dinah Shore, Lucille Ball, and Rowan and Martin. She then went on a nightclub tour and also starred on her own television special *Diana*. In 1972 she played Billie Holiday in the film *Lady Sings the Blues*.

Other films followed including *Mahogany* and *The Wiz*. She received a Tony Award for her Broadway show *An Evening with Diana Ross*. Her concert career continues and in 1979 she appeared at Radio City Music Hall and that same year signed a 2.52 million dollar contract for 72 performances at Resorts International in Atlantic City. She has had more number one records than any other artist in the history of the charts, and she recently signed a 20 million dollar contract with RCA Records. In 1981 she had a television special on CBS.

She lives with her three daughters in a 35-room house in Connecticut.

## NIPSEY RUSSELL
## Comedian

One of the first "stand-up" comedians to gain success with jokes drawn from the contemporary racial situation is Nipsey Russell. Long before similar material had found its way to the general public via television appearances by various black comedians, Russell was delighting Harlem audiences with his routines at Smalls Paradise and the Baby Grand.

Born in Atlanta, Georgia, Russell at the age of six began to tour the South as a child performer. During his final years in high school, he lived in Cincinnati, and later attended college there earning his B.A. in English in 1946 (with four years out for duty as an Army captain).

Russell had a running part in television's *Car 54, Where Are You?* and was a frequent guest on Arthur Godfrey's show. He first came to national attention on The Tonight Show when he was a guest of Orson Bean who was substituting for host Jack Paar. Paar subsequently had Russell on the show many times. He has also worked as a panelist on such shows as *Missing Links*.

In the 1970s, he co-hosted the television shows *The Wide World of Comedy* and the *Les Crane Show*. In the 1980s he was appearing in nightclubs and on cruises and doing television variety and quiz shows. Russell lives in Manhattan.

## HILDA SIMMS
### Actress

Hilda Simms was born Hilda Moses in Minneapolis in 1920, the oldest of 13 children. Her family was very poor, and she worked at many odd jobs to help out before she won a scholarship to the University of Minnesota. After she had been in school for a year and a half, she left to marry William Simms, and shortly afterward, accepted a teaching fellowship at Hampton Institute in Virginia where she also worked for her B.S. degree.

Having completed her course of study at Hampton, Simms left for New York City, working as a singer for several different radio stations before playing the lead in the 1944 production of *Anna Lucasta,* a role which was to make her famous.

The play was a production of the American Negro Theater of Harlem, and was first performed in a tiny theater in the basement of the 135th Street public library in New York. It was subsequently brought to Broadway, where opening night reviewers had high praise for the "beauty and intelligence" of Miss Simms' characterization.

The actress has an interest in writing (she has begun one novel) and has been an active worker in political campaigns. She became a featured columnist in *Tuesday* magazine. Recently she was director of Theater Therapy Addiction Research and Treatment Center.

## NINA SIMONE
### Singer, Pianist

Nurtured in the tradition of Billie Holiday and fortified as well by years of classical training, Nina Simone is one of the most original and versatile black concert performers to have come along in the past decade. Implicit in her work is a deep-seated racial pride which burns through her music and suffuses her audiences with its liberating intensity and driving force. Her singing style is too individual to classify simply as jazz, popular, folk, gospel, or any other style. Like her piano playing, it is fraught with elements from many recognizable idioms, all of which are blended and contrasted in a highly evocative and spellbinding manner.

Born Eunice Kathleen Waymon on February 21, 1935 in Tryon, North Carolina, Simone exhibited extraordinary virtuosity on the piano early in life but found herself hampered by lack of money to pursue proper training. A dedicated and unselfish teacher soon moved to overcome the difficulty, establishing a fund which enabled her outstanding pupil to attend high school in North Carolina, where young Eunice excelled academically, in extracurricular activities, and in her musical development. She continued her education later at Juilliard and at the Curtis Institute of Music, but was finally forced to support herself by teaching piano privately.

The turning point in her career came in 1954 when she found a job in an Atlantic City nightclub, ostensibly as a performer on the piano, not as a vocalist. Her smashing success in both capacities convinced her that show business was a worthy career for her unique talents. Her first hit record thereafter was a haunting version *I Loves You, Porgy*, from the score of Gershwin's celebrated *Porgy and Bess.* At later recording sessions, she discovered a further gift for composition, and thus has come to write more than 50 of her own songs, including the bitter and controversial lament, *Wild is the Wind.*

Since 1960, the year she was named Most Promising Singer of the Year, Simone has grown in stature as a concert and nightclub entertainer. She prefers the concert hall, where she feels she can "get more out of myself... call on every resource... give on a huge scale."

These widely acclaimed performances have placed her time and again among the top 10 performers in national and international jazz polls. In 1966, she was designated Woman of the Year by the Jazz at Home Club in New York City. The following year the National Association of Television and Radio Announcers named her Female Jazz Singer of the Year.

## NOBLE SISSLE
### Songwriter
### 1889-1975

Noble Sissle reaped his early successes teamed up with the great Eubie Blake. Sissle wrote the lyrics and sang them in performance; Blake wrote and played the music. Together they wrote the famous *I'm Just Wild about Harry*, which was picked up by the Truman campaign of 1948.

*Shuffle Along*, the first black musical with a love theme, made Sissle and Blake famous. Joining forces with the writing and comedy team of Miller and Lyles, Sissle and Blake wrote the words and music to over a dozen songs for the show. *Shuffle Along* became a huge success in the United States and Europe, where it had a prolonged tour.

As with most black performers in the early 1900s, Sissle

*The torrid and terrific, Tina Turner.*

and his troupe would have to travel as far as 20 or 30 miles out of their way from where they were performing in order to find a place to eat and sleep, since blacks were not welcome in the white hotels of the towns they played.

Other Sissle and Blake shows included *Keep Shufflin'* and *Chocolate Dandies*. Sissle attributed his business and popular decline to the increased acceptance of rock and roll music, but said his long popularity was due to "beautiful music."

Noble Sissle died December 17, 1975 at his home in Tampa, Florida.

## TINA TURNER
### Singer

Most of the most exciting performers in contemporary music, Tina Turner has become established as a popular singer with audiences who enjoy both rock as well as soul music. After performing with Ike Turner for years, she has been performing and touring on her own since 1976.

Tina was born Anna Mae Bullock in Nutbush, Tennessee on November 25, 1940. The daughter of a cotton plantation manager and his wife, she began singing in class talent shows at a very early age. She and her sister joined their then-divorced mother in St. Louis in the mid-1950s and began to visit local clubs where they met Ike Turner and his band, the Kings of Rhythm. After asking for months, she was finally allowed to sing with the band one night. Soon thereafter, she was singing with the band on occasional engagements.

In 1959, when the scheduled vocalist failed to appear at a recording session, Tina filled in and recorded Ike Turner's *Fool in Love*. In time, they married and formed the Ike and Tina Turner Revue. Within 10 years, the Ike and Tina Turner Revue had 15 albums and 60 singles to its credit.

Tina's vocal renditions captivated the group's audiences with their eroticism and soon the group had toured Japan, Africa and other continents as well. In 1971, the group won a Grammy Award for their recording, *Proud Mary*.

When she decided to separate from the band and Ike, she worked hard as a touring artist and built on the success of her solo album, *Private Dancer*.

## CICELY TYSON
### Actress

During the early 1970s Cicely Tyson emerged as America's leading black dramatic star. This she achieved with two sterling performances—as Rebecca, the wife of a southern sharecropper in the film *Sounder;* and as the lead in a television special, *The Autobiography of Miss Jane Pittman,* the story of an ex-slave who past her hundredth year, challenges racist authority by deliberately drinking from a "white only" water fountain as a paunchy white deputy sheriff looks on ominously.

Though both roles were of southern women, Cicely Tyson was born in New York City. She was raised strictly by a very religious, proper mother, who associated movies with sin and forbade Cicely to attend them. When 18, Cicely became a secretary, but one day she stood up before an office of fellow workers, announced that God did not put her on Earth to pound a typewriter and walked out.

*The gifted actress Cicely Tyson.*

Blessed with poise and natural grace, Cicely became a model, appearing on the cover of America's two foremost fashion magazines, *Vogue* and *Harper's Bazaar* in 1956. Interested in acting, she started to study drama and in 1959 appeared on a CBS culture series, *Camera Three,* with what is believed to be the first African natural hair style on television.

Her star rising, Cicely Tyson won a role in an off-Broadway production of Jean Genet's *The Blacks,* for which she received the 1962 Vernon Rice Award. She then played a lead part in the CBS-TV series *East Side, West Side.*

From this, Cicely Tyson moved into film parts in *The Comedians, The Heart Is a Lonely Hunter,* and others. Critical acclaim led to the role of Rebecca in *Sounder,* for which she was nominated for an Academy Award and named Best Actress by the National Society of Film Critics. She won an Emmy TV acting trophy for *Jane Pittman.*

More than most stars, Cicely Tyson demands to be judged solely on her professional ability, making little effort to garnish her image. She will not say whether or not she was married, remarks frankly that she is not sure pregnancy in an unmarried relationship is grounds for marriage, and refuses to confirm or deny that she herself has had a son and daughter out of wedlock. In 1974, she was the first actor, of any race or sex, to be honored with a day by the Harvard University Faculty Club, and in 1975 firmly declared that she would not participate in any film she regarded as black exploitation.

Her recent films have included *The Blue Bird, River Niger,* and *Wilma.* On television she did *Roots* and *King,* and portrayed Harriet Tubman in *A Woman Called Moses* and Chicago schoolteacher Marva Collins in a television movie.

In 1979, Marymount College presented her with an

honorary Doctor of Fine Arts. Tyson owns a house on Malibu Beach in California. In November 1981, she married jazz trumpeter Miles Davis in Amherst, Massachusetts.

### LESLIE UGGAMS
### Singer, actress

Once dubbed a black Shirley Temple, scintillating Leslie Uggams has been a popular performer since her childhood. Nevertheless, abiding undisputed fame did not come to the versatile entertainer until she opened on Broadway in the much-heralded musical *Hallelujah Baby*. The show was given the lift and verve it needed to survive by Uggams' dynamic and impressive performance.

Born in the Washington Heights section of New York City in May 1943, Uggams enjoyed a comfortable childhood. She made her singing debut at the age of six, performing with the choir of St. James Presbyterian Church in New York, and followed shortly thereafter with her acting debut in the television series *Beulah*. Uggams developed her poise and stage presence early in life, attending the Professional Children's School, where she was chosen student body president in her senior year.

Later she won $25,000 on the popular TV quiz show *Name That Tune,* gaining the opportunity, as well, to renew her interest in a singing career. In 1961, Uggams became a regular on the Mitch Miller show, a variety offering featuring old favorites. She was at the time the only black performer appearing regularly on network television.

Throughout the 1960s, Uggams appeared in numerous nightclubs and filled several supperclub and television engagements. Her big break came when she was signed as a replacement for Lena Horne in *Hallelujah Baby,* a show which represented a kind of musical chronicle of the civil rights movement. Billed as "pure sunshine" and worth the price of admission by herself, Uggams was elevated to instant stardom and received a Tony Award for her performance. On television she appeared as Kizzy in *Roots* and in *Backstairs at the White House*, a miniseries.

In 1965 Uggams married a white man, Grahame Pratt, and she has two children.

Uggams has written a beauty book (The Leslie Uggams Beauty Book) dedicated to her two early mentors, Harry Salter and Mitch Miller, both of the *Name That Tune* era. The pair had "nothing to do with her beauty," one New York reporter once pointed out, "but a great deal to do with its intelligent exploitation."

In May 1982 Leslie Uggams was appearing in a new Broadway show, *Blues in the Night*, at the Rialto Theater in New York City.

### BEN VEREEN
### Dancer, Actor

Ben Vereen was born in the Bedford-Stuyvesant section of Brooklyn, New York and attended the High School of Performing Arts in Manhattan. Vereen was also an active member of the Pentecostal Church. His dancing ability was uncovered almost accidentally after he had been sent to dance school by his mother. Vereen would have preferred playing stickball with neighborhood kids. Vereen has been called America's premier song and dance man and his talents were discovered by Sammy Davis Jr. while performing in the chorus of *Sweet Charity*.

Many have said that Vereen is the most gifted, energetic, and multifaceted entertainer since Davis. Vereen starred in the ABC comedy series *Tenspeed and Brown Shoe* and is known for his television specials. The most notable special was *Ben Vereen—His Roots*, which won seven Emmy Awards. He also portrayed Louis "Satchmo" Armstrong and received wide acclaim for his role of Chicken George in the original *Roots* and also for his performance in *Jubilee*.

Vereen is best known for his Broadway role in *Pippin,* which won him a Tony Award. He was also nominated for a Tony for his co-starring role in *Jesus Christ Superstar*.

He has appeared at the White House on several occasions, and during the 1980 inauguration of President Ronald Reagan Vereen came under fire from blacks after he appeared in blackface on national television.

### ADAM WADE
### Singer, Actor

Multitalented Adam Wade came to the performing arts via the basketball court and the laboratory of polio vaccine discoverer Dr. Jonas Salk, for whom he worked as a research assistant.

Born in Pittsburgh, he won a basketball scholarship to Virginia State College and later studied biochemistry at the University of Pennsylvania. Although he had been singing since childhood, his professional start did not come until he did a song-writing friend the favor of singing some of his lyrics to a New York recording agent. Liking the voice more than the words, the agent signed Wade in 1960 to sing *Tell Her for Me*, which became a hit and launched his career, followed by *Ruby* in 1961. After considerable early success as a vocalist, he turned to drama and has appeared in many stage, television, and movie roles. As host on the CBS show *Musical Chairs* he became the first black entertainer to host a daily game show. In the mid-1970s he also was preparing a nightclub act with two female vocalists.

### THEODORE WARD
### Playwright

One of the America's greatest living playwrights, Theodore Ward, has been virtually ignored by the theater establishment. Long an active advocate of racial equality and social justice, Ward's plays have consistently served as artistic witness of the history of black people in the United States.

When his play *Big White Fog* reached the "legitimate" stage in 1940, Ralph Ellison noted, "Seldom in literature or on stage has the inner dignity of an oppressed people struggling to affirm its nationhood risen so indestructibly, so magnificently, as in the Negro family portrayed in *Big White Fog*. The same words would ring true for most of Ward's more than 15 full-length dramas. Yet his work has appeared on Broadway just once: *Our Lan'* in 1947. Since that production, Ward has not had a nationally noticed production, in spite of numerous grants and awards, including the

Theatre Guild Award, a John Simon Guggenheim Fellowship, and the National Theatre Conference.

Born on September 15, 1902, in Thibodeaux, Louisiana, Ward was the son of a schoolteacher. Running away from home after the death of his mother, he spent much of his teens wandering from city to city, from coast to coast, working in menial employment.

Ward was most prolific during the years between 1930 and 1950. Besides his two best known works, *Big White Fog* and *Our Lan'*, Ward's other plays include The *Daubers*, a play about the social and political implications of drug abuse in a black middle-class family; *Charity*, a musical portrayal of the life of the famed slave performer Blind Tom; *John Brown; Even the Dead Arise; Whole Hog or Nothing;* and *The Creole*, based on a story by Frederick Douglass concerning a black revolt aboard a slave ship.

In 1980, Ward could be reached through Free So Theater, 1328 Dryades, New Orleans, Louisiana 70113.

## ETHEL WATERS
**Singer, Actress**
**1900-1977**

The distinguished career of Ethel Waters spanned half a century, and made its mark in virtually every entertainment medium—stage, screen, television, and recordings.

Ethel Waters was born on October 31, 1900, and spent most of her childhood in Chester, Pennsylvania. At the age of 17, she was singing professionally at the Lincoln Theatre in Baltimore. During this early phase of her career, she became the first woman to perform W. C. Handy's *St. Louis Blues* on stage.

After several years in nightclubs and vaudeville, she made her Broadway debut in the 1927 review *Africana*. In 1930, she appeared in *Blackbirds*, and in 1931 and 1932 she starred in *Rhapsody in Black*. The following year she was featured with Clifton Webb and Marilyn Miller in Irving Berlin's *As Thousands Cheer*. In 1935, she co-starred with Bea Lillie in *At Home Abroad*, and three years later, she played the lead in *Mamba's Daughters*.

In 1940, she created her greatest role in *Cabin in the Sky*, a triumph which she repeated in the 1943 movie version. Her other films include *Rufus Jones for President* (1931), *Tales of Manhattan* (1941), *Cairo* (1942), *Stage Door Canteen* (1943), and *Pinky* (1949).

Her autobiography, *His Eye Is on the Sparrow*, was a 1951 Book-of-the-Month Club selection. The title is taken from a song which she sang during her memorable performance in the 1950 stage success *Member of the Wedding*.

Ethel Waters sang at a worship service at the White House in 1971, and was invited again to attend the wedding of Tricia Nixon. In her obituary *The New York Times* noted, "In the last two decades of her life, her religious spirit came to the fore more and more and more. She was brought up as a Roman Catholic but said she was a Baptist, a Methodist, "everything that's help to people." Through the Billy Graham crusades she rededicated herself to Jesus. Waters died

*The legendary vaudeville team of Bert Williams and George Walker*

September 1, 1977 in Chatsworth, California, at the home of friends with whom she lived.

## BERT WILLIAMS
## Vaudevillian
## 1876-1922

The legendary Bert Williams is considered by many to be the greatest black vaudeville performer in the history of the American stage. His considerable success extended into the realm of musical comedy as well.

Born in 1876 in the Bahamas, Williams moved to New York with his family, and then on to California, where he graduated from high school. After studying civil engineering for a time, he decided instead to try his hand at show business.

In 1895, he teamed with George Walker to form a successful vaudeville team. Five years later, they opened in New York in *The Sons of Ham* and were acclaimed for the characterizations that became their stock-in-trade—Walker as a dandy, and Williams in blackface, complete with outlandish costumes and "Negro" comic dialect. The show ran for two years.

In 1902, their show *In Dahomey* was so popular that they took it to England, and met with equal success there. The partners continued to produce shows such as *The Policy Players, Bandanna Land, and Abyssinia* until Walker's death in 1909.

Thereafter, Williams worked as a featured single in the Ziegfeld Follies, touring America for 10 years in several versions of the show. His most famous songs were *Woodman, Spare That Tree; O, Death, Where is Thy Sting;* and *Nobody,* his own composition and trademark.

Williams died of pneumonia on March 4, 1922.

*Billy Dee Williams, a more than creditable actor.*

## BILLY DEE WILLIAMS
## Actor

A screen, television and stage actor with impressive credits, Billy Dee Williams achieved success by starring in some of the most commercially popular films ever released.

Born in Harlem on April 6, 1937, he grew up with an interest in becoming a painter, but had a small stage role at the age of seven. He was a withdrawn, overweight youngster who initially focused on plans to become a fashion illustrator. While studying on scholarship at the School of Fine Arts in the National Academy of Design, a CBS casting director helped him secure bit parts in several TV shows including *Lamp Unto My Feet* and *Look Up And Live*.

He then began to study acting under Sidney Poitier and Paul Mann at the Actors Workshop in Harlem. He made his film debut in *The Last Angry Man*, released in 1959 and then appeared on stage in *The Cool World, A Taste of Honey* and *The Blue Boy Is Black*.

Later, he appeared briefly on Broadway in *Hallelujah Baby* as well as several off-Broadway shows including *Ceremonies in Dark Old Men*.

Williams' next major film role was in the 1972 drama, *The Final Comedown*. In time, he would co-star in the acclaimed television movie, *Brian's Song*. Motown's Berry Gordy then signed Williams to a seven-year contract and he starred in *Lady Sings the Blues* with Diana Ross. He was well-received as a romantic hero and then went on to appear in several action films, starring with Ross again in *Mahogany*. His last movie for Gordy was *The Bingo Long Traveling All-Stars and Motor King*.

He would win his widest acclaim starring in two of George Lucas' *Star Wars* adventures, *The Empire Strikes Back* and *Return of the Jedi*. Movie roles in such action adventures as *Nighthawks* continued as well as starring roles in TV movies like *The Scott Joplin, Christmas Lilies of the Field* and the miniseries, *Chiefs*. When he was cast opposite Diahann Carroll in the prime time drama, *Dynasty*, his reputation as a romantic lead was solidified. By the end of the decade, he had continued to star in action films like *Oceans of Fire* and *Number One With A Bullet*.

## DEMOND WILSON
## Actor

Demond Wilson's mother admired Bill Robinson and wanted her son to become a famous dancer too. But the family flat in Harlem where he was born in 1947 had linoleum floors—and tap dancing destroyed the linoleum. So Demond was put in the bathroom, where the floor was covered with a harder, mosaic-type tile, and told to dance.

When he was 4, Demond's mother took him to try out for a part in the Broadway play *Green Pastures* starring William Marshall. He got the part—a cherub in heaven. After Wilson outgrew his mother's prodding he enrolled in Hunter College in New York where he studied drama and the arts. Two years later he dropped out to make some money, then he was

*Flip Wilson, one of the big names and truly original talents in comedy.*

drafted and sent to Vietnam.

After being discharged, Wilson went on tour with *Boys in the Band,* a play with a homosexual theme. "That was the one thing my folks weren't too happy about," said Wilson, "They were relieved when I got in my old car and drove to Hollywood."

Then things happened fast. Wilson won a part in *The Organization* starring Sidney Poitier, and then a role in a segment of *All in the Family* as a burglar. It was that role which led to his audition for the part of Lamont Sanford in the popular TV show Sanford and Son in which he co-starred with Redd Foxx. He also appeared in the TV situation comedy *Baby, I'm Back*, and in the mid-1970s, was appearing in Las Vegas with a new nightclub act.

## FLIP WILSON
### Comedian

Flip Wilson has reached the pinnacle of stardom in the entertainment world with a series of original routines and ethnic characters rivaled only by Bill Cosby. Wilson's hilarious monologues, seen on a number of network television shows, made him perhaps the most visible black comedian of the early 1970s.

Born on December 8, 1933 and named Clerow, he was the tenth in a family of 24 children, 18 of whom survived. The family was destitute with his father being a painter, and Wilson was a troublesome child during his youth in Jersey City. He ran away from reform school several times, and was ultimately raised in foster homes.

Wilson's comic talents first surfaced during a hitch in the Air Force. While in service, he was sent overseas to the Pacific theater, where he entertained his buddies with such preposterous routines as *The Sex Habits of the Coconut Crab.*

Back in civilian life, he became a bellhop and part-time showman, but constant economic pressure left him without adequate time to refine his spontaneous material. Opportunity struck in 1959 when a Miami businessman gave him $50 a week for a year, thus enabling him to concentrate on the evolution of a successful style.

For the next five years or so, Wilson was a regular at the Apollo in Harlem. In 1965 he began a series of nationwide appearances on the *Tonight Show*. Long-term contracts and several hit records have followed in quick sequence since then, and Wilson has become firmly established as one of the big names and truly innovative talents in the comedy profession.

With *The Flip Wilson Show* in the early seventies, he became the first black to have a weekly prime time TV show with his own name. He became famous for his original character creations such as "Geraldine." On January 31, 1972 he was on the cover of Time magazine. In 1976 he made his dramatic debut on TV in the ABC series *Six Million Dollar Man.*

Wilson has been national president of the American Cancer Society. In 1975 his common-law wife of 17 years and the mother of his four children filed for divorce in Florida.

In the early 1980s he was doing nightclubs and television specials. Wilson lives in California.

## STEVIE WONDER
### Singer, pianist, composer

Stevie Wonder was born in 1950 in Saginaw, Michigan. Blind since birth, Wonder began his professional career recording with Motown in Detroit. At the height of his career in the mid-1970s, Wonder had recorded more than 12 gold records. During the period from 1975 to 1976, Wonder received more singing awards than any other pop singer. He has recorded such hits as *I Call It Pretty Music, Fingertips,* and *Uptight*. He has also appeared in the movies *Bikini Beach* and *Muscle Beach Party.*

In the 1980s, Wonder began to speak out and lead demonstrations in Washington, D.C. to press for the birth date of Dr. Martin Luther King Jr. to be made a national holiday. His recording *Happy Birthday to You* became a part of the January 15th birth date of Dr. King and the record is played by disk jockeys across the country as part of the King memorial.

## PLAYS BY AND ABOUT BLACKS

| Title | Author | Date of Production |
|---|---|---|
| *The Black Doctor* | Ira Aldridge | 1847 |
| *The Brown Overcoat* | Victor Sejour | 1858 |
| *The Escape: or, A Leap for Freedom* | William Wells Brown | 1858 |
| *Caleb, the Degenerate* | Joseph Cotter, Sr. | 1901 |
| *Rachel* | Angelina Grimkea | 1916 |
| *Mine eyes Have Seen* | Alice Dunber Nelson | 1918 |
| *They that Sit in Darkness* | Mary Burrill | 1919 |
| *Balo* | Jean Toomer | 1924 |
| *Appearances* | Garland Anderson | 1925 |
| *The Church Fight* | Ruth Gaines-Shelton | 1925 |
| *A Sunday Morning in the South* | Georgia Douglass Johnson | 1925 |
| *For Unborn Children* | Myrtle Smith Livingston | 1926 |
| *'Cruiter* | John Matheus | 1926 |
| *Flight of the Natives* | Willis Richardson | 1927 |
| *The Purple Flower* | Marita Bonner | 1928 |
| *Meek Mose* | Frank Wilson | 1928 |
| *Undertow* | Eulalie Spence | 1929 |
| *Graven Images* | May Miller | 1929 |
| *Harlem* | Wallace Thurman with William Jordan Rapp | 1929 |
| *Job Hunters* | H. F. V. Edward | 1931 |
| *Run Little Children* | Hall Johnson with Lew Cooper | 1933 |
| *Louisiana* | Augustus Smith | 1933 |
| *Bad Man* | Randolph Edmonds | 1934 |
| *Legal Murder* | Dennis Donoghue | 1934 |
| *Little Ham* | Langston Hughes | 1935 |
| *Mulatto* | Langston Hughes | 1935 |
| *Don't You Want to Be Free?* | Langston Hughes | 1937 |
| *Natural Man* | Theodore Browne | 1937 |
| *Big White Fog* | Theodore Ward | 1938 |
| *Divine Comedy* | Owen Dodson | 1938 |
| *Limitations of Life* | Langston Hughes | 1938 |
| *Dry August* | Charles Sebree | 1938 |
| *Joy Exceeding Glory* | George Norford | 1938 |
| *Native Son* | Richard Wright and Paul Green | 1941 |
| *Walk Hard* | Abram Hill | 1944 |
| *District of Columbia* | Stanley Richards | 1945 |
| *On Strivers' Row* | Abram Hill | 1945 |
| *Our Lan'* | Theodore Ward | 1947 |
| *A Medal for Willie* | William Branch | 1951 |
| *Gold through the Trees* | Alice Childress | 1952 |
| *Take a Giant Step* | Louis Peterson | 1953 |
| *The Amen Corner* | James Baldwin | 1954 |
| *In Splendid Error* | William Branch | 1954 |
| *Mrs. Patterson* | Charles Sebree with | 1954 |
| *Trouble in Mind* | Alice Childress | 1955 |
| *A Land Beyond the River* | Loften Mitchell | 1956 |
| *Simply Heaven* | Langston Hughes | 1957 |
| *A Raison in the Sun* | Lorraine Hansberry | 1959 |
| *Fly Backward* | C. Bernard Jackson and James V. Hatch | 1960 |
| *The Drinking Gourd* | Lorraine Hansberry | 1960 |
| *Marcus in the High Grass* | Bill Gunn | 1960 |
| *Purlie Victorious* | Ossie Davis | 1961 |
| *Moon on a Rainbow* | Shawl Errol John | 1962 |
| *Tambourines to Glory* | Langston Hughes | 1963 |
| *Walk in Darkness* | William Hairston | 1963 |
| *The Slave* | Imamu Amiri Baraka | 1964 |
| *Blues for Mister Charlie* | James Baldwin | 1964 |
| *The Sign in Sidney Brustein's Window* | Lorraine Hansberry | 1964 |

*Bruce Strickland, Frozine Jo Thomas, Peggy Alston, and Carol Woods in the smash New Orleans musical* One Mo' Time.

| Title | Author | Date of Production |
|---|---|---|
| *Funnyhouse of a Negro* | Adrienne Kennedy | 1964 |
| *Dutchman* | Imamu Amiri Baraka | 1964 |
| *Star of the Morning* | Loften Mitchell | 1964 |
| *Day of Absence* | Douglas Turner Ward | 1965 |
| *The Owl Answers* | Adrienne Kennedy | 1965 |
| *The Zulu and the Zayda* | Ossie Davis | 1965 |
| *Goin' a Buffalo* | Ed Bullins | 1966 |
| *Who's Got His Own* | Ronald Milner | 1966 |
| *The Tumult and the Shouting* | Thomas Pawley | 1969 |
| *Daddy Goodness* | Richard Wright (produced posthumously) | 1968 |
| *Wine in the Wilderness* | Alice Childress | 1969 |
| *Black Love Song # 1* | Val Ferdinand | 1969 |
| *No Place to Be Somebody* | Charles Gordone | 1969 |
| *The Duplex* | Ed Bullins | 1969 |
| *Job Security* | Martie Charles | 1970 |
| *Ain Supposed to Die a Natural Death* | Melvin Van Peebles | 1971 |
| *Don' Play Us Cheap* | Melvin Van Peebles | 1972 |
| *Don't Bother Me, I Can't Cope* | Micki Grant | 1972 |
| *The River Niger* | Joseph Walker | 1973 |
| *Black Girl* | J. E. Franklin | 1973 |
| *My Sister, My Sister* | Ray Aranha | 1973 |
| *Short Eyes* | Miguel Pinero | 1974 |
| *The Sirens* | Richard Wesley | 1974 |
| *The Prodigal Sister* | J. (Jenny) E. Franklin; music by Micki Grant, lyrics by Micki Grant and J. E. Franklin | 1974 |
| *Sizwe Banzi Is Dead* | Athol Fugard, John Kani, Winston Ntshona | 1975 |
| *The Wiz* | William F. Brown, music and lyrics by Charles Smalls | 1975 |
| *Black Picture Show* | Bill Gunn | 1975 |
| *The Taking of Miss Janie* | Ed Bullins | 1975 |
| *The First Breeze of Summer* | Leslie Lee | 1975 |
| *Dr. Jazz* | Paul Carter Harrison | 1975 |
| *For Colored Girls Who Have Considered SuicideWhen the Rainbow Is Enuf* | Ntozake Shange | 1976 |
| *Bubbling Brown Sugar* | Loften Mitchell with Rosetta Le Noire; music by Duke Ellington | 1976 |
| *Your Arm's Too Short to Box With God* | Conceived by Vinnett Carroll; music and lyrics by Alex Bradford and Micki Grant | 1976 |
| *The Brownsville Raid* | Charles H. Fuller, Jr. | 1976 |
| *Eden* | Steve Carter | 1976 |
| *I'm Laughin' But I Ain't Tickled* | Vinnette Carroll and Micki Grant | 1976 |
| *Solders of Freedom* | Louis Rivers | 1977 |
| *Eubie* | Conceived by Julianne Boyd; music by Eubie Blake; lyrics by Noble Sissle, Anzy Razas, Johnny Brandon, F. E. Miller, Jim Europe | 1978 |
| *Timbuktu* | Luther Davis; music and lyrics by Robert Wright and George Forrest | 1978 |
| *Ain't Misbehavin'* | Richard Maltby, Jr.; music and lyrics by Fats Waller (posthumously) | 1978 |
| *Home* | Samm-Art Williams | 1979 |

*Melvin Van Peebles, seated, produced, directed, and stared in* Waltz of the Stork *with Bob Carten, C. J. Critt, and Mario Van Peebles.*

| Title | Author | Date of Production |
|---|---|---|
| *One Mo' Time* | Conceived by Vernel Bagneris | 1979 |
| *Comin' Uptown* | Philip Rose and Peter Udell; music by Gary Sherman; lyrics by Peter Udell | 1979 |
| *A Lesson from Aloes* | Athol Fugard | 1980 |
| *Sophisticated Ladies* | Duke Ellington (music); Donald McKayle (concept) | 1981 |
| *Lena Horne, The Lady and Her Music* | Musical direction by Harold Wheeler | 1981 |
| *Dreamgirls* | Tom Eyen; music by Henry Krieger; lyrics by Tom Eyen | 1981 |
| *A Soldiers Play* | Charles Fuller | 1982 |
| *Master Harold... and the Boys* | Athol Fugard | 1982 |
| *Waltz of the Stork* | Melvin Van Peebles | 1982 |
| *Mama, I Want To Sing* | Vy Higgensen | 1982 |
| *Amen Corner* | James Baldwin | 1983 |
| *The Tap Dance Kid* | Charles Blackwell | 1983 |
| *Fences* | August Wilson | 1984 |
| *Fraternity* | Jordan Budde | 1984 |
| *The Colored Museum* | George Wolfe | 1986 |
| *Moms* | Ben Caldwell | 1987 |
| *Don' t Get God Started* | Ron Milner | 1988 |
| *Black and Blue* | Claudio Segova | 1988 |
| *Sarafina!* | Mbongeni Ngema | 1988 |
| *Driving Miss Daisy* | Alfred Unry | 1987 |
| *I'm Not Rappaport* | Herb Gardner | 1985 |

## OTHER BLACK ENTERTAINERS

| Name | Category | Born |
|---|---|---|
| Mary Alice | Actress | 1941 |
| Jonelle Allen | Actress | 1944 |
| William Duncan Allen | Pianist | 1908 |
| Osceola Archer | Actress | 1920 |
| Peggy Alston | Singer/actress | n.a. |
| Joseph Attles | Actor | 1903 |
| Hinton Battle | Dancer/actor | n.a. |
| Cynthia Belgrave | Actress | 1900 |
| Fran Bennett | Actress | 1935 |
| Charles Blackwell | Actor | 1935 |
| Sherri Brewer | Actress | 1922 |
| Charles Brown | Actor | n.a. |
| Chelsea Brown | Actress | 1946 |
| George Stanford Brown | Actor | 1924 |
| Graham Brown | Actor | 1924 |
| Jim Brown | Actor | 1936 |
| Roscoe Lee Brown | Actor | 1925 |
| Betty E. Burghardt | Actress | 1922 |
| Vinie Burrows | Actor | 1925 |
| Gregg Burge | Dancer/actor | n.a. |
| Leon Bibb | Singer | 1926 |
| Jules Bledsoe | Singer | 1900 |
| Johnny Brown | Comic | 1945 |
| Dick Campbell | Actor | 1946 |
| Thelma Carpenter | Actor | 1922 |
| Ben Carter | Actor | 1912 |
| Alvin Childress | Actor | 1952 |
| Rolf Coleman | Actor | 1946 |
| Nell Carter | Singer/actress | n.a. |
| Adolph Caesar | Actor | n.a. |
| Brian Evaret Chandler | Actor | n.a. |
| Scatman Crothers | Comic | 1905 |
| Dorothy Dandridge | Actress | 1924 |
| Clifton Davis | Actor | 1945 |
| Peter DeAnda | Actor | 1941 |
| Carmen de Lavallade | Dancer | 1930 |
| Loretta Devine | Singer/actress | n.a. |
| Ivan Dixon | Actor | 1934 |
| Josie Dotson | Actor | 1936 |
| O. L. Duke | Actor | n.a. |
| Nat Dickerson | Singer | n.a. |
| Arthur Duncan | Dancer | 1945 |
| Roy Felix Eaton | Pianist | n.a. |
| Mercedes Ellington | Dancer/actress | n.a. |
| Mercer Ellington | Musician | n.a. |
| Lola Falana | Singer | c1944 |
| Step 'N' Fletchit | Comic | 1900 |
| Roger Furman | Actor | 1936 |
| Charles Gordone | Actor | 1925 |
| Louis Gossett | Actor | 1936 |
| Shirley Graham | Actress | 1904 |
| Micki Grant | Singer/composer | 1946 |
| Theresa Graves | Actress | 1945 |
| Roosevelt Grier | Actor | 1933 |
| Timmy Grimes | Comic | 1925 |
| Danny Glover | Actor | n.a. |
| Robert Guillaume | Actor/singer | 1927 |
| Dick Gregory | Comedian | 1932 |
| Charles Griffin | Actor | 1937 |
| Moses Gunn | Actor | 1929 |
| Ed Hall | Actor | 1931 |
| Juanita Hall | Actress | 1914 |

| Name | Category | Born |
|---|---|---|
| Ina Hartman | Actress | 1926 |
| Hilda Haynes | Actress | 1935 |
| Lloyd Haynes | Actor | 1926 |
| Sherman Hemsley | Actor | 1938 |
| George Hillman | Actor | 1934 |
| Maurice Hines | Dancer/actor | n.a. |
| Ernest Hogan | Comic | 1924 |
| Jennifer Holliday | Singer/actress | n.a. |
| Robert Hooks | Actor | 1937 |
| Ida Hubbard | Actress | 1900 |
| Phyllis Hyman | Singer/actress | n.a. |
| Judith Jamison | Dancer/actress | n.a. |
| Blind Lemon Jefferson | Singer | 1897 |
| Brent Jennings | Actor | n.a. |
| Dots Johnson | Actor | 1903 |
| Robert Earl Jones | Actor | 1900 |
| Woodie King | Actor | 1937 |
| George Kirby | Comic | 1939 |
| Eartha Kitt | Singer/actress | 1928 |
| Ted Lange | Actor | n.a. |
| Roger Lawson | Actor | 1942 |
| Rosetta Le Noire | Actress | 1911 |
| Eugene Lee | Actor | n.a. |
| Philip Lindsay | Actor | 1924 |
| Cleavon Little | Actor | 1939 |
| Avon Long | Dancer | 1910 |
| Aubrey Lyles | Actor | 1884 |
| Pigmeat Markham | Comic | 1900 |
| Julian Mayfield | Actor | 1928 |
| Whitman Mayo | Actor | 1904 |
| Barbara McNair | Singer | 1939 |
| Claudia McNeil | Actress | 1917 |
| Butterfly McQueen | Actress | 1911 |
| Theresa Merritt | Actress | 1903 |
| Flournoy Miller | Actor | 1887 |
| Zakas Mohoe | Actor | n.a. |
| Lynne Moody | Actress | 1902 |
| Manton Moreland | Comic | 1901 |
| Pauline Myers | Actress | 1900 |
| Denise Nicholas | Actress | 1946 |
| Maidie Norman | Actress | 1936 |
| Odetta | Singer | 1930 |

| Name | Category | Born |
|---|---|---|
| Ron O'Neal | Actor | 1937 |
| Judy Pace | Actress | 1950 |
| Cecil Perrin | Actor | 1945 |
| Lincoln T. Perry | Actor | 1902 |
| Walter Raines | Actor | 1940 |
| Sheryl Lee Randolph | Singer/actress | n.a. |
| Tracy Reed | Actor | 1900 |
| Beah Richards | Actress | 1900 |
| Larry Riley | Actor | n.a. |
| Roger Robinson | Actor | 1941 |
| Percy Rodriguez | Actor | 1925 |
| Sugar Chile Robinson | Pianist | 1939 |
| Diana Sands | Actress | 1934 |
| Harold Scott | | 1935 |
| Bobby Short | Pianist/singer | 1924 |
| Frank Silvera | Actor | 1914 |
| Nat Simmons | | 1901 |
| Muriel Smith | | 1923 |
| Bruce Strickland | Singer/actor | n.a. |
| Clarice Taylor | Actress | 1927 |
| Barbara Ann Teer | Actress | 1936 |
| Frozine Jo Thomas | Singer/actress | n.a. |
| Lois Towles | Pianist | n.a. |
| George Walker | Comic | 1873 |
| J. J. Walker | Actor/comedian | 1952 |
| Douglas Turner Ward | Actor | 1930 |
| Richard Ward | Actor | 1935 |
| Vernon Washington | Actor | 1927 |
| Charles Weldon | Actor | n.a. |
| Leigh Whipper | Actor | 1876 |
| Jane White | Actress | 1921 |
| Josh White | Singer | 1908 |
| Slappy White | Comic | 1930 |
| Napoleon Whiting | Actor | 1901 |
| Red Wilcher | Singer/actor | n.a. |
| Clarence Williams III | Actor | 1939 |
| Dooley Wilson | Actor | 1884 |
| Theodore Wilson | Actor | 1903 |
| Andre Womble | Actor | 1940 |
| Allie Woods | Actor | 1940 |
| Carol Woods | Singer/Actress | n.a. |

# BLACK CLASSICAL MUSICIANS: OUTSTANDING ARTISTS OF THE BLACK CLASSICAL TRADITION

**Composers ■ Conductors ■ Musicians ■ Singers**

The role of the African-American in the history of music is finally being given serious attention. Recent discoveries of excellent black symphonic music, both contemporary and two centuries old, have begun to ventilate the stereotype of black music as a limited program of spirituals, jazz, and the blues. Even more important, studies of comprehensive musicology (the study of music in relation to the culture and society in which it exists) are beginning to focus on the unique, non-European nature of African-American music.

African-American music looks back to Africa, not Europe, as the Old World. Whereas the European tradition often considers music in the realm of "art for art's sake," African music is first and foremost a social function. It is such an important part of daily life that ritual and social events cannot even happen without the exact and proper music. As a result, despite the lack of formal theory, both African music and the traditional African audience have always been among the world's most sophisticated.

Social functionalism, following Dr. Rene-Dominique de Lerma's analysis, has continued to be one of the chief characteristics of African-American music. Never sinking to the level of acoustical decoration, the music remains a key force of events; the Civil Rights movement could not have evolved as it did without the songs of the freedom marchers. Other characteristic elements of African-American music, according to Dr. de Lerma, are participant "confusion" (such as the interplay of audience, performer, composer, and arranger); the scale and barform phrasing of the blues; a sense of lively unity with the environment; "speaking" instruments (like Louis Armstrong's trumpet); and inspiration's intense need to find a voice. These are the non-European elements that give traditional African-American music its distinctive quality. This degree of complexity might seem exaggerated to students of the European tradition, but black composers have begun to display the sophistication of their musical heritage and also their individual creative talents in classical Western forms.

Black symphonic music falls into two categories: black-stream music, synonymous with Gunther Schuller's *Third Stream,* which is serious music influenced by the ethnic background described above; and traditional European music created by black composers. Until a few years ago, composers of either style were largely unknown, but the public relations efforts and researches of Paul Freeman, Dr. de Lerma, C. Edward Thomas and the Afro-American Music Opportunities Association have brought to light a great many first-rate symphonic compositions both old and new. Among the best black-stream pieces are William Grant Still's *Afro-American Symphony* (1931) and Ornette Coleman's *Skies of America.* Examples of black symphonic music in which there is no obvious contribution from the black heritage are the Chevalier de Saint Georges' *Symphonic Concertante* (1782) and Ulysses Kay's *Markings* (1966).

Organizations such as the Afro-American Music Opportunities Association and the Dance Theater of Harlem have been an integral part of classical music. The Afro-American Music Opportunities Association, in existence since 1969, was formed out of the need for more acknowledgment of black music and musicians. Since its formation, C. Edward Thomas has developed his concepts into viable and dynamic programs which have already substantially changed American musical sociology.

AAMOA has put out its own record label for nonsymphonic repertoires with the release of David Baker's *Sonata for Piano and String Quartet* in a performance which features Brazilian virtuoso Helena Freire. On March 18, 1974, the first four records of the Black Composers Series were formally released by Columbia Records. These discs featured works by the Chevalier de Saint-George, Samuel Coleridge-Taylor, William Grant Still, George Walker, Ulysses Kay, and Roque Cordero under the artistic direction of Paul Freeman. This Black Composer's Series grew out of an agreement between CBS and AAMOA for at least 12 recordings of some 20 black composers.

The Dance Theater of Harlem was founded by Arthur Mitchell not only to teach black children but to teach children, of all races, dance and especially the classical ballet. The company, formed following the assassination of Dr. Martin Luther King, Jr., has won international acclaim and is probably the youngest company appearing throughout the world. Mitchell, the founder and artistic director, attended New York City's High School of Performing Arts and was the first male graduate to receive the annual Dance Award from the school. Mitchell made his debut with the New York City ballet in 1955 in George Balanchine's "Western Symphony." Since its founding, Mitchell has built the company into a strong group with a repertoire that has the distinction of being unique and at the same time appealing to an audience both young and old, black and white.

In the 1970s two national black opera companies were formed. Opera/South was founded in 1970 by Sister Elise of the Catholic order the Sisters of the Blessed Sacrament and members of the Mississippi Inter-Collegiate Opera Guild (Jackson State University, Utica Junior College, and Tougaloo College). In addition to staging grand opera, the company performed operas by black composers including *Highway No. 1 USA* and *A Bayou Legend* (William Grant Still) and *Jubilee* and *The Juggler of Our Lady* (Ulysses Kay).

In 1974, Sister Elise with three co-founders Margaret Harris, Benjamin Matthews, and Wayne Sanders, organized Opera Ebony.

Performers with these two companies included conductors Leonard De Paur, Margaret Harris, and Everett Lee; pianist Wayne Sanders; and singers Donnie Ray Albert, William Brown, Alpha Floyd, Ester Hinds, Robert Mosley, Wilma Shakesnider, and Walter Turnbull (founder of The Boys Choir of Harlem).

Eileen Southern reports in *The Music of Black Americans*, "The Houston Opera Company's production in 1975 of the opera *Treemonisha* by Scott Joplin had an impact on the operatic world similar to that of Opera/South and Opera Ebony productions in that it served as a showcase for black talent and sent some of the singers to major opera companies."

No major American symphony orchestra has a black music director and only three have black conductors on their staffs, one of which is James De Priest, nephew of Marian Anderson, who conducts the Portland Symphony.

A survey by the National Urban League disclosed that of the nearly 5,000 musicians playing regularly in 56 leading orchestras, 70 were black. Only six of the 528 members of the Big Five orchestras—New York, Boston, Chicago, Cleveland and Philadelphia were black.

The Metropolitan Opera has 15 black artists on its roster plus two in the chorus. The New York City Opera has 11 black singers in principal roles with two conductors and one stage director. Prior to World War II, there were no black singers in any opera house in the United States, but now they are accepted almost anywhere. In the pit at the opera, as on symphony stages, blacks are still occasionally seen serving as extras but rarely given tenure.

San Francisco Symphony Orchestra tympanist Elayne Jones, the only black "first chair" player in a major American orchestra, had to file suit claiming contract violation on grounds of racism and sexism because she was denied tenure. She lost her case.

Over the past few years, there has been an awareness and a renewed interest in black classical music. Dominating the classic stage, however, are female singers . Simon Estes, in a January 3, 1982 *New York Times* interview, said, "When I tell people about this problem they say, 'Look, we have Leontyne Price, Shirley Verrett, Grace Bumbry, Martina Arroyo,' and I say, 'Yes, but how many black men?' 'Well..., I never thought of that.' They can't think of another black man singing major roles in opera. Yet there are probably eight black men who are qualified to do it right now."

Persons close to the opera scene as well as opera singers,

both male and female, agree that black men haven't made it as big in the field because of the sex image they portray. Most agree that at one time the black male was seen as virile and threatening to whites; such stereotypic attitudes have changed over the years, giving black males more opportunity in many areas of endeavor.

The formation of Opera Ebony provided an avenue for blacks to accept classical music. In the 1980s, the black composer and the classical musician can be appreciated more because of a long and varied heritage within the mainstream of American music.

In Harlem, the Harlem School of the Arts has been a vehicle through which black youngsters have been exposed to the classical arts. Many classical performers as well as jazz and pop musicians have participated in workshops at the school.

## OUTSTANDING ARTISTS: COMPOSERS, CONDUCTORS, MUSICIANS, SINGERS

### ADELE ADDISON
**Soprano**
**1925**

Adele Addison received her musical training at Westminster Choir College (Mus. B., 1946) and the University of Massachusetts (1963). After making her recital debut at Town Hall, New York City, in 1952, she went on many annual recital tours of the United States and Canada. In 1963, she made a tour of the Soviet Union under the cultural exchange program. She has appeared with the New England, New York City, and Washington opera companies. Her premiere performances include John La Montaine's *Fragments from the Song of Songs* with the New Haven Symphony (1959) and Poulenc's *Gloria* with the Boston Symphony (1961). She performed the soloist opening concert at Philharmonic Hall of Lincoln Center in 1962, and she is a trustee of Westminster Choir College.

### ROBERTA ALEXANDER
**Soprano**

*Opera* Magazine said of Roberta Alexander "... a soprano who, with a range of over two octaves, rich low notes and crystalline, brilliant top notes, excellent diction and clear execution of coloratura passages, should make a name for herself," and so she has.

She was born in Lynchburg, Virginia, grew up in Yellow Springs Ohio and currently makes her home in Amsterdam, Holland. She has a B.S. degree in Music Education from Central State University in Ohio and a Masters degree in Voice from the University of Michigan at Ann Arbor.

Her premier with the Metropolitan Opera came in 1983's fall season as Zerlina in Do*n Giovanni*. Other Met successes were as Bess in *Porgy and Bess* and in the title role of *Jenufa*.

In the summer of 1984, she made her debut at the Aix-en Provence Festival in France in Mozart's *La Finta Giardiniera*, and in 1985, in Vienna she performed as Cleopatra in Handel's *Giulio Cesare*. She has also performed Ilia in *Idomeneo* in West Berlin and *La Bohéme* in East Berlin. She has also performed extensively at the Netherlands Opera, the London Opera and here in America at the Santa Fe Opera in New Mexico and at the Houston Grand Opera in Texas. In 1987, she returned to the Met where she once again performed the role of Mimi in *La Bohéme*.

*Roberta Alexander, as Bess in* Porgy and Bess.

*Messo-soprano Betty Lou Allen recently appeared with the Santa Fe and Washington opera companies.*

## BETTY LOU ALLEN
### Mezzo-Soprano
### 1930

Born in Campbell, Ohio, Betty Lou Allen studied at Wilberforce University and toured with Leontyne Price as the Wilberforce Sisters. She continued her musical studies at the Hartford School of Music (1950) and the Berkshire Music Center (1951), and studied voice with Sarah Peck Moore, Paul Ulanowsky, and Zinka Milanov. Her New York debut was in Virgil Thompson's *Four Saints in Three Acts* with the New York City Opera Company (1953) and her formal opera debut was at the Teatro Colon, Buenos Aires (1964). She has been a soloist with major symphonies on many tours as well as in Bernstein's *Jeremiah* Symphony. She opened the Lyndon Baines Johnson Library Concert Hall (1971) and has appeared with the Santa Fe and Washington opera companies.

## MARIAN ANDERSON
### Contralto
### 1902

At the peak of her career, Marian Anderson was regarded as the world's greatest contralto. When she made her Town Hall debut in New York on December 31, 1935, Howard Taubman, the *New York Times* reviewer, described it as "music-making that probed too deep for words."

Marian Anderson was born on February 27, 1902 in Philadelphia and, as a young choir girl, demonstrated her vocal talents by singing parts from soprano, alto, tenor and bass. At the age of 19, she began studying with Giuseppe Boghetti and, four years later, appeared as soloist with the New York Philharmonic. After a short engagement with the Philadelphia Symphony Orchestra, she traveled to Europe on a scholarship granted by the National Association of Negro Musicians.

It was on Easter Sunday in 1939 that Miss Anderson gave what is perhaps her most memorable concert—singing on the steps of the Lincoln Memorial after having been barred from making an appearance at Constitution Hall by the Daughters of the American Revolution (DAR).

In 1955, after years of successful concert work, she made her Metropolitan Opera debut in Verdi's *A Masked Ball.* Two years later, a State Department tour took her around the world. In September of 1958, Miss Anderson was named to the U.S. delegation to the United Nations.

Now retired, she lives with her husband, Orpheus Fisher, in Danbury, Connecticut.

In 1982, when Marian Anderson celebrated her eightieth birthday, Grace Bumbry and Shirley Verrett sang at New York City's Carnegie Hall in tribute to Mrs. Anderson. Ms. Verrett hailed Mrs. Anderson as "a dream maker." Ms. Verrett and Ms. Bumbry are both former recipients of Marian Anderson scholarships.

## THOMAS J. ANDERSON
### Composer, Educator
### 1928

Thomas Jefferson Anderson was born in Coatesville, Pennsylvania. His mother was a musician, and as a teenager he toured with a jazz orchestra. His music shows influences from jazz, the post-Webern composers, and traditional African music.

Anderson studied at West Virginia State College (B.M. 1950), Pennsylvania State University (M.E. 1951), Aspen

*Martina Arroyo has sung with many of the world's major orchestras.*

School of Music, and University of Iowa (Ph.D. 1958). He was composer-in-residence with the Atlanta Symphony Orchestra on a grant from the Rockefeller Foundation during the 1969-1971 seasons.

The composer's most widely performed works have been *Chamber Symphony* (1968); *Squares* (1965), an essay for orchestra; and *Personals* (1966), a cantata for narrator, chorus, and brass ensemble. He has also written music for band (*In Memoriam Zach Walker* ), works for piano (*Watermelon* ) and various compositions for solo voice and for chorus. In all he has published some 50 pieces of music.

Dr. Anderson is currently (1988) chairman of the Music department at Tufts University in Medford Maine

## MARTINA ARROYO
### Soprano
### 1939

Martina Arroyo, a New York native, made her debut at the Metropolitan Opera in February 1965 in the title role of Aida and has since sung engagements with opera houses in Vienna, Berlin, Buenos Aires, London, and Hamburg. In addition to operatic appearances, she has also been a frequent guest soloist with many of the world's major orchestras.

In addition to Aida, Miss Arroyo's Metropolitan repertoire includes Donna Anna in *Don Giovanni,* Liu in *Turandot*, Leonora in *Il Trovatore,* Elsa in *Lohengrin,* and the title role of *Madame Butterfly*. These have been developed since 1958, the year she made her debut in Carnegie Hall in the American premiere of Pizzetti's *Murder in the Cathedral*. That same year she made her Metropolitan debut as the celestial voice in *Don Carlo*.

On opening night of the 1970-1971 Met opera season Miss Arroyo sang Elvira in *Ernani*, and she opened the 1971-1972 season as Elizabeth in *Don Carlo*.

Ms. Arroyo sang at the White House in 1977 sharing the bill with Andre Previn and Isaac Stern at a dinner for 26 heads of state marking the signing of the Panama Canal treaty, and in April 1987 she was guest artist for the New Mexico Symphony Orchestra where she sang the overture of Verdi's *La Forza del Destino* as well as several other numbers. Also in 1987, in Miss Arroyo's American tour, she performed in Puccinni's Turandot *in Cincinnati.* In 1988, she performed once again with New York's Met with performances in *Turandot*, *Cavalleria Rusticana* and *Aida*.

Summers, over the past several years, she has spent teaching and as well singing in various summer song festivals.

## JEROME ASHBY
### Horn

Jerome Ashby grew up in New York City and began violin lessons in grade school as an alternative to shop classes because "music classes had girls." At age 13 he was mesmerized by the sound of the horn but did not receive encouragement from teachers who indicated that the instrument was not for him. Undaunted, he studied for an entire summer and returned to school to take the first chair in the orchestra and qualify for entrance to the High School of Performing Arts in Manhattan. He studied privately with former Philharmonic Principal Horn James Chambers and during his student years at Juilliard Mr. Ashby supported himself playing in the pit of two Broadway shows—*Fiddler On The Roof* and *The King And I*. Prior to joining the Philharmonic in 1979 he was Principal Horn with the Symphony of the University of Mexico during which time he met his wife Patricia. The couple live in New Jersey and have three daughters, Elizabeth, Juanita, and Violeta.

## DAVID BAKER
### Composer
### 1931

David N. Baker, a composer of great promise, directs the jazz studies program at Indiana University. Born in Indianapolis, he obtained his B.A. and M.A. in music education from the university there. He taught music in the public schools of Indianapolis and at Indiana Central College and Lincoln University (Missouri) before returning to his alma mater as a faculty member. Baker has logged considerable experience with both jazz bands and college and municipal symphony orchestras. He was a member of Quincy Jones' All-Star Jazz Orchestra which toured Europe in 1961. Among his better known works is a cello sonata that Janos Starker plays. Paul Freeman has praised Baker's talent as that of a "black Bartok."

*Jerome Ashby plays the horn in symphony orchestras.*

*Priscilla Baskerville, a vigorous and dynamic performer.*

## PRISCILLA BASKERVILLE
### Lyric Soprano

The operatic and theatrical talents of Priscilla Baskerville have added another dynamic and vigorous dimension and excitement to the classic music scene. In an outdoor summer music festival in New York in which Met performers had to compete with a bad outdoor sound system, "Priscilla Baskerville sang Musetta as if microphones and loudspeakers were unnecessary impedimentia....her voice was big and gleaming." Her voice has also been called "exciting" and "sensuous."

A graduate of the Manhattan School of Music, she made her Metropolitan Opera debut as Bess in (1949) a then new production of *Porgy and Bess*. Priscilla Baskerville returned to the Met during the 1986-1987 season as Musetta in *La Bohéme. In* 1986 she was honored to perform at the White House singing selections from Gershwin classics. The evening was a tribute to Gershwin and was aired by PBS as "*In Performance at the White House*." Highlights of Miss Baskerville's 1986-1987 season included a debut with the New York City Opera in the world premiere of Anthony Davis' *Malcolm X*.

In 1988 Miss Baskerville gave "standout" performances as Serena in another new production of *Porgy and Bess* directed by Gotz Friedrich at the Berlin Opera (Theater des Westens). She also made a solo appearance with the Cincinnati Symphony, and sang excerpts from *Porgy and Bess* with the Philadelphia Orchestra and Dennis Russell Davies at the Saratoga Festival. In January, Miss Baskerville performed her first Giorgetta in *Il Tabbaro* in Miami followed by her first *Aida* for the Dayton Opera, more performances of *Porgy and Bess* in Berlin followed and later the Verdi *Requiem* with the Charleston Symphony. She returned to the Met during the 1989-1990 season as both Bess and Musetta. That same season Priscilla Baskerville sung the role of Elisabetta in Verdi's *Don Carlo* for the Indianapolis and Memphis Operas. The Brooklyn-born soprano spent the spring and summer of 1986 with the Houston Grand Opera tour of *Porgy and Bess*, which visited Modena, Italy, and the Theatre Musical de Paris/Chatelet.

While Miss Baskerville has sung with the Houston and Springfield Symphonies, she has also appeared on Broadway in *Sophisticated Ladies* (and on the original cast album), and also in the movie *Cotton Club*. In 1986 she made her debut with the Bel Canto Chorus of Milwaukee singing Orff's *Catulli Carmina* and Rossini's Petite Messe Solenelle.

## LEON BATES
### Pianist

A Philadelphia native Leon Bates began his musical studies at the age of six and demonstrated an early proficiency on both piano and violin. He studied at the Settlement School in Philadelphia with Irene Beck and later under Natalie Hinderas at Temple University where he earned a bachelor's degree in music. He has played with the Philadelphia and Cleveland Orchestras, the National American, San Francisco, Saint Louis and Detroit Symphonies, the Los Angeles

Philharmonic, and under James DePreist with the Oregon Symphony. He has played at the Kennedy Center in Washington, Carnegie Hall and Alice Tully Hall in New York. He made his New York Philharmonic debut during the 1987-1988 season. Internationally he has played with the Vienna Symphony Orchestra, the Strasbourg Symphony, the Dublin Symphony, the National Symphony Orchestra of Zimbabwe and the Orchestra Sinfonica del l'Accademia Nationale di Santa Cecilia in Rome. He performed the Gershwin *Concert in F* with the Basel Symphony and the performance was captured on a 'classical video' which was released for broadcast in Europe, Canada and the United States on the Bravo Network.

Among Mr. Bates' many awards are the National Association of Music Teachers Collegiate Artists Competition, the National Association of Negro Musicians Competition, the Philadelphia Orchestra Senior Auditions, the Symphony of the New World Competition, the Rhode Island International Competition and the National Endowment for the Arts Solo Recitalists Fellowship Grant.

Mr. Bates is on the faculty of the University of Delaware. He frequently gives master classes while on tour. He has recorded on the Orion and Performance Records labels.

## KATHLEEN BATTLE
**Soprano**

An active orchestral soloist, Kathleen Battle made her Met debut in 1977 as the Shepherd in *Tannhauser* and has also been heard there as Sophie in *Werther* and Blondchen in *The Abduction from the Seraglio.* She has sung with the symphonies of Chicago, Boston, and Cincinnati, as well as with the New York and Berlin Philharmonics. She is a graduate of the University of Cincinnati's Conservatory of Music. The 1980-1981 season included her first Metropolitan Opera performances of Elvira in *The Italian Girl in Algiers* as well as debuts with the Zurich Opera and the Lyric Opera of Chicago. In 1982, she received critical kudos for her Rosina in the Met's *Barber of Seville.* Ms. Battle was born in Portsmouth, Ohio.

In the 1987-88 season, Miss Battle returned to the Metropolitan Opera to sing the role of Zerbinetta in R. Strauss' *Ariadne auf Naxos* with Jessye Norman as Ariadne and Tatiana Troyanos as the Composer. Miss Battle will join the Metropolitan Opera on tour in Japan for performances as Susanna in Mozart's *Le Nozze di Figaro*, and for a joint concert with Placido Domingo. Miss Battle will also open the Metropolitan Opera's Parks season as Adina in L'Elisir d'Amore opposite the Nemorino of Luciano Pavarotti, during the summer of 1988.

Miss Battle appeared in a Gala New Year's Eve concert at Avery Fisher Hall with the New York Philharmonic under Zubin Mehta, which was televised on P.B.S. Her season also included the Brahms German Requiem with the Chicago Symphony Orchestra under Sir George Solti; Haydn's Creation with the Berlin Philharmonic.

## MARGARET BONDS
**Composer, Pianist**
**1913**

Margaret Bonds has written several scores for the stage as well as concert works. Born in Chicago, she was encouraged by her mother, a talented organist, to develop her musical gifts. After receiving an M.A. in music from Northwestern, she continued her studies at Juilliard. Her awards include a Rosenwald Fellowship, a Roy Harris Scholarship, and a Wanamaker Award. Her best known works are *Migration,* a ballet; *Spiritual Suite for Piano; Mass in D Minor; Three Dream Portraits;* and, of the many songs, "The Ballad of the Brown King" and "The Negro Speaks of Rivers."

## GWENDOLYN BRADLEY
**Soprano**

Gwendolyn Bradley was born in New York City but grew up in Bishopville, South Carolina. Ms. Bradley was a finalist in the 1977 Metropolitan Opera National Council auditions. She is a graduate of the North Carolina School of the Arts and attended both the Curtis Institute of Music and the Academy of Vocal Arts in Philadelphia and has studied with Margaret Harshaw and Seth McCoy. Ms. Bradley made her Metropolitan Opera debut as the Nightingale in the Met premiere of Raval's "L'Enfant et les Sortileges" in February 1981. Since making her professional operatic debut in 1976 with the Lake George Opera Festival as Nanetta in *Falstaff,* she has been heard as Titania in *A Midsummer Night's Dream* with the Central City Opera, Lakme with Opera/South, and Aurelia in *Rumpelstiltskin* with the Opera Company of Philadelphia. Ms. Bradley has sung with the Philadelphia Orchestra, the Kansas City Philharmonic, and the Charleston Symphony. During 1980-1981 she appeared with the Los Angeles Philharmonic at the Hollywood Bowl and with the Seattle Symphony. In addition to the

*Margaret Bonds plays her Spiritual Suite for Piano*

Metropolitan Opera she has performed with the Opera companies of Philadelphia, Cleveland and Michigan.

Highlights of recent seasons were a debut at the Hamburg Staatsoper as Blondchen and subsequent performances with that company as Zerbinetta, Adina in L'Elisir d'Amore and her first Susanna. Miss Bradley also performed Oscar in Un Ballo in Maschera for Radio France and sang the role of the Fiakermilli for a debut at Glyndebourne.

During season 1987-88, Miss Bradley's roles at the Metropolitan Opera included Olympia, which was televised on PBS' Live From the Met series, and also appears as the Woodbird in *Siegfried* a new Otto Schenk production conducted by James Levine. In Europe the soprano portrayed Zerbinetta at the Hamburg Staatsoper, and also repeated this role and Susanna in *Le nozze di Figaro* at the Deutsche Opera Berlin. Miss Bradley's previous success in Berlin resulted in this company's invitation to join the Deutsche Opera Berlin ensemble in September 1988 where she performed as Gilda in *Rigoletto*. As a soloist with orchestra, Miss Bradley appeared in an all Mozart concert at the Paris Opera, in Britten's *Spring Symphony* with the Orchestre Nationale de Paris, and in Mahler's Symphony No. 8 with the Columbus

## HAROLD J. BROWN
### Composer
### 1909

Harold J. Brown is a composer and choral conductor. He was born in Shellman, Georgia and received a B.A. degree from Fisk University in Nashville, Tennessee in 1923. He received his M.A. degree in 1931 from Indiana University. He has taught at Florida A & M College and at Southern University. Brown was music director at Karamu House and the Huntington Playhouse in Cleveland. He wrote the oratorio *The Saga of Rip Van Winkle* and *The African Chief*, a cantata.

*Gwendolyn Bradley, a soprano with a distinct sound.*

## GRACE BUMBRY
### Mezzo-soprano
### 1937

Grace Bumbry is the first black performer to have sung at the Wagner Festival in Bayreuth, Germany, and one of the few young singers who can boast of having been called to play a command performance at the White House. Miss Bumbry sang at a formal state dinner opening Washington's official social season in 1962 as a guest of the Kennedys and the nation.

A native of St. Louis, Missouri, Miss Bumbry, like many

*The brilliant singing of Grace Bumbry wins worldwide acclaim.*

black singers, had her first exposure to music in a church choir, singing with her brothers and her parents at the Union Memorial Methodist Church in St. Louis. After studying voice locally she won a nationwide talent contest in 1954, and went on, with scholarship aid, to study successively at Boston and Northwestern universities. At the latter school, she attended master classes in opera and lieder given by the famed singer and teacher Lotte Lehmann. Later competitions led to several important cash awards, as well as contacts with such important personages as Marian Anderson.

Beginning in 1959, Miss Bumbry traveled to various European countries, performing in the operatic capitals of the world. On July 23, 1961, Wieland Wagner, grandson of Richard Wagner, shocked many traditionalists by selecting Miss Bumbry to sing the role of Venus in *Tannhauser,* a role which conventionally calls for a figure of so-called Nordic beauty, usually a tall and voluptuous blond. Miss Bumbry proceeded to give a performance which won acclamation from both the harshest and the kindest of critics, all of whom praised her both for her physical radiance and her brilliant singing.

After her Bayreuth engagement, Miss Bumbry returned to the United States for a concert debut at Carnegie Hall. Her recital was only moderately successful, however. Over the years, critics seemed to question her ability to evolve as a full-fledged interpreter of German lieder, many preferring instead to view her as the possessor of a big voice whose calibre and quality are more suited for opera. To some extent, it would seem that she concurs in this analysis, being on record as having once said: "My style is really Verdi. This is my heart and soul."

In 1974, Miss Bumbry returned to the Met to sing Santuzza in *Cavalleria Rusticana.* She has since appeared successfully with various opera companies as Dalilah, Lady Macbeth, Medea, and other great dramatic roles, which have become her speciality.

On January 31,1982, Ms. Bumbry shared the stage with Shirley Verrett at Carnegie Hall in New York City to pay tribute to Marian Anderson on her eightieth birthday. Ms. Bumbry sang Adriana's entrance aria from Cilea's *Adriana Lecouvreur* entirely in mezza voice. On December 6, 1981, Ms. Bumbry had also appeared in a benefit concert at Carnegie Hall for Artists to End Hunger.

Bumbry entered an altogether new phase of her performance career when she joined Frank Sinatra in a Gala Benefit at New York's Waldorf Astoria and sang the pop ballad "Natalie" to great acclaim.

In the 1987/88 season Grace Bumbry returned to the San Francisco Opera as Abigaille in *Nabucco* and starred as Lady Macbeth in a new production of Macbeth in Los Angeles. She celebrated her 25th anniversary at the Royal Opera, Covent Garden with a series of performances of *Tosca* and appeared at the Vienna State Opera in the same role. Bumbry returned to Barcelona for La Gioconda and was also heard in *Cavalleria Rusticana* and *Don Carlos* at the Hamburg State Opera. She starred as Amneris in *Aida* at the Arena di Verona.

*Steve Cole, versatile singer-actor.*

**Steven Cole**
**Tenor**

Versatile tenor Steven Cole is a native of Baltimore, Maryland. He made his professional debut with the Boston Symphony on just two days notice singing Monsieur Triquet in *Eugene Onegin* conducted by Seiji Ozawa.

A specialist in operatic character roles, he has emerged as a major international singer-actor as a result of a succession of prestigious engagements that have included Goro in the Ken Russell production of *Madame Butterfly* at the Spoleto Festivals of Italy, Charleston, and Melbourne, Australia; the Dancing Master in *Ariadne auf Naxos* at the Aix-en-Provence Festival and the Nice Opera; the world premiere of *Medea* by Robert Wilson/Gavin Bryars for the Paris Opera; Pere Lilaque in Hans Werner Henze's *Boulevard Solitude* for the Avignon Festival; and *L'Incoronazione di Poppea* for the Lausanne Opera, Switzerland.

Steven Cole made his Metropolitan Opera debut in the fall of 1987 as the Dancing Master in *Ariadne auf Naxos* with Jessye Norman and Kathleen Battle, conducted by James Levine. Other operatic engagements for Mr. Cole in the 1988 season include *Falstaff* in Nice, *Turandot* in Cincinnati, and *Madame Butterfly* at the Victoria State Opera in Melbourne, Australia. In addition, he performed Handel's *Messiah* with the Phoenix Symphony Orchestra and the San Jose Symphony.

His 1986-87 season included *Madame Butterfly* with the Greensboro Opera, *Ariadne auf Naxos* and *The Merry Widow* in Nice, *Falstaff* in Lyon, *Boris Godunov* in Philadelphia, and *Porgy and Bess* with the North Carolina Symphony. Mr. Cole's European engagements last season continued with Monteverdi's *Orfeo* in Nantes and Angers, *Ariadne auf Naxos* in Lausanne, and *Der Rosenkavalier* in Aix-en-Provence.

*Samuel Coleridge-Taylor was a celebrated turn-of-the-century composer.*

## VINCENT COLE
### Tenor

Vincent Cole has received international acclaim for his performances on the operatic stage and with leading symphony orchestras in both the United States and Europe. Regarded as uncommonly versatile his operatic repertoire extends from the works of Monteverdi through Stravinsky.

*Vincent Cole, as des Grieux in Act I, Scene 1 of Massenet's "Manon."*

Cole made his Metropolitan Opera debut in 1987 as Alfred in *Die Fledermaus*. He also debuted in Stuttgart as Percy in a new production of *Anna Bolena* opposite Katia Ricciarelli, returned to the Nice Opera as Fenton in *Falstaff* and made his Teatro San Carlo, Naples debut as Riccardo in Bellini's *I Puritani*. Cole starred at the Seattle Opera in a new production of Gluck's *Orphee* specially mounted for him and made his Mostly Mozart Festival debut in August of 1988 under Gerald Schwarz. In 1988 he sang his first Don Ottavio in *Don Giovanni* at the Ravinia Festival under James Levine.

Also at home in Italian opera, his successful debut at The Vienna Staatsoper was as Alfredo in *La Traviata*, a role he first sang at the L'Opera de Montreal. At The New York City Opera he has sung Rodolfo in *La Bohème* (a role he also performed in Santa Fe, St. Louis and Minneapolis); the Duke in *Rigoletto* (also in Dallas and Winnipeg) and Pinkerton in *Madame Butterfly*. His German repertoire in this country has included *Flute* (New York, St. Louis); *Merry Wives of Windsor* (New York); *Die Fledermaus;* and *The Flying Dutchman* (Boston Opera).

Much of Mr. Cole's early music education came on a full scholarship to the Philadelphia Musical Academy. Mr. Cole continued his studies at the Curtis Institute with Margaret Harshaw. In 1976, he won The National Award in Chicago's prestigious WGN "Auditions of the Air," and in 1977 received the first prize "Weyerhauser Award" at The Metropolitan Opera National Auditions and grants from The Rockefeller Foundation. He has sung at the White House three times since 1977. Projects in 89/90 include *Gianni Schicchi* at the Metropolitan Opera, *Thais* for the Festival of Nil and *Fidelio* under Von Karajan at the Salzburg Festival.

Mr. Cole currently makes his home in New York City.

## SAMUEL COLERIDGE-TAYLOR
### Composer
### 1875-1912

Coleridge-Taylor was one of England's most celebrated composers at the turn of the century.

Born to a doctor from Sierra Leone and a British mother, he showed musical gifts at age five, and ten years later entered the Royal College of Music in London. There he studied with Sir Charles Wood and Sir Charles Villiers Stanford. Fame was his with the premiere of *Hiawatha's Wedding Feast.*

The beautiful aria "On away! Awake, Beloved," became one of the most popular and frequently recorded songs of the period.

In 1901, the Coleridge-Taylor Society was founded in Washington, D.C. specifically to study and perform his music. Harry Burleigh was one of the soloists to perform under the composer's baton soon after, along with a 200-voice choir, 52 musicians from the U.S. Marine Band, and the supplementary strings required by the *Hiawatha* music. The composer was very warmly received in this country. James Weldon Johnson and Booker T. Washington were among his friends, and he was President Theodore Roosevelt's guest at the White House.

*Philip Creech, an accomplished recitalist.*

## ROQUE CORDERO
### Composer, Educator
### 1917

Roque Cordero is respected as one of Latin America's most creative talents because of his abilities as a violinist, a conductor, and a composer who incorporates popular Panamanian forms into concert music.

Born in Panama, his interests developed from popular songwriting to classical music at the age of 17. Four years later he was appointed director of the Orquesta Sinfonica de la Union Musical in Panama, and he later joined the Orquesta Sinfonica de Panama as violist. In 1943, he began studying abroad. He was engaged by the University of Minnesota as Artistic Director of the Institute of Latin-American Studies, and after completing his course of study, was awarded a Guggenheim Fellowship. Dr. Cordero is presently music editor for the publishing company of Peer International Corporation and is professor of music at Illinois State University.

## PHILIP CREECH
### Tenor

Philip Creech is a native of Hempstead, New York and a graduate of Northwestern University. Creech performed with Margaret Hillis' Chicago Symphony Chorus from 1973 to 1975 and frequently appeared as tenor soloist. Since 1976 he has sung with the Chicago Symphony, the Boston Symphony, the New York Philharmonic, and the Cincinnati Symphony. Creech made his debut at the Salzburg Festival in 1979 singing in the Berlioz *Requiem.* He made his Metropolitan Opera debut in September 1979 as Beppe in the season's premiere of Leoncavallo's *Pagliacci*, and was heard later that season as Edmondo in the premiere and subsequent live overseas telecast of the new production of Puccini's *Manon Lescaut.* Creech has also appeared at the Met as Tonio in *Pagliacci.*

Mr. Creech made his recording debut in Stravinsky's *Les Noces,* with the Chicago Symphony on RCA Red Seal's *Music from Raviniar* series. He has recently recorded *Carmina Burana* with James Levine and the Chicago Symphony, which was released on the DGG label and became a best-seller and a Grammy Award winner.

Philip Creech is also recognized as an accomplished recitalist and has sung well over 100 recitals throughout the United States.

*James DePreist is the Music Director of the Oregon Symphony*

## OSCEOLA DAVIS
**Soprano**

Osceola Davis is a native of New Jersey and a graduate of the Philadelphia Musical Academy. She received further vocal training at the Curtis Institute of Music, where she sang Gilda in *Rigoletto* and Despina in *Cosig fan Tutte*. Ms. Davis went to Germany to sing with the Staatstheater am Gaertnerplatz in Munich, where her roles included Rosina in *The Barber of Seville,* Blondchen in *The Abduction from the Seraglio,* Olympia in *The Tales of Hoffman,* Esmeralda in *The Bartered Bride,* and Papagenain *The Magic Flute*. She returned to the United States in 1979.

## WILLIAM LEVI DAWSON
**Composer, Conductor**
**1898**

Born in Anniston, Alabama, Dawson attended Tuskegee Institute and later enrolled at the Hornes Institute for fine arts in Kansas City, Kansas. In 1927, he received an M.A. in music from the American Conservatory. One of Dawson's famous orchestral compositions, the *Negro Folk Symphony,* was premiered in 1934 by the Philadelphia Orchestra under the direction of Leopold Stokowski. Critics were moved by the music's "dramatic feeling," "directness of melodic speech," and "sumptuous orchestration." Inspired by Dvorak, Dawson's goal, in his own words, was "to write a symphony in the Negro folk idiom, based on authentic folk, but in the same symphonic form used by the composers of the (European) romantic-nationalist school."

## JAMES DEPREIST
**Conductor**
**1936**

A gifted and versatile musician, James DePreist has been active in several areas of music as a performer, composer, arranger, and conductor. It is in the last-named field that he has been most often acclaimed by musicians and critics alike as a young man of rare ability. This estimate was confirmed in 1965 when he was appointed assistant conductor of the New York Philharmonic.

Born in Philadelphia on November 21, 1936, DePreist studied piano and percussion from the age of 10, but did not decide on a musical career until he reached his early twenties. After graduating from high school, he entered the Wharton School of the University of Pennsylvania as a prelaw student, receiving a B.S. in 1958 and an M.A. in 1961.

DePreist also studied music history, the theory of harmony, and orchestration at the Philadelphia Conservatory of Music, and composition with the distinguished American composer Vincent Persichetti.

In 1962, the State Department sponsored a cultural exchange tour of the Near and the Far East, engaging DePreist as an American specialist in music. During this tour, DePreist was stricken with polio, paralyzed in both legs, and flown home for intensive therapy.

Within six months he had fought his way back to the point where he could walk with the aid of crutches and braces. Courage, determination, and talent carried him to the semifinals of the 1963 Dmitri Mitropoulos International Music Competition for Conductors.

After another overseas tour as conductor in residence in Thailand, DePreist returned to the United States, appearing with the Minneapolis International Symphony Orchestra, the New York Philharmonic, and the Philadelphia Orchestra.

In 1964, he recorded what is perhaps his most satisfying triumph, capturing first prize in the Mitropoulos International Competition. Another highlight of his career occurred on June 28, 1965 when he conducted Marian Anderson's farewell concert at Philadelphia's Robin Hood Dell.

He last led the New York Philharmonic during the 1984 Parks concerts. Currently Mr. De Priest is the Music Director of the Oregon Symphony. He is one of a select and talented circle of American-born and-trained conductors who have appeared with the nation's five premier orchestras—New York, Boston, Philadelphia, Cleveland and Chicago. He has also been guest conductor in most of the capitals of Europe and the United States.

## CHEVALIER DE SAINT-GEORGES
**Composer**
**1739-1799**

The Chevalier de Saint-Georges is considered to be the first man of African ancestry to have made a major impression on European music.

Born on the Caribbean island of Guadeloupe to an African-

*Dean Dixon conducted the New York Philharmonic Orchestra at the age of 26, making him the youngest person ever to do so.*

slave mother and a French father, he displayed early talent on the violin. He studied with Francois Gossec, whom he succeeded as concertmaster of the celebrated Concert des Amateurs in 1769. His musical output was enormous, including several operas, 11 symphonies concertantes, a dozen string quartets, 10 violin concertos, and other instrumental and vocal works. His hours away from the composing table were as full of life as his music. He was one of Europe's outstanding swordsmen, an expert swimmer and boxer, and colonel of an all-black regiment that included the father of Alexandre Dumas.

Saint-Georges is stylistically and chronologically pre-Classic. Within the frequent lypastel-hued hedonism of his music can be found the French progenitors of the string quartet and the basic architecture of the sonata form for violin and piano.

## DEAN DIXON
**Conductor**
**1915**

In 1941, Dean Dixon became the first black and, at 26, the youngest musician ever to conduct the New York Philharmonic Orchestra.

Dixon was born in Manhattan on January 10, 1915, and graduated from DeWitt Clinton High School in 1932. Exposed to classical music by his parents (as a small boy he was regularly taken to Carnegie Hall), Dixon formed his own amateur orchestra at the Harlem YMCA while he was still in high school.

On the basis of a successful violin audition, he was admitted to the Juilliard School where he received his B.S. in 1936. Three years later he acquired his masters from Columbia.

The Dean Dixon Symphony Society, which he had formed in 1932, began to receive financial support from the Harlem community in 1937, and in 1941, at the request of Eleanor Roosevelt, Dixon gave a concert at the Heckscher Theater. He was later signed by the musical director of NBC radio to conduct the network's summer symphony in two concerts. Two months after the NBC concerts he made his debut with the New York Philharmonic.

Dixon is currently (1988) director of the Frankfurt Orchestra in Frankfurt, Germany. He makes his home there although he makes occasional visits to the United States to conduct.

## MATTIWILDA DOBBS
**Coloratura Soprano**
**1925**

One of the world's most gifted coloratura sopranos is Mattiwilda Dobbs. Now residing in Sweden, where she is a national favorite, Miss Dobbs has gained international fame with a voice that has been described as one "of often miraculous beauty... fascinating ease and uncanny accuracy."

Born in Atlanta, Georgia on July 11, 1925, Miss Dobbs graduated from Spelman College in 1946 as class valedictorian, having majored in voice training. After studying Spanish at Columbia, where she received her master's degree, she went on to Paris for two years on a Whitney Fellowship.

In October 1950, competing against hundreds of singers from four continents, she won the International Music Competition held at Geneva. She made her professional debut in Paris, and then became the first black to sing a principal role at La Scala in Milan.

On March 8, 1954, she made her Town Hall debut in New York in the one-act opera *Ariadne auf Naxos,* and received a rousing ovation. A year later she repeated the success with her first concert recital on the same stage.

Since then, she has made numerous recordings, including *The Pearl Fishers* and *Zaidde,* and has toured the world with great success. She is currently a mainstay in the world of Swedish opera.

## RUDOLPH DUNBAR
**Composer**
**1917**

A native of British Guiana, Rudolph Dunbar received his musical education at the Institute of Musical Art in New York as well as in Paris and Leipzig. In addition to being a musical conductor, Dunbar is also a clarinetist. He made his debut with the NBC Symphony Orchestra in New York City and has conducted in Great Britain and throughout the United States. He is the author of *A Treatise on Clarinet Playing* and is known widely for the composition *Dance of the 20th Century.*

## TODD DUNCAN
**Actor, singer**
**1903**

Although thinking of himself primarily as a teacher, Todd Duncan has made notable contributions to the world of theater and concert.

Duncan was born into a well-to-do family in Danville, Kentucky on February 12, 1903. He graduated from Butler University in Indianapolis in 1925 and began a teaching career—first at a junior high school and then in Louisville at the Municipal College for Negroes.

In 1934, he appeared in New York in a single performance of an all-black version of the opera *Cavalleria Rusticana*. On the strength of this alone, he was auditioned less than a year later by George Gershwin, and received the role of Porgy in *Porgy and Bess*. He was such a success that he repeated his performance in the role in the 1938 and 1942 revivals of the play.

In 1940, he was a featured performer on Broadway in *Cabin in the Sky*. When the play closed, he headed for Hollywood to appear in the movie *Syncopation*. His concert repertoire includes German lieder and French and Italian songs. Duncan retired in 1965 after singing at President Lyndon B. Johnson's inaugural. Only once has he broken his retirement and that was in 1972 to sing the title role of *Job* at Washington's Kennedy Center. In 1978, Duncan was honored by the Washington Performing Arts Society with a dinner dance at the Sheraton Park Hotel. He still teaches voice in his home in Washington.

*Simon Estes, has been called the world's foremost bass-baritone.*

## SIMON ESTES
**Bass-Baritone**

Simon Estes was the first black man to sing at the Bayreuth Festival, appearing in the title role of a new production of *Der Fliegende Hollander,* a portrayal he repeated there in three subsequent seasons. A native of Centerville, Iowa, Estes attended the University of Iowa and received a full scholarship to Juilliard studying under Sergius Kagan and Christopher West. He won the Munich International Vocal Competition in 1965 and subsequently was the silver medalist in the Tchaikovsky Competition in 1966. Estes made his operatic debut as Ramfis in *Aida* at the Deutsche Oper Berlin and since then has appeared in most of the world's major opera houses, including La Scala, the Hamburg State Opera, the Bavarian State Opera of Munich, the Vienna State Opera, the Lyric Opera of Chicago, the San Francisco Opera, and the Zurich Opera. He made his debut at the Metropolitan Opera in 1982, foregoing the honor of singing the national anthem on baseball's opening day—the day of his Met debut. He has appeared as soloist with most of the world's leading symphony orchestras. Estes was heard with the National Symphony of Washington at the opening of the Kennedy Center's Concert Hall in 1971. Estes spent the early part of his career making a name for himself in Europe. The grandson of a slave, Estes has been called the world's foremost bass-baritone.

Mr. Estes' 1988-1989 season includes an impressive array of international engagements. In addition to performing *Simon Boccanegra* (conducted by Giuseppe Sinopoli) and *The Flying Dutchman* with the Deutsche Opera, Berlin, he appeared in productions of *The Flying Dutchman*, *Salome*, and *Macbeth* in Vienna; *Parsiafal* in Barcelona; *Tosca* in Hannover and Dusseldorf; and a new production of *Prince Igor* in Munich. Mr. Estes also performs recitals and orchestral engagements in numerous European cities, including Paris, Zurich, Brussels, Munich, Bonn, Madrid, and Bordeaux. His North American highlights include appearances with the Chicago Symphony Orchestra conducted by Sir George Solti, and the Montreal Symphony conducted by Charles Dutoit.

In addition to having recorded The *Flying Dutchman*, he has recorded Handel's *Messfah*, the Faure *Requiem*, and Beethoven's *Ninth Symphony*, all conducted by Sir Colin Davis. Other recordings include spirituals and highlights from *Porgy and Bess*. He records exclusively for Philips Classics

*Louis Moreau Gottschalk enjoyed international fame for his music.*

### LOUIS MOREAU GOTTSCHALK
**Composer, Pianist**
**1829**

Louis Moreau Gottschalk was, perhaps, the first black composer born in the United States to achieve international renown. Chopin praised his debut at the Salle Pleyel in April 1844, and Berlioz, with whom he studied, applauded his "sovereign power."

Born in New Orleans, Gottschalk was a violin prodigy at six years of age and later became a brilliant concert pianist. He was already something of a European matinee idol when he first appeared in New York, on February 10, 1853, and his romantic compositions enjoyed a wide vogue.

Although Gottschalk went to Paris when he was 13 to study with Halle, Stamaty, and Maleden, much of his music reflected the Creole environment of his early childhood. One of his best-known compositions, *La Bamboula,* is based on the sights and sounds of New Orleans' Congo Square. His autobiographical book, *Notes of a Pianist,* provides an interesting description of his background and method of composition.

### RERI GRIST
**Coloratura Soprano**

Reri Grist, one of America's best coloratura sopranos, has sung at most of the world's great opera houses, including La Scala, Vienna State, Britain's Royal Opera, and the Met.

Miss Grist first came to national attention in the role of Consuela in Leonard Bernstein's *West Side Story*, and compounded this success in a performance of Mahler's *Fourth Symphony* with the New York Philharmonic.

When Dr. Herbert Graf, the former stage director of the Met, left in 1960 to become Director of the Zurich Opera, he persuaded many operatic talents, including Miss Grist, to accompany him there. While in Europe, Miss Grist was asked by Stravinsky to sing under his baton in *Le Rossignol.* In July 1964 she made a successful debut at the renowned Salzburg Festival in Austria. She now resides in Austria, where she is a national favorite.

### HELEN EUGENIA HAGAN
**Pianist**
**1893-1964**

Born in Portsmouth, New Hampshire, Ms. Hagan is a graduate of the Yale University School of Music. She received a Samuel Simmons Sanford Fellowship to study two years abroad and made her New York City debut in Aeolian Hall. Ms. Hagan was later on the faculty at Bishop College in Dallas, Texas.

*Reri Grist as Sophie in Richard Strauss* Der Rosenkavalier.

## HILDA HARRIS
### Mezzo-soprano

Hilda Harris is a native of Warrenton, North Carolina and has been heard frequently with the New York City Opera where her roles include Cherubino in *The Marriage of Figaro*, Orsini in *Lucrezia Borgia*, Smeton in *Anna Bolena*, and Nicklausse in *Tales of Hoffman*. Ms. Harris has also sung with the San Diego Opera, the Pittsburgh Opera, and the companies of Miami, St. Paul, and Fort Worth. She made her Metropolitan debut as the Wardrobe Mistress/The Schoolboy in the 1976-1977 premiere of Alban Berg's *Lulu*. Ms. Harris is an active orchestral soloist, having been heard with the New York Philharmonic, the Pittsburg Symphony, the Buffalo Philharmonic, and the Houston Symphony, as well as with orchestras in England, Holland, Luxembourg, and Switzerland.

## ROLAND HAYES
### Tenor
### 1887-1977

The success of Roland Hayes in the concert field played a great part in broadening the opportunities later afforded such singers as Paul Robeson and Marian Anderson.

Hayes was born of former slave parents in Curryville, Georgia on June 3, 1887. His tenant-farmer father was crippled by an accident and died when Hayes was 12. Determined that her seven children would not share her illiteracy, Hayes' mother sent them to Chattanooga, Tennessee, where they set up a rotating system whereby one brother worked while the others attended school. Hayes was employed in a machine shop, but when his turn came to go to school he passed it up, continuing to supply the family income while he studied at night.

In 1917, he became the first black to give a recital in Boston's Symphony Hall. Three years later he traveled to London and gave a royal command performance, following this up with other successes on the continent. Over the years, his rich, delicate tenor voice was used to good advantage in programs blended from Negro spirituals, folk songs, operatic arias, and German lieder.

Hayes gave a well-received farewell concert at Carnegie Hall in New York on the occasion of his seventy-fifth birthday in 1962.

During his career, Hayes received many awards and citations including eight honorary degrees and the NAACP's Spingarn Medal for the most outstanding achievement among blacks in 1925.

Hayes died in Boston on January 1, 1977 at the age of 89.

## BARBARA HENDRICKS
### Soprano

Barbara Hendricks, after graduating from the University of Nebraska with a bachelor of science degree in chemistry and mathematics, attended The Juilliard School and received a B.A. in voice. She later studied with Jennie Tourel. She made her first appearance with the New York Philharmonic in 1976. That same year she made her operatic debut in *Poppea* with the San Francisco Opera and performed *Orfro* with the Netherlands Opera at the Holland Festival. She has since sung with the opera companies of Boston, Glyndebourne, Hamburg and Santa Fe. In 1978 she sang the role of Susannah in an all-star production of *The Marriage of Figaro* with the Berlin Opera conducted by Daniel Barenboim. She repeated the role at the Aix-en-Provence Festival in 1979 with Neville Marriner conducting and again in Berlin in 1981 under the direction of Karl Bohm. She has also appeared as Gilda in *Rigolletto* and Pamina in *Die Zaubernoflote,* and in 1982, she was Nanetta in a highly acclaimed production of Falstaff co-produced by the Los Angeles Philharmonic, Covent Garden and the Florence Opera under the baton of Carlo Maria Giulini. That Spring also marked her Paris Opera debut as Juliette in *Romeo and Juliette*. She has recorded on several different labels.

## BEN HOLT
### Baritone

A native of Washington, D.C., Mr. Holt attended the Oberlin Conservatory of Music and was a scholarship student at Juilliard School, where he worked with Sixten Ehrling, Tito Gobbi and Manuel Rosenthal. He studied in Luciano Pavarotti's master classes and coached extensively with renowned pianist and coach Martin Isepp. While at the San Francisco Opera's Merola Program in master classes of Elisabeth Schwarzkopf, he was honored with an invitation to study privately at her studio in Zurich. He made his

*Ben Holt, he studied with Luciano Pavarotti.*

Metropolitan debut during the 1985-1986 season and in 1988 made his debut with the New York City Opera in the title role of *Malcolm X* by Anthony Davis . There he also performed in *Faust*. During 1988, he sang *Porgy and Bess* with the Calgary Opera in Canada, starred in *Le Nozze di Figaro* with the Cincinnati Opera. His New York Philharmonic debut was during the 1987-1988 season.

He has played such roles as I Papageno in *The Magic Flute*, Falke in *Die Fledermaus* and Ismenor in Rameau's *Dardanus*, as well as appearing in de Falla's *La Vida Breve* with the National Symphony under Rafael Fruhbeck de Burgos, Faure's *Requiem* and Gershwin's *Porgy and Bess* with the New Haven Symphony and Opera/South's nationally televised *A Bayou Legend* by William Grant Still.

Mr. Holt is the winner of many competitions and awards, including the Joy of Singing Competition, Oratorio Society of New York, Independent Black Opera Singers, Washington International and D'Angelo Young Artists Competition. He has been the recipient of a Sullivan Foundation grant and has worked with Phyllis Curtin and John Shirley-Quirk on Tanglewood Fellowships.

## ISOLA JONES
### Mezzo-soprano

Since making her Met debut in 1977 as Olga in *Eugene Onegin,* Isola Jones has been heard there in more than a dozen roles, including Maddalena in *Rigoletto*, which was telecast "Live from the Met," Lola in *Cavalleria Rusticana,* Mercedes in *Carmen*, and a Musician in *Manon Lescaut,* which was also televised in the "Live from the Met" series. Ms. Jones is a native of Chicago and a graduate of Northwestern University. She has sung Carmen with the Stamford State Opera and has been heard at Santa Fe, with the symphonies of Chicago, Los Angeles, Cleveland, Boston, and at the Ravinia Festival.

## ULYSSES KAY
### Composer, Educator
### 1917

Ulysses Simpson Kay is a traditionally trained classical composer and the creator of eloquent symphonic music.

Born in Tucson, he won a scholarship to the Eastman School of Music and went on to study with Paul Hindemith at Yale and Otto Luening at Columbia. He spent the years 1942-1945 in the Navy, where he played with the bands, and 1949-1952 in Rome studying music as a Fulbright fellow. He has visited the Soviet Union on a cultural exchange program and is currently Distinguished Professor of Music at Herbert H. Lehman College in New York.

Kay is a prolific composer. His works for voice, chamber groups, and orchestra include *Choral Triptych, Six Dances* (for string orchestra), *Fantasy Variations* (for orchestra), *Sinfonia in E*, and *The Boor* (an opera). He regularly performs and records throughout the United States and Europe.

Although his uncle was King Oliver, the legendary cornet player, Kay believes that jazz is a much more limited medium than symphonic music, where "you can express everything."

*Ulysses Kay composes elegant symphonic music.*

## HENRY LEWIS
### Conductor
### 1933

Henry Lewis attracted worldwide attention in the 1970s because of his conductorial abilities. He was the first black conductor of a leading American symphony orchestra when he was named to head the New Jersey Symphony Orchestra. Lewis was also the first black person to conduct *La Bohème* at the Metropolitan Opera in New York. He has served as assistant conductor of the Los Angeles Philharmonic and also formed and conducted his own orchestra, the Los Angeles Chamber Orchestra.

## DOROTHY MAYNOR
### Soprano
### 1910

Within a short time after her debut at New York's Town Hall in 1939, soprano Dorothy Maynor was being acclaimed by critics as a leading American singer. Since then, she has appeared as a soloist with almost every major symphony orchestra in the United States, and has made concert tours in Europe, Canada, and Latin America.

Born Dorothy Leigh Mayner (she changed the spelling of her last name when she became a singer) on September 3, 1910 in Norfolk, Virginia, she was raised in an atmosphere of music and singing. Nevertheless, she was originally intent on becoming a home economics teacher and, with this in mind, entered Hampton Institute at the age of 14. She received her B.S. degree in 1933, and shortly afterwards was heard by the director of the Westminster Choir, who made it possible for her to receive a scholarship at Westminster Choir College in Princeton, New Jersey.

*Robert McFerrin singing the role of Valentin* in Faust.

In 1935, she graduated with a B.M. degree and left for New York to study voice. After four years of directing a choir and teaching, she felt that she was ready for her New York debut, which took place in November of 1939. She had previously received support from Serge Koussevitzky, the conductor of the Boston Symphony Orchestra, who had once heard her sing and exclaimed: "The whole world must hear her!"

Miss Maynor has made several recordings for RCA Victor, and has been a guest artist on both radio and television. When not on tour she lives in New York City with her husband, the Reverend Shelby A. Rooks of St. James Church.

In 1975, Miss Maynor was elected to the Metropolitan Opera's board of directors, becoming the first black to sit on the Met board. She is founder of the Harlem School of the Arts in St. James Presbyterian Church, which is pastored by her husband. The school is now a huge complex on St. Nicholas Avenue in New York's Harlem.

## ROBERT McFERRIN
**Baritone**
**1921**

Born in Marianna, Arkansas, Robert McFerrin studied at Fisk University (1940-1941), Chicago Municipal College (1941-1942; 1946-1948), and Kathryn Turney Long School (1953). He sang the title role in *Rigoletto* with the New England Opera Company (1950), was a baritone soloist in the Lewisohn Stadium Summer Concert Series (1954), and made his Metropolitan Opera debut with the role of Amonasro in *Aida* (1955). He has been a guest professor of voice at Sibelius Academy, Finland (1959) and served as a member of the voice faculty at Nelson School of Fine Arts in Nelson, B.C., Canada.

## MYRA MERRITT
**Soprano**

Myra Merritt, a native of Washington, D.C., is a member of the Metropolitan Opera company's Young Artist Program. Ms. Merritt is a graduate of the Peabody Conservatory of Music where she studied with Flora Wend. She has been heard with the Washington Opera as Fleurette in Offenbach's *Christopher Columbus* and in the title role of Lehar's *The Merry Widow*. In 1981, Ms. Merritt sang Musetta in *La Bohème* with the Houston Grand Opera and has been heard with them as both Clara and Lily in their New York performances of *Porgy and Bess*. She made her Metropolitan Opera debut in January 1982 as the Shepherd in *Tannhauser*.

## LEONA MITCHELL
**Soprano**

Leona Mitchell is a native of Enid, Oklahoma and a graduate of Oklahoma University and subsequently a winner of the San Francisco Kurt Herbert Adler Award. Ms. Mitchell has been heard with the San Francisco Opera, the Washington Opera Society, the Houston Opera, and at the Gran Teatro del Liceo in Barcelona as Mathilde in Rossini's *William Tell*. Her orchestral appearances include concerts with the Cleveland Orchestra, the London Symphony, and the New Jersey Symphony. During the summer of 1980 she sang Bess in the Cleveland Orchestra Blossom Festival production of *Porgy and Bess* and performed the same role in their subsequent recording of the work. Ms. Mitchell made her Metropolitan Opera debut as Micaela in *Carmen* in December 1975 and since then has been heard there as Lauretta in *Gianni Schicci*, Pamina in *The Magic Flute*, and Madame Lidoine in *Dialogues of the Carmelites*.

## MICHAEL MORGAN
**Conductor**

Michael Morgan appeared with the New York Philharmonic in September, 1986, in the Leonard Bernstein Young American Conductors concerts. From 1980 to 1987, he was Exxon/Arts Endowment assistant conductor of the Chicago Symphony Orchestra, were he is now affiliate artist conductor. Previously, he was apprentice conductor of the Buffalo Philharmonic under music director Julius Rudel. Mr. Morgan has appeared as a guest conductor with many of our nation's major orchestras. Earlier this season, he made his New York City Opera debut conducting multiple performances of *La Traviata* in New York, Wolftrap, and Taiwan.

In Europe, Mr. Morgan has led performances of the Vienna State Opera, the Deutsche Staatsoper in East Berlin, the Vienna Symphony Orchestra, Warsaw Philharmonic Orchestra, and Danish Radio Orchestra.

The many awards Mr. Morgan has earned include first

prizes in the 1980 Hans Swarowsky International Conductors Competition (Vienna), the Gino Marrinuzzi International Conductors Competition (San Remo, Italy) and the Baltimore Symphony Young Conductors Competition.

Born in Washington, D.C., in 1957, Mr. Morgan attended the Oberlin College Conservatory of Music. He pursued additional studies at the Vienna master classes of Witold Rowicki and at the Berkshire Music Center at Tanglewood where he was a conducting fellow and student of Seiji Ozawa and Gunther Schuller.

### JESSYE NORMAN
**Soprano**

Jessye Norman grew up in Augusta, Georgia and attended Howard University in Washington, D.C. on a full scholarship. Ms. Norman graduated from Howard in 1967 with a music degree. Following her graduation from Howard, Ms. Norman spent what she calls "an unhappy summer" at the Peabody Conservatory in Baltimore. However, according to the soprano she couldn't put up with the "rat race" there so she enrolled at the University of Michigan to study with Pierre Bernac, one of the world's top teachers of art song. Ms. Norman has spent a great deal of her time in Germany, and in 1969, she was signed to a three-year contract by the Deutsche Oper in West Berlin where she was immediately put into major parts. She made her debut as Elisabeth in *Tannhauser*. Soon after, she sang the Countess Almaviva opposite Dietrich Fisher-Dieskau in *The Marriage of Figaro*. Before her debut in Berlin, she had sung in the Howard University chorus and appeared in small recitals, contests, and auditions.

In 1982, she received an Honorary Doctor of Music degree from Howard University, was named Musician of the Year by High Fidelity Musical/America in 1982, and in 1983 received the Grand Prix du Disque Academie Charles Cros.

*Leona Mitchell, winner of the Kurt Herbert Adler Award in San Francisco.*

### COLERIDGE-TAYLOR PERKINSON
**Composer**
**1932**

Coleridge-Taylor Perkinson has been a figure in explorative musical movements in both Hollywood and New York.

Born in New York, Perkinson took graduate and postgraduate degrees from the Manhattan School of Music (1953, 1954), before going on to study at the Berkshire Music Center, the Mozarteum, and the Netherland Radio Union Hilversum. Becoming first composer-in-residence for the Negro Ensemble Company, he wrote the music for many plays, including Peter Weiss' *Song of the Lusitanian Bogey*, Ray McIver's *God Is a (Guess What?)*, and Errol Hill's *Man Better Man*. In 1965, when the Symphony of the New World was organized in New York, Perkinson was named associate conductor. His concert pieces include *Concerto for Violin and Orchestra* (1954) and *Attitudes* (1964), written for black opera star George Shirley. Perkinson has also composed music for television and radio programs, documentary films (*Cross-roads Africa* ), and ballet ensembles.

### JULIA PERRY
**Composer**
**1927**

Julia Perry, born in Akron, Ohio, studied composition, piano, and voice at the Westminster Choir School in Princeton, New Jersey. After taking her M.A. there, she continued her musical studies at Juilliard, at the Berkshire Music Center, and in Europe with Luigi Dallapiccola and Nadia Boulanger. Her best-known works are *Stabat Mater* (1951), for solo voice and string orchestra; *A Short Piece for Orchestra* (1952); *Pastoral* (1969), for flute and strings; and *Homunculus, C. F.* (1969), for soprano and percussion. She has also written two operas, *The Bottle* and *The Cask of Amontillado*.

### KARL HAMPTON PORTER
**Conductor**
**1939**

Karl Porter was born in Pittsburgh, Pennsylvania on April 25, 1939. As a youngster he had no knowledge or familiarity with classical music until he inadvertently turned the dial on his grandmother's old Philco radio and had his heart and soul captured by an Arturo Toscannini symphony orchestra radio program; he was about eight years of age at the time. Finding other classical radio programs were very difficult for young Karl, not only did he have difficulty spinning the radio dial to find the classics but his grandmother, whom he lived with, did not favor this type of music and controlled the programming to suit her taste. Karl was raised by his grandparents and they gave him little if any encouragement to his efforts to discover and develop in the classics. There was a piano in the home upon which Karl became self-taught, but when he began "banging on it" his grandmother gave the piano away to their church. While in elementary school he would walk 3 miles out of his way home to stop at the church and "pound away at the old piano."

During his high school years he played the saxophone and became totally self-taught on the bassoon and became so proficient that he played the instrument for the Pittsburgh Youth Symphony Orchestra and played first chair in the All-State band and orchestra. He obtained his musical education at the Carnegie-Mellon University in Pittsburgh, Pennsylvania (1958-60), the Peabody Conservatory in Baltimore, Maryland (1960-62), the Juilliard School of Music in New York ( 1962-63), the Domaine School for Conductors in Hancock, Maine ( 1961-63 ), the American Symphony Orchestra League's Institute for Conductors at Orkney Springs, Virginia, and the Berkshire Music Center at Tanglewood, Massachusetts (all on scholarship). At Baltimore's famed Peabody Institute he became the first African-American in the schools history to be elected President of the Student Council, and later, the first African-American bassoonist to play with a major symphony orchestra.

He played bassoon in various organizations, including the Denver Symphony Orchestra (1964-65), American Symphony (1960-61), Metropolitan Opera National Company orchestra (1964-65), Gil Evans's jazz band (1967-69) New Jersey Symphony, and Symphony of the New World. During the late 1960s he founded several groups in the Harlem community of New York; among them, the Harlem Youth Symphony (1968-70), Harlem Philharmonic Orchestra (1969), New Breed Brass Ensemble, Harlem String Quartet, and the Harlem Woodwind Quintet. Some of the musicians in these groups were non-professionals. In 1972, he started and developed the New York City Housing Authority Orchestra. Also during that year he became music director

*Orchestra conductor Karl Hampton Porter at rehearsal.*

for Josephine Baker. In 1971, he was appointed conductor of the Massapequa (New York) Symphony Society. His teaching experience included tenures at the Newark New Jersey Community Arts Center (1971) and the New York City Community College of the City University of New York (1972). From 1967 he also was active as a free-lance bassoonist and guest orchestral conductor. His honors included grants from the Rockefeller Foundation (1969), and the National Endowment for the Arts (1970).

## LEONTYNE PRICE
### Lyric Soprano
### 1927

Leontyne Price is one of the world's leading lyric sopranos. Her career in concerts and opera has brought her the praise of public and critics alike.

Miss Price was born in Laurel, Mississippi on February 10, 1927, and received her B.A. in 1948 from the College of Education and Industrial Arts (now Central State College) in Wilberforce, Ohio. She later accepted a scholarship to Juilliard where she studied with Florence Page Kimball.

After seeing her in the student production of Verdi's *Falstaff,* Virgil Thompson, the noted composer and critic, selected her to sing in the revival of his *Four Saints in Three Acts,* which was performed on Broadway for two weeks in 1952. She then played the role of Bess in the 1952 revival of *Porgy and Bess,* and continued in the part on a tour sponsored by the U.S. State Department.

During the run of *Porgy and Bess,* she introduced works by Stravinsky, Henri Saguet, John La Montaine and others at such places as the Metropolitan Museum in New York and Constitution Hall in Washington, D.C.

Miss Price made her Metropolitan debut in *Il Trovatore* on January 27, 1961. Since then, she has made numerous recordings of operas and operatic arias. She was married to the noted African-American bass baritone William Warfield.

In 1961, just one season after she had made her Met debut as Leonora in Verdi's *Il Trovatore,* Miss Price had her first Met opening in the title role of Puccini's *The Girl of the Golden West.* Since then, she has made numerous recordings of operas and operatic arias. She opened the new Metropolitan Opera House at Lincoln Center in Barber's *Antony and Cleopatra.*

In the world of opera, Miss Price ranks alongside Birgit Nilsson, Joan Sutherland, and Renata Tebaldi as one of the most esteemed and celebrated sopranos of the contemporary era. Her voice is said to be the perfect Verdi voice; her *Aida* is often regarded as the paragon against which all others should be measured.

On April 20, 1982 Miss Price opened the convention of the Daughters of the American Revolution in Constitution Hall with a concert honoring Marian Anderson. It was in 1939 that Miss Anderson was barred from appearing in Constitution Hall by the DAR, prompting Eleanor Roosevelt to resign in anger from the organization. In September 1981, Miss Price opened the 1981-1982 concert series at Rutgers University in New Brunswick, New Jersey, which marked her first New Jersey appearance after 15 years. In 1977, she was awarded the San Francisco Opera medal in honor of the twentieth anniversary of her debut with the company.

## FLORENCE QUIVAR
### Mezzo-soprano

A native of Philadelphia, Florence Quivar graduated from the Academy of Music and was a member of the Juilliard Opera Theater. She has been a soloist with practically all of the major symphony orchestras in the United States, including the New York Philharmonic, the Cleveland Orchestra, the Cincinnati Symphony, and the Boston Symphony. Ms. Quivar made her debut in New York in 1973 as soloist for Verdi's *Requiem* with the National Orchestral Association at Carnegie Hall, and has also sung that work with Giulini and the Los Angeles Philharmonic and with Muti and the Philadelphia Orchestra. Since Ms. Quivar's Metropolitan Opera debut as Marina during the 1977-1978 opening night performance of *Boris Godunov,* she has been heard there as Suzuki in *Madame Butterfly,* Fides in *Le Prophegte,* and Isabella in *L'Italiana in Algeri.*

*Leontyne Price is said to have the perfect Verdi voice.*

In 1983, she was invited by Zubin Mehta to perform with him and the Israel Philharmonic on a tour of the festivals of Caracas, Salzburg, Lucerne, London, Frankfurt, Bonn, Edinburgh and Florence. She has appeared in a gala Carnegie Hall concert performance of *Four Saints in Three Acts* in celebration of Virgil Thomson's 85th birthday, a Bach 300th birthday celebration at Alice Tully Hall with Gerard Schwarz, a concert with Kathleen Battle as part of the Great Performers series at Alice Tully Hall, and a nationally televised PBS "Gala of Stars" broadcast.

### PHILIPPA SCHUYLER
**Pianist**
**1932-1969**

Philippa Schuyler was at one time considered to be one of America's most outstanding musical prodigies. Remembered as a mature concert pianist who died tragically at the height of her powers, she first gained recognition for her piano artistry and original compositions as a child.

Born on August 21, 1932 in New York City, Miss Schuyler was already playing the piano at the age of two and began composing a year later. By the time she was eight, she had some 50 compositions to her credit. (Her published works include *Six Little Pieces* and *Eight Little Pieces*.)

At 12, her first symphonic composition, *Manhattan Nocturne*, was performed at Carnegie Hall, and the following year her scherzo, *Rumpelstiltskin*, was written and subsequently performed by the Dean Dixon Youth Orchestra, the Boston Pops, the New Haven Symphony Orchestra, and the New York Philharmonic. Miss Schuyler herself was a soloist with the last-named orchestra.

In 1953, she made her debut at Town Hall in New York. She then traveled in some 50 countries on good will concert tours sponsored by the U.S. State Department.

Gifted also as a writer, Miss Schuyler was the author of such books as *Adventures in Black and White* (1960), and *Who Killed the Congo?* (1962).

### GEORGE SHIRLEY
**Tenor**
**1934**

Tenor George Shirley has sung more than 20 leading roles at the Metropolitan since his debut there as Fernando in *Cosi Fan Tutte* on October 24, 1961.

Shirley, winner of the 1960-1961 Metropolitan Opera auditions, was born April 18, 1934 in Indianapolis, and moved to Detroit in 1940. There he began giving vocal recitals in churches, and decided on a musical career after playing baritone horn in the community band. In 1955, he graduated from Wayne State University in Detroit with a B.S. in musical education.

After his discharge from the Army in 1959 he began serious vocal studies with Themy S. Georgi. In June of that year he made his operatic debut as Eisenstein in Strauss's *Die Fledermaus*, performing with the Turnau Players in Woodstock. A year later he won the American Opera Auditions, whereupon he journeyed to Milan, Italy, making his opera debut there in Puccini's *La Bohème*.

*Tenor George Shirley sings over twenty roles with the Metropolitan Opera company.*

In 1961, his career was given tremendous impetus by his victory in the Metropolitan Opera auditions. Recording, opera, and television engagements were numerous that year. In 1963, he made his debut at Carnegie Hall with the Friends of French Opera, singing opposite Rita Gorr in Massenet's *La Navarraise*.

Since then, he has sung with several of the Met's leading divas, including Renata Tebaldi in *Simon Boccanegra* and Birgit Nilsson in *Salome*. In 1974, he sang the title role in Mozart's *Idomeneo* at the Glyndeburne Festival, and he has remained a favorite at the Met over the years.

By now, Shirley has so broadened and refined his repertory that he is at home in virtually every major opera culture in Europe. He has made several European tours, performing with the leading orchestras on the continent and at the most prestigious opera houses there.

In 1973, Shirley initiated a radio program on WQXR (N.Y.) entitled *Afro-American Artists in the Classical Field*.

**ANDREW SMITH**
**Baritone**

A native of Lexington, Kentucky, Andrew Smith received his bachelors degree from Kentucky State University and his masters from Roosevelt University. Smith also pursued doctoral studies at Northwestern University. He made his operatic debut in 1969 with Beverly Sills at Chicago's Grant Park Summer Festival in *La Traviata*. He has been heard with the Chicago Symphony, the Cleveland Orchestra, the Buffalo Philharmonic, and he toured with the Houston Grand Opera's production of *Porgy and Bess*. Smith is a member of the New York City Opera and made his Metropolitan Opera debut in the premiere of *Billy Budd*, singing the role of the First Mate.

**HALE SMITH**
**Composer, Teacher**

Hale Smith composes symphonic music whose elements stretch from avant-garde concepts of tone rows to erotic Brazilian dances.

Born in Cleveland, Ohio, Smith's musicianship was nurtured there at the Jeliffe's Karamu House, where he had the opportunity to write scores for such stage productions as Lorca's *Yerma* and *Blood Wedding, and Contours for Orchestra*. The latter, perhaps his best known work, builds its virile power by balancing abrasive, protesting brass against cool strings. Other works include *In Memoriam: Beryl Rubinstein* (chorus and chamber orchestra); *Epicedial Variations* (violin and piano); and *Music for Harp and Orchestra*.

**WILLIAM GRANT STILL**
**Composer**
**1895-1978**

William Grant Still was acclaimed as the "dean of African-American composers." He has numerous firsts to his credit, and his musical inspiration and skills united both classical and folk traditions.

Born in Woodville, Mississippi, Still received his early musical training at home. He attended Wilberforce University and then studied at the Oberlin Conservatory of Music and the New England Conservatory. Work with George W. Chadwick and Edgar Varese completed his formal studies.

Still's early work was as an arranger for jazz orchestras, but he soon turned to composition, making use of his jazz background in a more classical framework. It was the performance of his *Afro-American Symphony* in 1931 by the Rochester Philharmonic under Howard Hanson that brought him real recognition. This was the first time a major orchestra had performed a full-length piece by an African-American composer. In 1936, Still became the first African-American to conduct a major American orchestra when he gave a program of his own compositions at the Hollywood Bowl.

He won two Guggenheim Fellowships during his lifetime. One was in 1944 and the other in 1961. In 1939, he was invited to compose the theme song for New York's world's fair.

Still wrote seven operas as well as composing music for films (*Pennies from Heaven*), radio, and television (*Perry Mason* and *Gunsmoke*). His numerous serious works reflect many sides of African-American life. Stokowski called him "one of our greatest American composers."

Still died in December 1978 in a nursing home in Los Angeles at the age of 83.

**HOWARD SWANSON**
**Composer**
**1909-1978**

Howard Swanson was born in Atlanta and raised in Cleveland, where he studied at the Institute of Music. He was taught composition by Herbert Elwell. In 1938, he won a Rosenwald Fellowship to study with Nadia Boulanger in Paris. Returning to the United States, he devoted himself to composition, and in 1950, won wide acclaim as well as serious attention as an American composer when his *Short Symphony*, written in 1948, was performed by the New York Philharmonic with Dmitri Mitropoulos conducting. In 1952, this symphony won the New York Critics' Award. One of Swanson's well-known works is the song "The Negro Speaks of Rivers," based on a poem by Langston Hughes, which Marian Anderson has sung in recital.

Swanson died in 1978 at New York Hospital. In 1979, at the St. James Presbyterian Church in New York City a concert was given by the Triad Chorale as a memorial to him and William Grant Still.

**ARTHUR THOMPSON**
**Baritone**

Baritone Arthur Thompson is a graduate of the Hartt College of Music and the Juilliard School. He is a former member of the Metropolitan Opera Studio and has been heard with the Juilliard Opera Theater, the Chautauqua Opera, the Aspen Summer Opera, and the Yale Summer Opera Theater. Thompson has also been heard as a soloist with the St. Louis Symphony, the Miami Symphony, the Hartford Symphony, the Milwaukee Symphony, and the Pro Arte Chorale. He was also heard as St. Ignatius Loyola in Thomson's *Four Saints in Three Acts* during the first season of the Mini-Met in 1973. Thompson made his Metropolitan Opera debut in 1974 in *Madame Butterfly*, and has also been heard there in *Boris Godunov, Fidelio, Tosca, Lohengrin*, and *Otello*.

**SHIRLEY VERRETT**
**Mezzo-soprano**

Mezzo-soprano Shirley Verrett is a striking and talented recitalist and opera performer whose most electrifying role has been in the title role of Bizet's *Carmen*, which she has performed to rave notices in the great opera houses of the world.

Born of a musical family in New Orleans, Miss Verrett moved to California at the age of five, but had no formal voice training during her childhood largely because her father felt singing would involve his daughter in too precarious a career. Still, he offered his daughter the opportunity to sing

*Shirley Verrett as Cassandra in Berlioz' Les Troyens.*

in church choirs under his direction, and provided her with an ample education at Ventura College, where she majored in business administration. By 1954, she was a prosperous real estate agent, but her longing for an artistic career had become so acute that she decided to take voice lessons in Los Angeles and train her sights on the concert stage after all.

After winning a television talent show in 1955, she enrolled at the Juilliard School on a scholarship, taking her diploma in voice some six years later. Her debut at Town Hall in 1958 was not a sensational one, earning plaudits for her "sensitive, imaginative... comprehension," even as it inspired the conclusion that she was perhaps only an "earnest, conscientious" singer who was well coached and adequately prepared.

At Spoleto, Italy in 1962, she delivered an excellent *Carmen* and was praised for a "warm vibrant voice and earthy womanliness." A year later, she performed at Lincoln Center in New York, where her recital was said to be "simply without flaws, simply a great event in the annals of American music-making."

By 1964 her *Carmen* had improved so dramatically that the New York *Herald Tribune* critic was able to claim it as "the finest" performance "seen or heard in New York" for the past generation. Other performances in such roles as Orfeo in Gluck's *Orfeo ed Euridice*, Ulrica in Verdi's *Un Ballo de Maschera*, and recently Leonora in Beethoven's *Fidelio* have been met with comparable acclaim.

In 1982, Miss Verrett appeared with Grace Bumbry in a concert honoring Marian Anderson on her eightieth birthday. Miss Verrett sang the "Salce" and "Ave Maria" from Verdi's *Otello*. In September 1977, she appeared with conductor Zubin Mehta on WNET-TV's "Live From Lincoln Center." The *New York Times* has hailed Miss Verrett as "a singer of intelligence, beauty and good vocal endowment." Her yearly recital tours take her to the major music centers throughout the country.

During the 1986-1987 season the successes for Miss Verrett included a series of operas staged especially for her by the Paris Opera; Rossini's *Mose*, Cherubini's *Medee* and Gluck's *Iphigenie en Tauride* and *Alceste*. She made a triumphant return to the Metropolitan Opera in 1986 as Eboli in *Don Carlo* and also starred that year in a new production of Macbeth with the San Francisco Opera. In the 1987/88 season, Shirley Verrett made her long awaited Chicago Lyric Opera debut as Lucena in Il trovatore. She also opened the 1988 San Francisco Opera season as Selika in *L'Africaine*.

## GEORGE WALKER
**Concert Pianist, Educator**
**1922**

George Walker's music has a strong foundation in his distinguished career as a concert recitalist.

Born in Washington, D.C., he studied at Oberlin, the Curtis Institute of Music, and at the Eastman School, where he completed his doctorate. His teachers included Rudolf Serkin, Giancarlo Menotti, and Robert Casadesus. Following his well-received Town Hall debut in 1945, Walker gained 20 seasons of experience touring the United States, Canada, and Europe. He is currently a professor at Rutgers University in Newark.

Recently, Dr. Walker's compositions have inclined toward pointillistic and serial styles. However, the neoclassical disciplines which shaped his earlier works are still in evidence. His major works include the *Address for Orchestra, Gloria in Memoriam* for women's voices and organ, and *Variations for Orchestra,* which exemplifies his stylistic development.

## WILLIAM WARFIELD
### Baritone

One of the most distinguished concert baritones in the world today is William Warfield, who made his debut at New York's Town Hall in March 1950.

Warfield was born in West Helena, Arkansas, and later moved with his family to Rochester, New York, where he attended school. The son of a Baptist minister, he received early training in voice, organ, and piano and, in 1938, while a student at Washington Junior High School, won the vocal competition at the Music Educators National Convention in St. Louis.

He then studied at the Eastman School of Music and the University of Rochester, receiving his A.B. while in the Army, where he worked in intelligence because of his fluency in Italian, French, and German. At the close of World War II he returned to Eastman before spending a year traveling with the national company of *Call Me Mister*.

After his resounding New York debut in 1950, he made an unprecedented tour of Australia under the auspices of the Australian Broadcasting Commission. A year later he made his movie debut in *Show Boat*.

Warfield then appeared on several major television shows and starred in the NBC television version of *Green Pastures*. Between 1952 and 1959 he made five international tours under the auspices of the U.S. State Department.

His performances as Porgy in the various revivals of *Porgy and Bess* have made him the best-known singer in this role. He was married to Leontyne Price, the brilliant opera star whom he met during a Porgy and Bess production.

In 1966, he appeared in a revival of the Jerome Kern-Edna Ferber classic, *Showboat*. In 1971 he performed the role in Austria.

## ANDRE WATTS
### Pianist

One of America's most gifted young pianists, Andre Watts achieved a substantial degree of fame while playing under the baton of Leonard Bernstein of the New York Philharmonic.

Born in Nuremberg, Germany of a Hungarian mother and an American G.I. father, Watts spent the first eight years of his life on Army posts in Europe before moving to Philadelphia, his current place of residence. By the time he was nine, he was already good enough to perform as a soloist with the Philadelphia Orchestra.

At the age of 17, Watts appeared on television in one of Leonard Bernstein's Young People's Concerts and was a huge success. After graduating from Lincoln Prep. in Philadelphia, he enrolled at Baltimore's Peabody Conservatory of Music.

On one occasion, when Glenn Gould became ill just prior to a performance with the New York Philharmonic, Bernstein chose Watts as a last-minute replacement. At the conclusion of the concerto, Watts received a standing ovation not only from the audience but from the orchestra as well.

In June 1966, Watts made his debut in London, and a month later was the soloist for the two-day Philharmonic Stravinsky Festival at Lincoln Center.

In the 1970s, Watts gave a concert in Teheran as part of the coronation festivities for the then Shah of Iran, and later, at a state dinner for Congo's President Mobutu he was presented with the African republic's highest honor, the Order of the Zaire. Watts also performed at President Richard M. Nixon's inaugural concert.

## OLLY WILSON
### Composer
### 1937

Olly Wilson, one of the nation's leading young composers, won the first International Electronic Music Competition (Dartmouth, N.H., 1968) with his *Cetus*.

Born in St. Louis, Wilson's high school clarinet playing

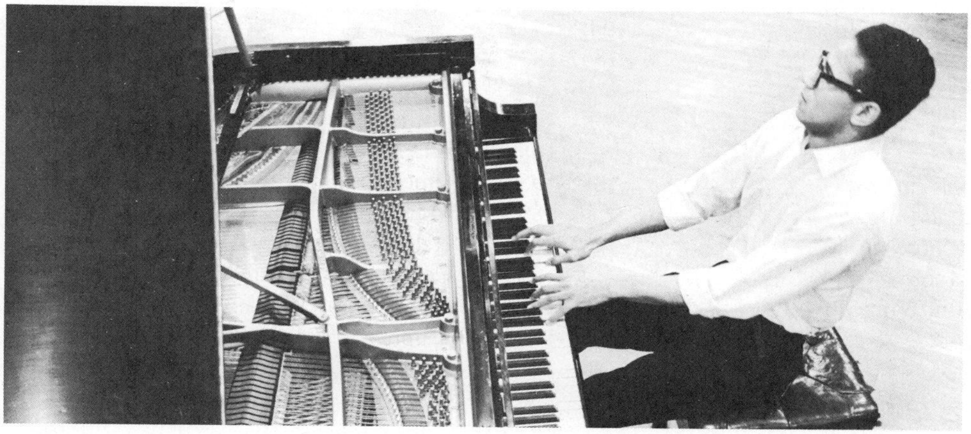

*Andre Watts, one of America's most gifted young pianists; at rehearsal with the New York Philharmonic .*

led to a scholarship at hometown Washington University. After taking a Ph.D. in composition at the State University of Iowa, he began focusing on electronic music at Illinois' Studio for Experimental Music. His practical experience has included playing double bass with symphony orchestras in St. Louis and Cedar Rapids, Iowa, and also with jazz groups. He has since spent a year of research in Africa, particularly Ghana, and is currently a faculty member at Berkeley.

Wilson's best-known works are the *Sextet* (1963), *Three Movements for Orchestra* (1964), and *Cetus* (1967). Even prior to turning to electronic sounds, Dr. Wilson's employment of traditional media stressed innovative sonorities, with such works as *Wry Fragments* (1961) for tenor and percussion, *And Death Shall Have No Dominion* (1963) for tenor and percussion, and *Chanson Innocent* (1965) for contralto and two bassoons. Wilson's style springs from his belief that an African-American composer's "reality" is different. He draws upon a wide spectrum of music not normally regarded as part of the Euro-American tradition.

## DANIEL J. WINDHAM
### Producer

In his position as Director of Educational Activities for the New York Philharmonic, Daniel J. Windham is responsible for the production of educational activities and concerts, including the Young People's Concerts of the Philharmonic. Prior to his Philharmonic appointment, Mr. Windham was Director of Education and Audience Development of the National Symphony Orchestra in Washington, D.C. He has also served as Director of Music Programs and Artists-in-Schools Coordinator for the District of Columbia Commission on the Arts and Humanities, and was for five years lecturer in Music History at Wellesley College. A baritone who has performed with the Boston Symphony, Boston Pops and the Opera Society of Washington, Mr. Windham has devised and narrated concerts for young people for the Boston Symphony, the Baltimore Symphony and for hundreds of educational programs around the country.

## OTHER NOTABLE CLASSICAL MUSICIANS

### Composers

| Name | Born |
|---|---|
| Alton Augustus Adams | 1889-? |
| Walter Anderson | 1915 |
| Thomas Green Bethune | 1849-1908 |
| Edward Boatner | 1898 |
| J. Harold Brown | 1902 |
| Harry Thacker Burleigh | 1866-1949 |
| Melville Charlton | 1880 |
| Edgar Rogie Clark | 1917 |
| Charles L. Cooke | 1891-1958 |
| Noel G. DeCosta | 1929 |
| Claude Brindis DeSala | ?-1912 |
| R. Nathaniel Dett | 1882-1943 |
| Carl Diton | 1886 |
| Shirley Lola Graham DuBois | 1906-1977 |
| Azalia Hackley | 1867-1922 |
| Margaret Harris | |
| Noral Holt | |
| Hall Johnson | 1888 |
| J. Rosamund Johnson | 1873-1954 |
| Penman Livingood | 1895 |
| Carman Leroy Moore | 1936 |
| Undine Smith Moore | 1905 |
| Clarence Cameron White | 1880-1960 |
| John Wesley Work | 1901-1967 |

### Concert Artists

| Name | Talent | Born |
|---|---|---|
| William Duncan Allen | Pianist | 1908 |
| Flora Batson Bergen | Soprano | 1865-? |
| Carol Brice | Singer | 1918 |
| Annie Wiggins Brown | Singer | 1915 |
| Terry Cook | Bass Baritone | |
| Mark S. Doss | Bass | |
| Lillian Fuanti | Singer | |
| Elizabeth Taylor Greenfield | Singer | 1809-1876 |
| Hazel Harrison | Pianist | 1881-? |
| Greogory Hopkins | Tenor | |
| Sissieretta Jones | Singer | 1868-1933 |
| Patricia Miller | Mezzo-Soprano | |
| Abbie Mitchell | Singer-actress | 1845-1924 |
| Nellie Brown Mitchell | Singer | |
| Etta Moten | Singer | |
| Othello Pumphrey | Singer | 1921 |
| Muriel Rahn | Singer | |
| Helen Thigpen | Singer | |
| Camilla E. Williams | Soprano | |
| Maria Selika Williams | Soprano | |
| Karen Williams | Soprano | |

# THE JAZZ SCENE

**The Medium and Its Background ■ Early Recordings and Improvisation ■ Jazz in the Twenties and Thirties ■ The Post WW II Period ■ A New Audience ■ The Varied Sounds of Jazz ■ Outstanding Jazz Artists**

In a time span of less than a century, the remarkable native American music called jazz has risen from obscure origins to become the most original form of musical expression of our times, loved, admired and played throughout the globe. Jazz has a long and rich ancestry. Its roots go back to the arrival of the first Africans on American soil and the encounter between native African and European musical traditions. Black music in America took many forms, including work songs, gospel and spirituals, and many and varied kinds of music for dancing.

By the late 19th century, a dance music called ragtime became very popular. Its heavily syncopated rhythms and sprightly melodies had a distinctly Afro-American flavor. Its greatest exponent was Scott Joplin (1868-1917) whose music was rediscovered in the 1970s. About the same time, a form of black American folk music called the blues coalesced into a 12-bar pattern that made it adaptable to popular song writing. The blues has a unique harmonic quality derived from a "flattening" of the third and seventh notes of the tempered scale, and while seemingly simple, lends itself to infinite variation. The blues had an impact not only on jazz, but later on such styles as rock and soul music, both of which would be unthinkable without the blues element.

It was when ragtime (primarily an instrumental music) and blues (at first primarily a vocal style) came together that jazz was born, and though this process was taking place in many parts of America, it was in New Orleans that the basic language of jazz first was spoken.

This was due not only to the rich musical tradition of this port city (with its international climate), but also because social conditions in New Orleans, while certainly not free from racist elements, were less restrictive and more open than in other large American cities of the time. Thus, there was much contact between musicians of varied ethnic background. Many histories of jazz mistakenly overemphasize the importance of the New Orleans red light district (called Storyville). While early jazz certainly was performed there, many other outlets for music-making existed. These included dances, parades, carnivals, and the traditional New Orleans funerals, for which a band would accompany the casket from church to cemetery with mournful strains, and then lead the march back to town with lively, peppy music including ragtime and early jazz.

Musicians from New Orleans began to tour the United States from about 1907 on, and had a big influence wherever they went. However, their intricate style of collective improvisation, in which each instrument in the band had its own specific role, was not so easily absorbed. It is another myth of jazz history that most of these early jazz players were a special breed of self-taught "naturals;" in fact, almost all of them had good basic musical training, and many could read music well.

*In New Orleans, bamboo drums and many-vowelled African chants made the music for exuberant and sensuous dance marathons.*

## Early Recordings and Improvisation

Jazz developed almost simultaneously with the phonograph, and without dissemination on records, it is unlikely that jazz would have spread as quickly as it did. By studying recorded performances, musicians anywhere could learn at least the rudiments of jazz, a spontaneous music in which improvisation played a considerable role. "Improvisation" is a much misunderstood concept. It does not mean inventing music on the spot, without guidelines. It does mean adding one's own personal ideas to a common musical text, and taking liberties as long as they fit within a shared framework. In addition, a jazz musician's personal style will be based on tonal qualities, a distinctive approach to rhythm and phrasing, and a vocabulary of melodic and thematic characteristics. Taken together, these ingredients are what makes it possible for a seasoned listener to almost immediately identify who is playing in a jazz performance, provided that the musician has developed his own personal style.

Ironically, the first New Orleans jazz to be recorded was performed by a white group, the Original Dixieland Jazz Band, in 1917. By then, black musicians had already made records, but they were not in a jazz idiom. It would take some five more years before the best black New Orleans players got to make records. In the meanwhile, however, some of them had already visited Europe, notably the great clarinetist and soprano saxophonist Sidney Bechet (1897-1959), who has been called the first great jazz soloist. But it was a somewhat younger New Orleanian, Louis Armstrong (1901-1971), who would have the biggest impact on the future of jazz.

Armstrong, who was brought to Chicago (by then the center of jazz activity) in 1922 by his mentor and fellow trumpeter Joe "King" Oliver (1885-1938) and made his first records there, came to New York two years later to join the band of Fletcher Henderson (1897-1952). This was the first musically significant big band in jazz. While most New Orleans jazz bands used an instrumentation of trumpet, trombone, clarinet, piano, guitar (or banjo), bass (string or brass) and drums, the early big bands used three trumpets, one or two trombones, three reeds (saxophonists doubling clarinet), and the same rhythm section instruments.

They employed written scores (called arrangements), but gave the soloists freedom to "improvise" their contributions.

Armstrong's arrival was a revelation to the Henderson band. His first solos on its records stand out like diamonds in a tin setting. What Louis brought to jazz was, first of all, his superior sense of rhythm that made other players sound stiff and clumsy in comparison. He discovered the rhythmic element called "swing" that sets jazz apart from other musics; a kind of rhythmic thrust that seems to float and soar. In addition, his sound on the trumpet was the biggest and most musically appealing yet heard, and he had exceptional range and powers of execution. Further, his gifts of melodic invention were so great that he can well be said to have laid the foundation for jazz as a medium for personal expression by an instrumental soloist.

One of his first Henderson colleagues to get the message was tenor saxophonist Coleman Hawkins (1904-1969), who soon created the first influential jazz style on his instrument. Also greatly affected was the band's chief arranger, Don Redman (1900-1964), who was the first to translate Louis' discoveries to big-band arranging. Many others followed suit, especially after Louis, now back in Chicago, began to make records with his own studio groups, the Hot Fives and Hot Sevens.

*Ads for the early jazz arrivals to New York City.*

## Jazz in the Twenties and Thirties

By the late 1920s, jazz had become a mainstay of American popular dance music and had spread to Europe as well. Black American musicians were touring world-wide, even in such exotic places as China and India, and wherever they went, their music left an imprint. Yet there was still quite a gap between jazz at its best and the more commercially acceptable versions of it. Not until the advent of the so-called "Swing Era" did unadulterated jazz reach a level of popular acceptance which, thus far, remains unmatched.

This was first of all due to the big bands, which had reached a new height of artistic maturity. This was in no small degree the result of the efforts of Duke Ellington (1899-1974), rightly called the greatest American composer. His unique band, for which he gradually created a perfect balance between written and improvised elements, not least due to such great soloists as Johnny Hodges (alto sax), Harry Carney (baritone sax), Barney Bigard (clarinet), Cootie Williams and Rex Stewart (trumpets), began a most important engagement at Harlem's famous Cotton Club in late 1927. Via appearances there, regular network radio broadcasts, and many recordings, Ellington's music was widely disseminated. His band visited Europe for the first time in 1933.

Other important work was done by Redman and by Benny Carter (b. 1907), a brilliant multi-instrumentalist and arranger-composer. Fletcher Henderson himself, had not previously arranged for his band, but began to do so in the early 1930s and soon became one of the best. Such efforts lay the foundation for the success of Benny Goodman (1909-1987), a white clarinetist and band leader, who commissioned the best black arrangers and also was the first white band leader to hire black musicians (pianist Teddy Wilson in early 1936; vibraphonist Lionel Hampton later that year).

By 1936, the Swing Era was under way. Black dance styles set at such places as Harlem's Savoy Ballroom swept the nation, and young people jitterbugged to the sounds of an astonishing number of excellent bands. Those led by Jimmie Lunceford and Count Basie (1905-1985) stood out among the many. The big bands spawned a host of gifted young players and also brought into the limelight many giants with established jazz reputations, such as Armstrong, who led his own big bands from 1929 to 1947.

*Joe "King" Oliver and the Creole Band introduced New Orleans Jazz to San Francisco in 1921.*

## The Post WW II Period

World War II brought economic and social changes that affected the big bands. Gasoline rationing impaired the constant touring that was one of their mainstays. The singers, whose popularity was first established through their work with the bands, became stars in their own right. After the war, the advent of television wrought fundamental changes in the ways people entertained themselves. Among the chief victims of the new stay-at-home trend was ballroom dancing. The big bands went into rapid decline, and only a handful maintained themselves, among them Ellington and Basie.

Meanwhile, the music itself had also undergone fundamental changes. The new generation of players who had come to maturity by way of big-band experiences were eager to express themselves at greater length than most big-band work permitted, and they were also coming up with new and potentially radical musical ideas.

The most advanced soloists of the Swing Era, such as Roy Eldridge (trumpet), Lester Young (tenor sax), Art Tatum (piano) and Sid Catlett (drums) had been extending the rhythmic, harmonic and technical resources of their instruments. Two young geniuses, both doomed to early death by tuberculosis, guitarist Charlie Christian (1916-1942), featured with Benny Goodman, and bassist Jimmy Blanton (1918-1942), featured with Duke Ellington, revolutionized the language of their respective instruments.

Christian was among the many notable players who participated in jam sessions (informal musical get-together) at Minton's Playhouse, a night club in Harlem, in the early 1940s. Here, where pianist Thelonious Monk and drummer Kenny Clarke were in the regular house band, experimentation took place that fed into the new jazz mainstream and led to the advent of modern jazz in 1944-45.

The chief creators of this new jazz language were trumpeter (and band leader-composer) Dizzy Gillespie and alto saxophonist-composer Charlie Parker, both of whom had put in time with leading big bands. While working together

*Jazz burst onto the New York City scene in the 1920s. Band leader Jelly Roll Morton was one of the first to appear in New York.*

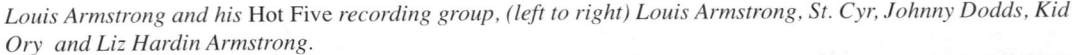

*Louis Armstrong and his* Hot Five *recording group, (left to right) Louis Armstrong, St. Cyr, Johnny Dodds, Kid Ory and Liz Hardin Armstrong.*

in the band of pianist Earl Hines (the father of modern jazz piano style) in 1943, they began to solidify their mutually compatible ideas. When they joined forces in a small group in 1945, on records and in person, bebop (as the new jazz style soon was called) came into first flowering.

Though bebop was solidly grounded in earlier jazz styles, it did not seem that way to the public, which often was unable to follow the intricate rhythmic and harmonic elaborations of the boppers. Furthermore, the bop musicians, unlike most of the jazz players who preceded them, were not interested in pleasing the public, but more concerned with creating music that fulfilled their own artistic ambitions. (Gillespie himself, however, was something of an exception , perhaps because his irrepressible sense of humor made him a natural entertainer).

### A New Audience

In any case, the advent of bop which had its beginnings in the Swing Era, went hand in hand with a change in the audience for jazz. By the mid-1930s, small clubs catering to jazz connoisseurs had begun to spring up in most larger urban areas. The biggest and most famous concentration was in New York, in two blocks on West 52nd Street, which soon became known as "Swing Street". In such clubs, musicians could perform for knowledgeable listeners without making musical compromises; most of them were too small for dancing, so people came strictly to listen. By this time, also, many people all over the world had become seriously interested in jazz. Some studied and documented its origins and history, others collected, researched and classified jazz records. Publications like *Downbeat* and *Metronome*, which catered to musicians and serious fans, sprang up. These magazines conducted polls and presented awards, as was also done, by 1944, by the prestigious *Esquire* magazine, which presented these awards at a huge all-star jazz concert on the stage of the Metropolitan Opera House in New York.

Jazz concerts had been a rarity in the 1920s. Then in 1938, Goodman staged one at Carnegie Hall , and from 1943, Duke Ellington gave an annual concert there. By the late 1940s, jazz concerts were regular events, among them the famous "Jazz at the Philharmonic" all-star tours. Thus, in many ways the stage was set for the acceptance, albeit in a limited way, of jazz as a music that no longer could be considered mere entertainment, or music primarily meant for dancing, but music having parity with "classical" music in its claim to serious artistic consideration.

(In this way, the foundation was laid for the advent of rock music, which filled the need for young people to have their own music to dance to at a time when jazz had largely abandoned them. Nevertheless, rock was resented by many jazz musicians and fans. Eventually, of course, rock itself spawned its own constituency of "serious" performers, commentators, and magazines).

Bebop was in turn succeeded by more radical new forms of jazz, though it has shown considerable staying power. In 1959, a young Texas-born alto saxophonist, Ornette Coleman, brought his adventurous quartet to New York, setting off a huge controversy with music that seemed to have abandoned most of the harmonic and structural principles of jazz as it had hitherto been known. In fact, Coleman's music was deeply rooted in the blues and in well-established improvisational jazz procedures and in time his music was accepted as part of the jazz tradition.

### The Varied Sounds of Jazz

By then, in the radical 1960s, so-called avant garde jazz was very much in evidence, in many and varied forms. The trumpeter Miles Davis, who had worked with Charlie Parker and also led his own very influential groups (one of them gave birth to a style known as cool jazz), hired a then little-known tenor saxophonist, John Coltrane, in 1956. With Coltrane, who also worked with Thelonious Monk, Davis introduced a modal approach (based on scales rather than harmonies) to jazz improvisation in 1958. Coltrane soon formed his own group, which took modality much further and extended improvisation, both in length and intensity, to a point of near-ecstasy. The pianist Cecil Taylor, a virtuoso of the keyboard, further stretched the boundaries of jazz. Davis himself experimented with electronics and rock and soul rhythms. The bassist and composer Charles Mingus, deeply influenced by Ellington and Parker, found new and imaginative ways of combining written and improvised jazz. Tenor saxophonist Sonny Rollins, while remaining rooted in traditional harmonic ground, expanded solo improvisation dramatically. And by the end of the 1960s, Albert Ayler, a tenor saxophonist with roots in rhythm-and-blues music, brought another new and intensely personal voice to jazz.

When Coltrane died suddenly in 1967, jazz was at the height of its experimental, expansionist stage, much of it inspired by the social and political upheavals of the time. By then, the term "free jazz" had begun to replace "avant garde," and many young musicians were following in the footsteps of Coltrane and other standard-bearers of innovation. But within a few years of Coltrane's passing, the storm quieted. There was some more experimentation, which was still going on within jazz in the late 1980s. Yet, by the early 1970s, it had become clear that the period of rapid and sometimes almost overpowering changes in jazz had come to an end.

In its place came a period of what might be called "peaceful coexistence" of many kinds of jazz. A goodly number of young musicians have turned to the rich tradition of jazz for inspiration, among them the gifted trumpeter Wynton Marsalis (also an expert classical player) and several other remarkable musicians from New Orleans, among them Wynton's slightly older brother Branford (tenor and soprano saxophones), trumpeter Terrence Blanshard, and alto saxophonist Donald Harrison. These young players reject both "fusion" with electronics and rock and the practices of "free jazz," and look to the bebop tradition and even to Armstrong and Ellington for inspiration. The many gifted players who emerged from Chicago's 1960s Association for the Advancement of Creative Musicians pursue their various approaches with stirring results, in such groups as the Art Ensemble of Chicago, The World Saxophone Quartet, and Lester Bowie's Brass Fantasy.

No one can predict where jazz will go next. After a long and remarkable period of intense innovation, the music seems to have reached a point where it is taking stock of its past while looking to the future. Whatever that future may bring, one thing is certain: the story of jazz is one of the most remarkable chapters in the history o£ 20th century artistic creativity, and names like Armstrong, Ellington and Parker are bound to loom large when that history is finally written.

Born in the crucible of slavery, jazz has become the universal song of freedom. (It's no coincidence that neither Hitler nor Stalin had any use for jazz and tried, unsuccessfully, to banish it.) Perhaps Thelonious Monk put it best when he said that "jazz and freedom go hand in hand."

*They came together one day in Harlem and this picture was taken.* The Golden Age of Jazz, *57 of the world's greatest jazz artists in one group sitting. At the top of the stairs center is 1. Hilton Jefferson and sitting on the curb with kids is 57. Count Basie—in between are 2.Benny Golson, 3. Art Farmer, 4. Wilbur Ware, 5. Art Blakey, 6. Chubby Jackson, 7. Johnny Griffin, 8. Dickey Wells, 9. Buck Clayton, 10. Taft Jordon, 11. Zutty Singleton, 12. Red Allen, 13. Tyree Glenn, 15. Sonny Greer, 16. Jay C. Higginbotham, 17. Jimmy Jones, 18. Charles Mingus, 19.Jo Jones, 20. Gene Krupa, 21. Max Cominsky, 22. George Wettling, 23. Bud Freeman, 24. Pee Wee Russell, 25. Ernie Wilkins, 26. Buster Bailey, 27. Osie Johnson, 28. Gigi Gryce, 29. Hank Jones, 30. Eddie Locke, 31. Horace Silver, 32. Lucky Roberts, 33. Maxine Sullivan, 34. Jimmy Rushing, 35. Joe Thomas, 36. Scoville Brown, 37. Stuff Smith, 38. Bill PCrump, 39. Coleman Hawkins, 40. Rudy Powell, 41. Oscar Pettiford, 42. Sahib Shihab, 43. Marian McPartland, 44. Sonny Rollins, 45. Lawrence Brown, 46. Mary Lou Williams, 47. Emmett Berry, 48. Thelonious Monk, 49. Vic Dickenson, 50. Milt Hinton, 51. Lester Young, 52. Rex Stewart, 53. J. C. Heard, 54. Gerry Mulligan, 55. Roy Eldridge and 56. Dizzy Gillespie.*

## OUTSTANDING JAZZ MUSICIANS

### MUHAL RICHARD ABRAMS
**Pianist, Composer, Band Leader**
**1930**

Born in Chicago, Abrams began his professional career in 1948, playing with many of the city's best musicians and bands. In 1961, he formed the Experimental Band, which soon became an informal academy for Chicago's most venturesome players. Under Abram's quiet but firm guidance, this grew into the Association for the Advancement of Creative Music, a cooperative that helped young musicians perform and promote their own music, that which could not be presented through established venues.

The AACM attracted such musicians as Roscoe Mitchell, Joseph Jarman, Lester Bowie, Malachi Favors and Don Moye, who would later achieve world-wide prominence as the Art Ensemble of Chicago, as well as other future leaders of avant garde jazz. Though he never so appointed himself, Abrams was the recognized leader and moral and spiritual force behind the AACM. In 1976, when his brood had come of age and mainly flown the coop, Abrams moved to New York and finally began to get some of the national and international recognition he had so long deserved. His work as a pianist and composer spans the entire range of the black musical tradition.

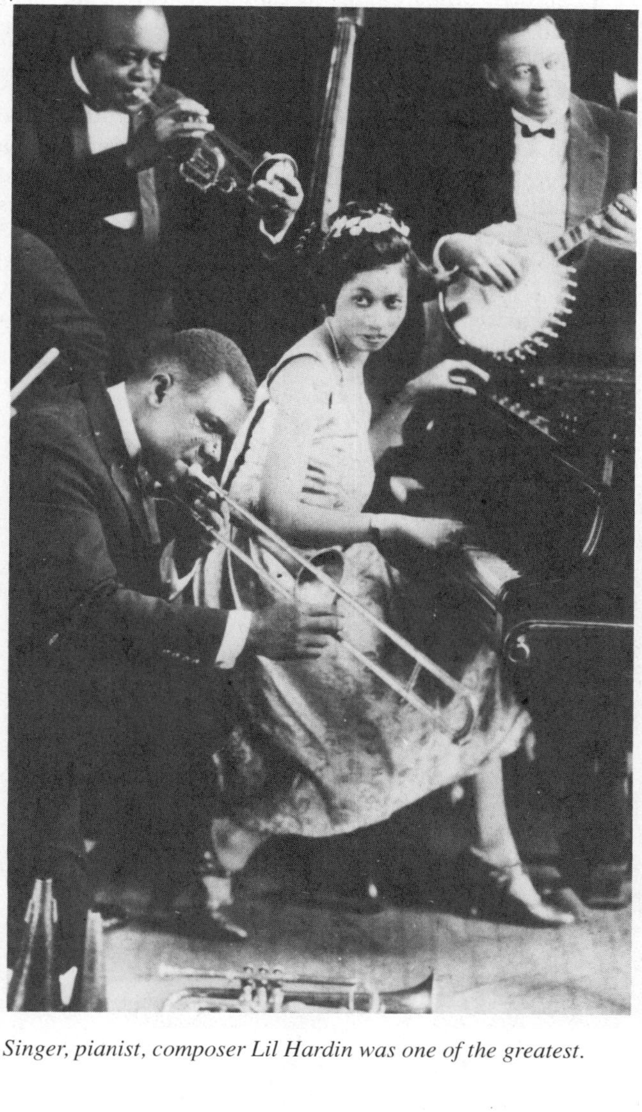

*Singer, pianist, composer Lil Hardin was one of the greatest.*

### LILIAN (LIL) HARDIN ARMSTRONG
**Piano, singer, composer**
**1898-1971**

Lil Armstrong, born in Memphis in 1898. Lil was a classically trained musician who received her music education at Fisk University. Her family moved from Memphis to Chicago somewhere around 1914 or 1915. One of her first jobs was selling sheet music in Jones music store in Chicago. It is said that she met Jelly Roll Morton while working there and it was Morton who influenced her style of hitting the notes "real heavy". She worked with the New Orleans Creole Jazz Band, The New Orleans Rhythm Kings, and King Oliver's Creole Jazz Band where she met her husband Louis Armstrong. Lil and Louie were married in 1924. She played and wrote music for many of Armstrong's Hot Five and Hot Seven concerts and recordings and helped Louie polish his raw brilliant talent. The Armstrongs were divorced in 1938. She also played in various bands and some combos of her own. Two of her songs "Bad Boy" and "Just For a Thrill" became big hits in the 60s. While playing at a Tribute to Louis Armstrong at Chicago's Civic Center Plaza Lilian Armstrong collapsed and died of a heart attack on July 7, 1971.

### LOUIS ARMSTRONG
**Trumpet**
**1900-1971**

Born in New Orleans at the turn of the century, Louis Armstrong was one of the most influential and durable of all jazz artists, and quite simply, one of the most famous people in the entire world.

On New Year's Eve in 1914, Armstrong was arrested in New Orleans for firing a pistol and sent to the Colored Waifs Home. It was there that he first learned to play the cornet. His skill increased with the experience he gained from playing in the Home's band. When he was finally released from the institution, he was already proficient enough with the instrument to begin playing for money.

Befriended by his idol, King Oliver, Armstrong quickly began to develop the jazz skills which he had, until then, been able to admire only from a distance. When Oliver left for Chicago in 1919, a place opened up for Armstrong as a member of the Kid Ory band in New Orleans.

In 1922, Oliver asked Armstrong to join him in Chicago as second cornet with his Creole Jazz Band. The duets between "Dippermouth" (as Armstrong was called) and "Papa Joe" (Oliver's nickname) soon became the talk of the Chicago music world.

*Louis Armstrong, mentor and model for generations of jazz musicians*

Two years later Armstrong joined the Fletcher Henderson band at the Roseland Ballroom in New York City. In 1925, he returned to Chicago to play with Erskine Tate, switching from cornet to trumpet, the instrument he played from then on. During the next four years he made a series of recordings which profoundly influenced the course of jazz.

In 1929, Armstrong returned to New York and there, in the revue "Hot Chocolates," scored his first triumph with a popular song (Fats Waller's "Ain't Misbehavin'?"). This success was a turning point in his career. He now began to front big bands, playing and singing popular songs rather than blues or original instrumentals.

In 1932, Armstrong headlined the show at the London Palladium, where he acquired the nickname "Satchmo". From 1933 to 1935 he toured Europe, returning to the United States to film *Pennies from Heaven* with Bing Crosby. He continued to evolve from the status of musician to that of entertainer, and his singing soon became as important as his playing. In 1947, he formed a small group, which was an immediate success. He continued to work in this context touring throughout the world.

Armstrong scored a tremendous success in 1964 with his record of "Hello Dolly," which bounced the Beatles from the top spot on the Top 40 list, a great feat in the age of rock. Though his health began to decline, he kept up his heavy schedule of international touring, and when he died in his sleep at home in Corona, Queens, two days after his 70th birthday, he had been preparing to resume work in spite of a serious heart attack suffered some three months before. "The music—it's my living and my life" was his motto.

Louis Armstrong's fame as an entertainer in the later stages of his extraordinary career sometimes made people forget that he remained a great musician to the end. More than any other artist, even the great Duke Ellington, Louis Armstrong symbolized the magic of jazz, a music unimaginable without his contribution. "You can't play a note on the horn that Louis hasn't already played," said Miles Davis. "I mean even modern." And Wynton Marsalis echoes that opinion.

In 1988, on the strength of its use in the film "Good Morning Vietnam," Armstrong's recording of "What A Wonderful World" became a surprise hit, climbing to number 11 on the Billboard chart.

*Early jazz forms were pioneered by Sidney Bechet on the soprano saxophone and clarinet.*

### WILLIAM (COUNT) BASIE
### Piano, Band leader
### 1904-1984

Count Basie is generally regarded as the leader of the best jazz band in the United States, and consequently, one of the major influences on jazz as a whole.

His musical career ranges from a boyhood spent watching the pit band at the local movie theater (he later learned the organ techniques of Fats Waller by crouching beside him in the Lincoln Theater in Harlem) to his dual triumphs in 1957 when his became the first American band to play a royal command performance for the Queen of England, and the first black jazz band ever to play at the Waldorf Astoria Hotel in New York City.

During the early 1920s, Basie toured in vaudeville. Stranded in Kansas City, he joined Walter Page's Blue Devils.(Jimmy Rushing was the singer.) After this band broke up, Basie joined Benny Moten, and in 1935, formed his own band at the Reno Club in Kansas City, where a local radio announcer soon dubbed him "Count."

At the urging of critic John Hammond, Basie brought his group to New York City in 1936. Within a year he had cut his first record and was well on his way to becoming an established presence in the jazz world.

The Basie trademark was a rhythm section, which featured Basie's own clean, spare piano style and outstanding soloists like Lester Young and Sweets Edison in the early years, and Lucky Thompson, J. J. Johnson, Clark Terry, and Benny Powell in the later period.

Except for the years 1950 and 1951 when he had a small group, Basie led a big band for more than 30 years. In some way immune to changing fashion, the Basie band completed numerous global tours and successful recording engagements without ever suffering an appreciable decline in its popularity. In 1974, on his seventieth birthday, the Count was honored at a "Royal Salute" party by virtually every big name in jazz.

Count Basie was honored at Radio City Music Hall in New York City in 1982. Among those honoring The Count were Dionne Warwick and Lena Horne.

### SIDNEY BECHET
### Soprano Saxophone
### 1897-1959

Sidney Bechet was the first jazzman to achieve recognition on the soprano saxophone, and also one of the first to win acceptance in classical circles as a serious musician.

In 1919, Bechet played in England and on the Continent with Will Marion Cook's Southern Syncopated Orchestra. Even before this, his clarinet and soprano sax had been heard in the bands of King Oliver and Freddie Keppard.

During the early 1920s Bechet made a series of records with Clarence Williams' Blue Five, worked briefly with Duke Ellington (one of his great admirers), and then returned to Europe. He came back to United States with Noble Sissle and expanded his career making many records. In 1949, he moved to France where he enjoyed the greatest success of his career. He died there in 1959. After his death, a statue of Bechet was erected in Anibes.

*Count Basie's light keyboard touch gave new style to the big bands.*

### ART BLAKEY
### Drummer, Band leader
### 1919

Aside from being one of the greatest drummers in jazz, Art Blakey is one of the music's foremost talent spotters. After early experience with Fletcher Henderson and Mary Lou Williams, he joined Billy Eckstine's band in 1944 and was in on the birth of bebop. After working with many of the greatest modern jazz musicians, he formed his own Jazz Messengers in 1954 with immediate success.

Since then and until this day, Blakey has hired and helped to stardom a vast number of gifted players, among them Horace Silver, Lee Morgan, Freddie Hubbard, Benny Golson, Woody Shaw, Wayne Shorter and Wynton Marsalis, to name but a very few. Blakey has one of the most powerful beats in jazz and has taken part in some of the finest recordings of the last 40 years. If you want to hear the stars of tomorrow, go listen to the Jazz Messengers.

### JIMMY BLANTON
### Bass
### 1918-1942

During his brief life, Jimmy Blanton changed the course of jazz history by originating a new way of playing the string bass. Playing the instrument as if it were a horn, he lifted it from rhythmic back-up to melodic focal point.

Born in St. Louis, Missouri, he played with Jeter Pillars and Fate Marable before joining Duke Ellington in 1939. Until this time the string bass rarely played anything but quarter notes in ensemble or solos, but Blanton began sliding into eighth-and sixteenth-note runs, introducing melodic and harmonic ideas that were totally new to the instrument. His skill put him in a different class from his predecessors, made him the first true master of the bass and demonstrated the instrument's unsuspected potential as a solo vehicle.

Blanton died of tuberculosis.

### BUDDY BOLDEN
**Cornet**
**1868-1931**

Buddy Bolden, a plasterer by trade, formed what may have been the first real jazz band in the 1890s in New Orleans. By the turn of the century, his cornet was so popular that he was often called upon to sit in with a number of bands on a single evening.

His cornet style was the starting point for a chain of musicians from King Oliver to Louis Armstrong to Dizzy Gillespie; put another way, from New Orleans to Chicago. Since his career predates the recording of jazz, the only lasting memorial to his talent lies in the oral tradition which carries on his legend, and in the known successes of his descendents.

Bolden was committed to East Louisiana State Hospital in 1907, and remained there until his death, never playing another note.

### RAY BROWN (RAYMOND MATTHEWS)
**Bass**
**1926**

Ray Brown is perhaps the most versatile bass player in jazz today and is in demand around the world. He was born in Pittsburgh in 1926. Early in 1951, he joined Oscar Peterson's Trio, an association that lasted 15 years. During this time, he and Peterson produced award-winning records and were in constant demand for concerts. Since leaving Peterson in 1966, Brown has joined forces with many famous artists, in live and recorded performances. He also works as a record producer and personal manager.

### BENNY CARTER
**Alto saxophone, trumpet, composer, band leader**
**1907**

Bennett Lester Carter made his professional debut in 1923, and sixty-five years later was still at the top of the jazz ranks as an instrumentalist, composer-arranger and leader. In 1988, he toured Europe, visited Japan with his own band, performed in Brazil for the first time in his career, and recorded three albums.

Admired and respected by generations of musicians, many of whom "went to school in his bands" (Sid Catlett, Miles Davis, J. J. Johnson, Max Roach and Teddy Wilson were some), Carter helped shape the language of big-band jazz. His scoring for saxophone sections was especially influential. On the alto saxophone, he and Johnny Hodges were the pace-setters before Charlie Parker and bebop. He has few peers as a trumpeter.

*Ray Charles breathes soul into jazz.*

*Alto sax virtuoso Ornette Coleman*

Carter was the first black composer to break the color barrier in the Hollywood film studios. He scored many major films and TV shows ("M-Squad"). The subject of one of the best biographies of a jazz artist ("Benny Carter: A Life in American Music"), Carter received an honorary doctorate in music from Princeton University, where he taught, in 1974.

**RAY CHARLES**
**Singer, Piano, Band Leader**
**1932**

Ray Charles is the vital link between contemporary jazz and the long-forgotten wellspring of early jazz. Charles uses what might be called a "down home" style to transmit contemporary musical ideas. He has succeeded to the point where he is one of the few musicians in our time to be acclaimed by jazz professionals and the general public alike.

Blinded at the age of six, Charles received his first musical training at a school for the blind in St. Augustine, Florida. Originally from Georgia, he left school at the age of 15 to play local engagements. Two years later, he formed a trio which had some success in the Northwest. In 1954, he organized a seven piece rhythm and blues group.

In 1957, his first LP was released, consisting of a potpourri of instrumentals drawn from pop, gospel, and modern jazz sources. His singing and piano playing found particular favor with a number of jazz artists who were reacting against what they felt was a growing tendency for jazz to become overscored and underfelt. In Charles, they saw an artist who had restored both a sense of "soul" and instrumental "funkiness" to the jazz idiom.

**CHARLIE CHRISTIAN**
**Electric Guitar**
**1917-1942**

Charlie Christian did for the electric guitar what Jimmy Blanton had done for the bass.

Christian joined Benny Goodman in 1939, and after only two years with the Goodman sextet, achieved great fame as the first electric guitarist to play single-string solos. In his after-hour activities at such Harlem clubs as Minton's, he was an early contributor to the jazz revolution which would one day come to be called Bop.(Christian is even credited by some with having coined the word.)

In 1941, he contracted tuberculosis, and the following year he died.

**KENNY CLARKE**
**(Liaqat Ali Salaam)**
**Drums**
**1914-1985**

Kenny Clarke was one of the "founding fathers" of the Bop movement. Along with Dizzy Gillespie, and Thelonious Monk, Clarke made Minton's in Harlem the late-hour haunt for jazz buffs and musicians alike in the 1940s.

A pioneer figure in the use of drums as a solo instrument and not just as a background presence, he was the first musician to move away from the blatant use of the bass drum to a more flexible style in which he maintained a steady rhythm on the top cymbal while "dropping bombs" with surprise bass-drum sounds.

From a musically inclined Pittsburgh family, Clarke studied vibes, piano, and trombone, as well as musical theory. His early professional experience was gained with Roy Eldridge and Edgar Hayes. (He traveled to Finland and Sweden with Hayes in 1937.)

In the early 1940s, he played with Teddy Hill and then moved into Minton's. Later he worked with Dizzy Gillespie, Coleman Hawkins, Tadd Dameron, and many others. In 1951, he toured with Billy Eckstine, and in the following year he helped organize the Modern Jazz Quartet, where he remained for the next three years. He moved to France in 1956 where he continued to work with a long list of visiting American talents, and co-led a fine 'big band' with Belgian pianist and arranger Frenchy Boland (1961-1972).

Clarke's integrated use of the drums with other soloists has become a staple of contemporary jazz.

## ORNETTE COLEMAN
## Alto Saxophone, Trumpet, Violin, Composer
## 1930

It has often been said that the Bop revolution in jazz marked the beginning of a new musical era, but the music of Ornette Coleman has called that generalization into question. For all its intricacies, its radical harmonic departures which shocked those who first heard them, and its extremely free adherence to melodic lines, Bop may well have been the end of an old era rather than the beginning of a new one, since the core of its uniqueness was built around the concept of improvisation based on chord patterns.

Ornette Coleman's style, however, represents a sharp break with this latter tradition. As a result of this, he has been dismissed by some musicians (as well as by much of the general jazz public) as little more than "a noisemaker."

Coleman is largely self-taught. His early professional experience was with rhythm and blues bands in New Orleans, his native Texas, and California. While working as an elevator operator in Los Angeles in the mid-1950s, Coleman undertook a textbook study of harmony and began composing.

Arguments raged when he completed his first major recording session in New York City in 1958. Some felt that the squeaks, bleats, and other sounds he produced with his plastic horn, not to mention the sounds he has later began to experiment with on trumpet,and violin, were meaningless. Others, (including John Lewis), were convinced that he is easily the most original and gifted jazz artist since Parker, Gillespie, and Monk.

As avant garde jazz evolved, Coleman gained more acceptance. He has performed his works with symphony orchestras and chamber groups, and since 1975, has also incorporated rock sounds and rhythms into his music.

## JOHN COLTRANE
## Tenor Saxophone
## 1926-1967

John Coltrane played tenor in a variety of settings during his musical career. In the 1940s, he was with a small combo featured in Philadelphia, then a U.S. Navy band playing in Hawaii, and, lastly, a rhythm and blues group. Throughout the 1950s, he saw service with some of the greats of contemporary jazz: Dizzy Gillespie, Miles Davis, and Thelonious Monk.

The music which Coltrane was creating—like that of Ornette Coleman, Archie Shepp, and others—was the subject of great controversy in its heyday. Coltrane used his tenor to produce harsh, strange sounds which defied easy categorization. The overall effect of his music was regarded as unpleasant and unnerving by many of his listeners, including those who have always felt they were truly open to jazz experimentation.

*Saxophonist John Coltrane won kudos with his revolutionary "sheets of sound" technique.*

Some have always maintained that Coltrane's music was "meaningless," a charge which at least one fellow musician, J. J. Johnson, took great pains to refute, professing to see in the Coltrane-Monk relationship a parallel with that of Parker and Gillespie.

For all of the difficulty which his music presents to fellow musicians and critics, and likewise to the general listening public, Coltrane has remained the most influential presence for young tenor men seeking to make their mark. The dissonance with which he was experimenting was a distinct keynote of jazz throughout the 1960s.

## MILES DAVIS
## Trumpet, Band Leader
## 1926

Miles Davis has played a major role in the transition from the hard, aggressive stance of Bop to the softer, more subtle in jazz.

As a teen-age musician in St. Louis in the early 1940s, Davis sat in with his idols Charlie Parker and Dizzy Gillespie when they passed through town with the Billy Eckstine Band.

In 1945, his well-to-do dentist father sent him to the Juilliard School of Music in New York. Within a short time, Davis was working the 52nd Street clubs with Parker and Coleman Hawkins, and touring with the bands of Billy Eckstine and Benny Carter.

In the late 1940s, Davis formed a nine-piece band , including Lee Konitz, Gerry Mulligan, John Lewis, and Max Roach. The group was a commercial failure, but had great impact on musicians.

Success came in 1956, the year after Davis had formed a quintet with John Coltrane featured on tenor sax, and the year in which he made his first record with arranger Gil Evans, "Miles Ahead." This was followed by two other collaborations with Evans, "Porgy and Bess" and "Sketches Of Spain," both landmarks in jazz. In 1958, came "Kind Of Blue," an album by a new sextet, still with Coltrane, but with Cannonball Adderley added on alto sax and Bill Evans on piano. which established modal improvisation in jazz and set the stage for Coltrane's explorations on his own.

*Miles Davis of the "Cool school."*

Davis continued to introduce new ideas and give exposure to new talent. By 1964, he had Wayne Shorter on saxophones, Herbie Hancock on piano, Ron Carter on bass and the sensational 18-year-old Tiny Williams on drums. This was a group that introduced new ideas, mostly in the realm of rhythmic and harmonic freedom. However, 1968 Davis got restless again, attracted by the possibilities of electronic instruments. Hancock, Chick Corea, Joe Zawinul and Keith Jarrett were among the keyboard players who contributed to the new stage of Miles, starting with the album "Bitches Brew."

Some of his many fans, and quite a few musicians, did not care for this new Miles, but characteristically, he couldn't have cared less. Going his own way, he gradually moved further away from jazz into contemporary black pop music, or rather, an unclassifiable and frequently changing music that appealed to a young audience not much interested in jazz as such. In the late 1970s, Miles became a cult figure, and his famous reserve (he had long been known for not acknowledging applause, walking off the stand when he wasn't playing, and being a difficult interview subject) was replaced by a new open manner that included smiling, waving to the audience and even shaking hands with those nearest the stage, and giving frequent and amiable interviews.

But those who now see Miles as a pop star lost to jazz ought to listen to his trumpet. No matter what the setting, it still speaks the language of jazz, creating beautiful sounds and melodies.

## ERIC DOLPHY
**Alto Sax, Bass Clarinet, Composer**
**1928-1964**

Eric Dolphy is greatly admired by musicians. Although his linear derivations were from Charlie Parker, his attack on alto sax and bass clarinet had a fierce bite that sprang from earlier jazz. His mastery of the bass clarinet has never been equaled.

Born in Los Angeles, his first recognition came with the Chico Hamilton quintet of 1958-1959. In 1960, he joined Charles Mingus in New York, and in 1961 he played many club dates with trumpeter Booker Little before joining John Coltrane for some historic tours, concerts, and recordings. Dolphy also played in a group with trumpeter Freddie Hubbard and recorded with Ornette Coleman, then experimenting with a plastic saxophone. In 1964, while on tour again with Mingus in Europe, he decided to stay abroad, where he recorded with Dutch, Scandinavian, and German rhythm sections. He died in Berlin of a heart attack possibly brought on by diabetes.

Dolphy was the winner of *Down Beat* magazine's New Star award for alto, flute, and miscellaneous instruments in 1961, and was elected to that magazine's Hall of Fame in 1965. His legacy includes many recordings for Prestige,

Blue Note, Impulse, and smaller companies, both as leader and side man.

Charles Mingus said of Dolphy that he had the "great capacity to talk in his music...He knew the level of language which very few musicians get down to."

## ROY (LITTLE JAZZ) ELDRIDGE
**Drums, Trumpet, Singer**
**1911**

Born in Pittsburgh, Roy Eldridge played his first "job" at the age of seven on drums. When he was 15 and had switched to trumpet, he ran away from home with a carnival band. After playing with some of the best bands in the midwest, he arrived in New York in 1931, impressing the locals with his speed and range and finding jobs with good bands. But it wasn't until 1935, with Teddy Hill, that he could be heard on records. By the next year, he was a star of Fletcher Henderson's band, and in 1937, he put together his own group and made some records that stood other trumpeters on their ears. One of them was young Dizzy Gillespie, who had been listening to Roy on the radio since 1935 and tried his best to copy him. By 1938, Roy was setting the pace for swing trumpeters, playing higher and faster than even Louis Armstrong had dared anyone to do, and making musical sense as well. The fact that he was also a good singer didn't hurt.

In 1941, Roy, now known in the world of music as "Little Jazz," took up an offer from drummer Gene Krupa to join his big band, thus becoming the first black musician to be featured in a white band not just as a special attraction (like Teddy Wilson and Lionel Hampton with the Benny Goodman Quartet, though Hamp sometimes took over the drum chair in the Goodman band as well) but as a member of the band's section. Duetting with girl singer Anita O'Day, Roy scored a smash hit for Krupa with "Let Me Off Uptown," while his instrumental feature "Rockin' Chair" was hailed as a jazz classic. Roy led his own big band for a while, but joined Artie Shaw, another white band, in 1944. A brief stint with his own big band followed, but small groups proved more viable. By 1949, Roy was a star of "Jazz At The Philharmonic," a touring concert group of famous players including, at that time, Charlie Parker, Lester Young and Buddy Rich. An offer to tour with a Benny Goodman small group brought him to Paris, where he stayed for a year and regained his confidence, a bit shaken by the advent of bebop and the trumpet innovations of his former disciple Gillespie. (Rivalry aside, the two always remained good friends and have often worked and recorded together.)

The 1950s and 1960s saw a long association with Coleman Hawkins; the two went together like ham and eggs. During this time Roy also backed Ella Fitzgerald and toured with JATP. A full decade, from 1970 on, found Little Jazz leading the house band at Jimmy Ryan's club in New York City, but a heart attack in 1980 put an end to his trumpet playing, though he still works occasionally as a singer and gives lectures and workshops on jazz.

No one is better qualified, for Roy Eldridge comprises, in his music and personality, the essence of jazz as a music that comes straight from, and goes straight to, the heart and soul.

Mr. Eldridge developed heart problems in 1980 and stopped playing the trumpet. He began to perform as a singer and a drummer and became a spokesman for jazz at schools and major jazz events. Roy Eldridge died after an illustrous career on February 26, 1989. He was 78-years-old.

*Duke Ellington- charm, sophistication, wit, and unlimited talent.*

## DUKE ELLINGTON
**Piano, Bandleader, Composer**
**1899-1974**

Duke Ellington is believed by many critics to have made the most pervasive contribution to the development of jazz. Though the lion's share of Ellington's public fame hinges on the numerous "standards" he composed, it is his work as the leader of a jazz orchestra for fifty years that won him the respect and admiration of fellow musicians throughout the world.

Ellington was born into a moderately well-to-do family in Washington, D.C. The name "Duke" was easily fitted to the dapper young man with the courtly manner. Ellington was offered a scholarship to the Pratt Institute of Fine Arts in New York City, but decided instead to play music.

In 1923, at the urging of Fats Waller, Ellington made a trip to New York City, working in Harlem for Bricktop (Ada Smith). He then became leader of his own group and moved to the Kentucky Club on Broadway.

In 1924, Ellington wrote his first score for *Chocolate Kiddies*, a show which ran for two years in Europe but never reached the U.S.A. From 1927 to 1932, Ellington and his orchestra remained at the Cotton Club on Lenox Avenue (except for a brief hiatus in 1930 when he appeared in his first movie, Amos and Andy's *Check and Double Check*).

During the Cotton Club period, Ellington's orchestral genius gained him a national reputation, particularly through his records and his network broadcasts. Brilliant performances by such soloists as Barney Bigard, Johnny Hodges, and Cootie Williams set the pace for many later jazz orchestrations—not his single-line melodies—which earned him the plaudits of his fellow musicians.

In 1927 Ellington introduced the wordless use of the voice as a jazz instrument, and in 1931 he broke through the traditional three-minute time limit set for commercial records. His later use of a miniature concerto context as a framework for compositions played by specific jazz soloists, and his creation of original works for concerts are among the other significant contributions he made to the jazz.

Through European tours begun in the 1930s, the Ellington sound was brought live to an international public which had, even then, long acclaimed his preeminence in the jazz domain. In 1943 his "Black, Brown and Beige" was regarded as the most important attempt to fuse jazz elements with formal concert idiom.

The roster of Ellington personnel through the years remains among the most impressive in the history of jazz—Ben Webster, Juan Tizol, Ray Nance, Oscar Pettiford, Louis Bellson, Harry Carney, Johnny Hodges, and many others.

The whole world of music was saddened by Ellington's death on May 24, 1974. Even today the Duke continues to exert a unique and powerful influence on jazz around the world, both through the music he left behind and through the galaxy of musicians who served in his great band.

*Dexter Gordon, the premier tenor saxophone stylist of bebop.*

### ELLA FITZGERALD
### Singer
### 1918

Ella Fitzgerald has emerged as the top female vocalist in virtually every poll conducted among jazz musicians during the last decade. No other jazz vocalist has been so unanimously acclaimed.

Discovered in 1934 by drummer-band leader Chick Webb during an amateur contest at Harlem's Apollo Theatre in New York City, she cut her first side with Webb a year later. In 1938, she recorded "A Tisket, A Tasket," a novelty number which brought her commercial success and made her name widely known among the general public. Among musicians, however, her reputation stemmed from her singular ability to use her voice like an instrument, improvising effortlessly in a clear style filled with rhythmic subtleties.

For more than 40 years Ella Fitzgerald has been the leading jazz interpreter of popular song.

### ERROLL GARNER
### Jazz Piano, Composer
### 1921-1977

A keyboard artist who played and composed by ear in the tradition of the founding fathers of jazz, Erroll Garner won the international acclaim of jazz lovers, music critics, and the general public. Strong and bouncy left-hand rhythms and beautiful melodies are the trademarks of his extremely enjoyable music. He was the best selling jazz pianist in the world.

Born in Pittsburgh, Garner grew up in a musical family and began picking out piano melodies before he was three years old. He started taking piano lessons at six, but his first and only piano teacher gave up on him when she realized he was playing all her assignments by ear instead of learning to read notes. At seven, he began playing regularly on Pittsburgh radio station KDKA. He dropped out of high school to play with a dance band and came to New York in 1939 as an accompanist for nightclub singer Ann Lewis. With guitarist Tiny Grimes and bassist Slam Stewart, he formed a trio which toured the East Coast. In 1946, he recorded "Laura," which sold a half million copies, and his fame began to grow. On March 27, 1950 he gave a solo recital at Cleveland's Music Hall, and in December a concert at New York's Town Hall. Gradually recitals and recording sessions took the place of nightclub performances.

Garner's most famous composition, "Misty" was a big hit for Johnny Mathis and Sarah Vaughn. His unique piano style has often been copied but never equaled.

### DIZZY GILLESPIE
**Trumpet, Band Leader**
**1917**

Dizzy Gillespie and Charlie Parker were the co-founders of the most revolutionary movement in jazz during the 1940S—the phenomenon known as Bop. The role which each played in this revolution has long been a subject of considerable debate. Billy Eckstine, whose band at one time included both Gillespie and Parker, has defined Parker's role more as instrumentalist, and Gillespie's more as writer and arranger. Whatever their particular contributions were, however, it cannot be disputed that the sum total of their ideas brought about a change in jazz which continues to the present time.

Gillespie studied harmony and theory at the Lauringburg Institute in North Carolina, and after moving to Philadelphia and gaining more professional experience there, he joined the Teddy Hill band where he replaced his early idol "Little Jazz" Roy Eldridge, who had moved to the Fletcher Henderson Orchestra.

He toured Europe with Teddy Hill in 1939, and when he returned to New York to play with Mercer Ellington and Cab Calloway, his bop experimentation was already beginning to develop and his career as arranger began. After working with Ella Fitzgerald, Benny Carter, Charlie Barnet, Earl Hines, and others, he joined Eckstine's band in 1944.

Since Bop has become internationally known, Gillespie has toured Europe, the Middle East, and Latin America with big bands and quintets, some of which have been subsidized by the U.S. State Department.

### EVANS TYREE GLENN
**Trombone**
**1912-1974**

Evans Tyree Glenn was one of the most accomplished jazz trombonists in the music world. He was born in Corsicana, Texas and played with many great bands during his career. Among the bands Glenn played with are those of Duke Ellington, Cab Calloway, Benny Carter, and Don Redman. The trombonist also formed his own groups and played many jazz engagements in the New York City area.

### DEXTER GORDON
**Tenor Saxophone, Band Leader**

Born in Los Angeles, the son of a prominent physician whose patients included famous jazz musicians, Dexter Gordon joined Lionel Hampton's newly formed big band in 1940. He was with Louis Armstrong in 1944, and later that year joined the Billy Eckstine Band. After freelancing in New York, he returned home and in 1946 recorded a "tenor battle," The Chase," with Wardell Gray, which became one of the biggest modern jazz hits. He then teamed up with Gray on and off until 1952, after which he temporarily disappeared from the jazz spotlight.

Gordon made a major comeback in the early 1960s with a series of much-acclaimed recordings. In 1962, he settled in Copenhagen, and the Danish capital became his headquarters for the next 14 years, though he made brief playing visits to his homeland. In 1977 he came home for good, forming his own group and winning many new fans. In 1986, he starred in the French feature film Round Midnight, in which his portrayal of a character based on Lester Young and Bud Powell won him an Oscar nomination as best actor. In 1988, he began work on an autobiography.

Dexter Gordon is the premier tenor saxophone stylist of bebop, but his strong, swinging music transcends categories. He greatly influenced young John Coltrane.

### JOHNNY GRIFFIN
**Tenor Saxophone**
**1928**

Johnny Griffin was born in Chicago and played with most of the prominent jazz personalities over the years. Among them have been Lionel Hampton, Art Blakey, Thelonious Monk, and Eddie Lockjaw Davis. Griffin, like many Chicago musicians, preferred to stay and play in the Windy City, and much of his early development took place there. In December 1962, he moved to Europe and played all over the continent. He lived in Paris in the late 1960s and later moved to Holland, where he owned a farm. In the late 1970s, Griffin moved back to the United States, celebrating the occasion with outstanding concerts and recordings with his friend Dexter Gordon.

### LIONEL HAMPTON
**Vibraphone**
**1909**

Lionel Hampton was the first jazz musician to feature the vibes, an instrument which has since come to play a vital role in jazz. His first recorded effort on the instrument was in 1930 on "Memories of You," which featured Louis Armstrong, then fronting the Les Hite band in California.

Hampton later left Hite's band to form his own Los Angeles group. When Benny Goodman heard him in 1936, he used him on a record date with Teddy Wilson and Gene Krupa, and then persuaded him to join on a permanent basis.

Hampton played with the Goodman Quartet until 1940, the year he formed his own big orchestra. The following year, it scored its first big hit: "Flyin' Home."

Hampton has enjoyed great success since the 1940s and 1950s in such places as Israel, Europe, Australia, and North Africa, and has continued to tour the world even as he past his eightieth birthday in 1989.

Lionel Hampton also has been active in the development of housing in the Harlem community of New York City. A complex of houses was named for his late wife, the Gladys Hampton Houses between Frederick Douglass Boulevard and St. Nicholas Avenue. Hampton was also honored in 1979 at the White House by President Reagan.

### HERBERT JEFFREY (HERBIE) HANCOCK
**Keyboards, Composer, Band Leader**
**1940**

Herbie Hancock was born in Chicago and has notably been associated with the piano, although in recent years he has turned to electronics as a vehicle of communication in his music: electric guitar, electric bass, electric piano, echoplex, phase shifter, and synthesizer. From 1963 to 1968, he traveled and played with Miles Davis, establishing himself as a composer and instrumentalist of the first rank. While with Davis, Hancock recorded with numerous other groups and became firmly established as a major jazz figure. He has won many awards, including *Down Beat* Jazzman of the Year in 1974 and *Cash Box* and *Playboy* Awards of the Year in 1974. Hancock has also written film scores and television specials. In 1972, Hancock moved to Los Angeles, where he continues to play and compose as he enjoys success and fame.

### W. C. HANDY
**Trumpet, Composer, Band Leader**
**1873-1958**

Although he began as a cornetist and band leader in the 1890s, W. C. Handy's fame as the "Father of the Blues" rests almost entirely on his work as a composer.

After studying at Kentucky Musical College, Handy toured with an assortment of musical groups, becoming the bandmaster of the Mahara Minstrels in 1896.

*Lionel Hampton, vibraphone virtuoso, is also great on drums.*

In 1909, during a political campaign in Memphis, Handy wrote *Mr. Crump,* a campaign song for E. H. "Boss" Crump. Three years later, the song was published as the *Memphis Blues.*

In 1914, Handy published his most famous song, *St. Louis Blues*, and that same year, also wrote *Yellow Dog Blues.* Some of his others which have become perennial favorites are *Joe Turner Blues* (1915); *Beale Street Blues* (1916); *Careless Love* (1921); and *Aunt Hagar's Blues* (1922).

In the 1920s, Handy became a music publisher in New York. Despite his failing sight, he remained active until his death in 1958. His songs extended beyond the world of jazz to find their way into the general field of popular music in innumerable forms. Their popularity continues unabated even today.

### COLEMAN HAWKINS
**Tenor Saxophone**
**1904-1969**

With the position occupied by the tenor saxophone in jazz today, it is difficult to imagine that until Coleman Hawkins came along, this instrument was not seriously considered as a suitable jazz vehicle. The full, rich tone which Hawkins brought to the tenor has helped make it one of the most vital instruments in the contemporary jazz ensemble.

When Hawkins took up the tenor at the age of nine, he had already had four years of training on piano and cello. He continued his studies at Washburn College in Topeka, Kansas and in 1922 toured with Mamie Smith's Jazz Hounds. In 1924, he began a 10-year stint with Fletcher Henderson's band.

Hawkins left Henderson in 1934 to tour England and the Continent, recording with Django Reinhardt, Benny Carter, and others. When he returned to the United States in 1939, he recorded his first commercial hit, "Body and Soul," with his own band.

Unlike many of his contemporaries, Hawkins was open to the experimentation of the young musicians of the 1940s. In 1944, for example, he formed an all-star band for the first Bop record session, and he gave help and encouragement to Dizzy Gillespie, Charlie Parker, Thelonious Monk and others he admired.

With the advent of the "cool school," Hawkins lapsed into temporary decline, but the warmth of his style has been recognized anew by scores of young musicians attempting to duplicate his "soul" sound.

### FLETCHER HENDERSON
**Band Leader, Arranger, Pianist**
**1897-1952**

Born in Georgia, the son of an educator, Fletcher Henderson came to New York in 1920 to study chemistry, but took a job to earn some extra money, as house pianist and musical director for Black Swan, the first black-owned and operated record company. Chemistry soon took a back seat, and in

1924 he was persuaded by some of his recording studio colleagues to audition with a band for a new club. They got the job, and soon graduated to the Roseland Ballroom on Broadway, where they resided for eight years, also touring and making hundreds of records.

The Henderson band was the first big band to play interesting jazz, and it became an incubator for some of the greatest stars of the day, among them Louis Armstrong, Coleman Hawkins and Benny Carter. It was the arranger and saxophonist Don Redman who shaped the bands early style. When he left in 1928, Carter and others, including Fletcher's younger brother Horace, also a pianist and arranger, took over. It was not until 1933 that Fletcher himself began to write full-time for his band, but he had such a talent for arranging that he soon became one of the architects of swing. Ironically, just as he hit his stride as a writer, his band fell on hard days, and for a brief while he gave it up and became a freelance arranger, contributing mightily to the library of the newly formed Benny Goodman Band.

Though he took up leading again soon, and had such greats as Ben Webster, Chu Berry and Roy Eldridge in his bands, he never again achieved the success of the 1920s.

### ALBERT (AL) HIBBLER
**Singer**
**1915**

Al Hibbler was born in Little Rock, Arkansas, and has been blind since birth. He was from early on influenced by Pha Terrell of the Andy Kirk band. Hibbler formed and led his own band in Texas and later joined Jay McShann's band in 1942. After leaving McShann, he freelanced in New York City, gaining national fame while touring with Duke Ellington from 1943 to 1951. Hibbler has a tonal quality once described by Ellington as "tonal pantomime." Hibbler still lives in New York and makes rare appearances.

### EARL (FATHA) HINES
**Piano, Band Leader**
**1903**

Except for increased technical proficiency, the piano style of Earl "Fatha" Hines has barely changed from what it was in the late 1920s.

Hailing from a Pittsburgh background musically rounded out by his trumpeter father and organist mother, Hines originally planned a concert career, but was soon caught up in the world of jazz. Forming his own trio while still in high school, he began to play in local clubs before moving on to Chicago in 1925.

While there, he made a series of records with Louis Armstrong's Hot Five, and soon became known as "the trumpet-style pianist." Because of the exciting single-note use of his right hand, the intricacy of his style was well beyond that of any of his contemporaries, and served as a touchstone for a succeeding generation of pianists.

In 1928, Hines formed his own band at the Grand Terrace in Chicago. For the next 20 years, this band served as a proving ground for the best instrumentalists and innovators of the period (from Bud Johnson and Walter Fuller in the early era, to Dizzy Gillespie and Charlie Parker in the later years).

From 1948 to 1951, Hines worked again with Armstrong, then played a long engagement in San Francisco. In 1963, a New York recital revitalized his career, and he enjoyed great success in Europe, Japan, and at home until his death.

*"Lady Day"—Billie Holiday*

### MILTON J. (MILT) HINTON
**Bass**
**1909**

Milt Hinton was born in Vicksburg, Mississippi and is considered one of the greatest of bass players. He has played with many top jazz artists, including Cab Calloway, Count Basie, Louis Armstrong, Teddy Wilson, and Benny Goodman. Hinton has appeared in concerts throughout the world and on numerous television shows, and has made more records than any other jazz musician. He is also an accomplished photographer.

### BILLIE HOLIDAY
**Singer**
**1915-1959**

Billie Holiday, dubbed "Lady Day" by Lester Young, was one of the greatest jazz singers

While still a young girl, she moved from her hometown of Baltimore to New York City, and in 1931, began her singing career in an assortment of Harlem night spots. In 1933, she cut her first sides with Benny Goodman, and from 1935 to 1939, established her reputation with a series of records made with Teddy Wilson. She also sang with the bands of

Count Basie and Artie Shaw.

In such classic records as "Strange Fruit" and "God Bless the Child," she departed from popular material to score her greatest artistic triumphs, depicting the harsh reality of Southern lynchings and the personal alienation she had experienced.

Miss Holiday died of lung congestion and other ailments in Metropolitan Hospital, New York City. Once addicted to drugs and alcohol, she had written in her 1956 autobiography, "All dope can do for you is kill you—and kill you the long, slow, hard way."

### J. J. JOHNSON
**Trombone, Composer**
**1924**

J. J. Johnson stands alone as the unchallenged master of the modern jazz trombone. He is the first musician to have adapted this instrument to the demanding techniques called for by the advent of Bop.

Early in his career, Johnson displayed such skill in performing high-speed and intricate solos that those who knew him only from records found it hard to believe that he was actually using a slide—and not a valve—trombone.

Johnson spent the 1940s touring with Benny Carter, Count Basie, Woody Herman, and Dizzy Gillespie. During these years, his trombone was as widely imitated as the trumpet and alto of Gillespie and Parker, respectively.

In the 1950s, Johnson retired for a time, only to return as partner of Kai Winding's *Jay and Kai Quintet*. This group soon began to tour Europe and the United States with great success.

Johnson's ability as a composer has also been widely praised. In 1959, he performed several of his works with the Monterey Festival Orchestra. He has also composed for films and TV.

### JAMES P. JOHNSON
**Piano, Composer**
**1894-1955**

James P. Johnson is less known than that of his most famous protege, Fats Waller, but Johnson nonetheless made a substantial contribution to the fields of jazz piano and popular show music.

Johnson was the master of the "stride piano," an instrumental style which derives its name from the strong, striding, left-hand style of the player. "Stride piano" came

*The one and only Earl (Fatha) Hines*

into its own during the 1920s, particularly in conjunction with the phenomenon known as the "rent party." Such a party was held for the purpose of raising rent money, and involved the payment of an admission fee which entitled a "patron" to food, drink, conviviality, and a stride piano session.

Duke Ellington and Count Basie were among the many who sharpened their skills in the rent party training ground. In fact, the influence of the stride piano was heard in popular music for the next two decades.

Johnson was also an early bridge between the worlds of jazz and Broadway. Numbered among his song hits are "If I Could Be With You," "Charleston," and "Runnin' Wild."

## SCOTT JOPLIN
### Composer
### 1868-1917

At the start of 1970, the name Scott Joplin was known only to connoisseurs of ragtime. His remains lay buried in an unmarked pauper's grave in New York City's Borough of Queens and his music had been consigned to oblivion.

Then, in 1970, Nonesuch Records released a recording of Joplin's rags on a classical label. The record pulled raves from critics of classical music, among them Harold Schomberg of the *New York Times.* In 1971, the New York City Public Library sponsored a concert of Joplin's work at Lincoln Center by pianists Mary Lou Williams, William Bolcom and Joshua Rifkin, and singers Barbara Christopher, Clamma Dale, and Michael Gordon. In 1972, a full-scale performance of Joplin's opera *Treemonisha* was staged by the Afro American Music Workshop in Atlanta. In 1973 Joplin rags were adapted for *The Sting,* a successful movie. By 1975, Scott Joplin's music was the rage of both the popular and classical music worlds, the former buying records and tapes of his rags by the millions, the latter seriously debating whether he should be rated with Ives and Gershwin in the top rank of American composers.

The popular success of Joplin's themes in *The Sting* obscures the key fact about his music and life; he was a serious composer of talent and versatility whose most earnest efforts were ignored and rejected because it was inconceivable to the American musical establishment that the black idiom, or indeed any black individual, could be associated with "serious" music. Thus, during his lifetime, Joplin was acclaimed as the King of Ragtime, but when he presumed to venture into the forms of grand opera, he was ignored and destroyed.

Joplin felt that rag would become the "classical" music of the United States, and that this would reflect an assimilation of African and American black folk themes with classical compositional devices into music with mixed urban and minstrel roots. Much of this view was accepted, tacitly at least, by established classical composers of his period, such as Igor Stravinsky, who wrote rag music, and Debussy, who wrote cakewalk music clearly modeled on rag.

Incredibly, rag, an interracial product of the American Midwest, was acceptable in concert halls only when composed by European whites.

Scott Joplin, whose father had been a slave, was born in Texas in 1868. He early displayed musical talent and was given piano lessons, free, by a local German music teacher. In his teens, he left home and became an itinerant pianist, playing in saloons and bordellos of Mississippi Rivertowns, then in St. Louis and Chicago, and then in Sedalia, Missouri, where he settled in 1894. In Sedalia, he worked in a honky tonk, studied harmony and composition at a local black college, and in 1897 composed "Maple Leaf Rag," which was published in 1899.

"Rag" was an instant success, rewarding Joplin sufficiently to allow him to leave the honky tonks, marry, and move to St. Louis where he taught and composed. In 1899, he wrote a long, choreographed song, "The Ragtime Dance," and in 1903 copyrighted his first opera, *A Guest of Honor,* which was in ragtime. Unusual for their time, neither was successful, but Joplin's short ragtime works continued to be in great demand.

In 1907, Joplin moved to New York where he started work on *Treemonisha,* a folk grand opera. Publishers would not consider such a thing, let alone one by a black pianist from the honky tonks of the Midwest, and Joplin had to publish *Treemonisha* at his own expense in 1911. However, he could not find a producer and his orchestration of it was lost. In 1916, in desperation, he unsuccessfully staged a piano version of *Treemonisha* in Harlem. Finally broken, and a victim of syphilis, Joplin was committed to a State Hospital

*Versatile guitarist B. B. King in concert.*

and died the next year.

For the next 55 years, Joplin's name and music were kept alive by a small band of disciples such as James Scott and Joseph Lamb, but much of his music, including *A Guest of Honor,* has been lost.

*Treemonisha,* Scott Joplin's major work—for 11 voices—consists of 27 set pieces, and overture, instrumental preludes to the second and third acts, arias, ensembles, recitative choruses—in short, it is a grand opera. It was originally composed for piano accompaniment only, then orchestrated by Joplin, probably in an attempt to improve its chances for acceptance (production). The music is evocative of standard opera of its period, Joplin's black heritage, and his genius for ragtime composition.

The story reflects Joplin's views, and that of many blacks and civil rights advocates of that time, that education of blacks was the most effective weapon against racism and prejudice.

In the story, Treemonisha is an 18-year-old orphan girl with an education, who becomes leader of recently freed slaves on a Southern plantation and refuses to allow her followers to punish their oppressors, because this would be unjust and a confirmation of ignorance. It clearly calls for blacks to acquire education and assert themselves.

## B. B. KING
**Singer-Guitar**
**1925**

B. B. King has become one of the most successful artists in the history of the blues. Each of his albums and singles have outsold each previous release and topped those of Bessie Smith, Robert Johnson, Big Bill Broonzy, and others.

B.B.'s career started when as a boy of 14 in Indianola, Mississippi, he met a preacher who played the guitar. B. B. soon owned his own guitar, which he bought for eight dollars, paid out of meager wages he earned working in the cotton fields. From that time on, B. B. spent his spare time singing and playing the guitar with other budding musicians in the town, and listening to itinerant blues guitarists who came to Indianola clubs. Although he loved tossing the blues, he had to do it away from home since such "lowdown" music was not sung in his religious household. In the early 1940s, he would travel to a nearby town where he would stand on street corners and play. Sometimes he'd come home with as much as 25 dollars.

After the war, B. B. hitchhiked to Memphis where a fellow musician, remembering him from Indianola, got him a performing job at the 16th Street Grill. He was paid 12 dollars a night, five nights a week, and room and board. B. B. then found a spot on a newly opened radio station in Memphis called WDIA. He played 10 minutes each afternoon, then became a disc jockey. The station named him "The Boy from Beale Street" and thereafter Riley B. King was known as "B.B."

B. B.'s first record was made in 1949 for RPM. He had a number one disc on the rhythm and blues charts in 1950 and has been known nationally ever since. A change of managers led to a new direction away from the "chitlin' circuit" and into prestigious "pop"-oriented clubs, colleges, and the fast-growing field of pop festivals.

*Rahsaan Kirk, a serious and creative innovator.*

A series of personal appearances on major television shows sparked his popularity. In 1969, B. B. toured Europe, starting with the Royal Albert Hall in London and continuing through England, France, Germany, Switzerland, Denmark, and Sweden. Returning to the United States, he joined a 14-city tour with the Rolling Stones.

He later performed at Carnegie Hall in New York. Shortly thereafter *Down Beat* magazine voted B. B. the number one blues artist in its annual International Critic's Poll.

## RAHSAAN ROLAND KIRK
**Composer; Flute, Tenor Sax, Manzello, etc.**
**1936-1977**

At first called "gimmicky" by the critics, Roland Kirk proved to be one of the most exciting jazz instrumentalists. His variety of instruments was matched only by the range of his improvisational styles, often switching in the middle of a number from a dissonant, Hawkins-like exploration to a tonal solo based on a conventional melody.

Born in Columbus, Ohio, Kirk was technically blind, having been able to see nothing but light from infancy. Educated at the Ohio State School for the Blind, he began picking up horns at the age of nine. At 19, while touring with Boyd Moore, he started experimenting with playing more than one instrument at one time. Finding obscure horns like the stritch and the manzello, he worked out a technique for playing three-part harmony through the use of trick fingering.

In 1960, Ramsey Lewis helped Kirk get his first recording date (with Argo Records). In 1961, he played with Charles Mingus' group, and later that year he went on the international circuit.

Among his many compositions are *Three for Dizzy; Hip Chops; The Business Ain't Nothin' but the Blues; From Bechet, Byas, & Fats;* and *Mystical Dreams.*

### JOHN LEWIS
### Pianist, Composer
### 1920

John Lewis has become an international force in the world of jazz as an arranger, conductor, composer, and instrumentalist.

Raised in a middle-class environment in Albuquerque, New Mexico, Lewis studied music and anthropology at the University of New Mexico until 1942. After three years in the Army, he went to New York City to become pianist and arranger with Dizzy Gillespie's band. Two years later at Carnegie Hall, Gillespie's band performed Lewis' first major work, "Toccata for Trumpet and Orchestra."

After a European tour with Gillespie, Lewis returned to the United States to play with Lester Young and Charlie Parker, and to arrange for Miles Davis. In 1952, after having finished his studies at the Manhattan School of Music, Lewis founded the group upon which a major part of his reputation rests: The Modern Jazz Quartet (MJQ). Throughout the 1950s, this group developed an international reputation in spite of some carping that its material was too charted to be truly called jazz.

Lewis has never confined his creativity to the MJQ but has constantly assumed a variety of roles, ranging from conducting in Germany to serving as music director of the highly acclaimed Monterey Jazz Festival.

### ABBEY LINCOLN
### Singer
### 1930

"This is a WOMAN singing, and more specifically it is a Negro woman, because part of this striking liberation of Abbey's singing has come from a renewed and urgent pride in herself as a Black Woman." This assessment of Abbey Lincoln's talent, style, and direction, made by critic Nat Hentoff, places her among the great jazz singers of our time.

Born Anna Marie Wooldridge in Chicago, Miss Lincoln graduated from Kalamazoo Central High School in Kalamazoo, Michigan and later studied music for a number of years in Hollywood under several prominent vocal and dramatic coaches.

She began her professional career in Jackson, Michigan in 1950. Since then she has performed in movies (*Nothing but a Man* ), made records (*Abbey Is Blue, Straight Ahead* ), played several prominent clubs, and appeared on nationwide television. More important, she has been hailed by many of the outstanding black jazz performers of our era, including Coleman Hawkins, Benny Carter, and Charles Mingus, as a singer to be classed with the likes of Billie Holiday.

### MELBA LISTON
### Arranger, Trombonist
### 1926

Melba Liston, who has played with the greatest names in jazz, is one of the very few female trombonists. Born in Kansas City, Missouri in 1926, Ms. Liston's family later moved to California. Her musical history began in 1937, when as a nine-year-old she played in a youth band under the tutelage of Alma Hightower. Ms. Liston continued her trombone studies, in addition to music composition, throughout high school. She got work with the Los Angeles Lincoln Theater upon graduation. She met band leader Gerald Wilson on the night club circuit, and he introduced her to Dizzy Gillespie, Count Basie, Duke Ellington, Charlie Parker and numerous others. By the late 1940s, she was playing alongside of John Coltrane and John Lewis in Dizzy's band, and later toured with Billie Holiday as her assistant musical director and arranger. When the Big Band era waned, Ms. Liston jumped off the music circuit and returned to California, where she passed a Board of Education examination and taught for four years. She was coaxed back into performing by Dizzy, and in the next 20 years, led an all-female jazz group, toured Europe with Quincy Jones, and did arrangements for Ellington, Basie, Dizzy and Diana Ross. In 1974, she went to Jamaica to explore reggae. When she returned to the U.S. in 1979, she formed Melba Liston and Company, in which she revived swing, bebop and contemporary compositions, many of which were her own. She is regarded as a brilliant and creative arranger and an exceptional trombonist by her peers.

### JIMMY LUNCEFORD
### Bandleader
### 1902-1947

"The Lunceford style"—although its originator himself never played an instrument while recording with his band (except flute in his record of *Liza* )—was one which influenced many band leaders and arrangers up to the 1950s, including Sonny Dunham, Sonny Burke, and Tommy Dorsey. The Lunceford band reigned with those of Duke Ellington, Count Basie, and Benny Goodman as the leading and most influential of the big jazz orchestras in the 1930s.

A native of Fulton, Missouri, Lunceford received his B.A. at Fisk University and later studied at City College in New York. After having become proficient on all reed instruments, Lunceford began his own career as a leader." in Memphis in 1927. By 1934, he was an established presence in the field of jazz. During the next decade, the Lunceford band was known as the best-disciplined and most showmanly black jazz ensemble in the nation.

The Lunceford vogue faded after 1942, by which time the band was already experiencing several changes of personnel. Lunceford died of a heart attack in 1947 while the band was on tour.

### WYNTON MARSALIS
### Trumpet, Band leader
### 1961

Born into a musical family in New Orleans (his father, Ellis Marsalis, is a prominent pianist and teacher; his brother Branford (b. 1960) is a well-known tenor and soprano saxophonist who leads his own groups and has worked with Sting, and several of his younger siblings also play), Wynton Marsalis was well schooled in both the jazz and classical traditions. At 17, he won an award at the prestigious Berkshire Music Center for his classical prowess; a year later, he left the Juiciness School of Music to join Art Blakey's Jazz Messengers.

After touring in Japan and the USA with Herbie Hancock and also recording with the pianist, he made his first own LP in 1981, formed his own group, and toured extensively. Soon he made a classical album, and in 1984 became the first instrumentalist to win simultaneous Grammy Awards as best jazz and classical soloist, with many other awards to follow. He also received a great deal of media coverage—more than any other serious young musician in recent memory.

A brilliant virtuoso of the trumpet with total command of any musical situation he chooses to place himself in, Marsalis has also made himself a potent spokesman for the highest musical standards in jazz, to which he is firmly and proudly committed. He has urged young musicians to acquaint themselves with the rich tradition of jazz and to avoid the pitfalls of "crossing over" to pop, fusion and rock. His own adherence to these principles and his stature as a player has made his words effective.

*Wynton Marsalis, a virtuoso of the trumpet.*

### CARMEN MCRAE
### Singer, Pianist
### 1922

As a singer/pianist, Carmen McRae has performed in concert halls and festivals throughout the United States, Europe and Japan. Born in Brooklyn in 1922, Ms. McRae's natural talent on the keyboards won her numerous music scholarships. During her teen years, she carefully studied the vocal style of Billie Holiday and incorporated it into her own style. An early highlight came when Miss Holiday recorded one of Ms. McRae's compositions, "Dream of Life." After finishing her education, Ms. McRae moved to Washington, D.C. and worked as a government clerk by day and a nightclub pianist/singer by night. In the early 1940s, she moved to Chicago to work with Benny Carter, Mercer Ellington and Count Basie. By 1954, she had gained enough attention through her jazz and pop recordings to be dubbed a "new star" by Downbeat magazine. She continues to grace music programs, and is considered a favorite addition to performances because of her harmonic sensitivity and exceptionally attuned musical knowledge.

### JIMMY MCGRIFF
### Organist
### 1936

Jazz organist James Harrell McGriff was born in Philadelphia and comes from a musical family. His father, Harrell, and his mother, Beatrice, both played the piano. By the time McGriff finished Roosevelt and Germantown high schools, he was playing bass, drums, sax, and vibes. Although he possessed excellent musical ability, McGriff thought that he was big enough to become a policeman and enrolled at the Penn Institute of Criminology in Philadelphia. However, while he was enrolled at the institute, he began to hang out in a club three miles from Philadelphia where Lynn Hope, Jimmy Smith, Donald Bailey, Lee Morgan, Don Gardner, Al Cass, and Eddie McFadden were playing. He was tempted to drop out of school and pursue a musical career—until he caught Smith, Cass, and Thornel Schwartz at a club in Trenton, New Jersey. He was hooked the first night he went in to listen. His records have been best sellers since the McGriff version of the Ray Charles tune "I Got a Woman" hit the international spotlight in 1962. His album *City Lights* in 1981 brought the total of McGriff 's compositions on record to an impressive number of 79. In the fall of 1981, McGriff was a participant in Norfolk State University's (Norfolk, Virginia) Eminent Scholars Program. McGriff has played clubs and concert dates all over the world.

*Pioneering bass player Charles Mingus, whose background includes classical training, took the bass from simple accompaniment and gave it a sophisticated contrapuntal role.*

## CHARLES MINGUS
**Bass, Composer**
**1922-1981**

Charles Mingus was to the young jazz musician of the 1960s what Charlie Parker and Dizzy Gillespie were to the same group in the two previous decades.

Mingus emerged from classical training in Los Angeles in solfeggio and trombone to become one of jazz's most original bassists. His musical background ranges from five years of study with H. Rheinschagen of the New York Philharmonic to professional stints with Louis Armstrong, Kid Ory, Lionel Hampton, Red Norvo, Charlie Parker, Stan Getz, Duke Ellington, Bud Powell, and Art Tatum (a roster which literally spans the entire history of jazz).

Mingus came into his own as a composer in the mid-1950s. His experiments were directed at expanding the arbitrary limitations he felt had been imposed on jazz. Some of the effects he created (including atonalities and dissonances) generated the sort of furor which greeted the advent of Bop a decade earlier.

In 1964, Mingus made his first appearance at the Monterey Jazz Festival with a specially assembled large band to play "Meditations." The powerful performance ranks as one of the high points in Mingus' career.

Mingus played little during the latter half of the 1960s, instead writing an autobiography called *Beneath the Underdog,* which was published in 1971. It spurred new interest in Mingus' music and he began to play again.

In February 1972, he made a comeback concert at Philharmonic Hall, appearing with a 20-piece band and several surprise guests and playing to a sell-out house. In 1974, he appeared at Carnegie Hall with Rahsaan Roland Kirk.

## THE MODERN JAZZ QUARTET

The Modern Jazz Quartet, formed in 1952, established the right of jazz to be performed on the world's great concert stages.

In 1957, the Quartet broke European barriers to jazz with a series of successful appearances in its staidest concert halls. This triumph was capped in 1970 when the MJQ was asked to preform in Venice's La Fenice opera house.

Another MJQ pioneering success includes the first solo jazz performance at the Berkshire Music Barn, in Massachusetts.

With one exception, in 1954, the Quartet has operated with the same personnel since its inception. In that year, drummer Connie Kay replaced Kenny Clarke. John Lewis is the pianist and musical director, Milt Jackson plays the vibraharp and is principal soloist, and Percy Heath rounds out the group on bass.

Though the Modern Jazz Quartet had disbanded in 1974, it was reunited by popular demand in 1981.

## THELONIOUS SPHERE MONK
**Piano, Composer**
**1917-1982**

Thelonious Monk's popularity with the general public dates largely from the middle 1950s. However, within the world of professional jazz musicians, his role as an important pioneer in the development of Bop had been acknowledged long before then.

Along with Charlie Parker and Dizzy Gillespie, Monk had been a vital member of the jazz revolution which took place in the early 1940s. Some musicians (among them Art Blakey) have felt that Monk actually predated his more renowned contemporaries. Monk's piano technique and his talent as a composer in the new idiom made him a leader in the development of modern jazz.

Aside from some brief work with the Lucky Millander band and Coleman Hawkins, Monk generally was leader of his own small groups. He has been called the most important jazz composer since Ellington. Many of his compositions (*Round About Midnight, Ruby My Dear* ) have become established jazz standards for sometime.

Monk was unique as both an instrumentalist and composer, maintaining his own musical integrity and his melodic originality.

Thelonious Monk died in Englewood, New Jersey in 1982.

### FERDINAND (JELLY ROLL) MORTON
**Piano**
**1890-1941**

Among the many controversial aspects of Jelly Roll Morton's life was his claim that he had "invented jazz in 1902." Although Morton's boast was often scorned by many, his talents as a soloist, composer, and arranger place him in the forefront of the early jazz innovators.

A pianist in New Orleans from 1905 until the close of the Storyville era, Morton lived in California from 1917 to 1922. Using the name "Morton's Red Hot Peppers" from 1926 to 1930, he cut a series of records which were to bring him a nation-wide reputation. During this period, Morton also became known for the diamond filling he wore in one of his teeth as a success symbol.

When jazz fashions changed in the 1930s, Morton fell into eclipse. By 1937 he was running an obscure nightclub in Washington, D.C.

In 1938, Morton made a number of recordings for the Library of Congress—playing, singing, and narrating the major incidents of his life and career. These recordings brought him renewed attention but within two years he had lapsed back into obscurity—this time in Los Angeles, where he died in 1941.

### THEODORE (FATS) NAVARRO
**Trumpet**
**1923-1950**

Fats Navarro was born in Key West, Florida. He started playing trumpet at age 13, and also played tenor sax. Navarro

*Formed in 1952, the Modern Jazz Quartet brought jazz to the world's great concert stages. MJQ's personnel were (left to right) John Lewis, Connie Kay, Percy Heath, and Milt Jackson.*

was first heard in the Northeast as a member of Andy Kirk's band from 1943 to 1944 when Dizzy Gillespie heard him and recommended him to Billy Eckstine, with whom he played for 18 months. In 1947-1948 Fats played with Illinois Jacquet, Lionel Hampton, and Coleman Hawkins. He also worked with Tadd Dameron in 1948-1949. Navarro was ranked with Dizzy Gillespie and Miles Davis as one of the greatest trumpet players of the boppers.

## JOSEPH (KING) OLIVER
**Cornet**
**1885-1938**

Joe Oliver first earned the sobriquet "King" in 1917 after winning a kind of "open combat" solo contest against the likes of Freddie Keppard, Manuel Perez, and a host of other cornetists who filled the Storyville nights with the first sounds of New Orleans jazz.

Strongly influenced by Buddy Bolden in the early part of his career, Oliver soon teamed up with Kid Ory and organized what was to become the leading jazz band in New Orleans.

During the Storyville era, Oliver met and befriended Louis Armstrong. Lacking a son of his own, he became Armstrong's "unofficial father," giving the boy his old horn, and sharing with him the musical knowledge which he had acquired over the years. In return, Armstrong treated him with great respect, referring to him always as "Papa Joe."

With the closing of Storyville, Oliver left for Chicago, whereupon Armstrong replaced him in Ory's band. By 1922, however, Oliver was in a position to summon Armstrong to play in his Creole Jazz Band as second cornetist.

In 1923, the Creole Jazz Band made the first series of recordings by a black jazz group, except for a few numbers by Kid Ory.

The duets of Oliver and Armstrong put Chicago on the jazz map of the United States. Some years later, however, changing tastes caused Oliver's music to decline in popularity so that, by the time he moved to New York in 1928, his best years were already behind him.

From 1932, Oliver toured mainly the South before finally settling in Savannah, Georgia, where he worked in a poolroom from 1936 until his death in 1938.

## EDWARD (KID) ORY
**Trombone, Band Leader**
**1886-1973**

Kid Ory's musical career is in many ways emblematic of the story of jazz itself. They both reached a high point in New Orleans during the first two decades of this century. They both moved north during the 1920s, only to lapse into obscurity in the 1930s before being revived in the next two decades.

Ory was the best known of the so-called tailgate trombonists. He led his own band in Los Angeles until 1924, when he moved to Chicago to play with King Oliver, Jelly Roll Morton and others. In 1926, with Louis Armstrong, he recorded his own composition "Muskrat Ramble."

He returned to the West Coast in 1929, and after playing for a time with local bands, retired to run a successful chicken ranch from 1930 to 1939. In the 1940s, he gradually returned to music with Barney Bigard, Bunk Johnson, and other New Orleans notables. When "Muskrat Ramble" was revived in 1956, Ory's name became known to a whole new generation.

He toured Europe successfully in 1956, and again in 1959, and spent his final years in Hawaii.

*Charlie Parker influenced the entire spectrum of jazz ideas.*

## CHARLIE (BIRD) PARKER
**Alto Saxophone**
**1920-1955**

The influence of Charlie Parker on the development of jazz has been felt not only in the realm of the alto saxophone, which he dominated, but on the whole spectrum of jazz ideas. The astounding innovations which he introduced melodically, harmonically, tonally, and rhythmically made it impossible for any jazz musician from the mid-1940s to the present time to develop his own style without reflecting some of Parker's tonal patterns, with or without acknowledgment.

Parker left school at 15 to become a professional, spending his early years with a group of fun-loving musicians in Kansas City, his hometown. After wandering about the Midwest for a time, Parker visited New York in 1939. Back in Kansas City he joined Jay McShann with whom he recorded his first sides two years later. It was at this time that Parker met Dizzy Gillespie, who was developing parallel ideas and who would become known as co-founder with Parker of the bop movement some four years later.

In the early 1940s, Parker played with the bands of Noble Sissle, Earl Hines, Cootie Williams, Andy Kirk, as well as the original Billy Eckstine band—the first big band formed expressly to feature the new jazz style in both solos and arrangements.

In 1945, Parker formally launched the bop movement by cutting a series of sides with Gillespie. Although Parker was soon revered by a host of younger musicians, his innovations met with a great deal of opposition from traditionalist jazz musicians and critics.

In 1946, Parker suffered a breakdown and was confined to a state hospital in California. Six months later he was back recording with Erroll Garner. From this point on until his death from a heart attack in 1955, he confined most of his activity to working with a quintet but also recorded and toured with a string section, and visited Europe in 1949 and 1950. He made his final appearance in 1955 at Bird land, the club which had been named in his honor.

**OSCAR PETERSON**
**Piano**
**1925**

Oscar Peterson began classical study of the piano at the age of six in his native Canada, and in less than a decade, was playing regularly on a local radio show.

In 1944, he became a featured soloist with Johnny Holmes, one of the top bands in Canada, and his reputation soon spread throughout the United States jazz world. He continued to resist offers from Jimmie Lunceford and others to tour the States, but in 1949 was persuaded by Norman Granz to come to New York City for a Carnegie Hall appearance. The following year he began to record and to tour the United States for Granz.

Peterson's international reputation stems from his annual European tours. His original group used bass (Ray Brown) and guitar (Barney Kessel, Herb Ellis), but when Ellis left in 1958, Peterson hired drummer Ed Thigpen to fill out the trio.

The initial reaction to Peterson in the United States was often one of curt dismissal. He was first thought of as nothing but a composite of other pianists, but gradually he came to be recognized as forming a creative bridge between two jazz generations—Swing and Bop—using the very best elements of both to make his own highly personal statement.

**OSCAR PETTIFORD**
**Bass**
**1922-1960**

Oscar Pettiford was the leading bassist in the modern era of jazz. Building his own style on the foundation established by the late Jimmy Blanton, Pettiford achieved renown as the most technically capable and melodically inventive bassist in the jazz world of the late 1940s.

Pettiford was born on an Indian reservation and raised in Minneapolis. Until he was 19, he toured with the family band (father and 11 children), and was well known in the Midwest. In 1943, Charlie Barnet heard him in Minneapolis and hired him to team up with bassist Chubby Jackson.

Pettiford left Barnet later that year, and led his own group on 52nd Street and also played with Coleman Hawkins, Duke Ellington, and Woody Herman.

Pettiford's fame grew during the 1950s through his recordings and his tours of Europe and the Orient. In 1958, he settled permanently in Europe, where he continued to work until his death in Copenhagen in 1960.

**BUD POWELL**
**Pianist, Composer**
**1924-1966**

Along with Charlie Parker and Dizzy Gillespie, with whom he often worked, Earl "Bud" Powell was one of the founding fathers of modern jazz. A piano prodigy, he had his first big-time job with trumpeter Cootie Williams's big band in 1943, and became involved in the "birth of bebop" at Minton's Playhouse in Harlem and on 52nd Street.

The first to transfer the melodic, harmonic and rhythmic innovations of bop to the piano keyboard, he set the style for modern jazz piano, though he was greatly influenced by Art Tatum as well. Although he suffered recurrently from mental instability from his early 20s until the end of his life, Powell was capable of long stretches of musical brilliance. He lived in Paris from 1959 to 1964, frequently working with his old

*Bud Powell; one of the fathers of modern jazz.*

*Restless innovator Dewey Redman.*

friend Kenny Clarke. More than 5000 people attended his funeral in Harlem. One of Powell's finest compositions and performances is the ironically titled "Un Poco Loco," but there was nothing crazy about his hugely influential playing.

### MA RAINEY
**Vocalist**
**1886-1939**

Ma Rainey, the "Mother of the Blues," who enveloped the 1920s with her powerful, message-oriented blues songs, is remembered as a genuine jazz pioneer. Born in Columbus, Georgia as Gertrude Pridgett, Ms. Rainey gave her first public performance as a twelve-year-old at the local Springer Opera House. At age eighteen, she married singer/dancer William "Pa" Rainey and the duo embarked on a long entertainment career. Around 1912, Ms. Rainey introduced a teen-aged Bessie Smith into her act, a move which was later seen as having a major impact on the blues/jazz singing styles. Ten years later, Ms. Rainey was recording with Fletcher Henderson, Louis Armstrong, Coleman Hawkins and racking up the biggest record sales at the time for Paramount Records. She stopped recording in the 1930s, but continued to tour the South for a few years, singing of the black experience. She retired from performances in 1935, and until her death four years later, managed two theaters she owned in Georgia. Her eloquent and communicative voice lives on in the more than one hundred recordings she made in her lifetime.

### DEWEY REDMAN
**Tenor Saxophone**
**1931**

Dewey Redman has spent most of his life in search of a greater knowledge of his instrument, the tenor saxophone, constantly reevaluating his relationship to his music.

Dewey was born in Ft. Worth, Texas, started playing the clarinet when he was 12, taking private lessons briefly for six months before he turned to self-instruction. At 15, he got a job with an eight-piece band that performed in church as the minister passed the collection plate.

At Prairie View A&M College, Dewey teamed up with a piano and bass player to work in local clubs, found a spot in the Prairie View "swing" band, and graduated in 1953 with a degree in industrial arts and a grasp on a new instrument he had worked on in college, the saxophone.

After a stint in the Army, Dewey obtained a masters degree in Education at North Texas State and taught school and directed school bands in West and South Texas.

In 1959, he moved to Los Angeles, where he found the music scene to be very cliquish, and then to San Francisco, where he remained for seven years, studying music, working out his own theories on chord progressions, improvisation and technique. In 1967, Dewey went to New York City, fell in with Ornette Coleman, who brought him into his quartet with Dave Izenson on bass and Ornette Coleman Jr. on the drums.

By 1973 Dewey was dividing his playing time between solo efforts and gigs with Ornette Coleman and Keith Jarrett and composition of *Peace Suite*, dedicated to the late Ralph Bunche.

### DON REDMAN
**Saxophone, Composer**
**1900-1964**

The first composer-arranger of consequence in the history of jazz, Don Redman was known in the 1920s as a brilliant instrumentalist on several kinds of saxophones. He also made many records with Bessie Smith, Louis Armstrong, and other top-ranking jazz artists.

Born in Piedmont, West Virginia in 1900, Redman was a child prodigy who played trumpet at the age of three, joined a band at six, and later studied harmony, theory, and composition at the Boston and Detroit conservatories. In 1924, he joined Fletcher Henderson's band as lead saxophonist and staff arranger, and in 1928 became leader of McKinney's Cotton Pickers.

During most of the 1930s, Redman led his own band, regarded as one of the leading black orchestras of the day, and the first to play a sponsored radio series. He also wrote for many other prominent bands, black and white.

In 1951, Redman became musical director for Pearl Bailey. From 1954 to 1955, he appeared in a small acting role in *House of Flowers* on Broadway. He continued to arrange and record until his death in 1964.

### MAXWELL (MAX) ROACH
**Percussion, Composer**
**1925**

Brooklyn-born Maxwell Roach was one of the key figures in the development of modern jazz. He was in the first group to play bebop on 52nd Street in New York, led by Dizzy

Gillespie in 1943-44, and later worked with Charlie Parker's finest group, in 1947-48. In 1954, he joined the brilliant young trumpeter Clifford Brown (1930-56) as co-leader of the Clifford Brown-Max Roach Quintet. Since Brown's untimely death in a car crash, Roach began to lead his own groups of various sizes and instrumentation (including interesting work with solo and choral voices, and an all percussion band, and a jazz quartet combined with a string quartet). His many compositions include We Insist-Freedom Now, a suite written with his then wife, the singer Abbey Lincoln, one of the first jazz works with a strong and direct political and social thrust.

A phenomenally gifted musician with a matchless percussion technique, Roach developed the drum solo to new heights of structural refinement; he has been an influence on every drummer to come along since the 1940s. A professor of music at the University of Massachusetts since 1972, Roach in 1988 became the first jazz artist to receive a MacArthur Fellowship, the most prestigious (and lucrative) award in the world of arts and letters. His daughter, Maxine, is a violinist, and they have worked and recorded together.

## SONNY ROLLINS
### Tenor Saxophonist, Band Leader
### 1929

Born and raised in New York City, Theodore Walter Rollins made his recording debut at 19, in such fast company as J. J. Johnson and Bud Powell. Distinctively personal from the start, his style developed through work with Thelonious Monk, Powell, Art Blakey and Miles Davis. In 1955, he joined the Clifford Brown-Max Roach Quintet. In 1959, he took two years off from active playing, studying and practising. When he reappeared at the helm of his own quartet in 1961, he surprised even those who already new the quality of his work with the power and conviction of his playing.

Since then, though briefly overshadowed by John Coltrane, Rollins has been the unchallenged. master of modern jazz tenor saxophone, with a sound and style totally his own. He often draws on his West Indian heritage for melodic and rhythmic inspiration and is one of the undisputed masters of extended improvisation, often playing all by himself as his group "lays out" in amazement, a feeling shared by his listeners.

## JIMMY RUSHING
### Singer
### 1903-1972

The song "Mister Five by Five," written in tribute to him, is an apt physical description of Jimmy Rushing, who was one of the greatest male jazz and blues singers.

Rushing played piano and violin as a boy, but entered music professionally as a singer in the after-hours world of California in 1925. Since then, Rushing was linked with leading bands and musicians: with Walter Page from 1927 to 1928; Benny Moten from 1929; and from 1936 to 1949 as a main stay of the famed Count Basie band.

Rushing formed his own small group when he left Basie and in the ensuing years worked most often as a "single." Following the rediscovery of the blues in the mid-1950s, Rushing regained wide spread popularity.

His nightclub and festival engagements were always successful, and his world tours, on his own and also with Benny Goodman, earned him critical acclaim and commercial success. His style has endured across four decades of jazz largely due to its great warmth, a sure, firm melodic line, and a swinging use of rhythm. Late in life, he appeared in a featured acting role in Gordon Parks' film *The Learning Tree*.

*With a personally distinctive modern jazz style and sound, Sonny Rollins is today's unchallenged master of the tenor sax.*

*Jimmy Rushing, the original "Mr. Five-by-Five," is often called the greatest male jazz vocalist.*

Jazz lost its premier male singer when Jimmy Rushing died on June 8, 1972.

### BESSIE SMITH
### Singer
### 1894-1937

They called her "The Empress Of the Blues," and she had no peers. Her magnificent voice, sense of the dramatic, clarity of diction (you never missed a word of what she sang) and incomparable time and phrasing set her apart from the competition and made her appeal as much to jazz lovers as to lovers of the blues. Her first record, "Down Hearted Blues," sold more than a million, in 1923, when only Caruso and Paul Whiteman were racking up those kind of figures.

By then, Bessie Smith had been singing professionally for some 15 years, but records by black singers had only been made from 1920 on, and only by much less earthy voices. She already had a big following and had appeared in big shows, so the timing was right—not least for Columbia Records, whom she pulled out of the red. Before long, she was backed by the best jazz players, including Louis Armstrong, and by 1925 starred in her own touring show, which traveled in its own private Pullman car. By 1927, she was the highest paid black artist in the world, and in 1929 she made a short film, "St. Louis Blues," that captures for posterity some of her magnetism as a stage performer. But tastes in music were changing rapidly, and though Bessie Smith added popular songs to her repertory (she'd always done some of those) and moved with the times, the Depression killed the business for jazz and blues records, and in 1931, Columbia dropped her and she was soon touring as a "single."

John Hammond brought her back to the studios in 1933. Her records were wonderful, her singing as powerful and swinging as ever, but they didn't sell and turned out to be her last. She still found plenty of work on the traveling circuit, but the money was not what it used to be. On the road early one morning in Mississippi, she was fatally injured in a collision. For years, it was held as a fact that she died because a white hospital refused to treat her, but this wasn't so. The hospital in which her right arm, almost severed from her body in the accident, was amputated was black, but she had already lost too much blood to survive. She was only 42. Had she lived, her star would surely have risen once more.

In 1968, Columbia reissued all of her records. She would have been pleased with the response. No one had come along who could match her when it came to singing the blues.

### MAXINE SULLIVAN
### Singer
### 1911-1987

Maxine Sullivan was born Marietta Williams in Homestead, Pennsylvania. Ms. Sullivan was doing radio work and performing with the Red Hot Peppers in Pittsburgh when she was discovered in 1936. Her first recording session resulted in the best seller, "Loch Lomond." Ms. Sullivan appeared with the John Kirby band in the 1930s and appeared in feature films and on radio. In 1952, she went into retirement for a period, but began singing again in 1958. Her career got back into high gear in 1965. She was particularly popular in Europe.

### ART TATUM
### Piano
### 1910-1956

He was a wizard of the keyboard. Nobody, not even the greatest classical virtuosi, surpassed his technique, but what made Art Tatum, nearly blind from birth, so very special was the musical imagination brought to life by his exceptional facility. Harmonically, he matched the boppers in sophistication—young Charlie Parker took a job as dishwasher in a club where Tatum worked so he could hear him every night. Rhythmically, he also anticipated modern jazz developments and could play rings around anyone, regardless of their instrument.

Though he enjoyed a full career, mostly as a soloist but also as leader of a trio (with electric guitar and bass, patterned on Nat King Cole's), and recorded quite prolifically, Tatum was born and died a bit too soon to benefit from the acceptance that came to jazz as a concert hall music. The concert hall, in which he rarely had the chance to perform, was Tatum's ideal medium. As it was, what he loved best was to play "after hours" for the edification of fellow musicians and perhaps in a challenge to some newcomer on the piano, whom he would cut down to size. When there were no rivals around, Tatum would challenge himself, setting seemingly impossible tempos or picking tunes with the toughest "changes.'

There was no one like Art Tatum, and there never will be. His records remain to keep generations of piano players from gaining too high an opinion of their own skills.

### SARAH VAUGHAN
### Singer
### 1924

Her voice is of such beauty, range and power, her ear so sure, her musicality so rare that Sarah Vaughan could have become

*Bessie Smith influenced most blues singers who followed her.*

an operatic star, had she wanted to. Fortunately, she went the way of jazz and has brought joy to the world since starting to sing professionally in 1943.

She had already sung in church in her native Newark and accompanied the choir on the piano (she plays it well, one reason why she is so sure footed harmonically) and tried a few pop songs at high school parties when, on a dare, she entered the Wednesday night amateur contest at Harlem's famed Apollo Theater. As in a fairy tale, Billy Eckstine happened to be backstage. He ran out front as soon as he heard that voice, and recommended the young lady (of course she won the contest, which meant a week's work at the Apollo) to his boss, band leader Earl Hines, who came, heard, and hired. In the Hines band of the time were Charlie Parker and Dizzy Gillespie. They and Sarah all left Hines when Eckstine decided to start his own band. By 1945, she'd made her first records under her own name. She also was the only singer to record with Bird and Dizzy together.

A year later, she started her solo career. Though she has had some big pop hits during her long and rich career, she never strayed from jazz for long. Incredibly, as she got older, she got better, losing none of her amazing top range and adding to the bottom while her mastery of interpretation also grew. Her fans call her "the Divine One." They're right on the mark.

## THOMAS (FATS) WALLER
### Composer, Piano, Singer
### 1904-1943

Weighing in at over 300 pounds and standing more than six feet tall, Tom Waller, a preacher's son (born in Greenwich Village in New York City), came by his nickname naturally. Big as he was, he was, as one of his many good friends said, "all music." His father wanted him to follow in his footsteps, but Fats liked the good times that came with playing the piano well, which he did almost from the start. At 15, he turned pro, backing singers in Harlem clubs and playing piano for silent movies. Wherever he went, people loved him, and he loved to spread joy. Few pianists, then or now, can match his terrific beat. He was also a master of the stride piano style. (He also loved to play Bach, especially on the organ, which he was the first to make into a jazz instrument, but that was seldom possible. One time it was—in Paris in 1932, when the world famous Marcel Dupre invited Fats to try out the organ at Notre Dame.

A talent for writing songs soon became evident. His first and biggest hit was "Ain't Misbehavin'", from 1929; others include "Honeysuckle Rose", "Blue Turning Gray Over You", and "The Jitterbug Waltz." He also wrote a "London Suite."

Fats was great on that new medium of the 1920s, the radio. He had an instant line of patter to go along with his great piano and carefree singing. He also made it to Hollywood. But his true medium was records. With his fine little group and occasional big band, he cut more than 500 sides between 1934 and his untimely death at 39 in 1943. He came across on records, and no matter how trite the tune, he turned it into a jazz gem. What cut Fats down in his prime was his appetite for huge quantities of food (he was capable of consuming two whole chickens at one sitting, or polishing off two full-size steak dinners and strong drink.) Ironically, his first complete Broadway musical (he'd written songs for many others) was becoming a hit as he started off for home from California, where he had just finished filming *Stormy Weather* which he almost stole from Lena Horne and Bill Robinson. He never arrived because pneumonia took him on a bitter cold December night just as the Superchief pulled into Kansas City.

But Fats wouldn't want tears. His power to make us laugh and marvel remains intact after almost half a century.

## DINAH WASHINGTON
### Vocalist
### 1924-1963

Dinah Washington's style defies categorization, but is seen as laying the groundwork for numerous rhythm and blues and jazz artists. Like many black singers, Ms. Washington got her start singing gospel; in her case, at St. Luke's Baptist Church on Chicago's South Side. She toured churches with her mother, playing the piano and singing solos, until another opportunity beckoned, an amateur talent contest at Chicago's Regal Theater. Her triumphant performance there led to performances at local nightclubs, and in 1943, the nineteen-year-old singer successfully auditioned for a slot in Lionel Hampton's band. She was soon discovered by composer Leonard Feather, and together Ms. Washington and Mr. Feather created several chart toppers, including "Baby Get Lost," "Salty Papa Blues," Evil Gal Blues," and "Homeward Bound." She gained legendary status with "What A Difference A Day Makes" and "Unforgettable." Ms. Washington proved to be such a versatile artist that she was acclaimed —and mourned when she died at age 39— by blues, jazz, gospel, pop, and rhythm and blues audiences alike. Aretha Franklin dedicated one of her early albums to Ms. Washington, labelling it simply "Unforgettable.

## BEN WEBSTER
**Tenor Saxophone**
**1909-1973**

Born in Kansas City, Ben Webster was at first a pianist, but switched to saxophone in his late teens. He worked with the family band led by Lester Young's father and with many other midwestern bands, and came to New York in 1931 with Benny Moten (whose pianist was Count Basie). After gaining a name among musicians as one of the most gifted disciples of Coleman Hawkins, he made many records and toured with many prominent bands (Fletcher Henderson, Cab Calloway, Teddy Wilson).

But it was when he joined Duke Ellington in 1939 that Webster really blossomed and soon became an influence in his own right. When he left Duke in 1943, he mainly led his own small groups, recorded prolifically, and also became one of the first black musicians to join a network radio musical staff. In 1964, he left on what had been planned as his first brief visit to Europe, but he never returned home. Settling in Copenhagen, he spent the final decade of his life as a revered and beloved elder statesman of jazz. During this period, his always masterful ballad playing ripened to full maturity, and his sound, ranging from a whisper to a gruff roar, one of the unsurpassed landmarks of classic jazz.

## MARY LOU WILLIAMS
**Pianist, Composer, Arranger**
**1910-1981**

Most women who have achieved fame in jazz have been singers, from Bessie Smith to Betty Carter. A singular exception to this rule was Mary Lou Williams, dubbed the "First Lady of Jazz."

Brought up in Pittsburgh, Atlanta-born Mary Elfrieda Scruggs had already performed in public at the age of six and was a pro by 13. Three years later she married saxophonist John Williams, with whom she made her record debut. When he joined Andy Kirk's band she took over the group. Soon, however, she was writing arrangements for Kirk, and in 1931, she became the band's pianist and musical director.

Though she also wrote for Benny Goodman and other bands, she stayed with Kirk until 1942, helping to make the band one of the swing era's best. Settling in New York, she led her own groups (sometimes all female) and began to compose longer works, including the "Zodiac Suite," performed at Town Hall in 1946. A champion of modern jazz, she gave advice and counsel to such rising stars as Dizzy Gillespie and Thelonious Monk. Miss Williams lived in England and France from 1952 to 1954. Back at home, she retired from music for some three years, but was coaxed out by Gillespie. Resuming her career, she toured widely, wrote several religious works including a Jazz Mass performed at St. Patrick's Cathedral, and in 1977 became artist in residence and teacher of jazz history and performance at Duke University, a position she held until her death. As pianist, composer and arranger, Mary Lou Williams ranks with the very best.

## TEDDY WILSON
**Pianist, Band Leader**
**1912-1986**

Theodore Wilson's father taught English and his mother was head librarian at Tuskegee Institute. He turned to music as a career while visiting relatives in Detroit in 1928, was

*"Fats" Waller; he had a good time with his music and people who hear it, jazz fan or not, love it as well.*

befriended by the great Art Tatum, played in Louis Armstrong's big band, and was brought to New York by Benny Carter in 1933.

Two years later, he began to make a series of records—which became classics—often with Billie Holiday and always with the greatest musicians of the time. Meanwhile, he was becoming famous as the first black jazzman to be featured with a white band leader, playing with the Benny Goodman Trio and Quartet. His marvelously clear, harmonically impeccable piano style was a big influence on the pianists of the swing era. His own big band, formed in 1939~ was excellent but not a commercial success. From 1940 on, he mostly led small groups or appeared as a soloist, touring world-wide and making hundreds of records. Though seriously ill, he continued to perform until a week before his death. Two of his three sons are professional musicians.

### LESTER (PREZ) YOUNG
### Tenor Saxophone
### 1909-1959

It was Lester Young who gave Billie Holiday the name "Lady Day" when both were with Count Basie, and it was Lady Day in turn who christened Lester Young "President" (later shortened to "Prez").

Young spent his youth on the carnival circuit in the Midwest with his musical family, choosing to concentrate on the tenor saxophone, only one of the many instruments he was able to play.

When Young took over Coleman Hawkin's chair in Fletcher Henderson's orchestra, he was criticized for not having the same style as his predecessor. As a result of this, he returned to Kansas City to play with Andy Kirk, and then with Count Basie from 1936 to 1940. During the Basie years, Young and Hawkins were the two most vital influences on the tenor as a jazz instrument. Hardly a tenor man from the middle 1940s through the 1950s achieved prominence without building on the foundations laid by Lester Young. Young is considered to be a major figure involved in the transition between the big, rich tenor style and the quiet, moody "cool school."

Young suffered a complete breakdown in 1956, and died three years later after having made a brief European comeback.

## OTHER NOTABLE JAZZMEN

| Name | Forte | Born |
|---|---|---|
| Cannonball Adderley | Sax, leader | 1928-1975 |
| Nat Adderley | Trumpet | 1931 |
| Red Allen | Trumpet | 1908-1969 |
| Albert Ammons | Piano | 1907-1949 |
| Gene Ammons | Tenor sax | 1925-1974 |
| Albert Ayler | Tenor sax | 1936 |
| Benny Bailey | Trumpet | 1925-1967 |
| Buster Bailey | Clarinet | 1902 |
| Dave Bailey | Drums | 1926 |
| Danny Barker | Guitar | 1909 |
| Denzil Best | Drums | 1917 |
| Leon "Chuck" Berry | Tenor sax | 1908-1941 |
| Barney Bigard | Clarinet | 1906 |
| Earl Bostic | Alto sax, composer | 1913-1965 |
| Lawrence Brown | Trombone | 1905 |
| Pete Brown | Alto sax | 1906 |
| Ray Bryant | Piano | 1931 |
| Donald Byrd | Trumpet | 1932 |
| Cab Calloway | Band leader | 1907 |
| Mutt Carey | Trumpet | 1892-1948 |
| Harry Carney | Baritone sax | 1910 |
| Bruno Carr | Drums | 1928 |
| Scoops Carry | Alto sax | 1915 |
| Ron Carter | Bass | 1937 |
| Al Casey | Guitar | 1915 |
| Buddy Catlett | Bass | 1933 |
| Sidney Catlett | Drums | 1910-1951 |
| Don Cherry | Trumpet | 1936 |
| Charlie Christian | Electric guitar | 1917-1942 |

| Name | Forte | Born |
|---|---|---|
| Buck Clayton | Trumpet | 1911 |
| Jimmy Cobb | Drums | 1929 |
| Cozy Cole | Drums | 1909-1981 |
| Bill Coleman | Trumpet | 1904-1981 |
| Hank Crawford | Alto sax | 1934 |
| Jimmy Crawford | Drums | 1910-1980 |
| Ted Curson | Trumpet | 1935 |
| Eddie (Lockjaw) Davis | Tenor sax | 1921 |
| Richard Davis | Bass | 1930 |
| Sidney DeParis | Trumpet | 1903-1967 |
| Johnny Dodds | Clarinet | 1892-1940 |
| Baby Dodds | Drums | 1898-1959 |
| Natty Dominique | Trumpet | 1896-1982 |
| Eddie Durham | Trombone, Guitar | 1906-1987 |
| Billy Eckstine | Vocalist | 1914 |
| Harry Edison | Trumpet | 1915 |
| Teddy Edwards | Tenor sax | 1924 |
| Ethel Ennis | Vocalist | 1934 |
| Booker Ervin | Tenor sax | 1930-1970 |
| Herschel Evans | Tenor sax | 1909-1939 |
| Tommy Flanagan | Piano | 1930 |
| Pops Foster | Bass | 1892-1969 |
| Gil Fuller | Composer, band leader | 1920 |
| Victor Gaskin | Bass | 1934 |
| Evans Tyree Glenn | Trombone | 1912-1974 |
| Wardell Gray | Tenor sax | 1921-1955 |
| Bennie Green | Trombone, composer | 1923-1977 |
| Grant Green | Guitar | 1911-1979 |
| Edmond Hall | Clarinet | 1901-1967 |

| Name | Forte | Born |
|---|---|---|
| Edmond Hall | Clarinet | 1901-1967 |
| Tubby Hall | Drums | 1895-1946 |
| Jimmy Hamilton | Clarinet | 1917 |
| Otto Hardwicke | Alto sax | 1904 |
| Eddie Harris | Tenor sax | 1934 |
| Barry Harris | Piano | 1929 |
| Jimmy Harrison | Trombone | 1900-1931 |
| Louis Hayes | Drums | 1937 |
| J. C. Heard | Drums | 1917-1988 |
| Percy Heath | Bass | 1923 |
| Joe Henderson | Tenor sax | 1937 |
| Jay C. Higginbotham | Trombone | 1906-1973 |
| Andrew Hill | Piano, composer | 1937 |
| Johnny Hodges | Alto sax | 1906-1970 |
| Red Holt | Drums | 1932 |
| Darnell Howard | Clarinet | 1892-1966 |
| Freddie Hubbard | Trumpet | 1938 |
| Paul Humphrey | Drums | 1935 |
| Bobby Hutcherson | Vibes | 1941 |
| Cliff Jackson | Piano | 1902-1970 |
| Quentin Jackson | Sax | 1909 |
| Hilton Jefferson | Alto sax | 1903-1968 |
| Bill Johnson | Bass | 1872-1972 |
| Budd Johnson | Tenor sax | 1910-1984 |
| Keg Johnson | Trombone | 1908-1967 |
| Lonnie Johnson | Guitar | 1889-1970 |
| Manzie Johnson | Drums | 1906-1971 |
| Pete Johnson | Piano | 1904-1967 |
| Elvin Jones | Drums | 1918 |
| Jo Jones | Drums | 1911-1985 |
| "Philly Jo" Jones | Drums | 1923 |
| Quincy Jones | Arranger, composer | 1933 |
| Thad Jones | Trumpet, Band leader | 1923-1986 |
| Connie Kay | Drums | 1927 |
| Wynton Kelly | Piano | 1931 |
| Al Killian | Trumpet | 1916-1950 |
| John Kirby | Bass, leader | 1908-1952 |
| Billy Kyle | Piano | 1914 |
| Tommy Ladnier | Trumpet | 1900-1939 |
| Yusef Lateef | Sax, band leader | 1921 |
| Harland Leonard | Sax, band leader | 1904 |
| John Levy | Bass | 1912 |
| Ed Lewis | Trumpet | 1909 |
| Meade Lux Lewis | Piano | 1905-1964 |
| Ramsey Lewis | Piano | 1935 |
| John Lindsay | Bass | 1894-1950 |
| Johnny Lytle | Piano | 1935 |
| Kaiser Marshall | Drums | 1902-1948 |
| Les McCann | Piano | 1935 |
| George Mitchell | Trumpet | 1899-? |
| Hank Mobley | Tenor sax | 1930 |
| Lee Morgan | Trumpet | 1938 |
| Benny Morton | Trombone | 1907 |
| Bennie Moten | Piano, leader | 1894-1935 |

| Name | Forte | Born |
|---|---|---|
| Tricky Sam Nanton | Trombone | 1904-1948 |
| Oliver Nelson | Sax, composer | 1932 |
| David Newman | Sax | 1933 |
| Frank Newton | Trumpet | 1906-1954 |
| Albert Nicholas | Clarinet | 1900 |
| Jimmy Noone | Clarinet | 1895-1944 |
| Jimmy Owens | Fluegelhorn | 1943 |
| Walter Page | Bass | 1900-1957 |
| John Patton | Organ | 1936 |
| Esther Phillips | Singer | 1935 |
| Tommy Potter | Bass | 1918-1988 |
| Bud Powell | Piano | 1924-1966 |
| Sammy Price | Piano | 1908-1984 |
| Russell Procope | Sax, clarinet | 1908-1981 |
| Lou Rawls | Singer | 1935 |
| Jerome Richardson | Sax | 1920 |
| Sam Rivers | Tenor sax, flute | 1930 |
| Luis Russell | Piano, band leader | 1902-1963 |
| Johnny St. Cyr | Banjo, guitar | 1890-1966 |
| Bud Scott | Banjo,guitar | 1890-1949 |
| Hazel Scott | Piano, singer | 1920-1981 |
| Shirley Scott | Organ, piano | 1934 |
| Bola Sete | Guitar, flute | 1928 |
| Charlie Shavers | Trumpet, arranger | 1917 |
| Orvell Shaw | Bass | 1923 |
| Archie Shepp | Tenor sax | 1937 |
| Wayne Shorter | Tenor sax, soprano sax | 1933 |
| Omer Simeon | Clarinet, alto sax | 1902-1959 |
| Tab Smith | Alto sax, arranger | 1909-1971 |
| Les Spann | Guitar, flute | 1932 |
| O'Neil Spencer | Drums, singer | 1909-1944 |
| Billy Strayhorn | Piano, composer | 1915-1967 |
| Buddy Tate | Tenor sax | 1915 |
| Art Taylor | Drums | 1929 |
| Cecil Taylor | Piano, arranger | 1933 |
| John Tchichai | Altosax | 1936 |
| Clark Terry | Trumpet, singer | 1920 |
| Walter Thomas | Tenor sax | 1907-1981 |
| "Lucky" Thompson | Tenor sax | 1924 |
| Stanley Turrentine | Tenor sax | 1934 |
| McCoy Tyner | Piano, composer | 1938 |
| Mal Waldron | Piano, composer | 1926 |
| Jack Washington | Baritone sax | 1912-1964 |
| Julius Watkins | French horn | 1921-1921 |
| Chick Webb | Drums, band leader | 1909-1934 |
| Randy Weston | Piano, composer | 1926 |
| Joe Williams | Singer | 1918 |
| Anthony Williams | Drums | 945 |
| Nancy Wilson | Vocalist | 1937 |
| Shadow Wilson | Drums | 1919 |
| Reggie Workman | Bass | 1937 |
| Gene Wright | Bass | 1923 |
| Lammar Wright, Sr. | Trumpet | 1907-1939 |
| Larry Young | Organ | 1940-1978 |

# THE BLACK IN FILMS

**A Survey of Blacks in Films (1902-1989) ■ Annotated List of Films with Black Themes or Actors**

In the early 1980s, black exploitation films were on the decline and fewer and fewer black stars were being featured in movies. This drew the concern of the NAACP, which mounted a protest against the film industry to get more blacks before the cameras. The NAACP's protest included urging blacks to boycott movie houses across the country. Subsequently, in the late 1980s more blacks were in major roles than ever before. By the end of the decade, signs of progress included Lou Gossett Jr.'s Academy Award for his role in "An Officer and a Gentleman" and Danny Glover, a skilled and accomplished actor was honored with a Golden Globe for his acting accomplishments. While there were fewer films with black themes, broad comedies attracted sizeable audiences with talents like Eddie Murphy starring in such films as "Beverly Hills Cop." Scores of actors were cast in recurring roles in such popular series like the "Police Academy" films. Films with a distinct character like the "The Color Purple" generated awards as well as dialogue about characterizations and dramatic impact. In addition, a new phenomenon of films by independent black film-makers like Spike Lee and Robert Townsend signaled an encouraging trend for newcomers with talent and skill as producers, directors and writers. More blacks were appearing on camera with veterans like Yaphet Kotto among the character actors who were cast in films time after time. For many observers, the fact that blacks were finally being selected for roles that did not specifically call for a black actor or actress was a symbolically small step that would lead to greater participation in the movie industry during the 1990s.

## A SURVEY OF BLACKS IN FILMS

Films of the pre-World War I period which featured black characters invariably fell into one or the other of two categories: the first was of the slapstick variety which portrayed blacks as clowns or fools; the second type was the sentimental melodrama full of laughing, hymn-singing slaves toiling contentedly for their benevolent masters. With very few exceptions, these roles were played not by black actors but by whites in blackface. Perhaps the most noteworthy film of this era was D. W. Griffith's 1915 production *The Birth of a Nation* , in which the portrayal of a black during the Reconstruction period as a corrupt, lawless villain invoked a storm of controversy and protest.

## The 1920s

After World War I the casting of blacks to depict blacks increased. But, far from portending any change in philosophy, the black servant, bellhop, maid, straight man—the black lackey—became an established vehicle for winning a few cheap laughs from the audience.

The motion picture industry was growing rapidly during the twenties, becoming America's prime mode of entertainment. During this era, there was little recognition that the movies were not only entertainment but an enormous propaganda machine that inordinately influenced the thinking and the behavior of its audience. Nothing in the movies during those early years did justice to the black American.

In 1922, with D. W. Griffith's *One Exciting Night*, a type had been born: the black as a blubbering, superstitious coward whose hair turned white at the approach of even the mildest form of danger. The other genre of black roles popular in the 1920s was the cannibalistic savage in jungle pictures about "darkest Africa." Probably the most true-to-life depiction of blacks in this period was in Hal Roach's "Our Gang" comedies in which black and white children played together naturally and generally as equals.

However, there was little serious attempt to tap the acting potential black actors possessed. In 1928, hope was kindled by Paul Sloane of Fox who was given the assignment of directing an all black motion picture for the studio entitled *Hearts in Dixie*. But with its premiere in 1929 there was new disappointment, as the same routine movie cliches regarding blacks were executed on a grand production scale. Lacking plot, story line, or sophistication, the movie was merely a succession of "darkies" picking cotton, praying, and getting together to sing spirituals. Later that year, King Vidor of MGM released *Hallelujah*, a more adept film that used several black actors. However, real thoughtfulness about life among black Americans was still lacking. The characters did not ring true. What was portrayed was more a white fantasy of the separated black society.

*Paul Robeson plays a porter who becomes a potentate in the classic* The Emperor Jones.

## The 1930s

Bad as it was, *Hallelujah* was nonetheless a milestone. The comment and criticism concerning the movie, both pro and con, had much influence on the work that followed, such as *Arrowsmith* in 1932, directed by the Hollywood great, John Ford. Clarence Brookes, a black actor, played a black physician who had a stature, sincerity, and ability the movie going public had been taught to associate with white heroes.

In 1933, Paul Robeson starred in *The Emperor Jones*, a major motion picture effort that failed financially but received excellent critical reviews.

For blacks, the advent of sound in motion pictures meant an endless parade of routines akin to those produced at the well-known Cotton Club in Harlem. The 1930s for the most part was an era of commercial exploitation, as singers, dancers, and jazz musicians from the New York stage and night club circuit appeared in countless Hollywood musicals, usually in all-Negro productions, or in segregated sequences in otherwise all-white films. Integrated jazz groups were never shown. Performers such as Cab Calloway, Louis Armstrong, Lena Horne, and Hazel Scott became box-office names, with the musical serving as a vehicle for the discovery and popularization of much significant black talent. At the same time, the myth of the Negro as the irrepressible "rhythm man" was reinforced—a myth which found its most demeaning expression in the grinning, shuffling, eye-rolling antics of Stepin Fetchit, Mantan Moreland, and Sleep "n' Eat, among others. Even black films made independently of the major studios by black or, on occasion, white producers followed Hollywood stereotypes of character and situation, although they at least utilized accurate local color motifs. Shoddily produced and acted, they made little effort to alter the already-distorted Negro film image.

The contributions of two directors, Mervyn Le Roy and Fritz Lang, offset these trends to some extent. In producing films which showed blacks to possess the qualities and emotions of ordinary human beings, or which dealt with the theme of intolerance, they prepared the way for more understanding treatment and more realistic themes in the years to come. Documentary films of the early 1940s also helped correct many Hollywood stereotypes by showing blacks at work, pursuing education, or in the armed services.

*Hollywood's romanticized version of the Old South spawned many black characters like those in* Carolina *(top); in* I Am a Fugitive from a Chain Gang *(bottom) blacks are portrayed with more human complexity and nobility.*

## The 1940s and the War

The new liberalism of the World War II years, with a concern for morale at home and support of the country's fighting men of all colors, had a corrective influence on the black's film image. In such pictures as *Of Mice and Men* and *Strange Incident* blacks appeared as dignified citizens, often as heroic or semi-heroic figures. Fewer films were made glorifying the Old South. The 1940s, also saw increasingly vocal protest by the black and the liberal press, and by such groups as the NAACP and the International Film and Radio Guild. Pressure from these sources did much to eliminate offensive dialogue and stereotypical roles and brought such major victories as the abandonment, in 1946, of plans for a new production of *Uncle Tom's Cabin.*

## After World War II

Gradually, following the war, the worst racial offenses began to disappear from the scene. The scatter brained maid, shuffle-foot janitor, and crazed savage had virtually disappeared. Black actors and actresses had begun to find roles worthy of their talent. In 1939, for example, Hattie McDaniel won an Academy award for her supporting role as a stereotyped "Mammy" in *Gone With the Wind.* By contrast, Sidney Poitier's 1965 best actor award was for a role (*Lilies of the Field*) which showed a black assuming his responsibilities with strength and skill in a natural, amicable relationship with a group of whites dependent on him.

Themes that were taboo well into the 1930s and beyond are now dealt with more frankly; where once it was daring to examine the color bar with a story about blacks "passing" for white, nowadays a number of films show interracial love affairs and marriages. Moreover, the contemporary urban, educated, black sophisticated in speech, dress, and tastes is more and more "visible" in both minor and major roles.

When blacks began to assert themselves with a more strident form of protest during the 1960s, the film industry took note. *Uptight* was based on the events in a major ghetto following the assassination of Martin Luther King. And as blacks forged ahead in the film industry, Gordon Parks led a quiet revolution, as he became the first black to direct a film (*The Learning Tree*) for a major studio. Then Melvin Van Peebles made an independent film, *The Night The Sun Came Out*, which grossed over $10 million. Soon more than 15 blacks had directed feature films for major studios or independent distributors and the industry had to acknowledge the impact of black performers and their following among moviegoing America.

Birth of the Blues *was a major 1941 musical.*

## The 1970s

In the early 1970s, the film industry started to produce movies in great quantity with the huge black moviegoing audience in mind. Almost all were action films with superheroes of the stud type. These films made huge sums of money and helped to rejuvenate a financially ailing Hollywood.

While Hollywood was gaining in benefits from what was to be called "The Black Film Boom," identity problems were emerging from the new films for black audience. By the summer of 1972, national media attention had been drawn towards the phenomenon which had acquired the label "blaxploitation."

Leaders of every major black organization—Jesse Jackson of PUSH, Roy Innis of CORE, Roy Wilkins of the NAACP, Ralph Abernathy of SCLC and Vernon Jordan of the Urban League—were condemning most of the films which dealt with the themes of violence and extolled unsavory characters such as pimps and drug dealers. Concern was also expressed by black intellectuals. Psychologist Alvin F. Poussaint, a Harvard professor, wrote of the films: "The same insidious message is there: blacks are violent, criminal, sexy savages who imitate the white man's ways as best they can."

## Blaxploitation Ends and New Era Begins

In Hollywood, some 400 concerned black artists working in the industry met to discuss the black image in contemporary films. The result: an organization was formed called The Coalition Against Blaxploitation. Its purpose: to meet with studio and industry union heads to improve the image of blacks on screen and their working lot in Hollywood as well.

In that time, new stars emerged, particularly popular athletes and pretty singers. They were followed by new producers and other personnel behind the cameras in production capacities.

In 1973, 10 films created primarily for black audiences were nominated for Academy Awards. In 1972, Isaac Hayes, a composer, won an Oscar for his theme song for *Shaft*.

The commercial success of these films was unexpected and very quickly—and expectedly—the industry responded with a profusion of similar films. In what could be described as a sudden explosion, there were scores of films boasting more blacks working before the cameras, and as a part of the crews, than Hollywood had ever witnessed at any time in its history. Virtually all of the superficial action-adventure films generated concern among critics and activists angry about the emphasis on black anti-heroes.

The phenomenon known as the black exploitation film boom virtually disappeared as quickly as it had arrived. Some observers had accurately predicted its demise, and soon it was obvious that audiences had begun to tire of the action, violence, and titillation. Some producers continued to release such low-budget projects over the next five years, but they were all rejected by theatergoers looking for something new and different.

During this period of transition, musicals and biographical dramas were released. If there was a new trend of movies with wide acceptance, it was reflected in a revival of the comedy genre—which had a history of negative acceptance among many blacks objecting to what they felt were stereotypic performances.

The films during the decade of the 1970s, however, proved to be successful entertainment, which appealed to a broad cross section of the moviegoing public, becoming unqualified commercial successes.

Specifically, the talents of a Hollywood veteran and an unpredictable neophyte meshed to established a trend that would continue successfully for years. The veteran—Sidney Poitier—had thrived through a precedent-setting career as an actor and was venturing into the world behind the camera as a director. The neophyte—Richard Pryor—had become a cult hero among the young as a tough-talking and hilarious street comic. When the two collaborated (with a gallery of other major black actors)in *Uptown Saturday Night*, a new era of black involvement in films was inaugurated. The film was a modest box office success, but it lead to separate career paths for the two principals reflective of increasing impact and power within the industry.

By 1980, Poitier and Pryor had reunited as director and actor in *Stir Crazy*, and the results were predictably successful. Poitier had grown over the previous decades to become the most prominent black presence in the movie industry. As he concentrated on a series of films, refining his expertise as a director, Pryor soon became one of Hollywood's top media

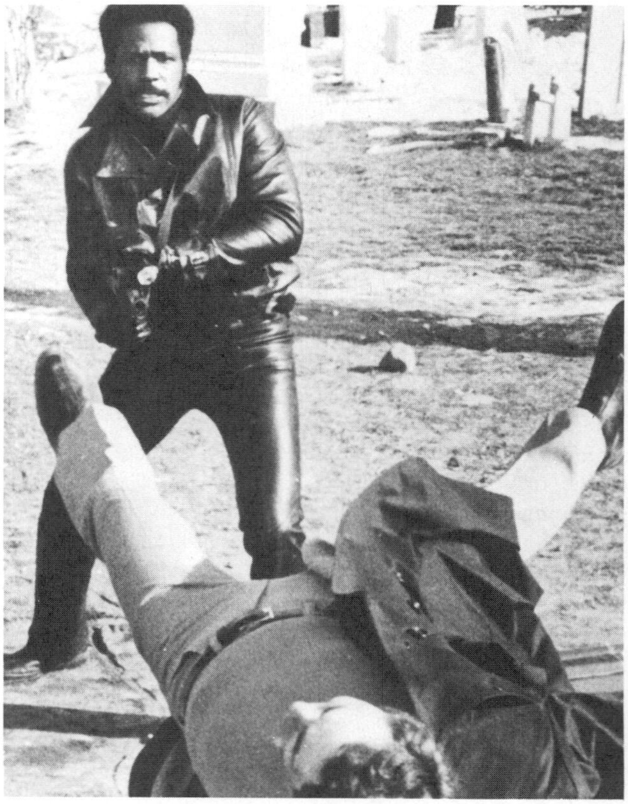

*Richard Roundtree in the 1971 action blockbuster* Shaft.

stars of the 1970s. In film after film, each presenting a role unique within itself, he emerged as a consistent box office draw and an increasingly popular performer.

The previously mentioned decline in the purely exploitational action films during this time resulted in a loss of work for such performers as the actor-athletes who had thrived on those movies. Blacks who had worked behind the cameras in positions ranging from producer and director to stunt man and cameraman were also hard-pressed to find regular employment.

In the constantly changing world of movies, however, new faces were being recruited and they were often experienced, stage-trained actors and actresses like James Earl Jones, Lou Gossett, Billy Dee Williams, Cicely Tyson, and Diahann Carroll.

As predominantly black projects became increasingly rare, these skilled performers were cast in films designed to appeal to audiences in general. Producers had realized that to gear a film solely for the black audience was self-defeating in terms of commercial success. Now the emphasis was on "crossover" films with mass appeal. So, in the space of some 10 years, the role of blacks on the screen had changed dramatically. The Hollywood-Beverly Hills chapter of the NAACP and the Black Film-Makers Hall of Fame sought to honor achievement and encourage a higher quality of performance in separate awards ceremonies.

And even in the absence of exploitation films, it was not necessarily a time of optimism. Hollywood's unsettling economic problems sharply reduced the number of films made. A lot of projects were left waiting and numerous talented people were forced to vie for painfully few roles. Yet it has been challenges such as this that have been accepted by each hopeful that ever came to Hollywood. And there was no indication that those among the generation of the 1980s would be any less determined to achieve their definition of success than the blacks who had preceded them.

Some Kind of Hero *once again demonstrated the enormous talent of Richard Pryor.*

As the decade came to a close, one trend remained strong. Just as Richard Pryor had succeeded with a string of films during the early decades, a new comic would achieve ever greater success on screen. Eddie Murphy, who had grown to achieve tremendous popularity on television's "Saturday Night Live," made a smooth transition into feature film work, starting with the movie, "48 Hours." When he created the role of Axel Foley in "Beverly Hills Cop," he became one of the top box office stars that year. In time, he had signed a major contract with Paramount and had gained the creative freedom to make his own films.

Comedy continued to have widespread appeal with movie audiences, and two independent filmmakers, Spike Lee, who brought the low-budget comedy about dating mores, "She's Gotta Have It" to the screen and Robert Townsend, who poked fun at Hollywood racial stereotypes in "Hollywood Shuffle," received acclaim in both the black community and the film-making community for their work. Based on the initial success of their debut films, they were able to move on and break into moviemaking on a larger scale.

Two films that were acclaimed for their effective film-making techniques, were hailed for their social consciousness on the one hand, but criticized within the black community by many who felt the true story of black heroism in adverse circumstances had not really been told.

"Cry Freedom," a Richard Attenborough film about South African activist Steve Biko and his friendship with a white reporter in the strife-torn country, was criticized for portraying the reporter as more of a hero than Biko. In the same token, "Mississippi Burning," loosely based on the killing and subsequent investigation surrounding three slain civil rights workers, was also accused of not accurately depicting the bravery of blacks in the deep South during the height of the civil rights era.

Yet, the industry did recognize the contributions of blacks during the decade, honoring Lou Gossett for his stirring performance as a Navy drill instructor in "An Officer and a Gentleman." "Purple Rain," with a music score by Prince, was a second film honored with an Oscar.

Finally, veteran Sidney Poitier, whose achievements as an actor and director were virtually without equal, was honored in 1989 with a dinner singling out his achievements during a career lasting over 20 years. The event, sponsored by the American Museum of the Moving Image, was one of the most highly regarded for a black since moviemaking began honoring its own.

The following is a list of representative films in which blacks have either starred, played feature roles, or otherwise made significant contributions.

## FILMS FEATURING BLACK ACTORS OR WITH BLACK THEMES: 1902-1989

***Off to Bloomingdale Asylum.*** 1902 (French). Produced by George Mealiegs. First appearance of Negroes in film. Slapstick comedy.

***The Wooing and Wedding of a Coon.*** 1905. All-Negro. Undisguised mockery of Negro couple.

***Fights of a Nation.*** **1905.** Negro depicted as cake-walker, buck-dancer, and razor-thrower.

***The Slave.*** Biograph, 1909. Directed by D. W. Griffith.

***The Sambo Series.*** 1909-1911. Produced by Sigmund Lubin. All-Negro comedies similar to Rastus series.

***The Rastus Series.*** About 1910. Produced by Sigmund Lubin. Series of all-Negro short comedies. Central character a Negro buffoon of small intelligence.

***The Judge's Story.*** Thanhauser, 1911. A Southern judge moves a jury to leniency for an accused Negro. Probably the first film to give a measure of sympathy to a Negro character.

***The Battle.*** Biograph, 1911. Directed by D. W. Griffith. The first of Griffith's glorifications of the Old South.

***The Dark Romance of a Tobacco Can.*** Essanay, 1911. A man is horrified to find the girl he proposes to is Negro.

***For Massa's Sake.*** Pathe, 1911. With Crane Wilbur. Devoted slave tries to sell himself to pay his master's gambling debts.

***The Debt.*** 1912. Tragedy of interracial love.

***In Slavery Days.*** Rex, 1913. Directed by Otis Turner. With Robert Z. Leonard, Margarita Fischer, Edna Maison. Wicked octoroon foiled.

***The Octoroon.*** 1913. From the play by Dion Boucicault. With Guy Coombes, Marguerite Courtot. The tragedy of whites with Negro blood.

***Coon Town Suffragettes.*** 1914. Produced by Sigmund Lubin. All-Negro. Southern "Mammys" try to keep their no-good husbands out of saloons.

***Dark Town Jubilee.*** 1914. The first attempt to star a Negro, in this case Bert Williams, the well-known New York vaudevillian. Badly received by white audiences.

***The Wages of Sin, The Broken Violin, etc.*** About 1914. Oscar Micheaux, independent producer. Series of all-Negro films.

***Uncle Tom's Cabin.*** World, 1914. Directed by William R. Daly. From the novel by Harriet Beecher Stowe. With Sam Lucas, Irving Cummings, Marie Eline, and a cast of Negro players. The featuring of Negro actor Sam Lucas, rather than a white actor in blackface, created a precedent. This was the third film version of the novel; the first, in 1909, directed by Edwin S. Porter, seriously distorted the abolitionist intent of the book into a sentimental tale about slaves who "know their place." In 1927, Negro actor Charles Gilpin left the filming of a new production over a dispute about the characterization of Uncle Tom.

***The Birth of a Nation.*** Epoch, 1915. Directed by D. W. Griffith. From the novel *The Clansman* by Thomas Dixon. With Mae Marsh, Lillian Gish, Henry B. Walthall, Robert Harron, Wallace Reid, George Seigmann, Walter Long, George Reed, Ralph Lewis, Elmo Lincoln, Elmer Clifton, Donald Crisp, Raoul Walsh, Joseph Henaberry, Eugene Pallette, Bessie Love, Jennie Lee, Howard Gaye, Tom Wilson, Erich von Stroheim, and others. Negroes as corrupt and brutal villains in Reconstruction-period South, with the Ku Klux Klan having a "just" triumph. The film caused a storm of indignation in the North, and was banned in some cities.

***The Nigger.*** Fox, 1915. From the novel by Edward Sheldon. With William Farnum.

*In the* Our Gang *comedies, the pint-sized heroes inhabit a world of mischief and pranks where race does not matter.*

***The "Our Gang" Comedies.*** Produced by Hal Roach. Negro children, including Farina, Stymie Beard, and Buckwheat, playing together with whites.

***The Greatest Thing in Life.*** 1918. Directed by D. W. Griffith. Includes an episode of a white soldier in World War I kissing his Negro comrade-in-arms as he died. Griffith was accused of planting the scene to appease critics of his racially biased *Birth of a Nation.*

***Ten Nights in a Bar-Room.*** Coloured Players Film Corporation, about 1920. All-Negro with Charles Gilpin.

***One Exciting Night.*** 1922. Directed by D. W. Griffith. First example of Negro as contemptible comic relief.

***Broken Chains.*** 1924. Shows Negro as a murderous agitator.

***The Florian Slappey Series.*** About 1925-1926. Written and produced by Octavus Roy Cohen, a Negro. All-Negro, "blackface" humor.

***Melancholy Dame.*** 1929. Written and directed by Octavus Roy Cohen. All-Negro with Evelyn Preer, Eddie Thompson, Spencer Williams.

***Hearts in Dixie.*** 1929. Directed by Paul Sloane. The first of Hollywood's All-Negro films, with Clarence Muse, Stepin Fetchit, Mildred Washington in stereotyped roles.

***Hallelujah.*** MGM, 1929. Directed by King Vidor. From the novel by Wanda Tuchock. All-Negro, with Daniel Haynes, Nina Mae McKinney, Victoria Spivey, William Fountain, Harry Gray, Fannie Belle de Knight, Everett McGarritty. Usual stereotypes, though not as extreme as in *Hearts in Dixie.* Had very favorable press.

***East of Borneo.*** Universal, 1932. Directed by George Melford. With Charles Bickford, Rose Hobart, Lupita Tovar, Noble Johnson. Typical Hollywood jungle film, in which Negro players were featured mostly as cannibals, head-hunters, and repulsive savages.

***The Black King.*** Southland, 1932. Directed by Bud Pollard. From the story by Donald Heywood. With Vivian Baber, Harry Gray, Knolly Mitchell, Mary Jane Watkins. One of the first big independent all-Negro film productions.

***Arrowsmith.*** 1932. Directed by John Ford. With Ronald Coleman, Clarence Brooks. Negro doctor given same stature as white doctor.

***I Am a Fugitive from a Chain Gang.*** Warners, 1932. Directed by Mervyn LeRoy. With Paul Muni, Everett Brown. Sympathetic, realistic portrayal of Negro prisoner.

***The Emperor Jones.*** Krimsky-Cochran, 1933. Directed by Dudley Murphy, under supervision of William C. DeMille. From the play by Eugene O'Neill. With Paul Robeson, Dudley Diggs, Frank Wilson, Rex Ingram, George Stamper, Fredi Washington, Ruby Elzy, Brandon Evans, Taylor Gordon. Significant in that it gave a Negro actor a leading part in a film also featuring whites. Dealt seriously with a Negro theme.

***Hypnotized.*** World Wide, 1933. Directed by Mack Sennett. With George Moran, Charlie Mack, Ernest Torrence, Wallace Ford, Maria Alba. Typical of comedies featuring well-known "blackface" minstrels.

***The Cabin in the Cotton.*** Warners, 1933. Directed by Michael Curtiz. From the novel by Henry Kroll. With Richard Barthelmess, Bette Davis, Dorothy Jordan, Henry B. Walthall, Clarence Muse, "Snowflake."

***Judge Priest.*** Fox, 1935. Directed by John Ford. With Will Rogers, Tom Brown, Anita Louise, Henry B. Walthall, Rochelle Hudson, Hattie McDaniel, Stepin Fetchit. A comedy drama about a judge who is not in conformance with a Southern town regarding blacks.

Carolina *was an extremely romanticized depiction of the Old South.*

***Helldorado.*** 1935. Directed by James Cruze. With Richard Arlen, Madge Evans, Ralph Bellamy, James Gleason, Henry B. Walthall, Stepin Fetchit. Negro frightened by a "ghost," the butt of the humor.

***Imitation of Life.*** Universal, 1935. Directed by John M. Stahl. From the novel by Fannie Hurst. With Claudette Colbert, Warren William, Ned Sparks, Louise Beavers, Fredi Washington, Rochelle Hudson, Sebie Hendricks, Dorothy Black, Alan Hale, Hazel Washington. A light-skinned Negro girl makes a desperate bid to pass as white. The film dealt seriously with this problem, but also had a "Mammy" role more in the foreground.

***So Red the Rose.*** Paramount, 1935. Directed by King Vidor. With Margaret Sullivan, Walter Connolly, Randolph Scott, Daniel Haynes, Clarence Muse. Depicts the revolt against slavery as the work of a few Negro opportunists misleading the contented masses.

***Show Boat.*** Universal, 1936. Directed by James Whale. From the operetta by Edna Ferber and Jerome Kern. With Irene Dunne, Paul Robeson, Allan Jones, Charles Winninger, Helen Morgan, Queenie Smith, Helen Westly, Donald Cook, Hattie McDaniel, Clarence Muse. A musical review and love story set on the Mississippi River in the 1880s.

***The Littlest Rebel.*** Twentieth-Century Fox, 1936. Directed by David Butler. With Shirley Temple, John Boles, Jack Holt, Bill Robinson, Karen Morley, Quinn Williams, Willie Best, Frank McGlynn Sr., Hannah Washington. Typical Hollywood Civil War picture, totally sympathetic to the South and Southerners.

***The Singing Kid.*** Warners, 1936. Directed by William Keighley. With Al Jolson, Sybil Jason, Allen Jenkins, Lyle Talbot, Wini Shaw, Edward Everett Horton, Cab Calloway. Negro shown in natural, friendly relationship with white.

***Spirit of Youth.*** Independent, 1937. With Joe Louis, Clarence Muse. Poor Negro fights his way to the top as a boxer.

***The Black Legion.*** Warners, 1937. Directed by Archie Mays. With Humphrey Bogart, Dick Foran, Erin O'Brien Moore, Ann Sheridan, Robert Barrat, Joseph Sawyer, Paul Harvey, Henry Brandon, John Litel. An attack on the Ku Klux Klan.

***The Green Pastures.*** Warners, 1937. Directed by William Keighley and Marc Connelly. All-Negro with Rex Ingram, Oscar Polk, Eddie Anderson, Frank Wilson, Ernest Whitman, William Cumby, Edna Mae Harris, Al Stokes, David Bethea, George Reed, Clinton Rosemond. Interprets the Negro idea of heaven. Did little to correct stereotypes, but gave many Negro actors chances for important roles.

***Pennies from Heaven.*** Columbia, 1937. Directed by Norman McLeod. With Bing Crosby, Madge Evans, Edith Fellowes, Donald Meek, John Gallaudet, Louis Armstrong, Charles Wilson. Musical.

***They Won't Forget.*** Warners, 1937. Directed by Mervyn LeRoy. Adapted from the Graham Greene novel *Deep in the Deep South*. With Claude Rains, Allyn Joslyn, Gloria Dickson, Edward Norris, Clinton Rosemond. Indictment of Southern values, including treatment of Negro.

***Mystery in Swing.*** Goldberg, independent, 1938. Produced and directed by Arthur Dreifuss. All-Negro with Monte Howley, Marguerite Whitten, Bob Webb, Sybil Lewis, Josephine Edwards, F. E. Miller, Haley Harding, Jess Lee Brooks. Murder of a famous jazz bandleader.

***One Mile from Heaven.*** Twentieth-Century Fox, 1938. Directed by Allan Dwan. With Claire Trevor, Sally Blane, Douglas Fowley, Fredi Washington, Bill Robinson, Eddie Anderson. Fredi Washington as Negro foster mother of a white child.

***Mr. Creeps.*** Toddy Pictures, 1938. All-Negro, with Mantan Moreland.

***The Adventures of Huckleberry Finn.*** MGM, 1939 (earlier production, 1932). Directed by Richard Thorpe. From the novel by Mark Twain. With Mickey Rooney, Walter Connolly, William Frawley, Rex Ingram, Lynne Carver, Elizabeth Risdon, Victor Kilian, Minor Watson, Clara Blandick.

***Harlem on the Prairie.*** Buell, 1939. Claimed as "the first independent all-Negro Western film."

***Gone with the Wind.*** Selznick, 1939. Directed by Victor Fleming. From the novel by Margaret Mitchell. With Vivien Leigh, Clark Gable, Leslie Howard, Olivia de Haviland, Thomas Mitchell, Evelyn Keyes, Barbara O'Neill, Hattie McDaniel, Butterfly McQueen, Oscar Polk, Adrian Morris, Ben Carter, Eddie "Rochester" Anderson. Negro depicted in "Mammy" and "Uncle Tom" tradition. Hattie McDaniel won an Academy Award for best supporting actress.

***Man About Town.*** Paramount, 1939. Directed by Mark Sandrich. With Jack Benny, Dorothy Lamour, Eddie "Rochester" Anderson, Binnie Barnes, Edward Arnold, Monty Woolley. Typical Benny-"Rochester" comedy of 1939-1944 period.

***Bronze Venus.*** Toddy Pictures, 1940. All-Negro, with Lena Horne, Ralph Cooper. The life of a great musical star.

***Chasing Trouble.*** Monogram, 1940. Directed by Howard Bretherton. From a screenplay by Mary McCarthy. With Frankie Darro, Mantan Moreland, Marjorie Reynolds, Milburn Stone, Cheryl Walker. White boy and Negro friend chase crooks together.

***One Tenth of Our Nation.*** American Film Centre, 1940. Directed by Henwar Rodakiewiecz. Documentary showing inadequate conditions of education among Negroes in the South.

***Of Mice and Men.*** Hal Roach, 1940. Directed by Lewis Milestone. From the book by John Steinbeck. With Burgess Meredith, Lon Chaney, Betty Field, Charles Bickford, Leigh Whipper. Dignified portrayal of Negro ranch worker.

***Maryland.*** Twentieth-Century Fox, 1940. Directed by Henry King. With Walter Brennan, Fay Bainter, Brenda Joyce, John Payne, Charlie Ruggles, Hattie McDaniel, Marjorie Weaver, Sydney Blackmer, Clarence Muse, George Reed, Ben Carter, Ernest Whitman, Zack Williams, Thaddeus Jones, Clinton Rosemond, Jesse Graves. Romance of the South with several Negro players featured prominently as comic relief.

***Murder on Lenox Avenue.*** Goldberg, independent, 1941. Directed by Arthur Dreifuss. All-Negro, with Mamie Smith, Alex Lovejoy, Dene Larry, Norman Astwood, Gus Smith, Edna Mae Harris, Alberta Perkins, George Williams. A murder mystery set in Harlem.

***A Place to Live.*** Philadelphia Housing Association, 1941. Directed by Irvin Lerner. Documentary on housing conditions among Negroes and whites in Philadelphia.

***Birth of the Blues.*** Paramount, 1941. Directed by Victor Scheitzinger. With Bing Crosby, Mary Martin, Brian Donlevy, Eddie "Rochester" Anderson, J. Carrol Naish, Warren Hymer, Horace MacMahon, Ruby Elzy. A musical review which features whites learning about blues.

***Affectionately Yours.*** Warners, 1941. Directed by Lloyd Bacon. With Merle Oberon, Dennis Morgan, Rita Hayworth, Ralph Bellamy, George Tobias, James Gleason, Hattie McDaniel, Butterfly McQueen. Good-natured "Mammy" types.

***In This Our Life.*** Warners, 1942. Directed by John Huston. From the novel by Ellen Glasgow. With Bette Davis, Olivia de Haviland, George Brent, Dennis Morgan, Charles Coburn, Frank Craven, Billie Burke, Lee Patrick, Hattie McDaniel, Ernest Anderson. Dignified portrayal of young Negro studying to be lawyer, victimized by Southern prejudice and injustice. Placed on Honor Roll of Race Relations for 1942.

***Henry Brown, Farmer.*** U.S. Department of Agriculture, 1942. Directed by Roger Barlow. Narration by Canada Lee. Documentary on the life of a Negro farmer in Alabama.

***Syncopation.*** RKO Radio, 1942. Directed by William Dieterle. With Adolphe Menjou, Jackie Cooper, Bonita Granville, George Bancroft, Ted North, Todd Duncan. Negro trumpet player teaches jazz to white girl. Sympathetic handling of race relations.

***Panama Hattie.*** MGM, 1943. Directed by Norman Z. McLeod. Based on the play by Herbert Fields and B. G. de Sylva. With Ann Sothern, Red Skelton, Rags Ragland, Ben Blue, Marsha Hunt, Virginia O'Brien, Carl Esmond, the Berry Brothers, Nyas, James and Warren, Lena Horne. Lena Horne's first major screen role.

***Stormy Weather.*** Twentieth-Century Fox, 1943. Directed by Andrew Stone. With Lena Horne, Bill Robinson, Cab Calloway, Katherine Dunham, Harold and Fayard Nicholas, Ada Brown, Dooley Wilson, Babe Wallace, Ernest Whitman, Zuttie Singleton,

F. E. Miller, Nicodemus Stewart. All-Negro musical.

***Dixie.*** Paramount, 1943. Directed by Edward Sutherland. With Bing Crosby, Dorothy Lamour, Billy de Wolfe, Marjorie Reynolds, Lynne Overman, Raymond Walburn, Eddie Foy Jr. Biography of Daniel Emmett, the first blackface minstrel and composer of "Dixie."

***Tales of Manhattan.*** Twentieth-Century Fox, 1943. Directed by Julian Duvivier. With Charles Boyer, Rita Hayworth, Ginger Rogers, Henry Fonda, Charles Laughton, Edward G. Robinson, Paul Robeson, Eddie "Rochester" Anderson, Ethel Waters, Clarence Muse. Paul Robeson, enticed back from his self-imposed exile in Britain to make this film, was so disturbed by his "darky" role he declared he would never again accept such a part in a Hollywood film.

***Cabin in the Sky.*** MGM, 1943. Directed by Vincente Minnelli. All-Negro, with Lena Horne, Eddie "Rochester" Anderson, Ethel Waters, Rex Ingram, Kenneth Spencer, Ernest Whitman, Mantan Moreland, Louis Armstrong, Oscar Polk, Buck and Bubbles, Duke Ellington, John Sublett, Willie Best. Musical fantasy. Brought prominence to Lena Horne and to Katherine Dunham ballet.

***Strange Incident.*** Twentieth-Century Fox, 1943. Directed by William Wellman. From the novel *The Oxbow Incident* by Walter V. T. Clark. With Henry Fonda, Dana Andrews, Anthony Quinn, and Leigh Whipper as Negro preacher who makes dignified, eloquent plea against lynching of white rustlers.

***Bataan.*** MGM, 1943. Directed by Tay Garnett. With Robert Taylor, George Murphy, Thomas Mitchell, Lee Bowman and Kenneth Spencer as a black G. I. Won special award from NAACP.

***Sahara.*** Columbia, 1944. Directed by Zoltan Korda. With Humphrey Bogart, Rex Ingram. Negro soldier in heroic role.

***Carnival in Rhythm.*** Warners, 1944. A short film devoted to Katherine Dunham and her Negro ballet.

***Lifeboat.*** Twentieth-Century Fox, 1944. Directed by Alfred Hitchcock. With Tallulah Bankhead, John Hodiak, Henry Hull, Walter Slezak, Canada Lee, Hume Cronyn, Mary Anderson, Heather Angel. Survivors in the lifeboat include an intelligent, heroic Negro.

***Dr. George Washington Carver.*** MGM, 1945. With Clinton Rosemond. Documentary based on the life and work of the Negro scientist.

***The House I Live In.*** MGM, 1945. With Frank Sinatra. A plea for racial tolerance; won special Academy Award.

***Jammin' the Blues.*** Warners, 1945. Directed and photographed by Gjon Mili. Semi-documentary of a "jam session" in a Negro club.

***We've Come a Long, Long Way.*** "Negro Marches On." 1945. Produced and directed by Jack Goldberg. Narration by Elder Michaux. A documentary cavalcade of the Negro race.

***Brewster's Millions.*** Edward Small, 1946. Directed by Alan Dwan. From the novel by George B. McCutcheon. With Dennis O'Keefe, Helen Walker, Eddie "Rochester" Anderson, June Havoc, Gail Patrick, Mischa Auer, Joseph Sawyer, John Litel, Herbert Dudley, Neil Hamilton. Film was banned in Memphis because Negro "acted too snappy and socialized too much with whites."

***Ziegfeld Follies.*** MGM, 1946. Directed by Vincente Minnelli. With William Powell, Virginia O'Brien, Lucille Ball, Esther Williams, James Melton, Marion Bell, Victor Moore, Fred Astaire, Lucille Bremer, Keenan Wynn, Lena Horne, Red Skelton, Judy Garland, Gene Kelly, Kathryn Grayson, Edward Arnold, Cyd Charisse, Robert Lewis, Avon Long. A musical review using as background the life of Florence Ziegfeld. Cute stereotype cameos performed by blacks.

***Saratoga Trunk.*** Warners, 1946. Directed by Sam Wood. From the novel by Edna Ferber. With Ingrid Bergman, Gary Cooper, Flora Robson. In a psychological throwback to earlier days, Flora Robson played an important role in "blackface."

***Mildred Pierce.*** Warners, 1946. Directed by Michael Curtiz. Based on the novel by James M. Cain. With Joan Crawford, Jack Carson, Zachary Scott, Eve Arden, Bruce Bennett, Ann Blyth, Lee Patrick, Butterfly McQueen, Moroni Olsen, Charles Trowbridge, Chester Clute. Butterfly McQueen in one of the "stupid maid" parts she subsequently announced she would no longer accept.

***The Brotherhood of Man.*** Brandon, 1946. A color cartoon based on *The Races of Mankind* by Ruth Benedict and Gene Weltfish. Anti-prejudice message.

***Till the End of Time.*** R.K.O. Radio, 1946. Directed by Edward Dmytryk. With Dorothy McGuire, Robert Mitchum, Guy Madison, Bill Williams, Tom Tully, Jean Porter, William Gargan. Subplot in which whites defend Negro against Fascist talk.

***Song of the South.*** R.K.O. Radio-Disney, 1947. Produced by Walt Disney. Based on the "Uncle Remus" stories. With Ruth Warrick, James Baskett, Lucille Watson, Hattie McDaniel, Luana Patten, Bobby Driscoll. NAACP and IFRG tried to stop the filming because of stereotyped character of Uncle Remus.

*Ethel Waters and Jeanne Crain have the leads in* Pinky, *a movie that attempts to deal with interpersonal race relations.*

***Uncle Tom's Cabana.*** MGM, 1947. Produced by Fred Quimby. Typical comedy short film emphasizing the stereotype.

***What a Guy.*** Toddy Pictures, 1947. All-Negro, with Ruby Dee.

***The Burning Cross.*** Somerset-Screen Guild, 1947. Directed by Walter Colmes. With Hank Daniels, Virginia Patton, Joel Fluellyn, Dick Rich, Raymond Bond, Mat Willis. Ku Klux Klan expose.

***The Jackie Robinson Story.*** 1948. With Jackie Robinson, Ruby Dee, Joel Fluellyn, Louise Beavers. The story of Robinson's breakthrough to the major leagues and his early playing career.

***Gangsters on the Loose.*** Toddy Pictures, 1948. All-Negro with Ralph Cooper. Teresa Thompson. Gangster picture about a double-crosser.

***The Betrayal.*** Released by Astor Pictures, 1948. Produced by Oscar Micheaux. All-Negro cast in this story about a young Negro farmer in South Dakota who refuses the love of a woman he believes is white—only to marry her after discovering she is Negro.

***Lost Boundaries.*** 1949. With Bill Greaves, Canada Lee, Beatrice Pearson. Concerns a New Hampshire physician "passing" for white, and his children who are unaware of their Negro blood.

***Home of the Brave.*** 1949. With James Edwards as a Negro soldier torn by discrimination and hatred.

***Pinky.*** 1949. With Ethel Waters, Jeanne Crain, Fred O'Neal, Kenny Washington, Nina Mae McKinney. A fair-skinned Negro girl refuses marriage with a white doctor.

***The Quiet One.*** 1949. With Estelle Evans, Sadie Stockton, Donald Thompson. The juvenile delinquency problem.

***Intruder in the Dust.*** 1949. From the story by William Faulkner. With Juano Hernandez. A Negro is accused of murdering a white man.

***Miracle in Harlem.*** 1949. Directed by Jack Kemp. Original screenplay and story by Vincent Valentini. All-Negro cast in this story about "murder and mayhem" in Harlem.

***Stars in My Crown.*** 1950. Produced by William H. Wright for MGM. Juano Hernandez as an aged Negro in this film about a parson in a Southern town after the Civil War.

***No Way Out.*** Twentieth-Century Fox, 1950. With Sidney Poitier, Bobby Darin, Linda Darnell, Mildred Joanne Smith, Fred O'Neal, Dots Johnson, Maude Simmons, Ruby Dee, Ossie Davis. The first Negro intern at a white hospital finds he must battle prejudice.

***Show Boat.*** 1951. "Ole Man River" is sung by William Warfield in this revival of the 1927 stage production and the 1929 movie.

***Bright Victory.*** 1951. With James Edwards. Concerns prejudice in a hospital for the blind once the white patients discover a blind Negro soldier is among them.

***Native Son.*** 1951. With Richard Wright, Gloria Madison, Willa Pearl Curtiss. The movie version of Richard Wright's novel.

***The Breaking Point.*** 1951. With Juano Hernandez. A white-Negro friendship.

***The Well.*** 1951. With Maidie Norman, Ernest Anderson, Christine Larson, Bill Walker, Alfred Grant, Benjamin Hamilton. Rescue operations for a Negro child trapped in a mine shaft.

***Tarzan's Perils.*** 1952. A Tarzan adventure film, with Dorothy Dandridge in the lead as African princess.

***Lydia Bailey.*** 1951. With Ken Renard, Juanita Moore, William Marshall. Story of Toussaint L'Ouverture, liberator of Haiti.

***To Live Together.*** 1951. A documentary produced by B'nai Brith. Depicts an interracial camp for Chicago children.

*Juano Hernandez (center) gives an extraordinary performance in the powerful, realistic drama* Intruder in the Dust.

***The Harlem Globetrotters.*** Columbia, 1951. With Thomas Gomez, Dorothy Dandridge, Bill Walker, Harlem Globetrotters team. Fiction plot, interspersed with Globetrotter games.

***Member of the Wedding.*** Paramount, 1951. Stars Ethel Waters opposite Julie Harris in the screen version of Carson McCullers' play. Miss Waters gives a powerful portrayal of a cook who befriends a troubled young girl.

***The Medium.*** 1951. Produced by Walter Lowenthal. Directed by Gian-Carlo Menotti, and based upon his play of the same name about a "phony" spiritualist. Leo Coleman, a Negro, plays the part of Toby, a mute gypsy boy.

***The Steel Helmet.*** Lippert Pictures, 1951. Produced by Samuel Fuller. Features James Edwards in a low-budget picture about the adventures of an American infantry patrol detailed to occupy a Korean temple and set up an observation post. Edwards plays the part of a Negro medic.

***Cry the Beloved Country.*** United Artists, 1952. Sidney Poitier along with Canada Lee in this screen version of Alan Paton's novel about South Africa.

***Red Ball Express.*** Universal, 1952. Sidney Poitier as a member of Korea's famed trucking outfit.

***Bright Road.*** MGM, 1953. Harry Belafonte, Dorothy Dandridge, Philip Hepburn in this story about a small, troubled boy and his schoolmaster.

***The Joe Louis Story.*** United Artists, 1953. Stars Hilda Simms, Coley Wallace, and others in a film based on the famous boxer's life.

***Go Man, Go.*** United Artists, 1954. Sidney Poitier as a member of the Harlem Globetrotters, along with Dane Clark and actual players on the team.

***New Faces.*** Twentieth-Century Fox, 1954. Eartha Kitt along with June Carroll, Ronny Graham, and others in this screen version of the Broadway musical.

*Canada Lee portrays a South African village priest in* Cry the Beloved Country.

***The Glenn Miller Story.*** Universal, 1955. Produced by Aaron Rosenberg. Louis Armstrong in this film biography of the famous bandleader.

***Trial.*** MGM, 1955. Produced by Charles Schnee; directed by Mark Robson. Based on the novel by Don Mankiewicz, the screen version concerns the defense of a Mexican who is tried on a murder charge in a California town. Juano Hernandez is the judge.

***Blackboard Jungle.*** MGM, 1956. Produced by Pandro S. Berman. Featuring Sidney Poitier in a film dealing with slum schools and juvenile delinquency.

***Good-bye, My Lady.*** Warner Brothers, 1956. Sidney Poitier in a supporting role as a young farmer who is involved in the problems confronting sharecroppers in the Louisiana swamp country. Brandon DeWilde and Phil Harris are also featured.

***Safari.*** Columbia, 1956. Produced by Adrian D. Worker. Features Earl Cameron, Orlando Martins, and Cy Grant in a story about hunting down the Mau Mau and life in Africa.

***That Certain Feeling.*** Paramount, 1956. Produced and directed by Norman Panama, Melvin Frank, I. A. L. Diamond, and William Altman. Based on the play *The King of Hearts* by Jean Kerr. Features Pearl Bailey as a lyrical maid (she sings two numbers) in a comedy farce.

***Edge of the City.*** United Artists. 1957. Sidney Poitier along with John Cassavetes and Jack Warden in a story about racial bigotry along the waterfront.

***Island in the Sun.*** 1957. Produced by Darryl F. Zanuck. Harry Belafonte stars opposite Joan Fontaine in this story of interracial romance written by Alec Waugh.

***Meet Me in Las Vegas.*** MGM, 1957. Produced by Joe Pasternak. Lena Horne is featured in this musical along with a host of other stars.

***Something of Value.*** MGM, 1957. Stars Sidney Poitier in the screen adaptation of the Robert Ruark novel about the Mau Mau revolt in Kenya.

Anna Lucasta *was a successful 1958 film with Eartha Kitt, Sammy Davis Jr., and Frederick O'Neal. Shown here is a scene from the play with Hilda Simms and Canada Lee, originally produced by the American Negro Theatre in Harlem.*

***The Benny Goodman Story.*** Universal, 1957. Produced by Aaron Rosenberg. Stars Sammy Davis Jr., Lionel Hampton, and Teddy Wilson in the life story of the famous jazzman.

***The Defiant Ones.*** United Artists, 1957. Produced by Stanley Kramer. Involves the trials of two escaped convicts—one white, the other Negro. Sidney Poitier opposite Tony Curtis.

***Anna Lucasta.*** United Artists, 1958. Produced by Sidney Harmon. Eartha Kitt, Sammy Davis Jr., Frederick O'Neal, Rex Ingram, Henry Morgan star in this film about the problems of a young woman who has left home to become a streetwalker.

***St. Louis Blues.*** Paramount, 1958. Produced by Robert Smith. All-Negro cast with Nat Cole, Eartha Kitt, Pearl Bailey, Cab Calloway, Ella Fitzgerald, Mahalia Jackson, Juano Hernandez, and Billy Preston in the life and times of W. C. Handy.

***The Decks Ran Red.*** 1958. Dorothy Dandridge opposite Curt Jurgens in a film which deals with life aboard a slave ship.

***The March of the Hawk.*** Universal-International, 1958. Sidney Poitier opposite Eartha Kitt in a story about the struggle for equality in Africa. Poitier plays a peaceful man at odds with his brother, the "hawk" who is dedicated to violence and war.

***Black Orpheus.*** A Lopert Films release, 1959. Produced by Sacha Gordine. All-Negro cast in this story of a young couple who fall suddenly and rapturously in love, only to be separated by death as in the ancient Greek legend.

***Night of the Quarter Moon.*** MGM, 1959. Produced by Albert Zugsmith. Stars Nat Cole, James Edwards, Marguerite Belafonte, and Billy Daniels in a story of interracial love.

***Odds Against Tomorrow.*** United Artists, 1959. Produced by Robert Wise. Stars Harry Belafonte, Carmen de Lavallade, along with Robert Ryan, Shelley Winters, and Ed Begley. Story of the planning and execution of a crime, with three men (one a Negro). Musical score written by John Lewis. Screenplay by John Oliver Killens.

***Porgy and Bess.*** Columbia, 1959. Produced by Samuel Goldwyn; directed by Otto Preminger. Based on the play by Dubose and Dorothy Heyward. Stars Sidney Poitier, Dorothy Dandridge, Sammy Davis Jr., Pearl Bailey, and others.

***Sapphire.*** J. Arthur Rank, 1959. Produced by Michael Ralph; directed by Basil Dearden. Featuring Earl Cameron, Gordon Heath, Harry Baird, Nigel Patrick, Yvonne Mitchell, Michael Craig, and Paul Massie in a mystery with racial overtones. (The murdered girl turns out to be a Negro.)

***Tamango.*** Hal Roach Release, 1959. Produced by Rene G. Vauttoux, Roland Gerard, Sig Shore, and Joe Harris. Based on the novel by Prosper Merimee, with Dorothy Dandridge, Curt Jurgens, Jean Servais, and Alex Cressah. Concerns the slave trade, and what happens on a slaver bound from Africa to Cuba.

***The Sound and the Fury.*** 1959. Produced by Jerry Wald. Features Ethel Waters along with Margaret Leighton, Joanne Woodward, Yul Brynner, and Jack Warden in the film version of the Faulkner novel. Miss Waters is Dilsey, the family cook.

***The World, the Flesh and the Devil.*** 1959. Stars Harry Belafonte, along with Inger Stevens and Mel Ferrer. An interracial theme in a story which takes place at the end of the world.

***All the Young Men.*** Columbia, 1960. Sidney Poitier, along with Alan Ladd and Mort Sahl, in this story about what happens to a small detachment of marines in Korea whose command is taken over by a Negro.

***Let No Man Write My Epitaph.*** Columbia, 1960. Produced by Boris D. Kaplan. Bernie Hamilton appears in this film version of Willard Motley's novel.

***Sergeant Rutledge.*** Warner Brothers, 1960. Produced and directed by John Ford. Stars Woody Strode in a tale of the Old West set in Arizona after the Civil War. The sergeant (Strode) is accused of violating and strangling a white girl, and of murdering her father, his commanding officer. Also features, Jeffrey Hunter, Constance Towers, and Billie Burke.

***Shadows.*** 1960. Directed by John Cassavetes. Focuses on the rootlessness of the urban Negro in Greenwich Village.

***Take a Giant Step.*** United Artists, 1960. Produced by Julius J. Epstein. Stars Johnny Nash, Ruby Dee, Frederick O'Neal, Beah Richards in the screen version of Louis Peterson's play about a young man growing up.

***The Adventures of Huckleberry Finn.*** MGM, 1960. Produced by Samuel Goldwyn Jr. Archie Moore plays Jim in this modern version of the Mark Twain novel.

***The Crowning Experience.*** Directed, produced, and presented by Moral Rearmament, 1960. All-Negro cast in the screen version of the life of Mary McLeod Bethune.

***A Raisin in the Sun.*** Columbia, 1961. Sidney Poitier, Claudia McNeil, Diana Sands in this film based on Lorraine Hansberry's award-winning play about an urban Negro family.

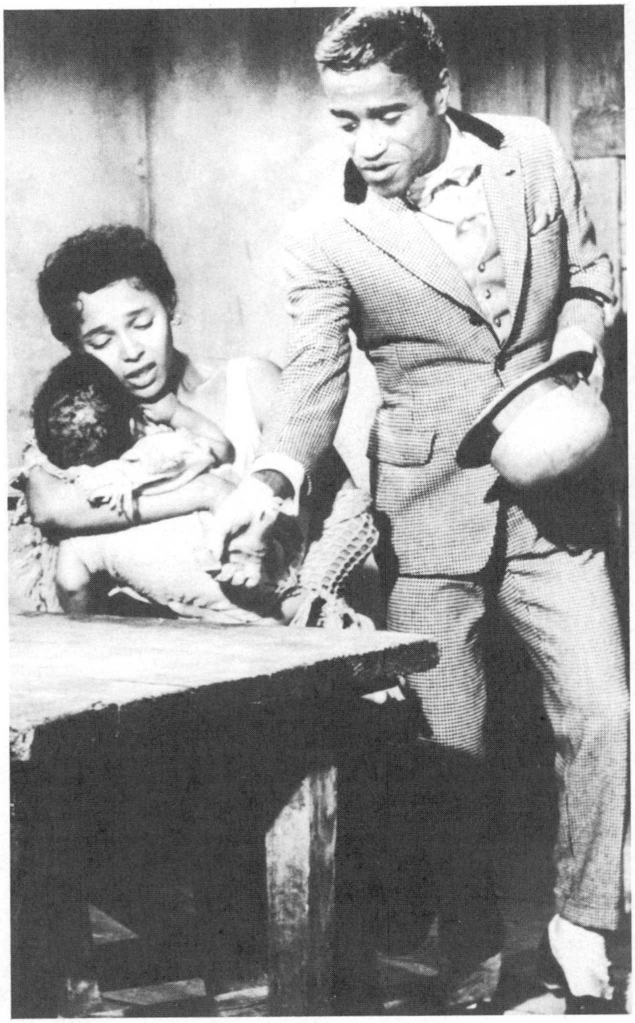

*Scene from the 1959 musical* Porgy and Bess.

***Biography of a Rookie.*** Wolper-Sterling Prod., 1961. Narrator, Mike Wallace. Story of the rise of Dodger baseball player Willie Davis to the major leagues.

***Guns of the Trees.*** 1961. Produced by Jonas Mekas. This film juxtaposes the lives of two married couples, one white, the other Negro.

***Paris Blues.*** United Artists, 1961. Sidney Poitier, Paul Newman, Joanne Woodward, Diahann Carroll in this film about two expatriate jazzmen living in Paris, and their romantic adventures with two American girls on the loose.

***The Intruder.*** 1961. Produced by Roger Gorman. Based on a novel by Charles Beaumont, this film concerns an anti-integrationist who goes to a small Southern town to arouse the townspeople against integration in the local schools.

***The Young One.*** 1961. Produced by George P. Werber. Stars Bernie Hamilton and Zachary Scott. A Negro (Hamilton) escapes to an isolated island over which Scott serves as a kind of warden.

***A Taste of Honey.*** Continental Pictures, 1962. Produced by Tony Richardson. Features Paul Danquah as the Negro sailor who gets involved with a young white girl. Also seen are Dora Bryan and Rita Tushingham.

***Carmen Jones.*** Twentieth-Century Fox, 1962. Produced and directed by Otto Preminger. Dorothy Dandridge, Harry Belafonte, Olga James, Pearl Bailey, and Diahann Carroll in this revised version of Bizet's opera.

***Oceans 11.*** 1962. Produced by Frank Sinatra. The famous "clan" with Sammy Davis Jr. in a prominent role as a member of a daring gang that plans to hold up Las Vegas nightspots.

***Pressure Point.*** United Artists, 1962. Sidney Poitier cast as a social worker who attempts to rehabilitate wrongdoer Bobby Darin.

***The Connection.*** 1962. Vivid screen portrayal of Negroes in the narcotics underworld. Based on Jack Gelber's play.

***An Affair of the Skin.*** 1963. Produced by Ben Maddow. Diana Sands as a Negro heroine in Greenwich Village. Featuring Viveca Lindfors, Kevin McCarthy.

***Convicts 4.*** Allied Artists, 1963. Produced by A. Ronald Lubin. Sammy Davis Jr. along with Richard Conte in a prominent role as a convict who contemplates escape.

***Gone Are the Days.*** 1963. Directed by Nicholas Webster. Based on the play *Purlie Victorious* by Ossie Davis.

***Sergeants 3.*** United Artists, 1963. Produced by Frank Sinatra. Stars Sammy Davis Jr., along with Sinatra and Peter Lawford, as members of a U.S. Cavalry unit which fights a number of frontier battles.

***The Cool World.*** 1963. Produced by Shirley Clarke. Based on Warren Miller's novel. An important film document about Negro life in Harlem.

***The Greenwich Village Story.*** 1963. Produced by Jack O'Connell. Features Negroes as background presences in party sequences, street and restaurant scenes and, in general, as part of the Village milieu.

***To Kill a Mockingbird.*** Universal, 1963. Produced by Alan J. Pakula; directed by Robert Mulligan. Based on Harper Lee's best selling novel of 1960, this film has Brock Peters and Estelle Evans in prominent roles. The story concerns the defense of a Negro on trial for allegedly raping a white girl.

***Black Like Me.*** 1964. Directed by Carl Lerner. Based on the novel of the same title by John Howard Griffin. A white man (James Whitmore) passes for Negro.

***Free, White and 21.*** American International, 1964. Directed by Larry Buchanan; stars Frederick O'Neal. Carefree, wild, abandoned whites and their world of tinsel and gold.

***Johnny Cool.*** United Artists, 1964. Producer-director William Asher. Based on the novel *The Kingdom of Johnny Cool* by John McPartland. Sammy Davis Jr. in the role of an "Educated," and sophisticated "hanger-on" in the underworld's gambling casinos. Plot turns on underworld life and intragang rivalry.

***Lilies of the Field.*** United Artists, 1964. Sidney Poitier as a traveling vagabond who befriends a group of nuns and wins their friendship and understanding.

***Living Between Two Worlds.*** 1964. Directed by Robert Johnson. Deals with a mother-son conflict within a Negro family in Los Angeles.

***Nothing but a Man.*** 1964. Produced by Michael Roemer. The award-winning story of a Negro laborer and his romance. Stars Ivan Dixon and Abbey Lincoln.

***One Potato, Two Potato.*** 1964. Directed by Larry Peerce. A love affair involving a Negro man and a white divorcee. The Negro is played by Bernie Hamilton.

***The Long Ships.*** Columbia, 1964. Sidney Poitier as a powerful sultan in a costume drama. Also features Richard Widmark.

***The Streets of Greenwood or Ivanhoe Donaldson.*** 1964. Directed by Harold Becher. A feature-length documentary illustrating the civil rights struggle in the United States.

***Cat Ballou.*** Columbia, 1965. Produced by Harold Hecht. Nat Cole is featured as a traveling minstrel.

***Major Dundee.*** Columbia, 1965. Produced by Jerry Bresher. Brock Peters is featured as a member of the U.S. Cavalry.

***None but the Brave.*** Warner Brothers, 1965. Produced and directed by Frank Sinatra. Rafer Johnson plays an Army officer on patrol in the South Pacific.

***Synanon.*** Columbia, 1965. Produced and directed by Richard Quine. Features Eartha Kitt, Bernie Hamilton, Chuck Connors, Stella Stevens, and Edmund O'Brien. The rehabilitation of drug addicts through the now-famous "Synanon" method.

***The Carpetbaggers.*** Paramount, 1965. Produced by Joseph E. Levine; based on the novel by Harold Robbins. Featuring Archie Moore in the role of Jedediah.

***The Greatest Story Ever Told.*** 1965. The story of the ministry of Christ. Sidney Poitier as the Ethiopian who is converted to Christianity.

***The Hill.*** 1965. Produced by Sidney Lumet. Features Ossie Davis as a West Indian soldier-prisoner known as Jacko King. Based on the play by Ray Rigby about a British detention camp in North Africa during World War II.

***The New Interns.*** Columbia, 1965. Ena Hartman in an important role as a nurse.

***The Pawnbroker.*** Landau, 1965. Produced by Worthington Miner. This film with Brock Peters, Juano Hernandez, and Rod Steiger depicts life in Harlem. One of the earliest films for which a Negro, Quincy Jones, wrote the musical score.

***A Man Called Adam.*** 1966. Produced by Sammy Davis Jr. Stars Sammy Davis Jr., along with Cicely Tyson, Ossie Davis, and Louis Armstrong in the story of a problem-ridden musician.

***Blues for Lovers.*** Twentieth-Century Fox, 1966. Produced by Alexander Salkind. Features Ray Charles along with his orchestra and singers in a story about a small boy's need for understanding.

***Booker T. Washington.*** Encyclopedia Britannica Films, 1966. Collaborator: John Hope Franklin. Tells the dramatic story of Washington's life and career.

***Duel at Diablo.*** 1966. Sidney Poitier plays a feared gunslinger in this Western.

***Hurry Sundown.*** 1966. Produced by Otto Preminger. Stars Diahann Carroll, Robert Hooks, Rex Ingram in a movie based on the best-selling novel.

***Our Man Flint.*** Twentieth-Century Fox, 1966. Ena Hartman has a featured role as bigwig's (Lee J. Cobb) secretary.

***Patch of Blue.*** MGM, 1966. Produced by Pandro S. Berman. A moving story about a blind girl befriended by a young Negro. Stars Sidney Poitier, Elizabeth Hartman, Shelley Winters, Ivan Dixon, Wallace Ford.

***Rio Conchos.*** Twentieth-Century Fox, 1966. Produced by David Weisbart. Ex-football star Jim Brown, now an actor, as U.S. Cavalry Sergeant Ben Franklin, one of four men out to recover stolen rifles.

***The Appaloosa.*** Universal, 1966. Frank Silvera in this modern Western starring Marlon Brando.

***The Cincinnati Kid.*** MGM, 1966. Produced by Martin Ransohoff, Cab Calloway in a prominent role as a traveling card shark in a film about top-flight poker players.

***The Girl Nobody Knew.*** Universal, 1966. Ena Hartman is cast as a sophisticated New Yorker who moves in top social circles.

***The Slender Thread.*** Paramount, 1966. Sidney Poitier opposite Anne Bancroft as the psychiatrist who saves her life.

***The Bedford Incident.*** 1966. Sidney Poitier along with Richard Widmark in a story about life on a U.S. warship.

***Dutchman.*** 1967. Produced by Gene Persson. Based on the off-Broadway play by Leroi Jones. Starring Shirley Knight and Al Freeman Jr.

***In the Heat of the Night.*** Mirisch Corporation, 1967. Director Norman Jewison presents a drama of racial hate and prejudice fictionally set in an ugly little Mississippi town. The stars Rod Steiger and Sidney Poitier (Virgil Tibbs) are well-realized characters. Quincy Jones composed the music and Ray Charles sang the title song.

***Now Is the Time.*** 1967. Carousel Films. 36 minutes. WCAU-TV, Philadelphia. Chronicles the history of the American Negro and his emergence from a 300-year old "pagan" slave state. Shows him as of 1968, a crucial year in which he demands his rights and equal status. Combines the sounds and rhythms of the violence of race riots with folk, rock, and hymnal music. Features the works of Langston Hughes, Countee Cullen, James Baldwin, Malcolm X, and Stokely Carmichael.

***Some of My Best Friends Are White.*** Robeck, 1967. Producer Michael Lathem. A provocative examination of America's racial problem as discussed from the point of view of the middle-class Negro involving his acceptance by society and the future of his children growing up in white suburbia. A BBC-TV Production.

***The Weapons of Gordon Parks.*** Color. 28 minutes. 1967. Contemporary-McGraw-Hill. The story of the internationally known black photographer seen at work, in his home, with his family, and on the streets of Harlem, as part of his past life is recreated. An inspiring and moving photographic essay. Directed by Warren Forma.

***The President's Analyst.*** Paramount, 1967. Screenwriter/director Theodore J. Flicker came up with this smartly filmed Hollywood comedy with a distinctly intellectual turn. Godfrey Cambridge featured alongside James Coburn. The story is a take-off on governmental security, automation, and international intrigue involving U.S. and foreign agents.

***A Time for Burning.*** 1967. Conceived, directed, and edited by William C. Jersey and Barbara Connell, this film deals with a crisis that actually occurred in Omaha, Nebraska, when a Lutheran minister tried to inspire church members to destroy the barriers existing between themselves and the Negro ghetto.

***Up the Down Staircase.*** Warner Brothers-Seven Arts, 1967. Director Robert Mulligan casts Jose Rodriguez in an adaptation of the best-selling novel about a big-city school system.

***To Sir, With Love.*** Columbia, 1967. Director James Clavell here paints a picture of a Negro teacher who takes a post in a tough London school and battles to reach rebellious youngsters. Starring Sidney Poitier.

***Doctor Doolittle.*** Twentieth-Century Fox, 1967. Director Richard Fleisher has multi-talented Geoffrey Holder in this musical based on a series of stories bearing the same title. The film is one big, colorful, imaginative burst of animal-people fun.

***Portrait of Jason.*** Filmmakers, 1967. Director Shirely Clarke's intimate marathon interview with a self-described male prostitute, himself a Negro. The star bares his soul in an all-night camera session for director Clarke. The film comes off as a first-rate socio-psychological documentary.

***The Dirty Dozen.*** MGM, 1967. Director Robert Aldrich has ex-football star Jim Brown in this tough, he-man, ribald film about war prisoners who are given a chance to redeem themselves by embarking on a perilous World War II mission.

***The Night of the Living Dead.*** Walter Reade, 1968. Director, George A. Romero. The story involves corpses reawakened by radiation who roam the countryside killing and devouring cities. Stars Duane Jones.

***The Scalphunters.*** United Artists, 1968. Directed by Sidney Pollack. Black power Western involving a fur trapper with a captured runaway slave stalking a scalphunting gang to retrieve stolen furs. A Negro, trying to gain his freedom by outwitting whites, proves that white supremacy isn't omnipotent. Ossie Davis is in this one along with Burt Lancaster.

***Guess Who's Coming to Dinner.*** Columbia Pictures, 1968. Director Stanley Kramer draws on a top-level cast which includes Sidney Poitier, Spencer Tracy, and Katherine Hepburn. The story deals with the question of interracial love and the problems of mixed marriage. The cast also includes Beah Richards.

*Ossie Davis and Burt Lancaster in a scene from* The Scalphunters.

The Last Man *dramatized black militancy in Philadelphia.*

Sweet Charity's *chorus line works out a song.*

***For Love of Ivy.*** Cinerama, 1968. Director Daniel Mann. This film stars Sidney Poitier, Abbey Lincoln, and Leon Bibb. A love affair between the luscious Ivy (Abbey Lincoln) and a suave businessman (Sidney Poitier). Quincy Jones composed the music.

***Negro Kingdoms.*** Color. 16 minutes. 1968. Atlantis. Reveals the high level of culture and society of slavery existing in West Africa prior to the era of slavery through treatment of the changing climate of Africa, trans-Saharan trade, the growth of Islam, and the story of medieval Mali and Ghana.

***If He Hollers, Let Him Go!.*** (Cinerama Releasing, 1968.) Theme of this film is injustice to a black man hunted down following his escape from prison for a crime he did not commit. Stars Raymond St. Jacques, Barbara McNair, Dana Wynter, and Kevin McCarthy.

***P. J.*** Universal, 1968. Rough, tough, violent private-eye story directed by John Gulleria with Brock Peters in a top-level role.

***Mingus.*** Filmmakers, 1968. Close-up of bass player and composer Charlie Mingus as he and his five-year-old daughter await eviction by the City of New York. The film is laced with intercuts of Mingus as a musician.

***Dark of the Sun.*** MGM, 1968. Director Jack Cardiff off to the Congo on a story involving killing, gore, and double-dealing. Jim Brown prominent in this one.

***Split Decision.*** Filmmakers, 1968. Fighter Jose Torres is followed in this film during preparations for his bout with Dick Tiger. The film manages to give some insight into the boxing profession.

***The Story of a Three Day Pass.*** Sigma III, 1968. Black director Melvin Van Peebles tells a story of a young Negro on a three-day pass in Paris, of his weekend encounter with a white girl, as well as some white buddies from camp. This film gives tremendous insight in the gap between what people feel and what they encounter.

***Robby.*** Bluewood, 1968. Writer/director Ralph C. Bluemke produces a sincere film about a white lad marooned on an island along with a Negro youngster. Both develop a friendship, only to be cruelly separated by racism after their rescue.

***The Biggest Bundle of Them All.*** MGM, 1968. Director Ken Annakin produced this big caper spoof featuring an aging, exiled gangster in Italy who leads gang of amateurs in carefully planned heist. Starring Godfrey Cambridge.

***Finian's Rainbow.*** Warner Brothers-Seven Arts, 1968. This long-time hit and favorite of Broadway's yesteryear is directed by Francis Ford Coppola and has a fresh movie look. Al Freeman Jr. with Fred Astaire, Petula Clark, Tommy Steele and a completely integrated cast.

***The Heart Is a Lonely Hunter.*** Warner Brothers-Seven Arts, 1968. Robert Ellis Miller directed this poignant film based on Carson McCullers' novel about loneliness in a Southern town. Cicely Tyson featured with Percy Rodrigues.

***Ice Station Zebra.*** MGM, 1968. Director John Sturges put Jim Brown in this suspenseful cold-war thriller about a U.S. nuclear war submarine on a secret mission to a polar region with an unknown saboteur aboard.

***The Split.*** MGM, 1968. Director Gordon Fleming stars Jim Brown as a tough criminal who decides on one last caper before retiring—robbing the Los Angeles Coliseum.

***Salt and Pepper.*** United Artists, 1968. Director Richard Donner put together this frantic comedy about London club owners caught in a plot to overthrow the British government. Peter Lawford is Pepper, and Sammy Davis Jr. is Salt.

***The Learning Tree.*** Warner Brothers-Seven Arts, 1969. Photojournalist-musician Gordon Parks with a reflective film based upon his novel about a Negro youngster growing up in Kansas in the 1920s. Parks also composed the music. Stars include Kyle Johnson, Alex Clarke, Estelle Evans, and Dana Elcar.

***The Last Man.*** Universal, 1969. Director Robert Alan Arthur cast Sidney Poitier as a hunted Negro militant in flight after a robbery to get funds for his movement fails. Also featuring Al Freeman Jr. and Leon Bibb.

***Float Like a Butterfly, Sting Like a Bee.*** Grove Films, 1969. Directed and filmed by William Klein, this film is a visually excellent, fascinating study of Cassius Clay, now Muhammad Ali. A factual biography with great moments from his ring career.

***Putney Swope.*** Cinema V, 1969. Director Robert Downey tells what happens when a group of Negroes takes over an ad agency. Arnold Johnson, Laura Greene, along with a huge amusing cast.

***Terry Whitmore for Example.*** Grove Films, 1969. Director Bill Brodie presents a young Negro who, after having won a medal for heroism as a marine in Vietnam, defects to Sweden.

***Ace High.*** Paramount, 1969. The world-famed Colizzi presents a western featuring intellectually attuned hombres, including Brock Peters.

***Death of a Gunfighter.*** Universal, 1969. A marvelous western with an interracial marriage theme. Involves a town marshal who kills too easily and alienates his town. Lena Horne as the wife, Richard Widmark as her husband.

***100 Rifles.*** Twentieth-Century Fox, 1969. Director Tom Gries presents a drama about the Mexican persecution of Yaqui Indians. The hero is Jim Brown and the heroine is Raquel Welch.

***Topaz.*** Alfred Hitchcock Universal Production Release, 1969. This is the film version of the Leon Uris best-selling novel of the same title dealing with international espionage. Roscoe Lee Browne plays the role of an espionage agent.

***Bye, Bye Braverman.*** Warner Brothers-Seven Arts, 1969. Director Sidney Lumet has Godfrey Cambridge in this film dealing with a slice of ethnic life in Brooklyn, New York.

***Slaves.*** Walter Reade, 1969. This controversial drama takes a bold look at the system of slavery as it occurred in the United States and stars Ossie Davis along with Dionne Warwick.

***Castle Keep.*** Columbia Pictures, 1969. Director Sydney Pollack casts Al Freeman, Jr. in this unusual war film about a small unit of U.S. servicemen who try to hold a castle against advancing Germans during World War II.

***Change of Mind.*** Cinerama Release, 1969. Director Robert Stephens casts Raymond St. Jacques in this film about the brain of a white district attorney transplanted into the brain of a Negro man.

***Two Gentlemen Sharing.*** American International Pictures, 1969. Director Ted Kotcheff put this film together about a young white man who shares a flat with an equally young Negro in London. An assortment of problems follows—equally shared by Robin Phillips and Hal Frederick.

***Sweet Charity.*** Universal, 1969. Director Bob Fosse made the transition from stage to screen with singular intelligence, imagination, and cinematic flair in this successful Broadway stage hit. Sammy Davis, Jr. is an appealing part of the action.

***Up Tight.*** Paramount, 1969. Director/producer Jules Dassin set his locale in Cleveland, Ohio, to tell an honest powerful drama of a poor, sincere Negro man caught in a changing world.

***The Informer.*** Screen version of the Liam O'Flaherty story, 1969. The very able cast includes Raymond St. Jacques, Julian Mayfield, Ruby Dee, Frank Silvera, and Roscoe Lee Browne. Booker T. Jones composed the music.

***Wild in the Streets.*** American International Pictures, 1969. Director Barry Shear put together this film about the explosive movement of the young to win the vote at age 15 and take over the U.S. government, with the "older generation" forcibly retired after age 35. Richard Pryor, comedian-turned-actor, plays a prominent role.

***Joanna.*** Twentieth-Century Fox, 1969. This well told British drama describes a world where life is free and easy. Its theme also covers an interracial love affair. Starring Glenna Forster Jones, Genevieve Waite, and Calvin Lockhart.

***The Comedians.*** MGM, 1969. Directed and produced by Peter Glenville. This film presents the sinister image of a rigid reign of terror in a Caribbean country under a black dictatorship. Negroes in top-level roles include Roscoe Lee Browne, George S. Brown, James Earl Jones, Raymond St. Jacques, and Cicely Tyson.

***Flame in the Streets.*** Atlantic, 1969 release (original 1962). Released again in 1969, this absorbing drama set in England deals with Negro and white civil, social, and labor relationships, and the double-edged problem of mixed marriage. Stars Earl Cameron, Sylvia Sims, John Wills, and Johnny Sekka.

***The Riot.*** Paramount, 1969. Director Buzz Kulik made this film on location at the Arizona State Prison. Starring Jim Brown in a story about a prison break.

***The Rievers.*** A Cinema Center Film Presentation, 1969. Director Mark Rydell based this film version on the Faulkner novel of the same title. The amusing story about the turn-of-the-century South co-starred Steve McQueen and Rupert Crosse, a Negro actor nominated for an Academy Award in a supporting role.

***Hello Dolly.*** Twentieth-Century Fox, 1969. Director Gene Kelly did the screen adaptation of this well-known Broadway play with finesse and great skill. The story hasn't changed. Dolly, a female jack-of-all-trades, is at it again. Barbra Streisand along with Walter Matthau, and Louis Armstrong.

***First World Festival of Negro Arts.*** Color, 20 minutes. Contemporary-McGraw-Hill, 1969. Scenes of the first World Festival of Negro Arts held at Dakar in 1966, showing music, dance, sculpture, painting and the reciprocal influence of Negro art and culture in relation to the Western world.

***I Have a Dream.*** 35 minutes. 1969. The biography of Martin Luther King made from newsreel footage of the civil rights movement during the 1950s and 1960s. Reveals his dedication to the movement and to the principles of nonviolence.

***Martin Luther King: The Man and the March.*** 83 minutes. 1969. Produced by Public Broadcast Laboratory of NET. A documentary on the late Doctor Martin Luther King Jr.'s "Poor People's March." Shows Dr. King conferring with aides, speaking at rallies and traveling as he solicits support for, and develops the operational details of, the March. Indicates the methods used by his aides to create interest and support on a local level and with other ethnic groups.

***Three in the Attic.*** American International Pictures, 1969. Director Richard Wilson. This film tells the story of a campus Don Juan kidnaped and held in the attic by three of his girlfriends. Judy Pace along with Christopher Jones.

***No Vietnamese Ever Called Me Nigger.*** Bob Maurice Paradigm, 1969. 68 minutes. Three black G. I.'s discuss their experiences in Vietnam, the racism that exists in the armed forces, and their dissatisfaction with life in the U.S. upon their return.

***The Watermelon Man.*** Columbia Pictures, 1970. Director Melvin Van Peebles (see also *The Story of a Three Day Pass*, 1969), in his American film debut, casts Godfrey Cambridge and Estelle Parsons in a film about a man who turns color overnight. What happens when that transformation becomes known to his associates and friends makes for a story perched on the fine edge between comedy and tragedy.

***The Angel Levine.*** United Artists, 1970. Jan Kadar directed this film which casts Harry Bellafonte as the angel opposite Zero Mostel whom he seeks to convince that he is for real.

*Jewish angel Harry Belafonte drinks Passover wine with a troubled Zero Mostel in* The Angel Levine.

*Diana Ross plays singer Billie Holiday in* The Lady Sings the Blues.

***Last of the Mobile Hot-Shots.*** Warner Brothers, 1970. A Sidney Lumet Production. The film version of *The Seven Descents of Myrtle,* a play by Tennessee Williams adapted for the screen by Gore Vidal, tells the story of two brothers; one white, one black and the women they both love. Filmed largely on location in and around Baton Rouge, Louisiana. Stars Robert Hooks, Lynn Redgrave, and James Coburn.

***My Sweet Charlie.*** Universal, 1970. Directed by Lamont Johnson, this boy-meets-girl story initially premiered on NBC. Stars Patty Duke and Al Freeman Jr.

***End of the Road.*** Allied Artists Film, 1970. Directed by Aram Avakian. This film stars James Earl Jones as Doctor D. in a story involving one man's attempt to straighten out his life, only to find more difficulty lies at the end of the road.

***Tick...Tick...Tick...*** MGM, 1970. Directed by Ralph Nelson. This drama stars Jim Brown, George Kennedy, and Frederic March and centers around the aftermath of a bitter election campaign for sheriff in a small rural county in the Deep South.

***Patton.*** Fox, 1970. A monumental performance by George C. Scott as World War II General George S. Patton. Karl Malden as General Bradley, along with the late James Edwards in his last film.

***Super Fly.*** Warner Brothers, 1971. Actor Ron O'Neal became a folk hero and a target of outrage simultaneously after playing a role as Priest in this sympathetic portrait of a drug pusher.

***Sweet Sweetback's Badasssss Song.*** Cinemation, 1971. Filmmaking Melvin Van Peebles involved himself in virtually every aspect of this X-rated film about the radicalization and subsequent revolt of a black stud. Controversial but independent and a precedent-setter.

***Shaft.*** MGM, 1971. Photogenic Richard Roundtree made his film debut with director Gordon Parks in this adventure tale about a black New York City private eye.

***Skin Game.*** Warner Brothers, 1971. Lou Gossett co-stars with James Garner in this film about two con men who take on town after town in the old West. Gossett plays a slave in this comedy, although he is actually a well-educated, but crooked man.

***Right On.*** Independent, 1971. Filmmakers Woody King and Herbert Danska filmed the Last Poets, an activist group of performers as they rapped about the black condition and intercut representative scenes of Harlem life in this documentary.

***The Organization.*** United Artists, 1971. Sidney Poitier portrays detective Tibbs again in this drama set in modern San Francisco. Barbara McNairco stars as his wife.

***Man and Boy.*** Levitt-Pickman, 1971. Bill Cosby invested huge sums of his own money to produce this film about a black family on the Western frontier. A pioneer effort and warm story.

***Honkey.*** Jack Harris Ent., 1971. Brenda Sykes starred in this tepid drama about an interracial teenage love affair that was more soap opera than anything else.

***The Bus Is Coming.*** Independent, 1971. K-Calb was the black production company that made this drama about a black Vietnam veteran who returns home to a racially tense town after his activist brother has been killed by police.

***Brother John.*** Columbia, 1971. Sidney Poitier plays the key role in this drama about a man who returns to a small Southern town for a funeral and confronts the establishment on a number of issues.

***Black Jesus.*** Cannon, 1971. Woody Strode stars in this Italian-made allegorical drama about a man who becomes a sacrificial lamb in an African struggle. The central figure is reminiscent of the Christ person.

The Watermelon Man *is a tragicomedy about a white man suddenly turning black.*

***Across 110th Street.*** United Artists, 1972. The emphasis is on crime in this heavy-handed drama about a territory war between the uptown and downtown mobs for control of the Harlem rackets. Yaphet Kotto in a key role as a police lieutenant.

***Black Gunn.*** Columbia, 1972. Jim Brown stars in this takeoff as a super-powerful operator who takes on established crime and wins handily.

***Trouble Man.*** Twentieth-Century Fox, 1972. Ivan Dixon made his film debut as a director working with actor Robert Hooks in this action film about a ghetto trouble shooter who free-lances and attempts to protect the community from outside gangsters.

***Farewell Uncle Tom.*** Cannon, 1972. An Italian-made film about slavery in the United States.

***Black Girl.*** Cinerama, 1972. Ossie Davis directed this film version of a successful off-Broadway play about the life in a black family. Emphasis was on the inter-relationship between three generations of women under one roof.

***Lady Sings the Blues.*** Paramount, 1972. Motown Records entered the movie business with this film and won five Academy Award nominations. Diana Ross made her film debut as singer Billie Holiday in one of the most important film biographies about a black character.

***Hickey and Boggs.*** United Artists, 1972. Bill Cosby teams with his old television co-star Robert Culp in this film about two aging private detectives and their careers. A rare screen role for Cosby.

***Hammer.*** United Artists, 1972. Fred Williamson stars in this film about a boxer who attempts to fight off corruption in boxing as well as keep his title in the ring.

***Sounder.*** Twentieth-Century Fox, 1972. Nominated for four Academy Awards, this film was based on a best-selling story and adapted for the screen by Lonne Elder III. Paul Winfield and Cicely Tyson starred as the parents of a depression era black family in the South. Both were nominated for their realistic portrayals.

***Melinda.*** MGM, 1972. Calvin Lockhart stars in this story about a black disc jockey who becomes involved in all kinds of intrigues and successfully solves the murder of his pretty girlfriend.

***Blacula.*** American International, 1972. A black version of the story about Count Dracula with William Marshall as the Count Mamuwalde (Blacula) who turns up in contemporary society and ventures forth in a journey of death but is ultimately exposed and killed.

***The Man.*** Paramount, 1972. James Earl Jones stars as the title character in this film version of the best-selling novel about the first black man to be elected president of the United States.

***Super Fly.*** Warner Brothers, 1972. A film probing deep inside a successful drug pusher and his relationship with his women. A controversial effort that was roundly criticized by those who felt the filmmakers left much to be desired.

***The Limit.*** Cannon, 1972. A Yaphet Kotto production written to shed light on the difficult task to handle: that of a black motorcycle policeman. The film awkwardly proposes several problems with no real resolution.

***The Final Comedown.*** New World, 1972. Billy Dee Williams stars in this drama about black revolution in the ghetto. Oscar Williams directed this film which was sponsored in part by grants from the American Film Institute.

***Black Rodeo.*** Cinerama, 1972. Basically a documentary on contemporary black cowboys in the rodeo circuit today. Also comments from various celebrities who have seen the cowboys at work.

***Come Back Charleston Blue.*** Warner Brothers, 1972. Television director Mark Warren makes his film debut with Raymond St. Jacques and Godfrey Cambridge recast as two Harlem detectives in this film based on novelist Chester Himes' books.

***Shaft's Big Score.*** MGM, 1972. The follow-up adventure of the handsome black private eye in New York City. A bag of money and a chase that involves virtually every mode of transportion in existence. Richard Roundtree stars.

***Malcolm X.*** Warner Brothers, 1972. An excellent documentary about the slain rights leader that was later nominated for an Academy Award.

***Top of the Heap.*** Fanfare, 1972. Actor Christopher St. John quickly becomes a writer and director in this film about the life of a big city black cop.

***The Legend of Nigger Charley.*** Paramount, 1972. A house slave on a Virginia plantation gets fed up and runs away to the West where he quickly adapts and becomes a hero. Fred Williamson stars.

***Buck and the Preacher.*** Columbia, 1972. Sidney Poitier made his directorial debut working on this Western in which he co-starred with Harry Belafonte and Ruby Dee.

***Cool Breeze.*** MGM, 1972. An unlikely team of bank thieves are the key players in this film which was fashioned after a 1950 drama. Thalmus Rasulala starred.

***Man and Boy.*** Levitt-Pickman, 1972. Bill Cosby produced and starred in this Western drama about a black family. Despite careful attention to make an important film, technical problems robbed the production of much of its potential.

***Georgia, Georgia.*** Cinerama, 1972. Diana Sands stars in this film about a black singer on tour in Europe. Made on location in Sweden by producer Jack Jordan, it was a milestone for efforts of blacks to work in Europe.

***Soul Soldier.*** Fanfare, 1972. Former Olympic winner Rafer Johnson among the cast in this poor film about life of the all-black cavalry on the Western frontier after the Civil War.

***Five on the Black Hand Side.*** United Artists, 1973. An off-Broadway play was the inspiration for this comedy about a black middle class family. Brock Peters made his co-producing debut and many of the original cast members became part of the film.

***Jimi Plays Berkeley.*** Independent, 1973. A documentary on rock singer Jimi Hendricks with specific emphasis on a concert he played at Berkeley.

***The Slams.*** MGM, 1973. Prison life is the background for this film about life in a penitentiary and an attempt is made to reveal some insight into how this unique society operates. Jim Brown stars.

***The Hit.*** Paramount, 1973. Billy Dee Williams is the key character in this story of a government agent who uses his expertise to track down the source of drug traffic in Europe and then wipe all the kingpins out of operation.

***Maurie.*** National General, 1973. Bernie Casey stars in the title role of this semi-fictional account of the life of basketball great Maurice Stokes, who was permanently incapacitated by a tragic accident at the height of his pro career. Well acted and well produced.

***Save the Children.*** Paramount, 1973. Filmed entirely on location at the 1972 PUSH Expo in Chicago, this music documentary featuring the finest black talent working at the time was a major effort that also featured as many talented blacks in the crucial positions behind the cameras, including director Stan Lathan.

***The Spook Who Sat by the Door.*** United Artists, 1973. Based on Sam Greenlee's powerful novel about black revolution, this action drama proved to be as potent on screen. Directed by Ivan Dixon with Lawrence Cook and J. A. Preston starring.

***Slaughter's Big Ripoff.*** American International, 1973. Jim Brown versus the Mafia is the theme in this action drama that pits Brown against a West Coast syndicate. A sequel to *Slaughter*.

***Scream Blacula Scream.*** American International, 1973. Modeled after the Dracula character, Blacula is played by William Marshall. He comes to life and terrorizes a contemporary town for several weeks before being discovered by a nosy investigator. A sequel to *Blacula*.

***Gordon's War.*** Twentieth-Century Fox, 1973. Ossie Davis and Paul Winfield team as director and star of this adventure film about a Vietnam veteran who returns home and seeks about to destroy drug dealers responsible for his wife's death by overdose.

***Cleopatra Jones.*** Warner Brothers, 1973. Former model Tamara Dobson is the leading lady in this film about an attractive drug fighter who becomes a community hero as much as an activist.

***The Soul of Nigger Charley.*** Paramount, 1973. A runaway slave becomes a folk hero in the West as he fights his way away from bounty hunters and helps out some Mexican allies. Fred Williamson stars.

***Ganja and Hess.*** Kelly-Jordan, 1973. Writer-director Bill Gunn is the key figure in this independently made and distributed production about a doctor's obsession with blood. Much more in heavily symbolic terms about the black experience. An extremely successful film at the Cannes festival.

***The Mack.*** Cinerama, 1973. Max Julian and Richard Pryor are the key figures in this portrait of a highly successful pimp and the lifestyle that he pursues. A significant collection of negative images and plenty of violence.

***Book of Numbers.*** Avco Embassy, 1973. Actor Raymond St. Jacques makes his directing and producing debut in this film based on the life of Southern society with an emphasis on numbers running. Good natured fun a major asset in this film based on a novel by Robert Dean Pharr.

***The Harder They Fall.*** New World, 1973. Reggae star Jimmy Cliff stars in this Jamaican-produced film about a singer and his encounters with the system. A first from the islands and a revealing portrait of Caribbean life.

***Wattstax.*** Columbia, 1973. A marathon concert covering a wide range of black music provides the basis for this concert and commentary film about the black experience in America. Comedian Richard Pryor and man on the street interviews are two unique features in this film, which was co-produced by Stax Records.

***Black Caesar.*** American International, 1973. The story of a ghetto youth who grows up to take over operation of Harlem mob activity once controlled by the Mafia. Fred Williamson's title character modeled after former Edward G. Robinson role.

***Black Mama, White Mama.*** American International, 1973. Filmed on location in the Philippines, this drama of a black and a white female convict who escape from jail handcuffed together reveals little more than a predictable chase and outcome.

***Trick Baby.*** Universal, 1973. A novel by Iceberg Slim was the inspiration for this film about two con men working the ghetto. Mel Stewart stars as the key team member who loses at the ultimate game of life.

***The Super Cops.*** United Artists, 1974. Based on the exploits of two real life renegade New York City cops who made some 400 drug arrests, this Gordon Parks Sr. directed adventure about drug warring in the ghetto marked the fourth film for the dean of black filmmaking.

***Thomasine and Bushrod.*** Columbia, 1974. Max Julian and Vonetta McGee are the key figures in this turn-of-the-century Western about a bank robbing team. Colorful characters and a sense of humor make this black-written and produced effort informative and entertaining.

***Conrack.*** Twentieth-Century Fox, 1974. Based on the true story of a white teacher who spends a school year on an isolated isle off the South Carolina coast, this warm drama featured local talent and many of the behind the camera artists who brought the black family film *Sounder* to the screen.

***Foxy Brown.*** American International, 1974. Pam Grier plays a nurse in this film of violence and sex. She avenges the death of her boyfriend by single-handedly taking on an entire crime syndicate and winning.

***Catch My Soul.*** Cinerama, 1974. Folk singer Richie Havens plays the key role of Othello in this filmed rock version of the famous Shakespearean play. An interesting idea that was an audience flop.

***The Black Six.*** Cinemation, 1974. Six mean looking professional football players make a formidable crime-fighting team in this poorly made drama and action film. Rosalind Miles co-stars.

***Three Tough Guys.*** Paramount, 1974. Film scorer Isaac Hayes stars as a fired police lieutenant who teams with a priest to solve a major ghetto murder. One of the first Italian-produced black films made in America.

***Blazing Saddles.*** Warner Brothers, 1974. A film of Mel Brooks which satirizes virtually everything possible in Hollywood Westerns. Cleavon Little stars as a black sheriff sent to work in racist town in a plot that ultimately backfires in the face of a corrupt state officer.

***Black Belt Jones.*** Warner Brothers, 1974. Jim Kelly, an actual Black Belt karate champ, plays the title role in this take-off on oriental martial arts films. Ex-Playboy Bunny Gloria Hendry co-stars in this action drama laced with humor.

***Hell Up In Harlem.*** American International, 1974. Fred Williamson stars as gangster Tommy Gibbs who uses all his ingenuity to regain control of the Harlem mob operations after they've been taken over by the white forces of evil. A sequel to *Black Caesar*.

***Sugar Hill.*** American International, 1974. Marki Bey stars as a young nightclub owner on a Caribbean isle whose boyfriend is slain. She seeks out the forces of voodoo to avenge his death. A rare black horror film.

***That Man Bolt.*** Universal, 1974. Ex-football player Fred Williamson stars as a high priced courier carrying a valuable prize from Hong Kong to Mexico. Pure James Bond story with exotic locales, pretty women, and lots of action.

***Willie Dynamite.*** Universal, 1974. The last film role for Diana Sands and the first directorial job for stage mentor Gil Moses. Roscoe Orman stars in the title role of an arrogant but doomed pimp and Miss Sands as a reformed prostitute converted to a social worker.

***Bone.*** Cannon, 1974. Yaphet Kotto stars as a frustrated rapist who invades and terrorizes the home of a wealthy but dishonest television personality and his insecure wife. Commercially unsuccessful satire on a very sensitive topic.

***Abby.*** American International, 1974. William Marshall and Carol Speed head the cast of this horror-oriented drama.

***Amazing Grace.*** United Artists, 1974. Slappy White and Moms Mabley make rare film appearances in this good-natured comedy.

***Claudine.*** Twentieth-Century Fox, 1974. Diahann Carroll and James Earl Jones head a stellar cast in this well-received romantic comedy.

***Black Belt Jones.*** Warner Bros, 1974. Jim Kelly and Gloria Hendry are featured in this action drama about a martial arts hero.

***The Education of Sonny Carson.*** Paramount, 1974. Rony Clanton stars in this sensitive drama about a ghetto youth whose life is a product of his surroundings.

***Lost in the Stars.*** American Film Theater, 1974. Brock Peters, Melba Moore, and Raymond St. Jacques appear in this film adaptation of a noted opera.

***The Take.*** Columbia, 1974. Billy Dee Williams stars in the central role of this drama about police activity.

***The Klansmen.*** Paramount, 1974. O. J. Simpson appears in this angry drama about hatred and violence in the South.

***Three The Hard Way.*** Allied Artists, 1974. Jim Brown, Fred Williamson, and Jim Kelly star in this action drama about three superheroes who take on corrupt forces. Gordon Parks Jr. directed.

***Together Brothers.*** Twentieth-Century Fox, 1974. Lincoln Kilpatrick stars in the suspense drama about a group of youngsters who take on a deadly villain in their community.

***Truck Turner.*** American International, 1974. Isaac Hayes takes a turn at acting, portraying a tough private investigator.

***Uptown Saturday Night.*** Warner Bros, 1974. Sidney Poitier stars and directs this light-hearted comedy with the able participation of such talents as Bill Cosby and Harry Belafonte.

***Boss Nigger.*** Dimension, 1975. Fred Williamson stars and serves as producer of this action drama typical of his tough-guy hero roles.

***Cornbread, Earl and Me.*** American International, 1975. Moses Gunn and Bernie Casey are among the stars of this sincere drama about the interaction between close friends.

***Cleopatra and the Casino of Gold.*** Warner Bros, 1975. Tamara Dobson appears as a tough lady who can hold her own as she uses charm and her wits to take on a challenging assignment.

***Aaron Loves Angela.*** Columbia. Gordon Parks Jr. directs this romantic drama which stars Kevin Hooks and Irene Cara as two urban young people.

***Cooley High.*** American International, 1975. Glynn Turman stars in this feature about life in a high school community of fascinating characters.

***Friday Foster.*** American International, 1975. Pam Grier and Yaphet Kotto star in this action drama about a femme private eye.

***Let's Do It Again.*** Warner Bros, 1975. Another Poitier-directed effort with Jimmy Walker among the newcomers to the cast that again included Bill Cosby in a comedy romp.

***Mahogony.*** Paramount, 1975. Diana Ross and Billy Dee Williams star in this romantic drama about a woman who fulfills her dream to become a celebrity fashion model.

***Mandingo.*** Paramount, 1975. Heavyweight boxer Ken Norton is among the cast of this racy drama about the goings-on at a plantation during slavery days.

***Sheba Baby.*** American International, 1975. Pam Grier headlines another action vehicle obviously conceived with her in mind.

***TNT Jackson.*** New World, 1975. Jeanne Bell stars in this drama whose title tells it all.

***Report to the Commissioner.*** United Artists, 1975. Yaphet Kotto stars as a police officer in this hard-hitting drama about a major case in New York City.

***Bingo Long and the Traveling All-Stars and Motor Kings.*** Universal, 1976. James Earl Jones, Billy Dee Williams, and Richard Pryor star in this humorous and often poignant drama about the early Negro baseball teams that barnstormed around the country.

***Car Wash.*** Universal, 1976. Richard Pryor had a cameo role in this rollicking comedy directed by Mark Warren depicting a day of activity in an establishment where a diverse group carries on the business.

***Countdown at Kusini.*** Columbia, 1976. Ossie Davis directed this drama about the politics of an African country.

***Drum.*** United Artists, 1976. Ken Norton and Yaphet Kotto star in this film which reverts to depicting an earlier generation of slave-era stereotypes.

***Mother, Jugs and Speed.*** Twentieth-Century Fox, 1976. Bill Cosby is one of the principals in this comedy about the operation of an ambulance service.

***Norman, Is That You?*** United Artists. Redd Foxx and Pearl Bailey star in this tepid comedy about a married couple whose son presents them with an unusual problem.

***Rocky.*** United Artists, 1976. Carl Weathers is featured as a ring antagonist in Sylvester Stallone's drama about a struggling boxer.

***Silver Streak.*** Twentieth-Century Fox, 1976. Richard Pryor teams with Gene Wilder in a comedy set aboard a cross-country train.

***Brothers.*** Warner Bros, 1977. Bernie Casey, Vonetta McGee, and Ron O'Neal are among the principals in this drama about black militancy.

***The Cassandra Crossing.*** ITC, 1977. O. J. Simpson worked with an international cast in this suspense drama about a train plagued with a potential disaster.

***The Deep.*** Columbia, 1977. Lou Gossett stars as a menacing presence on a Caribbean island who becomes a principal foe as a group of treasure hunters attempt to recover a fortune.

***The Greatest.*** Columbia, 1977. Paul Winfield starred among an all-star cast of actors including Muhammad Ali in a dramatization of the flamboyant boxing champ's life.

***Greased Lightning.*** Warner Bros, 1977. Richard Pryor and Pam Grier star in this drama based on the life of Wendell Scott, one of the nation's most prominent black racing car drivers.

***A Hero Ain't Nothing but a Sandwich.*** New World, 1977. The Alice Childress novel became the basis for this drama starring Paul Winfield and Cicely Tyson.

***A Piece of the Action.*** Warner Bros, 1977. Sidney Poitier directed this comedy after again assembling a team of prominent black actors including Bill Cosby, who again portrayed his sidekick.

***Short Eyes.*** Paramount, 1977. Nathan George was among the talented cast in this film adaptation of Miguel Pinero's acclaimed stage drama.

***Which Way Is Up?*** Universal, 1977. Richard Pryor starred in three different roles in this comedy-drama about compromise and sticking with convictions.

***Blue Collar.*** Universal, 1978. The plight of the working man is dramatized in this film which marked a departure from the roles Richard Pryor generally played.

*Comedian Richard Pryor plays a crazed Pharoh in the zany epic* Wholly Mosses!

***California Suite.*** Columbia, 1978. Bill Cosby and Richard Pryor star in this Neil Simon comedy about guests at a California hotel.

***The Boys in Company C.*** Columbia, 1978. Stan Shaw is among the principals in this gritty drama about a group of Marine recruits sent to fight in the Vietnam War.

***FM.*** Universal, 1978. Cleavon Little stars as a disc jockey at a small station battling to keep its successful format.

***Scott Joplin.*** Universal, 1978. Billy Dee Williams stars in the title role of this biographical drama about the noted ragtime composer.

***Apocalypse Now.*** United Artists, 1979. Albert Hall stars in a central role of this Francis Ford Coppola drama about the Vietnam War.

***The Fish That Saved Pittsburgh.*** United Artists, 1979. Julius Erving and Meadowlark Lemon star in this Gilbert Moses film about a sports phenomenon with humorous overtones.

***Richard Pryor in Concert.*** Independent, 1979. Filmed as Pryor performed, this straightforward film proved to be an unexpected hit.

***Rocky II.*** United Artists, 1979. Carl Weathers as a fighter going up against Sylvester Stallone as the great white hope.

***Airplane.*** Paramount, 1980. Kareem Abdul Jabbar found his way to the cockpit of a fictional airliner in this spoof on disaster films.

***All That Jazz.*** Twentieth-Century Fox, 1980. Ben Vereen stars as a Broadway performer in this acclaimed drama inspired by the career of a famous director.

***The Blues Brothers.*** Universal, 1980. Aretha Franklin, James Brown, and Cab Calloway are among the performers who make rare cameo appearances in this comedy about two men on the lam.

***Brubaker.*** Twentieth-Century Fox, 1980. Yaphet Kotto stars in this Robert Redford drama about a man attempting to expose corruption in a prison system.

***The Empire Strikes Back.*** Twentieth-Century Fox, 1980. Billy Dee Williams stars as one of the principal heroes in this tremendously successful sequel to the science fiction adventure *Star Wars.*

***Fame.*** United Artists, 1980. Irene Cara stands out among the talented young performers in this musical drama about youngsters attempting to excel at a performing arts high school.

***The Hunter.*** Paramount, 1980. LeVar Burton stars as a young fugitive who becomes a friend of the bounty hunter who picked him up in this drama that was Steve McQueen's last film.

***Stir Crazy.*** Columbia, 1980. Richard Pryor stars again with Gene Wilder about a mismatched pair of con men in this comedy directed by Sidney Poitier.

***Wholly Moses.*** Columbia, 1980. Richard Pryor stars with Dudley Moore in this comedy which unsuccessfully attempted to parody the noted biblical character.

***Bustin' Loose.*** Universal, 1981. Richard Pryor stars with Cicely Tyson in this heart-warming comedy about a man who transports a lively group of youngsters across the country by bus.

***Carbon Copy.*** Avco Embassy, 1981. Denzell Washington stars as the black son of a white man who is totally unprepared for this revelation years after his son's birth.

***Fort Apache The Bronx.*** Twentieth-Century Fox, 1981. Pam Grier stars as a deadly prostitute in this grim drama starring Paul Newman as a police officer working in a notorious Bronx ghetto.

***Nighthawks.*** Universal, 1981. Billy Dee Williams stars with Sylvester Stallone in a suspense drama about New York City police attempting to locate and apprehend a European terrorist.

***Body and Soul.*** Cannon, 1981. Leon Isaac Kennedy wrote this drama about a young boxer obviously inspired by a John Garfield film of a previous era. He stars in the central role with his wife Jayne Kennedy and Muhammad Ali also appearing.

***Ragtime.*** Paramount, 1981. Moses Gunn, Howard E. Rollins, and Debbie Allen appeared with James Cagney in an acclaimed adaptation of E. L. Doctorow's novel about life in New York when ragtime music would become a reflection of the turn-of-the-century epoch. Howard E. Rollins was nominated for an Academy Award for his performance.

***Penitentiary I and II.*** Gerry Gross Org., 1981, 1982. Leon Isaac Kennedy in these moving films about prison life and the struggles of a boxer.

***Some Kind of a Hero.*** United Artists, 1982. Richard Pryor stars with Olivia Cole and Lynn Moody about a returning Vietnam veteran adjusting to society.

***Live on Sunset Strip.*** Paramount Pictures Corp., 1982. Stars Richard Pryor in a solo stand-up routine.

***Amin, The Rise and Fall.*** Twin Continental, 1982. Joseph Olita stars as Idi Amin, former Ugandan president, showing how he ruled the country.

***Carbon Copy.*** Avco Embassy, 1981. Denzel Washington stars in this comedy as the black son of a white businessman, who unexpectedly shows up and shocks his father with news of paternity.

***48 Hours.*** Paramount, 1982. Eddie Murphy stars in a dramatic role as a wise-talking con who is let out of prison to team with a cop and solve a tough crime case.

***An Officer And A Gentleman.*** Paramount, 1982. Lou Gossett won an Oscar for Best Supporting Actor in his role as a tough Navy drill instructor at a school for flight recruits.

***Rocky III.*** MGM/UA, 1982. Carl Weathers and Mr. T flexed their muscles in this, the third in a series of boxing movies starring Sylvester Stallone.

***Say Amen Somebody.*** United Artists Classics, 1982. Thomas A. Dorsey and other pioneers of gospel music were featured in this well-received film about the origins of spiritual music in the black church.

***The Toy.*** Columbia, 1982. Richard Pryor joined Jackie Gleason in this comedy about a store employee who is chosen as a Christmas gift by a spoiled, rich child.

*One of the biggest hits of 1981,* Ragtime, *with Howard Rollins (center).*

*Oprah Winfrey in the 1986 drama* Native son.

***Streamers.*** United Artists, 1983. Adapted from a powerful stage play, this film dramatized a dialogue involving Vietnam veterans as they bared their souls and shared their agony about fighting in the war.

***Trading Places.*** Paramount, 1983. This Eddie Murphy vehicle featured the talents of the popular comic as he portrayed a street denizen who switches places with a wealthy scion.

***Best Defense.*** Paramount, 1984. Featured in another vehicle starring Dudley Moore, Eddie Murphy added his comedic talents in a story about defense department secrets.

***Beverly Hills Cop.*** Paramount, 1984. In one of the most popular films in his career, Eddie Murphy starred as a Detroit cop who upstages his counterparts in Beverly Hills and takes on the snobby establishment as he tries to find the killer of one of his best friends.

***The Cotton Club.*** Orion, 1984. Nominated for two Oscars, this stylized drama about the Jazz Age focused on the legendary nightclub. Gregory Hines, Lonette McKee, Maurice Hines, Novella Nelson and Charles "Honi" Coles were among the Francis Ford Coppola directed cast.

***The Gods Must Be Crazy.*** TLC Films, 1984. A popular independent foreign film about an African bushman who finds a Coke bottle and believes it is a gift from the Gods.

***Purple Rain.*** Warner Bros, 1984. Prince was the inspiration for this Oscar-winning film (Best Score), which featured performance segments and dramatized the story of a song man trying to make it to the top of the music business.

***Brewster's Millions.*** Universal, 1984. Richard Pryor starred in this remake of the 1946 comedy about a man in the unique position of trying to spend millions in a short period of time in order to keep an inheritance.

***Police Academy.*** Warner Bros, 1984. The first of a series of near-slapstick films about a group of misfits trying to become police officers featured Bubba Smith, Michael Winslow and what would be a repertory company starring in six related films.

***The Brother From Another Planet.*** Cinecom International, 1985. Joe Morton starred in this low-budget comedy about an alien who finds himself attempting to adapt to the lifestyle of Harlem.

***The Color Purple.*** Warner Bros, 1985. Alice Walker's Pulitzer Prize-winning novel provided the story for this Oscar-nominated drama directed by Steven Spielberg. Danny Glover, Whoopi Goldberg, Margaret Avery and Oprah Winfrey headed a strong black cast.

***Silverado.*** Columbia, 1985. Danny Glover joined a top cast of this rare western with four good guys who join forces to battle traditional bad guys.

***The Last Dragon.*** Tri-Star, 1985. Taimak and Vanity star in this light-hearted musical drama about a martial arts devotee who finds love while seeking to find a mythical master of his craft.

***White Nights.*** Columbia, 1985. Gregory Hines starred in this drama about two dancers who become the focal point of an international controversy as they attempt to break out from behind the Iron Curtain.

***Crossroads.*** Columbia, 1986. Joe Seneca stars as a legendary bluesman who finds a young white musician enamored with both his talent and roots as the two make a pilgrimage back to his Mississippi home.

***The Golden Child.*** Paramount, 1986. Eddie Murphy found this fantasy adventure about a young man's journey to locate the perfect child; one of his most controversial and least successful film projects.

***Jo Jo Dancer, Your Life Is Calling.*** Columbia, 1986. In a film generally acknowledged as autobiographical, Richard Pryor starred in this drama about the life of a young man aspiring to become a comedic performer.

***Mona Lisa.*** Handmade Films, 1986. Cathy Tyson starred as a call girl who has a tumultuous relationship with a small-time hood assigned to drive her around to her London assignments.

***Jumpin' Jack Flash.*** 20th Century-Fox, 1986. Whoopi Goldberg stars as a telephone company employee drawn into a drama when she makes inadvertent contact with a spy attempting to escape from enemy territory.

***Native Son.*** Cinecom, 1986. Oprah Winfrey starred in this drama based on Richard Wright's best-selling novel about a young man and the problems he faces after an unfortunate incident.

***Running Scared.*** Metro-Goldwyn-Mayer, 1986. Gregory Hines stars as part of a salt-and-pepper detective team working the streets of Chicago and elsewhere.

***She's Gotta Have It.*** Island Pictures, 1986. Spike Lee starred in and directed this comedy about the love life of a young woman and three men vying for her affections.

***Soul Man.*** New World, 1986. James Earl Jones has a featured role in this comedy about a young man who poses as a black student to win a minority college scholarship.

***Iron Eagle.*** Tri-Star, 1986. This adventure drama about a young man who flies a rescue mission to save his father starred Lou Gossett as the fighter pilot who makes the near-impossible trip a success.

***Beverly Hills COP II.*** Paramount, 1987. Eddie Murphy reprised his role as a Detroit detective with incredible success working outside of his usual inner city haunts in the fabled streets of Beverly Hills.

***Cry Freedom.*** Universal, 1987. A controversial drama about the racial problems in South Africa, this film featured Denzel Washington as activist Steven Biko who befriended a white journalist while attempting to work for dignity for his people.

***Critical Condition.*** Warner *Bros*, 1987. This Richard Pryor comedy about a criminal who finds freedom while in a hospital and attempts to impersonate a doctor, failed to capture the general public.

***Disorderlies.*** Warner Bros, 1987. The rap group, The Fat Boys, tried film acting in this comedy vehicle about their efforts to work as orderlies for a cranky millionaire.

***Eddie Murphy Raw.*** Paramount, 1987. A concert film with some of the comedians most vitriolic material, this movie was directed by Robert Townsend.

***Fatal Beauty.*** MGM, 1987. Whoopi Goldberg starred as a narcotics detective in this film with a message about drug abuse.

***Burglar.*** Warner Bros, 1987. In another vehicle, Whoopi Goldberg stars as a cat burglar who witnesses a murder and tries to solve the crime in order to clear herself.

***He's My Girl.*** Scotti Brothers, 1987. T. K. Carter stars in this limp comedy about a man who attempts to impersonate the girlfriend of a companion in order to avoid identification.

*Eddie Murphy goes on an adventure quest in* The Golden Child.

*Carl Weathers is a super-cop in the 1988 adveture-thriller* Action Jackson.

***Lethal Weapon.*** Warner Bros, 1987. Danny Glover stars as the veteran, stable partner in another salt-and-pepper detective team drama.

***Hollywood Shuffle.*** Samuel Goldwyn, 1987. Robert Townsend directed and starred in this independent comedy hailed as an entertaining sendup of Hollywood stereotypes.

***Matewan.*** Cinecom Pictures, 1987. James Earl Jones had a key role in this powerful drama about labor trouble in the coal mining regions of West Virginia in the 1920s.

***Street Smart.*** Cannon Films, 1987. Morgan Freeman received widespread accolades for his performance of a New York City pimp in this drama seen through the eyes of a magazine writer.

***Bird.*** Warner Bros 1988. Forest Whitaker starred in the title role of this drama reflecting Clint Eastwood's homage to jazz musician, Charlie Parker.

***Action Jackson.*** Warner Bros 1988. Carl Weathers starred with Vanity as a hero cop out to solve a series of crimes, even when it means taking on a corrupt but powerful industrialist.

***Coming To America.*** Paramount, 1988. Eddie Murphy and Arsenio Hall starred in this popular comedy about an African prince who comes to America looking for a mate.

***Iron Eagle II.*** Tri-Star 1988. Lou Gossett returns in his role as an air force general who trains a squadron of American and Soviet fighter pilots to face a determined foe.

***Leonard Part 6.*** Columbia 1988. Bill Cosby's fantasy comedy proved to be one of the most unsuccessful projects undertaken in an otherwise top-flight career.

***Little Nikita.*** Columbia, 1988. In one of his latter career starring roles, Sidney Poitier portrayed a government agent who befriends a youngster whose parents are caught up in international intrigue.

***Mississippi Burning.*** Orion, 1988. This film, inspired by an incident at the height of the civil rights movement of the 1960s, garnered widespread critical acclaim and spirited complaints from the black community for overlooking the role blacks played during that time.

***Off Limits.*** 20th Century Fox, 1988. Gregory Hines starred in another detective drama, again with a white partner, this time set during the Vietnam War as the two attempted to solve a string of slayings in Saigon.

***School Daze.*** Columbia 1988. Independent film-maker Spike Lee took on the life of students involved in college fraternity rituals and social lifestyles in this musical-oriented comedy.

***Shoot To Kill.*** *Columbia*, 1988. Sidney Poitier starred as a big-city policeman working with a guide in the wilderness to hunt down a ruthless killer.

***I'm Gonna Get You Sucka.*** United Artists, 1989 Jim Brown and Isaac Hayes were among the stars who joined in this good-natured parody of the black exploitation films of an earlier generation.

***Lean On Me.*** Warner Bros, 1989. Morgan Freeman starred in this drama about the true-life exploits of controversial New Jersey high school principal Joe Clark.

***The Mighty Quinn.*** Metro-Goldwyn-Mayer, 1989. Denzel Washington and Robert Townsend starred in this mystery drama set on a Caribbean island.

***Tap.*** Tri-Star, 1989. Sammy Davis Jr. and Gregory Hines starred in this film about two men whose lives are dedicated to the art of tap dancing.

***The Telephone.*** New World 1988. Whoopi Goldberg starred in this drama about an out-of-work actress with psychological problems.

# THE BLACK PRESS AND BROADCAST MEDIA

**A Survey of the Mass Media ■ Black Reporters on White Newspapers ■ Prominent Black Publishers and Journalists ■ Guide to Black Newspapers and Periodicals ■ Broadcast Media ■ Broadcast Personalities ■ Guide to Radio Stations with Black Programming**

Black representation and influence in America's print and broadcast media has shown tremendous increases from where it was thirty years, or even twenty years ago. There was a big increase in the number of black-operated and oriented radio stations, a rise in the major television networks and local affiliates featuring black themes such as *Tony Brown's Journal*, excellent locally hosted public affairs programs such as Gil Noble's *Positively Black* on New York's ABC TV and programming by Black Entertainment Television as well. Blacks also successfully challenged cases of discriminatory programming and employment by television and radio stations.

In addition, there was an increase in the number of black journalists and commentators employed by general interest newspapers and broadcasters. National syndicated columnist Carl Rowan continued to be heard on a number of radio stations across the country and other columnists such as William Raspberry, Tony Brown, Les Payne, Robert Maynard have become household names throughout the United States.

During this time period, there was an explosion of special interest magazines catering to blacks such as *Essence* and *Black Enterprise*,—which also has a share of an interested white audience—both of which are enjoying success. Other magazines made their debut but had to cease publication because of financial instability.

Since the 1970s, over 200 black newspapers ceased publication and until 1975, there was only one major black daily, *The Chicago Defender*. There are now three, the Chicago *Defender, The Atlanta Daily World* and *The Daily Challenge* in Brooklyn, New York.

In the late 1980s, there were more than 170 black weekly newspapers being published in 34 states and the District of Columbia.

In the early 1980s, there were 194 black weekly newspapers. Many newspapers could not survive because they lacked advertising revenue to sustain their publishing ventures.

Poor circulation and subscription sales also contributed to the demise of those publications. Many black newspapers that once published national editions such as *The Journal* and *Guide* in Norfolk, Virginia, The *Pittsburgh Courier* and *Afro-American* newspapers, all had to cease national distribution. The *National Leader*, published in Philadelphia also made an attempt at a national circulation but also had to cease publication.

During the early 1960s, the number of blacks on white publications were very few and they were household names because of the trails they blazed—the late Ted Poston and Nancy Hicks-Maynard of *The New York Post;* Hugh Wyatt,

Ted Francis and David Hardy of the *New York Daily News;* Wendell Smith of the *Chicago Daily News;* Gordon Parks of *Life Magazine*; William Brower of the *Toledo Blade*; Ernie Johnston, Jr. of the *Star-Ledger* in Newark, New Jersey; Luther Jackson, Harry Robinson and Rudy Johnson of the *Newark News;* William Hilliard of the *Portland Oregonian;* Albert Fitzpatrick of the *Akron Beacon Journal;* William Matney of the *Detroit Free Press;* Collins George of the *Detroit News;* Thomas Johnson, Gerald Frazier, Earl Caldwell, Charlayne Hunter Gault and Paul Delaney of *The New York Times;* Vernon Jarrett, columnist of the *Chicago Sun Times;* Chuck Stone, columnist of the *Philadelphia Daily News;* William J. Drummond of the *Los Angeles Times;* L. F. "Lu" Palmer of the *Chicago Daily News;* Austin Scott of the *Associated Press;* William Raspberry and Robert Maynard of the *Washington Post;* John Dotson of *Newsweek;* and Jack White of *Time* magazine. Many of the early blacks in the business received their training on black newspapers.

Black women made up a very small percentage on daily newspapers. Some of the early women reporters included Nancy Hicks-Maynard (*New York Post*); Charlayne Hunter-Gault (*The New York Times*); Barbara Reynolds (currently a *USA Today* editor); Jeannye Thornton (*Chicago Tribune*); Marilyn Duncan (*Memphis Commercial Appeal*); Almena Lomax (*San Francisco Examiner*); Jean Perry (*New York Daily News*); Angela Claire Parker (*Chicago Tribune*); and Betty Washington (*Chicago Daily News*).

In the 1980s, the number of black women reporters and editors increased tremendously on daily publications—many covering assignments that heretofore had been given to male reporters.

In the 1970s, there were 120 blacks on white publications but in the late 1980s, that number is close to 4,000. Despite the gains made by blacks in newsrooms across the country, there is still a per capita underrepresentation among the nation's reporters and broadcasters and particularly in editorial policy-making positions. Blacks account for about 1 percent of the editorial policy-making jobs on daily publications.

A survey conducted by the Dallas based company of Delden Associates for the American Newspaper Publishers Association reported that in the 1980s, U.S. daily newspaper staffs are 16 percent minority. That survey also disclosed that the greatest number of newspaper minority employees are located in general management (22 percent), circulation (19 percent), and production (19 percent).

In order to increase the number of blacks on newspapers, many publications have instituted an aggressive minority hiring program and active voluntary affirmative action programs.

In 1979, Robert Maynard became the first black editor-publisher of a daily newspaper, *The Oakland Tribune-East Bay Today* in Oakland, California. Maynard, through a group of investors, later bought the newspaper from the Gannett newspaper company and renamed it *The Oakland Tribune*. In 1981, Pam Johnson was named publisher of the *Ithaca Journal* in Ithaca, New York, becoming the first black female publisher in the United States.

## BLACK NEWSPAPERS AND JOURNALISTS

The black press in the United States is heir to a great, largely unheralded tradition. It began with the first black newspaper, *Freedom's Journal* (edited and published by Samuel Cornish and John B. Russwurm), which appeared in New York City on March 16, 1827. *Freedom's Journal* sought to plead the black case before the American public. *The North Star,* the newspaper of the celebrated abolitionist Frederick Douglass, dedicated itself to much the same cause when its first edition appeared in Rochester, New York on December 3, 1847.

Black journalism experienced a rapid growth in the era immediately following the Civil War. Several periodicals began publication, but more importantly, the "political" press came into its own, reflecting the black's new found awareness of himself.

By the 1880s, the black's ability to establish a substantial cultural environment in many cities of the North, led to the creation of a new wave of publications, including the Washington *Bee,* the Indianapolis *World,* the Philadelphia *Tribune,* the Cleveland *Gazette,* and the New York *Age*. By 1900, there were no less than three dailies, one each in Norfolk, Kansas City, and Washington, D.C.

Among famous black editors of this era were W. M. Trotter, editor of the Boston *Guardian,* a self-styled "radical" paper that showed no sympathy for the so-called conciliatory stance of Booker T. Washington, Robert S. Abbott whose Chicago *Defender* pioneered in the use of headlines and other techniques of mass circulation, and T. T. Fortune of the New York *Age,* who championed free public schools in an age when many opposed the idea.

The black press set the goal of keeping the black public informed of vital issues and creating an appropriate forum for voicing black sentiment on such issues, exposing political injustice and corruption, exhorting the black to become more aware of his achievements and the opportunities open to him. While on the one hand it demanded that society as a whole provide better schools, improved sanitation, and more comprehensive police protection, it likewise threw its support behind black self-help groups like the NAACP and the National Negro Business League.

Believing that urbanization, for all its drawbacks, still offered blacks more promise than a rural environment, the black press backed migration to the North as a means of escaping southern oppression. Most black papers were behind American involvement in World War I and sought actively to encourage blacks to fight for their country.

*The black press in America goes back to 1827 when Freedom's Journal was published by Samuel Cornish and John B. Russwurm. In 1975 there were over 100 black newspapers, and some 35 of them had a circulation exceeding 20,000 per issue.*

## Between the World Wars

Between the two World Wars, black journalists were major leaders and advocates in the civil rights cause. Roy Wilkins, for example, achieved prominence, and recognition by the NAACP, as a vigorous journalist in Minnesota and Missouri during the 1920s and early 1930s. In 1940, there were over 200 black newspapers, mostly weeklies with local readership, and about 120 black magazines in the country. The Pittsburgh *Courier*, a weekly, had the largest circulation, about 140,000 per issue.

Many of these papers did not regard America's entry into World War II as sufficient reason to relax their vigilance, especially when the armed forces' determination to maintain segregation became apparent. Some papers headlined news that commanders were refusing to accept black troops except in menial roles, and that blacks were victims of injustices on military bases and in nearby communities in many parts of the South. In 1942, the Justice Department threatened about 20 editors with sedition charges, and many black papers found it difficult to obtain newsprint. The NAACP negotiated an unofficial settlement in which black papers tamed their criticism and were able to obtain essential supplies.

## The 1950s and 1960s

After World War II black papers suffered from troubles similar to those that afflicted most of America's newspapers—competition for readers and advertisers from radio and television and increasing costs of operation. These problems were compounded by an increasing demand for black journalists from large metropolitan dailies, a demand that was spurred by government pressure and a realization among white publishers that it was absurd to have white reporters continually assigned to cover black communities.

Black papers simply could not compete with the salaries, prestige, and benefits offered by large metropolitan dailies. For example, in 1975, black papers commonly started reporters at salaries of $110 a week, while some major white papers paid salaries of $400 a week to reporters with a few months experience.

The presence of black journalists on major papers was a benefit to blacks as a whole, but black papers lost many of their most experienced and competent people.

In response to declining circulation, many papers sought almost entirely to entertain readers, concentrating on local social and crime news and omitting news of developments and issues important to blacks. Often, when they reported

*President Eisenhower addresses black leaders at a 1958 meeting sponsored by the National Newspaper Publishers' Association.*

such matters, accounts were based largely on rewrites of accounts in general newspapers or culled from radio and TV newscasts.

Criticism of papers with this orientation peaked in the later 1960s and early 1970s, when the political consciousness of blacks was ascending and black citizens began to recall the great contributions of black journalists from the days of Abolition through World War II. In response, the National Newspapers Publishers Association, a group representing some 30 black papers, scheduled workshops and trips abroad to acquaint editors and reporters with important news centers and news sources. A result was a trend to more progressive and interpretive reporting.

## The 1970s

Black papers were also enlivened in the 1960s and 1970s by a new breed of owners. Typical of the trend was the purchase in 1971 of the New York *Amsterdam News.*

A group of investors headed by lawyer-Wall Street broker Clarence B. Jones, organized under the name of Inner City Broadcasting, purchased the Harlem-based newspaper from its original owners. Jones served two years as editor and publisher. Immediately after Jones departed and was succeeded by general manager John L. Procope, the group exercised an option and gained full ownership of WBLS, one of the nation's rare FM stations with a "soul" format.

Sengstacke Enterprises, the largest black newspaper chain in the nation, also grew strongly in the last decade. Its Chairman, John H. Sengstacke, entered the newspaper business in the 1930s after studying both printing and business administration in college. As head of a chain of 11 newspapers, Sengstacke's group turned in $5 million in overall sales in 1973. Sengstacke's papers include The Chicago *Daily Defender*, the Memphis *Tri-State Defender,* and eight papers in the Pittsburgh Courier chain.

Chester L. Washington, the first black reporter on the *Los Angeles Times,* became head of the Los Angeles *Central News-Wave* Publications in 1974. With a total audience of 233,000 *News-Wave* is the largest black newspaper operation in any single metropolitan area. Washington's papers stress black news and rarely feature crime news.

In the 1970s, the Houston *Forward Times* and the Milwaukee *Courier* made a mark after only a few years of publishing. In 1973 the *Courier* earned a profit of $114,000 with a circulation of 13,000. Under publisher and owner Jerrel W. Jones, it won six editorial awards.

An older black paper, the *Baltimore Afro-American,* expanded from Baltimore to include editions catering to Newark, Philadelphia, Washington, D.C., and Richmond. The paper is run by John H. Murphy III, grandson of John Murphy Sr. who founded the paper in 1892.

However, in 1975, black newspapers presented a picture of mixed success. Despite the increases in ethnic and political consciousness that marked the decade, black newspapers, like other ethnic papers in the United States, remained largely marginal operations with small staffs and little advertising.

Only about 100 black newspapers were in existence in 1975 and only some 35 of these had a circulation exceeding 20,000 per issue. The largest of these, the weekly *Amsterdam News* of New York had a circulation of about 85,000 per issue in 1974, but still had to struggle along with an editorial staff of six.

Black newspapers remained largely dependent on black readers, many of whom were more responsive to the general press, with its daily coverage and variety of features, than to papers oriented to blacks. In 1975, no major black newspaper in the country reached more than 20% of the black community it catered to and the coverage of most was appreciably less. The *Amsterdam News,* for example, reached only about 10% of New York City's blacks.

## The 1980s

A number of newspapers that began publishing in the late 1960s and in the 1970s were out of business by the beginning of the 1980s mainly due to their inability to attract advertising, both locally and nationally, and because of general economic decline during that period.

*The Afro-American Building in Baltimore, Maryland, serves as headquarters for one of the nation's largest black newspaper chains.*

Most of the newspapers found that they couldn't survive solely on small business advertisements and they didn't have the capital to continue publishing and building circulation figures in order to attract the major advertisers. The local advertiser for the most part were unable to pay rates requested of large businesses and much of the national and big store chain advertising went to the white-run newspapers.

Major advertisers also began to watch their budget in that period of economic decline and placed their dollars where they felt they could get the most mileage-in major commercial newspapers.

Because much of the advertising went to major publications, newspapers such as the New York *Amsterdam News* and the *Afro-American* in Baltimore felt the impact. However, those newspapers as well as more of the older publishing publications were able to hold their regular lineage, but in many cases failed to attract new advertising.

Coupled with the fact that advertising was the focal point of survival, those publishers venturing into the newspaper field also found that they didn't have the necessary capital to survive. They needed money in order to promote their product in order to develop a readership which meant advertising dollars.

Many publishers starting newspapers didn't have that type of capital. Where as at one time black newspapers had a built-in readership in the black community, publishers in the 1970s and the 1980s were learning that a new upscale readership of young and educated blacks existed. They realized that readers of black newspapers had a need for more national and international coverage, especially news from the African continent. Many black newspapers failed to provide this coverage.

Therefore, black newspaper publishers began to take a hard look at how to make their publications survive and some went the route of developing "metros" or controlled circulation newspapers, commonly called "giveaways."

Through this method, publishers were able to increase their circulation and therefore compete for national advertisers. Dr. Carlton B. Goodlet, publisher of the San Francisco *Metro Reporter,* a string of newspapers on the West Coast, has been successful in such a venture.

Along with reassessing their circulation methods, many black newspapers began to take a look at their products editorially. Many publishers and editors began to deemphasize murders, sensationalist headlines, and blood and gut pictures found on the pages of many black publications. Instead, there were more community-oriented stories and picture coverage of African affairs.

In 1982, a national publication was born, *The National Leader*, however the newspaper subsequently folded because it could not attract advertising necessary to carry it as a national publication. Claude Lewis was the editor. Lewis had been an associate editor at the Philadelphia *Bulletin* before its demise earlier in 1982. The newspaper began publishing during the spring of 1982 and presented stories around the United States, Africa, and features and information about the black communities across the country.

The closing of *The Bulletin*, *The Chicago Daily News*, *The Washington Star*, and *The Cleveland Press* all had an impact upon the black community and placed additional demands on the black press to produce new newspapers. Black communities were learning that their outlet for news had been closed and black publications began to cover the communities more and present more news relevant to blacks. However, because of the closing of the major newspapers, it did not make a significant change in the advertising picture for black newspapers because much of the advertising went to other white run newspapers or to radio and television.

A Scarborough Report on black newspaper audience readership put out by the Amalgamated Publishers Inc. (API) stated that 82.2% of readers of API newspapers found that the publications dealt with subjects of special interest to them while 58.9% found subjects of special interest in daily publications. Of API newspapers readers, 69.9% stated that they found an understanding of their life in the publications; 40.4% found it in daily newspapers. API represents 88 leading, black community newspapers in 68 markets and the study represented only those markets within the top 50 metropolitan areas where there is an API newspaper.

## Black Reporters

Until the mid-1970s, the number of blacks on white publications numbered about 120 and during the latter part of the 1980s, the number had risen to close to 4,000 blacks.

Although the number has increased tremendously, blacks are still not adequately represented in huge numbers in policy-making positions on major newspapers. However, blacks do hold senior management positions,and serve as executive editors, managing editors, department editors, columnists, editorial writers and foreign correspondents. Despite the fact that blacks do hold those positions, the numbers do not correspond to the number of whites working on daily publications.

Many newspapers have at least one or more black reporters on their staff. The New York Post has only about a half dozen black reporters on its staff while the Washington Post and the New York Times have 50 or more black reporters which are employed in every category including vice president and senior management positions.

In 1981, Janet Cooke, a reporter for *The Washington Post,* won the Pulitzer Prize for her story on an 8-year-old drug addict, which later turned out to be a phony story. Her actions created a furor in newsrooms across the country and thus made the work of other black reporters suspect.

However, newspapers have begun an aggressive policy of hiring more blacks in newsrooms across the country, working through such organizations as the National Association of Black Journalists, job fairs sponsored across the United States by newspapers and through their own minority hiring programs.

In 1982, William Hilliard, who had been managing editor of the *Portland Oregonian,* was named editor to head editorial direction of the newspaper. Hilliard has also served on the Pulitzer Prize board along with other black journalists such as Bob Maynard, publisher of *The Oakland Tribune,* and Joel Dreyfuss of *Black Enterprise Magazine.*

Other blacks who are working in top management positions include Tom Greer of the Cleveland *Plain Dealer,* Jay Harris of the *Philadelphia Daily News,* Les Payne of *Newsday,* Nancy Hicks Maynard of *The Oakland Tribune* and Pam Johnson of the *Ithaca Journal.*

## Magazines

A significant development of the 1970s was the advent of a new class of special interest magazines. Johnson Publications was very much in the vanguard, with *Ebony Jr.*, a youthful version of its popular general interest magazine, *Ebony.* The company also converted *Tan*, a woman's magazine, into a successful show business and personality monthly called *Black Stars.*

*Essence* editor Ida Lewis departed from her position at that woman's digest and created *Encore*, a journal that appealed to a multi-racial audience with a format similar to three major news weeklies, *Time, Newsweek,* and *U.S. News and World Report. Encore* was one of the first of the news magazines to base itself in the black community, and also to develop its editorial approach appealing to a wide base in order to attract increased readership and advertising.

Earl G. Graves, a young businessman, embarked on a concept to publish a monthly digest of news, commentary, and informative articles for blacks interested in business enterprise. Heavily subsidized initially, *Black Enterprise* soon achieved prominence as one of the more sophisticated magazines in the country.

Another young man, Allan Barron, established *Black Sports*, a magazine geared to highlight the tremendous impact blacks have at all levels of competitive athletics. A spin-off of the publication was the Black Hall of Fame, which has become a prominent institution in the community.

*Players* magazine, a nationally distributed version of *Playboy*, started on the West Coast, flourished immediately, and built a substantial readership in both the black and general markets. *Soul Journey*, a monthly travel magazine began publishing and capitalized on the huge leisure market among blacks.

In 1981, a new national competitor to women-oriented *Essence*, called *Elam,* published for several months but ceased publication in 1982.

In Chicago, a magazine called *Black Family* began publishing in 1981 with Mary Ellen Strong as publisher.

Meanwhile, magazines such as *Black Enterprise* and *Essence* continued to show strong growth. *Black Enterprise* has become known for its list of the top 100 black companies and has become widely quoted in national publications.

*Essence* is considered the top in a field of women's magazines geared to black women and has steadily gained in its circulation since its inception. The magazine has added more departments relevant to the black woman of the 1980s.

Other magazines showing strong sales on newsstands during the 1980s included *Ebony Man* published by Johnson Publishing Company, *Dollar and Sense, Black Elegance, Class magazine, Ebony, Jet* and *American Visions.*

Although several other magazines made its debut during the 1980s, they soon ceased publication because of the financial resources necessary to keep the publications afloat. One magazine venture, *Emerge* had announced its debut in 1987 and had carried out extensive promotional plans only to have them scrapped because principals in the venture could not come up with funds to match those of the magazine's investors.

*The late Ted Paston reported for the New York Post.*

## BLACK REPORTERS, EDITORS, PHOTOGRAPHERS, AND COLUMNISTS ON MAJOR NEWSPAPERS

**Atlanta Constitution**
Tony Cooper
Linda Horton
Burnis Morris—Assistant City Editor
Ernest Reese—Sports

**Atlanta Journal**
Chet Fuller
John Head—Assistant City Editor
Clem Richardson
Prentiss Rogers—Sports
Angela Terrell

**Boston Globe**
Joanne Ball
Fred Biddle
Ron Borges
Paula Bouknight—Copy Editor/news
Cheryl Charles—Copy Editor sports
Steven Curwood
Michael Frisby—City Hall bureau chief
Desiree French
Renee Graham
Jesse Harris—Copy Editor news
Will Haygood
Ronald Hutson—Asst. to the Editor
Derrick Jackson—Columnist
Judy Jackson—Copy Editor Living
Keith Jenkins—Photographer
Larry Johnson—Cartoonist
Michelle Johnson—Asst. Night Editor
Robert Jordan—Columnist
Diane Lewis
Victor Lewis—Asst. National Foreign Editor
Wendy Maeda—Photographer
Lincoln Millstein—Business Editor
Gregory Moore—City Editor
Viola Osgood—Editorial writer
Elaine Ray—Copy Editor magazine
Alex Reid
Pam Reynolds—National reporter
John Robinson
Mary Sit
Arnold Stockard—Copy Editor/news
Tito Stevens—Copy Editor sports
Kathryn Tolbert—Foreign Editor
Michael Vega
Larry Whiteside
Jim Wilson—Photographer

**Chicago Sun-Times**
Lacy Banks
Maudlynd Ihejirika
Frederick Lowe
Leon Pitt
Tracy Robinson
Patricia Smith
Lillian Williams

**Chicago Tribune**
Monroe Anderson
Joyce Brown
Vernon Jarrett
Leanita McClain
John White

**Charlotte News**
Ramona Clark
Ted DeAdyler
Deborah Gates
Cassandra Lawton
David Porter—Assistant City Editor
Osker Spicer
Gail Westry—Copy Editor

**Detroit Free Press**
Bruce Britt
Donna Britt-Gibson
Andrea Ford
Brenda Gilchrist
Moses Harris
Kim Heron
Greg Huskisson
Luther Jackson III
Ben Johnson
Jackie Jones
Larry Olmstead
Ruth Seymour
Cassandra Spratling
Monte Trammer
Joyce Walker-Tyson
Susan Watson

**Detroit News**
Chauncey Bailey
Terry Cabell—Sports
Denise Crittenden
Larry Davis—Copy Editor news
Betty DeRamus—Columnist
Kirthmon Dozier Photographer
Terry Foster—Sports
Dave Grant
Bill Johnson—Editorial writer
Linda Jones
Luther Keith—Night City Editor
Pat McCaughan
Jim McFarlin—Entertainment writer
Darren Patterson—Copy Editor/sports
Connie Prater
Harold Robinson
Photographer
Arlena Sawyer—Copy Editor news
Denise Smith
Calvin Stovall—Business Editor
Monroe Walker
Allen Whitt—Asst. Sports Editor
Yolanda Woodlee

**Houston Chronicle**
James T. Campbell
Andrea Greene
Kendra Holyfield—Copy Editor
Norma Martin
Gina Seay
William Stickney—Sports

**Louisville Courier-Journal**
Mervin Aubespin
Marie Bradby
Leon Carter
Michael Days
Cheryl Devall
Angela Dotson
Keith Harriston
Donna Whitaker

**Los Angeles Times**
Chris Baker
Janet Clayton
Ron Harris
Charrise Jones
Pam Moreland
Gayle Pollard
Jube Shiver

**Newsday**
Michael Cottman
Merle English
Marilyn Milloy
Les Payne

**Louisville Times**
Bruce Branch
Michelle Chandler
Delma Francis
Clarence Matthews
Milford Reid

**New York Daily News**
Willie Anderson Photographer
Hollis Bernard
Sharon Broussard
Bryan Burwell—Sports
Natalie Byfield
Earl Caldwell—Columnist
Alan Carter—Entertainment writer
Richard Carter—Editorial Board/Columnist
Clarence Davis Photographer
Sheryl Everette
David Hardy

*Ron Smothers, journalist for the* New York Times.

New York Times *journalist, Paul Delany.*

Lyle Harris
James Harney
Robert Herbert—Columnist
Karen Hutner
Jared McAllister
Keith Moore
Rob Parker
Charles Seaton
Joan Shepard
Causewell Vaughan
Hollie West
Joyce White
Hugh Wyatt

**New York Post**
Florence Anthony—Entertainment writer
Romona Garnes
Michael George—Sports
Greg Morris
David Steele
Lenore Davis—Photographer

**New York Times**
Daryl Alexander—Asst. National Editor
Gerald Boyd
Gary Bradford—Copy Editor
Diane Camper—Editorial Board
Don Hogan Charles Photographer
Paul Delaney
Lee Daniels
Angela Dodson—Living Editor
Dwayne Draffin—Education Editor
C. Gerald Frazier—Arts and Culture writer
Howard French
Al Harvin—Sports
Jonathan Hicks
Julie Johnson—Washington Bureau
Shawn Kennedy
Warren Leary
Felicia Lee
Michel Marriott
Tom Morgan—Copy Editor
Kenneth Noble
Bill Rhoden—Sports
Yanick Rice—Copy Editor
Michael Ross—Copy Editor
Sheila Rule
E. R. Shipp
Calvin Sims
Pamela Smith—Copy Editor
Ronald Smothers—Atlanta Bureau
Brent Staples—Asst. Metro Editor
Don Terry
Reg Thomas—Copy Editor
Ruby Washington—Photographer
Isabel Wilkerson
Jim Wilson—Photographer
Lena Williams
Winston Williams
Don Wycliff—Editorial Board

**The Oakland Tribune**
Marilyn Bailey—Assistant City Editor
Sharon Bibb—Copy Editor
Mary Ellen Butler—Feature Editor
Gerald Davis
Skye Dent—Editorial Writer
Kenneth Green—Photographer
Juadine Henderson—Assistant City Editor
Denise Holt—Education Writer
Lonnie Isabel
Annette John—Sports Writer
Sidney Jones—Columnist
Will Jones—Assistant City Editor
Brenda Lane-Worthington Columnist
Robert Maynard—Editor, Publisher, President
Tina Pania—Copy Editor
Brenda Payton
Doris Worsham—Columnist

**Philadelphia Daily News**
Lorenzo Biggs
Joseph Blake
Prentice Cole
Wayne Faircloth
Juan Gonzalez
Frederick Lowe
Valerie Russ
Gene Seymour
Elmer Smith
Chuck Stone—Columnist
Leon Taylor
Linn Washington
Barnett Wright
Earni Young

**The Star-Ledger, Newark, New Jersey**
Bill Bright
Frederick W. Byrd
Kathy Barrett-Carter
Janice Carter
Kevin Dilworth
Bernadette Germain
Larry Hall—Columnist
Caryl Lucas
Lisa Peterson
Janice Phipps
Reginald Roberts
Lauren Robinson
Angela Stewart
Iris Taylor
Stanley Terrell—Editorial Writer
Chris Thorne—Sports
Joan Whitlow—Medical Editor
Kenneth Woody

**The Washington Post**
Jean Fox-Alston—Director, Newsroom Recruiting
David Aldridge—Sports
Claudette Arons—Copy Editor/Business and Finance
Jacqui Bates—Copy Editor Business and Finance
Warren Brown
Milton Coleman—Asst. Managing Editor
Anthony Cotton—Sports
Leon Dash—Investigative Reporter
Michael Ducile Photographer
Ellsworth Davis—Night Photo Editor
Herbert H. Denton
Cheryl Eaves—Asst. News Editor
Cornelius Foote
Dorothy Butler-Gilliam Columnist
Marcia S. Greene
Carla Hall—Style Section
Neil Henry
Graig Herndon—Photographer
Michael Hill—Television Guide section
Retha Hill
Vanessa Barnes-Hillian
Donald Huff—Sports
Gwen Ifill—National Correspondent
Athelia Knight
Leah Y. Latimer
Beverly Lawrence
Gary Lee—Foreign Correspondent
Matthew Lewis—Photography Department
Courtland Milloy Jr. Columnist
Jill Nelson—Magazine section
Carol Porter—Graphics
Rudolph Pyatt—Columnist, Business and Financial
William Raspberry columnist
Vincent E. Reed—Vice President, Communications
Keith Richburg—Foreign Correspondent/Pacific
Eugene Robinson—Foreign Correspondent
Jane Seaberry—Asst. Assignment Editor/Metro Desk
Fred Sweets—Photo Department
Jacqueline Trescott
Joseph D. Whitaker
Ronald D. White
Michael Wilborn—Sports
Juan Williams

## PROMINENT BLACK PUBLISHERS AND BROADCAST EXECUTIVES

### EARL G. GRAVES
**Publisher and Broadcast Executive**
**1935**

In the 1970s, Earl Graves emerged as one of America's leading publishers and exponents of black entrepreneurship. Within a few short years his magazine, *Black Enterprise*, was accepted as the authority on the progress of minorities in business and as an important advocate for an active, socially responsive, black middle class.

Born in Brooklyn, Graves graduated from Morgan State College. In 1966, he was hired to a position on the staff of Robert Kennedy, then Senator from New York. In 1968, he organized Earl Graves Associates, a firm which serves as a consultant on urban affairs, black economic development and publishes *Black Enterprise*.

Graves represented a new wave of blacks in publishing. His magazine is polished, topical, thorough, and distinctive in its own right.

He also has interests in radio as President of EGG Dallas Broadcasting, Inc., which operates KNOK-AM and KNOK-FM in Fort Worth, Texas.

*Earl Graves, rapidly becoming one of the most important publishers in the country.*

### RAGAN A. HENRY
**Broadcast and Newspaper Executive, Attorney**
**1934**

Ragan A. Henry, President of Broadcast Enterprises National, Inc. formerly was the publisher of *The National Leader*, a black national newspaper launched in May 1982, both of which had Philadelphia as its headquarters. Henry is also President of radio stations in several states and is a partner in the Philadelphia law firm of Wolf, Black, Schorr, and Solis-Cohen..

Henry was born in Sadiesville, Kentucky on February 2, 1934. He received his A.B. from Harvard College in 1956 and his L.L.B. from Harvard Law School in 1961. He also attended Temple University Graduate School in 1963. Prior to joining his current law firm, he had been a partner in the Philadelphia firm of Goodis, Greenfield, Henry and Edelstein from 1964 to 1977.

Henry has been a Visiting Professor at Syracuse University's S. I. Newhouse School of Communications since 1979 and was a lecturer at LaSalle College from 1971-1973. He serves on the boards of directors of Continental Bank, Abt Associates, Inc., National Association of Black Owned Broadcasters (President of the Board), LaSalle College, and the Hospital of the University of Pennsylvania. He had been chairman of the John McKee Scholarship Committee Fellowships, Noyes and Whitney Foundations.

### JOHN H. JOHNSON
**Publisher**
**1918**

One of the America's foremost businessmen, John H. Johnson sits at the head of the most prosperous and powerful black publishing company in the United States. Beginning with *Negro Digest* in 1942, and following with *Ebony* in 1945, Johnson built a chain of journalistic successes that now also includes *Jet, Ebony, Jr.*, and book publishing.

In the 1980s, Johnson began publishing *Ebony Man* and also became involved in other broadcasting ventures in addition to WJPC, a Chicago AM radio station. The widely acclaimed nationally syndicated television program, "Ebony/Jet Showcase" continued to draw a huge television audience.

Born in Arkansas City, Arkansas, Johnson, at age six, lost his father, a mill worker, and was raised by his mother and stepfather. His segregated schooling was obtained locally until the family moved to Chicago. Johnson attended DuSable High School in Chicago, excelling academically and in extracurricular activities, writing for the yearbook and school paper.

After graduation, an insurance executive heard a speech delivered by Johnson, and was so impressed he offered him a partial scholarship at the University of Chicago. After two years, however, Johnson quit classes, although he entered the Northwestern School of Commerce in 1938, studying for an additional two years before joining the Supreme Liberty

*John H. Johnson directs the most prosperous and powerful black publishing company in the United States.*

Life Insurance Company.

While running the company's house organ, it occurred to Johnson that a digest of weekly or monthly gathered news items of special interest and importance to the black community might achieve a wide black readership. The idea resulted in the creation of *Negro Digest*, a periodical containing both news reprints and feature articles. Of the latter, perhaps the most beneficial to circulation was Eleanor Roosevelt's contribution, "If I Were a Negro."

Buoyed by success, Johnson decided to approach the market with yet another offering, a pictorial magazine patterned after *Life*. The first issue of *Ebony* sold out its press run of 25,000 copies and soon became a permanent staple in the world of journalism, as big companies began to advertise regularly in it. Johnson ran ads for both consumer merchandise and ethnic products, mainly hair-and skin-conditioning items. The world of "special markets" was born.

In style, tone, and format, *Ebony* glamorized American life and appealed both to middle-class citizens who felt they were already participating in the milieu he described, and to poor blacks who modeled their aspirations on the world of fulfillment he so effectively created.

From its preoccupation with frothy glamor and eye-catching photographs, *Ebony* evolved over the years into a family-style magazine devoting much of its coverage to black success stories, show business personalities, and other unusual facets of black life. For a time, much of its material was so superficial and innocuous that it succeeded in alienating many black activists, but as its circulation grew and its outlook changed, it took a more aggressive editorial stance.

In addition to serving as President and Publisher of Johnson Publishing Company, Inc., Johnson is Chairman and Chief Executive Officer of Supreme Life Insurance Company, Chairman of WJPC-AM in Chicago, and President of Fashion Fair Cosmetics. He serves on the boards of directors of The Greyhound Corporation, Verex Corporation, Marina Bank, Supreme Life Insurance Company, and Zenith Radio Corporation. Johnson also serves as a Trustee for The Art Institute of Chicago and United Negro College Fund; on the Advisory Council, Harvard Graduate School of Business; as a Director, Chamber of Commerce of the United States, The Advertising Council, Junior Achievement, and Chicago USO. In 1972, Johnson was appointed to the Urban Transportation District of Chicago. He has received honorary doctoral degrees from 16 colleges and universities, and many honors and awards from civil and professional organizations.

## CLARENCE B. JONES
**Publisher and Lawyer**
**1931**

With a background in civil rights litigation, investment financing, publishing, and broadcasting, Clarence Jones is one of New York City's more influential and knowledgeable citizens.

Born in Philadelphia, Jones graduated from Columbia University and Boston University Law School and then practiced as an attorney, specializing in civil rights and copyright cases for a New York City law firm. During this period, he was counsel for Dr. Martin Luther King Jr. and the Southern Christian Leadership Conference. In 1968 and again in 1972, he served as a delegate from New York State to the Democratic Convention.

Jones was also an observer at Attica prison during the uprising there in 1971.

In 1971, Jones, as head of Inner City Broadcasting, led a group of investors in the purchase of the New York *Amsterdam News,* the nation's largest black newspaper. Inner City Broadcasting also owned radio station WLIB and has full ownership of WBLS-FM.

## JOHN H. MURPHY III
**Publisher**
**1916**

John Murphy III is the great-nephew of John Murphy Sr., founder of the Baltimore *Afro-American*, which John III now heads. Murphy was born in Baltimore and raised in Philadelphia where at the age of nine he started his newspaper career by covering an *Afro-American* delivery route.

In 1937, Murphy graduated from Temple University in Philadelphia with a degree in Business Administration. He immediately joined the *Afro-American* staff, working in both editorial and publishing capacities, under Dr. Carl Murphy, his uncle.

From 1961 to 1974, he was President of the *Afro-American Newspapers*, and since 1974 has been Chairman of the Board of Directors.

Murphy serves on the boards of Amalgamated Publishers, Inc., National Newspaper Publishers Association, Council on Equal Business Opportunities, National Aquarium at Baltimore, Provident Hospital, Baltimore School for the

Arts, and Baltimore City Literacy Commission. He is a former member of the U.S. Civil Rights Commission.

Murphy has received numerous honors and awards from civic, educational, charitable, and journalistic organizations.

### JOHN HERMAN HENRY SENGSTACKE
### Publisher
### 1912

A nephew of the great publisher Robert Abbott, John H. Sengstacke has achieved fame in his own right, and today heads several publishing companies.

Born in Savannah, Sengstacke received a B.A. from Hampton Institute in 1933. Upon graduation, he went to work with Robert Abbott, attended school to learn printing, and wrote editorials and articles for three Abbott papers. In 1934, he became Vice President and General Manager of the company.

During World War II, Sengstacke was an advisor to the U.S. Office of War Information, during a period of severe tension between the government and black press. He also presided over the Chicago rationing board.

In 1940, after the death of his uncle, Sengstacke became President of the Robert S. Abbott Publishing Company. In 1905, his uncle had founded the weekly *Defender*. In 1956, Sengstacke founded the *Daily Defender,* one of only three black dailies in the country. In 1940 he founded the Negro Newspaper Publishers Association, now known as the National Newspaper Publishers Association, and served six terms as president. Today he is president of Tri-State Defender, Inc., Florida Courier Publishing Company, New Pittsburgh Courier Publishing Company, and Amalgamated Publishers, Inc., and chairman of Michigan Chronicle Publishing Company and Sengstacke Enterprises, Inc., and treasurer of Chicago Defender Charities, Inc.

*John Sengstacke heads the mighty* Chicago Defender.

*Publisher John H. Murphy III in his office at the Baltimore Afro-American.*

Sengstacke has served in leadership positions with many professional, educational, and civic organizations, received a number of presidential appointments, and is the recipient of several academic awards. He is currently a trustee of Bethune-Cookman College, Chairman of the Board of Provident Hospital and Training School Association, member of the board of directors of the American Society of Newspaper Editors, on the Advisory Board of the Boy Scouts of America, and a principal in Chicago United.

### CHESTER LLOYD WASHINGTON
### Publisher

Chester L. Washington is a rare breed—a reporter who became a publishing executive. He is now publisher of *The Wave* newspapers, 12 newspapers, and 4 weekly news magazines, in Los Angeles.

Washington was born in Pittsburgh, where he completed his primary education, and was graduated from Pittsburgh's

Business High School. For several years he was employed by the Pittsburgh *Courier* as legal secretary for Robert L. Vann, then publisher of the *Courier*.

He earned his B.A. degree at Virginia Union University where he taught typewriting in Richmond's Evening High School, after winning the area's typewriting championship.

Following graduation from Virginia Union, Washington returned to the *Courier* where he eventually became secretary of The Courier Corporation.

In 1949, Washington became the first black full-time reporter for the *Mirror-News*, owned by the *Los Angeles Times*. While there he specialized in coverage of superior court cases.

In 1960, he went to the *Los Angeles Sentinel* as a reporter, covering the Civic Center. In 1961, he was promoted to editor and in 1965 was named editor-in-chief.

In September 1966, he purchased the *Central News* and *Southwest News*. Then, in 1971, the *Central News* and *Southwest News* were merged with the five newspapers of The Wave Publications, which became the Central News-Wave Publications. He created three additional weeklies for a total of 10. Central News-Wave Publications is now the largest black-owned newspaper chain in the United States. In 1979, it made its first appearance on the *Black Enterprise* magazine's list of the top 100 black owned businesses. The newspapers also have won several journalism awards.

Washington is chairman of the Los Angeles County Parks and Recreation Commission, was a member of the California State Bicentennial Commission, and serves on the Coliseum Commission. He is active in many educational, youth, and civic organizations. He participated in a speaking tour at colleges in Sweden under the auspices of the State Department, and was a member of the American Delegation to Israel. At dedication ceremonies in March 1982, the Western Avenue Golf Course in Los Angeles was renamed the Chester L. Washington Golf Course. The course hosts many well-known tournaments.

*William O. Walker, president of the National Newspaper Publishers Association, receives a citation from President Eishenhower for his contribution to American journalism.*

## FAMOUS PUBLISHERS OF THE PAST

### ROBERT S. ABBOTT
### Founder of the Chicago Defender
### 1870-1940

A founding father of black journalism in the United States, Robert S. Abbott realized a lifelong dream when the first issue of his Chicago *Defender* rolled off the presses on May 5, 1905.

A native of St. Simon Island, Georgia, Abbott studied at Beach Institute in Savannah, and later did his undergraduate work at Claflin College in Orangeburg, South Carolina. Some 12 years later, he took the advice of his stepfather, John J. Sengstacke, and learned the printing trade. Migrating to Chicago, he attended Kent Law School and took a job in a printing house until he completed his law studies in 1899.

After wandering around the country for a time, Abbott returned to Chicago and decided to devote all his energies to founding the *Defender*, which he initially sold on a door-to-door basis. Over the next 15 years, the paper's circulation climbed into the hundreds of thousands.

Abbott died in 1940, where upon the *Defender* was inherited by his nephew, John H. Sengstacke, who introduced a daily edition of the paper in 1956.

### JOHN HENRY MURPHY
### Founder, Baltimore Afro-American
### 1840-1922

John Henry Murphy was born a slave in Maryland. After his emancipation at the age of 23, he worked another 27 years in menial jobs. Then at age 50, inspired by a desire to represent the black cause with honor and integrity, Murphy launched the Baltimore *Afro-American,* which to this day remains a prominent force in the black community.

At first, Murphy set the paper's type himself, having acquired this skill during his forties. Throughout, he insisted that his paper maintain political and editorial independence. The paper grew and is now under the helm of Murphy's grandson, John H. Murphy III.

### JOHN B. RUSSWURM
### Co-Publisher, Freedom's Journal
### 1799-1851

John B. Russwurm is conventionally identified as the second black to have graduated from a U.S. college. Edward A. Jones graduated from Amherst some 11 days before he did in 1826.

Russwurm took his degree at Bowdoin in 1826, and by 1827 he was engaged in editing the first Negro newspaper, *Freedom's Journal.* His colleague in this effort was the Reverend Samuel E. Cornish, pastor of the African Presbyterian Church in New York. (The paper changed its name to *Rights of All* in 1830.)

In 1828, Russwurm migrated to Liberia, finding in the new colony a "promised land." He remained there until his death some 23 years later.

## A GUIDE TO BLACK NEWSPAPERS

*John Henry Murphy launched the* Afro-American *in 1890.*

### National Weekly Newspapers

*National Afro-American*
628 N. Eutaw Street
Baltimore, MD 21201
Circulation: 6,092

*Bilalian News*
(American Muslim Mission)
7801 S. Cottage Grove
Chicago, IL 60619
Circulation: 150,000

*New Courier*
315 E. Carson Street
PO Box 2939
Pittsburgh, PA 15230
Circulation: 7,956

*The National Leader*
1422 Chestnut Street
Philadelphia, PA 11902
Circulation:

### National Newspaper Supplements

*Black Monitor*
Black Media, Inc.
507 Fifth Avenue
New York, NY 10017
Circulation: 1,000,000
(cooperatively published supplement to 110 black newspapers)

*Dawn Magazine*
628 N. Eutaw Street
Baltimore, MD 21203
Circulation: 900,000
(distributed once a month in local and national black newspapers)

*National Scene*
L. H. Stanton
Publications, Inc.
507 Fifth Avenue

New York, NY 10017
Circulation: 792,773
(monthly supplement to 23 weekly newspapers)

## Daily Newspapers

*The Daily Challenge*
1368 Fulton Street
Brooklyn, NY 11216
Circulation: 72,500
(publishes every day except Saturday)

*Chicago Daily Defender*
Robert S. Abbott Publishing Co.
2400 S. Michigan
Chicago, IL 60616
Circulation: 17,349 (Monday-Friday)
18,250 (Saturday)

*Atlanta Daily World*
145 Auburn Avenue
Atlanta, GA 30335
Circulation: 18,500 (Mon., Tues., Thur., Fri.)
Cir. 22,500 (Sat.)

## Weekly Newspapers

### Alabama

**Birmingham**
*Times*
PO Box 10503
Birmingham, AL 35204
Cir. 36,000
205-251-5158

**Birmingham**
*World*
312 N. 17th St.
Birmingham, AL 35203
Cir. 9,200
205-251-6523

**Florence**
*Shoals News-Leader*
PO Box 427
Florence, AL 35631
Cir. 10,000
205-766-5542

**Mobile**
*Beacon*
PO Box 1407
2311 Coastarides St.
Mobile, AL 36633
Cir. 5,000
205-479-0629

**Mobile**
*Inner City News*
PO Box 1545
Mobile, AL 36633
Cir. 21,000
205-473-2767

**Montgomery**
*Times*
PO Box 9133
Montgomery, AL 36108
Cir. 5,000
205-264-7149

**Tuskgee**
*News*
PO Box 60
Tuskgee, AL 36083
Cir. 17,000
205-727-3020

### Arizona

**Phoenix**
*Arizona Informant*
1746 E. Madison St.
Phoenix, AZ 85034
Cir. 8,400
602-257-9300

**Phoenix**
*Press Weekly*
PO Box 8753
Phoenix, AZ 85066
Cir. 11,000
602-243-1857

### Arkansas

**Little Rock**
*Arkansas Weekly Sentinel*
PO Box 4520
Little Rock, AR 72214
Cir. 2,500
602-257-9300

**Little Rock**
*Statewide Mediator*
500 E. Markham, Suite 300
Little Rock, AR 72201
Cir. 51,749
602-243-1857

### California

**Bakersfield**
*Bakersfield News Observer*
1219 20th St.
Bakersfield, CA 93301
Cir. 20,000
805-324-9466

**Fresno**
*California Advocate*
PO Box 11826
450 Fresno St.
Fresno, CA 93775
Cir. 46,000
209-268-0941

**Los Angeles**
*Central News Wave Publications*
Publishes:
Culver City Wave
Hawthorne Wave, Inglewood
L A Central News
L A Mesa Wave, L A Southside Journal
L A Southwest News
L A SW Topics-Wave
L A SW Wave
L A SW Wave Star
LA SW Sun,
L A Tribune News Wave
2621 W. 54th St.
Los Angeles, CA 90043
Cir. 210,000
213-290-3000

**Los Angeles**
*Southeast News Press*
Publishes:
Firestone Park News
Herald-Dispatch
Watts Star Review
PO Box 19027
Los Angeles, CA 90019
Cir. 89,000
213-291-9486

**Los Angeles**
*Sentinel*
1112 E 43 St.
Los Angeles 90011
Cir. 30,000
213-232-3261

**Oakland**
*Alameda Pub Co*
Publishes:
*The Post* for
Berkeley
Oakland
Richmond
San Francisco
also *El Mundo*
Oakland Sea-side Post
PO Box 1350
Oakland, CA 94604
Cir. 150,000
415-763-1120

**Pasedena**
*Gazette Publications*
Publishes:
*The Gazette* for
Los Angeles,
Pasadena
San Fernando Valley
PO Box 93275
Pasedena, CA 91103
Cir. 65,000
818-584-9601

**Riverside**
*Black Voice News*
PO Box 1581
Riverside, CA 92502
Cir. 5,000
714-682-6070

**Sacramento**
*Observer*
PO Box 209
3540 4th Ave.
Sacramento, CA 95801
Cir. 92,800

**San Bernardino**
*Precinct Reporter*
1677 W. Baseline St.
San Bernardino, CA 92411
Cir. 30,000

**San Diego**
*Voice and Viewpoint News*
PO Box 95
4684 Federal Blvd.
San Diego, CA 92112
Cir. 10,000

**San Francisco**
*Reporter Publications*
Publishes:
*Metro Reporter* for
Berkeley,
Oakland
Peninsula
Richmond
San Francisco
San Joaquin,
San Jose
Vallejo/Fairfield
1366 Turk
San Francisco, CA 94115
Cir. 156,0000
415-931-5778

### Colorado

**Denver**
*Weekly News*
2547 Welton St.
Denver, CO 80205
Cir. 15,000
303-297-1131

### Connecticut

**Hartford**
*Hartford Inquirer* for
Bridgeport
Hartford
New Haven
Waterbury
Springfield
PO Box, CT 1260
Hartford 06101
Cir. 66,000
203-522-1462

### Delaware

**Wilmington**
*Delaware Valley Star*
1050 A.S. Market St.
Wilmington, DE 19801
Cir. 10,000

## District of Columbia

**Washington**
*Afro-American*
2002 11th St. N.W.
Washington, DC 20001
Cir. 10,100
202-332-0080

**Washington**
*Capital Spotlight*
1158 Nat'l Press Bldg
Washington, DC 20045
Cir. 50,000
202-628-0700

**Washington**
*Informer*
3117 M. L King SE
Washingotn, DC 20032
Cir. 45,000
202-561-4100

**Washington**
*New Observer*
811 Florida Ave. NW
Washington, DC 20001
Cir. 24,000
202-232-3060

## Florida

**Daytona Beach**
*Times*
PO Box 1110
Daytona Beach, FL 32015
Cir. 10,000
904-253-0321

**Fort Lauderdale**
*Gazette*
PO Box 5304
Fort Lauderdale, FL 33310
Cir. 21,000
305-523-5115

**Fort Pierce**
*Chronicle*
1527 Ave. D
Fort Pierce, FL 33450
Cir. 7,000
305-461-7093

**Jacksonville**
*Florida Star-News*
PO Box 40629
Jacksonville, FL 32203
Cir. 26,050
904-354-8880

**Jacksonville**
*Jacksonville Advocate*
860 Sorrento Road
Jacksonville, FL 32207
Cir. 5,000

**Miami**
*Florida Courier*
1466 N.W. 62 St.
Miami, FL 33147
Cir. 4,496

**Miami**
*The Liberty News*
North side Shopping Center
188 North Plaza
Miami, FL 33147

**Miami**
*Miami Times*
900 N.W. 54th St.
Miami, FL 33127
Cir. 24,160
305-757-1147

**Orlando**
*Florida Sun & Mirror*
PO Box 2488
Orlando, FL 32802
Cir. 5,000

**Orlando**
*Sun Review*
4020 W. Columbia St.
Orlando, FL 32805
Cir. 4,000

**Orlando**
*Times*
2393 W. Church St.
Orlando, FL 32805
Cir. 10,000
305-841-3052

**Pensacola**
*Pensacola Voice*
213 E. Young St.
Pensacola, FL 32503
Cir. 32,700
904-434-6963

**Riveria Beach**
*Gold Coast Star News*
PO Box 6002
206 No. Flagler Ave.
Riveria Beach, FL 33060
CIr. 7,500

**Sarasota**
*Weekly Bulletin*
PO Box 2560
Sarasota, FL 33578
Cir. 17,500
813-366-5821

**St. Petersburg**
*Weekly Challenger*
Suite C
2500 9th St. S.
St. Petersburg, FL 33705
Cir. 15,300
813-896-2922

**Tallahassee**
*Capitol Outlook*
PO Box 31
Tallahassee, FL 32302
Cir. 5,000
904-878-3895

**Tampa**
*News Reporter*
1610 N. Howard Ave.
Tampa, FL 33607
Cir. 5,759

**Tampa**
*Sentinel-Bulletin*
2207 21st Ave.
Tampa, FL 33601
Cir. 39,806
813-248-1921

**West Palm Beach**
*Florida Photo News*
PO Box 1583-46
601 Clematis St.
West Palm Beach, FL 33402
Cir. 2,288
305-833-4511

## Georgia

**Albany**
*Albany/Macon Times*
141 West Broad
Albany, GA 31705
Cir. 46,000

**Albany**
*Southwest Georgian*
PO Box 1943
Albany, GA 33701
Cir. 10,000
912-436-2156

**Albany**
*Times*
PO Box 528
Albany 31701
Cir. 5,000
912-432-7070

**Atlanta**
*The Atlanta Inquirer*
787 Parsons St. S.W.
Atlanta, GA 30314
Cir. 55,000
404-523-6086

**Atlanta**
*Atlanta People's Crusader*
551 Houston St. N. E.
Atlanta, GA 30312
Cir. 20,000

**Atlanta**
*Atlanta Voice*
PO Box 92405
Atlanta, GA 30312
Cir. 50,000
404-524-6426

**Augusta**
*Focus*
PO Box 10112
Augusta, GA 30903
Cir. 22,000
404-722-7327

**Augusta**
*Metro Co. Courier*
PO Box 2385
Augusta, GA 30903
Cir. 26,000
404-724-6556

**Augusta**
*News Review*
PO Box 953
Augusta, GA 30903
Cir. 3,025

**Columbus**
*Times*
2230 Buena Vista Rd.
Columbus, GA 31906
Cir. 20,000
404-324-2404

**Cordele**
*Southeastern News*
PO Box 461
Cordele, GA 31015
Cir. 20,000
912-237-6714

**Macon**
*Courier*
PO Box 52D
Macon, GA 31208
Cir. 7,500
912-745-7433

**Macon**
*Macon Times*
813 Forsythe
Macon, GA 31201
Cir. 32,000

**Savannah**
*Savannah Herald*
PO Box 41
803 Barnard St.
Savannah, GA 31402
Cir. 6,000
912-232-4505

**Savannah**
*Tribune*
PO Box 2066
Savannah,GA 31402
Cir. 6,000
912-233-6128

## Illinois

**Champaign**
*Spectrum*
Station A. PO Box 2285
Champaign, IL 61820

**Chicago**
*Chicago Metro News*
Suite 101
2600 S. Michigan Ave.
Chicago, IL 60616
Cir. 70,205
312-842-5950

**Chicago**
*Citizen Newspapers*
Publisher:
Chatham Citizen
Chicago Weekend
S End Citizen
412 E. 87 St.

Chicago, IL 60619
Cir. 65,000
312-487-7700

**Chicago**
*Independent Bulletin Newspapers*
2042 W. 95th St.
Chicago, IL 60643
Cir. 47,000
312-783-1040

**Chicago**
*New Crusader*
6429 Martin Luther King Dr.
Chicago, IL 60637
Cir. 39,411
312-752-2500

**Chicago**
*Observer*
6040 S. Harper
Chicago, IL 60637
Cir. 30,000
312-493-0557

**Chicago**
*Shoreland*
11740 S. Elizabeth St.
Chicago, IL 60643
Cir. 20,000

**Chicago**
*South Shore Scene*
7135 S. Jeffrey
Chicago, IL 60649
Cir. 80,000
312-667-0790

**Chicago**
*Westside Journal*
4 N. Cicero
Chicago, IL 60644
Cir. 60,000
312-287-7431

**Chicago Hts.**
*Standard Publishing*
Publishes:
*Chicago Standard*
*South Suburban Standard*
615 Halsted
Chicago Hts., IL 60411
Cir. 35,000
312-755-5021

**Chicago Hts.**
*Tri-City Journal*
1406 Park Ave.
Chicago, IL Hts.
Cir. 30,000

**Decatur**
*Decatur Voice*
3180 N. Woolford Rd. Rm. 31
Decatur, IL 62526
Cir. 5,000
217-423-2231

**East St. Louis**
*Monitor*
1501 State St.
East St. Louis, IL 62205
Cir. 17,000
618-271-0468

**Evanston**
*North Shore Examiner*
909 Pitner Ave.
Evanston, IL 60202

**Rockford**
*The Rockford Chronicle*
605 West State Street
Rockford, IL 61102

## Indiana

**Ft. Wayne**
*Ft. Wayne Frost Illustrated*
PO Box 10418
Ft. Wayne, IN 46852
Cir. 4,500
219-745-0552

**Gary**
*American*
PO Box 1199
Gary, IN 46407
Cir. 12,000
219-883-4903

**Gary**
*Gary Crusader*
1549 Broadway
Gary, IN 46407
Cir. 20,000
219-885-4357

**Gary**
*Info*
PO Box M 587
Gary, IN 46401
Cir. 19,000
219-882-5591

**Indianapolis**
*Herald*
723 N.W. St.
Indianapolis, IN 46205
Cir. 27,200

**Indianapolis**
*Indianapolis Recorder*
PO Box 18267
Indianapolis, IN 46218
Cir. 12,000
317-924-5143

## Iowa

**W. Des Moines**
*New Iowa Bystander*
PO Box 65640
W. Des Moines, IA 50265
Cir. 3,000

## Kansas

**Kansas City**
*Kansas City Globe*
1125 Grand Suite 1102
Kansas City, KS 64106
Cir. 19,000

**Kansas City**
*Kansas City Voice*
2727 N. 13th St.
Kansas City, KS 66104
Cir. 34,000

**Kansas City**
*State Globe*
PO Box 1309
Kansas City, KS 66104
Cir. 68,000
913-596-1008

**Wichita**
*Journal*
PO Box 3179
Wichita, KS 67201
Cir. 1,600
316-263-5277

## Kentucky

**Louisville**
*The Defender*
1720 Dixie Highway
Louisville, KY 40210
Cir. 2,000
502-772-2591

## Louisiana

**Alexandria**
*Alexandria News Weekly*
PO Box 608
Alexandria, LA 71301
Cir. 13,500
318-443-7664

**Baton Rouge**
*Community Leader*
1010 North Blvd.
Baton Rouge, LA 70802
Cir. 46,013
504-343-0544

**Baton Rouge**
*Baton Rouge Weekly Press*
PO Box 73579
Baton Rouge, LA 70807
Cir. 19,000
507-775-2002

**Monroe**
*Dispatch*
PO Box 4823
Monroe, LA 71211
Cir. 7,500
318-387-3001

**New Orleans**
*Black Data Weekly*
PO Box 51933
New Orleans, LA 70151
Cir. 15,000
504-821-9220

**New Orleans**
*Louisiana Weekly*
PO Box 53008
New Orleans, LA 70153
Cir. 10,000
504-524-5563

**Shreveport**
*Shreveport Ebony Tribune*
PO Box 3857
Shreveport, LA 71103.

**Shreveport**
*Shreveport Sun*
PO Box 9328
Shreveport, LA 71139
Cir. 5,500
318-631-6222

## Maryland

**Baltimore**
*Afro-American*
PO Box 1857
Baltimore, MD 21203
Cir. 30,000
301-728-8200

**Baltimore**
*African-American News & World Report*
325 E. 2nd St.
Baltimore, MD 21218
Cir. 10,000

## Massachusetts

**Boston**
*Bay State Banner*
925 Washington St.
Roxbury, MA 02124
Cir. 12,000
617-288-4900

**Boston**
*Greater News*
PO Box 497
BostonMA 02119
Cir. 13,500
617-445-7063

## Michigan

**Benton Harbor**
*Citizen*
PO Box 216
Benton Harbor, MI 49022
Cir. 42,000
616-927-1527

**Detroit**
*Michigan Chronicle*

479 Ledyard St.
Detroit, MI 48201
Cir. 28,000
313-963-5522

**Ecorse**
*Telegram*
4122 10th St.
Detroit, MI 48229
Cir. 12,000
313-928-2955

**Flint**
*Spokesman*
3604 W. Saginaw St.
Flint, MI 48405
Cir. 9,000

**Grand Rapids**
*Grand Rapids Times*
PO Box 7258
Grand Rapids, MI 49501
Cir. 12,000
616-245-8737

**Jackson**
*Jackson Blazer*
PO Box 806
Jackson, MI 49204
Cir. 6,400
517-787-0450

### Minnesota

**Minneapolis**
*Minneapolis Spokesman*
3744 4th Ave. S.
Minneapolis, MN 55409
Cir. 16,000
612-827-4021

**Minneapolis**
*St. Paul Recorder*
3744 4th Ave. S.
Minneapolis, MN 55409
Cir. 13,000
612-827-4021

**Minneapolis**
*Twin Cities Courier*
Suite 501
84 S. 6th St.
Minneapolis, MN 55402
Cir. 16,000
612-332-3211

### Mississippi

**Jackson**
*Jackson Advocate*
PO Box 3708
Jackson, MS 39207
Cir. 23,000
601-948-4122

**Meredian**
*Memo Digest*
PO Box 5782
Meredian, MS 39301
Cir. 3,000
601-693-2372

### Missouri

**Kansas City**
*Call*
PO Box 477
Kansas City, MO 64141
Cir. 35,000
816-842-3804

**Kansas City**
*Globe*
PO Box 090410
Kansas City, MO 64109
Cir. 30,000
816-842-3301

**St. Louis**
*St. Louis American*
4144 Lindell Blvd.
St. Louis, MO 63108
Cir. 31,000
314-533-8000

**St. Louis**
*St. Louis Argus*
4595 Martin Luther King Dr.
St. Louis, MO 63113
Cir. 17,000
314-531-1323

**St. Louis**
*St. Louis Crusader*
4371 Finney Ave.
St. Louis, MO 63113
Cir. 12,500
314-531-5860

**St. Louis**
*St. Louis Evening Whirl*
PO Box 5088
St. Louis, MO 63115
Cir. 40,000
314-383-3875

**St. Louis**
*St. Louis Metro-Sentinel*
Suite 206
3338 Olive St.
St. Louis, MO 63103
Cir. 50,000
314-531-2101

### Nebraska

**Omaha**
*Omaha Star*
2216 N. 24 St.
Omaha, NE 68110
Cir. 30,000
402-346-4041

### Nevada

**Las Vegas**
*Las Vegas Sentinel-Voice*
1201 S. Eastern Ave.
Las Vegas, NV 89104
Cir. 5,000
702-383-4030

**Reno**
*The Reno Observer*
328 E. Taylor
Reno, NV 89505
Cir. 5,000

### New Jersey

**East Orange**
*Grafrica News*
28 Emerson St.
East Orange, NJ 07018
Cir. 24,000

**Newark**
*New Jersey Afro-American*
Suites 200-201
11 Hill St.
Newark, NJ 07102
Cir. 4,405

**Newark**
*Newark/Essex Greater News*
585 Broad St.
Newark, NJ 07102
Cir. 50,000
201-643-3364

**Willingboro**
*Willingboro Tri-County News*
PO Box 248
Willingboro, NJ 08046
Cir. 10,000

### New York

**Brooklyn**
*Big Red-News*
1406 Fulton St.
Brooklyn, NY 11216
Cir. 59,000
718-638-6841

**Brooklyn**
*City Sun*
PO Box 560
Brooklyn, NY 11202
Cir. 25,000
718-624-5959

**Brooklyn**
*New York Recorder*
86 Bainbridge St.
Brooklyn, NY 11233
Cir. 45,000
718-493-4616

**Buffalo**
*Buffalo Challenger*
1303 Fillmore Ave.
Buffalo, NY 14211
Cir. 15,000
716-897-0422

**Buffalo**
*Buffalo Criterion*
625 William St.
Buffalo, NY 14206
Cir. 6,000
716-882-9570

**Buffalo**
*Buffalo Fine Print News*
Box 57
Buffalo, NY 14205
Cir. 32,000
716-855-3810

**Flushing**
*New York Voice*
78-36 Parsons Blvd.
Flushing, NY 11366
Cir. 68,000
718-591-6600

**Hastings-On-Hudson**
*Westchester County Press*
PO Box 173
Hastings-On-Hudson, NY 10706
Cir. 7,700
914-684-0006

**Hempstead**
*N.Y.-L.I. Courier*
507 Fulton Ave.
Hempstead, NY
Cir. 4,900

**New York City**
*The Black American*
545 8th Ave.
New York, NY 10018
Cir. 177,000
212-564-5110

**New York City**
*New York Amsterdam News*
2340 8th Ave.
New York, NY 10027
Cir. 40,000
212-678-6600

**New York City**
*Militant*
410 West St.
New York, NY 10014
Cir. 12,000
212-243-6392

**Poughkeepsie**
*Mid Hudson Herald*
15 Smith St.
Poughkeepsie, NY 12602
Cir. 4,500

**Rochester**
*Communicade*
PO Box 60739
Rochester, NY 14607
Cir. 3,000
716-235-6695

**Syracuse**
*The Impartial Citizen*
PO Box 98
1313 S. Saline St.
Syracuse, NY 13205
Cir. 3,000

**Uniondale L. I.**
*Courier*
PO Box 8
Uniondale, NY 11553
Cir. 6,000

## North Carolina

**Charlotte**
*Charlotte Post*
PO Box 30144
Charlotte, NC 28230
Cir. 11,000
704-376-0496

**Charlotte**
*Star of Zion*
PO Box 31005
Charlotte, NC 28231
Cir. 8,000
704-377-4329

**Durham**
*Carolina Times*
PO Box 3825
Durham, NC 27702
Cir. 6,500
919-682-2913

**Goldsboro**
*Metro Times*
PO Box 1935
Goldsboro, NC 27533
Cir. 8,000
919-734-0302

**Greensboro**
*Carolina Peacemaker*
PO Box 20853
Greensboro, NC 27420
Cir. 6,000
919-274-6210

**Raeford**
*Raeford Public Post*
PO Box 1093
Raeford, NC 28376
Cir. 1,000
919-875-8938

**Raleigh**
*The Carolinian*
PO Box 25308
Raleigh, NC 27611
Cir. 17,000
919-834-5558

**Statesville**
*Iredell County News*
PO Box 407
Statesville, NC 28677
Cir. 2,500
704-873-1054

**Wilmington**
*Wilmington Journal*
PO Box 1618
Wilmington, NC 28402
Cir. 9,000
919-762-5502

**Winston-Salem**
*Chronicle*
PO Box 3154
Winston-Salem, NC 27102
Cir. 5,000
919-722-8624

## Ohio

**Akron**
*Reporter*
PO Box 2042
Akron, OH 44309
Cir. 35,000
216-253-0007

**Bedford**
*Cleveland Metro*
22801 Aurora Rd.
Bedford, OH 44116
Cir. 55,000

**Cincinnati**
*Cincinnati Herald*
863 Lincoln Ave.
Cincinnati, OH 45206
Cir. 23,000
513-221-5440

**Cleveland**
*Call and Post* (separate editions for Cincinnati, Cleveland, and Columbus)
PO Box 6237
Cleveland, OH 44101
Cir. 54,000
216-791-7600

**Columbus**
*Columbus Onyx*
1312 East Broad St.
Columbus, OH 43205
Cir. 35,000

**Dayton**
*Jetstone News*
627 Salem Ave.
Dayton, OH 45406
Cir. 24,000

**Toledo**
*The Toledo Journal*
PO Box 2536
Toledo, OH 43606
Cir. 13,500
419-472-4521

**Youngstown**
*Buckeye Review*
PO Box 1436
632 Belmont Ave.
Youngstown, OH 44502
Cir. 5,000
216-743-2250

## Oklahoma

**Oklahoma City**
*Black Chronicle*
PO Box 17498
Oklahoma, OK City 73136
Cir. 27,000
405-424-4695

**Oklahoma City**
*Black Dispatch*
1301 North Eastern Ave.
Oklahoma City, OK 73117
Cir. 6,500

**Tulsa**
*Oklahoma Eagle*
PO Box 3267
Tulsa, OK 74101
Cir. 13,000
918-582-7124

## Oregon

**Portland**
*Observer*
PO Box 3137
Portland, OR 97208
Cir. 16,000
503-288-0033

**Portland**
*Skanner*
PO Box 5455
Portland, OR 97228
Cir. 20,000
503-287-3562

## Pennsylvania

**Philadelphia**
*Afro American*
427 S. Broad St.
Philadelphia, PA 19107
Cir. 842

**Philadelphia**
*New Observer*
511 N. Broad
Philadelphia, PA 19123
Cir. 20,000
215-922-5220

**Philadelphia**
*Nite Owl*
2806 W. Girard Ave.
Philadelphia, PA 19130
Cir. 10,000
215-232-2414

**Philadelphia**
*Philadelphia Spirit*
649 N. 52 St.
Philadelphia, PA 19131
Cir. 25,000
215-878-0270

**Philadelphia**
*Tribune*
520 S. 16th St.
Philadelphia, PA 19146
Cir. 92,000
215-893-4050

**Philadelphia**
*Nite Scene*
2951 N. 22 St.
Philadelphia, PA 19132
Cir. 75,000
215-229-8253

*Christopher J. Perry, founder of the* Philadelphia Tribune.

**Pittsburgh**
*Homewood Bruston News*
121 S. Highland Mall
Pittsburgh, PA 15206
Cir. 11,750

**Pittsburgh**
*New Courier*
PO Box 2939
Pittsburgh, PA 15230
Cir. 35,000
412-481-8302

## South Carolina

**Charleston**
*Charleston Chronicle*
PO Box 2548
Charleston, SC 29403
Cir. 6,000
803-723-2785

**Charleston**
*Coastal Times*
PO Box 1407
Charleston, SC 29403
Cir. 5,000
803-723-5318

**Columbia**
*Juju Publishing*
Publishes:
*Charleston Black Times*
*Columbia Black News*
*Florence Black Sun*
*Greenville Black Star*
*Orangeburg Black Voice*
*Sumter Black Post*
*Rock Hills Black Views*
PO Box 11128
Columbia, SC 29211
Cir. 60,000
803-799-5252

**Florence**
*The Key*
PO Box 491
Florence, SC 29503
Cir. 7,000

**Marion**
*Pee Dee Observer*
PO Box 39
Marion, SC 29571
Cir. 4,500
803-423-0809

**Orangeburg**
*Afro Weekly*
460 Sullen N. E.
Orangeburg, SC 29115
Cir. 3,000

## Tennessee

**Memphis**
*Mid-South Express*
918 S. Pkwy. E.
Memphis, TN 38106
Cir. 32,000
901-774-1405

**Memphis**
*Tri-State Defender*
PO Box 2065
Memphis, TN 38101
Cir. 30,000
901-523-1818

## Texas

**Austin**
*Capitol City Argus*
1309 E. 12 St.
Austin, TX 78702
Cir. 4,000
512-928-9427

**Austin**
*Villager*
1151 1/2 San Bernard St.
Austin, TX 78702
Cir. 6,000
512-476-0082

**Dallas**
*Dallas Weekly*
PO Box 15832
Dallas, TX 75215
Cir. 50,000
214-428-8958

**Dallas**
*Freedoms' Journal*
2814 S. Beckley
Dallas, TX 75224

**Dallas**
*Great Circle News*
3101 Forest Ave.
Dallas, TX 75215

**Dallas**
*Post Tribune*
PO Box 24727
Dallas, TX 75224
Cir. 16,000
214-946-7678

**Fort Worth**
*Fort Worth Como Monitore*
PO Box 885
5529 Wellesley Ave.
Fort Worth, TX 76101
Cir. 1,000

**Fort Worth**
*Fort Worth Mind*
1632 D.E. Berry St.
Fort Worth, TX 76119
Cir. 12,955

**Fort Worth**
*Metro Cities News*
3204 E. Rosedale Ave.
Fort Worth, TX 76105
Cir. 2,050

**Ft. Worth**
*Texas Times*
PO Box 1341
Ft. Worth, TX 76101
Cir. 10,000
817-926-4666

**Houston**
*Defender*
PO Box 8005
Houston, TX 77288
Cir. 16,000
713-663-7716

**Houston**
*Forward Times*
PO Box 8346
Houston, TX 77004
Cir. 30,000
713-526-4727

**Houston**
*Globe-Advocate*
PO Box 8147
3221 Southmore Blvd.
Houston, TX 77004
Cir. 10,000

**Lubbock**
*Southwest Digest*
PO Box 2553
Lubbock, TX 79408
Cir. 25,000
806-762-3612

**San Antonio**
*Register*
PO Box 1598
San Antonio, TX 78296
Cir. 10,000

**Texarkana**
*Texarkana Courier*
504 W. 3rd St.
PO Box 6066
Texarkana, TX

**Waco**
*Messenger*
Po Box 2087
Waco, TX 76703
Cir. 3,000
817-799-6911

## Virginia

**Charlottesville**
*Charlottesville-Albemarle Tribune*
PO Box 3428
Charlottesville, VA 22902
Cir. 4,000
703-979-0373

**Danville**
***Danville News & Observer***
PO Box 163
Danville, VA 24541
Cir. 5,000

**Norfolk**
*Journal/Guide*
PO Box 209
Norfolk 23501
Cir. 27,000
804-625-3686

**Richmond**
*Afro American*
301 East Clay St.
Richmond, VA 23219
Cir. 13,000
804-649-8478

**Roanoke**
*Tribune*
PO Box 6021
Roanoke, VA 24017
Cir. 5,000
703-343-0326

## Washington

**Seattle**
*Seattle Facts*
PO Box 22015
Seattle, WA 98122
Cir. 20,000

**Seattle**
*Medium*
PO Box 22047
Seattle, WA 98122
Cir. 50,000
206-323-3070

**Tacoma**
*Northwest Dispatch*
PO Box 5637
Tacoma, WA 98405
Cir. 10,000
206-272-7587

**Tacoma**
*True Citizen*
PO Box 5955
Tacoma, WA 98405
Cir. 14,000
206-627-1103

## Wisconsin

**Beloit**
*Chronicle*
PO Box 133
Beloit, WI 53511
Cir. 9,000
608-364-0166

**Milwaukee**
*Community Journal*
3612 N. Greenbay Ave.
Milwaukee, WI 53212
Cir. 40,000
414-265-6647

**Milwaukee**
*Courier Communications*
Publishes:
*Milwaukee Courier*
*Milwaukee Star*
*Racine Courier*
2431 W. Hopkins
Milwaukee, WI 53206
Cir. 60,000
414-445-2031

## A GUIDE TO BLACK PERIODICALS

### Magazines

***About Time***
30 Genessee Street
Rochester, NY 14611
Cir. 16,280
(monthly)

***Beauty Trade***
15 Columbus Circle
New York, NY 10022
Cir. 2,680,000
(monthly)

***Black Affairs***
Suite 1121 National Press Building
Washington, DC 20045
(bi-weekly)

***The Black Collegian***
1240 Broad Street
New Orleans, LA 70125
Cir. 254,818
(bi-monthly)

***Black Enterprise***
Earl G. Graves Publishing Co.
295 Madison Avenue
New York, NY 10027
Cir. 230,000
(monthly)

***Black Family***
332 North Michigan Avenue
Chicago, IL 60601

***Black News***
10 Claver Place
Brooklyn, NY 11238
(monthly)

***Black Odyssey***
J.F.F. Communications
114 E. 28 Street
New York, NY 11434
(monthly, travel and leisure magazine)

***Black Stars***
Johnson Publishing Co.
820 S. Michigan Avenue
Chicago, IL 60605
Cir. 200,000
(monthly; lifestyles of blacks who have achieved success, especially in the entertainment industry)

***Blac-Tress***
Harris Publications
79 Madison Avenue
New York, NY 10016
Cir. 150,000
(six times a year; beauty and hair fashions)

***Disco That***
250 West 57Th Street, Suite 224
New York, NY 10019

***Dollar and Sense***
840 E. 87 Street, Suite 202
Chicago, IL 60619
Cir. 91,476
(six times a year; Business magazine)

***Eagle & Swan***
Port Royal Communications Network
155 E. 55th Street
New York, NY 10022
Cir. 110,000
(six times a year; special interest for military service personnel)

***Ebony***
Johnson Publishing Co.
820 S. Michigan Avenue
Chicago, IL 60605
Cir. 1,250,000
(monthly;general interest picture article format)

***Encore***
Tanner Publications
155 E. 55th Street
New York, NY 10022
Cir. 170,000
(monthly)

***Equal Opportunity***
Equal Opportunity Publications, Inc.
Box 202
Centerport, NY 11721
Cir. 15,000
(three times a year; minority student magazine)

***Essence***
1550 Broadway
New York, NY 10036
Cir. 650,000
(monthly; women's magazine)

***First World***
1580 Avon Avenue, S.W.
Atlanta, GA 30311
Cir. 20,000
(quarterly)

***Freedomways***
799 Broadway
New York, NY 10003
Cir. 10,000
(quarterly; review of the Freedom Movement)

***Great Black Group:***
*Bronze Thrills*
*Jive*
*Help*
*Soul*
*Soul Confessions*
Sepia Publishing Corporation
1220 Harding Street
Fort Worth, TX 76102
Cir. 150,000
(monthly; true romance and confessional magazines)

***Jet***
Johnson Publishing Company
820 S. Michigan Avenue
Chicago, IL 60605
Cir. 700,000
(weekly; digest size national newsmagazine)

***Journal of Black Studies***
Sage Publications
275 S. Beverly Drive
Beverly Hills, CA 90212
(quarterly)

***Negro Traveler and Conventioneer***
11717 S. Vincennes
Chicago, IL 60643
Cir. 72,000
(bi-monthly; guide to travel)

***Players***
8060 Melrose Avenue
Los Angeles, CA 90046
Cir. 200,000
(monthly; black men's magazine)

***Sepia***
1220 Harding Boulevard
Fort Worth, TX 76102
Cir. 50,000
(monthly; topical and contemporary, oriented to young black families)

***Soul***
6331 Hollywood Boulevard
Los Angeles, CA 90028
Cir. 225,000
(bi-weekly; entertainment coverage for young blacks)

***Soul Teen***
Sepia Publishing Corporation
1220 Harding Street
Fort Worth, TX 76102
Cir. 50,000
(monthly; features and photos on black entertainment personalities)

***Uptown The Voice of Central Harlem***
Minisink Town House
646 Lenox Avenue
New York, NY 10037
(monthly)

### Association, Professional, and Collegiate Publications

***Afro-American Journal***
Martin Center
3561 N. College Avenue
Indianapolis, IN 46205
(quarterly)

***Afro-Americans in New York Life and History***
Afro-American Historical Association of the Niagara Frontier
Box 1663 Hertel Station
Buffalo, NY 14216
(semiannually)

***Atlanta University Bulletin***
Office of Public Relations
Atlanta University
Atlanta, GA 30314
Cir. 8,500
(semi-annually)

***Black American Literature Forum***
Indiana State University
School of Education
Terre Haute, IN 47809
(quarterly)

***Black Law Journal***
University of California at Los Angeles
School of Law
Los Angeles, CA 90024
Cir. 5,000
(three times a year)

***Black Male/Female Relationships***
Black Think Tank
1801 Bush Street
San Francisco, CA 94109
Cir. 10,000
(quarterly)

***Black News Digest***
Department of Labor Office of Information
200 Constitution Avenue, N.W.
Washington, DC 20210
Cir. 2,000
(weekly)

***Black Perspective in Music***
Foundation for Research in the Afro-American Creative Arts, Inc. Drawer I
Cambria Heights, NY 11411
Cir. 1,000
(semi-annually)

***Black Scholar (Journal of Black Studies and Research)***

Black World Foundation
Box 908
Sausalito, CA 94965
Cir. 25,000
(six times a year)

***Black Writers News***
4019 S. Vincennes Avenue
Chicago, IL 60653
Cir. 5,000
(quarterly)

***Campus Digest***
Tuskegee Institute
Bulletin Publishing Co.
Auburn, AL 36830
Cir. 4,000
(weekly)

***Core***
Congress of Racial Equality Magazine
1916-38 Park Avenue
New York, NY 10037

***Crisis***
National Association for the Advancement of Colored People
1790 Broadway
New York, NY 10019
Cir. 119,000
(monthly)

***Culture—A Journal of Black Consciousness***
Institute of Positive Education
7524 S. Cottage Grove Avenue
Chicago, IL 60619
Cir. 12,500
(quarterly; formerly Black Books Bulletin)

***Everybody***
Ruffin Publications
2514 N. 24 Street
Omaha, NE 68111
Cir. 94,198
(monthly)

*Popular black magazines include general interest* Ebony; Essence, *oriented toward the black woman; and* Encore, *a multiracial news digest.*

***Gold Torch***
Central State University
Wilberforce, OH 45384
Cir. 2,400
(weekly)

***Hampton Script***
Hampton Institute
Hampton, VA 23368
Cir. 2,800-3,000
(semiannually)

***Ivy Leaf***
Alpha Kappa Alpha Sorority
5211 S. Greenwood Avenue
Chicago, IL 60615
(quarterly)

***Journal of the National Medical Association***
292 Madison Avenue
New York, NY 10017
Cir. 24,000
(monthly)

***Journal of National Black Associations***
Charles Williams-Kerr Enterprises, Inc.
Box 2063
Hyattsville, MD 20784
(quarterly)

***Journal of Negro Education***
Howard University, Bureau of Educational Research
2400 Sixth Avenue N.W.
Washington, DC 20059
Cir. 3,000
(quarterly)

***Journal of Negro History***
Association for the Study of Afro-American Life and History
1407 14th Street N.W.
Washington, DC 20005
Cir. 6,500
(quarterly)

***Maroon Tiger***
Morehouse College
Atlanta, GA 30314
Cir. 2,000
(every three weeks)

***Morehouse College Bulletin; The Alumnus***
Morehouse College
Public Relations and Alumni Affairs
Atlanta, GA 30314
Cir. 6,500
(quarterly)

***Negro History Bulletin***
Association for the Study of Afro-American Life and History
1407 14th Street N.W.
Washington, DC 20005
Cir. 22,000
(bi-monthly)

***Southern Digest***
Southern University
Baton Rouge, LA 70813
Cir. 10,000
(weekly)

***Urban League Review***
(National Urban League Research Department)
Transaction Periodicals Consortium
Rutgers University
New Brunswick, NJ 08903
(semiannually)

## Religious Publications

***AME Church Review***
African Methodist Episcopal Church
468 Lincoln Drive N.W.
Atlanta, GA 30318
Cir. 4,500
(quarterly)

***American Baptist***
American Baptist Churches in the U.S.A.
Valley Forge, PA 19481
Cir. 122,000
(monthly)

***Baptist Leader***
Baptist Churches in the U.S.A.
Baptist Board of Educational Ministries
Valley Forge, PA 19481
Cir. 17,000
(monthly)

***Journal of Religious Thought***
Howard University Divinity School
2900 Van Ness Street N.W.
Washington, DC 20008
Cir. 400
(semiannually)

***Message***
Southern Publishing Association
1900 Elm Hill Pike
Nashville, TN 37202
Cir. 75,000-125,000
(bi-monthly)

***Star of Zion***
African Methodist Episcopal Zion Church
PO Box 31005
Charlotte, NC 20202
Cir. 6,200
(weekly)

***Voice of Mission***
African Methodist Episcopal Church
475 Riverside Drive
New York, NY 10027
Cir. 3,500
(monthly)

## TELEVISION

### The 1970s

The mid-1970s saw a mixed picture of black progress in television. Black performers and programs of interest to blacks were slowly increasing, but there were no black-owned conventional television stations in the United States. A black-led group in Detroit did hold a license and expected to start a station soon (WGPR), and Howard University was expected to launch a station in 1976. One cable-operating station in Gary, Indiana was black-owned.

Outside the continental United States, WSVI-TV in Christiansted, Virgin Islands, was owned by blacks.

The importance of black ownership was underscored by the paucity of black programming by the major networks. No network had, in 1975, a program concerned with the needs or history of the black community; such undertakings were restricted to special one-time efforts, like *The Autobiography of Miss Jane Pittman* 1974), a CBS venture which was nominated for nine Emmy Awards and won two.

Major network news programs also omitted blacks, especially programs of the question and answer type where reporters interview political leaders. Black journalists rarely appeared on CBS's *Face the Nation* or ABC's *Issues and Answers*.

Blacks were, however, given greater exposure as performers, in such light entertainment programs as *Good Times* and the *Flip Wilson Show*, and they did appear more frequently in local news programming. The 1974 season brought about a new comedy series, That's *My Mama,* starring Clifton Davis and Theresa Merritt, while *Sanford and Son* continued. In the adventure realm, former *Laugh-In* star Theresa Graves became the title character in a woman detective series entitled *Get Christie Love*.

Following the success of *Jane Pittman,* plays by Alice Childress and Lonnie Elder III-namely *Wedding Band* and *Ceremonies in Dark Old Men*-—were brought to the home screen.

In New York, WABC had been successful with the cultural affairs program *Like It Is* since 1967. A loss to blacks in the New York area was the decision by CBS, Channel 2, to drop Black Arts, a weekly 30-minute program devoted to the cultural and intellectual contributions of black Americans.

A strong record for black broadcasters and performers had been turned in by station WAGA, Atlanta.

### The 1980s

By the 1980s, television had become a dominant force in the lifestyle of most Americans, including blacks. No longer a luxury but a fixture in most households, it played for an average of nearly seven hours a day and generated a profound effect on those viewers who sought it for entertainment and information. As years passed, new records were being set as estimated audiences exceeded 100 million on popular entertainment and sports broadcasts.

For all of its inherent influence, there was perhaps no single industry more sensitive to the concerns of its huge, multifaceted constituency.

Though some groups and individuals had voiced anger over portrayals by black actors and actresses in such series as *Amos 'n' Andy*, *Beulah,* and *The Jack Benny Show,* it wasn't until the 1970s that a concerted effort evolved from several quarters. With the realization that the resolve of advocacy from the outside was not always sufficient to make an impression, blacks working within the industry began to work toward the goal of building a more representative minority presence in what went out over the airwaves as well as in the creative, technical, and management work force.

In addition, Benjamin Hooks and Tyrone Brown were able to add their voices to the minority cause as members of the Federal Communications Commission, the government body assigned to regulate the broadcast industry and insure that each broadcasting organization only receives a license as long as it continues to meet the needs of its viewing audience.

Commercial television touched the sensibilities of viewers through a combination of news presentations, entertainment programming, and the incessant commercials that keep the industry alive. With hour after hour spent by adults and

*A scene from NBC's powerful dramatization of the life of Martin Luther King, Jr., with Paul Winfield and Cicely Tyson.*

impressionable children day after day, many observers began to develop an increased awareness of the impact the medium was having on its viewers.

The first object of attention, of course, was the programming on the air. Of all the shows on the air starring or featuring blacks in prominent roles, situation comedies consistently proved to be the most popular with viewing audiences. Not every program proved successful, but series like *Sanford and Son,* often ranked as the top show of the week, and *The Jeffersons,* also a regular among the top 10 shows, were excellent examples.

As these series came and went, however, there was one major miniseries that captivated 130 million viewers for a solid week and certainly became the media story involving black television for the decade. The program was called *Roots* and for eight consecutive nights, in early 1977, it captured the interest of American viewers like few programs ever aired prior to that time. The dramatization of Alex Haley's best-selling book tracing his ancestry back to Africa, the program was praised for more than its entertainment value. Following its presentation, National Urban League director Vernon Jordan described Roots as "the single most spectacular educational experience in race relations in America."

The *Roots* experience certainly had a profound impact on the television industry as well as the American public. It was not only a symbol of pride but of hope that the drama's success might signal a shift in programming depicting the many aspects of the black experience in America. It was not long before most observers were disappointed.

When NBC-TV broadcast a powerful dramatization of the life of Dr. Martin Luther King Jr. a few months later (with the full cooperation of Coretta King), the program was roundly criticized by black leaders and failed to attract a substantial audience. Following a new trend of presenting programs about factual individuals, the networks presented television films about people like Harriet Tubman (*A Woman Called Moses*), Olympic gold medalist Wilma Rudolph (*Wilma*), and baseball great Satchel Paige (*Don't Look Back*). During this period there was also a dramatization of a sensational Deep South rape trial (*Judge Horton and the Scottsboro Boys*), and Cicely Tyson starred in *The Marva Collins Story*.

Alex Haley wrote a sequel to *Roots,* which picked up the story and traced his family tree into the twentieth century. While not as spectacularly successful as the initial presentation, it did attract a large audience. During this time, some of America's most prominent black stage-trained actors moved to Hollywood. When series like *Paris* with James Earl Jones and *The Lazarus Syndrome* starring Lou Gossett failed, however, there appeared to be a general rejection of blacks in serious roles.

From time to time, there were dramas written by blacks that garnered critical acclaim, if not substantial ratings success. Melvin Van Peebles wrote *The Sophisticated Gents* while Maya Angelou adapted her book, *I Know Why a Caged Bird Sings* and wrote *Sister, Sister*.

All the while, the new comedy series blossomed. *Sanford* was brought back for a brief unsuccessful run while new shows proliferated. Among the titles were *Good Times, One in a Million, What's Happening, That's My Mama, Baby, I'm Back, Benson, Diff'rent Strokes,* and *Gimme a Break*.

While there was concern about many of the previously mentioned programs, nothing rallied the black community to action like *Beulah Land*, an NBC miniseries about the Deep South during the antebellum period. Basically the story of a strong-willed woman who persevered through hardships before, during, and after the Civil War, the program ran into protests about its characterization of black slaves even as it was being filmed. As the highly publicized outcry grew, the network held meetings with concerned blacks and the program was postponed from the initial telecast time. It eventually did air (with moderate ratings success), but the episode marked an important time for blacks who had banded together and strongly expressed their discontent, bringing about some changes in the roles portrayed by black actors and actresses.

One of the issues raised during the *Beulah Land* controversy was that attacking television programming would have the ultimate effect of forcing black talent out of work when the protests succeeded. This was a sensitive issue since most black actors and actresses were out of work at any given time. Among many of television's most successful series, blacks were able to work in roles that did not emphasize their race. Ron Glass portrayed a detective in *Barney Miller*, Ted Lange an amiable bartender in *Love Boat*, and Madge Sinclair a nurse in *Trapper John, M.D.*

Yet there was a prevailing feeling that blacks were underrepresented in prime-time television. Daytime dramas, also known as soap operas, grew in audience interest—expanding from its traditional base of women at home to college students, professionals, and others. Here again, there were times when some of the 14 or so programs had no blacks in the casts at all.

*KNXT-TV, Los Angeles's* Insider Outsider *discusses vital civic issues each Sunday morning*

During the mid to latter part of the 1980s, more and more blacks were seen on television sitcoms, soap operas and variety and special programs.

The Cosby Show continued to pull in high ratings and became the top rated show on television. A spinoff of The Cosby Show, "A Different World," continued to draw a huge viewing audience. Other shows pulling in high ratings included "Amen" starring Sherman Helmsley and Clifton Davis, and "227" with Marla Gibbs, Hal Williams and Jackee.

Even though there were popular series like *Fat Albert* (inspired by the Bill Cosby characters) and *The Jackson Five* (based on the teen rock group) on Saturday morning children's television schedules, these animated series were the symbol of hope for more programming in this part of the weekly network schedules.

While the battle for more input continued in the entertainment realm, news grew to become more and more important on the networks as well. As surveys continued to indicate that more and more Americans were getting most of their awareness of world events from television, there were increased efforts to seek more black participation in news gathering and reporting.

On the network level, Max Robinson became the first black to become a regular co-anchor for an evening news program when he joined ABC-TV's *World News Tonight*. Bryant Gumble, a versatile sportscaster, also made news in early 1982 when he became the first black co-host for NBC's *Today* show. Irv Crosse, a former athlete, became a regular CBS sportscaster, providing expert commentary during the professional football season.

There are over 1,000 television stations in the United States—some affiliated with the networks, others independent, and still others part of the educational television operation. At the beginning of the 1980s, only eight of those stations were owned by blacks.

Several other television stations across the country also came under black ownership with one noticeable acquisition in Buffalo, New York where a group of investors which included businessman Bruce Llwellyan and basketball superstar Julius "Dr. J" Ervin added to the number of minority owned stations.

More black women were seen as anchors and reporters on major market television stations during this period. However there was a lack of males anchoring news either alongside a white male or a white female.

Black men seemingly have lost ground in television news and are exiting the industry. Many are finding themselves in dead-end jobs and are not finding television as attractive as it once was.

A high proportion of new hires have been women and in most cases they have been put into positions formerly held by men because they would work for lower pay.

However, despite the high proportion of hiring by television stations, stations with minority representation have stayed about the same from 1972 to 1986.

## Public Television

The hopes of many blacks for programming rested in programs like those produced on the local level. Tony Brown, former Dean of the Howard University School of Communications, continued to produce *The Tony Brown Journal*. The oldest and only black public affairs program in the country, it remained a victim to erratic scheduling in many cities. *For You Black Woman,* another syndicated program aimed at black women, suffered a similar fate. With all that the networks might do, the hope of many was that a valuable alternative would provide more of those black-produced programs to add a balance to the images that had become a way of life for so many black Americans.

*Bryant Gumble, anchorman of NBC's* Today Show.

## Cable Television

The most significant development in broadcasting and the one deemed to have the most impact on television in the future was the advent of cable or pay television. Conceived as an alternative to network television, the systems seemed initially geared to viewers with specialized tastes. Most prominent among the programming were movies, shown without commercials and material edited out by the networks when deemed objectionable.

Soon there was a network broadcasting sports 24 hours a day and another bringing news around the clock. As more systems began and diversified their programming, cable began to grow at an increasing pace. Soon, there was a discernible decline in network viewing.

Without question, cable will be a major, if not predominant, medium of the 1980s and beyond. There had been hope that blacks would be able to capitalize on the growing medium and become owners of cable systems since many of the early franchises were in large cities with significant black populations. When it became obvious that this was a lucrative market to be tapped, many large corporations seeking to diversify joined in competing for the chance to operate a system.

Still, some black-owned companies like Inner City Broadcasting in New York City have successfully bid for systems.

Black Entertainment Television distributes black programming to systems around the country and televises a mix of pubic service programming, news, entertainment and sports featuring football and basketball from Historically Black Colleges.

*Clarence Jones, lawyer, publisher, broadcast executive.*

Local cable companies have begun to televise public affairs programs, local meetings as well as variety programs and independent producers have begun to use the cable systems to develop their own programming. However prospective cable owners are finding that the biggest obstacle is in the funding, not only to buy the systems but to construct them and to operate them.

## RADIO

With a faithful and loyal audience, radio stations with programming geared for blacks—amounting to 100— appeared to be a prominent part of a thriving industry. In the mid-1970s, some 30 of those 100 stations were owned by blacks. By 1981, the total of black-owned radio stations had increased fourfold to 130. At that time, there were more than 9,000 stations (AM, FM, and FM educational) in the United States.

Proportionally, blacks were found to be a more frequent and responsive audience than whites. As a result, astute advertisers were able to tap into a lucrative marketplace, often at the expense of traditional avenues including black newspapers and magazines. Many major corporations were among those sought to reach the ever expanding black buying power traced back to the black community. By buying time on stations with proven popularity among blacks, they received just those returns they were seeking.

With soul and jazz music broadening its appeal into the white market, a new success in building audiences was noted. One of the more spectacular examples of the phenomenon occurred with WBLS-FM in New York. Owned by Inner City Broadcasting, it became the top station in New York for an extended period of time.

With proper management, radio stations proved to be a worthy investment. Owners of individual stations were able to buy into new markets and use their expertise to build viable broadcast corporations. The number of black-owned radio stations increased to close to 200 by the latter part of the 1980s. As more and more radio stations became available across the country, many radio station owners became owners of multiple stations.

As many of the stations grew from their limited local status, there was a parallel movement to cooperate in broadcasting efforts. The National Black Network was an important example of an effort to broaden the scope of local newscasts with national reporting with a black perspective. The Sheridan Broadcasting Network with 117 AM and FM affiliates plays a dominant role expanding the scope of national reporting into black communities across the country.

Clearly, the most successful enterprise involving blacks in all of the media, radio—despite obstacles that remain until today—will establish a pattern proving that responsible black ownership and programming can meet the needs of a diversified audience and lead to a medium that entertains and informs just the way it was conceived to do.

## RADIO AND TELEVISION PERSONAGES

### DENISE BAKER
### NBC News Correspondent

NBC News Correspondent Denise Baker joined the Northeast Bureau of NBC News in January 1981. Based in New York, Baker covers stories throughout the Northeast.

She joined NBC News in July 1979 as a correspondent in Pittsburgh, and until her move to New York, covered stories in the Pittsburgh area, western Pennsylvania, southwestern New York, West Virginia, Ohio, and Kentucky.

Before joining NBC News she was a correspondent for WETA-TV, the PBS station in Washington, D.C. (from April 1978) and covered local and national affairs. Among her assignments was anchoring the WETA special program *Who Killed King?*, telecast nationally on the PBS Network. For her work in public affairs she was nominated for two Emmy Awards.

She began her broadcasting career in September 1974, at WGN Radio in Chicago, where she produced the station's late-night talk program, "Extension 720," during which listeners phoned in their opinions on a variety of topics.

Baker was born in Chicago. She was graduated from Yale University with a B.A. degree in English and received her masters degree from the Medill School of Journalism at Northwestern University.

*J. Tuber Bolden Jr. is an executive with NBC-TV.*

### J. TABER BOLDEN JR.
### Vice President, Station Affairs
### NBC-TV

After serving three years as Station Manager of WRC-TV, the NBC television station in Washington, D.C., J. Taber Bolden Jr. was named to the newly created position of Vice President, Station Affairs, NBC Television Stations. The appointment was effective in December 1976.

Before joining WRC-TV, Bolden had been Director, Personnel of NBC Washington. He came to the network after working for RCA for 12 years. He began his career at NBC as an administrator of training in January 1968 and was later promoted to Director, Management Development, a position he held until his move to Washington.

Bolden started with RCA as a Training Specialist in the Engineering Personnel area in Camden, New Jersey, in 1955. In 1961 he moved to the RCA Aerospace Systems Division and held other positions until his move to NBC.

A native of Cleveland, Bolden received a B.A. degree in psychology from Boston University and a masters degree in education. He also did postgraduate study in behavioral science at Temple University.

### ANNA MONIQUE BOND
### NBC News

Anna Monique Bond began her WABC-TV New York career in November 1970 as an administrative assistant to the Director of Local News and Public Affairs.

Prior to her appointment as a reporter in August 1973, Bond was a WABC-TV news writer for the station's news program telecast during the early morning *A.M. New York* series. She also served as a part-time producer of weekend news programs, as a remote and field producer for various local news stories and features, and prepared news copy and edited film for presentation on the 6 and 11 o'clock editions of *Eyewitness News*.

Bond has also been a news researcher and assistant to the station's Vice President and General Manager and administrative assistant to the News and Public Affairs Director.

Bond joined NBC-TV in New York in 1982 and now co-anchors the local weekend news programs.

### ED BRADLEY
### Co-Editor, 60 Minutes
### CBS-TV

Ed Bradley replaced Dan Rather as a co-editor of *60 Minutes*, the weekly news magazine at the beginning of the 1981-1982 season. Prior to that, he had been a principal correspondent for CBS *Reports* since September 1978. From November 1976 until that time, he had served as CBS News White House Correspondent. In addition to CBS *Reports*, Bradley had been anchor of the CBS *Sunday Night News* from November 1976 to May 1981. Bradley's new duties included being co-anchor of CBS News daytime broadcast, *Up to the Minute*.

After working as a reporter for WDAS Radio in Philadelphia, Bradley was a reporter for WCBS Radio in New York. He joined CBS News as a stringer in the Paris Bureau in 1971. In a few months, he was transferred to the Saigon Bureau, where he remained until he was assigned to the CBS News Washington Bureau in June 1974. He had been named a correspondent in April 1973.

His documentary assignments include *What's Happened to Cambodia?, CBS Reports: The Boat People, The Boston Goes to China, and Blacks in America: With All Deliberate Speed?* His other assignments include reports broadcast on "CBS Evening News with Walter Cronkite," "CBS News Sunday Morning," and "CBS News Magazine."

A native of Pennsylvania, Bradley received a B.S. degree in education from Cheyney State College in Cheyney, Pennsylvania.

### JAROBIN GILBERT JR.
### Vice President, NBC-TV

Jarobin Gilbert Jr. was named to the newly created position of Vice President, NBC Television Network in February 1981. Previously, he was Vice President, Olympic Administration, and Director, Olympic Administration, NBC Sports. He had joined the company in November 1977 and was responsible for the coordination of planning for the network's 1980 Olympic coverage (ultimately canceled when President Carter called a boycott of the Moscow games).

*Ed Bradley, TV news journalist and co-editor of* 60 Minutes.

*Television news reporter Anna Bond covering an outdoor concert at Lincoln Center in New York City.*

*Mal Goode reported from the United Nations.*

Prior to joining NBC, Gilbert was associated with the US-USSR Trade and Economic Council in Moscow as a Director of Projects. He worked with the State Department/U.S. Information Agency before joining the US-USSR Council. An internationalist by training, he reads, writes, and speaks several languages including Russian, French, and German.

Gilbert is a graduate of Harvard University, where he emphasized linguistics and Slavic languages. He also studied international law and Soviet law at Columbia University.

## MAL GOODE
### ABC News Correspondent

Mal Goode had been with the *Pittsburgh Courier* 14 years when in 1962 he joined ABC to cover the United Nations. His first test was the Cuban missile crisis, just two months later, during which Goode distinguished himself with incisive TV and radio reports during the long hours of U.N. debate.

Goode was born in White Plains, Virginia; educated in the public schools of Homestead, Pennsylvania; and graduated from the University of Pittsburgh. He was employed for 12 years as a laborer in the steel mills while in high school and college and for five years after graduation. In 1936, he was appointed to a post in Juvenile Court and became Boys Work Director of the Centre Avenue Y.M.C.A., where he led the fight to eliminate discrimination in Pittsburgh branches of the Y.

Goode served with the Pittsburgh Housing Authority for six years and in 1948 joined the *Pittsburgh Courier*. The following year he started a career in radio with station KQV, doing a 15-minute news show two nights each week. In 1950, he started a five minute daily news program on WHOD.

Goode was named News Director of WHOD in 1952. He and his sister, the late Mary Dee, had the only brother-sister team in radio for six years. He was the first black to hold membership in the National Association of Radio and TV News Directors.

For two months, in 1963, he joined with three colleagues to conduct courses in journalism for 104 African students in seminars at Lagos, Nigeria; Addis Ababa, Ethiopia; and Dar es Salaam, Tanzania.

## GORDON GRAHAM
### NBC News Correspondent

Gordon Graham has been an NBC News correspondent in Washington, D.C., since January 1971, covering the House of Representatives and general assignments.

Between 1968 and 1971, he was a news reporter for two years for KNBC Television, Los Angeles. Prior to joining KNBC he was a reporter and writer for KRON, San Francisco.

Graham was born in Coshocton, Ohio, in 1936. He majored in broadcasting at Ohio University and was graduated with a B.F.A. degree in 1958. His first news job from 1962 to 1965 was with KGFJ, a Los Angeles radio station, first as a reporter, subsequently as a News Director.

*Bryant Gumbel, anchorman for NBC-TV's* Today.

### BRYANT GUMBLE
### Co-Anchor, Today
### NBC TV

Bryant Gumble was named co-anchor (with Jane Pauley) of *Today* in January 1981—the first black in such a regular position on the long-running NBC News morning program. In 1989 the team of Gumble and Pauley was still running strong.

Prior to that time, Gumble had made regular sports reports on *Today*, although his primary responsibilities were with NBC Sports as host of pregame programming during coverage of the National Football League, Major League Baseball, and other sports broadcasts.

He began his broadcasting career in October 1972 when he was named a weekend sportscaster for KNBC, the NBC station in Los Angeles. Within a year, he became weekday sportscaster and was appointed the station's Sports Director in 1976. He remained in that post until July 1980.

Prior to embarking on his career in television, Gumble was a sports writer. After submitting his first piece to *Black Sports* magazine in 1971, he was given additional free-lance assignments and was soon hired as a staff writer. Within eight months he was elevated to Editor-in-Chief.

A native of New Orleans, Gumble grew up in Chicago. He received a liberal arts degree from Bates College in Lewiston, Maine in 1970.

*Carol Jenkins reports the news on NBC-TV.*

### EUGENE D. JACKSON
### Broadcast Executive

Eugene D. Jackson is president of Unity Broadcasting Network in New York City, parent company of the National Black Network, and of four radio stations of which Jackson is also president—WDAS-AM and FM in Philadelphia and KATZ-AM and WZEN-FM in St. Louis.

Jackson was born in Wauhomis, Oklahoma on September 5, 1943. He received a B.S. degree from the University of Missouri at Rolla in 1967 and an M.S. from Columbia University in 1971.

Jackson serves on the boards of directors of the National Association of Broadcasters, the Council of Concerned Black Executives Freedom National Bank, and Trans Africa (1977). He was a member of the Council on Foreign Relations in 1978 and on the board of governors of the International Radio and TV Society from 1974 to 1976.

From 1969 to 1971, he directed major industry programs for the Interracial Council for Business Opportunity in New York City. He was a production and project engineer for the Black Economic Union in New York City from 1968 to 1969 and an industrial engineer for Colgate-Palmolive from 1967 to 1968.

### CAROL JENKINS
### NBC News

Carol Jenkins has learned the value of a broad knowledge during her experience as a network correspondent for ABC News, as a reporter and anchorwoman for WOR-TV, and since February, 1973 with WNBC-TV, where she was a general assignment reporter, and anchored the 1 A.M. news.

With WNBC-TV, Jenkins has also covered returning POWs and interviewed New York City Mayors Lindsay and Beame, Governors Rockefeller and Wilson, and Senators Javits and Buckley.

Jenkins was born in Montgomery Alabama, in 1944 and moved with her family to Jamaica, New York, when she was three. She attended Boston University where she received a B.A. She also has a M.A. from New York University.

Honors as a broadcaster include the Harlem Preparatory School Service Award (1971), Ophelia DeVore School, Outstanding Achievement Award (1972), and Alabama State University Alumni Association Outstanding Achievement Award (1972).

### JOHN JOHNSON
### ABC News

WABC-TV *Eyewitness News* reporter John Johnson was born in Harlem and grew up in the Bedford-Stuyvesant section of Brooklyn, New York. Johnson received his masters degree with honors from the City University of New York. After six years with the New York Board of Education as a teacher, dean of students, and assistant principal, he became Associate Professor of Fine Arts at Lincoln University. From Lincoln, Johnson won a fellowship to Indiana University to complete his Ph.D. in the Arts.

From 1968 to 1971, Johnson was with ABC network

*TV newsman John Johnson has won acclaim as a producer, writer, and director of network documentaries*

documentaries, during which time he rose from an associate producer to producer/director/writer. Included among his documentaries was the widely acclaimed *To All the World's Children*, narrated by Rod Steiger, for which Johnson won a Christopher Award for his directing.

Johnson has also won acclaim as writer/narrator for the Emmy Award-winning *People, Places and Things* program dealing with natural childbirth.

## ROYAL KENNEDY
## ABC News Chicago Correspondent

Royal Kennedy was named an ABC News Chicago Correspondent in April 1978. Kennedy had been a reporter for WMAQ-TV since June 1975. She was a general assignment reporter, anchored a consumer segment of the station's *Beat the System* series, and anchored local newscasts during the *Today* show telecasts on WMAQ.

She began her news career as a copy editor and researcher for *Playboy* magazine in Chicago in June 1969, and then joined WDSU-TV, New Orleans, in September 1971. She was a general assignment reporter and anchored local newscasts during the *Today* show.

Kennedy moved on to WKYC-TV, the NBC-owned station in Cleveland, in April 1973, to become a general assignment reporter, host of a weekly public affairs program, and anchor person for *Today* show local newscasts.

The recipient of numerous awards and honors, Kennedy won a Cleveland Emmy for "outstanding individual achievement" as a producer-reporter of a five-part series on rape. The rape series also earned her a citation for "excellence in reporting a legal issue" from the American Association of Trial Lawyers. She has also received a San Francisco State Journalism Award for a five-part series on abortion, which she produced and reported.

Kennedy majored in history at Ohio University. She attended Dartmouth College and studied journalism at Columbia University.

## EMERY KING
## NBC News Correspondent

As of April 1980, Emery King became an NBC News correspondent, based in Washington, D.C., on general assignment. Prior to joining NBC News, King had been a reporter covering politics and the Illinois State House for WBBM-TV, Chicago, since 1977. From 1973 until 1977, he was a reporter/anchor with WBBM News Radio in that city.

Between 1972 and 1973, King was with radio station WWCA in Gary, Indiana, as a reporter, and during the period from 1970 to 1972 he held the same post with radio station WJOB in Hammond, Indiana. From 1967 until 1971, he attended Purdue University studying speech and drama.

## LEON LEWIS
## Radio Commentator

The Peabody Award citation received by Harlem radio station WLIB in 1966 was a milestone in the career of dialogue jockey Leon Lewis, now Ombudsman for WMCA's *Call for Action*. The WLIB show hosted by Lewis consisted of any early evening talk marathon (*Community Opinion*) in which ghetto residents could voice their grievances, air their feelings, and, perhaps more importantly, take advantage of under publicized community services available to deal with specific problems.

Lewis frequently cultivated relationships with local legal, educational, and political experts who volunteered free advisory and consulting services. To their surprise and dismay, they often found themselves squirming nervously under a constant barrage of pointed questions. Lewis generally stayed out of the fray, except for an occasional quiet and philosophical remark that brought the confrontations to a satisfying close.

Still, by abating many tensions, WLIB, in the words of the Peabody citation, "gave Harlem a safety valve". It developed *Community Opinion*, a radio program permitting citizens of Harlem to voice their feelings, frankly and openly, via a hot line telephone interview, heard not only by the Negro community, but by the entire city.

*Leon Lewis opened the radio microphones to the Harlem Community.*

"In addition, the station provided details of how listeners could avail themselves of existing vital community service. At WLIB community involvement is more than just a station phrase." In recognition, WLIB received a Peabody Award for outstanding local radio education during 1966.

Veteran newsman Lewis, born in Troy, New York in 1917, has worked in a variety of radio and journalism jobs, including that of sales manager for an Albany station and circulation manager for the *Amsterdam News*. Glib and resourceful, he was not able to break into New York radio at first, but he found a ready career on the ethnic air waves.

After his success at WLIB, however, opportunity beckoned, and Lewis joined WMCA as Assistant Public Affairs Director in 1967. Over the years, several of his documentaries won prestigious journalism awards and even led to a teaching career at Fordham University.

Nothing seems to satisfy Lewis better than his early morning rendezvous with the unpredictable and fascinating potpourri of characters who vie for attention on his show, constantly seeking to either put him on the defensive or joke about his own idiosyncrasies.

For Lewis, though, there has always been a discernible mission to be accomplished at his secluded outpost. While at WLIB, he once found succinct words to sum it up: "The walls of the ghetto are so high," he said, "that people can't see in and they can't see out. I'd like to see those walls come tumbling down."

## ROBERT W. MATTHEWS
## NBC Radio News Manager

Robert W. Matthews, Manager, NBC Radio News, in Washington, D.C. supervises and coordinates the gathering of news stories for local and national presentation.

Prior to joining NBC News as Duty Manager in January 1969, Matthews was a reporter/assignment editor for CBS-TV News in New York. He began his career in television in 1964 as a reporter and weekend anchorman for WBAL-TV News, Baltimore. He later became News Manager, the first black newsman in the country to assume that post at a major TV station.

Matthews got his start in journalism in 1948 with the Afro-American Newspaper chain in Baltimore. His 15 years in various news posts with that organization culminated in his assignment as editor of the magazine section.

Before joining WEBB Radio in Baltimore in 1963 as news director, he worked for the Annapolis *Evening Capitol* and Baltimore *News-American* newspapers.

A native of Detroit, Matthews attended Lane College in Jackson, Tennessee, and Wayne State University in Detroit.

## GIL NOBLE
## ABC News

Channel 7's *Eyewitness News* late-night weekend anchorman Gil Noble has been honored with several professional awards, including an Emmy for hosting *Like It Is*.

In addition, Noble has been honored with the Golden Mike Award of the National Association of Television and Radio Artists, and the John B. Russwurm Award of the New York Urban League.

In 1975, Noble was artist in residence at Seton Hall University, Orange, New Jersey, where he teaches two courses, the first time a black journalist has appeared and become involved in the Communications Department at Seton Hall.

In October 1971, Noble hosted the first televised program ever devoted to sickle cell anemia. The *Like It Is* special, *Attica: The Unanswered Questions,* co-hosted by Noble and Geraldo Rivera, won a Tonge Shaeffer Award.

*Jazz: The American Art Form,* a documentary produced by Noble in October 1972, was another unprecedented step for black representation in the media.

Born and raised in Harlem, Noble taught himself to play the piano and became one of the leading pianists in New York City. He is a graduate of DeWitt Clinton High School in the Bronx and attended City College at night.

Noble spent two years in the Army Medical Corps. When back in New York, he worked as a clerk and occasionally as a male model. In 1962, he became a part-time announcer for WLIB-Radio. At this time, he also had a professional music combo, *The Gil Noble Trio,* which was playing at night clubs in New York. He auditioned for WABC-TV in 1967 and his first assignment was coverage of the Newark riots. His work there landed him the job and Noble has been reporting for Channel 7 ever since.

*Gil Noble of ABC-TV has a weekly news feature,* Like It Is, *as well as reporting duties.*

*Norma Quarles, NBC news correspondent based in Chicago.*

## NORMA QUARLES
## NBC News Correspondent

Norma Quarles became an NBC News correspondent based in Chicago in October 1978. She had been producing and reporting the *Urban Journal* series for *Newscenter 5* at WMAQ-TV for a year at that time.

Before joining WMAQ, Quarles was an award-winning reporter for *Newscenter 4* on WNBC-TV in New York, where she also anchored the early local news broadcasts during the *Today* show.

A native New Yorker and an alumna of Hunter College and City College of New York, Quarles worked as a buyer for a New York specialty shop before moving to Chicago where she became a licensed real estate broker. In 1965, she began her broadcast career in Chicago at WSDM Radio, working as a news reporter and disk jockey. She later returned to New York where she joined NBC in 1966 for a one-year training program. After three years with WKYC-TV in Cleveland, she was transferred to WNBC-TV where in 1973 she won a Front Page Award and a Sigma Delta Chi Deadline Club Award for her film story *The Stripper.*

## STANLEY ROBERTSON
## NBC Vice President

Stanley Robertson, Vice President, Motion Pictures for Television, NBC-TV joined NBC-TV in 1957 as a page and served in the Music Library and Music Rights Department.

In 1965, he was named Manager, Film Program Operations, West Coast. He was promoted to Director, Motion Pictures for Television, in March 1970, and elevated to Vice President in April 1971.

A native of Los Angeles, Robertson graduated from Los Angeles City College and then majored in telecommunications for three years at the University of Southern California. While at college he was a reporter for the Los Angeles *Sentinal* and an associate editor of *Ebony* magazine.

In 1975, Robertson was a member of the Board of Directors of the Hollywood Radio and Television Society and served on the Board of Governors, Hollywood Chapter, National Academy of Television Arts and Sciences.

### MAX ROBINSON
### ABC News Correspondent

Max Robinson joined ABC News in June 1978 as head of the National Desk in Chicago on *ABC News World News Tonight*. The new program premiered in July 1978. Robinson covers major news events that occur in the heartland of the nation and anchors the evening news from the Midwest. He is the first network anchorman to broadcast regularly from a city other than New York or Washington.

Robinson came to ABC News for WTOP-TV in Washington, D.C., where he had been anchoring the station's *Eyewitness News* since 1969. He also anchored news specials and public affairs programs for that station. He received widespread praise last year for his coverage of the Hanafi Muslim siege in the nation's capital.

Robinson had been a correspondent for WRC-TV in Washington from 1966 until 1969. There he anchored the *Today in Washington Early Morning News* and covered Capitol Hill, the White House, and the District Building.

He began his career as a studio floor director at WTOP-TV in 1965, becoming a news reporter shortly thereafter. He is the recipient of three Emmy Awards, the Capital Press Club Journalist of the Year Award, and the Ohio State Award, as well as an award from the National Education Association.

An accomplished painter, he has taught communicative arts and television production at Federal City College. He attended Oberlin College and learned Russian as a language specialist in the Air Force Language Institute at Indiana University.

Robinson helped found the Association of Black Journalists, a group whose efforts are aimed at encouraging blacks in journalism.

### BARBARA ROWAN
### NBC News Correspondent

Barbara Rowan has been a correspondent based in the Houston bureau since she joined NBC News in January 1981. Before that, she had been a reporter/anchor for WDIV-TV, the NBC affiliate in Detroit, from August 1978. She covered the Republican National Convention in that city in 1980.

Rowan was a reporter and weekend anchor for WDTN-TV, the NBC affiliate in Dayton, Ohio in 1977-1978, and covered the school desegregation hearings and the United Mineworkers' strike, among other stories. From September 1975 to August 1977, she was a reporter, anchor, and program host for WKBW-TV, the ABC affiliate in Buffalo, New York.

She has won numerous honors for her work in broadcasting, including the Michigan Education Association's School Bell Award in 1980 for "outstanding and objective reporting" of the lengthy Armada (Michigan) teachers' strike. In 1978, she won a Distinguished Service Award in Newscasting and Communication from St. Agnes Parish in Dayton. She received a Special Services Award in 1977 from the Western New York Chapter of the National Society for Autistic Children. In 1976, she won the Black Achievement in Industry Award from the Community Action Foundation in Buffalo, and was named Outstanding Woman of the Year by the Niagara Falls Professional and Businesswoman's Association.

### BERNARD SHAW
### CNN News Correspondent

Bernard Shaw is currently the Washington correspondent for the Cable News Network (CNN). Previously Shaw was with ABC News as Miami Bureau Chief in 1977. He later became a correspondent for the CBS News Washington Bureau. While at CBS he broke the story that Representative Wayne Hays would resign. He also did an exclusive interview

*Bernard Shaw is CNN's chief Washington correspondent.*

with Attorney General John Mitchell at the height of the Watergate scandal. Shaw filed a major report on marijuana for the *CBS Evening News,* following travel and research in the South and Midwest.

Shaw wrote and anchored radio newscasts and did the same on the *Washington Week* program. He was a special correspondent on the children's specials *What's an Election About* and *What the Oil Crisis Is About.*

Prior to joining CBS News, Shaw was a reporter for Group W, Westinghouse Broadcasting Company, based first in Chicago and then in Washington (1966-1971). Shaw served as Group W's White House Correspondent during the last year of the Johnson Administration (1968). His other assignments included local and national urban affairs, the struggles of the Mexican Americans and Puerto Ricans, and the plight of the American Indians in Billings, Montana. In 1966, he reported on the aftermath of the assassination of Dr. Martin Luther King Jr. in Memphis and his funeral in Atlanta.

Born in Chicago, Shaw attended the University of Illinois, Chicago Circle Campus, where he majored in history.

### PIERRE MONTEA (PEPE) SUTTON
### Broadcast Executive

Pierre Sutton is President of Inner City Broadcasting Corporation in New York City and President of its radio stations in New York and California. He is the son of Percy E. Sutton, chairman of the board of Inner City Broadcasting and former Borough President of Manhattan.

*Veteran executive producer Lem Tucker.*

*Bob Teague, NBC-TV special assignments reporter.*

Pierre Sutton was born in New York City on February 1, 1947. He received a B.A. degree from the University of Toledo in 1968 and attended New York University in 1972.

He began his career in 1971 as Vice President of Inner City Research and Analysis Corporation, was Executive Editor of the *New York Courier* newspaper in 1971-1972, served as Public Affairs Director for WLIB radio from 1972 to 1975, was Vice President of Inner City Broadcasting from 1975 to 1977, and became President in 1977.

During the past decade he has served as a board member of the Minority Investment Fund, First Vice President of the National Association of Black Owned Broadcasters, Chairman of the Harlem Boy Scouts, member of the board and executive committee of the New York City Marathon, a trustee of the Alvin Ailey Dance Foundation, a board member of the Better Business Bureau of Harlem, and a member of the board of the Hayden Planetarium.

### BOB TEAGUE
### NBC News

Bob Teague has been an anchorman for late night news, a moderator and panelist for interview programs, and a sportscaster.

Teague was born in Milwaukee in 1929. In 1950 he received a B.S. degree in journalism from the University of Wisconsin, where he starred in football.

Following his graduation, the *Milwaukee Journal* provided

a wide scope for his talents: he covered sports, wrote book reviews, and served as a reporter. At the *New York Times,* starting in 1956, Teague covered a variety of sports events.

He has been honored with the Amistad Award from the American Missionary Association "for his dignity and journalistic skill."

He has written three books, *Climate of Opinion* published in 1962, *Letters To A Black Boy* in 1968, and his autobiography was published in 1982.

### LEM TUCKER
### CBS News Correspondent

Lem Tucker joined ABC News in January 1972, from WOR-TV in New York where he was News Director and an executive producer for special news presentation. He was assigned to ABC News' Chicago Bureau, and was later transferred to ABC News headquarters in New York.

From 1965 through July 1970, Tucker was with NBC News where he was awarded an Emmy for his reporting on hunger in the United States, a series of seven reports broadcast during 1968 and 1969.

A native of Saginaw, Michigan, Tucker is a graduate of Central Michigan University. He served briefly as an administrative assistant to the Auditor General of Michigan before entering the Army in 1960. He was discharged in 1962 with the rank of first lieutenant and worked in the public relations department of Buick Motors in Flint, Michigan, before joining NBC News.

## A GUIDE TO BLACK BROADCAST MEDIA

### Television

#### California

**KSTS-TV 48**
National Group Television
N. John Douglass, President
2349 Bering Drive
San Jose, CA 95131

#### Washington, D.C.

**Channel 50**
Ted Ledbetter, President
6507 Chillum Place, N.W.
Washington, DC 20012

**WHMM-TV (PBS)**
(Noncommercial)
Arnold Wallace,
General Manager
Howard University
26004th Street, N.W.
Washington, DC 20059

#### Maine

**WVII-TV**
Dr. Jasper Williams Sr.,
Chairman Seaway Comm.
41 Farm Road
Bangor, ME 04401

#### Michigan

**WGPR-TV**
WGPR, Inc.
Dr. William V. Banks, Pres.
3146 East Jefferson Street
Detroit, MI 48207

#### Mississippi

**WLBT-TV**
TV-3, Inc.
Aaron Henry, Chairman
PO Box 1712
Jackson, MS 38205

#### New Jersey

**WRBV-TV**
Renaissance Broadcasting Co.
Donald McMeans, President
145 Tyler Drive
Willingboro, NJ 08046

#### New York

**WHEC-TV**
BENI
Ragan Henry, President
191 East Avenue
Rochester, NY 14604

#### Texas

**KLBK-TV**
PRIMA, Inc.
Dr. Robert Lee, President
7400 S. University Avenue
Lubbock, TX 79408

**KTXS-TV**
PRIMA, Inc.
Dr. Robert Lee, President
PO Box 2997
Abeline, TX 79604

#### Wisconsin

**WAEO-TV**
Dr. Jasper Williams Sr.,
Chairman Seaway Comm.
Box 858
S. Oneida Avenue
Rhinelander, WI 54501

*The charming Xerona Clayton works for Ted Turner's Atlanta station.*

## Professional Media Organizations

**Amalgamated Publishers, Inc.**
John H. Sengstacke, Pres.
45 West 45th Street
New York, NY 10036
(212) 489-1220

**Black Anti-Defamation Coalition**
Robert E. Price
Executive Director,
1765 N. Highland
Box 426
Los Angeles, CA 90028

**Black Awareness in Television**
David Rambeau
Executive Director,
13217 Livernois Avenue
Detroit, MI 48238
(313)931-3427

**The Black Filmmaker Foundation**
Denise Oliver
Executive Director,
1 Centre Street
WNYC-TV 26th Floor
New York, NY 10007
(212) 619-2480

**Black Media, Inc.**
Benjamin H. Wright, President
507 5th Avenue
Suite 1101
New York, NY 10017
(212)867-0983

**Black Owned Communication Alliance**
Terrie Williams,
Executive Director
PO Box 2757
Grand Central Station
New York, NY 10017
(212) 586-0370

**The BMI Cooperative**
Calvin Rolark, Chairman
PHC, 410 Central Park W.
New York, NY 10025
(212) 222-3555

**Broadcast Enterprises Nationwide Inc.**
Ragan A. Henry, Pres.
1422 Chestnut St.
8th Floor
Philadelphia, PA 19102
(215) 563-2910

**Capital Press Club**
Janet Dewert, President
PO Box 19403
Washington, DC 20036
(202)797-3746

**Delta Sigma Theta Telecommunications, Inc.**
Mrs. Lillian Benbow, Pres.
1951 Pembridge Place
Detroit, MI 48207
(313) 483-5460

**Minority Telecommunications Corp.**
Roy Thompson, Pres.
166 Madison Avenue
New York, NY 10016
(212)686-6850

**National Association of Black Journalists**
Bob Reid, Pres.
PO Box 2089
Washington, DC 20013
(202) 737-0277

**National Association of Black Owned Broadcasters**
Nate Boyer,
Executive Director
1629 K Street, N.W.
Suite 302
Washington, DC 20006
(202) 293-1137

**National Association of Media Women**
Ella Kay Mays, Pres.
157 W. 126th Street
New York, NY 10027
(212) 666-1320

**National Black Media Coalition**
Pluria Marshall, Chairman
1802 T Street, N.W.
Suite B
Washington, DC 20009
(202) 387-8155

**National Black Network**
Eugene Jackson, Pres.
1350 Avenue of the Americas
24th Floor
New York, NY 10019
(212) 586-0610

**National Black Programming Consortium, Inc.**
Mable Haddock,
Executive Director
700 Bryden Road
Suite 135
Columbus, OH 43215
(614) 461-1536

**National Newspaper Publishers Association**
Steve Davis
Executive Director
770 National Press Building
Washington, DC 20045
(202) 638-4473

**School of Communications**
Lionel C. Barrow, Dean,
Howard University
Washington, DC 20059
(202) 636-7491

**Sheridan Broadcasting Network**
Skip Finley, Pres.
1745 S. Jefferson Davis Highway
Suite 404
Arlington, VA 22202
(703) 685-2146

## Radio

### Alabama

**WAGG - AM**
William Manney, Gen. Mgr.
1523 5th Ave.
Birmingham, AL 35203

**WAJO - AM**
Ernest Palmaer, Pres.
Drawer 930
Marion, AL 36756

**WATV - AM**
Stuart Hepburn, Pres.
BOX 39054
Birmingham, AL 35208

**WARI**
PO Box 5962
Abbieville AL. 36303

**WIZB**
PO Box 5962
Abbieville AL. 36303

**WAYE - AM**
4650 Ave. W, Suite K
Steve Green, Gen. Mgr.
Birmingham, AL 35208

**WBCF- AM**
Benny Carle, Pres.
201 N. Pine St.
Countview Towers
Florence, AL 35630

**WBIL - AM/FM**
George Clay, Gen. Mgr.
PO Box 666
Tuskegee, AL 36083

**WBLX - FM**
Larry Williams, Gen. Mgr.
PO Box 1967
Mobile, AL 36601

**WENN - AM/FM**
A. G. Gaston, Pres.
1523 5th Ave.
Birmingham, AL 35203

**WEUP - AM**
Viola Garrett, Gen. Mgr.
2609 Jordan Lane, NW
Huntsville, AL 35806

**WJLD - AM**
Alfred Bell, Gen. Mgr.
1449 Spaulding Ishkooda Rd.
Birmingham, AL 35209

**WMGL**
PO Box 408
Garden AL 35902

**WORJ - FM**
Box 1259
Ozark, AL 36361
Steve McGowan, Pres.

**WQIM - FM**
Paul H. Downs, Pres.
2137 Campbell Road
Prattville, AL 36067

**WTAK - AM**
Peter Barber, Gen. Mgr.
Box 554
Huntsville, AL 35804

**WTQX - AM**
Bob Carl Bailey, Gen. Mgr.
PO. Box 1307
Selma, AL 36701

**WTUG - FM**
James Shaw, Gen. Mgr.
142 Skyland Blvd.
Tuscaloosa, AL 35405

**WTWG - AM**
Linda F. Spivey, Pres.
Box 3800-E
Birmingham, AL 35208

**WULA - AM**
Steve McGowan, Pres.
1354 S. Eufala Ave.
Box 531
Eufaula, AL 36027

**WVAS- FM**
Alabama State University
915 S. Jackson Street
Montgomery, AL 36195

**WXAL - AM**
Nan Jordan, Pres.
1028 U.S. Highway 80 E
Demopolis, AL 36732

**WXVI - AM**
Wes Attaway, Pres.
Box 4280
Montgomery, AL 36104

**WYLS - AM**
PO Box 687
York, AL 36925

**WZZA-AM**
Bob Carl Bailey, Pres.
PO Box 2562
Muscle Shoals, AL 35560

### Arkansas

**KADO - FM**
Floyd Bell, Pres.
303 W. Broad Street
Texarkana, AR 75501

**KCAT - AM**
J. B. Scanlon, Pres.
Box 8808
Pine Bluff, AR 71611

**KCLT**
PO Box 2870
W. Helena, AR. 73290

**KDEW - AM**
John Green, Pres.
PO Box 566
Dewitt, AR 72042

**KDJC - AM**
4 Canterbury Corner
Jacksonville, AR 72076

**KELD-AM**
2525 Northwest Ave.
Helena AR 71730

**KFMU - FM**
PO Box 430
Magnolia, AR 71753

**KITA - AM**
Gary Vaile, Gen. Mgr.
723 W. 14th Street
Little Rock, AR 72202

**KLAZ - FM**
Ron Curtis, Gen. Mgr.
1501 N. University
Little Rock, AR 72207

**KOKY - AM**
Ron Curtis, Gen. Mgr.
1501 N. University
Little Rock, AR 72207

**KSWH - FM**
Edwin Ryland, Gen. Mgr.
Henderson State University
HSU Box 7536
Arkadelphia, AR 71923

**KUCA - FM**
J. Wayne Lewis, Gen. Mgr.
Univ. of Central Arkansas
PO. Box A
Conway, AR 72032

**KWRF - AM**
Weldon Sledge, Pres.
Box 480
Warren, AR 71671

**KYDE - AM**
George S Ivory, Pres.
PO Box 5086
Pine Bluff, AR 71611

## California

**KACE - FM**
Jim Blakely, Gen. Mgr.
1710 East 111th Street
Los Angeles, CA 90059

**KBLX - FM**
Percy Sutton, Pres.
601 Ashby Avenue
Berkeley, CA 94701

**KDAY - AM**
Ed Kirby, Gen. Mgr.
1700 N. Alvarado
Los Angeles, CA 90026

**KDIA RAD10**
Gen. Mgr.
Gen. Mgr.
100 Swan Way
Oakland, CA 94621

**KFCF - FM**
Alex Vavoulis, Pres.
Box 4364
Fresno, CA 93744

**KFOX - FM**
Ed Roper, Pres.
123 Torrance Blvd.
Redondo Beach, CA 90277

**KGFJ - AM**
Percy Sutton, Pres.
1989 Riverside Drive
Los Angeles, CA 90039

**KIIS - FM & AM**
Ms. Lynn Anderson-Powell,
Gen. Mgr.
6255 Sunset Blvd.
Los Angeles, CA 90028

**KJLH - FM**
Steveland Morris, Pres.
3847 S. Crenshaw Blvd.
Los Angeles, CA 90008

**KJOP - AM**
John Pembroke, Pres.
15279 Hanford-Armona Road
Lemoore, CA 93245

**KJOY - AM**
Ort. J. Lofthus, Pres.
Box Y
Stockton, CA 95201

**KKGO - FM**
Saul Levine, Pres.
10880 Wilshire Blvd.,
Suite 2006
Los Angeles, CA 90024

**KKHR - FM**
George Nicholaw, Gen. Mgr.
6121 Sunset Blvd.
Los Angeles, CA 90028

**KLIP - AM**
Carlton Goodlett, Pres.
PO Box 129
Fowler, CA 93625

**KMEL- FM**
Rick Lee-Vice, Gen. Mgr.
2300 Stockton Street,
Suite 330
San Francisco, CA 94113

**KMPX-FM**
Lloyd Edwards, Pres.
655 Sutter St.
San Francisco, CA 94102

**KNAC - FM**
Ed Wright, Pres.
320 Pine Avenue, Suite 1000
Long Beach, CA 90802

**KNX RAD10**
George Nicholaw, Gen. Mgr.
6121 Sunset Blvd.
Los Angeles, CA 90028

**KPLM - FM**
Rose Casalan Pres.
1276 N. Palm Canyon Drive
Suite 106
Palm Springs, CA 92262

**KPOO - FM**
Joe Rudolph, Gen. Mgr.
Box 11008
San Francisco, CA 94101

**KPOP - FM**
William M. Cloutier,
Gen. Mgr.
Box 1110
Roseville, CA 95661

**KRE - AM**
Percy Sutton, Pres.
601 AshbyAvenue
Berkeley, CA 94710

**KSOL - FM**
Ken Shubat, Gen. Mgr.
1730 S. Amphlett Blvd.,
Suite 327
San Mateo, CA 94402

**KSTN - AM**
Knox LaRue, Pres.
2171 Ralph Avenue
Stockton, CA 95206

**KUOP - FM**
Richard Terry, Gen. Mgr.
3601 Pacific Avenue
Stockton, CA 95211

**KUTE - FM**
Percy Sutton, Pres.
5900 Wilshire Blvd.
Suite 33
Los Angeles, CA 90036

**KYNO - AM**
Wayne Decker, Pres.
2125 N. Barton
Fresno, CA 93703

**XHRM - FM**
Tip Calvin, Gen. Mgr.
4165 Market Street
San Diego, CA 92101

## Colorado

**KDKO - AM**
Rodney V Louden, Gen. Mgr.
7880 E. Berry Pl.
Littleton, CO 80111

**KEPC - FM**
John F Donahue, Gen. Mgr.
Pikes Peak Com. College
5675 S. Academy Blvd.
Colorado Springs, CO 80906

**KWBZ - FM**
3 West Princeton
Englewood, CO 80110

## Connecticut

**WKND - AM**
John N. Catlett, Gen. Mgr.
PO Box 1480
Windsor, CT 06095

**WNOU-FM**
Frank Jacobs, Pres.
PO Box 98
Willimatic, CT 06226

**WNAB- FM**
Harry Lawson, Pres.
474 E Washington Avenue
Bridgeport, CT 06608

**WNHC - AM**
Box 1340
New Haven, CT 06505

**WQTQ - FM**
Paul Robertson, Gen. Mgr.
Weaver High School
415 Grandy Street
Hartford, CT 06112

## District of Columbia

**WDCU - FM**
Dr. G. Godwin Oyewole,
Gen. Mgr.
University of the
District of Columbia
4200 Connecticut Ave., N.W.
Washington, DC 20008

**WDJY - FM**
E. Carlton Myers, Gen. Mgr.
5321 First Place, N.E.
Washington, DC 20011

**WHUR - FM**
James Watkins, Gen. Mgr.
Howard University
529 Bryant St., N.W.
Washington, DC 20059

**WKYS - FM**
Bartley Walsh, Gen. Mgr.
4001 Nebraska Avenue
Washington, DC 20016

**WOL - AM**
Dewey Hughes, Pres.
400 H Street, N.E.
Washington, DC 20002

**WPFW- FM**
Marita Rivero, Gen. Mgr.
700 H Street, N.W.
Washington, DC 20001-3794

**WUST - AM**
James Queen, Pres.
815 V Street, N.W.
Washington, DC 20001

**WYCB - AM**
Karen Jackson, Gen. Mgr.
1340 G Street, N.W.
Washington, DC 20007

## Florida

**WAMF - FM**
Dr. Walter Smith Pres.
314 Tucker Hall
Florida A & M University
Tallahassee, FL 32307

**WANM - AM**
Bob Badger, Gen. Mgr.
PO. Box 10174
Tallahassee, FL 32307

**WBCC- AM**
Glen Walker, Gen. Mgr.
Bethune Cookman University
640 2nd Avenue
Daytona Beach, FL 32015

**WBOP - AM**
Wayne Coleman, Gen. Mgr.
PO. Box 12764
Pensacola, FL 32575

**WCGL - AM**
Emily Timmons, Gen. Mgr.
4035 Atlantic Blvd.
Jacksonville, FL 32207

**WCHN - AM**
Alexander Rush,
Operations Manager
PO. Box 31680
Quincy, FL 32351

**WERD-AM**
Art Gilliam, Pres.
PO Box 2467
Jacksonville, FL 32203

**WDGM - FM**
Alexander Rush,
Operations Manager
Box 3168
109 Ridgeland Drive
Tallahassee, FL 32315

**WFYV-FM**
Ragan Henry, Pres.
9090 Hogan Rd.
Jacksonville, FL 32216

**WHQT - FM**
Chuck Goldmark, Gen. Mgr.
377 Alhambra
Miami, FL 33134

**WJAX AM/FM**
Bruce Webb, Gen. Mgr.
PO Box 1740
Jacksonville, FL 32201

**WMBM - AM**
Ed Margolis, Gen. Mgr.
814 First Street
Miami Beach, FL 33139

**WMIM - FM**
Major R. Bernard Pres.
PO Box 2830
Ocala, FL 32678

**WONE - FM**
Rodney J. Long, Pres.
6 East University
Gainesville, FL 32601

**WOKB - AM**
Arnold Schorr, Gen. Mgr.
111 S. Division Street
Orlando, FL 32805

**WORL - AM**
Harvey Tate, Gen. Mgr.
2001 N. Mercy Drive
Orlando, FL 32808

**WPDQ - AM**
Ragan Henry, Pres.
9090 Hogan Road
Jacksonville, FL 32216

**WPOM - AM**
Rodney G. Dore, Pres.
4286 Upthegrove Ln.
West Palm Beach, FL 33407

**WRBD - AM**
Robert F. Bell, Pres.
4431 Rock Island Rd.
Fort Lauderdale, FL 33319

**WRXB - AM**
J. Eugene Danzey, Pres.
3000 34th Street South,
Suite B-206
St. Petersburg, FL 33712

**WSWN - FM**
J. Eugene Danzey, Pres.
Box 593 Pohokee
Belle Glade, FL 33476

**WTHM - FM**
George Corwin, Gen. Mgr.
20938 S. Dixie Hwy.
Miami, FL 33189

**WTMP - AM**
Paul C. Major, Pres.
5207 Washington Blvd.
Tampa, FL 33601

**WWAB - AM**
Dee Van, Gen. Mgr.
1203 Chase Street,
Box 65
Lakeland, FL 33802

**WWSD - FM**
Ken Harmon, Gen. Mgr.
Box 630
Quincy, FL 32351

**WZAZ - AM**
Mark Picus, Pres.
300 West Tenn
Tallahassee, FL 32302

## Georgia

**WAOK - AM**
Ragan Henry, Pres.
120 Ralph McGill Blvd.,
Suite 1000
Atlanta, GA 30365-6901

**WBAF - AM**
Wimley Waters, Gen. Mgr.
Rt. 2 Box A
Barnesville, GA 30204

**WCLK - FM**
Elias Blake Jr. Pres.
Clarke College
240 Chestnut Street
Atlanta, GA 30314

**WDDO - AM**
Ben G. Porter, Jr., Pres.
Box 900
Macon, GA 31202

**WEAS - FM**
Bob Bryant, Gen. Mgr.
Box 1207
2403 Bonaventure Road
Savannah, GA 31414

**WFXA- FM**
Randy Sheffield, Gen. Mgr.
PO Box 1584
August, GA 30903

**WFXE - FM**
B. Ken Woodfin, Gen. Mgr.
Box 1100
Columbus, GA 31994

**WGOV - AM**
John Rodriquez, Gen. Mgr.
Box 1207
Valdosta, GA 31603

**WHYD - AM**
Lowell E. White, Gen. Mgr.
1825 Buena Vista Road
Columbus, GA 31906

**WIBB - AM**
D. A. Haight, Gen. Mgr.
Drawer 6517
Macon, GA 31213

**WIGO - FM**
Neil McElhaney, Gen. Mgr.
1422 W. Peachtree Street, NW
Atlanta, GA 30309

**WJGA - FM**
Don Earnhart, Gen. Mgr.
PO Box 3878
Jackson, GA 30233

**WJIZ - FM**
Bob Lee, Pres.
PO. Box 5226
Albany, GA 31706

**WLAG - AM**
Rick Ellis, Gen. Mgr.
304 Broom Street
La Grange, GA 30240

**WOKS - AM**
B. Ken Woodfin, Gen. Mgr.
115 14th Street
Columbus, GA 31902

**WPGA - AM/FM**
Lowell Register, Pres.
Drawer 980
Perry, GA 31069

**WQDE - AM**
Davis B. McGriff, Gen. Mgr.
2804 N. Jefferson
Albany, GA 31702

**WRDW - AM**
Terry L. Browen Pres.
Box 1405
Augusta, GA 30903

**WSNT - AM**
James Whaley, Gen. Mgr.
Box 150
Sandersville, GA 31802

**WSOK - AM**
Benjamin M. Tucker,
Gen. Mgr.
Box 1288
Savannah, GA 31498

**WTHB - AM**
Walter Brumbleloe, Gen. Mgr.
Box 1584
Augusta, GA 30903

**WTJH - AM**
Bea Goodbee, Gen. Mgr.
2146 Dodson Drive
East Point, GA 30364

**WTUF - FM**
Tom Plak, Gen. Mgr.
Box 45
Thomasville, GA 31792

**WVEE - FM**
C. B. Rogers, Gen. Mgr.
120 Ralph McGill Blvd.,
Suite 1000
Atlanta, GA 30365-6901

**WVFJ - AM**
Steve Williams, Gen. Mgr.
Box 510
Manchester, GA 31816

**WXAG - AM**
Michael Thurmond, Gen. Mgr.
2145 S. Milledge Avenue
Athens, GA 30605

**WXKO - AM**
Dollie D. Horton, Pres.
Box 1150
Fort Valley, GA 31030

**WXLL - AM**
Ralph Jennings, Gen. Mgr.
2218 B Chandler Rd.
Decatur, GA 30032

**WXRS - AM**
Lee Studstill, Gen. Mgr.

Box 1590
Swainsboro, GA 30401

**WYNR - AM**
Dick Boekeloo, Gen. Mgr.
Rt 6, Box 150
Brunswick, GA 31520

**WYZE - AM**
George Buck Pres.
111 Blvd. S.E.
Atlanta, GA 30312

## Illinois

**WARG - FM**
Tom Janiak, Gen. Mgr.
7329 W. 63rd Street
Summit, IL 60501

**WBEE - FM**
Charles Sherrell, II, Gen. Mgr.
35 E. Wacker
Chicago, IL 60601

**WBMX - FM**
Kernie Anderson, Gen. Mgr.
408 S. Oak Avenue
Oak Park, IL 60302

**WESL - AM**
Wendell Hansen, Gen. Mgr.
149 S. 8th Street
East St. Louis, IL 62201

**WGCI - FM**
Marv Dyson, Pres.
6 North Michigan Avenue
Chicago, IL 60602

**WJPC - AM**
John H.Johnson, Pres.
820 S. Michigan Avenue
Chicago, IL 60605

**WKRO - AM**
Robert Stout, Pres.
Box 311
Cairo, IL 62914

**WLUV - AM/FM**
Angelo Joseph Salvi, Pres.
PO Box 2201
Love Park, IL 61131

**WVON - AM**
Wesley W. South, Pres.
3350 S. Kedzie Ave.
Chicago, IL 60623

**WYOU - FM**
James Shepherd, Pres.
609 N. Jackson Street
Danville, IL 61832

**WXOL-AM**
Wesley South, Pres.
3350 South Kedzie Ave.
Chicago, IL 60623

## Indiana

**WGRT - FM**
Stephen Ross, Gen. Mgr.
Box 301
Danville, IN 46122

**WJEL - FM**
John King, Gen. Mgr.
1901 E. 86th Street
Indianapolis, IN 46240

**WLTH - AM**
Judy Burks, Gen. Mgr.
3669 Broadway
Gary, IN 46409

**WTLC - FM**
Ragan Henry, Pres.
2126 N. Meridian Street
Indianapolis, IN 46202

**WWCA - AM**
L. E. Willis, Sr., Pres.
545 Broadway
Gary, IN 46402

## Iowa

**KALA- FM**
Charles C. Shepler, Gen. Mgr.
Ambrose College
518 West Locust Street
Davenport, IA 52803

**KBBG - FM**
Harris Ceaser, Gen. Mgr.
527 Cottage Ave.
Waterloo, IA 50703

**KLNG - AM**
Bill Cunningham, Gen. Mgr.
1700 College Road
Council Bluffs, IA 51501

**KOJC - FM**
Robert Irwin, Pres.
PO Box 1405
Cedar Rapids, IA 52406

**KUCB - FM**
Charles Knox, Gen. Mgr.
801 Forest Avenue
Des Moines, IA 50314

## Kansas

**KBUZ - FM**
Gary Violet, Pres.
Strother Field
Winfield
Arkansas City, KS 67156

**KEYN - AM/FM**
Charlie Pride, Pres.
2829 Salina Avenue
Wichita, KS 67204

**KTPK FM**
M. Wilson, Pres.
910 First National Bank Tower
Topeka, KS 66603

## Kentucky

**WABD - AM**
Don Belyea, Gen. Mgr.
Box 521
Fort Campbell, KY 42223

**WCYN - FM**
Estil Reed Anderson, Pres.
Box 207
Cynthiana, KY 41031

**WJYL - FM**
Thomas P Lewis, Chairman
10213 Linn Station Rd.,
Suite 3
Louisville, KY 40223

**WLOU - AM**
Charles Mootry, Gen. Mgr.
2549 S. Third St.
Louisville, KY 40208

## Louisiana

**KBCE - FM**
Gus Lewis, Gen. Mgr.
Highway 1 South
PO Box 69
Boyce, LA 71409

**KCLF - AM**
4470 Winbourne Ave.
Baton Rouge, LA 70805

**KDKS - FM**
Vandelon Williams, Gen. Mgr.
2600 Jewella Avenue, Suite C
Shreveport, LA 71109

**KEZM - AM**
Patrick Manual, Gen. Mgr.
320 West Parrish Rd.
Sulphur, LA 70663

**KICB - AM**
Joshua Jackson, Pres.
123 Michael Allen Blvd.
Lafayette, LA 70501

**KLPL - AM**
Larry G. Wade, Gen. Mgr.
Box 231
Lake Providence, LA 71254

**KOKA - AM**
James A. Reeder
Managing Partner
1315 Milam Street
Shreveport, LA 71120

**KPWS - AM**
Barry Thompson, Gen. Mgr.
110 W. 3rd Street
PO Box 1561
Crawley, LA 70526

**KQXL - FM**
1676 Dallas Dr.
Baton Rouge, LA 70806

**KROF - AM**
Garland Bernard, Gen. Mgr.
Box 610, Hwy. 167N
Abbeville, LA 70510

**KTRY - AM/FM**
Henry Cotton, Pres.
Shelton Road
Bastrop, LA 7122Q

**KXZZ - AM**
Jim Nettles, Gen. Mgr.
PO Box 1725
Lake Charles, LA 70602

**KYEA - FM**
Chuck Morgan, Pres.
516 Martin St.
West Monroe, LA 71291

**KZMZ - FM**
Bill Lynch, Gen. Mgr.
601 Washington St.
Alexandria, LA 71301

**KZZM - AM**
Chris C. Kimbell, Jr, Pres.
Box 111 Johnson St.
Tallulah, LA 71282

**WBOK - AM/FM**
Alvin L. McCattry, Gen. Mgr.
3301 1/2 Tulane Avenue
PO Box 19085
New Orleans, LA 70176

**WQCK - FM**
Pat Tolle, Gen. Mgr.
PO Box 7934
Clinton, LA 70722

**WTKL - AM**
John Marver, Gen. Mgr.
7249 Florida Blvd., Suite 604
Baton Rouge, LA 70806

**WXOK - AM**
Le Carter, Gen. Mgr.
6819 Cezanne Ave.
Baton Rouge, LA 70896

**WYLD - AM/FM**
James J. Hutchinson, Jr., Pres.
2906 Tulane Avenue
New Orleans, LA 70119

## Maryland

**WANN - AM**
Morris Blum, Gen. Mgr.
PO Box 631
Annapolis, MD 21404

**WEAA - FM**
Alfred Stewart, Gen. Mgr.
Morgan State University
Hillen Road &
Coldspring Lane
Baltimore, MD 21239

**WEBB - AM**
Dorothy Brunson, Pres.
2018 Dennison Street
Baltimore, MD 21216

**WITH - AM**
Ragan Henry, Pres.
5 Light Street
Baltimore, MD 21202

**WJDY - AM**
J. P Connor, Gen. Mgr.
1633 N. Division Street
Salisbury, MD 21801

**WWIN - AM/FM**
H. Shelton Earp, Gen. Mgr.
2800 Matthews Street
Baltimore, MD 21218

**WXYV - FM**
Bob Abernethy, Gen. Mgr.
8001 Park Heights Avenue
Baltimore, MD 21208

## Massachusetts

**WACM - AM**
Sally Daboue, Gen. Mgr.
34 Sylvan St.
West Springfield, MA 01089

**WAIC - FM**
Glenn Linder, Gen. Mgr.
American International College
170 Wilbraham Rd.
Springfield, MA 01109

**WCUW- FM**
Dave Goldbert, Pres.
910 Main St.
Worcester, MA 06101

**WILD - AM**
Kendell Nash, Pres.
390 Commonwealth Ave.
Boston, MA 02215

**WLVG**
E. W. Jackson, Sr., Gen. Mgr.
1972 Mass. Avenue
Cambridge, MA 02140

**WNTN - AM**
Orestes Demetriades, Pres.
143 Rumford Avenue
Newton, MA 02166

**WPAA - FM**
George Cogan, Pres.
Phillips Academy
Andover, MA 01810

**WSCB FM**
Robert Albert, Gen. Mgr.
Springfield College
Box 1703
Springfield, MA 01109

**WXKS - FM**
Richard Balsbaugh, Gen. Mgr.
99 Revere Beach Pkwy.
Boston, MA 02155

## Michigan

**WCHB - AM**
Mrs. Mary Bell, Pres.
2994 E. Grand Blvd.
Detroit, MI 48202

**WCHB-FM**
Mrs.Mary Bell, Pres.
32790 Henry Ruff Rd.
Inkster, MI 48141

**WCXT - FM**
Mrs. Mary Bell, Pres.
220 Polk Road
Hart, MI 49420

**WDET- FM**
Caryn G. Mathes, Gen. Mgr.
5057 Woodward Avenue, 15th Floor
Detroit, MI 48202

**WDZZ- FM**
Vernon Merritt, Jr., Pres.
Box 9300
Flint, MI 48501

**WGPR-FM**
W. V. Banks, Pres.
3146 East Jefferson St.
Detroit, MI 48207

**WLBS-FM**
Percy Sutton, Pres.
15565 N'land Dr. E.
Room 200
Southfield, MI 48075

## Mississippi

**WALT - AM**
Bob Benson, Gen. Mgr.
Box 5797
Meridian, MS 39302

**WBAD - FM**
W. D. Jackson, Pres.
Box 4426
Greenville, MS 38701

**WCLD - FM**
J. R. Denton, Pres.
Drawer X
Cleveland, MS 38732

**WCPR - AM**
Robin Mathis, Pres.
Box 569
Houston, MS 38851

**WESY - AM**
William Jackson, Pres.
Box 5804
Greenville, MS 38701

**WFEZ - FM**
Box 1414
Meridian, MS 39301

**WHNY**
Robert Hamilton, Gen. Mgr.
Drawer E
McComb, MS 39648

**WJKX - AM**
Glen Murphy, Gen. Mgr.
4519 Jefferson Avenue
Pascagoula, MS 39563

**WJMG-FM**
Vernon C. Floyd, Gen. Mgr.
1204 Graveline St.
Hattiesburg, MS 39401

**WJMI - FM**
George Lund, Gen. Mgr.
Box 3320
Jackson, MS 39207

**WJSU - FM**
Anthony Dean, Gen. Mgr.
1400 Lynch Street
Jackson, MS 39217

**WJYV - AM**
Box 1539
Forest, MS 39074

**WJZZ-FM**
Mrs. Mary Bell, Pres.
2994 East Grand Blvd.
Detroit, MI 48202

**WKKY- FM**
Sam Farnham, Gen. Mgr.
Box 1789
Pascagoula-Moss Point, MS 39567

**WKWM-AM**
Richard Culpepper, Pres.
PO Box 828
Kentwood, MI 49508

**WKOZ - AM**
H. Mims Boswell, Jr., Pres.
Golf Course Rd.
Kosciusko, MS 39090

**WKPG - AM**
Box 481
Port Gibson, MS

**WKXI - AM**
Robert O'Brien, Gen. Mgr.
Box 9446
Jackson, MS 39206

**WMGO - AM**
Gene Dow, Gen. Mgr.
Box 182
Canton, MS 39046

**WMLC-AM**
Houston P. Smith, Gen. Mgr.
Box 1270
Monticello, MS 39654

**WMPR - FM**
Theodore Jones Pres.
Box 408
Tougaloo, MS 39174

**WNSL- FM**
Bob Holladay, Pres.
Box 1229
Laurel, MS 39441

**WOKJ - AM**
Richard Lange, Gen. Mgr.
Box 3320
Jackson, MS 39207

**WORV - AM**
Vernon C. Floyd, Pres.
1204 Graveline Street
Hattiesburg, MS 39401

**WPJJ - AM**
Joel Netherland, Pres.
Box 1048
Yazoo City, MS 39194

**WQBC - AM**
Frank Holifield, Jr, Pres.
Box 589
Vicksburg, MS 39180

**WQFX - FM**
Robert Snugg, Gen. Mgr.
2301 - 14th Street
Gulfport, MS 39501

**WQIC - AM**
Stan Torgerson, Pres.
Box 5353
Meridian, MS 39302

**WQIS - FM**
Bob Holladay, Gen. Mgr.
Box 1229
Laurel, MS 39441

**WROB - AM**
Jack King, Gen. Mgr.
Box 1336
West Point, MS 39773

**WSLL - AM**
Bob Cupit, Pres.
Box 310
Centerville, MS 69631

**WSWG - FM**
Keith Worrell Jr., Gen. Mgr.
Box 885
Greenwood, MS 38930

**WTAM - FM**
Carnell Tucker, Gen. Mgr.
Box 1570
Gulfport, MS 39501

**WXIY - FM**
Jerome Hughey, Pres.
Box 548
Bay Springs, MS 39422

**WYKC - AM**
Bob Evans, Jr., Pres.
Box 946
Grenada, MS 39801

**WMGO - AM**
Gene Dow, Gen. Mgr.
Box 182
Canton, MS 39046

**WMLC - AM**
Houston P. Smith, Gen. Mgr.
Box 1270
Monticello, MS 39654

**WMPR - FM**
Theodore Jones Pres.
Box 408
Tougaloo, MS 39174

**WNSL- FM**
Bob Holladay, Pres.
Box 1229
Laurel, MS 39441

**WOKJ - AM**
Richard Lange, Gen. Mgr.
Box 3320
Jackson, MS 39207

**WORV - AM**
Vernon C. Floyd, Gen. Mgr.
1204 Graveline Street
Hattiesburg, MS 39401

**WPJJ - AM**
Joel Netherland, Pres.
Box 1048
Yazoo City, MS 39194

**WQBC - AM**
Frank Holifield, Jr, Pres.
Box 589
Vicksburg, MS 39180

**WQFX - FM**
Robert Snugg, Gen. Mgr.
2301 - 14th Street
Gulfport, MS 39501

**WQIC - AM**
Stan Torgerson, Pres.
Box 5353
Meridian, MS 39302

**WQIS - FM**
Bob Holladay, Gen. Mgr.
Box 1229
Laurel, MS 39441

**WROB - AM**
Jack King, Gen. Mgr.
Box 1336
West Point, MS 39773

**WSLL - AM**
Bob Cupit, Pres.
Box 310
Centerville, MS 69631

**WSWG - FM**
Keith Worrell Jr., Gen. Mgr.
Box 885
Greenwood, MS 38930

**WTAM - FM**
Carnell Tucker, Gen. Mgr.
Box 1570
Gulfport, MS 39501

**WXIY - FM**
Jerome Hughey, Pres.
Box 548
Bay Springs, MS 39422

**WYKC - AM**
Bob Evans, Jr., Pres.
Box 946
Grenada, MS 39801

### Missouri

**KATZ - AM**
Eugene Jackson, Pres.
1139 Olive Street
St. Louis, MO 63101

**KCXL - AM**
Chuck Moore, Gen. Mgr.
810 E. 63rd Street
Kansas City, MO 64410

**KIRL - AM**
Johnny Roland, Pres.
3713 Highway 94 North
St. Charles, MO 63301

**KMJM - FM**
Barry Baker, Gen. Mgr.
532 DeBaliviere
St. Louis, MO 63112

**KPRS - FM**
John E. Carter, Gen. Mgr.
2440 Pershing Road
Kansas City, MO 64108

**KPRT - AM**
Andrew Carter, Pres.
2440 Pershing Road
Kansas City, MO 64108

**WZEN - FM**
Johnny Roland, Pres.
1139 Olive Street
St. Louis, MO 63101

### Nebraska

**KBWH - FM**
Jack Harris, Pres.
5829 North 60th Street
Omaha, NE 68104

**KCRO - AM**
Bill Butler, Gen. Mgr.
3615 Dodge Street
Omaha, NE 68131

**KYNN - AM**
Jim Carter, Gen. Mgr.
11128 John Galt Blvd.
Omaha, NE 68137

**KZUM - FM**
Lori Martin, Station Manager
941 "0" St., Suite B-2
Lincoln, NE 68508

**WOW - AM**
Ken Fearnow, Gen. Mgr.
615 N. 90th Street
Omaha, NE 68124

### Nevada

**KCEP - FM**
Ray E. Willis, Gen. Mgr.
330 W. Washington Avenue
Las Vegas, Nevada 89101

### New Jersey

**WBGO - FM**
Robert Ottenhoff, Gen. Mgr.
54 Park Place
Newark, NJ 07102

**WIMG - AM**
Janne Greenberg, Pres.
Box 2050
Princeton, NJ 08540

**WNJR - AM**
Jeri Warrick-Crisman, Pres.
1700 Union Avenue
Union, NJ 07083

**WSSJ - AM**
James N. Wade, Pres.
6th & Market Street
Camden, NJ 08101

**WUSS - AM**
John F. Hickman, Gen. Mgr.
15000 Absecon Avenue
Atlantic City, NJ 88401

**WWDJ - AM**
Joseph Batta, Gen. Mgr.
167 Main Street
Hackensack, NJ 07602

### New York

**WBLK - FM**
Franklin W. Lorenz, Pres.
420 Franklin Street
Buffalo, NY 14202

**WBLS- FM**
Percy Sutton, Pres.
801 Second Avenue
New York, NY 10017

**WDKX - FM**
Andrew A. Langston, Pres.
683 E. Main St.
Rochester, NY 14605

**WHCU - FM**
Rudy Paolangeli, Gen. Mgr.
Cornell University
212 Common East
Ithaca, NY 14850

**WIZR-FM**
Norman T.Pinkard, Chmn.
PO Box 307
Johnstown, 12095

**WKTU - FM**
Mel Karmazin, Pres.
655 Madison Avenue
New York, NY 10021

**WLIB - AM**
Percy Sutton, Chairman
801 2nd Avenue
New York, NY 10017

**WMYL-AM**
Norman T. Pinkard, Chmn.
PO Box 307
Johnstown, 12095

**WPNR - FM**
Jack Morgan, Gen. Mgr.
Utica College
Burrstone Road
Utica, NY 13502

**WRKS- FM**
Tony Gray, Gen Mgr.
1440 Broadway
New York, NY 10018

**WUCI - FM**
Ashemha Tarig, Pres.
117 Howley, Suite 203
Binghampton, NY 13901

**WUFO - AM**
Ron Davenport, Pres.
89 La Salle Avenue
Buffalo, NY 14214

**WWRL - AM**
Vince Sanders, Vice Pres.
41-30 58th Street
Woodside, NY 11377

### North Carolina

**WAAA - AM**
Mutter Evans, Pres.
Box 11197
Winston-Salem, NC 27116

**WAFR - FM**
Robert Spruill, Pres.
2501 Fayetteville St.
Durham, NC 27707

**WAIR - AM**
Nick P Patella, Gen. Mgr.
Box 2099
Winston-Salem, NC 27102

**WARR - AM**
Ralph Coleman, Pres.
Box 577
Warrenton, NC 27589

**WBMU - FM**
James E. Robinson, Pres.
2 Wall Street, Suite 111
Asheville, NC 28801

**WDUR - AM**
Richard G. Glover, Pres.
Box 2169
Durham, NC 27702

**WEAL - AM**
Morgan Rees Poag, Gen. Mgr.
Box 6626
Greensboro, NC 27405

**WEGG - AM**
J. B. Wilson, Sr., Pres.
Box 608
Rose Hill, NC 28458

**WENC - AM**
Doug Tyler, Gen. Mgr.
Box 709
Whiteville, NC 28472

**WFSS - FM**
Joseph Ross, Director
1200 Murchison Road
Fayetteville, NC 28301

**WGIV - AM**
Garfield Harris, Pres.
2520 Toomey Avenue
Charlotte, NC 28203

**WGSS - FM**
Doyle Russell, Gen. Mgr.
Box 393
Lumberton, NC 28358

**WIDU - AM**
W. B. Belche, Pres.
Drawer 2247
Fayetteville, NC 28302

**WIZS - AM**
Thomas J. Moore, Gen. Mgr.
Box 1299
Henderson, NC 27536

**WLLE - AM**
Prentice & Henry Moore, Owners
522 East Martin
Raleigh, NC 27601

**WNAA - FM**
Tony Welborne, Gen. Mgr.
A & T University
Greensboro, NC 27411

**WNDN - FM**
Jack Walls, Gen. Mgr.
Catawba College
Salisbury, NC 28144

**WOKN - FM**
Webster A. James, Gen. Mgr.
Box 2006
Goldsboro, NC 27533

**WPEG - FM**
William R. Rollins, Pres.
Box 128
Concord, NC 28431

**WQCC - AM**
Wayne Hammond, Gen. Mgr.
1402 E. Morehead Street
Charlotte, NC 28204

**WQDW- FM**
Tom Joyner, Pres.
Box 668
Kinston, NC 28501

**WQMG - FM**
M. Rees Poag, Pres.
Box 668
Kinston, NC 27536

**WRSV- FM**
W. A. Wynne, Jr., Pres.
Box 2267
Rocky Mount, NC 27801

**WSHA - FM**
Cathis Hall, Gen. Mgr.
Shaw University
118 E. South Street
Raleigh, NC 27116

**WSMX - AM**
Chuck Webster, Gen. Mgr.
500 Kinard Street
Winston Salem, NC 27101

**WSRC - AM**
James H. Mayes, Pres.
Box 1331
Durham, NC 27702

**WVBS - AM**
Danny Marshburn, Gen. Mgr.
Box 696
Burgaw, NC 28425

**WVOE - AM**
Margaret Reaves, Gen. Mgr.
PO. Box 328
Chadbourn, NC 28431

**WVSP - FM**
Walter Norflett, Gen. Mgr.
Box 365
Warrenton, NC 27589

**WWGM - AM**
J. D. Conner, Pres.
Box 3436
New Bern, NC 28560

**WWIL - AM**
James Capers, Vice Pres.
Box 3368
Wilmington, NC 27106

**WYRU - AM**
William Morgan, Pres.
Box 711
Red Springs, NC 28377

## Ohio

**WABQ - FM**
Mike Gallager, Gen. Mgr.
8000 Euclid Ave.
Cleveland, OH 44103

**WAIF - FM**
Robin Ford Gen. Mgr.
2525 Victory Pkwy.
Cincinnati, OH 45206

**WBLZ- FM**
Ragan Henry, Pres.
First Nat'l Bank Bldg.
Hamilton, OH 45011

**WCIN - AM**
Ragan Henry, Pres.
106 Glenwood Avenue
Cincinnati, OH 45217

**WCKX - FM**
Jack Harris, Pres.
696 E. Broad Street
Columbus, OH 43215

**WCXL FM**
Harold F. Parshall, Pres.
Box 362
Dayton, OH 45449

**WDAO - FM**
Jim Johnson, Gen. Mgr.
1400 Cincinnati St.
Dayton, OH 45408

**WDMT- FM**
Bill Becker Gen. Mgr.
14781 Sperry Rd.
Cleveland, OH 44065

**WELX - AM**
LaRue Turner, Pres.
Box 219
Xenia, OH 45385

**WJMO - AM**
Curtis Shaw Gen. Mgr.
11821 Euclid Avenue
Cleveland Hgts., OH 44106

**WSLN - FM**
Lori A. Berliner Gen. Mgr.
Ohio Wesleyan University
40 Slocum Hall
Delaware, OH 43015

**WVKO - AM**
Al Fetch, Vice Pres.
4401 Carriage Hill Lane
Columbus, OH 43220

**WVOI - AM**
Charles Welch Gen. Mgr.
Box 5408
Toledo, OH 43613

**WZAK - FM**
Xenophon Zapis, Pres.
1729 Superior Avenue, Suite 401
Cleveland, OH 44114

**WZZT - FM**
Mike Davis
PO Box 373
Johnstown, OH 43031

## Oklahoma

**KAEZ - FM**
James E. Miller, Pres.
PO Box 11333
Oklahoma City, OK 73136

**KALU - FM**
Dr. Ernest Holloway, Pres.
Langston University
Box 837
Langston, OK 73050

**KGOU - FM**
Bruce H. Hinson, Gen. Mgr.
University of Oklahoma
780 Van Vlett Oval
Norman, OK 73019

**KHIB - FM**
Southeastern State University
Durant, OK 74701

## Pennsylvania

**WAMO - AM/FM**
Ron Davenport, Pres.
1811 Blvd. of the Allies
Pittsburgh, PA 15219

**WCDL - AM**
Noble V. Blackwell, Pres.
127 Salem Road
Carbondale, PA 18407

**WLSP - FM**
Noble V. Blackwell, Pres.
127 Salem Road
Carbondale, PA 18407

**WDAS - AM/FM**
Eugene Jackson, Pres.
Belmont Avenue & Edgley Rd.
Philadelphia, PA 19131

**WHAT - AM/FM**
Dolly Banks, Pres.
3930 Conshohocken Avenue
Philadelphia, PA 19131

**WJAS - AM**
Amos Brown, 111, Gen. Mgr.
Crane Avenue
Pittsburgh, PA 15220

**WLAN - AM**
Samuel Adtdoerffer, Gen. Mgr.
252 N. Queen St.
Lancaster, PA 17603

**WRTI - FM**
Vincent C. Thomas, Gen. Mgr.
Temple University
2020 N. 13th Street
Philadelphia, PA 19122

**WUSL - FM**
Bruce H. Holberg, Pres.
440 Domino Lane
Philadelphia, PA 19128

**WVAM - AM/FM**
James Drayton, Pres.
2727 W. Albert Drive
Altoona, PA 16603

**WYIS - AM**
Samuel Hart, Pres.
186 Bridge S.
Phoenixville, PA 19460

## Rhode Island

**WHIM - AM**
Henry Hampton, Pres.
125 Eastern Avenue
East Providence, Rl 19460

## South Carolina

**WASC - AM**
James E. Harrison, Gen. Mgr.
Box 5686
Spartanburg, SC 29304

**WBSC - AM**
A. K. Harmon, Gen. Mgr.
Drawer 629
Bennettsville, SC 29512

**WCIG - FM**
James F. Ramsey, Pres.
Drawer 542
Mullins, SC 29574

**WDOG - AM**
H. Carl Gooding, Gen. Mgr.
Box 442
Allendale, SC 29810

**WDWQ-FM**
Mary Forbes, Chmn.
PO Box 903-904
St.George, SC 292022

**WDPN - FM**
6004 Two Notch Road
Columbia, SC 29204

**WGCD - AM**
Jerry Goodale, Gen. Mgr.
Box 746
Chester, SC 29706

**WHYZ - AM**
Thomas Hooper, Pres.
Box 4309
Greenville, SC 29608

**WOIC - AM**
I. S. Leevy Johnson, Pres.
PO. Box 565
Columbia, SC 29202

**WPAL - AM**
William Saunders, Pres.
Box 30999
Charleston, SC 29407

**WQIZ - AM**
Steve Judy, Gen. Mgr.
Box 903
St. George, SC 29477

**WQKI - AM**
Robert Newsham, Pres.
Box 777
St. Matthews, SC 29135

**WSSB - FM**
Gil Harris, Gen. Mgr.
South Carolina State College
PO Box 1915
Orangeburg, SC 29117

**WTWF- FM**
I. S. Levy Johnson, Pres.
Box 758
Moncks Corner, SC 29202

**WVBX**
Robert Cunningham, Pres.
1215 Church Street
Georgetown, SC 29440

**WVGB - AM**
Vivian Galloway, Pres.
806 Monson Street
Beaufort, SC 29902

**WWDM - FM**
Dan Mellette, Manager
Drawer 38
Sumter, SC 29150

**WWKT- FM**
Don H. LaDuke, Gen. Mgr.
Box 525
Kingstree, SC 29556

**WWWZ - FM**
Clifford Fletcher, Gen. Mgr.
Box 30669
Charleston, SC 29407

**WYNN - AM**
James N. Maurer, Gen. Mgr.
170 E. Palmetto Street
Box F-14
Florence, SC 29501

## Tennessee

**KRNB - FM**
E. W. Bie, Gen. Mgr.
Box 12107
Memphis, TN 38112

**KWAM - FM**
E. W. Bie, Gen. Mgr.
Box 12107
Memphis, TN 38112

**WBMX - AM**
T. Crawford, Pres.
2108 Prosser Road
Knoxville, TN 37914

**WDBL - AM**
Al Rider, Gen. Mgr.
Box 729
Beautiful Signal Hill
Springfield, TN 37172

**WDIA - AM**
Ernest Jackson, Jr., Gen. Mgr.
112 Union Avenue
Memphis, TN 38103

**WDXL - AM**
Ben Enochs, Pres.
Box 170
Lexington, TN 38351

**WHRK - FM**
Ernest Jackson, Jr., Gen. Mgr.
112 Union Avenue
Memphis, TN 38103

**WJTT - FM**
Michael Benns, Jr., Gen. Mgr.
621 O'Grady Dr.
Chattanooga, TN 37409

**WKDJ - AM**
Donald W. Boyles, Gen. Mgr.
112 Union Avenue
Memphis, TN 38103

**WLOK - AM**
A. Gilliam, Jr., Pres.
363 S. Second Street
Memphis, TN 38103

**WMAK - FM**
William H. Seaver, Gen. Mgr.
Box 24850
Hendersonville, TN 37202

**WNOO - AM**
Harold Cothran, Gen. Mgr.
1108 Hedricks Street
Chattanooga, TN 37406

**WRFN - FM**
Preston A. Blakely, Gen. Mgr.
Fisk University
906 17th Street
Naashville, TN 37203

**WTBG - FM**
Carlton Veirs, Pres.
Box 198
Brownsville, TN

**WVOL - AM**
1320 Brick Church Rd.
Berry Hill, TN 37207

## Texas

**KAPE - AM**
Sam Sitterle, Pres.
3900 M. L. King, Box 20107
San Antonio, TX 78220

**KAYC - AM/FM**
Vesta Brandt, Gen. Mgr.
Box 870
Beaumont, TX 77704

**KAZI - FM**
Jan Warfield, Gen. Mgr.
3112 B Manor Rd.
Austin, TX 78723

**KBWC - FM**
Melvin Jones, Gen. Mgr.
Wiley College
711 Rosborough Sprangs Rd.
Marshall, TX 75670

**KCOH - AM**
J. B.Coleman, Pres.
5011 Almeda Road
Houston, TX 77004

**KDLF - AM**
Billy James Hargis, Pres.
Box 545
Port Neches, TX 77651

**KGBC - AM**
Vandy Anderson, Gen. Mgr.
Box 1138
Galveston, TX 77550

**KHYS - FM**
James D. Smith, Gen. Mgr.
7700 Gulfway
Port Arthur, TX 77642

**KIIZ - AM**
Douglas C. Raab, Gen. Mgr.
Killeen, TX 76540

**KKDA - AM**
Haymen Childs, Pres.
Box 860
Grand Prairie, TX 75051

**KMJQ- FM**
Cecelia Scott, CEO
Box 22900
Houston, TX 77227

**KNOK-AM/FM**
Earl G. Graves, Pres.
3601 Kimbo St.
Fort Worth, TX 76111

**KSAX - AM**
William Chatment, Gen. Mgr.
Box 7116
Fort Worth, TX 76111

**KTSU - FM**
3101 Wheeler Ave.
Houston, TX 77004

**KTXC - AM**
Charles Porter, Gen. Mgr.
7700 Gulfway
Port Arthur, TX 77642
James D. Smith, Gen. Mgr.

**KZEY - AM**
Rick Reynolds, Pres.
Box 75712
Tyler, TX 75712

**KYOK - AM**
Don Rosette Gen. Mgr.
3001 LaBranch
Houston, TX 77004

## Virginia

**WANT - AM**
Ben Miles, Gen. Mgr.
1101 FrontStreet
Richmond, VA 23222

**WENZ-AM**
Tyrone Dickerson, Pres.
4719 Nine Mile Rd.
Richmond, VA 23901

**WBCI-FM**
Cicero M. Green, Jr., Pres.
PO Box 180
Williamsburg, VA 23185

**WBMG-AM**
Cicero M. Green, Jr., Pres.
PO Box 180
Williamsburg, VA 23185

**WFTH - AM**
Jack Johnson, Gen. Mgr.
2122 W. Cary Street
Richmond, VA 23331

**WILA - AM**
Francis McMillan, Pres.
PO. Box 3444
Danville, VA 24543

**WJJS - FM**
Edward W. Smith, Gen. Mgr.
8th & Church Streets
Lunchburg, VA 24504

**WINA - AM**
Colin Rose, Vice Pres.
Box 1230
Charlottesville, VA 22902

**WKIE - AM**
C. Cummings, Pres.
6001 Wilkinson Road
Richmond, VA 23227

**WKLV - AM**
Drawer 192
Blackstone, VA 23824

**WKRE - AM**
Richard Shingleton, Gen. Mgr.
PO. Box 220
Exmore, VA 23350

**WMYK - FM**
William E. Benns, II
Gen. Mgr.
168 Business Park Road
Virginia Beach, VA 23462

**WNOR - AM**
Jack M. Rattigan, Gen. Mgr.
700 Monticello Avenue
Norfolk, VA 23510

**WNWZ - AM**
Tyrone Dickerson, Pres.
4719 Nine Mile Road
Richmond, VA 23223

**WOWI - FM**
L. E. Willis, Sr., Pres.
1010 Park Avenue
Norfolk, VA 23504

**WPAK - AM**
Shirley Everette, Pres.
800 Old Plank Road
PO Box 494
Farmville, VA 23901

**WPCE - AM**
L. E. Willis, Sr., Pres.
1010 Park Avenue
Norfolk, VA 23504

**WPLZ - AM/FM**
Glenn R. Mahone, Pres.
3267 South Crater Rd.
Petersburg, VA 23805

**WRAP - AM**
William Jaeger, Vice Pres.
13 Downtown Plaza
Norfolk, VA 23501

**WSHV - FM**
Norman Talley, Gen. Mgr.
Box 216
South Hill, VA 23970

**WSSV - AM**
Gordon Finney, Gen. Mgr.
N. Walnut Hill Station
Petersburg, VA 23805

**WTOY AM**
Roanoke Valley
Broadcasting Inc.
26 E. Church Avenue
Roanoke, VA 24011

## Washington

**KNHC - FM**
Gregg Neilson, Gen. Mgr.
10750 30th Avenue, N.E.
Seattle, WA 98125

**KQIN - AM**
John Irons, Gen. Mgr.
Box 66160
Seattle, WA 98125

**KUJ - AM**
Kenneth M. Albridge,
Gen. Mgr.
Rt 5, Box 513
Walla Walla, WA 99362

**KYAC-AM**
Lloyd Edwards, Pres.
Seattle, WA 98101

## West Virginia

**WEYS - FM**
Robert Lipscomb, Pres.
One Bruce Street
Institute, WV 25112-0054

**WXIT - AM**
Frank Black, Pres.
136 Hight Street
Charleston, WV 25311

## Wisconsin

**WAWA - FM**
Mike Elliott, Gen. Mgr.
12800 Bluemound Rd.
Elmgrove, WI 53122

**WLUM - FM**
Mike Elliott, Gen. Mgr.
12800 Bluemound Road
Elm Grove, WI 53122

**WNOU-AM**
Jerrel W. Jones, Pres.
3815 N. Teutonia Ave.
Milwaukee, WI 53206

**WNOV - AM**
Jerrell W. Jones, Pres.
3815 N. Teutonia Avenue
Milwaukee, WI 53206

**WSSU - FM**
University of Wisconsin
Superior, WI 54880

# THE BLACK RELIGIOUS TRADITION

**A History of Black Religion in the United States ■ Black Denominations: The Baptists and the Methodists ■ Other Predominantly Black Churches ■ Black Participation in Predominantly White Churches ■ Roman Catholicism ■ Black Jews ■ Mormon Policy Toward Blacks ■ Black Churchmen ■ Gospel Music**

At the end of the 1980s, the church in the black community continued to remain strong and flourish. There was a strong and faithful core of believers who continued to remain active in worship and a wide variety of church activities. Both on the local level and within national organizations, there were positive signs of activity. Within the worship experience itself, there were innovations that reflected an appreciation of a changing world. Of course, on the local level, some churches were more successful than others and that success most often reflected leadership which acknowledged the necessity of meeting the needs—spiritual and otherwise—of church members in the 1980s.

There was a general acknowledgment that family worship of previous generations was not always the best approach for families in the 1980s. The traditional home, which had been a bedrock of black society as much as the black church, was now often splintered and fragmented. And progressive black churches of various denominations responded.

Churches began to provide nursery programs with trained staff for worship services, particularly on Sunday mornings. This provided an incentive to parents who might find difficulty worshipping with young infants. Increasingly, churches began to adopt "Children's Church" programs away from the main worship service so that youngsters might receive a ministry prepared especially for them.

During this time, there was evidence of growth. Some local churches found it necessary to schedule two Sunday morning worship services to accommodate all those who desired to attend on Sundays. And in many inner city communities, churches were able to purchase buildings ranging from abandoned synagogues and cathedrals to even huge, abandoned movie theaters and convert them for their worship services. In the larger cities across the country, it was not all unheard for churches to have several thousand members.

Meeting the needs of those in the local community remained a priority. Many local churches provided services ranging from hot meals during traditional holidays to clothing drives and food baskets to needy families. In the absence of other organized programs, churches developed numerous programs to meet the needs of senior citizens.

With safe and timely transportation a major concern for

many, most churches also acquired fleets of vans and buses to bring those in need to service and also get them safely home.

Realizing that there were large segments of the community who could not and were not attending services, most churches developed a variety of outreach services. First and foremost among them were regular services inside prisons, senior citizen centers and hospitals.

There was increased emphasis on outreach through broadcasting. Religious broadcasting increases several-fold during the 1980s with numerous stations across the country airing a full religious format. Other stations with programming geared to the black listener, also offered time for paid religious programming, particularly on Sunday mornings and evenings.

While nationally recognized evangelists and pastors were broadcasting to large audiences in targeted cities—using independent stations and cable networks, many local ministers were recording weekly services for taped broadcast in their local area.

In another new phenomenon, local black churches with the wherewithal began to establish religious schools and academies for children ranging from elementary to high school. This reflected the emphasis that large denominations had placed on education for decades by establishing colleges for black students who might have not been able to pursue a higher education otherwise.

In another established trend, black ministers continued to move from the pulpit into secular positions where their leadership skills could be put to work. In 1988,

Presidential candidate Jesse Jackson made history on several levels as he pursued the highest elected position in the land. There were many others like Congressman Floyd Flake, who remained a pastor at his New York City church after being elected to the U.S. House of Representatives. While some ministers chose to leave their church roots, others remained firm to their commitment to continue an active role in the religious world.

All in all, the black church remained a symbol of strength in the black community. Despite the problems raised by the highly-publicized errors of some leaders, it was obvious that the church served a need for those who came to worship—and other benefits, tangible and intangible, to the community it has continued to serve for generations.

## BLACK CHRISTIANITY IN THE EIGHTEENTH CENTURY

In the mid-eighteenth century, just before the signing of the Declaration of Independence, there were no black churches or church organizations in the colonies. A few sparsely organized congregations of free blacks met, often secretly, in diverse places, but there were few black Christians, the British largely having confined conversion efforts to Indians. One exception was the Quakers, as William Penn had established a monthly Friends meeting for blacks as far back as 1700.

Though Christian dissenters such as the Germantown Mennonites were important in the founding of the American colonies, and nonconformists such as George Fox and John Wesley were among the first articulate English-speaking foes of slavery, the tardy start of Christianity among blacks was to be expected. Two forces—religious indifference among white settlers and fear that Christian conversion of blacks would undermine white supremacy—were much more powerful than the ideals of a few Quakers and Mennonites.

Early colonizers were generally lethargic about organized religion; fewer than half belonged to churches. Many who did attend services eschewed evangelizing and tended to interpret their faith in terms of proper personal ethics rather than adherence to a formal doctrine or spreading of the gospel.

In such a setting, missionary work among heathen blacks, who were widely presumed by British settlers to have no soul, was scarcely a priority.

This was in contrast to Latin America where slaves were routinely converted to Catholicism. Indeed, the French *Code Noir* of 1685 required that slaves be baptized and provided religious instruction.

The colonists' religious indifference was compounded by several fears, one of which was that if blacks were allowed to congregate for church purposes, they would also want to congregate to plot rebellions. Moreover, if blacks were taught Christian doctrines of brotherhood and equality of all mankind before God, they would protest the precept that whites had a moral authority over blacks—something that was staunchly believed by white colonists in general and slaveholders in particular.

By the start of the eighteenth century, all southern states plus New York and New Jersey had enacted statutes which decreed that conversion to Christianity did not entitle slaves to freedom; Virginia was the first state to do so in 1669. Nevertheless, fears remained strong and the few missionaries who were interested in reaching black souls were opposed by slaveholders and usually denied access to slave quarters.

### The White Evangelists

In the 1740s, the religious environment of the colonies started to change drastically. Spurred by such formidable men as George Whitefield, an Anglican, and Gilbert Tennent, a Presbyterian, religious revivals were mounted from New England to Georgia.

The first of the colorful oratorical preachers—in the tradition that later was to include Billy Sunday and Billy

*Bishop Christopher Rush (left), eloquent orator and ardent abolitionist, laid the groundwork for expansion of the AME Zion church; Quakers like John Woolman (above right) treated slaves like brothers; Dr. Benjamin Rush (right) championed the black's right to education.*

Graham—George Whitefield traveled the length of the Eastern seaboard preaching that a decent orderly life of itself could not lead to salvation, that man must accept Christ or suffer an eternal, burning Hell. With his mastery of English and a booming voice that Benjamin Franklin estimated could reach 30,000 people in the open air, Whitefield shook the casual attitudes of colonial Protestants, and followed by the nearly equally eloquent Tennent, shattered the prevailing conservatism among the New World's religious leaders.

At first Whitefield opposed slavery, but he tempered his stance when he decided that an orphanage of his in Georgia could not survive without slave labor. He later owned slaves himself and was influential in the removal of proscriptions against slavery that had existed in Georgia.

Religious consciousness was revitalized with a new sense of reform and a new independence among laymen within the church structure itself. This spiritual climate bode well for the direction of the colonial seekers of independence and provided the groundwork for future abolitionist movements. Thus black religion in the United States is now being reexamined as an important force in the survival and growth of black culture in this country rather than merely as a means of "escapism" for people who suffered.

In addition, an increasing number of churchmen, white and black, also contend that features of worship found in many black churches, notably shouting-back participation by the congregation, musical improvisation, melodic license in hymn singing, and lack of inhibition with which these aspects of worship are carried out contain ingredients of spiritual freedom that dominant white churches have mistakenly rejected in their emphasis on formalistic worship and social respectability. Rock services and group participation by worshippers are now increasingly found among white congregations.

## Christianity and Slavery

During the mid-eighteenth century the "radical left" of the time, the anti-crown revolutionaries, were also making an impact against slavery by advancing the egalitarian precepts that were to provide the ideals of the war for independence. Such sentiments as "all men are by nature free and independent" and "have the right to life, liberty and the pursuit of happiness" did not persuade the framers of the Constitution to abolish slavery but did contribute greatly to the growth of abolitionist sentiment.

Egalitarian notions increasingly permeated church groups. By 1769, Dr. Samuel Hopkins, minister of the First Congregationalist Church at Newport, Rhode Island, declared the incompatibility of Christianity and slavery. Hopkins, who had been a slaveholder himself, made a house-to-house campaign to arouse abolitionist sentiment. In 1773, Hopkins and Ezra Stiles, who was later to become president of Yale University, conceived a project to train blacks as missionaries for work in Africa. Two slaves, Bristol Yamma and John Quaniero, were selected for this experiment, given freedom, and schooled in the divinities. Money for their manumission was raised through the congregation. In 1774, Yamma and Quaniero entered Princeton to further their studies, but the outbreak of the American Revolution caused the project to be canceled.

As the black and white populations of the mid-eighteenth-century colonies increased, there were only moderate increases in church membership. The greatest gains were made by the Baptists, Presbyterians, and Quakers.

Most important, a religious plurality and liberty to worship or not to worship had developed in the colonies. This crystallized into the constitutional concept that church and state be separate.

## THE FIRST BLACK CHURCHES

As the religious revival swept the country, white missionaries and ministers in the mid-eighteenth-century colonies moved through the South from plantation to plantation conducting services and providing religious training to blacks. Slaves were often used to assist white ministers, and on rare occasions a particularly able slave was purchased and freed to travel with a minister. However, although these black assistants grew to excel in their ministry, they could not hold the title of minister. Slaveholders insisted that black slaves not meet under their own leadership and successfully thwarted black religious workers from being elevated to the position of minister.

Because of segregation, blacks tended to gather in small groups and worship in their own style. For formal services, black freemen and members of the slave church congregations would request permission to use the white churches and were allowed to worship between the services for whites. Only a white preacher or minister was allowed to officiate, however.

The first effort for blacks to organize a church independently took place between 1773 and 1775 at Silver Bluff, South Carolina, 12 miles from Augusta, Georgia, with the creation of a black Baptist church. Leadership of this church was attributed to a Mr. Parmer, first name unknown. David George, another black, also served at Silver Bluff during its early days.

The slaveowner who allowed this group to organize was George Galphin, who became a patron of the congregation. Galphin, an anti-crown colonist, fled in 1778 when the British overran Georgia, and the church was temporarily disbanded. In 1781, after the Revolutionaries' victory, it was revived by the Reverend Jesse Peters.

A second black church was founded in Savannah, Georgia by George Liele, a former servant of a British officer who was previously a leader in the Silver Bluff Baptist church. Liele left with the British forces and successfully organized a church in Jamaica.

In 1780, the Freewill Baptists, formed in New Durham, New Hampshire, took an anti-slavery stance that was later to exempt them from William Lloyd Garrison's attacks on Protestants for indulging slavery. Garrison wrote:

*It gives me great pleasure to mention one Christian denomination that deserves to be excepted from the censures I have been compelled to bestow upon the rest. I allude to the Freewill Baptists who from the beginning refused to receive slaveholders into communion, and most of whom were prompt to espouse the doctrine of emancipation.*

By the late eighteenth century, Presbyterians were also beginning a renunciation of slavery. In 1787, resolutions in New York and Philadelphia were approved stating general principles in favor of the idea of "universal liberty, that prevail in America" and of the interest which many of the states had in promoting abolition of slavery. These Presbyterians also resolved that slaveholders would give slaves a "suitable education as may prepare them for better enjoyment of freedom."

Also in the 1780s, Bishop Coke of the Methodist (Baptist) Church was preaching that slavery was "the vilest [institution] that ever saw the sun." He urged General Washington to sign an anti-slavery petition and lend his influence to the cause of abolition. Washington declined to sign the petition but stated he was a member of the Assembly and that he would support such a resolution if it came to a hearing. It did not.

The changing attitudes of New England churchmen were significant. It is often forgotten that the Puritans were the first settlers to justify slavery theologically, with their view that slaves were the progeny of Ham and condemned to servitude forever.

*The Reverend Andrew Bryan (left) spread the Gospel in Georgia.*

*The Reverend Absalom Jones (below), a Philadelphia pastor and church organizer.*

## ADDITIONAL BLACK CHURCHES

### Black Catholics

Before the Civil War, black Catholics in the United States were largely confined to Baltimore, New Orleans, St. Augustine, and Key West, the Catholic Church in the United States having made little effort to convert blacks. However, Catholics increased conversion efforts after the Civil War and by the end of the nineteenth century there were some 200,000 black Catholics in the United States, and two papers devoted to their interests: the *St. Joseph's Advocate* of Baltimore, and the *American Catholic Tribune* of Cincinnati. The first black priest, ordained in 1886, was Augustus Tolton.

He was followed in Savannah by Andrew Bryan, a courageous and articulate man who was feared by whites. Bryan was often waylaid, assaulted, and beaten viciously. However, he continued his influential work, was ordained a minister, and died a natural death in 1812.

### Black Protestants

Blacks also organized churches in other parts of the South—in Petersburg, Virginia in 1776 and Richmond in 1780. These and other churches were formed by bold enterprising men such as Henry Evans, who established the first Methodist Church with an all-black congregation in Fayetteville, North Carolina in 1790. Evans, originally from Virginia, was a shoemaker by trade and born free. A devoted religious man, he settled in Fayetteville where he set out to help blacks of the area by bringing them closer to God. He was denied the right to preach by the town council and so was forced to hold his services secretly. However, Evans' honesty, integrity and earnest pleadings to the town council eventually convinced authorities to allow him to preach in the town. His church was incorporated into the black AME Zion Church in 1866.

*Right Reverend Richard Allen, first bishop of the AME church.*

One very prominent, respected black preacher of the time was black Harry Housier who traveled with Bishop Asbury of the Methodist Church. The Methodist Bishop Coke wrote in 1784: "I have had the pleasure of hearing Harry Housier preach several times. I sometimes give notice immediately after preaching that in a little while he will preach to the blacks, but the whites always stay to hear him."

A very prominent black minister of the late eighteenth century was John Chavis. Born free in North Carolina in 1763, Chavis was a soldier in the Revolutionary Army, attended Princeton University, and was appointed a minister by the Presbyterian Church to serve among blacks. He eventually set up a school where he taught both white and black students classics in preparation for college. Many of his students, such as Senator Charles Manly, in later years achieved status and recognition in government.

### Beginning of AME Church

The growing number of blacks within the Methodist denomination and a rigid set of segregationist standards moved blacks in the direction of formally organizing their own church. The first was to emerge in Philadelphia under the leadership of Richard Allen and Absalom Jones and to be known as the Bethel African Methodist Episcopal Church.

The Philadelphia Church was to start as a direct result of violence by whites. Absalom Jones, a thrifty black from Delaware who had bought his and his wife's freedom, worshipped with whites in St. George's Methodist Church, as did other Philadelphia blacks. One day in 1787 Jones was jerked from his knees while praying and ordered to move to the balcony. The upshot was that Jones, together with Richard Allen, started to organize independently. The immediate result, in 1787, was the Free African Society. Then in 1793 Allen formed the Bethel African Methodist Episcopal Church (AME) while Jones, ordained in the Episcopal Church in 1794, became pastor at St. Thomas' Episcopal Church.

The separate courses followed by Allen and Jones were the forerunners of a split in black Protestantism that prevails to this day. Jones followed a course close to the style and procedures of established white churches, while Allen set out to appeal almost solely to blacks by displaying empathy with their experience and views. Inevitably, the approach of the two groups was to part further, the churches affiliated with white denominations following a more staid, ceremonial course and forcefully preaching education and social benefits for blacks, while the latter tended to concentrate on the distinctiveness and emotions of blacks while often eschewing social protest.

However, it would be grossly misleading to assume that the latter group played no part in black political progress. Such great leaders as Martin Luther King Jr., Leon Sullivan, and Jesse Jackson were to emerge from such religious organizations.

Though Allen resisted help from whites, it was Methodist Bishop Asbury who obtained a church for him in 1793 and in 1799 ordained him a Deacon. The AME grew, sprouting branches in Pennsylvania, Maryland, Delaware, and New Jersey and by 1822 had moved south to Charleston.

## Beginning of AME Zion Church

In New York City, James Varick was to follow a course similar to Allen's. In 1796, members of the Methodist Episcopal Church in New York hired a house and started to hold separate meetings. In 1799, they formally organized their own church. In 1820, they officially seceded from the Methodist Church when that group refused to ordain Varick. Two years later Varick was elected Bishop of the AME Zion Church.

Similar patterns developed in other churches. For example, in Philadelphia in 1809 blacks, who were denied worship in a local Baptist church, formed an African Baptist Church under the leadership of a Reverend Burrows. Also in 1809, blacks established the Abyssinian Baptist Church, in Boston, under Thomas Paul.

## Recolonization

Black ministers in the early nineteenth century became involved in African recolonization efforts, some as missionaries. One of these, the Baptist Lott Cary went to Liberia in 1821 where he worked until his death seven years later.

Blacks such as Cary were ambivalent to recolonization. On the one hand, they saw it as a way of spreading the word of God, but on the other they felt it contrary to the best interests of blacks. One leading black who later supported recolonization was Bishop Daniel Payne of the AME Church, another was Alexander Crummell, an Episcopalian minister from New York City.

Other black churchmen favored recolonization and missionary work in the West Indies.

*Rural clergymen, post-Civil War.*

*Zealous Abolitionist William Lloyd Garrison was known as "The Great Liberator."*

## The Effect of Slave Revolts

The march of Christianity among blacks—always suspect to many whites—was soon to meet strong opposition in 1822, following suppression of Denmark Vesey's plot to revolt. White fears of the consequences of allowing blacks to organize for religious worship were stirred by the ingenuity of Vesey's planning and by the fact that Vesey himself was a member of the African Methodist Church. Numerous black churches in the South were forced to go underground, a step that was to further the "blackness" of black religions in the United States.

The Nat Turner revolt of 1830 resulted in further restrictions on the freedom of blacks to move about and organize. However, during the period from 1822 to the outbreak of the civil war in 1861, there was a substantial increase in the number of black Christian congregations and church organizations. Noteworthy increases occurred in the West where itinerant preachers spread the gospel. One of these, William Paul Quinn, a missionary of the AME, had set up nearly 50 churches with over 2,000 members by the early 1830's in Western Pennsylvania, Ohio, and Illinois. By 1836, the AME had 86 churches and nearly 8,000 members throughout the country, and during that year the first organization of black Baptist churches, the Providence Baptist Association, was formed in Ohio. By 1850, there were 150,000 black members of the Baptist Church.

## Christians and Abolition

Of great urgency during this time was the involvement of black and white churchmen in the abolitionist struggle, on both sides. Abolitionist leaders were, ironically, slow to accept black churchmen. In 1836, abolitionists vetoed a move to have a black minister address them. Many churches, pressured from both sides, adopted carefully developed fence-sitting positions. The Methodist Episcopal Church, which had condemned slavery in 1780, announced in 1836 that it had no wish to interfere in the relationship between master and slave as it then existed. In 1842, an Episcopal Convention in Pennsylvania adopted a resolution excluding representatives from black churches. In 1844, Methodists in the South seceded from their church when northern church leaders declared that a bishop could not own slaves.

Firmest opposition to slavery continued to come from Quakers, who sought to buy slaves in order to free them and who encouraged blacks to attend Friends meetings. Their stance was supported by individual ministers of conscience in all major churches who sought, often successfully, to encourage blacks to worship in their congregations and to send representatives to their conventions.

During the Civil War, Lincoln acknowledged the importance of religion to blacks when he appointed Henry McNeal Turner, an elder in the Methodist Episcopal Church, as Chaplain for the black 1st Regiment.

## Religion and Reconstruction

Black church membership expanded greatly after the Civil War. Greatest growth was achieved by the Baptists, who had 500,000 members by 1870. The Methodist Episcopal Church, while split into northern and southern divisions, also grew, with separate black church conferences emerging in the South. The African Methodist Episcopal Church, which had gone underground in the South in the Civil War, also grew. Membership in the African Methodist Episcopal Zion Church boomed from 25,000 in 1860 to 200,000 in 1870.

Meanwhile in the Catholic Church, Father Patrick Healy and James Augustine Healy, who were brothers, were to assume important posts, the former becoming president of Georgetown University in 1873, the latter a Bishop in 1875, and then an assistant to the papal throne.

## The Churches and Segregation

The history of black Christianity after the Civil War is also being subjected to reexamination. There is no doubt that churchmen, both white and black, adjusted to segregation efforts following Reconstruction and frequently encouraged it. Until recently, this has been almost universally regarded as a negative, retrogressive step, which furthered the humiliation and degradation of blacks and which was to be given legitimacy in the 1896 "separate but equal" decision of the U.S. Supreme Court.

In general, southern churches completely excluded blacks from both churches and church organizations. Northern churches often forced blacks to worship in separate and most unequal structures, and subordinated them within individual churches and church organizations, but not sharing the racial fanaticism then prevalent in the South, did not wish to suffer the diminution of church membership that would result from complete exclusion of blacks from church membership.

The reunification of the Methodist Church reflected the different concerns of northern and southern Protestants, the latter insisting on considerable independence as a condition of reunion.

However, in the latter part of the nineteenth century as in the 1970s, there were those who felt strongly that separation of the races was essential to the survival and self-respect of blacks. In many cases, black clergymen were a vital source of racial pride.

A comment by a black student at Tugaloo University, Mississippi in 1894, as reported by the Reverend A. F. Beard, D.D., secretary of the American Missionary Association, underscores the fact that charges against black churches for encouraging obsequiousness and acceptance of their low status were not altogether correct.

*I find the Negro lacks race pride. He despises his own makeup. Who of you ever heard any Negro say that he thought the general characteristics of his race were as becoming as those of other races? Nor are they. The Anglo-Saxon is proud of his race characteristics. The Indian is, also, but the Negro despises himself, and would be anything else than what God has made him. But how can we escape hell if we hate ourselves because we are Negroes, when this is the divine wisdom of a just God? We may talk about improving our homes by getting an education as much as we please, but we will never be anything until we have race pride, and try to carry out the great plan of God who made us and knew what is best for us. Let us be genuine Negroes, pure and good, and not desire a drop of other blood in our veins.*

*Wendell Phillips speaking against slavery on Boston Common.*

## THE TWENTIETH-CENTURY BLACK CHURCH

The influence of religious institutions among blacks probably peaked in the first decade of the twentieth century. With the start of the massive migration from the rural South to northern cities, the small community structures on which the church's authority rested were ruptured. Churches remained very important to blacks and to their adjustment to urban life, but their authority diminished. By 1926, the Congregationalist Church was to report that less than half of America's black population and less than one-third of blacks who lived in large northern cities had a religious affiliation.

Many black church leaders ascribed the decline in religious interest primarily to a national trend produced by rising acceptance of evolutionary and scientific interpretations of the meaning of existence and to the growing strength of Socialism and other anti-clerical political viewpoints. However, many black civil rights leaders and some church leaders themselves charged that churches, with what in the 1960s was to become labeled as "irrelevance," lacked interest in the day-to-day housing, employment, and education problems that plagued blacks.

### Christianity and Political Activism in the Sixties

Churches spawned some of the great leaders of the twentieth century, men such as Powell, King, Abernathy, and most recently Jesse Jackson. These ministers were to use their churches as a base for uniting blacks politically. In so doing, they did not eschew traditional Christian doctrines or organized religion but sought to ally Christian faith with social militancy. Religion to these men and other activist ministers was not a pacifier, but a spur to action. For, they maintained, if God was in man, then man was worthy of respect from others and by the law. To exploit human beings, be they black or white, was to deny God.

Dr. King took special pains to point out the compatibility between his activism and religious worship. His reconciliation of passive resistance with Christianity contributed substantially to his reputation as one of the great Americans of the twentieth century and his receipt of the Nobel Peace Prize. There was also in King's theology, as well as that of other postwar Christians, an affinity for Ghandian doctrines of nonviolence. King held staunchly to his pacifist views, in the face of black critics who considered nonviolence a failure, and in the mid 1960s became one of the first Americans to oppose military involvement in Vietnam, when he equated war and racism.

In addition to the rising activism of the black clergy, there were three other major postwar developments in black religion, each of which emerged strongly in the 1960s:

The growth of the Nation of Islam, frequently known as the Black Muslims.

The prominence received by the concept of the "Black Messiah, "as advanced by the Reverend Albert Cleague of Detroit.

The demands of blacks for monetary reparation from white-dominated religious groups.

### The Nation of Islam

From its outset during the 1920s and 1930s, the Nation of Islam stressed the superiority of blacks as a race. According to the founder of the religion, who was known at times under other names, variously as W. D. Fard, Farad Muhammad, Wally Farad, as well as F. Muhammad Ali, mankind was originally black, but people had a weak and evil side which was white. The two halves became separated and whites were given some 6,000 years to reign, until 1984, when blacks would again rule.

In the 1930s, Fard disappeared and was succeeded as head of the movement by Elijah Poole, who became known as Elijah Muhammad. Muhammad declared that Fard was Allah and that he, Muhammad, was Allah's messenger,

*James Forman delivering the 1969 Black Manifesto demanding $500,000 from white churches in reparation for the injustices of slavery and racism.*

selected by Allah to inform blacks of their heritage, rights, and responsibilities.

The Nation of Islam also differed from more conventional religions in the directness of its appeal to what some sociologists have come to call the "black underclass"—people who are unemployed, prison inmates, or living by their wits in the street.

Along with their doctrines of black integrity, the Nation preaches discipline, abstinence, honor, cleanliness, and self-sufficiency. By 1975, when Elijah Muhammad died, it had an estimated 160,000 members, operated several schools, a university, and thriving businesses in such fields as publishing, agriculture, food processing and retailing, and had earned the respect of whites and more theologically conservative blacks.

It was under the leadership of the now-retired Dr. Mohammed Abdul-Rauf that a reconciliation was made between the conventional Muslims and the Nation of Islam (Black Muslims). Dr. Abdul-Rauf, in private consultations, gained concessions from the Black Muslims to change practices that were not in conformity with the best traditions of Islam.

There are close to 3 million Muslims in the United States with a large concentration in the Washington, D.C. area. *The Muslim News* is the national publication.

## The Black Messiah

Another religious concept associated with black pride and the impoverished was the Black Messiah movement led by the Reverend Albert Cleague. Established in Detroit in the 1960s, Cleague's militant group asserted that there was no reason the Messiah could not be black and proceeded to challenge such groups as The United Church of Christ to allocate positions of responsibility in church hierarchies for black churchmen and to give substantial sums of church money for improvements of conditions in ghettos.

## Reparations

The move for reparations reflected a growing tendency for blacks to demand economic aid from white-dominated institutions. The most widely publicized demand for reparations was made by James Forman, head of the now-defunct Student Non-Violent Coordinating Committee, in 1968, when in the midst of Sunday services at New York City's Riverside Church, he strode to the pulpit and demanded $500 million as repayment to blacks for past abuses by white Americans.

The Council of Churches and other white-led churches responded by setting up organizations to advance funds to disadvantaged groups, but little money changed hands; the net effect of Forman's demand was to raise the consciousness of whites. Moreover, not all blacks supported Forman's view. The Reverend Joseph Jackson, head of the Black National Baptist Convention, for example, attacked the National Council of Churches for establishing a black development corporation in reaction to Forman's demands.

Blacks within major national and international church groups also challenged their leadership. In Chicago, black priests protested the appointment policy of the Archbishop. Blacks petitioned the Vatican for a separate rite for black Catholics in the United States. Dissension between white and black Catholics in the United States peaked in 1971 when the U.S. Conference of Catholic Bishops omitted funding for the National Office of Black Catholics.

In 1973, a black, The Most Reverend Joseph Lawson Howze, was named Auxiliary Bishop of Mississippi. Harold Perry, a Roman Catholic Bishop in Louisiana, is also black.

Enrollment of minorities in seminaries has slowly risen from 808 in 1970 to 1,061 in 1972. Hispanic enrollment in 1972 was 264, less than 1% of seminary population.

By contrast with established religions, racial conflict has long been rare and racial integration extensive among Pentecostal groups.

*Communities look to their pastors for both spiritual and temporal leadership.*

### Black Churches Remain Dominant

In 1980, the majority of America's black Christians continued to worship within churches that appealed primarily to blacks and generally had all-black congregations. A thread uniting these congregations and distinguishing them from white-dominated groups is the verbal feedback of congregations during sermons, the music of black hymns, the melodic license of members of the congregantion to improvise in church singing, and a greater tendency of black than white preachers in their fiery utterances to be positive, to offer hope more than to warn of damnation, and to avoid dwelling on the sins and dangers of religious or lay threats, such as "Socialists" or "intellectuals."

Once despised by theologians and intellectuals as crude and naive, the black church has increasingly become an object of respect and admiration. In part this is attributable to rising race consciousness among blacks and increasing respect among the general public for people willing, without embarrassment, "to do their thing." Also, awareness slowly dawned that there is probably no more truly black institution in the United States than the black church.

As Henry H. Mitchell observes:

*It is important to remember that there is a distinct black religious experience today because there was and is a distinct black experience in America and because that experience was given religious interpretation by men, most of whom were ignorant of the white tradition. Their interpretations were made on the basis of their African background and peculiar experience in America, as this experience could be articulated with their knowledge of the Bible. The theological world has therefore, a fresh datum of experience, far more free . . . [of European influences] than can be found elsewhere in America.*

Black churches have grown stronger because they served the needs of their congregations, both spiritually and socially. While the black church frequently has been accused of "otherworldly escapism," it is also true that the civil rights movement of the sixties would not have been possible without the leadership and facilities of the churches. The proof of this participation is seen in the multitude of churches that were burned and bombed and the religious leaders who were jailed and otherwise persecuted.

### The Black Church and Current Religious Conservatism

The rise of the "Moral Majority" movement in the 1980s was greeted with general ambivalence by black churches. In two major cities, black ministers headed up city-wide chapters of the Moral Majority and one black minister formed a national conservative organization of his own.

But while most black churches, specifically the Baptists, agree with the Moral Majority on such doctrinal matters as belief in God, The Holy Spirit, deity of Jesus Christ, the Fall of Man, doctrine of sin, salvation, and redemption, they diverge on issues such as racism and politics.

The Reverend Frank Madison Reid, Bishop in the African Methodist Church, summed up the major problem that blacks had with the Moral Majority: "There is a lot about the movement's inflexibility, intolerance and passion for annihilation that makes me think of the Great Inquisition and the Dark Ages." Church people must pray and think together.

The Reverend William Jones Jr., President of the National Black Minister's Conference, was even more succinct, in an open letter to Moral Majority leader Reverend Jerry Falwell: "You, Dr. Falwell, are a champion of the American system. I, sir, refuse to champion any system that historically and presently engages in the systematic demeaning, degrading and dehumanizing of millions of lives and is in conflict with the ethic espoused by Jesus of Nazareth." He noted that the John Birch Society and Ku Klux Klan were supporting the movement.

Thus it seemed as if there would be little outpouring of support for the Moral Majority by black churches; indeed, many black religious organizations, such as the Progressive National Convention, took official stands against the religious right as early as 1980.

## BLACK DENOMINATIONS

### Baptists: History and Worship

The Baptist church became a major force in black religious life in the years immediately following the Civil War. By 1870 (four years after North Carolina had launched the movement), Baptist state conventions had been organized throughout the South.

The Consolidated American Baptist Convention, organized in 1867 and lasting until 1880, represented the black's first attempt to create a national body independent of, and separate from, white-dominated groups. With the dissolution of this convention, three smaller ones sprang up: the Foreign Mission Baptist Convention of the U.S.A. (1880), the American National Baptist Convention (1880), and the American National Educational Baptist Convention (1893). These organizations were then united as the National Baptist Convention of the U.S.A.

The National Baptist Convention, U.S.A., Inc. is the parent convention of black Baptists. Its membership in 1981 was 6.3 million, up from 5.15 million in 1958. Dr. Joseph H. Jackson has been president of the Convention since 1953.

The National Baptist Convention of America was organized in 1880 and is usually referred to as the "unincorporated body." In 1981 it had a membership of 6,300,000. The Convention is based in Jacksonville, Florida. (Correspondence should be addressed to Albert E. Chew, 2823 North Houston, Fort Worth, TX 76106.)

## Directory and Officers of the National Baptist Convention, U.S.A., Inc. Through 1989

### Officers

President
Dr. T. J. Jemison
915 Spain St.
Baton Rouge, LA 70802
(504) 383-5401

Gen. Secretary
Dr. W. Franklyn Richardson
52 South 6th Ave.
Mt. Vernon, NY 10550
(914) 664-2676

Vice-President-at-large
Dr. C. A. Clark
902 N. Good St.
Dallas, TX 75204

Treasurer
Dr. Isaac Green
3068 Iowa St.
Pittsburgh, PA 15219
(412) 556-1437

Vice-Presidents
Dr. David Matthews
P 0 Box 627
Indianola, MS

Dr. A. E. Campbell
2500 Carnes Ave.
Memphis, TN 38114
and
Dr. Henry L. Lyons
Dr. E. Victor Hill
Dr. Allen Stanley

Asst. Secretaries
Dr. B. J. Whipper Sr.
15 Ninth St.
Charleston, SC 29403

Dr. Marshall F. Robinson
818 Summerfield St.
Mobile, AL 36617

Dr. Roger P. Derricotte
539 Roseville Ave.
Newark NJ 07107

Dr. McKinley Dukes
4223 S. Benton
Kansas City, MO 64130

Statistician
Dr. M L. Gabriel

Historiographer
Dr. Clarence Wagner

### Officers of Boards

Foreign Mission Board
Secretary
Dr. William J. Harvey, III701 S. 19th St.
Philadelphia, PA 19146

Home Mission Board
Exec. Secretary
Dr. Jerry Moore
1612 Buchanan St. N.W.
Washington, DC 20011

Sunday School Publishing Board
Exec. Director.
Mrs. C. N. Adkins
330 Charlotte Ave.
Nashville, TN 37201

B.T.U. Board
Secretary
Dr. Maynard Turner
412 4th Ave.
Nashville, TN 37219

Education Board
Chairperson
Dr. W. H. Brewster
903 Looney St.
Memphis, TN 38107

Evangelism Board
Dr. Manuel Scott
2600 S. Marsalis Ave.
Dallas, TX 75216

Laymen's Movement
President
Mr. Walter Cade
537 N. 82nd St.
Kansas City, KS 66112

Woman's Auxiliary Convention
President
Mrs. Mary 0. Ross
584 Arden Pk.
Detroit Ml 48202

Congress of Christian Education
President
Dr. T. Oscar Chappelle
1014 East Pine St.
Tulsa, OK 74106

### Periodical

National Baptist Voice (s-m)
Editor
Dr. Roscoe Cooper
2800 Third Ave.
Richmond, VA 23222
(804) 321-5115

*The Baptist church has been a major force in the religious life of African-Americans since the Civil War.*

## Directory and Officers of the National Baptist Convention of America Through 1989

**Officers**

President
E. Edward Jones
1450 Pierre Ave.
Shreveport LA 71103

Vice-Presidents
1st Vice-President
Dr. S. M. Lockridge
710 Crosby St.
San Diego CA 92113

2nd Vice-Pres
Dr. Albert Chew
2823 N. Houston St.
Ft. Worth TX 76106

3rd Vice-President
Dr. Wallace S. Hansfield
3100 E. 31st St.
Kansas City MO 64128

Corr. Secretary
Rev. Stephen Thurston
740 E 77th St.
Chicago IL 60619

Gen. Rec. Secretary
Dr. Clarence C. Pennywell
2016 Russell Rd.
Shrevepon LA 71107

Treasurer
Rev. Floyd N. Williams
5902 Bealt St., Houston
TX 77091

Historiographer
Rev. Marvin C. Griffin
1010 E. Tenth St.
Austin, TX 78702

Statistician
Rev. E. E. Stafford
6614 5. Western Ave.
Los Angeles CA 90047

Auditor
Rev. J. Carlton Allen
1639 Hays St.
San Antonio TX 78202
(512) 225-7907

Youth Advisor
Rev. B. W. Noble
636 N. Fourth St.
Muskogee OK 74401

Admn. Asst. to Pres.
Rev. Joe R. Gant
5823 Ledbetter,
Shrevepon LA 71108

Secretary of Finance
Rev. H. T. Johnson
2807 Tanner St.
Dallas TX 75215

**Other Organizations**

Education Board
Chairperson
Dr. T. B. Adams
609 S.W. 9th St.
Belle Glade, FL 33430

Exec. Secretary.
Dr. W. E. Hausey
3538 Jackson Ave.
New Orleans LA 70113

Foreign Mission Board
Chairperson
Rev. J. W. Toomer
1905 Amelia
Orlando, FL 32805

Exec. Secretary
Dr. Robert H. Wilson
P O Drawer 223655
Dallas TX 75222

Home Mission Board
Chairperson
Dr. Luke Mingo
3993 S. King Dr.
Chicago, IL 60653

Exec. Secretary
Dr. 0. B. Williams
3132 N. Vancouver Ave.
Portland, OR 97227

Evangelical Board
Chairperson
Rev. E. Potter
2403 Hewes
St., Gulfport, MS 52303

Exec. Secretary
Dr. F. H. Dunn Sr.
P O Box 51737
New Orleans, LA 70151

Baptist Training Union Board
Chairperson
Rev. A. Bernard
3069 Orchard St.
Indianapolis, IN 46218

Exec. Secretary
Dr. J. Royster Powell
5708 Wayne St.
Houston TX 77026

Benevolent Board
Chairperson
Rev. William Bowie Jr.
718 E. 40th St.
Houston, TX 77022

Sec. Treasurer
Rev. J. F. Hargrett
P O Box 5907
Orlando, FL 32855

Senior Women
#l President
Dr. Fannie C. Thompson
516 E. Waverly St.
Tucson, AZ 85705

Senior Women
#2 President
Dr. Hattie L. E. Williams
1166 Rapides Ave.
Alexandria, LA 71301

Junior Women
President
Sis. Frances Worthy
705 Carver Ave.
Waco, TX 76704

Brotherhood
President
Bro. Wayman Smith
1449 86th Ave.
Oakland, CA 94621

Ushers
President
Bro. Charles Walker
3167 Boulevard Pl.
Indianapolis, IN 46208

Young Men for Christ
President
Rev. Curtis L. Carter
2808 Crest Ave.
Austin, TX 78702

Youth
President
Rev. Previn Carr
302 E . Thunderbird Trail
Phoenix, AZ 85040

*Abolitionist periodicals raised public consciousness. Many of the early religious figures were spokesmen for the anti-slavery movement.*

*This Baptist church in Savannah was the second black place of worship to be built in the colonies.*

## Directory and Officers of the Progressive National Baptist Convention, Inc. Through 1989

**Officers**

President
Dr. J. Alfred Smith Sr.
Allen Temple Baptist Church
8500 A St.
Oakland, CA 94621

Gen. Secretary
Rev. C. J. Malloy Jr.
601 5Oth St., N.E.
Washington, DC 20019
(202) 396-0558

**Other Organizations**

Dept. of Christian Education
Secretary
Rev. C. B. Lucas
3815 W. Broadway
Louisville, KY 40211

Women's Auxiliary
Mrs. Goldie Hollie
537 66th St
Oakland CA 94609

Home Mission Bd.
Exec. Director
Rev. Archie LeMone
601 5Oth St., N.E.
Washington, DC 20019

Cong. of Christian Ed.
President
Dr. Pauline C. Reeder
788 E. 52nd St.
Brooklyn, NY 11203

Baptist F. M. Bureau
Dr. Ronald K. Hill
1678 Fairview Ave.
Willow Grove, PA 19090

**Periodical**

Baptist Progress (q)
Tabernacle Baptist Church 1477
Copley Rd.
Akron, OH 44320
Ed. Rev. Isaiah F. Paul

## Methodists: History and Worship

Large numbers of blacks joined the Methodist Church in prerevolutionary times. In some areas they were organized into separate congregations presided over by white preachers, while in others they participated in services on a segregated basis (occupying special seats, and taking communion only after their white counterparts had done so). Dissatisfaction with the latter system grew so pronounced that, by 1785, several influential members of Methodist churches in the North had voted to establish their own places of worship. The leader in this movement, Richard Allen, was himself a freedman and a convert to Methodism.

The black Methodist movement experienced its first flowering after the Civil War, at which time many rural churches in the South showed an inclination to accept its leadership. In part this phenomenon was due to the greater mobility enjoyed by the black—both preacher and convert—as a result of emancipation. Despite its growth, however, the Methodists never succeeded in matching the appeal generated by the Baptist movement. Nevertheless, the Methodists of today lay claim to more than 2 million members.

As in the case of the Baptists, Methodist worship has tended to reflect the religious mentality and spiritual expectations of the black masses. As such, it is usually evangelistic in tone and relies heavily on the dynamism and personality of the preacher, rather than on any strict adherence to articles of faith.

## The AME Church

In 1816, Richard Allen, then a deacon of Bethel Church, called together representatives of separate black churches which had been established in Delaware, Maryland, and New Jersey. The meeting resulted in the formation of the African Methodist Episcopal (AME) Church.

The AME Church, which has parishes in Africa, Canada, and the islands of the Caribbean as well as across the United States, has a membership of 1.9 million. The number of churches has declined sharply, from 6,000 in the 1970s to slightly more than 3,000 in the 1980s. Membership expanded by 800,000, however.

The AME's chief governing bodies are the General Conference, the Council of Bishops, and the General Board. The main work of the church is carried out through a number of lesser boards and departments in charge of such fields as missionary endeavor, education, and evangelism.

*Bishop Herbert Bell Shaw.*

## Directory and Officers of the African Methodist Episcopal (AME) Church Through 1989

**Officers**

Senior Bishop
Bishop Henry W. Murph
8939 Sepulveda Blvd.
Ste. 240
Los Angeles, CA 90045
(213) 216-7561

Gen. Secretary
A.M.E. Church
Dr. Richard Allen Chappelle Sr.
P O Box 183
St. Louis, MO 63166
(314) 534-6020

President
Council of Bishops
Bishop Remben E. Stokes
400 S. Zang Blvd.
Ste. 813
Dallas, TX 75208
(214) 941-9323

Sec. Council of Bishops
Bishop Cornelius E. Thomas
500 Eighth Ave. S.
Ste. 201
Nashville, TN 37203
(615) 242-6814

President Gen. Board
Bishop Frank M. Reid Jr.
2101 Magnolia
Birmingham, AL 35205
(205) 252-2612

Secretary Gen. Board
Dr. Richard Allen Chappelle Sr.
P O Box 183
St. Louis, MO 63166

Trea. A.M.E. Church
Dr. Joseph C. McKinney
2311 M St., N.W.
Washington, DC 20037
(202) 337-3930

Historiographer
Dr. Henderson Davis
P O Box 783,
Indianapolis, IN 46206
(317) 546-9654

Pres, Judical Council
Atty. P. A. Townsend
1010 Macvicar St.
Topeka, KS 66604

**Departments**

Missions
Dr. Frederick C. Harrison
475 Riverside Dr.
Rm. 1926
New York, NY 10115
(212) 870-2558

Church Extension
Secretary-Treasurer
Dr. Hercules Miles
3526 Dodier
St. Louis, MO 63107
(314) 534-4272

Christian Education
Secretary
Dr. Edgar Mack
500 8th Ave. S.
Nashville, TN 37203
(615) 242-1420

Sunday School Union
Sec-Treasurer
Dr. Lee Henderson
500 Eighth Ave., S.
Nashville, TN 37203
(615) 256-5882

Evangelism
Director
Yale B. Bruce
5728 Major Blvd.
Orlando, FL 82819
(305) 352-6515

Publications
Secretary-Treasurer
Dr. A. Lee Henderson
500 8th Ave., S.
Nashville, TN 37203
(615) 256 5882

Pension
Secretary-Treasurer
Dr. Joseph L. Jomer
500 8th Ave. S.
Nashville, TN 37203
(615) 256-7725

Finance Department
Dr. Joseph C. McKinney
2311 M St., N.W.
Washington, DC 20037
(202) 337-3930

Statistical Department
Dr. Richard A. Chappelle Sr.
P O Box 183
St. Louis, MO 63166
(314) 534-6020

Minimum Salary
Dr. Ezra M. Johnson
280 Hernando St.
Memphis, TN 38126
(901) 526-4281

Religious Literature Dept.
Sr., Editor-in-Chief
Dr. Cyrus S. Keller
P O Box 5327
St. Louis, MO 63115
(314) 535-8822

Women's Missionary Society
President
Mrs. Delores L. K. Williams
2311 M St., N.W.
Washington, DC 20037
(212) 337-1335

Lay Organization
Connectional President
Dr. Kathryn M. Brown
171 Ashby St.
Atlanta, GA 30314

**Periodicals**

A.M.E. Christian Recorder
Editor
Dr. Roben H. Reid
500 8th Ave., S.
Nashville, TN 37203
(615) 256-8548

A.M.E., Review
Dr. Jamye Coleman Williams
500 Eighth Ave., S.
Nashville, TN 37203
(615) 320-3500

Voice of Missions
Editor
Dr. Frederick C. Harnson
475 Riverside Dr.
Rm. 1920
New York, NY 10115

Women's Missionary Mag.
Mrs. Benha 0. Fordham
800 Risley Ave.
Pleasantville, NJ, 08232

Secret Chamber
Dr. Yale B. Bruce
5728 Major Blvd.
Orlando, FL 82819
(305) 352-6515

Journal of Christian Ed.
Dr. Edgar L. Mack
500 Eighth Ave., S.
Nashville, TN 37202
(615) 242-1420

**Bishops in the U.S.A.**

First District
Frank C. Cummings
5070 Parkside
Ste. 1410
Philadelphia, PA 19131
(215) 877-3771

Second District
John Hurst Adams
615 G St. S.W.
Washington, DC 20024
(202) 554-4351

Third District
Richard A. Hildebrand
700 Bryden Rd.
Ste. 135
Columbus, OH 43215
(614) 461-6496

Fourth District
Samuel S. Morris Jr.
4448 S. Michigan Ave.
P O Box 53539
Chicago, IL 60653
(312) 285-5500

Fifth District
Henry W. Murph
8939 S. Sepulveda
Ste. 240
Los Angeles, CA 90045
(213) 216-7561

Sixth District
Frederick Talbot
208 Auburn Ave. N.E.
Atlanta, GA 30303
(404) 659-2012

Seventh District
Frederick C. James
370 Forest Dr.
Ste. 402
Columbia, SC 29204

Eighth District
Donald G. Ming
2138 St. Bernard Ave.,
New Orleans, LA 70119
(504) 948-4251

Ninth District
Frank M. Reid Jr.
2101 Magnolia
Birmingham, AL 35205
(205) 252-2612

Tenth District
Remben E. Stokes
400 S. Zang Blvd.
Ste. 813
Dallas, TX 75208
(214) 941-9323

Eleventh District
Philip R. Cousin
P O Box 2140
Jacksonville, FL 32203
(904) 398-3797

Twelfth District
H. Hanford Brookins
604 Locust Ave. North
Little Rock AR 72114
(501) 375-4310

Thirteenth District
Cornelius Thomas
500 8th Ave., So.
Nashville, TN 37203
(615) 242-6814

Fourteenth District
Vernon R. Byrd
460 Waverly Pl.
Orange, NJ 07050
(201) 674-1177

Fifteenth District
Henry A. Belin Jr.
1358 Laboldi
Nashville, TN 37207
(615) 868-5272

Sixteenth District
James H. Mayo
6 Morningwood Ct.
Olney, MD 20232
(301) 774 3278

Seventeenth District
Robert L. Pruitt
7911 13th St. NW
Washington, DC 20012

Nineteenth District
John E. Hunter
22335 La Garonne
Southville, Ml 48075
(313) 559-7627

Ecumenical Officer
Vinton R. Anderson
7748 Peachtree Lane
University City, MO 63130
(314) 534-4278

**Retired Bishops**

D. Ward Nichols
2295 Seventh Ave.
New York, NY 10030
(516) 427-0225

Ernest L. Hickman
1320 Oakcrest Dr. S.W.
Atlanta, GA 30311
(404) 349-1336

Harrison J. Bryant
4000 Bedford Rd.
Baltimore, MD 21207
(301) 484-7508

H. Thomas Primm
2820 Monaco Parkway
Denver, CO 80207
(303) 335-9545

Huben N. Robinson
357 Arden Park
Detroit, Ml 48202
(313) 875-4967

Bishop Harold I. Bearden
644 Skipper Dr.
Atlanta, GA 30314
(404) 691-9642

*Powerful AME leader Daniel Coker later emigrated to Liberia.*

## The African Methodist Episcopal Zion Church

In 1796, Bishop Francis Asbury acceded to the request of black members of the Methodist Episcopal Church in New York for permission to hold meetings under their own auspices. Among those who participated in this movement were James Varick, Francis Jacobs, William Brown, Peter Williams, June Scott, Samuel Pontier, Thomas Miller, William Hamilton, Abraham Thompson, and William Miller. They fitted out an old building on Cross Street, between Mulberry and Orange streets, which had previously been used as a stable, as a place of worship. Thus was born the prototype of the African Methodist Episcopal Zion Church. The founders, however, did not declare their underlying purpose at once and withheld their new name from the public until 1799.

Prominent among those who attended the meeting in 1799, when it was decided to make public their purpose and declare the name of the first African Methodist Church in America, were George E. Moore, Thomas Sipkins, David Bias, George White, Thomas Cook, John Teesman, and George Collins, along with those named above. The first Board of Trustees consisted of Francis Jacobs, William Brown, Thomas Miller, Peter Williams, Thomas Sipkins, William Hamilton, and George Collins.

The first church frame was built in 1800 on the corner of Church and Leonard streets. A year later, on February 16, 1801, the church was officially incorporated. The General Conference of the Methodist Episcopal Church, through Reverend John McClaskey, recognized the new body on April 6, 1801.

The first elders elected in the AMEZ Church were Abraham Thompson and James Varick. These, with Leven Smith, were ordained elders June 17, 1821, by Reverend James Covel, D.D., Reverend Sylvester Hutchinson, and Reverend William Stilwell, elders of the Methodist Episcopal Church. Local deacons, ordained by the Methodist Episcopal Conference, officiated in the African Methodist Episcopal Zion Church prior to 1800.

The first Conference was held in Zion Church, New York, June 21, 1821. Reverend William Phoebus, of the Methodist Church, presided. At this Conference a form of "Limited Episcopacy" was established, and James Varick was elected the first Bishop—then called "Superintendent." The first Discipline for the African Methodist Episcopal Zion Church was adopted October 25, 1820.

The first attempt to effect the "Organic Union" of the African Methodist Episcopal and African Methodist Episcopal Zion churches was made August 17, 1820, at the residence of Mr. William Brown, Leonard Street, New York, by the officials of the African Methodist Episcopal Zion Church and Bishop Richard Allen. The merger was not accomplished, however.

The original title of the African Methodist Episcopal Zion Church was The African Methodist Episcopal Church, the word "Zion" being used only accommodatively. Since the sister church had adopted the same title, however, the General Conference of 1848 made the Zion a part of the corporate title to avoid confusion.

The policy of the church has been Episcopal Methodism in its entirety from its beginning. Changes have been minimal, except that in 1868 the limit of Episcopal tenure was extended during life on good behavior. The form of consecration also varied, and the imposition of hands was introduced.

This is the first Methodist church to admit women to all functions save ordination. It was also the only black Methodist church that declared against slavery, the measure being incorporated in its first Copy of Discipline, 1820. This action proved a means of keeping it out of the South until 1862-1863.

Latest figures (1979) place the membership at 1,125,176 up from 900,000 in 1970.

*This old painting shows Deacon Peter Williams, one of the founders of the AME Zion Church, standing in the doorway of New York's John Street Methodist Episcopal Church.*

## Directory and Officers of the African Methodist Episcopal Zion Church Through 1989

**Officers**

Senior Bishop
Bishop William Milton Smith
3753 Springhill Ave.
Mobile, AL 36608

Sec. Board of Bishops
Bishop Charles H. Foggie
200 Windermere Dr.
Pittsburgh, PA 15218

Asst. Secretary
Bishop John H. Milier Sr.
Springdale Estates,
8605 Caswell Ct.
Raleigh, NC 27612

**Other Agencies**

Gen. Secretary-Aud.
Rev. Earle E. Johnson
P O Box 32843
Charlotte, NC 28232
(704) 332-3851

Fin. Secretary
Ms. Madie L. Simpson
P O Box 31005,
Charlotte, NC 28230
(704) 333-4847

A.M.E. Zion Publishing House
Dr. Lem Long, Jr.
General Mgr.
P O Box 30714
Charlotte, NC 28230
(704) 334-9596

Dept. of Overseas Missions
Rev. Dr. Kermit J. DeGraffenreidt
Secretary-Treas.
475 Riverside Dr.
Ste. 1910
New York, NY 10115
(212) 870-2952

Dept. of Home Missions Pensions, and Relief
Secretary-Treas.
Rev. Dr. Jewett Walker
P O Box 30846
Charlotte, NC 28231
(704) 333-3179

Dept. of Christian Education
Secretary
Rev. G L. Blackwell
128 E. 58th St.
Chicago, IL 60637
(312) 667-0183

Dept. of Church School Literature
Editor
Ms. Mary A. Love
P 0 Box 31005
Charlotte, NC 28230
(704) 332-1034

Dept. of Church Extension
Sec. Treas.
Dr. Lem Long Jr.
P 0 Box 31005
Charlotte NC 28231
(704) 334-2519

Dept. of Evangelism
Director
Rev. J. Dallas Jenkins Sr.
4550 Laurel Dr.
Dayton, OH 45417
(513) 263-2411

Dept. of Public Relations
Director
Gregory R. Smith
344 Hawthorne Terr.
Mt. Vernon, NY 10550
(212) 234-1544

Woman's Home and Overseas Missionary Society
Gen. President
Mrs. Grace L. Holmes
2505 Linden Ave.,
Knoxville, TN
(615) 525-1523
Exec. Secretary
Mrs. Alcenia Harps
975 Reservoir Ave.
Norfolk, VA 23504
(804) 627-1727

Treasurer
Mrs. Gwendolyn B. Johnson
2011 Sterns Dr.
Los Angeles, CA 90034
(213) 939-9417

Conventional Lay Council
President
Dr. C. Dupont Rippy
1701 Patton Ave.
Charlotte, NC 28216

**Periodicals**

Star of Zion (w)
Editor
Rev. Morgan Tarm
P O Box 31005
Charlotte, NC 28230

Quarterly Review (q)
Editor
Dr. Jomm H. Satterwhite
1814 Tamarack St., N.W.
Washington, DC 20012
(202) 726-7308

*Black camp meeting in the rural South during Reconstruction—a time when church membership expanded greatly.*

*AMEZ Bishop Stephen Spottswood is the chairman of the National Board of Directors of the NAACP.*

Missionary Seer (m)
Editor
Rev. Kermit I. DeGraffenreidt
475 Riverside Dr.
Ste. 1910
New York NY 10115
(212) 870-2952

Church School Herald (q)
Editor
Ms. Mary A. Love
P O Box 31005
Charlotte, NC 28230

**Bishops**

First Episcopal District
Bishop William Milton Smith
3753 Springhill Ave.
Mobile, AL 30608
(205) 344-7769

Second Episcopal District
Bishop Alfred G. Durlston Jr.
Presidential Commons
A 521 City Line
and Presidential Blvd.
Philadelphia, PA 19131
(215) 877-2659

Third Episcopal District
Bishop Charles H. Foggie
1200 Windermere Dr.
Pittsburgh, PA 15218
(412) 245-5842

Fourth Episcopal District
Bishop J . Clinton Hoggard
1100 W. 42nd St.
Rm. 344
Indianapolis, IN 46208
(317) 925-1207

Fifth Episcopal District
Bishop Clinton R. Coleman
3513 Ellamont Rd.
Baltimore, MD 21215
(301) 466-2220

Sixth Episcopal District
Bishop Arthur Marshall Jr.
P O Box 41138
Ben Hill Station
Atlanta, GA 30331
(404) 344-6554

Seventh Episcopal District
Bishop John H. Miller,
Springdale Estates
8605 Caswell Ave.
Raleigh, NC 27612
(919) 787-1346

Eighth Episcopal District
Bishop Ruben L. Speaks
1238 Marshan St.
P 0 Box 986
Salkbury NC 28144
(704) 637-1471

Ninth Episcopal District
Bishop Herman L. Anderson
5700 Barrington Dr.
Charlotte, NC 28215
(704) 536-7251

Tenth Episcopal District
Bishop Cecil Bishop
5401 Broadwater St.
Temple Hin, MD 20748
(301) 894-2165

Eleventh Episcopal District
Bishop Richard L. Fkher
8015 Starfrord St.
St. Louis, MO 63130
(314) 727-4439

Twelfth Episcopal District
Bishop Alfred E. White
93 Ridgefield St.
Hartford, CT 06112

## The CME Church

The Christian Methodist Episcopal (CME) Church, known until 1956 as the Colored Methodist Episcopal Church, is the third largest black Methodist body in the United States.

Like many black churches, it came into being after the Civil War when some 250,000 segregated or otherwise restricted blacks belonging to the Methodist Episcopal (ME) Church South appealed to the General Conference for the right to form their own church.

In December 1870, the first General Conference of the CME Church was held in Jackson, Tennessee, where two black bishops—Henry Miles and Richard H. Vanderhorst—were elected. Since then, the two churches have cooperated in many ways, primarily in the field of education. (The CME Church operates three colleges, several secondary schools, and a seminary.)

Latest figures (1988) show a total inlcusive membership of 788,922.

*Bishop J. Clinton Hoggard, president of the Board of Bishops, A.M.E. Zion Church.*

## Directory and Officers of the Christian Methodist Episcopal Church Through 1989

**Officers**

Exec. Secretary
Dr. W. Clyde Williams
2805 Shoreland Dr.
Atlanta, GA 30331
(404) 344-6738

Secretary Gen. Conf.
Rev. Edgar L. Wade
P O Box 3403
Memphis, TN 38103

**Other Organizations**

Christian Education
Gen. Secretary
Dr. Ronald M. Cunningham
1474 Humber St.
Memphis, TN 38106
(901) 947-3144

Lay Ministry
Gen Secretary
Dr. I. Carlton Faulk
1222 Rose St.
Berkeley CA 94702
(415) 655-4106

Evangelism, Missions & Human Concerns
Gen. Secretary
Rev Raymond F. Williams
P O Box 9067
Silver Spring, MD 20906
(301) 598-2653

Finance
Secretary
Mr. Joseph C. Neal Jr.
P O Box 75085
Los Angeles, CA 90030
(213) 233-5050

Publications
Gen. Secretary
Rev. Lonnie L. Napier
P O Box 2018
Memphis TN 38101
(901) 947-3135

Personnel Services
Gen. Sec.
Dr. N. Charles Thomas.
P O Box 74
Memphis, TN 39101
(901) 947-3135

Women's Missionary Council
President
Dr. Thelma J. Dudley
P O Box 5245
Orlando, FL 35855
(305) 293-8186

**Periodicals**

Christian Index, The (bi-m)
Editor
Rev. L.L. Reddick III
P 0 Box 665
Memphis, TN 38101

Missionary Messenger, The (m)
Editor
Cora B. Williams
1634 Garden St.
Shreveport, LA 71101

**Bishops**

First District
Bishop William H. Graves
564 Frank Ave.
Memphis, TN 38101
(901) 947-6180

Second District
Bishop Othal H. Lakey
6322 Elwynne Dr.
Cincinnati, OH 45236
(513) 984-6825

Third District
Bishop Dotcy Isom Jr.
11470 Northway Dr.
St Louis, MO 63136
(314) 381-3111

Fourth District
Bishop Marshall Gilmore
109 Holcomb Dr.
Shreveport, LA 71103
(318) 222-6284

Firth District
Bishop Richard O. Bass
308 10th Ave.
W. Birmingham, AL 35204
(205) 252-3541

Sixth District
Bishop Joseph C. Coles Jr.
2780 Collier Dr.
Atlanta, GA 30018
(404) 794-0096

Seventh District
Bishop Oree Broomfield. Sr.
6524 16th St., N.W.
Washington, DC 20012
(202) 723-2660

Eighth District
Bishop C. D Coleman Sr.
2330 Sutter St.
Dallas, TX 75216
(214) 942-5781

Ninth District
Bishop E. Lynn Brown
P O Box 11276
Los Angeles, CA 90011
(213) 216-9278

Tenth District
Bishop Nathaniel L. Linsey
P O Box 170127
Atlanta, GA 30317

**Retired**

Bishop E. P. Murchison
4094 Windsor Castle Way
Decatur, GA 30034

Bishop Henry C. Bunton,
853 East Dempster Ave.
Memphis, TN 38106

Bishop Chester A. Kirkendoll
10 Hurtland
Jackson, TN 38305

Bishop P. Randolph Shy
894 Falcon Dr. S.W.
Atlanta, GA 30311

## The Bible Church of Christ, Inc.

The Bible Church of Christ was founded on March 1, 1961 by Bishop Roy Bryant Sr. Since that time it has grown to 6 churches including congregations in the U.S. and Jamaica. The church is trinitarian and accepts the Bible as the divinely inspired Word of God. Its doctrine includes miracles of healing and the baptism of the Holy Ghost.

Inclusive Membership has grown to 6,400, and their are 40 Ordained Clergy.

*Many black preachers have been blessed with great oratorical gifts.*

## Directory and Officers of The Bible Church of Christ Inc. Through 1989

**General Organization**

General Meeting: annual
Headquarters: 135R Morns Ave.,
Bronx, NY 10456
(212) 588-2284

**Officers**

President
Bishop Roy Bryant Sr.
3033 Gunther Ave.
Bronx, NY 10469
(212) 379-8080

Vice-President
Bishop Roy Bryant Jr.
34 Tuxedo Rd.
Montclair, NJ 07042
(201) 746-0063

Secretary
Sissieretta Bryant

Treasurer
Elder Artie Burney

**Executive Trustee Board**

Chairperson
Leon T. Mims
1358 Morris Ave.
Bronx, NY 10456
(212) 588-2284

Vice-Chairperson
Peggy Rawls
100 W. 2nd St.
Mount Vernon, NY 10550
(914) 664-4602

**Other Organizations**

Foreign Missions
President
Elder Diane Cooper

Home Missions
President
Evangelist Eleanor Samuel

Sunday Schools
Gen. Supt.
Elder Alice Jones

Evangelism
National President
Evangelist Gloria Gray Field

Representative
Evangelist Elizabeth Price

Youth
President
Deacon Tommy Robinson

Minister of Music
Leon T. Mims

Prison Ministry Team
President
Evangelist Martin Lowe

**Presiding Elders**

Elder Roland Mifflin
Diamond Acre
Dagsboro, DE 19939

Elder Larry Bryant
West Johnson Rd.
Clinton, NC 28328

Elder Jesse Alston
104 Waverly Ave.
Monticello, NY 12701

Elder Artie Burney Sr.
100 W. 2nd St.
Mount Vernon, NY 10550

Elder Anita Robinson
1358 Morris Ave.
Bronx, NY 10456

Elder Betty Gilliard
1069 Morris Ave.
Bronx, NY 10456

Bible School
President
Dr. Roy Bryant
1358 Morris Ave.
Bronx, NY 10456
(212) 588-2284

Bookstore
Manager
Elder Elizabeth Johnson
1358 Morris Ave.
Bronx, NY 10456
(212) 293-1928

**Periodical**

The Voice (q)
Editor
Montrose Bushrod
1358 Morris Ave.
Bronx NY 10456
(212) 588-2284

*"We Shall Overcome" is sung as a hymn during black congregational services.*

## The Church of God in Christ

The Church of God in Christ was founded in 1906 in Memphis, Tenn., and was organized by Bishop Charles Harrison Mason, a former Baptist minister who pioneered the embryonic stages of the Holiness movement beginning in 1895 in Mississippi.

The Church further developed when its founder organized four major departments between 1910-1916. These departments were (1) Women's Department, (2) Sunday School, (3) Young Peoples Willing Workers (YPWW), (4) Home and Foreign Mission.

Doctrinally, the Church is basically trinitarian. It teaches the infallibility of scripture, the need for regeneration and subsequent baptism of the Holy Ghost. It emphasizes the holiness as God's standard for Christian conduct. It recognizes as ordinances Holy Communion, Water Baptism, and Feet Washing. Its governmental structure is basically episcopal with the General Assembly being the Legislative body.

The Church is headquartered at Memphis, Tenn. The organization has experienced tremendous growth and expansion of its ministries under the present leadership of the Presiding Bishop, Bishop J. O. Patterson.

## Directory and Officers of the The Church of God in Christ Through 1989

National Headquarters
Mason Temple
939 Mason St.
Memphis, TN 38126

World Headquarters
272 South Main St.
Memphis, TN 38103
(901) 521-1163
or 527-1422

The Mother Church
Pentecostal Temple
2295 Danny Thomas Blvd.
Memphis, TN 38126
(901) 527-9202

**General Offices**

All located at
2725 Main St.
Memphis, TN 38103

Mail
P 0 Box 320
Memphis, TN 38101
(901) 525-2507

**Office of the Presiding Bishop**

Presiding Bishop
Most Rev. J. O. Patterson

Adm. Asst.
Elder J. 0. Patterson Jr.

Exec. Secretary
Mrs. Julia Mason Atkins

Secretary
Elder Alfred Z. Hall Jr.

Adjutant
Bishop F. E. Perry

Adjutant to the Presiding Bishop Dr. J. Delano Ellis II

Chief of Military and Institutional Chaplains
Bishop Ithiel Clemmons

**The General Board**

Presiding Bishop
Most Rev. J. 0. Patterson
1774 S. Parkway
E. Memphis, TN 38114

First Assistant Presiding Bishop
Rt. Rev. L. H. Ford
9401 M. L. King Drive
Chicago IL 60619

Second Assistant Presiding Bishop
Rt. Rev. F. D. Washington
1328 President St.
Brooklyn, NY 11213

Bishop J. D. Husband
P O Box 824
Atlanta, GA

Bishop C. L. Anderson Jr.
20485 Mendota
Detroit, MI 48221

Bishop L. R. Anderson
265 Ranch Trail West
Amherst, NY 14221

Bishop C. D. Owens
14 Van Velsor Pl.
Newark, NJ 07112

Bishop O. T. Jones Jr.
363 N. 60th St.
Philadelphia, PA 19139

Bishop Jacob Cohen
3120 N.W. 48th Terr.
Miami, FL 33142

Bishop P. A. Brooks
30945 Wendbrook Lane
Birmingham, MI 48010

Bishop S . L. Green
2416 Orcutt Ave.
Newport News, VA 23607

Bishop J. N. Haynes
6743 Talbot
Dallas, TX 75216

**Office of the General Secretary**
(901) 521-1163

General Secretary
Bishop G. R. Ross

Asst. Gen. Sec. for Reg.
Bishop E. Harris Moore

Asst. Gen. Sec. for Records
Bishop Herbert J. Williams
Dr. J. Delano Ellis II

Asst. to Gen. Sec. at Headquarters
Bishop A. LaDell Thomas
Coord. Dir. of Research and Survey
Elder Ronald A. Blumburg

**Office of the Financial Secretary**
(901) 744-0710

Secretary
Dr. S. Y. Burnett

Gen. Treasurer
Bishop Theodore Davis

Chmn. of Finance
Bishop Benjamin Crouch

**Office of the Board of Trustees**

Chairperson
Dr. Roger L. Jones

Secretary
Elder Warren Miller

Office of the Clergy Bureau
(901) 523-7045

Director
Elder Samuel Smith

Secretary
Mrs. Dorothy Motley

**Office of the Superintendent of Properties**
(901) 774-0710

Superintendent
Bishop W. L. Porter

Secretary
(not named at press)

**Office of the Counsel General**
(901) 527-4402

Counsel General
Bishop J. 0. Patterson Jr.
Assoc. Counsel
Attorney A. W. Willis

**Board of Publications**
(901) 526-3644

Chairperson
Bishop Roy L. H. Winbush

Secretary-Treasurer
Bishop Floyde E. Perry Jr.
Headquarters
Rep. Elder David Hail

Publishing House
(901) 521-0142

Manager
Mr. Hugheau Terry

**Department of Missions**
(901) 522-9221

President
Bishop Cariis L. Moody

Exec. Secretary
Elder Jesse W. Denny

**Department of Women**
(901) 522-9964

President-Gen. Supervisor
Dr. Mattie McGlothen

Asst. Supervisor
Mrs. Emma Crouch

Exec. Secretary
Mrs. Elizabeth C. Moore

Sec. of the Women's Convention
Mrs. Freddie J. Beli

Treasurer
Mrs. Mary L. Belvin

Fin. Secretary
Mrs. Olive Brown

**Department of Evangelism**

President
Dr. Edward L. Battles
4310 Steeplechase rail
Arlington, TX 76016
(817) 429-7166

**Department of Music**

President
Mrs. Mattie Moss Clark
18203 Sorrento
Detroit, MI 48235

Vice President
Mrs. Mattie Wigley
1726 S. Wellington
Memphis, TN 38106

**Department or Youth**

(Youth Congress)
President
Bishop C. H. Brewer
260 Roydon Rd.
New Haven, CT 06511

**Department of Sunday Schools**

Gen. Supt.
Bishop Cleveland W. Williams
270 Division St.
Derby, CT 06418

**United National Auxiliary Convention**
UNAC-5
Chairperson
Bishop Roy L. H. Winbush

Sec. of Exec. Committee
Bishop G. R. Ross

**Church of God in Christ Book Store**
2725 Main St.
Memphis, TN 38103
(901) 525-7334

**Charles Harrison Mason Foundation**
2725. Main St.
Memphis, TN 38103
(901) 525-2507

Chairperson
The Executive Advisory Board
President
Bishop, J. O. Patterson

Executive Director
Mrs. Julia Mason Atkins

Chmn., Bd. of Dir.
Bishop P. A. Brooks

Dir. of Fine Arts Scholarships
Mrs. Sara Jordan Powell

**Periodicals**

Whole Truth
Editor
Elder David Hall
P O Box 2017
Memphis, TN 38101

Sunday School Literature
Editor
Bishop Roy L. H. Winbush
Publishing House
Church of God in Christ
2725 Main St.
Memphis, TN 38103

Y.P.W.W. Topics
Editor
Elder James L. Whitehead, Jr.
67 Tennyson
Highland Park
MI 48203

Sunshine Band Topics
Editor
Mrs. Mildred Wells
648 Peart St.
Benton Harbor, MI 29022

Punty Guide
Editor
Mrs. Pearl McCullom
P 0 Box 1526
Gary, IN 46407

International Directory
930 Mason St.
Memphis, TN 38126.

The Pentecostal Interpreter
Editor
Bishop H. Jenkins Bell
P O Box 6118
Knoxville, TN 37914

The Voice of Missions
Editor
Ms. Jenifer James
1932 Dewey Ave.
Evanston, IL 60201

## Bible Way Church of Our Lord Jesus Christ World Wide, Inc.

This body was organized in 1957 in the Pentecostal tradition for the purpose of accelerating evangelistic and foreign missionary commitment and to effect a greater degree of collective leadership than was found in the body in which they had previously participated.

The doctrine is the same as that of the Church of Our Lord Jesus Christ of the Apostolic Faith, Inc. of which some of the churches and clergy were formerly members.

The growth of this organization has been very encouraging. There are approximately 300,000 members with 300 churches and missions located in Africa, England, Guyana, Trinidad, and Jamaica, and churches in 25 states in America.

The Bible Way Church WW is involved in humanitarian, as well as evangelical outreach, with concerns for urban housing and education and economic development.

*Marcus Garvey was, among his other achievements, a central figure in the Rastafarian faith.*

## Directory and Officers of the Bible Way Church of Our Lord Jesus Christ World Wide, Inc. Through 1989

**General Organization**

Headquarters:
1100 New Jersey Ave. N W.
Washington, DC 20001

**Officers**

Presiding Bishop
Smallwood E. Williams
4720 16th St., N.W.
Washington, DC 20011

Gen. Secretary
Bishop Edward William
5118 Clarendon Rd .
Brooklyn, NY 11226

**Periodicals**

The Bible Way News Voice (q)
Washington, DC

## The Lost-Found Nation Of Islam In The West: The Black Muslims

Pigeonholed in the 1960s as a fanatical anti-white separatist movement, the Black Muslims became, in the 1970s, a major economic and educational force in America's black community.

The Muslims are a religious organization in the sense that they worship a supreme being. (There is no God but Allah. Muhammad is His Apostle.) In addition, many of their admonitions and disciplines can be likened to the puritanism of some religious groups. Followers are expected to abstain from alcohol, tobacco, and cosmetics. Children are educated in sect-oriented schools.

After the assassination of Malcolm X, the Muslim organization was saddled with the reputation of being a fierce and fanatic hate group, fearlessly self-righteous and ready to seek vengeance and retribution for alleged wrongdoing. Since then, however, the fiery rhetoric of Elijah Muhammad has cooled, and the Messenger has displayed a keen interest in developing the Nation's economic self-sufficiency. Muslim's economic holdings extend throughout the United States and beyond, to the Caribbean and Central America.

In Chicago, where the Muslims are headquartered, The Nation manages publishing, trucking, egg, meat, baking, retailing, restaurant, and apparel manufacturing operations. Muslims also own modern cattle, dairy, poultry, and produce farms in Alabama, Georgia, and Michigan, having survived, in 1970, the poisoning of much of its Alabama herd. Value of the Nation's holdings is estimated at about $60 million.

Starting in the early 1970s, the Nation started to alter its membership base, expanding its appeal from prisons and ghetto streets to the black middle class. Much of the reason for this was the need for professional specialists to man its growing economic ventures. However, the Muslims still reject membership and offers of help from whites, even white governments. The Nation has refused help from the United States government but has borrowed $3 million from Libya to finance purchase of a temple in Chicago.

The Muslims also operate some 50 schools and colleges, from which whites are also excluded. The Muslim schools have an excellent reputation and frequently surpass public school systems in academic achievement.

## Rastafarians

Rastafarians, who wear their hair in matted "dreadlocks" and smoke marijuana as part of their faith, have grown in popularity in the United States and Britain since the sect was born in Jamaica in the 1930s. Members of the religion regard Ethiopian Emperor Haile Selassie, who died in 1975, as God.

Marcus Garvey, a Jamaican-born nationalist who advocated a back-to-Africa movement in the United States in the early 1920s, is also a central figure in the faith. Garvey founded the Universal Negro Improvement Association in Harlem in the 1920s with the message that "Africa was for the Africans" and urged blacks to look back to the motherland, where a black King would be crowned soon. He was deported to Jamaica in 1927.

In 1930, Lij Ras Tafari Makonnen ascended to the throne of Ethiopia and took the titles of His Imperial Majesty, Haile Selassie I, Power of the Holy Trinity, 225th Emperor of the 3,000 year-old Ethiopian Empire, Elect of God, Lord of Lords, King of Kings, Heir to the Throne of Solomon, and Conquesting Lion of the Tribe of Judah. Rastafarians hailed him as Jah, the living God on earth.

Today, Rastas differ on specific dogma, but they basically believe they are descended from black Hebrews exiled in Babylon and therefore are true Israelites. They also believe that Haile Selassie is the direct descendent of Solomon and Sheba, and that God is black.

Most white men, they believe, have been worshipping a dead god and have attempted to teach the blacks to do likewise. They believe the Bible was distorted by King James I and that the black race sinned and was punished by God with slavery. They view Ethiopia as Zion, the Western world as Babylon, and believe that one day they will return to Zion. They preach love, peace, and reconciliation between races but warn that Armageddon is now.

Rastas don't vote, tend to be vegetarians, abhor alcohol, and wear their hair in long, uncombed plaits called dreadlocks. The hair is never cut, since it is part of the spirit, nor is it ever combed.

They never use the word "last" because it expresses retrogression and a Rastaman can only go forward. Marijuana is the holy herb, regarded as a sacramental gift, and the Bible is quoted as proof of this: "And thou shalt eat the herb of the field" (Gen.3:18).

The movement in America grew rapidly in the fifties and sixties, and accelerated with the emergence of reggae musician Bob Marley, the first Rastafarian to become a pop superstar, and the 1966 visit of Selassie to Jamaica. Selassie died in 1975 and Marley died in 1981.

There are an estimated 50,000 Rastas in Britain and almost a million in the United States, approximately 80,000 of whom live in New York City, mainly in Brooklyn where there is a high concentration of West Indians and Haitians.

## OTHER PREDOMINANTLY BLACK CHURCHES

The following is a list of black churches and religious organizations now active in the United States. Inevitably, such a list can only offer a brief glimpse into the prevailing religious mood of the black churchgoer in the United States today.

The *African Orthodox Church* was founded in 1921 by Archbishop George Alexander McGuire, once a priest in the Protestant Episcopal Church. At first associated with the Marcus Garvey movement, this church is today an autonomous and independent body adhering to an "orthodox" confession of faith. Its nearly 6,000 members worship in some 25 to 30 churches. The organization's headquarters are at 122 West 129th Street, New York City.

The *African Union First Colored Methodist Protestant Church, Inc.* grew out of the Methodist Episcopal Church in 1805, although it did not become a distinct denomination until fully eight years later. Today, it has more than 30 churches and a membership of some 5,000. Headquarters for the organization are at 602 Spruce Street, Wilmington, Delaware.

The *Apostolic Overcoming Holy Church of God* was incorporated in Alabama in 1919. Evangelistic in purpose, it emphasizes sanctification, holiness, and the power of divine healing. As of 1956, it had a membership of 75,000 people in some 300 congregations. The headquarters of the organization are at 1807 S. Mott Drive, Mobile, Alabama.

*Christ's Sanctified Holy Church* was organized in 1903 from among the members of a Negro Methodist church. The last available figures put church membership at 600. This church, which holds its annual conference in September, has its headquarters at South Cutting Avenue and East Spencer Street in Jennings, Louisiana.

The *Church of Christ, Holiness, U.S.A.* was organized by Bishop C. P. Jones in 1896. The avowed mission of this body is to proclaim the gospel, seek the conversion of sinners, and perfect them in their Christian belief. Some 150 churches belong to this group, which has a membership of about 7,500. The organization, with headquarters at 329 East Monument Street, Jackson, Mississippi, has an annual national convention in August.

The *Church of God and Saints of Christ* was organized in 1896 in Lawrence, Kansas by William S. Crowdy, who held the belief that blacks were descended from the 10 lost tribes of Israel. Crowdy's followers today observe the Old Testament calendar, using Hebrew terminology for the months, and are sometimes referred to as "Black Jews." National headquarters for the organization were established in Philadelphia in 1900. In 1917 international headquarters were set up at Belleville, R.F.D. 1, Portsmouth, Virginia, site of the quadrennial general conference. The organization's more than 200 churches have a membership of some 38,000.

The *Church of God in Christ* was organized in Arkansas in 1895 by Elders C. P. Jones and C. H. Mason. Today, the organization has over 4,000 churches and a membership of better than 400,000. Annual conferences are held in the 5,000-seat Mason's Temple in Memphis, Tennessee. Headquarters are at 958 Mason Street, Memphis.

The *Church of the Living God* was founded in 1889 in Wrightsville, Arkansas by William Christian. Believers practice baptism by immersion, foot-washing, and the use of water in the dispensation of the sacrament. The churches—or temples as they are called—are organized along fraternal order lines. A national assembly is held by the group on the second Tuesday in October on a biennial basis. The close-to-300 churches in the movement claim a membership of over 43,000.

The *Churches of God, Holiness* were organized by K. H. Burruss in Georgia in 1914. Headquarters are at 170 Ashby Street, N.W., Atlanta, Georgia. Membership in the group's 40-odd churches totals some 25,000.

The black churches of the *Cumberland Presbyterian Church* were established with their own ecclesiastical organization in 1869. Nowadays, the general assembly of the Second Cumberland Presbyterian Church in U.S. (formerly Colored Cumberland Presbyterian Church) meets annually in June. Total membership in the church's more than 854 places of worship in the United States stands at some 94,574.

The *Fire Baptized Holiness Church* was organized in Atlanta, Georgia in 1898. Its headquarters today are at 556 Houston Street, Atlanta, Georgia. The general council for its 50-odd churches (membership, c. 1,000) meets annually.

The *Free Christian Zion Church of Christ* was organized in 1905 at Redemption, Arkansas by a company of black ministers who were associated with a variety of Methodist-inclined denominations. Church membership today stands at approximately 20,000. Headquarters for the organization, which has an annual general assembly in November, are in Nashville, Arkansas.

The *House of God, Which Is the Church of the Living God, the Pillar and Ground of the Truth, Inc.* was organized by R. A. R. Johnson in 1918. A small body which meets annually in October, it has about 100 churches and a membership approaching 2,500.

The *Independent AME Denomination* was founded in Jacksonville, Florida in 1907 by 12 elders who had withdrawn from the AME Church. Information on this body is scant, although it is known that, as of 1940, it had 12 churches and an inclusive membership of 1,000.

The *Kodesh Church of Immanuel* was founded in 1929 by the Reverend Frank R. Killings worth, leader of a group which had withdrawn from the African Methodist Episcopal Zion Church. According to its last report, it had five churches, and a membership of 326.

The *National Baptist Evangelical Life and Soul Saving Assembly of U.S.A.* was founded in 1921 by A. A. Banks, who envisioned that it would become a charitable, educational, and evangelical body. The church, with headquarters at 441 Monroe Avenue, Detroit, Michigan, has a general assembly for its close to 60,000 members who worship in some 260 churches across the United States.

The *National David Spiritual Temple of Christ Church Union (Inc.), U.S.A.* was organized in 1921 by the Most Reverend David William Short, originally a Baptist minister. The organization's headquarters are at 545 W. 92nd Street, Los Angeles, California. A national assembly is held annually in August. Membership has already passed 40,000.

The *National Primitive Baptist Convention of the U.S.A.*, founded in 1907, differs from similar bodies in its general opposition to the notion of extensive organization. Headquarters of this body are at 2116 Clinton Avenue, West, Huntsville, Alabama.

The *Reformed Methodist Union Episcopal Church* was founded in Charleston, South Carolina by a group which had withdrawn from the African Methodist Episcopal Church there. Doctrinally, this church closely resembles the Methodist Episcopal Church. Headquarters for the more than 30 churches are in Charleston, South Carolina. Membership is estimated at over 11,000. The church also has an annual general conference.

The *Reformed Zion Union Apostolic Church*, organized in 1869 at Boydton, Virginia by a minister of the AME Zion Church (Elder James R. Howell of New York), espouses doctrines which are generally in accord with those of the Methodist Episcopal Church. Its annual conference, held in August, is superseded by a quadrennial general conference, the last of which was held in 1966. It has over 50 churches, and a membership of about 16,000.

*Triumph the Church and Kingdom of God in Christ* was organized in 1902 in Georgia by the Elder E. D. Smith, who taught sanctification and the second coming of Christ. The church has quarterly and annual conferences, as well as a quadrennial international religious congress. Headquarters are at 213 Furrington Avenue, S.E., Atlanta, Georgia. Membership has grown rapidly in recent years, and is now approaching 60,000.

The *Union American Methodist Episcopal Church*, founded by Rev. Peter Spencer in Delaware in 1813, is reputed to be the first all-black Methodist denomination in the United States. Until 1850 the organization went by the name of the "Union Church of Africans." That year, however, a split occurred, whereupon the main body adopted the name by which it is currently known. The latest figures made available by the organization show it to have 256 churches and 27,560 members.

The *United Free Will Baptist Church* set up its organization in 1870, and has since maintained close ties with the Free Will Baptists. It has a general conference every three years and is headquartered at Kinston College, 1000 University Street, Kinston, North Carolina. Membership stands at about 100,000; churches number close to 900.

The *United Holy Church of America, Inc.* was founded in 1886 at Method, North Carolina. This body recognizes baptism by immersion and the Lord's Supper, and meets quadrennially. Its headquarters are at both 500 Gulley Street, Goldsboro, North Carolina and 31 Miami Avenue, Columbus, Ohio. Its membership is approaching 30,000, while its churches are nearing the 500 mark in number.

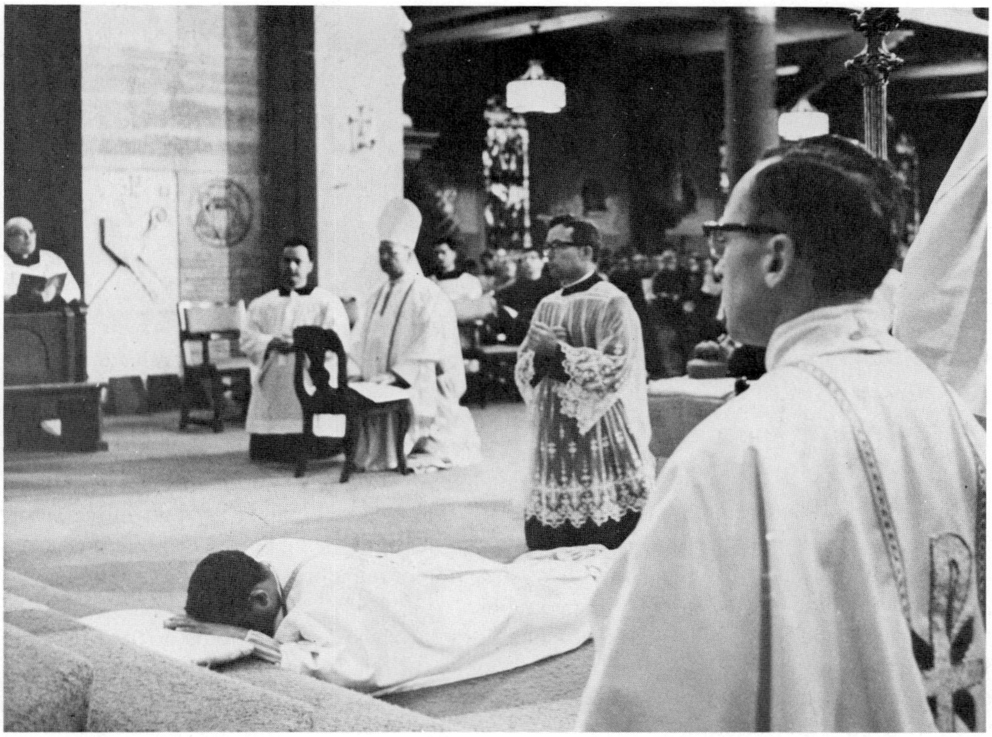

*The consecration of Bishop Harold R. Perry in New Orleans.*

## "WHITE CHURCHES"

The term "white churches" is used to identify those churches which, while having predominantly white congregations, have large numbers of black worshippers on a generally nonsegregated basis. Among others, these include: the Methodist Church (c. 370,000); the Protestant Episcopal Church (c. 78,000); Seventh Day Adventists (c. 50,000), and the Congregational Church (c. 38,000). Since not all churches base their tabulations of membership on a racial breakdown, it is hazardous to estimate the number of blacks in such churches, although a figure of 800,000 has been advanced.

Black members of "white churches" generally enjoy the rights of full participation. In the Methodist Church, for example, black bishops serve side by side and on an equal footing, with their white counterparts.

### Catholicism

Missionary activities have intensified, particularly since the early 1960s, resulting in a tripling of black membership; in 1982 the Catholic Office of Black Ministry reported a black membership of 1.3 million, up from 700,000 in 1963. The Catholic church thus became the fourth largest religious organization among American blacks, following the two Baptist conventions and the AME denomination.

Black participation in the church has not been without dissension. In the early 1970s, for example, blacks petitioned the Vatican for a separate rite for black Catholics in the United States. Later, black and white Catholics spoke out against each other when the U.S. Conference of Catholic Bishops omitted funding for the National Office of Black Catholics in 1971.

However, the church has sought to elevate black leaders: in 1966 Harold Robert Perry of Lake Charles, Louisiana, became the first black bishop; Joseph Lawson Howze followed in his footsteps in 1973. On February 10, 1982, New York City's Terence Cardinal Cooke created the posts of Episcopal Vicar for black community development and Vicar of Harlem, and named Emerson Moore, pastor of St. Charles Borromeo Church in Harlem, to handle the dual role. Moore thus became the nation's first black monsignor.

Black enrollment in seminaries has increased substantially: in 1970, 808 black students were reported in seminary studies; by 1980, the enrollment had reached 2,205. However, blacks still constitute only about 4.4% of the entire student population. Also, more than 600 of the students attend one of five predominantly black institutions.

### The Black Jews

There are believed to be approximately 44,000 so-called black Jews (they are actually more appropriately classified as members of Ethiopian Hebrew congregations) in the United States. These Jews, located in such cities as Philadelphia, Boston, Chicago, Los Angeles, and New York, are mainly natives of the West Indies or the American South, although they consistently trace their ancestry and heritage back to Africa. Clannish, and fully involved, the black Jews continue to live successfully in poor or lower middle-class neighborhoods, despite the high crime rates prevalent in settings such as these. Both their religious optimism and the strong parental authority exercised on offspring contribute to the inherent stability of the group. New York's Wentworth A. Matthew, leader of Harlem's Ethiopian Hebrew Congregation, credits the strength and solidarity of his group to the presence of a "towering" father figure and a tenacious mother who "sets the tone and the mood" of family life.

Like Jews everywhere, the Ethiopian Hebrew congregations observe the rituals and holidays stemming from ancient Jewish traditions. Thus they celebrate such joyous occasions as the liberation of the Jews from bondage in Egypt by reading the Passover stories and participating in the family *seder*.

Their form of worship, the *Sephardic,* originated with the Jews in Spain and Portugal and was carried by them to the lands of Latin America and the islands of the West Indies. Thus the Spanish influence is evident in the ethnic composition of the congregations, which often includes Spanish and Portuguese members.

Like many American Jews, the Ethiopians identify strongly with Israel. Despite the Jewish values which suffuse their lives, young blacks in the congregation are sensitive to pressures to identify with the black movement. In most cases, however, cultural and philosophical preoccupations continue to eclipse racial matters as concerns which unify and connect the community.

Race, however, is still an issue which tends to fragment the black Jews and becloud their status. Thus some black Jews seek to identify with the universal Jewish world, whose nationhood is centered in the state of Israel, while others, sensing the suspicion and uneasiness that might be generated by their presence in many areas of the white (including the Jewish) world, prefer to remain in small, unrelated clusters or decentralized factions.

Though many have worshipped as Jews for years, they often cannot produce the necessary documents required to prove to a rabinnical court their eligibility to call themselves Orthodox Jews. Some do not qualify as Jews in the strict religious sense of the term, being persons neither born of a Jewish mother nor brought into the faith by a properly ordained rabbi.

The isolation of the black Jews contributes to the difficulty of finding absolute verification of their Jewish origins. Most trace their forbears to West or East Africa and are linked in some way to the Ethiopian Jews known as Falashas.

*A black rabbi stands in front of his Bronx synagogue.*

### Mormonism

On January 9, 1970, Mormon leaders around the world were informed of church policy toward the black. The text of the official Mormon position follows:

*In view of confusion that has arisen, it was decided at a meeting of the first presidency and the quorum of the twelve to restate the position of the church with regard to the Negro both in society and in the church.*

*First, may we say that we know something of the suffering of those who are discriminated against in a denial of their civil rights and constitutional privileges. Our early history as a church is a tragic story of persecution and oppression.*

*Our people repeatedly were denied the protection of the law. They were driven and plundered, robbed and murdered by mobs who in many instances were aided and abetted by those sworn to uphold the law. We as a people have experienced the bitter fruits of civil discrimination and mob violence.*

*We believe that the Constitution of the United States was divinely inspired, that it was produced by "wise men" whom God raised up for this "very purpose," and that the principles embodied in the Constitution are so fundamental and important that, if possible, they should be extended "for the rights and protection" of all mankind.*

*In revelations received by the first prophet of the church in this dispensation, Joseph Smith the Lord made it clear that it is "not right that any man should be in bondage one to another." These words were spoken prior to the Civil War. From these and other revelations have sprung the church's deep and historic concern with man's free agency and our commitment to the sacred principles of the Constitution.*

*It follows, therefore, that we believe the Negro, as well as those of other races, should have his full constitutional privileges as a member of society, and we hope that members of the church everywhere will do their part as citizens to see that these rights are held inviolate. Each citizen must have equal opportunities and protection under the law with reference to civil rights.*

*However, matters of faith, conscience, and theology are not within the purview of the civil law. The first amendment to the Constitution specifically provides that "Congress shall make no law respecting an establishment of religion, or prohibiting the free exercise thereof."*

*The position of the Church of Jesus Christ of Latter-Day Saints affecting those of the Negro race who choose to join the church falls wholly within the category of religion. It has no bearing upon matters of civil rights. In no case or degree does it deny to the Negro his full privileges as a citizen of the nation.*

*This position has no relevancy whatever to those who do not wish to join the church. Those individuals, we suppose, do not believe in the divine origin and nature of the church, nor that we have the priesthood of God. Therefore, if they feel we have no priesthood, they should have no concern with any aspect of our theology on priesthood so long as that theology does not deny any man his constitutional privileges.*

*A word of explanation concerning the position of the church: The Church of Jesus Christ of Latter-Day Saints owes its origin, its existence, and its hope for the future to the principle of continuous revelation. "We believe all that God has revealed, all that He does now reveal, and we believe that He will yet reveal many great and important things pertaining to the Kingdom of God."*

*From the beginning of this dispensation, Joseph Smith and all succeeding presidents of the church have taught that Negroes, while spirit children of a common father, and the progeny of our earthly parents Adam and Eve, were not yet to receive the priesthood, for reasons which we believe are known to God, but which He has not made fully known to man.*

*Our living prophet, President David O. McKay, has said, "The seeming discrimination by the church toward the Negro is something which originated with man; but goes back into the beginning with God. Revelation assures us that this plan antedates man's mortal existence, extending back to man's pre-existent state."*

*President McKay has also said, "Sometime in God's eternal plan, the Negro will be given the right to hold the priesthood.*

*Until God reveals His will in this matter, to Him whom we sustain as a prophet, we are bound by that same will. Priesthood, when it is conferred on any man comes as a blessing from God, not of men.*

*We feel nothing but love, compassion, and the deepest appreciation for the rich talents, endowments, and the earnest strivings of our Negro brothers and sisters. We are eager to share them with men of all races the blessings of the gospel. We have no racially segregated congregations.*

*Were we the leaders of an enterprise created by ourselves and operated only according to our own earthly wisdom, it would be a simple thing to act according to popular will. But we believe that this work is directed by God and that the*

*Father Divine, founder of the Peace Mission Cult, and his wife (left) celebrating their wedding anniversary in 1954.*

*conferring of the priesthood must await His revelation. To do otherwise would be to deny the very premise on which the church is established.*

*We recognize that those who do not accept the principle of modern revelation may oppose our point of view. We repeat that such would not wish for membership in the church, and therefore the question of priesthood should hold no interest for them.*

*Without prejudice they should grant us the privilege afforded under the Constitution to exercise our chosen form of religion just as we must grant all others a similar privilege. They must recognize that the question of bestowing or withholding priesthood in the church is a matter of religion and not a matter of constitutional right.*

*We extend the hand of friendship to men everywhere and the hand of fellowship to all who wish to join the church and partake of the many rewarding opportunities to be found therein.*

This position stood until a landmark decision in 1978, when Church leader Spencer W. Kimball, after "hours of supplicating the Lord for divine guidance," had a revelation to allow "all males 12 years and older to be admitted to the priesthood."

On June 8, 1978, a letter went out to all general and local priesthood officers of the Church of Jesus Christ of Latter-Day Saints throughout the world:

*As we have witnessed the expansion of the work of the Lord over the earth, we have been grateful that people of many nations have responded to the message of the restored gospel, and have joined the Church in ever-increasing numbers. This, in turn, has inspired us with a desire to extend to every worthy member of the Church all of the privileges and blessings which the gospel affords.*

*Aware of the promises made by the prophets and presidents of the Church who have preceded us that at some time, in God's eternal plan, all of our brethren who are worthy may receive the priesthood, and witnessing the faithfulness of those from whom the priesthood has been withheld, we have pleaded long and earnestly in behalf of these, our faithful brethren, spending many hours in the Upper Room of the Temple supplicating the Lord for divine guidance.*

*He has heard our prayers, and by revelation has confirmed that the long-promised day has come when every faithful, worthy man in the Church may receive the holy priesthood, with power to exercise its divine authority, and enjoy with his loved ones every blessing that flows therefrom, including the blessings of the temple.*

*Accordingly, all worthy male members of the Church may be ordained to the priesthood without regard for race or color. Priesthood leaders are instructed to follow the policy of carefully interviewing all candidates for ordination to either the Aaronic or the Melchizeded Priesthood to insure that they meet the established standards for worthiness.*

*We declare with soberness that the Lord has now made known His will for the blessing of all His children throughout the earth who will hearken to the voice of His authorized servants, and prepare themselves to receive every blessing of the gospel.*

Two days after this announcement, Joseph Freeman Jr., 26, a Salt Lake City telephone repairman and father of three, became the first black man ordained to the priesthood.

Although there are more than four million Mormons worldwide, membership is not broken down by race or nationality; thus it is not known how many black men have been ordained since.

### Nonaffiliated Churches: The Evangelical Movement

One of the by-products of black migration from rural to urban areas has been the development of the so-called store front church, that is, one which serves those poor who are forced to live within the confines of what is known as "the inner city," or in other ghetto quarters. Such churches are usually set up in vacant stores which lend themselves readily to adaptation as appropriate meeting places. In some cases, such groups are affiliated with larger bodies; in others, they are individual units maintained by a single, self-appointed evangelist.

## BLACK CHURCHMEN

The pioneer minister of the early churches was not only responsible for the material needs of his congregation but was also a primary force in promoting its material welfare. By working with abolitionist societies, by helping to sponsor the Underground Railroad, and by directing a number of forums for the voicing of black protest sentiment, the black minister managed to establish his church as the focal point of every significant movement designed to improve the political and social status of his congregation.

Although the importance of black churchmen is said to be declining in importance today, several major contemporary figures—the Reverend Jesse Jackson and the Reverend Ralph Abernathy to name just two—continue to exert a good part of their influence on the national scene through the pulpit. Biographies of some of these people are contained in the Civil Rights section.

This section takes into account both the historical importance of the individual and the position he occupied within the framework of the religious belief he espoused.

*New York Minister W. Sterling Cary, president of the National Council of Churches.*

### RICHARD ALLEN
**Founder, African Methodist Episcopal (AME) Church**
**1760-1831**

For biography see Civil Rights section.

### JOHN M. BURGESS
**Former Bishop, Episcopal Diocese of Massachusetts**
**1909**

The Right Reverend Burgess, who earned the distinction of becoming the first black Episcopal bishop in the United States, was born in Grand Rapids, Michigan. He received both an A.B. and M.A. from Michigan University by 1931 and went on to graduate from the Episcopal Theological School in Cambridge, Massachusetts in 1934.

After serving in various posts, Reverend Burgess was named chaplain of Howard University in 1946 and canon of the Episcopal Cathedral in Washington, D.C. in 1951. Five years later he moved to Boston where he served as superintendent of the Episcopal City Mission until 1962, when he was appointed Suffragan Bishop. His historical moment came in 1970, with his election as Bishop of the Diocese, and he served in that post until 1976, when he retired and moved to Connecticut.

### W. STERLING CARY
**Former President, National Council of Churches**
**1927**

Once a prominent political activist and New York-based minister in the United Church of Christ, Reverend W. Sterling Cary became the first black president of the National Council of Churches in 1972. He served a three-year term, through 1974, and later moved to Illinois to become the Conference Minister for the Illinois Conference of the Church of Christ. He also served on the Church of Christ's governing board for many years until 1981.

Born in 1927 in Plainfield, New Jersey, Reverend Cary holds a B.A. from Morehouse College and a B.D. from the Union Theological Seminary. During his career, he earned a reputation for his antiwar positions and advocated extensive welfare reform, low-income housing, and strict enforcement of fair employment statutes. He also adhered to moderate theological positions and urged reconciliation between Christians who interpret the Bible conservatively and those who choose a more liberal path.

### GEORGE WYLIE CLINTON
**Bishop, AMEZ Church**
**1859-1921**

An activist who was buffeted about by the ebb and flow of black fortunes after the Civil War, George Wiley Clinton was born in Lancaster County, South Carolina and raised in the home of his grandparents with whom he and his mother lived, his father having died when Wiley was very young. In 1874, he entered South Carolina University, but he had to leave in 1877 when Governor Wade Hampton closed the school to blacks. He returned home to help his family harvest the season's crops and then became a teacher in a public school for blacks while studying law in the office of two lawyers in Lancaster. While doing so, he heeded advice in the writings of Blackstone, the great legal scholar, to study the Bible and in 1879 became a licensed preacher.

In 1891, Clinton returned to Brainard Institute in Chester, South Carolina to complete his formal education, teaching there to help pay his fees. In the 1890s, he became pastor of the John Wesley Church in Pittsburgh, and in 1896 he was consecrated a bishop in the AMEZ.

During his career, Bishop Clinton was a prominent writer on church and political matters. He participated in the Southern Sociological Congress and in work of the Federal Council of the Churches of Christ in America.

### FATHER DIVINE
**The Peace Mission Cult**
**1877-1965**

Father Divine was the founder of the Peace Mission Cult, a nonritualistic religious movement whose followers worshipped their leader as God incarnate on earth.

Mystery shrouds the early identity and real name of Father Divine. There is reason to believe he was born George Baker in 1877 on Hutchinson's Island in Georgia. Before the turn of the century, he lived in East Baltimore, where he preached in local Sunday schools. In 1907, he became a disciple of Sam Morris, a Pennsylvania black who called himself Father Jehovia. Two years later he switched over to John Hickerson's "Lift Ever, Die Never" group before returning to Georgia where he began his own campaign to promote himself as a "divine messenger."

Threatened by local authorities (he was once booked as

"John Doe, alias God"), Father Divine left Georgia in 1914 and later settled in New York City, where he worked as a kind of employment agent for the few followers still loyal to him. Calling his meeting place "Heaven," he soon attracted a larger following and moved to Sayville, Long Island, where he was once sentenced to six months in jail as a public nuisance.

Four days after his trial, the judge in his case died of a heart attack, whereupon Father Divine was quoted as having said: "I hated to do it." The ensuing publicity enhanced his popularity.

The Divine movement grew by leaps and bounds in the 1930s and 1940s, with "Father" speaking across the country and publicizing his views in the *New Day,* a weekly magazine published by his organization. In 1946, he married his "Sweet Angel," a 21-year-old Canadian stenographer known thereafter as Mother Divine.

In 1953, Father Divine acquired Woodmont, a 73-acre estate in lower Merion township on Philadelphia's Main Line. In later years he came to refer to it as the showcase of the "Kingdom of Peace."

Many believers in the Father Divine cult pointed with pride to the way their leader had provided them with food and lodging over the years, at prices well within the range of their pocketbooks. The low-cost service originated in the Depression years, and has continued to be a hallmark of the missions ever since then.

Spiritually, Father Divine fostered what amounted to a massive cooperative agency, based on the communal spirit of the Last Supper. Services included songs and impromptu sermons and were conducted without Scripture readings and the use of a clergy.

Father Divine himself died peacefully at Woodmont on September 10, 1965. His wife pledged to continue the work of the movement, whose property holdings were then estimated at $10 million.

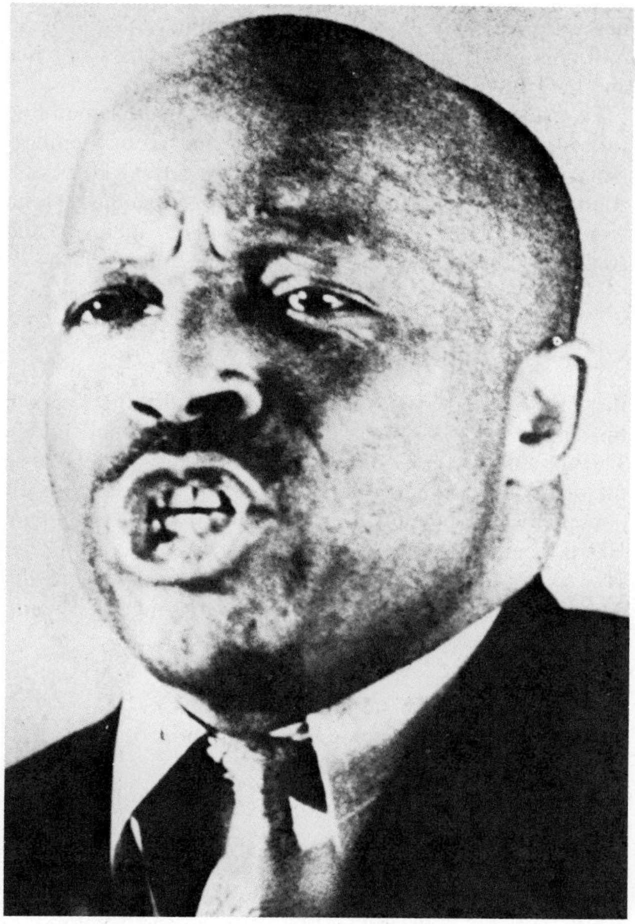

*Father Divine believed he could "produce God and shake the earth with it."*

## ELIJAH JOHN FISHER
## 1858-1915

Elijah Fisher exemplifies the great charismatic black preachers of the nineteenth and early twentieth centuries who, with very little formal education, built large religious institutions, counseled racial pride, and expounded the cause of blacks as a people.

Born in La Grange, Georgia, the youngest of eight boys in a family of 17 children, Fisher's father was an unordained preacher of a Baptist congregation that met in a white church. Fisher worked in a Baptist parsonage as a boy slave, and was taught to read by a former house slave and a white missionary. In his teens, he worked in mines in Alabama and then as a butler, all the while studying theology in his own time. Though losing a leg in an accident, Fisher in his early twenties became pastor of several small country churches, and then in 1889, of the Mount Olive Baptist Church in Atlanta. In that year, when past the age of 30, he enrolled in the Atlanta Baptist Seminary, later to become Morehouse College, passed his examinations, went on to preach in Nashville and then to Chicago where he led the Olive Baptist Church from 1902 until his death.

Throughout his life, Dr. Fisher continued his studies, preached from coast to coast, and involved the Church in youth work, food programs for poor people, and black-run businesses. An active member of the Republican party, Fisher strongly criticized blacks who advised their breathren to rely solely on the good will of whites and publicly criticized Booker T. Washington for not speaking out against lynching.

## REV. JAMES FORBES JR.
## Riverside Church

The Rev. James Forbes Jr. was named the first black man to be named senior pastor at New York City's Riverside Church. A professor of preaching at Union Theological Seminary for 12 years at the time of his appointment, the 53-year-old Forbes was nominated by church officials of the prestigious church, built in the 1920s, by John D. Rockefeller Jr.

The church, located on New York City's upper west side,

has a membership of 3,000 and an annual budget of $6 million. It is affiliated with the American Baptist Churches and the United Church of Christ.

Described as "the most prestigious pulpit in mainline Protestantism," the congregation is made up of members from various demonations. In describing Rev. Forbes, J. Richard Butler, head of the search committee said, "He is an eminent preacher, committed to pluralism, inclusity and social justice, key characteristics for our senior minister."

### REV. BARBARA HARRIS
### Bishop, Episcopal Church

Rev. Barbara Harris, 58, was elected as the first woman bishop in the 2,000-year tradition of the Episcopal church. The appointment became official in February, 1989 after a majority of 60 of the church's 118 U.S. bishops gave their consent for her elevation. A former public relations executive, Harris received support despite the concerns of some that her views were too liberal. Her supporters said that despite the lack of a college degree or seminary training, she would broaden the outreach of the church.

### JAMES AUGUSTINE HEALY
### First Black Catholic Bishop
### 1830-1900

James Augustine Healy was the first black Catholic bishop in the United States. For 25 years he presided over a diocese covering the states of Maine and New Hampshire.

A native of Macon, Georgia, Healy received his education in the North, first at Franklin Park Quaker School in Burlington, New York and later at Holy Cross in Worcester, Massachusetts. Healy graduated from the latter with first honors. Healy continued his studies abroad, and was ordained in Paris at Notre Dame Cathedral in 1854. He then returned to the United States.

Pastor of a predominantly Irish congregation which was at first reluctant to accept him, Bishop Healy performed his priestly duties with devotion and eventually won the respect and admiration of his parishioners—particularly after performing his office during a typhoid epidemic.

Thereafter, he was made an assistant to Bishop John Fitzpatrick of Boston, who appointed him chancellor and entrusted him with a wide variety of additional responsibilities. In 1875, he was named Bishop of Portland, Maine.

Bishop Healy died in 1900. (His brother, Patrick Francis Healy, was a Jesuit priest who served as president of Georgetown University from 1873 to 1882.)

*James A. Healy was the first black American to become a Roman Catholic bishop.*

### JOSEPH LAWSON HOWZE
### Auxiliary Bishop of Mississippi
### 1925

Born in Daphne, Alabama, Reverend Howze attended Junior College in Alabama, graduated with a B.S. in Education from Alabama State University, and taught sciences in the public schools of Mobile. During the 1940s, Howze increasingly questioned the desirability of a public school teaching career for himself and in 1950 entered Epiphany Apostolic College in Newburgh, New York. In 1959, he graduated from St. Bonaventure University, New York and entered the priesthood. In 1973, he was named to his current post, becoming the second black bishop presently in the Catholic Church, the other being Bishop Perry of Louisiana.

### JOSEPH H. JACKSON
### President, National Baptist Convention, U.S.A., Inc.

Dr. Joseph H. Jackson has been the leader of some 5 million U.S. black Baptists since 1953, the year he was elected to the presidency of the National Baptist Convention, U.S.A., Inc. Dr. Jackson has steered the organization into new spheres of influence, notably into a more activist role in the civil rights struggle.

One of the most ambitious ventures initiated under Dr. Jackson has been the Liberian land investment program whereby Baptists hope to develop extensive farms on some 100,000 acres of Liberian land, and thus raise additional funds to help sponsor their missionary labors in Africa. The Convention has also purchased 400 acres in Fayette County, Tennessee, and owns a Nashville publishing house with sales of close to $1 million annually.

Dr. Jackson holds a B.A. from Jackson College, an M.A. from Creighton University, and a B.D. from Rochester Colgate School of Divinity. He is a member of the Central

Committee of the World Council of Churches and a vice president of the World Baptist Alliance. He has visited Asia, Africa, Europe, and the Middle East, taped messages for the Voice of America, preached in Russia, written campaign literature for John F. Kennedy, and attended the 1962 Second Vatican Council in Rome. He is pastor of Olivet Baptist Church in Chicago.

### ISAAC LANE
### Bishop, Colored Methodist Church
### 1834-1937

A great religious leader and educator, whose life spanned more than a century, Isaac Lane was born a slave in Jackson, Tennessee. Self-educated, in 1856 he was granted a license to exhort, a category assigned blacks who were forbidden to preach, in the Methodist Episcopal Church, South.

Lane was ordained a minister in 1865 and in 1873 was made a bishop, at a salary so low he had to raise cotton to supplement his income and support his family, which contained 11 children. In the 1890s, he established Lane College in Jackson with $9,000 he himself raised.

### ARCHBISHOP EUGENE A. MARINO
### Archdiocese of Atlanta

He started off as an altar boy in Biloxi, Mississippi, but in 1988, Eugene A. Marino, who had been an auxiliary bishop of the Catholic Church, was named Archbishop of the Atlanta Diocese. The appointment of the 54-year-old prelate made him the spiritual leader of 156,000 Catholics (including about 10,000 blacks). His jurisdiction includes 64 parishes, 14 parochial elementary school, two parochial high schools and 95 diocesan priests, 100 religious order priests and 154 sisters involved in various responsibilities.

*Elijah Muhammad, perhaps the United States' most significant and controversial religious leader of the twentieth century.*

### ELIJAH MUHAMMAD
### Spiritual Leader of the Nation of Islam
### 1897-1975

Perhaps the United States' most significant and controversial religious leader of the twentieth century, Elijah Muhammad was born Elijah Poole in Sandersville, Georgia in 1897. His father, a Baptist preacher, had been a slave.

As a boy, Elijah worked as a sawmill helper and field boy, later as a laborer for the Southern Railroad and as a foreman for a brick company. At the age of 26, he moved with his wife and two children (he was to have eight children in all) to Detroit where he worked at several jobs, including one for Chevrolet.

In Detroit in 1930, Poole met Fard Muhammad, also known as W. D. Fard, who had founded the Black Nation of Islam. Poole soon became Fard's chief assistant and in 1932 went to Chicago where he established the Nation of Islam's Temple, Number Two, which soon became the largest. In 1934, he returned to Detroit. When Fard disappeared in that year, political and theological rivals accused Poole of foul play. He returned to Chicago where he organized his own movement, in which Fard was deified as Allah and Elijah (Poole) Muhammad became known as Allah's Messenger. This movement soon became known as the Black Muslims.

During World War II, Elijah Muhammad expressed support for Japan, on the basis of its being a nonwhite country, and was jailed for sedition. The time Muhammad served in prison was probably significant in his later, successful attempts to convert large numbers of black prison inmates, including Malcolm X, to the Nation of Islam. During the 1950s, and especially during the 1960s, the Nation grew under Muhammad's leadership, surviving internal differences between Muhammad and Malcolm X. In the late 1960s and early 1970s, Elijah Muhammad moderated the Nation's criticism of whites without compromising its message of black integrity. When Muhammad died in 1975, the Nation was an important religious, political, and economic force among America's blacks and in this country's major cities.

Elijah Muhammad was a leader whose significance was too great to assess shortly after his death. But some factors stand out. In many respects, Muhammad resembled the great black religious leaders of the late nineteenth and early twentieth centuries. He appealed to the racial consciousness and pride of blacks and he advocated discipline and abstinence in personal living. But he was clearly unique in three ways:

> His message on the virtues of being black was explicit and uncompromising.
>
> In addition to preaching the importance of self-sufficiency for blacks, he sought successfully through the Nation's schools and business enterprises to provide vehicles for attaining this self-sufficiency.

He built the first strong, national religious group in the United States that appealed primarily to the unemployed and underemployed city dweller. In his later years, Muhammad made some attempts to broaden the Nation's appeal to the growing black middle class, but a preponderance of the Nation's membership continued to come from the ranks of poor people who sought to live with pride and decency in America's black ghettos.

### THOMAS PAUL
### Baptist Leader
### 1773-1831

Thomas Paul is credited with having begun the movement to establish independent black Baptist churches in the United States.

Organizing a congregation of free blacks in a church on Jay Street in Boston (1805), Paul soon became so famous that he was invited to speak before white congregations in New York City where blacks were maintained as "segregated brethren." The First Baptist Church soon granted 16 of its members the right to organize a separate congregation under Paul's leadership. (It later became known as Abyssinian Baptist Church.)

Paul also carried his message to the Caribbean, spending six months in Haiti under the auspices of the Massachusetts Baptist Society. He later returned to the United States, continuing his work in the North until his death in 1831.

### HAROLD ROBERT PERRY
### Auxiliary Bishop of New Orleans

Harold Robert Perry was consecrated a Bishop of New Orleans on January 6, 1966—and thus became the first black Catholic bishop in the United States in the twentieth century.

One of six children, Perry was born the son of a rice-mill worker and a domestic cook in Lake Charles, Louisiana. He entered the Divine Word Seminary in Mississippi at the age of 13, was ordained a priest in 1944, and spent the next 14 years in parish work. In 1958, he was appointed rector of the seminary.

Louisiana has the largest concentration of black Catholics in the South, some 200,000 in all.

Perry is one of five black bishops now serving in Catholic parishes around the nation. Others include Joseph Howze in Biloxi, Mississippi; James Lyke in Cleveland, Ohio; Joseph Francis in Newark, New Jersey; and Eugene Marino in Washington, D. C.

### ADAM CLAYTON POWELL SR.
### Pastor, Abyssinian Baptist Church
### 1865-1953

Adam Clayton Powell Sr.—father of the late Harlem congressman—was largely responsible for building the Abyssinian Baptist Church into one of the most celebrated black congregations in the world.

Born in the backwoods of Virginia in 1865, Powell attended school locally, and between sessions, worked in the mines of West Virginia. After deciding to enter the ministry, he began his studies at Wayland Academy (now Virginia Union University), working his way through as a janitor and waiter. He later attended the Yale University School of Divinity and served as pastor of the Immanuel Baptist Church in New Haven.

Powell became pastor of Abyssinian in 1908—when it had a membership of only 1,600 and indebtedness of over $100,000. By 1921, the church had not been made solvent but was able to move into a $350,000 Gothic structure at its present location on 138th Street in Harlem.

During the depression Powell opened soup kitchens for Harlem residents and served thousands of meals. Later he and his son campaigned vigorously to expand job opportunities and city services in Harlem.

Powell retired from Abyssinian in 1937. He died in 1953, at which time the church was being pastored by his son.

### STEPHEN GILL SPOTTSWOOD
### 1897-1974

Bishop of the African Episcopal Zion Church from 1952 to 1972 and board chairman of the National Association for the Advancement of Colored People from 1961 until his death in 1974, Bishop Spottswood embodied the religious faith and intellectual incisiveness that has produced so many effective black religious activists.

Reverend Spottswood was born in Boston, attended Albright College, Gordon Divinity School, and then received a Doctor of Divinity from Yale University.

As a religious leader, Bishop Spottswood was president of the Ohio Council of Churches and served on the boards of numerous interfaith conferences as well as heading the AMEZ church. His activity with NAACP started in 1919, when he joined the organization. He was appointed to the national board in 1955. In 1971, he became the center of a political storm when he chastised the Nixon administration for its policies toward blacks and refused, under strong pressure from the administration, to retract his comments.

### GARDNER C. TAYLOR
### Concord Baptist Church of Christ
### 1918

Reverend Taylor is widely regarded as the dean of the nation's black preachers. He received a B.A. degree from Leland College in 1937 and B.D. degree from Oberlin Graduate School of Theology in Baton Rouge in 1940.

Reverend Taylor has long been a community activist. He demonstrated for civil rights with Martin Luther King in Brooklyn in the 1960s, and was one of 700 clergymen arrested during such demonstrations. He is the past president of the Council of Churches and past vice president of the Urban League in New York City.

Reverend Taylor has been the pastor at the Concord Baptist Church of Christ in Brooklyn for more than 30 years.

## GOSPEL MUSIC IN THE UNITED STATES

Gospel music, a function of the camp-meeting spiritual, blues, and jazz, has as its theme uninhibited praise and joyous worship of God. Major rhythms of gospel pieces are up-tempo and syncopated, but their melodies remain simple enough to enable large numbers of untrained musicians to master the playing and singing. Their harmonies are generally uncomplicated, although they have of late begun to show the influence of other musical forms.

The main performer in gospel is an outstanding soloist who is usually backed by a combination of singers able to provide him or her with a moving foundation on which to base improvisations. (This is, then, not unlike jazz where the group often forms a fabric around and through which the soloist may move.) Another major aspect of gospel is the highly repetitious "drive" which seeks to raise the fervor of the audience by building a hypnotic effect over it. The repeated phrases of the "drive" are intended to sway the listener and create a mood which mounts to an apex of power.

### Historical Roots

The rich, vibrant gospel music of the American black—an integral part of most traditional black religious services—can be grouped into two main styles or divisions: spirituals themselves, with their poignant and soulful quality ("Deep River," "Were You There," "Nobody Knows the Trouble I've Seen"), and camp-meeting songs, sung in part by a "leader" and then taken up by a "congregation," or chorus.

Along with traditional hymns, spirituals were sung during worship services in black Baptist or Methodist churches and were also heard in conjunction with the work songs which the black devised to help him through his wearisome field labors. The "field holler," a combination of yell and yodel developed by black slaves in the South, eventually became a component of solo blues, a musical diary through which blacks expressed despair and hopelessness.

Spirituals, hymns, and blues—these were the three ingredients which contributed most significantly to the development of gospel music in the post-Emancipation era. The black was free but remained a creature apart from the rest of humanity, still clinging to the single institution around which much of his social life revolved: the church.

Choral or communal singing in the black church soon came to be a highly organized practice. Certain arrangements of traditional spirituals then began to incorporate ideas from

*The Utterbach Concert Ensemble blends the fervor of gospel with classical and contemporary harmony.*

the blues idiom, together with a more syncopated, up-tempo style. In the early 1900s, a blues pianist, Thomas A. Dorsey, was sufficiently impressed by some of this music to write original tunes using this form. Dorsey was later responsible for popularizing it across the country by going on tour with Sallie Martin, a religious singer.

The leader-congregation style eventually gave way to the soloist-background method of performing. In this way, several soloists began to gain widespread fame for their artistic achievement. In the late 1930s, for example, Miss Roberta Martin of Chicago brought together several young soloists of varying styles and outstanding ability and formed a small, mixed group known as the Roberta Martin Singers. (This group is still in existence today.) Elsewhere in Chicago, Miss Mahalia Jackson was also on her way to becoming an international celebrity through her singular renditions of black gospel music. In the East, it was Clara Ward and the Ward Singers, given their original impetus by Mrs. Gertrude Ward. The Ward Singers introduced new techniques into their performances, employing all-female voices singing together in unusually high-pitched harmony and using synchronized theatrical motions and movements in their presentations.

## Postwar Trends

During World War II "jubilee" singing had a run of popularity, involving as it did male quartets who sang a type of arranged spiritual. Perhaps the most representative of these groups in this era was the Golden Gate Quartet. Radio appearances by such choral ensembles as The Wings Over Jordan group helped popularize the gospel style even further, making thousands of people more acutely aware of a coming musical trend. Soon, the recording industry (Apollo and Gotham records) took a more active interest in cultivating this brand of music. One of the first big recording successes for gospel was "Old Ship of Zion" by the Roberta Martin Singers, featuring the voice of Norsalus McKissick.

The music itself quickly became separated into two camps: gospel and quartet. Gospel included all-male, all-female, or mixed groups using piano or organ as accompanying instruments, whereas quartet involved all-male groups whose accompaniment was always provided by a guitarist. Gospel singers generally used colorful choir robes, whereas quartet groups were identified by conventional coat and trousers.

The first gospel recording which sold over a million copies—"Surely God Is Able" (Savoy Records)—was made during the late 1940s by Clara Ward and her group. Soon thereafter the Alex Bradford Singers recorded "Too Close to Heaven" (Specialty Records), a tune which approximated the success of "Surely." Gospel arrangers then began to pore through the pages of hymnals in search of appropriate material for the growing number of revivals, festivals, and other programs.

In the 1950s, the Davis Sisters came to dominate the gospel field, ushering in the era of "song battles" between competing groups which would try to outdo each other in the intensity and fervor of their performances. Some of the most popular tunes recorded by the Davis Sisters were "Jesus," "Reign in Jerusalem," "He'll Understand," "Plant My Feet on Higher Ground," and "Twelve Gates to the City." (Perhaps the arch rivals of the Davis Sisters during these years were the Gospel Harmonettes of Birmingham, led by Dorothy Love. Among the leading tunes recorded by the Harmonettes were "I'm Sealed," "You Must Be Born Again," "That's Enough," and "Lord, You've Been Good to Me.")

The leading quartet groups of this period included The Dixie Hummingbirds, The Nightingales, The Harmonizing Four, and The Soul Stirrers. (Sam Cooke, later to gain great fame in the popular music field, was once a regular performer with the last-named group, and had such hits as "Nearer to Thee" and "Touch the Hem of His Garment.")

## The Impact of Gospel

Gospel had profound effects on rock 'n' roll performers like Ray Charles and James Brown, both of whom retained the same inflections used by the gospel singer. In fact, many churches in which gospel music is sung have served as a kind of unintentional training ground for rock 'n' roll, popular, and jazz musicians whose trademark came to be called "soul."

Over the years, gospel forms have often been incorporated into more programmed arrangements in an effort to blend the fervor and excitement of the music itself with the form and texture of classical music.

Inevitably, gospel music achieved the international spotlight. Instrumental in this was Langston Hughes, whose singsong plays *Black Nativity, Jericho, Jim Crow*, and *Trumpets for the Lord* were successful abroad. In many respects, gospel's European success paralleled that of the Fisk Jubilee Singers, who toured Europe in 1870.

In the 1960s, gospel started to move from the churches into auditoriums across the country where jazz and folk music enthusiasts lined up to hear performances. Along with jazz and spirituals, gospel was recognized as a significant black contribution to American culture and the world of music.

The trend continued into the 1980s where such groups as The Winans, The Hawkins Family, Andre Crouch and other gospel artists had recorded music that was popular outside of the gospel community. A sign of recognition within the music recording industry was the fact that gospel singers now had their own category in being singled out for music awards.

While there was concern among some in the church, gospel singers became part of Broadway plays and other presentations outside of strictly gospel presentations. The trend of gospel singers to cross over and sing secular music continued with an unusual twist—some singers like Al Green left pop music and returned to his church roots, even so far as pastoring a church as well as recording gospel music.

Music had always been an integral part of the black worship experience and as the 1990s approached, there seemed to be strong indications that this would always remain the case—while a larger outside-the-church world continued to be a part of the following as well.

# NATIONAL BLACK ORGANIZATIONS

**A Brief History ■ Fraternities ■ Sororities ■ Professional Societies ■ Religious and Cooperative Associations ■ Lodges ■ Brotherhood ■ Benevolent Orders ■ Various Incorporated Groups**

During the 1970s and early 1980s, the tenor and orientation of black organizations increasingly reflected the desire of blacks to work on their own behalf, independent of control by whites, and to explore black history and heritage. Many organizations were also formed to develop and explore business opportunities for blacks, this in response to government programs encouraging minority entrepreneurship. However, traditional black groups of a professional and fraternal nature remained prominent as did racially integrated organizations with social and political objectives. Groups stressing economic progress by poor tenants, welfare recipients, and others, of all races increased in importance in the mid-1970s. Also notable in the 1970s was the increasing prominence of black women in positions of leadership. For example, Margaret Bush Wilson became board chairman of the National Association for the Advancement of Colored People. Another trend was the emergence of black caucuses within white groups. The most notable of these was the formation of the Congressional Black Caucus in the House of Representatives. Others appeared within such professional societies as the American Bar Association, to complement the efforts of groups consisting entirely of blacks.

Throughout their history on these shores, blacks have displayed a remarkable capacity to organize in pursuit of their political and personal objectives. The nature of these organizations of course has varied in terms of what was permitted, by whites, as well as what was sought by blacks.

Until the late eighteenth century, blacks were frequently forbidden by white laws and policies to organize in more than the most informal and limited sense. Thus black organizations that did exist were clandestine and unrecorded, and the first black organization in what is now the United States cannot be identified. Probably it was some camp of runaway slaves in Virginia in the seventeenth century. Some of these camps survived as independent communities for many years with their own government, rules, and procedures, and so certainly qualify as "organizations."

In the 1770s, following zealous efforts by white evangelists, a small number of blacks in South Carolina and Georgia were permitted to form their own churches (as discussed elsewhere in this volume). At about the same time, black slaves in New England were organizing, with sympathetic whites, to sue for their freedom in Massachusetts courts.

The Free African Society formed by Richard Allen in Philadelphia in 1787 is generally viewed as the United States' first black organization of note. In many respects, its orientation was a model for groups to follow. It was founded by a clergyman, in great part so blacks could worship without interference from harassing whites, but it soon became a factor in the education and political status of blacks. The influence of clergymen in lay black groups remains important to this day, with Reverends Jesse Jackson of Operation PUSH, Cecil Williams of the Glide Memorial Church, and John Lewis of the Voters Education Project, just three of many current examples.

In the nineteenth century, organizations concerned with issues important to blacks were invariably dominated by whites. Blacks had little influence in abolitionist and "back to Africa" efforts, though black leaders and heroes such as Paul Cuffe and Frederick Douglass did emerge.

During Reconstruction and into the early twentieth century a great many black groups were formed. The thrust of most was toward education, betterment, and religious training, and in many cases also a reassurance of whites that blacks posed no threat to the nation's segregationist order. Other organizations, however, such as the National Colored Farmers Alliance, sought, with unfortunately little success, to strengthen the economic and political position of blacks.

In the early twentieth century, led by W. E. B. DuBois, a black intelligentsia increasingly came to the fore, to struggle for the rights of blacks, first in the Niagara Movement founded in 1905, then in the National Association for the Advancement of Colored People, which succeeded it in 1910, and the Urban League shortly thereafter.

Less noted by historians, but of great significance during the early decades of this century was the formation and growth of professional, business, and labor groups such as the National Medical Association, the National Negro Business League, the National Newspaper Publishers Association, the Brotherhood of Sleeping Car Porters, and scores of others.

Though less publicized than civil rights and black power groups, they have also contributed enormously to the progress of blacks and it is such organizations as well as those with political objectives which are listed and briefly described in the ensuing pages.

## PROMINENT BLACK ORGANIZATIONS

(The Civil Rights, Legal, and Science sections each have additional organizations listed within the respective subdivisions.)

This section also lists some organizations which, while nonblack, focus on minority issues. These groups are set off by an asterisk.

**A Better Chance, Inc.**
739 Boylston Street
Boston, MA 02116
(617) 421-0950
Established in 1963, A Better Chance, Inc., recruits academically talented and highly motivated minority students, places them in outstanding private and public secondary schools and provides ongoing support and counsel to them during their enrollment.

**A. Philip Randolph Institute and A. Philip Randolph Educational Fund**
260 Park Avenue South
New York, NY 10010
(212) 533-8000
With 20,000 members in 180 local chapters and 12 state organizations, the A. Philip Randolph Institute works to heighten the political involvement of blacks at the local, state and national levels of government. The organization also seeks to increase black activity in the labor movement and to foster the development of trade unionism in the black community.

**Action Alliance of Black Managers**
PO Box 15636
Columbus, OH 43215
(614) 431-6050
The Alliance was formed for the purpose of providing networking opportunities for black professionals, politicians, technicians and entrepreneurs to widen the opportunities for individuals from each group. Organizers provide workshops, seminars and business-card exchanges as well as career conferences. The group is active with high school and college groups, encouraging young people to maximize their career potential.

**Afram Associates, Inc.**
68-72 East 131 Street
New York, NY 10037
(212) 690-7010
Afram Associates exists to develop a depository of information and research for use by the community's action groups; to reprint and circulate articles on critical social issues; to formulate and implement research about the problems of minority groups; to provide staff services to groups involved with consumers and the community and, ultimately, to promote self-understanding, self-determination, and true liberation.

**African American Institute**
833 United Nations Plaza
New York, NY 10017
(212) 661-0800
The institute's purpose is to strengthen African-American understanding, to inform America about Africa, and to help further African development.

**African American Museum of Nassau County**
110 North Franklin Street
Hempstead, NY 11550
(516) 485-0470
The Museum's mission is to promote the art history, and culture of African Americans on Long Island and in the diaspora.

**African American Museums Association**
420 7th Street, NW
Washington DC 20004
(202) 783-7744
Founded in 1978, AAMA is a membership organization of black museums and museum professionals. It exists to nurture the people who run museums in matters of organization, scholarship, publications publicity, information development and advancement. AAMA promotes unity among these various institutions and is constantly concerned that black museums have every opportunity to thrive and succeed.

**African American Scholars Council, Inc.**
1001 Connecticut Avenue NW, Suite 1119
Washington, DC 20036
(202) 785-4743

*The A. Philip Randolph Institute has been effective in labor conference rooms and in the streets as well, for encouraging people to take an active role in their communities.*

The council is an educational organization to promote social, economic, and human resources of the African continent.

**African Art Museum of the S.M.A. Fathers**
23 Bliss Avenue
Tenafly, New Jersey 07670
(201) 567-0450
The Museum hopes to increase appreciation of African art and the knowledge and understanding of the richness and variety of the cultures of African peoples.

**African Bibliographic Center, Inc.**
1346 Connecticut Avenue NW, #901
Washington, DC 20036
(202) 233-1392
The center exists to disseminate information on African affairs in the United States and abroad. The information is selected primarily on a "need to know" basis by print and electronic media forms.

**African Heritage Studies Association**
c/o Ofuctey Kudjoe Department of Political Studies
Queens College
65-30 Kissena Blvd.
Flushing, NY 11367
(718) 520-2878
The African Heritage Studies Association was founded in 1968 for the preservation of the historical and cultural heritage of African people throughout the world. The organization promotes trips to Africa, the Caribbean and South America, as well as workshops and seminars throughout the U.S. It provides scholarships for students and teachers. Its membership includes university and community groups from all parts of the U.S., Africa, the Caribbean and South America.

**African Methodist Episcopal Church**
2311 M Street, NW
Washington, DC 20037
(202) 337-3930
A.M.E. Church was founded by Richard Allen in 1787 at Bethel Church in Philadelphia. Today, the group's membership numbers 2.1 million in some 6,000 congregations. The organization's principal activities include serving the needy, feeding the hungry, housing the homeless and providing jobs. The A.M.E. "Christian Recorder," first published in the late 18th century, is the oldest continuing black, church periodical in the world.

**African Methodist Episcopal Zion Church**
1200 Windermere Drive
Pittsburgh, PA 15218
(412) 242-5842
Established in 1796, this organization now encompasses 2,500 churches and has an active membership of 1.5 million. The Church has founded and continues to support a number of institutions of higher learning—Livingstone College (with its affiliate, Hood Theological Seminary) and Lomax Hannon Junior College in North Carolina; Clinton Junior College in South Carolina, and Dinwiddy Institute in Virginia—and maintains missions here and abroad.

**Africare, Inc.**
1601 Connecticut Ave. NW
Washington D.C. 20009
(202) 462-3614
Africare, Inc., is a private, nonprofit organization dedicated to improving the quality of life in rural Africa through increased food production, water resources development, health care systems and refugee assistance. Founded in 1971, Africare's major objective is helping Africans to help themselves.

**Afro-American Book Source**
PO Box 851
Boston, MA 02120

(617) 445-9209
The Book Source exists to improve the ease of purchase and availability of books by, about or of special interest to Afro-Americans.

**Afro American Cultural Foundation**
394 Tarrytown Road
White Plains, NY 10607
(914) 761-4778
The purpose of the foundation is to improve the self-esteem of blacks, change the attitude of whites toward black people and their talents, to raise awareness of the potentials and problems of black people and help eliminate latent and induced prejudices.

**Afro-American Cultural and Historical Society**
1839 East 81 Street
Cleveland, OH 44104
(216) 795-3121
The Society was founded to build an International African and Afro-American Historical Society Museum and Library; erect monuments in Cleveland honoring Colonel Charles Young and Reverend John Malvin, Cleveland's first ordained black minister; and also to integrate textbooks in the school system and promote the study of Afro-American history; and obtain official national holidays honoring Harriet Tubman, Crispus Attucks, Colonel Young, Mary McLeod Bethune, and Dr. Martin Luther King Jr.

**Afro-American Historical and Genealogical Society**
PO Box 13086
"T" Street Station
Washington, DC 20009
(202) 668-2651
The Afro-American Historical and Genealogical Society was founded in 1977 to encourage scholarly research in Afro-American history and genealogy. The original 30 members, made up of anthropologists, historians, sociologists, genealogists and educators, worked with Alex Haley on the Kente Project, which conducted research into the genealogy of American blacks.

*Afro-American Music Opportunities Association Incorporated helps find professional placement for black musicians.*

**Afro-American Music Hall of Fame and Musicians, Inc.**
PO Box 390
Youngstown, OH 44505
(216) 746-7189
The Hall of Fame was established to ensure that the works of the Afro-Americans in the world of rhythm and blues, jazz, and gospel music will live on, to enlighten, to educate, and to entertain all those who visit the Hall of Fame so they will feel fulfillment and they will pass on the works of their ancestors and the Hall of Fame.

**Afro-American Music Opportunities Association, Inc.**
2909 Wayzata Boulevard
Minneapolis, MN 55405
(612) 377-3730
The Association exists to help place black performers in professional ensembles; black music specialists on college campuses; assist these individuals in educational opportunities, materials, and repertoire; assemble information on black music history and make it readily available to the public; serve as a repository and clearinghouse on all aspects of black music.

**Afro-American Patrolmen's League**
7126 South Jeffery Boulevard
Chicago, IL 60649
(312) 667-7384
The League seeks to elevate the image of black policemen, especially in the black community; seeks fair hiring and promotion practices of black police; represents needs of minority people to police departments; elevates police performance and acts as a check on unethical police practices; seeks to lessen danger and increase understanding between police and citizens; and improve relations between black and white police.

**Afro-American Resource Center**
PO Box 746
Howard University
Washington, DC 20059
(202) 636-7242
The Center disseminates information about (or related to) the black experience. It contains books, tapes, films and records, and serves the university community as well as the general public.

**Alabama A&M University**
Alumni Affairs Office
PO Box 348
Normal, AL 35762
(205) 859-7408
The objective of the Office of Alumni Affairs is to serve alumni and offer ways for alumni to serve the University and society.

**Alabama Legislative Black Caucus**
PO Box 45
Mobile, AL 36601
(205) 438-9509
Organized in 1974, the Alabama Legislative Black Caucus acts to help its black constituency better understand and make use of the Alabama State Legislature. The Caucus researches state conditions, as well as existing and pending legislation, with the purpose of making the state more responsive to blacks especially in the areas of employment, housing education and health.

**Alaska Black Caucus**
PO Box 3342
Anchorage AK 99510
(907) 276-2777
The Alaska Black Caucus was founded in 1975 by Mr. Overstreet and Ms. Berkley to develop an alliance with the National Congressional Black Caucus, to increase the effectiveness of black members in the state legislature and to make certain that black concerns were dealt with fairly. The organization is comprised of

*American Committee on Africa actively supports the struggle for freedom for the people of Africa.*

a cross section of the Alaskan community that includes blacks, whites and Hispanics.

**Alliance Enterprise Corporation**
1616 Walnut Street, Suite 802
Philadelphia, PA 19103
(215) 732-2812
To make the maximum contribution within capital resource limitations to the economic growth of the minority business community.

**Alpha Kappa Alpha Sorority, Inc.**
5656 S. Stony Island Ave.
Chicago, IL 60637
(312) 684-1282
Founded in 1980 at Howard University, Alpha Kappa Alpha is a social action organization of 100,000 members in 750 chapters. These chapters are located in 47 states, West Africa, the Bahamas, the Virgin Islands and Germany. The organization is dedicated to improving the quality of life through service with a global perspective.

**Alpha Phi Alpha Fraternity, Inc.**
4432 South King Drive
Chicago, IL 60053
(312) 373-1819
Founded in 1906 on the campus of Cornell University in Ithaca, NY, Alpha Phi Alpha Fraternity, Inc., is the oldest predominantly black Greek-letter organization in America. The organization has an active membership of 75,000 and 650 chapters in 45 states, the Caribbean, Africa, Europe and Asia. In addition to promoting academic excellence, the Fraternity has increasingly supported community service activities.

**Alpha Pi Chi Sorority**
PO Box 5639
St. Louis, MO 63121
(314) 382 0100
Founded in 1963 as a service organization, the Sorority has a membership of more than 1,300 in chapters throughout much of the U.S. The groups' fund-raising efforts have benefited several civil rights organizations and black charities. The Sorority has developed a showcase for talented youths called "Talent a Rama," which helps with fund-raising events for philanthropic causes and encourages the creative expressions of young people. Another national program has Sorority chapters "adopting" senior-citizen homes.

**American Association for Affirmative Action**
101 Administrative Building
Emory University
Atlanta, GA 30322
(404) 727-6017
More than 1,000 professionals, committed to the implementation of affirmative action and equal opportunity nation-wide, belong to this seven-year-old organization. AAAA serves as a liaison to private and government agencies involved with compliance in employment and education and disseminates materials relevant to these objectives. It also provides training in the AA/EEO area.

**American Association of Black Women Entrepreneurs**
814 Thayer Avenue Suite 202
Silver Spring, MD 20910
(301) 585-2232
The American Association of Black Women Entrepreneurs was formed in April, 1982, to provide black women business owners with an organization primarily concerned with their needs. The organization's 20 national chapters promote the interests of its

members through a variety of federal, state and local governmental business development programs as well as those of private industry. Members are provided with information, professional development training and networking, as well as a variety of programs aimed at increasing business skills.

**American Association of Blacks in Energy**
1220 "L" Street, NW Suite 605
Washington, DC 20005
(202) 898-0828
The Association is a nonprofit advisory organization formed in 1977 to assure that minority voices are heard in the development of a national energy policy. The Association is concerned with energy use, research, the ownership of energy resources and the development of energy technologies in the U.S. The 325 Association members work to increase the number of minority scientists, engineers and technicians in the energy field through seminars, recruiting and scholarships.

**American Bridge Association, Inc.**
555 Kappock Street #12G
Riverdale NY 10463
(212) 543-2911
Founded in 1933 to promote tournament bridge among blacks, the American Bridge Association has more than 6,100 members in some 175 chapters in 38 states. In addition to sponsoring national bridge tournaments the Association makes annual contributions to the National Association for the Advancement of Colored People, People United to Save Humanity and the United Negro College Fund, among others.

**American Committee on Africa**
164 Madison Avenue
New York, NY 10016
(212) 532-3700
The Committee was created to establish an organization in the United States fully sympathetic with and actively supporting the struggle for freedom of the people of Africa.

**American Council on Education, Office of Minority Concerns**
One Dupont Circle
Washington, DC 20035
(202) 939-9395
Founded in 1981 with a Ford Foundation Grant, the Office of Minority Concerns provides assistance to minority administrators in higher education around the country, including those in both predominantly white and historically black colleges and universities. The Office focuses on studying and improving the status of blacks, Hispanics, native Americans and Asian-Americans in the nation's system of higher education.

**American Health and Beauty Aids Institute**
111 East Wacker Drive
Suite 600
Chicago, IL 60601
(312) 644-6610
The American Health and Beauty Aids Institute was founded in 1981 as a trade association for minority-owned companies that manufacture ethnic health and beauty products. Representing 21 manufacturers and more than 100 associate members nation-wide, the Institute keeps its constituent groups up-to-date on trends, pricing, and government regulations, and makes recommendations for philanthropic gestures to community organizations.

**American Economic Association**
1313 Twenty-First Avenue South
Nashville, TN 37212
(615) 322-2595
The Association encourages economic research, especially historical and statistical study; issues publications on economic subjects; promotes perfect freedom of economic discussion.

**American League of Financial Institutions**
1511 "K" Street, NW
Suite 516
Washington DC 20005
(202) 628-5624
Founded in 1948, the American League of Financial Institutions comprises 75 black, Hispanic, Asian-American and women-owned or women-managed savings and loan institutions in 24 states and the District of Columbia. It promotes thrift and home ownership among minority groups and has programs to stimulate the growth of minority-owned S & L's. Membership assets for 1985 exceeded $5 billion. The League conducts research and directs plans for financing housing for minority groups. A deposit-generation program encourages businesses and investors to make deposits with insured ALFI members.

*Architect's model of the Amistad Research Center, the world's largest collection of African-American source material.*

**American Library Association Black Caucus**
Bureau of Academic and Research Libraries
99Washington Avenue
Albany, NY 12230
The Association serves as a clearinghouse for black librarians; reviews, analyzes, evaluates and recommends to the American Library Association actions on the needs of black librarians in the areas of recruitment, development, advancement, and general working conditions.

**American Society for Training and Development**
PO Box 5307
Madison, WI 53705
(608) 274-3440
A professional society devoted exclusively to the education, development, and expansion of the skills and standards of members in the training and development profession.

**American Society of Planning Officials**
1313 East 60 Street
Chicago, IL 60637
(312) 947-2560
The Society exixts to evolve the best techniques for guiding development in cities, regions, states, and the nation; facilitates communication among all groups in the planning field; and seeks to provide professional aid to the planner.

**Amistad Research Center**
Tulane University
New Orleans, LA 70118
(504) 865-5000
The center is a historical research library which collects primary source material on the histories and cultures of America's ethnic minorities. Its 8,000,000 manuscript pieces comprise the world's largest collection of original material on the Afro-American and on race relations in the United States. Although privately funded, the center is a public archive open to all students of American Ethnic history.

**Ancient Egyptian Arabic Order Nobles Mystic Shrine, Inc. (P.H.A.)**
Imperial Potentate
Linden Tower Professional Centre
Suite 710
2nd & Franklin Streets
Richmond, VA 23219
(804) 783-0020
AEAONMS is a world-wide charitable and benevolent organization that sponsors programs to curb delinquency and drug use among black youth, and lends support to education through scholarships. AEAONMS also funds medical research for the study of diseases that particularly affect blacks.

**Anderson Communications, Inc.**
1465 Westwood Avenue, SW
Atlanta, GA 30310
(404) 752-9353
Anderson Communications is a full service public relations and promotions firm which works with major corporations to develop programs with the black consumer market. Its subsidiary Anderson Media Services syndicates radio programs targeted at the black consumer market including Inspirations Across America and Focus On Women.

**Arkansas Black Legislative Caucus**
State Capitol
Little Rock, AR 72203
(501 ) 372-1924
Founded in 1979, the Arkansas Black Legislative Caucus was formed to uplift and improve the educational economic and social development of all people in Arkansas. The Caucus functions to make certain that black interests are not overlooked in legislative proceedings and it also acts to keep blacks in Arkansas informed on matters of special interest to the black community. The Caucus interacts with other black state legislative caucuses and with other black groups to keep its members and supporters current on national and regional issues.

**Arizona Contractors' Service Center, Inc.**
1800 North Central, Suite 201
Phoenix, AZ 85004
(602) 267-7541
The Center provides management assistance for minority contractors in the state of Arizona.

**Associated Publishers, Inc.**
1407 14th Street NW
Washington, DC 20005-3704
(202) 265-1441
The Associated Publishers is the oldest Afro-American Publisher in the US. It was founded by Dr. Carter G. Woodson, November 20, 1920 to do a general publishing on Afro-Americans. The publications are planned to cover the form of textbooks and popular treatises of every phase of Afro-American life and history.

**Association for Black Management in Health Care, Inc.**
120 Liberty Street
New York, NY 10006
(212) 682-5595
The Association provides economic development to health systems to advance the participation and involvement in service provision in health care delivery.

**Association for Multi-Cultural Counseling and Development**
5999 Stevenson Avenue
Alexandria, VA 22302
(702) 823-9800
A division of the American Association for Counseling and Development, the Association for Multi-Cultural Counseling and Development focuses on programs seeking to improve ethnic and racial empathy and understanding. Its activities are also designed to advance the state of personal growth and improve educational opportunities for persons of diverse cultural backgrounds.

**Association for the Integration of Management, Inc.**
280 Park Avenue West Building, 33F
New York, NY 10017
(212) 687-7075
The Association exists to achieve full participation in management by minority group men and women; to accelerate the movement of minority group men and women into key positions in management.

**Association for the Study of Afro-American Life and History**
1401 14th Street, NW
Washington DC 20005
(202) 667-2822
The Association for the Study of Afro-American Life and History was founded by Dr. Carter G. Woodson in 1915 for the purpose of collecting, preserving and promoting black history. The Association, with more than 139 branches, promotes an appreciation of Afro-American history, encourages an understanding of present status and works to enrich the promise of the future.

**Association of Black Admissions and Financial Aid Officers of the Ivy League and Sister Schools, Inc.**
PO Box 2114
Cambridge, MA 02238-0001
(617) 280-2521
ABAFAOILS, founded in 1970 is a professional educational organization for minority admissions and financial aid officers in the Ivy League and sister schools and the Massachusetts Institute

of Technology. The organization's primary goal is to improve methods of recruitment, selection and financial aid packaging for the minority student populations at these colleges.

**Association of Black Foundation Executives**
1828 "L" Street, NW
Suite 1200
Washington, DC 20036
(202) 466-6512
The Association of Black Foundation Executives was established in 1971 as a membership organization of men and women who are on the staffs or boards of corporate and foundation grants-making organizations. The Association came into being primarily to help corporations and foundations improve their performance in supporting blacks, and to address social economic, and educational problems. It also helps its members do their jobs more effectively.

**Association of Black Psychologists**
PO Box 55999
Washington, DC 20040-5999
(202) 722-0808
Established in 1968 and operating with 27 chapters nation-wide, this 800-member organization seeks to unite black professionals and students of psychology to enhance the psychological well-being of black people in America. It also seeks to influence the mental health of the black community through research and by developing policies on the local, state, and national levels.

**Association of Black Sociologists**
Department of Sociology
University of Michigan
Ann Arbor, MI 48109-1382
(313) 764-5561
Nearly 60 percent of all American blacks who have attained doctorates in sociology are members of this group, and these scholars hold faculty posts at more than 110 major colleges and universities. Within ABS, the membership works to facilitate research on the black experience and to publicize findings in professional journals.

**Association of Black Women in Higher Education, Inc.**
c/o UNCF
500 East 62nd Street
New York, NY 10021
(212) 644-9636
Founded in 1978, the Association of Black Women in Higher Education, Inc., was established to foster and expand the historically substantive role of black women in higher education. The Association is organized to provide a vehicle for supporting the aims and goals of black women in their professional development.

**Association of Minority Enterprises of New York**
165-40A Baisley Boulevard
Jamaica, NY 11434
(718) 341-0707
The Association of Minority Enterprises of New York was founded in 1975 as a support group for minority businesses. The Association functions to promote economic, commercial and industrial growth of more than 350 members across the state. It monitors government and industry vendor programs for minority businesses and holds its annual meeting in conjunction with New York State's Black and Puerto Rican Legislative Caucus.

**Association of Social and Behavioral Scientists**
Box 5522
Durham, NC 27707
(919) 684-3175
The Association exists to study the weakness in social science offerings with the view of recommending improvements; to think through some of the most difficult and perplexing problems confronting blacks from the black point of view, with the intent of working out satisfactory methods and plans for acquainting the student with and developing within him a philosophy and an attitude that will enable him to confront the baffling problems that he will face throughout life.

**Association of United Contractors of America, Inc.**
360 West 125 Street
New York, NY 10027
(212) 663-0900
The Association exists to help eliminate discrimination against minority groups in all phases of building construction and general business, thereby contributing to the general growth of the country through economic well-being and stability.

**Atlanta Associated Contractors and Trade Council, Inc.**
825 1/2 Cascade Avenue, S.W.
Atlanta, GA 30311
The Council exists to assist minority contractors in developing and creating new businesses; to improve those already in existence, to assist and/or encourage successful minority contractors in expanding existing business.

**Audience Development Committee**
PO Box 30
Manhattanville Station
New York, NY 10027
(212) 534-8776
AUDELCO was founded in 1977 by Vivian Robinson, then advertising manager of The New York Amsterdam News who wanted to help develop a greater appreciation among blacks for theatrical productions. Organized to help build a large and dependable audience for black theater and dance companies, AUDELCO also works to generate more recognition, understanding and acceptance of the arts in the black community.

**Bedford-Stuyvesant Restoration Corporation**
1368 Fulton Street
Brooklyn, NY 11216
(212) 636-1100
The Corporation provides for the social, physical, and economic redevelopment of the Bedford-Stuyvesant community.

**Beulah Youth Development Council**
PO Box 7243
Columbia, SC 29202
(803) 771-4197
Founded in 1981 "to help youth help themselves," the Council encourages young people to make the most of their education and other opportunities available to them. Soliciting funds from the public, the Council has set up internship programs, with stipends, that try to introduce young people to the world of work and to acquaint them with the duties and responsibilities of holding jobs and caring for families. The Council efforts are, for the most part, preventative, specializing in teenage pregnancy, alcohol and drug abuse prevention for teenagers. One Council program provides classroom instruction for students suspended from classes for violating school rules and awaiting school board hearings.

**Bancap Corporation**
420 Lexington Avenue
New York, NY 10017
(212) 684-6460
The Corporation supports the economic development of minority group members.

**Black Affairs Center, Inc.**
1200 Fifteenth Street, N.W., Suite 608
Washington, DC 20005
(202) 872-1787
The Center provides training, consultation, and applied survey

research and evaluation for individuals, educational institutions, organizations, public/private, communities, and religious groups. Adapts the use of behavioral science technology to meet the often neglected and overlooked needs of the African-American community.

**Black American Response to the African Community**
261 East Colorado Boulevard, #210
Pasadena CA 91101
(818) 584-0303
The organization was formed in 1984 in response to the famine in Africa by clergymen who believed that black Americans have a vested interest in that continent. The group raised money and shipped grain to hard-hit nations where many were in danger of starving, and subsequently developed long-range, permanent assistance programs to combat the causes of poor harvests, malnutrition and disease. The organization has organized a task force of medical students to train in medically underserviced areas.

**Black and Puerto Rican Legislative Caucus (New York)**
PO Box 2528
State Plaza Station
Albany, NY 12220
(518) 455-5347
The Black and Puerto Rican Legislative Caucus was established to maximize the political potential for New York State's minority populations. Currently there are 25 black and Puerto Rican legislators in New York.

**Black Arts National Diaspora, Inc.**
114-36 227 Street
Cambria Heights, NY 11411
(718) 528-5880
The BAND, was founded in 1982 to help service the needs for creative expressions of African Americans, although its doors are open to all groups. Working with hundreds of individuals and with scores of civil rights and community groups as well as educational institutions, BAND has produced a variety of programs, workshops and seminars on the arts, dance theater, photography, computer technology, video, history, music and science, among other topics.

**Black Awareness in Television**
13217 Livernois Street
Detroit, MI 48238
(313) 931-3427
Black Awareness in Television was founded in June, 1970, to communicate African American ideas to the general public, promote affirmative action in the media and assist black groups in their interactions with the electronics media.

**Black Caucus of the American Library Association**
157 "A" Milner Library
Illinois State University
Normal, IL 61761
Founded in 1970, the Caucus's more than 400 members meet twice yearly as members of the American Library Association. The group works to promote the professionalism and services of the library profession and to ensure that black librarians are an integral part of the national library system as well as a major resource to the black community. The Caucus monitors legislation affecting library systems on the national, state and municipal levels of government, actively recruits blacks into the profession and supports affirmative action policies.

**Black Child Development Institute, Inc.**
1028 Connecticut Avenue, N.W., Suite 514
Washington, DC 20036
(202) 659-4010
The institute was formed to ensure that every black child receives comprehensive developmental services; to assist black parents and communities in making policies and decisions that affect black children; to ensure that programs dealing with a black child are consistent with the reality of his experience and recognize the strengths of his family and community.

**Black Data Processing Associates**
PO Box 7466
Philadelphia, PA 19101
(215) 843-4120
The Associates was formed in 1976 to provide a network for blacks in the data processing industry and to help bring more minorities into the field of data processing. The Association has more than 500 members in 11 chapters nation-wide and it conducts educational programs for data processing personnel as well as minority entrepreneurs.

**Black Development Foundation, Inc.**
442 Pratt Street
Buffalo, NY 14204
(716) 855-1703
The Foundation exists to promote economic development in the city of Buffalo, specifically in the disadvantaged community; to mobilize local municipal governments and coordinate state and federal grants to further the economic aid.

**Black Economic Research Center**
112 West 120 Street
New York, NY 10027
(212) 666-0310
The Center hopes to focus attention and skills on the economic aspects of the black condition with a view toward discovering more effective ways of winning the full measure of dignity, security, power, and economic well-being for blacks.

**Black Economic Union of Greater Kansas City**
2502 Prospect Avenue
Kansas City, MO 64127
(816) 924-6789
The Union assists minorities in joining the "mainstream" of the American economy.

**Black Elected Democrats of Ohio**
Democratic Headquarters
88 East Broad Street
Suite 1920
Columbus, OH 43215
(614) 221-6563
Founded in 1967 by black state legislators, the organization has created a mechanism to help educate blacks and other minorities about the importance of citizen involvement in party politics in order to secure a fair share of government services for their communities.

**Black Emergency Cultural Coalition**
463 West Street
New York, NY 10014
(212) 924-6666
Action-oriented watchdog organization, the Coalition exists to implement rights and aspirations of artists; to encourage participation and employment of blacks in educational, curatorial, and policymaking areas of art institutions; to uphold the validity of art as an agent for social and cultural growth and change; to stimulate, develop, and sustain interest of black youth in the exploration of art.

**Black Filmmakers Foundation**
80 Eighth Avenue
Suite 1704
New York, NY 10011
(212) 924-1198
The Black Filmmakers Foundation was founded in 1978 to support and promote the independently produced film/video work of black producers. BFF distributes more than 70 films/videos to organizations and institutions throughout the U.S.

*Members of the Black Economic Research Center. Robert S. Brown (right) is staff leader.*

**Black Law Students Union**
Yale Law School
127 Wall Street
New Haven, CT 06520
(203) 486-2029
The Union promotes the interests of Afro-American and African students; focuses and articulates the viewpoints of black students; improves the quality of life for black students in law schools.

**Black Methodists for Church Renewal, Inc.**
890 Beckwith Street, S.W.
Atlanta, GA 30314
(404) 758-8118
The Black Methodists was established to assist in strengthening the black church within the predominantly white structure; to eradicate racism within the total society; and ensure that the church serves the total community and administers to the needs of the total person.

**Black Music Association**
Inner Visions
1500 Locust Street, Suite 1905
Philadelphia, PA 19102
(215) 545-8600
The Association exists to protect the interests of professionals in the music field. The BMA also funds scholarships for young musicians and provides education and career guidance.

**Black Psychiatrists of America**
25 West 11th Street
New York, NY 10011
(212) 242-4500
The organization serves as a resource for information and training on the special mental health needs of the black community and provides a network for its members.

**Black Resources, Inc.**
507 Fifth Avenue, Suite 803
New York, NY 10017
(212) 972-1260
The group is a resource on race-related matters for corporations, government agencies and institutions.

**Black Retail Action Group, Inc.**
PO Box 1192
Rockefeller Center Station
New York, NY 10185
(212) 308-6017
The Black Retail Action Group, Inc., was formed in 1970 to get more minorities interested in the field of retailing and also involved in the field at all levels. The Group holds work-shops, seminars and networking sessions periodically.

**Black Scholar**
PO Box 908
Sausalito, CA 94965
(415) 332-3130
The group publishes serious essays on topics of concern to the black community.

**Black Student Fund**
(202) 387-1414
The Black Student Fund (BSF) encourages black enrollment in Washington area independent schools. Its goals are to ensure that rigorous academic opportunities are available to black students and that these schools are both racially and economically diverse.

**Black United Front**
700 West Oakwood Boulevard
Chicago, IL 60053
(312) 268-7500
Founded in Brooklyn, NY, as an alternative civil rights group in June, 1980 the Front has concentrated within its 22 nationwide chapters on the promotion of quality education for black children, police and black community relations electoral politics, women's affairs, economic development, housing and international affairs. The group has established contacts with black nations in Africa and the Caribbean as well as the South Africa liberation movements. The group is developing programs to strengthen black families.

**Black Women in Church and Society**
c/o Inter Denominational Theological Center
671 Beckwith Street, SW
Atlanta, GA 30314
(404) 527-7740
Founded in 1981, black Women in Church and Society provides leadership training and develops support structures to help women in fulfilling responsibilities brought on by their increased participation in religious and non-religious activities in the U.S. and in the Third World. The center has developed a research-resource center, and a directory. The facilities of Black Women in Church and Society are open to the public.

**Black Women in Publishing, Inc.**
PO Box 6275
FDR Station
New York, NY 10150
(212) 645-4800 Ext. 3357
Black Women in Publishing was founded in 1979 to provide professional minority women in the publishing field with information, moral support and a network for exchanging ideas and improving skills. Black Women in Publishing is seeking to encourage other minority organizations in minority publishing around the country.

**Black Women's Community Development Foundation**
1028 Connecticut Avenue, N.W.,
Suite 1010
Washington, DC 20036
(202) 296-7565
The Foundation exists to foster communication among black women in the United States; for identification of issues and problems of particular relevance to black women and program development relevant to these issues; and for the operation of a Juvenile Justice Project, a community-based program for the personal development and counseling of young women referred to the Project by the courts.

**Black Women's Forum**
3870 Crenshaw Boulevard
Suite 210
Los Angeles, CA 90008
(213) 292-3009
With organized chapters in ten states and a membership of over 1,200 nation-wide BWF provides a platform for regular discussion of issues of concern to black women.

**Black Women's Network, Inc.**
PO Box 12072
Milwaukee, WI 53212
(414) 353-8925
Founded in 1979, this organization supports the goals and activities of professional business and volunteer groups on issues of concern to black women. The Network monitors legislation affecting black women and helps to organize support for relevant political and economic organizations. The Network has, in addition, monitored the development of cable television franchises in inner-city areas and lobbied to change policies that were not in the best interests of black women. The Network also helped to devise redistricting plans to guarantee minority political participation in urban centers.

**Blacks in Agriculture, Inc.**
817 14th Street
Sacramento CA 95814
(916) 444-2924
Blacks in Agriculture was founded in 1982 to inform blacks and other minorities of the opportunities in agriculture. Activities include educational programs for professional farmers and inexperienced youth. The organization also conducts public policy education classes and advocacy projects that address legislative issues affecting agriculture on state and national levels. The organization is active in voter registration in rural areas and assists minorities threatened with the loss of their farmlands. It offers technical and staff assistance to organizations and individuals and assists minorities with problems involving taxes, water and education.

**Blacks in Government**
1424 "K" Street, NW
Suite 604
Washington DC 20005
(202) 638-7767
Blacks in Government, founded in 1975 in Washington to promote the interests of black civil servants working in federal, state and local governments, has more than 100 chapters throughout the nation.

**Booker T. Washington Foundation**
1010 Massachusetts Avenue, NW
Suite 400
Washington, DC 20006
(202) 371-1300
The Booker T. Washington Foundation was established in 1967 by the National Business League, then under the direction of the late Berkley Burrell. With offices in 15 cities and in two foreign countries, the Foundation operates in five basic areas: resource development, international development and cooperation, science and technology telecommunications and public policy research.

**Bowie State University**
National Alumni Association
Bowie, MD 20715
(301) 632-1155
The purpose of the association is to advance the cause of education; to establish a mutually beneficial relationship between Bowie State Univ. and the National Alumni Association, Inc.; To financially aid students who wish to attend B. S. U.; and to financially aid B. S. U.

**Bridges Book Center**
African-American Research Library & Museum
1480 Main Street
Rahway, NJ 07065
(201) 381-2040
Resource Center
The Center has materials relating to the complete African-American Diaspora, as well as tours to Africa.

**Brotherhood of Sleeping Car Porters**
AFL, CIO, CLC
103 East 125 Street
New York, NY 10035
(212) 348-2245
The group is a railroad service union.

**Burger Wing Mesbic, Inc.**
PO Box 520783
Biscayne Annex Miami, FL 33152
(305) 274-7011
The group exists to finance minority-owned Burger Wing franchised restaurants throughout the United State.

**California Legislative Black Caucus**
State Capitol Room 4040
Sacramento, CA 95814
(916) 445-5215
While the Caucus focuses closely on the total legislative process in California, it also puts special concentration on the issues important to the under-represented minority in the state, making certain that their needs do not go unnoticed.

**Carats, Inc.**
c/o Martha C. Young
6236 N. 15th Street
Philadelphia, PA 19141
(215) 424-2212
Founded in 1975, The Carats, Inc., is an organization of more than 200 women and has chapters in 11 cities. The group promotes the social, educational and civic involvement of its membership. Each chapter is actively involved in diverse projects at the local level. The Carats fund-raising efforts have provided grants to many groups, as well as numerous individual scholarships to students.

**Career Expo Planning Committee, Inc.**
180 Cambridge Street
Boston MA 02114
(617) 227-7786
The Career Expo Planning Committee Inc., was founded in 1974 in Boston to address the special needs of minority students who were not taking full advantage of career planning facilities on their respective campuses. The organization acts as a liaison between minority students and prospective employers, and allots scholarships.

**Caribbean Action Lobby**
322 West Compton Boulevard
Compton, CA 90220
(213) 639 3641
The Caribbean Action Lobby was founded in 1981 by Congressman Mervyn M. Dymally, its Chairman, who is a native of Trinidad, to give voice to the Caribbean and the Caribbean-American concerns in Congress.

**Caribbean-American Chamber of Commerce and Industry, Inc.**
26 Court Street
Brooklyn, NY 11242
(718) 834-4544
The Chamber was formed in 1985 to promote economic development among Caribbean-American and other minority-owned businesses.

It provides information and services to develop the economic potential of minority entrepreneurs in the U. S. and in the Caribbean nations.

**Caribbean American Research Institute**
400 First Street, NW
Washington, DC 20001
(202) 639-8211
Formed in 1986, the Institute seeks, through its research and demonstration activities to develop closer relationships between the Caribbean and other selected Third World nations and the United States. Through research, the Institute seeks to collect and disseminate data and facts that will be instrumental in the economic development of minority communities in the U.S. and Caribbean nations. The Institute will provide technical assistance to assist with economic development efforts in these areas.

**Carrousels, Inc.**
2508 Schaaf Drive
Columbus, OH 43209
(614) 275-5804
Founded in 1956 in Columbus by Betty Brewer and Clenna L. Watson, The Carrousels, Inc., have worked to raise funds to support the work of numerous deserving charities while providing its members and their families with organized social activities. This has helped to build strong friendships while fostering congenial attitudes toward one another within the group's chapters located throughout the continental U.S.

**Center for Community Economic Development**
1878 Massachusetts Avenue
Cambridge, MA 02140
(617) 547-9695
The center was formed to promote community-based economic development; work on research which will have an impact on state and national policies for community-based economic development, and strengthen active projects in the field through publications and newsletter.

**Center for Venture Management**
811 East Wisconsin Avenue
Milwaukee, WI 53202
(414) 272-5421
The Center researches into the nature of new venture formation, into the nature of the entrepreneur, and into the ecology of new and small business.

**Chi Eta Phi Sorority, Inc.**
3029 13th Street, NW
Washington, DC 20009
(202) 723-3384
Founded in 1932, Chi Eta Phi Sorority, Inc., is an international organization of professional nurses. The Sorority encourages continuing education by providing scholarships for nursing students. National programs include a joint effort with the American Cancer Society in meeting the challenge of cancer among blacks and other minorities, recruitment and retention of black student nurses in nursing schools and participation with the Adolescent Pregnancy Child Watch, designed to help learn more about adolescent pregnancy and develop action agendas to prevent "children having children."

**Children's Defense Fund of the Washington Research Project**
1763 R Street, N.W.
Washington, DC 20009
(202) 483-1470
The Fund seeks to guarantee the right to an education for children who have been excluded or misclassified; protect children's right to privacy of records kept by various social agencies, with particular attention to guidelines for data banking and information retrieval systems; protect children from medical experimentation or other harmful research procedures and guarantee fair and humane services under the juvenile justice system.

**Chums, Inc.**
3000 Granada Avenue
Baltimore, MD 21207
(301) 448-0569
Chums, Inc., was founded in Norfolk, VA, by Mary Barnes, Joyce Brown and Theodora Cora in 1946, to stimulate foster and provide cultural activities among its members and within their communities. Local chapters work to improve both the outlook and the potential of black females, utilizing a variety of locally run educational and self-help programs. Chums contributes to national and local civil rights and community improvement groups and charities.

**Church of What's Happening Now**
832 Seventh Street, N.E.
Washington, DC 20002
(202) 547-8549
The Church seeks to apply freeing power of the gospel to those that are oppressed; to work with other ministers to get the church back into the forefront of the liberation struggle.

**Coalition of Black Trade Unionists**
PO Box 13055
Washington, DC 20009
(202) 452-4837
The Coalition seeks to get more blacks into labor while at the same time strengthening the trade union movement in order to improve the socioeconomic level of minorities.

**Coalition of 100 Black Women**
60 East 86th Street
New York, NY 10028
(212) 560-2840
The Coaliton exists to look into the root causes of institutionalized racism to determine ways and means by which change can be brought about; assess and analyze issues which affect black women specifically; seek effective solutions to major problems confronting blacks; attempt to equalize life results for blacks generally and black women specifically and bring about a commitment for change in the black communities in order to improve our society.

**College Service Bureau, Inc.**
1625 Eye Street, N.W., Suite 725
Washington, DC 20006
(202) 293-6366
The Bureau provides educational services to colleges and universities, assists organizations with identification of black professionals, without regard to race.

**Combined Opportunities, Inc.**
5050 North Broadway
Chicago, IL 60640
(312) 275-3871
The organization seeks to increase the participation of individuals from minority groups in the free enterprise system by providing investment loan funds to, and arranging or providing management assistance for, small businesses that are at least 51% owned and operated by minority individuals and organizations, presently restricted to the state of Illinois.

**Commission for Racial Justice United Church of Christ**
105 Madison Avenue
New York, NY 10016
(212) 683-5656
The Commission exists to increase the involvement of the United Church of Christ in the continuing struggle for racial justice and to assist in making this involvement relevant; assist the national black community and other minority groups to become self-determinative,

self-directed, and self-controlled whereby meaningful social change can be effected; assist the black constituency of the UCC to become effectively organized, thereby contributing to the empowerment of Black United Churches of Christ.

**Committee for a Free Mozambique**
616 West 116 Street
New York, NY 10027
(212) 662-2323
The Committee seeks to educate groups and people about the southern African struggle, especially as it relates to Mozambique and to American involvement in African colonialism.

**Community Law Offices**
176 East 106 Street
New York, NY 10029
(212) 369-2007
The offices provide for civil and criminal representation to poor persons who reside in the communities of Harlem and East Harlem.

**Community Tax Aid, Inc.**
Box 1040, Cathedral Station
New York, NY 10025
The Community gives free income tax service to low-income people (for example, less than $7,500 for a family of four) by volunteer professionals.

**Community Telecommunications Development Foundation**
1010 Massachusetts Avenue, NW
Washington, DC 20001
(202) 371-1300
The Foundation was started in 1980 by a coalition of minority organizations to promote the control and ownership by minorities of telecommunications facilities and networks. It serves as both a voice and a resource center for minorities on telecommunications issues. The minority community at large is also serviced by the Foundation through the production of satellite teleconferences on a variety of topics.

**Concerned Educators of Black Students**
c/o School of Education
Florida International University
Miami Campus
Miami, FL 33199
(305) 554-2768
The Concerned Educators of black Students was formed in 1976 to promote the improvement of reading for all students, but with particular emphasis on blacks.

**Conference of Minority Public Administrators ASPA**
1120 "G" Street, NW
Washington, DC 20005
(202) 393-7878
Founded in 1971, the Conference of Minority Public Administrators has more than a thousand professional administrators as members nation-wide. A section of the American Society for Public Administration, the Conference membership is dedicated to better government and to excellence in public service. Local chapters are involved in a variety of self-help efforts and in programs aimed at educating young people about careers in public service.

**Conference of Prince Hall Grand Masters**
6314 Pauline Drive
New Orleans, LA 70126
(504) 288-5394
Grand Lodge Leaders give broad guidance to the group's programs. The group contributes annually to the NAACP Legal and Educational Defense Fund, the Educational Defense Fund, the United Negro College Fund, the Urban League and the NAACP.

*The primary goal of Concerned Educators of Black Students is to improve reading skills.*

**Congress of Racial Equality**
1457 Flatbush Avenue
Brooklyn, NY 11210
(718) 434-3580
The Congress of Racial Equality was founded in Chicago in 1942 and played a major role in the direct action phase of the civil rights movement during the 1960s when its goals, its leaders say, were to attack the overt manifestations of racism and discrimination in America. Today, the organization seeks "to unearth covert, more subtle and unsuspecting forms of racism and discrimination, including reverse racism." CORE is active with nations in Africa and the Caribbean, and concentrates domestically on economic development education, job training and after-school programs.

**Congressional Black Associates, Inc.**
PO Box 23300
L'Enfant Plaza Station
Washington, DC 20026
(202) 225-4001
Founded in 1979 by a group of Black congressional staff members, the Congressional Black Associates, Inc., is made up of present and past employees of the U.S. House of Representatives, the Senate and other related agencies. The organization provides information and analyses on the workings of the federal government to its members and the community at large, through a variety of community programs, special projects and political education seminars. The group works to develop meaningful networking programs for its membership and the community.

**Congressional Black Caucus**
H 2344 House Annex N2

Washington, DC 20515
(202) 226-7790
The CBC serves as a catalyst for the economic, educational, and social concerns of black people and other underrepresented Americans. A yearly legislative agenda is drawn up outlining the major policies supported by the caucus. Among the policies supported by the CBC are full employment, national health care, education, minority business assistance, urban redevelopment, welfare reform, and international relations.

**Connecticut Afro-American Historical Society**
444 Orchard Street
New Haven, CT 06511
(203) 776-4907
The Society collects and archives materials relating to the history and achievements of African-Americans in the state of Connecticut; displays and promotes the study of such materials around the state in as many arenas as possible, and especially to schools; maintains a resource and research center for the study of black history in the state; and does the same, but to a lesser degree, for African-American and African history in general.

**Connecticut Legislative Black and Hispanic Caucus**
State Capitol
Hartford, CT 06101
(203) 777-4552
The Connecticut Legislative Black and Hispanic Caucus was formed in the mid-1970s to promote and assist minorities in becoming more actively involved in politics and in attaining political offices. The group pushes, in addition, to raise the economic potentials for minorities in the state.

**Continental Societies, Inc.**
9300 Wilmecote Avenue
Richmond, VA 23228
(804) 262-9328
With special interest in youths with special needs, this service organization of 29 chapters in the U.S. and one in Bermuda also has programs in the arts and the humanities. "Operation Awareness"/ HEER (Health, Education, Employment and Recreation) involves each chapter in fund-raising efforts to support local and national programs serving the needs of youth. The organization has been responsible for charitable gifts of more than half a million dollars to local groups, the United Negro College Fund and the NAACP Youth Education Fund.

**Delta Sigma Theta Sorority, Inc.**
1707 New Hampshire Avenue NW
Washington, DC 20009
(202) 483-5460
Delta Sigma Theta encourages academic excellence through scholarship assistance and endowments for distinguished professorships. The five-point program is focused on educational development, physical and mental health, political involvement and international awareness.

**Derocher Associates, Ltd.**
PO Box 3714
Silver Spring, MD 20901
(301) 384-6625
Derocher conducts minority executive recruitment primarily in technical areas.

**Dignity Institute of Technology**
PO Box 1670
San Francisco, CA 94101
(415) 524-7762
The Institute seeks to learn how many and what type of black scientists we have among us; allow a familiarization among black scientists; direct black minds in scientific areas; keep abreast of black students developing in scientific areas regardless of educational institution they may attend.

**Diuguid Fellowship Program**
795 Peachtree Street, N.W.
Suite 484
Atlanta, GA 30308
(404) 874-4891
The program seeks to help women whose career and professional goals have been deferred because of marriage or other reasons. Fellowships make funds available for one year of intensive retraining or concentrated study on a full-time or part-time basis. No racial or religious restrictions.

**Doll League, Inc.**
36 Stevens Street
Montclair, NJ 07042
(201) 744-2716
Formed in 1959, The Doll League functions as an advocate for improving the quality of life for disadvantaged children and young adults, with special emphasis in the areas of health care, education and the arts. The group has distributed dolls and other toys to children in schools, orphanages, hospitals and day-care centers. The League is affiliated with and makes contributions to numerous organizations, including the United Negro College Fund, the Fresh Air Fund, Meharry Medical College, The Dance Theater of Harlem and the Young Playwright Fund.

**Drifters, Inc.**
305 Wynn Street
Portsmouth VA 23701
(804) 465-3521
Founded in 1954, this group of professional women now includes 26 chapters and 500 members. Each chapter supports civic, charitable and educational projects within its own community. On the national level, the Drifters sponsor an annual scholarship program and has endowed revolving student loan funds programs.

**East Central Committee for Opportunity, Inc.**
Central Administration Building
Mayfield, GA 31059
(404) 465-3201
The Committee seeks to create new opportunities for employment; provide for capital accumulation; establish minority-owned businesses; develop new community services and mobilize indigenous persons within the community to effectively utilize all the resources available to them for the purpose of achieving a sound socioeconomic community.

**East Harlem Food Buying Federation**
237 East 104th Street
New York, NY 10024
(212) LE4-7900
This union of 11 food cooperatives, involving some 600 families, was organized in 1973 to provide top-quality fresh fruits and vegetables at prices 40% cheaper than retail supermarkets.

**Economic Development Corporation of Greater Detroit**
1501 Fisher Building
Detroit, MI 48202
(313) 873-9300
The Corporation exists to promote and assist minority economic development.

**EDGES Group, Inc.**
c/o F. W. Woolworth Co.
233 Broadway
New York, NY 10279
(212) 553-2365
The EDGES Group, Inc. is a nonprofit organization founded in 1969 to facilitate the entry of minorities into the private sector,

government and industry. The 100 active members focus on issues related to employment, affirmative action, and urban and community affairs. EDGES stands for employment, dissemination of information, group development, economic awareness and solving problems. "EDGE" chief concerns include a scholarship program, sponsoring youth in various areas of interest and helping to introduce minority vendors and suppliers of goods and services into the mainstream of American business.

**Enterprises Now, Inc.**
898 Beckwith Street, S.W.
Atlanta, GA 30314
(404) 753-1163
The group makes loans and investments in small minority businesses.

**Equal Opportunity Finance, Inc.**
224 East Broadway
Louisville, KY 40202
(502) 583-0601
The group seeks to help disadvantaged individuals begin, expand, or improve business operations. Loans, investments, and technical assistance are considered for minority or socially disadvantaged persons in the states of Kentucky, Ohio, Indiana, and West Virginia.

**Equitable Life Community Enterprises Corp.***
1285 Avenue of the Americas,
Location 15-M
New York, NY 10019
(212) 554-4978
The corporation invests in minority-owned companies that have been in existence three to five years and are located in New York State.

**Eric Clearinghouse on Urban Education***
Box 40
Teachers College,
Columbia University
New York, NY 10027
(212) 678-3437
A national information storage and retrieval system supported by the National Institute of Education of the U.S. Department of Education and Welfare. Its purposes are to provide ready access to educational literature for subsequent information analysis activities. ERIC Clearinghouse on Urban Education collects, evaluates, and disseminates published and unpublished materials concerning the education of urban children and youth.

**Eta Phi Beta Sorority Inc.**
1724 Mohawk Boulevard
Tulsa OK 74110
(918) 425-7717
Eta Phi Beta, founded in Detroit in 1942, is a national business and professional sorority with chapters throughout the U.S. and the Virgin Islands. The Sorority works to create congenial fellowship among business women and to assist them in building professional business careers through which they might compete with the best in the business. High school graduates are assisted with business and professional scholarships by the Sorority. The organization has a special national program to assist the mentally retarded.

**Executive Secretariat of the Organization of African Unity**
211 East 43 Street
New York, NY 10017
(212) 697-8334
The organization seeks to promote the unity and solidarity of the African states; coordinate and intensify cooperation and efforts to achieve a better life for people of Africa; eradicate all forms of colonialism from Africa; and promote international cooperation with regard to the United Nations Charter and the Universal Declaration of Human Rights.

**Fayetteville State University**
National Alumni Association, Inc.
PO Box 578
Fayetteville, NC 28302-0578
(919) 486-1473
The purpose of the Association is to cooperate with, and promote the policies of the administration of the Fayetteville State University in matters for the best interest of the institution, and graduates thereof; to preserve the history of the University; to act without profit as trustees of educational or charitable trusts; fund raising.

**Federation of Corporate Professionals**
1000 Connecticut Avenue, NW
Washington, DC 20036
(202) 452-1260
Organized in 1981 to serve as a national networking forum for black professional groups the Federation is a nonprofit corporation that implements programs to promote the business and professional interests of its member organizations.

**Federation of Masons of the World and Federation of Eastern Stars**
1017 East 11th Street
Austin, TX 78702
(512) 477-5380
The Federations support projects for the good of the public and also donate financially to disadvantaged students desiring to go to college.

**Federation of Southern Cooperatives Land Assistance Fund**
100 Edgewood Avenue #1228
Atlanta, GA 30303
(404) 763-1385
Founded in 1971 as the Emergency Land Fund, the organization changed its name in 1986 to the Federation of Southern Cooperatives Land Assistance Fund. The purpose continues to be that of addressing the crisis of black rural land loss in the South. The Fund provides legal, technical and financial services to black landowners.

**First National Black Historical Society of Kansas**
PO Box 2695
601 N. Water
Wichita, KS 67201
(316) 683-1247
A not-for-profit, nonpartisan educational and service corporation, its primary mission is to recognize, exhibit and foster the historical and cultural contributions of blacks to the city of Wichita, the state of Kansas and the nation.

**Florida Conference of Black State Legislators**
c/o Rep. Doug Jamerson
424 Central Avenue
St. Petersburg, FL 33701
(813) 821-6686
The Florida Conference of Black State Legislators was formed in 1982 to help provide a greater access to state government for the constituent groups represented by the black legislators.

**Florida Crown Minority Enterprise Small Business Investment Company**
604 Hogan Street
Jacksonville, FL 32202
(904) 353-6161
The company invests seed capital in businesses which are at least 51% owned by minorities—blacks, Indians, disadvantaged whites, Mexicans, Puerto Ricans, etc.

**Forsyth County Investment Company**
305 Pepper Building
Winston-Salem, NC 27101
(919) 724-3676

The Company provides venture capital financing and management consulting services to small concerns.

**Foundation for Research and Education in Sickle Cell Disease**
423 West 120 Street
New York, NY 10027
(212) 222-8500
The Foundation seeks to coordinate local activities with a national education program and to allocate funds for research on all levels.

**Free Southern Theater**
1328 Dryades Street
New Orleans, LA 70113
(504) 581-5091
The group seeks to use theater, a viable cultural form, to advance the struggles of black and oppressed people from the burden of exploitation and oppressive conditions, and to educate and motivate social change.

**Frontiers International**
5915 West Gerard Avenue
Philadelphia, PA 19151
(215) 476-4089
With a membership of 2,500, this club supports a broad cross-section of community projects. Each chapter operates autonomously, and the organization as a whole develops major projects, such as funding the medical battle against vitiligo, and programs geared toward youth.

**Gamma Phi Delta Sorority**
2657 West Grand Boulevard
Detroit, MI 48208
(313) 872-8597
The aims of the sorority are to encourage and finance the education and training of women and to support health projects for deprived and retarded children. Educational aid is also provided to needy students who do not benefit from the scholarship program.

**General Alumni Association of Fisk University, Inc.**
1000-17th Avenue, North
Nashville, TN 37208-3051
(615) 329-8596
The purposes of the association are to maintain and promote the loyalty of its alumni to Fisk University; to assist and promote the interest of Fisk University generally; to establish and administer fund-raising activities and related endeavors undertaken by the alumni; to assist in the starting and maintenance of affiliated local chapters of this corporation in the various states of the union and other parts of the world; to organize and mobilize the collective strength of the alumni and cooperate with the University in suggesting and carrying out programs designed to affect the continued growth and welfare of Fisk University; to advance the influence, interest and usefulness of Fisk University; and these ends to take and hold by bequest, devise, gift, grant, purchase, lease, or otherwise any property, real, personal, tangible or intangible, or any undivided interest therein without limitations as to amount or value, toward the overall purpose of best promoting the corporation and Fisk University.

**Genesis Personnel Service, Inc.**
10921 Reed Hartman HWY
Suite 324
Cincinnati, OH 45242
(513) 891-4433
Genesis recruits, refers and places qualified minorities in Fortune 500 companies across the country, with emphasis on degreed individuals with 1-2 years of experience.

**Georgia Legislative Black Caucus**
Georgia State Capitol Room 401 E2
PO Box 38028
Atlanta GA 30334
(404) 656-6372
With six Senators and 22 members of the House of Representatives, the Georgia Legislative Black Caucus is the largest state legislative Black caucus in the U.S. The Caucus has a full-time staff to manage the day-to-day affairs of the organization and to provide technical assistance and resources for its constituency. The Caucus functions to make certain that blacks in Georgia have up-to-date information on all agencies in state government.

**Girl Friends, Inc.**
3726 Eagle Street
Houston, TX 77004
(713) 748-4667
Since 1927 The Girl Friends, Inc., has carried out civic, cultural and charitable programs within the framework of a social club. Each chapter conducts fund-raising activities for projects that benefit its own community, but chapters also contribute to a National Project Fund for unified support of charitable institutions.

**Glide Memorial United Methodist Church**
Glide Urban Center
330 Ellis Street
San Francisco, CA 94102
(415) 771-6300
The Church's goals include creating change; making positive change possible; coalition building; celebrations; provide a free health clinic, food, housing, and transportation clinic; drug abuse and alcoholic referral and a program for prisoners presently confined or encountering reentry difficulties on release.

**Gospel Music Workshop of America**
PO Box 4632
Detroit, MI 48234
(313) 989-2340
Founded in 1966 to promote and perpetuate gospel and spiritual music, the Workshop has more than 18,000 members in 184 chapters around the country. Promoting local concerts in many American cities, the Workshop seeks to build a larger constituency for gospel and spiritual music while increasing the number of performing artists in the field.

**Grand United Order of Odd Fellows**
12th and Spruce Streets
Philadelphia, PA
(215) PE5-8774
The Order exists to provide charity and education.

**Greater Fairbanks Black Caucus (Alaska)**
PO Box 73009
Fairbanks, AK 99709
(907) 479-4697
The Greater Fairbanks Black Caucus was founded by Gladys M. Austin in 1975 to develop an alliance with the National Congressional Black Caucus and to increase the effectiveness of all black elected and appointed officials in Alaska. The founders wanted, in addition, to make certain that black concerns were given proper consideration at every government level in Alaska.

**Greater Philadelphia Venture Capital Corporation, Inc.**
Lewis Tower Building, Suite 920
22 South 15 Street
Philadelphia, PA 19102
(215) 734-3415
The Corporation seeks to provide long-term equity or seed capital and managerial assistance to minority-owned corporations in the Delaware Valley area.

**Gulf South Venture Corporation**
Commerce Building, Suite 1202
821 Gravier Street

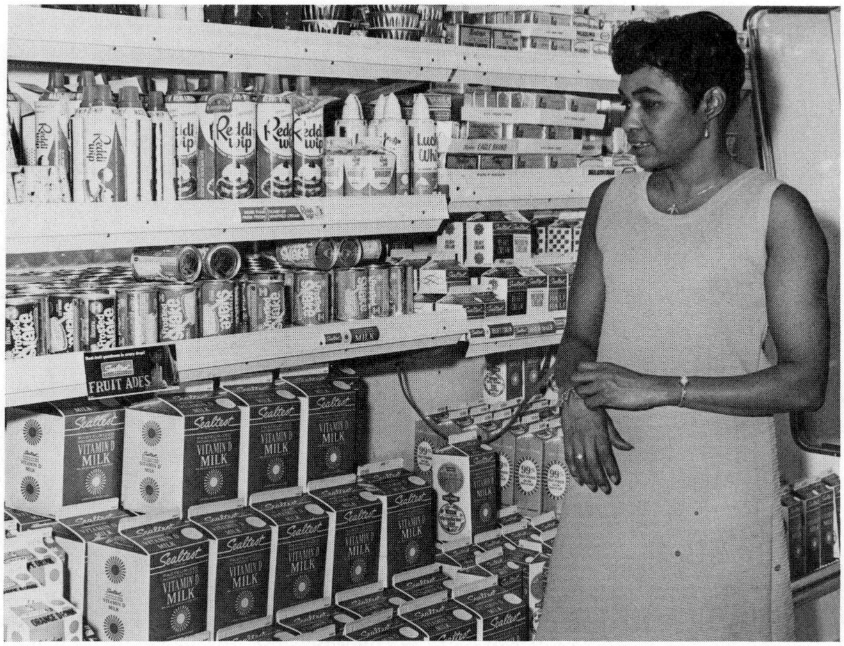


*Cora Walker heads the Harlem River Consumers Co-op, a neighborhood approach to marketing.*

New Orleans, LA 70112
(504) 523-7386
The Corporation provides venture capital to existing and emerging business enterprises in which American minorities own at least 51%, and promotes industrial economic development in the Gulf South region.

**Haitian & Co-Arts Association, Inc.**
165 Park Row, Suite 8-D
New York, NY 10038
(212) 732-9735
The Association was created by Andre Letellier, a Haitian-born U.S. citizen, to help eliminate hunger, eradicate disease, combat illiteracy, and promote multitrade development and vocational schools plus improve farming in the rural areas of Haiti.

**Harlem River Consumers Cooperative, Inc.**
270 Lenox Avenue
New York, NY 10027
(212) 472-7252
Harlem River was organized in 1969 to help blacks gain control of business in Harlem in order to provide food and housing at reasonable prices to the Harlem community.

**Holidays, Inc.**
3814 Grantley Road
Baltimore MD 21215
(301) 376-6890
Founded in 1965 to provide social and recreational activities for the members and their families, The Holidays is a bridge group organized in 18 chapters around the country which also promotes civic responsibilities among its members. This social/civic group, whose female members are called "holidays" and male members are called "labor days" has selected the United Negro College Fund as its principal charity.

**Howard Clark Associates**
507 White Horse
Haddon Heights, NJ 08035
(609) 547-7200
Howard Clark specializes in recruitment and placement of minority candidates nation-wide.

**Illinois Legislative Black Caucus**
c/o Rep. Carol Moseley Braun
109 State Capitol Building
Springfield, IL 62706
(217) 782-3201
Formed in the late 1970s, the Caucus works to ensure that issues of interests to blacks are dealt with fully and fairly in the legislature and that blacks in the state of Illinois are kept up to date on both the proceedings and the results.

**Imperial Court, Daughters of Isis**
Prichard Building, Room 404
Ninth Street and Sixth Avenue
Huntington, WV 25701
(304) 523-5241
To unite in one common bond of friendship the mother, wife, sister, daughter, and widow of all Nobles of the Mystic Shrine give true expression fraternally to the Ancient Tradition of the Order; practice charity and benevolence; promote general welfare and inculcate honor and integrity as symbolized in the Legend of the Egyptian Queen—"The Goddess of Isis."

**Improved Benevolent Protective Order of Elks of the World**
PO Box 159
Winton, NC 27986
(919) 358-7661
Through a variety of civic, educational, and religious programs, the organization has raised more than $100,000 yearly in scholarship assistance. Instruction in preventive medicine is also provided to its 450,000 members.

**Independence Capital Formation, Inc.**
3049 East Grand Boulevard
Detroit, MI 48202
(313) 875-7669
The group provides venture capital financing and assistance, particularly to the minority community.

**Indiana Black Legislative Caucus**
Room 4A7 State House
Indianapolis, IN 46204
(317) 232-9672

Founded in 1980, the Indiana Black Legislative Caucus was formed to be a focal point for black voters to impact on the political process and on state policies. The Caucus established a state-wide informational network to keep black voters informed and to encourage their participation in politics. The Caucus is a forum for ideas, dialogue action and analysis of the total political process in Indiana, and serves as the link between Indiana blacks and blacks in other states as well as the National Congressional Black Caucus. The Caucus creed is "to observe, educate, inspire, advocate and lead those most in need."

**Inner City Business Improvement Forum**
3049 East Grand Boulevard
Detroit, MI 48202
(313) 875-4700
The Forum promotes minority entrepreneurship by providing advisory, technical, managerial, loan packaging, financing assistance to help Detroit's black inner city become a strong economic entity.

**Institute of the Black World, Inc.**
87 Chestnut Street, S.W.
Atlanta, GA 30314
(404) 523-7805
A community of black scholar-activists convinced that blacks must move to control the definition of our past and present if we are to become masters of our future. Committed to doing tasks of research, analysis, and advocacy which will forward the struggles of the black community toward self-understanding, self-determination, and ultimate liberation.

**Inter America Travel Agents Society**
c/o Almeda Travel
1020 Holcombe Boulevard
Suite 1306
Houston, TX 77030
(713) 797-1001
ITAS was founded in 1960 by black travel agents from five cities who wanted to combine their efforts into an effective networking system that would improve both the outreach and incomes of each participant.

**International Alumni Association of Virginia Union University**
1500 N. Lombardy Street
Richmond, VA 23220
(804) 257-5720
The association promotes the growth and effectiveness of the alumni chapters so they can better support the university; and serves as a liason between the alumni and the university.

**International Association of Black Professional Fire Fighters**
PO Box 22005
Seattle WA 98122
(206) 228-8049
Founded in 1970 during a meeting of five black organizations of fire fighters, the International Association of Black Professional Fire Fighters was formed to address the special problems facing black fire fighters nation-wide. The organization seeks to increase the number of minority fire fighters nation-wide and to make certain that lessons in fire prevention reach inner-city residents. The Association also raises funds for the NAACP, the UNCF, and to combat sickle cell anemia.

**International Benevolent Society, Inc.**
PO Box 1276
837 Fifth Avenue
Columbus, GA 31901
(404) 322-5671
The International Benevolent Society, Inc., a social welfare organization, was founded in 1906 to minister to the needs of the sick and distressed and to provide burial funds. The IBS seeks to increase its financial assets through membership expansion and community economic development, thus becoming a more self-sustaining organization within the total community. Special programs include a scholarship fund, a social welfare program and an economic development program.

**International Black Writers**
PO Box 1030
Chicago, IL 60690
(312) 995-5195
This organization of authors and journalists was founded in 1970 to encourage black writers nation-wide to produce the factual and fictional a pieces that would reflect black ideas following the years of protest, demonstration and urban disorders during the 1960s.

**Interracial Council for Business Opportunity**
800 Second Avenue
New York, NY 10017
(212) 599-0677
The Interracial Council for Business Opportunity was created in 1963 to foster minority economic growth through business development. ICBO operates nationally and serves black, Hispanic, Indian and other minority groups. ICBO identifies and evaluates possible acquisitions, new business opportunities and expansion possibilities of existing minority firms. Through its management training program, ICBO offers the fundamentals of business operation.

**Iota Phi Lambda Sorority, Inc.**
1727 Chester Street
Savannah, GA 31401
(912) 236-0459
Iota Phi Lambda Sorority, Inc., was formed during the Depression in 1929, when the tentative gains made by black women in white-collar areas were being sharply eroded. The Sorority works with black women to develop the personal and competitive skills necessary to gain and maintain a place in the highly competitive business world.

**Iota Phi Theta Fraternity, Inc.**
PO Box 1459
Laurel, MD 20707
(301) 792-2192
A national social service organization, Iota Phi Theta Fraternity, Inc., was founded at Morgan State College in 1963. It has since grown to 69 chapters, 18 of which are on the graduate level, and its membership insists the fraternity is "building a tradition, not resting upon one!" Among the group's major charitable commitments are the NAACP Life Memberships, The National Federation of the Blind, Big Brothers of America and the United Negro College Fund.

**Iowa Legislative Black Caucus**
4929 Douglas Avenue
Suite 4
Des Moines, IA 50310
(515) 272-0196
The Caucus was founded to create positive legislative changes in the state and to help improve the general conditions of blacks in the state. It helps to make blacks aware of the political process and of the necessity to involve themselves in the political and business areas.

**Jack and Jill of America, Inc.**
1029 LaPleins Drive
East St. Louis, IL 62203
(618) 397-6314; (618) 398-4823
Jack and Jill provides educational, cultural, civic and social programs for minority youth. The organization, composed of parents, has also

*Wendell G. Freeland (left) and Eddie N. Williams head The Joint Center for Political Studies.*

operated the Jack and Jill Foundation since 1968. It has awarded more than $500,000 in grants to education and community projects.

**Jackie Robinson Foundation**
80-90 Eighth Avenue
New York, NY 10011
(212) 675-1511
Founded in 1973, the Foundation has grown from a small group of devoted family members and friends to a strong base of support from a host of talented volunteers, forward-looking corporations and institutions and outstanding scholarship recipients. Foundation programs to develop leadership and professional skills among minority and poor youth include an Education and Scholarship Program and a Seminar Sports Management Program.

**Joint Center for Political Studies**
1301 Pennsylvania Avenue, N.W.,
Suite 400
Washington, DC 20004
(202) 626-3500
The Center provides research, education, technical assistance, and information for the nation's black and other minority elected officials, and responds to minority-group aspirations to participate in the political process, and enhances the effectiveness of minorities at every level of government.

**J.U.G.S., Inc.**
101 Spring Street
Silver Spring, MD 20907
(301) 587-2807
Founded in Memphis in 1953, J.U.G.S. (Justice, Unity, Generosity and Service) is a national charitable organization of close to 200 business and professional women in chapters located in ten states. The membership has contributed hundreds of thousands of dollars to organizations serving the needs of abused and handicapped youth and the mentally retarded, among other groups.

**Kansas Black Legislative Caucus**
c/o Norman E. Justice
Legislative Services Room 511
South State Capitol Building
Topeka, KS 66612
(913) 296-2391
The Kansas Black Legislative Caucus was formed in the mid-1970s to monitor propose and take an active role in the legislative process with special emphasis on matters affecting the black community.

**Kappa Alpha Psi Fraternity, Inc.**
2320 North Broad Street
Philadelphia, PA 19132
(215) 228-7184
Kappa Alpha Psi Fraternity was founded at Indiana University in 1911 to encourage black achievement on college campuses by bringing black men of culture, patriotism and honor together for mutual support. The Fraternity maintains the Kappa Alpha Psi Foundation the Housing and Economic Development Corporation, the Active Chapter Housing Program, the Scholarships and Grants Program, a revolving loan fund and a job placement service.

**Karamu House, Inc.**
2355 East 89th Street
Cleveland, Ohio 44106
(216) 795-7070
Karamu House is a metropolitan center for the arts charged with serving people of all ages and races while adhering to and promoting high standards of excellence in the provision of education and training in the performing, visual and cultural arts. Karamu also accepts the unique responsibility of providing avenues and arenas for black artists to demonstrate, practice, share, communicate and further develop their skills and talents.

**Kentucky State University Alumni Association**
215 Hume Hall
Frankfurt, Kentucky 40601
(502) 227-6705
African American Historical and Cultural Society
Fort Mason C-165
San Francisco, CA 94123
(415) 441-0640
The association seeks to promote an understanding of the role that people of African descent have played in world history; collect materials depicting and recording the contributions made by African Americans to world history and American culture; provide the public with materials and information concerning African Americans; and establish and maintain an African-American cultural center in San Francisco.

**Knights of Peter Claver**
1821 Orleans Avenue
New Orleans, LA 70116
(504) 821-4225
The group promotes civic improvements; encourages Lady Apostolic and Catholic action; provides financial assistance to sick members; awards scholarships; fosters recreational assemblies and facilities.

**Lambda Kappa Mu Sorority, Inc.**
400 Kimber Road
Syracuse, NY 13224
(315) 446-6943
Founded by Florence K. Norman in New York City in 1937,

Lambda Kappa Mu promotes the ideals of sisterhood, personal achievement, scholarship and community service throughout the U.S. The Sorority provides community services that include the donation of scholarship monies to the United Negro College Fund, the National Urban League and the National Committee on Children and Youth. The Sorority publishes "The Acorn" and a newsletter.

**Lawyers' Committee for Civil Rights Under Law**
1400 "Eye" Street, NW
Washington, DC 20005
(202) 371-1212
The Lawyers' Committee for Civil Rights Under Law has since its founding in 1963 arranged volunteer legal assistance for the poor and for minorities on a nation-wide basis, representing cases ranging from discrimination suits to the misuse of federal funds.

**Leadership Conference on Civil Rights**
2027 Massachusetts Avenue, N.W.
Washington, DC 20036
(202) 667-1780
The Conference seeks an integrated, democratic, plural society, in which every individual is accorded equal rights, opportunities, and justice without regard to race, religion, ethnic origin, or sex; and in which every group is accorded an equal opportunity to enter fully into the general life of the society with mutual acceptance and regard for differences.

**Legislative Coalition Caucus (Utah)**
2609 South State Street
Salt Lake City, UT 84105
(801 ) 486-2323
Utah's Legislative Coalition Caucus was formed in 1982 to formulate legislation with special emphasis on the state's minority population and peoples of color. The Caucus co-sponsors events with black and Hispanic civil rights groups to promote minority involvement in politics and economics in Utah and to provide educational scholarships for deserving youths.

**Liberty House Cooperative**
PO Box 3468
Jackson, MS 39207
(601) 969-7522
The group seeks to provide work for poor rural Mississippians through craft cooperatives; publicize co-ops and market items nationally by means of mail-order catalog, and advertising in national magazines.

**Links, Inc.**
1200 Massachusetts Avenue, NW
Washington, DC 20005
(202) 842-8696
Links seeks to enrich the lives of its members and the community by promoting educational, civic, and cultural activities. Financial assistance is provided by The Links to the NAACP, the United Negro College Fund, and the National Urban League.

**Lokahi Pacific**
PO Box 767
Kihei, Maui, HI 96753
(808) 879-1517
Lokahi seeks to develop new skills, to broaden the county's economic base, and to increase the income level of the disadvantaged.

**Louisiana Legislative Black Caucus**
PO Box 44003
Baton Rouge, LA 70804
(504) 342-7342
The Louisiana Legislative Black Caucus functions to help blacks become more active and effective in dealing with state government. The Caucus monitors, promotes and supports legislation aimed at improving the condition of minorities in the state and works to keep its constituency aware of issues and events that will impact on blacks. Politics and economics have been major thrusts of the Caucus during recent years.

**Major L. Holland, Architect & Associates, P. C.**
111 South Main Street
Tuskegee, AL 36083-0547
(205) 727-4079
Major Holland provides architectural Services, i.e., programming, building design and construction.

**Mary Homes College**
PO Drawer 1257
West Point, MS 39773
(601) 494-6820
The college provides for the education of needy, worthy youth of whatever color, country, or creed in the service of humanity.

**Maryland Legislative Black Caucus**
516 North Charles Street
Baltimore, MD 21201
(301) 727-6212
The Maryland Legislative Black Caucus was founded in 1970 to build alliances between black legislators and also to build coalitions within the total legislature. The Caucus helps to maximize the effectiveness of the group in promoting legislation favored by blacks, particularly programs aimed at building the political and economic strengths of their constituencies.

**Massachusetts Legislative Black Caucus**
State House Room 56
Boston, MA 02133
(617) 722-2090
Founded-in the early 1970s, the Massachusetts Legislative Black Caucus is a nonprofit, nonpartisan organization that advocates on behalf of all minority citizens in the Commonwealth of Massachusetts.

**Medina Children's Service**
PO Box 22638
Seattle, WA 98122
(206) 461-4520
Medina prepares for adoption of black and biracial children of all ages by prospective families located in the Seattle area and facilitates placement of children with them.

**Merabush Museum, Inc.**
PO Box 752
Willingboro, NJ 08046
(609) 877-3177
The Museum was formed to establish a museum designed to educate society in the artistic and scientific contributions of the African American; to provide an environment for continual study and research in artistic and scientific contributions; to engender incentive for further and greater achievements by African Americans toward prosperous and peaceful development of the whole society. The fundamental goal of MERABASH MUSEUM, then is to enlighten the public about African Americans.

**Mesbic Financial Corporation of Dallas**
PO Box 6228
Dallas, TX 75222
(214) 632-0445
The Corporation exists to provide debt and equity capital and management assistance to selected businesses in the Dallas-Fort Worth area which are owned by disadvantaged small businessmen.

**Metropolitan Applied Research Center**
60 East 86 Street
New York, NY 10028

*The indefatigable Mother Waddles, whose Perpetual Mission cares for the needy without fanfare.*

(212) 628-7400
The Center serves as a catalyst for change and advocates for the poor and powerless in American cities.

**Metropolitan Contractors Association**
4450 Oakman Boulevard
Detroit, MI 48204
(313) 933-6470
The Association seeks to develop and administer educational programs for minority contractors.

**Michigan Legislative Black Caucus**
State Capitol
Lansing, MI 48909
(517) 373-0475
Black legislators in Michigan formed the Michigan Legislative Black Caucus in 1977 to better pursue the state-wide goals of blacks and other disadvantaged Americans. The Caucus conducts research and provides a network for the continual flow of information and ideas between Caucus members and their constituent groups.

**Minority Business Enterprise Legal Defense and Educational Fund, Inc.**
318 Massachusetts Avenue, NE
Washington, DC 20002
(202) 543-0040
The Minority Business Enterprise Legal Defense and Educational Fund, Inc., was organized in the public interest to provide information and legal assistance to help with the development of minority businesses nation-wide.

**Minority Contractors Assistance Project, Inc.**
1211 Connecticut Avenue, N.W.,
Suite 312
Washington, DC 20036
(202) 833-1840
The Project seeks to increase participation of minority groups in building industry; provide technical and financial assistance to local associations of minority contractors; multiply and upgrade at all skill levels the minority workforce in the construction industry; assist core city residents to participate in rebuilding of their own communities; expand minority opportunities in mortgage, surety brokerage, engineering, and other construction-related fields.

**Minority Equity Capital Company, Inc.**
470 Park Avenue South
New York, NY 10016
(212) 889-0880
The Company provides venture capital, equity-oriented investments in larger, ongoing minority-owned businesses where such an investment will aid businesses in undertaking major growth or expansion.

**Mississippi Legislative Black Caucus**
c/o 3500 Meadowlark Drive
Gulfport MS 39501
(601) 864-9319
Providing a networking system for each of the black legislators, the Caucus functions, in addition, as liaison to the National Black Caucus of State Legislators and the National Congressional Black Caucus. The Caucus keeps black residents up-to-date on the workings of the legislature and also keeps the black legislators alert to the priorities of blacks throughout the state.

**Missouri Legislative Black Caucus**
State Capitol Building Room 402 A
Jefferson City, MO 65101
(314) 751-2198
The Missouri Legislative Black Caucus was formed in 1967 as a primary force for developing political power for blacks throughout the state and especially within the state legislature. The Caucus monitors legislation that will impact on the black community and keeps black citizens informed concerning the progress of such legislation. The Caucus conducts research and helps to plan for appropriate legislative and administrative actions required to improve the quality of life for all state residents and especially for blacks.

**Modern Free and Accepted Masons of the World, Inc.**
PO Box 1072
Columbus GA 31902
(404) 322-3326
In this international fraternal organizations requirements for membership are good character, good health, and belief in a Supreme Being. The group was founded in 1917 to encourage Masons and Stars to set definite goals in life, to work through the

Modern Free brotherhood method and to train and educate leaders and specialists within the organization. Goals include building a strong economic base by pooling resources, investing in business and providing jobs for blacks.

**Moorland-Spingarn Research Center**
c/o Howard University
Washington, DC 20059
(202) 636-7237
Located on the campus of Howard University, the Moorland-Spingarn Research Center is one of the world's largest and most comprehensive repositories for collections documenting the history and culture of people of African descent in the Americas, Africa and Europe. Collections of documents on blacks at Howard date back to the 1870's; the Moorland-Spingarn Research Center was established in 1914 and reorganized in 1973.

**Most Worshipful National Grand Lodge Free and Accepted Ancient York Masons Prince Hall Origin, National Compact, U.S.A. Inc.**
26070 Tryon Road
Oakwood Village, OH 44146
(216) 232-9495
The organization's main thrust is giving generously each year to the United Negro College Fund. Scholarships are also granted to nonmembers of the organization and it also supports sickle cell anemia research.

**MWPHGL of Ohio, Free and Accepted Masons**
50 Hamilton Park
Columbus, OH 43203
(614) 221-6197
MWPHGL is a charitable and fraternal organization whose major charitable venture is the Grand Lodge Scholarship Program.

**Mother Waddles' Perpetual Mission**
3700 Gratiot
Detroit, MI 48207
(313) 925-0901
The mission was founded in 1957 to provide food, shelter, clothing, and medical care to the needy. Staffed by volunteers, and open 24 hours a day, it also offers religious services, day and evening classes, and counseling.

**Motor Enterprises, Inc.***
General Motors Corporation
13-152 General Motors Building 3044
West Grand Boulevard
Detroit, MI 48202
(313) 556-4273
The group provides financing to minority businessmen in communities where General Motors has plant operations. Along with financing, Motor Enterprises offers managerial and technical assistance to those businessmen granted loans.

**Museum of African-American Culture**
1403 Richland Street
Columbia, SC 29201
(803) 252-1450 or (803) 252-3964
The Museum preserves and presents to the public African-American culture.

**National Action Council for Minorities in Engineering, Inc.**
3 West 35th Street
New York, NY 10001
(212) 279-2626
The National Action Council for Minorities in Engineering Inc., was founded in 1980 to address the problem of the under-representation of blacks, Mexican-Americans, Puerto Ricans and Native Americans in the field of engineering. The Council supports pre-college and retention programs at many schools and provides scholarships.

**NAFEO**
Black Higher Education Center
Lovejoy Building
400 12th Street NE
Washington, DC 20002
(202) 543-9111
NAFEO serves as a voice for historically black colleges; clearinghouse of information on black colleges; coordinator in black higher education; and a presidential resource.

**National Alliance of Black School Educators**
1430 K. Street, N.W., Suite 702
Washington, DC 20005
(202) 638-7970
The Alliance seeks to make a strong commitment to the education of all children and black children in particular; to provide a coalition of black educators; create a forum for the exchange of ideas and techniques; identify and develop black professionals who will assume leadership positions in the education of black children.

**National Alliance of Postal and Federal Employees**
1628 11th Street, NW
Washington, DC 20001
(202) 939-6325
The Alliance seeks to promulgate better working conditions for blacks, minorities, and women in the Postal Service and federal government as well as to bring about constructive social change.

**National Association for Equal Opportunity in Higher Education**
2243 Wisconsin Avenue, N.W.
Washington, DC 20007
(202) 333-3855
The group seeks to promote the widest possible sensitivity to the complex factors involved and the institutional commitment required to create successful higher education programs for students from groups buffeted by the racism, exploitation, and neglect of the economic, educational, and social institutions of America.

**National Association for Sickle Cell Disease, Inc.**
4222 Wilshire Boulevard
Los Angeles CA 90010-3503
(213) 936-7205
Founded in 1971, the National Association for Sickle Cell Disease, Inc., is a nonprofit organization of community groups involved in sickle cell disease programs throughout the U.S., the Bahamas and Canada. The Association and its 86 affiliate groups provide education, screening, genetic counseling, referrals and technical assistance. The group also supports research.

**National Association for the Advancement of Colored People**
1790 Broadway
New York, NY 10019
(212) 245-2100
The NAACP seeks to end all barriers to racial justice and guarantee full equality of opportunity and achievement in the United States.

**NAACP Legal Defense and Educational Fund, Inc.**
Ten Columbus Circle
New York, NY 10019
(212) 586-8397
The Fund provides free legal assistance to people and organizations involved in racial discrimination suits. The fund also handles suits related to voting rights, housing, and education as well as the administration of criminal justice.

**National Association of Alumni and Friends**
Concordia College
1804 Green Street
Selma, AL 36701
(205) 875-1550

The Association seeks to promote Christian Education and a quality secular education; to establish a mutually beneficial relationship between the school and Alumni and Friends, and give gifts to perpetuate a valuable ministry.

**National Association of Black Accountants**
300 I Street, NE
Suite 107
Washington, DC 20002
(202) 543-6656
The exists to encourage members of minority groups to enter the profession of accounting; stimulate acquaintance and fellowship among members of minority groups; provide opportunities for members to increase their knowledge of accounting practices and individual capabilities.

**National Association of Black Catholic Administrators**
PO Box 29260
Washington, DC 20017
(301 ) 853-4579
The National Association of Black Catholic Administrators was established in 1975 by Father Jerome Robinson as "the conscience of the Catholic Church on issues relating to people of color." The NABCA has sought to provide an inner resource for the social and spiritual needs and necessities of black Catholics and has since evolved to address world issues of civil and human rights for over 500,000 Catholics in the local, national and international communities it serves.

**National Association of Black Consulting Engineers**
6406 Georgia Avenue, NW
Washington DC 20012
(202) 291-3550
The Association provides a stronger and more consistent voice for promoting the interests of black consulting engineers and has provided considerable support for the development of new opportunities in the federal minority business programs across the U.S.

**National Association of Black County Officials**
440 First Street, NW
Suite 412
Washington, DC 20001
The Association was formed in 1975 to provide the national organization structure for black county officials so they might review, share and develop responses to local and national issues affecting their constituency and county government.

**National Association of Black Journalists**
PO Box 2089
Washington, DC 20013
202) 737-0277
The Association provides an ongoing educational program for black journalists and assists them in upgrading their professional skills so that they may get into management positions.

**National Association of Black Manufacturers**
1910 K Street, N.W., Suite 600
Washington, DC 20006
(202) 785-5133
The group promotes the interests of all minority-owned manufacturing firms; seeks domestic and foreign markets for products of minority manufacturers; brings large industrial firms together with small business corporations; develops communication between NABM and other industrial associations, labor unions, and various governmental agencies; and encourages minority young people to enter industry.

**National Association of Black Reading and Language Educators**
PO Box 22614
Baltimore, MD 21203
(301) 732-4000

*The prestigious and very effective NAACP dates back to 1909. In this 1945 photo, the old National Offices show their wartime austerity.*

Founded in 1974, the Association is the principal umbrella organization for blacks in all fields concerned about improving literacy among African peoples throughout the world. Its members include individuals and organizations of educators, administrators and researchers, among the disciplines, working as professionals on all levels of the schools systems.

**National Association of Black Social Workers**
271 West 125th Street
Room 317
New York, NY 10027
(212) 749-0470
Committed to enhancing the social welfare of the black community and assisting the black social worker in his or her professional development, the National Association of Black Social Workers was established in 1968.

**National Association of Black Women Attorneys, Inc.**
1625 Fifth Street, N.W., Suite 626
Washington, DC 20001
(202) 393-7077
The group seeks to increase opportunities for minorities in the legal profession by expanding options of professionals and through scholarship assistance for students.

**National Association of Black and Minority Chambers of Commerce**
7700 Edgewater Drive
Suite 725
Oakland, CA 94621
(415) 639-7915
The Association was founded in 1983 in response to the need for an organization to address the need for minority business enterprise involvement in the travel and tourism industry. Its outreach expanded quickly to include chambers of commerce representing minority entrepreneurs in all kinds of legal commercial enterprises around the country.

**National Association of Black-Owned Broadcasters**
1730 M Street NW
Washington, DC 20036
(202) 463-8970
Founded in 1977, the Association provides information on the broadcast industry and the Federal Communications Commission to both the general public and to its 250 members. It lobbies government bodies and provides legal and research facilities for its membership.

**National Association of Blacks in Criminal Justice**
PO Box 28369
Washington, DC 20005
(202) 829-8860
This national membership organization, founded in 1973, is designed to examine and act upon the needs and concerns of blacks and other minorities as related to the administration of equal justice in the U.S. It seeks to coordinate efforts of individuals and organizations concerned with the elimination of injustices within the justice system.

**National Association of Colored Women's Clubs, Inc.**
5808 Sixteenth Street, N.W.
Washington, DC 20011
(202) 726-2044
The association exists to promote the education of women and girls; raise the standard of the home; work for moral, economic, social, and religious welfare of women and children; protect the rights of women and children who work; and obtain for all women the opportunity of reaching the highest standards in all fields of human endeavor.

**National Association of Health Services Executives**
551 Fifth Avenue
New York, NY 10017
(212) 867-0027
The Association in involved in the dissemination of information, educational material, job position clearing house, research in health care.

**National Association of Investment Companies**
915 15th Street, NW
Suite 700
Washington, DC 20005
(202) 347-8600
The National Association of Investment Companies was formerly known as the American Association of MESBICS (Minority Enterprises Business Investment Companies), an organization founded in 1971. The Association represents 82 venture capital firms and accepts as associates other individuals and organizations committed to the Association's goal of developing minority business.

**National Association of Market Developers, Inc.**
201 Ashby Street, N.W., Suite 306
Atlanta, GA 30314
(404) 688-9075
The association encourages young people to enter the marketing profession while at the same time promoting professionalism among its members through seminars and regional workshops.

**National Association of Media Women**
157 West 126th Street
New York, NY 10027
(212) 675-0975 or (212) 666-1320
This interracial organization with more than 500 members was founded in 1965 to provide a forum for women working in mass communications. NAMW members exchange ideas and share information at forums organized by individual chapters. NAMW also grants scholarships to students pursuing communications careers and gives awards.

**National Association of Milliners, Dressmakers and Tailors, Inc.**
157 West 126th Street
New York, NY 10027
(212) 666-1320
The NAMDT is a trade association of professionals in the fashion industry, students enrolled in fashion institutes and business people in such related fields as fashion design, alterations and fashion illustration. The purposes of the Association are the organization of members into a cooperative for group buying, the exchange of professional contacts and the sharing of technical expertise. NAMDT seeks to discover and encourage new talent, help put the small-business person on sound economic footing and increase the availability of American-made high-fashion merchandise. The Association also currently assists in the Building Fund of the Harlem Institute of Fashion and the Black Fashion Museum.

**National Association of Minority CPA Firms**
c/o Ralph Johnson & Co.
301 East Armor
Suite 300
Kansas City, MO 64111
(816) 756-2225
One hundred and fifty CPA firms with minority ownership comprise this organization, which was founded in 1971 to enhance the status of blacks and other minorities within the profession. The group is dedicated to increasing the number of minority accountants, upgrading professional standards among CPA's and fostering equal opportunity in the field by encouraging improved compliance with governmental guidelines. In addition, the Association functions as a clearinghouse for information relevant to its members.

**National Association of Minority Contractors**
806 15th Street, NW
Suite 340
Washington DC 20005
(202) 347-8259
Established in 1969, NAMC is the full-service, nonprofit Association representing black, female, Puerto Rican, Mexican-American, Native American and Asian-American construction contractors.

**National Association of Negro Business and Professional Women's Clubs**
1806 New Hampshire Avenue, NW
Washington, DC 20009
(202) 483-4206
A coalition of 300 local groups, this organization was established as a support network for black women in business and the professions. The Association is also committed to community service and conducts programs focusing on education, employment, health, housing and the problems of the elderly. Monitoring federal legislation and providing consumer education on these topics are also primary activities of the group. High priority is also given to leadership and education programs for youth, including a revolving student loan fund. The 12,000-member group also presents national and local awards for outstanding community service.

**National Association of Negro Musicians**
4330 Fullerton Street
Detroit, MI 48238
(313) 934-7448
Created as a communications network for black musicians, this organization disseminates music and job information and seeks to promote the appreciation of black music.

**National Association of Neighborhoods**
1651 Fuller Street, NW
Washington DC 20009
(202) 332-7766
Founded in 1975, this organization was formed to provide information, training and technical assistance to neighborhood groups nation-wide, as well as to inform constituent groups about legislation that would impact on neighborhoods.

**National Association of Planners**
Cable communications Resource Center
1900 L Street, N.W., Suite 205
Washington, DC 20036
The Association seeks to increase the numbers of minority persons participating in planning; make technical planning information and sources available to planners in minority communities; improve the quality and number of planning departments in black schools; make the planning profession and education more relevant to needs of minority communities; and develop a national communication system between minority planners.

**National Association of Real Estate Brokers**
1101 14th Street, NW
Suite 1000
Washington, DC 20009
(202) 289-6655
The National Association of Real Estate Brokers was founded in 1947 and is made up, for the most part, of black and other minority real estate professionals. It has a membership of 7,000 and stresses education and professionalism among its members and affiliates. Housing reform for minorities; seminars for real estate brokers in management, appraisal, development, and conversions.

**National Association of University Women**
1501 11Th Street, NW
Washington DC 20009
(202) 232-4844

*National Association of Black Social Workers' officers* (from left), *President Jay Chunn, Treasurer Lenora Delaney, Secretary Andreye Johnson, and Vice President Howard Brabson.*

The National Association of University Women was founded in 1923. The organization's major goals are to increase membership and provide community building service through the Assault on Illiteracy Program.

**National Association of Urban Bankers, Inc.**
111 East Wacker Drive
Suite 600
Chicago, IL 60601
(312) 644-6610
Founded in 1974, the National Association of Urban Bankers Inc., is an organization of 1,500 minority professionals in the banking industry and related financial fields. It seeks to provide educational technical and advisory assistance to minority businesses and students and provides scholarship awards for deserving students.

**National Bankers Association**
122 C Street, NW
Suite 240
Washington, DC 20001
(202) 783-3200
Founded in 1927, The National Bankers Association has a membership of 90 minority banks and is devoted to strengthening existing member banks, increasing their numbers, and ultimately increasing the economic impact of minority-owned banks in their communities. The Association uses education through seminars, conferences and conventions to achieve these goals.

**National Baptist Convention of America**
Second Missionary Baptist Church
954 Kings Road
Jacksonville, FL 32204
(904) 354-8268
The organization does missionary work in Africa, the Caribbean, and South America. Its primary effort is to support its evangelical work through education and fund raising.

**The National Baptist Convention, USA, Inc.**
52 South Sixth Avenue
Mt. Vernon, NY 10550
(914) 664-2676
The 7.5-million-member National Baptist Convention, U.S.A., Inc., with more than 30,000 churches, is frequently referred to as the largest black organization in the world. Founded in 1880, it was the parent organization to a number of smaller black Baptist church groups. The church leadership has worked during recent years to unite black organizations into a major national economic force.

**National Bar Association**
1225 11th Street, NW
Washington, DC 20001
(202) 842-3900
The National Bar Association was founded in 1925 and currently represents 10,500 lawyers in 64 affiliate chapters throughout the U.S. and the Virgin Islands. The Association works to ensure that equal justice prevails for all Americans. Its activities include legislative advocacy seminar development and technical assistance to members in specific legal areas.

**National Barristers' Wives, Inc.**
4580 Mt. Vernon Drive
Los Angeles, CA 90043
(213) 296-0627
Founded in 1951, the organization is comprised of spouses of attorneys and judges from the U.S. and Virgin Islands to promote a more cohesive relationship among the wives of persons in the legal profession on national and local levels. The programs sponsored by the group concentrate on civic, cultural, educational, political, social and economic matters and have included the provision of scholarships for deserving students as well as contributions to the NMCP Legal Defense and Education Fund, The UNCF, Child Advocacy Projects, Court Tour Programs and African Water Wells through Africare.

**National Beauty Culturists League, Inc.**
25 Logan Circle, N.W.
Washington, DC 20005
(202) 332-2695
The League was formed to upgrade professional standards in the cosmetology field while at the same time assuring equal opportunity through fair licensing and state regulation practices. Training courses in beauty and business techniques are also offered through the League.

**National Black Alcoholism Council, Inc.**
417 South Dearborn Street
Chicago, IL 60605
(312) 663-5780
The National Black Alcoholism Council, Inc., was formed in 1978 to address the problems and concerns related to alcoholism and alcohol abuse among black people. Another purpose was to increase public awareness about the multitude of concomitant issues associated with the immoderate uses of beverage alcohol.

**National Black Caucus of Local Elected Officials**
1301 Pennsylvania Avenue, N.W.,
Suite 400
Washington, DC 20004
(202) 626-3500
The Caucus was formed to have an impact upon the National League of Cities and The United States Conference of Mayors as well as other policymaking bodies that influence issues of concern to black people. Membership in the caucus represents 44 states and the District of Columbia.

**National Black Caucus of State Legislators**
1012 14th Street, Suite 706
Washington, DC 20005
(202) 347-6020; (301) 578-0400
The Caucus was designed to promote a more effective leadership among its members; also functions as an information resource and network for blacks in state legislatures.

**National Black Child Development Institute**
1463 Rhode Island Avenue, N.W.
Washington, DC 20005
(202) 387-1281
The Institute is dedicated to the enactment of public policies to better the welfare and development of black children.

**National Black Christian Education Resources Center**
Education for Christian Life and Mission
Division of Education and Ministry
National Council of Churches, in cooperation with JED* Black Church Education Team
475 Riverside Drive
New York, NY 10027
(212) 870-2772
The Center identifies, collecta, evaluatea, and disseminatea information about resources available for programs based on the black experience.

**National Black Coalition of Federal Aviation Employees**
PO Box 51741
Indianapolis, IN 46251
(317) 297-3597
The Coalition was founded in 1976 by black air-traffic controllers and was expanded a year later to include all black federal aviation employees eager to address the special problems of blacks in this industry. The Coalition seeks to make minority youths aware of

opportunities in aviation and encourage applicants to prepare themselves to take federal examinations for entry-level positions. They monitor Federal Aviation Administration regulations as well as job opportunities.

**National Black Health Planners Association**
2635 43rd Street, NW
Washington, DC 20007
(202) 232-6707
Founded in 1980, the Association seeks to improve the health of black Americans by addressing health-care delivery issues. There are more than 200 health planners active with the Association nation-wide. The group represents blacks' interests in the formulation of health policies laws and regulations. Its quarterly newsletter is called "Network."

**National Black MBA Association, Inc.**
111 East Wacker Drive
Suite 600
Chicago IL 60601
(312) 644-6610
An organization of 1,500 minority holders of advanced business degrees in 19 chapters throughout the U.S., the National Black MBA Association was established in 1970 to assist the entry of interested minorities into the business community.

**National Black Nurses Association**
PO Box 18358
Boston, MA 02118
(617) 266-9703
The Association serves as a job bank and recruits for the nursing field. The association also functions as an information resource for federal agencies concerned with health care. In addition, it monitors federal legislation.

**National Black Police Association**
PO Box 138
Jamaica, NY 11412
(516) 379-9549
Chartered in 1972, the association has three goals: (1) to improve the relationship between police departments, institutions, and black communities; (2) to recruit minority police officers across the country; and (3) to eliminate police corruption, brutality, and racial discrimination.

**National Black Programming Consortium**
1266 East Broad Street
Columbus, OH 43205
(614) 252-0921
The Consortium was founded in 1980 by blacks working in the television industry around the country to seek more positive portrayals of minorities. The Consortium collects distributes and co-produces programs that portray blacks positively in television and in films.

**National Black Public Relations Society**
c/o Burrell
20 North Michigan Avenue
Chicago, IL 60602
(312) 443-8600
The National Black Public Relations Society was formed in 1982 in Chicago to promote and to expand the opportunities for minorities in public relations.

**National Black Sisters' Conference**
3508 Fifth Avenue
Pittsburgh, PA 15213
(412) 621-9677
The Conference seeks to develop personal resources of individual sisters for the deepening of spirituality and promotion of unity and solidarity among black religious women; to importune our society to respond with Christian enthusiasm to the need for eradicating powerlessness and poverty by responsibly encouraging white people to address themselves to the roots of racism in their own social, professional, and spiritual milieu.

**National Black United Fund**
2090 Adam Clayton Powell Boulevard
Suite 821
New York, NY 10027
(212) 866-5400
The nonprofit Fund provides financial and technical support to projects that address the critical needs of black and minority communities throughout the U.S.

**National Black Women's Consciousness-Raising Association**
1906 North Charles Street
Baltimore MD 21218
(301) 685-9418
The NBWCRA was founded in 1975 in Baltimore by Louise Johnson to serve as a post-operative support group for women who have had gender-related surgery. The NBWCRA's concerns have expanded into other areas of interest to women, including the fields of business and education.

**National Brotherhood of Skiers**
PO Box 49097
Chicago, IL 60649
(312) 324-1488
Founded in 1973, the National Brotherhood of Skiers promotes both recreational and competitive skiing among minorities. Black youngsters from around the country participate in the organization's national effort to identify, develop and finance the training of future U.S. Ski Team members and Olympians.

**National Business League**
4324 Georgia Avenue, N.W.
Washington, DC 20011
(202) 726-6200
The League promotes commercial and financial development of blacks and other minorities in the United States; exposes problems of its members and provides technical assistance.

**National Catholic Conference for Interracial Justice**
1200 Varnum Street, NE
Washington, DC 20017
(202) 529-6480
Founded in 1960 by the Catholic Interracial Council of Chicago to be the Catholic vehicle for participation in the civil rights movement, the National Catholic Conference for Interracial Justice now encompasses 100 dioceses around the U.S. and includes approximately 4,500 members.

**National Caucus and Center on Black Aged, Inc.**
1424 K Street. NW
Suite 500
Washington DC 20005
(202) 637-8400
Founded in 1971, the National Caucus and Center on Black Aged, Inc., is concerned with the quality of life of older Black Americans. Advocacy on issues and legislation relevant to this group and research and program development and technical assistance for improving basic services are major NCBA activities.

**National Center for Voluntary Action**
1785 Massachusetts Avenue, N.W.
Washington, DC 20036
(202) 797-7800
The center strengthens volunteer services and organizations in their efforts to prevent and alleviate social problems; serves as a source of information on volunteer programs; assists in development of central community volunteer services; provides leadership in

education and training of volunteer leaders; encourages public awareness of voluntary action.

**National Coalition of 100 Black Women**
45 Rockefeller Plaza
New York, NY 10020
(212) 410-7511
The Coalition is an advocacy organization that seeks to empower black women to meet their diverse needs through programs stressing leadership development and networking while establishing links between the organization and the corporate and political sectors.

**National Committee Against Discrimination in Housing, Inc.**
1425 H Street, N.W., Suite 410
Washington, DC 20005
(202) 783-8150
The Committee exists to test equality of treatment of black and white housing applicants by real estate brokers and rental offices; gather evidence of racial discrimination by lending institutions; testify at hearings on behalf of state and municipal fair housing measures; combat misuses of local zoning to exclude low-income families; to create a local awareness of fair housing laws; and to stabilize interracial neighborhoods by counteracting block-busting techniques through person-to-person contact.

**National Committee for the Defense of Political Prisoners**
PO Box 1184
New York, NY 10027
The Committee was formed for the defense and support of blacks arrested or imprisoned for alleged political offenses or viewpoints.

**National Committee for Self-Development of People**
475 Riverside Drive, Room 1260
New York, NY 10027
(212) 870-2563
The Committee funds programs of community groups to increase self-determination, build relationships between subcommunities and surrounding economic, political, and social institutions. It seeks to avoid the dangers of paternalism and discourage individual alienation from social origins, and also attract other resources.

**National Conference of Black and Nonwhite Laymen and Staff of the YMCA**
100 North Arlington Avenue
East Orange, NJ 07017
(201) 673-5588
The Conference seeks to overcome the practices, procedures, and policies of the YMCA that subordinate nonwhites because of their race and provide the leadership for survival and future of the YMCA in nonwhite communities.

**National Conference of Black Churchmen**
Atlanta, GA
(404) 524-8010
The Conference was formed to unite black churches and black church people in efforts to unify, develop, and strengthen the black community; promulgate the vitality and life style of black families; enhance the contribution of black churches and black people in the larger religious fellowship across racial, national, denominational, and sectarian lines.

**National Conference of Black Lawyers**
126 West 119 Street
New York, NY 10026
(212) 866-3501
The Conference carries on a program of litigation, including defense of the politically unpopular and affirmative action suits on community issues; monitors governmental activity affecting the black community; serves the black bar through lawyer referral, job placement, legal education programs, watchdog activity on law school admission and curriculum; defends advocates facing judicial and bar sanctions.

**National Conference of Black Lawyers, Columbus, Ohio Chapter**
209 South High Street, Suite 212
Columbus, OH 43215
(614) 436-2956
The association seeks to facilitate the inclusion of minorities in the legal system as students and lawyers; to address legal, social and civic issues which directly and indirectly impact on minorities; to provide competent legal representation to minorities.

**National Conference of Black Mayors**
1430 Peachtree Street, N.E., Suite 318
Atlanta, GA 30309
(404) 892-0127
Formed in 1974, the NCBM works to channel greater financial aid and managerial resources into the communities served by black mayors. The organization places a great emphasis on sewage and water projects.

**National Conference of Black Political Scientists**
Department of History and Political Science
Albany State College
Albany, GA 31705
(912) 439-4870
The National Conference of Black Political Scientists was formed in 1969 on the campus of Southern University, Baton Rouge, LA, by political scientists concerned about the status of blacks in the discipline and that of the black community in general. Its primary goal has been to provide a forum for the exchange and dissemination of scholarly works on and about the struggles of blacks in the U.S. and abroad. The Conference sponsors a graduate assistance program to assist black students of political science.

**National Council for Equal Business Opportunity, Inc.**
1211 Connecticut Avenue, N.W., Suite 310
Washington, DC 20036
(202) 293-3960
The Council assists individuals, groups, and organizations in economic development projects; provides technical assistance and professional counseling of all types, including business planning for individuals, organizations and their members for the economic development of low-income or low-employment areas.

**National Council of Negro Women**
815 Second Avenue
New York, NY 10017
A 45-year-old organization focusing the resources and energies of its constituents on the social, economic, and political aspects of American life. Its program efforts for youth include career development and juvenile justice. Other important concerns of the organization are leadership development, women's history, and public health.

**National Dental Association**
5506 Connecticut Avenue, N.W., Suite 24
Washington, DC 20015
(202) 244-7555
The Association exists to promote the art and science of dentistry; raise the standards of the dental profession and of dental education; sponsor and work for enactment of just dental laws; promote betterment of public health; work persistently for elimination of religious and racial discrimination and segregation from American dental institutions, clinics, and organizations.

**National Economic Association**
c/o Dr. Gus T. Ridgel
Southern University
Baton Rouge, LA 70812
(504) 771-5150
Founded by black economists 15 years ago, the National Economic

Association aims to promote the professional careers of blacks within the field and increase the number of minority economists in America.

**National Fellowship Fund**
795 Peachtree Street, N.E.
Atlanta, GA 30308
(404) 874-4891
The Fund provides qualified black personnel for careers in higher education in the United States through the stimulation of doctoral study in the basic biological and physical sciences, humanities, and social sciences. Awards are available to black Americans who plan to continue on to the doctoral degree in preparation for a career in higher education.

**National Funeral Directors and Morticians Association**
734 West 79th Street
Chicago, IL 60620
(312) 487-3603
Founded in 1924, the NFDMA seeks to maintain high standards for the benefit of the public and their own business community. The organization conducts workshops and seminars, sponsors research, and represents the interests of its constituency before the various federal, state, and local governing bodies.

**National Insurance Association**
2400 S. Michigan Avenue
Chicago, IL 60616
(312) 842-5125
To improve professional standards within the insurance industry and bring about a better public understanding of its services, the group also provides technical assistance for its members and facilitates management and operating manpower development.

**National Medical Association**
1720 Massachusetts Avenue, N.W.
Washington, DC 20036
(202) 659-9623
The Association was formed to raise the standards of the medical profession and medical education; stimulate favorable relationships among all physicians; nurture growth and diffusion of medical knowledge; sponsor education of the public concerning all matters affecting public health; sponsor enactment of just medical laws and eliminate religious and racial discrimination and segregation from American medical institutions.

**National Medical Association Foundation, Inc.**
2109 E Street, N.W.
Washington, DC 20037
(202) 338-8266
The Foundation seeks to promote programs providing comprehensive health care and residential accommodations, together with related facilities, for inhabitants of the core cities of metropolitan areas and other medically deprived areas in the United States; improve the quality of medical care; enhance the image of the physician and demonstrate his or her concern for the health of the poor.

**National Medical Fellowships, Inc.**
250 West 57 Street
New York, NY 10019
(212) 246-4293
The group seeks to create more physicians from groups currently under-represented in medicine—blacks, American Indians, Puerto Ricans, and Mexican-Americans—by giving financial aid to medical students for those groups needing it.

**National Minority Business Campaign**
1016 Plymouth Avenue
Minneapolis, MN 55406
(612) 522-3323
The Campaign publishes a national directory of minority-owned firms.

**National Minority Suppliers Development Council, Inc.**
1412 Broadway
New York, NY 10018
(212) 944-2430
The Council was founded in 1972 to expand business opportunities for minority-owned companies and to encourage mutually beneficial economic links between minority suppliers and the public and private sectors. The organization's Business Consortium Fund, which became operational in 1986, will provide Council registered vendors with working capital of up to $250,000.

**National Museum of African Art**
Smithsonian Institution
950 Independence Ave. SW
Washington, DC 20560
(202) 357-4600
The National Museum of African Art is the only museum in the United States dedicated exclusively to the collection, exhibition, conservation and study of the arts of Africa south of the Sahara.

**National Naval Officers Association**
PO Box 42614
Washington, DC 20050-6214
(804) 547-0979
The National Naval Officers Association was formed in 1972 to promote the professional and career development of minority officers in the U.S. Navy, the U.S. Marine Corps and the U.S. Coast Guard. The organization is active in recruiting minority youths for careers in the naval services as well as providing speakers for community and educational groups.

**National Newspaper Publishers Association**
770 National Press Building
Washington, DC 20045
(202) 638-4473
The Association seeks to unify, strengthen, and improve the black press.

**National Office for Black Catholics**
734 Fifteenth Street, N.W.
Washington, DC 20005
(202) 347-4260
The Office seeks to enable black Catholics to assume greater responsibility for and participation in the Catholic Church; assist black Catholics and the Church in general; make an effective contribution to the needs of the total black community; and bring the Catholic Church to recognition and elimination of racism within its own structure and assume a more forceful stand against racism in America.

**National Optometric Association**
55 Marietta Street, N.W., Suite 1935
Atlanta, GA 30303
(404) 523-7028
The Association is involved in minority recruitment for the optometric profession; education of the public regarding the profession of optometry; and better primary optometric and health care delivery.

**National Organization of Black Chemists and Chemical Engineers**
c/o Atlanta University
360 Westview Drive
Atlanta, GA 30310
(212) 719-7859
The National Organization of Black Chemists and Chemical

Engineers was founded in 1973 to develop and carry out programs to assist blacks in realizing their full potential in the fields of chemistry and chemical engineering. Numbering more than 1,000 members in 14 national chapters, the organization's goals include the continued professional development of black scientists, support of black technical entrepreneurial ventures, the recruitment and retention of blacks in science and engineering-related university programs and community involvement of professionals to provide essential role models within the black community.

**National Organization of Black Law Enforcement Executives (NOBLE)**
908 Pennsylvania Avenue, SE
Washington, DC 20003
(202) 546-8811
NOBLE works for a greater community involvement in the criminal justice system and increases the sensitivity by law enforcement agencies to the problems of the black police officer and the black community.

**National Organization of Black Owned Broadcasters**
1730 M Street, NW
Suite 412
Washington, DC 20036
(202) 463-8970
NABOB is a trade association representing the interests of the black owners of radio and television stations across the country. NABOB has two principal objectives: first, to increase the number of black owner of radio and television stations, and second, to improve the business climate in which black owned radio and television stations operate, so that they can maximize their potential for financial success.

**National Organization of Minority Architects**
1730 "M" Street, NW
Suite 713
Washington, DC 20036
(202) 659-3918
NOMA seeks to foster communication among minority architects by forming a confederation of local membership groups. It serves as a members' clearinghouse for information and maintains rosters of qualified professionals for use by architectural firms and minority engineering, planning and contracting firms. The organization speaks for minority architects on political matters and issues affecting the physical development of communities. NOMA also seeks to motivate minority youth and play an active role in the education of new architects.

**National Pan-Hellenic Council**
2222 Albion Street
Nashville, TN 37208
(615) 329 1655
Founded in 1930 at Howard University, the Council was organized to coordinate activities of inter-collegiate Greek-letter sororities and fraternities active on black college campuses. In addition, the Council studies and makes recommendations to member organizations on legislation that would affect their groups and constituencies. The Council also makes recommendations for the involvement of Greek-letter organizations in programs designed to assist minority communities.

**National Pharmaceutical Association**
Howard University College of Pharmacy and Pharmacal Sciences
2300 Fourth Street, N.W.
Washington, DC 20059
(202) 636-6530
The Association was formed to provide an atmosphere to exchange ideas among minority pharmacists; continue education; stimulate positive community relationships for the minority pharmacist; contribute financially to charitable causes and promote enforcement and enactment of just health-care legislation.

**National Political Congress of Black Women, Inc.**
1825 "K" Street, NW
Suite 722
Washington, DC 20006
(202) 775-8650
The National Political Congress of Black Women, Inc. was founded in 1984 as an independent, nonpartisan political organization to encourage all black women to participate in the political process as voters, political candidates, policy makers, fund-raisers and political role models for younger people.

**National Scholarship Service and Fund for Negro Students**
1776 Broadway
New York, NY 10019
(212) 757-8100
The Fund provides to black and other high school juniors and seniors increased access to postsecondary institutions through a computerized college advisory and counseling service. Limited supplementary scholarship assistance is available to students who complete the application process and demonstrate need.

**National Sharecroppers Fund**
2128 Commonwealth Avenue
Charlotte, NC 28205
(704) 334-3051
The Fund helps low-income farm and other rural people develop programs and services they need to live a good life and remain on the land. NSF maintains an experimental farm and training center in Wadesboro, NC and legislative and research office in Washington, DC; provides services and technical help to cooperatives and other self-help groups in rural areas; and publishes reports and newsletters on developments of concern to rural people.

**National Small Business Association***
1225 Nineteenth Street, N.W.
Washington, DC 20036
(202) 296-7400
The Association demands revision of tax laws, adoption of a sound fiscal and economic policy, establishment of a fair management-labor policy; opposes growth of unnecessary government authority, regulations, and reports which burden the limited resources of independent business; promotes government policies that permit independent business to obtain its fair share of government contracts.

**National Smart Set**
140 West End Avenue, Apt. 12H
New York, NY 10023
Formed in 1937, the organization's programs benefit young people. The group also contributes to the United Negro College Fund annually.

**National Student Business League**
4324 Georgia Avenue NW
Washington, DC 20011
(202) 829-5900
The National Student Business League was founded in 1974 to serve as a communications center for black undergraduates in the business, finance, marketing, computer science and management

**The National United Affiliated Beverage Association**
5429 Market Street
Philadelphia PA 19139
(215) 748-5670
The National United Affiliated Beverage Association was formed in 1978 by the merger of two organizations, the National United License Beverage Association and the National Affiliated Beverage Association. The Association monitors liquor laws nationally and keeps its membership of local beverage retailers in each of the 50 states informed about national and state laws. The Association raises funds through its National Auxiliary NUABA Drive to benefit the UNCF and black economic development organizations.

*The National Sharecroppers Fund helps co-op farms compete with the large industrialized farm operation. Aerial photo shows the fund's experimental farm and training center in Anson County, North Carolina.*

**National United Church Ushers Association of America, Inc.**
1431 Sheppard Street, NW
Washington, DC 20011
(202) 722-1192
An interdenominational organization active in 32 states, the National United Church Ushers Association was founded in 1919 in Philadelphia by Elijah Hamilton to bring a uniform system of ushering to its membership.

**National Urban Affairs Council**
2350 Adam C. Powell Boulevard
New York, NY 10030
The Council's primary objective is to identify the common interests of the public and private sectors and the black community in order to promote mutual economic growth. The group sponsors a national job bank and a scholarship fund, monitors legislation affecting the Black community and serves as a liaison among black organizations.

**National Urban Coalition**
1201 Connecticut Avenue N.W., Suite 400
Washington, DC 20036
(202) 331-2400
The Coalition was designed to link the needs of the private job sector to more effective occupational education and training. Its aim is to build economically stronger and physically sounder urban neighborhoods around the country and to stabilize communities through the reduction of violence and delinquency.

**National Urban League**
500 East 62nd Street
New York, NY 10021
(212) 310-9000
The League seeks to achieve equal opportunity for all Americans, especially members of minority groups.

**National Welfare Rights Organization**
1420 N Street, N.W.
Washington, DC 20005
(202) 483-1531
The Organization seeks to secure those legal, economic, and human rights to which poor people are now entitled by federal law; to advocate for true welfare reform which will bring dignity, justice, and the right to self-determination to the poor.

**Negro Actors Guild, Inc.**
1674 Broadway
New York, NY 10019
(212) 245-4343
The Guild was designed to elevate, foster, and promote good fellowship and the spiritual welfare of actors and those connected with the theatrical profession; render service to members of the profession in time of illness and distress; champion and uphold the highest standards of the stage and elsewhere; and attend and support performances adhering to such standards.

**Negro Labor Committee**
312 West 125 Street
New York, NY 10027
(212) UN4-3295
The Committee organizes and guides black workers into bona fide trade unions and establish the solidarity of black and white labor.

**New Concept Self Development Center, Inc.**
636 West Kneeland Street
Milwaukee, WI 53212
(414) 271-7496
Since its founding in 1975, the New Concept Self Development Center has provided job training, family and mental health counseling and family planning to residents in Milwaukee County.

The Center has produced a series of books for minority parents on teaching human sexuality to their children. The organization has developed a specialty in teen pregnancy prevention and produced the Milwaukee Blue Ribbon Panel's report on Teenage Pregnancy Prevention.

**New Jersey Legislative Black Caucus**
State House
West State Street
Trenton, NJ 08625
(607) 292-7065
While the two female and five male legislators are all Democrats, the Caucus is organized to be nonpartisan and would welcome a Republican legislator. The Caucus concentrates on the total legislative program but puts special emphasis on the issues involving blacks, Hispanics, and the poor.

**New York City Task Force on Youth Motivation***
c/o St. Regis Paper Company
633 Third Avenue
New York, NY 10017
(212) 697-4400, Ext. 225
The Force seeks to inspire and encourage minority youths to stay in school and obtain their high school diploma.

**New York State Urban Development Corp.***
1345 Avenue of the Americas
New York, NY 10019
(212) 974-7000
The Corporation exists to help build low- and moderate-income housing.

**Nigerian American Friendship Fund**
c/o James E. Obi
1 Penn Plaza, # 4315
New York, NY 10119
(212) 560-5500
The Nigerian-American Friendship Society was founded in 1977 to develop and strengthen educational, cultural and commercial links between Nigeria and the U.S. A nonprofit, tax-exempt organization, it has diversified Nigerian and American membership, including academic, business, cultural, diplomatic and governmental leaders from both nations.

**North Carolina A&T State University Alumni Association, Inc.**
Office Of Alumni Affairs
1606 Salem Street
Grensboro, NC 27411
(919) 334-7583
The Association seeks to develop financial, volunteer, and moral support necessary to enable the University to accomplish its greater mission as an institution of higher learning; and further, to provide the means by which individuals may join in a united effort to insure the future growth and development of the NCA&T State University.

**North Carolina Legislative Black Caucus**
Room 539
Legislature Office Building
Raleigh, NC 27611
(919) 833-1931
The Caucus was developed in 1974 to initiate legislation important to the forward movement of blacks in North Carolina, as well as to monitor, study, and participate more effectively in the total legislative process for the state. In addition, the Caucus works to keep minorities and working people up-to-date on the activities of the legislature, and encourage an increase in the state's black voting power as a means to strengthen black involvement in education, economic development, labor and the job market.

**North Street Capital Corporation**
250 North Street
White Plains, NY 10625
(914) 631-3000
The Corporation helps businesses owned or controlled by socially and economically disadvantaged persons, and members of minority groups in particular. It is especially interested in those businesses (or business ideas) that show potential for bank financing.

**Northwest Black Public Elected and Appointed Officials (Alaska, Colorado, Idaho, Oregon, Washington and Wyoming)**
101 Municipal Bldg.
Seattle, WA 98104
(206) 625-2794
The Conference was formed in 1970 to provide information for blacks in the Northwestern states on the activities and reports coming out of the National Congressional Black Caucus. It has since been expanded to monitor governmental activities in the Northwest to make certain that blacks are kept aware of what is going on throughout the region.

**Office for the Advancement of Public Black Colleges**
One Dupont Circle, Suite 710
Washington, DC 20036
(202) 293-7120
This group, which is affiliated with the National Association of State University and Land Grant Colleges and the American Association of State Universities and Colleges, works to enhance public awareness of the contributions of those institutions to American society.

**Office of Human Rights**
American Personnel and Guidance Association
1607 New Hampshire Avenue, N.W.
Washington, DC 20009
(202) 483-4633
The Office develops a roster of resource people who are representative of and responsible to minority group communities.

**Oklahoma Legislative Black Caucus**
5909 North Terry
Oklahoma City, OK 73111
(405) 427-6000
Founded in 1981, the Oklahoma Legislative Black Caucus was developed to support the legislative goals of the state's black and minority communities and to keep these communities up to date and more actively involved in the total legislative process.

**Omega Psi Phi Fraternity**
2714 Georgia Avenue, N.W.
Washington, DC 20001
(202) 667-7158; (800) 424-2442
The 26,000-member organization formed at Howard University in 1911 undertakes civic and community service projects and also lends financial support to the NAACP as well as the United Negro College Fund.

**One Hundred Black Men**
100 East 22nd Street
New York, NY 10010
(212) 777-7070
Founded in 1965, this civic organization has over 500 members from business, professional and political sectors. Its purpose is to achieve meaningful gains for blacks in housing, education employment, health services government, and to improve the overall quality of life for minorities. One Hundred Black Men provides college scholarships for public high school graduates and helps to support institutions.

**Opera North**
4401 Conshohocken Avenue
Philadelphia, PA 19131
(215) 879-9029
Opera North was founded in 1974 as "Opera Ebony," the only minority opera company owned and operated by blacks. Its purpose is to provide additional opportunities for gifted minority singers instrumentalists, directors and conductors in the field of grand opera.

**Operation PUSH**
(People United to Save Humanity)
930 East 50 Street
Chicago, IL 60615
(312) 373-3366
PUSH's basic contention is that it does very little good to have the *right* to do certain things without the *ability*. We have the right to attend any school, to eat in any restaurant, stay in any motel, and live in any neighborhood, but we do not have the money to pay the tuition, the bill, or the house note. Operation PUSH addresses the economic question through research, education, and direct action.

**Opportunities Industrialization Centers of America, Inc.**
100 West Coulter Street
Philadelphia, PA
(215) 951-2200/2213
The Center provides training, counseling, and employment programs for developing vocational skills of community people regardless of race, creed, sex, or color within the broad field of industry.

**Opportunity Capital Corp.**
235 Montgomery Street, Suite 1226
San Francisco, CA 94104
(415) 392-5696
The corporation provides long-term equity financing for minority-owned businesses.

**Organization of Black Airline Pilots, Inc.**
PO Box 86
LaGuardia Airport
Flushing, NY 11371
(201) 568-8145
The Organization was formed in 1976 to make certain blacks and other minorities had a group that would keep them informed about opportunities for advancement within commercial aviation. It sponsors the Summer Flight Academy and provides scholarships for some of the teen-agers enrolled in flying programs. The Organization also provides speakers for schools and community groups to advise youths in career opportunities within the field of aviation.

**Pan American Contractors Service Center**
2211 East Missouri Avenue, Suite E-243
El Paso, TX 79903
(915) 545-2758
The Center provides investments in minority-owned businesses.

**Penn Center, Inc.**
PO Box 126
St. Helena Island, South Carolina 29920
(803) 838-2432 or 838-2235
The Center preserves the Sea Islands History, culture and environment through serving as a local, national and international educational resource center and acting as a catalyst for the development of programs for self-sufficiency.

**Pennsylvania Legislative Black Caucus**
203 South Office Bldg.
Harrisburg, PA 17120
(717) 738-1665
The Pennsylvania Legislative Black Caucus was formed in 1969 to serve as an informational vehicle for the advancement of the interests of minorities in the state. It monitors legislation and the legislative process as well as state agencies.

**Phelps Stokes Fund**
10 East 87th Street
New York, NY 10128
(212) 427-8100
The Phelps Stokes Fund was founded in 1911 by a grant from the estate of Caroline Phelps Stokes, to enhance educational opportunities for American blacks, Africans, American Indians and needy whites. The Fund develops and administers programs in education for its constituent groups. The Fund hosts numerous lectures, workshops and seminars.

**Phi Beta Sigma Fraternity, Inc.**
145 Kennedy Street, N.W.
Washington, DC 20011
(202) 726-5434
The 65,000-member fraternity established in 1914 promotes brotherhood and community service. The fraternity instills in its membership the desire to pursue scholastic excellence, and program support is given to education through scholarships and tutorial services.

**Phi Delta Kappa Sorority**
Mrs. Arthur Mae Norris, Supreme Basileus
1337 South Hall Street
Montgomery, AL 36106
(205) 262-0875
The sorority, founded in 1923 for the purpose of promoting sisterhood, encourages higher education among its membership and the community at large.

**Pioneer Capital Corporation**
1440 Broadway
New York, NY 10018
(212) 594-4860
The corporation provides investments in minority-owned companies.

**Progress Venture Capital Corp.**
1501 North Broad Street
Philadelphia, PA 19122
(215) PO 9-3484
The corporation provides capital and technical assistance to minority entrepreneurs.

**Progressive National Baptist Convention, Inc.**
601 50th Street, NE
Washington, DC 20019
(202) 396-0558
There are more than 1,000 churches with more than 1.5 million members throughout America that support and encourage missions, education, civil rights programs and stewardship development through membership in the PNBC.

**Resource Placement and Development, Inc.**
77 Maple Street
Springfield, MA 01105
(413) 733-3121
The group recruits minorities to match companies' employment opportunities.

**Rhode Island Caucus of State Black Legislators**
906 Narragansett Boulevard
Providence, RI 02905
(401) 941-1660
The Caucus lobbies where necessary and monitors state legislative proceedings with special emphasis on issues of housing, jobs, economic development, education and affirmative action programs

to guarantee that blacks, Hispanics and other minorities are dealt with fairly within the considerations of the state legislature.

**Rutgers Minority Investment Company**
92 New Street
Newark, NJ 07102
(201) 648-5287
The company is active in assisting and encouraging minority-owned small businesses.

**Schomburg Center for Research in Black Culture**
515 Lenox Avenue
New York, NY 10037
(212) 862-4000
One of the largest and best-known sources of black research, the Schomburg Center was founded as a New York City public library in 1926. It was based on the extensive private collection of books on black culture by the late Arthur A. Schomburg, a black man born in Puerto Rico. Located in the heart of Harlem, the ultra-modern facility counted close to 65,000 visitors in 1985. The collection of more than 100,000 books about Afro-Americans and people of African descent, plus numerous photographs, manuscripts, recordings and films, is available to scholars and researchers.

**Sedfre, Inc.**
315 Seventh Avenue, 7th Floor
New York, NY 10001
(212) 741-0800
Sedfre provides training and technical assistance to those organizations and institutions that are involved in all of the dimensions of community development.

**Seminole Employment Economic Development Corp.**
1011 South Sanford Avenue
PO Box 2076
Sanford, FL 32771
(305) 323-4360
Seminole provides opportunities for employment at the highest skill levels possible; develops new salable skills; reduces unemployment; curbs emigration; and develops managerial talent among the disadvantaged in the economic life of Seminole County.

**Seven Hills Neighborhood Houses**
701 Lincoln Park Drive
Cincinnati, OH 45203
(513) 721-2512
The Houses work with neighborhood residents who, in the search for a useful and satisfying life, have the least number of alternatives open to them by reason of color, discrimination, lack of educational training, minimal access to full employment, inadequate health facilities, few opportunities for home ownership, and too few resources to solve basic problems of survival in the city.

**Sickle Cell Anemia Foundation of Greater New York**
209 West 125th Street
New York, NY 10027
(212) 865-1201
The Sickle Cell Anemia Foundation of Greater New York was established in 1972 in the belief that education is the key to combating sickle cell disease within the black and Hispanic communities, where the blood disorders are most commonly found. While its programs of education, screening and genetic counseling are conducted for the most part in the New York Metropolitan area, the Foundation has provided information and advice to individuals and groups throughout much of the world. The Foundation also runs an ongoing blood bank, a research library facility and frequent educational programs for schools and community groups.

**Sigma Gamma Rho Sorority, Inc.**
7311 South Yates Boulevard
Chicago, IL 60649
(313) 731-4661
The Sorority encourages academic achievement while at the same time nurturing special talents and leadership ability. The sorority has as one of its goals promotion of community involvement among its membership.

**Sigma Pi Phi Fraternity ("The Boule")**
69 Fifth Avenue, Apt. 9G
New York, NY 10001
(212) 247-5850
The oldest black Greek letter fraternal society, Sigma Pi Phi

*Southern Africa Committee seeks to educate and highlight the many issues and problems of the entire southern regions of Africa including the apartheid policy of South Africa through it's publication* Africa.

fraternity has commitments to philanthropic and charitable causes. These funds are channeled through its tax-exempt foundation.

**Solomon Fuller Institute**
127 Mt. Auburn Street
Cambridge, MA 02138
(617) 661-9446
The Institute is dedicated to research and study, and devising methods of disseminating information which will have a positive effect on the mental health of all people, particularly black and other minority groups. Projects reflect a desire to improve and increase the conditions which will enable people to function and relate to each other so each person can realize his fullest, healthy potential.

**South Carolina Legislative Black Caucus**
432 B. Solomon Blatt Bldg.
Columbia, SC 29202
(803) 734-3061
Organized to promote and promulgate legislation needed for black advancement, the Caucus monitors the legislature and state agencies and keeps black residents informed through "report cards" seminars, workshops and a newsletter.

**Southern Africa Committee**
244 East 27 Street
New York, NY 10011
(212) 741-3480
Inform and activate people concerning the issues of Southern Africa through the monthly magazine AFRICA containing articles and information about military, political, economic, and social developments in South Africa, Zimbabwe (Rhodesia), Namibia, Angola, and the former Portuguese colonies of Mozambique and the new Republic of Guinea-Bissau.

**Southern Association of Black Administration Personnel**
District Administrative Officers
Florida Junior College at Jacksonville
Jacksonville, FL 32205
(904) 387-8346
The Association seeks to articulate needs of black students in higher education; research, develop, and coordinate recruiting techniques for black students in the South; investigate and develop economic resources for black students, and minimize attrition rates of black students in higher education.

**Southern Christian Leadership Conference**
334 Auburn Avenue, N.E.
Atlanta, GA 30303
(404) 522-1420
The Conference functions as an eleemosynary organization, more particularly to organize and maintain Christian guidance to help improve civic, religious, economic, and cultural conditions in the nation. This organization hopes to achieve its purposes through nonviolent direct action, lectures, dissemination of literature, and other means of public instruction.

**Southern California Minority Capital Corp.**
2651 South Western Avenue, Suite 303
Los Angeles, CA 90018
(213) 731-8211
The Corporation financially assists small businesses on a venture capital basis.

**Southern Fellowship Fund**
795 Peachtree Street, N.E., Suite 484
Atlanta, GA 30308
(404) 874-4891
The Fund provides a cadre of qualified persons for faculty and staff of colleges in the United States. Primary emphasis is placed on providing black talent, but others who are on the staff of black colleges and who have commitments to continuing careers in these institutions are eligible.

**Southern Poverty Law Center**
1001 South Hull Street
Montgomery, AL 36101
(205) 264-0286
The Center provides free legal aid for the financially handicapped. The group works with legal aid groups and with the local branches of the American Civil Liberties Union.

**Southern Regional Council, Inc.**
52 Fairlie Street, N.W.
Atlanta, GA 30303
(404) 522-8764
The Council seeks to alert, sensitize, educate, and mobilize Southerners on issues which will broaden opportunity and enhance quality of life for its people, primarily in areas of education, economic development, health, and housing.

**Southwest Virginia Community Development Fund**
401 First Street, N.W.
Roanoke, VA 24016
(703) 344-6624
The Fund seeks to reduce unemployment and underemployment in depressed areas through the creation of economically sound, community-owned industries that will hire and train unemployed and underemployed persons.

**Spaulding for Children**
36 Prospect St.
Westfield, NJ 07090
(201) 233-2282
The agency is a non-profit specialized adoption agency which finds adoptive homes for older and handicapped children.

**Student National Medical Association, Inc.**
1012 10th Street, NW
Washington DC 20001
(202) 371-1616
Established in 1964 by students at the Howard University and Meharry Medical Schools and members of the National Medical Association, the organization helps to recruit minority high school students for the medical profession, supports legislative initiatives for better health care, assists in the eradication of prejudicial practices in medical education and supports programs to improve urban and rural health care.

**Sulton Campbell & Associates, Chartered**
6031 Kansas Avenue, NW
Washington, DC 20011
(202) 882-0636
Sulton Campbel is an architectural, landscape architecture, urban design, and planning firm, dedicated to the revitalization of older urban communities.

**Tactics (Technical Assistance Consortium To Improve College Services)**
2001 S Street, N.W., Suite 503
Washington, DC 20009
(202) 232-7738
Tactics seeks to create and maintain a pool of deployable manpower capable of dealing with institutional problems identified by the colleges; assist colleges in efforts to strengthen academic programs; establish and maintain a closer interface between federal programs and institutions for their mutual benefit and ensure that colleges become knowledgeable about government and nongovernment funding programs.

**Tau Gamma Delta Sorority, Inc.**
2207 Baker Street

Baltimore, MD 21216
(301) 669-2421
The 38-year-old sorority of college-educated women encourages educational opportunities for young people through its National Service Project and scholarship program. The organization also assists charitable institutions.

**Tennessee Black Caucus of State Legislators**
105 War Memorial Bldg.
Nashville, TN 37219
(615) 741-3900
The Tennessee Black Caucus of State Legislators was formed in 1975 to formalize and strengthen the efforts of black legislators to address the concerns of black residents. The organization monitors the total legislative process and advises black voters with periodic reports and publications.

**Texas Legislative Black Caucus**
PO Box 2910
Austin, TX 78701
(512) 659-5008
The Texas Legislative Black Caucus was formed to provide an effective network for black legislators in order to keep the group informed and aware of the total Texas legislative process at all times. The Caucus also functions to communicate with black voters, assessing the priorities coming out of the black community and helping that community to understand and to accomplish goals within the legislative process.

**Third World Press**
7524-26 South Cottage Grove
Chicago, IL 60619
(321) 651-1095
The Press makes available low-priced, quality books that can be purchased in most bookstores; publishes works of social and political analysis, as well as creative and critical writing aimed at raising the consciousness of third-world people, wherever they may be.

**369th Veterans' Association, Inc.**
369th Regiment Armory
One 369th Plaza
New York, NY 10037
(212) 926-5800
Founded in 1953 by veterans of the 369th Anti-Aircraft Artillery and units affiliated with the 369th during World War II, the Association supports all patriotic endeavors of the U.S., works for the general welfare of communities in which its members reside and helps to build capable leaders for the future.

**Top Ladies of Distinction, Inc.**
PO Box 600504
Houston TX 77260
(713) 747-1541
Founded in 1964, Top Ladies of Distinction, Inc., is an international community service organization dedicated to alleviating the problems faced by teenagers. Its objectives include the enhancement of the status of women, service to senior citizens and community beautification. Scholarships are given to graduating top teens. TLOD also supports several civil rights, health and children's advocacy groups.

**Transafrica, Inc.**
1325 18th Street, N.W., Suite 202
Washington, DC 20036
(202) 223-9666
The organization is designed to promote an active U.S. policy on African and Caribbean issues. Transafrica also monitors federal legislation.

**Tuskegee Airmen, Inc.**
4217 American River Drive
Sacramento, CA 95864
(916) 485-4731
The Tuskegee Airmen, Inc., was founded in 1972 by veterans of the all-black group of U.S. Army Air Force personnel trained and stationed at Tuskegee Institute and Air Field during Work War II. With three regions and 22 chapters nation-wide and overseas, the membership of more than 2,000 includes new members interested in aviation and the aerospace industry as well as veterans. A watchdog for minority concerns in aerospace and aviation, the group also provides scholarship aid to students entering the field from a $1 million trust fund.

**Tuskegee Institute National Historic Site**
PO Drawer 10
Tuskegee Institute, AL 36088
(205) 727-3200
The Institute was formed to commemorate the lives and works of Drs. Booker T. Washington and George Washington Carver and the roles they played in the advancement of the Negro.

**Twenty-First Century Foundation**
411 West 148th Street
New York NY 10031
(212) 926-5762
Founded in 1971 by the economist Robert S. Browne, the Foundation is the only national public foundation devoted to assisting the work of black community-based organizations.

**United American Progress Association**
701 East 79th Street
Chicago, IL 60619
(312) 268-1873
This Association, founded in 1961, worked initially to build black businesses in the Chicago area but has since expanded to assist black entrepreneurs nation-wide. Business owners agree to provide quality goods and services to the black community, while residents pledge to support local black-owned firms. More than 400 individuals and organizations, including clubs, block associations, consumer groups and churches, are current members.

**United Black Church Appeal**
860 Forrest Avenue
Bronx, NY 10456
(212) 992-5315
The United Black Church Appeal was founded in 1980 as a non-denominational black church foundation with the purpose of awakening and organizing the power of the black clergy and the black church to provide greater leadership for the liberation of the black community. Its programs center on economic development, political power and strengthening black families and black churches. Programs have included the distribution of massive amounts of foodstuffs to the needy, action rallies against drugs in inner-city areas and the promotion of the development of a black Church Center that would include a Hall of Fame, museum and library dedicated to preserving the history and restoring the importance of the black Church.

**United Church of Christ, Commission for Racial Justice**
105 Madison Avenue, Rooms 1102-1120
New York, NY 10016
(212) 683-5656
Criminal justice, penal reform, consumer advocacy, higher education, black family life, community organization, and retarded offender advocacy are supported by the commission's interdenominational and ecumenical programs.

**United Golfers Association**
James Morrow, President
(Direct communications via local Professional
Golf Association offices.)

Founded in Stone, MA, in 1926, the association represents some 20,000 golfers in 89 golf clubs across the United States. A scholarship fund and junior golfer interest programs are emphasized.

**United Mortgage Bankers of America, Inc.**
840 East 87 Street
Chicago, IL 60619
(312) 994-7200
The group seeks to unite black persons interested in mortgage banking; exchange information and establish educational programs for recruiting blacks into banking.

**United Negro College Fund**
500 East 62nd Street
New York, NY 10021
(212) 644-9600
UNCF is the fund raising arm of 41 private, accredited, four-year institutions of higher learning, located in the southern region of the United States with the exception of one in Ohio.

**UNCF's National Alumni Council**
c/o UNCF
500 East 62nd Street
New York, NY 10021
(212) 644-9600
The Alumni Council was founded in 1946 and functions as the umbrella organization for the more than 200,000 alumni of the 43 UNCF-member colleges as well as the 45,000 students currently enrolled in those colleges. Council members help to raise funds for UNCF schools and recruit students and constitute an active network for the exchange of information useful to their schools and their own careers.

**United States Commission on Civil Rights***
1121 Vermont Avenue, N.W.
Washington, DC 20425
(202) 254-6600
The Commission investigates denials of voting rights; collects information about denials of equal protection of the laws under the Constitution; appraises federal laws and policies regarding equal protection of laws; serves as a national clearing house for information about denial of equal protection and submits reports, findings, and recommendations to the President and Congress.

**Urban Bankers Coalition**
c/o Robert Samuels
Manufacturers Hanover Trust
350 Park Avenue
New York, NY 10022
(212) 350-3109
The Coalition was formed to inform young people about opportunities in the banking industry; assist fellow employees to take advantage of opportunities for advancement in banking; promote economic improvement of the community and individuals through financial education and counseling.

**Urban Fund, Inc.**
1525 East 53 Street
Chicago, IL 60615
(312) 455-0080
The Fund provides equity financing of minority businesses in manufacturing and distribution.

**Urban Ventures, Inc.**
Tower Three, 18th Floor
825 South Bayshore Drive
Miami, FL 23131
(305) 371-4691
The group helps minority industry with business investments.

**US Black Engineer Magazine**
729 E. Pratt St., Suite 504
Baltimore, MD 21202
(301) 244-7101
The magazine promotes engineering and science.

**Venture Capital, Inc.**
PO Box 1434
Little Rock, AR 72203
(501) 374-9977
The group provides financing and management services for economically and socially oriented businesses.

**Veterans' Association, Inc.**
369th Regiment Armory
2366 Fifth Avenue
New York, NY 10037
(212) WA6-5800
The Associaion assists the men and women veterans in any problems that might arise; acquaints them with the veterans benefits available; participates in community activities, especially as they pertain to youth, and sponsors the Annual Dr. Martin Luther King Jr. Memorial Parade on Fifth Avenue in New York in May of each year.

**Virginia Legislative Black Caucus**
309 West Bute Street
Norfolk VA 23510
(804) 622-0803
Founded in 1969, the Virginia Legislative Black Caucus was developed to give blacks in the state a more organized state-wide effort to get legislation passed in their behalf and to help bring more

*The United Negro College Fund has sought to assist needy students with the funds to attend college. Bethune—Cookman College, pictured, is one of their associated schools.*

blacks into the political arena. The Caucus has kept blacks informed about issues that interest them and has developed legislative positions based on the priorities set by black voters.

**Voter Education Project, Inc.**
52 Fairlie Street, N.W.
Atlanta, GA 30303
(404) 522-7495
The project assists minority political participation in the 11 southern states—Alabama, Arkansas, Florida, Georgia, Louisiana, Mississippi, North Carolina, South Carolina, Tennessee, Texas, and Virginia; and provides assistance to black public officials in those states.

**Washington Task Force on African Affairs**
PO Box 13033
Washington, DC 20009
(202) 223-1392
The Task Force collects data and furnishes analyses relevant to United States-Africa relations; assures consideration of black America in U.S. policies and activities with respect to Africa; and methodically builds a constituency for African issues in the United States.

**Whitney M. Young, Jr. Academic and Intern Fellowship Program**
795 Peachtree Street, N.W., Suite 484
Atlanta, GA 30308
(404) 874-4891
The program exists to fittingly memorialize Whitney M. Young, Jr. by providing training and developmental opportunities for people in the areas of interracial cooperation; human resources; social services and corporate social responsibility in relationships with minorities.

**Winston-Salem State University National Alumni Association**
PO Box 13175
Winston-Salem, NC 27110
The principal purposes and aims of this organization shall be to foster and encourage loyalty and cooperation among graduates and former students; to cooperate with the faculty and administration of the University in improving and promoting its interests and perpetuating its principles; to encourage and emphasize close relationships with graduates and former students; and to encourage and foster meaningful financial support to the institution, its programs and student activities.

**Women's Auxiliary to the National Medical Association**
1627 Mill "B" Lane Avenue
Savannah, GA 31405
(601) 534-8686
The Association was formed to increase interest in the National Medical Association; to aid and encourage the medical profession in its effort to educate the public in matters of sanitation and health; to promote acquaintances among doctors' families.

**World Institute of Black Communications, Inc.**
10 Columbus Circle
New York, NY 10019
(212) 586-1771
Established in 1978 the nonprofit World Institute of Black Communications, Inc., is dedicated to broadening opportunities for African Americans in the communications media and promoting excellence in communications vehicles targeted to black audiences. The Institute sponsors the WIBC AAAA Scholarship Award for minority students interning in advertising agencies. It annually presents the CEBA Awards (Communications Excellence to Black Audiences) to advertisers, agencies and individuals whose advertisements and programs demonstrate excellence.

**Youth Pride, Inc.**
1536 You Street, N.W.
Washington, DC 20009
(202) 483-1900
The group seeks to reclaim the lives of young inner-city black men who come from hard-core problem-ridden levels of society. Pride does this by recruiting them from the streets, enrolling them in a work-study program for which they are salaried, and placing them with both public and private employers. YPI's basic philosophy is self-respect, self-help, and self-sufficiency.

**Zeta Delta Phi Sorority, Inc.**
PO Box 157
Bronx, NY 10469
(212) 407-8288
Zeta Delta Phi Sorority, Inc., was founded in 1962 and incorporated in 1964. The goal of the Sorority is to promote academic excellence and provide positive role models and encouragement to our youth. The Sorority selects a high school senior annually to receive a scholarship award.

**Zeta Phi Beta Sorority, Inc.**
1734 New Hampshire Avenue, N.W.
Washington, DC 20009
(202) 387-3103
The Sorority provides scholarships, service, and community action.

**Zion Non-Profit Charitable Trust**
Progress Plaza Shopping Center
1501 North Broad Street
Philadelphia, PA 19122
(215) 769-3484
The Trust exists to develop residential and commercial real estate; to build and manage residential, industrial, and commercial property;

# THE BLACK WOMAN

**Blacks and Women's Liberation ■ Historical Perspectives ■ Matriarchy and Current Trends ■ Outstanding Black Women**

Because women must work harder than men to achieve the same recognition and earn the same money, black women have, throughout their history on these shores, labored under a double burden. They have had to struggle for the emancipation of their race, while contending with prejudices and policies in American life that discriminate against women. Thus the rise of the women's movement in the early 1970s presented black women with a hard question: Is it productive to fight for the rights of minorities and women at the same time, or will involvement in one inevitably detract from success in the other? As debate on this continued into the 1980s, Representative Shirley Chisholm observed that in many respects it was more difficult to be a woman than a black. Aileen Fernandez became leader of what has probably been the women's movement's most potent force, the National Organization for Women (NOW).

Feminists, both black and white, pointed out that many of the nation's sexist laws and procedures exerted their most adverse effect on black women. Examples cited included anti-abortion laws, which have the effect of increasing the cost of abortions to astronomical prices that few black women can afford, state labor laws that deny certain "strenuous" well-paying jobs to women, and welfare laws that rupture homes by denying aid to families that contain an able-bodied male.

However, while granting validity to these points, many blacks, both men and women, were deeply disturbed by the women's movement. In part their concern stemmed from the focus of much of the movement. Many blacks felt that feminists were unduly preoccupied with the problems and career aspirations of professional whites to the neglect of pressing job, housing, health, and education problems suffered more by black than white women.

In addition, many blacks, among them psychiatrist Alvin Poussaint, charged that the women's liberation movement was being used to perpetuate discriminatory practices in employment; that white women were being hired for positions that could be filled by blacks, male or female.

Carrying this assertion further, many blacks contended that the women's liberation movement (and the environmentalist movement as well) was a national cop out, a retreat from the fight for racial justice to a less violent and controversial arena of justice for women. People supporting this view asserted that during the late 1960s and early 1970s the decline of the movement for racial justice and the rise of women's liberation coincided, until the latter gained preeminence in the consciences and priorities of the American government and public.

However, partisans of racial and sexual equality found much in common. In the summer of 1975, representatives of the two causes joined in the defense of Joanne Little, a North Carolina woman indicted for first degree murder after she killed a male prison guard whom she alleged had raped her while she was in jail pending an appeal of her conviction on a burglary charge.

It is ironic that black women were—and indeed still are—given special status as nurse and confidante to the children of white mothers they serve, while being deprived of the opportunity to shower the same appropriate attentions on their own children.

On many occasions, even before the Civil War, the two streams—black rights and women's rights—have merged. The battles for the black vote and the vote for women, for education of blacks and women, were often fought on the same ground. In the mid-nineteenth century, for instance, Frederick Douglass and the Forten sisters, all blacks, were fighting for black emancipation and the rights of women, and were aided in their work by a number of white abolitionists (e.g., Sarah and Angelina Grimkea). In Philadelphia and Boston especially, many black and white families united to form anti-slavery societies dedicated to the causes of emancipation and education.

After Emancipation, one of the first discernible trends among black women was the development of a strong club movement, designed to improve their overall welfare and increase opportunities open to them. At that time, such leading black educators as Fannie Jackson Coppin, Charlotte Hawkins Brown, and Nannie Helen Burroughs came into prominence, to be joined later by Mary McLeod Bethune and Mary Church Terrell, among others.

### Matriarchy and Current Trends

Much has been written of the matriarchal structure of black society, from the postwar era down to the present day. Whatever conclusions are drawn, there can be little doubt that the black woman has often been called upon to compensate for the failure (through no fault of his own) of the black man to find suitable, dependable employment in an intensely competitive and racist society. Cases in which women become the marginal family breadwinner—the sole financial support of the group—inevitably involve a reversal of traditional roles for both partners, and contribute in some measure to the hazards faced by the blacks.

Black women have strengthened their positions considerably in the twentieth century by their entry into more skilled and better-paying jobs made possible through higher educational achievement. As opportunities have opened up, the black woman has been quick to make the transition from low-paid, unskilled domestic, farm, and operative jobs to employment in clerical, professional, technical, sales, and service jobs. But in comparison to whites, black women still lag far behind. In an effort to increase upward mobility, many black women have opted for national women's movements. This has caused dissension among blacks who feel that the feminists have put the various black movements on the back burner of social priorities.

The social trends and economic troubles of the 1970s and 1980s have strained the fragile alliance between the women's and black movements. On one hand, such organizations as NOW participated importantly with blacks in equal opportunity litigation that improved the lot of both women and blacks, and blacks and women shared a concern about preachments from the radical right which sought to portray the aspirations of both groups as immoral. However, to many blacks, the priorities of feminists, such as the right to abortion and the Equal Rights Amendment, were subordinate to the issues of economic survival manifested by inflation, recessions, and the competition to blacks of both sexes presented by the rapid increase of white women in the nation's labor force.

## OUTSTANDING BLACK WOMEN

Whatever the pros and cons of the feminist cause for blacks as a whole, the number of prominent black women in American life has grown substantially. Many of these outstanding women have their biographies given below. Biographies of other prominent black women may be found in the sections of the *Almanac* devoted to their major fields or the section on Prominent Black Americans.

### MARGARET W. ALEXANDER
### College Administrator, Author

Director of black studies at Jackson State College in Mississippi, Margaret W. Alexander is also the author of many books, including the bestselling *Jubilee*, a novel about the Civil War. Born in Birmingham, she attended Northwestern University (B.A., English) and the University of Iowa (M.A. and Ph.D., English). Her writing has won many prizes, including the Yale Award for Younger Poets. She has taught college English since 1949.

### SADIE T. M. ALEXANDER
### Lawyer

Sadie Alexander set a series of precedents in pursuing her distinguished career as a lawyer. She was the first black woman to earn a Ph.D. degree in the United States and the first woman to earn a law degree from the University of Pennsylvania. In 1927, she became the first black woman to be admitted to the bar in the state of Pennsylvania.

Before graduating with honors from the University of Pennsylvania in 1918, Mrs. Alexander had acted as the associate editor of the university's law review. She then received a scholarship for a year's graduate study, and was also awarded the Frances S. Pepper Fellowship in Economics for the year 1920-1921.

Besides belonging to several church and law associations, Mrs. Alexander has served on the Board of Directors of the New York City branch of the National Urban League. The author of several articles, she was the editor of *Who's Who Among Negro Lawyers* in 1949.

Mrs. Alexander now lives in semi-retirement in Philadelphia.

### AUGUSTA BAKER
### Librarian, Children's Specialist

During her distinguished 37-year career with the New York Public Library, Augusta Baker rose to the position of Coordinator of Children's Services. Under her knowledgeable and sensitive leadership, library materials for juveniles were greatly expanded in both kind and degree. Although she retired from the library in 1974, she continues to teach the art of storytelling at Columbia University and to lecture at colleges around the country.

After taking her bachelors degree in library science from the State University of New York, Albany, in 1934, she founded the New York Public Library's James Weldon Johnson Memorial collection of children's books about black life. In addition to contributing to numerous professional journals, she is the author of *The Black Experience in Books for Children* and two collections of folk tales, *The Talking Tree and The Golden Lynx.* Her extensive knowledge of juvenile literature has made her an active consultant for NBC-TV's children's programming, as well as for the successful *Sesame Street* series.

The recipient of many professional honors, Mrs. Baker is associated with the New York Library Association and the American Library Association, where she has served on the Executive Board (1968-1972). In 1975, Mrs. Baker was elected to an honorary life membership in the American Library Association, one of only 55 such memberships awarded in the 100 years of the association's existence.

*Augusta Baker founded the New York Public Library's collection of children's books about African-American life.*

*Ida B. Wells Barnett spoke out in the South against lynching.*

### IDA B. WELLS BARNETT
### Anti-lynching Crusader
### 1864-1931

Born in Mississippi and educated at Rusk University, Ida Wells Barnett was one of the few women in the South who engaged in a vigorous campaign against the lynching practices common at that time. She was affiliated with several newspapers, most prominently as the editor of *Free Speech* in Memphis.

In 1895, her first pamphlet against lynching, *The Red Record*, was compiled. Mrs. Barnett also wrote several other pamphlets and articles during the years when her speaking engagements took her across the United States and to Europe as well.

After having become chairman of the Anti-Lynching Bureau of the National African Council, she organized and became the first president of the Negro Fellowship League in 1908. Five years later, her social work began to center in Chicago, where she was appointed probation officer. She left this post in 1915, having been elected Vice-president of the Chicago Equal Rights League. From then on, Mrs. Barnett devoted most of her time to civil rights activities.

She died in 1931.

### BRENETTA H. BARRETT
### State Official

Brenetta H. Barrett is currently director of Illinois' human resources administration. Prior to her appointment, she was national vice chairman for the 1972 First National Conference on Business Opportunities for Women. A native of Chicago, she attended Chicago Loop College and DePaul University.

She is a board member of the Illinois ACLU, and has served on the advisory board of the Illinois Citizens for Medical Control of Abortions.

### MARY TREADWELL BARRY
### Executive

Mary T. Barry is an executive and co-founder of the Pride corporations, which provide work-training, job placement, and business ownership opportunities for black youths and inner city black males. Born in Lexington, Ky., she studied at Fisk University, Ohio State University, and Antioch Law School in Columbia, Md. She is a member of the Washington, D.C. chapter of the National Association of Market Developers, Inc., the Washington, D.C. Citizens for Better Public Education, Inc., and the American Management Association.

### CHARLOTTA A. BASS
### Vice-Presidential Candidate
### 1890-1961

Chosen unanimously by the Progressive Party convention in 1952, Mrs. Charlotta A. Bass became the first black woman to run for the nation's second-highest political office—Vice President of the United States.

Born in Little Compton, R.I. in 1890, Mrs. Bass studied at Brown University, Columbia University, and U.C.L.A. While a resident of Los Angeles, Mrs. Bass was the editor and publisher of the California *Eagle*, the oldest black newspaper on the West Coast.

Until 1948, Mrs. Bass was a member of the Republican party, and had even served as Western Regional Director for Wendell Wilkie in his 1940 presidential campaign. In 1950, however, Mrs. Bass ran for Congress in the 14th District of Los Angeles on the ticket of the Progressive party, which she herself had helped found two years earlier.

During her newspaper career, she was known as a vigorous opponent of the Ku Klux Klan and an outspoken foe of discrimination in employment.

Mrs. Bass died in 1961.

### DAISY BATES
### Little Rock Integrationist

Mrs. Daisy Bates first captured the national spotlight in 1957 during the Little Rock crisis in which President Eisenhower was forced to use federal troops to effect the admission of nine black children to Central High School. As Arkansas president of the NAACP, Mrs. Bates submitted to arrest and other attempts at intimidation while standing firm in the struggle to integrate the school.

Born in Huttig, Ark., Mrs. Bates attended school in Memphis and later went to Philander Smith and Shorter colleges in Little Rock. She married L. Christopher Bates in 1941, the same year they organized a weekly newspaper, *The Arkansas State Press*, which has since become one of the most influential of its kind in the South. In 1946, Mrs. Bates and her husband were convicted on contempt charges for criticizing a Circuit Court trial, but the Arkansas Supreme Court later reversed the decision.

*Mary McLeod Bethune dedicated her career to teaching and government service.*

Mrs. Bates has recounted her integration experiences in her book *The Long Shadow of Little Rock*, published in 1962. Ever critical of discriminatory policies, she led a 1972 attack on Nixon's cut of OEO funds for Mitchellville, Ark., calling the budgetary measure a form of economic genocide. In March 1974, Mrs. Bates and the nine children who integrated Little Rock's white Central High School in 1957 were honored for their courage by the National Black Political Convention.

### Dr. MARY FRANCES BERRY
### Scholar, Educator, Activist

Mary Francis Berry was born in Nashville TN in 1938. After attending Howard University and receiving a B.A. in 1961 and an M.A. she went on to graduate studies at the University of Michigan where she received a doctorate in history and a Juristical Doctorate (law) in 1966.

Dr. Berry taught at the University of Michigan and at the University Of Maryland where she was director of Afro-American studies. Professor Berry joined the Howard University faculty in 1980, the same year she became a member of the U.S. Commission on Civil Rights. Earlier she served as U.S. Assistant Secretary for Education under President Jimmy Carter in the late 70s.

As a member of the U.S. Commission on Civil Rights, Dr. Berry, was an outspoken critic of the Reagan Administration's policies, particularly those of the Justice Department. As a result she was ousted from the Commission by Reagan in 1983, but subsequently reinstated by the courts.

Her writings are extensive considering her enormous time

*Ruth Bowen, founder of the nation's largest black-owned entertainment agency.*

consuming professional schedule. In 1971 she authored, Black *Resistance/ White Law: A History of Constitutional Racism in America* and co- authored *The Black Experience in America* in 1976. She has also written numerous articles and essays. Her fifth book, *Why ERA Failed: Politics, Women's Rights and Amending Process of the Constitution* was published by Indiana University Press in 1986. Previously, in 1974, she was editor of the *Journal of Negro History*.

Dr. Berry is one of the founders of the Free South Africa Movement.

Through her scholarship, profession and community activities Dr. Berry has accrued 15 honorary degrees.

## MARY McLEOD BETHUNE
### Administrator, Division of Negro Affairs, National Youth Administration (NYA)
### 1875-1955

Mary McLeod Bethune is such a major figure in black American history that no comprehensive discussion of it is possible without recalling her contributions.

Born on July 10,1875, she gained her special insight into the everyday problems of the average black youth while growing up on a farm in Mayesville, S.C. As a young woman, she spent some seven years at Scotia Seminary in North Carolina and later did further study at the Moody Bible Institute in Chicago—all this with the intention of eventually becoming a missionary. But when this proved impossible (her application for a post in Africa was turned down by the Presbyterian Board of Missions in New York), she turned instead to teaching.

Herbert Hoover was the first American president to utilize her abilities when, in 1930, he invited her to a White House Conference on Child Health and Protection. Franklin D. Roosevelt was quick to follow his predecessor's lead by asking her to serve on the Advisory Committee of one of the organizations he helped establish—the National Youth Administration (NYA). In 1935, after a year spent laying the foundations for the NYA, her work had so impressed the President that he was persuaded to setup an Office of Minority Affairs, with Mrs. Bethune as administrator. This established a precedent, for it was the first post of its kind ever to be held by an American black woman.

Congressional appropriations for the NYA continued from 1936 through 1944, and Mary Bethune's title was soon changed to the more specific one of Director of the Division of Negro Affairs. Her duties consisted largely in granting funds to deserving students (particularly blacks) who could not otherwise have continued graduate study.

During the 1930s, she was one of the leading figures (and the only woman) in the unofficial "Black Cabinet" which had begun the fight for advanced integration in the U.S. government.

In later years, Mrs. Bethune was instrumental in establishing what is now known as Bethune-Cookman College, a merger of her own school (The Daytona Educational and Industrial School for Negro Girls) with the Cookman Institute.

Mrs. Bethune died in 1955 at the age of 80. Though she had been the holder of many important awards—among them the 1935 Spingarn Medal—her greatest achievement was the legacy of a lifelong career dedicated to young people, one which won her worldwide recognition and acclaim.

## DOROTHY BOLDEN
### Labor Leader

Fighting for good job conditions and fair employment opportunities for domestic workers, Dorothy Bolden founded and serves as president of the National Domestic Workers Union. Her interest in improving home situations has also led her to become director of the Homemaking Skills Training Program in Atlanta. Born in Fulton County, Ga., she attended high school there before going on to study at the Chicago School of Dress Designers. She is on the board of directors of the Welfare Rights Organization, a member of the Atlanta Legal Aid Society, and a member of the League of Women Voters. Her homemaking skills project teaches consumer rights, nutrition, child care, budgeting, cooking, and housekeeping.

## RUTH J. BOWEN
### Booking Agent

Ruth J. Bowen is founder and president of Queen Booking Corp., New York City. Born in Danville, Va., and raised in

Brooklyn, N.Y., she studied business administration at New York University and UCLA.

After marrying Billy Bowen, one of the original Inkspots, she began to gain show business experience by handling her husband's business affairs. A friendship with Dinah Washington, who urged Mrs. Bowen to assume all her management responsibilities, led to the founding of Queen Booking, which has grown to be the largest black-owned entertainment agency in the country, grossing over $800,000 annually.

The only woman to head her own booking agency, Mrs. Bowen handles such talent as Stevie Wonder, Sammy Davis Jr., Aretha Franklin, Redd Foxx, Ray Charles, and Gladys Knight and the Pips. She is a member, and former president, of the Rinkydinks Club, and is a member of Operation Push.

*Vinie Burrows, a performing actress, is extremely active in civil affairs.*

## CHARLOTTE HAWKINS BROWN
**Educator**
**1882-1961**

Although she was raised and educated in Cambridge, Mass., Charlotte Hawkins made yearly visits with her parents to her birthplace in Henderson, N.C., and as she grew older, became interested in improving educational facilities for black people in the South.

With the aid of her benefactor, Alice Freeman Palmer, she received training as a teacher at Salem (Mass.) Normal School and at Wellesley College, later accepting a position from the American Missionary Association as a teacher in a small school near Sedalia, N.C.

Lack of funds, however, forced the Association to close the school in 1902. Conscious of the community's urgent need for educational facilities, Miss Hawkins decided to work in Sedalia without a salary, and to establish her own school there. By 1904, she had raised enough money to construct the first building of what was to become Palmer Memorial Institute. A mid-winter conflagration burned the school's wooden structure to the ground in 1917, but Mrs. Brown turned the disaster into an opportunity for further growth and improvement. With the assistance of loyal friends in both New England and North Carolina, she raised enough money to construct the sturdy brick buildings which are still in use.

In addition to her distinguished work as an educator, Mrs. Brown (she married Edward S. Brown in 1911) served as president of the Federation of Women's Clubs of North Carolina, and as vice-president of the National Association of Colored Women. She was also well-known as a lecturer on interracial subjects.

Mrs. Brown resigned as president of Palmer in 1952 but remained as director of finance until 1955. Mrs. Brown died in 1961 in Greensboro, N.C.

## DOROTHY LAVINIA BROWN
**Physician**

Dorothy L. Brown holds the positions of clinical professor of surgery at Meharry Medical College in Nashville, director of Student Health Service at Meharry and Fisk universities, and chief of surgery at Riverside Hospital. Born in Philadelphia, she spent the first 12 years of her life in a foster home. She is a graduate of Bennett College (B.A., 1941) and Meharry Medical College (M.D., 1948). As a member of Tennessee's legislature, Dr. Brown wrote and sponsored the state's only attempt at abortion reform, which was rejected, and she was then defeated in her own attempts for reelection. Dr. Brown enjoys the distinction of being the first black woman general surgeon in the South, and she was also the first single woman in Tennessee permitted to adopt a child. She is a fellow of the American College of Surgeons.

## HALLIE Q. BROWN
**Teacher, Elocutionist, Writer**
**1855?-1949**

A distinguished lecturer and elocutionist who traveled throughout the United States and several European countries, Hallie Q. Brown was born in Pittsburgh, but moved with her family at an early age to Ontario, Canada. Having completed her early education, she returned to the United States and attended Wilberforce College in Ohio, graduating with a B.S. degree in 1873.

Before she began her lecture tours with the Wilberforce Grand Concert Company, Miss Brown taught for several years at plantation schools in the South and later at Allen

University (South Carolina) and Tuskegee Institute (Alabama). She also returned to her alma mater to teach and serve as a trustee.

Between 1905 and 1912, Miss Brown served as president of both the Ohio State Federation of Women and National Association of Colored Women, establishing the latter organization's scholarship fund.

Miss Brown was the author of several books, among them *First Lessons in Public Speaking* and *Homespun Heroines and Other Women of Distinction*.

### NANNIE HELEN BURROUGHS
**Educator**
**1883-1961**

Nannie Helen Burroughs began her career as a bookkeeper and associate editor of the Philadelphia *Christian Banner,* but because of her long-standing interest in the church, decided after a year to leave her position with the paper in order to devote all her energies to social service.

Working for the Association of Colored Women, she organized the Women's Industrial Club in Louisville, which specialized in teaching domestic skills to black girls. In 1907 she began her work with the National Baptist Convention, playing an important role in founding the National Training School for Women and Girls, which opened in 1909 with her as president. Though most of her time was devoted to the school, Miss Burroughs was also particularly active as a member of both the National Association of Colored Women and the National Association for the Advancement of Colored People.

### VINIE BURROWS
**Performing Artist**

Vinie Burrows is a founding member of Women for Racial and Economic Equality. A native of New York City, Vinie Burrows began her theatrical career as a child actress with Helen Hayes on the New York stage. She has appeared both on and off Broadway with such stars as Ossie Davis, James Earl Jones, Mary Martin, Ben Gazzara, and Cicely Tyson. Ms. Burrows created a one-woman show, called *Walk Together Children*, which is an exploration of the black presence in America, using poetry, prose and song. The show has received rave reviews from the more than 900 colleges in the United States and in Holland, Sweden, Nigeria, Algeria, and Viet Nam.

Vinie Burrows has had feature articles published in national magazines and produces a weekly live radio show focusing on concerns of women. Her concern for political, economic, and social democracy is evidenced in her role as an NGO (Nongovernmental Organization) Permanent Representative to the United Nations where she is closely involved with women's issues, disarmament, and the struggle against apartheid.

### MADELYN CHENNAULT
**Educator, Psychologist**

One of the handful of black women in the United States qualifying for a license to practice clinical psychology, Madelyn Chennault is both Calloway Professor of Educational Psychology at Fort Valley (Ga.) State College and director of the school's forward-looking "crisis clinic." The clinic offers its services to members of the college and to the local community. Born in Atlanta, she took degrees from Morris Brown College, the University of Michigan, and Indiana University before completing her doctoral internship in clinical psychology at the University of Georgia. She belongs to the Association of Black Psychologists and the American Association of University Professors.

### MAY EDWARD CHINN
**Physician**
**1896-1980**

Dr. May Edward Chinn was born in 1876 in Great Barrington, Massachusetts. Her father was William Lafayette Chinn, a slave who escaped from the Chinn Plantation in Lancasta, Virginia in 1864. The Chinn family moved from Great Barrington in 1899.

In 1921, May passed tests at New York's Teachers College which qualified her for the music course there. She was a pianist and was an accompanist for Paul Robeson for a four-year period. While at Teachers College, she came to the attention of a professor through a paper she had written on sewage disposal, which ultimately led to medical studies.

In 1926, she was graduated from the Bellevue Hospital Medical College and was admitted to an internship at Harlem Hospital. Her early work in cancer detection earned her high professional praise and in 1944 she was invited to join the staff of the Strang Clinic, where she remained for 29 years. By 1978, Dr. Chinn had become a consultant to the Phelps-Stokes Fund where she remained until her death on December 1, 1980. Dr. Chinn was the recipient of numerous awards. Among them were the doctor of science degree from New York University and an honorary doctorate from Columbia University.

She was the first black female intern at Harlem Hospital and for many years the lone female doctor in Harlem.

### XERONA CLAYTON
**Television Producer and Hostess**

Xerona Clayton produces and hosts *The Xerona Clayton Show*, which focuses on current events from an activist viewpoint, on WAGA-TV in Atlanta. A native of Muskogee, Okla., she graduated from Tennessee State University (B.A., 1952) and taught in the public school systems of Chicago and Los Angeles before joining the Southern Christian Leadership Conference. Mrs. Clayton is a consultant for the Atlanta Model Cities Program and a member of American Women in Radio and Television and of the Atlanta Press Club.

### LENORA COLE-ALEXANDER
**Administrator**

Dr. Lenora Cole-Alexander is the ninth woman to head the Labor Department's Women's Bureau since it was created in 1920. As director, she is responsible for carrying out the agency's mandate to formulate standards and policies promoting the welfare of working women and to advance their employment opportunities. A native of Buffalo, New York, Dr. Cole-Alexander has been involved in a number of professional and community service activities. She has served on the boards or commissions of the Washington, D.C. Chamber of Commerce, the D.C. Rental Accommodations Commission, National Association of Student Personnel Administrators, National Council of Negro Women, American Council on Education, and Washington Opportunities for Women.

Dr. Cole-Alexander was educated at the State University of New York at Buffalo, where she received her bachelors degree in 1957 and her masters in 1969 and Ph.D. in 1974. Prior to being named to her Labor Department post, Dr. Cole-Alexander was vice president for student affairs at the University of the District of Columbia. She has also served as vice president for student life at American University in Washington, D.C. and was assistant to the vice president for student affairs and interim director, Cooperative College Center at the State University of New York in Buffalo from 1969 to 1973.

## MARVA N. COLLINS
### Educator

Marva N. Collins is well known for her educational work in Chicago, where she established her own school to teach slow learners. Mrs. Collins was the subject of a special television program in which Cicely Tyson played the role of the noted educator. Mrs. Collins, an Alabama native, taught in the Chicago school system for 14 years but became concerned with the type of education black youngsters were receiving. In 1975, she opened the Westside Preparatory School in her home and since then she has been teaching basic education to youngsters on Chicago's West Side. Mrs. Collins graduated from Chicago Teacher's College and is a recipient of the Watson Washburn Award for Excellence in Education.

## ANNA JULIA COOPER
### Educator
### 1858-1964

This noted educator was, as early as the age of 11, acting as a student-teacher at St. Augustine Normal School, the institution which she attended in her native city of Raleigh, N.C. She was later to return there to teach for two years after she had become a full professor.

Dr. Cooper married the Reverend G. A. C. Cooper in 1877, and four years later left for Oberlin College in Ohio, where she taught and continued to pursue her own studies at the same time. Upon graduation in 1885, she became a professor of modern languages and science at Wilberforce University. However, her primary work in the field of educational administration came during her 50-year association with the old M Street High School in Washington, D.C. (later to become Dunbar). She served there as both instructor and principal.

In addition to her career as a teacher, Dr. Cooper wrote *A Voice from the South,* a well-received book on the racial problem which appeared in 1892. In 1925, at the age of 66, she received a Ph.D. from the Sorbonne in Paris, and later became president of Frelinghuysen University, a school for unemployed blacks which she ran in her own home in Washington, D.C.

Dr. Cooper died on February 27, 1961, at the age of 105.

## LOUISE M. DARGANS
### Administrator

Louise M. Dargans became known as the "good right hand" of New York Congressman Adam Clayton Powell after joining his staff in 1946. Today, as Chief Clerk of the House Committee on Education and Labor, she is one of the two blacks who heads a committee staff, and the only woman employed as chief clerk of a House committee.

The youngest of nine children, Miss Dargans was born in Daytona Beach, Fla., and moved to New York with her parents at the age of seven. In 1938, she graduated from Hunter College and went on to work for the New York State Department of Labor, the Office of Price Administration, and the Internal Revenue Service.

## ANGELA DAVIS
### Political Activist

Born in Birmingham, Ala., Angela Davis grew up in a segregated middle-class neighborhood, which became known as "Dynamite Hill" because of the terrorist attacks of white nightriders. After taking part in the mid-1950s civil rights demonstrations, she won a scholarship to a progressive high school in New York City, which prepared her for Brandeis University, where her intellectual leftism was sharpened by philosopher Herbert Marcuse. After two years of advanced study in Germany, she returned to the United States because she felt she had to take an active political role here.

Earning her masters degree at the University of California, San Diego, she worked with SNCC, the Black Panthers, and the Communist Party, eventually joining the last in 1968. Shortly thereafter, she was hired by UCLA to teach philosophy and fired twice by the Board of Regents over the strong protests of faculty and students after FBI leaks had identified her as a Party member. Counted against her were the speeches she gave in the cause of the Soledad Brothers. Then, in 1970, guns she had legally bought were used in a courtroom shootout and she became a fugitive on the FBI's "Most Wanted" list. Captured two months later, she spent 16 months in jail before coming to trial for murder and conspiracy. Needing only 13 hours of deliberations, the jurors acquitted her of all charges in June 1972.

Since then she has focused on the long-range revolutionary goals that affect not only blacks but all working people of the United States. To this end she has helped organize the National Alliance Against Racist and Political Repression, which now has 20 chapters. Despite university pleas, the California Regents refuses to rehire her. Her autobiography, *Angela Davis,* was published in 1974.

## CHRISTINE R. DAVIS
## Publishing Executive

Christine Ray Davis was born in Nashville and began her education as a music major at Fisk University. However, she left Fisk in 1935 and completed her higher education at Tennessee State College, majoring in business administration.

Her first job was as secretary and research assistant in a Boston law firm. Later, she left for Washington, D.C., to become administrative assistant to Arthur W. Mitchell, the Democratic Congressman from Illinois. She held this position until 1942 when Mitchell retired, after which she began to work for his successor, William L. Dawson.

In 1949, Dawson became chairman of the Committee on Expenditures (now the Committee on Government Operations), and appointed Mrs. Davis chief clerk. When the Democrats won control of the House in 1954, Dawson appointed her Staff Director of the Committee.

Mrs. Davis has been the recipient of several awards for her work in government, among them the citation of "Outstanding Woman of the Year," given her by the National Council of Negro Women in 1949. She also holds the award for "distinguished achievement in government affairs" from the National Association of Colored Women's Clubs.

Mrs. Davis is now a member of the staff of *Tuesday* magazine.

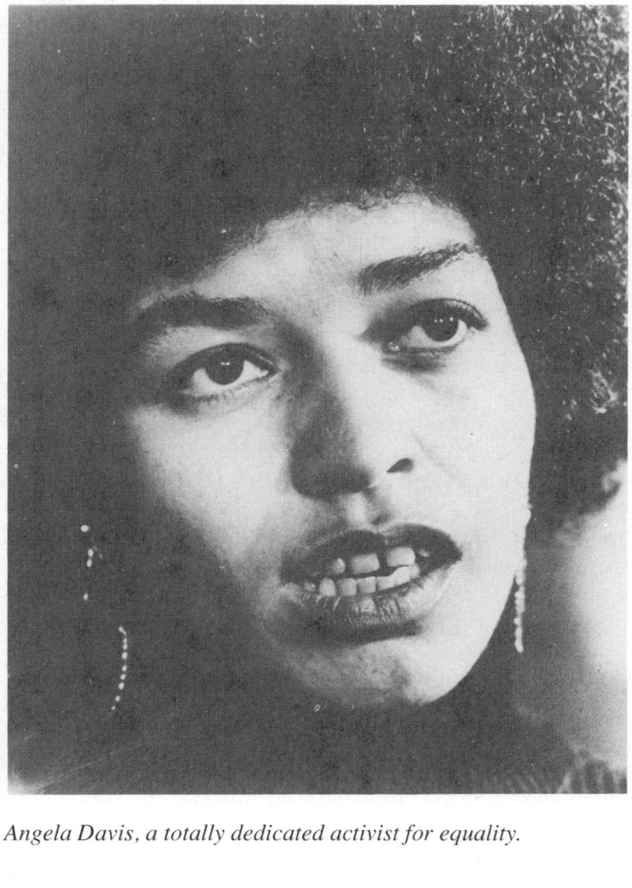

*Angela Davis, a totally dedicated activist for equality.*

## JULIETTE DERRICOTTE
## Educator
## 1897-1931

Raised in Athens, Ga., Juliette Derricotte was educated in the public schools there and at Talladega College, then a small school in Alabama operated by the American Missionary Association. Some 11 years after graduating from Talladega in 1918, Miss Derricotte became the first woman trustee of the college.

In the intervening years, she traveled across the United States, speaking at many colleges and educational conferences. In both 1924 and 1928, she was chosen to be a delegate representing American college students at the convention of the General Committee of the World's Student Christian Federation.

She later became the National Student Secretary for the Y.W.C.A. but resigned from this position in 1929 in order to become Dean of Women at Fisk University.

She died two years later in an automobile accident.

## DOROTHY B. FEREBEE
## Physician

A physician who received her medical degree with honors from Tufts Medical School in Massachusetts, Dr. Dorothy Ferebee has been active all her life in civic and social affairs. She began her medical career in Washington, D.C., where she served for several years on the Board of Directors of the Southeast Settlement House.

For seven summers, she worked among black sharecroppers in Mississippi on a health project which was sponsored by the Alpha Kappa Alpha Sorority. Dr. Ferebee later became president of this society, and also succeeded Mary McLeod Bethune as president of the National Council of Negro Women.

In 1951, Dr. Ferebee was sent by the U.S. Labor Department to study the problems of women in Germany, and she later visited Africa as a delegate to an international conference of women of African descent.

Besides maintaining her own medical practice, Dr. Ferebee acts as the head of the Student Health Service at Howard University and is a full professor of preventive medicine at the Howard School of Medicine.

## MARY HATWOOD FUTRELL
## Educator

Born on May 24, 1940, in Alta Vista, Virginia, Futrell graduated from Dunbar Public High School in Lynchburg, Virginia. She received her bachelor's degree in business education from Virginia State College, Petersburg, Virginia, and her master's degree from George Washington University in Washington, D.C. Futrell has also completed graduate work at the University of Maryland, the University of Virginia, and Virginia Polytechnic Institute and State University. In 1987, she received honorary doctorates from Eastern Michigan University and the University of Lowell, Massachusetts and in 1988, she received honorary degrees from North Carolina Central University and Xavier University.

*Mary Futrell, president of the National Education Association, dedicated to quality education for all and equal rights for women.*

A tireless educator, she has spent almost all of her adult professional life involved in providing or maintaining the quality of education provided youngsters in the nation's schools. By trade, a classroom teacher, who began her teaching career in Alexandria, Virginia, she has moved through the ranks, so to speak, to become president of the 1.9 million-member National Education Association, a position she has held since 1983. She was re-elected to an unprecedented third term as president of the NEA during the Association's 1987 convention.

In Alexandria, where she taught high school business education, Futrell was president of the Education Association of Alexandria, the local NEA affiliate, from 1973-75. She went on to become president of the Virginia Education Association serving two terms between 1976-78.

Throughout these years, Futrell was involved at the national level of the Association, serving on the NEA Board of Directors and on other national panels such as the NEA Task Force on School Volunteers.

Futrell also headed the NEA Human Relations Committee, was a member of the Special Committee on Attacks on Public Education, and served on the NEA's Freedom Hall Committee, a panel furthering the construction campaign efforts of the Martin Luther King, Jr. Center in Atlanta. She was a co-convener of the August 1983 observance of the 20th anniversary celebration of the historic march on Washington led by Dr. King.

Futrell is a member of the Select Committee on Education of Black Youth, a group of national black leaders in education, religion and politics working to develop a "National Manifesto" to aid minority youths.

Appointed to the Education Commission of the States by former Virginia Governor Charles Robb in 1982, Futrell was reappointed by Governor Gerald Baliles for a term that runs to 1990. Governor Baliles also named her to his Israel-Virginia Commission. She also has served on state advisory committees on career education (1977), the education of the handicapped (1977), civil rights (1978), and teacher certification (1977-82).

In 1985, *Ms* magazine named Futrell one of 12 "Women of the Year." *Ebony* magazine honored her as the outstanding black business and professional person for 1984, and cited her as one of the 100 most influential blacks in America for 1985, 1986, 1987, and 1988. The *Ladies Home Journal* in 1984 named the NEA president one of the country's 100 top women.

Futrell also has international credentials having traveled to many parts of the world in pursuit of education, human rights and women's rights. In 1980, she attended an international teachers' conference to combat racism, anti-Semitism and violations of human rights in Tel Aviv. In December 1982, she returned to observe Israeli schools and education methods at the invitation of the Israeli Teachers Union. In 1981, under the sponsorship of the Ford Foundation and the National committee on U.S.-China Relations, she joined a delegation of women leaders who were invited to visit the country by the All-China Women's Federation. In 1987, she led a 64-member NEA delegation to China as part of an educational exchange program. In 1982, Futrell also headed an NEA delegation to the French Syndicate National des Instituteurs et Professeurs de College (SNI- PEGC), one of the major teachers' unions in France, to study the country's education system and the activities of the union. In 1984, she led an NEA delegation that studied the Japanese education system and the operation of Japan's schools.

The Virginia Education Association recognized Futrell's socially oriented public service by awarding her the Fitz Turner Human Rights Award in 1976. The National Conference of Christians and Jews twice — in 1976 and 1986 — recognized her efforts in the field of human relations.

Futrell also served five years as president of ERAmerica, a national group dedicated to passage of the Equal Rights Amendment. She is a member of the Women's and Labor Councils of the Democratic National Committee and chairs NEA's independent Political Action Committe (NEA-PAC).

Futrell and her husband, Donald Futrell, also a classroom teacher, live in Lorton, Virginia.

## PHYLLIS T. GARLAND
### Journalist

Phyllis ("Phyl") Garland is a journalism professor at Columbia University in New York City. The former *Ebony* editor is an expert on black music and musicians and her book, *The*

*Former public administrator, Anna Arnold Hedgeman served at the federal, state, and municipal levels of government.*

*Sound of Soul: The Story of Black Music,* is used as a text in many high school and college music courses. Born in McKeesport, Pa., she studied journalism at Northwestern University. While writing for the Pittsburgh *Courier* newspaper, she received the 1962 Golden Quail award as "outstanding feature writer."

## GLORIA GASTON
### Diplomat

A career diplomat, Gloria Gaston is a member of the Foreign Services Office of the Department of State. She became the first black woman to occupy a post of major importance in the Agency for International Development (AID) when she was appointed Human Resources Development Officer for the Bureau of Latin America in 1970.

A graduate of the University of Washington (B.A., 1948), Miss Gaston has done graduate work at the New School for Social Research in New York City. Her first government assignment was as a Peace Corps liaison officer (1962-1964). Later she served in the Sudan with a Columbia research team gathering data on possible investment programs there.

Miss Gaston has also held a number of important posts with private organizations—among them the Bank Street College of Education, the National Conference of Christians and Jews, and the American Society of African Culture.

## REGINA GOFF
### Professor, Retired Public Official

A specialist in child development and welfare, Dr. Regina Goff has worked in the field of education for many years. From 1965 to 1971, she was Assistant Commissioner responsible for programs for the disadvantaged in the U.S. Office of Education, Washington, D.C.

Born in St. Louis in 1917, she received a B.A. in Education from Northwestern University in 1936, and later, both an M.A. and a Ph.D. in child development from Columbia University. She has taught both nursery school and kindergarten, and has served as chairman of the department of child development at Florida A & M, state supervisor of Negro elementary schools for the Florida Department of Education, and professor of education at Morgan State College in Baltimore.

In 1955, Dr. Goff was appointed consultant to the Ministry of Education in Iran by the International Cooperation Administration (now the Agency for International Development). In 1971 she accepted a professorship at the University of Maryland.

She is a member of the American Psychological Association and president of the Maryland Association of Teachers of Education.

## JESSIE P. GUZMAN
### Educator

The distinguished teaching career of Jessie P. Guzman, which began in 1918 in the schools of Greensboro, N.C., came to an end in 1965 when she retired as professor of history and director of the Department of Records and Research at Tuskegee Institute in Alabama.

A native of Savannah, Mrs. Guzman was educated at Clark College in Atlanta, Columbia University, and the University of Chicago. Before her appointment to the Tuskegee faculty in 1924, Mrs. Guzman had taught at Dillard University in New Orleans and had served as a secretary to the New York City Bible Society. She left Tuskegee after one year to join the faculty of Alabama State Teachers College in Montgomery, but returned to the former school in 1930 to begin an uninterrupted 34-year tenure there. She served as teacher, research assistant, and dean of women at Tuskegee prior to accepting the positions she held at the time of her retirement.

A leader in the civic affairs of her community, Mrs. Guzman has also written some 15 books, pamphlets, and articles. In 1947 and again in 1952, she was the editor of the *Negro Year Book*, and she later served as secretary to the Southern Conference Educational Fund and as director of the Tuskegee branch of the NAACP. She now lives in retirement in Tuskegee.

## ANNA ARNOLD HEDGEMAN
### Educator

After serving as an administrator in several political and social welfare organizations, Dr. Anna Arnold Hedgeman joined with her husband, Merritt A. Hedgeman, to establish

*Dorothy Height has done much for all women in her service as President of the National Council of Negro Women.*

the Hedgeman Consultant Service in 1967. Their clients include educational institutions, civic, business, and community organizations.

Born in Marshalltown, Ia., Dr. Hedgeman was educated at Hamline University, the University of Minnesota, and the New York School of Social Work. After teaching for two years in Mississippi, she worked in various executive capacities for the YMCAs of Ohio, Jersey City, New York, and Philadelphia for 12 years.

In 1944, she was named executive director of the National Council for the Fair Employment Practices Commission, a position which she held for four years. From 1949 to 1953 she served as assistant to the administrator of the Federal Security Agency (now the Department of Health, Education, and Welfare). In 1954, she became a member of New York Mayor Robert F. Wagner's cabinet with liaison responsibility for eight city departments. From 1963 to 1968 she served as associate director of the Department of Social Justice and director of ecumenical action for the National Council of Churches in 1967.

The recipient of many awards, Dr. Hedgeman is on the boards of the National Conference of Christians and Jews and the United Seamen's Service, and is a member of the National Urban League and the Community Council of New York.

## DOROTHY I. HEIGHT
### Administrator

Before becoming the fourth president of the National Council of Negro Women, Dorothy Height had for many years served as a member of the organization's Board of Directors, later becoming its executive director. Miss Height is also the Associate Director for Leadership Training Services for the Young Women's Christian Association of the United States. From 1952 to 1955 she served as a member of the Defense Advisory Committee on Women in the Services, having been appointed by General George C. Marshall.

A native of Richmond, Va., Miss Height holds a masters degree from New York University and has also studied at the New York School of Social Work. In the fall of 1952, she served as a visiting professor at the Delhi School of Social Work in New Delhi, India. Six years later, Miss Height was appointed to the Social Welfare Board of New York by Governor Averell Harriman, and was reappointed by Governor Nelson Rockefeller in 1961 for another five years.

In 1960, Miss Height was sent to five African countries by the Committee on Correspondence to make a study of women's organizations there. In addition to the presidency of the National Council of Negro Women, Miss Height also holds the office of vice-president of the National Council of Women of the United States.

In May 1973, she was elected president of Women in Community Services, Inc. Her recent accomplishments include designing a vast program sponsored by the Agency for International Development and serving as a chief architect for the 1974-1975 International Women's Year program.

## AILEEN C. HERNANDEZ
### Public Affairs Consultant

Aileen C. Hernandez is a consultant and lecturer on urban affairs and public relations. From 1965 to 1966, she was a commissioner on the U.S. Equal Employment Opportunity Commission.

Born in New York City, Mrs. Hernandez attended Howard University in Washington, D.C., where she was active in student civil rights work. In 1959, she received an M.A. from Los Angeles State College, and she has since studied at New York University, UCLA, and the University of Oslo in Norway.

She has had several years' experience with the educational program of the International Ladies Garment Workers Union on the West Coast, and in the summer of 1960, toured six Latin American countries under the auspices of the State Department, giving lectures on labor education and reporting on the position of minority groups in the United States.

Mrs. Hernandez is a member of several national organizations, including the NAACP, the Urban League, and Americans for Democratic Action. In 1961, she was selected "Woman of the Year" by the Community Relations Conference of Southern California. In 1971, she was elected president of NOW (the National Organization for Women).

*Aileen Hernandez, former president of the National Organization for Women (NOW).*

*Jean Blackwell Hutson, former curator of New York's prestigious Schomburg Library.*

## CHARLOTTE MOTON HUBBARD
### Public Official

Charlotte Hubbard has had a long and distinguished career in communications and politics. Appointed in May of 1964 as Deputy Assistant Secretary of State for Public Affairs, she served in the highest permanent federal position ever held by a black woman until her retirement in 1970.

Born in Hampton, Va., Mrs. Hubbard received a junior college certificate in home economics from Tuskegee Institute, a B.S. in education at Boston University, and did graduate work both at the latter school and at Bennington College. Before joining the government, she was an instructor and later an associate professor of physical education at Hampton Institute.

In 1942 Mrs.Hubbard—largely on the recommendation of Eleanor Roosevelt—was named recreation representative in what became the Department of Health, Education and Welfare, her main job being that of organizing communities where a particular need for welfare and recreational facilities existed.

Some 10 years later, Mrs. Hubbard became the first black person to be appointed to an important position with a television station (WTOP-TV) in Washington, D.C. From 1958 to 1963, she was public relations assistant of the United Givers Fund, an organization linking local and national welfare agencies.

She is a trustee of Southeastern College, on the board of governors of the Women's National Democratic Club, and on the board of directors of the Educational Community Association. In 1970, she was named one of the Foremost Women in Communications.

## JANE EDNA HUNTER
### Social Worker
### 1882-1971

Jane Hunter spent the early years of her life in her home state of South Carolina, before taking nurses training in Virginia and then migrating north in search of a better job. However, she had great difficulty finding suitable employment in Cleveland, and it was not until she met the secretary to the physician of John D. Rockefeller that she received any real help in securing a satisfactory position.

By this time, she was acutely aware of the need for an institution to aid other black women coming to Cleveland in search of employment. With this in mind, she called the first meeting of the Working Girls' Home Association (later renamed the Phyllis Wheatley Association) in 1911. Although the early years of the Association were ones of hardship, it was able to expand both its boarding facilities and other services after receiving a substantial grant from Rockefeller in 1917.

Although much of her time was occupied by her obligations to the Association, Miss Hunter was able to study law for four years at Baldwin Wallace College. She was admitted to the bar in 1925, after which she continued her work with the Association. Under her guidance, several similar organizations have been established in leading cities across the country.

Miss Hunter died in Cleveland in January 1971, at the age of 89. In her will she bequeathed $427,107 to aid young women in South Carolina.

### CHARLAYNE HUNTER-GAULT
### Journalist

Charlayne Hunter-Gault is an anchorwoman for WNET television news and was formerly a reporter for *The New York Times* and chief of that newspaper's Harlem bureau, which she founded in the late 1960s to make certain that reportage about black persons would begin to "provide stories about human beings rather than sociological stereotypes."

Born in Due West, S.C., she pioneered the admission of black women to the University of Georgia (B.A., journalism, 1963). By graduation time her writing style was fine enough to win her a berth on the staff of the prestigious *New Yorker* magazine as a "Talk of the Town" contributor and a short story writer. Leaving the magazine in 1967, she accepted a Russell Sage Fellowship at Washington University to pursue her studies in the social sciences and simultaneously began her career in media news, working with WRL/NBC News, Washington, D.C.

### JEAN BLACKWELL HUTSON
### Library Administrator

Jean Blackwell Hutson served as curator of the prestigious Schomburg Collection of Negro Life and History for more than 25 years. The Schomburg Collection is a special noncirculating library and autonomous research division within the New York Public Library system. The collection grew immensely under Mrs. Hutson's guidance, which reflects her expert acquisitions, alert reading of the expanding relevance of black studies materials, and internationalist outlook. The Schomburg now has vertical files, microfilm, tapes and records, and photographs in addition to books and periodicals from all over the world. It is the single most important repository on black culture and achievement in the United States.

A native of Summerfield, Fla., Mrs. Hutson earned her B.A. in 1935. A year later she received a B.S. from the Columbia School of Library Service. Her first assignment in the New York Public Library system was as branch librarian of Woodstock in the Bronx. She has been with Schomburg since 1948, although she took a leave of absence in 1964-1965 to serve as assistant librarian at the University of Ghana. After her return to New York, she served as chairman of the Harlem Cultural Council.

Mrs. Hutson has been a lecturer at City College and belongs to numerous organizations which cultivate interest in, and promote the study of, the heritage of Africa. These include the American Society of African Culture and the African Studies Association. Mrs. Hutson is a Delta, and a member of the NAACP, the National Urban League, and the American Library Association.

*Beverly Johnson, first black model to adorn the cover of Vogue.*

### BEVERLY JOHNSON
### Fashion Model

Beverly Johnson was considered one of the world's top high fashion models as well as an outspoken and career-minded young woman from Buffalo, N.Y. Smart enough to win a full academic scholarship to Boston's Northeastern University, she left for New York City after her freshman year to see if she'd find the instant modeling success her friends predicted. She did. Within two years she was a star in the high fashion world, and in August 1974 she landmarked the first black cover for *Vogue* magazine. Her professional dedication coupled with beautifully photogenic features and figure made her, during this time period, one of the most sought after mannequins. When a radio host commented that she was the "biggest black model in the business," she replied: "No, I'm not. I'm the biggest model—period."

### MAIDA SPRINGER KEMP
### Labor Leader

Maida Springer Kemp is a general organizer and member of the international staff of the International Ladies Garment Workers Union, and is a consultant for the African Labor History Center. Born in Panama City, Panama, she studied at Wellesley College, Rand School of Social Sciences in New York, and with the education department of the ILGWU. She joined the Dressmakers Union (AFL-CIO) in 1933, became a member of its executive board (1938-1942), and was a captain in the Women's Health Brigade (1942-1944). She served in East and West Africa as a representative in the Department of International Affairs, AFL-CIO, (1959-1965), was an ILGWU organizer in the Southwestern United States

(1965-1968), and organized the Midwestern Regional Office of the A. Philip Randolph Institute (1969-1972). She is vice president of the National Council of Negro Women, a member of the board of the DuSable History Museum, and a life member of the NAACP.

### ELIZABETH DUNCAN KOONTZ
### Educator, Government Official

Mrs. Elizabeth Duncan Koontz has devoted most of her professional life to the field of classroom education, having served as a teacher in the public schools of Salisbury, N.C., from 1938 to 1965, the year she became president of the 1.1-million-member National Education Association (NEA). A year later she was appointed Director of the Women's Bureau in the Department of Labor, and in a related assignment, named U.S. Delegate to the U.S. Commission on the Status of Women. Mrs. Koontz resigned her directorship in late 1972.

Early in her teaching career, she developed what became a lifelong interest in "supposedly mentally retarded" children, whom she herself generally classifies as slow learners needing only patience and understanding before they will develop the same rate of perception and level of skill as other less-neglected pupils.

Mrs. Koontz was once head of North Carolina's all-black NEA affiliate, as well as the Association's largest division, the 820,000-member Association of Classroom Teachers. Once in office as NEA head, she made it clear that she anticipated trouble as soon as teachers began to organize, agitate, and strike for higher pay and improved conditions. When the NEA did in fact stage strikes, she advised communities to adjust to teachers' demands and support bona fide attempts to upgrade the caliber of teaching candidates by making the profession more lucrative.

From 1975 until 1982, she served as Assistant State Schools Superintendent. She retired in 1982.

Her husband, a former math teacher died in 1986. They had no children. Elizabeth Koontz died Jan 5, 1989.

### LUCY LANEY
### Educator
### 1854-1933

Lucy Craft Laney, born a slave in Macon, Ga., rose to become the founder and principal of Haines Normal Institute in Georgia. Her work was made possible largely through the early efforts of her master's sister, who taught her to read at the age of four and later enabled her to enter Atlanta University.

After graduating from the first class there, Miss Laney taught for several years in the public schools of Savannah before accepting an invitation from the Presbyterian Board of Missions for Freedmen to start a private school in Atlanta. When the funds from the Board were not forthcoming, Miss Laney decided to raise the money for the school herself. In

*Elizabeth Koontz was appointed by President Richard Nixon as Director of the Women's Bureau of the Department of Labor. Mrs. Koontz and the President are flanked by George Shultz (right) and Arnold Weber (left).*

*Jewel Jackson McCabe, extensively involved with many vital social issues.*

1886, the school was first opened in the remodeled basement of a church, and though beset by financial difficulties, was able to accommodate over 200 pupils by its second year.

Such generous financial aid was received from Mrs. F. E. H. Haines of Milwaukee that it was soon decided to name the school after its benefactor. Further allocations from the Presbyterian Mission Board, together with donations of land from other sources, made it possible for Haines to expand from a one-room school to the prospering educational community of over 1,000 students which it is today.

## MARJORIE LAWSON
### Lawyer

In August of 1962, Marjorie M. Lawson became the first black woman to be appointed to a judgeship by a president of the United States, and the first black woman ever to be approved by the Senate for a statutory appointment. She resigned from the bench in 1965 and is now back in private practice.

Born in Pittsburgh in 1912, Mrs. Lawson graduated from the University of Michigan in 1933 and received a Certificate in Social Work there the next year. In 1939, she earned the Bachelor of Law degree from the Terrell Law School in Washington, D.C., and in 1950 from the Columbia University School of Law.

Admitted to the District of Columbia Bar in 1939, Mrs. Lawson engaged in private practice with her husband, Belford V. Lawson Jr., until the time of her appointment to the bench. She wrote a weekly public affairs column for 15 years for the Pittsburgh *Courier*.

She has held a variety of social work positions, often employing her capacity as a lawyer to act as counsel for families in the Juvenile Court of the District of Columbia. She has also been active in several organizations dealing with housing and employment problems, among them the National Urban League, and has held the post of Vice-President of the National Council of Women.

In 1958, Mrs. Lawson became race relations advisor to Senator John F. Kennedy, and upon his nomination for the presidency, was named director of civil rights for his campaign. In 1962, Kennedy named her to his Committee on Equal Employment Opportunity.

## MARIAN B. LOGAN
### Civil Rights Activist, Public Official

Marian B. Logan was appointed Chair of the New York City Commission on Human Rights by Mayor Abraham D. Beame on June 8, 1977. Commissioner Logan has a long and substantive record in the field of human rights, and is widely known for her leadership in the civil rights movement.

A civil rights activist since the movement's earliest days, Commissioner Logan served from 1960 through 1968 as Director of Special Projects for Dr. Martin Luther King Jr., acting as "troubleshooter" to put into effect diverse civil rights projects and to implement affirmative action programs in businesses, government agencies, labor unions, religious organizations and community groups. Commissioner Logan initiated some of the first fund-raising efforts in the 1950's in the Northeast for the student non-violent movement in the South, and later coordinated the recruitment and training of college students from across the country to prepare them for voter education and registration drives in Alabama, Georgia, and Mississippi.

Commissioner Logan has served since 1962 as Secretary to the Southern Christian Leadership Conference (SCLC) organizing activities among major civil rights groups. As a Coordinator of the massive Poor People's March on Washington in 1968, she was liaison between the Justice Department and SCLC for Resurrection City. Commissioner Logan has also appeared in many forums, speaking on behalf of civil rights and civil liberties.

Commissioner Logan's commitment to women's rights parallels her concern for racial justice. The National Council of Negro Women chose her in 1964 to participate in the first interracial team sent to Mississippi to build "a bridge of understanding between women in the South and those from across the U.S.A." In 1973, the Phelps Stokes Fund selected her as emissary on behalf of American black women to discuss women's rights with the national leadership of Africa. In 1979, Commissioner Logan was appointed as a special assistant to the New York State Department of transportation by then Governor Hugh Carey and reappointed by Governor Mario Cuomo; she resigned the position in 1986 to devote more time to her activities with charities. She is a founder and member of both the Bayard Rustin Foundation and the Jackie Robinson Foundation, organizations to which she contributes a great deal of time and effort. Among Commissioner Logan's other civic activities are: Advisory Board member, New York Urban League; Board member Medgar Evers Fund; Board member, National Council of Negro Women; member, and Coalition of 100 Black Women.

*Marion Logan has been involved in the civil rights movement since the effective era of the movement began in the 60s.*

### JEWELL JACKSON McCABE
### Community Affairs Specialist

Jewell Jackson McCabe is president of the National Coalition of 100 Black Women and is Director of WNET-TV/Thirteen's Government and Community Affairs Department in New York City. As director of that department, Ms. McCabe plays an important role in Thirteen's relations with federal, state, and city governments, and with major community relations organizations in the tri-state metropolitan area.

The daughter of broadcast pioneer Hal Jackson, Ms. McCabe, who attended Bard College, has been an active leader in civic and community affairs for a number of years. In her short career, Ms. McCabe has distinguished herself as an important spokesperson and role model for today's contemporary black woman. She has been recognized by several national organizations, including the Women's Equity Action League (WEAL), which is the leading national women's advocacy group, and the national YWCA, which saluted her for outstanding service on behalf of women in business. Ms. McCabe has become an advisor to leaders in the public and private sector related to minority issues and concerns. She serves on the boards of the National Urban Coalition, the Overseas Education Fund, Community Council of Greater New York, Lenox Hill Hospital, and the New York Urban League. She is also a member of the Board of Directors of Planned Parenthood of New York, the Women's Forum, and the Executive Committee of the Association for a Better New York, the Policy Committee of the New York Partnership chaired by David Rockefeller, and a Commissioner for the New York City Commission on the Status of Women.

### ERNESTINE McCLENDON
### Theatrical Agent

Ernestine McClendon Enterprises, named for its owner and founder, is a theatrical agency which represents several hundred well-known television, movie, stage, and radio actors, as well as writers, directors, and variety acts. Born in Norfolk, Va., Ms. McClendon began her career as a stage actress. Moving on to teaching, she organized the Harlem Workshop. She was the first theatrical agent to be recognized by all unions and was one of the major people responsible for getting blacks into television commercials. She won the Woman's Award (1969) and was named one of Two Thousand Women of Achievement (1970).

### ROSALIE J. McGUIRE
### Educator

Rosalie J. McGuire is president of the National Association of Negro Business and Professional Women's Clubs, Inc. Born in Baltimore, she studied at Morgan State College (B.A.), New York University (M.A.), and Johns Hopkins and Columbia universities. Entering the profession of education, she became principal of Bentalou Elementary School in Baltimore. She has been first vice president of the Maryland League of Women's Clubs, co-chairman of Baltimore's Provident Hospital Development Program, and national education chairperson and national first vice president of the NBPWC. Mrs. McGuire is on the board of directors of Provident Hospital and is a member of the National Council of Women of the United States and the President's Committee on the Employment of the Handicapped.

### MILDRED MITCHELL-BATEMAN
### Psychiatrist, Administrator

When Mildred Mitchell-Bateman became director of West Virginia's Department of Mental Health in 1962, she advanced the causes of both black and women's rights, becoming the country's first female mental health chief and the state's first black department head. She has shown her fitness for the post by increasing the number of West Virginia communities offering mental health services from four to 54, and by her success in obtaining much more Federal money for her state. Born in Cordele, Ga., she was

*Eleanor Holmes Norton, a former chairperson of the EEOC now a strong voice for civil rights as an attorney.*

a student at Johnson C. Smith University (B.S., 1941), Women's Medical College of Pennsylvania (M.D., 1946), and the Menninger School of Psychiatry (three-year residency, 1957). After internship in New York and private practice in Philadelphia, she transferred to Lakin State Hospital, where she worked as physician, clinic director, and superintendent, until assuming her present position.

## JEANNE NOBLE
### Educator, Guidance Expert

Dr. Jeanne Noble is a full professor at Brooklyn College School of Education in New York City, where she works with graduate students in the guidance and counseling programs. In July 1975, she was appointed by President Ford to the National Advisory Council on Professional Development.

A product of a poverty-stricken environment in Albany, Ga., she graduated from Howard University before going on to take two postgraduate degrees at the Teachers College of New York's Columbia University. Having specialized in guidance and developmental psychology, Dr. Noble returned to her hometown to teach social science at Albany State College. She later was a visiting professor at Tuskegee Institute and the University of Vermont, and has taught human relations at New York University.

With her extensive background in the fields of education and social service, Dr. Noble was well-equipped to accept Sargent Shriver's 1964 offer to head a committee in drawing up plans for the Girls' Job Corps. Her other activities in the field of social service include work with the Girl Scouts, HARYOU-ACT in Harlem, the National Social Welfare Assembly, and the President's Commission on the Status of Women. In 1975 she was chairperson for the Arts and Letters Committee of Delta Sigma Theta. In addition to publishing articles in several professional journals, she is author of *The Negro Woman's College Education.*

In 1963 Dr. Noble was named by *Ebony* magazine as "one of the 100 most influential Negroes of the Emancipation Centennial Year." She received the 1965 Bethune-Roosevelt Award for service in the field of education.

## ELEANOR HOLMES NORTON
### Attorney

Born in Washington, D.C., Eleanor Holmes Norton is a graduate of Antioch College and holds masters and law degrees from Yale University. In 1977, Mrs. Norton was appointed chairperson of the Equal Employment Opportunity

*Rosa Parks, some call her the mother of the 60s civil rights revolution. The resultant effect of her refusal to move to the back of the bus in 1955 was to start the dominoes to fall.*

Commission (EEOC). Mrs. Norton also has headed the New York City Human Rights Commission, a post she was appointed to in 1970. She has long included sex among the irrational factors which sometimes cause discrimination and has worked diligently to remove this consideration from the list of acceptable job criteria. She is a former teacher of black history and participated in the freedom marches as a SNCC worker. While chairman of the New York City Human Rights Commission, Mrs. Norton co-hosted a Sunday morning television program along with Art Rust Jr.

In 1968, while serving as a Civil Liberties Attorney, Mrs. Norton demonstrated her dedication to principle by pressing for the right of George Wallace to hold an outdoor rally at Shea Stadium. She followed through on her stand despite stiff opposition from the mayor and noisy protests from other liberal quarters.

### ESTELLE MASSEY OSBORNE
### Nurse

With her appointment in February of 1945 to the faculty of New York University, Estelle Osborne became the first black woman instructor at that school. She began her duties with the Department of Nursing Education in the spring of that year.

Prior to her appointment, Mrs. Osborne had already had a long career in nursing and allied fields. An instructor of nursing at Harlem and Lincoln hospitals from 1929 to 1931, she later served as director of the Freedmen's Nursing School and of the Homer Phillips School in St. Louis. She was also a consultant on the staff of the National Nursing Council for War Service.

Active throughout her life in public health organizations, Mrs. Osborne has also served as vice-president of the National Council of Negro Women. In 1943, the "Estelle Massey Scholarship" was established in her honor at Fisk University, and in 1946 she was the recipient of the Mary Mahoney Award in recognition of her contributions to nursing.

Mrs. Osborne is now retired and living in Queens, N.Y.

### ROSA PARKS
### Civil Rights Activist

There is about her name no discernible ring nor aura of distinction. There is about her dress and manner no singular, commanding, or memorable uniqueness. Her story, however, is one of the most inspirational to come out of the civil rights movement, a simple message to all that human dignity cannot interminably be undermined by brute force.

On the evening of December 1, 1955, Rosa Parks boarded a public bus in Montgomery, Ala., took a seat with the other passengers, and prepared to relax for 15 minutes or so before arriving home. As the bus began to fill up, however, the number of seats dwindled until, within a few minutes, there were none left. As soon as the white bus driver noticed that a black woman was occupying a seat in the "white" section of the bus while a white passenger was standing, he ordered the "offender" to the rear.

The "offender" did not make a scene when she refused. She did not scream; she did not whine; she did not threaten; she did not exhort. She simply did not move, thus forcing those who would force her to move to make the next move.

Rosa Parks was arrested, jailed, and brought to trial while the rest of the once quiescent black community refused to ride public buses. Mrs. Parks was the catalyst in the Montgomery boycott, the first public confrontation which brought the name of Martin Luther King Jr., into the ears of America.

Mrs. Parks paid dearly for her courage. Her husband, a barber, became ill from the pressure; the family ultimately moved to Detroit, where Parks resumed his profession. Mrs. Parks did sewing and alterations at home until she found a job as a dressmaker.

In Detroit, she has since become active in youth work, job guidance, cultural and recreational planning—the daily grind of a community activist. Dr. King, while he lived, once called her "the great fuse that led to the modern stride toward freedom." She made the stride while sitting still.

Mrs. Parks is presently a receptionist-secretary to Representative John Conyers. A religious person, she serves as deaconess of St. Matthews A.M.E. church in Detroit. She accepts many speaking engagements because she wants to help "young people grow, develop, and reach their potential."

### DOROTHY PORTER
### Library Administrator, Author

Dorothy Porter is former librarian of Howard University's Moorland-Spingarn Collection in Washington, D.C., which she shepherded to its enormous collection of more than 165,000 books and reference tools dealing with black history and culture. Born in Warrenton, Va., she studied at Howard University (A.B., 1928) and Columbia University (B.S., library science, 1931; M.S., 1932). She is the author of several articles on black history for various books and scholarly journals, a member of Phi Beta Kappa, and the winner of many awards, including a 1971 Distinguished Service Award from the student body of Howard's College of Liberal Arts. Since her retirement, she lives in Washington, D.C.

### ERSA H. POSTON
### Government Official

Ersa H. Poston, a top official with the Federal Civil Service Commission, was born in Paducah, Ky. and is a 1942 graduate of Kentucky State College. She received her M.A. degree in 1946 in social work from Atlanta University. Mrs. Poston was formerly director of the New York State Office of Economic Opportunity and in 1967 was appointed president of the New York Civil Service Commission. She began her career working in various youth programs and in 1964 was named confidential assistant to Governor Nelson Rockefeller. Mrs. Poston is a member of a number of organizations and has received many awards and citations for her community involvement.

*Bernice Fletcher Powell, president of the coalition of 100 Black Women of New York.*

## BERNICE FLETCHER POWELL
### Public Information Specialist

Bernice Fletcher Powell is president of the Coalition of 100 Black Women of New York, an organization of women from a cross section of the business, corporate, and private sector of the city. Born in Washington, D.C., Mrs. Powell is special assistant for public information, Women's Division of the Governor's Office of New York. She is a board member of the New York Urban League and is chairperson of the Riverside Church Video Project. Mrs. Powell received her B.A. from Wilson College and her M.S. from Columbia University Graduate School of Journalism.

## VIRGINIA ESTELLE RANDOLPH
### Social Worker
### 1876-1958

Concerned with the problems of youth, Virginia E. Randolph was both a teacher and a social worker in the area of juvenile affairs. Born of slave parents in Richmond, Va., she was able to receive an education at the Bacon School and the City Normal School, both in her native city. At the age of 16, she took her first teaching job in Goochland County, Va., holding it for three years before moving to a small schoolhouse in Henrico County.

In 1908, she accepted an important appointment as the first supervisor of the Jeanes Fund, a philanthropic organization established by Anna Jeanes, a Philadelphia Quaker, to finance black rural schools in the South. Having for many years emphasized the importance of vocational training for youth, Miss Randolph often worked in conjunction with the Richmond Juvenile and Domestic Relations Court and in 1926 received the Harmon Award in recognition of her outstanding social service.

She retired in 1948 as supervisor of education in Henrico County, and was honored the next year at an appreciation service given her by many educators of both races.

## LILLIAN ROBERTS
### Labor Leader

Lillian Roberts is the Commissioner of Labor for the New York State Labor Department. Mrs. Roberts was formerly the Associate Director of District Council 37 of the American Federation of State, County and Municipal Employees (AFSCME), AFL-CIO. As associate director of AFSCME, Mrs. Roberts headed the largest union in New York City. She was sworn in as Commissioner of Labor by New York Governor Hugh Carey on July 2, 1981. Mrs. Roberts began her career in 1945 in Chicago as a nurse's aide and operating room technician. During the years of 1958 and 1965, she was employed by AFSCME District Councils 19 and 34 to organize state mental health employees and volunteer hospital workers in Illinois.

In 1965, Mrs. Roberts came to New York City as Hospital Division Director for DC 37. Governor Carey named Mrs. Roberts a trustee of the State University of New York in 1979 and she has served as an International Vice President of the national AFSCME organization and at the Governor's request, she has served on the State Advisory Council on Substance Abuse.

She has been cited by a number of groups for her dedication to human rights and for her work in furthering minority-labor relations.

## LUCILLE MASON ROSE
### Civil Servant

New York City's Commissioner of Employment, Lucille Mason Rose oversees an agency which attempts to find skilled job openings and then train unskilled and uneducated workers to qualify for the jobs. Born in Richmond, Va., she came to Brooklyn's Bedford-Stuyvesant section as a young child when her family moved North. While attending Girls' High, she joined the local branch of the NAACP. She has always been a firm believer in diligent work and personal responsibility. When her husband enlisted in World War II, she enrolled as a welding trainee at the Brooklyn Navy Yard to earn money for their house mortgage.

In 1949, Mrs. Rose joined the Department of Social Services. She graduated from Brooklyn College at night in 1963 (B.A. economics), and was shortly thereafter appointed director of the Bedford-Stuyvesant field office of the city's Department of Labor. When the poverty programs centralized

*Lillian Roberts, Commissioner of the Labor Department for the State of New York.*

neighborhood employment services in 1966, Mrs. Rose became the first director of the Bedford-Stuyvesant Manpower Center. Mayor Lindsay appointed her first deputy commissioner of the Manpower and Development Agency in 1970, where she remained until November 1972, when she was named to be the city's employment chief.

Under Mrs. Rose's direction, the city's employment agency locates employment openings and then trains people on the job, a program which avoids the old pitfall of training workers for nonexistent jobs. "Our main concern," she says, "is to get poor people into jobs."

## BETTY SHABAZZ
## Community Activist

The widow of Malcolm X, Betty Shabazz is currently dedicating the major part of her energies to raising their children according to his principles and ideas. Born in Detroit, she studied at Tuskegee Institute, Brooklyn State Hospital School of Nursing (R.N.), and Jersey City State College (B.A., public health education; certified school nurse). She is a director of the African-American Foundation, the Day Care Council of Westchester County, and the Women's Service League; a trustee of the National Housewives League; and a co-chairman of the advisory board of the *Amsterdam News* newspaper. She lives in Mt. Vernon, N.Y.

## NAOMI SIMS
## Fashion Model

Naomi Sims manages to be both one of America's leading fashion models and a dedicated community worker. This diversity of talents can be traced back to her school days when she was a scholarship student at both the Fashion Institute of Technology and New York University (psychology). Born in Oxford, Mississippi, she was the first black model to appear in a television commercial, to grace the cover of a major women's magazine (*Ladies Home Journal),* and to be featured in *Vogue*. She has been on the cover of *Life*, and in 1969/70 was voted Model of the Year by International Famous Mannequins.

## SUSAN SMITH MC KINNEY STEWART
## Physician
## 1848-1918

Born in Brooklyn , in a house on the corner of Fulton St. and Buffalo Avenue, she was the daughter of a prosperous family. Her father was a successful pig farmer, who was listed in directories of the time as a pig merchant. She was the seventh of ten children. As a child, Susan was a serious student of music and studied under the tutelage of two famous organists of NYC. Her career interests shifted toward medicine and she eventually graduated from the New York Medical School for Women and Children in 1870, the third African American Women graduate in the US. and the first in NY State.

She practiced 24 years in Brooklyn as Dr. Susan Smith [1870-73] and as Dr. Susan Mc Kinney from 1874-95. Her office was located at 205 De Kalb Avenue, which is not too distant from the Bridget Street A.M.E. Church where she was choir director and not far from the 101 Park Avenue site of JHS 265 which was renamed in her honor on September 15, 1974.

Dr. Mc Kinney also maintained an office in Manhattan. She was a member of the medical staff of the NY Medical College and Hospital for Women at 213 W. 54 Street between Broadway and Seventh Ave., in 1882. During 1887-88, she did post-graduate study at L.I. Medical College Hospital in Brooklyn. She was one of the organizers and founders of the Brooklyn Woman's Homeopathic Hospital and Dispensary at Myrtle and Grand Avenues in 1881 and a member of the staff until 1895. The hospital was later renamed the Memorial Hospital for Women and Children and relocated to Prospect Paeade in Brooklyn.

Dr. Mc Kinney was a member of the Kings County Medical Society and the NY State Homeopathic Medical Society. She was the official physician to the Brooklyn

*Naomi Sims, a successful fashion model who has far more to offer than a pretty face.*

Home for Aged Colored People and served as a member of its governing board from 1892-1895. This home is still in operation at 1095 St. John's Place and received a grant to renovate in about 1979.

In 1911, she addressed the International Congress in London, England and lectured on colored women in America.

Her husband died when she was 48 years old. She remarried a US Army chaplain, Theophilus G. Steward and became licensed to practice medicine in both Nebraska and Montana.

In 1898, shortly before Chaplain Steward's retirement from the military, Dr. Mc Kinney Steward went to Ohio to become a member of the faculty and resident physician at Wilberforce University at Xenia. Upon his retirement, he joined her there on the faculty as a teacher of history.

Dr. Steward is buried in Greenwood Cemetery in Brooklyn.

### JUANITA STOUT
### Municipal Court Judge

The first woman ever to reach the bench in Pennsylvania is Juanita Kidd Stout, who was appointed Judge of the Philadelphia Municipal Court by Governor David L. Lawrence in September of 1959. In November of that year, Judge Stout ran in a city-wide election and won a 10-year term, thus becoming the nation's first elected black woman judge.

Judge Stout earned her Master of Laws and Doctor of Jurisprudence degrees at the University of Indiana, and was admitted to the bar in the District of Columbia in 1950 and in Philadelphia in 1954.

Since 1959 she has served as a judge of Philadelphia's Juvenile Court, a position which at times has proven to be a dangerous one. Her safety has often been threatened by those who feel that her methods of dealing with delinquent youth are too severe, but she also has many supporters who feel that her stringent measures have done much to reduce Philadelphia's delinquency rate.

### LYNNETTE DOBBINS TAYLOR
### Executive

Lynnette Dobbins Taylor is executive director of the international sorority Delta Sigma Theta, and is a member of the boards of directors of the National Friends of Public Broadcasting Corporation and the National Center for Voluntary Action. Born in Birmingham, she attended Alabama State Teachers College (B.S., 1939) and Wayne State University (M.S., 1948). In her career she has been New York editor of the *Chicago Defender* and the *Detroit Tribune*, principal of Roosevelt Elementary School, and a program analyst for the Office of Economic Opportunity. She is a director of college and youth activities for the American Red Cross and a member of the Public Committee on Truth in Lending Legislation.

### MARY CHURCH TERRELL
### Women's Rights Advocate
### 1863-1954

An active leader all her life in the campaign for equal rights, Mary Church Terrell was born the year the Emancipation Proclamation was issued and died only a few months after segregation had been declared unconstitutional by the *Brown* v. *Board of education* decision of 1954

A graduate of Oberlin College in 1884, Mrs. Terrell was appointed to the District of Columbia school board in 1895, and in the following year, became one of the charter members of the National Association of Colored Women. She was consistently active in politics, campaigning against the practice of segregation in the United States, and on several occasions acting as a delegate from her country to international conferences.

Born of ex-slave parents in Memphis, Mary Church Terrell chose to make her home in Washington, D.C., a city which remained segregated until 1953. In that year, she headed a committee of Washington citizens who demanded enforcement of a 75-year-old law prohibiting discrimination against "respectable persons" in restaurants. In the resulting test case, the U.S. Supreme Court ruled that the old law was still valid, thus paving the way for the beginning of integration in the public accommodations of the nation's capital.

A year later, having seen the initiation of a new policy which she herself had done much to bring about, Mary Church Terrell died in Annapolis, Md., at the age of 90.

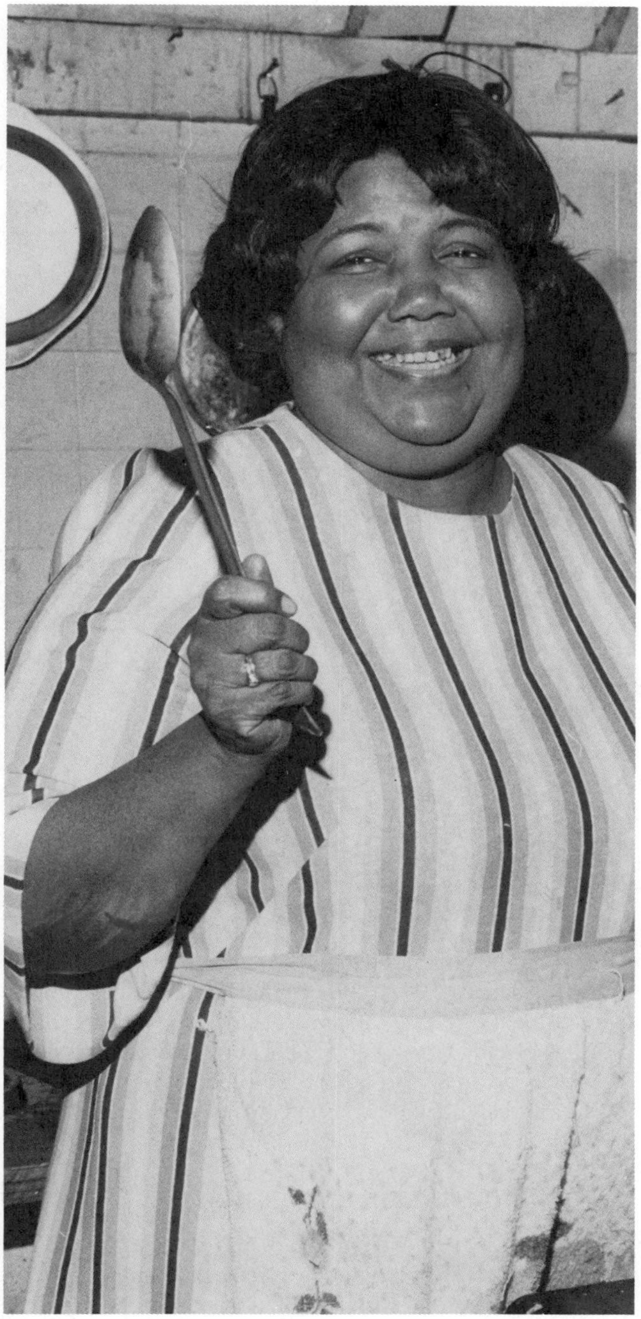

*Charleszetta Waddles, known as Mother Waddles, runs a soup kitchen in Detroit.*

## GLORIA E. A. TOOTE
### Attorney

Dr. Gloria E. A. Toote, regarded as a high-ranking black in the Republican Party, is a New York City attorney. Dr. Toote is a former teacher and was Assistant Secretary for Equal Opportunity of the Housing and Urban Development agency. She was also a HUD contract compliance officer. Dr. Toote is also founder, owner, and builder of Town Sound Studios and is a self-taught recording expert. She has been featured in the *Chicago Tribune, Ebony, Jet*, and the *Washington Post.*

## CHARLESZETTA WADDLES
### Clergywoman

Dedicated to religious and social action, Mother Charleszetta Waddles founded her Perpetual Mission in Detroit in 1957 to help the poor. The mission, which never closes its doors, offers food, shelter, clothing, medical care, and instruction to the needy.

Born in St. Louis, she moved to Detroit and married Payton Waddles, then a Ford Motor Company employee, and raised a family of 10 children. She founded her mission as a nonprofit, nondenominational, religious, charitable organization serving metropolitan Detroit. Staffed mainly by volunteers, the mission operates on funds from private contributions. Mother Waddles leads the worship and directs the social services. Perhaps she is known best for the kitchens she maintains on "Skid Row," where she serves approximately 7,500 meals each month at 35¢ per meal or free to those with no money. Her work has merited numerous humanitarian and outstanding community service awards, including letters of commendation from Vice Presidents Hubert Humphrey and Lyndon Johnson, and from President Richard Nixon. She has had her own radio and television programs and is advisory consultant to Detroit's Shelby Hotel.

Mother Waddles operates with the philosophy that the church should make itself relevant to the needs of the people, and that if a person needs assistance then it is up to the church, above all, to give it to him or her.

## MADAME C. J. WALKER
### Cosmetics Manufacturer
### 1869-1919

Madame C. J. Walker who, because of her innovations in the cosmetics business, was to become one of the wealthiest and most famous women of her race, experienced an early life of poverty and hardship. Born to ex-slave parents in Delta, La., Sarah McWilliams was orphaned at the age of seven, married at 14, and was left a widow with a small child at the age of 20.

Deciding to begin a new life, she traveled to St. Louis and worked as a laundress in order to send her daughter to school. In the 1890s, she married Charles J. Walker, and under the name of Madame C. J. Walker, subsequently made famous her new hair-styling formula.

In 1910, she went to Indianapolis to begin the manufacture of her hair preparations, later adding a complete line of toiletries and cosmetics to her products. As her business expanded, she established many Walker schools of beauty culture across the country. In the process, she became the first black woman millionaire.

Before her death in 1919, Madame Walker was well-known for her philanthropic activities. She made large bequests to the NAACP, the YMCA of St. Louis, Tuskegee Institute, and Bethune-Cookman College, and also stipulated in her will that two-thirds of the profits of her company should be given to charitable organizations.

Today, students from several foreign countries come to the United States to receive training at the Walker beauty schools, and over 2,000 agents represent the Walker system in the country and abroad.

## CORA WALKER
### Attorney, Businesswoman

Cora Walker is best known for bringing to Harlem a cooperative supermarket. Although some have tried to undermine the venture, it has drawn community support. Mrs. Walker was born in Charlotte, N.C., but grew up in the Bronx. She attended St. John's University in Brooklyn and went on to study law. Her public career has involved her in numerous legal and civic projects. Often quoted as a severe critic of the Harlem community, Mrs. Walker has come under fire from many political regulars who feel her views are distorted.

*Cora Walker, coordinator and legal counselor of the Harlem Co-op Supermarket.*

## MAGGIE LENA WALKER
### Banker
### 1867-1934

Born in Richmond, Va., Maggie L. Walker had no specific training for the banking career in which she was later to achieve such notable success. After graduating from high school, she taught for several years before starting as secretary to the Independent Order of St. Luke, a black organization in Virginia.

During this time, she helped establish branches of the Order throughout Virginia and West Virginia. In 1899, she became secretary-treasurer of the organization. Under her guidance, the Order was restored to financial solvency and grew to include an insurance concern and a banking establishment. The latter, which became known as the Consolidated Bank and Trust Company, functioned with Mrs. Walker serving as chairman of the board. She also established and supervised the *St. Luke Herald*, the newspaper which was the official organ of the Order of St. Luke.

A contributor to several charitable organizations, Mrs. Walker was also an organizer and president of the Council of Colored Women, a director of the NAACP, and a board member of the National Urban League.

She died in 1934.

## MARY DAWSON WALTERS
### Librarian

Associate professor of library administration at Ohio State University in Columbus, Mary Dawson Walters doubles as head of the library's acquisition department. The responsibilities of this position include keeping the library abreast of the latest advances in scholarship and allocating a budget of over $1 million a year. A native of Mitchell County, Ga., she is a graduate of Savannah State College (B.S., home economics, 1949) and Atlanta University (M.S., library science, 1957). When she accepted her present appointment in 1961, Mrs. Walters became the first black person to head one of Ohio State's library departments. She has received the Who's Who in Library Service Award (1965) and the Two Thousand Women of Achievement Award (1972).

## BENNETTA B. WASHINGTON
### Administrator

Dr. Bennetta B. Washington is special assistant to William H. Kolberg, assistant secretary of labor for manpower, U.S. Department of Commerce.

Born in Winston-Salem, N.C., she moved as a child to Washington, D.C., with her parents. She received both B.A. and M.A. degrees from Howard University, and later a Ph.D. in sociology from the Catholic University of America.

In 1941, she began working as a counselor in the public school system of Baltimore, leaving in 1944 to act as program director for young adults at the Phillis Wheatley Y.W.C.A. in Washington, D.C. From 1946 to 1965, Dr. Washington worked first as counselor in the Washington schools, then as principal of several different high schools.

In 1965, she was appointed Director of the Women's Job Corps, a branch of the Office of Economic Opportunity, where she remained until accepting her present post.

## FRANCES CRESS WELSING
**Psychiatrist**

Following in the Hippocratic footsteps of both her father and her grandfather, Frances Cress Welsing became a doctor. She is currently assistant professor of pediatrics at Freedmen's Hospital and Howard University School of Medicine in Washington, D.C. Born in Chicago, she received her training at Antioch College and Howard University School of Medicine. She is the author of *The Cress Theory of Color-Confrontation and Racism,* and is a member of the National Medical Association, the American Medical Association, and the American Psychiatric Association.

## GERALDINE WHITTINGTON
**Civil Servant**

During her secretarial career in government service, Geraldine Whittington was one of President Lyndon Johnson's traveling secretaries and later served in the Office of the Chief of Protocol.

Born in West River, Md., she began her career in 1950 as a secretary for the Veterans Administration. By 1961, she had become executive assistant to the Administrator of the Agency for International Development, and was called upon to work as a secretary to Ralph Durgan, special assistant to President John F. Kennedy. In 1963, she joined the staff of Bill Moyers, press secretary to Lyndon Johnson. In December of that year, President Johnson invited her to work with him during his subsequent campaign.

Retired after an illness, Miss Whittington now lives in Washington, D.C.

## MARGARET BUSH WILSON
**Civil Rights Activist**

Mrs. Margaret Bush Wilson is a St. Louis lawyer who has been in the civil rights and public service arena for a number of years. As chairman of the national board of the NAACP, Mrs. Wilson sits at the helm of the 450,000-member organization, the oldest and the largest civil rights body and often regarded as the most feared but yet most respected and the most consulted group in the world.

Mrs. Wilson has served as an assistant attorney general of Missouri, acting legal services specialist in the federal government's war against poverty, and other government positions. She has been associated with the NAACP virtually all her life and is a former president of the St. Louis branch. A member of the national board of directors since 1963, Mrs. Wilson is the first black woman to serve in the NAACP's top policy-making position.

Mrs. Wilson's determination to become a lawyer overshadowed her father's desires for her to merely enter one of the female professions such as nursing, teaching, or social work. Her father was a long-time NAACP member and the first successful black real estate broker in St. Louis.

Following Mrs. Wilson's graduation from Talladega College, where she majored in economics and mathematics, she returned to St. Louis where she entered the Lincoln

*Margaret Bush Wilson, former Chairman, National NAACP.*

University School of Law. Her first assignment following her admission to the Missouri bar in 1943 was to act as counsel for the Real Estate Brokers Association of St. Louis, of which her father was president. She obtained the association's corporate charter. She is a founder of the Model Housing Corporation in St. Louis, which was established to get federal funds in order to improve housing for poor people. Mrs. Wilson took part in a national board hearing in 1972 that resulted in overturning the Atlanta NAACP chapter's compromise policy of allowing that city's school system to remain partially segregated.

## JANE C. WRIGHT
**Surgeon, Educator**

Jane C. Wright is a noted surgeon and educator who was born in New York City. Dr. Wright was director of cancer chemotherapy research and instructor in research surgery at the State University of New York Downstate Medical Center and later became associate dean and professor of surgery at the hospital.

Dr. Wright succeeded her father, Dr. Louis Wright, at Harlem Hospital Cancer Research Foundation as director. As head of the foundation, Dr. Wright pioneered tests in the use of chemotherapy on tumors and other abnormal growths.

She received a B.A. degree from Smith College in Northampton, Mass. in 1942, and her M.D. degree in 1945 from New York Medical College.

Dr. Wright has also been an assistant resident in internal medicine at Bellevue Hospital in New York City, and was also chief medical resident at Harlem Hospital.

## NOTABLE BLACK WOMEN OF THE PAST

| Name | Career | Dates |
|---|---|---|
| Wilhelminia F. Adams | Political activist/ leader | 1905-1987 |
| Sarah Allen | Missionary pioneer | 1764-1849 |
| Caroline Still Anderson M.D. | Physician | 1849-1919 |
| Maria Louise Baldwin | Educator | 1856-1919 |
| Janie Porter Barrett | Educator | 1870-1949 |
| Delilah L. Beasley | Historian, journalist | 1871-1934 |
| Mother Matilda Beasley | Educator, social worker | 1834-1903 |
| Ann Marie Becraft | Educator | 1805-1833 |
| Rosa Dixon Bowser | Educator | 1885-1931 |
| Sue M. Brown | Club leader, organizer | 1877-1941 |
| Nannie Helen Burroughs | Founded Nat. Trade & Prof. School for Women & Girls Washington, D.C. | 1878?-1961 |
| Mary Ann Shadd Cary | Abolitionist, educator | 1823-1893 |
| Myrtle Foster Cook | Teacher, civic leader | 1870-1951 |
| Fannie Jackson Coppin | Teacher, missionary | 1835-1912 |
| Elizabeth Cotten | Housekeeper/ musician | 1892-1987 |
| Anna Murray Douglass | Underground railroad conductor | n.a.-1882 |
| Sarah Mapps Douglass | Abolitionist, educator | 1806-1882 |
| Alice Dunnigan | Chief corresp. Wash Bureau Assoc. Negro Press | 1906-1983 |
| Olivia Davidson | Washington Fund-raiser | 1859-1889 |
| Elleanor Eldridge | Writer | 1785-1845 |
| Mathilda A. Evans | Physician/ founded hospitals, clinics in SC' | 1874-1935 |
| Sarah H. Fayerweather | Underground railroad conductor | 1820-1870 |
| Dorothy B. Ferebee | Physician/educator | 1897-1980 |

| Name | Career | Dates |
|---|---|---|
| Susan E. Frazier | Woman's Guild Founder | 1866-1901 |
| Nora A. Gordon | Teacher, missionary | 1866-1901 |
| Ida Gray, M. D. | Dentist | 1867-n.a. |
| Charlotte F. Grimkea | Teacher, writer, poet | 1838-1914 |
| Emma Azalia Hackley | Teacher, creative artist | 1867-1922 |
| Maude Cuney Hare | Music teacher | 1874-1936 |
| Annie Wealthy Holland | Educator | 1871-1934 |
| Anna Elizabeth Hudlun | Social worker | 1840-1911 |
| Sophia A. Jones | Physician / Spelman faculty | 1885-1888 |
| Lucy Laney | Founder, Haines Institute, GA | 1854-1933 |
| Adella H. Logan | Educator | 1863-1915 |
| Victoria Matthews | Social worker | 1861-1898 |
| Emma G. Merrit | Educator | 1860-1933 |
| Gertrude Mossell | Newspaper editor | 1855-? |
| Mary Mossell | Teacher, missionary | 1853-1866 |
| Margaret Murray | Washington Woman's club organizer | 1865-1925 |
| Alice D. Nelson | Author, editor | 1875-1935 |
| Mary Jane Patterson | Educator | 1840-1894 |
| Mary Smith Kelsey | Peake Teacher | 1823-1862 |
| Frances E. L. Preston | Lecturer | 1844-1929 |
| Georgianna Putnam | Educator | 1839-1914 |
| Charlotta G. Pyles | Abolitionist | 1806-1880 |
| Sarah Remond, M.D. | Abolitionist, physician | 1815-n.a. |
| Georgia D. Rooks | Physician/ established Ob. facility GA | 1885-1977 |
| Josephine St. Pierre Ruffin | Woman's club organizer | 1842-1924 |
| Josephine Silone | Yates Educator, writer | 1852-1912 |
| Susie Shorter | Teacher, writer | 1859-1912 |
| Georgianna Simpson | Professor, linguistics | 1866-1944 |
| Amanda Berry Smith | African missionary | 1836-1915 |
| Sallie W. Stewart | Teacher, club woman | 1881-1951 |
| Mary B. Talbert | Educator, social reformer | 1866-1923 |
| Josephine Turpin | Washington Journalist, teacher | 1861-1949 |
| Susan Paul Vashon | Teacher, nurse | 1838-1912 |
| Lulu Williams | Teacher, social reformer | 1874-1945 |

# PROMINENT BLACK AMERICANS: BIOGRAPHIES OF NOTABLE MEN AND WOMEN

**Biographies of Notable Men and Women**
**■ Other Prominent Black Americans**

Increasingly important on the American scene are black men and women who are making day-to-day contributions to the social, cultural, and economic progress of the nation. The brief biographies given here offer a cross-sectional view of this burgeoning group. Although many of the people named here are distinguished, they are not so much celebrities as part of the fiber of the country. If they share one distinguishing characteristic, it is decision-making responsibility. The following selection does not intend to be inclusive, but to sketch a representative sample of the growing number of blacks enjoying the challenge of significant careers and assuming increasing responsibility for our national future.

### WILLIAM AIKEN
**Certified Public Accountant**

President of the National Association of Black Accountants, William Aiken is a partner in his own New York-based CPA firm of Aiken, Wilson & Brown. Born in New York City, in 1934, he is a member of the board of the Ethical-Fieldston Fund and the Business Advisory Board of the Borough of Manhattan Community College.

### MILTON BURK ALLEN
**Attorney**

As Maryland State Attorney for Baltimore, Milton Allen is the only black person elected chief prosecutor of a large American city. Born in Baltimore, in 1917, he graduated from Coppin State Teachers College in 1938, served as a naval officer in World War II, and obtained a law degree from Maryland University in 1948. After becoming one of Baltimore's most successful civil rights defense and criminal attorneys, he was selected in 1966 to chair the Baltimore Criminal Courts Committee and was elected chief prosecutor in 1970.

### JIM ANDERSON
**Community Development Activist, Actor**

Working to unite neighbors into functioning communities, Jim Anderson has developed several projects, including the East Harlem Food Buying Federation, which provides fresh

*Randall C. Bacon, considered by* Ebony *to be one of the 100 most influential blacks in America.*

produce to over 600 families in 11 separate neighborhood clubs at less than 60% of retail costs. Born in Harlem, in 1929, he has been a Golden Gloves boxer, a dock worker, and a principal actor with the Living Theatre.

## SARAH A. ANDERSON
### Legislator

Sarah A. Anderson was a member of the Pennsylvania House of Representatives for 18 years prior to her retirement in 1972. Her work led to the establishment, in 1964, of the state's Commission on the Status of Women She sponsored the Pennsylvania Equal Rights Amendment guaranteeing equal treatment to women.

## HANNAH DIGGS ATKINS
### Legislator

Oklahoma state representative Hannah Diggs Atkins plays an important role on the governor's Commission on Women. Born in Winston-Salem, N.C., in 1923, she was a law librarian at Oklahoma State Library before her electoral victory. She is the first black woman in Oklahoma history to chair a committee in the legislature.

## J. EDWARD ATKINSON
### Executive

J. Edward Atkinson directs public relations for the Carnation Co. in Los Angeles, where his functions include liaison work with black community groups. Born in Denver, in 1914, he is the author of *Black Dimensions in Contemporary American Art* (1971) and a member of the L. A. Mayor's Area Advisory Board.

## JAMES S. AVERY
### Executive

James S. Avery manages the giant Exxon Corporation's public relations programs in New York, New Jersey, and the six New England states. His responsibilities include developing liaison with government officials in his region. Born in Cranford, N.J., in 1923, he takes an active role in several civic and educative organizations and is grand basileus of Omega Psi Phi.

## JOHN A. AXAM
### Librarian

John A. Axam directs the mobile division of Philadelphia's Free Library. Through the Reader Development Program he founded, he supervises library service to institutions and to undereducated and young adults. Born in Cincinnati, in 1930, he is a member of the Pennsylvania Library Association and the board of the Crime Prevention Association.

## RANDALL C. BACON
### Administrator

Randall Bacon was employed by the Los Angeles County for over 23 years. After graduating from California State University at Los Angeles with a B.S. degree, he started work for the county as a clerk and through 12 promotions, was elevated to the position of Division Chief within the Chief Administrative Offices. In 1979, he accepted the position of Chief Administrative Officer of San Diego County, and later became the Director of Social Services for the County.

Most recently, in December of 1988, Bacon, once again has taken a position in Los Angeles and is now head of the department of general services. In this capacity, he will act as chief agent for the city bureaucracy. *Ebony* has called Bacon one of the 100 most influential blacks in America.

Bacon is a former Grand Polemarch of Kappa Alpha Psi, an important and influential fraternal organization. He is a member of the 44th Congressional District Advisory Committee; on the board of directors of the Southern California Association of Public Administrators; and on the executive council of the American Society of Public Administrators.

## WARREN H. BACON
### Administrator

Warren H. Bacon is a personnel executive for Chicago's Inland Steel Co. Born in Chicago in 1923, he is a member of

*James S. Avery, an executive with Exxon Corporation.*

the American Iron and Steel Institute, a director of Hyde Park Federal Savings & Loan Association of Chicago, and president of Urban Ventures, Inc., which aids minority entrepreneurs.

## JANET JONES BALLARD
## Educator

Janet Jones Ballard of Richmond, Virginia is national president of Alpha Kappa Alpha Sorority, Incorporated, which is the premiere Greek-letter organization for sororities. Alpha Kappa Alpha can boast of it's 800 chapters in the United States and abroad with a membership that includes 100,000 college-trained women in the United States, Germany, the Bahamas, the Virgin Islands and West Africa.

Mrs. Ballard became a member of Alpha Kappa Alpha Sorority in 1947 while a student at Virginia Union University. Since that time she has assumed increasing positions of responsibility with the organization and as a community leader. In 1969, she was elected president of the Upsilon Omega chapter in Richmond, Virginia. Her exemplary leadership came to the attention of the sorority and she was named President of the Year. Subsequent to that, she was elected Mid Atlantic Regional Director, a post that automatically placed her on the national board of directors of Alpha Kappa Alpha Sorority. Again, she distinguished herself as she was cited for outstanding leadership in that region. In 1986, she was elected to a 4-year term as president of the Sorority. Her theme for her tenure as President was to have a broad worldwide perspective on matters pertaining to increasing the quality of life for all.

In addition to extending the sorority's international scope, Mrs. Ballard has etched a five-point offensive to cement the sorority's support of historically black colleges and universities. The plan includes advocacy, recruitment of students, retention of students in the colleges, diversion of individual scholarship monies to students attending these schools, and increased national and chapter support of these colleges and universities.

Mrs. Ballard is presently Alumni Affairs Director and an Assistant Professor at Virginia State University in Petersburg, Virginia.

## DONALD J. BEAN
## Dentist

Dr. Donald J. Bean is the first black to be appointed by the New York State Board of Dental Examiners. The Board of Dental Examiners is composed of eleven dentists, three public representatives, and two dental hygienists. Dr. Bean is a product of the New York City Public School System and a graduate of Howard University College of Dentistry. He is

*Janet Jones Ballard, national president of Alpha Kappa Alpha Sorority, Inc., the premiere sorority.*

a past president of the Greater Metropolitan New York Dental Society and presently a member of the Board of Trustees of the National Dental Association. He also serves as a clinical instructor on the staff of New York Medical College and is responsible for the training of residents at Metropolitan Hospital and Bird S. Coler Hospital in New York City. His dental practice is in Jamaica, New York.

*Dr. Donald Bean, member of the New York State Board of Dental Examiners.*

### AL BELL
### Executive

Al Bell worked his way from an AM disc jockey to board chairman of Stax Records, Inc., in Memphis, Tenn. Born in Little Rock, Ark., in 1940, he is now one of the most powerful men in the American record industry. He also serves as executive vice president of Stax, which produces Isaac Hayes, the Staple Singers, and Rufus Thomas.

### EDWARD B. BELL
### Executive

Former professional football player Edward B. Bell is now an executive with Atlantic Richfield, where he coordinates urban marketing programs and activities for the merchandising department. Born in Philadelphia in 1931, he has been a guided missile instructor at Fort Monmouth, N.J., and a national treasurer of the National Association of Market Developers.

*Former baseball great Joe Black, now a vice president of Greyhound.*

### ANDREW BILLINGSLEY
### Educator

Author of *Black Families in White America*, Andrew Billingsley is the president of Morgan State College. Born in Marion, Ala., in 1926, he received degrees from Grinnel College, Boston University, the University of Michigan, and Brandeis. His concern for social welfare is shown by his work on the board of directors of the Council on Social Work Education, the Publications Advisory Commission, and the Child Welfare League of America.

### CAROLYN BILLINGSLEA
### Government official

Carolyn Billingslea works for the Internal Revenue Service as their assistant chief of examination for the Detroit district. Her position requires decisions on policies and planning of IRS operations. A graduate of Canisius College in Buffalo, N.Y., Ms. Billingslea is the second black female to hold the title of assistant examination chief, and is the only black female in the nation currently in that position.

### JOE BLACK
### Executive

In his corporate position as vice president of special markets for the Greyhound Corporation, Joe Black is responsible for the development and recommendation of policies, practices, programs, and procedures of marketing for the black

*Emma Blake, (right) the 1987 recipient of The Brooke Russell Astor Award, runs a soup kitchen in Harlem, New York City.*

consumer market. Born in Plainfield, N.J., in 1924, he became the first black pitcher in the big leagues in 1952 when he joined the Brooklyn Dodgers and was named the National League's Rookie of the Year. After a career in which he came to be considered one of the top relievers in the sport, he joined Greyhound in 1962, rapidly rising to important administrative posts. He is a member of the Task Force on Youth Motivation under the National Alliance of Businessmen (NAB) and of the National Association of Market Developers (NAMD).

## EMMA BLAKE
### Practical nurse

Since her retirement as a practical nurse a few years ago, Emma Blake, the 1987 recipient of The Brooke Russell Astor Award, has devoted her enormous energy and her reservoir of loving care to feeding the hungry and the homeless in central Harlem. Working with modest resources—including her own social security money—Ms. Blake feeds 150 people weekly, and when finances allow, provides food packages from the soup kitchen she runs at the New Hope Community Church on West 123rd Street. "I cannot see myself eating and living without feeling obligated to feed those who are hungry, " she says. Ms. Blake does her good work "surrounded by angels," she says, but she is clearly the archangel of the neighborhood. Ms. Blake, 68 years old, was born in McClellan, South Carolina and has been a resident of New York for 50 years. Her work has been recognized by the Citizens Committee's One City Award.

## JAMES BOGGS
### Author

Born in Marion Junction, Ala., in 1919, self-educated James Boggs worked in a Detroit automobile plant until he was 48 years old before deciding to quit his job and start writing "to project a vision of what we must do in this country to develop another way for man to live." His books *The American Revolution:Pages from a Negro Worker's Notebook* and *Racism and the Class Struggle* have become a fundamental part of the ideology of the black revolution.

## JAMES E. BOOKER
### Public Relations Consultant

After 18 years as an award-winning columnist and political editor on the *Amsterdam News*, James Booker formed his own firm to deal with the public relations aspects of civil rights, urban affairs, minority economic development, and government relations. Born in Riverhead, N.Y., in 1926, he is also a university lecturer and TV commentator.

## HILDAGARDEIS BOSWELL
### Legislator

Hildagardeis Boswell serves Maryland as a state representative and a specialist with the State Commission on Human Relations. Born in Daisytown, Pa., in 1934, she was nearly cheated of her election by fraud, but took her case to the courts and won an upset. She co-sponsored the controversial bill which proposes three-year renewable marriage contracts.

## MILLER W. BOYD
### Psychologist

Research psychologist Miller W. Boyd co-directs the Academy of Urban Service, Inc., in his home town of St. Louis. Born in 1934, he is a prolific psychological journal contributor, former director of Experiment in Higher Education, and a member of the National Association of

Education for Young Children and the National Council for Black Child Development.

### RAYMOND A. BROWN
### Attorney

Raymond A. Brown has been described by many as the "black F. Lee Bailey" and an associate in his law firm called him "the greatest lawyer in America." Raymond Brown tackles the tough ones, including some of the more socially and politically controversial figures of the time. He has represented Rubin (Hurricane) Carter, Imamu Amiri Baraka, Linden, N.J. Mayor and State Senator John T. Gregorio, former Camden, N.J. Mayor Angelo Errichetti, Sam (The Plumber) DeCavalcante, Angelo (Gyp) DeCarlo, and the Black Panther Party of New Jersey. The Montclair, N.J. resident, who has his law practice in Jersey City, also represents major corporations from time to time, although his specialty is criminal law.

Brown was born in Jacksonville, Florida, but grew up in Jersey City. He graduated from Florida A&M University where he played football, and finished Fordham Law School at night by working during the day. Brown has been a civil rights activist and was jailed in the 1960s along with Percy Sutton, lawyer and former Manhattan Borough President. He is a former president of the Jersey City branch of the NAACP, a board member of the Boy Scouts of America, and was a delegate to the White House Conference on Children in 1960 and to the White House Conference on the Aged in 1961. In 1967, Brown was appointed to the Commission on Civil Disorders to investigate the underlying causes of Newark and Plainfield race riots.

*Dr. Roscoe C. Brown Jr. is president of Bronx Community College.*

### ROSCOE C. BROWN JR.
### Educator

Roscoe C. Brown is president of Bronx Community College and was formerly director of the Institute of Afro-American Affairs at New York University. Born in Washington, D.C., in 1922, he was a squadron commander in the USAF, hosted the Emmy award winning TV series *Black Arts,* has more than 50 publications to his credit (including co-editing the first edition of *The Negro Almanac*), and is an active consultant for the city, state, and federal government.

### ROBERT S. BROWNE
### Economist

Robert S. Browne created and heads New York's Black Economic Research Center, which provides technical assistance to black economic development programs. A man of resolute principle, he renounced a promising career with the U.S. aid program in Cambodia (1955-1957) and Vietnam (1958-1961) and went on to give speeches against U.S. policies in Southeast Asia. Born in Chicago in 1924, he is vice president of the National Sharecroppers Fund and a member of the board of the American Commission on Africa.

### MANFORD BYRD JR.
### Administrator

Manford Byrd Jr. is deputy superintendent of the Chicago Public School System, which is the second largest in the country. Born in Brewton, Ala., in 1928, he began teaching in the Chicago schools in 1949. He is a trustee of Central College and a board member of Chicago State University and of the Joint Negro Appeal.

### LEROY CALLENDER
### Engineer

One of the nation's foremost consulting engineers, LeRoy Callender got his start at renowned Brooklyn Technical High School, graduating first in its architectural design class in 1950. After designing buildings for the U.S. Army in Korea, he graduated from the City College of New York, then worked on a nuclear power plant for the Consolidated Edison Company before forming his own firm in 1969. In 1975, Callender completed the first phase design of York College, a projected university in New York City, and formed a second company, Callender & Smith, which specializes in waterworks development.

**Dr. MARY SCHMIDT CAMPELL**
**City Official**

Dr. Mary Schmidt Campbell, the former executive director of the Studio Museum in Harlem, is New York City's commissioner of Cultural Affairs. She received a Bachelor of Arts in English Literature from Swarthmore College, a Master of Arts in Art History and her doctorate in Humanities from Syracuse University. She taught English Literature for two years at Nkumbi International College, a school for South African refugees in Zambia. She has lectured extensively on black American art, and maintains a special interest in artist Romare Bearden, on whom she wrote a definitive study for her doctorate, as well as a book for Oxford University Press. As Cultural Affairs commissioner, Dr. Campbell oversees a budget of $162 million, which funds institutions such as the Metropolitan Museum of Art, the New York Zoological Society, and the Studio Museum. She also oversees the allocation of support to more than 400 local arts groups. Her husband is Dr. George Campbell, a physicist at AT&T Bell Labs. They have two sons.

**THEOPHILUS CAVINESS**
**Clergyman**

The Reverend Caviness is pastor of Cleveland's Greater Abyssinia Baptist Church and president of that church's Federal Credit Union. Born in Marshall, Tex., in 1928, he serves as the historian and a member of the board of the National Baptist Convention, U.S.A., and is a member of the Zoning Board of Appeals of the City of Cleveland.

*Kenneth Clark spearheaded psychological research leading to civil rights reforms.*

**JAMES E. CHEEK**
**Educator**

James Cheek was named president of Howard University in 1969, becoming one of the youngest major American university heads. Born in Roanoke Rapids, N.C., in 1932, he obtained three theological degrees—from Shaw, Colgate, and Drew universities—but was interested in an academic rather than clerical career. In 1963 he became president of Shaw, rescued that institution from financial collapse, and acquired a reputation as one of academia's most gifted administrators and diplomats.

**CHARLES DARRETT CHURCHWELL**
**Administrator**

Charles Darrett Churchwell is associate provost of Miami University in Oxford, Ohio. Born in Dunnellon, Fla., he is an alumnus of Morehouse College, Atlanta University, and the University of Illinois. He is the author of *A History of Education for Librarianship, 1919-1939.*

**KENNETH BANCROFT CLARK**
**Psychologist, Social Critic**

Gifted scholar Kenneth B. Clark heads Clark, Phipps, Clark & Harris, Inc., an executive consulting firm specializing in affirmative action in race relations matters. Born in the Panama Canal Zone in 1914, he performed important psychological research cited by the Supreme Court in its 1954 ruling outlawing segregation in the schools. A regular contributor to professional journals, he is the author of *Dark Ghetto: Dilemmas of Social Power* and is one of the chief organizers behind Harlem Youth Opportunities Unlimited (HARYOU).

**RICHARD V. CLARKE**
**Entrepreneur**

The founder and president of Richard Clarke Associates, Inc., a pioneer firm in the recruitment of black executives, has a wide range of business successes to his credit. He publishes the magazines *Opportunities for the College Graduate* and *Contact*, operates Hallmark Holidays travel agency, and is a consultant to several federal, state, and private agencies.

**MAURICE LIONEL COLVIN**
**Administrator**

Maurice Colvin serves Corpus Christi, Tex., as administrative assistant to the city manager, the highest municipal post ever held there by a black, and is administrator of the Human Relations Committee. Born in Prairie View, Tex., in 1932, he became one of the original members (and chairman) of the Human Relations Committee, which coordinates programs against racial and ethnic discrimination.

## JAMES R. COWAN
**State Official**

James Cowan, M.D., is commissioner of health for the State of New Jersey. Born in Washington, D.C., in 1916, he became chief of surgery at the U.S. Army's 26th Station Hospital in Regensburg, Germany. He went on to a post as senior attending physician at East Orange General Hospital before becoming the first black state commissioner of health in the United States.

## ARNOLD (JERSEY JOE WOLCOTT) CREAM
**State Official**

Former world heavyweight champion Arnold Cream, who boxed under the name of Jersey Joe Wolcott, is Commissioner of Athletics for the State of New Jersey. Prior to that position, Jersey Joe was New Jersey's State Director of Special Olympics, a program involving sports projects for handicapped children. He had also been sheriff in his hometown of Camden, N.J. Born in 1914, he began his professional boxing career at 15, and finally, in 1951, he knocked out Ezzard Charles with a left hook to become, at 37, the oldest man ever to win the crown. A family man of strong religious beliefs, he uses his present post to help people.

## GEORGE W. CROCKETT JR.
**Jurist**

Now in his second term as Recorder's Court Judge in Detroit, George W. Crockett continues his distinguished career as an unswerving opponent of racism. Born in Jacksonville, Fla., he has been a senior attorney for the U.S. Department of Labor and a general counsel for the United Auto Workers-CIO. He was the lawyer in the case which opened the Atlanta union to black auto workers and has set several judicial precedents in cases involving black rights.

## WILLIE L. DANIELS
**Stockbroker**

Willie L. Daniels formed and directs Daniels & Bell, Inc., the first black member firm on the New York Stock Exchange. Born in Valdosta, Ga., he began working on Wall Street in 1960 and was ready in 1971 to open his own brokerage, which now holds two seats on the exchange and does business throughout the United States and Europe. He is a member of the Lawyers Club and a director of the Young Adult Institute & Workshop.

## GEORGIA M. DAVIS
**Legislator**

Georgia M. Davis enjoys the double distinction of being the first black and the first woman elected to the Kentucky State Senate, where she is chairwoman of the Subcommittee on Wages and Hours. Born in Springfield, Ky., in 1923, she owns a restaurant, a laundry, and a dry cleaning establishment. Always active in civil rights causes, she was a charter member of Allied Organizations for Civil Rights and an organizer of the Kentucky Christian Leadership Conference.

## C. C. DEJOIE JR.
**Executive**

C. C. Dejoie Jr., publishes the *Louisiana Weekly,* the only black newspaper in New Orleans, his hometown. Born in 1914, he entered the newspaper business in 1938 and has on-the-staff experience of all its aspects. He has been president and treasurer of the National Newspaper Publishers Association and is a member of the group that owns the New Orleans Saints football team.

## JAMES R. DUMPSON
**Administrator**

Professor James R. Dumpson is dean of Fordham University's Graduate School of Social Service. Born in 1909, his 25-year career in the New York Department of Welfare was capped by his appointment as city welfare commissioner in 1959. A member of many organizations and societies, he has been named to several presidential commissions on welfare, drug abuse, and child welfare.

*Former boxing champion Arnold "Jersey Joe Wolcott" Cream now heads New Jersey's Special Olympics Program.*

## ROY EATON
### Music Production Executive

Performer and music writer Roy Eaton is president of Roy Eaton Music in Roosevelt Island, New York. The versatile musician has made a number of radio and television appearances as a performer and writer, and has had articles published in several magazines. Roy Eaton is best known as a concert pianist and made his debut with the Chicago Symphony Orchestra in 1951, appearing the next year at New York City's Town Hall. Prior to forming his own company, Roy Eaton was vice president and music director of Benton and Bowles, Inc. At B&B, he was responsible for supervising the creation and production of all music for the agency's radio and television commercials. Among the well-known jingles he has composed are "Start the day a little bit better" for General Foods' Post Cereals and a jingle for Kent Cigarettes which is believed to be the first use of modern jazz in commercial jingles.

Roy Eaton holds baccalaureate degrees from both the Manhattan School of Music and CCNY, and a masters degree from The Manhattan School of Music. He has also taught music history at the U.S. Armed Forces Institute.

*Roy Eaton, versatile musician and president of Roy Eaton Music Corporation.*

## CHRISTOPHER FAIRFIELD EDLEY
### Administrator

Christopher Fairfield Edley serves as executive director of the United Negro College Fund. Born in Charleston, W.Va., in 1928, he has held a wide range of private and governmental legal posts and was program officer of the Ford Foundation from 1963-1973. Mr. Edley graduated magna cum laude from Howard University in 1949 and received his law degree from Harvard Law School in 1953. He is a board member of The Great Atlantic and Pacific Tea Company, The Bowery Savings Bank, American Airlines, C.I.T. Financial Corporation, and the National Bank of North America. In 1950, Mr. Edley was the recipient of the John Hay Whitney Fellowship and received the Distinguished Alumni Award from Howard University in 1979. He has also received a number of other honors and awards from colleges and fraternal organizations.

*Former New York City Welfare Commissioner James Dumpson is now a dean at Fordham University.*

## A. WILSON EDWARDS
### City Official

A. Wilson Edwards supervises the police and fire departments of Louisville, Ky. Born in Frankfort, Ky., in 1908, he began his career as a patrolman in 1935. He served as a security officer at the inaugurations of presidents Eisenhower and Johnson, and as a security advisor to President William V. S. Tubman of Liberia and Colonel Tran Minh Cong, police chief of Da Nang.

## NELSON JACK EDWARDS
### Union Official

As international vice president of the United Auto Workers, and a member of that union's International Executive Board,

Nelson Jack Edwards represents some 400,000 black and white workers in the automobile and aerospace industries. Born in Lowndes County, Ala., in 1917, he began his career at 17 with the Southern Oil Co., working 12 hours a day at $15 an hour. In 1936, he made the move to the UAW, was soon elected chairman of the overwhelmingly white Ford Motor local, and became the first black member of the UAW board in 1962.

**LLOYD CHARLES ELAM**
**Educator**

As president of Meharry Medical College in Nashville, Lloyd Charles Elam has devoted much of his energies to expanding the faculty, the physical plant, and student enrollment. Born in Little Rock, Ark., in 1928, he arrived at Meharry in 1961 to found and chair the department of psychiatry. He serves on the Advisory Committee to the National Academy of Sciences, the National Board of Medical Examiners, and the National Association for Equal Opportunity in Higher Education.

**JEAN R. ESQUERRE**
**Corporate Executive**

Jean R. Esquerre is assistant to the president of the Grumman Aerospace Corporation and Director of the corporation's Opportunity Development Department. Mr. Esquerre is responsible for Grumman's equal employment and Affirmative Action programs. Very active in civic affairs, Mr. Esquerre is a member of the Society of Automotive Engineers and the Alpha Phi Alpha Fraternity. He is past president of the Board of the Huntington Station Youth Development Association, former Labor and Industry Chairman of the Huntington Township branch of the NAACP, and president of the Urban League of Long Island. Mr. Esquerre was born in Yonkers, N.Y., and during World War II, served as a radio operator-gunner in the United States Army Air Force 477th B-25 Medium Bomber Group. He received a B.S. in Engineering Technology from Empire State College, State University of New York, and has studied mechanical engineering and industrial management at the City College of New York and New York University.

*Jean R. Esquerre is an executive with Grumman Aerospace Corporation.*

*W. Leonard Evans is president of Tuesday Publications.*

**W. LEONARD EVANS JR.**
**Publisher**

W. Leonard Evans Jr., is president of Chicago-based Tuesday Publications, Inc., which creates monthly magazine inserts for 22 major newspapers. Born in Louisville, Ky., in 1914, he was awarded Lincoln University's Citation of Merit for Outstanding Contributions to Journalism in 1968 and the National Newspaper Award from the Poor Richard Club in 1970. He is a member of the boards of the National Conference of Christians and Jews, the Advertising Council, Inc., Fisk University, and the University of Chicago.

**CLARENCE C. FINLEY**
**Executive**

As executive vice president of Burlington House Products

Group in New York, Clarence C. Finley is probably the most important black executive in the United States. Starting as a $12-a-week file clerk in 1942, he has risen to the second spot in a corporation that does over $250 million yearly business and employs nearly 7,000 people. He was born in Chicago.

**JAMES D. FOWLER**
**Executive**

As executive vice president and director of administration and marketing for ITT Consumer Financial Corporation, James D. Fowler oversees the company's compensation budget and development of marketing programs. Mr. Fowler, who lives in the Minneapolis area with his wife and two children, is an engineering graduate of West Point Military Academy. He earned his Master of Business Administration degree from the Rochester Institute of Technology.

**LUTHER H. FOSTER**
**Educator**

Luther H. Foster is the president of renowned Tuskegee Institute. Born in Lawrenceville, Va., in 1913, he pursued his education at Virginia State College, Harvard School of Business Administration, and the University of Chicago. Since becoming Tuskegee's president in 1953, he has augmented the college's buildings, strengthened its financial underpinning, and greatly increased service programs for the disadvantaged. He is a trustee of the United Negro College Fund.

**ERWIN A. FRANCE**
**City Official**

Erwin A. France serves Chicago as administrative assistant to the mayor and as director of Model Cities—the Chicago Committee on Urban Opportunity Program. Born in St. Louis, in 1938, he has divided his career between public service and higher education. Besides teaching at several universities, he has been director of the Chicago Youth Opportunity Centers and deputy director of the Illinois State Employment Service for the Chicago central city.

**FRANKIE M. FREEMAN**
**Attorney**

Frankie M. Freeman serves on the U.S. Commission on Civil Rights and is associate general counsel of the St. Louis Housing and Land Clearance Authorities. Born in Danville, Va., her career has included instructing business law at College Center of the Fingerlakes as well as practicing law. Often honored for her civil rights work, she is a member of several bar associations, the National Association of Housing and Redevelopment Officials, and the League of Women Voters.

**MARY E. FRIZZELL**
**Fraternal Leader**

Mary E. Frizzell is president of the Women's Missionary Society of the A.M.E. Church and has been involved in missionary work for nearly 25 years. Under her guidance, the missionary education department of the society has developed leadership courses in adult work, published inspirational literature, maintained a reference book service, and established a correspondence school. She was born in Mayfield, Ky.

**D. PARKE GIBSON**
**Marketing Specialist**

Author of *The $30 Billion Negro*, D. Parke Gibson heads his own national marketing and public relations consulting firm, which publishes monthly newsletters on black consumers and on race-related developments in corporation policies and communication. Born in Seattle, he is a member of the American Marketing Association, the National Association of Market Developers, and the Public Relations Society of America.

**SIMEON GOLAR**
**Judge**

Following an outstanding career as an administrator in New York City government, Simeon Golar was named a municipal judge in Queens. His position prior to judicial appointment was chairman of the NYC Housing Authority, where he regulated construction and management of low-income and middle-income housing in the metropolis. Born in Chester, S.C., in 1928, he attended City College of New York and New York University Law School. He is an officer of the National Association of Housing and Redevelopment Officials.

**BERRY GORDY JR.**
**Entrepreneur**

One of the great business successes, Berry Gordy Jr., parlayed an $800 loan into gigantic Motown Industries, which grosses over $50 million a year. Born in Detroit, Mich., he had 15 fights as a Golden Gloves featherweight before joining the U.S. Army in Korea. As president and board chairman of Motown, he has introduced many new artists to the public and to fame, including Smokey Robinson and the Miracles, the Temptations, the Four Tops, the Supremes, and Martha and the Vandellas.

**STANLEY E. GRAYSON**
**City Official**

As commissioner of the Department of Finance for the City of New York, Stanley E. Grayson heads the fourth largest taxing jurisdiction in the nation, following the Federal government, and the States of California and New York. Mr. Grayson, who has a law degree from the University of Michigan Law School and a Bachelor of Arts degree from the College of the Holy Cross, oversees a staff of 2,500 and a department which collects nearly $14 billion in revenues. Prior to his 1988 appointment as finance commissioner, Mr. Grayson served as commissioner of the non-profit Office of Financial Services Corporation, chairman of the city's Industrial Development Agency, and as a member of the law department of Metropolitan Life Insurance. Mr. Grayson, a native of Detroit, is a member of the American Bar, New York State Bar, and District of Columbia Bar Association. He is married and has one daughter.

### RICHARD T. GREENE
**Executive**

Richard T. Greene is president of the Carver Federal Savings Bank, the only black-owned and operated full-service savings institution in New York. He was recently nominated to be an industry director on the Federal Home Loan Bank Board of New York, which serves as a regulatory overseer of banking institutions in New York, New Jersey, Puerto Rico and the Virgin Islands. Mr. Greene is a graduate of Hampton University, Hampton, Va., with graduate studies at New York University, Wharton School of Banking and Finance, and the American Savings and Loan Institute. He has been president since 1969 of the Carver Federal Savings Bank, which is located in Harlem with branch offices in Manhattan, Brooklyn and Nassau County.

### BOOKER GRIFFIN
**Broadcast Journalist**

Media personality Booker Griffin is director of news and community relations at radio station KGFJ in Los Angeles and is a featured columnist for the *Los Angeles Sentinel* newspaper. His radio responsibilities include reviewing the news to be broadcast, designing community relations programs, and coordinating public service announcements and the station's services to listeners. He was born in Gary, Ind., in 1938.

*Ira D. Hall, assistant treasurer of IBM Corp. in Armonk, NY, and governor of the U. S. Postal Service in Washington, D. C.*

### GILROYE A. GRIFFIN JR.
**Executive**

Gilroye A. Griffin Jr., is a member of the board of directors of Kenyon & Eckhardt, a New York advertising agency. He also serves the firm as vice president of corporate administration and associate counsel. Born in Columbia, S.C., in 1938, he attended Dartmouth College and Columbia University. On the job he supervises all of the company's corporate and advertising legal matters and is director of personnel.

### JUNIUS GRIFFIN
**Executive**

Junius Griffin formed his own public relations firm in Hollywood, Calif., in 1972. Born in Stonega, Va., in 1929, he abandoned a promising career in journalism to become a public relations aide to Martin Luther King Jr., served as director of public relations for the SCLC, and was an executive of Motown Records. He is a member of the boards of trustees and of governors of the Martin Luther King Center for Social Change and a member of the board of the U.S. Commission on Civil Rights.

### IRA D. HALL
**Executive**

Stanford University MBA graduate Ira D. Hall holds two powerful positions. As assistant treasurer of the IBM Corporation in Armonk, N.Y., he oversees the corporation's financing, international treasury, and related management programs. As governor of the U.S. Postal Service in Washington, D.C., a presidential appointment, Mr. Hall is responsible for the selection of the Post Master General.

### CHARLES V. HAMILTON
**Educator**

Charles V. Hamilton heads New York's Metropolitan Applied Research Center (MARC), which was formed to research social problems related to community development. Born in Muskogee, Okla., in 1927, he taught at several universities and has published widely. His magazine credits include *The New York Times* magazine, *Harvard Educational Review,* and *Black World,* and he is the author of *The Black Preacher in America* (1972) and *The Black Experience in American Politics* (1973). He is vice president of the American Political Science Association.

### NATHAN HARE
**Publisher**

Author of *The Black Anglo-Saxon*, Nathan Hare is president and founder of The Black World Foundation and publisher of *The Black Scholar*. Born in Slick, Okla., in 1933, he has taught at Howard University and San Francisco College, where he was the country's first coordinator of a black studies program, and has published several articles in *Saturday Review*, *Ramparts*, *Black World*, *Newsweek*, and the *Times* of London. Mr. Hare was a professional fighter under the name Nat Harris. He is a member of the National Steering Committee of the African Liberation Day.

## BERNARD W. HARLESTON
### Educator

Dr. Bernard W. Harleston is the ninth president of the City College of New York. At CCNY, he has emphasized the importance of maintaining the college's 135-year-old tradition of academic excellence and service to the young people of New York City, particularly those who might not otherwise have attended college. A summa cum laude graduate of Howard University, Dr. Harleston received his doctorate in experimental psychology in 1955 from the University of Rochester, where he began his teaching career. He joined Tufts University as an assistant professor of psychology in 1956, but was away from the institution from 1968 to 1970, when he was provost and later acting president of Lincoln University in Pennsylvania. A member of Phi Beta Kappa, Dr. Harleston holds an honorary Doctor of Science degree from the University of Rochester and has received the John H. Franklin Award from the Tufts University African American Cultural Center in 1980. His articles on psychology and education have appeared in scholarly journals and his papers and lectures have been presented to many professional associations. Dr. Harleston was born in New York City.

## EDWARD W. HAWTHORNE
### Physician

A pioneer in the study of cardiac functioning and hypertension, Dr. Hawthorne has made important contributions to the research of high blood pressure, an affliction which strikes a far greater proportion of black than white Americans. Born in 1924, he is a graduate of Howard Medical School and took his Ph.D. in physiology from the University of Illinois. Named chairman of Howard's Physiology Department, he pioneered methods of recording heart functioning in conscious animals. In 1974, he was appointed chairman of the Hypertension Research Center's Advisory Committee of the National Heart and Lung Institute.

## OLLEN B. HINNANT
### Attorney

Ollen B. Hinnant is Assistant General Counsel of the Prudential Insurance Company in Newark, N.J. and is a member of the U.S. National Commission for the United Nations Educational, Scientific and Cultural Organization (UNESCO). Former President Gerald Ford also appointed Mr. Hinnant a member of the State Appeal Board of the Selective Service System of New Jersey. The Newark attorney is active in a number of organizations which include the Planned Parenthood Association of America, the American Bar Association, and the National Bar Association where he is chairperson of the Institutional Law Section. He has been named in editions of *Who's Who in the East*, *Who's Who in Black America*, and *Who's Who in New Jersey International Register of Profiles*. Mr. Hinnant was born in Lexington, Ky. and received his B.A. degree from Kentucky State University in Frankfort, Kentucky, and his J.D. degree from the University of Kentucky Law School in 1955, prior to undertaking postgraduate studies at New York University.

## J. CLINTON HOGGARD
### Clergyman

As bishop of the 6th Episcopal District of the African Methodist Episcopal Zion Church, J. Clinton Hoggard oversees the Indiana, Kentucky, North Alabama, and the East Tennessee-Virginia conferences. Born in Jersey City, N.J., he graduated from Rutgers University in 1939 and took a graduate B.D. degree at New York's Union Theological Seminary in 1942. From 1952 to 1972 he served as secretary-treasurer of the AMEZ's Department of Foreign Missions, during which time he earned an international reputation as a diligent and altruistic churchman, with a deep dedication to religious ideals. Consecrated a bishop in 1970, he is a member of the World Council of Churches, the National Council of Churches of Christ in the U.S.A., the NAACP, and the ACLU.

*Dr. Bernard W. Harleston is president of the City College of New York.*

NAACP General Counsel Nathaniel R. Jones.

## DONALD LEE HOLLOWELL
**Federal Executive**

As a regional director of the Equal Employment Opportunity Commission, Donald Lee Hollowell works to eliminate discriminatory hiring practices in the southeastern United States. Born in Wichita, Kan., in 1917, he began the private practice of law in Atlanta, Ga., in 1952, has handled several school desegregation and public accommodation cases, and was legal representative for Martin Luther King Jr., and Ralph D. Abernathy.

## RAYMOND W. HOOD
**Legislator**

Raymond W. Hood is Democratic party leader in the Michigan House of Representatives. Elected from the 14th District of Detroit, his hometown, he is chairman of the Public Health Committee, vice chairman of the Labor Committee, and a member of the Elections Committee and the Conservation and Recreation committees. Born in 1936, he was first elected in 1964, at which time he became the youngest black legislator in Michigan history.

## ROY DAVAGE HUDSON
**Educator**

President of Virginia's Hampton Institute since 1970, Roy Davage Hudson was formerly a pharmacology faculty member at the University of Michigan Medical School and served as an associate dean of Brown's Graduate School. Born in Chattanooga, Tenn., in 1930, he is a board member of the Virginia Peninsula Industrial Committee and the National Association for Equal Opportunity in Higher Education.

## NATHANIEL R. JONES
**Attorney**

General counsel of the National Association for the Advancement of Colored People, Nathaniel Jones was born in Youngstown, Ohio, in 1926. He obtained a Bachelor of Law Degree from Youngstown University in 1956, served as executive director of that city's Fair Employment Practices Commission, and then became an assistant United States Attorney for the Northern District of Ohio. In 1967, Jones was general counsel for President Lyndon Johnson's Commission on Civil Disorders (also known as the Kerner Commission). Named NAACP general counsel in 1969, Jones has earned distinction as a champion of black servicemen and has sparked major revisions in the United States military justice system.

## VIRGINIA L. JONES
**Librarian**

Virginia L. Jones, whose career as a librarian began at Louisville Municipal College in 1934, is director of Atlanta University's School of Library Sciences. Born in Cincinnati, Ohio, in 1912, she has been an instructor in library science and a university dean. A former president of the Association of American Library Schools, she sits on the executive board of the American Library Association and is a member of the President's Advisory Committee on Library Training and Research.

## FREDERICK DOUGLASS JORDAN
**Clergyman**

Bishop Frederick Douglass Jordan is ecumenical prelate of the A.M.E. Church. Born in Atlanta in 1901, he is chairman of the Commission on the Union of Black Methodist Churches and of the Commission on the Consultation on Church Union, and a member of the executive committee of the World Methodist Council and of the governing board of the National Council of the Churches of Christ in the U.S. He has been a leader in building up the A.M.E. Church in Africa.

## E. J. JOSEY
**Librarian**

E. J. Josey heads the New York State Education Department's Bureau of Academic and Research Libraries, where he charts the development of specialized research library services. Born in Norfolk, Va., in 1924, he organized the first

*Dr. Augusta Kappner, among her other achievements, was the first black woman to become president of the City University of New York.*

NAACP college chapter in the South in 1963 and was the first chairman of the Black Caucus of the American Library Association. He is the author of *What Black Librarians Are Saying* and *The Black Librarian in America*.

## DR. AUGUSTA SOUZA KAPPNER
### Educator

Dr. Augusta Souza Kappner, president of the Borough of Manhattan Community College, has held a number of important positions in New York City's academic world. She was the first black woman to become president of the City University of New York. She was professor and dean of Adult and Continuing Education at LaGuardia Community College, and served as director of admissions at the State University of New York at Stonybrook. She has held both teaching and administrative positions at Columbia University School of Social Work, New York City Community College, as well as Hunter College, where she earned her Master of Social Work degree and where she has been inducted into the university's "Hall of Fame." A graduate of Barnard College, Dr. Kappner received her Doctor of Social Welfare degree from Columbia University, specializing in social policy and planning. She resides in Manhattan.

## MICHELLE D. KOUROUMA
### Administrator

Michelle Doswell Kourouma is the executive director of the Atlanta-based National Conference of Black Mayors, Inc., which has more than 300 towns and cities as members. Her role is to assist the mayors in administrative tasks, budget analysis, fund-raising, and interfacing with corporate, federal, state and local officials. Ms. Kourouma earned a Bachelor of Science degree in Education at the State University of New York, College at Oswego, and has taught classes at the State University of New York College at New Paltz, Hofstra University, and Fairleigh Dickinson University. Prior to joining the NCBM in 1975, Ms. Kourouma was a project coordinator for The Project, Inc., a minority company contracted to conduct housing and community development activities for the City of Atlanta. Ms. Kourouma, who is married to Louis C. Williamson and the mother of two daughters, participated in the 1962 Operation Crossroads Africa program in Gambia.

*Michelle D. Kourouma, executive director of the Atlanta-based National Conference of Black Mayors, Inc.*

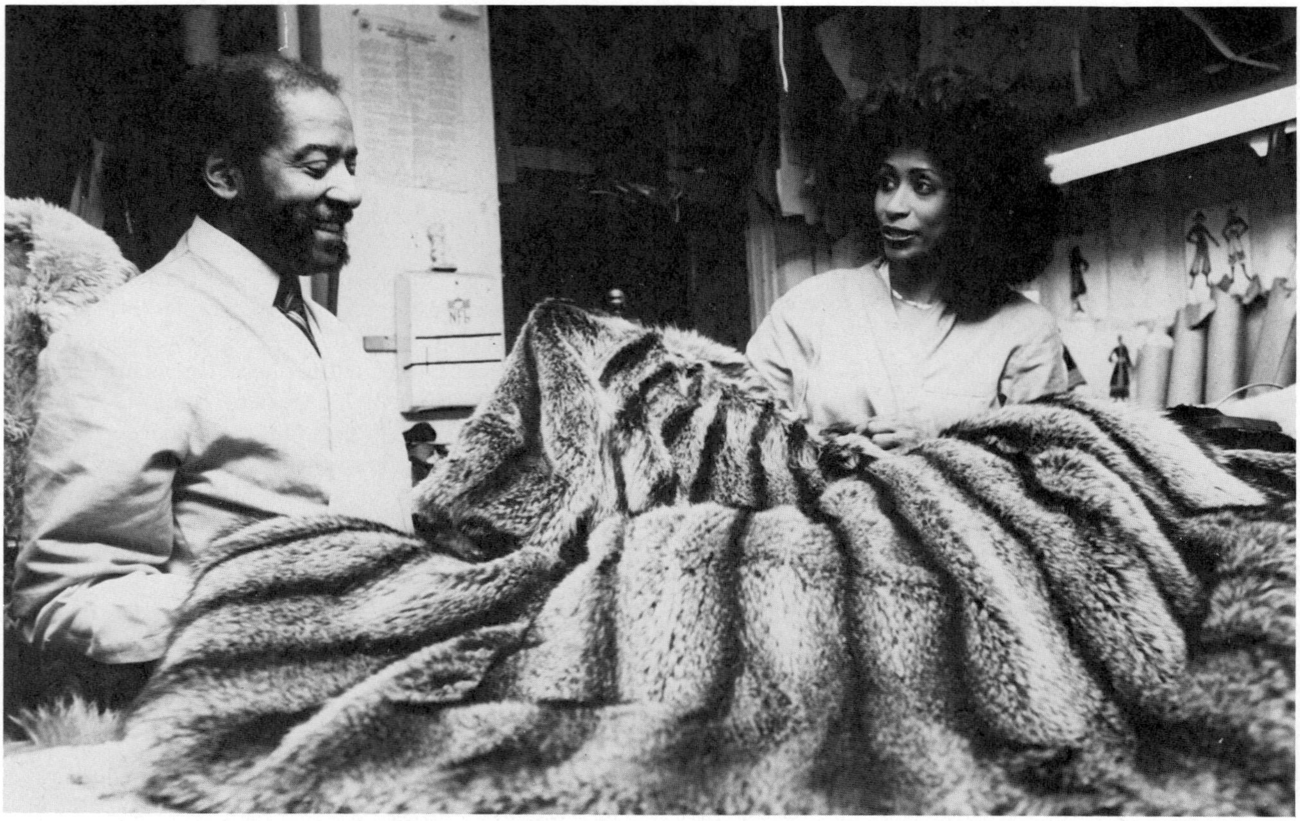

*James McQuay is the only black in wholesale-retail fur manufacturing to own his own business.*

### BARBARA LAMONT
### Television Newscaster

Barbara Lamont is co-host of New York City's WNEW-TV *Black News* and a key member of the channel's *10 O'clock News*. Born in 1925, she received the Newswoman's Guild Award for excellence in reporting in 1973 for her two documentaries, *Guyana* and *Brownstone Fever*. She is the author of *City People* and a Democratic district leader in Manhattan.

### HARRISON EDWARD LEE
### Educator

Professor Harrison Edward Lee is director of public relations at Prentiss Institute Jr. College in Mississippi. Born in Talladega, Ala., in 1922, he has taught at several colleges and is an accomplished poet as well as a journalist and news broadcaster. He is a member of the Voter's League and the NAACP.

### ROBERT O. LOWERY
### City Official

Robert O. Lowery became the first black fire commissioner of a major city when he was appointed to that post in New York City on January 1, 1966. Born in Buffalo, N.Y., in 1916, he joined the New York Fire Department in 1942 and worked his way up the ranks. His administration is noteworthy for its honesty, public education programs, and attempts to recruit minority personnel.

### ERNEST DUKE McNEIL
### Attorney

Ernest Duke McNeil is founder and senior partner of his own law firm and president of Chicago's Woodlawn Organization. Born in Memphis in 1936, he is co-founder of UHURU, a legal foundation, and of the Organization of Black American Culture, chairman of the Black Businessmen's Association, and president of Hustlers Discount Records. A recent candidate for mayor of Chicago, he was cited by Power, Inc., for Outstanding Contributions to Black Liberation in 1972.

### JAMES P. McQUAY
### Furrier

James McQuay is known as "The Black Furrier" because he is the only black in the wholesale-retail fur manufacturing business. McQuay opened his first store in Harlem with $460. It took him seven years to get to the point where he was making a living for himself. At the beginning Mr. McQuay did most of the manual labor himself, but as time went on and business picked up, he did less and less. Since 1963, Mr. McQuay has operated in the heart of the wholesale fur district in New York City, making custom-made coats, producing specialty items for several prestigious stores, and remodeling, repairing, and altering old furs. His clientele includes entertainers, politicians, community and business leaders from all over the nation. Mr. McQuay's designs are also in demand all across the nation for various fashion galas.

### L. PEARL MITCHELL
### Humanitarian

L. Pearl Mitchell is a former director of the NAACP and functionary of Alpha Kappa Alpha sorority. Born in Wilberforce, Ohio, she began teaching music in 1915, worked as a juvenile probation officer in Cleveland for 20 years, and served as director of membership drives for the NAACP. In 1965, she coordinated several AKA fund drives which raised nearly $500,000 in life memberships for the NAACP. Langston Hughes' poem "I dream" is dedicated to her.

### WINSTON E. MOORE
### State Official

Director of the Cook County (Chicago) Department of Corrections, Winston Moore was born in New Orleans in 1929. He obtained a B.S. from West Virginia State College and an M.S. in psychology from the University of Louisville. In 1961, he joined the Illinois Youth Commission as a psychologist and soon became a clinic director. In 1968, he was named warden of the Cook County Jail and was appointed Director of the county's penal system in 1969.

### RICHARD DAVID MORRISON
### Educator

Richard David Morrison is president of Alabama A & M University. Born in Utica, Miss., in 1910, he joined the college in 1937, rising to chairman of the Agriculture Division before being appointed college president in 1962. Since then, he has directed a fundamental reorganization of the school, gaining it full academic accreditation as a university, increasing student enrollment 60%, and constructing several new buildings.

### JOHN A. MORSELL
### Administrator

John A. Morsell serves both as assistant executive director of the NAACP and as a member of the New York City Board of Higher Education. Born in Pittsburgh in 1912, he became an eminent sociological researcher, focusing on racial integration and civil rights questions, before joining the NAACP in 1956. He is a Fellow of the American Sociological Association and a member of the American Association for Public Opinion Research.

### HUGO A. OWENS
### City Official, Dentist

A member of the Dental Staff of the Portsmouth, Va. General Hospital and president of the Portsmouth branch of the NAACP, Hugo A. Owens became the first black city councilman in Chesapeake County history in 1970, and has since been reelected to that post. Born in 1917, he served in the U.S. Army during World War II and graduated from Howard University Dental College in 1947. He is a formidable organizer of community action and public opinion.

### HENRY G. PARKS JR.
### Executive

Henry G. Parks Jr. is founder and president of H. G. Parks, Inc., the famous sausage makers in Baltimore. Born in Atlanta in 1916, he started his present company in 1951 and, within 20 years, had brought sales past the $10 million mark. He is a director of several corporations including Magnavox and First Pennsylvania.

### JOHN A. PEOPLES
### Educator

John A. Peoples was appointed president of Mississippi's Jackson State College in 1967. Born in Starkville, Miss., in 1926, he began his career in education as an instructor of mathematics in Gary, Ind., in 1951. His memberships include the Institute for Educational Management, the American Association for Higher Education, and HEW's Advisory Committee on Accreditation and Institutional Eligibility.

### CHANNING E. PHILLIPS
### Administrator

As president of the Housing Development Corp. in Washington, D.C., the Reverend Channing E. Phillips supervises the firm's real estate transactions and property management. Born in Brooklyn, N.Y., in 1928, he has taught at several colleges. At the 1968 Democratic National Convention in Chicago, he became the first black American ever nominated for the office of President of the United States.

### DARLENE WRIGHT POWELL
### Lawyer

Darlene Wright Powell handles general corporate law matters in the Washington, D.C. and mid-Atlantic region for Kaiser Permanente, one of the nation's largest health maintenance organizations. Her duties as associate regional counsel concern land use and zoning, commercial real estate, contract law and tax issues. Ms. Powell, who is married to attorney Clayton J. Powell, is a graduate of Cornell University and has a law degree from the University of Maryland.

### ERSA HINES POSTON
### State Official

Ersa Hines Poston became president of the New York State Civil Service Commission in 1967, taking on a department with 900 employees and a yearly budget of $10 million. Born in Paducah, Ky., in 1921, she began her career with the Hartford Tuberculosis and Health Association in 1946. She has been a confidential assistant to Governor Nelson Rockefeller and director of the New York State Office of Economic Opportunity.

*Reverend Samuel Proctor is pastor of New York's famous Abyssinian Baptist Church.*

**ALVIN POUSSAINT**
**Psychiatrist**

Alvin Poussaint is associate dean of students at the Harvard University Medical School, where he also teaches psychiatry. Born in New York City in 1934, he has taught at Tufts University Medical School, has written several articles as well as the book *Why Blacks Kill Blacks* (1972), and is one of the founding fellows of The Black Academy of Arts and Letters.

**JOHN L. PROCOPE**
**Editor, Publisher**

In 1974, John L. Procope took the reins as editor and publisher of the New York *Amsterdam News,* one of the nation's more important and prestigious black newspapers, with a circulation of 91,000. In an era marked by black newspaper failures, he has successfully redirected his paper's focus toward significant national events rather than concentrating on community events of limited appeal. A native of New York City, he attended Morgan State College and did graduate work in marketing at New York University.

**SAMUEL DeWITT PROCTOR**
**Clergyman**

Reverend Samuel DeWitt Proctor is pastor of New York's famous Abyssinian Baptist Church and is a professor of education at Rutgers University. Born in Norfolk, Va., in 1921, he was ordained in 1943 and has held several important posts in government, education, and the church. He is a trustee of Meharry Medical College, the National Urban League, and Ottawa University, and is the author of *The Young Negro in America, 1960-1980.*

**MAHLON T. PURYEAR**
**Administrator**

Mahlon T. Puryear is director of the Economic Development Department of the National Urban League. Born in Winston-Salem, N.C., in 1915, he has been a college teacher, a personnel counselor for Wright Aeronautical Corp., and has served in various capacities with the Urban League since 1951. In 1968, he became president of Manpower Consultants to direct their projected coordination of employer needs and school programs.

**ROYAL W. PURYEAR**
**Educator**

Royal W. Puryear is president of Miami's Florida Memorial College, an accredited Southern Association senior college which he built up from a two-year institution. Born in Winston-Salem, N.C., in 1912, he began his teaching career in the public schools of his hometown and has been associate pastor of St. John the Baptist Church in Dallas and president of Butler College in Tyler, Texas.

*Mahlon T. Puryear directs the Economic Development Department of the National Urban League.*

## ROY S. ROBERTS
**Executive**

Roy S. Roberts, who has been with General Motors Corporation since 1977, is currently GM's vice president of Personnel Administration and Development Staff. He began his automotive career as an instrument inspector and assembler with Lear Siegler, Inc. in 1959. He later joined GM as a salaried employee-in-training in Grand Rapids, Mich., and worked his way up from assistant superintendent to plant manager in 1981. He holds a business administration degree from Western Michigan University. In 1982, he completed the program for Management Development at Harvard Graduate School of Business, and in 1988 was awarded an honorary doctorate of Laws from Grand Valley State University. He is associated with the Detroit Zoological Society, and the United Foundation of Metropolitan Detroit.

## JAMES A. RUSSELL JR.
**Educator**

James A. Russell Jr., is president of Saint Paul's College in his hometown of Lawrenceville, Va. Born in 1917, he taught for many years at Hampton Institute, where he developed outstanding engineering and technology programs to train young black men and women for positions in industry. He has received several awards, including the 1971 Outstanding Educator of America.

*Stanley S. Scott, vice president, director of Corporate Relations and assistant to the Chairman of the Board of Philip Morris Companies, Inc.*

*Roy S. Roberts, General Motors Corporation's vice president of Personnel Administration and Development Staff.*

## STANLEY S. SCOTT
**Executive**

Stanley S. Scott has been an executive with Philip Morris Inc. since 1977. His most recent position, assigned in May 1987, is vice president, director of Corporate Relations and assistant to the Chairman of the Board of Philip Morris Companies, Inc., the parent company. Mr. Scott, a Korean War veteran, earned a Bachelor of Arts degree in Journalism from Lincoln University in Missouri. In his reporting career, he worked for the Atlanta Daily world, Memphis World, and for United Press International, where he was nominated for a Pulitzer Prize for his eye-witness account of the slaying of Malcolm X. He also worked as a radio reporter for Westinghouse Broadcasting Corporation in New York City, and as public relations director for the NAACP. In 1971, he was asked to join the Nixon White House staff as assistant director of communications, and later served as assistant to the President during the Ford Administration. In 1975, he was named assistant administrator to the State Department's Agency for International Development, which sent him on extensive travels to Europe and Africa. In addition to his work at Philip Morris, Mr. Scott served the Reagan Administration as a member of the Advisory Committee on Small and Minority Business Ownership, and the President's Commission on White House Fellowships. He is otherwise affiliated with St. Luke's/Roosevelt Hospital Center, North Carolina Central University School of Law, and the Smithsonian Institution's National Museum of African Art.

### LEANDER J. SHAW, JR.
### Justice, Florida Supreme Court

Leander J. Shaw, Jr., was appointed him to the Supreme Court of Florida in January of 1983 by Governor Graham.

Justice Shaw came to Tallahassee in 1957 as an assistant professor of law at Florida A & M University and was admitted to the Florida Bar in 1960. He is a member of the American Bar, National Bar, Florida Bar, Florida Government Bar, and Tallahassee Bar Associations and is admitted to practice in all Florida courts, the United States Southern District Court of Florida, the United States Circuit Court of Appeals for the Eleventh Circuit, and the United States Supreme Court.

Justice Shaw has an active background in community, civic, and church activities having received numerous awards for his outstanding service. He is the father of five children, and he and his wife, Vidya, live on Lake Iamonia in Leon County.

He attended public schools in Virginia and received his B.A. degree in 1952 from West Virginia State College in Institute, west Virginia. After serving in the Korean conflict as an artillery officer, he entered law school and earned his Juris Doctor degree in 1957 from Howard University in Washington, D.C. In 1986 he was awarded an honorary Doctor of Laws degree from West Virginia State College, Institute, West Virginia.

### FRED L. SHUTTLESWORTH
### Clergyman

The Reverend Fred L. Shuttlesworth serves as pastor of the Greater New Light Baptist Church in Cincinnati, Ohio, and is the national secretary of the Southern Christian Leadership Conference (SCLC). Born in Montgomery, Ala., in 1922, he organized the Alabama Christian Movement for Human Rights in 1952, and was an important aide to Martin Luther King Jr.

### WILLIAM E. SIMS
### Educator

William E. Sims has been president of Oklahoma's Langston University since 1970. Born in Chickasha, Okla., in 1921, he served in the U.S. Navy as a musician from 1942 to 1946 and taught public school in Tulsa, before joining the Langston faculty as a professor of music and band director in 1953. He is a member of the Adult Education Association and has worked with the Oklahoma Humanities Task Force.

### BETTE SMITH
### Executive

Bette Smith is president of Completion Bond Company, the most successful of four major completion-guarantee companies. Primarily serving the entertainment industry, Ms. Smith's company ensures that motion picture and television productions are produced and delivered on time, within budget. Her company, which was started in 1981, is based in Los Angeles, with offices in London, Paris, Rome, Toronto, and in Australia. Ms. Smith is a graduate of West Virginia University and was senior vice president with the Albert G. Rubin Insurance Agency in Los Angeles before striking out on her own. Since its inception, Completion Bond Company has insured more than $1 billion in aggregate production budgets.

### ASA T. SPAULDING SR.
### Executive

Asa T. Spaulding is president of his own consulting firm in Durham, N.C., which he formed in 1968 after retiring from the presidency of North Carolina Mutual Life Insurance Co., the largest black-controlled insurance company in the world. Born in Columbus County, N.C., in 1902, he worked at North Carolina Mutual for 36 years, was named the first black director of W. T. Grant Co. in 1964, and is an advisor to many governmental commissions and philanthropic organizations.

### EDWARD S. SPRIGGS
### Executive

Artist and author Edward S. Spriggs is the executive director of The Studio Museum of Contemporary Black Art in Harlem, New York City. Born in Cleveland in 1934, he has worked as a freelance graphic artist, a sound technician, and a film editor. A consultant to the New York State Council on the Arts, he edits *Black Dialogue* magazine, and is a member of the American Association of Museums and the International Council of Museums.

### WILLIAM H. STAFFORD
### Executive

As executive director of the New York Community Training Institute, Inc., William H. Stafford is a recognized leader in the development of programs to solve the problems of training men and women in the nation's poverty areas. Born in Valdosta, Ga., in 1929, he graduated from Kentucky State College and holds a masters degree from Adelphi University School of Social Work. Prior to his present position, he worked for several years with the New York City Youth Board and gave counseling in special manpower programs for the Board of Education and for Mobilization for Youth. He has been instrumental in developing many programs which operate in New York City's 26 poverty areas, providing training in management, comprehensive health, nontraditional degree programs, economic development, housing, management and maintenance, and board operations and institutional development.

### REMBERT EDWARDS STOKES
**Educator**

A.M.E. minister Rembert Edwards Stokes has been president of Wilberforce University since 1956. Born in Dayton, Ohio, in 1917, he was formerly dean of the school's Payne Theological Seminary. He is a trustee of the Cleveland Chapter of the National Conference of Christians and Jews and a member of the Ohio Mental Health Association, the National Council of Churches, and the American Association for the Advancement of Science.

### LEON HOWARD SULLIVAN
**Clergyman, Executive**

Founder and board chairman of the Opportunities Industrialization Centers of America, the Reverend Leon Sullivan was born in Charleston, W.Va., in 1922 and ordained a Baptist minister in 1941. In 1944, he was a prominent figure in A. Philip Randolph's successful threat to march on Washington to obtain jobs for blacks. During this period, Sullivan served as an aide to the Rev. Adam Clayton Powell Jr., while the latter was running for Congress. In 1951, Sullivan was named pastor of the Zion Baptist Church, Philadelphia, and in 1964 formed OIC, which soon became one of the largest and most prestigious job training organizations in the world. In 1971, Rev. Sullivan was named a director of General Motors.

### ALVIN I. THOMAS
**Educator**

President of Prairie View A & M College since 1966, Alvin I. Thomas had formerly served the school as industrial arts instructor, woodwork instructor, director of industrial education, and dean of the school of Industrial Education and Technology. Born in New Orleans in 1925, he has been a consultant for the public schools of Texas, Kansas, California, and Ohio, and for Dow Chemical, Litton Industries, and the U.S. Office of Education. He is a member of the National Education Association and the Texas Rural Development Commission.

### FRANKLIN THOMAS
**Attorney, Administrator**

Franklin Thomas, president of the Ford Foundation, is the first black person to head a major philanthropic organization. An attorney, Thomas served as president and chief executive officer of the Bedford-Stuyvesant Restoration Corporation in Brooklyn from 1967 to 1977, where he helped establish neighborhood businesses, renovate local residences, and create thousands of new jobs. Thomas was born in the Bedford-Stuyvesant section of Brooklyn in a stable working-class environment and was the only member of his family to go to college. As a youngster growing up in Bed-Stuy, Thomas avoided street gangs and became active in the Boy Scouts. He developed his skill in basketball on black-top courts and went on to Franklin K. Lane High School where he was captain and star of the basketball team. He also excelled academically. At Columbia University, Thomas starred on the basketball team and was voted the Ivy League's most valuable player in 1955 and 1956. He became the first black student to serve as captain of the team. In 1963 and 1964 Thomas worked as an adviser and attorney in the regional New York office of the Federal Housing and Home Finance Agency, and in 1964, was appointed assistant United States attorney for the Southern District of New York. Thomas was appointed deputy police commissioner of New York City in 1965, the fourth black man to serve in that position. He has served as a director or trustee of several organizations, including the John Hay Whitney Foundation, the Foreign Policy Study Foundation, and the Columbia Law School Alumni Association. Thomas has been on the boards of directors of such corporations as the Columbia Broadcasting System, the Aluminum Corporation of America, the Cummins Engine Company, Allied Stores Corporation, and the New York Life Insurance Corporation.

### JAMES S. THOMAS
**Clergyman**

Bishop James S. Thomas watches over the nearly 1,000 congregations of the United Methodist Church in Iowa and directs the Church's assistance programs. Born in Orangeburg, S.C., in 1919, he has been instrumental in

*William Toby, Regional Administrator of the Health Care Financing Administration in Region II.*

securing Church support for black private colleges, launching the program by which 11 black colleges of the Methodist Church gained accreditation from the Southern Association of Schools and Colleges.

### WILLIAM TOBY
### Administrator

William Toby, who holds a Masters Degree in International Development from Harvard University's John F. Kennedy School of Government, a Bachelor's Degree in Spanish Studies from West Virginia State College, has served as Regional Administrator of the Health Care Financing Administration of the Federal Government in Region II since the formation of this new agency on June 19, 1977.

Prior to this appointment, Mr. Toby was Regional Commissioner of HEW's Social and Rehabilitation Service (SRS) in Region II, with responsibility for medicaid, public assistance, and social service programs.

Before being named SRS Regional Commissioner, Mr. Toby had served New York City's Office of the Mayor as inter-governmental relations officer and held key positions with HEW and the National Urban League.

Mr. Toby has been the recipient of numerous awards. Among them, the John W. Davis Meritorious Achievement Award. Previously, an Appreciation Award from the International Health Economics and Management Institute, the U.S. Department of Health and Human Services' Award for Exceptional Achievement in controlling Medicaid costs in New York State.

Mr. Toby was born in Augusta, Georgia, on August 12, 1934 and later raised in New York City.

*Eugene Toomer is Vice President for Employee Relations at Alexander's Department Stores.*

### EUGENE A. TOOMER
### Executive

In his post as vice president for Employee Relations and Urban Affairs at Alexander's Department Stores, Eugene Toomer has been instrumental in implementing Equal Opportunity efforts and programs for 13 stores and more than 13,000 employees.Born in Macon, Georgia, in 1921, he earned his B.A. at Kentucky State University, where he was an all-American football player, and his M.A. at Wayne State University. He is on the executive board of Edges, on the board of directors of the Bronx-Manhattan Mental Health Association, and is the president of the Consumer Distribution Committee for Retail Industries. Mr. Toomer has also been very involved in community programs.

### WILLIAM H. TOWNSEND
### Legislator

A member of the Arkansas House of Representatives, William H. Townsend is also a practicing optometrist in Little Rock. Born near West Point, Miss., in 1914, he became the first black optometrist licensed in Arkansas in 1950, and is now president of the Arkansas Council on Human Relations, vice president of the Arkansas Optometric Association, and treasurer of Professional Services, Inc. He is a trustee of Mt. Zion Baptist Church in Little Rock.

### JACKIE VAUGHN III
### Legislator

Michigan state representative Jackie Vaughn III wrote his state's ground-breaking voting rights bill for 18-year-olds. Born in Birmingham, Ala., in 1939, he studied social science at Oxford University as a Fulbright Scholar and Fellow, and was the first black to be elected president of the Young Democrats of Michigan.

### JOHN THOMAS WALKER
### Clergyman

The Rt. Reverend John Thomas Walker, bishop of the Episcopal Diocese of Washington, D.C., was born in Barnesville, Ga., in 1925. Placing great emphasis on social and educational reform, he provides an active chairmanship to the Negro Student Fund. He is a member of the boards of trustees of Absalom Jones Theological Institute in Atlanta, St. Paul's School in New Hampshire, and the National Cathedral School for Girls in Washington, D.C.

### LUCIUS WALKER JR.
### Clergyman

The Reverend Lucius Walker Jr., is executive director of the Inter-religious Foundation for Community Organization in

*Reverend Wyatt Tee Walker advised New York Governor Nelson Rockefeller on urban affairs.*

New York City, which provides economic assistance for black community development. Born in Roselle, N.J., in 1930, he is a member of the Black Foundation Executives and sits on the board of trustees of Shaw University and over Newton Theological School.

### WYATT TEE WALKER
**Clergyman**

Former chief of staff to Martin Luther King Jr., the Reverend Wyatt Tee Walker is minister of the Canaan Baptist Church of Christ in New York City, and was urban affairs assistant to the governor of New York. Born in Brockton, Mass., in 1929, he has conducted sensitivity seminars on racial polarization for IBM, New York Bell Telephone Co., and Consolidated Edison. Under his direction the Canaan Baptist Church has grown physically and financially and has added several new social programs.

### WILLIAM J. L. WALLACE
**Educator**

William J. L. Wallace is president of West Virginia State College in Institute, W.Va. Born in Salisbury, N.C., in 1908, he is a member of the West Virginia Advisory Committee, the U.S. Commission on Civil Rights, and the Farmers Home Administration. He was awarded the Outstanding Civilian Service Medal of the Army in 1972. In 1987 he recieved the Martin Luther King, Jr. "Living the Dream" award for outstanding scholarship.

### WALTER WASHINGTON
**Educator**

Walter Washington is president of Alcorn A & M College in Lorman, Miss., the oldest land-grant college in the nation, where he has initiated a dynamic program of renovation and improvements. Born in Hazlehurst, Miss., in 1923, he is a member of the Mississippi Advisory Commission on Vocational Education, vice chairman of the secondary commission of the Southern Association of Colleges and Schools, and a member of the state board of directors of the Boy Scouts of America. He has served as a director for several public utilities as well as being on the board of directors of Blue Cross/Blue Shield of Mississippi. Among his many other activities he was a member of the presidential commission of the NCAA.

### LEVI WATKINS
**Educator**

Founder and former president of Owen College in Memphis, Levi Watkins former president of Alabama State University in Montgomery was also president of Bishop College in Dallas Texas. Bishop College was closed in 1988 because of the tremendous fall-off in enrollment at the school. Born in Montgomery, Ky., he was a vice president of the Alabama Commission on Higher Education and a member of the Advisory Board on Health and Environmental Quality.

### BARBARA M. WATSON
**Federal Official**

Barbara M. Watson is former administrator of the Bureau of Security and Consular Affairs of the U.S. State Department in Washington, D.C. Born in New York City in 1918, she has operated a successful modeling school, worked as an attorney with the New York City Board of Statutory Review, and was executive director of the New York City Commission to the United Nations (1964-1966). She is a member of the board of directors of the United Mutual Life Insurance Co.

### KENNETH L. WEBSTER
**Legislator**

Kenneth L. Webster is a member of the Maryland House of Delegates from Baltimore's 5th District and is also a community relations assistant for the Model Cities Housing Development. Born in Baltimore in 1935, he served in the Strategic Air Command and is a member of the Black United Front, the Baltimore Advisory Council of Vocational Education, and the New Democratic Coalition of Maryland.

*Social activist A. Cecil Williams of Celebrations and Involvement at San Francisco's Glide Memorial United Methodist Church.*

## LEONARD 12X WEIR
### Policeman

New York City patrolman Leonard 12X Weir is founder and president of the National Society of Afro-American Policemen. Born in New York in 1931, he has been a patrolman since 1959, and his current assignment is in the Internal Affairs Division, which investigates police corruption. He is a member of the Nation of Islam and the owner of a book and natural foods store.

## VERDA F. WELCOME
### Legislator

Verda F. Welcome is a state senator from Baltimore's 4th District. She was elected State Senator for her first term in 1963. Born in Lake Lure, N.C., she became the first woman and the first black to be elected to Baltimore's senate in 1963. She sponsored the 1967 "Miscegenation Bill" repealing the ban on interracial marriage and the 1968 bill to prohibit racial discrimination in the sale of new housing. Among her many awars is an achievement award from the National Council of Negro Women and an outstanding services award from Tau Gamma Delta.

## WILLIAM R. WILKES
### Clergyman

A.M.E. bishop William R. Wilkes is now responsible for the episcopal district of Kentucky and Tennessee. Born in Eatonton, Ga., in 1902, he has served the Church in many capacities. During his tenure as bishop of Ohio he was instrumental in adding many new buildings to the campus of Wilberforce University.

## A. CECIL WILLIAMS
### Clergyman

The Reverend A. Cecil Williams is minister of Celebrations and Involvement at the Glide Memorial United Methodist Church in San Francisco. Born in San Angelo, Tex., in 1929, he takes an initiatory role in multiracial social reform. He has served as co-chairman for the Congress of Racial Equality, is a trustee of the Martin Luther King Center for Social Change, and hosts a weekly TV public affairs program.

## CHANCELLOR WILLIAMS
### Educator

Dr. Chancellor Williams is a retired Howard University history professor who grew up in Bennettsville, S.C. As a child, Williams wanted to know more about the social positions of blacks in America and did a great deal of reading on the subject during his youth. Dr. Williams has written eight books, among them *The Destruction of Black Civilization: Great Issues of a Race from 4500 B.C. to 2000 A.D.* He has a B.A. in education and an M.A. degree in history, both from Howard University. His Ph.D. in history and sociology is from American University. Williams has spent his lifetime rediscovering the truth of the African past.

## HARDY WILLIAMS
**Legislator**

Democrat Hardy Williams was elected to the Pennsylvania legislature from his hometown of Philadelphia in 1970. An attorney with a private practice, he is a member of the Lawyers Committee for Civil Rights, the Philadelphia Council for Community Advancement, and Community Legal Services. He was born in 1931.

## NATHAN WRIGHT JR.
**Educator**

Professor Nathan Wright Jr. teaches urban affairs at the State University of New York in Albany. Born in Shreveport, La., in 1923, he is a prolific author, with more than 300 published articles to his credit. His award-winning books include *Black Power and Urban Unrest; What Black Educators Are Saying;* and *Ready to Riot*. He has been a columnist for the *Newark Star-Ledger*, chairman of the 1967 and 1968 National and International Conferences on Black Power in Newark and Philadelphia, and was one of the participants in the "Journey of Reconciliation" in CORE's 1967 freedom ride.

## OTHER PROMINENT BLACK AMERICANS

| Name | Occupation | Born |
|---|---|---|
| Adams, Albert W., Jr. | Administrator | 1948 |
| Adams, John D. | PR executive | 1943 |
| Alexander, Louis G. | Bank executive | 1910 |
| Alexander, William H. | Legislator, lawyer | 1930 |
| Allen, Aris T. | Legislator, physician | 1910 |
| Allen, George Louis | Businessman, legislator | 1910 |
| Allen, George M. | Legislator | 1933 |
| Allen, Willie | Clergyman | 1921 |
| Amory, Reginald L. | Engineer, educator | 1936 |
| Amos, Larry C. | Corporate attorney | 1935 |
| Anderson, Gloria L. | Educator | 1938 |
| Anderson, Marcellus J., Sr. | Businessman | 1900 |
| Anderson, Harold | manager | 1939 |
| Arlene, Herbert | Legislator | 1917 |
| Arnelle, Hugh J. | Attorney | 1933 |
| Artis, Anthony J. | Environmental engineer | 1951 |
| Atkins, Thomas I. | Legislator | 1939 |
| Bailey, Adrienne Y. | Foundation administrator, educator | 1944 |
| Barbee, Lloyd A. | Legislator | 1925 |
| Barnes, Eugene M. | Legislator | 1931 |
| Barnett, Brenetta Howell | State official | 1932 |
| Bates, Nathaniel | Mayor | 1931 |
| Bearden, Harold I. | Clergyman | 1910 |
| Bell, Thomas M. | Legislator, businessman | 1948 |
| Bennett, Marion D. | Clergyman, legislator | 1936 |
| Billington, Clyde | Legislator, realtor | 1934 |
| Bishop, Cecil | Clergyman | 1930 |
| Black, Leona R. | County official | 1924 |
| Blackwell, Lucien E. | Legislator | 1931 |
| Blackwell, Robert B. | Public official | 1921 |
| Blakeley, Ulysses B., Sr. | Clergyman | 1911 |
| Bodden, Wendell N. | Administrator | 1930 |
| Bolden, Darwin W. | Executive | 1932 |
| Bonner, Isaiah H. | Clergyman | 1890 |
| Boone, Charles H. | Marketing specialist | 1932 |
| Booth, L. Venchael | Clergyman | 1919 |
| Borders, William H. | Clergyman | 1905 |
| Bowen, William F. | Legislator | 1929 |
| Brailey, Troy | Legislator | 1916 |
| Branch, Dorothy S. | Clergy woman | 1922 |
| Brown, Eddie C. | Investment counselor | 1940 |
| Brown, Tony | Producer | 1933 |
| Caldwell, James F. | Tax counsel | 1930 |
| Cafritz, Peggy C. | TV executive | 1947 |
| Carr, Charles V. | Legislator, businessman | 1903 |
| Carter, James Y. | Legislator | 1915 |
| Carter, Matthew G. | Business executive | 1915 |
| Cashin, John L. Jr. | Dentist, politician | 1928 |
| Charbonnet, Louis, III | Legislator, businessman | 1939 |
| Cherry, Gwen S. | Legislator | 1923 |
| Chess, Sammie Jr. | Judge | 1934 |
| Chester, Joseph A., Sr. | Legislator | 1914 |
| Clark, Caesar A. W. | Clergyman | 1914 |
| Clark, Robert G. | Legislator | 1929 |
| Cleveland, Jones | Clergyman | 1931 |
| Clyburn, James E. | Gubernatorial aide | 1940 |
| Coleman, Charles A. | Administrator | 1921 |
| Colter, Cyrus J. | Public official | 1910 |
| Combs, Willa R. | Educator | 1925 |
| Common, Davita | Editor | 1949 |
| Compton, James W. | Administrator | 1939 |
| Connor, George C. Jr. | Legislator | 1921 |
| Cooper, Peggy | Attorney | 1947 |
| Copes, Glenda L. | Business executive | 1943 |
| Coston, Bessie | Administrator | 1916 |
| Cousins, William Jr. | Legislator, attorney | 1927 |
| Curls, Phillip B. | Legislator | 1942 |
| Daniel, David | Administrator | 1906 |
| Daniels, Hayzel B. | Jurist | 1907 |
| Darnell, Emma I. | City official | 1937 |
| Davis, Charles A. | Administrator | 1922 |
| Davis, Corneal A. | Legislator | 1900 |
| Davis, Edward D. | Businessman | 1904 |
| Davis, Normen Emanuel | Asso. exc. | 1941 |
| Dawkins, Maurice A. | Administrator | 1921 |
| Dean, James E. | Legislator | 1945 |
| Dean, Walter R. | Legislator | 1934 |

| Name | Occupation | Born |
|---|---|---|
| Dilday, William H., Jr. | Executive | 1937 |
| Dixon, Isaiah Jr. | Legislator | 1922 |
| Doss, Lawrence P. | Administrator | 1927 |
| Douglas, Herbert P., Jr. | Executive | 1922 |
| Douglass, Calvin A. | Legislator | 1909 |
| Douglass, John W. | Legislator | 1942 |
| Dunham, Robert | Restaurateur | 1932 |
| Dunmore, Albert J. | Administrator | 1915 |
| Edgill, John W. | Executive | 1921 |
| Edwards, Alfred L. | Federal official | 1920 |
| Edwards, George H. | Legislator | 1911 |
| Elliott, Daisy | Legislator | 1919 |
| Evans, Samuel L. | Administrator | 1902 |
| Ewell, Raymond W. | Legislator | 1928 |
| Fielding, Herbert V. | Legislator | 1923 |
| Fields, Charles L. | Executive | 1932 |
| Fierce, Hughlyn F. | Executive | 1932 |
| Fitzpatrick, William T. | Administrator | 1889 |
| Foggie, Samuel L. | Executive | 1927 |
| Frost, Wilson | City official | 1925 |
| Gardner, Betram E. | Banker | 1915 |
| Gaston, Arthur G., Sr. | Businessman | 1892 |
| Goode, Malvin R. | Media consultant | 1908 |
| Goward, Russell | Legislator | 1935 |
| Granger, Shelton B. | Civic official | 1921 |
| Graves, Curtis M. | Administrator | 1938 |
| Graves, Earl Gilbert | Executive | 1935 |
| Greene, Bill | Legislator | 1931 |
| Hamer, Fannie Lou | Community leader | 1917 |
| Hamilton, Paul L. | Curriculum specialist | 1941 |
| Hampton, Leroy | Executive | 1927 |
| Hancock, Wayman E., Jr. | Marketing representative | 1937 |
| Harris, Charles F. | Executive | 1934 |
| Harris, J. Robert | Marketing analyst | 1944 |
| Harris, Marion R. | Business ex. | 1934 |
| Hayes, Reginald C. | Executive | 1928 |
| Hernandez, Aileen Claile | Org. ex. | 1926 |
| Hicks, William H. | Legislator | 1925 |
| Hobson, Charles | Broadcast journalist | 1926 |
| Holloway, Ruth L. | Administrator | 1932 |
| Holmes, David S., Jr. | Legislator | 1914 |
| Holomon, Frank | Legislator | 1934 |
| Hoover, Odie W., Jr. | Clergyman | 1921 |
| Hunter, Clarence H. | Administrator | 1925 |
| Hunter, James | Executive | 1936 |
| Irby, Roy | Executive | 1918 |
| Jackson, George E. | Executive | 1931 |
| Jackson, Johnny, Jr. | Legislator | 1943 |
| Jackson, Samuel C. | Administrator | 1929 |
| Jarrett, Vernon D. | Journalist | 1921 |
| Jeffries, Leroy N. | Market consultant | 1911 |
| Jennings, Robert R. | Educator | 1950 |
| Johnson, George E. | Businessman | 1927 |
| Jones, Benjamin E. | Administrator | 1935 |
| Jones, Johnnie A. | Legislator | 1919 |
| Jones, Paul R. | Federal executive | 1930 |
| Jones, Sidney A. Jr. | Judge | 1909 |
| Jordon, Orchid I. | Legislator | 1910 |
| King, Edward B. Jr. | Executive | 1939 |
| Kornegay, Francis A. | Executive | 1913 |
| Lewis, Aubrey C. | Executive | 1937 |
| Lewis, Byron | Executive | 1931 |
| Lewis, Edward | Executive | 1940 |
| Lewis, Elma I. | Administrator | 1929 |
| Lewis, Elsie Makel | Educator | 1914 |
| Lyles, Leonard E. | Executive | 1936 |
| McClendon, Ernestine | Businesswoman | 1921 |
| McGee, Henry W. | Postal official | 1910 |
| McGuire, Rosalie J. | Educator | 1910 |
| McNeal, Dorothy M. | Social worker | 1922 |
| Melton, Mitchell W. | Legislator | 1943 |
| Moore, Daniel A. | Executive | 1935 |
| Moore, George A. | TV producer | 1914 |
| Moore, Hilliard T., Sr. | City official | 1925 |
| Norford, George E. | Administrator | 1918 |
| Owens, Jesse | Marketing executive | 1913 |
| Parker, Joseph C., Jr. | Trial lawyer | 1952 |
| Payton, Sallyanne | White House aide | 1943 |
| Rayford, Phillip L. | Ed. administrator | 1927 |
| Reynolds, Hobson R. | Administrator | 1898 |
| Rhodes, Joseph, Sr. | Legislator | 1947 |
| Richardson, George C. | Legislator | 1929 |
| Robertson, William B. | Legislator | 1933 |
| Robinson, William P. Sr. | Legislator | 1911 |
| Rollins, Joseph W., Jr. | Manpower expert | 1920 |
| Sanders, Charles L. | Consultant | 1938 |
| Sears, Arthur Jr. | Consultant | 1928 |
| Seymour, Frank M. | Businessman | 1916 |
| Sherwood, Kenneth N. | Businessman | 1930 |
| Simmons, Leonard | Public official | 1920 |
| Simmons, Sylvia J. | Educator | 1935 |
| Singleton, Mary L. | Legislator | 1926 |
| Smith, Herman B., Jr. | Administrator | 1927 |
| Smith, Kelly M., Sr. | Clergyman | 1920 |
| Smith, Nate | Library specialist | 1929 |
| Talbot, Gerald E. | State official | 1931 |
| Thomas, Franklin A. | Administrator | 1934 |
| Tucker, Dorothy M. | Psychologist, educator | 1942 |
| Vaughn, Jacqueline B. | Union official | 1935 |
| Wedgeworth, Robert, Jr. | Administrator | 1937 |
| Williams, Betty Smith | Nurse, educator | 1929 |
| Wilson, Margaret F. | Librarian | 1932 |
| Wright, Stephen J. | Educator | 1910 |
| Younger, Robert D. | Computer science | 1932 |

# BLACK FIRSTS: A COMPILATION OF INTERESTING DEBUT EVENTS

The following list of firsts describes a wide spectrum of pioneering events in African-American history. Many of the moments described possess considerable intrinsic significance — such as the first publication of a novel by a black author in 1853, or the selection of the first interracial jury in 1865 for the trial of ex-Confederate president Jefferson Davis—while other events listed are merely interesting. To all of these breakthroughs, great and small, an undeniable human interest attaches, for they tell of people who refused to accept old limitations. Seen as a whole, the list has an even greater importance, for it takes on a historical shape. From this perspective, the individual stories of courage and daring combine to reveal a very personal and nontheoretical chart of the progress of equal opportunity and black achievement in America. This section does not repeat many of the most important firsts in civil rights, science, the arts, and entertainment, which are dealt with at length in their respective sections of the *Almanac*, especially in the biographies of the individuals involved.

**1621** **William Tucker** becomes the first black child born in the American colonies. A native of Jamestown, Virginia, his birthright entails the same privileges of freedom and liberty enjoyed by the white children of the colony.

**1623** The first black in the colonies to be baptized a Christian is a child named **Anthony**, son of Isabel and William, who becomes a member of the Anglican Church in Jamestown.

**1783** **James Derham**, born a slave in Philadelphia in 1762, becomes the first black physician in the United States. After learning medicine, while serving as an assistant to his master (a doctor by profession), Derham purchased his freedom in 1783, and went on to develop a thriving practice with both black and white clientele. By 1788, he was considered to be one of the leading physicians in New Orleans. Dr. Benjamin Rush, a famous contemporary of Derham, once said of him: "I have conversed with him upon most of the acute and epidemic diseases of the country where he lives. I expected to have suggested some new medicines to him, but he suggested many more to me."

**1786** **Lemuel Haynes**, who served in the Revolution as a minuteman, becomes the first black minister with a white congregation.

**1795** First black missionary minister to work with Indians is **John Morront** of New York. He is ordained as a Methodist minister on May 15 in London, England. Among his converts to the Christian faith were a Cherokee chieftain and his daughter.

**1826** The first black college graduate, **John Russwurm**, receives his degree from Bowdoin College in Maine in

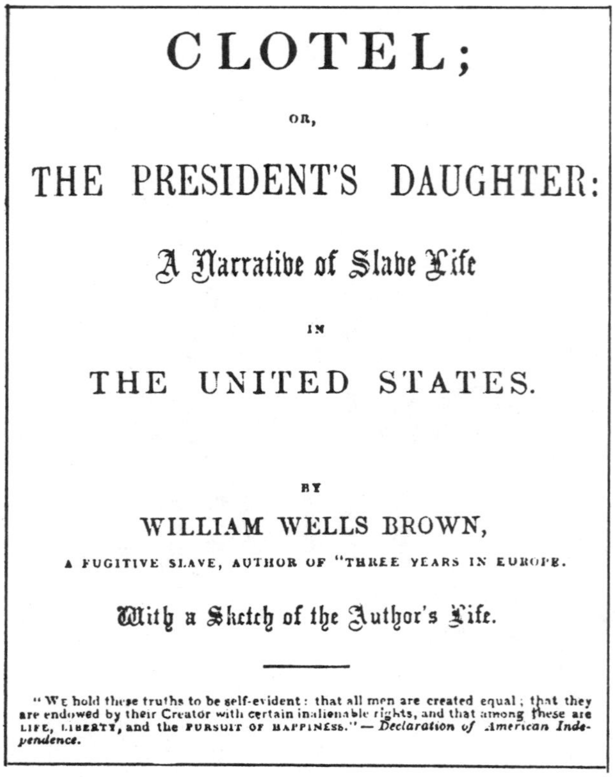

CLOTEL;

OR,

THE PRESIDENT'S DAUGHTER:

A Narrative of Slave Life

IN

THE UNITED STATES.

BY

WILLIAM WELLS BROWN,

A FUGITIVE SLAVE, AUTHOR OF "THREE YEARS IN EUROPE.

With a Sketch of the Author's Life.

"We hold these truths to be self-evident: that all men are created equal; that they are endowed by their Creator with certain inalienable rights, and that among these are LIFE, LIBERTY, and the PURSUIT OF HAPPINESS." — *Declaration of American Independence.*

*Title page of the first novel published by a black American author.*

1826. (This claim is disputed in some sources, which maintain that Edward A. Jones graduated from Amherst a few days earlier than Russwurm.) Russwurm was one of the editors of Freedom's Journal, the first black newspaper printed in the United States.

**1834** First black to obtain a patent from the U.S. Patent Office is **Henry Blair** of Greenosa, Maryland. Blair invented is a corn planter. He later invents a cotton seed planter.

**1845** First black lawyer to be formally admitted to the bar is **Macon B. Allen** after he passes the state bar examination in Worcester, Massachusetts. He had practiced law previously for two years in Maine, a state in which no license was required at the time.

**1853** First novel written by a black American and published is a work by **W. W. Brown**, entitled *Clotel A Tale of the Southern States*. The American edition is published by James Redfaith of Boston. The novel is 104 pages and sells for 10 cents.

**1854 John Mercer Langston,** who was born a slave in Virginia, is admitted to the Ohio bar. Langston is to become dean of Howard University and the first black to win elective office in the history of the United States.

**1860** First African-American baseball team to tour various parts of the country is called the **Brooklyn Excelsiors.** They play in cities of New York State (such as Troy, Buffalo, and New York) on a regular basis. On an irregular basis they play in various cities of the South and West.

**1861** The first black is wounded in the Civil War—65-year-old **Nicholas Biddle** of Pottsville, Pennsylvania. An escaped slave who has attached himself to a troop unit heading for the defense of Washington, D.C., he is stoned by an angry mob in Baltimore. His scalp cut to the bone, Biddle manages to escape further injury only with the aid of his white comrades-in-arms.

**1862 Mary Patterson** becomes the first black woman in the United States to earn an M.A. degree, awarded her by Oberlin College.

**1863** The first black to be appointed a chaplain in the U.S. Army is **Henry McNeal Turner**.

**1865 Martin R. Delany** becomes the first black to reach the rank of Major in the U.S. Army. A graduate of Howard University Medical School, Delany served in the Medical Corps. He was also a writer.

**1865** The first black school below the Mason Dixon Line is established in Lexington, Kentucky—in the same building over which the first Confederate flag was raised in Kentucky.

**1865** The selection of the first interracial jury indicts **Jefferson Davis,** former President of the Confederate States of America. On December 3, 1868 the case comes

*Bishop Henry Turner was the first black chaplin in the U.S. Army.*

to trial but is dismissed by President Johnson's amnesty proclamation on December 25, 1868.

**1865** **John Rock** becomes the first black admitted to practice before the Supreme Court.

**1865** The first black newspaper in the South—***The Colored American***—is published in Augusta, Georgia, edited by J. T. Shutten.

**1865** **John Rock** becomes the first black lawyer to be admitted to practice before the U.S. Supreme Court. His admittance is moved by Senator Charles Sumner of Massachusetts. Chief Justice Salmon P. Chase presides.

**1866** First black state representatives to sit in any state legislature are **Charles Lewis Mitchell** and **Edward Garrison Walker** of Boston. Both are elected at the same time to the Massachusetts State Legislature.

**1869** **Ebenezer Don Carlos Bassett**, believed to be the first black to receive an appointment in the diplomatic service, becomes U.S. Minister to Haiti.

**1870** **Richard Greener** is the first black to receive a degree from Harvard. Active as a teacher and editor, Greener is admitted to the South Carolina bar in 1876 and becomes dean of Howard's Law School in 1879.

**1872** The first black delegates to the presidential nominating convention of a major party appear at the Republican Convention in Philadelphia.

**1872** The first black midshipman to attend the U.S. Naval Academy is **Henry Conyers** of South Carolina. Conyers did not graduate, however, and left the academy on November 11, 1873.

**1872** The first black woman lawyer, **Charlotte E. Roy**, receives her degree from Howard University School of Law in Washington, D.C.

**1873** The first black municipal judge, **M. W. Gibbs**, is elected in Little Rock, Arkansas.

**1873** **Susan McKinney**, believed to be the first black woman to enter the medical profession formally, is certified as a physician. (Records at the medical college of the New York Infirmary indicate that Dr. Rebecca Cole was the first black woman physician in the United States, having practiced from 1872 to 1881.)

**1873** **William Monroe Trotter,** becomes Harvard University's first black Phi Beta Kappa and the founder of the Boston Guardian newspaper.

**1875** **Oscar Lewis**, is the first black jockey to win the Kentucky Derby. He rode Aristides at Churchill Downs in Louisville.

**1879** In Boston, **Mary E. Mattoney** is the first black woman to receive a diploma in nursing from New England Hospital for Women and Children.

**1882** The first daily newspaper to be owned by a black, *The Cairo Illinois Gazette*, is published by **W. S. Scott**.

**1884** **Moses Fleetwood Walker** becomes the first black major league baseball player, for Toledo in the American Association.

**1884** **John Roy Lynch** becomes the first black to preside over a national political convention, becoming temporary chairman of the Republican Party's national convention after being nominated by Henry Cabot Lodge of Massachusetts. The nomination was seconded by Theodore Roosevelt. Lynch received 424 votes; his opposition, George William Curtis, received 384.

**1884** The first black professional baseball team, the Cuban Giants, is formed in New York City by **Frank Thompson** from a group of black waiters at a Long Island hotel.

**1885** First black state legislator to represent a constituency in which the majority are white is **Bishop Benjamin William Arnett** of the AME Church. He represented Green County, Ohio from 1885 to 1887.

**1885** The first black Protestant Episcopal Bishop in the United States, the **Reverend Samuel David Ferguson**, is elected to the House of Bishops in 1884 and consecrated at Grace Church in New York City in 1885.

**1885** **Jonathan Jasper Wright** is the first black to be elected to the State Supreme Court of South Carolina. He had also been the first black to be admitted to the bar in Pennsylvania.

**1890** **Thomy Gafon**, a real estate speculator and moneylender in Louisiana, is probably the first black millionaire in the United States. The *Afro American Almanac* of 1896 complains that "in politics [Gafon was] rather more conservative than an old-fashioned planter and not at all desirous of seeing the colored people rule the state."

**1890** The first medical journal written for and by blacks is published in Jackson, Mississippi. The first editor of the publication is **Bandaburst Lynk, M.D.** The journal lasted 18 months.

**1890** **George Dixon** of Halifax, Nova Scotia, becomes the first black to win a world boxing title, when he beats Nunc Wallace in 18 rounds in London. Dixon was a bantam weight.

**1892** The first black college football game is played between **Biddle College** and **Livingstone College.** Biddle wins 4 to 0.

**1902** ***Off Bloomingdale Asylum***, a satirical comedy, is the first film to use blacks, the film is made in Paris, France.

**1903** **Lena Walker** becomes the first black woman bank president. Miss Walker was the founder and chief executive of the Saint Luke Penny Savings Bank in Richmond, Virginia.

**1908** The first black sorority, **Alpha Kappa Alpha,** is founded at Howard University in Washington, D.C.

**1910** First black to be awarded a coveted Rhodes Scholarship is **Alain Leroy Locke** of Philadelphia. Locke received his B.A. degree from Howard University in 1908 and under

*Fritz Pollard was the first black to play pro football for a major team.*

his Rhodes Scholarship he studied at Oxford University in England. Locke was a certified teacher in the Philadelphia school system.

**1916** **"Fritz" Pollard** from Brown University becomes the first black all-American football player.

**1918** First black Bishop of the Episcopal Church was **Edward Thomas Demley.**

**1918** The first black in the U.S. to earn a ship master's license and have the right to take command of a ship was **Hugh N. Mulzac**. Mulzac, however, could not find employment as a ships master and took jobs at sea as either a cook or steward for the next 24 years. He finally took command of a ship in 1942, a Liberty cargo vessel transporting troops and supplies into the war zones. His ship was the Booker T. Washington.

**1919** **Fritz Pollard** becomes the first black to play professional football for a major team, the Akron Indians. In 1916, Pollard had been the first black to play in the Rose Bowl, for Brown University.

**1923** The first black basketball team known as the **Renaissance** team was organized.

**1926** First black woman lawyer to practice before the U.S. Supreme Court is **Violette M. Anderson of Chicago.**

**1929** In the first black post season "bowl" football game in history, **the Prairie View Bowl,** Atlanta University defeats Prairie View 6 to 0.

**1931** **Estele Massey Osborne** became the first black recipient in the United States of a masters degree in nursing education. She is a 1931 graduate of Columbia's Teachers College.

**1933** The first transcontinental flight by black civilian pilots is made by **Charles Alfred Anderson** of Bryn Mawr, Pennsylvania and Albert Ernest Forsythe of Atlantic City.

**1935** **Mrs. Gertrude Elise Ayer**, the first black woman to serve as a school principal in the New York City public school system, is appointed to her post at P.S. 24 (Madison Avenue and 128th Street).

**1938** **Crystal Bird Fauset** becomes the first black woman elected to a state legislature in the United States, acquiring this distinction when she was named to the Pennsylvania House of Representatives on November 8, 1938. Miss Fauset died in 1965.

**1939** First black woman to become a judge, **Jane Matilda Bolin,** is appointed to the bench of the Court of Domestic Relations by Mayor Fiorello La Guardia of New York City.

**1940** First black to win an Oscar from the Academy of Motion Pictures Arts and Sciences is **Hattie McDaniel** as best supporting actress for her performance in *Gone with the Wind*. Star billing in the movie went to Clark Gable and Vivian Leigh.

**1940** **Benjamin O. Davis Sr.** is promoted to the rank of brigadier general in 1940, thus becoming the first black to hold this post in the U.S. Army. Born in 1877, career officer Davis made second lieutenant in 1901 and rose through the ranks until he was promoted to full colonel in 1930. He retired in 1948. (His son, Lieutenant General

*In 1940, Hattie Mc Daniel became the first black to win an Oscar.*

Benjamin O. Davis Jr. was formerly a general in the Air Force. His last assignment was as chief of staff of U.S. Forces in Korea, and Chief of Staff of the U.N. Commission there. After World War II, Davis was the first black to command an airbase—Godman Field in Kentucky. He became the first black general in the history of the Air Force on October 27, 1954.)

**1940** The first postage stamp honoring a black, the **Booker T. Washington** stamp, goes on sale at Tuskegee Institute. Valued at 10 cents, the stamp belongs to the Famous American Series and bears a picture of Washington's head. Its issuance comes at the culmination of a seven-year campaign which had originally been sponsored by Major R. R. Wright, president of the Citizens and Southern Bank and Trust Company of Philadelphia. (Seven years later, a stamp honoring George Washington Carver was issued on the fourth anniversary of the renowned scientist's death. The stamp is of three-cent denomination, and bears a picture of Carver's head.)

**1942 Bernard W. Robinson**, a medical student at Harvard, becomes the first black to be commissioned an officer in the U.S. Navy. Robinson was the first black ensign in the U.S. Naval Reserve.

**1943 Dr. W. E. B. DuBois** becomes the first black admitted to the National Institute of Arts and Letters. At the time of his admittance, Dr. DuBois headed the Department of Sociology at Atlanta University.

*Benjamin O. Davis Sr., was the first black brigadier general in the U.S. Army.*

*The first U.S. coin and stamps honoring black citizens were issued in the 1940's.*

**1943** The first Liberty Ship named for a black, the **George Washington Carver**, is launched from a New Jersey shipyard to begin its career of carrying war cargo to Europe during WW II.

**1944** The **USS Harmon** becomes the first fighting ship of the U.S. named for a black man. Leonard Roy Harmon won the Navy Cross for his heroism aboard the USS San Francisco in a battle with the Japanese near the Solomon Islands. Harmon died of wounds suffered during the engagement.

**1944** The first black accredited White House news correspondent is **Harry McAlpin**, who represented the *Daily World* of Atlanta, Georgia. He was, as well, the representative for the press service of the Negro Newspaper Publishers Association.

**1945** First black nurse to be commissioned in the Navy Reserve Corps is **Phyllis Mae Dolly**. Miss Dolly, a registered nurse from New York City was sworn in as an Ensign.

**1945** First black appointed as a Judge of the Custom's Court is **Irving Charles Mollison** of Chicago, Illinois.

**1946 Roy Campanella**, a catcher for Nashua, New Hampshire, in the New England League, becomes the first black to manage an organized baseball team on the field, when the regular manager Walt Alston is evicted from the field by the umpire. Nashua wins the game when a black pitcher, Don Newcombe, hits a pinch hit home run.

**1946** The first coin honoring a black was a 50 cents piece which bears a relief bust of **Booker T. Washington,** the founder of Tuskegee Institute. The coin was issued in May, 1946.

**1947 Dan Bankhead** of the Brooklyn Dodgers becomes

the first black pitcher in the major leagues. The first black pitcher in the American League follows in 1948. He is Leroy Satchell Paige whose age at the time is variously estimated between 41 and 54. Paige wins six, loses one, and has an earned run average of 2.47. Though of advanced years, Paige was to have many successful years in the major leagues and then in the minors before his final season with Portland in the Pacific Coast League in 1961.

**1947** **Louis Lautier**, Washington Bureau Chief of the Negro Newspaper Publishers Association, becomes the first black issued credentials for both the Senate and the House press galleries. Lautier is admitted to the galleries after a Senate Rules Committee overrode the refusal of the Standing Committee of Newspaper Correspondents to grant him the necessary credentials.

**1947** **John Lee** of Indianapolis, Indiana, becomes the first black commissioned officer in the Regular Navy. His first assignment upon being commissioned was on the USS *Kearsage*.

**1948** First appointed black clerk of the Supreme Court of the United States is **William Thaddeus Coleman Jr.** of Philadelphia. His appointment was made by Supreme Court Justice Felix Frankfurter.

**1948** First black commissioned officer in the Regular U.S. Marine Corps is **John Earl Rudder.**

**1949** **Wesley A. Brown** becomes the first black to graduate from the Naval Academy at Annapolis. **Henry O. Flipper** became the first black to graduate from West Point on June 15, 1877.

*Jessie L. Brown plays backgammon after becoming the first black U.S. Naval pilot.*

*Pulitzer Prize winner Gwendolyn Brooks.*

**1949** First black pilot in U.S. Naval Reserve is **Jesse Leroy Brown** from Hattiesburg, Virginia. On December 4, 1950 at Changjin Reservoir in Korea, Jesse Brown became the first black naval pilot to be killed in action.

**1949** **Dr. Peter Marshall Murray** of New York is the first black to be appointed to the American Medical Association's policy-making body.

**1949** **Jackie Robinson** becomes the first black baseball player to win his league's "Most Valuable Player" award while with the National League Brooklyn Dodgers. The first black to win the award three times was Roy Campanella of the Brooklyn Dodgers, in 1951, 1953, and 1955.

**1950** United Nations undersecretary **Ralph Bunche** becomes the first African-American to recieve a Noble Peace Prize.

**1950** **Gwendolyn Brooks** won the Pulitzer Prize for her volume of poetry. She was the first black woman to win the award and also the first black woman elected to the National Institute of Arts and Letters.

**1950** The first black judge of a Circuit Court of Appeals is **William Henry Hastie**, who was also the first black to be appointed governor of the American Virgin Islands.

**1950** The first black to play in organized hockey is **Arthur Dovington** with the Atlantic City Seagulls of the Eastern Amateur League. He played for only one season, 1950-1951.

*Coretta Scott King looks on as Ralph Bunche (left), the first black to receive a Nobel Peace Prize, congratulates Rev. Martin Luther King Jr. upon his becoming the second Nobel Prize recipient of his race.*

**1951** The first black Deputy Police Commissioner, **William L. Rowe,** is appointed to this position in New York by Mayor Vincent Impellitieri. He completed his term of service in 1954. Rowe was employed by the *Pittsburgh Courier* newspaper chain for some 16 years before entering government service. As an overseas correspondent he covered World War II from Guadalcanal to Tokyo and was cited for bravery in the Solomon Islands.

**1951** **Janet Collins** is the first black to dance for the Metropolitan Opera in New York. Miss Collins, signed by an agent of the company in 1951, made her debut in *Aida*.

**1954** **Dr. James Joshua Thomas** becomes the first black pastor of the Reformed Dutch Church. He is installed as minister of the Mott Haven Reformed Church in the Bronx, New York City.

**1954** The first black radio network, called the **National Negro Network,** begins programming. The New York outlet was station WOV. The first program of the network, a soap opera titled *The Story of Ruby Valentine,* starred Juanita Hall and was carried on 40 stations. The program, sponsored by Philip Morris and Pet Milk, ran five days a week.

**1955** The first black Methodist minister of an all-white congregation is **Reverend Simon Peter Montgomery** of Pineville, South Carolina. At that time he was appointed minister of the Mystic Methodist Church in Old Mystic, Connecticut.

**1956** The first athlete to high jump over seven feet is a black, **Charles Dumas**. The feat is performed at the Coliseum in Los Angeles. At the time Dumas was 19 and a freshman at Compton College.

**1958** The first black minister with two all-white congregations is the **Reverend Joseph Reed** Washington, who serves as minister of the Methodist Church in Newfield, Maine and in the Congregational Church of West Newfield. The distance between the two churches is three miles.

**1958** **Ruth Carol Taylor** becomes the first black airline stewardess. A graduate nurse from Ithaca, New York, Miss Taylor worked for Mohawk Airlines.

**1958** **Gloria Davey** sings Aida at New York's Metropolitan Opera and becomes the first black to appear in song at this celebrated palace of music.

**1959** **John McLendon** becomes the first black to coach an integrated professional basketball team, the Cleveland Pipers of the National Industrial Basketball League.

**1961** The first black appointed as a District Court judge is **James Benton Parsons**. Judge Parsons had been a Justice on the State Supreme Council of Illinois.

**1962** The first black warship commander, **Lieutenant**

*The first black coach for a major league sports team was Bill Russell in 1967.*

**Commander Samuel L. Gravely,** assumes command of the USS Falgout, a destroyer escort.

**1966 Emmett Ashford,** the first black umpire in the major leagues, makes his debut in the American League inaugural between the Cleveland Indians and the Washington Senators. Born in Los Angeles, Ashford attended Jefferson High School and Los Angeles City College. Before receiving his major league assignment at the age of 51 (four years before compulsory retirement age), Ashford had umpired in the Dominican Republic for three winter seasons (1958, 1959, 1964), and in several minor leagues as well, including the Pacific Coast League where he was Umpire-in-Chief as of September 1965.

**1967 Bill Russell**, star center of the world-champion Boston Celtics, becomes the first black to direct a major league sports team when he is named to succeed Red Auerbach as coach of the Boston basketball franchise.

**1968** Chairman of the District of Columbia Democratic delegation, **Reverend Channing Phillips**, a favorite son, is placed in nomination for President at the Democratic convention in Chicago. Phillips receives 67.5 votes. At the same time, the Peace and Freedom Party of New York State announces that Dick Gregory would run for this office on its ballot.

**1968 Archbishop Terence J. Cooke** names Reverend Harold A. Salmon the first black pastor in the N.Y. Archdiocese and Vicariate Delegate for Harlem in 1968. Reverend Salmon is put in charge of Harlem's largest parish, St. Charles Borromeo.

**1968 Henry Lewis** is the first black named director of an American orchestra (the Newark-based New Jersey Symphony). Other black conductors—Dean Dixon and Everett Lee—had found regular podiums in Europe. Lewis, however, was the first to be appointed in the United States.

**1968 Martin Briscoe** became the first black quaterback in pro-football.

**1969 Joseph L. Searles III** becomes the first black man proposed for a seat on the New York Stock Exchange. Searles, formerly an aide in the administration of New York City Mayor John Lindsay, had resigned to become one of the three floor traders, as well as a general partner, for Newburger, Loeb & Co.

**1969 Federal Judge A. Leon Higginbotham Jr.**, is elected a trustee of Yale University, the first black to be so honored. The judge, who succeeded New York's Mayor John Lindsay, defeated five other candidates in nationwide balloting in April and May 1969. Some 25,000 of Yale's 75,000 eligible alumni took part.

**1970 Chris Dickerson** becomes the first black man to win the title "Mr. America," one of 15 bodybuilding titles which Dickerson has earned. Among the others are Mr. California, Mr. Eastern America, Mr. Junior U.S.A. Born

*Judge A. Leon Higgenbotham was the first black elected as a trustee of Yale University.*

one of triplets in Montgomery, Alabama on August 25, 1939, Dickerson was an outstanding athlete throughout his school years, and showed an early interest in a singing career. The desire to improve his voice quality and breath control led him into bodybuilding in the mid-1960s.

**1970 Renard Edwards** becomes the first black musician to play for the Philadelphia Orchestra when he is hired as a violist for the 1970-1971 season. Edwards was formerly with the Symphony of the New World, an integrated orchestra one-third to one-half of whose members are blacks.

**1971 Dr. James Allen Colston** becomes the first black to head a college in New York State (and possibly the first to head a "predominantly white" college in the United States) when he is appointed president of the two-year Bronx Community College in New York City.

**1973 Thomas Bradley** of Los Angeles and **Coleman Young** of Detroit become the first blacks to be elected mayors of cities with populations exceeding one million.

**1974 J. Garfield Owens** became the first black pastor of an all-white congregation in San Antonio, Texas.

**1975** The U.S. Navy commissions **Dr. Donna P. Davis** as a lieutenant in the Navy's medical corps, making Lt. Davis the first black woman physician in the corps history.

**1975 Frank Robinson** becomes the first black man to manage a major league baseball team, and leads his Cleveland Indians to an opening-day victory over the New York Yankees, hitting a home run himself.

*The first black "Mr. America," Chris Dickerson.*

*Mayor Thomas Bradley of Los Angeles*

**1976 Attorney Ernest A. Finney Jr.** of Sumpter, South Carolina becomes the state's first black Circuit Court Judge. Finney was selected by fellow lawyers for the judgeship.

**1976 Dr. W. J. Yelder** becomes the first black principal at Selma, Alabama High School. The school board passed over Dr. Yelder in 1975 and appointed Roy Wilson, a white, to the position. However, Federal Judge Bernard Hand ordered the appointment of Yelder after a lengthy legal battle.

**1977 William Bryant** becomes the first black chief U.S. District Court Judge in Washington, D.C. Bryant, a former U.S. District Court judge, appointed by President Lyndon Johnson, had won early fame as a criminal lawyer. He argued the *Mallory* case before the Supreme Court, which led to the decision in which arrested criminal suspects must be presented before a magistrate as rapidly as possible.

**1978 Karen Farmer** becomes the first black member of the Daughters of the American Revolution. It was the DAR that refused to allow Marian Anderson to perform in concert in Washington, D.C. in 1939.

**1978 Right Reverend Emerson Moore Jr.** named first black monsignor of the Catholic Church in the United

*Roman Catholic archbishop Eugene Antonio Marino of the Atlanta archdiocese.*

States. Monsignor Moore is pastor of St. Charles Borromeo Church in New York City. He was ordained a priest in the historic St. Patrick's Cathedral in 1964.

**1979 John Glover** is named the first black FBI field office chief in charge of the Milwaukee, Wisconsin FBI office. Glover was the first black agent to be named an inspector at FBI headquarters in Washington, D.C.

**1979** U.S. Army **Second Lieutenant Marcella A. Hayes**, a graduate of the University of Wisconsin and the Army ROTC program, earns her aviator wings and becomes the first black woman pilot in U.S. armed services history.

**1979 Loren Monroe** becomes first black named as Michigan's state treasurer. Monroe was born in Thomasville, Georgia and holds degrees in law and accounting.

**1979 Audrey Neal** the first black woman or woman of any ethnic group to become a longshoreman on the eastern seaboard. Neal works at the Bayonne Military Ocean Terminal in New Jersey.

**1980 Dr. Levi Watkins Jr.** performs the first surgical implantation of the automatic implantable defibrillator in the human heart. The device corrects an ailment known as ventricular fibrillator, or arrhythmia, which prevents the heart from pumping blood.

**1981 Dr. Lenora Cole-Alexander** becomes the first black to head the U.S. Labor Department's Women's Bureau.

**1981 Pamela Johnson** is named publisher of the *Ithaca Journal* and becomes the first black woman to hold such a position with a major newspaper in the United States.

**1981 Dr. Ruth Love** became the first black to serve as superintendent of the Chicago school system. Before her appointment to this top post, Dr. Love held the same position in Oakland, California.

**1981 Lillian Roberts** is named the first black woman to head the New York State Labor Department. She was appointed commissioner of the department July 2, 1981.

**1983** Representing New York State, **Vanessa Williams** becomes the first black Miss America in the 62-year history of the Atlantic City pageant. The first runner-up is **Suzette Charles** representing New Jersey, who coincidentally is also black and also the first black Miss New Jersey.

**1985 Lt. Cmdr. Donnie Cochran** becomes the first black pilot in the U.S. Navy to fly with the Navy's elite special flying squadron the Blue Angels. The precision flight team was formed some 40 years ago and has performed its highly sophisticated aerobatics in air shows here and in Europe.

**1988 Eugene Antonio Marino** becomes the first black Roman Catholic archbishop in the United States as he is named archbishop of the Atlanta archdiocese. Marino was one of three auxiliary bishops in Washington, D.C.

**1988 Lee Roy Young**, a 14-year veteran of the Texas Department of Public Safety becomes the first Texas Ranger in the 165-year history of this famed state police force that, in legend, 'tamed' the early western frontier and whose 'daring heroic exploits' are enshrined forever in hundreds of grade B cowboy movies. Young, at a news conference, said that it was his dream to become a Texas Ranger ever since he was a little boy.

**1989** Former St. Louis Cardinal first baseman **Bill White** assumes office as president of the National League, becoming the first black to head a professional sports league.

**1989** Episcopal **Reverend Barbara Harris**, a black, becomes the first female bishop in the worldwide Anglican communion. The Anglican church decided in 1976 that women could be ordained as priests.

**1989 Rodney S. Patterson**, an ordained Baptist minister, starts the first "black" church in Vermont, which Ebony magazine has dubbed "the whitest state in America" due to its tiny black population. Patterson, who moved to Burlington, Vt., to join the staff at the University of Vermont, named the church the New Alpha Missionary Baptist Church.

# SLAVERY IN THE AMERICAS

**The Transatlantic Slave Trade ■ The Colonial United States: 1619-1787 ■ The Divided Nation: (1783-1865) ■ The Great Debate: Arguments for and against Slavery ■ Comparisons with Latin America and the Caribbean ■ Slave Conspiracies in the United States ■ Chronology of U.S. Slave Rebellions and Conspiracies, 1663-1863 ■ Leaders of Slave Revolts in the United States ■ Abolition of Slavery by Country and Date**

The transatlantic slave trade hoisted its first anchor in 1517 when Spain resolved to encourage the immigration to its American possessions by granting each loyal settler the right to own 12 black slaves. Time had already shown that the American Indian was unable to adjust to the rigors of European-administered slavery. Indians died in large numbers, either from disease or from the constant pressure of forced labor, but the African's will to live made him valuable. Most of these early slaves were sent to work on the plantations or in the mines of the Caribbean islands, or in Spanish and Portuguese holdings in South and Central America. Slavery gained its first foothold in the British colonies of North America in 1619, when the settlement of Jamestown, Va., bartered with a Dutch warship for 20 blacks captured from a Latin American slave ship.

While historical head counts vary, the number of black persons who reached lives of slavery in the New World is now put at around 10 million. Nearly 600,000 were brought in the sixteenth century, 2 million in the seventeenth century, 5 million in the eighteenth century, and 3 million in the nineteenth century. Added to these must be an enormous number who died between capture and their intended arrival in America. It is estimated that 15% died of disease on the noxiously overcrowded "Middle Passage" from Africa to the Caribbean, and another 30% during the brutal three-month training period in the West Indies before they were shipped on to the American mainland.

Although Spain and Portugal were the first powers to import slaves to their colonies, much of the traffic was conducted by the Dutch, French, and British. The majority of the slaves they transported came from the territories of the modern states of Senegal, Gambia, Guinea, Sierra Leone, Liberia, Upper Volta, Ivory Coast, Ghana, Togo, Benin, Nigeria, Cameroon, Gabon, the Congo Republic, and the Republic of the Congo. It is to these lands that most black people now living in the United States and North America can trace their ancestry.

## THE AFRICAN ROOTS OF SLAVERY

West Africa was the birthplace of three powerful tribal empires: Ghana, Mali, and Songhay. Despite their complexity and advancements, these societies retained the custom of slavery and commonly sold captives taken in war. As early as the ninth century, the Ghanaian king was trading slaves to Arab merchants for goods from the Mediterranean and the East. Although this early slave trade is now believed to have been a two-way affair, the balance gradually shifted. As the centuries passed, the mud-walled city of Timbuktu became both a university and the famous southern hub of trade across the Sahara. Horses, steel, and woven goods came south and were paid for by gold, ivory, cotton, and slaves.

When fifteenth-century Portuguese explorers became the first modern Europeans to reach West Africa by sea, they found slave trading was part of the social fabric, as it was back in Portugal. However, the opening of a direct sea route immediately changed things for the worse. Once the Portuguese began turning over guns for captives, the slave trade became a vicious trap. An African king could not refuse to raid for slaves or the traders would cut off his gun supply, making his own people defenseless before the raids of others. It was in this way that the great Mani-Çongo kingdom was brought to ruins. Furthermore, there was an immense difference between the slavery which the Europeans exported and that which had existed in black Africa.

African slavery was not a stigma of human inferiority. As in the ancient world, many slaves were men of accomplishment and learning. Most important, African slavery was not based on race. The gulf between master and slave could be bridged, and often was crossed within a few generations. Dahomean kings were known to choose the sons of slaves to succeed to the throne. West African slavery was more like medieval serfdom than the slavery that developed in the Americas. In these lands, where race became the badge of slavery, the slave's heaviest chain was the color of his skin. His condition became irrevocable for his life and the lives of his descendants, and enslavement began to be taken as a mark of racial inferiority. When, as happened in North America, a race was enslaved by another race, the gulf between master and slave became filled with terrors. Not the least terrible is the schizophrenic barbarization of the whites who grafted a primitive social relationship onto an industrial and civilized society.

*Before shipment to the colonies, Africans were inspected for sale into slavery by exporters (below); while awaiting shipment they were kept in sheds (above).*

## THE COLONIAL UNITED STATES: 1619-1787

Europeans who colonized the North American mainland generally intended to settle there for good. They brought their wives and children, and went about building a society for themselves. They were reluctant to import slaves directly from Africa, fearing them too savage and violent. The Caribbean islands, huge plantations where brutal work conditions were the norm, became a mid-station at which those blacks were "seasoned" for several months before completing the journey from Africa to the New World.

### From Indentured Servant to Slave

Many Europeans (chiefly of English, German, and Scotch-Irish ancestry) who immigrated to the colonies as laborers came as "indentured servants." They had voluntarily bound themselves over to the service of a master for a number of years in payment for passage and board. Most who came involuntarily were debtors and paupers who had been deported and were obliged to work seven years before achieving their freedom. Among them were some children who had been kidnapped, shipped to the colonies, and then sold into service.

The 20 blacks who landed at Jamestown in 1619 were accepted into the community as indentured servants. On the completion of their contracts, they automatically enjoyed the liberties and privileges of the "free laboring class," including the right to own property. Other blacks arrived, and some prospered. Anthony Johnson, who seems to have graduated from servant to freeman by 1622, was rich enough to import five servants of his own by 1651, for which he obtained 250 acres from the colony's government. A black carpenter, Richard Johnson, imported two white servants in 1654 and was given 100 acres. But these men were the exceptions, and the rule they proved was that a fissure was cracking open between black and white servitude.

Beginning in the 1640s, the black ceased to be regarded as a servant and came to be assigned the status of a "chattel slave"—one who remained a fixed item of personal property for the duration of his life. Of three runaways in 1640, two whites were sentenced to four extra years as servants, but a black was given a life term. By the 1650s black chattels were commonly being sold for life, and in 1661 the House of Burgesses formally recognized the institution of black slavery.

The erosion of black indentured servitude followed a similar course in the sister colony of Maryland, where the slave law passed in 1663 was even more specific. "All negroes," the law proclaimed, "or other slaves within the province, [and] all negroes (sic) to be hereafter imported, shall serve *durante vita.*"

With the passage of time, white indentured servants gradually disappeared from the colonial labor market, particularly after liberalized legislation enabled them to acquire freedom and land. This accelerated the flow of black workers into the colonies and encouraged planters to institutionalize the notion of perpetual black servitude. Practical considerations for such a move included the fact that black runaways could be detected more easily than fugitive whites. Moreover, since the incoming black was not a Christian, he was regarded as a product of a primitive, savage culture, and hence fit for nothing better than an animal's life of unbroken labor. Of course, even when the black later accepted Christianity, his status was in no way altered. As early as 1667 Virginia wrote into statute that "baptism doth not alter the condition of the person as to his bondage or freedom." Color remained the real cutting edge, and ultimately, in the mind of white colonists, color razored the black man from the ranks of humanity and cast him, once and for all, into the immutable role of slave.

*A new shipment of slaves is cataloged prior to delivery to a slave market in Colonial America.*

### The Spread of Slavery

Of the 13 original colonies, only Pennsylvania put up any sustained opposition to the use of slavery. Rhode Island had an anti-slavery ordinance on the books, but it was openly violated. And Massachusetts, the cradle of liberty, was actually the first colony to make perpetual bondage legal. Nevertheless, the conditions of slavery differed significantly from North to South.

The New England colonies played a principal role in the slave trade, but they had little reason to buy slaves themselves. By 1700 blacks amounted to only about 1,000 in a

*A slave canoe heading downstream to the coast.*

population of 90,000. As the economy of the area was diversified, so too were the occupations of the blacks. Many were skilled craftsmen, and there are records of black physicians. Furthermore, the Puritan heritage asserted itself in an Old Testament kind of slavery, which did not deny the slave's existence as a human being. Blacks could own property, they could testify in court against whites, and the law regulated the way a master could treat slaves.

The Mid-Atlantic states were familiar with small slaveholdings; slaves comprised 12% of the population of eighteenth-century New York. In addition to laboring on farms, they worked as domestics and craftsmen. Although the Quakers in Pennsylvania passed laws against the slave trade in 1688, 1693, and 1696—protesting that it violated the principles of Christianity and the rights of man—their statutes were overruled by Parliament in 1712. The behavior of slaves in these colonies was controlled, as in the South, by strict slave codes, under which the slaves were stripped of most rights. Slavery may have been mild in Pennsylvania, but the codes were enforced with frightening severity in New York.

The colonial South was divided into the tobacco-raising provinces of Virginia, Maryland, and North Carolina, and the huge rice and indigo plantations now comprising South Carolina and Georgia. Since tobacco was often raised on family farms, the slave population of the Chesapeake Bay area never reached the intense concentrations created in the deeper South. Terrified of uprisings, slaveholders devised ever harsher slave codes. A slave could not own anything, carry a weapon, or even leave his plantation without a written pass. There were many capital crimes, and small offenses were commonly punished by whipping, maiming, and branding. In the area where 90% of colonial blacks lived, a slave had no rights even to defend himself against a white man, and, as far north as Virginia, it was impossible for a white man to be convicted of the murder of a slave.

*Arab slave traders taking their captives overland to the coast for shipment. Resistance of any kind meant instant death.*

*James Otis argued that blacks had just as much right to freedom as whites, an unpopular view since much of the work in the colonies was done by slave labor. Black slaves are shown boiling out sugar cane on a colonial Plantation.*

## THE REVOLUTIONARY ERA AND THE CONSTITUTION

The spirit of revolution that gripped the American continent in the 1770s shook acceptance of slavery. Even the economic structure seemed open to change, for the declining fertility of the tobacco lands of Virginia, Maryland, and North Carolina was making the plantation system only marginally profitable. Until this time only the Quakers had consistently opposed slavery. Now their intensified efforts were swelled by the political events. The colonists, angered by the restrictions imposed upon them by the Crown, were practically forced by the logic of their own struggle to agitate also for the rights of blacks. These religious and political beliefs took philosophical sail in the ideals of the Enlightenment, which stressed natural rights and human liberty. Sentiments of racial egalitarianism began to permeate the colonies.

In his *Rights of the British Colonies* (1764), James Otis fearlessly proclaimed the black's right to be free. In 1773, Reverend Isaac Skillman carried the argument to the even more radical assertion that slaves should rebel against their masters. A year later Thomas Jefferson was describing the abolition of slavery as one of the goals of the colonists, and accusing Great Britain of blocking efforts to end the slave trade. Moved by these arguments, the Continental Congress passed a resolution not to import any slaves after December 1, 1775. Ultimately, Jefferson went so far as to include a violent denunciation of slavery in an early draft of the Declaration of Independence, but this clause was eliminated.

Throughout the Revolutionary War, only South Carolina and Georgia remained aggressively pro slavery, refusing to arm blacks even when their cultural pearl, Charleston, was burned by the British.

In the other new states, many blacks had been given their freedom in return for military service. After the war, manumission and anti-slavery activities increased. Slavery was banned in Pennsylvania (1789), Massachusetts (1783), Connecticut and Rhode Island (1784), New York (1785), and New Jersey (1786). In 1783, Jefferson convinced the Virginia legislature to make it legal for a slaveowner to free his slaves. When the Philadelphia Anti-slavery Society was reorganized in 1787, Benjamin Franklin surfaced as its president, and in that same year the Northwest Territory was closed to slavery. Unfortunately, that was the high-water mark. Despite these successes, and although there were 59,000 free blacks in the United States by 1790, the anti-slavery movement lost its revolutionary thrust.

The Constitution, which was written in 1787, was a setback for opponents of slavery. It provided for the extension of the slave trade for 20 years, for return of fugitive slaves to their owners, and for the famous "three-fifths compromise," by which five slaves were to be regarded as the equivalent of three nonslaves for purposes of taxation and representation. These deals succeeded in safeguarding pro-slavery interests.

## THE DIVIDED NATION: 1783-1865

From the defeat of Britain by the colonists to the outbreak of the Civil War, the young nation spent nearly 80 years trying to balance on the knife edge of slavery. Very few national decisions were taken without reference to this question, but all effort to preserve such a union proved vain. The difference between slavery and freedom was too great to compromise. The slaveholders did not release their power graciously, but the momentum of civilization was building against them, and the democratic ideals on which the United States had been founded eventually prevailed.

## The Growth of Slave Power

The strength of the slave states surged forward in 1793 when New Englander Eli Whitney invented the cotton gin. All the cotton a planter could grow suddenly brought high prices in the markets. Profits were so high that vast plantations were hacked from the wilderness, and armies of slaves were imported to work the fields. Congress enacted the first fugitive slave law in 1793, and the institutions of the Old South began pouring into the rich, virgin lap of the Gulf states.

The rate of growth was phenomenal. Between 1800 and 1859 the population of Mississippi, for example, grew from 3,489 slaves and 5,179 whites to 309,878 slaves and 295,718 whites. By mid-century the states of Georgia, Alabama, Mississippi, and Louisiana were annually producing 1,726,349 bales of cotton, 48,000,000 pounds of rice, and 226,098,000 pounds of sugar. Along with this economic wealth came political clout. Where cotton was king, slavery became the way of life for both plantation owner and field hand. By the outbreak of the Civil War, the slave population of the United States had reached a figure of 4,000,000 persons and nearly three-fourths of them were involved in cotton agriculture.

Although the African slave trade was technically discontinued in 1808, it is estimated that from that date until 1860, no less than 250,000 slaves were illegally imported. Also, nothing prevented slaves from being bartered across various districts of the country. The breeding of slaves for sale became a specialized business of the upper South. Virginia earned the sobriquet of the "Negro-raising state" by virtue of its export of over 6,000 slaves annually to such centers of trade as Baltimore, Washington, D.C., Charleston, Montgomery, Memphis, and New Orleans.

*In Virginia, the men cut the wheat with a two handed sickle as the women followed behind stacking the crop.*

## Slave Life

A lucky slave might work on a family-sized farm, or he might be a house servant, or he might have a kind master. That was the luckiest. But kind masters were rare. It was not in the nature of slavery, the wielding of absolute control over other human beings, to foster kindness. For the average slave, life was a grim business.

On the larger plantations slaves were divided into house servants and field hands. The former group was charged with such assorted tasks as caring for the grounds and garden, house cleaning, and maintaining the rigs and appliances. In many cases, house servants were allowed to learn trades (becoming smiths, brick masons, tailors, etc.) and to develop other skills (doctoring, child care, musicianship). Body slaves served their masters as valets and personal messengers, and from this intimacy real friendship sometimes developed. In any case, these were the aristocrats of slavery, and their daily lives had little in common with the faceless masses of field hands, who were forced to submit to the brutal monotony of sowing and reaping, planting and picking, without respite or prospect of change. If the plantation were large enough—containing, say, 25 slaves—the field hand's only contact with whites was through overseers, whose notorious cruelty was considered one of the necessary evils of slave owning. Many planters figured the best profits were made by working a slave to death in 8 or 10 years and then buying a new one. Even tenderhearted masters often had little contact with the field workers, and if the overseer returned a profit no questions were asked. Cruel and vicious brutality was commonplace.

*Sugar cane growing in Louisiana. Here the seed cane had been buried for the winter, in the spring it was plowed up and the men are removing the seed cane. The process is called "hooking up."*

The bare necessities—a roof over one's head, food on one's table, clothes on one's back—were all that a slave could expect for his life of drudgery. That roof was never much more than the leaky top of a windowless, mud-floored shack for a large family, and the food was often limited to a bucket of rice or corn a week with no meat. The only break in the routine occurred at Christmas time and on other holidays, or in those brief hours before the day's end when the slave might hunt, fish, or garden. In many places, slaves were given no free time at all, but forced to work 14 to 15 hours a day. Louisiana, the only state with a law on the subject, said that a slave could be worked 21 hours every day.

### Mansions as Prisons

Slave mistreatment resulted in an atmosphere of suspicion and terror. Masters lived in constant fear of an uprising. Although organized rebellions were rare, historical documents sparkle with reports of masters murdered and of dwellings burned down by angry slaves. The codes were made stricter, but no amount of protection could soften the jaws within which an owner lived—his inner guilt and the invisible anger which surrounded him. A slave had no free moments, every gesture was watched, but this means that whites had no free moments either. Inside its glittering plantation houses, the Old South was a nerve-wracked, armed camp, or as Frederick Law Olmstead called it, "a police state."

### Abolition

The abortive Nat Turner rebellion of 1831 became a turning point in the history of the black slave. From this point until the outbreak of the Civil War, the slave was relentlessly harassed. Manumission was almost completely suspended.

This period also marked a decline in the "repatriation" movement which had been sponsored largely by the American Colonization Society. The idea of returning free blacks to their "ancestral homeland" had been in part motivated by sincere humanitarian impulses, but it had also had its sinister side. By 1830, the more than 300,000 free blacks in the United States constituted an important element in the population, particularly in the South where their presence struck fear into the planter aristocracy. While Northerners contributed support and donations, Southern patrols were out threatening blacks who were unenthusiastic about emigrating to Liberia.

With the downplaying of repatriation, however, came the creation of the New England Anti-slavery Society and publication of the first issue of the crusading abolitionist journal, *The Liberator*. As colonization and manumission lost their momentum, abolition quickly sprang to the fore as a compelling moral alternative, drawing much of its strength from the dedication of an impressive array of leaders, including William Lloyd Garrison, Theodore Dwight Weld, James Forten, Robert Purvis, and David Ruggles. By 1833, the new American Anti-Slavery Society was demanding immediate abolition and stressing the rhetoric of racial equality.

In the South, abolition only hardened the already congealed opinion of the slaveholding class. Slavery, said such champions as Thomas Roderick Dew, was necessary for economic survival; it had enabled the white man to create a unique and progressive culture; it was even countenanced by Christianity as a means of converting the black pagan from heathenism. Above and beyond these rationalizations lay the ultimate racist ideology which has characterized the thinking of many whites. The black was, in their view, biologically inferior—a fact which they would at times assert without any seeming malice.

*Field hand slaves lived in windowless, one room cabins, propped on the ground atop several bricks under the main struts. Field hand slaves were called "mudsills" in the plantation society.*

## Toward War and Emancipation

As positions polarized and battle lines were drawn, the politics of the slavery question vaulted into the foreground of American life. The Fugitive Slave Act (1850), the Compromise of 1850, the publication of *Uncle Tom's Cabin* (1852), the Kansas-Nebraska Act (1854), the Dred Scott decision (1857), the Harpers Ferry raid (1859): these and countless other events were connected with the attempt to resolve the slavery issue.

"Slavery" and "Preservation of the Union" were the paramount issues of the Civil War. It can be said that both questions had to be resolved simultaneously, or not at all. However, Abraham Lincoln, elected to the presidency as a racial moderate in 1860, argued that the federal government had no right to prohibit slavery in the South, and that preserving the Union was the sole issue.

*If I could save the Union without freeing any slave, I would do it; if I could save it by freeing all the slaves, I would do it; and if I could save it by freeing some and leaving others alone, I would also do that. What I do about slavery and the colored race, I do because I believe it helps save the Union...*

As tension with the South mounted, Lincoln sponsored the Confiscation Act of 1861, which provided for the emancipation of slaves who had been used for insurrectionary purposes in the South. Within two years, free black regiments were responding to the Union slogan that they could at last fight for their own freedom.

By May 1862, Lincoln was prepared to move even closer to the position advocated by the Radical Republicans: complete abolition. In September of that year, the President issued a preliminary Emancipation Proclamation—holding out to slave owners the possibility of compensation, and continuing to suggest to freedmen the prospect of voluntary colonization in Africa.

On January 1, 1863, a further proclamation declared that all slaves living in the *seceded states* of the Confederacy were to be "thenceforward, and forever free." It conferred legal, though not actual, emancipation on three-fourths of the slave population, yet made no provisions for some 800,000 blacks living outside the South who remained technically enslaved. Constitutional emancipation did not come *for all slaves* until 1865 with the passage of the thirteenth amendment—the single, all-embracing legislative enactment which brought the United States steps closer to its motto: "Land of the Free."

The story of the black freedman during Reconstruction, and of the black population in general during the twentieth century, belongs to another province of American history. For our purposes, slavery as a *legal* concept ended in the year 1865, although its repercussions continue to plague our society down to our own time.

*A slave auction in a Confederate city, from an 1861 Harper's illustration.*

## THE GREAT DEBATE: ARGUMENTS FOR AND AGAINST SLAVERY

Civilized man has produced several arguments in favor of, or violently opposed to, the institution of slavery. We attempt here to indicate them in summary form.

### In Defense of Slavery

The established classes within most ancient and medieval societies assumed that certain groups of people were inherently inferior. In modern times, this theory is embodied in the term "white supremacy."

Agricultural and industrial surpluses could not be produced, nor could public works projects or cultural monuments be undertaken, without use of slave labor. Slavery was needed to create wealth and grandeur.

The advancement of culture, thought to be the natural province of the "leisure class," could not exist unless menial and commonplace services were provided by a laboring class.

Slave ownership was a primary attribute of power and distinction within certain societies.

Slavery afforded Christianity a means of converting the slave from paganism.

Slavery was profitable to those engaged in the trade. Their well-being was not isolated but contributed instead to the good fortune of others.

### In Opposition to Slavery

The inherent inferiority of any group of people cannot be scientifically demonstrated.

Slavery was morally indefensible, since it involved the denial of two inalienable rights: personal freedom and equality of birth.

Slavery was inhumane, awakening the most brutal instincts within the slave owner.

Slavery caused the physical, mental, and moral degradation of the slave.

Slavery was contrary to such Christian principles as brotherly love and the sanctity of the individual in the sight of God.

Slavery deprived the slave of a sense of identity and pride, causing him to lose confidence in his own capacities—intellectual and otherwise.

*Slaves being herded to a Deep South auction house.*

## COMPARISONS WITH LATIN AMERICA

Slavery in Spanish and Portuguese colonies was regulated by a code of laws that stretched back to Roman traditions and had been influenced by Church jurists. Instead of allowing considerable local autonomy, as the British did, the Iberian crowns regulated overseas affairs with a paternal hand. Slaves were numbered among the monarch's subjects, not simply considered property to be disposed of as the owner wished. The Church, accepting slavery as a labor system, zealously exercised her role as guardian of public morals to insure that slaves were treated as human beings. Not only was missionary activity intense, but human rights were upheld.

Many historians argue that the Latin American system was far more humane than that of the British colonies. While North American slaves were rarely given their freedom, manumission was a common practice in Latin countries, favored by both law and social approval. While North American jurists ruled that preventing the separate sale of family members would tamper with owners property rights—putting property higher than slave marriage—the South American church insisted that slave unions be sacramentalized, and Latin law forbade the separate sale of husband, wife, and children under the age of 10. While North American courts refrained from interfering in the master's nearly absolute power over his slaves, South American justice took an active role. Slave crimes were prosecuted in court, and if a slave was murdered the case was often tried as if the victim had been a free citizen. Mistreatment could not only cost the master fines but win freedom for the slave. Finally, South American slaves could own property and were guaranteed times in which they could work for themselves.

In retrospect, North American slaves were consistently regarded as objects, with both laws and customs pushing them deeper and deeper into the role of "thing," whereas South American societies made some effort to protect the slave's humanity.

The conclusion that Latin American slavery was more humane has been disputed, however. Certain historians point to the fact that in Brazil, the largest importer of slaves to the south, the death rate was much higher than in the United States, as were suicides, and that there was also intense dehumanization, many slaves being forced by owners to wear masks, a practice rare in the United States. These historians also cite the frequency of Latin American slave resistance, which sometimes took the form of wholesale insurrections. In the 1550s, for example, there were frequent outbreaks of violence in Cartagena (Colombia). During the seventeenth century, similar upheavals occurred in Bahia and Rio de Janeiro, despite the fact that blacks in these areas enjoyed a relative measure of well-being at that time. It may be suggested in reply that greater well-being, and the sharper sense of human rights it gave to the slaves, would encourage rebellion, whereas slaves who were absolutely suppressed would be unlikely to revolt.

One factor enhancing Brazil's reputation for humane slavery was the emergence of a mulatto class which, after emancipation, rose to a respectable and fairly secure place in Brazilian society, while in the United States mulattoes were defined out of the white world as bearers of black blood. A major cause of this exclusion was that blacks were always a minority in the English mainland colonies—never more than 20% of the overall population of what was to become the United States—while in Brazil, Europeans (especially European women) were always in the minority. As a result, white women on the northern continent were more influential within the social structure, and thus in a position to prevent widespread miscegenation. In Brazil, more European men had children by female slaves, and were more ready to acknowledge their offspring. Ultimately, it is hard to gauge how frequently the mixture of races occurred in the United States because of the social sanctions against it. Another difference between the American continents was that in the United States, despite notable exceptions, slaves were largely confined to agricultural labor, while in Latin America they were needed in skilled trades. In the north, these trades were mostly filled by whites and often rigidly segregated to preclude competition, a practice that worsened as abolition gained ground and after the collapse of Reconstruction.

### The Caribbean

Scholars are intrigued by the great disparity between slavery on the English islands of the Caribbean and slavery in the English provinces of the North American mainland. Caribbean slavery, after the discovery of the value of sugar around 1650, became one of the most brutal systems of servitude known to history. The death rate of blacks was enormous, as the grossest and most avaricious of Englishmen were attracted to the quick wealth and wild living style the islands then offered. By 1680, almost all the 40,000 slaves in Barbados worked for some 175 planters, and by 1700, in the West Indies, six major islands held some 270,000 black slaves under the control of a few hundred whites.

Wherever possible these overcrowded warrens spurred revolt. In Jamaica alone, there were six major uprisings between 1650 and 1700.

Of the English mainland colonies, South Carolina appears to have been closest in economy and style to Barbados and Jamaica. By 1700, as rice became an important crop and adventurers moved from the West Indies to develop it, blacks comprised a majority of the population.

Slavery, of course, developed differently over time and space, a fact often overlooked in the passions with which the "peculiar institution" has been attacked and defended. For example, in Virginia in the seventeenth century, slavery developed slowly, whites consistently outnumbering blacks by 6 and 7 to 1. White slaveholders often worked beside blacks and encouraged their mastery of trades to better contribute to the self-sufficient life style then prized in Virginia. However, skilled slaves were the most rebellious, the most able to plot, forage, and escape successfully, a factor that contributed to restrictions on the trades blacks could pursue and to limitations on manumission and the liberties of free blacks. It was these "mobile" blacks who stunned Virginia with the skill and intensity of the planned Prosser uprising of 1800.

## SLAVE CONSPIRACIES IN THE UNITED STATES

Slave rebellions in the West Indies were larger and more successful than those on the North American mainland. In the U.S. South, whites outnumbered blacks and maintained the solid front of a unified ruling class, unconcerned until the Civil War about invasion from the outside. The Indies were far less stable politically and militarily, and in many areas the population was overwhelmingly black. Thus large effective societies consisting of escaped slaves existed throughout the Caribbean. In some cases rebellious slaves had been trained to fight for their captors as soldiers, a factor that was rare in the United States.

However, the growing list of rebellions and communities of escaped blacks in the United States refutes for all time the picture of the American slave as docile and content.

Little is known specifically of slave revolts between the seventeenth and nineteenth centuries, and only three major uprisings have been documented. These were led by Prosser, Vesey, and Turner, whose brief biographies are listed below. A fourth famous revolt, Cinque's capture of the *Amistad*, occurred off the coast of Cuba.

Other slave leaders are known only remotely, by a name or placard, posted briefly on a pole or courthouse. From the skimpy records of available history, *The Negro Almanac* has compiled the following list of slave uprisings prior to the Civil War.

## CHRONOLOGY OF U.S. SLAVE REBELLIONS AND CONSPIRACIES, 1663-1863

**1663** A servant betrays the first serious plot of black slaves and white servants in Gloucester, Va.

**1687** A planned uprising by a group of slaves to take place during a funeral is quelled in northern Virginia.

**1691** Mingoe, an escaped slave from Middlesex County, and his followers attack a white settlement in Rappahannock County, Va., for food and ammunition.

**1711** Sebastian, an escaped slave, leads maroon attacks on a white South Carolina community. In 1729, an Indian hunter tracks and kills him.

**1712** A slave revolt in New York results in the death of nine whites and the execution of 21 slaves.

**1730** In Williamsburg, Va., a black rebellion is precipitated when a rumor circulates to the effect that all baptized persons would be set free.

**1739** Other revolts in South Carolina are squashed; Of a band on the way to St. Augustine, Fla., 44 perish in an ambush, and more than 30 of the slaves led by Cato at Stono River are killed. A third insurrection with no record of casualties takes place in Berkeley County, S.C.

**1741** Reports of a slave conspiracy in New York City lead to the execution of 31 slaves and five whites.

**1771** Bands of fugitive slaves commit robberies in Savannah and Ebenezer, leading to a joint effort by militiamen and Indians against them.

**1786** A band of slaves promised freedom for service by the British form a group called soldiers of the King of England and carry on guerrilla warfare on the banks of the Savannah River. Their settlement is attacked by militia from Georgia and South Carolina, with heavy casualties suffered.

**1792** In Chesterfield and Charles City counties, Va., maroons are tracked down after flurries of marauding. Ten runaways are captured with the help of dogs.

*Maroons banded together for the common defense, often the leaders were given arbitrary rank. Pictured here Leonard Parkinson, Captain of Maroons.*

Many runaway slaves slaves fled to the Dismal Swamp of North Carolina (left). Those who fled here established house camps such as the one above.

**1795** General of the Swamps, a maroon leader and five of his group are killed by a hunting party.

**1800** A conspiracy of Gabriel Prosser and some 1,000 followers is betrayed by two slaves. Gabriel and 15 others hang.

**1802** Tom Copper, leader of a maroon camp in Elizabeth City, North Carolina, instigates insubordination among the slave population.

**1811** A slave revolt in Louisiana is suppressed by U.S. troops.

**1811** A community of runaways settled in Cabarras County, N.C. who resolved to hold out against any force, is wiped out.

**1812** During July, 80 slaves escape from Georgia to go east to Florida, arousing them. In September, Captain Williams and 20 men, on their way to assist Colonel Smith, were routed, attacked, and killed by maroons and Indians.

**1813** In February, after numerous battles a black fort is destroyed.

**1816** A black fort on Appalachicola Bay is destroyed by cannon after a 10-day siege; 270 men, women, and children are killed.

**1816** In Ashepoo, S.C. a large maroon community which had carried on continuous plundering missions is defeated by Major-General Youngblood. Large numbers of blacks are killed and captured.

**1818** Andrey, alias Billy James, a.k.a. Abaellino, leader of some 30 runaway slaves, has a $100 reward posted on him for carrying on attacks in Princess Anne County, Va.

**1819** The slave outlaw Harry, leader of a runaway slave company, is killed by whites on an expedition against maroons. Harry had a reward of $200 on his head.

**1819** Slaves in Augusta, Ga., planned to burn the city. Their leader, Coco, also known as Coot, is caught and executed.

**1821** Rebellion led by Isam, alias General Jackson, takes place through concerted activities of maroon groups in Onslow, Carteret, and Bladen counties in North Carolina. A joint action is planned by outlaws, field hands, and some free blacks against slaveholders. It takes 300 militiamen 23 days to subdue the insurrection.

**1822** The Denmark Vesey conspiracy involving thousands of blacks in Charleston, S.C., and environs, is betrayed by a house slave. Four whites, and 131 blacks are arrested; 37 hang (including Vesey and five of his aides).

**1823** Bob Ferebee, an outlaw slave leader, is captured and executed.

**1827** In Mobile County, Ala., a maroon community built a stockade fort which falls after a three-day attack by armed slaveholders.

**1829** A race riot occurs in Cincinnati, Ohio. More than 1,000 blacks migrate to Canada.

**1830** Maroon communities cause insubordination in Sampson, Bladen, Onslow, New Hanover, and Dublin counties, N.C. According to one leader, Moses, an upris-

*Henry "Box" Brown escaped from Virginia in a crate 3 feet long, 2 1/2 feet deep, and 2 feet wide.*

ing is planned with considerable arms, ammunition, runners, and food supply.

**1831** The Nat Turner Revolt in Southampton County, Va. results in the death of 60 whites. Turner is captured and hanged.

**1836** Squire, the leader of a three-year-old group of maroons near New Orleans, is killed by a guard of soldiers.

**1841** A slave revolt occurs on *Creole*, a ship en route from Hampton, Va. to New Orleans. The slaves sail the vessel to the Bahamas, where they are granted asylum and emancipated.

**1859** John Brown and his followers (13 whites and five blacks) attack Harpers Ferry. Of the five blacks, two are killed, two are captured, and one escapes.

*The execution of Captain Ferrer under mutiny-leader Joseph Cinque's watchful eyes, from a* Harper's *etching. Defended in court by John Quincy Adams, the mutineers were set free and returned to Africa.*

## LEADERS OF SLAVE REVOLTS IN THE UNITED STATES

### GABRIEL PROSSER
### Slave Insurrectionist
### 1775?-1800

Little is known of the early life of Gabriel Prosser. Born around 1775, he was a coachman belonging to Thomas Prosser of Henrico County, Va.

The revolt which Prosser planned was remarkable not only for the skill of its organization but also for the large numbers of people who were to take part in it. The environs of Richmond, Va.—chosen as the site of the rebellion—had some 32,000 slaves, but only 8,000 whites, including a number of French and Quakers, groups which Prosser felt would be sympathetic to his cause.

Prosser planned the revolt for the end of August, reasoning that there would be plenty to eat at the harvest, and that his followers would thus be spared any shortage of important supplies. He intended to kill all slave owners but to spare the French, Quakers, elderly women, and children. Eventually, he hoped that the remaining 300,000 slaves in Virginia would follow his lead and take over the entire state.

The plans laid, it was decided to meet at the Old Brook Swamp outside of Richmond on the last night of August, and to martial forces there for the attack on the city. A severe rainstorm, however, made it impossible for many of the slaves to assemble, and the plot was betrayed by a pair of house slaves who did not wish their master killed.

Panic quickly swept Richmond, and martial law was declared. Most slaves implicated in the conspiracy were rounded up and hanged, at least until it became apparent that this procedure would soon decimate the area's slave population. Less severe sentences were then meted out by the courts.

Prosser himself was captured in the hold of the schooner *Mary* when it docked at Norfolk after a trip from Richmond. Brought back in chains, he was interrogated by the governor but refused to divulge any information on the nature of his plans or on the identities of his compatriots. Prosser was hanged on October 7, 1800.

### DENMARK VESEY
### Slave Insurrectionist
### 1767-1822

Another serious uprising of the nineteenth century was led by Denmark Vesey, a slave who for 20 years had sailed with his master, Captain Vesey, to the Virgin Islands and Haiti, the latter an independent island ruled by blacks.

Born in 1767, Vesey was sold by his master at an early age but later repurchased because he was an epileptic. Vesey enjoyed a considerable degree of mobility in his native Charleston, S.C., eventually securing his own freedom by paying his master $600 of a $1,500 sum won in a lottery. He later became a Methodist minister, using his church as a base from which to recruit supporters for his plan to take over Charleston—a plan set to go into operation on the second Sunday in July of 1822.

As in the case of Prosser, the Vesey plan was betrayed by a slave who alerted the white authorities of the city. Hundreds of blacks were quickly rounded up, and Vesey himself was taken prisoner after a two-day search.

Vesey, who was literate, was extremely adept at cross-examining witnesses at his trial but was unable to deny that his intended purpose was the overthrow of the city. Sentenced to death, he was hanged with some of his co-conspirators on July 2, 1822.

Some of Vesey's collaborators probably escaped to fight as maroons in the Carolinas.

### NAT TURNER
### Slave Insurrectionist
### 1800-1831

Nat Turner, the best-known of the three major slave revolutionaries, was strongly drawn by a kind of visionary mysticism through which he heard "voices" and believed in a special destiny. An avid reader of the Bible, he also prayed, fasted, and ultimately felt that God wanted him to conquer Southampton County in Virginia.

Recruiting a handful of conspirators, Turner struck isolated white homes within his immediate area, and within 48 hours, had built up his band to 60 armed men. Terrorizing the county, they killed 55 whites before deciding to attack the county seat of Jerusalem.

While en route, Turner's men were overtaken by a posse and dispersed, with Turner himself taking refuge in the forbidding confines of what was known as the Dismal Swamp. Remaining there for six weeks, he was finally captured, brought to trial, and along with 16 other blacks, sentenced to death by hanging.

*Nat Turner planning his insurrection.*

### JOSEPH CINQUE
### Amistad Mutineer
### 1811-1852

In Havana, Cuba, in 1839, Joseph Cinque, an African who had been sold into slavery there, was purchased by some Spaniards and put aboard a ship, the *Amistad,* for transportation to Puerto Principe. The *Amistad* was caught in a storm, and the crew exhausted itself keeping the ship afloat. Noting the opportunity, Cinque led the other slaves in seizing the ship. They killed the entire crew except for two men left alive to navigate. Cinque ordered a course set for Africa but had no knowledge of navigation and did not realize that his captives headed north rather than east. The ship was sighted off Long Island and taken to port in Connecticut, where the blacks were put in prison.

However, abolitionists took up their cause. Cinque was released and went on a lecture tour to raise funds for judicial appeals. Cinque spoke in the Mendi language, which was translated, and became known as an excellent speaker. In 1841, with John Quincy Adams presenting their case, the Supreme Court ruled that the slaves be released.

Together with five white missionaries, Cinque returned to Africa.

*Joseph Cinque, painted from life by Nathaniel Jocelyn.*

*When his short lived insurrection was over, Nat Turner hid in the Dismal Swamp. He was taken prisoner after six weeks of being on the run in the swamp.*

## ABOLITION OF SLAVERY BY COUNTRY AND DATE

The first European nation to abolish slavery in the New World was France (1794), which provided for the theoretical, if not actual, emancipation of all slaves in the French West Indies. The distinction of being the first nation in the Western Hemisphere actually to do away with slavery belongs to Haiti (1804). Slavery was abolished in England in 1772, and the British slave trade halted in 1807. It was not until 1833, however, that Parliament passed an act eliminating slavery, after payment of compensation to slave owners, in all British overseas possessions including Canada, the mainland colonies in Central and South America, and the island colonies in the Caribbean. The measure was not fully enforced until 1838.

On the Spanish and Portuguese mainland colonies the abolition of slavery was linked with the independence struggles of various subject territories. Slaves were freed in the United Provinces of Central America (1824); in Mexico (1829); in Latin America, to all intent and purpose, by 1855; in Cuba (1886); and in Brazil (1888). In Spain and Portugal themselves, slavery was declared illegal in 1872 and 1856, respectively.

England—1771 Legal decision; 1833 Act of Parliament
France—1794 (ineffectively enforced in colonies)
Haiti—1804
Jamaica—1804
British Colonies—1807 (measure enforced in 1838)
British Guiana—1827
Mexico—1829
Bolivia—1831
Uruguay—1842
West Indies—1842
Colombia—1851
Venezuela—1854
Paraguay—1862
United States—1865
Puerto Rico—1873
Cuba—1898
Brazil—1888
Spain—1872
Portugal—1856
Russia—1851
Peru—1860

*The effect of the Emancipation Proclamation was the start of an exodus north and west.*

# SUB-SAHARAN AFRICA: THE EMERGING NATIONS

**A Brief History ■ Africa—An Overview ■ Chronology (3000 B.C.-A.D. 1989) ■ Sub-Saharan Nations ■ North African Nations ■ European Dependencies**

With the independence of Angola, Mozambique and the Cape Verde Republic in the mid-1970s, all but one of Africa's 47 Sub-Saharan nations (i.e., Namibia) had achieved independence from their colonial rulers.In many of these new nations, events following independence were more tumultuous than the struggle for freedom itself. By 1985, there had been 90 coups d'etat, and nearly two-thirds of the new nations had experienced nonconstitutional changes in their governments. More than half had come under military rule.

Brutal dictators such as Amin of Uganda and Bokassa of the Central African Republic were eventually deposed by more moderate leaders. In other nations, notably Tanzania, Gambia, Botswana, Kenya and the Ivory Coast, there has been relatively stable leadership from the first days of independence.

Of all the former colonies, the 15 formerly French territories have been the most stable, receiving French support for their currencies and economies in return for commercial favors and military bases. Three former French colonies are among those African nations with the highest per capita incomes, including the Ivory Coast with $1,000 in 1986, the Congo with $1,320 in 1983, and Gabon, with Sub-Sahara's highest per capita income of $3,900 in 1987.

Ironically, though, by the mid-1980s, black Africans were generally eating less and struggling harder in their livelihoods than at the time of independence, some 25 years earlier. In fact, Africa was regarded in some circles as lagging so far behind the rest of the world that it was separated from the Asian and Latin American "Third World" and designated as the "Fourth World."

By the late 1980s, three war-torn areas were approaching peace. Chad had, at long last, dislodged Libyan forces from its northern section and by late 1988, had resumed diplomatic relations with Libya. A 13-year war between Morocco and Polisario Front guerillas for the dominion of Western Sahara was apparently coming to a close when both sides accepted an internationally monitored referendum to allow Western Sahara to determine its future. Namibia remained under South African rule, despite United Nations and world condemnation, but negotiations to establish self-rule there were also in progress by late 1988.

Internal fighting continued in earnest elsewhere, with rebels fighting government troops in Angola, Mozambique and Ethiopia.

The United States and the Soviet Union continued to expand their interests in Africa, including establishment of military facilities at strategic points along Africa's 19,000-

mile coastline, particularly in East Africa. By 1988, though, the Soviet's most solid stronghold was Ethiopia, a former U.S. ally. Nominally Marxist states such as Mozambique, Benin, the Congo, Ghana, Burkina Faso, Guinea and Mali were courting Western investment and aid, and were revising internal policies to include capitalistic private enterprise.

Because of its prolonged, extreme and rigid policies of racial segregation, the Union of South Africa remained a nation of profound interest to blacks in the United States. Neighboring countries formed a coalition called the "Front Line States," and unanimously condemned apartheid. In 1986, the U.S. Congress, overriding a veto by President Reagan, voted limited economic sanctions against South Africa. Although some reforms have been made—the repeal of the Mixed Marriages Act in 1985, for instance—the country remains in an emotionally explosive state.

## AFRICA—AN OVERVIEW

Sub-Saharan Africa encompasses some 9.3 million of Africa's 11.6 million square miles and 340 million of its 400 million inhabitants. It includes all but six most northern and most Arabic of the continent's nations: Egypt, Libya, Algeria, Tunisia, Morocco, and Western Sahara. Most of the area is situated in tropical latitudes and a great deal of it is desert.

In recent years archeologists have come to believe modern man originated in Africa some 2.5 million years ago and eventually expanded to other continents. Three racial groups, Bushmanoid, Pygmoid, and Negroid developed, with the latter becoming dominant through its skills in hunting, farming, and domesticating animals. A group classified linguistically as *Niger Congo* came to control much of Southern Africa. Other subgroups speaking Bantu extended to the East, dominating and almost eliminating the Pygmoid and Bushmanoid people.

During much of this period, Caucasoids moved from Europe and the Near East into North and Northeast Africa. Bedouins came in the seventh to tenth century, and between the tenth and eighteenth centuries large numbers of Moslems emigrated to East Africa.

Sophisticated societies developed, among them the Kush, between 700 B.C. and A.D. 200 and the ancient Ghana, Kanen, Mali Songhai, and the Haissa states. In the Congo, the Kingdoms of Lunda, Lula, Bushong, and Kongo were founded, probably between the sixteenth and eighteenth centuries. On the Guinea Coast, the city states of Benin, Ite, Oyo, Ashanti, and Yoruba date back to the fifteenth century. These states traded extensively in gold, ivory, salt, and livestock.

Significant trade with Europe started in the fifteenth century, with the slave trade an important part. An estimated 10 to 30 million people were sold into slavery by the mid-nineteenth century.

The interior of Africa was first exposed to Europeans in the eighteenth century by missionaries, traders, and adventurers. Their reports of Africa's resources eventually spurred European conquest and direct control of virtually all of Sub-Saharan Africa. Between 1879 and 1900 most of the continent was conquered. By 1900 only Ethiopia and Liberia, of the current 47 Sub-Saharan nations, were free of European control. The Union of South Africa achieved a large measure of independence in 1910 when the British granted it dominion status.

Freedom for black-dominated regions, however, was withheld until a decade after World War II. In 1957, independence movements started with a rush in Kenya, Ghana, and Guinea. (By 1980, only one, Namibia remained under foreign control.)

### Population

Sub-Saharan population is most heavily concentrated in Nigeria, southern Ghana, along the Gulf of Guinea, Benin and Togo, the Nile Valley, in northern Sudan, the East Africa highlands of Ethiopia, Kenya, and Tanzania, eastern Zaire, the eastern and southern coasts, and the inland High Veld of South Africa. The desert and mountain regions are largely uninhabited.

Population growth is rapid, estimated as 2.8% annually. The average African woman in 1985 was bearing 6.9 children in her lifetime. In Kenya, where the annual population growth is the highest in the world, the average woman has eight children. No African nation had an effective population control program in place by the mid-1980s, and common practices of having multiple wives, early marriages, and demonstrating masculine virility via pregnancy continued.

The urbanization rate is 11%, and until recently, 90% of Africa's people lived in rural areas. African cities with populations exceeding one million include Accra, Ghana; Addis Ababa, Ethiopia; Cape Town and Johannesburg, South Africa; Maputo, Mozambique; Ibadan and Lagos, Nigeria; Kinshasa, Zaire; and Alexandria and Cairo, Egypt.

Africa's most populous country is Nigeria, with an estimated 108 million inhabitants in 1987. Nigeria was the eighth most populous country in the world in 1987, but was expected to become the third most populous by 2100, with nearly 509 million inhabitants. Other major African populations expected by 2100 are Ethiopia (173 million), Zaire (139 million), Tanzania (119 million) and Kenya (116 million).

In addition to indigenous Africans, about 5 million people are of predominantly European descent, and 1 million are of Asian descent.

The diversity of Africa's people is underscored by the existence of more than 800 languages and dialects, only less than 10 of which are used by more than 1 million persons.

The United Nations reported in 1988 that infant and child mortality rates in Africa were rising, with the potential to strike 50 million children between 1985-2000. In every other country and region of the world, such mortality rates were dropping rapidly.

Diseases which were being vanquished elsewhere in the world were also continuing unabated in Africa. Major killers were malaria and diarrhea. The emergence of Acquired Immune Deficiency Syndrome (AIDS) on the continent was also documented. Known as the "slim" disease, AIDS struck mostly the African heterosexual population. Uganda was cited in 1987 as having the most identified cases: 15,000 infected persons in Kampala alone.

Literacy, while rising steadily in most other countries, was estimated at less than 50% in most African countries. Notable exceptions were Tanzania (79% literacy, the highest in black Africa), Gabon (65%), Mauritius (61%), Seychelles (65%), and Somalia (60%).

Life expectancy in Africa by 1980 was 43 years, although in select countries such as Kenya and South Africa, the average was on par with the rest of the developing world, at 53 years. Life expectancy in the United States, by comparison, was 73 years.

## Economy

Africa produces 95% of the world's diamonds and 65% of its gold. South Africa and Zimbabwe supply 99% of the world's chromate, while Zaire and Zambia are major producers of cobalt and copper. Nigeria, Gabon and Angola are major producers of oil while Guinea has major aluminum reserves.

However, poverty has become extreme, especially in arid or landlocked areas such as Burkina Faso, Burundi, Equatorial Guinea, Chad, Mali, Uganda, Zaire and Zambia.

Africa's total debt in 1983 was $9 billion. Depressed export earnings, particularly in oil, minerals, cocoa and tea, as well as mounting debt interest, combined to expand the total debt to $218 billion by the end of 1987.

Africa's overall per capita food production declined by 1.4% annually in the 1970s. Although agricultural reforms began to lift production by 1987, the potential for serious grain shortages by 1990 remained. In 1985, food production remained at least 1% behind annual population growth, and the continent imported at least two-fifths of its food. In 1978, the average daily food intake for Africans was very low—1,950 calories with 55 grams of protein—and these figures were declining.

Several factors have contributed to the continent's agricultural chaos.

In several African countries, the leaders opted to apply Marxist agricultural policies, such as collectivizing the farms, sharing tools and animals, and selling at controlled prices only to the government. In most countries, these policies wreaked havoc on agricultural production. In Ethiopia, for example, 10 years of Marxist policies had put its centuries-old agriculture in such disarray that the nation was helpless in the face of the 1984-85 drought and ensuing famine. By 1988, several African countries were discarding their Marxist policies; some slowly, by allowing such innovations as private enterprise; in other cases, dramatically, through changes in leadership.

In a few countries—Nigeria and Uganda, for instance—the leaders literally threw away the future of their people by personally mismanaging or squandering their nation's resources. Nigeria is hard pressed to rebuild its economy after the excesses of President Shagari; in Zaire, President Mobutu Seso Seko is reputed to be one of the world's richest men, while the average Zairean survives on $180 a year.

In some cases, countries unwisely tied their economies to a single export product, incurring disaster when that product's world marketability changed. Oil-producing Nigeria, for example, suffered severely during the oil glut of 1981. Zambia saw its fortunes decline with falling copper prices.

Another major problem in Africa is deforestation, which has continued unchecked for decades. By 1984, 18 African countries faced acute shortages of fuel wood, and virtual wastelands have been created near highly populated West African capitals such as Dakar, Ouagadougou and Niamey. Such scarcity takes a toll on day-to-day living: drinking water does not get boiled, huts are not heated at night; protein-rich soybeans are not introduced into diets because they require too much cooking. In Botswana, women walk as far as eight miles a day to gather wood. In the northern regions, loss of forest land is paving the way for the desertification of vast portions of grazing and agricultural areas. Three major rivers—the Nile, the Niger and the Senegal—are showing signs of drying up.

Transportation has also been a major stumbling block. Railroads, often the only lifeline for landlocked countries, have fallen victim to fluctuating economies and domestic warfare. Roads are scarce, and in many countries, amount to mere trails.

Finally, drought and famine have plagued the continent during the 1980s, especially in 1984-85. In addition to the "biblical famine" endured by Ethiopia, nearly a dozen other countries were gravely hurt by the lack of rainfall and failed crops.

## United Nations; Supranational Organizations

In 1980 all independent Sub-Saharan nations belonged to the United Nations, collectively comprising nearly 30% of the General Assembly's membership of 152.

The most notable African organization is the Organization of African Unity, formed in 1963. Based in Addis Ababa, the OAU seeks to form an African consensus on major world issues and to further the economic development of African nations. OAU has four important organizational components: an Assembly of Heads of State and Government; a Council of (Foreign) Ministers; the General Secretariat; and a Commission of Mediation, Conciliation and Arbitration.

As with other major international groups, the OAU has had little success in resolving major disputes, but remains important as a forum for dialogue and negotiation on major issues.

*A Boer prisoner farm in 1897—tribal chiefs were kept here.*

## CHRONOLOGY OF IMPORTANT EVENTS IN AFRICAN HISTORY: 3000 B.C.-A.D. 1982

**3000 B.C.** Tasili Frescoes, rock murals located in southeast Algeria, give evidence of an early black pastoral civilization (believed to date back to 6000 B.C.).

**1200 B.C.** The beginnings of Nok culture (in Nigeria): an advanced black civilization with a great tradition of terra cotta sculpture (lasting until 200 B.C.).

**1100 B.C.** The Phoenicians found the city of Utica in Tunisia.

**813 B.C.** The Phoenicians found the city of Carthage, a center of trade in North Africa and later a bitter rival of the Roman Empire.

**650 B.C.** The beginnings of the Kingdom of Axum in Ethiopia (lasting until A.D. 650.).

**631 B.C.** The Greeks found the city of Cyrene in North Africa.

**470 B.C.** Hanno of Carthage explores the coast of West Africa as far south as Sierra Leone.

**350 B.C.** Meroe, the capital of ancient Nubia, falls to Ethiopia.

**332 B.C.** Conquest of Egypt by Alexander the Great, who later builds the city of Alexandria.

**168 B.C.** Rome Colonizes Egypt.

**A.D. 100** Introduction of Christianity into North Africa.

**300** The beginnings of the kingdom of Ghana in the Western Sudan.

**320** Christianity is introduced in the Kingdom of Axum (present-day Ethiopia).

**800** Arab colonies are founded in Madagascar and Zanzibar; Arab expeditions are organized into East Africa in search of slaves.

**800** The zenith of the black kingdom of Ghana—extending from the Atlantic coast to Timbuktu, "the land of gold" (lasting until 1240).

**1000** The zenith of the Great Zimbabwe civilization of Rhodesia, site of a highly developed black culture marked by architectural wonders.

**1054** The beginnings of the conquest of West Africa by Moslem Berber tribes.

**1100** The zenith of the Songhai kingdom of West Africa, with its capital at Timbuktu.

**1147** The conquest of portions of North Africa by the Almohades, fierce Berber Moslems who establish hegemony over the region.

**1269** The fall of the Berber's North African Empire.

**1300-1500** The zenith of Ife, a holy city in Nigeria noted for its fine sculpture.

**1307** West Africa is ruled by the Mandingo Empire, successor to the Ghana and Songhai kingdoms.

**1350** The beginnings of Benin, seat of a royal court and Nigerian city famed for bronze sculpture (lasting until 1897).

**1400** A Baluba Kingdom emerges in the Congo.

**1415** The arrival of Portuguese in West Africa marks the beginnings (under Prince Henry the Navigator) of trade with, and exploration of, West Africa.

**1471** Portuguese begin mining of precious metal on "Gold Coast."

**1482** Portuguese colonize Angola.

**1488** Portuguese explorer, Bartholomew Diaz, reaches Cape of Good Hope at the southern tip of Africa.

**1491** Portuguese explorer, Vasco da Gama, rounds the Cape, and sails up the East African coast en route to Asia.

**1493-1529** The Mandingos are defeated by the Songhai Empire, headed by Askia Mohammed.

**1503-1507** Loe Africanus of Morocco explores the Sudan.

**1508-1515** Portuguese colonize Mozambique.

**1513-1517** Hausa states are conquered by Songhai Empire; blacks succeed Arabs, and form Hausa Confederation to carry on prosperous trade (West Africa).

**1571-1603** The zenith of Kanem (Bornu) Empire in Lake Chad region, West Africa.

**1590-1618** Songhai are defeated by Moroccans who gain control over much of West Africa.

**1592** England's Sir John Hawkins plays an active role in slave trade between Africa and the Americas.

**1618** Pedro Paez of Spain discovers the source of the Blue Nile in Ethiopia.

**1652** The Dutch found Cape Town, South Africa.

**1660** The Bambara Kingdom rises in Niger (West Africa).

**1672** England founds the Royal Africa Company for the cultivation of trade in West Africa.

**1697-1893** The Ashanti Kingdom (noted for its high-quality gold work) rises in what is now Ghana.

**1713** The Asiento Treaty enables British to monopolize slave trade to Latin America.

**1787** Great Britain acquires Sierra Leone (West Africa) through treaties with local chieftains.

**1795** England's Mungo Park explores Gambia, the Niger River regions, and the interior of West Africa.

**1807** Great Britain abolishes the slave trade.

**1808** Sierra Leone becomes a British Crown Colony, with Gambia falling under its administration.

**1814** Great Britain secures possession of the Cape of Good Hope through the Peace of Paris.

**1815** France, Spain, and Portugal abolish the slave trade.

**1821** Sierra Leone, the Gold Coast, and Gambia are united to form British West Africa.

**1822-1827** Hugh Clapperton and Dixon Denham explore the Sudan, Nigeria, and other territories in West Africa.

**1827** Rene Caillie of France reaches Timbuktu.

**1835-1837** The Great Boer Trek from the Cape Colony to the Transvaal (South Africa).

**1840-1870** Dr. David Livingstone explores Central Africa, discovering Lakes Ngami and Nyasa, and reaching the Upper Zambezi River.

**1845-1855** Heinrich Barth of Germany leads scientific expeditions into the Sahara and the Sudan.

**1847** Liberia becomes the first independent republic in Africa.

**1858** Richard Burton and John Speke of England discover Lake Tanganyika.

**1861-1864** Samuel Baker of England discovers Lake Albert and Murchison Falls and explores the Nile's tributaries in Ethiopia.

**1867-1871** Diamonds are discovered in South Africa; Kimberly becomes the center of the diamond industry and the mecca for fortune hunters.

**1869** Gustav Nachtigal of Germany explores the central Sahara.

**1871** Great Britain annexes the Orange Free State (South Africa).

**1873-1874** Great Britain conquers the Ashanti Kingdom of the Gold Coast region.

**1874-1889** Henry Morton Stanley explores the Congo River from its source to its mouth.

**1875-1883** Pierre de Brazza of France explores southern and western Africa; founds Brazzaville.

**1876** Exploitation of the Congo begins under King Leopold II of Belgium.

**1877** The Transvaal (South Africa) is annexed by Great Britain.

**1878-1890** Emin Pasha (Eduard Schnitzer) of Germany explores Central Africa.

**1879** The British-Zulu war begins, with British winning decisive victory at Ulundi.

**1880** Brazzaville is founded in the Congo by France.

**1881** Tunisia accepts status as French protectorate (Treaty of Bardo).

**1884** Germany annexes Southwest Africa, and establishes control over Cameroons and Togoland.

**1885** Germany proclaims a protectorate over Tanganyika.

**1886** Gold rush to Witwatersrand in southern Transvaal (South Africa).

**1888** The British East Africa Company is formed.

*A Portuguese sentry and Lorenzo Marquez tribesman in the 1890s.*

**1889** Germany relinquishes its claim on Uganda to Great Britain.

**1890-1897** Cecil Rhodes, British diamond tycoon, becomes leading empire-builder in Africa.

**1893** Great Britain establishes a protectorate over Ashanti Kingdom (West Africa) and Nyasaland (Central Africa).

**1896** Ethiopian forces, victorious in the Battle of Adua, force Italy to withdraw from Ethiopia.

**1896-1925** Carl E. Ackley of the United States explores various parts of Africa.

**1898-1899** France assigns the name "French West Africa" to its West African possessions.

**1899** Nigeria becomes a British protectorate.

**1899-1902** Great Britain defeats the Boers in South Africa, and annexes the Orange Free State and the Transvaal.

**1902** Louis Gentil of France explores portions of Morocco and the Atlas Mountains of North Africa.

**1904-1935** Leo Frobenius of Germany makes 12 expeditions into Africa.

**1905** Italy assumes control of Somaliland.

**1908** Belgium annexes the Congo Free State.

**1910** The Union of South Africa (composed of Cape of Good Hope and Natal provinces, Transvaal and Orange Free State) is formed, with Luis Botha as first premier.

**1911** Libya is annexed by Italy.

**1912** Partition of Africa is completed (only Ethiopia and Liberia independent).

**1914** France and Great Britain conquer the German colonies of Togo and Cameroons.

**1923** Rhodesia (named after Cecil B. Rhodes) is divided into Northern and Southern Rhodesia.

**1926** Firestone Rubber Company purchases one million acres of land in Liberia to be used in the development of rubber plantations.

**1930** Haile Selassie I is crowned as Emperor of Ethiopia.

**1935-1942** Ethiopia is invaded and conquered by Italy.

**1945** Mandated League of Nations territories are transferred to the control of the Trusteeship Council of the United Nations.

**1945-1966** Independence comes to Africa; European domination ends, except in Southern Africa.

**1946** India breaks diplomatic relations with the Union of South Africa because of alleged mistreatment of its Indian minority.

**1948** D.F. Malan and the National Party are elected in South Africa on apartheid platform.

**1950** Seretse Khama is sent into exile from Bechuanaland.

**1952** Independence for Libya (North Africa).

**1952-1960** Mau-Mau violence breaks out in Kenya (East Africa).

*In the streets of Luanda, Angolans celebrate their newly gained independence from Portugal.*

**1953** Egypt proclaims itself a republic.

**1954** A revolt begins in Algeria.

**1956** Tunisia and Morocco gain independence from France.

**1956** The Sudan proclaims itself a republic.

**1957** Ghana becomes the first independent "black dominion" in the British Commonwealth.

**1958** The first conference of independent African states convenes in Accra, Ghana.

**1958** Arch supporter of apartheid, Henrik Verwoerd, is elected Prime Minister of South Africa.

**1958** Guinea votes for independence from France, but the rest of French West Africa joins French Community.

**1960** Cameroon, Togo, Malagasy Republic, Congo (Leopoldville), Somali Republic, Dahomey, Niger, Upper Volta, Ivory Coast, Chad, Central African Republic, Congo (Brazzaville), Gabon, Senegal, Mali, Nigeria, and Mauritania, all attain independence.

**1960-1963** Tribal war and anarchy prevail in the Congo until United Nations forces restore order; Premier Patrice Lumumba is assassinated.

**1961** Independence for Tanganyika.

**1961** Death of Dag Hammarskjold, Secretary General of the UN, in a plane crash in Northern Rhodesia.

**1961** Sierra Leone becomes independent within the British Commonwealth.

**1962** Independence for Algeria, Burundi, Rwanda, and Uganda.

**1963** Independence for Kenya (with Jomo Kenyatta as prime minister) and Zanzibar.

**1964** Independence for Malawi and Zambia.

**1964** Tanzania (composed of Tanganyika and Zanzibar) are united under Julius Nyerere.

**1964** Moise Tshombe is named premier of the Congo.

**1965** Independence for Gambia.

**1965** Ahmed Ben Bella is overthrown in Algeria by Colonel Houari Boumedienne.

**1965** General Joseph Mobutu seizes power in Congo (Leopoldville); General Christophe Soglo ousts Sourou Migan-Apithy in Dahomey.

**1965** Rhodesia declares unilateral independence from Great Britain.

**1966** Colonel Jean-Bedel Bokassa overthrows President David Dacko of the Central African Republic; Lieutenant Colonel Sangoule Lamizane seizes power in Upper Volta.

**1966** Abubakar Tafawa Balewa, chief of state in Nigeria is assassinated; General Aguiyi Ironsi heads a caretaker military government.

**1966** Kwame Nkrumah overthrown in Ghana by Sandhurst-trained officers under the leadership of General Joseph A. Ankrah.

**1966** South African premier, Henrik Verwoerdis assassinated.

**1966** Independence for Basutoland (Lesotho) and for Bechuanaland (Botswana). Lesotho is ruled by Premier Leabua Jonathan, whereas Botswana has as its prime minister Seretse Khama.

**1967** Congolese President Joseph Mobutu nationalizes the Union Minere du Haut-Katanga, the Belgian mining concern which produces three-fourths of the nation's mineral exports, and accounts for nearly one-half of his government's revenues. The company, on the other hand, withholds more than 10 million dollars in royalties, and suspends its tax payments which normally run some two million dollars per month.1969 A new Rhodesian constitution severs all ties with Great Britain and institutionalizes white minority rule and racial supremacy for an indefinite period.

**1969** Kenya's Economic Planning Commissioner Tom Mboya is assassinated in Nairobi, sparking sporadic clashes between Luo tribesmen and members of the Kikuyu.

**1970** Two and a half years of civil war in Nigeria end with the capitulation of the Biafran secessionists to federal authorities in Lagos. At the time of the surrender, Biafra has shrunk to a 3,000-square-mile area with a population of three million. On May 30, 1967, at the time it declared its independence, Biafra consisted of a 30,000-square-mile area peopled by 14 million tribesmen, most of them Ibos. Announcement of the surrender is made by Maj. Gen. Philip Effiong, successor to Odumegwu Ojukwu who had fled the country. In an attempt to quell rumours of an impending bloodbath, Nigerian commander Major General Yakubu Gowon declares a general amnesty "for all those misled into attempting to disintegrate the country." Gowon calls the surrender "one of the greatest moments in the history of our nation, a great moment of victory for unity and national reconciliation." As he talks, a million Biafran refugees search the scorched and barren countryside for food and shelter; victims of the political struggle which has caused widespread famine and mass starvation. Relief offers from nations deemed hostile are rejected by General Gowon, but the General expresses "warm appreciation" for U.S. and British gestures. Withal, Biafra remains etched in the memory of Western man as a grim chapter of human horror and barbarism; a reminder that not even the cries of innocent children for food will prevent men from clashing doggedly over divergent points of view.

**1971** Strained relations between Rhodesia and Great Britain are relieved when the two countries restore normal relations in November. Rhodesian Prime Minister Ian Smith, had broken ties with the United Kingdom in 1965, when Britain objected that the nation's new constitution did not allow blacks sufficient rights.

**1972** Ghana's Prime Minister, Kafi A. Busia, is overthrown in a bloodless coup by Army officers during a visit by Busia to London for medical treatment. Leaders of the uprising, which was headed by Colonel Ignatius Kutu Achaempong, dissolve Parliament.

**1972** Black opposition to the Rhodesian government rises as it becomes apparent that Prime Minister Smith will do little to increase their representation in the nation's public and economic life.

**1972** President Amin of Uganda expels all Indians and Pakistanis who have British passports. Some 25,000 leave the country.

**1972** After 17 years, the civil war in Sudan between Moslem and Christian forces is unofficially ended. Arab Moslem factions had controlled the north of the country, Christian and Pagan forces the south.

**1972** Sheik Abeid Amani Karume of Zanzibar is assassinated by a commando team and succeeded in power by Aboud Jumbe. Though Zanzibar is part of Tanzania, Karume had been extremely powerful in his own domain. Jumbe had the support of Tanzanian President Nyerere.

**1972** Border disputes between Morocco and Algeria are officially resolved when King Hassan of Morocco and Algerian President Boumedienne sign a treaty in Rabat. Leaders of 23 African nations attended the event.

**1972** The government of the Union of South Africa bans student marches and meetings after students at Witwatersrand and Capetown Universities protest the nation's apartheid policies.

**1973** Egypt and the United States renew diplomatic relations after a break of six years. The "October War" between Egypt and Israel is stopped by cease fire and prisoners are exchanged in November. Also in November, Arab diplomats meeting in Algeria announce an oil embargo on countries supporting Israel and their intent to reduce oil production and exports. The embargo affects virtually all of Western Europe, Japan, and the United States. In December the price of oil is doubled. The embargo is lifted on all countries except the United States, Netherlands, and Denmark.

**1973** Large numbers of African nations break diplomatic ties with Israel, in efforts to firm relations with Arab countries.

**1974** The Ethiopian Army, in a coup, seizes Addis Ababa. Emperor Haile Selassie agrees to free political prisoners and accedes to a new constitution. Though the new leaders agree to let Selassie remain as Emperor, he is slowly stripped of his powers and then deposed. The Emperor had ruled Ethiopia for 58 years.

**1974** In August, at a conference in Algiers, Portugal agrees with African representatives to grant freedom to Portuguese Guinea and the Cape Verde Islands. Portuguese Guinea is to become Guinea Bissau. Cape Verde inhabitants are to vote on whether they wish to be independent or join Guinea Bissau. In September, at a meeting in Zambia, Portugal signs agreement with Frelimo (Front for the Liberation of Mozambique) that institutes a provisional government there, with freedom set for June 25,

*Victorious Major Gen. Yakubu Gowan became Nigerian Chief-of-State in 1970.*

*Odumegwu Ojukuwn, the former ruler of Nigeria, fled the country.*

1975. White settlers resist briefly, capturing the radio station, but give up when they are rebuffed by the Portuguese Army. Freedom is also promised to Angola, with a date set for November 1975.

**1975** Signs of change appear in the foreign policy of South Africa as Prime Minister Vorster visits many black African nations and seems to reduce support for the white government in Rhodesia. However, though blacks start to appear in South African athletic events, the policy of apartheid remains firm.

**1975** Numerous efforts for agreement between the Rhodesian government and black forces collapse, as Smith avoids transfer of power and black groups fight among themselves. By the summer of 1975 the days of absolute white rule in Rhodesia seem to be numbered.

**1975** An assassination attempt in June against President Mobutu of Zaire fails. Mobutu implies that the United States was behind the attempt.

**1975** After 470 years of colonial rule, on June 25, the Portuguese flag is lowered throughout Mozambique and what seems to be Africa's most Marxist government takes over. Samora Machel, 41-year-old Frelimo leader, is sworn in as President. Portugal affirms its intent to leave Angola, despite possibility of civil war there and rising emigration of white settlers.

**1976** Lieutenant Colonel Jean-Baptiste Bagaza, a Tutsi, leads a bloodless coup in Burundi and ousts President Michel Micombero, who was in his second term. Bagaza assumes the presidency two days after the coup, suspends the Constitution, and heads a 30-member Supreme Revolutionary Council.

**1976** The U.N. Security Council unanimously condemns South Africa's "illegal occupation" of Namibia and calls for free elections under U.N. supervision.

**1976** Murtala Ramat Muhammad, who assumed leadership in Nigeria following a coup in 1975, is assassinated during another coup attempt. Lieutenant General Olusegun Obasanjo succeeds the slain leader and captures and executes Muhammad's assassins.

**1976** The Republic of Seychelles is granted independence from Britain as a republic within the Commonwealth. A year later, the first president, James Mancham is ousted for what is termed "lavish spending."

**1976** Somalia leader, Mohamed Siad Barre, dissolves the Supreme Revolutionary Council and forms the Somali Revolutionary Socialist Party, as the nation's only legal party.

**1976** A third attempted coup against Sudan President Gafaar Muhammed al-Nimeiry leaves 1,000 rebels and loyal troops dead following a fierce battle in Khartoum. President Nimeiry blames Libyan President Muammar Qaddafy for instigating the attempt; Sudan breaks relations with Libya.

**1976** Morocco formally assumes control of the northern two-thirds of Western Sahara; Mauritania assumes the southern third while Polisario proclaims the establishment of an independent Saharan Arab Democratic Republic as government-in-exile. Mohammed Ould Ahmed is named Prime Minister.

**1977** Zairean refugees in Angola invade Zaire's Shaba Province, prompting President Mobutu Sese Seko to charge

Angola and the Soviet Union with the invasion. The regime of Agostinho Neto, the Soviet Union, and Cuba denied this, but in May 1978 another invasion takes place.

**1977** A small, but fierce, battle is fought at Cotonou in which Beninese exiles are repulsed by the forces of Major Mathieu Kerekou. A U.N. mission of inquiry later reports that the invaders had been flown in from Gabon which leads Kerekou to sharply criticize Gabonese President Bongo.

**1977** The Supreme Revolutionary Council in Burundi gives Lieutenant Colonel Jean-Baptiste Bagaza a mandate for a renewable five-year term and proposes its own dissolution and a return to civilian rule once the Tutsi-dominated political party, Unity and National Progress (UPRONA), has been restored.

**1977** President Marien N'Gouabi of the Congo is assassinated by a four-man hit squad and the power of the country shifts to an 11-member committee headed by Colonel Joachim Yhombi-Opango, who suspends the Constitution and reportedly seeks Western aid for the nation.

**1977** The Republic of Djibouti is born after more than 98% of the population votes for independence. Three days following the election, Issa leader Hassan Gouled is unanimously elected President. Two months later, Afar leader Ahmed Dini is named head of a 15-member Council of Ministers.

**1977** Somali rebels in Ethiopia's Ogaden Province cut the railway to Djibouti. There is fear that Somali will annex the tiny nation. Somali still considers Djibouti a "land to be redeemed" which makes relations between the nations strained.

**1977** King Hassan of Morocco sends 1,500 Moroccan troops to Zaire to help President Mobuto defeat an invasion force from Angola.

**1977** South Africa experiences the worst outbreak of racial violence since the Sharpeville riots in 1960. The bloodshed begins in the black township of Soweto outside Johannesburg, growing out of black student protests against the compulsory use of Afrikaans. As a result, many theaters and opera houses are desegregated.

**1977** Rioting intensifies in South Africa following the death of anti-apartheid activist Steven Biko from a head injury while in prison. The government invokes some of its strictest apartheid policies in two decades by closing down

*In the right foreground stands Kenya's Prime Minister Jomo Kenyatta, wearing a beaded cap. Other African leaders include (left to right: ) Milton Obote (Uganda), Cyrille Adoula (former premier of the Congo) and, at far right in traditional African dress, Kenneth Kaunda of Zambia. The occasion is the opening meeting of the Pan-African Movement for East and Central Africa.*

the leading black newspaper, arresting its editor, and banning a number of protest groups.

**1978** Algerian President Colonel Houari Boumedienne dies after a long illness. Chadli Bendjedid, secretary-general of the National Liberation Front, assumes the presidency. When Boumedienne took over the presidency in 1965, he sought to restore financial stability and maintain good economic and financial relations with France and the United States until 1967.

**1978** A 10-day "summit" meeting convenes at Camp David with U.S. President Jimmy Carter, Israeli Prime Minister Menachem Begin, and Egyptian President Anwar Sadat. The summit results in two documents—A Framework for Peace in the Middle East and A Framework for a Peace Treaty Between Israel and Egypt.

**1978** Kenya's President Jomo Kenyatta, known as "The Old Man," dies and is succeeded by Daniel Arap Moi, who had been vice president. Moi is declared president for the remainder of Kenyatta's five-year term and in 1979, he is reelected for another five-year term.

**1978** Libya breaks its relations with Egypt following the Camp David accord and fortifies their mutual border.

**1978** Nigeria's 12-year state of emergency ends and a ban on political party activity is lifted. In mid-1979 elections are held which place a number of federal representatives, state legislators, and state governors in power with Alhaji Shehu Shagari as president.

**1978** United States President Jimmy Carter's visit to Nigeria is the first to Africa by an American president since President Franklin Roosevelt stopped in Liberia during World War II.

**1978** Sierra Leone becomes a one-party state with a new Constitution adopted by referendum and Siaka Stevens is reelected president for a seven-year term.

**1979** Angola's President Agostinho Neto dies in Moscow, where he had been undergoing medical treatment. MPLA/Party of Labor Chairman Jose Eduardo dos Santos becomes president.

**1979** While Central African Republic's President Jean-Bedel Bokassa is in Libya, he is deposed by former President Dacko, aided by French military forces.

**1979** Colonel Joachim Yhombi-Opango of the Congo resigns under pressure from the Central Committee of the Congolese Labor Party. Late in 1979 he is arrested and demoted to a private soldier.

**1979** The President of Equatorial Guinea, Macie Nguema Biyogo, is deposed in a coup led by his nephew, Lieutenant Colonel Teodoro Obiang Nguema Mbazogo, who formed a Supreme Military Council. Macie was executed a month after being deposed for the crimes of genocide, treason, and embezzlement.

**1979** Protests over a price increase of rice lead to riots in Monrovia, Liberia, which result in more than 40 deaths, 500 injuries, and property damage estimated at $35 million. The government reversed itself and lowered the price of rice—a brief period of calm followed.

**1979** Colonel Mohamed Mahmoud Ould Ahmed Louly, President of Mauritania, concludes a peace treaty with Polisario, a Saharan independence group backed by Algeria by withdrawing Mauritanian troops. Moroccan troops immediately occupy the land.

**1979** A 171-member People's Assembly is elected in Somalia under a new constitution and Mohamed Siad Barre is confirmed as President for a six-year term.

**1979** Major General Maphevu Dlamini, who had been Prime Minister of Swaziland since 1976, dies. Prince Mandabala Fred Dlamini is designated as his successor.

**1979** The Amin regime is overthrown in Kampala following an invasian by Tanzanian and exiled Ugandan forces. Amin's eight-year reign had been a horror reminiscent of Hitler's purges in Germany.

**1979** Zambia endures several Rhodesian commando attacks, including an attack on Lusaka. However, later in the year, Zambia, Rhodesia (to be known as Zimbabwe), and Angola sign a pact to end support for each other's exiled opposition forces, as well as to cooperate with transportation needs.

**1979** In Rhodesia, white voters choose to ratify a new constitution which enfranchises all blacks, establishes a black majority Senate and Assembly, and changes the country's name to Zimbabwe.

**1979** Algerian President Chadli Bendjedid frees deposed President Ben Bella from a 14-year "house arrest."

**1980** President Ahmadou Ahidjo of Cameroon is elected to

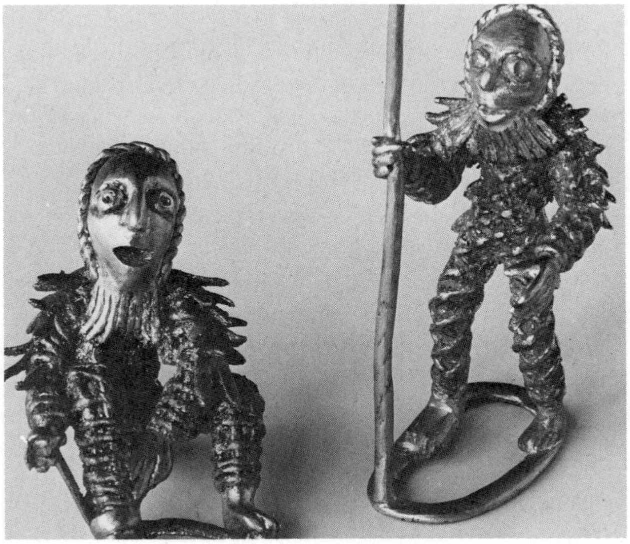

*These brass figurines from Cameroon were made by the lost-wax process, which has been practiced for many centuries in West Africa. Called Suah Dua ("jujumen" in English), the figures wear the fibered costumes used for religious ceremonies.*

*The haff-bearer of the King of Togoland, from a nineteenth-century engraving.*

a fifth term, having faced no organized opposition in his reelection efforts. In 1979 the Ahidjo administration had tried to mediate regional factions but in 1980, sought instead to protest Libya's participation in the disputes.

**1980** Algerian Minister of Executive Affairs Behzad Nabair persuades the Iranian government to retain the $3 billion in Iranian assets against which the banks had legal claims.

**1980** Fifty-two American hostages are released to Algerian custody and flown to Algiers en route to the United States. The release of the hostages coincided with the inauguration of President Ronald Reagan. President Reagan delegated former President Jimmy Carter to serve as the official U.S. representative to greet the released hostages.

**1980** The National People's Assembly adopted Cape Verde Island's first constitution, expected to be emulated in Guinea-Bissau's. Four days after Guinea-Bissau adopts a similar constitution, the mainland government under President Luis Cabral is overthrown in a military coup.

**1980** President Jean-Bedel Bokassa of the Central African Republic is sentenced to death for crimes that include murder, cannibalism, and embezzlement. President Dacko, however, undermines his own popularity on his second attempt at leadership by keeping several high ranking officials from the hated Bokassa regime in office and creating one-party rule again.

**1980** Civil war breaks out in Chad when Hissein Habre, who had been the Defense Minister, challenges President Goukhouni Queddei. During this period, some 80,000 civilians flee the capital of Ndjamena, the site of much of the fighting.

**1980** During a trip to France, Hassan Gouledof Djibouti asks that a truce in the Horn of Africa be made. Djibouti, as a neutral state, is willing to facilitate peace discussions between Somali and Ethiopia. He suggests regional agreements in nomadic migration, freedom of travel in the Ogaden, and joint economic development plans.

**1980** Guinea's President Sekou Toure barely escapes an assassination attempt which claims several lives and injures 30 bystanders. Following the assassination, he immediately calls Guineans to "remobilize" and "unite against intruders." In 1981 Toure is reelected president.

**1980** The Ivory Coast enters a slight recession, but anticipates renewed economic progress under the continued guidance of its president, Felix Houphouet-Boigny. The Ivory Coast has the reputation of being one of the most prosperous, highly developed and politically stable African countries. In the past two decades, the Ivory Coast has tripled its agricultural exports.

**1980** While Gabriel Baccus Matthews is awaiting trial after he had called for a general strike to overthrow the government in Liberia, a coup is held and President William R. Tolbert Jr. and more than two dozen government leaders are killed. Master Sergeant Samuel Doe, leader of the coup, frees Matthews and appoints him as foreign minister.

**1980** Libya gives military support in the Chadian civil war, thereby helping the Goukhouni Woddei government defeat insurgent forces.

**1980** King Hassan of Morocco, under pressure from other African leaders at the Organization of African Unity summit in Nairobi, Kenya, agrees to a cease fire with the Polisarios. It is decided that a referendum under international supervision be used to determine the future of the territory.

**1980** Niger attends the OAU emergency summit on Chad and joins the Central African Republic, Cameroon, Guinea, Senegal, Sudan, and Togo in calling for Libya's immediate withdrawal from Chad.

**1980** President Leopold Sedar Senghor of Senegal retires as leader of the Senegalese Progressive Union. He was considered one of the most highly respected intellectuals in Africa. He had been president since 1960.

*Afrikaaner guns and horses took away ancestral lands from primitive tribes.*

**1980** Robert Mugabe's Zimbabwe African National Union-Patriotic Front party wins 57 of the 80 Assembly seats reserved for blacks, and Joshua Nkomo's ZAPU-Patriotic Front wins another 20 seats, leaving three seats for Bishop Abel Muzorewa's council. Mugabe is sworn in as Prime Minister of Zimbabwe.

**1981** President Ronald Reagan asks Congress to repeal a 1976 ban on military aid to the tattered National Union for the Total Independence of Angola (UNITA) rebels, but Congress refuses partly because of lobbying pressures from American oil businesses which have interests in Angola's oil-rich Cabinda section.

**1981** The National People's Assembly of Cape Verde Islands reelects Aristides Pereira as President and revokes all constitutional provisions relating to a union with Guinea-Bissau. Earlier, the Cape Verde wing of the African Party for the Independence of Guinea and Cape Verde (PAIGC) cut its association with the Guinea-Bissau wing of the party and formed its own party, the African Party for the Independence of Cape Verde (PAICV).

**1981** President Dacko of the Central African Republic is elected to a six-year term by a slim margin. His opponents protest that the election was rigged and begin demonstrations against him.

**1981** General Andre Kolingba, commander of the Central African Republic Army, deposes President Dacko and places all political parties in suspension, declaring rule under the Military Committee of National Redress.

**1981** Egyptian President Anwar Sadat is assassinated in full view of thousands of Egyptians by a small force of terrorists. Sadat's assassins are captured, put on trial, and executed within five months.

**1981** The Reagan Administration closes the Libyan embassy in Washington, citing Libya's connection to international terrorism as the reason. Relations between the countries have not improved though U.S. oil companies remain active in Libya and some 2,000 U.S. citizens continue to work there.

**1981** Tanzania faces bankruptcy and the 18 million population is faced with daily shortages of staples such as bread, soap, and cooking oil.

**1981** Robert Mugabe of Zimbabwe dismisses Joshua Nkomo as Home Minister; Nkomo leaves in protest. Mugabe also discharges Edgar Tekere, the Planning Minister.

**1981** Jerry Rawlings, who had lost in a presidential balloting against Dr. Hilla Limann during a 1979 election in Ghana, leads a coup against Limann. Following the coup, Rawlings dismisses Ghana's parliament, bans political parties, and suspends the Constitution. Rawlings is an admirer of Libya's Muammar Qaddafi.

**1982** Negotiations are completed between Senegal and Gambia whereby the nations will unite in a confederation known as Senegambia. Public opinion in both countries is divided about the merger.

**1982** Kenya's President Daniel Arap Moi accuses the 100,000 Asians of "ruining the country's economy" and pledges to deport any Asians found hoarding or smuggling currency regardless of their citizenship in Kenya.

**1982** A previous U.S. policy is reversed by the Reagan Administration and support is stepped up for Morocco's King Hassan's government, in order to help stabilize that country and to reestablish American military bases there.

**1982** President Mobuto Sese Seko, who brought a degree of stability to impoverished Zaire renews diplomatic relations with Israel, saying that his representative would live in Jerusalem thereby giving tacit recognition of Israel's annexation of the controversial Holy City.

*A woman's detachment of the FRELIMO army that fought for Mozambique independence.*

**1982** Nigerian President Shenhu Shagari reportedly pardons ex-Biafran leader C. Odumegwu Ojukwu, paving the way for his return home from exile in the Ivory Coast where he has been a successful businessman due to the help of President Houghphet Boigny. Nigeria's Ambassador to the United Nation's and a close friend of Shagari, Alhaji Maitama Sule is said to have been instrumental in the pardon.

**1982** A wave of strikes across South Africa by some 10,000 African workers in the automobile and commercial sectors occurs the first of May. The key issues are mounting lay-offs due to recession and a demand for a minimum wage of $2 an hour.

**1982** President Arap Moi of Kenya, chairman of the Organization of African Unity (OAU), joins the president of Chad, Goukoni Oueddi, in asking the U.N. Security Council to help pay for the African peace-keeping force in troubled Chad. The force is made up of troops from Senegal, Nigeria, and Zaire and has been patrolling since 1981.

**1982** Zimbabwean officials announce that the country's capital city, Salisbury, will be renamed Harare, in honor of the second anniversary of the nation.

**1983** Nigerian President Shagari is overthrown by a group of senior military officials. Major General Muhammadu Buhari assumes power.

**1983** President Houphouet-Boigny of the Ivory Coast officially moves the nation's capital from Abidjan to his native village of Yamoussoukro. Actual relocation of the seat of government 166 miles inland does not take place for years.

**1984** Drought sweeps several countries, including Benin, Djibouti, Ghana, Ethiopia, Kenya, Mali, Mauritania, Mozambique, Niger, Somalia, and Sudan. Ethiopia alone suffers a death toll of 1 million, although the world responds with an unprecedented $3 billion in aid.

**1984** A gunman opens fire from the Libyan embassy in London and kills a female police constable. The British government evicts numerous Libyans, holds the embassy under siege for more than a week and ultimately breaks diplomatic relations with Libya.

**1984** Mauritania's President Haidalla was overthrown in a bloodless coup while attending a conference out of the country. Army chief of staff Colonel Maouya Sid'ahmed Taya assumes power.

**1984** Mozambique and South Africa sign the Nkomati Accord, which says that Mozambique will not harbor African National Congress guerillas and South Africa will not assist Renamo guerillas. Neither government appears to keep its word, however.

**1984** Somalia declares, after a visit from Kenyan President Daniel Moi, that it no longer has "as any claim" on Kenyan territory.

**1984** South African Anglican Bishop Desmond Tutu is awarded the Nobel Peace Prize.

**1984** Guinea's President Toure dies undergoing heart surgery in the United States. He is replaced, following brief power struggles, by Colonel Lansana Conte.

**1984** Upper Volta officially changes its name to Burkina Faso.

**1985** Tanzanian President Nyerere steps down, and Vice President Ali Hassan Mwinyi is elected president.

**1985** In an attempt to "stop the killing," Ugandan Brigadier Basilio Okello leads a coup against President Obote, forcing the latter to flee to Sudan. Lieutenant General Tito Okello is subsequently sworn in as leader. By the end of the year, he is ousted by National Resistance Army leader Yoweri Museveni, who is elected president.

**1985** Sierra Leone President Stevens retires and transfers power to Major General Joseph Momoh.

**1985** The United Nations agrees to henceforth call the Ivory Coast, Cote d'Ivoire.

**1985** South Africa abolishes the Mixed Marriages Act and lifts bans against multiracial political movements. This is seen as "too little, too late" and by mid-year, Pretoria must declare a state of emergency in 36 black townships because of the unrest.

**1985** Nigerian President Buhari is overthrown, replaced by a government headed by Major General Ibrahim Babangida.

**1985** The United States repeals the Clark Amendment and begins sending $15 million in annual aid to Jonas Savimbi's UNITA guerillas in Angola.

**1985** Sudan President Nimeiry is deposed while on a trip. Respected Islamic leader Sadiq el-Mahdi is later elected as prime minister.

**1985** The Zambian capital of Lusaka becomes the headquarters of African National Congress, which is outlawed in South Africa.

**1985** South African military forces invade the Botswanan capital of Gaborone and attack 10 havens for African National Congress members. Twelve persons are killed.

**1986** Uganda remains embroiled in bloody, internal fighting. International headlines are made by followers of a prostitute-turned-priestess Alice Lakwena, who urges them to run bare-chested into enemy gunfire.

**1986** The United States bombs military targets in the Libyan capital of Tripoli and Benghazi, after receiving "conclusive evidence" of Libya's role in the bombing at a West German disco.

**1986** The United States Congress, overriding President Reagan's veto, votes limited sanctions against South Africa.

**1986** After reneging again on a promise to hold free elections, Lesotho Prime Minister Jonathan is ousted in a bloodless coup. Major General Justin Lekhanya is sworn into power by King Moshoeshoe.

**1986** Nigerian playwright, poet and novelist Wole Soyinka becomes the first black to be awarded the Nobel Prize for Literature.

**1986** Mozambican leader Samore Machel is killed when his plane crashes on a return trip from Zambia. He is succeeded by Foreign Affairs Minister Joaquim Alberto Chissano.

**1986** Some 1,700 Cameroonians are killed in their sleep when a huge cloud of poisonous gas emerges from the volcanic Lake Nios.

**1986** Central African Republic dictator Bokassa returns from exile and is promptly arrested upon arrrival. He is put on trial, and given the death penalty, later the sentence is commuted to life in prison.

**1986** King Mswati, a teenager, becomes the world's youngest monarch when he comes to power in Swaziland, in order to quash power struggles.

**1986** Zimbabwe is estimated to be paying $1 million a day to keep 15,000 troops in Mozambique to fight off Renamo guerillas.

**1987** Uganda is cited as having the most AIDS victims on the African continent.

**1987** After years of encroachment in northern Chad, Libyan forces are routed by Chadian troops.

**1987** Zambian President Kaunda makes international news when he informs the International Monetary Fund that he will not subject his country to their austerity measures, and that he will no longer make interest payments.

**1987** When it is revealed that some $50 million in U.S. aid to Liberia is unaccounted for, the United States sends in 17 "financial experts" to oversee the books. President Doe is further informed that Liberia must either reform its economic policies or face cutoff of U.S. aid.

**1987** Burkina Faso's mercurial leader, Captain Thomas Sankara, is assassinated by his second-in-command, Captain Blaise Compaore, who assumes the presidency.

**1987** Burundi's President Bagaza is deposed while out of the country. Major Pierre Buyoya assumes the presidency.

**1987** General Zine Ben-Ali deposes the senile Tunisian President Bourguiba.

**1987** Niger President Kountche dies in a Paris hospital. Although the death is officially attributed to a brain tumor, other reports hold that he died of AIDS. Army Chief of Staff Colonel Ali Seibou is named president.

**1988** Hutus in Burundi, fearing a Tutsi massacre, preemptively kill several hundred Tutsis. The Tutsi-controlled government retaliates by killing between 5,000 and 20,000 Hutus.

**1988** Malawi is swamped by 750,000 refugees from Mozambique.

**1988** Morocco and Algeria resume diplomatic relations.

**1988** A major series of talks are held to decide the future of Namibia,—formerly South West Africa—but do not have concrete results.

**1988** Chad and Libya resume formal diplomatic relations, and agree to let United Nations and Organization of African Unity resolve their dispute over the Aozou Strip.

**1988** Morocco and Polisario guerillas agree to a United Nations and OAU proposal for a referendum on Western Sahara, to determine if the territory should be self-ruling or affiliated with Morocco.

**1988** Food riots in Algeria lead to between 200 and 400 deaths.

# SUB-SAHARAN AFRICA

## Angola

***Date of independence:*** November 11, 1975
***Area:*** 481,351 sq. miles
***Population:*** 8,000,000 (est. 1987)
***Capital:*** Luanda
***Monetary unit:*** Kwanza
***Nationality:*** Angolan
***Religion:*** 10% animist, 69% Catholic, 20% Protestant
***Language:*** Portuguese (official), native dialects
***Literacy:*** 20%
***Type of government:*** Republic
***Political parties/leaders:*** Popular Movement for Liberation of Angola-Labor Party (MPLA) (only legal party), National Union for the Total Independence of Angola (UNITA)
***Monetary conversion rate:*** 29.91 kwanza = $1 US (1987)
***Principal economic resources:*** Coffee, sisal, corn, cotton, sugar, oil, diamonds, tobacco, timber

### History at a Glance

The Congo River (the northern border of Angola) was discovered in 1482 by the Portuguese navigator Diogo Cao, who was followed by a number of other Portuguese explorers. Settlements were soon established, and by 1575, the town of Luanda had been founded. Except for a brief period between 1641 and 1648 during which it was under Dutch control, Angola has been one of Portugal's major overseas dominions and a primary source of tropical products and raw materials.

Until the abolition of the slave trade in 1836, Angola served as the chief supplier of slaves bound for Brazil and other parts of South America. The territory's boundaries were first fixed by an international treaty signed by the major European powers at the Berlin Conference of 1884-1885.

The tribes of the Angolan interior were gradually pacified during the first two decades of the 20th century, and by 1951, Portugal had imposed the status of an overseas province upon the territory. However, African representation in government and equal citizenship rights were slow in coming to Angola.

Guerrilla opposition to colonial rule erupted in 1961 and continued for 13 years despite fierce reprisals from Portuguese forces. In 1974, with Portugal itself in the midst of a revolt, Lisbon announced plans to relinquish control of the last of its African colonies.

At the time of the government turnover, three principal independence forces were operating in Angola: the Popular Movement for the Liberation of Angola (MPLA), led by Dr. Agostinho Neto, which controlled much of the central region plus oil-rich Cabinda; the National Front for the Liberation of Angola (FNLA), which had established a government-in-exile in Zaire in 1963 under the leadership of Holden Toberto and controlled most of the northeast section; and the National Union for the Total Independence of Angola (UNITA), which controlled the eastern part of Angola under

*On the day of independence from Portugal, marchers in Luanda raise their machetes in support of tne Popular Movement for the Liberation of Angola.*

the leadership of Dr. Jonas Savimbi.

The three groups initially signed a pact with Portuguese officials declaring Angola's independence on November 11, 1975. However, four months later, the MPLA forces, backed by Soviet weapons and advisors, established a new government under MPLA auspices and ousted the rival factions.

Two weeks later, FNLA-UNITA announced the formation of a rival Democratic People's Republic of Angola and claimed the central highlands city of Huambo as its capital.

Conflict grew between the factions, with the Soviets aiding the MPLA with some 18,000 Cuban troops and the United States sending aid to the FNLA group through Zaire.

In early February 1976, the MPLA captured Huambo and other key cities, forcing FNLA and UNITA to resort to guerrilla warfare. Meanwhile, the Organization of African Unity announced that the MPLA was formally admitted to its membership and on December 1, 1976, Angola, under MPLA rule, was also admitted to the United Nations.

On September 10, 1979 President Neto died in Moscow, where he had been undergoing medical treatment, and on September 21, MPLA-Party of Labor Chairman Jose Eduardo dos Santos became President.

FNLA forces dwindled to practically nothing, but the UNITA forces under Dr. Savimbi swelled, growing to 50,000 by 1985. Headquartered since 1980 in Jamba in southeast Angola, the UNITA forces held sway over about a third of the country by 1988. By then, Jamba was home to some 12,000 civilians and guerrillas, and was nearly self-sufficient in food. In addition to a few factories, UNITA forces also oversaw several hundred "mobile" schools to educate the next generation.

Despite government superiority in troops, which included 40,000 Cuban troops, 2,400 Soviet military advisors, and thousands of North Koreans, East Germans, and other Soviet bloc forces, UNITA troops handed them major defeats. By August 1988, peace talks were under negotiation. However, revelations about the arrival of 10,000 more Cubans and fresh military supplies put the talks on hold while both sides prepared for new offensives.

Angola has also been embroiled in numerous fights between groups in neighboring Namibia, South Africa and Zaire.

In March 1977, Zairian exiles in Angola invaded Zaire's Shaba Province, prompting Zairian President Mobutu to charge Angola with collaborating with the Soviet Union to invade Zaire. The Neto regime, the Soviet Union and Cuba denied this, but in May 1978, another invasion took place. This time, the United States and France joined Mobutu in protesting the invasion. Denials were again heard, but negotiations began, resulting in a nonaggression pact between the countries on October 12, 1979.

In the south, the dos Santos government has supported efforts by the South West Africa People's Organization (SWAPO) to wrest Namibia from South African control. By 1987, Cuban leader Fidel Castro had sent 37,000 Cuban troops to Angola to assist in its fights with UNITA and South Africa, while the Soviet Union poured in an estimated $1 billion in arms and supplies. In 1980, Angola sustained a three-week raid by South African troops.

In March 1981, President Reagan asked Congress to repeal the 1976 Clark Amendment, which forbade aid to anti-Marxist rebel forces. When Congress repealed the amendment in July 1985, the U.S. began sending $15 million in annual aid to UNITA.

Meanwhile, U.S. businesses, such as Chevron and the U.S. Export-Import Bank came under criticism for maintaining massive oil operations at Cabinda, and loaning $230 million to the Angolan government, respectively. The Chevron operations alone provided the Marxist government with $1 billion in 1986, which amounted to 90% of Angola's foreign exchange.

Although rich in natural and agricultural resources—Angola was once a food exporter—the country has remained economically devastated since its birth throes in the 1970s. The continuing civil war has paralyzed the economy, and the dos Santos government pays an estimated 60% to 80% of its revenues to sustain its thousands of troops. In 1986, it was reported that Angola gave $500 million a year to the Cuban government as payment for the Cuban troops stationed there.

The kwanza has been grossly devalued; in 1986, the cost of one egg was the equivalent of $10. In addition to oil, coffee production remained the government's economic hope.

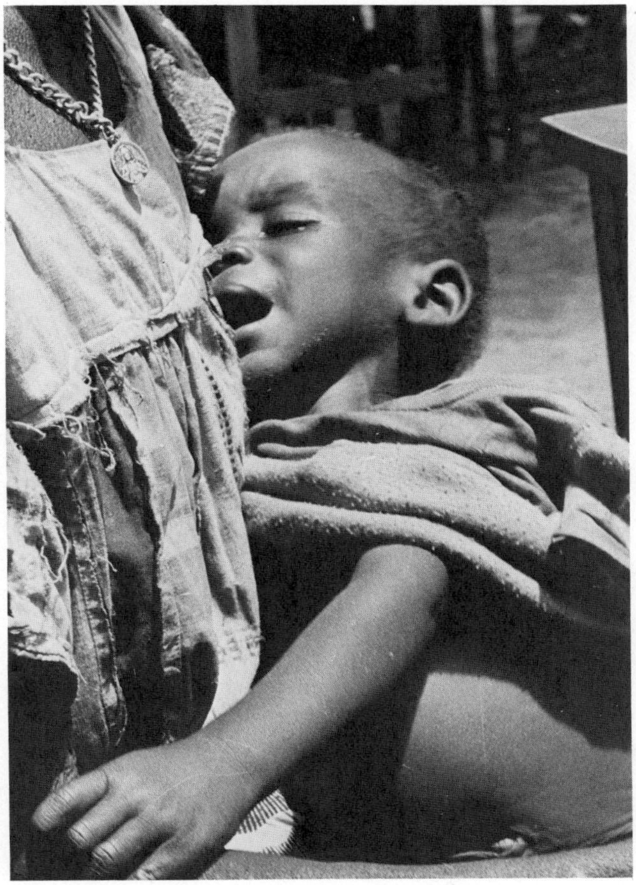

*This starving infant is one of the casualties of the Biafran War.*

### Benin (formerly Dahomey)

***Date of independence:*** August 1, 1980
***Area:*** 43,483 square miles
***Population:*** 4,300,000 (1987 est.)
***Capital:*** Porto-Novo (official); Coronou (de facto)
***Monetary unit:*** Franc CFA
***Nationality:*** Beninois
***Religion:*** 15% Islam, 15% Christian, 70% Animist
***Language:*** French (official), tribal dialects
***Literacy:*** 20%
***Type of government:*** Marxist one party state
***Political parties/leaders:*** People's Revolutionary Party of Benin (established 1975)
***Monetary conversion rate:*** 304.50 francs = $1 US (1987)
***Principal economic resources:*** Oil, palms, peanuts, cotton, coffee, tobacco, corn, rice, iron ore

#### History at a Glance

Founded in the 16th century, Benin was composed of small principalities, the most powerful of which was the Kingdom of Dahomey. In the 17th and 18th centuries, European powers established trading posts along the coast and traded arms and luxuries for slaves. At the height of its power, Dahomey (then much larger than it is today) exchanged ambassadors with the French court of King Louis XIV.

The Portuguese (who discovered Dahomey's ancient capital of Abomey) were soon followed by the Dutch, English, French and Spanish, all of whom shared a common interest: the slave trade.

So many thousands of slaves—their destinations Brazil or the Caribbean—were taken from Dahomey that it was called "the Slave Coast."

In the mid 19th century, France took measures to suppress the slave trade and imposed protectorate status on the territory. In 1904, Dahomey was made part of the Federation of French West Africa. The territory's first real stride toward independence occurred under the Constitution of 1947 when, as an overseas member of the French Union, it won the right to send representatives to the Chamber of Deputies in Paris. By 1952, a territorial assembly had been established. Four years later, under the *loi-cadre* (the Enabling Act which gave most of French West African territories a greater share in self-government), universal suffrage was instituted.

Dahomey accepted French President Charles de Gaulle's Constitution of 1958 and proclaimed itself an autonomous republic, with full membership in the French Community. Two years later, Dahomey opted for full independence, with Hubert Maga as President.

In the first of five coups in 10 years, the Maga government was deposed in 1963 by a military group led by General Christophe Soglo. Soglo stepped aside when a general election in January 1964 elected President Sourou-Migan Apithy, but took back the reins of power in 1965 after numerous political crises in the civilian government.

Soglo was himself deposed in December 1967 by a military coup led by Major Maurice Kouandete and an interim regime was established under Lieutenant Colonel Alphonse Alley.

When a general election attempted in May 1968 failed, former Foreign Minister Dr. Emile-Derlin Zinsou was appointed President of the civilian regime. However in December 1969, the Zinsou government was overthrown, again by Kouandete, and military rule remained until another election was attempted in May 1970.

This time the military forces established a Presidential Council made up of the country's three leading politicians: Justin Ahomadegbe and former Presidents Apithy and Maga.

Kouandete, in his third coup, tried to overthrow the triumvirate, but failed. Eight months later, however, another coup led by Major Mathieu Kerekou succeeded in abolishing the presidential council.

Kerekou announced that the country was to become a Marxist-Leninist state and significantly altered national economic and industrial operations. On November 30, 1975, Kerekou changed the name of the country to Benin after an African kingdom that flourished in the seventeenth century.

The Benin People's Revolutionary Party was established as the new one-party system and remains in power, although an illegal party, the Front for the Liberation and Rehabilitation of Dahomey, was also formed at the time of Kerekou's takeover.

A small, but fierce battle was fought at Cotonou in January 1977 in which Beninese exiles were repulsed by Kerekou's forces. A U.N. mission of inquiry later reported that the invaders had been flown in from Gabon, which led Kerekou to sharply criticize Gabonese President Bongo. Bongo immediately ordered some 6,000 Benin nationals expelled from that country.

A 1983 drought proved to be so devastating to crop harvests that virtually the entire country was declared a disaster area, and a major austerity drive was implemented. Two years later, many areas remained either stagnant or in recession.

In 1986, following student unrest and boycotts, the national assembly agreed to move control of transportation and consignment of goods from the state, where it had been for 10 years, to the private sector. Cabinet changes in 1987 which placed "pragmatists" in key positions were further evidence of the country's attempts to resolve its difficult economic circumstances.

Benin has maintained ties with both Western and communist governments, as well as neighbors such as Togo, Nigeria, Niger and Burkina Faso (formerly Upper Volta). Its centuries-old ties with France were reaffirmed in 1981 and 1983 when Kerekou met with French President Francois Mitterrand. Kerekou's relationship with Libyan Colonel Muammar Qaddafi, which had been close since 1980 when Kerekou converted to Islam during a state visit by Qaddafi, seemed to have cooled by the mid-1980s. In 1988, however, Benin was accused of allowing Libyan agents to use its territory as a base to foment terrorism in West Africa.

In 1985, Kerekou was redesignated to a five-year term as head of state.

Benin is one of the smallest and most densely populated states in Africa. It is primarily an agricultural state, with palm products, cotton, and groundnuts as principal exports.

## Botswana

***Date of independence:*** September 30, 1966
***Area:*** 222,000 square miles
***Population:*** 1,200,000 (est.1986)
***Capital:*** Gaborone
***Monetary unit:*** Pula
***Nationality:*** Botswana
***Religion:*** 49% Animist, 48% Christian
***Language:*** English (official), Tswana
***Literacy:*** 54%
***Type of government:*** Parliamentary republic
***Political parties/leaders:*** Botswana Democratic Party, Botswana National Front, Botswana People's Party, Botswana Independence Party, Botswana Liberal Party
***Monetary conversion rate:*** 1 71 pula=$1US (1987)
***Principal economic resources:*** Diamonds, copper, nickel, salt, coal, beef

### History at a Glance

Sparsely populated, landlocked Botswana, bordered by South Africa, Namibia, and Zimbabwe, has a democratic government and one of the best human rights records in Africa.

Largely covered by the Kalahari Desert, its principal industry has traditionally been cattle-raising. In the late 1960s, the discovery of major copper, nickel, and diamond deposits opened a highly profitable source of revenue. Although it began as one of the world's poorest countries, Botswana has steadily grown stronger economically. By the mid-1980s, it was producing more diamonds than South Africa, and in 1985, earned the equivalent of $562 million. By 1988, the per capita income was reported at $1,690, the highest in the region after South Africa. Tourism, in the form of safaris, also continued to flourish.

Botswana suffered a few setbacks in the 1980s. The world market for minerals slumped slightly, curtailing Botswana's export revenues. Then, in 1984-85, the country suffered a severe drought and famine. Heavy rains fell in 1986 but unleashed the worst infestation of locusts in 60 years, and crops were destroyed for the third year in a row. Lack of water remains a major problem.

Until his death on July 13, 1980, President (Sir) Seretse Khama sought to preserve Botswana's independence in African and world affairs, as well as an uncompromising anti-apartheid policy at home. He was succeeded by Dr. Quett Ketumile Masire, who had served as vice president and Minister of Finance and Development Planning since Botswana's independence. President Masire and Vice President Peter Mmusi were reappointed in September 1984.

Botswana's Foreign Minister Gaositwe Chiepe is one of two women who hold high office in Africa.

Although it is one of the six Front-Line States which oppose apartheid, Botswana is economically dependent on South Africa and does not support sanctions. It has maintained its neutrality by officially denying shelter to combatants of the African National Congress (ANC). However, Botswana's 1,500-mile border with South Africa proved impossible to patrol, and ANC members set up bases in Botswana for their bombing raids into South Africa.

In June 1985, South African military forces retaliated, storming the Botswanan capital of Gaborone and attacking 10 alleged ANC havens. Twelve persons were killed.

The raid heightened tensions between the two nations, with South Africa threatening future incursions. Masire moved to evict ANC members and received counter-intelligence training and substantial military equipment from Britain and the United States to safeguard Botswanan borders. The government also passed an unpopular National Security Act which gave police the power to arrest without a warrant.

In 1979, a highway connection with Zambia, financed with U.S. aid, gave Botswana "an opening to the north" and provided the country with its first communications link to a nation with African majority rule. Since then, Botswana has added 15,000 kilometers of roads, three airports, and a portion of the railway from South Africa to Zimbabwe.

Botswana formed its own central bank in 1979; however, its ties to South Africa remain strong; in 1988, 95% of its exports and 85% of its imports passed through South Africa. Unemployment, due to under-education of its population, continues to be a problem. Some 45,000 Botswanans work in South Africa, most of them in diamond mines.

## Burkina Faso
## (formerly Upper Volta)

***Date of independence:*** August 5, 1960, present name adopted Aug. 4, 1984
***Area:*** 105,869 square miles
***Population:*** 7,300,000 (est. 1987)
***Capital:*** Ouagadougou
***Monetary unit:*** CFA franc
***Nationality:*** Bukinabe
***Religion:*** 65% Animist, 25% Islam, 10% Catholic
***Language:*** French (official); tribal languages
***Literacy:*** 10%
***Type of government:*** Military
***Political parties/leaders:*** Democratic Union, Progressive Union, National Revolutionary Council, Patriotic League for Development
***Monetary conversion rate:*** 304.50 francs = $1 US (1987)
***Principal economic resources:*** Millet, sorghum, corn, rice, livestock, peanuts, sugar cane, cotton

### History at a Glance

The early history of Burkino Faso, which was known as Upper Volta from August 1960 to August 1983 is largely concerned with the exploits of the Mossi people who migrated from the east between the eleventh and thirteenth centuries. During the following two centuries, there is evidence indicating that the Mossi conducted highly successful raids on the wealthy trading cities along the Niger River. Checked eventually by the armed might of the Songhai Empire, the Mossi organized the territorial spoils they had acquired into the states of Tenkodogo, Yatenga, and Ouagadougou, each of which was ruled by a moro naba (king). Of the three reigning kingdoms, Ouagadougou was unquestionably the most powerful.

The Mossi finally settled down to a life of commerce, engaging profitably in the export of gold, kola nuts, and slaves. In the eighteenth century, the Ashanti, from Ghana, made significant military inroads into Mossi territory. The rest of it was conquered in 1896 by a French lieutenant in command of a single infantry battalion.

Governed at first as part of the Ivory Coast, Upper Volta was separated from this territory in 1969 and made a single administrative unit. In 1933, it was parceled up among Niger, French Sudan, and the Ivory Coast.

After World War II, however, Upper Volta was reconstituted as a separate territory in response to the wishes of the Mossi, and to curb the growth of the African Democratic Rally, an interterritorial political party which was gaining widespread support throughout West Africa. Upper Volta accepted the French Constitution of 1958, thereby becoming an autonomous unit within the French Community. Two years later, the territory became completely independent, although retaining close ties with metropolitan France.

In 1966, Maurice Yameogo, President of Upper Volta, was deposed by Lieutenant Colonel Sangoule Lamizan after several days of rioting in Ouagadougou concerning the issue of pay cuts for government employees.

Throughout the late 1960s, Chief of Staff Lamizana effectively headed the country and prevented any further erosion of its precarious financial position.

In 1970, Upper Volta returned to a constitutional government under Lamizana, but soon suffered two natural disasters: a severe drought in 1973 and famine in 1974. Political fighting between Lamizana and ex-President Ameogo resulted in Lamizana, with the Army, taking control of the government and dissolving the National Assembly and suspending the 1970 constitution. A new cabinet was formed in February 1974 with Lamizana continuing as both President and Prime Minister.

In yet another governmental reorganization in 1977, Lamizana announced that a constitutional referendum would take place soon with both presidential and legislative elections, though he would not stand as a candidate. On November 27, 1977, the majority of the population voted for democratic rule in the referendum. However, Lamizana reneged on his promise not to run for the presidency and won in the 1978 election.

Upper Volta had been one of two multiparty democracies (Senegal was the other) in French Africa, until November 25, 1980, when the regime was overthrown in a military coup led by former Foreign Minister Colonel Saye Zerbo.

Under Zerbo's rule, all political activity was banned, former leaders were arrested, and the constitution was suspended. The Military Committee of Reform for National Progress was formed and an 11-member "directing committee," headed by Zerbo, installed.

In November 1982, Zerbo's reign was ended in a coup which left Major Jean-Baptiste Ouedraogo as the national leader. Ouedraogo was overthrown in August 1983 in a rebellion led by the youthful former prime minister Captain Thomas Sankara.

Sankara, a Marxist-Leninist, immediately formed a National Revolutionary Council (CNR) with himself as chairman. He weathered two coup attempts and in 1984, renamed the country Burkina Faso, which has been said to mean "the land of upright men," or "the incorruptible country."

Sankara stressed self-sufficiency, and banned nightclubs, begging and prostitution. He also oversaw unorthodox policies such as the annual "tradition" of dissolving his cabinet, appointing new ministers and sending the former ministers to head agriculture and development projects.

Under Sankara, a 20-year land dispute between Burkina and Mali erupted into four days of bloodshed in December 1985, leaving a dozen persons dead. The International Court of Justice eventually awarded the two countries approximately equal portions of the disputed land. In September 1986, Burkina (along with Ghana) was also accused of masterminding a commando raid which tried to overturn the Togoese government of President Gnassingbe Eyadema.

On October 15, 1987, commandos led by Sankara's second command and "best friend," Captain Blaise Compaore, shot Sankara and 12 aides to death. Compaore assumed the presidency, calling Sankara a "renegade" and a "madman," and reportedly released a number of political prisoners jailed by Sankara. However, the nation mourned Sankara and within two weeks, a key army unit staged an unsuccessful rebellion against Compaore.

Under Sankara, Burkina sought good relations with neighbors, Ivory Coast, Niger and Senegal. The late leader met with French President Francois Mitterrand in 1986, shoring up French relations, important in view of the fact that half of Burkina's sizable foreign aid comes from France.

Burkina Faso is landlocked, contains virtually no raw materials, and in 1987, was listed as the third poorest nation in the world. Average per capita income was estimated at $140 in 1985. Around one-third of the population works in the more prosperous Ivory Coast. Located on the southern edge of the Sahara, Burkina has sustained major droughts in recent years, the most recent in 1984. It is largely dependent on foreign aid, listed as $230 million in 1983.

## Burundi

***Date of independence:*** July 1, 1962
***Area:*** 10,747 square miles
***Population:*** 5,000,000 (est. 1987)
***Capital:*** Bujumbura
***Monetary unit:*** Burundi franc
***Nationality:*** Burundi
***Religion:*** Catholic 78%, Protestant 5%, Islam 2%, Animist 15%
***Language:*** Kirundi and French (official), Swahili
***Literacy:*** 23%
***Type of government:*** Republic, military government, one-party socialist
**Political parties/leaders:** Unity for National Progress (only legitimate party)
***Monetary conversion rate:*** 93 francs=$1 US (1987)
***Principal economic resources:*** Coffee, tea, cotton, food crops

### History at a Glance

The early history of Burundi strongly parallels that of its northern neighbor, Rwanda. The first-known inhabitants of both regions were the Twa, a tribe of pygmy hunters who were gradually pushed back into the jungle by the agriculturally inclined Hutu, a Bantu people.

In the fifteenth century, the Tutsi (of Hamitic stock) entered the area from the northeast, establishing a caste-oriented, feudal society. Headed by an omnipotent chieftain, or mwami, the Tutsi became the ruling class and obliged the Hutu to tend the fields and produce food for everyone.

In 1858, the English explorers John Speke and Richard Burton became the first white men in the area when they crossed Burundi in search of the headwaters of the Nile River. Thirteen years later, Stanley and Livingstone landed at Usumbura and explored the Ruzizi River region. Ultimately, however, it was the Germans who succeeded in consolidating control over the territory as a result of agreements reached with other major European powers at the Berlin Conference (1884-1885).

During World War I, Belgium replaced Germany as the power administering the territory. In 1923, the League of Nations formalized this arrangement by granting the Belgian king a special mandate over the combined territory of Ruanda-Urundi. This mandate remained operative until 1946, at which the United Nations substituted a system of trusteeship.

By this time, it was clear that Ruanda and Urundi were developing along separate paths which would, without proper supervision, lead to a possible collision course. To the north, Ruanda seemed bent on a republic form of government; to the south, Urundi continued to favor a monarchical structure. In the 1961 elections, Urundi expressed its preference for a constitutional monarchy, headed by Prince Rwagasore, a son of the mwami. Later that same year, the prince was assassinated by rival nationalists.

The UN stepped into the ensuing power vacuum, recommending that a united Ruanda-Urundi declare itself independent by July 1, 1962. With one significant exception, the deadline and the conditions were met by both territories. Ruanda became the Republic of Rwanda; Urundi, the Kingdom of Burundi.

Underlying Burundi's internal history is its centuries-old tribal division between the Tutsis, known as "the tall ones" and the Hutus, "the short ones." Although the Tutsis comprise only 15% of the population, they have always held the most powerful positions in government, military and business, leaving the subservient jobs to the Hutus, which comprise 85% of the population. Critics have accused the Tutsis of "tribal apartheid," and, in fact, the Tutsis have long been wary of the Hutus: Hutu uprisings were successful in placing Hutus in power in neighboring Rwanda.

In 1966, Burundi's first king, Mwambutsa IV, was deposed by his son, Ntare V. In November 1966, Captain Michel Micombero, a Tutsi and commander of the government troops, deposed King Ntare, suspended the constitution, dissolved the National Assembly and assumed the presidency of the Tutsi-dominated Unity for National Progress party (UPRONA).

Micombero ruled for several years, surviving plots against him in 1969 and 1971. In 1972, when Ntare was executed after being promised safe-conduct into the country, the Hutus revolted and killed nearly 1,000 Tutsis.

Micombero and the army responded in what has been described as "a sustained campaign of selective genocide" and throughout April and May 1972, systematically slaughtered between 80,000 and 150,000 Hutus—virtually all the educated or prominent Hutus in the country.

On November 1, 1976, Lieutenant Colonel Jean-Baptiste Bagaza, a Tutsi, led a bloodless coup and ousted Micombero, who was in his second term. Bagaza assumed the presidency two days later, suspended the constitution, and headed a 30-member Supreme Revolutionary Council.

In 1977, the Council gave Bagaza a mandate for a renewable five-year term. It also proposed its own dissolution and a return to civilian rule, once the Tutsi-dominated UPRONA had been restored. In 1979, the Council was abolished and its functions were transferred to a Central Committee headed by the president. On October 22, 1982, elections were held for a new National Assembly and reconfirmation of Bagaza as chief executive. During a congress on July 25-27, 1984, Bagaza was named to a third presidential term.

Under Bagaza, the government turned hostile to the Catholic church, where a majority of Hutus worship. In 1985, more than 80 missionaries were expelled and others were imprisoned for publishing messages deemed "insulting" to the president. In 1987, the government imposed severe restrictions, abolishing Catholic parish councils, and forbidding weekly masses.

In September 1987, during a trip to Canada, Bagaza was ousted and replaced by military leader, Major Pierre Buyoya, a Tutsi and a Catholic. He immediately lifted restrictions against the church and freed political prisoners.

Another bloody Tutsi-Hutu massacre occurred in August 1988. Although the government estimated 5,000 dead, other reports placed the death toll at 20,000, with another 50,000, virtually all of them Hutus, fleeing to Rwanda. Most of the dead were Hutus.

Small, landlocked Burundi remains one of the 12 poorest countries in the world, with a per capita income of $130 in 1985. Coffee provides 85% of foreign earnings.

In 1977, Burundi, Rwanda and Zaire formed the Economic Community of the Great Lakes Countries in order to exploit gas deposits under Lake Kivu, and the fishing industry on Lake Tanganyika. In addition, Burundi is working with Rwanda, Tanzania and Uganda to build a rail network in the Kagera River Basin.

## Cameroon

***Date of independence:*** January 1,1960
***Area:*** 183,569 square miles
***Population:*** 8,650,000 (est.1981)
***Capital:*** Yaounde
***Monetary unit:*** Communaute Financiere Africaine (CFA) franc

***Nationality:*** Cameroonian
***Religion:*** 50% Animist, 25% Christian, 10% Muslim
***Language:*** English/French
***Literacy:*** South 40%, North 10%
***Type of government:*** One-party presidential regime
*Political parties/leaders:* Cameroonian National Union (established 1966)
***Monetary conversion rate:*** 212.7 CFA francs =$1 US (1979)
***Principal economic resources:*** Cocoa, coffee, timber, aluminum, cotton

## History at a Glance

The first European to explore any part of present-day Cameroon was Fernando Po, a Portuguese who arrived in the territory in 1472. (Po was followed by a number of Portuguese navigators who found the territory's main waterways overloaded with prawn, a crustacean known in their language as "camaraos.") Portuguese interests soon gave way to those of the English and the Germans.

Germany had already established trading posts and factories at various points along the West African coast before becoming interested in basing her African colonial empire in the Cameroons. In 1884, with the approval of England, she placed the territory under protectorate status. Prior to World War I, the Germans concentrated on developing the resources of the interior, cultivating banana and coffee plantations, building roads and railroads, and establishing a communications network.

During World War I, the German Cameroons were seized by French, British and Belgian troops. In 1915, the territory known as "New Cameroons" (an additional portion which had been ceded to Germany by France in 1911) was returned to France and incorporated into French Equatorial Africa. Later that year, the French and the British agreed to rule the rest of the territory jointly. New Cameroons remained part of French Equatorial Africa; the eastern sector became East Cameroon, while the western area adjoining Nigeria was dubbed British Cameroons.

Between the two world wars, the French contributed significantly to the development of the territory's resources, although they did little to encourage self-sustaining political institutions. In 1946, the territory was placed under international trusteeship and in 1957, France granted Cameroon full internal autonomy. A year later, the Cameroonian Legislative Assembly voted to declare the territory independent by 1960, with Ahmadou Ahidjo as chief of state. During this same period, John Foncha emerged as the key figure behind the independence movement in the British Cameroons. After a short period of unrest culminating with the appearance of French troops in East Cameroon, a national assembly was elected and Ahidjo was returned to office as president of the newly created Republic of Cameroon.

In 1961, the Northern British Cameroons were incorporated into the Republic of Nigeriaas the Sarduana Province, while the Southern British Cameroons joined the Cameroon Republic. After a constitution had finally been drafted and approved, the Cameroon Republic came into being as the combined states of East and West Cameroon. Ahidjo served as President of the republic; Foncha, as Vice-president.

Throughout the 1960s, Cameroon maintained close ties

*Farmers take their cattle to graze near the village of Mokolo in Cameroon.*

with France, its chief economic benefactor. Internationally, the country generally supported the Western bloc, although it signed economic and cultural agreements with the Soviet Union and its satellites.

In 1972 Cameroon's federal structure gave way to a unitary republic under a new constitution. Legislative power was placed in the hands of a 120 member National Assembly, elected directly.

As part of Ahidjo's plan to encourage a regime of national unity and social justice, a five-year economic plan was initiated in 1972. He faced no organized opposition and on April 5, 1980, was reelected to a fifth term as president. In November 1982, however, he unexpectedly announced his retirement, and handed the presidency to his longtime associate, Prime Minister Paul Biya. Their relationship later soured to the point where Biya sentenced Ahidjo to death in abstentia for plotting against him.

Biya was reelected in his own right on January 14, 1984, but had to quell a major uprising a few months later. In 1984, the National Assembly renamed the country the United Republic of Cameroon.

Cameroon is an unaligned nation, with a limited democracy; in 1986, for the first time in 20 years, elections were held with multiple candidates on the ballots. In the early 1980s, Cameroon got involved in the internal disputes of Chad, when 100,000 Chadian refugees fled into Cameroon's northern provinces.

Cameroon embraces capitalism and has pursued numerous business ventures with Americans. France is a major trading partner. In 1986, it restored diplomatic relations with Israel.

A natural disaster occurred on August 21, 1986, when a huge cloud of poisonous gas emerged from the volcanic Lake Nios and killed more than 1,700 persons in their sleep.

Cameroon's economy, which is primarily agricultural, has grown steadily. Per capita income in 1987 was $800. Cameroon is largely self-sufficient in basic foods, and is one of the leading exporters of cocoa, coffee and timber. It also sustains an off-shore oil business. The most important manufacturing industry is aluminum processing.

*Workmen arranging logs brought down the river to Lagos from the interior of the country. The lumber from these logs is for export. Many poor underdeveloped countries are totally dependent upon the export sale of their raw materials.*

## Cape Verde Islands (Santa Antas, Boa Vista, Sao Nicolau, Sao Vicente)

***Date of independence:*** July 5, 1975
***Area:*** 1,557 square miles
***Population:*** 300,000 (est. 1987)
***Capital:*** Praia
***Monetary unit:*** Cape Verde escudo
***Nationality:*** Cape Verdian
***Religion:*** Catholic 98%
***Language:*** Portuguese and crioula (blend of Portuguese and West African)
***Literacy:*** 37%
***Type of government:*** Republic (one-party socialist)
**Political parties/leaders:** African Party for the Independence of Cape Verde (PAICV)
***Monetary conversion rate:*** 72.04 escudos = $1 US (1987)
***Principal economic resources:*** Fish, bananas, salt, flour, corn

### History at a Glance

The Cape Verde Islands, uninhabited when they were discovered by the Portuguese in 1456, were first settled toward the end of the sixteenth century, when African slaves were brought in from Portuguese Guinea to work the land. In 1587, the islands were placed under the administration of a colonial governor.

For the next two centuries, the population of the islands grew steadily, particularly with the influx of Genoese and Spanish immigrants. Great Britain established a coaling station on the island of Sao Vicente in the eighteenth century, a move which also involved the founding of a settlement. On occasion, famine has caused some of the island's inhabitants to emigrate to the African mainland or to the United States.

Although Portuguese rule of the Cape Verde Islands was more benign than that of its other African possessions, rebellious uprisings started as early as 1956. Neighboring mainland country Guinea-Bissau rebels fought Portuguese troops and often the two countries found themselves allied against the common ruler.

When Portuguese rule of the islands finally ended in July 1975, it seemed appropriate to many that the islands would merge with Guinea-Bissau.

During the 1970s, two major independence movements developed: the mainland-based African Party for the Independence of Guinea and Cape Verde (PAIGC), which advocated the union of the islands and the mainland; and the Democratic Union of Cape Verde (UDCV), headed by Joao Baptista Monterio, which opposed a union.

When Cape Verde was liberated from Portuguese rule, a transitional government was set up via the election of a 56-member National People's Assembly. However, only members of the PAIGC participated in the election and it appeared that the majority of people wanted unification.

In July 1975, the Assembly elected Aristides Pereira, the secretary general of PAIGC as President of Cape Verde, and Major Pedro Pires, who had engineered independence agreements for both Guinea-Bissau and Cape Verde, was made Prime Minister. Later, the countries were governed through President Pereira as Secretary General and Guinea-Bissau's President Luis Cabral as Deputy Secretary.

Although a union between the two countries appeared inevitable, signs of trouble appeared in January 1977 when a Unity Council, formed to examine the means of unification, announced that it must move cautiously in order to establish "a common strategy of development."

On September 7, 1980, the National People's Assembly adopted Cape Verde's first constitution, which was expected to emulate Guinea-Bissau's. However, on November 14, 1980, four days after Guinea-Bissau adopted a similar constitution, the mainland government under Cabral was overthrown in a military coup. The reasons for this were partly because the black Guinea-Bissau people did not want to be dominated by the mostly mestizo population of Cape Verde.

Three weeks after the coup, Cape Verde's President Pereira pledged that his country would not interfere with the internal affairs of Guinea-Bissau, and on February 12, 1981, the National People's Assembly both reelected Pereira as President and revoked all constitutional provisions relating to a union with Guinea-Bissau. Earlier, the Cape Verde wing of the PAIGC cut its association with the Guinea-Bissau wing of the party and formed its own party, the African Party for the Independence of Cape Verde (PAICV).

Friendly relations were formally reestablished with Guinea-Bissau in July 1982.

The islands, located in the Sahel region, have experienced drought-like conditions since 1968. Lack of fresh water has crippled agriculture and kept the islands in poverty; in 1984, some 60% of food needs were imported. The once-plentiful trees, which gave the islands the "verde" (green) in their name, have virtually vanished.

The government has tried to energize domestic agriculture through various programs, one of the most controversial being a program to repatriate some 600,000 Cape Verdeans, many of whom are skilled laborers or absentee landlords. Fish, bananas, corn and salt are traditional export products. The average annual income per person in 1987 was $270.

Sanctions against South Africa affected Cape Verde's income, as well. The Cape Verde Airport on Sal Island, long a stop-over for international flights, used to receive $10 million in income from South African Airways. In 1987, that income fell to $7 million as the South African company cut back its flights. Despite the economic crisis, Cape Verde favored sanctions.

## Central African Republic

***Date of independence:*** August 13, 1960
***Area:*** 241,343 square miles
***Population:*** 2,000,000 (est. 1981)
***Capital:*** Bangui
***Monetary unit:*** CFA franc
***Nationality:*** Central African
***Religion:*** 40% Protestant, 28% Catholic, 24% Animist, 8% Muslim
***Language:*** French (official)
***Literacy:*** 5-10%
***Type of government:*** Democratic republic with a single party—presently under military rule
***Monetary conversion rate:*** 225.50 Communaute Financiere Africaine (CFA) =$1 US (1980)
***Principal economic resources:*** Cotton, coffee, peanuts, livestock, diamonds, titanium

### History at a Glance

The territory of what is now the landlocked Central African Republic was first settled by France in 1887 pursuant to the Berlin Conference (1884-1885), which had established French rights to all land lying beyond the right bank of the Congo River. Early French explorers of this region were particularly concerned with solidifying France's control over all territory between Brazzaville and Lake Chad. With this in mind they set up the first French outpost of any major consequence at Bangui (the site of the present capital) in 1889. Within five years, the territory had become the French colony of Ubangi-Shari, a name derived from its two main rivers. In 1905, Ubangi-Shari was united with Chad and, five years later, became one of the four territories constituting French Equatorial Africa.

During both world wars, the territory was effectively utilized as a base for French military operations—in the first case, against the Germans in the Cameroons and then in conjunction with the Free French forces active in Africa from 1940 to 1944.

Following World War II, Ubangi-Shari was granted a greater degree of autonomy, sending elected representatives to the French Senate and Chamber of Deputies in Paris. Under the 1946 constitution, all inhabitants of the region were officially designated as citizens of France. In 1958, Ubangi-Shari changed its name to the Central African Republic, and voted to join the French Community as an autonomous republic. Two years later, it voted for full independence with David Dacko as President.

Dacko introduced one-party rule and steered his regime toward a closer alignment with the government of Communist China. In 1964, this policy led to official recognition of the Chinese regime which, by then, had launched an ambitious program of economic aid in the Central African Republic.

On January 1, 1966, the Dacko regime was overthrown in a military coup led by colonel Jean-Bedel Bokassa, who proved to be one of Africa's most unpredictable and cruel leaders. In the 13 years he ruled this impoverished nation, Bokassa appointed himself President for Life, created—and later abolished—a Council of the Central African Revolution, changed the country's government from a republic to a parliamentary monarchy, crowned himself Emperor Bokassa I in a lavish ceremony, and survived numerous coup attempts, one of which involved his son-in-law. He brutally enforced martial law and was reported to have tortured and murdered school children who refused to wear official school uniforms in 1979.

Bokassa cut relations with China, but began a courtship with the Soviet bloc and Libya's Colonel Muammar Qaddafi. On September 21, 1979, while Bokassa was in Libya, he was deposed by former president Dacko, who was aided by French military forces.

The new government put Bokassa on trial in absentia, as the Emperor had fled to the Ivory Coast, and in December 1980, sentenced him to death for crimes that included murder, cannibalism, and embezzlement.

President Dacko, however, undermined his own popularity on his second attempt at leadership; he kept several high-ranking officials from the hated Bokassa regime in office and set up a one-party rule again.

In March 1981, Dacko was elected to a 6-year term as President by a slim margin, but opponents protested that the election was rigged and began demonstrations against him.

On September 1, 1981, General Andre Kolingba, Commander of the Central African Republic Army, deposed Dacko, placed all political parties in suspension, and declared rule under the Military Committee for National Recovery.

Kolingba survived several coup attempts, and in 1985, in keeping with pledges to return the country to civilian rule, dissolved the CMRN. He assumed the presidency and prime ministership, and headed a cabinet composed of both military and civilian members.

On October 23, 1986, Bokassa inexplicably returned to Bangui from exile in France and was immediately arrested. After a sensational six-month trial, he was found guilty and sentenced to death. On February 29, 1987, Kolingba commuted Bokassa's sentence to life in prison.

Farming, animal husbandry, and food processing are main sources of employment in Central African Republic. Diamond exports were the leading source of revenue in 1978-79 and uranium resources are still being tapped. However, economic diversification has been hampered by lack of transportation facilities and the fact that Bokassa squandered virtually all of the national treasury during his reign. The per capita income in 1984 was $270.

*This traditional ironworker makes arrows and farm tools.*

## Chad

***Date of independence:*** August 11, 1960
***Area:*** 495,752 square miles
***Population:*** 5,000,000 (1987 est.)
***Capital:*** N'Djamena
***Monetary unit:*** CFA franc
***Religion:*** Islam 44%, Christian 33%, Animist 23%
***Language:*** French (official), Arabic, Sara
***Literacy:*** 5-10%
***Type of government:*** Republic
***Political parties/leaders:*** National Union for Independence and Revolution, 6 other groups
***Monetary conversion rate:*** 304.50 francs = $1 US (1987)
***Principal economic resources:*** Cotton, cattle, fish, livestock, oil, uranium.

### History at a Glance

Ancient history records the existence of several African empires which flourished between the Niger River and the Upper Nile; the Baguirmi and Wadai Empires are known to have held sway within the boundaries of the present Chadian republic. In the fourteenth century Islamic invaders from North and West Africa penetrated as far south as Wadai, and used this land as a fertile hunting ground for the flourishing slave trade.

*Obtaining water from a hand-dug well.*

One of the long-range results of this human exploitation has been the development of a deep-seated hostility between Chadian blacks and their former Arab masters.

Initial European contact with the territory dates back to 1822, although exploration did not begin in earnest until 1853. During the 1890s, the French pushed their way northwards from the Middle Congo region, and by 1897 had reached the shores of Lake Chad itself. Before the turn of the century, boundaries had been fixed between adjacent French, British and German territories in the area.

In 1910, Chad became one of the territories constituting French Equatorial Africa, but its economy developed slowly due to the lack of markets for its produce. By 1930 it was already being affected adversely by the onset of the world depression.

During World War II, the colony rallied to the side of the Free French and became an important staging area for Allied troops earmarked for battle on the North African front. As a reward for its loyalty, Chad was granted a greater degree of autonomy in 1946, and began sending elected representatives to the French National Assembly. In 1958, Chad became a member state of the French Community.

An independence movement, led by the first Premier and President Francois Tombalbaye, gained complete freedom for Chad on August 11, 1960. A struggle for political control began. A coup in 1963 was rebuffed and a new constitution and government under President Tombalbaye was established. Dissatisfaction with his policies grew, however, and in 1966, the Chad National Liberation Front (Frolinat) was formed.

President Tombalbaye tried hard to keep his country together until his assassination on April 13, 1975 during a coup by army and police units. He was succeeded by General Felix Malloum, who received endorsement from a number of former opposition groups, except Frolinat.

Frolinat, under the military leadership of Hissein Habre, fought Libyan forces in northern Chad in June 1976, and later sought help from the Malloum regime. When Malloum refused assistance, Habre lost control of the main wing of the Frolinat to Goukhouni Oueddei, who in turn decided to cooperate with the Libyans. Frolinat launched several offensives against Chadian cities and by June 1978, was in control of the northern two-thirds of the country. This time, President Malloum treated the force with more seriousness and on August 29, announced the appointment of Habre as prime minister under a "basic charter of national reconciliation."

The honeymoon between Malloum and Habre was shortlived, and following an abortive coup against Malloum in February 1979, fighting broke out between the factions.

Nine rival groups met in Lagos, Nigeria in March 1979 and agreed to form a provisional government and named former Frolinat leader Oueddei as President. However, fighting broke out again in March 1980 when Habre, now the Defense Minister, challenged President Oueddei, and a bloody civil war began.

During this period, some 80,000 civilians fled the capital of N'Djamena, the site of much of the fighting.

Habre's forces, the Armed Forces of the North (FAN), secured the capital, but Libyan troops, in support of President Oueddei, attacked and captured the city in June 1980. Libyan troops, under instruction of Muammar Qaddafi, stormed into Chad throughout the rest of the year and beat back Habre's army—virtually annexing the entire country much to the consternation of the rest of the world, aware of Qaddafi's expansionist dreams.

French President Francois Mitterand first tried to woo President Oueddei from Qaddafi, offering him unconditional French aid to rebuild Chad's army and economy. Nigeria and Senegal also pledged to supply troops to Chad, as did, on a lesser scale, Zaire, Benin, and Gabon.

Finally, at the North-South Cancun Summit in Mexico in October 1981, President Mitterand publicly appealed for the Organization of African Unity to create a peace-keeping force to replace the Libyans in Chad.

This time, President Oueddei complied and served Qaddafi an eviction notice, calling for complete Libyan withdrawal from N'Djamena and evacuation of Chad within a year. Qaddafi had promised to withdraw if asked, and with the world watching, withdrew his 10,000 troops from all Chadian land except a narrow, uranium-rich tract of land in Northern Chad, called the Aozou Strip, which Libya has long claimed as its own.

Tensions and fighting continued through the early 1980s. In 1984, Libya invaded the north, ostensibly to assist Oueddei forces in their rebellion against the Habre government.

Some 70,000 northern Chadians opted to flee the Libyans and their accompanying influence. The Libyans prohibited the speaking of French, insisted on the exclusive use of the Libyan dinar as the legal tender, and the flying of Libyan flags in Chadian villages.

In September 1984, France and Libya signed a much-ballyhooed agreement to end foreign (i.e., their own) intervention in Chad, in order to allow Habre to fight it out with Oueddei. The French promptly withdrew their 3,000 troops to the Central African Republic, but were publicly humiliated when the Libyans reneged and kept their 3,000 troops in place.

For the next two years, Oueddei's forces "shared" northern Chad with the Libyans but relations were uneasy. By 1986, most of Oueddei's top supporters had defected to the Habre government and Oueddei himself was reportedly held prisoner in Libya.

In March 1987, Habre government troops delivered a series of crushing blows to the Libyan interlopers. One-third of the 14,500-man Libyan force was either killed or wounded, while Chadian losses were minimal. The Libyans fled, abandoning some $500 million in military equipment.

Habre kept the upper hand, reshuffling his cabinet to embrace now-humbled rebel leaders, and even extended an olive branch to Oueddei, who was now in Algiers. Oueddei refused the overture.

In August 1987, on the heels of their victory, Chadian forces chased the Libyans out of the disputed Aozou Strip, only to be bombed back out three weeks later. Habre appealed to the Organization of African Unity to either make a decision on territorial rights, or turn it over to the World Court. Meanwhile, Libya was busily beefing up its forces in Aozou by bringing in thousands of mercenaries from North Yemen and North Korea, fortifying its military operations there and even reassembling Chadian rebels with help from Oueddei.

In October 1988, Chad and Libya resumed diplomatic relations, and agreed to abide by international decisions regarding the Aozou.

Qaddafi is up for the chairmanship of the OAU and observers have speculated that he might be interested in improving his image. Others thought his congenial withdrawal was geared to allow Chad to plunge deeper into economic and political chaos, thus making a merger with Libya more palatable to the Chadians. Libya has kept Chad afloat with oil shipments and food supplies and President Habri would not be able to survive a complete severance in trade. The year long Libyan occupation also has served to keep Habre and numerous other factions in line.

Chad's economy is almost exclusively agricultural, with farming, livestock, and fish. Attempts at locating significant mineral deposits have been unsuccessful; the only known uranium and other mineral deposits are located in the northern-most region, which is occupied by Libya.

## Comoros

***Date of independence:*** July 6, 1975
***Area:*** 718 square miles
***Population:*** 400,000 (est.1987)
***Capital:*** Moroni
***Monetary unit:*** CFA franc
***Nationality:*** Comoran
***Religion:*** Islamic
***Language:*** French, Arabic, Swahili
***Literacy:*** 15%
***Type of government:*** 3 islands form independent republic; 4th island remains French territorial community
***Political parties/leaders:*** Federal Assembly, other parties
***Monetary conversion rate:*** 304.50 francs = $1 US (1987)
***Principal economic resources:*** Perfume essences, copra, coconuts, cloves, spices

### History at a Glance

The Comoros Islands—Grand Comoro, Anjouan, Moheli, and Mayotte—are volcanic islands in the Indian Ocean between Mozambique and Madagascar.

Through the centuries, the Comoros have been invaded by a succession of groups from the coast of Africa, Persian Gulf, Indonesia, and Madagascar and ruled by many Arab sultans. In 1505, Portuguese explorers came, and Arab migrants brought the Muslim faith. Between 1843 and 1912, France set up colonial rule over the Comoros, placing them under the administration of the Governor-General of Madagascar. Later, wealthy, French and Arab merchants established plantations on the islands.

Following a 1968 student strike, France decided to permit formation of legal political parties in the islands and within four years, pro-independence forces were strong. Under French approval, three of the Comoros Islands declared themselves independent on July 6, 1975 with Mayotte voting to remain under French administration. The main reason for this separation is that Mayotte's population is mostly Christian while the other islands are Muslim.

A month after independence, Justice Minister Ali Soilih staged a coup with the help of mercenaries and overthrew the nation's first president, Ahmed Abdallah. Soilih implemented drastic reforms, lowering the voting age to 14, destroying all records, and killing many Comorans. His socialist leanings did not please the population, however, and after two unsuccessful coup attempts, Soilih was desposed on May 13, 1978 by a revolt aided by some of the same mercenaries he had employed three years earlier.

Soilih was killed shortly thereafter, allegedly during an escape attempt.

After the coup, Ahmed Abdallah and Mohammed Ahmed formed a "military and political directorate" until a constitution and republic were formed on October 1. Ahmed stepped down two days later and Abdallah regained the presidency. Abdallah, who was unopposed, won reelection to a six-year term on September 30, 1984.

His administration has been unpopular, in part because of his suppression of political opposition. In September 1984, three exile groups accused Abdallah of "repressive actions" and in March 1985, a major coup was attempted, but defeated.

Tensions following the coup continue to cause problems, but the major effort of the government is to revive a stagnant economy and persuade Mayotte to join an economic federation. (Mayotte has 14% of Comoros' population.)

Comoros is one of the world's poorest and least developed nations. Besides its economic and political upheavals, a volcano on Grande Comore erupted in April 1976, causing havoc and dispossessing some 500 families.

Comoros is the leading producer of ylang-ylang, a critical element in perfume production, and the second largest producer of the world's vanilla supply. However, the country must still import 40% of its food. The per capita income in 1984 was $250.

## Congo

***Date of independence:*** August 15, 1960
***Area:*** 132,046 square miles
***Population:*** 2,100,000 (est. 1987)
***Capital:*** Brazzaville
***Monetary unit:*** CFA franc
***Nationality:*** Congolese
***Religion:*** Animist 48%, Christian 47%, Islam 2%
***Language:*** French (official), Lingala, Kikongo
***Literacy:*** 20%
***Type of government:*** Republic (military regime established September 1978)
**Political parties/leaders:** Congolese Labor Party, Colonel Denis Sassou-Nguessou
***Monetary conversion rate:*** 304.50 francs = $1US (1987)
***Principal economic resources:*** Sugar cane, wood, coffee, cocoa, crude oil, tobacco

*Delcommune dam supplies hydropower to the Congo's largest mining operation.*

### History at a Glance

During the sixteenth century, the territory of today's Congo (Brazzaville) Republic was part of the so-called Congo Empire, which is believed to have extended as far south as Angola. Prior to this time, the sole Europeans in the area had been the Portuguese who discovered the mouth of the Congo River in 1484.

France established numerous trading companies during the seventeenth century, showing particular interest in slaves and ivory as items of commerce. Following the abolition of the slave trade, France undertook the exploration of the interior, a task hampered by its dense forests and barely navigable rivers. In 1880, a local chieftain signed a treaty with French explorer Pierre Savorgnan de Brazza, placing his domain under the protection of France. Five years later, the major European powers recognized French claims to the entire region lying beyond the right bank of the Congo River. In 1908, France installed a governor-general in Brazzaville, the present-day capital of the republic. Two years later, Middle Congo (as it was then called) was made a separate colony within the framework of French Equatorial Africa.

In 1940 Middle Congo joined Chad in declaring its support of the Free French forces under the leadership of Charles de Gaulle. During the war, it played a valuable strategic role in accommodating troops ultimately bound for combat in various parts of the Sahara Desert.

By 1956 Middle Congo had achieved full local autonomy. Two years later, it became an independent state within the French Community, changing its name to the Congo Republic. Fulbert Youlou, the mayor of Brazzaville, was elected president in 1960, the same year the Congo opted for full independence. Youlou was deposed three years later in the wake of popular unrest following passage of a bill designed to institute one-party rule in the country.

Under Youlou's successor, Alphonse Massamba-Debat, the Congo cultivated close ties with China, and sought to implement a national policy which Debat characterized as "scientific socialism." When Debat introduced Cuban advisers, however, utilizing them as a kind of private militia, the regular army staged a coup d'etat in 1968, installing President Marien N'Gouabi as head of state.

During his eight years as president, N'Gouabi proclaimed a "people's republic" and formed the official party, the Congolese Labor Party, complete with constitution, in January 1970. Later, student unrest and alleged plots against the regime caused a shake-up and in 1973, the Constitution was rewritten and the post of prime minister reestablished.

President N'Gouabi was assassinated by a four-man hit squad on March 18, 1977, and the power of the country went to an 11-member committee headed by Colonel Joachim Yhombi-Opango, who suspended the Constitution and reportedly sought Western aid for the nation. Opango also had former president Massamba-Debat, who was accused of masterminding the N'Gouabi assassination, executed on March 25. Shortly thereafter, Opango named Major Denis Sassou-Nguesso as First Vice President of the Military Committee.

Opango's sympathy toward the West, however, earned

him enmity from his fellow party members and he resigned under pressure from the Central Committee of the Congolese Labor Party on February 5, 1979. He was later arrested and in late 1979 demoted to a private soldier. Meanwhile, Sassou-Nguesso was named President, a decision which was later confirmed by an election.

President Sassou-Nguesso has renewed relations with the Soviet Union, Cuba, and China, as well as the United States. He is on good terms with most of the Congo's neighbors, with the exception of Zaire, which has accused the Congo of both launching surreptitious guerrilla attacks against it as well as stockpiling weapons with Benin and Guinea.

A booming oil export business in the early 1980s helped boost the country's economy, but revenues slipped by 1985 when oil prices fell. The average per capita income in 1983 was $1,320.

Timber and potash are two other important resources, along with copper, lead and zinc.

## Djibouti

***Date of independence:*** June 27, 1977
***Area:*** 8,800 square miles
***Population:*** 300,000 (est. 1987)
***Capital:*** Djibouti
***Monetary unit:*** Djibouti franc
***Nationality:*** Afar or Issa
***Religion:*** 94% Muslim, 6% Christian
***Language:*** French (official), Somali, Afar, Arabic
***Literacy:*** 20%
***Type of government:*** Republic
***Political parties/leaders:*** Four major political parties
***Monetary conversion rate:*** 177.00 francs = $1 US (1986)
***Principal economic resources:*** Goats, sheep, camels

### History at a Glance

French control over this portion of Somaliland dates back to an omnibus treaty signed by France and a number of Danakil tribal chieftains in 1862. Seven years later, concurrent with the opening of the Suez Canal, a number of French development companies were established in the region. In 1896, France annexed the territory as a colony after having signed additional treaties with Danakil and Issa chieftains. The all-important railroad which links Addis Ababa (Ethiopia) to the sea was completed in 1917.

After World War II, French Somaliland became an overseas territory, and gained complete internal autonomy in 1956. Two years later, the local assembly voted to retain its territorial status.

In 1964, a conference of nonaligned nations placed the issue of French Somaliland on its agenda, and called upon France to grant the territory immediate independence. The Somalian delegate to the United Nations later asked that body to take up the same question, but political leaders within the territory itself rejected this proposal on the grounds that it involved "annexationist designs." Consequently, French Somaliland reaffirmed its loyalty to France.

In 1967, when the area voted to remain part of France, rioting erupted among Somalis who wished to join Somalia.

In 1972, President Pomidou of France affirmed that the country had direct ties with France. In 1975, a United Nations General Assembly resolution called on France to withdraw from the territory, and on May 8, 1977, the population voted for independence and approval of a list of 65 candidates for the Chamber of Deputies. On June 27, the territory became the Republic of Djibouti. President Hassan Gouled Aptidon, elected on the 1977 slate, was reelected to six-year terms in 1981 and 1987.

Djibouti faces internal conflicts stemming from its population of Afars, who favor Ethiopia, and Issas, who are Somali-oriented. Both Ethiopia and Somali have recognized Djibouti's independence, but covet the smaller land's strategic position at the entrance of the Red Sea. The Addis Ababa-Djibouti railroad, which terminates in the capital of Djibouti, carries about 60% of Ethiopia's exports over its 486 miles.

Internal security is maintained with the aid of a French garrison of more than 4,500 troops.

The drought of the mid-1980s affected the country, directly through agricultural hardships, and indirectly with refugees from Ethiopia and Somalia. The principal agricultural products remain goats, sheep and camels. The per capita income in 1984 was $270.

## Equatorial Guinea

***Date of independence:*** October 12, 1968
***Area:*** 10,830 square miles
***Population:*** 300,000 (est. 1987)
***Capital:*** Malabo
***Monetary unit:*** CFA franc
***Nationality:*** Equatorial Guinean
***Religion:*** 99% population nominally Christian
***Language:*** Spanish, Fang, French
***Literacy:*** 55%
***Type of government:*** Republic
***Political parties/leaders:*** La Transition (formerly National Unity Party of Workers), National Alliance for the Restoration of Democracy (in exile)
***Monetary conversion rate:*** 304.50 francs = $1 US (1987)
***Principal economic resources:*** Cocoa, wood, coffee

### History at a Glance

The Island of Fernando Poo, now known as Bioko was discovered by Fernao de Po of Portugal in 1471, at which time it was given the name Formosa. (Annobon, an island lying some 400 miles to the southwest, was discovered a year later.) Portugal ceded both islands to Spain in 1778. From 1827 to 1843, Great Britain received permission from Spain to use Fernando Poo as a base for hunting down slave-runners. During this period, a number of Sierra Leonean Creoles and West Indian Maroons were liberated on the island. In 1904, Fernando Poo and Rio Muni became known as the West African Territories and, later, as Spanish Guinea. This territory acquired the status of a province in 1960. Rio Muni was ceded to Spain by Portugal in 1778 and reconfirmed as a Spanish possession at the Berlin Conference

*Some children of Equatorial Guinea.*

(1884-1885). Spain, however, did not take over its administration until about 1900.

When the colonies sought independence in the late 1960s, progress was hampered by differences between mainland Fang, which wanted to sever all ties with Spain, and the island Bubi, which preferred a semi-autonomous government with connections to Spain. A compromise constitution was reached and passed by a people's election on August 11, 1968 by a 63% majority. During a presidential election a month later, a mainland Fang, Macias Nguema Biyogo, was elected president and on October 12, 1968, the nation, Equatorial Guinea was born.

In 1969, President Macia (who later changed his name to Macie) seized emergency power when a series of tribal rivalries engendered unrest. As Macie's cruel politics emerged, opposition arose and soon he was forced to squelch a major coup against him. During this time of turmoil, Macie executed more than 200 political enemies and hundreds of skilled workers, and forced most of the Spaniards still living in the country to flee. Macie quickly established a one-party state, and declared himself President for Life in July 1972.

During Macie's 11-year rule, which was supported by the Soviet bloc nations, Equatorial Guinea was dubbed the "Auschwitz of Africa." Macie was deposed on August 3, 1979 in a coup led by his nephew, Lieutenant Colonel Teodoro Obiang Nguema Mbasogo, who formed a Supreme Military Council. Macie was executed a month later for the crimes of genocide, treason, and embezzlement.

Obiang has since reopened churches, released all political prisoners, returned confiscated property, and sought to reconstruct the country with the help of Spain. When Spain balked, however, Obiang turned to the more receptive France, and by 1985, Equatorial Guinea had changed its currency and joined the 13-country African-franc monetary zone.

The economy of the nation is based on cocoa, timber, bananas, palm products and coffee. However, economic growth has remained stunted as a result of the mass murders of the majority of the nation's workers under the Macie tyranny. In 1988, South Africa was considering building a communications center on Bioko and assisting in the expansion of the airport.

Equatorial Guinea, which is switching from its traditional Spanish language to French, is one of the poorest countries in Africa, with an average per capita income of $172.

President Obiang outlawed all political parties in 1979 and has since resisted a few coup attempts, including a "family plot" conducted in 1986 by an uncle.

## Ethiopia

***Date of independence:*** September 12, 1974
***Area:*** 471,799 square miles
***Population:*** 45,500,000 (est. 1987)
***Capital:*** Addis Ababa
***Monetary unit:*** Birr
***Nationality:*** Ethiopian
***Religion:*** Ethiopian Orthodox 49%, Islam 31%, Animist 11%
***Language:*** Amharic (official), English
***Literacy:*** 15%
***Type of government:*** Military rule since 1974
***Political parties/leaders:*** Worker's Party of Ethiopia, 9 opposition groups
***Monetary conversion rate:*** 2.07 birr =$1 US (1987)
***Principal economic resources:*** Coffee, barley, wheat, corn, potash, salt, gold, copper, platinum

### History at a Glance

Ethiopia is one of the oldest nations in the world, and the oldest in Africa south of the Sahara Desert. Its original settlers, the Cushites, were descendants of the Galla and Sidama tribes which occupied the territory prior to 1000 B.C. From the tenth to the seventh centuries B.C., Semitic peoples from southern Arabia entered Ethiopia, and it is their offspring which became the lineal descendants of the Amhara and Tigrai tribes found there today. In the writings of the fifth century B.C. Greek historian Herodotus, one encounters a reference to the Ethiopians as "the most just men" and, even in Homer, they are spoken of as the "blameless race."

Traditionally, Menelik, the first son of King Solomon and the Queen of Sheba, is regarded as the founder of the Ethiopian Empire, which is said to date back to 1000 B.C. The earliest authenticated history of the area describes Ethiopia as a pagan empire with its capital at Axum.

Christianity was introduced in the fourth century A.D., and survived the onslaughts of Moslem hordes which in the seventh century imposed the religion of Islam on northeastern Africa. For a time, the Axum dynasty fell into decline and was threatened with extinction by the Zagwe dynasty which was founded by Takla Haimanot. In 1260, with the accession of Yekuma Amlak, the Axum line was restored and the reputed link with Solomon reestablished. Emperor Amda Seyon I later imposed Ethiopian rule over the Moslem principalities which had sprung up to the east and south.

In the sixteenth century, Moslem power reasserted itself when the Somalis (with the aid of the Ottoman Turks) began a holy war that threatened to engulf the entire kingdom. Though the Ethiopians received help from Portugal, they were saved largely due to the heroic exploits of their legendary emperor, Prester John.

The next three centuries, characterized by anarchy, cultural decadence, religious controversy, and other divisive influences, resulted in the partitioning of Ethiopia by a number of rival pretenders to the throne. Allegiance to a central government was not rekindled until 1855 when the Emperor Theodore II, himself a one-time petty chieftain, succeeded in subjugating a number of other dissident chieftains. However, when Theodore committed suicide in 1869, the country was once again plunged into strife.

In 1885, Italy capitalized on the discordant situation by capturing the seaport of Massawa, thus gaining a secure foothold in Eritrea. Menelik II, one of Ethiopia's great reform emperors, thereupon signed a face-saving treaty with Italy, maintaining that it was with his approval that a protectorate was being established over the country. Italy attempted to force the issue to total conquest by launching an invasion in 1895, but was forced to withdraw after a humiliating defeat.

Menelik II turned his energies to the development of the interior of his country—building a rail line, establishing more schools, improving communications and introducing postal service. After the death of Menelik in 1913, his successor Lij Yassu embraced the Moslem faith—a gesture which led to his being deposed by Ras Tafari Menkonnen, a grand-nephew of Menelik. Later Ras (prince) Tafarimade made Judith (Lij Yassu's aunt) empress, and assumed the role of regent until her death in 1930. He was then crowned as emperor in his own right, and ascended the throne as Haile Selassie I, the Lion of Judah.

Five years later, with the invasion of Ethiopia by Italy, he was forced to flee his country. His plea for international intervention, aired before the League of Nations, went largely unheeded, and he then took up his exile in Great Britain. On May 5, 1941, however, he triumphantly re-entered Addis Ababa at the head of a liberating army and was restored to his throne.

In 1952, with the approval of the United Nations, Eritrea was linked to Ethiopia as a federated state. Ten years later, its status was changed to that of an Ethiopian province.

During the postwar period, Ethiopia modernized its institutions somewhat. A liberalized constitution was put into effect, and Haile Selassie attempted to function as a kind of moderating influence between African nationalists on the one hand, and the last heirs to the European colonial tradition on the other.

In Ethiopia itself, a coup d'etat was attempted in 1960 by members of the Imperial Guard under the leadership of Crown Prince Asfa Wassan. The revolt was quickly crushed, and its chief leaders (with the exception of the Crown Prince, the emperor's son) were executed.

Throughout the 1960s, Ethiopia attempted to establish itself as a political headquarters and cultural center for the rest of emergent Africa. This is symbolized in the pride of Addis Ababa, the imposing edifice known as Africa Hall, headquarters of the Organization of African Unity and the United Nations Economic Commission for Africa.

Though a symbol of black culture and progress, Ethiopia remained in the grip of a feudal system in which over half the nation's rural population was required to turn over some three-fourths of their crops to landlords.

In 1974, Haile Selassie was overthrown by a military coup, which announced sweeping land reform measures. However, opposition from both large and small landlords threatened implementation.

Emperor Haile Selassie died at the age of 83 on August 27, 1975 while still in detention. Earlier, on March 21, Lieutenant Colonel Mengistu Haile-Mariam, leader of the Provisional Military Administrative Council (PMAC), decreed formal abolition of the monarchy with the intention of reorganizing Ethiopia by socialism.

A number of officials were executed for "counter-revolutionary crimes" and the Mengistu regime enacted an indiscriminate "red terror" from December 1977 to February 1978 in order to establish their control.

Following the 1974 coup, revolt in Eritrea escalated into full-scale war with Ethiopia and the Eritrean Independence Front, armed by Libya and other Arab states, demanded full independence. Some 22,000 government troops were sent into combat in February 1975, and thousands of deaths were reported in the ensuing months.

Somalian rebels supported Eritrea's fight, but when the Soviets diverted their support from Somalia to Ethiopia, the tide of war turned and by March 1978, badly beaten Somalis retreated to their homeland, leaving Eritrea still under Ethiopian control.

Mengistu's Marxist government, popularly called "the Dergue," has continued to face fierce opposition from separatist groups, and has retaliated at times without mercy. Ethiopian troops, in a major offensive in mid-1979 designed to wipe out Eritrean resistance, resorted to a "scorched earth" policy of poisoning water sources, killing livestock and firing indiscriminately into civilian areas.

In 1984-85, a major drought swept the Sahara and set the stage for a famine of "biblical" proportions in Ethiopia. More than seven million people faced starvation, and although the world responded with an unprecedented $3 billion in food and aid, an estimated one million Ethiopians perished. The United States alone sent 2 million tons of food. On July 13, 1985, an estimated one billion people watched an international rock concert called "Live Aid," which raised millions in famine relief; in America, sales of an all-star production of the song, "We Are The World," raised at least $45 million in aid.

Mengistu's government came under severe criticism for its handling of the aid. Food rotted on docks while military hardware from the Soviet Union was unloaded; a "port tax," which at times amounted to $50-a-ton, was imposed on ships bearing gift food, causing some large loads to be turned away. Uglier accusations had government officials refusing to give food to rebel-occupied areas, applying a Stalinist tactic of letting famine solve problems of political opposition. Even a government cover-up was cited: Two weeks before BBC television first aired its shocking footage of the thousands of emaciated, starving Ethiopians, the Marxist government had spent nearly $200 million in celebration of their 10-year anniversary.

The famine was followed by a government plan to resettle some 12.5 million peasants into collective farms in southern Ethiopia. This plan drew sharp criticism from abroad as being a ploy to "empty out" the northern, rebel-held areas. Later criticisms were directed at the farms themselves. Refugees described them as "concentration camps" where armed guards kept people from leaving, where disease, fostered by unsanitary conditions, ran rampant, and where food was provided only to those who worked. In 1985, M. Peter McPherson, director of the U.S. Agency for International Development, reported that as many people were dying in the resettlement program as perished in the worst days of the 1984 famine—an average of 100 fatalities a day. Several Ethiopian officials who defected in the 1980s, including Foreign Minister Goshu Wolde, confirmed such excesses.

As a result, several members of Congress called for economic sanctions against Ethiopia, and by 1988, in deference to this and other outside pressures, the Mengistu government scaled down its resettlement efforts.

The total numbers of Ethiopians fleeing drought, famine and government policies was estimated at 1.5 million in 1985, including one million who fled to drought-ravaged Sudan.

*Ethopians facing starvation collect their food rations in Makelle.*

By 1988, there was some indication that Mengistu's regime might be nearing its close. In the face of yet another crop failure and ensuing food shortage in 1988, he asked for millions in foreign aid, but expelled all foreign relief workers from rebel areas.

Despite the government's military superiority—Ethiopia's standing army of 250,000 soldiers, equipped with $2 billion in Soviet-made armaments, is the largest in black Africa—Mengistu's troops continued to be defeated by Eritrean and Tigrayan rebels. In 1987, at least a third of the country was described as "out of government control."

Warming relations between the United States and the Soviet Union under Mikhail Gorbachev led some to believe the Soviets could put pressure on Mengistu to "humanize" his policies.

Ethiopia is now one of the world's poorest countries, with a per capita income in 1985 of $110. Its principal export is coffee. Gold has been mined commercially, and deposits of copper, potash and natural gas have been discovered. Most technical and economic assistance is supplied by communist nations. In 1987, Mengistu claimed that "25 million metric tons of oil" had been found in the Ogaden Desert, long the target of a territorial dispute between Ethiopia and Somalia.

## Gabon

***Date of independence:*** August 17, 1960
***Area:*** 103,346 square miles
***Population:*** 1,200,000 (1987 est.)
***Capital:*** Libreville
***Monetary unit:*** CFA franc
***Nationality:*** Gabonese
***Religion:*** Catholic 64%, Protestant 18%, Animist, Islam
***Language:*** French (official), Fang
***Literacy:*** 65%
***Type of government:*** Republic (since 1964 one-party regime)
***Political parties/leaders:*** Gabonese Democratic Party
***Monetary conversion rate:*** 304.50 francs = $1 US (1987)
***Principal economic resources:*** Cocoa, coffee, timber, iron ore, oil, manganese

### History at a Glance

The first Europeans to visit and explore the territory of Gabon were the Portuguese, who arrived toward the end of the fifteenth century and established trading posts at the mouth of the Ogowe River. French missionaries followed soon after, only to be succeeded by groups of European slave traders.

By 1815, the slave trade had been abolished, thus obliging the French to concentrate on exploitation of the territory's other resources, notably her forests. This policy brought about the development of several coastal ports, and the signing of a number of treaties with local rulers. The French agreed to protect the interests of these chieftains in return for access to the regions they controlled.

At the Congress of Berlin (1884-1885), the major European powers agreed to recognize French control over the land lying beyond the right bank of the Congo River (subsequently known as the French Congo). Five years later, Gabon became a part of this region, although it did not come to exist as a distinct administrative entity until 1893. In 1910, it achieved colonial status within what was then called French Equatorial Africa.

After World War II, Gabon was made an Overseas Territory of the French Union, and given the right to be represented in the French Parliament by a senator and a deputy of its own choice. In 1958, the colony voted to become fully autonomous within the framework of the French Community, and two years later declared itself a fully independent republic, with Leon M'Ba as premier.

M'Ba was returned to office a year later, this time with the title of president of Gabon. In 1964, the Gabonese army temporarily overthrew the government, but the deposed M'Ba was reinstated by French President Charles de Gaulle who ordered French troops airlifted into Libreville to quell the rebellion.

In 1967, M'Ba died, and was replaced by Vice President Albert Bernard (later El Hadj Omar) Bongo. Under the one-party system established in March 1968, Mr. Bongo was consistently reelected, and by 1988, was in his fourth seven-year term. His extraordinarily long tenure was marred by a coup attempt by military officers in mid-1985.

Under Bongo's tight and prudent leadership, Gabon has grown into one of the most stable and prosperous nations in Black Africa. Electricity and piped water are commonplace. A bounteous oil supply, pumped and sold by a French-Gabonese company, has given Gabon one of the highest per capita incomes in sub Sahara Africa, measured at $3,900 in 1987.

Gabon's economic stability and strong emphasis on education—it had a literacy rate of 65% in 1987—as well as its relatively small population made it attractive for workers of other nations. Beginning in the 1980s, the Bongo government took measures to install educated Gabonese in white collar positions, and restrict major influxes of non-Gabonese. This caused a backlash, particularly from its northern neighbor, Cameroon, whose nationals participated in violent demonstrations at Libreville and Port-Gentil in 1981. Some 10,000 Cameroonians were subsequently expelled. Still, Gabon offered refuge to some 80,000 Equatorial Guineans who fled the Macie tyranny in the 1970s.

In foreign relations, Gabon has tried to become independent and self-sufficient, loosening the historical ties to France and cooling relations with other nations, such as Cuba and Libya. In 1988, with diminishing oil profits, the country was embarking on an austerity program. Additional revenues come from uranium, manganese, and iron reserves.

## The Gambia

***Date of independence:*** February 18, 1965, formed Senegambia Confederation with Senegal on December 17, 1981
***Area:*** 4,361 square miles
***Population:*** 790,000 (est. 1987)
***Capital:*** Banjul
***Monetary:*** Dalasi
***Nationality:*** Gambian
***Religion:*** Islam 85%, Animist 11%, Christian 2%
***Language:*** English (official), Mandinka, Wolof
***Literacy:*** 20%
***Type of government:*** Republic
***Political parties/leaders:*** People's Progressive Party, four opposition parties
***Monetary conversion rate:*** 7.45 dalasi = $1 US (1987)
***Principal economic resources:*** Peanuts, fish

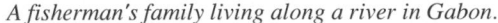

*A fisherman's family living along a river in Gabon.*

### History at a Glance

The Gambia is the smallest nation in Africa. The first reference to The Gambia in the historical records of antiquity occurs in the reports of voyages made by Carthaginian explorers. Hanno's writings lend support to the theory that an entrance was made into the Gambian estuary as far back as 450 B.C.

The first Europeans to set foot in The Gambia were led by Alvise de Cadamosto and Antoniotto Usodimare, both of whom were in the service of Portugal's Prince Henry the Navigator (1455).

Later, The Gambia became part of England's ambitious colonization schemes for West Africa, with a settlement being founded at Fort James, a small island some 20 miles from the mouth of the Gambia River. English merchants in increasing numbers were granted royal charters to trade in West Africa, often competing with their French counterparts. Not until the Treaty of Versailles (1783) did the English establish a clearcut priority in the area.

In 1821, The Gambia was placed under the control of a British colonial administration based in Sierra Leone. It became a colony in its own right until 1888 when it was provided with its own governor and legislative and executive councils.

The Gambia's path to independence in the 20th century was peaceful and gradual. The nation's present Constitution, introduced in 1960, established a representative assembly headed by a chief minister. Modeling its governmental institutions on those of Great Britain, Gambia achieved final independence on February 18, 1965 with Dawda K. Jawara as Prime Minister. On the first anniversary of its independence, The Gambia opted for a republican form of government. Jawara was reelected for five-year terms in 1972, 1977, 1982 and in March 1987.

The Gambia has avoided the extravagant and, at times, grandiose economic projects which have brought some of her more famous neighbors to the brink of financial ruin. Careful and deliberate, the tiny country has met its budget and staked out realistic, rather than improbable goals.

Like many African nations, The Gambia has been troubled by drought and inflation. While The Gambia has been losing a preferred market for its peanut crop due to Britain's joining the Common Market, direct involvement with the Common Market may well offset this potential loss. The per capita income in The Gambia was $250 in 1984.

In February 1982, following riots the previous year in Banjul which were put down with the help of Senegalese troops, negotiations were completed by which Senegal and The Gambia formed the Confederation of Senegambia.

Public opinion in both countries is divided as to the desirability of the merger—Gambians are concerned that their river-hugging nation will become just another province in Senegal, especially since the latter is 17 times larger in size and has a population 10 times larger than Gambia's.

Under the agreement, Senegal and Gambia will remain sovereign nations, but will integrate their security forces and communications networks and undertake an economic and monetary union. President Abdou Diouf of Senegal will be President of Senegambia and President Jawara will be Vice–President.

Integration has already been achieved by virtue of Gambia's small reserves; Senegal's 5,000 troops have already provided protection. Both nations are pro-West and have severed diplomatic ties with Libya.

As of 1988, the countries had not agreed on a monetary union: the Gambia still uses the dalasi, while Senegal used the CFA franc. There was one area of harmony, though: the first Miss Senegambia was crowned in February 1985.

## Ghana

***Date of independence:*** March 6,1957
***Area:*** 92,099 square miles
***Population:*** 13,900,000 (est.1987)
***Capital:*** Accra
***Monetary unit:*** New Cedi
***Religion:*** Christian 63%, Animist 21%, Islam 16%
***Language:*** English (official), Akan, Mole-Dagbani, Ewe languages
***Literacy:*** 45%
***Type of government:*** Republic
***Political parties/leaders:*** People's National Party, five opposition parties
***Monetary conversion rate:*** 153.00 cedi = $1 US (1987)
***Principal economic resources:*** Cocoa, timber, coconuts, coffee, rubber, gold, diamonds, bauxite, manganese, fish

### History at a Glance

Modern Ghana takes its name from an ancient African empire which flourished in the Western Sudan from the fourth through the twelfth centuries.

Ghana's first contact with the nations of Europe dates back to the 15th century when a band of Portuguese seafarers landed on the "Gold Coast," as it was then called, and began to trade in the area's plentiful gold dust. The Portuguese were followed by the Dutch, the Danes, the Swedes, the Prussians and, finally, by the English who in 1807 prohibited the lucrative slave trade which had begun to replace gold as the most profitable commodity in the territory.

The English remained the dominant European power in Ghana during the nineteenth century, although their hegemony was often threatened by frequent tribal uprisings of the powerful and well-organized Ashanti Confederation. Ashanti territory, however, was annexed by the English in 1900, and incorporated with the Northern Protectorates into the already-existing Gold Coast Colony. In 1922 Togoland, formerly under German control, was given to Great Britain, which administered this territory, too, as part of the Gold Coast.

After World War II, Ghana gradually came to have more say about its political destiny, first by participating actively in there writing of a constitution, then by electing its own representatives to a duly constituted parliament. On March 6, 1957, Ashanti, the Northern Protectorates, the Gold Coast and British Togoland declared their independence, adopted the name of Ghana, and immediately joined the British

*A tribal chief in Ghana.*

*A woman in traditional dress walks past the new state library in Accra, Ghana.*

Commonwealth. Officially, Ghana became a republic on July 1, 1960, continuing under the leadership of President Kwame Nkrumah, who held absolute power until he himself was overthrown on February 24, 1966 while on a visit to Red China.

The National Liberation Council then established a military government, installing J. A. Ankrah as head of state.

In July 1972, Colonel Ignatius K. Acheampong headed a group of military leaders who seized governing power from the civilian Prime Minister, Kofi A. Busia, while he was in London undergoing medical treatment.

However, Colonel Acheampong was forced to resign on July 5, 1978, and was immediately succeeded by his deputy, Lieutenant General Frederick Akuffo. Less than a year later, Akuffo was deposed in a coup led by junior military officers and an Armed Forces Revolutionary Council (AFRC) was established under Flight Lieutenant Jerry Rawlings, who had been undergoing a court martial for staging an unsuccessful coup a few months earlier.

Rawlings had former presidents Acheampong, Akuffo, and Brigadier Akwasi Afrifa executed in addition to a number of other high-ranking military and civilian officials, causing international protests.

Rawlings stepped aside when Dr. Hilla Limann of the People's National Party won a presidential balloting in July 1979, but led a coup against Limann on New Year's Eve 1981. He has since dismissed Ghana's parliament, banned political parties, and suspended the Constitution. Rawlings is a devout admirer of Libya's Muammar Qaddafi and sees Libya as a "revolutionary dream." He appears to be leading Ghana down a similar path, having established a "people's government" in early 1982.

Rawlings promptly renewed relations with Libya, and was later accused by exiled Ghanaians of masterminding the 1981 coup which brought Captain Thomas Sankara into power in neighboring Upper Volta, later renamed Burkina Faso. As ideological comrades, Rawlings and Sankara were making a 10-year plan to form a political union between their countries when Sankara was assassinated in 1987.

Domestic relations have been strained. Neighboring Togo has closed its border on occasion; in 1981, Togo accused Ghana of being behind a plot to overthrow Togolese President Eyadema. In 1985, Nigeria deported hundreds of thousands of Ghanaians as illegal aliens. Many died en route home and those that arrived, strained the Ghanaian economy. In 1985, Ghana recalled its ambassador to the Ivory Coast, after a soccer dispute.

Rawlings has escaped several coup attempts, including one in 1986 by exiles based in Brazil.

In 1985, drought and bushfires devastated crops. Cocoa exports, which were a massive 420,000 tons in the early 1960s, declined steadily until 1984, after which intense government effort revived it. Additional boosts from the International Monetary Fund and World Bank have helped reverse Ghana's slide into poverty in recent years. The average per capita income in 1984 was $380.

## Guinea

***Date of independence:*** October 2, 1958
***Area:*** 94,924 square miles
***Population:*** 6,400,000 (est.1987)
***Capital:*** Conakry
***Monetary unit:*** Guinea franc
***Nationality:*** Guinean
***Religion:*** Islam 69%, Animist 30%
***Language:*** French (official), several tribal dialects
***Literacy:*** 28%
***Type of government:*** Republic (one-party presidential regime)
***Political parties/leaders:*** Democratic Party of Guinea, National Liberation Front of Guinea (illegal)
***Monetary conversion rate:*** 340.00 francs = $1 US (1987)
***Principal economic resources:*** Palm oil, bananas, rice, coconuts, peanuts, bauxite, gold, diamonds

### History at a Glance

Modern-day Guinea is linked historically with the ancient Ghanian kingdom of West Africa. The territory is believed to have been ruled by a succession of dynasties, the most celebrated of which was headed by the Malinke chieftain, Sundiata, founder of the Mali Empire. The last Malinke emperor was deposed in the seventeenth century, some two centuries after the first Europeans (the Portuguese) had begun to explore the area.

Portuguese, French, and British traders were engaged in competitive trade along Guinea's coast long before the Peace of Paris (1814) secured for France the most advantageous position in the region. By 1849, the French had proclaimed a protectorate over the Guinea coast.

Opposition to French rule from the inhabitants of the interior was widespread during the last decades of the nineteenth century. In 1879, the famous Malinke chieftain, Almany Samoury Toure (a direct ancestor of Guinea's Sekou Toure), seized Kankan in the Upper Guinea region, and began terrorizing French settlers.

By that time, Guinea was being administered as a separate colony, its name having been changed from Rivieres du Sud to French Guinea. Up until World War I, a number of chieftains from the hinterlands continued to harass the colonial authorities, but this did not prevent the French from holding together the federation they had imposed on their West African territories.

The inhabitants of Guinea became French citizens in 1946, and won the right to vote in 1957. A year later, the electorate rejected an offer of independence within the French Community, preferring instead complete independence with Sekou Toure as President. The French immediately withdrew all economic and financial aid, and recalled the trained technical and administrative personnel needed to operate an efficient bureaucracy. For a time, Guinea received aid from the Soviet Union and China, although it has since been assisted by the United States and other Western

*Members of a U.N. commission cross over a makeshift bridge during Guinea-Bissau's struggle for independence from Portugal.*

nations as well. Since their independence, Guinea, Ghana, and Mali have been closely allied as members of the Union of African States.

Although an avowed Marxist, Toure has followed a foreign policy of nonalignment, and cultivated particularly close ties with Kwame Nkrumah (deposed as President of Ghana in 1966).

Toure offered Nkrumah a huge welcome after the latter entered Guinea in exile, naming him co-president.

After a serious internal crisis (a Portuguese-Guinean exile attack on its capital city—1970-1972) that decimated a large percentage of its governing class, Guinean President Toure turned to improving his nation's social and economic conditions. Ample supplies of natural resources such as bauxite and iron ore helped make his job easier. In 1975, Toure formed a company with Saudi Arabia, Kuwait, Egypt, and Libya to mine bauxite in the country's north.

Toure calls Guinea a "people's state" and has stressed the use of "national" languages as a replacement for French, has replaced the franc with the syli, has removed beggars from public view, and has included women in the governmental process.

He also has improved relations with Liberia, Sierra Leone, Nigeria, Cameroon, Algeria, and since 1978, Senegal and the Ivory Coast.

Despite peaceful overtures to other nations, on May 14, 1980, Toure barely escaped an assassination attempt which claimed the lives of others and injured 30 additional bystanders. Toure immediately called Guineans to "remobilize" and "unite against intruders." He was reelected President in 1981.

Toure's record-setting tenure as an African leader ended on March 26, 1984 when he died undergoing heart surgery in a U.S. hospital. Prime Minister Lansana Beavogui assumed office but was quietly ousted a week later, and Colonel Lansana Conte and Colonel Diarra Traore took over as president and prime minister, respectively. They freed some 1,000 political prisoners, lifted press restrictions, and restored freedom of speech and travel, as well as the name of the country to the Republic of Guinea.

Power struggles between Conte and Traore ensued, and on July 5, 1985, when Conte was out of the country, a coup attempt on behalf of Traore was attempted. Traore and others were tried and executed by mid-1986.

The Conte government has negotiated foreign investments from France and other Western countries; however, the economy remains plagued by soaring prices and low wages. Guinea is the world's second largest exporter of bauxite. Other assets are iron ore, gold, diamonds, uranium, oil, as well as bananas, coffee and peanuts. The per capita income in 1984 was $290.

*Committee on the decolonization of Africa meets in Conakry.*

## Guinea-Bissau

***Date of independence:*** September 10, 1974
***Area:*** 13,948 square miles
***Population:*** 900,000 (est. 1987)
***Capital:*** Bissau
***Monetary unit:*** Guinea-peso
***Nationality:*** Guinean
***Religion:*** Animist 65%, Islam 30%, Christian 5%
***Language:*** Portuguese, several tribal dialects
***Literacy:*** 3-5%
***Type of government:*** Political parties/leaders: Revolutionary Council, Major Joao Bernardo Vieira
***Monetary conversion rate:*** 170.47 pesos = $1 US (1987)
***Principal economic resources:*** Palm oil, rice, coconuts, peanuts, bauxite

### History at a Glance

Portuguese sailors first visited this portion of Guinea in 1446, some 100 years before it was to become a source of slaves. Cape Verdeans set up trading posts here and, by the nineteenth century, had imposed their administration over the entire territory. The tribes of the interior, however, were not fully subjugated until after World War I and only then with difficulty. Nationalism quickly grew during the Angola uprising of the 1960s.

Guinea-Bissau achieved *de facto* independence in 1974 with Portugal's other African colonies and was expected to unite with Cape Verde Islands under a common government.

For five years, measures toward unification were taken under the guidance of a mutually representative National People's Assembly. But, in November 1980, when a Cape Verde-based constitution was adopted in Guinea-Bissau under President Luis Cabral's leadership, Vice President Major Joao Bernardo Vieira led a military coup against Cabral, deposed him, and revoked the Constitution. Vieira immediately set up a Revolutionary Council with himself as Premier.

Cabral was denounced as having helped "corrupt the meaning of unity" between the two countries and was expected to be put on trial. Vieira, however, continued to entertain hopes that a unification between the two countries could be arranged. However, the Cape Verdeans quickly rejected the goal of unifying with the mainland.

Vieira's first years as president were rocky, with a major coup attempt repulsed in November 1985, and a major cabinet shake-up staged in 1986.

Guinea-Bissau accepted Soviet assistance during its struggles for independence, but after a 1978 disagreement with the Soviet Union over fishing rights, Vieira sought development aid from Western countries instead. The question of off-shore oil rights between Guinea and Guinea-Bissau was resolved by the World Court in 1985.

Peanuts are the major import of this impoverished country, with other important products including palm products, fish, cattle, sugar, cotton and tobacco. The per capita income in 1984 was $190.

*Armed with a spear, a watchman stands guard at the Ivory Coast Bouake Dam.*

## Ivory Coast

***Date of independence:*** August 7, 1960
***Area:*** 124,503 square miles
***Population:*** 10,800,000 (est. 1987)
***Capital:*** Abidjan (old), Yamassoukro, designated in March 1983
***Monetary unit:*** CFA franc
***Nationality:*** Ivorian
***Religion:*** Animist 44%, Christian 32%, Islam 24%
***Language:*** French (official), 60 native dialects (primarily Dioula)
***Literacy:*** **65%**
***Type of government:*** Republic (one-party presidential regime)
***Political parties/leaders:*** Democratic Party of the Ivory Coast, President Felix Houphouet-Boigny
***Monetary conversion rate:*** 304.50 francs = $1 US (1987)
***Principal economic resources:*** Coffee, cocoa, timber, palm oil, petroleum, iron ore

### History at a Glance

The first Europeans to establish themselves in what is today the Ivory Coast were the Portuguese, whose commercial activities date back to the fifteenth century. Other European nations (principally Holland and England) soon began to compete for their share of the thriving slave market, and for gold, ivory, and spices as well. With different aims in view, French missionaries established a foothold in this region by settling at Assinie in 1687.

It was not until the nineteenth century, however, that the economic exploitation of the Ivory Coast was begun in earnest. In 1842, France established a protectorate over the coastal region and built up a number of trading posts, primarily at Assinie and Grand Bassam. French control was gradually extended into the interior through a number of treaties signed with various local chieftains. In 1893, the territory was placed under the control of a French governor. The administrative organization and military pacification of the area engaged the energies of the French until 1912.

After World War I, the colony flourished as a producer of hardwoods, cocoa, coffee, and bananas. Both European planters and African cultivators shared in the wealth produced by these exports.

In 1933, France linked Upper Volta with the Ivory Coast in the hope of inducing the former territory to provide a source of cheap labor for the latter. The plan failed, however, and the Ivory Coast was soon returned to its original status.

At the close of World War II, the Ivory Coast officially became an overseas territory of the French Union. By 1956, it had gained self-autonomy; by 1958, it had become an independent republic and a member of the French Community; and by 1960, it had attained complete independence, as a republic headed by a popularly elected president, Felix Houphouet-Boigny.

Since then, the Ivory Coast has retained close economic ties with France, disavowing all help from countries with alleged communist affiliations. Foreign companies operate relatively free of intervention.

The Ivory Coast has relied heavily on foreign investment to modernize the capital, improve public health, and eliminate primitive housing.

Relying heavily on foreign investment and expertise, Boigny, in 1974, set as a goal a 7.7% increase in gross domestic product based on a $1 billion 5-year plan. Already the Bandama River dam at Kossou (which will provide irrigation for nearby farm communities and substantial fish catch) has been opened as a result of this program. A port at San Pedro in the undeveloped southwestern area was completed in 1971.

The Ivory Coast has earned the distinction of being one of the most prosperous, highly developed, and politically stable countries in Africa, having tripled its agricultural exports in the past two decades.

The 1980s were less kind to the land which had been praised as the "showcase" of sub Sahara Africa.

A global recession in 1982, which dropped coffee and cocoa prices worldwide, created an unaccustomed need for austerity in the Ivory Coast. Later, an energy crisis occurred when drought caused water levels in the hydroelectric dams

*Fishermen work on their nets at Abidjan, the principal port of Ivory Coast.*

to fall below normal levels.

In March 1983, Houphouet-Boigny's dream of turning his native village of Yamoussoukro into the national capital officially came true. However, the actual work of relocating the government from the coastal city Abidjan to Yamoussoukro, 166 miles inland, was delayed by lack of roads and recession conditions.

In November 1985, the United Nations agreed to a request that the Ivory Coast be henceforth known as Cote d'Ivoire, rather than the Ivory Coast or Costa de Marfil.

Houphouet-Boigny was reelected October 27, 1985 for a sixth five-year term. There has been considerable concern as to who will take over when he leaves office —aged 83 in 1988. Houphouet-Boigny is the oldest and longest-serving African head of state, having been Ivory Coast's only leader since the country gained independence in 1960.

An oil boom in the early 1980s attracted nearly 1.2 million job-seekers from rural areas, and in 1987, an estimated 3 million of the 10 million inhabitants were immigrants. The country was 85% self-sufficient in food in 1985, electricity was available in half the villages and water supplies were abundant. The annual per capita income had dropped slightly, to $720 in 1983, but had rebounded to around $1,000 by 1986.

## Kenya

***Date of independence:*** December 12, 1963
***Area:*** 224,960 square miles
***Population:*** 22,400,000 (est. 1981)
***Capital:*** Nairobi
***Monetary unit:*** Kenya shilling
***Religion:*** Protestant 27%, Catholic 26%, Animist 19%, Islam 6%
***Language:*** Swahili (official), English
***Literacy:*** 59%
***Type of government:*** Republic within Commonwealth
***Political parties/leaders:*** Kenya African National Union
***Monetary conversion rate:*** 16.23 shillings = $1 US (1987)
***Principal economic resources:*** Coffee, sisal, tea, cotton, livestock, wildlife

### History at a Glance

Archeological excavations in Kenya have unearthed bones, instruments, and several other artifacts (some of which may be 30,000 years old) in the Great Rift Valley. It has been determined that the earliest known inhabitants of the region buried their dead ceremoniously—a practice generally associated with relatively advanced cultures. Archeologists

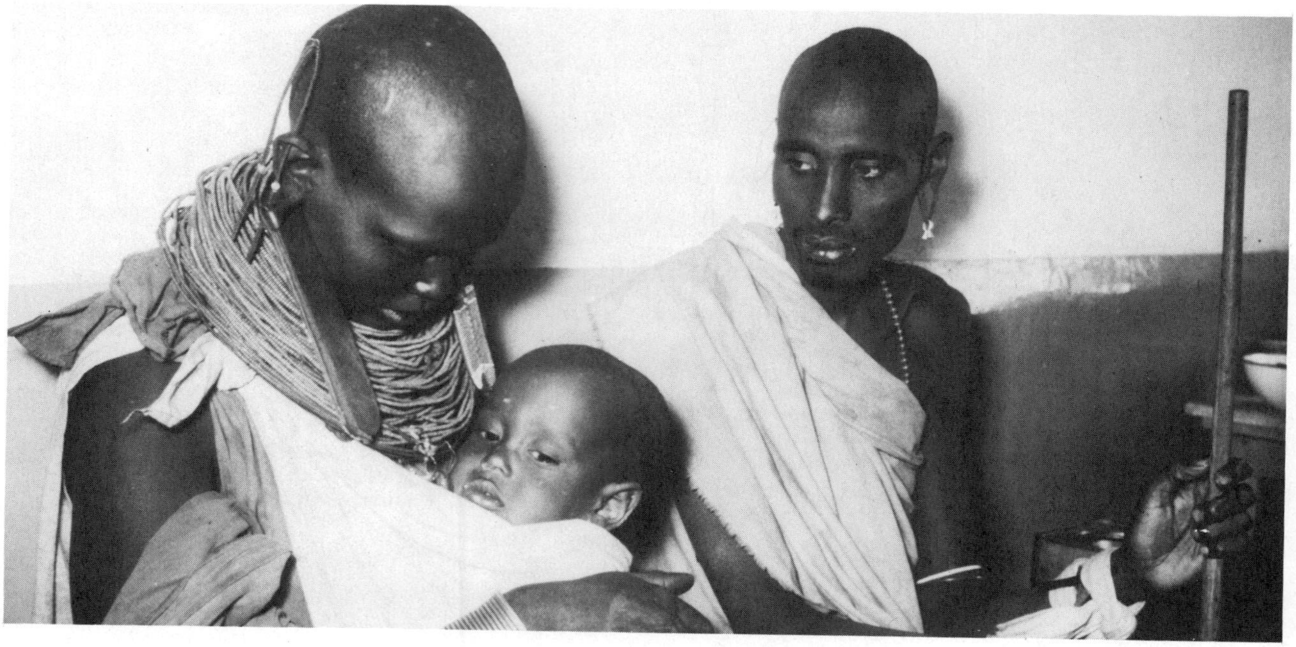

*A mother and father with their baby in a dispensary in Kenya.*

have also linked Kenya with an Iron Age civilization.

Long before the Portuguese arrived in Africa in the fifteenth century, the region was visited by Greek merchants and Arab slave traders. With the arrival of Vasco da Gama in 1498, the Portuguese established new trading posts and succeeded in suppressing Arab influence for the next two centuries. In 1729, however, the Arabs regained their influence, exercising sway for more than 150 years, during which time an Arab empire was established throughout East Africa.

European explorers again became active in the area in the nineteenth century, particularly the Englishmen Rebman and Kraft, and John Speke, who discovered Lake Victoria in 1858. During the next few decades, Great Britain and France put into effect what has been called the "spheres of influence policy" of partitioning East and Central Africa. In 1887, Great Britain obtained a lease on the main coastal dominion of the Sultan of Zanzibar, the island from which the Arabs exercised considerable control over Kenya. Eight years later, Kenya (including the Sultan's coastal strip) was declared a British protectorate.

Beginning in the twentieth century, settlement of the territory was undertaken on a large scale by the British, the South Africans, and Asians most of whom were from the Indian subcontinent. As a rule, white Europeans acquired exclusive rights over the most desirable land in Kenya: the so-called "White Highlands." After World War I, the protectorate became a British Crown Colony and the coastal strip was given the status of a protectorate.

During the next three decades, sharp divisions between the Crown, the settlers (both white and Indian), and the natives resulted in an explosive situation—culminating in 1952 with the outbreak of the "Mau Mau" rebellion. This uprising was characterized by savage butchery on all sides and eventually claimed some 12,000 lives. When the state of emergency was finally declared at an end in 1960, some 80,000 suspected "Mau Mau" members were in prison, including Jomo Kenyatta, convicted leader of the rebellion.

Majority rule by the Africans was in the process of being introduced even as the "Mau Mau" revolt raged. In 1954, however, Tom Mboya, leader of the elected Africans, expressed his dissatisfaction with the existing political arrangement and rejected a newly proposed constitution. In 1960, an African delegation finally accepted the British blueprint for a transitional government. A year later, Kenyatta was released from prison and quickly returned to the leadership of the Kenya African National Union (KANU). In 1963, KANU won control of the legislature, and with British approval introduced a program of internal self-government. In October of the same year, the Sultan of Zanzibar relinquished all rights to his mainland dominion. A month later, Kenya became an independent republic within the British Commonwealth with Kenyatta as President.

In 1969, Tom Mboya, the expected successor to Kenyatta, was assassinated, triggering a period of civil strife and abolition of the opposition party, Kenya People's Union. Opposition to the Kenyatta reign continued into the 1970s, with a few attempts to overthrow the government. Kenyatta and his Vice President, Daniel Arap Moi, were reelected in 1974, but not without political crises and the assassination of an opposition leader.

Kenyatta, who was known as "The Old Man," died in his bed at a rest home on August 22, 1978 and was immediately succeeded by Moi, who was later declared President for the remainder of Kenyatta's five-year term.

He was reelected to five-year terms in 1979 and 1983. The generally peaceful elections were marred by isolated rioting and post-election purges of non-members of the African National Union. Political unrest continued to grow and in 1986, Moi's government conducted a year-long crackdown on political dissent, drawing international criticism for human rights abuses.

Kenya's leading cash crops—coffee, tea, sisal, sugar and pyrethrum—which were adversely affected in the mid-1980s by falling world prices and drought, were starting to experience a rebound by 1986. The economy, however, continued to be strained by Kenya's maintenance of the world's highest rate of natural population increase (estimated at 4.2% in 1986, twice that of India). Unemployment has skyrocketed. In 1985, only 1.1 million of the nation's 9 million work-age adults were salaried employees.

Kenya has uneasy relations with neighbors Tanzania and Uganda, stemming from ideological differences, and has, in recent years, also found itself in the midst of Ethiopian and Somalian hostilities. Its relations with the United States have been strong: in 1983, Kenya was the largest African recipient of U.S. aid. The average per capita income in 1985 was $1,650.

Tourism was given a boost by the 1985 Academy Award-winning film, "Out of Africa." Although Kenyans did not find the film flattering, some 500,000 foreign tourists visited Kenya in 1985 alone.

*A Masai tribesman of the Kajiade District, Kenya.*

## Lesotho

***Date of independence:*** October 4, 1966
***Area:*** 11,720 square miles
***Population:*** 1,600,000 (est. 1981)
***Capital:*** Maseru
***Monetary unit:*** Loti
***Nationality:*** Basotho
***Religion:*** Catholic 44%, Lesotho Evangelical 30%, Anglican 12%
***Language:*** Sesotho (all population), English
***Literacy:*** 55%
***Type of government:*** Constitutional monarchy
***Political parties/leaders:*** Basotho National Party, four opposition parties
***Monetary conversion rate:*** 2.07 maloti = $1 US (1987)
***Principal economic resources:*** Corn,wheat, sorghum, barley, diamonds

### History at a Glance

An enclave within the Republic of South Africa, Lesotho, then known as Basutoland, first became a battleground in 1831, when Basuto tribes engaged in open warfare against the Boers who were advancing northward from South Africa. In 1867, having been defeated by the Boers, the Basuto asked for and received British protection in return for granting England full sovereignty rights. In 1964, Basutoland won internal autonomy and made known its intention of becoming independent as the Kingdom of Lesotho in October of 1966. Motlotlehi Moshoeshoe II is King. His son, Letsie David Seeiso, is the heir.

The reins of the "mountain kingdom," however, resided with Prime Minister Chief Leabua Jonathan, whose Basutoland National Party had emerged as the majority party.

From the beginning, a power struggle occurred between the king and Jonathan, which escalated into some rioting among supporters and a brief confinement of the king to his palace.

When elections held in 1970 indicated that the opposition Basotho Congress Party outpolled the Basutoland National Party, Jonathan declared the election invalid. He declared a state emergency, which lasted until July 1973, suspended the constitution, and temporarily jailed opposition leaders. King Moshoeshoe went into exile for two years.

Jonathan's regime remained unpopular and a coup against him was attempted in January 1974. This was followed by government-imposed internal restrictions, patterned after those in South Africa, including detention of individuals for 60 days without legal assistance.

From 1979 to 1982, Lesotho was rocked by military clashes between the government and the Lesotho Liberation Army, whose leader, Ntsu Mokhehle, claimed he was the rightful leader based on the 1970 election returns.

In January 1986, after reneging on a promise to hold elections, Jonathan was ousted in a bloodless coup led by Major General Justin Lekhanya, who pledged allegiance to King Moshoeshoe. He was sworn in by the king as chairman of a military council. Jonathan died some 16 months later.

Under the Jonathan regime, Lesotho maintained good

relations with Pretoria, while rejecting apartheid. Tensions grew, however, when it became clear that outlawed African National Congress (ANC) guerillas were using Lesotho as a base. In 1982, South African commandos entered Maseru and killed 27 ANC leaders. In 1986, South Africa tightened the screws further, imposing an economically crippling border blockade, which was only lifted after the Lekhanya-led coup.

Lekhanya later signed a pact with South Africa forbidding either country from planning or executing "acts of terrorism" against each other. A number of ANC supporters reportedly fled to Zambia and Zimbabwe following Lekhanya's takeover.

South Africa is Lesotho's main trading partner, employs 80% of the country's wage earners, and is the principal energy supplier. Diamonds yield about two-thirds of the country's export earnings, while the majority of the country is engaged in livestock and agriculture.

In October 1986, Lesotho signed an agreement with South Africa to dam the headwaters of the Orange River, thus providing Lesotho with its own hydroelectric power source. Also in 1986, Lesotho and Swaziland signed an agreement with South Africa which caused the South African rand to no longer be legal tender in the smaller countries. The average per capita income in 1984 was $520.

## Liberia

***Date of independence:*** July 26, 1847
***Area:*** 43,000 square miles
***Population:*** 2,400,000 (est. 1987)
***Capital:*** Monrovia
***Monetary unit:*** Liberian dollar
***Nationality:*** Liberian
***Religion:*** Animist 75%, Christian 10%, Islam 15%
***Language:*** English (official)
***Literacy:*** 35%
***Type of government:*** Highly centralized military rule
***Political parties/leaders:*** All suspended, but three parties remain in existence
***Monetary conversion rate:*** $1 = $1 US (1987)
***Principal economic resources:*** Rubber, rice, palm oil, iron ore, diamonds

### History at a Glance

Portuguese adventurers of the fifteenth century were most likely the first white men to see and explore the Liberian coast from Cape Mount to Cape Palmas.

The first permanent settlement of this territory at Cape Mesurado in 1822 was sponsored by the American Colonization Society, a private corporation which financed the return of free blacks to Africa. By 1839 the group of settlements which had sprung up in the interim found it mutually advantageous to join forces and to establish a commonwealth. Liberia's first governor was Thomas Buchanan, a cousin of James Buchanan, the fifteenth president of the United States. Eight years later, on July 26, the commonwealth proclaimed itself an independent republic.

*William U.S. Tubman, President of Liberia, being welcomed in Monrovia in 1963. In 1980 the Tubman family grip on Liberia was destroyed in a successful revolution.*

For the remainder of the nineteenth century, Liberia was ruthlessly carved up by a host of European nations, which were interested not only in exploiting its natural resources, but also in preventing it, as a nation of free blacks, from becoming a base for the dissemination of ideas politically dangerous to colonial territories in adjacent areas.

Soon after the turn of the century, the United States directly intervened to save Liberia from financial ruin, made imminent as a result of disastrous foreign loans negotiated largely through British concessionaires. Particularly hard-hit by the Depression of the 1930s, Liberia found itself further humiliated by an international scandal involving corrupt government officials who were condoning a thriving forced-labor trade.

Due to its strategic value, Liberia became an important base for Allied military operations in Africa during World War II. The country did not become financially solvent, however, until its defaulted loans were paid off by the Firestone Corporation, which then invested heavily in the development of many new rubber plantations. The wealth flowing from this booming industry has helped to improve public health and educational facilities in the country, which is now ruled, for the most part, by some 15,000 Americo-Liberian descendants.

Liberia's constitution is modeled on that of the United States. However, only African descendants may become citizens. Real estate ownership is permitted only to citizens.

According to some reliable historians, the "natives" of the interior have been exploited by the Americo-Liberians in much the same way as their forebearers had once been at the hands of southern slaveholders.

William V. S. Tubman, the President between 1943 and 1971, was a leading supporter of the concept of a West African common market.

In July 1971, President Tubman died following surgery and was succeeded by his long-time associate, Vice President William R. Tolbert Jr.

In the years under Tolbert, allegations of corruption and

misadministration grew. On April 14, 1979, protests over a price increase of rice led to riots in Monrovia resulting in more than 40 deaths, 500 injuries, and property damage estimated at $35 million. The government reversed itself and lowered the price of rice, and a brief period of calm followed.

Although Liberia had been a *de facto* one-party state since 1869, Tolbert decided to allow the People's Progressive Wing (PPP) to operate legally, under the leadership of Gabriel Baccus Matthews. When Matthews called for a general strike in February 1980 to overthrow the government, he was arrested and the PPP banned.

On April 12, 1980, before Matthews could come to trial, a coup was held by insurgents from the army, and Tolbert and more than two dozen government leaders were killed, as well as 400 others. Master Sergeant Samuel Doe, who had led the coup, established a People's Redemption Council (PRC), freed Matthews and appointed him Foreign Minister. Under the PRC, political activity was banned for the next four years.

Doe, who is unschooled, has been compared to modern-day despots such as Haiti's Jean-Claude "Baby Doc" Duvalier and the Philippine's Ferdinand Marcos. Doe has executed numerous opponents, including all the Tolbert administration officials and later his staunchest critic in the PRC, Major General Thomas Syen. Doe has successfully put down several coup attempts, including one involving political rival, Ellen Johnson-Sirleaf, a former executive with Citibank. Her imprisonment, release and rearrest generated international headlines in 1985. Like other opponents, she eventually fled the country.

A human rights group reported in 1986 that since Doe's takeover, the military has behaved lawlessly, citing several hundred instances where soldiers had been involved in arsons, looting, rape and unauthorized executions.

When Doe took over, he promised that the country would return to a civilian government, with a U.S.-style constitution and "free and fair" elections by April 1985. However, by the time elections were held in October 1985, he had disqualified several parties (and their candidates) and, amid widespread accusations of election fraud and military intimidation, was himself elected president.

Tales of graft and corruption have grown over the years. The United States, always a major contributor to the Liberian economy, had a record $434 million in aid to Liberia under the Reagan administration. When it was revealed in 1987 that some $50 million in U.S. aid was unaccounted for, Secretary of State George Shultz told the Doe administration in a visit that year to either reform its economic policies or face a cutoff in aid. The U.S. also insisted on sending in 17 "financial experts" to oversee the books and cosign checks. Media reports later revealed that at least $65 million in other funds could not be "watched" by the Americans, and money continued to disappear from those accounts while federal employees and school teachers went unpaid.

Liberia's economy has been chaotic due to mismanagement, and was described as "near-bankruptcy" by 1986. Iron ore has replaced rubber as the major source of export revenue, and three-fourths of the nation is engaged in agriculture. Per capita income in 1984 was $460.

Despite proselytization by Christians and Moslems, the majority of Liberians still believe in tribal religious rites, known as "juju", which involve witch doctors, and animal and even human sacrifice.

## Madagascar

***Date of independence:*** June 30, 1960
***Area:*** 226,657 square miles
***Population:*** 10,600,000 (est. 1987)
***Capital:*** Antananarivo
***Monetary unit:*** Malagasy franc
***Nationality:*** Malagasy
***Religion:*** Animist 47%, Catholic 26%, Protestant 23%, Islam 2%
***Language:*** Malagasy (official), French
***Literacy:*** 53%
***Type of government:*** Republic
***Political parties/leaders:*** National Front for the Defense of the Malagasy Socialist Revolution
***Monetary conversion rate:*** 787.09 francs = $1 US (1987)
***Principal economic resources:*** Rice, livestock, coffee, vanilla, sugar, cloves, graphite, chromium, coal

### History at a Glance

The language, customs, and culture of the Malagasy Republic (now known as Madagascar) are closely associated with those of other Indonesian peoples who are believed to have migrated in great numbers to the island even before the Christian era. Arab traders and African slaves began arriving in the seventh century A.D.

Portuguese explorers became aware of the island's existence in the fifteenth century. They were followed by French, Dutch, and English traders. In the seventeenth century, France attempted for a time to establish her own colonies in the southern portion of the island, but abandoned the area. This left open the way for Malagasy to become a popular pirate haunt. The famous Captain Kidd laid over on occasion.

By this time, the three main kingdoms on the island—the Merina, the Sakalava, and the Betsimisaraka—were establishing themselves in the central, western, and eastern reaches of the island. Near the end of the eighteenth century, the Merina kingdom, headed by its greatest ruler, Andrianampoinimerina, made a first attempt to extend its dominion over the entire island. Radama I not only continued in his father's footsteps, but went further—imposing a ban on the slave trade. Opposition to French influence hardened after the death of Radama I; Christian persecution intensified and European settlers were eventually obliged to leave the island altogether.

By 1885, France had reasserted itself in the territory with the establishment of a protectorate that was recognized in 1890 by Great Britain in return for French recognition of British control in Zanzibar. French forces occupied the capital in 1895, but did not stamp out opposition in the south until 10 years later.

The move toward independence showed signs of gaining

momentum in Madagascar as far back as the post-World War I decade. In 1940 British troops occupied the territory, maintaining themselves there until French administration could be restored under General de Gaulle's Free French government.

In 1946, Madagascar became an overseas territory of France, a move denounced by various nationalist elements. A bloody rebellion broke out against French rule in 1947. Before peace was restored a year later, some 60,000-90,000 Malagasy had lost their lives. Conservative business and political interests on the island gained support and, in 1958, succeeded in leading the territory to independence within the framework of the French Community. Two years later, the Malagasy Republic became a sovereign independent nation, retaining close ties with France.

The republic's first president, Philibert Tsiranana, leader of the pro-French Social Democratic Party, spent much of his time assuaging ethnic rivalries between the Merina people (Protestants) and the *cotiers* (Roman Catholics).

Tsiranana was ousted in a coup in May 1972. A referendum in October of the same year approved General Gabriel Ramanantsoa as head of a new government.

With unemployment and inflation high, General Ramanantsoa resigned on February 5, 1975. His leftist successor, Colonel Richard Ratsimandrava, was assassinated six days later by a machine gun ambush in Antananarivo.

On June 15, 1975, Commander Didier Ratsiraka was named President. He announced that the country would follow a socialist course and nationalized all banks, insurance companies, and mineral sources. The name of the country was changed to Madagascar on December 21, 1975.

The Ratsiraka regime has been plagued by at least two coup attempts, civil unrest, and scarcities of food and other essential commodities.

Since Ratsiraka came to power, Madagascar has moved away from its French and U.S. ties and drawn closer to the Soviet Union. In 1986, it accepted a $255 million Soviet loan and allowed construction of a major Soviet embassy. Madagascar lies some 300 miles off the coast of Mozambique, which has some 500 advisors from the Soviet Union, Cuba and North Korea, and is considered strategically important in view of Indian Ocean sea lanes.

Additional aid agreements have been made with a number of European countries, and Japan.

Madagascar, with Reunion and Comoros Islands, supplies three-quarters of the world's trade in vanilla. Per capita income in 1983 was $290.

*A woman farmer looks at her corn crop maintained by Malawi's agricultural program.*

## Malawi

***Date of independence:*** July 6, 1974
***Area:*** 45,747 square miles
***Population:*** 7,400,000 (est. 1987)
***Capital:*** Lilongwe
***Monetary unit:*** Kwacha
***Nationality:*** Malawian
***Religion:*** Christian 57%, Animist 19%, Islam 16%
***Language:*** Chichewa (official), English, Tombucka
***Literacy:*** 25%
***Type of government:*** One-party state
***Political parties/leaders:*** Malawi Congress Party, exile opposition groups
***Monetary conversion rate:*** 2.32 kwacha = $1 US (1987)
***Principal economic resources:*** Tobacco, tea, peanuts, sugar, cotton

### History at a Glance

Malawi, known as Nyasaland prior to its independence, was first settled by an agricultural people of Bantu origin who appeared in the Lake Nyasa area some 2,000 years ago and then moved southward to the Shire River Valley. Later migrations by the Yao and Nyanja peoples from the neighborhood of the southern Congo eventually led to population pressures and tribal conflicts in the lake Nyasa region.

The first European to sight the lake was probably a Portuguese, Casper Boccaro, in 1616, but discovery of it is credited to David Livingstone, the Scottish explorer who arrived there in 1859. By this time, Nyasaland was an important base for Arab slave traders, whose operations were not checked until a number of Christian missionaries appeared in the area.

British influence in Nyasaland reached its zenith during the last four decades of the nineteenth century. The African Lakes Company, having followed the missionaries into the territory in 1878, quickly became embroiled in sharp competition with the Arab ivory traders on the northern end of Lake Nyasa. By 1891 the British had fully consolidated their political position in the region and given it protectorate status.

Hostility to British colonial policies first manifested itself in Nyasaland in 1915 when John Chilembwe, an American-trained African religious leader, led an armed revolt which, though unsuccessful, helped crystallize the political aspirations of the African inhabitants. After World War II, Great Britain tried to establish a federation made up of its three important Central African territories—Northern Rhodesia, Southern Rhodesia, and Nyasaland. Despite its opposition to the idea, Nyasaland was forced in 1953 to join a move which fanned the growing flames of nationalist fervor in the territory. Nyasaland lost no time in protesting to the Queen herself that the federation was dominated by a white minority intent on institutionalizing the notion of perpetual European political superiority. Fearing likewise that the federation might achieve complete independence from Great Britain, Nyasaland became ripe for revolt—particularly with the return of Dr. H. Kamuzu Banda in 1958. Within a year, an uprising did occur, and several Africans were killed. As a consequence, the Nyasaland African Congress (NAC), the main nationalist party, was outlawed, and its leaders, including Dr. Banda, imprisoned.

In 1960, the British government accepted the fact-finding report of an investigating commission which maintained that the original uprising had been caused by popular dissatisfaction with the idea of federation.

Upon his release from prison, Dr. Banda formed the Malawi Congress Party (MCP) which won widespread support at the polls. This encouraged England to institute constitutional reforms leading to internal autonomy for Nyasaland, which seceded from the federation in 1963 and became an independent state, adopting the name "Malawi" a year later.

In 1967, Malawi took the initiative among black African republics in establishing trade relations with the white-dominated nations of southern Africa. Despite the criticism he incurred, Banda remained steadfast in his conviction that Malawi should trade "with the devil" if it becomes necessary to improve the economic status of the nation.

Under Banda, who was voted President for Life in 1971, and is thought to be in his late 80s, the government has been relatively stable and uncorrupted, although opposition groups operate out of neighboring Mozambique and Tanzania. Unlike his neighbors, Banda has kept full diplomatic relations with South Africa.

Major problems have involved transportation. Traditionally, the landlocked Malawi has trafficked some 90% of its imports and exports through the Mozambican ports of Beria and Nacala. However, civil unrest in Mozambique has kept those routes virtually closed for six years.

The other major trade route, to Durban, South Africa, via train and truck through Zimbabwe and Zambia, appears equally vulnerable. As such, Malawi has been working to develop a route to the north, through Tanzania, to its port of Dar es Salaam.

Important cash crops are tobacco, tea, peanuts, sugar and cotton. Developmental aid from the West has helped many Malawian farmers raise enough crops to feed their families and have a surplus for marketing. Still, the per capita income in 1982 was only $222. An influx of 750,000 Mozambican refugees in 1988 further strained the economy.

In 1986, Mozambican President Samora Machel was killed in a plane crash. Documentation later found in the plane revealed that Machel had been plotting with Zimbabwean officials to overthrow the Banda government.

## Mali

***Date of independence:*** September 22, 1960
***Area:*** 478,764 square miles
***Population:*** 8,400,000 (est.1987)
***Capital:*** Bamako
***Monetary unit:*** CFA Franc
***Nationality:*** Malian
***Religion:*** 90% Muslim, 9% Animist, 1% Christian
***Language:*** French (official), Mande, other dialects
***Literacy:*** less than 5%
***Type of government:*** Republic (civilian rule)
***Political parties/leaders:*** Mali People's Democratic Union. No other parties.
***Monetary conversion rate:*** 304.50 francs = $1 US (1987)
***Principal economic resources:*** Millet, sorghum, corn, rice, sugar, cotton, bauxite, iron ore

### History at a Glance

What is now known as Mali was, in the fourth century A.D., only a portion of the larger and far more influential empire of Ghana. By the eighth century, Ghana was known to the Moslem Arab world as the land of gold. It later became a source of wealth for Spain and North Africa before entering into a period of decline which culminated in its overthrow in the mid-thirteenth century by a Moslem empire named Mali.

Perhaps the most famous of Mali's many emperors was the fabled Mansa Musa, who conquered Timbuktu and the vast regions of the Middle Niger. On one of his pilgrimages to Mecca, he is reported to have taken along some 500 slaves and to have distributed 50,000 ounces of gold. On his return from Mecca, he brought with him a number of Moslem tutors and men of learning, and thus fostered the growth of Timbuktu as a center of medieval African scholarship.

Due to persistent pressure on its frontiers, Mali declined in power in the fourteenth and fifteenth centuries, eventually giving way to the Songhai kingdom of Gao which, in its turn, was overcome by armed hosts from Morocco. During the nineteenth century, the territory finally achieved a degree of unity under the banner of Islam, but this was short-lived due to French military intervention and the extension of French administrative control.

Mali was known at this time as the French Soudan, a vast and underdeveloped country which was to have little importance until World War II when it became a rallying point for the Free French. Even in 1958, the Soudan was still only one of the numerous French West African territories which accepted the de Gaulle Constitution and voted for membership in the French Community.

A year later, Soudan, Senegal, Dahomey, and Upper Volta drafted their own constitution calling for the creation of a Federation of Mali. Only Senegal and Soudan, however, ratified the document. Shortly thereafter, the Mali Federation appealed to France for recognition by, and complete sovereignty within, the French Community. Although this request was granted, the federation collapsed almost immediately, largely because of the sharp differences existing between key politicians in each territory.

Under the leadership of Modibo Keita, Mali declared itself an independent state and embarked on its own program of development.

In 1965, Bamako was the site of an epoch-making conference between the heads of state of Ghana, Algeria, and Mali, all nations desirous of creating a closely knit Pan African group to rival the French-oriented Afro-Malagasy Common Organization.

Keita subsequently set the nation on a course of alignment with the Chinese brand of "socialism." The economy fell completely into the hands of state enterprises, operated with the help of more than 1,000 technicians. This policy produced a counter-revolutionary fervor among a group of young Army officers who, in 1968, overthrew Keita and installed a National Liberation Committee, headed by Lieutenant Moussa Traore.

Mining and petroleum codes were revised in 1969 to encourage more systematic prospecting in extant resources of bauxite, uranium, iron ore, gold, manganese, and petroleum among others.

In the early 1970s, Chinese and Soviet influence waned in the country, French aid doubled, and France joined Mali's three-year economic plan.

Mali, a landlocked country, is mainly agricultural and pastoral. The Sahelian drought which struck sub-Saharan nations in 1973-1974 led to severe famine and mass starvation in Mali.

The drought was later followed by an equally devastating rainfall; 1.8 million Malians were affected, thousands were killed.

The country is run effectively by the army. General Traore was elected to a six-year term as President and Prime Minister in June 1979 and again in June 1985.

In 1974, traditional border disputes flared between Mali and her southern neighbor, Burkina Faso (formerly Upper Volta), and scores of Malians were killed. The scenario was repeated, with a smaller death toll, in December 1985 when a five-day war broke out. The land dispute was taken before the International Court of Justice, which eventually divided the land into approximately equal portions.

Mali was greatly affected by the 1984-85 drought, and survived mainly because of international food aid. Much of the livestock of its Tuareg herdsmen perished, while many farmlands fell victim to desertification. As a result, Mali remains one of the 12 poorest countries in the world, with a per capita income of $150 in 1983.

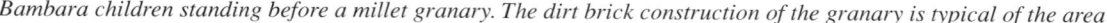

*Bambara children standing before a millet granary. The dirt brick construction of the granary is typical of the area.*

## Mauritania

***Date of independence:*** November 28, 1960
***Area:*** 397,953 square miles
***Population:*** 2,00,000 (est. 1987)
***Capital:*** Nouakchott
***Monetary unit:*** Ouguiya
***Nationality:*** Mauritanian
***Religion:*** 100% Muslim
***Language:*** French (official), Arabic
***Literacy:*** 17%
***Type of government:*** Republic
***Political parties/leaders:*** National Demcratic Union, Union for Progress and Fraternity
***Monetary conversion rate:*** 72.25 ouguiyas = $1 US (1987)
***Principal economic resources:*** Sugar cane, rice, iron ore, gypsum, fish

### History at a Glance

In its early history, Mauritania was the scene of successive waves of southward migration by Arabs and Berbers, both of whom conquered the indigenous black inhabitants. Perhaps the most important invaders were the nomadic Tuareg Berbers who often carried out raids on the Morocco-Ghana caravan route, and thus disrupted the commerce between the great black empires of the Western Sudan in the eleventh century. Islam became a potent force during the fourteenth and fifteenth centuries when Arab invaders from Egypt drove out the Berbers. Attracted by the gum trade, the Portuguese arrived in the fifteenth century, setting up trading posts along Mauritania's southern boundary—the Senegal River. For the next four centuries, the French slowly pushed their way northward from Senegal, and by signing appropriate treaties with several Moorish chieftains, came to exercise hegemony over most of the desert zone of Mauritania.

The French retaliated against the frequent raids of Moorish tribes early in the twentieth century by extending their authority over more and more of the territory. By 1909, they had added to the Adrar region, bordering on the Spanish Sahara, to their dominion. The territory of Mauritania was established as an administrative unit in 1920, at which time the city of Saint-Louis in Senegal was made its capital. At the same time, Mauritania became a part of French West Africa, a loosely knit federation set up in the French colonial holdings.

After World War II, Mauritania received the same colonial concessions from France as did the other territories in the region. In 1946 it assumed partial control of its own affairs through the election of its own assembly and sent representatives to the French National Assembly in Paris, as well as to the Assembly of the French Union. Work was begun on the new capital of Nouakchott in 1957. A year later, Mauritania approved the Constitution of the Fifth French Republic and decided in favor of membership within the French Community. Complete independence was not achieved until 1960.

Mauritania and Morocco planned to divide the territory of the former Spanish Sahara after the departure of Spain in November 1975. Although Mauritanian troops moved into the region, they were rebuffed by the Polisario, a Saharan independence group backed by Algeria. Mauritania broke diplomatic relations with Algeria in 1976 after Algeria recognized the area as an independent state.

Increased military spending and high casualties were incurred when Mauritania tried to maintain control of its southern third of Western Sahara and unrest grew on the home front. On July 10, 1978, President Moktar Ould Daddah was deposed in a bloodless coup and Lieutenant Colonel Mustapha Ould Salek installed as Head of State.

Western Sahara continued to occupy national interest and President Salek spent the next few months trying to get a "global settlement" concerning that desert territory, but was unsuccessful. In March 1979, he dismissed several leaders who were sympathetic to the Polisario and relinquished the office of Prime Minister to Lieutenant Colonel Ahmed Ould Bouceif, who was highly esteemed. Barely a month later, Bouceif was killed in an airplane crash and was succeeded on May 31 by Lieutenant Colonel Mohamed Khouna Ould Haidalla.

President Salek was forced to resign three days later and the ruling body, the Military Committee for National Salvation (CMNS), named Lieutenant Colonel Mahomed Mahmoud Ould Ahmed Louly as President.

Colonel Louly concluded a peace treaty with Polisario in August 1979 and ended hostilities by withdrawing Mauritanian troops. Moroccan troops immediately occupied the land.

Colonel Louly only held power for six months and then was removed by a junta on January 4, 1980 with Prime Minister Haidalla named President.

Under President Haidalla, economic reconstruction became a priority. The Sahelian drought of 1968-1974 devastated the land, wiping out 80% of the country's cattle, one-third of its camels and more than half the sheep and goats. Subsequent drought conditions wracked the country, so that by 1986, less than 25% of the northern population was still engaged in cattle-raising. Driven to the cities, modern Mauritanians now participate in the mining of iron ore, which accounts for 75% of the nation's export earnings. The average per capita income in 1983 was $450.

After surviving two coup attempts in 1981 and 1982, President Haidalla was overthrown in a bloodless coup in December 1984 while in Burundi attending a conference. Army chief of staff Colonel Maouya Sid'ahmed Taya assumed power as prime minister. All members of the ruling military committee, except the ousted Haidalla, retained their posts.

With military withdrawal from Western Sahara complete, and an economic program underway, Prime Minister Taya's major domestic problems revolved around ethnic and racial unrest. Although the CMNS outlawed slavery in 1980, the centuries-old tradition was dying hard, and by the mid-1980s, it was estimated that some 400,000 blacks, women and Harantines (mixed-race descendants of black slaves) were still in some form of bondage.

Sand dunes were beginning to pose a serious threat to the capital of Nouakchott by 1985.

## Mauritius

***Date of independence:*** March 12,1968
***Area:*** 790 square miles
***Population:*** 1,100,000 (est.1987)
***Capital:*** Port Louis
***Monetary unit:*** Mauritian rupee
***Nationality:*** Mauritian
***Religion:*** Hindu 46%, Christian 33%, Islam 16%
***Language:*** English (official), Hindi, Creole, Chinese
*Literacy:* 61%
***Type of government:*** Independent state, recognizes Elizabeth II as Chief of State
***Political parties/leaders:*** Independence Party, Mauritian Social Democratic Party, 5 opposition parties
***Monetary conversion rate:*** 12.86 rupees = $1 US (1987)
***Principal economic resources:*** Sugar cane, rice, cut diamonds, tobacco, iron ore

### History at a Glance

Mauritius is located in the Indian Ocean some 500 miles east of Madagascar. It was discovered by Portuguese sailors in the early sixteenth century and first settled by the Dutch who gave it its name in 1598. After the Dutch withdrew in 1710, the French claimed the island (renaming it Ile de France), but lost it to British forces in 1810. Four years later, British sovereignty was recognized by the Peace of Paris. With the abolition of slavery in the British Empire in 1834, Mauritius absorbed large numbers of migrant laborers from the Asian subcontinent.

In 1967, Mauritius became self-governing, with Mauritius Labor Party (MLP) leader Seewoosagur Ramgoolam appointed as Prime Minister. Opposition from the radical Mauritian Militant Movement (MMM) grew and in 1976, Ramgoolam remained in office by a slim majority. In balloting in June 1982, the incumbents all lost their seats and were replaced by MMM leaders Paul Berenger and Aneerood Jugnauth. Since tradition dictates that only a Hindu can be prime minister, Jugnauth assumed the top post, while Berenger, who is white, became finance minister.

Berenger's dictatorial and Marxist ways caused him and 11 other ministers to be ousted the next spring. Jugnauth and his supporters formed an alliance with leaders of other parties, and formed the less-radical Mauritian Socialist Movement.

The government was rocked by scandal in 1985 when four members of the alliance were found at an airport with nearly $1 million worth of heroin in their luggage. Jugnauth retained his post, but several members of the government resigned. Ramgoolam died in December 1985.

One of the most densely populated countries in the world, Mauritius has been a melting pot for the peoples of Africa, Asia and Europe. About 68% of the population is of Indian descent, blacks and Creoles (mixed race) make up 27%, and the remainder are of European or Chinese descent. Although they maintain their cultural diversities, Mauritians live in relative domestic peace.

Sugar exports, which once accounted for the bulk of foreign earnings, had dropped to about 35% of exports by 1986. Textile exports, meanwhile, swelled to about 50% of earnings, and tourism had become the third largest revenue source. The per capita income in 1983 was $1,000.

Mauritius is the only former British colony in Africa which still recognizes Queen Elizabeth II as its sovereign.

## Mozambique

***Date of independence:*** June 25, 1975
***Area:*** 302,328 square miles
***Population:*** 14,700,000 (est.1987)
***Capital:*** Maputo
***Monetary unit:*** Metical
***Nationality:*** Mozambican
***Religion:*** Animist 48%, Christian 17%, Islam 17%
***Language:*** Portuguese (official), many tribal dialects
***Literacy:*** 27% (1974)
***Type of government:*** One-party socialist
***Political parties/leaders:*** Mozambique Liberation Front, Mozambique National Resistance (RENAMO); three illegal parties
***Monetary conversion rate:*** 202.00 meticais = $1 US (1987)
***Principal economic resources:*** Cotton, cashew nuts, sugar, tea, copra, coal, iron ore

### History at a Glance

Mozambique was first visited by the Portuguese explorer Vasco da Gama in the course of his voyage to India and the Far East in 1498. Settlements along the coastal areas were established in the sixteenth century, during which time the slave trade also prospered. By 1878, this trade had been abolished and boundary settlements reached between adjacent British and German territories.

In 1951, the territory's status was changed to that of an overseas Portuguese province. African nationalism in Mozambique was slow to develop, with no definite trend in evidence until 1962 when the Mozambique Liberation Front (Frelimo) was formed. Fighting broke out in 1964.

At first, the Portuguese fragmented the rebels and forced them underground, but the guerrillas held on and led by the Frelimo movement, slowly gained the upperhand. In 1974, with guerrillas in control of much of the country, the Portuguese announced that they would depart in 1975. In June 1975, the Social Frelimo leader, Samora Machel, became president of an independent "people`s republic."

While not wracked with the degree of internal dissensions that plagued transition in Angola, Mozambique's young government faced many difficulties. Hopes for economic aid from Portugal dissipated after Portuguese holdings in Mozambique were "nationalized." Economic troubles were further aggravated by the flooding of the Limpopo River, emigration of some 240,000 of the nation's 250,000 Portuguese, and the implementation of Marxist-Leninist collective farming systems, which saw the decline of sugar and cotton production.

Aid came from China in 1974 and 1975, which supported Frelimo's 12,000-man army.

Mozambique enjoyed a brief period of cooperation with its landlocked neighbor, Rhodesia (later Zimbabwe) until internal fighting broke out there in 1976. While supporting Robert Mugabe's ZANU faction, Mozambique closed its border, thus blocking Rhodesia from ports along its 1,500-mile coastline on the Indian Ocean.

Mozambique paid dearly for its role as a "rear base" for Mugabe's guerillas during the Rhodesian civil war. Machel later estimated that Rhodesian forces attacked his nation 350 times, killed more than 1,000 Mozambicans and cost the country $550 million in revenues.

After Rhodesia achieved independence as Zimbabwe in 1980, rail and highway communications were resumed.

Marxist Mozambique has received aid from the Soviet Union, Cuba, East Germany and other Soviet bloc countries, as well as Western sources including the United States, United Kingdom, Brazil and Portugal.

Mozambique condemns apartheid in South Africa, but like other Front-Line states, has had to face economic realities, such as the employment of 61,000 of its citizens in South African mines, and transport and hydroelectric needs.

Tensions between the two nations have intensified in recent years, due to the growing strength of the main opposition group, Mozambique National Resistance (Renamo), which was formed in 1976 with the initial support of the white Rhodesian government of Ian Smith, and has been supported in recent years by South Africa.

In 1984, Pretoria signed the Nkomati Accord, which signaled its willingness to stop aiding Renamo if Mozambique would cease assistance to the outlawed African National Congress (ANC). Neither government appeared to have kept its word, however.

Renamo forces, which occupied 10% of the land and were 20,000 strong in 1988, pose a serious threat. In 1985, Zimbabwe sent in an estimated 10,000 troops to bolster the Frelimo army, which was 30,000 strong, and Tanzania also agreed to make troops available. Ironically, the United States, which has generously aided Jonas Savimbi's UNITA rebels in Angola, chose not to assist the Renamo rebels, and instead gave $40 million in aid to the Machel government in 1985.

The widely respected Machel perished at age 53 in a plane crash while returning to Mozambique from a strategy meeting in Zambia on October 19, 1986. The crash was initially condemned as a South African sabotage, but later inquiries laid the blame on human error and malfunction of the Soviet-made plane. The South African government later revealed that papers found at the crash site, which was on South African soil, showed that Zimbabwe and Mozambique were plotting an overthrow of the Malawi government. Malawi has given shelter to Renamo rebels and is the only sub-Saharan country to maintain full diplomatic relations with South Africa.

Machel was succeeded by Foreign Affairs Minister Joaquim Alberto Chissano.

A severe drought in 1981 destroyed the cash crops of cashews, sugar, cotton and tea. Drought, battles with Renamo, and transportation problems caused episodes of mass starvation and widespread poverty from 1983 on. Since the beginning of the civil war, which was 12 years old in 1988, some 1 million Mozambicans have been displaced, including 750,000 who have sought refuge in Malawi.

Coal, diamonds and bauxite are mined, but other mineral deposits remain untapped. The per capita income in 1983 was $150.

## Namibia

***Date of independence:***
***Area:*** 318,259 square miles
***Population:*** 1,240,000 (est. 1987)
***Capital:*** Windhoek
***Monetary unit:*** South African Rand
***Nationality:*** Namibian
***Religion:*** Christian, Animist
***Language:*** Afrikaans (principal), German, English
***Literacy:*** 100% whites, 28% non-whites
***Type of government:*** U.N. Mandate
***Political parties/leaders:*** South West African People's Organization (SWAPO), Democratic Turnhalle Alliance (DTA)
***Monetary conversion rate:*** 2.07 rands = $1 US (1987)
***Principal economic resources:*** Corn, millet, diamonds, copper, lead, zinc, fish

### History at a Glance

Great Britain was the first European nation to set foot in what is now the territory of Namibia, having gained control of a number of off shore islands, as well as the Walvis Bay region, by 1878. Germany established a protectorate over the mainland in 1884, acquired a number of trading concessions there, and established full administrative control in 1908.

Captured by South African troops in 1915, South West Africa became a South African mandated territory in 1920, retaining this status until the close of World War II, when South Africa sought unsuccessfully to annex the territory outright, rather than place it under the trusteeship of the United Nations as other colonial powers had done.

Soon thereafter, representatives of the African population in the territory were sent as petitioners to air their grievances before the United Nations. In 1962 Ethiopia and Liberia brought suit against South Africa before the International Court of Justice at The Hague, Netherlands, maintaining that the rights of the South-West African population had consistently been violated by the administering power.

On July 18, 1966, the Court dismissed the suit on the grounds that Ethiopia and Liberia did not have sufficient legal interest too obtain a judgment on the case's merits. This setback was regarded as a severe blow to the foes of apartheid.

The territory, governed by a South African administrator, is divided into the police zone (white settlement areas) and the reserve area (for native inhabitants only).

In 1966, the U.N. General Assembly declared that the South African mandate was terminated and, within a year, appointed a council to administer the territory until independence. In 1968, the territory was renamed Namibia.

South Africa, however, refused to relinquish administration, and instead maintained some 18,000 troops in the area.

In 1970, the U.N. Security Council condemned South Africa for its illegal control of the area and, in 1971, the International Court of Justice concurred.

In 1973, Ovamboland in the north received limited self-government. Ovambos constitute about half of Namibia's population.

In 1974, a U.N. Security Council resolution required South Africa to begin the transfer of power to the Namibians by May 30, 1975, or face U.N. action. South African Prime Minister Balthazar Vorster rejected the U.N. resolution, saying his government would not recognize nor negotiate with the black separatist South West Africa People's Organisation (SWAPO) as the sole representative of Namibia.

The U.N. has since condemned South Africa for its "illegal occupation," periodically called for free elections, and appointed U.N. commissioners for Namibia, but by 1988, had not taken military action.

Of the three dozen political parties in Namibia, SWAPO, formed in 1958, is the largest and most active nationalist group. Although it was recognized in the 1960s by the U.N. as the "authentic representative of the Namibian people," SWAPO has since been accused of conducting massacres on other tribes, and been labeled by opponents as a "terrorist guerilla organization with Marxist leanings." SWAPO operates from bases in Angola and in Ovamboland, where most of its supporters live; its leader is Sam Nujoma. In 1984, South Africa released SWAPO co-founder Herman Toivo ja Toivo from 16 years in prison.

The other major political group is the Democratic Turnhalle Alliance (DTA), which was established after the Turnhalle Conference in 1975. The DTA is a coalition of European, Coloured and African groups, and advocates a constitutional arrangement with equal ethnic representation.

Conferences were held at Windhoek during 1975 through 1977, each revising the proposed constitution. Turnhalle delegates, and later 95% of white voters in a referendum, approved of a draft constitution in March 1977. However, it was opposed by SWAPO, and Western diplomats from Canada, France, Germany, Britain and the United States, as racially imbalanced.

Preparation for a general election in 1978 continued amidst negotiations among opposition groups, Western diplomats, South Africa and neighboring countries. In the meantime, South African-appointed Administrator General Marthinus Steyn worked to dismantle the apartheid system, abolishing the Mixed Marriages Act and pass laws.

By the end of 1978, balloting was held, although SWAPO boycotted it. The DTA was declared the victor with 82% of the vote, and awarded 41 of the 50 seats on the newly formed Constituent Assembly.

South Africa agreed in 1979 to recognize the Constituent Assembly as a National Assembly, although it would not give it authority to change Namibia's status; meanwhile, fighting between South African troops and SWAPO intensified. The same year, then-President Neto of Angola proposed the creation of a 60-mile-wide demilitarized zone along the Angolan-Namibian border to prevent incursions, but this was never enacted.

Throughout the 1980s, South African forces battled SWAPO guerillas, who were fortified by Cuban troops stationed in Angola. International pressure was placed on South Africa to withdraw from Namibia, but Pretoria steadfastly refused to leave or allow U.N.-monitored free elections unless Cuban troops were first withdrawn from Angola.

In 1988, many South Africans were complaining about the $1 billion a year poured into Namibia, but despite intense multinational negotiations, including a major series of talks in August and September 1988, efforts to break the stalemate were not effective.

Namibia is rich in diamonds and uranium, as well as copper and other minerals. Per capita income was $700 in 1985.

## Niger

***Date of independence:*** August 3, 1960
***Area:*** 489,189 square miles
***Population:*** 6,674,000 (est.1987
***Capital:*** Niamey
***Monetary unit:*** CFA franc
***Nationality:*** Nigerien
***Religion:*** Islam 90%, Animist 10%, Christian 10%
***Language:*** French (official), many dialects
***Literacy:*** 10%
***Type of government:*** Republic (military regime since1974)
***Political parties/leaders:*** Banned
***Monetary conversion rate:*** 304.50 francs = $1 US (1987)
***Principal economic resources:*** Peanuts, cotton, livestock, sorghum, uranium, coal, iron

### History at a Glance

The territory known today as Niger was, for most of its early history, a crossroads of migration between white peoples of North Africa and black peoples of the Lake Chad region. The Kanem Bornu Empire was only one of several powerful states which emerged in this area during the eighth and ninth centuries. This empire was overthrown in the tenth century by the Hausa states which lay in the southern reaches of Niger, and by the Songhai Kingdom which held sway in the western half of the country until the sixteenth century, when it was itself destroyed by an invading Moroccan army.

The first European explorer in the area was the fabled Scot, Mungo Park (1805). Later Major Dixon Denham and Lieutenant Hugh Clapperton were sent by Great Britain to explore the Niger River and they reached Lake Chad after crossing the Sahara Desert from Tripoli.

By 1900, the French had pushed their way eastward despite fierce opposition from the Tuareg tribe. In 1901, Niger was declared a military district and became part of a larger territorial unit known as Haut-Senegal et Niger. Sporadic revolts continued right up until the eve of World War I, at which time they were quelled with the aid of British forces from Nigeria. In 1922, Niger was officially declared a French colony.

Due to its lack of strategic importance, the territory remained virtually unaffected by World War II. Nationalism and, with it, the growth of political parties became inevitable once France allowed her West African territories a greater share in self-government. In 1958, Niger approved the new French Constitution, and within two years had become a fully independent state.

The President of Niger, Hamani Diori, embarked upon an ambitious economic program which called for long-term cooperation with France. He survived one assassination attempt in April 1965. In 1970, he was reelected to a five year term.

A massive drought from 1968 to 1974 had devastating consequences for this landlocked nation; half of the 4 million population experienced starvation. The United States and other nations sent some 200,000 tons of food to Niger. However, when President Diori was accused of mishandling the relief supplies, discontent grew.

On April 15, 1974, President Diori was ousted by a military coup led by Lieutenant Colonel Seyni Kountche, who suspended both the Constitution and the only political party, the Niger Progressive Party. Kountche installed a 12-man military government and adopted diplomatic relations with a number of communist states while maintaining a conservative posture in regional affairs.

In 1980, Niger's attention was focused on the civil war in neighboring Chad, with concern about Libya's involvement. In December 1980, Niger attended the OAU emergency summit on Chad and joined the Central African Republic, Cameroon, Guinea, Senegal, the Sudan, and Togo in calling for Libya's immediate withdrawal from Chad.

Drought revisited the land in 1984, reducing the year's harvest by 60%. However, with foreign food aid and stored surpluses, Niger did not fall victim to mass starvation like Ethiopia.

The country's agriculture continued to be plagued by desertification and flooding, and in 1986, a major infestation of locusts. In 1985, the government introduced an "anti-corruption" campaign, and cracked down on misuse of government funds. Still, Niger remained one of the poorest countries in the world. Per capita income dropped from $340 in 1984 to around $200 in 1987.

Uranium continued to be a major export, despite low prices on the world market.

On November 10, 1987, Kountche died in a Paris hospital, and his cousin, Army chief of staff Colonel Ali Seibou was named president. Although Kountche officially died of a brain tumor, subsequent reports claimed he died of AIDS.

Kountche's death was seen as a loss to the West, as he had quietly kept Libyan expansionist forces in check, both in Niger and in neighboring Chad.

*Youngsters carrying fresh water accross the flooded streets of Say, in Niger.*

## Nigeria

***Date of independence:*** October 1, 1960
***Area:*** 356,667 square miles
***Population:*** 93,383,000 (est.1987)
***Capital:*** Abuja (as of 1989), formerly Lagos
***Monetary unit:*** Naira
***Religion:*** 47% Muslim, 34% Christian, 18% Animist
***Language:*** English (official), Hausa, Yoruba, Ibo
***Literacy:*** 25%
***Type of government:*** Federal republic (since 1979)
***Political parties/leaders:*** National Party of Nigeria, Nigerian People's Party, 3 minority parties
***Monetary conversion rate:*** 3.08 naira = $1 US (1987)
***Principal economic resources:*** Peanuts, cotton, cocoa, rubber, yams, cassava, livestock, oil, natural gas, coal, tin, processed rubber

### History at a Glance

Little is known of the early peoples who inhabited Nigeria. During the Middle Ages, Northern Nigeria was in contact with the kingdoms of the western Sudan and the nations lying to the north of the Sahara Desert as well. Islam was established as the major religion in Nigeria during the fifteenth century, by which time the Ife and Benin kingdoms were flourishing.

Contact between the coastal peoples of Nigeria and the nations of Europe was based upon the exploitation of slaves who were removed from the territory in astounding numbers. The British abolished the slave trade in 1807 and, with the discovery of the mouth of the Niger River in 1830, extended their economic influence into the interior. In 1861, they annexed the island of Lagos, an important center in the palm oil trade. Toward the end of the century, they swept into the eastern regions of Nigeria, establishing the Oil Rivers Protectorate (1885) and the Niger Coast Protectorate (1893).

British influence in Nigeria was formally recognized by the Berlin Conference of 1884-1885. Over the next 15 years, Great Britain gained control of an even more substantial piece of territory in Northern Nigeria, where a third protectorate was established.

In 1914, these separate administrative areas were combined into the Colony and Protectorate of Nigeria, introducing a system of indirect rule which enabled local chieftains to exercise a significant degree of control over their own affairs.

Nationalism became a potent force in Nigeria after World War II, primarily under the leadership of Nnamdi Azikiwe, Obafemi Awolowo, and Alhaji Sir Abubakar Tafawa Balewa. In 1960, Nigeria became a fully independent federation within the framework of the British Commonwealth, and three years later opted for a republican government.

Early in 1966, Nigeria was the scene of the bloodiest military coup any black African nation has suffered to date. Prime Minister Tafawa Balewa was assassinated and a military government headed by General J. Aguiyi-Ironsi seized power. This government abolished the existing constitution, eliminated the offices of president and prime minister, and dismissed the premiers of Nigeria's semi-autonomous regions (the Northern, the Western, the Eastern, and the Midwestern).

Later that year, Aguiyi-Ironsi was deposed by Lieutenant Colonel Yakubu Gowon, head of a new military junta. When anti-Ibo rioting began anew late in 1966, Ibos from all over the nation began flocking back to their homeland in the Eastern Region. Soon the new state of Biafra was created, and civil war engulfed the country.

In January 1970, after 31 months of civil war, the Republic of Biafra surrendered to the federal government, leaving an estimated 1 million persons, mostly inhabitants of the defeated state, homeless and starving. A massive international relief operation kept the death toll lower than might have been anticipated. The overall cost of the war was estimated at $840 million.

Gowon's nine-year rule ended on July 1975 when he was deposed in a bloodless coup while at an OAU summit in Uganda. By the beginning of August, a Supreme Military Council was reorganized as well as a 25-member Federal Executive Council, with coup leader Brigadier General Murtala Ramat Muhammad in position of leadership. Muhammad's rule was only temporary—he was assassinated on February 13, 1976, during a coup attempt. Lieutenant General Olusegun Obasanjo succeeded the slain leader as Chairman of the Supreme Military Council and captured and executed Muhammad's assassins.

*A minaret in Agades, Niger.*

*Teenagers draw water in a rural village in the Western Region of Nigeria, an oil-rich country battling widespread poverty.*

On March 31, 1978, President Carter came to visit—the first visit by an American President since President Franklin Roosevelt stopped in Liberia during World War II.

On September 12, 1978, Nigeria's 12-year state of emergency ended and a ban on political party activity was lifted.

Elections were held in mid-1979 which placed a number of federal representatives, state legislators, and state governors in power and Alhaji Shehu Shagari as President.

In October after the elections, power transferred peacefully from military to multiparty civilian rule and was hailed as a good example for other African states.

Shagari was personally popular, but his administration proved to be hopelessly corrupt, and nearly destroyed the economy with its gross overspending.

In December 1983, a group of senior military officers took over in a bloodless coup. Major General Muhammadu Buhari assumed power as chairman of the Supreme Military Council. He launched a "war on indiscipline," placed many government officials on trial for embezzlement, limited freedoms and reintroduced the death penalty.

Two years later, Buhari was himself deposed. The new government, headed by Major General Ibrahim Babangida, released political prisoners, lifted press restrictions and pledged a return to civilian rule by 1990. Babangida also decreed in 1986 that former politicians be barred from seeking office for 10 years.

Nigeria has been struggling to regain what government abuses have lost. Oil revenues fell from $25 billion in 1981 to $5 billion in 1986. In the face of a $20 billion world debt, austerity has been imposed on all lifestyles, except in agriculture, where a program is underway to make black Africa's most heavily populated country self-sufficient in food. The per capita income in 1987 was $800.

In 1985, Nigeria passed its first anti-drug laws, to combat a burgeoning heroin smuggling trade.

On October 16, 1986, Nigerian playwright, poet and novelist Wole Soyinka became the first black to win the Nobel Prize for Literature. The country was stunned a few days later, however, when Dele Giwa, the feisty editor of the country's largest news magazine was killed by a letter bomb. Other domestic problems included bloody religious riots and labor strikes.

## Rwanda

***Date of independence:*** July 1, 1962
***Area:*** 10,169 square miles
***Population:*** 6,700,000 (est. 1987)
***Capital:*** Kigali
***Monetary unit:*** Rwanda franc
***Nationality:*** Rwandan
***Religion:*** Catholic 56%, Protestant 12%, Islam 9%, Animist 23%
***Language:*** Kinyarwanda (official), French, Kiswahili
***Literacy:*** 49%
***Type of government:*** Republic
***Political parties/leaders:*** National Revolutionary Movement for Development (MRND)
***Monetary conversion rate:*** 81.51 francs = $1 US (1987)
***Principal economic resources:*** Coffee, tea, beans, potatoes, cassiterite, wolfram

### History at a Glance

The history of Rwanda, a tiny country adjacent to Zaire, has been largely one involving the strained relationship between the Tutsi and the Hutu tribes.

The Hutu comprise some 90% of the population, but have long been subjugated by the tall, disciplined Tutsi, sometimes referred to as Watusis.

A nomadic pastoral people, the Tutsi first entered Rwanda in the fifteenth century, subjugating its inhabitants, the Hutu and Twa. The Tutsi instituted a caste system and came to function as the feudal overlords of the Hutu tribe, which was composed mainly of farmers. The Twa slowly retired into the surrounding jungle in search of wild game.

The first white men to pass through Rwanda were the English explorers John Speke and Richard Burton, who crossed the territory in 1858 during their search for the southernmost source of the river Nile. In 1871, Stanley and

Livingstone landed at Usumbura (now in Burundi) after having first explored the Ruzizi River region. They were soon to be followed by German explorers and by Roman Catholic missionaries.

The status of both Rwanda (originally spelled Ruanda) and Burundi (then known as Urundi) was first determined by the Berlin Conference of 1884-1885. Ultimately, Rwanda was made a distinct colony by Germany and given its own administrative headquarters at Kigali.

Following World War I, Germany was forced to surrender this territory to Belgium, which was awarded a mandate over once-again-united Ruanda-Urundi by the League of Nations. In 1946, although it continued to be administered from the Belgian Congo, it was made a trust territory by the United Nations.

During the 1950s, fierce tribal clashes became more frequent in Ruanda-Urundi. The politically awakened Hutu tribe, in particular, grew more militant and self-assertive toward its aristocratic Tutsi overlords. In 1959, the Hutus succeeded in breaking the Tutsi-dominated monarchy, and thousands of Tutsis fled the country.

By mid-1960, Belgium found herself in the midst of withdrawing from both her African colonies: the Belgian Congo (now known as Zaire) and Rwanda.

An election held in Rwanda in 1960 gave the country's leadership to Gregoire Kayibanda and his Party for Hutu Emancipation. When the United Nations refused to recognize the 1960 election, a second one was held, under U.N. auspices, in September 1961, with the same result. Kayibanda was formally confirmed as president on October 26, 1961, and Rwanda gained full independence on July 1, 1962.

The Tutsis, who had retained a monarchist form of government in Burundi, tried to restore themselves to power in Rwanda in 1963, but were put down in bloody fighting. An estimated 10,000 people died, and more than 150,000 Tutsis fled the country.

Kayibanda, reelected in 1965 and 1969, was legally barred from seeking another term in 1973. When he tried to alter the constitution to allow another term, hostile elements arose and he was overthrown in a bloodless coup on July 5, 1973.

The new government, under the leadership of Major General Juvenal Habyarimana, suspended parts of the constitution and banned all political parties. In 1976, a new legal party, the National Revolutionary Movement for Development, was organized.

Under Habyarimana, Rwanda took a distinctly "anti-imperialist" turn and became the first African nation to break relations with Israel as a result of the October 1973 war. It has also supported liberation movements in South Africa, and opened closer relations with Burundi, Zaire, and Tanzania. Habyarimana was reconfirmed to five-year terms in 1978 and 1983.

In 1985, Rwanda gave shelter to some 26,000 Ugandans who were fleeing the Obote regime's excesses. In 1973 and 1988, when Tutsi-Hutu fighting broke out in Burundi, tens of thousands of Hutus fled to Rwanda.

Rwanda is the most densely populated state in Africa due mainly to the population's strict Catholic beliefs about family planning. It is one of Africa's poorest countries, with a per capita income in 1983 of $270. Coffee and tea are the leading cash exports, and many Rwandan farmers grow a species of flower (chrysanthemum) which is processed into an insecticide.

Rwanda is famed for a species of rare mountain gorilla. In late 1985, headlines were made when Dr. Dian Fossey, the internationally respected American naturalist who had studied these gorillas, was found slain in her cabin in Rwanda.The 1988 movie, *Gorilla's In The Mist,* documents her life in Rwanda.

## Sao Tome and Principe

***Date of independence:*** July 10, 1975
***Area:*** 372 square miles
***Population:*** 100,000 (est. 1987)
***Capital:*** Sao Tome
***Monetary unit:*** Dobra
***Nationality:*** Sao Tomean
***Religion:*** Roman Catholic, Evangelical, Seventh Day Adventist
***Language:*** Portuguese (official)
***Literacy:*** 54%
***Type of government:*** Republic
***Political parties/leaders:*** Unicameral Popular Assembly is the supreme organ of the state and designates the President No other political parties
***Monetary conversion rate:*** 35.89 dobras = $1 US (1987)
***Principal economic resources:*** Cocoa, coconut, palm oil, coffee, bananas, copra

### History at a Glance

Most of the people inhabiting Sao Tome and Principe are descendants of the original Portuguese colonists and African slaves from Gabon and other parts of the Guinea coast as far south as Angola. The Angolares, descendants of Angolan slaves shipwrecked in the sixteenth century, live along the south and west coast of Sao Tome. They have been joined there by a large number of migrant laborers who have come from other Portuguese territories on the mainland for the purpose of working on the numerous plantations scattered through the islands.

The islands are located about 125 miles west of the African coast in the Gulf of Guinea.

Independence was granted on July 12, 1975 as part of Portugal's dissolution of its African possessions. Most of the Europeans on the islands left at this time.

Dr. Manuel Pinto da Costa assumed the presidency with the support of the Movement for the Liberation of Sao Tome and Principe (MLSTP). A constitution was approved on December 12, 1975 which named a Popular Assembly as the supreme organ of the state, but neither Assembly members nor da Costa have undergone reelection. Opposition groups are largely exiled in Angola, Gabon and Portugal.

A Marxist, da Costa set about socializing the country's resources, including the lucrative cocoa plantations. Under state management, however, productions dropped from

11,586 tons in 1983 to 3,000 tons in 1987. After food riots broke out, da Costa returned the plantations to private control.

For many years, da Costa enjoyed warm relations with the Soviet Union and Cuba, which have strong interests to the south in Angola. As of 1986, about 750 Cuban and Soviet Union troops were stationed in Sao Tome as "protectors." In 1988, da Costa was tipped off by Angola President Jose Eduardo dos Santos about a coup attempt, and arrested the rebel leader and 40 others when they landed on the island.

Recently, though, da Costa opened up to Western interests, visiting Washington, D.C., and several European capitals. A close friend is Albert-Bernard Bongo, the pro-Western president of Gabon.

Foreign aid, much of it from Western sources, accounted for more than 40% of the gross national product in 1986. The same year, Sao Tome ended an accord with the Soviet Union for use of its excellent fishing waters, and initiated one with the European Community. The per capita income in 1984 was $330.

## Senegal

***Date of independence:*** On August 20, 1960, formed Senegambia Confederation with The Gambia on December 17, 1981
***Area:*** 75,750 square miles
***Population:*** 6,800,000 (est. 1987)
***Capital:*** Dakar
***Monetary unit:*** CFA franc
***Nationality:*** Senegalese
***Religion:*** Islam 91%, Christian 6%, Animist
***Language:*** French(official), Wolof vernacular
***Literacy:*** 10%
***Type of government:*** Republic
***Political parties/leaders:*** Socialist Party, Senegalese Democratic Party, African Independence Party
***Monetary conversion rate:*** 304.50 francs = $1 US (1987)
***Principal economic resources:*** Peanuts, millet, cotton, rice, sorghum

### History at a Glance

Parts of what is today Senegal were at different times ruled by the empires of Tekrur, Ghana, and Mali, the last of which reached the zenith of its power in the fourteenth century.

The first Europeans to arrive in this general area—along the Cape Verde peninsula and in the estuary of the Gambia River—were the Portuguese, who were soon followed by the English and the French. French activity was concentrated around the trading post of Saint Louis and the island of Goree, just outside the city of Dakar.

In the nineteenth century, the French began cultivating peanuts in the valleys of Senegal, and this crop came to be the staple of a predominantly agricultural economy.

On the political front, four large municipalities (Saint Louis, Goree, Dakar, and Rufisque) won the right to choose a single deputy to be seated in the French parliament. However, the first African deputy was not elected until 1914. At the end of World War II, Senegal, as part of the French Union, was permitted to send two representatives to the Chamber of Deputies in Paris.

In 1946, a constitution was drawn up, and a territorial assembly established. By 1957, universal suffrage had been introduced. A year later, Senegal ratified the new Constitution of French president de Gaulle, thus becoming an autonomous republic within the French Community.

Senegal joined the short-lived Mali Federation in 1959, only to withdraw a year later when the Legislative Assembly declared the country independent.

Leopold Sedar Senghor, who was leader of the Senegalese Progressive Union and considered to be one of the most highly respected intellectuals in Africa, served as President from 1960 until his retirement in 1980. Senghor's tenure was not wholly peaceful—he survived at least one coup attempt—but he supervised three revisions of the constitution, reinstituted the post of prime minister and in 1976, passed an amendment sanctioning three political parties, each with a prescribed ideology. Although he was reelected for a fourth five-year term in 1978, Senghor announced his resignation in November 1980. Abdou Diouf, who had served as Prime Minister for 11 years, succeeded him on January 2, 1981, and was reelected to five-year terms in February 1983 and 1988. He also served as head of the Organization of African Unity.

By the end of 1981, Senegal and The Gambia had formed the Confederation of Senegambia, wherein "each... shall maintain its independence and sovereignty." As Senegalese President, Diouf served as president of the Senegambia cabinet, while Gambian President Alhaji Sir Dawda Jawara became vice president. A joint council of ministers, composed of six Senegalese and five Gambians, met in early 1983 to create nine areas of planned cooperation, including formation of military police and a Senegambian army which would be mobilized by both presidents.

The confederation came about as a result of an August 1981 uprising in the Gambian capital of Banjul, which was put down by 2,000 Senegalese troops, acting at Jawara's request.

One problem which remained unresolved by 1988 was the monetary difference: The Gambia, which uses the dalasi, was reluctant to join Senegal in the French-backed CFA franc zone.

In Senegal, Diouf has fought to lift his country from the economic ravages of Sahelian drought, desertification and massive debt. In 1986, the Diama Dam was built with $100 million of foreign aid on the Senegal River, which forms the border with Mauritania to the north.

Domestically, Diouf's socialist government has allowed political diversification, including the formation of the opposition, five-party Senegalese Democratic Alliance. Diouf's reelection in 1988, however, was greeted by the worst rioting in 20 years, when he defeated Senegalese Democratic Party leader Abdoulaye Wade.

Diouf has also had to put down secessionist forces in Senegal's southern Creole/Portuguese-speaking region which desire separation from the more self-serving, French-speaking northern region.

In 1987, plans were underway to create a museum on the

A fisherman with his fishing net at the Senegal River.

island of Goree, off the coast of Dakar, to commemorate the millions of Africans which were shipped to slavery in the New World from its shores.

Senegal is formally unaligned but pro-Western and retains close ties with France. It has participated in several African development groups and strengthened relations with Gambia, Liberia, Guinea, and the Ivory Coast.

Severe droughts in recent years forced the government to apply stringent economic policies which in turn have sparked student unrest and demonstrations. Peanuts remain the principal export, accounting for one-third of the country's exports, but successive poor harvests have necessitated foreign assistance. Per capita income was $490 in 1985 but had fallen to $338 by 1988.

## Seychelles

***Date of independence:*** June 29, 1976
***Area:*** 171 square miles
***Population:*** 65,490 (est. 1987)
***Capital:*** Victoria
***Monetary unit:*** Seychelles rupee
***Religion:*** 90% Roman Catholic
***Language:*** English (official), Creole
***Literacy:*** 65%
***Type of government:*** Republic
***Political parties/leaders:*** Seychelles People's United Party
***Monetary conversion rate:*** 6.23 rupees = $1 US (1987)
***Principal economic resources:*** Cinnamon, coconut, fish

### History at a Glance

Discovered by Portugal in 1505, the Seychelles became a pirates' base until they were settled by France in the mid-eighteenth century. In 1794, Great Britain took control of the islands and, by 1810, had made them a dependency of the British colony of Mauritius. Four years later, at the signing of the Peace of Paris, the French officially ceded them to Great Britain. In 1903, the Seychelles became a separate colony, with a governor as well as executive and legislative councils.

Though blessed with a pleasant climate, the Seychelles are very poor. Unemployment has risen as plantations have increasingly mechanized. The annual birthrate, 38 per 1,000, is very high.

The Republic of Seychelles consists of 92 islands in the Indian Ocean northeast of Madagascar.

They were seized from France by the British in 1810 and remained a colony until independence was granted on June 29, 1976. The state is an independent republic within the Commonwealth.

The first president, James Mancham, was ousted in abstentia on June 5, 1977, after a year-long rule marked by "lavish spending." Albert Rene assumed power, backed by the guns of Tanzanian troops secretly flown in for the occasion.

Rene was confirmed in office for a five-year term in 1979 and again in June 1984. However, he has spent most of his time in office derailing coup attempts against him.

In November 1979, he denounced a coup attempt "from abroad" and arrested nearly 100 Seychellois, including two high-ranking government officials. In November 1981, another major coup was attempted, this one led by Colonel Michael "Mad Mike" Hoare, an Irishman who has been involved in numerous African destabilization efforts. In 1986, another assassination attempt was discovered, which involved the Seychellois minister of defense, who later fled to England.

Rene received troops from North Korea in 1984 and currently uses some 125 North Koreans as bodyguards.

Copra accounts for about two-thirds of the export earnings followed by fish and cinnamon. Tourism has increased due to the opening of an international airport on the main island of Mahe. However, the overall economy has remained depressed and nearly one-third of the population has emigrated.

## Sierra Leone

***Date of independence:*** April 27,1961
***Area:*** 27,699 square miles
***Population:*** 3,900,000 (est.1987)
***Capital:*** Freetown
***Monetary unit:*** Leone
***Nationality:*** Sierra Leonean
***Religion:*** Animist 52%, Islam 40%, Christian 9%
***Language:*** English (official), (unofficial) Mende, Temne, Krio dialects
***Literacy:*** 25%
***Type of government:*** Republic (presidential regime)
***Political parties/leaders:*** All People's Congress
***Monetary conversion rate:*** 43.10 leones = $1 US (1987)

***Principal economic resources:*** Diamonds, bauxite, chromite, iron ore, coffee, cocoa, ginger, rice

### History at a Glance

Founded in 1787 by Granville Sharp, an English abolitionist, Sierra Leone was first settled by black slaves who had been brought to England and freed there.

Granted a royal charter in 1799, Sierra Leone ("The Province of Freedom") was first governed by a town council, complete with a mayor and aldermen. However, after several attacks on the settlement by hostile tribes, Great Britain decided to bring the colony under the direct administration of the Crown. When the English parliament ruled the slave trade illegal in 1807, Sierra Leone came to be utilized as a base from which slave runners could be hunted down.

The frontiers of Sierra Leone were not settled until late in the nineteenth century. At this time, the hinterlands of the territory were declared a British protectorate, a move which caused considerable tribal unrest. The Mende and Temne peoples in particular were opposed to a hut tax imposed by the officials of the Crown.

In 1924 the Constitution under which the colony had been governed was revised to provide for the election of three Sierra Leoneans to posts on the Legislative Council. Again, in 1951, a new Constitution was promulgated, ushering in a system of party rule through a duly elected African majority, whose decisions, however, were still subject to the veto of an English resident. Five years later, the Legislative Council gave way to a House of Representatives, consisting of 39 members and 12 chiefs.

In 1958, Dr. Milton Margai formed the first Cabinet, and three years later the country achieved full independence within the British Commonwealth. Prime Minister Margai died in 1964 and was succeeded by his brother, Albert, who was overthrown in 1967 by Dr. Siaka Stevens, head of the All People's Congress. Stevens was temporarily overthrown by an army coup, but was reinstated in 1968.

For the next several years, the Stevens regime battled with opponents, declaring states of emergency, banning political parties, and nearly succumbing to various coup attempts. In a constitutional referendum in 1978, the country was finally declared a one-party state and Stevens was elected to a seven-year term.

In 1985, the 80-year-old Stevens retired, and transferred power to Major General Joseph S. Momoh, who was later confirmed in a single-party balloting.

Momoh has been criticized for not cracking down on government corruption left over from the Stevens regime, and for not reviving the economy. A trap laid for him in March 1987 was avoided due to a tipster. He has also faced internal unrest posed by an influx of Lebanese Shiite Moslem emigrants, who fight with Lebanese Christians.

Momoh has been successful in curtailing some of the diamond smuggling which has cost the country an estimated $100 million in export revenue. The nation's unique currency, greatly devalued in recent years, has been another source of trouble: Sierra Leoneans have been more likely to smuggle their rice, diamonds, and gold to neighboring countries in order to earn more marketable cash. The per capita income in 1983 was $380.

In 1987, Momah was pursuing France to sign an agreement to utilize Sierra Leone's excellent fishing grounds. So far, the Soviet Union has enjoyed a virtual monopoly on the waters.

## Somalia

***Date of independence:*** July 1, 1960
***Area:*** 246,199 square miles
***Population:*** 4,700,000 (est. 1987) plus 500,000 to 850,000 refugees from Ethiopia
***Capital:*** Mogadishu
***Monetary unit:*** Somali shilling
***Nationality:*** Somali
***Religion:*** Islam
***Language:*** Somali, Arabic, Italian, English
***Literacy:*** 60%
***Type of government:*** Republic
***Political parties/leaders:*** Somali Revolutionary Socialist Party (since 1976)
***Monetary conversion rate:*** 6,295 Somali shillings = $1 (1980)
***Principal economic resources:*** Livestock, bananas, sorghum, peanuts, sugar cane, cotton, maize

### History at a Glance

The ancient Egyptians visited Somalia (Land of Aromatics) during the pre-Christian era in search of incense and aromatic herbs.

From A.D. 900 to 1400 the eastern coast of the territory was part of the Zenj Empire, which fell in the fifteenth century to Portugal. Later, Arabs from Muscat and Oman asserted their control over Somalia's major coastal centers, to be replaced in the nineteenth century by the Sultan of Zanzibar.

European contact with this region dates back to 1839, the year that Aden came under the domination of Great Britain. Effective control was not established, however, until the English signed between 1884 and 1886, a number of "protectorate" treaties with various Somali chieftains in the north. The Italians, meanwhile, began to expand into Southern Somalia in 1885, establishing administrative control and consolidating their territory by extensive military operations. Great Britain first began to administer her protectorate through the Colonial Office in 1905, and was embroiled in conflict with a rebellious local chief until 1920.

From 1934 to 1936, Italy used Somalia as a staging area for the invasion of Ethiopia, establishing at the same time a colonial government to administer most of Somalia, as well as Ogaden (the eastern portion of Ethiopia and the home of many Somalis).

During World War II, Italian troops occupied British Somaliland, but they lost control of this region with their defeat in 1941 at the hands of the British. Italian Somaliland was itself occupied by British troops until 1950, at which time it was returned to Italy under a 10-year trusteeship arrangement. By then, the United Nations had already decided that Italian Somaliland should receive its independence by 1960. (In 1954, matters had been complicated somewhat by the transference of a portion of British controlled Ogaden to Ethiopia.) Unification of the two territories and their subsequent independence was achieved in 1960.

Since then, Somali-inhabited sections of both Kenya and Ethiopia have repeatedly expressed a desire to be reunited with Somalia. In 1953, diplomatic relations were severed with Kenya over this issue, and two years later, fighting broke out with Ethiopia over much the same question. As might be expected, Somalia has also advocated self-determination for the inhabitants of French Somaliland, including the port of Djibouti, terminus of the Ethiopian railroad.

In 1967, a popular election put President Abdirashid Ali Shermarke in office and Mohammed Haji Ibrahim Egal as Prime Minister. These two men guided Somalia in to Western-oriented relationships and conciliation with neighboring states.

However, a 1969 coup led by Major General Mohammed Siad Barre ended in Shermarke's assassination and a reorganization of the country along socialist lines. Soon foreign banks and other foreign-controlled establishments were nationalized and local governments were introduced in eight regions and 48 districts.

On July 1, 1976, Barre dissolved the Supreme Revolutionary Council, which had been instituted at the time of the coup, and formed the Somali Revolutionary Socialist Party, the nation's only legal party. In late 1979, a 171-member People's Assembly was elected under a new Constitution and Barre was confirmed as President. He was reelected to a second seven-year term in December 1986. By 1988, his poor health and advancing age gave rise to speculation as to how long he could remain in office.

At the start of his tenure, Barre maintained close ties with the Soviet Union, allowing the Soviets to build a naval base at Berbera in return for assistance in building up Somalia's 9,000-man army. Meanwhile, the Soviet Union chose to ignore the decades-old rivalry between Somalia and Ethiopia, and poured money into Ethiopia's new Marxist regime of Lieutenant Colonel Mengistu Haile-Mariam.

In 1977, Somalia openly backed rebels in Ethiopia's Ogaden desert, who were struggling to overthrow Ethiopia's claim to the land. The Soviet Union took Ethiopia's side, and cut off military aid to Somalia. Somalia retaliated by expelling some 1,500 Soviet personnel and breaking diplomatic relations with a number of Soviet bloc countries.

Eventually, after full-scale fighting, Somalia conceded defeat in the Ogaden and in March 1978, accepted some $13 million in U.S. food aid. Military aid was withheld until Somalia relinquished claims to northern Kenya, the Ogaden and the Republic of Djibouti, all of which were contained in the so-called "Greater Somalia." In 1979, although the Somalian constitution still called for the "liberation of Somali territories under colonial occupation," the Somalis promised not to intervene militarily in dissident activities. Border relations with Ethiopia remained tense, but in 1984, Barre agreed, following a visit from Kenyan President Daniel Moi, that Somalia no longer "had any claim" to Kenyan territory.

Beginning in January 1980, the U.S. has poured billions of dollars of military and economic aid into Somalia, in return for bases for U.S. planes and ships. In 1986, relations with the Soviet Union were "normalized."

In 1984-85, Somalia was swamped by some 500,000 to 850,000 Ethiopians fleeing drought and mass starvation, and later, the forced villagization policies of Mengistu.

Somalia is the world's largest producer of incense, which was sold around $36 a kilo in 1987. Due to drought, refugee influx and civil strife, the country has made no substantive economic growth in the past two decades. Per capita income in 1983 was $228.

## South Africa

***Date of independence:*** 1934
***Area:*** 471,445 square miles
***Population:*** 34,400,000 (est.1987)
***Capital:*** Pretoria
***Monetary unit:*** Rand
***Nationality:*** South African
***Religion:*** Dutch Reformed 40%, Anglican 11%, Catholic 8%, other Christian 25%, Hindu, Islam
***Language:*** English, Afrikaans, 9 Bantu dialects
***Literacy:*** Whites 100%, blacks 50%
***Type of government:*** Republic
***Political parties/leaders:*** National Party, four white opposition parties, 11 non-white parties
***Monetary conversion rate:*** **2.07 rands = $1 US (1987)**
***Principal economic resources:*** Corn, wool, wheat, sugar cane, gold, diamonds, platinum, uranium

### History at a Glance

Fossils discovered in South Africa lend evidence to speculation that the country is one of the earliest homes of mankind. Before Bartholomew Diaz of Portugal discovered the Cape of Good Hope in 1488, this huge area was inhabited by Bushmen, nomadic hunters confined to the western uplands, and by Hottentots, a pastoral people settled largely in its southern and eastern coastal sectors. At the same time, however, there was increased migration from the north by Bantu-speaking peoples who today live primarily in "reserves" set aside for them by the government.

On Christmas Day in 1497, Vasco da Gama discovered Natal, bordering on the Mozambique Channel, but South Africa itself did not come to be settled by Europeans until 1652. In that year, Jan van Riebeeck brought the first colonists into the Cape of Good Hope region under the sponsorship of the Dutch East India Company. The settlers began to import slaves from West Africa almost immediately, and with the scarcity of European women, eventually entered into mixed marriages which produced the so-called Cape Colored people. The Dutch, who were known as Boers, or "farmers," were soon joined by French, Scandinavian, and German immigrants who adopted the name "Afrikaaners" to distinguish themselves from the rest of the population.

The first contacts with Bantu-speaking Africans were

*Mourners at Lagna Township in Uitenhage on the International Day for the Elimination of Racial Discrimination, a commemorative day for those killed by South African police.*

made along the Great Fish River in the 1730s. By 1778, boundaries had been set up to separate the settlers from the Africans. Within the year, the first Kaffir War had broken out between the Xhosa tribesmen and the colonists.

In 1795, Great Britain took charge of the Cape region, and by 1815, pursuant to the Treaty of Vienna, had extended official control over the territory. English settlers began arriving in 1820. From the outset, England granted the free "Cape Colored" people the same legal and political privileges as white people, and in fact, abolished slavery in 1834. Two years later, the Dutch (Boers), alienated by these policies, undertook their great northward trek, defeating Bantu tribesmen in the interior, to found the Natal, Transvaal, and Orange Free State territories.

The British, however, followed close on the heels of the Boers annexing Natal in 1843, Kaffraria in 1847, Griqualand West in 1874, Bechuanaland in 1885, and Zululand and Tongaland in 1887. In 1848, the Orange Free State was taken over by the British, only to regain its independence six years later. The Transvaal was made independent in 1852, annexed in 1877, and returned to independence in 1881, the same year in which Swaziland achieved this status.

Despite the preponderance of British political influence, economic factors in the territory accounted for much of its social development during the nineteenth century. The growth of the sugar cane plantations in Natal led to the importation of thousands of east Indians who worked off their period of indenture and then remained in the territory as tradesmen and fishermen. The discovery of diamonds along the Orange and Vaal Rivers (1868) and of gold on the Witwatersrand (1886) hastened the fanatically systematic creation of separate white and black communities. Within the white communities, however, friction between the Dutch farmers and the "outsiders" (English and others) soon led to armed conflict, culminating in the Boer War, which was won by the British in 1902.

The Union of South Africa was formed in 1910 and consisted of the two Boer republics, which by then had been granted self-government by the British, and the Cape and Natal provinces. In 1926, South Africa was given equal legal status with Great Britain, and the right to associate freely with the sovereign members of the British Commonwealth.

Despite the restoration of peace, Boer-English relations continued to be marked by wholesale bitterness and recrimination. Two political parties emerged—the Unionists on the one hand advocating cooperation with Great Britain and the Boer supremacists (the group in power today) who ultimately conceived and executed the policy of "apartheid," or separate racial development.

During both world wars, Boer nationalists attempted to prevent South Africa from participating on the Allied side. They first managed to consolidate effective control over the country in 1948, the year in which Prime Minister Daniel Malan came to power. Since then, white-supremacist policies have become even more firmly entrenched, particularly now that industrial development has brought a tremendous improvement in the living standards of white South Africans.

In 1959, the Nationalists passed the Promotion of Bantu Self-Government Act which provided for the creation of eight separate autonomous states for blacks only. Two years later, concurrent with its withdrawal from the British Commonwealth, South Africa opted for a republican form of government, although its constitution barely changed.

South Africa continued to refine its program of apartheid, turning a deaf ear to the protests of the United Nations, the rest of Africa, and most of the civilized world. The state, then headed by Prime Minister Hendrik F. Verwoerd, had taken stern measures to suppress all forms of political opposition, censoring the press and other media, imprisoning citizens for up to six months with no formal charges and without a trial—in short, declaring all forms of objectionable activity as communist-inspired.

Late in 1966, Prime Minister Verwoerd was assassinated by Dimitrio Tsafendas, a white, who, ironically, thought that Verwoerd was doing too much for the black population.

Under Prime Minister Balthazar J. Vorster, South Africa strengthened its defense establishment in anticipation of stepped-up guerrilla activity and possible sea and air attacks emanating from its black neighbors to the North. At the same time, the United Nations sought desperately to take control of South West Africa (now Namibia) due to South Africa's imposition of apartheid there, but had been unable to dislodge the republic from the mandated territory.

The late 1960s and early 1970s were an economic boom time for South Africa, though two-thirds of the national income went to the white fifth of the population.

A critical issue in the 1970s and 1980s has been the future of South West Africa, a former German territory that has

*Black youth of Langa Township.*

been ruled by South Africa since World War I. Local leaders appealed for help from the United Nations to gain independence under the name Namibia, and the country came under U.N. jurisdiction by a 1966 General Assembly resolution. However, South Africa has refused to relinquish the country to its most powerful nationalist group, the South West Africa People's Organization (SWAPO), and instead installed 18,000 troops there. South Africa was later ousted from the United Nations and remains barred from the General Assembly to date.

Other crises in the 1970s which attracted South African military intervention included the Marxist Angolan government's battle with Dr. Jonas Savimbi's UNITA guerillas. Cuba bolstered the Angolan troops while South Africa aided UNITA. On the other side of the continent, unrest in Zimbabwe (formerly Rhodesia) escalated and military aid was given to assist the failing Ian Smith government.

In 1977, South Africa experienced the worst outbreak of racial violence since the Sharpeville riots in 1960. The bloodshed, which began in the black township of Soweto, a suburb of Johannesburg, grew out of black student protests against the compulsory use of Afrikaans as the language of instruction. As a result, many theaters and opera houses were desegregated, though the Vorster government gave no indication of wanting to end apartheid restrictions altogether. Instead, it insisted that the blacks in South Africa are not segregated because of their race but rather because they represent distinct "nations" to which special political and constitutional arrangements should be made. It was in accordance with this philosophy that independence was granted to the "homelands" of Transkei in October 1976, Bophuthatswana in December 1977, Venda in September 1979, and Ciskei in 1981. An attempt to overthrow the president of Bophuthatswana in February 1988 was put down by South African troops.

Rioting intensified greatly after September 12, 1977, after the controversial death of anti-apartheid activist Steven Biko, when it was discovered that he died from a head injury while in prison. As a result, the government invoked some of its strictest policies in two decades, closing down the leading black newspaper, arresting its editor, and banning a number of protest groups.

Prime Minister Vorster was forced to resign on June 4, 1979, following a scandal involving $11 million which was supposed to have been used to buy *The Washington Star* for propaganda purposes.

Prime Minister Pieter W. Botha, designated by the National Party in 1978, officially elected in 1984, and reelected in May 1987, has steadily yielded ground to apartheid's opponents, but has resisted giving legitimate political power to the nation's black majority.

In 1984, Anglican Bishop Desmond Tutu, a black, was awarded the Nobel Peace Prize for his anti-apartheid stance.

In 1985, the government abolished the Mixed Marriages Act, and lifted bans against multiracial political movements. Still, the efforts were seen as "too little, too late," and riots

*A girl winnows hand-threshed rice at a U.N. agricultural station designed to promote modern methods of farming among primitive tribesmen. The Sudanese government has set up a number of such experimental farms to raise the living standard of the population.*

broke out. In July 1985, a state of emergency was declared in 35 black townships, and a policy of detaining individuals without trial was implemented. By 1988, an estimated 20,000 to 30,000 persons had been incarcerated under that rule, with perhaps 1,500 left to languish in custody.

In the January 1986 opening of Parliament, Botha shocked the council by declaring, "We have outgrown the outdated colonial system of paternalism, as well as the outdated concept of apartheid." Efforts to dismantle apartheid, including ending pass laws, continued at an unacceptably slow pace, and in June, riots broke out on the anniversary of the 1976 Soweto uprising.

Numerous nations have cut trade with South Africa because of its apartheid practices and occupation of Namibia. In 1986, the United States Congress, overriding a veto by President Reagan, voted limited economic sanctions against South Africa, including forbidding landing rights to South Africa Airlines. Some U.S. businesses, bowing to pressure, began to divest themselves of South African holdings. European Community members voted to ban a variety of South African imports.

Domestically, most of South Africa's neighbors have declared themselves "Front-Line" States, and called for black majority rule in South Africa. Due, however, to their impoverished economies and trade route dependencies with South Africa, many of these countries have not been able to effect economic sanctions. Instead, several have given tacit shelter to the outlawed ANC rebels. South African forces have, in turn, violated national borders to bomb and raid ANC camps in Zimbabwe, Zambia, Mozambique and elsewhere.

Black South Africans have retaliated by striking, including a three-week walkout in August 1987 involving some 300,000 gold miners. That strike did not bear good fruit: some 35,000 miners were dismissed, union demands were not met, and the government curtailed union influence. More effective was a rent strike in 1988, imposed by Soweto residents, which had cost the township more than $100 million after 20 months.

South Africa is the first African country to experience the full force of the Industrial Revolution. Its gold mines supply about two-thirds of the gold produced by non-communist countries. Other important mineral products include diamonds, copper, asbestos, chrome and platinum.

Agriculturally, South Africa is self-sufficient in most foods. Its principal deficiency is oil, although that is mitigated by large coal reserves.

After a stagnant period in the mid-1980s, South Africa's economy began to grow by 1987. Gold export earnings of $8 billion in 1986 and other mineral export revenues kept the economy relatively immune to outside sanctions.

Per capita incomes continued to be disproportionate by race: for example, in 1988, the average monthly wage of a black miner was $153, as compared to $765 of a white miner.

### South African Dependency of Bophuthatswana

***Date of independence:*** December 6, 1977
***Area:*** 15,571 square miles
***Population:*** 1,500,000 (est. 1987)
***Capital:*** Mmabatho
***Monetary unit:*** South African rand
***Religion:*** Methodist, Lutheran, Anglican
***Language:*** Setswana, also English, Africaan
***Political party:*** Bophuthatswana Democratic Party
***Monetary conversion rate:*** 2.07 rands = $1 US (1987)
***Principal economic resource:*** Platinum

### South African Dependency of Transkei

***Date of independence:*** October 26,1976
***Area:*** 15,831 square miles
***Population:*** 2,830,000 (est.1987)
***Capital:*** Umtata
***Monetary unit:*** South African rand
***Religion:*** 66% Christian, 24% Animist
***Language:*** Xhosa, English, Africaan
***Political parties:*** Transkei Congress Party, two opposition parties
***Monetary conversion rate:*** 2.07 rands = $1 US (1987)
***Principal economic resources:*** Tea, beans,corn, sorghum, timber

### South African Dependency of Venda

***Date of independence:*** September 13, 1979
***Area:*** 2,861 square miles
***Population:*** 450,000 (est. 1987)
***Capital:*** Thohoyandou
***Monetary unit:*** South African rand
***Religion:*** Christian, tribal
***Language:*** English, Africaans, Luvenda
***Political parties:*** Venda National Party, Venda Independence Party (opposition)

***Monetary conversion rate:*** 2.07 rands = $1 US (1987)
***Principal economic resources:*** Meat, tea, fruit, timber, graphite

### Sudan

***Date of independence:*** January 1, 1956
***Area:*** 967,494 square miles
***Population:*** 23,500,000 (est.1981)
***Capital:*** Khartoum
***Monetary unit:*** Sudanese pound
***Religion:*** 73% Sunni Muslim, 23% Pagan, 4% Christian
***Language:*** Arabic (official), Nubian, English
***Literacy:*** 20%
***Type of government:*** Republic (under military control since May 1969)
***Political parties/leaders:*** Umma Party, Democratic Unionist Party, 7 other parties, one insurgent group
***Monetary conversion rate:*** 2.50 pounds = $1 US (1987)
***Principal economic resources:*** Cotton, peanuts, sesame seeds, gum Arabic, sorghum, wheat, sugar cane

#### History at a Glance

Sudanese history reflects the country's natural division between the predominantly Arab North (which for centuries has lived in close contact with the civilizations of Egypt, Rome, Byzantium, and Turkey) and the black-dominated South (which has been virtually isolated from significant contact with North African and Near Eastern culture).

In antiquity, the center of Sudan lay in what is today the eastern portion of the territory—that is, in the vicinity of the kingdom of Meroe (750 B.C.-A.D. 300) which even ruled Egypt for a time.

Beginning in the ninth century A.D., nomadic tribes from neighboring Egypt penetrated other areas of the Sudan, intermarrying with the indigenous peoples of the Upper Nile region. From 1500 to 1820, control over most of central and northern Sudan rested with a confederation of tribes ruled and administered by the "Black Sultans" of the Funj dynasty.

In 1820, Sudan was conquered by the Ottoman viceroy of Egypt, Mohammed Ali. Some 50 years passed before the Khedive Ismail led a campaign against the slave trade, and as a result, moved down the Nile into the Southern Sudan.

Soon after, several Sudanese tribes rallied to the side of Muhammad Ahmad, who proclaimed himself the Mahdi, a religious leader believed to be acting under the inspiration of Allah, and led a number of Sudanese tribes in a successful revolt against Anglo-Egyptian rule. The Mahdi took possession of Khartoum and put to death the British governor, General Charles Gordon. In 1898, Anglo-Egyptian forces under General Kitchener defeated the Mahdi's successor in the battle of Obdurman. British rule was then established through a nominal Anglo-Egyptian condominium (a jointly ruled territory) which remained in effect until 1955.

Sudanese nationalism became a force after World War I, when differences were growing more pronounced between Moslem Northerners and the black tribes of the South who were falling under the influence of Christian missionaries and the British educational system. The split gradually widened between those seeking union with Egypt and those advocating the establishment of a separate state.

During World War II, British-led Sudanese troops complied an outstanding combat record, particularly against superior and better equipped Italian forces. Later, several schemes for a unified state encompassing the entire Nile Valley were advanced, but agreement was not reached by the negotiating parties, Great Britain, Egypt, and the Sudan, until 1953, the year Egypt's King Farouk was deposed.

The new republic of Sudan came into being three years later. Within a short time, the government had launched its Arabization-of-the-South program which had widespread repercussions, leading to the eventual overthrow of the existing parliamentary regime by a military junta headed by Lieutenant General Ibrahim Abbud. In 1964, a popular revolution swept the army aside, but by this time the question of Sudanese unity threatened to plunge the nation into civil war.

Though secessionist activity subsided in the late 1960s, the Sudan was still troubled by internal turmoil and a growing financial deficit. The nation relinquished American aid in 1967 after breaking ties with the United States over the Arab-Israeli war. Two years later, a military coup headed by Gafaar Muhammed al-Nimeiry took over and set a socialist course.

A constitutional calm crept into the Sudan with al-Nimeiry's inauguration as President in 1971. Though beset by both communist and pro-Egyptian elements, Nimeiry has managed to pursue a moderate course. Three southern provinces of the country were given their own regional government, thus ending long-standing guerrilla warfare in this area.

In 1972, the Sudan resumed diplomatic relations with the United States, and stressed friendly relations with Ethiopia, Uganda, and its other neighbors. This shift in focus led to a decline in its friendship with Egypt.

In 1973, the United States Ambassador and charge d'affaires and a Belgian diplomat were killed by "Black September" Palestinian terrorists. The terrorists were convicted by a Sudanese court, but later freed by the Sudanese government and turned over to a Palestinian group in Egypt.

Numerous internal problems, including persistent charges of corruption, led to six cabinet reorganizations between 1970 and 1975.

In 1976, a third attempted coup against President Nimeiry left 1,000 rebels and loyal troops dead after a fierce battle in Khartoum. President Nimeiry blamed Libyan President Muammar Qaddafi for instigating the attempt and Sudan broke relations with Libya. Firing squads later executed 81 convicted rebels. President Nimeiry also charged the Soviets with complicity in the attempt and expelled 90 Soviet advisors.

Tensions between Egypt and Sudan had been strong, but in February 1974 an agreement coordinating political and economic strategies between the countries was signed. In 1979, Sudan distinguished itself by not breaking relations with Egypt, although, like all other Arab countries, it rejected the Egyptian-Israeli peace treaty.

In 1982, Sudan signed a "charter of integration" with

Egypt which would unite the two countries at some unspecified date.

In February 1983, Nimeiry was reelected president. His regime grew increasingly unpopular—a particularly hated move was to impose Islamic laws on the Christian and animist populations. In April 1985, in the 16th year of his rule, Nimeiry was deposed while on a trip to the United States. General Abd al-Rahman Siwar Al-Dahab, who led the military coup, became head of a Transitional Military Council. General elections were held the next year, which saw the elevation of the respected Islamic leader and Umma Party head, Sadiq el-Mahdi, to prime minister.

El-Mahdi has remained on good terms with the United States, despite a 15-year friendship with Libyan leader Qaddafi.

Major problems faced the new government. Of foremost concern was the ongoing civil war between the Arabic north and Christian-and-animist south, where people call themselves "Africans." Other ethnic divisions caused tensions. In 1984, it was estimated that Sudan encompassed 56 different ethnic groups using 115 languages.

Economic problems mushroomed, with foreign debt hitting $9 billion by 1984. The 1984-85 famine affected more than four million Sudanese and added one million Ethiopians to the multitude of refugees already sheltered in Sudanese borders. Ironically, impoverished Sudan was described in 1985 as harboring the third largest refugee population in the world, following Pakistan and Somalia.

Cotton has been a major cash crop followed by gum arabic, of which Sudan produces four-fifths of the world's supply.

Sudan's civil war has stalled two important projects: the procurement of some 200 million barrels of proven oil reserves located in the south, and the Jonglei Canal Project, a vast irrigation system along the Nile. The per capita income in 1984 was $320.

The summer of 1988 brought additional disasters: huge swarms of locusts destroyed five million acres of croplands in western Sudan, and unleashed another major famine. Elsewhere, severe flooding occurred. In Khartoum alone, 800,000 people lost their homes to water. Also in 1988, reports surfaced about the ongoing enslavement of Dinka men, women and children by Arabs in the north.

## Swaziland

***Date of independence:*** September 6,1968
***Area:*** 6,703 square miles
***Population:*** 700,000 (est.1987)
***Capital:*** Mbabane
***Monetary unit:*** Lilangeni
***Nationality:*** Swazi
***Religion:*** 77% Christian, 27% Animist
***Language:*** English, Siswati (both official)
***Literacy:*** 25%
***Type of government:*** Monarchy
***Political parties/leaders:*** King Mswati III
***Monetary conversion rate:*** 2.07 emalangeni = $1 US (1987)
***Principal economic resources:*** Corn, livestock, sugar cane, citrus fruits, cotton, rice, pineapple

### History at a Glance

Swaziland was settled in the early nineteenth century by the Swazi, a people of Bantu stock who had been driven from their homelands in northern Zululand by the Zulus. Swazi independence was guaranteed by Great Britain in 1881, and three years later by the Republic of South Africa. In 1890, a British-South African-Swazi government was established, with South Africa declaring a protectorate over the territory four years later. After the Boer War, Swaziland was administered by the governor of Transvaal. In 1907, it was placed under the control of the British High Commissioner for South Africa.

In 1967, Swaziland won a measure of self-government under a new constitution and, a year later, achieved full independence under King Sobhuza II. In 1972, Swaziland held its first general election since independence in 1968. A hint of opposition crept into the political pattern of the country, though it was not strong enough to keep the ruling Imbokodvo National Movement from forming another one-party government. The INM favors heightened cooperation with its neighbor, South Africa.

Major General Maphevu Dlamini, who had served as Prime Minister since 1976, died on October 25, 1979. Prince Mandabala Fred Dlamini was designated his successor a month later.

King Sobhuza, who died on August 21, 1982, at age 83, was the world's longest reigning monarch, having technically begun his rule as a 1-year-old.

Following his death, his son, 15-year-old Prince Makhosetive was named successor. In the interim before the crown prince was installed as King Mswati III in 1986, a number of palace power struggles took place. Various people were installed and deposed, including King Sobhuza's senior wife, Queen Regent Dzeliwe Shongwe. In 1983, Prince Bhekimpi Dlamini succeeded Prince Fred Dlamini as prime minister, and later the prince's mother, Queen Regent Notmbi Thwala, was named head of state.

When he finally came to power, two years ahead of schedule, King Mswati, now the world's youngest monarch, quickly consolidated his power and named Prince Sotsha Dlamini as his prime minister.

King Mswati followed in his father's footsteps, maintaining good relations with South Africa as well as diplomatic relations with Mozambique.

The economy is quite diversified, considering the country's small size and population. Production of iron ore, which once accounted for a quarter of the export earnings, virtually ceased by the end of the 1970s. Coal mining, on the other hand, is increasing and additional minerals such as tin, barites, and silica have been found in some abundance. In 1986, three-quarters of Swaziland's revenue came from trade with South Africa, and some 16,000 Swazi citizens worked in the larger country.

In light of international economic sanctions imposed against South Africa, there was some discussion of Swaziland becoming a "back door" for trade, in a situation similar to that of Hong Kong serving as an outlet for China.

### Tanzania

***Date of independence:*** December 9,1961
***Area:*** 364,898 square miles
***Population:*** 23,500,000 (est.1987)
***Capital:*** Dar es Salaam
***Monetary unit:*** Shilling
***Religion:*** Islam 60%, Christian 25%, Animist 15%
***Language:*** English (official), Swahili, local languages
***Literacy:*** 79%
***Type of government:*** Republic (single party)
***Political parties/leaders:*** Revolutionary Party of Tanzania No other recognized parties.
***Monetary conversion rate:*** 55.30 shillings = $1 US (1987)
***Principal economic resources:*** Sugar, maize, rice, wheat, cotton, coffee, iron, coal, natural gas

#### History at a Glance

Since 1959 Tanzania has been able to claim the distinction of being the aboriginal home of mankind. It was in this year that Dr. L. S. B. Leakey discovered *homozinjanthropus* in the Olduvai Gorge near Serengeti National Park. Knowledge of the early history of the region is scant, although it is certain that East Africa as a whole was involved in trade with Greece, Arabia, Persia, India, and even China.

The coastal region of Tanzania, then known as Tanganyika, first attracted Arab colonists from Oman in the eighth century A.D. and Persian settlers a century later. For the next 500 years, a number of coastal towns enjoyed considerable commercial prosperity. During this period, Islam gained a secure foothold along the coast and the Swahili language and culture developed among the Bantu tribes of the region.

Portugal came on the scene in the sixteenth century, wresting the Indian Ocean trade from the Arabs and conquering the coastal towns under the latter's control. The Portuguese themselves were driven from their coastal holdings during the next two centuries by Arab slave traders based on the nearby island of Zanzibar and loyal to the Omani sultans. The height of Arab influence on the mainland occurred in the nineteenth century under the Imam Seyyid Said. The plantation system introduced by Zanzibar around 1840 led to an extension of the slave trade which brought about considerable tribal unrest and warfare.

The first Europeans to explore the interior of Tanzania were the Englishmen Burton and Speke, who crossed the territory in 1857 in search of the headwaters of the Nile River. After the Berlin Conference of 1884-1885, Germany established a protectorate extending over the areas of Rwanda and Burundi (German East Africa). In 1890, Germany purchased a portion of the coast from the Sultan of Zanzibar, and gradually began to extend its influence farther into the interior, encountering stiff resistance from the African population. The Germans established plantations, built railways, improved communications, and substituted a system of forced labor for the slave trade.

After Germany's defeat in World War I, Tanzania was mandated to Great Britain by the League of Nations and retained this status until it was taken over by the United Nations after World War II.

By 1954 African nationalism had reached such a fever pitch in the territory that the Tanganyika African National Union (TANU) petitioned the United Nations to persuade Great Britain to establish a timetable for the specific steps leading to independence. In September 1960, Julius Nyerere became Tanganyika's chief minister. By the end of 1961 the territory had become fully independent.

Meanwhile, Zanzibar and its sister island, Pemba, had likewise begun to press Great Britain for autonomy. In 1964, shortly after Zanzibar had won its independence under an Arab-controlled government, a popular revolt was staged by the African-supported Afro-Shirazi Party (ASP). Both the sultan and the prime minister were deposed, and a republican government headed by Abeid Amani Karume was installed.

Three months later, Zanzibar merged with Tanganyika, creating what was at first called the United Republic of Tanganyika and Zanzibar and has since come to be known as Tanzania.

In 1972, after assassins killed Karume, Nyerere appointed the more-moderate Aboud Jumbe to be the ASP leader as well as first vice president of Tanzania.

In 1974-75, Nyerere began implementing a Chinese-inspired socialist economic plan, called "ujamaa," at the grass-roots level, moving some 11 million peasants into 8,000 collective villages. In 1977, TANU and ASP merged to form the Revolutionary Party of Tanzania (CCM).

The "ujamaa" program was curtailed by 1978 as fighting finally broke out between Tanzania and Uganda. Tensions had been building since 1972, when General Idi Amin came to power in Uganda. Tanzanian youths applying for work in Uganda had been disappearing, and before long, Ugandan rebels had set up bases in Tanzania.

Ugandan troops invaded Tanzania in November 1978, and were fiercely counter-attacked by 40,000 Tanzanian troops and 3,000 Ugandan exiles. By January 1979, a full-scale war had developed, which ended when the Tanzanian forces pushed north to successfully capture the Ugandan capital of Kampala in April. Amin fled to Libya.

Nyerere ordered some 20,000 Tanzanian soldiers to remain in Uganda until President Milton Obote, who had been deposed by Amin and was in exile in Tanzania, could be confirmed in national elections in December 1980. By the summer of 1981, all Tanzanians had been withdrawn.

The six-month war, later estimated to have cost $500 million, drained the Tanzanian economy and the nation's 18 million people faced daily shortages of such staples as bread and cooking oil.

Vice President Jumbe remained in office until January 1984, when he resigned. Zanzibar-born Ali Hassan Mwinyi was named as his replacement.

Meanwhile, the 63-year-old Nyerere, sometimes called the "George Washington of Tanzani," declared his intention to step down when his term expired. In 1985, in what was hailed as a "rare, peaceful transition of power," Mwinyi was elected as president of Tanzania.

Mwinyi, a pragmatic socialist, faced enormous economic problems, including a $2.6 billion international debt, floundering agricultural production, decline in the once-lucrative oil production, and entrenched government corruption. He reformed several of Nyerere's agricultural policies (some with Nyerere's blessing), allowing for private enterprise. By 1987, Tanzania's economy was at last growing faster than its population.

Major exports include coffee, cotton and sisal. Oil production was helped by the completion of the Tanzam Railway, which links Dar es Salaam and the Zambian copper belt. Cloves continued to account for 95% of Zanzibar's foreign exchange earnings. The per capita income was $210 in 1985.

Notable achievements under Nyerere, who in 1988 was continuing to play a role in Tanzania's government, included Africa's highest literacy rate of 79%, clean tap water to much of the nation, and frequent medical outposts. Average life expectancy grew from 30 years to 51 years.

Tanzania has no relations with South Africa, but reopened its border with Kenya in 1984 after a lengthy, acrimonious period.

Tourism was also being advanced for both the mainland and the islands. Tanzania is home to three of Africa's best known lakes (Victoria, Tanganyika, and Nyasa); Mount Kilimanjaro, the highest peak on the continent at 19,340 feet; and the famous Serengeti Plains.

A woman potter in Togoland.

## Togo

***Date of independence:*** April 27, 1960
***Area:*** 21,622 squaremiles
***Population:*** 3,200,000 (est. 1987)
***Capital:*** Lome
***Monetary unit:*** CFA franc
***Nationality:*** Togolese
***Religion:*** Animist 46%, Christian 37%, Islam 17%
***Language:*** French (official), four major African languages are spoken
***Literacy:*** 18%, 54.9% of school age children
***Type of government:*** Republic (under military rule since 1967)
***Political parties/leaders:*** Rally of the Togolese People
***Monetary conversion rate:*** 304.50 francs = $1 US (1987)
***Principal economic resources:*** Yams, manioc, millet, sorghum, cocoa, coffee, rice

### History at a Glance

Togo was first settled by the Ewe people, who migrated there from the Niger Valley between the twelfth and the fourteenth centuries.

During the next two centuries, the territory was frequently visited by the Portuguese, who instituted a thriving slave trade in Grand Popo and Petit Popo, two of Togo's coastal villages. The Portuguese were then displaced, first by the French, who established trading posts in the area, and then by the Germans, who ultimately won control over the territory by signing a treaty with the chief of Togo, then only a village on the coast. The Germans later applied the name Togo to the entire territory.

The Togolese capital of Lome was established in 1897 and, within a few years, boundary settlements had been arranged with England and France. These agreements paid scant attention to existing tribal unities, with the result that a number of groups found themselves simultaneously incorporated into three distinct colonial areas—Ghana, Togo, and Dahomey.

During World War I, England took over control of the coastal areas (British Togoland), whereas France administered Togo's interior (French Togoland). In 1922 the League of Nations sanctioned this wartime arrangement.

In 1945, England and France relinquished their holds on Togo to the United Nations. Two years later, the Ewe people sent the first of a number of petitions to the United Nations requesting assistance in the achievement of tribal and national unification. After nine years of debate (differences had to be resolved not only between England and France, but also between a number of conflicting tribes), a plebiscite was held in British Togoland, which was incorporated into the Republic of Ghana when that nation became independent in 1957.

French Togoland voted for full autonomy within the French Community, a decision opposed at first by the United

Nations. In 1960 the Republic of Togo became a sovereign nation, with Sylvanus Olympio as Prime Minister. When Olympio was assassinated in 1963, Nicholas Grunitzky, living in exile in Dahomey at the time, became Prime Minister.

President Etienne (later "Africanized" to Gnassingbe) Eyadema, seized power in 1967 through a military coup. He immediately banned all political parties until 1969, when he established the Rally of the Togolese People (RTP) as the legitimate party.

Eyadema was elected president in 1972 by "popular referendum," which so pleased him that he released all political prisoners. He has been reelected to subsequent seven-year terms in December 1979 and 1986.

Eyadema has been subjected to a number of coup attempts, including one in 1977 led by professional mercenaries, and another in September 1986 carried out by insurgents from Ghana. The latter episode caused the Ghana-Togo border to be closed briefly, while Togo called upon French military support.

Togo is one of the smallest and poorest African countries, with a per capita income near $300 in 1986.

Coffee, cocoa, and most recently, cotton are its primary exports. Phosphates are the most important mining activity, and a substantial amount of smuggling between Togo and Ghana enhances the country's meager economy. (Authorities have estimated that as much as a third of Togo's cocoa exports begin in Ghana, but are smuggled into Togo in exchange for luxury items.)

## Uganda

***Date of independence:*** October 9, 1962
***Area:*** 91,133 square miles
***Population:*** 15,500,000 (est.1987)
***Capital:*** Kampala
***Monetary unit:*** Uganda shilling
***Nationality:*** Ugandan
***Religion:*** Christian 63%, Animist 31%, Islam 6%
***Language:*** English (official), Luganda, Swahili
***Literacy:*** 52%
***Type of government:*** Republic
***Political parties/leaders:*** Uganda People's Congress, three opposition parties
***Monetary conversion rate:*** 1,400 shillings = $1 US (1987)
***Principal economic resources:*** Coffee, tea, cotton, tobacco, sugar, copper

### History at a Glance

According to the testimony of contemporary archeologists, tiny landlocked Uganda was the site of a highly developed African civilization long before European explorers opened up this portion of the African continent. Africans of Bantu stock built up a relatively advanced Iron Age civilization there. It remained intact until Hamitic peoples from the northeast overcame the Bantu.

The two mightiest kingdoms in the area were the Buganda to the north and the Bunyoro to the south. Arab slave traders took advantage of the clash between these two groups, which reached a climactic stage in the mid-nineteenth century.

In 1862, John Hanning Speke and Captain J. A. Grant explored the territory for Great Britain, as did Samuel Baker who discovered Lake Albert. Baker later returned to Uganda as a foreign agent for Egypt which had its own expansionist interests in the regions of the lower Nile. In 1875, Henry Stanley arrived in Uganda, and was followed by Christian missionaries seeking to win favor with the Kabaka (the king of Buganda).

In 1894, consistent with the role it had assigned itself in the carving up of Africa into different "spheres of influence," Great Britain established a formal protectorate over Buganda. In 1900, Sir Harry Johnstone negotiated the Uganda Agreement, giving the Buganda Kingdom a privileged position within the British-controlled territory. A year later, similar agreements were concluded with the kingdoms of Toro and Ankole.

In the first decade of the twentieth century, Sir Hesketh Bell, the British commissioner, drafted a program designed to assist development of cotton as a staple crop. Thus Uganda was spared the upheaval which later afflicted neighboring Kenya, where the predominant system of free speculation in land allowed white Europeans to win control of the choicest land and to establish a plantation-based economy.

On October 9, 1962, Uganda achieved independence within the British Commonwealth, with a national government representing the four traditional kingdoms. Sir Edward Mutesa II was elected president in October 1963.

In 1966, Prime Minister A. Milton Obote, leader of the Uganda People's Congress (UPC), overthrew Mutesa and suspended the constitution. By 1969, now-president Obote had unified or driven away leaders of the kingdoms, established a one-party state with a socialist program, and banned political parties. He also initiated what would be the hallmarks of Ugandan regimes for the next 15 years: unlicensed torture and murder of political enemies, and government theft of resources.

In 1971, Major General Idi Amin, the 43-year-old commander in chief of the army and air force, seized power while Obote was away at a conference.

For the next eight years, Amin presented a charming demeanor to the world while privately overseeing one of the bloodiest dictatorships in history.

In 1972, he banned foreign tourists, expelled most of the country's 75,000 Asian Indians, and put cronies in charge of the businesses, who bled them dry. He pampered the army and secret police with houses, cars, money and tanks. In turn, they committed between 300,000 and 500,000 murders for him. Amin's victims included political and tribal foes as well as Jews (he once said Hitler had the "right to burn six million Jews.")

Tensions between Uganda and Tanzania heightened during the 1970s, and when Ugandan troops chased rebels in Tanzania in the fall of 1978, Tanzanian President Nyerere retaliated with ferocity. A full-scale war ensued, and by April 1979, some 40,000 Tanzanian troops, aided by Ugandan exiles, captured Kampala. Amin fled to Libya where he stayed for years before moving to Saudi Arabia in the mid-1980s.

Tanzanian troops remained for a year to ensure the return to power of Obote, who had been in exile in Tanzania. He was reelected in December 1980 by a newly established National Assembly.

Bloodshed continued for the next five years. Obote's National Liberation Army fought an entrenched National Resistance Army (NRA), led by Yoweri Museveni. By 1985, an estimated 600,000 persons had been killed by one of the armies, and 200,00 others had become refugees.

On July 25, 1985, in an effort to "stop the killing," Brigadier Basilio Okello led a senior officer's coup against Obote, forcing the president to flee to Sudan. The National Assembly was abolished, a military council was formed with Lieutenant General Tito Okello sworn in as chairman, and all guerilla groups, including former Amin soldiers, were invited to join Okello's army. Only NRA leader Museveni and his forces declined.

Peace was still not at hand. For the next six months, the army under Okello continued to loot, rob and rape. In one instance, government troops massacred 300 Kampalans.

By December 1985, the Okello regime had negotiated a power-sharing accord with the NRA rebels. However, on January 4, 1986, Museveni launched a surprise attack against the government and within four weeks, was himself sworn in as president.

Museveni vowed to end the 15 years of terror suffered under Obote and Amin. He released more than 1,600 political prisoners, and set up a Commission of Inquiry to conduct public hearings on atrocities. Soldiers in Museveni's army found guilty of committing crimes were punished. Museveni later met with General Okello, absolved him of atrocities committed by troops under his command, and invited him to return from exile in Tanzania. No such olive branch was offered to Obote, who in 1988 remained in exile in Zambia, and was still wanted for trial for his crimes.

However, Museveni, a Marxist who is friendly with Libya, Cuba and North Korea, has not won any human rights plaudits. In mid-1986, civil war broke out and Museveni's troops killed thousands of political opponents, including anti-communist rebels; bands of soldiers still aligned with Amin, Obote or Okello; and followers of a prostitute-turned-priestess named Alice Lakwena.

Economic reform in the once prosperous nation has been sluggish. Inflation remained extraordinarily high—an average pay check in 1988 bought a bunch of bananas; a month's worth of wages ($6) only bought three days worth of food. As a result, widespread corruption, theft and graft continued to plague the economy. Coffee continued to account for more than 90% of exports.

Uganda's relations with neighbors remain uneasy. Landlocked Uganda's major trading route has traditionally gone through Kenya. Kenya leader Daniel Moi, who dislikes Museveni's socialism and suspects Uganda could become a springboard for subversion, has given refuge to some 2,000 exiles. He has occasionally closed the border to prevent Ugandan troops from pursuing rebels into Kenya.

A final spectre of death had appeared on Uganda's horizon by 1987: Uganda was cited as having the most AIDS victims on the African continent, with an estimated 15,000 persons infected in Kampala alone.

## Zaire

***Date of independence:*** June 30, 1960
***Area:*** 905,562 square miles
***Population:*** 32,780,000 (est. 1987)
***Capital:*** Kinshasa
***Monetary unit:*** Zaire
***Nationality:*** Zairian
***Religion:*** Catholic 48%, Protestant 29%, Islam 10%
***Language:*** French, English, Lingala, Swahili, Kikongo, Chiluba (all official)
***Literacy:*** 40% male, 15% female
***Type of government:*** Republic
***Political parties/leaders:*** Popular Movement of the Revolution, four exile groups
***Monetary conversion rate:*** 88.38 zaire = $1 US (1987)
***Principal economic resources:*** Coffee, palm oil, rubber, tea, cotton, copper, cobalt, zinc, industrial diamonds, manganese, tin, gold

### History at a Glance

The first known inhabitants of the Congo are believed to have been pygmy tribes who eventually came to be dominated by Bantu and Nilotic groups engaged in sedentary agriculture.

In 1482, the Portuguese explorer Diago Cao visited the mouth of the Congo River, but the world became aware of the potential wealth of the territory only after Henry Stanley made his fabled trip down the Congo River in 1877. Rumors of great riches induced King Leopold II of Belgium to commission Stanley to conduct further explorations and sign commercial treaties with local chieftains for access to the region. Within a year Leopold had formed the International Association of the Congo, a development company in which he himself was the chief stockholder. At the Berlin Conference of 1884-1885, the major European powers recognized the Independent State of the Congo, with Leopold as its absolute monarch. However, a subsequent scandal concerning the treatment accorded Congolese mine and plantation workers forced the king to transfer his territory to Belgium in 1908. Rechristened the Belgian Congo, the territory was sufficiently stable to campaign against the Germans during World War I.

The Belgian Congolese did not agitate for self-rule until after World War II. In 1959, rioting broke out in Leopoldville (now Kinshasa) and soon spread. Belgium initially advocated a slow timetable for self-rule for the giant nation, which had no national political organization, and sustained more than 200 splinter groups, divided along religious, tribal and regional lines. The Belgians eventually accepted June 30, 1960 as the date for complete independence.

The Belgian Congo's first week of freedom saw the collapse of its national authority. Intertribal fighting broke out and Belgian civil servants and professionals fled en masse. The army rebelled against its European officers and mutinied against the central government, headed by President Joseph Kasavubu. Less than two weeks later, separatist leader Moise Tshombe announced that the mineral-rich Katanga Province (now known as Shaba) was seceding. Tshombe's audacious move was supported by Belgium, who sent troops to Katanga.

Faced with chaos, the new republic (which became Zaire in 1971) appealed to the United Nations, which responded with massive aid and a multinational armed force.

A struggle shaped up between Kasavubu and adherents of the Belgian-appointed first prime minister, Patrice Lumumba, a militant nationalist. When the U.N. forces did not move to dislodge the Belgian troops in Katanga, Lumumba called on the Soviet Union to help. Kasavubu promptly dismissed Lumumba, who in turn declared himself as the legal central government.

Two weeks later, on September 14, 1960, army Colonel Joseph Mobutu, who later adopted the African name Mobutu Sese Seko, inserted himself into the Kasavubu government as a relevant power. On December 2, Lumumba was captured en route to his stronghold in Stanleyville by Kasavubu forces. A month and a half later, he was delivered to the Katanga secessionists, where he died under undetermined circumstances.

The next two years were occupied by the Katanga problem. U.N. Secretary-General Dag Hammarskjold was killed in an air crash in September 1961 en route to a meeting with Tshombe. Tshombe finally agreed to end Katanga's secession at the end of 1962, and a measure of unity returned to the country.

Lumumba's followers continued to be a thorn in the side of the Kasavubu government. Led by Christophe Gbenye, they set up a "government in exile" across the river, in the Congolese capital of Brazzaville, and aided by weapons from communist China and the Soviet Union, conducted guerilla raids into Zaire. Incidents of butchery and pillaging grew in number and severity, missionaries were slain, and innocent civilians were indiscriminately slaughtered. The rebels eventually took over Stanleyville (now known as Kisangani) and consolidated power over much of the eastern territory.

Zairian forces, aided by Belgian paratroopers, eventually liberated Stanleyville, but drew protests from the communist bloc and nonaligned African countries. The U.N. forces withdrew in 1964.

In the summer of 1964, Tshombe returned to Zaire and was sworn in as the new premier. Within the year, however, Kasavubu ousted him from office.

For years, Mobutu, now a general, had been watching the Kasavubu-Tshombe rivalry, and in December of 1965, decided to act. He deposed Kasavubu, canceled the scheduled presidential elections and installed himself as head of a "regime of exception."

Mobutu put down two major challenges to his authority in 1966 and 1967. By 1969, three rebel leaders, including Tshombe, were dead, and in 1970, Mobutu was elected president.

With the exception of the Popular Movement of the Revolution (MPR), all political parties have been outlawed since 1965. Mobutu, as president of the MPR, has easily won seven-year terms in 1977 and 1984.

An estimated 400,000 Zairians died in the 1960s, in civil wars and attempted secessions.

Mobutu's first actions including nationalizing much of the economy, barring religious instruction in schools and decreeing the adoption of African names. He took the name Mobutu Sese Seko, and the country was officially renamed Zaire in 1971.

He also expelled diplomats and technicians from Soviet bloc nations, and invited the United States, South Africa and Japan to invest in Zaire, in order to replace Belgian interests.

Struggles for control of the Shaba Province continued, with rebel invasions in 1977 and 1978. The first attack was repulsed with 1,500 troops from Morocco, airlifted to Zaire by France. A second invasion on May 15, 1978, saw the capture of the mining town of Kolwezi and slaughter of 300 blacks and 100 Europeans. This time France and Belgium troops intervened, and President Carter sent in military aid. A seven-nation African security force was formed following the bloodshed to protect the Shaba region until August 1979.

Relations with neighboring countries have been mixed. Mobutu backed the losers in the Angolan civil war of 1975-76, and only reluctantly acknowledged the victory of the Soviet-backed Popular Movement for the Liberation of Angola. Relations improved in 1979 when Mobutu and Angolan President Agostinho Neto exchanged visits; however, Mobutu has been accused of sheltering members of UNITA, who are fighting to overthrow the Angolan government. The countries share a 1,250-mile border.

Zaire sent troops to assist the Habre government of Chad in 1983, and joined Burundi and Rwanda in forming the Economic Community of the Great Lakes Countries. Relations with Zambia have been cordial despite a boundary dispute. Zaire reopened relations with Israel in 1981, and has maintained good relations with the U.S., who uses a military base in southern Zaire.

As president, Mobutu has governed with a firm hand with a 60,000-man army and secret police organization to back him up. Corruption and mismanagement have permeated his government, and he has been accused of amassing a fortune in European banks while most of Zaire's 40 million people suffer from lack of food. He has many enemies; at least a dozen rebel groups are in exile, and Amnesty International reported in 1986 that arrest and torture of political opponents "is used frequently."

Mobutu has enforced a number of personal quirks. All Zairians must address each other as "Citizen." Western clothing is banned, and instead, the populace is encouraged to wear a high-necked outfit designed by Mobutu, called "Mobutu suits." The president, who likes to be called "The Guide," often wears a leopardskin hat.

The Shaba region holds the world's richest diamond, copper and zinc deposits and is the largest known cobalt reserve, supplying 60% of the world's cobalt. In 1975, offshore oil was discovered.

Revenues from these have been used to repay foreign debt,

which was $4.5 billion in 1986. As such, the country lives in dire poverty. The average annual income was $186 in 1988.

Agriculture production has declined so much that the once self-sufficient Zaire must now import 60% of its food. The Belgians left Africa's best network of roads in 1960; by 1987, only 12,000 of the 85,000 miles were passable. Inflation hit 100% in 1979 and fell to 37% in 1980.

Zaire's elite are quickly identified with their Mercedes, imported foods and air-conditioned houses; the majority of people live in slums, surviving on tea bread via outright thievery and a thriving black market.

## Zambia

***Date of independence:*** October 24, 1964
***Area:*** 290,585 square miles
***Population:*** 7,100,000 (est.1987)
***Capital:*** Lusaka
***Monetary unit:*** Kwacha
***Nationality:*** Zambian
***Religion:*** 82% Animist, 17% Christian, 1% Hindu, less than 1% Muslim
***Language:*** English (official), tribal languages
***Literacy:*** 55%
***Type of government:*** One-party state
***Political parties/leaders:*** United National Independence Party
***Monetary conversion rate:*** 8.99 kwachas = $1 US (1987)
***Principal economic resources:*** Maize, tobacco, cotton, sugar cane, copper, zinc, lead, cobalt, coal

### History at a Glance

Archeological discoveries in the Gwembe Valley near Lusaka in 1964 uncovered such artifacts as copper wire, pottery specimens, and iron gongs dating to the ninth century. It is also believed that the people of this period, 850-1000, were skilled in the art of weaving cloth.

The first European to explore the territory was the Scotsman David Livingstone. He was followed by representatives of the British South Africa Company which gradually edged its way across the Zambezi River until, by 1924, it had extended its influence as far north as the Belgian Congo (now known as Zaire).

Since the mineral wealth of Northern Rhodesia, as it was then called, was not immediately apparent, the British did not feel it necessary to give the territory colonial status, particularly since it was under the direct jurisdiction of the Colonial Office. In 1925, however, the rich ore deposits in what is today known as the Copper Belt were discovered, and Europeans flocked northward.

The political tactics of the European settler had a twofold objective: to minimize the authority of the British Crown in the territory, and at the same time, to prevent Africans from uniting.

The political strength of Africans crystallized slowly in Northern Rhodesia. It was not until 1948 that they won the right to be represented by non-Europeans. Five years later, the British government decided to include the territory in a newly created federation, consisting of Northern and Southern Rhodesia and Nyasaland.

In 1959, an investigating commission of the Crown reported that the majority of the population in both Northern Rhodesia and Nyasaland were violently opposed to union with Southern Rhodesia on the grounds that racial discrimination was institutionalized there. The European-dominated United Federal Party (UFP) contested the findings of the commission, and took issue with the pro-African United National Independence Party (UNIP) over the question of dissolving the federation.

With the eventual withdrawal of Nyasaland (now known as Malawi), relations between the two Rhodesias became even more strained, and the federation was officially dissolved in 1963. A year later, Northern Rhodesia became independent as Zambia, with Kenneth Kaunda as its premier. President Kaunda was popularly elected to subsequent five-year terms in 1968, 1973, 1978 and 1983.

Under Kaunda, Zambia evolved from a British-type democracy stressing private enterprise into a socialistic, one-party nation in which the government controlled the most important industries and the disposition of much of the country's labor force.

Copper production was so prosperous in the 1960s that Zambia virtually tied its national economy to that single source, to the neglect of its agriculture and other assets. Zambians flocked to the cities, taking civil servant jobs in a bloated government.

World copper prices started to fall by 1973, and by 1975, the market collapsed. Within a few more years, the price of a pound of copper had fallen from $1.40 to 68 cents, and it now cost Zambia more to mine copper than to sell it.

This fact, coupled with the realization that the most accessible copper deposits would be exhausted by 2000, forced Zambian leaders to regroup and diversify. An austerity plan was in place by 1984, and emphasis was being placed on production of maize and other cash crops. A massive foreign debt, around $5.1 billion in 1987, threatened to strangle the economy.

Kaunda's government has faced major problems in recent years. When he removed subsidies on a corn staple in late 1986, food riots broke out. Kaunda quickly relented; when he tried to raise prices on fuel a few months later, he was likewise forced to back down. Unemployment has grown and labor strikes have occurred with more frequency. Per capita income, which was $630 in 1981, had fallen to $200 in 1987.

By May 1987, Kaunda decided his country simply could not withstand the strict austerity measures proposed by the International Monetary Fund, and rejected them. His decision, as well as a declaration that Zambia would no longer make interest payments, sparked international debate about foreign lenders who give millions to impoverished nations with the expectation that the debts would be repaid, with interest, in a few years.

In domestic relations, Zambia has taken strong actions against South Africa. For years, landlocked Zambia had sent more than 80% of its exports through South African trade routes. In 1986, however, Zambia joined the sanctions war against South Africa, and refused to trade directly with them. At the same time, Zambia signed an agreement with China to bolster construction on its only other significant trade exit, the inefficient and often-sabotaged Tanzania-Zambia (TAZARA) Railway.

In 1985, the Zambian capital of Lusaka also became the headquarters of the outlawed African National Congress (ANC). In 1987, South African troops raided ANC camps in Lusaka, killing a few citizens, and drawing international condemnation.

Although Kaunda's rule has been marked by political stability for many years, there was growing disenchantment with him by 1988. However, no candidate nor political group was seen as capable of preventing him from winning another five-year term.

## Zimbabwe

***Date of independence:*** As Southern Rhodesia on November 11, 1965, as Republic of Zimbabwe on April 18, 1980
***Area:*** 150,803 square miles
***Population:*** 8,576,000 (est. 1987)
***Capital:*** **Harare** (April 1982)
***Monetary unit:*** Zimbabwe dollar
***Nationality:*** Zimbabwean
***Religion:*** Syncretic (Christian-Animist) 50%, Christian 25%, Animist 24%
***Language:*** English (official), Shona and Ndebele
***Literacy:*** 25-30% black, nearly 100% white
***Type of government:*** Independent (British style democracy)
***Political parties/leaders:*** Zimbabwe African National Union, Patriotic Front, Rhodesian Front, eight other political parties
***Monetary conversion rate:*** **1 dollar** = $1.64 US (1987)
***Principal economic resources:*** Tobacco, corn, sugar, cotton, livestock, gold, copper, cobalt, nickel, tin

### History at a Glance

The Rhodesian plateau is believed to have been settled some 2,000 years ago by a group of farmers who had mastered the use of iron. After the eighth century A.D., descendants of this group began trading gold and ivory with the Arabs on the east coast of Africa. The great stone structures of Zimbabwe near Fort Victoria, were probably built between the eleventh and fifteenth centuries, shortly before the Vakaranga tribe moved northward to establish a state which extended over the northern and eastern Rhodesian plateau and the Mozambique lowlands.

The Portuguese were the first Europeans in the region, arriving between 1514 and 1569. At the end of the seventeenth century, the Monomatapa tribe and their Portuguese overlords were defeated by the Changamires who then held sway until the nineteenth century, the time of the great Zulu emigration from Natal. This emigration ushered in the era of Matabele rule at much the same time that David Livingstone, the Scottish missionary and explorer, was opening up the entire region to European exploitation. Livingstone's reports in 1875-1876 were chiefly responsible for the establishment of two Scottish missions in the territory of Nyasaland.

British entry into this region precipitated a series of conflicts with the Portuguese who had laid claim to the whole of Central Africa in the hope of linking Angola on the west with Mozambique on the east. Cecil B. Rhodes, holder of the controlling interest in the diamond mines of South Africa, sent his agents into the territory to obtain mining concessions from a number of the local chieftains. In 1888 Lobengula, the powerful and legendary chief of the Matabele, signed such a treaty with the British, thus preventing Portuguese or Boer (South African) penetration. Within a year, the discovery of extensive gold deposits enabled Rhodes to acquire a charter giving him the right to form the British South Africa Company and to exploit the area.

In 1890, the company sent a group of European settlers into Mashonaland, where they founded the town of Salisbury, site of the present capital. Meanwhile, Lobengula had granted Edward A. Lippert, a German concessionaire, the sole right to dispose of land in territory he controlled. This did not stop Rhodes from buying the concession and from continuing to send in settlers until 1893, the year of the unsuccessful Matabele rebellion. In 1897, a Mashona uprising was crushed by the British, and Rhodes was able to promote the development of the territory without interference.

For the next 20 years, conflicts arose between the settlers who sought an increasing degree of self-government and the British South Africa Company, which was subject only to the supervisory control of the high commissioner in South Africa. In 1922, the settlers finally won the right to establish a government separate from that of South Africa. A year later, the territory was annexed to the Crown, a move which made British subjects of all African inhabitants.

Southern Rhodesia (as it was then called) then divided its total land mass into two basic areas: mining and industrial regions (for European settlement), and native reserves and forest lands (for Africans only). Through this system, the Europeans received some 52 million acres of the choicest land.

After World War II, European settlers in neighboring Northern Rhodesia and Nyasaland merged into a federation embracing the three territories. The Federation of Rhodesia and Nyasaland came into being in 1953, and had a stormy life for the 10 years it survived. African resentment in Nyasaland flared into violence in 1959, during which time a state of emergency was declared in Nyasaland and Northern Rhodesia, African-controlled governments came into being and succeeded in getting Great Britain to agree to independence talks.

In 1962, the UN General Assembly censured Southern Rhodesia in an official resolution calling for the passage of a new constitution there. This pressure only led to the creation of a right-wing, white-supremacist government headed by Prime Minister Ian Smith, who was to defy Great Britain late in 1965 by declaring unilateral independence and withdrawing from the British Commonwealth. Economic sanctions imposed in 1966 by Great Britain and other members of the United Nations did not succeed in breaking the determination of Rhodesia's minority to maintain its hold on the country.

Three years later, the predominantly white electorate of Rhodesia voted overwhelmingly in a referendum to abandon all pretext at professing loyalty to the Queen and to support a constitution guaranteeing white supremacy indefinitely.

Rhodesian black nationalists, based in neighboring Zambia, intensified guerrilla actions in the early 1970s. The Smith government held out effectively, but in 1974 the success of the Frelimo Movement in Mozambique changed the picture drastically. Some 80% of Rhodesia's exports had traditionally passed through Mozambique to such ports as Beira and Lourenco Marques on the Indian Ocean. Also, with the Portuguese preparing to leave Mozambique, the government of South Africa began slowly to withdraw police and military forces it had dispatched to the aid of the Smith government and seemed to pressure Smith to reach an accord with black leaders. Smith made overtures to black groups in early 1975 and discussions of a new constitution, granting blacks greater power, started.

Divisions between Rhodesian blacks—Bishop Abel Muzorewa of the African National Congress and Ndabangi Sithole of the Zimbabwe African National Union as moderates versus Robert Mugabe and Joshua Nkomo of the Patriotic Front as advocates of guerrilla force—intensified in 1977. By July, white Rhodesian residents were fleeing by the hundreds and the economy began to falter.

On March 3, 1978, Smith, Muzorewa, Sithole, and Chief Jeremiah Chirau signed an agreement to transfer power to the black majority by December 31, and constituted themselves as an Executive Council with Smith as Prime Minister. However, the Patriotic Front Leaders denounced this action and no recognition was granted.

On January 30, 1979, white voters chose to ratify the new Constitution which enfranchised all blacks, established a black majority Senate and Assembly, and changed the country's name to Zimbabwe. Muzorewa's party received more than 67% of the vote although the Patriotic Front members lobbied for a boycott.

A turnabout in power came in February 29, 1980 when Mugabe's ZANU-Patriotic Front party won 57 of the 80 Assembly seats reserved for blacks and Nkomo's ZAPU-Patriotic Front won another 20 seats—leaving only three seats for Muzorewa's council. Mugabe was sworn in as Prime Minister on April 18, 1980. Reverend Canaan Sodindo Banana, the only nominated candidate, was sworn in for a six-year term on April 18.

On April 18, 1982, Zimbabwe officials announced that the country's capital city, Salisbury, would be renamed Harare in honor of the second anniversary of the nation.

Prime Minister Mugabe was reconfirmed after an election in July 1985; President Banana entered a second-six-year term in April 1986.

Mugabe, a Marxist, is striving to establish a one-party state by 1990, and has worked to unite the many factions still in Zimbabwe. His methods of quelling dissident activity, in Matabeleland especially, have drawn criticism from international human rights groups, and opposition parties flourish in exile.

Western aid has been generous. Britain initially offered a two-year $165 million aid program, while the United States gave $15 million for rural rehabilitation and $2 million to rebuild rural clinics. In 1981 alone, Mugabe had received $1.8 billion in Western aid to use over the next three years.

Relations between Zimbabwe and the U.S. later soured. In September 1983, Zimbabwe refused to condemn the Soviet shoot-down of a Korean Air Lines passenger jet; two months later, it co-sponsored resolutions condemning the U.S. for invading Grenada. By 1986, the U.S. expressed its displeasure with Zimbabwe by cutting its annual $20 million in aid to $7 million, and later, withdrawing its ambassador for seven months.

As a member of the "Front-Line" states, Mugabe has strongly attacked South Africa's apartheid policies. As a landlocked country, however, Zimbabwe has remained dependent on South African trade. South Africa purchases many of Zimbabwe's products and 90% of Zimbabwean exports go through South Africa.

These economic realities have prevented Zimbabwe from employing full sanctions against South Africa, and in 1987, a planned boycott had to be shelved.

In the meantime, Zimbabwe has shored up relations with neighboring Mozambique and its important railroad to the sea, in preparation to stage a full-out "economic war" with South Africa. The friendship was not consummated without cost: by 1986, Mugabe was spending enormous amounts of money to keep 15,000 troops in Mozambique as backups for the Marxist Frelimo government. In 1987, Mozambican anti-communist Renamo rebels retaliated by attacking Zimbabwe.

Also in 1987, a Mugabe plan came to light, which would see the annexation of a portion of Mozambique, bounded by the Zambezi River to the north and the Save River to the south, in order to provide Zimbabwe with access to the sea. Mozambican President Joseph Chissano, desperate to secure control of his country, was reportedly receptive to the idea. The name of the new federation would be "Mozamabwe."

The same year, Mugabe spent $300 million to buy 10 Soviet MiGs, which raised eyebrows but were determined to be of "defensive use" only.

Zimbabwe is well endowed with natural resources, and exports tobacco, sugar, asbestos, chrome and copper. Its agricultural programs have prospered, but have not outstripped the population growth; as such, malnutrition is still a major problem. In 1986, the government was promoting family planning with contraceptives.

By 1987, only 2% of the population was white. Many of these eschewed politics, and held prominent positions in business. Uneasy racial feelings persisted, and were heightened in 1986 when 16 white missionaries and their children were axed to death in Matabeleland. Random murders of white farmers also continued in 1988.

## FRENCH AFRICAN DEPENDENCIES

### Reunion

***Area:*** 970 square miles
***Population:*** 515,000 (est. 1986)
***Capital:*** Saint Denis
***Monetary unit:*** CFA franc
***Language:*** Creole
***Principal economic resources:*** Sugar cane, geranium, vetiver

#### History at a Glance

Located 450 miles east of Malagasy, Reunion was an uninhabited volcanic island at the time of its discovery in 1528 by Pedro de Mascarenhas, a Portuguese explorer. By 1649, it had fallen under the control of France and was called "Bourbon Island." Having served originally as a French penal colony, it was later settled by blacks, Malays, Indo-Chinese, Chinese, and Malabar Indians.

In 1665, the French East India Company established an outpost there. Coffee, which by 1715 had become the major agricultural staple of the island, was replaced in importance after 1800 by sugar cane.

Reunion, which received its present name in 1793, was made an overseas department of France in 1947.

A prefect appointed in Paris administers Reunion together with an elected general council. Reunion sends three Deputies and two Senators to the French Parliament in Paris.

In addition to sugar cane, Reunion's principal exports are vanilla, bananas and perfume essences. Its gross national product in 1983 was an impressive $2.06 billion.

*Although Algeria is in the process of modernizing at a rapid pace, as is most of North Africa, many Algerian shepherds still follow a traditional lifestyle.*

## SPANISH AFRICAN DEPENDENCIES

### Spanish North Africa (consisting of Ceuta and Melilla)

***Area:*** 12 square miles
***Population:*** 165,000
***Language:*** Spanish
***Principal economic resources:*** Fish, tourism

#### History at a Glance

Built on the site of an ancient Phoenician colony, Ceuta is believed to have been the locale of one of the fabled Pillars of Hercules. It was taken over from the Arabs by Portugal in 1415, only to fall under Spanish control in 1580. Melilla, the site of the initial uprising which launched the Spanish Civil War in 1936, has belonged to Spain since 1496. Both Ceuta and Melilla are part of Metropolitan Spain, and the population is predominantly Spanish.

## UNITED KINGDOM AFRICAN DEPENDENCIES

### St. Helena (Tristan da Cunha, Ascension Island, and Gough, Nightingale, and Inaccessible Islands)

***Area:*** 47 square miles
***Population:*** 6,000
***Capital:*** Jamestown
***Monetary unit:*** British pound
***Language:*** English
***Principal economic resources:*** Hemp, timber, vegetables, flax

#### History at a Glance

St. Helena, located in the Atlantic 1,200 miles west of the African continent, was sighted by the Portuguese explorer Juan de Nova Castelle in 1502, but was first claimed by the Dutch in 1633. By 1659, it was garrisoned by the British East India Company which withstood an armed attack by the Dutch in 1673.

Perhaps St. Helena's major claim to fame is the fact that Napoleon was exiled there in 1815, the year of his disastrous defeat at Waterloo. He remained there until his death in 1821.

In 1834, St. Helena became a British Crown Colony. It is now administered by a governor, who is assisted by executive and advisory councils.

## COUNTRIES OF NORTH AFRICA

### Algeria

***Date of independence:*** July 3, 1962
***Area:*** 919,591 square miles
***Population:*** 23,000,000 (est. 1987)

***Capital:*** Algiers
***Monetary unit:*** Dinar
***Nationality:*** Algerian
***Religion:*** 99% Muslim, 1% Christian and Hebrew
***Language:*** Arabic (official), French, Berber dialects
***Literacy:*** 46%
***Type of government:*** Republic
***Political parties/leaders:*** National Liberation Front, President Bendjedid Chadli
***Monetary conversion rate:*** 4.66 dinars = $1 US (1987)
***Principal economic resources:*** Oil, natural gas, wheat, barley, grapes, citrus fruits

## History at a Glance

Algeria (ancient Numidia) did not exist as a unified territory until 1848, at which time the French finally subdued the Berber inhabitants from whom they had originally taken much of the fertile land along the coastal area. (Before this, Algeria had been ruled by Carthage, Rome, and a succession of Arab invaders, the most powerful of whom had established a Moorish empire uniting Algeria with Morocco and Spain.)

Effective control of Berber outposts in the Sahara region was not achieved by the French until the first decade of the twentieth century. During World War II, many Algerian nationalists cooperated with the Allies in the hope of gaining a greater degree of autonomy. Having failed in this, a group of discontented factions united in 1954 under the banner of two revolutionary associations: the *Front de Liberation Nationale* (FLN) and the *Mouvement Nationale Algerien* (MNA). Both groups, though at odds with each other, began to undermine French interests in the territory—first by terrorism and subversion, and ultimately, by open revolt.

Politically, this revolt was instrumental in bringing about the fall of the Fourth French Republic in 1958 and the rise to power of Charles de Gaulle, hero of the French resistance during World War II and the man to whom the army and the *colons* (European colonists in Algeria) looked to as their savior. This group, which centralized its opposition to the Algerian nationalists in the Secret Army Organization (OAS), eventually (though unsuccessfully) sought to overthrow de Gaulle when he advocated negotiations with the FLN and self-determination for Algeria. Ultimately, the following choices were open to the rebels: absolute independence (with no ties to the mother country); incorporation into France as an overseas province; or federal autonomy involving closer ties with France. Algeria chose self-determination in a 1961 referendum, and a year later voted for the third of the above alternatives.

A cease fire was achieved in 1962, followed by the formation of a sovereign state headed by Premier Youssef Ben Khedda. He in turn was overthrown by a military coup d'etat which supported Ahmed Ben Bella, then Vice-Premier. Elected on a single-party slate in 1962, Ben Bella announced that Algeria would follow a socialist course of development, with a non-aligned foreign policy.

In 1965, Ben Bella was deposed in a bloodless, army-backed coup by Colonel Houari Boumedienne, President and Defense Minister.

Boumedienne sought to restore financial stability and maintain good economic and financial relations with France and the United States until 1967, when Algeria joined the war against Israel and entered the Arab bloc. Thereafter, Algeria received most of its developmental support from the Soviet Union.

Algeria expanded petroleum and natural gas exports, with the United States as its chief trading partner, until 1976. However, in 1977 and 1978, like other oil-exporting countries, Algeria slowed its general industrial expansion and turned to increasing its oil and gas output and reviving agricultural livelihoods.

Boumedienne died in December 1978 after a long illness, and Bendjedid Chadli , Secretary-General of the National Liberation Front, assumed the presidency. On July 4, 1979, Chadli freed former President Ben Bella, who had been imprisoned for the past 14 years. Bendjedid was reelected to a second five-year term in January 1984.

Algeria played a key role in the release of the 52 American hostages in Iran. Algerian Minister of Executive Affairs Behzad Nabavi was a chief negotiator between the United States and Iran, and helped achieve a critical breakthrough on January 17, 1980 when he persuaded the Iranians to allow U.S. banks to retain the $3.7 billion in Iranian assets against which the banks had legal claims.

The hostages were released three days later to Algerian custody and flown to Algiers, where they were greeted for the first time in 444 days by U.S. officials.

Relations with the United States continued to warm, with Bendjedid making an official visit to the U.S. in 1982.

One area of conflict for the U.S. and Algeria was the question of Western Sahara. U.S.-Morocco relations have always been strong, and the U.S. tacitly approved when, in late 1975, Morocco annexed the former Spanish colony of Western Sahara. Algeria, however, opposed the annexation and sent troops and supplies to bolster the Polisario Front guerillas who took up arms against Morocco for self-determination of the territory. Algeria and Morocco broke diplomatic relations in 1975.

When Algeria sought to purchase military arms from the U.S. in 1982, it raised delicate questions, since the U.S. was also selling weapons to Morocco. In the end, Algeria contracted to buy about $50,000 worth of supplies.

In its domestic relations, Algeria has watched Libya closely. In 1984, Libya and Morocco signed a treaty of union. The next year, Bendjedid made a public proposal to merge all North African Arab nations, from Libya to Mauritania, into a single union. His only stipulation was that Western Sahara be included as a separate component. Libya then asked Algeria to form a political union with it, which Algeria came close to accepting. In November 1987, however, Algeria declined the Libyan offer and instead suggested that Libya join a 1983 friendship treaty with Algeria, Tunisia and Mauritania. By 1988, nothing concrete had been finalized.

Internal Algerian problems included a galloping birthrate; an overcentralized, socialistic economy; and a growing Islamic fundamentalist movement whose ranks have been swelled by discontented young Algerians who cannot find work.

In 1986, non-Islamic students rioted in Algeria's third largest city, Constantine, because Islamic questions were added to final exams. Police repression of Islamic students escalated to include fundamentalist groups thought to be particularly subversive, and some 200 activists were put on trial.

By the mid-1980s, Bendjedid was encouraging private enterprise to boost the nation's agriculture, which in 1985 met half the country's food needs. In the meantime, he was forced to implement austerity measures in the face of low oil revenues, which accounted for 97% of Algeria's foreign exchange.

The austerity measures and farm reforms worked quickly. By 1987, Algeria's cereal crops alone were covering 40% of the country's food needs. Bendjedid's popularity, however, especially among the growing population under 30 years of age, was not particularly strong. Food riots broke out in the fall of 1988, leaving dozens dead.

In May 1988, Algeria and Morocco resumed diplomatic relations which left the Polisario efforts in Western Sahara in jeopardy. By September 1988, however, the 13-year war in Western Sahara seemed to be at a close when the guerillas and Morocco both accepted a United Nation's proposal to hold a referendum to determine whether the territory should be independent or affiliated with Morocco.

## Egypt

***Date of independence:*** June 18, 1953
***Area:*** 386,659 square miles
***Population:*** 52,000,000 (est.1987)
***Capital:*** Cairo
***Monetary unit:*** Egyptian pound
***Religion:*** Islam 93%, Christian 7%
***Language:*** Arabic (official)
***Literacy:*** 50%
***Type of government:*** Republic (under presidential rule)
***Political parties/leaders:*** National Democratic Party, three opposition parties, several illegal groups
***Monetary conversion rate:*** 1 pound = $1.43 US (1987)
***Principal economic resources:*** Cotton, wheat, rice, corn, manganese, oil, gold, nickel, tungsten

### History at a Glance

The site of one of the world's oldest civilizations, Egypt was a name in recorded history long before its upper and lower kingdoms were united (c. 3200 B.C.). The "golden age" of Egypt was reached during the eighteenth dynasty, about 1570 B.C., at which time the New Empire superceded it. As this kingdom weakened, invasion by foreign conquerors, particularly the Assyrians, the Persians (525 B.C.), and the Macedonians under Alexander the Great (332 B.C.), became more and more devastating.

For the next three centuries, Egypt was effectively ruled by the Ptolemaic dynasty which fell to Rome in 31 B.C. when Caius Octavius, later to become the Emperor Augustus, defeated the combined forces of Cleopatra and Marc Antony at the Battle of Actium.

In A.D. 340, Egypt was made part of the Eastern Roman Empire (Byzantium). Three centuries later, it fell under Arab control and became a center of the Islamic world. Arab domination was not ended until 1250 when the Mamelukes, slaves of non-Arabic stock, gained supremacy, only to be engulfed in their own turn by the Ottoman Empire, centered in Constantinople (1517). In 1798, the armies of Napoleon Bonaparte occupied Egypt, but within three years, were ousted by British and Turkish forces. In 1805, the Ottoman Turks appointed Mohammed Ali pasha, or governor, of the territory. Backed by the power of the Turks, he was able, by 1811, to eliminate the last vestiges of Mameluke influence in Egypt. The dynasty which Mohammed Ali founded eventually proved to be Egypt's last royal line.

The nineteenth century was a time of ambitious planning in Egypt. Land reform and improved methods for cotton cultivation were introduced, and construction was begun on the Suez Canal, linking the Mediterranean with the Red Sea. With the opening of the canal in 1869, Egypt became a transportation center of international significance—so much so that, in 1882, Great Britain sent in troops to quell a threatened rebellion. In the process, Britain also took over the government, solidifying her rule over all territory as far south as the Sudan.

With the outbreak of World War I, Great Britain established a protectorate over this area as well. By 1922, Egypt had won back a degree of sovereignty. Britain continued, however, to exercise control over foreign affairs, defense, communications, and the Anglo-Egyptian Sudan to the South.

Between the wars, Egyptian nationalism was centered in the Ward Party, first led by Sa'ad Zaghul Pasha and later by Dahas Pasha. In 1936, the year Farouk I ascended the throne, an Anglo-Egyptian treaty was signed under which Britain restricted its occupation forces to specified areas, mainly along the Suez Canal route.

During World War II, Cairo became the Middle Eastern headquarters for British forces and a key military staging ground for the Allies. In 1948, fighting broke out between Egypt and Israel which had only just acquired its independence. After nine months, in which the Egyptians were severely beaten, a truce was declared, but army dissatisfaction continued to smolder. In 1952, a group called the Society of Free Officers revolted against the monarchy. Led by General Mohammed Naguib, though the guiding genius was Colonel Gamal Abdel Nasser, the coup forced Farouk to abdicate and led to the establishment of a republic on June 18, 1953. Within a year, Nasser had gained absolute control of the country, and entered into a series of agreements with the Unted States, Great Britain, and other U.N. members to help build a new dam at Aswan. Nasser also negotiated with the Soviet Union for economic aid and arms shipments, a move which finally caused the United States to withhold promised financial assistance. Nasser, however, countered this move by seizing and nationalizing the Suez Canal on July 26, 1956. This action was followed by an Israeli invasion of the Sinai Peninsula, and by British and French military intervention in the Port Sa'id area. However, a Soviet ultimatum, backed in part by the United States, led to the forced withdrawal of these troops and to the subsequent restoration of peace and order by UN forces.

In 1958, Egypt and Syria combined their states into a single entity—the United Arab Republic (UAR), a federation under one chief of state, governed by a common legislature and defended by a unified army. That same year, Yemen joined the federation which came to be known as the United Arab States (UAS). The union lasted until 1961, when the Syrian army revolted, causing the withdrawal of Syria from the federation. By the end of the year, Egypt had broken off relations with Yemen as well.

In May 1967, at the insistence of Nasser, the U.N. peacekeeping force was withdrawn. Shortly thereafter, on June 5, Israeli forces struck and by June 10 had occupied the entire Sinai Peninsula and reached the Suez Canal, when a cease fire instituted by the United Nations halted hostilities. In August 1970, Egypt and Israel agreed to a cease fire, though clashes along the Canal were to continue. In September, Nasser died and was succeeded by Anwar el Sadat.

Despite increased hopes for peace, tensions persisted as Egypt and her Arab allies, notably Syria, Iraq, Algeria, and Libya, sought unsuccessfully to obtain an Israeli withdrawal to her 1967 boundaries. In October 1973, Egyptian forces attacked again, along with the Syrians on Israel's northern frontier. After initial successes by Egypt, the Israelis again prevailed, occupying the town of Suez. A disengagement agreement was reached in January 1974, under which Israel withdrew from the Suez Canal's west bank.

In February 1974, Egypt and the United States reestablished diplomatic relations, which had been broken in 1967. In July 1975, extremely intense and sensitive negotiations regarding the degree and speed of Israeli withdrawal from the Sinai had been underway for over a year, with Egypt demanding complete withdrawal from all its occupied land and Israel seeking to maintain a measure of occupation in some of Sinai's strategic areas.

U. S. Secretary of State Henry Kissinger pursued "shuttle diplomacy" between Cairo and Jerusalem to expand areas of agreement. Israel yielded on the possession of the Mitla and Giddi passes in the Sinai and the Abu Rudeis oil field in the peninsula. Both sides agreed to annual renewal of the U.N. peacekeeping force in the Sinai and allowed the United States to assume a mediating position.

Sadat received blistering accusations from Arab countries who perceived his actions with Israel as betrayal, but in 1977 Saudi Arabia and other Arabian Gulf states agreed to lend Egypt $1.5 billion. Sadat also gained U.S. aid to combat a 30% inflation rate and serious unemployment.

A 1976 referendum gave Sadat the right to run for a second six-year term and he achieved a 99.9% vote of approval.

Sadat garnered both praise and anger when he flew to Jerusalem at the invitation of Prime Minister Menachem Begin to plead for peace before Israel's Knesset on November 20, 1977. Among the members of the Arab world, only Morocco, Tunisia, Sudan, and Oman voiced support.

Egypt's own Foreign Minister Ismail Fahmy resigned in

*Until very recently most of the agricultural work in the United Arab Republic was done by traditional ancient methods.*

***This typical Libyan farmer still farms the ancient way as he uses a camel to plough his fields.***

disgust. Negotiations lagged in Jerusalem after several weeks, and the Egyptian contingent returned home. The major problem had been Israel's refusal to discuss the ultimate status of the West Bank and Gaza Strip, which Sadat had proposed to be placed under Jordanian and Egyptian administration, respectively.

Progress for peace remained bogged down until 1978 when a historic 10-day "summit" at Camp David was convened by U.S. President Carter. The meeting of Begin, Sadat, and Carter resulted in two documents—A Framework for Peace in the Middle East and Framework for a Peace Treaty Between Israel and Egypt—signed by the leaders at the White House on September 17, 1978. Negotiations continued in order to work out details and a timetable for the treaty, and on March 26, 1979, the completed treaty was signed; a month later the 31-year state of war between Egypt and Israel was officially ended.

In reaction, the Arab League convened in Baghdad to approve resolutions to isolate Egypt. By midyear, all League members except Oman, Somalia, and Sudan had severed relations with the Sadat regime and Cairo was suspended from numerous Arab groups.

Egypt weathered the tactics, thanks to the nominal participation of Saudi Arabia and increased economic aid from Western countries including France, West Germany, and Japan.

Undercurrent tensions in Egypt remained, exploding in July 1981 when Sadat was assassinated in full view of thousands of Egyptians by a small force of terrorists. Anwar el-Sadat died during the ambush and the assassins were captured, put on trial, and executed within five months.

Under the leadership of Mohamed Hossny Mubarak, who was sworn in as president for a six-year term on October 14, 1982, Egypt has faced problems with a floundering economy, drifting foreign policy and a growing religious imbroglio.

Islamic fundamentalism have long pushed for the incorporation of strict Islamic law, known as "sharia," into Egyptian law. Non-Moslems and Egypt's 6 million Coptic Christians have understandably been distressed by such overtures, since they would be reduced to second-class citizens. Under sharia, for example, Christians are regarded as infidels and cannot have leadership positions, own property nor build nor repair churches.

The Mubarak government has also gone head to head with Koran-based law over the issue of multiple marriages. In 1979, Sadat passed a law which required a husband to notify his wife if he planned to take a second wife; she then had the option of divorcing him within the year and retaining their living quarters—a valuable asset in Egypt's overcrowded cities. Prior to 1979, a husband only had to say "I divorce you" three times to eject his wife from his life and his home.

In 1985, Sadat's law was struck down, generating strong protests from many Egyptian women, including Jihan Sadat, the late leader's widow, that women would again live at the mercy of their husband. The 1979 law was quickly reinstated by the Mubarak government, but it pointedly noted that it would make "no encroachment on a man's right to polygamy."

Egyptian women have long considered having babies as the best way to keep their husband, and by 1986, with 150,000 newborns arriving each month, Egypt's population was literally exploding. Family planning measures, in place since the 1970s, were having little effect and the population was expected to hit 66 million by 2000.

Such a population explosion was straining an economy already weakened by declining oil prices. A three-year drought in the mid-1980s also imperiled the population by lowering the level of the Aswan Dam's huge reservoir and threatening its vital hydroelectric power. In 1986, $10 million worth of food was being imported daily; however, efforts were underway to revitalize farming in the still-fertile Nile Valley.

Other problems included a bloated bureaucracy of 12 million civil servants and foreign debt exceeding $33 billion. Tourism, once a major source of revenue, also had dropped by the mid-1980s following an increase in terrorism in the Middle East. In 1985 alone, Egypt figured in three fatal hijacking incidents. Per capita income in 1984 was $500.

In February 1986, some 20,000 police conscripts rioted for two days in protest of being treated like slaves by senior officers. More than 100 persons were killed.

Although Egypt's relations with some Arab nations had

warmed since the Camp David accords, they remained strained with the more radical Libya and Syria, due to Egypt's continued relations with Israel. Mubarak has also steered a course of cordial nonalignment with the Soviet Union and the United States.

## Libya

***Date of independence:*** December 24, 1951
***Area:*** 679,358 square miles
***Population:*** 3,800,000 (est. 1987)
***Capital:*** Tripoli
***Monetary unit:*** Dinar
***Nationality:*** Libyan
***Religion:*** 97% Muslim
***Language:*** Arabic, Italian, English
***Literacy:*** 50%
***Type of government:*** Republic (Constitutional overhaul in 1977)
***Political parties/leaders:*** Banned
***Monetary conversion rate:*** 1 dinar = $3.29 US (1987)
***Principal economic resources:*** Wheat, barley, olives, dates, oil, natural gas

### History at a Glance

Both Carthage and Rome left their imprint on Libya in the pre-Christian era—Carthage along the Tripolitania coast, then Greece in the portion known as Cyrenaica. By the third century B.C., Rome had replaced Greece as the dominant power in the region, and with the destruction of Carthage, went on to become the sole empire builder throughout most of North Africa.

In the third century A.D., with Rome already in a state of decline, Emperor Diocletian assigned Tripolitania to the western part of the Roman Empire and Cyrenaica to the eastern portion of it. By 431, however, Rome could no longer protect these outlying territories, and they were overrun by hordes of Vandal invaders. In the sixth century, Emperor Justinian's military commander, Belisarius, conquered the territory and placed it under the suzerainty of the Byzantine Empire. The first of what were to become frequent Arab invasions occurred in 643, the year which ushered in three centuries of almost continuous religious and dynastic conflicts. During this period, Tripolitania manifested a tendency to identify itself with the Western world, whereas Cyrenaica became more closely associated with Egypt to the east.

In 1510, Tripoli was seized by the Spanish who were in turn overcome by Ottoman Turks. From 1711 to 1835, Libyan territory was controlled by the Karamanli family, which wrested virtual autonomy from the Turks whose capital was in Constantinople. Ultimately, the Turks regained their power, only to lose it again to Italy in 1911. Over the next two decades, the Italians worked their way inland with marked effectiveness.

During World War II, Libya was occupied by Italian, German, and finally British and Free French forces. When the war ended, the United Nations voted to create an independent state—a decision which was put into effect two years later with the establishment of a federated kingdom embracing Tripolitania and Cyrenaica (now known as Fezzan and Barquah).

*Carpet weavers at the school of Popular Arts in Teutan, Morocco.*

Libya was once considered a country largely devoid of natural resources, but in the late 1950s with the discovery of oil, this desert nation became a rapidly growing world power. In 1979, Libya had the highest per capita gross national product ($8,000) of any African nation.

After the discovery of oil, Libya's foreign policy was formed: anti-Western sentiments were voiced, especially regarding foreign-dominated petroleum companies and the presence of foreign military bases on Libyan soil.

The period following the June 1967 Arab-Israeli conflict saw a succession of prime ministers. In September 1968, while King Idris I was abroad, Colonel Muammar Qaddafi seized control of the government and established a revolutionary regime under the military-controlled Revolutionary Command Council (RCC).

The new regime employed a combination of puritanical

*Moroccan folklore produces many master musicians and dancers*

Islamic codes and radical Arab nationalism. By 1970 Western military bases were evacuated and the Italian and Jewish communities forced to leave. The regime also began to acquire shares in the nation's oil industry and by 1976, controlled about two thirds of production.

Under Qaddafi, Libya has made a strong commitment to Arab unity, total war against Israel, and shown a willingness to use oil as a political weapon. It has given support to many radical Islamic, terrorist, and dissident groups around the world, including Uganda's Idi Amin, Polisario of Western Sahara, and the Palestinian Liberation Organization. Libya broke relations with Egypt following the Camp David accords in 1978 and fortified their mutual border.

The most blatant military action, however, came in December 1980, when Libya gave military support in the Chadian civil war, helping the Goukhouni Woddei government defeat insurgent forces. Equally ignominious was the 2,000-man Libyan army sent in 1979 to Uganda to assist Amin against Ugandan rebels and Tanzanian forces. Qaddafi later offered asylum to the ousted Amin and his family.

The U.S. Embassy in Tripoli has been closed since February 7, 1979, and four Libyan embassy members were expelled from Washington in May after they were accused of threatening Libyan students in America. On July 14, a scandal erupted when it was revealed that Billy Carter, brother of President Carter, had registered as a Libyan agent. A Senate investigation was launched when it was further revealed that Carter had taken $220,000 from Libyan officials.

Libya, which was renamed in 1977 as the Socialist People's Libyan Arab Hamahiriya, has continued to play friend and host to the world's radicals and terrorist organizations. In 1983, Brazil found huge arms shipments in Libyan planes en route to Nicaragua; Libya had ostensibly been sending medical supplies. In 1984, Britain evicted four Libyans and held the Libyan embassy under siege when an unidentified gunman opened fire from the embassy and killed a female police constable. Both countries withdrew their envoys and ended diplomatic relations. In March 1987, radical Palestinian leaders met in Tripoli for what was dubbed "a convention of terrorists."

Qaddafi has long held a goal of building a continent-wide Islamic Saharan state. Among his many attempts to obtain this goal have been failed mergers with Egypt, Sudan and Syria (1969); with Egypt and Syria (1971); with Egypt (1972); with Tunisia (1974); with Syria (1980); with Chad (1981) and with Morocco (1984).

Following a spate of terrorist actions, Qaddafi was blamed when in December 1985, Palestinian gunmen attacked airports in Rome and Vienna, with several fatalities. The United States, which had closed its embassy in Tripoli in 1981, froze all Libyan government assets in U.S. banks, advised U.S. citizens to evacuate the country, and ordered a series of air and sea maneuvers in the Gulf of Sidra. On April 14, 1986, U.S. bombers attacked Libyan military targets in Tripoli and Benghazi. The attack, President Reagan explained, was prompted by "conclusive evidence" that Libya had ordered the bombing of a West German disco nine days earlier which cost several people their lives. Although Qaddafi pledged to avenge the U.S. attack, in fact, it appeared that Libyan-sponsored offensives around the world were curtailed.

The mercurial Arab leader suffered yet another international humiliation a year later, when in March 1987, Chadian forces under President Hissein Habre, chased Libyan forces out of northern Chad. The Libyans fled, abandoning nearly $1 billion worth of armaments, and regrouped long enough to prevent their eviction from the contested Aozou Strip, along Chad's northern border. In October 1988, Libya and Chad formally ended their 15-year war and restored diplomatic ties. Libya retained control of the mineral-rich Aozou Strip for the time being, but both nations pledged to abide by United Nations and Organization of Africa Unity committee decisions regarding their respective claims to the land.

Libya's sole natural resource has been oil, discovered in the late 1950s. Exploitation of oil grew to the extent that by 1980, Libya enjoyed the highest per capita income in Africa: more than $8,600.

World market conditions later conspired to reduce export revenues, and Libya's oil income fell from $20 billion in 1980 to $5 billion in 1986. Agriculture, never a strong suit, was hampered by poor rainfall and lack of laborers. Main crops included barley, wheat, olives, dates and citrus. In September 1988, Qaddafi announced plans to build a $25 billion "Great Man-Made River" of "Concrete Nile," to pump water from underground aquifers in the Sahara through pipes to farmland along the Mediterranean coast. Some 270 miles of the 1,140-mile pipeline had been completed by the end of 1988.

*A Saharan refugee camp near Zag, southern Morocco, during the dispute to oust Spanish colonial rule.*

### Morocco

***Date of independence:*** March 2, 1956
***Area:*** 269,756 square miles, including some 97,343 square miles of Western Sahara
***Population:*** 24,600,000 (est. 1987)
***Capital:*** Rabat
***Monetary unit:*** Dirham
***Nationality:*** Moroccan
***Religion:*** 98.7% Islam, 1.1% Christian, 0.2% Jewish
***Language:*** Arabic (official), French, Berber dialects
*Literacy:* 28%
***Type of government:*** Constitutional monarchy
***Political parties/leaders:*** National Assembly of Independents, nine other parties
***Monetary conversion rate:*** 8.49 dirhams = $1 US (1987)
***Principal economic resources:*** Phosphates, iron, manganese, barley, wheat, citrus fruits, fish, silver, lead, coal and several other minor minerals

### History at a Glance

Morocco shares with the rest of North Africa a long history of domination by foreign powers, but differs from its neighbors in that it was never completely overrun by either Rome or the Ottoman Empire.

In ancient times, the Berbers, the earliest known inhabitants of Morocco, were invaded by Phoenicians and Carthaginians. In the early centuries of the Christian era, they suffered the same fate at the hands of the Vandals, Byzantines, and Arabs. In 683, Morocco fell under the influence of Islam, but, for all its unifying effect, religion did not succeed in the next four centuries in eliminating conflict between numerous petty chieftains.

From the eleventh to the thirteenth centuries, Morocco was ruled by the Almoravid, Almohade, and Marinid dynasties and enjoyed a period of relative political stability and intellectual development. Under the Sa'adi kings, Morocco experienced its period of greatest prosperity. Its strong army protected it from Turkish invasions while its own spoils of victory enabled it to build a magnificent capital at Marrakesh.

By the middle of the sixteenth century, however, Spain and England controlled most of the country's major seaports. Were it not for the tenacity of the Filali dynasty, these nations would certainly have attempted to gain control of the interior as well. The Filali king Mawlay Isma'il (1672-1727) managed for a time to preserve Moroccan independence by driving the Spanish from Lavache and the English from Tangier.

The establishment of diplomatic relations with France in 1682 led to an expansion of Moroccan trade during the following two centuries and, ultimately, to French military occupation (1844). In 1860, Spain invaded and occupied northern Morocco, necessitating the signing in 1880 of an international agreement to guarantee Morocco's territorial integrity. By 1904, however, France and Spain had secretly agreed to divide up all of Morocco between themselves. Two years later, the Act of Algeciras established the principle of commercial equality for European nations trading in the region, although policing of the act's provisions was left to France and Spain. In 1912, Morocco was divided into French Morocco (a protectorate with Rabat as its capital), Spanish Morocco (a protectorate with Tetuan as its capital), Southern Morocco (administered as part of Spanish Sahara), and the international zone of Tangier.

In 1921, Berber nationalism reached fever pitch, culminating in the Rif War during which Abd el-Krim inflicted several crucial defeats on both the French and Spanish before himself being captured and exiled in 1926.

Guerrilla fighting continued until 1934.

During World War II, Allied forces landed in Morocco, where they were soon joined by large detachments of Moroccan troops who fought on the side of the Free French. At the war's end, Sultan Sidi Mohammed demanded independence for his country, but was exiled instead in 1952—a gesture which triggered massive anti-French demonstrations lasting for nearly two years. With her already humiliating defeat in Indo-China, France was now forced to loosen her grip on Morocco, to allow Sidi Mohammed to return in 1955 and to grant the territory (including Tangier and the French and Spanish zones) complete independence a year later. Muhammad V then ascended the throne as the first modern-day king of Morocco.

After his death in 1961, the King was succeeded by his son, Hassan II, who faced an uphill battle to win popular support and maintain a stable government. In the early 1970s, he survived two separate assassination attempts.

A new constitution was accepted by a popular referendum in 1972, but change in the political process has been slow.

Early in 1969 Morocco persuaded Spain to surrender the tiny enclave of Ifni on the Mediterranean, signed an accord minimizing political and military frictions with its leftist neighbor Algeria, and worked out terms with the European Common Market to achieve associate status. Morocco has further asked Spain to give up offshore oil prospecting rights to Couta and Melilla, two Spanish enclaves on Morocco's north coast.

The country's major concern in recent years has been the Moroccan takeover of Western Sahara. In 1975 tens of thousands of Moroccans crossed into Spanish Sahara to give evidence that the northern party of that territory was historically part of Morocco. At the same time, Mauritania occupied the southern half of the land in defiance of Spanish threats to resist such a takeover. In November 1975, Spain relinquished claims to Spanish Sahara and struck a deal with Morocco and Mauritania: Morocco would administer the northern two-thirds and Mauritania would takeover the southern third.

However, when the two countries moved to establish their dominion in February 1976, Polisario, an independence group, declared a government-in-exile in Algeria. Within two years, Polisario undermined Mauritania's rule in western Sahara and Mauritania renounced its claims on the territory. Moroccan troops immediately invaded the southern third of the country and to date continue to fight Polisario forces.

King Hassan maintained firm day-to-day military control while his popularity soared. The 21 million Moroccans believe so strongly in Morocco's historic claims to Western Sahara that they firmly united behind King Hassan as never before during his reign.

In September 1988, the 13-year war in Western Sahara, which had cost more than 10,000 people their lives, seemed to be nearing an end. Both Morocco and Polisario agreed to a proposed independent referendum from the United Nations and the Organization of African Unity. Morocco agreed to reduce its troops in the territory, and Polisario's fighters agreed to be quartered under U.N. supervision.

One problem facing the U.N. referendum, however, was deciding who could vote. Under the U.N. plan, only those born in the territory were eligible to vote. Polisario claimed that 165,000 Western Saharans were living as exiles and should be allowed to take part, but Morocco disputed that claim. Conversely, a Moroccan claim that many who lived in the Moroccan-occupied section of the country were eligible was rejected by Polisario, which insisted that many of those were Moroccan immigrants, not native-born Western Saharans.

Other notable events occurred in 1977, when King Hassan sent 1,500 Moroccan troops to Zaire to help President Mobutu Sese Seko defeat an invasion from Angola. In 1986, King Hassan invited Israeli Prime Minister Shimon Peres to talk about the Middle East. Although no major event came of the two-day meeting, Syria and Libya both denounced Hassan as committing "an act of treason."

Agriculturally, a low-growth period from 1980-1984 was followed by bumper crops in 1986. Although yields fell slightly in 1987, Morocco finally became a net food exporter. Twenty-five years of dam building has brought more than 800,000 hectares under irrigation, a boon to a country bounded by desert. The per capita income in 1983 was $750.

Resolution of the Western Sahara conflict will give a major boost to the Moroccan economy—by 1988, the government was spending an estimated $2 million a day on the war.

*The improvement of agriculture is one of the major priorities of virtually every North African country.*

### Western Sahara

***Date of independence:*** **Spanish dominion ended February 28, 1976; Morocco and Mauritania assumed responsibility**
***Area:*** **102,000 square miles**
***Population:*** **101,000**
***Capital:*** **El Aioun**
***Monetary unit:*** **Moroccan and Mauritanian currencies**
***Nationality:*** **Saharan**
***Religion:*** **Muslim**
***Language:*** **Hassaniya Arabic**
***Literacy:*** **Saharans 5%, Moroccans 20%**
***Type of government:*** **Undetermined (Under Moroccan administrative control)**
***Political party:*** **Polisario**
***Monetary conversion rate:*** **4.33 dirhams = $1 (1980)**
***Principal economic resources:*** **Phosphates**

#### History at a Glance

For centuries, the territory now known as Western Sahara has been the home of desert nomads. Its coastline was first annexed by Spain in 1884, with penetration further inland by the 1930s.

Morocco, with longstanding historical rights to Western Sahara, sent thousands of soldiers to attack the territory in 1957 immediately after achieving its own independence. That invasion was quelled by Spanish and French forces and assistance from Western Sahara territorial divisions of Saguia el Hamra and Rio de Oro.

Interest in the land again heightened in 1963 with the discovery of one of the world's richest phosphate deposits in Bu Craa. During the next 12 years, Morocco pressured Spain to relinquish claims to Western Sahara, using a United Nations referendum, guerrilla activity, and a legal challenge in the International Court of Justice. Meanwhile, newly independent Mauritania lobbied from the south with claims to parts of Western Sahara.

Bowing to pressure, Spain formally announced its intention to give up claims to the land in May 1975 and in a Madrid conference in November of that year, administrative control of the territory was divided between Morocco and Mauritania—excising Western Sahara's eastern neighbor, Algeria.

As might have been expected, some inhabitants of Western Sahara felt the country should be self-governing, and in the fall of 1975 they formed the Popular Front for the Liberation of Saguia el Hamra and Rio de Oro (Polisario).

On February 28, 1976, Morocco formally assumed control of the northern two-thirds of Western Sahara; Mauritania assumed control of the southern third. Meanwhile, Polisario proclaimed the establishment of an independent Saharan Arab Democratic Republic, as government-in-exile and named Mohammed Ould Ahmed as Prime Minister.

Several months later, a World Court ruling said that Moroccan and Mauritania claims to the region were limited and had little bearing on the question of self-determination. Nevertheless, in November 1976 Morocco's King Hassan ordered 300,000 unarmed Moroccans to enter the territory in what was called "The Green March."

Polisario moved its headquarters from Mauritania to a more sympathetic Algeria, where it flourished in safety and received supplies from Libya. In July 1978, Polisario showed its strength by contributing to the overthrow of Mauritania's President Moktar Ould Dadda. A year later, Mauritania, beset by domestic troubles, renounced claims to Western Sahara at a conference held in Algeria, with Polisario officials in attendance.

Morocco seized the opportunity and sent troops into the southern third of the country, in effect annexing the entire country. Polisario in turn launched raids into Morocco itself, starting the first of many hit-and-run skirmishes.

Much of Western Sahara's nomadic population has been forced to either join Polisario refugee camps in Algeria or flee the region. The rest live in a few coastal towns, but little now remains of the nomadic lifestyle.

There are an estimated 15,000 Polisario fighters, who claim a "liberated zone" 30 miles from the Algerian town of Tindouf. Meanwhile, some 85,000 Moroccan troops stand watch behind a 400-mile long, 20-foot-high sand wall, fortified by land mines, which protects the Western Saharan capital of El Aioun and the northern regions, richest in phosphates.

The Polisario has been using Soviet-made weapons and missiles to drive out the Moroccans while King Hassan has sought military aid from the West. Since 1980, an uneasy truce has been called. However, military observers say negotiations for peace are remote and the situation is in a stalemate.

The Polisario has worked to gain recognition from other African countries, and by 1980 received a diplomatic nod from 45 nations.

### Tunisia

***Date of independence:*** March 20, 1956
***Area:*** 63,170 square miles
***Population:*** 7,300,000 (est. 1987)
***Capital:*** Tunis
***Monetary unit:*** Dinar
***Nationality:*** Tunisian
***Religion:*** 98% Muslim, 1% Christian, 1%Jewish
***Language:*** Arabic (official), French
***Literacy:*** 64%
***Type of government:*** Republic
***Political parties/leaders:*** Destourian Socialist Party, three legal parties, four major illegal parties
***Monetary conversionrate:*** 1 dinar = $1.22 US (1987)
***Principal economic resources:*** Wheat, olives, citrus fruits, grapes, dates, oil, phosphates

#### History at a Glance

Tunisia is the site of the ancient empire of Carthage, which once vied with Rome for power in the Mediterranean and in North Africa, but was finally defeated in 146 B.C. in the last of the three Punic Wars. Tunisia was occupied by the Vandals in the fifth century A.D.; by the Byzantines a century later; and by the Arabs for many centuries thereafter. The Arabs used Tunisia as a base from which to extend their power and the religion of Islam south and west into sub-Sahara Africa, and northward to Sicily.

The Turks seized Tunisia in 1574, holding it for three centuries, during which the territory was ruled by governors from Istanbul or by descendants of the Husayn dynasty.

In the late nineteenth century, France imposed a protectorate over the territory by armed force. By 1880, Great Britain, Italy, and France had established a control commission to supervise Tunisia's tottering finances. Once France had a clear field, though, she proceeded with a program of heavy investments which helped Tunisia modernize itself. In return, she benefited from Tunisia's unstinting loyalty during World War I.

Tunisian nationalism was an outgrowth of a moderate reform movement begun by the Destour Party in the 1920s. Led by Habib Bourguiba, the Neo-Destour Party of the next decade was activist in character, and able to negotiate with France from a position of strength after World War II.

In 1951, the French rejected a Tunisian demand for internal autonomy, a decision which touched off a wave of unrest punctuated by terrorism. In 1955, a Franco-Tunisian treaty was signed in Paris, and a year later Tunisia was granted full independence. A new constitution went into effect in 1959, and Bourguiba became first president.

Two years later, Tunisia attempted a blockade of the French naval base at Bizerte, a move which provoked the armed intervention of France and led to the massacre of several Tunisian civilians. Tension eased gradually and, in 1963, the base was evacuated by France.

Since then, Tunisia has nationalized all foreign-owned land in an effort to initiate a program of internal reform. In response, the French withdrew their technical experts, suspended financial aid, and eliminated export subsidies. The United States took up part of the slack by donating surplus grain, and by supporting a large public works program.

Tunisia ended its traditionally neutral role in the Arab world when it joined with the majority of Arab League members in condemning Egypt for signing a peace treaty with Israel. After Egypt was expelled from the League in 1979, Tunis became the headquarters for the League. Difficult relations with neighboring Algeria were smoothed over in 1979, but Tunisia broke all ties with Libya after its mining town of Gafsa was seized in 1980 by insurgents who were allegedly trained in Libya.

Over the next six years, Tunisia and Libya achieved rapprochement several times, only to see the relationship deteriorate again. Food riots in 1984 which left scores of people dead were blamed on Libyan influence. Tunis finally suspended relations with Tripoli in September 1985.

For 30 years, Bourguiba headed the only legal party in Tunisia, the Socialist Destourian Party. In the late 1970s, he was forced by internal pressures to recognize other parties, but in other areas of concern, he remained intractable and authoritarian. Voted President for Life in 1974, Bourguiba grew increasingly unpopular as the country faced a staggering birth rate, 20% unemployment and an increase in radical Islamic movements.

In October 1987, Bourguiba dismissed his prime minister, Rachid Sfar, and appointed General Zine el-Abidine Ben Ali in his place. It was presumed that the general would assist Bourguiba in putting down the fundamentalist movement, which had associations with the terrorist Islamic Jihad and Iran. Ben Ali's appointment came a week after seven fundamentalists were sentenced to death and 69 others to prison for planting bombs and conspiring against the government.

The next month, however, Ben Ali deposed Bourguiba, charging that the elderly statesman was planning numerous trials and wanted "12 to 15 fundamentalists hanged within the week." Such a plan, Ben Ali said in announcing why he assumed the presidency, demonstrated the "senility" of the 84-year-old Bourguiba, and would have caused national strife if carried out. Bourguiba was placed under house arrest in his palace, where he remained under doctors' care in 1988.

Ben Ali, who abolished the "President for Life" concept, indicated he planned to remain in office until the next scheduled elections in 1991. A "partial election" which brought new members to the Central Committee was held in August 1988.

He has continued to treat the fundamentalists carefully, giving amnesty to nearly 2,500 prisoners in December 1987, but keeping certain leaders in jail, in remembrance of the attempted coup earlier that year. In other areas, Ben Ali loosened restrictions on the press and political activity, and spoke in favor of the emancipation of Tunisian women, who already enjoy the most liberated lifestyle of any women in the Arab world.

Relations between Tunisia and Libya once again warmed, with visa restrictions lifted in March 1988.

Tunisia's greatest problem in the late 1980s continued to be its economy, which was plagued by a decline in oil prices, a foreign debt of $7 billion, and low productivity. Although the per capita income in 1986 was $1,000, unemployment continued to be high, especially among Tunisians under 25 years of age, who in 1987, made up 60% of the population. Many of the unemployed young people were high school or college graduates. Tunisia claims the first steel mill in northwest Africa.

A drought in 1987, which forced the country to purchase millions of dollars worth of grain, was followed in April 1988 by the worst locust invasion in 30 years.

# BLACKS IN THE WESTERN HEMISPHERE

**North America ■ South America ■ Central America ■ The Caribbean ■ Independent Nations ■ French American Dependencies ■ Netherlands American Dependencies ■ United Kingdom American Dependencies ■ United States Dependencies**

The status of blacks in the Western Hemisphere can be divided broadly into three categories. In the English-speaking countries of the United States and Canada, blacks comprise an identifiable minority. On many islands of the Caribbean blacks are a majority of the population, and sometimes, as on Barbados and Jamaica, an overwhelming majority. In other areas, notably on the continental mainland from Mexico south to Argentina, blacks have largely been absorbed into the mainstream of their country's population.

South Americans who are predominantly a mixture of black and Indian are known as Zambos. Those who are primarily a mixture of Caucasian and American Indian are known as mestizos, and those who are a mixture of Caucasian and black are, as in the United States, referred to as mulattoes. In tens of millions of cases, the Latin American is a mixture of all three strains. Because intermarriage has been accepted in so much of Latin America, black consciousness and racial, political, and cultural activity as such is minimal. Our description of these countries is brief. We give somewhat more space to Mexico and Canada because of their proximity to the United States and to other nations where the black presence is apparent and significant. However, it should not be thought that blacks have played a minor role in the history of other countries. Blacks, both slave and free, were prominent in the armies of Bolivar and San Martin in the liberation of South America from Spain. Bolivar was an avid opponent of slavery, and as slavery was culminated in Latin America—in contrast to feelings in the United States of America—there was little bitterness or resistance to the incorporation of blacks into the social fabric of the countries in which they lived.

## NORTH AMERICA

### Canada

Blacks comprise a minuscule portion of Canada's population, less than 25,000, or 0.1% of the total. Though the income and living conditions of Canada's blacks are much lower than those of its whites, Canada's major race problem reflects in its treatment of the Indians and Eskimos, who total about 200,000 and whose life expectancy is little more than half that of whites.

Blacks were prominent in the early seventeenth-century explorations and development of Canada by French explorers and Jesuit missionaries. The first slaves were Indians. The first black slave is believed to have been a native of Madagascar (Malagasy) and to have been sold to a French resident of Quebec in 1628. As French Canada expanded, slaves were purchased in the United States.

In 1749, the British brought slaves to Halifax, and slavery was legalized in British Canada in 1762. Slavery increased shortly thereafter, when the British took all of Canada in the French and Indian Wars. Many British fleeing from the revolutionary colonies to the south after 1775 brought slaves with them.

British slave codes were more severe than the French, under whom slaves could marry, own property, and maintain parental rights.

However, the British were not to sustain slavery for long. London had divided Canada into two governments, Upper Canada and Lower Canada. The governor of Upper Canada, Colonel James Simcoe, an ardent abolitionist, induced the areas's legislature to pass laws forbidding importation of slaves and freeing every slave born in the area by the age of 25. As a result, slavery in Upper Canada soon collapsed.

North America

Similar legislation was not enacted in Lower Canada, but by 1800 the Courts, through complex legal decisions, established the principle that a slave could leave his master whenever he wished. In the Maritime Provinces, courts also acted so as to eliminate slavery in fact if not in theory. Slavery was formally abolished in Canada in 1833.

Meanwhile, starting slowly in the eighteenth century, Canada was becoming a haven for slaves fleeing across her southern borders. Slaves who had served with the British in the American War for Independence came to Halifax from New York in large numbers in 1782 and 1783. Though many were to migrate to Freetown on the West Coast of Africa, others stayed. In 1826, Canada defied the United States and formally refused to return fugitive slaves. In 1829, the legislature of Lower Canada announced that every slave that entered the Province was immediately free, a declaration that gave impetus to the underground railroad and stimulated moves for resettlement by blacks in Canada.

The passage of the Fugitive Slave Act in 1850 meant that any escaped slave who remained in the U.S.A. was to be returned to his owner. Within a year after passage of the Law, some 10,000 slaves arrived in Canada, welcomed by a majority of Canadians who provided communities and services for them. In 1858, Canada served as a refuge for John Brown to plan his attack on Harpers Ferry.

Blacks were accepted into the mainstream of Canadian life, were allowed to choose separate or integrated schools, were elected to local office and served as officers in the Canadian Army. Black laborers contributed substantially to the expansion of the Canadian Pacific Railroad, as immigrants from Eastern and Southern Europe were to contribute to the development of railroads in the United States. Black skilled laborers were much in demand. By 1861, at the outbreak of the U.S. Civil War, there were 50,000 blacks in Canada, some pioneering above the Arctic Circle.

However, after the Civil War, feelings of fear and jealousy that had been festering among white Canadians led to discrimination in employment and schools. Blacks started to re-emigrate to the U.S.A. in large numbers, feeling that, with slavery outlawed there, a bright future awaited them. By 1871, the black population of Canada dipped to about 20,000. It has remained at about that level since.

In 1984, a leading Jewish organization issued a scathing report on bigotry in Canada, citing rising incidents of vandalism against Jewish institutions, anti-Catholic literature and cases of discrimination against black workers.

In April 1985, Section 15 of the Canadian Charter of Rights went into effect. The amendment to the then-three-year-old constitution stipulated that each Canadian "is equal before and under the law and has the right to equal protection and equal benefit of the law without discrimination... based on race, national or ethnic origin, color, religion, sex, age or mental or physical disability."

(The Canadian Constitution and Charter of Rights came

under Canadian control on April 17, 1982, when Queen Elizabeth II signed away Britain's control over such affairs. The French-Canadian province of Quebec, which is led by a separatist government, refuses to recognize the Constitution.)

Since then, public school systems have launched a drive to teach human rights in schools in order to promote cultural understanding and tolerance. Canada, the most sparsely populated country in the world with 1.5 persons per square mile, has become a haven for so many refugees that it has earned awards for "outstanding achievement" from human rights organizations. In fact, so many immigrants from Asia, Africa, the Caribbean and elsewhere have moved to Canada, that the established British-Caucasian population has expressed fears it will become extinct (assimilated) within 100 years. Toronto alone has become one of the world's most cosmopolitan cities with more than 100 cultural or ethnic groups among its 2.5 million population.

A number of Canada's blacks continue to live in rural areas settled by escaped slaves, but the majority live in or near major cities in the East. Earlier slaves and migrants from the U.S.A. have been joined by blacks from the West Indies.

### Mexico

Blacks accompanied the Spanish as conquerors to Mexico in the sixteenth century, and later were brought in large numbers as slaves. It is estimated that there were 150,000 black slaves in Mexico in the sixteenth century. One of the earlier slaves, Estevanico, is credited with opening up the northern interior lands of what is now New Mexico and Arizona, to Spanish conquest.

The use of slavery dropped sharply in the eighteenth and early nineteenth centuries. In 1829, Mexico abolished slavery in all its states except Texas, allowing it to remain there to pacify the United States. As slavery in the United States moved westward into Texas, Mexico became a haven for escaped slaves who slipped into the heart of the country and blended with the population.

Since the sixteenth century, Mexico's blacks have intermarried with Indians and whites so that their African heritage is no longer clearly identifiable. Some 100,000 blacks, about 0.5% of the population, do live in Mexico, mostly in the port cities of Vera Cruz and Acapulco. Blacks in lesser density live in Mexico City and in border cities across the Rio Grande River from Texas.

## SOUTH AMERICA

### Argentina

Blacks comprise a very small portion of the population of Argentina, which is one of South America's most Europeanized countries. Black population is estimated at about 30,000. In part, this low figure represents absorption of blacks into the general population.

### Bolivia

About 2% of the population of Bolivia is classified as black. Cultural factors, primarily those involving the Spanish and Indian populations, are of greater import in this country than the race question. Two-thirds of the population is Indian.

### Brazil

Brazil is the "melting pot" of South America. The Brazilian heritage is a compound of several diverse elements, blacks from Africa, Asians from Japan, Caucasians from Europe, mostly Portugal, and the country's aboriginal population. Official figures indicate that about 11% of Brazil's population of 140 million is black, another 26% is of mixed origins, 62% is European. However, the numbers of Brazilians with some African descent may be considerably greater, since children of mixed black and European parentage were commonplace during the days of slavery.

Slavery was introduced into Brazil in the 1530s, expanded greatly after 1540, when sugar became important, and grew most rapidly between 1580 and 1640, when Spain controlled the country. Estimates of the total number of slaves brought to Brazil varies from 6 to 20 million. Slavery did not finally

South America

end in Brazil until 1888.

Blacks in Brazil occasionally succeeded in establishing their own states within the country, the most famous being Palmares, which survived from 1630 to 1697, and at its peak had a population of 20,000. Palmares was a Kingdom with a capital, a well-developed economy and a remarkably efficient and courageous army. In the 19th century, Moslem blacks frequently came near to controlling the post city of Bahia.

Though slavery in Brazil was often extremely brutal, and the death rate of blacks on sugar, coffee and cotton plantations was enormous, large numbers of Africans achieved freedom. About 25% of Brazil's blacks were free during slavery.

During the nineteenth century, free blacks intermarried so rapidly their numbers fell from about 400,000 in 1800 to 20,000 by 1888 when slavery was finally abolished. Free blacks enjoyed full legal equality both during the period of slavery and after it was abolished.

In Brazil slaves who served masters in cities were often allowed to seek part-time and temporary employment elsewhere. They were able to read and write and develop employable skills. Blacks became important to the development and economy of the country and some became prominent in public life. Nilo Pecanha served as vice-president and briefly as president of Brazil in the first decade of this century. Blacks also achieved fame in Brazil's intellectual and artistic life.

Brazil is the only large South American country that has a sizable number of churches, periodicals and cultural groups oriented to blacks.

## Chile

Blacks have been less important to the development of Chile than to other South American nations, though black soldiers did fight in San Martin's Army in the nineteenth century when he liberated Chile from Spain. About two-thirds of Chile's population is of mixed European and Spanish ancestry, about one-third is European. The black population is less than 5,000.

## Colombia

Colombia's population typifies the Spanish, African and Indian mixture found in South America with perhaps a larger proportion of African stock than is evidenced in most other countries on the South American mainland—a factor that is largely due to the country's location on the Caribbean Sea. The territory that now comprises Colombia was one of the first locations in South America to which black slaves were brought in the sixteenth century. Blacks reside mostly along the coastal areas and in Colombia's tropical valleys. Blacks are noted in Colombia for their conspicuous contribution to its armed forces.

*On Saturday of each week, Indians from neighboring towns converge on Otavalo, Ecuador. They come to sell their wares, to replenish their larders and to meet socially with friends.*

### Ecuador

About 10% of Ecuador's 10 million people are classified as black. The rest of the population is composed of some 40% Indian, 40% mestizo and 10% Caucasian, and mostly resides along the Atlantic coast.

### Paraguay

Paraguay's 3 million inhabitants are largely a mixture of European and Guarani Indian. Blacks make up about 15,000 or approximately 0.5% of the population.

### Peru

Black slave-soldiers accompanied Pizarro in his sixteenth-century conquest of Peru and saved subsequent conquistadores from defeat by the Indians. In the eighteenth century, blacks made up over one-fifth of the population of Lima. Peru was the last nation in Spanish South America to abolish slavery, not doing so until 1855. Today some 550,000 of Peru's 20 million inhabitants are regarded as black.

### Uruguay

Uruguay is widely regarded as South America's most Europeanized country. About 15,000 of its 3 million inhabitants are black and Uruguay's proportion of mulattoes and mestizos is perhaps the lowest in South America.

### Venezuela

About 900,000 of Venezuela's 17 million people are black and another 500,000 are Zambos. In the sixteenth and seventeenth centuries, Caracas was a major center for the import of slaves. In the early nineteenth century, blacks and mulattoes comprised more than half of the population of The Captaincy General of Caracas, as Venezuela was known then. Blacks remain a significant part of the country because of its proximity to the Caribbean and employment opportunities that have been available in this oil-rich nation.

## CENTRAL AMERICA

### Belize—formerly British Honduras

About 60% of the inhabitants of Belize are of mixed black-white parentage, including Carib Blacks (Garifunas), Creoles, who are descendants of African slaves and settlers, and mestizos, who are descended from Spanish and Mayan Indians.

Most blacks are of West Indian origin.

### Costa Rica

Only 2% of the population of Costa Rica is black. Most blacks are of Jamaican origin and, together with a small number of mulattoes, are settled in the Limon Province.

### El Salvador

Less than 5,000 of El Salvador's 5 million inhabitants are classified as black.

### Guatemala

The relatively few blacks and mulattoes in Guatemala inhabit the Caribbean and Pacific lowland areas.

### Honduras

Some 2% of the Honduras population is black. The dominant strain is a mixture of Spanish and Indian blood.

### Nicaragua

Blacks comprise some 9% of the population in sparsely inhabited Nicaragua. They are settled mainly along the Miskito Coast.

### Panama

Roughly 70% of the inhabitants of Panama are classified as mestizo or mulatto—i.e., mixed white and Indian, or mixed white and black. In part this reflects large numbers of blacks brought to Panama to build the Panama Canal. (See United States Dependencies: Panama Canal Zone.)

Central America

Caribbean Islands

## THE CARIBBEAN

The end of slavery in the Caribbean in the 1830s did little to help the area's blacks. Still dependent for a living on the plantation-type economy dominant in the area, blacks tended in large numbers to enter into debt-ridden, subordinate relations with landowners, much like the tenant farming system many American blacks were forced into after the Civil War. Some blacks, however, taking advantage of the short labor supply in West Indian towns and cities, moved to urban areas where they acquired skills and higher living standards. On many islands, they filled lower civil service posts and became sources of manpower to the police and military. In some cases, a few blacks eventually worked their way into their island's upper social strata, themselves becoming landowners and public officials. But the vast majority remained impoverished. This was also true in Haiti, despite the fact that blacks owned the land and ran the government. Most holdings there were, and are, remain very small. Since its freedom, Haiti has largely been ruled by a mulatto elite.

In the 1860s, denial of suffrage to all but a few blacks, and on some islands, large scale importation of cheap contract labor from India, led to unsuccessful rebellions by blacks. One rebellion in Jamaica was ruthlessly suppressed at a cost of thousands of lives and burning of black neighborhoods.

Economic conditions, education and political rights slowly improved until the end of World War II, when Britain, facing the need of dissolving most of its Empire, and prodded by black West Indians, started to grant independence to most of its Caribbean territory. A Federation of the West Indies, containing Jamaica, Trinidad and Tobago and Barbados, was formed in 1958, but could not function well over the great distances between the islands, and was dissolved in 1962.

Despite freedom, most Caribbean nations continue to suffer from an inequitable distribution of wealth, a matter which in turn induces large scale emigration of educated blacks. Many of these contributed substantially to the development of the United States. John Russwurm, Marcus Garvey, and Claude McKay were immigrants from the British West Indies.

Poor living standards have also created large amounts of emigration to Britain and the United States. In the eastern part of the United States, Jamaicans are frequently imported to perform short term agricultural jobs, such as apple picking in Vermont. In 1975, unemployment in Jamaica was about 20% of its workforce.

The following territories are discussed in this section.

Bahama Islands
Barbados
Cuba
Dominican Republic
Guyana (in South America)
Haiti
Jamaica
Trinidad and Tobago
French American Dependencies
French Guiana (in South America)
Guadeloupe
Martinique
Netherlands American Dependencies
Netherlands Antilles
Surinam (in South America)
United Kingdom American Dependencies
Bermuda
British Virgin Islands

Cayman Islands
Leeward Islands
Turks and Caicos Islands
Windward Islands
United States Dependencies
Corn Islands
Panama Canal Zone
Puerto Rico
Swan Islands
Virgin Islands of the U.S.

### Barbados

***Date of independence:*** November 30, 1966
***Area:*** 166 square miles
***Population:*** 260,000 (January 1987)
***Capital:*** Bridgetown
***Monetary unit:*** Barbados dollar
***Ethnic divisions:*** 80% African, 17% mixed, 4% European
***Religion:*** 70% Anglican, Roman Catholic, Methodist, Moravian
***Language:*** English
***Literacy***: Over 96%
***Type of government:*** Independent sovereign state within the Commonwealth since November 1966 recognizing Elizabeth II as Chief of State
***Political parties leaders:*** Barbados Labor Party (BLP), Democratic Labor Party (DLP), Errol Barrow
***Monetary conversion rate:*** 2.01 Barbados dollars = U.S. $1 (1987)
***Principal economic resources:*** Tourism, sugar milling, light manufacturing

#### History at a Glance

The most easterly of the Caribbean Islands, Barbados was originally the home of the Arawak Indians, although it was probably uninhabited when the first British settlers arrived in 1627. Barbados is an island in the Atlantic located some 300 miles north of Venezuela. It is only 21 miles long and at its widest point is 14 miles across. Land patents were granted to members of the English nobility but returned to the Crown in 1652. Slavery was legally abolished in 1834, the last of the slaves liberated four years later.

The constitution of Barbados, among the oldest in the Commonwealth, is based largely on convention. Universal adult suffrage was introduced in 1951, elected ministers in 1954, a cabinet system in 1958, and full internal autonomy in 1961. The bicameral legislature was headed by a Crown-appointed governor, who in turn appointed a premier empowered to name a five-member cabinet.

Called the "Little England" of the Caribbean, Barbados played a leading role in the West Indies Federation (1958-1962) and supplied the organization's only prime minister, Sir Grantley Adams.

Barbados achieved independence in November 1966, electing Democratic Labor Party leader and premier Errol Barrow as prime minister that month. Barrow was reelected in 1971, but was unseated at the end of his term by Sir Grantley's son, J. M. "Tom" Adams, leader of the Barbados Labour Party.

Prime Minister Adams, a conservative, guided the island until his death in March 1985, when he was succeeded by his deputy, Bernard St. John. In May elections the next year, however, Mr. St. John lost to the more liberal Mr. Barrow, who will remain in office until the 1991 elections.

Barbados has enjoyed a stable and flourishing economy, with per capita income at $4,000 in 1984. It has the highest population density in the Western Hemisphere, with 16,500 persons per square mile.

### Cuba

***Date of independence:*** May 20, 1902
***Area:*** 44,218 square miles
***Population:*** 10,100,000 (January 1987)
***Capital:*** Havana
***Monetary unit:*** Peso (noncommercial rate December 1980)
***Ethnic divisions:*** 51% Mulatto, 37% white, 11% Negro, 1% Chinese
***Religion:*** At least 85% nominally Roman Catholic before Castro assumed power
***Language:*** Spanish
***Literacy:*** About 96%
***Type of government:*** Communist state
***Political parties/leaders:*** Cuban Communist Party (PCC), First Secretary Fidel Castro Ruz, Second Secretary Raul Castro Ruz
***Monetary conversion rate:*** 1 Peso = U.S. $1.38 (nominal)
***Principal economic resources:*** Sugar milling, petroleum refining, food and tobacco processing, textiles, chemicals, paper and wood products, metals

#### History at a Glance

Cuba was discovered by Christopher Columbus during his first voyage to America. In 1511, the Spanish appointed a governor, Diego Velasquez, who established Santiago as the capital and founded Havana just south of where it lies today. By 1523, the African slave had become a familiar sight on the island. Yet, during this period, Cuba was of even greater importance as an embarkation point for Spanish explorers bound for the Central and South American mainlands. The treasures of Mexico obtained by the conquistadores invariably passed through Havana on their way back to Europe, with the result that the northern coast of Cuba was often despoiled by French and English pirates preying on Spanish shipping. In 1762 the English occupied Havana and held Cuba for nearly a year before returning it to Spain in exchange for Florida. The English occupation encouraged a greater spirit of national unity and stimulated free trade.

Most of Spanish America managed to win independence in the early decades of the nineteenth century, but not Cuba. In 1868, Carlos Manuel de Cespedes, a wealthy planter, granted his slaves their freedom and agitated for revolution against Spain. For the next decade or so, guerrillas were holed up in the hills of eastern Cuba, but their efforts against the combined strength of the colonial government and the Spanish army proved fruitless. In 1892, while in exile in the United States, Jose Marti founded the Cuban Revolutionary Party and three years later, issued the famous *grito de Baire* (call to arms). The insurrection lasted for three years, though Marti was killed in the initial engagement against Spanish forces.

The cause of the revolutionaries aroused considerable sympathy in the United States, both in private and official circles. Consequently, it hardly came as a surprise when the United States declared war on Spain after the U.S. battleship Maine was blown up in Havana harbor on February 15, 1898. Spanish resistance on both land and sea was easily overcome and Cuba was declared independent.

The United States, however, did force Cuba to ratify the Platt Amendment which specified that it could intervene in the island's internal affairs in the event it became necessary to insure the maintenance of law and order. In addition to this, much of Cuba's wealth, natural and otherwise, was soon in the hands of a number of American absentee owners. Revolts against Yankee imperialism brought about the periodic intervention of U.S. Marines—in 1906, 1912, and again in 1920. Finally, in 1934, during the first administration of Franklin D. Roosevelt, the Platt Amendment was abrogated. (The United States, however, retained possession of a naval base at Guantanamo Bay.)

During World War I, Cuba enjoyed a brief period of prosperity due to the growth of its gold reserves, but sugar prices soon declined, giving rise to widespread unemployment and national hardship. In 1925, Gerardo Machado began an eight-year reign as dictator. His successor was overthrown in 1934 by an army sergeant, Fulgencio Batista y Zaldivar. More clever than his predecessor, Batista held power by installing puppet presidents whom he then deposed at will. In 1940, he had himself elected president and allowed a new constitution to be passed. After his four-year term was over, he continued, nonetheless, to be a potent force in Cuban politics—a fact borne out by his seizure of power in 1952.

On July 26, 1953, a group of young firebrands staged an abortive raid on the army barracks at Fort Moncada. Led by Fidel Castro, the uprising was quickly suppressed and Castro himself thrown into prison. He was released under a 1954 presidential amnesty, only to begin the immediate organization of what he came to term the sequel to the "26th of July" movement. Two years later, he and a small group of revolutionary forces (including his trusted aide Ernesto "Che" Guevara of Argentina) landed in Oriente province, where they holed up in the Sierra Maestra Mountains. The rebellion spread across the island and, within three years, Batista has been forced into exile. The "26th of July" movement swept Castro into power as premier in 1959.

Members of the revolutionary cabinet then undertook to rule the country by decree, ostensibly until those reforms to which the movement had been dedicated could be put into effect. Castro himself disavowed ties with Communism.

By 1960, however, the government plunged ahead with a comprehensive scheme of land expropriation, one which affected U.S. property holdings with disturbing frequency. Anti-Communist cabinet members were soon purged and Cuba became a base for other Latin American revolutionary movements.

In 1961, the United States, at this time still Cuba's chief hemispheric customer, decided to sever diplomatic relations with the Castro regime. The Cuban government countered this move by nationalizing U.S. oil refineries for having refused to process Soviet crude oil, whereupon the United States decided in its turn to eliminate Cuba's sugar quota. Trade and general relations with Soviet-bloc nations and Communist China offset some of the deficit incurred by the loss of U.S. markets. Late in 1960, Castro labeled Cuba a socialist country, and within a year, declared himself to be a follower of Marxist-Leninist doctrine.

In 1961, a group of Cuban exiles—financed, trained, and organized by the Central Intelligence Agency—undertook an amphibious invasion of the island at the Bay of Pigs. Within three days, however, Cuban military forces defeated the invaders, taking some 1,200 men prisoner. (The captives were later used by Castro as human barter for U.S. supplies.)

By 1962, all major means of production and distribution, as well as communication and other public services, were in the hands of the state.

That same year, evidence gathered from U.S. aerial reconnaissance photographs of Cuba established that the Soviet Union had begun to install ballistic missiles capable of reaching American soil. Moving decisively, President Kennedy quickly initiated a blockade of the island and issued an ultimatum calling for the immediate withdrawal of all such offensive weapons. This action brought the world to the brink of war, averted only after the Soviets backed down in the face of Kennedy's demand.

Castro remained in control, however, and continued to spread revolutionary propaganda throughout the rest of Latin America. In 1965, he instituted a program whereby all Cubans wishing to go to the United States (excepting those males eligible for military service) would be permitted to do so.

Castro has since reported that 1970 was a turning point in Cuban affairs. Viewing a decade of revolution, he assured the people that agricultural programs would continue to put plenty of food on their tables and on the shelves of their stores. He also maintained that Cuban industry was making remarkable strides and would bring the country out of its underdeveloped status before 1975.

In 1973, Cuba and the U.S. signed an agreement providing for extradition of hijackers of planes or vessels brought by Americans to Cuba or by Cubans to the U.S.

In 1975, there were hints that the United States and Cuba might soon resume diplomatic and trade relations. Cuba's efforts to direct other Latin American nations toward a Communist path had largely failed and her foreign policy appeared more moderate. Many Latin American nations that had broken relations with Cuba indicated a wish to restore them and Senators Pell and Javits of the United States had made a visit to Cuba and then introduced a resolution in the Senate asking President Ford to try to improve relations with Cuba. Secretary of State Kissinger also hinted at interest in friendlier relations.

*The government of the Dominican Republic hopes eventually to replace the improvised homes in the foreground with better standard public housing as in the background.*

However, prospects for normalization were clouded by reports that in the early 1960s, the United States Central Intelligence Agency had sought to have Fidel Castro assassinated and that perhaps the Cuban government had been involved in the 1963 assassination of President Kennedy.

In 1980, both foreign and domestic issues were dominated by the massive emigration of Cuban citizens mainly orchestrated by the Castro regime. Touching off the exodus was the influx of 10,000 Cubans into the Peruvian embassy at Havana after the government had withdrawn its police guard following a dispute over the right of political asylum.

In 1984, the U.S. insisted Cuba take back some 2,700 "undesirables"—criminals and mentally ill persons—that had come with the boatlift, and send, in return, some 3,000 political prisoners. Castro quashed this suggestion as well as a U.S. appeal to allow 27,000 Cubans to emigrate annually when the U.S. began its anti-communist "Radio Marti" broadcasting in May 1985. By 1987, however, Castro agreed to accept the "undesirables" back and allow the 27,000 to leave, providing they meet qualifications and could pay an "exit fee" anywhere from $3,000 to $40,000.

While Cuba has courted South American countries such as Brazil and Uruguay, most of its neighbors give it wide berth. Cuba has maintained good relations with Libya, Iran and North Korea, and has routinely sent thousands of Cuban troops to bolster Marxist governments elsewhere, such as in Angola, Nicaragua and Ethiopia.

By the mid-1980s, the Soviet Union was reportedly subsidizing Cuba by about $4 billion a year, and joblessness on the island had tripled from 1981 to 1985. An attempt to form a Solidarity-style union in 1982 ended with arrests and death sentences for the five union leaders. In the late 1980s, Castro came under fire from the United Nations for keeping some 15,000 "political prisoners," the highest number per capita in the world. Castro avoided a U.N. investigation by releasing several hundred prisoners, and loosening some prison restrictions.

Sugar is still a major export, most of which is purchased by Soviet satellite countries; in fact, in 1980, 75% of Cuba's trade was with the Soviet Union. Production of other traditional exports, coffee and tobacco, were down, and Cubans have lived under a rationing program for years.

## Dominican Republic

***Date of independence:*** February 27, 1809
***Area:*** 18,816 sq. miles
***Population:*** 6,300,000
***Capital:*** Santo Domingo
***Monetary unit:*** Peso
***Ethnic divisions:*** 73% Mulatto, 16% white, 11% black
***Religion:*** 95% Roman Catholic
***Language:*** Spanish
***Literacy:*** 68%
***Type of government:*** Republic
***Political parties/leaders:*** Social Christian Reformist Party
***Monetary conversion rate:*** 3.17 pesos = U.S. $1.00 (1987)

***Principal economic resources:*** Tourism, sugar, sugar processing, nickel mining, bauxite mining, gold mining, textiles, cement

## History at a Glance

The eastern portion of the island of Hispaniola, the portion which forms today's Dominican Republic, was originally known as Quisqueya—"mother of all lands." It was first settled by the warlike Carib Indians, who were succeeded by the peace-loving and agriculturally inclined Arawaks.

In 1492, Christopher Columbus became the first European to land on the island, claiming it for Spain. Within the next two decades, Hispaniola became a base from which Spain initiated her conquest of the New World. By 1517 cattle and horses were being raised on the island and sugar cane had become the staple of its agricultural economy. At that time, the population was estimated to be about 60,000, a substantial portion of which were black slaves. The discovery of Mexico and Peru, the ravages of a smallpox epidemic, and the excesses of Dutch, English, and French buccaneers, led to a sharp population decline and Hispaniola soon outlived its usefulness as a staging ground for the Spanish conquests.

In 1697, Spain was forced by the Treaty of Ryswick to acknowledge French dominion over the western third of the island (Haiti). A century later it also lost control of the eastern two-thirds of Hispaniola (Santo Domingo) in the aftermath of a slave uprising. Toussaint L'Ouverture, the liberator of Haiti, conquered Santo Domingo in 1801, but the Dominicans, fearing the Haitian's rule, backed a French force which soon succeeded in overcoming them. Haiti achieved independence in 1804, but Saint Domingue (as it was rechristened by the French) remained under French control until 1809 when Juan Sanchez Ramirez defeated the French at Palo Hincado and proclaimed the founding of the first Dominican Republic.

Spain regained control of this territory under the Treaty of Paris (1814), but in 1821 another republic was founded, this time by Jose Munez de Caceres. Within a year, however, Santo Domingo was once again overrun by Haiti, which occupied the territory for some 22 years, a period marked by the departure of most land-owning whites, fierce racial and cultural animosities, and an atmosphere heavy with oppression and violence. In 1884, a secret group known as La Trinitaria organized a successful revolt which once more restored the independent republic of Santo Domingo.

During the next 20 years Dominican history ran an unpredictable course, punctuated by petty internecine rivalries, further threatened invasions by Haiti, and several changes of government. In 1861, President General Santana invited Spain to annex the country, and during the next four years, it was administered as a Spanish colony. Spanish troops withdrew in 1865, ushering in still another period of almost continuous revolution and widespread governmental corruption.

In 1870, Santo Domingo was on the verge of being annexed by the United States, but the U.S. Senate refused to ratify the necessary treaty. By 1905, the country teetered on the brink of bankruptcy and political chaos and the United States assumed control of Dominican customs. In 1915, following a presidential assassination and the overthrow of several chief executives, the United States set up an economic council to stabilize the island's economy. A year later, a military government under Captain H. S. Knapp was established. This government remained in power until 1924 when Dominican sovereignty was restored and U.S. forces withdrew. (The customs control mission remained until 1941.)

In 1930, Rafael Leonidas Trujillo Molina was elected president and ushered in a 30-year period of rule during which Santo Domingo became his personal property. Aided by his family, Trujillo became an absolute dictator who quashed all attempts at resistance by murder, imprisonment, and other grisly forms of intimidation. Reelected in 1934, 1940, and 1947, Trujillo did manage to improve economic conditions in his country, achieve administrative stability, balance the budget and free the nation from domestic and foreign debt. In the process, however, he accumulated an enormous private fortune, estimated at from 900 million to 1.5 billion dollars.

In 1961, Trujillo was assassinated and a wave of terror swept the island as his son, Air Force General Rafael Trujillo Martinez, seized power. Special investigators from the Organization of American States (OAS) reported that the new repressions were even more ruthless than the old.

Over the next four years, the influence of the Trujillo family was eradicated. The country was ruled by two presidents, two councils of state, and two juntas. Coup and counter-coup verged on the order of the day. The situation was further complicated by near-war with Haiti and by guerrilla activity sponsored by pro-Castro Dominicans.

In 1965, the ruling civilian junta was overthrown in a military uprising which triggered a civil war involving rebel forces laced with Castroite supporters and hard-core Communists. Almost at once the United States intervened militarily, ostensibly on the grounds that it was protecting American nationals. In May of that year an inter-American contingent was created by the Organization of American States and dispatched to the scene to serve as an occupational force. The major factions agreed on the installation of Hector Garcia-Godoy as provisional president in the summer of 1965. A year later Joaquin Balaguer was elected president, where upon U.S. combat troops were withdrawn.

Balaguer, who was reelected in 1970, kept the nominal allegiance of the military, but at a high price. The national budget allocated more than 17% of its expenditures to military upkeep. The expansion of the U.S. sugar quota helped the country, but political unrest, labor problems, and dwindling tourism offset much of the gain from this source. About two-thirds of the Republic's population is mulatto and mestizo, about 12% is black.

Silvestre Antonio Guzman Fernandez of the Dominican Revolutionary Party succeeded Dr. Joaquin Balaguer following an election on May 16, 1978. Fernandez has been applauded for many sweeping reforms while in office. He has also met resistance especially from his own Dominican Revolutionary Party (PRD), concerning maneuvering for the 1982 election. Although he stated that he would not seek another term, Fernandez has made no effort to implement a 1978 PRD campaign pledge to seek a constitutional amendment that would bar reelection. In 1979, Fernandez ousted his principal rival, Salvador Jorge Blanco, as president of the party.

In May 1982, Blanco returned to political power, wresting the presidency of both the PRD and the country from President Guzman. Two months later, Guzman committed suicide.

In 1986, President Blanco was narrowly defeated by the elderly and nearly blind former president Joaquin Balaguer and his Social Christian Reformist Party.

President Balaguer has had to grapple with low sugar prices, financial disarray inherited from previous administrations, and drug trafficking by military leaders and others. In 1987, after being named in a corruption investigation, Blanco sought political asylum in Venezuela. The PRD has splintered into three factions.

The Dominican Republic's troubles have been further increased by an influx of several thousand Haitians, fleeing their country's political bloodshed and poverty. Under Balaguer, however, some 200,000 jobs have been created in public works projects, tomatoes are supplanting sugar as a principal cash crop and tourism is rising.

## Guyana (formerly British Guiana)

***Date of independence:*** May 26, 1966
***Area:*** 83,000 square miles
***Population:*** 1,000,000 (January 1987)
***Capital:*** Georgetown
***Monetary unit:*** Guyana dollar
***Ethnic divisions:*** 51% East Indians, 43% Negro and Negro mixed, 4% Amerindian, 2% white/Chinese
***Religion:*** 57% Christian, 33% Hindu, 9% Muslim, 1% other
***Language:*** English
***Literacy:*** 86%
***Type of government:*** Republic within Common wealth
***Political parties/leaders:*** People's National Congress (PNC), People's Progressive Party (PPP), Cheddi Jagan, Working People's Alliance (WPA), Rupert Roopnarine, Walter Omawale, Eusi Kwayana, United Force (UF) Feilden Singh
***Monetary conversion rate:*** 10.00 dollars = $1 US (1987)
***Principal economic resources:*** Bauxite mining, alumina production, sugar and rice milling, timber

### History at a Glance

Spanish sailors first charted the coastline of what is now Guyana in 1499, but the territory was not settled until 1620, by the Dutch West Indies Company. By 1746, the Dutch had founded settlements in Essequibo, Demerara, and Berbice. But they lost control of these areas to the English—first in 1796, then in 1803, and finally, in 1814. The colony of British Guiana was formed in 1831.

With the abolition of slavery in 1837, most blacks settled down on the land they had worked or migrated to the towns. The aristocratic planter class exerted pressure on the government for the importation of indentured servants from India to work on the plantations. Today most of the sugar workers are East Indians, where as the urban population is predominantly of African origin—a factor of great importance in current political trends in the country.

In 1928, British Guiana was granted a limited representative government along with a new constitution. In 1953, another constitution was put into effect, calling for the establishment of a bicameral legislature and an increase in the elected majority of the lower house. Because of charges of Communist subversion, however, England suspended the elections, instituting instead an interim government which ruled until 1957 when new elections were held. Victory went to the People's Progressive Party (PPP), headed by Dr. Cheddi Jagan, who was named minister of trade and industry.

In 1961, British Guiana was granted full autonomy. That same year, elections held under still another constitution resulted again in a majority victory for the PPP which controlled the Legislative Assembly. A year later, Dr. Jagan, by then the premier, submitted an austerity program calling for compulsory savings and for a property tax. Announcement of this program triggered a violent general strike, which could not be put down until British troops arrived on the scene.

In 1963, there was further unrest with the passage of a labor relations bill which appeared to make it possible for Dr. Jagan to favor the interests of certain unions. Racial friction heightened between the East Indian followers of Dr. Jagan and the black-dominated urban population, many of whom occupied civil service posts. Strikes and even more violent upheavals seriously affected Guiana's economy and large losses were suffered by the sugar and bauxite industries.

Late in 1964 the People's National Congress (PNC), headed by Forbes Burnham, wrested control from the PPP by winning the national elections. The PNC, however, was only able to form a government with the aid of the United Force Party, a right-wing, business-oriented group, encouraging close ties with the West. British Guiana became independent under its new name of Guyana on May 26, 1966, with Burnham remaining in power as the duly elected prime minister. Guyana was declared a republic in 1970.

Guyana then became involved in a feud with its western neighbor, Venezuela, which laid claim to more than half the entire territory of the new republic. The dispute was officially resolved for a period of 12 years, by an agreement in 1970. In 1974 Forbes Burnham was still Prime Minister.

In October 1980, Prime Minister Burnham became president and Ptolemy Reid became prime minister as a new constitution went into effect. Neither man remained in office for long. Reid, suffering from ill health, was succeeded by Hugh Desmond Hoyte in August 1984. The next year, President Burnham died undergoing surgery, and Hoyte was elected to a five-year term amid accusations of ballot fraud. Hamilton Green, leader of the People's National Congress, succeeded Hoyte as prime minister.

Guyana gained widespread attention in 1978 when 911 persons died in a mass murder-suicide at a remote settlemen' in Guyana founded by a sect from the United States known as the People's Temple led by Reverend Jim Jones. Jones, on November 19, 1978 had ordered his followers to die (the victims were either shot or forced to drink poisoned Kool-Aid) after his aides had killed U.S. Representative Leo J. Ryan of California. Three journalists who were with Ryan were also killed.

In 1984, five Canadians and one American were charged with plotting to assassinate President Burnham and others in his administration.

Guyana has struggled with a "virtually bankrupt" economy, 85% of which is under state control. It is also embroiled in land disputes with Venezuela and Suriname. Under Burnham and Hoyte, the country courted Soviet interests, however, lately relations with the U.S. and Caribbean nations have improved.

## Haiti

***Date of independence:*** January 1, 1804
***Area:*** 10,714 square miles
***Population:*** 6,200,000 (1987)
***Capital:*** Port-au-Prince
***Monetary unit:*** Gourde
***Ethnic divisions:*** Over 90% Negro, nearly 10% Mulatto, few whites
***Religion:*** 10%Protestant, 75% to 80% Roman Catholic (of which an overwhelming majority also practice voodoo)
***Language:*** French (official) spoken by only 10% of the population; all speak Creole
***Literacy:*** 10 to 12%
***Type of government:*** Republic
***Political parties/leaders:*** National Unity Party, Haitian Christian Democratic Party, Haitian Christian Democratic Party of June 27, Haitian National Christian Party, United Haitian Communist Party (PUCH), illegal (communist)
***Monetary conversion rate:*** 5 Gourdes = U.S. $ 1 (December 1987)
***Principal economic resources:*** Sugar refining, textiles, flour milling, cement manufacturing, bauxite mining, tourism, light assembly industries

### History at a Glance

Christopher Columbus discovered the island of Hispaniola (the western half of which is today called Haiti) in 1492 and established a settlement on the north coast near the present city of Cap Haitien. The Spanish colonists lost little time in wiping out the island's Indian inhabitants, a policy which eventually made it necessary for the Spanish crown to import slaves from Africa for plantation labor.

By 1625, French privateers, operating from the island of Tortuga, were successful in expelling the Spanish along the northern coast and paving the way for French colonies to spring up. With sugar as the basis of the plantation economy, the French brought more and more slaves from West Africa. In 1697, under the Treaty of Ryswick, Spain ceded the

*A student at a large ceramics center in Port-au-Prince molds an urn by hand.*

western portion of Hispaniola to France. Under French rule, St. Domingue (as this area was then called) became one of the most prosperous territories in the Caribbean.

By the eighteenth century, four distinct social groupings had emerged on the island: the white French planter; the Creole; the freed black and the black slave. The Creoles—sandwiched, as it were, between the white and black—found themselves striving desperately for the privileges accorded the white minority while living in fear of being overrun by the blacks.

It was not until the French Revolution in 1789 that the explosive potential, inherent in such a social situation, began to reveal itself. Haiti's half a million black slaves became increasingly imbued with a desire for freedom. In 1791, an uprising was suppressed by the French, but the movement never lost its momentum due largely to the fervor and genius of a self-educated slave and former soldier, Toussaint L'Ouverture. Within two years, Toussaint had conquered the entire island, promulgated a new constitution, and abolished slavery. In 1802, however, a huge force sent by Napoleon recaptured the island. Toussaint himself was betrayed and, after being taken prisoner, was shipped to France where he died.

However, his successor, Jean Jacques Dessalines, another black general who had risen in the ranks, continued this struggle and overcame the French forces in 1803. A year later, Dessalines proclaimed the independence of St. Domingue and restored to it the original Indian name of Haiti ("land of mountains"), in the process taking for himself the title of emperor.

Haiti became the first independent republic in Latin America. France lost control of Santo Domingo, the eastern portion of the island, in 1808.

Haiti's history has been marred by a number of cruel and corrupt administrations, and tensions between the black and mulatto population. U.S. military forces occupied the country from 1915 to 1934. The 1940s saw the succession of seven black presidents, until 1957, when Francois Duvalier won the presidential election. "Papa Doc," as he was later called, turned the presidency into a dictatorship and had himself declared "President for Life" in 1964.

Until his death in April 1971, "Papa Doc" ruled the population through terrorism, employing the wiles of voodoo priests who reportedly could turn a person into a "zombie," and the strength of a 30,000-strong secret police force known as "Tontons Macoutes" or "bogeymen." Critics of the government frequently met with imprisonment, torture or death, and thousands fled the island.

In 1971, as "Papa Doc" planned, his "President for Life" mantle passed to his son, Jean-Claude Duvalier. The younger Duvalier, known as "Baby Doc," made a few reforms in the mid-1970s in order to gain U.S. aid. However, a period of liberalization ended in 1980, followed by a resurgence in repressive laws and attacks by the Tontons Macoutes.

By the 1980s, after more than 20 years of combined rule, the Duvaliers had succeeded in reducing Haiti to one of the hemisphere's poorest countries while earning personal reputations as reckless spendthrifts. When elections in the early 1980s failed to dislodge "Baby Doc," riots broke out in protest of food shortages, police brutality, and political and human rights abuses. Despite government attempts to quell the Haitians' unrest, the rioting continued, and in February 1986, "Baby Doc," his wife, Michelle, and their family fled to France. Army Chief of Staff Gen. Henri Namphy assumed power and formed a provisional government.

It has been estimated that at least 50,000 people were killed by the Duvaliers and that the family expropriated between $300 million and $800 million from the economy.

Gen. Namphy maintained an uneasy rule until elections in January 1988, when exiled political leader Leslie Manigat was chosen as president. (Elections held on November 29, 1987 were shattered when bands of Tontons Macoutes attacked voters; 34 persons were hacked or shot to death.) After Manigat's election, lawlessness continued and in July Namphy deposed Manigat and assumed power. By the end of September, Namphy was himself deposed in a coup and replaced by Lt. Gen. Prosper Avril.

Haitians today exist in extreme poverty, living in slums and shanties with rampant disease. Unemployment remains around 50%. Tourism, once a major source of revenue, suffered immeasurably when in 1982 Haitians were

*Throughout the Caribbean the loading of bananas is a common sight.*

designated as a high risk group for Acquired Immune Deficiency Syndrome (AIDS). In 1988, the U.S. narcotics investigators cited Haiti as the "busiest cocaine transfer point in the Caribbean."

## Jamaica

***Date of independence:*** August 6, 1962
***Area:*** 4,411 square miles
***Population:*** 2,300,000
***Capital:*** Kingston
***Monetary unit:*** Jamaican dollar
***Ethnic divisions:*** African 76%, Afro-European 15.1%, Chinese and Afro-Chinese 1.2%, East Indian and Afro-East Indian, 3.4%, White 3.2%, others 0.9%
***Religion:*** Predominantly protestant, some Roman Catholic and spiritualist cults
***Language:*** English
***Literacy:*** Although government claims 82%, only about half are functionally illiterate
***Type of government:*** Independent state within the Commonwealth
***Political parties/leaders:*** Jamaica Labor Party (JLP), People's National Party (PNP), Michael Manley
***Monetary conversion rate:*** 5.48 Jamaican dollars = $1 US (1987)
***Principal economic resources:*** Bauxite mining, textiles, food processing, light manufacturing, tourism, bananas, rum

### History at a Glance

Jamaica was discovered by Christopher Columbus on May 2, 1494, on his second voyage to the New World. Some 15 years later, it was settled by the Spanish who systematically exterminated its original inhabitants, the Arawak Indians, replacing them with slaves brought from Africa to work the plantations. The name Jamaica was derived from an Arawak Indian word, Xaymaca. Jamaica is the third largest island in the Caribbean and the largest and most populous of the independent Commonwealth nations in the area.

The English conquered the island in 1655, at which time a group of slaves (the Maroons) fled into the interior, where they established a number of strongholds from which they made sporadic raids on the English settlers. This situation lasted until 1740, the year the Maroons were granted virtual autonomy over their own lands.

Jamaica soon became a base of operations for buccaneers raiding the Spanish Main. On the whole, however, the English continued to maintain a slave-operated plantation economy based on such crops as sugar, cocoa, and coffee. With the abolition of slavery in 1834, the settlers were forced to recruit other sources of cheap labor, resorting to the importation of East Indian and Chinese farm hands. In 1846 the removal of the tariff protection for colonial produce entering the British market set off a violent dispute between the planter-dominated Jamaican legislature and the Crown on the one hand, and the planter-dominated administration and the Jamaican freedmen on the other. This conflict culminated in the Morant Bay uprising of 1865, which led to the imposition of Crown-colony status one year later. The growth of banana cultivation, improvement of internal transportation and communication, and reform in the political administration improved the status of the islanders somewhat, but insurmountable barriers continued to separate most groups within Jamaican society, which was largely class-centered.

The Depression of the 1930s aggravated already-existing problems to such an extent that England felt it necessary to dispatch a royal investigating commission to the island. The commission's report led to the drafting of the 1944 constitution which permitted Jamaicans a wider degree of self-government.

Cabinet government was introduced in 1953, five years before the island became a member of the West Indies Federation. Jamaica withdrew from this organization in 1961. Full self-government came in 1959; independence within the British Commonwealth was achieved three years later. Thereafter, the Prime Minister was Sir Alexander Bustamante, leader of the Jamaican Labour Party (JLP). Bustamante was succeeded in office in 1967 by Hugh Shearer.

In 1972, Michael Manley of the People's National Party defeated the People's Labor Party to become Prime Minister. In 1975, Manley was host to a meeting of British Commonwealth Prime Ministers in Kingston, at which time he affirmed Jamaica's intent to remain in the Commonwealth. He has been trying to forge closer ties with Africa through such means as inviting leaders like Julius Nyerere of Tanzania to visit Jamaica and encouraging the appointment of a research fellow in linguistics to trace surviving African influences in Jamaican English.

In international affairs, Manley described Jamaica as a "third world" nation suffering from the ever-present problem of receiving low prices for exports of raw materials and having to pay steeply rising prices for imports of manufactured goods from industrially advanced countries.

Prime Minister Edward Philip George Seaga of the Jamaica Labour Party succeeded Manley following an election on October 30, 1980. The magnitude of the JLP victory was a function of the poor economic situation that had developed in the last couple of years while Manley ruled. There had been a decline in bauxite earnings along with an escalating oil import cost which generated an inflation rate exceeding 25%. There also had been a 33% unemployment rate plus a cumulative decline of 16% in the Gross National Product since 1974. Soon after the election, Seaga issued a call for a "Marshall Plan" to aid Jamaica and other Caribbean countries.

Seaga has strengthened ties to the U.S., advocating the Reagan Administration's Caribbean Basin Initiative in 1981 and assisting in the 1983 U.S. invasion in Grenada in October 1983. Seaga has also been instrumental in the formation of the Caribbean Democratic Union, which enlists conservative parties in the island nations to resist socialist influences.

Seaga ran into trouble, however, when he tried to buck the austerity measures imposed by international bankers, to

Christopher Columbus discovered Trinidad in 1498.

which Jamaica was at least $70 million in debt. In 1987, the International Monetary Fund agreed to refinance a $3.3 million debt, to allow the country to regain economic footing. These plans were placed in disarray, however, by severe flooding in 1986 and Hurricane Gilbert, which devastated the island in September 1988.

## Trinidad and Tobago

***Date of independence:*** August 31, 1962
***Area:*** 1,980 square miles
***Population:*** 1,200,000 (January 1987)
***Capital:*** Port-of-Spain
***Monetary unit:*** Trinidad and Tobago dollar
***Ethnic divisions:*** 43% black, 40% East Indian, 14% mixed, 1% white, 2% other
***Religion:*** 26.8% Protestant, 31.2% Roman Catholic, 23.0% Hindu, 6.0% Muslim, 13.0% unknown
***Language:*** English
***Literacy:*** 95%
***Type of government:*** Independent state
***Political parties/leaders:*** People's National Movement, United Labor Front (ULF), Democratic Labor Party (DLP), Democratic Action Congress (DAC), West Indian National Party (WINP)
***Monetary conversion rate:*** 3.60 dollars = $1 US (1987)
Principal economic resources: Oil, asphalt, cocoa, sugar, molasses, rum, tourism

### History at a Glance

Christopher Columbus discovered Trinidad and Tobago on July 31,1498, bestowing the name "La Trinidad" (Spanish for "The Trinity") on the larger of the two islands. A Spanish governor was placed in charge of Trinidad in 1522, at which time the island became a supply station for ships en route to South America. Settlers attempting to colonize Trinidad during these years met with opposition from the Carib Indians and from British buccaneers then active in the Caribbean. Sir Walter Raleigh, for example, burned St. Joseph in 1595.

In time, however, the Spanish did manage to establish settlements and introduce a plantation-based economy heavily dependent on slave labor from West Africa. In 1725, a severe blight all but wiped out the cocoa crop, and agriculture was at a virtual standstill for the next 50 years. In 1783, the Spanish government began inviting immigrants of other nationalities to help colonize the islands, an offer which attracted many Frenchmen who acquired free land grants. (The distinctive French-Creole flavor in today's Trinidad is directly traceable to this influx of French settlers.)

Trinidad was captured by the British in 1797 and formally ceded to Great Britain by Spain five years later (The Treaty of Amiens).

In the nineteenth century sugar proved to be the island's agricultural staple. Cultivation of this crop was made possible by the utilization of slave labor. When slavery was abolished in 1834, the landowners resorted to the importation of more than 150,000 Hindu and Moslem "contract workers" from India. A good number of them remained in Trinidad once their contracts had expired, finding work in the cocoa industry which experienced a revival in the late nineteenth century. Since then, sugar and petroleum have grown in importance.

After its discovery by Columbus, Tobago too went virtually ignored until 1616, when colonists from Great Britain first appeared among the island's Carib Indian inhabitants. England gained permanent possession of Tobago in 1814 and ruled it for much of the nineteenth century from the Windward Island of Grenada. Tobago became a Crown Colony in 1877 and was linked to Trinidad, also a crown colony, in 1888. Since then, it has remained associated with the latter in all phases of its political, economic, and social development.

*A Trinidad constable pauses on the principal street of Port-of-Spain.*

*The offices of Tobago's premier occupy a nineteenth-century mansion.*

Independence was granted Trinidad and Tobago jointly in 1962, with Dr. Eric Williams serving the new nation both as prime minister and head of the majority party, the People's National Movement. In 1970, Trinidad was rocked by Black Power demonstrations and a mutiny in its armed forces, both of which were overcome by the government.

Williams died unexpectedly on March 29, 1981. George Chambers was immediately invested as Williams' interim successor. On May 9,1981, Chambers was formally elected leader of the People's National Movement. Williams had led the country for a quarter of a century and prior to his death there had been no obvious successor to him. Williams had insisted that anyone designated as a successor should be selected for party, not personal, responsibility.

In the December 1986 elections, Chambers and his PNM were swept from office by Arthur N. R. Robinson and his opposition group, the National Alliance for Reconstruction. Prime Minister Robinson was expected to reverse the economic slide—he had campaigned on the slogan, "Stop the thieving"—but soon found that not only were the island treasuries empty, but the government was in arrears for several hundred million dollars. The austerity measures he was forced to impose quickly ended the NAR's "honeymoon" period with the populace.

# FRENCH AMERICAN DEPENDENCIES

## French Guiana

***Area:*** 35,135 square miles
***Population:*** 78,000 (January 1984)
***Capital:*** Cayenne
***Monetary unit:*** Franc
***Ethnic divisions:*** 95% black or mulatto, 5% Caucasian, 10,000 East Indian, Chinese
***Religion:*** Roman Catholic
***Language:*** French
***Literacy:*** 73%
***Type of government:*** Overseas department and region of France
***Political parties/leaders:*** Guianese Socialist Party, Rally for the Republic (RPR)
***Monetary conversion rate:*** 6.09 French francs = $1 US (1987)
***Principal economic resources:*** Timber, rum, gold mining, production of rosewood essence, space center

### History at a Glance

French Guiana first was colonized in 1604 and was formally awarded to France in 1667 by the Peace of Breda. During the French Revolution, it served both as a penal colony and a place of exile. The territory's permanent borders were not settled until 1854.

Since 1947, French Guiana has been an overseas department of France, represented in the French parliament by one senator and one deputy. The territory of Inini, included within it, has a status equivalent to that of a Parisian *arrondissement* (an administrative district).

Most of the inhabitants are mulattoes. There are several tribes of aboriginal Indians in the interior. Most descendants of free or fugitive black slaves have settled along the rivers and coastal lowlands. In recent years, some 20,000 refugees have entered French Guiana from Suriname.

French Guiana is north of Brazil and east of Suriname on the northeast coast of South America. In 1958, French Guiana accepted the new Constitution of the French Fifth Republic, while remaining an Overseas Department of the French Republic.

## Guadeloupe (Basse-Terre, Grand Terre)

***Area:*** 687 square miles
***Population:*** 317,000 (January 1987)
***Capital:*** Basse-Terre
***Monetary unit:*** Franc
***Ethnic divisions:*** 90% black or mulatto, less than 5% East Indian, 5% Caucasian, Lebanese, Chinese
***Religion:*** Roman Catholic
***Language:*** French, creole, patois
***Literacy:*** Over 70%
***Type of government:*** Overseas department and region of France
***Political parties/leaders:*** Rassemblement Pour la Republique (RPR)
***Monetary conversion rate:*** 6.09 French francs = $1 US (1987)
***Principal economic resources:*** Bananas, rum, sugar cane, fishing, tourism, agricultural processing

### History at a Glance

Guadeloupe was discovered by Christopher Columbus in 1493 during his second voyage to the New World. A permanent colony was established there by France in 1635. Since then, with the exception of two brief periods during which the island was occupied by Great Britain, Guadeloupe has been in the hands of the French. An overseas department of France since 1946, it is represented in Paris by three deputies and two senators.

The inhabitants of Guadeloupe are either black or a mixture of black and the French settlers who first arrived in the seventeenth century.

Fervent demonstrations for independence erupted in 1967. In response, France increased its economic and educational subsidies to Guadeloupe. Militant groups continued to attack the status quo during the 1980s.

Guadeloupe is located 300 miles southeast of Puerto Rico and consists of the twin islands of Basse-Terre and Grande-Terre and five dependencies—Marie-Galante, Les Saintes, LaDesirade, St. Barthelemy, and the northern half of St. Martin.

*An open-air market in the Caribbean.*

### Martinique

***Area:*** 425 square miles
***Population:*** 312,000 (Jan. 1987)
***Capital:*** Fort-de-France
***Monetary unit:*** Franc
***Ethnic divisions:*** 90% African and African-Caucasian-Indian mixture, less than 5% East Indian, Lebanese, Chinese, 5% Caucasian
***Religion:*** 95% Roman Catholic, 5% Hindu and Pagan African
***Language:*** French, creole, patois
***Literacy:*** Over 70%
***Type of government:*** Overseas department of France
***Political parties/leaders:*** Rassemblement Pour la Republique, (RPR), Emile Maurice; Progressive Party of Martinique (PPM), Aime Cesaire; Communist Party of Martinique (PCM); Democratic Union of Martinique, and Federation of the Left
***Monetary conversion rate:*** 6.09 French francs = $1 US (1987)
***Principal economic resources:*** Tourism, bananas, sugar, rum, fishing

#### History at a Glance

Christopher Columbus discovered Martinique in 1502. It was first colonized by the French in 1635 and has remained under the control of France for all but two short periods of its history: from 1762 to 1763, during the Seven Years War and from 1794 to 1815, during the Napoleonic Wars. In both instances, Great Britain temporarily occupied the island.

In 1902, Mount Pelee erupted and completely destroyed the city of St. Pierre, together with its 30,000 inhabitants.

Martinique is represented in the French parliament by three deputies and two senators. An appointed prefect is chief administrator and is assisted by a 36-member general council. The island has been an overseas department of France since 1946.

Martinique is in the Lesser Antilles and about 300 miles northeast of Venezuela. A new Constitution of the French Fifth Republic was approved in 1958 and Martinique has since remained an Overseas Department of the French Republic. The people of Martinique are mostly black, or of Carib Indian or European descent.

## NETHERLANDS AMERICAN DEPENDENCIES

### Netherlands Antilles

***Area:*** 308 square miles
***Population:*** 190,000 (Jan. 1987)
***Capital:*** Willemstad, Curacao
***Monetary unit:*** Netherlands Antilles guilder
***Ethnic divisions:*** Racial mixture with African, Caribbean Indian, European, Latin and Oriental influences, negroid characteristics dominant on Curacao, Indian on Aruba
***Religion:*** Roman Catholic, sizable Protestant and smaller Jewish minorities
***Language:*** Officially Dutch; Papiamento, a Spanish Portuguese-Dutch-English dialect with English widely spoken
***Literacy:*** 95%
***Type of government:*** A territory within the Kingdom of the Netherlands
***Political parties/leaders:*** Indigenous to each island
***Monetary conversion rate:*** 2.28 guilders = $1 US (1987)
***Principal economic resources:*** Oil (Aruba and Curacao), boat building (Saba), cotton, sugar, cane (Saint Maarten), agriculture (St. Eustatius), tourism

#### History at a Glance

Curacao, the largest of the Netherlands Antilles, was discovered in 1499 by Aloso de Ojeda and Amerigo Vespucci, but Spain did not begin colonizing the island until 1527. In 1634 the Dutch, under Johannes van Walkeeck, seized the islands, including Aruba and Bonaire and installed Peter Stuyvesant as governor. During the Napoleonic Wars, the English occupied them, but they were restored to the Netherlands in 1816.

Saba was first occupied by the Dutch in the seventeenth century, while St. Eustatius, in the hands of the Dutch since 1632, served as a supply depot for England's American colonies before and during the Revolutionary War. (It is traditionally credited with having been the first foreign post to render a salute to the American flag in 1776.) The island changed hands several times before being permanently restored to the Netherlands in 1841. Saint Maarten, occupied by the Dutch and French in 1648, was later divided between them.

The people are mostly a mixture of black, Indian, Spanish, and Dutch strains.

The Netherlands Antilles, a part of the kingdom of the Netherlands, has had complete internal autonomy since 1954. Executive power is wielded by a governor who represents the Dutch sovereign. The current governor, Dr. Rene Romer, was invested in October 1983, while the Prime Minister Dominico F. Martina of the New Antilles Movement took office in November 1985 after defeating the incumbent Maria Liberia Peters of the National Peoples Party.

Aruba was given separate status within the kingdom January 1, 1986, which translated into a 21% revenue loss to the island coalition. Prime Minister J.H.A. Eman of the Aruba Peoples Party was sworn into office the same day.

## Suriname (Formerly Dutch Guiana)

***Area:*** 63,251 square miles
***Population:*** 400,000 (1987)
***Date of Independence:*** November 25, 1975.
***Capital:*** Paramaribo
***Monetary unit:*** Suriname guilder
***Ethnic divisions:*** 40% Creole (black and mixed), 37% Hindustani, 15% Javanese, 2.6% American Indian, 1.7% Chinese, 1.7% European
***Religion:***
***Language:*** Dutch (official), English (widely spoken)
***Literacy:*** 80%
***Type of government:*** Parliamentary democracy with military participation
Political parties/leaders: Bruma (principal leftist party), Progressive Party, Javanese Farmers Party, Reformed Progressive Party
***Monetary conversion rate:*** 2.57 guilders = $1 US (1987)
***Principal economic resources:*** Bauxite, lumbering, rice, sugar cane, citrus fruits, coconuts, bananas

### History at a Glance

In the sixteenth century Spaniards in search of gold were the first Europeans to set foot on Suriname, but they left when no treasure was found. In 1625 the British, French, and Dutch began to vie for control of the territory. Under the Treaty of Breda (1667), Great Britain agreed to cede it to the Netherlands in return for the colony of New Amsterdam (later New York). Dutch control, however, was not recognized by other European powers until the Treaty of Paris at the end of the Napoleonic Wars.

In 1954, Suriname was granted full internal autonomy in accordance with the provisions of a new statute put into effect by the king of the Netherlands. (This charter united the Netherlands, Suriname, and the Netherlands Antilles on a basis of equality and as constituents by a governor who is assisted by a cabinet and by an elected legislative council.)

The black inhabitants of Suriname, representing about 40% of the population, are descendants of fugitive slaves who were imported from Africa before 1865. Other major groups include: Indians (from the Asian subcontinent), Indonesians; Creoles (persons of mixed descent), and aboriginal Indians.

The first prime minister, Henck A. E. Arron, was deposed by a military junta called the National Military Council (NMC) on February 25, 1980, and replaced by Dr. Henk Chin A Sen.

Prime Minister Chin, who later became president, was thwarted in his plans for democracy by Lieutenant Colonel Desi Bouterse, who led the 1980 coup. In 1982, Chin resigned and was replaced by L. F. Ramdat-Misier. Changes in government over the years have been followed by rumors of coups and imposition of martial law. In 1985, Suriname's *de facto* leader, Bouterse, was named Commander-in-chief of the Army and Head of Government, and President Ramdat-Misier was reconfirmed in his post. A new prime minister, Jules Wijdenbosch, was confirmed in February 1987.

*A flower vendor carries her wares in a basket on her head.*

The government has faced a number of domestic problems in recent years. Since 1980, Suriname has contested its western neighbor, Guyana, for rights to a 6,000-square-mile tract of land which is rich in bauxite. Another imbroglio was a $1.5 billion loan from the Netherlands which was to have been dispensed to Suriname over a 10-year period. Due to the leftward tilt of the country after the coup, the Dutch withdrew the loan. When Suriname sought to receive money and aid from Cuba and Libya, Brazil threatened to invade Suriname. In 1986, a serious threat to the military government was posed by Ronny Brunswijk and his guerilla force, composed mainly of "Bush Negroes," a hardy ethnic group descended from African slaves. Some 20,000 people fled to French Guiana to escape government reprisals.

In November 1987, Suriname held elections for a civilian government. Ramsewak Shankar was elected to a five-year term as president, and Henck Arron as vice president. Bouterse and the military were expected to continue to have influence over the country, which by the late 1980s, faced a blighted economy, food shortages, and burgeoning black market.

# UNITED KINGDOM AMERICAN DEPENDENCIES

## Bermuda

***Area:*** 21 square miles
***Population:*** 58,000 (January 1986)
***Capital:*** Hamilton
***Monetary unit:*** Bermuda dollar
***Ethnic divisions:*** 60% black, 40% white
Religion: 47.5% Church of England, 38.2% other Protestant, 10.2% Catholic, 4.1% other
***Language:*** English
***Literacy:*** Virtually 100%
***Type of government:*** British colony
***Political parties/leaders:*** United Bermuda Party (UBP), J. David Gibbons; Progressive Labor Party (PLP), Lois Browne Evans
***Monetary conversion rate:*** 1 Bermuda dollar = U.S. $1
***Principal economic resources:*** Tourism, finance

### History at a Glance

Discovered in 1515 by the Spaniard Juan de Bermudez, Bermuda was first settled by a group of British colonists who had been shipwrecked in 1609 while en route to Virginia. The islands were officially acquired by the British Crown in 1684.

In modern times, the British have established a naval base on Ireland Island, while the United States has leased sites for military bases on two other islands.

A Crown Colony, Bermuda has the oldest British colonial legislature. It is administered by a governor who represents the sovereign and is assisted by a nine-member executive council. The British maintain control over foreign affairs and the Bermudan police.

The current population breakdown lists 60% as black or mixed and 40% as white.

In 1973, the governor Sir Richard Sharples and an aide were assassinated and a state of emergency was declared. Motives for the crime remain obscure. However, there was much rioting in December 1977 after two blacks had been hanged for a series of murders, including the assassination of the Governor. British troops were called in to restore order.

## British Virgin Islands

***Area:*** 59 square miles
***Population:*** 12,000
***Capital:*** Road Town
***Monetary unit:*** U.S. dollar
***Language:*** English
***Principal economic resources:*** Fish, livestock, tourism

*Fishing trainees aboard the Alcyon, a ship of the Caribbean Fishery Development Project.*

*Road construction in Barbados, also called the "Little England" of the Caribbean.*

### History at a Glance

Great Britain obtained title to these 40-odd islands and islets in 1666 and, until 1960, administered them as part of the Leeward Islands. At present, the government is headed by a Crown-appointed administrator who is assisted by both executive and legislative councils.

The administration of the British Virgin Islands is headed by a governor, James Alfred Davidson, and its representative institutions include a mainly elected Legislative Council and an appointed Executive Council. The governor chooses the chief minister from the legislature. H. Lavity Stoutt is currently chief minister.

Almost the entire population is of African descent.

## Cayman Islands (Grand Cayman, Little Cayman, Cayman Brac)

***Area:*** 100 square miles
***Population:*** 23,000
***Capital:*** Georgetown
***Monetary unit:*** Cayman Islands dollar
***Language:*** English
***Principal economic resources:*** The Caymans' traditional sources of revenue, fishing and tourism, have been superseded by offshore banking services in recent years. By 1980, some 325 banks and 12,000 companies had registered in the islands.

### History at a Glance

Christopher Columbus discovered the Cayman Islands in 1503, naming them "Tortugas" due to the profusion of turtles in the surrounding waters.

Once it became clear that the Spanish did not intend to colonize them, the British sent in settlers from nearby Jamaica. The islands remained a dependency of Jamaica until its independence in 1959, when they became subject to a new constitution providing for a Crown-appointed administrator, a legislative assembly, and an executive council.

One out of every five Cayman Islanders is classified as black; approximately half of the population is of mixed blood; the rest is European.

## Leeward Islands (Antigua, Anguilla, Barbuda, Redonda, St. Christopher-Nevis, Montserrat)

***Area:*** 356 square miles
***Population:*** 61,000
***Language:*** English
***Principal economic resources:*** Agriculture, tourism, sugar

### History at a Glance

When the Leeward Islands were discovered by Christopher Columbus in 1493, they were inhabited by Carib Indians. St. Kitts was the first English settlement in the Caribbean (1623); Nevis was colonized five years later and Montserrat in 1632. The French captured some of the islands in 1666 and again in 1782, but they were returned to the British under the Treaty of Versailles (1783).

Significant constitutional changes were first introduced in the nineteenth century, particularly after the abolition of the slave trade (1808). Although suffrage was extended, the small farmer and the laboring class still found themselves not truly represented.

In 1956, the separate colonies were united to form the territory of the Leeward Islands, and two years later were incorporated into the Federation of the West Indies which lasted until 1962.

Today each territorial unit has a Crown-appointed administrator, as well as executive and legislative councils.

Most of the population is an intermixture of European settlers and the descendants of West African slaves.

In 1967, Antigua and a St. Christopher Nevis-Anguilla Federation were granted full control of their domestic affairs.

Antigua and Barbuda became independent members of the Commonwealth in November 1981. St. Christopher-Nevis followed suit in September 1983.

## Bahama Islands

***Date of independence:*** July 10, 1973
***Area:*** 5,380 square miles
***Population:*** 249,000
***Capital:*** Nassau (New Providence Island)

***Monetary unit:*** Bahamian dollar
***Ethnic divisions:*** 80% black, 10% white, 10% mixed
***Religion:*** 29% Baptist, 23% Church of England, 23% Roman Catholic, 7% Methodist
***Language:*** English
***Literacy:*** 89%
***Type of government:*** Independent Commonwealth since July 1973 which recognizes Elizabeth II as chief of state
***Political parties/leaders:*** Progressive Liberal Party, Lynden O. Pindling; Bahamian Democratic Party (BDP) Henry Bostwick; Free National Movement (FNM), Cecil Wallace-Whitfield
***Monetary conversion rate:*** 1 Bahamian dollar (B$1)=U.S. $1
***Principal economic resources:*** Tourism, cement, oil refining, lumber, salt production, rum, aragonite, pharmaceuticals, spiral weld, steel pipe

### History at a Glance

Christopher Columbus first set foot in the New World on the island of San Salvador (now called Watling's Island) in the Bahamas on October 12, 1492. The first settlers of the Bahamas, however, were British who came from Bermuda in the seventeenth century. British companies subsequently brought in large numbers of African slaves to work the plantations. The first royal governor, appointed in 1717, made the islands safe for colonization by permanently driving off the many pirates, among them the notorious Bluebeard, who had utilized the Bahamas as a base of operation. The islands were claimed by the French in the eighteenth century, then captured by the Spanish in 1781. The English, however, quickly regained control of them via the Treaty of Paris (1783).

During the U.S. Civil War, confederate blockade runners operated out of the Bahamas, as did rum runners during the American prohibition era. In 1940, the United States established naval bases in the area.

The Bahamas are administered by a governor, who is assisted by legislative and executive councils. The constitution has existed virtually unchanged since 1729.

On July 10, 1973, the Bahamas obtained their independence and assumed the status of an independent member of the British Commonwealth. Lynden O. Pindling of the Progressive Liberal Party is Prime Minister. Following an overwhelming election by the Progressive Liberal Party in 1968, the Bahamas gained greater autonomy. Sir Pindling was reappointed following general elections in 1977 and 1982.

The Bahamas, since World War II, has become established as an important center of banking and finance. Its banking laws promise anonymity as does Switzerland, and the islands house more than 300 financial institutions. It is a popular tax haven, since the Bahamas do not extract corporate, capital gains or personal income taxes. Tourism provides employment for two-thirds of the population and draws an estimated 2.5 million visitors a year. As a result, the Bahamas are flourishing, with a gross domestic product of $2 billion and a per capita income of $7,600 by the mid-1980s.

The Bahamas make up an archipelago of some 700 islands plus uninhabited inlets (2,400), as well as cays 50 miles off Florida's coast. Twenty-two of the islands are inhabited, the most important being New Providence where Nassau is located.

## Turks (Grand Turk; Salt Cay) and Caicos (South Caicos, North Caicos) Islands

***Area:*** 166 square miles
***Population:*** 10,000 (1987)
***Capital:*** Grand Turk
***Language:*** English
***Principal economic resources:*** Salt, crayfish, sisal, conch products

### History at a Glance

Though discovered by Ponce de Leon in 1512, the Turks and Caicos Islands remained uninhabited until 1678, when the Bermudians settled there to mine salt. They were expelled by the Spanish in 1710, but soon returned, only to survive several Spanish and French attacks.

In 1848, the islands became a separate colony under the administration of Jamaica before being annexed by the latter in 1873. They were again separated from Jamaica when it became independent in 1962. Since then they have been administered by a British resident who is assisted by an executive council and a legislative assembly.

Most of the inhabitants are either of African or mixed descent.

In 1987, prominent citizens of these impoverished islands suggested that Canada annex them and position them as sort of a "Canadian sunshine province." A similar proposal the year before was shot down by the Canadian External Affairs Department, which predicted racial tensions between the island's mostly black populace and the mostly white Canadian tourists. In fact, in early 1987, violence did break out when proprietors of a Club Med resort on the island of Providenciales tried to exclude all blacks from the island.

The islands are loath to leave Britain's protectorship, despite its few advantages, due to their 30% unemployment rates.

## Windward Islands (Dominica, Grenada, Saint Lucia, Saint Vincent)

***Area:*** 825 square miles
***Population:*** 400,000
***Principal economic resources:*** Livestock, fish
***Language:*** English
***Monetary unit:*** Caribbean Dollar
***Monetary conversion rate:*** 2.70 = $1 US (1987)

### History at a Glance

The Windward Islands were inhabited by Indians when they were discovered by Columbus in 1493. Later settled by the English, they soon became a battle ground between the indigenous Caribs, the English, and the French. Carib opposition was, to all intent and purpose, eliminated toward the beginning of the eighteenth century, when the remaining Indians were deported to areas near Honduras. During much the same period, Great Britain won important territorial concessions under the Treaty of Versailles (1783) and at the Congress of Vienna (1815).

Africans worked the fields until slavery was abolished, at which time they were replaced by East Indians and Portuguese. Despite the introduction of limited voting rights, the descendants of the land-working class remained essentially unrepresented until the twentieth century.

In 1956, the four territories—Dominica, Grenada, Saint Lucia, and Saint Vincent—were combined to form the Windward Islands, and two years later incorporated into the Federation of the West Indies (dissolved in 1962).

The islands are governed by a Crown-appointed administrator, aided by executive and legislative councils.

The population is an intermixture of European settlers, the descendants of West African slaves, and Carib Indians.

In 1967, Dominica, Grenada, and St. Lucia were granted self-government with Britain retaining control of foreign affairs. St. Vincent received similar status in 1969.

In 1975, Grenada became an independent member of the Commonwealth. The other islands soon followed suit, with Dominica in 1978, St. Lucia in February 1979, and St. Vincent and the Grenadines in November 1979.

When Grenada joined the Commonwealth, the unpopular Sir Eric Gairy was designated as prime minister. Gairy was perceived as a dangerous eccentric and the ensuing public uneasiness fostered the growth of a People's Alliance, formed of three opposition groups. In March 1979, while Gairy was out of the country, "New Jewel Movement" leader Maurice Bishop led a coup and formed a People's Revolutionary Government.

Four years later, when Bishop failed to adopt a hard-line alliance with the Soviet Union, he was arrested and executed on the orders of Deputy Prime Minister Bernard Coard and Gen. Hudson Austin, commander of the People's Revolutionary Army.

The murder of Bishop prompted Governor General Sir Paul Scoon to ask for intervention by the Organization of Eastern Caribbean States, and on October 25, 1983, U.S. troops landed on Grenada and captured the leadership. Further investigation on the island revealed massive caches of arms and military materiel, and hundreds of Cubans and Soviet bloc "advisors." Islanders viewed the invasion as a "liberation," and requested that a contingent of U.S. troops stay on the island until mid-1985. Herbert A. Blaize was installed as prime minister of a parliamentary regime in December 1984. Since then, Grenada has received millions in aid from the U.S., the World Bank, and European countries. As a result, there has been a resurgence in nutmeg, cocoa and banana crop production, fishing and tourism. However, unemployment continues to hover around 30%

In Dominica, Mary Eugenia Charles was sworn in as prime minister, and reappointed in 1985. Disaster came to that island in 1979 and 1980 when hurricanes devastated the banana industry.

## UNITED STATES DEPENDENCIES

### Corn Islands

***Area:*** 4 square miles
***Language:*** English
***Principal economic resources:*** Coconuts

#### History at a Glance

The Corn Islands (Great Corn and Little Corn) were leased to the United States by Nicaragua in 1916 as a means of protecting a contemplated canal across the latter country. The lease was signed for a 99-year period.

### Panama Canal Zone

***Area:*** 560 square miles (372 are land)
***Population:*** 45,000
***Language:*** English, Spanish
***Principal economic resources:*** Canal operations

#### History at a Glance

The Canal Zone is a 50-mile-long, five-mile-wide strip lying between the Atlantic and Pacific Oceans, on both sides of the Panama Canal. It was granted in perpetuity to the United States by virtue of a United States-Panamanian treaty signed in 1903.

Since 1959 the residents of the zone (half of whom were born in the continental United States, the rest from Panama or the zone itself ) had grown vehement in their demands for its restoration to Panama. On occasion, student demonstrations flared to the point of violence before being suppressed.

The canal was operated by the U.S.-owned Panama Canal Company under the terms of the Panama Canal Act of 1950. The governor of the zone was also the president of the company. Canal Zone legislation remained in the hands of the U.S. Congress.

By 1967, U.S. and Panamanian negotiators produced draft treaties that would provide for Panamanian participation in canal management, profit-sharing between Panama and the United States, and a measure of dual sovereignty. The treaties were obstructed by the forceful overthrow of Panamanian President Arnulfo Arias in 1968, and in 1970 Panama repudiated the treaty. In 1973, the United States vetoed a United Nations Security Council resolution that would have called for negotiation of a new treaty that recognized Panamanian sovereignty. However, in 1974 the two countries entered negotiations which would eventually hand over control to Panama and in the meantime increase Panamanian influence and revenues.

Two treaties were signed in Washington on September 7, 1977 and though Panama endorsed it in a plebiscite on October 23, the treaties were barely approved by the U.S. Senate on March 16 and April 18, 1978. During a visit to Panama by President Carter on June 16, 1978, documents of the ratification were exchanged. There was a delay in the implementation of the treaties due to a U.S. Senate stipulation that ratification would not be deemed complete until passage of enabling legislation by the Congress or until March 31, 1979, or which ever was first. On October 1, 1979, the American flag was lowered within the Canal Zone and the administrative authority for the canal was then formally transferred to a binational Panama Canal Commission.

In 1986, a panel composed of Japanese, U.S. and Panamanian interests began a four-year study to consider either upgrading or augmenting the canal.

## Puerto Rico (Culebra, Mona, Vieques)

***Area:*** 3,435 square miles
***Population:*** 3,300,000 (1987)
***Capital:*** San Juan
***Religion:*** Roman Catholic
***Language:*** Spanish, English
***Type of government:*** Democracy
***Political parties/leaders:*** Popular Democratic Parrty, New Progressive Parrty, Puerto Rican Socialist Party, Puerto Rican Independence Party
***Principal economic resources:*** Coffee, tobacco, sugar cane, tourism, dairy farming, manufacturing industries

### History at a Glance

Discovered by Columbus in 1493 on his second voyage to the New World, Puerto Rico was soon conquered by the Spaniard Ponce de Leon, who was appointed governor of the island in 1509. The indigenous Carib Indians, almost all of whom were utilized by the Spaniards as plantation laborers, were eventually wiped out—to be replaced in 1513 by African slaves. Puerto Rico was held by the English in 1598 and San Juan was besieged by the Dutch in 1625. Otherwise, Spanish control remained unchallenged until the Spanish-American War.

The island was captured by U.S. forces during this conflict and ceded outright to the United States under the Treaty of Paris (1898). In 1900, Congress established a local

*More than 25,000 persons in Panama are estimated to be working full- or part-time in domestic industries or family-type shops, using such raw materials as leather (above).*

*One of Puerto Rico's most fascinating and famed points of interest is El Morro, which rises dramatically from the sea at the northwest tip of old San Juan.*

administration—with a governor appointed by the American president, an executive council, and an elected house of delegates. Puerto Ricans were granted U.S. citizenship in 1917.

After World War II, Congress provided that the governor of the island be an elected official, where upon, in 1948, Luis Munoz Marin was chosen for this office. In 1950, a further act of Congress enabled Puerto Rico to draft its own constitution and, in three years, it became a U.S. Commonwealth.

Since then, Puerto Rican politics have been dominated by the Popular Democratic Party. Marin's handpicked successor, Roberto Sanchez Villela, was elected in January 1965. This party is committed to the retention of Commonwealth status. Emigration to the mainland, a major factor in the 1950s, has declined in recent years. Despite the preponderance of popular support for the Democrats, two other parties have managed to gain some foothold: the Statehood Republican Party, which advocates statehood for the island, and the Independence Party, which seeks complete independence for Puerto Rico. In a 1967 referendum, Puerto Rico voted to remain a Commonwealth.

Many Puerto Ricans today are of mixed black and Spanish ancestry. For the most part, the original Indian inhabitants of the island were exterminated in the sixteenth century.

In 1968, Luis A. Ferre, long an advocate of statehood, was elected governor of the island as a candidate of the New Progressive Party. Ferre made it clear, however, that statehood would depend on a separate plebiscite which would be run apart from the general election.

In the late 1960s and early 1970s, Puerto Rico came increasingly to resemble the United States, especially in the area of San Juan which was being disrupted more and more often by road and office building construction and some of the Western Hemisphere's most spectacular traffic jams. Labor disputes intensified in 1974, leading to sabotage of large sections of the island's water supply. However, the relatively unexplored portion of the island's center, the Cordillera Central, remained relatively undeveloped and an example of tropical lushness where the brilliant flamboya blooms in cone-shaped symmetry from tall trees, and oranges and grapefruit grow waiting to be picked on trees alongside the roads.

In 1979, former governor Rafael Hernandez Colon was designated as the gubernatorial candidate by the Popular Democratic Party for the 1980 election. The PPD called for administration by the Commonwealth of most of the transferred federal funds, the right to negotiate international trade agreements and to create a 200-mile economic zone in order to ensure local control of marine resources and potential offshore petroleum deposits. The New Progressive Party won the governorship by 0.3% of the votes cast with Carlos Romero Barcelo assuming office. Barcelo had been expected to call for a 1981 plebiscite on statehood, but after his election he decided to defer plans on the issue.

Puerto Rico has grown from an impoverished island with

a per capita income of $121 in 1940 to an industrial center, with a 1988 per capita income of $5,368, the highest in the hemisphere after the United States and Canada. Its successes with industry—which accounts for 63% of the country's income—have earned it the reputation as being a "model" for the Caribbean. Problems, however, still exist with inflation, public debt and unemployment.

## Swan Islands

***Area:*** 4 square miles
***Population:*** Less than 100 (on Big Swan)
***Language:*** English
***Principal economic resources:*** Guano

### History at a Glance

The Swan Islands (Big Swan and Little Swan) were discovered in the early sixteenth century, and have been in the possession of the United States since 1863, although the Central American republic of Honduras has laid claim to them. The islands, now the site of a lighthouse and a radio station, are believed to be a base of operations for the Central Intelligence Agency.

Following years of dispute, in 1971 the United States signed a treaty which recognized Honduran sovereignty over the islands. On September 1, 1972, the treaty ratifications were exchanged.

## Virgin Islands (St. Croix, St. Thomas, St. John)

***Date of independence:***
***Area:*** 133 square miles
***Population:*** 170,000 (1985)
***Capital:*** Charlotte Amalie
***Ethnic divisions:*** 80% black or mulatto
***Language:*** English
***Principal economic resources:*** Fish, tourism, rum

### History at a Glance

Discovered by Christopher Columbus in 1493, the Virgin Islands (an archipelago of 74 islands) is now divided into two distinct clusters; the U.S. Virgin Islands (three main islands, 65 islets) and the British Virgin Islands (six main islands).

The American group was originally settled by the Danish West India Company, which first colonized St. Thomas in 1672. In 1683, St. John was likewise claimed by this company, and by 1733, St. Croix had been acquired from France. Some 20 years later, the holdings of this company were taken over by the Danish crown, which then reconstituted them as a royal colony, The Danish West Indies.

The United States bought the territory from Denmark in 1917 for some 25 million dollars and granted citizenship to its inhabitants 10 years later. In 1931, its administration was transferred from the U.S. Navy Department to the Department of the Interior.

Limited self-government for the territory dates back to 1936, although the internal administration of the islands continues to be in the hands of a governor appointed by the President of the United States. (The first black governor, William H. Hastie, was appointed in 1946.) Under the terms of the 1954 Revised Organic Act of the Virgin Islands, local legislative power rests in the hands of a unicameral chamber composed of 11 popularly elected senators.

Under the terms of the constitution now in effect, the United States retains the authority to introduce and enact legislation to govern the territory. The courts are also controlled by the United States, with an American district judge serving as the territory's highest judicial officer.

Pursuant to a bill passed by Congress in 1968, the governor of the island is an elected, rather than an appointed, official. Dr. Melvin Evans, the first native black governor, came to office in mid-1969. In 1970, Dr. Evans was elected governor in the Virgin Islands' first popular election.

In 1972, the Virgin Islands were granted the right to send one nonvoting delegate to the House of Representatives. Island residents enjoy the same rights as mainlanders with the exception that they may not vote in a presidential election.

In 1973 and 1974, simmering economic and racial problems erupted, with fervent Black Power agitation and a series of murders disturbing the area's tranquility and tourism.

There has been no significant agitation for independence, with formal constitutions rejected by the islanders in 1964, 1971 and 1979. Governor Alexander Farrelly assumed office after elections in November 1986.

A 20-year economic growth plus an increase in the principal industry, tourism, has brought jobs and luxury items to the islands. On the downside, rising property values now threaten to price the Thomians out of their homeland. Crime and drug trafficking have burgeoned, as well, and at least two organized crime families have made strong inroads into the society there.

# A SELECTED BIBLIOGRAPHY

**General ■ Africa ■ Biography ■ Culture and Society ■ Economics ■ Education ■ History ■ Juvenile ■ Literature ■ Music ■ Politics**

Recent years have seen a great increase in the publication of material dealing with blacks and civil rights. Because so many new books and articles have been published in these areas since 1982, the following bibliography does not repeat the listings already printed in previous editions of *The Negro Almanac*, and the reader interested in basic source material should not neglect those volumes. Furthermore, to make the torrent of new information easier to handle and to help the student encounter a sufficiently large selection of current material on any given subject, this bibliography has been subdivided into 11 areas: General, Africa, Biography, Culture and Society, Economics, Education, History, Juvenile, Literature, Music, and Politics. The materials included were compiled by Ernest Kaiser, former curator of the Schomburg Collection of the New York Public Library. Subject breakdown of the books was completed by the *Almanac* staff. Other important bibliographies are *A Bibliography of Black Literature*, available from the Office of Adult Services of the New York Public Library; *The Black Experience in Children's Books*, selected by Barbara Rolluck, available from the Office of Branch Libraries, New York Public Library; *The Negro in the United States: A Selected Bibliography*, compiled by Dorothy Porter, available from the Superintendent of Documents/U.S. Government Printing Office/Washington, D.C.; and *A Bibliography of Negro History and Culture for Young Readers*, compiled by Miles M. Jackson, available from the Unversity of Pennsylvania Press.

## General

This section encompasses a potpourri of subjects, including religion, sports, cooking, and art.


### A

*A Guide to Black Organizations, 1984-85*. Philip Morris, Public Affairs Dept., 120 Park Ave., New York 10017.

### B

*Black Resource Guide, The 1987 edition*. Black Resource Guide, Inc., 501 Oneida Pl. NW, Washington, DC 20011.

*Blackbook 1984: International Reference Guide*. National Publications Sales Agency, 1610 E. 79 St., Chicago 60649.

*Burrelle's Black Media Directory 1983-84*. Burrelle's Media Directories, 75 E. Northfield Road, Livington, NJ 07039.

### D

Davis, Marianna W. (editor). *Contributions of Black Women to America*. Kenday Press, PO Box 3097, Columbia, SC 29230.

### E

*Encyclopedia of Black America*. Edited by W. Augustus Low and Virgil A. Clift. NY: McGraw-Hill.

### F

*Facts About Blacks, 1980-81 (6th edition).* Leroy W. Jeffries and Assoc., Suite 876, 3540 Wilshire Blvd., Los Angeles 90010

### G

Gubert, Betty Kaplan. *Early Black Bibliographies, 1863-1918.* NY: Garland Publishing.

*Guide to Scholarly Journals in Black Studies.* Chicago Center for Afro-American Studies and Research Programs, PO Box 7610, Chicago 60680.

### H

Hill, George H. *Black Media in America: A Resource Guide.* Boston: G. K. Hall.

Hill, George H. *Civil Rights Organizations and Leaders: An Annotated Bibliography.* Garland Publishing, Inc., 136 Madison Ave., New York 10016.

### J

Johnson & Johnson. *Who's What & Where.* Davstar Publishing Co., 21405 Lostine Ave., Carson, CA 90745.

### M

Matney, William C. and Dwight L. Johnson. *America's Black Population: 1970 to 1982: A Statistical View.* U.S. Dept. of Commerce, Bureau of Census.

### N

Newman, Richard. *Black Access: A Bibliography of Afro-American Bibliographies.* Westport, CT: Greenwood Press.

### P

Ploski, Harry A. and James Williams. *The Negro Almanac: A Reference Work on the Afro-American.* NY: John Wiley & Sons. 1983.

## Africa

### A

Achebe, Chirua. *Anthills of the Savannah.* NY: Anchor Press/Doubleday. 1988.

Achebe, Chinua and C. L. Innes (editors). *African Short Stories.* Portsmouth, NH: Heinemann Educational Books.

*Africa South of the Sahara 1981-1982.* 11th edition. xxiv, 1585 pp. 28 maps. London: Europa Publications. Available in US from Gale Research, Book Tower, Detroit, MI 48226.

*African Furniture & Household Objects.* Bloomington: Indiana Univ. Press in association with the American Federation of the Arts.

Archer, Robert and Antoine Bouillon. *The South African Game: Sport and Racism.* Lawrence Hill, Westport, CT.

Asante, Molefi Kete. *The Afrocentric Idea.* Philadelphia, PA: Temple Univ. Press. 1987.

Astrow, Andre. *Zimbabwe: A Revolution that Lost Its Way?* London: Zed Press.

### B

Babu, Abdul Rahman Mohamed. *African Socialism or Socialist Africa?* Lawrence Hill, Westport, CT.

Ball, Nicole. *World Hunger: A Guide to the Economic and Political Dimensions.* ABC-Clio Press, Box 4397, Santa Barbara, CA 93103.

Bebey, Francis. *King Albert (translated from the French).* Lawrence Hill, 520 Riverside Ave., Westport, CT 06880.

Becker, Peter. *The Pathfinders: The Saga of Exploration in Southern Africa.* NY: Viking Press.

Beckwith, Carol and Marian von Offelen. *Nomads of Niger.* NY: Harry N. Abrams.

Benson, Mary. *Nelson Mandela: The Man and His Movement.* NY: W. W. Norton. 1986.

Bernal, Martin. *Black Athena: The Afro-Asiatic Roots of Classical Civilization. Volume I: The Fabricatino of Ancient Greece, 1785-1985.* New Brunswick, NJ: Rutgers Univ. Press. 1987.

Brink, Andre. *A Chain of Voices.* William Morrow.

Brown, Lloyd W. *Women Writers in Black Africa.* Westport, CT: Greenwood Press.

### C

Cawl, Faarax M. J. *Ignorance Is the Enemy of Love.* Westport, CT: Lawrence Hill.

Coetzee, J. M. *Waiting for the Barbarians.* Penguin Books, New York.

Cooper, Allan D. *U.S. Economic Power and Political Influence in Namibia, 1700-1920.* Westview Press, 5500 Central Ave., Boulder, CO 80301.

Courlander, Harold. *The Master of the Forge: A West African Odyssey.* NY: Crown Publishers.

Crapanzano, Vincent. *Waiting: The Whites of South Africa.* NY: Random House.

Crisp, J. *The Story of an African Working Class: Ghanaian Miners' Struggles, 1870-1980.* Biblio Distribution Center, Totowa, NJ.

Cromwell, Adelaide. *Dynamics of the African-Afro-American Connection: From Dependency to Self-Reliance.* Washington, DC: Howard Univ. Press. 1986.

Crowder, Michael (editor). *The Cambridge Encyclopedia of Africa.* Cambridge Univ. Press.

Cutufelli, Maria Rosa. *Women of Africa: Roots of Oppression.* London: Zed Press.

### D

Davis, Stephen M. *Apartheid's Rebels: Inside South Africa's Hidden War.* New Haven: Yale Univ. Press. 1987.

Delius, Peter. *The Land Belongs to Us: The Pedi Polity, the Boers and the British in the Nineteenth Century Transvaal.* Univ. of Calif. Press.

Delury, George E. (editor). *World Encyclopedia of Political Systems & Parties: Vol. I — Afghanistan - Mozambique; Vol. II — Nepal - Zimbabwe and Smaller Countries and Microstates.* Facts on File, 460 Park Ave. South, New York 10016.

Dem, Tidiane. *Masseni.* Louisiana State Univ. Press.

Doyal, Lesley with Imogene Pennell. *The Political Enemy of Health.* South End Press, Box 68, Astor Sta., Boston, MA 02123.

Du Boulay, Shirley. *Tutu: Voice of the Voiceless.* Grand Rapids, MI: Wm. B. Eerdmans. 1988.

### E

Ebersohn, Wessel. *Store Up the Anger.* NY: Doubleday.

Eltis, David. *Economic Growth and the Ending of the Transatlantic Slave Trade.* NY: Oxford Univ. Press. 1987.

*Encyclopedia of the Third World (1982 revised edition).* Facts on File, 460 Park Ave. South, New York 10016.

*Exhibition of Photographs: Southern Africa: The Imprisoned Society.*

International Defense and Aid Fund for Southern Africa, 104 Newgate St., London EC1.

F

Falola, Tovin and Julius Ihonvbere. *The Rise and Fall of Nigeria's Second Republic, 1979-84.* Zed Press/Biblio Distribution Centre, 81 Adams Dr., Totowa, NJ 07512.

Finnegan, William. *Dateline Soweto: Travels With Black South African Reporters.* NY: Harper & Row. 1988.

G

Galperin, Georgi. *Ethiopia: Population, Resources, Economy.* Imported Publications.

*Gavshon's Crisis in Africa: Battleground of East and West.* NY: Penguin Books.

Gibbons, Arnold. *Information, Ideology and Communication: The New Nations' Perspectives on an Intellectual Revolution.* Univ. Press of America, 4720 Boston Way, Lanham, MD 20706.

Gibbs, James. *Wole Soyinka: Modern Dramatist.* NY: Grove Press. 1985.

Glaze, Anita J. *Art and Death in a Senufo Village.* Bloomington: Indiana Univ. Press.

Gleason, Judith (editor). *Leaf and Bone: African Praise Poems.* NY: Viking Press.

Golden, Marita. *Migrations of the Heart: A Personal Odyssey.* NY: Anchor Press/Doubleday.

Goodwin, June. *Cry Amandla!: South African Women and the Question of Power.* Holmes & Meier Africana Publishing Co. 30 Irving Place, New York 10003.

Gordimer, Nadine. *July's People.* NY: Viking Press.

*Grass Roots Leadership in Colonial West Africa.* Tarikh magazine, Vol. 7, No. 1, 1981. Published for the Historical Society of Nigeria by Longman Group; in the U.S. by Humanities Press, 171 First Ave., Atlantic Highlands, NJ 07716.

Gruber, Ruth. *Rescue: The Exodus of the Ethiopian Jews.* NY: Atheneum. 1987.

H

Harris, Joseph E. (editor). *Global Dimensions of the African Diaspora.* Howard Univ. Press.

Hodges, Tony. *Historical Dictionary of Western Sahara.* Scarecrow Press, Metuchen, NJ 08840.

Houston, Drusilla Dunjee. *The Wonderful Ethiopians of the Ancient Cushite Empire.* Black Classic Press, PO Box 13414-1A, Baltimore, MD 21203.

Hovey, Gail. *Namibia's Stolen Wealth: North American Investment and South African Occupation.* The Africa Fund, 198 Broadway, New York 10038.

Howard, Joseph H. *Gifts From Ile Ife: African Impact on the Americas.* Black History Museum Umum Publishers, Box 15057, Philadelphia, PA 19130.

I

Iliffe, John. *The African Poor: A History.* NY: Cambridge Univ. Press. 1987.

J

Jackson, Prof. Henry F. *From the Congo to Soweto: U.S. Foreign Policy Toward Africa Since 1960.* William Morrow.

Jeyifo, Biodun. *The Truthful Lie: Essays in a Sociology of African Drama.* New Beacon Books, 76 Stroud Green Road, London N4 3EN, England.

K

Keller, Edmund J. *Revolutionary Ethiopia: From Empire to People's Republic.* Bloomington: Indiana Univ. Press. 1988.

Klein, Herbert S. *African Slavery in Latin America and the Caribbean.* NY: Oxford Univ. Press. 1987.

Konig, Barbara. *Namibia: The Ravages of War.* International Defense & Aid Fund for Southern Africa, PO Box 17, Cambridge, MA 02138.

Kornegay, Francis A. *Reagan, Congress and the Changing African Constituency.* Greenwood Press, Westport, CT., or Vantage Press, NY.

Kpomassie, Tete-Michel. *An African in Greenland.* Harcourt Brace Jovanovich.

Kurian, George. *Atlas of the Third World.* Facts on File, 460 Park Ave. South, New York 10016.

L

Leakey, Mary. *Africa's Vanishing Art: The Rock Paintings of Tanzania.* NY: Doubleday. 1985.

Leape, Jonathan, Bo Baskin and Stefan Underhill (editors). *Business In the Shadow of Apartheid: U.S. Firms in South Africa.* Lexington, MA: Lexington Books/D.C. Heath.

Leonard, Richard. *South Africa at War: White Power and the Crisis in Southern Africa.* Westport, CT: Lawrence Hill.

Lewis, David Levering. *The Race to Fashoda: European Colonialism and African Resistance in the Scramble for Africa.* NY: Weidenfeld & Nicolson. 1988.

Love, Janice. *The U.S. Anti-Apartheid Movement: Local Activism in Global Politics.* NY: Praeger Publishers.

Lynch, Hollis (editor). *Black Africa.* Arno Press. 1973.

M

Madunagu, E. *Nigeria: The Economy and the People — The Political Economy of State Robbery and Its Popular Democratic Negation.* New Beacon Books.

Madunagu, E. *Problems of Socialism: The Nigerian Challenge.* Lawrence Hill, Westport, CT.

Magubane, Bernard and Nzongola-Ntalaja (editors). *Proletarianization and Class Struggle in Africa.* Synthesis Publications, Dept. 118, 2703 Folsom St., San Francisco 94110.

Magubane, Peter. *Black Child.* A. A. Knopf.

Makeba, Miriam with James Hall. *Makeba: My Story.* NY: New American Library. 1987.

Mandela, Winnie. *"A Piece of My Soul" from Part of My Soul Went With Him.* NY: W.W. Norton. 1985.

Marcus, Harold G. *Haile Selassie I: The Formative Years, 1892-1936.* Berkeley: Univ. of Calif. Press. 1986.

Meredith, Martin. *In the Name of Apartheid: South Africa in the Postwar Period.* NY: Harper & Row. 1988.

Mason, Clifford. *The Case of the Ashanti Gold.* NY: St. Martin's Publishing Co. 1985.

Mathabane, Mark. *Kaffir Boy.* NY: New American Library. 1986.

Mathabane, Mark. *Kaffir Boy in America.* NY: Charles Scribner's Sons. 1989.

Mazrui, Ali A. *The Africans: A Triple Heritage.* Boston: Little Brown. 1986.

McCarthy, Michael. *Dark Continent: Africa As Seen by Americans.* Westport, CT: Greenwood Press.

McNaughton, Patrick R. *The Mande Blacksmiths: Knowledge, Power and Art in West Africa.* Bloomington: Indiana Univ. Press. 1988.

Meredith, Martin *In the Name of Apartheid: South Africa in the Postwar Period.* NY: Harper & Row. 1988.

Meredith, Martin. *The First Dance of Freedom: Black Africa in the Postwar Era.* NY: Harper & Row. 1985 or 86.

Miller, Joseph C. *The Way of Death: Mexican Capitalism and the Angolan Slave Trade, 1730-1830.* Madison: Univ. of Wisconsin Press. 1989.

Mockler, Anthony. *Haile Selassie's War: The Italian-Ethiopian Campaign, 1935-1941.* NY: Random House.

Moikobu, Josephine Moraa. *Blood and Flesh: Black American and African Identifications.* Westport, CT: Greenwood Press.

Moleah, Alfred T. *Namibia: The Struggle for Liberation.* Disa Press, PO Box 9284, Wilmington, DE 19809.

Moore, Gerald and Ulli Beier (editors). *The Penguin Book of Modern African Poetry.* NY: Penguin Books.

Mphahlele, Es'kia. *Chirundu.* Westport, CT: Lawrence Hill.

Mphahlele, Es'Kia. *Renewal Time.* Readers International. 1989.

Mudimbe, V. Y. *Before the Birth of the Moon.* Translated by Marjolijn de Jager. NY: Fireside/Simon & Schuster. 1989.

Murphy, Joseph. *Santeria: An African Religion in America.* Boston: Beacon Press. 1986.

## N

Naidoo, Indres with Albie Sachs. *Robben Island: Ten Years as a Political Prisoner in South Africa's Most Notorious Penitentiary.* NY: Vintage Books.

Nayra, Atiya. *Kuhl-Khaal: Five Egyptian Women Tell Their Stories.* Syracuse (NY) Univ. Press.

Nkomo, M. O. *Student Culture and Activism in Black South African Universities: The Roots of Resistance.* Greenwood Press.

Nkosi, Lewis. *Mating Birds.* NY: St. Martin's Press. 1986.

Nolutshungu, Sam. *Changing South Africa: Political Consideration.* Holmes & Meier, 30 Irving Place, New York City.

Noer, Thomas J. *Cold War and Black Liberation: The United States and White Rule in Africa, 1948-1968.* Columbia: Univ. of Missouri Press. 1984.

Nunley, John W. *Moving With the Face of The Devil: Art and Politics in Urban West Africa.* Champaign: Univ. of Illinois Press. 1987.

Nyang, Sulayman S. *Ali A. Mazrui: The Man and His Works.* Brunswick Publishing Co., Box 555, Lawrenceville, VA 23868.

Nyang, Professor Sulayman S. *Islam, Christianity and African Identity.* Amana Books, 58 Elliot St., Brattleboro, VT 05301.

## O

Offiong, Daniel A. *Imperialism and Dependency: Obstacles to African Development.* Washington, DC: Howard Univ. Press.

## P

*Papyrus Ebers: The First Medical Book in the World.* Translated from the German version by Cyril P. Bryan in 1931.

Parpart, Jane L. *Labor and Capital on the African Copperbelt.* Philadelphia, PA: Temple Univ. Press.

Paton, Alan. *Ah, But Your Land Is Beautiful.* Charles Scribner's Sons.

Pheko, Motsuko. *Apartheid: The Story of An Oppressed People.* Montreal, Canada: Black Rose Press. 1988.

Plumpp, Sterling. (editor). *Somehow We Survive: An Anthology of South African Writing.* Thunder's Mouth Press, 242 W. 104 St., 5RW, New York 10025.

Polshikov, P. I. *Capital Accumulation and Economic Growth in Developing Africa.* Imported Publications, 320 W. Ohio St., Chicago 60610.

Pomeroy, William. *Apartheid, Imperialism and African Freedom.* NY: International Publishers. 1986.

## R

Ramsamy, Sam. *Apartheid: The Real Hurdle: Sport in South Africa & the International Boycott.* International Defense & Aid Fund for Southern Africa, Box 17, Cambridge, MA 02138.

Ramsamy, Sam. *South Africa: Challenge and Hope.* American Friends Service Committee, 1501 Cherry St., Philadelphia 19102.

Ramusi, Molapatene Collins and Ruth S. Turner. *Soweto, My Love.* NY: Holt, Rinehart & Winston. 1988.

Ransford, Oliver. *"Bid the Sickness Cease": Disease in the History of Black Africa.*

Robertson, Claire C. and Martin A. Klein (editors). *Women and Slavery in Africa.* Madison: Univ. of Wisconsin Press. 1984.

Robinson, Pearl T. and Elliott P. Skinner (editors). *Toward the Decolonization of African Literature: Vol. I.*

Robinson, Pearl T. and Elliott P. Skinner (editors). *Transformation and Resiliency in Africa.*

Rogge, John R. *Too Many, Too Long: Sudan's Twenty-Year Refugee Dilemma.* Rowman & Allenheld, 81 Adams Dr., Totowa, NJ 07512.

## S

Salaam, Yusef A. *Capoeira: African Brazilian Karate.* Salaam, 167 W. 136 St., Apt. 5, New York 10030.

Saul, John S. (editor). *A Difficult Road: The Transition to Socialism in Mozambique.* NY: Monthly Review Press.

Serote, Mongane. *To Every Birth Its Blood.* NY: Thunder's Mouth Press. 1989.

Shachtman, Tom (text) and Donn Renn (photographs). *Growing Up Masai.* Macmillan.

Shostak, Marjorie. *Nisa: The Life and Words of a "Kung Woman".* Vintage Books.

Simon, Jack and Ray. *Class & Colour in South Africa 1850-1950.* International Defense & Aid Fund for Southern Africa, PO Box 17, Cambridge, MA 02138.

Southall, Roger. *South Africa's Transkei: The Political Economy of an Independent Bantustan.* Monthly Review Press.

Soyinka, Wole. *Ake: The Years of Childhood.* NY: Aventura. 1985.

Soyinka, Wole. *Mandela's Earth and Other Poems.* NY: Random House. 1988.

Stavriano, L. S. *Global Rift: The Third World Comes of Age.* William Morrow.

## T

Terborg-Penn, Rosalyn, Sharon Harley and Andrea Benton Rushing (editors). *Women in Africa and the African Diaspora.* Washington, DC: Howard Univ. Press. 1986.

*Third World Atlas.* Taylor & Francis, Inc., 242 Cherry St., Philadelphia 19106.

Tutuola, Yoruba Amos. *The Witch-Herbalist of the Remote Town.* Boston: Faber & Faber.

## U

Ungar, Sanford J. *Africa: The People and Politics of an Emerging Continent.* NY: Simon & Schuster.

Usman, Ysufu Bala. *For The Liberation of Nigeria.* New Beacon Books.

## V

Valkenier, Elizabeth Krindl. *The Soviet Union and the Third World: An Economic Bind.* NY: Praeger Publishers.

van der Post, Laurens and Jane Taylor. *Testament to the Bushmen.* NY: Viking Press.

### W

Whitaker, Jennifer Seymour. *How Can Africa Survive?* NY: Harper & Row. 1988.

Willan, Brian. *Sol Plaatje, South African Nationalist, 1876-1932*. Berkeley: Univ. of Calif. Press.

Woronoff, Jon (editor). *The African Historical Dictionaries*. Metuchen, NJ: Scarecrow Press.

### Y

Ya-Otto, John, et al. *Battlefront Namibia*. Lawrence Hill, Westport, C

Zell, Hans M., et al. (editors). *A New Reader's Guide to African Literature*. NY: Africana Publishing Co./Holmes & Meier.


## Biography

The following works include biographies and autobiographies for both the general audience and for juveniles.


### A

Abbott, Elizabeth. *Haiti: The Duvaliers and Their Legacy*. NY: McGraw-Hill. 1988.

Abdul-Jabbar, Kareem and Peter Knobler. *Giant Steps: The Autobiography of Kareem Abdul-Jabbar*. NY: Bantam Books. 1985.

Abe, K. *Jazz Giants: A Visual Retrospective*. NY: Billboard. 1988.

Adler, Bill. *The Cosby Wit: His Life and Humor*. NY: Critics Choice Paper. 1987.

Allen, Cleveland James. *Brazilian Odyssey: Memoirs of a United Nations Specialist*. Dorrance & Co., Cricket Terrace Center, Ardmore, PA 19003.

Allen, Dick and Tim Whitaker. *Crash: The Life and Times of Dick Allen*. NY: Ticknor & Fields. 1989.

Allen, Maury. *Jackie Robinson: A Life Remembered*. NY: Franklin Watts. 1987.

Allen, Maury. *Mr. October: The Reggie Jackson Story*.

Alpers, Edward A. and Pierre-Michel Fontaine (editors). *Walter Rodney: Revolutionary and Scholar: A Tribute*. Center for Afro-American Studies, Univ. of Calif., Los Angeles, 405 Hilgard Ave., 3111 Campbell Hall, Los Angeles 90024.

Andrews, William L. (editor). *Critical Essays on W.E.B. DuBois*. Boston: G. K. Hall. 1985.

Andrews, William L. (editor). *Sisters of the Spirit: Three Black Women's Autobiographies of the Nineteenth Century*. Bloomington: Indiana Univ. Press. 1988.

Andrews, William L. *To Tell a Free Story: The First Century of Afro-American Autobiography, 1760-1865*. Champaign: Univ. of Illinois Press. 1986.

Ansbro, John J. *Martin Luther King, Jr.: The Making of a Mind*. Orbis Books, Maryknoll, NY 10545.

Anson, Robert Sam. *Best Intentions: The Education and Killing of Edmund Perry*. NY: Random House. 1987.

Aptheker, Herbert. *From Tennessee Slave to St. Louis Entrepreneur: The Autobiography of James Thomas*. Univ. of Missouri Press, PO Box 1653, Hagerstown, MD 21741.

Arvey, Verna. *In One Lifetime*. Univ. of Missouri Press, PO Box 1653, Hagerstown, MD 21741.

Ashe, Arthur (with Neil Amdur). *Off the Court*. NY: New American Library.

Astor, Gerald (editor). *The Baseball Hall of Fame 50th Anniversary Book*. Englewood Cliffs, NJ: Prentice-Hall. 1988.

### B

Baker, William J. *Jesse Owens: An American Life*. NY: Free Press/Macmillan. 1986.

Ballard, Allen B. *One More Day's Journey: The Story of a Family and a People*. NY: McGraw-Hill.

Balliett, Whitney. *Jelly Roll, Jabbo and Fats: 19 Portraits in Jazz*. NY: Oxford Univ. Press.

Baraka, Amiri. *The Autobiography of LeRoi Jones*. NY: Freundlich Books. 1984

Barkey, Danny. Edited by Alyn Shipton. *A Life In Jazz*. NY: Oxford Univ. Press. 1987.

Barrow Jr., Joe Louis and Barbara Munder. *Joe Louis: 50 Years An American Hero*. Foreword by Arthur Ashe, Jr. NY: McGraw-Hill. 1988.

Basie, Count as told to Albert Murray. *Good Morning Blues: The Autobiography of Count Basie*. NY: Random House.

Baylor, Don with Carroll Smith. *Nothing But the Truth: A Baseball Life*. NY: St. Martin's Press. 1989.

Bego, Mark. *Michael!* NY: Pinnacle Books.

Berger, Morroe, et al. *Benny Carter: A Life in American Music*. Metuchen, NJ: Scarecrow Press.

Bernhardt, Clyde E. B. (as told to Sheldon Harris). *I Remember: Eighty Years of Black Entertainment, Big Bands and the Blues*. Philadelphia: Univ. of Pennsylvania Press. 1986.

Berry, Chuck. *The Autobiography of Chuck Berry*. NY: Harmony Books. 1985.

Berry, Leonidas H. *I Wouldn't Take Nothin' For My Journey: Two Centuries of an Afro-American Minister's Family*. Chicago: Johnson Publishing Co.

Bigard, Barney (edited by Barry Martin). *With Louis and the Duke: The Autobiography of a Jazz Clarinetist*. NY: Oxford University Press. 1986, 1988.

Bishop, Maurice. *Maurice Bishop Speaks: The Grenada Revolution 1979-83*. NY: Pathfinder Press.

Blancq, Charles. *Sonny Rollins: The Journey of a Jazzman*. Boston: G.K. Hall/Twayne. 1983.

Blassingame, John W. *Frederick Douglass: The Clarion Voice*. Washington, DC: Supt. of Documents.

Bream, Ion. *Prince: Inside the Purple Reign*. NY: Collier/Macmillan.

Brignano, Russell C. *Black Americans in Autobiography: An Annotated Bibliography of Autobiographies and Autobiographical Books Written Since the Civil War*. Durham, NC: Duke Univ. Press. 1984.

Brown, James with Bruce Tucker. *James Brown: The Godfather of Soul*. NY: Macmillan. 1985.

Brown, Sterling. *Sterling A. Brown: A Umum Tribute, edited by the Black History Museum Committee*. Black History Museum Umum Publishers, PO Box 15057, Philadelphia, PA 19130.

Buckley, Gail Lumet. *The Hornes: An American Family*. NY: A. A. Knopf, 1986.

Buhle, Paul (editor). *C. L. R. James: His Life and Work*. NY: Schocken Books. 1987.

Buhle, Paul (editor). *C. L. R. James: The Author as Revolutionary*. NY: Verso/Routledge. 1988.

*Bulletin of Bibliography*. Meckler Publishing, 11 Ferry Lane West, Westport, CT 06880.

Bushell, Garvin (as told to Mark Tucker). *Jazz From the Beginning*. Ann Arbor: Univ. of Michigan Press. 1988.

### C

Calderon, Erma with Leonard Ray Teel. *Erma: A Black Woman Remembers: 1912-1980*. NY: Random House.

Carew, Rod et al. *Rod Carew's Art & Science of Hitting.* NY: Viking Press.

Carr, Ian. *Miles Davis: A Biography.* NY: William Morrow.

Cazort, Jean E. and Constance Tibbs Hobson. *Born to Play: The Life and Career of Hazel Harrison.* Westport, CT: Greenwood Press. 1983.

Chambers, Jack. *Milestones 2: The Music and Times of Miles Davis Since 1960.* NY: Beech Tree/Morrow. 1985.

Charleston, Blacksmith. Edited by John Michael Vlach. *The Work of Philip Simmons.* Athens: Univ. of Georgia Press.

Chavers-Wright, Madrue. *The Guarantee: P. W. Chavers: Banker, Entrepreneur, Philanthropist in Chicago's Black Belt of the Twenties.* Order from: The Guarantee-Wright, Box 502, Bronx, NY 10467. 1985.

Cheney, Anne. *Lorraine Hansberry.* Boston: G.K. Hall/Twayne.

Chilton, John. *Sidney Bechet: The Wizard of Jazz.* NY: Oxford Univ. Press. 1988.

Chilton, John. *Who's Who of Jazz.* NY: Oxford Univ. Press.

Clayton, Buck (with Nancy Miller Elliot). *Buck Clayton's Jazz World.* Introduction by Humphrey Lyttleton. NY: Oxford Univ. Press. 1987.

Collier, James Lincoln. *Duke Ellington.* NY: Oxford Univ. Press. 1987.

Collier, James Lincoln. *Louis Armstrong: An American Genius.* Oxford Univ. Press. 1983.

Cone, James H. *My Soul Looks Back.* Abingdon Press, 201 Eighth Ave. S., Box 801, Nashville, TN 37202.

Cooper, Wayne F. *Claude McKay, Rebel Sojourner in the Harlem Renaissance: A Biography.* Baton Rouge: Louisiana State Univ. Press. 1986.

## D

Dabney, Virginius. *The Jefferson Scandals.* NY: Dodd, Mead.

Davis, Allison. *Leadership, Love & Aggression. As the Twig is Bent: The Psychological Factors in the Making of Four Black Leaders.* NY: Harcourt Brace Jovanovich.

Davis, Angela. *Angela Davis: An Autobiography.* A new introduction. NY: International Publishers. 1988.

Davis, Lenwood G. *A Paul Robeson Research Guide: A Selected, Annotated Bibliography.* Westport, CT: Greenwood Press.

Davis, Lenwood G. and Marsha L. Moore. *Joe Louis: A Bibliography of Articles, Books, Pamphlets, Records and Archival Materials.* Greenwood Press.

Davis, Lenwood G. (compiler) with Marsha L. Moore. *Malcolm X: A Selected Bibliography.* Westport, CT: Greenwood Press.

Davis Jr., Sammy (with Jane and Burt Boyar). *Why Me? The Sammy Davis Jr. Story.* NY: Farrar, Straus & Giroux. 1989.

Davis, Stephen. *Bob Marley.* NY: Doubleday/Dolphin.

Delany, Samuel R. *The Motion of Light in Water: Sex & Science Fiction Writing in the East Village, 1957-1965.* NY; Arbor House/Morrow. 1988.

DeMarco, Joseph P. *The Social Thought of W.E.B. DuBois.* Lanham, MD: Univ. Press of America. 1983.

Devaney, John. *Carl Lewis: An American Hero.* NY: Bantam Books.

Dickerson, Eric and Steve Delsohn. *On The Run.* Chicago: Contemporary Books. 1986.

Duberman, Martin Bauml. *Paul Robeson: A Biography.* NY: A. A. Knopf. 1989.

DuBois, W.E.B. *An ABC of Color.* International Publishers, 381 Park Ave. S., New York 10016.

DuBois, W.E.B. Edited by Herbert Aptheker. *Contributions by W.E.B. DuBois in Government Publications and Proceedings.* Kraus International Publications, Route 100, Milwood, NY 10546.

DuBois, W.E.B. Edited by Herbert Aptheker. *W.E.B. DuBois & The Struggle Against Racism in the World.* Centre Against Apartheid, United Nations Secretariat, Room 2794, New York 10013. July 1983.

## F

Farmer, James. *Lay Bare the Heart: An Autobiography of the Civil Rights Movement.* Arbor House Publishing, 235 E. 45 St., New York 10017.

Farnsworth, Robert M. *Melvin B. Tolson (1898-1966): Plain Talk and Poetic Prophecy.* Univ. of Missouri Press, PO Box 1653, Hagerstown, MD 27141.

Faulkner, Audrey O., et al. *When I Was Comin' Up: An Oral History of Aged Blacks.* Archon Books/Shoe String Press, Hamden, CT.

Feguson, James. *Papa Doc, Baby Doc: Haiti and the Duvaliers.* NY: Basil Blackwell. 1987.

Feldman, Jim. *Prince.* NY: Ballantine Books.

Fields, Mamie Garvin, with Karen Fields. *Lemon Stamp and Other Places: A Carolina Memoir.* NY: The Free Press/Macmillan.

Fissinger, Laura. *Tina Turner.* NY: Ballantine Books.

Fletcher, Marvin E. *America's First Black General: Benjamin O. Davis, Sr., 1880-1970.* Introduction by Benjamin O. Davis, Jr. Lawrence, KS: Univ. Press of Kansas. 1989.

Foner, Philip S. (editor). *Paul Robeson Speaks; Writings, Speeches, Interviews, 1918-1974.* Brunner/Mazel, New York. 1978.

Franklin, John Hope. *George Washington Williams: A Biography.* Chicago: Univ. of Chicago Press. 1985, 1987.

Franklin, John Hope and August Meier (editors). *Black Leaders of the Twentieth Century.* Urbana: Univ. of Illinois Press.

Frazier, Walt with Neil Offen. *Walt Frazier: One Magic Season and a Basketball Life.* NY: Times Books. 1988.

Freedomways editors. *Paul Robeson:* The Great Forerunner. NY: International Publishers. 1985.

Frommer, Harvey. *Rickey & Robinson: The Men Who Broke Baseball's Color Barrier.* Macmillan.

## G

Gabbin, Joanne V. *Sterling A. Brown: Building the Black Aesthetic Tradition.* Westport, CT: Greenwood Press.

Gabel, Leona C. *From Slavery to the Sorbonne and Beyond: The Life and Writings of Anna J. Cooper.* Edited with an introduction by Sidney Kaplan. Smith College Studies in History, Vol. 49, Northampton, MA. 1982.

Garrow, David J. *Bearing the Cross: Martin Luther King, Jr. and the Southern Christian Leadership Conference.* NY: William Morrow. 1986.

Garrow, David J. *The FBI and Martin Luther King, Jr.: From "SOLO" to Memphis.* NY: W. W. Norton.

Garvey, Marcus. *The Poetical Works of Marcus Garvey.* Edited by Tony Martin. The Majority Press, PO Box 538, Dover, MA 02030.

Gendzier, Irene L. *Frantz Fanon: A Critical Study.* NY: Grove Press.

George, Don. *Sweet Man: The Real Duke Ellington.* NY: G. P. Putnam's Sons.

George, Nelson. *The Michael Jackson Story.* NY: Dell Publishing Co. 1984-1987.

Giddins, Gary. *Celebrating Bird: The Triumph of Charlie Parker.* NY: Beech Tree/Morrow. 1986, 1987.

Giddins, Gary. *Satchmo.* NY: Dolphin/Doubleday. 1989.

Goldman, Vivien (text). Photos by Adrian Boot. *Bob Marley: Soul Rebel— Natural Mystic.* NY: St. Martin's Press.

Gooden, Dwight. *Rookie: The Story of My First Year in the Major Leagues.* NY: Doubleday.

Goreau, Lauraine. *Just Mahalia, Baby.* Pelican Publishing, PO Box 189, Gretna, LA 70053.

Gourse, Leslie. *Every Day: The Story of Joe Williams.* NY: DaCapo Press. 1986.

Green, Jeffrey P. *Edmund Thornton Jenkins: The Life and Times of an*

*American Black Composer, 1894-1926.* Greenwood Press.

Green, Mildred Denby. *Black Women Composers: A Genesis.* Boston: Twayne/G.K. Hall.

Gwynn, Tony. *Tony!* Chicago: Contemporary Books. 1986.

## H

Hammer, Robert D. *Derek Wolcott.* Boston: G. K. Hall/Twayne.

Haney, Lynn. *Naked At the Feast: A Biography of Josephine Baker.* NY: Dodd, Mead. 1981.

Harlan, Louis R. *Booker T. Washington: The Wizard of Tuskegee, 1901-1915.* NY: Oxford Univ. Press.

Harris, William J. *The Poetry and Politics of Amiri Baraka: The Jazz Aesthetic.* Columbia: Univ. of Missouri Press.

Harrison, Daphne Duval. *Black Pearls: Blues Queens of the 1920s.* New Brunswick, NJ: Rutgers Univ. Press. 1988.

Haskins, James. *Mabel Mercer: A Life.* NY: Atheneum Publishers. 1988.

Haskins, James and Kathleen Benson. *Lena.* NY: Stein and Day.

Haskins, Jim and N. R. Mitgang. *Mr. Bojangles: The Biography of Bill Robinson.* NY: William Morrow. 1988.

Haskins, James. *Katherine Dunham.* Coward McCann Geoghegan.

Haskins, James. *Sugar Ray Leonard.* Lothrop, Lee & Shepard.

Hatch, Roger D. and Frank E. Watkins (editors). *Reverend Jesse L. Jackson: Straight From the Heart.* Philadelphia: Fortress Press. 1988.

Hatcher, John. *From the Auroral Darkness: The Life and Poetry of Robert Hayden.* George Ronald Books, PO Box 447, St. Louis, MO 63166.

Henderson, David. *Jimi Hendrix: Voodoo Child of the Aquarian Age.* NY: Doubleday.

Henderson, David. *'Scuse Me While I Kiss the Sky: The Life of Jimi Hendrix.* NY: Bantam Books.

Hill, Robert A. and Barbara Bair (editors). *Marcus Garvey: Life and Lessons.* Berkeley: Univ. of Calif. Press. 1987.

Hinton, Milt with David G. Berger. *Bass Line: The Stories and Photographs of Milt Hinton.* Philadelphia: Temple Univ. Press. 1988.

Hodges, Willis Augustus. *Free Man of Color. The Autobiography of Wilis Augustus Hodges.* Edited by Willard B. Gatewood, Jr. Knoxville: Univ. of Tennessee Press.

Hogan, Lawrence D. *A Black National News Service: The Associated Negro Press and Claude Barnett, 1919-1945.* Cranbury, NJ: Fairleigh Dickinson Univ. Press.

Holmes, Lowell D. and John W. Thomson. *Jazz Greats: Getting Better With Age.* NY: Holmes & Meier Publishers. 1986.

Honeyford, Paul. *The Thrill of Michael Jackson.* NY: Quill/William Morrow.

Honig, Donald. *Mays, Mantle, Snider: A Celebration.* NY: Macmillan. 1987.

Horne, Gerald C. *Black and Red: W.E.B. DuBois and the Afro-American Response to the Cold War, 1944-1963.* Albany: State Univ. of NY Press. 1986.

Hoskins, Lotte (compiler). *"I Have a Dream": The Quotations of Martin Luther King, Jr.* Grosset & Dunlap, 1968.

Hull, Gloria T. (editor). *Give Us Each Day: The Diary of Alice Dunbar-Nelson.* NY: W. W. Norton. 1985, 1986.

Humez, Jean McMahon (editor). *Gifts of Power: The Writings of Rebecca Jackson, Black Visionary, Shaker Eldress.* Amherst: Univ. of Massachusetts Press.

Hunton, Dorothy. *Alphaeus Hunton: The Unsung Valiant.* Order from: Dorothy Hunton, 100-23 93rd Ave., Richmond Hill, NY 11418. 1986.

Hurston, Zora Neale. *Dust Tracks On a Road: An Autobiography.* New introduction by Robert E. Hemenway. Champaign: Univ. of Illinois Press.

Hutchinson, Louise D. *Anna J. Cooper: A Voice from the South.* 1981.

## I

Ivory, Steven. *Prince.* Perigee Books, Putnam Publishing Group, 200 Madison Ave., New York.

Ivory, Steven. *Tina.* NY: Perigee Books.

## J

Jackson, Jesse. *A Time to Speak: The Autobiography of Rev. Jesse Jackson.* NY: Simon & Schuster. 1988.

Jackson, Michael. *Moon Walk.* NY: Doubleday. 1988.

Jackson, Reggie (with Mike Lupica). *Reggie: The Autobiography.* NY: Villard Books/Random House. 1984.

James, C. L. R. *The Future in the Present; Spheres of Existence; At the Rendezvous of Victory: Selected Writings (3 Vols.).* Westport, CT: Lawrence Hill. 1977, 1980, 1983.

Johnson, Buzz. *"I Think of My Mother": Notes on the Life and Times of Claudia Jones.* Karia Press, BCM Karia, London WC1N3XX.

Johnson, John H. (with Lerone Bennett, Jr.). *Succeeding Against the Odds: The Autobiography of John H. Johnson.* NY: Warner Books. 1989.

Johnson, Michael P. and James L. Roark. *Black Masters: A Free Family of Color in the Old South.* NY: W. W. Norton.

Johnson, Michael P. and James L. Roark (editors). *No Chariot Let Down.* Univ. of North Carolina Press.

Jones, Bessie. *For the Ancestors: Autobiographical Memories.* Collected and edited by John Stewart. Champaign, IL: Univ. of Illinois Press. 1983.

Joseph, Pleasant (Cousin Joe) and Harriet J. Ottenkeimer. *Cousin Joe: Blues From New Orleans.* Chicago: Univ. of Chicago Press. 1987.

## K

King Jr., Martin Luther. *Speeches, Sermons and Correspondence.* 12 vols. Edited by Clayborne Carson.

Knight, Curtis. *Jimi: Jimi Hendrix Anthology.* Cimino Publications, Farmingdale, NY.

Kondrashov, Stanislav. *The Life and Death of Martin Luther King.* Moscow: Progress Publishers.

Kosof, Anna. *Jesse Jackson.* NY: Franklin Watts. 1988.

Krech III, Shepard. *Praise the Bridge That Carries You Over: The Life of Joseph Sutton.* Cambridge, MA: Schenkman Publishing Co.

Kremer, Gary R. *George Washington Carver in His Own Words.* Columbia: Univ. of Missouri Press. 1984.

## L

Laraborrelli, J. Randy. *Diana.* NY: Doubleday/Dolphin. 1985.

Latham, Caroline. *Michael Jackson Thrill.* NY: Zebra Books.

Lester, Julius. *Lovesong: Becoming a Jew.* NY: Henry Holt & Co. 1987.

Levinson, David. *Michael Jackson: The Victory Tour.* Crescent Publishing, 5410 Wilshire Blvd. #400, Los Angeles, CA 90036.

Lewis, Samella. *The Art of Elizabeth Catlett.* Claremont, CA: Hancraft Studios. 1984.

Lieb, Sandra R. *Mother of the Blues; A Study of Ma Rainey.* Amherst: Univ. of Mass. Press.

Lightfoot, Claude M. *Chicago Slums to World Politics: Autobiography of Claude M.* Lightfoot, edited by Timothy V. Johnson. NY: New Outlook Publishers. 1986.

Lightfoot, Sara Lawrence. *Balm in Gilead: Journey of a Healer.* Reading, MA: Addison-Wesley Publishing Co. 1988.

*Like It Is: Arthur E. Thomas Interviews Leaders on Black America.* Elsevier-Dutton, 2 Park Ave., New York 10016.

Linnemann, Russell J. (editor). *Alain Locke: Reflections on a Modern Renaissance Man.* Baton Rouge, Louisiana State Univ. Press.

Litwack, Leon and August Meier (editors). *Black Leaders of the Nineteenth Century.* Champaign, IL: Univ. of Illinois Press. 1987.

Logan, Rayford W. and Michael R. Winston (editors). *Dictionary of American Negro Biography.* W. W. Norton, 500 Fifth Ave., New York 10110.

## M

Majors, Monroe A. *Noted Negro Women.* NY: Arno Press.

Manning, Kenneth R. *Black Apollo of Science: The Life of Ernest Everett Just.* NY: Oxford Univ. Press. 1983.

Marable, Manning. *W.E.B. DuBois: Black Radical Democrat.* Boston: Twayne/G.K. Hall. 1986, 1987.

Martin, Tony. *Literary Garveyism: Garvey, Black Arts and the Harlem Renaissance.* The Majority Press.

Martin, Tony. *Marcus Garvey, Hero: A First Biography.* The Majority Press.

Martin Jr., Waldo E. *The Mind of Frederick Douglass.* Chapel Hill: Univ. of N.C. Press.

Maynard, Olga. *Judith Jamison: Aspects of a Dancer.* NY: Doubleday.

Mays, Willie with Lou Sahadi. *Say Hey: The Autobiography of Willie Mays.* NY: Simon & Schuster. 1988.

McDonnel, Robert W. *The Papers of W.E.B. DuBois (1877-1963)* 1979: A Guide. 1981, Microfilming Corp. of America, 1620 Hawkins Ave., Box 10, Sanford, NC 27330.

McGovern, James R. *Black Eagle: General Daniel "Chappie" James, Jr.* University: Univ. of Alabama Press.

McMurry, Linda O. *George Washington Carver: Scientist and Symbol.* NY: Oxford Univ. Press.

McMurry, Linda O. *Recorder of the Black Experience: Monroe Nathan Work.* Baton Rouge: Louisiana State Univ. Press.

McNeil, Genna Rae. *Groundwork: Charles Hamilton Houston and the Struggle for Civil Rights.* Foreword by Judge A. Leon Higginbotham, Jr. Philadelphia: Univ. of Pennsylvania Press.

Mead, Chris. Champion. *Joe Louis: Black Hero in White America.* NY: Charles Scribner's Sons. 1985. Illus; NY: Penguin Books. 1986.

Miller, Carroll L. *Role Model Blacks, Known But Little Known Role Models of Successful Blacks.* Accelerated Development, 2515 W. Jackson, Muncie, IN 47303.

Mills, Bart. *Tina.* NY: Warner Books.

Moore, Jack B. W.E.B. DuBois. G. K. Hall/Twayne.

Mr. T. *The Man With the Gold: An Autobiography by Mr. T.* NY: St. Martin's Press. 1984.

## N

Nathan, David. *Lionel Richie: An Illustrated Biography.* NY: McGraw-Hill. 1986.

Nazel Jr., Joseph G. *Jackie Robinson: First of a Chosen Few: A Biography.* Holloway House, 8060 Melrose Ave., Los Angeles 90046.

Nazel, Joseph. *Paul Robeson: Biography of a Proud Man.* Los Angeles: Holloway House.

Neilson, Kenneth P. *The World of Langston Hughes Music: A Bibliography of Musical Settings of Langston Hughes' Work With Recordings and Other Listings.* The Author, 100-25 205 Pl., Hollis, NY 11423.

Newman, Richard. *Lemuel Haynes: A Bio-Bibliography.* Lambeth Press, 143 E. 37 St., NYC 10016.

Nisenson, Eric. *'Round About Midnight: A Portrait of Miles Davis.* NY: Dial Press.

## O

Oates, Stephen B. *Let the Trumpet Sound: The Life of Martin Luther King, Jr.* NY: Harper & Row.

O'Daniel, Therman (editor). *Jean Toomer: A Critical Evaluation.* Washington, DC: Howard Univ. Press.

Ojo-Ade, Femi. *Rene Maran: The Black Frenchman: A Bio-Critical Study.* Three Continents Press, 1346 Connecticut Ave., NW #1131, Washington, DC 20036.

## P

Panger, Daniel. *Black Ulysses.* Athens: Ohio Univ. Press.

Parkinson, Wenda. *"This Gilded African.": Toussaint L'Ouverture.* London: Quartet; Boston: Charles Riven Books.

Peisch, Jeffrey. *Stevie Wonder.* NY: Ballantine Books.

Perinbam, B. Marie. *Holy Violence: The Revolutionary Thought of Frantz Fanon, An Intellectual Biography.* Three Continents Press, 1346 Connecticut Ave., #1131, Washington, DC 20036.

Pleasant, Henry. *The Great American Popular Singers: Their Lives, Careers & Art.* NY: Simon & Schuster.

Plotzik, Roberta. *Lionel Ritchie.* NY: Dell Publishing.

Porter, Lewis. *Lester Young.* Boston: Twayne/G. K. Hall.

Priestley, Brian. *Mingus: A Critical Biography.* NY: Quartet Books; NY: Da Capo Press reprint.

## R

Rabinowitz, Howard N. (editor). *Southern Black Leaders of the Reconstruction Era.* Univ. of Illinois Press.

Rampersad, Arnold. *The Art and Imagination of W.E.B. DuBois.* Cambridge, MA: Harvard Univ. Press. 1979.

Rampersad, Arnold. *The Life of Langston Hughes: Vol. I, 1902-1941, I, Too, Sing America; Vol. II, 1941-1967, I Dream a World.* NY: Oxford Univ. Press. 1986, 1988.

Rashad, Ahmad (with Peter Body). *Rashad: Vikes, Mikes and Something on the Backside.* NY: Viking Books. 1988.

Ritchie, Andrew. *Major Taylor: The Extraordinary Career of a Champion Bicycle Racer.* San Francisco, CA: Bicycle Books/Kampmann & Co. Illus. 1988.

Ritter, Lawrence S. and Donald Honig. *The 100 Greatest Baseball Players of All Time.*

Ritz, David. *Divided Soul: The Life of Marvin Gaye.* NY: McGraw-Hill.

Roberts, Randy. *Papa Jack: Jack Johnson and the Era of White Hopes.* NY: Free Press. 1983.

Robeson, Paul. *Here I Stand.* Introduction by Sterling Stuckey. Boston: Beacon Press. 1988.

Robeson, Susan. *The Whole World in His Hands: A Pictorial Biography of Paul Robeson.* Secaucus, NJ: Citadel Press. 1985.

Robinson, Frank and Benny Stainback. *Extra Innings.* NY: McGraw-Hill. 1988.

Robinson, Smokey with David Ritz. *Smokey: Inside My Life.* NY: McGraw-Hill. 1989.

Rosengarten, Theodore. *All Gods Dangers: The Life of Nate Shaw.* Random House/Vintage Books.

Rouse, Jacqueline Anne. *Lugenia Burns Hope: Black Southern Reformer.* Athens, GA: Univ. of Georgia Press. 1988.

Rudwick, Elliott M. *W.E.B. DuBois: Voice of the Black Protest Movement.* Champaign: Univ. of Illinois Press.

Rust, Jr., Art and Edna. *Art Rust's Illustrated History of the Black Athlete.* NY: Doubleday.

## S

Sawyer, Charles. *B. B. King: The Authorized Biography.* London: Quartet; NY: DaCapo. 1982.

Scally, Sister Anthony (compiler). *Carter G. Woodson: A Bio-Bibliography.*

Westport, CT: Greenwood Press.

Schilpp, Madelon Golden and Sharon M. Murphy. *Great Women of the Press*. Carbondale: Southern Illinois Univ. Press.

Schulke, F. and P. O. McPhee. *King Remembered: (A Biography, A Photo Essay and A Tribute)*. NY: W. W. Norton. 1986.

Sedwick, Judith. *Women of Courage*. 1984.

Sewell, George A. and Margaret L. Dwight. *Mississippi Black History Makers*. Univ. Press of Miss., 3825 Ridgewood Road, Jackson 392311.

Shakur, Assata. *Assata: An Autobiography*. Westport, CT: Lawrence Hill. 1987.

Sinnette, Elinor Des Verney. *Arthur Alfonso Schomburg, Black Bibliophile and Collector, A Biography*. Detroit: New York Public Library and Wayne State Univ. Press. 1989.

Smith, Ada (Bricktop). *Bricktop with James Haskins*. NY: Atheneum.

Smith Jr., Luther E. *Howard Thurman: The Mystic as Prophet*. Washington, DC: University Press of America. 1983.

Smith, Ronald L. *Cosby*. NY: St. Martin's Press. 1986.

Snowden, The Reverend John Baptist, The Reverend Thomas Baptist Snowden and Houston D. Snowden. *From Whence Cometh*. NY: Vantage Press.

Soyinka, Wole. *Ake: The Years of Childhood*. NY: Random House.

Spady, James G. (editor). *William L. Dawson: A Umum Tribute and a Marvelous Journey*. Creative Artists' Workshop, 940 E. Washington Lane, Philadelphia 19138.

Spradling, Mary Mace (editor). *In Black and White*. Detroit, MI: Gale Research Co. 1985.

Sterling, Dorothy. *Black Foremothers: Three Lives*. NY: Feminist Press. 1988 (2nd ed.)

Stone, Eddie. *Jesse Jackson: A Biography*. Los Angeles, CA: Holloway House. 1979, 1988.

Sugar, Bert Randolph. *100 Greatest Boxers of All Times*. Revised edition. NY: W. H. Smith Publishers. 1983.

Suggs, Henry Lewis. *P. B. Young, Newspaperman: Race, Politics and Journalism in the New South, 1910-62*. Charlottesville, VA: Univ. Press of VA. 1988.

### T

Taraborrelli, J. Randy. *Diana*. Doubleday/Dolphin.

Tarry, Ellen. *The Other Toussaint*. St. Paul Press, 59 E. 43 St., New York.

Taylor, Frank C. with Gerald Cook. *Alberta Hunter: A Celebration in Blues*. NY: McGraw-Hill. 1987.

Taylor, Lawrence with David Falkner. *LT: Living on the Edge*. NY: Times Books. 1987.

Thomas, Duane and Paul Zimmerman. *Duane Thomas and the Fall of America's Team*. NY: Warner Books. 1988.

Toperoff, Sam. *Sugar Ray Leonard and Other Noble Warriors*. NY: McGraw-Hill. 1987.

Travis, Dempsey J. *An Autobiography of Black Chicago*. Urban Research Institute, 840 E. 87 St., Chicago 60619.

T'Shaka, Oba. *The Political Legacy of Malcolm X*. Third World Press, 7524 S. Cottage Grove, Chicago 60619.

Turner, Tina. *I, Tina: My Life Story*. NY: William Morrow. 1984 or 5.

Turner, W. Burghardt and Joyce Moore Turner (editors). *Richard B. Moore: Caribbean Militant in Harlem: Collected Writings 1920-1972*. Bloomington, IN: Indiana Univ. Press. 1988.

Tweedle, John (photographer). *A Lasting Impression: A Collection of Photographs of Martin Luther King, Jr.* Compiled and edited by Hermene D. Hartman. Foreword by Rev. Jesse L. Jackson. Columbia: Univ. of South Carolina Press.

Tygiel, Jules. *Baseball's Great Experiment: Jackie Robinson and His Legacy*. NY: Oxford Univ. Press.

### W

Waldron, Robert. *Oprah!* NY: St. Martin's Press. 1987, 1988.

Walker, Herschel and Terry Todd. *Herschel Walker's Basic Training*. NY: Doubleday.

Walker, Juliet E. K. *Free Frank: A Black Pioneer on the Antebellum Frontier*. Lexington: Univ. Press of Kentucky.

Walter, John C. *The Harlem Fox: J. Raymond Jones and Tammany, 1920-1970*. Ithaca, NY: State Univ. of New York Press. 1988.

Ware, Gilbert. *William Hastie: Grace Under Pressure*. NY: Oxford Univ. Press. 1985.

Warner, Malcolm-Jamal. *Theo and Me: Growing Up Okay*. NY: Dutton Books. 1988.

Weisbrot, Robert. *Father Devine and the Struggle for Racial Equality*. Champaign: Univ. of Illinois Press.

Welch, Chris. *Hendrix: A Biography*. NY: Putnam Publishing Group.

West, Hollie I. *Afro-American Culture and Traditions*. Washington, DC: Howard Univ. Press.

Wheat, Ellen Harkins. *Jacob Lawrence, American Painter*. Seattle: Univ. of Washington Press and the Seattle Art Museum. 1986.

White, Charles. *The Life and Times of Little Richard: The Quasar of Rock*. NY: Harmony Books/Crown. 1984.

White, Charles. *Those Incredible Jackson Boys*. Sharon Publications, Cresskill, NJ.

White, Timothy. *Catch a Fire: The Life of Bob Marley*. NY: Holt, Rinehart & Winston.

Whitney, Malika Lee and Dermott Hussey. *Bob Marley: Reggae King of the World*. NY: E. P. Dutton.

Wilkins, Roger. *A Man's Life: An Autobiography*. NY: Simon & Schuster. 1982.

Wilkins, Roger. (with Tom Mathews). *Standing Fast: The Autobiography of Roy Wilkins*. NY: Viking Press. 1982.

Williams, Brett. *John Henry: A Bio-Bibliography*. Westport, CT: Greenwood Press.

Williams, Thomas Edgar. *Silverstreet*. Smithtown, NY: Exposition Press.

Wilson, Mary. *Dreamgirl: My Life as a Supreme*. NY: St. Martin's Press. 1986, 1987.

Winfield, Dave with Tom Parker. *Winfield: A Player's Life*. NY: W. W. Norton. 1988.

Witherspoon, William Roger. *Martin Luther King, Jr.: To The Mountaintop*. NY: Doubleday. 1985.

*Words of Martin Luther King Jr., The*. Selected by Coretta Scott King. Newmarket.

Wynn, Ron. *Tina: The Tina Turner Story*. NY: Collier/Macmillan.

### Y

Yarbrough, Tinsley E. *A Passion For Justice: J. Waties Waring and Civil Rights*. NY: Oxford Univ. Press. 1987.

Young, Al. *Bodies & Soul—Musical Memoirs*. Creative Arts Book Co., 839 Bancroft Way, Berkeley, CA 94710.

### Z

Zinsser, William. *Willie and Dwike: An American Profile*. NY: Harper & Row.

## Culture and Society

Books in this category are related to race, racism, racial struggle, civil rights, sociology, psychology, prison, police and other present-day issues of social consequence. See also the History and Politics bibliographies.

## A

Adamcyzk, Alice J. *Black Dance: An Annotated Bibliography.* NY: Garland Publishing, Inc. 1989.

## B

Baldwin, James. *The Evidence of Things Not Seen.* NY: Holt, Rinehart & Winston. 1985.

Ballard, Allen B. *One More Day's Journey: The Story of a Family and a People.* NY: McGraw-Hill. 1985.

Barlow, William. *"Looking Up at Dawn.": The Emergence of Blues Culture.* Philadelphia: Temple Univ. Press. 1987.

Baugh, John. *Black Street Speech: Its History, Structure and Survival.* Austin: Univ. of Texas Press. 1983.

Berkley, George. *On Being Black & Healthy: How Black Americans Can Lead Longer and Healthier Lives.* Prentice-Hall, Englewood Cliffs, NJ.

Bogle, Donald. *Blacks in American Films and Television: An Illustrated Encyclopedia by.* NY: Viking Press. 1989.

Bogle, Donald. *Toms, Coons, Mulattos, Mammies and Bucks: An Interpretive History of Blacks in American Films.* NY: Viking Press. 1989.

Borchert, James. *Alley Life in Washington: Family, Community, Religion and Folklife in the City, 1850-1970.* Champaign: Univ. of Illinois Press.

Boskin, Joseph. *Sambo: The Rise & Demise of an American Jester.* NY: Oxford Univ. Press. 1986.

Boykin, A. Wade, Anderson Franklin and J. F. Yates (Editors). *Research Directions of Black Psychologists.* Russell Sage Foundation, New York City.

Bringhurst, Newell G. *Saints, Slaves and Blacks: The Changing Place of Black People in Mormonism.* Westport, CT: Greenwood Press. Illus. 1981.

Bruce, Janet. *The Kansas City Monarchs: Champions of Black Baseball.* Lawrence: Univ. Press of Kansas.

## C

Cham, Mbye B. and Claire Andrade-Watkins (editors). *Black Frames: Critical Perspectives on Independent Black Cinema.* Cambridge, MA: MIT Press. 1988.

Christmas, Rachel Jackson and Walter Christmas. *Fielding's Bermuda and the Bahamas.* NY: William Morrow. 1987.

Cox, Joseph Mason Andrew. *Great Black Men of Masonry 1723-1982.* Blue Diamond Press, 801 Tilden St., Bronx, NY 10467.

Creel, Margaret Washington. *A Peculiar People: Slave Religion and Community Culture Among the Gullahs.* NY: NY Univ. Press. 1986.

## D

Davis, Lenwood G. and Belinda S. Daniels (compilers). *Black Athletes in the United States: A Bibliography of Books, Articles, Autobiographies, and Biographies on Black Professional Athletes in the United States, 1800-1981.* Westport, CT: Greenwood Press.

Davis, Lenwood G. *Religious Broadcasting, 1922-1983: A Selectively Annotated Bibliography* (with George Hill). Garland Publishing, 136 Madison Ave., New York 10016.

DeCarava, Roy (photographs) and Langston Hughes (text). *The Sweet Flypaper of Life.* Washington, DC: Howard Univ. Press.

Dunham, Katherine. *Dances of Haiti.* CAAS Publications, Univ. of Calif., Los Angeles, 405 Hillgard Ave., 3111 Campbell Hall, Los Angeles 99024.

## E

Emery, Lynne F. *Black Dance in the United States from 1619 to 1970.* Dance Horizons, 1801 E. 26 St., Brooklyn, NY

## F

Fabre, Genevieve. *Drumbeats, Masks and Metaphor: Contemporary Afro-American Theatre.* Harvard Univ. Press.

Farabee, James. *A Guide to Beautiful Skin for Black Men & Women.* Doubleday.

Fardan, Dorothy Blake. *Understanding Self and Society: An Islamic Perspective.* NY: Philosophical Library.

Farley, Reynolds and Walter R. Allen. *The Color Line and the Quality of Life: The Problems of the Twentieth Century.* NY: Russell Sage Foundation. 1987.

Fax, Elton C. *Elyuchin.* Moscow: Progress Publishers. Distributed by Imported Publications, 320 W. Ohio St., Chicago 60610. Available from Unity Book Center, 235 W. 23 St., New York.

Fields, Mike. *Getting It Together: The Black Man's Guide to Good Grooming and Fashion.* NY: Dodd, Mead.

Folb, Edith A. *Runnin' Down Some Lines: The Language and Culture of Black Teenagers.* Cambridge, MA: Harvard Univ. Press.

Fox, Ted. *Show Time at the Apollo.* NY: Holt, Rinehart and Winston.

Freeman, Roland L. *Southern Roads/City Pavements.* International Center of Photography, 1130 Fifth Ave., New York City.

## G

Gibbs, Pj. *Black Collectibles Sold in America.* Paducah, KY: Collector Books. 1987.

Grosvenor, Vertamae Smart. *Vibration Cooking or the Travel Notes of a Geechee Girl.* NY: Ballantine Books. 1986.

## H

*Harlem Renaissance: Art of Black America.* NY: Harry N. Abrams, Inc. 1987.

Haskins, James. *Black Theater in America.* Thomas Y. Crowell.

Hill, Errol. *Shakespeare in Sable: A History of Black Shakespearean Actors.* Amherst: Univ. of Massachusetts Press.

Hill, George H. and Sylvia Saverson Hill (compilers). *Blacks on Television: A Selectively Annotated Bibliography.* Metuchen, NJ: Scarecrow Press.

Holder, Geoffrey. *A.D.A.M.* NY: Viking Press. 1986.

Honour, Hugh. *The Image of the Black in Western Art. Vol. 4: From the American Revolution to World War I. Part 1, Slaves and Liberators; Part 2, Black Models and White Myths.* Cambridge: Harvard Univ. Press. 1989.

Hoskins, Charles Lwanga. *Black Episcopalians in Georgia: Strife, Struggle and Salvation.* The Author, St. Matthew's Episcopal Church, 1401 W. Broad St., Savannah 31401.

Humez, Jean McMahon. *Gifts of Power: The Writings of Rebecca Jackson, Black Visionary, Shaker Eldress.* Amherst: Univ. of Mass. Press.

Hurt Jr., James E. and Warren D. St. James (editors). *The National Assembly of Black Church Organizations.* Black Churches of America Publication, Inc., 307 Prospect Ave. 7F, Hackensack, NJ 07601.

## I

Igoe, Lynn Moody with James Igoe. *250 Years of Afro-American Art: An Annotated Bibliography.* Foreword by Camille Billops. NY: R. R. Bowker.

*Images of Dignity: A Retrospective of the Works of Charles White.* (Catalog of an exhibition at the Studio Museum in Harlem, 144 W. 125 St., New York 10027, June 20 to Aug. 31, 1982).

### J

James, C.L.R. *Beyond a Boundary.* NY: Pantheon Books.

Johnson, Beverly. *Beverly Johnson's Guide to a Life of Health and Beauty.* NY: Times Books.

Johnson, John H. *Fact Not Fiction in Harlem.* Northern Type Printing. Glen Cove, NY.

Jones, Reginald L. (editor). *Black Psychology.* NY: Harper & Row.

Jones-Jackson, Patricia. *When Roots Die: Endangered Traditions on the Sea Islands.* Foreword by Charles Joyner. Athens: Univ. of GA Press. 1987.

Joyce, Donald Franklin (compiler). *Blacks in the Humanities, 1750-1984: A Selected Annotated Bibliography.* Westport, CT: Greenwood Press. 1986.

### K

Kellner, Bruce (editor). *The Harlem Renaissance: A Historical Dictionary for the Era.* Westport, CT: Greenwood Press.

King Jr., Woodie. *Black Theatre: Present Condition.* Woodie King Assoc., 417 Convent Ave., New York 10031.

Kochman, Thomas. *Black and White Styles in Conflict.* Univ. of Chicago Press.

### L

Landry, Bart. *The New Black Middle Class.* Berkeley: Univ. of Calif. Press. 1988.

Lanker, Brian. *I Dream a World: Portraits of Black Women Who Changed America.* Stewart, Taban & Chang. 1989.

Lapchick, Richard. *Broken Promises: Racism in American Sports.* NY: St. Martins/Marek Book.

Lewis, Edna. *In Pursuit of Flavor.* NY: A. A. Knopf. 1988.

Lynch, Edie. *With Glory I So Humbly Stand.* NY: Vantage Press.

### M

MacDonald, J. Fred. *Black & White TV: Afro-Americans in Television Since 1948.* Chicago: Nelson-Hall Publishers.

Mancini, Janet K. *Strategic Styles: Coping in the Inner City.* University Press of New England, Box 979, Hanover, NH 03755.

McBride, Davis. *Integrating the City of Medicine: Blacks in Philadelphia Health Care, 1910-1965.* Philadelphia: Temple Univ. Press.

McDaniel, George W. *Hearth and Home: Preserving a People's Culture.* Philadelphia, PA.: Temple Univ. Press.

Mintz, Sidney W. and Sally Price (editors). *Caribbean Contours.* Baltimore, MD: Johns Hopkins Univ. Press.

Moore, Sylvia (editor). *Yesterday and Tomorrow: California Women Artists.* NY: Midmarch Arts Press. 1989.

Moutoussamy-Ashe, Jeanne. *Daufuskie Island: A Photographic Essay.* Foreword by Alex Haley. Columbia: Univ. of South Carolina Press. 1982.

### O

Ostler, S. and S. Springer. *Winnin' Times: The Magical Journey of the Los Angeles Lakers.* NY: Macmillan.

### P

Paris, Arthur E. *Black Pentecostalism: Southern Religion in an Urban World.* Amherst: Univ. of Massachusetts Press.

Pasteur, Alfred B. and Ivory L. Toldson. *Roots of Soul: The Psychology of Black Expressiveness.* NY: Anchor Press/Doubleday.

Peterson, Robert. *Only the Ball Was White.* NY: McGraw-Hill.

### R

Reiterman, Tim with John Jacobs. *Raven: The Untold Story of the Rev. Jim Jones and His People.* NY: E. P. Dutton.

Rogosin, Donn. *Invisible Men: Life in Baseball's Negro Leagues.* Atheneum.

Rose, Dan. *Black American Street Life: South Philadelphia, 1969-1971.* Philadelphia: Univ. of PA Press. 1987.

Roy De Carava. *Photographs.* Friends of Photography, Carmel, CA.

Rust, Jr., Art and Edna. *Recollections of a Baseball Junkie.* NY: William Morrow.

### S

Sanders, Leslie Catherine. *The Development of Black Theater in America: From Shadows to Selves.* Baton Rouge, LA: LA State Univ. Press. 1988.

Seale, Bobby. *Barbecue'n With Bobby.* Philadelphia: Ten Speed Press. 1988.

Sims, Naomi. *All About Hair Care for the Black Woman.* Doubleday.

Smitherman-Donaldson, Geneva and Teun A. van Dijk (editors). *Discourse and Discrimination.* Detroit: Wayne State Univ. Press. 1988.

Snorgrass, J. William and Gloria T. Woody. *Blacks and Media: A Selected, Annotated bibliography, 1962-1982.* Gainesville: University Presses of Florida.

Staples, Robert. *Black Masculinity: The Black Man's Role in American Society.* Blackscholar Press, Box 7106, San Francisco 94120.

Stingley, Darryl and Mark Mulvoy. *Happy to Be Alive.* Beaufort Books, 9 E. 40 St., New York, 10016.

### T

Teague, Bob. *Live and Off-Color: News Biz.* NY: A & W Publishers. 1982.

Traguth, Fred. *Modern Jazz Dance.*

### W

Wepman, Dennis, Ronald B. Newman and Murray B. Binderman (editors). *The Life: The Lore and Folk Poetry of the Black Hustler.* Philadelphia: Univ. of Pennsylvania Press.

Williams, Mance. *Black Theatre in the 1960s and 1970s: A Historical-Critical Analysis of the Movement.* Westport, CT: Greenwood Press.

Williamson, Joel. *New People: Miscegenation and Mulattoes in the United States.* NY: New York Univ. Press. 1984.

Willis, Deborah. *Black Photographers 1840-1940: An Illustrated Bio-Bibliography.* NY: Garland Publishing, Inc. 1985.

Willis, Deborah. *An Illustrated Bio-Bibliography of Black Photographers, 1940-1987.* NY: Garland Publishing, Inc. 1988.

Wilson, Emily Herring. *Hope and Dignity: Older Black Women of the South.* Photographs by Susan Mullally. Foreword by Maya Angelou. Philadelphia: Temple Univ. Press.

Woll, Allen. *Dictionary of Black Theatre: Broadway, Off-Broadway and Selected Harlem Theatre.* Westport, CT: Greenwood Press.


## Economics

Listed in this category are books related to jobs, business, economic philosophy, and specialized economic issues.


### A

Alexis, Marcus, George H. Haines and Leonard S. Simon. *Black Consumer*

*Profiles: Food Purchasing in the Inner City.* Ann Arbor: Univ. of Michigan.

America Jr., Richard F. *Developing the Afro-American Economy.* Lexington Books, 125 Spring St., Lexington, MA 02173.

**B**

Bates, Timothy and William D. Bradford. *Financing Black Economic Development.* Academic Press, 111 Fifth Ave., New York City 10003.

Belau, Hugo Alain. *Hunger in America: The Growing Epidemic.* A report by the Physicians' Task Force on Hunger in America, New York Times, Feb. 27, 1985, p. A12.

Boston, Thomas D. *Race, Class and Conservatism.* Winchester, MA: Univ. in Hyman. 1988.

Botsch, Robert Emil. *We Shall Not Overcome: Populism and Southern Blue-Collar Workers.* Chapel Hill: Univ. of North Carolina Press.

**D**

Daniel, Cletus. *Bitter Harvest: A History of California Farmworkers, 1870-1941.* Ithaca, NY: Cornell Univ. Press.

Davis, George and Gregg Watson. *Black Life in Corporate America: Swimming in the Mainstream.* NY: Anchor Press/Doubleday. 1982.

Dickerson, Dennis C. *Out of the Crucible: Black Steelworkers in Western Pennsylvania, 1875-1980.* Ithaca, NY: State Univ. of New York Press. 1986.

**E**

Ellwood, David T. *Poor Support: Poverty in the American Family.* NY: Basic Books. 1988.

*Ending Hunger: An Idea Whose Time Has Come.* The Hunger Project.

**F**

Farley, Reynolds. *Blacks & Whites: Narrowing the Gap?* Cambridge: Harvard Univ. Press. 1984, 1986.

Foner, Philip S. *Organized Labor & The Black Worker, 1619-1981.* NY: International Publishers.

Foner, Philip S., Ronald L. Lewis and Robert Cvornyek (editors). *The Black Worker: The Era Since the AFL-CIO Merger 1955-1980.* Philadelphia: Temple Univ. Press.

**G**

Goldfarb, Ronald L. *Migrant Farm Workers: A Caste of Despair.* Ames: Iowa State Univ. Press.

**H**

Hall, Donald L. *Actuality Management: A Concept for the Effective Utilization of All Human Resources in Organizations.* Julian Richardson Assoc., 540 McAllister St., San Francisco 94102.

Harrington, Michael. *The New American Poverty.* NY: Holt, Rinehart & Winston.

Harris, William H. *The Harder We Run: Black Workers Since the Civil War.* NY: Oxford Univ. Press.

Hill, George H. *Black Business and Economics: A Bibliography.* Garland Publishing, 136 Madison ave., New York 10016.

Hirsch, Arnold R. *Making the Second Ghetto: Race & Housing in Chicago, 1940-1960.* Cambridge Univ. Press.

**I**

*Images of Labor* edited by Moe Foner. NY: Pilgrim Press.

**K**

Katzman, David M. *Seven Days a Week: Women and Domestic Service in Industrializing America.* Urbana: Univ. of Illinois Press.

Kozol, Jonathan. *Rachel and Her Children: Homeless Families in America.* NY: Crown Publishers. 1988.

**L**

Lake, Robert W. *The New Suburbanites: Race and Housing in the Suburbs.* Center For Urban Policy Research, Rutgers Univ., Box 489, Piscataway, NJ 08854.

**M**

Mangum, Garth L. and Stephen F. Seniger. *Coming of Age in the Ghetto: A Dilemma of Youth Unemployment.* Baltimore, MD: Johns Hopkins Univ. Press.

Manuel, Ron C. (editor). *Minority Aging: Sociological and Social Psychological Issues.* Westport, CT: Greenwood Press.

McElvaine, Robert S. (editor). *Down & Out in the Great Depression. Letters From the Forgotten Man.* Chapel Hill: Univ. of North Carolina Press.

Monroe, Sylvester and Peter Goldman. *Brothers: Black and Poor—A True Story of Courage and Survival.* NY: Newsweek/Morrow. 1988.

Moore Jr., Jesse T. *A Search for Equality: The National Urban League, 1910-1961.* University Park: Pennsylvania State Univ. press.

Murray, Charles. *Losing Ground: American Social Policy, 1950-1980.* NY: Basic Books.

**N**

Nivens, Beatryce. *The Black Woman's Career Guide.* Anchor/Doubleday.

**P**

Physicians Task Force. *Hunger in America: The Growing Epidemic.* Middletown, CT: Wesleyan Univ. Press.

**R**

*Resources for Affirmative Action: An Annotated Directory for Books, Periodicals, Films, Training Aids, and Consultants on Equal Opportunity.* Edited by Joan Bartczak Cannon and Ed Smith. Garrett Park Press, Garrett Park, MD 20896.

Rollins, Judith. *Between Women: Domestics and Their Employers.* Philadelphia: Temple Univ. Press. 1985.

**S**

Segal, Geraldine R. *Blacks in the Law: Philadelphia and the Nation.* Foreword by Judge A. Leon Higginbotham, Jr. Philadelphia: Univ. of Pennsylvania Press.

Sims, Naomi. *All About Success for the Black Woman.*

Stallard, Karin, Barbara Ehrenreich and Holly Sklar. *Poverty in the American Dream: Women & Children First.* Institute for New Communications, South End Press, 302 Columbus Ave., Boston 02116.

Stone, Deborah A. *The Disabled State.* Philadelphia: Temple Univ. Press.

**T**

Turner, William H. and Edward J. Cabbell (editors). *Blacks in Appalachia.* Lexington: Univ. Press of Kentucky.

### W

Wilson, Joseph (compiler and editor). *Black Labor in America, 1865-1983: A Selected Annotated Bibliography.* Westport, CT: Greenwood Press. 1985.

Wilson, William Julius. *The Truly Disadvantaged: The Inner City, The Underclass and Public Policy.* Chicago: Univ. of Chicago Press. 1987.

Work, John W. *Race, Economics and Corporate America.* Scholarly Resources, 1508 Pennsylvania Ave., Wilmington, DE 19806.


## Education

Books in this category are related directly to the education process and schooling.


### A

Aldridge, Dan. *The Aldridge Historically Black College Guide.* Detroit, MI. 1983.

Anderson, James D. *The Education of Blacks in the South, 1860-1935.* Chapel Hill: Univ. of North Carolina Press. 1986.

### B

Beckham, Barry (editor). *The Black Student's Guide to Colleges.* NY: E.P. Dutton.

Beriak, Ann and Harold. *Dilemmas of Schooling.* NY: Methuen.

Brooks, Charlotte K. (editor). *Tapping Potential: English and Language Arts for the Black Learner.* National Council of Teachers of English, 1111 Kenyon Road, Urbana, IL 61801.

Brooks, Lyman Beecher. *Upward: A History of Norfolk State University.* Washington, DC: Howard Univ. Press.

### C

Carter, Candy (Editor). *Non-Native and Nonstandard Dialect Students: Classroom Practices in Teaching English, 1982-1983.*

Chunn II, Jay C., Patricia J. Dunston and Fariyal Ross-Sheriff (editors). *Mental Health and People of Color: Curriculum Development and Change.* Washington, DC: Howard Univ. Press.

Comer, James P. *School Power.* NY: Free Press.

### D

Davis, James P. *How To Make It Through Law School: A Guide for Minority and Disadvantaged Students.* Conch Magazine Ltd. Publishers, 102 Normal Ave., Buffalo, NY 14213.

Dilworth, Mary E. *Teachers' Totter: A Report on Teacher Certification Issues.* Washington, DC: Howard Univ. Institute for the Study of Educational Policy.

*Directory of Historically Black Colleges and Universities in the United States (15th ed., 1984).* Washington, DC: National Alliance of Business under contract to U.S. Dept. of Education.

### E

Exum, William H. *Paradoxes of Protest: Black Student Activism in a White University.* Philadelphia: Temple Univ. Press.

### F

Fancher, Raymond E. *The Intelligence Men: Makers of the IQ Controversy.* NY: W.W. Norton.

Foner, Philip S. and Josephine F. Pacheco. *Three Who Dared: Prudence Crandall, Margaret Douglass, Myrtilla Miner— Champions of Antebellum Black Education.* Westport, CT: Greenwood Press.

### G

Gaillard, Frye. *The Dream Long Deferred.* Chapel Hill: Univ. of NC Press. 1988.

Gallot, Mildred B. G. *A History of Grambling State University.* Lanham, MD: Univ. Press of America. 1985.

Griffin, Paul R. *Black Theology as the Foundation of Three Methodist Colleges: The Educational Views and Labors of Daniel Payne, Joseph Price, Isaac Lane.* Lanham, MD: Univ. Press of America. 1984.

### H

Haber, Louis. *Women Pioneers of Science.* NY: Harcourt Brace Jovanovich.

Haynes, III, Floyd W. *Structures of Dominance and the Political Economy of Black Higher Education in a Technocratic Era: A Theoretical Framework.* Institute for the Study of Educational Policy, Howard Univ., Washington, DC 20008.

Hochschild, Jennifer L. *The New American Dilemma: Liberal Democracy and School Desegregation.* Yale Univ. Press, 1984.

Hochschild, Jennifer L. *Thirty Years After Brown.* Joint Center for Political Studies, 1301 Pennsylvania Ave., NW #400, Washington, DC 20004.

Huckaby, Elizabeth. *Crisis at Central High: Little Rock, 1957-58.* Baton Rouge: Louisiana State Univ. Press. 1982.

### J

Johnson, Evelyn Adelaide. *History of Elizabeth City State University: A Story of Survival.* NY: Vantage Press.

Jones, Faustine C. *A Traditional Model of Educational Excellence: Dunbar High School of Little Rock, Arkansas.* Howard Univ. Press.

### K

Kozol, Jonathan. *Illiterate America.* NY: Doubleday.

Kunjufu, Jawanza. *Developing Positive Self-Images & Discipline in Black Children.* Chicago: African-American Images.

### L

Lightfoot, Sara Lawrence. *The Good High School: Portraits of Character and Culture.* NY: Basic Books.

Lukas, J. Anthony. *Common Ground: A Turbulent Decade in the Lives of Three American Families.* NY: A. A. Knopf.

### M

McCaul, Robert L. *The Black Struggle for Public Schooling in Nineteenth Century Illinois.* Carbondale, IL: Southern Illinois Univ. Press. 1987.

Metcalf, George R. *From Little Rock to Boston: The History of School Desegregation.* Westport, CT: Greenwood Press.

Morris, J. Kenneth. *Elizabeth Evelyn Wright, 1872-1906: Founder of Voorhees College.* University Press, Sewanee, TN 37375.

Morris, Lorenzo, et al. *4th ISEP Status Report.*

Morris, Robert C. *Reading, 'Riting and Reconstruction: The Education of Freedmen in the South, 1861-1870.* Chicago: Univ. of Chicago Press.

### N

National Education Assn. and the Council on Interracial Books for Children. *Teaching Guide on the Ku Klux Klan.*

*New Moton Guide to American Colleges With a Black Heritage, The.* Moton Institute, PO Box 1070, Gloucester, VA 23061. 1982 second edition.

Newman, Richard. *Afro-American Education, 1907-1932: A Bibliographical Index.* Lambert Press.

### O

Owens, David. *None of the Above: The Myth of Scholastic Aptitude.* Boston: Houghton Mifflin.

### P

Payne, Charles M. *Getting What WE Ask For: The Ambiguity of Success and Failure in Urban Education.* Greenwood Press.

Pilgrim, David. *Deception by Stratagem: Segregation in Public Higher Education.* Wynham Hall Press, Box 877, Bristol, IN 46507.

Piliawsky, Monte. *Exit 13: Oppression and Racism in Academia.* South End Press, 302 Columbus Ave., Boston 02116.

Preer, Jean L. *Lawyers v. Educators: Black Colleges and Desegregation in Public Higher Education.* Greenwood Press, Westport, CT.

### R

Rebell, Michael A. and Arthur R. Black. *Equality and Education: Federal Civil Rights Enforcement in the New York City School System.* Princeton, NJ: Princeton Univ. Press.

Rossell, Christine H. and Willis D. Hawley (editors). *The Consequences of School Desegregation.* Philadelphia: Temple Univ. Press.

### S

Smith, Ed. *Black Students in Interracial Schools: A Guide for Students, Teachers, and Parents.* Garrett Park Press, Garrett Park, MD 20896.

Stanfield, John H. *Philanthropy and Jim Crow in American Social Science.* Greenwood Press.

Stikes, C. Skully. *Black Students in Higher Education.* Carbondale: Southern Illinois Univ. Press.

Summerville, James. *Educating Black Doctors: A History of Meharry Medical College.* Univ. of Alabama Press, PO Box 2877, University, AL 35486.

Swanson, Kathryn. *Affirmative Action and Preferential Admission to Higher Education: An Annotated Bibliography.* Scarecrow Press, Metuchen, NJ.

### T

Tamarkin, Civia and Marva Collins. *Marva Collins' Way.* Published by J.P. Tarcher and distributed by Houghton Mifflin, Boston. 1982.

Tobin, McLean. *The Black Female Ph.D.: Education and Career Development.* Washington, DC: Univ. Press of America.

Tollett, Kenneth S. *Black Colleges As Instruments of Affirmative Action.*

Tollett, Kenneth S. *The Right to Education: Reaganism, Reaganomics Or Human Capital?* Institute for the Study of Educational Policy, Howard Univ., Washington, DC.

### W

Weinberg, Meyer. *The Search For Quality Integrated Education: Policy and Research on Minority Students in School and College.* Westport, CT: Greenwood Press.

Wolters, Raymond. *The Burden of Brown: Thirty Years of School Desegregation.* Knoxville: Univ. of Tennessee Press.

## History

Books listed here are either specifically about history or have a general historical perspective.

### A

Afro-American Historical and Cultural Museum, The *Of Color, Humanitas and Statehood: The Black Experience in Pennsylvania Over Three Centuries 1681-1981.* 7th & Arch Sts., Philadelphia 19106.

Anderson, Eric. *Race and Politics in North Carolina: The Black Second.* Baton Rouge: Louisiana State Univ. Press.

Aptheker, Bettina. *Woman's Legacy: Essays on Race, Sex & Class in American History.* Amherst: Univ. of Mass. Press. 1983.

Aptheker, Herbert. *Abolitionism: A Revolutionary Movement.* Boston: G. K. Hall. 1989.

Aptheker, Herbert. *"We Will Be Free": Advertisements for Runaways and the Reality of American Slavery.* Occasional Paper No. 1, Ethnic Studies Program, Univ. of Santa Clara, Santa Clara, CA 95053.

Ashe Jr., Arthur R. with Kip Branch, Ocania Chalk and Francis Harris. *A Hard Road to Glory: A History of the African-American Athlete. Vol. I, 1619-1918. Vol. II, 1919-1945. Vol. III, 1946 to the Present.* NY: Warner Books. 1988. Illus.

### B

Bateman, Fred and Thomas Weiss. *A Deplorable Scarcity: The Failure of Industrialization in the Slave Economy.* Chapel Hill: Univ. of North Carolina Press.

Bennett Jr., Lerone. *Before the Mayflower: A History of Black America.* Chicago: Johnson Publishing Co. 1982.

Berlin, Ira, et al. (editors). *Freedom: A Documentary History of Emancipation 1861-1867: Selected from the Holdings of the National Archives of the United States: Series II: The Black Military Experience.* NY: Cambridge Univ. Press.

Berry, Mary Frances and John W. Blassingame. *Long Memory: The Black Experience in America.* NY: Oxford Univ. Press.

Bethel, Elizabeth Rauh. *Promiseland: A Century of Life in a Negro Community.* Philadelphia: Temple Univ. Press.

*Black Worker: The Era of Post-War Prosperity and the Great Depression, The 1920-1936 (Volume VI).* Edited by Philip S. Foner and Ronald L. Lewis. Philadelphia: Temple Univ. Press.

Blackburn, Robin. *The Overthrow of Colonial Slavery 1776-1848.* NY: Verso. 1989.

Blackett, R.J.M. *Building an Antislavery Wall: Black Americans in the Atlantic Abolitionist Movement, 1830-1860.* Louisiana State Univ. Press.

Blakely, Allison. *Russia and the Negro: Blacks in Russian History and Thought.* Washington, DC: Howard Univ. Press.

Blassingame, John W., Mae G. Henderson and Jessica M. Dunn. *Antislavery Newspapers and Periodicals. Vol. V 1861-1871: An Annotated Index.* Boston: G.K. Hall.

Blassingame, John W., Mae G. Henderson and Jessica M. Dunn (editors). *Antislavery Newspapers and Periodicals. Volume III, 1836-1854: An Annotated Index of Letters in the Friend of Man, Pennsylvania Freeman, Advocate of Freedom and American & Foreign Anti-Slavery Reporter.* Boston: G. K. Hall.

Blockson, Charles L. *The Underground Railroad.* NY: Prentice Hall Press. 1987.

Blockson, Charles L. *The Underground Railroad in Pennsylvania.* Flame International, P.O. Box 5336, Jacksonville, NC 28540.

Bole, John B. *Black Southerners, 1619-1869.* Lexington: Univ. Press of Kentucky.

Bullock, Penelope L. *The Afro-American Periodical Press 1838-1909.* Baton Rouge: Louisiana State Univ. Press.

### C

Carnegie, Mary Elizabeth. *The Path We Tread: Blacks in Nursing 1854-*

*1984*. Philadelphia: J. B. Lippincott. 1986.

Cassity, Michael J. *Chains of Fear: American Race Relations Since Reconstruction*. Westport, CT: Greenwood Press.

Cimprich, John. *Slavery's End in Tennessee, 1861-1865*. University, AL: Univ. of Alabama Press. 1985.

Conrad, Robert Edgar. *Children of God's Fire: A Documentary History of Black Slavery in Brazil*. Princeton, NJ: Princeton Univ. Press.

Cottrol, Robert J. *The Afro-Yankees: The Black Community of Providence, Rhode Island From Colonial Times to 1860*. Westport, CT: Greenwood Press. 1982.

Coughtry, Jay. *The Notorious Triangle: Rhode Island and the African Slave Trade, 1700-1807*. Philadelphia: Temple Univ. Press.

Counter, Allen and David L. Evans. *I Sought My Brother: An Afro-American Reunion*. Foreword by Alex Haley. Cambridge: MIT Press.

Crow, Jeffrey and Flora J. Hatley (editors). *Black Americans in North Carolina and the South*. Chapel Hill: Univ. of N.C. Press.

*Crusader, The 1918-1922*. (Organ of the African Blood Brotherhood.) NY: Garland Publishing. 1987.

Curry, Leonard P. *The Free Black in Urban America, 1800-1850: The Shadow of the Dream*. Chicago: Univ. of Chicago Press. 1985.

## D

Dabbs, Henry E. *Black Brass: Black Generals and Admirals in the Armed Forces of the United States*. Afro-American Heritage House Publishers, Century Office Park, 200 Craig Road, Freehold, NJ 07728.

Davis, David Brion. *Slavery and Human Progress*. NY: Oxford Univ. Press.

Davis-Harris, Jeannette G. *Springfield's Ethnic Heritage: The Black Community*. 1982.

Davis, Lenwood G. and George Hill (compilers). *Blacks in the American Armed Forces, 1776-1983: A Bibliography*. Westport, CT: Greenwood Press.

Davis, Lenwood G. *Black-Jewish Relations in the United States, 1752-1984: A Selected Bibliography*. Greenwood Press.

Davis, Lenwood G. with Janet L. Sims-Wood. *The Ku Klux Klan: A Bibliography*. Greenwood Press.

Davis, Marianna W. (editor). *South Carolina Blacks and Native Americans: 1776-1976*. Columbia, SC: State Human Affairs Commission, 1976.

Davis, Ronald L. F. *Good and Faithful Labor: From Slavery to Sharecropping in the Natchez District, 1860-1890*. Greenwood Press.

Davis, Thomas J. *A Rumor of Revolt: The "Great Negro Plot" In Colonial New York*. NY: Free Press.

DeSane, John. *Analogies and Black History: A Programmed Approach*. De Sane and Assoc., PO Box 1069, Teaneck, NJ 07666.

Digg, Ellen Irene. *Black Chronology from 4000 B.C. to the Abolition of the Slave Trade*. Boston: G.K. Hall.

Dixon, Phil. *Black in Baseball, 1857-1955: A Pictorial History*. Kansas City, MO: Amercon Publishing. 1988.

Drago, Edmund L. *Black Politicians and Reconstruction in Georgia: A Splendid Failure*. Baton Rouge: Louisiana State Univ. Press.

DuBois, W.E.B. *Against Racism: Unpublished Essays, Papers, Addresses, 1887-1961*. Edited by Herbert Aptheker. Amherst: Univ. of Mass. Press. 1985.

## E

Edwards, Paul and James Walvin (editors). *Black Personalities in the Era of the Slave Trade*. Louisiana State Univ.

## F

Fehrenbacher, Don E. *Slavery, Law and Politics: The Dred Scott Case in Historical Perspective*. NY: Oxford Univ. Press, an abridged edition of the 1978 book titled *The Dred Scott Case: Its Significance in American Law and Politics*.

Fields, Barbara Jeanne. *Slavery and Freedom on the Middle Ground: Maryland During the Nineteenth Century*. New Haven, CT: Yale Univ. Press. 1986.

Filler, Louis. *The Rise and Fall of Slavery in America*. Jerome S. Ozer Publisher, 340 Tenafly Road, Englewood, NJ 07631.

Fladeland, Betty. *Abolitionists and Working-Class Problems in the Age of Industrialization*. Baton Rouge: LA State Univ. Press.

Fletcher, Marvin E. *The Black Soldier and Officer in the United States Army, 1891-1917*. Columbia: Univ. of Missouri Press. 1985.

Foner, Eric. *Nothing But Freedom: Emancipation and Its Legacy*. Louisiana State Univ. Press.

Foner, Eric. *Reconstruction: America's Unfinished Revolution, 1863-1877*. NY: Harper and Row. 1988.

Foner, Philip S. (editor). *Black Socialist Preacher: The Teachings of Reverend George Washington Woodbey and His Disciple Reverend George W. Slater, Jr.* Synthesis Publications, Dept. 118, 2703 Folsom St., San Francisco 94110.

Foner, Philip S. *History of Black Americans, vols. 2 and 3*. Greenwood Press.

Fox-Genovese, Elizabeth. *Within the Plantation Household: Black and White Women of the Old South*. Chapel Hill: Univ. of North Carolina Press. 1988.

Franklin, John Hope and Alfred A. Moss, Jr. *From Slavery to Freedom: A History of Negro Americans*. NY: A. A. Knopf. 1987.

Franklin, V. P. *Black Self-Determination: A Cultural History of the Faith of the Fathers*. Westport, CT: Lawrence Hill & Co.

Fraser, Jr., Walter J. and Winfred B. Moore, Jr. (editors). *The Southern Enigma: Essays on Race, Class and Folk Culture*. Westport, CT: Greenwood Press.

Fredrickson, George M. *The Arrogance of Race: Historical Perspectives on Slavery, Racism and Social Inequality*. Middleton, CT: Wesleyan Univ. Press. 1989.

*Free Black Heads of Households in the New York State Federal Census, 1790-1830*. Edited by Alice Eichholz and James M. Rose. Gale Research, Book Tower, Detroit 48226.

## G

Gaspar, David Barry. *Bondmen and Rebels: A Study of Master-Slave Relations in Antigua with Implications for Colonial British America*. Baltimore, MD: Johns Hopkins Univ. Press.

Gilman, Sander L. *On Blackness Without Blacks: Essays on the Image of the Black in Germany*. Boston: G. K. Hall.

Glasrud, Bruce A. and Alan M. Smith (editors). *Race Relations in British North America, 1607-1783*. Chicago: Nelson-Hall.

Graham, Leroy. *Baltimore: The Nineteenth Century Black Capital*. Lanham, MD: Univ. Press of America. 1982.

Greene, Robert Ewell. *Black Courage: Documentation of Black Participation in the American Revolutionary War*.

## H

Harding, Vincent. *There is a River: The Black Struggle for Freedom in America*. NY: Harcourt Brace Jovanovich.

Hayden, Robert C. *Faith, Culture and Leadership: A History of the Black Church in Boston*. Boston Branch NAACP, 451 Massachusetts Ave., Boston 02118.

Hill, Daniel G. *The Freedom Seekers: Blacks in Early Canada*. Book Society of Canada, Box 200, Agincourt, Ontario M1S 3B6.

Hine, Darlene Clark (editor). *The State of Afro-American History: Past, Present and Future*. Baton Rouge: Louisiana State Univ. Press. 1988.

Holtzclaw, Robert Fulton. *Black Magnolias: A History of Black*

*Mississippians.* Keeble Press, 3634 Winchell Road, Shaker Heights, OH 44122.

Hughes, Langston, Milton Meltzer and C. Eric Lincoln. *A Pictorial History of Black Americans.* NY: Crown Publishers. 1983.

Hyman, Mark. *Blacks Who Died for Jesus: A History Book.* Corrective Black History Books, Box 12020, Philadelphia, PA 19108.

## J

Jacob, Donald M. *Index to the American Slave: A Composite Autobiography.* Westport, CT: Greenwood Press.

Jacobs, Harriet A. *Incidents in the Life of a Slave Girl, Written by Herself.* Edited by Jean Fagan Yellin. Cambridge: Harvard Univ. Press. 1987.

Johanse, Bruce E. *Forgotten Founders: Benjamin Franklin, the Iroquois, and the Rationale for the American Revolution.* Gambit, 27 N. Main St., Meeting House Green, Ipswich, MA 01958.

Johnson, Daniel M. and Rex R. Campbell. *Black Migration in America: A Social Demographic History.* Durham, NC: Duke Univ. Press.

Johnson, Michael P. and James L. Roark (editors). *No Chariot Let Down: Charleston's Free People of Color on the Eve of the Civil War.* Univ. of N.C. Press.

Jones, Howard. *Mutiny on the Amistad: The Saga of a Slave Revolt and Its Impact on American Abolition, Law and Diplomacy.* NY: Oxford Univ. Press. 1986.

Jones, Jacqueline. *Labor of Love, Labor of Sorrow: Black Women, Work and the Family from Slavery to the Present.* NY: Basic Books.

Joyce, Donald Franklin. *Gatekeepers of Black Culture: Black-Owned Book Publishing in the United States, 1817-1981.* Westport, CT: Greenwood Press.

Joyner, Charles. *Down by the Riverside: A South Carolina Slave Community.* Champaign: Univ. of Illinois Press.

## K

Kaplan, Sidney. *The Black Soldier of the Civil War in Literature and Art. The Chancellor's Lecture Series, 1979-1980.* Amherst: Univ. of Massachusetts.

Katz, William Loren. *Black Indians: A Hidden Heritage.* NY: Atheneum. 1986.

Katz, William Loren. *The Black West.* Seattle, WA: Open Hand Publishing, Inc. 1987.

Katz, William Loren. *The Invisible Empire: The Ku Klux Klan Impact on History.* Seattle, WA: Open Hand Publishing, Inc. 1986.

Kemble, Frances Anne. *Journal of a Residence on a Georgian Plantation in 1838-1839.* Univ. of Georgia Press, Athens 30602.

Kornweibel, Jr., Theodore (editor). *In Search of the Promised Land: Essays in Black Urban History.* Port Washington, NY: Kennikat Press.

## L

Lamon, Lester C. *Blacks in Tennessee 1791-1970.* Knoxville: Univ. of Tennessee Press.

Lane, Roger. *Roots & Violence in Black Philadelphia: 1860-1900.* Cambridge: Harvard Univ. Press. 1988.

Lawson, Michael L. *Damned Indians: The Pick-Sloan Plan and the Missouri River Sioux, 1944-1980.* Univ. of Oklahoma Press, Norman.

Lesy, Michael. *Bearing Witness: A Photographic Chronicle of American Life, 1860-1945.* NY: Pantheon Books.

Lewis, David Levering. *When Harlem Was in Vogue.* NY: A. A. Knopf.

Libby, Jean. *Black Voices From Harpers Ferry: Osborne Anderson and the John Brown Raid.* Published by the author in Palo Alto, CA, as a special limited edition in 1979.

Lofton, John. *Denmark Vesey's Revolt: The Slave Plot that Lit a Fuse to Fort Sumter.* Kent, OH: Kent State Univ. Press.

## M

Marable, Manning. *Blackwater: Historical Studies in Race, Class Consciousness and Revolution.* Black Praxis Press, 4527 Germantown Pike, Dayton, OH 45418. 1978.

Marable, Manning. *From the Grassroots: Social and Political Essays Towards Afro-American Liberation.* Black Praxis Press, 4527 Germantown Pike, Dayton, OH 45418. 1976.

Marable, Manning. *How Capitalism Underdeveloped Black America: Problems in Race, Political Economy and Society.* South End Press, 302 Columbus Ave., Boston 02116. 1982.

Martin, B. Edman. *All We Want Is Make Us Free: La Amistad and the Reform Abolitionists.* Lanham, MD: Univ. Press of America. 1986.

Mays, Joe H. *Black Americans and Their Contributions Toward Union Victory in the American Civil War.* Lanham, MD: Univ. Press of America. 1984.

McKenzie, Edna. *Freedom in the Midst of a Slave Society.* Washington, DC: University Press of America.

McPherson, James M. *Battle Cry of Freedom: The Civil War Era.* NY: Oxford Univ. Press. 1988.

Mellon, James (editor). *Bullwhip Days; The Slaves Remember.* NY: Weidenfeld & Nicolson. 1988.

Miller, Joseph C. *Slavery: A Worldwide Bibliography, 1900-1982.* White Plains, NY: Kraus International Publications.

Mintz, Sidney W. *Sweetness and Power: The Place of Sugar in Modern History.* NY: Viking Press.

Moore, Robert B. and Beryle Banfield. *Reconstruction: The Promise and Betrayal of Democracy.* Council on Interracial Books for Children, 1841 Broadway, New York 10023.

Mumford, Esther Hall. *Seattle's Black Victorians 1852-1901.* Ananse Press, PO Box 22565, Seattle, WA 98122.

## N

Nalty, Bernard C. *Strength For the Fight: A History of Black Americans in the Military.* NY: The Free Press/Macmillan. 1986.

Nash, Gary B. *Forging Freedom: The Formation of Philadelphia's Black Community, 1720-1840.* Cambridge: Harvard Univ. Press. 1988.

## O

Oakes, James. *The Ruling Race: A History of American Slaveholders.* NY: Vintage Books.

Olson, James S. *Slave Life in America: A Historiography and Selected Bibliography.* Lanham, MD: Univ. Press of America. 1983.

## P

Painter, Nell Irvin. *Standing at Armageddon: The United States, 1877-1919.* NY: W. W. Norton. 1987.

Patterson, Orlando. *Slavery and Social Death: A Comparative Study.* Cambridge, MA; Harvard Univ. Press.

Piersen, William D. *Black Yankees: The Development of an Afro-American Subculture in Eighteenth-Century New England.* Amherst: Univ. of Mass. Press. 1987.

Price, Richard. *First Time: The Historical Vision of an Afro-American People.* Baltimore, MD: Johns Hopkins Univ. Press. 1984.

Price, Sally and Richard. *Afro-American Arts of the Suriname Rain Forest.* Berkeley: Univ. of Calif. Press.

## Q

Quarles, Benjamin. *Black Mosaic: Essays in Afro-American History and Historiography.* Amherst: Univ. of Mass. Press. 1988.

Quarles, Benjamin. *The Negro in the Civil war.* New introduction by William S. McFeely. NY: DaCapo Press. 1989.

**R**

Rable, George C. *But There Was No Peace: The Role of Violence in the Politics of Reconstruction.* Univ. of Georgia Press, Athens 30602.

Rachleff, Peter J. *Black Labor in the South: Richmond, Virginia, 1865-1890.* Philadelphia: Temple Univ. Press.

Rawley, James A. *The Transatlantic Slave Trade: A History.* NY: W. W. Norton.

Ripley, C. Peter (editor), et al. *The Black Abolitionist Papers: Vol. I, The British Isles, 1830-1865; Vol. II, Canada, 1830-1865.* Chapel Hill: Univ. of NC Press. 1985, 1987.

Rodney, Walter. *A History of the Guyanese Working People, 1881-1905.* Introduction by George Lamming. Baltimore, MD: Johns Hopkins Univ. Press. 1982.

Rogers, J.A. *Your History: From the Beginning of Time to the Present.* Black Classic Press, Box 13414—1A, Baltimore, MD 21203.

Rose, Willie Lee. *Slavery and Freedom.* W. W. Frehling (editor). NY: Oxford Univ. Press.

Ruck, Rob. *Sandlot Seasons: Sport in Black Pittsburgh.* Champaign: Univ. of Illinois Press. 1987.

Rust, Jr., Edna and Art. *Art Rust's Illustrated History of the Black Athlete.* NY: Doubleday. 1985.

**S**

San Sertima, Ivan (editor). *Black Women in Antiquity. Journal of African Civilizations (Vol. 6, No. 1, April 1984).* Africana Studies Dept., Beck Hall, Rutgers Univ., New Brunswick, NJ 08903.

Sears, Richard D. *The Day of Small Things: Abolitionism in the Midst of Slavery.* Lanham, Md: Univ. Press of America. 1986.

Sernett, Milton C. (editor). *Afro-American Religious History: A Documentary Witness.* Durham, NC: Duke Univ. Press. 1985.

Shapiro, Herbert. *White Violence and Black Response: From Reconstruction to Montgomery.* Amherst: Univ. of Mass. Press. 1988.

Sherwood, Marika. *Many Struggles: West Indian Workers and Service Personnel in Britain 1939-45.* Karia Press, BCM Karia, London WC1 N3XX.

Snowden, Jr., Frank M. *Before Color Prejudice: The Ancient View of Blacks.* Cambridge, MA: Harvard Univ. Press.

Smith, Edward D. *Climbing Jacob's Ladder: The Rise of Black Churches in Eastern American Cities, 1740-1877.* Washington, DC: Smithsonian Institution Press. 1988.

Smith, Graham. *When Jim Crow Met John Bull: Black American Soldiers in World War II Britain.* NY: St. Martin's Press. 1988.

Smith: John David. *Black Slavery in the Americas: An Interdisciplinary Bibliography, 1865-1980.* Westport, CT: Greenwood Press.

Sobel, Mechal. *The World They Made Together: Black and White Values in Eighteenth Century Virginia.* Princeton, NJ: Princeton Univ. Press. 1988.

Starling, Marion Wilson. *The Slave Narrative: Its Place in American History.* Boston: G. K. Hall.

Sterling, Dorothy (editor). *We Are Your Sisters: Black Women in the Nineteenth Century.* NY: W. W. Norton. 1984.

**T**

Takaki, Ronald T. *Iron Cages: Race and Culture in Nineteenth-Century America.* Seattle: Univ. of Washington Press.

*Tarikh Magazine* (No. 26, Vol. 7, No. 2, 1982) published for the Historical Society of Nigeria by Longman and by Humanities Press in the U.S.

Turner, Jonathan H., Royce Singleton, Jr. and David Musick. *Oppression: A Socio-History of Black-White Relations in America.* Chicago: Nelson Hall.

**V**

van der Zee, John. *Bound Over: Indentured Servitude and American Conscience.* NY: Simon and Schuster.

Van Sertima, Ivan (editor). *Blacks in Science: Ancient and Modern.*

Volney, C. F. *The Ruins or Meditation on the Revolutions of Empires: And the Law of Nature.*

**W**

Walvin, James (editor). *Slavery and British Society, 1776-1846.* Baton Rouge: Louisiana State Univ. Press.

Wesley, Charles Harris. *The History of the National Association of Colored Women's Clubs: A Legacy of Service.* Nat'l. Assn. of Colored Women's Clubs, 5808 16th St., NW, Washington, DC 20011.

Wheeler, Edward L. *Uplifting the Race: The Black Minister in the New South, 1865-1902.* Lanham, MD: Univ. Press of America. 1986.

Willa, Davis W. and Richard Newman (editors). *Black Apostles at Home and Abroad: Afro-Americans and the Christian Mission from the Revolution to Reconstruction.* Boston: G. K. Hall.

Williams, David. *Hit Hard.* NY: Bantam Books.

Williamson, Joel. *The Crucible of Race: Black-White Relations in the American South Since Emancipation.* NY: Oxford Univ. Press.

Wink, Robin W. *The Blacks in Canada: A History.* New Haven, CT: Yale University Press, 1971.

Winston, Betty. *The Africans.* NY: Dell Publishing.

Wood, Betty. *Slavery in Colonial Georgia, 1730-1775.* Univ. of Georgia Press, Athens 30602.

Wright, George C. *Life Behind a Veil: Blacks in Louisville, Kentucky, 1865-1930.* Baton Rouge: Louisiana State Univ. Press. 1985.

Wyatt-Brown, Bertram. *Southern Honor: Ethics and Behavior in the Old South.* NY: Oxford Univ. Press.

## Juvenile

This section lists works written specifically for elementary, junior high, and high school students.

**A**

Adoff, Arnold. *All the Colors of the Race: Poems.* Illustrated by John Steptoe. NY: Lothrop, Lee & Shepard.

**B**

Blau, Zena Smith. *Black Children/White Children.* NY: Free Press.

Boyd, Candy Dawson. *Breadsticks and Blessing Places.* NY: Macmillan.

Bryan, Ashley. *I'm Going to Sing: Black American Spirituals. (Vol. 2)* NY: Atheneum Publishers.

**C**

Caine, Jeannette. *Just Us Women.* Harper Junior Books.

Childress, Alice. *Rainbow Jordan.* NY: Coward, McCann & Geoghegan.

Collier, James Lincoln and Christopher. *Jump Ship to Freedom.* NY: Delacorte Press.

Council on Interracial Books for Children, The. 1841 Broadway, New York 10023. *"The Depiction of South Africa in U.S. Teaching Materials for Children."*

Council on Interracial Books for Children, The. *1985 Catalog: Resources to Counter Racism, Sexism and Other Forms of Bias in School and Society.*

**D**

Dennis, Donna and Susan Willmarth. *Black History for Beginners.*

Distributed by W. W. Norton, New York.

### E

Ehrlich, Scott. *Paul Robeson: Singer and Actor.* NY: Chelsea House Publishers. 1988.

### F

Feelings, Tom and Eloise Greenfield. *Daydreamers.* NY: Dial Press. 1981.

Frank, Daniel B. *Deep Blue Funk and Other Stories: Portraits of Teenage Parents.* Univ. of Chicago Press.

### H

Hale, Janice E. *Black Children: Their Roots, Culture and Learning Styles.* Brigham Young Univ. Press, 205 UPB, Provo, UT 84602.

Hamilton, Virginia. *Anthony Burns: The Defeat and Triumph of a Fugitive Slave.* NY: A. A. Knopf. 1988.

Hamilton, Virginia. *Junius Over Far.* NY: Harper & Row Junior Books.

Hamilton, Virginia. *Sweet Whispers, Brother Rush.* NY: Putnam/Philomel Books.

Hamilton, Virginia. *The Gathering.* NY: Greenwillow Books.

Hamilton, Virginia. *Willie Bea and the Time the Martians Landed.* NY: Greenwillow Books/Morrow.

Hancock, Sibyl. *Famous Firsts of Black Americans.* Pelican Publishing Co., PO Box 189, Gretna, LA 70053.

Hunter, Kirstin. *Lou in the Limelight.* NY: Charles Scribner's Sons. 1982.

### J

Jackson, Barbara D. *We Are the Children of the Great Ancient Africans.* The author. 792 Columbus Ave., #11A, New York 10025.

Jakoubek, Robert E. *Adam Clayton Powell, Jr.: Political Leader.* NY: Chelsea House Publishers.

Jaquith, Priscilla. *Bo Rabbit Smart for True: Folktales from the Gullah.* Putnam's Sons.

### L

Lens, Sidney. *Strikemakers & Strikebreakers.* NY: Lodestar Books.

Lester, Julius. *This Strange New Feeling.* NY: Dial Press.

### M

McKissack, Patricia C. *Mirandy and Brother Wind.* Illustrated by Jerry Pinkney. NY: A. A. Knopf. 1988.

Meltzer, Milton (editor). *The Black Americans: A History in Their Own Words.* NY: Crowell Junior Books 1983.

Michaels, Barbara and Bettye White (editors). *Apples on a Stick: The Folklore of Black Children.* Coward-McCann. Illustrated by Jerry Pinkney.

### R

Rollock, Barbara. *Black Authors and Illustrators of Children's Books: A Biographical Dictionary.* NY: Garland Publishing Co. 1986, 1988.

Rollock, Barbara. *The Black Experience in Children's Books.*

### S

Scioscia, Mary. *Bicycle Rider.* Harper Junior Books.

Sims, Rudine. *Shadow and Substance: Afro-American Experience in Contemporary Children's Fiction.* National Council of Teachers of English, 1111 Kenyon Road, Urbana, IL 61801.

Strickland, Dorothy S. *Listen Children.* Bantam Skylark Books.

Suransky, Valerie Polakow. *The Erosion of Childhood.* Univ. of Chicago Press.

### T

Thomas, Ianthe. *Willie Blows a Mean Horn.* NY: Harper & Row.

Thomas, Joyce Carol. *Marked by Fire.* Avon.

Toma, David. *Toma Tells it Straight—With Love.* Books in Focus, 160 E. 38 St. #31B, New York 10016.

*Two Ways to Count to Ten. A Liberian Folktale.* Retold by Ruby Dee. Illustrated by Susan Meddaugh. NY: Henry Holt. 1988.

### W

Walker, Alice. *To Hell With Dying.* San Diego, CA: Harcourt Brace Jovanovich. 1987.

Wilson, Merzie. *Merzette Coloring Book.* The Author. 4221 Otter St., Philadelphia, PA 19104.

### Z

Zaslavsky, Claudia. *Preparing Young Children for Math: A Book of Games.* NY: Shocken Books.

Zaslavsky, Claudia. *Tic Tac Toe.* Crowell Junior Books.

Zemach, Margot. *Jake and Honeybunch Go to Heaven.* Farrar, Straus & Giroux.

## Literature

This list contains both literary criticism and works of fiction, including novels, poetry, and drama.

### A

Abraham, Roger D. (editor). *Afro-American Folk Tales: Stories From Black Traditions in the New World.* NY: Pantheon Books.

Abrahams, Peter. *Hard Rain.* NY: E.P. Dutton. 1988.

*Afro-American Journal of Philosophy, Vol. I, Nos. 1-4, 1982-1983.* Percy Johnston, editor. Afro American Philosophy Assn., c/o Dasein Literary Society, G.P.O. Box 2121, New York 10116.

Ai (Florence Anthony). *Sin.* Boston: Houghton Mifflin. 1987.

Andrews, Raymond. *Baby Sweet's.* Dial Press.

Aptheker, Herbert. *The Literary Legacy of W.E.B. DuBois.* Millwood, NY: Kraus International Organization. 1989.

Arnold, A. James. *Modernism and Negritude: The Poetry and Poetics of Aime Cesaire.* Cambridge: Harvard Univ. Press.

### B

Baker, Houston. *Blues, Ideology and Afro-American Literature: A Vernacular Theory.* Univ. of Chicago Press.

Baldwin, James. *Notes of a Native Son.* Boston: Beacon Press.

Baldwin, James. *Price of the Ticket: Collected Nonfiction 1948-1985, The.* NY: St. Martin's/Marek.

Ball, Wendy and Tony Martin. *Rare Afro-Americana: A Reconstruction of the Adger Library.* Boston: G. K. Hall.

Baraka, Amin and Amiri Baraka (editors). *Confirmation: An Anthology of African American Women.* NY: Quill/Morrow. 1983.

Barry, Lynda. *The Good Times Are Killing Me.* Real Comet Press. 1988.

Beckham, Barry. *Double Dunk.* Los Angeles: Holloway House.

Bell, Bernard W. *The Afro-American Novel and Its Tradition.* Amherst: Univ. of Mass. Press. 1988.

Birtha, Becky. *Literature by Black Women.* The Author, 1933 Chestnut St., Philadelphia 19103.

Bogus, S. Diane. *Sapphire's Sampler: An Anthology of Poetry, Prose and Drama.* WIM Publications, Box 367, College Corner, OH 45003.

Brathwaite, Edward K. *History of the Voice: The Development of Nation Language in Anglophone Caribbean Poetry.* New Beacon Books, 76 Stroud Green Road, London N4 3EN.

Branch, Kip. *Gnawing At My Soul.* NY: Richard Marek; distributed by G. P. Putnam's Sons.

Britton, Mariah (editor). *Long Journey Home: Anthology of Poems.* Meta Press, 730 E. 219 St., Bronx, NY 10467.

Brown, Cecil M. *Days Without Weather.* NY: Farrar, Straus & Giroux.

Bruck, Peter and Wolfgang Karrer (editors). *The Afro-American Novel Since 1960.* Humanities Press, Atlantic Highlands, NJ 07716.

Bulkin, Elly and Joan Larkin (editors). *Lesbian Poetry: An Anthology.* Persephone Press, Box 7222, Watertown, MA 02172.

Bunge, Nancy. *Finding the Words: Interviews with Writers Who Teach.* Ohio Univ. Press/Swallow Press, Athens, OH 45701.

Butcher, Philip (editor). *The Ethnic Image in Modern American Literature: 1900-1950.* Washington, DC: Howard Univ. Press.

Butler, Octavia E. *Wild Seed.* NY: Doubleday.

## C

Campbell, George. *First Poems: A New Edition with Additional Poems.* Garland Publishing.

Carby, Hazel V. *Reconstructing Womanhood: The Emergence of the Afro-American Woman Novelist.* NY: Oxford University Press. 1987.

Cartier, Xam Wilson. *Be-Bop, Re-Bop.* NY: Available/Ballantine Books. 1987.

Cesaire, Aime. *The Collected Poetry.* Univ. of Calif. Press, Berkeley.

Charters, Samuel. *Louisiana Black.* NY: Marion Boyars/Kampmann. 1986.

Chestnutt, Charles W. *The Short Fiction of Charles W. Chesnutt.* Edited by Sylvia Lyons Render. Washington: Howard Univ. Press.

Christian, Barbara. *Black Feminist Criticism: Perspectives on Black Women Writers.* NY: Pergamon Press.

Clark, Edward. *Black Writers in New England: A Bibliography with Biographical Notes of Books by and About Afro-American Writers Associated with New England.* National Park Service, Boston.

Clarke, Austin. *Growing Up Stupid Under the Union Jack.* Havana, Cuba: Ediciones Casa de las Americas.

Clifton, Lucille. *Good Woman: Poems and a Memoir 1969-1980.* Brockport, NY: BOA Editions. 1988 or 89.

Coke, Michael G. *Afro-American Literature in the Twentieth Century: The Achievement of Intimacy.* New Haven: Yale Univ. Press.

*Contemporary Literary Criticism - Vol. 17: Excerpts From Criticism of the Works of Today's Novelists, Poets, Playwrights, Short Story Writers, Film-Makers, and Other Creative Writers.* Edited by Sharon R. Gunton. Gale Research Co., Book Tower, Detroit, MI 48226.

Cousins, Linda (editor). *Ancient Black Youth and Elders Reborn: Anthology of the Poetry, Short Stories, Oral Histories and Deeper Thoughts of African-American Youth and Elders.* Universal Black Writers Press, Box 5, Radio City Sta., New York 10101.

Cousins, Linda (editor). *Black and in Brooklyn: Creators and Creations.* University Black Writers Press, PO Box 5, Radio City Sta., New York City 10125.

Cudjoe, Selwyn R. *Resistance and Caribbean Literature.* Athens: Ohio Univ. Press.

## D

Dalphinis, Morgan. *Caribbean & African Languages: Social History, Language, Literature and Education.* Karia Press.

Dathorne, O. R. *Dark Ancestor: The Literature of the Black Man in the Caribbean.* Baton Rouge: Louisiana State Univ. Press.

Davis, Arthur P. and J. Saunders Redding. *Cavalcade: Negro American Writing from 1760 to the Present. 1983.*

Davis, Charles T. and Henry Louis Gates Jr. (editors). *The Slave's Narrative.* NY: Oxford Univ. Press.

Davis, Charles T. and Michel Fabre. *Richard Wright: A Primary Bibliography.* Boston: G. K. Hall.

Davis, Charles T. *Black Is the Color of the Cosmos: Essays on Afro-American Literature and Culture, 1942-1981.* NY: Garland Publishing Co.

Davis, Thadious M. *Faulkner's "Negro": Art and the Southern Context.* Baton Rouge: Louisiana State Univ. Press.

Davis, T. M. and T. Harris. *Afro-American Writers After 1955: Dramatists and Prose Writers.* Gale Research Co.

Davis, Thadious M. and Trudier Harris (editors). *Afro-American Fiction Writers After 1955.* Detroit: Gale Research Co.

Delany, Samuel R. *The Bridge of Lost Desire.* NY: Arbor House/Morrow. 1988.

Dent, Tom. *Blue Lights and River Songs.* Lotus Press, PO Box 21607, Detroit, MI 48221.

De Veaux, Alexis. *Blue Heat: A Portfolio of Poems and Drawings.* Diva Publishing, 135 Eastern Pkwy. 8K, Brooklyn, NY 11238.

Dixon, Melvin. *Ride Out the Wilderness: Geography and Identity in Afro-American Literature.* Champaign: Univ. of Illinois Press. 1987.

Dodd, Mead. *Complete Poems of Paul Laurence Dunbar, The 1980.*

*Drum Magazine. Vol. 11, No. 1.* May 1981. Amherst: Univ. of Mass.

*Drum Magazine, Vol. 12, No. 1, Spring 1982 and Vol. 13, Nos. 1 and 2, Summer 1983.*

DuBois, W.E.B. *Creative Writings by W.E.B. DuBois: A Pageant, Poems, Short Stories and Playlets.* Edited by Herbert Aptheker. Kraus International Publications, 1 Water St., White Plains, 10601.

DuBois, W.E.B. *The Suppression of the African Slave Trade to the United States of America, 1638-1870; The Souls of Black Folk; Dusk of Dawn;* Essays edited by Nathan I. Huggins (all in one volume). The Library of America, 5 Norden Lane, Huntington Station, NY 11746. 1986.

Dunbar, Paul Laurence. *The Sport of the Gods.* Introduction by Kenny J. Williams. NY: Dodd, Mead.

## E

Edwards-Yearwood, Grace. *In the Shadow of the Peacock.* NY: McGraw-Hill. 1988.

Ellis, Trey. *Platitudes.* NY: Vintage Contemporaries. 1988.

Ellison, Ralph. *Going to the Territory.* NY: Random House. 1986.

Evans, Mari (editor). *Black Women Writers (1950-1980): A Critical Evaluation.* NY: Anchor Press/Doubleday. 1984.

Evans, Mari. *Nightstar: Poems from 1973-1978.* Nelson Stevens collages. Center for Afro-American Studies, Univ. of Calif., Los Angeles.

## F

Feuser, Willfried F. (editor). *Jazz and Palm Wine.* Three Continents Press, 1346 Connecticut Ave., #1131, Washington, DC 20036.

Field, Julia. *Slow Coins: Minted by Julia Fields.* Three Continents Press.

1646 Conn. Ave., NW, Washington. DC, 20036.

*Fire II*, Vol. 9, Feb. 1983.

Forrest, Leon. *Two Wings To Veil My Face*. Random House.

Fowler, Carolyn (compiler). *Black Arts and Black Aesthetics— A Bibliography*. The Author, Atlanta Univ., Atlanta, GA.

## G

Gaess, Roger (editor). *Leaving the Bough: 50 American Poets of the 80s*. International Publishers.

Gales Jr., Henry Louis. *The Signifying Monkey: A Theory of Afro-American Literary Criticism*. NY: Oxford Univ. Press. 1988.

Gates Jr., Henry Louis (editor). *Black Literature and Literary Theory*. Methuen, Inc., 733 Third Ave., New York.

Gibson, Donald B. *The Politics of Literary Expression: A Study of Major Black Writers*. Westport, CT: Greenwood Press.

Giovanni, Nikki. *Those Who Ride the Night Winds*. NY: William Morrow.

Grant, C. D. *Keeping Time*. Blind Beggar Press, 2059 McGraw Ave., Bronx, NY 10462.

Gunn, Bill. *Rhinestone Sharecropping*. Cannon/Reed, 2140 Shattuck Ave. #311, Berkeley, CA 94704.

Guy, Rosa. *A Measure of Time*. NY: Holt, Rinehart and Winston. 1983.

Guy, Rosa. *Bird At My Window*. London: Allison and Busby. NY: Schocken Books.

## H

Hall, Gloria T. *Color, Sex & Poetry: Three Women Writers of the Harlem Renaissance*. Bloomington: Indiana Univ. Press. 1987.

Harris, Leonard (editor). *Philosophy Born of Struggle: Anthology of Afro-American Philosophy From 1917*. Kendall/Hunt Publishing Co., 2460 Kerper Blvd., Dubuque, IA 52001.

Harris, Trudier. *Black Women in the Fiction of James Baldwin*. Univ. of Tenn. Press, Box 6525, Ithaca, NY 14850.

Harris, Trudier. *From Mammies to Militants: Domestics in Black American Literature*. Philadelphia: Temple Univ. Press.

Harris, T. and T. M. Davis (editors). *Afro-American Poets Since 1955*. Gale Research Co.

Harris, Wilson. *The Guyana Quartet*. Boston: Faber & Faber.

Himes, Chester. *Cotton Comes to Harlem*. NY: Allison & Busby/ Schocken Books.

Hull, Gloria T., et al. (editors). *But Some of Us Are Brave: Black Women's Studies*. Feminist Press, Box 334, Old Westbury, NY 11568.

## I

Ikonne, Chidi. *From DuBois to Van Vechten: The Early New Negro Literature, 1903-1926*. Westport, CT: Greenwood Press

## J

Jackson, Clyde Owen. *Come Like the Benediction: A Tribute to Tuskegee Institute and Other Essays*. Smithtown, NY: Exposition Press.

Jaye, Michael C. and Ann Chalmers Watts (editors). *Literature and the Urban Experience: Essays on the City and Literature*. New Brunswick, NJ: Rutgers Univ. Press.

Johnson, Charles. *Being & Race: Black Writing Since 1970*. Bloomington: Indiana Univ. Press. 1988.

Johnson, Charles. *Oxherding Tale*. Bloomington: Indiana Univ. Press.

Jones, Gayl. *Song for Anninho*. Detroit: Lotus Press.

Jones, Gayl. *Palmares: The Soul of the Black Liberation Army*. Julian Richardson Assoc.

Jones, Nettie. *Mischief Makers*. NY: Weidenfeld & Nicolson. 1989.

## K

Kellner, Bruce (editor). *"Keep A-Inchin' Along": Selected Writings of Carl Van Vechten about Black Arts and Letters. Greenwood Press.*

Kilgore, James C. *African Violet: Poems for a Black Woman: New and Selected Poems*. Lotus Press, PO Box 21607, Detroit, MI 48221.

Kincaid, Jamaica. *A Small Place*. NY: Farrar, Straus & Giroux. 1988.

Kincaid, Jamaica. *At The Bottom of the River*. Farrar, Straus & Giroux.

King, Anita (comp. and editor). *Quotations in Black*. Westport, CT: Greenwood Press.

## L

Lee, Andrea. *Sarah Philips*. NY: Random House.

Leonard, Walter J. *A Collection of Inspired Black Poetry*. WJBL Enterprises, PO Box 30537, Bethesda, MD 20814.

Lester, Julis. *Do Lord Remember Me: A Novel*. NY: Holt, Rinehart and Winston.

Lincoln, C. Eric. *The Avenue, Clayton City*. NY: William Morrow. 1988.

Long, Richard A. and Eugenia W. Collier (editors). *Afro-American Writing: An Anthology of Prose and Poetry*. Pennsylvania State University Press, University Park 16802.

Lorde, Audre. *Chosen Poems— Old and New*. W. W. Norton.

Lorde, Audre. *Zami: A New Spelling of My Name*. Persephone Press, PO Box 7222, Watertown, MA 02172.

## M

Madgett, Naomi Long. *Phantom Nightingale: Juvenilia: Poems 1934-1943*.

Madhubuti, Haki R. *Earthquakes and Sunrise Missions: Poetry and Essays of Black Renewal, 1973-1983*. Third World Press, 7524 S. Cottage Grove, Chicago 60619.

Major, Clarence. *Such Was the Season*. San Francisco, CA: Mercury House. 1987.

Marshall, Paule. *Praisesong for the Widow*. NY: G. P. Putnam's Sons.

McAlpine-Watson, Carole. *Prologue: The Novels of Black American Women, 1891-1965*. Westport, CT: Greenwood Press.

McKnight, Reginald. *Moustapha's Eclipse*. Pittsburgh: Univ. of Pittsburgh Press. 1988.

McMillan, Terry. *Mama*. Boston: Houghton Mifflin. 1987.

Middleton, Listervelt. *We Be Creosote People*. Seamon Publications, 1305 Lorick Ave., Columbia, SC 29205.

Miller, R. Baxter (editor). *Black American Literature and Humanism*. Univ. Press of Kentucky, Lexington 40506.

Moraga, Cherrie and Gloria Evangelina Anzaldua (editors). *This Bridge Called My Back: Writings by Radical Women of Color*. Persephone Press, Box 7222, Watertown, MA 02172.

Morrison, Toni. *Beloved*. NY: A. A. Knopf. 1987.

Moses, Louise Jane. *Shadow Castings: A Book of Poetry*. The Author, Brockman Gallery, 4334 Degnan, Los Angeles, CA 90008.

## N

Nadel, Alan. *Invisible Criticism: Ralph Ellison and the American Canon*. Iowa City, IA: Univ. of Iowa Press. 1988.

Naipaul, Shiva. *Beyond the Dragon's Mouth*. Viking.

Naylor, Gloria. *Mama Day*. NY: TicKnor & Fields. 1988.

Naylor, Gloria. *The Women of Brewster Place*. NY: Viking Press.

Nemiroff, Robert (editor). *Lorraine Hansberry: The Collected Last Plays: Les Blancs, The Drinking Gourd, What Use Are Flowers?* NY: Plume/New American Library.

## O

O'Daniel, Therman B. (editor). *Jean Toomer: A Critical Evaluation.* Washington, DC: Howard Univ. Press.

Okantah, Mwatabu S. *Afreeka Brass.* Cleveland State Univ. Poetry Center, Cleveland, OH 44115.

## P

Page, James A. and Jae Minroh. *Selected Black American, African and Caribbean Authors: A Bio-Bibliography.* Libraries Unlimited, PO Box 263, Littleton, CO 80160.

Parker, Pat. *Movement in Black: The Collected Poetry of Pat Parker.* Crossing Press, Trumansburg, NY 14886.

Parks, Gordon. *Shannon: A Novel.* Boston: Little Brown.

Payne, Ladell. *Black Novelists and the Southern Literary Tradition.* Athens: Univ. of Georgia Press.

Penkower, Monty. *The Federal Writers' Project: A Study in Government Patronage of the Arts.* Univ. of Illinois Press.

Perry, Margaret. *The Harlem Renaissance: An Annotated Bibliography and Commentary.* Garland Publishing, 136 Madison Ave., New York 10016.

Phillips, Waldo. *Proflective Poetry Book V.* Sociomation Communication Center, Route 4, Box 265, Waco TX 76705.

Phinazee, Annette L. (editor). *The Black Librarian in the Southeast: Reminiscences, Activities, Challenges.* North Carolina Central Univ. Alumni Assn., Box 19795, Durham 27707.

Prescott, Peter S. (editor). *The Norton Book of American Short Stories.* NY: W. W. Norton. 1988.

## R

Redding, J. Saunders. *Stranger and Alone.* Foreword by Pancho Savery. Boston, MA: Northeastern Univ. Press. 1989.

Reed, Ishmael. *God Made Alaska for the Indians: Selected Essays.* NY: Garland Press.

Reed, Ishmael. *The Terrible Threes.* NY: Atheneum Publishers. 1989.

Royster, Philip M. *Songs and Dances: Selected Poems.*

## S

*Schomburg Library of Nineteenth Century Black Women Writers, The* (30 volumes of fiction, poetry, autobiography, biography, essays and journalism). Henry Louis Gates, Jr. general editor. NY: Oxford Univ. Press. 1988.

Schwarz-Bart, Simone. *Between Two Worlds.* Translated from the French by Barbara Bray. NY: Harper & Row.

Shange, Ntozake. *A Daughter's Geography.* St. Martin's Press.

Shange, Ntozake. *Sassafrass, Cypress & Indigo.* NY: St. Martin's Press.

Shockley, Ann Allen. *Afro-American Women Writers 1746-1933: An Anthology and Critical Guide.* Boston: G. K. Hall. 1988; NY: New American Library. 1989.

Shockley, Ann Allen. *Say Jesus and Come to Me.* NY: Avon.

Simcox, Helen Earle. *Dear Dark Faces: Portraits of a People.* Lotus Press, PO Box 21607, Detroit, MI 48221.

Smith, Barbara (editor). *Home Girls: A Black Feminist Anthology.* Kitchen Table: Women of Color Press, PO Box 2753, Rockefeller Center Sta., New York 10185.

Smith, Valerie. *Self-Discovery and Authority in Afro-American Narrative.* Cambridge: Harvard Univ. Press. 1987.

*Steppingstones: A Literary Anthology Toward Liberation* (a quarterly journal). PO Box 1856, New York 10027.

Stetson, Erlene (editor). *Black Sister: Poetry by Black American Women, 1746-1980.* Bloomington: Indiana Univ. Press.

## T

Tait, George Edward. *At War: Selected Poems of George Edward Tait.* Papyri Press, 1944 Madison Ave., New York 10035.

Tate, Claudia. *Black Women Writers at Work.* NY: Continuum Publishing Corp. 1983.

Thelwell, Michael. *Duties, Pleasures and Conflicts: Essays in Struggle.* Introduction by James Baldwin. Amherst: University of Mass. Press. 1987.

Thomas, Joyce Carol. *Bright Shadow.* Avon/Flare Books, Dept. FL, Box 767, Dresden, TN 38225. 1983.

*Thunder & Honey. Dec. 1984—Jan. 1985.* Blacksun Publications, PO Box 1386, Atlanta, GA 30310.

Tolson, Melvin B. *Caviar and Cabbage: Selected Columns by Melvin B. Tolson from the "Washington Tribune," 1937-1944.* Edited by Robert M. Farnsworth. Columbia: Univ. of Missouri Press.

Tracy, Steven C. *Langston Hughes and the Blues.* Champaign: Univ. of Illinois Press. 1988.

## W

Walcott, Derek. *Collected Poems 1948-1984.* NY: Farrar, Straus, Giroux. 1987.

Walcott, Derek. *Poems of the Caribbean.* Limited Editions Club, 551 Fifth Ave., New York 10017.

Walcott, Derek. *The Arkansas Testament.* NY: Farrar, Strauss & Giroux. 1988.

Walcott, Derek. *The Fortunate Traveller.* NY: Farrar Straus & Giroux.

Walker, Alice. *In Search of Our Mothers' Gardens: Womanist Prose.* San Diego, CA: Harcourt Brace Jovanovich. 1983, 1984.

Walker, Alice. *Living By The Word: Selected Writings 1973-1987.* San Diego, CA: Harcourt Brace Jovanovich. 1988.

Walker, Alice. *The Color Purple.* San Diego, CA: Harcourt Brace Jovanovich. 1982, 1983, 1986.

Walker, Alice. *The Temple of My Familiar.* San Francisco, CA: Harcourt Brace Jovanovich. 1989.

Walker, Margaret and Nikki Giovanni. *A Poetic Equation: Conversations Between Nikki Giovanni and Margaret Walker.* 1983.

Warner, Keith Q. *Kaiso! The Trinidad Calypso: A Study of the Calypso as Oral Literature.* Three Continents Press, 1346 Conn. Ave. #1131, Washington DC 20036.

Weixlmann, Joe, et al. (editors). *Studies in Black American Literature: Black American Prose Theory, Vol. I.* The Penkevill Publishing Co., Box 212, Greenwood, FL 32443.

Welburn, Ron. *Heartland: Selected Poems.* Lotus Press.

White, Vernessa C. *Afro-American and East German Fiction: A Comparative Study of Alienation, Identity and the Development of Self.* Peter Lang Publishers, 34 E. 39 St., New York 10016.

Wideman, John Edgar. *Sent For You Yesterday.* NY: Bard/Avon Books.

Williams, John A. *Click Song.* Boston: Houghton Mifflin.

Williams, June Vanleer. *Will the Real You Please Stand Up?* Dorrance & Co., 828 Lancaster Ave., Bryn Mawr, PA 19010.

Williams, Sherley Anne. *Dessa Rose.* NY: William Morrow. 1986.

Wilson, Harriet L. *Our Nig: Or Sketches From the Life of a Free Black.* NY: Vintage Books. 1983.

Wilson, Harris. *The Womb of Space: The Cross-Cultural Imagination.* Westport, CT: Greenwood Press.

Wright, Jay. *The Double Invention of Komo.* Austin: Univ. of Texas Press.

## Y

Yerby, Frank. *Devil Seed.* NY: Doubleday.

## Music


### B

Balliett, Whitney. *American Musicians: Fifty-Six Portraits in Jazz.* NY: Oxford Univ. Press. 1986.

Balliett, Whitney. *American Singers: Twenty-Seven Portraits in Song* (expanded edition). NY: Oxford Univ. Press. 1988.

Baraka, Amiri. *The Music: Reflections on Jazz & Blues.* NY: William Morrow. 1987.

Bastin, Bruce. *Red River Blues: The Blues Tradition in the Southeast.* Champaign: Univ. of Illinois Press. 1986.

Berendt, Joachim E. *Jazz Book: From Ragtime to Fusion and Beyond.* Lawrence Hill, 520 Riverside Ave., Westport, CT 06880.

Bianco, David. *Heat Wave.* Ann Arbor, MI: Pierian Press. 1988.

Brooks, Tilford. *America's Black Musical Heritage.* Englewood Cliffs, NJ: Prentice-Hall.

Broughton, Viv. *Black Gospel: An Illustrated History of the Gospel Sound.* Distributed by Sterling Publishing Co., 2 Park Ave., New York 10016.

Broven, John. *Rhythm & Blues in New Orleans.* Gretna, LA: Pelican Publishing Co. 1983.

Brown, Rae Linda. *Music, Printed and Manuscript, in the James Weldon Johnson Memorial Collection of Negro Arts and Letters.* Yale University: An Annotated Catalog. NY: Garland Publishing.

### D

Davensbourg, Joe. *Jazz Odyssey: The Autobiography of Joe Davensbourg as told to Peter Vacher.* Baton Rouge, LA: LA State Univ. Press. 1988.

Davis, Francis. *In The Moment: Jazz in the 80s.* NY: Oxford University Press. 1986.

Davis, Stephen and Peter Simon. *Reggae International.* Published by Rogner & Barnard, New York City; distributed by Random House, NY.

de Lerma, Dominique-Rene. *Bibliography of Black Music Volume 4: Theory, Education, and Related Studies.* Westport, CT: Greenwood Press.

### E

Evans, David. *Big Road Blues: Tradition and Creativity in the Folk Blues.* NY: DaCapo Press. 1987.

### F

Feather, Leonard. *The Jazz Years: Earwitness to an Era.* NY: DaCapo Press. 1987.

Finkelstein, Sidney. *Jazz: A People's Music.* NY: International Publishers. 1989.

Frith, Simon. *Sound Effects: Youth, Leisure, and the Politics of Rock 'N' Roll.* NY: Pantheon Books.

### G

George, Nelson, et al. *Fresh: Hip Hop Don't Stop.* NY: Random House. 1985.

George, Nelson. *The Death of Rhythm and Blues.* NY: Pantheon Books. 1988.

George, Nelson. *Where Did Our Love Go: The Rise & Fall of the Motown Sound.* NY: St. Martin's Press. 1985, 1987.

Giddins, Gary. *Rhythm-A-Ning Jazz: Tradition and Innovation in the 80s.* NY: Oxford Univ. Press. 1986.

Gioia, Ted. *The Imperfect Art: Reflections on Jazz and Modern Culture.* NY: Oxford Univ. Press. 1988.

Grime, Kitty. *Jazz Voices.* Quartet Books/Merrimack.

Guralnick, Peter. *Feel Like Going Home: Portraits in Blues & Rock 'n' Roll.* NY: Random House/Vintage.

Guralnick, Peter. *The Listener's Guide to the Blues.* Facts on File, New York City.

### H

Handy, D. Antoinette. *Black Women in American Bands & Orchestras.* Metuchen, NJ: Scarecrow Press.

Handy, D. Antoinette. *The International Sweethearts of Rhythm.* Metuchen, NJ: Scarecrow Press.

Hasse, John Edward (editor). *Ragtime: Its History, Composers and Music.* NY: Schirmer/Macmillan.

Haydon, G. and D. Marks (editors). *Repercussions: A Celebration of African-American Music.* London: Century.

Hebdige, Dick. *Cut 'N' Mix: Culture, Identity and Caribbean Music.* NY: Methuen. 1987.

Hirshey, Gerri. *Nowhere to Run: The Story of Soul Music.* NY: Times Books.

### J

Jackson, Irene V. (Compiler and editor). *Lift Every Voice and Sing: A Collection of Afro-American Spirituals and Other Songs.* The Church Hymnal Corp., 800 Second Ave., New York 10017.

James, Burnett. *Billie Holiday.* Spellmount Ltd., England; NY: Hippocrene Books.

### K

Keepnews, Orrin. *The View From Within: Jazz Writings, 1948-1987.* NY: Oxford Univ. Press. 1988.

### L

Leonard, Neil. *Jazz: Myth and Religion.* NY: Oxford Univ. Press. 1987.

Litweiler, John. *The Freedom Principle: Jazz After 1958.* NY: William Morrow. 1984.

Longstreet, Stephen. *Storyville to Harlem: Fifty Years in the Jazz Scene.* New Brunswick, NJ: Rutgers Univ. Press. 1985.

Lornell, Kip. *"Happy in the Service of the Lord": Afro-American Gospel Quartets in Memphis.* Champaign: Univ. of Illinois Press. 1988.

### M

McKee, Margaret and Fred Chisenhall. *Beale, Black & Blue: Life and Music on Black America's Main Street.* Baton Rouge: Louisiana State Univ. Press.

### N

*New Grove Dictionary of Jazz, The.* Edited by Barry Kernfeld. London: Macmillan Publishers; distributed by Grove's Dictionaries of Music, Washington, DC 1988.

### O

Oliver, Paul. *Songsters and Saints: Vocal Traditions on Race Records.* NY: Cambridge Univ. Press.

Oliver, Paul, Max Harrison and William Bolcom. *The New Grove Dictionary of Music and Musicians: Gospel, Blues and Jazz.* NY: W. W. Norton. 1987.

Omar, Adisa Maina. *'60 to '80: Songs for the Black Struggle.* Aku Press, 3636 16th St., Box B1227, Washington, DC 20010.

## P

Palmer, Robert. *Deep Blues*. NY: Viking Press.

Pearson Jr., Nathan W. *Goin' To Kansas City*. Champaign: Univ. of Illinois Press. 1988.

Placksin, Sally. *American Women in Jazz: 1900 to the Present: Their Words, Lives and Music*. Seaview Books, 1655 Broadway, New York City.

## S

Sallis, James (editor). *Jazz Guitars*. William Morrow/Quill.

Savage, Jr., William W. *Singing Cowboys and All That Jazz: A Short History of Popular Music in Oklahoma*. Norman: Univ. of Oklahoma Press.

Schiffman, Jack. *Harlem Heyday: A Pictorial History of Modern Black Show Business and the Apollo Theatre*. Prometheus Books, 700 E. Amherst St., Buffalo, NY 14215.

Schuller, Gunther. *The Swing Era: The Development of Jazz, 1933-1945*. NY: Oxford Univ. Press. 1988.

Shaw, Arnold. *Black Popular Music in America From the Spirituals, Minstrels & Ragtime to Soul, Disco & Hip Hop*. NY: Schirmer Books. 1986.

Shaw, Arnold. *Honkers & Shouters*. NY: Collier/Macmillan. 1986.

Shaw, Arnold. *The Jazz Age: Popular Music in the 1920s*. NY: Oxford Univ. Press. 1987.

Shaw, Arnold. *The Rockin' 50s*. NY: DaCapo Press. 1987.

Southern, Eileen. *Biographical Dictionary of Afro-American and African Musicians*. Westport, CT: Greenwood Press.

Spivey, Donald. *Union and the Black Musician: The Narrative of William Everett Samuels and Chicago*. Lanham, MD: Univ. Press of America. 1984.

## T

Taraborrelli, J. Randy. *Motown: Hot Wax, City Cool & Solid Gold*. NY: Doubleday. 1985.

Taylor, Arthur. *Notes and Tones*. NY: Perigee Books. 1982.

Taylor, Billy. *Jazz Piano: A Jazz History*. Dubuque, Iowa: Wm. C. Brown Co., 1982.

Titon, Jeff Todd. *Early Downhome Blues: A Musical and Cultural Analysis*. Champaign: Univ. of Illinois Press. 1979.

## W

Waller, Don. *The Motown Story*. NY: Charles Scribner's Sons. 1985.

*We Are The World: The Photos, the Music and the Inside Story of One of the Most Historic Events in American Popular Music*. NY: Perigee Books.

Williams, Otis (with Patricia Romanowski). *Temptations*. NY: Putnam Publishing Group. 1988.

## Y

Yorke, Ritchie. *The History of Rock 'N' Roll*. NY: Methuen, Inc. 1982.

Young, Al. *Things Ain't What They Used to Be: Musical Memoirs*. Berkeley, CA: Donald S. Ellis/Creative Arts Books. 1987.


# Politics

These books relate to political philosophy, political acts, and consequences, or politicians.


## A

Alston, Jacquelyn G. *Comparative Nationalism: Definitions, Interpretations and the Black American and British West African Experience to 1947*. Historical Dimensions Press, Box 12042, Washington, DC 20005.

American Civil Liberties Union. *Voting Rights in the South: Ten Years of Litigation Challenging Continuing Discrimination Against Minorities by Laughlin McDonald, director, ACLU Southern Regional Office*. ACLU, 132 W. 43 St., New York 10036.

Arditti, Rita, et al. editors. *Science and Liberation*. Boston: South End Press.

Ashmore, Harry S. *Hearts and Minds: The Anatomy of Racism from Roosevelt to Reagan*. NY: McGraw-Hill.

## B

Baldwin, James. *Evidence of Things Not Seen, The*. NY: Holt, Rinehart and Winston.

Ball, Howard, et al. *Compromised Compliance: Implementation of the 1965 Voting Rights Act*. Westport, CT: Greenwood Press.

Baraka, Amiri. *Daggers and Javelins: Essays, 1974-1979*. NY: William Morrow.

Barker, Lucius J. *Our Time Has Come: A Delegate's Diary of Jesse Jackson's 1984 Presidential Campaign*. Champaign, IL: Univ. of Illinois Press. 1988.

Barnes, Catherine A. *Journey From Jim Crow: The Desegregation of Southern Transit*. Irvington, NY: Columbia Univ. Press. 1985.

Beckford, George and Michael Witter. *Small Garden...Bitter Weed: Struggle and Change in Jamaica*. Westport, CT: Lawrence Hill.

Bell, Derrick. *And We Are Not Saved: The Elusive Quest for Racial Justice*. NY: Basic Books. 1987.

Bermanzohn, Paul C. and Sally A. *The True Story of the Greensboro Massacre*. Cesar Cauce Publishers, P. O. Box 389, 39 Bowery, New York 10002.

Berry, Mary Frances. *Why ERA Failed: Politics, Women's Rights and the Amending Process*. Bloomington: Indiana Univ. Press. 1986.

*Black Elected Officials: A National Roster (15th Edition)*. 1986. Joint Center for Political Studies, Suite 400, 1301 Pennsylvania Ave., NW, Washington, DC 20004.

*Black Elected Officials: A National Roster 1985*. UNIPUB, Box 1222, Ann Arbor, MI 48106.

*Black Immigration and Ethnicity in the United States: An Annotated Bibliography*. Edited by the Center for Afroamerican and African Studies, Univ. of Michigan, Ann Arbor. Greenwood Press.

Blauner, Bob. *Black Lives, White Lives: Three Decades of Race Relations in America*. Berkeley, CA: Univ. of Calif. Press. 1988.

Bloom, Jack M. *Class, Race and the Civil Rights Movement: The Changing Political Economy of Southern Racism*. Bloomington, IN: Indiana Univ. Press. 1987.

Branch, Taylor. *Parting the Waters: America in the King Years 1954-63*. NY: Simon & Schuster. 1988.

Browning, Rufus P., Dale R. Marshall and David H. Tabb. *Protest Is Not Enough: The Struggle of Blacks and Hispanics for Equality in Urban Politics*. Berkeley: Univ. of Calif. Press. 1985.

Bush, Rod (editor). *The New Black Vote: Politics and Power in Four American Cities*. Synthesis Publications, Dept. 127, 2703 Folsom St., San Francisco, CA 94110.

## C

Cagin, Seth and Philip Dray. *We Are Not Afraid: The Story of Goodman, Schwerner and Chaney and the Civil Rights Campaign for Mississippi*. NY: Macmillan. 1988.

Capeci Jr., Dominic J. *Race Relations in Wartime Detroit: The Sojourner Truth Housing Controversy of 1942*. Philadelphia: Temple Univ. Press.

Carson, Clayborne. *In Struggle: SNCC and the Black Awakening of the*

*1960's.* Cambridge, MA: Harvard Univ. Press. 1981.

Carton, Paul. *Mobilizing the Black Community: The Effects of Personal Contact Campaigning on Black Voters.* Joint Center for Political Studies, 1301 Pennsylvania Ave., NW #400, Washington, DC 20004.

Childs, John Brown. *Leadership, Conflict and Cooperation in Afro-American Social Thought.* Philadelphia: Temple Univ. Press.

Clausen, Edwin G. and Jack Bermingham (editors). *Pluralism, Racism, and Public Policy: The Search for Equality.* Boston: G. K. Hall.

Collins, Carol C. (editor). *Black Progress: Reality or Illusion?* NY: Facts on File.

*Contemporary Black Thought: Alternative Analyses in Social and Behavioral Science.* Edited by Molefi Kete Asante and Abdulai S. Vandi. Sage Publications, 275 S. Beverly Dr., Beverly Hills, CA 90212.

Cross, Theodore. *The Black Power Imperative: Racial Inequality and the Politics of Non-Violence.* Faulkner Books, 870 Seventh Ave., New York 10019.

Cruse, Harold. *Plural But Equal.* NY: William Morrow. 1988.

Cudjoe, Selwyn R. *Movement of the People: Essays on Independence.* Calaloux Research Associates, PO Box 6803, Ithaca, NY 14850.

Cudjoe, Selwyn R. *Grenada: Two Essays.* Calaloux Publications, PO Box 6803, Ithaca, NY 14850.

Custer, Dick (editor). *They Should Have Served That Cup of Coffee: 7 Radicals Remember the 60s.* Boston: South End Press.

## D

*Dangerous Waters* (40-page booklet, 1988). National Interreligous Commission on Civil Rights, 1442 N. Farwell Ave. #210, Milwaukee, WI 53202.

Davidson, Chandler (editor). *Minority Vote Dilution.* Washington, DC: Howard Univ. Press.

Davis, Angela. *Women, Culture and Politics.* NY: Random House. 1989.

## E

Edelman, Marian Wright. *Families in Peril: An Agenda for Social Change.* Cambridge: Harvard Univ. Press. 1986.

Ellsworth, Scott. *Death in a Promised Land: The Tulsa Race Riot of 1921.* Foreword by John Hope Franklin. Baton Rouge: Louisiana State Univ. Press.

Ezekiel, Raphael S. *Voices From the Corner: Poverty and Racism in the Inner City.* Philadelphia, PA: Temple Univ. Press.

## F

Fairclough, Adam. *To Redeem the Soul of America: The Southern Christian Leadership Conference and Martin Luther King Jr.* Athens: Univ. of GA Press. 1987.

Faw, Bob and Nancy Skelton. *Thunder in America: The Improbable Presidential Campaign of Jesse Jackson in 1984.* Foreword by Dan Rather. Austin: Texas Monthly Press. 1986; NY: Paperjacks. 1988.

Fernandez, John P. *Racism and Sexism in Corporate Life: Changing Values in American Business.* Lexington, MA: Lexington Books.

Finch, Minnie. *The NAACP: Its Fight for Justice.* Foreword by James Farmer. Metuchen, NJ: Scarecrow Press.

Foner, Philip S. and James S. Allen (editors). *American Communism and Black Americans: A Documentary History, 1919-1929.* Philadelphia: Temple Univ. Press. 1987.

Forman, James R. *Self-Determination & The African-American People.* Open Hand Publishing, 5 Securities Bldg., 1904 3rd Ave., Seattle, WA 98101.

Fuller, Chet. *I Hear Them Calling My Name: A Journey Through the New South.* Boston: Houghton Mifflin.

Fusfeld, Daniel R. and Timothy Bates. *The Political Economy of the Urban Ghetto.* Carbondale: Southern Illinois Univ. Press.

## G

Gaillard, Frye. *Race, Rock and Religion: Profiles From a Southern Journalist.* The East Woods Press, 429 East Blvd., Charlotte, NC 28203.

George Jr., Herman. *American Race Relations Theory: A Review of Four Models.* University Press of America, 4720 Boston Way, Lanham, MD 20706.

Gerlach, Larry. *Blazing Crosses in Zion.* Logan: Utah State Univ. Press.

Giddings, Paula. *When and Where I Enter: The Impact of Black Women on Race and Sex in America.* NY: William Morrow. 1984.

Gilmore, William C. *The Grenada Intervention: Analysis and Documentation.* NY: Facts on File.

Glasgow, Douglas G. *The Black Underclass: Poverty, Unemployment and the Entrapment of Ghetto Youth.* NY: Random House.

Gossett, Thomas F. *Uncle Tom's Cabin and American Culture.* Dallas: Southern Methodist Univ. Press.

*Grenada: The Peaceful Revolution.* Epica Task Force. 1470 Irving St., NW, Washington, DC 20010.

Gwalthney, John Langston. *Drylongso: A Self-Portrait of Black America.* NY: Random House. 1983.

## H

Hall, Gus. *Fighting Racism: Selected Writings.* NY: International Publishers.

Harding, Rosemarie and Vincent. *A Way of Faith, A Time For Courage.* National Organization for an American Revolution, Box 2617, Philadelphia, PA 19121.

Harris, Fred R. and Roger W. Wilkins (editors). *Quiet Riots: Race and Poverty in the U.S. The Kerner Report Twenty Years Later.* NY: Pantheon Books. 1988.

Haskins, Ethelbert. *The Crisis in Afro-American Leadership.* Buffalo, NY: Prometheus Books. 1988.

Hatch, Roger D. *Beyond Opportunity: Jesse Jackson's Vision for America.* Philadelphia: Fortress Press. 1988.

Hermann, Janet S. *The Pursuit of a Dream.* NY: Oxford Univ. Press.

Hogan, Lloyd. *Principles of Black Political Economy.* Routledge & Kegan Paul, 9 Park St., Boston, MA 02135.

Hooks, Bell. *Ain't I A Woman: Black Women and Feminism.* South End Press, Box 68, Astor Sta., Boston 02123.

Hooks, Bell. *Feminist Theory: From Margin to Center.* South End Press, 302 Columbus Ave., Boston, MA 02116.

Horne, Gerald C. *Communist Front: The Civil Rights Congress, 1946-1956.* Cranbury, NJ: Fairleigh Dickinson Univ. Press. 1987.

House, Ernest R. *Jesse Jackson and the Politics of Charisma: The Rise and Fall of the PUSH/Excel Program.* Boulder, CO: Westview Press. 1988.

Hull, Gloria T., Patricia Bell Scott and Barbara Smith (editors). *But Some of Us Are Brave: Black Women's Studies.* Feminist Press, Box 334, Old Westbury, NY 11568.

## I

Irwin, Victoria (text). *We The Homeless: Portraits of America's Displaced People.* Photographs by Stephanie Hollyman. NY: Philosophical Library. 1989.

## J

Janiewski, Dolores E. *Sisterhood Denied: Race, Gender and Class in a New South Community.* Philadelphia: Temple Univ. Press.

Jordan, June. *On Call: Political Essays.* Boston: South End Press.

## K

Kaufman, Jonathan. *Broken Alliance: The Turbulent Times Between Blacks and Jews in America.* NY: Charles Scribner's Sons. 1988.

King Charles. *Fire in My Bones.* Grand Rapids, MI: Wm. B. Eerdmans Publishing Co.

King, Mary. *Freedom Song: A Personal Story of the 1960s Civil Rights Movement.* NY: William Morrow. 1987, 1988.

King, Mel. *Chain of Change: Struggles for Black Community Development.* Boston: South End Press.

Kirby, John B. *Black Americans in the Roosevelt Era.* Knoxville: Univ. of Tennessee Press.

Kunjufu, Jawanza. *Countering the Conspiracy to Destroy Black Boys.* AFRO-AM, Inc., 910 S. Michigan Ave. #556, Chicago 60605.

## L

Lauren, Paul Gordon. *Power and Prejudice: The Politics and Diplomacy of Racial Discrimination.* Boulder, CO: Westview Press. 1988.

Lawson, Steven F. *In Pursuit of Power: Southern Blacks and Electoral Politics, 1965-1982.* NY: Columbia Univ. Press.

Leinen, Stephen. *Black Police, White Society.* NY: New York Univ. Press. 1984.

Liebman, Lance (editor). *Ethnic Relations in America.* Englewood Cliffs, NJ: Prentice-Hall.

Lincoln, C. Eric. *Race, Religion and the Continuing American Dilemma.* NY: Hill and Wang.

## M

Magee, Doug. *Slow Coming Dark: Interviews on Death Row.* Pilgrim Press, 36-01 43 Ave., Long Island City, NY 11101.

Marable, Manning. *Black American Politics: From the Washington Marches to Jesse Jackson.* NY: Verso/Routledge. 1988.

Marable, Manning. *Race, Reform & Rebellion: The Second Reconstruction in Black America.* Jackson, MS: Univ. Press of Mississippi. 1984.

*Marcus Garvey and Universal Negro Improvement Association Papers, The.* Berkeley: Univ. of Calif. Press. 1980s.

Marefu, Majani. *A Guide to Pan Afrikan Culture and History.* Jamia Consultants Cooperative, Box 236, Philadelphia, PA 29050.

Marsh, Clifton E. *From Black Muslims to Muslims: The Transition From Separation to Islam, 1930-1980.* Metuchen, NJ: Scarecrow Press.

Maison, Mark. *Communists in Harlem During the Depression.* Champaign: Univ. of Illinois Press. 1983.

McAdam, Doug. *Freedom Summer.* NY: Oxford Univ. Press. 1988.

McAdam, Doug. *Political Process and the Development of Black Insurgency, 1930-1970.* Chicago: Univ. of Chicago Press. 1985.

McClain, Leanita. *A Foot in Each World: Essays and Articles on Race, Politics, Crime, Family and Education.* Evanson, IL: Northwestern Univ. Press. 1986.

Moraga, Cherrie and Gloria E. Anzaldua (editors). *The Bridge Called My Back: Writings by Radical Women of Color.* Persephone Press, Watertown, MA.

Moses, Wilson Jeremiah. *Black Messiahs and Uncle Toms.* University Park: Pennsylvania State Univ. Press.

Morris, Aldon D. *The Origins of the Civil Rights Movement: Black Communities Organizing for Change.* NY: Free Press/Macmillan.

Mostovets, Nikolai V. *A Man of Unflinching Courage.* Moscow: Polizdat Publishers.

## N

*National Urban League. The State of Black America 1989.* National Urban League, 500 E. 62 St., New York 10021.

Norrell, Robert J. *Reaping the Whirlwind: The Civil Rights Movement in Tuskegee.* NY: A. A. Knopf. 1986.

## O

O'Shaughnessy, Hugh. *Grenada: An Eye-Witness Account of the U.S. Invasion and the Caribbean History that Provoked It.* NY: Dodd, Mead.

## P

Paquin, Lyonel. *The Haitians: Class and Color Politics.* The Author, 207 W. 96 St., New York 10025.

Perkins, John. *With Justice for All.* Regal Books, 2300 Knoll Dr., Ventura, CA 93003.

Pinckney, Alphonse. *The Myth of Black Progress.* NY: Cambridge Univ. Press.

*Policy Framework for Racial Justice, A.* Joint Center for Political Studies, 1301 Pennsylvania Ave., NW, Washington, DC 20004.

Pomerance, Allen. *The Repeal of the Blues: How Black Entertainers Influenced Civil Rights.* Secaucus, NJ: Citadel Press. 1988.

*Proceedings of the Black National and State Conventions, 1865-1870.* Volume I, edited by Philip S. Foner and George E. Walker. Philadelphia: Temple Univ. Press. 1986.

## Q

Quinn, Richard and Thomas Landers. *Jesse Jackson and the Politics of Race.* Foreword by Rev. Ralph Abernathy. Ottawa, IL: Green Hill Publishing (distributed by Kampmann). 1985.

## R

Reed Jr., Adolph L. (editor). *Race, Politics and Culture: Critical Essays on the Radicalism of the 1960s.* Westport, CT: Greenwood Press. 1985.

Reed Jr., Adolph L. *The Jesse Jackson Phenomenon: The Crisis of Purpose in Afro-American Politics.* New Haven, CT: Yale Univ. Press. 1986.

Reich, Michael. *Racial Inequality: A Political-Economic Analysis.* PA: Princeton Univ. Press.

Rice, Mitchell F. and Woodrow Jones, Jr. (editors). *Contemporary Public Policy Perspectives and Black Americans: Issues in an Era of Retrenchment Politics.* Westport, CT: Greenwood Press.

Ringer, Benjamin B. *"We the People" and Others: Duality and America's Treatment of Its Racial Minorities.* NY: Methuen.

Rose, Thomas and John Greenya. *Black Leaders: Then and Now: A Personal History of Students Who led the Civil Rights Movement in the 1960's—And What Happened to Them.* Garrett Park, MD: Garrett Park Press.

Rothschild, Mary A. *A Case of Black and White: Northern Volunteers and the Southern Freedom Summers, 1964-1965.* Westport, CT: Greenwood Press.

Rozier, John. *Black Boss: Political Revolution in a Georgia County.* Athens: Univ. of Georgia Press.

## S

Scharf, Lois and Joan M. Jensen (editors). *Decades of Discontent: The Women's Movement, 1920-1940.* Westport, CT: Greenwood Press.

Schlesinger, Stephen and Stephen Kinzer. *Bitter Fruit: The Untold Story of the American Coup in Guatemala.* Introduction by Harrison Salisbury. NY: Doubleday.

Schuman, Howard, Charlotte Steel and Lawrence Bobo. *Racial Attitudes in America: Trends and Interpretations.* Cambridge: Harvard Univ. Press. 1988.

Siegal, Loren and David Landau. *No Justice for the Poor: How Cutbacks*

*Are Destroying Legal Services.* American Civil Liberties Union, 132 W. 43 St., New York 10036.

Sivanandan, A. *A Different Hunger: Writings on Black Resistance.* London: Pluto Press.

Smead, Howard. *Blood Justice: The Lynching of Mack Charles Parker.* NY: Oxford Univ. Press. 1986.

Sowell, Thomas. *A Conflict of Visions: Ideological Origins of Political Struggles.* NY: William Morrow. 1988.

Sowell, Thomas. *Civil Rights: Rhetoric or Reality?* NY: William Morrow.

Sowell, Thomas. *The Economics and Politics of Race: An International Perspective.* NY: William Morrow.

Stein, Judith. *The World of Marcus Garvey: Race and Class in Modern Society.* Baton Rouge: Louisiana State Univ. Press. 1986.

## T

Terry, Wallace. *Bloods: An Oral History of the Vietnam War by Black Veterans.* NY: Random House. 1984.

Thiong'o, Ngugi wa. *Barrel of a Pen: Resistance to Oppression in Neo-Colonial Kenya.* New Beacon Books, 76 Stroud Green Road, London N4 3EN, England.

Thompson, Jerry. *My Life in the Klan: A True Story by the First Investigative Reporter to Infiltrate the Ku Klux Klan.* NY: G. P. Putnam's Sons.

## W

Walker, Rev. Wyatt Tee. *Road to Damascus.* NY: M. L. King Fellows Press.

Walton, Jr., Hayes. *When the Marching Stopped: The Politics of Civil Rights Regulatory Agencies.* Ithaca, NY: State Univ. of New York Press. 1988.

Washburn, Patrick S. *A Question of Sedition: The Federal Government's Investigation of the Black Press During World War II.* NY: Oxford Univ. Press. 1986.

Weisbord, Robert G. and Richard Kazarian, Jr. *Israel in the Black American Perspective.* Greenwood Press.

Weisbrot, Robert. *Father Divine and the Struggle for Racial Equality.* Champaign: University of Illinois Press. 1983.

Weiss, Nancy J. *Farewell to the Party of Lincoln: Black Politics in the Age of FDR.* Princeton, NJ: Princeton Univ. Press.

West, Cornel. *Prophesy Deliverance! An Afro-American Revolutionary Christianity.* Westminster Press, 925 Chestnut St., Philadelphia, PA 19107.

Whitfield, Stephen J. *A Death in the Delta: The Story of Emmett Till.* NY: The Free Press. 1989.

Williams, Juan. *Eyes on the Prize: America's Civil Rights Years, 1954-1965.* Introduction by Julian Bond. NY: Viking Press. 1986.

Williams, Walter E. *The State Against Blacks.* NY: McGraw-Hill.

Williamson, Joel. *The Crucible of Race: Black-White Relations in the American South Since Emancipation.* NY: Oxford Univ. Press. 1984.

*Woman's Nature: Rationalizations of Inequality.* Edited by Marion Lowe and Ruth Hubbard. Pergamon Press, Maxwell House, Fairview Park, Elmsford, NY 10523.

Woody, Bette. *Managing Crisis Cities: The New Black Leadership and the Politics of Resource Allocation.* Westport, CT: Greenwood Press.

Wright, Bruce. *Black Robes, White Justice.* Secaucus, NJ: Lyle Stuart Publishers. 1987.

# APPENDIX

## List of Tables
## List of Charts
## Spingarn Medalists

## LIST OF CHARTS

## SPINGARN MEDALISTS

1915 Ernest E. Just—professor of physiology—For research in biology.

1916 Charles Young—Major, U.S. Army—For service in Liberia.

1917 Harry T. Burleigh—composer, pianist, singer—For excellence in creative music.

1918 William S. Braithwaite—poet, critic, editor—For distinguished achievement in literature.

1919 Archibald H. Grimke—former U.S. Consul, president of the American Negro Academy, president of the Washington, D.C. NAACP—For seventy years of distinguished service to his race and country.

1920 William E. B. DuBois—author, editor of *The Crisis*—For founding the Pan-African Congress.

1921 Charles S. Gilpin—actor—For his notable performance in the title role of *The Emperor Jones*.

1922 Mary B. Talbert—former president of the National Association of Colored Women—For service to her race and restoration of Frederick Douglass' home.

1923 George Washington Carver—head of research at Tuskegee Institute—For distinguished research in agricultural chemistry.

1924 Roland Hayes—singer—For great musical artistry.

1925 James Weldon Johnson—former U.S. Consul, former editor and secretary of the NAACP—For distinguished achievement in writing, diplomacy, and public service.

1926 Carter G. Woodson—historian and educator—For 10 years devoted service in collecting and publishing the records of the black in America.

1927 Anthony Overton—businessman—For gaining his insurance company the right to conduct business in the state of New York.

1928 Charles W. Chesnutt—author—For pioneer work as a novelist depicting the life and struggle of black Americans.

1929 Mordecai Wyatt Johnson—former president of Howard University—For his success as first black president of the leading black university in America.

1930 Henry A. Hunt—school principal—For 25 years of devoted service to rural blacks in Georgia.

1931 Richard Berry Harrison—actor—For his performance in *Green Pastures*.

1932 Robert Russa Moton—president of Tuskegee Institute—For active leadership as an educator and spokesman—For the rights of black Americans.

1933 Max Yergan—YMCA secretary in South Africa—For 10 years of selfless work as a missionary.

1934 William Taylor Burwell Williams—dean of Tuskegee Institute—For contributions to black education.

1935 Mary McLeod Bethune—founder and president of Bethune-Cookman College—For courage and perseverance in black education.

1936 John Hope—president of Atlanta University—For distinguished leadership as chief administrator of Atlanta University.

1937 Walter White—executive secretary of the NAACP—For the successful fight for a federal anti-lynching bill

1938 No award given.

1939 Marian Anderson—contralto—For musical achievements

1940 Louis T. Wright—physician and surgeon—For contributions in medicine

1941 Richard Wright—novelist—For his book *Native Son*.

1942 A. Philip Randolph—labor leader, president of the Brotherhood of Sleeping Car Porters—For leadership in labor organization.

1943 William H. Hastie—jurist, educator—For a distinguished career in law and the fight for racial justice

1944 Charles Drew—scientist—For outstanding work in blood plasma research

1945 Paul Robeson—singer, actor—For distinguished achievement in the theater and on the concert stage

1946 Thurgood Marshall—special counsel for the NAACP—For service as a lawyer arguing cases before the Supreme Court

1947 Percy Julian—research chemist, educator—For discoveries in chemistry.

1948 Channing H. Tobias—minister, educator—For contributions as a spokesman for civil liberties

1949 Ralph J. Bunche—diplomat—For distinguished contributions to Gunnar Myrdal's study, *An American Dilemma*

1950 Charles Hamilton Houston—lawyer, chairman of the NAACP Legal Committee—For leadership in the legal profession

1951 Mabel Keaton Staupers—nurse—For efforts to gain equal opportunity for black nurses.

1952 Harry T. Moore [posthumous award]—state leader of the Florida NAACP—For courage in the struggle for black political equality.

1953 Paul R. Williams—architect—For his contributions as a creative designer and architect.

1954 Theodore K. Lawless—physician, educator—For research work in the field of dermatology.

1955 Carl Murphy—editor, publisher—For leading the attempt to secure equality for blacks in employment, education and recreation.

1956 Jack Roosevelt Robinson—athlete—For sportsmanship and work with young blacks.

1957 Martin Luther King, Jr.—minister, civil rights leader—For brilliant leadership in the cause of civil rights.

1958 Daisy Bates and the Little Rock Nine—publisher and student group—For their efforts to achieve equal educational rights in the state of Arkansas.

1959 Edward Kennedy (Duke) Ellington—composer, musician, orchestra leader—For outstanding achievements in music.

1960 Langston Hughes—poet, author, playwright—For major contributions to literature.

1961 Kenneth B. Clark—psychologist—For psychological research and its application to civil rights.

1962 Robert C. Weaver—economist, government administrator—For public service and pioneering "open housing".

1963 Medgar Wiley Evers [posthumous award]—field secretary of the NAACP, civil rights leader—For steadfast dedication to civil rights causes in Mississippi.

1964 Roy Wilkins—Executive Director of the NAACP, civil rights leader—For dedication, exceptional leadership, and courage in pursuit of democratic principles.

1965 Leontyne Price—soprano—For extraordinary achievements as a musical artist.

1966 John H. Johnson—publisher, businessman—For outstanding contributions to black America through enterprise, ingenuity and imagination in publishing.

1967 Edward W. Brooke III—Senator from Massachusetts—For a distinguished career as a public servant.

1968 Sammy Davis, Jr.—entertainer—For superb and diverse talent and commitment to civil rights.

1969 Clarence Mitchell, Jr.—director of the Washington Bureau of the NAACP—For selfless efforts in the cause of racial justice.

1970 Jacob Lawrence—artist, educator—For excellently portraying the life and history of black Americans.

1971 Leon Howard Sullivan—minister—For inspiration and resourcefulness in improving the economic conditions of blacks.

1972 Gordon Parks—photographer, filmmaker, writer—For outstanding achievements in many art forms.

1973 Wilson C. Riles—educator—For leadership in education and devotion to integrated living in a multiracial society.

1974 Damon J. Keith—jurist—For steadfast defense of constitutional principles and distinguished public service.

1975 Henry Aaron—For singular achievements in baseball and contributions as a citizen to the American community.

1976 Alvin Ailey—dancer, choreographer, and artistic director—In recognition of his international preeminence in the field of dance—For his development of one of the world's premiere dance companies.

1977 Alexander Palmer Haley—author, biographer, and lecturer—For his incomparable, exhaustive research and literary skill which was combined in *Roots*.—or his unsurpassed effectiveness in portraying the legendary story of an American of African descent—and for his role in presenting the survival story of a black American family, for inspiration to black youth, for the enlightenment of the general public.

1978 Andrew Jackson Young—diplomat, cabinet member, civil rights activist, minister—For the deftness with which he handled relations between this nation and other countries through the offices of the United Nations—for his major role in raising the consciousness of American citizens to the significance in world affairs of the massive African continent, for exemplary service as United States Congressman.

1979 Rosa L. Parks—community activist—A tribute to the quiet courage and determination exemplified on December 1, 1955, when she refused to surrender her seat on a Montgomery, Alabama bus to a white male passenger, and in recognition of her personal dedication since that time to the cause of civil rights.

1980 Rayford W. Logan—educator, historian, author—For his prodigious efforts to set before the world the black American's continuing struggle against the forces of oppression and inhumanity and for his equally penetrating monographs on conditions which adversely affect the people of Africa and Haiti.

1981 Coleman Alexander Young—public servant, labor leader, civil rights activist—In recognition of his singular accomplishments as mayor of the City of Detroit since 1973, guiding that city from the brink of bankruptcy to becoming a model of renaissance—establishing an unparalleled record of affirmative action programs, crime reduction, improved police-community relations and urban revitalization.

1982 Benjamin E. Mays—educator, civil rights activist, and past president of Morehouse College. In appreciation of his singular achievement of conjoining spiritual and moral leadership with prescient social vision—For continuing devotion to the highest standards of excellence for his students and youth in general—for his enduring and uncompromising advocacy of human and civil rights—and in recognition of his intellectual honesty and compelling integrity in all circumstances.

1983 Lena Horne—artist, humanitarian and living symbol of excellence—In recognition of her eminently distinguished career in the entertainment world of theater, motion pictures, television, radio and recordings—for her continuous contribution to enhancement of the self-image of black citizens throughout this nation and elsewhere—for her unfaltering dedication and commitment to the principles of equality and justice for all.

1984 Tom Bradley—government executive, public servant, humanist—In salutation to a lifetime of growth and achievement, from a sharecropper's cabin in the cotton fields of Calvert, Texas, to four terms as Chief Executive of the nation's second largest city.

1985 William H. Cosby, Jr.—humorist, artist, educator, family man and humanitarian—For his perseverance and preparation for a spectacular career nurtured in a Philadelphia ghetto, honed in athletic competition, refined through continuous pursuit of educational goals to broaden, then focus his insights—and in salutation and appreciation of his televised projection of American family qualities

1986 Benjamin Lawson Hooks—Executive Director, National Association for the Advancement of Colored People—In recognition of a superlative, evolutionary career as a lawyer, minister, jurist, scholar, orator, national public servant, social innovator—in tribute to his precedent setting accomplishments as the first black public defender of his native Memphis, Tennessee, and as the first black appointed by a United States president to the Federal Communications Commission .

1987 Percy Ellis Sutton—Public servant, businessman, community leader—In recognition of unqualified successes as patriot, lawyer, national and international civil rights' guardian, public official and pioneering businessman—for his evolutionary career accomplishments as New York State Legislator, 12-year president of the Borough of Manhattan.

1988 Frederick Douglass Patterson—Educator, Doctor of Veterinary Medicine, visionary and humanitarian—In tribute to a quietly spectacular career anchored in the bedrock belief that human productivity and well-being in a free society are the end products of determination and self-preparation—in salutation of his efforts in the establishment, in 1943, of the United Negro College Fund—for his critical leadership in gaining acceptance of black flying personnel into the United States Air Force; and for his long persistent leadership while serving on academic and corporate directorates with an unfettered vision of the future.

## Picture Credits

AAMO 1336—AAR 1026—ABC 926—ABC 927, 932, 945, 1211, 1214, 1215, 1280, 1282, 1284, 1286, 1379—ACA 1337—AD 1401—ADB 954—AF 1239—AH 1394—AL 1029—AMEZ 1310—AN 238, 272, 277, 303, 940, 967, 1323—ANS 1374—AP 242, 284, 939, 944, 953, 958, 979, 1324—APR 297, 560, 1335—AR 1138, 1139, 1218—ARC 1338—ARP 217, 578, 578, 617, 703, 1034, 1055, 1058—ASP 1257, 1265, 1270—ATL 199, 764—AUY 1231—AZC 1314—BAA 1263—BE 1261—BERC 1342—BL 287, 1375—BM 32, 39, 194, 661, 693, 748—BMH 1331—BSG 1065—BT 992—BXM 1056—CA 1176, 177, 1179, 1182, 1187—CBS 1156, 1279—CCNY 722—CD 1263—CEBS 1345—CGJ 153—CH 280—CN 930, 931, 937, 1316—CNN 1285—CORE 558—CP 1240, 1246, 1249—CR 1212—CRS 1071—CS 1086—D 1205, 1206—DEL 157, 452, 1256, 1264—DM 1000, 1049—DPL 193, 204, 227—ED 297, 565—EP 1131, 1146—ES 993—FM 1384—FS 213—GF 568, 1262, 1395, 1410—GM 1415—GP 582—GPS 1033—GS 1009—H 113, 734, 735, 808, 950—HB 982—HBC 1050—HBE 1059—HEW 692, 696, 698, 699, 700, 701, 1380—HF 1051—HFC 583—HI 231—HLC 1198—HM 2, 7, 8, 9, 15, 19, 108, 110, 121, 122, 190, 218, 222, 470, 800,828, 842, 1302, 1434, 1436, 1436, 1438, 1438, 1444, 1460, 1461—HRCC 1349—HTL 404—HW 9, 10, 13, 127, 134, 134, 145, 187, 188, 215, 220, 226, 226, 320, 321, 367, 371, 372, 373, 373, 378, 411, 411, 413, 472, 724, 725, 726, 809, 835, 836, 839, 840, 842, 1116, 1196, 1313, 1315, 1448—JC 393, 394, 396, 396, 414, 415, 416, 425, 429—JCPS 65, 82, 84, 282, 1351—JEB 1028—JFKL 374, 559, 737—JIR 1198, 1200, 1201, 1202, 1204, 1208, 1209, 1217, 1219, 1220, 1221, 1223, 1226—JJ 1062—JRE 1060—K 1128—KF 1398—KNXT 1275—KP 1387—LBJL 45, 375—LBS 935—LC 4, 4, 6, 6, 8, 11, 16, 109, 116, 123, 130, 133, 135, 202, 211, 212, 230, 232, 236, 299, 300, 402, 403, 405, 406, 406, 554, 555, 555, 556, 557, 733, 733, 796, 797, 799, 799, 799, 800, 801, 803, 804, 805, 806, 807, 807, 808, 810, 813, 817, 818, 819, 821, 822, 822, 823, 823, 824, 827, 838, 844, 844, 845, 847, 848, 860, 1117, 1181, 1308, 1309, 1424, 1434, 1435, 1439, 1445—LCL 1172, 1173, 1174, 1174, 1175, 1178, 1180, 1183, 1184, 1185, 1193—LHG 1064—LIT 814—LIW 556—LM 983—LOR 1252—MAA 1026, 1035—MB 1411—MCMY 1162—MEA 1031—MGM 234, 1232—MHS 14—ML 197, 474, 832, 833, 834, 837, 1441, 1443—MMS 1072, 1073—MO 1171, 1178, 1186, 1189, 1190, 1192—MR 1329—MW 276, 1353—NA 797, 798, 859—NA 860, 1532, 1533—NAACP 43, 66, 73, 94, 166, 238, 261, 302, 315, 316, 317, 318, 323, 405, 521, 708, 977, 1014, 1318, 1355—NAACP/DL 506, 516, 694, 28, 269, 310—NABSW 1357—NASA 1080, 1093, 1094, 1095, 1098, 1099—NBC 960,

964, 1123, 1139, 1144, 1153, 1154, 1158, 1164, 1274, 1276, 1278, 1279, 1280, 1281, 1284, 1286—NBWM 1091—NC 68—NCM 1411—NET 175, 271, 289, 326, 771, 978—NFL 932—NGSL 815—NPG 112, 120, 235—NPS 208, 95—NSF 1363—NUL 59, 179, 262, 263, 414—NWPL. 1126—NYDL 1391—NYHS 191, 1016—NYPL 3, 12, 119, 203, 225, 286, 332, 332, 802, 810, 811, 812, 819, 824, 825, 826, 999, 1120, 1176, 1183, 1197, 1213, 1225, 1299, 1299, 1299, 1300, 1301, 1327, 1328, 1444, 1445, 1446, 1447, 1447—NYPO 1258—NYT 1259, 1260, 1388—NYU 1402—PB 1382—PB 1383—PE 342—PM 1151, 1163, 1231, 1233, 1245, 1250, 1251, 1415—PR 31—PSI 922—PW 1056—RB 1403—RHO 1053—RM 1419—RR 564—RS 1125, 1147—SAC 1222, 1366—SAS 1148—SBG 1149—SC 20, 22, 55, 225, 407, 408, 732, 986, 995, 1040, 1043, 1067, 1079, 1082, 1087, 1087, 1088, 1088, 1089, 1089, 1092, 1108, 1111, 1111, 1114, 1117, 1118, 1119, 1300, 1311, 1312, 1321, 1373, 1424—SCLC 161—SCU 923—SH 997—SLS 1166—SWG 949—TCF 1160, 1237—TI 149, 186, 723, 1081—TL 26—TR 982—TRI 1141, 1142—UA 1129, 1239, 1242, 1245—UB 750, 754, 757, 758—UN 184, 446, 447, 619, 1462, 1464, 1465, 1470, 1471, 1473, 1474, 1476, 1478, 1480, 1481, 1483, 1483, 1484, 1485, 1486, 1487, 1488, 1489, 1490, 1492, 1492, 1499, 1500, 1501, 1504, 1507, 1508, 1509, 1513, 1520, 1523, 1524, 1525, 1526, 1527, 1528, 1532, 1535, 1536, 1539, 1542, 1543, 1545, 1546, 1546, 1547, 1549, 1550, 1551, 1554,1555—UNCF 736, 745, 752, 760, 1369—UO 224—UP 1136, 1243, 1243—UPI 42, 47, 52, 172, 239, 245, 254, 265, 275, 285, 288, 292, 326, 328, 331, 344, 555, 561, 564, 723, 729, 730, 738, 741, 864, 915, 916, 917, 924, 924, 925, 941, 943, 951, 958, 962, 966, 969, 1121, 1157, 1277, 1304, 1404, 1426—USAF 849, 886, 888, 891, 900, 901, 910—USAR 21, 71, 201, 846, 850, 851, 853, 854, 862, 863, 864, 866, 869, 873, 892, 893, 895, 896, 897, 902, 905, 1427—USDD 852—USMA 879, 880—USMC 155, 852, 856, 868, 904—USN 26, 623, 855, 865, 899, 909, 910, 1428—USNA 883, 884—USSC 187, 205, 843—USWD 845, 846, 846, 861—UTA 877—VAN 1074—WAGA 1287—WB 1070, 1231—WH 80, 164, 168, 445—WLIB 1283—WM 1048, 1051, 1052—WMA 1135, 207—WW 27, 29, 29, 30, 31, 33, 34, 34, 35, 36, 37, 42, 45, 46, 46, 47, 48, 51, 60, 68, 82, 93, 95, 97, 98, 101, 103, 106, 159, 180, 189, 245, 257, 264, 278, 295, 313, 324, 330, 345, 370, 376, 399, 442, 454, 566, 587, 606, 652, 951, 970, 1159, 1383, 1385, 1388, 1393, 1432—YUL 260

## Key to Picture Credits

AAMO—Afro-American Music Opportunities Association.
AAR—Abby Aldrich Rockefeller Collection
ABCO—Associated Bookkeeping Co.
ABCR—ABC Records
ABC—American BroadcastingCompany
ABE—Adult Basic Education
ACA—American Committee on Africa
ADB—A.D. Bernstein
AD—Ann Day
AH—A. Hanson
AH—Alfred Hathaway, Jr.
AL—Arthur Lavine
AM—New York Amsterdam News
ANS—A. N. Schurlock
APR—A. Philip Randolph Institute
ARC—Amistad Research Center
ARP—Andy Roy
AR—Atlantic Records
ASCAP—American Society of Composers, Authors and Publishers
ASP—Associated Publishers
ATL—Atlanta University
AUY— Autrey Studios
AU—Atlantic Records
AW—Alex Williamson
BAA—Baltimore Afro-American
BA—Bettmann Archive
BBC—Hatch, Billops Collection
BCM—Brooklyn Children's Museum
BC—Brooklyn College
BERC—Black economic Research Center
BE—Black Enterprise
BL—Blackstone
BMA—Bill Mackey
BMH—Bill Mitchell
BMI—Broadcast Music Incorporated
BM—Brooklyn Museum
BNR—Blue Note Records
BOC—Bowdoin College
BSG—Bernice Steinbaum Gallery
BTM—Bethune Museum
BT—Bert Andrewes
BXN—Bronx Museum
CA—Columbia Artists
CBS—Columbia BroadcastingSystem
CCNY—City College of New York
CD—Chicago Defender
CEFS—Chamba Educational Film Services
CF—Craig Fisher
CGJ—Consulate General of Jamaica
CH—Chester Higgons Jr.
CL—Cecil Layne
CMB—Chase Manhattan Bank
CN—Carl Nesfield
COSM—Collection Old Slave Mart Museum
CP—Columbia Pictures
CRE—Cinerama Releasing
CRS—Coreen Simpson
CR—Columbia Records
CS—Conway Studios
DEL—Dwight Eiisenhower Library
DEL—Eisenhower Library
DFS—David Frost Show
DHWU—Drug and Hospital Workers Union
DIA—Detroit Institute of Arts
DL—David LeShay
DM—Dodd, Mead & Co.
DPL—Denver Public Library
DRTT—Dick Raphael
DU—Dillard University
D—Downbeat
ED—Ed druck
EEC—Electric Engine Co., Phila.
EP—Epic Records
ES—Edward Spring
E—El l i nger
FDI—Frederick Douglass Institute, D.C.
FDRL—Franklin Delano Roosevelt Library
FF—Ford Foundation
FHS—Frederick H. Simmons
FL—Frank Lerner
FM—Ford Model Agency
FR—Folkways Records
FS—Fort Shaw
F—Fox Films
GC—Geoffrey Clements
GF—George Frye
GM—General Motors
GPS—Galbreath Photo Service
GP—Gwenn Phillips
GRM—Griswold Museum
GS—George Schless
HBC—Hatch-Billips Collection
HBE—Henry Beville
HB—Harper Brothers
HEW—U.S. Dept. of Health, Education and Welfare
HFC—H.F. Henderson Corp.
HF—Harmon Foundation
HH—Harlem Hospital
HI—Hampton Institute
HLC—Harris Levine Collection
HM—Harper's Monthly
HRCC—Harlem River Consumers Co-op
HS—Headstart
HTL—Harry Truman Library
HW—Harper's Weekly
IP—International Pictures
I—Impulse
JA—Joe Alper
JCPS—Joint Center for Political Studies
JC—Jamacian Consulate
JDS—John D. Schiff
JEB—J. Edward Bailey
JEC—J. Ekstrom Cordier
JET—J.E. Taylor
JFKL—John Fitzgerald Kennedy Library
JIR—Jazz Institute of Rutgers University
JJ—Jan Jachniewicz
JK—Jill Krementz
JM—Jim Marshall
JP—Jyme Productions
JRE—J.R. Eyerman
JVD—James Van Deilee
Key to Picture Credits
KF—Kay Frantrenty
KNX—KNX-TV
KP—Kerr Photographers
K— Kegstone
LBJL—Lyndon B. Johnson Library
LBS—LBS Communications
LCL—Lincoln Center Library
LC—Library of Congress
LHG—Liz Harris Gallery
LIT—London International Times
LIW—Leslie's Illustrated Weekly
LM—Larry McLucas
LOR—Lorimer Films
LP—Learning Process
LSM—Louisiana State Museum
MAA—Museum of African Art
MB—Marlis Momber
MCNY—Museum of the City of New York
MEA—Mary Ellen Andrews
ME—Mecury Records
MGM—Metro-Goldwyn-Mayer

MJG—Martha Jackson Gallery
MKM—Monte Kay Management
MK—Monte Kay
ML—Morgan Library
MMA—Metropolitan Museum of Art
MMBM—Mary McCleod Bethune Museum
MMS—Marvin and Morgan Smith
MOV— Movietone
MO—Metropolitan Opera
MR—Merrill Roberts
MSC—Morgan State College
MS—Michael Sullivan
MW—Milton Williams
MW—Mother Waddles Perpetual Mission
M—Macmillan
NAACP—National Association for the Advancement of Colored People
NABSW—National Association of Black Social Workers
NASA—National Aeronautic and Space Administration
NA—National Archives
NBC—National Broadcasting Company
NBN—National Black Network
NBWM—New Bedford Whaling Museum
NCM—National Conference of Black Mayors
NC—Nancy Crampton
ND—University of Notre Dame
NET—National Educational Television
NGSL—National Geographic Society Library
NHA—Negro History Association
NPG—NatioNal Portrait Museum
NPS—National Park Service
NSF—National Sharecroppers Fund Training
NSN—Newark Star News
NUL—National Urban League
NWPL—Newark Public Library
NYCB—New York City Balle~
NYDL—New York State Department of Labor
NYDN—New York Daily News
NYGS—New York Graphic Society
NYHS—New York Historical Society
NYPL—New York Public Library
NYPO—New York Post
NYT—New York Times
NYT—New York Times
NYU—New York University
PB—Pach Brothers
PE—Penning Studio
PM—Philip Morris
PP—Paramount Pictures
PSI—Professional Service Inc.
PS—Pilgrim Society
PW—Printmakers Workshop
P—Philips
RB—Raimondo Boriea
RHO—R.H. Osterman
RH—Random House
RM—Rolond Mitchell
RR—Rocky Robertson
RS—Ron Scherl
SAC—Shaw Artists Corp.
SAS—SAS Inc.
SA—Shaw Artists
SBG—S.A. Seidenberg
SCHS—South Carolina Historical Society
SCK—A.N. Schurlock
SCLC—Southern Christian Leadership Conference
SCU—Scott Cunningham
SC—Schomburg Collection
SH—"Spike" Harris
SLC—St. Louis Cardinals
SLPD—St. Louis Post Dispatch
SLS—S. L. Schulman
Sl—Smithsonian Institute
SL—Sunday Leisure
SSA—Schulment Associates
SWG—Shell's Wide World of Golf
TCF—20th Century-Fox
TIA—Theatre in America
TL—Truman Library
Tl—Tuskegee Institute
TMC—Taft Museum, Cinn.
TRI—Tri-Star Pictures
TR—Todd Reed
T—Time
UA—United Artists
UB—Upward Bound
UL—University of Louisville
UNCF—United Negro College Fund
UNI—Uniroyal
UN—United Nations
UO—University of Oklahoma
UPI—United Press International
UP—Universal Pictures
USAF—United States Air Force
USAR—United States Army
USDD—U.S. Department of Defense
USMA— U.S. Military Academy
USMC—United States Marine Corps
USNA—U.S. Naval Academy
USN—United States Navy
USSC—United States Signal Corps
USWD—United States War Department
UTA—University of Texas Archives
VAN—Van Der Zee Estate
WAGA—WAGA-TV
WB—Warner Brothers
WH—White House
WLIB—WLIB Radio
WMA—William Morris Agency
WM—Whitney Museum
WP—West Point Museum
WR—Winold Reiss
WW—World Wide
YU—Yale University Library
ZP—Zodiac Photographers

# INDEX

## — B —

## — C —

## — D —

## — E —

## — F —

## — H —

## — I —



## — J —

## — K —



## — L —

## — M —

## — N —

**—O—**

## — P —

## — Q —



## — R —

**—S—**

## — T —

## — U —

**—Y—**



**—Z—**